COLLINS
PAPERBACK
FRENCH
DICTIONARY

COLLINS
PAPERBACK
FRENCH
DICTIONARY
FRENCH ▶ ENGLISH   ENGLISH ▶ FRENCH

HarperCollins*Publishers*

second edition/deuxième édition 1995

© **HarperCollins Publishers 1995**
© **William Collins Sons & Co. Ltd. 1988**

HarperCollins Publishers
P.O. Box, Glasgow G4 0NB, Great Britain
ISBN 0 00 470210 7 (Paperback)
ISBN 0 00 470729 X (College)

Pierre-Henri Cousin • Lorna Sinclair Knight
Jean-François Allain • Catherine E. Love

contributors to second edition/deuxième édition
Megan Thomson
Cécile Aubinière-Robb • Harry Campbell
Keith Foley • Janet Gough • Jean-Benoît Ormal-Grenon

editorial staff/secrétariat de rédaction
Elspeth Anderson • Susan Dunsmore

series editor/collection dirigée par
Lorna Sinclair Knight
editorial management/chef de projet
Vivian Marr

Dépôt légal:avril 1995
Achevé d'imprimer en avril 1995

Typeset by Morton Word Processing Ltd, Scarborough

Printed in Great Britain by
HarperCollins Manufacturing, Glasgow

TABLE DES MATIÈRES   CONTENTS

INTRODUCTION

Vous désirez apprendre l'anglais ou approfondir des connaissances déjà solides. Vous voulez vous exprimer en anglais, lire ou rédiger des textes anglais ou converser avec des interlocuteurs anglophones. Que vous soyez lycéen, étudiant, touriste, homme ou femme d'affaires, vous venez de choisir le compagnon de travail idéal pour vous exprimer et pour communiquer en anglais, oralement ou par écrit. Résolument pratique et moderne, votre dictionnaire fait une large place au vocabulaire de tous les jours, aux domaines de l'actualité, des affaires, de la bureautique et du tourisme. Comme dans tous nos dictionnaires, nous avons mis l'accent sur la langue contemporaine et sur les expressions idiomatiques.

MODE D'EMPLOI

Vous trouverez ci-dessous quelques explications sur la manière dont les informations sont présentées dans votre dictionnaire. Notre objectif: vous donner un maximum d'informations sans pour autant sacrifier la clarté.

Les articles

Voici les différents éléments dont est composé un article type dans votre dictionnaire:

Transcription phonétique

La prononciation des mots figure, entre crochets, immédiatement après l'entrée. Comme la plupart des dictionnaires modernes, nous avons opté pour le système dit "alphabet phonétique international". Vous trouverez ci-dessous, aux pages xii et xiii, une liste complète des caractères utilisés dans ce système.

Données grammaticales

Les mots appartiennent tous à une catégorie grammaticale donnée: substantif, verbe, adjectif, adverbe, pronom, article, conjonction, préposition, abréviation. Les substantifs peuvent être singuliers ou pluriels et, en français, masculins ou féminins. Les verbes peuvent être transitifs, intransitifs, pronominaux (ou réfléchis) ou encore impersonnels. La catégorie grammaticale des mots est indiquée en *italiques*, immédiatement après le mot.

Souvent un mot se subdivise en plusieurs catégories grammaticales. Ainsi le français **creux** peut-il être un adjectif ou un nom masculin; et l'anglais **early** peut-il être soit un adverbe, soit un adjectif. De même le verbe **fumer** est parfois transitif ("fumer un cigare"), parfois intransitif ("défense de fumer"). Pour vous permettre de trouver plus rapidement le sens que vous cherchez, et pour aérer la présentation, nous avons séparé les différentes catégories grammaticales par un losange noir ♦.

Subdivisions sémantiques

La plupart des mots ont plus d'un sens; ainsi **bouchon** peut être un objet servant à boucher une bouteille, ou, dans un sens figuré, un embouteillage. D'autres mots se traduisent différemment selon le contexte dans lequel ils sont employés: **couler** se traduira en anglais "to leak" ou "to sink" selon qu'il s'agit d'un stylo ou d'un bateau. Pour vous permettre de choisir la bonne traduction dans tous les contextes, nous avons subdivisé les articles en catégories de sens; ces catégories sont introduites par une "indication d'emploi" entre parenthèses et en *italiques*. Pour les exemples ci-dessus, les articles se présenteront donc comme suit:

> **bouchon** *nm* (*en liège*) cork; (*autre matière*) stopper; (*fig: embouteillage*) hold-up

> **couler** *vi* to flow, run; (*fuir: stylo, récipient*) to leak; (*sombrer: bateau*) to sink

De même certains mots changent de sens lorsqu'ils sont employés dans un domaine spécifique, comme par exemple **puce** que nous employons généralement dans son acception de "petit insecte sauteur", mais qui est aussi un terme d'informatique. Pour montrer à l'utilisateur quelle traduction choisir, nous avons donc ajouté, en italiques majuscules entre parenthèses, une indication de domaine, à savoir dans ce cas particulier (*INFORMATIQUE*), que nous avons abrégé pour gagner de la place en (*INFORM*):

puce *nf* flea; (*INFORM*) chip.

Une liste complète des abréviations dont nous nous sommes servis dans ce dictionnaire figure ci-dessous, aux pages x et xi.

Traductions

La plupart des mots français se traduisent par un seul mot anglais, et vice-versa, comme dans les exemples ci-dessus. Parfois cependant il n'y a pas d'équivalent exact dans la langue d'arrivée et nous avons donné un équivalent approximatif, indiqué par le signe ≈; c'est le cas par exemple pour le mot **baccalauréat** dont l'équivalent anglais est "GCE A-levels": il ne s'agit pas d'une traduction à proprement parler puisque nos deux systèmes scolaires sont différents:

baccalauréat *nm* ≈ GCE A-levels

Parfois il est impossible même de trouver un équivalent approximatif. C'est le cas par exemple pour les noms de plats régionaux, comme le plat languedocien suivant:

cassoulet *nm sausage and bean hotpot*

L'explication remplace ici une traduction (qui n'existe pas); pour plus de clarté, cette explication, ou glose, est donnée en *italiques*.

Souvent aussi, on ne peut traduire isolément un mot, ou une acception particulière d'un mot. La traduction anglaise de **copain**, par exemple, est "mate, pal", cependant **être copain avec** se traduit "to be pally with". Même une expression toute simple comme **doigt de pied** nécessite une traduction séparée, en l'occurrence "toe" (et non "footfinger"). C'est là que votre dictionnaire se révélera particulièrement utile et complet, car il contient un maximum de composés, de phrases et d'expressions idiomatiques.

Registre

En français, vous saurez instinctivement quand dire **j'en ai assez** et quand dire **j'en ai marre** ou **j'en ai ras le bol**. Mais lorsque vous essayez de comprendre quelqu'un qui s'exprime en anglais, ou de vous exprimer vous-même en anglais, il est particulièrement important de savoir ce qui est poli et ce qui l'est moins. Nous avons donc ajouté l'indication (*col*) (= *colloquial*) aux expressions de langue familière dans la partie anglais-français; les expressions particulièrement grossières se voient dotées d'un point d'exclamation supplémentaire (*col!*), vous incitant à une prudence accrue. Notez également que dans la partie français-anglais, les traductions qui appartiennent au registre vulgaire sont suivies d'un point d'exclamation entre parenthèses.

Mots-clés

Une importance particulière a été accordée aux mots qui figurent dans le texte sous la mention *MOT-CLÉ*, tels que **être** et **faire** ou leurs équivalents anglais **be** et **do.** Ils constituent en effet les éléments de base de la langue. Ce petit coup de pouce supplémentaire vous permettra d'utiliser ces termes complexes en toute confiance.

Notes culturelles

Les articles séparés du texte principal par deux lignes horizontales décrivent certaines caractéristiques culturelles des pays francophones et anglophones. Les médias, l'éducation, la politique et les fêtes figurent parmi les sujets traités. Exemple: **quality papers, honours degree, Assemblée nationale** et **Toussaint.**

INTRODUCTION

You may be starting French for the first time, or you may wish to extend your knowledge of the language. Perhaps you want to read and study French books, newspapers and magazines, or perhaps simply have a conversation with French speakers. Whatever the reason, whether you're a student, a tourist or want to use French for business, this is the ideal book to help you understand and communicate. This modern, user-friendly dictionary gives priority to everyday vocabulary and the language of current affairs, business, computing and tourism, and, as in all Collins dictionaries, the emphasis is firmly placed on contemporary language and expressions.

HOW TO USE THE DICTIONARY

Below you will find an outline of how information is presented in your dictionary. Our aim is to give you the maximum amount of detail in the clearest and most helpful way.

Entries

A typical entry in your dictionary will be made up of the following elements:

Phonetic transcription

Phonetics appear in square brackets immediately after the headword. They are shown using the International Phonetic Alphabet (IPA), and a complete list of the symbols used in this system can be found on pages xii and xiii.

Grammatical information

All words belong to one of the following parts of speech: noun, verb, adjective, adverb, pronoun, article, conjunction, preposition, abbreviation. Nouns can be singular or plural and, in French, masculine or feminine. Verbs can be transitive, intransitive, reflexive or impersonal. Parts of speech appear in *italics* immediately after the phonetic spelling of the headword. The gender of the translation also appears in *italics* immediately following the key element of the translation.

Often a word can have more than one part of speech. Just as the English word **chemical** can be an adjective or a noun, the French word **rose** can be an adjective ("pink") or a feminine noun ("rose"). In the same way the verb **to walk** is sometimes transitive, ie it takes an object ("to walk the dog") and sometimes intransitive, ie it doesn't take an object ("to walk to school"). To help you find the meaning you are looking for quickly and for clarity of presentation, the different part of speech categories are separated by a black lozenge ♦.

Meaning divisions

Most words have more than one meaning. Take, for example, **punch** which can be, amongst other things, a blow with the fist or an object used for making holes. Other words are translated differently depending on the context in which they are used. The transitive verb **to roll up**, for example, can be translated by "rouler" or "retrousser" depending on *what* it is you are rolling up. To help you select the most appropriate translation in every context, entries are divided according to meaning. Different meanings are introduced by an "indicator" in *italics* and in brackets. Thus, the examples given above will be shown as follows:

> **punch** n (*blow*) coup m de poing; (*tool*) poinçon m

> **roll up** vt (*carpet, cloth, map*) rouler; (*sleeves*) retrousser

Likewise, some words can have a different meaning when used to talk about a specific subject area or field. For example, **bishop**, which we generally use to mean a high-ranking clergyman, is also the name of a chess piece. To show English speakers which translation to use, we have added "subject field labels" in capitals and in brackets, in this case (*CHESS*):

> **bishop** *n* évêque *m*; (*CHESS*) fou *m*

Field labels are often shortened to save space. You will find a complete list of abbreviations used in the dictionary on pages x and xi.

Translations

Most English words have a direct translation in French and vice versa, as shown in the examples given above. Sometimes, however, no exact equivalent exists in the target language. In such cases we have given an approximate equivalent, indicated by the sign ≈. An example is **National Insurance**, the French equivalent of which is "Sécurité Sociale". There is no exact equivalent since the systems of the two countries are quite different:

> **National Insurance** *n* (*BRIT*) ≈ Sécurité Sociale

On occasion it is impossible to find even an approximate equivalent. This may be the case, for example, with the names of types of food:

> **mince pie** *n sorte de tarte aux fruits secs*

Here the translation (which doesn't exist) is replaced by an explanation. For increased clarity the explanation, or "gloss", is shown in *italics*.

It is often the case that a word, or a particular meaning of a word, cannot be translated in isolation. The translation of **Dutch**, for example, is "hollandais(e), néerlandais(e)". However, the phrase **to go Dutch** is rendered by "partager les frais". Even an expression as simple as **washing powder** needs a separate translation since it translates as "lessive (en poudre)", not "poudre à laver". This is where your dictionary will prove to be particularly informative and useful since it contains an abundance of compounds, phrases and idiomatic expressions.

Levels of formality and familiarity

In English you instinctively know when to say **I don't have any money** and when to say **I'm broke** or **I'm a bit short of cash**. When you are trying to understand someone who is speaking French, however, or when you yourself try to speak French, it is important to know what is polite and what is less so, and what you can say in a relaxed situation but not in a formal context. To help you with this, on the French-English side we have added the label (*fam*) to show that a French meaning or expression is colloquial, while those meanings or expressions which are vulgar are given an exclamation mark (*fam!*), warning you they can cause serious offence. Note also that on the English-French side, translations which are vulgar are followed by an exclamation mark in brackets.

Key words

Words labelled in the text as *KEYWORDS*, such as **be** and **do** or their French equivalents **être** and **faire**, have been given special treatment because they form the basic elements of the language. This extra help will ensure that you know how to use these complex words with confidence.

Cultural information

Entries which appear separated from the main text by a line above and below them explain aspects of culture in French and English-speaking countries. Subject areas covered include politics, education, media and national festivals, for example **Assemblée nationale**, **baccalauréat**, **BBC** and **Hallowe'en**.

ABRÉVIATIONS

ABBREVIATIONS

abréviation	**ab(b)r**	abbreviation
adjectif, locution adjective	**adj**	adjective, adjectival phrase
administration	**ADMIN**	administration
adverbe, locution adverbiale	**adv**	adverb, adverbial phrase
agriculture	**AGR**	agriculture
anatomie	**ANAT**	anatomy
architecture	**ARCHIT**	architecture
l'automobile	**AUT(O)**	the motor car and motoring
aviation, voyages aériens	**AVIAT**	flying, air travel
biologie	**BIO(L)**	biology
botanique	**BOT**	botany
anglais de Grande-Bretagne	**BRIT**	British English
cinéma	**CINÉ, CINE**	cinema
langue familière (! emploi vulgaire)	**col(!)**	colloquial usage (! particularly offensive)
commerce, finance, banque	**COMM**	commerce, finance, banking
informatique	**COMPUT**	computing
conjonction	**conj**	conjunction
construction	**CONSTR**	building
nom utilisé comme adjectif, ne peut s'employer ni comme attribut, ni après le nom qualifié	**cpd**	compound element: noun used as an adjective and which cannot follow the noun it qualifies
cuisine, art culinaire	**CULIN**	cookery
déterminant: article, adjectif démonstratif ou indéfini etc	**dét, det**	determiner: article, demonstrative etc.
économie	**ECON**	economics
électricité, électronique	**ELEC**	electricity, electronics
exclamation, interjection	**excl**	exclamation, interjection
féminin	**f**	feminine
langue familière (! emploi vulgaire)	**fam (!)**	colloquial usage (! particularly offensive)
emploi figuré	**fig**	figurative use
(verbe anglais) dont la particule est inséparable du verbe	**fus**	(phrasal verb) where the particle cannot be separated from the main verb
dans la plupart des sens; généralement	**gén, gen**	in most or all senses; generally
géographie, géologie	**GEO**	geography, geology
géométrie	**GEOM**	geometry
histoire	**HIST**	history
informatique	**INFORM**	computing
invariable	**inv**	invariable
irrégulier	**irrég, irreg**	irregular
domaine juridique	**JUR**	law
grammaire, linguistique	**LING**	grammar, linguistics
masculin	**m**	masculine
mathématiques, algèbre	**MATH**	mathematics, calculus
médecine	**MÉD, MED**	medical term, medicine
masculin ou féminin, suivant le sexe	**m/f**	either masculine or feminine depending on sex
domaine militaire, armée	**MIL**	military matters
musique	**MUS**	music
nom	**n**	noun

ABRÉVIATIONS

ABBREVIATIONS

navigation, nautisme	**NAVIG, NAUT**	sailing, navigation
nom non comptable: ne peut s'utiliser au pluriel	**no pl**	collective (uncountable) noun: is not used in the plural
adjectif ou nom numérique	**num**	numeral adjective or noun
	o.s.	oneself
péjoratif	**péj, pej**	derogatory, pejorative
photographie	**PHOT(O)**	photography
physiologie	**PHYSIOL**	physiology
pluriel	**pl**	plural
politique	**POL**	politics
participe passé	**pp**	past participle
préposition	**prép, prep**	preposition
psychologie, psychiatrie	**PSYCH**	psychology, psychiatry
temps du passé	**pt**	past tense
quelque chose	**qch**	
quelqu'un	**qn**	
religions, domaine ecclésiastique	**REL**	religions, church service
	sb	somebody
enseignement, système scolaire et universitaire	**SCOL**	schooling, schools and universities
singulier	**sg**	singular
	sth	something
subjonctif	**sub**	subjunctive
sujet (grammatical)	**su(b)j**	(grammatical) subject
techniques, technologie	**TECH**	technical term, technology
télécommunications	**TEL**	telecommunications
théâtre	**THÉÂT, THEAT**	theatre
télévision	**TV**	television
typographie	**TYP(O)**	typography, printing
anglais des USA	**US**	American English
verbe	**vb**	verb
verbe ou groupe verbal à fonction intransitive	**vi**	verb or phrasal verb used intransitively
verbe ou groupe verbal à fonction transitive	**vt**	verb or phrasal verb used transitively
zoologie	**ZOOL**	zoology
marque déposée	®	registered trademark
indique une équivalence culturelle	≈	introduces a cultural equivalent
	'	no liaison before aspirate h

TRANSCRIPTION PHONÉTIQUE

Consonnes

_p_ou_p_ée	p	_p_u_pp_y
_b_om_b_e	b	_b_a_b_y
_t_en_t_e _th_ermal	t	_t_en_t_
_d_in_d_e	d	_d_a_dd_y
_c_o_q_ _qu_i _k_épi	k	_c_ork _k_iss _ch_ord
_g_ag ba_gu_e	g	_g_ag _gu_ess
_s_ale _c_e na_t_ion	s	_s_o ri_c_e _k_i_ss_
_z_éro ro_s_e	z	cou_s_in bu_zz_
ta_ch_e _ch_at	ʃ	_sh_eep _s_ugar
gilet _j_uge	ʒ	plea_s_ure bei_g_e
	tʃ	_ch_ur_ch_
	dʒ	_j_u_dg_e _g_eneral
_f_er _ph_are	f	_f_arm ra_ff_le
_v_al_v_e	v	_v_ery re_v_
	θ	_th_in ma_th_s
	ð	_th_at o_th_er
_l_ent sa_ll_e	l	_l_itt_l_e ba_ll_
_rar_e _r_ent_r_er	ʀ	
	r	_r_at ra_r_e
_m_a_m_an fe_mm_e	m	_m_u_mm_y co_m_b
_n_on _n_o_nn_e	n	_n_o ra_n_
a_gn_eau vi_gn_e	ɲ	
	ŋ	si_ng_ing ba_n_k
_h_op!	h	_h_at re_h_eat
_y_eux pai_ll_e p_i_ed	j	_y_et
n_ou_er _ou_i	w	_w_all be_w_ail
_hu_ile l_u_i	ɥ	
	x	lo_ch_

Consonants

Divers / Miscellaneous

pour l'anglais: le r final se prononce en liaison devant une voyelle	*	
pour l'anglais: précède la syllabe accentuée	'	in French transcription: no liaison before aspirate h

En règle générale, la prononciation est donnée entre crochets après chaque entrée. Toutefois, du côté anglais-français et dans le cas des expressions composées de deux ou plusieurs mots non réunis par un trait d'union et faisant l'objet d'une entrée séparée, la prononciation doit être cherchée sous chacun des mots constitutifs de l'expression en question.

PHONETIC TRANSCRIPTION

Voyelles

NB. La mise en équivalence de certains sons n'indique qu'une ressemblance approximative.

Vowels

NB. The pairing of some vowel sounds only indicates approximate equivalence.

ici vie lyre	i iː	heel bead
	ɪ	hit pity
jouer été	e	
lait jouet merci	ɛ	set tent
plat amour	a æ	bat apple
bas pâte	ɑ ɑː	after car calm
	ʌ	fun cousin
le premier	ə	over above
beurre peur	œ	
peu deux	ø əː	urn fern work
or homme	ɔ	wash pot
mot eau gauche	o ɔː	born cork
genou roue	u	full soot
	uː	boon lewd
rue urne	y	

Diphtongues

Diphthongs

ɪə	beer tier
ɛə	tear fair there
eɪ	date plaice day
aɪ	life buy cry
au	owl foul now
əu	low no
ɔɪ	boil boy oily
uə	poor tour

Nasales

Nasal Vowels

matin plein	ɛ̃
brun	œ̃
sang an dans	ɑ̃
non pont	ɔ̃

In general, we give the pronunciation of each entry in square brackets after the word in question. However, on the English-French side, where the entry is composed of two or more unhyphenated words, each of which is given elsewhere in this dictionary, you will find the pronunciation of each word in its alphabetical position.

FRENCH VERB FORMS

1 Participe présent *2* Participe passé *3* Présent *4* Imparfait *5* Futur *6* Conditionnel *7* Subjonctif présent

acquérir *1* acquérant *2* acquis *3* acquiers, acquérons, acquièrent *4* acquérais *5* acquerrai *7* acquière

ALLER *1* allant *2* allé *3* vais, vas, va, allons, allez, vont *4* allais *5* irai *6* irais *7* aille

asseoir *1* asseyant *2* assis *3* assieds, asseyons, asseyez, asseyent *4* asseyais *5* assiérai *7* asseye

atteindre *1* atteignant *2* atteint *3* atteins, atteignons *4* atteignais *7* atteigne

AVOIR *1* ayant *2* eu *3* ai, as, a, avons, avez, ont *4* avais *5* aurai *6* aurais *7* aie, aies, ait, ayons, ayez, aient

battre *1* battant *2* battu *3* bats, bat, battons *4* battais *7* batte

boire *1* buvant *2* bu *3* bois, buvons, boivent *4* buvais *7* boive

bouillir *1* bouillant *2* bouilli *3* bous, bouillons *4* bouillais *7* bouille

conclure *1* concluant *2* conclu *3* conclus, concluons *4* concluais *7* conclue

conduire *1* conduisant *2* conduit *3* conduis, conduisons *4* conduisais *7* conduise

connaître *1* connaissant *2* connu *3* connais, connaît, connaissons *4* connaissais *7* connaisse

coudre *1* cousant *2* cousu *3* couds, cousons, cousez, cousent *4* cousais *7* couse

courir *1* courant *2* couru *3* cours, courons *4* courais *5* courrai *7* coure

couvrir *1* couvrant *2* couvert *3* couvre, couvrons *4* couvrais *7* couvre

craindre *1* craignant *2* craint *3* crains, craignons *4* craignais *7* craigne

croire *1* croyant *2* cru *3* crois, croyons, croient *4* croyais *7* croie

croître *1* croissant *2* crû, crue, crus, crues *3* croîs, croissons *4* croissais *7* croisse

cueillir *1* cueillant *2* cueilli *3* cueille, cueillons *4* cueillais *5* cueillerai *7* cueille

devoir *1* devant *2* dû, due, dus, dues *3* dois, devons, doivent *4* devais *5* devrai *7* doive

dire *1* disant *2* dit *3* dis, disons, dites, disent *4* disais *7* dise

dormir *1* dormant *2* dormi *3* dors, dormons *4* dormais *7* dorme

écrire *1* écrivant *2* écrit *3* écris, écrivons *4* écrivais *7* écrive

ÊTRE *1* étant *2* été *3* suis, es, est, sommes, êtes, sont *4* étais *5* serai *6* serais *7* sois, sois, soit, soyons, soyez, soient

FAIRE *1* faisant *2* fait *3* fais, fais, fait, faisons, faites, font *4* faisais *5* ferai *6* ferais *7* fasse

falloir *2* fallu *3* faut *4* fallait *5* faudra *7* faille

FINIR *1* finissant *2* fini *3* finis, finis, finit, finissons, finissez, finissent *4* finissais *5* finirai *6* finirais *7* finisse

fuir *1* fuyant *2* fui *3* fuis, fuyons, fuient *4* fuyais *7* fuie

joindre *1* joignant *2* joint *3* joins, joignons *4* joignais *7* joigne

lire *1* lisant *2* lu *3* lis, lisons *4* lisais *7* lise

luire *1* luisant *2* lui *3* luis, luisons *4* luisais *7* luise

maudire *1* maudissant *2* maudit *3* maudis, maudissons *4* maudissait *7* maudisse

mentir *1* mentant *2* menti *3* mens, mentons *4* mentais *7* mente

mettre *1* mettant *2* mis *3* mets, mettons *4* mettais *7* mette

mourir *1* mourant *2* mort *3* meurs, mourons, meurent *4* mourais *5* mourrai *7* meure

naître *1* naissant *2* né *3* nais, naît, naissons *4* naissais *7* naisse

offrir *1* offrant *2* offert *3* offre, offrons *4* offrais *7* offre

PARLER *1* parlant *2* parlé *3* parle, parles, parle, parlons, parlez, parlent *4* parlais, parlais, parlait, parlions, parliez, parlaient *5* parlerai, parleras, parlera, parlerons, parlerez, parleront *6* parlerais, parlerais, parlerait, parlerions, parleriez, parleraient *7*

1 Participe présent **2** Participe passé **3** Présent **4** Imparfait **5** Futur **6** Conditionnel **7** Subjonctif présent

parle, parles, parle, parlions, parliez, parlent *impératif* parle! parlez!

partir *1* partant *2* parti *3* pars, partons *4* partais *7* parte

plaire *1* plaisant *2* plu *3* plais, plaît, plaisons *4* plaisais *7* plaise

pleuvoir *1* pleuvant *2* plu *3* pleut, pleuvent *4* pleuvait *5* pleuvra *7* pleuve

pourvoir *1* pourvoyant *2* pourvu *3* pourvois, pourvoyons, pourvoient *4* pourvoyais *7* pourvoie

pouvoir *1* pouvant *2* pu *3* peux, peut, pouvons, peuvent *4* pouvais *5* pourrai *7* puisse

prendre *1* prenant *2* pris *3* prends, prenons, prennent *4* prenais *7* prenne

prévoir *like voir* *5* prévoirai

RECEVOIR *1* recevant *2* reçu *3* reçois, reçois, reçoit, recevons, recevez, reçoivent *4* recevais *5* recevrai *6* recevrais *7* reçoive

RENDRE *1* rendant *2* rendu *3* rends, rends, rend, rendons, rendez, rendent *4* rendais *5* rendrai *6* rendrais *7* rende

résoudre *1* résolvant *2* résolu *3* résous, résout, résolvons *4* résolvais *7* résolve

rire *1* riant *2* ri *3* ris, rions *4* riais *7* rie

savoir *1* sachant *2* su *3* sais, savons, savent *4* savais *5* saurai *7* sache

impératif sache, sachons, sachez

servir *1* servant *2* servi *3* sers, servons *4* servais *7* serve

sortir *1* sortant *2* sorti *3* sors, sortons *4* sortais *7* sorte

souffrir *1* souffrant *2* souffert *3* souffre, souffrons *4* souffrais *7* souffre

suffire *1* suffisant *2* suffi *3* suffis, suffisons *4* suffisais *7* suffise

suivre *1* suivant *2* suivi *3* suis, suivons *4* suivais *7* suive

taire *1* taisant *2* tu *3* tais, taisons *4* taisais *7* taise

tenir *1* tenant *2* tenu *3* tiens, tenons, tiennent *4* tenais *5* tiendrai *7* tienne

vaincre *1* vainquant *2* vaincu *3* vaincs, vainc, vainquons *4* vainquais *7* vainque

valoir *1* valant *2* valu *3* vaux, vaut, valons *4* valais *5* vaudrai *7* vaille

venir *1* venant *2* venu *3* viens, venons, viennent *4* venais *5* viendrai *7* vienne

vivre *1* vivant *2* vécu *3* vis, vivons *4* vivais *7* vive

voir *1* voyant *2* vu *3* vois, voyons, voient *4* voyais *5* verrai *7* voie

vouloir *1* voulant *2* voulu *3* veux, veut, voulons, veulent *4* voulais *5* voudrai *7* veuille *impératif* veuillez

LE VERBE ANGLAIS

present	pt	pp	present	pt	pp
arise	arose	arisen	drive	drove	driven
awake	awoke	awoken	dwell	dwelt	dwelt
be (am, is, are; being)	was, were	been	eat	ate	eaten
			fall	fell	fallen
			feed	fed	fed
bear	bore	born(e)	feel	felt	felt
beat	beat	beaten	fight	fought	fought
become	became	become	find	found	found
befall	befell	befallen	flee	fled	fled
begin	began	begun	fling	flung	flung
behold	beheld	beheld	fly	flew	flown
bend	bent	bent	forbid	forbad(e)	forbidden
beset	beset	beset	forecast	forecast	forecast
bet	bet, betted	bet, betted	forget	forgot	forgotten
bid (at auction, cards)	bid	bid	forgive	forgave	forgiven
			forsake	forsook	forsaken
			freeze	froze	frozen
bid (say)	bade	bidden	get	got	got, (us) gotten
bind	bound	bound			
bite	bit	bitten	give	gave	given
bleed	bled	bled	go (goes)	went	gone
blow	blew	blown	grind	ground	ground
break	broke	broken	grow	grew	grown
breed	bred	bred	hang	hung	hung
bring	brought	brought	hang (execute)	hanged	hanged
build	built	built			
burn	burnt, burned	burnt, burned	have	had	had
			hear	heard	heard
burst	burst	burst	hide	hid	hidden
buy	bought	bought	hit	hit	hit
can	could	(been able)	hold	held	held
cast	cast	cast	hurt	hurt	hurt
catch	caught	caught	keep	kept	kept
choose	chose	chosen	kneel	knelt, kneeled	knelt, kneeled
cling	clung	clung			
come	came	come	know	knew	known
cost	cost	cost	lay	laid	laid
cost (work out price of)	costed	costed	lead	led	led
			lean	leant, leaned	leant, leaned
creep	crept	crept	leap	leapt, leaped	leapt, leaped
cut	cut	cut			
deal	dealt	dealt	learn	learnt, learned	learnt, learned
dig	dug	dug			
do (3rd person: he/she/it does)	did	done	leave	left	left
			lend	lent	lent
			let	let	let
			lie (lying)	lay	lain
draw	drew	drawn	light	lit, lighted	lit, lighted
dream	dreamed, dreamt	dreamed, dreamt	lose	lost	lost
			make	made	made
drink	drank	drunk	may	might	—

present	pt	pp	present	pt	pp
mean	meant	meant	speed	sped,	sped,
meet	met	met		speeded	speeded
mistake	mistook	mistaken	spell	spelt,	spelt,
mow	mowed	mown,		spelled	spelled
		mowed	spend	spent	spent
must	(had to)	(had to)	spill	spilt,	spilt,
pay	paid	paid		spilled	spilled
put	put	put	spin	spun	spun
quit	quit,	quit,	spit	spat	spat
	quitted	quitted	spoil	spoiled,	spoiled,
read	read	read		spoilt	spoilt
rid	rid	rid	spread	spread	spread
ride	rode	ridden	spring	sprang	sprung
ring	rang	rung	stand	stood	stood
rise	rose	risen	steal	stole	stolen
run	ran	run	stick	stuck	stuck
saw	sawed	sawed,	sting	stung	stung
		sawn	stink	stank	stunk
say	said	said	stride	strode	stridden
see	saw	seen	strike	struck	struck
seek	sought	sought	strive	strove	striven
sell	sold	sold	swear	swore	sworn
send	sent	sent	sweep	swept	swept
set	set	set	swell	swelled	swollen,
sew	sewed	sewn			swelled
shake	shook	shaken	swim	swam	swum
shear	sheared	shorn,	swing	swung	swung
		sheared	take	took	taken
shed	shed	shed	teach	taught	taught
shine	shone	shone	tear	tore	torn
shoot	shot	shot	tell	told	told
show	showed	shown	think	thought	thought
shrink	shrank	shrunk	throw	threw	thrown
shut	shut	shut	thrust	thrust	thrust
sing	sang	sung	tread	trod	trodden
sink	sank	sunk	wake	woke,	woken,
sit	sat	sat		waked	waked
slay	slew	slain	wear	wore	worn
sleep	slept	slept	weave	wove	woven
slide	slid	slid	weave	weaved	weaved
sling	slung	slung	*(wind)*		
slit	slit	slit	wed	wedded,	wedded,
smell	smelt,	smelt,		wed	wed
	smelled	smelled	weep	wept	wept
sow	sowed	sown,	win	won	won
		sowed	wind	wound	wound
speak	spoke	spoken	wring	wrung	wrung
			write	wrote	written

LES NOMBRES

NUMBERS

un (une)	**1**	one
deux	**2**	two
trois	**3**	three
quatre	**4**	four
cinq	**5**	five
six	**6**	six
sept	**7**	seven
huit	**8**	eight
neuf	**9**	nine
dix	**10**	ten
onze	**11**	eleven
douze	**12**	twelve
treize	**13**	thirteen
quatorze	**14**	fourteen
quinze	**15**	fifteen
seize	**16**	sixteen
dix-sept	**17**	seventeen
dix-huit	**18**	eighteen
dix-neuf	**19**	nineteen
vingt	**20**	twenty
vingt et un (une)	**21**	twenty-one
vingt-deux	**22**	twenty-two
trente	**30**	thirty
quarante	**40**	forty
cinquante	**50**	fifty
soixante	**60**	sixty
soixante-dix	**70**	seventy
soixante et onze	**71**	seventy-one
soixante-douze	**72**	seventy-two
quatre-vingts	**80**	eighty
quatre-vingt-un (-une)	**81**	eighty-one
quatre-vingt-dix	**90**	ninety
quatre-vingt-onze	**91**	ninety-one
cent	**100**	a hundred
cent un (une)	**101**	a hundred and one
trois cents	**300**	three hundred
trois cent un (une)	**301**	three hundred and one
mille	**1 000**	a thousand
un million	**1 000 000**	a million

LES NOMBRES

NUMBERS

premier (première), 1er	first, 1st
deuxième, 2e or 2ème	second, 2nd
troisième, 3e or 3ème	third, 3rd
quatrième	fourth, 4th
cinquième	fifth, 5th
sixième	sixth, 6th
septième	seventh
huitième	eighth
neuvième	ninth
dixième	tenth
onzième	eleventh
douzième	twelfth
treizième	thirteenth
quatorzième	fourteenth
quinzième	fifteenth
seizième	sixteenth
dix-septième	seventeenth
dix-huitième	eighteenth
dix-neuvième	nineteenth
vingtième	twentieth
vingt-et-unième	twenty-first
vingt-deuxième	twenty-second
trentième	thirtieth
centième	hundredth
cent-unième	hundred-and-first
millième	thousandth

L'HEURE

THE TIME

quelle heure est-il?	what time is it?
il est ...	it's ...

minuit	midnight
une heure (du matin)	one o'clock (in the morning) , one (am)
une heure cinq	five past one
une heure dix	ten past one
une heure et quart	a quarter past one, one fifteen
une heure vingt-cinq	twenty-five past one, one twenty-five
une heure et demie, une heure trente	half past one, one thirty
deux heures moins vingt-cinq, une heure trente-cinq	twenty-five to two, one thirty-five
deux heures moins vingt, une heure quarante	twenty to two, one forty
deux heures moins le quart, une heure quarante-cinq	a quarter to two, one forty-five
deux heures moins dix, une heure cinquante	ten to two, one fifty
midi	twelve o'clock, midday, noon
deux heures (de l'après-midi)	two o'clock (in the afternoon), two (pm)
sept heures (du soir)	seven o'clock (in the evening), seven (pm)

à quelle heure?	at what time?

à minuit	at midnight
à sept heures	at seven o'clock
à une heure	at one o'clock
dans vingt minutes	in twenty minutes
il y a dix minutes	ten minutes ago

LA DATE

THE DATE

aujourd'hui	today
demain	tomorrow
après-demain	the day after tomorrow
hier	yesterday
avant-hier	the day before yesterday
la veille	the day before, the previous day
le lendemain	the next or following day

le matin	morning
le soir	evening
ce matin	this morning
ce soir	this evening
cet après-midi	this afternoon
hier matin	yesterday morning
hier soir	yesterday evening
demain matin	tomorrow morning
demain soir	tomorrow evening
dans la nuit du samedi au dimanche	during Saturday night, during the night of Saturday to Sunday
il viendra samedi	he's coming on Saturday
le samedi	on Saturdays
tous les samedis	every Saturday
samedi passé *ou* dernier	last Saturday
samedi prochain	next Saturday
samedi en huit	a week on Saturday
samedi en quinze	a fortnight *or* two weeks on Saturday
du lundi au samedi	from Monday to Saturday
tous les jours	every day
une fois par semaine	once a week
une fois par mois	once a month
deux fois par semaine	twice a week
il y a une semaine *ou* huit jours	a week ago
il y a quinze jours	a fortnight *or* two weeks ago
l'année passée *ou* dernière	last year
dans deux jours	in two days
dans huit jours *ou* une semaine	in a week
dans quinze jours	in a fortnight *or* two weeks
le mois prochain	next month
l'année prochaine	next year

quel jour sommes-nous?	*what day is it?*
le 1er/24 octobre 1996	the 1st/24th of October 1996, October 1st/24th 1996
en 1996	in 1996
mille neuf cent quatre-vingt seize	nineteen ninety-six
44 av. J.-C.	44 BC
14 apr. J.-C.	14 AD
au XIXe (siècle)	in the nineteenth century
dans les années trente	in the thirties
il était une fois ...	once upon a time ...

Français-Anglais
French-English

A a

A, a [ɑ] *nm inv* A, a ♦ *abr* = **anticyclone, are**;
(= *ampère*) amp; (= *autoroute*) ≈ M (*BRIT*); **A
comme Anatole** A for Andrew (*BRIT*) *ou*
Able (*US*); **de a à z** from a to z; **prouver qch
par a + b** to prove sth conclusively.

a [a] *vb voir* **avoir**.

====================== *MOT-CLÉ*

à [a] (*à + le* = **au**, *à + les* = **aux**) *prép* **1** (*endroit,
situation*) at, in; **être ~ Paris/au Portugal** to
be in Paris/Portugal; **être ~ la maison/~
l'école** to be at home/at school; **~ la
campagne** in the country; **c'est ~ 10 km/~
20 minutes (d'ici)** it's 10 km/20 minutes
away
2 (*direction*) to; **aller ~ Paris/au Portugal** to
go to Paris/Portugal; **aller ~ la maison/~
l'école** to go home/to school; **~ la campagne**
to the country
3 (*temps*): **~ 3 heures/minuit** at 3 o'clock/
midnight; **au printemps** in the spring; **au
mois de juin** in June; **au départ** at the start,
at the outset; **~ demain/la semaine
prochaine!** see you tomorrow/next week!; **~
visites de 5 heures ~ 6 heures** visiting from
5 to *ou* till 6 o'clock
4 (*attribution, appartenance*) to; **le livre est ~
Paul/~ lui/~ nous** this book is Paul's/his/
ours; **donner qch ~ qn** to give sth to sb; **un
ami ~ moi** a friend of mine; **c'est ~ moi de
le faire** it's up to me to do it
5 (*moyen*) with; **se chauffer au gaz** to have
gas heating; **~ bicyclette** on a *ou* by bicycle;
~ la main/machine by hand/machine; **~ la
télévision/la radio** on television/the radio
6 (*provenance*) from; **boire ~ la bouteille** to
drink from the bottle
7 (*caractérisation, manière*): **l'homme aux
yeux bleus** the man with the blue eyes; **~ la
russe** the Russian way; **glace ~ la framboise**
raspberry ice cream
8 (*but, destination*): **tasse ~ café** coffee cup;
maison ~ vendre house for sale; **problème
~ régler** problem to sort out
9 (*rapport, évaluation, distribution*): **100 km/
unités ~ l'heure** 100 km/units per *ou* an
hour; **payé ~ l'heure** paid by the hour; **cinq**

~ six five to six
10 (*conséquence, résultat*): **~ ce qu'il prétend**
according to him; **~ leur grande surprise**
much to their surprise; **~ nous trois nous
n'avons pas su le faire** we couldn't do it
even between the three of us; **ils sont
arrivés ~ 4** 4 of them arrived (together).

Å *abr* (= *Angström*) A *ou* Å.
A2 *abr* (= *Antenne 2*) French TV channel.
AB *abr* = **assez bien**.
abaissement [abɛsmɑ̃] *nm* lowering; pulling
down.
abaisser [abese] *vt* to lower, bring down;
(*manette*) to pull down; (*fig*) to debase; to
humiliate; **s'~** *vi* to go down; (*fig*) to demean
o.s.; **s'~ à faire/à qch** to stoop *ou* descend to
doing/to sth.
abandon [abɑ̃dɔ̃] *nm* abandoning; deserting;
giving up; withdrawal; surrender,
relinquishing; (*fig*) lack of constraint;
relaxed pose *ou* mood; **être à l'~** to be in a
state of neglect; **laisser à l'~** to abandon.
abandonné, e [abɑ̃dɔne] *adj* (*solitaire*)
deserted; (*route, usine*) disused; (*jardin*)
abandoned.
abandonner [abɑ̃dɔne] *vt* to leave, abandon,
desert; (*projet, activité*) to abandon, give up;
(*SPORT*) to retire *ou* withdraw from; (*céder*)
to surrender, relinquish; **s'~** *vi* to let o.s. go;
s'~ à (*paresse, plaisirs*) to give o.s. up to; **~
qch à qn** to give sth up to sb.
abasourdir [abazurdir] *vt* to stun, stagger.
abat [aba] *etc vb voir* **abattre**.
abat-jour [abaʒur] *nm inv* lampshade.
abats [aba] *vb voir* **abattre** ♦ *nmpl* (*de bœuf,
porc*) offal *sg* (*BRIT*), entrails (*US*); (*de volaille*)
giblets.
abattage [abataʒ] *nm* cutting down, felling.
abattant [abatɑ̃] *vb voir* **abattre** ♦ *nm* leaf, flap.
abattement [abatmɑ̃] *nm* (*physique*)
enfeeblement; (*moral*) dejection,
despondency; (*déduction*) reduction; **~ fiscal**
≈ tax allowance.
abattis [abati] *vb voir* **abattre** ♦ *nmpl* giblets.
abattoir [abatwar] *nm* abattoir (*BRIT*),
slaughterhouse.

abattre [abatʀ(ə)] *vt* (*arbre*) to cut down, fell; (*mur, maison*) to pull down; (*avion, personne*) to shoot down; (*animal*) to shoot, kill; (*fig: physiquement*) to wear out, tire out; (: *moralement*) to demoralize; **s'~** *vi* to crash down; **s'~ sur** (*suj: pluie*) to beat down on; (: *coups, injures*) to rain down on; **~ ses cartes** (*aussi fig*) to lay one's cards on the table; **~ du travail** *ou* **de la besogne** to get through a lot of work.

abattu, e [abaty] *pp de* **abattre** ♦ *adj* (*déprimé*) downcast.

abbatiale [abasjal] *nf* abbey (*church*).

abbaye [abei] *nf* abbey.

abbé [abe] *nm* priest; (*d'une abbaye*) abbot; **M l'~** Father.

abbesse [abɛs] *nf* abbess.

abc, ABC [abese] *nm* alphabet primer; (*fig*) rudiments *pl*.

abcès [apsɛ] *nm* abscess.

abdication [abdikasjɔ̃] *nf* abdication.

abdiquer [abdike] *vi* to abdicate ♦ *vt* to renounce, give up.

abdomen [abdɔmɛn] *nm* abdomen.

abdominal, e, aux [abdɔminal, -o] *adj* abdominal ♦ *nmpl*: **faire des abdominaux** to do exercises for the stomach muscles.

abécédaire [abesedɛʀ] *nm* alphabet primer.

abeille [abɛj] *nf* bee.

aberrant, e [abɛʀɑ̃, -ɑ̃t] *adj* absurd.

aberration [abɛʀasjɔ̃] *nf* aberration.

abêtir [abetiʀ] *vt* to make morons (*ou* a moron) of.

abêtissant, e [abetisɑ̃, -ɑ̃t] *adj* stultifying.

abhorrer [abɔʀe] *vt* to abhor, loathe.

abîme [abim] *nm* abyss, gulf.

abîmer [abime] *vt* to spoil, damage; **s'~** *vi* to get spoilt *ou* damaged; (*fruits*) to spoil; (*tomber*) to sink, founder; **s'~ les yeux** to ruin one's eyes *ou* eyesight.

abject, e [abʒɛkt] *adj* abject, despicable.

abjurer [abʒyʀe] *vt* to abjure, renounce.

ablatif [ablatif] *nm* ablative.

ablation [ablasjɔ̃] *nf* removal.

ablutions [ablysjɔ̃] *nfpl*: **faire ses ~** to perform one's ablutions.

abnégation [abnegasjɔ̃] *nf* (self-)abnegation.

aboie [abwa] *etc vb voir* **aboyer**.

aboiement [abwamɑ̃] *nm* bark, barking *no pl*.

aboierai [abwajəʀe] *etc vb voir* **aboyer**.

abois [abwa] *nmpl*: **aux ~** at bay.

abolir [abɔliʀ] *vt* to abolish.

abolition [abɔlisjɔ̃] *nf* abolition.

abolitionniste [abɔlisjɔnist(ə)] *adj, nmf* abolitionist.

abominable [abɔminabl(ə)] *adj* abominable.

abomination [abɔminasjɔ̃] *nf* abomination.

abondamment [abɔ̃damɑ̃] *adv* abundantly.

abondance [abɔ̃dɑ̃s] *nf* abundance; (*richesse*) affluence; **en ~** in abundance.

abondant, e [abɔ̃dɑ̃, -ɑ̃t] *adj* plentiful, abundant, copious.

abonder [abɔ̃de] *vi* to abound, be plentiful; **~ en** to be full of, abound in; **~ dans le sens de qn** to concur with sb.

abonné, e [abɔne] *nm/f* subscriber; season ticket holder ♦ *adj*: **être ~ à un journal** to subscribe to *ou* have a subscription to a periodical; **être ~ au téléphone** to be on the (tele)phone.

abonnement [abɔnmɑ̃] *nm* subscription; (*pour transports en commun, concerts*) season ticket.

abonner [abɔne] *vt*: **s'~ à** to subscribe to, take out a subscription to.

abord [abɔʀ] *nm*: **être d'un ~ facile** to be approachable; **être d'un ~ difficile** (*personne*) to be unapproachable; (*lieu*) to be hard to reach *ou* difficult to get to; **de prime ~**, **au premier ~** at first sight; **d'~** *adv* first; **tout d'~** first of all.

abordable [abɔʀdabl(ə)] *adj* (*personne*) approachable; (*marchandise*) reasonably priced; (*prix*) affordable, reasonable.

abordage [abɔʀdaʒ] *nm* boarding.

aborder [abɔʀde] *vi* to land ♦ *vt* (*sujet, difficulté*) to tackle; (*personne*) to approach; (*rivage etc*) to reach; (*NAVIG: attaquer*) to board; (: *heurter*) to collide with.

abords [abɔʀ] *nmpl* surroundings.

aborigène [abɔʀiʒɛn] *nm* aborigine, native.

Abou Dhabî, Abu Dhabî [abudabi] *nm* Abu Dhabi.

aboulique [abulik] *adj* totally lacking in willpower.

aboutir [abutiʀ] *vi* (*négociations etc*) to succeed; (*abcès*) to come to a head; **~ à/dans/sur** to end up at/in/on.

aboutissants [abutisɑ̃] *nmpl voir* **tenants**.

aboutissement [abutismɑ̃] *nm* success; (*de concept, projet*) successful realization; (*d'années de travail*) successful conclusion.

aboyer [abwaje] *vi* to bark.

abracadabrant, e [abʀakadabʀɑ̃, -ɑ̃t] *adj* incredible, preposterous.

abrasif, ive [abʀazif, -iv] *adj, nm* abrasive.

abrégé [abʀeʒe] *nm* summary; **en ~** in a shortened *ou* abbreviated form.

abréger [abʀeʒe] *vt* (*texte*) to shorten, abridge; (*mot*) to shorten, abbreviate; (*réunion, voyage*) to cut short, shorten.

abreuver [abʀœve] *vt* to water; (*fig*): **~ qn de** to shower *ou* swamp sb with; (*injures etc*) to shower sb with; **s'~** *vi* to drink.

abreuvoir [abʀœvwaʀ] *nm* watering place.

abréviation [abʀevjasjɔ̃] *nf* abbreviation.

abri [abʀi] *nm* shelter; **à l'~** under cover; **être/se mettre à l'~** to be/get under cover *ou* shelter; **à l'~ de** sheltered from; (*fig*) safe from.

Abribus [abʀibys] *nm* ® bus shelter.

abricot [abʀiko] *nm* apricot.

abricotier [abʀikɔtje] *nm* apricot tree.

abrité, e [abʀite] *adj* sheltered.

abriter [abʀite] vt to shelter; (*loger*) to accommodate; **s'~** to shelter, take cover.

abrogation [abʀɔgasjɔ̃] nf (*JUR*) repeal, abrogation.

abroger [abʀɔʒe] vt to repeal, abrogate.

abrupt, e [abʀypt] adj sheer, steep; (*ton*) abrupt.

abruti, e [abʀyti] nm/f (*fam*) idiot, moron.

abrutir [abʀytiʀ] vt to daze; (*fatiguer*) to exhaust; (*abêtir*) to stupefy.

abrutissant, e [abʀytisɑ̃, -ɑ̃t] adj (*bruit, travail*) stupefying.

abscisse [apsis] nf X axis, abscissa.

absence [apsɑ̃s] nf absence; (*MÉD*) blackout; (*distraction*) mental blank; **en l'~ de** in the absence of.

absent, e [apsɑ̃, -ɑ̃t] adj absent; (*chose*) missing, lacking; (*distrait: air*) vacant, faraway ♦ nm/f absentee.

absentéisme [apsɑ̃teism(ə)] nm absenteeism.

absenter [apsɑ̃te]: **s'~** vi to take time off work; (*sortir*) to leave, go out.

abside [apsid] nf (*ARCHIT*) apse.

absinthe [apsɛ̃t] nf (*boisson*) absinth(e); (*BOT*) wormwood, absinth(e).

absolu, e [apsɔly] adj absolute; (*caractère*) rigid, uncompromising ♦ nm (*PHILOSOPHIE*): **l'~** the Absolute; **dans l'~** in the absolute, in a vacuum.

absolument [apsɔlymɑ̃] adv absolutely.

absolution [apsɔlysjɔ̃] nf absolution; (*JUR*) dismissal (*of case*).

absolutisme [apsɔlytism(ə)] nm absolutism.

absolvais [apsɔlvɛ] etc vb voir **absoudre**.

absorbant, e [apsɔʀbɑ̃, -ɑ̃t] adj absorbent; (*tâche*) absorbing, engrossing.

absorbé, e [apsɔʀbe] adj absorbed, engrossed.

absorber [apsɔʀbe] vt to absorb; (*gén MÉD: manger, boire*) to take; (*ÉCON: firme*) to take over, absorb.

absorption [apsɔʀpsjɔ̃] nf absorption.

absoudre [apsudʀ(ə)] vt to absolve; (*JUR*) to dismiss.

absous, oute [apsu, -ut] pp de **absoudre**.

abstenir [apstəniʀ]: **s'~** vi (*POL*) to abstain; **s'~ de qch/de faire** to refrain from sth/from doing.

abstention [apstɑ̃sjɔ̃] nf abstention.

abstentionnisme [apstɑ̃sjɔnism(ə)] nm abstaining.

abstentionniste [apstɑ̃sjɔnist(ə)] nm abstentionist.

abstenu, e [apstəny] pp de **abstenir**.

abstiendrai [apstjɛ̃dʀe], **abstiens** [apstjɛ̃] etc voir **abstenir**.

abstinence [apstinɑ̃s] nf abstinence; **faire ~** to abstain (*from meat on Fridays*).

abstint [apstɛ̃] etc vb voir **abstenir**.

abstraction [apstʀaksjɔ̃] nf abstraction; **faire ~ de** to set ou leave aside; **~ faite de ...** leaving aside ....

abstraire [apstʀɛʀ] vt to abstract; **s'~ (de)** (*s'isoler*) to cut o.s. off (from).

abstrait, e [apstʀɛ, -ɛt] pp de **abstraire** ♦ adj abstract ♦ nm: **dans l'~** in the abstract.

abstraitement [apstʀɛtmɑ̃] adv abstractly.

abstrayais [apstʀɛjɛ] etc vb voir **abstraire**.

absurde [apsyʀd(ə)] adj absurd ♦ nm absurdity; (*PHILOSOPHIE*): **l'~** absurd; **par l'~** ad absurdio.

absurdité [apsyʀdite] nf absurdity.

abus [aby] nm (*excès*) abuse, misuse; (*injustice*) abuse; **~ de confiance** breach of trust; (*détournement de fonds*) embezzlement; **~ de pouvoir** abuse of power.

abuser [abyze] vi to go too far, overstep the mark ♦ vt to deceive, mislead; **s'~** vi (*se méprendre*) to be mistaken; **~ de** vt (*force, droit*) to misuse; (*alcool*) to take to excess; (*violer, duper*) to take advantage of.

abusif, ive [abyzif, -iv] adj exorbitant; (*punition*) excessive; (*pratique*) improper.

abusivement [abyzivmɑ̃] adv exorbitantly; excessively; improperly.

AC sigle f (= appellation contrôlée) guarantee of quality of wine.

acabit [akabi] nm: **du même ~** of the same type.

acacia [akasja] nm (*BOT*) acacia.

académicien, ne [akademisjɛ̃, -ɛn] nm/f academician.

académie [akademi] nf (*société*) learned society; (*école: d'art, de danse*) academy; (*ART: nu*) nude; (*SCOL: circonscription*) ≈ regional education authority; **l'A~ (française)** the French Academy.

---

*The **Académie française** was founded by Cardinal Richelieu in 1635 during the reign of Louis XIII. It consists of forty elected scholars and writers who are known as "les Quarante" or "les Immortels". One of the Académie's functions is to regulate the development of the French language and its recommendations are frequently the subject of lively public debate. It has produced several editions of its famous dictionary and also awards various literary prizes.*

---

académique [akademik] adj academic.

Acadie [akadi] nf: **l'~** the Maritime Provinces.

acadien, ne [akadjɛ̃, -ɛn] adj Acadian, of ou from the Maritime Provinces.

acajou [akaʒu] nm mahogany.

acariâtre [akaʀjɑtʀ(ə)] adj sour(-tempered) (*BRIT*), cantankerous.

accablant, e [akɑblɑ̃, -ɑ̃t] adj (*témoignage, preuve*) overwhelming.

accablement [akɑbləmɑ̃] nm deep despondency.

accabler [akable] vt to overwhelm, overcome; (*suj: témoignage*) to condemn, damn; **~ qn d'injures** to heap ou shower abuse on sb; **~**

qn de travail to overburden sb with work;
accablé de dettes/soucis weighed down
with debts/cares.
accalmie [akalmi] *nf* lull.
accaparant, e [akaparɑ̃, -ɑ̃t] *adj* that takes up
all one's time *ou* attention.
accaparer [akapaʀe] *vt* to monopolize; (*suj:
travail etc*) to take up (all) the time *ou*
attention of.
accéder [aksede]: **~ à** *vt* (*lieu*) to reach; (*fig:
pouvoir*) to accede to; (: *poste*) to attain;
(*accorder: requête*) to grant, accede to.
accélérateur [akseleʀatœʀ] *nm* accelerator.
accélération [akseleʀasjɔ̃] *nf* speeding up;
acceleration.
accéléré [akseleʀe] *nm*: **en ~** (*CINÉ*) speeded
up.
accélérer [akseleʀe] *vt* (*mouvement, travaux*) to
speed up ♦ *vi* (*AUTO*) to accelerate.
accent [aksɑ̃] *nm* accent; (*inflexions
expressives*) tone (of voice); (*PHONÉTIQUE,
fig*) stress; **aux ~s de** (*musique*) to the
strains of; **mettre l'~ sur** (*fig*) to stress; **~
aigu/grave/circonflexe** acute/grave/
circumflex accent.
accentuation [aksɑ̃tɥasjɔ̃] *nf* accenting;
stressing.
accentué, e [aksɑ̃tɥe] *adj* marked,
pronounced.
accentuer [aksɑ̃tɥe] *vt* (*LING: orthographe*) to
accent; (: *phonétique*) to stress, accent; (*fig*)
to accentuate, emphasize; (: *effort, pression*)
to increase; **s'~** *vi* to become more marked
ou pronounced.
acceptable [akseptabl(ə)] *adj* satisfactory,
acceptable.
acceptation [akseptasjɔ̃] *nf* acceptance.
accepter [aksepte] *vt* to accept; (*tolérer*): **~
que qn fasse** to agree to sb doing; **~ de faire**
to agree to do.
acception [aksepsjɔ̃] *nf* meaning, sense; **dans
toute l'~ du terme** in the full sense *ou*
meaning of the word.
accès [akse] *nm* (*à un lieu, INFORM*) access;
(*MÉD*) attack; (: *de toux*) fit, bout ♦ *nmpl*
(*routes etc*) means of access, approaches;
d'~ facile/malaisé easily/not easily
accessible; **donner ~ à** (*lieu*) to give access
to; (*carrière*) to open the door to; **avoir ~
auprès de qn** to have access to sb; **l'~ aux
quais est interdit aux personnes non munies
d'un billet** ticket-holders only on platforms,
no access to platforms without a ticket; **~
de colère** fit of anger; **~ de joie** burst of joy.
accessible [aksesibl(ə)] *adj* accessible;
(*personne*) approachable; (*livre, sujet*): **~ à qn**
within the reach of sb; (*sensible*): **~ à la
pitié/l'amour** open to pity/love.
accession [aksesjɔ̃] *nf*: **~ à** accession to; (*à un
poste*) attainment of; **~ à la propriété** home-
ownership.
accessit [aksesit] *nm* (*SCOL*) ≈ certificate of

merit.
accessoire [akseswaʀ] *adj* secondary, of
secondary importance; (*frais*) incidental
♦ *nm* accessory; (*THÉÂT*) prop.
accessoirement [akseswaʀmɑ̃] *adv*
secondarily; incidentally.
accessoiriste [akseswaʀist(ə)] *nm/f* (*TV, CINÉ*)
property man/woman.
accident [aksidɑ̃] *nm* accident; **par ~** by
chance; **~ de parcours** mishap; **~ de la route**
road accident; **~ du travail** accident at
work; industrial injury *ou* accident; **~s de
terrain** unevenness of the ground.
accidenté, e [aksidɑ̃te] *adj* damaged *ou*
injured (in an accident); (*relief, terrain*)
uneven; hilly.
accidentel, le [aksidɑ̃tel] *adj* accidental.
accidentellement [aksidɑ̃telmɑ̃] *adv* (*par
hasard*) accidentally; (*mourir*) in an accident.
accise [aksiz] *nf*: **droit d'~(s)** excise duty.
acclamation [aklamasjɔ̃] *nf*: **par ~** (*vote*) by
acclamation; **~s** *nfpl* cheers, cheering *sg*.
acclamer [aklame] *vt* to cheer, acclaim.
acclimatation [aklimatasjɔ̃] *nf*
acclimatization.
acclimater [aklimate] *vt* to acclimatize; **s'~** *vi*
to become acclimatized.
accointances [akwɛ̃tɑ̃s] *nfpl*: **avoir des ~ avec**
to have contacts with.
accolade [akɔlad] *nf* (*amicale*) embrace;
(*signe*) brace; **donner l'~ à qn** to embrace
sb.
accoler [akɔle] *vt* to place side by side.
accommodant, e [akɔmɔdɑ̃, -ɑ̃t] *adj*
accommodating, easy-going.
accommodement [akɔmɔdmɑ̃] *nm*
compromise.
accommoder [akɔmɔde] *vt* (*CULIN*) to
prepare; (*points de vue*) to reconcile; **~ qch à**
(*adapter*) to adapt sth to; **s'~ de** to put up
with; (*se contenter de*) to make do with; **s'~ à**
(*s'adapter*) to adapt to.
accompagnateur, trice [akɔ̃paɲatœʀ, -tʀis]
nm/f (*MUS*) accompanist; (*de voyage*) guide;
(: *de voyage organisé*) courier; (*d'enfants*)
accompanying adult.
accompagnement [akɔ̃paɲmɑ̃] *nm* (*MUS*)
accompaniment; (*MIL*) support.
accompagner [akɔ̃paɲe] *vt* to accompany, be
ou go *ou* come with; (*MUS*) to accompany;
s'~ de to bring, be accompanied by.
accompli, e [akɔ̃pli] *adj* accomplished.
accomplir [akɔ̃pliʀ] *vt* (*tâche, projet*) to carry
out; (*souhait*) to fulfil; **s'~** *vi* to be fulfilled.
accomplissement [akɔ̃plismɑ̃] *nm* carrying
out; fulfilment (*BRIT*), fulfillment (*US*).
accord [akɔʀ] *nm* (*entente, convention, LING*)
agreement; (*entre des styles, tons etc*)
harmony; (*consentement*) agreement,
consent; (*MUS*) chord; **donner son ~** to give
one's agreement; **mettre 2 personnes d'~** to
make 2 people come to an agreement,

reconcile 2 people; **se mettre d'**~ to come to an agreement (with each other); **être d'**~ to agree; **être d'**~ **avec qn** to agree with sb; **d'**~**!** OK!, right!; **d'un commun** ~ of one accord; ~ **parfait** (*MUS*) tonic chord.

accord-cadre, *pl* **accords-cadres** [akɔʀkadʀ(ə)] *nm* framework *ou* outline agreement.

accordéon [akɔʀdeɔ̃] *nm* (*MUS*) accordion.

accordéoniste [akɔʀdeɔnist(ə)] *nm/f* accordionist.

accorder [akɔʀde] *vt* (*faveur, délai*) to grant; (*attribuer*): ~ **de l'importance/de la valeur à qch** to attach importance/value to sth; (*harmoniser*) to match; (*MUS*) to tune; **s'**~ to get on together; (*être d'accord*) to agree; (*couleurs, caractères*) to go together, match; (*LING*) to agree; **je vous accorde que** ... I grant you that ....

accordeur [akɔʀdœʀ] *nm* (*MUS*) tuner.

accoster [akɔste] *vt* (*NAVIG*) to draw alongside; (*personne*) to accost ♦ *vi* (*NAVIG*) to berth.

accotement [akɔtmɑ̃] *nm* (*de route*) verge (*BRIT*), shoulder; ~ **stabilisé/non stabilisé** hard shoulder/soft verge *ou* shoulder.

accoter [akɔte] *vt*: ~ **qch contre/à** to lean *ou* rest sth against/on; **s'**~ **contre/à** to lean against/on.

accouchement [akuʃmɑ̃] *nm* delivery, (child)birth; (*travail*) labour (*BRIT*), labor (*US*); ~ **à terme** delivery at (full) term; ~ **sans douleur** natural childbirth.

accoucher [akuʃe] *vi* to give birth, have a baby; (*être en travail*) to be in labour (*BRIT*) *ou* labor (*US*) ♦ *vt* to deliver; ~ **d'un garçon** to give birth to a boy.

accoucheur [akuʃœʀ] *nm*: (**médecin**) ~ obstetrician.

accoucheuse [akuʃøz] *nf* midwife.

accouder [akude]: **s'**~ *vi*: **s'**~ **à/contre/sur** to rest one's elbows on/against/on; **accoudé à la fenêtre** leaning on the windowsill.

accoudoir [akudwaʀ] *nm* armrest.

accouplement [akupləmɑ̃] *nm* coupling; mating.

accoupler [akuple] *vt* to couple; (*pour la reproduction*) to mate; **s'**~ to mate.

accourir [akuʀiʀ] *vi* to rush *ou* run up.

accoutrement [akutʀəmɑ̃] *nm* (*péj*) getup (*BRIT*), outfit.

accoutrer [akutʀe] (*péj*) *vt* to do *ou* get up; **s'**~ to do *ou* get o.s. up.

accoutumance [akutymɑ̃s] *nf* (*gén*) adaptation; (*MÉD*) addiction.

accoutumé, e [akutyme] *adj* (*habituel*) customary, usual; **comme à l'**~**e** as is customary *ou* usual.

accoutumer [akutyme] *vt*: ~ **qn à qch/faire** to accustom sb to sth/to doing; **s'**~ **à** to get accustomed *ou* used to.

accréditer [akʀedite] *vt* (*nouvelle*) to

substantiate; ~ **qn (auprès de)** to accredit sb (to).

accro [akʀo] *nm/f* (*fam*: = *accroché(e)*) addict.

accroc [akʀo] *nm* (*déchirure*) tear; (*fig*) hitch, snag; **sans** ~ without a hitch; **faire un** ~ **à** (*vêtement*) to make a tear in, tear; (*fig: règle etc*) to infringe.

accrochage [akʀoʃaʒ] *nm* hanging (up); hitching (up); (*AUTO*) (minor) collision; (*MIL*) encounter, engagement; (*dispute*) clash, brush.

accroche-cœur [akʀoʃkœʀ] *nm* kiss-curl.

accrocher [akʀoʃe] *vt* (*suspendre*): ~ **qch à** to hang sth (up) on; (*attacher: remorque*): ~ **qch à** to hitch sth (up) to; (*heurter*) to catch; to hit; (*déchirer*): ~ **qch (à)** to catch sth (on); (*MIL*) to engage; (*fig*) to catch, attract ♦ *vi* to stick, get stuck; (*fig: pourparlers etc*) to hit a snag; (*plaire: disque etc*) to catch on; **s'**~ (*se disputer*) to have a clash *ou* brush; (*ne pas céder*) to hold one's own, hang on in (*fam*); **s'**~ **à** (*rester pris à*) to catch on; (*agripper, fig*) to hang on *ou* cling to.

accrocheur, euse [akʀoʃœʀ, -øz] *adj* (*vendeur, concurrent*) tenacious; (*publicité*) eye-catching; (*titre*) catchy, eye-catching.

accroire [akʀwaʀ] *vt*: **faire** *ou* **laisser** ~ **à qn qch/que** to give sb to believe sth/that.

accroîs [akʀwa], **accroissais** [akʀwasɛ] *etc vb voir* **accroître**.

accroissement [akʀwasmɑ̃] *nm* increase.

accroître [akʀwatʀ(ə)] *vt*, **s'**~ *vi* to increase.

accroupi, e [akʀupi] *adj* squatting, crouching (down).

accroupir [akʀupiʀ]: **s'**~ *vi* to squat, crouch (down).

accru, e [akʀy] *pp de* **accroître**.

accu [aky] *nm* (*fam*: = *accumulateur*) accumulator, battery.

accueil [akœj] *nm* welcome; (*endroit*) reception (desk); (: *dans une gare*) information kiosk; **comité/centre d'**~ reception committee/centre.

accueillant, e [akœjɑ̃, -ɑ̃t] *adj* welcoming, friendly.

accueillir [akœjiʀ] *vt* to welcome; (*loger*) to accommodate.

acculer [akyle] *vt*: ~ **qn à** *ou* **contre** to drive sb back against; ~ **qn dans** to corner sb in; ~ **qn à** (*faillite*) to drive sb to the brink of.

accumulateur [akymylatœʀ] *nm* accumulator, battery.

accumulation [akymylɑsjɔ̃] *nf* accumulation; **chauffage/radiateur à** ~ (night-)storage heating/heater.

accumuler [akymyle] *vt* to accumulate, amass; **s'**~ *vi* to accumulate; to pile up.

accusateur, trice [akyzatœʀ, -tʀis] *nm/f* accuser ♦ *adj* accusing; (*document, preuve*) incriminating.

accusatif [akyzatif] *nm* (*LING*) accusative.

accusation [akyzɑsjɔ̃] *nf* (*gén*) accusation;

(*JUR*) charge; (*partie*): **l'**~ the prosecution; **mettre en** ~ to indict; **acte d'**~ bill of indictment.

accusé, e [akyze] *nm/f* accused; (*prévenu(e)*) defendant ♦ *nm*: ~ **de réception** acknowledgement of receipt.

accuser [akyze] *vt* to accuse; (*fig*) to emphasize, bring out; (: *montrer*) to show; **s'**~ *vi* (*s'accentuer*) to become more marked; ~ **qn de** to accuse sb of; (*JUR*) to charge sb with; ~ **qn/qch de qch** (*rendre responsable*) to blame sb/sth for sth; **s'**~ **de qch/d'avoir fait qch** to admit sth/having done sth; to blame *o.s.* for sth/for having done sth; ~ **réception de** to acknowledge receipt of; ~ **le coup** (*aussi fig*) to be visibly affected.

acerbe [asɛrb(ə)] *adj* caustic, acid.

acéré, e [asere] *adj* sharp.

acétate [asetat] *nm* acetate.

acétique [asetik] *adj*: **acide** ~ acetic acid.

acétone [asetɔn] *nf* acetone.

acétylène [asetilɛn] *nm* acetylene.

ACF *sigle m* (= *Automobile Club de France*) ≈ AA (*BRIT*), ≈ AAA (*US*).

ach. *abr* = **achète**.

achalandé, e [aʃalɑ̃de] *adj*: **bien/mal** ~ well-/poorly stocked.

acharné, e [aʃarne] *adj* (*lutte, adversaire*) fierce, bitter; (*travail*) relentless, unremitting.

acharnement [aʃarnəmɑ̃] *nm* fierceness; relentlessness.

acharner [aʃarne]: **s'**~ *vi*: **s'**~ **sur** to go at fiercely, hound; **s'**~ **contre** to set o.s. against; to dog, pursue; (*suj: malchance*) to hound; **s'**~ **à faire** to try doggedly to do; to persist in doing.

achat [aʃa] *nm* buying *no pl*; (*article acheté*) purchase; **faire l'**~ **de** to buy, purchase; **faire des** ~**s** to do some shopping, buy a few things.

acheminement [aʃminmɑ̃] *nm* conveyance.

acheminer [aʃmine] *vt* (*courrier*) to forward, dispatch; (*troupes*) to convey, transport; (*train*) to route; **s'**~ **vers** to head for.

acheter [aʃte] *vt* to buy, purchase; (*soudoyer*) to buy, bribe; ~ **qch à** (*marchand*) to buy *ou* purchase sth from; (*ami etc: offrir*) to buy sth for; ~ **à crédit** to buy on credit.

acheteur, euse [aʃtœr, -øz] *nm/f* buyer; shopper; (*COMM*) buyer; (*JUR*) vendee, purchaser.

achevé, e [aʃve] *adj*: **d'un ridicule** ~ thoroughly *ou* absolutely ridiculous; **d'un comique** ~ absolutely hilarious.

achèvement [aʃɛvmɑ̃] *nm* completion, finishing.

achever [aʃve] *vt* to complete, finish; (*blessé*) to finish off; **s'**~ *vi* to end.

achoppement [aʃɔpmɑ̃] *nm*: **pierre d'**~ stumbling block.

acide [asid] *adj* sour, sharp; (*ton*) acid, biting;

(*CHIMIE*) acid(ic) ♦ *nm* acid.

acidifier [asidifje] *vt* to acidify.

acidité [asidite] *nf* sharpness; acidity.

acidulé, e [asidyle] *adj* slightly acid; **bonbons** ~**s** acid drops (*BRIT*), ≈ lemon drops (*US*).

acier [asje] *nm* steel; ~ **inoxydable** stainless steel.

aciérie [asjeri] *nf* steelworks *sg*.

acné [akne] *nf* acne.

acolyte [akɔlit] *nm* (*péj*) associate.

acompte [akɔ̃t] *nm* deposit; (*versement régulier*) instalment; (*sur somme due*) payment on account; (*sur salaire*) advance; **un** ~ **de 100 F** 100 F on account.

acoquiner [akɔkine]: **s'**~ **avec** *vt* (*péj*) to team up with.

Açores [asɔr] *nfpl*: **les** ~ the Azores.

à-côté [akote] *nm* side-issue; (*argent*) extra.

à-coup [aku] *nm* (*du moteur*) (hic)cough; (*fig*) jolt; **sans** ~**s** smoothly; **par** ~**s** by fits and starts.

acoustique [akustik] *nf* (*d'une salle*) acoustics *pl*; (*science*) acoustics *sg* ♦ *adj* acoustic.

acquéreur [akerœr] *nm* buyer, purchaser; **se porter/se rendre** ~ **de qch** to announce one's intention to purchase/to purchase sth.

acquérir [akerir] *vt* to acquire; (*par achat*) to purchase, acquire; (*valeur*) to gain; (*résultats*) to achieve; **ce que ses efforts lui ont acquis** what his efforts have won *ou* gained (for) him.

acquiers [akjɛr] *etc vb voir* **acquérir**.

acquiescement [akjɛsmɑ̃] *nm* acquiescence, agreement.

acquiescer [akjese] *vi* (*opiner*) to agree; (*consentir*): ~ (**à qch**) to acquiesce *ou* assent (to sth).

acquis, e [aki, -iz] *pp de* **acquérir** ♦ *nm* (accumulated) experience; (*avantage*) gain ♦ *adj* (*voir* **acquérir**) acquired; gained; achieved; **être** ~ **à** (*plan, idée*) to be in full agreement with; **son aide nous est** ~**e** we can count on *ou* be sure of his help; **tenir qch pour** ~ to take sth for granted.

acquisition [akizizjɔ̃] *nf* acquisition; (*achat*) purchase; **faire l'**~ **de** to acquire; to purchase.

acquit [aki] *vb voir* **acquérir** ♦ *nm* (*quittance*) receipt; **pour** ~ received; **par** ~ **de conscience** to set one's mind at rest.

acquittement [akitmɑ̃] *nm* acquittal; payment, settlement.

acquitter [akite] *vt* (*JUR*) to acquit; (*facture*) to pay, settle; **s'**~ **de** to discharge; (*promesse, tâche*) to fulfil (*BRIT*), fulfill (*US*), carry out.

âcre [ɑkr(ə)] *adj* acrid, pungent.

âcreté [ɑkrəte] *nf* acridness, pungency.

acrimonie [akrimɔni] *nf* acrimony.

acrobate [akrɔbat] *nm/f* acrobat.

acrobatie [akrɔbasi] *nf* (*art*) acrobatics *sg*; (*exercice*) acrobatic feat; ~ **aérienne** aerobatics *sg*.

acrobatique [akʀɔbatik] *adj* acrobatic.
acronyme [akʀɔnim] *nm* acronym.
Acropole [akʀɔpɔl] *nf*: l'~ the Acropolis.
acrylique [akʀilik] *adj, nm* acrylic.
acte [akt(ə)] *nm* act, action; (*THÉÂT*) act; ~**s**
nmpl (*compte-rendu*) proceedings; **prendre** ~
de to note, take note of; **faire** ~ **de présence**
to put in an appearance; **faire** ~ **de**
candidature to submit an application; ~
d'accusation charge (*BRIT*), bill of
indictment; ~ **de baptême** baptismal
certificate; ~ **de mariage/naissance**
marriage/birth certificate; ~ **de vente** bill
of sale.
acteur [aktœʀ] *nm* actor.
actif, ive [aktif, -iv] *adj* active ♦ *nm* (*COMM*)
assets *pl*; (*LING*) active (voice); (*fig*): **avoir à**
son ~ to have to one's credit; (*fig*): **avoir à**
people in employment; **mettre à son** ~ to
add to one's list of achievements; l'~ **et le**
passif assets and liabilities; **prendre une**
part active à qch to take an active part in
sth; **population active** working population.
action [aksjɔ̃] *nf* (*gén*) action; (*COMM*) share;
une bonne/mauvaise ~ a good/an unkind
deed; **mettre en** ~ to put into action; **passer**
à l'~ to take action; **sous l'**~ **de** under the
effect of; l'~ **syndicale** (the) union action;
un film d'~ an action film *ou* movie; ~ **en**
diffamation libel action; ~ **de grâce(s)** (*REL*)
thanksgiving.
actionnaire [aksjɔnɛʀ] *nm/f* shareholder.
actionner [aksjɔne] *vt* to work; to activate; to
operate.
active [aktiv] *adj f voir* **actif**.
activement [aktivmɑ̃] *adv* actively.
activer [aktive] *vt* to speed up; (*CHIMIE*) to
activate; **s'**~ *vi* (*s'affairer*) to bustle about; (*se*
hâter) to hurry up.
activisme [aktivism(ə)] *nm* activism.
activiste [aktivist(ə)] *nm/f* activist.
activité [aktivite] *nf* activity; **en** ~ (*volcan*)
active; (*fonctionnaire*) in active life;
(*militaire*) on active service.
actrice [aktʀis] *nf* actress.
actualiser [aktɥalize] *vt* to actualize; (*mettre à*
jour) to bring up to date.
actualité [aktɥalite] *nf* (*d'un problème*)
topicality; (*événements*): l'~ current events;
les ~**s** (*CINÉ, TV*) the news; l'~ **politique/**
sportive the political/sports *ou* sporting
news; **les** ~**s télévisées** the television news;
d'~ topical.
actuel, le [aktɥɛl] *adj* (*présent*) present;
(*d'actualité*) topical; (*non virtuel*) actual; **à**
l'**heure** ~**le** at this moment in time, at the
moment.
actuellement [aktɥɛlmɑ̃] *adv* at present, at
the present time.
acuité [akɥite] *nf* acuteness.
acuponcteur, acupuncteur [akypɔ̃ktœʀ] *nm*
acupuncturist.

acuponcture, acupuncture [akypɔ̃ktyʀ] *nf*
acupuncture.
adage [adaʒ] *nm* adage.
adagio [ada(d)ʒjo] *adv, nm* adagio.
adaptable [adaptabl(ə)] *adj* adaptable.
adaptateur, trice [adaptatœʀ, -tʀis] *nm/f*
adapter.
adaptation [adaptɑsjɔ̃] *nf* adaptation.
adapter [adapte] *vt* to adapt; **s'**~ (**à**) (*suj:*
personne) to adapt (to); (: *objet, prise etc*) to
apply (to); ~ **qch à** (*approprier*) to adapt sth
to (fit); ~ **qch sur/dans/à** (*fixer*) to fit sth
on/into/to.
addenda [adɛ̃da] *nm inv* addenda.
Addis-Ababa [adisababa], **Addis-Abeba**
[adisababa] *n* Addis Ababa.
additif [aditif] *nm* additional clause;
(*substance*) additive; ~ **alimentaire** food
additive.
addition [adisjɔ̃] *nf* addition; (*au café*) bill.
additionnel, le [adisjɔnɛl] *adj* additional.
additionner [adisjɔne] *vt* to add (up); **s'**~ *vi* to
add up; ~ **un produit d'eau** to add water to a
product.
adduction [adyksjɔ̃] *nf* (*de gaz, d'eau*)
conveyance.
ADEP *sigle f* (= *Agence nationale pour le*
développement de l'éducation permanente)
national body which promotes adult
education.
adepte [adɛpt(ə)] *nm/f* follower.
adéquat, e [adekwa, -at] *adj* appropriate,
suitable.
adéquation [adekwɑsjɔ̃] *nf* appropriateness;
(*LING*) adequacy.
adhérence [adeʀɑ̃s] *nf* adhesion.
adhérent, e [adeʀɑ̃, -ɑ̃t] *nm/f* (*de club*)
member.
adhérer [adeʀe] *vi* (*coller*) to adhere, stick; ~ **à**
(*coller*) to adhere *ou* stick to; (*se rallier à:*
parti, club) to join; to be a member of;
(: *opinion, mouvement*) to support.
adhésif, ive [adezif, -iv] *adj* adhesive, sticky
♦ *nm* adhesive.
adhésion [adezjɔ̃] *nf* (*à un club*) joining;
membership; (*à une opinion*) support.
ad hoc [adɔk] *adj* ad hoc.
adieu, x [adjø] *excl* goodbye ♦ *nm* farewell;
dire ~ **à qn** to say goodbye *ou* farewell to
sb; **dire** ~ **à qch** (*renoncer*) to say *ou* wave
goodbye to sth.
adipeux, euse [adipø, -øz] *adj* bloated, fat;
(*ANAT*) adipose.
adjacent, e [adʒasɑ̃, -ɑ̃t] *adj*: ~ (**à**) adjacent
(to).
adjectif [adʒɛktif] *nm* adjective; ~ **attribut**
adjectival complement; ~ **épithète**
attributive adjective.
adjectival, e, aux [adʒɛktival, -o] *adj*
adjectival.
adjoignais [adʒwaɲɛ] *etc vb voir* **adjoindre**.
adjoindre [adʒwɛ̃dʀ(ə)] *vt*: ~ **qch à** to attach

sth to; (*ajouter*) to add sth to; ~ **qn à**
(*personne*) to appoint sb as an assistant to;
(*comité*) to appoint sb to, attach sb to; **s'~** *vt*
(*collaborateur etc*) to take on, appoint.
adjoint, e [adʒwɛ̃, -wɛ̃t] *pp de* **adjoindre ♦** *nm/f*
assistant; **directeur** ~ assistant manager.
adjonction [adʒɔ̃ksjɔ̃] *nf* (*voir adjoindre*)
attaching; addition; appointment.
adjudant [adʒydɑ̃] *nm* (*MIL*) warrant officer;
~-chef ≈ warrant officer 1st class (*BRIT*),
≈ chief warrant officer (*US*).
adjudicataire [adʒydikatɛʀ] *nm/f* successful
bidder, purchaser; (*pour travaux*) successful
tenderer (*BRIT*) *ou* bidder (*US*).
adjudicateur, trice [adʒydikatœʀ, -tʀis] *nm/f*
(*aux enchères*) seller.
adjudication [adʒydikasjɔ̃] *nf* sale by auction;
(*pour travaux*) invitation to tender (*BRIT*) *ou*
bid (*US*).
adjuger [adʒyʒe] *vt* (*prix, récompense*) to
award; (*lors d'une vente*) to auction (off); **s'~**
vt to take for o.s; **adjugé!** (*vendu*) gone!,
sold!
adjurer [adʒyʀe] *vt:* ~ **qn de faire** to implore
ou beg sb to do.
adjuvant [adʒyvɑ̃] *nm* (*médicament*) adjuvant;
(*additif*) additive; (*stimulant*) stimulant.
admettre [admɛtʀ(ə)] *vt* (*visiteur, nouveau-
venu*) to admit, let in; (*candidat: SCOL*) to
pass; (*TECH: gaz, eau, air*) to admit; (*tolérer*) to
allow, accept; (*reconnaître*) to admit,
acknowledge; (*supposer*) to suppose;
j'admets que ... I admit that ...; **je n'admets
pas que tu fasses cela** I won't allow you to
do that; **admettons que ...** let's suppose that
...; **admettons** let's suppose so.
administrateur, trice [administʀatœʀ, -tʀis]
nm/f (*COMM*) director; (*ADMIN*)
administrator; ~ **délégué** managing
director; ~ **judiciaire** receiver.
administratif, ive [administʀatif, -iv] *adj*
administrative ♦ *nm* person in
administration.
administration [administʀasjɔ̃] *nf*
administration; **l'A~** ≈ the Civil Service.
administré, e [administʀe] *nm/f* ≈ citizen.
administrer [administʀe] *vt* (*firme*) to manage,
run; (*biens, remède, sacrement etc*) to
administer.
admirable [admiʀabl(ə)] *adj* admirable,
wonderful.
admirablement [admiʀabləmɑ̃] *adv*
admirably.
admirateur, trice [admiʀatœʀ, -tʀis] *nm/f*
admirer.
admiratif, ive [admiʀatif, -iv] *adj* admiring.
admiration [admiʀasjɔ̃] *nf* admiration; **être en**
~ **devant** to be lost in admiration before.
admirativement [admiʀativmɑ̃] *adv*
admiringly.
admirer [admiʀe] *vt* to admire.
admis, e [admi, -iz] *pp de* **admettre**.

admissibilité [admisibilite] *nf* eligibility;
admissibility, acceptability.
admissible [admisibl(ə)] *adj* (*candidat*) eligible;
(*comportement*) admissible, acceptable;
(*JUR*) receivable.
admission [admisjɔ̃] *nf* admission; **tuyau d'~**
intake pipe; **demande d'~** application for
membership; **service des ~s** admissions.
admonester [admɔnɛste] *vt* to admonish.
ADN *sigle m* (= *acide désoxyribonucléique*) DNA.
ado [ado] *nm/f* (*fam: = adolescent(e)*)
adolescent, teenager.
adolescence [adɔlesɑ̃s] *nf* adolescence.
adolescent, e [adɔlesɑ̃, -ɑ̃t] *nm/f* adolescent,
teenager.
adonner [adɔne]: **s'~ à** *vt* (*sport*) to devote o.s.
to; (*boisson*) to give o.s. over to.
adopter [adɔpte] *vt* to adopt; (*projet de loi etc*)
to pass.
adoptif, ive [adɔptif, -iv] *adj* (*parents*)
adoptive; (*fils, patrie*) adopted.
adoption [adɔpsjɔ̃] *nf* adoption; **son pays/sa
ville d'~** his adopted country/town.
adorable [adɔʀabl(ə)] *adj* adorable.
adoration [adɔʀasjɔ̃] *nf* adoration; (*REL*)
worship; **être en** ~ **devant** to be lost in
adoration before.
adorer [adɔʀe] *vt* to adore; (*REL*) to worship.
adosser [adose] *vt:* ~ **qch à** *ou* **contre** to stand
sth against; **s'~ à** *ou* **contre** to lean with
one's back against; **être adossé à** *ou* **contre**
to be leaning with one's back against.
adoucir [adusiʀ] *vt* (*goût, température*) to make
milder; (*avec du sucre*) to sweeten; (*peau,
voix, eau*) to soften; (*caractère, personne*) to
mellow; (*peine*) to soothe, allay; **s'~** *vi* to
become milder; to soften; to mellow.
adoucissement [adusismɑ̃] *nm* becoming
milder; sweetening; softening; mellowing;
soothing.
adoucisseur [adusisœʀ] *nm:* ~ (**d'eau**) water
softener.
adr. *abr* = **adresse, adresser**.
adrénaline [adʀenalin] *nf* adrenaline.
adresse [adʀɛs] *nf* (*voir adroit*) skill, dexterity;
(*domicile, INFORM*) address; **à l'~ de** (*pour*)
for the benefit of.
adresser [adʀese] *vt* (*lettre: expédier*) to send;
(*: écrire l'adresse sur*) to address; (*injure,
compliments*) to address; ~ **qn à un docteur/
bureau** to refer *ou* send sb to a doctor/an
office; ~ **la parole à qn** to speak to *ou*
address sb; **s'~ à** (*parler à*) to speak to,
address; (*s'informer auprès de*) to go and see,
go and speak to; (*: bureau*) to enquire at;
(*suj: livre, conseil*) to be aimed at.
Adriatique [adʀijatik] *nf:* **l'~** the Adriatic.
adroit, e [adʀwa, -wat] *adj* (*joueur, mécanicien*)
skilful (*BRIT*), skillful (*US*), dext(e)rous
(*politicien etc*) shrewd, skilled.
adroitement [adʀwatmɑ̃] *adv* skilfully (*BRIT*),
skillfully (*US*), dext(e)rously; shrewdly.

AdS *sigle f* = *Académie des Sciences*.
aduler [adyle] *vt* to adulate.
adulte [adylt(ə)] *nm/f* adult, grown-up ◊ *adj* (*personne, attitude*) adult, grown-up; (*chien, arbre*) fully-grown, mature; **l'âge** ~ adulthood; **formation/film pour** ~**s** adult training/film.
adultère [adyltɛʀ] *adj* adulterous ◊ *nm/f* adulterer/adulteress ◊ *nm* (*acte*) adultery.
adultérin, e [adylteʀɛ̃, -in] *adj* born of adultery.
advenir [advəniʀ] *vi* to happen; **qu'est-il advenu de?** what has become of?; **quoi qu'il advienne** whatever befalls *ou* happens.
adventiste [advɑ̃tist(ə)] *nm/f* (*REL*) Adventist.
adverbe [advɛʀb(ə)] *nm* adverb; ~ **de manière** adverb of manner.
adverbial, e, aux [advɛʀbjal, -o] *adj* adverbial.
adversaire [advɛʀsɛʀ] *nm/f* (*SPORT, gén*) opponent, adversary; (*MIL*) adversary, enemy.
adverse [advɛʀs(ə)] *adj* opposing.
adversité [advɛʀsite] *nf* adversity.
AE *sigle m* (= *adjoint d'enseignement*) *non-certificated teacher*.
AELE *sigle f* (= *Association européenne de libre-échange*) EFTA (= *European Free Trade Association*).
AEN *sigle f* (= *Agence pour l'énergie nucléaire*) ≈ AEA (= *Atomic Energy Authority*).
aérateur [aeʀatœʀ] *nm* ventilator.
aération [aeʀɑsjɔ̃] *nf* airing; (*circulation de l'air*) ventilation; **conduit d'**~ ventilation shaft; **bouche d'**~ air vent.
aéré, e [aeʀe] *adj* (*pièce, local*) airy, well-ventilated; (*tissu*) loose-woven; **centre** ~ outdoor centre.
aérer [aeʀe] *vt* to air; (*fig*) to lighten; **s'**~ *vi* to get some (fresh) air.
aérien, ne [aeʀjɛ̃, -ɛn] *adj* (*AVIAT*) air *cpd*, aerial; (*câble, métro*) overhead; (*fig*) light; **compagnie** ~**ne** airline (company); **ligne** ~**ne** airline.
aérobic [aeʀɔbik] *nf* aerobics *sg*.
aérobie [aeʀɔbi] *adj* aerobic.
aéro-club [aeʀɔklœb] *nm* flying club.
aérodrome [aeʀɔdʀɔm] *nm* airfield, aerodrome.
aérodynamique [aeʀɔdinamik] *adj* aerodynamic, streamlined ◊ *nf* aerodynamics *sg*.
aérofrein [aeʀɔfʀɛ̃] *nm* air brake.
aérogare [aeʀɔgaʀ] *nf* airport (buildings); (*en ville*) air terminal.
aéroglisseur [aeʀɔglisœʀ] *nm* hovercraft.
aérogramme [aeʀɔgʀam] *nm* air letter, aerogram(me).
aéromodélisme [aeʀɔmɔdelism(ə)] *nm* model aircraft making.
aéronaute [aeʀɔnot] *nm/f* aeronaut.
aéronautique [aeʀɔnotik] *adj* aeronautical

◊ *nf* aeronautics *sg*.
aéronaval, e [aeʀɔnaval] *adj* air and sea *cpd* ◊ *nf*: **l'A**~**e** ≈ the Fleet Air Arm (*BRIT*), ≈ the Naval Air Force (*US*).
aéronef [aeʀɔnɛf] *nm* aircraft.
aérophagie [aeʀɔfaʒi] *nf* aerophagy.
aéroport [aeʀɔpɔʀ] *nm* airport; ~ **d'embarquement** departure airport.
aéroporté, e [aeʀɔpɔʀte] *adj* airborne, airlifted.
aéroportuaire [aeʀɔpɔʀtɥɛʀ] *adj* of an *ou* the airport, airport *cpd*.
aéropostal, e, aux [aeʀɔpɔstal, -o] *adj* airmail *cpd*.
aérosol [aeʀɔsɔl] *nm* aerosol.
aérospatial, e, aux [aeʀɔspasjal, -o] *adj* aerospace ◊ *nf* the aerospace industry.
aérostat [aeʀɔsta] *nm* aerostat.
aérotrain [aeʀɔtʀɛ̃] *nm* hovertrain.
AF *sigle fpl* = **allocations familiales** ◊ *sigle f* (*Suisse*) = *Assemblée fédérale*.
AFAT [afat] *sigle m* (= *Auxiliaire féminin de l'armée de terre*) *member of the women's army*.
affabilité [afabilite] *nf* affability.
affable [afabl(ə)] *adj* affable.
affabulateur, trice [afabylatœʀ, -tʀis] *nm/f* storyteller.
affabulation [afabylɑsjɔ̃] *nf* invention, fantasy.
affabuler [afabyle] *vi* to make up stories.
affacturage [afaktyʀaʒ] *nm* factoring.
affadir [afadiʀ] *vt* to make insipid *ou* tasteless.
affaiblir [afebliʀ] *vt* to weaken; **s'**~ *vi* to weaken, grow weaker; (*vue*) to grow dim.
affaiblissement [afeblismɑ̃] *nm* weakening.
affaire [afɛʀ] *nf* (*problème, question*) matter; (*criminelle, judiciaire*) case; (*scandaleuse etc*) affair; (*entreprise*) business; (*marché, transaction*) (business) deal, (piece of) business *no pl*; (*occasion intéressante*) good deal, bargain; ~**s** *nfpl* affairs; (*activité commerciale*) business *sg*; (*effets personnels*) things, belongings; **tirer qn/se tirer d'**~ to get sb/o.s. out of trouble; **ceci fera l'**~ this will do (nicely); **avoir** ~ **à** (*comme adversaire*) to be faced with; (*en contact*) to be dealing with; **tu auras** ~ **à moi!** (*menace*) you'll have me to contend with!; **c'est une** ~ **de goût/d'argent** it's a question *ou* matter of taste/money; **c'est l'**~ **d'une minute/heure** it'll only take a minute/an hour; **ce sont mes** ~**s** (*cela me concerne*) that's my business; **toutes** ~**s cessantes** forthwith; **les** ~**s étrangères** (*POL*) foreign affairs.
affairé, e [afeʀe] *adj* busy.
affairer [afeʀe]: **s'**~ *vi* to busy o.s., bustle about.
affairisme [afeʀism(ə)] *nm* (political) racketeering.
affaissement [afɛsmɑ̃] *nm* subsidence; collapse.

affaisser [afese]: **s'~** *vi* (*terrain, immeuble*) to subside, sink; (*personne*) to collapse.

affaler [afale]: **s'~** *vi*: **s'~ dans/sur** to collapse *ou* slump into/onto.

affamé, e [afame] *adj* starving, famished.

affamer [afame] *vt* to starve.

affectation [afɛktasjɔ̃] *nf* (*voir affecter*) allotment; appointment; posting; (*voir affecté*) affectedness.

affecté, e [afɛkte] *adj* affected.

affecter [afɛkte] *vt* (*émouvoir*) to affect, move; (*feindre*) to affect, feign; (*telle ou telle forme etc*) to take on, assume; **~ qch à** to allocate *ou* allot sth to; **~ qn à** to appoint sb to; (*diplomate*) to post sb to; **~ qch de** (*de coefficient*) to modify sth by.

affectif, ive [afɛktif, -iv] *adj* emotional, affective.

affection [afɛksjɔ̃] *nf* affection; (*mal*) ailment; **avoir de l'~ pour** to feel affection for; **prendre en ~** to become fond of.

affectionner [afɛksjɔne] *vt* to be fond of.

affectueusement [afɛktɥøzmɑ̃] *adv* affectionately.

affectueux, euse [afɛktɥø, -øz] *adj* affectionate.

afférent, e [afeʀɑ̃, -ɑ̃t] *adj*: **~ à** pertaining *ou* relating to.

affermir [afɛʀmiʀ] *vt* to consolidate, strengthen.

aff. étr. *abr* (= *Affaires étrangères*) *voir* **affaire**.

affichage [afiʃaʒ] *nm* billposting, billsticking; (*électronique*) display; **"~ interdit"** "stick no bills", "billsticking prohibited"; **~ à cristaux liquides** liquid crystal display, LCD; **~ numérique** *ou* **digital** digital display.

affiche [afiʃ] *nf* poster; (*officielle*) (public) notice; (*THÉÂT*) bill; **être à l'~** (*THÉÂT*) to be on; **tenir l'~** to run.

afficher [afiʃe] *vt* (*affiche*) to put up, post up; (*réunion*) to put up a notice about; (*électroniquement*) to display; (*fig*) to exhibit, display; **s'~** (*péj*) to flaunt o.s.; **"défense d'~"** "stick no bills".

affichette [afiʃɛt] *nf* small poster *ou* notice.

affilé, e [afile] *adj* sharp.

affilée [afile]: **d'~** *adv* at a stretch.

affiler [afile] *vt* to sharpen.

affiliation [afiljasjɔ̃] *nf* affiliation.

affilié, e [afilje] *adj*: **être ~ à** to be affiliated to ♦ *nm/f* affiliated party *ou* member.

affilier [afilje] *vt*: **s'~ à** to become affiliated to.

affiner [afine] *vt* to refine; **s'~** *vi* to become (more) refined.

affinité [afinite] *nf* affinity.

affirmatif, ive [afiʀmatif, -iv] *adj* affirmative ♦ *nf*: **répondre par l'affirmative** to reply in the affirmative; **dans l'affirmative** (*si oui*) if (the answer is) yes ..., if he does (*ou* you do *etc*) ....

affirmation [afiʀmasjɔ̃] *nf* assertion.

affirmativement [afiʀmativmɑ̃] *adv* affirma-

tively, in the affirmative.

affirmer [afiʀme] *vt* (*prétendre*) to maintain, assert; (*autorité etc*) to assert; **s'~** to assert o.s.; to assert itself.

affleurer [aflœʀe] *vi* to show on the surface.

affliction [afliksjɔ̃] *nf* affliction.

affligé, e [afliʒe] *adj* distressed, grieved; **~ de** (*maladie, tare*) afflicted with.

affligeant, e [afliʒɑ̃, -ɑ̃t] *adj* distressing.

affliger [afliʒe] *vt* (*peiner*) to distress, grieve.

affluence [aflyɑ̃s] *nf* crowds *pl*; **heures d'~** rush hour *sg*; **jours d'~** busiest days.

affluent [aflyɑ̃] *nm* tributary.

affluer [aflye] *vi* (*secours, biens*) to flood in, pour in; (*sang*) to rush, flow.

afflux [afly] *nm* flood, influx; rush.

affolant, e [afɔlɑ̃, -ɑ̃t] *adj* terrifying.

affolé, e [afɔle] *adj* panic-stricken, panicky.

affolement [afɔlmɑ̃] *nm* panic.

affoler [afɔle] *vt* to throw into a panic; **s'~** *vi* to panic.

affranchir [afʀɑ̃ʃiʀ] *vt* to put a stamp *ou* stamps on; (*à la machine*) to frank (*BRIT*), meter (*US*); (*esclave*) to enfranchise, emancipate; (*fig*) to free, liberate; **s'~ de** to free o.s. from; **machine à ~** franking machine, postage meter.

affranchissement [afʀɑ̃ʃismɑ̃] *nm* franking (*BRIT*), metering (*US*); freeing; (*POSTES: prix payé*) postage; **tarifs d'~** postage rates.

affres [afʀ(ə)] *nfpl*: **dans les ~ de** in the throes of.

affréter [afʀete] *vt* to charter.

affreusement [afʀøzmɑ̃] *adv* dreadfully, awfully.

affreux, euse [afʀø, -øz] *adj* dreadful, awful.

affriolant, e [afʀijɔlɑ̃, -ɑ̃t] *adj* tempting, enticing.

affront [afʀɔ̃] *nm* affront.

affrontement [afʀɔ̃tmɑ̃] *nm* (*MIL, POL*) clash, confrontation.

affronter [afʀɔ̃te] *vt* to confront, face; **s'~** to confront each other.

affubler [afyble] *vt* (*péj*): **~ qn de** to rig *ou* deck sb out in; (*surnom*) to attach to sb.

affût [afy] *nm* (*de canon*) gun carriage; **à l'~ (de)** (*gibier*) lying in wait (for); (*fig*) on the look-out (for).

affûter [afyte] *vt* to sharpen, grind.

afghan, e [afgɑ̃, -an] *adj* Afghan.

Afghanistan [afganistɑ̃] *nm*: **l'~** Afghanistan.

afin [afɛ̃]: **~ que** *conj* so that, in order that; **~ de faire** in order to do, so as to do.

AFNOR [afnɔʀ] *sigle f* (= *Association française de normalisation*) *industrial standards authority*.

a fortiori [afɔʀsjɔʀi] *adv* all the more, a fortiori.

AFP *sigle f* = *Agence France-Presse*.

AFPA *sigle f* = *Association pour la formation professionnelle des adultes*.

africain, e [afʀikɛ̃, -ɛn] *adj* African ♦ *nm/f*:

A~, **e** African.

afrikaans [afʀikɑ̃] *nm*, *adj inv* Afrikaans.

Afrikaner [afʀikanɛʀ] *nm/f* Afrikaner.

Afrique [afʀik] *nf*: **l'~** Africa; **l'~** **australe/du** **Nord/du Sud** southern/North/South Africa.

afro [afʀo] *adj inv*: **coupe ~** afro hairstyle ♦ *nm/f*: **A~** Afro.

afro-américain, e [afʀoameʀikɛ̃, -ɛn] *adj* Afro-American.

afro-asiatique [afʀoazjatik] *adj* Afro-Asian.

AG *sigle f* = *assemblée générale*.

ag. *abr* = *agence*.

agaçant, e [agasɑ̃, -ɑ̃t] *adj* irritating, aggravating.

agacement [agasmɑ̃] *nm* irritation, aggravation.

agacer [agase] *vt* to pester, tease; (*involontairement*) to irritate, aggravate; (*aguicher*) to excite, lead on.

agapes [agap] *nfpl* (*humoristique*: *festin*) feast.

agate [agat] *nf* agate.

AGE *sigle f* = *assemblée générale extraordinaire*.

âge [ɑʒ] *nm* age; **quel ~ as-tu?** how old are you?; **une femme d'un certain ~** a middle-aged woman, a woman who is getting on (in years); **bien porter son ~** to wear well; **prendre de l'~** to be getting on (in years), grow older; **limite d'~** age limit; **dispense d'~** special exemption from age limit; **troisième ~** (*période*) retirement; (*personnes âgées*) senior citizens; **l'~ ingrat** the awkward *ou* difficult age; **~ légal** legal age; **~ mental** mental age; **l'~ mûr** maturity, middle age; **~ de raison** age of reason.

âgé, e [ɑʒe] *adj* old, elderly; **~ de 10 ans** 10 years old.

agence [aʒɑ̃s] *nf* agency, office; (*succursale*) branch; **~ immobilière** estate agent's (office) (*BRIT*), real estate office (*US*); **~ matrimoniale** marriage bureau; **~ de placement** employment agency; **~ de publicité** advertising agency; **~ de voyages** travel agency.

agencé, e [aʒɑ̃se] *adj*: **bien/mal ~** well/badly put together; well/badly laid out *ou* arranged.

agencement [aʒɑ̃smɑ̃] *nm* putting together; arrangement, laying out.

agencer [aʒɑ̃se] *vt* to put together; (*local*) to arrange, lay out.

agenda [aʒɛ̃da] *nm* diary.

agenouiller [aʒnuje]: **s'~** *vi* to kneel (down).

agent [aʒɑ̃] *nm* (*aussi*: **~ de police**) policeman; (*ADMIN*) official, officer; (*fig: élément, facteur*) agent; **~ d'assurances** insurance broker; **~ de change** stockbroker; **~ commercial** sales representative; **~ immobilier** estate agent (*BRIT*), realtor (*US*); **~ (secret)** (secret) agent.

agglo [aglo] *nm* (*fam*) = **aggloméré**.

aggloméré [aglɔmeʀa] *nm* (*GÉO*) agglomerate.

agglomération [aglɔmeʀasjɔ̃] *nf* town; (*AUTO*) built-up area; **l'~ parisienne** the urban area of Paris.

aggloméré [aglɔmeʀe] *nm* (*bois*) chipboard; (*pierre*) conglomerate.

agglomérer [aglɔmeʀe] *vt* to pile up; (*TECH*: *bois, pierre*) to compress; **s'~** *vi* to pile up.

agglutiner [aglytine] *vt* to stick together; **s'~** *vi* to congregate.

aggravant, e [agʀavɑ̃, -ɑ̃t] *adj*: **circonstances ~es** aggravating circumstances.

aggravation [agʀavɑsjɔ̃] *nf* worsening, aggravation; increase.

aggraver [agʀave] *vt* to worsen, aggravate; (*JUR*: *peine*) to increase; **s'~** *vi* to worsen; **~ son cas** to make one's case worse.

agile [aʒil] *adj* agile, nimble.

agilement [aʒilmɑ̃] *adv* nimbly.

agilité [aʒilite] *nf* agility, nimbleness.

agio [aʒjo] *nm* (bank) charges *pl*.

agir [aʒiʀ] *vi* (*se comporter*) to behave, act; (*faire quelque chose*) to act, take action; (*avoir de l'effet*) to act; **il s'agit de** it's a matter *ou* question of; it is about; (*il importe que*): **il s'agit de faire** we (*ou* you *etc*) must do; **de quoi s'agit-il?** what is it about?

agissements [aʒismɑ̃] *nmpl* (*gén péj*) schemes, intrigues.

agitateur, trice [aʒitatœʀ, -tʀis] *nm/f* agitator.

agitation [aʒitɑsjɔ̃] *nf* (hustle and) bustle; (*trouble*) agitation, excitement; (*politique*) unrest, agitation.

agité, e [aʒite] *adj* (*remuant*) fidgety, restless; (*troublé*) agitated, perturbed; (*journée*) hectic; (*mer*) rough; (*sommeil*) disturbed, broken.

agiter [aʒite] *vt* (*bouteille, chiffon*) to shake; (*bras, mains*) to wave; (*préoccuper, exciter*) to trouble, perturb; **s'~** *vi* to bustle about; (*dormeur*) to toss and turn; (*enfant*) to fidget; (*POL*) to grow restless; **"~ avant l'emploi"** "shake before use".

agneau, x [aɲo] *nm* lamb; (*toison*) lambswool.

agnelet [aɲlɛ] *nm* little lamb.

agnostique [agnɔstik] *adj*, *nm/f* agnostic.

agonie [agɔni] *nf* mortal agony, death pangs *pl*; (*fig*) death throes *pl*.

agonir [agɔniʀ] *vt*: **~ qn d'injures** to hurl abuse at sb.

agoniser [agɔnize] *vi* to be dying; (*fig*) to be in its death throes.

agrafe [agʀaf] *nf* (*de vêtement*) hook, fastener; (*de bureau*) staple; (*MÉD*) clip.

agrafer [agʀafe] *vt* to fasten; to staple.

agrafeuse [agʀaføz] *nf* stapler.

agraire [agʀɛʀ] *adj* agrarian; (*mesure, surface*) land *cpd*.

agrandir [agʀɑ̃diʀ] *vt* (*magasin, domaine*) to extend, enlarge; (*trou*) to enlarge, make bigger; (*PHOTO*) to enlarge, blow up; **s'~** *vi* to be extended; to be enlarged.

agrandissement [agʀɑ̃dismɑ̃] *nm* extension;

enlargement; (*photographie*) enlargement.
agrandisseur [agʀɑ̃disœʀ] *nm* (*PHOTO*)
enlarger.
agréable [agʀeabl(ə)] *adj* pleasant, nice.
agréablement [agʀeabləmɑ̃] *adv* pleasantly.
agréé, e [agʀee] *adj*: **concessionnaire** ~
registered dealer; **magasin** ~ registered
dealer('s).
agréer [agʀee] *vt* (*requête*) to accept; ~ **à** *vt* to
please, suit; **veuillez** ~ ... (*formule
épistolaire*) yours faithfully.
agrég [agʀeg] *nf* (*fam*) = **agrégation**.
agrégat [agʀega] *nm* aggregate.
agrégation [agʀegasjɔ̃] *nf* highest teaching
diploma in France.

The **agrégation**, colloquially known as the
agrég, is a prestigious competitive
examination for the recruitment of secondary
education teachers in France. The number of
candidates always far exceeds the number of
posts available. Most teachers of **classes
préparatoires** and university lecturers hold the
agrégation; see also **CAPES**.

---

agrégé, e [agʀeʒe] *nm/f* holder of the
agrégation.
agréger [agʀeʒe]: **s'**~ *vi* to aggregate.
agrément [agʀemɑ̃] *nm* (*accord*) consent,
approval; (*attraits*) charm, attractiveness;
(*plaisir*) pleasure; **voyage/jardin d'**~
pleasure trip/garden.
agrémenter [agʀemɑ̃te] *vt*: ~ **(de)** to
embellish (with), adorn (with).
agrès [agʀɛ] *nmpl* (gymnastics) apparatus *sg*.
agresser [agʀese] *vt* to attack.
agresseur [agʀesœʀ] *nm* aggressor.
agressif, ive [agʀesif, -iv] *adj* aggressive.
agression [agʀesjɔ̃] *nf* attack; (*POL, MIL,
PSYCH*) aggression.
agressivement [agʀesivmɑ̃] *adv* aggressively.
agressivité [agʀesivite] *nf* aggressiveness.
agreste [agʀɛst(ə)] *adj* rustic.
agricole [agʀikɔl] *adj* agricultural, farm *cpd*.
agriculteur, trice [agʀikyltœʀ, -tʀis] *nm/f*
farmer.
agriculture [agʀikyltyʀ] *nf* agriculture;
farming.
agripper [agʀipe] *vt* to grab, clutch; (*pour
arracher*) to snatch, grab; **s'**~ **à** to cling (on)
to, clutch, grip.
agro-alimentaire [agʀɔalimɑ̃tɛʀ] *adj* farming
cpd ♦ *nm*: **l'**~ agribusiness.
agronome [agʀɔnɔm] *nm/f* agronomist.
agronomie [agʀɔnɔmi] *nf* agronomy.
agronomique [agʀɔnɔmik] *adj* agronomic(al).
agrumes [agʀym] *nmpl* citrus fruit(s).
aguerrir [ageʀiʀ] *vt* to harden; **s'**~ **(contre)** to
become hardened (to).
aguets [agɛ]: **aux** ~ *adv*: **être aux** ~ to be on
the look-out.
aguichant, e [agiʃɑ̃, -ɑ̃t] *adj* enticing.

aguicher [agiʃe] *vt* to entice.
aguicheur, euse [agiʃœʀ, -øz] *adj* enticing.
ah [ɑ] *excl* ah!; ~ **bon?** really?, is that so?; ~
mais ... yes, but ...; ~ **non!** oh no!
ahuri, e [ayʀi] *adj* (*stupéfait*) flabbergasted;
(*idiot*) dim-witted.
ahurir [ayʀiʀ] *vt* to stupefy, stagger.
ahurissant, e [ayʀisɑ̃, -ɑ̃t] *adj* stupefying,
staggering, mind-boggling.
ai [e] *vb voir* **avoir**.
aide [ɛd] *nm/f* assistant ♦ *nf* assistance, help;
(*secours financier*) aid; **à l'**~ **de** with the help
ou aid of; **aller à l'**~ **de qn** to go to sb's aid,
go to help sb; **venir en** ~ **à qn** to help sb,
come to sb's assistance; **appeler (qn) à l'**~
to call for help (from sb); **à l'**~**!** help!; ~ **de
camp** *nm* aide-de-camp; ~ **comptable** *nm*
accountant's assistant; ~ **électricien** *nm*
electrician's mate; ~ **familiale** *nf* mother's
help, ≈ home help; ~ **judiciaire** *nf* legal aid;
~ **de laboratoire** *nm/f* laboratory assistant; ~
ménagère *nf* ≈ home help; ~ **sociale** *nf*
(*assistance*) state aid; ~ **soignant, e** *nm/f*
auxiliary nurse; ~ **technique** *nf* ≈ VSO
(*BRIT*), ≈ Peace Corps (*US*).
aide-mémoire [ɛdmemwaʀ] *nm inv* (key facts)
handbook.
aider [ede] *vt* to help; ~ **à qch** to help
(towards) sth; ~ **qn à faire qch** to help sb to
do sth; **s'**~ **de** (*se servir de*) to use, make use
of.
aie [ɛ] *etc vb voir* **avoir**.
aïe [aj] *excl* ouch!
AIEA *sigle f* (= *Agence internationale de l'énergie
nucléaire*) IAEA (= *International Atomic Energy
Agency*).
aïeul, e [ajœl] *nm/f* grandparent, grandfather/
grandmother; (*ancêtre*) forebear.
aïeux [ajø] *nmpl* grandparents; forebears,
forefathers.
aigle [ɛgl(ə)] *nm* eagle.
aiglefin [ɛgləfɛ̃] *nm* = **églefin**.
aigre [ɛgʀ(ə)] *adj* sour, sharp; (*fig*) sharp,
cutting; **tourner à l'**~ to turn sour.
aigre-doux, -douce [ɛgʀədu, -dus] *adj* (*fruit*)
bitter-sweet; (*sauce*) sweet and sour.
aigrefin [ɛgʀəfɛ̃] *nm* swindler.
aigrelet, te [ɛgʀəlɛ, -ɛt] *adj* (*taste*) sourish;
(*voix, son*) sharpish.
aigrette [ɛgʀɛt] *nf* (*plume*) feather.
aigreur [ɛgʀœʀ] *nf* sourness; sharpness; ~**s
d'estomac** heartburn *sg*.
aigri, e [ɛgʀi] *adj* embittered.
aigrir [egʀiʀ] *vt* (*personne*) to embitter;
(*caractère*) to sour; **s'**~ *vi* to become
embittered; to sour; (*lait etc*) to turn
sour.
aigu, ë [egy] *adj* (*objet, arête*) sharp, pointed;
(*son, voix*) high-pitched, shrill; (*note*) high
(-pitched); (*douleur, intelligence*) acute,
sharp.
aigue-marine, *pl* aigues-marines [ɛgmaʀin]

nf aquamarine.

aiguillage [egɥijaʒ] *nm* (*RAIL*) points *pl*.

aiguille [egɥij] *nf* needle; (*de montre*) hand; ~ **à tricoter** knitting needle.

aiguiller [egɥije] *vt* (*orienter*) to direct; (*RAIL*) to shunt.

aiguillette [egɥijɛt] *nf* (*CULIN*) aiguillette.

aiguilleur [egɥijœR] *nm* (*RAIL*) pointsman; ~ **du ciel** air traffic controller.

aiguillon [egɥijɔ̃] *nm* (*d'abeille*) sting; (*fig*) spur, stimulus.

aiguillonner [egɥijɔne] *vt* to spur *ou* goad on.

aiguiser [egize] *vt* to sharpen, grind; (*fig*) to stimulate; (: *esprit*) to sharpen; (: *sens*) to excite.

aiguisoir [egizwaR] *nm* sharpener.

aïkido [ajkido] *nm* aikido.

ail [aj] *nm* garlic.

aile [ɛl] *nf* wing; (*de voiture*) wing (*BRIT*), fender (*US*); **battre de l'**~ (*fig*) to be in a sorry state; **voler de ses propres** ~s to stand on one's own two feet; ~ **libre** hang-glider.

ailé, e [ele] *adj* winged.

aileron [ɛlRɔ̃] *nm* (*de requin*) fin; (*d'avion*) aileron.

ailette [ɛlɛt] *nf* (*TECH*) fin; (: *de turbine*) blade.

ailier [elje] *nm* (*SPORT*) winger.

aille [aj] *etc vb voir* **aller**.

ailleurs [ajœR] *adv* elsewhere, somewhere else; **partout/nulle part** ~ everywhere/nowhere else; **d'**~ *adv* (*du reste*) moreover, besides; **par** ~ *adv* (*d'autre part*) moreover, furthermore.

ailloli [ajɔli] *nm* garlic mayonnaise.

aimable [ɛmabl(ə)] *adj* kind, nice; **vous êtes bien** ~ that's very nice *ou* kind of you, how kind (of you)!

aimablement [ɛmabləmɑ̃] *adv* kindly.

aimant [ɛmɑ̃] *nm* magnet.

aimant, e [ɛmɑ̃, -ɑ̃t] *adj* loving, affectionate.

aimanté, e [ɛmɑ̃te] *adj* magnetic.

aimanter [ɛmɑ̃te] *vt* to magnetize.

aimer [eme] *vt* to love; (*d'amitié, affection, par goût*) to like; (*souhait*): **j'aimerais ... I** would like ...; **s'**~ to love each other; to like each other; **je n'aime pas beaucoup Paul** I don't like Paul much, I don't care much for Paul; ~ **faire qch** to like doing sth, to like to do sth; **aimeriez-vous que je vous accompagne?** would you like me to come with you?; **j'aimerais (bien) m'en aller** I should (really) like to go; **bien** ~ **qn/qch** to like sb/sth; **j'aime mieux Paul (que Pierre)** I prefer Paul (to Pierre); **j'aime mieux** *ou* **autant vous dire que** I may as well tell you that; **j'aimerais autant** *ou* **mieux y aller maintenant** I'd sooner *ou* rather go now; **j'aime assez aller au cinéma** I quite like going to the cinema.

aine [ɛn] *nf* groin.

aîné, e [ene] *adj* elder, older; (*le plus âgé*) eldest, oldest ♦ *nm/f* oldest child *ou* one, oldest boy *ou* son/girl *ou* daughter; ~s *nmpl*

(*fig: anciens*) elders; **il est mon** ~ **(de 2 ans)** he's (2 years) older than me, he's 2 years my senior.

aînesse [enɛs] *nf*: **droit d'**~ birthright.

ainsi [ɛ̃si] *adv* (*de cette façon*) like this, in this way, thus; (*ce faisant*) thus, so; ~ **que** (*comme*) (just) as; (*et aussi*) as well as; **pour** ~ **dire** so to speak, as it were; ~ **donc** and so; ~ **soit-il** (*REL*) so be it; **et** ~ **de suite** and so on (and so forth).

aïoli [ajɔli] *nm* = **ailloli**.

air [ɛR] *nm* air; (*mélodie*) tune; (*expression*) look, air; (*atmosphère, ambiance*): **dans l'**~ in the air (*fig*); **prendre de grands** ~s **(avec qn)** to give o.s. airs (with sb); **en l'**~ (up) into the air; **tirer en l'**~ to fire shots in the air; **paroles/menaces en l'**~ idle words/threats; **prendre l'**~ to get some (fresh) air; (*avion*) to take off; **avoir l'**~ **triste** to look *ou* seem sad; **avoir l'**~ **de qch** to look like sth; **avoir l'**~ **de faire** to look as though one is doing, appear to be doing; **courant d'**~ draught (*BRIT*), draft (*US*); **le grand** ~ the open air; **mal de l'**~ air-sickness; **tête en l'**~ scatterbrain; ~ **comprimé** compressed air; ~ **conditionné** air-conditioning.

airbag [ɛRbag] *nm* air bag.

aire [ɛR] *nf* (*zone, fig, MATH*) area; (*nid*) eyrie (*BRIT*), aerie (*US*); ~ **d'atterrissage** landing strip; landing patch; ~ **de jeu** play area; ~ **de lancement** launching site; ~ **de stationnement** parking area.

airelle [ɛRɛl] *nf* bilberry.

aisance [ɛzɑ̃s] *nf* ease; (*COUTURE*) easing, freedom of movement; (*richesse*) affluence; **être dans l'**~ to be well-off *ou* affluent.

aise [ɛz] *nf* comfort ♦ *adj*: **être bien** ~ **de/que** to be delighted to/that; ~s *nfpl*: **aimer ses** ~s to like one's (creature) comforts; **prendre ses** ~s to make o.s. comfortable; **frémir d'**~ to shudder with pleasure; **être à l'**~ *ou* **à son** ~ to be comfortable; (*pas embarrassé*) to be at ease; (*financièrement*) to be comfortably off; **se mettre à l'**~ to make o.s. comfortable; **être mal à l'**~ *ou* **à son** ~ to be uncomfortable; (*gêné*) to be ill at ease; **mettre qn à l'**~ to put sb at his (*ou* her) ease; **mettre qn mal à l'**~ to make sb feel ill at ease; **à votre** ~ please yourself, just as you like; **en faire à son** ~ to do as one likes; **en prendre à son** ~ **avec qch** to be free and easy with sth, do as one likes with sth.

aisé, e [eze] *adj* easy; (*assez riche*) well-to-do, well-off.

aisément [ezemɑ̃] *adv* easily.

aisselle [ɛsɛl] *nf* armpit.

ait [ɛ] *vb voir* **avoir**.

ajonc [aʒɔ̃] *nm* gorse *no pl*.

ajouré, e [aʒuRe] *adj* openwork *cpd*.

ajournement [aʒuRnəmɑ̃] *nm* adjournment; deferment, postponement.

ajourner [aʒuRne] *vt* (*réunion*) to adjourn;

(*décision*) to defer, postpone; (*candidat*) to refer; (*conscrit*) to defer.

ajout [aʒu] *nm* addition.

ajouter [aʒute] *vt* to add; (*INFORM*) to append; ~ **à** *vt* (*accroître*) to add to; **s'**~ **à** to add to; ~ **que** to add that; ~ **foi à** to lend *ou* give credence to.

ajustage [aʒystaʒ] *nm* fitting.

ajusté, e [aʒyste] *adj*: **bien** ~ (*robe etc*) close-fitting.

ajustement [aʒystəmɑ̃] *nm* adjustment.

ajuster [aʒyste] *vt* (*régler*) to adjust; (*vêtement*) to alter; (*arranger*): ~ **sa cravate** to adjust one's tie; (*coup de fusil*) to aim; (*cible*) to aim at; (*adapter*): ~ **qch à** to fit sth to.

ajusteur [aʒystœr] *nm* metal worker.

al *abr* = **année-lumière**.

alaise [alɛz] *nf* = **alèse**.

alambic [alɑ̃bik] *nm* still.

alambiqué, e [alɑ̃bike] *adj* convoluted, overcomplicated.

alangui, e [alɑ̃gi] *adj* languid.

alanguir [alɑ̃giʀ]: **s'**~ *vi* to grow languid.

alarmant, e [alaʀmɑ̃, -ɑ̃t] *adj* alarming.

alarme [alaʀm(ə)] *nf* alarm; **donner l'**~ to give *ou* raise the alarm; **jeter l'**~ to cause alarm.

alarmer [alaʀme] *vt* to alarm; **s'**~ *vi* to become alarmed.

alarmiste [alaʀmist(ə)] *adj* alarmist.

Alaska [alaska] *nm*: **l'**~ Alaska.

albanais, e [albanɛ, -ɛz] *adj* Albanian ♦ *nm* (*LING*) Albanian ♦ *nm/f*: **A**~, **e** Albanian.

Albanie [albani] *nf*: **l'**~ Albania.

albâtre [albɑtʀ(ə)] *nm* alabaster.

albatros [albatʀos] *nm* albatross.

albigeois, e [albiʒwa, -waz] *adj* of *ou* from Albi.

albinos [albinos] *nm/f* albino.

album [albɔm] *nm* album; ~ **à colorier** colouring book; ~ **de timbres** stamp album.

albumen [albymɛn] *nm* albumen.

albumine [albymin] *nf* albumin; **avoir** *ou* **faire de l'**~ to suffer from albuminuria.

alcalin [alkalɛ̃, -in] *adj* alkaline.

alchimie [alʃimi] *nf* alchemy.

alchimiste [alʃimist(ə)] *nm* alchemist.

alcool [alkɔl] *nm*: **l'**~ alcohol; **un** ~ a spirit, a brandy; ~ **à brûler** methylated spirits (*BRIT*), wood alcohol (*US*); ~ **à 90°** surgical spirit; ~ **camphré** camphorated alcohol; ~ **de prune** *etc* plum *etc* brandy.

alcoolémie [alkɔlemi] *nf* blood alcohol level.

alcoolique [alkɔlik] *adj, nm/f* alcoholic.

alcoolisé, e [alkɔlize] *adj* alcoholic.

alcoolisme [alkɔlism(ə)] *nm* alcoholism.

alco(o)test [alkɔtɛst] *nm* ® (*objet*) Breathalyser ®; (*test*) breath-test; **faire subir l'**~ **à qn** to Breathalyze ® sb.

alcôve [alkov] *nf* alcove, recess.

aléas [alea] *nmpl* hazards.

aléatoire [aleatwaʀ] *adj* uncertain; (*INFORM, STATISTIQUE*) random.

alémanique [alemanik] *adj*: **la Suisse** ~ German-speaking Switzerland.

ALENA [alena] *sigle m* (= *Accord de libre-échange nord-américain*) NAFTA (= *North American Free Trade Agreement*).

alentour [alɑ̃tuʀ] *adv* around (about); ~**s** *nmpl* surroundings; **aux** ~**s de** in the vicinity *ou* neighbourhood of, around about; (*temps*) around about.

Aléoutiennes [aleusjɛn] *nfpl*: **les (îles)** ~ the Aleutian Islands.

alerte [alɛʀt(ə)] *adj* agile, nimble; (*style*) brisk, lively ♦ *nf* alert; warning; **donner l'**~ to give the alert; **à la première** ~ at the first sign of trouble *ou* danger; ~ **à la bombe** bomb scare.

alerter [alɛʀte] *vt* to alert.

alèse [alɛz] *nf* (*drap*) undersheet, drawsheet.

aléser [aleze] *vt* to ream.

alevin [alvɛ̃] *nm* alevin, young fish.

alevinage [alvinaʒ] *nm* fish farming.

Alexandrie [alɛksɑ̃dʀi] *n* Alexandria.

alexandrin [alɛksɑ̃dʀɛ̃] *nm* alexandrine.

alezan, e [alzɑ̃, -an] *adj* chestnut.

algarade [algaʀad] *nf* row, dispute.

algèbre [alʒɛbʀ(ə)] *nf* algebra.

algébrique [alʒebʀik] *adj* algebraic.

Alger [alʒe] *n* Algiers.

Algérie [alʒeʀi] *nf*: **l'**~ Algeria.

algérien, ne [alʒeʀjɛ̃, -ɛn] *adj* Algerian ♦ *nm/f*: **A**~, **ne** Algerian.

algérois, e [alʒeʀwa, -waz] *adj* of *ou* from Algiers ♦ *nm*: **l'A**~ (*région*) the Algiers region.

algorithme [algɔʀitm(ə)] *nm* algorithm.

algue [alg(ə)] *nf* (*gén*) seaweed *no pl*; (*BOT*) alga (*pl* -ae).

alias [aljas] *adv* alias.

alibi [alibi] *nm* alibi.

aliénation [aljenasjɔ̃] *nf* alienation.

aliéné, e [aljene] *nm/f* insane person, lunatic (*péj*).

aliéner [aljene] *vt* to alienate; (*bien, liberté*) to give up; **s'**~ *vi* to alienate.

alignement [aliɲmɑ̃] *nm* alignment, lining up; **à l'**~ in line.

aligner [aliɲe] *vt* to align, line up; (*idées, chiffres*) to string together; (*adapter*): ~ **qch sur** to bring sth into alignment with; **s'**~ (*soldats etc*) to line up; **s'**~ **sur** (*POL*) to align o.s. with.

aliment [alimɑ̃] *nm* food; ~ **complet** whole food.

alimentaire [alimɑ̃tɛʀ] *adj* food *cpd*; (*péj: besogne*) done merely to earn a living; **produits** ~**s** foodstuffs, foods.

alimentation [alimɑ̃tasjɔ̃] *nf* feeding; supplying, supply; (*commerce*) food trade; (*produits*) groceries *pl*; (*régime*) diet; (*INFORM*) feed; ~ (**générale**) (general) grocer's; ~ **de base** staple diet; ~ **en feuilles/en continu/en papier** form/stream/

sheet feed.

alimenter [alimɑ̃te] *vt* to feed; (*TECH*): ~ **(en)** to supply (with), feed (with); (*fig*) to sustain, keep going.

alinéa [alinea] *nm* paragraph; "**nouvel ~**" "new line".

aliter [alite]: **s'~** *vi* to take to one's bed; **infirme alité** bedridden person *ou* invalid.

alizé [alize] *adj, nm*: **(vent)** ~ trade wind.

allaitement [alɛtmɑ̃] *nm* feeding; ~ **maternel/au biberon** breast-/bottle-feeding; ~ **mixte** mixed feeding.

allaiter [alete] *vt* (*suj: femme*) to (breast-)feed, nurse; (*suj: animal*) to suckle; ~ **au biberon** to bottle-feed.

allant [alɑ̃] *nm* drive, go.

alléchant, e [aleʃɑ̃, -ɑ̃t] *adj* tempting, enticing.

allécher [aleʃe] *vt*: ~ **qn** to make sb's mouth water; to tempt sb, entice sb.

allée [ale] *nf* (*de jardin*) path; (*en ville*) avenue, drive; ~**s et venues** comings and goings.

allégation [alegasjɔ̃] *nf* allegation.

alléger [aleʒe] *vt* (*voiture*) to make lighter; (*chargement*) to lighten; (*souffrance*) to alleviate, soothe.

allégorie [alegɔʀi] *nf* allegory.

allégorique [alegɔʀik] *adj* allegorical.

allègre [alɛgʀ(ə)] *adj* lively, jaunty (*BRIT*); (*personne*) gay, cheerful.

allégresse [alegʀɛs] *nf* elation, gaiety.

allegretto [al(l)egʀɛt(t)o] *adv, nm* allegretto.

allegro [al(l)egʀo] *adv, nm* allegro.

alléguer [alege] *vt* to put forward (as proof *ou* an excuse).

Allemagne [aləmaɲ] *nf*: **l'~** Germany; **l'~ de l'Est/Ouest** East/West Germany; **l'~ fédérale (RFA)** the Federal Republic of Germany (FRG).

allemand, e [almɑ̃, -ɑ̃d] *adj* German ♦ *nm* (*LING*) German ♦ *nm/f*: **A~, e** German; **A~ de l'Est/l'Ouest** East/West German.

aller [ale] *nm* (*trajet*) outward journey; (*billet*): ~ **(simple)** single (*BRIT*) *ou* one-way ticket; ~ **(et) retour (AR)** (*trajet*) return trip *ou* journey (*BRIT*), round trip (*US*); (*billet*) return (*BRIT*) *ou* round-trip (*US*) ticket ♦ *vi* (*gén*) to go; ~ **à** (*convenir*) to suit; (*suj: forme, pointure etc*) to fit; **cela me va** (*couleur*) that suits me; (*vêtement*) that suits me; that fits me; (*projet, disposition*) that suits me, that's fine *ou* OK by me; ~ **à la chasse/ pêche** to go hunting/fishing; ~ **avec** (*couleurs, style etc*) to go (well) with; **je vais le faire/me fâcher** I'm going to do it/to get angry; ~ **voir/chercher qn** to go and see/look for sb; **comment allez-vous?** how are you?; **comment ça va?** how are you?; (*affaires etc*) how are things?; **ça va? — oui (ça va)!** how are things? — fine!; **ça va (comme ça)** that's fine (as it is); **il va bien/mal** he's well/not well, he's fine/ill; **ça va bien/mal** (*affaires etc*)

it's going well/not going well; **tout va bien** everything's fine; **ça ne va pas!** (*mauvaise humeur etc*) that's not on!, hey, come on!; **ça ne va pas sans difficultés** it's not without difficulties; ~ **mieux** to be better; **il y va de leur vie** their lives are at stake; **se laisser** ~ to let o.s. go; **s'en** ~ *vi* (*partir*) to be off, go, leave; (*disparaître*) to go away; ~ **jusqu'à** to go as far as; **ça va de soi, ça va sans dire** that goes without saying; **tu y vas un peu fort** you're going a bit (too) far; **allez!** go on!; come on!; **allons-y!** let's go!; **allez, au revoir** right *ou* OK then, bye-bye!

allergène [alɛʀʒɛn] *nm* allergen.

allergie [alɛʀʒi] *nf* allergy.

allergique [alɛʀʒik] *adj* allergic; ~ **à** allergic to.

allez [ale] *vb voir* **aller**.

alliage [aljaʒ] *nm* alloy.

alliance [aljɑ̃s] *nf* (*MIL, POL*) alliance; (*mariage*) marriage; (*bague*) wedding ring; **neveu par** ~ nephew by marriage.

allié, e [alje] *nm/f* ally; **parents et** ~**s** relatives and relatives by marriage.

allier [alje] *vt* (*métaux*) to alloy; (*POL, gén*) to ally; (*fig*) to combine; **s'~** to become allies; (*éléments, caractéristiques*) to combine; **s'~ à** to become allied to *ou* with.

alligator [aligatɔʀ] *nm* alligator.

allitération [aliteʀasjɔ̃] *nf* alliteration.

allô [alo] *excl* hullo, hallo.

allocataire [alɔkatɛʀ] *nm/f* beneficiary.

allocation [alɔkasjɔ̃] *nf* allowance; ~ **(de) chômage** unemployment benefit; ~ **(de) logement** rent allowance; ~**s familiales** ≈ child benefit *no pl*; ~**s de maternité** maternity allowance.

allocution [alɔkysjɔ̃] *nf* short speech.

allongé, e [alɔ̃ʒe] *adj* (*étendu*): **être** ~ to be stretched out *ou* lying down; (*long*) long; (*étiré*) elongated; (*oblong*) oblong; **rester** ~ to be lying down; **mine** ~**e** long face.

allonger [alɔ̃ʒe] *vt* to lengthen, make longer; (*étendre: bras, jambe*) to stretch (out); (*sauce*) to spin out, make go further; **s'~** *vi* to get longer; (*se coucher*) to lie down, stretch out; ~ **le pas** to hasten one's step(s).

allouer [alwe] *vt*: ~ **qch à** to allocate sth to, allot sth to.

allumage [alymaʒ] *nm* (*AUTO*) ignition.

allume-cigare [alymsigaʀ] *nm inv* cigar lighter.

allume-gaz [alymgɑz] *nm inv* gas lighter.

allumer [alyme] *vt* (*lampe, phare, radio*) to put *ou* switch on; (*pièce*) to put *ou* switch the light(s) on in; (*feu, bougie, cigare, pipe, gaz*) to light; (*chauffage*) to put on; **s'~** *vi* (*lumière, lampe*) to come *ou* go on; ~ **(la lumière** *ou* **l'électricité)** to put on the light.

allumette [alymɛt] *nf* match; (*morceau de bois*) matchstick; (*CULIN*): ~ **au fromage** cheese straw; ~ **de sûreté** safety match.

allumeuse [alymøz] *nf* (*péj*) tease (*woman*).
allure [alyʀ] *nf* (*vitesse*) speed; (*: à pied*) pace; (*démarche*) walk; (*maintien*) bearing; (*aspect, air*) look; **avoir de l'~** to have style *ou* a certain elegance; **à toute ~** at top *ou* full speed.
allusion [alyzjɔ̃] *nf* allusion; (*sous-entendu*) hint; **faire ~ à** to allude *ou* refer to; to hint at.
alluvions [alyvjɔ̃] *nfpl* alluvial deposits, alluvium *sg*.
almanach [almana] *nm* almanac.
aloès [alɔɛs] *nm* (*BOT*) aloe.
aloi [alwa] *nm*: **de bon/mauvais ~** of genuine/doubtful worth *ou* quality.

================= *MOT-CLÉ*

alors [alɔʀ] *adv* **1** (*à ce moment-là*) then, at that time; **il habitait ~ à Paris** he lived in Paris at that time; **jusqu'~** up till *ou* until then
2 (*par conséquent*) then; **tu as fini? ~ je m'en vais** have you finished? I'm going then
3 (*expressions*): **~? quoi de neuf?** well *ou* so? what's new?; **et ~?** so (what)?; **ça ~!** (well) really!
~ que *conj* **1** (*au moment où*) when, as; **il est arrivé alors que je partais** he arrived as I was leaving
2 (*pendant que*) while, when; **~ qu'il était à Paris, il a visité ...** while *ou* when he was in Paris, he visited ...
3 (*tandis que*) whereas, while; **~ que son frère travaillait dur, lui se reposait** while his brother was working hard, HE would rest.

alouette [alwɛt] *nf* (sky)lark.
alourdir [aluʀdiʀ] *vt* to weigh down, make heavy; **s'~** *vi* to grow heavy *ou* heavier.
aloyau [alwajo] *nm* sirloin.
alpaga [alpaga] *nm* (*tissu*) alpaca.
alpage [alpaʒ] *nm* high mountain pasture.
Alpes [alp(ə)] *nfpl*: **les ~** the Alps.
alpestre [alpɛstʀ(ə)] *adj* alpine.
alphabet [alfabɛ] *nm* alphabet; (*livre*) ABC (book), primer.
alphabétique [alfabetik] *adj* alphabetic(al); **par ordre ~** in alphabetical order.
alphabétisation [alfabetizɑsjɔ̃] *nf* literacy teaching.
alphabétiser [alfabetize] *vt* to teach to read and write; (*pays*) to eliminate illiteracy in.
alphanumérique [alfanymeʀik] *adj* alphanumeric.
alpin, e [alpɛ̃, -in] *adj* (*plante etc*) alpine; (*club*) climbing.
alpinisme [alpinism(ə)] *nm* mountaineering, climbing.
alpiniste [alpinist(ə)] *nm/f* mountaineer, climber.
Alsace [alzas] *nf*: **l'~** Alsace.
alsacien, ne [alzasjɛ̃, -ɛn] *adj* Alsatian.
altercation [altɛʀkɑsjɔ̃] *nf* altercation.

alter ego [altɛʀego] *nm* alter ego.
altérer [altere] *vt* (*faits, vérité*) to falsify, distort; (*qualité*) to debase, impair; (*données*) to corrupt; (*donner soif à*) to make thirsty; **s'~** *vi* to deteriorate; to spoil.
alternance [altɛʀnɑ̃s] *nf* alternation; **en ~** alternately; **formation en ~** sandwich course.
alternateur [altɛʀnatœʀ] *nm* alternator.
alternatif, ive [altɛʀnatif, -iv] *adj* alternating ♦ *nf* alternative.
alternativement [altɛʀnativmɑ̃] *adv* alternately.
alterner [altɛʀne] *vt* to alternate ♦ *vi*: **~ (avec)** to alternate (with); **(faire) ~ qch avec qch** to alternate sth with sth.
Altesse [altɛs] *nf* Highness.
altier, ière [altje, -jɛʀ] *adj* haughty.
altimètre [altimɛtʀ(ə)] *nm* altimeter.
altiport [altipɔʀ] *nm* mountain airfield.
altiste [altist(ə)] *nm/f* viola player, violist.
altitude [altityd] *nf* altitude, height; **à 1 000 m d'~** at a height *ou* an altitude of 1000 m; **en ~** at high altitudes; **perdre/prendre de l'~** to lose/gain height; **voler à haute/basse ~** to fly at a high/low altitude.
alto [alto] *nm* (*instrument*) viola ♦ *nf* (contr)alto.
altruisme [altʀɥism(ə)] *nm* altruism.
altruiste [altʀɥist(ə)] *adj* altruistic.
aluminium [alyminjɔm] *nm* aluminium (*BRIT*), aluminum (*US*).
alun [alœ̃] *nm* alum.
alunir [alyniʀ] *vi* to land on the moon.
alunissage [alynisaʒ] *nm* (moon) landing.
alvéole [alveɔl] *nm ou f* (*de ruche*) alveolus.
alvéolé, e [alveɔle] *adj* honeycombed.
AM *sigle f* = **assurance maladie**.
amabilité [amabilite] *nf* kindness; **il a eu l'~ de** he was kind *ou* good enough to.
amadou [amadu] *nm* touchwood, amadou.
amadouer [amadwe] *vt* to coax, cajole; (*adoucir*) to mollify, soothe.
amaigrir [amegʀiʀ] *vt* to make thin *ou* thinner.
amaigrissant, e [amegʀisɑ̃, -ɑ̃t] *adj*: **régime ~** slimming (*BRIT*) *ou* weight-reduction (*US*) diet.
amalgame [amalgam] *nm* amalgam; (*fig: de gens, d'idées*) hotch-potch, mixture.
amalgamer [amalgame] *vt* to amalgamate.
amande [amɑ̃d] *nf* (*de l'amandier*) almond; (*de noyau de fruit*) kernel; **en ~** (*yeux*) almond *cpd*, almond-shaped.
amandier [amɑ̃dje] *nm* almond (tree).
amanite [amanit] *nf* (*BOT*) *mushroom of the genus Amanita*; **~ tue-mouches** fly agaric.
amant [amɑ̃] *nm* lover.
amarre [amaʀ] *nf* (*NAVIG*) (mooring) rope *ou* line; **~s** *nfpl* moorings.
amarrer [amaʀe] *vt* (*NAVIG*) to moor; (*gén*) to make fast.
amaryllis [amaʀilis] *nf* amaryllis.

amas [amɑ] nm heap, pile.
amasser [amase] vt to amass; **s'~** vi to pile up, accumulate; (foule) to gather.
amateur [amatœʀ] nm amateur; **en ~** (péj) amateurishly; **musicien/sportif ~** amateur musician/sportsman; **~ de musique/sport** etc music/sport etc lover.
amateurisme [amatœʀism(ə)] nm amateurism; (péj) amateurishness.
Amazone [amazɔn] nf: **l'~** the Amazon.
amazone [amazɔn] nf horsewoman; **en ~** sidesaddle.
Amazonie [amazɔni] nf: **l'~** Amazonia.
ambages [ɑ̃baʒ]: **sans ~** adv without beating about the bush, plainly.
ambassade [ɑ̃basad] nf embassy; (mission): **en ~** on a mission.
ambassadeur, drice [ɑ̃basadœʀ, -dʀis] nm/f ambassador/ambassadress.
ambiance [ɑ̃bjɑ̃s] nf atmosphere; **il y a de l'~** everyone's having a good time.
ambiant, e [ɑ̃bjɑ̃, -ɑ̃t] adj (air, milieu) surrounding; (température) ambient.
ambidextre [ɑ̃bidɛkstʀ(ə)] adj ambidextrous.
ambigu, ë [ɑ̃bigy] adj ambiguous.
ambiguïté [ɑ̃bigɥite] nf ambiguousness no pl, ambiguity.
ambitieux, euse [ɑ̃bisjø, -øz] adj ambitious.
ambition [ɑ̃bisjɔ̃] nf ambition.
ambitionner [ɑ̃bisjɔne] vt to have as one's aim ou ambition.
ambivalent, e [ɑ̃bivalɑ̃, -ɑ̃t] adj ambivalent.
amble [ɑ̃bl(ə)] nm: **aller l'~** to amble.
ambre [ɑ̃bʀ(ə)] nm: **~ (jaune)** amber; **~ gris** ambergris.
ambré, e [ɑ̃bʀe] adj (couleur) amber; (parfum) ambergris-scented.
ambulance [ɑ̃bylɑ̃s] nf ambulance.
ambulancier, ière [ɑ̃bylɑ̃sje, -jɛʀ] nm/f ambulanceman/woman (BRIT), paramedic (US).
ambulant, e [ɑ̃bylɑ̃, -ɑ̃t] adj travelling, itinerant.
âme [ɑm] nf soul; **rendre l'~** to give up the ghost; **bonne ~** (aussi ironique) kind soul; **un joueur/tricheur dans l'~** a gambler/cheat through and through; **~ sœur** kindred spirit.
amélioration [ameljɔʀasjɔ̃] nf improvement.
améliorer [ameljɔʀe] vt to improve; **s'~** vi to improve, get better.
aménagement [amenaʒmɑ̃] nm fitting out; laying out; development; **~s** nmpl developments; **l'~ du territoire** ≈ town and country planning; **~s fiscaux** tax adjustments.
aménager [amenaʒe] vt (agencer: espace, local) to fit out; (: terrain) to lay out; (: quartier, territoire) to develop; (installer) to fix up, put in; **ferme aménagée** converted farmhouse.
amende [amɑ̃d] nf fine; **mettre à l'~** to penalize; **faire ~ honorable** to make

amends.
amendement [amɑ̃dmɑ̃] nm (JUR) amendment.
amender [amɑ̃de] vt (loi) to amend; (terre) to enrich; **s'~** vi to mend one's ways.
amène [amɛn] adj affable; **peu ~** unkind.
amener [amne] vt to bring; (causer) to bring about; (baisser: drapeau, voiles) to strike; **s'~** vi (fam) to show up, turn up; **~ qn à qch/à faire** to lead sb to sth/to do.
amenuiser [amənɥize]: **s'~** vi to dwindle; (chances) to grow slimmer, lessen.
amer, amère [amɛʀ] adj bitter.
amèrement [amɛʀmɑ̃] adv bitterly.
américain, e [ameʀikɛ̃, -ɛn] adj American ♦ nm (LING) American (English) ♦ nm/f: **A~, e** American; **en vedette ~e** as a special guest (star).
américaniser [ameʀikanize] vt to Americanize.
américanisme [ameʀikanism(ə)] nm Americanism.
amérindien, ne [ameʀɛ̃djɛ̃, -ɛn] adj Amerindian, American Indian.
Amérique [ameʀik] nf America; **l'~ centrale** Central America; **l'~ latine** Latin America; **l'~ du Nord** North America; **l'~ du Sud** South America.
Amerloque [amɛʀlɔk] nm/f (fam) Yank, Yankee.
amerrir [ameʀiʀ] vi to land (on the sea); (capsule spatiale) to splash down.
amerrissage [ameʀisaʒ] nm landing (on the sea); splash-down.
amertume [amɛʀtym] nf bitterness.
améthyste [ametist(ə)] nf amethyst.
ameublement [amœbləmɑ̃] nm furnishing; (meubles) furniture; **articles d'~** furnishings; **tissus d'~** soft furnishings, furnishing fabrics.
ameuter [amøte] vt (badauds) to draw a crowd of; (peuple) to rouse, stir up.
ami, e [ami] nm/f friend; (amant/maîtresse) boyfriend/girlfriend ♦ adj: **pays/groupe ~** friendly country/group; **être (très) ~ avec qn** to be (very) friendly with sb; **être ~ de l'ordre** to be a lover of order; **un ~ des arts** a patron of the arts; **un ~ des chiens** a dog lover; **petit ~/petite ~e** (fam) boyfriend/girlfriend.
amiable [amjabl(ə)]: **à l'~** adv (JUR) out of court; (gén) amicably.
amiante [amjɑ̃t] nm asbestos.
amibe [amib] nf amoeba (pl -ae).
amical, e, aux [amikal, -o] adj friendly ♦ nf (club) association.
amicalement [amikalmɑ̃] adv in a friendly way; (formule épistolaire) regards.
amidon [amidɔ̃] nm starch.
amidonner [amidɔne] vt to starch.
amincir [amɛ̃siʀ] vt (objet) to thin (down); **s'~** vi to get thinner ou slimmer; **~ qn** to make

sb thinner *ou* slimmer.
amincissant, e [amɛ̃sisɑ̃, -ɑ̃t] *adj* slimming.
aminé, e [amine] *adj*: **acide ~** amino acid.
amiral, aux [amiʀal, -o] *nm* admiral.
amirauté [amiʀote] *nf* admiralty.
amitié [amitje] *nf* friendship; **prendre en ~** to take a liking to; **faire** *ou* **présenter ses ~s à qn** to send sb one's best wishes; **~s** (*formule épistolaire*) (with) best wishes.
ammoniac [amɔnjak] *nm*: (**gaz**) **~** ammonia.
ammoniaque [amɔnjak] *nf* ammonia (water).
amnésie [amnezi] *nf* amnesia.
amnésique [amnezik] *adj* amnesic.
Amnesty International [amnɛsti-] *n* Amnesty International.
amniocentèse [amnjosɛ̃tɛz] *nf* amniocentesis.
amnistie [amnisti] *nf* amnesty.
amnistier [amnistje] *vt* to amnesty.
amocher [amɔʃe] *vt* (*fam*) to mess up.
amoindrir [amwɛ̃dʀiʀ] *vt* to reduce.
amollir [amɔliʀ] *vt* to soften.
amonceler [amɔ̃sle] *vt*, **s'~** *vi* to pile *ou* heap up; (*fig*) to accumulate.
amoncellement [amɔ̃sɛlmɑ̃] *nm* piling *ou* heaping up; accumulation; (*tas*) pile, heap; accumulation.
amont [amɔ̃]: **en ~** *adv* upstream; (*sur une pente*) uphill; **en ~ de** *prép* upstream from; uphill from, above.
amoral, e, aux [amɔʀal, -o] *adj* amoral.
amorce [amɔʀs(ə)] *nf* (*sur un hameçon*) bait; (*explosif*) cap; (*tube*) primer; (: *contenu*) priming; (*fig: début*) beginning(s), start.
amorcer [amɔʀse] *vt* to bait; to prime; (*commencer*) to begin, start.
amorphe [amɔʀf(ə)] *adj* passive, lifeless.
amortir [amɔʀtiʀ] *vt* (*atténuer: choc*) to absorb, cushion; (*bruit, douleur*) to deaden; (*COMM: dette*) to pay off, amortize; (: *mise de fonds, matériel*) to write off; **~ un abonnement** to make a season ticket pay (for itself).
amortissable [amɔʀtisabl(ə)] *adj* (*COMM*) that can be paid off.
amortissement [amɔʀtismɑ̃] *nm* (*de matériel*) writing off; (*d'une dette*) paying off.
amortisseur [amɔʀtisœʀ] *nm* shock absorber.
amour [amuʀ] *nm* love; (*liaison*) love affair, love; (*statuette etc*) cupid; **un ~ de** a lovely little; **faire l'~** to make love.
amouracher [amuʀaʃe]: **s'~ de** *vt* (*péj*) to become infatuated with.
amourette [amuʀɛt] *nf* passing fancy.
amoureusement [amuʀøzmɑ̃] *adv* lovingly.
amoureux, euse [amuʀø, -øz] *adj* (*regard, tempérament*) amorous; (*vie, problèmes*) love *cpd*; (*personne*): **~ (de qn)** in love (with sb) ♦ *nm/f* lover ♦ *nmpl* courting couple(s); **tomber ~ de qn** to fall in love with sb; **être ~ de qch** to be passionately fond of sth; **un ~ de la nature** a nature lover.
amour-propre, *pl* **amours-propres** [amuʀpʀɔpʀ(ə)] *nm* self-esteem.

amovible [amɔvibl(ə)] *adj* removable, detachable.
ampère [ɑ̃pɛʀ] *nm* amp(ere).
ampèremètre [ɑ̃pɛʀmɛtʀ(ə)] *nm* ammeter.
amphétamine [ɑ̃fetamin] *nf* amphetamine.
amphi [ɑ̃fi] *nm* (*SCOL fam*: = *amphithéâtre*) lecture hall *ou* theatre.
amphibie [ɑ̃fibi] *adj* amphibious.
amphibien [ɑ̃fibjɛ̃] *nm* (*ZOOL*) amphibian.
amphithéâtre [ɑ̃fiteɑtʀ(ə)] *nm* amphitheatre; (*d'université*) lecture hall *ou* theatre.
amphore [ɑ̃fɔʀ] *nf* amphora.
ample [ɑ̃pl(ə)] *adj* (*vêtement*) roomy, ample; (*gestes, mouvement*) broad; (*ressources*) ample; **jusqu'à plus ~ informé** (*ADMIN*) until further details are available.
amplement [ɑ̃pləmɑ̃] *adv* amply; **~ suffisant** ample, more than enough.
ampleur [ɑ̃plœʀ] *nf* scale, size; extent, magnitude.
ampli [ɑ̃pli] *nm* (*fam*: = *amplificateur*) amplifier, amp.
amplificateur [ɑ̃plifikatœʀ] *nm* amplifier.
amplification [ɑ̃plifikɑsjɔ̃] *nf* amplification; expansion, increase.
amplifier [ɑ̃plifje] *vt* (*son, oscillation*) to amplify; (*fig*) to expand, increase.
amplitude [ɑ̃plityd] *nf* amplitude; (*des températures*) range.
ampoule [ɑ̃pul] *nf* (*électrique*) bulb; (*de médicament*) phial; (*aux mains, pieds*) blister.
ampoulé, e [ɑ̃pule] *adj* (*péj*) pompous, bombastic.
amputation [ɑ̃pytɑsjɔ̃] *nf* amputation.
amputer [ɑ̃pyte] *vt* (*MÉD*) to amputate; (*fig*) to cut *ou* reduce drastically; **~ qn d'un bras/pied** to amputate sb's arm/foot.
Amsterdam [amstɛʀdam] *n* Amsterdam.
amulette [amylɛt] *nf* amulet.
amusant, e [amyzɑ̃, -ɑ̃t] *adj* (*divertissant, spirituel*) entertaining, amusing; (*comique*) funny, amusing.
amusé, e [amyze] *adj* amused.
amuse-gueule [amyzgœl] *nm inv* appetizer, snack.
amusement [amyzmɑ̃] *nm* (*voir amusé*) amusement; (*voir amuser*) entertaining, amusing; (*jeu etc*) pastime, diversion.
amuser [amyze] *vt* (*divertir*) to entertain, amuse; (*égayer, faire rire*) to amuse; (*détourner l'attention de*) to distract; **s'~** *vi* (*jouer*) to amuse o.s., play; (*se divertir*) to enjoy o.s., have fun; (*fig*) to mess around; **s'~ de qch** (*trouver comique*) to find sth amusing; **s'~ avec** *ou* **de qn** (*duper*) to make a fool of sb.
amusette [amyzɛt] *nf* idle pleasure, trivial pastime.
amuseur [amyzœʀ] *nm* entertainer; (*péj*) clown.
amygdale [amidal] *nf* tonsil; **opérer qn des ~s** to take sb's tonsils out.

amygdalite [amidalit] *nf* tonsillitis.

AN *sigle f* = **Assemblée nationale.**

an [ã] *nm* year; **être âgé de** *ou* **avoir 3 ~s** to be 3 (years old); **en l'~ 1980** in the year 1980; **le jour de l'~, le premier de l'~, le nouvel ~** New Year's Day.

anabolisant [anabɔlizã] *nm* anabolic steroid.

anachronique [anakʀɔnik] *adj* anachronistic.

anachronisme [anakʀɔnism(ə)] *nm* anachronism.

anaconda [anakɔ̃da] *nm* (*ZOOL*) anaconda.

anaérobie [anaeʀɔbi] *adj* anaerobic.

anagramme [anagʀam] *nf* anagram.

ANAH *sigle f* = **Agence nationale pour l'amélioration de l'habitat.**

anal, e, aux [anal, -o] *adj* anal.

analgésique [analʒezik] *nm* analgesic.

anallergique [analɛʀʒik] *adj* hypoallergenic.

analogie [analɔʒi] *nf* analogy.

analogique [analɔʒik] *adj* (*LOGIQUE*: *raisonnement*) analogical; (*calculateur, montre etc*) analogue; (*INFORM*) analog.

analogue [analɔg] *adj*: **~ (à)** analogous (to), similar (to).

analphabète [analfabɛt] *nm/f* illiterate.

analphabétisme [analfabetism(ə)] *nm* illiteracy.

analyse [analiz] *nf* analysis; (*MÉD*) test; **faire l'~ de** to analyse; **une ~ approfondie** an in-depth analysis; **en dernière ~** in the last analysis; **avoir l'esprit d'~** to have an analytical turn of mind; **~ grammaticale** grammatical analysis, parsing (*SCOL*).

analyser [analize] *vt* to analyse; (*MÉD*) to test.

analyste [analist(ə)] *nm/f* analyst; (*psychanalyste*) (psycho)analyst.

analyste-programmeur, euse, *pl* **analystes-programmeurs, euses** [analist-pʀɔgʀamœʀ, -øz] *nm/f* systems analyst.

analytique [analitik] *adj* analytical.

analytiquement [analitikmã] *adv* analytically.

ananas [anana] *nm* pineapple.

anarchie [anaʀʃi] *nf* anarchy.

anarchique [anaʀʃik] *adj* anarchic.

anarchisme [anaʀʃism(ə)] *nm* anarchism.

anarchiste [anaʀʃist(ə)] *adj* anarchistic ♦ *nm/f* anarchist.

anathème [anatɛm] *nm*: **jeter l'~ sur, lancer l'~ contre** to anathematize, curse.

anatomie [anatɔmi] *nf* anatomy.

anatomique [anatɔmik] *adj* anatomical.

ancestral, e, aux [ɑ̃sɛstʀal, -o] *adj* ancestral.

ancêtre [ɑ̃sɛtʀ(ə)] *nm/f* ancestor; (*fig*): **l'~ de** the forerunner of.

anche [ɑ̃ʃ] *nf* reed.

anchois [ɑ̃ʃwa] *nm* anchovy.

ancien, ne [ɑ̃sjɛ̃, -ɛn] *adj* old; (*de jadis, de l'antiquité*) ancient; (*précédent, ex-*) former, old ♦ *nm* (*mobilier ancien*): **l'~** antiques *pl* ♦ *nm/f* (*dans une tribu etc*) elder; **un ~ ministre** a former minister; **mon ~ne voiture** my previous car; **être plus ~ que qn dans une**

maison to have been in a firm longer than sb; (*dans l'hiérarchie*) to be senior to sb in a firm; **~ combattant** ex-serviceman; **~ (élève)** (*SCOL*) ex-pupil (*BRIT*), alumnus (*US*).

anciennement [ɑ̃sjɛnmã] *adv* formerly.

ancienneté [ɑ̃sjɛnte] *nf* oldness; antiquity; (*ADMIN*) (length of) service; seniority.

ancrage [ɑ̃kʀaʒ] *nm* anchoring; (*NAVIG*) anchorage; (*CONSTR*) anchor.

ancre [ɑ̃kʀ(ə)] *nf* anchor; **jeter/lever l'~** to cast/weigh anchor; **à l'~** at anchor.

ancrer [ɑ̃kʀe] *vt* (*CONSTR*) to anchor; (*fig*) to fix firmly; **s'~** *vi* (*NAVIG*) to (cast) anchor.

andalou, ouse [ɑ̃dalu, -uz] *adj* Andalusian.

Andalousie [ɑ̃daluzi] *nf*: **l'~** Andalusia.

andante [ɑ̃dɑ̃t] *adv, nm* andante.

Andes [ɑ̃d] *nfpl*: **les ~** the Andes.

Andorre [ɑ̃dɔʀ] *nf* Andorra.

andouille [ɑ̃duj] *nf* (*CULIN*) *sausage made of chitterlings*; (*fam*) clot, nit.

andouillette [ɑ̃dujɛt] *nf* *small andouille.*

âne [ɑn] *nm* donkey, ass; (*péj*) dunce, fool.

anéantir [aneɑ̃tiʀ] *vt* to annihilate, wipe out; (*fig*) to obliterate, destroy; (*déprimer*) to overwhelm.

anecdote [anɛkdɔt] *nf* anecdote.

anecdotique [anɛkdɔtik] *adj* anecdotal.

anémie [anemi] *nf* anaemia.

anémié, e [anemje] *adj* anaemic; (*fig*) enfeebled.

anémique [anemik] *adj* anaemic.

anémone [anemɔn] *nf* anemone; **~ de mer** sea anemone.

ânerie [ɑnʀi] *nf* stupidity; (*parole etc*) stupid *ou* idiotic comment *etc*.

anéroïde [aneʀɔid] *adj voir* **baromètre.**

ânesse [ɑnɛs] *nf* she-ass.

anesthésie [anɛstezi] *nf* anaesthesia; **sous ~** under anaesthetic; **~ générale/locale** general/local anaesthetic; **faire une ~ locale à qn** to give sb a local anaesthetic.

anesthésier [anɛstezje] *vt* to anaesthetize.

anesthésique [anɛstezik] *adj* anaesthetic.

anesthésiste [anɛstezist(ə)] *nm/f* anaesthetist.

anfractuosité [ɑ̃fʀaktɥozite] *nf* crevice.

ange [ɑ̃ʒ] *nm* angel; **être aux ~s** to be over the moon; **~ gardien** guardian angel.

angélique [ɑ̃ʒelik] *adj* angelic(al) ♦ *nf* angelica.

angelot [ɑ̃ʒlo] *nm* cherub.

angélus [ɑ̃ʒelys] *nm* angelus; (*cloches*) evening bells *pl*.

angevin, e [ɑ̃ʒvɛ̃, -in] *adj* of *ou* from Anjou; of *ou* from Angers.

angine [ɑ̃ʒin] *nf* sore throat, throat infection; **~ de poitrine** angina (pectoris).

angiome [ɑ̃ʒjom] *nm* angioma.

anglais, e [ɑ̃glɛ, -ɛz] *adj* English ♦ *nm* (*LING*) English ♦ *nm/f*: **A~, e** Englishman/woman; **les A~** the English; **filer à l'~e** to take French leave; **à l'~e** (*CULIN*) boiled.

anglaises [ɑ̃glɛz] *nfpl* (*cheveux*) ringlets.

angle [ɑ̃gl(ə)] *nm* angle; (*coin*) corner; ~
droit/obtus/aigu/mort right/obtuse/acute/
dead angle.
Angleterre [ɑ̃glətɛʀ] *nf*: **l'**~ England.
anglican, e [ɑ̃glikɑ̃, -ɑn] *adj, nm/f* Anglican.
anglicanisme [ɑ̃glikanism(ə)] *nm*
Anglicanism.
anglicisme [ɑ̃glisism(ə)] *nm* anglicism.
angliciste [ɑ̃glisist(ə)] *nm/f* English scholar;
(*étudiant*) student of English.
anglo... [ɑ̃glɔ] *préfixe* Anglo-, anglo(-).
anglo-américain, e [ɑ̃glɔameʀikɛ̃, -ɛn] *adj*
Anglo-American ♦ *nm* (*LING*) American
English.
anglo-arabe [ɑ̃glɔaʀab] *adj* Anglo-Arab.
anglo-canadien, ne [ɑ̃glɔkanadjɛ̃, -ɛn] *adj*
Anglo-Canadian ♦ *nm* (*LING*) Canadian
English.
anglo-normand, e [ɑ̃glɔnɔʀmɑ̃, -ɑ̃d] *adj*
Anglo-Norman; **les îles** ~**es** the Channel
Islands.
anglophile [ɑ̃glɔfil] *adj* anglophilic.
anglophobe [ɑ̃glɔfɔb] *adj* anglophobic.
anglophone [ɑ̃glɔfɔn] *adj* English-speaking.
anglo-saxon, ne [ɑ̃glɔsaksɔ̃, -ɔn] *adj* Anglo-
Saxon.
angoissant, e [ɑ̃gwasɑ̃, -ɑ̃t] *adj* harrowing.
angoisse [ɑ̃gwas] *nf*: **l'**~ anguish *no pl*.
angoissé, e [ɑ̃gwase] *adj* anguished;
(*personne*) full of anxieties *ou* hang-ups
(*fam*).
angoisser [ɑ̃gwase] *vt* to harrow, cause
anguish to ♦ *vi* to worry, fret.
Angola [ɑ̃gɔla] *nm*: **l'**~ Angola.
angolais, e [ɑ̃gɔlɛ, -ɛz] *adj* Angolan.
angora [ɑ̃gɔʀa] *adj, nm* angora.
anguille [ɑ̃gij] *nf* eel; ~ **de mer** conger (eel); **il
y a** ~ **sous roche** (*fig*) there's something
going on, there's something beneath all
this.
angulaire [ɑ̃gylɛʀ] *adj* angular.
anguleux, euse [ɑ̃gylø, -øz] *adj* angular.
anhydride [anidʀid] *nm* anhydride.
anicroche [anikʀɔʃ] *nf* hitch, snag.
animal, e, aux [animal, -o] *adj, nm* animal; ~
domestique/sauvage domestic/wild animal.
animalier [animalje] *adj*: **peintre** ~ animal
painter.
animateur, trice [animatœʀ, -tʀis] *nm/f* (*de
télévision*) host; (*de music-hall*) compère; (*de
groupe*) leader, organizer; (*CINÉ: technicien*)
animator.
animation [animɑsjɔ̃] *nf* (*voir animé*)
busyness; liveliness; (*CINÉ: technique*)
animation; (*activité*): ~**s** activities; **centre
d'**~ ≈ community centre.
animé, e [anime] *adj* (*rue, lieu*) busy, lively;
(*conversation, réunion*) lively, animated;
(*opposé à inanimé, aussi LING*) animate.
animer [anime] *vt* (*ville, soirée*) to liven up,
enliven; (*mettre en mouvement*) to drive;
(*stimuler*) to drive, impel; **s'**~ *vi* to liven up,

come to life.
animosité [animozite] *nf* animosity.
anis [ani] *nm* (*CULIN*) aniseed; (*BOT*) anise.
anisette [anizɛt] *nf* anisette.
Ankara [ɑ̃kaʀa] *n* Ankara.
ankyloser [ɑ̃kiloze]: **s'**~ *vi* to get stiff,
ankylose.
annales [anal] *nfpl* annals.
anneau, x [ano] *nm* ring; (*de chaîne*) link;
(*SPORT*): **exercices aux** ~**x** ring exercises.
année [ane] *nf* year; **souhaiter la bonne** ~ **à
qn** to wish sb a Happy New Year; **tout au
long de l'**~ all year long; **d'une** ~ **à l'autre**
from one year to the next; **d'**~ **en** ~ from
year to year; **l'**~ **scolaire/fiscale** the school/
tax year.
année-lumière, *pl* années-lumières
[anelymjɛʀ] *nf* light year.
annexe [anɛks(ə)] *adj* (*problème*) related;
(*document*) appended; (*salle*) adjoining ♦ *nf*
(*bâtiment*) annex(e); (*de document, ouvrage*)
annex, appendix; (*jointe à une lettre, un
dossier*) enclosure.
annexer [anɛkse] *vt* to annex; **s'**~ (*pays*) to
annex; ~ **qch à** (*joindre*) to append sth to.
annexion [anɛksjɔ̃] *nf* annexation.
annihiler [aniile] *vt* to annihilate.
anniversaire [anivɛʀsɛʀ] *nm* birthday; (*d'un
événement, bâtiment*) anniversary ♦ *adj*: **jour**
~ anniversary.
annonce [anɔ̃s] *nf* announcement; (*signe,
indice*) sign; (*aussi*: ~ **publicitaire**)
advertisement; (*CARTES*) declaration; ~
personnelle personal message; **les petites**
~**s** the small *ou* classified ads.
annoncer [anɔ̃se] *vt* to announce; (*être le signe
de*) to herald; (*CARTES*) to declare; **je vous
annonce que** ... I wish to tell you that ...; **s'**~
bien/difficile to look promising/difficult; ~
la couleur (*fig*) to lay one's cards on the
table.
annonceur, euse [anɔ̃sœʀ, -øz] *nm/f* (*TV,
RADIO: speaker*) announcer; (*publicitaire*)
advertiser.
annonciateur, trice [anɔ̃sjatœʀ, -tʀis] *adj*: ~
d'un événement presaging an event.
Annonciation [anɔ̃sjɑsjɔ̃] *nf*: **l'**~ (*REL*) the
Annunciation; (*jour*) Annunciation Day.
annotation [anɔtɑsjɔ̃] *nf* annotation.
annoter [anɔte] *vt* to annotate.
annuaire [anɥɛʀ] *nm* yearbook, annual; ~
téléphonique (telephone) directory,
phone book.
annuel, le [anɥɛl] *adj* annual, yearly.
annuellement [anɥɛlmɑ̃] *adv* annually,
yearly.
annuité [anɥite] *nf* annual instalment.
annulaire [anɥlɛʀ] *nm* ring *ou* third finger.
annulation [anɥlɑsjɔ̃] *nf* cancellation;
annulment; quashing, repeal.
annuler [anɥle] *vt* (*rendez-vous, voyage*) to
cancel, call off; (*mariage*) to annul;

(*jugement*) to quash (*BRIT*), repeal (*US*); (*résultats*) to declare void; (*MATH, PHYSIQUE*) to cancel out; **s'**~ to cancel each other out.

anoblir [anɔbliʀ] *vt* to ennoble.

anode [anɔd] *nf* anode.

anodin, e [anɔdɛ̃, -in] *adj* harmless; (*sans importance*) insignificant, trivial.

anomalie [anɔmali] *nf* anomaly.

ânon [anɔ̃] *nm* baby donkey; (*petit âne*) little donkey.

ânonner [anɔne] *vi, vt* to read in a drone; (*hésiter*) to read in a fumbling manner.

anonymat [anɔnima] *nm* anonymity; **garder l'**~ to remain anonymous.

anonyme [anɔnim] *adj* anonymous; (*fig*) impersonal.

anonymement [anɔnimmɑ̃] *adv* anonymously.

anorak [anɔʀak] *nm* anorak.

anorexie [anɔʀɛksi] *nf* anorexia.

anorexique [anɔʀɛksik] *adj, nm/f* anorexic.

anormal, e, aux [anɔʀmal, -o] *adj* abnormal; (*insolite*) unusual, abnormal.

anormalement [anɔʀmalmɑ̃] *adv* abnormally; unusually.

ANPE *sigle f* (= *Agence nationale pour l'emploi*) national employment agency (*functions include job creation*).

anse [ɑ̃s] *nf* handle; (*GÉO*) cove.

antagonisme [ɑ̃tagɔnism(ə)] *nm* antagonism.

antagoniste [ɑ̃tagɔnist(ə)] *adj* antagonistic ♦ *nm* antagonist.

antan [ɑ̃tɑ̃]: **d'**~ *adj* of yesteryear, of long ago.

antarctique [ɑ̃taʀktik] *adj* Antarctic ♦ *nm*: **l'A**~ the Antarctic; **le cercle A**~ the Antarctic Circle; **l'océan A**~ the Antarctic Ocean.

antécédent [ɑ̃tesedɑ̃] *nm* (*LING*) antecedent; ~**s** *nmpl* (*MÉD etc*) past history *sg*; ~**s professionnels** record, career to date.

antédiluvien, ne [ɑ̃tedilyvjɛ̃, -ɛn] *adj* (*fig*) ancient, antediluvian.

antenne [ɑ̃tɛn] *nf* (*de radio, télévision*) aerial; (*d'insecte*) antenna (*pl* -ae), feeler; (*poste avancé*) outpost; (*petite succursale*) sub-branch; **sur l'**~ on the air; **passer à/avoir l'**~ to go/be on the air; **2 heures d'**~ 2 hours' broadcasting time; **hors** ~ off the air; ~ **chirurgicale** (*MIL*) advance surgical unit.

antépénultième [ɑ̃tepenyltjɛm] *adj* antepenultimate.

antérieur, e [ɑ̃teʀjœʀ] *adj* (*d'avant*) previous, earlier; (*de devant*) front; ~ **à** prior *ou* previous to; **passé/futur** ~ (*LING*) past/future anterior.

antérieurement [ɑ̃teʀjœʀmɑ̃] *adv* earlier; (*précédemment*) previously; ~ **à** prior *ou* previous to.

antériorité [ɑ̃teʀjɔʀite] *nf* precedence (*in time*).

anthologie [ɑ̃tɔlɔʒi] *nf* anthology.

anthracite [ɑ̃tʀasit] *nm* anthracite ♦ *adj*: (**gris**)

~ charcoal (grey).

anthropologie [ɑ̃tʀɔpɔlɔʒi] *nf* anthropology.

anthropologue [ɑ̃tʀɔpɔlɔg] *nm/f* anthropologist.

anthropomorphisme [ɑ̃tʀɔpɔmɔʀfism(ə)] *nm* anthropomorphism.

anthropophage [ɑ̃tʀɔpɔfaʒ] *adj* cannibalistic.

anthropophagie [ɑ̃tʀɔpɔfaʒi] *nf* cannibalism, anthropophagy.

anti... [ɑ̃ti] *préfixe* anti....

antiaérien, ne [ɑ̃tiaeʀjɛ̃, -ɛn] *adj* anti-aircraft; **abri** ~ air-raid shelter.

antialcoolique [ɑ̃tialkɔlik] *adj* anti-alcohol; **ligue** ~ temperance league.

antiatomique [ɑ̃tiatɔmik] *adj*: **abri** ~ fallout shelter.

antibiotique [ɑ̃tibjɔtik] *nm* antibiotic.

antibrouillard [ɑ̃tibʀujaʀ] *adj*: **phare** ~ fog lamp.

antibruit [ɑ̃tibʀɥi] *adj inv*: **mur** ~ (*sur autoroute*) sound-muffling wall.

antibuée [ɑ̃tibɥe] *adj inv*: **dispositif** ~ demister; **bombe** ~ demister spray.

anticancéreux, euse [ɑ̃tikɑ̃seʀø, -øz] *adj* cancer *cpd*.

anticasseur(s) [ɑ̃tikɑsœʀ] *adj*: **loi/mesure** ~ law/measure against damage done by demonstrators.

antichambre [ɑ̃tiʃɑ̃bʀ(ə)] *nf* antechamber, anteroom; **faire** ~ to wait (for an audience).

antichar [ɑ̃tiʃaʀ] *adj* antitank.

antichoc [ɑ̃tiʃɔk] *adj* shockproof.

anticipation [ɑ̃tisipasjɔ̃] *nf* anticipation; (*COMM*) payment in advance; **par** ~ in anticipation, in advance; **livre/film d'**~ science fiction book/film.

anticipé, e [ɑ̃tisipe] *adj* (*règlement, paiement*) early, in advance; (*joie etc*) anticipated, early; **avec mes remerciements** ~**s** thanking you in advance *ou* anticipation.

anticiper [ɑ̃tisipe] *vt* to anticipate, foresee; (*paiement*) to pay *ou* make in advance ♦ *vi* to look *ou* think ahead; (*en racontant*) to jump ahead; (*prévoir*) to anticipate; ~ **sur** to anticipate.

anticlérical, e, aux [ɑ̃tikleʀikal, -o] *adj* anticlerical.

anticoagulant, e [ɑ̃tikɔagylɑ̃, -ɑ̃t] *adj, nm* anticoagulant.

anticolonialisme [ɑ̃tikɔlɔnjalism(ə)] *nm* anticolonialism.

anticonceptionnel, le [ɑ̃tikɔ̃sɛpsjɔnɛl] *adj* contraceptive.

anticonformisme [ɑ̃tikɔ̃fɔʀmism(ə)] *nm* nonconformism.

anticonstitutionnel, le [ɑ̃tikɔ̃stitysjɔnɛl] *adj* unconstitutional.

anticorps [ɑ̃tikɔʀ] *nm* antibody.

anticyclone [ɑ̃tisiklɔn] *nm* anticyclone.

antidater [ɑ̃tidate] *vt* to backdate, predate.

antidémocratique [ɑ̃tidemɔkʀatik] *adj* antidemocratic; (*peu démocratique*)

undemocratic.
antidérapant, e [ɑ̃tideʀapɑ̃, -ɑ̃t] *adj* nonskid.
antidopage [ɑ̃tidɔpaʒ], **antidoping** [ɑ̃tidɔpiŋ] *adj (lutte)* antidoping; *(contrôle)* dope *cpd*.
antidote [ɑ̃tidɔt] *nm* antidote.
antienne [ɑ̃tjɛn] *nf (fig)* chant, refrain.
antigang [ɑ̃tigɑ̃g] *adj inv*: **brigade** ~ commando unit.
antigel [ɑ̃tiʒɛl] *nm* antifreeze.
antigène [ɑ̃tiʒɛn] *nm* antigen.
antigouvernemental, e, aux [ɑ̃tiguvɛʀnəmɑ̃tal, -o] *adj* antigovernment.
Antigua et Barbude [ɑ̃tigaebaʀbyd] *nf* Antigua and Barbuda.
antihistaminique [ɑ̃tiistaminik] *nm* antihistamine.
anti-inflammatoire [ɑ̃tiɛ̃flamatwaʀ] *adj* anti-inflammatory.
anti-inflationniste [ɑ̃tiɛ̃flɑsjɔnist(ə)] *adj* anti-inflationary.
antillais, e [ɑ̃tijɛ, -ɛz] *adj* West Indian.
Antilles [ɑ̃tij] *nfpl*: **les** ~ the West Indies; **les Grandes/Petites** ~ the Greater/Lesser Antilles.
antilope [ɑ̃tilɔp] *nf* antelope.
antimilitarisme [ɑ̃timilitaʀism(ə)] *nm* antimilitarism.
antimilitariste [ɑ̃timilitaʀist(ə)] *adj* antimilitarist.
antimissile [ɑ̃timisil] *adj* antimissile.
antimite(s) [ɑ̃timit] *adj, nm*: **(produit)** ~ mothproofer, moth repellent.
antinucléaire [ɑ̃tinykleɛʀ] *adj* antinuclear.
antioxydant [ɑ̃tiɔksidɑ̃] *nm* antioxidant.
antiparasite [ɑ̃tipaʀazit] *adj (RADIO, TV)* anti-interference; **dispositif** ~ suppressor.
antipathie [ɑ̃tipati] *nf* antipathy.
antipathique [ɑ̃tipatik] *adj* unpleasant, disagreeable.
antipelliculaire [ɑ̃tipelikylɛʀ] *adj* anti-dandruff.
antiphrase [ɑ̃tifʀaz] *nf*: **par** ~ ironically.
antipodes [ɑ̃tipɔd] *nmpl (GÉO)*: **les** ~ the antipodes; *(fig)*: **être aux** ~ **de** to be the opposite extreme of.
antipoison [ɑ̃tipwazɔ̃] *adj inv*: **centre** ~ poison centre.
antipoliomyélitique [ɑ̃tipɔljɔmjelitik] *adj* polio *cpd*.
antiprotectionniste [ɑ̃tipʀɔtɛksjɔnist(ə)] *adj* free-trade.
antiquaire [ɑ̃tikɛʀ] *nm/f* antique dealer.
antique [ɑ̃tik] *adj* antique; *(très vieux)* ancient, antiquated.
antiquité [ɑ̃tikite] *nf (objet)* antique; **l'A**~ Antiquity; **magasin/marchand d'**~**s** antique shop/dealer.
antirabique [ɑ̃tiʀabik] *adj* rabies *cpd*.
antiraciste [ɑ̃tiʀasist(ə)] *adj* antiracist, antiracialist.
antireflet [ɑ̃tiʀəflɛ] *adj inv (verres)* antireflective.

antirépublicain, e [ɑ̃tiʀepyblikɛ̃, -ɛn] *adj* antirepublican.
antirides [ɑ̃tiʀid] *adj (crème)* antiwrinkle.
antirouille [ɑ̃tiʀuj] *adj inv*: **peinture** ~ antirust paint; **traitement** ~ rustproofing.
antisémite [ɑ̃tisemit] *adj* anti-Semitic.
antisémitisme [ɑ̃tisemitism(ə)] *nm* anti-Semitism.
antiseptique [ɑ̃tisɛptik] *adj, nm* antiseptic.
antisocial, e, aux [ɑ̃tisɔsjal, -o] *adj* antisocial.
antispasmodique [ɑ̃tispasmɔdik] *adj, nm* antispasmodic.
antisportif, ive [ɑ̃tispɔʀtif, -iv] *adj* unsporting; *(hostile au sport)* against sport, anti-sport.
antitétanique [ɑ̃titetanik] *adj* tetanus *cpd*.
antithèse [ɑ̃titɛz] *nf* antithesis.
antitrust [ɑ̃titʀœst] *adj inv (loi, mesures)* antimonopoly.
antituberculeux, euse [ɑ̃titybɛʀkylø, -øz] *adj* tuberculosis *cpd*.
antitussif, ive [ɑ̃titysif, -iv] *adj* antitussive, cough *cpd*.
antivariolique [ɑ̃tivaʀjɔlik] *adj* smallpox *cpd*.
antivol [ɑ̃tivɔl] *adj, nm*: **(dispositif)** ~ antitheft device; *(pour vélo)* padlock.
antonyme [ɑ̃tɔnim] *nm* antonym.
antre [ɑ̃tʀ(ə)] *nm* den, lair.
anus [anys] *nm* anus.
Anvers [ɑ̃vɛʀ] *n* Antwerp.
anxiété [ɑ̃ksjete] *nf* anxiety.
anxieusement [ɑ̃ksjøzmɑ̃] *adv* anxiously.
anxieux, euse [ɑ̃ksjø, -øz] *adj* anxious, worried; **être** ~ **de faire** to be anxious to do.
AOC *sigle f (= Appellation d'origine contrôlée) guarantee of quality of wine.*

> **AOC** *is the highest French wine classification. It indicates that the wine meets strict requirements concerning the vineyard of origin, the type of vine grown, the method of production, and the volume of alcohol present; see also* **vin***.*

aorte [aɔʀt(ə)] *nf* aorta.
août [u] *nm* August; *voir aussi* **juillet**.
aoûtien, ne [ausjɛ̃, -ɛn] *nm/f* August holiday-maker.
AP *sigle f* = **Assistance publique**.
apaisant, e [apɛzɑ̃, -ɑ̃t] *adj* soothing.
apaisement [apɛzmɑ̃] *nm* calming; soothing; *(aussi POL)* appeasement; ~**s** *nmpl* soothing reassurances; *(pour calmer)* pacifying words.
apaiser [apeze] *vt (colère)* to calm, quell, soothe; *(faim)* to appease, assuage; *(douleur)* to soothe; *(personne)* to calm (down), pacify; **s'**~ *vi (tempête, bruit)* to die down, subside.
apanage [apanaʒ] *nm*: **être l'**~ **de** to be the privilege *ou* prerogative of.
aparté [apaʀte] *nm (THÉÂT)* aside; *(entretien)* private conversation; **en** ~ *adv* in an aside

(*BRIT*); (*entretien*) in private.

apartheid [apaʀtɛd] *nm* apartheid.

apathie [apati] *nf* apathy.

apathique [apatik] *adj* apathetic.

apatride [apatʀid] *nm/f* stateless person.

Apennins [apɛnɛ̃] *nmpl*: **les** ~ the Apennines.

apercevoir [apɛʀsəvwaʀ] *vt* to see; **s'**~ **de** *vt* to notice; **s'**~ **que** to notice that; **sans s'en** ~ without realizing *ou* noticing.

aperçu, e [apɛʀsy] *pp de* **apercevoir** ♦ *nm* (*vue d'ensemble*) general survey; (*intuition*) insight.

apéritif, ive [apeʀitif, -iv] *adj* which stimulates the appetite ♦ *nm* (*boisson*) aperitif; (*réunion*) (pre-lunch *ou* -dinner) drinks *pl*; **prendre l'**~ to have drinks (before lunch *ou* dinner) *ou* an aperitif.

apesanteur [apəzɑ̃tœʀ] *nf* weightlessness.

à-peu-près [apøpʀɛ] *nm inv* (*péj*) vague approximation.

apeuré, e [apœʀe] *adj* frightened, scared.

aphasie [afazi] *nf* aphasia.

aphone [afɔn] *adj* voiceless.

aphorisme [afɔʀism(ə)] *nm* aphorism.

aphrodisiaque [afʀɔdizjak] *adj*, *nm* aphrodisiac.

aphte [aft(ə)] *nm* mouth ulcer.

aphteuse [aftøz] *adj f*: **fièvre** ~ foot-and-mouth disease.

à-pic [apik] *nm* cliff, drop.

apicole [apikɔl] *adj* beekeeping *cpd*.

apiculteur, trice [apikyltœʀ, -tʀis] *nm/f* beekeeper.

apiculture [apikyltyʀ] *nf* beekeeping, apiculture.

apitoiement [apitwamɑ̃] *nm* pity, compassion.

apitoyer [apitwaje] *vt* to move to pity; ~ **qn sur qn/qch** to move sb to pity for sb/over sth; **s'**~ **(sur qn/qch)** to feel pity *ou* compassion (for sb/over sth).

ap. J.-C. *abr* (= *après Jésus-Christ*) AD.

APL *sigle f* (= *aide personnalisée au logement*) type of loan for house purchase.

aplanir [aplaniʀ] *vt* to level; (*fig*) to smooth away, iron out.

aplati, e [aplati] *adj* flat, flattened.

aplatir [aplatiʀ] *vt* to flatten; **s'**~ *vi* to become flatter; (*écrasé*) to be flattened; (*fig*) to lie flat on the ground; (: *fam*) to fall flat on one's face; (: *péj*) to grovel.

aplomb [aplɔ̃] *nm* (*équilibre*) balance, equilibrium; (*fig*) self-assurance; (: *péj*) nerve; **d'**~ *adv* steady; (*CONSTR*) plumb.

apocalypse [apɔkalips(ə)] *nf* apocalypse.

apocalyptique [apɔkaliptik] *adj* (*fig*) apocalyptic.

apocryphe [apɔkʀif] *adj* apocryphal.

apogée [apɔʒe] *nm* (*fig*) peak, apogee.

apolitique [apɔlitik] *adj* (*indifférent*) apolitical; (*indépendant*) unpolitical, non-political.

apologie [apɔlɔʒi] *nf* praise; (*JUR*) vindication.

apoplexie [apɔplɛksi] *nf* apoplexy.

a posteriori [apɔsteʀjɔʀi] *adv* after the event, with hindsight, a posteriori.

apostolat [apɔstɔla] *nm* (*REL*) apostolate, discipleship; (*gén*) evangelism.

apostolique [apɔstɔlik] *adj* apostolic.

apostrophe [apɔstʀɔf] *nf* (*signe*) apostrophe; (*appel*) interpellation.

apostropher [apɔstʀɔfe] *vt* (*interpeller*) to shout at, address sharply.

apothéose [apɔteoz] *nf* pinnacle (of achievement); (*MUS etc*) grand finale.

apothicaire [apɔtikɛʀ] *nm* apothecary.

apôtre [apotʀ(ə)] *nm* apostle, disciple.

Appalaches [apalaʃ] *nmpl*: **les** ~ the Appalachian Mountains.

appalachien, ne [apalaʃjɛ̃, -ɛn] *adj* Appalachian.

apparaître [apaʀɛtʀ(ə)] *vi* to appear ♦ *vb avec attribut* to appear, seem.

apparat [apaʀa] *nm*: **tenue/dîner d'**~ ceremonial dress/dinner.

appareil [apaʀɛj] *nm* (*outil, machine*) piece of apparatus, device; (*électrique etc*) appliance; (*politique, syndical*) machinery; (*avion*) (aero)plane (*BRIT*), (air)plane (*US*), aircraft *inv*; (*téléphonique*) telephone; (*dentier*) brace (*BRIT*), braces (*US*); ~ **digestif/reproducteur** digestive/reproductive system *ou* apparatus; **l'**~ **productif** the means of production; **qui est à l'**~? who's speaking?; **dans le plus simple** ~ in one's birthday suit; ~ **(photographique)** camera; ~ **24 x 36** *ou* **petit format** 35 mm camera.

appareillage [apaʀɛjaʒ] *nm* (*appareils*) equipment; (*NAVIG*) casting off, getting under way.

appareiller [apaʀeje] *vi* (*NAVIG*) to cast off, get under way ♦ *vt* (*assortir*) to match up.

appareil-photo, *pl* **appareils-photos** [apaʀɛjfɔto] *nm* camera.

apparemment [apaʀamɑ̃] *adv* apparently.

apparence [apaʀɑ̃s] *nf* appearance; **malgré les** ~**s** despite appearances; **en** ~ apparently, seemingly.

apparent, e [apaʀɑ̃, -ɑ̃t] *adj* visible; (*évident*) obvious; (*superficiel*) apparent; **coutures** ~**es** topstitched seams; **poutres** ~**es** exposed beams.

apparenté, e [apaʀɑ̃te] *adj*: ~ **à** related to; (*fig*) similar to.

apparenter [apaʀɑ̃te]: **s'**~ **à** *vt* to be similar to.

apparier [apaʀje] *vt* (*gants*) to pair, match.

appariteur [apaʀitœʀ] *nm* attendant, porter (*in French universities*).

apparition [apaʀisjɔ̃] *nf* appearance; (*surnaturelle*) apparition; **faire son** ~ to appear.

appartement [apaʀtəmɑ̃] *nm* flat (*BRIT*), apartment (*US*).

appartenance [apaʀtənɑ̃s] *nf*: ~ **à** belonging to, membership of.

appartenir [apartəniʀ]: ~ **à** *vt* to belong to; (*faire partie de*) to belong to, be a member of; **il lui appartient de** it is up to him to.

appartiendrai [apartjɛ̃dʀe], **appartiens** [apartjɛ̃] *etc voir* **appartenir**.

apparu, e [apaʀy] *pp de* **apparaître**.

appas [apɑ] *nmpl* (*d'une femme*) charms.

appât [apɑ] *nm* (*PÊCHE*) bait; (*fig*) lure, bait.

appâter [apɑte] *vt* (*hameçon*) to bait; (*poisson, fig*) to lure, entice.

appauvrir [apovʀiʀ] *vt* to impoverish; **s'~** *vi* to grow poorer, become impoverished.

appauvrissement [apovʀismɑ̃] *nm* impoverishment.

appel [apɛl] *nm* call; (*nominal*) roll call; (*: SCOL*) register; (*MIL: recrutement*) call-up; (*JUR*) appeal; **faire ~ à** (*invoquer*) to appeal to; (*avoir recours à*) to call on; (*nécessiter*) to call for, require; **faire *ou* interjeter ~** (*JUR*) to appeal, lodge an appeal; **faire l'~** to call the roll; to call the register; **indicatif d'~** call sign; **numéro d'~** (*TÉL*) number; **produit d'~** (*COMM*) loss leader; **sans ~** (*fig*) final, irrevocable; **~ d'air** in-draught; **~ d'offres** (*COMM*) invitation to tender; **faire un ~ de phares** to flash one's headlights; **~ (téléphonique)** (tele)phone call.

appelé [aple] *nm* (*MIL*) conscript.

appeler [aple] *vt* to call; (*TÉL*) to call, ring; (*faire venir: médecin etc*) to call, send for; (*fig: nécessiter*) to call for, demand; **~ au secours** to call for help; **~ qn à l'aide *ou* au secours** to call to sb for help; **~ qn à un poste/des fonctions** to appoint sb to a post/assign duties to sb; **être appelé à** (*fig*) to be destined to; **~ qn à comparaître** (*JUR*) to summon sb to appear; **en ~ à** to appeal to; **s'~: elle s'appelle Gabrielle** her name is Gabrielle, she's called Gabrielle; **comment ça s'appelle?** what is it *ou* that called?

appellation [apelɑsjɔ̃] *nf* designation, appellation; **vin d'~ contrôlée** "appellation contrôlée" wine, *wine guaranteed of a certain quality*.

appelle [apɛl] *etc vb voir* **appeler**.

appendice [apɛ̃dis] *nm* appendix.

appendicite [apɑ̃disit] *nf* appendicitis.

appentis [apɑ̃ti] *nm* lean-to.

appert [apɛʀ] *vb*: **il ~ que** it appears that, it is evident that.

appesantir [apzɑ̃tiʀ]: **s'~** *vi* to grow heavier; **s'~ sur** (*fig*) to dwell at length on.

appétissant, e [apetisɑ̃, -ɑ̃t] *adj* appetizing, mouth-watering.

appétit [apeti] *nm* appetite; **couper l'~ à qn** to take away sb's appetite; **bon ~!** enjoy your meal!

applaudimètre [aplodimɛtʀ(ə)] *nm* applause meter.

applaudir [aplodiʀ] *vt* to applaud ♦ *vi* to applaud, clap; **~ à** *vt* (*décision*) to applaud, commend.

applaudissements [aplodismɑ̃] *nmpl* applause *sg*, clapping *sg*.

applicable [aplikabl(ə)] *adj* applicable.

applicateur [aplikatœʀ] *nm* applicator.

application [aplikɑsjɔ̃] *nf* application; (*d'une loi*) enforcement; **mettre en ~** to implement.

applique [aplik] *nf* wall lamp.

appliqué, e [aplike] *adj* (*élève etc*) industrious, assiduous; (*science*) applied.

appliquer [aplike] *vt* to apply; (*loi*) to enforce; (*donner: gifle, châtiment*) to give; **s'~** *vi* (*élève etc*) to apply o.s.; **s'~ à** (*loi, remarque*) to apply to; **s'~ à faire qch** to apply o.s. to doing sth, take pains to do sth; **s'~ sur** (*coïncider avec*) to fit over.

appoint [apwɛ̃] *nm* (extra) contribution *ou* help; **avoir/faire l'~** (*en payant*) to have/give the right change *ou* money; **chauffage d'~** extra heating.

appointements [apwɛ̃tmɑ̃] *nmpl* salary *sg*, stipend (*surtout REL*).

appointer [apwɛ̃te] *vt*: **être appointé à l'année/au mois** to be paid yearly/monthly.

appontage [apɔ̃taʒ] *nm* landing (*on an aircraft carrier*).

appontement [apɔ̃tmɑ̃] *nm* landing stage, wharf.

apponter [apɔ̃te] *vi* (*avion, hélicoptère*) to land.

apport [apɔʀ] *nm* supply; (*argent, biens etc*) contribution.

apporter [apɔʀte] *vt* to bring; (*preuve*) to give, provide; (*modification*) to make; (*suj: remarque*) to contribute, add.

apposer [apoze] *vt* to append; (*sceau etc*) to affix.

apposition [apozisjɔ̃] *nf* appending; affixing; (*LING*): **en ~** in apposition.

appréciable [apʀesjabl(ə)] *adj* (*important*) appreciable, significant.

appréciation [apʀesjɑsjɔ̃] *nf* appreciation; estimation, assessment; **~s** *nfpl* (*avis*) assessment *sg*, appraisal *sg*.

apprécier [apʀesje] *vt* to appreciate; (*évaluer*) to estimate, assess; **j'apprécierais que tu ...** I should appreciate (it) if you ....

appréhender [apʀeɑ̃de] *vt* (*craindre*) to dread; (*arrêter*) to apprehend; **~ que** to fear that; **~ de faire** to dread doing.

appréhensif, ive [apʀeɑ̃sif, -iv] *adj* apprehensive.

appréhension [apʀeɑ̃sjɔ̃] *nf* apprehension.

apprendre [apʀɑ̃dʀ(ə)] *vt* to learn; (*événement, résultats*) to learn of, hear of; **~ qch à qn** (*informer*) to tell sb (of) sth; (*enseigner*) to teach sb sth; **tu me l'apprends!** that's news to me!; **~ à faire qch** to learn to do sth; **~ à qn à faire qch** to teach sb to do sth.

apprenti, e [apʀɑ̃ti] *nm/f* apprentice; (*fig*) novice, beginner.

apprentissage [apʀɑ̃tisaʒ] *nm* learning; (*COMM, SCOL: période*) apprenticeship; **école *ou* centre d'~** training school *ou* centre;

faire l'~ de qch (*fig*) to be initiated into sth.

apprêt [aprɛ] *nm* (*sur un cuir, une étoffe*) dressing; (*sur un mur*) size; (*sur un papier*) finish; **sans ~** (*fig*) without artifice, unaffectedly.

apprêté, e [aprete] *adj* (*fig*) affected.

apprêter [aprete] *vt* to dress, finish; **s'~** *vi*: **s'~ à qch/à faire qch** to prepare for sth/for doing sth.

appris, e [apri, -iz] *pp de* **apprendre**.

apprivoisé, e [aprivwaze] *adj* tame, tamed.

apprivoiser [aprivwaze] *vt* to tame.

approbateur, trice [aprɔbatœr, -tris] *adj* approving.

approbatif, ive [aprɔbatif, -iv] *adj* approving.

approbation [aprɔbasjɔ̃] *nf* approval; **digne d'~** (*conduite, travail*) praiseworthy, commendable.

approchant, e [aprɔʃɑ̃, -ɑ̃t] *adj* similar, close; **quelque chose d'~** something similar.

approche [aprɔʃ] *nf* approaching; (*arrivée, attitude*) approach; **~s** *nfpl* (*abords*) surroundings; **à l'~ du bateau/de l'ennemi** as the ship/enemy approached *ou* drew near; **l'~ d'un problème** the approach to a problem; **travaux d'~** (*fig*) manoeuvrings.

approché, e [aprɔʃe] *adj* approximate.

approcher [aprɔʃe] *vi* to approach, come near ◆ *vt* (*vedette, artiste*) to come close to, approach; (*rapprocher*): **~ qch (de qch)** to bring *ou* put *ou* move sth near (to sth); **~ de** *vt* to draw near to; (*quantité, moment*) to approach; **s'~ de** *vt* to approach, go *ou* come *ou* move near to; **approchez-vous** come *ou* go nearer.

approfondi, e [aprɔfɔ̃di] *adj* thorough, detailed.

approfondir [aprɔfɔ̃dir] *vt* to deepen; (*question*) to go further into; **sans ~** without going too deeply into it.

appropriation [aprɔprijasjɔ̃] *nf* appropriation.

approprié, e [aprɔprije] *adj*: **~ (à)** appropriate (to), suited to.

approprier [aprɔprije] *vt* (*adapter*) adapt; **s'~** *vt* to appropriate, take over.

approuver [apruve] *vt* to agree with; (*autoriser: loi, projet*) to approve, pass; (*trouver louable*) to approve of; **je vous approuve entièrement/ne vous approuve pas** I agree with you entirely/don't agree with you; **lu et approuvé** (read and) approved.

approvisionnement [aprɔvizjɔnmɑ̃] *nm* supplying; (*provisions*) supply, stock.

approvisionner [aprɔvizjɔne] *vt* to supply; (*compte bancaire*) to pay funds into; **~ qn en** to supply sb with; **s'~** *vi*: **s'~ dans un certain magasin/au marché** to shop in a certain shop/at the market; **s'~ en** to stock up with.

approximatif, ive [aprɔksimatif, -iv] *adj* approximate, rough; (*imprécis*) vague.

approximation [aprɔksimɑsjɔ̃] *nf* approximation.

approximativement [aprɔksimativmɑ̃] *adv* approximately, roughly; vaguely.

appt *abr* = **appartement**.

appui [apɥi] *nm* support; **prendre ~ sur** to lean on; (*objet*) to rest on; **point d'~** fulcrum; (*fig*) something to lean on; **à l'~ de** (*pour prouver*) in support of; **à l'~** *adv* to support one's argument; **l'~ de la fenêtre** the windowsill, the window ledge.

appuie [apɥi] *etc vb voir* **appuyer**.

appui-tête, appuie-tête [apɥitɛt] *nm inv* headrest.

appuyé, e [apɥije] *adj* (*regard*) meaningful; (: *insistant*) intent, insistent; (*excessif: politesse, compliment*) exaggerated, overdone.

appuyer [apɥije] *vt* (*poser*): **~ qch sur/contre/à** to lean *ou* rest sth on/against/on; (*soutenir: personne, demande*) to support, back (up) ◆ *vi*: **~ sur** (*bouton, frein*) to press, push; (*mot, détail*) to stress, emphasize; (*suj: chose: peser sur*) to rest (heavily) on, press against; **s'~ sur** *vt* to lean on; (*compter sur*) to rely on; **s'~ sur qn** to lean on sb; **~ contre** (*toucher: mur, porte*) to lean *ou* rest against; **~ à droite** *ou* **sur sa droite** to bear (to the) right; **~ sur le champignon** to put one's foot down.

apr. *abr* = **après**.

âpre [ɑpr(ə)] *adj* acrid, pungent; (*fig*) harsh; (*lutte*) bitter; **~ au gain** grasping, greedy.

après [aprɛ] *prép* after ◆ *adv* afterwards; **2 heures ~** 2 hours later; **~ qu'il est** *ou* **soit parti/avoir fait** after he left/having done; **courir ~ qn** to run after sb; **crier ~ qn** to shout at sb; **être toujours ~ qn** (*critiquer etc*) to be always on at sb; **~ quoi** after which; **d'~** *prép* (*selon*) according to; **d'~ lui** according to him; **d'~ moi** in my opinion; **~ coup** *adv* after the event, afterwards; **~ tout** *adv* (*au fond*) after all; **et (puis) ~?** so what?

après-demain [apredmɛ̃] *adv* the day after tomorrow.

après-guerre [apregɛr] *nm* post-war years *pl*; **d'~** *adj* post-war.

après-midi [apremidi] *nm ou nf inv* afternoon.

après-rasage [aprerɑzaʒ] *nm inv*: **(lotion) ~** after-shave (lotion).

après-ski [apreski] *nm inv* (*chaussure*) snow boot; (*moment*) après-ski.

après-vente [aprevɑ̃t] *adj inv* after-sales *cpd*.

âpreté [ɑprəte] *nf* (*voir* **âpre**) pungency; harshness; bitterness.

à-propos [aprɔpo] *nm* (*d'une remarque*) aptness; **faire preuve d'~** to show presence of mind, do the right thing; **avec ~** suitably, aptly.

apte [apt(ə)] *adj*: **~ à qch/faire qch** capable of sth/doing sth; **~ (au service)** (*MIL*) fit (for service).

aptitude [aptityd] *nf* ability, aptitude.

apurer [apyʀe] *vt* (*COMM*) to clear.
aquaculture [akwakyltyʀ] *nf* fish farming.
aquaplanage [akwaplanaʒ] *nm* (*AUTO*) aquaplaning.
aquaplane [akwaplan] *nm* (*planche*) aquaplane; (*sport*) aquaplaning.
aquaplaning [akwaplaniŋ] *nm* aquaplaning.
aquarelle [akwaʀɛl] *nf* (*tableau*) watercolour (*BRIT*), watercolor (*US*); (*genre*) watercolo(u)rs *pl*, aquarelle.
aquarelliste [akwaʀelist(ə)] *nm/f* painter in watercolo(u)rs.
aquarium [akwaʀjɔm] *nm* aquarium.
aquatique [akwatik] *adj* aquatic, water *cpd*.
aqueduc [akdyk] *nm* aqueduct.
aqueux, euse [akø, -øz] *adj* aqueous.
aquilin [akilɛ̃] *adj m*: **nez** ~ aquiline nose.
AR *sigle m* (= *accusé de réception*): **lettre/paquet avec** ~ ≈ recorded delivery letter/parcel; (*AVIAT, RAIL etc*) = **aller (et) retour** ♦ *abr* (*AUTO*) = **arrière**.
arabe [aʀab] *adj* Arabic; (*désert, cheval*) Arabian; (*nation, peuple*) Arab ♦ *nm* (*LING*) Arabic ♦ *nm/f*: **A**~ Arab.
arabesque [aʀabɛsk(ə)] *nf* arabesque.
Arabie [aʀabi] *nf*: **l'**~ Arabia; **l'**~ **Saoudite** *ou* **Séoudite** Saudi Arabia.
arable [aʀabl(ə)] *adj* arable.
arachide [aʀaʃid] *nf* groundnut (plant); (*graine*) peanut, groundnut.
araignée [aʀeɲe] *nf* spider; ~ **de mer** spider crab.
araser [aʀɑze] *vt* to level; (*en rabotant*) to plane (down).
aratoire [aʀatwaʀ] *adj*: **instrument** ~ ploughing implement.
arbalète [aʀbalɛt] *nf* crossbow.
arbitrage [aʀbitʀaʒ] *nm* refereeing; umpiring; arbitration.
arbitraire [aʀbitʀɛʀ] *adj* arbitrary.
arbitrairement [aʀbitʀɛʀmɑ̃] *adv* arbitrarily.
arbitre [aʀbitʀ(ə)] *nm* (*SPORT*) referee; (: *TENNIS, CRICKET*) umpire; (*fig*) arbiter, judge; (*JUR*) arbitrator.
arbitrer [aʀbitʀe] *vt* to referee; to umpire; to arbitrate.
arborer [aʀbɔʀe] *vt* to bear, display; (*avec ostentation*) to sport.
arborescence [aʀbɔʀesɑ̃s] *nf* tree structure.
arboricole [aʀbɔʀikɔl] *adj* (*animal*) arboreal; (*technique*) arboricultural.
arboriculture [aʀbɔʀikyltyʀ] *nf* arboriculture; ~ **fruitière** fruit (tree) growing.
arbre [aʀbʀ(ə)] *nm* tree; (*TECH*) shaft; ~ **à cames** (*AUTO*) camshaft; ~ **fruitier** fruit tree; ~ **généalogique** family tree; ~ **de Noël** Christmas tree; ~ **de transmission** (*AUTO*) driveshaft.
arbrisseau, x [aʀbʀiso] *nm* shrub.
arbuste [aʀbyst(ə)] *nm* small shrub, bush.
arc [aʀk] *nm* (*arme*) bow; (*GÉOM*) arc; (*ARCHIT*) arch; ~ **de cercle** arc of a circle; **en** ~ **de**

cercle *adj* semi-circular.
arcade [aʀkad] *nf* arch(way); ~**s** *nfpl* arcade *sg*, arches; ~ **sourcilière** arch of the eyebrows.
arcanes [aʀkan] *nmpl* mysteries.
arc-boutant, *pl* **arcs-boutants** [aʀkbutɑ̃] *nm* flying buttress.
arc-bouter [aʀkbute]: **s'**~ *vi*: **s'**~ **contre** to lean *ou* press against.
arceau, x [aʀso] *nm* (*métallique etc*) hoop.
arc-en-ciel, *pl* **arcs-en-ciel** [aʀkɑ̃sjɛl] *nm* rainbow.
archaïque [aʀkaik] *adj* archaic.
archaïsme [aʀkaism(ə)] *nm* archaism.
archange [aʀkɑ̃ʒ] *nm* archangel.
arche [aʀʃ(ə)] *nf* arch; ~ **de Noé** Noah's Ark.
archéologie [aʀkeɔlɔʒi] *nf* arch(a)eology.
archéologique [aʀkeɔlɔʒik] *adj* arch(a)eological.
archéologue [aʀkeɔlɔg] *nm/f* arch(a)eologist.
archer [aʀʃe] *nm* archer.
archet [aʀʃɛ] *nm* bow.
archétype [aʀketip] *nm* archetype.
archevêché [aʀʃəveʃe] *nm* archbishopric; (*palais*) archbishop's palace.
archevêque [aʀʃəvɛk] *nm* archbishop.
archi... [aʀʃi] *préfixe* (*très*) dead, extra.
archibondé, e [aʀʃibɔ̃de] *adj* chock-a-block (*BRIT*), packed solid.
archiduc [aʀʃidyk] *nm* archduke.
archiduchesse [aʀʃidyʃɛs] *nf* archduchess.
archipel [aʀʃipɛl] *nm* archipelago.
archisimple [aʀʃisɛ̃pl(ə)] *adj* dead easy *ou* simple.
architecte [aʀʃitɛkt(ə)] *nm* architect.
architectural, e, aux [aʀʃitɛktyʀal, -o] *adj* architectural.
architecture [aʀʃitɛktyʀ] *nf* architecture.
archive [aʀʃiv] *nf* file; ~**s** *nfpl* archives.
archiver [aʀʃive] *vt* to file.
archiviste [aʀʃivist(ə)] *nm/f* archivist.
arçon [aʀsɔ̃] *nm voir* **cheval**.
arctique [aʀktik] *adj* Arctic ♦ *nm*: **l'A**~ the Arctic; **le cercle A**~ the Arctic Circle; **l'océan A**~ the Arctic Ocean.
ardemment [aʀdamɑ̃] *adv* ardently, fervently.
ardent, e [aʀdɑ̃, -ɑ̃t] *adj* (*soleil*) blazing; (*fièvre*) raging; (*amour*) ardent, passionate; (*prière*) fervent.
ardeur [aʀdœʀ] *nf* blazing heat; (*fig*) fervour, ardour.
ardoise [aʀdwaz] *nf* slate.
ardu, e [aʀdy] *adj* arduous, difficult; (*pente*) steep, abrupt.
are [aʀ] *nm* are, 100 square metres.
arène [aʀɛn] *nf* arena; (*fig*): **l'**~ **politique/littéraire** the political/literary arena; ~**s** *nfpl* bull-ring *sg*.
arête [aʀɛt] *nf* (*de poisson*) bone; (*d'une montagne*) ridge; (*GÉOM etc*) edge (*where two faces meet*).
arg. *abr* = **argus**.

argent [aʀʒɑ̃] *nm* (*métal*) silver; (*monnaie*) money; (*couleur*) silver; **en avoir pour son ~** to get value for money; **gagner beaucoup d'~** to earn a lot of money; **~ comptant** (hard) cash; **~ liquide** ready money, (ready) cash; **~ de poche** pocket money.

argenté, e [aʀʒɑ̃te] *adj* silver(y); (*métal*) silver-plated.

argenter [aʀʒɑ̃te] *vt* to silver(-plate).

argenterie [aʀʒɑ̃tʀi] *nf* silverware; (*en métal argenté*) silver plate.

argentin, e [aʀʒɑ̃tɛ̃, -in] *adj* (*son*) silvery; (*d'Argentine*) Argentinian, Argentine ♦ *nm/f*: **A~, e** Argentinian, Argentine.

Argentine [aʀʒɑ̃tin] *nf*: **l'~** Argentina, the Argentine.

argile [aʀʒil] *nf* clay.

argileux, euse [aʀʒilø, -øz] *adj* clayey.

argot [aʀɡo] *nm* slang.

> Initially **argot** was the jargon of the criminal underworld, characterized by colourful images and distinctive intonation and designed to confuse the outsider. Some French authors write in argot and contribute to its diffusion and development. More generally, the special vocabulary used by any social or professional group is also known as argot.

argotique [aʀɡɔtik] *adj* slang *cpd*; (*très familier*) slangy.

arguer [aʀɡɥe]: **~ de** *vt* to put forward as a pretext *ou* reason; **~ que** to argue that.

argument [aʀɡymɑ̃] *nm* argument.

argumentaire [aʀɡymɑ̃tɛʀ] *nm* list of sales points; (*brochure*) sales leaflet.

argumentation [aʀɡymɑ̃tɑsjɔ̃] *nf* (*fait d'argumenter*) arguing; (*ensemble des arguments*) argument.

argumenter [aʀɡymɑ̃te] *vi* to argue.

argus [aʀɡys] *nm* guide to second-hand car etc prices.

arguties [aʀɡysi] *nfpl* pettifoggery *sg* (*BRIT*), quibbles.

aride [aʀid] *adj* arid.

aridité [aʀidite] *nf* aridity.

arien, ne [aʀjɛ̃, -ɛn] *adj* Arian.

aristocrate [aʀistɔkʀat] *nm/f* aristocrat.

aristocratie [aʀistɔkʀasi] *nf* aristocracy.

aristocratique [aʀistɔkʀatik] *adj* aristocratic.

arithmétique [aʀitmetik] *adj* arithmetic(al) ♦ *nf* arithmetic.

armada [aʀmada] *nf* (*fig*) army.

armagnac [aʀmaɲak] *nm* armagnac.

armateur [aʀmatœʀ] *nm* shipowner.

armature [aʀmatyʀ] *nf* framework; (*de tente etc*) frame; (*de corset*) bone; (*de soutien-gorge*) wiring.

arme [aʀm(ə)] *nf* weapon; (*section de l'armée*) arm; **~s** *nfpl* weapons, arms; (*blason*) (coat of) arms; **les ~s** (*profession*) soldiering *sg*; **à ~s égales** on equal terms; **en ~s** up in arms;

passer par les **~s** to execute (by firing squad); **prendre/présenter les ~s** to take up/present arms; **se battre à l'~ blanche** to fight with blades; **~ à feu** firearm.

armé, e [aʀme] *adj* armed; **~ de** armed with.

armée [aʀme] *nf* army; **~ de l'air** Air Force; **l'~ du Salut** the Salvation Army; **~ de terre** Army.

armement [aʀməmɑ̃] *nm* (*matériel*) arms *pl*, weapons *pl*; (: *d'un pays*) arms *pl*, armament; (*action d'équiper: d'un navire*) fitting out; **~s nucléaires** nuclear armaments; **course aux ~s** arms race.

Arménie [aʀmeni] *nf*: **l'~** Armenia.

arménien, ne [aʀmenjɛ̃, -ɛn] *adj* Armenian ♦ *nm* (*LING*) Armenian ♦ *nm/f*: **A~, ne** Armenian.

armer [aʀme] *vt* to arm; (*arme à feu*) to cock; (*appareil-photo*) to wind on; **~ qch de** to fit sth with; (*renforcer*) to reinforce sth with; **~ qn de** to arm *ou* equip sb with; **s'~ de** to arm o.s. with.

armistice [aʀmistis] *nm* armistice; **l'A~** ≈ Remembrance (*BRIT*) *ou* Veterans (*US*) Day.

armoire [aʀmwaʀ] *nf* (tall) cupboard; (*penderie*) wardrobe (*BRIT*), closet (*US*); **~ à pharmacie** medicine chest.

armoiries [aʀmwari] *nfpl* coat of arms *sg*.

armure [aʀmyʀ] *nf* armour *no pl*, suit of armour.

armurerie [aʀmyʀʀi] *nf* arms factory; (*magasin*) gunsmith's (shop).

armurier [aʀmyʀje] *nm* gunsmith; (*MIL, d'armes blanches*) armourer.

ARN *sigle m* (= *acide ribonucléique*) RNA.

arnaque [aʀnak] *nf*: **de l'~** daylight robbery.

arnaquer [aʀnake] *vt* to do (*fam*), swindle; **se faire ~** to be had (*fam*) *ou* done.

arnaqueur [aʀnakœʀ] *nm* swindler.

arnica [aʀnika] *nm*: (**teinture d'**)**~** arnica.

aromates [aʀɔmat] *nmpl* seasoning *sg*, herbs (and spices).

aromathérapie [aʀɔmateʀapi] *nf* aromatherapy.

aromatique [aʀɔmatik] *adj* aromatic.

aromatiser [aʀɔmatize] *vt* to flavour.

arôme [aʀom] *nm* aroma; (*d'une fleur etc*) fragrance.

arpège [aʀpɛʒ] *nm* arpeggio.

arpentage [aʀpɑ̃taʒ] *nm* (land) surveying.

arpenter [aʀpɑ̃te] *vt* to pace up and down.

arpenteur [aʀpɑ̃tœʀ] *nm* land surveyor.

arqué, e [aʀke] *adj* arched; (*jambes*) bow *cpd*, bandy.

arr. *abr* = **arrondissement**.

arrachage [aʀaʃaʒ] *nm*: **~ des mauvaises herbes** weeding.

arraché [aʀaʃe] *nm* (*SPORT*) snatch; **obtenir à l'~** (*fig*) to snatch.

arrache-pied [aʀaʃpje]: **d'~** *adv* relentlessly.

arracher [aʀaʃe] *vt* to pull out; (*page etc*) to tear off, tear out; (*déplanter: légume*) to lift;

(*: herbe, souche*) to pull up; (*bras etc: par explosion*) to blow off; (*: par accident*) to tear off; **s'~** *vt* (*article très recherché*) to fight over; **~ qch à qn** to snatch sth from sb; (*fig*) to wring sth out of sb, wrest sth from sb; **~ qn à** (*solitude, rêverie*) to drag sb out of; (*famille etc*) to tear ou wrench sb away from; **se faire ~ une dent** to have a tooth out ou pulled (*US*); **s'~ de** (*lieu*) to tear o.s. away from; (*habitude*) to force o.s. out of.

arraisonner [aʀɛzɔne] *vt* to board and search.

arrangeant, e [aʀɑ̃ʒɑ̃, -ɑ̃t] *adj* accommodating, obliging.

arrangement [aʀɑ̃ʒmɑ̃] *nm* arrangement.

arranger [aʀɑ̃ʒe] *vt* to arrange; (*réparer*) to fix, put right; (*régler*) to settle, sort out; (*convenir à*) to suit, be convenient for; **s'~** (*se mettre d'accord*) to come to an agreement ou arrangement; (*s'améliorer: querelle, situation*) to be sorted out; (*se débrouiller*): **s'~ pour que ...** to arrange things so that ...; **je vais m'~** I'll manage; **ça va s'~** it'll sort itself out; **s'~ pour faire** to make sure that ou see to it that one can do.

arrangeur [aʀɑ̃ʒœʀ] *nm* (*MUS*) arranger.

arrestation [aʀɛstɑsjɔ̃] *nf* arrest.

arrêt [aʀɛ] *nm* stopping; (*de bus etc*) stop; (*JUR*) judgment, decision; (*FOOTBALL*) save; **~s** *nmpl* (*MIL*) arrest *sg*; **être à l'~** to be stopped, have come to a halt; **rester** ou **tomber en ~ devant** to stop short in front of; **sans ~** without stopping, non-stop; (*fréquemment*) continually; **~ d'autobus** bus stop; **~ facultatif** request stop; **~ de mort** capital sentence; **~ de travail** stoppage (of work).

arrêté, e [aʀete] *adj* (*idées*) firm, fixed ♦ *nm* order, decree; **~ municipal** ≈ bylaw, byelaw.

arrêter [aʀete] *vt* to stop; (*chauffage etc*) to turn off, switch off; (*COMM: compte*) to settle; (*COUTURE: point*) to fasten off; (*fixer: date etc*) to appoint, decide on; (*criminel, suspect*) to arrest; **s'~** *vi* to stop; (*s'interrompre*) to stop o.s.; **~ de faire** to stop doing; **arrête de te plaindre** stop complaining; **ne pas ~ de faire** to keep on doing; **s'~ de faire** to stop doing; **s'~ sur** (*suj: choix, regard*) to fall on.

arrhes [aʀ] *nfpl* deposit *sg*.

arrière [aʀjɛʀ] *nm* back; (*SPORT*) fullback ♦ *adj inv*: **siège/roue ~** back ou rear seat/wheel; **~s** *nmpl* (*fig*): **protéger ses ~s** to protect the rear; **à l'~** *adv* behind, at the back; **en ~** *adv* behind; (*regarder*) back, behind; (*tomber, aller*) backwards; **en ~ de** *prép* behind.

arriéré, e [aʀjere] *adj* (*péj*) backward ♦ *nm* (*d'argent*) arrears *pl*.

arrière-boutique [aʀjɛʀbutik] *nf* back shop.

arrière-cour [aʀjɛʀkuʀ] *nf* backyard.

arrière-cuisine [aʀjɛʀkɥizin] *nf* scullery.

arrière-garde [aʀjɛʀɡaʀd(ə)] *nf* rearguard.

arrière-goût [aʀjɛʀɡu] *nm* aftertaste.

arrière-grand-mère, *pl* **arrière-grand-mères** [aʀjɛʀɡʀɑ̃mɛʀ] *nf* great-grandmother.

arrière-grand-père, *pl* **arrière-grands-pères** [aʀjɛʀɡʀɑ̃pɛʀ] *nm* great-grandfather.

arrière-grands-parents [aʀjɛʀɡʀɑ̃paʀɑ̃] *nmpl* great-grandparents.

arrière-pays [aʀjɛʀpei] *nm inv* hinterland.

arrière-pensée [aʀjɛʀpɑ̃se] *nf* ulterior motive; (*doute*) mental reservation.

arrière-petite-fille, *pl* **arrière-petites-filles** [aʀjɛʀpətitfij] *nf* great-granddaughter.

arrière-petit-fils, *pl* **arrière-petits-fils** [aʀjɛʀpətifis] *nm* great-grandson.

arrière-petits-enfants [aʀjɛʀpətizɑ̃fɑ̃] *nmpl* great-grandchildren.

arrière-plan [aʀjɛʀplɑ̃] *nm* background; **d'~** *adj* (*INFORM*) background *cpd*.

arriérer [aʀjere]: **s'~** *vi* (*COMM*) to fall into arrears.

arrière-saison [aʀjɛʀsɛzɔ̃] *nf* late autumn.

arrière-salle [aʀjɛʀsal] *nf* back room.

arrière-train [aʀjɛʀtʀɛ̃] *nm* hindquarters *pl*.

arrimer [aʀime] *vt* to stow; (*fixer*) to secure, fasten securely.

arrivage [aʀivaʒ] *nm* arrival.

arrivant, e [aʀivɑ̃, -ɑ̃t] *nm/f* newcomer.

arrivée [aʀive] *nf* arrival; (*ligne d'arrivée*) finish; **~ d'air/de gaz** air/gas inlet; **courrier à l'~** incoming mail; **à mon ~** when I arrived.

arriver [aʀive] *vi* to arrive; (*survenir*) to happen, occur; **j'arrive!** (I'm) just coming!; **il arrive à Paris à 8 h** he gets to ou arrives in Paris at 8; **~ à destination** to arrive at one's destination; **~ à** (*atteindre*) to reach; **~ à (faire) qch** (*réussir*) to manage (to do) sth; **~ à échéance** to fall due; **en ~ à faire** to end up doing, get to the point of doing; **il arrive que** it happens that; **il lui arrive de faire** he sometimes does.

arrivisme [aʀivism(ə)] *nm* ambition, ambitiousness.

arriviste [aʀivist(ə)] *nm/f* go-getter.

arrogance [aʀɔɡɑ̃s] *nf* arrogance.

arrogant, e [aʀɔɡɑ̃, -ɑ̃t] *adj* arrogant.

arroger [aʀɔʒe]: **s'~** *vt* to assume (without right); **s'~ le droit de ...** to assume the right to ....

arrondi, e [aʀɔ̃di] *adj* round ♦ *nm* roundness.

arrondir [aʀɔ̃diʀ] *vt* (*forme, objet*) to round; (*somme*) to round off; **s'~** *vi* to become round(ed); **~ ses fins de mois** to supplement one's pay.

arrondissement [aʀɔ̃dismɑ̃] *nm* (*ADMIN*) ≈ district.

arrosage [aʀozaʒ] *nm* watering; **tuyau d'~** hose(pipe).

arroser [aʀoze] *vt* to water; (*victoire etc*) to celebrate (over a drink); (*CULIN*) to baste.

arroseur [aʀozœʀ] *nm* (*tourniquet*) sprinkler.

arroseuse [aʀozøz] *nf* water cart.

arrosoir [aʀozwaʀ] *nm* watering can.

arrt *abr* = **arrondissement**.

arsenal, aux [aʀsənal, -o] nm (NAVIG) naval dockyard; (MIL) arsenal; (fig) gear, paraphernalia.

arsenic [aʀsənik] nm arsenic.

art [aʀ] nm art; **avoir l'~ de faire** (fig: personne) to have a talent for doing; **les ~s** the arts; **livre/critique d'~** art book/critic; **objet d'~** objet d'art; **~ dramatique** dramatic art; **~s martiaux** martial arts; **~s et métiers** applied arts and crafts; **~s ménagers** home economics sg; **~s plastiques** plastic arts.

art. abr = **article**.

artère [aʀtɛʀ] nf (ANAT) artery; (rue) main road.

artériel, le [aʀteʀjɛl] adj arterial.

artériosclérose [aʀteʀjɔskleʀoz] nf arteriosclerosis.

arthrite [aʀtʀit] nf arthritis.

arthrose [aʀtʀoz] nf (degenerative) osteoarthritis.

artichaut [aʀtiʃo] nm artichoke.

article [aʀtikl(ə)] nm article; (COMM) item, article; (INFORM) record, item; **faire l'~** (COMM) to do one's sales spiel; **faire l'~ de** (fig) to sing the praises of; **à l'~ de la mort** at the point of death; **~ défini/indéfini** definite/indefinite article; **~ de fond** (PRESSE) feature article; **~s de bureau** office equipment; **~s de voyage** travel goods ou items.

articulaire [aʀtikylɛʀ] adj of the joints, articular.

articulation [aʀtikylasjɔ̃] nf articulation; (ANAT) joint.

articulé, e [aʀtikyle] adj (membre) jointed; (poupée) with moving joints.

articuler [aʀtikyle] vt to articulate; **s'~ (sur)** (ANAT, TECH) to articulate (with); **s'~ autour de** (fig) to centre around ou on, turn on.

artifice [aʀtifis] nm device, trick.

artificiel, le [aʀtifisjɛl] adj artificial.

artificiellement [aʀtifisjɛlmɑ̃] adv artificially.

artificier [aʀtifisje] nm pyrotechnist.

artificieux, euse [aʀtifisjø, -øz] adj guileful, deceitful.

artillerie [aʀtijʀi] nf artillery, ordnance.

artilleur [aʀtijœʀ] nm artilleryman, gunner.

artisan [aʀtizɑ̃] nm artisan, (self-employed) craftsman; **l'~ de la victoire/du malheur** the architect of victory/of the disaster.

artisanal, e, aux [aʀtizanal, -o] adj of ou made by craftsmen; (péj) cottage industry cpd, unsophisticated.

artisanalement [aʀtizanalmɑ̃] adv by craftsmen.

artisanat [aʀtizana] nm arts and crafts pl.

artiste [aʀtist(ə)] nm/f artist; (THÉÂT, MUS) artist, performer; (: de variétés) entertainer.

artistique [aʀtistik] adj artistic.

artistiquement [aʀtistikmɑ̃] adv artistically.

aryen, ne [aʀjɛ̃, -ɛn] adj Aryan.

AS sigle fpl (ADMIN) = **assurances sociales**

♦ sigle f (SPORT: = Association sportive)
≈ FC (= Football Club).

as vb [a] voir **avoir** ♦ nm [ɑs] ace.

a/s abr (= aux soins de) c/o.

ASBL sigle f (= association sans but lucratif) non-profit-making organization.

asc. abr = **ascenseur**.

ascendance [asɑ̃dɑ̃s] nf (origine) ancestry; (ASTROLOGIE) ascendant.

ascendant, e [asɑ̃dɑ̃, -ɑ̃t] adj upward ♦ nm influence; **~s** nmpl ascendants.

ascenseur [asɑ̃sœʀ] nm lift (BRIT), elevator (US).

ascension [asɑ̃sjɔ̃] nf ascent; climb; **l'A~** (REL) the Ascension; (: jour férié) Ascension (Day); **(île de) l'A~** Ascension Island.

La fête de l'**Ascension** is a public holiday in France. Falling on a Thursday, usually in May, the holiday provides the opportunity for many French people also to take Friday off work and enjoy a long weekend; see also **faire le pont**.

ascète [asɛt] nm/f ascetic.

ascétique [asetik] adj ascetic.

ascétisme [asetism(ə)] nm asceticism.

ascorbique [askɔʀbik] adj: **acide ~** ascorbic acid.

ASE sigle f (= Agence spatiale européenne) ESA (= European Space Agency).

asepsie [asɛpsi] nf asepsis.

aseptique [asɛptik] adj aseptic.

aseptiser [asɛptize] vt to sterilize; (plaie) to disinfect.

asexué, e [asɛksɥe] adj asexual.

asiatique [azjatik] adj Asian, Asiatic ♦ nm/f: **A~** Asian.

Asie [azi] nf: **l'~** Asia.

asile [azil] nm (refuge) refuge, sanctuary; (POL): **droit d'~** (political) asylum; (pour malades, vieillards etc) home; **accorder l'~ politique à qn** to grant ou give sb political asylum; **chercher/trouver ~ quelque part** to seek/find refuge somewhere.

asocial, e, aux [asɔsjal, -o] adj antisocial.

aspect [aspɛ] nm appearance, look; (fig) aspect, side; (LING) aspect; **à l'~ de** at the sight of.

asperge [aspɛʀʒ(ə)] nf asparagus no pl.

asperger [aspɛʀʒe] vt to spray, sprinkle.

aspérité [aspeʀite] nf excrescence, protruding bit (of rock etc).

aspersion [aspɛʀsjɔ̃] nf spraying, sprinkling.

asphalte [asfalt(ə)] nm asphalt.

asphyxiant, e [asfiksjɑ̃, -ɑ̃t] adj suffocating; **gaz ~** poison gas.

asphyxie [asfiksi] nf suffocation, asphyxia, asphyxiation.

asphyxier [asfiksje] vt to suffocate, asphyxiate; (fig) to stifle; **mourir asphyxié** to die of suffocation ou asphyxiation.

aspic [aspik] nm (ZOOL) asp; (CULIN) aspic.

aspirant, e [aspiʀɑ̃, -ɑ̃t] *adj*: **pompe ~e** suction pump ♦ *nm* (*NAVIG*) midshipman.

aspirateur [aspiʀatœʀ] *nm* vacuum cleaner, hoover ®.

aspiration [aspiʀɑsjɔ̃] *nf* inhalation; sucking (up); drawing up; **~s** *nfpl* (*ambitions*) aspirations.

aspirer [aspiʀe] *vt* (*air*) to inhale; (*liquide*) to suck (up); (*suj: appareil*) to suck *ou* draw up; **~ à** *vt* to aspire to.

aspirine [aspiʀin] *nf* aspirin.

assagir [asaʒiʀ] *vt*, **s'~** *vi* to quieten down, sober down.

assaillant, e [asajɑ̃, -ɑ̃t] *nm/f* assailant, attacker.

assaillir [asajiʀ] *vt* to assail, attack; **~ qn de** (*questions*) to assail *ou* bombard sb with.

assainir [aseniʀ] *vt* to clean up; (*eau, air*) to purify.

assainissement [asenismɑ̃] *nm* cleaning up; purifying.

assaisonnement [asɛzɔnmɑ̃] *nm* seasoning.

assaisonner [asɛzɔne] *vt* to season; **bien assaisonné** highly seasoned.

assassin [asasɛ̃] *nm* murderer; assassin.

assassinat [asasina] *nm* murder; assassination.

assassiner [asasine] *vt* to murder; (*surtout POL*) to assassinate.

assaut [aso] *nm* assault, attack; **prendre d'~** to (take by) storm, assault; **donner l'~ (à)** to attack; **faire ~ de** (*rivaliser*) to vie with *ou* rival each other in.

assèchement [asɛʃmɑ̃] *nm* draining, drainage.

assécher [aseʃe] *vt* to drain.

ASSEDIC [asedik] *sigle f* (= *Association pour l'emploi dans l'industrie et le commerce*) *unemployment insurance scheme.*

assemblage [asɑ̃blaʒ] *nm* assembling; (*MENUISERIE*) joint; **un ~ de** (*fig*) a collection of; **langage d'~** (*INFORM*) assembly language.

assemblée [asɑ̃ble] *nf* (*réunion*) meeting; (*public, assistance*) gathering; assembled people; (*POL*) assembly; (*REL*): **l'~ des fidèles** the congregation; **l'A~ nationale (AN)** the (French) National Assembly.

> *The* **Assemblée nationale** *is the lower house of the French parliament, the upper house being the* **Sénat**. *It sits at the Palais Bourbon in Paris and consists of 577* **députés** *elected every five years; see also* **élection**.

assembler [asɑ̃ble] *vt* (*joindre, monter*) to assemble, put together; (*amasser*) to gather (together), collect (together); **s'~** *vi* to gather, collect.

assembleur [asɑ̃blœʀ] *nm* assembler, fitter; (*INFORM*) assembler.

assener, asséner [asene] *vt*: **~ un coup à qn** to deal sb a blow.

assentiment [asɑ̃timɑ̃] *nm* assent, consent; (*approbation*) approval.

asseoir [aswaʀ] *vt* (*malade, bébé*) to sit up; (*personne debout*) to sit down; (*autorité, réputation*) to establish; **s'~** *vi* to sit (o.s.) up; to sit (o.s.) down; **faire ~ qn** to ask sb to sit down; **~ qch sur** to build sth on; (*appuyer*) to base sth on.

assermenté, e [asɛʀmɑ̃te] *adj* sworn, on oath.

assertion [asɛʀsjɔ̃] *nf* assertion.

asservir [asɛʀviʀ] *vt* to subjugate, enslave.

asservissement [asɛʀvismɑ̃] *nm* (*action*) enslavement; (*état*) slavery.

assesseur [asesœʀ] *nm* (*JUR*) assessor.

asseyais [asɛjɛ] *etc vb voir* **asseoir**.

assez [ase] *adv* (*suffisamment*) enough, sufficiently; (*passablement*) rather, quite, fairly; **~!** enough!, that'll do!; **~/pas ~ cuit** well enough done/underdone; **est-il ~ fort/rapide?** is he strong/fast enough *ou* sufficiently strong/fast?; **il est passé ~ vite** he went past rather *ou* quite *ou* fairly fast; **~ de pain/livres** enough *ou* sufficient bread/books; **vous en avez ~?** have you got enough?; **en avoir ~ de qch** (*en être fatigué*) to have had enough of sth; **travailler ~** to work sufficiently (hard), work (hard) enough.

assidu, e [asidy] *adj* assiduous, painstaking; (*régulier*) regular; **~ auprès de qn** attentive towards sb.

assiduité [asidɥite] *nf* assiduousness, painstaking; regularity; attentiveness; **~s** *nfpl* assiduous attentions.

assidûment [asidymɑ̃] *adv* assiduously, painstakingly; attentively.

assied [asje] *etc vb voir* **asseoir**.

assiégé, e [asjeʒe] *adj* under siege, besieged.

assiéger [asjeʒe] *vt* to besiege, lay siege to; (*suj: foule, touristes*) to mob, besiege.

assiérai [asjeʀe] *etc vb voir* **asseoir**.

assiette [asjet] *nf* plate; (*contenu*) plate(ful); (*équilibre*) seat; (*de colonne*) seating; (*de navire*) trim; **~ anglaise** assorted cold meats; **~ creuse** (soup) dish, soup plate; **~ à dessert** dessert *ou* side plate; **~ de l'impôt** basis of (tax) assessment; **~ plate** (dinner) plate.

assiettée [asjete] *nf* plateful.

assignation [asiɲɑsjɔ̃] *nf* assignation; (*JUR*) summons; (: *de témoin*) subpoena; **~ à résidence** compulsory order of residence.

assigner [asiɲe] *vt*: **~ qch à** to assign *ou* allot sth to; (*valeur, importance*) to attach sth to; (*somme*) to allocate sth to; (*limites*) to set *ou* fix sth to; (*cause, effet*) to ascribe *ou* attribute sth to; **~ qn à** (*affecter*) to assign sb to; **~ qn à résidence** (*JUR*) to give sb a compulsory order of residence.

assimilable [asimilabl(ə)] *adj* easily assimilated *ou* absorbed.

assimilation [asimilɑsjɔ̃] *nf* assimilation, absorption.

assimiler [asimile] *vt* to assimilate, absorb; (*comparer*): ~ **qch/qn à** to liken *ou* compare sth/sb to; **s'**~ *vi* (*s'intégrer*) to be assimilated *ou* absorbed; **ils sont assimilés aux infirmières** (*ADMIN*) they are classed as nurses.

assis, e [asi, -iz] *pp de* **asseoir** ♦ *adj* sitting (down), seated ♦ *nf* (*CONSTR*) course; (*GÉO*) stratum (*pl* -a); (*fig*) basis (*pl* bases), foundation; ~ **en tailleur** sitting cross-legged.

assises [asiz] *nfpl* (*JUR*) assizes; (*congrès*) (annual) conference.

assistanat [asistana] *nm* assistantship; (*à l'université*) probationary lectureship.

assistance [asistɑ̃s] *nf* (*public*) audience; (*aide*) assistance; **porter** *ou* **prêter** ~ **à qn** to give sb assistance; **A**~ **publique (AP)** *public health service*; **enfant de l'A**~ **(publique)** (*formerly*) child in care; ~ **technique** technical aid.

assistant, e [asistɑ̃, -ɑ̃t] *nm/f* assistant; (*d'université*) probationary lecturer; **les** ~**s** *nmpl* (*auditeurs etc*) those present; ~**e sociale** social worker.

assisté, e [asiste] *adj* (*AUTO*) power assisted ♦ *nm/f* person receiving aid from the State.

assister [asiste] *vt* to assist; ~ **à** *vt* (*scène, événement*) to witness; (*conférence, séminaire*) to attend, be (present) at; (*spectacle, match*) to be at, see.

association [asɔsjɑsjɔ̃] *nf* association; (*COMM*) partnership; ~ **d'idées/images** association of ideas/images.

associé, e [asɔsje] *nm/f* associate; (*COMM*) partner.

associer [asɔsje] *vt* to associate; ~ **qn à** (*profits*) to give sb a share of; (*affaire*) to make sb a partner in; (*joie, triomphe*) to include sb in; ~ **qch à** (*joindre, allier*) to combine sth with; **s'**~ *vi* to join together; (*COMM*) to form a partnership ♦ *vt* (*collaborateur*) to take on (as a partner); **s'**~ **à** to be combined with; (*opinions, joie de qn*) to share in; **s'**~ **à** *ou* **avec qn pour faire** to join (forces) *ou* join together with sb to do.

assoie [aswa] *etc vb voir* **asseoir**.

assoiffé, e [aswafe] *adj* thirsty; (*fig*): ~ **de** (*sang*) thirsting for; (*gloire*) thirsting after.

assoirai [asware], **assois** [aswa] *etc vb voir* **asseoir**.

assolement [asɔlmɑ̃] *nm* (systematic) rotation of crops.

assombrir [asɔ̃bʀiʀ] *vt* to darken; (*fig*) to fill with gloom; **s'**~ *vi* to darken; (*devenir nuageux, fig: visage*) to cloud over; (*fig*) to become gloomy.

assommer [asɔme] *vt* (*étourdir, abrutir*) to knock out, stun; (*fam: ennuyer*) to bore stiff.

Assomption [asɔ̃psjɔ̃] *nf*: **l'**~ the Assumption.

> **La fête de l'Assomption** *on August 15 is a national holiday in France. Traditionally, large numbers of holidaymakers set out on this date, frequently causing chaos on French roads; see also* faire le pont.

assorti, e [asɔʀti] *adj* matched, matching; **fromages/légumes** ~**s** assorted cheeses/vegetables; ~ **à** matching; ~ **de** accompanied with; (*conditions, conseils*) coupled with; **bien/mal** ~ well/ill-matched.

assortiment [asɔʀtimɑ̃] *nm* (*choix*) assortment, selection; (*harmonie de couleurs, formes*) arrangement; (*COMM: lot, stock*) selection.

assortir [asɔʀtiʀ] *vt* to match; **s'**~ to go well together, match; ~ **qch à** to match sth with; ~ **qch de** to accompany sth with; **s'**~ **de** to be accompanied by.

assoupi, e [asupi] *adj* dozing, sleeping; (*fig*) (be)numbed; (*sens*) dulled.

assoupir [asupiʀ]: **s'**~ *vi* (*personne*) to doze off; (*sens*) to go numb.

assoupissement [asupismɑ̃] *nm* (*sommeil*) dozing; (*fig: somnolence*) drowsiness.

assouplir [asupliʀ] *vt* to make supple, soften; (*membres, corps*) to limber up, make supple; (*fig*) to relax; (: *caractère*) to soften, make more flexible; **s'**~ *vi* to soften; to limber up; to relax; to become more flexible.

assouplissement [asuplismɑ̃] *nm* softening; limbering up; relaxation; **exercices d'**~ limbering up exercises.

assourdir [asuʀdiʀ] *vt* (*bruit*) to deaden, muffle; (*suj: bruit*) to deafen.

assourdissant, e [asuʀdisɑ̃, -ɑ̃t] *adj* (*bruit*) deafening.

assouvir [asuviʀ] *vt* to satisfy, appease.

assoyais [aswajɛ] *etc vb voir* **asseoir**.

ASSU [asy] *sigle f* = Association du sport scolaire et universitaire.

assujetti, e [asyʒeti] *adj*: ~ **(à)** subject (to); (*ADMIN*): ~ **à l'impôt** subject to tax(ation).

assujettir [asyʒetiʀ] *vt* to subject, subjugate; (*fixer: planches, tableau*) to secure, fix securely; ~ **qn à** (*règle, impôt*) to subject sb to.

assujettissement [asyʒetismɑ̃] *nm* subjection, subjugation.

assumer [asyme] *vt* (*fonction, emploi*) to assume, take on; (*accepter: conséquence, situation*) to accept.

assurance [asyʀɑ̃s] *nf* (*certitude*) assurance; (*confiance en soi*) (self-)confidence; (*contrat*) insurance (policy); (*secteur commercial*) insurance; **prendre une** ~ **contre** to take out insurance *ou* an insurance policy against; ~ **contre l'incendie** fire insurance; ~ **contre le vol** insurance against theft; **société d'**~, **compagnie d'**~**s** insurance company; ~

maladie **(AM)** health insurance; ~ **au tiers** third party insurance; ~ **tous risques** (*AUTO*) comprehensive insurance; ~**s sociales (AS)** ≈ National Insurance (*BRIT*), ≈ Social Security (*US*).

assurance-vie, *pl* **assurances-vie** [asyʀɑsvi] *nf* life assurance *ou* insurance.

assurance-vol, *pl* **assurances-vol** [asyʀɑsvɔl] *nf* insurance against theft.

assuré, e [asyʀe] *adj* (*victoire etc*) certain, sure; (*démarche, voix*) assured, (self-) confident; (*certain*): ~ **de** confident of; (*ASSURANCES*) insured ♦ *nm/f* insured (person); ~ **social** ≈ member of the National Insurance (*BRIT*) *ou* Social Security (*US*) scheme.

assurément [asyʀemɑ] *adv* assuredly, most certainly.

assurer [asyʀe] *vt* (*COMM*) to insure; (*stabiliser*) to steady, stabilize; (*victoire etc*) to ensure, make certain; (*frontières, pouvoir*) to make secure; (*service, garde*) to provide, operate; ~ **qch à qn** (*garantir*) to secure *ou* guarantee sth for sb; (*certifier*) to assure sb of sth; ~ **à qn que** to assure you that that is not the case/is the case; ~ **qn de** to assure sb of; ~ **ses arrières** (*fig*) to be sure one has something to fall back on; **s'~ (contre)** (*COMM*) to insure o.s. (against); **s'~ de/que** (*vérifier*) to make sure of/that; **s'~ (de)** (*aide de qn*) to secure; **s'~ sur la vie** to take out a life insurance; **s'~ le concours/la collaboration de qn** to secure sb's aid/collaboration.

assureur [asyʀœʀ] *nm* insurance agent; (*société*) insurers *pl*.

Assyrie [asiʀi] *nf*: **l'~** Assyria.

assyrien, ne [asiʀjɛ, -ɛn] *adj* Assyrian ♦ *nm/f*: **A~, ne** Assyrian.

astérisque [asteʀisk(ə)] *nm* asterisk.

astéroïde [asteʀɔid] *nm* asteroid.

asthmatique [asmatik] *adj* asthmatic.

asthme [asm(ə)] *nm* asthma.

asticot [astiko] *nm* maggot.

asticoter [astikɔte] *vt* (*fam*) to needle, get at.

astigmate [astigmat] *adj* (*MÉD: personne*) astigmatic, having an astigmatism.

astiquer [astike] *vt* to polish, shine.

astrakan [astʀakɑ] *nm* astrakhan.

astral, e, aux [astʀal, -o] *adj* astral.

astre [astʀ(ə)] *nm* star.

astreignant, e [astʀɛɲɑ, -ɑt] *adj* demanding.

astreindre [astʀɛdʀ(ə)] *vt*: ~ **qn à qch** to force sth upon sb; ~ **qn à faire** to compel *ou* force sb to do; **s'~ à** to compel *ou* force o.s. to.

astringent, e [astʀɛʒɑ, -ɑt] *adj* astringent.

astrologie [astʀɔlɔʒi] *nf* astrology.

astrologique [astʀɔlɔʒik] *adj* astrological.

astrologue [astʀɔlɔg] *nm* astrologer.

astronaute [astʀɔnot] *nm/f* astronaut.

astronautique [astʀɔnotik] *nf* astronautics *sg*.

astronome [astʀɔnɔm] *nm/f* astronomer.

astronomie [astʀɔnɔmi] *nf* astronomy.

astronomique [astʀɔnɔmik] *adj* astronomic(al).

astrophysicien, ne [astʀɔfizisjɛ, -ɛn] *nm/f* astrophysicist.

astrophysique [astʀɔfizik] *nf* astrophysics *sg*.

astuce [astys] *nf* shrewdness, astuteness; (*truc*) trick, clever way; (*plaisanterie*) wisecrack.

astucieusement [astysjøzmɑ] *adv* shrewdly, cleverly, astutely.

astucieux, euse [astysjø, -øz] *adj* shrewd, clever, astute.

asymétrique [asimetʀik] *adj* asymmetric(al).

AT *sigle m* (= *Ancien Testament*) OT.

atavisme [atavism(ə)] *nm* atavism, heredity.

atelier [atəlje] *nm* workshop; (*de peintre*) studio.

atermoiements [atɛʀmwamɑ] *nmpl* procrastination *sg*.

atermoyer [atɛʀmwaje] *vi* to temporize, procrastinate.

athée [ate] *adj* atheistic ♦ *nm/f* atheist.

athéisme [ateism(ə)] *nm* atheism.

Athènes [atɛn] *n* Athens.

athénien, ne [atenjɛ, -ɛn] *adj* Athenian.

athlète [atlɛt] *nm/f* (*SPORT*) athlete; (*costaud*) muscleman.

athlétique [atletik] *adj* athletic.

athlétisme [atletism(ə)] *nm* athletics *sg*; **faire de l'~** to do athletics; **tournoi d'~** athletics meeting.

Atlantide [atlɑtid] *nf*: **l'~** Atlantis.

atlantique [atlɑtik] *adj* Atlantic ♦ *nm*: **l'(océan) A~** the Atlantic (Ocean).

atlantiste [atlɑtist(ə)] *adj*, *nm/f* Atlanticist.

Atlas [atlɑs] *nm*: **l'~** the Atlas Mountains.

atlas [atlɑs] *nm* atlas.

atmosphère [atmɔsfɛʀ] *nf* atmosphere.

atmosphérique [atmɔsfeʀik] *adj* atmospheric.

atoll [atɔl] *nm* atoll.

atome [atom] *nm* atom.

atomique [atɔmik] *adj* atomic, nuclear; (*usine*) nuclear; (*nombre, masse*) atomic.

atomiseur [atɔmizœʀ] *nm* atomizer.

atomiste [atɔmist(ə)] *nm/f* (*aussi*: **savant, ingénieur** *etc* ~) atomic scientist.

atone [atɔn] *adj* lifeless; (*LING*) unstressed, unaccented.

atours [atuʀ] *nmpl* attire *sg*, finery *sg*.

atout [atu] *nm* trump; (*fig*) asset; (: *plus fort*) trump card; "~ **pique/trèfle**" "spades/clubs are trumps".

ATP *sigle f* (= *Association des tennismen professionnels*) ATP (= *Association of Tennis Professionals*) ♦ *sigle mpl* (= *arts et traditions populaires*): **musée des** ~ ≈ folk museum.

âtre [ɑtʀ(ə)] *nm* hearth.

atroce [atʀɔs] *adj* atrocious, horrible.

atrocement [atʀɔsmɑ] *adv* atrociously, horribly.

atrocité [atʀɔsite] *nf* atrocity.
atrophie [atʀɔfi] *nf* atrophy.
atrophier [atʀɔfje]: **s'~** *vi* to atrophy.
atropine [atʀɔpin] *nf* (CHIMIE) atropine.
attabler [atable]: **s'~** *vi* to sit down at (the)
table; **s'~ à la terrasse** to sit down (at a
table) on the terrace.
attachant, e [ataʃɑ̃, -ɑ̃t] *adj* engaging,
likeable.
attache [ataʃ] *nf* clip, fastener; (*fig*) tie; **~s** *nfpl*
(*relations*) connections; **à l'~** (*chien*) tied up.
attaché, e [ataʃe] *adj*: **être ~ à** (*aimer*) to be
attached to ♦ *nm* (ADMIN) attaché; **~ de
presse/d'ambassade** press/embassy
attaché; **~ commercial** commercial attaché.
attaché-case [ataʃekɛz] *nm inv* attaché case
(BRIT), briefcase.
attachement [ataʃmɑ̃] *nm* attachment.
attacher [ataʃe] *vt* to tie up; (*étiquette*) to
attach, tie on; (*souliers*) to do up ♦ *vi* (*poêle,
riz*) to stick; **s'~** (*robe etc*) to do up; **s'~ à**
(*par affection*) to become attached to; **s'~ à
faire qch** to endeavour to do sth; **~ qch à** to
tie *ou* fasten *ou* attach sth to; **~ qn à** (*fig:
lier*) to attach sb to; **~ du prix/de
l'importance à** to attach great value/attach
importance to.
attaquant [atakɑ̃] *nm* (MIL) attacker; (SPORT)
striker, forward.
attaque [atak] *nf* attack; (*cérébrale*) stroke;
(*d'épilepsie*) fit; **être/se sentir d'~** to be/feel
on form; **~ à main armée** armed attack.
attaquer [atake] *vt* to attack; (*en justice*) to
bring an action against, sue; (*travail*) to
tackle, set about ♦ *vi* to attack; **s'~ à** to
attack; (*épidémie, misère*) to tackle, attack.
attardé, e [ataʀde] *adj* (*passants*) late; (*enfant*)
backward; (*conceptions*) old-fashioned.
attarder [ataʀde]: **s'~** *vi* (*sur qch, en chemin*) to
linger; (*chez qn*) to stay on.
atteignais [ateɲɛ] *etc vb voir* **atteindre.**
atteindre [atɛ̃dʀ(ə)] *vt* to reach; (*blesser*) to
hit; (*contacter*) to reach, contact, get in
touch with; (*émouvoir*) to affect.
atteint, e [atɛ̃, -ɛ̃t] *pp de* **atteindre** ♦ *adj* (MÉD):
être ~ de to be suffering from ♦ *nf* attack;
hors d'~e out of reach; **porter ~e à** to strike
a blow at, undermine.
attelage [atlaʒ] *nm* (*de remorque etc*) coupling
(BRIT), (trailer) hitch (US); (*animaux*) team;
(*harnachement*) harness; (: *de bœufs*) yoke.
atteler [atle] *vt* (*cheval, bœufs*) to hitch up;
(*wagons*) to couple; **s'~ à** (*travail*) to buckle
down to.
attelle [atɛl] *nf* splint.
attenant, e [atnɑ̃, -ɑ̃t] *adj*: **~ (à)** adjoining.
attendant [atɑ̃dɑ̃]: **en ~** *adv* (*dans l'intervalle*)
meanwhile, in the meantime.
attendre [atɑ̃dʀ(ə)] *vt* to wait for; (*être destiné
ou réservé à*) to await, be in store for ♦ *vi* to
wait; **je n'attends plus rien (de la vie)** I
expect nothing more (from life); **attendez**

que je réfléchisse wait while I think; **s'~ à**
(*ce que*) (*escompter*) to expect (that); **je ne
m'y attendais pas** I didn't expect that; **ce
n'est pas ce à quoi je m'attendais** that's not
what I expected; **~ un enfant** to be
expecting a baby; **~ de pied ferme** to wait
determinedly; **~ de faire/d'être** to wait until
one does/is; **~ que** to wait until; **~ qch de** to
expect sth of; **faire ~ qn** to keep sb waiting;
se faire ~ to keep people (*ou* us *etc*)
waiting; **en attendant** *adv voir* **attendant.**
attendri, e [atɑ̃dʀi] *adj* tender.
attendrir [atɑ̃dʀiʀ] *vt* to move (to pity);
(*viande*) to tenderize; **s'~ (sur)** to be moved
ou touched (by).
attendrissant, e [atɑ̃dʀisɑ̃, -ɑ̃t] *adj* moving,
touching.
attendrissement [atɑ̃dʀismɑ̃] *nm* (*tendre*)
emotion; (*apitoyé*) pity.
attendrisseur [atɑ̃dʀisœʀ] *nm* tenderizer.
attendu, e [atɑ̃dy] *pp de* **attendre** ♦ *adj* long-
awaited; (*prévu*) expected ♦ *nm*: **~s reasons**
adduced for a judgment; **~ que** *conj*
considering that, since.
attentat [atɑ̃ta] *nm* (*contre une personne*)
assassination attempt; (*contre un bâtiment*)
attack; **~ à la bombe** bomb attack; **~ à la
pudeur** (*exhibitionnisme*) indecent exposure
no pl; (*agression*) indecent assault *no pl*.
attente [atɑ̃t] *nf* wait; (*espérance*) expectation;
contre toute ~ contrary to (all)
expectations.
attenter [atɑ̃te]: **~ à** *vt* (*liberté*) to violate; **~ à
la vie de qn** to make an attempt on sb's life;
~ à ses jours to make an attempt on one's
life.
attentif, ive [atɑ̃tif, -iv] *adj* (*auditeur*)
attentive; (*soin*) scrupulous; (*travail*) careful;
~ à paying attention to; (*devoir*) mindful of;
~ à faire careful to do.
attention [atɑ̃sjɔ̃] *nf* attention; (*prévenance*)
attention, thoughtfulness *no pl*; **mériter ~** to
be worthy of attention; **à l'~ de** for the
attention of; **porter qch à l'~ de qn** to bring
sth to sb's attention; **attirer l'~ de qn sur
qch** to draw sb's attention to sth; **faire ~ (à)**
to be careful (of); **faire ~ (à ce) que** to be *ou*
make sure that; **~! careful!**, watch!, watch
ou mind (BRIT) out!; **~, si vous ouvrez cette
lettre** (*sanction*) just watch out, if you open
that letter; **~, respectez les consignes de
sécurité** be sure to observe the safety
instructions.
attentionné, e [atɑ̃sjone] *adj* thoughtful,
considerate.
attentisme [atɑ̃tism(ə)] *nm* wait-and-see
policy.
attentiste [atɑ̃tist(ə)] *adj* (*politique*) wait-and-
see ♦ *nm/f* believer in a wait-and-see policy.
attentivement [atɑ̃tivmɑ̃] *adv* attentively.
atténuant, e [atenɥɑ̃, -ɑ̃t] *adj*: **circonstances
~es** extenuating circumstances.

atténuer [atenɥe] *vt* to alleviate, ease; (*diminuer*) to lessen; (*amoindrir*) to mitigate the effects of; **s'~** *vi* to ease; (*violence etc*) to abate.

atterrer [atere] *vt* to dismay, appal.

atterrir [aterir] *vi* to land.

atterrissage [aterisaʒ] *nm* landing; **~ sur le ventre/sans visibilité/forcé** belly/blind/forced landing.

attestation [atɛstasjɔ̃] *nf* certificate, testimonial; **~ médicale** doctor's certificate.

attester [atɛste] *vt* to testify to, vouch for; (*démontrer*) to attest, testify to; **~ que** to testify that.

attiédir [atjedir]: **s'~** *vi* to become lukewarm; (*fig*) to cool down.

attifé, e [atife] *adj* (*fam*) got up (*BRIT*), decked out.

attifer [atife] *vt* to get (*BRIT*) *ou* do up, deck out.

attique [atik] *nm*: **appartement en ~** penthouse (flat (*BRIT*) *ou* apartment (*US*)).

attirail [atiraj] *nm* gear; (*péj*) paraphernalia.

attirance [atirɑ̃s] *nf* attraction; (*séduction*) lure.

attirant, e [atirɑ̃, -ɑ̃t] *adj* attractive, appealing.

attirer [atire] *vt* to attract; (*appâter*) to lure, entice; **~ qn dans un coin/vers soi** to draw sb into a corner/towards one; **~ l'attention de qn** to attract sb's attention; **~ l'attention de qn sur qch** to draw sb's attention to sth; **~ des ennuis à qn** to make trouble for sb; **s'~ des ennuis** to bring trouble upon o.s., get into trouble.

attiser [atize] *vt* (*feu*) to poke (up), stir up; (*fig*) to fan the flame of, stir up.

attitré, e [atitre] *adj* qualified; (*agréé*) accredited, appointed.

attitude [atityd] *nf* attitude; (*position du corps*) bearing.

attouchements [atuʃmɑ̃] *nmpl* touching *sg*; (*sexuels*) fondling *sg*, stroking *sg*.

attractif, ive [atraktif, -iv] *adj* attractive.

attraction [atraksjɔ̃] *nf* attraction; (*de cabaret, cirque*) number.

attrait [atrɛ] *nm* appeal, attraction; (*plus fort*) lure; **~s** *nmpl* attractions; **éprouver de l'~ pour** to be attracted to.

attrape [atrap] *nf voir* **farce**.

attrape-nigaud [atrapnigo] *nm* con.

attraper [atrape] *vt* to catch; (*habitude, amende*) to get, pick up; (*fam: duper*) to take in (*BRIT*), con.

attrayant, e [atrɛjɑ̃, -ɑ̃t] *adj* attractive.

attribuer [atribɥe] *vt* to award; (*rôle, tâche*) to allocate, assign; (*imputer*): **~ qch à** to attribute sth to, ascribe sth to, put sth down to; **s'~** *vt* (*s'approprier*) to claim for o.s.

attribut [atriby] *nm* attribute; (*LING*) complement.

attribution [atribysjɔ̃] *nf* (*voir attribuer*) awarding; allocation, assignment; attribution; **~s** *nfpl* (*compétence*) attributions; **complément d'~** (*LING*) indirect object.

attristant, e [atristɑ̃, -ɑ̃t] *adj* saddening.

attrister [atriste] *vt* to sadden; **s'~ de qch** to be saddened by sth.

attroupement [atrupmɑ̃] *nm* crowd, mob.

attrouper [atrupe]: **s'~** *vi* to gather.

au [o] *prép* + *dét voir* **à**.

aubade [obad] *nf* dawn serenade.

aubaine [obɛn] *nf* godsend; (*financière*) windfall; (*COMM*) bonanza.

aube [ob] *nf* dawn, daybreak; (*REL*) alb; **à l'~** at dawn *ou* daybreak; **à l'~ de** (*fig*) at the dawn of.

aubépine [obepin] *nf* hawthorn.

auberge [obɛrʒ(ə)] *nf* inn; **~ de jeunesse** youth hostel.

aubergine [obɛrʒin] *nf* aubergine (*BRIT*), eggplant (*US*).

aubergiste [obɛrʒist(ə)] *nm/f* inn-keeper, hotel-keeper.

auburn [obœrn] *adj inv* auburn.

aucun, e [okœ̃, -yn] *dét* no, *tournure négative +* any; (*positif*) any ♦ *pron* none, *tournure négative +* any; (*positif*) any(one); **il n'y a ~ livre** there isn't any book, there is no book; **je n'en vois ~ qui** I can't see any which, I (can) see none which; **~ homme** no man; **sans ~ doute** without any doubt; **sans ~e hésitation** without hesitation; **plus qu'~ autre** more than any other; **plus qu'~ de ceux qui ...** more than any of those who ...; **en ~e façon** in no way at all; **~ des deux** neither of the two; **~ d'entre eux** none of them; **d'~s** (*certains*) some.

aucunement [okynmɑ̃] *adv* in no way, not in the least.

audace [odas] *nf* daring, boldness; (*péj*) audacity; **il a eu l'~ de ...** he had the audacity to ...; **vous ne manquez pas d'~!** you're not lacking in nerve *ou* cheek!

audacieux, euse [odasjø, -øz] *adj* daring, bold.

au-dedans [odədɑ̃] *adv*, *prép* inside.

au-dehors [odəɔr] *adv*, *prép* outside.

au-delà [odla] *adv* beyond ♦ *nm*: **l'~** the hereafter; **~ de** *prép* beyond.

au-dessous [odsu] *adv* underneath; below; **~ de** *prép* under(neath), below; (*limite, somme etc*) below, under; (*dignité, condition*) below.

au-dessus [odsy] *adv* above; **~ de** *prép* above.

au-devant [odvɑ̃]: **~ de** *prép*: **aller ~ de** to go (out) and meet; (*souhaits de qn*) to anticipate.

audible [odibl(ə)] *adj* audible.

audience [odjɑ̃s] *nf* audience; (*JUR: séance*) hearing; **trouver ~ auprès de** to arouse much interest among, get the (interested) attention of.

audimat [odimat] *nm* (*taux d'écoute*) ratings *pl*.

audiogramme [odjɔgʀam] *nm* audiogramme.
audio-visuel, le [odjɔvizɥɛl] *adj* audio-visual ♦ *nm* (*équipement*) audio-visual aids *pl*; (*méthodes*) audio-visual methods *pl*; **l'~** radio and television.
auditeur, trice [oditœʀ, -tʀis] *nm/f* (*à la radio*) listener; (*à une conférence*) member of the audience, listener; **~ libre** unregistered student (*attending lectures*), auditor (*US*).
auditif, ive [oditif, -iv] (*mémoire*) auditory; **appareil ~** hearing aid.
audition [odisjɔ̃] *nf* (*ouïe, écoute*) hearing; (*JUR: de témoins*) examination; (*MUS, THÉÂT: épreuve*) audition.
auditionner [odisjɔne] *vt, vi* to audition.
auditoire [oditwaʀ] *nm* audience.
auditorium [oditɔʀjɔm] *nm* (public) studio.
auge [oʒ] *nf* trough.
augmentation [ɔgmɑ̃tɑsjɔ̃] *nf* (*action*) increasing; raising; (*résultat*) increase; **~ (de salaire)** rise (in salary) (*BRIT*), (pay) raise (*US*).
augmenter [ɔgmɑ̃te] *vt* to increase; (*salaire, prix*) to increase, raise, put up; (*employé*) to increase the salary of, give a (salary) rise (*BRIT*) *ou* (pay) raise (*US*) to ♦ *vi* to increase; **~ de poids/volume** to gain (in) weight/volume.
augure [ɔgyʀ] *nm* soothsayer, oracle; **de bon/mauvais ~** of good/ill omen.
augurer [ɔgyʀe] *vt*: **~ qch de** to foresee sth (coming) from *ou* out of; **~ bien de** to augur well for.
auguste [ɔgyst(ə)] *adj* august, noble, majestic.
aujourd'hui [oʒuʀdɥi] *adv* today; **~ en huit/quinze** a week/two weeks today, a week/two weeks from now; **à dater** *ou* **partir d'~** from today('s date).
aumône [omon] *nf* alms *sg* (*pl inv*); **faire l'~** (**à qn**) to give alms (to sb); **faire l'~ de qch à qn** (*fig*) to favour sb with sth.
aumônerie [omonʀi] *nf* chaplaincy.
aumônier [omonje] *nm* chaplain.
auparavant [oapaʀavɑ̃] *adv* before(hand).
auprès [opʀɛ]: **~ de** *prép* next to, close to; (*recourir, s'adresser*) to; (*en comparaison de*) compared with, next to; (*dans l'opinion de*) in the opinion of.
auquel [okɛl] *prép* + *pron voir* **lequel**.
aurai [oʀɛ] *etc vb voir* **avoir**.
auréole [oʀeɔl] *nf* halo; (*tache*) ring.
auréolé, e [oʀeɔle] *adj* (*fig*): **~ de gloire** crowned with *ou* in glory.
auriculaire [oʀikylɛʀ] *nm* little finger.
aurore [oʀɔʀ] *nf* dawn, daybreak; **~ boréale** northern lights *pl*.
ausculter [oskylte] *vt* to sound.
auspices [ospis] *nmpl*: **sous les ~ de** under the patronage *ou* auspices of; **sous de bons/mauvais ~** under favourable/unfavourable auspices.
aussi [osi] *adv* (*également*) also, too; (*de comparaison*) as ♦ *conj* therefore, consequently; **~ fort que** as strong as; **lui ~** (*sujet*) he too; (*objet*) him too; **~ bien que** (*de même que*) as well as.
aussitôt [osito] *adv* straight away, immediately; **~ que** as soon as; **~ envoyé** as soon as it is (*ou* was) sent; **~ fait** no sooner done.
austère [ostɛʀ] *adj* austere; (*sévère*) stern.
austérité [osteʀite] *nf* austerity; **plan/budget d'~** austerity plan/budget.
austral, e [ostʀal] *adj* southern; **l'océan A~** the Antarctic Ocean; **les Terres A~es** Antarctica.
Australie [ostʀali] *nf*: **l'~** Australia.
australien, ne [ostʀaljɛ̃, -ɛn] *adj* Australian ♦ *nm/f*: **A~, ne** Australian.
autant [otɑ̃] *adv* so much; (*comparatif*): **~ (que)** as much (as); (*nombre*) as many (as); **~ (de)** so much (*ou* many); as much (*ou* many); **n'importe qui aurait pu en faire ~** anyone could have done the same *ou* as much; **~ partir** we (*ou* you *etc*) may as well leave; **~ ne rien dire** best not say anything; **~ dire que** ... one might as well say that ...; **fort ~ que courageux** as strong as he is brave; **il n'est pas découragé pour ~** he isn't discouraged for all that; **pour ~ que** *conj* assuming, as long as; **d'~** *adv* accordingly, in proportion; **d'~ plus/mieux (que)** all the more/the better (since).
autarcie [otaʀsi] *nf* autarky, self-sufficiency.
autel [otɛl] *nm* altar.
auteur [otœʀ] *nm* author; **l'~ de cette remarque** the person who said that; **droit d'~** copyright.
auteur-compositeur [otœʀkɔ̃pozitœʀ] *nm/f* composer-songwriter.
authenticité [otɑ̃tisite] *nf* authenticity.
authentifier [otɑ̃tifje] *vt* to authenticate.
authentique [otɑ̃tik] *adj* authentic, genuine.
autiste [otist] *adj* autistic.
auto [oto] *nf* car; **~s tamponneuses** bumper cars, dodgems.
auto... [oto] *préfixe* auto..., self-.
autobiographie [otobjɔgʀafi] *nf* autobiography.
autobiographique [otobjɔgʀafik] *adj* autobiographical.
autobus [otobys] *nm* bus.
autocar [otokaʀ] *nm* coach.
autocensure [otosɑ̃syʀ] *nf* self-censorship.
autochtone [otokton] *nm/f* native.
autocollant, e [otokɔlɑ̃, -ɑ̃t] *adj* self-adhesive; (*enveloppe*) self-seal ♦ *nm* sticker.
auto-couchettes [otokuʃɛt] *adj inv*: **train ~** car sleeper train, motorail ® train (*BRIT*).
autocratique [otokʀatik] *adj* autocratic.
autocritique [otokʀitik] *nf* self-criticism.
autocuiseur [otokwizœʀ] *nm* (*CULIN*) pressure cooker.
autodéfense [otodefɑ̃s] *nf* self-defence;

groupe d'~ vigilante committee.
autodétermination [ɔtɔdetɛRminasjɔ̃] *nf* self-determination.
autodidacte [ɔtɔdidakt(ə)] *nm/f* self-taught person.
autodiscipline [ɔtɔdisiplin] *nf* self-discipline.
autodrome [ɔtɔdRom] *nm* motor-racing stadium.
auto-école [ɔtɔekɔl] *nf* driving school.
autofinancement [ɔtɔfinãsmã] *nm* self-financing.
autogéré, e [ɔtɔʒeRe] *adj* self-managed, managed internally.
autogestion [ɔtɔʒɛstjɔ̃] *nf* joint worker-management control.
autographe [ɔtɔgRaf] *nm* autograph.
autoguidé, e [ɔtɔgide] *adj* self-guided.
auto-immun, e [ɔtɔimœ̃, -yn] *adj* autoimmune.
automate [ɔtɔmat] *nm* (*robot*) automaton; (*machine*) (automatic) machine.
automatique [ɔtɔmatik] *adj, nm* automatic; **l'~** (*TÉL*) ≈ direct dialling.
automatiquement [ɔtɔmatikmã] *adv* automatically.
automatisation [ɔtɔmatizasjɔ̃] *nf* automation.
automatiser [ɔtɔmatize] *vt* to automate.
automatisme [ɔtɔmatism(ə)] *nm* automatism.
automédication [ɔtɔmedikasjɔ̃] *nf* self-medication.
automitrailleuse [ɔtɔmitRajøz] *nf* armoured car.
automnal, e, aux [ɔtɔnal, -o] *adj* autumnal.
automne [ɔtɔn] *nm* autumn (*BRIT*), fall (*US*).
automobile [ɔtɔmɔbil] *adj* motor *cpd* ♦ *nf* (motor) car; **l'~** motoring; (*industrie*) the car *ou* automobile (*US*) industry.
automobiliste [ɔtɔmɔbilist(ə)] *nm/f* motorist.
autonettoyant, e [ɔtɔnɛtwajã, -ãt] *adj*: **four ~** self-cleaning oven.
autonome [ɔtɔnɔm] *adj* autonomous; (*INFORM*) stand-alone; **(en mode) ~** off line.
autonomie [ɔtɔnɔmi] *nf* autonomy; (*POL*) self-government, autonomy; **~ de vol** range.
autonomiste [ɔtɔnɔmist(ə)] *nm/f* separatist.
autoportrait [ɔtɔpɔRtRɛ] *nm* self-portrait.
autopsie [ɔtɔpsi] *nf* post-mortem (examination), autopsy.
autopsier [ɔtɔpsje] *vt* to carry out a post-mortem *ou* an autopsy on.
autoradio [ɔtɔRadjo] *nf* car radio.
autorail [ɔtɔRaj] *nm* railcar.
autorisation [ɔtɔRizasjɔ̃] *nf* permission, authorization; (*papiers*) permit; **donner à qn l'~ de** to give sb permission to, authorize sb to; **avoir l'~ de faire** to be allowed *ou* have permission to do, be authorized to do.
autorisé, e [ɔtɔRize] *adj* (*opinion, sources*) authoritative; (*permis*): **~ à faire** authorized *ou* permitted to do; **dans les milieux ~s** in official circles.
autoriser [ɔtɔRize] *vt* to give permission for,

authorize; (*fig*) to allow (of), sanction; **~ qn à faire** to give permission to sb to do, authorize sb to do.
autoritaire [ɔtɔRitɛR] *adj* authoritarian.
autoritarisme [ɔtɔRitaRism(ə)] *nm* authoritarianism.
autorité [ɔtɔRite] *nf* authority; **faire ~** to be authoritative; **~s constituées** constitutional authorities.
autoroute [ɔtɔRut] *nf* motorway (*BRIT*), expressway (*US*); **~ de l'information** (*TEL*) information highway.
autoroutier, ière [ɔtɔRutje, -jɛR] *adj* motorway *cpd* (*BRIT*), expressway *cpd* (*US*).
autosatisfaction [ɔtɔsatisfaksjɔ̃] *nf* self-satisfaction.
auto-stop [ɔtɔstɔp] *nm*: **l'~** hitch-hiking; **faire de l'~** to hitch-hike; **prendre qn en ~** to give sb a lift.
auto-stoppeur, euse [ɔtɔstɔpœR, -øz] *nm/f* hitch-hiker, hitcher (*BRIT*).
autosuffisant, e [ɔtɔsyfizã, -ãt] *adj* self-sufficient.
autosuggestion [ɔtɔsygʒɛstjɔ̃] *nf* autosuggestion.
autour [otuR] *adv* around; **~ de** *prép* around; (*environ*) around, about; **tout ~** *adv* all around.

═══════════════════════════ *MOT-CLÉ*

autre [otR(ə)] *adj* **1** (*différent*) other, different; **je préférerais un ~ verre** I'd prefer another *ou* a different glass; **d'~s verres** different glasses; **se sentir ~** to feel different; **la difficulté est ~** the difficulty is *ou* lies elsewhere
2 (*supplémentaire*) other; **je voudrais un ~ verre d'eau** I'd like another glass of water
3: **~ chose** something else; **~ part** somewhere else; **d'~ part** on the other hand
♦ *pron* **1**: **un ~** another (one); **nous/vous ~s** us/you; **d'~s** others; **l'~** the other (one); **les ~s** the others; (*autrui*) others; **l'un et l'~** both of them; **ni l'un ni l'~** neither of them; **se détester l'un l'~/les uns les ~s** to hate each other *ou* one another; **d'une semaine/minute à l'~** from one week/minute *ou* moment to the next; (*incessamment*) any week/minute *ou* moment now; **de temps à ~** from time to time; **entre ~s** among other things
2 (*expressions*): **j'en ai vu d'~s** I've seen worse; **à d'~s!** pull the other one!

autrefois [otRəfwa] *adv* in the past.
autrement [otRəmã] *adv* differently; (*d'une manière différente*) in another way; (*sinon*) otherwise; **je n'ai pas pu faire ~** I couldn't do anything else, I couldn't do otherwise; **~ dit** in other words; (*c'est-à-dire*) that is to say.
Autriche [otRiʃ] *nf*: **l'~** Austria.

autrichien, ne [otʀiʃjɛ̃, -ɛn] *adj* Austrian
♦ *nm/f:* **A~, ne** Austrian.
autruche [otʀyʃ] *nf* ostrich; **faire l'~** (*fig*) to
bury one's head in the sand.
autrui [otʀɥi] *pron* others.
auvent [ovɑ̃] *nm* canopy.
auvergnat, e [ɔvɛʀɲa, -at] *adj* of *ou* from the
Auvergne.
Auvergne [ɔvɛʀɲ(ə)] *nf:* **l'~** the Auvergne.
aux [o] *prép* + *dét voir* **à.**
auxiliaire [ɔksiljɛʀ] *adj, nm/f* auxiliary.
auxquels, auxquelles [okɛl] *prép* + *pron voir*
lequel.
AV *sigle m* (*BANQUE*: = *avis de virement*) *advice
of bank transfer* ♦ *abr* (*AUTO*) = **avant.**
av. *abr* (= *avenue*) Av(e).
avachi, e [avaʃi] *adj* limp, flabby; (*chaussure,
vêtement*) out-of-shape; (*personne*): ~ **sur
qch** slumped on *ou* across sth.
avais [avɛ] *etc vb voir* **avoir.**
aval [aval] *nm* (*accord*) endorsement, backing;
(*GÉO*): **en** ~ downstream, downriver; (*sur
une pente*) downhill; **en** ~ **de** downstream *ou*
downriver from; downhill from.
avalanche [avalɑ̃ʃ] *nf* avalanche; ~ **poudreuse**
powder snow avalanche.
avaler [avale] *vt* to swallow.
avaliser [avalize] *vt* (*plan, entreprise*) to back,
support; (*COMM, JUR*) to guarantee.
avance [avɑ̃s] *nf* (*de troupes etc*) advance;
(*progrès*) progress; (*d'argent*) advance;
(*opposé à retard*) lead; being ahead of
schedule; ~**s** *nfpl* overtures; (*amoureuses*)
advances; **une** ~ **de 300 m/4 h** (*SPORT*) a
300 m/4 hour lead; **(être) en** ~ (to be) early;
(*sur un programme*) (to be) ahead of
schedule; **on n'est pas en** ~! we're kind of
late!; **être en** ~ **sur qn** to be ahead of sb;
d'~, à l'~, par ~ in advance; ~ **(du) papier**
(*INFORM*) paper advance.
avancé, e [avɑ̃se] *adj* advanced; (*travail etc*)
well on, well under way; (*fruit, fromage*)
overripe ♦ *nf* projection; overhang; **il est** ~
pour son âge he is advanced for his age.
avancement [avɑ̃smɑ̃] *nm* (*professionnel*)
promotion; (*de travaux*) progress.
avancer [avɑ̃se] *vi* to move forward, advance;
(*projet, travail*) to make progress; (*être en
saillie*) to overhang; to project; (*montre,
réveil*) to be fast; (: *d'habitude*) to gain ♦ *vt* to
move forward, advance; (*argent*) to
advance; (*montre, pendule*) to put forward;
(*faire progresser: travail etc*) to advance, move
on; **s'~** *vi* to move forward, advance; (*fig*) to
commit o.s.; (*faire saillie*) to overhang; to
project; **j'avance (d'une heure)** I'm (an hour)
fast.
avanies [avani] *nfpl* snubs (*BRIT*), insults.
avant [avɑ̃] *prép* before ♦ *adv:* **trop/plus** ~ too
far/further forward ♦ *adj inv:* **siège/roue** ~
front seat/wheel ♦ *nm* front; (*SPORT: joueur*)
forward; ~ **qu'il parte/de partir** before he

leaves/leaving; ~ **qu'il (ne) pleuve** before it
rains (*ou* rained); ~ **tout** (*surtout*) above all;
à l'~ (*dans un véhicule*) in (the) front; **en** ~
adv forward(s); **en** ~ **de** *prép* in front of; **aller
de l'~** to steam ahead (*fig*), make good
progress.
avantage [avɑ̃taʒ] *nm* advantage; (*TENNIS*): ~
service/dehors advantage *ou* van (*BRIT*) *ou*
ad (*US*) in/out; **tirer** ~ **de** to take advantage
of; **vous auriez** ~ **à faire** you would be well-
advised to do, it would be to your
advantage to do; **à l'~ de qn** to sb's
advantage; **être à son** ~ to be at one's best;
~**s en nature** benefits in kind; ~**s sociaux**
fringe benefits.
avantager [avɑ̃taʒe] *vt* (*favoriser*) to favour;
(*embellir*) to flatter.
avantageux, euse [avɑ̃taʒø, -øz] *adj*
attractive; (*intéressant*) attractively priced;
(*portrait, coiffure*) flattering; **conditions
avantageuses** favourable terms.
avant-bras [avɑ̃bʀa] *nm inv* forearm.
avant-centre [avɑ̃sɑ̃tʀ(ə)] *nm* centre-forward.
avant-coureur [avɑ̃kuʀœʀ] *adj inv* (*bruit etc*)
precursory; **signe** ~ advance indication *ou*
sign.
avant-dernier, ière [avɑ̃dɛʀnje, -jɛʀ] *adj, nm/f*
next to last, last but one.
avant-garde [avɑ̃gaʀd(ə)] *nf* (*MIL*) vanguard;
(*fig*) avant-garde; **d'~** avant-garde.
avant-goût [avɑ̃gu] *nm* foretaste.
avant-hier [avɑ̃tjɛʀ] *adv* the day before
yesterday.
avant-poste [avɑ̃pɔst(ə)] *nm* outpost.
avant-première [avɑ̃pʀəmjɛʀ] *nf* (*de film*)
preview; **en** ~ as a preview, in a preview
showing.
avant-projet [avɑ̃pʀɔʒɛ] *nm* preliminary
draft.
avant-propos [avɑ̃pʀɔpo] *nm* foreword.
avant-veille [avɑ̃vɛj] *nf:* **l'~** two days before.
avare [avaʀ] *adj* miserly, avaricious ♦ *nm/f*
miser; ~ **de compliments** stingy *ou* sparing
with one's compliments.
avarice [avaʀis] *nf* avarice, miserliness.
avaricieux, euse [avaʀisjø, -øz] *adj* miserly,
niggardly.
avarié, e [avaʀje] *adj* (*viande, fruits*) rotting,
going off (*BRIT*); (*NAVIG: navire*) damaged.
avaries [avaʀi] *nfpl* (*NAVIG*) damage *sg*.
avatar [avataʀ] *nm* misadventure;
(*transformation*) metamorphosis (*pl* -phoses).
avec [avɛk] *prép* with; (*à l'égard de*) to(wards),
with ♦ *adv* (*fam*) with it (*ou* him *etc*); ~
habileté/lenteur skilfully/slowly; ~ **eux/ces
maladies** with them/these diseases; ~ **ça**
(*malgré ça*) for all that; **et** ~ **ça?** (*dans un
magasin*) anything *ou* something else?
avenant, e [avnɑ̃, -ɑ̃t] *adj* pleasant ♦ *nm*
(*ASSURANCES*) additional clause; **à l'~** *adv* in
keeping.
avènement [avɛnmɑ̃] *nm* (*d'un roi*) accession,

succession; (*d'un changement*) advent; (*d'une politique, idée*) coming.

avenir [avniʀ] *nm*: **l'**~ the future; **à l'**~ in future; **sans** ~ with no future, without a future; **carrière/politicien d'**~ career/politician with prospects *ou* a future.

Avent [avɑ̃] *nm*: **l'**~ Advent.

aventure [avɑ̃tyʀ] *nf*: **l'**~ adventure; **une** ~ an adventure; (*amoureuse*) an affair; **partir à l'**~ to go off in search of adventure; (*au hasard*) to go where one's fancy takes one; **roman/film d'**~ adventure story/film.

aventurer [avɑ̃tyʀe] *vt* (*somme, réputation, vie*) to stake; (*remarque, opinion*) to venture; **s'**~ *vi* to venture; **s'**~ **à faire qch** to venture into sth.

aventureux, euse [avɑ̃tyʀø, -øz] *adj* adventurous, venturesome; (*projet*) risky, chancy.

aventurier, ière [avɑ̃tyʀje, -jɛʀ] *nm/f* adventurer ♦ *nf* (*péj*) adventuress.

avenu, e [avny] *adj*: **nul et non** ~ null and void.

avenue [avny] *nf* avenue.

avéré, e [aveʀe] *adj* recognized, acknowledged.

avérer [aveʀe]: **s'**~ *vb avec attribut*: **s'**~ **faux/coûteux** to prove (to be) wrong/expensive.

averse [avɛʀs(ə)] *nf* shower.

aversion [avɛʀsjɔ̃] *nf* aversion, loathing.

averti, e [avɛʀti] *adj* (well-)informed.

avertir [avɛʀtiʀ] *vt*: ~ **qn (de qch/que)** to warn sb (of sth/that); (*renseigner*) to inform sb (of sth/that); ~ **qn de ne pas faire qch** to warn sb not to do sth.

avertissement [avɛʀtismɑ̃] *nm* warning.

avertisseur [avɛʀtisœʀ] *nm* horn, siren; ~ **(d'incendie)** (fire) alarm.

aveu, x [avø] *nm* confession; **passer aux** ~**x** to make a confession; **de l'**~ **de** according to.

aveuglant, e [avœglɑ̃, -ɑ̃t] *adj* blinding.

aveugle [avœgl(ə)] *adj* blind ♦ *nm/f* blind person; **les** ~**s** the blind; **test en (double)** ~ (double) blind test.

aveuglement [avœgləmɑ̃] *nm* blindness.

aveuglément [avœglemɑ̃] *adv* blindly.

aveugler [avœgle] *vt* to blind.

aveuglette [avœglɛt]: **à l'**~ groping one's way along; (*fig*) in the dark, blindly.

avez [ave] *vb voir* **avoir**.

aviateur, trice [avjatœʀ, -tʀis] *nm/f* aviator, pilot.

aviation [avjɑsjɔ̃] *nf* (*secteur commercial*) aviation; (*sport, métier de pilote*) flying; (*MIL*) air force; **terrain d'**~ airfield; ~ **de chasse** fighter force.

aviculteur, trice [avikyltœʀ, -tʀis] *nm/f* poultry farmer; bird breeder.

aviculture [avikyltyʀ] *nf* (*de volailles*) poultry farming.

avide [avid] *adj* eager; (*péj*) greedy, grasping; ~ **de** (*sang etc*) thirsting for; ~ **d'honneurs/**

d'argent greedy for honours/money; ~ **de connaître/d'apprendre** eager to know/learn.

avidité [avidite] *nf* eagerness; greed.

avilir [aviliʀ] *vt* to debase.

avilissant, e [avilisɑ̃, -ɑ̃t] *adj* degrading.

aviné, e [avine] *adj* drunken.

avion [avjɔ̃] *nm* (aero)plane (*BRIT*), (air)plane (*US*); **aller (quelque part) en** ~ to go (somewhere) by plane, fly (somewhere); **par** ~ by airmail; ~ **de chasse** fighter; ~ **de ligne** airliner; ~ **à réaction** jet (plane).

avion-cargo [avjɔ̃kaʀgo] *nm* air freighter.

avion-citerne [avjɔ̃sitɛʀn(ə)] *nm* air tanker.

aviron [aviʀɔ̃] *nm* oar; (*sport*): **l'**~ rowing.

avis [avi] *nm* opinion; (*notification*) notice; (*COMM*): ~ **de crédit/débit** credit/debit advice; **à mon** ~ in my opinion; **je suis de votre** ~ I share your opinion, I am of your opinion; **être d'**~ **que** to be of the opinion that; **changer d'**~ to change one's mind; **sauf** ~ **contraire** unless you hear to the contrary; **sans** ~ **préalable** without notice; **jusqu'à nouvel** ~ until further notice; ~ **de décès** death announcement.

avisé, e [avize] *adj* sensible, wise; **être bien/mal** ~ **de faire** to be well-/ill-advised to do.

aviser [avize] *vt* (*voir*) to notice, catch sight of; (*informer*): ~ **qn de/que** to advise *ou* inform *ou* notify sb of/that ♦ *vi* to think about things, assess the situation; **s'**~ **de qch/que** to become suddenly aware of sth/that; **s'**~ **de faire** to take it into one's head to do.

aviver [avive] *vt* (*douleur, chagrin*) to intensify; (*intérêt, désir*) to sharpen; (*colère, querelle*) to stir up; (*couleur*) to brighten up.

av. J.-C. *abr* (= *avant Jésus-Christ*) BC.

avocat, e [avɔka, -at] *nm/f* (*JUR*) ≈ barrister (*BRIT*), lawyer; (*fig*) advocate, champion ♦ *nm* (*CULIN*) avocado (pear); **se faire l'**~ **du diable** to be the devil's advocate; **l'**~ **de la défense/partie civile** the counsel for the defence/plaintiff; ~ **d'affaires** business lawyer; ~ **général** assistant public prosecutor.

avocat-conseil, *pl* **avocats-conseils** [avɔkakɔ̃sɛj] *nm* ≈ barrister (*BRIT*).

avocat-stagiaire, *pl* **avocats-stagiaires** [avɔkastaʒjɛʀ] *nm* ≈ barrister doing his articles (*BRIT*).

avoine [avwan] *nf* oats *pl*.

━━━━━━━━━━━━━━━━━━━━ *MOT-CLÉ*

avoir [avwaʀ] *nm* assets *pl*, resources *pl*; (*COMM*) credit; ~ **fiscal** tax credit
♦ *vt* **1** (*posséder*) to have; **elle a 2 enfants/une belle maison** she has (got) 2 children/a lovely house; **il a les yeux bleus** he has (got) blue eyes
2 (*éprouver*): **qu'est-ce que tu as?, qu'as-tu?** what's wrong?, what's the matter?; *voir aussi* **faim, peur** *etc*
3 (*âge, dimensions*) to be; **il a 3 ans** he is 3

(years old); **le mur a 3 mètres de haut** the wall is 3 metres high

4 (*fam: duper*) to do, have; **on vous a eu!** you've been done *ou* had!

5: en ~ contre qn to have a grudge against sb; **en ~ assez** to be fed up; **j'en ai pour une demi-heure** it'll take me half an hour; **n'~ que faire de qch** to have no use for sth

♦ *vb aux* **1** to have; **~ mangé/dormi** to have eaten/slept; **hier je n'ai pas mangé** I didn't eat yesterday

2 (*avoir +à +infinitif*): **~ à faire qch** to have to do sth; **vous n'avez qu'à lui demander** you only have to ask him; **tu n'as pas à me poser des questions** it's not for you to ask me questions

♦ *vb impers* **1**: **il y a** (+ *singulier*) there is; (+ *pluriel*) there are; **qu'y-a-t-il?, qu'est-ce qu'il y a?** what's the matter?, what is it?; **il doit y avoir une explication** there must be an explanation; **il n'y a qu'à ...** we (*ou* you *etc*) will just have to ...; **il ne peut y en ~ qu'un** there can only be one

2 (*temporel*): **il y a 10 ans** 10 years ago; **il y a 10 ans/longtemps que je le connais** I've known him for 10 years/a long time; **il y a 10 ans qu'il est arrivé** it's 10 years since he arrived.

avoisinant, e [avwazinɑ̃, -ɑ̃t] *adj* neighbouring.

avoisiner [avwazine] *vt* to be near *ou* close to; (*fig*) to border *ou* verge on.

avons [avɔ̃] *vb voir* **avoir.**

avortement [avɔʀtəmɑ̃] *nm* abortion.

avorter [avɔʀte] *vi* (*MÉD*) to have an abortion; (*fig*) to fail; **faire ~** to abort; **se faire ~** to have an abortion.

avorton [avɔʀtɔ̃] *nm* (*péj*) little runt.

avouable [avwabl(ə)] *adj* respectable; **des pensées non ~s** unrepeatable thoughts.

avoué, e [avwe] *adj* avowed ♦ *nm* (*JUR*) ≈ solicitor (*BRIT*), lawyer.

avouer [avwe] *vt* (*crime, défaut*) to confess (to) ♦ *vi* (*se confesser*) to confess; (*admettre*) to admit; **~ avoir fait/que** to admit *ou* confess to having done/that; **~ que oui/non** to admit that that is so/not so; **s'~ vaincu** to admit defeat.

avril [avʀil] *nm* April; *voir aussi* **juillet.**

The traditional prank on April 1 in France involves placing a cut-out paper fish, known as a **poisson d'avril,** *on the back of one's victim, without being caught.*

---

axe [aks(ə)] *nm* axis (*pl* axes); (*de roue etc*) axle; (*prolongement*): **dans l'~ de** directly in line with; (*fig*) main line; **~ routier** trunk road, main road.

axer [akse] *vt*: **~ qch sur** to centre sth on.

axial, e, aux [aksjal, -o] *adj* axial.

axiome [aksjom] *nm* axiom.

ayant [ɛjɑ̃] *vb voir* **avoir** ♦ *nm*: **~ droit** assignee; **~ droit à** (*pension etc*) person eligible for *ou* entitled to.

ayons [ɛjɔ̃] *etc vb voir* **avoir.**

azalée [azale] *nf* azalea.

Azerbaïdjan [azɛʀbaidʒɑ̃] *nm* Azerbaijan.

azerbaïdjanais, e [azɛʀbaidʒanɛ, -ɛz] *adj* Azerbaijani ♦ *nm* (*LING*) Azerbaijani ♦ *nm/f:* **A~, e** Azerbaijani.

azimut [azimyt] *nm* azimuth; **tous ~s** *adj* (*fig*) omnidirectional.

azote [azɔt] *nm* nitrogen.

azoté, e [azɔte] *adj* nitrogenous.

AZT *sigle m* (= *azidothymidine*) AZT.

aztèque [aztɛk] *adj* Aztec.

azur [azyʀ] *nm* (*couleur*) azure, sky blue; (*ciel*) sky, skies *pl*.

azyme [azim] *adj*: **pain ~** unleavened bread.

B b

B, b [be] *nm inv* B, b ♦ *abr* = *bien*; **B comme Bertha** B for Benjamin (*BRIT*) *ou* Baker (*US*).

BA *sigle f* (= *bonne action*) good deed.

baba [baba] *adj inv*: **en être ~** (*fam*) to be flabbergasted ♦ *nm*: **~ au rhum** rum baba.

babil [babi] *nm* prattle.

babillage [babijaʒ] *nm* chatter.

babiller [babije] *vi* to prattle, chatter; (*bébé*) to babble.

babines [babin] *nfpl* chops.

babiole [babjɔl] *nf* (*bibelot*) trinket; (*vétille*) trifle.

bâbord [bɑbɔʀ] *nm*: **à** *ou* **par ~** to port, on the port side.

babouin [babwɛ̃] *nm* baboon.

baby-foot [babifut] *nm inv* table football.

Babylone [babilɔn] *n* Babylon.

babylonien, ne [babilɔnjɛ̃, -ɛn] *adj* Babylonian.

baby-sitter [babisitœʀ] *nm/f* baby-sitter.

baby-sitting [babisitiŋ] *nm* baby-sitting.

bac [bak] *nm* (*SCOL*) = **baccalauréat;** (*bateau*) ferry; (*récipient*) tub; (*: PHOTO etc*) tray; (*: INDUSTRIE*) tank; **~ à glace** ice-tray; **~ à légumes** vegetable compartment *ou* rack.

baccalauréat [bakalɔʀea] *nm* ≈ GCE A-levels *pl* (*BRIT*), ≈ high school diploma (*US*).

In France the **baccalauréat** *or* **bac** *is the school-leaving certificate taken at a lycée at the age of seventeen or eighteen after seven years of secondary education. A variety of subject combinations is available, although in* *all cases a broad range of subjects is studied. Holders of the certificate are entitled to go on to university.*

bâche [bɑʃ] *nf* tarpaulin, canvas sheet.

bachelier, ière [baʃəlje, -jɛʀ] *nm/f* holder of the baccalauréat.

bâcher [bɑʃe] *vt* to cover (with a canvas sheet *ou* a tarpaulin).

bachot [baʃo] *nm* = **baccalauréat**.

bachotage [baʃɔtaʒ] *nm* (*SCOL*) cramming.

bachoter [baʃɔte] *vi* (*SCOL*) to cram (for an exam).

bacille [basil] *nm* bacillus (*pl* -i).

bâcler [bɑkle] *vt* to botch (up).

bacon [bekɔn] *nm* bacon.

bactéricide [bakteʀisid] *nm* (*MÉD*) bactericide.

bactérie [bakteʀi] *nf* bacterium (*pl* -ia).

bactérien, ne [bakteʀjɛ̃, -ɛn] *adj* bacterial.

bactériologie [bakteʀjɔlɔʒi] *nf* bacteriology.

bactériologique [bakteʀjɔlɔʒik] *adj* bacteriological.

bactériologiste [bakteʀjɔlɔʒist(ə)] *nm/f* bacteriologist.

badaud, e [bado, -od] *nm/f* idle onlooker, stroller.

baderne [badɛʀn(ə)] *nf* (*péj*): **(vieille)** ~ old fossil.

badge [badʒ(ə)] *nm* badge.

badigeon [badiʒɔ̃] *nm* distemper; colourwash.

badigeonner [badiʒɔne] *vt* to distemper; to colourwash; (*péj: barbouiller*) to daub; (*MÉD*) to paint.

badin, e [badɛ̃, -in] *adj* light-hearted, playful.

badinage [badinaʒ] *nm* banter.

badine [badin] *nf* switch (*stick*).

badiner [badine] *vi:* ~ **avec qch** to treat sth lightly; **ne pas** ~ **avec qch** not to trifle with sth.

badminton [badmintɔn] *nm* badminton.

BAFA [bafa] *sigle m* (= *Brevet d'aptitude aux fonctions d'animation*) *diploma for youth leaders and workers.*

baffe [baf] *nf* (*fam*) slap, clout.

Baffin [bafin] *nf:* **terre de** ~ Baffin Island.

baffle [bafl(ə)] *nm* baffle (board).

bafouer [bafwe] *vt* to deride, ridicule.

bafouillage [bafujaʒ] *nm* (*fam: propos incohérents*) jumble of words.

bafouiller [bafuje] *vi, vt* to stammer.

bâfrer [bɑfʀe] *vi, vt* (*fam*) to guzzle, gobble.

bagage [bagaʒ] *nm:* ~**s** luggage *sg*, baggage *sg*; ~ **littéraire** (stock of) literary knowledge; ~**s à main** hand-luggage.

bagarre [bagaʀ] *nf* fight, brawl; **il aime la** ~ he loves a fight, he likes fighting.

bagarrer [bagaʀe]: **se** ~ *vi* to (have a) fight.

bagarreur, euse [bagaʀœʀ, -øz] *adj* pugnacious ♦ *nm/f:* **il est** ~ he loves a fight.

bagatelle [bagatɛl] *nf* trifle, trifling sum (*ou* matter).

Bagdad, Baghdâd [bagdad] *n* Baghdad.

bagnard [baɲaʀ] *nm* convict.

bagne [baɲ] *nm* penal colony; **c'est le** ~ (*fig*) it's forced labour.

bagnole [baɲɔl] *nf* (*fam*) car, wheels *pl* (*BRIT*).

bagout [bagu] *nm* glibness; **avoir du** ~ to have the gift of the gab.

bague [bag] *nf* ring; ~ **de fiançailles** engagement ring; ~ **de serrage** clip.

baguenauder [bagnode]: **se** ~ *vi* to trail around, loaf around.

baguer [bage] *vt* to ring.

baguette [bagɛt] *nf* stick; (*cuisine chinoise*) chopstick; (*de chef d'orchestre*) baton; (*pain*) stick of (French) bread; (*CONSTR: moulure*) beading; **mener qn à la** ~ to rule sb with a rod of iron; ~ **magique** magic wand; ~ **de sourcier** divining rod; ~ **de tambour** drumstick.

Bahamas [baamas] *nfpl:* **les (îles)** ~ the Bahamas.

Bahrein [baʀɛn] *nm* Bahrain *ou* Bahrein.

bahut [bay] *nm* chest.

bai, e [bɛ] *adj* (*cheval*) bay.

baie [bɛ] *nf* (*GÉO*) bay; (*fruit*) berry; ~ **(vitrée)** picture window.

baignade [bɛɲad] *nf* (*action*) bathing; (*bain*) bathe; (*endroit*) bathing place.

baigné, e [beɲe] *adj:* ~ **de** bathed in; (*trempé*) soaked with; (*inondé*) flooded with.

baigner [beɲe] *vt* (*bébé*) to bath ♦ *vi:* ~ **dans son sang** to lie in a pool of blood; ~ **dans la brume** to be shrouded in mist; **se** ~ *vi* to go swimming *ou* bathing; (*dans une baignoire*) to have a bath; **ça baigne!** (*fam*) everything's great!

baigneur, euse [beɲœʀ, -øz] *nm/f* bather ♦ *nm* (*poupée*) baby doll.

baignoire [beɲwaʀ] *nf* bath(tub); (*THÉÂT*) ground-floor box.

bail, baux [baj, bo] *nm* lease; **donner** *ou* **prendre qch à** ~ to lease sth.

bâillement [bɑjmɑ̃] *nm* yawn.

bâiller [bɑje] *vi* to yawn; (*être ouvert*) to gape.

bailleur [bajœʀ] *nm:* ~ **de fonds** sponsor, backer; (*COMM*) sleeping *ou* silent partner.

bâillon [bɑjɔ̃] *nm* gag.

bâillonner [bɑjɔne] *vt* to gag.

bain [bɛ̃] *nm* (*dans une baignoire, PHOTO, TECH*) bath; (*dans la mer, une piscine*) swim; **costume de** ~ bathing costume (*BRIT*), swimsuit; **prendre un** ~ to have a bath; **se mettre dans le** ~ (*fig*) to get into (the way of) it *ou* things; ~ **de bouche** mouthwash; ~ **de foule** walkabout; ~ **de pieds** footbath; (*au bord de la mer*) paddle; ~ **de siège** hip bath; ~ **de soleil** sunbathing *no pl*; **prendre un** ~ **de soleil** to sunbathe; ~**s de mer** sea bathing *sg*; ~**s(-douches) municipaux** public baths.

bain-marie, *pl* **bains-marie** [bɛ̃maʀi] *nm* double boiler; **faire chauffer au** ~ (*boîte etc*) to immerse in boiling water.

baïonnette [bajɔnɛt] *nf* bayonet; (*ÉLEC*):

douille à ~ bayonet socket; **ampoule à** ~ bulb with a bayonet fitting.

baisemain [bɛzmɛ̃] *nm* kissing a lady's hand.

baiser [beze] *nm* kiss ♦ *vt* (*main, front*) to kiss; (*fam!*) to screw (*!*).

baisse [bɛs] *nf* fall, drop; (*COMM*): "~ **sur la viande**" "meat prices down"; **en** ~ (*cours, action*) falling; **à la** ~ downwards.

baisser [bese] *vt* to lower; (*radio, chauffage*) to turn down; (*AUTO: phares*) to dip (*BRIT*), lower (*US*) ♦ *vi* to fall, drop, go down; **se** ~ *vi* to bend down.

bajoues [baʒu] *nfpl* chaps, chops.

bal [bal] *nm* dance; (*grande soirée*) ball; ~ **costumé/masqué** fancy-dress/masked ball; ~ **musette** dance (*with accordion accompaniment*).

balade [balad] *nf* walk, stroll; (*en voiture*) drive; **faire une** ~ to go for a walk *ou* stroll; to go for a drive.

balader [balade] *vt* (*traîner*) to trail around; **se** ~ *vi* to go for a walk *ou* stroll; to go for a drive.

baladeur [baladœʀ] *nm* personal stereo.

baladeuse [baladøz] *nf* inspection lamp.

baladin [baladɛ̃] *nm* wandering entertainer.

balafre [balafʀ(ə)] *nf* gash, slash; (*cicatrice*) scar.

balafrer [balafʀe] *vt* to gash, slash.

balai [balɛ] *nm* broom, brush; (*AUTO: d'essuie-glace*) blade; (*MUS: de batterie etc*) brush; **donner un coup de** ~ to give the floor a sweep; ~ **mécanique** carpet sweeper.

balai-brosse, *pl* **balais-brosses** [balɛbʀɔs] *nm* (long-handled) scrubbing brush.

balance [balɑ̃s] *nf* (*à plateaux*) scales *pl*; (*de précision*) balance; (*COMM, POL*): ~ **des comptes** *ou* **paiements** balance of payments; (*signe*): **la B**~ Libra, the Scales; **être de la B**~ to be Libra; ~ **commerciale** balance of trade; ~ **des forces** balance of power; ~ **romaine** steelyard.

balancelle [balɑ̃sɛl] *nf* garden hammock-seat.

balancer [balɑ̃se] *vt* to swing; (*lancer*) to fling, chuck; (*renvoyer, jeter*) to chuck out ♦ *vi* to swing; **se** ~ *vi* to swing; (*bateau*) to rock; (*branche*) to sway; **se** ~ **de qch** (*fam*) not to give a toss about sth.

balancier [balɑ̃sje] *nm* (*de pendule*) pendulum; (*de montre*) balance wheel; (*perche*) (balancing) pole.

balançoire [balɑ̃swaʀ] *nf* swing; (*sur pivot*) seesaw.

balayage [balɛjaʒ] *nm* sweeping; scanning.

balayer [balɛje] *vt* (*feuilles etc*) to sweep up, brush up; (*pièce, cour*) to sweep; (*chasser*) to sweep away *ou* aside; (*suj: radar*) to scan; (*: phares*) to sweep across.

balayette [balɛjɛt] *nf* small brush.

balayeur, euse [balɛjœʀ, -øz] *nm/f* roadsweeper ♦ *nf* (*engin*) roadsweeper.

balayures [balɛjyʀ] *nfpl* sweepings.

balbutiement [balbysimɑ̃] *nm* (*paroles*) stammering *no pl*; ~**s** *nmpl* (*fig: débuts*) first faltering steps.

balbutier [balbysje] *vi, vt* to stammer.

balcon [balkɔ̃] *nm* balcony; (*THÉÂT*) dress circle.

baldaquin [baldakɛ̃] *nm* canopy.

Bâle [bɑl] *n* Basle *ou* Basel.

Baléares [baleaʀ] *nfpl*: **les** ~ the Balearic Islands.

baleine [balɛn] *nf* whale; (*de parapluie*) rib; (*de corset*) bone.

baleinier [balenje] *nm* (*NAVIG*) whaler.

baleinière [balenjɛʀ] *nf* whaleboat.

balisage [balizaʒ] *nm* (*signaux*) beacons *pl*; buoys *pl*; runway lights *pl*; signs *pl*, markers *pl*.

balise [baliz] *nf* (*NAVIG*) beacon, (marker) buoy; (*AVIAT*) runway light, beacon; (*AUTO, SKI*) sign, marker.

baliser [balize] *vt* to mark out (with beacons *ou* lights *etc*).

balistique [balistik] *adj* (*engin*) ballistic ♦ *nf* ballistics.

balivernes [balivɛʀn(ə)] *nfpl* twaddle *sg* (*BRIT*), nonsense *sg*.

balkanique [balkanik] *adj* Balkan.

Balkans [balkɑ̃] *nmpl*: **les** ~ the Balkans.

ballade [balad] *nf* ballad.

ballant, e [balɑ̃, -ɑ̃t] *adj* dangling.

ballast [balast] *nm* ballast.

balle [bal] *nf* (*de fusil*) bullet; (*de sport*) ball; (*du blé*) chaff; (*paquet*) bale; (*fam: franc*) franc; ~ **perdue** stray bullet.

ballerine [balʀin] *nf* ballet dancer; (*chaussure*) pump, ballerina.

ballet [balɛ] *nm* ballet; (*fig*): ~ **diplomatique** diplomatic to-ings and fro-ings.

ballon [balɔ̃] *nm* (*de sport*) ball; (*jouet, AVIAT, de bande dessinée*) balloon; (*de vin*) glass; ~ **d'essai** (*météorologique*) pilot balloon; (*fig*) feeler(s); ~ **de football** football; ~ **d'oxygène** oxygen bottle.

ballonner [balɔne] *vt*: **j'ai le ventre ballonné** I feel bloated.

ballon-sonde, *pl* **ballons-sondes** [balɔ̃sɔ̃d] *nm* sounding balloon.

ballot [balo] *nm* bundle; (*péj*) nitwit.

ballottage [balɔtaʒ] *nm* (*POL*) second ballot.

ballotter [balɔte] *vi* to roll around; (*bateau etc*) to toss ♦ *vt* to shake *ou* throw about; to toss; **être ballotté entre** (*fig*) to be shunted between; (*: indécis*) to be torn between.

ballottine [balɔtin] *nf* (*CULIN*): ~ **de volaille** meat loaf made with poultry.

ball-trap [baltʀap] *nm* (*appareil*) trap; (*tir*) clay pigeon shooting.

balluchon [balyʃɔ̃] *nm* bundle (of clothes).

balnéaire [balneɛʀ] *adj* seaside *cpd*.

balnéothérapie [balneɔteʀapi] *nf* spa bath therapy.

BALO *sigle m* (= *Bulletin des annonces légales*

obligatoires) ≈ Public Notices (*in newspapers etc*).

balourd, e [baluʀ, -uʀd(ə)] *adj* clumsy ♦ *nm/f* clodhopper.

balourdise [baluʀdiz] *nf* clumsiness; (*gaffe*) blunder.

balte [balt] *adj* Baltic ♦ *nm/f*: **B~** native of the Baltic States.

baltique [baltik] *adj* Baltic ♦ *nf*: **la (mer) B~** the Baltic (Sea).

baluchon [balyʃɔ̃] *nm* = **balluchon**.

balustrade [balystʀad] *nf* railings *pl*, handrail.

bambin [bɑ̃bɛ̃] *nm* little child.

bambou [bɑ̃bu] *nm* bamboo.

ban [bɑ̃] *nm* round of applause, cheer; **être/ mettre au ~ de** to be outlawed/to outlaw from; **le ~ et l'arrière-~ de sa famille** every last one of his relatives; **~s (de mariage)** banns, bans.

banal, e [banal] *adj* banal, commonplace; (*péj*) trite; **four/moulin ~** village oven/mill.

banalisé, e [banalize] *adj* (*voiture de police*) unmarked.

banalité [banalite] *nf* banality; (*remarque*) truism, trite remark.

banane [banan] *nf* banana.

bananeraie [banɑnʀɛ] *nf* banana plantation.

bananier [bananje] *nm* banana tree; (*bateau*) banana boat.

banc [bɑ̃] *nm* seat, bench; (*de poissons*) shoal; **~ des accusés** dock; **~ d'essai** (*fig*) testing ground; **~ de sable** sandbank; **~ des témoins** witness box; **~ de touche** dugout.

bancaire [bɑ̃kɛʀ] *adj* banking, bank *cpd*.

bancal, e [bɑ̃kal] *adj* wobbly; (*personne*) bow-legged; (*fig: projet*) shaky.

bandage [bɑ̃daʒ] *nm* bandaging; (*pansement*) bandage; **~ herniaire** truss.

bande [bɑ̃d] *nf* (*de tissu etc*) strip; (*MÉD*) bandage; (*motif, dessin*) stripe; (*CINÉ*) film; (*INFORM*) tape; (*RADIO, groupe*) band; (*péj*): **une ~ de** a bunch *ou* crowd of; **par la ~** in a roundabout way; **donner de la ~** to list; **faire ~ à part** to keep to o.s.; **~ dessinée (BD)** strip cartoon (*BRIT*), comic strip; **~ magnétique** magnetic tape; **~ perforée** punched tape; **~ de roulement** (*de pneu*) tread; **~ sonore** sound track; **~ de terre** strip of land; **~ Velpeau** ® (*MÉD*) crêpe bandage.

The **bande dessinée** *or* **BD** *enjoys a huge following in France amongst adults as well as children, with the strip cartoon being accorded both literary and artistic status. An international show takes place at Angoulême at the end of January every year. Astérix, Tintin, Lucky Luke and Gaston Lagaffe are among the most famous cartoon characters.*

---

bandé, e [bɑ̃de] *adj* bandaged; **les yeux ~s** blindfold.

bande-annonce, *pl* **bandes-annonces** [bɑ̃danɔ̃s] *nf* (*CINÉ*) trailer.

bandeau, x [bɑ̃do] *nm* headband; (*sur les yeux*) blindfold; (*MÉD*) head bandage.

bandelette [bɑ̃dlɛt] *nf* strip of cloth, bandage.

bander [bɑ̃de] *vt* to bandage; (*muscle*) to tense; (*arc*) to bend ♦ *vi* (*fam!*) to have a hard on (*!*); **~ les yeux à qn** to blindfold sb.

banderole [bɑ̃dʀɔl] *nf* banderole; (*dans un défilé etc*) streamer.

bande-son, *pl* **bandes-son** [bɑ̃dsɔ̃] *nf* (*CINÉ*) soundtrack.

bande-vidéo, *pl* **bandes-vidéo** [bɑ̃dvideo] *nf* video tape.

bandit [bɑ̃di] *nm* bandit.

banditisme [bɑ̃ditism(ə)] *nm* violent crime, armed robberies *pl*.

bandoulière [bɑ̃duljɛʀ] *nf*: **en ~** (slung *ou* worn) across the shoulder.

Bangkok [bɑ̃kɔk] *n* Bangkok.

Bangladesh [bɑ̃ɡladɛʃ] *nm*: **le ~** Bangladesh.

banjo [bɑ̃(d)ʒo] *nm* banjo.

banlieue [bɑ̃ljø] *nf* suburbs *pl*; **lignes/quartiers de ~** suburban lines/areas; **trains de ~** commuter trains.

banlieusard, e [bɑ̃ljøzaʀ, -aʀd(ə)] *nm/f* suburbanite.

bannière [banjɛʀ] *nf* banner.

bannir [baniʀ] *vt* to banish.

banque [bɑ̃k] *nf* bank; (*activités*) banking; **~ des yeux/du sang** eye/blood bank; **~ d'affaires** merchant bank; **~ de dépôt** deposit bank; **~ de données** (*INFORM*) data bank; **~ d'émission** bank of issue.

banqueroute [bɑ̃kʀut] *nf* bankruptcy.

banquet [bɑ̃kɛ] *nm* (*de club*) dinner; (*de noces*) reception; (*d'apparat*) banquet.

banquette [bɑ̃kɛt] *nf* seat.

banquier [bɑ̃kje] *nm* banker.

banquise [bɑ̃kiz] *nf* ice field.

bantou, e [bɑ̃tu] *adj* Bantu.

baptême [batɛm] *nm* (*sacrement*) baptism; (*cérémonie*) christening, baptism; (*d'un navire*) launching; (*d'une cloche*) consecration, dedication; **~ de l'air** first flight.

baptiser [batize] *vt* to christen; to baptize; to launch; to consecrate, dedicate.

baptismal, e, aux [batismal, -o] *adj*: **eau ~e** baptismal water.

baptiste [batist(ə)] *adj, nm/f* Baptist.

baquet [bakɛ] *nm* tub, bucket.

bar [baʀ] *nm* bar; (*poisson*) bass.

baragouin [baʀaɡwɛ̃] *nm* gibberish.

baragouiner [baʀaɡwine] *vi* to gibber, jabber.

baraque [baʀak] *nf* shed; (*fam*) house; **~ foraine** fairground stand.

baraqué, e [baʀake] *adj* well-built, hefty.

baraquements [baʀakmɑ̃] *nmpl* huts (*for refugees, workers etc*).

baratin [baʀatɛ̃] *nm* (*fam*) smooth talk, patter.

baratiner [baʀatine] *vt* to chat up.

baratte [baʀat] *nf* churn.
Barbade [baʀbad] *nf*: **la ~** Barbados.
barbant, e [baʀbɑ̃, -ɑ̃t] *adj* (*fam*) deadly (boring).
barbare [baʀbaʀ] *adj* barbaric ♦ *nm/f* barbarian.
Barbarie [baʀbaʀi] *nf*: **la ~** the Barbary Coast.
barbarie [baʀbaʀi] *nf* barbarism; (*cruauté*) barbarity.
barbarisme [baʀbaʀism(ə)] *nm* (*LING*) barbarism.
barbe [baʀb(ə)] *nf* beard; (**au nez et**) **à la ~ de qn** (*fig*) under sb's very nose; **quelle ~!** (*fam*) what a drag *ou* bore!; **~ à papa** candy-floss (*BRIT*), cotton candy (*US*).
barbecue [baʀbəkju] *nm* barbecue.
barbelé [baʀbəle] *nm* barbed wire *no pl*.
barber [baʀbe] *vt* (*fam*) to bore stiff.
barbiche [baʀbiʃ] *nf* goatee.
barbichette [baʀbiʃɛt] *nf* small goatee.
barbiturique [baʀbityʀik] *nm* barbiturate.
barboter [baʀbɔte] *vi* to paddle, dabble ♦ *vt* (*fam*) to filch.
barboteuse [baʀbɔtøz] *nf* rompers *pl*.
barbouiller [baʀbuje] *vt* to daub; (*péj: écrire, dessiner*) to scribble; **avoir l'estomac barbouillé** to feel queasy *ou* sick.
barbu, e [baʀby] *adj* bearded.
barbue [baʀby] *nf* (*poisson*) brill.
Barcelone [baʀsəlɔn] *n* Barcelona.
barda [baʀda] *nm* (*fam*) kit, gear.
barde [baʀd(ə)] *nf* (*CULIN*) piece of fat bacon ♦ *nm* (*poète*) bard.
bardé, e [baʀde] *adj*: **~ de médailles** *etc* bedecked with medals *etc*.
bardeaux [baʀdo] *nmpl* shingle *no pl*.
barder [baʀde] *vt* (*CULIN: rôti, volaille*) to bard ♦ *vi* (*fam*): **ça va ~** sparks will fly, things are going to get hot.
barème [baʀɛm] *nm* scale; (*liste*) table; **~ des salaires** salary scale.
barge [baʀʒ] *nf* barge.
barguigner [baʀgiɲe] *vi*: **sans ~** without (any) humming and hawing and shilly-shallying.
baril [baʀil] *nm* (*tonneau*) barrel; (*de poudre*) keg.
barillet [baʀijɛ] *nm* (*de revolver*) cylinder.
bariolé, e [baʀjɔle] *adj* many-coloured, rainbow-coloured.
barman [baʀman] *nm* barman.
baromètre [baʀɔmɛtʀ(ə)] *nm* barometer; **~ anéroïde** aneroid barometer.
baron [baʀɔ̃] *nm* baron.
baronne [baʀɔn] *nf* baroness.
baroque [baʀɔk] *adj* (*ART*) baroque; (*fig*) weird.
baroud [baʀud] *nm*: **~ d'honneur** gallant last stand.
baroudeur [baʀudœʀ] *nm* (*fam*) fighter.
barque [baʀk(ə)] *nf* small boat.
barquette [baʀkɛt] *nf* small boat-shaped tart; (*récipient: en aluminium*) tub; (*: en bois*) basket.

barracuda [baʀakyda] *nm* barracuda.
barrage [baʀaʒ] *nm* dam; (*sur route*) roadblock, barricade; **~ de police** police roadblock.
barre [baʀ] *nf* (*de fer etc*) rod, bar; (*NAVIG*) helm; (*écrite*) line, stroke; (*DANSE*) barre; (*niveau*): **la livre a franchi la ~ des 10 frs** the pound has broken the 10 frs barrier; (*JUR*): **comparaître à la ~** to appear as a witness; **être à** *ou* **tenir la ~** (*NAVIG*) to be at the helm; **coup de ~** (*fig*): **c'est le coup de ~!** it's daylight robbery!; **j'ai le coup de ~!** I'm all in!; **~ fixe** (*GYM*) horizontal bar; **~ de mesure** (*MUS*) bar line; **~ à mine** crowbar; **~s parallèles/asymétriques** (*GYM*) parallel/asymmetric bars.
barreau, x [baʀo] *nm* bar; (*JUR*): **le ~** the Bar.
barrer [baʀe] *vt* (*route etc*) to block; (*mot*) to cross out; (*chèque*) to cross (*BRIT*); (*NAVIG*) to steer; **se ~** *vi* (*fam*) to clear off.
barrette [baʀɛt] *nf* (*pour cheveux*) (hair) slide (*BRIT*) *ou* clip (*US*); (*REL: bonnet*) biretta; (*broche*) brooch.
barreur [baʀœʀ] *nm* helmsman; (*aviron*) coxswain.
barricade [baʀikad] *nf* barricade.
barricader [baʀikade] *vt* to barricade; **se ~ chez soi** (*fig*) to lock o.s. in.
barrière [baʀjɛʀ] *nf* fence; (*obstacle*) barrier; (*porte*) gate; **la Grande B~** the Great Barrier Reef; **~ de dégel** (*ADMIN: on roadsigns*) no heavy vehicles - road liable to subsidence due to thaw; **~s douanières** trade barriers.
barrique [baʀik] *nf* barrel, cask.
barrir [baʀiʀ] *vi* to trumpet.
baryton [baʀitɔ̃] *nm* baritone.
BAS *sigle m* (= *bureau d'aide sociale*) ≈ social security office (*BRIT*), ≈ Welfare office (*US*).
bas, basse [bɑ, bɑs] *adj* low; (*action*) low, ignoble ♦ *nm* (*vêtement*) stocking; (*partie inférieure*): **le ~ de** the lower part *ou* foot *ou* bottom of ♦ *nf* (*MUS*) bass ♦ *adv* low; (*parler*) softly; **plus ~** lower down; more softly; (*dans un texte*) further on, below; **la tête basse** with lowered head; (*fig*) with head hung low; **avoir la vue basse** to be short-sighted; **au ~ mot** at the lowest estimate; **enfant en ~ âge** infant, young child; **en ~** down below; at (*ou* to) the bottom; (*dans une maison*) downstairs; **en ~ de** at the bottom of; **de ~ en haut** upwards; from the bottom to the top; **des hauts et des ~** ups and downs; **un ~ de laine** (*fam: économies*) money under the mattress (*fig*); **mettre ~** *vi* to give birth; **à ~ la dictature!** down with dictatorship!; **~ morceaux** (*viande*) cheap cuts.
basalte [bazalt(ə)] *nm* basalt.
basané, e [bazane] *adj* tanned, bronzed; (*immigré etc*) swarthy.
bas-côté [bakote] *nm* (*de route*) verge (*BRIT*),

shoulder (*US*); (*d'église*) (side) aisle.
bascule [baskyl] *nf*: **(jeu de)** ~ seesaw;
(balance à) ~ scales *pl*; **fauteuil à** ~ rocking
chair; **système à** ~ tip-over device; rocker
device.
basculer [baskyle] *vi* to fall over, topple
(over); (*benne*) to tip up ♦ *vt* (*aussi:* **faire** ~)
to topple over; to tip out, tip up.
base [baz] *nf* base; (*POL*): **la** ~ the rank and
file, the grass roots; (*fondement, principe*)
basis (*pl* bases); **jeter les** ~**s de** to lay the
foundations of; **à la** ~ **de** (*fig*) at the root of;
sur la ~ **de** (*fig*) on the basis of; **de** ~ basic;
à ~ **de café** *etc* coffee *etc* -based; ~ **de
données** (*INFORM*) database; ~ **de lancement**
launching site.
base-ball [bɛzbol] *nm* baseball.
baser [baze] *vt*: ~ **qch sur** to base sth on; **se** ~
sur (*données, preuves*) to base one's
argument on; **être basé à/dans** (*MIL*) to be
based at/in.
bas-fond [bafɔ̃] *nm* (*NAVIG*) shallow; ~**s** *nmpl*
(*fig*) dregs.
BASIC [bazik] *nm* BASIC.
basilic [bazilik] *nm* (*CULIN*) basil.
basilique [bazilik] *nf* basilica.
basket(-ball) [baskɛt(bol)] *nm* basketball.
baskets [baskɛt] *nfpl* (*chaussures*) trainers
(*BRIT*), sneakers (*US*).
basketteur, euse [baskɛtœʀ, -øz] *nm/f*
basketball player.
basquaise [baskɛz] *adj f* Basque ♦ *nf*: **B**~
Basque.
basque [bask(ə)] *adj, nm* (*LING*) Basque ♦ *nm/f*:
B~ Basque; **le Pays** ~ the Basque country.
basques [bask(ə)] *nfpl* skirts; **pendu aux** ~ **de
qn** constantly pestering sb; (*mère etc*)
hanging on sb's apron strings.
bas-relief [baʀəljɛf] *nm* bas-relief.
basse [bas] *adj f, nf* voir **bas**.
basse-cour, *pl* **basses-cours** [baskuʀ] *nf*
farmyard; (*animaux*) farmyard animals.
bassement [basmɑ̃] *adv* basely.
bassesse [bases] *nf* baseness; (*acte*) base act.
basset [basɛ] *nm* (*ZOOL*) basset (hound).
bassin [basɛ̃] *nm* (*cuvette*) bowl; (*pièce d'eau*)
pond, pool; (*de fontaine, GÉO*) basin; (*ANAT*)
pelvis; (*portuaire*) dock; ~ **houiller** coalfield.
bassine [basin] *nf* basin; (*contenu*) bowl,
bowlful.
bassiner [basine] *vt* (*plaie*) to bathe; (*lit*) to
warm with a warming pan; (*fam: ennuyer*) to
bore; (*: importuner*) to bug, pester.
bassiste [basist(ə)] *nm/f* (double) bass player.
basson [basɔ̃] *nm* bassoon.
bastide [bastid] *nf* (*maison*) country house (*in
Provence*); (*ville*) walled town (*in SW France*).
bastingage [bastɛ̃gaʒ] *nm* (ship's) rail.
bastion [bastjɔ̃] *nm* (*aussi fig, POL*) bastion.
bas-ventre [bavɑ̃tʀ(ə)] *nm* (lower part of the)
stomach.
bât [ba] *nm* packsaddle.

bataille [bataj] *nf* battle; **en** ~ (*en travers*) at
an angle; (*en désordre*) awry; ~ **rangée**
pitched battle.
bataillon [batajɔ̃] *nm* battalion.
bâtard, e [batar, -ard(ə)] *adj* (*enfant*)
illegitimate; (*fig*) hybrid ♦ *nm/f* illegitimate
child, bastard (*péj*) ♦ *nm* (*BOULANGERIE*)
≈ Vienna loaf; **chien** ~ mongrel.
batavia [batavja] *nf* ≈ Webb lettuce.
bateau, x [bato] *nm* boat; (*grand*) ship ♦ *adj inv*
(*banal, rebattu*) hackneyed; ~ **de pêche/à
moteur** fishing/motor boat.
bateau-citerne [batositɛʀn(ə)] *nm* tanker.
bateau-mouche [batomuʃ] *nm* (passenger)
pleasure boat (*on the Seine*).
bateau-pilote [batopilɔt] *nm* pilot ship.
bateleur, euse [batlœʀ, -øz] *nm/f* street
performer.
batelier, ière [batəlje, -jɛʀ] *nm/f* ferryman/
woman.
bat-flanc [baflɑ̃] *nm inv* raised boards for
sleeping, in cells, army huts etc.
bâti, e [bati] *adj* (*terrain*) developed ♦ *nm* (*armature*) frame; (*COUTURE*) tacking; **bien** ~
(*personne*) well-built.
batifoler [batifɔle] *vi* to frolic *ou* lark about.
batik [batik] *nm* batik.
bâtiment [batimɑ̃] *nm* building; (*NAVIG*) ship,
vessel; (*industrie*): **le** ~ the building trade.
bâtir [batiʀ] *vt* to build; (*COUTURE: jupe, ourlet*)
to tack; **fil à** ~ (*COUTURE*) tacking thread.
bâtisse [batis] *nf* building.
bâtisseur, euse [batisœʀ, -øz] *nm/f* builder.
batiste [batist(ə)] *nf* (*COUTURE*) batiste,
cambric.
bâton [batɔ̃] *nm* stick; **mettre des** ~**s dans les
roues à qn** to put a spoke in sb's wheel; **à** ~**s
rompus** informally; ~ **de rouge (à lèvres)**
lipstick; ~ **de ski** ski stick.
bâtonnet [batɔnɛ] *nm* short stick *ou* rod.
bâtonnier [batɔnje] *nm* (*JUR*) ≈ President of
the Bar.
batraciens [batʀasjɛ̃] *nmpl* amphibians.
battage [bataʒ] *nm* (*publicité*) (hard) plugging.
battant, e [batɑ̃, -ɑ̃t] *vb voir* **battre** ♦ *adj*: **pluie**
~**e** lashing rain ♦ *nm* (*de cloche*) clapper; (*de
volets*) shutter, flap; (*de porte*) side; (*fig:
personne*) fighter; **porte à double** ~ double
door; **tambour** ~ briskly.
batte [bat] *nf* (*SPORT*) bat.
battement [batmɑ̃] *nm* (*de cœur*) beat;
(*intervalle*) interval (*between classes, trains
etc*); ~ **de paupières** blinking *no pl* (of
eyelids); **un** ~ **de 10 minutes, 10 minutes de**
~ 10 minutes to spare.
batterie [batʀi] *nf* (*MIL, ÉLEC*) battery; (*MUS*)
drums *pl*, drum kit; ~ **de cuisine** kitchen
utensils *pl*; (*casseroles etc*) pots and pans *pl*;
une ~ **de tests** a string of tests.
batteur [batœʀ] *nm* (*MUS*) drummer; (*appareil*)
whisk.
batteuse [batøz] *nf* (*AGR*) threshing machine.

battoir [batwaʀ] *nm* (*à linge*) beetle (*for laundry*); (*à tapis*) (carpet) beater.

battre [batʀ(ə)] *vt* to beat; (*suj: pluie, vagues*) to beat *ou* lash against; (*œufs etc*) to beat up, whisk; (*blé*) to thresh; (*cartes*) to shuffle; (*passer au peigne fin*) to scour ♦ *vi* (*cœur*) to beat; (*volets etc*) to bang, rattle; **se ~** *vi* to fight; **~ la mesure** to beat time; **~ en brèche** (*MIL: mur*) to batter; (*fig: théorie*) to demolish; (*: institution etc*) to attack; **~ son plein** to be at its height, be going full swing; **~ pavillon britannique** to fly the British flag; **~ des mains** to clap one's hands; **~ des ailes** to flap its wings; **~ de l'aile** (*fig*) to be in a bad way *ou* in bad shape; **~ la semelle** to stamp one's feet; **~ en retraite** to beat a retreat.

battu, e [baty] *pp de* **battre** ♦ *nf* (*chasse*) beat; (*policière etc*) search, hunt.

baud [bo(d)] *nm* baud.

baudruche [bodʀyʃ] *nf*: **ballon en ~** (toy) balloon; (*fig*) windbag.

baume [bom] *nm* balm.

bauxite [boksit] *nf* bauxite.

bavard, e [bavaʀ, -aʀd(ə)] *adj* (very) talkative; gossipy.

bavardage [bavaʀdaʒ] *nm* chatter *no pl*; gossip *no pl*.

bavarder [bavaʀde] *vi* to chatter; (*indiscrètement*) to gossip; (*: révéler un secret*) to blab.

bavarois, e [bavaʀwa, -waz] *adj* Bavarian ♦ *nm ou nf* (*CULIN*) bavarois.

bave [bav] *nf* dribble; (*de chien etc*) slobber, slaver (*BRIT*), drool (*US*); (*d'escargot*) slime.

baver [bave] *vi* to dribble; to slobber, slaver (*BRIT*), drool (*US*); (*encre, couleur*) to run; **en ~** (*fam*) to have a hard time (of it).

bavette [bavɛt] *nf* bib.

baveux, euse [bavø, -øz] *adj* dribbling; (*omelette*) runny.

Bavière [bavjɛʀ] *nf*: **la ~** Bavaria.

bavoir [bavwaʀ] *nm* (*de bébé*) bib.

bavure [bavyʀ] *nf* smudge; (*fig*) hitch; blunder.

bayer [baje] *vi*: **~ aux corneilles** to stand gaping.

bazar [bazaʀ] *nm* general store; (*fam*) jumble.

bazarder [bazaʀde] *vt* (*fam*) to chuck out.

BCBG *sigle a* (= *bon chic bon genre*) ≈ preppy.

BCG *sigle m* (= *bacille Calmette-Guérin*) BCG.

bcp *abr* = **beaucoup**.

BD *sigle f* = **bande dessinée**; (= *base de données*) DB.

bd *abr* = **boulevard**.

b.d.c. *abr* (*TYPO*: = *bas de casse*) l.c.

béant, e [beɑ̃, -ɑ̃t] *adj* gaping.

béarnais, e [beaʀnɛ, -ɛz] *adj* of *ou* from the Béarn.

béat, e [bea, -at] *adj* showing open-eyed wonder; (*sourire etc*) blissful.

béatitude [beatityd] *nf* bliss.

beau (bel), belle, beaux [bo, bɛl] *adj* beautiful, lovely; (*homme*) handsome ♦ *nf* (*SPORT*) decider ♦ *adv*: **il fait ~** the weather's fine ♦ *nm*: **avoir le sens du ~** to have an aesthetic sense; **le temps est au ~** the weather is set fair; **un ~ geste** (*fig*) a fine gesture; **un ~ salaire** a good salary; **un ~ gâchis/rhume** a fine mess/nasty cold; **en faire/dire de belles** to do/say (some) stupid things; **le ~ monde** high society; **~ parleur** smooth talker; **un ~ jour** one (fine) day; **de plus belle** more than ever, even more; **bel et bien** well and truly; (*vraiment*) really (and truly); **le plus ~ c'est que ...** the best of it is that ...; **c'est du ~!** that's great, that is!; **on a ~ essayer** however hard *ou* no matter how hard we try; **il a ~ jeu de protester** etc it's easy for him to protest etc; **faire le ~** (*chien*) to sit up and beg.

beauceron, ne [bosʀɔ̃, -ɔn] *adj* of *ou* from the Beauce.

════════════════ *MOT-CLÉ*

beaucoup [boku] *adv* **1** a lot; **il boit ~** he drinks a lot; **il ne boit pas ~** he doesn't drink much *ou* a lot

2 (*suivi de plus, trop etc*) much, a lot, far; **il est ~ plus grand** he is much *ou* a lot *ou* far taller

3: **~ de** (*nombre*) many, a lot of; (*quantité*) a lot of; **pas ~ de** (*nombre*) not many, not a lot of; (*quantité*) not much, not a lot of; **~ d'étudiants/de touristes** a lot of *ou* many students/tourists; **~ de courage** a lot of courage; **il n'a pas ~ d'argent** he hasn't got much *ou* a lot of money; **il n'y a pas ~ de touristes** there aren't many *ou* a lot of tourists

4: **de ~** by far

♦ *pron*: **~ le savent** lots of people know that.

beau-fils, *pl* **beaux-fils** [bofis] *nm* son-in-law; (*remariage*) stepson.

beau-frère, *pl* **beaux-frères** [bofʀɛʀ] *nm* brother-in-law.

beau-père, *pl* **beaux-pères** [bopɛʀ] *nm* father-in-law; (*remariage*) stepfather.

beauté [bote] *nf* beauty; **de toute ~** beautiful; **en ~** *adv* with a flourish, brilliantly.

beaux-arts [bozaʀ] *nmpl* fine arts.

beaux-parents [bopaʀɑ̃] *nmpl* wife's/husband's family *sg ou pl*, in-laws.

bébé [bebe] *nm* baby.

bébé-éprouvette, *pl* **bébés-éprouvette** [bebeepʀuvɛt] *nm* test-tube baby.

bec [bɛk] *nm* beak, bill; (*de plume*) nib; (*de cafetière etc*) spout; (*de casserole etc*) lip; (*d'une clarinette etc*) mouthpiece; (*fam*) mouth; **clouer le ~ à qn** (*fam*) to shut sb up; **ouvrir le ~** (*fam*) to open one's mouth; **~ de gaz** (street) gaslamp; **~ verseur** pouring lip.

bécane [bekan] *nf* (*fam*) bike.

bécarre [bekaʀ] *nm* (*MUS*) natural.
bécasse [bekas] *nf* (*ZOOL*) woodcock; (*fam*) silly goose.
bec-de-cane, *pl* **becs-de-cane** [bɛkdəkan] *nm* (*poignée*) door handle.
bec-de-lièvre, *pl* **becs-de-lièvre** [bɛkdəljɛvʀ(ə)] *nm* harelip.
béchamel [beʃamɛl] *nf*: (**sauce**) ~ white sauce, bechamel sauce.
bêche [bɛʃ] *nf* spade.
bêcher [beʃe] *vt* (*terre*) to dig; (*personne: critiquer*) to slate; (*: snober*) to look down on.
bêcheur, euse [beʃœʀ, -øz] *adj* (*fam*) stuck-up ♦ *nm/f* fault-finder; (*snob*) stuck-up person.
bécoter [bekɔte]: **se** ~ *vi* to smooch.
becquée [beke] *nf*: **donner la** ~ **à** to feed.
becqueter [bɛkte] *vt* (*fam*) to eat.
bedaine [bədɛn] *nf* paunch.
bédé [bede] *nf* (*fam*: = *bande dessinée*) strip cartoon (*BRIT*), comic strip.
bedeau, x [bədo] *nm* beadle.
bedonnant, e [bədɔnɑ̃, -ɑ̃t] *adj* paunchy, potbellied.
bée [be] *adj*: **bouche** ~ gaping.
beffroi [befʀwa] *nm* belfry.
bégaiement [begɛmɑ̃] *nm* stammering, stuttering.
bégayer [begeje] *vt*, *vi* to stammer.
bégonia [begɔnja] *nm* (*BOT*) begonia.
bègue [bɛg] *nm/f*: **être** ~ to have a stammer.
bégueule [begœl] *adj* prudish.
béguin [begɛ̃] *nm*: **avoir le** ~ **de** *ou* **pour** to have a crush on.
beige [bɛʒ] *adj* beige.
beignet [bɛɲɛ] *nm* fritter.
bel [bɛl] *adj m voir* **beau**.
bêler [bele] *vi* to bleat.
belette [bəlɛt] *nf* weasel.
belge [bɛlʒ(ə)] *adj* Belgian ♦ *nm/f*: **B**~ Belgian.

La fête nationale belge, *on July 21, is the anniversary of Leopold of Saxe-Coburg Gotha becoming King Leopold I in 1831.*

Belgique [bɛlʒik] *nf*: **la** ~ Belgium.
Belgrade [bɛlgʀad] *n* Belgrade.
bélier [belje] *nm* ram; (*engin*) (battering) ram; (*signe*): **le B**~ Aries, the Ram; **être du B**~ to be Aries.
Bélize [beliz] *nm*: **le** ~ Belize.
bellâtre [bɛlɑtʀ(ə)] *nm* dandy.
belle [bɛl] *adj f*, *nf voir* **beau**.
belle-famille, *pl* **belles-familles** [bɛlfamij] *nf* (*fam*) in-laws *pl*.
belle-fille, *pl* **belles-filles** [bɛlfij] *nf* daughter-in-law; (*remariage*) stepdaughter.
belle-mère, *pl* **belles-mères** [bɛlmɛʀ] *nf* mother-in-law; (*remariage*) stepmother.
belle-sœur, *pl* **belles-sœurs** [bɛlsœʀ] *nf* sister-in-law.
belliciste [belisist(ə)] *adj* warmongering.
belligérance [beliʒeʀɑ̃s] *nf* belligerence.

belligérant, e [beliʒeʀɑ̃, -ɑ̃t] *adj* belligerent.
belliqueux, euse [belikø, -øz] *adj* aggressive, warlike.
belote [bəlɔt] *nf* belote (*card game*).
belvédère [bɛlvedɛʀ] *nm* panoramic viewpoint (*or small building there*).
bémol [bemɔl] *nm* (*MUS*) flat.
ben [bɛ̃] *excl* (*fam*) well.
bénédiction [benediksjɔ̃] *nf* blessing.
bénéfice [benefis] *nm* (*COMM*) profit; (*avantage*) benefit; **au** ~ **de** in aid of.
bénéficiaire [benefisjɛʀ] *nm/f* beneficiary.
bénéficier [benefisje] *vi*: ~ **de** to enjoy; (*profiter*) to benefit by *ou* from; (*obtenir*) to get, be given.
bénéfique [benefik] *adj* beneficial.
Bénélux [benelyks] *nm*: **le** ~ Benelux, the Benelux countries.
benêt [bənɛ] *nm* simpleton.
bénévolat [benevɔla] *nm* voluntary service *ou* work.
bénévole [benevɔl] *adj* voluntary, unpaid.
bénévolement [benevɔlmɑ̃] *adv* voluntarily.
Bengale [bɛ̃gal] *nm*: **le** ~ Bengal; **le golfe du** ~ the Bay of Bengal.
bengali [bɛ̃gali] *adj* Bengali, Bengalese ♦ *nm* (*LING*) Bengali.
Bénin [benɛ̃] *nm*: **le** ~ Benin.
bénin, igne [benɛ̃, -iɲ] *adj* minor, mild; (*tumeur*) benign.
bénir [beniʀ] *vt* to bless.
bénit, e [beni, -it] *adj* consecrated; **eau** ~**e** holy water.
bénitier [benitje] *nm* stoup, font (*for holy water*).
benjamin, e [bɛ̃ʒamɛ̃, -in] *nm/f* youngest child; (*SPORT*) under-13.
benne [bɛn] *nf* skip; (*de téléphérique*) (cable) car; ~ **basculante** tipper (*BRIT*), dump *ou* dumper truck.
benzine [bɛ̃zin] *nf* benzine.
béotien, ne [beɔsjɛ̃, -ɛn] *nm/f* philistine.
BEP *sigle m* (= *Brevet d'études professionnelles*) school-leaving diploma, taken at approx. 18 years.
BEPA [bepa] *sigle m* (= *Brevet d'études professionnelles agricoles*) school-leaving diploma in agriculture, taken at approx. 18 years.
BEPC *sigle m* (= *Brevet d'études du premier cycle*) former school certificate (taken at approx. 16 years).
béquille [bekij] *nf* crutch; (*de bicyclette*) stand.
berbère [bɛʀbɛʀ] *adj* Berber ♦ *nm* (*LING*) Berber ♦ *nm/f*: **B**~ Berber.
bercail [bɛʀkaj] *nm* fold.
berceau, x [bɛʀso] *nm* cradle, crib.
bercer [bɛʀse] *vt* to rock, cradle; (*suj: musique etc*) to lull; ~ **qn de** (*promesses etc*) to delude sb with.
berceur, euse [bɛʀsœʀ, -øz] *adj* soothing ♦ *nf* (*chanson*) lullaby.

BERD [bɛʀd] *sigle f* (= *Banque européenne pour la reconstruction et le développement*) EBRD.

béret (basque) [beʀɛ(bask(ə))] *nm* beret.

bergamote [bɛʀgamɔt] *nf* (*BOT*) bergamot.

berge [bɛʀʒ(ə)] *nf* bank.

berger, ère [bɛʀʒe, -ɛʀ] *nm/f* shepherd/ shepherdess; ~ **allemand** (*chien*) alsatian (dog) (*BRIT*), German shepherd (dog) (*US*).

bergerie [bɛʀʒəʀi] *nf* sheep pen.

bergeronnette [bɛʀʒəʀɔnɛt] *nf* wagtail.

béribéri [beʀibeʀi] *nm* beriberi.

Berlin [bɛʀlɛ̃] *n* Berlin; ~-**Est/-Ouest** East/ West Berlin.

berline [bɛʀlin] *nf* (*AUTO*) saloon (car) (*BRIT*), sedan (*US*).

berlingot [bɛʀlɛ̃go] *nm* (*emballage*) carton (*pyramid shaped*); (*bonbon*) lozenge.

berlinois, e [bɛʀlinwa, -waz] *adj* of *ou* from Berlin ♦ *nm/f*: **B~, e** Berliner.

berlue [bɛʀly] *nf*: **j'ai la** ~ I must be seeing things.

bermuda [bɛʀmyda] *nm* (*short*) Bermuda shorts.

Bermudes [bɛʀmyd] *nfpl*: **les (îles)** ~ Bermuda.

Berne [bɛʀn(ə)] *n* Bern.

berne [bɛʀn(ə)] *nf*: **en** ~ at half-mast; **mettre en** ~ to fly at half-mast.

berner [bɛʀne] *vt* to fool.

bernois, e [bɛʀnwa, -waz] *adj* Bernese.

berrichon, ne [beʀiʃɔ̃, -ɔn] *adj* of *ou* from the Berry.

besace [bəzas] *nf* beggar's bag.

besogne [bəzɔɲ] *nf* work *no pl*, job.

besogneux, euse [bəzɔɲø, -øz] *adj* hard-working.

besoin [bəzwɛ̃] *nm* need; (*pauvreté*): **le** ~ need, want; **le** ~ **d'argent/de gloire** the need for money/glory; ~**s** (*naturels*) nature's needs; **faire ses** ~**s** to relieve o.s.; **avoir** ~ **de qch/ faire qch** to need sth/to do sth; **il n'y a pas** ~ **de (faire)** there is no need to (do); **au** ~, **si** ~ **est** if need be; **pour les** ~**s de la cause** for the purpose in hand.

bestial, e, aux [bɛstjal, -o] *adj* bestial, brutish ♦ *nmpl* cattle.

bestiole [bɛstjɔl] *nf* (tiny) creature.

bétail [betaj] *nm* livestock, cattle *pl*.

bétaillère [betajɛʀ] *nf* livestock truck.

bête [bɛt] *nf* animal; (*bestiole*) insect, creature ♦ *adj* stupid, silly; **les** ~**s** (the) animals; **chercher la petite** ~ to nit-pick; ~ **noire** pet hate, bugbear (*BRIT*); ~ **sauvage** wild beast; ~ **de somme** beast of burden.

bêtement [bɛtmɑ̃] *adv* stupidly; **tout** ~ quite simply.

Bethléem [bɛtleɛm] *n* Bethlehem.

bêtifier [betifje] *vi* to talk nonsense.

bêtise [betiz] *nf* stupidity; (*action, remarque*) stupid thing (to say *ou* do); (*bonbon*) *type of mint sweet* (*BRIT*) *ou candy* (*US*); **faire/dire une** ~ to do/say something stupid.

béton [betɔ̃] *nm* concrete; **(en)** ~ (*fig: alibi, argument*) cast iron; ~ **armé** reinforced concrete; ~ **précontraint** prestressed concrete.

bétonner [betɔne] *vt* to concrete (over).

bétonnière [betɔnjɛʀ] *nf* cement mixer.

bette [bɛt] *nf* (*BOT*) (Swiss) chard.

betterave [bɛtʀav] *nf* (*rouge*) beetroot (*BRIT*), beet (*US*); ~ **fourragère** mangel-wurzel; ~ **sucrière** sugar beet.

beugler [bøgle] *vi* to low; (*péj: radio etc*) to blare ♦ *vt* (*péj: chanson etc*) to bawl out.

Beur [bœʀ] *adj, nm/f* second-generation Arab immigrant.

> **Beur** *is the term used to refer to a person born in France of North African immigrant parents. It is not a racist term and is often used by the media, anti-racist groups and second-generation North Africans themselves. The word itself comes from* **verlan***.*

beurre [bœʀ] *nm* butter; **mettre du** ~ **dans les épinards** (*fig*) to add a little to the kitty; ~ **de cacao** cocoa butter; ~ **noir** brown butter (sauce).

beurrer [bœʀe] *vt* to butter.

beurrier [bœʀje] *nm* butter dish.

beuverie [bœvʀi] *nf* drinking session.

bévue [bevy] *nf* blunder.

Beyrouth [beʀut] *n* Beirut.

Bhoutan [butɑ̃] *nm*: **le** ~ Bhutan.

bi... [bi] *préfixe* bi..., two-.

Biafra [bjafʀa] *nm*: **le** ~ Biafra.

biafrais, e [bjafʀɛ, -ɛz] *adj* Biafran.

biais [bjɛ] *nm* (*moyen*) device, expedient; (*aspect*) angle; (*bande de tissu*) piece of cloth cut on the bias; **en** ~, **de** ~ (*obliquement*) at an angle; (*fig*) indirectly.

biaiser [bjeze] *vi* (*fig*) to sidestep the issue.

biathlon [biatlɔ̃] *nm* biathlon.

bibelot [biblo] *nm* trinket, curio.

biberon [bibʀɔ̃] *nm* (feeding) bottle; **nourrir au** ~ to bottle-feed.

bible [bibl(ə)] *nf* bible.

bibliobus [biblijɔbys] *nm* mobile library van.

bibliographie [biblijɔgʀafi] *nf* bibliography.

bibliophile [biblijɔfil] *nm/f* book-lover.

bibliothécaire [biblijɔtekɛʀ] *nm/f* librarian.

bibliothèque [biblijɔtɛk] *nf* library; (*meuble*) bookcase; ~ **municipale** public library.

biblique [biblik] *adj* biblical.

bicarbonate [bikaʀbɔnat] *nm*: ~ **(de soude)** bicarbonate of soda.

bicentenaire [bisɑ̃tnɛʀ] *nm* bicentenary.

biceps [bisɛps] *nm* biceps.

biche [biʃ] *nf* doe.

bichonner [biʃɔne] *vt* to groom.

bicolore [bikɔlɔʀ] *adj* two-coloured (*BRIT*), two-colored (*US*).

bicoque [bikɔk] *nf* (*péj*) shack, dump.

bicorne [bikɔʀn(ə)] *nm* cocked hat.

bicyclette [bisiklɛt] *nf* bicycle.
bidasse [bidas] *nm* (*fam*) squaddie (*BRIT*).
bide [bid] *nm* (*fam: ventre*) belly; (*THÉÂT*) flop.
bidet [bidɛ] *nm* bidet.
bidirectionnel, le [bidirɛksjɔnɛl] *adj* bidirectional.
bidoche [bidɔʃ] *nf* (*fam*) meat.
bidon [bidɔ̃] *nm* can ♦ *adj inv* (*fam*) phoney.
bidonnant, e [bidɔnɑ̃, -ɑ̃t] *adj* (*fam*) hilarious.
bidonville [bidɔ̃vil] *nm* shanty town.
bidule [bidyl] *nm* (*fam*) thingamajig.
bielle [bjɛl] *nf* connecting rod; (*AUTO*) track rod.
biélorusse [bjelɔrys] *adj* Belarussian ♦ *nm/f*: **B~** Belarussian.
Biélorussie [bjelɔrysi] *nf* Belorussia.

═══════════════ *MOT-CLÉ*

bien [bjɛ̃] *nm* **1** (*avantage, profit*): **faire le ~** to do good; **faire du ~ à qn** to do sb good; **ça fait du ~ de faire** it does you good to do; **dire du ~ de** to speak well of; **c'est pour son ~** it's for his own good; **changer en ~** to change for the better; **le ~ public** the public good; **vouloir du ~ à qn** (*vouloir aider*) to have sb's (best) interests at heart; **je te veux du ~** (*pour mettre en confiance*) I don't wish you any harm
2 (*possession, patrimoine*) possession, property; **son ~ le plus précieux** his most treasured possession; **avoir du ~** to have property; **~s (de consommation** *etc*) (consumer *etc*) goods; **~s durables** (consumer) durables
3 (*moral*): **le ~** good; **distinguer le ~ du mal** to tell good from evil
♦ *adv* **1** (*de façon satisfaisante*) well; **elle travaille/mange ~** she works/eats well; **aller** *or* **se porter ~** to be well; **croyant ~ faire, je/il ...** thinking I/he was doing the right thing, I/he ...
2 (*valeur intensive*) quite; **~ jeune** quite young; **~ assez** quite enough; **~ mieux** (very) much better; **~ du temps/des gens** quite a time/a number of people; **j'espère ~ y aller** I do hope to go; **je veux ~ le faire** (*concession*) I'm quite willing to do it; **il faut ~ le faire** it has to be done; **il y a ~ 2 ans** at least 2 years ago; **il semble ~ que** it really seems that; **peut-être ~** it could well be; **aimer ~** to like; **Paul est ~ venu, n'est-ce pas?** Paul HAS come, hasn't he?; **où peut-il ~ être passé?** where on earth can he have got to?
3 (*conséquence, résultat*): **si ~ que** with the result that; **on verra ~** we'll see; **faire ~ de ...** to be right to ...
♦ *excl* right!, OK!, fine!; **eh ~!** well!; **(c'est) ~ fait!** it serves you right! (*ou* him *etc*) right!; **~ sûr!, ~ entendu!** certainly!, of course!
♦ *adj inv* **1** (*en bonne forme, à l'aise*): **je me sens ~, je suis ~** I feel fine; **je ne me sens**

pas **~, je ne suis pas ~** I don't feel well; **on est ~ dans ce fauteuil** this chair is very comfortable
2 (*joli, beau*) good-looking; **tu es ~ dans cette robe** you look good in that dress
3 (*satisfaisant*) good; **elle est ~, cette maison/secrétaire** it's a good house/she's a good secretary; **c'est très ~ (comme ça)** it's fine (like that); **ce n'est pas si ~ que ça** it's not as good *ou* great as all that; **c'est ~?** is that all right?
4 (*moralement*) right; (: *personne*) good, nice; (*respectable*) respectable; **ce n'est pas ~ de ...** it's not right to ...; **elle est ~, cette femme** she's a nice woman, she's a good sort; **des gens ~s** respectable people
5 (*en bons termes*): **être ~ avec qn** to be on good terms with sb.

bien-aimé, e [bjɛ̃neme] *adj, nm/f* beloved.
bien-être [bjɛ̃nɛtr(ə)] *nm* well-being.
bienfaisance [bjɛ̃fəzɑ̃s] *nf* charity.
bienfaisant, e [bjɛ̃fəzɑ̃, -ɑ̃t] *adj* (*chose*) beneficial.
bienfait [bjɛ̃fɛ] *nm* act of generosity, benefaction; (*de la science etc*) benefit.
bienfaiteur, trice [bjɛ̃fɛtœr, -tris] *nm/f* benefactor/benefactress.
bien-fondé [bjɛ̃fɔ̃de] *nm* soundness.
bien-fonds [bjɛ̃fɔ̃] *nm* property.
bienheureux, euse [bjɛ̃nœrø, -øz] *adj* happy; (*REL*) blessed, blest.
biennal, e, aux [bjenal, -o] *adj* biennial.
bien-pensant, e [bjɛ̃pɑ̃sɑ̃, -ɑ̃t] *adj* right-thinking ♦ *nm/f*: **les ~s** right-minded people.
bien que [bjɛ̃k(ə)] *conj* although.
bienséance [bjɛ̃seɑ̃s] *nf* propriety, decorum *no pl*; **les ~s** (*convenances*) the proprieties.
bienséant, e [bjɛ̃seɑ̃, -ɑ̃t] *adj* proper, seemly.
bientôt [bjɛ̃to] *adv* soon; **à ~** see you soon.
bienveillance [bjɛ̃vɛjɑ̃s] *nf* kindness.
bienveillant, e [bjɛ̃vɛjɑ̃, -ɑ̃t] *adj* kindly.
bienvenu, e [bjɛ̃vny] *adj* welcome ♦ *nm/f*: **être le ~/la ~e** to be welcome ♦ *nf*: **souhaiter la ~e à** to welcome; **~e à** welcome to.
bière [bjɛr] *nf* (*boisson*) beer; (*cercueil*) bier; **~ blonde** lager; **~ brune** brown ale; **~ (à la) pression** draught beer.
biffer [bife] *vt* to cross out.
bifteck [biftɛk] *nm* steak.
bifurcation [bifyrkasjɔ̃] *nf* fork (*in road*); (*fig*) new direction.
bifurquer [bifyrke] *vi* (*route*) to fork; (*véhicule*) to turn off.
bigame [bigam] *adj* bigamous.
bigamie [bigami] *nf* bigamy.
bigarré, e [bigare] *adj* multicoloured (*BRIT*), multicolored (*US*); (*disparate*) motley.
bigarreau, x [bigaro] *nm* type of cherry.
bigleux, euse [biglø, -øz] *adj* (*fam: qui louche*) cross-eyed; (: *qui voit mal*) short-sighted; **il est complètement ~** he's as blind as a bat.

bigorneau, x [bigɔʀno] nm winkle.
bigot, e [bigo, -ɔt] (péj) adj bigoted ♦ nm/f bigot.
bigoterie [bigɔtʀi] nf bigotry.
bigoudi [bigudi] nm curler.
bigrement [bigʀəmɑ̃] adv (fam) fantastically.
bijou, x [biʒu] nm jewel.
bijouterie [biʒutʀi] nf (magasin) jeweller's (shop) (BRIT), jewelry store (US); (bijoux) jewellery, jewelry.
bijoutier, ière [biʒutje, -jɛʀ] nm/f jeweller (BRIT), jeweler (US).
bikini [bikini] nm bikini.
bilan [bilɑ̃] nm (COMM) balance sheet(s); (annuel) end of year statement; (fig) (net) outcome; (: de victimes) toll; **faire le ~ de** to assess; to review; **déposer son ~** to file a bankruptcy statement; **~ de santé** (MÉD) check-up; **~ social** statement of a firm's policies towards its employees.
bilatéral, e, aux [bilateʀal, -o] adj bilateral.
bilboquet [bilbɔkɛ] nm (jouet) cup-and-ball game.
bile [bil] nf bile; **se faire de la ~** (fam) to worry o.s. sick.
biliaire [biljɛʀ] adj biliary.
bilieux, euse [biljø, -øz] adj bilious; (fig: colérique) testy.
bilingue [bilɛ̃g] adj bilingual.
bilinguisme [bilɛ̃gɥism(ə)] nm bilingualism.
billard [bijaʀ] nm billiards sg; (table) billiard table; **c'est du ~** (fam) it's a cinch; **passer sur le ~** (fam) to have an (ou one's) operation; **~ électrique** pinball.
bille [bij] nf ball; (du jeu de billes) marble; (de bois) log; **jouer aux ~s** to play marbles.
billet [bijɛ] nm (aussi: **~ de banque**) (bank)note; (de cinéma, de bus etc) ticket; (courte lettre) note; **~ à ordre** ou **de commerce** (COMM) promissory note, IOU; **~ d'avion/de train** plane/train ticket; **~ circulaire** round-trip ticket; **~ doux** love letter; **~ de faveur** complimentary ticket; **~ de loterie** lottery ticket; **~ de quai** platform ticket.
billetterie [bijɛtʀi] nf ticket office; (distributeur) ticket dispenser; (BANQUE) cash dispenser.
billion [biljɔ̃] nm billion (BRIT), trillion (US).
billot [bijo] nm block.
BIMA sigle m = Bulletin d'information du ministère de l'agriculture.
bimbeloterie [bɛ̃blɔtʀi] nf (objets) fancy goods.
bimensuel, le [bimɑ̃sɥɛl] adj bimonthly, twice-monthly.
bimestriel, le [bimɛstʀijɛl] adj bimonthly, two-monthly.
bimoteur [bimɔtœʀ] adj twin-engined.
binaire [binɛʀ] adj binary.
biner [bine] vt to hoe.
binette [binɛt] nf (outil) hoe.

binoclard, e [binɔklaʀ, -aʀd(ə)] (fam) adj specky ♦ nm/f four-eyes.
binocle [binɔkl(ə)] nm pince-nez.
binoculaire [binɔkylɛʀ] adj binocular.
binôme [binom] nm binomial.
bio... [bjɔ] préfixe bio....
biochimie [bjɔʃimi] nf biochemistry.
biochimique [bjɔʃimik] adj biochemical.
biochimiste [bjɔʃimist(ə)] nm/f biochemist.
biodégradable [bjɔdegʀadabl(ə)] adj biodegradable.
biodiversité [bjodivɛʀsite] nf biodiversity.
bioéthique [bjɔetik] nf bioethics sg.
biographe [bjɔgʀaf] nm/f biographer.
biographie [bjɔgʀafi] nf biography.
biographique [bjɔgʀafik] adj biographical.
biologie [bjɔlɔʒi] nf biology.
biologique [bjɔlɔʒik] adj biological.
biologiste [bjɔlɔʒist(ə)] nm/f biologist.
biomasse [bjomas] nf biomass.
biopsie [bjɔpsi] nf (MÉD) biopsy.
biosphère [bjɔsfɛʀ] nf biosphere.
biotope [bjɔtɔp] nm biotope.
bipartisme [bipaʀtism(ə)] nm two-party system.
bipartite [bipaʀtit] adj (POL) two-party, bipartisan.
bipède [bipɛd] nm biped, two-footed creature.
biphasé, e [bifaze] adj (ÉLEC) two-phase.
biplace [biplas] adj, nm (avion) two-seater.
biplan [biplɑ̃] nm biplane.
bique [bik] nf nanny goat; (péj) old hag.
biquet, te [bikɛ, -ɛt] nm/f: **mon ~** (fam) my lamb.
BIRD [biʀd] sigle f (= Banque internationale pour la reconstruction et le développement) IBRD.
biréacteur [biʀeaktœʀ] nm twin-engined jet.
birman, e [biʀmɑ̃, -an] adj Burmese.
Birmanie [biʀmani] nf: **la ~** Burma.
bis, e [bi, biz] adj (couleur) greyish brown ♦ adv [bis]: **12 ~** 12a ou A ♦ excl, nm [bis] encore ♦ nf (baiser) kiss; (vent) North wind.
bisaïeul, e [bizajœl] nm/f great-grandfather/great-grandmother.
bisannuel, le [bizanɥɛl] adj biennial.
bisbille [bisbij] nf: **être en ~ avec qn** to be at loggerheads with sb.
Biscaye [biske] nf: **le golfe de ~** the Bay of Biscay.
biscornu, e [biskɔʀny] adj crooked; (bizarre) weird(-looking).
biscotte [biskɔt] nf (breakfast) rusk.
biscuit [biskɥi] nm biscuit (BRIT), cookie (US); (gateau) sponge cake; **~ à la cuiller** sponge finger.
biscuiterie [biskɥitʀi] nf biscuit manufacturing.
bise [biz] adj f, nf voir **bis**.
biseau, x [bizo] nm bevelled edge; **en ~** bevelled.
biseauter [bizote] vt to bevel.
bisexué, e [bisɛksɥe] adj bisexual.

bisexuel, le [bisɛksɥɛl] *adj, nm/f* bisexual.
bismuth [bismyt] *nm* bismuth.
bison [bizɔ̃] *nm* bison.
bisou [bizu] *nm (fam)* kiss.
bisque [bisk(ə)] *nf*: ~ **d'écrevisses** shrimp bisque.
bissectrice [bisɛktʀis] *nf* bisector.
bisser [bise] *vt (faire rejouer: artiste, chanson)* to encore; *(rejouer: morceau)* to give an encore of.
bissextile [bisɛkstil] *adj*: **année** ~ leap year.
bistouri [bisturi] *nm* lancet.
bistre [bistʀ(ə)] *adj (couleur)* bistre; *(peau, teint)* tanned.
bistro(t) [bistʀo] *nm* bistro, café.
BIT *sigle m* (= *Bureau international du travail*) ILO.
bit [bit] *nm (INFORM)* bit.
biterrois, e [bitɛʀwa, -waz] *adj* of *ou* from Béziers.
bitte [bit] *nf*: ~ **d'amarrage** bollard *(NAUT)*.
bitume [bitym] *nm* asphalt.
bitumer [bityme] *vt* to asphalt.
bivalent, e [bivalā, -āt] *adj* bivalent.
bivouac [bivwak] *nm* bivouac.
bizarre [bizaʀ] *adj* strange, odd.
bizarrement [bizaʀmā] *adv* strangely, oddly.
bizarrerie [bizaʀʀi] *nf* strangeness, oddness.
blackbouler [blakbule] *vt (à une élection)* to blackball.
blafard, e [blafaʀ, -aʀd(ə)] *adj* wan.
blague [blag] *nf (propos)* joke; *(farce)* trick; **sans** ~! no kidding!; ~ **à tabac** tobacco pouch.
blaguer [blage] *vi* to joke ♦ *vt* to tease.
blagueur, euse [blagœʀ, -øz] *adj* teasing ♦ *nm/f* joker.
blair [blɛʀ] *nm (fam)* conk.
blaireau, x [blɛʀo] *nm (ZOOL)* badger; *(brosse)* shaving brush.
blairer [blɛʀe] *vt*: **je ne peux pas le** ~ I can't bear *ou* stand him.
blâmable [blɑmabl(ə)] *adj* blameworthy.
blâme [blɑm] *nm* blame; *(sanction)* reprimand.
blâmer [blɑme] *vt (réprouver)* to blame; *(réprimander)* to reprimand.
blanc, blanche [blɑ̃, blɑ̃ʃ] *adj* white; *(non imprimé)* blank; *(innocent)* pure ♦ *nm/f* white, white man/woman ♦ *nm (couleur)* white; *(linge)*: **le** ~ whites *pl*; *(espace non écrit)* blank; *(aussi*: ~ **d'œuf)** (egg-)white; *(aussi*: ~ **de poulet)** breast, white meat; *(aussi*: **vin** ~) white wine ♦ *nf (MUS)* minim *(BRIT)*, half-note *(US)*; *(fam: drogue)* smack; **d'une voix blanche** in a toneless voice; **aux cheveux** ~**s** white-haired; **le** ~ **de l'œil** the white of the eye; **laisser en** ~ to leave blank; **chèque en** ~ blank cheque; **à** ~ *adv (chauffer)* white-hot; *(tirer, charger)* with blanks; **saigner à** ~ to bleed white; ~ **cassé** off-white.
blanc-bec, *pl* **blancs-becs** [blɑ̃bɛk] *nm* greenhorn.

blanchâtre [blɑ̃ʃɑtʀ(ə)] *adj (teint, lumière)* whitish.
blancheur [blɑ̃ʃœʀ] *nf* whiteness.
blanchir [blɑ̃ʃiʀ] *vt (gén)* to whiten; *(linge, fig: argent)* to launder; *(CULIN)* to blanch; *(fig: disculper)* to clear ♦ *vi* to grow white; *(cheveux)* to go white; **blanchi à la chaux** whitewashed.
blanchissage [blɑ̃ʃisaʒ] *nm (du linge)* laundering.
blanchisserie [blɑ̃ʃisʀi] *nf* laundry.
blanchisseur, euse [blɑ̃ʃisœʀ, -øz] *nm/f* launderer.
blanc-seing, *pl* **blancs-seings** [blɑ̃sɛ̃] *nm* signed blank paper.
blanquette [blɑ̃kɛt] *nf (CULIN)*: ~ **de veau** veal in a white sauce, blanquette de veau.
blasé, e [blaze] *adj* blasé.
blaser [blaze] *vt* to make blasé.
blason [blazɔ̃] *nm* coat of arms.
blasphémateur, trice [blasfematœʀ, -tʀis] *nm/f* blasphemer.
blasphématoire [blasfematwaʀ] *adj* blasphemous.
blasphème [blasfɛm] *nm* blasphemy.
blasphémer [blasfeme] *vi* to blaspheme ♦ *vt* to blaspheme against.
blatte [blat] *nf* cockroach.
blazer [blazɛʀ] *nm* blazer.
blé [ble] *nm* wheat; ~ **en herbe** wheat on the ear; ~ **noir** buckwheat.
bled [blɛd] *nm (péj)* hole; *(en Afrique du Nord)*: **le** ~ the interior.
blême [blɛm] *adj* pale.
blêmir [blemiʀ] *vi (personne)* to (turn) pale; *(lueur)* to grow pale.
blennorragie [blenɔʀaʒi] *nf* blennorrhoea.
blessant, e [blesā, -āt] *adj* hurtful.
blessé, e [blese] *adj* injured ♦ *nm/f* injured person, casualty; **un** ~ **grave, un grand** ~ a seriously injured *ou* wounded person.
blesser [blese] *vt* to injure; *(délibérément: MIL etc)* to wound; *(suj: souliers etc, offenser)* to hurt; **se** ~ to injure o.s.; **se** ~ **au pied** *etc* to injure one's foot *etc*.
blessure [blesyʀ] *nf* injury; wound.
blet, te [blɛ, blɛt] *adj* overripe.
blette [blɛt] *nf* = **bette**.
bleu, e [blø] *adj* blue; *(bifteck)* very rare ♦ *nm (couleur)* blue; *(novice)* greenhorn; *(contusion)* bruise; *(vêtement: aussi*: ~**s)** overalls *pl (BRIT)*, coveralls *pl (US)*; **avoir une peur** ~**e** to be scared stiff; **zone** ~**e** ≈ restricted parking area; **fromage** ~ blue cheese; **au** ~ *(CULIN)* au bleu; ~ **(de lessive)** ≈ blue bag; ~ **de méthylène** *(MÉD)* methylene blue; ~ **marine/nuit/roi** navy/midnight/royal blue.
bleuâtre [bløɑtʀ(ə)] *adj (fumée etc)* bluish, blueish.
bleuet [bløɛ] *nm* cornflower.
bleuir [bløiʀ] *vt, vi* to turn blue.

bleuté – bol

bleuté, e [bløte] *adj* blue-shaded.

blindage [blɛ̃daʒ] *nm* armo(u)r-plating.

blindé, e [blɛ̃de] *adj* armoured (*BRIT*), armored (*US*); (*fig*) hardened ♦ *nm* armoured *ou* armored car; (*char*) tank.

blinder [blɛ̃de] *vt* to armour (*BRIT*), armor (*US*); (*fig*) to harden.

blizzard [blizaʀ] *nm* blizzard.

bloc [blɔk] *nm* (*de pierre etc*, *INFORM*) block; (*de papier à lettres*) pad; (*ensemble*) group, block; **serré à ~** tightened right down; **en ~** as a whole; wholesale; **faire ~** to unite; **~ opératoire** operating *ou* theatre block; **~ sanitaire** toilet block; **~ sténo** shorthand notebook.

blocage [blɔkaʒ] *nm* (*voir bloquer*) blocking; jamming; freezing; (*PSYCH*) hang-up.

bloc-cuisine, *pl* **blocs-cuisines** [blɔkkɥizin] *nm* kitchen unit.

bloc-cylindres, *pl* **blocs-cylindres** [blɔksilɛ̃dʀ(ə)] *nm* cylinder block.

bloc-évier, *pl* **blocs-éviers** [blɔkevje] *nm* sink unit.

bloc-moteur, *pl* **blocs-moteurs** [blɔkmɔtœʀ] *nm* engine block.

bloc-notes, *pl* **blocs-notes** [blɔknɔt] *nm* note pad.

blocus [blɔkys] *nm* blockade.

blond, e [blɔ̃, -ɔ̃d] *adj* fair; (*plus clair*) blond; (*sable, blés*) golden ♦ *nm/f* fair-haired *ou* blond man/woman; **~ cendré** ash blond.

blondeur [blɔ̃dœʀ] *nf* fairness; blondness.

blondin, e [blɔ̃dɛ̃, -in] *nm/f* fair-haired *ou* blond child *ou* young person.

blondinet, te [blɔ̃dinɛ, -ɛt] *nm/f* blondy.

blondir [blɔ̃diʀ] *vi* (*personne, cheveux*) to go fair *ou* blond.

bloquer [blɔke] *vt* (*passage*) to block; (*pièce mobile*) to jam; (*crédits, compte*) to freeze; (*personne, négociations etc*) to hold up; (*regrouper*) to group; **~ les freins** to jam on the brakes.

blottir [blɔtiʀ]: **se ~** *vi* to huddle up.

blousant, e [bluzɑ̃, ɑ̃t] *adj* blousing out.

blouse [bluz] *nf* overall.

blouser [bluze] *vi* to blouse out.

blouson [bluzɔ̃] *nm* blouson (jacket); **~ noir** (*fig*) ≈ rocker.

blue-jean(s) [bludʒin(s)] *nm* jeans.

blues [bluz] *nm* blues *pl*.

bluet [blyɛ] *nm* = **bleuet**.

bluff [blœf] *nm* bluff.

bluffer [blœfe] *vi, vt* to bluff.

BN *sigle f* = *Bibliothèque nationale*.

BNP *sigle f* = *Banque nationale de Paris*.

boa [bɔa] *nm* (*ZOOL*): **~ (constricteur)** boa (constrictor); (*tour de cou*) (feather *ou* fur) boa.

bobard [bɔbaʀ] *nm* (*fam*) tall story.

bobèche [bɔbɛʃ] *nf* candle-ring.

bobine [bɔbin] *nf* (*de fil*) reel; (*de machine à coudre*) spool; (*de machine à écrire*) ribbon;

(*ÉLEC*) coil; **~ (d'allumage)** (*AUTO*) coil; **~ de pellicule** (*PHOTO*) roll of film.

bobo [bobo] *nm* (*aussi fig*) sore spot.

bob(sleigh) [bɔb(slɛg)] *nm* bob(sleigh).

bocage [bɔkaʒ] *nm* (*GÉO*) bocage, *farmland criss-crossed by hedges and trees*; (*bois*) grove, copse (*BRIT*).

bocal, aux [bɔkal, -o] *nm* jar.

bock [bɔk] *nm* (beer) glass; (*contenu*) glass of beer.

bœuf [bœf, *pl* bø] *nm* ox (*pl* oxen), steer; (*CULIN*) beef; (*MUS: fam*) jam session.

bof [bɔf] *excl* (*fam: indifférence*) don't care!; (: *pas terrible*) nothing special.

Bogota [bɔgɔta] *n* Bogotá.

bogue [bɔg] *nf* (*BOT*) husk ♦ *nm* (*ORDIN*) bug.

Bohème [bɔɛm] *nf*: **la ~** Bohemia.

bohème [bɔɛm] *adj* happy-go-lucky, unconventional.

bohémien, ne [bɔemjɛ̃, -ɛn] *adj* Bohemian ♦ *nm/f* gipsy.

boire [bwaʀ] *vt* to drink; (*s'imprégner de*) to soak up; **~ un coup** to have a drink.

bois [bwa] *vb voir* **boire** ♦ *nm* wood; (*ZOOL*) antler; (*MUS*): **les ~** the woodwind; **de ~, en ~** wooden; **~ vert** green wood; **~ mort** deadwood; **~ de lit** bedstead.

boisé, e [bwaze] *adj* woody, wooded.

boiser [bwaze] *vt* (*galerie de mine*) to timber; (*chambre*) to panel; (*terrain*) to plant with trees.

boiseries [bwazʀi] *nfpl* panelling *sg*.

boisson [bwasɔ̃] *nf* drink; **pris de ~** drunk, intoxicated; **~s alcoolisées** alcoholic beverages *ou* drinks; **~s non alcoolisées** soft drinks.

boit [bwa] *vb voir* **boire**.

boîte [bwat] *nf* box; (*fam: entreprise*) firm, company; **aliments en ~** canned *ou* tinned (*BRIT*) foods; **~ de sardines/petits pois** can *ou* tin (*BRIT*) of sardines/peas; **mettre qn en ~** (*fam*) to have a laugh at sb's expense; **~ d'allumettes** box of matches; (*vide*) matchbox; **~ de conserves** can *ou* tin (*BRIT*) (of food); **~ crânienne** cranium; **~ à gants** glove compartment; **~ aux lettres** letter box, mailbox (*US*); (*INFORM*) mailbox; **~ à musique** musical box; **~ noire** (*AVIAT*) black box; **~ de nuit** night club; **~ à ordures** dustbin (*BRIT*), trash can (*US*); **~ postale (BP)** PO box; **~ de vitesses** gear box.

boiter [bwate] *vi* to limp; (*fig*) to wobble; (*raisonnement*) to be shaky.

boiteux, euse [bwatø, -øz] *adj* lame; wobbly; shaky.

boîtier [bwatje] *nm* case; (*d'appareil-photo*) body; **~ de montre** watch case.

boitiller [bwatije] *vi* to limp slightly, have a slight limp.

boive [bwav] *etc vb voir* **boire**.

bol [bɔl] *nm* bowl; (*contenu*): **un ~ de café** *etc* a bowl of coffee *etc*; **un ~ d'air** a breath of fresh air; **en avoir ras le ~** (*fam*) to have had a bellyful.

bolée [bɔle] *nf* bowlful.

boléro [bɔleʀo] *nm* bolero.

bolet [bɔlɛ] *nm* boletus (mushroom).

bolide [bɔlid] *nm* racing car; **comme un ~** like a rocket.

Bolivie [bɔlivi] *nf*: **la ~** Bolivia.

bolivien, ne [bɔlivjɛ̃, -ɛn] *adj* Bolivian ♦ *nm/f*: **B~, ne** Bolivian.

bolognais, e [bɔlɔɲɛ, -ɛz] *adj* Bolognese.

Bologne [bɔlɔɲ] *n* Bologna.

bombance [bɔ̃bɑ̃s] *nf*: **faire ~** to have a feast, revel.

bombardement [bɔ̃baʀdəmɑ̃] *nm* bombing.

bombarder [bɔ̃baʀde] *vt* to bomb; **~ qn de** (*cailloux, lettres*) to bombard sb with; **~ qn directeur** to thrust sb into the director's seat.

bombardier [bɔ̃baʀdje] *nm* (*avion*) bomber; (*aviateur*) bombardier.

bombe [bɔ̃b] *nf* bomb; (*atomiseur*) (aerosol) spray; (*ÉQUITATION*) riding cap; **faire la ~** (*fam*) to go on a binge; **~ atomique** atomic bomb; **~ à retardement** time bomb.

bombé, e [bɔ̃be] *adj* rounded; (*mur*) bulging; (*front*) domed; (*route*) steeply cambered.

bomber [bɔ̃be] *vi* to bulge; (*route*) to camber ♦ *vt*: **~ le torse** to swell out one's chest.

================================= *MOT-CLÉ*

bon, bonne [bɔ̃, bɔn] *adj* **1** (*agréable, satisfaisant*) good; **un ~ repas/restaurant** a good meal/restaurant; **être ~ en maths** to be good at maths

2 (*charitable*): **être ~ (envers)** to be good (to), to be kind (to); **vous êtes trop ~** you're too kind

3 (*correct*) right; **le ~ numéro/moment** the right number/moment

4 (*souhaits*): **~ anniversaire** happy birthday; **~ voyage** have a good trip; **bonne chance** good luck; **bonne année** happy New Year; **bonne nuit** good night

5 (*approprié*): **~ à/pour** fit to/for; **~ à jeter** fit for the bin; **c'est ~ à savoir** that's useful to know; **à quoi ~ (...)?** what's the point *ou* use (of ...)?

6 (*intensif*): **ça m'a pris 2 bonnes heures** it took me a good 2 hours; **un ~ nombre de** a good number of

7: **~ enfant** *adj inv* accommodating, easygoing; **bonne femme** (*péj*) woman; **de bonne heure** early; **~ marché** cheap; **~ mot** witticism; **pour faire ~ poids** ... to make up for it ...; **~ sens** common sense; **~ vivant** jovial chap; **bonnes œuvres** charitable works, charities; **bonne sœur** nun

♦ *nm* **1** (*billet*) voucher; (*aussi*: **~ cadeau**) gift voucher; **~ de caisse** cash voucher; **~ d'essence** petrol coupon; **~ à tirer** pass for

press; **~ du Trésor** Treasury bond

2: **avoir du ~** to have its good points; **il y a du ~ dans ce qu'il dit** there's some sense in what he says; **pour de ~** for good

♦ *nm/f*: **un ~ à rien** a good-for-nothing

♦ *adv*: **il fait ~** it's *ou* the weather is fine; **sentir ~** to smell good; **tenir ~** to stand firm; **juger ~ de faire** ... to think fit to do ...

♦ *excl* right!, good!; **ah ~?** really?; **~, je reste** right, I'll stay; *voir aussi* **bonne**.

bonasse [bɔnas] *adj* soft, meek.

bonbon [bɔ̃bɔ̃] *nm* (boiled) sweet.

bonbonne [bɔ̃bɔn] *nf* demijohn; carboy.

bonbonnière [bɔ̃bɔnjɛʀ] *nf* sweet (*BRIT*) *ou* candy (*US*) box.

bond [bɔ̃] *nm* leap; (*d'une balle*) rebound, ricochet; **faire un ~** to leap in the air; **d'un seul ~** in one bound, with one leap; **~ en avant** (*fig: progrès*) leap forward.

bonde [bɔ̃d] *nf* (*d'évier etc*) plug; (: *trou*) plughole; (*de tonneau*) bung; bunghole.

bondé, e [bɔ̃de] *adj* packed (full).

bondieuserie [bɔ̃djøzʀi] *nf* (*péj: objet*) religious knick-knack.

bondir [bɔ̃diʀ] *vi* to leap; **~ de joie** (*fig*) to jump for joy; **~ de colère** (*fig*) to be hopping mad.

bonheur [bɔnœʀ] *nm* happiness; **avoir le ~ de** to have the good fortune to; **porter ~ (à qn)** to bring (sb) luck; **au petit ~** haphazardly; **par ~** fortunately.

bonhomie [bɔnɔmi] *nf* goodnaturedness.

bonhomme [bɔnɔm], *pl* **bonshommes** [bɔ̃zɔm] *nm* fellow ♦ *adj* good-natured; **un vieux ~** an old chap; **aller son ~ de chemin** to carry on in one's own sweet way; **~ de neige** snowman.

boni [bɔni] *nm* profit.

bonification [bɔnifikasjɔ̃] *nf* bonus.

bonifier [bɔnifje] *vt*, **se ~** *vi* to improve.

boniment [bɔnimɑ̃] *nm* patter *no pl*.

bonjour [bɔ̃ʒuʀ] *excl*, *nm* hello; (*selon l'heure*) good morning (*ou* afternoon); **donner** *ou* **souhaiter le ~ à qn** to bid sb good morning *ou* afternoon.

Bonn [bɔn] *n* Bonn.

bonne [bɔn] *adj f*, *nf voir* **bon**.

bonne-maman, *pl* **bonnes-mamans** [bɔnmamɑ̃] granny, grandma, gran.

bonnement [bɔnmɑ̃] *adv*: **tout ~** quite simply.

bonnet [bɔnɛ] *nm* bonnet, hat; (*de soutien-gorge*) cup; **~ d'âne** dunce's cap; **~ de bain** bathing cap; **~ de nuit** nightcap.

bonneterie [bɔnɛtʀi] *nf* hosiery.

bon-papa, *pl* **bons-papas** [bɔ̃papa] *nm* grandpa, grandad.

bonsoir [bɔ̃swaʀ] *excl* good evening.

bonté [bɔ̃te] *nf* kindness *no pl*; **avoir la ~ de** to be kind *ou* good enough to.

bonus [bɔnys] *nm* (*assurances*) no-claims bonus.

bonze [bɔ̃z] *nm* (*REL*) bonze.
boomerang [bumʀɑ̃g] *nm* boomerang.
boots [buts] *nfpl* boots.
borborygme [bɔʀbɔʀigm(ə)] *nm* rumbling noise.
bord [bɔʀ] *nm* (*de table, verre, falaise*) edge; (*de rivière, lac*) bank; (*de route*) side; (*de vêtement*) edge, border; (*de chapeau*) brim; (**monter**) **à ~** (to go) on board; **jeter par-dessus ~** to throw overboard; **le commandant/les hommes du ~** the ship's master/crew; **du même ~** (*fig*) of the same opinion; **au ~ de la mer/route** at the seaside/roadside; **être au ~ des larmes** to be on the verge of tears; **virer de ~** (*NAVIG*) to tack; **sur les ~s** (*fig*) slightly; **de tous ~s** on all sides; **~ du trottoir** kerb (*BRIT*), curb (*US*).
bordage [bɔʀdaʒ] *nm* (*NAVIG*) planking *no pl*; plating *no pl*.
bordeaux [bɔʀdo] *nm* Bordeaux ♦ *adj inv* maroon.
bordée [bɔʀde] *nf* broadside; **une ~ d'injures** a volley of abuse; **tirer une ~** to go on the town.
bordel [bɔʀdɛl] *nm* brothel; (*fam!*) bloody (*BRIT*) *ou* goddamn (*US*) mess (*!*) ♦ *excl* hell!
bordelais, e [bɔʀdəlɛ, -ɛz] *adj* of *ou* from Bordeaux.
border [bɔʀde] *vt* (*être le long de*) to border, line; (*garnir*): **~ qch de** to line sth with; to trim sth with; (*qn dans son lit*) to tuck up.
bordereau, x [bɔʀdəʀo] *nm* docket, slip.
bordure [bɔʀdyʀ] *nf* border; (*sur un vêtement*) trim(ming), border; **en ~ de** on the edge of.
boréal, e, aux [bɔʀeal, -o] *adj* boreal, northern.
borgne [bɔʀɲ(ə)] *adj* one-eyed; **hôtel ~** shady hotel; **fenêtre ~** obstructed window.
bornage [bɔʀnaʒ] *nm* (*d'un terrain*) demarcation.
borne [bɔʀn(ə)] *nf* boundary stone; (*aussi*: **~ kilométrique**) kilometre-marker, ≈ milestone; **~s** *nfpl* (*fig*) limits; **dépasser les ~s** to go too far; **sans ~(s)** boundless.
borné, e [bɔʀne] *adj* narrow; (*obtus*) narrow-minded.
Bornéo [bɔʀneo] *nm*: **le ~** Borneo.
borner [bɔʀne] *vt* (*délimiter*) to limit; (*limiter*) to confine; **se ~ à faire** to content o.s. with doing; to limit o.s. to doing.
bosniaque [bɔznjak] *adj* Bosnian ♦ *nm/f*: **B~** Bosnian.
Bosnie [bɔsni] *nf* Bosnia.
bosnien, ne [bɔznjɛ̃, -ɛn] *adj* Bosnian ♦ *nm/f*: **B~, ne** Bosnian.
Bosphore [bɔsfɔʀ] *nm*: **le ~** the Bosphorus.
bosquet [bɔskɛ] *nm* copse (*BRIT*), grove.
bosse [bɔs] *nf* (*de terrain etc*) bump; (*enflure*) lump; (*du bossu, du chameau*) hump; **avoir la ~ des maths** *etc* to have a gift for maths *etc*; **il a roulé sa ~** he's been around.

bosseler [bɔsle] *vt* (*ouvrer*) to emboss; (*abîmer*) to dent.
bosser [bɔse] *vi* (*fam*) to work; (: *dur*) to slog (hard) (*BRIT*), slave (away).
bosseur, euse [bɔsœʀ, -øz] *nm/f* (hard) worker, slogger (*BRIT*).
bossu, e [bɔsy] *nm/f* hunchback.
bot [bo] *adj m*: **pied ~** club foot.
botanique [bɔtanik] *nf* botany ♦ *adj* botanic(al).
botaniste [bɔtanist(ə)] *nm/f* botanist.
Botswana [bɔtswana] *nm*: **le ~** Botswana.
botte [bɔt] *nf* (*soulier*) (high) boot; (*ESCRIME*) thrust; (*gerbe*): **~ de paille** bundle of straw; **~ de radis/d'asperges** bunch of radishes/asparagus; **~s de caoutchouc** wellington boots.
botter [bɔte] *vt* to put boots on; (*donner un coup de pied à*) to kick; (*fam*): **ça me botte** I fancy that.
bottier [bɔtje] *nm* bootmaker.
bottillon [bɔtijɔ̃] *nm* bootee.
bottin [bɔtɛ̃] *nm* ® directory.
bottine [bɔtin] *nf* ankle boot.
botulisme [bɔtylism(ə)] *nm* botulism.
bouc [buk] *nm* goat; (*barbe*) goatee; **~ émissaire** scapegoat.
boucan [bukɑ̃] *nm* din, racket.
bouche [buʃ] *nf* mouth; **une ~ à nourrir** a mouth to feed; **les ~s inutiles** the non-productive members of the population; **faire du ~ à ~ à qn** to give sb the kiss of life (*BRIT*), give sb mouth-to-mouth resuscitation; **de ~ à oreille** confidentially; **pour la bonne ~** (*pour la fin*) till last; **faire venir l'eau à la ~** to make one's mouth water; **~ cousue!** mum's the word!; **~ d'aération** air vent; **~ de chaleur** hot air vent; **~ d'égout** manhole; **~ d'incendie** fire hydrant; **~ de métro** métro entrance.
bouché, e [buʃe] *adj* (*flacon etc*) stoppered; (*temps, ciel*) overcast; (*carrière*) blocked; (*péj: personne*) thick; (*trompette*) muted; **avoir le nez ~** to have a blocked(-up) nose.
bouchée [buʃe] *nf* mouthful; **ne faire qu'une ~ de** (*fig*) to make short work of; **pour une ~ de pain** (*fig*) for next to nothing; **~s à la reine** chicken vol-au-vents.
boucher [buʃe] *nm* butcher ♦ *vt* (*pour colmater*) to stop up; to fill up; (*obstruer*) to block (up); **se ~** (*tuyau etc*) to block up, get blocked up; **se ~ le nez** to hold one's nose.
bouchère [buʃɛʀ] *nf* butcher; (*femme du boucher*) butcher's wife.
boucherie [buʃʀi] *nf* butcher's (shop); (*métier*) butchery; (*fig*) slaughter, butchery.
bouche-trou [buʃtʀu] *nm* (*fig*) stop-gap.
bouchon [buʃɔ̃] *nm* (*en liège*) cork; (*autre matière*) stopper; (*fig: embouteillage*) holdup; (*PÊCHE*) float; **~ doseur** measuring cap.
bouchonner [buʃɔne] *vt* to rub down ♦ *vi* to form a traffic jam.

bouchot [buʃo] *nm* mussel bed.
bouclage [buklaʒ] *nm* sealing off.
boucle [bukl(ə)] *nf* (*forme, figure, aussi INFORM*) loop; (*objet*) buckle; ~ (**de cheveux**) curl; ~ **d'oreilles** earring.
bouclé, e [bukle] *adj* curly; (*tapis*) uncut.
boucler [bukle] *vt* (*fermer: ceinture etc*) to fasten; (*: magasin*) to shut; (*terminer*) to finish off; (*: circuit*) to complete; (*budget*) to balance; (*enfermer*) to shut away; (*: condamné*) to lock up; (*: quartier*) to seal off ♦ *vi* to curl; **faire** ~ (*cheveux*) to curl; ~ **la boucle** (*AVIAT*) to loop the loop.
bouclette [buklɛt] *nf* small curl.
bouclier [buklije] *nm* shield.
bouddha [buda] *nm* Buddha.
bouddhisme [budism(ə)] *nm* Buddhism.
bouddhiste [budist(ə)] *nm/f* Buddhist.
bouder [bude] *vi* to sulk ♦ *vt* (*chose*) to turn one's nose up at; (*personne*) to refuse to have anything to do with.
bouderie [budʀi] *nf* sulking *no pl*.
boudeur, euse [budœʀ, -øz] *adj* sullen, sulky.
boudin [budɛ̃] *nm* (*CULIN*) black pudding; (*TECH*) roll; ~ **blanc** white pudding.
boudiné, e [budine] *adj* (*doigt*) podgy; (*serré*): ~ **dans** (*vêtement*) bulging out of.
boudoir [budwaʀ] *nm* boudoir; (*biscuit*) sponge finger.
boue [bu] *nf* mud.
bouée [bwe] *nf* buoy; (*de baigneur*) rubber ring; ~ (**de sauvetage**) lifebuoy; (*fig*) lifeline.
boueux, euse [bwø, -øz] *adj* muddy ♦ *nm* refuse (*BRIT*) *ou* garbage (*US*) collector.
bouffant, e [bufɑ̃, -ɑ̃t] *adj* puffed out.
bouffe [buf] *nf* (*fam*) grub, food.
bouffée [bufe] *nf* puff; ~ **de chaleur** (*gén*) blast of hot air; (*MÉD*) hot flush (*BRIT*) *ou* flash (*US*); ~ **de fièvre/de honte** flush of fever/shame; ~ **d'orgueil** fit of pride.
bouffer [bufe] *vi* (*fam*) to eat; (*COUTURE*) to puff out ♦ *vt* (*fam*) to eat.
bouffi, e [bufi] *adj* swollen.
bouffon, ne [bufɔ̃, -ɔn] *adj* farcical, comical ♦ *nm* jester.
bouge [buʒ] *nm* (*bar louche*) (low) dive; (*taudis*) hovel.
bougeoir [buʒwaʀ] *nm* candlestick.
bougeotte [buʒɔt] *nf*: **avoir la** ~ to have the fidgets.
bouger [buʒe] *vi* to move; (*dent etc*) to be loose; (*changer*) to alter; (*agir*) to stir ♦ *vt* to move; **se** ~ (*fam*) to move (oneself).
bougie [buʒi] *nf* candle; (*AUTO*) spark(ing) plug.
bougon, ne [bugɔ̃, -ɔn] *adj* grumpy.
bougonner [bugɔne] *vi, vt* to grumble.
bougre [bugʀ(ə)] *nm* chap; (*fam*): **ce** ~ **de** ... that confounded ....
boui-boui [bwibwi] *nm* (*fam*) greasy spoon.
bouillabaisse [bujabɛs] *nf* type of fish soup.

bouillant, e [bujɑ̃, -ɑ̃t] *adj* (*qui bout*) boiling; (*très chaud*) boiling (hot); (*fig: ardent*) hotheaded; ~ **de colère** *etc* seething with anger *etc*.
bouille [buj] *nf* (*fam*) mug.
bouilleur [bujœʀ] *nm*: ~ **de cru** (home) distiller.
bouillie [buji] *nf* gruel; (*de bébé*) cereal; **en** ~ (*fig*) crushed.
bouillir [bujiʀ] *vi* to boil ♦ *vt* (*aussi*: **faire** ~: *CULIN*) to boil; ~ **de colère** *etc* to seethe with anger *etc*.
bouilloire [bujwaʀ] *nf* kettle.
bouillon [bujɔ̃] *nm* (*CULIN*) stock *no pl*; (*bulles, écume*) bubble; ~ **de culture** culture medium.
bouillonnement [bujɔnmɑ̃] *nm* (*d'un liquide*) bubbling; (*des idées*) ferment.
bouillonner [bujɔne] *vi* to bubble; (*fig*) to bubble up; (*torrent*) to foam.
bouillotte [bujɔt] *nf* hot-water bottle.
boulanger, ère [bulɑ̃ʒe, -ɛʀ] *nm/f* baker ♦ *nf* (*femme du boulanger*) baker's wife.
boulangerie [bulɑ̃ʒʀi] *nf* bakery, baker's (shop); (*commerce*) bakery; ~ **industrielle** bakery.
boulangerie-pâtisserie, *pl* **boulangeries-pâtisseries** [bulɑ̃ʒʀipɑtisʀi] *nf* baker's and confectioner's (shop).
boule [bul] *nf* (*gén*) ball; (*pour jouer*) bowl; (*de machine à écrire*) golf ball; **roulé en** ~ curled up in a ball; **se mettre en** ~ (*fig*) to fly off the handle, blow one's top; **perdre la** ~ (*fig: fam*) to go off one's rocker; ~ **de gomme** (*bonbon*) gum(drop), pastille; ~ **de neige** snowball; **faire** ~ **de neige** (*fig*) to snowball.
bouleau, x [bulo] *nm* (silver) birch.
bouledogue [buldɔg] *nm* bulldog.
bouler [bule] *vi* (*fam*): **envoyer** ~ **qn** to send sb packing; **je me suis fait** ~ (*à un examen*) they flunked me.
boulet [bulɛ] *nm* (*aussi*: ~ **de canon**) cannonball; (*de bagnard*) ball and chain; (*charbon*) (coal) nut.
boulette [bulɛt] *nf* ball.
boulevard [bulvaʀ] *nm* boulevard.
bouleversant, e [bulvɛʀsɑ̃, -ɑ̃t] *adj* (*récit*) deeply distressing; (*nouvelle*) shattering.
bouleversé, e [bulvɛʀse] *adj* (*ému*) deeply distressed; shattered.
bouleversement [bulvɛʀsəmɑ̃] *nm* (*politique, social*) upheaval.
bouleverser [bulvɛʀse] *vt* (*émouvoir*) to overwhelm; (*causer du chagrin à*) to distress; (*pays, vie*) to disrupt; (*papiers, objets*) to turn upside down, upset.
boulier [bulje] *nm* abacus; (*de jeu*) scoring board.
boulimie [bulimi] *nf* bulimia; compulsive eating.
boulimique [bulimik] *adj* bulimic.
boulingrin [bulɛ̃gʀɛ̃] *nm* lawn.

bouliste [bulist(ə)] *nm/f* bowler.

boulocher [buloʃe] *vi* (*laine etc*) to develop little snarls.

boulodrome [bulodrom] *nm* bowling pitch.

boulon [bulɔ̃] *nm* bolt.

boulonner [bulɔne] *vt* to bolt.

boulot [bulo] *nm* (*fam: travail*) work.

boulot, te [bulo, -ɔt] *adj* plump, tubby.

boum [bum] *nm* bang ♦ *nf* party.

bouquet [bukɛ] *nm* (*de fleurs*) bunch (of flowers), bouquet; (*de persil etc*) bunch; (*parfum*) bouquet; (*fig*) crowning piece; **c'est le ~!** that's the last straw!; **~ garni** (*CULIN*) bouquet garni.

bouquetin [buktɛ̃] *nm* ibex.

bouquin [bukɛ̃] *nm* (*fam*) book.

bouquiner [bukine] *vi* (*fam*) to read.

bouquiniste [bukinist(ə)] *nm/f* bookseller.

bourbeux, euse [buʀbø, -øz] *adj* muddy.

bourbier [buʀbje] *nm* (quag)mire.

bourde [buʀd(ə)] *nf* (*erreur*) howler; (*gaffe*) blunder.

bourdon [buʀdɔ̃] *nm* bumblebee.

bourdonnement [buʀdɔnmɑ̃] *nm* buzzing *no pl*, buzz; **avoir des ~s d'oreilles** to have a buzzing (noise) in one's ears.

bourdonner [buʀdɔne] *vi* to buzz; (*moteur*) to hum.

bourg [buʀ] *nm* small market town (*ou* village).

bourgade [buʀgad] *nf* township.

bourgeois, e [buʀʒwa, -waz] *adj* (*péj*) ≈ (upper) middle class; bourgeois; (*maison etc*) very comfortable ♦ *nm/f* (*autrefois*) burgher.

bourgeoisie [buʀʒwazi] *nf* ≈ upper middle classes *pl*; bourgeoisie; **petite ~** middle classes.

bourgeon [buʀʒɔ̃] *nm* bud.

bourgeonner [buʀʒɔne] *vi* to bud.

Bourgogne [buʀgɔɲ] *nf*: **la ~** Burgundy ♦ *nm*: **b~** burgundy (wine).

bourguignon, ne [buʀgiɲɔ̃, -ɔn] *adj* of *ou* from Burgundy, Burgundian; **bœuf ~** bœuf bourguignon.

bourlinguer [buʀlɛ̃ge] *vi* to knock about a lot, get around a lot.

bourrade [buʀad] *nf* shove, thump.

bourrage [buʀaʒ] *nm* (*papier*) jamming; **~ de crâne** brainwashing; (*SCOL*) cramming.

bourrasque [buʀask(ə)] *nf* squall.

bourratif, ive [buʀatif, -iv] *adj* filling, stodgy.

bourre [buʀ] *nf* (*de coussin, matelas etc*) stuffing.

bourré, e [buʀe] *adj* (*rempli*): **~ de** crammed full of; (*fam: ivre*) pickled, plastered.

bourreau, x [buʀo] *nm* executioner; (*fig*) torturer; **~ de travail** workaholic, glutton for work.

bourrelé, e [buʀle] *adj*: **être ~ de remords** to be racked by remorse.

bourrelet [buʀlɛ] *nm* draught (*BRIT*) *ou* draft

(*US*) excluder; (*de peau*) fold *ou* roll (of flesh).

bourrer [buʀe] *vt* (*pipe*) to fill; (*poêle*) to pack; (*valise*) to cram (full); **~ de** to cram (full) with, stuff with; **~ de coups** to hammer blows on, pummel; **~ le crâne à qn** to pull the wool over sb's eyes; (*endoctriner*) to brainwash sb.

bourricot [buʀiko] *nm* small donkey.

bourrique [buʀik] *nf* (*âne*) ass.

bourru, e [buʀy] *adj* surly, gruff.

bourse [buʀs(ə)] *nf* (*subvention*) grant; (*porte-monnaie*) purse; **sans ~ délier** without spending a penny; **la B~** the Stock Exchange; **~ du travail** ≈ trades union council (regional headquarters).

boursicoter [buʀsikɔte] *vi* (*COMM*) to dabble on the Stock Market.

boursier, ière [buʀsje, -jɛʀ] *adj* (*COMM*) Stock Market *cpd* ♦ *nm/f* (*SCOL*) grant-holder.

boursouflé, e [buʀsufle] *adj* swollen, puffy; (*fig*) bombastic, turgid.

boursoufler [buʀsufle] *vt* to puff up, bloat; **se ~** *vi* (*visage*) to swell *ou* puff up; (*peinture*) to blister.

boursouflure [buʀsuflyʀ] *nf* (*du visage*) swelling, puffiness; (*de la peinture*) blister; (*fig: du style*) pomposity.

bous [bu] *vb voir* **bouillir**.

bousculade [buskylad] *nf* (*hâte*) rush; (*poussée*) crush.

bousculer [buskyle] *vt* to knock over; to knock into; (*fig*) to push, rush.

bouse [buz] *nf*: **~ (de vache)** (cow) dung *no pl* (*BRIT*), manure *no pl*.

bousiller [buzije] *vt* (*fam*) to wreck.

boussole [busɔl] *nf* compass.

bout [bu] *vb voir* **bouillir** ♦ *nm* bit; (*extrémité: d'un bâton etc*) tip; (: *d'une ficelle, table, rue, période*) end; **au ~ de** at the end of, after; **au ~ du compte** at the end of the day; **pousser qn à ~** to push sb to the limit (of his patience); **venir à ~ de** to manage to finish (off) *ou* overcome; **à ~** to end to end; **à tout ~ de champ** at every turn; **d'un ~ à l'autre, de ~ en ~** from one end to the other; **à ~ portant** at point-blank range; **un ~ de chou** (*enfant*) a little tot; **~ d'essai** (*CINÉ etc*) screen test; **~ filtre** filter tip.

boutade [butad] *nf* quip, sally.

boute-en-train [butɑ̃tʀɛ̃] *nm inv* live wire (*fig*).

bouteille [butɛj] *nf* bottle; (*de gaz butane*) cylinder.

boutiquaire [butikɛʀ] *adj*: **niveau ~** shopping level.

boutique [butik] *nf* shop (*BRIT*), store (*US*); (*de grand couturier, de mode*) boutique.

boutiquier, ière [butikje, -jɛʀ] *nm/f* shopkeeper (*BRIT*), storekeeper (*US*).

boutoir [butwaʀ] *nm*: **coup de ~** (*choc*) thrust; (*fig: propos*) barb.

bouton [butɔ̃] *nm* (*de vêtement, électrique etc*)

button; (*BOT*) bud; (*sur la peau*) spot; (*de porte*) knob; ~ **de manchette** cuff-link; ~ **d'or** buttercup.

boutonnage [butɔnaʒ] *nm* (*action*) buttoning(-up); **un manteau à double** ~ a coat with two rows of buttons.

boutonner [butɔne] *vt* to button up, do up; **se** ~ to button one's clothes up.

boutonneux, euse [butɔnø, -øz] *adj* spotty.

boutonnière [butɔnjɛʀ] *nf* buttonhole.

bouton-poussoir, *pl* **boutons-poussoirs** [butɔ̃puswaʀ] *nm* pushbutton.

bouton-pression, *pl* **boutons-pression** [butɔ̃pʀesjɔ̃] *nm* press stud, snap fastener.

bouture [butyʀ] *nf* cutting; **faire des** ~**s** to take cuttings.

bouvreuil [buvʀœj] *nm* bullfinch.

bovidé [bɔvide] *nm* bovine.

bovin, e [bɔvɛ̃, -in] *adj* bovine ♦ *nm*: ~**s** cattle.

bowling [boliŋ] *nm* (tenpin) bowling; (*salle*) bowling alley.

box [bɔks] *nm* lock-up (garage); (*de salle, dortoir*) cubicle; (*d'écurie*) loose-box; **le** ~ **des accusés** the dock.

box(-calf) [bɔks(kalf)] *nm inv* box calf.

boxe [bɔks(ə)] *nf* boxing.

boxer [bɔkse] *vi* to box ♦ *nm* [bɔksɛʀ] (*chien*) boxer.

boxeur [bɔksœʀ] *nm* boxer.

boyau, x [bwajo] *nm* (*corde de raquette etc*) (cat) gut; (*galerie*) passage(way); (narrow) gallery; (*pneu de bicyclette*) tubeless tyre ♦ *nmpl* (*viscères*) entrails, guts.

boycottage [bɔjkɔtaʒ] *nm* (*d'un produit*) boycotting.

boycotter [bɔjkɔte] *vt* to boycott.

BP *sigle f* = **boîte postale**.

BPAL *sigle f* (= *base de plein air et de loisir*) open-air leisure centre.

BPF *sigle* (= *bon pour francs*) *printed on cheques before space for amount to be inserted.*

brabançon, ne [bʀabɑ̃sɔ̃, -ɔn] *adj* of *ou* from Brabant.

Brabant [bʀabɑ̃] *nm*: **le** ~ Brabant.

bracelet [bʀaslɛ] *nm* bracelet.

bracelet-montre [bʀaslɛmɔ̃tʀ(ə)] *nm* wristwatch.

braconnage [bʀakɔnaʒ] *nm* poaching.

braconner [bʀakɔne] *vi* to poach.

braconnier [bʀakɔnje] *nm* poacher.

brader [bʀade] *vt* to sell off, sell cheaply.

braderie [bʀadʀi] *nf* clearance sale; (*par des particuliers*) ≈ car boot sale (*BRIT*), ≈ garage sale (*US*); (*magasin*) discount store; (*sur marché*) cut-price (*BRIT*) *ou* cut-rate (*US*) stall.

braguette [bʀagɛt] *nf* fly, flies *pl* (*BRIT*), zipper (*US*).

braillard, e [bʀajaʀ, -aʀd] *adj* (*fam*) bawling, yelling.

braille [bʀaj] *nm* Braille.

braillement [bʀajmɑ̃] *nm* (*cri*) bawling *no pl*, yelling *no pl*.

brailler [bʀaje] *vi* to bawl, yell ♦ *vt* to bawl out, yell out.

braire [bʀɛʀ] *vi* to bray.

braise [bʀɛz] *nf* embers *pl*.

braiser [bʀeze] *vt* to braise; **bœuf braisé** braised steak.

bramer [bʀame] *vi* to bell; (*fig*) to wail.

brancard [bʀɑ̃kaʀ] *nm* (*civière*) stretcher; (*bras, perche*) shaft.

brancardier [bʀɑ̃kaʀdje] *nm* stretcher-bearer.

branchages [bʀɑ̃ʃaʒ] *nmpl* branches, boughs.

branche [bʀɑ̃ʃ] *nf* branch; (*de lunettes*) side (-piece).

branché, e [bʀɑ̃ʃe] *adj* (*fam*) switched-on, trendy ♦ *nm/f* (*fam*) trendy.

branchement [bʀɑ̃ʃmɑ̃] *nm* connection.

brancher [bʀɑ̃ʃe] *vt* to connect (up); (*en mettant la prise*) to plug in; ~ **qn/qch sur** (*fig*) to get sb/sth launched onto.

branchies [bʀɑ̃ʃi] *nfpl* gills.

brandade [bʀɑ̃dad] *nf* brandade (*cod dish*).

brandebourgeois, e [bʀɑ̃dəbuʀʒwa, -waz] *adj* of *ou* from Brandenburg.

brandir [bʀɑ̃diʀ] *vt* (*arme*) to brandish, wield; (*document*) to flourish, wave.

brandon [bʀɑ̃dɔ̃] *nm* firebrand.

branlant, e [bʀɑ̃lɑ̃, -ɑ̃t] *adj* (*mur, meuble*) shaky.

branle [bʀɑ̃l] *nm*: **mettre en** ~ to set swinging; **donner le** ~ **à** to set in motion.

branle-bas [bʀɑ̃lba] *nm inv* commotion.

branler [bʀɑ̃le] *vi* to be shaky, be loose ♦ *vt*: ~ **la tête** to shake one's head.

braquage [bʀakaʒ] *nm* (*fam*) stick-up, hold-up; (*AUTO*): **rayon de** ~ turning circle.

braque [bʀak] *nm* (*ZOOL*) pointer.

braquer [bʀake] *vi* (*AUTO*) to turn (the wheel) ♦ *vt* (*revolver etc*): ~ **qch sur** to aim sth at, point sth at; (*mettre en colère*): ~ **qn** to antagonize sb, put sb's back up; ~ **son regard sur** to fix one's gaze on; **se** ~ *vi*: **se** ~ **(contre)** to take a stand (against).

bras [bʀa] *nm* arm; (*de fleuve*) branch ♦ *nmpl* (*fig: travailleurs*) labour *sg* (*BRIT*), labor *sg* (*US*), hands; ~ **dessus** ~ **dessous** arm in arm; **à** ~ **raccourcis** with fists flying; **à tour de** ~ with all one's might; **baisser les** ~ to give up; ~ **droit** (*fig*) right hand man; ~ **de fer** arm-wrestling; **une partie de** ~ **de fer** (*fig*) a trial of strength; ~ **de levier** lever arm; ~ **de mer** arm of the sea, sound.

brasero [bʀazeʀo] *nm* brazier.

brasier [bʀazje] *nm* blaze, (blazing) inferno; (*fig*) inferno.

Brasilia [bʀazilja] *n* Brasilia.

bras-le-corps [bʀalkɔʀ]: **à** ~ *adv* (a)round the waist.

brassage [bʀasaʒ] *nm* (*de la bière*) brewing; (*fig*) mixing.

brassard [bʀasaʀ] *nm* armband.

brasse [bʀas] nf (nage) breast-stroke; (mesure) fathom; ~ **papillon** butterfly(-stroke).

brassée [bʀase] nf armful; **une ~ de** (fig) a number of.

brasser [bʀase] vt (bière) to brew; (remuer: salade) to toss; (: cartes) to shuffle; (fig) to mix; ~ **l'argent/les affaires** to handle a lot of money/business.

brasserie [bʀasʀi] nf (restaurant) bar (selling food), brasserie; (usine) brewery.

brasseur [bʀasœʀ] nm (de bière) brewer; ~ **d'affaires** big businessman.

brassière [bʀasjɛʀ] nf (baby's) vest (BRIT) ou undershirt (US); (de sauvetage) life jacket.

bravache [bʀavaʃ] nm blusterer, braggart.

bravade [bʀavad] nf: **par ~** out of bravado.

brave [bʀav] adj (courageux) brave; (bon, gentil) good, kind.

bravement [bʀavmɑ̃] adv bravely; (résolument) boldly.

braver [bʀave] vt to defy.

bravo [bʀavo] excl bravo! ♦ nm cheer.

bravoure [bʀavuʀ] nf bravery.

BRB sigle f (POLICE: = Brigade de répression du banditisme) ≈ serious crime squad.

break [bʀɛk] nm (AUTO) estate car (BRIT), station wagon (US).

brebis [bʀəbi] nf ewe; ~ **galeuse** black sheep.

brèche [bʀɛʃ] nf breach, gap; **être sur la ~** (fig) to be on the go.

bredouille [bʀəduj] adj empty-handed.

bredouiller [bʀəduje] vi, vt to mumble, stammer.

bref, brève [bʀɛf, bʀɛv] adj short, brief ♦ adv in short ♦ nf (voyelle) short vowel; (information) brief news item; **d'un ton ~** sharply, curtly; **en ~** in short, in brief; **à ~ délai** shortly.

brelan [bʀəlɑ̃] nm: **un ~** three of a kind; **un ~ d'as** three aces.

breloque [bʀəlɔk] nf charm.

brème [bʀɛm] nf bream.

Brésil [bʀezil] nm: **le ~** Brazil.

brésilien, ne [bʀeziljɛ̃, -ɛn] adj Brazilian ♦ nm/f: **B~, ne** Brazilian.

bressan, e [bʀesɑ̃, -an] adj of ou from Bresse.

Bretagne [bʀətaɲ] nf: **la ~** Brittany.

bretelle [bʀətɛl] nf (de fusil etc) sling; (de vêtement) strap; (d'autoroute) slip road (BRIT), entrance ou exit ramp (US); ~**s** nfpl (pour pantalon) braces (BRIT), suspenders (US); ~ **de contournement** (AUTO) bypass; ~ **de raccordement** (AUTO) access road.

breton, ne [bʀətɔ̃, -ɔn] adj Breton ♦ nm (LING) Breton ♦ nm/f: **B~, ne** Breton.

breuvage [bʀœvaʒ] nm beverage, drink.

brève [bʀɛv] adj f, nf voir **bref**.

brevet [bʀəvɛ] nm diploma, certificate; ~ **(d'invention)** patent; ~ **d'apprentissage** certificate of apprenticeship; ~ **(des collèges)** school certificate, taken at approx. 16 years.

breveté, e [bʀəvte] adj patented; (diplômé) qualified.

breveter [bʀəvte] vt to patent.

bréviaire [bʀevjɛʀ] nm breviary.

BRGM sigle m = Bureau de recherches géologiques et minières.

briard, e [bʀijaʀ, -aʀd(ə)] adj of ou from Brie. ♦ nm (chien) briard.

bribes [bʀib] nfpl bits, scraps; (d'une conversation) snatches; **par ~** piecemeal.

bric [bʀik]: **de ~ et de broc** adv with any old thing.

bric-à-brac [bʀikabʀak] nm inv bric-a-brac, jumble.

bricolage [bʀikɔlaʒ] nm: **le ~** do-it-yourself (jobs); (péj) patched-up job.

bricole [bʀikɔl] nf (babiole, chose insignifiante) trifle; (petit travail) small job.

bricoler [bʀikɔle] vi to do odd jobs; (en amateur) to do DIY jobs; (passe-temps) to potter about ♦ vt (réparer) to fix up; (mal réparer) to tinker with; (trafiquer: voiture etc) to doctor, fix.

bricoleur, euse [bʀikɔlœʀ, -øz] nm/f handyman/woman, DIY enthusiast.

bride [bʀid] nf bridle; (d'un bonnet) string, tie; **à ~ abattue** flat out, hell for leather; **tenir en ~** to keep in check; **lâcher la ~ à, laisser la ~ sur le cou à** to give free rein to.

bridé, e [bʀide] adj: **yeux ~s** slit eyes.

brider [bʀide] vt (réprimer) to keep in check; (cheval) to bridle; (CULIN: volaille) to truss.

bridge [bʀidʒ(ə)] nm bridge.

brie [bʀi] nm Brie (cheese).

brièvement [bʀijɛvmɑ̃] adv briefly.

brièveté [bʀijɛvte] nf brevity.

brigade [bʀigad] nf squad; (MIL) brigade.

brigadier [bʀigadje] nm (POLICE) ≈ sergeant; (MIL) bombardier; corporal.

brigadier-chef, pl brigadiers-chefs [bʀigadjeʃɛf] nm ≈ lance-sergeant.

brigand [bʀigɑ̃] nm brigand.

brigandage [bʀigɑ̃daʒ] nm robbery.

briguer [bʀige] vt to aspire to; (suffrages) to canvass.

brillamment [bʀijamɑ̃] adv brilliantly.

brillant, e [bʀijɑ̃, -ɑ̃t] adj brilliant; bright; (luisant) shiny, shining ♦ nm (diamant) brilliant.

briller [bʀije] vi to shine.

brimade [bʀimad] nf vexation, harassment no pl; bullying no pl.

brimbaler [bʀɛ̃bale] vb = bringuebaler.

brimer [bʀime] vt to harass; to bully.

brin [bʀɛ̃] nm (de laine, ficelle etc) strand; (fig): **un ~ de** a bit of; **un ~ mystérieux** etc (fam) a weeny bit mysterious etc; ~ **d'herbe** blade of grass; ~ **de muguet** sprig of lily of the valley; ~ **de paille** wisp of straw.

brindille [bʀɛ̃dij] nf twig.

bringue [bʀɛ̃g] nf (fam): **faire la ~** to go on a binge.

bringuebaler [bʀɛ̃gbale] *vi* to shake (about)
♦ *vt* to cart about.
brio [bʀijo] *nm* brilliance; (*MUS*) brio; **avec ~**
brilliantly, with panache.
brioche [bʀijɔʃ] *nf* brioche (bun); (*fam: ventre*)
paunch.
brioché, e [bʀijɔʃe] *adj* brioche-style.
brique [bʀik] *nf* brick; (*fam*) 10,000 francs
♦ *adj inv* brick red.
briquer [bʀike] *vt* (*fam*) to polish up.
briquet [bʀikɛ] *nm* (cigarette) lighter.
briqueterie [bʀiktʀi] *nf* brickyard.
bris [bʀi] *nm*: ~ **de clôture** (*JUR*) breaking in;
~ **de glaces** (*AUTO*) breaking of windows.
brisant [bʀizɑ̃] *nm* reef; (*vague*) breaker.
brise [bʀiz] *nf* breeze.
brisé, e [bʀize] *adj* broken; ~ **(de fatigue)**
exhausted; **d'une voix ~e** in a voice broken
with emotion; **pâte ~e** shortcrust pastry.
brisées [bʀize] *nfpl*: **aller** *ou* **marcher sur les ~**
de qn to compete with sb in his own
province.
brise-glace(s) [bʀizglas] *nm inv* (*navire*)
icebreaker.
brise-jet [bʀizʒɛ] *nm inv* tap swirl.
brise-lames [bʀizlam] *nm inv* breakwater.
briser [bʀize] *vt* to break; **se ~** *vi* to break.
brise-tout [bʀiztu] *nm inv* wrecker.
briseur, euse [bʀizœʀ, -øz] *nm/f*: ~ **de grève**
strike-breaker.
brise-vent [bʀizvɑ̃] *nm inv* windbreak.
bristol [bʀistɔl] *nm* (*carte de visite*) visiting
card.
britannique [bʀitanik] *adj* British ♦ *nm/f*: **B~**
Briton, British person; **les B~s** the British.
broc [bʀo] *nm* pitcher.
brocante [bʀokɑ̃t] *nf* (*objets*) secondhand
goods *pl*, junk; (*commerce*) secondhand
trade; junk dealing.
brocanteur, euse [bʀokɑ̃tœʀ, -øz] *nm/f*
junkshop owner; junk dealer.
brocart [bʀokaʀ] *nm* brocade.
broche [bʀoʃ] *nf* brooch; (*CULIN*) spit; (*fiche*)
spike, peg; (*MÉD*) pin; **à la ~** spit-roasted,
roasted on a spit.
broché, e [bʀoʃe] *adj* (*livre*) paper-backed;
(*tissu*) brocaded.
brochet [bʀoʃɛ] *nm* pike *inv*.
brochette [bʀoʃɛt] *nf* skewer; ~ **de**
décorations row of medals.
brochure [bʀoʃyʀ] *nf* pamphlet, brochure,
booklet.
brocoli [bʀokoli] *nm* broccoli.
brodequins [bʀodkɛ̃] *nmpl* (*de marche*) (lace-
up) boots.
broder [bʀode] *vt* to embroider ♦ *vi*: ~ **(sur des**
faits *ou* **une histoire)** to embroider the facts.
broderie [bʀodʀi] *nf* embroidery.
bromure [bʀomyʀ] *nm* bromide.
broncher [bʀɔ̃ʃe] *vi*: **sans ~** without flinching,
without turning a hair.
bronches [bʀɔ̃ʃ] *nfpl* bronchial tubes.

bronchite [bʀɔ̃ʃit] *nf* bronchitis.
broncho-pneumonie [bʀɔ̃kɔpnømɔni] *nf*
broncho-pneumonia *no pl*.
bronzage [bʀɔ̃zaʒ] *nm* (*hâle*) (sun)tan.
bronze [bʀɔ̃z] *nm* bronze.
bronzé, e [bʀɔ̃ze] *adj* tanned.
bronzer [bʀɔ̃ze] *vt* to tan ♦ *vi* to get a tan; **se ~**
to sunbathe.
brosse [bʀos] *nf* brush; **donner un coup de ~ à**
qch to give sth a brush; **coiffé en ~** with a
crewcut; ~ **à cheveux** hairbrush; ~ **à dents**
toothbrush; ~ **à habits** clothesbrush.
brosser [bʀose] *vt* (*nettoyer*) to brush; (*fig:*
tableau etc) to paint; to draw; **se ~** to brush
one's clothes; **se ~ les dents** to brush one's
teeth; **tu peux te ~!** (*fam*) you can sing for
it!
brou [bʀu] *nm*: ~ **de noix** (*pour bois*) walnut
stain; (*liqueur*) walnut liqueur.
brouette [bʀuɛt] *nf* wheelbarrow.
brouhaha [bʀuaa] *nm* hubbub.
brouillage [bʀujaʒ] *nm* (*d'une émission*)
jamming.
brouillard [bʀujaʀ] *nm* fog; **être dans le ~** (*fig*)
to be all at sea.
brouille [bʀuj] *nf* quarrel.
brouillé, e [bʀuje] *adj* (*fâché*): **il est ~ avec ses**
parents he has fallen out with his parents;
(*teint*) muddy.
brouiller [bʀuje] *vt* to mix up; to confuse;
(*RADIO*) to cause interference to;
(: *délibérément*) to jam; (*rendre trouble*) to
cloud; (*désunir: amis*) to set at odds; **se ~** *vi*
(*ciel, vue*) to cloud over; (*détails*) to become
confused; **se ~ (avec)** to fall out (with); ~
les pistes to cover one's tracks; (*fig*) to
confuse the issue.
brouillon, ne [bʀujɔ̃, -ɔn] *adj* disorganized,
unmethodical ♦ *nm* (first) draft; **cahier de ~**
rough (work) book.
broussailles [bʀusaj] *nfpl* undergrowth *sg*.
broussailleux, euse [bʀusajø, -øz] *adj* bushy.
brousse [bʀus] *nf*: **la ~** the bush.
brouter [bʀute] *vt* to graze on ♦ *vi* to graze;
(*AUTO*) to judder.
broutille [bʀutij] *nf* trifle.
broyer [bʀwaje] *vt* to crush; ~ **du noir** to be
down in the dumps.
bru [bʀy] *nf* daughter-in-law.
brucelles [bʀysɛl] *nfpl*: **(pinces)** ~ tweezers.
brugnon [bʀyɲɔ̃] *nm* nectarine.
bruine [bʀɥin] *nf* drizzle.
bruiner [bʀɥine] *vb impers*: **il bruine** it's
drizzling, there's a drizzle.
bruire [bʀɥiʀ] *vi* (*eau*) to murmur; (*feuilles,*
étoffe) to rustle.
bruissement [bʀɥismɑ̃] *nm* murmuring; rus-
tling.
bruit [bʀɥi] *nm*: **un ~** a noise, a sound; (*fig:*
rumeur) a rumour (*BRIT*), a rumor (*US*); **le ~**
noise; **pas/trop de ~** no/too much noise;
sans ~ without a sound, noiselessly; **faire du**

~ to make a noise; ~ **de fond** background noise.

bruitage [bʀɥitaʒ] *nm* sound effects *pl*.

bruiteur, euse [bʀɥitœʀ, -øz] *nm/f* sound-effects engineer.

brûlant, e [bʀylɑ̃, -ɑ̃t] *adj* burning (hot); (*liquide*) boiling (hot); (*regard*) fiery; (*sujet*) red-hot.

brûlé, e [bʀyle] *adj* (*fig: démasqué*) blown; (: *homme politique etc*) discredited ♦ *nm*: **odeur de** ~ smell of burning.

brûle-pourpoint [bʀylpuʀpwɛ̃]: **à** ~ *adv* point-blank.

brûler [bʀyle] *vt* to burn; (*suj: eau bouillante*) to scald; (*consommer: électricité, essence*) to use; (*feu rouge, signal*) to go through (without stopping) ♦ *vi* to burn; (*jeu*): **tu brûles** you're getting warm *ou* hot; **se** ~ to burn o.s.; to scald o.s.; **se** ~ **la cervelle** to blow one's brains out; ~ **les étapes** to make rapid progress; (*aller trop vite*) to cut corners; ~ **(d'impatience) de faire qch** to burn with impatience to do sth, be dying to do sth.

brûleur [bʀylœʀ] *nm* burner.

brûlot [bʀylo] *nm* (*CULIN*) flaming brandy; **un** ~ **de contestation** (*fig*) a hotbed of dissent.

brûlure [bʀylyʀ] *nf* (*lésion*) burn; (*sensation*) burning *no pl*, burning sensation; ~**s d'estomac** heartburn *sg*.

brume [bʀym] *nf* mist.

brumeux, euse [bʀymø, -øz] *adj* misty; (*fig*) hazy.

brumisateur [bʀymizatœʀ] *nm* atomizer.

brun, e [bʀœ̃, -yn] *adj* brown; (*cheveux, personne*) dark ♦ *nm* (*couleur*) brown ♦ *nf* (*cigarette*) cigarette made of dark tobacco; (*bière*) ≈ brown ale, stout.

brunâtre [bʀynɑtʀ(ə)] *adj* brownish.

brunch [bʀœntʃ] *nm* brunch.

Brunei [bʀynei] *nm*: **le** ~ Brunei.

brunir [bʀyniʀ] *vi* (*aussi*: **se** ~) to get a tan ♦ *vt* to tan.

brushing [bʀœʃiŋ] *nm* blow-dry.

brusque [bʀysk(ə)] *adj* (*soudain*) abrupt, sudden; (*rude*) abrupt, brusque.

brusquement [bʀyskəmɑ̃] *adv* (*soudainement*) abruptly, suddenly.

brusquer [bʀyske] *vt* to rush.

brusquerie [bʀyskəʀi] *nf* abruptness, brusqueness.

brut, e [bʀyt] *adj* raw, crude, rough; (*diamant*) uncut; (*soie, minéral, INFORM: données*) raw; (*COMM*) gross ♦ *nf* brute; (**champagne**) ~ brut champagne; (**pétrole**) ~ crude (oil).

brutal, e, aux [bʀytal, -o] *adj* brutal.

brutalement [bʀytalmɑ̃] *adv* brutally.

brutaliser [bʀytalize] *vt* to handle roughly, manhandle.

brutalité [bʀytalite] *nf* brutality *no pl*.

brute [bʀyt] *adj f, nf voir* **brut**.

Bruxelles [bʀysɛl] *n* Brussels.

bruxellois, e [bʀysɛlwa, -waz] *adj* of *ou* from

Brussels ♦ *nm/f*: **B**~, **e** inhabitant *ou* native of Brussels.

bruyamment [bʀɥijamɑ̃] *adv* noisily.

bruyant, e [bʀɥijɑ̃, -ɑ̃t] *adj* noisy.

bruyère [bʀyjɛʀ] *nf* heather.

BT *sigle m* (= *Brevet de technicien*) *vocational training certificate, taken at approx. 18 years.*

BTA *sigle m* (= *Brevet de technicien agricole*) *agricultural training certificate, taken at approx. 18 years.*

BTP *sigle mpl* (= *Bâtiments et travaux publics*) *public buildings and works sector.*

BTS *sigle m* (= *Brevet de technicien supérieur*) *vocational training certificate taken at end of 2-year higher education course.*

BU *sigle f* = *Bibliothèque universitaire*.

bu, e [by] *pp de* **boire**.

buanderie [bɥɑ̃dʀi] *nf* laundry.

Bucarest [bykaʀɛst] *n* Bucharest.

buccal, e, aux [bykal, -o] *adj*: **par voie** ~**e** orally.

bûche [byʃ] *nf* log; **prendre une** ~ (*fig*) to come a cropper (*BRIT*), fall flat on one's face; ~ **de Noël** Yule log.

bûcher [byʃe] *nm* pyre; bonfire ♦ *vi* (*fam: étudier*) to swot (*BRIT*), grind (*US*) ♦ *vt* to swot up (*BRIT*), cram.

bûcheron [byʃʀɔ̃] *nm* woodcutter.

bûchette [byʃɛt] *nf* (*de bois*) stick, twig; (*pour compter*) rod.

bûcheur, euse [byʃœʀ, -øz] *nm/f* (*fam: étudiant*) swot (*BRIT*), grind (*US*).

bucolique [bykɔlik] *adj* bucolic, pastoral.

Budapest [bydapɛst] *n* Budapest.

budget [bydʒɛ] *nm* budget.

budgétaire [bydʒetɛʀ] *adj* budgetary, budget *cpd*.

budgétiser [bydʒetize] *vt* to budget (for).

buée [bɥe] *nf* (*sur une vitre*) mist; (*de l'haleine*) steam.

Buenos Aires [bwenɔzɛʀ] *n* Buenos Aires.

buffet [byfɛ] *nm* (*meuble*) sideboard; (*de réception*) buffet; ~ (**de gare**) (station) buffet, snack bar.

buffle [byfl(ə)] *nm* buffalo.

buis [bɥi] *nm* box tree; (*bois*) box(wood).

buisson [bɥisɔ̃] *nm* bush.

buissonnière [bɥisɔnjɛʀ] *adj f*: **faire l'école** ~ to play truant (*BRIT*), skip school.

bulbe [bylb(ə)] *nm* (*BOT, ANAT*) bulb; (*coupole*) onion-shaped dome.

bulgare [bylgaʀ] *adj* Bulgarian ♦ *nm* (*LING*) Bulgarian ♦ *nm/f*: **B**~ Bulgarian, Bulgar.

Bulgarie [bylgaʀi] *nf*: **la** ~ Bulgaria.

bulldozer [buldozɛʀ] *nm* bulldozer.

bulle [byl] *adj, nm*: (**papier**) ~ manil(l)a paper ♦ *nf* bubble; (*de bande dessinée*) balloon; (*papale*) bull; ~ **de savon** soap bubble.

bulletin [byltɛ̃] *nm* (*communiqué, journal*) bulletin; (*papier*) form; (: *de bagages*) ticket; (*SCOL*) report; ~ **d'informations** news bulletin; ~ **météorologique** weather report; ~ **de naissance** birth certificate; ~ **de salaire** pay slip; ~ **de santé** medical bulletin; ~ **(de vote)** ballot paper.

buraliste [byʀalist(ə)] *nm/f* (*de bureau de tabac*) tobacconist; (*de poste*) clerk.

bure [byʀ] *nf* homespun; (*de moine*) frock.

bureau, x [byʀo] *nm* (*meuble*) desk; (*pièce, service*) office; (~ **de change** (*foreign*) exchange office *ou* bureau; ~ **d'embauche** ≈ job centre; ~ **d'études** design office; ~ **de location** box office; ~ **de placement** employment agency; ~ **de poste** post office; ~ **de tabac** tobacconist's (shop), smoke shop (*US*); ~ **de vote** polling station.

bureaucrate [byʀokʀat] *nm* bureaucrat.

bureaucratie [byʀokʀasi] *nf* bureaucracy.

bureaucratique [byʀokʀatik] *adj* bureaucratic.

bureautique [byʀɔtik] *nf* office automation.

burette [byʀɛt] *nf* (*de mécanicien*) oilcan; (*de chimiste*) burette.

burin [byʀɛ̃] *nm* cold chisel; (*ART*) burin.

buriné, e [byʀine] *adj* (*fig: visage*) craggy, seamed.

Burkina(-Faso) [byʀkina(faso)] *nm*: **le ~** Burkina Faso.

burlesque [byʀlɛsk(ə)] *adj* ridiculous; (*LITTÉRATURE*) burlesque.

burnous [byʀnu(s)] *nm* burnous.

Burundi [buʀundi] *nm*: **le ~** Burundi.

BUS *sigle m* = *Bureau universitaire de statistiques*.

bus *vb* [by] *voir* **boire** ♦ *nm* [bys] (*véhicule, aussi INFORM*) bus.

busard [byzaʀ] *nm* harrier.

buse [byz] *nf* buzzard.

busqué, e [byske] *adj*: **nez ~** hook(ed) nose.

buste [byst(ə)] *nm* (*ANAT*) chest; (*: de femme*) bust; (*sculpture*) bust.

bustier [bystje] *nm* (*soutien-gorge*) long-line bra.

but [by] *vb voir* **boire** ♦ *nm* (*cible*) target; (*fig*) goal, aim; (*FOOTBALL etc*) goal; **de ~ en blanc** point-blank; **avoir pour ~ de faire** to aim to do; **dans le ~ de** with the intention of.

butane [bytan] *nm* butane; (*domestique*) calor gas ®(*BRIT*), butane.

buté, e [byte] *adj* stubborn, obstinate ♦ *nf* (*ARCHIT*) abutment; (*TECH*) stop.

buter [byte] *vi*: ~ **contre** *ou* **sur** to bump into; (*trébucher*) to stumble against ♦ *vt* to antagonize; **se ~** *vi* to get obstinate, dig in one's heels.

buteur [bytœʀ] *nm* striker.

butin [bytɛ̃] *nm* booty, spoils *pl*; (*d'un vol*) loot.

butiner [bytine] *vi* to gather nectar.

butor [bytɔʀ] *nm* (*fig*) lout.

butte [byt] *nf* mound, hillock; **être en ~ à** to be exposed to.

buvable [byvabl(ə)] *adj* (*eau, vin*) drinkable; (*MÉD: ampoule etc*) to be taken orally; (*fig:*

roman etc) reasonable.

buvais [byvɛ] *etc vb voir* **boire**.

buvard [byvaʀ] *nm* blotter.

buvette [byvɛt] *nf* refreshment room *ou* stall; (*comptoir*) bar.

buveur, euse [byvœʀ, -øz] *nm/f* drinker.

buvons [byvɔ̃] *etc vb voir* **boire**.

BVP *sigle m* (= *Bureau de vérification de la publicité*) advertising standards authority.

Byzance [bizɑ̃s] *n* Byzantium.

byzantin, e [bizɑ̃tɛ̃, -in] *adj* Byzantine.

BZH *abr* (= *Breizh*) Brittany.

C c

C, c [se] *nm inv* C, c ♦ *abr* (= *centime*) c; (= *Celsius*) C; **C comme Célestin** C for Charlie.

c' [s] *dét voir* **ce**.

CA *sigle m* = **chiffre d'affaires, conseil d'administration, corps d'armée** ♦ *sigle f* = **chambre d'agriculture**.

ca *abr* (= *centiare*) 1 m^2.

ça [sa] *pron* (*pour désigner*) this; (*: plus loin*) that; (*comme sujet indéfini*) it; ~ **m'étonne que** it surprises me that; ~ **va?** how are you?; how are things?; (*d'accord?*) OK?, all right?; ~ **alors!** (*désapprobation*) well!, really!; (*étonnement*) heavens!; **c'est ~** that's right.

çà [sa] *adv*: ~ **et là** here and there.

cabale [kabal] *nf* (*THÉÂT, POL*) cabal, clique.

caban [kabɑ̃] *nm* reefer jacket, donkey jacket.

cabane [kaban] *nf* hut, cabin.

cabanon [kabanɔ̃] *nm* chalet; (*country*) cottage.

cabaret [kabaʀɛ] *nm* night club.

cabas [kaba] *nm* shopping bag.

cabestan [kabɛstɑ̃] *nm* capstan.

cabillaud [kabijo] *nm* cod *inv*.

cabine [kabin] *nf* (*de bateau*) cabin; (*de plage*) (beach) hut; (*de piscine etc*) cubicle; (*de camion, train*) cab; (*d'avion*) cockpit; ~ **(d'ascenseur)** lift cage; ~ **d'essayage** fitting room; ~ **de projection** projection room; ~ **spatiale** space capsule; ~ **(téléphonique)** call *ou* (tele)phone box, (tele)phone booth.

cabinet [kabinɛ] *nm* (*petite pièce*) closet; (*de médecin*) surgery (*BRIT*), office (*US*); (*de notaire etc*) office; (*: clientèle*) practice; (*POL*) cabinet; (*d'un ministre*) advisers *pl*; ~**s** *nmpl* (*w.-c.*) toilet *sg*, loo *sg* (*fam BRIT*); ~ **d'affaires** business consultants' (bureau), business partnership; ~ **de toilette** toilet; ~ **de travail** study.

câble [kɑbl(ə)] nm cable; **le ~** (TV) cable television, cablevision (US).

câblé, e [kɑble] adj (fam) switched on; (TECH) linked to cable television.

câbler [kɑble] vt to cable; **~ un quartier** (TV) to put cable television into an area.

câblogramme [kɑblɔgʀam] nm cablegram.

cabosser [kabɔse] vt to dent.

cabot [kabo] nm (péj: chien) mutt.

cabotage [kabɔtaʒ] nm coastal navigation.

caboteur [kabɔtœʀ] nm coaster.

cabotin, e [kabɔtɛ̃, -in] nm/f (péj: personne maniérée) poseur; (: acteur) ham ♦ adj dramatic, theatrical.

cabotinage [kabɔtinaʒ] nm playacting; third-rate acting, ham acting.

cabrer [kabʀe]: **se ~** vi (cheval) to rear up; (avion) to nose up; (fig) to revolt, rebel; to jib.

cabri [kabʀi] nm kid.

cabriole [kabʀijɔl] nf caper; (gymnastique etc) somersault.

cabriolet [kabʀijɔlɛ] nm convertible.

CAC [kak] sigle f (= Compagnie des agents de change): **indice ~** ≈ FT index (BRIT), ≈ Dow Jones average (US).

caca [kaka] nm (langage enfantin) pooh; (couleur): **~ d'oie** greeny-yellow; **faire ~** (fam) to do a pooh.

cacahuète [kakaɥɛt] nf peanut.

cacao [kakao] nm cocoa (powder); (boisson) cocoa.

cachalot [kaʃalo] nm sperm whale.

cache [kaʃ] nm mask, card (for masking) ♦ nf hiding place.

cache-cache [kaʃkaʃ] nm: **jouer à ~** to play hide-and-seek.

cache-col [kaʃkɔl] nm scarf (pl scarves).

cachemire [kaʃmiʀ] nm cashmere ♦ adj: **dessin ~** paisley pattern; **le C~** Kashmir.

cache-nez [kaʃne] nm inv scarf (pl scarves), muffler.

cache-pot [kaʃpo] nm inv flower-pot holder.

cache-prise [kaʃpʀiz] nm inv socket cover.

cacher [kaʃe] vt to hide, conceal; **~ qch à qn** to hide ou conceal sth from sb; **se ~** to hide; to be hidden ou concealed; **il ne s'en cache pas** he makes no secret of it.

cache-sexe [kaʃsɛks] nm inv G-string.

cachet [kaʃɛ] nm (comprimé) tablet; (sceau: du roi) seal; (: de la poste) postmark; (rétribution) fee; (fig) style, character.

cacheter [kaʃte] vt to seal; **vin cacheté** vintage wine.

cachette [kaʃɛt] nf hiding place; **en ~** on the sly, secretly.

cachot [kaʃo] nm dungeon.

cachotterie [kaʃɔtʀi] nf mystery; **faire des ~s** to be secretive.

cachottier, ière [kaʃɔtje, -jɛʀ] adj secretive.

cachou [kaʃu] nm: **pastille de ~** cachou (sweet).

cacophonie [kakɔfɔni] nf cacophony, din.

cacophonique [kakɔfɔnik] adj cacophonous.

cactus [kaktys] nm cactus.

c-à-d abr (= c'est-à-dire) i.e.

cadastre [kadastʀ(ə)] nm land register.

cadavéreux, euse [kadaveʀø, -øz] adj (teint, visage) deathly pale.

cadavérique [kadaveʀik] adj deathly (pale), deadly pale.

cadavre [kadavʀ(ə)] nm corpse, (dead) body.

caddie [kadi] nm (supermarket) trolley.

cadeau, x [kado] nm present, gift; **faire un ~ à qn** to give sb a present ou gift; **faire ~ de qch à qn** to make a present of sth to sb, give sb sth as a present.

cadenas [kadna] nm padlock.

cadenasser [kadnase] vt to padlock.

cadence [kadɑ̃s] nf (MUS) cadence; (: rythme) rhythm; (de travail etc) rate; **~s** nfpl (en usine) production rate sg; **en ~** rhythmically; in time.

cadencé, e [kadɑ̃se] adj rhythmic(al); **au pas ~** (MIL) in quick time.

cadet, te [kadɛ, -ɛt] adj younger; (le plus jeune) youngest ♦ nm/f youngest child ou one, youngest boy ou son/girl ou daughter; **il est mon ~ de deux ans** he's 2 years younger than me, he's 2 years my junior; **les ~s** (SPORT) the minors (15 - 17 years); **le ~ de mes soucis** the least of my worries.

cadrage [kadʀaʒ] nm framing (of shot).

cadran [kadʀɑ̃] nm dial; **~ solaire** sundial.

cadre [kadʀ(ə)] nm frame; (environnement) surroundings pl; (limites) scope ♦ nm/f (ADMIN) managerial employee, executive ♦ adj: **loi ~** outline ou blueprint law; **~ moyen/supérieur** (ADMIN) middle/senior management employee, junior/senior executive; **rayer qn des ~s** to discharge sb; to dismiss sb; **dans le ~ de** (fig) within the framework ou context of.

cadrer [kadʀe] vi: **~ avec** to tally ou correspond with ♦ vt (CINÉ, PHOTO) to frame.

cadreur, euse [kadʀœʀ, -øz] nm/f (CINÉ) cameraman/woman.

caduc, uque [kadyk] adj obsolete; (BOT) de-ciduous.

CAF sigle f (= Caisse d'allocations familiales) family allowance office.

caf abr (= coût, assurance, fret) cif.

cafard [kafaʀ] nm cockroach; **avoir le ~** to be down in the dumps, be feeling low.

cafardeux, euse [kafaʀdø, -øz] adj (personne, ambiance) depressing, melancholy.

café [kafe] nm coffee; (bistro) café ♦ adj inv coffee cpd; **~ crème** coffee with cream; **~ au lait** white coffee; **~ noir** black coffee; **~ en grains** coffee beans; **~ en poudre** instant coffee; **~ tabac** tobacconist's or newsagent's also serving coffee and spirits; **~ liégeois** coffee ice cream with whipped cream.

café-concert, *pl* **cafés-concerts** [kafekɔ̃sɛʀ] *nm* (*aussi:* **caf'conc'**) *café with a cabaret.*
caféine [kafein] *nf* caffeine.
cafétéria [kafeteʀja] *nf* cafeteria.
café-théâtre, *pl* **cafés-théâtres** [kafeteatʀ(ə)] *nm café used as a venue by (experimental) theatre groups.*
cafetier, ière [kaftje, -jɛʀ] *nm/f* café-owner ♦ *nf* (*pot*) coffee-pot.
cafouillage [kafujaʒ] *nm* shambles *sg.*
cafouiller [kafuje] *vi* to get in a shambles; (*machine etc*) to work in fits and starts.
cage [kaʒ] *nf* cage; ~ (**des buts**) goal; **en** ~ in a cage, caged up *ou* in; ~ **d'ascenseur** lift shaft; ~ **d'escalier** (stair)well; ~ **thoracique** rib cage.
cageot [kaʒo] *nm* crate.
cagibi [kaʒibi] *nm* shed.
cagneux, euse [kaɲø, -øz] *adj* knock-kneed.
cagnotte [kaɲɔt] *nf* kitty.
cagoule [kagul] *nf* cowl; hood; (*SKI etc*) cagoule.
cahier [kaje] *nm* notebook; (*TYPO*) signature; (*revue*): ~**s** journal; ~ **de revendications/doléances** list of claims/grievances; ~ **de brouillons** roughbook, jotter; ~ **des charges** specification; ~ **d'exercices** exercise book.
cahin-caha [kaɛ̃kaa] *adv:* **aller** ~ to jog along; (*fig*) to be so-so.
cahot [kao] *nm* jolt, bump.
cahoter [kaɔte] *vi* to bump along, jog along.
cahoteux, euse [kaɔtø, -øz] *adj* bumpy.
cahute [kayt] *nf* shack, hut.
caïd [kaid] *nm* big chief, boss.
caillasse [kajas] *nf* (*pierraille*) loose stones *pl.*
caille [kaj] *nf* quail.
caillé, e [kaje] *adj:* **lait** ~ curdled milk, curds *pl.*
caillebotis [kajbɔti] *nm* duckboard.
cailler [kaje] *vi* (*lait*) to curdle; (*sang*) to clot; (*fam*) to be cold.
caillot [kajo] *nm* (*blood*) clot.
caillou, x [kaju] *nm* (little) stone.
caillouter [kajute] *vt* (*chemin*) to metal.
caillouteux, euse [kajutø, -øz] *adj* stony; pebbly.
cailloutis [kajuti] *nm* (*petits graviers*) gravel.
caïman [kaimɑ̃] *nm* cayman.
Caïmans [kaimɑ̃] *nfpl:* **les** ~ the Cayman Islands.
Caire [kɛʀ] *nm:* **le** ~ Cairo.
caisse [kɛs] *nf* box; (*où l'on met la recette*) cashbox; (: *machine*) till; (*où l'on paye*) cash desk (*BRIT*), checkout counter; (: *au supermarché*) checkout; (*de banque*) cashier's desk; (*TECH*) case, casing; **faire sa** ~ (*COMM*) to count the takings; ~ **claire** (*MUS*) side *ou* snare drum; ~ **éclair** express checkout; ~ **enregistreuse** cash register; ~ **d'épargne** (*CE*) savings bank; ~ **noire** slush fund; ~ **de retraite** pension fund; ~ **de sortie** checkout; *voir* **grosse**.

caissier, ière [kesje, -jɛʀ] *nm/f* cashier.
caisson [kɛsɔ̃] *nm* box, case.
cajoler [kaʒɔle] *vt* to wheedle, coax; to surround with love and care, make a fuss of.
cajoleries [kaʒɔlʀi] *nfpl* coaxing *sg*, flattery *sg.*
cajou [kaʒu] *nm* cashew nut.
cake [kɛk] *nm* fruit cake.
CAL *sigle m* (= *Comité d'action lycéen*) *pupils' action group seeking to reform school system.*
cal [kal] *nm* callus.
cal. *abr* = **calorie.**
calamar [kalamaʀ] *nm* = **calmar.**
calaminé, e [kalamine] *adj* (*AUTO*) coked up.
calamité [kalamite] *nf* calamity, disaster.
calandre [kalɑ̃dʀ(ə)] *nf* radiator grill; (*machine*) calender, mangle.
calanque [kalɑ̃k] *nf* rocky inlet.
calcaire [kalkɛʀ] *nm* limestone ♦ *adj* (*eau*) hard; (*GÉO*) limestone *cpd.*
calciné, e [kalsine] *adj* burnt to ashes.
calcium [kalsjɔm] *nm* calcium.
calcul [kalkyl] *nm* calculation; **le** ~ (*SCOL*) arithmetic; ~ **différentiel/intégral** differential/integral calculus; ~ **mental** mental arithmetic; ~ (**biliaire**) (gall)stone; ~ (**rénal**) (kidney) stone; **d'après mes** ~**s** by my reckoning.
calculateur [kalkylatœʀ] *nm*, **calculatrice** [kalkylatʀis] *nf* calculator.
calculé, e [kalkyle] *adj:* **risque** ~ calculated risk.
calculer [kalkyle] *vt* to calculate, work out, reckon; (*combiner*) to calculate; ~ **qch de tête** to work sth out in one's head.
calculette [kalkylɛt] *nf* (pocket) calculator.
cale [kal] *nf* (*de bateau*) hold; (*en bois*) wedge, chock; ~ **sèche** *ou* **de radoub** dry dock.
calé, e [kale] *adj* (*fam*) clever, bright.
calebasse [kalbɑs] *nf* calabash, gourd.
calèche [kalɛʃ] *nf* horse-drawn carriage.
caleçon [kalsɔ̃] *nm* pair of underpants, trunks *pl;* ~ **de bain** bathing trunks *pl.*
calembour [kalɑ̃buʀ] *nm* pun.
calendes [kalɑ̃d] *nfpl:* **renvoyer aux** ~ **grecques** to postpone indefinitely.
calendrier [kalɑ̃dʀije] *nm* calendar; (*fig*) timetable.
cale-pied [kalpje] *nm inv* toe clip.
calepin [kalpɛ̃] *nm* notebook.
caler [kale] *vt* to wedge, chock up ♦ (*son moteur/véhicule*) to stall (one's engine/vehicle); **se** ~ **dans un fauteuil** to make o.s. comfortable in an armchair.
calfater [kalfate] *vt* to caulk.
calfeutrage [kalføtʀaʒ] *nm* draughtproofing (*BRIT*), draftproofing (*US*).
calfeutrer [kalføtʀe] *vt* to (make) draughtproof (*BRIT*) *ou* draftproof (*US*); **se** ~ to make o.s. snug and comfortable.
calibre [kalibʀ(ə)] *nm* (*d'un fruit*) grade; (*d'une*

arme) bore, calibre (*BRIT*), caliber (*US*); (*fig*) calibre, caliber.

calibrer [kalibʀe] *vt* to grade.

calice [kalis] *nm* (*REL*) chalice; (*BOT*) calyx.

calicot [kaliko] *nm* (*tissu*) calico.

calife [kalif] *nm* caliph.

Californie [kalifɔʀni] *nf*: la ~ California.

californien, ne [kalifɔʀnjɛ̃, -ɛn] *adj* Californian.

califourchon [kalifuʀʃɔ̃]: à ~ *adv* astride; à ~ sur astride, straddling.

câlin, e [kɑlɛ̃, -in] *adj* cuddly, cuddlesome; tender.

câliner [kɑline] *vt* to fondle, cuddle.

câlineries [kɑlinʀi] *nfpl* cuddles.

calisson [kalisɔ̃] *nm* diamond-shaped sweet or candy made with ground almonds.

calleux, euse [kalø, -øz] *adj* horny, callous.

calligraphie [kaligʀafi] *nf* calligraphy.

callosité [kalozite] *nf* callus.

calmant [kalmɑ̃] *nm* tranquillizer, sedative; (*contre la douleur*) painkiller.

calmar [kalmaʀ] *nm* squid.

calme [kalm(ə)] *adj* calm, quiet ♦ *nm* calm(ness), quietness; **sans perdre son** ~ without losing one's cool *ou* calmness; ~ **plat** (*NAVIG*) dead calm.

calmement [kalməmɑ̃] *adv* calmly, quietly.

calmer [kalme] *vt* to calm (down); (*douleur, inquiétude*) to ease, soothe; **se** ~ to calm down.

calomniateur, trice [kalɔmnjatœʀ, -tʀis] *nm/f* slanderer; libeller.

calomnie [kalɔmni] *nf* slander; (*écrite*) libel.

calomnier [kalɔmnje] *vt* to slander; to libel.

calomnieux, euse [kalɔmnjø, -øz] *adj* slanderous; libellous.

calorie [kalɔʀi] *nf* calorie.

calorifère [kalɔʀifɛʀ] *nm* stove.

calorifique [kalɔʀifik] *adj* calorific.

calorifuge [kalɔʀifyʒ] *adj* (heat-)insulating, heat-retaining.

calot [kalo] *nm* forage cap.

calotte [kalɔt] *nf* (*coiffure*) skullcap; (*gifle*) slap; **la** ~ (*péj: clergé*) the cloth, the clergy; ~ **glaciaire** icecap.

calque [kalk(ə)] *nm* (*aussi:* **papier** ~) tracing paper; (*dessin*) tracing; (*fig*) carbon copy.

calquer [kalke] *vt* to trace; (*fig*) to copy exactly.

calvados [kalvados] *nm* Calvados (*apple brandy*).

calvaire [kalvɛʀ] *nm* (*croix*) wayside cross, calvary; (*souffrances*) suffering, martyrdom.

calvitie [kalvisi] *nf* baldness.

camaïeu [kamajø] *nm*: (**motif en**) ~ monochrome motif.

camarade [kamaʀad] *nm/f* friend, pal; (*POL*) comrade.

camaraderie [kamaʀadʀi] *nf* friendship.

camarguais, e [kamaʀgɛ, -ɛz] *adj* of *ou* from the Camargue.

Camargue [kamaʀg] *nf*: la ~ the Camargue.

cambiste [kɑ̃bist(ə)] *nm* (*COMM*) foreign exchange dealer, exchange agent.

Cambodge [kɑ̃bɔdʒ] *nm*: le ~ Cambodia.

cambodgien, ne [kɑ̃bɔdʒjɛ̃, -ɛn] *adj* Cambodian ♦ *nm/f*: **C~, ne** Cambodian.

cambouis [kɑ̃bwi] *nm* dirty oil *ou* grease.

cambré, e [kɑ̃bʀe] *adj*: **avoir les reins** ~**s** to have an arched back; **avoir le pied très** ~ to have very high arches *ou* insteps.

cambrer [kɑ̃bʀe] *vt* to arch; **se** ~ to arch one's back; ~ **la taille** *ou* **les reins** to arch one's back.

cambriolage [kɑ̃bʀijɔlaʒ] *nm* burglary.

cambrioler [kɑ̃bʀijɔle] *vt* to burgle (*BRIT*), burglarize (*US*).

cambrioleur, euse [kɑ̃bʀijɔlœʀ, -øz] *nm/f* burglar.

cambrure [kɑ̃bʀyʀ] *nf* (*du pied*) arch; (*de la route*) camber; ~ **des reins** small of the back.

cambuse [kɑ̃byz] *nf* storeroom.

came [kam] *nf*: **arbre à** ~**s** camshaft; **arbre à** ~**s en tête** overhead camshaft.

camée [kame] *nm* cameo.

caméléon [kameleɔ̃] *nm* chameleon.

camélia [kamelja] *nm* camellia.

camelot [kamlo] *nm* street pedlar.

camelote [kamlɔt] *nf* rubbish, trash, junk.

camembert [kamɑ̃bɛʀ] *nm* Camembert (*cheese*).

caméra [kameʀa] *nf* (*CINÉ, TV*) camera; (*d'amateur*) cine-camera.

caméraman [kameʀaman] *nm* cameraman/woman.

Cameroun [kamʀun] *nm*: le ~ Cameroon.

camerounais, e [kamʀunɛ, -ɛz] *adj* Cameroonian.

caméscope [kameskɔp] ® *nm* camcorder.

camion [kamjɔ̃] *nm* lorry (*BRIT*), truck; (*plus petit, fermé*) van; (*charge*): ~ **de sable/cailloux** lorry-load (*BRIT*) *ou* truck-load of sand/stones; ~ **de dépannage** breakdown (*BRIT*) *ou* tow (*US*) truck.

camion-citerne, *pl* **camions-citernes** [kamjɔ̃sitɛʀn(ə)] *nm* tanker.

camionnage [kamjɔnaʒ] *nm* haulage (*BRIT*), trucking (*US*); **frais/entreprise de** ~ haulage costs/business.

camionnette [kamjɔnɛt] *nf* (small) van.

camionneur [kamjɔnœʀ] *nm* (*entrepreneur*) haulage contractor (*BRIT*), trucker (*US*); (*chauffeur*) lorry (*BRIT*) *ou* truck driver; van driver.

camisole [kamizɔl] *nf*: ~ (**de force**) straitjacket.

camomille [kamɔmij] *nf* camomile; (*boisson*) camomile tea.

camouflage [kamuflaʒ] *nm* camouflage.

camoufler [kamufle] *vt* to camouflage; (*fig*) to conceal, cover up.

camouflet [kamuflɛ] *nm* (*fam*) snub.
camp [kɑ̃] *nm* camp; (*fig*) side; ~ **de nudistes/
vacances** nudist/holiday camp; ~ **de
concentration** concentration camp.
campagnard, e [kɑ̃paɲaʀ, -aʀd(ə)] *adj* country
cpd ♦ *nm/f* countryman/woman.
campagne [kɑ̃paɲ] *nf* country, countryside;
(*MIL, POL, COMM*) campaign; **en** ~ (*MIL*) in the
field; **à la** ~ in/to the country; **faire** ~ **pour** to
campaign for; ~ **électorale** election
campaign; ~ **de publicité** advertising
campaign.
campanile [kɑ̃panil] *nm* (*tour*) bell tower.
campé, e [kɑ̃pe] *adj*: **bien** ~ (*personnage,
tableau*) well-drawn.
campement [kɑ̃pmɑ̃] *nm* camp, encampment.
camper [kɑ̃pe] *vi* to camp ♦ *vt* (*chapeau etc*) to
pull *ou* put on firmly; (*dessin*) to sketch; **se
~ devant** to plant o.s. in front of.
campeur, euse [kɑ̃pœʀ, -øz] *nm/f* camper.
camphre [kɑ̃fʀ(ə)] *nm* camphor.
camphré, e [kɑ̃fʀe] *adj* camphorated.
camping [kɑ̃piŋ] *nm* camping; (**terrain de**) ~
campsite, camping site; **faire du** ~ to go
camping; **faire du** ~ **sauvage** to camp rough.
camping-car [kɑ̃piŋkaʀ] *nm* caravanette,
camper (*US*).
campus [kɑ̃pys] *nm* campus.
camus, e [kamy, -yz] *adj*: **nez** ~ pug nose.
Canada [kanada] *nm*: **le** ~ Canada.
canadair [kanadɛʀ] *nm* ® fire-fighting plane.
canadien, ne [kanadjɛ̃, -ɛn] *adj* Canadian
♦ *nm/f*: **C~, ne** Canadian ♦ *nf* (*veste*) fur-lined
jacket.
canaille [kanɑj] *nf* (*péj*) scoundrel; (*populace*)
riff-raff ♦ *adj* raffish, rakish.
canal, aux [kanal, -o] *nm* canal; (*naturel*)
channel; (*ADMIN*): **par le** ~ **de** through (the
medium of), via; ~ **de distribution/
télévision** distribution/television channel; ~
de Panama/Suez Panama/Suez Canal.
canalisation [kanalizɑsjɔ̃] *nf* (*tuyau*) pipe.
canaliser [kanalize] *vt* to canalize; (*fig*) to
channel.
canapé [kanape] *nm* settee, sofa; (*CULIN*)
canapé, open sandwich.
canapé-lit, *pl* **canapés-lits** [kanapeli] *nm* sofa
bed.
canaque [kanak] *adj* of *ou* from New
Caledonia ♦ *nm/f*: **C~** native of New
Caledonia.
canard [kanaʀ] *nm* duck.
canari [kanaʀi] *nm* canary.
Canaries [kanaʀi] *nfpl*: **les (îles)** ~ the Canary
Islands, the Canaries.
cancaner [kɑ̃kane] *vi* to gossip (maliciously);
(*canard*) to quack.
cancanier, ière [kɑ̃kanje, -jɛʀ] *adj* gossiping.
cancans [kɑ̃kɑ̃] *nmpl* (malicious) gossip *sg*.
cancer [kɑ̃sɛʀ] *nm* cancer; (*signe*): **le C~**
Cancer, the Crab; **être du C~** to be Cancer;
il a un ~ he has cancer.

cancéreux, euse [kɑ̃seʀø, -øz] *adj* cancerous;
(*personne*) suffering from cancer.
cancérigène [kɑ̃seʀiʒɛn] *adj* carcinogenic.
cancérologue [kɑ̃seʀɔlɔg] *nm/f* cancer
specialist.
cancre [kɑ̃kʀ(ə)] *nm* dunce.
cancrelat [kɑ̃kʀəla] *nm* cockroach.
candélabre [kɑ̃delɑbʀ(ə)] *nm* candelabrum;
(*lampadaire*) street lamp, lamppost.
candeur [kɑ̃dœʀ] *nf* ingenuousness,
guilelessness.
candi [kɑ̃di] *adj inv*: **sucre** ~ (sugar-)candy.
candidat, e [kɑ̃dida, -at] *nm/f* candidate; (*à un
poste*) applicant, candidate.
candidature [kɑ̃didatyʀ] *nf* candidacy;
application; **poser sa** ~ to submit an
application, apply.
candide [kɑ̃did] *adj* ingenuous, guileless,
naïve.
cane [kan] *nf* (female) duck.
caneton [kantɔ̃] *nm* duckling.
canette [kanɛt] *nf* (*de bière*) (flip-top) bottle;
(*de machine à coudre*) spool.
canevas [kanva] *nm* (*COUTURE*) canvas (for
tapestry work); (*fig*) framework, structure.
caniche [kaniʃ] *nm* poodle.
caniculaire [kanikylɛʀ] *adj* (*chaleur, jour*)
scorching.
canicule [kanikyl] *nf* scorching heat;
midsummer heat, dog days *pl*.
canif [kanif] *nm* penknife, pocket knife.
canin, e [kanɛ̃, -in] *adj* canine ♦ *nf* canine
(tooth), eye tooth; **exposition** ~**e** dog show.
caniveau, x [kanivo] *nm* gutter.
cannabis [kanabis] *nm* cannabis.
canne [kan] *nf* (walking) stick; ~ **à pêche**
fishing rod; ~ **à sucre** sugar cane; **les** ~**s
blanches** (*les aveugles*) the blind.
canné, e [kane] *adj* (*chaise*) cane *cpd*.
cannelé, e [kanle] *adj* fluted.
cannelle [kanɛl] *nf* cinnamon.
cannelure [kanlyʀ] *nf* fluting *no pl*.
canner [kane] *vt* (*chaise*) to make *ou* repair
with cane.
cannibale [kanibal] *nm/f* cannibal.
cannibalisme [kanibalism(ə)] *nm* cannibalism.
canoë [kanɔe] *nm* canoe; (*sport*) canoeing; ~
(**kayak**) kayak.
canon [kanɔ̃] *nm* (*arme*) gun; (*HIST*) cannon;
(*d'une arme: tube*) barrel; (*fig*) model; (*MUS*)
canon ♦ *adj*: **droit** ~ canon law; ~ **rayé** rifled
barrel.
cañon [kaɲɔ̃] *nm* canyon.
canonique [kanɔnik] *adj*: **âge** ~ respectable
age.
canoniser [kanɔnize] *vt* to canonize.
canonnade [kanɔnad] *nf* cannonade.
canonnier [kanɔnje] *nm* gunner.
canonnière [kanɔnjɛʀ] *nf* gunboat.
canot [kano] *nm* boat, ding(h)y; ~
pneumatique rubber *ou* inflatable ding(h)y;
~ **de sauvetage** lifeboat.

canotage [kanɔtaʒ] *nm* rowing.
canoter [kanɔte] *vi* to go rowing.
canoteur, euse [kanɔtœʀ, -øz] *nm/f* rower.
canotier [kanɔtje] *nm* boater.
Cantal [kɑ̃tal] *nm*: **le ~** Cantal.
cantate [kɑ̃tat] *nf* cantata.
cantatrice [kɑ̃tatʀis] *nf* (opera) singer.
cantilène [kɑ̃tilɛn] *nf* (MUS) cantilena.
cantine [kɑ̃tin] *nf* canteen; (*réfectoire d'école*) dining hall.
cantique [kɑ̃tik] *nm* hymn.
canton [kɑ̃tɔ̃] *nm* district (*consisting of several communes*); (*en Suisse*) canton.

---
*In France the **canton** is the administrative
division represented by a councillor in the
Conseil général. It comprises a number of
communes and is, in turn, a subdivision of the
arrondissement. In Switzerland the cantons are
the 23 sovereign political divisions comprising
the Swiss confederation.*

---

cantonade [kɑ̃tɔnad] : **à la ~** *adv* to everyone in general; (*crier*) from the rooftops.
cantonais, e [kɑ̃tɔnɛ, -ɛz] *adj* Cantonese ♦ *nm* (LING) Cantonese.
cantonal, e, aux [kɑ̃tɔnal, -o] *adj* cantonal, ≈ district.
cantonnement [kɑ̃tɔnmɑ̃] *nm* (*lieu*) billet; (*action*) billeting.
cantonner [kɑ̃tɔne] *vt* (MIL) to billet (BRIT), quarter; to station; **se ~ dans** to confine o.s. to.
cantonnier [kɑ̃tɔnje] *nm* roadmender.
canular [kanylaʀ] *nm* hoax.
CAO *sigle f* (= *conception assistée par ordinateur*) CAD.
caoutchouc [kautʃu] *nm* rubber; **~ mousse** foam rubber; **en ~** rubber *cpd*.
caoutchouté, e [kautʃute] *adj* rubberized.
caoutchouteux, euse [kautʃutø, -øz] *adj* rubbery.
CAP *sigle m* (= *Certificat d'aptitude professionnelle*) *vocational training certificate taken at secondary school*.
cap [kap] *nm* (GÉO) cape; headland; (*fig*) hurdle; watershed; (NAVIG): **changer de ~** to change course; **mettre le ~ sur** to head *ou* steer for; **doubler** *ou* **passer le ~** (*fig*) to get over the worst; **Le C~** Cape Town; **le ~ de Bonne Espérance** the Cape of Good Hope; **le ~ Horn** Cape Horn; **les îles du C~ Vert** (*aussi*: **le C~-Vert**) the Cape Verde Islands.
capable [kapabl(ə)] *adj* able, capable; **~ de qch/faire** capable of sth/doing; **il est ~ d'oublier** he could easily forget; **spectacle/ livre ~ d'intéresser** show/book liable *ou* likely to be of interest.
capacité [kapasite] *nf* (*compétence*) ability; (JUR, INFORM, *d'un récipient*) capacity; **~ (en droit)** *basic legal qualification*.

caparaçonner [kapaʀasɔne] *vt* (*fig*) to clad.
cape [kap] *nf* cape, cloak; **rire sous ~** to laugh up one's sleeve.
capeline [kaplin] *nf* wide-brimmed hat.
CAPES [kapɛs] *sigle m* (= *Certificat d'aptitude au professorat de l'enseignement du second degré*) *secondary teaching diploma*.

---
*The **CAPES** is a competitive examination for
the recruitment of French secondary school
teachers. It is taken after the **licence**.
Successful candidates become fully-qualified
teachers (professeurs certifiés); see also
agrégation.*

---

capésien, ne [kapesjɛ̃, -ɛn] *nm/f person who holds the CAPES.*
CAPET [kapɛt] *sigle m* (= *Certificat d'aptitude au professorat de l'enseignement technique*) *technical teaching diploma*.
capharnaüm [kafaʀnaɔm] *nm* shambles *sg*.
capillaire [kapilɛʀ] *adj* (*soins, lotion*) hair *cpd*; (*vaisseau etc*) capillary; **artiste ~** hair artist *ou* designer.
capillarité [kapilaʀite] *nf* capillary action.
capilliculteur [kapilikyltœʀ] *nm* hair-care specialist.
capilotade [kapilɔtad]: **en ~** *adv* crushed to a pulp; smashed to pieces.
capitaine [kapitɛn] *nm* captain; **~ des pompiers** fire chief (BRIT), fire marshal (US); **~ au long cours** master mariner.
capitainerie [kapitɛnʀi] *nf* (*du port*) harbour (BRIT) *ou* harbor (US) master's (office).
capital, e, aux [kapital, -o] *adj* major; of paramount importance; fundamental; (JUR) capital ♦ *nm* capital; (*fig*) stock; asset ♦ *nf* (*ville*) capital; (*lettre*) capital (letter) ♦ *nmpl* (*fonds*) capital *sg*, money *sg*; **les sept péchés capitaux** the seven deadly sins; **peine ~e** capital punishment; **~ (social)** authorized capital; **~ d'exploitation** working capital.
capitaliser [kapitalize] *vt* to amass, build up; (COMM) to capitalize ♦ *vi* to save.
capitalisme [kapitalism(ə)] *nm* capitalism.
capitaliste [kapitalist(ə)] *adj, nm/f* capitalist.
capiteux, euse [kapitø, -øz] *adj* (*vin, parfum*) heady; (*sensuel*) sensuous, alluring.
capitonnage [kapitɔnaʒ] *nm* padding.
capitonné, e [kapitɔne] *adj* padded.
capitonner [kapitɔne] *vt* to pad.
capitulation [kapitylɑsjɔ̃] *nf* capitulation.
capituler [kapityle] *vi* to capitulate.
caporal, aux [kapɔʀal, -o] *nm* lance corporal.
caporal-chef, *pl* **caporaux-chefs** [kapɔʀalʃɛf, kapɔʀo-] *nm* corporal.
capot [kapo] *nm* (AUTO) bonnet (BRIT), hood (US) ♦ *adj inv* (CARTES): **être ~** to lose without taking a single trick.
capote [kapɔt] *nf* (*de voiture*) hood (BRIT), top

(*US*); (*de soldat*) greatcoat; ~ **(anglaise)** (*fam*) rubber, condom.

capoter [kapɔte] *vi* to overturn; (*négociations*) to founder.

câpre [kɑpʀ(ə)] *nf* caper.

caprice [kapʀis] *nm* whim, caprice; passing fancy; ~**s** *nmpl* (*de la mode etc*) vagaries; **faire un** ~ to throw a tantrum; **faire des** ~**s** to be temperamental.

capricieux, euse [kapʀisjø, -øz] *adj* capricious; whimsical; temperamental.

Capricorne [kapʀikɔʀn] *nm*: **le** ~ Capricorn, the Goat; **être du** ~ to be Capricorn.

capsule [kapsyl] *nf* (*de bouteille*) cap; (*amorce*) primer; cap; (*BOT etc, spatiale*) capsule.

captage [kaptaʒ] *nm* (*d'une émission de radio*) picking-up; (*d'énergie, d'eau*) harnessing.

capter [kapte] *vt* (*ondes radio*) to pick up; (*eau*) to harness; (*fig*) to win, capture.

capteur [kaptœʀ] *nm*: ~ **solaire** solar collector.

captieux, euse [kapsjø, -øz] *adj* specious.

captif, ive [kaptif, -iv] *adj, nm/f* captive.

captivant, e [kaptivɑ̃, -ɑ̃t] *adj* captivating.

captiver [kaptive] *vt* to captivate.

captivité [kaptivite] *nf* captivity; **en** ~ in captivity.

capture [kaptyʀ] *nf* capture, catching *no pl*; catch.

capturer [kaptyʀe] *vt* to capture, catch.

capuche [kapyʃ] *nf* hood.

capuchon [kapyʃɔ̃] *nm* hood; (*de stylo*) cap, top.

capucin [kapysɛ̃] *nm* Capuchin monk.

capucine [kapysin] *nf* (*BOT*) nasturtium.

Cap-Vert [kabvɛʀ] *nm*: **le** ~ Cape Verde.

caquelon [kaklɔ̃] *nm* (*ustensile de cuisson*) fondue pot.

caquet [kakɛ] *nm*: **rabattre le** ~ **à qn** to bring sb down a peg or two.

caqueter [kakte] *vi* (*poule*) to cackle; (*fig*) to prattle.

car [kaʀ] *nm* coach (*BRIT*), bus ♦ *conj* because, for; ~ **de police** police van; ~ **de reportage** broadcasting *ou* radio van.

carabine [kaʀabin] *nf* carbine, rifle; ~ **à air comprimé** airgun.

carabiné, e [kaʀabine] *adj* violent; (*cocktail, amende*) stiff.

Caracas [kaʀakas] *n* Caracas.

caracoler [kaʀakɔle] *vi* to caracole, prance.

caractère [kaʀaktɛʀ] *nm* (*gén*) character; **en** ~**s gras** in bold type; **en petits** ~**s** in small print; **en** ~**s d'imprimerie** in block capitals; **avoir du** ~ to have character; **avoir bon/ mauvais** ~ to be good-/ill-natured *ou* tempered; ~ **de remplacement** wild card (*INFORM*); ~**s/seconde** (**cps**) characters per second (cps).

caractériel, le [kaʀaktɛʀjɛl] *adj* (*enfant*) (emotionally) disturbed ♦ *nm/f* problem child; **troubles** ~**s** emotional problems.

caractérisé, e [kaʀaktɛʀize] *adj*: **c'est une grippe/de l'insubordination** ~**e** it is a clear(-cut) case of flu/insubordination.

caractériser [kaʀaktɛʀize] *vt* to characterize; **se** ~ **par** to be characterized *ou* distinguished by.

caractéristique [kaʀaktɛʀistik] *adj, nf* characteristic.

carafe [kaʀaf] *nf* decanter; carafe.

carafon [kaʀafɔ̃] *nm* small carafe.

caraïbe [kaʀaib] *adj* Caribbean; **les C**~**s** *nfpl* the Caribbean (Islands); **la mer des C**~**s** the Caribbean Sea.

carambolage [kaʀɑ̃bɔlaʒ] *nm* multiple crash, pileup.

caramel [kaʀamɛl] *nm* (*bonbon*) caramel, toffee; (*substance*) caramel.

caraméliser [kaʀamelize] *vt* to caramelize.

carapace [kaʀapas] *nf* shell.

carapater [kaʀapate]: **se** ~ *vi* to take to one's heels, scram.

carat [kaʀa] *nm* carat; **or à 18** ~**s** 18-carat gold.

caravane [kaʀavan] *nf* caravan.

caravanier [kaʀavanje] *nm* caravanner.

caravaning [kaʀavaniŋ] *nm* caravanning; (*emplacement*) caravan site.

caravelle [kaʀavɛl] *nf* caravel.

carbonate [kaʀbɔnat] *nm* (*CHIMIE*): ~ **de soude** sodium carbonate.

carbone [kaʀbɔn] *nm* carbon; (*feuille*) carbon, sheet of carbon paper; (*double*) carbon (copy).

carbonique [kaʀbɔnik] *adj*: **gaz** ~ carbon dioxide; **neige** ~ dry ice.

carbonisé, e [kaʀbɔnize] *adj* charred; **mourir** ~ to be burned to death.

carboniser [kaʀbɔnize] *vt* to carbonize; (*brûler complètement*) to burn down, reduce to ashes.

carburant [kaʀbyʀɑ̃] *nm* (motor) fuel.

carburateur [kaʀbyʀatœʀ] *nm* carburettor.

carburation [kaʀbyʀasjɔ̃] *nf* carburation.

carburer [kaʀbyʀe] *vi* (*moteur*): **bien/mal** ~ to be well/badly tuned.

carcan [kaʀkɑ̃] *nm* (*fig*) yoke, shackles *pl*.

carcasse [kaʀkas] *nf* carcass; (*de véhicule etc*) shell.

carcéral, e, aux [kaʀseʀal, -o] *adj* prison *cpd*.

carcinogène [kaʀsinɔʒɛn] *adj* carcinogenic.

cardan [kaʀdɑ̃] *nm* universal joint.

carder [kaʀde] *vt* to card.

cardiaque [kaʀdjak] *adj* cardiac, heart *cpd* ♦ *nm/f* heart patient; **être** ~ to have a heart condition.

cardigan [kaʀdigɑ̃] *nm* cardigan.

cardinal, e, aux [kaʀdinal, -o] *adj* cardinal ♦ *nm* (*REL*) cardinal.

cardiologie [kaʀdjɔlɔʒi] *nf* cardiology.

cardiologue [kaʀdjɔlɔg] *nm/f* cardiologist, heart specialist.

cardio-vasculaire [kaʀdjɔvaskylɛʀ] *adj*

cardiovascular.

cardon [kaʀdɔ̃] *nm* cardoon.

carême [kaʀɛm] *nm*: **le C~** Lent.

carence [kaʀɑ̃s] *nf* incompetence, inadequacy; (*manque*) deficiency; ~ **vitaminique** vitamin deficiency.

carène [kaʀɛn] *nf* hull.

caréner [kaʀene] *vt* (*NAVIG*) to careen; (*carrosserie*) to streamline.

caressant, e [kaʀɛsɑ̃, -ɑ̃t] *adj* affectionate; caressing, tender.

caresse [kaʀɛs] *nf* caress.

caresser [kaʀese] *vt* to caress, stroke, fondle; (*fig: projet, espoir*) to toy with.

cargaison [kaʀgɛzɔ̃] *nf* cargo, freight.

cargo [kaʀgo] *nm* cargo boat, freighter; ~ **mixte** cargo and passenger ship.

cari [kaʀi] *nm* = curry.

caricatural, e, aux [kaʀikatyʀal, -o] *adj* caricatural, caricature-like.

caricature [kaʀikatyʀ] *nf* caricature; (*politique etc*) (satirical) cartoon.

caricaturer [kaʀikatyʀe] *vt* (*personne*) to caricature; (*politique etc*) to satirize.

caricaturiste [kaʀikatyʀist(ə)] *nm/f* caricaturist; (*satirical*) cartoonist.

carie [kaʀi] *nf*: **la ~ (dentaire)** tooth decay; **une ~** a bad tooth.

carié, e [kaʀje] *adj*: **dent ~e** bad *ou* decayed tooth.

carillon [kaʀijɔ̃] *nm* (*d'église*) bells *pl*; (*de pendule*) chimes *pl*; (*de porte*): ~ **(électrique)** (electric) door chime *ou* bell.

carillonner [kaʀijone] *vi* to ring, chime, peal.

caritatif, ive [kaʀitatif, -iv] *adj* charitable.

carlingue [kaʀlɛ̃g] *nf* cabin.

carmélite [kaʀmelit] *nf* Carmelite nun.

carmin [kaʀmɛ̃] *adj inv* crimson.

carnage [kaʀnaʒ] *nm* carnage, slaughter.

carnassier, ière [kaʀnasje, -jɛʀ] *adj* carnivorous ♦ *nm* carnivore.

carnation [kaʀnɑsjɔ̃] *nf* complexion; ~**s** *nfpl* (*PEINTURE*) flesh tones.

carnaval [kaʀnaval] *nm* carnival.

carné, e [kaʀne] *adj* meat *cpd*, meat-based.

carnet [kaʀnɛ] *nm* (*calepin*) notebook; (*de tickets, timbres etc*) book; (*d'école*) school report; (*journal intime*) diary; ~ **d'adresses** address book; ~ **de chèques** cheque book (*BRIT*), checkbook (*US*); ~ **de commandes** order book; ~ **de notes** (*SCOL*) (school) report; ~ **à souches** counterfoil book.

carnier [kaʀnje] *nm* gamebag.

carnivore [kaʀnivɔʀ] *adj* carnivorous ♦ *nm* carnivore.

Carolines [kaʀolin] *nfpl*: **les ~** the Caroline Islands.

carotide [kaʀotid] *nf* carotid (artery).

carotte [kaʀot] *nf* (*aussi fig*) carrot.

Carpates [kaʀpat] *nfpl*: **les ~** the Carpathians, the Carpathian Mountains.

carpe [kaʀp(ə)] *nf* carp.

carpette [kaʀpɛt] *nf* rug.

carquois [kaʀkwa] *nm* quiver.

carre [kaʀ] *nf* (*de ski*) edge.

carré, e [kaʀe] *adj* square; (*fig: franc*) straightforward ♦ *nm* (*de terrain, jardin*) patch, plot; (*NAVIG: salle*) wardroom; (*MATH*) square; (*CARTES*): ~ **d'as/de rois** four aces/ kings; **élever un nombre au ~** to square a number; **mètre/kilomètre ~** square metre/ kilometre; ~ **de soie** silk headsquare *ou* headscarf; ~ **d'agneau** loin of lamb.

carreau, x [kaʀo] *nm* (*en faïence etc*) (floor) tile; (*wall*) tile; (*de fenêtre*) (window) pane; (*motif*) check, square; (*CARTES: couleur*) diamonds *pl*; (: *carte*) diamond; **tissu à ~x** checked fabric; **papier à ~x** squared paper.

carrefour [kaʀfuʀ] *nm* crossroads *sg*.

carrelage [kaʀlaʒ] *nm* tiling; (*tiled*) floor.

carreler [kaʀle] *vt* to tile.

carrelet [kaʀlɛ] *nm* (*poisson*) plaice.

carreleur [kaʀlœʀ] *nm* (*floor*) tiler.

carrément [kaʀemɑ̃] *adv* (*franchement*) straight out, bluntly; (*sans détours, sans hésiter*) straight; (*nettement*) definitely; **il l'a ~ mis à la porte** he threw him straight out.

carrer [kaʀe]: **se ~** *vi*: **se ~ dans un fauteuil** to settle o.s. comfortably *ou* ensconce o.s. in an armchair.

carrier [kaʀje] *nm*: **(ouvrier) ~** quarryman, quarrier.

carrière [kaʀjɛʀ] *nf* (*de roches*) quarry; (*métier*) career; **militaire de ~** professional soldier; **faire ~ dans** to make one's career in.

carriériste [kaʀjeʀist(ə)] *nm/f* careerist.

carriole [kaʀjɔl] *nf* (*péj*) old cart.

carrossable [kaʀosabl(ə)] *adj* suitable for (motor) vehicles.

carrosse [kaʀos] *nm* (horse-drawn) coach.

carrosserie [kaʀosʀi] *nf* body, bodywork *no pl* (*BRIT*); (*activité, commerce*) coachwork (*BRIT*), (car) body manufacturing; **atelier de ~** (*pour réparations*) body shop, panel beaters' (yard) (*BRIT*).

carrossier [kaʀosje] *nm* coachbuilder (*BRIT*), (car) body repairer; (*dessinateur*) car designer.

carrousel [kaʀuzɛl] *nm* (*ÉQUITATION*) carousel; (*fig*) merry-go-round.

carrure [kaʀyʀ] *nf* build; (*fig*) stature.

cartable [kaʀtabl(ə)] *nm* (*d'écolier*) satchel, (school)bag.

carte [kaʀt(ə)] *nf* (*de géographie*) map; (*marine, du ciel*) chart; (*de fichier, d'abonnement etc, à jouer*) card; (*au restaurant*) menu; (*aussi*: ~ **postale**) (post)card; (*aussi*: ~ **de visite**) (visiting) card; **avoir/donner ~ blanche** to have/give carte blanche *ou* a free hand; **tirer les ~s à qn** to read sb's cards; **jouer aux ~s** to play cards; **jouer ~s sur table** (*fig*) to put one's cards on the table; **à la ~** (*au restaurant*) à la carte; ~ **bancaire** cash card;

~ **à circuit imprimé** printed circuit; ~ **à puce** smartcard; ~ **de crédit** credit card; ~ **d'état-major** ≈ Ordnance (*BRIT*) *ou* Geological (*US*) Survey map; **la ~ grise** (*AUTO*) ≈ the (car) registration document; ~ **d'identité** identity card; ~ **jeune** young person's railcard; ~ **perforée** punch(ed) card; ~ **de séjour** residence permit; ~ **routière** road map; **la ~ verte** (*AUTO*) the green card; **la ~ des vins** the wine list.

cartel [kaʀtɛl] *nm* cartel.

carte-lettre, *pl* **cartes-lettres** [kaʀtəletʀ(ə)] *nf* letter-card.

carte-mère, *pl* **cartes-mères** [kaʀtəmɛʀ] *nf* (*INFORM*) mother board.

carter [kaʀtɛʀ] *nm* (*AUTO: d'huile*) sump (*BRIT*), oil pan (*US*); (*: de la boîte de vitesses*) casing; (*de bicyclette*) chain guard.

carte-réponse, *pl* **cartes-réponses** [kaʀt(ə)ʀepɔ̃s] *nf* reply card.

cartésien, ne [kaʀtezjɛ̃, -ɛn] *adj* Cartesian.

Carthage [kaʀtaʒ] *n* Carthage.

carthaginois, e [kaʀtaʒinwa, -waz] *adj* Carthaginian.

cartilage [kaʀtilaʒ] *nm* (*ANAT*) cartilage.

cartilagineux, euse [kaʀtilaʒinø, -øz] *adj* (*viande*) gristly.

cartographe [kaʀtɔgʀaf] *nm/f* cartographer.

cartographie [kaʀtɔgʀafi] *nf* cartography, map-making.

cartomancie [kaʀtɔmɑ̃si] *nf* fortune-telling, card-reading.

cartomancien, ne [kaʀtɔmɑ̃sjɛ̃, -ɛn] *nm/f* fortune-teller (*with cards*).

carton [kaʀtɔ̃] *nm* (*matériau*) cardboard; (*boîte*) (cardboard) box; (*d'invitation*) invitation card; (*ART*) sketch; cartoon; **en ~** cardboard *cpd*; **faire un ~** (*au tir*) to have a go at the rifle range; to score a hit; ~ (**à dessin**) portfolio.

cartonnage [kaʀtɔnaʒ] *nm* cardboard (packing).

cartonné, e [kaʀtɔne] *adj* (*livre*) hardback, cased.

carton-pâte [kaʀtɔ̃pɑt] *nm* pasteboard; **de ~** (*fig*) cardboard *cpd*.

cartouche [kaʀtuʃ] *nf* cartridge; (*de cigarettes*) carton.

cartouchière [kaʀtuʃjɛʀ] *nf* cartridge belt.

cas [kɑ] *nm* case; **faire peu de ~/grand ~ de** to attach little/great importance to; **le ~ échéant** if need be; **en aucun ~** on no account, under no circumstances (whatsoever); **au ~ où** in case; **dans ce ~** in that case; **en ~ de besoin** if need be; **en ~ d'urgence** in an emergency; **en ce ~** in that case; **en tout ~** in any case, at any rate; ~ **de conscience** matter of conscience; ~ **de force majeure** case of absolute necessity; (*ASSURANCES*) act of God; ~ **limite** borderline case; ~ **social** social problem.

Casablanca [kazablɑ̃ka] *n* Casablanca.

casanier, ière [kazanje, -jɛʀ] *adj* stay-at-home.

casaque [kazak] *nf* (*de jockey*) blouse.

cascade [kaskad] *nf* waterfall, cascade; (*fig*) stream, torrent.

cascadeur, euse [kaskadœʀ, -øz] *nm/f* stuntman/girl.

case [kɑz] *nf* (*hutte*) hut; (*compartiment*) compartment; (*pour le courrier*) pigeonhole; (*de mots croisés, d'échiquier*) square; (*sur un formulaire*) box.

casemate [kazmat] *nf* blockhouse.

caser [kaze] *vt* (*mettre*) to put; (*loger*) to put up; (*péj*) to find a job for; (*to marry off*); **se ~** (*personne*) to settle down.

caserne [kazɛʀn(ə)] *nf* barracks.

casernement [kazɛʀnəmɑ̃] *nm* barrack buildings *pl*.

cash [kaʃ] *adv*: **payer ~** to pay cash down.

casier [kazje] *nm* (*à journaux etc*) rack; (*de bureau*) filing cabinet; (*: à cases*) set of pigeonholes; (*case*) compartment; pigeonhole; (*: à clef*) locker; (*PÊCHE*) lobster pot; ~ **à bouteilles** bottle rack; ~ **judiciaire** police record.

casino [kazino] *nm* casino.

casque [kask(ə)] *nm* helmet; (*chez le coiffeur*) (hair-)dryer; (*pour audition*) (head-)phones *pl*, headset; **les C~s bleus** the UN peace-keeping force.

casquer [kaske] *vi* (*fam*) to cough up, stump up (*BRIT*).

casquette [kaskɛt] *nf* cap.

cassable [kasabl(ə)] *adj* (*fragile*) breakable.

cassant, e [kasɑ̃, -ɑ̃t] *adj* brittle; (*fig*) brusque, abrupt.

cassate [kasat] *nf*: (**glace**) ~ **cassata**.

cassation [kasasjɔ̃] *nf*: **se pourvoir en ~** to lodge an appeal; **recours en ~** appeal to the Supreme Court.

casse [kɑs] *nf* (*pour voitures*): **mettre à la ~** to scrap, send to the breakers (*BRIT*); (*dégâts*): **il y a eu de la ~** there were a lot of breakages; (*TYPO*): **haut/bas de ~** upper/lower case.

cassé, e [kɑse] *adj* (*voix*) cracked; (*vieillard*) bent.

casse-cou [kɑsku] *adj inv* daredevil, reckless; **crier ~ à qn** to warn sb (*against a risky undertaking*).

casse-croûte [kɑskʀut] *nm inv* snack.

casse-noisette(s) [kɑsnwazɛt], **casse-noix** [kɑsnwa] *nm inv* nutcrackers *pl*.

casse-pieds [kɑspje] *adj, nm/f inv* (*fam*): **il est ~, c'est un ~** he's a pain (in the neck).

casser [kɑse] *vt* to break; (*ADMIN: gradé*) to demote; (*JUR*) to quash; (*COMM*): ~ **les prix** to slash prices; ~ *vi* to break; (*fam*) to go, leave ♦ *vt*: **se ~ la jambe/une jambe** to break one's leg/a leg; **à tout ~** fantastic, brilliant; **se ~ net** to break clean off.

casserole [kasʀɔl] *nf* saucepan; **à la** ~ (*CULIN*) braised.

casse-tête [kastɛt] *nm inv* (*fig*) brain teaser; (*difficultés*) headache (*fig*).

cassette [kasɛt] *nf* (*bande magnétique*) cassette; (*coffret*) casket; ~ **numérique** digital compact cassette.

casseur [kasœʀ] *nm* hooligan; rioter.

cassis [kasis] *nm* blackcurrant; (*de la route*) dip, bump.

cassonade [kasɔnad] *nf* brown sugar.

cassoulet [kasulɛ] *nm* sausage and bean hotpot.

cassure [kasyʀ] *nf* break, crack.

castagnettes [kastaɲet] *nfpl* castanets.

caste [kast(ə)] *nf* caste.

castillan, e [kastijɑ̃, -an] *adj* Castilian ♦ *nm* (*LING*) Castilian.

Castille [kastij] *nf*: **la** ~ Castile.

castor [kastɔʀ] *nm* beaver.

castrer [kastʀe] *vt* (*mâle*) to castrate; (*femelle*) to spay; (*cheval*) to geld; (*chat, chien*) to doctor (*BRIT*), fix (*US*).

cataclysme [kataklism(ə)] *nm* cataclysm.

catacombes [katakɔ̃b] *nfpl* catacombs.

catadioptre [katadjɔptʀ(ə)] *nm* = **cataphote**.

catafalque [katafalk(ə)] *nm* catafalque.

catalan, e [katalɑ̃, -an] *adj* Catalan, Catalonian ♦ *nm* (*LING*) Catalan.

Catalogne [katalɔɲ] *nf*: **la** ~ Catalonia.

catalogue [katalɔg] *nm* catalogue.

cataloguer [katalɔge] *vt* to catalogue, list; (*péj*) to put a label on.

catalyse [kataliz] *nf* catalysis.

catalyser [katalize] *vt* to catalyze.

catalyseur [katalizœʀ] *nm* catalyst.

catalytique [katalitik] *adj* catalytic.

catamaran [katamaʀɑ̃] *nm* (*voilier*) catamaran.

cataphote [katafɔt] *nm* reflector.

cataplasme [kataplasm(ə)] *nm* poultice.

catapulte [katapylt(ə)] *nf* catapult.

catapulter [katapylte] *vt* to catapult.

cataracte [kataʀakt(ə)] *nf* cataract; **opérer qn de la** ~ to operate on sb for a cataract.

catarrhe [kataʀ] *nm* catarrh.

catarrheux, euse [kataʀø, -øz] *adj* catarrhal.

catastrophe [katastʀɔf] *nf* catastrophe, disaster; **atterrir en** ~ to make an emergency landing; **partir en** ~ to rush away.

catastropher [katastʀɔfe] *vt* (*personne*) to shatter.

catastrophique [katastʀɔfik] *adj* catastrophic, disastrous.

catch [katʃ] *nm* (all-in) wrestling.

catcheur, euse [katʃœʀ, -øz] *nm/f* (all-in) wrestler.

catéchiser [kateʃize] *vt* to indoctrinate; to lecture.

catéchisme [kateʃism(ə)] *nm* catechism.

catéchumène [katekymɛn] *nm/f* catechumen, *person attending religious instruction prior to baptism.*

catégorie [kategɔʀi] *nf* category; (*BOUCHERIE*): **morceaux de première/deuxième** ~ prime/second cuts.

catégorique [kategɔʀik] *adj* categorical.

catégoriquement [kategɔʀikmɑ̃] *adv* categorically.

catégoriser [kategɔʀize] *vt* to categorize.

caténaire [katenɛʀ] *nf* (*RAIL*) catenary.

cathédrale [katedʀal] *nf* cathedral.

cathéter [katetɛʀ] *nm* (*MÉD*) catheter.

cathode [katɔd] *nf* cathode.

cathodique [katɔdik] *adj*: **rayons** ~**s** cathode rays; **tube/écran** ~ cathode-ray tube/screen.

catholicisme [katɔlisism(ə)] *nm* (Roman) Catholicism.

catholique [katɔlik] *adj, nm/f* (Roman) Catholic; **pas très** ~ a bit shady *ou* fishy.

catimini [katimini]: **en** ~ *adv* on the sly, on the quiet.

catogan [katɔgɑ̃] *nm* bow (*tying hair on neck*).

Caucase [kokaz] *nm*: **le** ~ the Caucasus (Mountains).

caucasien, ne [kokazjɛ̃, -ɛn] *adj* Caucasian.

cauchemar [koʃmaʀ] *nm* nightmare.

cauchemardesque [koʃmaʀdɛsk(ə)] *adj* nightmarish.

caudal, e, aux [kodal, -o] *adj* caudal, tail *cpd*.

causal, e [kozal] *adj* causal.

causalité [kozalite] *nf* causality.

causant, e [kozɑ̃, -ɑ̃t] *adj* chatty, talkative.

cause [koz] *nf* cause; (*JUR*) lawsuit, case; brief; **faire** ~ **commune avec qn** to take sides with sb; **être** ~ **de** to be the cause of; **à** ~ **de** because of, owing to; **pour** ~ **de** on account of; owing to; (**et**) **pour** ~ and for (a very) good reason; **être en** ~ (*intérêts*) to be at stake; (*personne*) to be involved; (*qualité*) to be in question; **mettre en** ~ to implicate; to call into question; **remettre en** ~ to challenge, call into question; **c'est hors de** ~ it's out of the question; **en tout état de** ~ in any case.

causer [koze] *vt* to cause ♦ *vi* to chat, talk.

causerie [kozʀi] *nf* talk.

causette [kozɛt] *nf*: **faire la** *ou* **un brin de** ~ to have a chat.

caustique [kostik] *adj* caustic.

cauteleux, euse [kotlø, -øz] *adj* wily.

cautériser [koteʀize] *vt* to cauterize.

caution [kosjɔ̃] *nf* guarantee, security; deposit; (*JUR*) bail (bond); (*fig*) backing, support; **payer la** ~ **de qn** to stand bail for sb; **se porter** ~ **pour qn** to stand security for sb; **libéré sous** ~ released on bail; **sujet à** ~ unconfirmed.

cautionnement [kosjɔnmɑ̃] *nm* (*somme*) guarantee, security.

cautionner [kosjɔne] *vt* to guarantee; (*soutenir*) to support.

cavalcade [kavalkad] *nf* (*fig*) stampede.

cavale [kaval] *nf*: **en ~** on the run.
cavalerie [kavalʀi] *nf* cavalry.
cavalier, ière [kavalje, -jɛʀ] *adj* (*désinvolte*)
offhand ♦ *nm/f* rider; (*au bal*) partner ♦ *nm*
(*ÉCHECS*) knight; **faire ~ seul** to go it alone;
allée *ou* **piste cavalière** riding path.
cavalièrement [kavaljɛʀmɑ̃] *adv* offhandedly.
cave [kav] *nf* cellar; (*cabaret*) (cellar)
nightclub ♦ *adj*: **yeux ~s** sunken eyes; **joues**
~s hollow cheeks.
caveau, x [kavo] *nm* vault.
caverne [kavɛʀn(ə)] *nf* cave.
caverneux, euse [kavɛʀnø, -øz] *adj*
cavernous.
caviar [kavjaʀ] *nm* caviar(e).
cavité [kavite] *nf* cavity.
Cayenne [kajɛn] *n* Cayenne.
CB [sibi] *sigle f* (= *citizens' band, canaux*
banalisés) CB.
CC *sigle m* = **corps consulaire, compte courant.**
CCI *sigle f* = **Chambre de commerce et**
d'industrie.
CCP *sigle m* = **compte chèque postal.**
CD *sigle m* (= *chemin départemental*) secondary
road, ≈ B road (*BRIT*); (= *compact disc*) CD;
(= *comité directeur*) steering committee;
(*POL*) = **corps diplomatique.**
CDD *sigle m* (= *contrat à durée déterminée*)
fixed-term contract.
CDF, CdF *sigle mpl* (= *Charbonnages de France*)
national coal board.
CDI *sigle m* (= *Centre de documentation et*
d'information) school library; (= *contrat à*
durée indéterminée) permanent *ou* open-
ended contract.
CD-I *sigle m* (= *compact disc interactif*) CD-I®.
CD-Rom [sederɔm] *nm inv* (= *Compact Disc Read*
Only Memory) CD-Rom.
CDS *sigle m* (= *Centre des démocrates sociaux*)
political party.
CE *sigle f* (= *Communauté européenne*) EC;
(*COMM*) = **caisse d'épargne** ♦ *sigle m*
(*INDUSTRIE*) = **comité d'entreprise**; (*SCOL*)
= **cours élémentaire.**

════════════════════ *MOT-CLÉ*

ce, cette [sə, sɛt] (*devant nm* **cet** + *voyelle ou h*
aspiré; pl **ces**) *dét* (*proximité*) this; these *pl*;
(*non-proximité*) that; those *pl*; **cette maison**
(-ci/là) this/that house; **cette nuit** (*qui vient*)
tonight; (*passée*) last night
♦ *pron* **1**: **c'est** it's, it is; **c'est petit/grand/un**
livre it's *ou* it is small/big/a book; **c'est un**
peintre he's *ou* he is a painter; **ce sont des**
peintres they're *ou* they are painters; **c'est**
le facteur *etc* (*à la porte*) it's the postman
etc; **qui est-ce?** who is it?; (*en désignant*) who
is he/she?; **qu'est-ce?** what is it?; **c'est toi**
qui lui as parlé it was you who spoke to him
2: **c'est que**: **c'est qu'il est lent/qu'il n'a pas**
faim the fact is, he's slow/he's not hungry
3 (*expressions*): **c'est ça** (*correct*) that's it,

that's right; **c'est toi qui le dis!** that's what
YOU say!; *voir aussi* **c'est-à-dire; -ci; est-ce**
que; n'est-ce pas.
4: **~ qui, ~ que** what; (*chose qui*): **il est bête,**
~ qui me chagrine he's stupid, which
saddens me; **tout ~ qui bouge** everything
that *ou* which moves; **tout ~ que je sais** all I
know; **~ dont j'ai parlé** what I talked about;
~ que c'est grand! it's so big!

CEA *sigle m* (= *Commissariat à l'énergie*
atomique) ≈ AEA (= *Atomic Energy Authority*)
(*BRIT*), ≈ AEC (= *Atomic Energy Commission*)
(*US*).
CECA [seka] *sigle f* (= *Communauté européenne*
du charbon et de l'acier) ECSC (= *European*
Coal and Steel Community).
ceci [səsi] *pron* this.
cécité [sesite] *nf* blindness.
céder [sede] *vt* to give up ♦ *vi* (*pont, barrage*) to
give way; (*personne*) to give in; **~ à** to yield
to, give in to.
CEDEX [sedɛks] *sigle m* (= *courrier d'entreprise à*
distribution exceptionnelle) *accelerated postal*
service for bulk users.
cédille [sedij] *nf* cedilla.
cèdre [sɛdr(ə)] *nm* cedar.
CEE *sigle f* (= *Communauté économique*
européenne) EEC.
CEG *sigle m* (= *Collège d'enseignement général*)
≈ junior secondary school (*BRIT*), ≈ junior
high school (*US*).
CEI *sigle f* (= *Communauté des États*
indépendants) CIS.
ceindre [sɛ̃dr(ə)] *vt* (*mettre*) to put on, don;
(*entourer*): **~ qch de qch** to put sth round
sth.
ceinture [sɛ̃tyʀ] *nf* belt; (*taille*) waist; (*fig*)
ring; belt; circle; **~ de sauvetage** lifebelt; **~**
de sécurité safety *ou* seat belt; **~ (de**
sécurité) à enrouleur inertia reel seat belt;
~ verte green belt.
ceinturer [sɛ̃tyʀe] *vt* (*saisir*) to grasp (round
the waist); (*entourer*) to surround.
ceinturon [sɛ̃tyʀɔ̃] *nm* belt.
cela [səla] *pron* that; (*comme sujet indéfini*) it; **~**
m'étonne que it surprises me that; **quand/**
où ~? when/where (was that)?
célébrant [selebrɑ̃] *nm* (*REL*) celebrant.
célébration [selebrasjɔ̃] *nf* celebration.
célèbre [selɛbr(ə)] *adj* famous.
célébrer [selebre] *vt* to celebrate; (*louer*) to
extol.
célébrité [selebrite] *nf* fame; (*star*) celebrity.
céleri [sɛlri] *nm*: **~(-rave)** celeriac; **~ (en**
branche) celery.
célérité [selerite] *nf* speed, swiftness.
céleste [selɛst(ə)] *adj* celestial; heavenly.
célibat [seliba] *nm* celibacy; bachelor/
spinsterhood.
célibataire [selibatɛʀ] *adj* single, unmarried
♦ *nm/f* bachelor/unmarried *ou* single woman;

mère ~ single *ou* unmarried mother.
celle, celles [sɛl] *pron voir* **celui.**
cellier [selje] *nm* storeroom.
cellophane [selɔfan] *nf* ® cellophane.
cellulaire [selylɛʀ] *adj* (*BIO*) cell *cpd*, cellular; **voiture** *ou* **fourgon** ~ prison *ou* police van; **régime** ~ confinement.
cellule [selyl] *nf* (*gén*) cell; ~ (**photo-électrique**) electronic eye.
cellulite [selylit] *nf* cellulite.
celluloïd [selyloid] *nm* ® Celluloid.
cellulose [selyloz] *nf* cellulose.
celte [sɛlt(ə)], **celtique** [sɛltik] *adj* Celt, Celtic.

=== *MOT-CLÉ*

celui, celle [səlɥi, sɛl] (*mpl* **ceux**, *fpl* **celles**) *pron*
1: ~**-ci/là, celle-ci/là** this one/that one; **ceux-ci, celles-ci** these (ones); **ceux-là, celles-là** those (ones); ~ **de mon frère** my brother's; ~ **du salon/du dessous** the one in (*ou* from) the lounge/below
2: ~ **qui bouge** the one which *ou* that moves; (*personne*) the one who moves; ~ **que je vois** the one (which *ou* that) I see; (*personne*) the one (whom) I see; ~ **dont je parle** the one I'm talking about
3 (*valeur indéfinie*): ~ **qui veut** whoever wants.

cénacle [senakl(ə)] *nm* (literary) coterie *ou* set.
cendre [sɑ̃dʀ(ə)] *nf* ash; ~**s** (*d'un foyer*) ash(es), cinders; (*volcaniques*) ash *sg*; (*d'un défunt*) ashes; **sous la** ~ (*CULIN*) in (the) embers.
cendré, e [sɑ̃dʀe] *adj* (*couleur*) ashen; (*piste*) ~**e** cinder track.
cendreux, euse [sɑ̃dʀø, -øz] *adj* (*terrain, substance*) cindery; (*teint*) ashen.
cendrier [sɑ̃dʀije] *nm* ashtray.
cène [sɛn] *nf*: **la** ~ (Holy) Communion; (*ART*) the Last Supper.
censé, e [sɑ̃se] *adj*: **être** ~ **faire** to be supposed to do.
censément [sɑ̃semɑ̃] *adv* supposedly.
censeur [sɑ̃sœʀ] *nm* (*SCOL*) deputy-head (*BRIT*), vice-principal (*US*); (*CINÉ, POL*) censor.
censure [sɑ̃syʀ] *nf* censorship.
censurer [sɑ̃syʀe] *vt* (*CINÉ, PRESSE*) to censor; (*POL*) to censure.
cent [sɑ̃] *num* a hundred, one hundred; **pour** ~ (%) per cent (%); **faire les** ~ **pas** to pace up and down.
centaine [sɑ̃tɛn] *nf*: **une** ~ (**de**) about a hundred, a hundred or so; (*COMM*) a hundred; **plusieurs** ~**s** (**de**) several hundred; **des** ~**s** (**de**) hundreds (of).
centenaire [sɑ̃tnɛʀ] *adj* hundred-year-old ♦ *nm/f* centenarian ♦ *nm* (*anniversaire*) centenary.
centième [sɑ̃tjɛm] *num* hundredth.

centigrade [sɑ̃tigʀad] *nm* centigrade.
centigramme [sɑ̃tigʀam] *nm* centigramme.
centilitre [sɑ̃tilitʀ(ə)] *nm* centilitre (*BRIT*), centiliter (*US*).
centime [sɑ̃tim] *nm* centime.
centimètre [sɑ̃timɛtʀ(ə)] *nm* centimetre (*BRIT*), centimeter (*US*); (*ruban*) tape measure, measuring tape.
centrafricain, e [sɑ̃tʀafʀikɛ̃, -ɛn] *adj* of *ou* from the Central African Republic.
central, e, aux [sɑ̃tʀal, -o] *adj* central ♦ *nm*: ~ (**téléphonique**) (telephone) exchange ♦ *nf*: ~**e d'achat** (*COMM*) central buying service; ~**e électrique/nucléaire** electric/nuclear power station; ~**e syndicale** group of affiliated trade unions.
centralisation [sɑ̃tʀalizasjɔ̃] *nf* centralization.
centraliser [sɑ̃tʀalize] *vt* to centralize.
centralisme [sɑ̃tʀalism(ə)] *nm* centralism.
centraméricain, e [sɑ̃tʀamerikɛ̃, -ɛn] *adj* Central American.
centre [sɑ̃tʀ(ə)] *nm* centre (*BRIT*), center (*US*); ~ **commercial/sportif/culturel** shopping/sports/arts centre; ~ **aéré** outdoor centre; ~ **d'apprentissage** training college; ~ **d'attraction** centre of attraction; ~ **de gravité** centre of gravity; ~ **d'enfouissement des déchets** landfill site; ~ **hospitalier** hospital complex; ~ **de tri** (*POSTES*) sorting office; ~**s nerveux** (*ANAT*) nerve centres.
centrer [sɑ̃tʀe] *vt* to centre (*BRIT*), center (*US*) ♦ *vi* (*FOOTBALL*) to centre the ball.
centre-ville, *pl* **centres-villes** [sɑ̃tʀəvil] *nm* town centre (*BRIT*) *ou* center (*US*), downtown (area) (*US*).
centrifuge [sɑ̃tʀifyʒ] *adj*: **force** ~ centrifugal force.
centrifuger [sɑ̃tʀifyʒe] *vt* to centrifuge.
centrifugeuse [sɑ̃tʀifyʒøz] *nf* (*pour fruits*) juice extractor.
centripète [sɑ̃tʀipɛt] *adj*: **force** ~ centripetal force.
centrisme [sɑ̃tʀism(ə)] *nm* centrism.
centriste [sɑ̃tʀist(ə)] *adj, nm/f* centrist.
centuple [sɑ̃typl(ə)] *nm*: **le** ~ **de qch** a hundred times sth; **au** ~ a hundredfold.
centupler [sɑ̃typle] *vi, vt* to increase a hundredfold.
CEP *sigle m* = **Certificat d'études (primaires).**
cep [sɛp] *nm* (vine) stock.
cépage [sepaʒ] *nm* (type of) vine.
cèpe [sɛp] *nm* (edible) boletus.
cependant [səpɑ̃dɑ̃] *adv* however, nevertheless.
céramique [seʀamik] *adj* ceramic ♦ *nf* ceramic; (*art*) ceramics *sg*.
céramiste [seʀamist(ə)] *nm/f* ceramist.
cerbère [sɛʀbɛʀ] *nm* (*fig: péj*) bad-tempered doorkeeper.
cerceau, x [sɛʀso] *nm* (*d'enfant, de tonnelle*) hoop.
cercle [sɛʀkl(ə)] *nm* circle; (*objet*) band, hoop;

décrire un ~ (*avion*) to circle; (*projectile*) to describe a circle; **~ d'amis** circle of friends; **~ de famille** family circle; **~ vicieux** vicious circle.

cercler [sɛʀkle] *vt*: **lunettes cerclées d'or** gold-rimmed glasses.

cercueil [sɛʀkœj] *nm* coffin.

céréale [seʀeal] *nf* cereal.

céréalier, ière [seʀealje, -jɛʀ] *adj* (*production, cultures*) cereal *cpd*.

cérébral, e, aux [seʀebʀal, -o] *adj* (*ANAT*) cerebral, brain *cpd*; (*fig*) mental, cerebral.

cérémonial [seʀemɔnjal] *nm* ceremonial.

cérémonie [seʀemɔni] *nf* ceremony; **~s** *nfpl* (*péj*) fuss *sg*, to-do *sg*.

cérémonieux, euse [seʀemɔnjø, -øz] *adj* ceremonious, formal.

CERES [seʀɛs] *sigle m* (= *Centre d'études, de recherches et d'éducation socialiste*) (*formerly*) *intellectual section of the French Socialist party*.

cerf [sɛʀ] *nm* stag.

cerfeuil [sɛʀfœj] *nm* chervil.

cerf-volant [sɛʀvɔlɑ̃] *nm* kite; **jouer au ~** to fly a kite.

cerisaie [səʀizɛ] *nf* cherry orchard.

cerise [səʀiz] *nf* cherry.

cerisier [səʀizje] *nm* cherry (tree).

CERN [sɛʀn] *sigle m* (= *Centre européen de recherche nucléaire*) CERN.

cerné, e [sɛʀne] *adj*: **les yeux ~s** with dark rings *ou* shadows under the eyes.

cerner [sɛʀne] *vt* (*MIL etc*) to surround; (*fig: problème*) to delimit, define.

cernes [sɛʀn(ə)] *nfpl* (dark) rings, shadows (under the eyes).

certain, e [sɛʀtɛ̃, -ɛn] *adj* certain; (*sûr*): **~ (de/que)** certain *ou* sure (of/ that) ♦ *dét* certain; **d'un ~ âge** past one's prime, not so young; **un ~ temps** (quite) some time; **sûr et ~** absolutely certain; **~s** *pron* some.

certainement [sɛʀtɛnmɑ̃] *adv* (*probablement*) most probably *ou* likely; (*bien sûr*) certainly, of course.

certes [sɛʀt(ə)] *adv* admittedly; of course; indeed (yes).

certificat [sɛʀtifika] *nm* certificate; **C~ d'études (primaires) (CEP)** former school leaving certificate (taken at the end of primary education); **C~ de fin d'études secondaires (CFES)** school leaving certificate.

certifié, e [sɛʀtifje] *adj*: **professeur ~** qualified teacher; (*ADMIN*): **copie ~e conforme (à l'original)** certified copy (of the original).

certifier [sɛʀtifje] *vt* to certify, guarantee; **~ à qn que** to assure sb that, guarantee to sb that; **~ qch à qn** to guarantee sth to sb.

certitude [sɛʀtityd] *nf* certainty.

cérumen [seʀymɛn] *nm* (ear)wax.

cerveau, x [sɛʀvo] *nm* brain; **~ électronique** electronic brain.

cervelas [sɛʀvəla] *nm* saveloy.

cervelle [sɛʀvɛl] *nf* (*ANAT*) brain; (*CULIN*) brain(s); **se creuser la ~** to rack one's brains.

cervical, e, aux [sɛʀvikal, -o] *adj* cervical.

cervidés [sɛʀvide] *nmpl* cervidae.

CES *sigle m* (= *Collège d'enseignement secondaire*) ≈ (junior) secondary school (*BRIT*), ≈ junior high school (*US*).

ces [se] *dét voir* **ce**.

césarienne [sezaʀjɛn] *nf* caesarean (*BRIT*) *ou* cesarean (*US*) (section).

cessantes [sesɑ̃t] *adj fpl*: **toutes affaires ~** forthwith.

cessation [sesasjɔ̃] *nf*: **~ des hostilités** cessation of hostilities; **~ de paiements/ commerce** suspension of payments/trading.

cesse [sɛs]: **sans ~** *adv* continually, constantly; continuously; **il n'avait de ~ que** he would not rest until.

cesser [sese] *vt* to stop ♦ *vi* to stop, cease; **~ de faire** to stop doing; **faire ~** (*bruit, scandale*) to put a stop to.

cessez-le-feu [seselfø] *nm inv* ceasefire.

cession [sesjɔ̃] *nf* transfer.

c'est [sɛ] *pron* + *vb voir* **ce**.

c'est-à-dire [sɛtadiʀ] *adv* that is (to say); (*demander de préciser*): **~?** what does that mean?; **~ que ...** (*en conséquence*) which means that ...; (*manière d'excuse*) well, in fact ....

CET *sigle m* (= *Collège d'enseignement technique*) (*formerly*) technical school.

cet [sɛt] *dét voir* **ce**.

cétacé [setase] *nm* cetacean.

cette [sɛt] *dét voir* **ce**.

ceux [sø] *pron voir* **celui**.

cévenol, e [sevnɔl] *adj* of *ou* from the Cévennes region.

cf. *abr* (= *confer*) cf, cp.

CFAO *sigle f* (= *conception de fabrication assistée par ordinateur*) CAM.

CFC *sigle mpl* (= *chlorofluorocarbures*) CFC.

CFDT *sigle f* (= *Confédération française et démocratique du travail*) trade union.

CFES *sigle m* = **Certificat de fin d'études secondaires**.

CFF *sigle m* (= *Chemin de fer fédéral*) Swiss railways.

CFL *sigle m* (= *Chemin de fer luxembourgeois*) Luxembourg railways.

CFP *sigle m* = *Centre de formation professionnelle* ♦ *sigle f* = *Compagnie française des pétroles*.

CFTC *sigle f* (= *Confédération française des travailleurs chrétiens*) trade union.

CGC *sigle f* (= *Confédération générale des cadres*) management union.

CGPME *sigle f* = *Confédération générale des petites et moyennes entreprises*.

CGT *sigle f* (= *Confédération générale du travail*) trade union.

CH *abr* (= *Confédération helvétique*) CH.

ch. *abr* = **charges, chauffage, cherche**.

chacal [ʃakal] nm jackal.
chacun, e [ʃakœ̃, -yn] pron each; (indéfini) everyone, everybody.
chagrin, e [ʃagʀɛ̃, -in] adj morose ♦ nm grief, sorrow; **avoir du** ~ to be grieved ou sorrowful.
chagriner [ʃagʀine] vt to grieve, distress; (contrarier) to bother, worry.
chahut [ʃay] nm uproar.
chahuter [ʃayte] vt to rag, bait ♦ vi to make an uproar.
chahuteur, euse [ʃaytœʀ, -øz] nm/f rowdy.
chai [ʃɛ] nm wine and spirit store(house).
chaîne [ʃɛn] nf chain; (RADIO, TV) channel; (INFORM) string; **~s** nfpl (liens, asservissement) fetters, bonds; **travail à la** ~ production line work; **réactions en** ~ chain reactions; **faire la** ~ to form a (human) chain; ~ **alimentaire** food chain; ~ **compacte** music centre; ~ **d'entraide** mutual aid association; ~ **(haute-fidélité ou hi-fi)** hi-fi system; ~ **(de montage ou de fabrication)** production ou assembly line; ~ **(de montagnes)** (mountain) range; ~ **de solidarité** solidarity network; ~ **(stéréo ou audio)** stereo (system).
chaînette [ʃɛnɛt] nf (small) chain.
chaînon [ʃɛnɔ̃] nm link.
chair [ʃɛʀ] nf flesh ♦ adj: **(couleur)** ~ flesh-coloured; **avoir la** ~ **de poule** to have goosepimples ou gooseflesh; **bien en** ~ plump, well-padded; **en** ~ **et en os** in the flesh; ~ **à saucisses** sausage meat.
chaire [ʃɛʀ] nf (d'église) pulpit; (d'université) chair.
chaise [ʃɛz] nf chair; ~ **de bébé** high chair; ~ **électrique** electric chair; ~ **longue** deckchair.
chaland [ʃalɑ̃] nm (bateau) barge.
châle [ʃɑl] nm shawl.
chalet [ʃalɛ] nm chalet.
chaleur [ʃalœʀ] nf heat; (fig) warmth; fire, fervour (BRIT), fervor (US); heat; **en** ~ (ZOOL) on heat.
chaleureusement [ʃalœʀøzmɑ̃] adv warmly.
chaleureux, euse [ʃalœʀø, -øz] adj warm.
challenge [ʃalɑ̃ʒ] nm contest, tournament.
challenger [ʃalɑ̃ʒɛʀ] nm (SPORT) challenger.
chaloupe [ʃalup] nf launch; (de sauvetage) lifeboat.
chalumeau, x [ʃalymo] nm blowlamp (BRIT), blowtorch.
chalut [ʃaly] nm trawl (net); **pêcher au** ~ to trawl.
chalutier [ʃalytje] nm trawler; (pêcheur) trawlerman.
chamade [ʃamad] nf: **battre la** ~ to beat wildly.
chamailler [ʃamaje]: **se** ~ vi to squabble, bicker.
chamarré, e [ʃamaʀe] adj richly brocaded.
chambard [ʃɑ̃baʀ] nm rumpus.

chambardement [ʃɑ̃baʀdəmɑ̃] nm: **c'est le grand** ~ everything has been (ou is being) turned upside down.
chambarder [ʃɑ̃baʀde] vt to turn upside down.
chamboulement [ʃɑ̃bulmɑ̃] nm disruption.
chambouler [ʃɑ̃bule] vt to disrupt, turn upside down.
chambranle [ʃɑ̃bʀɑ̃l] nm (door) frame.
chambre [ʃɑ̃bʀ(ə)] nf bedroom; (TECH) chamber; (POL) chamber, house; (JUR) court; (COMM) chamber; federation; **faire** ~ **à part** to sleep in separate rooms; **stratège/ alpiniste en** ~ armchair strategist/ mountaineer; ~ **à un lit/deux lits** single/ twin-bedded room; ~ **pour une/deux personne(s)** single/double room; ~ **d'accusation** court of criminal appeal; ~ **d'agriculture** body responsible for the agricultural interests of a département; ~ **à air** (de pneu) (inner) tube; ~ **d'amis** spare ou guest room; ~ **de combustion** combustion chamber; ~ **de commerce et d'industrie (CCI)** chamber of commerce and industry; ~ **à coucher** bedroom; **la C**~ **des députés** the Chamber of Deputies, ≈ the House (of Commons) (BRIT), ≈ the House of Representatives (US); ~ **forte** strongroom; ~ **froide** ou **frigorifique** cold room; ~ **à gaz** gas chamber; ~ **d'hôte** ≈ bed and breakfast (in private home); ~ **des machines** engine-room; ~ **des métiers (CM)** chamber of commerce for trades; ~ **meublée** bedsit(ter) (BRIT), furnished room; ~ **noire** (PHOTO) dark room.
chambrée [ʃɑ̃bʀe] nf room.
chambrer [ʃɑ̃bʀe] vt (vin) to bring to room temperature.
chameau, x [ʃamo] nm camel.
chamois [ʃamwa] nm chamois ♦ adj: **(couleur)** ~ fawn, buff.
champ [ʃɑ̃] nm (aussi INFORM) field; (PHOTO): **dans le** ~ in the picture; **prendre du** ~ to draw back; **laisser le** ~ **libre à qn** to leave sb a clear field; ~ **d'action** sphere of operation(s); ~ **de bataille** battlefield; ~ **de courses** racecourse; ~ **d'honneur** field of honour; ~ **de manœuvre** (MIL) parade ground; ~ **de mines** minefield; ~ **de tir** shooting ou rifle range; ~ **visuel** field of vision.
Champagne [ʃɑ̃paɲ] nf: **la** ~ Champagne, the Champagne region.
champagne [ʃɑ̃paɲ] nm champagne.
champenois, e [ʃɑ̃pənwa, -waz] adj of ou from Champagne; (vin): **méthode** ~**e** champagne-type.
champêtre [ʃɑ̃pɛtʀ(ə)] adj country cpd, rural.
champignon [ʃɑ̃piɲɔ̃] nm mushroom; (terme générique) fungus (pl -i); (fam: accélérateur) accelerator, gas pedal (US); ~ **de couche** ou **de Paris** button mushroom; ~ **vénéneux** toadstool, poisonous mushroom.

champion, ne [ʃɑ̃pjɔ̃, -ɔn] *adj, nm/f* champion.
championnat [ʃɑ̃pjɔna] *nm* championship.
chance [ʃɑ̃s] *nf*: **la ~** luck; **une ~** a stroke *ou* piece of luck *ou* good fortune; (*occasion*) a lucky break; **~s** *nfpl* (*probabilités*) chances; **avoir de la ~** to be lucky; **il a des ~s de gagner** he has a chance of winning; **il y a de fortes ~s pour que Paul soit malade** it's highly probable that Paul is ill; **bonne ~!** good luck!; **encore une ~ que tu viennes!** it's lucky you're coming; **je n'ai pas de ~** I'm out of luck; (*toujours*) I never have any luck; **donner sa ~ à qn** to give sb a chance.
chancelant, e [ʃɑ̃slɑ̃, -ɑ̃t] *adj* (*personne*) tottering; (*santé*) failing.
chanceler [ʃɑ̃sle] *vi* to totter.
chancelier [ʃɑ̃səlje] *nm* (*allemand*) chancellor; (*d'ambassade*) secretary.
chancellerie [ʃɑ̃sɛlʀi] *nf* (*en France*) ministry of justice; (*en Allemagne*) chancellery; (*d'ambassade*) chancery.
chanceux, euse [ʃɑ̃sø, -øz] *adj* lucky, fortunate.
chancre [ʃɑ̃kʀ(ə)] *nm* canker.
chandail [ʃɑ̃daj] *nm* (thick) jumper *ou* sweater.
Chandeleur [ʃɑ̃dlœʀ] *nf*: **la ~** Candlemas.
chandelier [ʃɑ̃dəlje] *nm* candlestick; (*à plusieurs branches*) candelabra.
chandelle [ʃɑ̃dɛl] *nf* (tallow) candle; (*TENNIS*): **faire une ~** to lob; (*AVIAT*): **monter en ~** to climb vertically; **tenir la ~** to play gooseberry; **dîner aux ~s** candlelight dinner.
change [ʃɑ̃ʒ] *nm* (*COMM*) exchange; **opérations de ~** (foreign) exchange transactions; **contrôle des ~s** exchange control; **gagner/perdre au ~** to be better/ worse off (for it); **donner le ~ à qn** (*fig*) to lead sb up the garden path.
changeant, e [ʃɑ̃ʒɑ̃, -ɑ̃t] *adj* changeable, fickle.
changement [ʃɑ̃ʒmɑ̃] *nm* change; **~ de vitesse** (*dispositif*) gears *pl*; (*action*) gear change.
changer [ʃɑ̃ʒe] *vt* (*modifier*) to change, alter; (*remplacer, COMM, rhabiller*) to change ♦ *vi* to change, alter; **se ~** to change (o.s.); **~ de** (*remplacer: adresse, nom, voiture etc*) to change one's; (*échanger, alterner: côté, place, train etc*) to change + *npl*; **~ d'air** to get a change of air; **~ de couleur/direction** to change colour/direction; **~ d'idée** to change one's mind; **~ de place avec qn** to change places with sb; **~ de vitesse** (*AUTO*) to change gear; **~ qn/qch de place** to move sb/sth to another place; **~ (de train *etc*)** to change (trains *etc*); **~ qch en** to change sth into.
changeur [ʃɑ̃ʒœʀ] *nm* (*personne*) moneychanger; **~ automatique** change machine; **~ de disques** record changer,
autochange.
chanoine [ʃanwan] *nm* canon.
chanson [ʃɑ̃sɔ̃] *nf* song.
chansonnette [ʃɑ̃sɔnɛt] *nf* ditty.
chansonnier [ʃɑ̃sɔnje] *nm* cabaret artist (*specializing in political satire*); (*recueil*) song book.
chant [ʃɑ̃] *nm* song; (*art vocal*) singing; (*d'église*) hymn; (*de poème*) canto; (*TECH*): **posé de *ou* sur ~** placed edgeways; **~ de Noël** Christmas carol.
chantage [ʃɑ̃taʒ] *nm* blackmail; **faire du ~** to use blackmail; **soumettre qn à un ~** to blackmail sb.
chantant, e [ʃɑ̃tɑ̃, -ɑ̃t] *adj* (*accent, voix*) sing-song.
chanter [ʃɑ̃te] *vt, vi* to sing; **~ juste/faux** to sing in tune/out of tune; **si cela lui chante** (*fam*) if he feels like it *ou* fancies it.
chanterelle [ʃɑ̃tʀɛl] *nf* chanterelle (*edible mushroom*).
chanteur, euse [ʃɑ̃tœʀ, -øz] *nm/f* singer; **~ de charme** crooner.
chantier [ʃɑ̃tje] *nm* (building) site; (*sur une route*) roadworks *pl*; **mettre en ~** to start work on; **~ naval** shipyard.
chantilly [ʃɑ̃tiji] *nf voir* **crème**.
chantonner [ʃɑ̃tɔne] *vi, vt* to sing to oneself, hum.
chantre [ʃɑ̃tʀ(ə)] *nm* (*fig*) eulogist.
chanvre [ʃɑ̃vʀ(ə)] *nm* hemp.
chaos [kao] *nm* chaos.
chaotique [kaɔtik] *adj* chaotic.
chap. *abr* (= *chapitre*) ch.
chapardage [ʃapaʀdaʒ] *nm* pilfering.
chaparder [ʃapaʀde] *vt* to pinch.
chapeau, x [ʃapo] *nm* hat; (*PRESSE*) introductory paragraph; **~!** well done!; **~ melon** bowler hat; **~ mou** trilby; **~x de roues** hub caps.
chapeauter [ʃapote] *vt* (*ADMIN*) to head, oversee.
chapelain [ʃaplɛ̃] *nm* (*REL*) chaplain.
chapelet [ʃaplɛ] *nm* (*REL*) rosary; (*fig*): **un ~ de** a string of; **dire son ~** to tell one's beads.
chapelier, ière [ʃapəlje, -jɛʀ] *nm/f* hatter; milliner.
chapelle [ʃapɛl] *nf* chapel; **~ ardente** chapel of rest.
chapellerie [ʃapɛlʀi] *nf* (*magasin*) hat shop; (*commerce*) hat trade.
chapelure [ʃaplyʀ] *nf* (dried) breadcrumbs *pl*.
chaperon [ʃapʀɔ̃] *nm* chaperon.
chaperonner [ʃapʀɔne] *vt* to chaperon.
chapiteau, x [ʃapito] *nm* (*ARCHIT*) capital; (*de cirque*) marquee, big top.
chapitre [ʃapitʀ(ə)] *nm* chapter; (*fig*) subject, matter; **avoir voix au ~** to have a say in the matter.
chapitrer [ʃapitʀe] *vt* to lecture, reprimand.
chapon [ʃapɔ̃] *nm* capon.
chaque [ʃak] *dét* each, every; (*indéfini*) every.

char [ʃaʀ] nm (à foin etc) cart, waggon; (de carnaval) float; ~ **(d'assaut)** tank.

charabia [ʃaʀabja] nm (péj) gibberish, gobbledygook (BRIT).

charade [ʃaʀad] nf riddle; (mimée) charade.

charbon [ʃaʀbɔ̃] nm coal; ~ **de bois** charcoal.

charbonnage [ʃaʀbɔnaʒ] nm: **les ~s de France** the (French) Coal Board sg.

charbonnier [ʃaʀbɔnje] nm coalman.

charcuterie [ʃaʀkytʀi] nf (magasin) pork butcher's shop and delicatessen; (produits) cooked pork meats pl.

charcutier, ière [ʃaʀkytje, -jɛʀ] nm/f pork butcher.

chardon [ʃaʀdɔ̃] nm thistle.

chardonneret [ʃaʀdɔnʀɛ] nm goldfinch.

charentais, e [ʃaʀɑ̃tɛ, -ɛz] adj of ou from Charente ♦ nf (pantoufle) slipper.

charge [ʃaʀʒ(ə)] nf (fardeau) load; (explosif, ÉLEC, MIL, JUR) charge; (rôle, mission) responsibility; ~**s** nfpl (du loyer) service charges; **à la ~ de** (dépendant de) dependent upon, supported by; (aux frais de) chargeable to, payable by; **j'accepte, à ~ de revanche** I accept, provided I can do the same for you (in return) one day; **prendre en ~** to take charge of; (suj: véhicule) to take on; (dépenses) to take care of; ~ **utile** (AUTO) live load; (COMM) payload; ~**s sociales** social security contributions.

chargé [ʃaʀʒe] adj (voiture, animal, personne) laden; (fusil, batterie, caméra) loaded; (occupé: emploi du temps, journée) busy, full; (estomac) heavy, full; (langue) furred; (décoration, style) heavy, ornate ♦ nm: ~ **d'affaires** chargé d'affaires; ~ **de cours** ≈ lecturer; ~ **de** (responsable de) responsible for.

chargement [ʃaʀʒəmɑ̃] nm (action) loading; charging; (objets) load.

charger [ʃaʀʒe] vt (voiture, fusil, caméra, INFORM) to load; (batterie) to charge ♦ vi (MIL etc) to charge; **se ~ de** vt to see to, take care of; ~ **qn de qch/faire qch** to give sb the responsibility for sth/of doing sth; to put sb in charge of sth/doing sth; **se ~ de faire qch** to take it upon o.s. to do sth.

chargeur [ʃaʀʒœʀ] nm (dispositif: d'arme à feu) magazine; (: PHOTO) cartridge; ~ **de batterie** (ÉLEC) battery charger.

chariot [ʃaʀjo] nm trolley; (charrette) waggon; (de machine à écrire) carriage; ~ **élévateur** fork-lift truck.

charisme [kaʀism(ə)] nm charisma.

charitable [ʃaʀitabl(ə)] adj charitable; kind.

charité [ʃaʀite] nf charity; **faire la ~** to give to charity; to do charitable works; **faire la ~ à** to give (something) to; **fête/vente de ~** fête/sale in aid of charity.

charivari [ʃaʀivaʀi] nm hullabaloo.

charlatan [ʃaʀlatɑ̃] nm charlatan.

charlotte [ʃaʀlɔt] nf (CULIN) charlotte.

charmant, e [ʃaʀmɑ̃, -ɑ̃t] adj charming.

charme [ʃaʀm(ə)] nm charm; ~**s** nmpl (appas) charms; **c'est ce qui en fait le ~** that is its attraction; **faire du ~** to be charming, turn on the charm; **aller ou se porter comme un ~** to be in the pink.

charmer [ʃaʀme] vt to charm; **je suis charmé de** I'm delighted to.

charmeur, euse [ʃaʀmœʀ, -øz] nm/f charmer; ~ **de serpents** snake charmer.

charnel, le [ʃaʀnɛl] adj carnal.

charnier [ʃaʀnje] nm mass grave.

charnière [ʃaʀnjɛʀ] nf hinge; (fig) turning-point.

charnu, e [ʃaʀny] adj fleshy.

charogne [ʃaʀɔɲ] nf carrion no pl; (fam!) bastard (!).

charolais, e [ʃaʀɔlɛ, -ɛz] adj of ou from the Charolais.

charpente [ʃaʀpɑ̃t] nf frame(work); (fig) structure, framework; (carrure) build, frame.

charpenté, e [ʃaʀpɑ̃te] adj: **bien ou solidement ~** (personne) well-built; (texte) well-constructed.

charpenterie [ʃaʀpɑ̃tʀi] nf carpentry.

charpentier [ʃaʀpɑ̃tje] nm carpenter.

charpie [ʃaʀpi] nf: **en ~** (fig) in shreds ou ribbons.

charretier [ʃaʀtje] nm carter; **de ~** (péj: langage, manières) uncouth.

charrette [ʃaʀɛt] nf cart.

charrier [ʃaʀje] vt to carry (along); to cart, carry ♦ vi (fam) to exaggerate.

charrue [ʃaʀy] nf plough (BRIT), plow (US).

charte [ʃaʀt(ə)] nf charter.

charter [tʃaʀtœʀ] nm (vol) charter flight; (avion) charter plane.

chasse [ʃas] nf hunting; (au fusil) shooting; (poursuite) chase; (aussi: ~ **d'eau**) flush; **la ~ est ouverte** the hunting season is open; **la ~ est fermée** it is the close (BRIT) ou closed (US) season; **aller à la ~** to go hunting; **prendre en ~, donner la ~ à** to give chase to; **tirer la ~ (d'eau)** to flush the toilet, pull the chain; ~ **aérienne** aerial pursuit; ~ **à courre** hunting; ~ **à l'homme** manhunt; ~ **gardée** private hunting grounds pl; ~ **sous-marine** underwater fishing.

châsse [ʃas] nf reliquary, shrine.

chassé-croisé, pl chassés-croisés [ʃasekʀwaze] nm (DANSE) chassé-croisé; (fig) mix-up (where people miss each other in turn).

chasse-neige [ʃasnɛʒ] nm inv snowplough (BRIT), snowplow (US).

chasser [ʃase] vt to hunt; (expulser) to chase away ou out, drive away ou out; (dissiper) to chase ou sweep away; to dispel, drive away.

chasseur, euse [ʃasœʀ, -øz] nm/f hunter ♦ nm (avion) fighter; (domestique) page (boy), messenger (boy); ~ **d'images** roving photographer; ~ **de têtes** (fig) headhunter; ~**s**

alpins mountain infantry.

chassieux, euse [ʃasjø, -øz] *adj* sticky, gummy.

châssis [ʃasi] *nm* (*AUTO*) chassis; (*cadre*) frame; (*de jardin*) cold frame.

chaste [ʃast(ə)] *adj* chaste.

chasteté [ʃastəte] *nf* chastity.

chasuble [ʃazybl(ə)] *nf* chasuble; **robe** ~ pinafore dress (*BRIT*), jumper (*US*).

chat [ʃa] *nm* cat; ~ **sauvage** wildcat.

châtaigne [ʃatɛɲ] *nf* chestnut.

châtaignier [ʃatɛɲe] *nm* chestnut (tree).

châtain [ʃatɛ̃] *adj inv* chestnut (brown); (*personne*) chestnut-haired.

château, x [ʃato] *nm* castle; ~ **d'eau** water tower; ~ **fort** stronghold, fortified castle; ~ **de sable** sandcastle.

châtelain, e [ʃatlɛ̃, -ɛn] *nm/f* lord/lady of the manor ♦ *nf* (*ceinture*) chatelaine.

châtier [ʃatje] *vt* to punish, castigate; (*fig: style*) to polish, refine.

chatière [ʃatjɛʀ] *nf* (*porte*) cat flap.

châtiment [ʃatimɑ̃] *nm* punishment, castigation; ~ **corporel** corporal punishment.

chatoiement [ʃatwamɑ̃] *nm* shimmer(ing).

chaton [ʃatɔ̃] *nm* (*ZOOL*) kitten; (*BOT*) catkin; (*de bague*) bezel; stone.

chatouillement [ʃatujmɑ̃] *nm* (*gén*) tickling; (*dans le nez, la gorge*) tickle.

chatouiller [ʃatuje] *vt* to tickle; (*l'odorat, le palais*) to titillate.

chatouilleux, euse [ʃatujø, -øz] *adj* ticklish; (*fig*) touchy, over-sensitive.

chatoyant, e [ʃatwajɑ̃, -ɑ̃t] *adj* (*reflet, étoffe*) shimmering; (*couleurs*) sparkling.

chatoyer [ʃatwaje] *vi* to shimmer.

châtrer [ʃatʀe] *vt* (*mâle*) to castrate; (*femelle*) to spay; (*cheval*) to geld; (*chat, chien*) to doctor (*BRIT*), fix (*US*); (*fig*) to mutilate.

chatte [ʃat] *nf* (she-)cat.

chatterton [ʃatɛʀtɔn] *nm* (*ruban isolant*: *ÉLEC*) (adhesive) insulating tape.

chaud, e [ʃo, -od] *adj* (*gén*) warm; (*très chaud*) hot; (*fig: félicitations*) hearty; (*discussion*) heated; **il fait** ~ it's warm; it's hot; **manger** ~ to have something hot to eat; **avoir** ~ to be warm; to be hot; **tenir** ~ to keep hot; **ça me tient** ~ it keeps me warm; **tenir au** ~ to keep in a warm place; **rester au** ~ to stay in the warm.

chaudement [ʃodmɑ̃] *adv* warmly; (*fig*) hotly.

chaudière [ʃodjɛʀ] *nf* boiler.

chaudron [ʃodʀɔ̃] *nm* cauldron.

chaudronnerie [ʃodʀɔnʀi] *nf* (*usine*) boilerworks; (*activité*) boilermaking; (*boutique*) coppersmith's workshop.

chauffage [ʃofaʒ] *nm* heating; ~ **au gaz/à l'électricité/au charbon** gas/electric/solid fuel heating; ~ **central** central heating; ~ **par le sol** underfloor heating.

chauffagiste [ʃofaʒist(ə)] *nm* (*installateur*) heating engineer.

chauffant, e [ʃofɑ̃, -ɑ̃t]: **couverture** ~**e** electric blanket; **plaque** ~**e** hotplate.

chauffard [ʃofaʀ] *nm* (*péj*) reckless driver; roadhog; (*après un accident*) hit-and-run driver.

chauffe-bain [ʃofbɛ̃] *nm* = **chauffe-eau.**

chauffe-biberon [ʃofbibʀɔ̃] *nm* (baby's) bottle warmer.

chauffe-eau [ʃofo] *nm inv* water heater.

chauffe-plats [ʃofpla] *nm inv* dish warmer.

chauffer [ʃofe] *vt* to heat ♦ *vi* to heat up, warm up; (*trop chauffer: moteur*) to overheat; **se** ~ (*se mettre en train*) to warm up; (*au soleil*) to warm o.s.

chaufferie [ʃofʀi] *nf* boiler room.

chauffeur [ʃofœʀ] *nm* driver; (*privé*) chauffeur; **voiture avec/sans** ~ chauffeur-driven/self-drive car.

chauffeuse [ʃoføz] *nf* fireside chair.

chauler [ʃole] *vt* (*mur*) to whitewash.

chaume [ʃom] *nm* (*du toit*) thatch; (*tiges*) stubble.

chaumière [ʃomjɛʀ] *nf* (thatched) cottage.

chaussée [ʃose] *nf* road(way); (*digue*) causeway.

chausse-pied [ʃospje] *nm* shoe-horn.

chausser [ʃose] *vt* (*bottes, skis*) to put on; (*enfant*) to put shoes on; (*suj: soulier*) to fit; ~ **du 38/42** to take size 38/42; ~ **grand/bien** to be big-/well-fitting; **se** ~ to put one's shoes on.

chausse-trappe [ʃostʀap] *nf* trap.

chaussette [ʃosɛt] *nf* sock.

chausseur [ʃosœʀ] *nm* (*marchand*) footwear specialist, shoemaker.

chausson [ʃosɔ̃] *nm* slipper; (*de bébé*) bootee; ~ **(aux pommes)** (apple) turnover.

chaussure [ʃosyʀ] *nf* shoe; (*commerce*): **la** ~ the shoe industry *ou* trade; ~**s basses** flat shoes; ~**s montantes** ankle boots; ~**s de ski** ski boots.

chaut [ʃo] *vb*: **peu me** ~ it matters little to me.

chauve [ʃov] *adj* bald.

chauve-souris, *pl* chauves-souris [ʃovsuʀi] *nf* bat.

chauvin, e [ʃovɛ̃, -in] *adj* chauvinistic; jingoistic.

chauvinisme [ʃovinism(ə)] *nm* chauvinism; jingoism.

chaux [ʃo] *nf* lime; **blanchi à la** ~ whitewashed.

chavirer [ʃaviʀe] *vi* to capsize, overturn.

chef [ʃɛf] *nm* head, leader; (*patron*) boss; (*de cuisine*) chef; **au premier** ~ extremely, to the nth degree; **de son propre** ~ on his *ou* her own initiative; **général/commandant en** ~ general-/commander-in-chief; ~ **d'accusation** (*JUR*) charge, count (of indictment); ~ **d'atelier** (shop) foreman; ~ **de bureau** head clerk; ~ **de clinique** senior hospital lecturer; ~ **d'entreprise** company head; ~ **d'équipe** team leader; ~ **d'état** head of state; ~ **de famille** head of the family; ~ **de file** (*de parti etc*) leader; ~ **de gare** station master; ~ **d'orchestre** conductor (*BRIT*), leader (*US*); ~ **de rayon** department(al) supervisor; ~ **de service** departmental head.

chef-d'œuvre, *pl* **chefs-d'œuvre** [ʃɛdœvʀ(ə)] *nm* masterpiece.

chef-lieu, *pl* **chefs-lieux** [ʃɛfljø] *nm* county town.

cheftaine [ʃɛftɛn] *nf* (guide) captain.

cheik(h) [ʃɛk] *nm* sheik.

chemin [ʃəmɛ̃] *nm* path; (*itinéraire, direction, trajet*) way; **en** ~, ~ **faisant** on the way; ~ **de fer** railway (*BRIT*), railroad (*US*); **par** ~ **de fer** by rail; **les** ~**s de fer** the railways (*BRIT*), the railroad (*US*); ~ **de terre** dirt track.

cheminée [ʃəmine] *nf* chimney; (*à l'intérieur*) chimney piece, fireplace; (*de bateau*) funnel.

cheminement [ʃəminmɑ̃] *nm* progress; course.

cheminer [ʃəmine] *vi* to walk (along).

cheminot [ʃəmino] *nm* railwayman (*BRIT*), railroad worker (*US*).

chemise [ʃəmiz] *nf* shirt; (*dossier*) folder; ~ **de nuit** nightdress.

chemiserie [ʃəmizʀi] *nf* (gentlemen's) outfitters'.

chemisette [ʃəmizɛt] *nf* short-sleeved shirt.

chemisier [ʃəmizje] *nm* blouse.

chenal, aux [ʃənal, -o] *nm* channel.

chenapan [ʃənapɑ̃] *nm* (*garnement*) rascal; (*péj: vaurien*) rogue.

chêne [ʃɛn] *nm* oak (tree); (*bois*) oak.

chenet [ʃənɛ] *nm* fire-dog, andiron.

chenil [ʃənil] *nm* kennels *pl*.

chenille [ʃənij] *nf* (*ZOOL*) caterpillar; (*AUTO*) caterpillar track; **véhicule à** ~**s** tracked vehicle, caterpillar.

chenillette [ʃənijɛt] *nf* tracked vehicle.

cheptel [ʃɛptɛl] *nm* livestock.

chèque [ʃɛk] *nm* cheque (*BRIT*), check (*US*); **faire/toucher un** ~ to write/cash a cheque; **par** ~ by cheque; ~ **barré/sans provision** crossed (*BRIT*)/bad cheque; ~ **en blanc** blank cheque; ~ **au porteur** cheque to bearer; ~ **postal** post office cheque, ≈ giro cheque (*BRIT*); ~ **de voyage** traveller's cheque.

chèque-cadeau, *pl* **chèques-cadeaux** [ʃɛkkado] *nm* gift token.

chèque-repas, *pl* **chèques-repas** [ʃɛkʀəpɑ], **chèque-restaurant,** *pl* **chèques-restaurant** [ʃɛkʀɛstɔʀɑ̃] *nm* ≈ luncheon voucher.

chéquier [ʃekje] *nm* cheque book (*BRIT*), checkbook (*US*).

cher, ère [ʃɛʀ] *adj* (*aimé*) dear; (*coûteux*) expensive, dear ♦ *adv*: **coûter/payer** ~ to cost/pay a lot ♦ *nf*: **la bonne chère** good food; **cela coûte** ~ it's expensive, it costs a lot of

money; **mon** ~, **ma chère** my dear.

chercher [ʃɛʀʃe] *vt* to look for; (*gloire etc*) to seek; (*INFORM*) to search; ~ **des ennuis/la bagarre** to be looking for trouble/a fight; **aller** ~ to go for, go and fetch; ~ **à faire** to try to do.

chercheur, euse [ʃɛʀʃœʀ, -øz] *nm/f* researcher, research worker; ~ **de** seeker of; hunter of; ~ **d'or** gold digger.

chère [ʃɛʀ] *adj f, nf voir* **cher.**

chèrement [ʃɛʀmɑ̃] *adv* dearly.

chéri, e [ʃeʀi] *adj* beloved, dear; **(mon)** ~ darling.

chérir [ʃeʀiʀ] *vt* to cherish.

cherté [ʃɛʀte] *nf*: **la** ~ **de la vie** the high cost of living.

chérubin [ʃeʀybɛ̃] *nm* cherub.

chétif, ive [ʃetif, -iv] *adj* puny, stunted.

cheval, aux [ʃəval, -o] *nm* horse; (*AUTO*): ~ **(vapeur) (CV)** horsepower *no pl*; **50 chevaux (au frein)** 50 brake horsepower, 50 b.h.p.; **10 chevaux (fiscaux)** 10 horsepower (*for tax purposes*); **faire du** ~ to ride; **à** ~ on horseback; **à** ~ **sur** astride, straddling; (*fig*) overlapping; ~ **d'arçons** vaulting horse; ~ **à bascule** rocking horse; ~ **de bataille** charger; (*fig*) hobby-horse; ~ **de course** race horse; **chevaux de bois** (*des manèges*) wooden (fairground) horses; (*manège*) merry-go-round.

chevaleresque [ʃəvalʀɛsk(ə)] *adj* chivalrous.

chevalerie [ʃəvalʀi] *nf* chivalry; knighthood.

chevalet [ʃəvalɛ] *nm* easel.

chevalier [ʃəvalje] *nm* knight; ~ **servant** escort.

chevalière [ʃəvaljɛʀ] *nf* signet ring.

chevalin, e [ʃəvalɛ̃, -in] *adj* of horses, equine; (*péj*) horsy; **boucherie** ~**e** horse-meat butcher's.

cheval-vapeur, *pl* **chevaux-vapeur** [ʃəvalvapœʀ, ʃəvo-] *nm voir* **cheval.**

chevauchée [ʃəvoʃe] *nf* ride; cavalcade.

chevauchement [ʃəvoʃmɑ̃] *nm* overlap.

chevaucher [ʃəvoʃe] *vi* (*aussi:* **se** ~) to overlap (each other) ♦ *vt* to be astride, straddle.

chevaux [ʃəvo] *nmpl voir* **cheval.**

chevelu, e [ʃəvly] *adj* with a good head of hair, hairy (*péj*).

chevelure [ʃəvlyʀ] *nf* hair *no pl*.

chevet [ʃəvɛ] *nm*: **au** ~ **de qn** at sb's bedside; **lampe de** ~ bedside lamp.

cheveu, x [ʃəvø] *nm* hair ♦ *nmpl* (*chevelure*) hair *sg*; **avoir les** ~**x courts/en brosse** to have short hair/a crew cut; **se faire couper les** ~**x** to get *ou* have one's hair cut; **tiré par les** ~**x** (*histoire*) far-fetched.

cheville [ʃəvij] *nf* (*ANAT*) ankle; (*de bois*) peg; (*pour enfoncer une vis*) plug; **être en** ~ **avec qn** to be in cahoots with sb; ~ **ouvrière** (*fig*) kingpin.

chèvre [ʃɛvʀ(ə)] *nf* (she-)goat; **ménager la** ~ **et**

le chou to try to please everyone.
chevreau, x [ʃəvʀo] *nm* kid.
chèvrefeuille [ʃɛvʀəfœj] *nm* honeysuckle.
chevreuil [ʃəvʀœj] *nm* roe deer *inv*; (*CULIN*) venison.
chevron [ʃəvʀɔ̃] *nm* (*poutre*) rafter; (*motif*) chevron, v(-shape); **à ~s** chevron-patterned; (*petits*) herringbone.
chevronné, e [ʃəvʀɔne] *adj* seasoned, experienced.
chevrotant, e [ʃəvʀɔtɑ̃, -ɑ̃t] *adj* quavering.
chevroter [ʃəvʀɔte] *vi* (*personne, voix*) to quaver.
chevrotine [ʃəvʀɔtin] *nf* buckshot *no pl*.
chewing-gum [ʃwiŋɡɔm] *nm* chewing gum.

═══════════════════════════ *MOT-CLÉ*

chez [ʃe] *prép* **1** (*à la demeure de*) at; (: *direction*) to; **~ qn** at/to sb's house *ou* place; **~ moi** at home; (*direction*) home **2** (*à l'entreprise de*): **il travaille ~ Renault** he works for Renault, he works at Renault('s) **3** (+*profession*) at; (: *direction*) to; **~ le boulanger/dentiste** at *ou* to the baker's/dentist's **4** (*dans le caractère, l'œuvre de*) in; **~ les renards/Racine** in foxes/Racine; **~ les Français** among the French; **~ lui, c'est un devoir** for him, it's a duty
♦ *nm inv*: **mon ~ moi/ton ~ toi** *etc* my/your *etc* home *ou* place.

chez-soi [ʃeswa] *nm inv* home.
Chf. cent. *abr* (= *chauffage central*) c.h.
chiadé, e [ʃjade] *adj* (*fam*: *fignolé, soigné*) wicked.
chialer [ʃjale] *vi* (*fam*) to blubber; **arrête de ~!** stop blubbering!
chiant, e [ʃjɑ̃, -ɑ̃t] *adj* (*fam!*) bloody annoying (*BRIT*), damn annoying (*US*); **qu'est-ce qu'il est ~!** he's such a bloody pain! (*!*).
chic [ʃik] *adj inv* chic, smart; (*généreux*) nice, decent ♦ *nm* stylishness; **avoir le ~ de** *ou* **pour** to have the knack of *ou* for; **de ~** *adv* off the cuff; **~!** great!, terrific!
chicane [ʃikan] *nf* (*obstacle*) zigzag; (*querelle*) squabble.
chicaner [ʃikane] *vi* (*ergoter*): **~ sur** to quibble about.
chiche [ʃiʃ] *adj* (*mesquin*) niggardly, mean; (*pauvre*) meagre (*BRIT*), meager (*US*) ♦ *excl* (*en réponse à un défi*) you're on!; **tu n'es pas ~ de lui parler!** you wouldn't (dare) speak to her!
chichement [ʃiʃmɑ̃] *adv* (*pauvrement*) meagrely (*BRIT*), meagerly (*US*); (*mesquinement*) meanly.
chichi [ʃiʃi] *nm* (*fam*) fuss; **faire des ~s** to make a fuss.
chicorée [ʃikɔʀe] *nf* (*café*) chicory; (*salade*) endive; **~ frisée** curly endive.
chicot [ʃiko] *nm* stump.
chien [ʃjɛ̃] *nm* dog; (*de pistolet*) hammer;

temps de ~ rotten weather; **vie de ~** dog's life; **couché en ~ de fusil** curled up; **~ d'aveugle** guide dog; **~ de chasse** gun dog; **~ de garde** guard dog; **~ policier** police dog; **~ de race** pedigree dog; **~ de traîneau** husky.
chiendent [ʃjɛ̃dɑ̃] *nm* couch grass.
chien-loup, *pl* **chiens-loups** [ʃjɛ̃lu] *nm* wolfhound.
chienne [ʃjɛn] *nf* (she-)dog, bitch.
chier [ʃje] *vi* (*fam!*) to crap (*!*), shit (*!*); **faire ~ qn** (*importuner*) to bug sb; (*causer des ennuis à*) to piss sb around (*!*); **se faire ~** (*s'ennuyer*) to be bored rigid.
chiffe [ʃif] *nf*: **il est mou comme une ~, c'est une ~ molle** he's spineless *ou* wet.
chiffon [ʃifɔ̃] *nm* (piece of) rag.
chiffonné, e [ʃifɔne] *adj* (*fatigué: visage*) worn-looking.
chiffonner [ʃifɔne] *vt* to crumple, crease; (*tracasser*) to concern.
chiffonnier [ʃifɔnje] *nm* ragman, rag-and-bone man; (*meuble*) chiffonier.
chiffrable [ʃifʀabl(ə)] *adj* numerable.
chiffre [ʃifʀ(ə)] *nm* (*représentant un nombre*) figure; numeral; (*montant, total*) total, sum; (*d'un code*) code, cipher; **~s romains/arabes** roman/arabic figures *ou* numerals; **en ~s ronds** in round figures; **écrire un nombre en ~s** to write a number in figures; **~ d'affaires** (*CA*) turnover; **~ de ventes** sales figures.
chiffrer [ʃifʀe] *vt* (*dépense*) to put a figure to, assess; (*message*) to (en)code, cipher ♦ *vi*: **~ à, se ~ à** to add up to.
chignole [ʃiɲɔl] *nf* drill.
chignon [ʃiɲɔ̃] *nm* chignon, bun.
chiite [ʃiit] *adj* Shiite ♦ *nm/f*: **C~** Shiite.
Chili [ʃili] *nm*: **le ~** Chile.
chilien, ne [ʃiljɛ̃, -ɛn] *adj* Chilean ♦ *nm/f*: **C~, ne** Chilean.
chimère [ʃimɛʀ] *nf* (wild) dream; pipe dream, idle fancy.
chimérique [ʃimeʀik] *adj* (*utopique*) fanciful.
chimie [ʃimi] *nf* chemistry.
chimio [ʃimjo], **chimiothérapie** [ʃimjoteʀapi] *nf* chemotherapy.
chimique [ʃimik] *adj* chemical; **produits ~s** chemicals.
chimiste [ʃimist(ə)] *nm/f* chemist.
chimpanzé [ʃɛ̃pɑ̃ze] *nm* chimpanzee.
chinchilla [ʃɛ̃ʃila] *nm* chinchilla.
Chine [ʃin] *nf*: **la ~** China; **la ~ libre, la république de ~** the Republic of China, Nationalist China (*Taiwan*).
chine [ʃin] *nm* rice paper; (*porcelaine*) china (vase).
chiné, e [ʃine] *adj* flecked.
chinois, e [ʃinwa, -waz] *adj* Chinese; (*fig: péj*) pernickety, fussy ♦ *nm* (*LING*) Chinese ♦ *nm/f*: **C~, e** Chinese.
chinoiserie(s) [ʃinwazʀi] *nf(pl)* (*péj*) red tape, fuss.

chiot [ʃjo] *nm* pup(py).
chiper [ʃipe] *vt* (*fam*) to pinch.
chipie [ʃipi] *nf* shrew.
chipolata [ʃipɔlata] *nf* chipolata.
chipoter [ʃipɔte] *vi* (*manger*) to nibble; (*ergoter*) to quibble, haggle.
chips [ʃips] *nfpl* (*aussi*: **pommes ~**) crisps (*BRIT*), (potato) chips (*US*).
chique [ʃik] *nf* quid, chew.
chiquenaude [ʃiknod] *nf* flick, flip.
chiquer [ʃike] *vi* to chew tobacco.
chiromancie [kirɔmɑ̃si] *nf* palmistry.
chiromancien, ne [kirɔmɑ̃sjɛ̃, -ɛn] *nm/f* palmist.
chiropracteur [kirɔpraktœr] *nm*,
chiropraticien, ne [kirɔpratisjɛ̃, -ɛn] *nm/f* chiropractor.
chirurgical, e, aux [ʃiryrʒikal, -o] *adj* surgical.
chirurgie [ʃiryrʒi] *nf* surgery; **~ esthétique** cosmetic *ou* plastic surgery.
chirurgien [ʃiryrʒjɛ̃] *nm* surgeon; **~ dentiste** dental surgeon.
chiure [ʃjyr] *nf*: **~s de mouche** fly specks.
ch.-l. *abr* = **chef-lieu**.
chlore [klɔr] *nm* chlorine.
chloroforme [klɔrɔfɔrm(ə)] *nm* chloroform.
chlorophylle [klɔrɔfil] *nf* chlorophyll.
chlorure [klɔryr] *nm* chloride.
choc [ʃɔk] *nm* impact; shock; crash; (*moral*) shock; (*affrontement*) clash ♦ *adj*: **prix ~** amazing *ou* incredible price/prices; **de ~** (*troupe, traitement*) shock *cpd*; (*patron etc*) high-powered; **~ opératoire/nerveux** post-operative/nervous shock; **~ en retour** return shock; (*fig*) backlash.
chocolat [ʃɔkɔla] *nm* chocolate; (*boisson*) (hot) chocolate; **~ à cuire** cooking chocolate; **~ au lait** milk chocolate; **~ en poudre** drinking chocolate.
chocolaté, e [ʃɔkɔlate] *adj* chocolate *cpd*, chocolate-flavoured.
chocolaterie [ʃɔkɔlatri] *nf* (*fabrique*) chocolate factory.
chocolatier, ière [ʃɔkɔlatje, -jɛr] *nm/f* chocolate maker.
chœur [kœr] *nm* (*chorale*) choir; (*OPÉRA, THÉÂT*) chorus; (*ARCHIT*) choir, chancel; **en ~** in chorus.
choir [ʃwar] *vi* to fall.
choisi, e [ʃwazi] *adj* (*de premier choix*) carefully chosen; select; **textes ~s** selected writings.
choisir [ʃwazir] *vt* to choose; (*entre plusieurs*) to choose, select; **~ de faire qch** to choose *ou* opt to do sth.
choix [ʃwa] *nm* choice; selection; **avoir le ~** to have the choice; **je n'avais pas le ~** I had no choice; **de premier ~** (*COMM*) class *ou* grade one; **de ~** choice *cpd*, selected; **au ~** as you wish *ou* prefer; **de mon/son ~** of my/his *ou* her choosing.

choléra [kɔlera] *nm* cholera.
cholestérol [kɔlɛsterɔl] *nm* cholesterol.
chômage [ʃomaʒ] *nm* unemployment; **mettre au ~** to make redundant, put out of work; **être au ~** to be unemployed *ou* out of work; **~ partiel** short-time working; **~ structurel** structural unemployment; **~ technique** lay-offs *pl*.
chômer [ʃome] *vi* to be unemployed, be idle; **jour chômé** public holiday.
chômeur, euse [ʃomœr, -øz] *nm/f* unemployed person, person out of work.
chope [ʃɔp] *nf* tankard.
choquant, e [ʃɔkɑ̃, -ɑ̃t] *adj* shocking.
choquer [ʃɔke] *vt* (*offenser*) to shock; (*commotionner*) to shake (up).
choral, e [kɔral] *adj* choral ♦ *nf* choral society, choir.
chorégraphe [kɔregraf] *nm/f* choreographer.
chorégraphie [kɔregrafi] *nf* choreography.
choriste [kɔrist(ə)] *nm/f* choir member; (*OPÉRA*) chorus member.
chorus [kɔrys] *nm*: **faire ~** (**avec**) to voice one's agreement (with).
chose [ʃoz] *nf* thing ♦ *nm* (*fam*: *machin*) thingamajig ♦ *adj inv*: **être/se sentir tout ~** (*bizarre*) to be/feel a bit odd; (*malade*) to feel out of sorts; **dire bien des ~s à qn** to give sb's regards to sb; **parler de ~(s) et d'autre(s)** to talk about one thing and another; **c'est peu de ~** it's nothing much.
chou, x [ʃu] *nm* cabbage ♦ *adj inv* cute; **mon petit ~** (my) sweetheart; **faire ~ blanc** to draw a blank; **feuille de ~** (*fig*: *journal*) rag; **~ à la crème** cream bun (*made of choux pastry*); **~ de Bruxelles** Brussels sprout.
choucas [ʃuka] *nm* jackdaw.
chouchou, te [ʃuʃu, -ut] *nm/f* (*SCOL*) teacher's pet.
chouchouter [ʃuʃute] *vt* to pet.
choucroute [ʃukrut] *nf* sauerkraut; **~ garnie** sauerkraut with cooked meats and potatoes.
chouette [ʃwɛt] *nf* owl ♦ *adj* (*fam*) great, smashing.
chou-fleur, *pl* **choux-fleurs** [ʃuflœr] *nm* cauliflower.
chou-rave, *pl* **choux-raves** [ʃurav] *nm* kohlrabi.
choyer [ʃwaje] *vt* to cherish; to pamper.
CHR *sigle m* = **Centre hospitalier régional**.
chrétien, ne [kretjɛ̃, -ɛn] *adj*, *nm/f* Christian.
chrétiennement [kretjɛnmɑ̃] *adv* in a Christian way *ou* spirit.
chrétienté [kretjɛ̃te] *nf* Christendom.
Christ [krist] *nm*: **le ~** Christ; **c~** (*crucifix etc*) figure of Christ; **Jésus ~** Jesus Christ.
christianiser [kristjanize] *vt* to convert to Christianity.
christianisme [kristjanism(ə)] *nm* Christianity.

Christmas [kʀistmas] *nf:* (l'île) ~ Christmas Island.
chromatique [kʀɔmatik] *adj* chromatic.
chrome [kʀom] *nm* chromium; (*revêtement*) chrome, chromium.
chromé, e [kʀome] *adj* chrome-plated, chromium-plated.
chromosome [kʀɔmozom] *nm* chromosome.
chronique [kʀɔnik] *adj* chronic ♦ *nf* (*de journal*) column, page; (*historique*) chronicle; (*RADIO, TV*): **la ~ sportive/théâtrale** the sports/theatre review; **la ~ locale** local news and gossip.
chroniqueur [kʀɔnikœʀ] *nm* columnist; chronicler.
chrono [kʀɔno] *nm* (*fam*) = **chronomètre.**
chronologie [kʀɔnɔlɔʒi] *nf* chronology.
chronologique [kʀɔnɔlɔʒik] *adj* chronological.
chronologiquement [kʀɔnɔlɔʒikmã] *adv* chronologically.
chronomètre [kʀɔnɔmɛtʀ(ə)] *nm* stopwatch.
chronométrer [kʀɔnɔmetʀe] *vt* to time.
chronométreur [kʀɔnɔmetʀœʀ] *nm* timekeeper.
chrysalide [kʀizalid] *nf* chrysalis.
chrysanthème [kʀizãtɛm] *nm* chrysanthemum.
CHU *sigle m* (= *Centre hospitalo-universitaire*) ≈ (teaching) hospital.
chu, e [ʃy] *pp de* **choir.**
chuchotement [ʃyʃɔtmã] *nm* whisper.
chuchoter [ʃyʃɔte] *vt, vi* to whisper.
chuintement [ʃɥɛ̃tmã] *nm* hiss.
chuinter [ʃɥɛ̃te] *vi* to hiss.
chut *excl* [ʃyt] sh! ♦ *vb* [ʃy] *voir* **choir.**
chute [ʃyt] *nf* fall; (*de bois, papier: déchet*) scrap; **la ~ des cheveux** hair loss; **faire une ~ (de 10 m)** to fall (10 m); **~s de pluie/neige** rain/snowfalls; **~ (d'eau)** waterfall; **~ du jour** nightfall; **~ libre** free fall; **~ des reins** small of the back.
Chypre [ʃipʀ] *nm:* **le ~** Cyprus.
chypriote [ʃipʀiɔt] *adj, nmf* = **cypriote.**
-ci, ci- [si] *adv voir* **par, ci-contre, ci-joint** *etc* ♦ *dét:* **ce garçon-ci/-là** this/that boy; **ces femmes-ci/-là** these/those women.
CIA *sigle f* CIA.
cial *abr* = **commercial.**
ciao [tʃao] *excl* (*fam*) (bye-)bye.
ci-après [siapʀe] *adv* hereafter.
cibiste [sibist(ə)] *nm* CB enthusiast.
cible [sibl(ə)] *nf* target.
cibler [sible] *vt* to target.
ciboire [sibwaʀ] *nm* ciborium (*vessel*).
ciboule [sibul] *nf* (large) chive.
ciboulette [sibulɛt] *nf* (small) chive.
ciboulot [sibulo] *nm* (*fam*) head, nut; **il n'a rien dans le ~** he's got nothing between his ears.
cicatrice [sikatʀis] *nf* scar.
cicatriser [sikatʀize] *vt* to heal; **se ~** to heal (up), form a scar.

ci-contre [sikɔ̃tʀ(ə)] *adv* opposite.
CICR *sigle m* (= *Comité international de la Croix-Rouge*) ICRC.
ci-dessous [sidəsu] *adv* below.
ci-dessus [sidəsy] *adv* above.
ci-devant [sidəvã] *nmf inv* aristocrat who lost his/her title in the French Revolution.
CIDEX *sigle m* (= *Courrier individuel à distribution exceptionnelle*) system which groups letter boxes in country areas, rather than each house having its letter box at its front door.
CIDJ *sigle m* (= *Centre d'information et de documentation de la jeunesse*) careers advisory service.
cidre [sidʀ(ə)] *nm* cider.
cidrerie [sidʀəʀi] *nf* cider factory.
CIDUNATI [sidynati] *sigle m* (= *Comité interprofessionnel de défense de l'union nationale des artisans et travailleurs indépendants*) union of self-employed craftsmen.
Cie *abr* (= *compagnie*) Co.
ciel [sjɛl] *nm* sky; (*REL*) heaven; **~s** *nmpl* (*PEINTURE etc*) skies; **cieux** *nmpl* sky *sg*, skies; (*REL*) heaven *sg*; **à ~ ouvert** open-air; (*mine*) opencast; **tomber du ~** (*arriver à l'improviste*) to appear out of the blue; (*être stupéfait*) to be unable to believe one's eyes; **C~!** good heavens!; **~ de lit** canopy.
cierge [sjɛʀʒ(ə)] *nm* candle; **~ pascal** Easter candle.
cieux [sjø] *nmpl voir* **ciel.**
cigale [sigal] *nf* cicada.
cigare [sigaʀ] *nm* cigar.
cigarette [sigaʀɛt] *nf* cigarette; **~ (à) bout filtre** filter cigarette.
ci-gît [siʒi] *adv* here lies.
cigogne [sigɔɲ] *nf* stork.
ciguë [sigy] *nf* hemlock.
ci-inclus, e [siɛ̃kly, -yz] *adj, adv* enclosed.
ci-joint, e [siʒwɛ̃, -ɛ̃t] *adj, adv* enclosed; **veuillez trouver ~** please find enclosed.
cil [sil] *nm* (eye)lash.
ciller [sije] *vi* to blink.
cimaise [simɛz] *nf* picture rail.
cime [sim] *nf* top; (*montagne*) peak.
ciment [simã] *nm* cement; **~ armé** reinforced concrete.
cimenter [simãte] *vt* to cement.
cimenterie [simãtʀi] *nf* cement works *sg*.
cimetière [simtjɛʀ] *nm* cemetery; (*d'église*) churchyard; **~ de voitures** scrapyard.
cinéaste [sineast(ə)] *nmf* film-maker.
ciné-club [sineklœb] *nm* film club; film society.
cinéma [sinema] *nm* cinema; **aller au ~** to go to the cinema *ou* pictures *ou* movies; **~ d'animation** cartoon (film).
cinémascope [sinemaskɔp] *nm* ® Cinemascope ®.
cinémathèque [sinematɛk] *nf* film archives *pl ou* library.

cinématographie [sinematɔgʀafi] *nf* cinematography.

cinématographique [sinematɔgʀafik] *adj* film *cpd*, cinema *cpd*.

cinéphile [sinefil] *nm/f* film buff.

cinérama [sineʀama] *nm* ®: **en** ~ in Cinerama ®.

cinétique [sinetik] *adj* kinetic.

cing(h)alais, e [sɛ̃galɛ, -ɛz] *adj* Sin(g)halese.

cinglant, e [sɛ̃glɑ̃, -ɑ̃t] *adj (propos, ironie)* scathing, biting; *(échec)* crushing.

cinglé, e [sɛ̃gle] *adj (fam)* crazy.

cingler [sɛ̃gle] *vt* to lash; *(fig)* to sting ♦ *vi (NAVIG)*: ~ **vers** to make *ou* head for.

cinq [sɛ̃k] *num* five.

cinquantaine [sɛ̃kɑ̃tɛn] *nf*: **une** ~ **(de)** about fifty; **avoir la** ~ *(âge)* to be around fifty.

cinquante [sɛ̃kɑ̃t] *num* fifty.

cinquantenaire [sɛ̃kɑ̃tnɛʀ] *adj, nm/f* fifty-year-old.

cinquantième [sɛ̃kɑ̃tjɛm] *num* fiftieth.

cinquième [sɛ̃kjɛm] *num* fifth.

cinquièmement [sɛ̃kjɛmmɑ̃] *adv* fifthly.

cintre [sɛ̃tʀ(ə)] *nm* coat-hanger; *(ARCHIT)* arch; **plein** ~ semicircular arch.

cintré, e [sɛ̃tʀe] *adj* curved; *(chemise)* fitted, slim-fitting.

CIO *sigle m (= Comité international olympique)* IOC *(= International Olympic Committee)*.

cirage [siʀaʒ] *nm (shoe)* polish.

circoncis, e [siʀkɔ̃si, -iz] *adj* circumcized.

circoncision [siʀkɔ̃sizjɔ̃] *nf* circumcision.

circonférence [siʀkɔ̃feʀɑ̃s] *nf* circumference.

circonflexe [siʀkɔ̃flɛks(ə)] *adj*: **accent** ~ circumflex accent.

circonlocution [siʀkɔ̃lɔkysjɔ̃] *nf* circumlocution.

circonscription [siʀkɔ̃skʀipsjɔ̃] *nf* district; ~ **électorale** *(d'un député)* constituency; ~ **militaire** military area.

circonscrire [siʀkɔ̃skʀiʀ] *vt* to define, delimit; *(incendie)* to contain; *(propriété)* to mark out; *(sujet)* to define.

circonspect, e [siʀkɔ̃spɛkt] *adj* circumspect, cautious.

circonspection [siʀkɔ̃spɛksjɔ̃] *nf* circumspection, caution.

circonstance [siʀkɔ̃stɑ̃s] *nf* circumstance; *(occasion)* occasion; **œuvre de** ~ occasional work; **air de** ~ fitting air; **tête de** ~ appropriate demeanour *(BRIT)* ou demeanor *(US)*; ~**s atténuantes** mitigating circumstances.

circonstancié, e [siʀkɔ̃stɑ̃sje] *adj* detailed.

circonstanciel, le [siʀkɔ̃stɑ̃sjɛl] *adj*: **complément/proposition** ~**(le)** adverbial phrase/clause.

circonvenir [siʀkɔ̃vniʀ] *vt* to circumvent.

circonvolutions [siʀkɔ̃vɔlysjɔ̃] *nfpl* twists, convolutions.

circuit [siʀkɥi] *nm (trajet)* tour, (round) trip; *(ÉLEC, TECH)* circuit; ~ **automobile** motor circuit; ~ **de distribution** distribution network; ~ **fermé** closed circuit; ~ **intégré** integrated circuit.

circulaire [siʀkylɛʀ] *adj, nf* circular.

circulation [siʀkylɑsjɔ̃] *nf* circulation; *(AUTO)*: **la** ~ (the) traffic; **bonne/mauvaise** ~ good/ bad circulation; **mettre en** ~ to put into circulation.

circulatoire [siʀkylatwaʀ] *adj*: **avoir des troubles** ~**s** to have problems with one's circulation.

circuler [siʀkyle] *vi* to drive (along); to walk along; *(train etc)* to run; *(sang, devises)* to circulate; **faire** ~ *(nouvelle)* to spread (about), circulate; *(badauds)* to move on.

cire [siʀ] *nf* wax; ~ **à cacheter** sealing wax.

ciré [siʀe] *nm* oilskin.

cirer [siʀe] *vt* to wax, polish.

cireur [siʀœʀ] *nm* shoeshine-boy.

cireuse [siʀøz] *nf* floor polisher.

cireux, euse [siʀø, -øz] *adj (fig: teint)* sallow, waxen.

cirque [siʀk(ə)] *nm* circus; *(arène)* amphitheatre *(BRIT)*, amphitheater *(US)*; *(GÉO)* cirque; *(fig: désordre)* chaos, bedlam; *(: chichis)* carry-on.

cirrhose [siʀoz] *nf*: ~ **du foie** cirrhosis of the liver.

cisailler [sizaje] *vt* to clip.

cisaille(s) [sizaj] *nf(pl)* (gardening) shears *pl*.

ciseau, x [sizo] *nm*: ~ **(à bois)** chisel ♦ *nmpl* (pair of) scissors; **sauter en** ~**x** to do a scissors jump; ~ **à froid** cold chisel.

ciseler [sizle] *vt* to chisel, carve.

ciselure [sizlyʀ] *nf* engraving; *(bois)* carving.

Cisjordanie [sisʒɔʀdani] *nf*: **la** ~ the West Bank (of Jordan).

citadelle [sitadɛl] *nf* citadel.

citadin, e [sitadɛ̃, -in] *nm/f* city dweller ♦ *adj* town *cpd*, city *cpd*, urban.

citation [sitɑsjɔ̃] *nf (d'auteur)* quotation; *(JUR)* summons *sg*; *(MIL: récompense)* mention.

cité [site] *nf* town; *(plus grande)* city; ~ **ouvrière** (workers') housing estate; ~ **universitaire** students' residences *pl*.

cité-dortoir, *pl* **cités-dortoirs** [sitedɔʀtwaʀ] *nf* dormitory town.

cité-jardin, *pl* **cités-jardins** [siteʒaʀdɛ̃] *nf* garden city.

citer [site] *vt (un auteur)* to quote (from); *(nommer)* to name; *(JUR)* to summon; ~ **(en exemple)** *(personne)* to hold up (as an example); **je ne veux** ~ **personne** I don't want to name names.

citerne [sitɛʀn(ə)] *nf* tank.

cithare [sitaʀ] *nf* zither.

citoyen, ne [sitwajɛ̃, -ɛn] *nm/f* citizen.

citoyenneté [sitwajɛnte] *nf* citizenship.

citrique [sitʀik] *adj*: **acide** ~ citric acid.

citron [sitʀɔ̃] *nm* lemon; ~ **pressé** (fresh) lemon juice; ~ **vert** lime.

citronnade [sitʀɔnad] *nf* lemonade.

citronné, e [sitʀɔne] *adj* (*boisson*) lemon-flavoured (*BRIT*) *ou* -flavored (*US*); (*eau de toilette*) lemon-scented.
citronnelle [sitʀɔnɛl] *nf* citronella.
citronnier [sitʀɔnje] *nm* lemon tree.
citrouille [sitʀuj] *nf* pumpkin.
cive(s) [siv] *nf(pl)* (*BOT*) chive(s); (*CULIN*) chives.
civet [sivɛ] *nm* stew; ~ **de lièvre** jugged hare.
civette [sivɛt] *nf* (*BOT*) chives *pl*; (*ZOOL*) civet (cat).
civière [sivjɛʀ] *nf* stretcher.
civil, e [sivil] *adj* (*JUR, ADMIN, poli*) civil; (*non militaire*) civilian ♦ *nm* civilian; **en** ~ in civilian clothes; **dans le** ~ in civilian life.
civilement [sivilmɑ̃] *adv* (*poliment*) civilly; **se marier** ~ to have a civil wedding.
civilisation [sivilizasjɔ̃] *nf* civilization.
civilisé, e [sivilize] *adj* civilized.
civiliser [sivilize] *vt* to civilize.
civilité [sivilite] *nf* civility; **présenter ses** ~**s** to present one's compliments.
civique [sivik] *adj* civic; **instruction** ~ (*SCOL*) civics *sg*.
civisme [sivism(ə)] *nm* public-spiritedness.
cl. *abr* (= *centilitre*) cl.
clafoutis [klafuti] *nm* batter pudding (*containing fruit*).
claie [klɛ] *nf* grid, riddle.
clair, e [klɛʀ] *adj* light; (*chambre*) light, bright; (*eau, son, fig*) clear ♦ *adv*: **voir** ~ to see clearly ♦ *nm*: **mettre au** ~ (*notes etc*) to tidy up; **tirer qch au** ~ to clear sth up, clarify sth; **bleu** ~ light blue; **pour être** ~ so as to make it plain; **y voir** ~ (*comprendre*) to understand, see; **le plus** ~ **de son temps/argent** the better part of his time/money; **en** ~ (*non codé*) in clear; ~ **de lune** moonlight.
claire [klɛʀ] *nf*: (**huître de**) ~ fattened oyster.
clairement [klɛʀmɑ̃] *adv* clearly.
claire-voie [klɛʀvwa]: **à** ~ *adj* letting the light through; openwork *cpd*.
clairière [klɛʀjɛʀ] *nf* clearing.
clair-obscur, *pl* **clairs-obscurs** [klɛʀɔpskyʀ] *nm* half-light; (*fig*) uncertainty.
clairon [klɛʀɔ̃] *nm* bugle.
claironner [klɛʀɔne] *vt* (*fig*) to trumpet, shout from the rooftops.
clairsemé, e [klɛʀsəme] *adj* sparse.
clairvoyance [klɛʀvwajɑ̃s] *nf* clear-sightedness.
clairvoyant, e [klɛʀvwajɑ̃, -ɑ̃t] *adj* perceptive, clear-sighted.
clam [klam] *nm* (*ZOOL*) clam.
clamer [klame] *vt* to proclaim.
clameur [klamœʀ] *nf* clamour (*BRIT*), clamor (*US*).
clan [klɑ̃] *nm* clan.
clandestin, e [klɑ̃dɛstɛ̃, -in] *adj* clandestine, covert; (*POL*) underground, clandestine; **passager** ~ stowaway.
clandestinement [klɑ̃dɛstinmɑ̃] *adv* secretly;

s'embarquer ~ to stow away.
clandestinité [klɑ̃dɛstinite] *nf*: **dans la** ~ (*en secret*) under cover; (*en se cachant: vivre*) underground; **entrer dans la** ~ to go underground.
clapet [klapɛ] *nm* (*TECH*) valve.
clapier [klapje] *nm* (*rabbit*) hutch.
clapotement [klapɔtmɑ̃] *nm* lap(ping).
clapoter [klapɔte] *vi* to lap.
clapotis [klapɔti] *nm* lap(ping).
claquage [klakaʒ] *nm* pulled *ou* strained muscle.
claque [klak] *nf* (*gifle*) slap; (*THÉÂT*) claque ♦ *nm* (*chapeau*) opera hat.
claquement [klakmɑ̃] *nm* (*de porte: bruit répété*) banging; (*: bruit isolé*) slam.
claquemurer [klakmyʀe]: **se** ~ *vi* to shut o.s. away, closet o.s.
claquer [klake] *vi* (*drapeau*) to flap; (*porte*) to bang, slam; (*coup de feu*) to ring out ♦ *vt* (*porte*) to slam, bang; (*doigts*) to snap; **elle claquait des dents** her teeth were chattering; **se** ~ **un muscle** to pull *ou* strain a muscle.
claquettes [klakɛt] *nfpl* tap-dancing *sg*.
clarification [klaʀifikasjɔ̃] *nf* (*fig*) clarification.
clarifier [klaʀifje] *vt* (*fig*) to clarify.
clarinette [klaʀinɛt] *nf* clarinet.
clarinettiste [klaʀinetist(ə)] *nm/f* clarinettist.
clarté [klaʀte] *nf* lightness; brightness; (*d'un son, de l'eau*) clearness; (*d'une explication*) clarity.
classe [klɑs] *nf* class; (*SCOL: local*) class(room); (*: leçon*) class; (*: élèves*) class, form; **1ère/2ème** ~ 1st/2nd class; **un (soldat de) deuxième** ~ (*MIL: armée de terre*) ≈ private (soldier); (*: armée de l'air*) ≈ aircraftman (*BRIT*), ≈ airman basic (*US*); **de** ~ luxury *cpd*; **faire ses** ~**s** (*MIL*) to do one's (recruit's) training; **faire la** ~ (*SCOL*) to be a *ou* the teacher; to teach; **aller en** ~ to go to school; **aller en** ~ **verte/de neige/de mer** to go to the countryside/skiing/to the seaside with the school; ~ **ouvrière** working class; ~ **préparatoire** *class which prepares students for the Grandes Écoles entry exams*; ~ **sociale** social class; ~ **touriste** economy class.

Classes préparatoires *is the term given to the two years of intensive study required to sit the competitive entry examinations into the* **grandes écoles**. *They are extremely demanding post-*baccalauréat *courses, usually taken in a* **lycée**. *Schools which provide such classes are more highly regarded than those which do not.*

---

classement [klɑsmɑ̃] *nm* classifying; filing; grading; closing; (*rang: SCOL*) place; (*: SPORT*) placing; (*liste: SCOL*) class list (in order of merit); (*: SPORT*) placings *pl*; **premier au** ~ **général** (*SPORT*) first overall.

classer [klɑse] vt (idées, livres) to classify; (papiers) to file; (candidat, concurrent) to grade; (personne: juger: péj) to rate; (JUR: affaire) to close; **se ~ premier/dernier** to come first/last; (SPORT) to finish first/last.
classeur [klɑsœʀ] nm (cahier) file; (meuble) filing cabinet; **~ à feuillets mobiles** ring binder.
classification [klasifikɑsjɔ̃] nf classification.
classifier [klasifje] vt to classify.
classique [klasik] adj classical; (sobre: coupe etc) classic(al); (habituel) standard, classic ♦ nm classic; classical author; **études ~s** classical studies, classics.
claudication [klodikɑsjɔ̃] nf limp.
clause [kloz] nf clause.
claustrer [klostʀe] vt to confine.
claustrophobie [klostʀɔfɔbi] nf claustrophobia.
clavecin [klavsɛ̃] nm harpsichord.
claveciniste [klavsinist(ə)] nm/f harpsichordist.
clavicule [klavikyl] nf clavicle, collarbone.
clavier [klavje] nm keyboard.
clé ou **clef** [kle] nf key; (MUS) clef; (de mécanicien) spanner (BRIT), wrench (US) ♦ adj: **problème/position ~** key problem/position; **mettre sous ~** to place under lock and key; **prendre la ~ des champs** to run away, make off; **prix ~s en main** (d'une voiture) on-the-road price; (d'un appartement) price with immediate entry; **~ de sol/de fa/d'ut** treble/bass/alto clef; **livre/film etc à ~** book/film etc in which real people are depicted under fictitious names; **à la ~** (à la fin) at the end of it all; **~ anglaise = ~ à molette**; **~ de contact** ignition key; **~ à molette** adjustable spanner (BRIT) ou wrench, monkey wrench; **~ de voûte** keystone.
clématite [klematit] nf clematis.
clémence [klemɑ̃s] nf mildness; leniency.
clément, e [klemɑ̃, -ɑ̃t] adj (temps) mild; (indulgent) lenient.
clémentine [klemɑ̃tin] nf (BOT) clementine.
clenche [klɑ̃ʃ] nf latch.
cleptomane [klɛptɔman] nm/f = **kleptomane**.
clerc [klɛʀ] nm: **~ de notaire** ou **d'avoué** lawyer's clerk.
clergé [klɛʀʒe] nm clergy.
clérical, e, aux [kleʀikal, -o] adj clerical.
cliché [kliʃe] nm (PHOTO) negative; print; (TYPO) (printing) plate; (LING) cliché.
client, e [klijɑ̃, -ɑ̃t] nm/f (acheteur) customer, client; (d'hôtel) guest, patron; (du docteur) patient; (de l'avocat) client.
clientèle [klijɑ̃tɛl] nf (du magasin) customers pl, clientèle; (du docteur, de l'avocat) practice; **accorder sa ~ à** to give one's custom to; **retirer sa ~ à** to take one's business away from.
cligner [kliɲe] vi: **~ des yeux** to blink (one's eyes); **~ de l'œil** to wink.
clignotant [kliɲɔtɑ̃] nm (AUTO) indicator.
clignoter [kliɲɔte] vi (étoiles etc) to twinkle; (lumière: à intervalles réguliers) to flash; (: vaciller) to flicker; (yeux) to blink.
climat [klima] nm climate.
climatique [klimatik] adj climatic.
climatisation [klimatizɑsjɔ̃] nf air conditioning.
climatisé, e [klimatize] adj air-conditioned.
climatiseur [klimatizœʀ] nm air conditioner.
clin d'œil [klɛ̃dœj] nm wink; **en un ~** in a flash.
clinique [klinik] adj clinical ♦ nf nursing home, (private) clinic.
clinquant, e [klɛ̃kɑ̃, -ɑ̃t] adj flashy.
clip [klip] nm (pince) clip; (vidéo) pop (ou promotional) video.
clique [klik] nf (péj: bande) clique, set; **prendre ses ~s et ses claques** to pack one's bags.
cliqueter [klikte] vi to clash; (ferraille, clefs, monnaie) to jangle, jingle; (verres) to chink.
cliquetis [klikti] nm jangle, jingle; chink.
clitoris [klitɔʀis] nm clitoris.
clivage [klivaʒ] nm cleavage; (fig) rift, split.
cloaque [klɔak] nm (fig) cesspit.
clochard, e [klɔʃaʀ, -aʀd(ə)] nm/f tramp.
cloche [klɔʃ] nf (d'église) bell; (fam) clot; (chapeau) cloche (hat); **~ à fromage** cheese-cover.
cloche-pied [klɔʃpje]: **à ~** adv on one leg, hopping (along).
clocher [klɔʃe] nm church tower; (en pointe) steeple ♦ vi (fam) to be ou go wrong; **de ~** (péj) parochial.
clocheton [klɔʃtɔ̃] nm pinnacle.
clochette [klɔʃɛt] nf bell.
clodo [klɔdo] nm (fam: = clochard) tramp.
clone [klɔn] nm clone.
clope [klɔp] nm ou f (fam) fag (BRIT), cigarette.
clopin-clopant [klɔpɛ̃klɔpɑ̃] adv hobbling along; (fig) so-so.
clopiner [klɔpine] vi to hobble along.
cloporte [klɔpɔʀt(ə)] nm woodlouse (pl -lice).
cloque [klɔk] nf blister.
cloqué, e [klɔke] adj: **étoffe ~e** seersucker.
cloquer [klɔke] vi (peau, peinture) to blister.
clore [klɔʀ] vt to close; **~ une session** (INFORM) to log out.
clos, e [klo, -oz] pp de **clore** ♦ adj voir **maison, huis, vase** ♦ nm (enclosed) field.
clôt [klo] vb voir **clore**.
clôture [klotyʀ] nf closure, closing; (barrière) enclosure, fence.

clôturer [klotyʀe] *vt* (*terrain*) to enclose, close off; (*festival, débats*) to close.

clou [klu] *nm* nail; (*MÉD*) boil; ~**s** *nmpl* = **passage clouté**; **pneus à ~s** studded tyres; **le ~ du spectacle** the highlight of the show; **~ de girofle** clove.

clouer [klue] *vt* to nail down (*ou* up); (*fig*): ~ **sur/contre** to pin to/against.

clouté, e [klute] *adj* studded.

clown [klun] *nm* clown; **faire le ~** (*fig*) to clown (about), play the fool.

clownerie [klunʀi] *nf* clowning *no pl*; **faire des ~s** to clown around.

CLT *sigle f* = *Compagnie Luxembourgeoise de Télévision.*

club [klœb] *nm* club.

CM *sigle f* = **chambre des métiers** ♦ *sigle m* = **conseil municipal**; (*SCOL*) = **cours moyen**.

cm. *abr* (= *centimètre*) cm.

CNAT *sigle f* (= *Commission nationale d'aménagement du territoire*) *national development agency.*

CNC *sigle m* (= *Conseil national de la consommation*) *national consumers' council.*

CNCL *sigle f* (= *Commission nationale de la communication et des libertés*) *independent broadcasting authority.*

CNDP *sigle m* = *Centre national de documentation pédagogique.*

CNE *sigle f* (= *Caisse nationale d'épargne*) *national savings bank.*

CNEC *sigle m* (= *Centre national de l'enseignement par correspondance*) ≈ *Open University.*

CNIL *sigle f* (= *Commission nationale de l'informatique et des libertés*) *board which enforces law on data protection.*

CNIT *sigle m* (= *Centre national des industries et des techniques*) *exhibition centre in Paris.*

CNJA *sigle m* (= *Centre national des jeunes agriculteurs*) *farmers' union.*

CNL *sigle f* (= *Confédération nationale du logement*) *consumer group for housing.*

CNP *sigle f* (= *Caisse nationale de prévoyance*) *savings bank.*

CNPF *sigle m* (= *Conseil national du patronat français*) *national council of French employers.*

CNRS *sigle m* = *Centre national de la recherche scientifique.*

c/o *abr* (= *care of*) c/o.

coagulant [kɔagylɑ̃] *nm* (*MÉD*) coagulant.

coaguler [kɔagyle] *vi, vt*, **se ~** *vi* to coagulate.

coaliser [kɔalize]: **se ~** *vi* to unite, join forces.

coalition [kɔalisjɔ̃] *nf* coalition.

coasser [kɔase] *vi* to croak.

coauteur [kɔotœʀ] *nm* co-author.

coaxial, e, aux [kɔaksjal, -o] *adj* coaxial.

cobalt [kɔbalt] *nm* cobalt.

cobaye [kɔbaj] *nm* guinea-pig.

COBOL, Cobol [kɔbɔl] *nm* COBOL, Cobol.

cobra [kɔbʀa] *nm* cobra.

coca [kɔka] *nm* ® Coke ®.

cocagne [kɔkaɲ] *nf*: **pays de ~** land of plenty; **mât de ~** greasy pole (*fig*).

cocaïne [kɔkain] *nf* cocaine.

cocarde [kɔkaʀd(ə)] *nf* rosette.

cocardier, ière [kɔkaʀdje, -jɛʀ] *adj* jingoistic, chauvinistic; militaristic.

cocasse [kɔkas] *adj* comical, funny.

coccinelle [kɔksinɛl] *nf* ladybird (*BRIT*), ladybug (*US*).

coccyx [kɔksis] *nm* coccyx.

cocher [kɔʃe] *nm* coachman ♦ *vt* to tick off; (*entailler*) to notch.

cochère [kɔʃɛʀ]

cochon, ne [kɔʃɔ̃, -ɔn] *nm* pig ♦ *nm/f* (*péj: sale*) (filthy) pig; (*: méchant*) swine ♦ *adj* (*fam*) dirty, smutty; ~ **d'Inde** guinea-pig; ~ **de lait** (*CULIN*) sucking pig.

cochonnaille [kɔʃɔnaj] *nf* (*péj: charcuterie*) (cold) pork.

cochonnerie [kɔʃɔnʀi] *nf* (*fam: saleté*) filth; (*: marchandises*) rubbish, trash.

cochonnet [kɔʃɔnɛ] *nm* (*BOULES*) jack.

cocker [kɔkɛʀ] *nm* cocker spaniel.

cocktail [kɔktɛl] *nm* cocktail; (*réception*) cocktail party.

coco [kɔko] *nm voir* **noix**; (*fam*) bloke (*BRIT*), dude (*US*).

cocon [kɔkɔ̃] *nm* cocoon.

cocorico [kɔkɔʀiko] *excl, nm* cock-a-doodle-do.

cocotier [kɔkɔtje] *nm* coconut palm.

cocotte [kɔkɔt] *nf* (*en fonte*) casserole; **ma ~** (*fam*) sweetie (*fam*); ~ **(minute)** ® pressure cooker; ~ **en papier** paper shape.

cocu [kɔky] *nm* cuckold.

code [kɔd] *nm* code; **se mettre en ~(s)** to dip (*BRIT*) *ou* dim (*US*) one's (head)lights; ~ **à barres** bar code; ~ **de caractère** (*INFORM*) character code; ~ **civil** Common Law; ~ **machine** machine code; ~ **pénal** penal code; ~ **postal** (*numéro*) postcode (*BRIT*), zip code (*US*); ~ **de la route** highway code; ~ **secret** cipher.

codéine [kɔdein] *nf* codeine.

coder [kɔde] *vt* to (en)code.

codétenu, e [kɔdetny] *nm/f* fellow prisoner *ou* inmate.

codicille [kɔdisil] *nm* codicil.

codifier [kɔdifje] *vt* to codify.

codirecteur, trice [kɔdiʀɛktœʀ, -tʀis] *nm/f* co-director.

coéditeur, trice [kɔeditœʀ, -tʀis] *nm/f* co-publisher; (*rédacteur*) co-editor.

coefficient [kɔefisjɑ̃] *nm* coefficient; ~ **d'erreur** margin of error.

coéquipier, ière [kɔekipje, -jɛʀ] *nm/f* team-mate, partner.

coercition [kɔɛʀsisjɔ̃] *nf* coercion.

cœur [kœʀ] *nm* heart; (*CARTES: couleur*) hearts *pl*; (*: carte*) heart; (*CULIN*): ~ **de laitue/d'artichaut** lettuce/artichoke heart; (*fig*): ~ **du débat** heart of the debate; ~ **de l'été**

height of summer; ~ **de la forêt** depths *pl* of the forest; **affaire de** ~ love affair; **avoir bon** ~ to be kind-hearted; **avoir mal au** ~ to feel sick; **contre** *ou* **sur son** ~ to one's breast; **opérer qn à** ~ **ouvert** to perform open-heart surgery on sb; **recevoir qn à** ~ **ouvert** to welcome sb with open arms; **parler à** ~ **ouvert** to open one's heart; **de tout son** ~ with all one's heart; **avoir le** ~ **gros** *ou* **serré** to have a heavy heart; **en avoir le** ~ **net** to be clear in one's own mind (about it); **par** ~ by heart; **de bon** ~ willingly; **avoir à** ~ **de faire** to be very keen to do; **cela lui tient à** ~ that's (very) close to his heart; **prendre les choses à** ~ to take things to heart; **à** ~ **joie** to one's heart's content; **être de tout** ~ **avec qn** to be (completely) in accord with sb.

coexistence [kɔɛgzistɑ̃s] *nf* coexistence.

coexister [kɔɛgziste] *vi* to coexist.

coffrage [kɔfʀaʒ] *nm* (*CONSTR: dispositif*) form(work).

coffre [kɔfʀ(ə)] *nm* (*meuble*) chest; (*coffre-fort*) safe; (*d'auto*) boot (*BRIT*), trunk (*US*); **avoir du** ~ (*fam*) to have a lot of puff.

coffre-fort, *pl* **coffres-fortes** [kɔfʀəfɔʀ] *nm* safe.

coffrer [kɔfʀe] *vt* (*fam*) to put inside, lock up.

coffret [kɔfʀɛ] *nm* casket; ~ **à bijoux** jewel box.

cogérant, e [kɔʒeʀɑ̃, -ɑ̃t] *nm/f* joint manager/ manageress.

cogestion [kɔʒestjɔ̃] *nf* joint management.

cogiter [kɔʒite] *vi* to cogitate.

cognac [kɔɲak] *nm* brandy, cognac.

cognement [kɔɲmɑ̃] *nm* knocking.

cogner [kɔɲe] *vi* to knock, bang; **se** ~ to bump o.s.

cohabitation [kɔabitasjɔ̃] *nf* living together; (*POL, JUR*) cohabitation.

cohabiter [kɔabite] *vi* to live together.

cohérence [kɔeʀɑ̃s] *nf* coherence.

cohérent, e [kɔeʀɑ̃, -ɑ̃t] *adj* coherent.

cohésion [kɔezjɔ̃] *nf* cohesion.

cohorte [kɔɔʀt(ə)] *nf* troop.

cohue [kɔy] *nf* crowd.

coi, coite [kwa, kwat] *adj*: **rester** ~ to remain silent.

coiffe [kwaf] *nf* headdress.

coiffé, e [kwafe] *adj*: **bien/mal** ~ with tidy/ untidy hair; ~ **d'un béret** wearing a beret; ~ **en arrière** with one's hair brushed *ou* combed back; ~ **en brosse** with a crew cut.

coiffer [kwafe] *vt* (*fig*) to cover, top; ~ **qn** to do sb's hair; ~ **qn d'un béret** to put a beret on sb; **se** ~ to do one's hair; to put on a *ou* one's hat.

coiffeur, euse [kwafœʀ, -øz] *nm/f* hairdresser ♦ *nf* (*table*) dressing table.

coiffure [kwafyʀ] *nf* (*cheveux*) hairstyle, hairdo; (*chapeau*) hat, headgear *no pl*; (*art*): **la** ~ hairdressing.

coin [kwɛ̃] *nm* corner; (*pour graver*) die; (*pour coincer*) wedge; (*poinçon*) hallmark; **l'épicerie du** ~ the local grocer; **dans le** ~ (*aux alentours*) in the area, around about; locally; **au** ~ **du feu** by the fireside; **du** ~ **de l'œil** out of the corner of one's eye; **regard en** ~ side(ways) glance; **sourire en** ~ half-smile.

coincé, e [kwɛ̃se] *adj* stuck, jammed; (*fig: inhibé*) inhibited, with hang-ups.

coincer [kwɛ̃se] *vt* to jam; (*fam*) to catch (out); to nab; **se** ~ to get stuck *ou* jammed.

coïncidence [kɔɛ̃sidɑ̃s] *nf* coincidence.

coïncider [kɔɛ̃side] *vi*: ~ (**avec**) to coincide (with); (*correspondre: témoignage etc*) to correspond *ou* tally (with).

coin-coin [kwɛ̃kwɛ̃] *nm inv* quack.

coing [kwɛ̃] *nm* quince.

coït [kɔit] *nm* coitus.

coite [kwat] *adj f voir* **coi**.

coke [kɔk] *nm* coke.

col [kɔl] *nm* (*de chemise*) collar; (*encolure, cou*) neck; (*de montagne*) pass; ~ **du fémur** neck of the thighbone; ~ **roulé** polo-neck; ~ **de l'utérus** cervix.

coléoptère [kɔleɔptɛʀ] *nm* beetle.

colère [kɔlɛʀ] *nf* anger; **une** ~ a fit of anger; **être en** ~ (**contre qn**) to be angry (with sb); **mettre qn en** ~ to make sb angry; **se mettre en** ~ to get angry.

coléreux, euse [kɔleʀø, -øz] *adj*, **colérique** [kɔleʀik] *adj* quick-tempered, irascible.

colibacille [kɔlibasil] *nm* colon bacillus.

colibacillose [kɔlibasiloz] *nf* colibacillosis.

colifichet [kɔlifiʃɛ] *nm* trinket.

colimaçon [kɔlimasɔ̃] *nm*: **escalier en** ~ spiral staircase.

colin [kɔlɛ̃] *nm* hake.

colin-maillard [kɔlɛ̃majaʀ] *nm* (*jeu*) blind man's buff.

colique [kɔlik] *nf* diarrhoea (*BRIT*), diarrhea (*US*); (*douleurs*) colic (pains *pl*); (*fam: personne ou chose ennuyeuse*) pain.

colis [kɔli] *nm* parcel; **par** ~ **postal** by parcel post.

colistier, ière [kɔlistje, -jɛʀ] *nm/f* fellow candidate.

colite [kɔlit] *nf* colitis.

coll. *abr* = **collection**; (= *collaborateurs*): **et** ~ **et al.**

collaborateur, trice [kɔlabɔʀatœʀ, -tʀis] *nm/f* (*aussi POL*) collaborator; (*d'une revue*) contributor.

collaboration [kɔlabɔʀasjɔ̃] *nf* collaboration.

collaborer [kɔlabɔʀe] *vi* to collaborate; ~ **à** to collaborate on; (*revue*) to contribute to.

collage [kɔlaʒ] *nm* (*ART*) collage.

collagène [kɔlaʒɛn] *nm* collagen.

collant, e [kɔlɑ̃, -ɑ̃t] *adj* sticky; (*robe etc*) clinging, skintight; (*péj*) clinging ♦ *nm* (*bas*) tights *pl*.

collatéral, e, aux [kɔlateʀal, -o] *nm/f* collateral.

collation [kɔlasjɔ̃] *nf* light meal.
colle [kɔl] *nf* glue; (*à papiers peints*) (wallpaper) paste; (*devinette*) teaser, riddle; (*SCOL fam*) detention; ~ **forte** superglue ®.
collecte [kɔlɛkt(ə)] *nf* collection; **faire une** ~ to take up a collection.
collecter [kɔlɛkte] *vt* to collect.
collecteur [kɔlɛktœʀ] *nm* (*égout*) main sewer.
collectif, ive [kɔlɛktif, -iv] *adj* collective; (*visite, billet etc*) group *cpd* ♦ *nm*: ~ **budgétaire** mini-budget (*BRIT*), mid-term budget; **immeuble** ~ block of flats.
collection [kɔlɛksjɔ̃] *nf* collection; (*ÉDITION*) series; **pièce de** ~ collector's item; **faire (la)** ~ **de** to collect; (**toute**) **une** ~ **de** ... (*fig*) a (complete) set of ....
collectionner [kɔlɛksjɔne] *vt* (*tableaux, timbres*) to collect.
collectionneur, euse [kɔlɛksjɔnœʀ, -øz] *nm/f* collector.
collectivement [kɔlɛktivmɑ̃] *adv* collectively.
collectiviser [kɔlɛktivize] *vt* to collectivize.
collectivisme [kɔlɛktivism(ə)] *nm* collectivism.
collectiviste [kɔlɛktivist(ə)] *adj* collectivist.
collectivité [kɔlɛktivite] *nf* group; **la** ~ the community, the collectivity; **les** ~**s locales** local authorities.
collège [kɔlɛʒ] *nm* (*école*) (secondary) school; (*assemblée*) body; ~ **électoral** electoral college; ~ **d'enseignement secondaire (CES)** ≈ junior secondary school (*BRIT*), ≈ junior high school (*US*).

The **collège** *is a state secondary school for children aged between eleven and fifteen. Pupils follow a nationally prescribed curriculum consisting of a common core and various subjects. Schools are free to arrange their own timetable and choose their own teaching methods. Before leaving the collège, pupils are assessed by examination and course work for their* **brevet des collèges**.

---

collégial, e, aux [kɔleʒjal, -o] *adj* collegiate.
collégien, ne [kɔleʒjɛ̃, -ɛn] *nm/f* secondary school pupil (*BRIT*), high school student (*US*).
collègue [kɔlɛg] *nm/f* colleague.
coller [kɔle] *vt* (*papier, timbre*) to stick (on); (*affiche*) to stick up; (*appuyer, placer contre*): ~ **son front à la vitre** to press one's face to the window; (*enveloppe*) to stick down; (*morceaux*) to stick ou glue together; (*fam: mettre, fourrer*) to stick, shove; (*SCOL fam*) to keep in, give detention to ♦ *vi* (*être collant*) to be sticky; (*adhérer*) to stick; ~ **qch sur** to stick (*ou paste ou glue*) sth on(to); ~ **à** to stick to; (*fig*) to cling to.
collerette [kɔlʀɛt] *nf* ruff; (*TECH*) flange.
collet [kɔlɛ] *nm* (*piège*) snare, noose; (*cou*): **prendre qn au** ~ to grab sb by the throat; ~

monté *adj inv* straight-laced.
colleter [kɔlte] *vt* (*adversaire*) to collar, grab by the throat; **se** ~ **avec** to wrestle with.
colleur [kɔlœʀ] *nm*: ~ **d'affiches** bill-poster.
collier [kɔlje] *nm* (*bijou*) necklace; (*de chien, TECH*) collar; ~ (**de barbe**), **barbe en** ~ narrow beard along the line of the jaw; ~ **de serrage** choke collar.
collimateur [kɔlimatœʀ] *nm*: **être dans le** ~ (*fig*) to be in the firing line; **avoir qn/qch dans le** ~ (*fig*) to have sb/sth in one's sights.
colline [kɔlin] *nf* hill.
collision [kɔlizjɔ̃] *nf* collision, crash; **entrer en** ~ (**avec**) to collide (with).
colloque [kɔlɔk] *nm* colloquium, symposium.
collusion [kɔlyzjɔ̃] *nf* collusion.
collutoire [kɔlytwaʀ] *nm* (*MÉD*) oral medication; (*en bombe*) throat spray.
collyre [kɔliʀ] *nm* (*MÉD*) eye lotion.
colmater [kɔlmate] *vt* (*fuite*) to seal off; (*brèche*) to plug, fill in.
Cologne [kɔlɔɲ] *n* Cologne.
colombage [kɔlɔ̃baʒ] *nm* half-timbering; **une maison à** ~**s** a half-timbered house.
colombe [kɔlɔ̃b] *nf* dove.
Colombie [kɔlɔ̃bi] *nf*: **la** ~ Colombia.
colombien, ne [kɔlɔ̃bjɛ̃, -ɛn] *adj* Colombian ♦ *nm/f*: **C**~, ne Colombian.
colon [kɔlɔ̃] *nm* settler; (*enfant*) boarder (*in children's holiday camp*).
côlon [kolɔ̃] *nm* colon (*MÉD*).
colonel [kɔlɔnɛl] *nm* colonel; (*armée de l'air*) group captain.
colonial, e, aux [kɔlɔnjal, -o] *adj* colonial.
colonialisme [kɔlɔnjalism(ə)] *nm* colonialism.
colonialiste [kɔlɔnjalist(ə)] *adj, nm/f* colonialist.
colonie [kɔlɔni] *nf* colony; ~ (**de vacances**) holiday camp (*for children*).
colonisation [kɔlɔnizasjɔ̃] *nf* colonization.
coloniser [kɔlɔnize] *vt* to colonize.
colonnade [kɔlɔnad] *nf* colonnade.
colonne [kɔlɔn] *nf* column; **se mettre en** ~ **par deux/quatre** to get into twos/fours; **en** ~ **par deux** in double file; ~ **de secours** rescue party; ~ (**vertébrale**) spine, spinal column.
colonnette [kɔlɔnɛt] *nf* small column.
colophane [kɔlɔfan] *nf* rosin.
colorant [kɔlɔʀɑ̃] *nm* colo(u)ring.
coloration [kɔlɔʀasjɔ̃] *nf* colour(ing) (*BRIT*), color(ing) (*US*); **se faire faire une** ~ (*chez le coiffeur*) to have one's hair dyed.
coloré, e [kɔlɔʀe] *adj* (*fig*) colo(u)rful.
colorer [kɔlɔʀe] *vt* to colour (*BRIT*), color (*US*); **se** ~ *vi* to turn red; to blush.
coloriage [kɔlɔʀjaʒ] *nm* colo(u)ring.
colorier [kɔlɔʀje] *vt* to colo(u)r (in); **album à** ~ colouring book.
coloris [kɔlɔʀi] *nm* colo(u)r, shade.
coloriste [kɔlɔʀist(ə)] *nm/f* colo(u)rist.
colossal, e, aux [kɔlɔsal, -o] *adj* colossal, huge.
colosse [kɔlɔs] *nm* giant.

colostrum [kɔlɔstʀɔm] *nm* colostrum.
colporter [kɔlpɔʀte] *vt* to hawk, peddle.
colporteur, euse [kɔlpɔʀtœʀ, -øz] *nm/f*
hawker, pedlar.
colt [kɔlt] *nm* revolver, Colt ®.
coltiner [kɔltine] *vt* to lug about.
colza [kɔlza] *nm* rape(seed).
coma [kɔma] *nm* coma; **être dans le** ~ to be in
a coma.
comateux, euse [kɔmatø, -øz] *adj* comatose.
combat [kɔ̃ba] *vb voir* **combattre** ♦ *nm* fight;
fighting *no pl*; ~ **de boxe** boxing match; ~ **de
rues** street fighting *no pl*; ~ **singulier** single
combat.
combatif, ive [kɔ̃batif, -iv] *adj* with a lot of
fight.
combativité [kɔ̃bativite] *nf* fighting spirit.
combattant [kɔ̃batɑ̃] *vb voir* **combattre** ♦ *nm*
combatant; (*d'une rixe*) brawler; **ancien** ~
war veteran.
combattre [kɔ̃batʀ(ə)] *vi* to fight ♦ *vt* to fight;
(*épidémie, ignorance*) to combat, fight
(against).
combien [kɔ̃bjɛ̃] *adv* (*quantité*) how much;
(*nombre*) how many; (*exclamatif*) how; ~ **de**
how much; how many; ~ **de temps** how
long, how much time; ~ **coûte/pèse ceci?**
how much does this cost/weigh?; **vous
mesurez** ~**?** what size are you?; **ça fait** ~ **en
largeur?** how wide is that?
combinaison [kɔ̃binɛzɔ̃] *nf* combination;
(*astuce*) device, scheme; (*de femme*) slip;
(*d'aviateur*) flying suit; (*d'homme-grenouille*)
wetsuit; (*bleu de travail*) boilersuit (*BRIT*),
coveralls *pl* (*US*).
combine [kɔ̃bin] *nf* trick; (*péj*) scheme, fiddle
(*BRIT*).
combiné [kɔ̃bine] *nm* (*aussi:* ~ **téléphonique**)
receiver; (*SKI*) combination (event);
(*vêtement de femme*) corselet.
combiner [kɔ̃bine] *vt* to combine; (*plan,
horaire*) to work out, devise.
comble [kɔ̃bl(ə)] *adj* (*salle*) packed (full) ♦ *nm*
(*du bonheur, plaisir*) height; ~**s** *nmpl*
(*CONSTR*) attic *sg*, loft *sg*; **de fond en** ~ from
top to bottom; **pour** ~ **de malchance** to
cap it all; **c'est le** ~**!** that beats everything!,
that takes the biscuit! (*BRIT*); **sous les** ~**s** in
the attic.
combler [kɔ̃ble] *vt* (*trou*) to fill in; (*besoin,
lacune*) to fill; (*déficit*) to make good;
(*satisfaire*) to gratify, fulfil (*BRIT*),
fulfill (*US*); ~ **qn de joie** to fill sb with joy;
~ **qn d'honneurs** to shower sb with
honours.
combustible [kɔ̃bystibl(ə)] *adj* combustible
♦ *nm* fuel.
combustion [kɔ̃bystjɔ̃] *nf* combustion.
COMECON [kɔmekɔn] *sigle m* Comecon.
comédie [kɔmedi] *nf* comedy; (*fig*) playacting
no pl; **jouer la** ~ (*fig*) to put on an act; ~
musicale musical.

Founded in 1680 by Louis XIV, the **Comédie
française** *is the French national theatre.
Subsidized by the state, the company performs
mainly in the Palais Royal in Paris and
concentrates on staging classical French
plays.*

---

comédien, ne [kɔmedjɛ̃, -ɛn] *nm/f* actor/
actress; (*comique*) comedy actor/actress,
comedian/comedienne; (*fig*) sham.
COMES [kɔmɛs] *sigle m = Commissariat à
l'énergie solaire.*
comestible [kɔmɛstibl(ə)] *adj* edible; ~**s** *nmpl*
foods.
comète [kɔmɛt] *nf* comet.
comice [kɔmis] *nm:* ~ **agricole** agricultural
show.
comique [kɔmik] *adj* (*drôle*) comical; (*THÉÂT*)
comic ♦ *nm* (*artiste*) comic, comedian; **le** ~
de qch the funny *ou* comical side of sth.
comité [kɔmite] *nm* committee; **petit** ~ select
group; ~ **directeur** management committee;
~ **d'entreprise (CE)** works council; ~ **des
fêtes** festival committee.
commandant [kɔmɑ̃dɑ̃] *nm* (*gén*)
commander, commandant; (*MIL: grade*)
major; (: *armée de l'air*) squadron leader;
(*NAVIG*) captain; ~ (**de bord**) (*AVIAT*) captain.
commande [kɔmɑ̃d] *nf* (*COMM*) order;
(*INFORM*) command; ~**s** *nfpl* (*AVIAT etc*)
controls; **passer une** ~ (**de**) to put in an order (for); **sur** ~ to order; ~ **à distance** remote control; **véhicule à double** ~
vehicle with dual controls.
commandement [kɔmɑ̃dmɑ̃] *nm* command;
(*ordre*) command, order; (*REL*)
commandment.
commander [kɔmɑ̃de] *vt* (*COMM*) to order;
(*diriger, ordonner*) to command; ~ **à** (*MIL*) to
command; (*contrôler, maîtriser*) to have
control over; ~ **à qn de faire** to command *ou*
order sb to do.
commanditaire [kɔmɑ̃ditɛʀ] *nm* sleeping
(*BRIT*) *ou* silent (*US*) partner.
commandite [kɔmɑ̃dit] *nf:* (**société en**) ~
limited partnership.
commanditer [kɔmɑ̃dite] *vt* (*COMM*) to
finance, back; to commission.
commando [kɔmɑ̃do] *nm* commando (squad).

============================== *MOT-CLÉ*

comme [kɔm] *prép* **1** (*comparaison*) like; **tout**
~ **son père** just like his father; **fort** ~ **un
bœuf** as strong as an ox; **joli** ~ **tout** ever so
pretty
2 (*manière*) like; **faites-le** ~ **ça** do it like this,
do it this way; ~ **ça ou cela on n'aura pas
d'ennuis** that way we won't have any
problems; ~ **ci**, ~ **ça** so-so, middling;
comment ça va? — ~ **ça** how are things? —
OK; ~ **on dit** as they say

3 (*en tant que*) as a; **donner** ~ **prix** to give as a prize; **travailler** ~ **secrétaire** to work as a secretary
4: ~ **quoi** (*d'où il s'ensuit que*) which shows that; **il a écrit une lettre** ~ **quoi il ...** he's written a letter saying that ...
5: ~ **il faut** *phr adv* properly; *phr adj* (*correct*) proper, correct
♦ *conj* **1** (*ainsi que*) as; **elle écrit** ~ **elle parle** she writes as she talks; ~ **si** as if
2 (*au moment où, alors que*) as; **il est parti** ~ **j'arrivais** he left as I arrived
3 (*parce que, puisque*) as, since; ~ **il était en retard, il ...** as he was late, he ...
♦ *adv:* ~ **il est fort/c'est bon!** he's so strong/ it's so good!; **il est malin** ~ **c'est pas permis** he's as smart as anything.

commémoratif, ive [kɔmemɔratif, -iv] *adj* commemorative; **un monument** ~ a memorial.
commémoration [kɔmemɔrasjɔ̃] *nf* commemoration.
commémorer [kɔmemɔre] *vt* to commemorate.
commencement [kɔmɑ̃smɑ̃] *nm* beginning, start, commencement; ~**s** *nmpl* (*débuts*) beginnings.
commencer [kɔmɑ̃se] *vt* to begin, start, commence; (*être placé au début de*) to begin ♦ *vi* to begin, start, commence; ~ **à** *ou* **de faire** to begin *ou* start doing; ~ **par qch** to begin with sth; ~ **par faire qch** to begin by doing sth.
commensal, e, aux [kɔmɑ̃sal, -o] *nm/f* companion at table.
comment [kɔmɑ̃] *adv* how; ~**?** (*que dites-vous*) (I beg your) pardon?; ~**!** what! ♦ *nm:* **le** ~ **et le pourquoi** the whys and wherefores; **et** ~**!** and how!; ~ **donc!** of course!; ~ **faire?** how will we do it?; ~ **se fait-il que?** how is it that?
commentaire [kɔmɑ̃tɛr] *nm* comment; remark; ~ (**de texte**) (*SCOL*) commentary; ~ **sur image** voice-over.
commentateur, trice [kɔmɑ̃tatœr, -tris] *nm/f* commentator.
commenter [kɔmɑ̃te] *vt* (*jugement, événement*) to comment (up)on; (*RADIO, TV: match, manifestation*) to cover, give a commentary on.
commérages [kɔmeraʒ] *nmpl* gossip *sg*.
commerçant, e [kɔmɛrsɑ̃, -ɑ̃t] *adj* commercial; trading; (*rue*) shopping *cpd*; (*personne*) commercially shrewd ♦ *nm/f* shopkeeper, trader.
commerce [kɔmɛrs(ə)] *nm* (*activité*) trade, commerce; (*boutique*) business; **le petit** ~ small shopowners *pl*, small traders *pl*; **faire** ~ **de** to trade in; (*fig: péj*) to trade on; **chambre de** ~ Chamber of Commerce; **livres de** ~ (account) books; **vendu dans le** ~

sold in the shops; **vendu hors-**~ sold directly to the public; ~ **en** *ou* **de gros/ détail** wholesale/retail trade; ~ **intérieur/ extérieur** home/foreign trade.
commercer [kɔmɛrse] *vi:* ~ **avec** to trade with.
commercial, e, aux [kɔmɛrsjal, -o] *adj* commercial, trading; (*péj*) commercial ♦ *nm:* **les commerciaux** the commercial people.
commercialisable [kɔmɛrsjalizabl(ə)] *adj* marketable.
commercialisation [kɔmɛrsjalizasjɔ̃] *nf* marketing.
commercialiser [kɔmɛrsjalize] *vt* to market.
commère [kɔmɛr] *nf* gossip.
commettant [kɔmetɑ̃] *vb voir* **commettre** ♦ *nm* (*JUR*) principal.
commettre [kɔmɛtr(ə)] *vt* to commit; **se** ~ to compromise one's good name.
commis [kɔmi] *vb voir* **commettre** ♦ *nm* (*de magasin*) (shop) assistant (*BRIT*), sales clerk (*US*); (*de banque*) clerk; ~ **voyageur** commercial traveller (*BRIT*) *ou* traveler (*US*).
commis, e [kɔmi, -iz] *pp de* **commettre**.
commisération [kɔmizerasjɔ̃] *nf* commiseration.
commissaire [kɔmisɛr] *nm* (*de police*) ≈ (police) superintendent (*BRIT*), ≈ (police) captain (*US*); (*de rencontre sportive etc*) steward; ~ **du bord** (*NAVIG*) purser; ~ **aux comptes** (*ADMIN*) auditor.
commissaire-priseur, *pl* **commissaires-priseurs** [kɔmisɛrprizœr] *nm* (official) auctioneer.
commissariat [kɔmisarja] *nm* police station; (*ADMIN*) commissionership.
commission [kɔmisjɔ̃] *nf* (*comité, pourcentage*) commission; (*message*) message; (*course*) errand; ~**s** *nfpl* (*achats*) shopping *sg*; ~ **d'examen** examining board.
commissionnaire [kɔmisjɔnɛr] *nm* delivery boy (*ou* man); messenger; (*TRANSPORTS*) (forwarding) agent.
commissure [kɔmisyr] *nf:* **les** ~**s des lèvres** the corners of the mouth.
commode [kɔmɔd] *adj* (*pratique*) convenient, handy; (*facile*) easy; (*air, personne*) easy-going; (*personne*): **pas** ~ awkward (to deal with) ♦ *nf* chest of drawers.
commodité [kɔmɔdite] *nf* convenience.
commotion [kɔmɔsjɔ̃] *nf:* ~ (**cérébrale**) concussion.
commotionné, e [kɔmɔsjɔne] *adj* shocked, shaken.
commuer [kɔmɥe] *vt* to commute.
commun, e [kɔmœ̃, -yn] *adj* common; (*pièce*) communal, shared; (*réunion, effort*) joint ♦ *nf* (*ADMIN*) commune, ≈ district; (*: urbaine*) ≈ borough; ~**s** *nmpl* (*bâtiments*) outbuildings; **cela sort du** ~ it's out of the ordinary; **le** ~

des mortels the common run of people; **sans ~e mesure** incomparable; **être ~ à** (*suj: chose*) to be shared by; **en ~** (*faire*) jointly; **mettre en ~** to pool, share; **peu ~** unusual; **d'un ~ accord** of one accord; with one accord.

communal, e, aux [kɔmynal, -o] *adj* (*ADMIN*) of the commune, ≈ (*district ou borough*) council *cpd*.

communard, e [kɔmynaʀ, -aʀd(ə)] *nm/f* (*HIST*) Communard; (*péj: communiste*) commie.

communautaire [kɔmynoteʀ] *adj* community *cpd*.

communauté [kɔmynote] *nf* community; (*JUR*): **régime de la ~** communal estate settlement.

commune [kɔmyn] *adj f, nf voir* **commun**.

communément [kɔmynemɑ̃] *adv* commonly.

Communes [kɔmyn] *nfpl* (*BRIT: parlement*) Commons.

communiant, e [kɔmynjɑ̃, -ɑ̃t] *nm/f* communicant; **premier ~** child taking his first communion.

communicant, e [kɔmynikɑ̃, -ɑ̃t] *adj* communicating.

communicatif, ive [kɔmynikatif, -iv] *adj* (*personne*) communicative; (*rire*) infectious.

communication [kɔmynikɑsjɔ̃] *nf* communication; **~ (téléphonique)** (telephone) call; **avoir la ~ (avec)** to get *ou* be through (to); **vous avez la ~** you're through; **donnez-moi la ~ avec** put me through to; **mettre qn en ~ avec qn** (*en contact*) to put sb in touch with sb; (*au téléphone*) to connect sb with sb; **~ interurbaine** long-distance call; **~ en PCV** reverse charge (*BRIT*) *ou* collect (*US*) call; **~ avec préavis** personal call.

communier [kɔmynje] *vi* (*REL*) to receive communion; (*fig*) to be united.

communion [kɔmynjɔ̃] *nf* communion.

communiqué [kɔmynike] *nm* communiqué; **~ de presse** press release.

communiquer [kɔmynike] *vt* (*nouvelle, dossier*) to pass on, convey; (*maladie*) to pass on; (*peur etc*) to communicate; (*chaleur, mouvement*) to transmit ♦ *vi* to communicate; **~ avec** (*suj: salle*) to communicate with; **se ~ à** (*se propager*) to spread to.

communisant, e [kɔmynizɑ̃, -ɑ̃t] *adj* communistic ♦ *nm/f* communist sympathizer.

communisme [kɔmynism(ə)] *nm* communism.

communiste [kɔmynist(ə)] *adj, nm/f* communist.

commutateur [kɔmytatœʀ] *nm* (*ÉLEC*) (change-over) switch, commutator.

commutation [kɔmytasjɔ̃] *nf* (*INFORM*): **~ de messages** message switching; **~ de paquets** packet switching.

Comores [kɔmɔʀ] *nfpl*: **les (îles) ~** the

Comoros (Islands).

comorien, ne [kɔmɔʀjɛ̃, -ɛn] *adj* of *ou* from the Comoros.

compact, e [kɔ̃pakt] *adj* dense; compact.

compagne [kɔ̃paɲ] *nf* companion.

compagnie [kɔ̃paɲi] *nf* (*firme, MIL*) company; (*groupe*) gathering; (*présence*): **la ~ de qn** sb's company; **homme/femme de ~** escort; **tenir ~ à qn** to keep sb company; **fausser ~ à qn** to give sb the slip, slip *ou* sneak away from sb; **en ~ de** in the company of; **Dupont et ~, Dupont et Cie** Dupont and Company, Dupont and Co; **~ aérienne** airline (company).

compagnon [kɔ̃paɲɔ̃] *nm* companion; (*autrefois: ouvrier*) craftsman; journeyman.

comparable [kɔ̃paʀabl(ə)] *adj*: **~ (à)** comparable (to).

comparaison [kɔ̃paʀɛzɔ̃] *nf* comparison; (*métaphore*) simile; **en ~ (de)** in comparison (with); **par ~ (à)** by comparison (with).

comparaître [kɔ̃paʀɛtʀ(ə)] *vi*: **~ (devant)** to appear (before).

comparatif, ive [kɔ̃paʀatif, -iv] *adj, nm* comparative.

comparativement [kɔ̃paʀativmɑ̃] *adv* comparatively; **~ à** by comparison with.

comparé, e [kɔ̃paʀe] *adj*: **littérature** *etc* **~e** comparative literature *etc*.

comparer [kɔ̃paʀe] *vt* to compare; **~ qch/qn à** *ou* **et** (*pour choisir*) to compare sth/sb with *ou* and; (*pour établir une similitude*) to compare sth/sb to *ou* and.

comparse [kɔ̃paʀs(ə)] *nm/f* (*péj*) associate, stooge.

compartiment [kɔ̃paʀtimɑ̃] *nm* compartment.

compartimenté, e [kɔ̃paʀtimɑ̃te] *adj* partitioned; (*fig*) compartmentalized.

comparu, e [kɔ̃paʀy] *pp de* **comparaître**.

comparution [kɔ̃paʀysjɔ̃] *nf* appearance.

compas [kɔ̃pa] *nm* (*GÉOM*) (pair of) compasses *pl*; (*NAVIG*) compass.

compassé, e [kɔ̃pase] *adj* starchy, formal.

compassion [kɔ̃pasjɔ̃] *nf* compassion.

compatibilité [kɔ̃patibilite] *nf* compatibility.

compatible [kɔ̃patibl(ə)] *adj*: **~ (avec)** compatible (with).

compatir [kɔ̃patiʀ] *vi*: **~ (à)** to sympathize (with).

compatissant, e [kɔ̃patisɑ̃, -ɑ̃t] *adj* sympathetic.

compatriote [kɔ̃patʀijɔt] *nm/f* compatriot, fellow countryman/woman.

compensateur, trice [kɔ̃pɑ̃satœʀ, -tʀis] *adj* compensatory.

compensation [kɔ̃pɑ̃sɑsjɔ̃] *nf* compensation; (*BANQUE*) clearing; **en ~** in *ou* as compensation.

compensé, e [kɔ̃pɑ̃se] *adj*: **semelle ~e** platform sole.

compenser [kɔ̃pɑ̃se] *vt* to compensate for, make up for.

compère [kɔ̃pɛʀ] *nm* accomplice; fellow musician *ou* comedian *etc*.
compétence [kɔ̃petɑ̃s] *nf* competence.
compétent, e [kɔ̃petɑ̃, -ɑ̃t] *adj* (*apte*) competent, capable; (*JUR*) competent.
compétitif, ive [kɔ̃petitif, -iv] *adj* competitive.
compétition [kɔ̃petisjɔ̃] *nf* (*gén*) competition; (*SPORT: épreuve*) event; **la ~** competitive sport; **être en ~ avec** to be competing with; **la ~ automobile** motor racing.
compétitivité [kɔ̃petitivite] *nf* competitiveness.
compilateur [kɔ̃pilatœʀ] *nm* (*INFORM*) compiler.
compiler [kɔ̃pile] *vt* to compile.
complainte [kɔ̃plɛ̃t] *nf* lament.
complaire [kɔ̃plɛʀ]: **se ~** *vi*: **se ~ dans/parmi** to take pleasure in/in being among.
complaisais [kɔ̃plɛze] *etc vb voir* **complaire**.
complaisamment [kɔ̃plɛzamɑ̃] *adv* kindly; complacently.
complaisance [kɔ̃plɛzɑ̃s] *nf* kindness; (*péj*) indulgence; (*: fatuité*) complacency; **attestation de ~** *certificate produced to oblige a patient etc*; **pavillon de ~** flag of convenience.
complaisant, e [kɔ̃plɛzɑ̃, -ɑ̃t] *vb voir* **complaire** ♦ *adj* (*aimable*) kind; obliging; (*péj*) accommodating; (*: fat*) complacent.
complaît [kɔ̃plɛ] *vb voir* **complaire**.
complément [kɔ̃plemɑ̃] *nm* complement; (*reste*) remainder; (*LING*) complement; **~ d'information** (*ADMIN*) supplementary *ou* further information; **~ d'agent** agent; **~ (d'objet) direct/indirect** direct/indirect object; **~ (circonstanciel) de lieu/temps** adverbial phrase of place/time; **~ de nom** possessive phrase.
complémentaire [kɔ̃plemɑ̃tɛʀ] *adj* complementary; (*additionnel*) supplementary.
complet, ète [kɔ̃plɛ, -ɛt] *adj* complete; (*plein: hôtel etc*) full ♦ *nm* (*aussi:* **~-veston**) suit; **au (grand) ~** all together.
complètement [kɔ̃plɛtmɑ̃] *adv* (*en entier*) completely; (*absolument: fou, faux etc*) absolutely; (*à fond: étudier etc*) fully, in depth.
compléter [kɔ̃plete] *vt* (*porter à la quantité voulue*) to complete; (*augmenter*) to complement, supplement; to add to; **se ~** (*personnes*) to complement one another; (*collection etc*) to become complete.
complexe [kɔ̃plɛks(ə)] *adj* complex ♦ *nm* (*PSYCH*) complex, hang-up; (*bâtiments*): **~ hospitalier/industriel** hospital/industrial complex.
complexé, e [kɔ̃plɛkse] *adj* mixed-up, hung-up.
complexité [kɔ̃plɛksite] *nf* complexity.
complication [kɔ̃plikasjɔ̃] *nf* complexity, intricacy; (*difficulté, ennui*) complication; **~s** *nfpl* (*MÉD*) complications.

complice [kɔ̃plis] *nm* accomplice.
complicité [kɔ̃plisite] *nf* complicity.
compliment [kɔ̃plimɑ̃] *nm* (*louange*) compliment; **~s** *nmpl* (*félicitations*) congratulations.
complimenter [kɔ̃plimɑ̃te] *vt*: **~ qn (sur** *ou* **de)** to congratulate *ou* compliment sb (on).
compliqué, e [kɔ̃plike] *adj* complicated, complex, intricate; (*personne*) complicated.
compliquer [kɔ̃plike] *vt* to complicate; **se ~** *vi* (*situation*) to become complicated; **se ~ la vie** to make life difficult *ou* complicated for o.s.
complot [kɔ̃plo] *nm* plot.
comploter [kɔ̃plɔte] *vi, vt* to plot.
complu, e [kɔ̃ply] *pp de* **complaire**.
comportement [kɔ̃pɔʀtəmɑ̃] *nm* behaviour (*BRIT*), behavior (*US*); (*TECH: d'une pièce, d'un véhicule*) behavio(u)r, performance.
comporter [kɔ̃pɔʀte] *vt* to be composed of, consist of, comprise; (*être équipé de*) to have; (*impliquer*) to entail, involve; **se ~** *vi* to behave; (*TECH*) to behave, perform.
composant [kɔ̃pozɑ̃] *nm* component, constituent.
composante [kɔ̃pozɑ̃t] *nf* component.
composé, e [kɔ̃poze] *adj* (*visage, air*) studied; (*BIO, CHIMIE, LING*) compound ♦ *nm* (*CHIMIE, LING*) compound; **~ de** made up of.
composer [kɔ̃poze] *vt* (*musique, texte*) to compose; (*mélange, équipe*) to make up; (*faire partie de*) to make up, form; (*TYPO*) to (type)set ♦ *vi* (*SCOL*) to sit *ou* do a test; (*transiger*) to come to terms; **se ~ de** to be composed of, be made up of; **~ un numéro** (*au téléphone*) to dial a number.
composite [kɔ̃pozit] *adj* heterogeneous.
compositeur, trice [kɔ̃pozitœʀ, -tʀis] *nm/f* (*MUS*) composer; (*TYPO*) compositor, typesetter.
composition [kɔ̃pozisjɔ̃] *nf* composition; (*SCOL*) test; (*TYPO*) (type)setting, composition; **de bonne ~** (*accommodant*) easy to deal with; **amener qn à ~** to get sb to come to terms; **~ française** (*SCOL*) French essay.
compost [kɔ̃pɔst] *nm* compost.
composter [kɔ̃pɔste] *vt* to date-stamp; to punch.
composteur [kɔ̃pɔstœʀ] *nm* date stamp; punch; (*TYPO*) composing stick.
compote [kɔ̃pɔt] *nf* stewed fruit *no pl*; **~ de pommes** stewed apples.
compotier [kɔ̃pɔtje] *nm* fruit dish *ou* bowl.
compréhensible [kɔ̃pʀeɑ̃sibl(ə)] *adj* comprehensible; (*attitude*) understandable.
compréhensif, ive [kɔ̃pʀeɑ̃sif, -iv] *adj* understanding.
compréhension [kɔ̃pʀeɑ̃sjɔ̃] *nf* understanding; comprehension.
comprendre [kɔ̃pʀɑ̃dʀ(ə)] *vt* to understand; (*se composer de*) to comprise, consist of;

(*inclure*) to include; **se faire** ~ to make o.s. understood; to get one's ideas across; **mal** ~ to misunderstand.

compresse [kɔ̃prɛs] *nf* compress.

compresser [kɔ̃prese] *vt* to squash in, crush together.

compresseur [kɔ̃presœr] *adj m voir* **rouleau.**

compressible [kɔ̃presibl(ə)] *adj* (*PHYSIQUE*) compressible; (*dépenses*) reducible.

compression [kɔ̃presjɔ̃] *nf* compression; (*d'un crédit etc*) reduction.

comprimé, e [kɔ̃prime] *adj:* **air** ~ compressed air ♦ *nm* tablet.

comprimer [kɔ̃prime] *vt* to compress; (*fig: crédit etc*) to reduce, cut down.

compris, e [kɔ̃pri, -iz] *pp de* **comprendre** ♦ *adj* (*inclus*) included; ~? understood?, is that clear?; ~ **entre** (*situé*) contained between; **la maison** ~**e/non** ~**e, y/non** ~ **la maison** including/excluding the house; **service** ~ service (charge) included; **100 F tout** ~ 100 F all inclusive *ou* all-in.

compromettant, e [kɔ̃prɔmetɑ̃, -ɑ̃t] *adj* compromising.

compromettre [kɔ̃prɔmɛtr(ə)] *vt* to compromise.

compromis [kɔ̃prɔmi] *vb voir* **compromettre** ♦ *nm* compromise.

compromission [kɔ̃prɔmisjɔ̃] *nf* compromise, deal.

comptabiliser [kɔ̃tabilize] *vt* (*valeur*) to post; (*fig*) to evaluate.

comptabilité [kɔ̃tabilite] *nf* (*activité, technique*) accounting, accountancy; (*d'une société: comptes*) accounts *pl*, books *pl*; (*: service*) accounts office *ou* department; ~ **à partie double** double-entry book-keeping.

comptable [kɔ̃tabl(ə)] *nm/f* accountant ♦ *adj* accounts *cpd*, accounting.

comptant [kɔ̃tɑ̃] *adv:* **payer** ~ to pay cash; **acheter** ~ to buy for cash.

compte [kɔ̃t] *nm* count, counting; (*total, montant*) count, (right) number; (*bancaire, facture*) account; ~**s** *nmpl* accounts, books; (*fig*) explanation *sg;* **ouvrir un** ~ to open an account; **rendre des** ~**s à qn** (*fig*) to be answerable to sb; **faire le** ~ **de** to count up, make a count of; **tout** ~ **fait** on the whole; **à ce** ~**-là** (*dans ce cas*) in that case; (*à ce train-là*) at that rate; **en fin de** ~ (*fig*) all things considered, weighing it all up; **au bout du** ~ in the final analysis; **à bon** ~ at a favourable price; (*fig*) lightly; **avoir son** ~ (*fig: fam*) to have had it; **pour le** ~ **de** on behalf of; **pour son propre** ~ for one's own benefit; **sur le** ~ **de qn** (*à son sujet*) about sb; **travailler à son** ~ to work for oneself; **mettre qch sur le** ~ **de qn** (*le rendre responsable*) to attribute sth to sb; **prendre qch à son** ~ to take responsibility for sth; **trouver son** ~ **à qch** to do well out of sth; **régler un** ~ (*s'acquitter de qch*) to settle an

account; (*se venger*) to get one's own back; **rendre** ~ (**à qn**) **de qch** to give (sb) an account of sth; **tenir** ~ **de qch** to take sth into account; ~ **tenu de** taking into account; ~ **chèque(s)** current account; ~ **chèque postal (CCP)** Post Office account; ~ **client** (*sur bilan*) accounts receivable; ~ **courant (CC)** current account; ~ **de dépôt** deposit account; ~ **d'exploitation** operating account; ~ **fournisseur** (*sur bilan*) accounts payable; ~ **à rebours** countdown; ~ **rendu** account, report; (*de film, livre*) review; *voir aussi* **rendre.**

compte-gouttes [kɔ̃tgut] *nm inv* dropper.

compter [kɔ̃te] *vt* to count; (*facturer*) to charge for; (*avoir à son actif, comporter*) to have; (*prévoir*) to allow, reckon; (*tenir compte de, inclure*) to include; (*penser, espérer*): ~ **réussir/revenir** to expect to succeed/return ♦ *vi* to count; (*être économe*) to economize; (*être non négligeable*) to count, matter; (*valoir*): ~ **pour** to count for; (*figurer*): ~ **parmi** to be *ou* rank among; ~ **sur** to count (up)on; ~ **avec qch/qn** to reckon with *ou* take account of sth/sb; ~ **sans qch/qn** to reckon without sth/sb; **sans** ~ **que** besides which; **à** ~ **du 10 janvier** (*COMM*) (as) from 10th January.

compte-tours [kɔ̃ttur] *nm inv* rev(olution) counter.

compteur [kɔ̃tœr] *nm* meter; ~ **de vitesse** speedometer.

comptine [kɔ̃tin] *nf* nursery rhyme.

comptoir [kɔ̃twar] *nm* (*de magasin*) counter; (*de café*) counter, bar; (*colonial*) trading post.

compulser [kɔ̃pylse] *vt* to consult.

comte, comtesse [kɔ̃t, kɔ̃tɛs] *nm/f* count/ countess.

con, ne [kɔ̃, kɔn] *adj* (*fam!*) bloody (*BRIT*) *ou* damned stupid (*!*).

concasser [kɔ̃kase] *vt* (*pierre, sucre*) to crush; (*poivre*) to grind.

concave [kɔ̃kav] *adj* concave.

concéder [kɔ̃sede] *vt* to grant; (*défaite, point*) to concede; ~ **que** to concede that.

concentration [kɔ̃sɑ̃trasjɔ̃] *nf* concentration.

concentrationnaire [kɔ̃sɑ̃trasjɔnɛr] *adj* of *ou* in concentration camps.

concentré [kɔ̃sɑ̃tre] *nm* concentrate; ~ **de tomates** tomato purée.

concentrer [kɔ̃sɑ̃tre] *vt* to concentrate; **se** ~ to concentrate.

concentrique [kɔ̃sɑ̃trik] *adj* concentric.

concept [kɔ̃sɛpt] *nm* concept.

concepteur, trice [kɔ̃sɛptœr, -tris] *nm/f* designer.

conception [kɔ̃sɛpsjɔ̃] *nf* conception; (*d'une machine etc*) design.

concernant [kɔ̃sɛrnɑ̃] *prép* (*se rapportant à*) concerning; (*en ce qui concerne*) as regards.

concerner [kɔ̃sɛrne] *vt* to concern; **en ce qui**

me concerne as far as I am concerned; **en ce qui concerne ceci** as far as this is concerned, with regard to this.

concert [kɔ̃sɛʀ] *nm* concert; **de** ~ *adv* in unison; together.

concertation [kɔ̃sɛʀtɑsjɔ̃] *nf (échange de vues)* dialogue; *(rencontre)* meeting.

concerter [kɔ̃sɛʀte] *vt* to devise; **se** ~ *vi (collaborateurs etc)* to put our *(ou* their *etc)* heads together, consult (each other).

concertiste [kɔ̃sɛʀtist(ə)] *nm/f* concert artist.

concerto [kɔ̃sɛʀto] *nm* concerto.

concession [kɔ̃sesjɔ̃] *nf* concession.

concessionnaire [kɔ̃sesjɔnɛʀ] *nm/f* agent, dealer.

concevable [kɔ̃svabl(ə)] *adj* conceivable.

concevoir [kɔ̃svwaʀ] *vt (idée, projet)* to conceive (of); *(méthode, plan d'appartement, décoration etc)* to plan, design; *(enfant)* to conceive; **maison bien/mal conçue** well-/ badly-designed *ou* -planned house.

concierge [kɔ̃sjɛʀʒ(ə)] *nm/f* caretaker; *(d'hôtel)* head porter.

conciergerie [kɔ̃sjɛʀʒəʀi] *nf* caretaker's lodge.

concile [kɔ̃sil] *nm* council, synod.

conciliable [kɔ̃siljabl(ə)] *adj (opinions etc)* reconcilable.

conciliabules [kɔ̃siljabyl] *nmpl* (private) discussions, confabulations *(BRIT)*.

conciliant, e [kɔ̃siljɑ̃, -ɑ̃t] *adj* conciliatory.

conciliateur, trice [kɔ̃siljatœʀ, -tʀis] *nm/f* mediator, go-between.

conciliation [kɔ̃siljɑsjɔ̃] *nf* conciliation.

concilier [kɔ̃silje] *vt* to reconcile; **se** ~ **qn/ l'appui de qn** to win sb over/sb's support.

concis, e [kɔ̃si, -iz] *adj* concise.

concision [kɔ̃sizjɔ̃] *nf* concision, conciseness.

concitoyen, ne [kɔ̃sitwajɛ̃, -ɛn] *nm/f* fellow citizen.

conclave [kɔ̃klav] *nm* conclave.

concluant, e [kɔ̃klyɑ̃, -ɑ̃t] *vb voir* **conclure** ♦ *adj* conclusive.

conclure [kɔ̃klyʀ] *vt* to conclude; *(signer: accord, pacte)* to enter into; *(déduire)*: ~ **qch de qch** to deduce sth from sth; ~ **à l'acquittement** to decide in favour of an acquittal; ~ **au suicide** to come to the conclusion *(ou (JUR)* to pronounce) that it is a case of suicide; ~ **un marché** to clinch a deal; **j'en conclus que** from that I conclude that.

conclusion [kɔ̃klyzjɔ̃] *nf* conclusion; ~**s** *nfpl (JUR)* submissions; findings; **en** ~ in conclusion.

concocter [kɔ̃kɔkte] *vt* to concoct.

conçois [kɔ̃swa], **conçoive** [kɔ̃swav] *etc vb voir* **concevoir**.

concombre [kɔ̃kɔ̃bʀ(ə)] *nm* cucumber.

concomitant, e [kɔ̃kɔmitɑ̃, -ɑ̃t] *adj* concomitant.

concordance [kɔ̃kɔʀdɑ̃s] *nf* concordance; **la** ~ **des temps** *(LING)* the sequence of tenses.

concordant, e [kɔ̃kɔʀdɑ̃, -ɑ̃t] *adj (témoignages, versions)* corroborating.

concorde [kɔ̃kɔʀd(ə)] *nf* concord.

concorder [kɔ̃kɔʀde] *vi* to tally, agree.

concourir [kɔ̃kuʀiʀ] *vi (SPORT)* to compete; ~ **à** *vt (effet etc)* to work towards.

concours [kɔ̃kuʀ] *vb voir* **concourir** ♦ *nm* competition; *(SCOL)* competitive examination; *(assistance)* aid, help; **recrutement par voie de** ~ recruitment by (competitive) examination; **apporter son** ~ **à** to give one's support to; ~ **de circonstances** combination of circumstances; ~ **hippique** horse show; *voir* **hors.**

concret, ète [kɔ̃kʀɛ, -ɛt] *adj* concrete.

concrètement [kɔ̃kʀɛtmɑ̃] *adv* in concrete terms.

concrétisation [kɔ̃kʀetizɑsjɔ̃] *nf* realization.

concrétiser [kɔ̃kʀetize] *vt* to realize; **se** ~ *vi* to materialize.

conçu, e [kɔ̃sy] *pp de* **concevoir.**

concubin, e [kɔ̃kybɛ̃, -in] *nm/f (JUR)* cohabitant.

concubinage [kɔ̃kybinaʒ] *nm (JUR)* cohabitation.

concupiscence [kɔ̃kypisɑ̃s] *nf* concupiscence.

concurremment [kɔ̃kyʀamɑ̃] *adv* concurrently; jointly.

concurrence [kɔ̃kyʀɑ̃s] *nf* competition; **jusqu'à** ~ **de** up to; ~ **déloyale** unfair competition.

concurrencer [kɔ̃kyʀɑ̃se] *vt* to compete with; **ils nous concurrencent dangereusement** they are a serious threat to us.

concurrent, e [kɔ̃kyʀɑ̃, -ɑ̃t] *adj* competing ♦ *nm/f (SPORT, ÉCON etc)* competitor; *(SCOL)* candidate.

concurrentiel, le [kɔ̃kyʀɑ̃sjɛl] *adj* competitive.

conçus [kɔ̃sy] *vb voir* **concevoir.**

condamnable [kɔ̃danabl(ə)] *adj (action, opinion)* reprehensible.

condamnation [kɔ̃danɑsjɔ̃] *nf (action)* condemnation; sentencing; *(peine)* sentence; conviction; ~ **à mort** death sentence.

condamné, e [kɔ̃dane] *nm/f (JUR)* convict.

condamner [kɔ̃dane] *vt (blâmer)* to condemn; *(JUR)* to sentence; *(porte, ouverture)* to fill in, block up; *(malade)* to give up (hope for); *(obliger)*: ~ **qn à qch/à faire** to condemn sb to sth/to do; ~ **qn à 2 ans de prison** to sentence sb to 2 years' imprisonment; ~ **qn à une amende** to impose a fine on sb.

condensateur [kɔ̃dɑ̃satœʀ] *nm* condenser.

condensation [kɔ̃dɑ̃sɑsjɔ̃] *nf* condensation.

condensé [kɔ̃dɑ̃se] *nm* digest.

condenser [kɔ̃dɑ̃se] *vt*, **se** ~ *vi* to condense.

condescendance [kɔ̃desɑ̃dɑ̃s] *nf* condescension.

condescendant, e [kɔ̃desɑ̃dɑ̃, -ɑ̃t] *adj*

(*personne, attitude*) condescending.
condescendre [kɔ̃desɑ̃dʀ(ə)] *vi*: ~ **à** to condescend to.
condiment [kɔ̃dimɑ̃] *nm* condiment.
condisciple [kɔ̃disipl(ə)] *nm/f* school fellow, fellow student.
condition [kɔ̃disjɔ̃] *nf* condition; ~**s** *nfpl* (*tarif, prix*) terms; (*circonstances*) conditions; **sans** ~ *adj* unconditional ◊ *adv* unconditionally; **sous** ~ **que** on condition that; **à** ~ **de** *ou* **que** provided that; **en bonne** ~ in good condition; **mettre en** ~ (*SPORT etc*) to get fit; (*PSYCH*) to condition (mentally); ~**s de vie** living conditions.
conditionnel, le [kɔ̃disjɔnɛl] *adj* conditional ◊ *nm* conditional (tense).
conditionnement [kɔ̃disjɔnmɑ̃] *nm* (*emballage*) packaging; (*fig*) conditioning.
conditionner [kɔ̃disjɔne] *vt* (*déterminer*) to determine; (*COMM: produit*) to package; (*fig: personne*) to condition; **air conditionné** air conditioning; **réflexe conditionné** conditioned reflex.
condoléances [kɔ̃dɔleɑ̃s] *nfpl* condolences.
conducteur, trice [kɔ̃dyktœʀ, -tʀis] *adj* (*ÉLEC*) conducting ◊ *nm/f* (*AUTO etc*) driver; (*machine*) operator ◊ *nm* (*ÉLEC etc*) conductor.
conduire [kɔ̃dɥiʀ] *vt* (*véhicule, passager*) to drive; (*délégation, troupeau*) to lead; **se** ~ *vi* to behave; ~ **vers/à** to lead towards/to; ~ **qn quelque part** to take sb somewhere; to drive sb somewhere.
conduit, e [kɔ̃dɥi, -it] *pp de* **conduire** ◊ *nm* (*TECH*) conduit, pipe; (*ANAT*) duct, canal.
conduite [kɔ̃dɥit] *nf* (*en auto*) driving; (*comportement*) behaviour (*BRIT*), behavior (*US*); (*d'eau, de gaz*) pipe; **sous la** ~ **de** led by; ~ **forcée** pressure pipe; ~ **à gauche** left-hand drive; ~ **intérieure** saloon (car).
cône [kon] *nm* cone; **en forme de** ~ cone-shaped.
conf. *abr* (= *confort*): **tt** ~ all mod cons (*BRIT*).
confection [kɔ̃fɛksjɔ̃] *nf* (*fabrication*) making; (*COUTURE*): **la** ~ the clothing industry, the rag trade (*fam*); **vêtement de** ~ ready-to-wear *ou* off-the-peg garment.
confectionner [kɔ̃fɛksjɔne] *vt* to make.
confédération [kɔ̃fedeʀasjɔ̃] *nf* confederation.
conférence [kɔ̃feʀɑ̃s] *nf* (*exposé*) lecture; (*pourparlers*) conference; ~ **de presse** press conference; ~ **au sommet** summit (conference).
conférencier, ière [kɔ̃feʀɑ̃sje, -jɛʀ] *nm/f* lecturer.
conférer [kɔ̃feʀe] *vt*: ~ **à qn** (*titre, grade*) to confer on sb; ~ **à qch/qn** (*aspect etc*) to endow sth/sb with, give (to) sth/sb.
confesser [kɔ̃fese] *vt* to confess; **se** ~ *vi* (*REL*) to go to confession.
confesseur [kɔ̃fesœʀ] *nm* confessor.

confession [kɔ̃fɛsjɔ̃] *nf* confession; (*culte: catholique etc*) denomination.
confessionnal, aux [kɔ̃fesjɔnal, -o] *nm* confessional.
confessionnel, le [kɔ̃fesjɔnɛl] *adj* denominational.
confetti [kɔ̃feti] *nm* confetti *no pl*.
confiance [kɔ̃fjɑ̃s] *nf* confidence, trust; faith; **avoir** ~ **en** to have confidence *ou* faith in, trust; **faire** ~ **à** to trust; **en toute** ~ with complete confidence; **de** ~ trustworthy, reliable; **mettre qn en** ~ to win sb's trust; **vote de** ~ (*POL*) vote of confidence; **inspirer** ~ **à** to inspire confidence in; ~ **en soi** self-confidence; *voir* **question**.
confiant, e [kɔ̃fjɑ̃, -ɑ̃t] *adj* confident; trusting.
confidence [kɔ̃fidɑ̃s] *nf* confidence.
confident, e [kɔ̃fidɑ̃, -ɑ̃t] *nm/f* confidant/confidante.
confidentiel, le [kɔ̃fidɑ̃sjɛl] *adj* confidential.
confidentiellement [kɔfidɑ̃sjɛlmɑ̃] *adv* in confidence, confidentially.
confier [kɔ̃fje] *vt*: ~ **à qn** (*objet en dépôt, travail etc*) to entrust to sb; (*secret, pensée*) to confide to sb; **se** ~ **à qn** to confide in sb.
configuration [kɔ̃figyʀasjɔ̃] *nf* configuration, layout; (*INFORM*) configuration.
configurer [kɔ̃figyʀe] *vt* to configure.
confiné, e [kɔ̃fine] *adj* enclosed; (*air*) stale.
confiner [kɔ̃fine] *vt*: ~ **à** to confine to; (*toucher*) to border on; **se** ~ **dans** *ou* **à** to confine o.s. to.
confins [kɔ̃fɛ̃] *nmpl*: **aux** ~ **de** on the borders of.
confirmation [kɔ̃fiʀmasjɔ̃] *nf* confirmation.
confirmer [kɔ̃fiʀme] *vt* to confirm; ~ **qn dans une croyance/ses fonctions** to strengthen sb in a belief/his duties.
confiscation [kɔ̃fiskasjɔ̃] *nf* confiscation.
confiserie [kɔ̃fizʀi] *nf* (*magasin*) confectioner's *ou* sweet shop (*BRIT*), candy store (*US*); ~**s** *nfpl* (*bonbons*) confectionery *sg*, sweets, candy *no pl*.
confiseur, euse [kɔ̃fizœʀ, -øz] *nm/f* confectioner.
confisquer [kɔ̃fiske] *vt* to confiscate.
confit, e [kɔ̃fi, -it] *adj*: **fruits** ~**s** crystallized fruits ◊ *nm*: ~ **d'oie** potted goose.
confiture [kɔ̃fityʀ] *nf* jam; ~ **d'oranges** (orange) marmalade.
conflagration [kɔ̃flagʀasjɔ̃] *nf* cataclysm.
conflictuel, le [kɔ̃fliktɥɛl] *adj* full of clashes *ou* conflicts.
conflit [kɔ̃fli] *nm* conflict.
confluent [kɔ̃flyɑ̃] *nm* confluence.
confondre [kɔ̃fɔ̃dʀ(ə)] *vt* (*jumeaux, faits*) to confuse, mix up; (*témoin, menteur*) to confound; **se** ~ *vi* to merge; **se** ~ **en excuses** to offer profuse apologies, apologize profusely; ~ **qch/qn avec qch/qn d'autre** to mistake sth/sb for sth/sb else.
confondu, e [kɔ̃fɔ̃dy] *pp de* **confondre** ◊ *adj*

(*stupéfait*) speechless, overcome; **toutes catégories** ~**es** taking all categories together.
conformation [kɔ̃fɔʀmɑsjɔ̃] *nf* conformation.
conforme [kɔ̃fɔʀm(ə)] *adj*: ~ **à** (*en accord avec*) in accordance with, in keeping with; (*identique à*) true to; **copie certifiée** ~ (*ADMIN*) certified copy; ~ **à la commande** as per order.
conformé, e [kɔ̃fɔʀme] *adj*: **bien** ~ well-formed.
conformément [kɔ̃fɔʀmemɑ̃] *adv*: ~ **à** in accordance with.
conformer [kɔ̃fɔʀme] *vt*: ~ **qch à** to model sth on; **se** ~ **à** to conform to.
conformisme [kɔ̃fɔʀmism(ə)] *nm* conformity.
conformiste [kɔ̃fɔʀmist(ə)] *adj, nm/f* conformist.
conformité [kɔ̃fɔʀmite] *nf* conformity; agreement; **en** ~ **avec** in accordance with.
confort [kɔ̃fɔʀ] *nm* comfort; **tout** ~ (*COMM*) with all mod cons (*BRIT*) *ou* modern conveniences.
confortable [kɔ̃fɔʀtabl(ə)] *adj* comfortable.
confortablement [kɔ̃fɔʀtabləmɑ̃] *adv* comfortably.
conforter [kɔ̃fɔʀte] *vt* to reinforce, strengthen.
confrère [kɔ̃fʀɛʀ] *nm* colleague; fellow member.
confrérie [kɔ̃fʀeʀi] *nf* brotherhood.
confrontation [kɔ̃fʀɔ̃tɑsjɔ̃] *nf* confrontation.
confronté, e [kɔ̃fʀɔ̃te] *adj*: ~ **à** confronted by, facing.
confronter [kɔ̃fʀɔ̃te] *vt* to confront; (*textes*) to compare, collate.
confus, e [kɔ̃fy, -yz] *adj* (*vague*) confused; (*embarrassé*) embarrassed.
confusément [kɔ̃fyzemɑ̃] *adv* (*distinguer, ressentir*) vaguely; (*parler*) confusedly.
confusion [kɔ̃fyzjɔ̃] *nf* (*voir confus*) confusion; embarrassment; (*voir confondre*) confusion; mixing up; (*erreur*) confusion; ~ **des peines** (*JUR*) concurrency of sentences.
congé [kɔ̃ʒe] *nm* (*vacances*) holiday; (*arrêt de travail*) time off *no pl*; leave *no pl*; (*MIL*) leave *no pl*; (*avis de départ*) notice; **en** ~ on holiday; off (work); on leave; **semaine/jour de** ~ week/day off; **prendre** ~ **de qn** to take one's leave of sb; **donner son** ~ **à** to hand *ou* give in one's notice to; ~ **de maladie** sick leave; ~ **de maternité** maternity leave; ~**s payés** paid holiday *ou* leave.
congédier [kɔ̃ʒedje] *vt* to dismiss.
congélateur [kɔ̃ʒelatœʀ] *nm* freezer, deep freeze.
congélation [kɔ̃ʒelɑsjɔ̃] *nf* freezing; (*de l'huile*) congealing.
congeler [kɔ̃ʒle] *vt*, **se** ~ *vi* to freeze.
congénère [kɔ̃ʒenɛʀ] *nm/f* fellow (bear *ou* lion *etc*), fellow creature.
congénital, e, aux [kɔ̃ʒenital, -o] *adj* congenital.

congère [kɔ̃ʒɛʀ] *nf* snowdrift.
congestion [kɔ̃ʒɛstjɔ̃] *nf* congestion; ~ **cérébrale** stroke; ~ **pulmonaire** congestion of the lungs.
congestionner [kɔ̃ʒɛstjɔne] *vt* to congest; (*MÉD*) to flush.
conglomérat [kɔ̃glɔmeʀa] *nm* conglomerate.
Congo [kɔ̃go] *nm*: **le** ~ (*pays, fleuve*) the Congo.
congolais, e [kɔ̃gɔlɛ, -ɛz] *adj* Congolese ◆ *nm/f*: **C**~, **e** Congolese.
congratuler [kɔ̃gʀatyle] *vt* to congratulate.
congre [kɔ̃gʀ(ə)] *nm* conger (eel).
congrégation [kɔ̃gʀegɑsjɔ̃] *nf* (*REL*) congregation; (*gén*) assembly; gathering.
congrès [kɔ̃gʀɛ] *nm* congress.
congressiste [kɔ̃gʀesist(ə)] *nm/f* delegate, participant (at a congress).
congru, e [kɔ̃gʀy] *adj*: **la portion** ~**e** the smallest *ou* meanest share.
conifère [kɔnifɛʀ] *nm* conifer.
conique [kɔnik] *adj* conical.
conjecture [kɔ̃ʒɛktyʀ] *nf* conjecture, speculation *no pl*.
conjecturer [kɔ̃ʒɛktyʀe] *vt, vi* to conjecture.
conjoint, e [kɔ̃ʒwɛ̃, -wɛ̃t] *adj* joint ◆ *nm/f* spouse.
conjointement [kɔ̃ʒwɛ̃tmɑ̃] *adv* jointly.
conjonctif, ive [kɔ̃ʒɔ̃ktif, -iv] *adj*: **tissu** ~ connective tissue.
conjonction [kɔ̃ʒɔ̃ksjɔ̃] *nf* (*LING*) conjunction.
conjonctivite [kɔ̃ʒɔ̃ktivit] *nf* conjunctivitis.
conjoncture [kɔ̃ʒɔ̃ktyʀ] *nf* circumstances *pl*; **la** ~ (**économique**) the economic climate *ou* situation.
conjoncturel, le [kɔ̃ʒɔ̃ktyʀɛl] *adj*: **variations/tendances** ~**les** economic fluctuations/trends.
conjugaison [kɔ̃ʒygɛzɔ̃] *nf* (*LING*) conjugation.
conjugal, e, aux [kɔ̃ʒygal, -o] *adj* conjugal; married.
conjugué, e [kɔ̃ʒyge] *adj* combined.
conjuguer [kɔ̃ʒyge] *vt* (*LING*) to conjugate; (*efforts etc*) to combine.
conjuration [kɔ̃ʒyʀɑsjɔ̃] *nf* conspiracy.
conjuré, e [kɔ̃ʒyʀe] *nm/f* conspirator.
conjurer [kɔ̃ʒyʀe] *vt* (*sort, maladie*) to avert; (*implorer*): ~ **qn de faire qch** to beseech *ou* entreat sb to do sth.
connais [kɔnɛ], **connaissais** [kɔnɛsɛ] *etc vb voir* **connaître**.
connaissance [kɔnɛsɑ̃s] *nf* (*savoir*) knowledge *no pl*; (*personne connue*) acquaintance; (*conscience, perception*) consciousness; ~**s** *nfpl* knowledge *no pl*; **être sans** ~ to be unconscious; **perdre/reprendre** ~ to lose/regain consciousness; **à ma/sa** ~ to (the best of) my/his knowledge; **faire** ~ **avec qn** *ou* **la** ~ **de qn** (*rencontrer*) to meet sb; (*apprendre à connaître*) to get to know sb; **avoir** ~ **de** to be aware of; **prendre** ~ **de**

(*document etc*) to peruse; **en ~ de cause** with full knowledge of the facts; **de ~** (*personne, visage*) familiar.

connaissant [kɔnɛsɑ̃] *etc vb voir* **connaître.**

connaissement [kɔnɛsmɑ̃] *nm* bill of lading.

connaisseur, euse [kɔnɛsœR, -øz] *nm/f* connoisseur ◆ *adj* expert.

connaître [kɔnɛtR(ə)] *vt* to know; (*éprouver*) to experience; (*avoir*) to have; to enjoy; **~ de nom/vue** to know by name/sight; **se ~** to know each other; (*soi-même*) to know o.s.; **ils se sont connus à Genève** they (first) met in Geneva; **s'y ~ en qch** to know about sth.

connasse [kɔnas] *nf* (*fam!*) stupid bitch (*!*) *ou* cow (*!*).

connecté, e [kɔnɛkte] *adj* (*INFORM*) on line.

connecter [kɔnɛkte] *vt* to connect.

connerie [kɔnRi] *nf* (*fam*) (bloody) stupid (*BRIT*) *ou* damn-fool (*US*) thing to do *ou* say.

connexe [kɔnɛks(ə)] *adj* closely related.

connexion [kɔnɛksjɔ̃] *nf* connection.

connivence [kɔnivɑ̃s] *nf* connivance.

connotation [kɔnɔtasjɔ̃] *nf* connotation.

connu, e [kɔny] *pp de* **connaître** ◆ *adj* (*célèbre*) well-known.

conque [kɔ̃k] *nf* (*coquille*) conch (shell).

conquérant, e [kɔ̃keRɑ̃, -ɑ̃t] *nm/f* conqueror.

conquérir [kɔ̃keRiR] *vt* to conquer, win.

conquerrai [kɔ̃kɛRRe] *etc vb voir* **conquérir.**

conquête [kɔ̃kɛt] *nf* conquest.

conquière, conquiers [kɔ̃kjɛR] *etc vb voir* **conquérir.**

conquis, e [kɔ̃ki, -iz] *pp de* **conquérir.**

consacrer [kɔ̃sakRe] *vt* (*REL*): **~ qch (à)** to consecrate sth (to); (*fig: usage etc*) to sanction, establish; (*employer*): **~ qch à** to devote *ou* dedicate sth to; **se ~ à qch/faire** to dedicate *ou* devote o.s. to sth/to doing.

consanguin, e [kɔ̃sɑ̃gɛ̃, -in] *adj* between blood relations; **frère ~** half-brother (*on father's side*); **mariage ~** intermarriage.

consciemment [kɔ̃sjamɑ̃] *adv* consciously.

conscience [kɔ̃sjɑ̃s] *nf* conscience; (*perception*) consciousness; **avoir/prendre ~ de** to be/become aware of; **perdre/reprendre ~** to lose/regain consciousness; **avoir bonne/mauvaise ~** to have a clear/guilty conscience; **en (toute) ~** in all conscience; **~ professionnelle** professional conscience.

consciencieux, euse [kɔ̃sjɑ̃sjø, -øz] *adj* conscientious.

conscient, e [kɔ̃sjɑ̃, -ɑ̃t] *adj* conscious; **~ de** aware *ou* conscious of.

conscription [kɔ̃skRipsjɔ̃] *nf* conscription.

conscrit [kɔ̃skRi] *nm* conscript.

consécration [kɔ̃sekRasjɔ̃] *nf* consecration.

consécutif, ive [kɔ̃sekytif, -iv] *adj* consecutive; **~ à** following upon.

consécutivement [kɔ̃sekytivmɑ̃] *adv* consecutively; **~ à** following on.

conseil [kɔ̃sɛj] *nm* (*avis*) piece of advice, advice *no pl*; (*assemblée*) council; (*expert*): **~**

en recrutement recruitment consultant ◆ *adj*: **ingénieur-~** consulting engineer, engineering consultant; **tenir ~** to hold a meeting; to deliberate; **donner un ~** *ou* **des ~s à qn** to give sb (a piece of) advice; **demander ~ à qn** to ask sb's advice; **prendre ~ (auprès de qn)** to take advice (from sb); **~ d'administration (CA)** board (of directors); **~ de classe** (*SCOL*) meeting of teachers, parents and class representatives to discuss pupils' progress; **~ de discipline** disciplinary committee; **~ général** regional council; **~ de guerre** court-martial; **le ~ des ministres** ≈ the Cabinet; **~ municipal (CM)** town council; **~ régional** regional board of elected representatives; **~ de révision** recruitment *ou* draft (*US*) board.

> *Each **département** has an elected body called a **Conseil général** made up of **conseillers généraux** each of whom represents a **canton** and is elected for a six year term. Half of the council's membership is elected every three years. The remit of the Conseil général is to administer matters affecting the département, including personnel, transport infrastructure, housing, school grants and economic development.*

conseiller¹ [kɔ̃seje] *vt* (*personne*) to advise; (*méthode, action*) to recommend, advise; **~ qch à qn** to recommend sth to sb; **~ à qn de faire qch** to advise sb to do sth.

conseiller², ère [kɔ̃seje, -ɛR] *nm/f* adviser; **~ général** regional councillor; **~ matrimonial** marriage guidance counsellor; **~ municipal** town councillor.

consensuel, le [kɔ̃sɑ̃sɥɛl] *adj* consensual.

consensus [kɔ̃sɛ̃sys] *nm* consensus.

consentement [kɔ̃sɑ̃tmɑ̃] *nm* consent.

consentir [kɔ̃sɑ̃tiR] *vt*: **~ (à qch/faire)** to agree *ou* consent (to sth/to doing); **~ qch à qn** to grant sth to sb.

conséquence [kɔ̃sekɑ̃s] *nf* consequence, outcome; **~s** *nfpl* consequences, repercussions; **en ~** (*donc*) consequently; (*de façon appropriée*) accordingly; **ne pas tirer à ~** to be unlikely to have any repercussions; **sans ~** unimportant; **de ~** important.

conséquent, e [kɔ̃sekɑ̃, -ɑ̃t] *adj* logical, rational; (*fam: important*) substantial; **par ~** consequently.

conservateur, trice [kɔ̃sɛRvatœR, -tRis] *adj* conservative ◆ *nm/f* (*POL*) conservative; (*de musée*) curator.

conservation [kɔ̃sɛRvasjɔ̃] *nf* retention; keeping; preserving; preservation.

conservatisme [kɔ̃sɛRvatism(ə)] *nm* conservatism.

conservatoire [kɔ̃sɛRvatwaR] *nm* academy; (*ÉCOLOGIE*) conservation area.

conserve [kɔsɛʀv(ə)] *nf (gén pl)* canned *ou* tinned (*BRIT*) food; ~**s de poisson** canned *ou* tinned (*BRIT*) fish; **en** ~ canned, tinned (*BRIT*); **de** ~ (*ensemble*) in concert; (*naviguer*) in convoy.

conservé, e [kɔsɛʀve] *adj:* **bien** ~ (*personne*) well-preserved.

conserver [kɔsɛʀve] *vt (faculté)* to retain, keep; (*habitude*) to keep up; (*amis, livres*) to keep; (*préserver, aussi CULIN*) to preserve; **se** ~ *vi (aliments)* to keep; "~ **au frais**" "store in a cool place".

conserverie [kɔsɛʀvəʀi] *nf* canning factory.

considérable [kɔsideʀabl(ə)] *adj* considerable, significant, extensive.

considération [kɔsideʀasjɔ̃] *nf* consideration; (*estime*) esteem, respect; ~**s** *nfpl (remarques)* reflections; **prendre en** ~ to take into consideration *ou* account; **ceci mérite** ~ this is worth considering; **en** ~ **de** given, because of.

considéré, e [kɔsideʀe] *adj* respected; **tout bien** ~ all things considered.

considérer [kɔsideʀe] *vt* to consider; (*regarder*) to consider, study; ~ **qch comme** to regard sth as.

consigne [kɔsiɲ] *nf (COMM)* deposit; (*de gare*) left luggage (office) (*BRIT*), checkroom (*US*); (*punition: SCOL*) detention; (*: MIL*) confinement to barracks; (*ordre, instruction*) instructions *pl*; ~ **automatique** left-luggage locker; ~**s de sécurité** safety instructions.

consigné, e [kɔsiɲe] *adj (COMM: bouteille, emballage*) returnable; **non** ~ non-returnable.

consigner [kɔsiɲe] *vt (note, pensée)* to record; (*marchandises*) to deposit; (*punir: MIL*) to confine to barracks; (*: élève*) to put in detention; (*COMM*) to put a deposit on.

consistance [kɔsistɑ̃s] *nf* consistency.

consistant, e [kɔsistɑ̃, -ɑ̃t] *adj* thick; solid.

consister [kɔsiste] *vi:* ~ **en/dans/à faire** to consist of/in/in doing.

consœur [kɔsœʀ] *nf (lady)* colleague; fellow member.

consolation [kɔsɔlasjɔ̃] *nf* consolation *no pl*, comfort *no pl*.

console [kɔsɔl] *nf* console; ~ **graphique** *ou* **de visualisation** (*INFORM*) visual display unit, VDU; ~ **de jeux vidéo** games console.

consoler [kɔsɔle] *vt* to console; **se** ~ (**de qch**) to console o.s. (for sth).

consolider [kɔsɔlide] *vt* to strengthen, reinforce; (*fig*) to consolidate; **bilan consolidé** consolidated balance sheet.

consommateur, trice [kɔsɔmatœʀ, -tʀis] *nm/f (ÉCON)* consumer; (*dans un café*) customer.

consommation [kɔsɔmasjɔ̃] *nf* consumption; (*JUR*) consummation; (*boisson*) drink; ~ **aux 100 km** (*AUTO*) (fuel) consumption per 100 km, ≈ miles per gallon (mpg), ≈ gas mileage (*US*); **de** ~ (*biens, société*) consumer *cpd*.

consommé, e [kɔsɔme] *adj* consummate ♦ *nm* consommé.

consommer [kɔsɔme] *vt (suj: personne)* to eat *ou* drink, consume; (*suj: voiture, usine, poêle*) to use, consume; (*JUR*) to consummate ♦ *vi (dans un café*) to (have a) drink.

consonance [kɔsɔnɑ̃s] *nf* consonance; **nom à** ~ **étrangère** foreign-sounding name.

consonne [kɔsɔn] *nf* consonant.

consortium [kɔsɔʀsjɔm] *nm* consortium.

consorts [kɔsɔʀ] *nmpl:* **et** ~ (*péj*) and company, and his bunch *ou* like.

conspirateur, trice [kɔspiʀatœʀ, -tʀis] *nm/f* conspirator, plotter.

conspiration [kɔspiʀasjɔ̃] *nf* conspiracy.

conspirer [kɔspiʀe] *vi* to conspire, plot; ~ **à** (*tendre à*) to conspire to.

conspuer [kɔspɥe] *vt* to boo, shout down.

constamment [kɔstamɑ̃] *adv* constantly.

constance [kɔstɑ̃s] *nf* permanence, constancy; (*d'une amitié*) steadfastness; **travailler avec** ~ to work steadily; **il faut de la** ~ **pour la supporter** (*fam*) you need a lot of patience to put up with her.

constant, e [kɔstɑ̃, -ɑ̃t] *adj* constant; (*personne*) steadfast ♦ *nf* constant.

Constantinople [kɔstɑ̃tinɔpl(ə)] *n* Constantinople.

constat [kɔsta] *nm (d'huissier)* certified report (*by bailiff*); (*de police*) report; (*observation*) (observed) fact, observation; (*affirmation*) statement; ~ (**à l'amiable**) (*jointly agreed*) *statement for insurance purposes.*

constatation [kɔstatasjɔ̃] *nf* noticing; certifying; (*remarque*) observation.

constater [kɔstate] *vt (remarquer)* to note, notice; (*ADMIN, JUR: attester*) to certify; (*dégâts*) to note; ~ **que** (*dire*) to state that.

constellation [kɔstelasjɔ̃] *nf* constellation.

constellé, e [kɔstele] *adj:* ~ **de** (*étoiles*) studded *ou* spangled with; (*taches*) spotted with.

consternant, e [kɔstɛʀnɑ̃ -ɑ̃t] *adj (nouvelle)* dismaying; (*attristant, étonnant: bêtise*) appalling.

consternation [kɔstɛʀnasjɔ̃] *nf* consternation, dismay.

consterner [kɔstɛʀne] *vt* to dismay.

constipation [kɔstipasjɔ̃] *nf* constipation.

constipé, e [kɔstipe] *adj* constipated; (*fig*) stiff.

constituant, e [kɔstitɥɑ̃, -ɑ̃t] *adj (élément)* constituent; **assemblée** ~**e** (*POL*) constituent assembly.

constitué, e [kɔstitɥe] *adj:* ~ **de** made up *ou* composed of; **bien** ~ of sound constitution; well-formed.

constituer [kɔstitɥe] *vt (comité, équipe)* to set up, form; (*dossier, collection*) to put together, build up; (*suj: éléments, parties: composer*) to make up, constitute; (*représenter, être*) to constitute; **se** ~ **prisonnier** to give o.s. up; **se**

~ **partie civile** to bring an independent action for damages.

constitution [kɔ̃stitysjɔ̃] nf setting up; building up; (composition) composition, make-up; (santé, POL) constitution.

constitutionnel, le [kɔ̃stitysjɔnɛl] adj constitutional.

constructeur [kɔ̃stryktœr] nm manufacturer, builder.

constructif, ive [kɔ̃stryktif, -iv] adj (positif) constructive.

construction [kɔ̃stryksjɔ̃] nf construction, building.

construire [kɔ̃stryiʀ] vt to build, construct; se ~: **l'immeuble s'est construit très vite** the building went up ou was built very quickly.

consul [kɔ̃syl] nm consul.

consulaire [kɔ̃sylɛʀ] adj consular.

consulat [kɔ̃syla] nm consulate.

consultant, e [kɔ̃syltɑ̃, -ɑ̃t] adj consultant.

consultatif, ive [kɔ̃syltatif, -iv] adj advisory.

consultation [kɔ̃syltasjɔ̃] nf consultation; **~s** nfpl (POL) talks; **être en ~** (délibération) to be in consultation; (médecin) to be consulting; **aller à la ~** (MÉD) to go to the surgery (BRIT) ou doctor's office (US); **heures de ~** (MÉD) surgery (BRIT) ou office (US) hours.

consulter [kɔ̃sylte] vt to consult ♦ vi (médecin) to hold surgery (BRIT), be in (the office) (US); se ~ to confer.

consumer [kɔ̃syme] vt to consume; se ~ vi to burn; **se ~ de chagrin/douleur** to be consumed with sorrow/grief.

consumérisme [kɔ̃symeʀism(ə)] nm consumerism.

contact [kɔ̃takt] nm contact; **au ~ de** (air, peau) on contact with; (gens) through contact with; **mettre/couper le ~** (AUTO) to switch on/off the ignition; **entrer en ~** (fils, objets) to come into contact, make contact; **se mettre en ~ avec** (RADIO) to make contact with; **prendre ~ avec** (relation d'affaires, connaissance) to get in touch ou contact with.

contacter [kɔ̃takte] vt to contact, get in touch with.

contagieux, euse [kɔ̃taʒjø, -øz] adj contagious; infectious.

contagion [kɔ̃taʒjɔ̃] nf contagion.

container [kɔ̃tɛnɛʀ] nm container.

contamination [kɔ̃taminasjɔ̃] nf infection; contamination.

contaminer [kɔ̃tamine] vt (par un virus) to infect; (par des radiations) to contaminate.

conte [kɔ̃t] nm tale; **~ de fées** fairy tale.

contemplatif, ive [kɔ̃tɑ̃platif, -iv] adj contemplative.

contemplation [kɔ̃tɑ̃plasjɔ̃] nf contemplation; (REL, PHILOSOPHIE) meditation.

contempler [kɔ̃tɑ̃ple] vt to contemplate, gaze at.

contemporain, e [kɔ̃tɑ̃pɔʀɛ̃, -ɛn] adj, nm/f contemporary.

contenance [kɔ̃tnɑ̃s] nf (d'un récipient) capacity; (attitude) bearing, attitude; **perdre ~** to lose one's composure; **se donner une ~** to give the impression of composure; **faire bonne ~ (devant)** to put on a bold front (in the face of).

conteneur [kɔ̃tnœʀ] nm container; **~ (de bouteilles)** bottle bank.

conteneurisation [kɔ̃tnœʀizasjɔ̃] nf containerization.

contenir [kɔ̃tniʀ] vt to contain; (avoir une capacité de) to hold; **se ~** (se retenir) to control o.s. ou one's emotions, contain o.s.

content, e [kɔ̃tɑ̃, -ɑ̃t] adj pleased, glad; **~ de** pleased with; **je serais ~ que tu ...** I would be pleased if you ....

contentement [kɔ̃tɑ̃tmɑ̃] nm contentment, satisfaction.

contenter [kɔ̃tɑ̃te] vt to satisfy, please; (envie) to satisfy; **se ~ de** to content o.s. with.

contentieux [kɔ̃tɑ̃sjø] nm (COMM) litigation; (: service) litigation department; (POL etc) contentious issues pl.

contenu, e [kɔ̃tny] pp de **contenir** ♦ nm (d'un bol) contents pl; (d'un texte) content.

conter [kɔ̃te] vt to recount, relate; **en ~ de belles à qn** to tell tall stories to sb.

contestable [kɔ̃tɛstabl(ə)] adj questionable.

contestataire [kɔ̃tɛstatɛʀ] adj (journal, étudiant) anti-establishment ♦ nm/f (anti-establishment) protester.

contestation [kɔ̃tɛstasjɔ̃] nf questioning, contesting; (POL): **la ~** anti-establishment activity, protest.

conteste [kɔ̃tɛst(ə)]: **sans ~** adv unquestionably, indisputably.

contesté, e [kɔ̃tɛste] adj (roman, écrivain) controversial.

contester [kɔ̃tɛste] vt to question, contest ♦ vi (POL, gén) to protest, rebel (against established authority).

conteur, euse [kɔ̃tœʀ, -øz] nm/f story-teller.

contexte [kɔ̃tɛkst(ə)] nm context.

contiendrai [kɔ̃tjɛ̃dʀe], **contiens** [kɔ̃tjɛ̃] etc vb voir **contenir**.

contigu, ë [kɔ̃tigy] adj: **~ (à)** adjacent (to).

continent [kɔ̃tinɑ̃] nm continent.

continental, e, aux [kɔ̃tinɑ̃tal, -o] adj continental.

contingences [kɔ̃tɛ̃ʒɑ̃s] nfpl contingencies.

contingent [kɔ̃tɛ̃ʒɑ̃] nm (MIL) contingent; (COMM) quota.

contingenter [kɔ̃tɛ̃ʒɑ̃te] vt (COMM) to fix a quota on.

contins [kɔ̃tɛ̃] etc vb voir **contenir**.

continu, e [kɔ̃tiny] adj continuous; **(courant) ~** direct current, DC.

continuation [kɔ̃tinyasjɔ̃] nf continuation.

continuel, le [kɔ̃tinyɛl] adj (qui se répète) constant, continual; (continu) continuous.

continuellement [kɔ̃tinɥɛlmɑ̃] *adv*
continually; continuously.
continuer [kɔ̃tinɥe] *vt* (*travail, voyage etc*) to
continue (with), carry on (with), go on with;
(*prolonger: alignement, rue*) to continue ♦ *vi*
(*pluie, vie, bruit*) to continue, go on;
(*voyageur*) to go on; **se ~** *vi* to carry on; **~ à**
ou **de faire** to go on *ou* continue doing.
continuité [kɔ̃tinɥite] *nf* continuity;
continuation.
contondant, e [kɔ̃tɔ̃dɑ̃, -ɑ̃t] *adj*: **arme ~e**
blunt instrument.
contorsion [kɔ̃tɔʀsjɔ̃] *nf* contortion.
contorsionner [kɔ̃tɔʀsjɔne]: **se ~** *vi* to contort
o.s., writhe about.
contorsionniste [kɔ̃tɔʀsjɔnist(ə)] *nm/f*
contortionist.
contour [kɔ̃tuʀ] *nm* outline, contour; **~s** *nmpl*
(*d'une rivière etc*) windings.
contourner [kɔ̃tuʀne] *vt* to bypass, walk (*ou*
drive) round.
contraceptif, ive [kɔ̃tʀasɛptif, -iv] *adj, nm*
contraceptive.
contraception [kɔ̃tʀasɛpsjɔ̃] *nf* contraception.
contracté, e [kɔ̃tʀakte] *adj* (*muscle*) tense,
contracted; (*personne: tendu*) tense, tensed
up; **article ~** (*LING*) contracted article.
contracter [kɔ̃tʀakte] *vt* (*muscle etc*) to tense,
contract; (*maladie, dette, obligation*) to
contract; (*assurance*) to take out; **se ~** *vi*
(*métal, muscles*) to contract.
contraction [kɔ̃tʀaksjɔ̃] *nf* contraction.
contractuel, le [kɔ̃tʀaktɥɛl] *adj* contractual
♦ *nm/f* (*agent*) traffic warden; (*employé*)
contract employee.
contradiction [kɔ̃tʀadiksjɔ̃] *nf* contradiction.
contradictoire [kɔ̃tʀadiktwaʀ] *adj*
contradictory, conflicting; **débat ~** (open)
debate.
contraignant, e [kɔ̃tʀɛɲɑ̃, -ɑ̃t] *vb voir*
contraindre ♦ *adj* restricting.
contraindre [kɔ̃tʀɛ̃dʀ(ə)] *vt*: **~ qn à faire** to
force *ou* compel sb to do.
contraint, e [kɔ̃tʀɛ̃, -ɛ̃t] *pp de* **contraindre** ♦ *adj*
(*mine, air*) constrained, forced ♦ *nf*
constraint; **sans ~e** unrestrainedly,
unconstrainedly.
contraire [kɔ̃tʀɛʀ] *adj, nm* opposite; **~ à**
contrary to; **au ~** *adv* on the contrary.
contrairement [kɔ̃tʀɛʀmɑ̃] *adv*: **~ à** contrary
to, unlike.
contralto [kɔ̃tʀalto] *nm* contralto.
contrariant, e [kɔ̃tʀaʀjɑ̃, -ɑ̃t] *adj* (*personne*)
contrary, perverse; (*incident*) annoying.
contrarier [kɔ̃tʀaʀje] *vt* (*personne*) to annoy,
bother; (*fig*) to impede; to thwart, frustrate.
contrariété [kɔ̃tʀaʀjete] *nf* annoyance.
contrasse [kɔ̃tʀast(ə)] *nm* contrast.
contraster [kɔ̃tʀaste] *vt, vi* to contrast.
contrat [kɔ̃tʀa] *nm* contract; (*fig: accord, pacte*)
agreement; **~ de travail** employment
contract.

contravention [kɔ̃tʀavɑ̃sjɔ̃] *nf* (*infraction*): **~ à**
contravention of; (*amende*) fine; (*PV pour
stationnement interdit*) parking ticket; **dresser
~ à** (*automobiliste*) to book; to write out a
parking ticket for.
contre [kɔ̃tʀ(ə)] *prép* against; (*en échange*) (in
exchange) for; **par ~** on the other hand.
contre-amiral, aux [kɔ̃tʀamiʀal, -o] *nm* rear
admiral.
contre-attaque [kɔ̃tʀatak] *nf* counterattack.
contre-attaquer [kɔ̃tʀatake] *vi* to counter-
attack.
contre-balancer [kɔ̃tʀəbalɑ̃se] *vt* to counterbalance; (*fig*) to offset.
contrebande [kɔ̃tʀəbɑ̃d] *nf* (*trafic*)
contraband, smuggling; (*marchandise*)
contraband, smuggled goods *pl*; **faire la ~ de**
to smuggle.
contrebandier, ière [kɔ̃tʀəbɑ̃dje, -jɛʀ] *nm/f*
smuggler.
contrebas [kɔ̃tʀəba]: **en ~** *adv* (down) below.
contrebasse [kɔ̃tʀəbas] *nf* (double) bass.
contrebassiste [kɔ̃tʀəbasist(ə)] *nm/f* (double)
bass player.
contre-braquer [kɔ̃tʀəbʀake] *vi* to steer into a
skid.
contrecarrer [kɔ̃tʀəkaʀe] *vt* to thwart.
contrechamp [kɔ̃tʀəʃɑ̃] *nm* (*CINÉ*) reverse
shot.
contrecœur [kɔ̃tʀəkœʀ]: **à ~** *adv*
(be)grudgingly, reluctantly.
contrecoup [kɔ̃tʀəku] *nm* repercussions *pl*;
par ~ as an indirect consequence.
contre-courant [kɔ̃tʀəkuʀɑ̃]: **à ~** *adv* against
the current.
contredire [kɔ̃tʀədiʀ] *vt* (*personne*) to
contradict; (*témoignage, assertion, faits*) to
refute; **se ~** to contradict o.s.
contredit, e [kɔ̃tʀədi, -it] *pp de* **contredire**
♦ *nm*: **sans ~** without question.
contrée [kɔ̃tʀe] *nf* region; land.
contre-écrou [kɔ̃tʀekʀu] *nm* lock nut.
contre-enquête [kɔ̃tʀɑ̃kɛt] *nf* counter-
inquiry.
contre-espionnage [kɔ̃tʀɛspjɔnaʒ] *nm*
counter-espionage.
contre-exemple [kɔ̃tʀɛgzɑ̃pl(ə)] *nf* counter-
example.
contre-expertise [kɔ̃tʀɛkspɛʀtiz] *nf* second
(expert) assessment.
contrefaçon [kɔ̃tʀəfasɔ̃] *nf* forgery; **~ de
brevet** patent infringement.
contrefaire [kɔ̃tʀəfɛʀ] *vt* (*document, signature*)
to forge, counterfeit; (*personne, démarche*)
to mimic; (*dénaturer: sa voix etc*) to disguise.
contrefait, e [kɔ̃tʀəfɛ, -ɛt] *pp de* **contrefaire**
♦ *adj* misshapen, deformed.
contrefasse [kɔ̃tʀəfas], **contreferai**
[kɔ̃tʀəfʀe] *etc vb voir* **contrefaire**.
contre-filet [kɔ̃tʀəfilɛ] *nm* (*CULIN*) sirloin.
contreforts [kɔ̃tʀəfɔʀ] *nmpl* foothills.
contre-haut [kɔ̃tʀəo]: **en ~** *adv* (up) above.

contre-indication [kɔ̃tʀɛ̃dikɑsjɔ̃] nf contraindication.

contre-indiqué, e [kɔ̃tʀɛ̃dike] adj (MÉD) contraindicated.

contre-interrogatoire [kɔ̃tʀɛ̃teʀɔgatwaʀ] nm: **faire subir un ~ à qn** to cross-examine sb.

contre-jour [kɔ̃tʀaʒuʀ]: **à ~** adv against the light.

contremaître [kɔ̃tʀəmɛtʀ(ə)] nm foreman.

contre-manifestant, e [kɔ̃tʀəmanifɛstɑ̃, -ɑ̃t] nm/f counter-demonstrator.

contre-manifestation [kɔ̃tʀəmanifɛstɑsjɔ̃] nf counter-demonstration.

contremarque [kɔ̃tʀəmaʀk(ə)] nf (ticket) pass-out ticket.

contre-offensive [kɔ̃tʀɔfɑ̃siv] nf counter-offensive.

contre-ordre [kɔ̃tʀɔʀdʀ(ə)] nm = **contrordre**.

contrepartie [kɔ̃tʀəpaʀti] nf compensation; **en ~** in compensation; in return.

contre-performance [kɔ̃tʀəpɛʀfɔʀmɑ̃s] nf below-average performance.

contrepèterie [kɔ̃tʀəpɛtʀi] nf spoonerism.

contre-pied [kɔ̃tʀəpje] nm (inverse, opposé): **le ~ de ...** the exact opposite of ...; **prendre le ~ de** to take the opposing view of; to take the opposite course to; **prendre qn à ~** (SPORT) to wrong-foot sb.

contre-plaqué [kɔ̃tʀəplake] nm plywood.

contre-plongée [kɔ̃tʀəplɔ̃ʒe] nf low-angle shot.

contrepoids [kɔ̃tʀəpwa] nm counterweight, counterbalance; **faire ~** to act as a counterbalance.

contrepoil [kɔ̃tʀəpwal]: **à ~** adv the wrong way.

contrepoint [kɔ̃tʀəpwɛ̃] nm counterpoint.

contrepoison [kɔ̃tʀəpwazɔ̃] nm antidote.

contrer [kɔ̃tʀe] vt to counter.

contre-révolution [kɔ̃tʀəʀevɔlysjɔ̃] nf counter-revolution.

contre-révolutionnaire [kɔ̃tʀəʀevɔlysjɔnɛʀ] nm/f counter-revolutionary.

contresens [kɔ̃tʀəsɑ̃s] nm misinterpretation; (mauvaise traduction) mistranslation; (absurdité) nonsense no pl; **à ~** adv the wrong way.

contresigner [kɔ̃tʀəsiɲe] vt to countersign.

contretemps [kɔ̃tʀətɑ̃] nm hitch, contretemps; **à ~** adv (MUS) out of time; (fig) at an inopportune moment.

contre-terrorisme [kɔ̃tʀətɛʀɔʀism(ə)] nm counter-terrorism.

contre-terroriste [kɔ̃tʀətɛʀɔʀist(ə)] nm/f counter-terrorist.

contre-torpilleur [kɔ̃tʀətɔʀpijœʀ] nm destroyer.

contrevenant, e [kɔ̃tʀəvnɑ̃, -ɑ̃t] vb voir **contrevenir** ♦ nm/f offender.

contrevenir [kɔ̃tʀəvniʀ]: **~ à** vt to contravene.

contre-voie [kɔ̃tʀəvwa]: **à ~** adv (en sens inverse) on the wrong track; (du mauvais côté) on the wrong side.

contribuable [kɔ̃tʀibɥabl(ə)] nm/f taxpayer.

contribuer [kɔ̃tʀibɥe]: **~ à** vt to contribute towards.

contribution [kɔ̃tʀibysjɔ̃] nf contribution; **les ~s** (bureaux) the tax office; **mettre à ~** to call upon; **~s directes/indirectes** direct/indirect taxation.

contrit, e [kɔ̃tʀi, -it] adj contrite.

contrôlable [kɔ̃tʀolabl(ə)] adj (maîtrisable: situation, débit) controllable; (alibi, déclarations) verifiable.

contrôle [kɔ̃tʀol] nm checking no pl, check; supervision; monitoring; (test) test, examination; **perdre le ~ de son véhicule** to lose control of one's vehicle; **~ des changes** (COMM) exchange controls; **~ continu** (SCOL) continuous assessment; **~ d'identité** identity check; **~ des naissances** birth control; **~ des prix** price control.

contrôler [kɔ̃tʀole] vt (vérifier) to check; (surveiller) to supervise; to monitor, control; (maîtriser, COMM: firme) to control; **se ~** to control o.s.

contrôleur, euse [kɔ̃tʀolœʀ, -øz] nm/f (de train) (ticket) inspector; (de bus) (bus) conductor/tress; **~ de la navigation aérienne** air traffic controller; **~ financier** financial controller.

contrordre [kɔ̃tʀɔʀdʀ(ə)] nm counter-order, countermand; **sauf ~** unless otherwise directed.

controverse [kɔ̃tʀɔvɛʀs(ə)] nf controversy.

controversé, e [kɔ̃tʀɔvɛʀse] adj (personnage, question) controversial.

contumace [kɔ̃tymas]: **par ~** adv in absentia.

contusion [kɔ̃tyzjɔ̃] nf bruise, contusion.

contusionné, e [kɔ̃tyzjɔne] adj bruised.

conurbation [kɔnyʀbasjɔ̃] nf conurbation.

convaincant, e [kɔ̃vɛ̃kɑ̃, -ɑ̃t] vb voir **convaincre** ♦ adj convincing.

convaincre [kɔ̃vɛ̃kʀ(ə)] vt: **~ qn (de qch)** to convince sb (of sth); **~ qn (de faire)** to persuade sb (to do); **~ qn de** (JUR: délit) to convict sb of.

convaincu, e [kɔ̃vɛ̃ky] pp de **convaincre** ♦ adj: **d'un ton ~** with conviction.

convainquais [kɔ̃vɛ̃kɛ] etc vb voir **convaincre**.

convalescence [kɔ̃valesɑ̃s] nf convalescence; **maison de ~** convalescent home.

convalescent, e [kɔ̃valesɑ̃, -ɑ̃t] adj, nm/f convalescent.

convenable [kɔ̃vnabl(ə)] adj suitable; (décent) acceptable, proper; (assez bon) decent, acceptable; adequate, passable.

convenablement [kɔ̃vnabləmɑ̃] adv (placé, choisi) suitably; (s'habiller, s'exprimer) properly; (payé, logé) decently.

convenance [kɔ̃vnɑ̃s] nf: **à ma/votre ~** to my/your liking; **~s** nfpl proprieties.

convenir [kɔ̃vniʀ] vt to be suitable; **~ à** to suit; **il convient de** it is advisable to;

(*bienséant*) it is right *ou* proper to; ~ **de** (*bien-fondé de qch*) to admit (to), acknowledge; (*date, somme etc*) to agree upon; ~ **que** (*admettre*) to admit that, acknowledge the fact that; ~ **de faire qch** to agree to do sth; **il a été convenu que** it has been agreed that; **comme convenu** as agreed.

convention [kɔ̃vɑ̃sjɔ̃] *nf* convention; ~**s** *nfpl* (*convenances*) convention *sg*, social conventions; **de** ~ conventional; ~ **collective** (*ÉCON*) collective agreement.

conventionnalisme [kɔ̃vɑ̃sjɔnalism(ə)] *nm* (*des idées*) conventionality.

conventionné, e [kɔ̃vɑ̃sjɔne] *adj* (*ADMIN*) *applying charges laid down by the state.*

conventionnel, le [kɔ̃vɑ̃sjɔnɛl] *adj* conventional.

conventionnellement [kɔ̃vɑ̃sjɔnɛlmɑ̃] *adv* conventionally.

conventuel, le [kɔ̃vɑ̃tɥɛl] *adj* monastic; monastery *cpd*; conventual, convent *cpd*.

convenu, e [kɔ̃vny] *pp de* **convenir** ♦ *adj* agreed.

convergent, e [kɔ̃vɛʀʒɑ̃, -ɑ̃t] *adj* convergent.

converger [kɔ̃vɛʀʒe] *vi* to converge; ~ **vers** *ou* **sur** to converge on.

conversation [kɔ̃vɛʀsasjɔ̃] *nf* conversation; **avoir de la** ~ to be a good conversationalist.

converser [kɔ̃vɛʀse] *vi* to converse.

conversion [kɔ̃vɛʀsjɔ̃] *nf* conversion; (*SKI*) kick turn.

convertible [kɔ̃vɛʀtibl(ə)] *adj* (*ÉCON*) convertible; (*canapé*) ~ sofa bed.

convertir [kɔ̃vɛʀtiʀ] *vt*: ~ **qn (à)** to convert sb (to); ~ **qch en** to convert sth into; **se** ~ **(à)** to be converted (to).

convertisseur [kɔ̃vɛʀtisœʀ] *nm* (*ÉLEC*) converter.

convexe [kɔ̃vɛks(ə)] *adj* convex.

conviction [kɔ̃viksjɔ̃] *nf* conviction.

conviendrai [kɔ̃vjɛ̃dʀe], **conviens** [kɔ̃vjɛ̃] *etc vb voir* **convenir**.

convier [kɔ̃vje] *vt*: ~ **qn à** (*dîner etc*) to (cordially) invite sb to; ~ **qn à faire** to urge sb to do.

convint [kɔ̃vɛ̃] *etc vb voir* **convenir**.

convive [kɔ̃viv] *nm/f* guest (*at table*).

convivial, e [kɔ̃vivjal] *adj* (*INFORM*) user-friendly.

convocation [kɔ̃vɔkasjɔ̃] *nf* (*voir convoquer*) convening, convoking; summoning; invitation; (*document*) notification to attend; summons *sg*.

convoi [kɔ̃vwa] *nm* (*de voitures, prisonniers*) convoy; (*train*) train; ~ **(funèbre)** funeral procession.

convoiter [kɔ̃vwate] *vt* to covet.

convoitise [kɔ̃vwatiz] *nf* covetousness; (*sexuelle*) lust, desire.

convoler [kɔ̃vɔle] *vi*: ~ **(en justes noces)** to be wed.

convoquer [kɔ̃vɔke] *vt* (*assemblée*) to convene, convoke; (*subordonné, témoin*) to summon; (*candidat*) to ask to attend; ~ **qn (à)** (*réunion*) to invite sb (to attend).

convoyer [kɔ̃vwaje] *vt* to escort.

convoyeur [kɔ̃vwajœʀ] *nm* (*NAVIG*) escort ship; ~ **de fonds** security guard.

convulsé, e [kɔ̃vylse] *adj* (*visage*) distorted.

convulsif, ive [kɔ̃vylsif, -iv] *adj* convulsive.

convulsions [kɔ̃vylsjɔ̃] *nfpl* convulsions.

coopérant [kɔɔpeʀɑ̃] *nm* ≈ person doing Voluntary Service Overseas (*BRIT*), ≈ member of the Peace Corps (*US*).

coopératif, ive [kɔɔpeʀatif, -iv] *adj*, *nf* co-operative.

coopération [kɔɔpeʀasjɔ̃] *nf* co-operation; (*ADMIN*): **la C**~ ≈ Voluntary Service Overseas (*BRIT*) *ou* the Peace Corps (*US*) (*done as alternative to military service*).

coopérer [kɔɔpeʀe] *vi*: ~ **(à)** to co-operate (in).

coordination [kɔɔʀdinasjɔ̃] *nf* coordination.

coordonnateur, trice [kɔɔʀdɔnatœʀ, -tʀis] *adj* coordinating ♦ *nm/f* coordinator.

coordonné, e [kɔɔʀdɔne] *adj* coordinated ♦ *nf* (*LING*) coordinate clause; ~**s** *nmpl* (*vêtements*) coordinates; ~**es** *nfpl* (*MATH*) coordinates; (*détails personnels*) address, phone number, schedule *etc*; whereabouts.

coordonner [kɔɔʀdɔne] *vt* to coordinate.

copain, copine [kɔpɛ̃, kɔpin] *nm/f* mate (*BRIT*), pal ♦ *adj*: **être** ~ **avec** to be pally with.

copeau, x [kɔpo] *nm* shaving; (*de métal*) turning.

Copenhague [kɔpənag] *n* Copenhagen.

copie [kɔpi] *nf* copy; (*SCOL*) script, paper; exercise; ~ **certifiée conforme** certified copy; ~ **papier** (*INFORM*) hard copy.

copier [kɔpje] *vt*, *vi* to copy; ~ **sur** to copy from.

copieur [kɔpjœʀ] *nm* (photo)copier.

copieusement [kɔpjøzmɑ̃] *adv* copiously.

copieux, euse [kɔpjø, -øz] *adj* copious, hearty.

copilote [kɔpilɔt] *nm* (*AVIAT*) co-pilot; (*AUTO*) co-driver, navigator.

copinage [kɔpinaʒ] *nm*: **obtenir qch par** ~ to get sth through contacts.

copine [kɔpin] *nf voir* **copain**.

copiste [kɔpist(ə)] *nm/f* copyist, transcriber.

coproduction [kɔpʀɔdyksjɔ̃] *nf* coproduction, joint production.

copropriétaire [kɔpʀɔpʀijetɛʀ] *nm/f* co-owner.

copropriété [kɔpʀɔpʀijete] *nf* co-ownership, joint ownership; **acheter en** ~ to buy on a co-ownership basis.

copulation [kɔpylasjɔ̃] *nf* copulation.

copyright [kɔpiʀajt] *nm* copyright.

coq [kɔk] *nm* cock, rooster ♦ *adj inv* (*BOXE*): **poids** ~ bantamweight; ~ **de bruyère** grouse; ~ **du village** (*fig: péj*) ladykiller.

coq-à-l'âne [kɔkalan] *nm inv* abrupt change of subject.

coque [kɔk] *nf (de noix, mollusque)* shell; *(de bateau)* hull; **à la ~** *(CULIN)* (soft-)boiled.
coquelet [kɔklɛ] *nm (CULIN)* cockerel.
coquelicot [kɔkliko] *nm* poppy.
coqueluche [kɔklyʃ] *nf* whooping-cough; *(fig)*: **être la ~ de qn** to be sb's flavour of the month.
coquet, te [kɔkɛ, -ɛt] *adj* appearance-conscious; *(joli)* pretty.
coquetier [kɔktje] *nm* egg-cup.
coquettement [kɔkɛtmɑ̃] *adv (s'habiller)* attractively; *(meubler)* prettily.
coquetterie [kɔkɛtʀi] *nf* appearance-conciousness.
coquillage [kɔkijaʒ] *nm (mollusque)* shellfish *inv*; *(coquille)* shell.
coquille [kɔkij] *nf* shell; *(TYPO)* misprint; **~ de beurre** shell of butter; **~ d'œuf** *adj (couleur)* eggshell; **~ de noix** nutshell; **~ St Jacques** scallop.
coquillettes [kɔkijɛt] *nfpl* pasta shells.
coquin, e [kɔkɛ̃, -in] *adj* mischievous, roguish; *(polisson)* naughty ♦ *nm/f (péj)* rascal.
cor [kɔʀ] *nm (MUS)* horn; *(MÉD)*: **~ (au pied)** corn; **réclamer à ~ et à cri** to clamour for; **~ anglais** cor anglais; **~ de chasse** hunting horn.
corail, aux [kɔʀaj, -o] *nm* coral *no pl*.
Coran [kɔʀɑ̃] *nm*: **le ~** the Koran.
coraux [kɔʀo] *pl de* **corail**.
corbeau, x [kɔʀbo] *nm* crow.
corbeille [kɔʀbɛj] *nf* basket; *(BOURSE)*: **la ~** ≈ the floor (of the Stock Exchange); **~ de mariage** *(fig)* wedding presents *pl*; **~ à ouvrage** work-basket; **~ à pain** bread-basket; **~ à papier** waste paper basket *ou* bin.
corbillard [kɔʀbijaʀ] *nm* hearse.
cordage [kɔʀdaʒ] *nm* rope; **~s** *nmpl (de voilure)* rigging *sg*.
corde [kɔʀd(ə)] *nf* rope; *(de violon, raquette, d'arc)* string; *(trame)*: **la ~** the thread; *(ATHLÉTISME, AUTO)*: **la ~** the rails *pl*; **les ~s** *(BOXE)* the ropes; **les (instruments à) ~s** *(MUS)* the strings, the stringed instruments; **semelles de ~** rope soles; **tenir la ~** *(ATHLÉTISME, AUTO)* to be in the inside lane; **tomber des ~s** to rain cats and dogs; **tirer sur la ~** to go too far; **la ~ sensible** the right chord; **usé jusqu'à la ~** threadbare; **~ à linge** washing *ou* clothes line; **~ lisse** (climbing) rope; **~ à nœuds** knotted climbing rope; **~ raide** tightrope; **~ à sauter** skipping rope; **~s vocales** vocal cords.
cordeau, x [kɔʀdo] *nm* string, line; **tracé au ~** as straight as a die.
cordée [kɔʀde] *nf (d'alpinistes)* rope, roped party.
cordelière [kɔʀdəljɛʀ] *nf* cord (belt).
cordial, e, aux [kɔʀdjal, -o] *adj* warm, cordial ♦ *nm* cordial, pick-me-up.

cordialement [kɔʀdjalmɑ̃] *adv* cordially, heartily; *(formule épistolaire)* (kind) regards.
cordialité [kɔʀdjalite] *nf* warmth, cordiality.
cordillère [kɔʀdijɛʀ] *nf*: **la ~ des Andes** the Andes cordillera *ou* range.
cordon [kɔʀdɔ̃] *nm* cord, string; **~ sanitaire/de police** sanitary/police cordon; **~ littoral** sandbank, sandbar; **~ ombilical** umbilical cord.
cordon-bleu [kɔʀdɔ̃blø] *adj, nm/f* cordon bleu.
cordonnerie [kɔʀdɔnʀi] *nf* shoe repairer's *ou* mender's (shop).
cordonnier [kɔʀdɔnje] *nm* shoe repairer *ou* mender, cobbler.
cordouan, e [kɔʀduɑ̃, -an] *adj* Cordovan.
Cordoue [kɔʀdu] *n* Cordoba.
Corée [kɔʀe] *nf*: **la ~ du Sud/du Nord** South/North Korea; **la République (démocratique populaire) de ~** the (Democratic People's) Republic of Korea.
coréen, ne [kɔʀeɛ̃, -ɛn] *adj* Korean ♦ *nm (LING)* Korean ♦ *nm/f*: **C~, ne** Korean.
coreligionnaire [kɔʀəliʒjɔnɛʀ] *nm/f* fellow Christian/Muslim/Jew *etc*.
Corfou [kɔʀfu] *n* Corfu.
coriace [kɔʀjas] *adj* tough.
coriandre [kɔʀjɑ̃dʀ(ə)] *nf* coriander.
Corinthe [kɔʀɛ̃t] *n* Corinth.
cormoran [kɔʀmɔʀɑ̃] *nm* cormorant.
cornac [kɔʀnak] *nm* elephant driver.
corne [kɔʀn(ə)] *nf* horn; *(de cerf)* antler; *(de la peau)* callus; **~ d'abondance** horn of plenty; **~ de brume** *(NAVIG)* foghorn.
cornée [kɔʀne] *nf* cornea.
corneille [kɔʀnɛj] *nf* crow.
cornélien, ne [kɔʀneljɛ̃, -ɛn] *adj (débat etc)* where love and duty conflict.
cornemuse [kɔʀnəmyz] *nf* bagpipes *pl*; **joueur de ~** piper.
corner *nm* [kɔʀnɛʀ] *(FOOTBALL)* corner (kick) ♦ *vb* [kɔʀne] *vt (pages)* to make dog-eared ♦ *vi (klaxonner)* to blare out.
cornet [kɔʀnɛ] *nm (paper)* cone; *(de glace)* cornet, cone; **~ à pistons** cornet.
cornette [kɔʀnɛt] *nf* cornet *(headgear)*.
corniaud [kɔʀnjo] *nm (chien)* mongrel; *(péj)* twit, clot.
corniche [kɔʀniʃ] *nf (de meuble, neigeuse)* cornice; *(route)* coast road.
cornichon [kɔʀniʃɔ̃] *nm* gherkin.
Cornouailles [kɔʀnwaj] *nf(pl)* Cornwall.
cornue [kɔʀny] *nf* retort.
corollaire [kɔʀɔlɛʀ] *nm* corollary.
corolle [kɔʀɔl] *nf* corolla.
coron [kɔʀɔ̃] *nm* mining cottage; mining village.
coronaire [kɔʀɔnɛʀ] *adj* coronary.
corporation [kɔʀpɔʀasjɔ̃] *nf* corporate body; *(au Moyen-Âge)* guild.
corporel, le [kɔʀpɔʀɛl] *adj* bodily; *(punition)* corporal; **soins ~s** care *sg* of the body.
corps [kɔʀ] *nm (gén)* body; *(cadavre)* (dead)

body; **à son ~ défendant** against one's will;
à ~ perdu headlong; **perdu ~ et biens** lost
with all hands; **prendre ~** to take shape;
faire ~ avec to be joined to; to form one
body with; **~ d'armée (CA)** army corps; **~
de ballet** corps de ballet; **~ constitués** (*POL*)
constitutional bodies; **le ~ consulaire (CC)**
the consular corps; **~ à ~** *adv* hand-to-hand
♦ *nm* clinch; **le ~ du délit** (*JUR*) corpus
delicti; **le ~ diplomatique (CD)** the
diplomatic corps; **le ~ électoral** the
electorate; **le ~ enseignant** the teaching
profession; **~ étranger** (*MÉD*) foreign body;
~ expéditionnaire task force; **~ de garde**
guardroom; **~ législatif** legislative body; **le
~ médical** the medical profession.

corpulence [kɔʀpylɑ̃s] *nf* build; (*embonpoint*)
stoutness (*BRIT*), corpulence; **de forte ~** of
large build.

corpulent, e [kɔʀpylɑ̃, -ɑ̃t] *adj* stout (*BRIT*),
corpulent.

corpus [kɔʀpys] *nm* (*LING*) corpus.

correct, e [kɔʀɛkt] *adj* (*exact*) accurate,
correct; (*bienséant, honnête*) correct;
(*passable*) adequate.

correctement [kɔʀɛktəmɑ̃] *adv* accurately;
correctly; adequately.

correcteur, trice [kɔʀɛktœʀ, -tʀis] *nm/f* (*SCOL*)
examiner, marker; (*TYPO*) proofreader.

correctif, ive [kɔʀɛktif, -iv] *adj* corrective
♦ *nm* (*mise au point*) rider, qualification.

correction [kɔʀɛksjɔ̃] *nf* (*voir corriger*)
correction; marking; (*voir correct*)
correctness; (*rature, surcharge*) correction,
emendation; (*coups*) thrashing; **~ sur écran**
(*INFORM*) screen editing; **~ (des épreuves)**
proofreading.

correctionnel, le [kɔʀɛksjɔnɛl] *adj* (*JUR*):
tribunal ~ ≈ criminal court.

corrélation [kɔʀelɑsjɔ̃] *nf* correlation.

correspondance [kɔʀɛspɔ̃dɑ̃s] *nf*
correspondence; (*de train, d'avion*)
connection; **ce train assure la ~ avec l'avion
de 10 heures** this train connects with the 10
o'clock plane; **cours par ~** correspondence
course; **vente par ~** mail-order business.

correspondancier, ière [kɔʀɛspɔ̃dɑ̃sje, -jɛʀ]
nm/f correspondence clerk.

correspondant, e [kɔʀɛspɔ̃dɑ̃, -ɑ̃t] *nm/f*
correspondent; (*TÉL*) person phoning (*ou*
being phoned).

correspondre [kɔʀɛspɔ̃dʀ(ə)] *vi* (*données,
témoignages*) to correspond, tally;
(*chambres*) to communicate; **~ à** to
correspond to; **~ avec qn** to correspond
with sb.

Corrèze [kɔʀɛz] *nf*: **la ~** the Corrèze.

corrézien, ne [kɔʀezjɛ̃, -ɛn] *adj* of *ou* from the
Corrèze.

corrida [kɔʀida] *nf* bullfight.

corridor [kɔʀidɔʀ] *nm* corridor, passage.

corrigé [kɔʀiʒe] *nm* (*SCOL*) correct version;
fair copy.

corriger [kɔʀiʒe] *vt* (*devoir*) to correct, mark;
(*texte*) to correct, emend; (*erreur, défaut*) to
correct, put right; (*punir*) to thrash; **~ qn de**
(*défaut*) to cure sb of; **se ~ de** to cure o.s. of.

corroborer [kɔʀɔbɔʀe] *vt* to corroborate.

corroder [kɔʀɔde] *vt* to corrode.

corrompre [kɔʀɔ̃pʀ(ə)] *vt* (*dépraver*) to
corrupt; (*acheter: témoin etc*) to bribe.

corrompu, e [kɔʀɔ̃py] *adj* corrupt.

corrosif, ive [kɔʀozif, -iv] *adj* corrosive.

corrosion [kɔʀozjɔ̃] *nf* corrosion.

corruption [kɔʀypsjɔ̃] *nf* corruption; bribery.

corsage [kɔʀsaʒ] *nm* (*d'une robe*) bodice;
(*chemisier*) blouse.

corsaire [kɔʀsɛʀ] *nm* pirate, corsair;
privateer.

corse [kɔʀs(ə)] *adj* Corsican ♦ *nm/f*: **C~**
Corsican ♦ *nf*: **la C~** Corsica.

corsé, e [kɔʀse] *adj* vigorous; (*café etc*) full-
flavoured (*BRIT*) *ou* -flavored (*US*); (*goût*)
full; (*fig*) spicy; tricky.

corselet [kɔʀsəlɛ] *nm* corselet.

corser [kɔʀse] *vt* (*difficulté*) to aggravate;
(*intrigue*) to liven up; (*sauce*) to add spice to.

corset [kɔʀsɛ] *nm* corset; (*d'une robe*) bodice;
~ orthopédique surgical corset.

corso [kɔʀso] *nm*: **~ fleuri** procession of floral
floats.

cortège [kɔʀtɛʒ] *nm* procession.

cortisone [kɔʀtizon] *nf* (*MÉD*) cortisone.

corvée [kɔʀve] *nf* chore, drudgery *no pl*; (*MIL*)
fatigue (duty).

cosaque [kɔzak] *nm* cossack.

cosignataire [kɔsiɲatɛʀ] *adj, nm/f* cosignatory.

cosinus [kɔsinys] *nm* (*MATH*) cosine.

cosmétique [kɔsmetik] *nm* (*pour les cheveux*)
hair-oil; (*produit de beauté*) beauty care
product.

cosmétologie [kɔsmetolɔʒi] *nf* beauty care.

cosmique [kɔsmik] *adj* cosmic.

cosmonaute [kɔsmɔnot] *nm/f* cosmonaut,
astronaut.

cosmopolite [kɔsmɔpɔlit] *adj* cosmopolitan.

cosmos [kɔsmɔs] *nm* outer space; cosmos.

cosse [kɔs] *nf* (*BOT*) pod, hull.

cossu, e [kɔsy] *adj* opulent-looking, well-to-
do.

Costa Rica [kɔstaʀika] *nm*: **le ~** Costa Rica.

costaricien, ne [kɔstaʀisjɛ̃, -ɛn] *adj* Costa
Rican ♦ *nm/f*: **C~, ne** Costa Rican.

costaud, e [kɔsto, -od] *adj* strong, sturdy.

costume [kɔstym] *nm* (*d'homme*) suit; (*de
théâtre*) costume.

costumé, e [kɔstyme] *adj* dressed up.

costumier, ière [kɔstymje, -jɛʀ] *nm/f*
(*fabricant, loueur*) costumier; (*THÉÂT*)
wardrobe master/mistress.

cotangente [kɔtɑ̃ʒɑ̃t] *nf* (*MATH*) cotangent.

cotation [kɔtɑsjɔ̃] *nf* quoted value.

cote [kɔt] *nf* (*en Bourse etc*) quotation; quoted

value; (*d'un cheval*): **la ~ de** the odds *pl* on; (*d'un candidat etc*) rating; (*mesure: sur une carte*) spot height; (*: sur un croquis*) dimension; (*de classement*) (classification) mark; reference number; **avoir la ~** to be very popular; **inscrit à la ~** quoted on the Stock Exchange; **~ d'alerte** danger *ou* flood level; **~ mal taillée** (*fig*) compromise; **~ de popularité** popularity rating.

coté, e [kɔte] *adj*: **être ~** to be listed *ou* quoted; **être ~ en Bourse** to be quoted on the Stock Exchange; **être bien/mal ~** to be highly/poorly rated.

côte [kot] *nf* (*rivage*) coast(line); (*pente*) slope; (*: sur une route*) hill; (*ANAT*) rib; (*d'un tricot, tissu*) rib, ribbing *no pl*; **à ~** *adv* side by side; **la C~** (**d'Azur**) the (French) Riviera; **la C~ d'Ivoire** the Ivory Coast.

côté [kote] *nm* (*gén*) side; (*direction*) way, direction; **de chaque ~** (**de**) on each side of; **de tous les ~s** from all directions; **de quel ~ est-il parti?** which way *ou* in which direction did he go?; **de ce/de l'autre ~** this/the other way; **d'un ~** ... **de l'autre ~** (*alternative*) on (the) one hand ... on the other (hand); **du ~ de** (*provenance*) from; (*direction*) towards; **du ~ de Lyon** (*proximité*) near Lyons; **du ~ gauche** on the left-hand side; **de ~** *adv* sideways; on one side; to one side; aside; **laisser de ~** to leave on one side; **mettre de ~** to put on one side, put aside; **de mon ~** (*quant à moi*) for my part; **à ~** *adv* (right) nearby; beside; next door; (*d'autre part*) besides; **à ~ de** beside; next to; (*fig*) in comparison to; **à ~** (**de la cible**) off target, wide (of the mark); **être aux ~s de** to be by the side of.

coteau, x [kɔto] *nm* hill.

côtelé, e [kotle] *adj* ribbed; **pantalon en velours ~** corduroy trousers *pl*.

côtelette [kotlɛt] *nf* chop.

coter [kɔte] *vt* (*BOURSE*) to quote.

coterie [kɔtʀi] *nf* set.

côtier, ière [kotje, -jɛʀ] *adj* coastal.

cotisation [kɔtizasjɔ̃] *nf* subscription, dues *pl*; (*pour une pension*) contributions *pl*.

cotiser [kɔtize] *vi*: **~ (à)** to pay contributions (to); (*à une association*) to subscribe (to); **se ~** to club together.

coton [kɔtɔ̃] *nm* cotton; **~ hydrophile** cotton wool (*BRIT*), absorbent cotton (*US*).

cotonnade [kɔtɔnad] *nf* cotton (fabric).

Coton-Tige [kɔtɔ̃tiʒ] *nm* ® cotton bud ®.

côtoyer [kotwaje] *vt* to be close to; (*rencontrer*) to rub shoulders with; (*longer*) to run alongside; (*fig: friser*) to be bordering *ou* verging on.

cotte [kɔt] *nf*: **~ de mailles** coat of mail.

cou [ku] *nm* neck.

couac [kwak] *nm* (*fam*) bum note.

couard, e [kwaʀ, -aʀd(ə)] *adj* cowardly.

couchage [kuʃaʒ] *nm voir* **sac**.

couchant [kuʃɑ̃] *adj*: **soleil ~** setting sun.

couche [kuʃ] *nf* (*strate: gén*, *GÉO*) layer, stratum (*pl* -a); (*de peinture, vernis*) coat; (*de poussière, crème*) layer; (*de bébé*) nappy (*BRIT*), diaper (*US*); **~ d'ozone** ozone layer; **~s** *nfpl* (*MÉD*) confinement *sg*; **~s sociales** social levels *ou* strata.

couché, e [kuʃe] *adj* (*étendu*) lying down; (*au lit*) in bed.

couche-culotte, *pl* **couches-culottes** [kuʃkylɔt] *nf* (plastic-coated) disposable nappy (*BRIT*) *ou* diaper (*US*).

coucher [kuʃe] *nm* (*du soleil*) setting ♦ *vt* (*personne*) to put to bed; (*: loger*) to put up; (*objet*) to lay on its side; (*écrire*) to inscribe, couch ♦ *vi* (*dormir*) to sleep, spend the night; **~ avec qn** to sleep with sb, go to bed with sb; **se ~** *vi* (*pour dormir*) to go to bed; (*pour se reposer*) to lie down; (*soleil*) to set, go down; **à prendre avant le ~** (*MÉD*) take at night *ou* before going to bed; **~ de soleil** sunset.

couchette [kuʃɛt] *nf* couchette; (*de marin*) bunk.

coucheur [kuʃœʀ] *nm*: **mauvais ~** awkward customer.

couci-couça [kusikusa] *adv* (*fam*) so-so.

coucou [kuku] *nm* cuckoo ♦ *excl* peek-a-boo.

coude [kud] *nm* (*ANAT*) elbow; (*de tuyau, de la route*) bend; **~ à ~** *adv* shoulder to shoulder, side by side.

coudée [kude] *nf*: **avoir ses ~s franches** (*fig*) to have a free rein.

cou-de-pied, *pl* **cous-de-pied** [kudpje] *nm* instep.

coudoyer [kudwaje] *vt* to brush past *ou* against; (*fig*) to rub shoulders with.

coudre [kudʀ(ə)] *vt* (*bouton*) to sew on; (*robe*) to sew (up) ♦ *vi* to sew.

couenne [kwan] *nf* (*de lard*) rind.

couette [kwɛt] *nf* duvet, (continental) quilt; **~s** *nfpl* (*cheveux*) bunches.

couffin [kufɛ̃] *nm* Moses basket; (straw) basket.

couilles [kuj] *nfpl* (*fam!*) balls (*!*).

couiner [kwine] *vi* to squeal.

coulage [kulaʒ] *nm* (*COMM*) loss of stock (*due to theft or negligence*).

coulant, e [kulɑ̃, -ɑ̃t] *adj* (*indulgent*) easy-going; (*fromage etc*) runny.

coulée [kule] *nf* (*de lave, métal en fusion*) flow; **~ de neige** snowslide.

couler [kule] *vi* to flow, run; (*fuir: stylo, récipient*) to leak; (*sombrer: bateau*) to sink ♦ *vt* (*cloche, sculpture*) to cast; (*bateau*) to sink; (*fig*) to ruin, bring down; (*: passer*): **~ une vie heureuse** to enjoy a happy life; **se ~ dans** (*interstice etc*) to slip into; **faire ~** (*eau*) to run; **faire ~ un bain** to run a bath; **il a coulé une bielle** (*AUTO*) his big end went; **~ de source** to follow on naturally; **~ à pic** to sink *ou* go straight to the bottom.

couleur [kulœʀ] *nf* colour (*BRIT*), color (*US*);

(*CARTES*) suit; ~**s** *nfpl* (*du teint*) colo(u)r *sg*; **les ~s** (*MIL*) the colo(u)rs; **en ~s** (*film*) in colo(u)r; **télévision en ~s** colo(u)r television; **de ~** (*homme, femme*) colo(u)red; **sous ~ de** on the pretext of.

couleuvre [kulœvʀ(ə)] *nf* grass snake.

coulisse [kulis] *nf* (*TECH*) runner; ~**s** *nfpl* (*THÉÂT*) wings; (*fig*): **dans les ~s** behind the scenes; **porte à ~** sliding door.

coulisser [kulise] *vi* to slide, run.

couloir [kulwaʀ] *nm* corridor, passage; (*de bus*) gangway; (: *sur la route*) bus lane; (*SPORT*: *de piste*) lane; (*GÉO*) gully; ~ **aérien** air corridor *ou* lane; ~ **de navigation** shipping lane.

coulpe [kulp(ə)] *nf*: **battre sa ~** to repent openly.

coup [ku] *nm* (*heurt, choc*) knock; (*affectif*) blow, shock; (*agressif*) blow; (*avec arme à feu*) shot; (*de l'horloge*) chime; stroke; (*SPORT*) stroke; shot; blow; (*fam: fois*) time; (*ÉCHECS*) move; ~ **de coude/genou** nudge (with the elbow)/with the knee; **à ~s de hache/marteau** (hitting) with an axe/a hammer; ~ **de tonnerre** clap of thunder; ~ **de sonnette** ring of the bell; ~ **de crayon/pinceau** stroke of the pencil/brush; **donner un ~ de balai** to sweep up, give the floor a sweep; **donner un ~ de chiffon** to go round with the duster; **avoir le ~** (*fig*) to have the knack; **être dans le/hors du ~** to be/not to be in on it; **boire un ~** to have a drink; **d'un seul ~** (*subitement*) suddenly; (*à la fois*) at one go; in one blow; **du ~** so (you see); **du premier ~** first time *ou* go, at the first attempt; **du même ~** at the same time; **à ~ sûr** definitely, without fail; **après ~** afterwards; ~ **sur ~** in quick succession; **être sur un ~** to be on to something; **sur le ~** outright; **sous le ~ de** (*surprise etc*) under the influence of; **tomber sous le ~ de la loi** to constitute a statutory offence; **à tous les ~s** every time; **il a raté son ~** he missed his turn; **pour le ~** for once; ~ **bas** (*fig*): **donner un ~ bas à** **qn** to hit sb below the belt; ~ **de chance** stroke of luck; ~ **de chapeau** (*fig*) pat on the back; ~ **de couteau** stab (of a knife); ~ **dur** hard blow; ~ **d'éclat** (great) feat; ~ **d'envoi** kick-off; ~ **d'essai** first attempt; ~ **d'état** coup d'état; ~ **de feu** shot; ~ **de filet** (*POLICE*) haul; ~ **de foudre** (*fig*) love at first sight; ~ **fourré** stab in the back; ~ **franc** free kick; ~ **de frein** (sharp) braking *no pl*; ~ **de fusil** rifle shot; ~ **de grâce** coup de grâce; ~ **du lapin** (*AUTO*) whiplash; ~ **de main**: **donner un ~ de main à** **qn** to give sb a (helping) hand; ~ **de maître** master stroke; ~ **d'œil** glance; ~ **de pied** kick; ~ **de poing** punch; ~ **de soleil** sunburn *no pl*; ~ **de téléphone** phone call; ~ **de tête** (*fig*) (sudden) impulse; ~ **de théâtre** (*fig*) dramatic turn of events; ~ **de vent** gust of wind; **en ~ de vent** (*rapidement*) in a

tearing hurry.

coupable [kupabl(ə)] *adj* guilty; (*pensée*) guilty, culpable ♦ *nm/f* (*gén*) culprit; (*JUR*) guilty party; ~ **de** guilty of.

coupant, e [kupɑ̃, -ɑ̃t] *adj* (*lame*) sharp; (*fig: voix, ton*) cutting.

coupe [kup] *nf* (*verre*) goblet; (*à fruits*) dish; (*SPORT*) cup; (*de cheveux, de vêtement*) cut; (*graphique, plan*) (cross) section; **être sous la ~ de** to be under the control of; **faire des ~s sombres dans** to make drastic cuts in.

coupé, e [kupe] *adj* (*communications, route*) cut, blocked; (*vêtement*): **bien/mal ~** well/badly cut ♦ *nm* (*AUTO*) coupé.

coupe-circuit [kupsiʀkɥi] *nm inv* cutout, circuit breaker.

coupée [kupe] *nf* (*NAVIG*) gangway.

coupe-feu [kupfø] *nm inv* firebreak.

coupe-gorge [kupɡɔʀʒ(ə)] *nm inv* cut-throats' den.

coupe-ongles [kupɔ̃ɡl(ə)] *nm inv* (*pince*) nail clippers; (*ciseaux*) nail scissors.

coupe-papier [kuppapje] *nm inv* paper knife.

couper [kupe] *vt* to cut; (*retrancher*) to cut (out), take out; (*route, courant*) to cut off; (*appétit*) to take away; (*fièvre*) to take down, reduce; (*vin, cidre*) to blend; (: *à table*) to dilute (with water) ♦ *vi* to cut; (*prendre un raccourci*) to take a short-cut; (*CARTES: diviser le paquet*) to cut; (: *avec l'atout*) to trump; **se ~** (*se blesser*) to cut o.s.; (*en témoignant etc*) to give o.s. away; ~ **l'appétit à qn** to spoil sb's appetite; ~ **la parole à qn** to cut sb short; ~ **les vivres à qn** to cut off sb's vital supplies; ~ **le contact** *ou* **l'allumage** (*AUTO*) to turn off the ignition; ~ **les ponts avec qn** to break with sb; **se faire ~ les cheveux** to have *ou* get one's hair cut.

couperet [kupʀɛ] *nm* cleaver, chopper.

couperosé, e [kupʀoze] *adj* blotchy.

couple [kupl(ə)] *nm* couple; ~ **de torsion** torque.

coupler [kuple] *vt* to couple (together).

couplet [kuplɛ] *nm* verse.

coupleur [kuplœʀ] *nm*: ~ **acoustique** acoustic coupler.

coupole [kupɔl] *nf* dome; cupola.

coupon [kupɔ̃] *nm* (*ticket*) coupon; (*de tissu*) remnant; roll.

coupon-réponse, *pl* **coupons-réponses** [kupɔ̃ʀepɔ̃s] *nm* reply coupon.

coupure [kupyʀ] *nf* cut; (*billet de banque*) note; (*de journal*) cutting; ~ **de courant** power cut.

cour [kuʀ] *nf* (*de ferme, jardin*) (court)yard; (*d'immeuble*) back yard; (*JUR, royale*) court; **faire la ~ à qn** to court sb; ~ **d'appel** appeal court (*BRIT*), appellate court (*US*); ~ **d'assises** court of assizes, ≈ Crown Court (*BRIT*); ~ **de cassation** final court of appeal; ~ **des comptes** (*ADMIN*) revenue court; ~ **martiale** court-martial; ~ **de récréation** (*SCOL*) schoolyard, playground.

courage [kuʀaʒ] *nm* courage, bravery.
courageusement [kuʀaʒøzmã] *adv* bravely,
courageously.
courageux, euse [kuʀaʒø, -øz] *adj* brave,
courageous.
couramment [kuʀamã] *adv* commonly;
(*parler*) fluently.
courant, e [kuʀã, -ãt] *adj* (*fréquent*) common;
(*COMM, gén: normal*) standard; (*en cours*)
current ♦ *nm* current; (*fig*) movement;
trend; **être au ~ (de)** (*fait, nouvelle*) to know
(about); **mettre qn au ~ (de)** (*fait, nouvelle*) to
tell sb (about); (*nouveau travail etc*) to teach
sb the basics (of), brief sb (about); **se tenir
au ~ (de)** (*techniques etc*) to keep o.s. up-to-
date (on); **dans le ~ de** (*pendant*) in the
course of; **~ octobre** *etc* in the course of
October *etc*; **le 10 ~** (*COMM*) the 10th inst; **~
d'air** draught (*BRIT*), draft (*US*); **~ électrique**
(electric) current, power.
courbature [kuʀbatyʀ] *nf* ache.
courbaturé, e [kuʀbatyʀe] *adj* aching.
courbe [kuʀb(ə)] *adj* curved ♦ *nf* curve; **~ de
niveau** contour line.
courber [kuʀbe] *vt* to bend; **~ la tête** to bow
one's head; **se ~** *vi* (*branche etc*) to bend,
curve; (*personne*) to bend (down).
courbette [kuʀbɛt] *nf* low bow.
coure [kuʀ] *etc vb voir* **courir**.
coureur, euse [kuʀœʀ, -øz] *nm/f* (*SPORT*)
runner (*ou* driver); (*péj*) womanizer/
manhunter; **~ cycliste/automobile** racing
cyclist/driver.
courge [kuʀʒ(ə)] *nf* (*BOT*) gourd; (*CULIN*)
marrow.
courgette [kuʀʒɛt] *nf* courgette (*BRIT*),
zucchini (*US*).
courir [kuʀiʀ] *vi* (*gén*) to run; (*se dépêcher*) to
rush; (*fig: rumeurs*) to go round; (*COMM:
intérêt*) to accrue ♦ *vt* (*SPORT: épreuve*) to
compete in; (*risque*) to run; (*danger*) to face;
~ les cafés/bals to do the rounds of the
cafés/dances; **le bruit court que** the rumour
is going round that; **par les temps qui
courent** at the present time; **~ après qn** to
run after sb, chase (after) sb; **laisser ~** to
let things alone; **faire ~ qn** to make sb run
around (all over the place); **tu peux
(toujours) ~!** you've got a hope!
couronne [kuʀɔn] *nf* crown; (*de fleurs*) wreath,
circlet; **~ (funéraire ou mortuaire)** (funeral)
wreath.
couronnement [kuʀɔnmã] *nm* coronation,
crowning; (*fig*) crowning achievement.
couronner [kuʀɔne] *vt* to crown.
courons [kuʀɔ̃], **courrai** [kuʀe] *etc vb voir*
courir.
courre [kuʀ] *vb voir* **chasse**.
courrier [kuʀje] *nm* mail, post; (*lettres à écrire*)
letters *pl*; (*rubrique*) column; **qualité ~** letter
quality; **long/moyen ~** *adj* (*AVIAT*) long-/
medium-haul; **~ du cœur** problem page; **~**

électronique electronic mail, E-mail.
courroie [kuʀwa] *nf* strap; (*TECH*) belt; **~ de
transmission/de ventilateur** driving/fan
belt.
courrons [kuʀɔ̃] *etc vb voir* **courir**.
courroucé, e [kuʀuse] *adj* wrathful.
cours [kuʀ] *vb voir* **courir** ♦ *nm* (*leçon*) lesson;
class; (*série de leçons*) course; (*cheminement*)
course; (*écoulement*) flow; (*avenue*) walk;
(*COMM*) rate; price; (*BOURSE*) quotation;
donner libre ~ à to give free expression to;
avoir ~ (*monnaie*) to be legal tender; (*fig*) to
be current; (*SCOL*) to have a class *ou*
lecture; **en ~** (*année*) current; (*travaux*) in
progress; **en ~ de route** on the way; **au ~ de**
in the course of, during; **le ~ du change** the
exchange rate; **~ d'eau** waterway; **~
élémentaire (CE)** *2nd and 3rd years of
primary school*; **~ moyen (CM)** *4th and 5th
years of primary school*; **~ préparatoire**
≈ infants' class (*BRIT*), ≈ 1st grade (*US*); **~
du soir** night school.
course [kuʀs(ə)] *nf* running; (*SPORT: épreuve*)
race; (*trajet: du soleil*) course; (*: d'un
projectile*) flight; (*: d'une pièce mécanique*)
travel; (*excursion*) outing; climb; (*d'un taxi,
autocar*) journey, trip; (*petite mission*)
errand; **~s** *nfpl* (*achats*) shopping *sg*;
(*HIPPISME*) races; **faire les** *ou* **ses ~s** to go
shopping; **jouer aux ~s** to bet on the races;
à bout de ~ (*épuisé*) exhausted; **~
automobile** car race; **~ de côte** (*AUTO*) hill
climb; **~ par étapes** *ou* **d'étapes** race in
stages; **~ d'obstacles** obstacle race; **~ à
pied** walking race; **~ de vitesse** sprint; **~s
de chevaux** horse racing.
coursier, ière [kuʀsje, -jɛʀ] *nm/f* courier.
court, e [kuʀ, kuʀt(ə)] *adj* short ♦ *adv* short
♦ *nm*: **~ (de tennis)** (tennis) court; **tourner ~**
to come to a sudden end; **couper ~ à** to cut
short; **à ~ de** short of; **prendre qn de ~** to
catch sb unawares; **pour faire ~** briefly, to
cut a long story short; **ça fait ~** that's not
very long; **tirer à la ~e paille** to draw lots;
faire la ~e échelle à qn to give sb a leg up;
~ métrage (*CINÉ*) short (film).
court-bouillon, *pl* **courts-bouillons**
[kuʀbujɔ̃] *nm* court-bouillon.
court-circuit, *pl* **courts-circuits** [kuʀsiʀkyi]
nm short-circuit.
court-circuiter [kuʀsiʀkyite] *vt* (*fig*) to bypass.
courtier, ière [kuʀtje, -jɛʀ] *nm/f* broker.
courtisan [kuʀtizã] *nm* courtier.
courtisane [kuʀtizan] *nf* courtesan.
courtiser [kuʀtize] *vt* to court, woo.
courtois, e [kuʀtwa, -waz] *adj* courteous.
courtoisement [kuʀtwazmã] *adv* courteously.
courtoisie [kuʀtwazi] *nf* courtesy.
couru, e [kuʀy] *pp de* **courir** ♦ *adj* (*spectacle etc*)
popular; **c'est ~ (d'avance)!** (*fam*) it's a safe
bet!
cousais [kuzɛ] *etc vb voir* **coudre**.

couscous [kuskus] *nm* couscous.
cousin, e [kuzɛ̃, -in] *nm/f* cousin ♦ *nm* (*ZOOL*) mosquito; ~ **germain** first cousin.
cousons [kuzɔ̃] *etc vb voir* **coudre.**
coussin [kusɛ̃] *nm* cushion; ~ **d'air** (*TECH*) air cushion.
cousu, e [kuzy] *pp de* **coudre** ♦ *adj*: ~ **d'or** rolling in riches.
coût [ku] *nm* cost; **le ~ de la vie** the cost of living.
coûtant [kutɑ̃] *adj m*: **au prix ~** at cost price.
couteau, x [kuto] *nm* knife; ~ **à cran d'arrêt** flick-knife; ~ **de cuisine** kitchen knife; ~ **à pain** bread knife; ~ **de poche** pocket knife.
couteau-scie, *pl* **couteaux-scies** [kutosi] *nm* serrated(-edged) knife.
coutelier, ière [kutəlje, -jɛR] *adj*: **l'industrie ~ière** the cutlery industry ♦ *nm/f* cutler.
coutellerie [kutɛlRi] *nf* cutlery shop; cutlery.
coûter [kute] *vt* to cost ♦ *vi*: ~ **à qn** to cost sb a lot; ~ **cher** to be expensive; **se** ~ **cher à qn** (*fig*) to cost sb dear *ou* dearly; **combien ça coûte?** how much is it?, what does it cost?; **coûte que coûte** at all costs.
coûteux, euse [kutø, -øz] *adj* costly, expensive.
coutume [kutym] *nf* custom; **de ~** usual, customary.
coutumier, ière [kutymje, -jɛR] *adj* customary: **elle est coutumière du fait** that's her usual trick.
couture [kutyR] *nf* sewing; dress-making; (*points*) seam.
couturier [kutyRje] *nm* fashion designer, couturier.
couturière [kutyRjɛR] *nf* dressmaker.
couvée [kuve] *nf* brood, clutch.
couvent [kuvɑ̃] *nm* (*de sœurs*) convent; (*de frères*) monastery; (*établissement scolaire*) convent (school).
couver [kuve] *vt* to hatch; (*maladie*) to be sickening for ♦ *vi* (*feu*) to smoulder (*BRIT*), smolder (*US*); (*révolte*) to be brewing; ~ **qn/qch des yeux** to look lovingly at sb/sth; (*convoiter*) to look longingly at sb/sth.
couvercle [kuvɛRkl(ə)] *nm* lid; (*de bombe aérosol etc, qui se visse*) cap, top.
couvert, e [kuvɛR, -ɛRt(ə)] *pp de* **couvrir** ♦ *adj* (*ciel*) overcast; (*coiffé d'un chapeau*) wearing a hat ♦ *nm* place setting; (*place à table*) place; (*au restaurant*) cover charge; ~**s** *nmpl* place settings; cutlery *sg*; ~ **de** covered with *ou* in; **bien ~** (*habillé*) well wrapped up; **mettre le ~** to lay the table; **à ~** under cover; **sous le ~ de** under the shelter of; (*fig*) under cover of.
couverture [kuvɛRtyR] *nf* (*de lit*) blanket; (*de bâtiment*) roofing; (*de livre, fig: d'un espion etc, ASSURANCES*) cover; (*PRESSE*) coverage; **de ~** (*lettre etc*) covering; ~ **chauffante** electric blanket.
couveuse [kuvøz] *nf* (*à poules*) sitter, brooder;

(*de maternité*) incubator.
couvre [kuvR(ə)] *etc vb voir* **couvrir.**
couvre-chef [kuvRəʃɛf] *nm* hat.
couvre-feu, x [kuvRəfø] *nm* curfew.
couvre-lit [kuvRəli] *nm* bedspread.
couvre-pieds [kuvRəpje] *nm inv* quilt.
couvreur [kuvRœR] *nm* roofer.
couvrir [kuvRiR] *vt* to cover; (*dominer, étouffer: voix, pas*) to drown out; (*erreur*) to cover up; (*ZOOL: s'accoupler à*) to cover; **se** ~ (*ciel*) to cloud over; (*s'habiller*) to cover up, wrap up; (*se coiffer*) to put on one's hat; (*par une assurance*) to cover o.s.; **se** ~ **de** (*fleurs, boutons*) to become covered in.
cover-girl [kɔvœRgœRl] *nf* model.
cow-boy [kobɔj] *nm* cowboy.
coyote [kɔjɔt] *nm* coyote.
CP *sigle m* = **cours préparatoire.**
CPAM *sigle f* (= *Caisse primaire d'assurances maladie*) *health insurance office.*
cps *abr* (= *caractères par seconde*) cps.
cpt *abr* = **comptant.**
CQFD *abr* (= *ce qu'il fallait démontrer*) QED (= *quod erat demonstrandum*).
CR *sigle m* = **compte rendu.**
crabe [kRab] *nm* crab.
crachat [kRaʃa] *nm* spittle *no pl*, spit *no pl*.
craché, e [kRaʃe] *adj*: **son père tout ~** the spitting image of his (*ou* her) father.
cracher [kRaʃe] *vi* to spit ♦ *vt* to spit out; (*fig: lave etc*) to belch (out); ~ **du sang** to spit blood.
crachin [kRaʃɛ̃] *nm* drizzle.
crachiner [kRaʃine] *vi* to drizzle.
crachoir [kRaʃwaR] *nm* spittoon; (*de dentiste*) bowl.
crachotement [kRaʃɔtmɑ̃] *nm* crackling *no pl*.
crachoter [kRaʃɔte] *vi* (*haut-parleur, radio*) to crackle.
crack [kRak] *nm* (*intellectuel*) whizzkid; (*sportif*) ace; (*poulain*) hot favourite (*BRIT*) *ou* favorite (*US*).
Cracovie [kRakɔvi] *n* Cracow.
cradingue [kRadɛ̃g] *adj* (*fam*) disgustingly dirty, filthy-dirty.
craie [kRɛ] *nf* chalk.
craignais [kRɛɲɛ] *etc vb voir* **craindre.**
craindre [kRɛ̃dR(ə)] *vt* to fear, be afraid of; (*être sensible à: chaleur, froid*) to be easily damaged by; ~ **de/que** to be afraid of/that; **je crains qu'il (ne) vienne** I am afraid he may come.
crainte [kRɛ̃t] *nf* fear; **de ~ de/que** for fear of/that.
craintif, ive [kRɛ̃tif, -iv] *adj* timid.
craintivement [kRɛ̃tivmɑ̃] *adv* timidly.
cramer [kRame] *vi* (*fam*) to burn.
cramoisi, e [kRamwazi] *adj* crimson.
crampe [kRɑ̃p] *nf* cramp; ~ **d'estomac** stomach cramp.
crampon [kRɑ̃pɔ̃] *nm* (*de semelle*) stud; (*ALPINISME*) crampon.

cramponner [kʀɑ̃pɔne]: **se** ~ *vi*: **se** ~ **(à)** to hang *ou* cling on (to).

cran [kʀɑ̃] *nm* (*entaille*) notch; (*de courroie*) hole; (*courage*) guts *pl*; ~ **d'arrêt** safety catch; ~ **de mire** bead; ~ **de sûreté** safety catch.

crâne [kʀɑn] *nm* skull.

crâner [kʀɑne] *vi* (*fam*) to swank, show off.

crânien, ne [kʀɑnjɛ̃, -ɛn] *adj* cranial, skull *cpd*, brain *cpd*.

crapaud [kʀapo] *nm* toad.

crapule [kʀapyl] *nf* villain.

crapuleux, euse [kʀapylø, -øz] *adj*: **crime** ~ villainous crime.

craquelure [kʀaklyʀ] *nf* crack; crackle *no pl*.

craquement [kʀakmɑ̃] *nm* crack, snap; (*du plancher*) creak, creaking *no pl*.

craquer [kʀake] *vi* (*bois, plancher*) to creak; (*fil, branche*) to snap; (*couture*) to come apart, burst; (*fig*) to break down, fall apart; (: *être enthousiasmé*) to go wild ♦ *vt*: ~ **une allumette** to strike a match.

crasse [kʀas] *nf* grime, filth ♦ *adj* (*fig: ignorance*) crass.

crasseux, euse [kʀasø, øz] *adj* filthy.

crassier [kʀasje] *nm* slag heap.

cratère [kʀatɛʀ] *nm* crater.

cravache [kʀavaʃ] *nf* (*riding*) crop.

cravacher [kʀavaʃe] *vt* to use the crop on.

cravate [kʀavat] *nf* tie.

cravater [kʀavate] *vt* to put a tie on; (*fig*) to grab round the neck.

crawl [kʀol] *nm* crawl.

crawlé, e [kʀole] *adj*: **dos** ~ backstroke.

crayeux, euse [kʀɛjø, -øz] *adj* chalky.

crayon [kʀɛjɔ̃] *nm* pencil; (*de rouge à lèvres etc*) stick, pencil; **écrire au** ~ to write in pencil; ~ **à bille** ball-point pen; ~ **de couleur** crayon; ~ **optique** light pen.

crayon-feutre, *pl* **crayons-feutres** [kʀɛjɔ̃føtʀ(ə)] *nm* felt(-tip) pen.

crayonner [kʀɛjɔne] *vt* to scribble, sketch.

CRDP *sigle m* (= *Centre régional de documentation pédagogique*) *teachers' resource centre*.

créance [kʀeɑ̃s] *nf* (*COMM*) (financial) claim, (recoverable) debt; **donner** ~ **à qch** to lend credence to sth.

créancier, ière [kʀeɑ̃sje, -jɛʀ] *nm/f* creditor.

créateur, trice [kʀeatœʀ, -tʀis] *adj* creative ♦ *nm/f* creator; **le C~** (*REL*) the Creator.

créatif, ive [kʀeatif, -iv] *adj* creative.

création [kʀeasjɔ̃] *nf* creation.

créativité [kʀeativite] *nf* creativity.

créature [kʀeatyʀ] *nf* creature.

crécelle [kʀesɛl] *nf* rattle.

crèche [kʀɛʃ] *nf* (*de Noël*) crib; (*garderie*) crèche, day nursery.

In France the Christmas crib (**crèche**) *usually contains figurines representing a miller, a wood-cutter and other villagers in addition to the Holy Family and the traditional cow, donkey and shepherds. Figurines representing the magi are added to the nativity scene at Epiphany; see also* **fête des Rois**.

crédence [kʀedɑ̃s] *nf* (small) sideboard.

crédibilité [kʀedibilite] *nf* credibility.

crédible [kʀedibl(ə)] *adj* credible.

CREDIF [kʀedif] *sigle m* (= *Centre de recherche et d'étude pour la diffusion du français*) *official body promoting use of the French language*.

crédit [kʀedi] *nm* (*gén*) credit; ~**s** *nmpl* funds; **payer/acheter à** ~ to pay/buy on credit *ou* on easy terms; **faire** ~ **à qn** to give sb credit; ~ **municipal** pawnshop; ~ **relais** bridging loan.

crédit-bail, *pl* **crédits-bails** [kʀedibaj] *nm* (*ÉCON*) leasing.

créditer [kʀedite] *vt*: ~ **un compte (de)** to credit an account (with).

créditeur, trice [kʀeditœʀ, -tʀis] *adj* in credit, credit *cpd* ♦ *nm/f* customer in credit.

credo [kʀedo] *nm* credo, creed.

crédule [kʀedyl] *adj* credulous, gullible.

crédulité [kʀedylite] *nf* credulity, gullibility.

créer [kʀee] *vt* to create; (*THÉÂT: pièce*) to produce (for the first time); (: *rôle*) to create.

crémaillère [kʀemajɛʀ] *nf* (*RAIL*) rack; (*tige crantée*) trammel; **direction à** ~ (*AUTO*) rack and pinion steering; **pendre la** ~ to have a house-warming party.

crémation [kʀemasjɔ̃] *nf* cremation.

crématoire [kʀematwaʀ] *adj*: **four** ~ crematorium.

crématorium [kʀematɔʀjɔm] *nm* crematorium.

crème [kʀɛm] *nf* cream; (*entremets*) cream dessert ♦ *adj inv* cream; **un (café)** ~ ≈ a white coffee; ~ **chantilly** whipped cream, crème Chantilly; ~ **fouettée** whipped cream; ~ **glacée** ice cream; ~ **à raser** shaving cream.

crémerie [kʀemʀi] *nf* dairy; (*tearoom*) teashop.

crémeux, euse [kʀemø, -øz] *adj* creamy.

crémier, ière [kʀemje, -jɛʀ] *nm/f* dairyman/woman.

créneau, x [kʀeno] *nm* (*de fortification*) crenel(le); (*fig, aussi COMM*) gap, slot; (*AUTO*): **faire un** ~ to reverse into a parking space (*between cars alongside the kerb*).

créole [kʀeɔl] *adj, nm/f* Creole.

créosote [kʀeozɔt] *nf* creosote.

crêpe [kʀɛp] *nf* (*galette*) pancake ♦ *nm* (*tissu*) crêpe; (*de deuil*) black mourning crêpe; (*ruban*) black armband (*ou* hatband *ou* ribbon); **semelle (de)** ~ crêpe sole; ~ **de Chine** crêpe de Chine.

crêpé, e [kʀepe] *adj* (*cheveux*) backcombed.

crêperie [kʀepʀi] *nf* pancake shop *ou* restaurant.

crépi [kʀepi] *nm* roughcast.

crépir [kʀepiʀ] *vt* to roughcast.
crépitement [kʀepitmɑ̃] *nm* (*du feu*) crackling *no pl*; (*d'une arme automatique*) rattle *no pl*.
crépiter [kʀepite] *vi* to sputter, splutter, crackle.
crépon [kʀepɔ̃] *nm* seersucker.
CREPS [kʀɛps] *sigle m* (= *Centre régional d'éducation physique et sportive*) ≈ sports *ou* leisure centre.
crépu, e [kʀepy] *adj* frizzy, fuzzy.
crépuscule [kʀepyskyl] *nm* twilight, dusk.
crescendo [kʀeʃɛndo] *nm, adv* (*MUS*) crescendo; *aller* ~ (*fig*) to rise higher and higher, grow ever greater.
cresson [kʀesɔ̃] *nm* watercress.
Crète [kʀɛt] *nf*: **la** ~ Crete.
crête [kʀɛt] *nf* (*de coq*) comb; (*de vague, montagne*) crest.
crétin, e [kʀetɛ̃, -in] *nm/f* cretin.
crétois, e [kʀetwa, -waz] *adj* Cretan.
cretonne [kʀatɔn] *nf* cretonne.
creuser [kʀøze] *vt* (*trou, tunnel*) to dig; (*sol*) to dig a hole in; (*bois*) to hollow out; (*fig*) to go (deeply) into; **ça creuse** that gives you a real appetite; **se** ~ **(la cervelle)** to rack one's brains.
creuset [kʀøze] *nm* crucible; (*fig*) melting pot; (*severe*) test.
creux, euse [kʀø, -øz] *adj* hollow ♦ *nm* hollow; (*fig: sur graphique etc*) trough; **heures creuses** slack periods; off-peak periods; **le** ~ **de l'estomac** the pit of the stomach.
crevaison [kʀəvɛzɔ̃] *nf* puncture, flat.
crevant, e [kʀəvɑ̃, -ɑ̃t] *adj* (*fam: fatigant*) knackering; (:*très drôle*) priceless.
crevasse [kʀəvas] *nf* (*dans le sol*) crack, fissure; (*de glacier*) crevasse; (*de la peau*) crack.
crevé, e [kʀəve] *adj* (*fam: fatigué*) worn out, dead beat.
crève-cœur [kʀɛvkœʀ] *nm inv* heartbreak.
crever [kʀəve] *vt* (*papier*) to tear, break; (*tambour, ballon*) to burst ♦ *vi* (*pneu*) to burst; (*automobiliste*) to have a puncture (*BRIT*) *ou* a flat (tire) (*US*); (*abcès, outre, nuage*) to burst (open); (*fam*) to die; **cela lui a crevé un œil** it blinded him in one eye; ~ **l'écran** to have real screen presence.
crevette [kʀəvɛt] *nf*: ~ **(rose)** prawn; ~ **grise** shrimp.
CRF *sigle f* (= *Croix-Rouge française*) French Red Cross.
cri [kʀi] *nm* cry, shout; (*d'animal: spécifique*) cry, call; **à grands** ~**s** at the top of one's voice; **c'est le dernier** ~ (*fig*) it's the latest fashion.
criant, e [kʀijɑ̃, -ɑ̃t] *adj* (*injustice*) glaring.
criard, e [kʀijaʀ, -aʀd(ə)] *adj* (*couleur*) garish, loud; (*voix*) yelling.
crible [kʀibl(ə)] *nm* riddle; (*mécanique*) screen, jig; **passer qch au** ~ to put sth through a riddle; (*fig*) to go over sth with a fine-tooth comb.

criblé, e [kʀible] *adj*: ~ **de** riddled with.
cric [kʀik] *nm* (*AUTO*) jack.
cricket [kʀikɛt] *nm* cricket.
criée [kʀije] *nf*: **(vente à la)** ~ (sale by) auction.
crier [kʀije] *vi* (*pour appeler*) to shout, cry (out); (*de peur, de douleur etc*) to scream, yell; (*fig: grincer*) to squeal, screech ♦ *vt* (*ordre, injure*) to shout (out), yell (out); **sans** ~ **gare** without warning; ~ **grâce** to cry for mercy; ~ **au secours** to shout for help.
crieur, euse [kʀijœʀ, -øz] *nm/f*: ~ **de journaux** newspaper seller.
crime [kʀim] *nm* crime; (*meurtre*) murder.
Crimée [kʀime] *nf*: **la** ~ the Crimea.
criminaliste [kʀiminalist(ə)] *nm/f* specialist in criminal law.
criminalité [kʀiminalite] *nf* criminality, crime.
criminel, le [kʀiminɛl] *adj* criminal ♦ *nm/f* criminal; murderer; ~ **de guerre** war criminal.
criminologie [kʀiminɔlɔʒi] *nf* criminology.
criminologiste [kʀiminɔlɔʒist(ə)] *nm/f* criminologist.
criminologue [kʀiminɔlɔg] *nm/f* criminologist.
crin [kʀɛ̃] *nm* hair *no pl*; (*fibre*) horsehair; **à tous** ~**s, à tout** ~ diehard, out-and-out.
crinière [kʀinjɛʀ] *nf* mane.
crique [kʀik] *nf* creek, inlet.
criquet [kʀikɛ] *nm* grasshopper.
crise [kʀiz] *nf* crisis (*pl* crises); (*MÉD*) attack; fit; ~ **cardiaque** heart attack; ~ **de foi** crisis of belief; ~ **de foie** bilious attack; ~ **de nerfs** attack of nerves.
crispant, e [kʀispɑ̃, -ɑ̃t] *adj* annoying, irritating.
crispation [kʀispasjɔ̃] *nf* (*spasme*) twitch; (*contraction*) contraction; tenseness.
crispé, e [kʀispe] *adj* tense, nervous.
crisper [kʀispe] *vt* to tense; (*poings*) to clench; **se** ~ to tense; to clench; (*personne*) to get tense.
crissement [kʀismɑ̃] *nm* crunch; rustle; screech.
crisser [kʀise] *vi* (*neige*) to crunch; (*tissu*) to rustle; (*pneu*) to screech.
cristal, aux [kʀistal, -o] *nm* crystal ♦ *nmpl* (*objets*) crystal(ware) *sg*; ~ **de plomb** (lead) crystal; ~ **de roche** rock-crystal; **cristaux de soude** washing soda *sg*.
cristallin, e [kʀistalɛ̃, -in] *adj* crystal-clear ♦ *nm* (*ANAT*) crystalline lens.
cristalliser [kʀistalize] *vi, vt*, **se** ~ *vi* to crystallize.
critère [kʀitɛʀ] *nm* criterion (*pl* -ia).
critiquable [kʀitikabl(ə)] *adj* open to criticism.
critique [kʀitik] *adj* critical ♦ *nm/f* (*de théâtre, musique*) critic ♦ *nf* criticism; (*THÉÂT etc*: *article*) review; **la** ~ (*activité*) criticism; (*personnes*) the critics *pl*.
critiquer [kʀitike] *vt* (*dénigrer*) to criticize;

(*évaluer, juger*) to assess, examine (critically).

croasser [kʀɔase] *vi* to caw.

croate [kʀɔat] *adj* Croatian ♦ *nm* (*LING*) Croat, Croatian.

Croatie [kʀɔasi] *nf*: **la ~** Croatia.

croc [kʀo] *nm* (*dent*) fang; (*de boucher*) hook.

croc-en-jambe, *pl* **crocs-en-jambe** [kʀɔkɑ̃jɑ̃b] *nm*: **faire un ~ à qn** to trip sb up.

croche [kʀɔʃ] *nf* (*MUS*) quaver (*BRIT*), eighth note (*US*); **double ~** semiquaver (*BRIT*), sixteenth note (*US*).

croche-pied [kʀɔʃpje] *nm* = **croc-en-jambe**.

crochet [kʀɔʃɛ] *nm* hook; (*clef*) picklock; (*détour*) detour; (*BOXE*): **~ du gauche** left hook; (*TRICOT: aiguille*) crochet hook; (*: technique*) crochet; **~s** *nmpl* (*TYPO*) square brackets; **vivre aux ~s de qn** to live *ou* sponge off sb.

crocheter [kʀɔʃte] *vt* (*serrure*) to pick.

crochu, e [kʀɔʃy] *adj* hooked; claw-like.

crocodile [kʀɔkɔdil] *nm* crocodile.

crocus [kʀɔkys] *nm* crocus.

croire [kʀwaʀ] *vt* to believe; **~ qn honnête** to believe sb (to be) honest; **se ~ fort** to think one is strong; **~ que** to believe *ou* think that; **vous croyez?** do you think so?; **~ être/faire** to think one is/does; **~ à, ~ en** to believe in.

croîs [kʀwa] *etc vb voir* **croître**.

croisade [kʀwazad] *nf* crusade.

croisé, e [kʀwaze] *adj* (*veston*) double-breasted ♦ *nm* (*guerrier*) crusader ♦ *nf* (*fenêtre*) window, casement; **~e d'ogives** intersecting ribs; **à la ~e des chemins** at the crossroads.

croisement [kʀwazmɑ̃] *nm* (*carrefour*) crossroads *sg*; (*BIO*) crossing; crossbreed.

croiser [kʀwaze] *vt* (*personne, voiture*) to pass; (*route*) to cross, cut across; (*BIO*) to cross ♦ *vi* (*NAVIG*) to cruise; **~ les jambes/bras** to cross one's legs/fold one's arms; **se ~** (*personnes, véhicules*) to pass each other; (*routes*) to cross, intersect; (*lettres*) to cross (in the post); (*regards*) to meet; **se ~ les bras** (*fig*) to twiddle one's thumbs.

croiseur [kʀwazœʀ] *nm* cruiser (*warship*).

croisière [kʀwazjɛʀ] *nf* cruise; **vitesse de ~** (*AUTO etc*) cruising speed.

croisillon [kʀwazijɔ̃] *nm*: **motif/fenêtre à ~s** lattice pattern/window.

croissais [kʀwasɛ] *etc vb voir* **croître**.

croissance [kʀwasɑ̃s] *nf* growing, growth; **troubles de la ~** growing pains; **maladie de ~** growth disease; **~ économique** economic growth.

croissant, e [kʀwasɑ̃, -ɑ̃t] *vb voir* **croître** ♦ *adj* growing; rising ♦ *nm* (*à manger*) croissant; (*motif*) crescent; **~ de lune** crescent moon.

croître [kʀwatʀ(ə)] *vi* to grow; (*lune*) to wax.

croix [kʀwa] *nf* cross; **en ~** *adj, adv* in the form of a cross; **la C~ Rouge** the Red Cross.

croquant, e [kʀɔkɑ̃, -ɑ̃t] *adj* crisp, crunchy ♦ *nm/f* (*péj*) yokel, (country) bumpkin.

croque-madame [kʀɔkmadam] *nm inv* toasted cheese sandwich with a fried egg on top.

croque-mitaine [kʀɔkmitɛn] *nm* bog(e)y-man (*pl* -men).

croque-monsieur [kʀɔkməsjø] *nm inv* toasted ham and cheese sandwich.

croque-mort [kʀɔkmɔʀ] *nm* (*péj*) pallbearer.

croquer [kʀɔke] *vt* (*manger*) to crunch; to munch; (*dessiner*) to sketch ♦ *vi* to be crisp *ou* crunchy; **chocolat à ~** plain dessert chocolate.

croquet [kʀɔkɛ] *nm* croquet.

croquette [kʀɔkɛt] *nf* croquette.

croquis [kʀɔki] *nm* sketch.

cross(-country), *pl* **cross(-countries)** [kʀɔs(kuntʀi)] *nm* cross-country race *ou* run; cross-country racing *ou* running.

crosse [kʀɔs] *nf* (*de fusil*) butt; (*de revolver*) grip; (*d'évêque*) crook, crosier; (*de hockey*) hockey stick.

crotale [kʀɔtal] *nm* rattlesnake.

crotte [kʀɔt] *nf* droppings *pl*; **~!** (*fam*) damn!

crotté, e [kʀɔte] *adj* muddy, mucky.

crottin [kʀɔtɛ̃] *nm*: **~ (de cheval)** (horse) dung *ou* manure.

croulant, e [kʀulɑ̃, -ɑ̃t] *nm/f* (*fam*) old fogey.

crouler [kʀule] *vi* (*s'effondrer*) to collapse; (*être délabré*) to be crumbling.

croupe [kʀup] *nf* croup, rump; **en ~** pillion.

croupier [kʀupje] *nm* croupier.

croupion [kʀupjɔ̃] *nm* (*d'un oiseau*) rump; (*CULIN*) parson's nose.

croupir [kʀupiʀ] *vi* to stagnate.

CROUS [kʀus] *sigle m* (= *Centre régional des œuvres universitaires et scolaires*) students' representative body.

croustade [kʀustad] *nf* (*CULIN*) croustade.

croustillant, e [kʀustijɑ̃, -ɑ̃t] *adj* crisp; (*fig*) spicy.

croustiller [kʀustije] *vi* to be crisp *ou* crusty.

croûte [kʀut] *nf* crust; (*du fromage*) rind; (*de vol-au-vent*) case; (*MÉD*) scab; **en ~** (*CULIN*) in pastry, in a pie; **~ aux champignons** mushrooms on toast; **~ au fromage** cheese on toast *no pl*; **~ de pain** (*morceau*) crust (of bread); **~ terrestre** earth's crust.

croûton [kʀutɔ̃] *nm* (*CULIN*) crouton; (*bout du pain*) crust, heel.

croyable [kʀwajabl(ə)] *adj* believable, credible.

croyais [kʀwaje] *etc vb voir* **croire**.

croyance [kʀwajɑ̃s] *nf* belief.

croyant, e [kʀwajɑ̃, -ɑ̃t] *vb voir* **croire** ♦ *adj*: **être/ne pas être ~** to be/not to be a believer ♦ *nm/f* believer.

Crozet [kʀɔzɛ] *n*: **les îles ~** the Crozet Islands.

CRS *sigle fpl* (= *Compagnies républicaines de sécurité*) state security police force ♦ *sigle m* member of the CRS.

cru, e [kʀy] *pp de* **croire** ♦ *adj* (*non cuit*) raw;

(_lumière, couleur_) harsh; (_description_) crude; (_paroles, langage: franc_) blunt; (: _grossier_) crude ♦ _nm_ (_vignoble_) vineyard; (_vin_) wine ♦ _nf_(_d'un cours d'eau_) swelling, rising; **de son (propre)** ~ (_fig_) of his own devising; **monter à** ~ to ride bareback; **du** ~ local; **en** ~**e** in spate.

crû [kʀy] _pp de_ **croître**.

cruauté [kʀyote] _nf_ cruelty.

cruche [kʀyʃ] _nf_ pitcher, (earthenware) jug.

crucial, e, aux [kʀysjal, -o] _adj_ crucial.

crucifier [kʀysifje] _vt_ to crucify.

crucifix [kʀysifi] _nm_ crucifix.

crucifixion [kʀysifiksjɔ̃] _nf_ crucifixion.

cruciforme [kʀysifɔʀm(ə)] _adj_ cruciform, cross-shaped.

cruciverbiste [kʀysivɛʀbist(ə)] _nm/f_ crossword puzzle enthusiast.

crudité [kʀydite] _nf_ crudeness _no pl_; harshness _no pl_; ~**s** _nfpl_ (_CULIN_) mixed salads (_as hors-d'œuvre_).

crue [kʀy] _nf voir_ **cru**.

cruel, le [kʀyɛl] _adj_ cruel.

cruellement [kʀyɛlmɑ̃] _adv_ cruelly.

crûment [kʀymɑ̃] _adv_ (_voir cru_) harshly; bluntly; crudely.

crus, crûs [kʀy] _etc vb voir_ **croire; croître**.

crustacés [kʀystase] _nmpl_ shellfish.

crypte [kʀipt(ə)] _nf_ crypt.

CSA _sigle f_ (= _Conseil supérieur de l'audiovisuel_) _French broadcasting regulatory body_, ≈ IBA (_BRIT_), ≈ FCC (_US_).

CSCE _sigle f_ = _Conférence sur la sécurité et la coopération en Europe_) CSCE.

cse _abr_ = **cause**.

CSEN _sigle f_ (= _Confédération des syndicats de l'éducation nationale_) _group of teachers' unions_.

CSG _sigle f_ (= _contribution sociale généralisée_) _supplementary social security contribution in aid of the underprivileged_.

Cte _abr_ = **Comtesse**.

CU _sigle f_ = _communauté urbaine_.

Cuba [kyba] _nm_: **le** ~ Cuba.

cubage [kybaʒ] _nm_ cubage, cubic content.

cubain, e [kybɛ̃, -ɛn] _adj_ Cuban ♦ _nm/f_: **C~, e** Cuban.

cube [kyb] _nm_ cube; (_jouet_) brick, building block; **gros** ~ powerful motorbike; **mètre** ~ cubic metre; **2 au** ~ **= 8** 2 cubed is 8; **élever au** ~ to cube.

cubique [kybik] _adj_ cubic.

cubisme [kybism(ə)] _nm_ cubism.

cubiste [kybist(ə)] _adj, nm/f_ cubist.

cubitus [kybitys] _nm_ ulna.

cueillette [kœjɛt] _nf_ picking, gathering; harvest _ou_ crop (of fruit).

cueillir [kœjiʀ] _vt_ (_fruits, fleurs_) to pick, gather; (_fig_) to catch.

cuiller _ou_ **cuillère** [kɥijɛʀ] _nf_ spoon; ~ **à café** coffee spoon; (_CULIN_) ≈ teaspoonful; ~ **à soupe** soup spoon; (_CULIN_) ≈ tablespoonful.

cuillerée [kɥijʀe] _nf_ spoonful; (_CULIN_): ~ **à soupe/café** tablespoonful/teaspoonful.

cuir [kɥiʀ] _nm_ leather; (_avant tannage_) hide; ~ **chevelu** scalp.

cuirasse [kɥiʀas] _nf_ breastplate.

cuirassé [kɥiʀase] _nm_ (_NAVIG_) battleship.

cuire [kɥiʀ] _vt_ (_aliments_) to cook; (_au four_) to bake; (_poterie_) to fire ♦ _vi_ to cook; (_picoter_) to smart, sting, burn; **bien cuit** (_viande_) well done; **trop cuit** overdone; **pas assez cuit** underdone; **cuit à point** medium done; done to a turn.

cuisant, e [kɥizɑ̃, -ɑ̃t] _vb voir_ **cuire** ♦ _adj_ (_douleur_) smarting, burning; (_fig: souvenir, échec_) bitter.

cuisine [kɥizin] _nf_ (_pièce_) kitchen; (_art culinaire_) cookery, cooking; (_nourriture_) cooking, food; **faire la** ~ to cook.

cuisiné, e [kɥizine] _adj_: **plat** ~ ready-made meal _ou_ dish.

cuisiner [kɥizine] _vt_ to cook; (_fam_) to grill ♦ _vi_ to cook.

cuisinette [kɥizinɛt] _nf_ kitchenette.

cuisinier, ière [kɥizinje, -jɛʀ] _nm/f_ cook ♦ _nf_ (_poêle_) cooker.

cuisis [kɥizi] _etc vb voir_ **cuire**.

cuissardes [kɥisaʀd] _nfpl_ (_de pêcheur_) waders; (_de femme_) thigh boots.

cuisse [kɥis] _nf_(_ANAT_) thigh; (_CULIN_) leg.

cuisson [kɥisɔ̃] _nf_ cooking; (_de poterie_) firing.

cuissot [kɥiso] _nm_ haunch.

cuistre [kɥistʀ(ə)] _nm_ prig.

cuit, e [kɥi, -it] _pp de_ **cuire** ♦ _nf_ (_fam_): **prendre une** ~ to get plastered _ou_ smashed.

cuivre [kɥivʀ(ə)] _nm_ copper; **les** ~**s** (_MUS_) the brass; ~ **rouge** copper; ~ **jaune** brass.

cuivré, e [kɥivʀe] _adj_ coppery; (_peau_) bronzed.

cul [ky] _nm_ (_fam!_) arse (_BRIT !_), ass (_US !_), bum (_BRIT_); ~ **de bouteille** bottom of a bottle.

culasse [kylas] _nf_ (_AUTO_) cylinder-head; (_de fusil_) breech.

culbute [kylbyt] _nf_ somersault; (_accidentelle_) tumble, fall.

culbuter [kylbyte] _vi_ to (take a) tumble, fall (head over heels).

culbuteur [kylbytœʀ] _nm_ (_AUTO_) rocker arm.

cul-de-jatte, _pl_ **culs-de-jatte** [kydʒat] _nm/f_ legless cripple.

cul-de-sac, _pl_ **culs-de-sac** [kydsak] _nm_ cul-de-sac.

culinaire [kylinɛʀ] _adj_ culinary.

culminant, e [kylminɑ̃, -ɑ̃t] _adj_: **point** ~ highest point; (_fig_) height, climax.

culminer [kylmine] _vi_ to reach its highest point; to tower.

culot [kylo] _nm_ (_d'ampoule_) cap; (_effronterie_) cheek, nerve.

culotte [kylɔt] _nf_ (_de femme_) panties _pl_, knickers _pl_ (_BRIT_); (_d'homme_) underpants _pl_; (_pantalon_) trousers _pl_ (_BRIT_), pants _pl_ (_US_); ~ **de cheval** riding breeches _pl_.

culotté, e [kylɔte] _adj_ (_pipe_) seasoned; (_cuir_)

mellowed; (*effronté*) cheeky.
culpabiliser [kylpabilize] *vt*: ~ **qn** to make sb feel guilty.
culpabilité [kylpabilite] *nf* guilt.
culte [kylt(ə)] *adj*: **livre/film** ~ cult film/book ♦ *nm* (*religion*) worship; (*hommage, vénération*) worship; (*protestant*) service.
cultivable [kyltivabl(ə)] *adj* cultivable.
cultivateur, trice [kyltivatœr, -tris] *nm/f* farmer.
cultivé, e [kyltive] *adj* (*personne*) cultured, cultivated.
cultiver [kyltive] *vt* to cultivate; (*légumes*) to grow, cultivate.
culture [kyltyr] *nf* cultivation; growing; (*connaissances etc*) culture; (**champs de**) ~**s** land(s) under cultivation; ~ **physique** physical training.
culturel, le [kyltyrɛl] *adj* cultural.
culturisme [kyltyrism(ə)] *nm* body-building.
culturiste [kyltyrist(ə)] *nm/f* body-builder.
cumin [kymɛ̃] *nm* (*CULIN*) caraway seeds *pl*; cumin.
cumul [kymyl] *nm* (*voir cumuler*) holding (*ou* drawing) concurrently; ~ **de peines** sentences to run consecutively.
cumulable [kymylabl(ə)] *adj* (*fonctions*) which may be held concurrently.
cumuler [kymyle] *vt* (*emplois, honneurs*) to hold concurrently; (*salaires*) to draw concurrently; (*JUR: droits*) to accumulate.
cupide [kypid] *adj* greedy, grasping.
cupidité [kypidite] *nf* greed.
curable [kyrabl(ə)] *adj* curable.
Curaçao [kyraso] *n* Curaçao ♦ *nm*: **c**~ curaçao.
curare [kyrar] *nm* curare.
curatif, ive [kyratif, -iv] *adj* curative.
cure [kyr] *nf* (*MÉD*) course of treatment; (*REL*) cure, ≈ living; presbytery, ≈ vicarage; **faire une** ~ **de fruits** to go on a fruit cure *ou* diet; **faire une** ~ **thermale** to take the waters; **n'avoir** ~ **de** to pay no attention to; ~ **d'amaigrissement** slimming course; ~ **de repos** rest cure; ~ **de sommeil** sleep therapy *no pl*.
curé [kyre] *nm* parish priest; **M le** ~ ≈ Vicar.
cure-dent [kyrdɑ̃] *nm* toothpick.
curée [kyre] *nf* (*fig*) scramble for the pickings.
cure-ongles [kyrɔ̃gl(ə)] *nm inv* nail cleaner.
cure-pipe [kyrpip] *nm* pipe cleaner.
curer [kyre] *vt* to clean out; **se** ~ **les dents** to pick one's teeth.
curetage [kyrtaʒ] *nm* (*MÉD*) curettage.
curieusement [kyrjøzmɑ̃] *adv* oddly.
curieux, euse [kyrjø, -øz] *adj* (*étrange*) strange, curious; (*indiscret*) curious, inquisitive; (*intéressé*) inquiring, curious ♦ *nmpl* (*badauds*) onlookers, bystanders.
curiosité [kyrjozite] *nf* curiosity, inquisitiveness; (*objet*) curio(sity); (*site*) unusual feature *ou* sight.

curiste [kyrist(ə)] *nm/f* person taking the waters at a spa.
curriculum vitae (CV) [kyrikylɔmvite] *nm inv* curriculum vitae (CV).
curry [kyri] *nm* curry; **poulet au** ~ curried chicken, chicken curry.
curseur [kyrsœr] *nm* (*INFORM*) cursor; (*de règle*) slide; (*de fermeture-éclair*) slider.
cursif, ive [kyrsif, -iv] *adj*: **écriture cursive** cursive script.
cursus [kyrsys] *nm* degree course.
curviligne [kyrviliɲ] *adj* curvilinear.
cutané, e [kytane] *adj* cutaneous, skin *cpd*.
cuti-réaction [kytireaksjɔ̃] *nf* (*MÉD*) skin-test.
cuve [kyv] *nf* vat; (*à mazout etc*) tank.
cuvée [kyve] *nf* vintage.
cuvette [kyvɛt] *nf* (*récipient*) bowl, basin; (*du lavabo*) (wash)basin; (*des w.-c.*) pan; (*GÉO*) basin.
CV *sigle m* (*AUTO*) = **cheval vapeur**; (*ADMIN*) = **curriculum vitae**.
CVS *sigle adj* (= *corrigées des variations saisonnières*) seasonally adjusted.
cx *abr* (= *coefficient de pénétration dans l'air*) drag coefficient.
cyanure [sjanyr] *nm* cyanide.
cybernétique [sibɛrnetik] *nf* cybernetics *sg*.
cyclable [siklabl(ə)] *adj*: **piste** ~ cycle track.
cyclamen [siklamɛn] *nm* cyclamen.
cycle [sikl(ə)] *nm* cycle; (*SCOL*): **premier/second** ~ ≈ middle/upper school (*BRIT*), ≈ junior/senior high school (*US*).
cyclique [siklik] *adj* cyclic(al).
cyclisme [siklism(ə)] *nm* cycling.
cycliste [siklist(ə)] *nm/f* cyclist ♦ *adj* cycle *cpd*; **coureur** ~ racing cyclist.
cyclo-cross [siklokros] *nm* (*SPORT*) cyclo-cross; (*épreuve*) cyclo-cross race.
cyclomoteur [siklomotœr] *nm* moped.
cyclomotoriste [siklomotorist(ə)] *nm/f* moped rider.
cyclone [siklon] *nm* hurricane.
cyclotourisme [sikloturism(ə)] *nm* (bi)cycle touring.
cygne [siɲ] *nm* swan.
cylindre [silɛ̃dr(ə)] *nm* cylinder; **moteur à 4** ~**s en ligne** straight-4 engine.
cylindrée [silɛ̃dre] *nf* (*AUTO*) (cubic) capacity; **une (voiture de) grosse** ~ a big-engined car.
cylindrique [silɛ̃drik] *adj* cylindrical.
cymbale [sɛ̃bal] *nf* cymbal.
cynique [sinik] *adj* cynical.
cyniquement [sinikmɑ̃] *adv* cynically.
cynisme [sinism(ə)] *nm* cynicism.
cyprès [siprɛ] *nm* cypress.
cypriote [siprijɔt] *adj* Cypriot ♦ *nm/f*: **C**~ Cypriot.
cyrillique [sirilik] *adj* Cyrillic.
cystite [sistit] *nf* cystitis.
cytise [sitiz] *nm* laburnum.
cytologie [sitolɔʒi] *nf* cytology.

Dd

D, d [de] *nm inv* D, d ♦ *abr:* **D** (*MÉTÉO:*
= *dépression*) low, depression; **D comme**
Désiré D for David (*BRIT*) *ou* Dog (*US*); *voir*
système.

d' *prép, dét voir* **de.**

Dacca [daka] *n* Dacca.

dactylo [daktilo] *nf* (*aussi:* ~**graphe**) typist;
(*aussi:* ~**graphie**) typing, typewriting.

dactylographier [daktilɔgʀafje] *vt* to type
(out).

dada [dada] *nm* hobby-horse.

dadais [dadɛ] *nm* ninny, lump.

dague [dag] *nf* dagger.

dahlia [dalja] *nm* dahlia.

dahoméen, ne [daɔmeɛ̃, -ɛn] *adj* Dahomean.

Dahomey [daɔme] *nm:* **le** ~ Dahomey.

daigner [deɲe] *vt* to deign.

daim [dɛ̃] *nm* (fallow) deer *inv*; (*peau*)
buckskin; (*imitation*) suede.

dais [dɛ] *nm* (*tenture*) canopy.

Dakar [dakaʀ] *n* Dakar.

dal. *abr* (= *décalitre*) dal.

dallage [dalaʒ] *nm* paving.

dalle [dal] *nf* slab; (*au sol*) paving stone,
flag(stone); **que** ~ nothing at all, damn all
(*BRIT*).

daller [dale] *vt* to pave.

dalmate [dalmat] *adj* Dalmatian.

Dalmatie [dalmasi] *nf:* **la** ~ Dalmatia.

dalmatien, ne [dalmasjɛ̃, -ɛn] *nm/f* (*chien*)
Dalmatian.

daltonien, ne [daltɔnjɛ̃, -ɛn] *adj* colour-blind
(*BRIT*), color-blind (*US*).

daltonisme [daltɔnism(ə)] *nm* colour (*BRIT*) *ou*
color (*US*) blindness.

dam [dam] *nm:* **au grand** ~ **de** much to the
detriment (*ou* annoyance) of.

Damas [dama] *n* Damascus.

damas [dama] *nm* (*étoffe*) damask.

damassé, e [damase] *adj* damask *cpd*.

dame [dam] *nf* lady; (*CARTES, ÉCHECS*) queen;
~**s** *nfpl* (*jeu*) draughts *sg* (*BRIT*), checkers *sg*
(*US*); **les (toilettes des)** ~**s** the ladies'
(toilets); ~ **de charité** benefactress; ~ **de**
compagnie lady's companion.

dame-jeanne, *pl* **dames-jeannes** [damʒan]
nf demijohn.

damer [dame] *vt* to ram *ou* pack down; ~ **le**
pion à (*fig*) to get the better of.

damier [damje] *nm* draughtboard (*BRIT*),
checkerboard (*US*); (*dessin*) check (pattern);
en ~ check.

damner [dane] *vt* to damn.

dancing [dɑ̃siŋ] *nm* dance hall.

dandiner [dɑ̃dine]: **se** ~ *vi* to sway about; (*en*
marchant) to waddle along.

Danemark [danmaʀk] *nm:* **le** ~ Denmark.

danger [dɑ̃ʒe] *nm* danger; **mettre en** ~ to
endanger, put in danger; **être en** ~ **de mort**
to be in peril of one's life; **être hors de** ~ to
be out of danger.

dangereusement [dɑ̃ʒʀøzmɑ̃] *adv*
dangerously.

dangereux, euse [dɑ̃ʒʀø, -øz] *adj* dangerous.

danois, e [danwa, -waz] *adj* Danish ♦ *nm* (*LING*)
Danish ♦ *nm/f:* **D**~, **e** Dane.

═══════════════════════════ *MOT-CLÉ*

dans [dɑ̃] *prép* **1** (*position*) in; (*à l'intérieur de*)
inside; **c'est** ~ **le tiroir/le salon** it's in the
drawer/lounge; ~ **la boîte** in *ou* inside the
box; **marcher** ~ **la ville/la rue** to walk about
the town/along the street; **je l'ai lu** ~ **le**
journal I read it in the newspaper; **être** ~ **les**
meilleurs to be among *ou* one of the best

2 (*direction*) into; **elle a couru** ~ **le salon** she
ran into the lounge

3 (*provenance*) out of, from; **je l'ai pris** ~ **le**
tiroir/salon I took it out of *ou* from the
drawer/lounge; **boire** ~ **un verre** to drink
out of *ou* from a glass

4 (*temps*) in; ~ **2 mois** in 2 months, in 2
months' time

5 (*approximation*) about; ~ **les 20 F** about
20 F.

dansant, e [dɑ̃sɑ̃, -ɑ̃t] *adj:* **soirée** ~**e** evening
of dancing; (*bal*) dinner dance.

danse [dɑ̃s] *nf:* **la** ~ dancing; (*classique*)
(ballet) dancing; **une** ~ a dance; ~ **du ventre**
belly dancing.

danser [dɑ̃se] *vi, vt* to dance.

danseur, euse [dɑ̃sœʀ, -øz] *nm/f* ballet
dancer; (*au bal etc*) dancer; (: *cavalier*)
partner; ~ **de claquettes** tap-dancer; **en**
danseuse (*à vélo*) standing on the pedals.

Danube [danyb] *nm:* **le** ~ the Danube.

DAO *sigle m* (= *dessin assisté par ordinateur*)
CAD.

dard [daʀ] *nm* sting (*organ*).

Dardanelles [daʀdanɛl] *nfpl:* **les** ~ the
Dardanelles.

darder [daʀde] *vt* to shoot, send forth.

dare-dare [daʀdaʀ] *adv* in double quick time.

Dar-es-Salaam, Dar-es-Salam [daʀɛsalam] *n*
Dar-es-Salaam.

darne [daʀn] *nf* steak (*of fish*).

darse [daʀs(ə)] *nf* sheltered dock (*in a*
Mediterranean port).

dartre [daʀtʀ(ə)] *nf* (*MÉD*) sore.

datation [datasjɔ̃] *nf* dating.

date [dat] *nf* date; **faire** ~ to mark a milestone;
de longue ~ *adj* longstanding; ~ **de**
naissance date of birth; ~ **limite** deadline;

(*d'un aliment: aussi:* ~ **limite de vente**) sell-by date.

dater [date] *vt, vi* to date; ~ **de** to date from, go back to; **à** ~ **de** (as) from.

dateur [datœʀ] *nm* (*de montre*) date indicator; **timbre** ~ date stamp.

datif [datif] *nm* dative.

datte [dat] *nf* date.

dattier [datje] *nm* date palm.

daube [dob] *nf*: **bœuf en** ~ beef casserole.

dauphin [dofɛ̃] *nm* (*ZOOL*) dolphin; (*du roi*) dauphin; (*fig*) heir apparent.

Dauphiné [dofine] *nm*: **le** ~ the Dauphiné.

dauphinois, e [dofinwa, -waz] *adj* of *ou* from the Dauphiné.

daurade [dɔʀad] *nf* sea bream.

davantage [davɑ̃taʒ] *adv* more; (*plus longtemps*) longer; ~ **de** more; ~ **que** more than.

DB *sigle f* (*MIL*) = division blindée.

DCA *sigle f* (= défense contre avions*) anti-aircraft defence.

DCC *sigle f* ® (= digital compact cassette*) DCC ®.

DCT *sigle m* (= diphtérie coqueluche tétanos*) DPT.

DDASS [das] *sigle f* (= Direction départementale d'action sanitaire et sociale*) ≈ DHSS (= Department of Health and Social Security*) (*BRIT*), ≈ SSA (= Social Security Administration*) (*US*).

DDT *sigle m* (= dichloro-diphénol-trichloréthane*) DDT.

════════ *MOT-CLÉ*

de (**d'**) (*de +le* = **du**, *de +les* = **des**) *prép* **1** (*appartenance*) of; **le toit** ~ **la maison** the roof of the house; **la voiture d'Elisabeth/**~ **mes parents** Elizabeth's/my parents' car **2** (*provenance*) from; **il vient** ~ **Londres** he comes from London; ~ **Londres à Paris** from London to Paris; **elle est sortie du cinéma** she came out of the cinema **3** (*moyen*) with; **je l'ai fait** ~ **mes propres mains** I did it with my own two hands **4** (*caractérisation, mesure*): **un mur** ~ **brique/bureau d'acajou** a brick wall/mahogany desk; **un billet** ~ **50 F** a 50 F note; **une pièce** ~ **2 m** ~ **large** *ou* **large** ~ **2 m** a room 2 m wide, a 2m-wide room; **un bébé** ~ **10 mois** a 10-month-old baby; **12 mois** ~ **crédit/travail** 12 months' credit/work; **elle est payée 20 F** ~ **l'heure** she's paid 20 F an hour *ou* per hour; **augmenter** ~ **10 F** to increase by 10 F; **3 jours** ~ **libres** 3 free days, 3 days free; **un verre d'eau** a glass of water; **il mange** ~ **tout** he'll eat anything **5** (*rapport*) from; ~ **4 à 6** from 4 to 6 **6** (*de la part de*): **estimé** ~ **ses collègues** respected by his colleagues **7** (*cause*): **mourir** ~ **faim** to die of hunger; **rouge** ~ **colère** red with fury **8** (*vb +de +infin*) to; **il m'a dit** ~ **rester** he told me to stay **9** (*en apposition*): **cet imbécile** ~ **Paul** that idiot Paul; **le terme** ~ **franglais** the term "franglais"

♦ *dét* **1** (*phrases affirmatives*) some (*souvent omis*); **du vin,** ~ **l'eau, des pommes** (some) wine, (some) water, (some) apples; **des enfants sont venus** some children came; **pendant des mois** for months **2** (*phrases interrogatives et négatives*) any; **a-t-il du vin?** has he got any wine?; **il n'a pas** ~ **pommes/d'enfants** he hasn't (got) any apples/children, he has no apples/children.

dé [de] *nm* (*à jouer*) die *ou* dice (*pl* dice); (*aussi:* ~ **à coudre**) thimble; ~**s** *nmpl* (*jeu*) (game of) dice; **un coup de** ~**s** a throw of the dice; **couper en** ~**s** (*CULIN*) to dice.

DEA *sigle m* (= Diplôme d'études approfondies*) post-graduate diploma.

dealer [dilœʀ] *nm* (*fam*) (drug) pusher.

déambulateur [deɑ̃bylatœʀ] *nm* zimmer ®.

déambuler [deɑ̃byle] *vi* to stroll about.

déb. *abr* = **débutant**; (*COMM*) = à débattre.

débâcle [debakl(ə)] *nf* rout.

déballage [debalaʒ] *nm* (*de marchandises*) display (*of loose goods*); (*fig: fam*) outpourings *pl*.

déballer [debale] *vt* to unpack.

débandade [debɑ̃dad] *nf* scattering; (*déroute*) rout.

débander [debɑ̃de] *vt* to unbandage.

débaptiser [debatize] *vt* (*rue*) to rename.

débarbouiller [debaʀbuje] *vt* to wash; **se** ~ **to** wash (one's face).

débarcadère [debaʀkadɛʀ] *nm* landing stage (*BRIT*), wharf.

débardeur [debaʀdœʀ] *nm* docker, stevedore; (*maillot*) slipover, tank top.

débarquement [debaʀkəmɑ̃] *nm* unloading, landing; disembarcation; (*MIL*) landing; **le D**~ the Normandy landings.

débarquer [debaʀke] *vt* to unload, land ♦ *vi* to disembark; (*fig*) to turn up.

débarras [debaʀa] *nm* lumber room; (*placard*) junk cupboard; (*remise*) outhouse; **bon** ~**!** good riddance!

débarrasser [debaʀase] *vt* to clear ♦ *vi* (*enlever le couvert*) to clear away; ~ **qn de** (*vêtements, paquets*) to relieve sb of; (*habitude, ennemi*) to rid sb of; ~ **qch de** (*fouillis etc*) to clear sth of; **se** ~ **de** *vt* to get rid of; to rid o.s. of.

débat [deba] *vb voir* **débattre** ♦ *nm* discussion, debate; ~**s** *nmpl* (*POL*) proceedings, debates.

débattre [debatʀ(ə)] *vt* to discuss, debate; **se** ~ *vi* to struggle.

débauchage [deboʃaʒ] *nm* (*licenciement*) laying off (of staff); (*par un concurrent*) poaching.

débauche [deboʃ] *nf* debauchery; **une** ~ **de** (*fig*) a profusion of; (: *de couleurs*) a riot of.

débauché, e [deboʃe] *adj* debauched ♦ *nm/f* profligate.

débaucher [deboʃe] *vt* (*licencier*) to lay off, dismiss; (*salarié d'une autre entreprise*) to poach; (*entraîner*) to lead astray, debauch; (*inciter à la grève*) to incite.

débile [debil] *adj* weak, feeble; (*fam: idiot*) dim-witted ♦ *nm/f*: ~ **mental, e** mental defective.

débilitant, e [debilitɑ̃, -ɑ̃t] *adj* debilitating.

débilité [debilite] *nf* debility; (*fam: idiotie*) stupidity; ~ **mentale** mental debility.

débiner [debine]: **se** ~ *vi* to do a bunk (*BRIT*), clear out.

débit [debi] *nm* (*d'un liquide, fleuve*) (rate of) flow; (*d'un magasin*) turnover (of goods); (*élocution*) delivery; (*bancaire*) debit; **avoir un** ~ **de 10 F** to be 10 F in debit; ~ **de boissons** drinking establishment; ~ **de tabac** tobacconist's (shop) (*BRIT*), tobacco *ou* smoke shop (*US*).

débiter [debite] *vt* (*compte*) to debit; (*liquide, gaz*) to yield, produce, give out; (*couper: bois, viande*) to cut up; (*vendre*) to retail; (*péj: paroles etc*) to come out with, churn out.

débiteur, trice [debitœʀ, -tʀis] *nm/f* debtor ♦ *adj* in debit; (*compte*) debit *cpd*.

déblai [deblɛ] *nm* (*nettoyage*) clearing; ~**s** *nmpl* (*terre*) earth; (*décombres*) rubble.

déblaiement [deblɛmɑ̃] *nm* clearing; **travaux de** ~ earth moving *sg*.

déblatérer [deblateʀe] *vi*: ~ **contre** to go on about.

déblayer [debleje] *vt* to clear; ~ **le terrain** (*fig*) to clear the ground.

déblocage [deblɔkaʒ] *nm* (*des prix, cours*) unfreezing.

débloquer [deblɔke] *vt* (*frein, fonds*) to release; (*prix*) to unfreeze ♦ *vi* (*fam*) to talk rubbish.

débobiner [debɔbine] *vt* to unwind.

déboires [debwaʀ] *nmpl* setbacks.

déboisement [debwazmɑ̃] *nm* deforestation.

déboiser [debwaze] *vt* to clear of trees; (*région*) to deforest; **se** ~ *vi* (*colline, montagne*) to become bare of trees.

déboîter [debwate] *vt* (*AUTO*) to pull out; **se** ~ **le genou** *etc* to dislocate one's knee *etc*.

débonnaire [debɔnɛʀ] *adj* easy-going, good-natured.

débordant, e [debɔʀdɑ̃, -ɑ̃t] *adj* (*joie*) unbounded; (*activité*) exuberant.

débordé, e [debɔʀde] *adj*: **être** ~ **de** (*travail, demandes*) to be snowed under with.

débordement [debɔʀdəmɑ̃] *nm* overflowing.

déborder [debɔʀde] *vi* to overflow; (*lait etc*) to boil over ♦ *vt* (*MIL, SPORT*) to outflank; ~ (**de**) **qch** (*dépasser*) to extend beyond sth; ~ **de** (*joie, zèle*) to be brimming over with *ou* bursting with.

débouché [debuʃe] *nm* (*pour vendre*) outlet; (*perspective d'emploi*) opening; (*sortie*): **au** ~

de la vallée where the valley opens out (onto the plain).

déboucher [debuʃe] *vt* (*évier, tuyau etc*) to unblock; (*bouteille*) to uncork, open ♦ *vi*: ~ **de** to emerge from, come out of; ~ **sur** to come out onto; to open out onto; (*fig*) to arrive at, lead up to.

débouler [debule] *vi* to go (*ou* come) tumbling down; (*sans tomber*) to come careering down ♦ *vt*: ~ **l'escalier** to belt down the stairs.

déboulonner [debulɔne] *vt* to dismantle; (*fig: renvoyer*) to dismiss; (*: détruire le prestige de*) to discredit.

débours [debuʀ] *nmpl* outlay.

débourser [debuʀse] *vt* to pay out, lay out.

déboussoler [debusɔle] *vt* to disorientate, disorient.

debout [dəbu] *adv*: **être** ~ (*personne*) to be standing, stand; (*: levé, éveillé*) to be up (and about); (*chose*) to be upright; **être encore** ~ (*fig: en état*) to be still going; to be still standing; to be still up; **mettre qn** ~ to get sb to his feet; **mettre qch** ~ to stand sth up; **se mettre** ~ to get up (on one's feet); **se tenir** ~ to stand; ~! get up!; **cette histoire ne tient pas** ~ this story doesn't hold water.

débouter [debute] *vt* (*JUR*) to dismiss; ~ **qn de sa demande** to dismiss sb's petition.

déboutonner [debutɔne] *vt* to undo, unbutton; **se** ~ *vi* to come undone *ou* unbuttoned.

débraillé, e [debʀaje] *adj* slovenly, untidy.

débrancher [debʀɑ̃ʃe] *vt* (*appareil électrique*) to unplug; (*téléphone, courant électrique*) to disconnect, cut off.

débrayage [debʀejaʒ] *nm* (*AUTO*) clutch; (*: action*) disengaging the clutch; (*grève*) stoppage; **faire un double** ~ to double-declutch.

débrayer [debʀeje] *vi* (*AUTO*) to declutch, disengage the clutch; (*cesser le travail*) to stop work.

débridé, e [debʀide] *adj* unbridled, unrestrained.

débrider [debʀide] *vt* (*cheval*) to unbridle; (*CULIN: volaille*) to untruss.

débris [debʀi] *nm* (*fragment*) fragment ♦ *nmpl* (*déchets*) pieces, debris *sg*; rubbish *sg* (*BRIT*), garbage *sg* (*US*).

débrouillard, e [debʀujaʀ, -aʀd(ə)] *adj* smart, resourceful.

débrouillardise [debʀujaʀdiz] *nf* smartness, resourcefulness.

débrouiller [debʀuje] *vt* to disentangle, untangle; (*fig*) to sort out, unravel; **se** ~ *vi* to manage.

débroussailler [debʀusaje] *vt* to clear (of brushwood).

débusquer [debyske] *vt* to drive out (from cover).

début [deby] *nm* beginning, start; ~**s** *nmpl* beginnings; (*de carrière*) début *sg*; **faire ses**

~**s** to start out; **au** ~ in *ou* at the beginning, at first; **au** ~ **de** at the beginning *ou* start of; **dès le** ~ from the start.

débutant, e [debytã, -ãt] *nm/f* beginner, novice.

débuter [debyte] *vi* to begin, start; *(faire ses débuts)* to start out.

deçà [dəsa]: **en** ~ **de** *prép* this side of; **en** ~ *adv* on this side.

décacheter [dekaʃte] *vt* to unseal, open.

décade [dekad] *nf (10 jours)* (period of) ten days; *(10 ans)* decade.

décadence [dekadãs] *nf* decadence; decline.

décadent, e [dekadã, -ãt] *adj* decadent.

décaféiné, e [dekafeine] *adj* decaffeinated, caffeine-free.

décalage [dekalaʒ] *nm* move forward *ou* back; shift forward *ou* back; *(écart)* gap; *(désaccord)* discrepancy; ~ **horaire** time difference (between time zones), time-lag.

décalaminer [dekalamine] *vt* to decoke.

décalcification [dekalsifikasjɔ̃] *nf* decalcification.

décalcifier [dekalsifje]: **se** ~ *vr* to decalcify.

décalcomanie [dekalkɔmani] *nf* transfer.

décaler [dekale] *vt (dans le temps: avancer)* to bring forward; *(: retarder)* to put back; *(changer de position)* to shift forward *ou* back; ~ **de 10 cm** to move forward *ou* back by 10 cm; ~ **de 2 h** to bring *ou* move forward 2 hours; to put back 2 hours.

décalitre [dekalitʀ(ə)] *nm* decalitre *(BRIT)*, decaliter *(US)*.

décalogue [dekalɔg] *nm* Decalogue.

décalquer [dekalke] *vt* to trace; *(par pression)* to transfer.

décamètre [dekamɛtʀ(ə)] *nm* decametre *(BRIT)*, decameter *(US)*.

décamper [dekãpe] *vi* to clear out *ou* off.

décan [dekã] *nm (ASTROLOGIE)* decan.

décanter [dekãte] *vt* to (allow to) settle (and decant); **se** ~ *vi* to settle.

décapage [dekapaʒ] *nm* stripping; scouring; sanding.

décapant [dekapã] *nm* acid solution; scouring agent; paint stripper.

décaper [dekape] *vt* to strip; *(avec abrasif)* to scour; *(avec papier de verre)* to sand.

décapiter [dekapite] *vt* to behead; *(par accident)* to decapitate; *(fig)* to cut the top off; *(: organisation)* to remove the top people from.

décapotable [dekapɔtabl(ə)] *adj* convertible.

décapoter [dekapɔte] *vt* to put down the top of.

décapsuler [dekapsyle] *vt* to take the cap *ou* top off.

décapsuleur [dekapsylœʀ] *nm* bottle-opener.

décarcasser [dekarkase] *vt*: **se** ~ **pour qn/ pour faire qch** *(fam)* to slog one's guts out for sb/to do sth.

décathlon [dekatlɔ̃] *nm* decathlon.

décati, e [dekati] *adj* faded, aged.

décédé, e [desede] *adj* deceased.

décéder [desede] *vi* to die.

décelable [des(ə)labl(ə)] *adj* discernible.

déceler [desle] *vt* to discover, detect; *(révéler)* to indicate, reveal.

décélération [deseleʀasjɔ̃] *nf* deceleration.

décélérer [deseleʀe] *vi* to decelerate, slow down.

décembre [desãbʀ(ə)] *nm* December; *voir aussi* **juillet**.

décemment [desamã] *adv* decently.

décence [desãs] *nf* decency.

décennal, e, aux [desenal, -o] *adj (qui dure dix ans)* having a term of ten years, ten-year; *(qui revient tous les dix ans)* ten-yearly.

décennie [deseni] *nf* decade.

décent, e [desã, -ãt] *adj* decent.

décentralisation [desãtʀalizasjɔ̃] *nf* decentralization.

décentraliser [desãtʀalize] *vt* to decentralize.

décentrer [desãtʀe] *vt* to decentre; **se** ~ to move off-centre.

déception [desɛpsjɔ̃] *nf* disappointment.

décerner [desɛʀne] *vt* to award.

décès [desɛ] *nm* death, decease; **acte de** ~ death certificate.

décevant, e [desvã, -ãt] *adj* disappointing.

décevoir [desvwaʀ] *vt* to disappoint.

déchaîné, e [deʃene] *adj* unbridled, raging.

déchaînement [deʃɛnmã] *nm (de haine, violence)* outbreak, outburst.

déchaîner [deʃene] *vt (passions, colère)* to unleash; *(rires etc)* to give rise to, arouse; **se** ~ *vi* to be unleashed; *(rires)* to burst out; *(se mettre en colère)* to fly into a rage; **se** ~ **contre qn** to unleash one's fury on sb.

déchanter [deʃãte] *vi* to become disillusioned.

décharge [deʃaʀʒ(ə)] *nf (dépôt d'ordures)* rubbish tip *ou* dump; *(électrique)* electrical discharge; *(salve)* volley of shots; **à la** ~ **de** in defence of.

déchargement [deʃaʀʒəmã] *nm* unloading.

décharger [deʃaʀʒe] *vt (marchandise, véhicule)* to unload; *(ÉLEC)* to discharge; *(arme: neutraliser)* to unload; *(: faire feu)* to discharge, fire; ~ **qn de** *(responsabilité)* to relieve sb of, release sb from; ~ **sa colère (sur)** to vent one's anger (on); ~ **sa conscience** to unburden one's conscience; **se** ~ **dans** *(se déverser)* to flow into; **se** ~ **d'une affaire sur qn** to hand a matter over to sb.

décharné, e [deʃaʀne] *adj* bony, emaciated, fleshless.

déchaussé, e [deʃose] *adj (dent)* loose.

déchausser [deʃose] *vt (personne)* to take the shoes off; *(skis)* to take off; **se** ~ to take off one's shoes; *(dent)* to come *ou* work loose.

dèche [dɛʃ] *nf (fam)*: **être dans la** ~ to be flat broke.

déchéance [deʃeɑ̃s] *nf* (*déclin*) degeneration, decay, decline; (*chute*) fall.

déchet [deʃɛ] *nm* (*de bois, tissu etc*) scrap; (*perte: gén COMM*) wastage, waste; **~s** *nmpl* (*ordures*) refuse *sg*, rubbish *sg* (*BRIT*), garbage *sg* (*US*); **~s radioactifs** radioactive waste.

déchiffrage [deʃifRaʒ] *nm* sight-reading.

déchiffrer [deʃifRe] *vt* to decipher.

déchiqueté, e [deʃikte] *adj* jagged(-edged), ragged.

déchiqueter [deʃikte] *vt* to tear *ou* pull to pieces.

déchirant, e [deʃiRɑ̃, -ɑ̃t] *adj* heart-breaking, heart-rending.

déchiré, e [deʃiRe] *adj* torn; (*fig*) heart-broken.

déchirement [deʃiRmɑ̃] *nm* (*chagrin*) wrench, heartbreak; (*gén pl: conflit*) rift, split.

déchirer [deʃiRe] *vt* to tear, rip; (*mettre en morceaux*) to tear up; (*pour ouvrir*) to tear off; (*arracher*) to tear out; (*fig*) to tear apart; **se ~** *vi* to tear, rip; **se ~ un muscle/tendon** to tear a muscle/tendon.

déchirure [deʃiRyR] *nf* (*accroc*) tear, rip; **~ musculaire** torn muscle.

déchoir [deʃwaR] *vi* (*personne*) to lower o.s., demean o.s; **~ de** to fall from.

déchu, e [deʃy] *pp de* **déchoir** ♦ *adj* fallen; (*roi*) deposed.

décibel [desibɛl] *nm* decibel.

décidé, e [deside] *adj* (*personne, air*) determined; **c'est ~** it's decided; **être ~ à faire** to be determined to do.

décidément [desidemɑ̃] *adv* undoubtedly; really.

décider [deside] *vt*: **~ qch** to decide on sth; **~ de faire/que** to decide to do/that; **~ qn (à faire qch)** to persuade *ou* induce sb (to do sth); **~ de qch** to decide upon sth; (*suj: chose*) to determine sth; **se ~** *vi* (*personne*) to decide, make up one's mind; (*problème, affaire*) to be resolved; **se ~ à qch** to decide on sth; **se ~ à faire** to decide *ou* make up one's mind to do; **se ~ pour qch** to decide on *ou* in favour of sth.

décideur [desidœR] *nm* decision-maker.

décilitre [desilitR(ə)] *nm* decilitre (*BRIT*), deciliter (*US*).

décimal, e, aux [desimal, -o] *adj, nf* decimal.

décimalisation [desimalizɑsjɔ̃] *nf* decimalization.

décimaliser [desimalize] *vt* to decimalize.

décimer [desime] *vt* to decimate.

décimètre [desimɛtR(ə)] *nm* decimetre (*BRIT*), decimeter (*US*); **double ~** (20 cm) ruler.

décisif, ive [desizif, -iv] *adj* decisive; (*qui l'emporte*): **le facteur/l'argument ~** the deciding factor/argument.

décision [desizjɔ̃] *nf* decision; (*fermeté*) decisiveness, decision; **prendre une ~** to make a decision; **prendre la ~ de faire** to take the decision to do; **emporter** *ou* **faire la ~** to be decisive.

déclamation [deklamɑsjɔ̃] *nf* declamation; (*péj*) ranting, spouting.

déclamatoire [deklamatwaR] *adj* declamatory.

déclamer [deklame] *vt* to declaim; (*péj*) to spout ♦ *vi*: **~ contre** to rail against.

déclarable [deklaRabl(ə)] *adj* (*marchandise*) dutiable; (*revenus*) declarable.

déclaration [deklaRɑsjɔ̃] *nf* declaration; registration; (*discours: POL etc*) statement; (*compte rendu*) report; **fausse ~** misrepresentation; **~ (d'amour)** declaration; **~ de décès** registration of death; **~ de guerre** declaration of war; **~ (d'impôts)** statement of income, tax declaration, ≈ tax return; **~ (de sinistre)** (insurance) claim; **~ de revenus** statement of income.

déclaré, e [deklaRe] *adj* (*juré*) avowed.

déclarer [deklaRe] *vt* to declare, announce; (*revenus, employés, marchandises*) to declare; (*décès, naissance*) to register; (*vol etc: à la police*) to report; **se ~** *vi* (*feu, maladie*) to break out; **~ la guerre** to declare war.

déclassé, e [deklɑse] *adj* relegated, downgraded; (*matériel*) (to be) sold off.

déclassement [deklɑsmɑ̃] *nm* relegation, downgrading; (*RAIL etc*) change of class.

déclasser [deklɑse] *vt* to relegate, downgrade; (*déranger: fiches, livres*) to get out of order.

déclenchement [deklɑ̃ʃmɑ̃] *nm* release; setting off.

déclencher [deklɑ̃ʃe] *vt* (*mécanisme etc*) to release; (*sonnerie*) to set off, activate; (*attaque, grève*) to launch; (*provoquer*) to trigger off; **se ~** *vi* to release itself; to go off.

déclencheur [deklɑ̃ʃœR] *nm* release mechanism.

déclic [deklik] *nm* trigger mechanism; (*bruit*) click.

déclin [deklɛ̃] *nm* decline.

déclinaison [deklinɛzɔ̃] *nf* declension.

décliner [dekline] *vi* to decline ♦ *vt* (*invitation*) to decline, refuse; (*responsabilité*) to refuse to accept; (*nom, adresse*) to state; (*LING*) to decline; **se ~** (*LING*) to decline.

déclivité [deklivite] *nf* slope, incline; **en ~** sloping, on the incline.

décloisonner [deklwazɔne] *vt* to decompartmentalize.

déclouer [deklue] *vt* to unnail.

décocher [dekɔʃe] *vt* to hurl; (*flèche, regard*) to shoot.

décoction [dekɔksjɔ̃] *nf* decoction.

décodage [dekɔdaʒ] *nm* deciphering, decoding.

décoder [dekɔde] *vt* to decipher, decode.

décodeur [dekɔdœR] *nm* decoder.

décoiffé, e [dekwafe] *adj*: **elle est toute ~e** her hair is in a mess.

décoiffer [dekwafe] *vt*: **~ qn** to disarrange *ou*

mess up sb's hair; to take sb's hat off; **se ~** to take off one's hat.
décoincer [dekwɛ̃se] *vt* to unjam, loosen.
déçois [deswa] *etc*, **déçoive** [deswav] *etc vb voir* **décevoir**.
décolérer [dekɔleʀe] *vi*: **il ne décolère pas** he's still angry, he hasn't calmed down.
décollage [dekɔlaʒ] *nm* (*AVIAT, ÉCON*) takeoff.
décollé, e [dekɔle] *adj*: **oreilles ~es** sticking-out ears.
décollement [dekɔlmɑ̃] *nm* (*MÉD*): **~ de la rétine** retinal detachment.
décoller [dekɔle] *vt* to unstick ♦ *vi* to take off; (*projet, entreprise*) to take off, get off the ground; **se ~** *vi* to come unstuck.
décolleté, e [dekɔlte] *adj* low-necked, low-cut; (*femme*) wearing a low-cut dress ♦ *nm* low neck(line); (*épaules*) (bare) neck and shoulders; (*plongeant*) cleavage.
décolleter [dekɔlte] *vt* (*vêtement*) to give a low neckline to; (*TECH*) to cut.
décolonisation [dekɔlɔnizasjɔ̃] *nf* decolonization.
décoloniser [dekɔlɔnize] *vt* to decolonize.
décolorant [dekɔlɔʀɑ̃] *nm* decolorant, bleaching agent.
décoloration [dekɔlɔʀasjɔ̃] *nf*: **se faire faire une ~** (*chez le coiffeur*) to have one's hair bleached *ou* lightened.
décoloré, e [dekɔlɔʀe] *adj* (*vêtement*) faded; (*cheveux*) bleached.
décolorer [dekɔlɔʀe] *vt* (*tissu*) to fade; (*cheveux*) to bleach, lighten; **se ~** *vi* to fade.
décombres [dekɔ̃bʀ(ə)] *nmpl* rubble *sg*, debris *sg*.
décommander [dekɔmɑ̃de] *vt* to cancel; (*invités*) to put off; **se ~** to cancel, cry off.
décomposé, e [dekɔ̃poze] *adj* (*pourri*) decomposed; (*visage*) haggard, distorted.
décomposer [dekɔ̃poze] *vt* to break up; (*CHIMIE*) to decompose; (*MATH*) to factorize; **se ~** *vi* to decompose.
décomposition [dekɔ̃pozisjɔ̃] *nf* breaking up; decomposition; factorization; **en ~** (*organisme*) in a state of decay, decomposing.
décompresser [dekɔ̃pʀese] *vi* (*fam: se détendre*) to unwind.
décompresseur [dekɔ̃pʀesœʀ] *nm* decompressor.
décompression [dekɔ̃pʀesjɔ̃] *nf* decompression.
décomprimer [dekɔ̃pʀime] *vt* to decompress.
décompte [dekɔ̃t] *nm* deduction; (*facture*) breakdown (of an account), detailed account.
décompter [dekɔ̃te] *vt* to deduct.
déconcentration [dekɔ̃sɑ̃tʀasjɔ̃] *nf* (*des industries etc*) dispersal; **~ des pouvoirs** devolution.
déconcentré, e [dekɔ̃sɑ̃tʀe] *adj* (*sportif etc*) who has lost (his/her) concentration.

déconcentrer [dekɔ̃sɑ̃tʀe] *vt* (*ADMIN*) to disperse; **se ~** *vi* to lose (one's) concentration.
déconcertant, e [dekɔ̃sɛʀtɑ̃, -ɑ̃t] *adj* disconcerting.
déconcerter [dekɔ̃sɛʀte] *vt* to disconcert, confound.
déconditionner [dekɔ̃disjɔne] *vt*: **~ l'opinion américaine** to change the way the Americans have been forced to think.
déconfit, e [dekɔ̃fi, -it] *adj* crestfallen, downcast.
déconfiture [dekɔ̃fityʀ] *nf* collapse, ruin; (*morale*) defeat.
décongélation [dekɔ̃ʒelasjɔ̃] *nf* defrosting, thawing.
décongeler [dekɔ̃ʒle] *vt* to thaw (out).
décongestionner [dekɔ̃ʒɛstjɔne] *vt* (*MÉD*) to decongest; (*rues*) to relieve congestion in.
déconnecter [dekɔnɛkte] *vt* to disconnect.
déconner [dekɔne] *vi* (*fam!: en parlant*) to talk (a load of) rubbish (*BRIT*) *ou* garbage (*US*); (*: faire des bêtises*) to muck about; **sans ~** no kidding.
déconseiller [dekɔ̃seje] *vt*: **~ qch (à qn)** to advise (sb) against sth; **~ à qn de faire** to advise sb against doing; **c'est déconseillé** it's not advised *ou* advisable.
déconsidérer [dekɔ̃sideʀe] *vt* to discredit.
décontamination [dekɔ̃taminasjɔ̃] *nf* decontamination.
décontaminer [dekɔ̃tamine] *vt* to decontaminate.
décontenancer [dekɔ̃tnɑ̃se] *vt* to disconcert, discountenance.
décontracté, e [dekɔ̃tʀakte] *adj* relaxed.
décontracter [dekɔ̃tʀakte] *vt*, **se ~** *vi* to relax.
décontraction [dekɔ̃tʀaksjɔ̃] *nf* relaxation.
déconvenue [dekɔ̃vny] *nf* disappointment.
décor [dekɔʀ] *nm* décor; (*paysage*) scenery; **~s** *nmpl* (*THÉÂT*) scenery *sg*, decor *sg*; (*CINÉ*) set *sg*; **changement de ~** (*fig*) change of scene; **entrer dans le ~** (*fig*) to run off the road; **en ~ naturel** (*CINÉ*) on location.
décorateur, trice [dekɔʀatœʀ, -tʀis] *nm/f* (interior) decorator; (*CINÉ*) set designer.
décoratif, ive [dekɔʀatif, -iv] *adj* decorative.
décoration [dekɔʀasjɔ̃] *nf* decoration.
décorer [dekɔʀe] *vt* to decorate.
décortiqué, e [dekɔʀtike] *adj* shelled; hulled.
décortiquer [dekɔʀtike] *vt* to shell; (*riz*) to hull; (*fig*) to dissect.
décorum [dekɔʀɔm] *nm* decorum; etiquette.
décote [dekɔt] *nf* tax relief.
découcher [dekuʃe] *vi* to spend the night away.
découdre [dekudʀ(ə)] *vt* (*vêtement, couture*) to unpick, take the stitching out of; (*bouton*) to take off; **se ~** *vi* to come unstitched; (*bouton*) to come off; **en ~** (*fig*) to fight, do battle.
découler [dekule] *vi*: **~ de** to ensue *ou* follow

from.

découpage [dekupaʒ] *nm* cutting up; carving; (*image*) cut-out (figure); ~ **électoral** division into constituencies.

découper [dekupe] *vt* (*papier, tissu etc*) to cut up; (*volaille, viande*) to carve; (*détacher: manche, article*) to cut out; **se** ~ **sur** (*ciel, fond*) to stand out against.

découplé, e [dekuple] *adj*: **bien** ~ well-built, well-proportioned.

découpure [dekupyʀ] *nf*: ~**s** (*morceaux*) cut-out bits; (*d'une côte, arête*) indentations, jagged outline *sg*.

décourageant, e [dekuʀaʒɑ̃, ɑ̃t] *adj* discouraging; (*personne, attitude*) discouraging, negative.

découragement [dekuʀaʒmɑ̃] *nm* discouragement, despondency.

décourager [dekuʀaʒe] *vt* to discourage, dishearten; (*dissuader*) to discourage, put off; **se** ~ *vi* to lose heart, become discouraged; ~ **qn de faire/de qch** to discourage sb from doing/from sth, put sb off doing/sth.

décousu, e [dekuzy] *pp de* **découdre** ♦ *adj* unstitched; (*fig*) disjointed, disconnected.

découvert, e [dekuvɛʀ, -ɛʀt(ə)] *pp de* **découvrir** ♦ *adj* (*tête*) bare, uncovered; (*lieu*) open, exposed ♦ *nm* (*bancaire*) overdraft ♦ *nf* discovery; **à** ~ *adv* (*MIL*) exposed, without cover; (*fig*) openly ♦ *adj* (*COMM*) overdrawn; **à visage** ~ openly; **aller à la ~e de** to go in search of.

découvrir [dekuvʀiʀ] *vt* to discover, (*apercevoir*) to see; (*enlever ce qui couvre ou protège*) to uncover; (*montrer, dévoiler*) to reveal; **se** ~ to take off one's hat; (*se déshabiller*) to take something off; (*au lit*) to uncover o.s.; (*ciel*) to clear; **se** ~ **des talents** to find hidden talents in o.s.

décrasser [dekʀase] *vt* to clean.

décrêper [dekʀepe] *vt* (*cheveux*) to straighten.

décrépi, e [dekʀepi] *adj* peeling; with roughcast rendering removed.

décrépit, e [dekʀepi, -it] *adj* decrepit.

décrépitude [dekʀepityd] *nf* decrepitude; decay.

decrescendo [dekʀeʃɛndo] *nm* (*MUS*) decrescendo; **aller** ~ (*fig*) to decline, be on the wane.

décret [dekʀɛ] *nm* decree.

décréter [dekʀete] *vt* to decree; (*ordonner*) to order.

décret-loi [dekʀɛlwa] *nm* statutory order.

décrié, e [dekʀije] *adj* disparaged.

décrire [dekʀiʀ] *vt* to describe; (*courbe, cercle*) to follow, describe.

décrisper [dekʀispe] *vt* to defuse.

décrit, e [dekʀi, -it] *pp de* **décrire**.

décrivais [dekʀivɛ] *etc vb voir* **décrire**.

décrochement [dekʀɔʃmɑ̃] *nm* (*d'un mur etc*) recess.

décrocher [dekʀɔʃe] *vt* (*dépendre*) to take

down; (*téléphone*) to take off the hook; (: *pour répondre*): ~ (**le téléphone**) to pick up *ou* lift the receiver; (*fig: contrat etc*) to get, land ♦ *vi* to drop out; to switch off; **se** ~ *vi* (*tableau, rideau*) to fall down.

décrois [dekʀwa] *etc vb voir* **décroître**.

décroiser [dekʀwaze] *vt* (*bras*) to unfold; (*jambes*) to uncross.

décroissant, e [dekʀwasɑ̃, -ɑ̃t] *vb voir* **décroître** ♦ *adj* decreasing, declining, diminishing; **par ordre** ~ in descending order.

décroître [dekʀwatʀ(ə)] *vi* to decrease, decline, diminish.

décrotter [dekʀɔte] *vt* (*chaussures*) to clean the mud from; **se** ~ **le nez** to pick one's nose.

décru, e [dekʀy] *pp de* **décroître**.

décrue [dekʀy] *nf* drop in level (of the waters).

décrypter [dekʀipte] *vt* to decipher.

déçu, e [desy] *pp de* **décevoir** ♦ *adj* disappointed.

déculotter [dekylɔte] *vt*: ~ **qn** to take off *ou* down sb's trousers; **se** ~ to take off *ou* down one's trousers.

déculpabiliser [dekylpabilize] *vt* (*personne*) to relieve of guilt; (*chose*) to decriminalize.

décuple [dekypl(ə)] *nm*: **le** ~ **de** ten times; **au** ~ tenfold.

décupler [dekyple] *vt, vi* to increase tenfold.

déçut [desy] *etc vb voir* **décevoir**.

dédaignable [dedɛɲabl(ə)] *adj*: **pas** ~ not to be despised.

dédaigner [dedeɲe] *vt* to despise, scorn; (*négliger*) to disregard, spurn; ~ **de faire** to consider it beneath one to do, not deign to do.

dédaigneusement [dedɛɲøzmɑ̃] *adv* scornfully, disdainfully.

dédaigneux, euse [dedɛɲø, -øz] *adj* scornful, disdainful.

dédain [dedɛ̃] *nm* scorn, disdain.

dédale [dedal] *nm* maze.

dedans [dədɑ̃] *adv* inside; (*pas en plein air*) indoors, inside ♦ *nm* inside; **au** ~ on the inside; inside; **en** ~ (*vers l'intérieur*) inwards; *voir aussi* **là**.

dédicace [dedikas] *nf* (*imprimée*) dedication; (*manuscrite, sur une photo etc*) inscription.

dédicacer [dedikase] *vt*: ~ (**à qn**) to sign (for sb), autograph (for sb), inscribe (to sb).

dédié, e [dedje] *adj*: **ordinateur** ~ dedicated computer.

dédier [dedje] *vt* to dedicate.

dédire [dediʀ]: **se** ~ *vi* to go back on one's word; (*se rétracter*) to retract, recant.

dédit, e [dedi, -it] *pp de* **dédire** ♦ *nm* (*COMM*) forfeit, penalty.

dédommagement [dedɔmaʒmɑ̃] *nm* compensation.

dédommager [dedɔmaʒe] *vt*: ~ **qn** (**de**) to compensate sb (for); (*fig*) to repay sb (for).

dédouaner [dedwane] *vt* to clear through customs.

dédoublement [dedubləmɑ̃] *nm* splitting; (*PSYCH*): ~ **de la personnalité** split *ou* dual personality.

dédoubler [deduble] *vt* (*classe, effectifs*) to split (into two); (*couverture etc*) to unfold; (*manteau*) to remove the lining of; ~ **un train/les trains** to run a relief train/additional trains; **se** ~ *vi* (*PSYCH*) to have a split personality.

dédramatiser [dedramatize] *vt* (*situation*) to defuse; (*événement*) to play down.

déductible [dedyktibl(ə)] *adj* deductible.

déduction [dedyksjɔ̃] *nf* (*d'argent*) deduction; (*raisonnement*) deduction, inference.

déduire [dedɥiʀ] *vt*: ~ **qch (de)** (*ôter*) to deduct sth (from); (*conclure*) to deduce *ou* infer sth (from).

déesse [deɛs] *nf* goddess.

DEFA *sigle m* (= *Diplôme d'État relatif aux fonctions d'animation*) *diploma for senior youth leaders*.

défaillance [defajɑ̃s] *nf* (*syncope*) blackout; (*fatigue*) (sudden) weakness *no pl*; (*technique*) fault, failure; (*morale etc*) weakness; ~ **cardiaque** heart failure.

défaillant, e [defajɑ̃, -ɑ̃t] *adj* defective; (*JUR*: *témoin*) defaulting.

défaillir [defajiʀ] *vi* to faint; to feel faint; (*mémoire etc*) to fail.

défaire [defɛʀ] *vt* (*installation, échafaudage*) to take down, dismantle; (*paquet etc, nœud, vêtement*) to undo; (*bagages*) to unpack; (*ouvrage*) to undo, unpick; (*cheveux*) to take out; **se** ~ *vi* to come undone; **se** ~ **de** *vt* (*se débarrasser de*) to get rid of; (*se séparer de*) to part with; ~ **le lit** (*pour changer les draps*) to strip the bed; (*pour se coucher*) to turn back the bedclothes.

défait, e [defɛ, -ɛt] *pp de* **défaire** ♦ *adj* (*visage*) haggard, ravaged ♦ *nf* defeat.

défaites [defɛt] *vb voir* **défaire**.

défaitisme [defetism(ə)] *nm* defeatism.

défaitiste [defetist(ə)] *adj, nm/f* defeatist.

défalcation [defalkasjɔ̃] *nf* deduction.

défalquer [defalke] *vt* to deduct.

défasse [defas] *etc vb voir* **défaire**.

défausser [defose] *vt* to get rid of; **se** ~ *vi* (*CARTES*) to discard.

défaut [defo] *nm* (*moral*) fault, failing, defect; (*d'étoffe, métal*) fault, flaw, defect; (*manque, carence*): ~ **de** lack of; shortage of; (*INFORM*) bug; ~ **de la cuirasse** (*fig*) chink in the armour (*BRIT*) *ou* armor (*US*); **en** ~ at fault; in the wrong; **faire** ~ (*manquer*) to be lacking; **à** ~ *adv* failing that; **à** ~ **de** for lack *ou* want of; **par** ~ (*JUR*) in his (*ou* her *etc*) absence.

défaveur [defavœʀ] *nf* disfavour (*BRIT*), disfavor (*US*).

défavorable [defavɔʀabl(ə)] *adj* unfavourable (*BRIT*), unfavorable (*US*).

défavoriser [defavɔʀize] *vt* to put at a disadvantage.

défectif, ive [defɛktif, -iv] *adj*: **verbe** ~ defective verb.

défection [defɛksjɔ̃] *nf* defection, failure to give support *ou* assistance; failure to appear; **faire** ~ (*d'un parti etc*) to withdraw one's support, leave.

défectueux, euse [defɛktɥø, -øz] *adj* faulty, defective.

défectuosité [defɛktɥozite] *nf* defectiveness *no pl*; (*défaut*) defect, fault.

défendable [defɑ̃dabl(ə)] *adj* defensible.

défendeur, eresse [defɑ̃dœʀ, -dʀɛs] *nm/f* (*JUR*) defendant.

défendre [defɑ̃dʀ(ə)] *vt* to defend; (*interdire*) to forbid; ~ **à qn qch/de faire** to forbid sb sth/to do; **il est défendu de cracher** spitting (is) prohibited *ou* is not allowed; **c'est défendu** it is forbidden; **se** ~ **to defend o.s.; il se défend** (*fig*) he can hold his own; **ça se défend** (*fig*) it holds together; **se** ~ **de/contre** (*se protéger*) to protect o.s. from/against; **se** ~ **de** (*se garder de*) to refrain from; (*nier*): **se** ~ **de vouloir** to deny wanting.

défenestrer [defənɛstʀe] *vt* to throw out of the window.

défense [defɑ̃s] *nf* defence (*BRIT*), defense (*US*); (*d'éléphant etc*) tusk; **ministre de la** ~ Minister of Defence (*BRIT*), Defence Secretary; **la** ~ **nationale** defence, the defence of the realm (*BRIT*); **la** ~ **contre avions** anti-aircraft defence; "~ **de fumer/cracher**" "no smoking/spitting", "smoking/spitting prohibited"; **prendre la** ~ **de qn** to stand up for sb; ~ **des consommateurs** consumerism.

défenseur [defɑ̃sœʀ] *nm* defender; (*JUR*) counsel for the defence.

défensif, ive [defɑ̃sif, -iv] *adj, nf* defensive; **être sur la défensive** to be on the defensive.

déféquer [defeke] *vi* to defecate.

déferai [defʀe] *etc vb voir* **défaire**.

déférence [defeʀɑ̃s] *nf* deference.

déférent, e [defeʀɑ̃, -ɑ̃t] *adj* (*poli*) deferential, deferent.

déférer [defeʀe] *vt* (*JUR*) to refer; ~ **à** *vt* (*requête, décision*) to defer to; ~ **qn à la justice** to hand sb over to justice.

déferlant, e [defɛʀlɑ̃, -ɑ̃t] *adj*: **vague** ~**e** breaker.

déferlement [defɛʀləmɑ̃] *nm* breaking; surge.

déferler [defɛʀle] *vi* (*vagues*) to break; (*fig*) to surge.

défi [defi] *nm* (*provocation*) challenge; (*bravade*) defiance; **mettre qn au** ~ **de faire qch** to challenge sb to do sth; **relever un** ~ to take up *ou* accept a challenge.

défiance [defjɑ̃s] *nf* mistrust, distrust.

déficeler [defisle] *vt* (*paquet*) to undo, untie.

déficience [defisjɑ̃s] *nf* deficiency.

déficient, e [defisjɑ̃, -ɑ̃t] *adj* deficient.

déficit [defisit] *nm* (*COMM*) deficit; (*PSYCH etc*: *manque*) defect; ~ **budgétaire** budget deficit; **être en** ~ to be in deficit.

déficitaire [defisitɛʀ] *adj* (*année, récolte*) bad; **entreprise/budget** ~ business/budget in deficit.

défier [defje] *vt* (*provoquer*) to challenge; (*fig*) to defy, brave; **se** ~ **de** (*se méfier de*) to distrust, mistrust; ~ **qn de faire** to challenge *ou* defy sb to do; ~ **qn à** to challenge sb to; ~ **toute comparaison/concurrence** to be incomparable/unbeatable.

défigurer [defigyʀe] *vt* to disfigure; (*suj: boutons etc*) to mar *ou* spoil (the looks of); (*fig: œuvre*) to mutilate, deface.

défilé [defile] *nm* (*GÉO*) (narrow) gorge *ou* pass; (*soldats*) parade; (*manifestants*) procession, march; **un** ~ **de** (*voitures, visiteurs etc*) a stream of.

défiler [defile] *vi* (*troupes*) to march past; (*sportifs*) to parade; (*manifestants*) to march; (*visiteurs*) to pour, stream; **se** ~ *vi* (*se dérober*) to slip away, sneak off; **faire** ~ (*bande, film*) to put on; (*INFORM*) to scroll.

défini, e [defini] *adj* definite.

définir [definiʀ] *vt* to define.

définissable [definisabl(ə)] *adj* definable.

définitif, ive [definitif, -iv] *adj* (*final*) final, definitive; (*pour longtemps*) permanent, definitive; (*sans appel*) final, definite ♦ *nf*: **en définitive** eventually; (*somme toute*) when all is said and done.

définition [definisjɔ̃] *nf* definition; (*de mots croisés*) clue; (*TV*) (picture) resolution.

définitivement [definitivmɑ̃] *adv* definitively; permanently; definitely.

défit [defi] *etc vb voir* **défaire**.

déflagration [deflagʀasjɔ̃] *nf* explosion.

déflation [deflɑsjɔ̃] *nf* deflation.

déflationniste [deflɑsjɔnist(ə)] *adj* deflationniste, deflationary.

déflecteur [deflɛktœʀ] *nm* (*AUTO*) quarterlight (*BRIT*), deflector (*US*).

déflorer [deflɔʀe] *vt* (*jeune fille*) to deflower; (*fig*) to spoil the charm of.

défoncé, e [defɔ̃se] *adj* smashed in; broken down; (*route*) full of potholes ♦ *nm/f* addict.

défoncer [defɔ̃se] *vt* (*caisse*) to stave in; (*porte*) to smash in *ou* down; (*lit, fauteuil*) to burst (the springs of); (*terrain, route*) to rip *ou* plough up; **se** ~ *vi* (*se donner à fond*) to give it all one's got.

défont [defɔ̃] *vb voir* **défaire**.

déformant, e [defɔʀmɑ̃, -ɑ̃t] *adj*: **glace** ~**e** *ou* **miroir** ~ distorting mirror.

déformation [defɔʀmɑsjɔ̃] *nf* loss of shape; deformation; distortion; ~ **professionnelle** conditioning by one's job.

déformer [defɔʀme] *vt* to put out of shape; (*corps*) to deform; (*pensée, fait*) to distort; **se** ~ *vi* to lose its shape.

défoulement [defulmɑ̃] *nm* release of tension; unwinding.

défouler [defule]: **se** ~ *vi* (*PSYCH*) to work off one's tensions, release one's pent-up feelings; (*gén*) to unwind, let off steam.

défraîchi, e [defʀeʃi] *adj* faded; (*article à vendre*) shop-soiled.

défraîchir [defʀeʃiʀ]: **se** ~ *vi* to fade; to become shop-soiled.

défrayer [defʀeje] *vt*: ~ **qn** to pay sb's expenses; ~ **la chronique** to be in the news; ~ **la conversation** to be the main topic of conversation.

défrichement [defʀiʃmɑ̃] *nm* clearance.

défricher [defʀiʃe] *vt* to clear (for cultivation).

défriser [defʀize] *vt* (*cheveux*) to straighten; (*fig*) to annoy.

défroisser [defʀwase] *vt* to smooth out.

défroque [defʀɔk] *nf* cast-off.

défroqué [defʀɔke] *nm* former monk (*ou* priest).

défroquer [defʀɔke] *vi* (*aussi*: **se** ~) to give up the cloth, renounce one's vows.

défunt, e [defœ̃, -œ̃t] *adj*: **son** ~ **père** his late father ♦ *nm/f* deceased.

dégagé, e [degaʒe] *adj* clear; (*ton, air*) casual, jaunty.

dégagement [degaʒmɑ̃] *nm* emission; freeing; clearing; (*espace libre*) clearing; passage; clearance; (*FOOTBALL*) clearance; **voie de** ~ slip road; **itinéraire de** ~ alternative route (*to relieve traffic congestion*).

dégager [degaʒe] *vt* (*exhaler*) to give off, emit; (*délivrer*) to free, extricate; (*MIL: troupes*) to relieve; (*désencombrer*) to clear; (*isoler, mettre en valeur*) to bring out; (*crédits*) to release; **se** ~ *vi* (*odeur*) to emanate, be given off; (*passage, ciel*) to clear; ~ **qn de** (*engagement, parole etc*) to release *ou* free sb from; **se** ~ **de** (*fig: engagement etc*) to get out of; (: *promesse*) to go back on.

dégaine [degɛn] *nf* awkward way of walking.

dégainer [degene] *vt* to draw.

dégarni, e [degaʀni] *adj* bald.

dégarnir [degaʀniʀ] *vt* (*vider*) to empty, clear; **se** ~ *vi* to empty; to be cleaned out *ou* cleared; (*tempes, crâne*) to go bald.

dégâts [dega] *nmpl* damage *sg*; **faire des** ~ to damage.

dégauchir [degoʃiʀ] *vt* (*TECH*) to surface.

dégazer [degaze] *vi* (*pétrolier*) to clean its tanks.

dégel [deʒɛl] *nm* thaw; (*fig: des prix etc*) unfreezing.

dégeler [deʒle] *vt* to thaw (out); (*fig*) to unfreeze ♦ *vi* to thaw (out); **se** ~ *vi* (*fig*) to thaw out.

dégénéré, e [deʒeneʀe] *adj, nm/f* degenerate.

dégénérer [deʒeneʀe] *vi* to degenerate; (*empirer*) to go from bad to worse; (*devenir*): ~ **en** to degenerate into.

dégénérescence [deʒeneʀesɑ̃s] *nf* degeneration.

dégingandé, e [deʒɛ̃gɑ̃de] *adj* gangling, lanky.

dégivrage [deʒivʀaʒ] *nm* defrosting; de-icing.

dégivrer [deʒivʀe] *vt* (*frigo*) to defrost; (*vitres*) to de-ice.

dégivreur [deʒivʀœʀ] *nm* defroster; de-icer.

déglinguer [deglɛ̃ge] *vt* to bust.

déglutir [deglytiʀ] *vt*, *vi* to swallow.

déglutition [deglytisjɔ̃] *nf* swallowing.

dégonflé, e [degɔ̃fle] *adj* (*pneu*) flat; (*fam*) chicken ♦ *nm/f* (*fam*) chicken.

dégonfler [degɔ̃fle] *vt* (*pneu, ballon*) to let down, deflate ♦ *vi* (*désenfler*) to go down; **se** ~ *vi* (*fam*) to chicken out.

dégorger [degɔʀʒe] *vi* (*CULIN*): **faire** ~ to leave to sweat; (*aussi*: **se** ~: *rivière*): ~ **dans** to flow into ♦ *vt* to disgorge.

dégoter [degɔte] *vt* (*fam*) to dig up, find.

dégouliner [deguline] *vi* to trickle, drip; ~ **de** to be dripping with.

dégoupiller [degupije] *vt* (*grenade*) to take the pin out of.

dégourdi, e [deguʀdi] *adj* smart, resourceful.

dégourdir [deguʀdiʀ] *vt* to warm (up); **se** ~ **(les jambes)** to stretch one's legs.

dégoût [degu] *nm* disgust, distaste.

dégoûtant, e [degutɑ̃, -ɑ̃t] *adj* disgusting.

dégoûté, e [degute] *adj* disgusted; ~ **de** sick of.

dégoûter [degute] *vt* to disgust; **cela me dégoûte** I find this disgusting *ou* revolting; ~ **qn de qch** to put sb off sth; **se** ~ **de** to get *ou* become sick of.

dégoutter [degute] *vi* to drip; ~ **de** to be dripping with.

dégradant, e [degʀadɑ̃, -ɑ̃t] *adj* degrading.

dégradation [degʀadasjɔ̃] *nf* reduction in rank; defacement; degradation, debasement; deterioration; (*aussi*: ~**s**: *dégâts*) damage *no pl*.

dégradé, e [degʀade] *adj* (*couleur*) shaded off; (*teintes*) faded; (*cheveux*) layered ♦ *nm* (*PEINTURE*) gradation.

dégrader [degʀade] *vt* (*MIL*: *officier*) to degrade; (*abîmer*) to damage, deface; (*avilir*) to degrade, debase; **se** ~ *vi* (*relations, situation*) to deteriorate.

dégrafer [degʀafe] *vt* to unclip, unhook, unfasten.

dégraissage [degʀesaʒ] *nm* (*ÉCON*) cutbacks *pl*; ~ **et nettoyage à sec** dry cleaning.

dégraissant [degʀesɑ̃] *nm* spot remover.

dégraisser [degʀese] *vt* (*soupe*) to skim; (*vêtement*) to take the grease marks out of; (*ÉCON*) to cut back; (*: entreprise*) to slim down.

degré [dəgʀe] *nm* degree; (*d'escalier*) step; **brûlure au 1er/2ème** ~ 1st/2nd degree burn; **équation du 1er/2ème** ~ linear/quadratic equation; **le premier** ~ (*SCOL*) primary level; **alcool à 90** ~**s** surgical spirit; **vin de 10** ~**s** 10° wine (*on Gay-Lussac scale*); **par** ~**(s)** *adv* by degrees, gradually.

dégressif, ive [degʀesif, -iv] *adj* on a decreasing scale, degressive; **tarif** ~ decreasing rate of charge.

dégrèvement [degʀɛvmɑ̃] *nm* tax relief.

dégrever [degʀəve] *vt* to grant tax relief to; to reduce the tax burden on.

dégriffé, e [degʀife] *adj* (*vêtement*) sold without the designer's label.

dégringolade [degʀɛ̃gɔlad] *nf* tumble; (*fig*) collapse.

dégringoler [degʀɛ̃gɔle] *vi* to tumble (down); (*fig: prix, monnaie etc*) to collapse.

dégriser [degʀize] *vt* to sober up.

dégrossir [degʀosiʀ] *vt* (*bois*) to trim; (*fig*) to work out roughly; (*: personne*) to knock the rough edges off.

déguenillé, e [degnije] *adj* ragged, tattered.

déguerpir [degɛʀpiʀ] *vi* to clear off.

dégueulasse [degœlas] *adj* (*fam*) disgusting.

dégueuler [degœle] *vi* (*fam*) to puke, throw up.

déguisé, e [degize] *adj* disguised; dressed up; ~ **en** disguised (*ou* dressed up) as.

déguisement [degizmɑ̃] *nm* disguise; (*habits: pour s'amuser*) dressing-up clothes; (*: pour tromper*) disguise.

déguiser [degize] *vt* to disguise; **se** ~ **(en)** (*se costumer*) to dress up (as); (*pour tromper*) to disguise o.s. (as).

dégustation [degystasjɔ̃] *nf* tasting; sampling; savouring (*BRIT*), savoring (*US*); (*séance*): ~ **de vin(s)** wine-tasting.

déguster [degyste] *vt* (*vins*) to taste; (*fromages etc*) to sample; (*savourer*) to enjoy, savour (*BRIT*), savor (*US*).

déhancher [deɑ̃ʃe]: **se** ~ *vi* to sway one's hips; to lean (one's weight) on one hip.

dehors [dəɔʀ] *adv* outside; (*en plein air*) outdoors, outside ♦ *nm* outside ♦ *nmpl* (*apparences*) appearances, exterior *sg*; **mettre** *ou* **jeter** ~ to throw out; **au** ~ outside; (*en apparence*) outwardly; **au** ~ **de** outside; **de** ~ from outside; **en** ~ outside; outwards; **en** ~ **de** apart from.

déifier [deifje] *vt* to deify.

déjà [deʒa] *adv* already; (*auparavant*) before, already; **as-tu** ~ **été en France?** have you been to France before?; **c'est** ~ **pas mal** that's not too bad (at all); **c'est** ~ **quelque chose** (at least) it's better than nothing; **quel nom,** ~**?** what was the name again?

déjanter [deʒɑ̃te]: **se** ~ *vi* (*pneu*) to come off the rim.

déjà-vu [deʒavy] *nm*: **c'est du** ~ there's nothing new in that.

déjeté, e [deʒte] *adj* lop-sided, crooked.

déjeuner [deʒœne] *vi* to (have) lunch; (*le matin*) to have breakfast ♦ *nm* lunch; (*petit déjeuner*) breakfast; ~ **d'affaires** business lunch.

déjouer [deʒwe] *vt* to elude; to foil, thwart.

déjuger [deʒyʒe]: **se** ~ *vi* to go back on one's opinion.

delà [dəla] *adv*: **par** ~, **en** ~ **(de)**, **au** ~ **(de)** beyond.

délabré, e [delabre] *adj* dilapidated, broken-down.

délabrement [delabrəmã] *nm* decay, dilapidation.

délabrer [delabre]: **se** ~ *vi* to fall into decay, become dilapidated.

délacer [delase] *vt* to unlace, undo.

délai [dele] *nm* (*attente*) waiting period; (*sursis*) extension (of time); (*temps accordé: aussi*: ~**s**) time limit; **sans** ~ without delay; **à bref** ~ shortly, very soon; at short notice; **dans les** ~**s** within the time limit; **un** ~ **de 30 jours** a period of 30 days; **comptez un** ~ **de livraison de 10 jours** allow 10 days for delivery.

délaissé, e [delese] *adj* abandoned, deserted; neglected.

délaisser [delese] *vt* (*abandonner*) to abandon, desert; (*négliger*) to neglect.

délassant, e [delasã, -ãt] *adj* relaxing.

délassement [delasmã] *nm* relaxation.

délasser [delase] *vt* (*reposer*) to relax; (*divertir*) to divert, entertain; **se** ~ *vi* to relax.

délateur, trice [delatœr, -tris] *nm/f* informer.

délation [delasjɔ̃] *nf* denouncement, informing.

délavé, e [delave] *adj* faded.

délayage [deleʒaʒ] *nm* mixing; thinning down.

délayer [deleje] *vt* (*CULIN*) to mix (with water *etc*); (*peinture*) to thin down; (*fig*) to pad out, spin out.

delco [dɛlko] *nm* ® (*AUTO*) distributor; **tête de** ~ distributor cap.

délectation [delɛktasjɔ̃] *nf* delight.

délecter [delɛkte]: **se** ~ *vi*: **se** ~ **de** to revel *ou* delight in.

délégation [delegasjɔ̃] *nf* delegation; ~ **de pouvoir** delegation of power.

délégué, e [delege] *adj* delegated ♦ *nm/f* delegate; representative; **ministre** ~ **à** minister with special responsibility for.

déléguer [delege] *vt* to delegate.

délestage [delɛstaʒ] *nm*: **itinéraire de** ~ alternative route (*to relieve traffic congestion*).

délester [delɛste] *vt* (*navire*) to unballast; ~ **une route** to relieve traffic congestion on a road by diverting traffic.

Delhi [dɛli] *n* Delhi.

délibérant, e [deliberã, -ãt] *adj*: **assemblée** ~**e** deliberative assembly.

délibératif, ive [deliberatif, -iv] *adj*: **avoir voix délibérative** to have voting rights.

délibération [deliberasjɔ̃] *nf* deliberation.

délibéré, e [delibere] *adj* (*conscient*) deliberate; (*déterminé*) determined, resolute; **de propos** ~ (*à dessein, exprès*) intentionally.

délibérément [deliberemã] *adv* deliberately; (*résolument*) resolutely.

délibérer [delibere] *vi* to deliberate.

délicat, e [delika, -at] *adj* delicate; (*plein de tact*) tactful; (*attentionné*) thoughtful; (*exigeant*) fussy, particular; **procédés peu** ~**s** unscrupulous methods.

délicatement [delikatmã] *adv* delicately; (*avec douceur*) gently.

délicatesse [delikatɛs] *nf* delicacy; tactfulness; thoughtfulness; ~**s** *nfpl* attentions, consideration *sg*.

délice [delis] *nm* delight.

délicieusement [delisjøzmã] *adv* deliciously; delightfully.

délicieux, euse [delisjø, -øz] *adj* (*au goût*) delicious; (*sensation, impression*) delightful.

délictueux, euse [deliktɥø, -øz] *adj* criminal.

délié, e [delje] *adj* nimble, agile; (*mince*) slender, fine ♦ *nm*: **les** ~**s** the upstrokes (*in handwriting*).

délier [delje] *vt* to untie; ~ **qn de** (*serment etc*) to free *ou* release sb from.

délimitation [delimitasjɔ̃] *nf* delimitation.

délimiter [delimite] *vt* to delimit.

délinquance [delɛ̃kãs] *nf* criminality; ~ **juvénile** juvenile delinquency.

délinquant, e [delɛ̃kã, -ãt] *adj*, *nm/f* delinquent.

déliquescence [delikesãs] *nf*: **en** ~ in a state of decay.

déliquescent, e [delikesã, -ãt] *adj* decaying.

délirant, e [delirã, -ãt] *adj* (*MÉD: fièvre*) delirious; (*imagination*) frenzied; (*fam: déraisonnable*) crazy.

délire [delir] *nm* (*fièvre*) delirium; (*fig*) frenzy; (*: folie*) lunacy.

délirer [delire] *vi* to be delirious; (*fig*) to be raving.

délit [deli] *nm* (criminal) offence; ~ **de droit commun** violation of common law; ~ **de fuite** failure to stop after an accident; ~ **d'initiés** insider dealing *ou* trading; ~ **de presse** violation of the press laws.

délivrance [delivrãs] *nf* freeing, release; (*sentiment*) relief.

délivrer [delivre] *vt* (*prisonnier*) to (set) free, release; (*passeport, certificat*) to issue; ~ **qn de** (*ennemis*) to set sb free from, deliver *ou* free sb from; (*fig*) to rid sb of.

déloger [deloʒe] *vt* (*locataire*) to turn out; (*objet coincé, ennemi*) to dislodge.

déloyal, e, aux [delwajal, -o] *adj* (*personne, conduite*) disloyal; (*procédé*) unfair.

Delphes [dɛlf] *n* Delphi.

delta [dɛlta] *nm* (*GÉO*) delta.

deltaplane [dɛltaplan] *nm* ® hang-glider.

déluge [delyʒ] *nm* (*biblique*) Flood, Deluge; (*grosse pluie*) downpour, deluge; (*grand nombre*): ~ **de** flood of.

déluré, e [delyʀe] *adj* smart, resourceful; (*péj*) forward, pert.

démagnétiser [demaɲetize] *vt* to demagnetize.

démagogie [demagɔʒi] *nf* demagogy.

démagogique [demagɔʒik] *adj* demagogic, popularity-seeking; (*POL*) vote-catching.

démagogue [demagɔg] *adj* demagogic ♦ *nm* demagogue.

démaillé, e [demaje] *adj* (*bas*) laddered (*BRIT*), with a run (*ou* runs).

demain [dəmɛ̃] *adv* tomorrow; ~ **matin/soir** tomorrow morning/evening; ~ **midi** tomorrow at midday; **à ~!** see you tomorrow!

demande [dəmɑ̃d] *nf* (*requête*) request; (*revendication*) demand; (*ADMIN, formulaire*) application; (*ÉCON*) **la** ~ demand; **"~s d'emploi"** "situations wanted"; **à la ~ générale** by popular request; ~ **en mariage** (marriage) proposal; **faire sa** ~ **(en mariage)** to propose (marriage); ~ **de naturalisation** application for naturalization; ~ **de poste** job application.

demandé, e [dəmɑ̃de] *adj* (*article etc*): **très** ~ (very) much in demand.

demander [dəmɑ̃de] *vt* to ask for; (*question: date, heure, chemin*) to ask; (*requérir, nécessiter*) to require, demand; ~ **qch à qn** to ask sb for sth, ask sb sth; **ils demandent 2 secrétaires et un ingénieur** they're looking for 2 secretaries and an engineer; ~ **la main de qn** to ask for sb's hand (in marriage); ~ **pardon à qn** to apologize to sb; ~ **à** *ou* **de voir/faire** to ask to see/ask if one can do; ~ **à qn de faire** to ask sb to do; ~ **que/pourquoi** to ask that/why; **se** ~ **si/pourquoi** *etc* to wonder if/why *etc*; (*sens purement réfléchi*) to ask o.s. if/why *etc*; **on vous demande au téléphone** you're wanted on the phone, there's someone for you on the phone; **il ne demande que ça** that's all he wants; **je ne demande pas mieux** I'm asking nothing more; **il ne demande qu'à faire** all he wants is to do.

demandeur, euse [dəmɑ̃dœʀ, -øz] *nm/f*: ~ **d'emploi** job-seeker.

démangeaison [demɑ̃ʒɛzɔ̃] *nf* itching.

démanger [demɑ̃ʒe] *vi* to itch; **la main me démange** my hand is itching; **l'envie** *ou* **ça me démange de faire** I'm itching to do.

démantèlement [demɑ̃tɛlmɑ̃] *nm* breaking up.

démanteler [demɑ̃tle] *vt* to break up; to demolish.

démaquillant [demakijɑ̃] *nm* make-up remover.

démaquiller [demakije] *vt*: **se** ~ to remove one's make-up.

démarcage [demaʀkaʒ] *nm* = **démarquage**.

démarcation [demaʀkasjɔ̃] *nf* demarcation.

démarchage [demaʀʃaʒ] *nm* (*COMM*) door-to-door selling.

démarche [demaʀʃ(ə)] *nf* (*allure*) gait, walk; (*intervention*) step; approach; (*fig: intellectuelle*) thought processes *pl*; approach; **faire** *ou* **entreprendre des ~s** to take action; **faire des ~s auprès de qn** to approach sb.

démarcheur, euse [demaʀʃœʀ, -øz] *nm/f* (*COMM*) door-to-door salesman/woman; (*POL etc*) canvasser.

démarquage [demaʀkaʒ] *nm* marking down.

démarque [demaʀk(ə)] *nf* (*COMM: d'un article*) mark-down.

démarqué, e [demaʀke] *adj* (*FOOTBALL*) unmarked; (*COMM*) reduced; **prix ~s** marked-down prices.

démarquer [demaʀke] *vt* (*prix*) to mark down; (*joueur*) to stop marking; **se** ~ *vi* (*SPORT*) to shake off one's marker.

démarrage [demaʀaʒ] *nm* starting *no pl*, start; ~ **en côte** hill start.

démarrer [demaʀe] *vt* to start up ♦ *vi* (*conducteur*) to start (up); (*véhicule*) to move off; (*travaux, affaire*) to get moving; (*coureur: accélérer*) to pull away.

démarreur [demaʀœʀ] *nm* (*AUTO*) starter.

démasquer [demaske] *vt* to unmask; **se** ~ to unmask; (*fig*) to drop one's mask.

démâter [demɑte] *vt* to dismast ♦ *vi* to be dismasted.

démêlant, e [demɛlɑ̃, -ɑ̃t] *adj*: **baume** ~, **crème ~e** (hair) conditioner.

démêler [demele] *vt* to untangle, disentangle.

démêlés [demele] *nmpl* problems.

démembrement [demɑ̃bʀəmɑ̃] *nm* dismemberment.

démembrer [demɑ̃bʀe] *vt* to dismember.

déménagement [demenaʒmɑ̃] *nm* (*du point de vue du locataire etc*) move; (*: du déménageur*) removal (*BRIT*), moving (*US*); **entreprise/ camion de** ~ removal (*BRIT*) *ou* moving (*US*) firm/van.

déménager [demenaʒe] *vt* (*meubles*) to (re)move ♦ *vi* to move (house).

déménageur [demenaʒœʀ] *nm* removal man (*BRIT*), (furniture) mover (*US*); (*entrepreneur*) furniture remover.

démence [demɑ̃s] *nf* madness, insanity; (*MÉD*) dementia.

démener [demne]: **se** ~ *vi* to thrash about; (*fig*) to exert o.s.

dément, e [demɑ̃, -ɑ̃t] *vb voir* **démentir** ♦ *adj* (*fou*) mad (*BRIT*), crazy; (*fam*) brilliant, fantastic.

démenti [demɑ̃ti] *nm* refutation.

démentiel, le [demɑ̃sjɛl] *adj* insane.

démentir [demɑ̃tiʀ] *vt* (*nouvelle, témoin*) to refute; (*suj: faits etc*) to belie, refute; ~ **que** to deny that; **ne pas se** ~ not to fail, keep up.

démerder [demɛʀde]: **se** ~ *vi* (*fam!*) to bloody well manage for o.s.

démériter [demeʀite] *vi*: ~ **auprès de qn** to come down in sb's esteem.

démesure [deməzyʀ] *nf* immoderation, immoderateness.

démesuré, e [deməzyʀe] *adj* immoderate, disproportionate.

démesurément [deməzyʀemɑ̃] *adv* disproportionately.

démettre [demɛtʀ(ə)] *vt*: ~ **qn de** (*fonction, poste*) to dismiss sb from; **se** ~ **(de ses fonctions)** to resign (from) one's duties; **se** ~ **l'épaule** *etc* to dislocate one's shoulder *etc*.

demeurant [dəmœʀɑ̃]: **au** ~ *adv* for all that.

demeure [dəmœʀ] *nf* residence; **dernière** ~ (*fig*) last resting place; **mettre qn en** ~ **de faire** to enjoin *ou* order sb to do; **à** ~ *adv* permanently.

demeuré, e [dəmœʀe] *adj* backward ♦ *nm/f* backward person.

demeurer [dəmœʀe] *vi* (*habiter*) to live; (*séjourner*) to stay; (*rester*) to remain; **en** ~ **là** (*suj: personne*) to leave it at that; (*: choses*) to be left at that.

demi, e [dəmi] *adj*: **et** ~: **trois heures/ bouteilles et** ~**es** three and a half hours/ bottles, three hours/bottles and a half ♦ *nm* (*bière*: = 0.25 litre) ≈ half-pint; (*FOOTBALL*) half-back; **il est 2 heures/midi et** ~**e** it's half past 2/12; ~ **de mêlée/d'ouverture** (*RUGBY*) scrum/fly half; **à** ~ *adv* half-; **ouvrir à** ~ to half-open; **faire les choses à** ~ to do things by halves; **à la** ~**e** (*heure*) on the half-hour.

demi... [dəmi] *préfixe* half-, semi..., demi-.

demi-bas [dəmibɑ] *nm inv* (*chaussette*) knee-sock.

demi-bouteille [dəmibutɛj] *nf* half-bottle.

demi-cercle [dəmisɛʀkl(ə)] *nm* semicircle; **en** ~ *adj* semicircular ♦ *adv* in a semicircle.

demi-douzaine [dəmiduzɛn] *nf* half-dozen, half a dozen.

demi-finale [dəmifinal] *nf* semifinal.

demi-finaliste [dəmifinalist(ə)] *nm/f* semifinalist.

demi-fond [dəmifɔ̃] *nm* (*SPORT*) medium-distance running.

demi-frère [dəmifʀɛʀ] *nm* half-brother.

demi-gros [dəmigʀo] *nm inv* wholesale trade.

demi-heure [dəmijœʀ] *nf*: **une** ~ a half-hour, half an hour.

demi-jour [dəmiʒuʀ] *nm* half-light.

demi-journée [dəmiʒuʀne] *nf* half-day, half a day.

démilitariser [demilitaʀize] *vt* to demilitarize.

demi-litre [dəmilitʀ(ə)] *nm* half-litre (*BRIT*), half-liter (*US*), half a litre *ou* liter.

demi-livre [dəmilivʀ(ə)] *nf* half-pound, half a pound.

demi-longueur [dəmilɔ̃gœʀ] *nf* (*SPORT*) half-length, half a length.

demi-lune [dəmilyn]: **en** ~ *adj inv* semicircular.

demi-mal [dəmimal] *nm*: **il n'y a que** ~ there's not much harm done.

demi-mesure [dəmiməzyʀ] *nf* half-measure.

demi-mot [dəmimo]: **à** ~ *adv* without having to spell things out.

déminer [demine] *vt* to clear of mines.

démineur [deminœʀ] *nm* bomb disposal expert.

demi-pension [dəmipɑ̃sjɔ̃] *nf* half-board; **être en** ~ (*SCOL*) to take school meals.

demi-pensionnaire [dəmipɑ̃sjɔnɛʀ] *nm/f* (*SCOL*) half-boarder.

demi-place [dəmiplas] *nf* half-price; (*TRANSPORTS*) half-fare.

démis, e [demi, -iz] *pp de* **démettre** ♦ *adj* (*épaule etc*) dislocated.

demi-saison [dəmisɛzɔ̃] *nf*: **vêtements de** ~ spring *ou* autumn clothing.

demi-sel [dəmisɛl] *adj inv* slightly salted.

demi-sœur [dəmisœʀ] *nf* half-sister.

demi-sommeil [dəmisɔmɛj] *nm* doze.

demi-soupir [dəmisupiʀ] *nm* (*MUS*) quaver (*BRIT*) *ou* eighth note (*US*) rest.

démission [demisjɔ̃] *nf* resignation; **donner sa** ~ to give *ou* hand in one's notice, hand in one's resignation.

démissionnaire [demisjɔnɛʀ] *adj* outgoing ♦ *nm/f* person resigning.

démissionner [demisjɔne] *vi* (*de son poste*) to resign, give *ou* hand in one's notice.

demi-tarif [dəmitaʀif] *nm* half-price; (*TRANSPORTS*) half-fare.

demi-ton [dəmitɔ̃] *nm* (*MUS*) semitone.

demi-tour [dəmituʀ] *nm* about-turn; **faire un** ~ (*MIL etc*) to make an about-turn; **faire** ~ to turn (and go) back; (*AUTO*) to do a U-turn.

démobilisation [demɔbilizasjɔ̃] *nf* demobilization; (*fig*) demotivation, demoralization.

démobiliser [demɔbilize] *vt* to demobilize; (*fig*) to demotivate, demoralize.

démocrate [demɔkʀat] *adj* democratic ♦ *nm/f* democrat.

démocrate-chrétien, ne [demɔkʀatkʀetjɛ̃, -ɛn] *nm/f* Christian Democrat.

démocratie [demɔkʀasi] *nf* democracy; ~ **populaire/libérale** people's/liberal democracy.

démocratique [demɔkʀatik] *adj* democratic.

démocratiquement [demɔkʀatikmɑ̃] *adv* democratically.

démocratisation [demɔkʀatizasjɔ̃] *nf* democratization.

démocratiser [demɔkʀatize] *vt* to democratize.

démodé, e [demɔde] *adj* old-fashioned.

démoder [demɔde]: **se** ~ *vi* to go out of fashion.

démographe [demɔgʀaf] *nm/f* demographer.

démographie [demɔgʀafi] *nf* demography.

démographique [demɔgʀafik] *adj* demographic; **poussée** ~ increase in population.

demoiselle [dəmwazɛl] *nf (jeune fille)* young lady; *(célibataire)* single lady, maiden lady; ~ **d'honneur** bridesmaid.

démolir [demɔliʀ] *vt* to demolish; *(fig: personne)* to do for.

démolisseur [demɔlisœʀ] *nm* demolition worker.

démolition [demɔlisjɔ̃] *nf* demolition.

démon [demɔ̃] *nm* demon, fiend; evil spirit; *(enfant turbulent)* devil, demon; **le** ~ **du jeu/des femmes** a mania for gambling/women; **le D**~ the Devil.

démonétiser [demɔnetize] *vt* to demonetize.

démoniaque [demɔnjak] *adj* fiendish.

démonstrateur, trice [demɔ̃stʀatœʀ, -tʀis] *nm/f* demonstrator.

démonstratif, ive [demɔ̃stʀatif, -iv] *adj, nm (aussi LING)* demonstrative.

démonstration [demɔ̃stʀasjɔ̃] *nf* demonstration; *(aérienne, navale)* display.

démontable [demɔ̃tabl(ə)] *adj* folding.

démontage [demɔ̃taʒ] *nm* dismantling.

démonté, e [demɔ̃te] *adj (fig)* raging, wild.

démonte-pneu [demɔ̃təpnø] *nm* tyre lever *(BRIT)*, tire iron *(US)*.

démonter [demɔ̃te] *vt (machine etc)* to take down, dismantle; *(pneu, porte)* to take off; *(cavalier)* to throw, unseat; *(fig: personne)* to disconcert; **se** ~ *vi (personne)* to lose countenance.

démontrable [demɔ̃tʀabl(ə)] *adj* demonstrable.

démontrer [demɔ̃tʀe] *vt* to demonstrate, show.

démoralisant, e [demɔʀalizɑ̃, -ɑ̃t] *adj* demoralizing.

démoralisateur, trice [demɔʀalizatœʀ, -tʀis] *adj* demoralizing.

démoraliser [demɔʀalize] *vt* to demoralize.

démordre [demɔʀdʀ(ə)] *vi*: **ne pas** ~ **de** to refuse to give up, stick to.

démouler [demule] *vt (gâteau)* to turn out.

démoustiquer [demustike] *vt* to clear of mosquitoes.

démultiplication [demyltiplikasjɔ̃] *nf* reduction; reduction ratio.

démuni, e [demyni] *adj (sans argent)* impoverished; ~ **de** without, lacking in.

démunir [demyniʀ] *vt*: ~ **qn de** to deprive sb of; **se** ~ **de** to part with, give up.

démuseler [demyzle] *vt* to unmuzzle.

démystifier [demistifje] *vt* to demystify.

démythifier [demitifje] *vt* to demythologize.

dénatalité [denatalite] *nf* fall in the birth rate.

dénationalisation [denasjɔnalizasjɔ̃] *nf* denationalization.

dénationaliser [denasjɔnalize] *vt* to denationalize.

dénaturé, e [denatyʀe] *adj (alcool)* denaturized; *(goûts)* unnatural.

dénaturer [denatyʀe] *vt (goût)* to alter (completely); *(pensée, fait)* to distort, misrepresent.

dénégations [denegasjɔ̃] *nfpl* denials.

déneigement [denɛʒmɑ̃] *nm* snow clearance.

déneiger [deneʒe] *vt* to clear snow from.

déni [deni] *nm*: ~ **(de justice)** denial of justice.

déniaiser [denjeze] *vt*: ~ **qn** to teach sb about life.

dénicher [denife] *vt* to unearth.

dénicotinisé, e [denikɔtinize] *adj* nicotine-free.

denier [dənje] *nm (monnaie)* formerly, a coin of small value; *(de bas)* denier; ~ **du culte** contribution to parish upkeep; ~**s publics** public money; **de ses (propres)** ~**s** out of one's own pocket.

dénier [denje] *vt* to deny; ~ **qch à qn** to deny sb sth.

dénigrement [denigʀəmɑ̃] *nm* denigration; **campagne de** ~ smear campaign.

dénigrer [denigʀe] *vt* to denigrate, run down.

dénivelé, e [denivle] *adj (chaussée)* on a lower level ♦ *nm* difference in height.

déniveler [denivle] *vt* to make uneven; to put on a lower level.

dénivellation [denivɛlasjɔ̃] *nf*, **dénivellement** [denivɛlmɑ̃] *nm* difference in level; *(pente)* ramp; *(creux)* dip.

dénombrer [denɔ̃bʀe] *vt (compter)* to count; *(énumérer)* to enumerate, list.

dénominateur [denɔminatœʀ] *nm* denominator; ~ **commun** common denominator.

dénomination [denɔminasjɔ̃] *nf* designation, appellation.

dénommé, e [denɔme] *adj*: **le** ~ **Dupont** the man by the name of Dupont.

dénommer [denɔme] *vt* to name.

dénoncer [denɔ̃se] *vt* to denounce; **se** ~ to give o.s. up, come forward.

dénonciation [denɔ̃sjasjɔ̃] *nf* denunciation.

dénoter [denɔte] *vt* to denote.

dénouement [denumɑ̃] *nm* outcome, conclusion; *(THÉÂT)* dénouement.

dénouer [denwe] *vt* to unknot, undo.

dénoyauter [denwajote] *vt* to stone; **appareil à** ~ stoner.

dénoyauteur [denwajotœʀ] *nm* stoner.

denrée [dɑ̃ʀe] *nf* commodity; *(aussi:* ~ **alimentaire)** food(stuff).

dense [dɑ̃s] *adj* dense.

densité [dɑ̃site] *nf* denseness; *(PHYSIQUE)* density.

dent [dɑ̃] *nf* tooth *(pl* teeth); **avoir/garder une** ~ **contre qn** to have/hold a grudge against sb; **se mettre qch sous la** ~ to eat sth; **être sur les** ~**s** to be on one's last legs; **faire ses** ~**s** to teethe, cut (one's) teeth; **en** ~**s de scie** serrated; *(irrégulier)* jagged; **avoir les** ~**s longues** *(fig)* to be ruthlessly ambitious; ~

de lait/sagesse milk/wisdom tooth.
dentaire [dɑ̃tɛʀ] *adj* dental; **cabinet** ~ dental
surgery; **école** ~ dental school.
denté, e [dɑ̃te] *adj*: **roue** ~**e** cog wheel.
dentelé, e [dɑ̃tle] *adj* jagged, indented.
dentelle [dɑ̃tɛl] *nf* lace *no pl*.
dentelure [dɑ̃tlyʀ] *nf* (*aussi*: ~**s**) jagged
outline.
dentier [dɑ̃tje] *nm* denture.
dentifrice [dɑ̃tifʀis] *adj, nm*: **(pâte)** ~
toothpaste; **eau** ~ mouthwash.
dentiste [dɑ̃tist(ə)] *nm/f* dentist.
dentition [dɑ̃tisjɔ̃] *nf* teeth *pl*, dentition.
dénucléariser [denykleaʀize] *vt* to make
nuclear-free.
dénudé, e [denyde] *adj* bare.
dénuder [denyde] *vt* to bare; **se** ~ (*personne*)
to strip.
dénué, e [denɥe] *adj*: ~ **de** lacking in; (*intérêt*)
devoid of.
dénuement [denymɑ̃] *nm* destitution.
dénutrition [denytʀisjɔ̃] *nf*
undernourishment.
déodorant [deɔdɔʀɑ̃] *nm* deodorant.
déodoriser [deɔdɔʀize] *vt* to deodorize.
déontologie [deɔ̃tɔlɔʒi] *nf* code of ethics;
(*professionnelle*) (professional) code of
practice.
dép. *abr* (*ADMIN*: = *département*) dept;
(= *départ*) dep.
dépannage [depanaʒ] *nm*: **service/camion de**
~ (*AUTO*) breakdown service/truck.
dépanner [depane] *vt* (*voiture, télévision*) to fix,
repair; (*fig*) to bail out, help out.
dépanneur [depanœʀ] *nm* (*AUTO*) breakdown
mechanic; (*TV*) television engineer.
dépanneuse [depanøz] *nf* breakdown lorry
(*BRIT*), tow truck (*US*).
dépareillé, e [depaʀeje] *adj* (*collection, service*)
incomplete; (*gant, volume, objet*) odd.
déparer [depaʀe] *vt* to spoil, mar.
départ [depaʀ] *nm* leaving *no pl*, departure;
(*SPORT*) start; (*sur un horaire*) departure; **à**
son ~ when he left; **au** ~ (*au début*) initially,
at the start; **courrier au** ~ outgoing mail.
départager [depaʀtaʒe] *vt* to decide between.
département [depaʀtəmɑ̃] *nm* department.

*France is divided into 96 administrative units
called **départements**. These local government
divisions are headed by a state-appointed
préfet, and administered by an elected **Conseil
général**. Départements are usually named after
prominent geographical features such as rivers
or mountain ranges; see also **DOM-TOM**.*

départemental, e, aux [depaʀtəmɑ̃tal, -o] *adj*
departmental.
départementaliser [depaʀtəmɑ̃talize] *vt* to
devolve authority to.
départir [depaʀtiʀ]: **se** ~ **de** *vt* to abandon,
depart from.

dépassé, e [depase] *adj* superseded,
outmoded; (*fig*) out of one's depth.
dépassement [depasmɑ̃] *nm* (*AUTO*)
overtaking *no pl*.
dépasser [depase] *vt* (*véhicule, concurrent*) to
overtake; (*endroit*) to pass, go past; (*somme,
limite*) to exceed; (*fig: en beauté etc*) to
surpass, outshine; (*être en saillie sur*) to jut
out above (*ou* in front of); (*dérouter*): **cela
me dépasse** it's beyond me ♦ *vi* (*AUTO*) to
overtake; (*jupon*) to show; **se** ~ to excel o.s.
dépassionner [depasjɔne] *vt* (*débat etc*) to
take the heat out of.
dépaver [depave] *vt* to remove the
cobblestones from.
dépaysé, e [depeize] *adj* disorientated.
dépaysement [depeizmɑ̃] *nm* disorientation;
change of scenery.
dépayser [depeize] *vt* (*désorienter*) to
disorientate; (*changer agréablement*) to
provide with a change of scenery.
dépecer [depəse] *vt* (*suj: boucher*) to joint, cut
up; (*suj: animal*) to dismember.
dépêche [depɛʃ] *nf* dispatch; ~
(télégraphique) telegram, wire.
dépêcher [depeʃe] *vt* to dispatch; **se** ~ *vi* to
hurry; **se** ~ **de faire qch** to hasten to do sth,
hurry (in order) to do sth.
dépeindre [depɛ̃dʀ(ə)] *vt* to depict.
dépénalisation [depenalizasjɔ̃] *nf*
decriminalization.
dépendance [depɑ̃dɑ̃s] *nf* (*interdépendance*)
dependence *no pl*, dependency; (*bâtiment*)
outbuilding.
dépendant, e [depɑ̃dɑ̃, -ɑ̃t] *vb voir* **dépendre**
♦ *adj* (*financièrement*) dependent.
dépendre [depɑ̃dʀ(ə)] *vt* (*tableau*) to take
down; ~ **de** *vt* to depend on; (*financièrement
etc*) to be dependent on; (*appartenir*) to
belong to.
dépens [depɑ̃] *nmpl*: **aux** ~ **de** at the expense
of.
dépense [depɑ̃s] *nf* spending *no pl*, expense,
expenditure *no pl*; (*fig*) consumption; (: *de
temps, de forces*) expenditure; **pousser qn à
la** ~ to make sb incur an expense; ~
physique (physical) exertion; ~ **de temps**
investment of time; ~**s de fonctionnement**
revenue expenditure; ~**s d'investissement**
capital expenditure; ~**s publiques** public
expenditure.
dépenser [depɑ̃se] *vt* to spend; (*gaz, eau*) to
use; (*fig*) to expend, use up; **se** ~ (*se fatiguer*)
to exert o.s.
dépensier, ière [depɑ̃sje, -jɛʀ] *adj*: **il est** ~
he's a spendthrift.
déperdition [depɛʀdisjɔ̃] *nf* loss.
dépérir [depeʀiʀ] *vi* (*personne*) to waste away;
(*plante*) to wither.
dépersonnaliser [depɛʀsɔnalize] *vt* to
depersonalize.
dépêtrer [depetʀe] *vt*: **se** ~ **de** (*situation*) to

extricate o.s. from.

dépeuplé, e [depœple] *adj* depopulated.

dépeuplement [depœpləmɑ̃] *nm* depopulation.

dépeupler [depœple] *vt* to depopulate; **se ~** to be depopulated.

déphasage [defazaʒ] *nm* (*fig*) being out of touch.

déphasé, e [defaze] *adj* (*ÉLEC*) out of phase; (*fig*) out of touch.

déphaser [defaze] *vt* (*fig*) to put out of touch.

dépilation [depilasjɔ̃] *nf* hair loss; hair removal.

dépilatoire [depilatwaʀ] *adj* depilatory, hair-removing.

dépiler [depile] *vt* (*épiler*) to depilate, remove hair from.

dépistage [depistaʒ] *nm* (*MÉD*) screening.

dépister [depiste] *vt* to detect; (*MÉD*) to screen; (*voleur*) to track down; (*poursuivants*) to throw off the scent.

dépit [depi] *nm* vexation, frustration; **en ~ de** *prép* in spite of; **en ~ du bon sens** contrary to all good sense.

dépité, e [depite] *adj* vexed, frustrated.

dépiter [depite] *vt* to vex, frustrate.

déplacé, e [deplase] *adj* (*propos*) out of place, uncalled-for; **personne ~e** displaced person.

déplacement [deplasmɑ̃] *nm* moving; shifting; transfer; (*voyage*) trip, travelling *no pl* (*BRIT*), traveling *no pl* (*US*); **en ~** away (on a trip); **~ d'air** displacement of air; **~ de vertèbre** slipped disc.

déplacer [deplase] *vt* (*table, voiture*) to move, shift; (*employé*) to transfer, move; **se ~** *vi* (*objet*) to move; (*organe*) to become displaced; (*personne: bouger*) to move, walk; (*: voyager*) to travel ♦ *vt* (*vertèbre etc*) to displace.

déplaire [deplɛʀ] *vi*: **ceci me déplaît** I don't like this, I dislike this; **il cherche à nous ~** he's trying to displease us *ou* be disagreeable to us; **se ~ quelque part** to dislike it *ou* be unhappy somewhere.

déplaisant, e [deplɛzɑ̃, -ɑ̃t] *vb voir* **déplaire** ♦ *adj* disagreeable, unpleasant.

déplaisir [deplɛziʀ] *nm* displeasure, annoyance.

déplaît [deplɛ] *vb voir* **déplaire**.

dépliant [deplijɑ̃] *nm* leaflet.

déplier [deplije] *vt* to unfold; **se ~** (*parachute*) to open.

déplisser [deplise] *vt* to smooth out.

déploiement [deplwamɑ̃] *nm* (*voir déployer*) deployment; display.

déplomber [deplɔ̃be] *vt* (*caisse, compteur*) to break (open) the seal of.

déplorable [deplɔʀabl(ə)] *adj* deplorable; lamentable.

déplorer [deplɔʀe] *vt* (*regretter*) to deplore; (*pleurer sur*) to lament.

déployer [deplwaje] *vt* to open out, spread; (*MIL*) to deploy; (*montrer*) to display, exhibit.

déplu [deply] *pp de* **déplaire**.

dépointer [depwɛ̃te] *vi* to clock out.

dépoli, e [depɔli] *adj*: **verre ~** frosted glass.

dépolitiser [depɔlitize] *vt* to depoliticize.

dépopulation [depɔpylasjɔ̃] *nf* depopulation.

déportation [depɔʀtasjɔ̃] *nf* deportation.

déporté, e [depɔʀte] *nm/f* deportee; (*1939-45*) concentration camp prisoner.

déporter [depɔʀte] *vt* (*POL*) to deport; (*dévier*) to carry off course; **se ~** *vi* (*voiture*) to swerve.

déposant, e [depozɑ̃, -ɑ̃t] *nm/f* (*épargnant*) depositor.

dépose [depoz] *nf* taking out; taking down.

déposé, e [depoze] *adj* registered; *voir aussi* **marque**.

déposer [depoze] *vt* (*gén: mettre, poser*) to lay down, put down, set down; (*à la banque, à la consigne*) to deposit; (*caution*) to put down; (*passager*) to drop (off), set down; (*démonter: serrure, moteur*) to take out; (*: rideau*) to take down; (*roi*) to depose; (*ADMIN: faire enregistrer*) to file; to register ♦ *vi* to form a sediment *ou* deposit; (*JUR*): **~ (contre)** to testify *ou* give evidence (against); **se ~** *vi* to settle; **~ son bilan** (*COMM*) to go into (voluntary) liquidation.

dépositaire [depozitɛʀ] *nm/f* (*JUR*) depository; (*COMM*) agent; **~ agréé** authorized agent.

déposition [depozisjɔ̃] *nf* (*JUR*) deposition.

déposséder [deposede] *vt* to dispossess.

dépôt [depo] *nm* (*à la banque, sédiment*) deposit; (*entrepôt, réserve*) warehouse, store; (*gare*) depot; (*prison*) cells *pl*; **~ d'ordures** rubbish (*BRIT*) *ou* garbage (*US*) dump, tip (*BRIT*); **~ de bilan** (voluntary) liquidation; **~ légal** registration of copyright.

dépoter [depɔte] *vt* (*plante*) to take from the pot, transplant.

dépotoir [depɔtwaʀ] *nm* dumping ground, rubbish (*BRIT*) *ou* garbage (*US*) dump; **~ nucléaire** nuclear (waste) dump.

dépouille [depuj] *nf* (*d'animal*) skin, hide; (*humaine*): **~ (mortelle)** mortal remains *pl*.

dépouillé, e [depuje] *adj* (*fig*) bare, bald; **~ de** stripped of; lacking in.

dépouillement [depujmɑ̃] *nm* (*de scrutin*) count, counting *no pl*.

dépouiller [depuje] *vt* (*animal*) to skin; (*spolier*) to deprive of one's possessions; (*documents*) to go through, peruse; **~ qn/ qch de** to strip sb/sth of; **~ le scrutin** to count the votes.

dépourvu, e [depuʀvy] *adj*: **~ de** lacking in, without; **au ~** *adv*: **prendre qn au ~** to catch sb unawares.

dépoussiérer [depusjeʀe] *vt* to remove dust from.

dépravation [depʀavasjɔ̃] *nf* depravity.

dépravé, e [depʀave] *adj* depraved.

dépraver [depʀave] *vt* to deprave.
dépréciation [depʀesjɑsjɔ̃] *nf* depreciation.
déprécier [depʀesje] *vt*, **se** ~ *vi* to depreciate.
déprédations [depʀedɑsjɔ̃] *nfpl* damage *sg*.
dépressif, ive [depʀesif, -iv] *adj* depressive.
dépression [depʀesjɔ̃] *nf* depression; ~ **(nerveuse)** (nervous) breakdown.
déprimant, e [depʀimɑ̃, -ɑ̃t] *adj* depressing.
déprime [depʀim] *nf (fam)*: **la** ~ depression.
déprimé, e [depʀime] *adj (découragé)* depressed.
déprimer [depʀime] *vt* to depress.
déprogrammer [depʀɔgʀame] *vt (supprimer)* to cancel.
DEPS *sigle (= dernier entré premier sorti)* LIFO *(= last in first out)*.
dépt *abr (= département)* dept.
dépuceler [depysle] *vt (fam)* to take the virginity of.

================================ *MOT-CLÉ*

depuis [dəpɥi] *prép* **1** *(point de départ dans le temps)* since; **il habite Paris** ~ **1983/l'an dernier** he has been living in Paris since 1983/last year; ~ **quand?** since when? ~ **quand le connaissez-vous?** how long have you known him?; ~ **lors** since then
2 *(temps écoulé)* for; **il habite Paris** ~ **5 ans** he has been living in Paris for 5 years; **je le connais** ~ **3 ans** I've known him for 3 years; ~ **combien de temps êtes-vous ici?** how long have you been here?
3 *(lieu)*: **il a plu** ~ **Metz** it's been raining since Metz; **elle a téléphoné** ~ **Valence** she rang from Valence
4 *(quantité, rang)* from; ~ **les plus petits jusqu'aux plus grands** from the youngest to the oldest
♦ *adv (temps)* since (then); **je ne lui ai pas parlé** ~ I haven't spoken to him since (then); ~ **que** *conj* (ever) since; ~ **qu'il m'a dit ça** (ever) since he said that to me

================================

dépuratif, ive [depyʀatif, -iv] *adj* depurative, purgative.
députation [depytɑsjɔ̃] *nf* deputation; *(fonction)* position of deputy, ≈ parliamentary seat *(BRIT)*, ≈ seat in Congress *(US)*.
député, e [depyte] *nm/f (POL)* deputy, ≈ Member of Parliament *(BRIT)*, ≈ Congressman/woman *(US)*.
députer [depyte] *vt* to delegate; ~ **qn auprès de** to send sb (as a representative) to.
déracinement [deʀasinmɑ̃] *nm (gén)* uprooting; *(d'un préjugé)* eradication.
déraciner [deʀasine] *vt* to uproot.
déraillement [deʀajmɑ̃] *nm* derailment.
dérailler [deʀaje] *vi (train)* to be derailed, go off *ou* jump the rails; *(fam)* to be completely off the track; **faire** ~ to derail.
dérailleur [deʀajœʀ] *nm (de vélo)* dérailleur

gears *pl*.
déraison [deʀɛzɔ̃] *nf* unreasonableness.
déraisonnable [deʀɛzɔnabl(ə)] *adj* unreasonable.
déraisonner [deʀɛzɔne] *vi* to talk nonsense, rave.
dérangement [deʀɑ̃ʒmɑ̃] *nm (gêne, déplacement)* trouble; *(gastrique etc)* disorder; *(mécanique)* breakdown; **en** ~ *(téléphone)* out of order.
déranger [deʀɑ̃ʒe] *vt (personne)* to trouble, bother, disturb; *(projets)* to disrupt, upset; *(objets, vêtements)* to disarrange; **se** ~ to put o.s. out; *(se déplacer)* to (take the trouble to) come *(ou* go) out; **est-ce que cela vous dérange si ...?** do you mind if ...?; **ça te dérangerait de faire ...?** would you mind doing ...?; **ne vous dérangez pas** don't go to any trouble; don't disturb yourself.
dérapage [deʀapaʒ] *nm* skid, skidding *no pl*; going out of control.
déraper [deʀape] *vi (voiture)* to skid; *(personne, semelles, couteau)* to slip; *(fig: économie etc)* to go out of control.
dératé, e [deʀate] *nm/f*: **courir comme un** ~ to run like the clappers.
dératiser [deʀatize] *vt* to rid of rats.
déréglé, e [deʀegle] *adj (mœurs)* dissolute.
dérèglement [deʀɛglmɑ̃] *nm* upsetting *no pl*, upset.
déréglementation [deʀɛglmɑ̃tɑsjɔ̃] *nf* deregulation.
dérégler [deʀegle] *vt (mécanisme)* to put out of order, cause to break down; *(estomac)* to upset; **se** ~ *vi* to break down, go wrong.
dérider [deʀide] *vt*, **se** ~ *vi* to brighten *ou* cheer up.
dérision [deʀizjɔ̃] *nf* derision; **tourner en** ~ to deride; **par** ~ in mockery.
dérisoire [deʀizwaʀ] *adj* derisory.
dérivatif [deʀivatif] *nm* distraction.
dérivation [deʀivɑsjɔ̃] *nf* derivation; diversion.
dérive [deʀiv] *nf (de dériveur)* centre-board; **aller à la** ~ *(NAVIG, fig)* to drift; ~ **des continents** *(GÉO)* continental drift.
dérivé, e [deʀive] *adj* derived ♦ *nm (LING)* derivative; *(TECH)* by-product ♦ *nf (MATH)* derivative.
dériver [deʀive] *vt (MATH)* to derive; *(cours d'eau etc)* to divert ♦ *vi (bateau)* to drift; ~ **de** to derive from.
dériveur [deʀivœʀ] *nm* sailing dinghy.
dermatite [dɛʀmatit] *nf* dermatitis.
dermato [dɛʀmato] *nm/f (fam: = dermatologue)* dermatologist.
dermatologie [dɛʀmatɔlɔʒi] *nf* dermatology.
dermatologue [dɛʀmatɔlɔg] *nm/f* dermatologist.
dermatose [dɛʀmatoz] *nf* dermatosis.
dermite [dɛʀmit] *nf* = **dermatite**.
dernier, ière [dɛʀnje, -jɛʀ] *adj (dans le temps,*

l'espace) last; (*le plus récent: gén avant n*) latest, last; (*final, ultime: effort*) final; (*échelon, grade*) top, highest ♦ *nm* (*étage*) top floor; **lundi/le mois** ~ last Monday/month; **du** ~ **chic** extremely smart; **le** ~ **cri** the last word (in fashion); **les** ~**s honneurs** the last tribute; **le** ~ **soupir: rendre le** ~ **soupir** to breathe one's last; **en** ~ *adv* last; **ce** ~, **cette dernière** the latter.

dernièrement [dɛʀnjɛʀmɑ̃] *adv* recently.

dernier-né, dernière-née [dɛʀnjene, dɛʀnjɛʀne] *nm/f* (*enfant*) last-born.

dérobade [deʀɔbad] *nf* side-stepping *no pl.*

dérobé, e [deʀɔbe] *adj* (*porte*) secret, hidden; **à la** ~**e** surreptitiously.

dérober [deʀɔbe] *vt* to steal; (*cacher*): ~ **qch à (la vue de) qn** to conceal *ou* hide sth from sb('s view); **se** ~ *vi* (*s'esquiver*) to slip away; (*fig*) to shy away; **se** ~ **sous** (*s'effondrer*) to give way beneath; **se** ~ **à** (*justice, regards*) to hide from; (*obligation*) to shirk.

dérogation [deʀɔgasjɔ̃] *nf* (special) dispensation.

déroger [deʀɔʒe]: ~ **à** *vt* to go against, depart from.

dérouiller [deʀuje] *vt*: **se** ~ **les jambes** to stretch one's legs.

déroulement [deʀulmɑ̃] *nm* (*d'une opération etc*) progress.

dérouler [deʀule] *vt* (*ficelle*) to unwind; (*papier*) to unroll; **se** ~ *vi* to unwind; to unroll, come unrolled; (*avoir lieu*) to take place; (*se passer*) to go.

déroutant, e [deʀutɑ̃, -ɑ̃t] *adj* disconcerting.

déroute [deʀut] *nf* (*MIL*) rout; (*fig*) total collapse; **mettre en** ~ to rout; **en** ~ routed.

dérouter [deʀute] *vt* (*avion, train*) to reroute, divert; (*étonner*) to disconcert, throw (out).

derrick [deʀik] *nm* derrick (*over oil well*).

derrière [dɛʀjɛʀ] *adv, prép* behind ♦ *nm* (*d'une maison*) back; (*postérieur*) behind, bottom; **les pattes de** ~ the back legs, the hind legs; **par** ~ from behind; (*fig*) in an underhand way, behind one's back.

derviche [dɛʀviʃ] *nm* dervish.

DES *sigle m* (= *diplôme d'études supérieures*) university post-graduate degree.

des [de] *dét, prép + dét voir* **de**.

dès [dɛ] *prép* from; ~ **que** *conj* as soon as; ~ **à présent** here and now; ~ **son retour** as soon as he was (*ou* is) back; ~ **réception** on receipt; ~ **lors** *adv* from then on; ~ **lors que** *conj* from the moment (that).

désabusé, e [dezabyze] *adj* disillusioned.

désaccord [dezakɔʀ] *nm* disagreement.

désaccordé, e [dezakɔʀde] *adj* (*MUS*) out of tune.

désacraliser [desakʀalize] *vt* to deconsecrate; (*fig: profession, institution*) to take the mystique out of.

désaffecté, e [dezafɛkte] *adj* disused.

désaffection [dezafɛksjɔ̃] *nf*: ~ **pour**

estrangement from.

désagréable [dezagʀeable(ə)] *adj* unpleasant, disagreeable.

désagréablement [dezagʀeabləmɑ̃] *adv* disagreeably, unpleasantly.

désagrégation [dezagʀegasjɔ̃] *nf* disintegration.

désagréger [dezagʀeʒe]: **se** ~ *vi* to disintegrate, break up.

désagrément [dezagʀemɑ̃] *nm* annoyance, trouble *no pl.*

désaltérant, e [dezalteʀɑ̃, -ɑ̃t] *adj* thirst-quenching.

désaltérer [dezalteʀe] *vt*: **se** ~ to quench one's thirst; **ça désaltère** it's thirst-quenching, it quenches your thirst.

désamorcer [dezamɔʀse] *vt* to remove the primer from; (*fig*) to defuse; (: *prévenir*) to forestall.

désappointé, e [dezapwɛ̃te] *adj* disappointed.

désapprobateur, trice [dezapʀɔbatœʀ, -tʀis] *adj* disapproving.

désapprobation [dezapʀɔbasjɔ̃] *nf* disapproval.

désapprouver [dezapʀuve] *vt* to disapprove of.

désarçonner [dezaʀsɔne] *vt* to unseat, throw; (*fig*) to throw, nonplus (*BRIT*), disconcert.

désargenté, e [dezaʀʒɑ̃te] *adj* impoverished.

désarmant, e [dezaʀmɑ̃, -ɑ̃t] *adj* disarming.

désarmé, e [dezaʀme] *adj* (*fig*) disarmed.

désarmement [dezaʀməmɑ̃] *nm* disarmament.

désarmer [dezaʀme] *vt* (*MIL, aussi fig*) to disarm; (*NAVIG*) to lay up; (*fusil*) to unload; (: *mettre le cran de sûreté*) to put the safety catch on ♦ *vi* (*pays*) to disarm; (*haine*) to wane; (*personne*) to give up.

désarrimer [dezaʀime] *vt* to shift.

désarroi [dezaʀwa] *nm* helplessness, disarray.

désarticulé, e [dezaʀtikyle] *adj* (*pantin, corps*) dislocated.

désarticuler [dezaʀtikyle] *vt*: **se** ~ to contort (o.s.).

désassorti, e [dezasɔʀti] *adj* unmatching, unmatched; (*magasin, marchand*) sold out.

désastre [dezastʀ(ə)] *nm* disaster.

désastreux, euse [dezastʀø, -øz] *adj* disastrous.

désavantage [dezavɑ̃taʒ] *nm* disadvantage; (*inconvénient*) drawback, disadvantage.

désavantager [dezavɑ̃taʒe] *vt* to put at a disadvantage.

désavantageux, euse [dezavɑ̃taʒø, -øz] *adj* unfavourable, disadvantageous.

désaveu [dezavø] *nm* repudiation; (*déni*) disclaimer.

désavouer [dezavwe] *vt* to disown, repudiate, disclaim.

désaxé, e [dezakse] *adj* (*fig*) unbalanced.

désaxer [dezakse] *vt* (*roue*) to put out of true; (*personne*) to throw off balance.

desceller [desele] *vt* (*pierre*) to pull free.
descendance [desɑ̃dɑ̃s] *nf* (*famille*)
descendants *pl*, issue; (*origine*) descent.
descendant, e [desɑ̃dɑ̃, -ɑ̃t] *vb voir* **descendre**
♦ *nm/f* descendant.
descendeur, euse [desɑ̃dœʀ, -øz] *nm/f* (*SPORT*)
downhiller.
descendre [desɑ̃dʀ(ə)] *vt* (*escalier, montagne*)
to go (*ou* come) down; (*valise, paquet*) to take
ou get down; (*étagère etc*) to lower; (*fam:*
abattre) to shoot down; (*: boire*) to knock
back ♦ *vi* to go (*ou* come) down; (*passager:*
s'arrêter) to get out, alight; (*niveau,*
température) to go *ou* come down, fall, drop;
(*marée*) to go out; ~ **à pied/en voiture** to
walk/drive down, go down on foot/by car; ~
de (*famille*) to be descended from; ~ **du**
train to get out of *ou* off the train; ~ **d'un**
arbre to climb down from a tree; ~ **de**
cheval to dismount, get off one's horse; ~ **à**
l'hôtel to stay at a hotel; ~ **dans la rue**
(*manifester*) to take to the streets; ~ **en ville**
to go into town, go down town.
descente [desɑ̃t] *nf* descent, going down;
(*chemin*) way down; (*SKI*) downhill (race); **au**
milieu de la ~ halfway down; **freinez dans**
les ~s use the brakes going downhill; ~ **de**
lit bedside rug; ~ **(de police)** (police) raid.
descriptif, ive [dɛskʀiptif, -iv] *adj* descriptive
♦ *nm* explanatory leaflet.
description [dɛskʀipsjɔ̃] *nf* description.
désembourber [dezɑ̃buʀbe] *vt* to pull out of
the mud.
désembourgeoiser [dezɑ̃buʀʒwaze] *vt*: ~ **qn**
to get sb out of his (*ou* her) middle-class
attitudes.
désembuer [dezɑ̃bɥe] *vt* to demist.
désemparé, e [dezɑ̃paʀe] *adj* bewildered,
distraught; (*bateau, avion*) crippled.
désemparer [dezɑ̃paʀe] *vi*: **sans** ~ without
stopping.
désemplir [dezɑ̃pliʀ] *vi*: **ne pas** ~ to be always
full.
désenchanté, e [dezɑ̃ʃɑ̃te] *adj* disenchanted,
disillusioned.
désenchantement [dezɑ̃ʃɑ̃tmɑ̃] *nm*
disenchantment, disillusion.
désenclaver [dezɑ̃klave] *vt* to open up.
désencombrer [dezɑ̃kɔ̃bʀe] *vt* to clear.
désenfler [dezɑ̃fle] *vi* to become less swollen.
désengagement [dezɑ̃gaʒmɑ̃] *nm* (*POL*)
disengagement.
désensabler [dezɑ̃sable] *vt* to pull out of the
sand.
désensibiliser [dezɑ̃sibilize] *vt* (*MÉD*) to
desensitize.
désenvenimer [dezɑ̃vnime] *vt* (*plaie*) to
remove the poison from; (*fig*) to take the
sting out of.
désépaissir [dezepesiʀ] *vt* to thin (out).
déséquilibre [dezekilibʀ(ə)] *nm* (*position*): **être**
en ~ to be unsteady; (*fig: des forces, du*

budget) imbalance; (*PSYCH*) unbalance.
déséquilibré, e [dezekilibʀe] *nm/f* (*PSYCH*)
unbalanced person.
déséquilibrer [dezekilibʀe] *vt* to throw off
balance.
désert, e [dezɛʀ, -ɛʀt(ə)] *adj* deserted ♦ *nm*
desert.
déserter [dezɛʀte] *vi, vt* to desert.
déserteur [dezɛʀtœʀ] *nm* deserter.
désertion [dezɛʀsjɔ̃] *nf* desertion.
désertique [dezɛʀtik] *adj* desert *cpd*; (*inculte*)
barren, empty.
désescalade [dezɛskalad] *nf* (*MIL*) de-
escalation.
désespérant, e [dezɛspeʀɑ̃, -ɑ̃t] *adj* hopeless,
despairing.
désespéré, e [dezɛspeʀe] *adj* desperate;
(*regard*) despairing; **état** ~ (*MÉD*) hopeless
condition.
désespérément [dezɛspeʀemɑ̃] *adv*
desperately.
désespérer [dezɛspeʀe] *vt* to drive to despair
♦ *vi*, **se** ~ *vi* to despair; ~ **de** to despair of.
désespoir [dezɛspwaʀ] *nm* despair; **être** *ou*
faire le ~ **de qn** to be the despair of sb; **en** ~
de cause in desperation.
déshabillé, e [dezabije] *adj* undressed ♦ *nm*
négligée.
déshabiller [dezabije] *vt* to undress; **se** ~ to
undress (o.s.).
déshabituer [dezabitɥe] *vt*: **se** ~ **de** to get out
of the habit of.
désherbant [dezɛʀbɑ̃] *nm* weed-killer.
désherber [dezɛʀbe] *vt* to weed.
déshérité, e [dezeʀite] *adj* disinherited ♦ *nm/f*:
les ~s (*pauvres*) the underprivileged, the
deprived.
déshériter [dezeʀite] *vt* to disinherit.
déshonneur [dezɔnœʀ] *nm* dishonour (*BRIT*),
dishonor (*US*), disgrace.
déshonorer [dezɔnɔʀe] *vt* to dishonour (*BRIT*),
dishonor (*US*), bring disgrace upon; **se** ~ to
bring dishono(u)r on o.s.
déshumaniser [dezymanize] *vt* to
dehumanize.
déshydratation [dezidʀatasjɔ̃] *nf*
dehydration.
déshydraté, e [dezidʀate] *adj* dehydrated.
déshydrater [dezidʀate] *vt* to dehydrate.
desiderata [dezideʀata] *nmpl* requirements.
design [dizajn] *adj* (*mobilier*) designer *cpd* ♦ *nm*
(*industrial*) design.
désignation [deziɲasjɔ̃] *nf* naming,
appointment; (*signe, mot*) name,
designation.
designer [dizajnɛʀ] *nm* designer.
désigner [deziɲe] *vt* (*montrer*) to point out,
indicate; (*dénommer*) to denote, refer to;
(*nommer: candidat etc*) to name, appoint.
désillusion [dezilyzjɔ̃] *nf* disillusion(ment).
désillusionner [dezilyzjɔne] *vt* to disillusion.
désincarné, e [dezɛ̃kaʀne] *adj* disembodied.

désinence–dessiller

désinence [dezinɑ̃s] nf ending, inflexion.
désinfectant, e [dezɛ̃fɛktɑ̃, -ɑ̃t] adj, nm disinfectant.
désinfecter [dezɛ̃fɛkte] vt to disinfect.
désinfection [dezɛ̃fɛksjɔ̃] nf disinfection.
désinformation [dezɛ̃fɔRmasjɔ̃] nf disinformation.
désintégration [dezɛ̃tegRasjɔ̃] nf disintegration.
désintégrer [dezɛ̃tegRe] vt, se ~ vi to disintegrate.
désintéressé, e [dezɛ̃teRese] adj (généreux, bénévole) disinterested, unselfish.
désintéressement [dezɛ̃teRɛsmɑ̃] nm (générosité) disinterestedness.
désintéresser [dezɛ̃teRese] vt: se ~ (de) to lose interest (in).
désintérêt [dezɛ̃teRɛ] nm (indifférence) disinterest.
désintoxication [dezɛ̃tɔksikasjɔ̃] nf treatment for alcoholism (ou drug addiction); faire une cure de ~ to have ou undergo treatment for alcoholism (ou drug addiction).
désintoxiquer [dezɛ̃tɔksike] vt to treat for alcoholism (ou drug addiction).
désinvolte [dezɛ̃vɔlt(ə)] adj casual, off-hand.
désinvolture [dezɛ̃vɔltyR] nf casualness.
désir [deziR] nm wish; (fort, sensuel) desire.
désirable [deziRabl(ə)] adj desirable.
désirer [deziRe] vt to want, wish for; (sexuellement) to desire; je désire ... (formule de politesse) I would like ...; il désire que tu l'aides he would like ou he wants you to help him; ~ faire to want ou wish to do; ça laisse à ~ it leaves something to be desired.
désireux, euse [deziRø, -øz] adj: ~ de faire anxious to do.
désistement [dezistəmɑ̃] nm withdrawal.
désister [deziste]: se ~ vi to stand down, withdraw.
désobéir [dezɔbeiR] vi: ~ (à qn/qch) to disobey (sb/sth).
désobéissance [dezɔbeisɑ̃s] nf disobedience.
désobéissant, e [dezɔbeisɑ̃, -ɑ̃t] adj disobedient.
désobligeant, e [dezɔbliʒɑ̃, -ɑ̃t] adj disagreeable, unpleasant.
désobliger [dezɔbliʒe] vt to offend.
désodorisant [dezɔdɔRizɑ̃] nm air freshener, deodorizer.
désodoriser [dezɔdɔRize] vt to deodorize.
désœuvré, e [dezœvRe] adj idle.
désœuvrement [dezœvRəmɑ̃] nm idleness.
désolant, e [dezɔlɑ̃, -ɑ̃t] adj distressing.
désolation [dezɔlasjɔ̃] nf (affliction) distress, grief; (d'un paysage etc) desolation, devastation.
désolé, e [dezɔle] adj (paysage) desolate; je suis ~ I'm sorry.
désoler [dezɔle] vt to distress, grieve; se ~ to be upset.

désolidariser [desɔlidaRize] vt: se ~ de ou d'avec to dissociate o.s. from.
désopilant, e [dezɔpilɑ̃, -ɑ̃t] adj screamingly funny, hilarious.
désordonné, e [dezɔRdɔne] adj untidy, disorderly.
désordre [dezɔRdR(ə)] nm disorder(liness), untidiness; (anarchie) disorder; ~s nmpl (POL) disturbances, disorder sg; en ~ in a mess, untidy.
désorganiser [dezɔRganize] vt to disorganize.
désorienté, e [dezɔRjɑ̃te] adj disorientated; (fig) bewildered.
désorienter [dezɔRjɑ̃te] vt (fig) to confuse.
désormais [dezɔRmɛ] adv in future, from now on.
désosser [dezɔse] vt to bone.
despote [dɛspɔt] nm despot; (fig) tyrant.
despotique [dɛspɔtik] adj despotic.
despotisme [dɛspɔtism(ə)] nm despotism.
desquamer [deskwame]: se ~ vi to flake off.
desquels, desquelles [dekɛl] prép + pron voir lequel.
DESS sigle m (= Diplôme d'études supérieures spécialisées) post-graduate diploma.
dessaisir [deseziR] vt: ~ un tribunal d'une affaire to remove a case from a court; se ~ de vt to give up, part with.
dessaler [desale] vt (eau de mer) to desalinate; (CULIN: morue etc) to soak; (fig fam: délurer) ~ qn to teach sb a thing or two ♦ vi (voilier) to capsize.
Desse abr = duchesse.
desséché, e [deseʃe] adj dried up.
dessèchement [desɛʃmɑ̃] nm drying out; dryness; hardness.
dessécher [deseʃe] vt (terre, plante) to dry out, parch; (peau) to dry out; (volontairement: aliments etc) to dry, dehydrate; (fig: cœur) to harden; se ~ vi to dry out; (peau, lèvres) to go dry.
dessein [desɛ̃] nm design; dans le ~ de with the intention of; à ~ intentionally, deliberately.
desseller [desele] vt to unsaddle.
desserrer [deseRe] vt to loosen; (frein) to release; (poing, dents) to unclench; (objets alignés) to space out; ne pas ~ les dents not to open one's mouth.
dessert [desɛR] vb voir desservir ♦ nm dessert, pudding.
desserte [desɛRt(ə)] nf (table) side table; (transport): la ~ du village est assurée par autocar there is a coach service to the village; chemin ou voie de ~ service road.
desservir [desɛRviR] vt (ville, quartier) to serve; (: suj: voie de communication) to lead into; (suj: vicaire: paroisse) to serve; (nuire à: personne) to do a disservice to; (débarrasser): ~ (la table) to clear the table.
dessiller [desije] vt (fig): ~ les yeux à qn to open sb's eyes.

dessin [desɛ̃] *nm* (*œuvre, art*) drawing; (*motif*) pattern, design; (*contour*) (out)line; **le ~ industriel** draughtsmanship (*BRIT*), draftsmanship (*US*); **~ animé** cartoon (film); **~ humoristique** cartoon.

dessinateur, trice [desinatœr, -tris] *nm/f* drawer; (*de bandes dessinées*) cartoonist; (*industriel*) draughtsman (*BRIT*), draftsman (*US*); **dessinatrice de mode** fashion designer.

dessiner [desine] *vt* to draw; (*concevoir: carrosserie, maison*) to design; (*suj: robe: taille*) to show off; **se ~** *vi* (*forme*) to be outlined; (*fig: solution*) to emerge.

dessoûler [desule] *vt, vi* to sober up.

dessous [dəsu] *adv* underneath, beneath ♦ *nm* underside; (*étage inférieur*): **les voisins du ~** the downstairs neighbours ♦ *nmpl* (*sous-vêtements*) underwear *sg*; (*fig*) hidden aspects; **en ~** underneath; below; (*fig: en catimini*) slyly, on the sly; **par ~** underneath; below; **de ~ le lit** from under the bed; **au-~** *adv* below; **au-~ de** *prép* below; (*peu digne de*) beneath; **au-~ de tout** the (absolute) limit; **avoir le ~** to get the worst of it.

dessous-de-bouteille [dəsudbutɛj] *nm* bottle mat.

dessous-de-plat [dəsudpla] *nm inv* tablemat.

dessous-de-table [dəsudtabl(ə)] *nm* (*fig*) bribe, under-the-counter payment.

dessus [dəsy] *adv* on top; (*collé, écrit*) on it ♦ *nm* top; (*étage supérieur*): **les voisins/ l'appartement du ~** the upstairs neighbours/flat; **en ~** above; **par ~** *adv* over it ♦ *prép* over; **au-~** above; **au-~ de** above; **avoir/prendre le ~** to have/get the upper hand; **reprendre le ~** to get over it; **bras ~ bras dessous** arm in arm; **sens ~ dessous** upside down; *voir* **ci-**; **là-**.

dessus-de-lit [dəsydli] *nm inv* bedspread.

déstabiliser [destabilize] *vt* (*POL*) to destabilize.

destin [dɛstɛ̃] *nm* fate; (*avenir*) destiny.

destinataire [dɛstinatɛr] *nm/f* (*POSTES*) addressee; (*d'un colis*) consignee; (*d'un mandat*) payee; **aux risques et périls du ~** at owner's risk.

destination [dɛstinasjɔ̃] *nf* (*lieu*) destination; (*usage*) purpose; **à ~ de** (*avion etc*) bound for; (*voyageur*) bound for, travelling to.

destinée [dɛstine] *nf* fate; (*existence, avenir*) destiny.

destiner [dɛstine] *vt*: **~ qn à** (*poste, sort*) to destine sb for, intend sb to + *verbe*; **~ qn/qch à** (*prédestiner*) to mark sb/sth out for, destine sb/sth to + *verbe*; **~ qch à** (*envisager d'affecter*) to intend to use sth for; **~ qch à qn** (*envisager de donner*) to intend to give sth to sb, intend sb to have sth; (*adresser*) to intend sth for sb; **se ~ à l'enseignement** to intend to become a teacher; **être destiné à** (*sort*) to be destined to + *verbe*; (*usage*) to be

intended *ou* meant for; (*suj: sort*) to be in store for.

destituer [dɛstitɥe] *vt* to depose; **~ qn de ses fonctions** to relieve sb of his duties.

destitution [dɛstitɥsjɔ̃] *nf* deposition.

destructeur, trice [dɛstryktœr, -tris] *adj* destructive.

destructif, ive [dɛstryktif, -iv] *adj* destructive.

destruction [dɛstryksjɔ̃] *nf* destruction.

déstructuré, e [destryktyre] *adj*: **vêtements ~s** casual clothes.

déstructurer [destryktyre] *vt* to break down, take to pieces.

désuet, ète [desɥɛ, -ɛt] *adj* outdated, outmoded.

désuétude [desɥetyd] *nf*: **tomber en ~** to fall into disuse, become obsolete.

désuni, e [dezyni] *adj* divided, disunited.

désunion [dezynjɔ̃] *nf* disunity.

désunir [dezynir] *vt* to disunite; **se ~** *vi* (*athlète*) to get out of one's stride.

détachable [detaʃabl(ə)] *adj* (*coupon etc*) tear-off *cpd*; (*capuche etc*) detachable.

détachant [detaʃɑ̃] *nm* stain remover.

détaché, e [detaʃe] *adj* (*fig*) detached ♦ *nm/f* (*représentant*) person on secondment (*BRIT*) *ou* a posting.

détachement [detaʃmɑ̃] *nm* detachment; (*fonctionnaire, employé*): **être en ~** to be on secondment (*BRIT*) *ou* a posting.

détacher [detaʃe] *vt* (*enlever*) to detach, remove; (*délier*) to untie; (*ADMIN*): **~ qn (auprès de** *ou* **à)** to send sb on secondment (to) (*BRIT*), post sb (to); (*MIL*) to detail; (*vêtement: nettoyer*) to remove the stains from; **se ~** *vi* (*tomber*) to come off; to come out; (*se défaire*) to come undone; (*SPORT*) to pull *ou* break away; (*se délier: chien, prisonnier*) to break loose; **se ~ sur** to stand out against; **se ~ de** (*se désintéresser*) to grow away from.

détail [detaj] *nm* detail; (*COMM*): **le ~** retail; **prix de ~** retail price; **au ~** *adv* (*COMM*) retail; (: *individuellement*) separately; **donner le ~ de** to give a detailed account of; (*compte*) to give a breakdown of; **en ~** in detail.

détaillant, e [detajɑ̃, -ɑ̃t] *nm/f* retailer.

détaillé, e [detaje] *adj* (*récit*) detailed.

détailler [detaje] *vt* (*COMM*) to sell retail; to sell separately; (*expliquer*) to explain in detail; to detail; (*examiner*) to look over, examine.

détaler [detale] *vi* (*lapin*) to scamper off; (*fam: personne*) to make off, scarper (*fam*).

détartrant [detartrɑ̃] *nm* descaling agent (*BRIT*), scale remover.

détartrer [detartre] *vt* to descale; (*dents*) to scale.

détaxe [detaks(ə)] *nf* (*réduction*) reduction in tax; (*suppression*) removal of tax;

(*remboursement*) tax refund.

détaxer [detakse] *vt* (*réduire*) to reduce the tax on; (*ôter*) to remove the tax on.

détecter [detɛkte] *vt* to detect.

détecteur [detɛktœʀ] *nm* detector, sensor; ~ **de mensonges** lie detector; ~ **(de mines)** mine detector.

détection [detɛksjɔ̃] *nf* detection.

détective [detɛktiv] *nm* (*BRIT: policier*) detective; ~ **(privé)** private detective *ou* investigator.

déteindre [detɛ̃dʀ(ə)] *vi* to fade; (*fig*): ~ **sur** to rub off on.

déteint, e [detɛ̃, -ɛ̃t] *pp de* **déteindre**.

dételer [dɛtle] *vt* to unharness; (*voiture, wagon*) to unhitch ♦ *vi* (*fig: s'arrêter*) to leave off (working).

détendeur [detɑ̃dœʀ] *nm* (*de bouteille à gaz*) regulator.

détendre [detɑ̃dʀ(ə)] *vt* (*fil*) to slacken, loosen; (*relaxer: personne, atmosphère*) to relax; (*: situation*) to relieve; **se** ~ to lose its tension; to relax.

détendu, e [detɑ̃dy] *adj* relaxed.

détenir [detniʀ] *vt* (*fortune, objet, secret*) to be in possession of, have (in one's possession); (*prisonnier*) to detain, hold; (*record*) to hold; ~ **le pouvoir** to be in power.

détente [detɑ̃t] *nf* relaxation; (*POL*) détente; (*d'une arme*) trigger; (*d'un athlète qui saute*) spring.

détenteur, trice [detɑ̃tœʀ, -tʀis] *nm/f* holder.

détention [detɑ̃sjɔ̃] *nf* (*voir détenir*) possession; detention; holding; ~ **préventive** (pre-trial) custody.

détenu, e [detny] *pp de* **détenir** ♦ *nm/f* prisoner.

détergent [detɛʀʒɑ̃] *nm* detergent.

détérioration [deteʀjɔʀasjɔ̃] *nf* damaging; deterioration.

détériorer [deteʀjɔʀe] *vt* to damage; **se** ~ *vi* to deteriorate.

déterminant, e [detɛʀminɑ̃, -ɑ̃t] *adj*: **un facteur** ~ a determining factor ♦ *nm* (*LING*) determiner.

détermination [detɛʀminasjɔ̃] *nf* determining; (*résolution*) decision; (*fermeté*) determination.

déterminé, e [detɛʀmine] *adj* (*résolu*) determined; (*précis*) specific, definite.

déterminer [detɛʀmine] *vt* (*fixer*) to determine; (*décider*): ~ **qn à faire** to decide sb to do; **se** ~ **à faire** to make up one's mind to do.

déterminisme [detɛʀminism(ə)] *nm* determinism.

déterré, e [detɛʀe] *nm/f*: **avoir une mine de** ~ to look like death warmed up (*BRIT*) *ou* warmed over (*US*).

déterrer [detɛʀe] *vt* to dig up.

détersif, ive [detɛʀsif, -iv] *adj, nm* detergent.

détestable [detɛstabl(ə)] *adj* foul, detestable.

détester [detɛste] *vt* to hate, detest.

détiendrai [detjɛ̃dʀe], **détiens** [detjɛ̃] *etc vb voir* **détenir**.

détonant, e [detɔnɑ̃, -ɑ̃t] *adj*: **mélange** ~ explosive mixture.

détonateur [detɔnatœʀ] *nm* detonator.

détonation [detɔnasjɔ̃] *nf* detonation, bang, report (of a gun).

détoner [detɔne] *vi* to detonate, explode.

détonner [detɔne] *vi* (*MUS*) to go out of tune; (*fig*) to clash.

détordre [detɔʀdʀ(ə)] *vt* to untwist, unwind.

détour [detuʀ] *nm* detour; (*tournant*) bend, curve; (*fig: subterfuge*) roundabout means; **au** ~ **de chemin** at the bend in the path; **sans** ~ (*fig*) plainly.

détourné, e [detuʀne] *adj* (*sentier, chemin, moyen*) roundabout.

détournement [detuʀnəmɑ̃] *nm* diversion, rerouting; ~ **d'avion** hijacking; ~ **(de fonds)** embezzlement *ou* misappropriation (of funds); ~ **de mineur** corruption of a minor.

détourner [detuʀne] *vt* to divert; (*avion*) to divert, reroute; (*: par la force*) to hijack; (*yeux, tête*) to turn away; (*de l'argent*) to embezzle, misappropriate; **se** ~ to turn away; ~ **la conversation** to change the subject; ~ **qn de son devoir** to divert sb from his duty; ~ **l'attention (de qn)** to distract *ou* divert (sb's) attention.

détracteur, trice [detʀaktœʀ, -tʀis] *nm/f* disparager, critic.

détraqué, e [detʀake] *adj* (*machine, santé*) broken-down ♦ *nm/f* (*fam*): **c'est un** ~ he's unhinged.

détraquer [detʀake] *vt* to put out of order; (*estomac*) to upset; **se** ~ *vi* to go wrong.

détrempe [detʀɑ̃p] *nf* (*ART*) tempera.

détrempé, e [detʀɑ̃pe] *adj* (*sol*) sodden, waterlogged.

détremper [detʀɑ̃pe] *vt* (*peinture*) to water down.

détresse [detʀɛs] *nf* distress; **en** ~ (*avion etc*) in distress; **appel/signal de** ~ distress call/signal.

détriment [detʀimɑ̃] *nm*: **au** ~ **de** to the detriment of.

détritus [detʀitys] *nmpl* rubbish *sg*, refuse *sg*, garbage *sg* (*US*).

détroit [detʀwa] *nm* strait; **le** ~ **de Bering** *ou* **Behring** the Bering Strait; **le** ~ **de Gibraltar** the Straits of Gibraltar; **le** ~ **du Bosphore** the Bosphorus; **le** ~ **de Magellan** the Strait of Magellan, the Magellan Strait.

détromper [detʀɔ̃pe] *vt* to disabuse; **se** ~: **détrompez-vous** don't believe it.

détrôner [detʀone] *vt* to dethrone, depose; (*fig*) to oust, dethrone.

détrousser [detʀuse] *vt* to rob.

détruire [detʀɥiʀ] *vt* to destroy; (*fig: santé, réputation*) to ruin; (*documents*) to shred.

détruit, e [detʀɥi, -it] *pp de* **détruire**.

dette [dɛt] *nf* debt; ~ **publique** *ou* **de l'État**

national debt.
DEUG [døg] *sigle m = Diplôme d'études universitaires générales.*

French students sit their **DEUG** *after two years of university study. Students can leave university after the DEUG, which may be awarded with distinction, or proceed to the* **licence***. The certificate obtained specifies the principal subject area studied.*

---

deuil [dœj] *nm* (*perte*) bereavement; (*période*) mourning; (*chagrin*) grief; **porter le ~ to** wear mourning; **prendre le/être en ~ to** go into/be in mourning.
DEUST [dœst] *sigle m = Diplôme d'études universitaires scientifiques et techniques.*
deux [dø] *num* two; **les ~** both; **ses ~ mains** both his hands, his two hands; **à ~ pas a** short distance away; **tous les ~ mois** every two months, every other month; **~ points** colon *sg.*
deuxième [døzjɛm] *num* second.
deuxièmement [døzjɛmmɑ̃] *adv* secondly, in the second place.
deux-pièces [døpjɛs] *nm inv* (*tailleur*) two-piece (suit); (*de bain*) two-piece (swimsuit); (*appartement*) two-roomed flat (*BRIT*) *ou* apartment (*US*).
deux-roues [døʀu] *nm* two-wheeled vehicle.
deux-temps [døtɑ̃] *adj* two-stroke.
devais [dəvɛ] *etc vb voir* **devoir**.
dévaler [devale] *vt* to hurtle down.
dévaliser [devalize] *vt* to rob, burgle.
dévalorisant, e [devalɔʀizɑ̃, -ɑ̃t] *adj* depreciatory.
dévalorisation [devalɔʀizɑsjɔ̃] *nf* depreciation.
dévaloriser [devalɔʀize] *vt*, **se ~** *vi* to depreciate.
dévaluation [devalɥasjɔ̃] *nf* depreciation; (*ÉCON: mesure*) devaluation.
dévaluer [devalɥe] *vt*, **se ~** *vi* to devalue.
devancer [dəvɑ̃se] *vt* to be ahead of; (*distancer*) to get ahead of; (*arriver avant*) to arrive before; (*prévenir*) to anticipate; **~ l'appel** (*MIL*) to enlist before call-up.
devancier, ière [dəvɑ̃sje, -jɛʀ] *nm/f* precursor.
devant [dəvɑ̃] *vb voir* **devoir** ♦ *adv* in front; (*à distance: en avant*) ahead ♦ *prép* in front; ahead of; (*avec mouvement: passer*) past; (*fig*) before, in front of; (*: face à*) faced with, in the face of; (*: vu*) in view of ♦ *nm* front; **prendre les ~s** to make the first move; **de ~** (*roue, porte*) front; **les pattes de ~** the front legs, the forelegs; **par ~** (*boutonner*) at the front; (*entrer*) the front way; **par-~ notaire** in the presence of a notary; **aller au-~ de qn** to go out to meet sb; **aller au-~ de** (*désirs de qn*) to anticipate; **aller au-~ des ennuis** *ou* **difficultés** to be asking for trouble.
devanture [dəvɑ̃tyʀ] *nf* (*façade*) (shop) front;

(*étalage*) display; (shop) window.
dévastateur, trice [devastatœʀ, -tʀis] *adj* devastating.
dévastation [devastɑsjɔ̃] *nf* devastation.
dévaster [devaste] *vt* to devastate.
déveine [devɛn] *nf* rotten luck *no pl.*
développement [devlɔpmɑ̃] *nm* development.
développer [devlɔpe] *vt*, **se ~** *vi* to develop.
devenir [dəvniʀ] *vb avec attribut* to become; **~ instituteur** to become a teacher; **que sont-ils devenus?** what has become of them?
devenu, e [dəvny] *pp de* **devenir**.
dévergondé, e [devɛʀɡɔ̃de] *adj* wild, shameless.
dévergonder [devɛʀɡɔ̃de] *vt*, **se ~** *vi* to get into bad ways.
déverrouiller [devɛʀuje] *vt* to unbolt.
devers [dəvɛʀ] *adv*: **par ~ soi** to oneself.
déverser [devɛʀse] *vt* (*liquide*) to pour (out); (*ordures*) to tip (out); **se ~ dans** (*fleuve, mer*) to flow into.
déversoir [devɛʀswaʀ] *nm* overflow.
dévêtir [devetiʀ] *vt*, **se ~** *vi* to undress.
devez [dəve] *vb voir* **devoir**.
déviation [devjasjɔ̃] *nf* deviation; (*AUTO*) diversion (*BRIT*), detour (*US*); **~ de la colonne (vertébrale)** curvature of the spine.
dévider [devide] *vt* to unwind.
dévidoir [devidwaʀ] *nm* reel.
deviendrai [dəvjɛ̃dʀe], **deviens** [dəvjɛ̃] *etc vb voir* **devenir**.
dévier [devje] *vt* (*fleuve, circulation*) to divert; (*coup*) to deflect ♦ *vi* to veer (off course); (**faire**) **~** (*projectile*) to deflect; (*véhicule*) to push off course.
devin [dəvɛ̃] *nm* soothsayer, seer.
deviner [dəvine] *vt* to guess; (*prévoir*) to foretell, foresee; (*apercevoir*) to distinguish.
devinette [dəvinɛt] *nf* riddle.
devint [dəvɛ̃] *etc vb voir* **devenir**.
devis [dəvi] *nm* estimate, quotation; **~ descriptif/estimatif** detailed/preliminary estimate.
dévisager [devizaʒe] *vt* to stare at.
devise [dəviz] *nf* (*formule*) motto, watchword; (*ÉCON: monnaie*) currency; **~s** *nfpl* (*argent*) currency *sg.*
deviser [dəvize] *vi* to converse.
dévisser [devise] *vt* to unscrew, undo; **se ~** *vi* to come unscrewed.
de visu [devizy] *adv*: **se rendre compte de qch ~** to see sth for o.s.
dévitaliser [devitalize] *vt* (*dent*) to remove the nerve from.
dévoiler [devwale] *vt* to unveil.
devoir [dəvwaʀ] *nm* duty; (*SCOL*) piece of homework, homework *no pl*; (*: en classe*) exercise ♦ *vt* (*argent, respect*): **~ qch (à qn)** to owe (sb) sth; (*suivi de l'infinitif: obligation*): **il doit le faire** he has to do it, he must do it; (*: fatalité*): **cela devait arriver un jour** it was bound to happen; (*: intention*): **il doit partir**

demain he is (due) to leave tomorrow; (: *probabilité*): **il doit être tard** it must be late; **se faire un ~ de faire qch** to make it one's duty to do sth; **~s de vacances** homework set for the holidays; **se ~ de faire qch** to be duty bound to do sth; **je devrais faire** I ought to *ou* should do; **tu n'aurais pas dû** you ought not to have *ou* shouldn't have; **comme il se doit** (*comme il faut*) as is right and proper.

dévolu, e [devɔly] *adj*: **~ à** allotted to ♦ *nm*: **jeter son ~ sur** to fix one's choice on.

devons [dəvɔ̃] *vb voir* **devoir**.

dévorant, e [devɔʀɑ̃, -ɑ̃t] *adj* (*faim, passion*) raging.

dévorer [devɔʀe] *vt* to devour; (*suj: feu, soucis*) to consume; **~ qn/qch des yeux** *ou* **du regard** (*fig*) to eye sb/sth intently; (: *convoitise*) to eye sb/sth greedily.

dévot, e [devo, -ɔt] *adj* devout, pious ♦ *nm/f* devout person; **un faux ~** a falsely pious person.

dévotion [devɔsjɔ̃] *nf* devoutness; **être à la ~ de qn** to be totally devoted to sb; **avoir une ~ pour qn** to worship sb.

dévoué, e [devwe] *adj* devoted.

dévouement [devumɑ̃] *nm* devotion, dedication.

dévouer [devwe]: **se ~** *vi* (*se sacrifier*): **se ~ (pour)** to sacrifice o.s. (for); (*se consacrer*): **se ~ à** to devote *ou* dedicate o.s. to.

dévoyé, e [devwaje] *adj* delinquent.

dévoyer [devwaje] *vt* to lead astray; **se ~** *vi* to go off the rails; **~ l'opinion publique** to influence public opinion.

devrai [dəvʀe] *etc vb voir* **devoir**.

dextérité [dɛksteʀite] *nf* skill, dexterity.

dfc *abr* (= *désire faire connaissance*) *in personal column of newspaper*.

DG *sigle m* = **directeur général**.

dg. *abr* (= *décigramme*) dg.

DGE *sigle f* (= *Dotation globale d'équipement*) *state contribution to local government budget*.

DGSE *sigle f* (= *Direction générale des services extérieurs*) ≈ MI6 (*BRIT*), ≈ CIA (*US*).

DI *sigle f* (*MIL*) = **division d'infanterie**.

dia [dja] *abr* = **diapositive**.

diabète [djabɛt] *nm* diabetes *sg*.

diabétique [djabetik] *nm/f* diabetic.

diable [djɑbl(ə)] *nm* devil; **une musique du ~** an unholy racket; **il fait une chaleur du ~** it's fiendishly hot; **avoir le ~ au corps** to be the very devil.

diablement [djɑbləmɑ̃] *adv* fiendishly.

diableries [djɑbləʀi] *nfpl* (*d'enfant*) devilment *sg*, mischief *sg*.

diablesse [djɑblɛs] *nf* (*petite fille*) little devil.

diablotin [djɑblɔtɛ̃] *nm* imp; (*pétard*) cracker.

diabolique [djɑbɔlik] *adj* diabolical.

diabolo [djɑbɔlo] *nm* (*jeu*) diabolo; (*boisson*) lemonade and fruit cordial; **~(-menthe)** lemonade and mint cordial.

diacre [djakʀ(ə)] *nm* deacon.

diadème [djadɛm] *nm* diadem.

diagnostic [djagnɔstik] *nm* diagnosis *sg*.

diagnostiquer [djagnɔstike] *vt* to diagnose.

diagonal, e, aux [djagɔnal, -o] *adj, nf* diagonal; **en ~e** diagonally; **lire en ~e** (*fig*) to skim through.

diagramme [djagʀam] *nm* chart, graph.

dialecte [djalɛkt(ə)] *nm* dialect.

dialectique [djalɛktik] *adj* dialectic(al).

dialogue [djalɔg] *nm* dialogue; **~ de sourds** dialogue of the deaf.

dialoguer [djalɔge] *vi* to converse; (*POL*) to have a dialogue.

dialoguiste [djalɔgist(ə)] *nm/f* dialogue writer.

dialyse [djaliz] *nf* dialysis.

diamant [djamɑ̃] *nm* diamond.

diamantaire [djamɑ̃tɛʀ] *nm* diamond dealer.

diamétralement [djametʀalmɑ̃] *adv* diametrically; **~ opposés** (*opinions*) diametrically opposed.

diamètre [djamɛtʀ(ə)] *nm* diameter.

diapason [djapazɔ̃] *nm* tuning fork; (*fig*): **être/se mettre au ~ (de)** to be/get in tune (with).

diaphane [djafan] *adj* diaphanous.

diaphragme [djafʀagm(ə)] *nm* (*ANAT, PHOTO*) diaphragm; (*contraceptif*) diaphragm, cap; **ouverture du ~** (*PHOTO*) aperture.

diapo [djapo], **diapositive** [djapozitiv] *nf* transparency, slide.

diaporama [djapɔrama] *nm* slide show.

diapré, e [djapʀe] *adj* many-coloured (*BRIT*), many-colored (*US*).

diarrhée [djaʀe] *nf* diarrhoea (*BRIT*), diarrhea (*US*).

diatribe [djatʀib] *nf* diatribe.

dichotomie [dikɔtɔmi] *nf* dichotomy.

dictaphone [diktafɔn] *nm* Dictaphone ®.

dictateur [diktatœʀ] *nm* dictator.

dictatorial, e, aux [diktatɔʀjal, -o] *adj* dictatorial.

dictature [diktatyʀ] *nf* dictatorship.

dictée [dikte] *nf* dictation; **prendre sous ~** to take down (*sth dictated*).

dicter [dikte] *vt* to dictate.

diction [diksjɔ̃] *nf* diction, delivery; **cours de ~** speech production lesson(s).

dictionnaire [diksjɔnɛʀ] *nm* dictionary; **~ géographique** gazetteer.

dicton [diktɔ̃] *nm* saying, dictum.

didacticiel [didaktisjɛl] *nm* educational software.

didactique [didaktik] *adj* didactic.

dièse [djɛz] *nm* (*MUS*) sharp.

diesel [djezɛl] *nm, adj inv* diesel.

diète [djɛt] *nf* diet; **être à la ~** to be on a diet.

diététicien, ne [djetetisjɛ̃, -ɛn] *nm/f* dietician.

diététique [djetetik] *nf* dietetics *sg* ♦ *adj*: **magasin ~** health food shop (*BRIT*) *ou* store (*US*).

dieu, x [djø] *nm* god; **D~** God; **le bon D~** the good Lord; **mon D~**! good heavens!

diffamant, e [difamɑ̃, -ɑ̃t] *adj* slanderous, defamatory; libellous.

diffamation [difamɑsjɔ̃] *nf* slander; (*écrite*) libel; **attaquer qn en ~** to sue sb for slander (*ou* libel).

diffamatoire [difamatwaʀ] *adj* slanderous, defamatory; libellous.

diffamer [difame] *vt* to slander, defame; to libel.

différé [difeʀe] *adj* (*INFORM*): **traitement ~** batch processing; **crédit ~** deferred credit ♦ *nm* (*TV*): **en ~** (pre-)recorded.

différemment [difeʀamɑ̃] *adv* differently.

différence [difeʀɑ̃s] *nf* difference; **à la ~ de** unlike.

différenciation [difeʀɑ̃sjɑsjɔ̃] *nf* differentiation.

différencier [difeʀɑ̃sje] *vt* to differentiate; **se ~ vi** (*organisme*) to become differentiated; **se ~ de** to differentiate o.s. from; (*être différent*) to differ from.

différend [difeʀɑ̃] *nm* difference (of opinion), disagreement.

différent, e [difeʀɑ̃, -ɑ̃t] *adj*: **~ (de)** different (from); **~s objets** different *ou* various objects; **à ~es reprises** on various occasions.

différentiel, le [difeʀɑ̃sjɛl] *adj, nm* differential.

différer [difeʀe] *vt* to postpone, put off ♦ *vi*: **~ (de)** to differ (from); **~ de faire** (*tarder*) to delay doing.

difficile [difisil] *adj* difficult; (*exigeant*) hard to please, difficult (to please); **faire le** *ou* **la ~** to be hard to please, be difficult.

difficilement [difisilmɑ̃] *adv* (*marcher, s'expliquer etc*) with difficulty; **~ lisible/ compréhensible** difficult *ou* hard to read/ understand.

difficulté [difikylte] *nf* difficulty; **en ~** (*bateau, alpiniste*) in trouble *ou* difficulties; **avoir de la ~ à faire** to have difficulty (in) doing.

difforme [difɔʀm(ə)] *adj* deformed, misshapen.

difformité [difɔʀmite] *nf* deformity.

diffracter [difʀakte] *vt* to diffract.

diffus, e [dify, -yz] *adj* diffuse.

diffuser [difyze] *vt* (*chaleur, bruit, lumière*) to diffuse; (*émission, musique*) to broadcast; (*nouvelle, idée*) to circulate; (*COMM: livres, journaux*) to distribute.

diffuseur [difyzœʀ] *nm* diffuser; distributor.

diffusion [difyzjɔ̃] *nf* diffusion; broadcast(ing); circulation; distribution.

digérer [diʒeʀe] *vt* (*suj: personne*) to digest; (*: machine*) to process; (*fig: accepter*) to stomach, put up with.

digeste [diʒɛst(ə)] *adj* easily digestible.

digestible [diʒɛstibl(ə)] *adj* digestible.

digestif, ive [diʒɛstif, -iv] *adj* digestive ♦ *nm* (after-dinner) liqueur.

digestion [diʒɛstjɔ̃] *nf* digestion.

digit [didʒit] *nm*: **~ binaire** binary digit.

digital, e, aux [diʒital, -o] *adj* digital.

digitale [diʒital] *nf* digitalis, foxglove.

digne [diɲ] *adj* dignified; **~ de** worthy of; **~ de foi** trustworthy.

dignitaire [diɲitɛʀ] *nm* dignitary.

dignité [diɲite] *nf* dignity.

digression [digʀesjɔ̃] *nf* digression.

digue [dig] *nf* dike, dyke; (*pour protéger la côte*) sea wall.

dijonnais, e [diʒɔnɛ, -ɛz] *adj* of *ou* from Dijon ♦ *nm/f*: **D~, e** inhabitant *ou* native of Dijon.

diktat [diktat] *nm* diktat.

dilapidation [dilapidɑsjɔ̃] *nf* (*voir vb*) squandering; embezzlement, misappropriation.

dilapider [dilapide] *vt* to squander, waste; (*détourner: biens, fonds publics*) to embezzle, misappropriate.

dilater [dilate] *vt* to dilate; (*gaz, métal*) to cause to expand; (*ballon*) to distend; **se ~ vi** to expand.

dilemme [dilɛm] *nm* dilemma.

dilettante [diletɑ̃t] *nm/f* dilettante; **en ~** in a dilettantish way.

dilettantisme [diletɑ̃tism(ə)] *nm* dilettant(e)ism.

diligence [diliʒɑ̃s] *nf* stagecoach, diligence; (*empressement*) despatch; **faire ~** to make haste.

diligent, e [diliʒɑ̃, -ɑ̃t] *adj* prompt and efficient; diligent.

diluant [dilɥɑ̃] *nm* thinner(s).

diluer [dilɥe] *vt* to dilute.

dilution [dilysjɔ̃] *nf* dilution.

diluvien, ne [dilyvjɛ̃, -ɛn] *adj*: **pluie ~ne** torrential rain.

dimanche [dimɑ̃ʃ] *nm* Sunday; **le ~ des Rameaux/de Pâques** Palm/Easter Sunday; *voir aussi* **lundi**.

dîme [dim] *nf* tithe.

dimension [dimɑ̃sjɔ̃] *nf* (*grandeur*) size; (*gén pl: cotes, MATH: de l'espace*) dimension.

diminué, e [diminɥe] *adj* (*personne: physiquement*) run-down; (*: mentalement*) less alert.

diminuer [diminɥe] *vt* to reduce, decrease; (*ardeur etc*) to lessen; (*personne: physiquement*) to undermine; (*dénigrer*) to belittle ♦ *vi* to decrease, diminish.

diminutif [diminytif] *nm* (*LING*) diminutive; (*surnom*) pet name.

diminution [diminysjɔ̃] *nf* decreasing, diminishing.

dînatoire [dinatwaʀ] *adj*: **goûter ~** ≈ high tea (*BRIT*); **apéritif ~** ≈ evening buffet.

dinde [dɛ̃d] *nf* turkey; (*femme stupide*) goose.

dindon [dɛ̃dɔ̃] *nm* turkey.

dindonneau, x [dɛ̃dɔno] *nm* turkey poult.

dîner [dine] *nm* dinner ♦ *vi* to have dinner; **~**

d'affaires/de famille business/family dinner.
dînette [dinɛt] nf (jeu): **jouer à la ~** to play at tea parties.
dingue [dɛ̃g] adj (fam) crazy.
dinosaure [dinozɔʀ] nm dinosaur.
diocèse [djɔsɛz] nm diocese.
diode [djɔd] nf diode.
diphasé, e [difaze] adj (ÉLEC) two-phase.
diphtérie [diftɛʀi] nf diphtheria.
diphtongue [diftɔ̃g] nf diphthong.
diplomate [diplɔmat] adj diplomatic ♦ nm diplomat; (fig: personne habile) diplomatist; (CULIN: gâteau) dessert made of sponge cake, candied fruit and custard, ≈ trifle (BRIT).
diplomatie [diplɔmasi] nf diplomacy.
diplomatique [diplɔmatik] adj diplomatic.
diplôme [diplom] nm diploma certificate; (examen) (diploma) examination.
diplômé, e [diplome] adj qualified.
dire [diʀ] nm: **au ~ de** according to; **leur ~s** what they say ♦ vt to say; (secret, mensonge) to tell; **~ l'heure/la vérité** to tell the time/the truth; **dis pardon/merci** say sorry/thank you; **~ qch à qn** to tell sb sth; **~ à qn qu'il fasse** ou **de faire** to tell sb to do; **~ que** to say that; **on dit que** they say that; **comme on dit** as they say; **on dirait que** it looks (ou sounds etc) as though; **on dirait du vin** you'd ou one would think it was wine; **que dites-vous de** (penser) what do you think of; **si cela lui dit** if he feels like it, if he fancies it; **cela ne me dit rien** that doesn't appeal to me; **à vrai ~** truth to tell; **pour ainsi ~** so to speak; **cela va sans ~** that goes without saying; **dis donc!, dites donc!** (pour attirer l'attention) hey!; (au fait) by the way; **et ~ que ...** and to think that ...; **ceci** ou **cela dit** that being said; (à ces mots) whereupon; **c'est dit, voilà qui est dit** so that's settled; **il n'y a pas à ~** there's no getting away from it; **c'est ~ si ...** that just shows that ...; **c'est beaucoup/peu ~** that's saying a lot/not saying much; **se ~** (à soi-même) to say to oneself; (se prétendre): **se ~ malade** etc to say (that) one is ill etc; **ça se dit ... en anglais** that is ... in English; **cela ne se dit pas comme ça** you don't say it like that; **se ~ au revoir** to say goodbye (to each other).
direct, e [diʀɛkt] adj direct ♦ nm (train) through train; **en ~** (émission) live; **train/bus ~** express train/bus.
directement [diʀɛktəmɑ̃] adv directly.
directeur, trice [diʀɛktœʀ, -tʀis] nm/f (d'entreprise) director; (de service) manager/eress; (d'école) head(teacher) (BRIT), principal (US); **comité ~** management ou steering committee; **~ général** general manager; **~ de thèse** ≈ PhD supervisor.
direction [diʀɛksjɔ̃] nf management; conducting; supervision; (AUTO) steering; (sens) direction; **sous la ~ de** (MUS)

conducted by; **en ~ de** (avion, train, bateau) for; **"toutes ~s"** (AUTO) "all routes".
directive [diʀɛktiv] nf directive, instruction.
directorial, e, aux [diʀɛktɔʀjal, -o] adj (bureau) director's; manager's; head teacher's.
directrice [diʀɛktʀis] adj f, nf voir **directeur.**
dirent [diʀ] vb voir **dire.**
dirigeable [diʀiʒabl(ə)] adj, nm: **(ballon) ~** dirigible.
dirigeant, e [diʀiʒɑ̃, -ɑ̃t] adj managerial; (classes) ruling ♦ nm/f (d'un parti etc) leader; (d'entreprise) manager, member of the management.
diriger [diʀiʒe] vt (entreprise) to manage, run; (véhicule) to steer; (orchestre) to conduct; (recherches, travaux) to supervise, be in charge of; (braquer: regard, arme): **~ sur** to point ou level ou aim at; (fig: critiques): **~ contre** to aim at; **se ~** (s'orienter) to find one's way; **se ~ vers** ou **sur** to make ou head for.
dirigisme [diʀiʒism(ə)] nm (ÉCON) state intervention, interventionism.
dirigiste [diʀiʒist(ə)] adj interventionist.
dis [di], **disais** [dizɛ] etc vb voir **dire.**
discal, e, aux [diskal, -o] adj (MÉD): **hernie ~e** slipped disc.
discernement [disɛʀnəmɑ̃] nm discernment, judgment.
discerner [disɛʀne] vt to discern, make out.
disciple [disipl(ə)] nm/f disciple.
disciplinaire [disiplinɛʀ] adj disciplinary.
discipline [disiplin] nf discipline.
discipliné, e [disipline] adj (well-)disciplined.
discipliner [disipline] vt to discipline; (cheveux) to control.
discobole [diskɔbɔl] nm/f discus thrower.
discographie [diskɔgʀafi] nf discography.
discontinu, e [diskɔ̃tiny] adj intermittent; (bande: sur la route) broken.
discontinuer [diskɔ̃tinɥe] vi: **sans ~** without stopping, without a break.
disconvenir [diskɔ̃vniʀ] vi: **ne pas ~ de qch/que** not to deny sth/that.
discophile [diskɔfil] nm/f record enthusiast.
discordance [diskɔʀdɑ̃s] nf discordance; conflict.
discordant, e [diskɔʀdɑ̃, -ɑ̃t] adj discordant; conflicting.
discorde [diskɔʀd(ə)] nf discord, dissension.
discothèque [diskɔtɛk] nf (disques) record collection; (: dans une bibliothèque): **~ (de prêt)** record library; (boîte de nuit) disco(thèque).
discourais [diskuʀɛ] etc vb voir **discourir.**
discourir [diskuʀiʀ] vi to discourse, hold forth.
discours [diskuʀ] vb voir **discourir** ♦ nm speech; **~ direct/indirect** (LING) direct/indirect ou reported speech.
discourtois, e [diskuʀtwa, waz] adj

discourteous.

discrédit [diskʀedi] *nm*: **jeter le ~ sur** to discredit.

discréditer [diskʀedite] *vt* to discredit.

discret, ète [diskʀɛ, -ɛt] *adj* discreet; (*fig: musique, style*) unobtrusive; (*: endroit*) quiet.

discrètement [diskʀɛtmɑ̃] *adv* discreetly.

discrétion [diskʀesjɔ̃] *nf* discretion; **à la ~ de qn** at sb's discretion; in sb's hands; **à ~** (*boisson etc*) unlimited, as much as one wants.

discrétionnaire [diskʀesjɔnɛʀ] *adj* discretionary.

discrimination [diskʀiminasjɔ̃] *nf* discrimination; **sans ~** indiscriminately.

discriminatoire [diskʀiminatwaʀ] *adj* discriminatory.

disculper [diskylpe] *vt* to exonerate.

discussion [diskysjɔ̃] *nf* discussion.

discutable [diskytabl(ə)] *adj* (*contestable*) doubtful; (*à débattre*) debatable.

discuté, e [diskyte] *adj* controversial.

discuter [diskyte] *vt* (*contester*) to question, dispute; (*débattre: prix*) to discuss ♦ *vi* to talk; (*ergoter*) to argue; **~ de** to discuss.

dise [diz] *etc vb voir* **dire**.

disert, e [dizɛʀ, -ɛʀt(ə)] *adj* loquacious.

disette [dizɛt] *nf* food shortage.

diseuse [dizøz] *nf*: **~ de bonne aventure** fortuneteller.

disgrâce [disgʀɑs] *nf* disgrace; **être en ~** to be in disgrace.

disgracié, e [disgʀasje] *adj* (*en disgrâce*) disgraced.

disgracieux, euse [disgʀasjø, -øz] *adj* ungainly, awkward.

disjoindre [diʒwɛ̃dʀ(ə)] *vt* to take apart; **se ~** *vi* to come apart.

disjoint, e [diʒwɛ̃, -wɛ̃t] *pp de* **disjoindre** ♦ *adj* loose.

disjoncteur [diʒɔ̃ktœʀ] *nm* (*ÉLEC*) circuit breaker.

dislocation [dislɔkasjɔ̃] *nf* dislocation.

disloquer [dislɔke] *vt* (*membre*) to dislocate; (*chaise*) to dismantle; (*troupe*) to disperse; **se ~** *vi* (*parti, empire*) to break up; **se ~ l'épaule** to dislocate one's shoulder.

disons [dizɔ̃] *etc vb voir* **dire**.

disparaître [dispaʀɛtʀ(ə)] *vi* to disappear; (*à la vue*) to vanish, disappear; to be hidden *ou* concealed; (*être manquant*) to go missing, disappear; (*se perdre: traditions etc*) to die out; (*personne: mourir*) to die; **faire ~** (*objet, tache, trace*) to remove; (*personne*) to get rid of.

disparate [dispaʀat] *adj* disparate; (*couleurs*) ill-assorted.

disparité [dispaʀite] *nf* disparity.

disparition [dispaʀisjɔ̃] *nf* disappearance.

disparu, e [dispaʀy] *pp de* **disparaître** ♦ *nm/f* missing person; (*défunt*) departed; **être porté ~** to be reported missing.

dispendieux, euse [dispɑ̃djø, -øz] *adj* extravagant, expensive.

dispensaire [dispɑ̃sɛʀ] *nm* community clinic.

dispense [dispɑ̃s] *nf* exemption; (*permission*) special permission; **~ d'âge** special exemption from age limit.

dispenser [dispɑ̃se] *vt* (*donner*) to lavish, bestow; (*exempter*): **~ qn de** to exempt sb from; **se ~ de** *vt* to avoid, get out of.

disperser [dispɛʀse] *vt* to scatter; (*fig: son attention*) to dissipate; **se ~** *vi* to scatter; (*fig*) to dissipate one's efforts.

dispersion [dispɛʀsjɔ̃] *nf* scattering; (*des efforts*) dissipation.

disponibilité [dispɔnibilite] *nf* availability; (*ADMIN*): **être en ~** to be on leave of absence; **~s** *nfpl* (*COMM*) liquid assets.

disponible [dispɔnibl(ə)] *adj* available.

dispos [dispo] *adj m*: (**frais et**) **~** fresh (as a daisy).

disposé, e [dispoze] *adj* (*d'une certaine manière*) arranged, laid-out; **bien/mal ~** (*humeur*) in a good/bad mood; **bien/mal ~ pour** *ou* **envers qn** well/badly disposed towards sb; **~ à** (*prêt à*) willing *ou* prepared to.

disposer [dispoze] *vt* (*arranger, placer*) to arrange; (*inciter*): **~ qn à qch/faire qch** to dispose *ou* incline sb towards sth/to do sth ♦ *vi*: **vous pouvez ~** you may leave; **~ de** *vt* to have (at one's disposal); **se ~ à faire** to prepare to do, be about to do.

dispositif [dispozitif] *nm* device; (*fig*) system, plan of action; set-up; (*d'un texte de loi*) operative part; **~ de sûreté** safety device.

disposition [dispozisjɔ̃] *nf* (*arrangement*) arrangement, layout; (*humeur*) mood; (*tendance*) tendency; **~s** *nfpl* (*mesures*) steps, measures; (*préparatifs*) arrangements; (*de loi, testament*) provisions; (*aptitudes*) bent *sg*, aptitude *sg*; **à la ~ de qn** at sb's disposal.

disproportion [dispʀɔpɔʀsjɔ̃] *nf* disproportion.

disproportionné, e [dispʀɔpɔʀsjɔne] *adj* disproportionate, out of all proportion.

dispute [dispyt] *nf* quarrel, argument.

disputer [dispyte] *vt* (*match*) to play; (*combat*) to fight; (*course*) to run; **se ~** *vi* to quarrel, have a quarrel; (*match, combat, course*) to take place; **~ qch à qn** to fight with sb for *ou* over sth.

disquaire [diskɛʀ] *nm/f* record dealer.

disqualification [diskalifikasjɔ̃] *nf* disqualification.

disqualifier [diskalifje] *vt* to disqualify; **se ~** *vi* to bring discredit on o.s.

disque [disk(ə)] *nm* (*MUS*) record; (*INFORM*) disk, disc; (*forme, pièce*) disc; (*SPORT*) discus; **~ compact** compact disc; **~ compact interactif** CD-I ®; **~ dur** hard disk; **~ d'embrayage** (*AUTO*) clutch plate; **~ laser** compact disc; **~ de stationnement** parking disc; ~ **système** system disk.

disquette [diskɛt] *nf* diskette, floppy (disk); ~ **(à) simple/double densité** single/double density disk; ~ **une face/double face** single-/double-sided disk.

dissection [disɛksjɔ̃] *nf* dissection.

dissemblable [disɑ̃blabl(ə)] *adj* dissimilar.

dissemblance [disɑ̃blɑ̃s] *nf* dissimilarity, difference.

dissémination [diseminasjɔ̃] *nf* (*voir vb*) scattering; dispersal; (*des armes*) proliferation.

disséminer [disemine] *vt* to scatter; (*troupes: sur un territoire*) to disperse.

dissension [disɑ̃sjɔ̃] *nf* dissension; ~**s** *nfpl* dissension.

disséquer [diseke] *vt* to dissect.

dissertation [disɛrtasjɔ̃] *nf* (*SCOL*) essay.

disserter [disɛrte] *vi*: ~ **sur** to discourse upon.

dissidence [disidɑ̃s] *nf* (*concept*) dissidence; **rejoindre la** ~ to join the dissidents.

dissident, e [disidɑ̃, -ɑ̃t] *adj, nm/f* dissident.

dissimilitude [disimilityd] *nf* dissimilarity.

dissimulateur, trice [disimyltœr, -tris] *adj* dissembling ♦ *nm/f* dissembler.

dissimulation [disimylasjɔ̃] *nf* concealing; (*duplicité*) dissimulation; ~ **de bénéfices/de revenus** concealment of profits/income.

dissimulé, e [disimyle] (*personne: secret*) secretive; (*: fourbe, hypocrite*) deceitful.

dissimuler [disimyle] *vt* to conceal; **se** ~ to conceal o.s.; to be concealed.

dissipation [disipasjɔ̃] *nf* squandering; unruliness; (*débauche*) dissipation.

dissipé, e [disipe] *adj* (*indiscipliné*) unruly.

dissiper [disipe] *vt* to dissipate; (*fortune*) to squander, fritter away; **se** ~ *vi* (*brouillard*) to clear, disperse; (*doutes*) to disappear, melt away; (*élève*) to become undisciplined *ou* unruly.

dissociable [disɔsjabl(ə)] *adj* separable.

dissocier [disɔsje] *vt* to dissociate; **se** ~ *vi* (*éléments, groupe*) to break up, split up; **se** ~ **de** (*groupe, point de vue*) to dissociate o.s. from.

dissolu, e [disɔly] *adj* dissolute.

dissoluble [disɔlybl(ə)] *adj* (*POL: assemblée*) dissolvable.

dissolution [disɔlysjɔ̃] *nf* dissolving; (*POL, JUR*) dissolution.

dissolvant, e [disɔlvɑ̃, -ɑ̃t] *vb voir* **dissoudre** ♦ *nm* (*CHIMIE*) solvent; ~ **(gras)** nail polish remover.

dissonant, e [disɔnɑ̃, -ɑ̃t] *adj* discordant.

dissoudre [disudr(ə)] *vt*, **se** ~ *vi* to dissolve.

dissous, oute [disu, -ut] *pp de* **dissoudre**.

dissuader [disɥade] *vt*: ~ **qn de faire/de qch** to dissuade sb from doing/from sth.

dissuasif, ive [disɥazif, iv] *adj* dissuasive.

dissuasion [disɥazjɔ̃] *nf* dissuasion; **force de** ~ deterrent power.

distance [distɑ̃s] *nf* distance; (*fig: écart*) gap; **à**

~ **at** *ou* **from a distance**; (*mettre en marche, commander*) by remote control; **(situé) à** ~ (*INFORM*) remote; **tenir qn à** ~ to keep sb at a distance; **se tenir à** ~ to keep one's distance; **à une** ~ **de 10 km, à 10 km de** ~ 10 km away, at a distance of 10 km; **à 2 ans de** ~ with a gap of 2 years; **prendre ses** ~**s** to space out; **garder ses** ~**s** to keep one's distance; **tenir la** ~ (*SPORT*) to cover the distance, last the course; ~ **focale** (*PHOTO*) focal length.

distancer [distɑ̃se] *vt* to outdistance, leave behind.

distancier [distɑ̃sje]: **se** ~ *vi* to distance o.s.

distant, e [distɑ̃, -ɑ̃t] *adj* (*réservé*) distant, aloof; (*éloigné*) distant, far away; ~ **de** (*lieu*) far away *ou* a long way from; ~ **de 5 km (d'un lieu)** 5 km away (from a place).

distendre [distɑ̃dr(ə)] *vt*, **se** ~ *vi* to distend.

distillation [distilasjɔ̃] *nf* distillation, distilling.

distillé, e [distile] *adj*: **eau** ~**e** distilled water.

distiller [distile] *vt* to distil; (*fig*) to exude; to elaborate.

distillerie [distilri] *nf* distillery.

distinct, e [distɛ̃(kt), distɛ̃kt(ə)] *adj* distinct.

distinctement [distɛ̃ktəmɑ̃] *adv* distinctly.

distinctif, ive [distɛ̃ktif, -iv] *adj* distinctive.

distinction [distɛ̃ksjɔ̃] *nf* distinction.

distingué, e [distɛ̃ge] *adj* distinguished.

distinguer [distɛ̃ge] *vt* to distinguish; **se** ~ *vi* (*s'illustrer*) to distinguish o.s.; (*différer*): **se** ~ **(de)** to distinguish o.s. *ou* be distinguished (from).

distinguo [distɛ̃go] *nm* distinction.

distorsion [distɔrsjɔ̃] *nf* (*gén*) distorsion; (*fig: déséquilibre*) disparity, imbalance.

distraction [distraksjɔ̃] *nf* (*manque d'attention*) absent-mindedness; (*oubli*) lapse (in concentration *ou* attention); (*détente*) diversion, recreation; (*passe-temps*) distraction, entertainment.

distraire [distrɛr] *vt* (*déranger*) to distract; (*divertir*) to entertain, divert; (*détourner: somme d'argent*) to divert, misappropriate; **se** ~ to amuse *ou* enjoy o.s.

distrait, e [distrɛ, -ɛt] *pp de* **distraire** ♦ *adj* absent-minded.

distraitement [distrɛtmɑ̃] *adv* absent-mindedly.

distrayant, e [distrɛjɑ̃, -ɑ̃t] *vb voir* **distraire** ♦ *adj* entertaining.

distribanque [distribɑ̃k] *nm* cash dispenser.

distribuer [distribɥe] *vt* to distribute; to hand out; (*CARTES*) to deal (out); (*courrier*) to deliver.

distributeur [distribytœr] *nm* (*AUTO, COMM*) distributor; (*automatique*) (vending) machine; ~ **de billets** (*RAIL*) ticket machine; (*BANQUE*) cash dispenser.

distribution [distribysjɔ̃] *nf* distribution; (*postale*) delivery; (*choix d'acteurs*) casting;

circuits de ~ (*COMM*) distribution network; ~ **des prix** (*SCOL*) prize giving.
district [distrik(t)] *nm* district.
dit, e [di, dit] *pp de* **dire ♦** *adj* (*fixé*): **le jour** ~ the arranged day; (*surnommé*): **X,** ~ **Pierrot** X, known as *ou* called Pierrot.
dites [dit] *vb voir* **dire.**
dithyrambique [ditiʀɑ̃bik] *adj* eulogistic.
DIU *sigle m* (= *dispositif intra-utérin*) IUD.
diurétique [djyʀetik] *adj, nm* diuretic.
diurne [djyʀn(ə)] *adj* diurnal, daytime *cpd.*
divagations [divagasjɔ̃] *nfpl* ramblings; ravings.
divaguer [divage] *vi* to ramble; (*malade*) to rave.
divan [divɑ̃] *nm* divan.
divan-lit [divɑ̃li] *nm* divan (bed).
divergence [diveʀʒɑ̃s] *nf* divergence; **des ~s d'opinion au sein de ...** differences of opinion within ....
divergent, e [diveʀʒɑ̃, -ɑ̃t] *adj* divergent.
diverger [diveʀʒe] *vi* to diverge.
divers, e [diveʀ, -eʀs(ə)] *adj* (*varié*) diverse, varied; (*différent*) different, various **♦** *dét* (*plusieurs*) various, several; (*frais*) ~ (*COMM*) sundries, miscellaneous (expenses); *"~"* (*rubrique*) "miscellaneous".
diversement [diveʀsəmɑ̃] *adv* in various *ou* diverse ways.
diversification [diveʀsifikasjɔ̃] *nf* diversification.
diversifier [diveʀsifje] *vt,* **se** ~ *vi* to diversify.
diversion [diveʀsjɔ̃] *nf* diversion; **faire** ~ to create a diversion.
diversité [diveʀsite] *nf* diversity, variety.
divertir [diveʀtiʀ] *vt* to amuse, entertain; **se** ~ to amuse *ou* enjoy o.s.
divertissant, e [diveʀtisɑ̃, -ɑ̃t] *adj* entertaining.
divertissement [diveʀtismɑ̃] *nm* entertainment; (*MUS*) divertimento, divertissement.
dividende [dividɑ̃d] *nm* (*MATH, COMM*) dividend.
divin, e [divɛ̃, -in] *adj* divine; (*fig: excellent*) heavenly, divine.
divinateur, trice [divinatœʀ, -tʀis] *adj* perspicacious.
divinatoire [divinatwaʀ] *adj* (*art, science*) divinatory; **baguette** ~ divining rod.
diviniser [divinize] *vt* to deify.
divinité [divinite] *nf* divinity.
divisé, e [divize] *adj* divided.
diviser [divize] *vt* (*gén, MATH*) to divide; (*morceler, subdiviser*) to divide (up), split (up); **se** ~ **en** to divide into; ~ **par** to divide by.
diviseur [divizœʀ] *nm* (*MATH*) divisor.
divisible [divizibl(ə)] *adj* divisible.
division [divizjɔ̃] *nf* (*gén*) division; ~ **du travail** (*ÉCON*) division of labour.
divisionnaire [divizjɔnɛʀ] *adj*: **commissaire** ~

≈ chief superintendent (*BRIT*), ≈ police chief (*US*).
divorce [divɔʀs(ə)] *nm* divorce.
divorcé, e [divɔʀse] *nm/f* divorcee.
divorcer [divɔʀse] *vi* to get a divorce, get divorced; ~ **de** *ou* **d'avec qn** to divorce sb.
divulgation [divylgasjɔ̃] *nf* disclosure.
divulguer [divylge] *vt* to divulge, disclose.
dix [di, dis, diz] *num* ten.
dix-huit [dizɥit] *num* eighteen.
dix-huitième [dizɥitjɛm] *num* eighteenth.
dixième [dizjɛm] *num* tenth.
dix-neuf [diznœf] *num* nineteen.
dix-neuvième [diznœvjɛm] *num* nineteenth.
dix-sept [disɛt] *num* seventeen.
dix-septième [disɛtjɛm] *num* seventeenth.
dizaine [dizɛn] *nf* (*10*) ten; (*environ 10*): **une** ~ (**de**) about ten, ten or so.
Djakarta [dʒakaʀta] *n* Djakarta.
Djibouti [dʒibuti] *n* Djibouti.
dl *abr* (= *décilitre*) dl.
DM *abr* (= *Deutschmark*) DM.
dm. *abr* (= *décimètre*) dm.
do [do] *nm* (*note*) C; (*en chantant la gamme*) do(h).
docile [dɔsil] *adj* docile.
docilement [dɔsilmɑ̃] *adv* docilely.
docilité [dɔsilite] *nf* docility.
dock [dɔk] *nm* dock; (*hangar, bâtiment*) warehouse.
docker [dɔkɛʀ] *nm* docker.
docte [dɔkt(ə)] *adj* (*péj*) learned.
docteur [dɔktœʀ] *nm* doctor; ~ **en médecine** doctor of medicine.
doctoral, e, aux [dɔktɔʀal, -o] *adj* pompous, bombastic.
doctorat [dɔktɔʀa] *nm*: ~ (**d'Université**) ≈ doctorate; ~ **d'État** ≈ PhD; ~ **de troisième cycle** ≈ doctorate.
doctoresse [dɔktɔʀɛs] *nf* lady doctor.
doctrinaire [dɔktʀinɛʀ] *adj* doctrinaire; (*sentencieux*) pompous, sententious.
doctrinal, e, aux [dɔktʀinal, o] *adj* doctrinal.
doctrine [dɔktʀin] *nf* doctrine.
document [dɔkymɑ̃] *nm* document.
documentaire [dɔkymɑ̃tɛʀ] *adj, nm* documentary.
documentaliste [dɔkymɑ̃talist(ə)] *nm/f* archivist; (*PRESSE, TV*) researcher.
documentation [dɔkymɑ̃tasjɔ̃] *nf* documentation, literature; (*PRESSE, TV: service*) research.
documenté, e [dɔkymɑ̃te] *adj* well-informed, well-documented; well-researched.
documenter [dɔkymɑ̃te] *vt*: **se** ~ (**sur**) to gather information *ou* material (on *ou* about).
Dodécanèse [dɔdekanɛz] *nm* Dodecanese (Islands).
dodeliner [dɔdline] *vi*: ~ **de la tête** to nod one's head gently.
dodo [dɔdo] *nm*: **aller faire** ~ to go to beddy-

dodu – donneur

byes.
dodu, e [dɔdy] *adj* plump.
dogmatique [dɔgmatik] *adj* dogmatic.
dogmatisme [dɔgmatism(ə)] *nm* dogmatism.
dogme [dɔgm(ə)] *nm* dogma.
dogue [dɔg] *nm* mastiff.
doigt [dwa] *nm* finger; **à deux ~s de** within an
ace (*BRIT*) *ou* an inch of; **un ~ de lait/whisky**
a drop of milk/whisky; **désigner** *ou* **montrer**
du ~ to point at; **au ~ et à l'œil** to the letter;
connaître qch sur le bout du ~ to know sth
backwards; **mettre le ~ sur la plaie** (*fig*) to
find the sensitive spot; **~ de pied** toe.
doigté [dwate] *nm* (*MUS*) fingering; (*fig:
habileté*) diplomacy, tact.
doigtier [dwatje] *nm* fingerstall.
dois [dwa] *etc vb voir* **devoir**.
doive [dwav] *etc vb voir* **devoir**.
doléances [dɔleɑ̃s] *nfpl* complaints;
(*réclamations*) grievances.
dolent, e [dɔlɑ̃, -ɑ̃t] *adj* doleful, mournful.
dollar [dɔlaʁ] *nm* dollar.
dolmen [dɔlmɛn] *nm* dolmen.
DOM [deɔɛm, dɔm] *sigle m ou mpl*
= *Département(s) d'outre-mer*.

France has four overseas départements or
DOMs: *French Guiana, Guadeloupe,
Martinique and Réunion. Since 1982 each of
these has also had regional status. France also
has five overseas territories or* **TOMs**: *Austral
and Antarctic French territories, French
Polynesia, Mayotte, New Caledonia and Wallis
and Futuna. Citizens of both DOMs and TOMs
have French nationality.*

---

domaine [dɔmɛn] *nm* estate, property; (*fig*)
domain, field; **tomber dans le ~ public** (*livre
etc*) to be out of copyright; **dans tous les ~s**
in all areas.
domanial, e, aux [dɔmanjal, -o] *adj* national,
state *cpd*.
dôme [dom] *nm* dome.
domestication [dɔmɛstikasjɔ̃] *nf* (*voir
domestiquer*) domestication; harnessing.
domesticité [dɔmɛstisite] *nf* (*domestic*) staff.
domestique [dɔmɛstik] *adj* domestic ♦ *nm/f*
servant, domestic.
domestiquer [dɔmɛstike] *vt* to domesticate;
(*vent, marées*) to harness.
domicile [dɔmisil] *nm* home, place of
residence; **à ~** at home; **élire ~ à** to take up
residence in; **sans ~ fixe** of no fixed abode;
~ conjugal marital home; **~ légal** domicile.
domicilié, e [dɔmisilje] *adj*: **être ~ à** to have
one's home in *ou* at.
dominant, e [dɔminɑ̃, -ɑ̃t] *adj* dominant; (*plus
important*) predominant ♦ *nf* (*caractéristique*)
dominant characteristic; (*couleur*) dominant
colour.
dominateur, trice [dɔminatœʁ, -tʁis] *adj*
dominating; (*qui aime à dominer*)

domineering.
domination [dɔminɑsjɔ̃] *nf* domination.
dominer [dɔmine] *vt* to dominate; (*passions
etc*) to control, master; (*surpasser*) to
outclass, surpass; (*surplomber*) to tower
above, dominate ♦ *vi* to be in the dominant
position; **se ~** to control o.s.
dominicain, e [dɔminikɛ̃, -ɛn] *adj* Dominican.
dominical, e, aux [dɔminikal, -o] *adj* Sunday
cpd, dominical.
Dominique [dɔminik] *nf*: **la ~** Dominica.
domino [dɔmino] *nm* domino; **~s** *nmpl* (*jeu*)
dominoes *sg*.
dommage [dɔmaʒ] *nm* (*préjudice*) harm,
injury; (*dégâts, pertes*) damage *no pl*; **c'est ~**
de faire/que it's a shame *ou* pity to do/that;
~s corporels physical injury.
dommages-intérêts [dɔmaʒ(əz)ɛ̃teʁɛ] *nmpl*
damages.
dompter [dɔ̃te] *vt* to tame.
dompteur, euse [dɔ̃tœʁ, -øz] *nm/f* trainer; (*de
lion*) liontamer.
DOM-TOM [dɔmtɔm] *sigle m ou mpl* =
*Département(s) d'outre-mer/Territoire(s)
d'outre-mer*.
don [dɔ̃] *nm* (*cadeau*) gift; (*charité*) donation;
(*aptitude*) gift, talent; **avoir des ~s pour** to
have a gift *ou* talent for; **faire ~ de** to make
a gift of; **~ en argent** cash donation.
donateur, trice [dɔnatœʁ, -tʁis] *nm/f* donor.
donation [dɔnɑsjɔ̃] *nf* donation.
donc [dɔ̃k] *conj* therefore, so; (*après une
digression*) so, then; (*intensif*): **voilà ~ la
solution** so there's the solution; **je disais ~
que ...** as I was saying, ...; **venez ~ dîner à la
maison** do come for dinner; **allons ~!** come
now!; **faites ~** go ahead.
donjon [dɔ̃ʒɔ̃] *nm* keep.
don Juan [dɔ̃ʒɥɑ̃] *nm* Don Juan.
donnant, e [dɔnɑ̃, -ɑ̃t] *adj*: **~, ~** fair's fair.
donne [dɔn] *nf* (*CARTES*): **il y a mauvaise** *ou*
fausse ~ there's been a misdeal.
donné, e [dɔne] *adj* (*convenu*) given; (*pas cher*)
dirt cheap, very cheap ♦ *nf* (*MATH, INFORM,
gén*) datum (*pl* data); **c'est ~** it's a gift; **étant
~ ... given ....**
donner [dɔne] *vt* to give; (*vieux habits etc*) to
give away; (*spectacle*) to put on; (*film*) to
show; **~ qch à qn** to give sb sth, give sth to
sb; **~ sur** (*suj: fenêtre, chambre*) to look (out)
onto; **~ dans** (*piège etc*) to fall into; **faire ~
l'infanterie** (*MIL*) to send in the infantry; **~
l'heure à qn** to tell sb the time; **~ le ton** (*fig*)
to set the tone; **~ à penser/entendre que ...**
to make one think/give one to understand
that ...; **se ~ à fond (à son travail)** to give
one's all (to one's work), devote o.s. heart
and soul (to one's work); **se ~ du mal** *ou* **de
la peine (pour faire qch)** to go to a lot of
trouble (to do sth); **s'en ~ à cœur joie** (*fam*)
to have a great time (of it).
donneur, euse [dɔnœʁ, -øz] *nm/f* (*MÉD*) donor;

(*CARTES*) dealer; ~ **de sang** blood donor.

=============================== *MOT-CLÉ*

dont [dɔ̃] *pron relatif* **1** (*appartenance: objets*) whose, of which; (: *êtres animés*) whose; **la maison ~ le toit est rouge** the house the roof of which is red, the house whose roof is red; **l'homme ~ je connais la sœur** the man whose sister I know

2 (*parmi lesquel(le)s*): **2 livres, ~ l'un est ... 2** books, one of which is ...; **il y avait plusieurs personnes, ~ Gabrielle** there were several people, among them Gabrielle; **10 blessés, ~ 2 grièvement** 10 injured, 2 of them seriously

3 (*complément d'adjectif, de verbe*): **le fils ~ il est si fier** the son he's so proud of; **ce ~ je parle** what I'm talking about; **la façon ~ il l'a fait** the way (in which) he did it.

donzelle [dɔ̃zɛl] *nf* (*péj*) young madam.
dopage [dɔpaʒ] *nm* doping.
dopant [dɔpɑ̃] *nm* dope.
doper [dɔpe] *vt* to dope; **se ~** to take dope.
doping [dɔpiŋ] *nm* doping; (*excitant*) dope.
dorade [dɔrad] *nf* = **daurade**.
doré, e [dɔre] *adj* golden; (*avec dorure*) gilt, gilded.
dorénavant [dɔrenavɑ̃] *adv* from now on, henceforth.
dorer [dɔre] *vt* (*cadre*) to gild; (**faire**) ~ (*CULIN*) to brown; (: *gâteau*) to glaze; **se ~ au soleil** to sunbathe; ~ **la pilule à qn** to sugar the pill for sb.
dorloter [dɔrlɔte] *vt* to pamper, cosset (*BRIT*); **se faire ~** to be pampered *ou* cosseted.
dormant, e [dɔrmɑ̃, -ɑ̃t] *adj*: **eau ~e** still water.
dorme [dɔrm(ə)] *etc vb voir* **dormir**.
dormeur, euse [dɔrmœr, -øz] *nm/f* sleeper.
dormir [dɔrmir] *vi* to sleep; (*être endormi*) to be asleep; ~ **à poings fermés** to sleep very soundly.
dorsal, e, aux [dɔrsal, -o] *adj* dorsal; *voir* **rouleau**.
dortoir [dɔrtwar] *nm* dormitory.
dorure [dɔryr] *nf* gilding.
doryphore [dɔrifɔr] *nm* Colorado beetle.
dos [do] *nm* back; (*de livre*) spine; **"voir au ~"** "see over"; **robe décolletée dans le ~** low-backed dress; **de ~** from the back, from behind; ~ **à ~** back to back; **sur le ~** on one's back; **à ~ de chameau** riding on a camel; **avoir bon ~** to be a good excuse; **se mettre qn à ~** to turn sb against one.
dosage [dozaʒ] *nm* mixture.
dos-d'âne [dodɑn] *nm* humpback; **pont en ~** humpbacked bridge.
dose [doz] *nf* (*MÉD*) dose; **forcer la ~** (*fig*) to overstep the mark.
doser [doze] *vt* to measure out; (*mélanger*) to mix in the correct proportions; (*fig*) to

expend in the right amounts *ou* proportions; to strike a balance between.
doseur [dozœr] *nm* measure; **bouchon ~** measuring cap.
dossard [dosar] *nm* number (*worn by competitor*).
dossier [dosje] *nm* (*renseignements, fichier*) file; (*enveloppe*) folder, file; (*de chaise*) back; (*PRESSE*) feature; **le ~ social/monétaire** (*fig*) the social/financial question; ~ **suspendu** suspension file.
dot [dɔt] *nf* dowry.
dotation [dɔtasjɔ̃] *nf* block grant; endowment.
doté, e [dɔte] *adj*: ~ **de** equipped with.
doter [dɔte] *vt*: ~ **qn/qch de** to equip sb/sth with.
douairière [dwɛrjɛr] *nf* dowager.
douane [dwan] *nf* (*poste, bureau*) customs *pl*; (*taxes*) (customs) duty; **passer la ~** to go through customs; **en ~** (*marchandises, entrepôt*) bonded.
douanier, ière [dwanje, -jɛr] *adj* customs *cpd*
♦ *nm* customs officer.
doublage [dublaʒ] *nm* (*CINÉ*) dubbing.
double [dubl(ə)] *adj, adv* double ♦ *nm* (*2 fois plus*): **le ~ (de)** twice as much (*ou* many) (as), double the amount (*ou* number) (of); (*autre exemplaire*) duplicate, copy; (*sosie*) double; (*TENNIS*) doubles *sg*; **voir ~** to see double; **en ~ (exemplaire)** in duplicate; **faire ~ emploi** to be redundant; **à ~ sens** with a double meaning; **à ~ tranchant** two-edged; ~ **carburateur** twin carburettor; **à ~s commandes** dual-control; ~ **messieurs/ mixte** men's/mixed doubles *sg*; ~ **toit** (*de tente*) fly sheet; ~ **vue** second sight.
doublé, e [duble] *adj* (*vêtement*): ~ **(de)** lined (with).
doublement [dubləmɑ̃] *nm* doubling; twofold increase ♦ *adv* doubly; (*pour deux raisons*) in two ways, on two counts.
doubler [duble] *vt* (*multiplier par 2*) to double; (*vêtement*) to line; (*dépasser*) to overtake, pass; (*film*) to dub; (*acteur*) to stand in for
♦ *vi* to double, increase twofold; **se ~ de** to be coupled with; ~ **(la classe)** (*SCOL*) to repeat a year; ~ **un cap** (*NAVIG*) to round a cape; (*fig*) to get over a hurdle.
doublure [dublyr] *nf* lining; (*CINÉ*) stand-in.
douce [dus] *adj f voir* **doux**.
douceâtre [dusɑtr(ə)] *adj* sickly sweet.
doucement [dusmɑ̃] *adv* gently; (*à voix basse*) softly; (*lentement*) slowly.
doucereux, euse [dusrø, -øz] *adj* (*péj*) sugary.
douceur [dusœr] *nf* softness; sweetness; mildness; gentleness; ~**s** *nfpl* (*friandises*) sweets (*BRIT*), candy *sg* (*US*); **en ~** gently.
douche [duʃ] *nf* shower; ~**s** *nfpl* shower room *sg*; **prendre une ~** to have *ou* take a shower; ~ **écossaise** (*fig*), ~ **froide** (*fig*) let-down.

doucher – droit

doucher [duʃe] *vt:* ~ **qn** to give sb a shower; (*mouiller*) to drench sb; (*fig*) to give sb a telling-off; **se** ~ to have *ou* take a shower.
doudoune [dudun] *nf* padded jacket; (*fam*) boob.
doué, e [dwe] *adj* gifted, talented; ~ **de** endowed with; **être** ~ **pour** to have a gift for.
douille [duj] *nf* (*ÉLEC*) socket; (*de projectile*) case.
douillet, te [dujɛ, -ɛt] *adj* cosy; (*péj*) soft.
douleur [dulœʀ] *nf* pain; (*chagrin*) grief, distress; **ressentir des** ~**s** to feel pain; **il a eu la** ~ **de perdre son père** he suffered the grief of losing his father.
douloureux, euse [duluʀø, -øz] *adj* painful.
doute [dut] *nm* doubt; **sans** ~ *adv* no doubt; (*probablement*) probably; **sans nul** *ou* **aucun** ~ without (a) doubt; **hors de** ~ beyond doubt; **nul** ~ **que** there's no doubt that; **mettre en** ~ to call into question; **mettre en** ~ **que** to question whether.
douter [dute] *vt* to doubt; ~ **de** *vt* (*allié*) to doubt, have (one's) doubts about; (*résultat*) to be doubtful of; ~ **que** to doubt whether *ou* if; **j'en doute** I have my doubts; **se** ~ **de qch/que** to suspect sth/that; **je m'en doutais** I suspected as much; **il ne se doutait de rien** he didn't suspect a thing.
douteux, euse [dutø, -øz] *adj* (*incertain*) doubtful; (*discutable*) dubious, questionable; (*péj*) dubious-looking.
douve [duv] *nf* (*de château*) moat; (*de tonneau*) stave.
Douvres [duvʀ(ə)] *n* Dover.
doux, douce [du, dus] *adj* (*lisse, moelleux, pas vif: couleur, non calcaire: eau*) soft; (*sucré, agréable*) sweet; (*peu fort: moutarde etc, clément: climat*) mild; (*pas brusque*) gentle; **en douce** (*partir etc*) on the quiet.
douzaine [duzɛn] *nf* (*12*) dozen; (*environ 12*): **une** ~ (**de**) a dozen or so, twelve or so.
douze [duz] *num* twelve; **les D**~ (*membres de la CEE*) the Twelve.
douzième [duzjɛm] *num* twelfth.
doyen, ne [dwajɛ̃, -ɛn] *nm/f* (*en âge, ancienneté*) most senior member; (*de faculté*) dean.
DPLG *sigle* (= *diplômé par le gouvernement*) *extra certificate for architects, engineers etc*.
Dr *abr* (= *docteur*) Dr.
dr. *abr* (= *droit(e)*) R, r.
draconien, ne [dʀakɔnjɛ̃, -ɛn] *adj* draconian, stringent.
dragage [dʀagaʒ] *nm* dredging.
dragée [dʀaʒe] *nf* sugared almond; (*MÉD*) (sugar-coated) pill.
dragéifié, e [dʀaʒeifje] *adj* (*MÉD*) sugar-coated.
dragon [dʀagɔ̃] *nm* dragon.
drague [dʀag] *nf* (*filet*) dragnet; (*bateau*) dredger.

draguer [dʀage] *vt* (*rivière: pour nettoyer*) to dredge; (*: pour trouver qch*) to drag; (*fam*) to try and pick up, chat up (*BRIT*) ♦ *vi* (*fam*) to try and pick sb up, chat sb up (*BRIT*).
dragueur [dʀagœʀ] *nm* (*aussi:* ~ **de mines**) minesweeper; (*fam*): **quel** ~! he's a great one for picking up girls!
drain [dʀɛ̃] *nm* (*MÉD*) drain.
drainage [dʀɛnaʒ] *nm* drainage.
drainer [dʀene] *vt* to drain; (*fig: visiteurs, région*) to drain off.
dramatique [dʀamatik] *adj* dramatic; (*tragique*) tragic ♦ *nf* (*TV*) (television) drama.
dramatisation [dʀamatizasjɔ̃] *nf* dramatization.
dramatiser [dʀamatize] *vt* to dramatize.
dramaturge [dʀamatyʀʒ(ə)] *nm* dramatist, playwright.
drame [dʀam] *nm* (*THÉÂT*) drama; (*catastrophe*) drama, tragedy; ~ **familial** family drama.
drap [dʀa] *nm* (*de lit*) sheet; (*tissu*) woollen fabric; ~ **de plage** beach towel.
drapé [dʀape] *nm* (*d'un vêtement*) hang.
drapeau, x [dʀapo] *nm* flag; **sous les** ~**x** with the colours (*BRIT*) *ou* colors (*US*), in the army.
draper [dʀape] *vt* to drape; (*robe, jupe*) to arrange.
draperies [dʀapʀi] *nfpl* hangings.
drap-housse, *pl* **draps-housses** [dʀaus] *nm* fitted sheet.
drapier [dʀapje] *nm* (*woollen*) cloth manufacturer; (*marchand*) clothier.
drastique [dʀastik] *adj* drastic.
dressage [dʀɛsaʒ] *nm* training.
dresser [dʀese] *vt* (*mettre vertical, monter: tente*) to put up, erect; (*fig: liste, bilan, contrat*) to draw up; (*animal*) to train; **se** ~ *vi* (*falaise, obstacle*) to stand; (*avec grandeur, menace*) to tower (up); (*personne*) to draw o.s. up; ~ **l'oreille** to prick up one's ears; ~ **la table** to set *ou* lay the table; ~ **qn contre qn d'autre** to set sb against sb else; ~ **un procès-verbal** *ou* **une contravention à qn** to book sb.
dresseur, euse [dʀɛsœʀ, -øz] *nm/f* trainer.
dressoir [dʀɛswaʀ] *nm* dresser.
dribbler [dʀible] *vt, vi* (*SPORT*) to dribble.
drille [dʀij] *nm*: **joyeux** ~ cheerful sort.
drogue [dʀɔg] *nf* drug; **la** ~ drugs *pl*; ~ **dure/douce** hard/soft drugs *pl*.
drogué, e [dʀɔge] *nm/f* drug addict.
droguer [dʀɔge] *vt* (*victime*) to drug; (*malade*) to give drugs to; **se** ~ (*aux stupéfiants*) to take drugs; (*péj: de médicaments*) to dose o.s. up.
droguerie [dʀɔgʀi] *nf* ≈ hardware shop (*BRIT*) *ou* store (*US*).
droguiste [dʀɔgist(ə)] *nm* ≈ keeper (*ou* owner) of a hardware shop *ou* store.
droit, e [dʀwa, dʀwat] *adj* (*non courbe*) straight; (*vertical*) upright, straight; (*fig: loyal, franc*) upright, straight(forward);

(*opposé à gauche*) right, right-hand ♦ *adv* straight ♦ *nm* (*prérogative, BOXE*) right; (*taxe*) duty, tax; (: *d'inscription*) fee; (*lois, branche*): **le ~ law** ♦ *nf* (*POL*) right (wing); (*ligne*) straight line; **~ au but** *ou* **au fait/cœur** straight to the point/heart; **avoir le ~ de** to be allowed to; **avoir ~ à** to be entitled to; **être en ~ de** to have a *ou* the right to; **faire ~ à** to grant, accede to; **être dans son ~ to** be within one's rights; **à bon ~** (*justement*) with good reason; **de quel ~?** by what right?; **à qui de ~** to whom it may concern; **à ~ on** the right; (*direction*) (to the) right; **à ~e de** to the right of; **de ~e** (*POL*) right-wing; **~ d'auteur** copyright; **avoir ~ de cité (dans)** (*fig*) to belong (to); **~ coutumier** common law; **~ de regard** right of access *ou* inspection; **~ de réponse** right to reply; **~ de visite** (right of) access; **~ de vote** (right to) vote; **~s d'auteur** royalties; **~s de douane** customs duties; **~s de l'homme** human rights; **~s d'inscription** enrolment *ou* registration fees.

droitement [dʀwatmɑ̃] *adv* (*agir*) uprightly.

droitier, ière [dʀwatje, -jɛʀ] *nm/f* right-handed person.

droiture [dʀwatyʀ] *nf* uprightness, straightness.

drôle [dʀol] *adj* (*amusant*) funny, amusing; (*bizarre*) funny, peculiar; **un ~ de ...** (*bizarre*) a strange *ou* funny ...; (*intensif*) an incredible ..., a terrific ....

drôlement [dʀolmɑ̃] *adv* funnily; peculiarly; (*très*) terribly, awfully; **il fait ~ froid** it's awfully cold.

drôlerie [dʀolʀi] *nf* funniness; funny thing.

dromadaire [dʀɔmadɛʀ] *nm* dromedary.

dru, e [dʀy] *adj* (*cheveux*) thick, bushy; (*pluie*) heavy ♦ *adv* (*pousser*) thickly; (*tomber*) heavily.

drugstore [dʀœgstɔʀ] *nm* drugstore.

druide [dʀɥid] *nm* Druid.

ds *abr* = **dans**.

DST *sigle f* (= *Direction de la surveillance du territoire*) *internal security service*, ≈ MI5 (*BRIT*)

DT *sigle m* (= *diphtérie tétanos*) *vaccine*.

DTCP *sigle m* (= *diphtérie tétanos coqueluche polio*) *vaccine*.

DTP *sigle m* (= *diphtérie tétanos polio*) *vaccine*.

DTTAB *sigle m* (= *diphtérie tétanos typhoïde A et B*) *vaccine*.

du [dy] *prép* + *dét, dét voir* **de**.

dû, due [dy] *pp de* **devoir** ♦ *adj* (*somme*) owing, owed; (: *venant à échéance*) due; (*causé par*): **~ à** due to ♦ *nm* due; (*somme*) dues *pl*.

dualisme [dɥalism(ə)] *nm* dualism.

Dubaï, Dubay [dybaj] *n* Dubai.

dubitatif, ive [dybitatif, -iv] *adj* doubtful, dubious.

Dublin [dyblɛ̃] *n* Dublin.

duc [dyk] *nm* duke.

duché [dyʃe] *nm* dukedom, duchy.

duchesse [dyʃɛs] *nf* duchess.

DUEL [dyɛl] *sigle m* = *Diplôme universitaire d'études littéraires*.

duel [dɥɛl] *nm* duel.

DUES [dyes] *sigle m* = *Diplôme universitaire d'études scientifiques*.

duettiste [dɥetist(ə)] *nm/f* duettist.

duffel-coat [dœfœlkot] *nm* duffelcoat.

dûment [dymɑ̃] *adv* duly.

dumping [dœmpiŋ] *nm* dumping.

dune [dyn] *nf* dune.

Dunkerque [dœkɛʀk] *n* Dunkirk.

duo [dɥo] *nm* (*MUS*) duet; (*fig: couple*) duo, pair.

dupe [dyp] *nf* dupe ♦ *adj*: **(ne pas) être ~ de** (not) to be taken in by.

duper [dype] *vt* to dupe, deceive.

duperie [dypʀi] *nf* deception, dupery.

duplex [dyplɛks] *nm* (*appartement*) split-level apartment, duplex; (*TV*): **émission en ~** link-up.

duplicata [dyplikata] *nm* duplicate.

duplicateur [dyplikatœʀ] *nm* duplicator; **~ à alcool** spirit duplicator.

duplicité [dyplisite] *nf* duplicity.

duquel [dykɛl] *prép* + *pron voir* **lequel**.

dur, e [dyʀ] *adj* (*pierre, siège, travail, problème*) hard; (*lumière, voix, climat*) harsh; (*sévère*) hard, harsh; (*cruel*) hard(-hearted); (*porte, col*) stiff; (*viande*) tough ♦ *adv* hard ♦ *nf*: **à la ~e** rough; **mener la vie ~e à qn** to give sb a hard time; **~ d'oreille** hard of hearing.

durabilité [dyʀabilite] *nf* durability.

durable [dyʀabl(ə)] *adj* lasting.

durablement [dyʀabləmɑ̃] *adv* for the long term.

durant [dyʀɑ̃] *prép* (*au cours de*) during; (*pendant*) for; **~ des mois, des mois ~** for months.

durcir [dyʀsiʀ] *vt, vi*, **se ~** *vi* to harden.

durcissement [dyʀsismɑ̃] *nm* hardening.

durée [dyʀe] *nf* length; (*d'une pile etc*) life; (*déroulement: des opérations etc*) duration; **pour une ~ illimitée** for an unlimited length of time; **de courte ~** (*séjour, répit*) brief, short-term; **de longue ~** (*effet*) long-term; **pile de longue ~** long-life battery.

durement [dyʀmɑ̃] *adv* harshly.

durent [dyʀ] *vb voir* **devoir**.

durer [dyʀe] *vi* to last.

dureté [dyʀte] *nf* (*voir dur*) hardness; harshness; stiffness; toughness.

durillon [dyʀijɔ̃] *nm* callus.

durit [dyʀit] *nf* ® (car radiator) hose.

DUT *sigle m* = *Diplôme universitaire de technologie*.

dut [dy] *etc vb voir* **devoir**.

duvet [dyvɛ] *nm* down; (*sac de couchage en*) **~** down-filled sleeping bag.

duveteux, euse [dyvtø, -øz] *adj* downy.

dynamique [dinamik] *adj* dynamic.

dynamiser [dinamize] *vt* to pep up, enliven; (*équipe, service*) to inject some dynamism into.

dynamisme [dinamism(ə)] *nm* dynamism.

dynamite [dinamit] *nf* dynamite.

dynamiter [dinamite] *vt* to (blow up with) dynamite.

dynamo [dinamo] *nf* dynamo.

dynastie [dinasti] *nf* dynasty.

dysenterie [disɑ̃tʀi] *nf* dysentery.

dyslexie [disleksi] *nf* dyslexia, word blindness.

dyslexique [disleksik] *adj* dyslexic.

dyspepsie [dispɛpsi] *nf* dyspepsia.

E e

E, e [ə] *nm inv* E, e ♦ *abr* (= *Est*) E; **E comme Eugène** E for Edward (*BRIT*) *ou* Easy (*US*).

EAO *sigle m* (= *enseignement assisté par ordinateur*) CAL (= *computer-aided learning*).

EAU *sigle mpl* (= *Émirats arabes unis*) UAE (= *United Arab Emirates*).

eau, x [o] *nf* water ♦ *nfpl* waters; **prendre l'~** (*chaussure etc*) to leak, let in water; **prendre les ~x** to take the waters; **faire ~** to leak; **tomber à l'~** (*fig*) to fall through; **à l'~ de rose** slushy, sentimental; **~ bénite** holy water; **~ de Cologne** eau de Cologne; **~ courante** running water; **~ distillée** distilled water; **~ douce** fresh water; **~ de Javel** bleach; **~ lourde** heavy water; **~ minérale** mineral water; **~ oxygénée** hydrogen peroxide; **~ plate** still water; **~ de pluie** rainwater; **~ salée** salt water; **~ de toilette** toilet water; **~x ménagères** dirty water (*from washing up etc*); **~x territoriales** territorial waters; **~x usées** liquid waste.

eau-de-vie, *pl* **eaux-de-vie** [odvi] *nf* brandy.

eau-forte, *pl* **eaux-fortes** [ofɔʀt(ə)] *nf* etching.

ébahi, e [ebai] *adj* dumbfounded, flabbergasted.

ébahir [ebaiʀ] *vt* to astonish, astound.

ébats [eba] *vb voir* **ébattre** ♦ *nmpl* frolics, gambols.

ébattre [ebatʀ(ə)]: **s'~** *vi* to frolic.

ébauche [eboʃ] *nf* (*rough*) outline, sketch.

ébaucher [eboʃe] *vt* to sketch out, outline; (*fig*): **~ un sourire/geste** to give a hint of a smile/make a slight gesture; **s'~** *vi* to take shape.

ébène [ebɛn] *nf* ebony.

ébéniste [ebenist(ə)] *nm* cabinetmaker.

ébénisterie [ebenistʀi] *nf* cabinetmaking;

(*bâti*) cabinetwork.

éberlué, e [ebɛʀlɥe] *adj* astounded, flabbergasted.

éblouir [ebluiʀ] *vt* to dazzle.

éblouissant, e [ebluisɑ̃, -ɑ̃t] *adj* dazzling.

éblouissement [ebluismɑ̃] *nm* dazzle; (*faiblesse*) dizzy turn.

ébonite [ebɔnit] *nf* vulcanite.

éborgner [ebɔʀɲe] *vt*: **~ qn** to blind sb in one eye.

éboueur [ebwœʀ] *nm* dustman (*BRIT*), garbageman (*US*).

ébouillanter [ebujɑ̃te] *vt* to scald; (*CULIN*) to blanch; **s'~** to scald o.s.

éboulement [ebulmɑ̃] *nm* falling rocks *pl*, rock fall; (*amas*) heap of boulders *etc*.

ébouler [ebule]: **s'~** *vi* to crumble, collapse.

éboulis [ebuli] *nmpl* fallen rocks.

ébouriffé, e [eburife] *adj* tousled, ruffled.

ébouriffer [eburife] *vt* to tousle, ruffle.

ébranlement [ebʀɑ̃lmɑ̃] *nm* shaking.

ébranler [ebʀɑ̃le] *vt* to shake; (*rendre instable: mur, santé*) to weaken; **s'~** *vi* (*partir*) to move off.

ébrécher [ebʀeʃe] *vt* to chip.

ébriété [ebʀijete] *nf*: **en état d'~** in a state of intoxication.

ébrouer [ebʀue]: **s'~** *vi* (*souffler*) to snort; (*s'agiter*) to shake o.s.

ébruiter [ebʀɥite] *vt*, **s'~** *vi* to spread.

ébullition [ebylisjɔ̃] *nf* boiling point; **en ~** boiling; (*fig*) in an uproar.

écaille [ekɑj] *nf* (*de poisson*) scale; (*de coquillage*) shell; (*matière*) tortoiseshell; (*de roc etc*) flake.

écaillé, e [ekɑje] *adj* (*peinture*) flaking.

écailler [ekɑje] *vt* (*poisson*) to scale; (*huître*) to open; **s'~** *vi* to flake *ou* peel (off).

écarlate [ekaʀlat] *adj* scarlet.

écarquiller [ekaʀkije] *vt*: **~ les yeux** to stare wide-eyed.

écart [ekaʀ] *nm* gap; (*embardée*) swerve; (*saut*) sideways leap; (*fig*) deviation; **à l'~** *adv* out of the way; **à l'~ de** *prép* away from; (*fig*) out of; **faire le grand ~** (*DANSE, GYMNASTIQUE*) to do the splits; **~ de conduite** misdemeanour.

écarté, e [ekaʀte] *adj* (*lieu*) out-of-the-way, remote; (*ouvert*): **les jambes ~es** legs apart; **les bras ~s** arms outstretched.

écarteler [ekaʀtəle] *vt* to quarter; (*fig*) to tear.

écartement [ekaʀtəmɑ̃] *nm* space, gap; (*RAIL*) gauge.

écarter [ekaʀte] *vt* (*séparer*) to move apart, separate; (*éloigner*) to push back, move away; (*ouvrir: bras, jambes*) to spread, open; (*: rideau*) to draw (back); (*éliminer: candidat, possibilité*) to dismiss; (*CARTES*) to discard; **s'~** *vi* to part; (*personne*) to move away; **s'~ de** to wander from.

ecchymose [ekimoz] *nf* bruise.

ecclésiastique [eklezjastik] *adj* ecclesiastical

♦ *nm* ecclesiastic.

écervelé, e [esɛʀvəle] *adj* scatterbrained, featherbrained.

ECG *sigle m* (= *électrocardiogramme*) ECG.

échafaud [eʃafo] *nm* scaffold.

échafaudage [eʃafodaʒ] *nm* scaffolding; (*fig*) heap, pile.

échafauder [eʃafode] *vt* (*plan*) to construct.

échalas [eʃala] *nm* stake, pole; (*personne*) beanpole.

échalote [eʃalɔt] *nf* shallot.

échancré, e [eʃɑ̃kʀe] *adj* (*robe, corsage*) low-necked; (*côte*) indented.

échancrure [eʃɑ̃kʀyʀ] *nf* (*de robe*) scoop neckline; (*de côte, arête rocheuse*) indentation.

échange [eʃɑ̃ʒ] *nm* exchange; **en ~** in exchange; **en ~ de** in exchange *ou* return for; **libre ~** free trade; **~ de lettres/ politesses/vues** exchange of letters/ civilities/views; **~s commerciaux** trade; **~s culturels** cultural exchanges.

échangeable [eʃɑ̃ʒabl(ə)] *adj* exchangeable.

échanger [eʃɑ̃ʒe] *vt*: **~ qch (contre)** to exchange sth (for).

échangeur [eʃɑ̃ʒœʀ] *nm* (*AUTO*) interchange.

échantillon [eʃɑ̃tijɔ̃] *nm* sample.

échantillonnage [eʃɑ̃tijɔnaʒ] *nm* selection of samples.

échappatoire [eʃapatwaʀ] *nf* way out.

échappée [eʃape] *nf* (*vue*) vista; (*CYCLISME*) breakaway.

échappement [eʃapmɑ̃] *nm* (*AUTO*) exhaust; **~ libre** cutout.

échapper [eʃape]: **~ à** *vt* (*gardien*) to escape (from); (*punition, péril*) to escape; **~ à qn** (*détail, sens*) to escape sb; (*objet qu'on tient: aussi:* **~ des mains de qn**) to slip out of sb's hands; **laisser ~** to let fall; (*cri etc*) to let out; **s'~** *vi* to escape; **l'~ belle** to have a narrow escape.

écharde [eʃaʀd(ə)] *nf* splinter (of wood).

écharpe [eʃaʀp(ə)] *nf* scarf (*pl* scarves); (*de maire*) sash; (*MÉD*) sling; **prendre en ~** (*dans une collision*) to hit sideways on.

écharper [eʃaʀpe] *vt* to tear to pieces.

échasse [eʃas] *nf* stilt.

échassier [eʃasje] *nm* wader.

échauder [eʃode] *vt*: **se faire ~** (*fig*) to get one's fingers burnt.

échauffement [eʃofmɑ̃] *nm* overheating; (*SPORT*) warm-up.

échauffer [eʃofe] *vt* (*métal, moteur*) to overheat; (*fig: exciter*) to fire, excite; **s'~** *vi* (*SPORT*) to warm up; (*discussion*) to become heated.

échauffourée [eʃofuʀe] *nf* clash, brawl; (*MIL*) skirmish.

échéance [eʃeɑ̃s] *nf* (*d'un paiement: date*) settlement date; (*: somme due*) financial commitment(s); (*fig*) deadline; **à brève/ longue ~** *adj* short-/long-term ♦ *adv* in the short/long term.

échéancier [eʃeɑ̃sje] *nm* schedule.

échéant [eʃeɑ̃]: **le cas ~** *adv* if the case arises.

échec [eʃɛk] *nm* failure; (*ÉCHECS*): **~ et mat/au roi** checkmate/check; **~s** *nmpl* (*jeu*) chess *sg*; **mettre en ~** to put in check; **tenir en ~** to hold in check; **faire ~ à** to foil, thwart.

échelle [eʃɛl] *nf* ladder; (*fig, d'une carte*) scale; **à l'~** de on the scale of; **sur une grande/ petite ~** on a large/small scale; **faire la courte ~ à qn** to give sb a leg up; **~ de corde** rope ladder.

échelon [eʃlɔ̃] *nm* (*d'échelle*) rung; (*ADMIN*) grade.

échelonner [eʃlɔne] *vt* to space out, spread out; (*versement*) **échelonné** (payment) by instalments.

écheveau, x [ɛʃvo] *nm* skein, hank.

échevelé, e [eʃəvle] *adj* tousled, dishevelled; (*fig*) wild, frenzied.

échine [eʃin] *nf* backbone, spine.

échiner [eʃine]: **s'~** *vi* (*se fatiguer*) to work o.s. to the bone.

échiquier [eʃikje] *nm* chessboard.

écho [eko] *nm* echo; **~s** *nmpl* (*potins*) gossip *sg*, rumours; (*PRESSE: rubrique*) "news in brief"; **rester sans ~** (*suggestion etc*) to come to nothing; **se faire l'~ de** to repeat, spread about.

échographie [ekɔgʀafi] *nf* ultrasound (scan).

échoir [eʃwaʀ] *vi* (*dette*) to fall due; (*délais*) to expire; **~ à** *vt* to fall to.

échoppe [eʃɔp] *nf* stall, booth.

échouer [eʃwe] *vi* to fail; (*débris etc : sur la plage*) to be washed up; (*aboutir: personne dans un café etc*) to arrive ♦ *vt* (*bateau*) to ground; **s'~** *vi* to run aground.

échu, e [eʃy] *pp de* **échoir** ♦ *adj* due, mature.

échut [eʃy] *etc vb voir* **échoir**.

éclabousser [eklabuse] *vt* to splash; (*fig*) to tarnish.

éclaboussure [eklabusyʀ] *nf* splash; (*fig*) stain.

éclair [eklɛʀ] *nm* (*d'orage*) flash of lightning, lightning *no pl*; (*PHOTO: de flash*) flash; (*fig*) flash, spark; (*gâteau*) éclair.

éclairage [eklɛʀaʒ] *nm* lighting.

éclairagiste [eklɛʀaʒist(ə)] *nm/f* lighting engineer.

éclaircie [eklɛʀsi] *nf* bright *ou* sunny interval.

éclaircir [eklɛʀsiʀ] *vt* to lighten; (*fig*) to clear up, clarify; (*CULIN*) to thin (down); **s'~** *vi* (*ciel*) to brighten up, clear; (*cheveux*) to go thin; (*situation etc*) to become clearer; **s'~ la voix** to clear one's throat.

éclaircissement [eklɛʀsismɑ̃] *nm* clearing up, clarification.

éclairer [eklɛʀe] *vt* (*lieu*) to light (up); (*personne: avec une lampe de poche etc*) to light the way for; (*fig: instruire*) to enlighten; (*: rendre comprehensible*) to shed light on ♦ *vt* **~ mal/bien** to give a poor/good light; **s'~** *vi* *(phare, rue)* to light up; *(situation etc)* to become clearer; **s'~ à la bougie/l'électricité** to use candlelight/have electric lighting.

éclaireur, euse [eklɛʀœʀ, -øz] *nm/f (scout)* (boy) scout/(girl) guide ♦ *nm (MIL)* scout; **partir en ~** to go off to reconnoitre.

éclat [ekla] *nm (de bombe, de verre)* fragment; *(du soleil, d'une couleur etc)* brightness, brilliance; *(d'une cérémonie)* splendour; *(scandale)*: **faire un ~** to cause a commotion; **action d'~** outstanding action; **voler en ~s** to shatter; **des ~s de verre** broken glass; flying glass; **~ de rire** burst *ou* roar of laughter; **~ de voix** shout.

éclatant, e [eklatɑ̃, -ɑ̃t] *adj* brilliant, bright; *(succès)* resounding; *(revanche)* devastating.

éclater [eklate] *vi (pneu)* to burst; *(bombe)* to explode; *(guerre, épidémie)* to break out; *(groupe, parti)* to break up; **~ de rire/en sanglots** to burst out laughing/sobbing.

éclectique [eklɛktik] *adj* eclectic.

éclipse [eklips(ə)] *nf* eclipse.

éclipser [eklipse] *vt* to eclipse; **s'~** *vi* to slip away.

éclopé, e [eklope] *adj* lame.

éclore [eklɔʀ] *vi (œuf)* to hatch; *(fleur)* to open (out).

éclosion [eklozjɔ̃] *nf* blossoming.

écluse [eklyz] *nf* lock.

éclusier [eklyzje] *nm* lock keeper.

éco- [eko] *préfixe* eco-.

écœurant, e [ekœʀɑ̃, -ɑ̃t] *adj* sickening; *(gâteau etc)* sickly.

écœurement [ekœʀmɑ̃] *nm* disgust.

écœurer [ekœʀe] *vt*: **~ qn** to make sb feel sick; *(fig: démoraliser)* to disgust sb.

école [ekɔl] *nf* school; **aller à l'~** to go to school; **faire ~** to collect a following; **les grandes ~s** prestige university-level colleges with competitive entrance examinations; **~ maternelle** nursery school; **~ primaire** primary *(BRIT)* ou grade *(US)* school; **~ secondaire** secondary *(BRIT)* ou high *(US)* school; **~ privée/publique/ élémentaire** private/state/elementary school; **~ de dessin/danse/musique** art/ dancing/music school; **~ hôtelière** catering college; **~ normale (d'instituteurs) (ENI)** *primary school teachers' training college*; **~ normale supérieure (ENS)** *grande école for training secondary school teachers*; **~ de secrétariat** secretarial college.

> *Nursery school* **(l'école maternelle)** *is publicly funded in France and, though not compulsory, is attended by most children between the ages of two and six. Statutory education begins with primary school* **(l'école primaire)** *from the age of six to ten or eleven; see also* **collège, lycée.**

écolier, ière [ekɔlje, -jɛʀ] *nm/f* schoolboy/girl.

écolo [ekɔlo] *nm/f (fam)* ecologist ♦ *adj* ecological.

écologie [ekɔlɔʒi] *nf* ecology; *(sujet scolaire)* environmental studies *pl*.

écologique [ekɔlɔʒik] *adj* ecological; environmental.

écologiste [ekɔlɔʒist(ə)] *nm/f* ecologist; environmentalist.

éconduire [ekɔ̃dɥiʀ] *vt* to dismiss.

économat [ekɔnɔma] *nm (fonction)* bursarship *(BRIT)*, treasurership *(US)*; *(bureau)* bursar's office *(BRIT)*, treasury *(US)*.

économe [ekɔnɔm] *adj* thrifty ♦ *nm/f (de lycée etc)* bursar *(BRIT)*, treasurer *(US)*.

économétrie [ekɔnɔmetʀi] *nf* econometrics *sg*.

économie [ekɔnɔmi] *nf (vertu)* economy, thrift; *(gain: d'argent, de temps etc)* saving; *(science)* economics *sg*; *(situation économique)* economy; **~s** *nfpl (pécule)* savings; **une ~ de temps/d'argent** a saving in time/of money; **~ dirigée** planned economy; **~ de marché** market economy.

économique [ekɔnɔmik] *adj (avantageux)* economical; *(ÉCON)* economic.

économiquement [ekɔnɔmikmɑ̃] *adv* economically; **les ~ faibles** *(ADMIN)* the low-paid, people on low incomes.

économiser [ekɔnɔmize] *vt, vi* to save.

économiste [ekɔnɔmist(ə)] *nm/f* economist.

écoper [ekɔpe] *vi* to bale out; *(fig)* to cop it; **~ (de)** *vt* to get.

écorce [ekɔʀs(ə)] *nf* bark; *(de fruit)* peel.

écorcer [ekɔʀse] *vt* to bark.

écorché, e [ekɔʀʃe] *adj*: **~ vif** flayed alive ♦ *nm* cut-away drawing.

écorcher [ekɔʀʃe] *vt (animal)* to skin; *(égratigner)* to graze; **~ une langue** to speak a language brokenly; **s'~ le genou** *etc* to scrape *ou* graze one's knee *etc*.

écorchure [ekɔʀʃyʀ] *nf* graze.

écorner [ekɔʀne] *vt (taureau)* to dehorn; *(livre)* to make dog-eared.

écossais, e [ekɔsɛ, -ɛz] *adj (lacs, tempérament)* Scottish, Scots; *(whisky, confiture)* Scotch; *(écharpe, tissu)* tartan ♦ *nm (LING)* Scots; *(: gaélique)* Gaelic; *(tissu)* tartan (cloth) ♦ *nm/f*: **É~, e** Scot, Scotsman/woman; **les É~** the Scots.

écosser [ekɔse] *vt* to shell.

écosystème [ekosistɛm] *nm* ecosystem.

écot [eko] *nm*: **payer son ~** to pay one's share.

écoulement [ekulmɑ̃] *nm (de faux billets)* circulation; *(de stock)* selling.

écouler [ekule] *vt* to dispose of; **s'~** *vi (eau)* to flow (out); *(foule)* to drift away; *(jours, temps)* to pass (by).

écourter [ekuʀte] *vt* to curtail, cut short.

écoute [ekut] *nf (NAVIG: cordage)* sheet; *(RADIO, TV)*: **temps/heure d'~** (listening *ou* viewing) time/ hour; **heure de grande ~** peak listening *ou* viewing time; **prendre l'~** to tune in; **rester à l'~ (de)** to stay listening (to) *ou* tuned in (to); **~s téléphoniques**

phone tapping *sg*.
écouter [ekute] *vt* to listen to.
écouteur [ekutœʀ] *nm* (*TÉL*) (additional)
earpiece; **~s** *nmpl* (*RADIO*) headphones,
headset *sg*.
écoutille [ekutij] *nf* hatch.
écr. *abr* = **écrire**.
écrabouiller [ekʀabuje] *vt* to squash, crush.
écran [ekʀɑ̃] *nm* screen; (*INFORM*) VDU,
screen; **~ de fumée/d'eau** curtain of
smoke/water; **porter à l'~** (*CINÉ*) to adapt for
the screen; **le petit ~** television, the small
screen.
écrasant, e [ekʀazɑ̃, -ɑ̃t] *adj* overwhelming.
écraser [ekʀaze] *vt* to crush; (*piéton*) to run
over; (*INFORM*) to overwrite; **se faire ~** to be
run over; **écrase(-toi)!** shut up!; **s'~ (au sol)**
to crash; **s'~ contre** to crash into.
écrémer [ekʀeme] *vt* to skim.
écrevisse [ekʀəvis] *nf* crayfish *inv*.
écrier [ekʀije]: **s'~** *vi* to exclaim.
écrin [ekʀɛ̃] *nm* case, box.
écrire [ekʀiʀ] *vt, vi* to write ♦ *vi*: **ça s'écrit
comment?** how is it spelt?; **~ à qn que** to
write and tell sb that; **s'~** to write to one
another.
écrit, e [ekʀi, -it] *pp de* **écrire** ♦ *adj*: **bien/mal ~**
well/badly written ♦ *nm* document; (*examen*)
written paper; **par ~** in writing.
écriteau, x [ekʀito] *nm* notice, sign.
écritoire [ekʀitwaʀ] *nf* writing case.
écriture [ekʀityʀ] *nf* writing; (*COMM*) entry;
~s *nfpl* (*COMM*) accounts, books; **l'É~
(sainte), les É~s** the Scriptures.
écrivain [ekʀivɛ̃] *nm* writer.
écrivais [ekʀive] *etc vb voir* **écrire**.
écrou [ekʀu] *nm* nut.
écrouer [ekʀue] *vt* to imprison;
(*provisoirement*) to remand in custody.
écroulé, e [ekʀule] *adj* (*de fatigue*) exhausted;
(*par un malheur*) overwhelmed; **~ (de rire)** in
stitches.
écroulement [ekʀulmɑ̃] *nm* collapse.
écrouler [ekʀule]: **s'~** *vi* to collapse.
écru, e [ekʀy] *adj* (*toile*) raw, unbleached;
(*couleur*) off-white, écru.
écu [eky] *nm* (*bouclier*) shield; (*monnaie:
ancienne*) crown; (*: de la CEE*) ecu.
écueil [ekœj] *nm* reef; (*fig*) pitfall; stumbling
block.
écuelle [ekɥɛl] *nf* bowl.
éculé, e [ekyle] *adj* (*chaussure*) down-at-heel;
(*fig: péj*) hackneyed.
écume [ekym] *nf* foam; (*CULIN*) scum; **~ de
mer** meerschaum.
écumer [ekyme] *vt* (*CULIN*) to skim; (*fig*) to
plunder ♦ *vi* (*mer*) to foam; (*fig*) to boil with
rage.
écumoire [ekymwaʀ] *nf* skimmer.
écureuil [ekyʀœj] *nm* squirrel.
écurie [ekyʀi] *nf* stable.
écusson [ekysɔ̃] *nm* badge.

écuyer, ère [ekɥije, -ɛʀ] *nm/f* rider.
eczéma [ɛgzema] *nm* eczema.
éd. *abr* = **édition**.
édam [edam] *nm* (*fromage*) edam.
edelweiss [edɛlvajs] *nm inv* edelweiss.
éden [edɛn] *nm* Eden.
édenté, e [edɑ̃te] *adj* toothless.
EDF *sigle f* (= *Électricité de France*) national
electricity company.
édifiant, e [edifjɑ̃, -ɑ̃t] *adj* edifying.
édification [edifikasjɔ̃] (*d'un bâtiment*)
building, erection.
édifice [edifis] *nm* building, edifice.
édifier [edifje] *vt* to build, erect; (*fig*) to edify.
édiles [edil] *nmpl* city fathers.
Édimbourg [edɛ̃buʀ] *n* Edinburgh.
édit [edi] *nm* edict.
édit. *abr* = **éditeur**.
éditer [edite] *vt* (*publier*) to publish; (*: disque*)
to produce; (*préparer: texte, INFORM*) to edit.
éditeur, trice [editœʀ, -tʀis] *nm/f* publisher;
editor.
édition [edisjɔ̃] *nf* editing *no pl*; (*série
d'exemplaires*) edition; (*industrie du livre*): **l'~**
publishing; **~ sur écran** (*INFORM*) screen
editing.
édito [edito] *nm* (*fam: éditorial*) editorial,
leader.
éditorial, aux [editɔʀjal, -o] *nm* editorial,
leader.
éditorialiste [editɔʀjalist(ə)] *nm/f* editorial *ou*
leader writer.
édredon [edʀədɔ̃] *nm* eiderdown.
éducateur, trice [edykatœʀ, -tʀis] *nm/f*
teacher; **~ spécialisé** specialist teacher.
éducatif, ive [edykatif, -iv] *adj* educational.
éducation [edykasjɔ̃] *nf* education; (*familiale*)
upbringing; (*manières*) (good) manners *pl*;
bonne/mauvaise ~ good/bad upbringing;
sans ~ bad-mannered, ill-bred; **l'É~
(nationale)** ≈ the Department for
Education; **~ permanente** continuing
education; **~ physique** physical education.
édulcorer [edylkɔʀe] *vt* to sweeten; (*fig*) to
tone down.
éduquer [edyke] *vt* to educate; (*élever*) to
bring up; (*faculté*) to train; **bien/mal éduqué**
well/badly brought up.
EEG *sigle m* (= *électroencéphalogramme*) EEG.
effacé, e [efase] *adj* (*fig*) retiring, unassuming.
effacer [efase] *vt* to erase, rub out; (*bande
magnétique*) to erase; (*INFORM: fichier, fiche*)
to delete, erase; **s'~** *vi* (*inscription etc*) to
wear off; (*pour laisser passer*) to step aside;
~ le ventre to pull one's stomach in.
effarant, e [efaʀɑ̃, -ɑ̃t] *adj* alarming.
effaré, e [efaʀe] *adj* alarmed.
effarement [efaʀmɑ̃] *nm* alarm.
effarer [efaʀe] *vt* to alarm.
effarouchement [efaʀuʃmɑ̃] *nm* alarm.
effaroucher [efaʀuʃe] *vt* to frighten *ou* scare
away; (*personne*) to alarm.

effectif, ive [efɛktif, -iv] *adj* real; effective
♦ *nm* (*MIL*) strength; (*SCOL*) total number of
pupils, size; ~**s** numbers, strength *sg*;
(*COMM*) manpower *sg*; **réduire l'~ de** to
downsize.

effectivement [efɛktivmã] *adv* effectively;
(*réellement*) actually, really; (*en effet*)
indeed.

effectuer [efɛktɥe] *vt* (*opération, mission*) to
carry out; (*déplacement, trajet*) to make,
complete; (*mouvement*) to execute, make;
s'~ to be carried out.

efféminé, e [efemine] *adj* effeminate.

effervescence [efɛrvesɑ̃s] *nf* (*fig*): **en ~** in a
turmoil.

effervescent, e [efɛrvesɑ̃, -ɑ̃t] *adj* (*cachet,
boisson*) effervescent; (*fig*) agitated, in a
turmoil.

effet [efɛ] *nm* (*résultat, artifice*) effect;
(*impression*) impression; (*COMM*) bill; (*JUR*:
d'une loi, d'un jugement): **applied retrospectively**; ~**s** *nmpl* (*vêtements
etc*) things; ~ **de style/couleur/lumière**
stylistic/colour/lighting effect; ~**s de voix**
dramatic effects with one's voice; **faire de
l'~** (*médicament, menace*) to have an effect,
be effective; **sous l'~ de** under the effect
of; **donner de l'~ à une balle** (*TENNIS*) to put
some spin on a ball; **à cet ~** to that end; **en
~** *adv* indeed; ~ (**de commerce**) bill of
exchange; ~ **de serre** greenhouse effect; ~**s
spéciaux** (*CINÉ*) special effects.

effeuiller [efœje] *vt* to remove the leaves (*ou*
petals) from.

efficace [efikas] *adj* (*personne*) efficient;
(*action, médicament*) effective.

efficacité [efikasite] *nf* efficiency;
effectiveness.

effigie [efiʒi] *nf* effigy; **brûler qn en ~** to burn
an effigy of sb.

effilé, e [efile] *adj* slender; (*pointe*) sharp;
(*carrosserie*) streamlined.

effiler [efile] *vt* (*cheveux*) to thin (out); (*tissu*)
to fray.

effilocher [efilɔʃe]: **s'~** *vi* to fray.

efflanqué, e [eflɑ̃ke] *adj* emaciated.

effleurement [eflœrmã] *nm*: **touche à ~**
touch-sensitive control *ou* key.

effleurer [eflœre] *vt* to brush (against); (*sujet*)
to touch upon; (*suj: idée, pensée*): ~ **qn** to
cross sb's mind.

effluves [eflyv] *nmpl* exhalation(s).

effondré, e [efɔ̃dre] *adj* (*abattu: par un malheur,
échec*) overwhelmed.

effondrement [efɔ̃drəmã] *nm* collapse.

effondrer [efɔ̃dre]: **s'~** *vi* to collapse.

efforcer [efɔrse]: **s'~ de** *vt*: **s'~ de faire** to try
hard to do.

effort [efɔr] *nm* effort; **faire un ~** to make an
effort; **faire tous ses ~s** to try one's
hardest; **faire l'~ de ...** to make the effort to
...; **sans ~** *adj* effortless ♦ *adv* effortlessly; ~

de mémoire attempt to remember; ~ **de
volonté** effort of will.

effraction [efraksjɔ̃] *nf* breaking-in;
s'introduire par ~ dans to break into.

effrangé, e [efrɑ̃ʒe] *adj* fringed; (*effiloché*)
frayed.

effrayant, e [efrɛjã, -ãt] *adj* frightening,
fearsome; (*sens affaibli*) dreadful.

effrayer [efrɛje] *vt* to frighten, scare; (*rebuter*)
to put off; **s'~ (de)** to be frightened *ou*
scared (by).

effréné, e [efrene] *adj* wild.

effritement [efritmã] *nm* crumbling; erosion;
slackening off.

effriter [efrite]: **s'~** *vi* to crumble; (*monnaie*)
to be eroded; (*valeurs*) to slacken off.

effroi [efrwa] *nm* terror, dread *no pl*.

effronté, e [efrɔ̃te] *adj* insolent.

effrontément [efrɔ̃temã] *adv* insolently.

effronterie [efrɔ̃tri] *nf* insolence.

effroyable [efrwajabl(ə)] *adj* horrifying,
appalling.

effusion [efyzjɔ̃] *nf* effusion; **sans ~ de sang**
without bloodshed.

égailler [egaje]: **s'~** *vi* to scatter, disperse.

égal, e, aux [egal, -o] *adj* (*identique, ayant les
mêmes droits*) equal; (*plan: surface*) even,
level; (*constant: vitesse*) steady; (*équitable*)
even ♦ *nm/f* equal; **être ~ à** (*prix, nombre*) to
be equal to; **ça lui est ~** it's all the same to
him, it doesn't matter to him, he doesn't
mind; **c'est ~, ...** all the same, ...; **sans ~**
matchless, unequalled; **à l'~ de** (*comme*)
just like; **d'~ à ~** as equals.

également [egalmã] *adv* equally; evenly;
steadily; (*aussi*) too, as well.

égaler [egale] *vt* to equal.

égalisateur, trice [egalizatœr, -tris] *adj*
(*SPORT*): **but ~** equalizing goal, equalizer.

égalisation [egalizasjɔ̃] *nf* (*SPORT*)
equalization.

égaliser [egalize] *vt* (*sol, salaires*) to level
(out); (*chances*) to equalize ♦ *vi* (*SPORT*) to
equalize.

égalitaire [egalitɛr] *adj* egalitarian.

égalitarisme [egalitarism(ə)] *nm*
egalitarianism.

égalité [egalite] *nf* equality; evenness;
steadiness; (*MATH*) identity; **être à ~ (de
points)** to be level; ~ **de droits** equality of
rights; ~ **d'humeur** evenness of temper.

égard [egar] *nm*: ~**s** *nmpl* consideration *sg*; **à
cet ~** in this respect; **à certains ~s/tous ~s**
in certain respects/all respects; **eu ~ à** in
view of; **par ~ pour** out of consideration
for; **sans ~ pour** without regard for; **à l'~
de** *prép* towards; (*en ce qui concerne*)
concerning, as regards.

égaré, e [egare] *adj* lost.

égarement [egarmã] *nm* distraction;
aberration.

égarer [egare] *vt* (*objet*) to mislay;

(*moralement*) to lead astray; **s'~** *vi* to get lost, lose one's way; (*objet*) to go astray; (*fig: dans une discussion*) to wander.

égayer [egeje] *vt* (*personne*) to amuse; (: *remonter*) to cheer up; (*récit, endroit*) to brighten up, liven up.

Égée [eʒe] *adj*: **la mer** ~ the Aegean (Sea).

égéen, ne [eʒeɛ̃, -ɛn] *adj* Aegean.

égérie [eʒeʀi] *nf*: **l'~ de qn/qch** the brains behind sb/sth.

égide [eʒid] *nf*: **sous l'~ de** under the aegis of.

églantier [eglɑ̃tje] *nm* wild *ou* dog rose (-bush).

églantine [eglɑ̃tin] *nf* wild *ou* dog rose.

églefin [egləfɛ̃] *nm* haddock.

église [egliz] *nf* church.

égocentrique [egɔsɑ̃tʀik] *adj* egocentric, self-centred.

égocentrisme [egɔsɑ̃tʀism(ə)] *nm* egocentricity.

égoïne [egɔin] *nf* handsaw.

égoïsme [egɔism(ə)] *nm* selfishness, egoism.

égoïste [egɔist(ə)] *adj* selfish, egoistic ♦ *nm/f* egoist.

égoïstement [egɔistəmɑ̃] *adv* selfishly.

égorger [egɔʀʒe] *vt* to cut the throat of.

égosiller [egozije]: **s'~** *vi* to shout o.s. hoarse.

égotisme [egɔtism(ə)] *nm* egotism, egoism.

égout [egu] *nm* sewer; **eaux d'~** sewage.

égoutier [egutje] *nm* sewer worker.

égoutter [egute] *vt* (*linge*) to wring out; (*vaisselle, fromage*) to drain ♦ *vi*, **s'~** *vi* to drip.

égouttoir [egutwaʀ] *nm* draining board; (*mobile*) draining rack.

égratigner [egʀatiɲe] *vt* to scratch; **s'~** to scratch o.s.

égratignure [egʀatiɲyʀ] *nf* scratch.

égrener [egʀəne] *vt*: ~ **une grappe**, ~ **des raisins** to pick grapes off a bunch; **s'~** *vi* (*fig: heures etc*) to pass by; (: *notes*) to chime out.

égrillard, e [egʀijaʀ, -aʀd(ə)] *adj* ribald, bawdy.

Égypte [eʒipt] *nf*: **l'~** Egypt.

égyptien, ne [eʒipsjɛ̃, -ɛn] *adj* Egyptian ♦ *nm/f*: **É~, ne** Egyptian.

égyptologue [eʒiptɔlɔg] *nm/f* Egyptologist.

eh [e] *excl* hey!; ~ **bien** well.

éhonté, e [eɔ̃te] *adj* shameless, brazen (*BRIT*).

éjaculation [eʒakylasjɔ̃] *nf* ejaculation.

éjaculer [eʒakyle] *vi* to ejaculate.

éjectable [eʒɛktabl(ə)] *adj*: **siège** ~ ejector seat.

éjecter [eʒɛkte] *vt* (*TECH*) to eject; (*fam*) to kick *ou* chuck out.

éjection [eʒɛksjɔ̃] *nf* ejection.

élaboration [elabɔʀasjɔ̃] *nf* elaboration.

élaboré, e [elabɔʀe] *adj* (*complexe*) elaborate.

élaborer [elabɔʀe] *vt* to elaborate; (*projet, stratégie*) to work out; (*rapport*) to draft.

élagage [elagaʒ] *nm* pruning.

élaguer [elage] *vt* to prune.

élan [elɑ̃] *nm* (*ZOOL*) elk, moose; (*SPORT: avant le saut*) run up; (*de véhicule ou objet en mouvement*) momentum; (*fig: de tendresse etc*) surge; **prendre son ~/de l'~** to take a run up/gather speed; **perdre son** ~ to lose one's momentum.

élancé, e [elɑ̃se] *adj* slender.

élancement [elɑ̃smɑ̃] *nm* shooting pain.

élancer [elɑ̃se]: **s'~** *vi* to dash, hurl o.s.; (*fig: arbre, clocher*) to soar (upwards).

élargir [elaʀʒiʀ] *vt* to widen; (*vêtement*) to let out; (*JUR*) to release; **s'~** *vi* to widen; (*vêtement*) to stretch.

élargissement [elaʀʒismɑ̃] *nm* widening; letting out.

élasticité [elastisite] *nf* (*aussi ÉCON*) elasticity; ~ **de l'offre/de la demande** flexibility of supply/demand.

élastique [elastik] *adj* elastic ♦ *nm* (*de bureau*) rubber band; (*pour la couture*) elastic *no pl*.

élastomère [elastɔmɛʀ] *nm* elastomer.

Elbe [ɛlb] *nf*: **l'île d'~** (the Island of) Elba; (*fleuve*): **l'~** the Elbe.

eldorado [ɛldɔʀado] *nm* Eldorado.

électeur, trice [elɛktœʀ, -tʀis] *nm/f* elector, voter.

électif, ive [elɛktif, -iv] *adj* elective.

élection [elɛksjɔ̃] *nf* election; ~**s** *nfpl* (*POL*) election(s); **sa terre/patrie d'~** one's chosen land/country, the land/country of one's choice; ~ **partielle** ≈ by-election; ~**s législatives/présidentielles** general/ presidential election *sg*.

Élections législatives *are held in France every five years to elect* députés *to the* Assemblée nationale. *The President is elected in the* élections présidentielles, *held every seven years. Elections are by universal direct suffrage and two rounds of voting take place. Elections take place on a Sunday.*

électoral, e, aux [elɛktɔʀal, -o] *adj* electoral, election *cpd*.

électoralisme [elɛktɔʀalism(ə)] *nm* electioneering.

électorat [elɛktɔʀa] *nm* electorate.

électricien, ne [elɛktʀisjɛ̃, -ɛn] *nm/f* electrician.

électricité [elɛktʀisite] *nf* electricity; **allumer/ éteindre l'~** to put on/off the light; ~ **statique** static electricity.

électrification [elɛktʀifikasjɔ̃] *nf* (*RAIL*) electrification; (*d'un village etc*) laying on of electricity.

électrifier [elɛktʀifje] *vt* (*RAIL*) to electrify.

électrique [elɛktʀik] *adj* electric(al).

électriser [elɛktʀize] *vt* to electrify.

électro... [elɛktʀɔ] *préfixe* electro....

électro-aimant [elɛktʀɔɛmɑ̃] *nm* electromagnet.

électrocardiogramme [elɛktʀɔkaʀdjɔgʀam]

nm electrocardiogram.
électrocardiographe [elɛktʀɔkaʀdjɔgʀaf] *nm* electrocardiograph.
électrochoc [elɛktʀɔʃɔk] *nm* electric shock treatment.
électrocuter [elɛktʀɔkyte] *vt* to electrocute.
électrocution [elɛktʀɔkysjɔ̃] *nf* electrocution.
électrode [elɛktʀɔd] *nf* electrode.
électro-encéphalogramme [elɛktʀɔ-ɑ̃sefalɔgʀam] *nm* electroencephalogram.
électrogène [elɛktʀɔʒɛn] *adj:* **groupe ~** generating set.
électrolyse [elɛktʀɔliz] *nf* electrolysis *sg.*
électromagnétique [elɛktʀɔmaɲetik] *adj* electromagnetic.
électroménager [elɛktʀɔmenaʒe] *adj:* **appareils ~s** domestic (electrical) appliances ♦ *nm:* **l'~** household appliances.
électron [elɛktʀɔ̃] *nm* electron.
électronicien, ne [elɛktʀɔnisjɛ̃, -ɛn] *nm/f* electronics (*BRIT*) *ou* electrical (*US*) engineer.
électronique [elɛktʀɔnik] *adj* electronic ♦ *nf* (*science*) electronics *sg.*
électronucléaire [elɛktʀɔnykleɛʀ] *adj* nuclear power *cpd* ♦ *nm:* **l'~** nuclear power.
électrophone [elɛktʀɔfɔn] *nm* record player.
électrostatique [elɛktʀɔstatik] *adj* electrostatic ♦ *nf* electrostatics *sg.*
élégamment [elegamɑ̃] *adv* elegantly.
élégance [elegɑ̃s] *nf* elegance.
élégant, e [elegɑ̃, -ɑ̃t] *adj* elegant; (*solution*) neat, elegant; (*attitude, procédé*) courteous, civilized.
élément [elemɑ̃] *nm* element; (*pièce*) component, part; **~s** *nmpl* (*aussi: rudiments*) elements.
élémentaire [elemɑ̃tɛʀ] *adj* elementary; (*CHIMIE*) elemental.
éléphant [elefɑ̃] *nm* elephant; **~ de mer** elephant seal.
éléphanteau, x [elefɑ̃to] *nm* baby elephant.
éléphantesque [elefɑ̃tɛsk(ə)] *adj* elephantine.
élevage [ɛlvaʒ] *nm* breeding; (*de bovins*) cattle breeding *ou* rearing; (*ferme*) cattle farm.
élévateur [elevatœʀ] *nm* elevator.
élévation [elevasjɔ̃] *nf* (*gén*) elevation; (*voir élever*) raising; (*voir s'élever*) rise.
élevé, e [ɛlve] *adj* (*prix, sommet*) high; (*fig: noble*) elevated; **bien/mal ~** well-/ill-mannered.
élève [elɛv] *nm/f* pupil; **~ infirmière** student nurse.
élever [ɛlve] *vt* (*enfant*) to bring up, raise; (*bétail, volaille*) to breed; (*abeilles*) to keep; (*hausser: taux, niveau*) to raise; (*fig: âme, esprit*) to elevate; (*édifier: monument*) to put up, erect; **s'~** *vi* (*avion, alpiniste*) to go up; (*niveau, température, aussi: cri etc*) to rise; (*survenir: difficultés*) to arise; **s'~ à** (*suj: frais, dégâts*) to amount to, add up to; **s'~ contre** to rise up against; **~ une protestation/**

critique to raise a protest/make a criticism; **~ la voix** to raise one's voice; **~ qn au rang de** to raise *ou* elevate sb to the rank of; **~ un nombre au carré/au cube** to square/cube a number.
éleveur, euse [elvœʀ, -øz] *nm/f* stock breeder.
elfe [ɛlf(ə)] *nm* elf.
élidé, e [elide] *adj* elided.
élider [elide] *vt* to elide.
éligibilité [eliʒibilite] *nf* eligibility.
éligible [eliʒibl(ə)] *adj* eligible.
élimé, e [elime] *adj* worn (thin), threadbare.
élimination [eliminɑsjɔ̃] *nf* elimination.
éliminatoire [eliminatwaʀ] *adj* eliminatory; (*SPORT*) disqualifying ♦ *nf* (*SPORT*) heat.
éliminer [elimine] *vt* to eliminate.
élire [eliʀ] *vt* to elect; **~ domicile à** to take up residence in *ou* at.
élision [elizjɔ̃] *nf* elision.
élite [elit] *nf* elite; **tireur d'~** crack rifleman; **chercheur d'~** top-notch researcher.
élitisme [elitism(ə)] *nm* elitism.
élitiste [elitist(ə)] *adj* elitist.
élixir [eliksiʀ] *nm* elixir.
elle [ɛl] *pron* (*sujet*) she; (: *chose*) it; (*complément*) her; it; **~s** (*sujet*) they; (*complément*) them; **~-même** herself; itself; **~-s-mêmes** themselves; *voir* **il.**
ellipse [elips(ə)] *nf* ellipse; (*LING*) ellipsis *sg.*
elliptique [eliptik] *adj* elliptical.
élocution [elɔkysjɔ̃] *nf* delivery; **défaut d'~** speech impediment.
éloge [elɔʒ] *nm* praise (*gén no pl*); **faire l'~ de** to praise.
élogieusement [elɔʒjøzmɑ̃] *adv* very favourably.
élogieux, euse [elɔʒjø, -øz] *adj* laudatory, full of praise.
éloigné, e [elwaɲe] *adj* distant, far-off.
éloignement [elwaɲmɑ̃] *nm* removal; putting off; estrangement; (*fig: distance*) distance.
éloigner [elwaɲe] *vt* (*objet*): **~ qch (de)** to move *ou* take sth away (from); (*personne*): **~ qn (de)** to take sb away *ou* remove sb (from); (*échéance*) to put off, postpone; (*soupçons, danger*) to ward off; **s'~ (de)** (*personne*) to go away (from); (*véhicule*) to move away (from); (*affectivement*) to become estranged (from).
élongation [elɔ̃gasjɔ̃] *nf* strained muscle.
éloquence [elɔkɑ̃s] *nf* eloquence.
éloquent, e [elɔkɑ̃, -ɑ̃t] *adj* eloquent.
élu, e [ely] *pp de* **élire** ♦ *nm/f* (*POL*) elected representative.
élucider [elyside] *vt* to elucidate.
élucubrations [elykybʀasjɔ̃] *nfpl* wild imaginings.
éluder [elyde] *vt* to evade.
élus [ely] *etc vb voir* **élire.**
élusif, ive [elyzif, -iv] *adj* elusive.
Élysée [elize] *nm:* (**le palais de) l'~** the Élysée palace; **les Champs ~s** the Champs Élysées.

---

*The **palais de l'Élysée**, situated in the heart of Paris off the Champs-Élysées, is the official residence of the French President. Built in the eighteenth century, it has been used in its present role since 1876. L'**Élysée** is frequently used to mean the presidency itself.*

émacié, e [emasje] *adj* emaciated.

émail, aux [emaj, -o] *nm* enamel.

émaillé, e [emaje] *adj* enamelled; (*fig*): ~ **de** dotted with.

émailler [emaje] *vt* to enamel.

émanation [emanɑsjɔ̃] *nf* emanation; **être l'~ de** to emanate from; to proceed from.

émancipation [emɑ̃sipɑsjɔ̃] *nf* emancipation.

émancipé, e [emɑ̃sipe] *adj* emancipated.

émanciper [emɑ̃sipe] *vt* to emancipate; **s'~** (*fig*) to become emancipated *ou* liberated.

émaner [emane]: ~ **de** *vt* to emanate from; (*ADMIN*) to proceed from.

émarger [emaʀʒe] *vt* to sign; ~ **de 1 000 F à un budget** to receive 1000 F out of a budget.

émasculer [emaskyle] *vt* to emasculate.

emballage [ɑ̃balaʒ] *nm* wrapping; packing; (*papier*) wrapping; (*carton*) packaging.

emballer [ɑ̃bale] *vt* to wrap (up); (*dans un carton*) to pack (up); (*fig: fam*) to thrill (to bits); **s'~** *vi* (*moteur*) to race; (*cheval*) to bolt; (*fig: personne*) to get carried away.

emballeur, euse [ɑ̃balœʀ, -øz] *nm/f* packer.

embarcadère [ɑ̃baʀkadɛʀ] *nm* landing stage (*BRIT*), pier.

embarcation [ɑ̃baʀkɑsjɔ̃] *nf* (small) boat, (small) craft *inv*.

embardée [ɑ̃baʀde] *nf* swerve; **faire une ~** to swerve.

embargo [ɑ̃baʀgo] *nm* embargo; **mettre l'~ sur** to put an embargo on, embargo.

embarquement [ɑ̃baʀkəmɑ̃] *nm* embarkation; loading; boarding.

embarquer [ɑ̃baʀke] *vt* (*personne*) to embark; (*marchandise*) to load; (*fam*) to cart off; (*: arrêter*) to nick ♦ *vi* (*passager*) to board; (*NAVIG*) to ship water; **s'~** *vi* to board; **s'~ dans** (*affaire, aventure*) to embark upon.

embarras [ɑ̃baʀa] *nm* (*obstacle*) hindrance; (*confusion*) embarrassment; (*ennuis*): **être dans l'~** to be in a predicament *ou* an awkward position; (*gêne financière*) to be in difficulties; ~ **gastrique** stomach upset.

embarrassant, e [ɑ̃baʀasɑ̃, -ɑ̃t] *adj* cumbersome; embarrassing; awkward.

embarrassé, e [ɑ̃baʀase] *adj* (*encombré*) encumbered; (*gêné*) embarrassed; (*explications etc*) awkward.

embarrasser [ɑ̃baʀase] *vt* (*encombrer*) to clutter (up); (*gêner*) to hinder, hamper; (*fig*) to cause embarrassment to; to put in an awkward position; **s'~ de** to burden o.s. with.

embauche [ɑ̃boʃ] *nf* hiring; **bureau d'~**

labour office.

embaucher [ɑ̃boʃe] *vt* to take on, hire; **s'~ comme** to get (o.s.) a job as.

embauchoir [ɑ̃boʃwaʀ] *nm* shoetree.

embaumer [ɑ̃bome] *vt* to embalm; (*parfumer*) to fill with its fragrance; ~ **la lavande** to be fragrant with (the scent of) lavender.

embellie [ɑ̃beli] *nf* bright spell, brighter period.

embellir [ɑ̃beliʀ] *vt* to make more attractive; (*une histoire*) to embellish ♦ *vi* to grow lovelier *ou* more attractive.

embellissement [ɑ̃belismɑ̃] *nm* embellishment.

embêtant, e [ɑ̃bɛtɑ̃, -ɑ̃t] *adj* annoying.

embêtement [ɑ̃bɛtmɑ̃] *nm* problem, difficulty; ~**s** *nmpl* trouble *sg*.

embêter [ɑ̃bete] *vt* to bother; **s'~** *vi* (*s'ennuyer*) to be bored; **il ne s'embête pas!** (*ironique*) he does all right for himself!

emblée [ɑ̃ble]: **d'~** *adv* straightaway.

emblème [ɑ̃blɛm] *nm* emblem.

embobiner [ɑ̃bɔbine] *vt* (*enjôler*): ~ **qn** to get round sb.

emboîtable [ɑ̃bwatabl(ə)] *adj* interlocking.

emboîter [ɑ̃bwate] *vt* to fit together; **s'~ dans** to fit into; **s'~** (*l'un dans l'autre*) to fit together; ~ **le pas à qn** to follow in sb's footsteps.

embolie [ɑ̃bɔli] *nf* embolism.

embonpoint [ɑ̃bɔ̃pwɛ̃] *nm* stoutness (*BRIT*), corpulence; **prendre de l'~** to grow stout (*BRIT*) *ou* corpulent.

embouché, e [ɑ̃buʃe] *adj*: **mal ~** foul-mouthed.

embouchure [ɑ̃buʃyʀ] *nf* (*GÉO*) mouth; (*MUS*) mouthpiece.

embourber [ɑ̃buʀbe]: **s'~** *vi* to get stuck in the mud; (*fig*): **s'~ dans** to sink into.

embourgeoiser [ɑ̃buʀʒwaze]: **s'~** *vi* to adopt a middle-class outlook.

embout [ɑ̃bu] *nm* (*de canne*) tip; (*de tuyau*) nozzle.

embouteillage [ɑ̃butejaʒ] *nm* traffic jam, (traffic) holdup (*BRIT*).

embouteiller [ɑ̃buteje] *vt* (*suj: véhicules etc*) to block.

emboutir [ɑ̃butiʀ] *vt* (*TECH*) to stamp; (*heurter*) to crash into, ram.

embranchement [ɑ̃bʀɑ̃ʃmɑ̃] *nm* (*routier*) junction; (*classification*) branch.

embrancher [ɑ̃bʀɑ̃ʃe] *vt* (*tuyaux*) to join; ~ **qch sur** to join sth to.

embraser [ɑ̃bʀaze]: **s'~** *vi* to flare up.

embrassade [ɑ̃bʀasad] *nf* (*gén pl*) hugging and kissing *no pl*.

embrasse [ɑ̃bʀas] *nf* (*de rideau*) tie-back, loop.

embrasser [ɑ̃bʀase] *vt* to kiss; (*sujet, période*) to embrace, encompass; (*carrière*) to embark on; (*métier*) to go in for, take up; ~ **du regard** to take in (*with eyes*); **s'~** to kiss (each other).

embrasure [ɑ̃bʀɑzyʀ] *nf*: **dans l'~ de la porte** in the door(way).

embrayage [ɑ̃bʀɛjaʒ] *nm* clutch.

embrayer [ɑ̃bʀeje] *vi* (*AUTO*) to let in the clutch ♦ *vt* (*fig: affaire*) to set in motion; **~ sur qch** to begin on sth.

embrigader [ɑ̃bʀigade] *vt* to recruit.

embrocher [ɑ̃bʀɔʃe] *vt* to (put on a) spit (*ou* skewer).

embrouillamini [ɑ̃bʀujamini] *nm* (*fam*) muddle.

embrouillé, e [ɑ̃bʀuje] *adj* (*affaire*) confused, muddled.

embrouiller [ɑ̃bʀuje] *vt* (*fils*) to tangle (up); (*fiches, idées, personne*) to muddle up; **s'~** *vi* to get in a muddle.

embroussaillé, e [ɑ̃bʀusaje] *adj* overgrown, scrubby; (*cheveux*) bushy, shaggy.

embruns [ɑ̃bʀœ̃] *nmpl* sea spray *sg*.

embryologie [ɑ̃bʀijɔlɔʒi] *nf* embryology.

embryon [ɑ̃bʀijɔ̃] *nm* embryo.

embryonnaire [ɑ̃bʀijɔnɛʀ] *adj* embryonic.

embûches [ɑ̃byʃ] *nfpl* pitfalls, traps.

embué, e [ɑ̃bɥe] *adj* misted up; **yeux ~s de larmes** eyes misty with tears.

embuscade [ɑ̃byskad] *nf* ambush; **tendre une ~ à** to lay an ambush for.

embusqué, e [ɑ̃byske] *adj* in ambush ♦ *nm* (*péj*) shirker, skiver (*BRIT*).

embusquer [ɑ̃byske] *vt*: **s'~** *vi* to take up position (for an ambush).

éméché, e [emeʃe] *adj* tipsy, merry.

émeraude [ɛmʀod] *nf* emerald ♦ *adj inv* emerald-green.

émergence [emɛʀʒɑ̃s] *nf* (*fig*) emergence.

émerger [emɛʀʒe] *vi* to emerge; (*faire saillie, aussi fig*) to stand out.

émeri [ɛmʀi] *nm*: **toile** *ou* **papier ~** emery paper.

émérite [emeʀit] *adj* highly skilled.

émerveillement [emɛʀvɛjmɑ̃] *nm* wonderment.

émerveiller [emɛʀveje] *vt* to fill with wonder; **s'~ de** to marvel at.

émet [emɛ] *etc vb voir* **émettre**.

émétique [emetik] *nm* emetic.

émetteur, trice [emɛtœʀ, -tʀis] *adj* transmitting; (*poste*) ~ transmitter.

émetteur-récepteur, *pl* **émetteurs-récepteurs** [emetœʀʀesɛptœʀ] *nm* transceiver.

émettre [emɛtʀ(ə)] *vt* (*son, lumière*) to give out, emit; (*message etc: RADIO*) to transmit; (*billet, timbre, emprunt, chèque*) to issue; (*hypothèse, avis*) to voice, put forward; (*vœu*) to express ♦ *vi*: **~ sur ondes courtes** to broadcast on short wave.

émeus [emø] *etc vb voir* **émouvoir**.

émeute [emøt] *nf* riot.

émeutier, ière [emøtje, -jɛʀ] *nm/f* rioter.

émeuve [emœv] *etc vb voir* **émouvoir**.

émietter [emjete] *vt* (*pain, terre*) to crumble;

(*fig*) to split up, disperse; **s'~** *vi* (*pain, terre*) to crumble.

émigrant, e [emigʀɑ̃, -ɑ̃t] *nm/f* emigrant.

émigration [emigʀasjɔ̃] *nf* emigration.

émigré, e [emigʀe] *nm/f* expatriate.

émigrer [emigʀe] *vi* to emigrate.

émincer [emɛ̃se] *vt* (*CULIN*) to slice thinly.

éminemment [eminamɑ̃] *adv* eminently.

éminence [eminɑ̃s] *nf* distinction; (*colline*) knoll, hill; **Son É~** His Eminence; **~ grise** éminence grise.

éminent, e [eminɑ̃, -ɑ̃t] *adj* distinguished.

émir [emiʀ] *nm* emir.

émirat [emiʀa] *nm* emirate; **les É~s arabes unis (EAU)** the United Arab Emirates (UAE).

émis, e [emi, -iz] *pp de* **émettre**.

émissaire [emisɛʀ] *nm* emissary.

émission [emisjɔ̃] *nf* (*voir* **émettre**) emission; transmission; issue; (*RADIO, TV*) programme, broadcast.

émit [emi] *etc vb voir* **émettre**.

emmagasinage [ɑ̃magazinaʒ] *nm* storage; storing away.

emmagasiner [ɑ̃magazine] *vt* to (put into) store; (*fig*) to store up.

emmailloter [ɑ̃majɔte] *vt* to wrap up.

emmanchure [ɑ̃mɑ̃ʃyʀ] *nf* armhole.

emmêlement [ɑ̃mɛlmɑ̃] *nm* (*état*) tangle.

emmêler [ɑ̃mele] *vt* to tangle (up); (*fig*) to muddle up; **s'~** to get into a tangle.

emménagement [ɑ̃menaʒmɑ̃] *nm* settling in.

emménager [ɑ̃menaʒe] *vi* to move in; **~ dans** to move into.

emmener [ɑ̃mne] *vt* to take (with one); (*comme otage, capture*) to take away; **~ qn au concert** to take sb to a concert.

emment(h)al [emɛtal] *nm* (*fromage*) Emmenthal.

emmerder [ɑ̃mɛʀde] (*fam!*) *vt* to bug, bother; **s'~** *vi* (*s'ennuyer*) to be bored stiff; **je t'emmerde!** to hell with you!

emmitoufler [ɑ̃mitufle] *vt* to wrap up (warmly); **s'~** to wrap (o.s.) up (warmly).

emmurer [ɑ̃myʀe] *vt* to wall up, immure.

émoi [emwa] *nm* (*agitation, effervescence*) commotion; (*trouble*) agitation; **en ~** (*sens*) excited, stirred.

émollient, e [emɔljɑ̃, -ɑ̃t] *adj* (*MÉD*) emollient.

émoluments [emɔlymɑ̃] *nmpl* remuneration *sg*, fee *sg*.

émonder [emɔ̃de] *vt* (*arbre etc*) to prune; (*amande etc*) to blanch.

émotif, ive [emɔtif, -iv] *adj* emotional.

émotion [emɔsjɔ̃] *nf* emotion; **avoir des ~s** (*fig*) to get a fright; **donner des ~s à** to give a fright to; **sans ~** without emotion, coldly.

émotionnant, e [emɔsjɔnɑ̃, -ɑ̃t] *adj* upsetting.

émotionnel, le [emɔsjɔnɛl] *adj* emotional.

émotionner [emɔsjɔne] *vt* to upset.

émoulu, e [emuly] *adj*: **frais ~ de** fresh from, just out of.

émoussé, e [emuse] _adj_ blunt.

émousser [emuse] _vt_ to blunt; _(fig)_ to dull.

émoustiller [emustije] _vt_ to titillate, arouse.

émouvant, e [emuvɑ̃, -ɑ̃t] _adj_ moving.

émouvoir [emuvwaʀ] _vt (troubler)_ to stir, affect; _(toucher, attendrir)_ to move; _(indigner)_ to rouse; _(effrayer)_ to disturb, worry; **s'~** _vi_ to be affected; to be moved; to be roused; to be disturbed _ou_ worried.

empailler [ɑ̃paje] _vt_ to stuff.

empailleur, euse [ɑ̃pajœʀ, -øz] _nm/f (d'animaux)_ taxidermist.

empaler [ɑ̃pale] _vt_ to impale.

empaquetage [ɑ̃paktaʒ] _nm_ packing, packaging.

empaqueter [ɑ̃pakte] _vt_ to pack up.

emparer [ɑ̃paʀe]: **s'~ de** _vt (objet)_ to seize, grab; _(comme otage, MIL)_ to seize; _(suj: peur etc)_ to take hold of.

empâter [ɑ̃pɑte]: **s'~** _vi_ to thicken out.

empattement [ɑ̃patmɑ̃] _nm (AUTO)_ wheelbase; _(TYPO)_ serif.

empêché, e [ɑ̃peʃe] _adj_ detained.

empêchement [ɑ̃peʃmɑ̃] _nm_ (unexpected) obstacle, hitch.

empêcher [ɑ̃peʃe] _vt_ to prevent; **~ qn de faire** to prevent _ou_ stop sb (from) doing; **~ que qch (n')arrive/qn (ne) fasse** to prevent sth from happening/sb from doing; **il n'empêche que** nevertheless, be that as it may; **il n'a pas pu s'~ de rire** he couldn't help laughing.

empêcheur [ɑ̃peʃœʀ] _nm_: **~ de danser en rond** spoilsport, killjoy _(BRIT)_.

empeigne [ɑ̃peɲ] _nf_ upper _(of shoe)_.

empennage [ɑ̃penaʒ] _nm (AVIAT)_ tailplane.

empereur [ɑ̃pʀœʀ] _nm_ emperor.

empesé, e [ɑ̃pəze] _adj (fig)_ stiff, starchy.

empeser [ɑ̃pəze] _vt_ to starch.

empester [ɑ̃peste] _vt (lieu)_ to stink out ♦ _vi_ to stink, reek; **~ le tabac/le vin** to stink _ou_ reek of tobacco/wine.

empêtrer [ɑ̃petʀe] _vt_: **s'~ dans** _(fils etc, aussi fig)_ to get tangled up in.

emphase [ɑ̃faz] _nf_ pomposity, bombast; **avec ~** pompously.

emphatique [ɑ̃fatik] _adj_ emphatic.

empiècement [ɑ̃pjɛsmɑ̃] _nm (COUTURE)_ yoke.

empierrer [ɑ̃pjeʀe] _vt (route)_ to metal.

empiéter [ɑ̃pjete]: **~ sur** _vt_ to encroach upon.

empiffrer [ɑ̃pifʀe]: **s'~** _vi (péj)_ to stuff o.s.

empiler [ɑ̃pile] _vt_ to pile (up), stack (up); **s'~** _vi_ to pile up.

empire [ɑ̃piʀ] _nm_ empire; _(fig)_ influence; **style E~** Empire style; **sous l'~ de** in the grip of.

empirer [ɑ̃piʀe] _vi_ to worsen, deteriorate.

empirique [ɑ̃piʀik] _adj_ empirical.

empirisme [ɑ̃piʀism(ə)] _nm_ empiricism.

emplacement [ɑ̃plasmɑ̃] _nm_ site; **sur l'~ de** on the site of.

emplâtre [ɑ̃plɑtʀ(ə)] _nm_ plaster; _(fam)_ twit.

emplette [ɑ̃plɛt] _nf_: **faire l'~ de** to purchase;

~s shopping _sg_; **faire des ~s** to go shopping.

emplir [ɑ̃pliʀ] _vt_ to fill; **s'~ (de)** to fill (with).

emploi [ɑ̃plwa] _nm_ use; _(COMM, ÉCON)_: **l'~** employment; _(poste)_ job, situation; **d'~ facile** easy to use; **le plein ~** full employment; **~ du temps** timetable, schedule.

emploie [ɑ̃plwa] _etc vb voir_ **employer**.

employé, e [ɑ̃plwaje] _nm/f_ employee; **~ de bureau/banque** office/bank employee _ou_ clerk; **~ de maison** domestic (servant).

employer [ɑ̃plwaje] _vt (outil, moyen, méthode, mot)_ to use; _(ouvrier, main-d'œuvre)_ to employ; **s'~ à qch/à faire** to apply _ou_ devote o.s. to sth/to doing.

employeur, euse [ɑ̃plwajœʀ, -øz] _nm/f_ employer.

empocher [ɑ̃pɔʃe] _vt_ to pocket.

empoignade [ɑ̃pwaɲad] _nf_ row, set-to.

empoigne [ɑ̃pwaɲ] _nf_: **foire d'~** free-for-all.

empoigner [ɑ̃pwaɲe] _vt_ to grab; **s'~** _(fig)_ to have a row _ou_ set-to.

empois [ɑ̃pwa] _nm_ starch.

empoisonnement [ɑ̃pwazɔnmɑ̃] _nm_ poisoning; _(fam: ennui)_ annoyance, irritation.

empoisonner [ɑ̃pwazɔne] _vt_ to poison; _(empester: air, pièce)_ to stink out; _(fam)_: **~ qn** to drive sb mad; **s'~** to poison o.s.; **~ l'atmosphère** _(aussi fig)_ to poison the atmosphere; **il nous empoisonne l'existence** he's the bane of our life.

empoissonner [ɑ̃pwasɔne] _vt (étang, rivière)_ to stock with fish.

emporté, e [ɑ̃pɔʀte] _adj (personne, caractère)_ fiery.

emportement [ɑ̃pɔʀtəmɑ̃] _nm_ fit of rage, anger _no pl_.

emporte-pièce [ɑ̃pɔʀtəpjɛs] _nm inv (TECH)_ punch; **à l'~** _adj (fig)_ incisive.

emporter [ɑ̃pɔʀte] _vt_ to take (with one); _(en dérobant ou enlevant, emmener: blessés, voyageurs)_ to take away; _(entraîner)_ to carry away _ou_ along; _(arracher)_ to tear off; _(suj: rivière, vent)_ to carry away; _(MIL: position)_ to take; _(avantage, approbation)_ to win; **s'~** _vi (de colère)_ to fly into a rage, lose one's temper; **la maladie qui l'a emporté** the illness which caused his death; **l'~** to gain victory; **l'~ (sur)** to get the upper hand (of); _(méthode etc)_ to prevail (over); **boissons à ~** take-away drinks.

empoté, e [ɑ̃pɔte] _adj (maladroit)_ clumsy.

empourpré, e [ɑ̃puʀpʀe] _adj_ crimson.

empreint, e [ɑ̃pʀɛ̃, -ɛ̃t] _adj_: **~ de** marked with; tinged with ♦ _nf (de pied, main)_ print; _(fig)_ stamp, mark; **~e (digitale)** fingerprint.

empressé, e [ɑ̃pʀese] _adj_ attentive; _(péj)_ overanxious to please, overattentive.

empressement [ɑ̃pʀesmɑ̃] _nm_ eagerness.

empresser [ɑ̃pʀese]: **s'~** _vi_: **s'~ auprès de qn** to surround sb with attentions; **s'~ de faire**

to hasten to do.

emprise [ɑ̃pʀiz] *nf* hold, ascendancy; **sous l'~ de** under the influence of.

emprisonnement [ɑ̃pʀizɔnmɑ̃] *nm* imprisonment.

emprisonner [ɑ̃pʀizɔne] *vt* to imprison, jail.

emprunt [ɑ̃pʀœ̃] *nm* borrowing *no pl*, loan (*from debtor's point of view*); (*LING etc*) borrowing; **nom d'~** assumed name; **~ d'État** government *ou* state loan; **~ public à 5%** 5% public loan.

emprunté, e [ɑ̃pʀœ̃te] *adj* (*fig*) ill-at-ease, awkward.

emprunter [ɑ̃pʀœ̃te] *vt* to borrow; (*itinéraire*) to take, follow; (*style, manière*) to adopt, assume.

emprunteur, euse [ɑ̃pʀœ̃tœʀ, -øz] *nm/f* borrower.

empuantir [ɑ̃pɥɑ̃tiʀ] *vt* to stink out.

EMT *sigle f* (= *éducation manuelle et technique*) handwork as a school subject.

ému, e [emy] *pp de* **émouvoir** ♦ *adj* excited; touched; moved.

émulation [emylasjɔ̃] *nf* emulation.

émule [emyl] *nm/f* imitator.

émulsion [emylsjɔ̃] *nf* emulsion; (*cosmétique*) (water-based) lotion.

émut [emy] *etc vb voir* **émouvoir**.

EN *sigle f* (= *Éducation nationale*) *voir* **éducation**.

═══════════════════════ *MOT-CLÉ*

en [ɑ̃] *prép* **1** (*endroit, pays*) in; (*direction*) to; **habiter ~ France/ville** to live in France/ town; **aller ~ France/ville** to go to France/ town

2 (*moment, temps*) in; **~ été/juin** in summer/June; **~ 3 jours/20 ans** in 3 days/20 years

3 (*moyen*) by; **~ avion/taxi** by plane/taxi

4 (*composition*) made of; **c'est ~ verre** it's (made of) glass; **un collier ~ argent** a silver necklace; **~ 2 volumes/une pièce** in 2 volumes/one piece

5 (*description, état*): **une femme (habillée) ~ rouge** a woman (dressed) in red; **peindre qch ~ rouge** to paint sth red; **~ T/étoile** T-/ star-shaped; **~ chemise/chaussettes** in one's shirt sleeves/socks; **~ soldat** as a soldier; **~ civil** in civilian clothes; **cassé ~ plusieurs morceaux** broken into several pieces; **~ réparation** being repaired, under repair; **~ vacances** on holiday; **~ bonne santé** healthy, in good health; **~ deuil** in mourning; **le même ~ plus grand** the same but *ou* only bigger

6 (*avec gérondif*) while; on; **~ dormant** while sleeping, as one sleeps; **~ sortant** on going out, as he *etc* went out; **sortir ~ courant** to run out; **~ apprenant la nouvelle, il s'est évanoui** he fainted at the news *ou* when he heard the news

7 (*matière*): **fort ~ math** good at maths;

**expert ~ expert in

8 (*conformité*): **~ tant que** as; **~ bon politicien, il ...** good politician that he is, he ..., like a good *ou* true politician, he ...; **je te parle ~ ami** I'm talking to you as a friend

♦ *pron* **1** (*indéfini*): **j'~ ai/veux** I have/want some; **~ as-tu?** have you got any?; **je n'~ veux pas** I don't want any; **j'~ ai 2** I've got 2; **combien y ~ a-t-il?** how many (of them) are there?; **j'~ ai assez** I've got enough (of it *ou* them); (*j'en ai marre*) I've had enough; **où ~ étais-je?** where was I?

2 (*provenance*) from there; **j'~ viens** I've come from there

3 (*cause*): **il ~ est malade/perd le sommeil** he is ill/can't sleep because of it

4 (*de la part de*): **elle ~ est aimée** she is loved by him (*ou* them *etc*)

5 (*complément de nom, d'adjectif, de verbe*): **j'~ connais les dangers** I know its *ou* the dangers; **j'~ suis fier/ai besoin** I am proud of it/need it; **il ~ est ainsi** *ou* **de même pour moi** it's the same for me, same here.

ENA [ena] *sigle f* (= *École nationale d'administration*) *grande école for training civil servants.*

énarque [enaʀk(ə)] *nm/f* former ENA student.

encablure [ɑ̃kablyʀ] *nf* (*NAVIG*) cable's length.

encadrement [ɑ̃kadʀəmɑ̃] *nm* framing; training; (*de porte*) frame; **~ du crédit** credit restrictions.

encadrer [ɑ̃kadʀe] *vt* (*tableau, image*) to frame; (*fig: entourer*) to surround; (*personnel, soldats etc*) to train; (*COMM: crédit*) to restrict.

encadreur [ɑ̃kadʀœʀ] *nm* (picture) framer.

encaisse [ɑ̃kɛs] *nf* cash in hand; **~ or/ métallique** gold/gold and silver reserves.

encaissé, e [ɑ̃kese] *adj* (*vallée*) steep-sided; (*rivière*) with steep banks.

encaisser [ɑ̃kese] *vt* (*chèque*) to cash; (*argent*) to collect; (*fig: coup, défaite*) to take.

encaisseur [ɑ̃kesœʀ] *nm* collector (*of debts etc*).

encan [ɑ̃kɑ̃] *nm*: **à l'~** *adv* by auction.

encanailler [ɑ̃kanaje]: **s'~** *vi* to become vulgar *ou* common; to mix with the riff-raff.

encart [ɑ̃kaʀ] *nm* insert; **~ publicitaire** publicity insert.

encarter [ɑ̃kaʀte] *vt* to insert.

en-cas [ɑ̃ka] *nm inv* snack.

encastrable [ɑ̃kastʀabl(ə)] *adj* (*four, élément*) that can be built in.

encastré, e [ɑ̃kastʀe] *adj* (*four, baignoire*) built-in.

encastrer [ɑ̃kastʀe] *vt*: **~ qch dans** (*mur*) to embed sth in(to); (*boîtier*) to fit sth into; **s'~ dans** to fit into; (*heurter*) to crash into.

encaustiquage [ɑ̃kɔstikaʒ] *nm* polishing, waxing.

encaustique [ɑ̃kɔstik] *nf* polish, wax.
encaustiquer [ɑ̃kɔstike] *vt* to polish, wax.
enceinte [ɑ̃sɛ̃t] *adj f:* ~ **(de 6 mois)** (6 months) pregnant ♦ *nf (mur)* wall; *(espace)* enclosure; ~ **(acoustique)** speaker.
encens [ɑ̃sɑ̃] *nm* incense.
encenser [ɑ̃sɑ̃se] *vt* to (in)cense; *(fig)* to praise to the skies.
encensoir [ɑ̃sɑ̃swar] *nm* thurible (*BRIT*), censer.
encéphalogramme [ɑ̃sefalɔgram] *nm* encephalogram.
encercler [ɑ̃sɛrkle] *vt* to surround.
enchaîné [ɑ̃ʃene] *nm (CINÉ)* link shot.
enchaînement [ɑ̃ʃɛnmɑ̃] *nm (fig)* linking.
enchaîner [ɑ̃ʃene] *vt* to chain up; *(mouvements, séquences)* to link (together) ♦ *vi* to carry on.
enchanté, e [ɑ̃ʃɑ̃te] *adj (ravi)* delighted; *(ensorcelé)* enchanted; ~ **(de faire votre connaissance)** pleased to meet you, how do you do?
enchantement [ɑ̃ʃɑ̃tmɑ̃] *nm* delight; *(magie)* enchantment; **comme par** ~ as if by magic.
enchanter [ɑ̃ʃɑ̃te] *vt* to delight.
enchanteur, teresse [ɑ̃ʃɑ̃tœr, -trɛs] *adj* enchanting.
enchâsser [ɑ̃ʃase] *vt:* ~ **qch (dans)** to set sth (in).
enchère [ɑ̃ʃɛr] *nf* bid; **faire une** ~ to (make a) bid; **mettre/vendre aux** ~s to put up for (sale by)/sell by auction; **les** ~s **montent** the bids are rising; **faire monter les** ~s *(fig)* to raise the bidding.
enchérir [ɑ̃ʃerir] *vi:* ~ **sur qn** *(aux enchères, aussi fig)* to outbid sb.
enchérisseur, euse [ɑ̃ʃerisœr, -øz] *nm/f* bidder.
enchevêtrement [ɑ̃ʃvɛtrəmɑ̃] *nm* tangle.
enchevêtrer [ɑ̃ʃvetre] *vt* to tangle (up).
enclave [ɑ̃klav] *nf* enclave.
enclaver [ɑ̃klave] *vt* to enclose, hem in.
enclencher [ɑ̃klɑ̃ʃe] *vt (mécanisme)* to engage; *(fig: affaire)* to set in motion; **s'**~ *vi* to engage.
enclin, e [ɑ̃klɛ̃, -in] *adj:* ~ **à qch/à faire** inclined *ou* prone to sth/to do.
enclore [ɑ̃klɔr] *vt* to enclose.
enclos [ɑ̃klo] *nm* enclosure; *(clôture)* fence.
enclume [ɑ̃klym] *nf* anvil.
encoche [ɑ̃kɔʃ] *nf* notch.
encoder [ɑ̃kɔde] *vt* to encode.
encodeur [ɑ̃kɔdœr] *nm* encoder.
encoignure [ɑ̃kɔɲyr] *nf* corner.
encoller [ɑ̃kɔle] *vt* to paste.
encolure [ɑ̃kɔlyr] *nf (tour de cou)* collar size; *(col, cou)* neck.
encombrant, e [ɑ̃kɔ̃brɑ̃, -ɑ̃t] *adj* cumbersome, bulky.
encombre [ɑ̃kɔ̃br(ə)]: **sans** ~ *adv* without mishap *ou* incident.
encombré, e [ɑ̃kɔ̃bre] *adj (pièce, passage)* cluttered; *(lignes téléphoniques)* engaged;

(marché) saturated.
encombrement [ɑ̃kɔ̃brəmɑ̃] *nm (d'un lieu)* cluttering (up); *(d'un objet: dimensions)* bulk.
encombrer [ɑ̃kɔ̃bre] *vt* to clutter (up); *(gêner)* to hamper; **s'**~ **de** *(bagages etc)* to load *ou* burden o.s. with; ~ **le passage** to block *ou* obstruct the way.
encontre [ɑ̃kɔ̃tr(ə)]: **à l'**~ **de** *prép* against, counter to.
encorbellement [ɑ̃kɔrbɛlmɑ̃] *nm:* **fenêtre en** ~ oriel window.
encorder [ɑ̃kɔrde] *vt:* **s'**~ *(ALPINISME)* to rope up.

═══════════════════════ *MOT-CLÉ*

encore [ɑ̃kɔr] *adv* **1** *(continuation)* still; **il y travaille** ~ he's still working on it; **pas** ~ not yet
2 *(de nouveau)* again; **j'irai** ~ **demain** I'll go again tomorrow; ~ **une fois** (once) again; ~ **un effort** one last effort; ~ **deux jours** two more days
3 *(intensif)* even, still; ~ **plus fort/mieux** even louder/better, louder/better still; **hier** ~ even yesterday; **non seulement ..., mais** ~ ... not only ..., but also ...; ~! *(insatisfaction)* not again!; **quoi** ~? what now?
4 *(restriction)* so *ou* then, only; ~ **pourrais-je le faire si ...** even so, I might be able to do it if ...; **si** ~ if only
encore que *conj* although.

encourageant, e [ɑ̃kuraʒɑ̃, -ɑ̃t] *adj* encouraging.
encouragement [ɑ̃kuraʒmɑ̃] *nm* encouragement; *(récompense)* incentive.
encourager [ɑ̃kuraʒe] *vt* to encourage; ~ **qn à faire qch** to encourage sb to do sth.
encourir [ɑ̃kurir] *vt* to incur.
encrasser [ɑ̃krase] *vt* to foul up; *(AUTO etc)* to soot up.
encre [ɑ̃kr(ə)] *nf* ink; ~ **de Chine** Indian ink; ~ **indélébile** indelible ink; ~ **sympathique** invisible ink.
encrer [ɑ̃kre] *vt* to ink.
encreur [ɑ̃krœr] *adj m:* **rouleau** ~ inking roller.
encrier [ɑ̃krije] *nm* inkwell.
encroûter [ɑ̃krute]: **s'**~ *vi (fig)* to get into a rut, get set in one's ways.
encyclique [ɑ̃siklik] *nf* encyclical.
encyclopédie [ɑ̃siklɔpedi] *nf* encyclopaedia (*BRIT*), encyclopedia (*US*).
encyclopédique [ɑ̃siklɔpedik] *adj* encyclopaedic (*BRIT*), encyclopedic (*US*).
endémique [ɑ̃demik] *adj* endemic.
endetté, e [ɑ̃dete] *adj* in debt; *(fig):* **très** ~ **envers qn** deeply indebted to sb.
endettement [ɑ̃dɛtmɑ̃] *nm* debts *pl*.
endetter [ɑ̃dete] *vt,* **s'**~ *vi* to get into debt.
endeuiller [ɑ̃dœje] *vt* to plunge into mourning; **manifestation endeuillée par**

event over which a tragic shadow was cast
by.

endiablé, e [ãdjable] *adj* furious; (*enfant*)
boisterous.

endiguer [ãdige] *vt* to dyke (up); (*fig*) to
check, hold back.

endimancher [ãdimãʃe] *vt*: **s'~** to put on one's
Sunday best; **avoir l'air endimanché** to be all
done up to the nines (*fam*).

endive [ãdiv] *nf* chicory *no pl.*

endocrine [ãdɔkrin] *adj f*: **glande ~** endocrine
(gland).

endoctrinement [ãdɔktrinmã] *nm*
indoctrination.

endoctriner [ãdɔktrine] *vt* to indoctrinate.

endolori, e [ãdɔlɔri] *adj* painful.

endommager [ãdɔmaʒe] *vt* to damage.

endormant, e [ãdɔrmã, -ãt] *adj* dull, boring.

endormi, e [ãdɔrmi] *pp de* **endormir** ♦ *adj*
(*personne*) asleep; (*fig: indolent, lent*)
sluggish; (*engourdi: main, pied*) numb.

endormir [ãdɔrmir] *vt* to put to sleep; (*suj:
chaleur etc*) to send to sleep; (*MÉD: dent, nerf*)
to anaesthetize; (*fig: soupçons*) to allay; **s'~**
vi to fall asleep, go to sleep.

endoscope [ãdɔskɔp] *nm* (*MÉD*) endoscope.

endoscopie [ãdɔskɔpi] *nf* endoscopy.

endosser [ãdose] *vt* (*responsabilité*) to take,
shoulder; (*chèque*) to endorse; (*uniforme,
tenue*) to put on, don.

endroit [ãdrwa] *nm* place; (*localité*): **les gens
de l'~** the local people; (*opposé à l'envers*)
right side; **à cet ~** in this place; **à l'~** right
side out; the right way up; (*vêtement*) the
right way out; **à l'~ de** *prép* regarding, with
regard to; **par ~s** in places.

enduire [ãdɥir] *vt* to coat; **~ qch de** to coat
sth with.

enduit, e [ãdɥi, -it] *pp de* **enduire** ♦ *nm* coating.

endurance [ãdyrãs] *nf* endurance.

endurant, e [ãdyrã, -ãt] *adj* tough, hardy.

endurcir [ãdyrsir] *vt* (*physiquement*) to
toughen; (*moralement*) to harden; **s'~** *vi* to
become tougher, to become hardened.

endurer [ãdyre] *vt* to endure, bear.

énergétique [enɛrʒetik] *adj* (*ressources etc*)
energy *cpd*; (*aliment*) energizing.

énergie [enɛrʒi] *nf* (*PHYSIQUE*) energy; (*TECH*)
power; (*fig: physique*) energy; (*: morale*)
vigour, spirit; **~ éolienne/solaire** wind/solar
power.

énergique [enɛrʒik] *adj* energetic; vigorous;
(*mesures*) drastic, stringent.

énergiquement [enɛrʒikmã] *adv*
energetically; drastically.

énergisant, e [enɛrʒizã, -ãt] *adj* energizing.

énergumène [enɛrgymɛn] *nm* rowdy
character *ou* customer.

énervant, e [enɛrvã, -ãt] *adj* irritating.

énervé, e [enɛrve] *adj* nervy, on edge; (*agacé*)
irritated.

énervement [enɛrvəmã] *nm* nerviness;

irritation.

énerver [enɛrve] *vt* to irritate, annoy; **s'~** *vi* to
get excited, get worked up.

enfance [ãfãs] *nf* (*âge*) childhood; (*fig*)
infancy; (*enfants*) children *pl*; **c'est l'~ de
l'art** it's child's play; **petite ~** infancy;
souvenir/ami d'~ childhood memory/friend;
retomber en ~ to lapse into one's second
childhood.

enfant [ãfã] *nm/f* child (*pl* children); **~
adoptif/naturel** adopted/natural child; **bon
~** *adj* good-natured, easy-going; **~ de chœur**
nm (*REL*) altar boy; **~ prodige** child prodigy;
~ unique only child.

enfanter [ãfãte] *vi* to give birth ♦ *vt* to give
birth to.

enfantillage [ãfãtijaʒ] *nm* (*péj*) childish
behaviour *no pl.*

enfantin, e [ãfãtɛ̃, -in] *adj* childlike; (*péj*)
childish; (*langage*) child *cpd.*

enfer [ãfɛr] *nm* hell; **allure/bruit d'~**
horrendous speed/noise.

enfermer [ãfɛrme] *vt* to shut up; (*à clef,
interner*) to lock up; **s'~** to shut o.s. away;
s'~ à clé to lock o.s. in; **s'~ dans la
solitude/le mutisme** to retreat into
solitude/silence.

enferrer [ãfɛre] : **s'~** *vi*: **s'~ dans** to tangle o.s.
up in.

enfiévré, e [ãfjevre] *adj* (*fig*) feverish.

enfilade [ãfilad] *nf*: **une ~ de** a series *ou* line
of; **prendre des rues en ~** to cross directly
from one street into the next.

enfiler [ãfile] *vt* (*vêtement*): **~ qch** to slip sth
on, slip into sth; (*insérer*): **~ qch dans** to
stick sth into; (*rue, couloir*) to take; (*perles*)
to string; (*aiguille*) to thread; **s'~ dans** to
disappear into.

enfin [ãfɛ̃] *adv* at last; (*en énumérant*) lastly;
(*de restriction, résignation*) still; (*eh bien*) well;
(*pour conclure*) in a word.

enflammé, e [ãflame] *adj* (*torche, allumette*)
burning; (*MÉD: plaie*) inflamed; (*fig: nature,
discours, déclaration*) fiery.

enflammer [ãflame] *vt* to set fire to; (*MÉD*) to
inflame; **s'~** *vi* to catch fire; to become
inflamed.

enflé, e [ãfle] *adj* swollen; (*péj: style*)
bombastic, turgid.

enfler [ãfle] *vi* to swell (up); **s'~** *vi* to swell.

enflure [ãflyr] *nf* swelling.

enfoncé, e [ãfɔ̃se] *adj* staved-in, smashed-in;
(*yeux*) deep-set.

enfoncement [ãfɔ̃smã] *nm* (*recoin*) nook.

enfoncer [ãfɔ̃se] *vt* (*clou*) to drive in; (*faire
pénétrer*): **~ qch dans** to push (*ou* drive) sth
into; (*forcer: porte*) to break open; (*: plancher*)
to cause to cave in; (*défoncer: côtes etc*) to
smash; (*fam: surpasser*) to lick, beat (hollow)
♦ *vi* (*dans la vase etc*) to sink in; (*sol, surface
porteuse*) to give way; **s'~** *vi* to sink; **s'~
dans** to sink into; (*forêt, ville*) to disappear

into; ~ **un chapeau sur la tête** to cram *ou* jam a hat on one's head; ~ **qn dans la dette** to drag sb into debt.

enfouir [ɑ̃fwiʀ] *vt* (*dans le sol*) to bury; (*dans un tiroir etc*) to tuck away; **s'**~ **dans/sous** to bury o.s. in/under.

enfourcher [ɑ̃fuʀʃe] *vt* to mount; ~ **son dada** (*fig*) to get on one's hobby-horse.

enfourner [ɑ̃fuʀne] *vt* to put in the oven; (*poterie*) to put in the kiln; ~ **qch dans** to shove *ou* stuff sth into; **s'**~ **dans** (*suj: personne*) to dive into.

enfreignais [ɑ̃fʀɛɲɛ] *etc vb voir* **enfreindre**.

enfreindre [ɑ̃fʀɛ̃dʀ(ə)] *vt* to infringe, break.

enfuir [ɑ̃fɥiʀ]: **s'**~ *vi* to run away *ou* off.

enfumer [ɑ̃fyme] *vt* to smoke out.

enfuyais [ɑ̃fɥijɛ] *etc vb voir* **enfuir**.

engagé, e [ɑ̃gaʒe] *adj* (*littérature etc*) engagé, committed.

engageant, e [ɑ̃gaʒɑ̃, -ɑ̃t] *adj* attractive, appealing.

engagement [ɑ̃gaʒmɑ̃] *nm* taking on, engaging; starting; investing; (*promesse*) commitment; (*MIL: combat*) engagement; (*: recrutement*) enlistment; (*SPORT*) entry; **prendre l'**~ **de faire** to undertake to do; **sans** ~ (*COMM*) without obligation.

engager [ɑ̃gaʒe] *vt* (*embaucher*) to take on, engage; (*commencer*) to start; (*lier*) to bind, commit; (*impliquer, entraîner*) to involve; (*investir*) to invest, lay out; (*faire intervenir*) to engage; (*SPORT: concurrents, chevaux*) to enter; (*inciter*): ~ **qn à faire** to urge sb to do; (*faire pénétrer*): ~ **qch dans** to insert sth into; ~ **qn à qch** to urge sth on sb; **s'**~ to get taken on; (*MIL*) to enlist; (*promettre, politiquement*) to commit o.s.; (*débuter*) to start (up); **s'**~ **à faire** to undertake to do; **s'**~ **dans** (*rue, passage*) to enter, turn into; (*s'emboîter*) to engage into; (*fig: affaire, discussion*) to enter into, embark on.

engazonner [ɑ̃gazɔne] *vt* to turf.

engeance [ɑ̃ʒɑ̃s] *nf* mob.

engelure [ɑ̃ʒlyʀ] *nf* chilblain.

engendrer [ɑ̃ʒɑ̃dʀe] *vt* to father; (*fig*) to create, breed.

engin [ɑ̃ʒɛ̃] *nm* machine; instrument; vehicle; (*péj*) gadget; (*AVIAT: avion*) aircraft *inv*; (*: missile*) missile; ~ **blindé** armoured vehicle; ~ **(explosif)** (explosive) device; ~**s (spéciaux)** missiles.

englober [ɑ̃glɔbe] *vt* to include.

engloutir [ɑ̃glutiʀ] *vt* to swallow up; (*fig: dépenses*) to devour; **s'**~ to be engulfed.

englué, e [ɑ̃glye] *adj* sticky.

engoncé, e [ɑ̃gɔ̃se] *adj:* ~ **dans** cramped in.

engorgement [ɑ̃gɔʀʒəmɑ̃] *nm* blocking; (*MÉD*) engorgement.

engorger [ɑ̃gɔʀʒe] *vt* to obstruct, block; **s'**~ *vi* to become blocked.

engouement [ɑ̃gumɑ̃] *nm* (sudden) passion.

engouffrer [ɑ̃gufʀe] *vt* to swallow up, devour;

s'~ **dans** to rush into.

engourdi, e [ɑ̃guʀdi] *adj* numb.

engourdir [ɑ̃guʀdiʀ] *vt* to numb; (*fig*) to dull, blunt; **s'**~ *vi* to go numb.

engrais [ɑ̃gʀɛ] *nm* manure; ~ **(chimique)** (chemical) fertilizer; ~ **organique/inorganique** organic/inorganic fertilizer.

engraisser [ɑ̃gʀɛse] *vt* to fatten (up); (*terre: fertiliser*) to fertilize ♦ *vi* (*péj*) to get fat(ter).

engranger [ɑ̃gʀɑ̃ʒe] *vt* (*foin*) to bring in; (*fig*) to store away.

engrenage [ɑ̃gʀənaʒ] *nm* gears *pl*, gearing; (*fig*) chain.

engueuler [ɑ̃gœle] *vt* (*fam*) to bawl at *ou* out.

enguirlander [ɑ̃giʀlɑ̃de] *vt* (*fam*) to give sb a bawling out, bawl at.

enhardir [ɑ̃aʀdiʀ]: **s'**~ *vi* to grow bolder.

ENI [eni] *sigle f* = **école normale (d'instituteurs)**

énième [ɛnjɛm] *adj* = **nième**.

énigmatique [enigmatik] *adj* enigmatic.

énigmatiquement [enigmatikmɑ̃] *adv* enigmatically.

énigme [enigm(ə)] *nf* riddle.

enivrant, e [ɑ̃nivʀɑ̃, -ɑ̃t] *adj* intoxicating.

enivrer [ɑ̃nivʀe] *vt:* **s'**~ to get drunk; **s'**~ **de** (*fig*) to become intoxicated with.

enjambée [ɑ̃ʒɑ̃be] *nf* stride; **d'une** ~ with one stride.

enjamber [ɑ̃ʒɑ̃be] *vt* to stride over; (*suj: pont etc*) to span, straddle.

enjeu, x [ɑ̃ʒø] *nm* stakes *pl*.

enjoindre [ɑ̃ʒwɛ̃dʀ(ə)] *vt:* ~ **à qn de faire** to enjoin *ou* order sb to do.

enjôler [ɑ̃ʒole] *vt* to coax, wheedle.

enjôleur, euse [ɑ̃ʒolœʀ, -øz] *adj* (*sourire, paroles*) winning.

enjolivement [ɑ̃ʒɔlivmɑ̃] *nm* embellishment.

enjoliver [ɑ̃ʒɔlive] *vt* to embellish.

enjoliveur [ɑ̃ʒɔlivœʀ] *nm* (*AUTO*) hub cap.

enjoué, e [ɑ̃ʒwe] *adj* playful.

enlacer [ɑ̃lase] *vt* (*étreindre*) to embrace, hug; (*suj: lianes*) to wind round, entwine.

enlaidir [ɑ̃lediʀ] *vt* to make ugly ♦ *vi* to become ugly.

enlevé, e [ɑ̃lve] *adj* (*morceau de musique*) played brightly.

enlèvement [ɑ̃lɛvmɑ̃] *nm* removal; (*rapt*) abduction, kidnapping; **l'**~ **des ordures ménagères** refuse collection.

enlever [ɑ̃lve] *vt* (*ôter: gén*) to remove; (*: vêtement, lunettes*) to take off; (*: MÉD: organe*) to remove; (*emporter: ordures etc*) to collect, take away; (*kidnapper*) to abduct, kidnap; (*obtenir: prix, contrat*) to win; (*MIL: position*) to take; (*morceau de piano etc*) to execute with spirit *ou* brio; (*prendre*): ~ **qch à qn** to take sth (away) from sb; **s'**~ *vi* (*tache*) to come out *ou* off; **la maladie qui nous l'a enlevé** (*euphémisme*) the illness which took him from us.

enliser [ɑ̃lize]: **s'**~ *vi* to sink, get stuck; (*dialogue etc*) to get bogged down.

enluminure [ɑ̃lyminyʀ] *nf* illumination.

ENM *sigle f* (= *École nationale de la magistrature*) *grande école for law students*.

enneigé, e [ɑ̃neʒe] *adj* snowy; (*col*) snowed-up; (*maison*) snowed-in.

enneigement [ɑ̃nɛʒmɑ̃] *nm* depth of snow, snowfall; **bulletin d'~** snow report.

ennemi, e [ɛnmi] *adj* hostile; (*MIL*) enemy *cpd* ♦ *nm/f* enemy; **être ~ de** to be strongly averse *ou* opposed to.

ennième [ɛnjɛm] *adj* = **nième**.

ennoblir [ɑ̃nɔbliʀ] *vt* to ennoble.

ennui [ɑ̃nɥi] *nm* (*lassitude*) boredom; (*difficulté*) trouble *no pl*; **avoir des ~s** to have problems; **s'attirer des ~s** to cause problems for o.s.

ennuie [ɑ̃nɥi] *etc vb voir* **ennuyer**.

ennuyé, e [ɑ̃nɥije] *adj* (*air, personne*) preoccupied, worried.

ennuyer [ɑ̃nɥije] *vt* to bother; (*lasser*) to bore; **s'~** *vi* to be bored; **s'~ de** (*regretter*) to miss; **si cela ne vous ennuie pas** if it's no trouble to you.

ennuyeux, euse [ɑ̃nɥijø, -øz] *adj* boring, tedious; (*agaçant*) annoying.

énoncé [enɔ̃se] *nm* terms *pl*; wording; (*LING*) utterance.

énoncer [enɔ̃se] *vt* to say, express; (*conditions*) to set out, lay down, state.

énonciation [enɔ̃sjasjɔ̃] *nf* statement.

enorgueillir [ɑ̃nɔʀgœjiʀ]: **s'~ de** *vt* to pride o.s. on; to boast.

énorme [enɔʀm(ə)] *adj* enormous, huge.

énormément [enɔʀmemɑ̃] *adv* enormously, tremendously; **~ de neige/gens** an enormous amount of snow/number of people.

énormité [enɔʀmite] *nf* enormity, hugeness; (*propos*) outrageous remark.

en part. *abr* (= *en particulier*) esp.

enquérir [ɑ̃keʀiʀ]: **s'~ de** *vt* to inquire about.

enquête [ɑ̃kɛt] *nf* (*de journaliste, de police*) investigation; (*judiciaire, administrative*) inquiry; (*sondage d'opinion*) survey.

enquêter [ɑ̃kete] *vi* to investigate; to hold an inquiry; (*faire un sondage*): **~ (sur)** to do a survey (on), carry out an opinion poll (on).

enquêteur, euse *ou* **trice** [ɑ̃ketœʀ, -øz, -tʀis] *nm/f* officer in charge of an investigation; person conducting a survey; pollster.

enquiers, enquière [ɑ̃kjɛʀ] *etc vb voir* **enquérir**.

enquiquiner [ɑ̃kikine] *vt* to rile, irritate.

enquis, e [ɑ̃ki, -iz] *pp de* **enquérir**.

enraciné, e [ɑ̃ʀasine] *adj* deep-rooted.

enragé, e [ɑ̃ʀaʒe] *adj* (*MÉD*) rabid, with rabies; (*furieux*) furiously angry; (*fig*) fanatical; **~ de** wild about.

enrageant, e [ɑ̃ʀaʒɑ̃, -ɑ̃t] *adj* infuriating.

enrager [ɑ̃ʀaʒe] *vi* to be furious, be in a rage; **faire ~ qn** to make sb wild with anger.

enrayer [ɑ̃ʀeje] *vt* to check, stop; **s'~** *vi* (*arme à feu*) to jam.

enrégimenter [ɑ̃ʀeʒimɑ̃te] *vt* (*péj*) to enlist.

enregistrement [ɑ̃ʀʒistʀəmɑ̃] *nm* recording; (*ADMIN*) registration; **~ des bagages** (*à l'aéroport*) baggage check-in; **~ magnétique** tape-recording.

enregistrer [ɑ̃ʀʒistʀe] *vt* (*MUS, INFORM etc*) to record; (*remarquer, noter*) to note, record; (*COMM: commande*) to note, enter; (*fig: mémoriser*) to make a mental note of; (*ADMIN*) to register; (*aussi: faire ~: bagages: par train*) to register; (*: à l'aéroport*) to check in.

enregistreur, euse [ɑ̃ʀʒistʀœʀ, -øz] *adj* (*machine*) recording *cpd* ♦ *nm* (*appareil*): **~ de vol** (*AVIAT*) flight recorder.

enrhumé, e [ɑ̃ʀyme] *adj*: **il est ~** he has a cold.

enrhumer [ɑ̃ʀyme]: **s'~** *vi* to catch a cold.

enrichir [ɑ̃ʀiʃiʀ] *vt* to make rich(er); (*fig*) to enrich; **s'~** to get rich(er).

enrichissant, e [ɑ̃ʀiʃisɑ̃, -ɑ̃t] *adj* instructive.

enrichissement [ɑ̃ʀiʃismɑ̃] *nm* enrichment.

enrober [ɑ̃ʀɔbe] *vt*: **~ qch de** to coat sth with; (*fig*) to wrap sth up in.

enrôlement [ɑ̃ʀolmɑ̃] *nm* enlistment.

enrôler [ɑ̃ʀole] *vt* to enlist; **s'~ (dans)** to enlist (in).

enroué, e [ɑ̃ʀwe] *adj* hoarse.

enrouer [ɑ̃ʀwe]: **s'~** *vi* to go hoarse.

enrouler [ɑ̃ʀule] *vt* (*fil, corde*) to wind (up); **s'~** to coil up; **~ qch autour de** to wind sth (a)round.

enrouleur, euse [ɑ̃ʀulœʀ, -øz] *adj* (*TECH*) winding ♦ *nm voir* **ceinture**.

enrubanné, e [ɑ̃ʀybane] *adj* trimmed with ribbon.

ENS *sigle f* = **école normale supérieure**.

ensabler [ɑ̃sable] *vt* (*port, canal*) to silt up, sand up; (*embarcation*) to strand (on a sandbank); **s'~** *vi* to silt up; to get stranded.

ensacher [ɑ̃saʃe] *vt* to pack into bags.

ENSAM *sigle f* (= *École nationale supérieure des arts et métiers*) *grande école for engineering students*.

ensanglanté, e [ɑ̃sɑ̃glɑ̃te] *adj* covered with blood.

enseignant, e [ɑ̃sɛɲɑ̃, -ɑ̃t] *adj* teaching ♦ *nm/f* teacher.

enseigne [ɑ̃sɛɲ] *nf* sign ♦ *nm*: **~ de vaisseau** lieutenant; **à telle ~ que** so much so that; **être logés à la même ~** (*fig*) to be in the same boat; **~ lumineuse** neon sign.

enseignement [ɑ̃sɛɲmɑ̃] *nm* teaching; **~ ménager** home economics; **~ primaire** primary (*BRIT*) *ou* grade school (*US*) education; **~ secondaire** secondary (*BRIT*) *ou* high school (*US*) education.

enseigner [ɑ̃sɛɲe] *vt, vi* to teach; **~ qch à qn/ à qn que** to teach sb sth/sb that.

ensemble [ɑ̃sɑ̃bl(ə)] *adv* together ♦ *nm* (*assemblage, MATH*) set; (*totalité*): **l'~ du/de la** the whole *ou* entire; (*vêtement féminin*)

ensemble, suit; (*unité, harmonie*) unity; (*résidentiel*) housing development; **aller** ~ to go together; **impression/idée d'** ~ overall *ou* general impression/idea; **dans l'** ~ (*en gros*) on the whole; **dans son** ~ overall, in general; ~ **vocal/musical** vocal/musical ensemble.

ensemblier [ɑ̃sɑ̃blije] *nm* interior designer.

ensemencer [ɑ̃smɑ̃se] *vt* to sow.

enserrer [ɑ̃seʀe] *vt* to hug (tightly).

ENSET [ɛnsɛt] *sigle f* (= *École normale supérieure de l'enseignement technique*) *grande école for training technical teachers*.

ensevelir [ɑ̃sǝvliʀ] *vt* to bury.

ensilage [ɑ̃silaʒ] *nm* (*aliment*) silage.

ensoleillé, e [ɑ̃sɔleje] *adj* sunny.

ensoleillement [ɑ̃sɔlɛjmɑ̃] *nm* period *ou* hours *pl* of sunshine.

ensommeillé, e [ɑ̃sɔmeje] *adj* sleepy, drowsy.

ensorceler [ɑ̃sɔʀsǝle] *vt* to enchant, bewitch.

ensuite [ɑ̃sɥit] *adv* then, next; (*plus tard*) afterwards, later; ~ **de quoi** after which.

ensuivre [ɑ̃sɥivʀ(ǝ)]: **s'** ~ *vi* to follow, ensue; **il s'ensuit que ...** it follows that ...; **et tout ce qui s'ensuit** and all that goes with it.

entaché, e [ɑ̃taʃe] *adj*: ~ **de** marred by; ~ **de nullité** null and void.

entacher [ɑ̃taʃe] *vt* to soil.

entaille [ɑ̃taj] *nf* (*encoche*) notch; (*blessure*) cut; **se faire une** ~ to cut o.s.

entailler [ɑ̃taje] *vt* to notch; to cut; **s'** ~ **le doigt** to cut one's finger.

entamer [ɑ̃tame] *vt* to start; (*hostilités, pourparlers*) to open; (*fig: altérer*) to make a dent in; to damage.

entartrer [ɑ̃taʀtʀe]: **s'** ~ *vi* to fur up; (*dents*) to become covered with plaque.

entassement [ɑ̃tɑsmɑ̃] *nm* (*tas*) pile, heap.

entasser [ɑ̃tɑse] *vt* (*empiler*) to pile up, heap up; (*tenir à l'étroit*) to cram together; **s'** ~ *vi* to pile up; to cram; **s'** ~ **dans** to cram into.

entendement [ɑ̃tɑ̃dmɑ̃] *nm* understanding.

entendre [ɑ̃tɑ̃dʀ(ǝ)] *vt* to hear; (*comprendre*) to understand; (*vouloir dire*) to mean; (*vouloir*): ~ **être obéi/que** to intend *ou* mean to be obeyed/that; **j'ai entendu dire que** I've heard (it said) that; **je suis heureux de vous l'~ dire** I'm pleased to hear you say it; ~ **parler de** to hear of; **laisser** ~ **que, donner à** ~ **que** to let it be understood that; ~ **raison** to see sense, listen to reason; **qu'est- ce qu'il ne faut pas** ~! whatever next!; **j'ai mal entendu** I didn't catch what was said; **je vous entends très mal** I can hardly hear you; **s'** ~ *vi* (*sympathiser*) to get on; (*se mettre d'accord*) to agree; **s'** ~ **à qch/à faire** (*être compétent*) to be good at sth/doing; **ça s'entend** (*est audible*) it's audible; **je m'entends** I mean; **entendons-nous!** let's be clear what we mean.

entendu, e [ɑ̃tɑ̃dy] *pp de* **entendre** ♦ *adj* (*réglé*)

agreed; (*au courant: air*) knowing; **étant** ~ **que** since (it's understood *ou* agreed that); **(c'est)** ~ all right, agreed; **c'est** ~ (*concession*) all right, granted; **bien** ~ of course.

entente [ɑ̃tɑ̃t] *nf* (*entre amis, pays*) understanding, harmony; (*accord, traité*) agreement, understanding; **à double** ~ (*sens*) with a double meaning.

entériner [ɑ̃teʀine] *vt* to ratify, confirm.

entérite [ɑ̃teʀit] *nf* enteritis *no pl*.

enterrement [ɑ̃tɛʀmɑ̃] *nm* burying; (*cérémonie*) funeral, burial; (*cortège funèbre*) funeral procession.

enterrer [ɑ̃teʀe] *vt* to bury.

entêtant, e [ɑ̃tɛtɑ̃, -ɑ̃t] *adj* heady.

entêté, e [ɑ̃tete] *adj* stubborn.

en-tête [ɑ̃tɛt] *nm* heading; (*de papier à lettres*) letterhead; **papier à** ~ headed notepaper.

entêtement [ɑ̃tɛtmɑ̃] *nm* stubbornness.

entêter [ɑ̃tete]: **s'** ~ *vi*: **s'** ~ (**à faire**) to persist (in doing).

enthousiasmant, e [ɑ̃tuzjasmɑ̃, -ɑ̃t] *adj* exciting.

enthousiasme [ɑ̃tuzjasm(ǝ)] *nm* enthusiasm; **avec** ~ enthusiastically.

enthousiasmé, e [ɑ̃tuzjasme] *adj* filled with enthusiasm.

enthousiasmer [ɑ̃tuzjasme] *vt* to fill with enthusiasm; **s'** ~ (**pour qch**) to get enthusiastic (about sth).

enthousiaste [ɑ̃tuzjast(ǝ)] *adj* enthusiastic.

enticher [ɑ̃tiʃe]: **s'** ~ **de** *vt* to become infatuated with.

entier, ière [ɑ̃tje, -jɛʀ] *adj* (*non entamé, en totalité*) whole; (*total, complet*) complete; (*fig: caractère*) unbending, averse to compromise ♦ *nm* (*MATH*) whole; **en** ~ totally; in its entirety; **se donner tout** ~ **à qch** to devote o.s. completely to sth; **lait** ~ full-cream milk; **pain** ~ wholemeal bread; **nombre** ~ whole number.

entièrement [ɑ̃tjɛʀmɑ̃] *adv* entirely, completely, wholly.

entité [ɑ̃tite] *nf* entity.

entomologie [ɑ̃tɔmɔlɔʒi] *nf* entomology.

entonner [ɑ̃tɔne] *vt* (*chanson*) to strike up.

entonnoir [ɑ̃tɔnwaʀ] *nm* (*ustensile*) funnel; (*trou*) shell-hole, crater.

entorse [ɑ̃tɔʀs(ǝ)] *nf* (*MÉD*) sprain; (*fig*): ~ **à la loi/au règlement** infringement of the law/rule; **se faire une** ~ **à la cheville/au poignet** to sprain one's ankle/wrist.

entortiller [ɑ̃tɔʀtije] *vt* (*envelopper*): ~ **qch dans/avec** to wrap sth in/with; (*enrouler*): ~ **qch autour de** to twist *ou* wind sth (a)round; (*fam*): ~ **qn** to get (a)round sb; (: *duper*) to hoodwink sb (*BRIT*), trick sb; **s'** ~ **dans** (*draps*) to roll o.s. up in; (*fig: réponses*) to get tangled up in.

entourage [ɑ̃tuʀaʒ] *nm* circle; family (circle); (*d'une vedette etc*) entourage; (*ce qui enclôt*) surround.

entouré, e [ɑ̃tuʀe] *adj* (*recherché, admiré*) popular; ~ **de** surrounded by.

entourer [ɑ̃tuʀe] *vt* to surround; (*apporter son soutien à*) to rally round; ~ **de** to surround with; (*trait*) to encircle with; **s'**~ **de** to surround o.s. with; **s'**~ **de précautions** to take all possible precautions.

entourloupette [ɑ̃tuʀlupɛt] *nf* mean trick.

entournures [ɑ̃tuʀnyʀ] *nfpl*: **gêné aux** ~ in financial difficulties; (*fig*) a bit awkward.

entracte [ɑ̃tʀakt(ə)] *nm* interval.

entraide [ɑ̃tʀɛd] *nf* mutual aid *ou* assistance.

entraider [ɑ̃tʀede]: **s'**~ *vi* to help each other.

entrailles [ɑ̃tʀaj] *nfpl* entrails; (*humaines*) bowels.

entrain [ɑ̃tʀɛ̃] *nm* spirit; **avec** ~ (*répondre, travailler*) energetically; **faire qch sans** ~ to do sth half-heartedly *ou* without enthusiasm.

entraînant, e [ɑ̃tʀɛnɑ̃, -ɑ̃t] *adj* (*musique*) stirring, rousing.

entraînement [ɑ̃tʀɛnmɑ̃] *nm* training; (*TECH*): ~ **à chaîne/galet** chain/wheel drive; **manquer d'**~ to be unfit; ~ **par ergots/ friction** (*INFORM*) tractor/friction feed.

entraîner [ɑ̃tʀene] *vt* (*tirer: wagons*) to pull; (*charrier*) to carry *ou* drag along; (*TECH*) to drive; (*emmener: personne*) to take (off); (*mener à l'assaut, influencer*) to lead; (*SPORT*) to train; (*impliquer*) to entail; (*causer*) to lead to, bring about; ~ **qn à faire** (*inciter*) to lead sb to do; **s'**~ (*SPORT*) to train; **s'**~ **à qch/à faire** to train o.s. for sth/to do.

entraîneur [ɑ̃tʀenœʀ] *nm* (*SPORT*) coach, trainer; (*HIPPISME*) trainer.

entraîneuse [ɑ̃tʀenøz] *nf* (*de bar*) hostess.

entrapercevoir [ɑ̃tʀapɛʀsəvwaʀ] *vt* to catch a glimpse of.

entrave [ɑ̃tʀav] *nf* hindrance.

entraver [ɑ̃tʀave] *vt* (*circulation*) to hold up; (*action, progrès*) to hinder, hamper.

entre [ɑ̃tʀ(ə)] *prép* between; (*parmi*) among(st); **l'un d'**~ **eux/nous** one of them/us; **le meilleur d'**~ **eux/nous** the best of them/us; **ils préfèrent rester** ~ **eux** they prefer to keep to themselves; ~ **autres (choses)** among other things; ~ **nous,** ... between ourselves ..., between you and me ...; **ils se battent** ~ **eux** they are fighting among(st) themselves.

entrebâillé, e [ɑ̃tʀəbaje] *adj* half-open, ajar.

entrebâillement [ɑ̃tʀəbajmɑ̃] *nm*: **dans l'**~ (**de la porte**) in the half-open door.

entrebâiller [ɑ̃tʀəbaje] *vt* to half open.

entrechat [ɑ̃tʀəʃa] *nm* leap.

entrechoquer [ɑ̃tʀəʃɔke]: **s'**~ *vi* to knock *ou* bang together.

entrecôte [ɑ̃tʀəkot] *nf* entrecôte *ou* rib steak.

entrecoupé, e [ɑ̃tʀəkupe] *adj* (*paroles, voix*) broken.

entrecouper [ɑ̃tʀəkupe] *vt*: ~ **qch de** to interesperse sth with; ~ **un récit/voyage de** to interrupt a story/journey with; **s'**~ (*traits, lignes*) to cut across each other.

entrecroiser [ɑ̃tʀəkʀwaze] *vt*, **s'**~ *vi* to intertwine.

entrée [ɑ̃tʀe] *nf* entrance; (*accès: au cinéma etc*) admission; (*billet*) (admission) ticket; (*CULIN*) first course; (*COMM: de marchandises*) entry; (*INFORM*) entry, input; ~**s** *nfpl*: **avoir ses** ~**s chez** *ou* **auprès de** to be a welcome visitor to; **d'**~ *adv* from the outset; **erreur d'**~ input error; **"**~ **interdite"** "no admittance *ou* entry"; ~ **des artistes** stage door; ~ **en matière** introduction; ~ **en scène** entrance; ~ **de service** service entrance.

entrefaites [ɑ̃tʀəfɛt]: **sur ces** ~ *adv* at this juncture.

entrefilet [ɑ̃tʀəfilɛ] *nm* (*article*) paragraph, short report.

entregent [ɑ̃tʀəʒɑ̃] *nm*: **avoir de l'**~ to have an easy manner.

entre-jambes [ɑ̃tʀəʒɑ̃b] *nm inv* crotch.

entrelacement [ɑ̃tʀəlasmɑ̃] *nm*: **un** ~ **de** ... a network of ....

entrelacer [ɑ̃tʀəlase] *vt*, **s'**~ *vi* to intertwine.

entrelarder [ɑ̃tʀəlaʀde] *vt* to lard; (*fig*): **entrelardé de** interspersed with.

entremêler [ɑ̃tʀəmele] *vt*: ~ **qch de** to (inter)mingle sth with.

entremets [ɑ̃tʀəmɛ] *nm* (cream) dessert.

entremetteur, euse [ɑ̃tʀəmɛtœʀ, -øz] *nm/f* go-between.

entremettre [ɑ̃tʀəmɛtʀ(ə)]: **s'**~ *vi* to intervene.

entremise [ɑ̃tʀəmiz] *nf* intervention; **par l'**~ **de** through.

entrepont [ɑ̃tʀəpɔ̃] *nm* steerage; **dans l'**~ in steerage.

entreposer [ɑ̃tʀəpoze] *vt* to store, put into storage.

entrepôt [ɑ̃tʀəpo] *nm* warehouse.

entreprenant, e [ɑ̃tʀəpʀənɑ̃, -ɑ̃t] *vb voir* **entreprendre** ♦ *adj* (*actif*) enterprising; (*trop galant*) forward.

entreprendre [ɑ̃tʀəpʀɑ̃dʀ(ə)] *vt* (*se lancer dans*) to undertake; (*commencer*) to begin *ou* start (upon); (*personne*) to buttonhole; ~ **qn sur un sujet** to tackle sb on a subject; ~ **de faire** to undertake to do.

entrepreneur [ɑ̃tʀəpʀənœʀ] *nm*: ~ **(en bâtiment)** (building) contractor; ~ **de pompes funèbres** funeral director, undertaker.

entreprenne [ɑ̃tʀəpʀɛn] *etc vb voir* **entreprendre.**

entrepris, e [ɑ̃tʀəpʀi, -iz] *pp de* **entreprendre** ♦ *nf* (*société*) firm, business; (*action*) undertaking, venture.

entrer [ɑ̃tʀe] *vi* to go (*ou* come) in, enter ♦ *vt* (*INFORM*) to input, enter; **(faire)** ~ **qch dans** to get sth into; ~ **dans** (*gén*) to enter; (*pièce*) to go (*ou* come) into, enter; (*club*) to join;

(*heurter*) to run into; (*partager: vues, craintes de qn*) to share; (*être une composante de*) to go into; (*faire partie de*) to form part of; ~ **au couvent** to enter a convent; ~ **à l'hôpital** to go into hospital; ~ **dans le système** (*INFORM*) to log in; ~ **en fureur** to become angry; ~ **en ébullition** to start to boil; ~ **en scène** to come on stage; **laisser** ~ **qn/qch** to let sb/sth in; **faire** ~ (*visiteur*) to show in.

entresol [ɑ̃tʀəsɔl] *nm* entresol, mezzanine.

entre-temps [ɑ̃tʀətɑ̃] *adv* meanwhile, (in the) meantime.

entretenir [ɑ̃tʀətniʀ] *vt* to maintain; (*amitié*) to keep alive; (*famille, maîtresse*) to support, keep; ~ **qn (de)** to speak to sb (about); **s'~ (de)** to converse (about); ~ **qn dans l'erreur** to let sb remain in ignorance.

entretenu, e [ɑ̃tʀətny] *pp de* **entretenir** ♦ *adj* (*femme*) kept; **bien/mal** ~ (*maison, jardin*) well/badly kept.

entretien [ɑ̃tʀətjɛ̃] *nm* maintenance; (*discussion*) discussion, talk; (*audience*) interview; **frais d'~** maintenance charges.

entretiendrai [ɑ̃tʀətjɛ̃dʀe], **entretiens** [ɑ̃tʀətjɛ̃] *etc vb voir* **entretenir**.

entretuer [ɑ̃tʀətɥe]: **s'~** *vi* to kill one another.

entreverrai [ɑ̃tʀəveʀe], **entrevit** [ɑ̃tʀəvi] *etc vb voir* **entrevoir**.

entrevoir [ɑ̃tʀəvwaʀ] *vt* (*à peine*) to make out; (*brièvement*) to catch a glimpse of.

entrevu, e [ɑ̃tʀəvy] *pp de* **entrevoir** ♦ *nf* meeting; (*audience*) interview.

entrouvert, e [ɑ̃tʀuveʀ, -ɛʀt(ə)] *pp de* **entrouvrir** ♦ *adj* half-open.

entrouvrir [ɑ̃tʀuvʀiʀ] *vt*, **s'~** *vi* to half open.

énumération [enymeʀasjɔ̃] *nf* enumeration.

énumérer [enymeʀe] *vt* to list, enumerate.

énurésie [enyʀezi] *nf* enuresis.

envahir [ɑ̃vaiʀ] *vt* to invade; (*suj: inquiétude, peur*) to come over.

envahissant, e [ɑ̃vaisɑ̃, -ɑ̃t] *adj* (*péj: personne*) interfering, intrusive.

envahissement [ɑ̃vaismɑ̃] *nm* invasion.

envahisseur [ɑ̃vaisœʀ] *nm* (*MIL*) invader.

envasement [ɑ̃vɑzmɑ̃] *nm* silting up.

envaser [ɑ̃vɑze]: **s'~** *vi* to get bogged down (in the mud).

enveloppe [ɑ̃vlɔp] *nf* (*de lettre*) envelope; (*TECH*) casing; outer layer; **mettre sous** ~ to put in an envelope; ~ **autocollante** self-seal envelope; ~ **budgétaire** budget; ~ **à fenêtre** window envelope.

envelopper [ɑ̃vlɔpe] *vt* to wrap; (*fig*) to envelop, shroud; **s'~ dans un châle/une couverture** to wrap o.s. in a shawl/blanket.

envenimer [ɑ̃vnime] *vt* to aggravate; **s'~** *vi* (*plaie*) to fester; (*situation, relations*) to worsen.

envergure [ɑ̃vɛʀgyʀ] *nf* (*d'un oiseau, avion*) wingspan; (*fig: étendue*) scope; (: *valeur*) calibre.

enverrai [ɑ̃veʀe] *etc vb voir* **envoyer**.

envers [ɑ̃vɛʀ] *prép* towards, to ♦ *nm* other side; (*d'une étoffe*) wrong side; **à l'~** upside down; back to front; (*vêtement*) inside out; ~ **et contre tous** *ou* **tout** against all opposition.

enviable [ɑ̃vjabl(ə)] *adj* enviable; **peu** ~ unenviable.

envie [ɑ̃vi] *nf* (*sentiment*) envy; (*souhait*) desire, wish; (*tache sur la peau*) birthmark; (*filet de peau*) hangnail; **avoir** ~ **de** to feel like; (*désir plus fort*) to want; **avoir** ~ **de faire** to feel like doing; to want to do; **avoir** ~ **que** to wish that; **donner** ~ **à qn l'~ de faire** to make sb want to do; **ça lui fait** ~ he would like that.

envier [ɑ̃vje] *vt* to envy; ~ **qch à qn** to envy sb sth; **n'avoir rien à** ~ **à** to have no cause to be envious of.

envieux, euse [ɑ̃vjø, -øz] *adj* envious.

environ [ɑ̃viʀɔ̃] *adv*: ~ **3 h/2 km, 3 h/2 km** ~ (around) about 3 o'clock/2 km, 3 o'clock/2 km or so.

environnant, e [ɑ̃viʀɔnɑ̃, -ɑ̃t] *adj* surrounding.

environnement [ɑ̃viʀɔnmɑ̃] *nm* environment.

environnementaliste [ɑ̃viʀɔnmɑ̃talist(ə)] *nm/f* environmentalist.

environner [ɑ̃viʀɔne] *vt* to surround.

environs [ɑ̃viʀɔ̃] *nmpl* surroundings; **aux** ~ **de** around.

envisageable [ɑ̃vizaʒabl(ə)] *adj* conceivable.

envisager [ɑ̃vizaʒe] *vt* (*examiner, considérer*) to view, contemplate; (*avoir en vue*) to envisage; ~ **de faire** to consider *ou* contemplate doing.

envoi [ɑ̃vwa] *nm* sending; (*paquet*) parcel, consignment; ~ **contre remboursement** (*COMM*) cash on delivery.

envoie [ɑ̃vwa] *etc vb voir* **envoyer**.

envol [ɑ̃vɔl] *nm* takeoff.

envolée [ɑ̃vɔle] *nf* (*fig*) flight.

envoler [ɑ̃vɔle]: **s'~** *vi* (*oiseau*) to fly away *ou* off; (*avion*) to take off; (*papier, feuille*) to blow away; (*fig*) to vanish (into thin air).

envoûtant, e [ɑ̃vutɑ̃, -ɑ̃t] *adj* enchanting.

envoûtement [ɑ̃vutmɑ̃] *nm* bewitchment.

envoûter [ɑ̃vute] *vt* to bewitch.

envoyé, e [ɑ̃vwaje] *nm/f* (*POL*) envoy; (*PRESSE*) correspondent ♦ *adj*: **bien** ~ (*remarque, réponse*) well-aimed.

envoyer [ɑ̃vwaje] *vt* to send; (*lancer*) to hurl, throw; ~ **une gifle/un sourire à qn** to aim a blow/flash a smile at sb; ~ **les couleurs** to run up the colours; ~ **chercher** to send for; ~ **par le fond** (*bateau*) to send to the bottom.

envoyeur, euse [ɑ̃vwajœʀ, -øz] *nm/f* sender.

enzyme [ɑ̃zim] *nf ou m* enzyme.

éolien, ne [eɔljɛ̃, -ɛn] *adj* wind *cpd*; **pompe ~ne** windpump.

EOR *sigle m* (= *élève officier de réserve*) ≈ military cadet.

éosine [eɔzin] *nf* eosin (*antiseptic used in France to treat skin ailments*).

épagneul, e [epaɲœl] *nm/f* spaniel.

épais, se [epɛ, -ɛs] *adj* thick.

épaisseur [epɛsœR] *nf* thickness.

épaissir [epesiR] *vt*, **s'~** *vi* to thicken.

épaississement [epesismã] *nm* thickening.

épanchement [epãʃmã] *nm*: **~ de sinovie** water on the knee; **~s** *nmpl* (*fig*) (sentimental) outpourings.

épancher [epãʃe] *vt* to give vent to; **s'~** *vi* to open one's heart; (*liquide*) to pour out.

épandage [epãdaʒ] *nm* manure spreading.

épanoui, e [epanwi] *adj* (*éclos, ouvert, développé*) blooming; (*radieux*) radiant.

épanouir [epanwiR]: **s'~** *vi* (*fleur*) to bloom, open out; (*visage*) to light up; (*fig: se développer*) to blossom (out); (: *mentalement*) to open up.

épanouissement [epanwismã] *nm* blossoming; opening up.

épargnant, e [epaRɲã, -ãt] *nm/f* saver, investor.

épargne [epaRɲ(ə)] *nf* saving; **l'~-logement** property investment.

épargner [epaRɲe] *vt* to save; (*ne pas tuer ou endommager*) to spare ♦ *vi* to save; **~ qch à qn** to spare sb sth.

éparpillement [epaRpijmã] *nm* (*de papier*) scattering; (*des efforts*) dissipation.

éparpiller [epaRpije] *vt* to scatter; (*pour répartir*) to disperse; (*fig: efforts*) to dissipate; **s'~** *vi* to scatter; (*fig*) to dissipate one's efforts.

épars, e [epaR, -aRs(ə)] *adj* (*maisons*) scattered; (*cheveux*) sparse.

épatant, e [epatã, -ãt] *adj* (*fam*) super, splendid.

épaté, e [epate] *adj*: **nez ~** flat nose (with wide nostrils).

épater [epate] *vt* to amaze; (*impressionner*) to impress.

épaule [epol] *nf* shoulder.

épaulé-jeté, *pl* **épaulés-jetés** [epoleʒəte] *nm* (*SPORT*) clean-and-jerk.

épaulement [epolmã] *nm* escarpment; (*mur*) retaining wall.

épauler [epole] *vt* (*aider*) to back up, support; (*arme*) to raise (to one's shoulder) ♦ *vi* to (take) aim.

épaulette [epolɛt] *nf* (*MIL*, *d'un veston*) epaulette; (*de combinaison*) shoulder strap.

épave [epav] *nf* wreck.

épée [epe] *nf* sword.

épeler [eple] *vt* to spell.

éperdu, e [epɛRdy] *adj* (*personne*) overcome; (*sentiment*) passionate; (*fuite*) frantic.

éperdument [epɛRdymã] *adv* (*aimer*) wildly; (*espérer*) fervently.

éperlan [epɛRlã] *nm* (*ZOOL*) smelt.

éperon [epRɔ̃] *nm* spur.

éperonner [epRɔne] *vt* to spur (on); (*navire*) to ram.

épervier [epɛRvje] *nm* (*ZOOL*) sparrowhawk; (*PÊCHE*) casting net.

éphèbe [efɛb] *nm* beautiful young man.

éphémère [efemɛR] *adj* ephemeral, fleeting.

éphéméride [efemerid] *nf* block *ou* tear-off calendar.

épi [epi] *nm* (*de blé, d'orge*) ear; **~ de cheveux** tuft of hair; **stationnement/se garer en ~** parking/to park at an angle to the kerb.

épice [epis] *nf* spice.

épicé, e [epise] *adj* highly spiced, spicy; (*fig*) spicy.

épicéa [episea] *nm* spruce.

épicentre [episɑ̃tR(ə)] *nm* epicentre.

épicer [epise] *vt* to spice; (*fig*) to add spice to.

épicerie [episRi] *nf* (*magasin*) grocer's shop; (*denrées*) groceries *pl*; **~ fine** delicatessen (shop).

épicier, ière [episje, -jɛR] *nm/f* grocer.

épicurien, ne [epikyRjɛ̃, -ɛn] *adj* epicurean.

épidémie [epidemi] *nf* epidemic.

épidémique [epidemik] *adj* epidemic.

épiderme [epidɛRm(ə)] *nm* skin, epidermis.

épidermique [epidɛRmik] *adj* skin *cpd*, epidermic.

épier [epje] *vt* to spy on, watch closely; (*occasion*) to look out for.

épieu, x [epjø] *nm* (hunting-)spear.

épigramme [epigRam] *nf* epigram.

épigraphe [epigRaf] *nf* epigraph.

épilation [epilasjɔ̃] *nf* removal of unwanted hair.

épilatoire [epilatwaR] *adj* depilatory, hair-removing.

épilepsie [epilɛpsi] *nf* epilepsy.

épileptique [epilɛptik] *adj*, *nm/f* epileptic.

épiler [epile] *vt* (*jambes*) to remove the hair from; (*sourcils*) to pluck; **s'~ les jambes** to remove the hair from one's legs; **s'~ les sourcils** to pluck one's eyebrows; **se faire ~** to get unwanted hair removed; **crème à ~** hair-removing *ou* depilatory cream; **pince à ~** eyebrow tweezers.

épilogue [epilɔg] *nm* (*fig*) conclusion, dénouement.

épiloguer [epilɔge] *vi*: **~ sur** to hold forth on.

épinard [epinaR] *nm* (*aussi*: **~s**) spinach *sg*.

épine [epin] *nf* thorn, prickle; (*d'oursin etc*) spine, prickle; **~ dorsale** backbone.

épineux, euse [epinø, -øz] *adj* thorny, prickly.

épinglage [epɛ̃glaʒ] *nm* pinning.

épingle [epɛ̃gl(ə)] *nf* pin; **tirer son ~ du jeu** to play one's game well; **tiré à quatre ~s** well turned-out; **monter qch en ~** to build sth up, make a thing of sth (*fam*); **~ à chapeau** hatpin; **~ à cheveux** hairpin; **virage en ~ à cheveux** hairpin bend; **~ de cravate** tie pin; **~ de nourrice** *ou* **de sûreté** *ou* **double** safety pin, nappy (*BRIT*) *ou* diaper (*US*) pin.

épingler [epɛ̃gle] *vt* (*badge, décoration*): **~ qch sur** to pin sth on(to); (*COUTURE: tissu, robe*) to pin together; (*fam*) to catch, nick.

épinière [epinjɛʀ] *adj f voir* **moelle**.
Épiphanie [epifani] *nf* Epiphany.
épique [epik] *adj* epic.
épiscopal, e, aux [episkɔpal, -o] *adj* episcopal.
épiscopat [episkɔpa] *nm* bishopric, episcopate.
épisiotomie [epizjɔtɔmi] *nf* (*MÉD*) episiotomy.
épisode [epizɔd] *nm* episode; **film/roman à ~s** serialized film/novel, serial.
épisodique [epizɔdik] *adj* occasional.
épisodiquement [epizɔdikmɑ̃] *adv* occasionally.
épissure [episyʀ] *nf* splice.
épistémologie [epistemɔlɔʒi] *nf* epistemology.
épistolaire [epistɔlɛʀ] *adj* epistolary; **être en relations ~s avec qn** to correspond with sb.
épitaphe [epitaf] *nf* epitaph.
épithète [epitɛt] *nf* (*nom, surnom*) epithet; **adjectif ~** attributive adjective.
épître [epitʀ(ə)] *nf* epistle.
éploré, e [eplɔʀe] *adj* in tears, tearful.
épluchage [eplyʃaʒ] *nm* peeling; (*de dossier etc*) careful reading *ou* analysis.
épluche-légumes [eplyʃlegym] *nm inv* potato peeler.
éplucher [eplyʃe] *vt* (*fruit, légumes*) to peel; (*comptes, dossier*) to go over with a fine-tooth comb.
éplucheur [eplyʃœʀ] *nm* (automatic) peeler.
épluchures [eplyʃyʀ] *nfpl* peelings.
épointer [epwɛ̃te] *vt* to blunt.
éponge [epɔ̃ʒ] *nf* sponge; **passer l'~ (sur)** (*fig*) to let bygones be bygones (with regard to); **jeter l'~** (*fig*) to throw in the towel; **~ métallique** scourer.
éponger [epɔ̃ʒe] *vt* (*liquide*) to mop *ou* sponge up; (*surface*) to sponge; (*fig: déficit*) to soak up, absorb; **s'~ le front** to mop one's brow.
épopée [epɔpe] *nf* epic.
époque [epɔk] *nf* (*de l'histoire*) age, era; (*de l'année, la vie*) time; **d'~** *adj* (*meuble*) period *cpd*; **à cette ~** at this (*ou* that) time *ou* period; **faire ~** to make history.
épouiller [epuje] *vt* to pick lice off; (*avec un produit*) to delouse.
époumoner [epumɔne]: **s'~** *vi* to shout (*ou* sing) o.s. hoarse.
épouse [epuz] *nf* wife (*pl* wives).
épouser [epuze] *vt* to marry; (*fig: idées*) to espouse; (: *forme*) to fit.
époussetage [epustaʒ] *nm* dusting.
épousseter [epuste] *vt* to dust.
époustouflant, e [epustuflɑ̃, -ɑ̃t] *adj* staggering, mind-boggling.
époustoufler [epustufle] *vt* to flabbergast, astound.
épouvantable [epuvɑ̃tabl(ə)] *adj* appalling, dreadful.
épouvantablement [epuvɑ̃tabləmɑ̃] *adj* terribly, dreadfully.
épouvantail [epuvɑ̃taj] *nm* (*à moineaux*) scarecrow; (*fig*) bog(e)y; bugbear.
épouvante [epuvɑ̃t] *nf* terror; **film d'~** horror film.
épouvanter [epuvɑ̃te] *vt* to terrify.
époux [epu] *nm* husband ♦ *nmpl*: **les ~** the (married) couple, the husband and wife.
éprendre [epʀɑ̃dʀ(ə)]: **s'~ de** *vt* to fall in love with.
épreuve [epʀœv] *nf* (*d'examen*) test; (*malheur, difficulté*) trial, ordeal; (*PHOTO*) print; (*TYPO*) proof; (*SPORT*) event; **à l'~ des balles/du feu** (*vêtement*) bulletproof/fireproof; **à toute ~** unfailing; **mettre à l'~** to put to the test; **~ de force** trial of strength; (*fig*) showdown; **~ de résistance** test of resistance; **~ de sélection** (*SPORT*) heat.
épris, e [epʀi, -iz] *vb voir* **éprendre** ♦ *adj*: **~ de** in love with.
éprouvant, e [epʀuvɑ̃, -ɑ̃t] *adj* trying.
éprouvé, e [epʀuve] *adj* tested, proven.
éprouver [epʀuve] *vt* (*tester*) to test; (*mettre à l'épreuve*) to put to the test; (*marquer, faire souffrir*) to afflict, distress; (*ressentir*) to experience.
éprouvette [epʀuvɛt] *nf* test tube.
EPS *sigle f* (= *Éducation physique et sportive*) ≈ PE.
épuisant, e [epɥizɑ̃, -ɑ̃t] *adj* exhausting.
épuisé, e [epɥize] *adj* exhausted; (*livre*) out of print.
épuisement [epɥizmɑ̃] *nm* exhaustion; **jusqu'à ~ des stocks** while stocks last.
épuiser [epɥize] *vt* (*fatiguer*) to exhaust, wear *ou* tire out; (*stock, sujet*) to exhaust; **s'~** *vi* to wear *ou* tire o.s. out, exhaust o.s.; (*stock*) to run out.
épuisette [epɥizɛt] *nf* landing net; shrimping net.
épuration [epyʀasjɔ̃] *nf* purification; purging; refinement.
épure [epyʀ] *nf* working drawing.
épurer [epyʀe] *vt* (*liquide*) to purify; (*parti, administration*) to purge; (*langue, texte*) to refine.
équarrir [ekaʀiʀ] *vt* (*pierre, arbre*) to square (off); (*animal*) to quarter.
équateur [ekwatœʀ] *nm* equator; **(la république de) l'É~** Ecuador.
équation [ekwɑsjɔ̃] *nf* equation; **mettre en ~** to equate; **~ du premier/second degré** simple/quadratic equation.
équatorial, e, aux [ekwatɔʀjal, -o] *adj* equatorial.
équatorien, ne [ekwatɔʀjɛ̃, -ɛn] *adj* Ecuadorian ♦ *nm/f*: **É~, ne** Ecuadorian.
équerre [ekɛʀ] *nf* (*à dessin*) (set) square; (*pour fixer*) brace; **en ~** at right angles; **à l'~, d'~** straight; **double ~** T-square.
équestre [ekɛstʀ(ə)] *adj* equestrian.
équeuter [ekøte] *vt* (*CULIN*) to remove the stalk(s) from.
équidé [ekide] *nm* (*ZOOL*) member of the

horse family.
équidistance [ekɥidistɑ̃s] *nf*: à ~ **(de)** equidistant (from).
équidistant, e [ekɥidistɑ̃, -ɑ̃t] *adj*: ~ **(de)** equidistant (from).
équilatéral, e, aux [ekɥilateʀal, -o] *adj* equilateral.
équilibrage [ekilibʀaʒ] *nm* (*AUTO*): ~ **des roues** wheel balancing.
équilibre [ekilibʀ(ə)] *nm* balance; (*d'une balance*) equilibrium; ~ **budgétaire** balanced budget; **garder/perdre l'**~ to keep/lose one's balance; **être en** ~ to be balanced; **mettre en** ~ to make steady; **avoir le sens de l'**~ to be well-balanced.
équilibré, e [ekilibʀe] *adj* (*fig*) well-balanced, stable.
équilibrer [ekilibʀe] *vt* to balance; **s'**~ (*poids*) to balance; (*fig: défauts etc*) to balance each other out.
équilibriste [ekilibʀist(ə)] *nm/f* tightrope walker.
équinoxe [ekinɔks] *nm* equinox.
équipage [ekipaʒ] *nm* crew; **en grand** ~ in great array.
équipe [ekip] *nf* team; (*bande: parfois péj*) bunch; **travailler par** ~**s** to work in shifts; **travailler en** ~ to work as a team; **faire** ~ **avec** to team up with; ~ **de chercheurs** research team; ~ **de secours** *ou* **de sauvetage** rescue team.
équipé, e [ekipe] *adj* (*cuisine etc*) equipped, fitted(-out) ♦ *nf* escapade.
équipement [ekipmɑ̃] *nm* equipment; ~**s** *nmpl* amenities, facilities; installations; **biens/ dépenses d'**~ capital goods/expenditure; **ministère de l'É**~ department of public works; ~**s sportifs/collectifs** sports/ community facilities *ou* resources.
équiper [ekipe] *vt* to equip; (*voiture, cuisine*) to equip, fit out; ~ **qn/qch de** to equip sb/sth with; **s'**~ (*sportif*) to equip o.s., kit o.s. out.
équipier, ière [ekipje, -jɛʀ] *nm/f* team member.
équitable [ekitabl(ə)] *adj* fair.
équitablement [ekitabləmɑ̃] *adv* fairly, equitably.
équitation [ekitasjɔ̃] *nf* (horse-)riding; **faire de l'**~ to go (horse-)riding.
équité [ekite] *nf* equity.
équivaille [ekivaj] *etc vb voir* **équivaloir**.
équivalence [ekivalɑ̃s] *nf* equivalence.
équivalent, e [ekivalɑ̃, -ɑ̃t] *adj, nm* equivalent.
équivaloir [ekivalwaʀ]: ~ **à** *vt* to be equivalent to; (*représenter*) to amount to.
équivaut [ekivo] *etc vb voir* **équivaloir**.
équivoque [ekivɔk] *adj* equivocal, ambiguous; (*louche*) dubious ♦ *nf* ambiguity.
érable [eʀabl(ə)] *nm* maple.
éradication [eʀadikasjɔ̃] *nf* eradication.
éradiquer [eʀadike] *vt* to eradicate.

érafler [eʀafle] *vt* to scratch; **s'**~ **la main/les jambes** to scrape *ou* scratch one's hand/ legs.
éraflure [eʀaflyʀ] *nf* scratch.
éraillé, e [eʀaje] *adj* (*voix*) rasping, hoarse.
ère [ɛʀ] *nf* era; **en l'an 1050 de notre** ~ in the year 1050 A.D.
érection [eʀɛksjɔ̃] *nf* erection.
éreintant, e [eʀɛ̃tɑ̃, -ɑ̃t] *adj* exhausting.
éreinté, e [eʀɛ̃te] *adj* exhausted.
éreintement [eʀɛ̃tmɑ̃] *nm* exhaustion.
éreinter [eʀɛ̃te] *vt* to exhaust, wear out; (*fig: critiquer*) to slate; **s'**~ (**à faire qch/à qch**) to wear o.s. out (doing sth/with sth).
ergonomie [ɛʀgɔnɔmi] *nf* ergonomics *sg*.
ergonomique [ɛʀgɔnɔmik] *adj* ergonomic.
ergot [ɛʀgo] *nm* (*de coq*) spur; (*TECH*) lug.
ergoter [ɛʀgɔte] *vi* to split hairs, argue over details.
ergoteur, euse [ɛʀgɔtœʀ, -øz] *nm/f* hairsplitter.
ériger [eʀiʒe] *vt* (*monument*) to erect; ~ **qch en principe/loi** to make sth a principle/law; **s'**~ **en critique (de)** to set o.s. up as a critic (of).
ermitage [ɛʀmitaʒ] *nm* retreat.
ermite [ɛʀmit] *nm* hermit.
éroder [eʀɔde] *vt* to erode.
érogène [eʀɔʒɛn] *adj* erogenous.
érosion [eʀozjɔ̃] *nf* erosion.
érotique [eʀɔtik] *adj* erotic.
érotiquement [eʀɔtikmɑ̃] *adv* erotically.
érotisme [eʀɔtism(ə)] *nm* eroticism.
errance [ɛʀɑ̃s] *nf* wandering.
errant, e [ɛʀɑ̃, -ɑ̃t] *adj*: **un chien** ~ a stray dog.
erratum, a [ɛʀatɔm, -a] *nm* erratum (*pl* -a).
errements [ɛʀmɑ̃] *nmpl* misguided ways.
errer [ɛʀe] *vi* to wander.
erreur [ɛʀœʀ] *nf* mistake, error; (*INFORM: de programme*) bug; (*morale*): ~**s** *nfpl* errors; **être dans l'**~ to be wrong; **induire qn en** ~ to mislead sb; **par** ~ by mistake; **sauf** ~ unless I'm mistaken; **faire** ~ to be mistaken; ~ **de date** mistake in the date; ~ **de fait** error of fact; ~ **d'impression** (*TYPO*) misprint; ~ **judiciaire** miscarriage of justice; ~ **de jugement** error of judgment; ~ **matérielle** *ou* **d'écriture** clerical error; ~ **tactique** tactical error.
erroné, e [ɛʀɔne] *adj* wrong, erroneous.
ersatz [ɛʀzats] *nm* substitute, ersatz; ~ **de café** coffee substitute.
éructer [eʀykte] *vi* to belch.
érudit, e [eʀydi, -it] *adj* erudite, learned ♦ *nm/f* scholar.
érudition [eʀydisjɔ̃] *nf* erudition, scholarship.
éruptif, ive [eʀyptif, -iv] *adj* eruptive.
éruption [eʀypsjɔ̃] *nf* eruption; (*cutanée*) outbreak; (: *boutons*) rash; (*fig: de joie, colère, folie*) outburst.
es [ɛ] *vb voir* **être**.
ès [ɛs] *prép*: **licencié** ~ **lettres/sciences** ≈ Bachelor of Arts/Science; **docteur** ~

lettres ≈ doctor of philosophy, PhD.
E/S *abr* (= *entrée/sortie*) I/O (= *in/out*).
esbroufe [ɛsbʀuf] *nf*: **faire de l'~** to have people on.
escabeau, x [ɛskabo] *nm* (*tabouret*) stool; (*échelle*) stepladder.
escadre [ɛskadʀ(ə)] *nf* (*NAVIG*) squadron; (*AVIAT*) wing.
escadrille [ɛskadʀij] *nf* (*AVIAT*) flight.
escadron [ɛskadʀɔ̃] *nm* squadron.
escalade [ɛskalad] *nf* climbing *no pl*; (*POL etc*) escalation.
escalader [ɛskalade] *vt* to climb, scale.
escalator [ɛskalatɔʀ] *nm* escalator.
escale [ɛskal] *nf* (*NAVIG*) call; (: *port*) port of call; (*AVIAT*) stop(over); **faire ~ à** to put in at, call in at; to stop over at; **~ technique** (*AVIAT*) refuelling stop.
escalier [ɛskalje] *nm* stairs *pl*; **dans l'~** *ou* **les ~s** on the stairs; **descendre l'~** *ou* **les ~s** to go downstairs; **~ mécanique** *ou* **roulant** escalator; **~ de secours** fire escape; **~ de service** backstairs; **~ à vis** *ou* **en colimaçon** spiral staircase.
escalope [ɛskalɔp] *nf* escalope.
escamotable [ɛskamɔtabl(ə)] *adj* (*train d'atterrissage, antenne*) retractable; (*table, lit*) fold-away.
escamoter [ɛskamɔte] *vt* (*esquiver*) to get round, evade; (*faire disparaître*) to conjure away; (*dérober: portefeuille etc*) to snatch; (*train d'atterrissage*) to retract; (*mots*) to miss out.
escapade [ɛskapad] *nf*: **faire une ~** to go on a jaunt; (*s'enfuir*) to run away *ou* off.
escarbille [ɛskaʀbij] *nf* bit of grit.
escarcelle [ɛskaʀsɛl] *nf*: **faire tomber dans l'~** (*argent*) to bring in.
escargot [ɛskaʀgo] *nm* snail.
escarmouche [ɛskaʀmuʃ] *nf* (*MIL*) skirmish; (*fig: propos hostiles*) angry exchange.
escarpé, e [ɛskaʀpe] *adj* steep.
escarpement [ɛskaʀpəmɑ̃] *nm* steep slope.
escarpin [ɛskaʀpɛ̃] *nm* flat(-heeled) shoe.
escarre [ɛskaʀ] *nf* bedsore.
Escaut [ɛsko] *nm*: **l'~** the Scheldt.
escient [ɛsjɑ̃] *nm*: **à bon ~** advisedly.
esclaffer [ɛsklafe]: **s'~** *vi* to guffaw.
esclandre [ɛsklɑ̃dʀ(ə)] *nm* scene, fracas.
esclavage [ɛsklavaʒ] *nm* slavery.
esclavagiste [ɛsklavaʒist(ə)] *adj* pro-slavery ♦ *nm/f* supporter of slavery.
esclave [ɛsklav] *nm/f* slave; **être ~ de** (*fig*) to be a slave of.
escogriffe [ɛskɔgʀif] *nm* (*péj*) beanpole.
escompte [ɛskɔ̃t] *nm* discount.
escompter [ɛskɔ̃te] *vt* (*COMM*) to discount; (*espérer*) to expect, reckon upon; **~ que** to reckon *ou* expect that.
escorte [ɛskɔʀt(ə)] *nf* escort; **faire ~ à** to escort.
escorter [ɛskɔʀte] *vt* to escort.

escorteur [ɛskɔʀtœʀ] *nm* (*NAVIG*) escort (ship).
escouade [ɛskwad] *nf* squad; (*fig: groupe de personnes*) group.
escrime [ɛskʀim] *nf* fencing; **faire de l'~** to fence.
escrimer [ɛskʀime]: **s'~** *vi*: **s'~ à faire** to wear o.s. out doing.
escrimeur, euse [ɛskʀimœʀ, -øz] *nm/f* fencer.
escroc [ɛskʀo] *nm* swindler, con-man.
escroquer [ɛskʀɔke] *vt*: **~ qn (de qch)/qch à qn** to swindle sb (out of sth)/sth out of sb.
escroquerie [ɛskʀɔkʀi] *nf* swindle.
ésotérique [ɛzɔteʀik] *adj* esoteric.
espace [ɛspas] *nm* space; **~ publicitaire** advertising space; **~ vital** living space.
espacé, e [ɛspase] *adj* spaced out.
espacement [ɛspasmɑ̃] *nm*: **~ proportionnel** proportional spacing (*on printer*).
espacer [ɛspase] *vt* to space out; **s'~** *vi* (*visites etc*) to become less frequent.
espadon [ɛspadɔ̃] *nm* swordfish *inv*.
espadrille [ɛspadʀij] *nf* rope-soled sandal.
Espagne [ɛspaɲ(ə)] *nf*: **l'~** Spain.
espagnol, e [ɛspaɲɔl] *adj* Spanish ♦ *nm* (*LING*) Spanish ♦ *nm/f*: **E~, e** Spaniard.
espagnolette [ɛspaɲɔlɛt] *nf* (*window*) catch; **fermé à l'~** resting on the catch.
espalier [ɛspalje] *nm* (*arbre fruitier*) espalier.
espèce [ɛspɛs] *nf* (*BIO, BOT, ZOOL*) species *inv*; (*gén: sorte*) sort, kind, type; (*péj*): **~ de maladroit/de brute!** you clumsy oaf/you brute!; **~s** *nfpl* (*COMM*) cash *sg*; (*REL*) species; **de toute ~** of all kinds *ou* sorts; **en l'~** *adv* in the case in point; **payer en ~s** to pay (in) cash; **cas d'~** individual case; **l'~ humaine** humankind.
espérance [ɛspeʀɑ̃s] *nf* hope; **~ de vie** life expectancy.
espéranto [ɛspeʀɑ̃to] *nm* esperanto.
espérer [ɛspeʀe] *vt* to hope for; **j'espère (bien)** I hope so; **~ que/faire** to hope that/to do; **~ en** to trust in.
espiègle [ɛspjɛgl(ə)] *adj* mischievous.
espièglerie [ɛspjɛgləʀi] *nf* mischievousness; (*tour, farce*) piece of mischief, prank.
espion, ne [ɛspjɔ̃, -ɔn] *nm/f* spy; **avion ~** spy plane.
espionnage [ɛspjɔnaʒ] *nm* espionage, spying; **film/roman d'~** spy film/novel.
espionner [ɛspjɔne] *vt* to spy (up)on.
espionnite [ɛspjɔnit] *nf* spy mania.
esplanade [ɛsplanad] *nf* esplanade.
espoir [ɛspwaʀ] *nm* hope; **l'~ de qch/de faire qch** the hope of sth/of doing sth; **avoir bon ~ que ...** to have high hopes that ...; **garder l'~ que ...** to remain hopeful that ...; **un ~ de la boxe/du ski** one of boxing's/skiing's hopefuls, one of the hopes of boxing/skiing; **sans ~** *adj* hopeless.
esprit [ɛspʀi] *nm* (*pensée, intellect*) mind; (*humour, ironie*) wit; (*mentalité, d'une loi etc,*

fantôme etc) spirit; **l'~ d'équipe/de compétition** team/competitive spirit; **faire de l'~** to try to be witty; **reprendre ses ~s** to come to; **perdre l'~** to lose one's mind; **avoir bon/mauvais ~** to be of a good/bad disposition; **avoir l'~ à faire qch** to have a mind to do sth; **avoir l'~ critique** to be critical; **~ de contradiction** contrariness; **~ de corps** esprit de corps; **~ de famille** family loyalty; **l'~ malin** (*le diable*) the Evil One; **~s chagrins** faultfinders.

esquif [ɛskif] *nm* skiff.

esquimau, de, x [ɛskimo, -od] *adj* Eskimo ♦ *nm* (*LING*) Eskimo; (*glace*): **E~** ® ice lolly (*BRIT*), popsicle (*US*) ♦ *nm/f*: **E~, de** Eskimo; **chien ~** husky.

esquinter [ɛskɛ̃te] *vt* (*fam*) to mess up; **s'~** *vi*: **s'~ à faire qch** to knock o.s. out doing sth.

esquisse [ɛskis] *nf* sketch; **l'~ d'un sourire/ changement** a hint of a smile/of change.

esquisser [ɛskise] *vt* to sketch; **s'~** *vi* (*amélioration*) to begin to be detectable; **~ un sourire** to give a hint of a smile.

esquive [ɛskiv] *nf* (*BOXE*) dodging; (*fig*) sidestepping.

esquiver [ɛskive] *vt* to dodge; **s'~** *vi* to slip away.

essai [ɛsɛ] *nm* trying; (*tentative*) attempt, try; (*RUGBY*) try; (*LITTÉRATURE*) essay; **~s** *nmpl* (*AUTO*) trials; **à l'~** on a trial basis; **~ gratuit** (*COMM*) free trial.

essaim [ɛsɛ̃] *nm* swarm.

essaimer [eseme] *vi* to swarm; (*fig*) to spread, expand.

essayage [esejaʒ] *nm* (*d'un vêtement*) trying on, fitting; **salon d'~** fitting room; **cabine d'~** fitting room (*cubicle*).

essayer [eseje] *vt* (*gén*) to try; (*vêtement, chaussures*) to try (on); (*restaurant, méthode, voiture*) to try (out) ♦ *vi* to try; **~ de faire** to try *ou* attempt to do; **s'~ à faire** to try one's hand at doing; **essayez un peu!** (*menace*) just you try!

essayeur, euse [esejœr, -øz] *nm/f* (*chez un tailleur etc*) fitter.

essayiste [esejist(ə)] *nm/f* essayist.

ESSEC [ɛsɛk] *sigle f* (= *École supérieure des sciences économiques et sociales*) *grande école for management and business studies.*

essence [esɑ̃s] *nf* (*de voiture*) petrol (*BRIT*), gas(oline) (*US*); (*extrait de plante, PHILOSOPHIE*) essence; (*espèce: d'arbre*) species *inv*; **prendre de l'~** to get (some) petrol *ou* gas; **par ~** (*essentiellement*) essentially; **~ de citron/rose** lemon/rose oil; **~ de térébenthine** turpentine.

essentiel, le [esɑ̃sjɛl] *adj* essential ♦ *nm*: **l'~ d'un discours/d'une œuvre** the essence of a speech/work of art; **emporter l'~** to take the essentials; **c'est l'~** (*ce qui importe*) that's the main thing; **l'~ de** (*la majeure partie*) the

main part of.

essentiellement [esɑ̃sjɛlmɑ̃] *adv* essentially.

esseulé, e [esœle] *adj* forlorn.

essieu, x [esjø] *nm* axle.

essor [esɔr] *nm* (*de l'économie etc*) rapid expansion; **prendre son ~** (*oiseau*) to fly off.

essorage [esɔraʒ] *nm* wringing out; spindrying; spinning; shaking.

essorer [esɔre] *vt* (*en tordant*) to wring (out); (*par la force centrifuge*) to spin-dry; (*salade*) to spin; (*: en secouant*) to shake dry.

essoreuse [esɔrøz] *nf* mangle, wringer; (*à tambour*) spin-dryer.

essouffler [esufle] *vt* to make breathless; **s'~** *vi* to get out of breath; (*fig: économie*) to run out of steam.

essuie [esɥi] *etc vb voir* **essuyer.**

essuie-glace [esɥiglas] *nm* windscreen (*BRIT*) *ou* windshield (*US*) wiper.

essuie-mains [esɥimɛ̃] *nm inv* hand towel.

essuierai [esɥire] *etc vb voir* **essuyer.**

essuie-tout [esɥitu] *nm inv* kitchen paper.

essuyer [esɥije] *vt* to wipe; (*fig: subir*) to suffer; **s'~** (*après le bain*) to dry o.s.; **~ la vaisselle** to dry up, dry the dishes.

est [ɛ] *vb voir* **être** ♦ *nm* [ɛst]: **l'~** the east ♦ *adj inv* east; (*région*) east(ern); **à l'~** in the east; (*direction*) to the east, east(wards); **à l'~ de** (to the) east of; **les pays de l'E~** the eastern countries.

estafette [ɛstafɛt] *nf* (*MIL*) dispatch rider.

estafilade [ɛstafilad] *nf* gash, slash.

est-allemand, e [ɛstalmɑ̃, -ɑ̃d] *adj* East German.

estaminet [ɛstaminɛ] *nm* tavern.

estampe [ɛstɑ̃p] *nf* print, engraving.

estamper [ɛstɑ̃pe] *vt* (*monnaies etc*) to stamp; (*fam: escroquer*) to swindle.

estampille [ɛstɑ̃pij] *nf* stamp.

est-ce que [ɛskə] *adv*: **~ c'est cher/c'était bon?** is it expensive/was it good?; **quand est-ce qu'il part?** when does he leave?, when is he leaving?; **où est-ce qu'il va?** where's he going?; **qui est-ce qui fait ça?** who knows him/did that?; *voir aussi* **que.**

este [ɛst(ə)] *adj* Estonian ♦ *nm/f*: **E~** Estonian.

esthète [ɛstɛt] *nm/f* aesthete.

esthéticienne [ɛstetisjɛn] *nf* beautician.

esthétique [ɛstetik] *adj* (*sens, jugement*) aesthetic; (*beau*) attractive, aesthetically pleasing ♦ *nf* aesthetics *sg*; **l'~ industrielle** industrial design.

esthétiquement [ɛstetikmɑ̃] *adv* aesthetically.

estimable [ɛstimabl(ə)] *adj* respected.

estimatif, ive [ɛstimatif, -iv] *adj* estimated.

estimation [ɛstimasjɔ̃] *nf* valuation; assessment; **d'après mes ~s** according to my calculations.

estime [ɛstim] *nf* esteem, regard; **avoir de l'~ pour qn** to think highly of sb.

estimer [ɛstime] *vt* (*respecter*) to esteem, hold

in high regard; (*expertiser*) to value; (*évaluer*) to assess, estimate; (*penser*): ~ **que/être** to consider that/o.s. to be; **s'~ satisfait/heureux** to feel satisfied/happy; **j'estime la distance à 10 km** I reckon the distance to be 10 km.

estival, e, aux [ɛstival, -o] *adj* summer *cpd*; **station ~e** (summer) holiday resort.

estivant, e [ɛstivɑ̃, -ɑ̃t] *nm/f* (summer) holiday-maker.

estoc [ɛstɔk] *nm*: **frapper d'~ et de taille** to cut and thrust.

estocade [ɛstɔkad] *nf* death-blow.

estomac [ɛstɔma] *nm* stomach; **avoir mal à l'~** to have stomach ache; **avoir l'~ creux** to have an empty stomach.

estomaqué, e [ɛstɔmake] *adj* flabbergasted.

estompe [ɛstɔ̃p] *nf* stump; (*dessin*) stump drawing.

estompé, e [ɛstɔ̃pe] *adj* blurred.

estomper [ɛstɔ̃pe] *vt* (*ART*) to shade off; (*fig*) to blur, dim; **s'~** *vi* (*sentiments*) to soften; (*contour*) to become blurred.

Estonie [ɛstɔni] *nf*: **l'~** Estonia.

estonien, ne [ɛstɔnjɛ̃, -ɛn] *adj* Estonian ♦ *nm* (*LING*) Estonian ♦ *nm/f*: **E~, ne** Estonian.

estrade [ɛstrad] *nf* platform, rostrum.

estragon [ɛstragɔ̃] *nm* tarragon.

estropié, e [ɛstrɔpje] *nm/f* cripple.

estropier [ɛstrɔpje] *vt* to cripple, maim; (*fig*) to twist, distort.

estuaire [ɛstɥɛʀ] *nm* estuary.

estudiantin, e [ɛstydjɑ̃tɛ̃, -in] *adj* student *cpd*.

esturgeon [ɛstyʀʒɔ̃] *nm* sturgeon.

et [e] *conj* and; ~ **lui?** what about him?; ~ **alors?**, ~ **(puis) après?** so what?; (*ensuite*) and then?

ét. *abr* = **étage**.

ETA [eta] *sigle m* (*POL*) ETA.

étable [etabl(ə)] *nf* cowshed.

établi, e [etabli] *adj* established ♦ *nm* (work)bench.

établir [etabliʀ] *vt* (*papiers d'identité, facture*) to make out; (*liste, programme*) to draw up; (*gouvernement, artisan etc: aider à s'installer*) to set up, establish; (*entreprise, atelier, camp*) to set up; (*réputation, usage, fait, culpabilité, relations*) to establish; (*SPORT: record*) to set; **s'~** *vi* (*se faire: entente etc*) to be established; **s'~** (**à son compte**) to set up in business; **s'~ à/près de** to settle in/near.

établissement [etablismɑ̃] *nm* making out; drawing up; setting up, establishing; (*entreprise, institution*) establishment; ~ **de crédit** credit institution; ~ **hospitalier** hospital complex; ~ **industriel** industrial plant, factory; ~ **scolaire** school, educational establishment.

étage [etaʒ] *nm* (*d'immeuble*) storey (*BRIT*), story (*US*), floor; (*de fusée*) stage; (*GÉO: de culture, végétation*) level; **au 2ème** ~ on the 2nd (*BRIT*) *ou* 3rd (*US*) floor; **à l'~** upstairs;

maison à deux ~s two-storey *ou* -story house; **de bas** ~ *adj* low-born; (*médiocre*) inferior.

étager [etaʒe] *vt* (*cultures*) to lay out in tiers; **s'~** *vi* (*prix*) to range; (*zones, cultures*) to lie on different levels.

étagère [etaʒɛʀ] *nf* (*rayon*) shelf; (*meuble*) shelves *pl*, set of shelves.

étai [etɛ] *nm* stay, prop.

étain [etɛ̃] *nm* tin; (*ORFÈVRERIE*) pewter *no pl*.

étais [etɛ] *etc vb voir* **être**.

étal [etal] *nm* stall.

étalage [etalaʒ] *nm* display; (*vitrine*) display window; **faire** ~ **de** to show off, parade.

étalagiste [etalaʒist(ə)] *nm/f* window-dresser.

étale [etal] *adj* (*mer*) slack.

étalement [etalmɑ̃] *nm* spreading; (*échelonnement*) staggering.

étaler [etale] *vt* (*carte, nappe*) to spread (out); (*peinture, liquide*) to spread; (*échelonner: paiements, dates, vacances*) to spread, stagger; (*exposer: marchandises*) to display; (*richesses, connaissances*) to parade; **s'~** *vi* (*liquide*) to spread out; (*fam*) to come a cropper (*BRIT*), fall flat on one's face; **s'~ sur** (*suj: paiements etc*) to be spread over.

étalon [etalɔ̃] *nm* (*mesure*) standard; (*cheval*) stallion; **l'~-or** the gold standard.

étalonner [etalɔne] *vt* to calibrate.

étamer [etame] *vt* (*casserole*) to tin(plate); (*glace*) to silver.

étamine [etamin] *nf* (*BOT*) stamen; (*tissu*) butter muslin.

étanche [etɑ̃ʃ] *adj* (*récipient; aussi fig*) watertight; (*montre, vêtement*) waterproof; ~ **à l'air** airtight.

étanchéité [etɑ̃ʃeite] *nf* watertightness; airtightness.

étancher [etɑ̃ʃe] *vt* (*liquide*) to stop (flowing); ~ **sa soif** to quench *ou* slake one's thirst.

étançon [etɑ̃sɔ̃] *nm* (*TECH*) prop.

étançonner [etɑ̃sɔne] *vt* to prop up.

étang [etɑ̃] *nm* pond.

étant [etɑ̃] *vb voir* **être, donné**.

étape [etap] *nf* stage; (*lieu d'arrivée*) stopping place; (: *CYCLISME*) staging point; **faire** ~ **à** to stop off at; **brûler les ~s** (*fig*) to cut corners.

état [eta] *nm* (*POL, condition*) state; (*d'un article d'occasion etc*) condition, state; (*liste*) inventory, statement; (*condition: professionnelle*) profession, trade; (: *sociale*) status; **en mauvais** ~ in poor condition; **en** ~ **(de marche)** in (working) order; **remettre en** ~ to repair; **hors d'~** out of order; **être en ~/hors d'~ de faire** to be in a state/in no fit state to do; **en tout** ~ **de cause** in any event; **être dans tous ses ~s** to be in a state; **faire** ~ **de** (*alléguer*) to put forward; **en** ~ **d'arrestation** under arrest; ~ **de grâce** (*REL*) state of grace; (*fig*) honeymoon period; **en** ~ **de grâce** (*fig*) inspired; **en** ~ **d'ivresse** under the influence of drink; ~ **de choses**

(*situation*) state of affairs; ~ **civil** civil status; (*bureau*) registry office; ~ **d'esprit** frame of mind; ~ **des lieux** inventory of fixtures; ~ **de santé** state of health; ~ **de siège/d'urgence** state of siege/emergency; ~ **de veille** (*PSYCH*) waking state; ~**s d'âme** moods; **les É~s barbaresques** the Barbary States; **les É~s du Golfe** the Gulf States; ~**s de service** service record *sg*.

étatique [etatik] *adj* state *cpd*, State *cpd*.

étatisation [etatizasjɔ̃] *nf* nationalization.

étatiser [etatize] *vt* to bring under state control.

étatisme [etatism(ə)] *nm* state control.

étatiste [etatist(ə)] *adj* (*doctrine etc*) of state control ♦ *nm/f* partisan of state control.

état-major, *pl* **états-majors** [etamaʒɔʀ] *nm* (*MIL*) staff; (*d'un parti etc*) top advisers *pl*; (*d'une entreprise*) top management.

État-providence [etapʀɔvidɑ̃s] *nm* welfare state.

États-Unis [etazyni] *nmpl*: **les ~ (d'Amérique)** the United States (of America).

étau, x [eto] *nm* vice (*BRIT*), vise (*US*).

étayer [eteje] *vt* to prop *ou* shore up; (*fig*) to back up.

et c(a)etera [ɛtseteʀa], **etc.** *adv* et cetera, and so on, etc.

été [ete] *pp de* **être** ♦ *nm* summer; **en ~** in summer.

éteignais [etɛɲɛ] *etc vb voir* **éteindre**.

éteignoir [etɛɲwaʀ] *nm* (candle) snuffer; (*péj*) killjoy, wet blanket.

éteindre [etɛ̃dʀ(ə)] *vt* (*lampe, lumière, radio, chauffage*) to turn *ou* switch off; (*cigarette, incendie, bougie*) to put out, extinguish; (*JUR: dette*) to extinguish; **s'~** *vi* to go off; to go out; (*mourir*) to pass away.

éteint, e [etɛ̃, -ɛ̃t] *pp de* **éteindre** ♦ *adj* (*fig*) lacklustre, dull; (*volcan*) extinct; **tous feux ~s** (*AUTO: rouler*) without lights.

étendard [etɑ̃daʀ] *nm* standard.

étendre [etɑ̃dʀ(ə)] *vt* (*appliquer: pâte, liquide*) to spread; (*déployer: carte etc*) to spread out; (*sur un fil: lessive, linge*) to hang up *ou* out; (*bras, jambes, par terre: blessé*) to stretch out; (*diluer*) to dilute, thin; (*fig: agrandir*) to extend; (*fam: adversaire*) to floor; **s'~** *vi* (*augmenter, se propager*) to spread; (*terrain, forêt etc*): **s'~ jusqu'à/de ...** à to stretch as far as/from ... to; **s'~ (sur)** (*s'allonger*) to stretch out (upon); (*se coucher*) to lie down (on); (*fig: expliquer*) to elaborate *ou* enlarge (upon).

étendu, e [etɑ̃dy] *adj* extensive ♦ *nf* (*d'eau, de sable*) stretch, expanse; (*importance*) extent.

éternel, le [etɛʀnɛl] *adj* eternal; **les neiges ~les** perpetual snow.

éternellement [etɛʀnɛlmɑ̃] *adv* eternally.

éterniser [etɛʀnize]: **s'~** *vi* to last for ages; (*personne*) to stay for ages.

éternité [etɛʀnite] *nf* eternity; **il y a** *ou* **ça fait**

une ~ **que** it's ages since; **de toute ~** from time immemorial.

éternuement [etɛʀnymɑ̃] *nm* sneeze.

éternuer [etɛʀnɥe] *vi* to sneeze.

êtes [ɛt] *vb voir* **être**.

étêter [etete] *vt* (*arbre*) to poll(ard); (*clou, poisson*) to cut the head off.

éther [etɛʀ] *nm* ether.

éthéré, e [etere] *adj* ethereal.

Éthiopie [etjɔpi] *nf*: **l'~** Ethiopia.

éthiopien, ne [etjɔpjɛ̃, -ɛn] *adj* Ethiopian.

éthique [etik] *adj* ethical ♦ *nf* ethics *sg*.

ethnie [ɛtni] *nf* ethnic group.

ethnique [ɛtnik] *adj* ethnic.

ethnographe [ɛtnɔgʀaf] *nm/f* ethnographer.

ethnographie [ɛtnɔgʀafi] *nf* ethnography.

ethnographique [ɛtnɔgʀafik] *adj* ethnographic(al).

ethnologie [ɛtnɔlɔʒi] *nf* ethnology.

ethnologique [ɛtnɔlɔʒik] *adj* ethnological.

ethnologue [ɛtnɔlɔg] *nm/f* ethnologist.

éthylique [etilik] *adj* alcoholic.

éthylisme [etilism(ə)] *nm* alcoholism.

étiage [etjaʒ] *nm* low water.

étiez [etje] *vb voir* **être**.

étincelant, e [etɛ̃slɑ̃, -ɑ̃t] *adj* sparkling.

étinceler [etɛ̃sle] *vi* to sparkle.

étincelle [etɛ̃sɛl] *nf* spark.

étioler [etjɔle]: **s'~** *vi* to wilt.

étions [etjɔ̃] *vb voir* **être**.

étique [etik] *adj* skinny, bony.

étiquetage [etiktaʒ] *nm* labelling.

étiqueter [etikte] *vt* to label.

étiquette [etikɛt] *vb voir* **étiqueter** ♦ *nf* label; (*protocole*): **l'~** etiquette.

étirer [etiʀe] *vt* to stretch; (*ressort*) to stretch out; **s'~** *vi* (*personne*) to stretch; (*convoi, route*): **s'~ sur** to stretch out over.

étoffe [etɔf] *nf* material, fabric; **avoir l'~ d'un chef** *etc* to be cut out to be a leader *etc*; **avoir de l'~** to be a forceful personality.

étoffer [etɔfe] *vt*, **s'~** *vi* to fill out.

étoile [etwal] *nf* star ♦ *adj*: **danseuse** *ou* **danceur** ~ leading dancer; **la bonne/ mauvaise ~ de qn** sb's lucky/unlucky star; **à la belle ~** (out) in the open; ~ **filante** shooting star; ~ **de mer** starfish; ~ **polaire** pole star.

étoilé, e [etwale] *adj* starry.

étole [etɔl] *nf* stole.

étonnamment [etɔnamɑ̃] *adv* amazingly.

étonnant, e [etɔnɑ̃, -ɑ̃t] *adj* surprising.

étonné, e [etɔne] *adj* surprised.

étonnement [etɔnmɑ̃] *nm* surprise; **à mon grand ~** ... to my great surprise *ou* amazement ....

étonner [etɔne] *vt* to surprise; **s'~ que/de** to be surprised that/at; **cela m'étonnerait (que)** (*j'en doute*) I'd be (very) surprised (if).

étouffant, e [etufɑ̃, -ɑ̃t] *adj* stifling.

étouffé, e [etufe] *adj* (*asphyxié*) suffocated; (*assourdi: cris, rires*) smothered ♦ *nf*: **à l'~e**

(*CULIN: poisson, légumes*) steamed; (*: viande*) braised.

étouffement [etufmɑ̃] *nm* suffocation.

étouffer [etufe] *vt* to suffocate; (*bruit*) to muffle; (*scandale*) to hush up ♦ *vi* to suffocate; (*avoir trop chaud; aussi fig*) to feel stifled; **s'**~ *vi* (*en mangeant etc*) to choke.

étouffoir [etufwaʀ] *nm* (*MUS*) damper.

étourderie [etuʀdəʀi] *nf* heedlessness *no pl*; thoughtless blunder; **faute d'**~ careless mistake.

étourdi, e [etuʀdi] *adj* (*distrait*) scatterbrained, heedless.

étourdiment [etuʀdimɑ̃] *adv* rashly.

étourdir [etuʀdiʀ] *vt* (*assommer*) to stun, daze; (*griser*) to make dizzy *ou* giddy.

étourdissant, e [etuʀdisɑ̃, -ɑ̃t] *adj* staggering.

étourdissement [etuʀdismɑ̃] *nm* dizzy spell.

étourneau, x [etuʀno] *nm* starling.

étrange [etʀɑ̃ʒ] *adj* strange.

étrangement [etʀɑ̃ʒmɑ̃] *adv* strangely.

étranger, ère [etʀɑ̃ʒe, -ɛʀ] *adj* foreign; (*pas de la famille, non familier*) strange ♦ *nm/f* foreigner; stranger ♦ *nm:* **l'**~ foreign countries; **à l'**~ abroad; **de l'**~ from abroad; ~ **à** (*mal connu*) unfamiliar to; (*sans rapport*) irrelevant to.

étrangeté [etʀɑ̃ʒte] *nf* strangeness.

étranglé, e [etʀɑ̃gle] *adj:* **d'une voix** ~**e** in a strangled voice.

étranglement [etʀɑ̃gləmɑ̃] *nm* (*d'une vallée etc*) constriction, narrow passage.

étrangler [etʀɑ̃gle] *vt* to strangle; (*fig: presse, libertés*) to stifle; **s'**~ *vi* (*en mangeant etc*) to choke; (*se resserrer*) to make a bottleneck.

étrave [etʀav] *nf* stem.

================== *MOT-CLÉ*

être [ɛtʀ(ə)] *nm* being; ~ **humain** human being ♦ *vb +attrib* **1** (*état, description*) to be; **il est instituteur** he is *ou* he's a teacher; **vous êtes grand/intelligent/fatigué** you are *ou* you're tall/clever/tired

2 (*+à: appartenir*) to be; **le livre est à Paul** the book is Paul's *ou* belongs to Paul; **c'est à moi/eux** it is *ou* it's mine/theirs

3 (*+de: provenance*): **il est de Paris** he is from Paris; (*: appartenance*): **il est des nôtres** he is one of us

4 (*date*): **nous sommes le 10 janvier** it's the 10th of January (today)

♦ *vi* to be; **je ne serai pas ici demain** I won't be here tomorrow

♦ *vb aux* **1** to have; to be; ~ **arrivé/allé** to have arrived/gone; **il est parti** he has left, he has gone

2 (*forme passive*) to be; ~ **fait par** to be made by; **il a été promu** he has been promoted

3 (*+à +inf: obligation, but*): **c'est à réparer** it needs repairing; **c'est à essayer** it should be tried; **il est à espérer que ...** it is *ou* it's to be

hoped that ...

♦ *vb impers* **1**: **il est** +*adjectif* it is +*adjective*; **il est impossible de le faire** it's impossible to do it

2 (*heure, date*): **il est 10 heures, c'est 10 heures** it is *ou* it's 10 o'clock

3 (*emphatique*): **c'est moi** it's me; **c'est à lui de le faire** it's up to him to do it; *voir aussi* **est-ce que, n'est-ce pas, c'est-à-dire, ce.**

étreindre [etʀɛ̃dʀ(ə)] *vt* to clutch, grip; (*amoureusement, amicalement*) to embrace; **s'**~ to embrace.

étreinte [etʀɛ̃t] *nf* clutch, grip; embrace; **resserrer son** ~ **autour de** (*fig*) to tighten one's grip on *ou* around.

étrenner [etʀene] *vt* to use (*ou* wear) for the first time.

étrennes [etʀɛn] *nfpl* (*cadeaux*) New Year's present; (*gratifications*) ≈ Christmas box *sg*, ≈ Christmas bonus.

étrier [etʀije] *nm* stirrup.

étriller [etʀije] *vt* (*cheval*) to curry; (*fam: battre*) to slaughter (*fig*).

étriper [etʀipe] *vt* to gut; (*fam*): ~ **qn** to tear sb's guts out.

étriqué, e [etʀike] *adj* skimpy.

étroit, e [etʀwa, -wat] *adj* narrow; (*vêtement*) tight; (*fig: serré*) close, tight; **à l'**~ cramped; ~ **d'esprit** narrow-minded.

étroitement [etʀwatmɑ̃] *adv* closely.

étroitesse [etʀwatɛs] *nf* narrowness; ~ **d'esprit** narrow-mindedness.

Étrurie [etʀyʀi] *nf:* **l'**~ Etruria.

étrusque [etʀysk(ə)] *adj* Etruscan.

étude [etyd] *nf* studying; (*ouvrage, rapport, MUS*) study; (*de notaire: bureau*) office; (*: charge*) practice; (*SCOL: salle de travail*) study room; ~**s** *nfpl* (*SCOL*) studies; **être à l'**~ (*projet etc*) to be under consideration; **faire des** ~**s (de droit/médecine)** to study (law/medicine); ~**s secondaires/supérieures** secondary/higher education; ~ **de cas** case study; ~ **de faisabilité** feasibility study; ~ **de marché** (*ÉCON*) market research.

étudiant, e [etydjɑ̃, -ɑ̃t] *adj, nm/f* student.

étudié, e [etydje] *adj* (*démarche*) studied; (*système*) carefully designed; (*prix*) keen.

étudier [etydje] *vt, vi* to study.

étui [etɥi] *nm* case.

étuve [etyv] *nf* steamroom; (*appareil*) sterilizer.

étuvée [etyve]: **à l'**~ *adv* braised.

étymologie [etimɔlɔʒi] *nf* etymology.

étymologique [etimɔlɔʒik] *adj* etymological.

eu, eue [y] *pp de* **avoir.**

EU(A) *sigle mpl* (= *États-Unis (d'Amérique)*) US(A).

eucalyptus [økaliptys] *nm* eucalyptus.

Eucharistie [økaʀisti] *nf:* **l'**~ the Eucharist, the Lord's Supper.

eucharistique [økaʀistik] *adj* eucharistic.

euclidien, ne [øklidjɛ̃, -ɛn] *adj* Euclidian.

eugénique [øʒenik] *adj* eugenic ♦ *nf* eugenics *sg.*
eugénisme [øʒenism(ə)] *nm* eugenics *sg.*
euh [ø] *excl* er.
eunuque [ønyk] *nm* eunuch.
euphémique [øfemik] *adj* euphemistic.
euphémisme [øfemism(ə)] *nm* euphemism.
euphonie [øfɔni] *nf* euphony.
euphorbe [øfɔRb(ə)] *nf* (*BOT*) spurge.
euphorie [øfɔRi] *nf* euphoria.
euphorique [øfɔRik] *adj* euphoric.
euphorisant, e [øfɔRizɑ̃, -ɑ̃t] *adj* exhilarating.
Euphrate [øfRat] *nm*: **l'~** the Euphrates *sg.*
eurafricain, e [øRafRikɛ̃, -ɛn] *adj* Eurafrican.
eurasiatique [øRazjatik] *adj* Eurasiatic.
Eurasie [øRazi] *nf*: **l'~** Eurasia.
eurasien, ne [øRazjɛ̃, -ɛn] *adj* Eurasian.
EURATOM [øRatɔm] *sigle f* Euratom.
eurent [yR(ə)] *vb voir* **avoir**.
euro- [øRo] *préfixe* Euro-.
eurocrate [øRɔkRat] *nm/f* (*péj*) Eurocrat.
eurodevise [øRɔdəviz] *nf* Eurocurrency.
eurodollar [øRodɔlaR] *nm* Eurodollar.
euromonnaie [øRɔmɔnɛ] *nf* Eurocurrency.
Europe [øRɔp] *nf*: **l'~** Europe; **l'~ centrale** Central Europe; **l'~ verte** European agriculture.
européanisation [øRɔpeanizɑsjɔ̃] *nf* Europeanization.
européaniser [øRɔpeanize] *vt* to Europeanize.
européen, ne [øRɔpeɛ̃, -ɛn] *adj* European ♦ *nm/f*: **E~, ne** European.
eurosceptique [øRɔsɛptik] *nm/f* Eurosceptic.
Eurovision [øRovizjɔ̃] *nf* Eurovision; **émission en ~** Eurovision broadcast.
eus [y] *etc vb voir* **avoir**.
euthanasie [øtanazi] *nf* euthanasia.
eux [ø] *pron* (*sujet*) they; (*objet*) them; **~, ils ont fait ...** THEY did ....
EV *abr* (= en ville) used on mail to be delivered by hand, courier etc within the same town.
évacuation [evakɥɑsjɔ̃] *nf* evacuation.
évacué, e [evakɥe] *nm/f* evacuee.
évacuer [evakɥe] *vt* (*salle, région*) to evacuate, clear; (*occupants, population*) to evacuate; (*toxine etc*) to evacuate, discharge.
évadé, e [evade] *adj* escaped ♦ *nm/f* escapee.
évader [evade]: **s'~** *vi* to escape.
évaluation [evalɥɑsjɔ̃] *nf* assessment, evaluation.
évaluer [evalɥe] *vt* to assess, evaluate.
évanescent, e [evanesɑ̃, -ɑ̃t] *adj* evanescent.
évangélique [evɑ̃ʒelik] *adj* evangelical.
évangélisation [evɑ̃ʒelizɑsjɔ̃] *nf* evangelization.
évangéliser [evɑ̃ʒelize] *vt* to evangelize.
évangéliste [evɑ̃ʒelist(ə)] *nm* evangelist.
évangile [evɑ̃ʒil] *nm* gospel; (*texte de la Bible*): **É~** Gospel; **ce n'est pas l'É~** (*fig*) it's not gospel.
évanoui, e [evanwi] *adj* in a faint; **tomber ~** to faint.

évanouir [evanwiR]: **s'~** *vi* to faint, pass out; (*disparaître*) to vanish, disappear.
évanouissement [evanwismɑ̃] *nm* (*syncope*) fainting fit; (*MÉD*) loss of consciousness.
évaporation [evapɔRɑsjɔ̃] *nf* evaporation.
évaporé, e [evapɔRe] *adj* giddy, scatterbrained.
évaporer [evapɔRe]: **s'~** *vi* to evaporate.
évasé, e [evaze] *adj* (*jupe etc*) flared.
évaser [evaze] *vt* (*tuyau*) to widen, open out; (*jupe, pantalon*) to flare; **s'~** *vi* to widen, open out.
évasif, ive [evazif, -iv] *adj* evasive.
évasion [evazjɔ̃] *nf* escape; **littérature d'~** escapist literature; **~ des capitaux** (*ÉCON*) flight of capital; **~ fiscale** tax avoidance.
évasivement [evazivmɑ̃] *adv* evasively.
évêché [eveʃe] *nm* (*fonction*) bishopric; (*palais*) bishop's palace.
éveil [evɛj] *nm* awakening; **être en ~** to be alert; **mettre qn en ~, donner l'~ à qn** to arouse sb's suspicions; **activités d'~** early-learning activities.
éveillé, e [eveje] *adj* awake; (*vif*) alert, sharp.
éveiller [eveje] *vt* to (a)waken; **s'~** *vi* to (a)waken; (*fig*) to be aroused.
événement [evɛnmɑ̃] *nm* event.
éventail [evɑ̃taj] *nm* fan; (*choix*) range; **en ~** fanned out; fan-shaped.
éventaire [evɑ̃tɛR] *nm* stall, stand.
éventé, e [evɑ̃te] *adj* (*parfum, vin*) stale.
éventer [evɑ̃te] *vt* (*secret, complot*) to uncover; (*avec un éventail*) to fan; **s'~** *vi* (*parfum, vin*) to go stale.
éventrer [evɑ̃tRe] *vt* to disembowel; (*fig*) to tear *ou* rip open.
éventualité [evɑ̃tɥalite] *nf* eventuality; possibility; **dans l'~ de** in the event of; **parer à toute ~** to guard against all eventualities.
éventuel, le [evɑ̃tɥɛl] *adj* possible.
éventuellement [evɑ̃tɥɛlmɑ̃] *adv* possibly.
évêque [evɛk] *nm* bishop.
Everest [ɛvRɛst] *nm*: **(mont) ~** (Mount) Everest.
évertuer [evɛRtɥe]: **s'~** *vi*: **s'~ à faire** to try very hard to do.
éviction [eviksjɔ̃] *nf* ousting, supplanting; (*de locataire*) eviction.
évidemment [evidamɑ̃] *adv* obviously.
évidence [evidɑ̃s] *nf* obviousness; (*fait*) obvious fact; **se rendre à l'~** to bow before the evidence; **nier l'~** to deny the evidence; **à l'~** evidently; **de toute ~** quite obviously *ou* evidently; **en ~** conspicuous; **mettre en ~** to bring to the fore.
évident, e [evidɑ̃, -ɑ̃t] *adj* obvious, evident; **ce n'est pas ~** (*cela pose des problèmes*) it's not (all that) straightforward, it's not as simple as all that.
évider [evide] *vt* to scoop out.
évier [evje] *nm* (kitchen) sink.
évincement [evɛ̃smɑ̃] *nm* ousting.

évincer [evɛ̃se] *vt* to oust, supplant.
évitable [evitabl(ə)] *adj* avoidable.
évitement [evitmɑ̃] *nm*: **place d'~** (*AUTO*) passing place.
éviter [evite] *vt* to avoid; **~ de faire/que qch ne se passe** to avoid doing/sth happening; **~ qch à qn** to spare sb sth.
évocateur, trice [evɔkatœʀ, -tʀis] *adj* evocative, suggestive.
évocation [evɔkasjɔ̃] *nf* evocation.
évolué, e [evɔlɥe] *adj* advanced; (*personne*) broad-minded.
évoluer [evɔlɥe] *vi* (*enfant, maladie*) to develop; (*situation, moralement*) to evolve, develop; (*aller et venir: danseur etc*) to move about, circle.
évolutif, ive [evɔlytif, -iv] *adj* evolving.
évolution [evɔlysjɔ̃] *nf* development; evolution; **~s** *nfpl* movements.
évolutionnisme [evɔlysjɔnism(ə)] *nm* evolutionism.
évoquer [evɔke] *vt* to call to mind, evoke; (*mentionner*) to mention.
ex. *abr* (= *exemple*) ex.
ex- [ɛks] *préfixe* ex-.
exacerbé, e [ɛgzasɛʀbe] *adj* (*orgueil, sensibilité*) exaggerated.
exacerber [ɛgzasɛʀbe] *vt* to exacerbate.
exact, e [ɛgzakt] *adj* (*précis*) exact, accurate, precise; (*correct*) correct; (*ponctuel*) punctual; **l'heure ~e** the right *ou* exact time.
exactement [ɛgzaktəmɑ̃] *adv* exactly, accurately, precisely; correctly; (*c'est cela même*) exactly.
exaction [ɛgzaksjɔ̃] *nf* (*d'argent*) exaction; (*gén pl: actes de violence*) abuse(s).
exactitude [ɛgzaktityd] *nf* exactitude, accurateness, precision.
ex aequo [ɛgzeko] *adj* equally placed; **classé 1er** *ou* placed equal first.
exagération [ɛgzaʒeʀasjɔ̃] *nf* exaggeration.
exagéré, e [ɛgzaʒeʀe] *adj* (*prix etc*) excessive.
exagérément [ɛgzaʒeʀemɑ̃] *adv* excessively.
exagérer [ɛgzaʒeʀe] *vt* to exaggerate ♦ *vi* (*abuser*) to go too far; (*dépasser les bornes*) to overstep the mark; (*déformer les faits*) to exaggerate; **s'~ qch** to exaggerate sth.
exaltant, e [ɛgzaltɑ̃, -ɑ̃t] *adj* exhilarating.
exaltation [ɛgzaltasjɔ̃] *nf* exaltation.
exalté, e [ɛgzalte] *adj* (over)excited ♦ *nm/f* (*péj*) fanatic.
exalter [ɛgzalte] *vt* (*enthousiasmer*) to excite, elate; (*glorifier*) to exalt.
examen [ɛgzamɛ̃] *nm* examination; (*SCOL*) exam, examination; **à l'~** (*dossier, projet*) under consideration; (*COMM*) on approval; **~ blanc** mock exam(ination); **~ de la vue** sight test.
examinateur, trice [ɛgzaminatœʀ, -tʀis] *nm/f* examiner.
examiner [ɛgzamine] *vt* to examine.

exaspérant, e [ɛgzaspeʀɑ̃, -ɑ̃t] *adj* exasperating.
exaspération [ɛgzaspeʀasjɔ̃] *nf* exasperation.
exaspéré, e [ɛgzaspeʀe] *adj* exasperated.
exaspérer [ɛgzaspeʀe] *vt* to exasperate; (*aggraver*) to exacerbate.
exaucer [ɛgzose] *vt* (*vœu*) to grant, fulfil; **~ qn** to grant sb's wishes.
ex cathedra [ɛkskatedʀa] *adj, adv* ex cathedra.
excavateur [ɛkskavatœʀ] *nm* excavator, mechanical digger.
excavation [ɛkskavasjɔ̃] *nf* excavation.
excavatrice [ɛkskavatʀis] *nf* = **excavateur**.
excédent [ɛksedɑ̃] *nm* surplus; **en ~** surplus; **payer 600 F d'~** (*de bagages*) to pay 600 francs excess luggage; **~ de bagages** excess luggage; **~ commercial** trade surplus.
excédentaire [ɛksedɑ̃tɛʀ] *adj* surplus, excess.
excéder [ɛksede] *vt* (*dépasser*) to exceed; (*agacer*) to exasperate; **excédé de fatigue** exhausted; **excédé de travail** worn out with work.
excellence [ɛksɛlɑ̃s] *nf* excellence; (*titre*) Excellency; **par ~** par excellence.
excellent, e [ɛksɛlɑ̃, -ɑ̃t] *adj* excellent.
exceller [ɛksele] *vi*: **~ (dans)** to excel (in).
excentricité [ɛksɑ̃tʀisite] *nf* eccentricity.
excentrique [ɛksɑ̃tʀik] *adj* eccentric; (*quartier*) outlying ♦ *nm/f* eccentric.
excentriquement [ɛksɑ̃tʀikmɑ̃] *adv* eccentrically.
excepté, e [ɛksɛpte] *adj, prép*: **les élèves ~s, ~ les élèves** except for *ou* apart from the pupils; **~ si/quand** except if/when; **~ que** except that.
excepter [ɛksɛpte] *vt* to except.
exception [ɛksɛpsjɔ̃] *nf* exception; **faire ~** to be an exception; **faire une ~** to make an exception; **sans ~** without exception; **à l'~ de** except for, with the exception of; **d'~** (*mesure, loi*) special, exceptional.
exceptionnel, le [ɛksɛpsjɔnɛl] *adj* exceptional; (*prix*) special.
exceptionnellement [ɛksɛpsjɔnɛlmɑ̃] *adv* exceptionally; (*par exception*) by way of an exception, on this occasion.
excès [ɛksɛ] *nm* surplus ♦ *nmpl* excesses; **à l'~** (*méticuleux, généreux*) to excess; **avec ~** to excess; **sans ~** in moderation; **tomber dans l'~ inverse** to go to the opposite extreme; **~ de langage** immoderate language; **~ de pouvoir** abuse of power; **~ de vitesse** speeding *no pl*, exceeding the speed limit; **~ de zèle** overzealousness *no pl*.
excessif, ive [ɛksesif, -iv] *adj* excessive.
excessivement [ɛksesivmɑ̃] *adv* (*trop: cher*) excessively, inordinately; (*très: riche, laid*) extremely, incredibly; **manger/boire ~** to eat/drink to excess.
exciper [ɛksipe]: **~ de** *vt* to plead.
excipient [ɛksipjɑ̃] *nm* (*MÉD*) inert base,

excipient.

exciser [ɛksize] *vt* (*MÉD*) to excise.

excision [ɛksizjɔ̃] *nf* (*MÉD*) excision; (*rituelle*) circumcision.

excitant, e [ɛksitɑ̃, -ɑ̃t] *adj* exciting ♦ *nm* stimulant.

excitation [ɛksitasjɔ̃] *nf* (*état*) excitement.

excité, e [ɛksite] *adj* excited.

exciter [ɛksite] *vt* to excite; (*suj: café etc*) to stimulate; **s'~** *vi* to get excited; **~ qn à** (*révolte etc*) to incite sb to.

exclamation [ɛksklamasjɔ̃] *nf* exclamation.

exclamer [ɛksklame]: **s'~** *vi* to exclaim.

exclu, e [ɛkskly] *pp de* **exclure** ♦ *adj*: **il est/n'est pas ~ que** ... it's out of the question/not impossible that ...; **ce n'est pas exclu** it's not impossible, I don't rule that out.

exclure [ɛksklyʀ] *vt* (*faire sortir*) to expel; (*ne pas compter*) to exclude, leave out; (*rendre impossible*) to exclude, rule out.

exclusif, ive [ɛksklyzif, -iv] *adj* exclusive; **avec la mission exclusive/dans le but ~ de** ... with the sole mission/aim of ...; **agent ~** sole agent.

exclusion [ɛksklyzjɔ̃] *nf* expulsion; **à l'~ de** with the exclusion *ou* exception of.

exclusivement [ɛksklyzivmɑ̃] *adv* exclusively.

exclusivité [ɛksklyzivite] *nf* exclusiveness; (*COMM*) exclusive rights *pl*; **film passant en ~ à** film showing only at.

excommunier [ɛkskɔmynje] *vt* to excommunicate.

excréments [ɛkskʀemɑ̃] *nmpl* excrement *sg*, faeces.

excréter [ɛkskʀete] *vt* to excrete.

excroissance [ɛkskʀwasɑ̃s] *nf* excrescence, outgrowth.

excursion [ɛkskyʀsjɔ̃] *nf* (*en autocar*) excursion, trip; (*à pied*) walk, hike; **faire une ~** to go on an excursion *ou* a trip; to go on a walk *ou* hike.

excursionniste [ɛkskyʀsjɔnist(ə)] *nm/f* tripper; hiker.

excusable [ɛkskyzabl(ə)] *adj* excusable.

excuse [ɛkskyz] *nf* excuse; **~s** *nfpl* apology *sg*, apologies; **faire des ~s** to apologize; **faire ses ~s** to offer one's apologies; **mot d'~** (*SCOL*) note from one's parent(s) (*to explain absence etc*); **lettre d'~s** letter of apology.

excuser [ɛkskyze] *vt* to excuse; **~ qn de qch** (*dispenser*) to excuse sb from sth; **s'~ (de)** to apologize (for); **"excusez-moi"** "I'm sorry"; (*pour attirer l'attention*) "excuse me"; **se faire ~** to ask to be excused.

exécrable [ɛgzekʀabl(ə)] *adj* atrocious.

exécrer [ɛgzekʀe] *vt* to loathe, abhor.

exécutant, e [ɛgzekytɑ̃, -ɑ̃t] *nm/f* performer.

exécuter [ɛgzekyte] *vt* (*prisonnier*) to execute; (*tâche etc*) to execute, carry out; (*MUS: jouer*) to perform, execute; (*INFORM*) to run; **s'~** *vi* to comply.

exécuteur, trice [ɛgzekytœʀ, -tʀis] *nm/f* (*testamentaire*) executor ♦ *nm* (*bourreau*) executioner.

exécutif, ive [ɛgzekytif, -iv] *adj, nm* (*POL*) executive.

exécution [ɛgzekysjɔ̃] *nf* execution; carrying out; **mettre à ~** to carry out.

exécutoire [ɛgzekytwaʀ] *adj* (*JUR*) (legally) binding.

exégèse [ɛgzeʒɛz] *nf* exegesis.

exégète [ɛgzeʒɛt] *nm* exegete.

exemplaire [ɛgzɑ̃plɛʀ] *adj* exemplary ♦ *nm* copy.

exemple [ɛgzɑ̃pl(ə)] *nm* example; **par ~** for instance, for example; (*valeur intensive*) really!; **sans ~** (*bêtise, gourmandise etc*) unparalleled; **donner l'~** to set an example; **prendre ~ sur** to take as a model; **à l'~ de** just like; **pour l'~** (*punir*) as an example.

exempt, e [ɛgzɑ̃, -ɑ̃t] *adj*: **~ de** (*dispensé de*) exempt from; (*sans*) free from; **~ de taxes** tax-free.

exempter [ɛgzɑ̃te] *vt*: **~ de** to exempt from.

exercé, e [ɛgzɛʀse] *adj* trained.

exercer [ɛgzɛʀse] *vt* (*pratiquer*) to exercise, practise; (*faire usage de: prérogative*) to exercise; (*effectuer: influence, contrôle, pression*) to exert; (*former*) to exercise, train ♦ *vi* (*médecin*) to be in practice; **s'~** (*sportif, musicien*) to practise; (*se faire sentir: pression etc*): **s'~ (sur ou contre)** to be exerted (on); **s'~ à faire qch** to train o.s. to do sth.

exercice [ɛgzɛʀsis] *nm* practice; exercising; (*tâche, travail*) exercise; (*COMM, ADMIN: période*) accounting period; **l'~** (*sportive etc*) exercise; (*MIL*) drill; **en ~** (*juge*) in office; (*médecin*) practising; **dans l'~ de ses fonctions** in the discharge of his duties; **~s d'assouplissement** limbering-up (exercises).

exergue [ɛgzɛʀg(ə)] *nm*: **mettre en ~** (*inscription*) to inscribe; **porter en ~** to be inscribed with.

exhalaison [ɛgzalɛzɔ̃] *nf* exhalation.

exhaler [ɛgzale] *vt* (*parfum*) to exhale; (*souffle, son, soupir*) to utter, breathe; **s'~** *vi* to rise (up).

exhausser [ɛgzose] *vt* to raise (up).

exhausteur [ɛgzostœʀ] *nm* extractor fan.

exhaustif, ive [ɛgzostif, -iv] *adj* exhaustive.

exhiber [ɛgzibe] *vt* (*montrer: papiers, certificat*) to present, produce; (*péj*) to display, flaunt; **s'~** (*personne*) to parade; (*suj: exhibitionniste*) to expose o.s.

exhibitionnisme [ɛgzibisjɔnism(ə)] *nm* exhibitionism.

exhibitionniste [ɛgzibisjɔnist(ə)] *nm/f* exhibitionist.

exhortation [ɛgzɔʀtasjɔ̃] *nf* exhortation.

exhorter [ɛgzɔʀte] *vt*: **~ qn à faire** to urge sb to do.

exhumer [ɛgzyme] *vt* to exhume.

exigeant, e [ɛgziʒɑ̃, -ɑ̃t] *adj* demanding; (*péj*)

hard to please.
exigence [εgziʒɑ̃s] *nf* demand, requirement.
exiger [εgziʒe] *vt* to demand, require.
exigible [εgziʒibl(ə)] *adj* (COMM, JUR) payable.
exigu, ë [εgzigy] *adj* cramped, tiny.
exiguïté [εgzigɥite] *nf* (d'un lieu) cramped nature.
exil [εgzil] *nm* exile; **en** ~ in exile.
exilé, e [εgzile] *nm/f* exile.
exiler [εgzile] *vt* to exile; **s'**~ to go into exile.
existant, e [εgzistɑ̃, -ɑ̃t] *adj* (actuel, présent) existing.
existence [εgzistɑ̃s] *nf* existence; **dans l'**~ in life.
existentialisme [εgzistɑ̃sjalism(ə)] *nm* existentialism.
existentiel, le [εgzistɑ̃sjɛl] *adj* existential.
exister [εgziste] *vi* to exist; **il existe un/des** there is a/are (some).
exode [εgzɔd] *nm* exodus.
exonération [εgzɔneʁɑsjɔ̃] *nf* exemption.
exonéré, e [εgzɔneʁe] *adj*: ~ **de TVA** zero-rated (for VAT).
exonérer [εgzɔneʁe] *vt*: ~ **de** to exempt from.
exorbitant, e [εgzɔʁbitɑ̃, -ɑ̃t] *adj* exorbitant.
exorbité, e [εgzɔʁbite] *adj*: **yeux** ~**s** bulging eyes.
exorciser [εgzɔʁsize] *vt* to exorcize.
exorde [εgzɔʁd(ə)] *nm* introduction.
exotique [εgzɔtik] *adj* exotic.
exotisme [εgzɔtism(ə)] *nm* exoticism.
expansif, ive [εkspɑ̃sif, -iv] *adj* expansive, communicative.
expansion [εkspɑ̃sjɔ̃] *nf* expansion.
expansionniste [εkspɑ̃sjɔnist(ə)] *adj* expansionist.
expansivité [εkspɑ̃sivite] *nf* expansiveness.
expatrié, e [εkspatʁije] *nm/f* expatriate.
expatrier [εkspatʁije] *vt* (argent) to take ou send out of the country; **s'**~ to leave one's country.
expectative [εkspεktativ] *nf*: **être dans l'**~ to be waiting to see.
expectorant, e [εkspεktɔʁɑ̃, -ɑ̃t] *adj*: **sirop** ~ expectorant (syrup).
expectorer [εkspεktɔʁe] *vi* to expectorate.
expédient [εkspedjɑ̃] *nm* (parfois péj) expedient; **vivre d'**~**s** to live by one's wits.
expédier [εkspedje] *vt* (lettre, paquet) to send; (troupes, renfort) to dispatch; (péj: travail etc) to dispose of, dispatch.
expéditeur, trice [εkspediter, -tʁis] *nm/f* (POSTES) sender.
expéditif, ive [εkspeditif, -iv] *adj* quick, expeditious.
expédition [εkspedisjɔ̃] *nf* sending; (scientifique, sportive, MIL) expedition; ~ **punitive** punitive raid.
expéditionnaire [εkspedisjɔnεʁ] *adj*: **corps** ~ (MIL) task force.
expérience [εkspeʁjɑ̃s] *nf* (de la vie, des choses) experience; (scientifique)

experiment; **avoir de l'**~ to have experience, be experienced; **avoir l'**~ **de** to have experience of; **faire l'**~ **de qch** to experience sth; ~ **de chimie/d'électricité** chemical/electrical experiment.
expérimental, e, aux [εkspeʁimɑ̃tal, -o] *adj* experimental.
expérimentalement [εkspeʁimɑ̃talmɑ̃] *adv* experimentally.
expérimenté, e [εkspeʁimɑ̃te] *adj* experienced.
expérimenter [εkspeʁimɑ̃te] *vt* (machine, technique) to test out, experiment with.
expert, e [εkspεʁ, -εʁt(ə)] *adj*: ~ **en** expert in ♦ *nm* (spécialiste) expert; ~ **en assurances** insurance valuer.
expert-comptable, *pl* **experts-comptables** [εkspεʁkɔ̃tabl(ə)] *nm* ≈ chartered (BRIT) ou certified public (US) accountant.
expertise [εkspεʁtiz] *nf* valuation; assessment; valuer's (ou assessor's) report; (JUR) (forensic) examination.
expertiser [εkspεʁtize] *vt* (objet de valeur) to value; (voiture accidentée etc) to assess damage to.
expier [εkspje] *vt* to expiate, atone for.
expiration [εkspiʁɑsjɔ̃] *nf* expiry (BRIT), expiration; breathing out *no pl*.
expirer [εkspiʁe] *vi* (prendre fin, littéraire: mourir) to expire; (respirer) to breathe out.
explétif, ive [εkspletif, -iv] *adj* (LING) expletive.
explicable [εksplikabl(ə)] *adj*: **pas** ~ inexplicable.
explicatif, ive [εksplikatif, -iv] *adj* (mot, texte, note) explanatory.
explication [εksplikɑsjɔ̃] *nf* explanation; (discussion) discussion; ~ **de texte** (SCOL) critical analysis (of a text).
explicite [εksplisit] *adj* explicit.
explicitement [εksplisitmɑ̃] *adv* explicitly.
expliciter [εksplisite] *vt* to make explicit.
expliquer [εksplike] *vt* to explain; ~ (**à qn**) **comment/que** to point out ou explain (to sb) how/that; **s'**~ (se faire comprendre: personne) to explain o.s.; (discuter) to discuss things; (se disputer) to have it out; (comprendre): **je m'explique son retard/absence** I understand his lateness/absence; **son erreur s'explique** one can understand his mistake.
exploit [εksplwa] *nm* exploit, feat.
exploitable [εksplwatabl(ə)] *adj* (gisement etc) that can be exploited; ~ **par une machine** machine-readable.
exploitant [εksplwatɑ̃] *nm* farmer.
exploitation [εksplwatɑsjɔ̃] *nf* exploitation; running; (entreprise): ~ **agricole** farming concern.
exploiter [εksplwate] *vt* to exploit; (entreprise, ferme) to run, operate.
exploiteur, euse [εksplwatœʁ, -øz] *nm/f* (péj) exploiter.

explorateur, trice [ɛksplɔʀatœʀ, -tʀis] *nm/f* explorer.

exploration [ɛksplɔʀasjɔ̃] *nf* exploration.

explorer [ɛksplɔʀe] *vt* to explore.

exploser [ɛksploze] *vi* to explode, blow up; (*engin explosif*) to go off; (*fig: joie, colère*) to burst out, explode; (: *personne: de colère*) to explode, flare up; **faire** ~ (*bombe*) to explode, detonate; (*bâtiment, véhicule*) to blow up.

explosif, ive [ɛksplozif, -iv] *adj, nm* explosive.

explosion [ɛksplozjɔ̃] *nf* explosion; ~ **de joie/ colère** outburst of joy/rage; ~ **démographique** population explosion.

exponentiel, le [ɛkspɔnɑ̃sjɛl] *adj* exponential.

exportateur, trice [ɛkspɔʀtatœʀ, -tʀis] *adj* exporting ♦ *nm* exporter.

exportation [ɛkspɔʀtasjɔ̃] *nf* export.

exporter [ɛkspɔʀte] *vt* to export.

exposant [ɛkspozɑ̃] *nm* exhibitor; (*MATH*) exponent.

exposé, e [ɛkspoze] *nm* (*écrit*) exposé; (*oral*) talk ♦ *adj:* ~ **au sud** facing south, with a southern aspect; **bien** ~ well situated; **très** ~ very exposed.

exposer [ɛkspoze] *vt* (*montrer: marchandise*) to display; (: *peinture*) to exhibit, show; (*parler de: problème, situation*) to explain, expose, set out; (*mettre en danger, orienter: maison etc*) to expose; ~ **qn/qch à** to expose sb/sth to; ~ **sa vie** to risk one's life; **s'**~ **à** (*soleil, danger*) to expose o.s. to; (*critiques, punition*) to lay o.s. open to.

exposition [ɛkspozisjɔ̃] *nf* (*voir exposer*) displaying; exhibiting; explanation, exposition; exposure; (*voir exposé*) aspect, situation; (*manifestation*) exhibition; (*PHOTO*) exposure; (*introduction*) exposition.

exprès [ɛksprɛ] *adv* (*délibérément*) on purpose; (*spécialement*) specially; **faire** ~ **de faire qch** to do sth on purpose.

exprès, esse [ɛksprɛs] *adj* (*ordre, défense*) express, formal ♦ *adj inv, adv* (*POSTES*) express; **envoyer qch en** ~ to send sth express.

express [ɛksprɛs] *adj, nm:* **(café)** ~ espresso; **(train)** ~ fast train.

expressément [ɛksprɛsemɑ̃] *adv* expressly, specifically.

expressif, ive [ɛksprɛsif, -iv] *adj* expressive.

expression [ɛksprɛsjɔ̃] *nf* expression; **réduit à sa plus simple** ~ reduced to its simplest terms; **liberté/moyens d'**~ freedom/means of expression; ~ **toute faite** set phrase.

expressionnisme [ɛksprɛsjɔnism(ə)] *nm* expressionism.

expressivité [ɛksprɛsivite] *nf* expressiveness.

exprimer [ɛksprime] *vt* (*sentiment, idée*) to express; (*faire sortir: jus, liquide*) to press out; **s'**~ *vi* (*personne*) to express o.s.

expropriation [ɛksprɔprijasjɔ̃] *nf* expropriation; **frapper d'**~ to put a compulsory purchase order on.

exproprier [ɛksprɔprije] *vt* to buy up (*ou* buy the property of) by compulsory purchase, expropriate.

expulser [ɛkspylse] *vt* (*d'une salle, d'un groupe*) to expel; (*locataire*) to evict; (*FOOTBALL*) to send off.

expulsion [ɛkspylsjɔ̃] *nf* expulsion; eviction; sending off.

expurger [ɛkspyʀʒe] *vt* to expurgate, bowdlerize.

exquis, e [ɛkski, -iz] *adj* (*gâteau, parfum, élégance*) exquisite; (*personne, temps*) delightful.

exsangue [ɛksɑ̃g] *adj* bloodless, drained of blood.

exsuder [ɛksyde] *vt* to exude.

extase [ɛkstaz] *nf* ecstasy; **être en** ~ to be in raptures.

extasier [ɛkstazje]: **s'**~ *vi:* **s'**~ **sur** to go into raptures over.

extatique [ɛkstatik] *adj* ecstatic.

extenseur [ɛkstɑ̃sœʀ] *nm* (*SPORT*) chest expander.

extensible [ɛkstɑ̃sibl(ə)] *adj* extensible.

extensif, ive [ɛkstɑ̃sif, -iv] *adj* extensive.

extension [ɛkstɑ̃sjɔ̃] *nf* (*d'un muscle, ressort*) stretching; (*MÉD*) **à l'**~ in traction; (*fig*) extension; expansion.

exténuant [ɛkstenɥɑ̃, -ɑ̃t] *adj* exhausting.

exténuer [ɛkstenɥe] *vt* to exhaust.

extérieur, e [ɛksteʀjœʀ] *adj* (*de dehors: porte, mur etc*) outer, outside; (: *commerce, politique*) foreign; (: *influences, pressions*) external; (*au dehors: escalier, w.-c.*) outside; (*apparent: calme, gaieté etc*) outer ♦ *nm* (*d'une maison, d'un récipient etc*) outside, exterior; (*d'une personne: apparence*) exterior; (*d'un pays, d'un groupe social*): **l'**~ the outside world; **à l'**~ (*dehors*) outside; (*fig: à l'étranger*) abroad.

extérieurement [ɛksteʀjœʀmɑ̃] *adv* (*de dehors*) on the outside; (*en apparence*) on the surface.

extérioriser [ɛksteʀjɔʀize] *vt* to exteriorize.

extermination [ɛkstɛʀminasjɔ̃] *nf* extermination, wiping out.

exterminer [ɛkstɛʀmine] *vt* to exterminate, wipe out.

externat [ɛkstɛʀna] *nm* day school.

externe [ɛkstɛʀn(ə)] *adj* external, outer ♦ *nm/f* (*MÉD*) non-resident medical student, extern (*US*); (*SCOL*) day pupil.

extincteur [ɛkstɛ̃ktœʀ] *nm* (fire) extinguisher.

extinction [ɛkstɛ̃ksjɔ̃] *nf* extinction; (*JUR: d'une dette*) extinguishment; ~ **de voix** (*MÉD*) loss of voice.

extirper [ɛkstiʀpe] *vt* (*tumeur*) to extirpate; (*plante*) to root out, pull up; (*préjugés*) to eradicate.

extorquer [ɛkstɔʀke] *vt* (*de l'argent, un renseignement*): ~ **qch à qn** to extort sth from sb.

extorsion [ɛkstɔʀsjɔ̃] *nf*: ~ **de fonds** extortion of money.

extra [ɛkstʀa] *adj inv* first-rate; (*marchandises*) top-quality ♦ *nm inv* extra help ♦ *préfixe* extra(-).

extraction [ɛkstʀaksjɔ̃] *nf* extraction.

extrader [ɛkstʀade] *vt* to extradite.

extradition [ɛkstʀadisjɔ̃] *nf* extradition.

extra-fin, e [ɛkstʀafɛ̃, -in] *adj* extra-fine.

extra-fort, e [ɛkstʀafɔʀ] *adj* extra strong.

extraire [ɛkstʀɛʀ] *vt* to extract.

extrait, e [ɛkstʀɛ, -ɛt] *pp de* **extraire** ♦ *nm* (*de plante*) extract; (*de film, livre*) extract, excerpt; ~ **de naissance** birth certificate.

extra-lucide [ɛkstʀalysid] *adj*: **voyante** ~ clairvoyant.

extraordinaire [ɛkstʀaɔʀdinɛʀ] *adj* extraordinary; (*POL, ADMIN*) special; **ambassadeur** ~ ambassador extraordinary; **assemblée** ~ extraordinary meeting; **par** ~ by some unlikely chance.

extraordinairement [ɛksʀaɔʀdinɛʀmɑ̃] *adv* extraordinarily.

extrapoler [ɛkstʀapɔle] *vt, vi* to extrapolate.

extra-sensoriel, le [ɛkstʀasɑ̃sɔʀjɛl] *adj* extrasensory.

extra-terrestre [ɛkstʀatɛʀɛstʀ(ə)] *nm/f* extraterrestrial.

extra-utérin, e [ɛkstʀaytɛʀɛ̃, -in] *adj* extra-uterine.

extravagance [ɛkstʀavagɑ̃s] *nf* extravagance *no pl*; extravagant behaviour *no pl*.

extravagant, e [ɛkstʀavagɑ̃, -ɑ̃t] *adj* (*personne, attitude*) extravagant; (*idée*) wild.

extraverti, e [ɛkstʀavɛʀti] *adj* extrovert.

extrayais [ɛkstʀɛjɛ] *etc vb voir* **extraire**.

extrême [ɛkstʀɛm] *adj, nm* extreme; (*intensif*): **d'une** ~ **simplicité/brutalité** extremely simple/brutal; **d'un** ~ **à l'autre** from one extreme to another; **à l'**~ **in** the extreme; **à l'**~ **rigueur** in the absolute extreme.

extrêmement [ɛkstʀɛmmɑ̃] *adv* extremely.

extrême-onction, *pl* **extrêmes-onctions** [ɛkstʀɛmɔ̃ksjɔ̃] *nf* (*REL*) last rites *pl*, Extreme Unction.

Extrême-Orient [ɛkstʀɛmɔʀjɑ̃] *nm*: **l'**~ the Far East.

extrême-oriental, e, aux [ɛkstʀɛmɔʀjɑ̃tal, -o] *adj* Far Eastern.

extrémisme [ɛkstʀemism(ə)] *nm* extremism.

extrémiste [ɛkstʀemist(ə)] *adj, nm/f* extremist.

extrémité [ɛkstʀemite] *nf* (*bout*) end; (*situation*) straits *pl*, plight; (*geste désespéré*) extreme action; ~**s** *nfpl* (*pieds et mains*) extremities; **à la dernière** ~ (*à l'agonie*) on the point of death.

extroverti, e [ɛkstʀɔvɛʀti] *adj* = **extraverti**.

exubérance [ɛgzybeʀɑ̃s] *nf* exuberance.

exubérant, e [ɛgzybeʀɑ̃, -ɑ̃t] *adj* exuberant.

exulter [ɛgzylte] *vi* to exult.

exutoire [ɛgzytwaʀ] *nm* outlet, release.

ex-voto [ɛksvɔto] *nm inv* ex-voto.

eye-liner [ajlajnœʀ] *nm* eyeliner.

Ff

F, f [ɛf] *nm inv* F, f ♦ *abr* = **féminin**; (= *franc*) fr.; (= *Fahrenheit*) F; (= *frère*) Br(o).; (= *femme*) W; (*appartement*): **un F2/F3** a 2-/3-roomed flat (*BRIT*) *ou* apartment (*US*); **F comme François** F for Frederick (*BRIT*) *ou* Fox (*US*).

fa [fa] *nm inv* (*MUS*) F; (*en chantant la gamme*) fa.

fable [fɑbl(ə)] *nf* fable; (*mensonge*) story, tale.

fabricant [fabʀikɑ̃] *nm* manufacturer, maker.

fabrication [fabʀikasjɔ̃] *nf* manufacture, making.

fabrique [fabʀik] *nf* factory.

fabriquer [fabʀike] *vt* to make; (*industriellement*) to manufacture, make; (*construire: voiture*) to manufacture, build; (*: maison*) to build; (*fig: inventer: histoire, alibi*) to make up; (*fam*): **qu'est-ce qu'il fabrique?** what is he up to?; ~ **en série** to mass-produce.

fabulateur, trice [fabylatœʀ, -tʀis] *nm/f*: **c'est un** ~ he fantasizes, he makes up stories.

fabulation [fabylasjɔ̃] *nf* (*PSYCH*) fantasizing.

fabuleusement [fabyløzmɑ̃] *adv* fabulously, fantastically.

fabuleux, euse [fabylø, -øz] *adj* fabulous, fantastic.

fac [fak] *abr f* (*fam*: = *faculté*) Uni (*BRIT fam*), ≈ college (*US*).

façade [fasad] *nf* front, façade; (*fig*) façade.

face [fas] *nf* face; (*fig: aspect*) side ♦ *adj*: **le côté** ~ heads; **perdre/sauver la** ~ to lose/save face; **regarder qn en** ~ to look sb in the face; **la maison/le trottoir d'en** ~ the house/pavement opposite; **en** ~ **de** *prép* opposite; (*fig*) in front of; **de** ~ *adv* from the front; **face on;** ~ **à** *prép* facing; (*fig*) faced with, in the face of; **faire** ~ **à** to cope with; **faire** ~ **à la demande** (*COMM*) to meet the demand; ~ **à** ~ *adv* facing each other ♦ *nm inv* encounter.

face-à-main, *pl* **faces-à-main** [fasamɛ̃] *nm* lorgnette.

facéties [fasesi] *nfpl* jokes, pranks.

facétieux, euse [fasesjø, -øz] *adj* mischievous.

facette [fasɛt] *nf* facet.

fâché, e [fɑʃe] *adj* angry; (*désolé*) sorry.

fâcher [fɑʃe] *vt* to anger; **se** ~ *vi* to get angry; **se** ~ **avec** (*se brouiller*) to fall out with.

fâcherie [fɑʃʀi] *nf* quarrel.

fâcheusement [fɑʃøzmɑ̃] *adv* unpleasantly;

(*impressionné etc*) badly; **avoir ~ tendance à** to have an irritating tendency to.

fâcheux, euse [faʃø, -øz] *adj* unfortunate, regrettable.

facho [faʃo] *adj, nm/f* (*fam*: = *fasciste*) fascist.

facial, e, aux [fasjal, -o] *adj* facial.

faciès [fasjɛs] *nm* (*visage*) features *pl*.

facile [fasil] *adj* easy; (*accommodant*) easy-going; **~ d'emploi** (*INFORM*) user-friendly.

facilement [fasilmɑ̃] *adv* easily.

facilité [fasilite] *nf* easiness; (*disposition, don*) aptitude; (*moyen, occasion, possibilité*): **il a la ~ de rencontrer les gens** he has every opportunity to meet people; **~s** *nfpl* facilities; (*COMM*) terms; **~s de crédit** credit terms; **~s de paiement** easy terms.

faciliter [fasilite] *vt* to make easier.

façon [fasɔ̃] *nf* (*manière*) way; (*d'une robe etc*) making-up; cut; (: *main-d'œuvre*) labour (*BRIT*), labor (*US*); (*imitation*): **châle ~ cachemire** cashmere-style shawl; **~s** *nfpl* (*péj*) fuss *sg*; **faire des ~s** (*péj: être affecté*) to be affected; (: *faire des histoires*) to make a fuss; **de quelle ~?** (in) what way?; **sans ~** *adv* without fuss ♦ *adj* unaffected; **d'une autre ~** in another way; **en aucune ~** in no way; **de ~ à so** as to; **de ~ à ce que, de (telle) ~ que** so that; **de toute ~** anyway, in any case; **(c'est une) ~ de parler** it's a way of putting it; **travail à ~** tailoring.

façonner [fasɔne] *vt* (*fabriquer*) to manufacture; (*travailler: matière*) to shape, fashion; (*fig*) to mould, shape.

fac-similé [faksimile] *nm* facsimile.

facteur, trice [faktœʀ, -tʀis] *nm/f* postman/woman (*BRIT*), mailman/woman (*US*) ♦ *nm* (*MATH, gén*) factor; **~ d'orgues** organ builder; **~ de pianos** piano maker; **~ rhésus** rhesus factor.

factice [faktis] *adj* artificial.

faction [faksjɔ̃] *nf* (*groupe*) faction; (*MIL*) guard *ou* sentry (duty); watch; **en ~** on guard; standing watch.

factionnaire [faksjɔnɛʀ] *nm* guard, sentry.

factoriel, le [faktɔʀjɛl] *adj, nf* factorial.

factotum [faktɔtɔm] *nm* odd-job man, dogsbody (*BRIT*).

factuel, le [faktɥɛl] *adj* factual.

facturation [faktyʀasjɔ̃] *nf* invoicing; (*bureau*) invoicing (office).

facture [faktyʀ] *nf* (*à payer: gén*) bill; (: *COMM*) invoice; (*d'un artisan, artiste*) technique, workmanship.

facturer [faktyʀe] *vt* to invoice.

facturier, ière [faktyʀje, -jɛʀ] *nm/f* invoice clerk.

facultatif, ive [fakyltatif, -iv] *adj* optional; (*arrêt de bus*) request *cpd*.

faculté [fakylte] *nf* (*intellectuelle, d'université*) faculty; (*pouvoir, possibilité*) power.

fadaises [fadɛz] *nfpl* twaddle *sg*.

fade [fad] *adj* insipid.

fading [fadiŋ] *nm* (*RADIO*) fading.

fagot [fago] *nm* (*de bois*) bundle of sticks.

fagoté, e [fagɔte] *adj* (*fam*): **drôlement ~** oddly dressed.

faible [fɛbl(ə)] *adj* weak; (*voix, lumière, vent*) faint; (*élève, copie*) poor; (*rendement, intensité, revenu etc*) low ♦ *nm* weak point; (*pour quelqu'un*) weakness, soft spot; **~ d'esprit** feeble-minded.

faiblement [fɛbləmɑ̃] *adv* weakly; (*peu: éclairer etc*) faintly.

faiblesse [fɛblɛs] *nf* weakness.

faiblir [febliʀ] *vi* to weaken; (*lumière*) to dim; (*vent*) to drop.

faïence [fajɑ̃s] *nf* earthenware *no pl*; (*objet*) piece of earthenware.

faignant, e [fɛɲɑ̃, -ɑ̃t] *nm/f* = **fainéant, e**.

faille [faj] *vb voir* **falloir** ♦ *nf* (*GÉO*) fault; (*fig*) flaw, weakness.

failli, e [faji] *adj, nm/f* bankrupt.

faillible [fajibl(ə)] *adj* fallible.

faillir [fajiʀ] *vi*: **j'ai failli tomber/lui dire** I almost *ou* nearly fell/told him; **~ à une promesse/un engagement** to break a promise/an agreement.

faillite [fajit] *nf* bankruptcy; (*échec: d'une politique etc*) collapse; **être en ~** to be bankrupt; **faire ~** to go bankrupt.

faim [fɛ̃] *nf* hunger; (*fig*): **~ d'amour/de richesse** hunger *ou* yearning for love/wealth; **avoir ~** to be hungry; **rester sur sa ~** (*aussi fig*) to be left wanting more.

fainéant, e [fɛneɑ̃, -ɑ̃t] *nm/f* idler, loafer.

fainéantise [fɛneɑ̃tiz] *nf* idleness, laziness.

========================= *MOT-CLÉ*

faire [fɛʀ] *vt* **1** (*fabriquer, être l'auteur de*) to make; (*produire*) to produce; (*construire: maison, bateau*) to build; **~ du vin/une offre/un film** to make wine/an offer/a film; **~ du bruit** to make a noise

2 (*effectuer: travail, opération*) to do; **que faites-vous?** (*quel métier etc*) what do you do?; (*quelle activité: au moment de la question*) what are you doing?; **que ~?** what are we going to do?, what can be done (about it)?; **~ la lessive/le ménage** to do the washing/the housework

3 (*études*) to do; (*sport, musique*) to play; **~ du droit/du français** to do law/French; **~ du rugby/piano** to play rugby/the piano; **~ du cheval/du ski** to go riding/skiing

4 (*visiter*): **~ les magasins** to go shopping; **~ l'Europe** to tour *ou* do Europe

5 (*simuler*): **~ le malade/l'ignorant** to act the invalid/the fool

6 (*transformer, avoir un effet sur*): **~ de qn un frustré/avocat** to make sb frustrated/a lawyer; **ça ne me fait rien** (*m'est égal*) I don't care *ou* mind; (*me laisse froid*) it has no effect on me; **ça ne fait rien** it doesn't matter; **~ que** (*impliquer*) to mean that

7 (*calculs, prix, mesures*): **2 et 2 font 4** 2 and 2 are *ou* make 4; **ça fait 10 m/15 F** it's 10 m/ 15 F; **je vous le fais 10 F** I'll let you have it for 10 F
8 (*vb +de*): **qu'a-t-il fait de sa valise/de sa sœur?** what has he done with his case/his sister?
9: ne ~ que: il ne fait que critiquer (*sans cesse*) all he (ever) does is criticize; (*seulement*) he's only criticizing
10 (*dire*) to say; **vraiment? fit-il** really? he said
11 (*maladie*) to have; **~ du diabète/de la tension** to have diabetes *sg*/high blood pressure
♦ *vi* **1** (*agir, s'y prendre*) to act, do; **il faut ~ vite** we (*ou* you *etc*) must act quickly; **comment a-t-il fait pour?** how did he manage to?; **faites comme chez vous** make yourself at home; **je n'ai pas pu ~ autrement** there was nothing else I could do
2 (*paraître*) to look; **~ vieux/démodé** to look old/old-fashioned; **ça fait bien** it looks good; **tu fais jeune dans cette robe** that dress makes you look young(er)
♦ *vb substitut* to do; **ne le casse pas comme je l'ai fait** don't break it as I did; **je peux le voir? — faites!** can I see it? — please do!; **remets-le en place — je viens de le ~** put it back in its place — I just have (done)
♦ *vb impers* **1**: **il fait beau** *etc* the weather is fine *etc*; *voir aussi* **jour; froid** *etc*
2 (*temps écoulé, durée*): **ça fait 2 ans qu'il est parti** it's 2 years since he left; **ça fait 2 ans qu'il y est** he's been there for 2 years
♦ *vb semi-aux* **1**: **~ +***infinitif* (*action directe*) to make; **~ tomber/bouger qch** to make sth fall/move; **~ démarrer un moteur/chauffer de l'eau** to start up an engine/heat some water; **cela fait dormir** it makes you sleep; **~ travailler les enfants** to make the children work *ou* get the children to work; **il m'a fait traverser la rue** he helped me to cross the road
2 (*indirectement, par un intermédiaire*): **~ réparer qch** to get *ou* have sth repaired; **~ punir les enfants** to have the children punished; **il m'a fait ouvrir la porte** he got me to open the door
se ~ *vi* **1** (*vin, fromage*) to mature
2: cela se fait beaucoup/ne se fait pas it's done a lot/not done
3 (*+nom ou pron*): **se ~ une jupe** to make o.s. a skirt; **se ~ des amis** to make friends; **se ~ du souci** to worry; **se ~ des illusions** to delude o.s.; **se ~ beaucoup d'argent** to make a lot of money; **il ne s'en fait pas** he doesn't worry
4 (*+adj*) (*devenir*): **se ~ vieux** to be getting old; (*délibérément*): **se ~ beau** to do o.s. up
5: se ~ à (*s'habituer*) to get used to; **je n'arrive pas à me ~ à la nourriture/au climat**

I can't get used to the food/climate
6 (*+infinitif*): **se ~ examiner la vue/opérer** to have one's eyes tested/have an operation; **se ~ couper les cheveux** to get one's hair cut; **il va se ~ tuer/punir** he's going to get himself killed/get (himself) punished; **il s'est fait aider** he got somebody to help him; **il s'est fait aider par Simon** he got Simon to help him; **se ~ ~ un vêtement** to get a garment made for o.s.
7 (*impersonnel*): **comment se fait-il/faisait-il que?** how is it/was it that?; **il peut se ~ que nous utilisions ...** it's possible that we could use ...

faire-part [fɛʀpaʀ] *nm inv* announcement (*of birth, marriage etc*).
fair-play [fɛʀplɛ] *adj inv* fair.
fais [fɛ] *vb voir* **faire.**
faisabilité [fəzabilite] *nf* feasibility.
faisable [fəzabl(ə)] *adj* feasible.
faisais [fəzɛ] *etc vb voir* **faire.**
faisan, e [fəzɑ̃, -an] *nm/f* pheasant.
faisandé, e [fəzɑ̃de] *adj* high (*bad*); (*fig péj*) corrupt, decadent.
faisceau, x [fɛso] *nm* (*de lumière etc*) beam; (*de branches etc*) bundle.
faiseur, euse [fəzœʀ, -øz] *nm/f* (*gén: péj*): **~ de manier** *ou* **~ de ♦** *nm* (*bespoke*) tailor; **~ d'embarras** fusspot; **~ de projets** schemer.
faisons [fəzɔ̃] *etc vb voir* **faire.**
faisselle [fɛsɛl] *nf* cheese strainer.
fait [fɛ] *vb voir* **faire ♦** *nm* (*événement*) event, occurrence; (*réalité, donnée*) fact; **le ~ que/ de manger** the fact that/of eating; **être le ~ de** (*causé par*) to be the work of; **être au ~ (de)** to be informed (of); **mettre qn au ~** to inform sb, put sb in the picture; **au ~** (*à propos*) by the way; **en venir au ~** to get to the point; **de ~** *adj* (*opposé à: de droit*) de facto ♦ *adv* in fact; **du ~ de ceci/qu'il a menti** because of *ou* on account of this/his having lied; **de ce ~** therefore, for this reason; **en ~** in fact; **en ~ de repas** by way of a meal; **prendre ~ et cause pour qn** to support sb, side with sb; **prendre qn sur le ~** to catch sb in the act; **dire à qn son ~** to give sb a piece of one's mind; **hauts ~s** (*exploits*) exploits; **~ d'armes** feat of arms; **~ divers** (*short*) news item; **les ~s et gestes de qn** sb's actions *ou* doings.
fait, e [fɛ, fɛt] *pp de* **faire ♦** *adj* (*mûr: fromage, melon*) ripe; (*maquillé: yeux*) made-up; (*vernis: ongles*) painted, polished; **un homme ~** a grown man; **tout(e) ~(e)** (*préparé à l'avance*) ready-made; **c'en est ~ de notre tranquillité** that's the end of our peace; **c'est bien ~** (*pour lui ou eux etc*) it serves him (*ou* them *etc*) right.
faîte [fɛt] *nm* top; (*fig*) pinnacle, height.
faites [fɛt] *vb voir* **faire.**

faîtière [fɛtjɛʀ] nf (de tente) ridge pole.
fait-tout nm inv, **faitout** nm [fɛtu] stewpot.
fakir [fakiʀ] nm (THÉÂT) wizard.
falaise [falɛz] nf cliff.
falbalas [falbala] nmpl fripperies, frills.
fallacieux, euse [falasjø, -øz] adj (raisonnement) fallacious; (apparences) deceptive; (espoir) illusory.
falloir [falwaʀ] vb impers: **il faut faire les lits** we (ou you etc) have to ou must make the beds; **il faut que je fasse les lits** I have to ou must make the beds; **il a fallu qu'il parte** he had to leave; **il faudrait qu'elle rentre** she ought to go home; **il va ~ 100 F** we'll (ou I'll etc) need 100 F; **il doit ~ du temps** that must take time; **il vous faut tourner à gauche après l'église** you have to turn left past the church; **nous avons ce qu'il (nous) faut** we have what we need; **il faut qu'il ait oublié** he must have forgotten; **il a fallu qu'il l'apprenne** he would have to hear about it; **il ne fallait pas** (pour remercier) you shouldn't have (done); **faut le faire!** (it) takes some doing! ♦ **s'en ~: il s'en est fallu de 100 F/5 minutes** we (ou they etc) were 100 F short/5 minutes late (ou early); **il s'en faut de beaucoup qu'il soit ...** he is far from being ...; **il s'en est fallu de peu que cela n'arrive** it very nearly happened; **ou peu s'en faut** or just about, or as good as; **comme il faut** adj proper ♦ adv properly.
fallu [faly] pp de **falloir**.
falot, e [falo, -ɔt] adj dreary, colourless (BRIT), colorless (US) ♦ nm lantern.
falsification [falsifikasjɔ̃] nf falsification.
falsifier [falsifje] vt to falsify.
famé, e [fame] adj: **mal ~** disreputable, of ill repute.
famélique [famelik] adj half-starved.
fameux, euse [famø, -øz] adj (illustre: parfois péj) famous; (bon: repas, plat etc) first-rate, first-class; (intensif): **un ~ problème** etc a real problem etc; **pas ~** not great, not much good.
familial, e, aux [familjal, -o] adj family cpd ♦ nf (AUTO) family estate car (BRIT), station wagon (US).
familiariser [familjaʀize] vt: **~ qn avec** to familiarize sb with; **se ~ avec** to familiarize o.s. with.
familiarité [familjaʀite] nf familiarity; informality; **~s** nfpl familiarities; **~ avec** (sujet, science) familiarity with.
familier, ière [familje, -jɛʀ] adj (connu, impertinent) familiar; (dénotant une certaine intimité) informal, friendly; (LING) informal, colloquial ♦ nm regular (visitor).
familièrement [familjɛʀmɑ̃] adv (sans façon: s'entretenir) informally; (cavalièrement) familiarly.
famille [famij] nf family; **il a de la ~ à Paris** he has relatives in Paris.

famine [famin] nf famine.
fan [fan] nm/f fan.
fana [fana] adj, nm/f (fam) = **fanatique**.
fanal, aux [fanal, -o] nm beacon; lantern.
fanatique [fanatik] adj: **~ (de)** fanatical (about) ♦ nm/f fanatic.
fanatisme [fanatism(ə)] nm fanaticism.
fane [fan] nf top.
fané, e [fane] adj faded.
faner [fane]: **se ~** vi to fade.
faneur, euse [fanœʀ, -øz] nm/f haymaker ♦ nf (TECH) tedder.
fanfare [fɑ̃faʀ] nf (orchestre) brass band; (musique) fanfare; **en ~** (avec bruit) noisily.
fanfaron, ne [fɑ̃faʀɔ̃, -ɔn] nm/f braggart.
fanfaronnades [fɑ̃faʀɔnad] nfpl bragging no pl.
fanfreluches [fɑ̃fʀəlyʃ] nfpl trimming no pl.
fange [fɑ̃ʒ] nf mire.
fanion [fanjɔ̃] nm pennant.
fanon [fanɔ̃] nm (de baleine) plate of baleen; (repli de peau) dewlap, wattle.
fantaisie [fɑ̃tezi] nf (spontanéité) fancy, imagination; (caprice) whim; extravagance; (MUS) fantasia ♦ adj: **bijou (de) ~** (piece of) costume jewellery (BRIT) ou jewelry (US); **pain (de) ~** fancy bread.
fantaisiste [fɑ̃tezist(ə)] adj (péj) unorthodox, eccentric ♦ nm/f (de music-hall) variety artist ou entertainer.
fantasmagorique [fɑ̃tasmagɔʀik] adj phantasmagorical.
fantasme [fɑ̃tasm(ə)] nm fantasy.
fantasmer [fɑ̃tasme] vi to fantasize.
fantasque [fɑ̃task(ə)] adj whimsical, capricious; fantastic.
fantassin [fɑ̃tasɛ̃] nm infantryman.
fantastique [fɑ̃tastik] adj fantastic.
fantoche [fɑ̃tɔʃ] nm (péj) puppet.
fantomatique [fɑ̃tɔmatik] adj ghostly.
fantôme [fɑ̃tom] nm ghost, phantom.
FAO sigle f (= Food and Agricultural Organization) FAO.
faon [fɑ̃] nm fawn (deer).
faramineux, euse [faʀaminø, -øz] adj (fam) fantastic.
farandole [faʀɑ̃dɔl] nf farandole.
farce [faʀs(ə)] nf (viande) stuffing; (blague) (practical) joke; (THÉÂT) farce; **faire une ~ à qn** to play a (practical) joke on sb; **~s et attrapes** jokes and novelties.
farceur, euse [faʀsœʀ, -øz] nm/f practical joker; (fumiste) clown.
farci, e [faʀsi] adj (CULIN) stuffed.
farcir [faʀsiʀ] vt (viande) to stuff; (fig): **~ qch de** to stuff sth with; **se ~** (fam): **je me suis farci la vaisselle** I've got stuck ou landed with the washing-up.
fard [faʀ] nm make-up; **~ à joues** blusher.
fardeau, x [faʀdo] nm burden.
farder [faʀde] vt to make up; (vérité) to disguise; **se ~** to make o.s. up.
farfelu, e [faʀfəly] adj wacky (fam), hare-

brained.
farfouiller [faʀfuje] _vi (péj)_ to rummage around.
fariboles [faʀibɔl] _nfpl_ nonsense _no pl._
farine [faʀin] _nf_ flour; ~ **de blé** wheatflour; ~ **de maïs** cornflour (_BRIT_), cornstarch (_US_); ~ **lactée** (_pour bouillie_) gruel.
fariner [faʀine] _vt_ to flour.
farineux, euse [faʀinø, -øz] _adj (sauce, pomme)_ floury ♦ _nmpl (aliments)_ starchy foods.
farniente [faʀnjɛnte] _nm_ idleness.
farouche [faʀuʃ] _adj_ shy, timid; (_sauvage_) savage, wild; (_violent_) fierce.
farouchement [faʀuʃmɑ̃] _adv_ fiercely.
fart [faʀ(t)] _nm_ (ski) wax.
farter [faʀte] _vt_ to wax.
fascicule [fasikyl] _nm_ volume.
fascinant, e [fasinɑ̃, -ɑ̃t] _adj_ fascinating.
fascination [fasinasjɔ̃] _nf_ fascination.
fasciner [fasine] _vt_ to fascinate.
fascisant, e [faʃizɑ̃, -ɑ̃t] _adj_ fascistic.
fascisme [faʃism(ə)] _nm_ fascism.
fasciste [faʃist(ə)] _adj, nm/f_ fascist.
fasse [fas] _etc vb voir_ **faire**.
faste [fast(ə)] _nm_ splendour (_BRIT_), splendor (_US_) ♦ _adj:_ **c'est un jour** ~ it's his (_ou_ our _etc_) lucky day.
fastidieux, euse [fastidjø, -øz] _adj_ tedious, tiresome.
fastueux, euse [fastɥø, -øz] _adj_ sumptuous, luxurious.
fat [fa] _adj m_ conceited, smug.
fatal, e [fatal] _adj_ fatal; (_inévitable_) inevitable.
fatalement [fatalmɑ̃] _adv_ inevitably.
fatalisme [fatalism(ə)] _nm_ fatalism.
fataliste [fatalist(ə)] _adj_ fatalistic.
fatalité [fatalite] _nf (destin)_ fate; (_coïncidence_) fateful coincidence; (_caractère inévitable_) inevitability.
fatidique [fatidik] _adj_ fateful.
fatigant, e [fatigɑ̃, -ɑ̃t] _adj_ tiring; (_agaçant_) tiresome.
fatigue [fatig] _nf_ tiredness, fatigue; (_détérioration_) fatigue; **les ~s du voyage** the wear and tear of the journey.
fatigué, e [fatige] _adj_ tired.
fatiguer [fatige] _vt_ to tire, make tired; (_TECH_) to put a strain on, strain; (_fig: importuner_) to wear out ♦ _vi (moteur)_ to labour (_BRIT_), labor (_US_), strain; **se** ~ _vi_ to get tired; to tire o.s. (out); **se** ~ **à faire qch** to tire o.s. out doing sth.
fatras [fatʀa] _nm_ jumble, hotchpotch.
fatuité [fatɥite] _nf_ conceitedness, smugness.
faubourg [fobuʀ] _nm_ suburb.
faubourien, ne [fobuʀjɛ̃, -ɛn] _adj (accent)_ working-class.
fauché, e [foʃe] _adj (fam)_ broke.
faucher [foʃe] _vt (herbe)_ to cut; (_champs, blés_) to reap; (_fig_) to cut down; to mow down; (_fam: voler_) to pinch, nick.

faucheur, euse [foʃœʀ, -øz] _nm/f_ reaper, mower.
faucille [fosij] _nf_ sickle.
faucon [fokɔ̃] _nm_ falcon, hawk.
faudra [fodʀa] _etc vb voir_ **falloir**.
faufil [fofil] _nm (COUTURE)_ tacking thread.
faufilage [fofilaʒ] _nm (COUTURE)_ tacking.
faufiler [fofile] _vt_ to tack, baste; **se** ~ _vi:_ **se** ~ **dans** to edge one's way into; **se** ~ **parmi/entre** to thread one's way among/between.
faune [fon] _nf (ZOOL)_ wildlife, fauna; (_fig péj_) set, crowd ♦ _nm_ faun; ~ **marine** marine (animal) life.
faussaire [fosɛʀ] _nm/f_ forger.
fausse [fos] _adj f voir_ **faux**.
faussement [fosmɑ̃] _adv (accuser)_ wrongly, wrongfully; (_croire_) falsely, erroneously.
fausser [fose] _vt (objet)_ to bend, buckle; (_fig_) to distort; ~ **compagnie à qn** to give sb the slip.
fausset [fosɛ] _nm:_ **voix de** ~ falsetto voice.
fausseté [foste] _nf_ wrongness; falseness.
faut [fo] _vb voir_ **falloir**.
faute [fot] _nf (erreur)_ mistake, error; (_péché, manquement_) misdemeanour; (_FOOTBALL etc_) offence; (_TENNIS_) fault; (_responsabilité_): **par la** ~ **de** through the fault of, because of; **c'est de sa/ma** ~ it's his/my fault; **être en** ~ to be in the wrong; **prendre qn en** ~ to catch sb out; ~ **de** (_temps, argent_) for _ou_ through lack of; ~ **de mieux** for want of anything _ou_ something better; **sans** ~ _adv_ without fail; ~ **de frappe** typing error; ~ **d'inattention** careless mistake; ~ **d'orthographe** spelling mistake; ~ **professionnelle** professional misconduct _no pl._
fauteuil [fotœj] _nm_ armchair; ~ **à bascule** rocking chair; ~ **club** (big) easy chair; ~ **d'orchestre** seat in the front stalls (_BRIT_) _ou_ the orchestra (_US_); ~ **roulant** wheelchair.
fauteur [fotœʀ] _nm:_ ~ **de troubles** trouble-maker.
fautif, ive [fotif, -iv] _adj (incorrect)_ incorrect, inaccurate; (_responsable_) at fault, in the wrong; (_coupable_) guilty ♦ _nm/f_ culprit.
fauve [fov] _nm_ wildcat; (_peintre_) Fauve ♦ _adj (couleur)_ fawn.
fauvette [fovɛt] _nf_ warbler.
fauvisme [fovism(ə)] _nm (ART)_ Fauvism.
faux¹ [fo] _nf_ scythe.
faux², fausse [fo, fos] _adj (inexact)_ wrong; (_piano, voix_) out of tune; (_falsifié_) fake, forged; (_sournois, postiche_) false ♦ _adv (MUS)_ out of tune ♦ _nm (copie)_ fake, forgery; (_opposé au vrai_): **le** ~ falsehood; **le** ~ **numéro/la fausse clé** the wrong number/key; **faire fausse route** to go the wrong way; **faire** ~ **bond à qn** to let sb down; ~ **ami** (_LING_) faux ami; ~ **col** detachable collar; ~ **départ** (_SPORT, fig_) false start; ~ **frais** _nmpl_ extras, incidental expenses; ~ **frère** (_fig péj_) false friend; ~ **mouvement** awkward

movement; ~ **nez** false nose; ~ **nom** assumed name; ~ **pas** tripping *no pl*; (*fig*) faux pas; ~ **témoignage** (*délit*) perjury; **fausse alerte** false alarm; **fausse clé** skeleton key; **fausse couche** (*MÉD*) miscarriage; **fausse joie** vain joy; **fausse note** wrong note.

faux-filet [fofilɛ] *nm* sirloin.

faux-fuyant [fofɥijɑ̃] *nm* equivocation.

faux-monnayeur [fomɔnɛjœʀ] *nm* counterfeiter, forger.

faux-semblant [fosɑ̃blɑ̃] *nm* pretence (*BRIT*), pretense (*US*).

faux-sens [fosɑ̃s] *nm* mistranslation.

faveur [favœʀ] *nf* favour (*BRIT*), favor (*US*); **traitement de** ~ preferential treatment; **à la** ~ **de** under cover of; (*grâce à*) thanks to; **en** ~ **de** in favo(u)r of.

favorable [favɔʀabl(ə)] *adj* favo(u)rable.

favori, te [favɔʀi, -it] *adj, nm/f* favo(u)rite.

favoris [favɔʀi] *nmpl* (*barbe*) sideboards (*BRIT*), sideburns.

favoriser [favɔʀize] *vt* to favour (*BRIT*), favor (*US*).

favoritisme [favɔʀitism(ə)] *nm* (*péj*) favo(u)ritism.

fayot [fajo] *nm* (*fam*) crawler.

FB *abr* (= *franc belge*) BF, FB.

FBI *sigle m* FBI.

FC *sigle m* (= *Football Club*) FC.

fébrile [febʀil] *adj* feverish, febrile; **capitaux** ~**s** (*ÉCON*) hot money.

fébrilement [febʀilmɑ̃] *adv* feverishly.

fécal, e, aux [fekal, -o] *adj voir* **matière.**

FECOM [fekɔm] *sigle m* (= *Fonds européen de coopération militaire*) EMCF.

fécond, e [fekɔ̃, -ɔ̃d] *adj* fertile.

fécondation [fekɔ̃dasjɔ̃] *nf* fertilization.

féconder [fekɔ̃de] *vt* to fertilize.

fécondité [fekɔ̃dite] *nf* fertility.

fécule [fekyl] *nf* potato flour.

féculent [fekylɑ̃] *nm* starchy food.

fédéral, e, aux [fedeʀal, -o] *adj* federal.

fédéralisme [fedeʀalism(ə)] *nm* federalism.

fédéraliste [fedeʀalist(ə)] *adj* federalist.

fédération [fedeʀasjɔ̃] *nf* federation.

fée [fe] *nf* fairy.

féerie [feʀi] *nf* enchantment.

féerique [feʀik] *adj* magical, fairytale *cpd*.

feignant, e [fɛɲɑ̃, -ɑ̃t] *nm/f* = **fainéant, e.**

feindre [fɛ̃dʀ(ə)] *vt* to feign ♦ *vi* to dissemble; ~ **de faire** to pretend to do.

feint, e [fɛ̃, fɛ̃t] *pp de* **feindre** ♦ *adj* feigned ♦ *nf* (*SPORT*: *escrime*) feint; (: *football, rugby*) dummy (*BRIT*), fake (*US*); (*fam*: *ruse*) sham.

feinter [fɛ̃te] *vi* (*SPORT*: *escrime*) to feint; (: *football, rugby*) to dummy (*BRIT*), fake (*US*) ♦ *vt* (*fam*: *tromper*) to fool.

fêlé, e [fele] *adj* (*aussi fig*) cracked.

fêler [fele] *vt* to crack.

félicitations [felisitasjɔ̃] *nfpl* congratulations.

félicité [felisite] *nf* bliss.

féliciter [felisite] *vt*: ~ **qn (de)** to congratulate sb (on).

félin, e [felɛ̃, -in] *adj* feline ♦ *nm* (big) cat.

félon, ne [felɔ̃, -ɔn] *adj* perfidious, treacherous.

félonie [feloni] *nf* treachery.

fêlure [felyʀ] *nf* crack.

femelle [fəmɛl] *adj* (*aussi ÉLEC, TECH*) female ♦ *nf* female.

féminin, e [feminɛ̃, -in] *adj* feminine; (*sexe*) female; (*équipe, vêtements etc*) women's; (*parfois péj: homme*) effeminate ♦ *nm* (*LING*) feminine.

féminiser [feminize] *vt* to feminize; (*rendre efféminé*) to make effeminate; **se** ~ *vi*: **cette profession se féminise** this profession is attracting more women.

féminisme [feminism(ə)] *nm* feminism.

féministe [feminist(ə)] *adj, nf* feminist.

féminité [feminite] *nf* femininity.

femme [fam] *nf* woman; (*épouse*) wife (*pl* wives); **être très** ~ to be very much a woman; **devenir** ~ to attain womanhood; ~ **d'affaires** businesswoman; ~ **de chambre** chambermaid; ~ **fatale** femme fatale; ~ **au foyer** housewife; ~ **d'intérieur** (real) homemaker; ~ **de ménage** domestic help, cleaning lady; ~ **du monde** society woman; ~**-objet** sex object; ~ **de tête** determined, intellectual woman.

fémoral, e, aux [femɔʀal, -o] *adj* femoral.

fémur [femyʀ] *nm* femur, thighbone.

FEN [fɛn] *sigle f* (= *Fédération de l'Éducation nationale*) teachers' trades union.

fenaison [fənɛzɔ̃] *nf* haymaking.

fendillé, e [fɑ̃dije] *adj* (*terre etc*) crazed.

fendre [fɑ̃dʀ(ə)] *vt* (*couper en deux*) to split; (*fissurer*) to crack; (*fig: traverser*) to cut through; to push one's way through; **se** ~ *vi* to crack.

fendu, e [fɑ̃dy] *adj* (*sol, mur*) cracked; (*jupe*) slit.

fenêtre [fənɛtʀ(ə)] *nf* window; ~ **à guillotine** sash window.

fennec [fenɛk] *nm* fennec.

fenouil [fənuj] *nm* fennel.

fente [fɑ̃t] *nf* slit; (*fissure*) crack.

féodal, e, aux [feɔdal, -o] *adj* feudal.

féodalisme [feɔdalism(ə)] *nm* feudalism.

féodalité [feɔdalite] *nf* feudalism.

fer [fɛʀ] *nm* iron; (*de cheval*) shoe; ~**s** *pl* (*MÉD*) forceps; **mettre aux** ~**s** (*enchaîner*) to put in chains; **au** ~ **rouge** with a red-hot iron; **santé/main de** ~ iron constitution/hand; ~ **à cheval** horseshoe; **en** ~ **à cheval** (*fig*) horseshoe-shaped; ~ **forgé** wrought iron; ~ **à friser** curling tongs; ~ **de lance** spearhead; ~ (**à repasser**) iron; ~ **à souder** soldering iron.

ferai [fəʀe] *etc vb voir* **faire.**

fer-blanc [fɛʀblɑ̃] *nm* tin(plate).

ferblanterie [fɛʀblɑ̃tʀi] *nf* tinplate making;

(produit) tinware.
ferblantier [fɛʀblɑ̃tje] *nm* tinsmith.
férié, e [feʀje] *adj*: **jour** ~ public holiday.
férir [feʀiʀ]: **sans coup** ~ *adv* without meeting any opposition.
fermage [fɛʀmaʒ] *nm* tenant farming.
ferme [fɛʀm(ə)] *adj* firm ♦ *adv (travailler etc)* hard; *(discuter)* ardently ♦ *nf (exploitation)* farm; *(maison)* farmhouse; **tenir** ~ to stand firm.
fermé, e [fɛʀme] *adj* closed, shut; *(gaz, eau etc)* off; *(fig: personne)* uncommunicative; *(: milieu)* exclusive.
fermement [fɛʀməmɑ̃] *adv* firmly.
ferment [fɛʀmɑ̃] *nm* ferment.
fermentation [fɛʀmɑ̃tɑsjɔ̃] *nf* fermentation.
fermenter [fɛʀmɑ̃te] *vi* to ferment.
fermer [fɛʀme] *vt* to close, shut; *(cesser l'exploitation de)* to close down, shut down; *(eau, lumière, électricité, robinet)* to put off, turn off; *(aéroport, route)* to close ♦ *vi* to close, shut; to close down, shut down; **se** ~ *vi (yeux)* to close, shut; *(fleur, blessure)* to close up; ~ **à clef** to lock; ~ **au verrou** to bolt; ~ **les yeux (sur qch)** *(fig)* to close one's eyes (to sth); **se** ~ **à** *(pitié, amour)* to close one's heart *ou* mind to.
fermeté [fɛʀməte] *nf* firmness.
fermette [fɛʀmɛt] *nf* farmhouse.
fermeture [fɛʀmətyʀ] *nf (voir fermer)* closing; shutting; closing *ou* shutting down; putting *ou* turning off; *(dispositif)* catch; fastening, fastener; **heure de** ~ *(COMM)* closing time; **jour de** ~ *(COMM)* day on which the shop *(etc)* is closed; ~ **éclair** ® *ou* **à glissière** zip (fastener) *(BRIT)*, zipper.
fermier, ière [fɛʀmje, -jɛʀ] *nm/f* farmer ♦ *nf (femme de fermier)* farmer's wife ♦ *adj*: **beurre/cidre** ~ farm butter/cider.
fermoir [fɛʀmwaʀ] *nm* clasp.
féroce [feʀɔs] *adj* ferocious, fierce.
férocement [feʀɔsmɑ̃] *adv* ferociously.
férocité [feʀɔsite] *nf* ferocity, ferociousness.
ferons [fəʀɔ̃] *etc vb voir* **faire**.
ferraille [fɛʀaj] *nf* scrap iron; **mettre à la** ~ to scrap; **bruit de** ~ clanking.
ferrailler [fɛʀaje] *vi* to clank.
ferrailleur [fɛʀajœʀ] *nm* scrap merchant.
ferrant [fɛʀɑ̃] *adj m voir* **maréchal**.
ferré, e [fɛʀe] *adj (chaussure)* hobnailed; *(canne)* steel-tipped; ~ **sur** *(fam: savant)* well up on.
ferrer [fɛʀe] *vt (cheval)* to shoe; *(chaussure)* to nail; *(canne)* to tip; *(poisson)* to strike.
ferreux, euse [fɛʀø, -øz] *adj* ferrous.
ferronnerie [fɛʀɔnʀi] *nf* ironwork; ~ **d'art** wrought iron work.
ferronnier [fɛʀɔnje] *nm* craftsman in wrought iron; *(marchand)* ironware merchant.
ferroviaire [fɛʀɔvjɛʀ] *adj* rail *cpd*, railway *cpd (BRIT)*, railroad *cpd (US)*.
ferrugineux, euse [fɛʀyʒinø, -øz] *adj*
ferruginous.
ferrure [fɛʀyʀ] *nf* (ornamental) hinge.
ferry(-boat) [fɛʀe(bot)] *nm* ferry.
fertile [fɛʀtil] *adj* fertile; ~ **en incidents** eventful, packed with incidents.
fertilisant [fɛʀtilizɑ̃] *nm* fertilizer.
fertilisation [fɛʀtilizɑsjɔ̃] *nf* fertilization.
fertiliser [fɛʀtilize] *vt* to fertilize.
fertilité [fɛʀtilite] *nf* fertility.
féru, e [feʀy] *adj*: ~ **de** with a keen interest in.
férule [feʀyl] *nf*: **être sous la** ~ **de qn** to be under sb's (iron) rule.
fervent, e [fɛʀvɑ̃, -ɑ̃t] *adj* fervent.
ferveur [fɛʀvœʀ] *nf* fervour *(BRIT)*, fervor *(US)*.
fesse [fɛs] *nf* buttock; **les** ~**s** the bottom *sg*, the buttocks.
fessée [fese] *nf* spanking.
fessier [fesje] *nm (fam)* behind.
festin [fɛstɛ̃] *nm* feast.
festival [fɛstival] *nm* festival.
festivalier [fɛstivalje] *nm* festival-goer.
festivités [fɛstivite] *nfpl* festivities, merrymaking *sg*.
feston [fɛstɔ̃] *nm (ARCHIT)* festoon; *(COUTURE)* scallop.
festoyer [fɛstwaje] *vi* to feast.
fêtard [fɛtaʀ] *nm (péj)* high liver, merrymaker.
fête [fɛt] *nf (religieuse)* feast; *(publique)* holiday; *(en famille etc)* celebration; *(kermesse)* fête, fair, festival; *(du nom)* feast day, name day; **faire la** ~ to live it up; **faire** ~ **à qn** to give sb a warm welcome; **se faire une** ~ **de** to look forward to; **ça va être sa** ~! *(fam)* he's going to get it!; **jour de** ~ holiday; **les** ~**s (de fin d'année)** the festive season; **la salle/le comité des** ~**s** the village hall/festival committee; **la** ~ **des Mères/Pères** Mother's/Father's Day; ~ **de charité** charity fair *ou* fête; ~ **foraine** (fun)fair; ~ **mobile** movable feast (day); **la F**~ **Nationale** the national holiday.

La fête de la Musique is a music festival which has taken place annually since 1981 on June 21. Throughout France local musicians perform free of charge in parks, streets and squares.

Fête-Dieu [fɛtdjø] *nf*: **la** ~ Corpus Christi.
fêter [fete] *vt* to celebrate; *(personne)* to have a celebration for.
fétiche [fetiʃ] *nm* fetish; **animal** ~, **objet** ~ mascot.
fétichisme [fetiʃism(ə)] *nm* fetishism.
fétichiste [fetiʃist(ə)] *adj* fetishist.
fétide [fetid] *adj* fetid.
fétu [fety] *nm*: ~ **de paille** wisp of straw.
feu¹ [fø] *adj inv*: ~ **son père** his late father.
feu², x [fø] *nm (gén)* fire; *(signal lumineux)* light; *(de cuisinière)* ring; *(sensation de*

brûlure) burning (sensation); ~**x** *nmpl* fire *sg*; *(AUTO)* (traffic) lights; **tous ~x éteints** *(NAVIG, AUTO)* without lights; **au ~!** *(incendie)* fire!; **à ~ doux/vif** over a slow/ brisk heat; **à petit ~** *(CULIN)* over a gentle heat; *(fig)* slowly; **faire ~** to fire; **ne pas faire long ~** *(fig)* not to last long; **commander le ~** *(MIL)* to give the order to (open) fire; **tué au ~** *(MIL)* killed in action; **mettre à ~** *(fusée)* to fire off; **pris entre deux ~x** caught in the crossfire; **en ~** on fire; **être tout ~ tout flamme (pour)** *(passion)* to be aflame with passion (for); *(enthousiasme)* to be fired with enthusiasm (for); **prendre ~** to catch fire; **mettre le ~ à** to set fire to, set on fire; **faire du ~** to make a fire; **avez-vous du ~?** *(pour cigarette)* have you got a light?; ~ **rouge/ vert/orange** *(AUTO)* red/green/amber *(BRIT) ou* yellow *(US)* light; **donner le ~ vert à qch/qn** *(fig)* to give sth/sb the go-ahead *ou* green light; ~ **arrière** *(AUTO)* rear light; ~ **d'artifice** firework; *(spectacle)* fireworks *pl*; ~ **de camp** campfire; ~ **de cheminée** chimney fire; ~ **de joie** bonfire; ~ **de paille** *(fig)* flash in the pan; ~**x de brouillard** *(AUTO)* fog lights *ou* lamps; ~**x de croisement** *(AUTO)* dipped *(BRIT) ou* dimmed *(US)* headlights; ~**x de position** *(AUTO)* sidelights; ~**x de route** *(AUTO)* headlights (on full *(BRIT) ou* high *(US)* beam); ~**x de stationnement** parking lights.

feuillage [fœjaʒ] *nm* foliage, leaves *pl*.

feuille [fœj] *nf (d'arbre)* leaf *(pl* leaves); ~ **(de papier)** sheet (of paper); **rendre ~ blanche** *(SCOL)* to give in a blank paper; ~ **d'or/de métal** gold/metal leaf; ~ **de chou** *(péj: journal)* rag; ~ **d'impôts** tax form; ~ **de maladie** medical expenses claim form; ~ **morte** dead leaf; ~ **de paye** pay slip; ~ **de présence** attendance sheet; ~ **de température** temperature chart; ~ **de vigne** *(BOT)* vine leaf; *(sur statue)* fig leaf; ~ **volante** loose sheet.

feuillet [fœjɛ] *nm* leaf *(pl* leaves), page.

feuilletage [fœjtaʒ] *nm (aspect feuilleté)* flakiness.

feuilleté, e [fœjte] *adj (CULIN)* flaky; *(verre)* laminated.

feuilleter [fœjte] *vt (livre)* to leaf through.

feuilleton [fœjtɔ̃] *nm* serial.

feuillette [fœjɛt] *etc vb voir* **feuilleter**.

feuillu, e [fœjy] *adj* leafy ♦ *nm* broad-leaved tree.

feulement [følmɑ̃] *nm* growl.

feutre [føtʀ(ə)] *nm* felt; *(chapeau)* felt hat; *(stylo)* felt-tip(ped) pen.

feutré, e [føtʀe] *adj* feltlike; *(pas, voix)* muffled.

feutrer [føtʀe] *vt* to felt; *(fig: bruits)* to muffle ♦ *vi*, **se ~** *vi (tissu)* to felt.

feutrine [føtʀin] *nf* (lightweight) felt.

fève [fɛv] *nf* broad bean; *(dans la galette des Rois)* charm *(hidden in cake eaten on Twelfth Night)*.

février [fevʀije] *nm* February; *voir aussi* **juillet**.

fez [fɛz] *nm* fez.

FF *abr (= franc français)* FF.

FFA *sigle fpl (= Forces françaises en Allemagne)* French forces in Germany.

FFI *sigle fpl = Forces françaises de l'intérieur (1942-45)* ♦ *sigle m* member of the FFI.

FFL *sigle fpl (= Forces françaises libres)* Free French Army.

Fg *abr = * **faubourg**.

FGA *sigle m (= Fonds de garantie automobile)* fund financed through insurance premiums, to compensate victims of uninsured losses.

FGEN *sigle f (= Fédération générale de l'éducation nationale)* teachers' trade union.

fi [fi] *excl*: **faire ~ de** to snap one's fingers at.

fiabilité [fjabilite] *nf* reliability.

fiable [fjabl(ə)] *adj* reliable.

fiacre [fjakʀ(ə)] *nm* (hackney) cab *ou* carriage.

fiançailles [fjɑ̃saj] *nfpl* engagement *sg*.

fiancé, e [fjɑ̃se] *nm/f* fiancé/fiancée ♦ *adj*: **être ~ (à)** to be engaged (to).

fiancer [fjɑ̃se]: **se ~** *vi*: **se ~ (avec)** to become engaged (to).

fiasco [fjasko] *nm* fiasco.

fibranne [fibʀan] *nf* bonded fibre *ou* fiber *(US)*.

fibre [fibʀ(ə)] *nf* fibre, fiber *(US)*; **avoir la ~ paternelle/militaire** to be a born father/ soldier; ~ **optique** optical fibre *ou* fiber; ~ **de verre** fibreglass *(BRIT)*, fiberglass *(US)*, glass fibre *ou* fiber.

fibreux, euse [fibʀø, -øz] *adj* fibrous; *(viande)* stringy.

fibrome [fibʀom] *nm (MÉD)* fibroma.

ficelage [fislaʒ] *nm* tying (up).

ficelé, e [fisle] *adj (fam)*: **être mal ~** *(habillé)* to be badly got up; **bien/mal ~** *(conçu: roman, projet)* well/badly put together.

ficeler [fisle] *vt* to tie up.

ficelle [fisɛl] *nf* string *no pl*; *(morceau)* piece *ou* length of string; *(pain)* stick of French bread; ~**s** *pl (fig)* strings; **tirer sur la ~** *(fig)* to go too far.

fiche [fiʃ] *nf (carte)* (index) card; *(INFORM)* record; *(formulaire)* form; *(ÉLEC)* plug; ~ **de paye** pay slip; ~ **signalétique** *(POLICE)* identification card; ~ **technique** data sheet, specification *ou* spec sheet.

ficher [fiʃe] *vt (dans un fichier)* to file; *(: POLICE)* to put on file; *(fam)* to do; *(: donner)* to give; *(: mettre)* to stick *ou* shove; *(planter)*: ~ **qch dans** to stick *ou* drive sth into; ~ **qn à la porte** *(fam)* to chuck sb out; **fiche(-moi) le camp** *(fam)* clear off; **fiche-moi la paix** *(fam)* leave me alone; **se ~ dans** *(s'enfoncer)* to get stuck in, embed itself in; **se ~ de** *(fam)* to make fun of; not to care about.

fichier [fiʃje] *nm (gén, INFORM)* file; *(à cartes)* card index; ~ **actif** *ou* **en cours d'utilisation**

(*INFORM*) active file; ~ **d'adresses** mailing list; ~ **d'archives** (*INFORM*) archive file.

fichu, e [fiʃy] *pp de* **ficher** (*fam*) ♦ *adj* (*fam*: fini, inutilisable) bust, done for; (: *intensif*) wretched, darned ♦ *nm* (*foulard*) (head)scarf (*pl* -scarves); **être ~ de** to be capable of; **mal ~** feeling lousy; useless; **bien ~** great.

fictif, ive [fiktif, -iv] *adj* fictitious.

fiction [fiksjɔ̃] *nf* fiction; (*fait imaginé*) invention.

fictivement [fiktivmɑ̃] *adv* fictitiously.

fidèle [fidɛl] *adj*: ~ **(à)** faithful (to) ♦ *nm/f* (*REL*): **les ~s** the faithful; (*à l'église*) the congregation.

fidèlement [fidɛlmɑ̃] *adv* faithfully.

fidélité [fidelite] *nf* faithfulness.

Fidji [fidʒi] *nfpl*: **(les îles)** ~ Fiji.

fiduciaire [fidysjɛʀ] *adj* fiduciary; **héritier ~** heir, trustee; **monnaie ~** flat money.

fief [fjɛf] *nm* fief; (*fig*) preserve; stronghold.

fieffé, e [fjefe] *adj* (*ivrogne, menteur*) arrant, out-and-out.

fiel [fjɛl] *nm* gall.

fiente [fjɑ̃t] *nf* (bird) droppings *pl*.

fier¹ [fje]: **se ~ à** *vt* to trust.

fier², fière [fjɛʀ] *adj* proud; ~ **de** proud of; **avoir fière allure** to cut a fine figure.

fièrement [fjɛʀmɑ̃] *adv* proudly.

fierté [fjɛʀte] *nf* pride.

fièvre [fjɛvʀ(ə)] *nf* fever; **avoir de la ~/39 de ~** to have a high temperature/a temperature of 39°C; ~ **typhoïde** typhoid fever.

fiévreusement [fjevʀøzmɑ̃] *adv* (*fig*) feverishly.

fiévreux, euse [fjevʀø, -øz] *adj* feverish.

FIFA [fifa] *sigle f* (= *Fédération internationale de Football association*) FIFA.

fifre [fifʀ(ə)] *nm* fife; (*personne*) fife-player.

fig *abr* (= *figure*) fig.

figer [fiʒe] *vt* to congeal; (*fig: personne*) to freeze, root to the spot; **se ~** *vi* to congeal; to freeze; (*institutions etc*) to become set, stop evolving.

fignoler [fiɲɔle] *vt* to put the finishing touches to.

figue [fig] *nf* fig.

figuier [figje] *nm* fig tree.

figurant, e [figyʀɑ̃, -ɑ̃t] *nm/f* (*THÉÂT*) walk-on; (*CINÉ*) extra.

figuratif, ive [figyʀatif, -iv] *adj* representational, figurative.

figuration [figyʀasjɔ̃] *nf* walk-on parts *pl*; extras *pl*.

figure [figyʀ] *nf* (*visage*) face; (*image, tracé, forme, personnage*) figure; (*illustration*) picture, diagram; **faire ~ de** to look like; **faire bonne ~** to put up a good show; **faire triste ~** to be a sorry sight; ~ **de rhétorique** figure of speech.

figuré, e [figyʀe] *adj* (*sens*) figurative.

figurer [figyʀe] *vi* to appear ♦ *vt* to represent; **se ~ que** to imagine that; **figurez-vous que**

... would you believe that ...?

figurine [figyʀin] *nf* figurine.

fil [fil] *nm* (*brin, fig: d'une histoire*) thread; (*du téléphone*) cable, wire; (*textile de lin*) linen; (*d'un couteau: tranchant*) edge; **au ~ des années** with the passing of the years; **au ~ de l'eau** with the stream *ou* current; **de ~ en aiguille** one thing leading to another; **ne tenir qu'à un ~** (*vie, réussite etc*) to hang by a thread; **donner du ~ à retordre à qn** to make life difficult for sb; **donner/recevoir un coup de ~** to make/get a phone call; ~ **à coudre** (sewing) thread *ou* yarn; ~ **dentaire** dental floss; ~ **électrique** electric wire; ~ **de fer** wire; ~ **de fer barbelé** barbed wire; ~ **à pêche** fishing line; ~ **à plomb** plumbline; ~ **à souder** soldering wire.

filament [filamɑ̃] *nm* (*ÉLEC*) filament; (*de liquide*) trickle, thread.

filandreux, euse [filɑ̃dʀø, -øz] *adj* stringy.

filant, e [filɑ̃, -ɑ̃t] *adj*: **étoile ~e** shooting star.

filasse [filas] *adj inv* white blond.

filature [filatyʀ] *nf* (*fabrique*) mill; (*policière*) shadowing *no pl*, tailing *no pl*; **prendre qn en ~** to shadow *ou* tail sb.

fil-de-fériste [fildəfeʀist(ə)] *nm/f* high-wire artist.

file [fil] *nf* line; ~ (**d'attente**) queue (*BRIT*), line (*US*); **prendre la ~** to join the (end of the) queue *ou* line; **prendre la ~ de droite** (*AUTO*) to move into the right-hand lane; **se mettre en ~** to form a line; (*AUTO*) to get into lane; **stationner en double ~** (*AUTO*) to double-park; **à la ~** *adv* (*d'affilée*) in succession; (*à la suite*) one after another; **à la** *ou* **en ~ indienne** in single file.

filer [file] *vt* (*tissu, toile, verre*) to spin; (*dérouler: câble etc*) to pay *ou* let out; (*prendre en filature*) to shadow, tail; (*fam: donner*): ~ **qch à qn** to slip sb sth ♦ *vi* (*bas, maille, liquide, pâte*) to run; (*aller vite*) to fly past *ou* by; (*fam: partir*) to make off; ~ **à l'anglaise** to take French leave; ~ **doux** to behave o.s., toe the line; ~ **un mauvais coton** to be in a bad way.

filet [filɛ] *nm* net; (*CULIN*) fillet; (*d'eau, de sang*) trickle; **tendre un ~** (*suj: police*) to set a trap; ~ (**à bagages**) (*RAIL*) luggage rack; ~ (**à provisions**) string bag.

filetage [filtaʒ] *nm* threading; thread.

fileter [filte] *vt* to thread.

filial, e, aux [filjal, -o] *adj* filial ♦ *nf* (*COMM*) subsidiary; affiliate.

filiation [filjasjɔ̃] *nf* filiation.

filière [filjɛʀ] *nf*: **passer par la ~** to go through the (administrative) channels; **suivre la ~** to work one's way up (through the hierarchy).

filiforme [filifɔʀm(ə)] *adj* spindly; threadlike.

filigrane [filigʀan] *nm* (*d'un billet, timbre*) watermark; **en ~** (*fig*) showing just beneath the surface.

filin [filɛ̃] *nm* (*NAVIG*) rope.

fille [fij] nf girl; (opposé à fils) daughter; **vieille ~** old maid; **~ de joie** prostitute; **~ de salle** waitress.

fille-mère, pl **filles-mères** [fijmɛʀ] nf unmarried mother.

fillette [fijɛt] nf (little) girl.

filleul, e [fijœl] nm/f godchild, godson/daughter.

film [film] nm (pour photo) (roll of) film; (œuvre) film, picture, movie; (couche) film; **~ muet/parlant** silent/talking picture ou movie; **~ alimentaire** clingfilm; **~ d'animation** animated film; **~ policier** thriller.

filmer [filme] vt to film.

filon [filɔ̃] nm vein, lode; (fig) lucrative line, moneyspinner.

filou [filu] nm (escroc) swindler.

fils [fis] nm son; **~ de famille** moneyed young man; **~ à papa** (péj) daddy's boy.

filtrage [filtʀaʒ] nm filtering.

filtrant, e [filtʀɑ̃, -ɑ̃t] adj (huile solaire etc) filtering.

filtre [filtʀ(ə)] nm filter; **"~ ou sans ~?"** (cigarettes) "tipped or plain?"; **~ à air** air filter.

filtrer [filtʀe] vt to filter; (fig: candidats, visiteurs) to screen ♦ vi to filter (through).

fin¹ [fɛ̃] nf end; **~s** nfpl (but) ends; **à (la) ~ mai, ~ mai** at the end of May; **en ~ de semaine** at the end of the week; **prendre ~** to come to an end; **toucher à sa ~** to be drawing to a close; **mettre ~ à** to put an end to; **mener à bonne ~** to bring to a successful conclusion; **à cette ~** to this end; **à toutes ~s utiles** for your information; **à la ~** in the end, eventually; **sans ~** adj endless ♦ adv endlessly; **~ de non-recevoir** (JUR, ADMIN) objection; **~ de section** (de ligne d'autobus) (fare) stage.

fin², e [fɛ̃, fin] adj (papier, couche, fil) thin; (cheveux, poudre, pointe, visage) fine; (taille) neat, slim; (esprit, remarque) subtle; shrewd ♦ adv (moudre, couper) finely ♦ nm: **vouloir jouer au plus ~ (avec qn)** to try to outsmart sb ♦ nf (alcool) liqueur brandy; **c'est ~!** (ironique) how clever!; **~ prêt/soûl** quite ready/drunk; **un ~ gourmet** a gourmet; **un ~ tireur** a crack shot; **avoir la vue/l'ouïe ~e** to have sharp eyes/ears, have keen eyesight/hearing; **or/linge/vin ~** fine gold/linen/wine; **le ~ fond de** the very depths of; **le ~ mot de** the real story behind; **la ~e fleur de** the flower of; **une ~e mouche** (fig) a sharp customer; **~es herbes** mixed herbs.

final, e [final] adj, nf final ♦ nm (MUS) finale; **quarts de ~e** quarter finals; **8èmes/16èmes de ~e** 2nd/1st round (in 5 round knock-out competition).

finalement [finalmɑ̃] adv finally, in the end; (après tout) after all.

finaliste [finalist(ə)] nm/f finalist.

finalité [finalite] nf (but) aim, goal; (fonction) purpose.

finance [finɑ̃s] nf finance; **~s** nfpl (situation financière) finances; (activités financières) finance sg; **moyennant ~** for a fee ou consideration.

financement [finɑ̃smɑ̃] nm financing.

financer [finɑ̃se] vt to finance.

financier, ière [finɑ̃sje, -jɛʀ] adj financial ♦ nm financier.

financièrement [finɑ̃sjɛʀmɑ̃] adv financially.

finasser [finase] vi (péj) to wheel and deal.

finaud, e [fino, -od] adj wily.

fine [fin] adj f, nf voir **fin, e**.

finement [finmɑ̃] adv thinly; finely; neatly; slimly; subtly; shrewdly.

finesse [fines] nf thinness; fineness; neatness, slimness; subtlety; shrewdness; **~s** nfpl (subtilités) niceties; finer points.

fini, e [fini] adj finished; (MATH) finite; (intensif): **un menteur ~** a liar through and through ♦ nm (d'un objet manufacturé) finish.

finir [finiʀ] vt to finish ♦ vi to finish, end; **~ quelque part** to end ou finish up somewhere; **~ de faire** to finish doing; (cesser) to stop doing; **~ par faire** to end ou finish up doing; **il finit par m'agacer** he's beginning to get on my nerves; **en pointe/tragédie** to end in a point/in tragedy; **en ~ avec** to be ou have done with; **à n'en plus ~** (route, discussions) never-ending; **il va mal ~** he will come to a bad end; **c'est bientôt fini?** (reproche) have you quite finished?

finish [finiʃ] nm (SPORT) finish.

finissage [finisaʒ] nm finishing.

finisseur, euse [finisœʀ, -øz] nm/f (SPORT) strong finisher.

finition [finisjɔ̃] nf finishing; finish.

finlandais, e [fɛ̃lɑ̃dɛ, -ɛz] adj Finnish ♦ nm/f: **F~, e** Finn.

Finlande [fɛ̃lɑ̃d] nf: **la ~** Finland.

finnois, e [finwa, -waz] adj Finnish ♦ nm (LING) Finnish.

fiole [fjɔl] nf phial.

fiord [fjɔʀ(d)] nm = fjord.

fioriture [fjɔʀityʀ] nf embellishment, flourish.

fioul [fjul] nm fuel oil.

firent [fiʀ] vb voir **faire**.

firmament [fiʀmamɑ̃] nm firmament, skies pl.

firme [fiʀm(ə)] nf firm.

fis [fi] vb voir **faire**.

fisc [fisk] nm tax authorities pl, ≈ Inland Revenue (BRIT), ≈ Internal Revenue Service (US).

fiscal, e, aux [fiskal, -o] adj tax cpd, fiscal.

fiscaliser [fiskalize] vt to subject to tax.

fiscaliste [fiskalist(ə)] nm/f tax specialist.

fiscalité [fiskalite] nf tax system; (charges) taxation.

fissible [fisibl(ə)] adj fissile.

fission [fisjɔ̃] nf fission.

fissure [fisyʀ] nf crack.

fissurer [fisyʀe] *vt*, **se ~** *vi* to crack.
fiston [fistɔ̃] *nm (fam)* son, lad.
fit [fi] *vb voir* **faire**.
FIV *sigle f* (= *fécondation in vitro*) IVF.
fixage [fiksaʒ] *nm (PHOTO)* fixing.
fixateur [fiksatœʀ] *nm (PHOTO)* fixer; (*pour cheveux*) hair cream.
fixatif [fiksatif] *nm* fixative.
fixation [fiksɑsjɔ̃] *nf* fixing; fastening; setting; (*de ski*) binding; (*PSYCH*) fixation.
fixe [fiks(ə)] *adj* fixed; (*emploi*) steady, regular ♦ *nm (salaire)* basic salary; **à heure ~** at a set time; **menu à prix ~** set menu.
fixé, e [fikse] *adj (heure, jour)* appointed; **être ~ (sur)** to have made up one's mind (about); to know for certain (about).
fixement [fiksəmɑ̃] *adv* fixedly, steadily.
fixer [fikse] *vt (attacher):* **~ qch (à/sur)** to fix *ou* fasten sth (to/onto); (*déterminer*) to fix, set; (*CHIMIE, PHOTO*) to fix; (*poser son regard sur*) to look hard at, stare at; **se ~** (*s'établir*) to settle down; **~ son choix sur qch** to decide on sth; **se ~ sur** (*suj: attention*) to focus on.
fixité [fiksite] *nf* fixedness.
fjord [fjɔʀ(d)] *nm* fjord, fiord.
fl. *abr* (= *fleuve*) r, R; (= *florin*) fl.
flacon [flakɔ̃] *nm* bottle.
flagada [flagada] *adj inv (fam: fatigué)* shattered.
flagellation [flaʒɛlɑsjɔ̃] *nf* flogging.
flageller [flaʒele] *vt* to flog, scourge.
flageoler [flaʒɔle] *vi* to have knees like jelly.
flageolet [flaʒɔlɛ] *nm (MUS)* flageolet; (*CULIN*) dwarf kidney bean.
flagornerie [flagɔʀnəʀi] *nf* toadying, fawning.
flagorneur, euse [flagɔʀnœʀ, -øz] *nm/f* toady, fawner.
flagrant, e [flagʀɑ̃, -ɑ̃t] *adj* flagrant, blatant; **en ~ délit** in the act, in flagrante delicto.
flair [flɛʀ] *nm* sense of smell; (*fig*) intuition.
flairer [fleʀe] *vt (humer)* to sniff (at); (*détecter*) to scent.
flamand, e [flamɑ̃, -ɑ̃d] *adj* Flemish ♦ *nm* (*LING*) Flemish ♦ *nm/f:* **F~, e** Fleming; **les F~s** the Flemish.
flamant [flamɑ̃] *nm* flamingo.
flambant [flɑ̃bɑ̃] *adv:* **~ neuf** brand new.
flambé, e [flɑ̃be] *adj (CULIN)* flambé ♦ *nf* blaze; (*fig*) flaring-up, explosion.
flambeau, x [flɑ̃bo] *nm* (flaming) torch; **se passer le ~** (*fig*) to hand down the (*ou* a) tradition.
flambée [flɑ̃be] *nf (feu)* blaze; (*COMM*): **~ des prix** (sudden) shooting up of prices.
flamber [flɑ̃be] *vi* to blaze (up) ♦ *vt (poulet)* to singe; (*aiguille*) to sterilize.
flambeur, euse [flɑ̃bœʀ, -øz] *nm/f* big-time gambler.
flamboyant, e [flɑ̃bwajɑ̃, -ɑ̃t] *adj* blazing; flaming.
flamboyer [flɑ̃bwaje] *vi* to blaze (up); (*fig*) to flame.

flamenco [flamɛnko] *nm* flamenco.
flamingant, e [flamɛ̃gɑ̃, -ɑ̃t] *adj* Flemish-speaking ♦ *nm/f:* **F~, e** Flemish speaker; (*POL*) Flemish nationalist.
flamme [flam] *nf* flame; (*fig*) fire, fervour; **en ~s** on fire, ablaze.
flammèche [flamɛʃ] *nf* (flying) spark.
flammerole [flamʀɔl] *nf* will-o'-the-wisp.
flan [flɑ̃] *nm (CULIN)* custard tart *ou* pie.
flanc [flɑ̃] *nm* side; (*MIL*) flank; **~ de colline** on the hillside; **prêter le ~ à** (*fig*) to lay o.s. open to.
flancher [flɑ̃ʃe] *vi (cesser de fonctionner)* to fail, pack up; (*armée*) to quit.
Flandre [flɑ̃dʀ(ə)] *nf:* **la ~** (*aussi:* **les ~s**) Flanders.
flanelle [flanɛl] *nf* flannel.
flâner [flɑne] *vi* to stroll.
flânerie [flɑnʀi] *nf* stroll.
flâneur, euse [flɑnœʀ, -øz] *adj* idle ♦ *nm/f* stroller.
flanquer [flɑ̃ke] *vt* to flank; (*fam: jeter*): **~ par terre/à la porte** to fling to the ground/chuck out; (: *donner*): **~ la frousse à qn** to put the wind up sb, give sb an awful fright.
flapi, e [flapi] *adj* dog-tired.
flaque [flak] *nf (d'eau)* puddle; (*d'huile, de sang etc*) pool.
flash, *pl* **flashes** [flaʃ] *nm (PHOTO)* flash; **~ (d'information)** newsflash.
flasque [flask(ə)] *adj* flabby ♦ *nf (flacon)* flask.
flatter [flate] *vt* to flatter; (*caresser*) to stroke; **se ~ de qch** to pride o.s. on sth.
flatterie [flatʀi] *nf* flattery.
flatteur, euse [flatœʀ, -øz] *adj* flattering ♦ *nm/f* flatterer.
flatulence [flatylɑ̃s], **flatuosité** [flatɥozite] *nf* (*MÉD*) flatulence, wind.
FLB *abr* (= *franco long du bord*) FAS ♦ *sigle m* (*POL*) = Front de libération de la Bretagne.
FLC *sigle m* = Front de libération de la Corse.
fléau, x [fleo] *nm* scourge, curse; (*de balance*) beam; (*pour le blé*) flail.
fléchage [fleʃaʒ] *nm (d'un itinéraire)* signposting.
flèche [flɛʃ] *nf* arrow; (*de clocher*) spire; (*de grue*) jib; (*trait d'esprit, critique*) shaft; **monter en ~** (*fig*) to soar, rocket; **partir en ~** (*fig*) to be off like a shot; **à ~ variable** (*avion*) swing-wing *cpd*.
flécher [fleʃe] *vt* to arrow, mark with arrows.
fléchette [fleʃɛt] *nf* dart; **~s** *nfpl (jeu)* darts *sg*.
fléchir [fleʃiʀ] *vt (corps, genou)* to bend; (*fig*) to sway, weaken ♦ *vi (poutre)* to sag, bend; (*fig*) to weaken, flag; (: *baisser: prix*) to fall off.
fléchissement [fleʃismɑ̃] *nm* bending; sagging; flagging; (*de l'économie*) dullness.
flegmatique [flɛgmatik] *adj* phlegmatic.
flegme [flɛgm(ə)] *nm* composure.
flemmard, e [flemaʀ, -aʀd(ə)] *nm/f* lazybones *sg*, loafer.
flemme [flɛm] *nf (fam):* **j'ai la ~ de faire** I can't**

be bothered to do.

flétan [fletɑ̃] *nm* (*ZOOL*) halibut.

flétrir [fletʀiʀ] *vt* to wither; (*stigmatiser*) to condemn (in the most severe terms); **se ~** *vi* to wither.

fleur [flœʀ] *nf* flower; (*d'un arbre*) blossom; **être en ~** (*arbre*) to be in blossom; **tissu à ~s** flowered *ou* flowery fabric; **la (fine) ~ de** (*fig*) the flower of; **être ~ bleue** to be soppy *ou* sentimental; **à ~ de terre** just above the ground; **faire une ~ à qn** to do sb a favour (*BRIT*) *ou* favor (*US*); **~ de lis** fleur-de-lis.

fleurer [flœʀe] *vt*: **~ la lavande** to have the scent of lavender.

fleuret [flœʀɛ] *nm* (*arme*) foil; (*sport*) fencing.

fleurette [flœʀɛt] *nf*: **conter ~ à qn** to whisper sweet nothings to sb.

fleuri, e [flœʀi] *adj* in flower *ou* bloom; surrounded by flowers; (*fig: style*) flowery; (*: teint*) glowing.

fleurir [flœʀiʀ] *vi* (*rose*) to flower; (*arbre*) to blossom; (*fig*) to flourish ♦ *vt* (*tombe*) to put flowers on; (*chambre*) to decorate with flowers.

fleuriste [flœʀist(ə)] *nm/f* florist.

fleuron [flœʀɔ̃] *nm* jewel (*fig*).

fleuve [flœv] *nm* river; **roman-~** saga; **discours-~** interminable speech.

flexibilité [flɛksibilite] *nf* flexibility.

flexible [flɛksibl(ə)] *adj* flexible.

flexion [flɛksjɔ̃] *nf* flexing, bending; (*LING*) inflection.

flibustier [flibystje] *nm* buccaneer.

flic [flik] *nm* (*fam: péj*) cop.

flingue [flɛ̃g] *nm* (*fam*) shooter.

flipper *nm* [flipœʀ] pinball (machine) ♦ *vi* [flipe] (*fam: être déprimé*) to feel down, be on a downer; (*: être exalté*) to freak out.

flirt [flœʀt] *nm* flirting; (*personne*) boyfriend, girlfriend.

flirter [flœʀte] *vi* to flirt.

FLN *sigle m* = *Front de libération nationale (during the Algerian war)*.

FLNKS *sigle m* (= *Front de libération nationale kanak et socialiste*) *political movement in New Caledonia*.

flocon [flɔkɔ̃] *nm* flake; (*de laine etc: boulette*) flock; **~s d'avoine** oatflakes, porridge oats.

floconneux, euse [flɔkɔnø, -øz] *adj* fluffy, fleecy.

flonflons [flɔ̃flɔ̃] *nmpl* blare *sg*.

flopée [flɔpe] *nf*: **une ~ de** loads of.

floraison [flɔʀɛzɔ̃] *nf* (*voir fleurir*) flowering; blossoming; flourishing.

floral, e, aux [flɔʀal, -o] *adj* floral, flower *cpd*.

floralies [flɔʀali] *nfpl* flower show *sg*.

flore [flɔʀ] *nf* flora.

Florence [flɔʀɑ̃s] *n* (*ville*) Florence.

florentin, e [flɔʀɑ̃tɛ̃, -in] *adj* Florentine.

floriculture [flɔʀikyltyʀ] *nf* flower-growing.

florissant, e [flɔʀisɑ̃, -ɑ̃t] *vb voir fleurir* ♦ *adj* flourishing; (*santé, teint, mine*) blooming.

flot [flo] *nm* flood, stream; (*marée*) flood tide; **~s** *nmpl* (*de la mer*) waves; **être à ~** (*NAVIG*) to be afloat; (*fig*) to be on an even keel; **à ~s** (*couler*) in torrents; **entrer à ~s** to stream *ou* pour in.

flottage [flɔtaʒ] *nm* (*du bois*) floating.

flottaison [flɔtɛzɔ̃] *nf*: **ligne de ~** waterline.

flottant, e [flɔtɑ̃, -ɑ̃t] *adj* (*vêtement*) loose (-fitting); (*cours, barème*) floating.

flotte [flɔt] *nf* (*NAVIG*) fleet; (*fam*) water; rain.

flottement [flɔtmɑ̃] *nm* (*fig*) wavering, hesitation; (*ÉCON*) floating.

flotter [flɔte] *vi* to float; (*nuage, odeur*) to drift; (*drapeau*) to fly; (*vêtements*) to hang loose ♦ *vb impers* (*fam: pleuvoir*): **il flotte** it's raining ♦ *vt* to float; **faire ~** to float.

flotteur [flɔtœʀ] *nm* float.

flottille [flɔtij] *nf* flotilla.

flou, e [flu] *adj* fuzzy, blurred; (*fig*) woolly (*BRIT*), vague; (*non ajusté: robe*) loose (-fitting).

flouer [flue] *vt* to swindle.

FLQ *abr* (= *franco long du quai*) FAQ.

fluctuant, e [flyktɥɑ̃, -ɑ̃t] *adj* (*prix, cours*) fluctuating; (*opinions*) changing.

fluctuation [flyktɥasjɔ̃] *nf* fluctuation.

fluctuer [flyktɥe] *vi* to fluctuate.

fluet, te [flyɛ, -ɛt] *adj* thin, slight; (*voix*) thin.

fluide [flɥid] *adj* fluid; (*circulation etc*) flowing freely ♦ *nm* fluid; (*force*) (mysterious) power.

fluidifier [flɥidifje] *vt* to make fluid.

fluidité [flɥidite] *nf* fluidity; free flow.

fluor [flyɔʀ] *nm* fluorine.

fluoré, e [flyɔʀe] *adj* fluoridated.

fluorescent, e [flyɔʀesɑ̃, -ɑ̃t] *adj* fluorescent.

flûte [flyt] *nf* (*aussi*: **~ traversière**) flute; (*verre*) flute glass; (*pain*) long loaf (*pl* loaves); **petite ~** piccolo (*pl* -s); **~!** drat it!; **~ (à bec)** recorder; **~ de Pan** panpipes *pl*.

flûtiste [flytist(ə)] *nm/f* flautist, flute player.

fluvial, e, aux [flyvjal, -o] *adj* river *cpd*, fluvial.

flux [fly] *nm* incoming tide; (*écoulement*) flow; **le ~ et le reflux** the ebb and flow.

fluxion [flyksjɔ̃] *nf*: **~ de poitrine** pneumonia.

FM *sigle f* (= *frequency modulation*) FM.

Fme *abr* (= *femme*) W.

FMI *sigle m* (= *Fonds monétaire international*) IMF.

FN *sigle m* (= *Front national*) ≈ NF (= *National Front*).

FNAC [fnak] *sigle f* (= *Fédération nationale des achats des cadres*) chain of discount shops (*hi-fi, photo etc*).

FNAH *sigle m* = *Fonds national d'amélioration de l'habitat*.

FNEF [fnɛf] *sigle f* (= *Fédération nationale des étudiants de France*) student union.

FNSEA *sigle f* (= *Fédération nationale des syndicats d'exploitants agricoles*) farmers' union.

FO *sigle f* (= *Force ouvrière*) *trades union*.

foc [fɔk] *nm* jib.

focal, e, aux [fɔkal, -o] *adj* focal ♦ *nf* focal length.

focaliser [fɔkalize] *vt* to focus.

foehn [føn] *nm* foehn, föhn.

fœtal, e, aux [fetal, -o] *adj* fetal, foetal (*BRIT*).

fœtus [fetys] *nm* fetus, foetus (*BRIT*).

foi [fwa] *nf* faith; **sous la ~ du serment** under *ou* on oath; **ajouter ~ à** to lend credence to; **faire ~** (*prouver*) to be evidence; **digne de ~** reliable; **sur la ~ de** on the word *ou* strength of; **être de bonne/mauvaise ~** to be in good faith/not to be in good faith; **ma ~!** well!

foie [fwa] *nm* liver; **~ gras** foie gras.

foin [fwɛ̃] *nm* hay; **faire les ~s** to make hay; **faire du ~** (*fam*) to kick up a row.

foire [fwaʀ] *nf* fair; (*fête foraine*) (fun) fair; (*fig: désordre, confusion*) bear garden; **faire la ~** to whoop it up; **~ (exposition)** trade fair.

fois [fwa] *nf* time; **une/deux ~** once/twice; **trois/vingt ~** three/twenty times; **2 ~ 2 2** times 2; **deux/quatre ~ plus grand (que)** twice/four times as big (as); **une ~** (*passé*) once; (*futur*) sometime; **une (bonne) ~ pour toutes** once and for all; **encore une ~** again, once more; **il était une ~** once upon a time; **une ~ que c'est fait** once it's done; **une ~ parti** once he (*ou* I *etc*) had left; **des ~** (*parfois*) sometimes; **si des ~ ...** (*fam*) if ever ...; **non mais des ~!** (*fam*) (now) look here!; **à la ~** (*ensemble*) (all) at once; **à la ~ grand et beau** both tall and handsome.

foison [fwazɔ̃] *nf*: **une ~ de** an abundance of; **à ~** *adv* in plenty.

foisonnant, e [fwazɔnɑ̃, -ɑ̃t] *adj* teeming.

foisonnement [fwazɔnmɑ̃] *nm* profusion, abundance.

foisonner [fwazɔne] *vi* to abound; **~ en** *ou* **de** to abound in.

fol [fɔl] *adj m voir* **fou**.

folâtre [fɔlɑtʀ(ə)] *adj* playful.

folâtrer [fɔlɑtʀe] *vi* to frolic (about).

folichon, ne [fɔliʃɔ̃, -ɔn] *adj*: **ça n'a rien de ~** it's not a lot of fun.

folie [fɔli] *nf* (*d'une décision, d'un acte*) madness, folly; (*état*) madness, insanity; (*acte*) folly; **la ~ des grandeurs** delusions of grandeur; **faire des ~s** (*en dépenses*) to be extravagant.

folklore [fɔlklɔʀ] *nm* folklore.

folklorique [fɔlklɔʀik] *adj* folk *cpd*; (*fam*) weird.

folle [fɔl] *adj f, nf voir* **fou**.

follement [fɔlmɑ̃] *adv* (*très*) madly, wildly.

follet [fɔlɛ] *adj m*: **feu ~** will-o'-the-wisp.

fomentateur, trice [fɔmɑ̃tatœʀ, -tʀis] *nm/f* agitator.

fomenter [fɔmɑ̃te] *vt* to stir up, foment.

foncé, e [fɔ̃se] *adj* dark; **bleu ~** dark blue.

foncer [fɔ̃se] *vt* to make darker; (*CULIN: moule etc*) to line ♦ *vi* to go darker; (*fam: aller vite*) to tear *ou* belt along; **~ sur** to charge at.

fonceur, euse [fɔ̃sœʀ, -øz] *nm/f* whizz kid.

foncier, ière [fɔ̃sje, -jɛʀ] *adj* (*honnêteté etc*) basic, fundamental; (*malhonnêteté*) deep-rooted; (*COMM*) real estate *cpd*.

foncièrement [fɔ̃sjɛʀmɑ̃] *adv* basically; (*absolument*) thoroughly.

fonction [fɔ̃ksjɔ̃] *nf* (*rôle*, MATH, LING) function; (*emploi, poste*) post, position; **~s** (*professionnelles*) duties; **entrer en ~s** to take up one's post *ou* duties; to take up office; **voiture de ~** company car; **être ~ de** (*dépendre de*) to depend on; **en ~ de** (*par rapport à*) according to; **faire ~ de** to serve as; **la ~ publique** the state *ou* civil (*BRIT*) service.

fonctionnaire [fɔ̃ksjɔnɛʀ] *nm/f* state employee *ou* official; (*dans l'administration*) ≈ civil servant (*BRIT*).

fonctionnariser [fɔ̃ksjɔnaʀize] *vt* (*ADMIN: personne*) to give the status of a state employee to.

fonctionnel, le [fɔ̃ksjɔnɛl] *adj* functional.

fonctionnellement [fɔ̃ksjɔnɛlmɑ̃] *adv* functionally.

fonctionnement [fɔ̃ksjɔnmɑ̃] *nm* working; functioning; operation.

fonctionner [fɔ̃ksjɔne] *vi* to work, function; (*entreprise*) to operate, function; **faire ~** to work, operate.

fond [fɔ̃] *nm voir aussi* **fonds**; (*d'un récipient, trou*) bottom; (*d'une salle, scène*) back; (*d'un tableau, décor*) background; (*opposé à la forme*) content; (*petite quantité*): **un ~ de verre** a drop; (*SPORT*): **le ~** long distance (running); **course/épreuve de ~** long-distance race/trial; **au ~ de** at the bottom of; at the back of; **aller au ~ des choses** to get to the root of things; **le ~ de sa pensée** his (*ou* her) true thoughts *ou* feelings; **sans ~** *adj* bottomless; **envoyer par le ~** (*NAVIG: couler*) to sink, scuttle; **à ~** *adv* (*connaître, soutenir*) thoroughly; (*appuyer, visser*) right down *ou* home; **à ~ (de train)** *adv* (*fam*) full tilt; **dans le ~, au ~** *adv* (*en somme*) basically, really; **de ~ en comble** *adv* from top to bottom; **~ sonore** background noise; background music; **~ de teint** (make-up) foundation.

fondamental, e, aux [fɔ̃damɑ̃tal, -o] *adj* fundamental.

fondamentalement [fɔ̃damɑ̃talmɑ̃] *adv* fundamentally.

fondamentalisme [fɔ̃damɑ̃talism(ə)] *nm* fundamentalism.

fondamentaliste [fɔ̃damɑ̃talist(ə)] *adj, nm/f* fundamentalist.

fondant, e [fɔ̃dɑ̃, -ɑ̃t] *adj* (*neige*) melting; (*poire*) that melts in the mouth; (*chocolat*) fondant.

fondateur, trice [fɔ̃datœʀ, -tʀis] *nm/f* founder; **membre ~** founder (*BRIT*) *ou* founding (*US*) member.

fondation [fɔ̃dɑsjɔ̃] *nf* founding; (*établissement*) foundation; **~s** *nfpl* (*d'une maison*) foundations; **travail de ~** foundation works *pl*.

fondé, e [fɔ̃de] *adj* (*accusation etc*) well-founded ♦ *nm:* **~ de pouvoir** authorized representative; **mal ~** unfounded; **être ~ à croire** to have grounds for believing *ou* good reason to believe.

fondement [fɔ̃dmɑ̃] *nm* (*derrière*) behind; **~s** *nmpl* foundations; **sans ~** *adj* (*rumeur etc*) groundless, unfounded.

fonder [fɔ̃de] *vt* to found; (*fig*): **~ qch sur** to base sth on; **se ~ sur** (*suj: personne*) to base o.s. on; **~ un foyer** (*se marier*) to set up home.

fonderie [fɔ̃dʀi] *nf* smelting works *sg*.

fondeur, euse [fɔ̃dœʀ, -øz] *nm/f* (*skieur*) long-distance skier ♦ *nm:* (*ouvrier*) **~ caster**.

fondre [fɔ̃dʀ(ə)] *vt* to melt; (*dans l'eau: sucre, sel*) to dissolve; (*fig: mélanger*) to merge, blend ♦ *vi* to melt; to dissolve; (*fig*) to melt away; (*se précipiter*): **~ sur** to swoop down on; **se ~** *vi* (*se combiner, se confondre*) to merge into each other; to dissolve; **~ en larmes** to dissolve into tears.

fondrière [fɔ̃dʀijɛʀ] *nf* rut.

fonds [fɔ̃] *nm* (*de bibliothèque*) collection; (*COMM*): **~ (de commerce)** business; (*fig*): **~ de probité** *etc* fund of integrity *etc* ♦ *nmpl* (*argent*) funds; **à ~ perdus** *adv* with little or no hope of getting the money back; **être en ~** to be in funds; **mise de ~** investment, (capital) outlay; **F~ monétaire international (FMI)** International Monetary Fund (IMF); **~ de roulement** *nm* float.

fondu, e [fɔ̃dy] *adj* (*beurre, neige*) melted; (*métal*) molten ♦ *nm* (*CINÉ*): **~ (enchaîné)** dissolve ♦ *nf* (*CULIN*) fondue.

fongicide [fɔ̃ʒisid] *nm* fungicide.

font [fɔ̃] *vb voir* **faire**.

fontaine [fɔ̃tɛn] *nf* fountain; (*source*) spring.

fontanelle [fɔ̃tanɛl] *nf* fontanelle.

fonte [fɔ̃t] *nf* melting; (*métal*) cast iron; **la ~ des neiges** the (spring) thaw.

fonts baptismaux [fɔ̃batismo] *nmpl* (baptismal) font *sg*.

foot(ball) [fut(bol)] *nm* football, soccer.

footballeur, euse [futbolœʀ, -øz] *nm/f* footballer (*BRIT*), football *ou* soccer player.

footing [futiŋ] *nm* jogging; **faire du ~** to go jogging.

for [fɔʀ] *nm:* **dans** *ou* **en son ~ intérieur** in one's heart of hearts.

forage [fɔʀaʒ] *nm* drilling, boring.

forain, e [fɔʀɛ̃, -ɛn] *adj* fairground *cpd* ♦ *nm* (*marchand*) stallholder; (*acteur etc*) fairground entertainer.

forban [fɔʀbɑ̃] *nm* (*pirate*) pirate; (*escroc*) crook.

forçat [fɔʀsa] *nm* convict.

force [fɔʀs(ə)] *nf* strength; (*puissance: surnaturelle etc*) power; (*PHYSIQUE, MÉCANIQUE*) force; **~s** *nfpl* (*physiques*) strength *sg*; (*MIL*) forces; (*effectifs*): **d'importantes ~s de police** large contingents of police; **avoir de la ~** to be strong; **être à bout de ~** to have no strength left; **à la ~ du poignet** (*fig*) by the sweat of one's brow; **à ~ de faire** by dint of doing; **arriver en ~** (*nombreux*) to arrive in force; **cas de ~ majeure** case of absolute necessity; (*ASSURANCES*) act of God; **~ de la nature** natural force; **de ~** *adv* forcibly, by force; **de toutes mes/ses ~s** with all my/his strength; **par la ~** using force; **par la ~ des choses/d'habitude** by force of circumstances/habit; **à toute ~** (*absolument*) at all costs; **faire ~ de rames/voiles** to ply the oars/cram on sail; **être de ~ à faire** to be up to doing; **de première ~** first class; **la ~ armée** (*les troupes*) the army; **~ d'âme** fortitude; **~ de frappe** strike force; **~ d'inertie** force of inertia; **la ~ publique** the authorities responsible for public order; **~s d'intervention** (*MIL, POLICE*) peace-keeping force *sg*; **les ~s de l'ordre** the police.

forcé, e [fɔʀse] *adj* forced; (*bain*) unintended; (*inévitable*): **c'est ~!** it's inevitable!, it HAS to be!

forcément [fɔʀsemɑ̃] *adv* necessarily; inevitably; (*bien sûr*) of course.

forcené, e [fɔʀsəne] *adj* frenzied ♦ *nm/f* maniac.

forceps [fɔʀsɛps] *nm* forceps *pl*.

forcer [fɔʀse] *vt* (*contraindre*): **~ qn à faire** to force sb to do; (*porte, serrure, plante*) to force; (*moteur, voix*) to strain ♦ *vi* (*SPORT*) to overtax o.s.; **se ~ à faire qch** to force o.s. to do sth; **~ la dose/l'allure** to overdo it/increase the pace; **~ l'attention/le respect** to command attention/respect; **~ la consigne** to bypass orders.

forcing [fɔʀsiŋ] *nm* (*SPORT*): **faire le ~** to pile on the pressure.

forcir [fɔʀsiʀ] *vi* (*grossir*) to broaden out; (*vent*) to freshen.

forclore [fɔʀklɔʀ] *vt* (*JUR: personne*) to debar.

forclusion [fɔʀklyzjɔ̃] *nf* (*JUR*) debarment.

forer [fɔʀe] *vt* to drill, bore.

forestier, ière [fɔʀɛstje, -jɛʀ] *adj* forest *cpd*.

foret [fɔʀɛ] *nm* drill.

forêt [fɔʀɛ] *nf* forest; **Office National des F~s** (*ADMIN*) ≈ Forestry Commission (*BRIT*), ≈ National Forest Service (*US*); **la F~ Noire** the Black Forest.

foreuse [fɔʀøz] *nf* (electric) drill.

forfait [fɔʀfɛ] *nm* (*COMM*) fixed *ou* set price; all-in deal *ou* price; (*crime*) infamy; **déclarer ~** to withdraw; **gagner par ~** to win by a walkover; **travailler à** ~ to work for a lump sum.

forfaitaire [fɔʀfɛtɛʀ] *adj* set; inclusive.

forfait-vacances, *pl* **forfaits-vacances** [fɔʀfɛvakɑ̃s] *nm* package holiday.

forfanterie [fɔʀfɑ̃tʀi] *nf* boastfulness *no pl*.

forge [fɔʀʒ(ə)] *nf* forge, smithy.

forgé, e [fɔʀʒe] *adj:* ~ **de toutes pièces** (*histoire*) completely fabricated.

forger [fɔʀʒe] *vt* to forge; (*fig: personnalité*) to form; (*: prétexte*) to contrive, make up.

forgeron [fɔʀʒəʀɔ̃] *nm* (black)smith.

formaliser [fɔʀmalize] *se* ~ *vi*: **se** ~ **(de)** to take offence (at).

formalisme [fɔʀmalism(ə)] *nm* formality.

formalité [fɔʀmalite] *nf* formality.

format [fɔʀma] *nm* size; **petit** ~ small size; (*PHOTO*) 35 mm (film).

formater [fɔʀmate] *vt* (*disque*) to format; **non formaté** unformatted.

formateur, trice [fɔʀmatœʀ, -tʀis] *adj* formative.

formation [fɔʀmasjɔ̃] *nf* forming; (*éducation*) training; (*MUS*) group; (*MIL, AVIAT, GÉO*) formation; **la** ~ **permanente** *ou* **continue** continuing education; **la** ~ **professionnelle** vocational training.

forme [fɔʀm(ə)] *nf* (*gén*) form; (*d'un objet*) shape, form; ~**s** *nfpl* (*bonnes manières*) proprieties; (*d'une femme*) figure *sg*; **en** ~ **de poire** pear-shaped, in the shape of a pear; **sous** ~ **de** in the form of; in the guise of; **sous** ~ **de cachets** in the form of tablets; **être en (bonne** *ou* **pleine)** ~, **avoir la** ~ (*SPORT etc*) to be on form; **en bonne et due** ~ in due form; **pour la** ~ for the sake of form; **sans autre** ~ **de procès** (*fig*) without further ado; **prendre** ~ to take shape.

formel, le [fɔʀmɛl] *adj* (*preuve, décision*) definite, positive; (*logique*) formal.

formellement [fɔʀmɛlmɑ̃] *adv* (*interdit*) strictly.

former [fɔʀme] *vt* (*gén*) to form; (*éduquer: soldat, ingénieur etc*) to train; **se** ~ to form; to train.

formidable [fɔʀmidabl(ə)] *adj* tremendous.

formidablement [fɔʀmidabləmɑ̃] *adv* tremendously.

formol [fɔʀmɔl] *nm* formalin, formol.

formosan, e [fɔʀmozɑ̃, -an] *adj* Formosan.

Formose [fɔʀmoz] *nm* Formosa.

formulaire [fɔʀmylɛʀ] *nm* form.

formulation [fɔʀmylasjɔ̃] *nf* (*voir vb*) formulation; expression.

formule [fɔʀmyl] *nf* (*gén*) formula; (*formulaire*) form; **selon la** ~ **consacrée** as one says; ~ **de politesse** polite phrase; (*en fin de lettre*) letter ending.

formuler [fɔʀmyle] *vt* (*émettre: réponse, vœux*) to formulate; (*expliciter: sa pensée*) to express.

forniquer [fɔʀnike] *vi* to fornicate.

FORPRONU [fɔʀpʀɔny] *sigle f* (= *Force de protection des Nations unies*) UNPROFOR.

fort, e [fɔʀ, fɔʀt(ə)] *adj* strong; (*intensité, rendement*) high, great; (*corpulent*) large; (*doué*): **être** ~ **(en)** to be good (at) ♦ *adv* (*serrer, frapper*) hard; (*sonner*) loud(ly); (*beaucoup*) greatly, very much; (*très*) very ♦ *nm* (*édifice*) fort; (*point fort*) strong point, forte; (*gén pl: personne, pays*): **le** ~, **les** ~**s** the strong; **c'est un peu** ~! it's a bit much!; **à plus** ~**e raison** even more so, all the more reason; **avoir** ~ **à faire avec qn** to have a hard job with sb; **se faire** ~ **de faire** to claim one can do; ~ **bien/peu** very well/few; **au plus** ~ **de** (*au milieu de*) in the thick of, at the height of; ~**e tête** rebel.

fortement [fɔʀtəmɑ̃] *adv* strongly; (*s'intéresser*) deeply.

forteresse [fɔʀtəʀɛs] *nf* fortress.

fortifiant [fɔʀtifjɑ̃] *nm* tonic.

fortifications [fɔʀtifikasjɔ̃] *nfpl* fortifications.

fortifier [fɔʀtifje] *vt* to strengthen, fortify; (*MIL*) to fortify; **se** ~ *vi* (*personne, santé*) to grow stronger.

fortin [fɔʀtɛ̃] *nm* (small) fort.

fortiori [fɔʀtjɔʀi]: **à** ~ *adv* all the more so.

FORTRAN [fɔʀtʀɑ̃] *nm* FORTRAN.

fortuit, e [fɔʀtɥi, -it] *adj* fortuitous, chance *cpd*.

fortuitement [fɔʀtɥitmɑ̃] *adv* fortuitously.

fortune [fɔʀtyn] *nf* fortune; **faire** ~ to make one's fortune; **de** ~ *adj* makeshift; (*compagnon*) chance *cpd*.

fortuné, e [fɔʀtyne] *adj* wealthy, well-off.

forum [fɔʀɔm] *nm* forum.

fosse [fos] *nf* (*grand trou*) pit; (*tombe*) grave; **la** ~ **aux lions/ours** the lions' den/bear pit; ~ **commune** common *ou* communal grave; ~ **(d'orchestre)** (orchestra) pit; ~ **à purin** cesspit; ~ **septique** septic tank; ~**s nasales** nasal fossae.

fossé [fose] *nm* ditch; (*fig*) gulf, gap.

fossette [fosɛt] *nf* dimple.

fossile [fosil] *nm* fossil ♦ *adj* fossilized, fossil *cpd*.

fossilisé, e [fosilize] *adj* fossilized.

fossoyeur [foswajœʀ] *nm* gravedigger.

fou (fol), folle [fu, fɔl] *adj* mad, crazy; (*déréglé etc*) wild, erratic; (*mèche*) stray; (*herbe*) wild; (*fam: extrême, très grand*) terrific, tremendous ♦ *nm/f* madman/woman ♦ *nm* (*du roi*) jester, fool; (*ÉCHECS*) bishop; ~ **à lier,** ~ **furieux (folle furieuse)** raving mad; **être** ~ **de** to be mad *ou* crazy about; (*chagrin, joie, colère*) to be wild with; **faire le** ~ to play *ou* act the fool; **avoir le** ~ **rire** to have the giggles.

foucade [fukad] *nf* caprice.

foudre [fudʀ(ə)] *nf* lightning; ~**s** *nfpl* (*fig: colère*) wrath *sg*.

foudroyant, e [fudʀwajɑ̃, -ɑ̃t] *adj* devastating; (*maladie, poison*) violent.

foudroyer [fudʀwaje] *vt* to strike down; ~ **qn du regard** to look daggers at sb; **il a été foudroyé** he was struck by lightning.

fouet [fwɛ] *nm* whip; (*CULIN*) whisk; **de plein ~** *adv* head on.

fouettement [fwɛtmɑ̃] *nm* lashing *no pl*.

fouetter [fwete] *vt* to whip; to whisk.

fougasse [fugas] *nf* type of flat pastry.

fougère [fuʒɛʀ] *nf* fern.

fougue [fug] *nf* ardour (*BRIT*), ardor (*US*), spirit.

fougueusement [fugøzmɑ̃] *adv* ardently.

fougueux, euse [fugø, -øz] *adj* fiery, ardent.

fouille [fuj] *nf* search; ~**s** *nfpl* (*archéologiques*) excavations; **passer à la ~** to be searched.

fouillé, e [fuje] *adj* detailed.

fouiller [fuje] *vt* to search; (*creuser*) to dig; (*: suj: archéologue*) to excavate; (*approfondir: étude etc*) to go into ♦ *vi* (*archéologue*) to excavate; ~ **dans/parmi** to rummage in/among.

fouillis [fuji] *nm* jumble, muddle.

fouine [fwin] *nf* stone marten.

fouiner [fwine] *vi* (*péj*): ~ **dans** to nose around *ou* about in.

fouineur, euse [fwinœʀ, -øz] *adj* nosey ♦ *nm/f* nosey parker, snooper.

fouir [fwiʀ] *vt* to dig.

fouisseur, euse [fwisœʀ, -øz] *adj* burrowing.

foulage [fulaʒ] *nm* pressing.

foulante [fulɑ̃t] *adj f*: **pompe ~** force pump.

foulard [fulaʀ] *nm* scarf (*pl* scarves).

foule [ful] *nf* crowd; **une ~ de** masses of; **venir en ~** to come in droves.

foulée [fule] *nf* stride; **dans la ~ de** on the heels of.

fouler [fule] *vt* to press; (*sol*) to tread upon; **se ~** *vi* (*fam*) to overexert o.s.; **se ~ la cheville** to sprain one's ankle; ~ **aux pieds** to trample underfoot.

foulure [fulyʀ] *nf* sprain.

four [fuʀ] *nm* oven; (*de potier*) kiln; (*THÉÂT: échec*) flop; **allant au ~** ovenproof.

fourbe [fuʀb(ə)] *adj* deceitful.

fourberie [fuʀbəʀi] *nf* deceit.

fourbi [fuʀbi] *nm* (*fam*) gear, junk.

fourbir [fuʀbiʀ] *vt*: ~ **ses armes** (*fig*) to get ready for the fray.

fourbu, e [fuʀby] *adj* exhausted.

fourche [fuʀʃ(ə)] *nf* pitchfork; (*de bicyclette*) fork.

fourcher [fuʀʃe] *vi*: **ma langue a fourché** it was a slip of the tongue.

fourchette [fuʀʃɛt] *nf* fork; (*STATISTIQUE*) bracket, margin.

fourchu, e [fuʀʃy] *adj* split; (*arbre etc*) forked.

fourgon [fuʀgɔ̃] *nm* van; (*RAIL*) wag(g)on; ~ **mortuaire** hearse.

fourgonnette [fuʀgɔnɛt] *nf* (delivery) van.

fourmi [fuʀmi] *nf* ant; **avoir des ~s** (*fig*) to have pins and needles.

fourmilière [fuʀmiljɛʀ] *nf* ant-hill; (*fig*) hive of activity.

fourmillement [fuʀmijmɑ̃] *nm* (*démangeaison*) pins and needles *pl*; (*grouillement*) swarming *no pl*.

fourmiller [fuʀmije] *vi* to swarm; ~ **de** to be teeming with, be swarming with.

fournaise [fuʀnɛz] *nf* blaze; (*fig*) furnace, oven.

fourneau, x [fuʀno] *nm* stove.

fournée [fuʀne] *nf* batch.

fourni, e [fuʀni] *adj* (*barbe, cheveux*) thick; (*magasin*): **bien ~ (en)** well stocked (with).

fournil [fuʀni] *nm* bakehouse.

fournir [fuʀniʀ] *vt* to supply; (*preuve, exemple*) to provide, supply; (*effort*) to put in; ~ **qch à qn** to supply sth to sb, supply *ou* provide sb with sth; ~ **qn en** (*COMM*) to supply sb with; **se ~ chez** to shop at.

fournisseur, euse [fuʀnisœʀ, -øz] *nm/f* supplier.

fourniture [fuʀnityʀ] *nf* supply(ing); ~**s** *nfpl* supplies; ~**s de bureau** office supplies, stationery; ~**s scolaires** school stationery.

fourrage [fuʀaʒ] *nm* fodder.

fourrager [fuʀaʒe] *vi*: ~ **dans/parmi** to rummage through/among.

fourrager, ère [fuʀaʒe, -ɛʀ] *adj* fodder *cpd* ♦ *nf* (*MIL*) fourragère.

fourré, e [fuʀe] *adj* (*bonbon, chocolat*) filled; (*manteau, botte*) fur-lined ♦ *nm* thicket.

fourreau, x [fuʀo] *nm* sheath; (*de parapluie*) cover; **robe/jupe ~** figure-hugging dress/skirt.

fourrer [fuʀe] *vt* (*fam*): ~ **qch dans** to stick *ou* shove sth into; **se ~ dans/sous** to get into/under; **se ~ dans** (*une mauvaise situation*) to land o.s. in.

fourre-tout [fuʀtu] *nm inv* (*sac*) holdall; (*péj*) junk room (*ou* cupboard); (*fig*) rag-bag.

fourreur [fuʀœʀ] *nm* furrier.

fourrière [fuʀjɛʀ] *nf* pound.

fourrure [fuʀyʀ] *nf* fur; (*sur l'animal*) coat; **manteau/col de ~** fur coat/collar.

fourvoyer [fuʀvwaje]: **se ~** *vi* to go astray, stray; **se ~ dans** to stray into.

foutre [futʀ(ə)] *vt* (*fam!*) = **ficher** (*fam*).

foutu, e [futy] *adj* (*fam!*) = **fichu**.

foyer [fwaje] *nm* (*de cheminée*) hearth; (*fig*) seat, centre; (*famille*) family; (*domicile*) home; (*local de réunion*) (social) club; (*résidence*) hostel; (*salon*) foyer; (*OPTIQUE, PHOTO*) focus; **lunettes à double ~** bi-focal glasses.

FP *sigle f* (= *franchise postale*) *exemption from postage*.

FPA *sigle f* (= *Formation professionnelle pour adultes*) adult education.

FPLP *sigle m* (= *Front populaire de la libération de la Palestine*) PFLP (= *Popular Front for the Liberation of Palestine*).

FR3 [ɛfɛʀtʀwa] *sigle f* (= *France Régions 3*) *TV channel*.

fracas [fʀaka] *nm* din; crash.
fracassant, e [fʀakasɑ̃, -ɑ̃t] *adj* sensational, staggering.
fracasser [fʀakase] *vt* to smash; **se ~ contre** *ou* **sur** to crash against.
fraction [fʀaksjɔ̃] *nf* fraction.
fractionnement [fʀaksjɔnmɑ̃] *nm* division.
fractionner [fʀaksjɔne] *vt* to divide (up), split (up).
fracture [fʀaktyʀ] *nf* fracture; **~ du crâne** fractured skull; **~ de la jambe** broken leg.
fracturer [fʀaktyʀe] *vt* (*coffre, serrure*) to break open; (*os, membre*) to fracture.
fragile [fʀaʒil] *adj* fragile, delicate; (*fig*) frail.
fragiliser [fʀaʒilize] *vt* to weaken, make fragile.
fragilité [fʀaʒilite] *nf* fragility.
fragment [fʀagmɑ̃] *nm* (*d'un objet*) fragment, piece; (*d'un texte*) passage, extract.
fragmentaire [fʀagmɑ̃tɛʀ] *adj* sketchy.
fragmenter [fʀagmɑ̃te] *vt* to split up.
frai [fʀɛ] *nm* spawn; (*ponte*) spawning.
fraîche [fʀɛʃ] *adj f voir* **frais**.
fraîchement [fʀɛʃmɑ̃] *adv* (*sans enthousiasme*) coolly; (*récemment*) freshly, newly.
fraîcheur [fʀɛʃœʀ] *nf* (*voir frais*) coolness; freshness.
fraîchir [fʀɛʃiʀ] *vi* to get cooler; (*vent*) to freshen.
frais, fraîche [fʀɛ, fʀɛʃ] *adj* (*air, eau, accueil*) cool; (*petit pois, œufs, nouvelles, couleur, troupes*) fresh; **le voilà ~!** he's in a (right) mess! ♦ *adv* (*récemment*) newly, fresh(ly); **il fait ~** it's cool; **servir ~** chill before serving, serve chilled ♦ *nm*: **mettre au ~** to put in a cool place; **prendre le ~** to take a breath of cool air ♦ *nmpl* (*débours*) expenses; (*COMM*) costs; charges; **faire des ~** to spend; to go to a lot of expense; **faire les ~ de** to bear the brunt of; **faire les ~ de la conversation** (*parler*) to do most of the talking; (*en être le sujet*) to be the topic of conversation; **il en a été pour ses ~** he could have spared himself the trouble; **rentrer dans ses ~** to recover one's expenses; **~ de déplacement** travel(ling) expenses; **~ d'entretien** upkeep; **~ généraux** overheads; **~ de scolarité** school fees, tuition (*US*).
fraise [fʀɛz] *nf* strawberry; (*TECH*) countersink (bit); (*de dentiste*) drill; **~ des bois** wild strawberry.
fraiser [fʀeze] *vt* to countersink; (*CULIN: pâte*) to knead.
fraiseuse [fʀezøz] *nf* (*TECH*) milling machine.
fraisier [fʀezje] *nm* strawberry plant.
framboise [fʀɑ̃bwaz] *nf* raspberry.
framboisier [fʀɑ̃bwazje] *nm* raspberry bush.
franc, franche [fʀɑ̃, fʀɑ̃ʃ] *adj* (*personne*) frank, straightforward; (*visage*) open; (*net: refus, couleur*) clear; (: *coupure*) clean; (*intensif*) downright; (*exempt*): **~ de port** post free, postage paid; (*zone, port*) free;

(*boutique*) duty-free ♦ *adv*: **parler ~** to be frank *ou* candid ♦ *nm* franc.
français, e [fʀɑ̃sɛ, -ɛz] *adj* French ♦ *nm* (*LING*) French ♦ *nm/f*: **F~, e** Frenchman/woman; **les F~** the French.
franc-comtois, e, *mpl* **francs-comtois** [fʀɑ̃kɔ̃twa, -waz] *adj* of *ou* from (the) Franche-Comté.
France [fʀɑ̃s] *nf*: **la ~** France; **en ~** in France.
Francfort [fʀɑ̃kfɔʀ] *n* Frankfurt.
franche [fʀɑ̃ʃ] *adj f voir* **franc**.
Franche-Comté [fʀɑ̃ʃkɔ̃te] *nf* Franche-Comté.
franchement [fʀɑ̃ʃmɑ̃] *adv* (*voir franc*) frankly; clearly; (*tout à fait*) downright ♦ *excl* well, really!
franchir [fʀɑ̃ʃiʀ] *vt* (*obstacle*) to clear, get over; (*seuil, ligne, rivière*) to cross; (*distance*) to cover.
franchisage [fʀɑ̃ʃizaʒ] *nm* (*COMM*) franchising.
franchise [fʀɑ̃ʃiz] *nf* frankness; (*douanière, d'impôt*) exemption; (*ASSURANCES*) excess; (*COMM*) franchise; **~ de bagages** baggage allowance.
franchissable [fʀɑ̃ʃisabl(ə)] *adj* (*obstacle*) surmountable.
francilien, ne [fʀɑ̃siljɛ̃, -ɛn] *adj* of *ou* from the Île-de-France region ♦ *nm/f*: **F~, ne** person from the Île-de-France region.
franciscain, e [fʀɑ̃siskɛ̃, -ɛn] *adj* Franciscan.
franciser [fʀɑ̃size] *vt* to gallicize, Frenchify.
franc-jeu [fʀɑ̃ʒø] *nm*: **jouer ~** to play fair.
franc-maçon, *pl* **francs-maçons** [fʀɑ̃masɔ̃] *nm* Freemason.
franc-maçonnerie [fʀɑ̃masɔnʀi] *nf* Freemasonry.
franco [fʀɑ̃ko] *adv* (*COMM*): **~ (de port)** postage paid.
franco... [fʀɑ̃ko] *préfixe* franco-.
franco-canadien [fʀɑ̃kokanadjɛ̃] *nm* (*LING*) Canadian French.
francophile [fʀɑ̃kɔfil] *adj* Francophile.
francophobe [fʀɑ̃kɔfɔb] *adj* Francophobe.
francophone [fʀɑ̃kɔfɔn] *adj* French-speaking ♦ *nm/f* French speaker.
francophonie [fʀɑ̃kɔfɔni] *nf* French-speaking communities *pl*.
franco-québécois [fʀɑ̃kokebekwa] *nm* (*LING*) Quebec French.
franc-parler [fʀɑ̃paʀle] *nm inv* outspokenness.
franc-tireur [fʀɑ̃tiʀœʀ] *nm* (*MIL*) irregular; (*fig*) freelance.
frange [fʀɑ̃ʒ] *nf* fringe; (*cheveux*) fringe (*BRIT*), bangs (*US*).
frangé, e [fʀɑ̃ʒe] *adj* (*tapis, nappe*): **~ de** trimmed with.
frangin [fʀɑ̃ʒɛ̃] *nm* (*fam*) brother.
frangine [fʀɑ̃ʒin] *nf* (*fam*) sis, sister.
frangipane [fʀɑ̃ʒipan] *nf* almond paste.
franglais [fʀɑ̃glɛ] *nm* Franglais.
franquette [fʀɑ̃kɛt]: **à la bonne ~** *adv* without any fuss.

frappant, e [fʀapɑ̃, -ɑ̃t] adj striking.

frappe [fʀap] nf (d'une dactylo, pianiste, machine à écrire) touch; (BOXE) punch; (péj) hood, thug.

frappé, e [fʀape] adj (CULIN) iced; ~ **de panique** panic-stricken; ~ **de stupeur** thunderstruck, dumbfounded.

frapper [fʀape] vt to hit, strike; (étonner) to strike; (monnaie) to strike, stamp; **se** ~ vi (s'inquiéter) to get worked up; ~ **à la porte** to knock at the door; ~ **dans ses mains** to clap one's hands; ~ **du poing sur** to bang one's fist on; ~ **un grand coup** (fig) to strike a blow.

frasques [fʀask(ə)] nfpl escapades; **faire des** ~**s** to get up to mischief.

fraternel, le [fʀatɛʀnɛl] adj brotherly, fraternal.

fraternellement [fʀatɛʀnɛlmɑ̃] adv in a brotherly way.

fraterniser [fʀatɛʀnize] vi to fraternize.

fraternité [fʀatɛʀnite] nf brotherhood.

fratricide [fʀatʀisid] adj fratricidal.

fraude [fʀod] nf fraud; (SCOL) cheating; **passer qch en** ~ to smuggle sth in (ou out); ~ **fiscale** tax evasion.

frauder [fʀode] vi, vt to cheat; ~ **le fisc** to evade paying tax(es).

fraudeur, euse [fʀodœʀ, -øz] nm/f person guilty of fraud; (candidat) candidate who cheats; (au fisc) tax evader.

frauduleux, euse [fʀodylø, -øz] adj fraudulent.

frauduleusement [fʀodyløzmɑ̃] adv fraudulently.

frayer [fʀeje] vt to open up, clear ♦ vi to spawn; (fréquenter): ~ **avec** to mix ou associate with; **se** ~ **un passage dans** to clear o.s. a path through, force one's way through.

frayeur [fʀejœʀ] nf fright.

fredaines [fʀədɛn] nfpl mischief sg, escapades.

fredonner [fʀədɔne] vt to hum.

freezer [fʀizœʀ] nm freezing compartment.

frégate [fʀegat] nf frigate.

frein [fʀɛ̃] nm brake; **mettre un** ~ **à** (fig) to put a brake on, check; **sans** ~ (sans limites) unchecked; ~ **à main** handbrake; ~ **moteur** engine braking; ~**s à disques** disc brakes; ~**s à tambour** drum brakes.

freinage [fʀɛnaʒ] nm braking; **distance de** ~ braking distance; **traces de** ~ tyre (BRIT) ou tire (US) marks.

freiner [fʀene] vi to brake ♦ vt (progrès etc) to check.

frelaté, e [fʀəlate] adj adulterated; (fig) tainted.

frêle [fʀɛl] adj frail, fragile.

frelon [fʀəlɔ̃] nm hornet.

freluquet [fʀəlykɛ] nm (péj) whippersnapper.

frémir [fʀemiʀ] vi (de froid, de peur) to tremble, shiver; (de joie) to quiver; (eau) to

(begin to) bubble.

frémissement [fʀemismɑ̃] nm shiver; quiver; bubbling no pl.

frêne [fʀɛn] nm ash (tree).

frénésie [fʀenezi] nf frenzy.

frénétique [fʀenetik] adj frenzied, frenetic.

frénétiquement [fʀenetikmɑ̃] adv frenetically.

fréon [fʀeɔ̃] nm ® Freon ®.

fréquemment [fʀekamɑ̃] adv frequently.

fréquence [fʀekɑ̃s] nf frequency.

fréquent, e [fʀekɑ̃, -ɑ̃t] adj frequent.

fréquentable [fʀekɑ̃tabl(ə)] adj: **il est peu** ~ he's not the type one can associate oneself with.

fréquentation [fʀekɑ̃tɑsjɔ̃] nf frequenting; seeing; ~**s** nfpl company sg.

fréquenté, e [fʀekɑ̃te] adj: **très** ~ (very) busy; **mal** ~ patronized by disreputable elements.

fréquenter [fʀekɑ̃te] vt (lieu) to frequent; (personne) to see; **se** ~ to see a lot of each other.

frère [fʀɛʀ] nm brother ♦ adj: **partis/pays** ~**s** sister parties/countries.

fresque [fʀɛsk(ə)] nf (ART) fresco.

fret [fʀɛ] nm freight.

fréter [fʀete] vt to charter.

frétiller [fʀetije] vi to wriggle; to quiver; ~ **de la queue** to wag its tail.

fretin [fʀətɛ̃] nm: **le menu** ~ the small fry.

freudien, ne [fʀødjɛ̃, -ɛn] adj Freudian.

freux [fʀø] nm (ZOOL) rook.

friable [fʀijabl(ə)] adj crumbly.

friand, e [fʀijɑ̃, -ɑ̃d] adj: ~ **de** very fond of ♦ nm (CULIN) small minced-meat (BRIT) ou ground-meat (US) pie; (: sucré) small almond cake.

friandise [fʀijɑ̃diz] nf sweet.

fric [fʀik] nm (fam) cash, bread.

fricassée [fʀikase] nf fricassee.

fric-frac [fʀikfʀak] nm break-in.

friche [fʀiʃ]: **en** ~ adj, adv (lying) fallow.

friction [fʀiksjɔ̃] nf (massage) rub, rub-down; (chez le coiffeur) scalp massage; (TECH, fig) friction.

frictionner [fʀiksjɔne] vt to rub (down); to massage.

frigidaire [fʀiʒidɛʀ] nm ® refrigerator.

frigide [fʀiʒid] adj frigid.

frigidité [fʀiʒidite] nf frigidity.

frigo [fʀigo] nm (= frigidaire) fridge.

frigorifier [fʀigɔʀifje] vt to refrigerate; (fig: personne) to freeze.

frigorifique [fʀigɔʀifik] adj refrigerating.

frileusement [fʀiløzmɑ̃] adv with a shiver.

frileux, euse [fʀilø, -øz] adj sensitive to (the) cold; (fig) overcautious.

frimas [fʀima] nmpl wintry weather sg.

frime [fʀim] nf (fam): **c'est de la** ~ it's all put on; **pour la** ~ just for show.

frimer [fʀime] vi to put on an act.

frimeur, euse [fʀimœʀ, -øz] nm/f poser.

frimousse [fʀimus] _nf_ (sweet) little face.
fringale [fʀɛ̃gal] _nf_: **avoir la** ~ to be ravenous.
fringant, e [fʀɛ̃gɑ̃, -ɑ̃t] _adj_ dashing.
fringues [fʀɛ̃g] _nfpl_ (_fam_) clothes, gear _no pl._
fripé, e [fʀipe] _adj_ crumpled.
friperie [fʀipʀi] _nf_ (_commerce_) secondhand clothes shop; (_vêtements_) secondhand clothes.
fripes [fʀip] _nfpl_ secondhand clothes.
fripier, ière [fʀipje, -jɛʀ] _nm/f_ secondhand clothes dealer.
fripon, ne [fʀipɔ̃, -ɔn] _adj_ roguish, mischievous ♦ _nm/f_ rascal, rogue.
fripouille [fʀipuj] _nf_ scoundrel.
frire [fʀiʀ] _vt_ (_aussi:_ **faire** ~), _vi_ to fry.
Frisbee [fʀizbi] _nm_ ® Frisbee ®.
frise [fʀiz] _nf_ frieze.
frisé, e [fʀize] _adj_ curly, curly-haired ♦ _nf_: (**chicorée**) ~**e** curly endive.
friser [fʀize] _vt_ to curl; (_fig: surface_) to skim, graze; (: _mort_) to come within a hair's breadth of; (: _hérésie_) to verge on ♦ _vi_ (_cheveux_) to curl; (_personne_) to have curly hair; **se faire** ~ to have one's hair curled.
frisette [fʀizɛt] _nf_ little curl.
frisotter [fʀizɔte] _vi_ (_cheveux_) to curl tightly.
frisquet [fʀiskɛ] _adj m_ chilly.
frisson [fʀisɔ̃], **frissonnement** [fʀisɔnmɑ̃] _nm_ shudder, shiver; quiver.
frissonner [fʀisɔne] _vi_ (_personne_) to shudder, shiver; (_feuilles_) to quiver.
frit, e [fʀi, fʀit] _pp de_ **frire** ♦ _adj_ fried ♦ _nf_: (**pommes**) ~**es** chips (_BRIT_), French fries.
friterie [fʀitʀi] _nf_ ≈ chip shop (_BRIT_), ≈ hamburger stand (_US_).
friteuse [fʀitøz] _nf_ chip pan (_BRIT_), deep (fat) fryer.
friture [fʀityʀ] _nf_ (_huile_) (deep) fat; (_plat_): ~ (**de poissons**) fried fish; (_RADIO_) crackle, crackling _no pl_; ~**s** _nfpl_ (_aliments frits_) fried food _sg._
frivole [fʀivɔl] _adj_ frivolous.
frivolité [fʀivɔlite] _nf_ frivolity.
froc [fʀɔk] _nm_ (_REL_) habit; (_fam: pantalon_) trousers _pl_, pants _pl._
froid, e [fʀwa, fʀwad] _adj_ cold ♦ _nm_ cold; (_absence de sympathie_) coolness _no pl_; **il fait** ~ it's cold; **avoir** ~ to be cold; **prendre** ~ to catch a chill _ou_ cold; **à** ~ _adv_ (_démarrer_) (from) cold; (**pendant**) **les grands** ~**s** (in) the depths of winter, (during) the cold season; **jeter un** ~ (_fig_) to cast a chill; **être en** ~ **avec** to be on bad terms with; **battre** ~ **à qn** to give sb the cold shoulder.
froidement [fʀwadmɑ̃] _adv_ (_accueillir_) coldly; (_décider_) coolly.
froideur [fʀwadœʀ] _nf_ coolness _no pl._
froisser [fʀwase] _vt_ to crumple (up), crease; (_fig_) to hurt, offend; **se** ~ _vi_ to crumple, crease; to take offence (_BRIT_) _ou_ offense (_US_); **se** ~ **un muscle** to strain a muscle.
frôlement [fʀolmɑ̃] _nm_ (_contact_) light touch.

frôler [fʀole] _vt_ to brush against; (_suj: projectile_) to skim past; (_fig_) to come within a hair's breadth of, come very close to.
fromage [fʀɔmaʒ] _nm_ cheese; ~ **blanc** soft white cheese; ~ **de tête** pork brawn.
fromager, ère [fʀɔmaʒe, -ɛʀ] _nm/f_ cheese merchant ♦ _adj_ (_industrie_) cheese _cpd._
fromagerie [fʀɔmaʒʀi] _nf_ cheese dairy.
froment [fʀɔmɑ̃] _nm_ wheat.
fronce [fʀɔ̃s] _nf_ (_de tissu_) gather.
froncement [fʀɔ̃smɑ̃] _nm_: ~ **de sourcils** frown.
froncer [fʀɔ̃se] _vt_ to gather; ~ **les sourcils** to frown.
frondaison [fʀɔ̃dɛzɔ̃] _nf_ foliage.
fronde [fʀɔ̃d] _nf_ sling; (_fig_) rebellion, rebelliousness.
frondeur, euse [fʀɔ̃dœʀ, -øz] _adj_ rebellious.
front [fʀɔ̃] _nm_ forehead, brow; (_MIL, MÉTÉOROLOGIE, POL_) front; **avoir le** ~ **de faire** to have the effrontery _ou_ front to do; **de** ~ _adv_ (_se heurter_) head-on; (_rouler_) together (_i.e. 2 or 3 abreast_); (_simultanément_) at once; **faire** ~ **à** to face up to; ~ **de mer** (sea) front.
frontal, e, aux [fʀɔ̃tal, -o] _adj_ frontal.
frontalier, ière [fʀɔ̃talje, -jɛʀ] _adj_ border _cpd_, frontier _cpd_ ♦ _nm/f_: (**travailleurs**) ~**s** workers who cross the border to go to work, commuters from across the border.
frontière [fʀɔ̃tjɛʀ] _nf_ (_GÉO, POL_) frontier, border; (_fig_) frontier, boundary.
frontispice [fʀɔ̃tispis] _nm_ frontispiece.
fronton [fʀɔ̃tɔ̃] _nm_ pediment; (_de pelote basque_) (front) wall.
frottement [fʀɔtmɑ̃] _nm_ rubbing, scraping; ~**s** _nmpl_ (_fig: difficultés_) friction _sg._
frotter [fʀɔte] _vi_ to rub, scrape ♦ _vt_ to rub; (_pour nettoyer_) to rub (up); (: _avec une brosse_) to scrub; ~ **une allumette** to strike a match; **se** ~ **à qn** to cross swords with sb; **se** ~ **à qch** to come up against sth; **se** ~ **les mains** (_fig_) to rub one's hands (gleefully).
frottis [fʀɔti] _nm_ (_MÉD_) smear.
frottoir [fʀɔtwaʀ] _nm_ (_d'allumettes_) friction strip; (_pour encaustiquer_) (long-handled) brush.
frou-frou, _pl_ **frous-frous** [fʀufʀu] _nm_ rustle.
frousse [fʀus] _nf_ (_fam: peur_): **avoir la** ~ to be in a blue funk.
fructifier [fʀyktifje] _vi_ to yield a profit; **faire** ~ to turn to good account.
fructueux, euse [fʀyktɥø, -øz] _adj_ fruitful; profitable.
frugal, e, aux [fʀygal, -o] _adj_ frugal.
frugalement [fʀygalmɑ̃] _adv_ frugally.
frugalité [fʀygalite] _nf_ frugality.
fruit [fʀɥi] _nm_ fruit _gén no pl_; ~**s de mer** (_CULIN_) seafood(s); ~**s secs** dried fruit _sg._
fruité, e [fʀɥite] _adj_ (_vin_) fruity.
fruiterie [fʀɥitʀi] _nf_ (_boutique_) greengrocer's (_BRIT_), fruit (and vegetable) store (_US_).
fruitier, ière [fʀɥitje, -jɛʀ] _adj_: **arbre** ~ fruit tree ♦ _nm/f_ fruiterer (_BRIT_), fruit

merchant (*US*).

fruste [fʀyst(ə)] *adj* unpolished, uncultivated.

frustrant, e [fʀystʀɑ̃, -ɑ̃t] *adj* frustrating.

frustration [fʀystʀasjɔ̃] *nf* frustration.

frustré, e [fʀystʀe] *adj* frustrated.

frustrer [fʀystʀe] *vt* to frustrate; (*priver*): ~ **qn de qch** to deprive sb of sth.

FS *abr* (= *franc suisse*) FS, SF.

FSE *sigle m* (= *foyer socio-éducatif*) community home.

FTP *sigle mpl* (= *Francs-tireurs et partisans*) *Communist Resistance in 1940-45.*

fuchsia [fyʃja] *nm* fuchsia.

fuel(-oil) [fjul(ɔjl)] *nm* fuel oil; (*pour chauffer*) heating oil.

fugace [fygas] *adj* fleeting.

fugitif, ive [fyʒitif, -iv] *adj* (*lueur, amour*) fleeting; (*prisonnier etc*) runaway ♦ *nm/f* fugitive, runaway.

fugue [fyg] *nf* (*d'un enfant*) running away *no pl*; (*MUS*) fugue; **faire une** ~ to run away, abscond.

fuir [fɥiʀ] *vt* to flee from; (*éviter*) to shun ♦ *vi* to run away; (*gaz, robinet*) to leak.

fuite [fɥit] *nf* flight; (*écoulement*) leak, leakage; (*divulgation*) leak; **être en** ~ to be on the run; **mettre en** ~ to put to flight; **prendre la** ~ to take flight.

fulgurant, e [fylgyʀɑ̃, -ɑ̃t] *adj* lightning *cpd*, dazzling.

fulminant, e [fylminɑ̃, -ɑ̃t] *adj* (*lettre, regard*) furious; ~ **de colère** raging with anger.

fulminer [fylmine] *vi*: ~ (**contre**) to thunder forth (against).

fumant, e [fymɑ̃, -ɑ̃t] *adj* smoking; (*liquide*) steaming; **un coup** ~ (*fam*) a master stroke.

fumé, e [fyme] *adj* (*CULIN*) smoked; (*verre*) tinted ♦ *nf* smoke; **partir en** ~**e** to go up in smoke.

fume-cigarette [fymsigaʀɛt] *nm inv* cigarette holder.

fumer [fyme] *vi* to smoke; (*liquide*) to steam ♦ *vt* to smoke; (*terre, champ*) to manure.

fumerie [fymʀi] *nf*: ~ **d'opium** opium den.

fumerolles [fymʀɔl] *nfpl* gas and smoke (*from volcano*).

fûmes [fym] *vb voir* **être**.

fumet [fymɛ] *nm* aroma.

fumeur, euse [fymœʀ, -øz] *nm/f* smoker; (**compartiment**) ~**s** smoking compartment.

fumeux, euse [fymø, -øz] *adj* (*péj*) woolly (*BRIT*), hazy.

fumier [fymje] *nm* manure.

fumigation [fymigasjɔ̃] *nf* fumigation.

fumigène [fymiʒɛn] *adj* smoke *cpd*.

fumiste [fymist(ə)] *nm* (*ramoneur*) chimney sweep ♦ *nm/f* (*péj: paresseux*) shirker; (*charlatan*) phoney.

fumisterie [fymistəʀi] *nf* (*péj*) fraud, con.

fumoir [fymwaʀ] *nm* smoking room.

funambule [fynɑ̃byl] *nm* tightrope walker.

funèbre [fynɛbʀ(ə)] *adj* funeral *cpd*; (*fig*)

doleful; funereal.

funérailles [fyneʀɑj] *nfpl* funeral *sg*.

funéraire [fyneʀɛʀ] *adj* funeral *cpd*, funerary.

funeste [fynɛst(ə)] *adj* disastrous; deathly.

funiculaire [fynikylɛʀ] *nm* funicular (railway).

FUNU [fyny] *sigle f* (= *Force d'urgence des Nations unies*) UNEF (= *United Nations Emergency Forces*).

fur [fyʀ]: **au** ~ **et à mesure** *adv* as one goes along; **au** ~ **et à mesure que** as; **au** ~ **et à mesure de leur progression** as they advance (*ou* advanced).

furax [fyʀaks] *adj inv* (*fam*) livid.

furent [fyʀ] *vb voir* **être**.

furet [fyʀɛ] *nm* ferret.

fureter [fyʀte] *vi* (*péj*) to nose about.

fureur [fyʀœʀ] *nf* fury; (*passion*): ~ **de passion** for; **faire** ~ to be all the rage.

furibard, e [fyʀibaʀ, -aʀd(ə)] *adj* (*fam*) livid, absolutely furious.

furibond, e [fyʀibɔ̃, -ɔ̃d] *adj* livid, absolutely furious.

furie [fyʀi] *nf* fury; (*femme*) shrew, vixen; **en** ~ (*mer*) raging.

furieusement [fyʀjøzmɑ̃] *adv* furiously.

furieux, euse [fyʀjø, -øz] *adj* furious.

furoncle [fyʀɔ̃kl(ə)] *nm* boil.

furtif, ive [fyʀtif, -iv] *adj* furtive.

furtivement [fyʀtivmɑ̃] *adv* furtively.

fus [fy] *vb voir* **être**.

fusain [fyzɛ̃] *nm* (*BOT*) spindle-tree; (*ART*) charcoal.

fuseau, x [fyzo] *nm* (*pantalon*) (ski-)pants *pl*; (*pour filer*) spindle; **en** ~ (*jambes*) tapering; (*colonne*) bulging; ~ **horaire** time zone.

fusée [fyze] *nf* rocket; ~ **éclairante** flare.

fuselage [fyzlaʒ] *nm* fuselage.

fuselé, e [fyzle] *adj* slender; (*galbé*) tapering.

fuser [fyze] *vi* (*rires etc*) to burst forth.

fusible [fyzibl(ə)] *nm* (*ÉLEC: fil*) fuse wire; (: *fiche*) fuse.

fusil [fyzi] *nm* (*de guerre, à canon rayé*) rifle, gun; (*de chasse, à canon lisse*) shotgun, gun; ~ **à deux coups** double-barrelled rifle *ou* shotgun; ~ **sous-marin** spear-gun.

fusilier [fyzilje] *nm* (*MIL*) rifleman.

fusillade [fyzijad] *nf* gunfire *no pl*, shooting *no pl*; (*combat*) gun battle.

fusiller [fyzije] *vt* to shoot; ~ **qn du regard** to look daggers at sb.

fusil-mitrailleur, pl fusils-mitrailleurs [fyzimitʀajœʀ] *nm* machine gun.

fusion [fyzjɔ̃] *nf* fusion, melting; (*fig*) merging; (*COMM*) merger; **en** ~ (*métal, roches*) molten.

fusionnement [fyzjɔnmɑ̃] *nm* merger.

fusionner [fyzjɔne] *vi* to merge.

fustiger [fystiʒe] *vt* to denounce.

fut [fy] *vb voir* **être**.

fût [fy] *vb voir* **être** ♦ *nm* (*tonneau*) barrel, cask; (*de canon*) stock; (*d'arbre*) bole, trunk; (*de colonne*) shaft.

futaie [fytɛ] *nf* forest, plantation.
futé, e [fyte] *adj* crafty.
fûtes [fyt] *vb voir* **être**.
futile [fytil] *adj* (*inutile*) futile; (*frivole*) frivolous.
futilement [fytilmɑ̃] *adv* frivolously.
futilité [fytilite] *nf* futility; frivolousness; (*chose futile*) futile pursuit (*ou* thing *etc*).
futon [fytɔ̃] *nm* futon.
futur, e [fytyʀ] *adj*, *nm* future; **son ~ époux** her husband-to-be; **au ~** (*LING*) in the future.
futuriste [fytyʀist(ə)] *adj* futuristic.
futurologie [fytyʀɔlɔʒi] *nf* futurology.
fuyant, e [fɥijɑ̃, -ɑ̃t] *vb voir* **fuir** ♦ *adj* (*regard etc*) evasive; (*lignes etc*) receding; (*perspective*) vanishing.
fuyard, e [fɥijaʀ, -aʀd(ə)] *nm/f* runaway.
fuyons [fɥijɔ̃] *etc vb voir* **fuir**.

G g

G, g [ʒe] *nm inv* G, g ♦ *abr* (= *gramme*) g; (= *gauche*) L, l; **G comme Gaston** G for George; **le G7** (*POL*) the G7 nations, the Group of Seven.
gabardine [gabaʀdin] *nf* gabardine.
gabarit [gabaʀi] *nm* (*fig: dimension, taille*) size; (*: valeur*) calibre; (*TECH*) template; **du même ~** (*fig*) of the same type, of that ilk.
gabegie [gabʒi] *nf* (*péj*) chaos.
Gabon [gabɔ̃] *nm*: **le ~** Gabon.
gabonais, e [gabɔnɛ, -ɛz] *adj* Gabonese.
gâcher [gaʃe] *vt* (*gâter*) to spoil, ruin; (*gaspiller*) to waste; (*plâtre*) to temper; (*mortier*) to mix.
gâchette [gaʃɛt] *nf* trigger.
gâchis [gaʃi] *nm* (*désordre*) mess; (*gaspillage*) waste *no pl*.
gadget [gadʒɛt] *nm* thingumajig; (*nouveauté*) gimmick.
gadin [gadɛ̃] *nm* (*fam*): **prendre un ~** to come a cropper (*BRIT*).
gadoue [gadu] *nf* sludge.
gaélique [gaelik] *adj* Gaelic ♦ *nm* (*LING*) Gaelic.
gaffe [gaf] *nf* (*instrument*) boat hook; (*fam: erreur*) blunder; **faire ~** (*fam*) to watch out.
gaffer [gafe] *vi* to blunder.
gaffeur, euse [gafœʀ, -øz] *nm/f* blunderer.
gag [gag] *nm* gag.
gaga [gaga] *adj* (*fam*) gaga.
gage [gaʒ] *nm* (*dans un jeu*) forfeit; (*fig: de fidélité*) token; **~s** *nmpl* (*salaire*) wages; (*garantie*) guarantee *sg*; **mettre en ~** to

pawn; **laisser en ~** to leave as security.
gager [gaʒe] *vt*: **~ que** to bet *ou* wager that.
gageure [gaʒyʀ] *nf*: **c'est une ~** it's attempting the impossible.
gagnant, e [gaɲɑ̃, -ɑ̃t] *adj*: **billet/numéro ~** winning ticket/number ♦ *adv*: **jouer ~** (*aux courses*) to be bound to win ♦ *nm/f* winner.
gagne-pain [gaɲpɛ̃] *nm inv* job.
gagne-petit [gaɲpəti] *nm inv* low wage earner.
gagner [gaɲe] *vt* (*concours, procès, pari*) to win; (*somme d'argent, revenu*) to earn; (*aller vers, atteindre*) to reach; (*s'emparer de*) to overcome; (*envahir*) to spread to; (*se concilier*): **~ qn** to win sb over ♦ *vi* to win; (*fig*) to gain; **~ du temps/de la place** to gain time/save space; **~ sa vie** to earn one's living; **~ du terrain** (*aussi fig*) to gain ground; **~ qn de vitesse** (*aussi fig*) to outstrip sb; **~ à faire** (*s'en trouver bien*) to be better off doing; **il y gagne** it's in his interest, it's to his advantage.
gagneur [gaɲœʀ] *nm* winner.
gai, e [ge] *adj* cheerful; (*livre, pièce de théâtre*) light-hearted; (*un peu ivre*) merry.
gaiement [gemɑ̃] *adv* cheerfully.
gaieté [gete] *nf* cheerfulness; **~s** *nfpl* (*souvent ironique*) delights; **de ~ de cœur** with a light heart.
gaillard, e [gajaʀ, -aʀd(ə)] *adj* (*robuste*) sprightly; (*grivois*) bawdy, ribald ♦ *nm/f* (*strapping*) fellow/wench.
gaillardement [gajaʀdəmɑ̃] *adv* cheerfully.
gain [gɛ̃] *nm* (*revenu*) earnings *pl*; (*bénéfice: gén pl*) profits *pl*; (*au jeu: gén pl*) winnings *pl*; (*fig: de temps, place*) saving; (*: avantage*) benefit; (*: lucre*) gain; **avoir ~ de cause** to win the case; (*fig*) to be proved right; **obtenir ~ de cause** (*fig*) to win out.
gaine [gɛn] *nf* (*corset*) girdle; (*fourreau*) sheath; (*de fil électrique etc*) outer covering.
gaine-culotte, *pl* **gaines-culottes** [gɛnkylɔt] *nf* pantie girdle.
gainer [gene] *vt* to cover.
gala [gala] *nm* official reception; **soirée de ~** gala evening.
galamment [galamɑ̃] *adv* courteously.
galant, e [galɑ̃, -ɑ̃t] *adj* (*courtois*) courteous, gentlemanly; (*entreprenant*) flirtatious, gallant; (*aventure, poésie*) amorous; **en ~e compagnie** (*homme*) with a lady friend; (*femme*) with a gentleman friend.
galanterie [galɑ̃tʀi] *nf* gallantry.
galantine [galɑ̃tin] *nf* galantine.
Galapagos [galapagɔs] *nfpl*: **les (îles) ~** the Galapagos Islands.
galaxie [galaksi] *nf* galaxy.
galbe [galb(ə)] *nm* curve(s); shapeliness.
galbé, e [galbe] *adj* (*jambes*) (well-)rounded; **bien ~** shapely.
gale [gal] *nf* (*MÉD*) scabies *sg*; (*de chien*) mange.
galéjade [galeʒad] *nf* tall story.

galère [galɛʀ] nf galley.

galérer [galeʀe] vi (fam) to work hard, slave (away).

galerie [galʀi] nf gallery; (THÉÂT) circle; (de voiture) roof rack; (fig: spectateurs) audience; ~ **marchande** shopping mall; ~ **de peinture** (private) art gallery.

galérien [galeʀjɛ̃] nm galley slave.

galet [galɛ] nm pebble; (TECH) wheel; ~**s** nmpl pebbles, shingle sg.

galette [galɛt] nf (gâteau) flat pastry cake; (crêpe) savoury pancake; **la ~ des Rois** cake traditionally eaten on Twelfth Night.

galeux, euse [galø, -øz] adj: **un chien ~** a mangy dog.

Galice [galis] nf: **la ~** Galicia (in Spain).

Galicie [galisi] nf: **la ~** Galicia (in Central Europe).

galiléen, ne [galileɛ̃, -ɛn] adj Galilean.

galimatias [galimatja] nm (péj) gibberish.

galipette [galipɛt] nf: **faire des ~s** to turn somersaults.

Galles [gal] nfpl: **le pays de ~** Wales.

gallicisme [galisism(ə)] nm French idiom; (tournure fautive) gallicism.

gallois, e [galwa, -waz] adj Welsh ♦ nm (LING) Welsh ♦ nm/f: **G~, e** Welshman/woman.

gallo-romain, e [galoʀɔmɛ̃, -ɛn] adj Gallo-Roman.

galoche [galɔʃ] nf clog.

galon [galɔ̃] nm (MIL) stripe; (décoratif) piece of braid; **prendre du ~** to be promoted.

galop [galo] nm gallop; **au ~** at a gallop; ~ **d'essai** (fig) trial run.

galopade [galɔpad] nf stampede.

galopant, e [galɔpɑ̃, -ɑ̃t] adj: **inflation ~e** galloping inflation; **démographie ~e** exploding population.

galoper [galɔpe] vi to gallop.

galopin [galɔpɛ̃] nm urchin, ragamuffin.

galvaniser [galvanize] vt to galvanize.

galvaudé, e [galvode] adj (expression) hackneyed; (mot) clichéd.

galvauder [galvode] vt to debase.

gambade [gɑ̃bad] nf: **faire des ~s** to skip ou frisk about.

gambader [gɑ̃bade] vi to skip ou frisk about.

gamberger [gɑ̃bɛʀʒe] (fam) vi to (have a) think ♦ vt to dream up.

Gambie [gɑ̃bi] nf: **la ~** (pays) Gambia; (fleuve) the Gambia.

gamelle [gamɛl] nf mess tin; billy can; (fam): **ramasser une ~** to fall flat on one's face.

gamin, e [gamɛ̃, -in] nm/f kid ♦ adj mischievous, playful.

gaminerie [gaminʀi] nf mischievousness, playfulness.

gamme [gam] nf (MUS) scale; (fig) range.

gammé, e [game] adj: **croix ~e** swastika.

Gand [gɑ̃] n Ghent.

gang [gɑ̃g] nm gang.

Gange [gɑ̃ʒ] nm: **le ~** the Ganges.

ganglion [gɑ̃glijɔ̃] nm ganglion; (lymphatique) gland; **avoir des ~s** to have swollen glands.

gangrène [gɑ̃gʀɛn] nf gangrene; (fig) corruption; corrupting influence.

gangster [gɑ̃gstɛʀ] nm gangster.

gangstérisme [gɑ̃gstɛʀism(ə)] nm gangsterism.

gangue [gɑ̃g] nf coating.

ganse [gɑ̃s] nf braid.

gant [gɑ̃] nm glove; **prendre des ~s** (fig) to handle the situation with kid gloves; **relever le ~** (fig) to take up the gauntlet; ~ **de crin** massage glove; ~ **de toilette** (face) flannel (BRIT), face cloth; ~**s de boxe** boxing gloves; ~**s de caoutchouc** rubber gloves.

ganté, e [gɑ̃te] adj: ~ **de blanc** wearing white gloves.

ganterie [gɑ̃tʀi] nf glove trade; (magasin) glove shop.

garage [gaʀaʒ] nm garage; ~ **à vélos** bicycle shed.

garagiste [gaʀaʒist(ə)] nm/f (propriétaire) garage owner; (mécanicien) garage mechanic.

garant, e [gaʀɑ̃, -ɑ̃t] nm/f guarantor ♦ nm guarantee; **se porter ~ de** to vouch for; to be answerable for.

garantie [gaʀɑ̃ti] nf guarantee, warranty; (gage) security, surety; **(bon de) ~** guarantee ou warranty slip; ~ **de bonne exécution** performance bond.

garantir [gaʀɑ̃tiʀ] vt to guarantee; (protéger): ~ **de** to protect from; **je vous garantis que** I can assure you that; **garanti pure laine/2 ans** guaranteed pure wool/for 2 years.

garce [gaʀs] nf (péj) bitch.

garçon [gaʀsɔ̃] nm boy; (célibataire) bachelor; (jeune homme) boy, lad; (aussi: ~ **de café**) waiter; ~ **boucher/coiffeur** butcher's/ hairdresser's assistant; ~ **de courses** messenger; ~ **d'écurie** stable lad; ~ **manqué** tomboy.

garçonnet [gaʀsɔnɛ] nm small boy.

garçonnière [gaʀsɔnjɛʀ] nf bachelor flat.

garde [gaʀd(ə)] nm (de prisonnier) guard; (de domaine etc) warden; (soldat, sentinelle) guardsman ♦ nf guarding; looking after; (soldats, BOXE, ESCRIME) guard; (faction) watch; (d'une arme) hilt; (TYPO: aussi: **page** ou **feuille de ~**) flyleaf; (: collée) endpaper; **de ~** adj, adv on duty; **monter la ~** to stand guard; **être sur ses ~s** to be on one's guard; **mettre en ~** to warn; **mise en ~** warning; **prendre ~** (à) to be careful (of); **avoir la ~ des enfants** (après divorce) to have custody of the children; ~ **champêtre** nm rural policeman; ~ **du corps** nm bodyguard; ~ **d'enfants** nf child minder; ~ **forestier** nm forest warden; ~ **mobile** nm, nf mobile guard; ~ **des Sceaux** nm ≈ Lord Chancellor (BRIT), ≈ Attorney General (US); ~ **à vue** nf (JUR) ≈ police custody.

garde-à-vous [gaʀdavu] _nm inv:_ **être/se mettre
au** ~ to be at/stand to attention; ~ **(fixe)!**
(_MIL_) attention!
garde-barrière, _pl_ **gardes-barrière(s)**
[gaʀdəbaʀjɛʀ] _nm/f_ level-crossing keeper.
garde-boue [gaʀdəbu] _nm inv_ mudguard.
garde-chasse, _pl_ **gardes-chasse(s)**
[gaʀdəʃas] _nm_ gamekeeper.
garde-côte [gaʀdəkot] _nm_ (_vaisseau_)
coastguard boat.
garde-feu [gaʀdəfø] _nm inv_ fender.
garde-fou [gaʀdəfu] _nm_ railing, parapet.
garde-malade, _pl_ **gardes-malade(s)**
[gaʀdəmalad] _nf_ home nurse.
garde-manger [gaʀdmɑ̃ʒe] _nm inv_ (_boîte_) meat
safe; (_placard_) pantry, larder.
garde-meuble [gaʀdəmœbl(ə)] _nm_ furniture
depository.
garde-pêche [gaʀdəpɛʃ] _nm inv_ (_personne_)
water bailiff; (_navire_) fisheries protection
ship.
garder [gaʀde] _vt_ (_conserver_) to keep; (: _sur soi:
vêtement, chapeau_) to keep on; (_surveiller:
enfants_) to look after; (: _immeuble, lieu,
prisonnier_) to guard; **se** ~ _vi_ (_aliment: se
conserver_) to keep; **se** ~ **de faire** to be
careful not to do; ~ **le lit/la chambre** to stay
in bed/indoors; ~ **le silence** to keep silent _ou_
quiet; ~ **la ligne** to keep one's figure; ~ **à
vue** to keep in custody; **pêche/chasse
gardée** private fishing/hunting (ground).
garderie [gaʀdəʀi] _nf_ day nursery, crèche.
garde-robe [gaʀdəʀɔb] _nf_ wardrobe.
gardeur, euse [gaʀdœʀ, -øz] _nm/f_ (_de vaches_)
cowherd; (_de chèvres_) goatherd.
gardian [gaʀdjɑ̃] _nm_ cowboy (_in the Camargue_).
gardien, ne [gaʀdjɛ̃, -ɛn] _nm/f_ (_garde_) guard;
(_de prison_) warder; (_de domaine, réserve_)
warden; (_de musée etc_) attendant; (_de phare,
cimetière_) keeper; (_d'immeuble_) caretaker;
(_fig_) guardian; ~ **de but** goalkeeper; ~ **de
nuit** night watchman; ~ **de la paix**
policeman.
gardiennage [gaʀdjɛnaʒ] _nm_ (_emploi_)
caretaking; **société de** ~ security firm.
gardon [gaʀdɔ̃] _nm_ roach.
gare [gaʀ] _nf_ (_railway_) station, train station
(_US_) ♦ _excl:_ ~ **à** ... mind ...!, watch out for ...!;
~ **à ne pas** ... mind you don't ...; ~ **à toi!**
watch out!; **sans crier** ~ without warning; ~
maritime harbour station; ~ **routière** coach
(_BRIT_) _ou_ bus station; (_camions_) haulage
(_BRIT_) _ou_ trucking (_US_) depot; ~ **de triage**
marshalling yard.
garenne [gaʀɛn] _nf voir_ **lapin**.
garer [gaʀe] _vt_ to park; **se** ~ to park; (_pour
laisser passer_) to draw into the side.
gargantuesque [gaʀgɑ̃tɥɛsk(ə)] _adj_
gargantuan.
gargariser [gaʀgaʀize]: **se** ~ _vi_ to gargle; **se** ~
de (_fig_) to revel in.
gargarisme [gaʀgaʀism(ə)] _nm_ gargling _no pl_;

(_produit_) gargle.
gargote [gaʀgɔt] _nf_ cheap restaurant, greasy
spoon (_fam_).
gargouille [gaʀguj] _nf_ gargoyle.
gargouillement [gaʀgujmɑ̃] _nm_ = **gargouillis.**
gargouiller [gaʀguje] _vi_ (_estomac_) to rumble;
(_eau_) to gurgle.
gargouillis [gaʀguji] _nm_ (_gén pl: voir vb_)
rumbling; gurgling.
garnement [gaʀnəmɑ̃] _nm_ rascal, scallywag.
garni, e [gaʀni] _adj_ (_plat_) served with
vegetables (_and chips or pasta or rice_) ♦ _nm_
(_appartement_) furnished accommodation _no
pl_ (_BRIT_) _ou_ accommodations _pl_ (_US_).
garnir [gaʀniʀ] _vt_ to decorate; (_remplir_) to fill;
(_recouvrir_) to cover; **se** ~ _vi_ (_pièce, salle_) to fill
up; ~ **qch de** (_orner_) to decorate sth with; to
trim sth with; (_approvisionner_) to fill _ou_
stock sth with; (_protéger_) to fit sth with;
(_CULIN_) to garnish sth with.
garnison [gaʀnizɔ̃] _nf_ garrison.
garniture [gaʀnityʀ] _nf_ (_CULIN: légumes_)
vegetables _pl_; (: _persil etc_) garnish; (: _farce_)
filling; (_décoration_) trimming; (_protection_)
fittings _pl_; ~ **de cheminée** mantelpiece
ornaments _pl_; ~ **de frein** (_AUTO_) brake
lining; ~ **intérieure** (_AUTO_) interior trim; ~
périodique sanitary towel (_BRIT_) _ou_ napkin
(_US_).
garrigue [gaʀig] _nf_ scrubland.
garrot [gaʀo] _nm_ (_MÉD_) tourniquet; (_torture_)
garrotte.
garrotter [gaʀote] _vt_ to tie up; (_fig_) to muzzle.
gars [gɑ] _nm_ lad; (_type_) guy.
Gascogne [gaskɔɲ] _nf:_ **la** ~ Gascony.
gascon, ne [gaskɔ̃, -ɔn] _adj_ Gascon ♦ _nm:_ **G**~
(_hâbleur_) braggart.
gas-oil [gazɔjl] _nm_ diesel oil.
gaspillage [gaspijaʒ] _nm_ waste.
gaspiller [gaspije] _vt_ to waste.
gaspilleur, euse [gaspijœʀ, -øz] _adj_ wasteful.
gastrique [gastʀik] _adj_ gastric, stomach _cpd_.
gastro-entérite [gastʀoɑ̃teʀit] _nf_ (_MÉD_)
gastro-enteritis.
gastro-intestinal, e, aux [gastʀoɛ̃tɛstinal, -o]
adj gastrointestinal.
gastronome [gastʀonɔm] _nm/f_ gourmet.
gastronomie [gastʀonɔmi] _nf_ gastronomy.
gastronomique [gastʀonɔmik] _adj:_ **menu** ~
gourmet menu.
gâteau, x [gɑto] _nm_ cake ♦ _adj inv_ (_fam: trop
indulgent_): **papa-/maman-**~ doting father/
mother; ~ **d'anniversaire** birthday cake; ~
de riz ≈ rice pudding; ~ **sec** biscuit.
gâter [gɑte] _vt_ to spoil; **se** ~ _vi_ (_dent, fruit_) to go
bad; (_temps, situation_) to change for the
worse.
gâterie [gɑtʀi] _nf_ little treat.
gâteux, euse [gɑtø, -øz] _adj_ senile.
gâtisme [gɑtism(ə)] _nm_ senility.
GATT [gat] _sigle m_ (= _General Agreement on
Tariffs and Trade_) GATT.

gauche [goʃ] *adj* left, left-hand; *(maladroit)* awkward, clumsy ♦ *nf* (POL) left (wing); *(BOXE)* left; **à ~** on the left; *(direction)* (to the) left; **à ~ de** (on *ou* to the) left of; **à la ~ de** to the left of; **de ~** (POL) left-wing.

gauchement [goʃmɑ̃] *adv* awkwardly, clumsily.

gaucher, ère [goʃe, -ɛʀ] *adj* left-handed.

gaucherie [goʃʀi] *nf* awkwardness, clumsiness.

gauchir [goʃiʀ] *vt (planche, objet)* to warp; *(fig: fait, idée)* to distort.

gauchisant, e [goʃizɑ̃, -ɑ̃t] *adj* with left-wing tendencies.

gauchisme [goʃism(ə)] *nm* leftism.

gauchiste [goʃist(ə)] *adj, nm/f* leftist.

gaufre [gofʀ(ə)] *nf (pâtisserie)* waffle; *(de cire)* honeycomb.

gaufrer [gofʀe] *vt (papier)* to emboss; *(tissu)* to goffer.

gaufrette [gofʀɛt] *nf* wafer.

gaufrier [gofʀije] *nm (moule)* waffle iron.

Gaule [gol] *nf*: **la ~** Gaul.

gaule [gol] *nf (perche)* (long) pole; *(canne à pêche)* fishing rod.

gauler [gole] *vt (arbre)* to beat *(using a long pole to bring down fruit etc)*; *(fruits)* to beat down *(with a pole)*.

gaullisme [golism(ə)] *nm* Gaullism.

gaulliste [golist(ə)] *adj, nm/f* Gaullist.

gaulois, e [golwa, -waz] *adj* Gallic; *(grivois)* bawdy ♦ *nm/f*: **G~, e** Gaul.

gauloiserie [golwazʀi] *nf* bawdiness.

gausser [gose]: **se ~ de** *vt* to deride.

gaver [gave] *vt* to force-feed; *(fig)*: **~ de** to cram with, fill up with; *(personne)*: **se ~ de** to stuff o.s. with.

gay [gɛ] *adj, nm (fam)* gay.

gaz [gaz] *nm inv* gas; **mettre les ~** (AUTO) to put one's foot down; **chambre/masque à ~** gas chamber/mask; **~ en bouteille** bottled gas; **~ butane** Calor gas ® (BRIT), butane gas; **~ carbonique** carbon dioxide; **~ hilarant** laughing gas; **~ lacrymogène** tear gas; **~ naturel** natural gas; **~ de ville** town gas (BRIT), manufactured domestic gas.

gaze [gaz] *nf* gauze.

gazéifié, e [gazeifje] *adj* carbonated, aerated.

gazelle [gazɛl] *nf* gazelle.

gazer [gaze] *vt* to gas ♦ *vi (fam)* to be going *ou* working well.

gazette [gazɛt] *nf* news sheet.

gazeux, euse [gazø, -øz] *adj* gaseous; *(eau)* sparkling; *(boisson)* fizzy.

gazoduc [gazɔdyk] *nm* gas pipeline.

gazole [gazɔl] *nm* = **gas-oil**.

gazomètre [gazɔmɛtʀ(ə)] *nm* gasometer.

gazon [gazɔ̃] *nm (herbe)* turf, grass; *(pelouse)* lawn.

gazonner [gazɔne] *vt (terrain)* to grass over.

gazouillement [gazujmɑ̃] *nm (voir vb)* chirping; babbling.

gazouiller [gazuje] *vi (oiseau)* to chirp; *(enfant)* to babble.

gazouillis [gazuji] *nmpl* chirp *sg*.

GB *sigle f* (= *Grande Bretagne*) GB.

gd *abr* (= *grand*) L.

GDF *sigle m* (= *Gaz de France*) national gas company.

geai [ʒɛ] *nm* jay.

géant, e [ʒeɑ̃, -ɑ̃t] *adj* gigantic, giant; *(COMM)* giant-size ♦ *nm/f* giant.

geignement [ʒɛɲmɑ̃] *nm* groaning, moaning.

geindre [ʒɛ̃dʀ(ə)] *vi* to groan, moan.

gel [ʒɛl] *nm* frost; *(de l'eau)* freezing; *(fig: des salaires, prix)* freeze; freezing; *(produit de beauté)* gel.

gélatine [ʒelatin] *nf* gelatine.

gélatineux, euse [ʒelatinø, -øz] *adj* jelly-like, gelatinous.

gelé, e [ʒəle] *adj* frozen ♦ *nf* jelly; *(gel)* frost; **~ blanche** hoarfrost, white frost.

geler [ʒəle] *vt, vi* to freeze; **il gèle** it's freezing.

gélule [ʒelyl] *nf* capsule.

gelures [ʒəlyʀ] *nfpl* frostbite *sg*.

Gémeaux [ʒemo] *nmpl*: **les ~** Gemini, the Twins; **être des ~** to be Gemini.

gémir [ʒemiʀ] *vi* to groan, moan.

gémissement [ʒemismɑ̃] *nm* groan, moan.

gemme [ʒɛm] *nf* gem(stone).

gémonies [ʒemɔni] *nfpl*: **vouer qn aux ~** to subject sb to public scorn.

gén. *abr* (= *généralement*) gen.

gênant, e [ʒɛnɑ̃, -ɑ̃t] *adj (objet)* awkward, in the way; *(histoire, personne)* embarrassing.

gencive [ʒɑ̃siv] *nf* gum.

gendarme [ʒɑ̃daʀm(ə)] *nm* gendarme.

gendarmer [ʒɑ̃daʀme]: **se ~** *vi* to kick up a fuss.

gendarmerie [ʒɑ̃daʀməʀi] *nf* military police force in countryside and small towns; their police station or barracks.

gendre [ʒɑ̃dʀ(ə)] *nm* son-in-law.

gène [ʒɛn] *nm* (BIO) gene.

gêne [ʒɛn] *nf (à respirer, bouger)* discomfort, difficulty; *(dérangement)* bother, trouble; *(manque d'argent)* financial difficulties *pl ou* straits *pl*; *(confusion)* embarrassment; **sans ~** *adj* inconsiderate.

gêné, e [ʒene] *adj* embarrassed; *(dépourvu d'argent)* short (of money).

généalogie [ʒenealɔʒi] *nf* genealogy.

généalogique [ʒenealɔʒik] *adj* genealogical.

gêner [ʒene] *vt (incommoder)* to bother; *(encombrer)* to hamper; *(bloquer le passage)* to be in the way of; *(déranger)* to bother; *(embarrasser)*: **~ qn** to make sb feel ill-at-ease; **se ~** to put o.s. out; **ne vous gênez pas!** *(ironique)* go right ahead!, don't mind me!; **je vais me ~!** *(ironique)* why should I care?

général, e, aux [ʒeneʀal, -o] *adj, nm* general ♦ *nf*: **(répétition) ~e** final dress rehearsal; **en ~** usually, in general; **à la satisfaction ~e** to everyone's satisfaction.

généralement [ʒeneralmɑ̃] *adv* generally.

généralisable [ʒeneralizabl(ə)] *adj* generally applicable.

généralisation [ʒeneralizɑsjɔ̃] *nf* generalization.

généraliser [ʒeneralize] *vt*, *vi* to generalize; **se** ~ *vi* to become widespread.

généraliste [ʒeneralist(ə)] *nmf* (*MÉD*) general practitioner, GP.

généralité [ʒeneralite] *nf*: **la** ~ **des** ... the majority of ...; ~**s** *nfpl* generalities; (*introduction*) general points.

générateur, trice [ʒeneratœr, -tris] *adj*: ~ **de** which causes *ou* brings about ♦ *nf* (*ÉLEC*) generator.

génération [ʒenerɑsjɔ̃] *nf* (*aussi INFORM*) generation.

généreusement [ʒenerøzmɑ̃] *adv* generously.

généreux, euse [ʒenerø, -øz] *adj* generous.

générique [ʒenerik] *adj* generic ♦ *nm* (*CINÉ*, *TV*) credits *pl*, credit titles *pl*.

générosité [ʒenerozite] *nf* generosity.

Gênes [ʒɛn] *n* Genoa.

genèse [ʒənɛz] *nf* genesis.

genêt [ʒənɛ] *nm* (*BOT*) broom *no pl*.

généticien, ne [ʒenetisjɛ̃, -ɛn] *nmf* geneticist.

génétique [ʒenetik] *adj* genetic ♦ *nf* genetics *sg*.

génétiquement [ʒenetikmɑ̃] *adv* genetically.

gêneur, euse [ʒɛnœr, -øz] *nmf* (*personne qui gêne*) obstacle; (*importun*) intruder.

Genève [ʒənɛv] Geneva.

genevois, e [ʒənəvwa, -waz] *adj* Genevan.

genévrier [ʒənevrije] *nm* juniper.

génial, e, aux [ʒenjal, -o] *adj* of genius; (*fam*) fantastic, brilliant.

génie [ʒeni] *nm* genius; (*MIL*): **le** ~ ≈ the Engineers *pl*; **avoir du** ~ to have genius; ~ **civil** civil engineering; ~ **génétique** genetic engineering.

genièvre [ʒənjɛvr(ə)] *nm* (*BOT*) juniper (tree); (*boisson*) geneva; **grain de** ~ juniper berry.

génisse [ʒenis] *nf* heifer; **foie de** ~ ox liver.

génital, e, aux [ʒenital, -o] *adj* genital.

génitif [ʒenitif] *nm* genitive.

génocide [ʒenɔsid] *nm* genocide.

génois, e [ʒenwa, -waz] *adj* Genoese ♦ *nf* (*gâteau*) ≈ sponge cake.

genou, x [ʒnu] *nm* knee; **à** ~**x** on one's knees; **se mettre à** ~**x** to kneel down.

genouillère [ʒənujɛr] *nf* (*SPORT*) kneepad.

genre [ʒɑ̃r] *nm* (*espèce, sorte*) kind, type, sort; (*allure*) manner; (*LING*) gender; (*ART*) genre; (*ZOOL etc*) genus; **se donner du** ~ to give o.s. airs; **avoir bon** ~ to have style; **avoir mauvais** ~ to be ill-mannered.

gens [ʒɑ̃] *nmpl* (*f in some phrases*) people *pl*; **les** ~ **d'Église** the clergy; **les** ~ **du monde** society people; ~ **de maison** domestics.

gentiane [ʒɑ̃sjan] *nf* gentian.

gentil, le [ʒɑ̃ti, -ij] *adj* kind; (*enfant: sage*) good; (*sympa: endroit etc*) nice; **c'est très** ~ **à vous** it's very kind *ou* good *ou* nice of you.

gentilhommière [ʒɑ̃tijɔmjɛr] *nf* (small) manor house *ou* country seat.

gentillesse [ʒɑ̃tijɛs] *nf* kindness.

gentillet, te [ʒɑ̃tijɛ, -ɛt] *adj* nice little.

gentiment [ʒɑ̃timɑ̃] *adv* kindly.

génuflexion [ʒenyflɛksjɔ̃] *nf* genuflexion.

géodésique [ʒeodezik] *adj* geodesic.

géographe [ʒeɔɡraf] *nmf* geographer.

géographie [ʒeɔɡrafi] *nf* geography.

géographique [ʒeɔɡrafik] *adj* geographical.

geôlier [ʒolje] *nm* jailer.

géologie [ʒeɔlɔʒi] *nf* geology.

géologique [ʒeɔlɔʒik] *adj* geological.

géologiquement [ʒeɔlɔʒikmɑ̃] *adv* geologically.

géologue [ʒeɔlɔɡ] *nmf* geologist.

géomètre [ʒeɔmɛtr(ə)] *nmf*: **(arpenteur-)** ~ (land) surveyor.

géométrie [ʒeɔmetri] *nf* geometry; **à** ~ **variable** (*AVIAT*) swing-wing.

géométrique [ʒeɔmetrik] *adj* geometric.

géophysique [ʒeofizik] *nf* geophysics *sg*.

géopolitique [ʒeopolitik] *nf* geopolitics *sg*.

Géorgie [ɡeɔrʒi] *nf*: **la** ~ (*URSS, USA*) Georgia; **la** ~ **du Sud** South Georgia.

géorgien, ne [ɡeɔrʒjɛ̃, -ɛn] *adj* Georgian.

géostationnaire [ʒeostasjɔnɛr] *adj* geostationary.

géothermique [ʒeɔtɛrmik] *adj*: **énergie** ~ geothermal energy.

gérance [ʒerɑ̃s] *nf* management; **mettre en** ~ to appoint a manager for; **prendre en** ~ to take over (the management of).

géranium [ʒeranjɔm] *nm* geranium.

gérant, e [ʒerɑ̃, -ɑ̃t] *nmf* manager/manageress; ~ **d'immeuble** managing agent.

gerbe [ʒɛrb(ə)] *nf* (*de fleurs, d'eau*) spray; (*de blé*) sheaf (*pl* sheaves); (*fig*) shower, burst.

gercé, e [ʒɛrse] *adj* chapped.

gercer [ʒɛrse] *vi*, **se** ~ *vi* to chap.

gerçure [ʒɛrsyr] *nf* crack.

gérer [ʒere] *vt* to manage.

gériatrie [ʒerjatri] *nf* geriatrics *sg*.

gériatrique [ʒerjatrik] *adj* geriatric.

germain, e [ʒɛrmɛ̃, -ɛn] *adj*: **cousin** ~ first cousin.

germanique [ʒɛrmanik] *adj* Germanic.

germaniste [ʒɛrmanist(ə)] *nmf* German scholar.

germe [ʒɛrm(ə)] *nm* germ.

germer [ʒɛrme] *vi* to sprout; (*semence, aussi fig*) to germinate.

gérondif [ʒerɔ̃dif] *nm* gerund; (*en latin*) gerundive.

gérontologie [ʒerɔ̃tɔlɔʒi] *nf* gerontology.

gérontologue [ʒerɔ̃tɔlɔɡ] *nmf* gerontologist.

gésier [ʒezje] *nm* gizzard.

gésir [ʒezir] *vi* to be lying (down); *voir aussi* **ci-gît**.

gestation [ʒɛstɑsjɔ̃] *nf* gestation.

geste [ʒɛst(ə)] *nm* gesture; move; motion; **il fit un ~ de la main pour m'appeler** he signed to me to come over, he waved me over; **ne faites pas un ~** (*ne bougez pas*) don't move.

gesticuler [ʒɛstikyle] *vi* to gesticulate.

gestion [ʒɛstjɔ̃] *nf* management; **~ des disques** (*INFORM*) housekeeping; **~ de fichier(s)** (*INFORM*) file management.

gestionnaire [ʒɛstjɔnɛʀ] *nm/f* administrator; **~ de fichier** (*INFORM*) file manager.

geyser [ʒɛzɛʀ] *nm* geyser.

Ghana [gana] *nm*: **le ~** Ghana.

ghanéen, ne [ganeɛ̃, -ɛn] *adj* Ghanaian.

ghetto [gɛto] *nm* ghetto.

gibecière [ʒibsjɛʀ] *nf* (*de chasseur*) gamebag; (*sac en bandoulière*) shoulder bag.

gibelotte [ʒiblɔt] *nf* rabbit fricassee in white wine.

gibet [ʒibɛ] *nm* gallows *pl*.

gibier [ʒibje] *nm* (*animaux*) game; (*fig*) prey.

giboulée [ʒibule] *nf* sudden shower.

giboyeux, euse [ʒibwajø, -øz] *adj* well-stocked with game.

Gibraltar [ʒibʀaltaʀ] *nm* Gibraltar.

gibus [ʒibys] *nm* opera hat.

giclée [ʒikle] *nf* spurt, squirt.

gicler [ʒikle] *vi* to spurt, squirt.

gicleur [ʒiklœʀ] *nm* (*AUTO*) jet.

GIE *sigle m* = **groupement d'intérêt économique.**

gifle [ʒifl(ə)] *nf* slap (in the face).

gifler [ʒifle] *vt* to slap (in the face).

gigantesque [ʒigɑ̃tɛsk(ə)] *adj* gigantic.

gigantisme [ʒigɑ̃tism(ə)] *nm* (*MÉD*) gigantism; (*des mégalopoles*) vastness.

gigaoctet [ʒigaɔktɛ] *nm* gigabyte.

GIGN *sigle m* (= *Groupe d'intervention de la gendarmerie nationale*) special crack force of the gendarmerie, ≈ SAS (*BRIT*).

gigogne [ʒigɔɲ] *adj*: **lits ~s** truckle (*BRIT*) *ou* trundle (*US*) beds; **tables/poupées ~s** nest of tables/dolls.

gigolo [ʒigɔlo] *nm* gigolo.

gigot [ʒigo] *nm* leg (of mutton *ou* lamb).

gigoter [ʒigɔte] *vi* to wriggle (about).

gilet [ʒilɛ] *nm* waistcoat; (*pull*) cardigan; (*de corps*) vest; **~ pare-balles** bulletproof jacket; **~ de sauvetage** life jacket.

gin [dʒin] *nm* gin.

gingembre [ʒɛ̃ʒɑ̃bʀ(ə)] *nm* ginger.

gingivite [ʒɛ̃ʒivit] *nf* inflammation of the gums, gingivitis.

ginseng [ʒinsɛŋ] *nm* ginseng.

girafe [ʒiʀaf] *nf* giraffe.

giratoire [ʒiʀatwaʀ] *adj*: **sens ~** roundabout.

girofle [ʒiʀɔfl(ə)] *nm*: **clou de ~** clove.

giroflée [ʒiʀɔfle] *nf* wallflower.

girolle [ʒiʀɔl] *nf* chanterelle.

giron [ʒiʀɔ̃] *nm* (*genoux*) lap; (*fig: sein*) bosom.

Gironde [ʒiʀɔ̃d] *nf*: **la ~** the Gironde.

girophare [ʒiʀɔfaʀ] *nm* revolving (flashing) light.

girouette [ʒiʀwɛt] *nf* weather vane *ou* cock.

gis [ʒi], **gisais** [ʒizɛ] *etc vb voir* **gésir.**

gisement [ʒizmɑ̃] *nm* deposit.

gît [ʒi] *vb voir* **gésir.**

gitan, e [ʒitɑ̃, -an] *nm/f* gipsy.

gîte [ʒit] *nm* home; shelter; (*du lièvre*) form; **~ (rural)** (country) holiday cottage *ou* apartment.

gîter [ʒite] *vi* (*NAVIG*) to list.

givrage [ʒivʀaʒ] *nm* icing.

givrant, e [ʒivʀɑ̃, -ɑ̃t] *adj*: **brouillard ~** freezing fog.

givre [ʒivʀ(ə)] *nm* (hoar)frost.

givré, e [ʒivʀe] *adj*: **citron ~/orange ~e** lemon/orange sorbet (*served in fruit skin*).

glabre [glabʀ(ə)] *adj* hairless; (*menton*) clean-shaven.

glaçage [glasaʒ] *nm* (*au sucre*) icing; (*au blanc d'œuf, de la viande*) glazing.

glace [glas] *nf* ice; (*crème glacée*) ice cream; (*verre*) sheet of glass; (*miroir*) mirror; (*de voiture*) window; **~s** *nfpl* (*GÉO*) ice sheets, ice *sg*; **de ~** (*fig: accueil, visage*) frosty, icy; **rester de ~** to remain unmoved.

glacé, e [glase] *adj* icy; (*boisson*) iced.

glacer [glase] *vt* to freeze; (*boisson*) to chill, ice; (*gâteau*) to ice (*BRIT*), frost (*US*); (*papier, tissu*) to glaze; (*fig*): **~ qn** to chill sb; (*fig*) to make sb's blood run cold.

glaciaire [glasjɛʀ] *adj* (*période*) ice *cpd*; (*relief*) glacial.

glacial, e [glasjal] *adj* icy.

glacier [glasje] *nm* (*GÉO*) glacier; (*marchand*) ice-cream maker.

glacière [glasjɛʀ] *nf* icebox.

glaçon [glasɔ̃] *nm* icicle; (*pour boisson*) ice cube.

gladiateur [gladjatœʀ] *nm* gladiator.

glaïeul [glajœl] *nm* gladiola.

glaire [glɛʀ] *nf* (*MÉD*) phlegm *no pl*.

glaise [glɛz] *nf* clay.

glaive [glɛv] *nm* two-edged sword.

gland [glɑ̃] *nm* (*de chêne*) acorn; (*décoration*) tassel; (*ANAT*) glans.

glande [glɑ̃d] *nf* gland.

glander [glɑ̃de] *vi* (*fam*) to fart around (*BRIT !*), screw around (*US !*).

glaner [glane] *vt, vi* to glean.

glapir [glapiʀ] *vi* to yelp.

glapissement [glapismɑ̃] *nm* yelping.

glas [glɑ] *nm* knell, toll.

glauque [glok] *adj* dull blue-green.

glissade [glisad] *nf* (*par jeu*) slide; (*chute*) slip; (*dérapage*) skid; **faire des ~s** to slide.

glissant, e [glisɑ̃, -ɑ̃t] *adj* slippery.

glisse [glis] *nf*: **sports de ~** sports involving sliding or gliding (*eg skiing, surfing, windsurfing*).

glissement [glismɑ̃] *nm* sliding; (*fig*) shift; **~ de terrain** landslide.

glisser [glise] *vi* (*avancer*) to glide *ou* slide

along; (*coulisser, tomber*) to slide; (*déraper*) to slip; (*être glissant*) to be slippery ♦ *vt:* ~ **qch sous/dans/à** to slip sth under/into/to; ~ **sur** (*fig: détail etc*) to skate over; **se** ~ **dans/entre** to slip into/between.

glissière [glisjɛʀ] *nf* slide channel; **à** ~ (*porte, fenêtre*) sliding; ~ **de sécurité** (*AUTO*) crash barrier.

glissoire [gliswaʀ] *nf* slide.

global, e, aux [glɔbal, -o] *adj* overall.

globalement [glɔbalmɑ̃] *adv* taken as a whole.

globe [glɔb] *nm* globe; **sous** ~ under glass; ~ **oculaire** eyeball; **le** ~ **terrestre** the globe.

globe-trotter [glɔbtʀɔtœʀ] *nm* globe-trotter.

globule [glɔbyl] *nm* (*du sang*): ~ **blanc/rouge** white/red corpuscle.

globuleux, euse [glɔbylø, -øz] *adj:* **yeux** ~ protruding eyes.

gloire [glwaʀ] *nf* glory; (*mérite*) distinction, credit; (*personne*) celebrity.

glorieux, euse [glɔʀjø, -øz] *adj* glorious.

glorifier [glɔʀifje] *vt* to glorify, extol; **se** ~ **de** to glory in.

gloriole [glɔʀjɔl] *nf* vainglory.

glose [gloz] *nf* gloss.

glossaire [glɔsɛʀ] *nm* glossary.

glotte [glɔt] *nf* (*ANAT*) glottis.

glouglouter [gluglute] *vi* to gurgle.

gloussement [glusmɑ̃] *nm* (*de poule*) cluck; (*rire*) chuckle.

glousser [gluse] *vi* to cluck; (*rire*) to chuckle.

glouton, ne [glutɔ̃, -ɔn] *adj* gluttonous, greedy.

gloutonnerie [glutɔnʀi] *nf* gluttony.

glu [gly] *nf* birdlime.

gluant, e [glɥɑ̃, -ɑ̃t] *adj* sticky, gummy.

glucide [glysid] *nm* carbohydrate.

glucose [glykoz] *nm* glucose.

gluten [glytɛn] *nm* gluten.

glycérine [gliseʀin] *nf* glycerine.

glycine [glisin] *nf* wisteria.

GMT *sigle adj* (= *Greenwich Mean Time*) GMT.

gnangnan [ɲɑ̃ɲɑ̃] *adj inv* (*fam: livre, film*) soppy.

GNL *sigle m* (= *gaz naturel liquéfié*) LNG (= *liquefied natural gas*).

gnôle [njol] *nf* (*fam*) booze *no pl*; **un petit verre de** ~ a drop of the hard stuff.

gnome [gnom] *nm* gnome.

gnon [ɲɔ̃] *nm* (*fam: coup de poing*) bash; (: *marque*) dent.

GO *sigle fpl* (= *grandes ondes*) LW ♦ *sigle m* (= *gentil organisateur*) *title given to leaders on Club Méditerranée holidays; extended to refer to easy-going leader of any group.*

go [go]: **tout de** ~ *adv* straight out.

goal [gol] *nm* goalkeeper.

gobelet [gɔblɛ] *nm* (*en métal*) tumbler; (*en plastique*) beaker; (*à dés*) cup.

gober [gɔbe] *vt* to swallow.

goberger [gɔbɛʀʒe]: **se** ~ *vi* to cosset o.s.

Gobi [gɔbi] *n:* **désert de** ~ Gobi Desert.

godasse [gɔdas] *nf* (*fam*) shoe.

godet [gɔdɛ] *nm* pot; (*COUTURE*) unpressed pleat.

godiller [gɔdije] *vi* (*NAVIG*) to scull; (*SKI*) to wedeln.

goéland [gɔelɑ̃] *nm* (sea)gull.

goélette [gɔelɛt] *nf* schooner.

goémon [gɔemɔ̃] *nm* wrack.

gogo [gɔgo] *nm* (*péj*) mug, sucker; **à** ~ *adv* galore.

goguenard, e [gɔgnaʀ, -aʀd(ə)] *adj* mocking.

goguette [gɔgɛt] *nf:* **en** ~ on the binge.

goinfre [gwɛ̃fʀ(ə)] *nm* glutton.

goinfrer [gwɛ̃fʀe]: **se** ~ *vi* to make a pig of o.s.; **se** ~ **de** to guzzle.

goitre [gwatʀ(ə)] *nm* goitre.

golf [gɔlf] *nm* (*jeu*) golf; (*terrain*) golf course; ~ **miniature** miniature golf.

golfe [gɔlf(ə)] *nm* gulf; bay; **le** ~ **d'Aden** the Gulf of Aden; **le** ~ **de Gascogne** the Bay of Biscay; **le** ~ **du Lion** the Gulf of Lions; **le** ~ **Persique** the Persian Gulf.

golfeur, euse [gɔlfœʀ, -øz] *nm/f* golfer.

gominé, e [gɔmine] *adj* slicked down.

gomme [gɔm] *nf* (*à effacer*) rubber (*BRIT*), eraser; (*résine*) gum; **boule** *ou* **pastille de** ~ throat pastille.

gommé, e [gɔme] *adj:* **papier** ~ gummed paper.

gommer [gɔme] *vt* (*effacer*) to rub out (*BRIT*), erase; (*enduire de gomme*) to gum.

gond [gɔ̃] *nm* hinge; **sortir de ses** ~**s** (*fig*) to fly off the handle.

gondole [gɔ̃dɔl] *nf* gondola; (*pour l'étalage*) shelves *pl*, gondola.

gondoler [gɔ̃dɔle]: **se** ~ *vi* to warp, buckle; (*fam: rire*) to hoot with laughter; to be in stitches.

gondolier [gɔ̃dɔlje] *nm* gondolier.

gonflable [gɔ̃flabl(ə)] *adj* inflatable.

gonflage [gɔ̃flaʒ] *nm* inflating, blowing up.

gonflé, e [gɔ̃fle] *adj* swollen; (*ventre*) bloated; (*fam: culotté*): **être** ~ to have a nerve.

gonflement [gɔ̃fləmɑ̃] *nm* inflation; (*MÉD*) swelling.

gonfler [gɔ̃fle] *vt* (*pneu, ballon*) to inflate, blow up; (*nombre, importance*) to inflate ♦ *vi* (*pied etc*) to swell (up); (*CULIN: pâte*) to rise.

gonfleur [gɔ̃flœʀ] *nm* air pump.

gong [gɔ̃g] *nm* gong.

gonzesse [gɔ̃zɛs] *nf* (*fam*) chick, bird (*BRIT*).

goret [gɔʀɛ] *nm* piglet.

gorge [gɔʀʒ(ə)] *nf* (*ANAT*) throat; (*poitrine*) breast; (*GÉO*) gorge; (*rainure*) groove; **avoir mal à la** ~ to have a sore throat; **avoir la** ~ **serrée** to have a lump in one's throat.

gorgé, e [gɔʀʒe] *adj:* ~ **de** filled with; (*eau*) saturated with ♦ *nf* mouthful; sip; gulp; **boire à petites/grandes** ~**es** to take little sips/big gulps.

gorille [gɔʀij] *nm* gorilla; (*fam*) bodyguard.

gosier [gozje] *nm* throat.

gosse [gɔs] *nm/f* kid.
gothique [gɔtik] *adj* gothic.
gouache [gwaʃ] *nf* gouache.
gouaille [gwaj] *nf* street wit, cocky humour (*BRIT*) *ou* humor (*US*).
goudron [gudrɔ̃] *nm* (*asphalte*) tar(mac) (*BRIT*), asphalt; (*du tabac*) tar.
goudronner [gudrɔne] *vt* to tar(mac) (*BRIT*), asphalt.
gouffre [gufr(ə)] *nm* abyss, gulf.
goujat [guʒa] *nm* boor.
goujon [guʒɔ̃] *nm* gudgeon.
goulée [gule] *nf* gulp.
goulet [gulɛ] *nm* bottleneck.
goulot [gulo] *nm* neck; **boire au ~** to drink from the bottle.
goulu, e [guly] *adj* greedy.
goulûment [gulymɑ̃] *adv* greedily.
goupille [gupij] *nf* (*metal*) pin.
goupiller [gupije] *vt* to pin (together).
goupillon [gupijɔ̃] *nm* (*REL*) sprinkler; (*brosse*) bottle brush; **le ~** (*fig*) the cloth, the clergy.
gourd, e [gur, gurd(ə)] *adj* numb (with cold); (*fam*) oafish.
gourde [gurd(ə)] *nf* (*récipient*) flask; (*fam*) (clumsy) clot *ou* oaf.
gourdin [gurdɛ̃] *nm* club, bludgeon.
gourmand, e [gurmɑ̃, -ɑ̃d] *adj* greedy.
gourmandise [gurmɑ̃diz] *nf* greed; (*bonbon*) sweet (*BRIT*), piece of candy (*US*).
gourmet [gurmɛ] *nm* epicure.
gourmette [gurmɛt] *nf* chain bracelet.
gourou [guru] *nm* guru.
gousse [gus] *nf* (*de vanille etc*) pod; **~ d'ail** clove of garlic.
gousset [gusɛ] *nm* (*de gilet*) fob.
goût [gu] *nm* taste; (*fig: appréciation*) taste, liking; **le (bon) ~** good taste; **de bon ~** in good taste, tasteful; **de mauvais ~** in bad taste, tasteless; **avoir bon/mauvais ~** (*aliment*) to taste nice/nasty; (*personne*) to have good/bad taste; **avoir du/manquer de ~** to have/lack taste; **avoir du ~ pour** to have a liking for; **prendre ~ à** to develop a taste *ou* a liking for.
goûter [gute] *vt* (*essayer*) to taste; (*apprécier*) to enjoy ♦ *vi* to have (afternoon) tea ♦ *nm* (afternoon) tea; **~ à** to taste, sample; **~ de** to have a taste of; **~ d'enfants/ d'anniversaire** children's tea/birthday party.
goutte [gut] *nf* drop; (*MÉD*) gout; (*alcool*) nip (*BRIT*), tot (*BRIT*), drop (*US*); **~s** *nfpl* (*MÉD*) drops; **~ à ~** *adv* a drop at a time; **tomber ~ à ~** to drip.
goutte-à-goutte [gutagut] *nm inv* (*MÉD*) drip; **alimenter au ~** to drip-feed.
gouttelette [gutlɛt] *nf* droplet.
goutter [gute] *vi* to drip.
gouttière [gutjɛr] *nf* gutter.
gouvernail [guvɛrnaj] *nm* rudder; (*barre*) helm, tiller.
gouvernant, e [guvɛrnɑ̃, -ɑ̃t] *adj* ruling *cpd*

♦ *nf* housekeeper; (*d'un enfant*) governess.
gouverne [guvɛrn(ə)] *nf*: **pour sa ~** for his guidance.
gouvernement [guvɛrnəmɑ̃] *nm* government.
gouvernemental, e, aux [guvɛrnəmɑ̃tal, -o] *adj* (*politique*) government *cpd*; (*journal, parti*) pro-government.
gouverner [guvɛrne] *vt* to govern; (*diriger*) to steer; (*fig*) to control.
gouverneur [guvɛrnœr] *nm* governor; (*MIL*) commanding officer.
goyave [gɔjav] *nf* guava.
GPL *sigle m* (= *gaz de pétrole liquéfié*) LPG (= *liquefied petroleum gas*).
GQG *sigle m* (= *grand quartier général*) GHQ.
grabataire [grabatɛr] *adj* bedridden ♦ *nm/f* bedridden invalid.
grâce [gras] *nf* grace; (*faveur*) favour; (*JUR*) pardon; **~s** *nfpl* (*REL*) grace *sg*; **de bonne/ mauvaise ~** with (a) good/bad grace; **dans les bonnes ~s de qn** in favour with sb; **faire ~ à qn de qch** to spare sb sth; **rendre ~(s) à** to give thanks to; **demander ~** to beg for mercy; **droit de ~** right of reprieve; **recours en ~** plea for pardon; **~ à** *prép* thanks to.
gracier [grasje] *vt* to pardon.
gracieusement [grasjøzmɑ̃] *adv* graciously, kindly; (*gratuitement*) freely; (*avec grâce*) gracefully.
gracieux, euse [grasjø, -øz] *adj* (*charmant, élégant*) graceful; (*aimable*) gracious, kind; **à titre ~** free of charge.
gracile [grasil] *adj* slender.
gradation [gradasjɔ̃] *nf* gradation.
grade [grad] *nm* (*MIL*) rank; (*SCOL*) degree; **monter en ~** to be promoted.
gradé [grade] *nm* (*MIL*) officer.
gradin [gradɛ̃] *nm* (*dans un théâtre*) tier; (*de stade*) step; **~s** *nmpl* (*de stade*) terracing *no pl* (*BRIT*), standing area; **en ~s** terraced.
graduation [graduasjɔ̃] *nf* graduation.
gradué, e [gradue] *adj* (*exercices*) graded (for difficulty); (*thermomètre, verre*) graduated.
graduel, le [graduɛl] *adj* gradual, progressive.
graduer [gradue] *vt* (*effort etc*) to increase gradually; (*règle, verre*) to graduate; (*exercices*) to increase in difficulty.
graffiti [grafiti] *nmpl* graffiti.
grain [grɛ̃] *nm* (*gén*) grain; (*de chapelet*) bead; (*NAVIG*) squall; (*averse*) heavy shower; (*fig: petite quantité*): **un ~ de** a touch of; **~ de beauté** beauty spot; **~ de café** coffee bean; **~ de poivre** peppercorn; **~ de poussière** speck of dust; **~ de raisin** grape.
graine [grɛn] *nf* seed; **mauvaise ~** (*mauvais sujet*) bad lot; **une ~ de voyou** a hooligan in the making.
graineterie [grɛntri] *nf* seed merchant's (shop).
grainetier, -ière [grɛntje, -jɛr] *nm/f* seed merchant.

graissage [gʀɛsaʒ] *nm* lubrication, greasing.
graisse [gʀɛs] *nf* fat; (*lubrifiant*) grease; ~ **saturée** saturated fat.
graisser [gʀese] *vt* to lubricate, grease; (*tacher*) to make greasy.
graisseux, euse [gʀesø, -øz] *adj* greasy; (*ANAT*) fatty.
grammaire [gʀamɛʀ] *nf* grammar.
grammatical, e, aux [gʀamatikal, -o] *adj* grammatical.
gramme [gʀam] *nm* gramme.
grand, e [gʀɑ̃, gʀɑ̃d] *adj* (*haut*) tall; (*gros, vaste, large*) big, large; (*long*) long; (*sens abstraits*) great ♦ *adv*: ~ **ouvert** wide open; **un** ~ **buveur** a heavy drinker; **un** ~ **homme** a great man; **son** ~ **frère** his big *ou* older brother; **avoir** ~ **besoin de** to be in dire *ou* desperate need of; **il est** ~ **temps de** it's high time to; **il est assez** ~ **pour** he's big *ou* old enough to; **voir** ~ to think big; **en** ~ on a large scale; **au** ~ **air** in the open (air); **les** ~**s blessés/brûlés** the severely injured/burned; **de** ~ **matin** at the crack of dawn; ~ **écart** splits *pl*; ~ **ensemble** housing scheme; ~ **jour** broad daylight; ~ **livre** (*COMM*) ledger; ~ **magasin** department store; ~ **malade** very sick person; ~ **public** general public; ~**e personne** grown-up; ~**e surface** hypermarket, superstore; ~**es écoles** *prestige university-level colleges with competitive entrance examinations*; ~**es lignes** (*RAIL*) main lines; ~**es vacances** summer holidays.

> *The **grandes écoles** are prestigious French establishments of tertiary education preparing students for specific careers. Students who have undertaken two years study after the* baccalauréat *in the* classes préparatoires *are recruited by competitive entry examination. The grandes écoles have a strong corporate identity and provide the intellectual, administrative and political elite of the country.*

grand-angle, *pl* **grands-angles** [gʀɑ̃tɑ̃gl(ə)] *nm* (*PHOTO*) wide-angle lens.
grand-angulaire, *pl* **grands-angulaires** [gʀɑ̃tɑ̃gylɛʀ] *nm* (*PHOTO*) wide-angle lens.
grand-chose [gʀɑ̃ʃoz] *nm/f inv*: **pas** ~ not much.
Grande-Bretagne [gʀɑ̃dbʀətaɲ] *nf*: **la** ~ (Great) Britain; **en** ~ in (Great) Britain.
grandement [gʀɑ̃dmɑ̃] *adv* (*tout à fait*) greatly; (*largement*) easily; (*généreusement*) lavishly.
grandeur [gʀɑ̃dœʀ] *nf* (*dimension*) size; (*fig: ampleur, importance*) magnitude; (*: gloire, puissance*) greatness; ~ **nature** *adj* life-size.
grand-guignolesque [gʀɑ̃giɲɔlɛsk(ə)] *adj* gruesome.
grandiloquent, e [gʀɑ̃dilɔkɑ̃, -ɑ̃t] *adj* bombastic, grandiloquent.

grandiose [gʀɑ̃djoz] *adj* (*paysage, spectacle*) imposing.
grandir [gʀɑ̃diʀ] *vi* (*enfant, arbre*) to grow; (*bruit, hostilité*) to increase, grow ♦ *vt*: ~ **qn** (*suj: vêtement, chaussure*) to make sb look taller; (*fig*) to make sb grow in stature.
grandissant, e [gʀɑ̃disɑ̃, -ɑ̃t] growing.
grand-mère, *pl* **grand(s)-mères** [gʀɑ̃mɛʀ] *nf* grandmother.
grand-messe [gʀɑ̃mɛs] *nf* high mass.
grand-oncle, *pl* **grands-oncles** [gʀɑ̃tɔ̃kl(ə), gʀɑ̃zɔ̃kl(ə)] *nm* great-uncle.
grand-peine [gʀɑ̃pɛn]: **à** ~ *adv* with (great) difficulty.
grand-père, *pl* **grands-pères** [gʀɑ̃pɛʀ] *nm* grandfather.
grand-route [gʀɑ̃ʀut] *nf* main road.
grand-rue [gʀɑ̃ʀy] *nf* high street.
grands-parents [gʀɑ̃paʀɑ̃] *nmpl* grandparents.
grand-tante, *pl* **grand(s)-tantes** [gʀɑ̃tɑ̃t] *nf* great-aunt.
grand-voile [gʀɑ̃vwal] *nf* mainsail.
grange [gʀɑ̃ʒ] *nf* barn.
granit(e) [gʀanit] *nm* granite.
granitique [gʀanitik] *adj* granite; (*terrain*) granitic.
granule [gʀanyl] *nm* small pill.
granulé [gʀanyle] *nm* granule.
granuleux, euse [gʀanylø, -øz] *adj* granular.
graphe [gʀaf] *nm* graph.
graphie [gʀafi] *nf* written form.
graphique [gʀafik] *adj* graphic ♦ *nm* graph.
graphisme [gʀafism(ə)] *nm* graphic arts *pl*; graphics *sg*; (*écriture*) handwriting.
graphiste [gʀafist(ə)] *nm/f* graphic designer.
graphologie [gʀafɔlɔʒi] *nf* graphology.
graphologue [gʀafɔlɔg] *nm/f* graphologist.
grappe [gʀap] *nf* cluster; ~ **de raisin** bunch of grapes.
grappiller [gʀapije] *vt* to glean.
grappin [gʀapɛ̃] *nm* grapnel; **mettre le** ~ **sur** (*fig*) to get one's claws on.
gras, se [gʀɑ, gʀɑs] *adj* (*viande, soupe*) fatty; (*personne*) fat; (*surface, main, cheveux*) greasy; (*terre*) sticky; (*toux*) loose, phlegmy; (*rire*) throaty; (*plaisanterie*) coarse; (*crayon*) soft-lead; (*TYPO*) bold ♦ *nm* (*CULIN*) fat; **faire la** ~**se matinée** to have a lie-in (*BRIT*), sleep late; **matière** ~**se** fat (content).
gras-double [gʀadubl(ə)] *nm* (*CULIN*) tripe.
grassement [gʀasmɑ̃] *adv* (*généreusement*): ~ **payé** handsomely paid; (*grossièrement: rire*) coarsely.
grassouillet, te [gʀasujɛ, -ɛt] *adj* podgy, plump.
gratifiant, e [gʀatifjɑ̃, -ɑ̃t] *adj* gratifying, rewarding.
gratification [gʀatifikasjɔ̃] *nf* bonus.
gratifier [gʀatifje] *vt*: ~ **qn de** to favour (*BRIT*) *ou* favor (*US*) sb with; to reward sb with; (*sourire etc*) to favo(u)r sb with.

gratin [gratɛ̃] nm (CULIN) cheese- (ou crumb-) topped dish; (: croûte) topping; **au ~ au gratin; tout le ~ parisien** all the best people of Paris.

gratiné, e [gratine] adj (CULIN) au gratin; (fam) hellish ♦ nf (soupe) onion soup au gratin.

gratis [gratis] adv, adj free.

gratitude [gratityd] nf gratitude.

gratte-ciel [gratsjɛl] nm inv skyscraper.

grattement [gratmɑ̃] nm (bruit) scratching (noise).

gratte-papier [gratpapje] nm inv (péj) penpusher.

gratter [grate] vt (frotter) to scrape; (enlever) to scrape off; (bras, bouton) to scratch; **se ~** to scratch o.s.

grattoir [gratwar] nm scraper.

gratuit, e [gratɥi, -ɥit] adj (entrée) free; (billet) free, complimentary; (fig) gratuitous.

gratuité [gratɥite] nf being free (of charge); gratuitousness.

gratuitement [gratɥitmɑ̃] adv (sans payer) free; (sans preuve, motif) gratuitously.

gravats [grava] nmpl rubble sg.

grave [grav] adj (dangereux: maladie, accident) serious, bad; (sérieux: sujet, problème) serious, grave; (personne, air) grave, solemn; (voix, son) deep, low-pitched ♦ nm (MUS) low register; **ce n'est pas ~!** it's all right, don't worry; **blessé ~** seriously injured person.

graveleux, euse [gravlø, -øz] adj (terre) gravelly; (fruit) gritty; (contes, propos) smutty.

gravement [gravmɑ̃] adv seriously; badly; gravely.

graver [grave] vt (plaque, nom) to engrave; (fig): **~ qch dans son esprit/sa mémoire** to etch sth in one's mind/memory.

graveur [gravœr] nm engraver.

gravier [gravje] nm (loose) gravel no pl.

gravillons [gravijɔ̃] nmpl gravel sg, loose chippings ou gravel.

gravir [gravir] vt to climb (up).

gravitation [gravitasjɔ̃] nf gravitation.

gravité [gravite] nf (voir grave) seriousness; gravity; (PHYSIQUE) gravity.

graviter [gravite] vi: **~ autour de** to revolve around.

gravure [gravyr] nf engraving; (reproduction) print; plate.

GRE sigle f (= garantie contre les risques à l'exportation) ≈ service provided by ECGD (= Export Credit Guarantees Department).

gré [gre] nm: **à son ~** adj to his liking ♦ adv as he pleases; **au ~ de** according to, following; **contre le ~ de qn** against sb's will; **de son (plein) ~** of one's own free will; **de ~ ou de force** whether one likes it or not; **de bon ~** willingly; **bon ~ mal ~** like it or not; willy-nilly; **de ~ à ~** (COMM) by mutual agreement; **savoir (bien) ~ à qn de qch** to

be (most) grateful to sb for sth.

grec, grecque [grɛk] adj Greek; (classique: vase etc) Grecian ♦ nm (LING) Greek ♦ nm/f: **G~, Grecque** Greek.

Grèce [grɛs] nf: **la ~** Greece.

gredin, e [grədɛ̃, -in] nm/f rogue, rascal.

gréement [gremɑ̃] nm rigging.

greffe [grɛf] nf graft; transplant ♦ nm (JUR) office.

greffer [grefe] vt (BOT, MÉD: tissu) to graft; (MÉD: organe) to transplant.

greffier [grefje] nm clerk of the court.

grégaire [greger] adj gregarious.

grège [grɛʒ] adj: **soie ~** raw silk.

grêle [grɛl] adj (very) thin ♦ nf hail.

grêlé, e [grele] adj pockmarked.

grêler [grele] vb impers: **il grêle** it's hailing ♦ vt: **la région a été grêlée** the region was damaged by hail.

grêlon [grelɔ̃] nm hailstone.

grelot [grəlo] nm little bell.

grelottant, e [grələtɑ̃, -ɑ̃t] adj shivering, shivery.

grelotter [grələte] vi (trembler) to shiver.

Grenade [grənad] n Granada ♦ nf (île) Grenada.

grenade [grənad] nf (explosive) grenade; (BOT) pomegranate; **~ lacrymogène** tear gas grenade.

grenadier [grənadje] nm (MIL) grenadier; (BOT) pomegranate tree.

grenadine [grənadin] nf grenadine.

grenat [grəna] adj inv dark red.

grenier [grənje] nm (de maison) attic; (de ferme) loft.

grenouille [grənuj] nf frog.

grenouillère [grənujɛr] nf (de bébé) leggings; (: combinaison) sleepsuit.

grenu, e [grəny] adj grainy, grained.

grès [grɛ] nm (roche) sandstone; (poterie) stoneware.

grésil [grezi] nm (fine) hail.

grésillement [grezijmɑ̃] nm sizzling; crackling.

grésiller [grezije] vi to sizzle; (RADIO) to crackle.

grève [grɛv] nf (d'ouvriers) strike; (plage) shore; **se mettre en/faire ~** to go on/be on strike; **~ bouchon** partial strike (in key areas of a company); **~ de la faim** hunger strike; **~ perlée** go-slow (BRIT), slowdown (US); **~ sauvage** wildcat strike; **~ de solidarité** sympathy strike; **~ surprise** lightning strike; **~ sur le tas** sit down strike; **~ tournante** strike by rota; **~ du zèle** work-to-rule (BRIT), slowdown (US).

grever [grəve] vt (budget, économie) to put a strain on; **grevé d'impôts** crippled by taxes; **grevé d'hypothèques** heavily mortgaged.

gréviste [grevist(ə)] nm/f striker.

gribouillage [gribujaʒ] nm scribble, scrawl.

gribouiller [gribuje] vt to scribble, scrawl ♦ vi

to doodle.

gribouillis [gʀibuji] *nm (dessin)* doodle; *(action)* doodling *no pl*; *(écriture)* scribble.

grief [gʀijɛf] *nm* grievance; **faire ~ à qn de** to reproach sb for.

grièvement [gʀijɛvmɑ̃] *adv* seriously.

griffe [gʀif] *nf* claw; *(fig)* signature; *(: d'un couturier, parfumeur)* label, signature.

griffé, e [gʀife] *adj* designer(-label) *cpd*.

griffer [gʀife] *vt* to scratch.

griffon [gʀifɔ̃] *nm (chien)* griffon.

griffonnage [gʀifɔnaʒ] *nm* scribble.

griffonner [gʀifɔne] *vt* to scribble.

griffure [gʀifyʀ] *nf* scratch.

grignoter [gʀiɲɔte] *vt, vi* to nibble.

gril [gʀil] *nm* steak *ou* grill pan.

grillade [gʀijad] *nf* grill.

grillage [gʀijaʒ] *nm (treillis)* wire netting; *(clôture)* wire fencing.

grillager [gʀijaʒe] *vt (objet)* to put wire netting on; *(périmètre, jardin)* to put wire fencing around.

grille [gʀij] *nf (portail)* (metal) gate; *(clôture)* railings *pl*; *(d'égout)* (metal) grate; *(fig)* grid.

grille-pain [gʀijpɛ̃] *nm inv* toaster.

griller [gʀije] *vt (aussi:* **faire ~**: *pain)* to toast; *(: viande)* to grill *(BRIT)*, broil *(US)*; *(: café)* to roast; *(fig: ampoule etc)* to burn out, blow; **~ un feu rouge** to jump the lights *(BRIT)*, run a stoplight *(US)* ♦ *vi (brûler)* to be roasting.

grillon [gʀijɔ̃] *nm (ZOOL)* cricket.

grimace [gʀimas] *nf* grimace; *(pour faire rire)*: **faire des ~s** to pull *ou* make faces.

grimacer [gʀimase] *vi* to grimace.

grimacier, ière [gʀimasje, -jɛʀ] *adj*: **c'est un enfant ~** that child is always pulling faces.

grimer [gʀime] *vt* to make up.

grimoire [gʀimwaʀ] *nm (illisible)* unreadable scribble; *(livre de magie)* book of magic spells.

grimpant, e [gʀɛ̃pɑ̃, -ɑ̃t] *adj*: **plante ~e** climbing plant, climber.

grimper [gʀɛ̃pe] *vi, vt* to climb ♦ *nm*: **le ~** *(SPORT)* rope-climbing; **~ à/sur** to climb (up)/climb onto.

grimpeur, euse [gʀɛ̃pœʀ, -øz] *nm/f* climber.

grinçant, e [gʀɛ̃sɑ̃, -ɑ̃t] *adj* grating.

grincement [gʀɛ̃smɑ̃] *nm* grating (noise); creaking (noise).

grincer [gʀɛ̃se] *vi (porte, roue)* to grate; *(plancher)* to creak; **~ des dents** to grind one's teeth.

grincheux, euse [gʀɛ̃ʃø, -øz] *adj* grumpy.

gringalet [gʀɛ̃galɛ] *adj m* puny ♦ *nm* weakling.

griotte [gʀijɔt] *nf* Morello cherry.

grippal, e, aux [gʀipal, -o] *adj (état)* flu-like.

grippe [gʀip] *nf* flu, influenza; **avoir la ~** to have (the) flu; **prendre qn/qch en ~** *(fig)* to take a sudden dislike to sb/sth.

grippé, e [gʀipe] *adj*: **être ~** to have (the) flu; *(moteur)* to have seized up *(BRIT)* ou jammed.

gripper [gʀipe] *vt, vi* to jam.

grippe-sou [gʀipsu] *nm/f* penny pincher.

gris, e [gʀi, gʀiz] *adj* grey *(BRIT)*, gray *(US)*; *(ivre)* tipsy ♦ *nm (couleur)* grey *(BRIT)*, gray *(US)*; **il fait ~** it's a dull *ou* grey day; **faire ~e mine** to look miserable *ou* morose; **faire ~e mine à qn** to give sb a cool reception.

grisaille [gʀizaj] *nf* greyness *(BRIT)*, grayness *(US)*, dullness.

grisant, e [gʀizɑ̃, -ɑ̃t] *adj* intoxicating, exhilarating.

grisâtre [gʀizɑtʀ(ə)] *adj* greyish *(BRIT)*, grayish *(US)*.

griser [gʀize] *vt* to intoxicate; **se ~ de** *(fig)* to become intoxicated with.

griserie [gʀizʀi] *nf* intoxication.

grisonnant, e [gʀizɔnɑ̃, -ɑ̃t] *adj* greying *(BRIT)*, graying *(US)*.

grisonner [gʀizɔne] *vi* to be going grey *(BRIT)* ou gray *(US)*.

Grisons [gʀizɔ̃] *nmpl*: **les ~** Graubünden.

grisou [gʀizu] *nm* firedamp.

gris-vert [gʀivɛʀ] *adj* grey-green.

grive [gʀiv] *nf (ZOOL)* thrush.

grivois, e [gʀivwa, -waz] *adj* saucy.

grivoiserie [gʀivwazʀi] *nf* sauciness.

Groenland [gʀɔɛnlɑ̃d] *nm*: **le ~** Greenland.

groenlandais, e [gʀɔɛnlɑ̃dɛ, -ɛz] *adj* of ou from Greenland ♦ *nm/f*: **G~, e** Greenlander.

grog [gʀɔg] *nm* grog.

groggy [gʀɔgi] *adj inv* dazed.

grogne [gʀɔɲ] *nf* grumble.

grognement [gʀɔɲmɑ̃] *nm* grunt; growl.

grogner [gʀɔɲe] *vi* to growl; *(fig)* to grumble.

grognon, ne [gʀɔɲɔ̃, -ɔn] *adj* grumpy, grouchy.

groin [gʀwɛ̃] *nm* snout.

grommeler [gʀɔmle] *vi* to mutter to o.s.

grondement [gʀɔ̃dmɑ̃] *nm* rumble; growl.

gronder [gʀɔ̃de] *vi (canon, moteur, tonnerre)* to rumble; *(animal)* to growl; *(fig: révolte)* to be brewing ♦ *vt* to scold.

groom [gʀum] *nm* page, bellhop *(US)*.

gros, se [gʀo, gʀos] *adj* big, large; *(obèse)* fat; *(problème, quantité)* great; *(travaux, dégâts)* extensive; *(large: trait, fil)* thick, heavy ♦ *adv*: **risquer/gagner ~** to risk/win a lot ♦ *nm* *(COMM)*: **le ~** the wholesale business; **écrire ~** to write in big letters; **prix de ~** wholesale price; **par ~ temps/~se mer** in rough weather/heavy seas; **le ~ de** the main body of; *(du travail etc)* the bulk of; **en avoir ~ sur le cœur** to be upset; **en ~** roughly; *(COMM)* wholesale; **~ intestin** large intestine; **~ lot** jackpot; **~ mot** coarse word, vulgarity; **~ œuvre** shell (of building); **~ plan** *(PHOTO)* close-up; **~ porteur** wide-bodied aircraft, jumbo (jet); **~ sel** cooking salt; **~ titre** headline; **~se caisse** big drum.

groseille [gʀozɛj] *nf*: **~ (rouge)/(blanche)** red/ white currant; **~ à maquereau** gooseberry.

groseillier [gʀozeje] *nm* red *ou* white currant

bush; gooseberry bush.

grosse [gʀos] *adj f voir* **gros** ♦ *nf* (*COMM*) gross.

grossesse [gʀosɛs] *nf* pregnancy; ~ **nerveuse** phantom pregnancy.

grosseur [gʀosœʀ] *nf* size; fatness; (*tumeur*) lump.

grossier, ière [gʀosje, -jɛʀ] *adj* coarse; (*travail*) rough; crude; (*évident: erreur*) gross.

grossièrement [gʀosjɛʀmɑ̃] *adv* coarsely; roughly; crudely; (*en gros*) roughly.

grossièreté [gʀosjɛʀte] *nf* coarseness; rudeness.

grossir [gʀosiʀ] *vi* (*personne*) to put on weight; (*fig*) to grow, get bigger; (*rivière*) to swell ♦ *vt* to increase; (*exagérer*) to exaggerate; (*au microscope*) to magnify, enlarge; (*suj: vêtement*): ~ **qn** to make sb look fatter.

grossissant, e [gʀosisɑ̃, -ɑ̃t] *adj* magnifying, enlarging.

grossissement [gʀosismɑ̃] *nm* (*optique*) magnification.

grossiste [gʀosist(ə)] *nm/f* wholesaler.

grosso modo [gʀosomɔdo] *adv* roughly.

grotesque [gʀotɛsk(ə)] *adj* grotesque.

grotte [gʀot] *nf* cave.

grouiller [gʀuje] *vi* (*foule*) to mill about; (*fourmis*) to swarm about; ~ **de** to be swarming with.

groupe [gʀup] *nm* group; **cabinet de** ~ group practice; **médecine de** ~ group practice; ~ **électrogène** generator; ~ **de pression** pressure group; ~ **sanguin** blood group; ~ **scolaire** school complex.

groupement [gʀupmɑ̃] *nm* grouping; (*groupe*) group; ~ **d'intérêt économique (GIE)** ≈ trade association.

grouper [gʀupe] *vt* to group; (*ressources, moyens*) to pool; **se** ~ to get together.

groupuscule [gʀupyskyl] *nm* clique.

gruau [gʀyo] *nm*: **pain de** ~ wheaten bread.

grue [gʀy] *nf* crane; **faire le pied de** ~ (*fam*) to hang around (waiting), kick one's heels (*BRIT*).

gruger [gʀyʒe] *vt* to cheat, dupe.

grumeaux [gʀymo] *nmpl* (*CULIN*) lumps.

grumeleux, euse [gʀymlø, -øz] *adj* (*sauce etc*) lumpy; (*peau etc*) bumpy.

grutier [gʀytje] *nm* crane driver.

gruyère [gʀyjɛʀ] *nm* gruyère (*BRIT*) *ou* Swiss cheese.

Guadeloupe [gwadlup] *nf*: **la** ~ Guadeloupe.

guadeloupéen, ne [gwadlupeɛ̃, -ɛn] *adj* Guadelupian.

Guatémala [gwatemala] *nm*: **le** ~ Guatemala.

guatémalien, ne [gwatemaljɛ̃, -ɛn] *adj* Guatemalan.

guatémaltèque [gwatemaltɛk] *adj* Guatemalan.

GUD [gyd] *sigle m* (= *Groupe Union Défense*) *student union*.

gué [ge] *nm* ford; **passer à** ~ to ford.

guenilles [gənij] *nfpl* rags.

guenon [gənɔ̃] *nf* female monkey.

guépard [gepaʀ] *nm* cheetah.

guêpe [gɛp] *nf* wasp.

guêpier [gepje] *nm* (*fig*) trap.

guère [gɛʀ] *adv* (*avec adjectif, adverbe*): **ne ... ~** hardly; (*avec verbe*): **ne ... ~** *tournure négative +* much; hardly ever; *tournure négative +* (very) long; **il n'y a ~ que/de** there's hardly anybody (*ou* anything) but/hardly any.

guéridon [geʀidɔ̃] *nm* pedestal table.

guérilla [geʀija] *nf* guerrilla warfare.

guérillero [geʀijeʀo] *nm* guerrilla.

guérir [geʀiʀ] *vt* (*personne, maladie*) to cure; (*membre, plaie*) to heal ♦ *vi* (*personne*) to recover, be cured; (*plaie, chagrin*) to heal; ~ **de** to be cured of, recover from; ~ **qn de** to cure sb of.

guérison [geʀizɔ̃] *nf* curing; healing; recovery.

guérissable [geʀisabl(ə)] *adj* curable.

guérisseur, euse [geʀisœʀ, -øz] *nm/f* healer.

guérite [geʀit] *nf* (*MIL*) sentry box; (*sur un chantier*) (workman's) hut.

Guernesey [gɛʀnɔze] *nf* Guernsey.

guernesiais, e [gɛʀnəzje, -ɛz] *adj* of *ou* from Guernsey.

guerre [gɛʀ] *nf* war; (*méthode*): ~ **atomique/ de tranchées** atomic/trench warfare *no pl*; **en** ~ at war; **faire la** ~ **à** to wage war against; **de** ~ **lasse** (*fig*) tired of fighting *ou* resisting; **de bonne** ~ fair and square; ~ **civile/mondiale** civil/world war; ~ **froide/ sainte** cold/holy war; ~ **d'usure** war of attrition.

guerrier, ière [gɛʀje, -jɛʀ] *adj* warlike ♦ *nm/f* warrior.

guerroyer [gɛʀwaje] *vi* to wage war.

guet [gɛ] *nm*: **faire le** ~ to be on the watch *ou* look-out.

guet-apens, *pl* **guets-apens** [gɛtapɑ̃] *nm* ambush.

guêtre [gɛtʀ(ə)] *nf* gaiter.

guetter [gete] *vt* (*épier*) to watch (intently); (*attendre*) to watch (out) for; (: *pour surprendre*) to be lying in wait for.

guetteur [getœʀ] *nm* look-out.

gueule [gœl] *nf* mouth; (*fam: visage*) mug; (: *bouche*) gob (!), mouth; **ta** ~! (*fam*) shut up!; ~ **de bois** (*fam*) hangover.

gueule-de-loup, *pl* **gueules-de-loup** [gœldəlu] *nf* snapdragon.

gueuler [gœle] *vi* (*fam*) to bawl.

gueuleton [gœltɔ̃] *nm* (*fam*) blowout (*BRIT*), big meal.

gueux [gø] *nm* beggar; (*coquin*) rogue.

gui [gi] *nm* mistletoe.

guibole [gibɔl] *nf* (*fam*) leg.

guichet [giʃɛ] *nm* (*de bureau, banque*) counter, window; (*d'une porte*) wicket, hatch; **les** ~**s** (*à la gare, au théâtre*) the ticket office; **jouer à** ~**s fermés** to play to a full house.

guichetier, ière [giʃtje, -jɛʀ] *nm/f* counter

clerk.

guide [gid] *nm* guide; (*livre*) guide(book) ♦ *nf*
(*fille scout*) (girl) guide (*BRIT*), girl scout
(*US*); ~**s** *nfpl* (*d'un cheval*) reins.

guider [gide] *vt* to guide.

guidon [gidɔ̃] *nm* handlebars *pl*.

guigne [giɲ] *nf* (*fam*): **avoir la** ~ to be jinxed.

guignol [giɲɔl] *nm* ≈ Punch and Judy show;
(*fig*) clown.

guillemets [gijmɛ] *nmpl*: **entre** ~ in inverted
commas *ou* quotation marks; ~ **de**
répétition ditto marks.

guilleret, te [gijrɛ, -ɛt] *adj* perky, bright.

guillotine [gijɔtin] *nf* guillotine.

guillotiner [gijɔtine] *vt* to guillotine.

guimauve [gimov] *nf* (*BOT*) marshmallow;
(*fig*) sentimentality, sloppiness.

guimbarde [gɛ̃baʁd(ə)] *nf* old banger (*BRIT*),
jalopy.

guindé, e [gɛ̃de] *adj* stiff, starchy.

Guinée [gine] *nf*: **la (République de)** ~ (the
Republic of) Guinea; **la** ~ **équatoriale**
Equatorial Guinea.

Guinée-Bissau [ginebiso] *nf*: **la** ~ Guinea-
Bissau.

guinéen, ne [gineɛ̃, -ɛn] *adj* Guinean.

guingois [gɛ̃gwa]: **de** ~ *adv* askew.

guinguette [gɛ̃gɛt] *nf* open-air café or dance
hall.

guirlande [giʁlɑ̃d] *nf* garland; (*de papier*)
paper chain; ~ **lumineuse** (fairy (*BRIT*))
lights *pl*; ~ **de Noël** tinsel *no pl*.

guise [giz] *nf*: **à votre** ~ as you wish *ou* please;
en ~ **de** by way of.

guitare [gitaʁ] *nf* guitar.

guitariste [gitaʁist(ə)] *nm/f* guitarist, guitar
player.

gustatif, ive [gystatif, -iv] *adj* gustatory; *voir*
papille.

guttural, e, aux [gytyʁal, -o] *adj* guttural.

guyanais, e [gɥijanɛ, -ɛz] *adj* Guyanese,
Guyanan; (*français*) Guianese, Guianan.

Guyane [gɥijan] *nf*: **la** ~ Guyana; **la** ~
(française) (French) Guiana.

gvt *abr* (= *gouvernement*) govt.

gymkhana [ʒimkana] *nm* rally; ~ **motocycliste**
(motorbike) scramble (*BRIT*), motocross.

gymnase [ʒimnɑz] *nm* gym(nasium).

gymnaste [ʒimnast(ə)] *nm/f* gymnast.

gymnastique [ʒimnastik] *nf* gymnastics *sg*;
(*au réveil etc*) keep-fit exercises *pl*; ~
corrective remedial gymnastics.

gynécologie [ʒinekɔlɔʒi] *nf* gynaecology
(*BRIT*), gynecology (*US*).

gynécologique [ʒinekɔlɔʒik] *adj*
gynaecological (*BRIT*), gynecological (*US*).

gynécologue [ʒinekɔlɔg] *nm/f* gynaecologist
(*BRIT*), gynecologist (*US*).

gypse [ʒips(ə)] *nm* gypsum.

gyrophare [ʒiʁɔfaʁ] *nm* (*sur une voiture*)
revolving (flashing) light.

H h

H, h [aʃ] *nm inv* H, h ♦ *abr* (= *homme*) M;
(= *hydrogène*) H; (= *heure*): **à l'heure** ~ at
zero hour; **bombe** ~ H bomb; **H comme**
Henri H for Harry (*BRIT*) *ou* How (*US*).

ha. *abr* (= *hectare*) ha.

hab. *abr* = **habitant.**

habile [abil] *adj* skilful; (*malin*) clever.

habilement [abilmɑ̃] *adv* skilfully; cleverly.

habileté [abilte] *nf* skill, skilfulness,
cleverness.

habilité, e [abilite] *adj*: ~ **à faire** entitled to do,
empowered to do.

habiliter [abilite] *vt* empower, entitle.

habillage [abijaʒ] *nm* dressing.

habillé, e [abije] *adj* dressed; (*chic*) dressy;
(*TECH*): ~ **de** covered with; encased in.

habillement [abijmɑ̃] *nm* clothes *pl*;
(*profession*) clothing industry.

habiller [abije] *vt* to dress; (*fournir en*
vêtements) to clothe; **s'**~ to dress (o.s.); (*se*
déguiser, mettre des vêtements chic) to dress
up; **s'**~ **de/en** to dress in/dress up as; **s'**~
chez/à to buy one's clothes from/at.

habilleuse [abijøz] *nf* (*CINÉ, THÉÂT*) dresser.

habit [abi] *nm* outfit; ~**s** *nmpl* (*vêtements*)
clothes; ~ (**de soirée**) tails *pl*; evening dress;
prendre l'~ (*REL: entrer en religion*) to enter
(holy) orders.

habitable [abitabl(ə)] *adj* (in)habitable.

habitacle [abitakl(ə)] *nm* cockpit; (*AUTO*)
passenger cell.

habitant, e [abitɑ̃, -ɑ̃t] *nm/f* inhabitant; (*d'une*
maison) occupant, occupier; **loger chez l'**~
to stay with the locals.

habitat [abita] *nm* housing conditions *pl*; (*BOT,*
ZOOL) habitat.

habitation [abitasjɔ̃] *nf* living; (*demeure*)
residence, home; (*maison*) house; ~**s à**
loyer modéré (HLM) low-rent, state-owned
housing, ≈ council housing *sg* (*BRIT*),
≈ public housing units (*US*).

habité, e [abite] *adj* inhabited; lived in.

habiter [abite] *vt* to live in; (*suj: sentiment*) to
dwell in ♦ *vi*: ~ **à/dans** to live in *ou* at/in; ~
chez *ou* **avec qn** to live with sb; ~ **16 rue**
Montmartre to live at number 16 rue
Montmartre; ~ **rue Montmartre** to live in
rue Montmartre.

habitude [abityd] *nf* habit; **avoir l'**~ **de faire** to
be in the habit of doing; **avoir l'**~ **des**
enfants to be used to children; **prendre l'**~
de faire qch to get into the habit of doing

sth; **perdre une** ~ to get out of a habit; **d'**~ usually; **comme d'**~ as usual; **par** ~ out of habit.

habitué, e [abitɥe] *adj*: **être** ~ **à** to be used *ou* accustomed to ♦ *nm/f* regular visitor; (*client*) regular (customer).

habituel, le [abitɥɛl] *adj* usual.

habituellement [abitɥɛlmɑ̃] *adv* usually.

habituer [abitɥe] *vt*: ~ **qn à** to get sb used to; **s'**~ **à** to get used to.

'hâbleur, euse ['ɑblœʀ, -øz] *adj* boastful.

'hache ['aʃ] *nf* axe.

'haché, e ['aʃe] *adj* minced (*BRIT*), ground (*US*); (*persil*) chopped; (*fig*) jerky.

'hache-légumes ['aʃlegym] *nm inv* vegetable chopper.

'hacher ['aʃe] *vt* (*viande*) to mince (*BRIT*), grind (*US*); (*persil*) to chop; ~ **menu** to mince *ou* grind finely; **to chop finely.**

'hachette ['aʃɛt] *nf* hatchet.

'hache-viande ['aʃvjɑ̃d] *nm inv* (meat) mincer (*BRIT*) *ou* grinder (*US*); (*couteau*) (meat) cleaver.

'hachis ['aʃi] *nm* mince *no pl* (*BRIT*), hamburger meat (*US*); ~ **de viande** minced (*BRIT*) *ou* ground (*US*) meat.

'hachisch ['aʃiʃ] *nm* hashish.

'hachoir ['aʃwaʀ] *nm* chopper; (meat) mincer (*BRIT*) *ou* grinder (*US*); (*planche*) chopping board.

'hachurer ['aʃyʀe] *vt* to hatch.

'hachures ['aʃyʀ] *nfpl* hatching *sg.*

'hagard, e ['agaʀ, -aʀd(ə)] *adj* wild, distraught.

'haie ['ɛ] *nf* hedge; (*SPORT*) hurdle; (*fig: rang*) line, row; **200 m** ~**s** 200 m hurdles; ~ **d'honneur** guard of honour.

'haillons ['ajɔ̃] *nmpl* rags.

'haine ['ɛn] *nf* hatred.

'haineux, euse ['ɛnø, -øz] *adj* full of hatred.

'haïr ['aiʀ] *vt* to detest, hate; **se** ~ to hate each other.

'hais ['ɛ], **'haïs** ['ai] *etc vb voir* **haïr.**

'haïssable ['aisabl(ə)] *adj* detestable.

Haïti [aiti] *n* Haiti.

haïtien, ne [aisjɛ̃, -ɛn] *adj* Haitian.

'halage ['alaʒ] *nm*: **chemin de** ~ towpath.

'hâle ['ɑl] *nm* (sun)tan.

'hâlé, e ['ɑle] *adj* (sun)tanned, sunburnt.

haleine [alɛn] *nf* breath; **perdre** ~ to get out of breath; **à perdre** ~ until one is gasping for breath; **avoir mauvaise** ~ to have bad breath; **reprendre** ~ to get one's breath back; **hors d'**~ out of breath; **tenir en** ~ to hold spellbound; (*en attente*) to keep in suspense; **de longue** ~ *adj* long-term.

'haler ['ale] *vt* to haul in; (*remorquer*) to tow.

'haleter ['alte] *vi* to pant.

'hall ['ol] *nm* hall.

hallali [alali] *nm* kill.

'halle ['al] *nf* (covered) market; ~**s** *nfpl* central food market *sg.*

'hallebarde ['albaʀd] *nf* halberd; **il pleut des**

~**s** (*fam*) it's bucketing down.

hallucinant, e [alysinɑ̃, -ɑ̃t] *adj* staggering.

hallucination [alysinasjɔ̃] *nf* hallucination.

hallucinatoire [alysinatwaʀ] *adj* hallucinatory.

halluciné, e [alysine] *nm/f* person suffering from hallucinations; (*fou*) (raving) lunatic.

hallucinogène [a(l)lysinɔʒɛn] *adj* hallucinogenic ♦ *nm* hallucinogen.

'halo ['alo] *nm* halo.

halogène [alɔʒɛn] *nm*: **lampe (à)** ~ halogen lamp.

'halte ['alt(ə)] *nf* stop, break; (*escale*) stopping place; (*RAIL*) halt ♦ *excl* stop!; **faire** ~ to stop.

'halte-garderie, pl 'haltes-garderies ['altgaʀdəʀi] *nf* crèche.

haltère [altɛʀ] *nm* (*à boules, disques*) dumbbell, barbell; (**poids et**) ~**s** weightlifting.

haltérophile [alteʀɔfil] *nm/f* weightlifter.

haltérophilie [alteʀɔfili] *nf* weightlifting.

'hamac ['amak] *nm* hammock.

'Hambourg ['ɑbuʀ] *n* Hamburg.

'hamburger ['ɑbuʀgœʀ] *nm* hamburger.

'hameau, x ['amo] *nm* hamlet.

hameçon [amsɔ̃] *nm* (fish) hook.

'hampe ['ɑp] *nf* (*de drapeau etc*) pole; (*de lance*) shaft.

'hamster ['amstɛʀ] *nm* hamster.

'hanche ['ɑʃ] *nf* hip.

'hand-ball ['ɑdbal] *nm* handball.

'handballeur, euse ['ɑdbalœʀ, -øz] *nm/f* handball player.

'handicap ['ɑdikap] *nm* handicap.

'handicapé, e ['ɑdikape] *adj* handicapped ♦ *nm/f* physically (*ou* mentally) handicapped person; ~ **moteur** spastic.

'handicaper ['ɑdikape] *vt* to handicap.

'hangar ['ɑgaʀ] *nm* shed; (*AVIAT*) hangar.

'hanneton ['antɔ̃] *nm* cockchafer.

'Hanovre ['anɔvʀ(ə)] *n* Hanover.

'hanovrien, ne ['anɔvʀjɛ̃, -ɛn] *adj* Hanoverian.

'hanter ['ɑte] *vt* to haunt.

'hantise ['ɑtiz] *nf* obsessive fear.

'happer ['ape] *vt* to snatch; (*suj: train etc*) to hit.

'harangue ['aʀɑg] *nf* harangue.

'haranguer ['aʀɑge] *vt* to harangue.

'haras ['aʀɑ] *nm* stud farm.

'harassant, e ['aʀasɑ̃, -ɑ̃t] *adj* exhausting.

'harcèlement ['aʀsɛlmɑ̃] *nm* harassment; ~ **sexuel** sexual harassment.

'harceler ['aʀsəle] *vt* (*MIL, CHASSE*) to harass, harry; (*importuner*) to plague.

'hardes ['aʀd(ə)] *nfpl* rags.

'hardi, e ['aʀdi] *adj* bold, daring.

'hardiesse ['aʀdjɛs] *nf* audacity; **avoir la** ~ **de** to have the audacity *ou* effrontery to.

'harem ['aʀɛm] *nm* harem.

'hareng ['aʀɑ] *nm* herring.

'hargne ['aʀɲ(ə)] *nf* aggressivity,

aggressiveness.

ʼhargneusement [ˈaʀɲøzmɑ̃] _adv_ belligerently, aggressively.

ʼhargneux, -euse [ˈaʀɲø, -øz] _adj (propos, personne)_ belligerent, aggressive; _(chien)_ fierce.

ʼharicot [ˈaʀiko] _nm_ bean; ~ **blanc/rouge** haricot/kidney bean; ~ **vert** French (_BRIT_) _ou_ green bean.

harmonica [aʀmɔnika] _nm_ mouth organ.

harmonie [aʀmɔni] _nf_ harmony.

harmonieux, euse [aʀmɔnjø, -øz] _adj_ harmonious.

harmonique [aʀmɔnik] _adj, nm ou nf_ harmonic.

harmoniser [aʀmɔnize] _vt_ to harmonize; **s'**~ _(couleurs, teintes)_ to go well together.

harmonium [aʀmɔnjɔm] _nm_ harmonium.

ʼharnaché, e [ˈaʀnaʃe] _adj (fig)_ rigged out.

ʼharnachement [ˈaʀnaʃmɑ̃] _nm (habillement)_ rig-out; _(équipement)_ harness, equipment.

ʼharnacher [ˈaʀnaʃe] _vt_ to harness.

ʼharnais [ˈaʀnɛ] _nm_ harness.

ʼharo [ˈaʀo] _nm_: **crier** ~ **sur qn/qch** to inveigh against sb/sth.

ʼharpe [ˈaʀp(ə)] _nf_ harp.

ʼharpie [ˈaʀpi] _nf_ harpy.

ʼharpiste [ˈaʀpist(ə)] _nm/f_ harpist.

ʼharpon [ˈaʀpɔ̃] _nm_ harpoon.

ʼharponner [ˈaʀpɔne] _vt_ to harpoon; _(fam)_ to collar.

ʼhasard [ˈazaʀ] _nm_: **le** ~ chance, fate; **un** ~ a coincidence; _(aubaine, chance)_ a stroke of luck; **au** ~ _(sans but)_ aimlessly; _(à l'aveuglette)_ at random, haphazardly; **par** ~ by chance; **comme par** ~ as if by chance; **à tout** ~ on the off chance; _(en cas de besoin)_ just in case.

ʼhasarder [ˈazaʀde] _vt (mot)_ to venture; _(fortune)_ to risk; **se** ~ **à faire** to risk doing, venture to do.

ʼhasardeux, euse [ˈazaʀdø, -øz] _adj_ hazardous, risky; _(hypothèse)_ rash.

ʼhaschisch [ˈaʃiʃ] _nm_ hashish.

ʼhâte [ˈɑt] _nf_ haste; **à la** ~ hurriedly, hastily; **en** ~ posthaste, with all possible speed; **avoir** ~ **de** to be eager _ou_ anxious to.

ʼhâter [ˈɑte] _vt_ to hasten; **se** ~ to hurry; **se** ~ **de** to hurry _ou_ hasten to.

ʼhâtif, ive [ˈɑtif, -iv] _adj (travail)_ hurried; _(décision)_ hasty; _(légume)_ early.

ʼhâtivement [ˈɑtivmɑ̃] _adv_ hurriedly; hastily.

ʼhauban [ˈobɑ̃] _nm (NAVIG)_ shroud.

ʼhausse [ˈos] _nf_ rise, increase; _(de fusil)_ backsight adjuster; **à la** ~ upwards; **en** ~ rising.

ʼhausser [ˈose] _vt_ to raise; ~ **les épaules** to shrug (one's shoulders); **se** ~ **sur la pointe des pieds** to stand (up) on tiptoe _ou_ tippytoe (_US_).

ʼhaut, e [ˈo, ˈot] _adj_ high; _(grand)_ tall; _(son, voix)_ high(-pitched) ♦ _adv_ high ♦ _nm_ top (part); **de 3 m de** ~, ~ **de 3 m** 3 m high, 3 m

in height; **en** ~**e montagne** high up in the mountains; **en** ~ **lieu** in high places; **à** ~**e voix, (tout)** ~ aloud, out loud; **des** ~**s et des bas** ups and downs; **du** ~ **de** from the top of; **tomber de** ~ to fall from a height; _(fig)_ to have one's hopes dashed; **dire qch bien** ~ to say sth plainly; **prendre qch de (très)** ~ to react haughtily to sth; **traiter qn de** ~ to treat sb with disdain; **de** ~ **en bas** from top to bottom; downwards; ~ **en couleur** _(chose)_ highly coloured; _(personne)_: **un personnage** ~ **en couleur** a colourful character; **plus** ~ higher up, further up; _(dans un texte)_ above; _(parler)_ louder; **en** ~ up above; at _(ou_ to) the top; _(dans une maison)_ upstairs; **en** ~ **de** at the top of; ~ **les mains!** hands up!, stick 'em up!; **la** ~**e couture/coiffure** haute couture/coiffure; ~**e fidélité** hi-fi, high fidelity; **la** ~**e finance** high finance; ~**e trahison** high treason.

ʼhautain, e [ˈotɛ̃, -ɛn] _adj (personne, regard)_ haughty.

ʼhautbois [ˈobwa] _nm_ oboe.

ʼhautboïste [ˈoboist(ə)] _nm/f_ oboist.

ʼhaut-de-forme, _pl_ **ʼhauts-de-forme** [ˈodfɔʀm(ə)] _nm_ top hat.

ʼhaute-contre, _pl_ **ʼhautes-contre** [ˈotkɔ̃tʀ(ə)] _nf_ counter-tenor.

ʼhautement [ˈotmɑ̃] _adv (ouvertement)_ openly; _(supérieurement)_: ~ **qualifié** highly qualified.

ʼhauteur [ˈotœʀ] _nf_ height; _(GÉO)_ height, hill; _(fig)_ loftiness; haughtiness; **à** ~ **de** up to (the level of); **à** ~ **des yeux** at eye level; **à la** ~ **de** _(sur la même ligne)_ level with; by; _(fig)_ equal to; **à la** ~ _(fig)_ up to it, equal to the task.

ʼHaute-Volta [ˈotvɔlta] _nf_: **la** ~ Upper Volta.

ʼhaut-fond, _pl_ **ʼhauts-fonds** [ˈofɔ̃] _nm_ shallow.

ʼhaut-fourneau, _pl_ **ʼhauts-fourneaux** [ˈofuʀno] _nm_ blast _ou_ smelting furnace.

ʼhaut-le-cœur [ˈolkœʀ] _nm inv_ retch, heave.

ʼhaut-le-corps [ˈolkɔʀ] _nm inv_ start, jump.

ʼhaut-parleur, _pl_ **ʼhaut-parleurs** [ˈopaʀlœʀ] _nm_ (loud)speaker.

ʼhauturier, ière [ˈotyʀje, -jɛʀ] _adj (NAVIG)_ deep-sea.

ʼhavanais, e [ˈavanɛ, -ɛz] _adj_ of _ou_ from Havana.

ʼHavane [ˈavan] _nf_: **la** ~ Havana ♦ _nm_: **ʼh**~ _(cigare)_ Havana.

ʼhâve [ˈɑv] _adj_ gaunt.

ʼhavrais, e [ˈavʀɛ, -ɛz] _adj_ of _ou_ from Le Havre.

ʼhavre [ˈavʀ(ə)] _nm_ haven.

ʼhavresac [ˈavʀəsak] _nm_ haversack.

Hawaï [awai] _n_ Hawaii; **les îles** ~ the Hawaiian Islands.

hawaïen, ne [awajɛ̃, -ɛn] _adj_ Hawaiian ♦ _nm_ (_LING_) Hawaiian.

ʼHaye [ˈɛ] _n_: **la** ~ the Hague.

ʼhayon [ˈɛjɔ̃] _nm_ tailgate.

HCR *sigle m* (= *Haut-Commissariat des Nations unies pour les réfugiés*) UNHCR.

hdb. *abr* (= *heures de bureau*) o.h. (= *office hours*).

'hé ['e] *excl* hey!

hebdo [ɛbdo] *nm* (*fam*) weekly.

hebdomadaire [ɛbdɔmadɛʀ] *adj*, *nm* weekly.

hébergement [ebɛʀʒəmɑ̃] *nm* accommodation, lodging; taking in.

héberger [ebɛʀʒe] *vt* to accommodate, lodge; (*réfugiés*) to take in.

hébété, e [ebete] *adj* dazed.

hébétude [ebetyd] *nf* stupor.

hébraïque [ebʀaik] *adj* Hebrew, Hebraic.

hébreu, x [ebʀø] *adj m*, *nm* Hebrew.

Hébrides [ebʀid] *nf*: **les ~** the Hebrides.

HEC *sigle fpl* (= *École des hautes études commerciales*) *grande école for management and business studies*.

hécatombe [ekatɔ̃b] *nf* slaughter.

hectare [ɛktaʀ] *nm* hectare, 10,000 square metres.

hecto... [ɛkto] *préfixe* hecto....

hectolitre [ɛktɔlitʀ(ə)] *nm* hectolitre.

hédoniste [edɔnist(ə)] *adj* hedonistic.

hégémonie [eʒemɔni] *nf* hegemony.

'hein ['ɛ̃] *excl* eh?; (*sollicitant l'approbation*): **tu m'approuves, ~?** so I did the right thing then?; **Paul est venu, ~?** Paul came, did he?; **que fais-tu, ~?** hey! what are you doing?

'hélas ['elɑs] *excl* alas! ♦ *adv* unfortunately.

'héler ['ele] *vt* to hail.

hélice [elis] *nf* propeller.

hélicoïdal, e, aux [elikɔidal, -o] *adj* helical; helicoid.

hélicoptère [elikɔptɛʀ] *nm* helicopter.

hélio(gravure) [eljɔgʀavyʀ] *nf* heliogravure.

héliomarin, e [eljɔmaʀɛ̃, -in] *adj*: **centre ~** *centre offering sea and sun therapy*.

héliotrope [eljɔtʀɔp] *nm* (*BOT*) heliotrope.

héliport [elipɔʀ] *nm* heliport.

héliporté, e [elipɔʀte] *adj* transported by helicopter.

hélium [eljɔm] *nm* helium.

hellénique [elenik] *adj* Hellenic.

hellénisant, e [elenizɑ̃, -ɑ̃t], **helléniste** [elenist(ə)] *nm/f* hellenist.

Helsinki [ɛlzinki] *n* Helsinki.

helvète [ɛlvɛt] *adj* Helvetian ♦ *nm/f*: **H~** Helvetian.

Helvétie [ɛlvesi] *nf*: **la ~** Helvetia.

helvétique [ɛlvetik] *adj* Swiss.

hématologie [ematɔlɔʒi] *nf* (*MÉD*) haematology.

hématome [ematom] *nm* haematoma.

hémicycle [emisikl(ə)] *nm* semicircle; (*POL*): **l'~** *the benches* (*in French parliament*).

hémiplégie [emipleʒi] *nf* paralysis of one side, hemiplegia.

hémisphère [emisfɛʀ] *nf*: **~ nord/sud** northern/southern hemisphere.

hémisphérique [emisfeʀik] *adj* hemispherical.

hémoglobine [emɔglɔbin] *nf* haemoglobin (*BRIT*), hemoglobin (*US*).

hémophile [emɔfil] *adj* haemophiliac (*BRIT*), hemophiliac (*US*).

hémophilie [emɔfili] *nf* haemophilia (*BRIT*), hemophilia (*US*).

hémorragie [emɔʀaʒi] *nf* bleeding *no pl*, haemorrhage (*BRIT*), hemorrhage (*US*); **~ cérébrale** cerebral haemorrhage; **~ interne** internal bleeding *ou* haemorrhage.

hémorroïdes [emɔʀɔid] *nfpl* piles, haemorrhoids (*BRIT*), hemorrhoids (*US*).

hémostatique [emɔstatik] *adj* haemostatic (*BRIT*), hemostatic (*US*).

'henné ['ene] *nm* henna.

'hennir ['eniʀ] *vi* to neigh, whinny.

'hennissement ['enismɑ̃] *nm* neighing, whinnying.

'hep ['ɛp] *excl* hey!

hépatite [epatit] *nf* hepatitis, liver infection.

héraldique [eʀaldik] *adj* heraldry.

herbacé, e [ɛʀbase] *adj* herbaceous.

herbage [ɛʀbaʒ] *nm* pasture.

herbe [ɛʀb(ə)] *nf* grass; (*CULIN, MÉD*) herb; **en ~** unripe; (*fig*) budding; **touffe/brin d'~** clump/blade of grass.

herbeux, euse [ɛʀbø, -øz] *adj* grassy.

herbicide [ɛʀbisid] *nm* weed-killer.

herbier [ɛʀbje] *nm* herbarium.

herbivore [ɛʀbivɔʀ] *nm* herbivore.

herboriser [ɛʀbɔʀize] *vi* to collect plants.

herboriste [ɛʀbɔʀist(ə)] *nm/f* herbalist.

herboristerie [ɛʀbɔʀistʀi] *nf* (*magasin*) herbalist's shop; (*commerce*) herb trade.

herculéen, ne [ɛʀkyleɛ̃, -ɛn] *adj* (*fig*) herculean.

'hère ['ɛʀ] *nm*: **pauvre ~** poor wretch.

héréditaire [eʀeditɛʀ] *adj* hereditary.

hérédité [eʀedite] *nf* heredity.

hérésie [eʀezi] *nf* heresy.

hérétique [eʀetik] *nm/f* heretic.

'hérissé, e ['eʀise] *adj* bristling; **~ de** spiked with; (*fig*) bristling with.

'hérisser ['eʀise] *vt*: **~ qn** (*fig*) to ruffle sb; **se ~** *vi* to bristle, bristle up.

'hérisson ['eʀisɔ̃] *nm* hedgehog.

héritage [eʀitaʒ] *nm* inheritance; (*fig*) heritage; (*: legs*) legacy; **faire un (petit) ~** to come into (a little) money.

hériter [eʀite] *vi*: **~ de qch (de qn)** to inherit sth (from sb); **~ de qn** to inherit sb's property.

héritier, ière [eʀitje, -jɛʀ] *nm/f* heir/heiress.

hermaphrodite [ɛʀmafʀɔdit] *adj* (*BOT, ZOOL*) hermaphrodite.

hermétique [ɛʀmetik] *adj* (*à l'air*) airtight; (*à l'eau*) watertight; (*fig: écrivain, style*) abstruse; (*: visage*) impenetrable.

hermétiquement [ɛʀmetikmɑ̃] *adv* hermetically.

hermine [ɛʀmin] *nf* ermine.

'**hernie** ['ɛrni] *nf* hernia.
héroïne [eRɔin] *nf* heroine; (*drogue*) heroin.
héroïnomane [eRɔinɔman] *nmf* heroin addict.
héroïque [eRɔik] *adj* heroic.
héroïquement [eRɔikmɑ̃] *adv* heroically.
héroïsme [eRɔismɔ(ə)] *nm* heroism.
'**héron** ['eR3] *nm* heron.
'**héros** ['eRo] *nm* hero.
herpès [ɛRpɛs] *nm* herpes.
'**herse** ['ɛRs(ə)] *nf* harrow; (*de château*) portcullis.
hertz [ɛRts] *nm* (*ÉLEC*) hertz.
hertzien, ne [ɛRtsjɛ̃, -ɛn] *adj* (*ÉLEC*) Hertzian.
hésitant, e [ezitɑ̃, -ɑ̃t] *adj* hesitant.
hésitation [ezitɑsjɔ̃] *nf* hesitation.
hésiter [ezite] *vi*: ~ (**à faire**) to hesitate (to do); ~ **sur qch** to hesitate over sth.
hétéro [eteRo] *adj inv* (= *hétérosexuel(le)*) hetero.
hétéroclite [eteRɔklit] *adj* heterogeneous; (*objets*) sundry.
hétérogène [eteRɔʒɛn] *adj* heterogeneous.
hétérosexuel, le [eteRɔsɛkɥɛl] *adj* heterosexual.
'**hêtre** ['ɛtR(ə)] *nm* beech.
heure [œR] *nf* hour; (*SCOL*) period; (*moment, moment fixé*) time; **c'est l'**~ it's time; **pourriez-vous me donner l'**~, **s'il vous plaît?** could you tell me the time, please?; **quelle** ~ **est-il?** what time is it?; **2** ~**s (du matin)** 2 o'clock (in the morning); **à la bonne** ~! (*parfois ironique*) splendid!; **être à l'**~ to be on time; (*montre*) to be right; **le bus passe à l'**~ the bus runs on the hour; **mettre à l'**~ to set right; **100 km à l'**~ ≈ 60 miles an *ou* per hour; **à toute** ~ at any time; **24** ~**s sur 24** round the clock, 24 hours a day; **à l'**~ **qu'il est** at this time (of day); (*fig*) now; **à l'**~ **actuelle** at the present time; **sur l'**~ at once; **pour l'**~ for the time being; **d'**~ **en** ~ from one hour to the next; (*régulièrement*) hourly; **d'une** ~ **à l'autre** from hour to hour; **de bonne** ~ early; **2** ~**s de marche/travail** 2 hours' walking/work; **une** ~ **d'arrêt** an hour's break *ou* stop; ~ **d'été** summer time (*BRIT*), daylight saving time (*US*); ~ **de pointe** rush hour; ~**s de bureau** office hours; ~**s supplémentaires** overtime *sg*.
heureusement [œRøzmɑ̃] *adv* (*par bonheur*) fortunately, luckily; ~ **que** ... it's a good job that ..., fortunately ....
heureux, euse [œRø, -øz] *adj* happy; (*chanceux*) lucky, fortunate; (*judicieux*) felicitous, fortunate; **être** ~ **de qch** to be pleased *ou* happy about sth; **être** ~ **de faire/que** to be pleased *ou* happy to do/that; **s'estimer** ~ **de qch/que** to consider o.s. fortunate with/that; **encore** ~ **que** ... just as well that ....
'**heurt** ['œR] *nm* (*choc*) collision; ~**s** *nmpl* (*fig*) clashes.
'**heurté, e** ['œRte] *adj* (*fig*) jerky, uneven;

(: *couleurs*) clashing.
'**heurter** ['œRte] *vt* (*mur*) to strike, hit; (*personne*) to collide with; (*fig*) to go against, upset; **se** ~ (*couleurs, tons*) to clash; **se** ~ **à** to collide with; (*fig*) to come up against; ~ **qn de front** to clash head-on with sb.
'**heurtoir** ['œRtwaR] *nm* door knocker.
hévéa [evea] *nm* rubber tree.
hexagonal, e, aux [ɛgzagɔnal, -o] *adj* hexagonal; (*français*) French (*see note at hexagone*).
hexagone [ɛgzagɔn] *nm* hexagon; (*la France*) France (*because of its roughly hexagonal shape*).
HF *sigle f* (= *haute fréquence*) HF.
hiatus [jatys] *nm* hiatus.
hibernation [ibɛRnɑsjɔ̃] *nf* hibernation.
hiberner [ibɛRne] *vi* to hibernate.
hibiscus [ibiskys] *nm* hibiscus.
'**hibou, x** ['ibu] *nm* owl.
'**hic** ['ik] *nm* (*fam*) snag.
'**hideusement** ['idøzmɑ̃] *adv* hideously.
'**hideux, euse** ['idø, -øz] *adj* hideous.
hier [jɛR] *adv* yesterday; ~ **matin/soir/midi** yesterday morning/evening/at midday; **toute la journée d'**~ all day yesterday; **toute la matinée d'**~ all yesterday morning.
'**hiérarchie** ['jeRaRʃi] *nf* hierarchy.
'**hiérarchique** ['jeRaRʃik] *adj* hierarchic.
'**hiérarchiquement** ['jeRaRʃikmɑ̃] *adv* hierarchically.
'**hiérarchiser** ['jeRaRʃize] *vt* to organize into a hierarchy.
'**hiéroglyphe** ['jeRɔglif] *nm* hieroglyphic.
'**hiéroglyphique** ['jeRɔglifik] *adj* hieroglyphic.
'**hi-fi** ['ifi] *nf inv* hi-fi.
hilarant, e [ilaRɑ̃, -ɑ̃t] *adj* hilarious.
hilare [ilaR] *adj* mirthful.
hilarité [ilaRite] *nf* hilarity, mirth.
Himalaya [imalaja] *nm*: **l'**~ the Himalayas *pl*.
himalayen, ne [imalajɛ̃, -ɛn] *adj* Himalayan.
hindou, e [ɛ̃du] *adj*, *nmf* Hindu; (*Indien*) Indian.
hindouisme [ɛ̃duismɔ(ə)] *nm* Hinduism.
Hindoustan [ɛ̃dustɑ̃] *nm*: **l'**~ Hindustan.
'**hippie** ['ipi] *nmf* hippy.
hippique [ipik] *adj* equestrian, horse *cpd*.
hippisme [ipism(ə)] *nm* (horse-)riding.
hippocampe [ipɔkɑ̃p] *nm* sea horse.
hippodrome [ipɔdRom] *nm* racecourse.
hippophagique [ipɔfaʒik] *adj*: **boucherie** ~ horse butcher's.
hippopotame [ipɔpɔtam] *nm* hippopotamus.
hirondelle [iRɔ̃dɛl] *nf* swallow.
hirsute [iRsyt] *adj* (*personne*) hairy; (*barbe*) shaggy; (*tête*) tousled.
hispanique [ispanik] *adj* Hispanic.
hispanisant, e [ispanizɑ̃, -ɑ̃t], **hispaniste** [ispanist(ə)] *nmf* Hispanist.
hispano-américain, e [ispanɔameRikɛ̃, -ɛn] *adj* Spanish-American.
hispano-arabe [ispanɔaRab] *adj* Hispano-

Moresque.

'hisser ['ise] *vt* to hoist, haul up; **se ~ sur** to haul o.s. up onto.

histoire [istwaʀ] *nf (science, événements)* history; *(anecdote, récit, mensonge)* story; *(affaire)* business *no pl*; *(chichis: gén pl)* fuss *no pl*; **~s** *nfpl (ennuis)* trouble *sg*; **l'~ de France** French history, the history of France; **l'~ sainte** biblical history; **une ~ de** *(fig)* a question of.

histologie [istɔlɔʒi] *nf* histology.

historien, ne [istɔʀjɛ̃, -ɛn] *nm/f* historian.

historique [istɔʀik] *adj* historical; *(important)* historic ♦ *nm (exposé, récit):* **faire l'~ de** to give the background to.

historiquement [istɔʀikmɑ̃] *adv* historically.

'hit-parade ['itpaʀad] *nm:* **le ~** the charts.

HIV *sigle m (= human immunodeficiency virus)* HIV.

hiver [ivɛʀ] *nm* winter; **en ~** in winter.

hivernal, e, aux [ivɛʀnal, -o] *adj (de l'hiver)* winter *cpd; (comme en hiver)* wintry.

hivernant, e [ivɛʀnɑ̃, -ɑ̃t] *n* winter holiday-maker.

hiverner [ivɛʀne] *vi* to winter.

HLM *sigle m ou f (= habitations à loyer modéré)* low-rent, state-owned *housing;* **un(e) ~** ≈ a council flat *(ou house)* (BRIT), ≈ a public housing unit (US).

Hme *abr (= homme)* M.

HO *abr (= hors œuvre)* labour not included *(on invoices).*

'hobby ['ɔbi] *nm* hobby.

'hochement ['ɔʃmɑ̃] *nm:* **~ de tête** nod; shake of the head.

'hocher ['ɔʃe] *vt:* **~ la tête** to nod; *(signe négatif ou dubitatif)* to shake one's head.

'hochet ['ɔʃɛ] *nm* rattle.

'hockey ['ɔkɛ] *nm:* **~ (sur glace/gazon)** (ice/field) hockey.

'hockeyeur, euse ['ɔkɛjœʀ, -øz] *nm/f* hockey player.

'holà ['ɔla] *nm:* **mettre le ~ à qch** to put a stop to sth.

'holding ['ɔldiŋ] *nm* holding company.

'hold-up ['ɔldœp] *nm inv* hold-up.

'hollandais, e ['ɔlɑ̃dɛ, -ɛz] *adj* Dutch ♦ *nm (LING)* Dutch ♦ *nm/f:* **H~, e** Dutchman/woman; **les H~** the Dutch.

'Hollande ['ɔlɑ̃d] *nf:* **la ~** Holland ♦ *nm:* **h~** *(fromage)* Dutch cheese.

holocauste [ɔlɔkost(ə)] *nm* holocaust.

hologramme [ɔlɔgʀam] *nm* hologram.

'homard ['ɔmaʀ] *nm* lobster.

homéopathe [ɔmeɔpat] *n* homoeopath.

homéopathie [ɔmeɔpati] *nf* homoeopathy.

homéopathique [ɔmeɔpatik] *adj* homoeopathic.

homérique [ɔmeʀik] *adj* Homeric.

homicide [ɔmisid] *nm* murder ♦ *nm/f* murderer/eress; **~ involontaire** manslaughter.

hommage [ɔmaʒ] *nm* tribute; **~s** *nmpl:* **présenter ses ~s** to pay one's respects; **rendre ~ à** to pay tribute *ou* homage to; **en ~ de** as a token of; **faire ~ de qch à qn** to present sb with sth.

homme [ɔm] *nm* man; *(espèce humaine):* **l'~** man, mankind; **~ d'affaires** businessman; **~ des cavernes** caveman; **~ d'Église** churchman, clergyman; **~ d'État** statesman; **~ de loi** lawyer; **~ de main** hired man; **~ de paille** stooge; **l'~ de la rue** the man in the street; **~ à tout faire** odd-job man.

homme-grenouille, *pl* **hommes-grenouilles** [ɔmgʀənuj] *nm* frogman.

homme-orchestre, *pl* **hommes-orchestres** [ɔmɔʀkɛstʀ(ə)] *nm* one-man band.

homme-sandwich, *pl* **hommes-sandwichs** [ɔmsɑ̃dwitʃ] *nm* sandwich (board) man.

homo [ɔmo] *adj, nm/f* = **homosexuel.**

homogène [ɔmɔʒɛn] *adj* homogeneous.

homogénéisé, e [ɔmɔʒeneize] *adj:* **lait ~** homogenized milk.

homogénéité [ɔmɔʒeneite] *nf* homogeneity.

homologation [ɔmɔlɔgasjɔ̃] *nf* ratification, official recognition.

homologue [ɔmɔlɔg] *nm/f* counterpart, opposite number.

homologué, e [ɔmɔlɔge] *adj (SPORT)* officially recognized, ratified; *(tarif)* authorized.

homologuer [ɔmɔlɔge] *vt (JUR)* to ratify; *(SPORT)* to recognize officially, ratify.

homonyme [ɔmɔnim] *nm (LING)* homonym; *(d'une personne)* namesake.

homosexualité [ɔmɔsɛksɥalite] *nf* homosexuality.

homosexuel, le [ɔmɔsɛksɥɛl] *adj* homosexual.

'Honduras ['ɔ̃dyʀas] *nm:* **le ~** Honduras.

'hondurien, ne ['ɔ̃dyʀjɛ̃, -ɛn] *adj* Honduran.

'Hong-Kong ['ɔ̃gkɔ̃g] *n* Hong Kong.

'hongre ['ɔ̃gʀ(ə)] *adj (cheval)* gelded ♦ *nm* gelding.

'Hongrie ['ɔ̃gʀi] *nf:* **la ~** Hungary.

'hongrois, e ['ɔ̃gʀwa, -waz] *adj* Hungarian ♦ *nm (LING)* Hungarian ♦ *nm/f:* **'H~, e** Hungarian.

honnête [ɔnɛt] *adj (intègre)* honest; *(juste, satisfaisant)* fair.

honnêtement [ɔnɛtmɑ̃] *adv* honestly.

honnêteté [ɔnɛtte] *nf* honesty.

honneur [ɔnœʀ] *nm* honour; *(mérite):* **l'~ lui revient** the credit is his; **à qui ai-je l'~?** to whom have I the pleasure of speaking?; **"j'ai l'~ de ..."** "I have the honour of ..."; **en l'~ de** *(personne)* in honour of; *(événement)* on the occasion of; **faire ~ à** *(engagements)* to honour; *(famille, professeur)* to be a credit to; *(fig: repas etc)* to do justice to; **être à l'~** to be in the place of honour; **être en ~** to be in favour; **membre d'~** honorary member; **table d'~** top table.

Honolulu [ɔnɔlyly] *n* Honolulu.

honorable [ɔnɔRabl(ə)] *adj* worthy,
honourable; (*suffisant*) decent.
honorablement [ɔnɔRabləmɑ̃] *adv*
honourably; decently.
honoraire [ɔnɔRɛR] *adj* honorary; ~**s** *nmpl*
fees; (*professeur* ~ professor emeritus.
honorer [ɔnɔRe] *vt* to honour; (*estimer*) to hold
in high regard; (*faire honneur à*) to do credit
to; ~ **qn de** to honour sb with; **s'**~ **de** to
pride o.s. upon.
honorifique [ɔnɔRifik] *adj* honorary.
'honte ['ɔ̃t] *nf* shame; **avoir** ~ **de** to be
ashamed of; **faire** ~ **à qn** to make sb (feel)
ashamed.
'honteusement ['ɔ̃tøzmɑ̃] *adv* ashamedly;
shamefully.
'honteux, euse ['ɔ̃tø, -øz] *adj* ashamed;
(*conduite, acte*) shameful, disgraceful.
hôpital, aux [ɔpital, -o] *nm* hospital.
'hoquet ['ɔkɛ] *nm* hiccough; **avoir le** ~ to have
(the) hiccoughs.
'hoqueter ['ɔkte] *vi* to hiccough.
horaire [ɔRɛR] *adj* hourly ♦ *nm* timetable,
schedule; ~**s** *nmpl* (*heures de travail*) hours; ~
flexible *ou* **mobile** *ou* **à la carte** *ou* **souple**
flex(i)time.
'horde ['ɔRd(ə)] *nf* horde.
'horions ['ɔRjɔ̃] *nmpl* blows.
horizon [ɔRizɔ̃] *nm* horizon; (*paysage*)
landscape, view; **sur l'**~ on the skyline *ou*
horizon.
horizontal, e, aux [ɔRizɔ̃tal, -o] *adj* horizontal
♦ *nf*: **à l'**~**e** on the horizontal.
horizontalement [ɔRizɔ̃talmɑ̃] *adv*
horizontally.
horloge [ɔRlɔʒ] *nf* clock; **l'**~ **parlante** the
speaking clock; ~ **normande** grandfather
clock; ~ **physiologique** biological clock.
horloger, ère [ɔRlɔʒe, -ɛR] *nm/f* watchmaker;
clockmaker.
horlogerie [ɔRlɔʒRi] *nf* watchmaking;
watchmaker's (shop); clockmaker's (shop);
pièces d'~ watch parts *ou* components.
'hormis ['ɔRmi] *prép* save.
hormonal, e, aux [ɔRmɔnal, -o] *adj* hormonal.
hormone [ɔRmɔn] *nf* hormone.
horodaté, e [ɔRɔdate] *adj* (*ticket*) time- and
date-stamped; (*stationnement*) pay and
display.
horodateur, trice [ɔRɔdatœR, -tRis] *adj*
(*appareil*) for stamping the time and date
♦ *nm/f* (parking) ticket machine.
horoscope [ɔRɔskɔp] *nm* horoscope.
horreur [ɔRœR] *nf* horror; **avoir** ~ **de** to loathe,
detest; **quelle** ~! how awful!; **cela me fait** ~
I find that awful.
horrible [ɔRibl(ə)] *adj* horrible.
horriblement [ɔRibləmɑ̃] *adv* horribly.
horrifiant, e [ɔRifjɑ̃, -ɑ̃t] *adj* horrifying.
horrifier [ɔRifje] *vt* to horrify.
horrifique [ɔRifik] *adj* horrific.
horripilant, e [ɔRipilɑ̃, -ɑ̃t] *adj* exasperating.

horripiler [ɔRipile] *vt* to exasperate.
'hors ['ɔR] *prép* except (for); ~ **de** out of; ~
ligne, ~ **pair** outstanding; ~ **de propos**
inopportune; ~ **série** (*sur mesure*) made-to-
order; (*exceptionnel*) exceptional; ~ **service**
(HS), ~ **d'usage** out of service; **être** ~ **de soi**
to be beside o.s.
'hors-bord ['ɔRbɔR] *nm inv* outboard motor;
(*canot*) speedboat (with outboard motor).
'hors-concours ['ɔRkɔ̃kuR] *adj inv* ineligible to
compete; (*fig*) in a class of one's own.
'hors-d'œuvre ['ɔRdœvR(ə)] *nm inv* hors
d'œuvre.
'hors-jeu ['ɔRʒø] *nm inv* being offside *no pl*.
'hors-la-loi ['ɔRlalwa] *nm inv* outlaw.
'hors-piste(s) ['ɔRpist] *nm inv* (*SKI*) cross-
country.
hors-taxe [ɔRtaks] *adj* (*sur une facture, prix*)
excluding VAT; (*boutique, marchandises*)
duty-free.
'hors-texte ['ɔRtɛkst(ə)] *nm inv* plate.
hortensia [ɔRtɑ̃sja] *nm* hydrangea.
horticole [ɔRtikɔl] *adj* horticultural.
horticulteur, trice [ɔRtikyltœR, -tRis] *nm/f*
horticulturalist (*BRIT*), horticulturist (*US*).
horticulture [ɔRtikyltyR] *nf* horticulture.
hospice [ɔspis] *nm* (*de vieillards*) home; (*asile*)
hospice.
hospitalier, ière [ɔspitalje, -jɛR] *adj*
(*accueillant*) hospitable; (*MÉD: service, centre*)
hospital *cpd*.
hospitalisation [ɔspitalizɑsjɔ̃] *nf*
hospitalization.
hospitaliser [ɔspitalize] *vt* to take (*ou* send) to
hospital, hospitalize.
hospitalité [ɔspitalite] *nf* hospitality.
hospitalo-universitaire [ɔspitalɔynivɛRsitɛR]
adj: **centre** ~ **(CHU)** ≈ (teaching) hospital.
hostie [ɔsti] *nf* host (*REL*).
hostile [ɔstil] *adj* hostile.
hostilité [ɔstilite] *nf* hostility; ~**s** *nfpl*
hostilities.
hôte [ot] *nm* (*maître de maison*) host; (*client*)
patron; (*fig*) inhabitant, occupant ♦ *nm/f*
(*invité*) guest; ~ **payant** paying guest.
hôtel [otɛl] *nm* hotel; **aller à l'**~ to stay in a
hotel; ~ **(particulier)** (private) mansion; ~
de ville town hall.
hôtelier, ière [otəlje, -jɛR] *adj* hotel *cpd* ♦ *nm/f*
hotelier, hotel-keeper.
hôtellerie [otɛlRi] *nf* (*profession*) hotel
business; (*auberge*) inn.
hôtesse [otɛs] *nf* hostess; ~ **de l'air** air
hostess (*BRIT*) *ou* stewardess; ~ **(d'accueil)**
receptionist.
'hotte ['ɔt] *nf* (*panier*) basket (*carried on the
back*); (*de cheminée*) hood; ~ **aspirante**
cooker hood.
'houblon ['ublɔ̃] *nm* (*BOT*) hop; (*pour la bière*)
hops *pl*.
'houe ['u] *nf* hoe.
'houille ['uj] *nf* coal; ~ **blanche** hydroelectric

power.

'**houiller, ère** ['uje, -ɛʀ] *adj* coal *cpd*; (*terrain*) coal-bearing ♦ *nf* coal mine.

'**houle** ['ul] *nf* swell.

'**houlette** ['ulɛt] *nf*: **sous la ~ de** under the guidance of.

'**houleux, euse** ['ulø, -øz] *adj* heavy, swelling; (*fig*) stormy, turbulent.

'**houppe** ['up] *nf*, '**houppette** ['upɛt] *nf* powder puff; (*cheveux*) tuft.

'**hourra** ['uʀa] *nm* cheer ♦ *excl* hurrah!

'**houspiller** ['uspije] *vt* to scold.

'**housse** ['us] *nf* cover; (*pour protéger provisoirement*) dust cover; (*pour recouvrir à neuf*) loose *ou* stretch cover; ~ (**penderie**) hanging wardrobe.

'**houx** ['u] *nm* holly.

HS *abr* = **hors service**.

HT *abr* = **hors taxe**.

'**hublot** ['yblo] *nm* porthole.

'**huche** ['yʃ] *nf*: ~ **à pain** bread bin.

'**huées** ['ɥe] *nfpl* boos.

'**huer** ['ɥe] *vt* to boo; (*hibou, chouette*) to hoot.

huile [ɥil] *nf* oil; (*ART*) oil painting; (*fam*) bigwig; **mer d'~** (*très calme*) glassy sea, sea of glass; **faire tache d'~** (*fig*) to spread; ~ **d'arachide** groundnut oil; ~ **essentielle** essential oil; ~ **de foie de morue** cod-liver oil; ~ **de ricin** castor oil; ~ **solaire** suntan oil; ~ **de table** salad oil.

huiler [ɥile] *vt* to oil.

huilerie [ɥilʀi] *nf* (*usine*) oil-works.

huileux, euse [ɥilø, -øz] *adj* oily.

huilier [ɥilje] *nm* (oil and vinegar) cruet.

huis [ɥi] *nm*: **à ~ clos** in camera.

huissier [ɥisje] *nm* usher; (*JUR*) ≈ bailiff.

'**huit** ['ɥi(t)] *num* eight; **samedi en ~** a week on Saturday; **dans ~ jours** in a week('s time).

'**huitaine** ['ɥitɛn] *nf*: **une ~ de** about eight, eight or so; **une ~ de jours** a week or so.

'**huitante** ['ɥitɑ̃t] *num* (*Suisse*) eighty.

'**huitième** ['ɥitjɛm] *num* eighth.

huître [ɥitʀ(ə)] *nf* oyster.

'**hululement** ['ylylmɑ̃] *nm* hooting.

'**hululer** ['ylyle] *vi* to hoot.

humain, e [ymɛ̃, -ɛn] *adj* human; (*compatissant*) humane ♦ *nm* human (being).

humainement [ymɛnmɑ̃] *adv* humanly; humanely.

humanisation [ymanizɑsjɑ̃] *nf* humanization.

humaniser [ymanize] *vt* to humanize.

humaniste [ymanist(ə)] *nm/f* (*LING*) classicist; humanist.

humanitaire [ymanitɛʀ] *adj* humanitarian.

humanitarisme [ymanitaʀism(ə)] *nm* humanitarianism.

humanité [ymanite] *nf* humanity.

humanoïde [ymanɔid] *nm/f* humanoid.

humble [œ̃bl(ə)] *adj* humble.

humblement [œ̃bləmɑ̃] *adv* humbly.

humecter [ymɛkte] *vt* to dampen; **s'~ les lèvres** to moisten one's lips.

'**humer** ['yme] *vt* to inhale; (*pour sentir*) to smell.

humérus [ymeʀys] *nm* (*ANAT*) humerus.

humeur [ymœʀ] *nf* mood; (*tempérament*) temper; (*irritation*) bad temper; **de bonne/ mauvaise ~** in a good/bad mood; **être d'~ à faire qch** to be in the mood for doing sth.

humide [ymid] *adj* (*linge*) damp; (*main, yeux*) moist; (*climat, chaleur*) humid; (*saison, route*) wet.

humidificateur [ymidifikatœʀ] *nm* humidifier.

humidifier [ymidifje] *vt* to humidify.

humidité [ymidite] *nf* humidity; dampness; **traces d'~** traces of moisture *ou* damp.

humiliant, e [ymiljɑ̃, -ɑ̃t] humiliating.

humiliation [ymiljasjɔ̃] *nf* humiliation.

humilier [ymilje] *vt* to humiliate; **s'~ devant qn** to humble o.s. before sb.

humilité [ymilite] *nf* humility.

humoriste [ymɔʀist(ə)] *nm/f* humorist.

humoristique [ymɔʀistik] *adj* humorous; humoristic.

humour [ymuʀ] *nm* humour; **avoir de l'~** to have a sense of humour; ~ **noir** sick humour.

humus [ymys] *nm* humus.

'**huppé, e** ['ype] *adj* crested; (*fam*) posh.

'**hurlement** ['yʀləmɑ̃] *nm* howling *no pl*, howl; yelling *no pl*, yell.

'**hurler** ['yʀle] *vi* to howl, yell; (*fig: vent*) to howl; (: *couleurs etc*) to clash; ~ **à la mort** (*suj: chien*) to bay at the moon.

hurluberlu [yʀlybɛʀly] *nm* (*péj*) crank ♦ *adj* cranky.

'**hutte** ['yt] *nf* hut.

hybride [ibʀid] *adj* hybrid.

hydratant, e [idʀatɑ̃, -ɑ̃t] *adj* (*crème*) moisturizing.

hydrate [idʀat] *nm*: ~**s de carbone** carbohydrates.

hydrater [idʀate] *vt* to hydrate.

hydraulique [idʀolik] *adj* hydraulic.

hydravion [idʀavjɔ̃] *nm* seaplane, hydroplane.

hydro... [idʀo] *préfixe* hydro....

hydrocarbure [idʀɔkaʀbyʀ] *nm* hydrocarbon.

hydrocution [idʀɔkysjɔ̃] *nf* immersion syncope.

hydro-électrique [idʀɔelɛktʀik] *adj* hydroelectric.

hydrogène [idʀɔʒɛn] *nm* hydrogen.

hydroglisseur [idʀɔglisœʀ] *nm* hydroplane.

hydrographie [idʀɔgʀafi] *nf* (*fleuves*) hydrography.

hydrophile [idʀɔfil] *adj voir* **coton**.

hyène [jɛn] *nf* hyena.

hygiène [iʒjɛn] *nf* hygiene; ~ **intime** personal hygiene.

hygiénique [iʒenik] *adj* hygienic.

hymne [imn(ə)] *nm* hymn; ~ **national** national anthem.

hyper... [ipɛʀ] *préfixe* hyper....

hypermarché [ipɛʀmaʀʃe] *nm* hypermarket.

hypermétrope [ipɛrmetrɔp] *adj* long-sighted.
hypernerveux, euse [ipɛrnɛrvø, -øz] *adj* highly-strung.
hypersensible [ipɛrsɑ̃sibl(ə)] *adj* hypersensitive.
hypertendu, e [ipɛrtɑ̃dy] *adj* having high blood pressure, hypertensive.
hypertension [ipɛrtɑ̃sjɔ̃] *nf* high blood pressure, hypertension.
hypertrophié, e [ipɛrtrɔfje] *adj* hypertrophic.
hypnose [ipnoz] *nf* hypnosis.
hypnotique [ipnɔtik] *adj* hypnotic.
hypnotiser [ipnɔtize] *vt* to hypnotize.
hypnotiseur [ipnɔtizœr] *nm* hypnotist.
hypnotisme [ipnɔtism(ə)] *nm* hypnotism.
hypocondriaque [ipɔkɔ̃drijak] *adj* hypochondriac.
hypocrisie [ipɔkrizi] *nf* hypocrisy.
hypocrite [ipɔkrit] *adj* hypocritical ♦ *nm/f* hypocrite.
hypocritement [ipɔkritmɑ̃] *adv* hypocritically.
hypotendu, e [ipɔtɑ̃dy] *adj* having low blood pressure, hypotensive.
hypotension [ipɔtɑ̃sjɔ̃] *nf* low blood pressure, hypotension.
hypoténuse [ipɔtenyz] *nf* hypotenuse.
hypothécaire [ipɔtekɛr] *adj* hypothecary; **garantie/prêt** ~ mortgage security/loan.
hypothèque [ipɔtɛk] *nf* mortgage.
hypothéquer [ipɔteke] *vt* to mortgage.
hypothermie [ipɔtɛrmi] *nf* hypothermia.
hypothèse [ipɔtɛz] *nf* hypothesis; **dans l'**~ **où** assuming that.
hypothétique [ipɔtetik] *adj* hypothetical.
hypothétiquement [ipɔtetikmɑ̃] *adv* hypothetically.
hystérectomie [isterɛktɔmi] *nf* hysterectomy.
hystérie [isteri] *nf* hysteria; ~ **collective** mass hysteria.
hystérique [isterik] *adj* hysterical.
Hz *abr* (= *Hertz*) Hz.

I i

I, i [i] *nm inv* I, i; **I comme Irma** I for Isaac (*BRIT*) *ou* Item (*US*).
IAC *sigle f* (= *insémination artificielle entre conjoints*) AIH.
IAD *sigle f* (= *insémination artificielle par donneur extérieur*) AID.
ibère [ibɛr] *adj* Iberian ♦ *nm/f*: **I**~ Iberian.
ibérique [iberik] *adj*: **la péninsule** ~ the Iberian peninsula.
ibid. [ibid] *abr* (= *ibidem*) ibid., ib.
iceberg [isbɛrg] *nm* iceberg.
ici [isi] *adv* here; **jusqu'**~ as far as this; (*temporel*) until now; **d'**~ **là** by then; (*en attendant*) in the meantime; **d'**~ **peu** before long.
icône [ikon] *nf* (*aussi INFORM*) icon.
iconoclaste [ikɔnɔklast(ə)] *nm/f* iconoclast.
iconographie [ikɔnɔgrafi] *nf* iconography; (*illustrations*) (collection of) illustrations.
id. [id] *abr* (= *idem*) id.
idéal, e, aux [ideal, -o] *adj* ideal ♦ *nm* ideal; (*système de valeurs*) ideals *pl*.
idéalement [idealmɑ̃] *adv* ideally.
idéalisation [idealizasjɔ̃] *nf* idealization.
idéaliser [idealize] *vt* to idealize.
idéalisme [idealism(ə)] *nm* idealism.
idéaliste [idealist(ə)] *adj* idealistic ♦ *nm/f* idealist.
idée [ide] *nf* idea; (*illusion*): **se faire des** ~**s** to imagine things, get ideas into one's head; **avoir dans l'**~ **que** to have an idea that; **mon** ~**, c'est que ...** I suggest that ..., I think that ...; **à l'**~ **de/que** at the idea of/that, at the thought of/that; **je n'ai pas la moindre** ~ I haven't the faintest idea; **avoir** ~ **que** to have an idea that; **avoir des** ~**s larges/ étroites** to be broad-/narrow-minded; **venir à l'**~ **de qn** to occur to sb; **en voilà des** ~**s!** the very idea!; ~ **fixe** idée fixe, obsession; ~**s noires** black *ou* dark thoughts; ~**s reçues** accepted ideas *ou* wisdom.
identifiable [idɑ̃tifjabl(ə)] *adj* identifiable.
identification [idɑ̃tifikasjɔ̃] *nf* identification.
identifier [idɑ̃tifje] *vt* to identify; ~ **qch/qn à** to identify sth/sb with; **s'**~ **à** (*héros etc*) to identify with sb/sth.
identique [idɑ̃tik] *adj*: ~ (**à**) identical (to).
identité [idɑ̃tite] *nf* identity; ~ **judiciaire** (*POLICE*) ≈ Criminal Records Office.
idéogramme [ideogram] *nm* ideogram.
idéologie [ideɔlɔʒi] *nf* ideology.
idéologique [ideɔlɔʒik] *adj* ideological.
idiomatique [idjɔmatik] *adj*: **expression** ~ idiom, idiomatic expression.
idiome [idjom] *nm* (*LING*) idiom.
idiot, e [idjo, idjɔt] *adj* idiotic ♦ *nm/f* idiot.
idiotie [idjɔsi] *nf* idiocy; (*propos*) idiotic remark *etc*.
idiotisme [idjɔtism(ə)] *nm* idiom, idiomatic phrase.
idoine [idwan] *adj* fitting.
idolâtrer [idɔlatre] *vt* to idolize.
idolâtrie [idɔlatri] *nf* idolatry.
idole [idɔl] *nf* idol.
IDS *sigle f* (= *Initiative de défense stratégique*) SDI.
idylle [idil] *nf* idyll.
idyllique [idilik] *adj* idyllic.
if [if] *nm* yew.
IFOP [ifɔp] *sigle m* (= *Institut français d'opinion*

publique) French market research institute.

IGF *sigle m* (= *impôt sur les grandes fortunes*) wealth tax.

IGH *sigle m* = *immeuble de grande hauteur.*

gloo [iglu] *nm* igloo.

IGN *sigle m* = *Institut géographique national.*

gnare [iɲaʀ] *adj* ignorant.

gnifuge [iɲifyʒ] *adj* fireproofing ♦ *nm* fireproofing (substance).

gnifuger [iɲify3e] *vt* to fireproof.

gnoble [iɲɔbl(ə)] *adj* vile.

gnominie [iɲɔmini] *nf* ignominy; (*acte*) ignominious *ou* base act.

gnominieux, euse [iɲɔminjø, øz] *adj* ignominious.

gnorance [iɲɔʀɑ̃s] *nf* ignorance; **dans l'~ de** in ignorance of, ignorant of.

gnorant, e [iɲɔʀɑ̃, -ɑ̃t] *adj* ignorant ♦ *nm/f*: **faire l'~** to pretend one doesn't know; **~ de** ignorant of, not aware of; **~ en** ignorant of, knowing nothing of.

gnoré, e [iɲɔʀe] *adj* unknown.

gnorer [iɲɔʀe] *vt* (*ne pas connaître*) not to know, be unaware *ou* ignorant of; (*être sans expérience de: plaisir, guerre etc*) not to know about, have no experience of; (*bouder: personne*) to ignore; **j'ignore comment/si** I do not know how/if; **~ que** to be unaware that, not to know that; **je n'ignore pas que ...** I'm not forgetting that ..., I'm not unaware that ...; **je l'ignore** I don't know.

IGPN *sigle f* (= *Inspection générale de la police nationale*) *police disciplinary body.*

IGS *sigle f* (= *Inspection générale des services*) *police disciplinary body for Paris.*

iguane [igwan] *nm* iguana.

il [il] *pron* he; (*animal, chose, en tournure impersonnelle*) it; *NB: en anglais les navires et les pays sont en général assimilés aux femelles, et les bébés aux choses, si le sexe n'est pas spécifié;* **~s** they; **~ neige** it's snowing; *voir aussi* **avoir.**

île [il] *nf* island; **les Î~s** the West Indies; **l'~ de Beauté** Corsica; **l'~ Maurice** Mauritius; **les ~s anglo- normandes** the Channel Islands; **les ~s Britanniques** the British Isles; **les ~s Cocos** *ou* **Keeling** the Cocos *ou* Keeling Islands; **les ~s Cook** the Cook Islands; **les ~s Scilly** the Scilly Isles, the Scillies; **les ~s Shetland** the Shetland Islands, Shetland; **les ~s Sorlingues** = **les ~s Scilly**; **les ~s Vierges** the Virgin Islands.

iliaque [iljak] *adj* (*ANAT*): **os/artère ~** iliac bone/artery.

illégal, e, aux [ilegal, -o] *adj* illegal, unlawful (*ADMIN*).

illégalement [ilegalmɑ̃] *adv* illegally.

illégalité [ilegalite] *nf* illegality; unlawfulness; **être dans l'~** to be outside the law.

illégitime [ileʒitim] *adj* illegitimate; (*optimisme, sévérité*) unjustified, unwarranted.

illégitimement [ileʒitimmɑ̃] *adv* illegitimately.

illégitimité [ileʒitimite] *nf* illegitimacy; **gouverner dans l'~** to rule illegally.

illettré, e [iletʀe] *adj*, *nm/f* illiterate.

illicite [ilisit] *adj* illicit.

illicitement [ilisitmɑ̃] *adv* illicitly.

illico [iliko] *adv* (*fam*) pronto.

illimité, e [ilimite] *adj* (*immense*) boundless, unlimited; (*congé, durée*) indefinite, unlimited.

illisible [ilizibl(ə)] *adj* illegible; (*roman*) unreadable.

illisiblement [ilizibləmɑ̃] *adv* illegibly.

illogique [ilɔʒik] *adj* illogical.

illogisme [ilɔʒism(ə)] *nm* illogicality.

illumination [ilyminɑsjɔ̃] *nf* illumination, floodlighting; (*inspiration*) flash of inspiration; **~s** *nfpl* illuminations, lights.

illuminé, e [ilymine] *adj* lit up; illuminated, floodlit ♦ *nm/f* (*fig: péj*) crank.

illuminer [ilymine] *vt* to light up; (*monument, rue: pour une fête*) to illuminate, floodlight; **s'~** *vi* to light up.

illusion [ilyzjɔ̃] *nf* illusion; **se faire des ~s** to delude o.s.; **faire ~** to delude *ou* fool people; **~ d'optique** optical illusion.

illusionner [ilyzjɔne] *vt* to delude; **s'~ (sur qn/qch)** to delude o.s. (about sb/sth).

illusionnisme [ilyzjɔnism(ə)] *nm* conjuring.

illusionniste [ilyzjɔnist(ə)] *nm/f* conjuror.

illusoire [ilyzwaʀ] *adj* illusory, illusive.

illustrateur [ilystʀatœʀ] *nm* illustrator.

illustratif, ive [ilystʀatif, -iv] *adj* illustrative.

illustration [ilystʀɑsjɔ̃] *nf* illustration; (*d'un ouvrage: photos*) illustrations *pl*.

illustre [ilystʀ(ə)] *adj* illustrious, renowned.

illustré, e [ilystʀe] *adj* illustrated ♦ *nm* illustrated magazine; (*pour enfants*) comic.

illustrer [ilystʀe] *vt* to illustrate; **s'~** to become famous, win fame.

îlot [ilo] *nm* small island, islet; (*de maisons*) block; (*petite zone*): **un ~ de verdure** an island of greenery, a patch of green.

ils [il] *pron voir* **il.**

image [imaʒ] *nf* (*gén*) picture; (*comparaison, ressemblance, OPTIQUE*) image; **~ de** picture *ou* image of; **~ d'Épinal** (social) stereotype; **~ de marque** brand image; (*d'une personne*) (public) image; (*d'une entreprise*) corporate image; **~ pieuse** holy picture.

imagé, e [imaʒe] *adj* full of imagery.

imaginable [imaʒinabl(ə)] *adj* imaginable; **difficilement ~** hard to imagine.

imaginaire [imaʒinɛʀ] *adj* imaginary.

imaginatif, ive [imaʒinatif, -iv] *adj* imaginative.

imagination [imaʒinɑsjɔ̃] *nf* imagination; (*chimère*) fancy, imagining; **avoir de l'~** to be imaginative, have a good imagination.

imaginer [imaʒine] *vt* to imagine; (*croire*): **qu'allez-vous ~ là?** what on earth are you thinking of?; (*inventer: expédient, mesure*) to devise, think up; **s'~** *vt* (*se figurer: scène etc*) to imagine, picture; **s'~ à 60 ans** to picture *ou* imagine o.s. at 60; **s'~ que** to imagine that; **s'~ pouvoir faire qch** to think one can do sth; **j'imagine qu'il a voulu plaisanter** I suppose he was joking; ~ **de faire** (*se mettre dans l'idée de*) to dream up the idea of doing.

imbattable [ɛ̃batabl(ə)] *adj* unbeatable.

imbécile [ɛ̃besil] *adj* idiotic ♦ *nm/f* idiot; (*MÉD*) imbecile.

imbécillité [ɛ̃besilite] *nf* idiocy; imbecility; idiotic action (*ou* remark *etc*).

imberbe [ɛ̃bɛʀb(ə)] *adj* beardless.

imbiber [ɛ̃bibe] *vt*: ~ **qch de** to moisten *ou* wet sth with; **s'~ de** to become saturated with; **imbibé(e) d'eau** (*chaussures, étoffe*) saturated; (*terre*) waterlogged.

imbriqué, e [ɛ̃bʀike] *adj* overlapping.

imbriquer [ɛ̃bʀike]: **s'~** *vi* to overlap (each other); (*fig*) to become interlinked *ou* interwoven.

imbroglio [ɛ̃bʀɔljo] *nm* imbroglio.

imbu, e [ɛ̃by] *adj*: ~ **de** full of; ~ **de soi-même/sa supériorité** full of oneself/one's superiority.

imbuvable [ɛ̃byvabl(ə)] *adj* undrinkable.

imitable [imitabl(ə)] *adj* imitable; **facilement ~** easily imitated.

imitateur, trice [imitatœʀ, -tʀis] *nm/f* (*gén*) imitator; (*MUSIC-HALL: d'une personnalité*) impersonator.

imitation [imitɑsjɔ̃] *nf* imitation; impersonation; **sac ~ cuir** bag in imitation *ou* simulated leather; **à l'~ de** in imitation of.

imiter [imite] *vt* to imitate; (*personne*) to imitate, impersonate; (*contrefaire: signature, document*) to forge, copy; (*ressembler à*) to look like; **il se leva et je l'imitai** he got up and I did likewise.

imm. *abr* = **immeuble**.

immaculé, e [imakyle] *adj* spotless, immaculate; **l'I~e Conception** (*REL*) the Immaculate Conception.

immanent, e [imanɑ̃, -ɑ̃t] *adj* immanent.

immangeable [ɛ̃mɑ̃ʒabl(ə)] *adj* inedible, uneatable.

immanquable [ɛ̃mɑ̃kabl(ə)] *adj* (*cible*) impossible to miss; (*fatal, inévitable*) bound to happen, inevitable.

immanquablement [ɛ̃mɑ̃kabləmɑ̃] *adv* inevitably.

immatériel, le [imateʀjɛl] *adj* ethereal; (*PHILOSOPHIE*) immaterial.

immatriculation [imatʀikylɑsjɔ̃] *nf* registration.

immatriculer [imatʀikyle] *vt* to register; **faire/se faire ~** to register; **voiture immatriculée dans la Seine** car with a Seine registration (number).

immature [imatyʀ] *adj* immature.

immaturité [imatyʀite] *nf* immaturity.

immédiat, e [imedja, -at] *adj* immediate ♦ *nm*: **dans l'~** for the time being; **dans le voisinage ~ de** in the immediate vicinity of.

immédiatement [imedjatmɑ̃] *adv* immediately.

immémorial, e, aux [imemɔʀjal, -o] *adj* ancient, age-old.

immense [imɑ̃s] *adj* immense.

immensément [imɑ̃semɑ̃] *adv* immensely.

immensité [imɑ̃site] *nf* immensity.

immerger [imɛʀʒe] *vt* to immerse, submerge; (*câble etc*) to lay under water; (*déchets*) to dump at sea; **s'~** *vi* (*sous-marin*) to dive, submerge.

immérité, e [imeʀite] *adj* undeserved.

immersion [imɛʀsjɔ̃] *nf* immersion.

immettable [ɛ̃mɛtabl(ə)] *adj* unwearable.

immeuble [imœbl(ə)] *nm* building ♦ *adj* (*JUR*) immovable, real; ~ **locatif** block of rented flats (*BRIT*), rental building (*US*); ~ **de rapport** investment property.

immigrant, e [imigʀɑ̃, -ɑ̃t] *nm/f* immigrant.

immigration [imigʀɑsjɔ̃] *nf* immigration.

immigré, e [imigʀe] *nm/f* immigrant.

immigrer [imigʀe] *vi* to immigrate.

imminence [iminɑ̃s] *nf* imminence.

imminent, e [iminɑ̃, -ɑ̃t] *adj* imminent, impending.

immiscer [imise]: **s'~** *vi*: **s'~ dans** to interfere in *ou* with.

immixtion [imiksjɔ̃] *nf* interference.

immobile [imɔbil] *adj* still, motionless; (*pièce de machine*) fixed; (*fig*) unchanging; **rester/se tenir ~** to stay/keep still.

immobilier, ière [imɔbilje, -jɛʀ] *adj* property *cpd*, in real property ♦ *nm*: **l'~** the property *ou* the real estate business.

immobilisation [imɔbilizɑsjɔ̃] *nf* immobilization; **~s** *nfpl* (*JUR*) fixed assets.

immobiliser [imɔbilize] *vt* (*gén*) to immobilize; (*circulation, véhicule, affaires*) to bring to a standstill; **s'~** (*personne*) to stand still; (*machine, véhicule*) to come to a halt *ou* a standstill.

immobilisme [imɔbilism(ə)] *nm* strong resistance *ou* opposition to change.

immobilité [imɔbilite] *nf* immobility.

immodéré, e [imɔdeʀe] *adj* immoderate, inordinate.

immodérément [imɔdeʀemɑ̃] *adv* immoderately.

immoler [imɔle] *vt* to sacrifice.

immonde [imɔ̃d] *adj* foul; (*sale: ruelle, taudis*) squalid.

immondices [imɔ̃dis] *nfpl* (*ordures*) refuse *sg*; (*saletés*) filth *sg*.

immoral, e, aux [imɔʀal, -o] *adj* immoral.

immoralisme [imɔʀalism(ə)] *nm* immoralism.

immoralité [imɔʀalite] *nf* immorality.

immortaliser [imɔʀtalize] *vt* to immortalize.

immortel, le [imɔʀtɛl] *adj* immortal ♦ *nf* (*BOT*)

everlasting (flower).

immuable [imyabl(ə)] *adj (inébranlable)* immutable; *(qui ne change pas)* unchanging; *(personne):* ~ **dans ses convictions** immoveable (in one's convictions).

immunisation [imynizasjɔ̃] *nf* immunization.

immuniser [imynize] *vt (MÉD)* to immunize; ~ **qn contre** to immunize sb against; *(fig)* to make sb immune to.

immunitaire [imynitɛʀ] *adj* immune.

immunité [imynite] *nf* immunity; ~ **diplomatique** diplomatic immunity; ~ **parlementaire** parliamentary privilege.

immunologie [imynɔlɔʒi] *nf* immunology.

immutabilité [imytabilite] *nf* immutability.

impact [ɛ̃pakt] *nm* impact; **point d'**~ point of impact.

impair, e [ɛ̃pɛʀ] *adj* odd ♦ *nm* faux pas, blunder; **numéros** ~**s** odd numbers.

impalpable [ɛ̃palpabl(ə)] *adj* impalpable.

impaludation [ɛ̃palydasjɔ̃] *nf* inoculation against malaria.

imparable [ɛ̃paʀabl(ə)] *adj* unstoppable.

impardonnable [ɛ̃paʀdɔnabl(ə)] *adj* unpardonable, unforgivable; **vous êtes** ~ **d'avoir fait cela** it's unforgivable of you to have done that.

imparfait, e [ɛ̃paʀfɛ, -ɛt] *adj* imperfect ♦ *nm (LING)* imperfect (tense).

imparfaitement [ɛ̃paʀfɛtmɑ̃] *adv* imperfectly.

impartial, e, aux [ɛ̃paʀsjal, -o] *adj* impartial, unbiased.

impartialité [ɛ̃paʀsjalite] *nf* impartiality.

impartir [ɛ̃paʀtiʀ] *vt:* ~ **qch à qn** to assign sth to sb; *(dons)* to bestow sth upon sb; **dans les délais impartis** in the time allowed.

impasse [ɛ̃pas] *nf* dead-end, cul-de-sac; *(fig)* deadlock; **être dans l'**~ *(négociations)* to have reached deadlock; ~ **budgétaire** budget deficit.

impassibilité [ɛ̃pasibilite] *nf* impassiveness.

impassible [ɛ̃pasibl(ə)] *adj* impassive.

impassiblement [ɛ̃pasibləmɑ̃] *adv* impassively.

impatiemment [ɛ̃pasjamɑ̃] *adv* impatiently.

impatience [ɛ̃pasjɑ̃s] *nf* impatience.

impatient, e [ɛ̃pasjɑ̃, -ɑ̃t] *adj* impatient; ~ **de faire qch** keen *ou* impatient to do sth.

impatienter [ɛ̃pasjɑ̃te] *vt* to irritate, annoy; **s'**~ *vi* to get impatient; **s'**~ **de/contre** to lose patience at/with, grow impatient at/with.

impayable [ɛ̃pejabl(ə)] *adj (drôle)* priceless.

impayé, e [ɛ̃peje] *adj* unpaid, outstanding.

impeccable [ɛ̃pekabl(ə)] *adj* faultless, impeccable; *(propre)* spotlessly clean; *(chic)* impeccably dressed; *(fam)* smashing.

impeccablement [ɛ̃pekabləmɑ̃] *adv* impeccably.

impénétrable [ɛ̃penetʀabl(ə)] *adj* impenetrable.

impénitent, e [ɛ̃penitɑ̃, -ɑ̃t] *adj* unrepentant.

impensable [ɛ̃pɑ̃sabl(ə)] *adj* unthinkable, unbelievable.

imper [ɛ̃pɛʀ] *nm* (= *imperméable*) mac.

impératif, ive [ɛ̃peʀatif, -iv] *adj* imperative; *(JUR)* mandatory ♦ *nm (LING)* imperative; ~**s** *nmpl* requirements; demands.

impérativement [ɛ̃peʀativmɑ̃] *adv* imperatively.

impératrice [ɛ̃peʀatʀis] *nf* empress.

imperceptible [ɛ̃pɛʀsɛptibl(ə)] *adj* imperceptible.

imperceptiblement [ɛ̃pɛʀsɛptibləmɑ̃] *adv* imperceptibly.

imperdable [ɛ̃pɛʀdabl(ə)] *adj* that cannot be lost.

imperfectible [ɛ̃pɛʀfɛktibl(ə)] *adj* which cannot be perfected.

imperfection [ɛ̃pɛʀfɛksjɔ̃] *nf* imperfection.

impérial, e, aux [ɛ̃peʀjal, -o] *adj* imperial ♦ *nf* upper deck; **autobus à** ~**e** double-decker bus.

impérialisme [ɛ̃peʀjalism(ə)] *nm* imperialism.

impérialiste [ɛ̃peʀjalist(ə)] *adj* imperialist.

impérieusement [ɛ̃peʀjøzmɑ̃] *adv:* **avoir** ~ **besoin de qch** to have urgent need of sth.

impérieux, euse [ɛ̃peʀjø, -øz] *adj (caractère, ton)* imperious; *(obligation, besoin)* pressing, urgent.

impérissable [ɛ̃peʀisabl(ə)] *adj* undying, imperishable.

imperméabilisation [ɛ̃pɛʀmeabilizasjɔ̃] *nf* waterproofing.

imperméabiliser [ɛ̃pɛʀmeabilize] *vt* to waterproof.

imperméable [ɛ̃pɛʀmeabl(ə)] *adj* waterproof; *(GÉO)* impermeable; *(fig):* ~ **à** impervious to ♦ *nm* raincoat; ~ **à l'air** airtight.

impersonnel, le [ɛ̃pɛʀsɔnɛl] *adj* impersonal.

impertinemment [ɛ̃pɛʀtinamɑ̃] *adv* impertinently.

impertinence [ɛ̃pɛʀtinɑ̃s] *nf* impertinence.

impertinent, e [ɛ̃pɛʀtinɑ̃, -ɑ̃t] *adj* impertinent.

imperturbable [ɛ̃pɛʀtyʀbabl(ə)] *adj (personne)* imperturbable; *(sang-froid)* unshakeable; **rester** ~ to remain unruffled.

imperturbablement [ɛ̃pɛʀtyʀbabləmɑ̃] *adv* imperturbably; unshakeably.

impétrant, e [ɛ̃petʀɑ̃, -ɑ̃t] *nm/f (JUR)* applicant.

impétueux, euse [ɛ̃petɥø, -øz] *adj* fiery.

impétuosité [ɛ̃petɥozite] *nf* fieriness.

impie [ɛ̃pi] *adj* impious, ungodly.

impiété [ɛ̃pjete] *nf* impiety.

impitoyable [ɛ̃pitwajabl(ə)] *adj* pitiless, merciless.

impitoyablement [ɛ̃pitwajabləmɑ̃] *adv* mercilessly.

implacable [ɛ̃plakabl(ə)] *adj* implacable.

implacablement [ɛ̃plakabləmɑ̃] *adv* implacably.

implant [ɛ̃plɑ̃] *nm (MÉD)* implant.

implantation [ɛ̃plɑ̃tasjɔ̃] *nf* establishment; settling; implantation.

implanter [ɛ̃plɑ̃te] *vt* (*usine, industrie, usage*) to establish; (*colons etc*) to settle; (*idée, préjugé*) to implant; **s'~ dans** to be established in; to settle in; to become implanted in.

implémenter [ɛ̃plemɑ̃te] *vt* to implement.

implication [ɛ̃plikasjɔ̃] *nf* implication.

implicite [ɛ̃plisit] *adj* implicit.

implicitement [ɛ̃plisitmɑ̃] *adv* implicitly.

impliquer [ɛ̃plike] *vt* to imply; **~ qn (dans)** to implicate sb (in).

implorant, e [ɛ̃plɔRɑ̃, -ɑ̃t] *adj* imploring.

implorer [ɛ̃plɔRe] *vt* to implore.

imploser [ɛ̃plɔze] *vi* to implode.

implosion [ɛ̃plɔzjɔ̃] *nf* implosion.

impoli, e [ɛ̃pɔli] *adj* impolite, rude.

impoliment [ɛ̃pɔlimɑ̃] *adv* impolitely.

impolitesse [ɛ̃pɔlites] *nf* impoliteness, rudeness; (*propos*) impolite *ou* rude remark.

impondérable [ɛ̃pɔ̃deRabl(ə)] *nm* imponderable.

impopulaire [ɛ̃pɔpylɛR] *adj* unpopular.

impopularité [ɛ̃pɔpylaRite] *nf* unpopularity.

importable [ɛ̃pɔRtabl(ə)] *adj* (*COMM: marchandise*) importable; (*vêtement: immettable*) unwearable.

importance [ɛ̃pɔRtɑ̃s] *nf* importance; **avoir l'~** to be important; **sans ~** unimportant; **d'~** important, considerable; **quelle ~?** what does it matter?

important, e [ɛ̃pɔRtɑ̃, -ɑ̃t] *adj* important; (*en quantité*) considerable, sizeable; (*: gamme, dégâts*) extensive; (*péj: airs, ton*) self-important ♦ *nm*: **l'~** the important thing.

importateur, trice [ɛ̃pɔRtatœR, -tRis] *adj* importing ♦ *nm/f* importer; **pays ~ de blé** wheat-importing country.

importation [ɛ̃pɔRtasjɔ̃] *nf* import; introduction; (*produit*) import.

importer [ɛ̃pɔRte] *vt* (*COMM*) to import; (*maladies, plantes*) to introduce ♦ *vi* (*être important*) to matter; **~ à qn** to matter to sb; **il importe de** it is important to; **il importe qu'il fasse** he must do, it is important that he should do; **peu m'importe** I don't care; **peu importe** it doesn't matter; **peu importe (que)** it doesn't matter (if); **peu importe le prix** never mind the price; *voir aussi* **n'importe**.

import-export [ɛ̃pɔRɛkspɔR] *nm* import-export business.

importun, e [ɛ̃pɔRtœ̃, -yn] *adj* irksome, importunate; (*arrivée, visite*) inopportune, ill-timed ♦ *nm* intruder.

importuner [ɛ̃pɔRtyne] *vt* to bother.

imposable [ɛ̃pozabl(ə)] *adj* taxable.

imposant, e [ɛ̃pozɑ̃, -ɑ̃t] *adj* imposing.

imposé, e [ɛ̃poze] *adj* (*soumis à l'impôt*) taxed; (*GYM etc: figures*) set.

imposer [ɛ̃poze] *vt* (*taxer*) to tax; (*REL*): **~ les mains** to lay on hands; **~ qch à qn** to impose sth on sb; **s'~** (*être nécessaire*) to be

imperative; (*montrer sa proéminence*) to stand out, emerge; (*artiste: se faire connaître*) to win recognition, come to the fore; **en ~** to be imposing; **~ à** to impress; **ça s'impose** it's essential, it's vital.

imposition [ɛ̃pozisjɔ̃] *nf* (*ADMIN*) taxation.

impossibilité [ɛ̃posibilite] *nf* impossibility; **être dans l'~ de faire** to be unable to do, find it impossible to do.

impossible [ɛ̃posibl(ə)] *adj* impossible ♦ *nm*: **l'~** the impossible; **à faire** impossible to do; **il m'est ~ de le faire** it is impossible for me to do it, I can't possibly do it; **faire l'~ (pour que)** to do one's utmost (so that); **si, par ~ ...** if, by some miracle ....

imposteur [ɛ̃pɔstœR] *nm* impostor.

imposture [ɛ̃pɔstyR] *nf* imposture, deception.

impôt [ɛ̃po] *nm* tax; (*taxes*) taxation, taxes *pl*; **~s** *nmpl* (*contributions*) (income) tax *sg*; **payer 1 000 F d'~s** to pay 1,000 F in tax; **~ direct/indirect** direct/indirect tax; **~ sur le chiffre d'affaires** tax on turnover; **~ foncier** land tax; **~ sur la fortune** wealth tax; **~ sur les plus-values** capital gains tax; **~ sur le revenu** income tax; **~ sur le RPP** personal income tax; **~ sur les sociétés** tax on companies; **~s locaux** rates, local taxes (*US*), ≈ council tax (*BRIT*).

impotence [ɛ̃pɔtɑ̃s] *nf* disability.

impotent, e [ɛ̃pɔtɑ̃, -ɑ̃t] *adj* disabled.

impraticable [ɛ̃pRatikabl(ə)] *adj* (*projet*) impracticable, unworkable; (*piste*) impassable.

imprécation [ɛ̃pRekasjɔ̃] *nf* imprecation.

imprécis, e [ɛ̃pResi, -iz] *adj* (*contours, souvenir*) imprecise, vague; (*tir*) inaccurate, imprecise.

imprécision [ɛ̃pResizjɔ̃] *nf* imprecision.

imprégner [ɛ̃pReɲe] *vt* (*tissu, tampon*): **~ (de)** to soak *ou* impregnate (with); (*lieu, air*): **~ (de)** to fill (with); (*suj: amertume, ironie*) to pervade; **s'~ de** to become impregnated with; to be filled with; (*fig*) to absorb.

imprenable [ɛ̃pRənabl(ə)] *adj* (*forteresse*) impregnable; **vue ~** unimpeded outlook.

impresario [ɛ̃pResaRjo] *nm* manager, impresario.

impression [ɛ̃pResjɔ̃] *nf* impression; (*d'un ouvrage, tissu*) printing; (*PHOTO*) exposure; **faire bonne ~** to make a good impression; **donner une ~ de/l'~ que** to give the impression of/that; **avoir l'~ de/que** to have the impression of/that; **faire ~** to make an impression; **~s de voyage** impressions of one's journey.

impressionnable [ɛ̃pResjɔnabl(ə)] *adj* impressionable.

impressionnant, e [ɛ̃pResjɔnɑ̃, -ɑ̃t] *adj* impressive; upsetting.

impressionner [ɛ̃pResjɔne] *vt* (*frapper*) to impress; (*troubler*) to upset; (*PHOTO*) to expose.

impressionnisme [ɛ̃pʀesjɔnism(ə)] *nm* impressionism.

impressionniste [ɛ̃pʀesjɔnist(ə)] *adj, nm/f* impressionist.

imprévisible [ɛ̃pʀevizibl(ə)] *adj* unforeseeable; (*réaction, personne*) unpredictable.

imprévoyance [ɛ̃pʀevwajɑ̃s] *nf* lack of foresight.

imprévoyant, e [ɛ̃pʀevwajɑ̃, -ɑ̃t] *adj* lacking in foresight; (*en matière d'argent*) improvident.

imprévu, e [ɛ̃pʀevy] *adj* unforeseen, unexpected ♦ *nm* unexpected incident; l'~ the unexpected; **en cas d'**~ if anything unexpected happens; **sauf** ~ barring anything unexpected.

imprimante [ɛ̃pʀimɑ̃t] *nf* (*INFORM*) printer; ~ **à bulle d'encre** bubblejet printer; ~ **à jet d'encre** ink-jet printer; ~ **à laser** laser printer; ~ (**ligne par) ligne** line printer; ~ **à marguerite** daisy-wheel printer; ~ **matricielle** dot-matrix printer; ~ **thermique** thermal printer.

imprimé [ɛ̃pʀime] *nm* (*formulaire*) printed form; (*POSTES*) printed matter *no pl*; (*tissu*) printed fabric; **un** ~ **à fleurs/pois** (*tissu*) a floral/polka-dot print.

imprimer [ɛ̃pʀime] *vt* to print; (*INFORM*) to print (out); (*apposer: visa, cachet*) to stamp; (*empreinte etc*) to imprint; (*publier*) to publish; (*communiquer: mouvement, impulsion*) to impart, transmit.

imprimerie [ɛ̃pʀimʀi] *nf* printing; (*établissement*) printing works *sg*; (*atelier*) printing house, printery.

imprimeur [ɛ̃pʀimœʀ] *nm* printer; **imprimeur-éditeur/-libraire** printer and publisher/ bookseller.

improbable [ɛ̃pʀɔbabl(ə)] *adj* unlikely, improbable.

improductif, ive [ɛ̃pʀɔdyktif, -iv] *adj* unproductive.

impromptu, e [ɛ̃pʀɔ̃pty] *adj* impromptu; (*départ*) sudden.

imprononçable [ɛ̃pʀɔnɔ̃sabl(ə)] *adj* unpronounceable.

impropre [ɛ̃pʀɔpʀ(ə)] *adj* inappropriate; ~ **à** unsuitable for.

improprement [ɛ̃pʀɔpʀəmɑ̃] *adv* improperly.

impropriété [ɛ̃pʀɔpʀijete] *nf*: ~ (**de langage**) incorrect usage *no pl*.

improvisation [ɛ̃pʀɔvizasjɔ̃] *nf* improvization.

improvisé, e [ɛ̃pʀɔvize] *adj* makeshift, improvized; (*jeu etc*) scratch, improvized; **avec des moyens** ~**s** using whatever comes to hand.

improviser [ɛ̃pʀɔvize] *vt, vi* to improvize; **s'**~ (*secours, réunion*) to be improvized; **s'**~ **cuisinier** to (decide to) act as cook; ~ **qn cuisinier** to get sb to act as cook.

improviste [ɛ̃pʀɔvist(ə)]: **à l'**~ *adv* unexpectedly, without warning.

imprudemment [ɛ̃pʀydamɑ̃] *adv* carelessly; unwisely, imprudently.

imprudence [ɛ̃pʀydɑ̃s] *nf* carelessness *no pl*; imprudence *no pl*; act of carelessness; foolish *ou* unwise action.

imprudent, e [ɛ̃pʀydɑ̃, -ɑ̃t] *adj* (*conducteur, geste, action*) careless; (*remarque*) unwise, imprudent; (*projet*) foolhardy.

impubère [ɛ̃pybɛʀ] *adj* below the age of puberty.

impubliable [ɛ̃pyblijabl(ə)] *adj* unpublishable.

impudemment [ɛ̃pydamɑ̃] *adv* impudently.

impudence [ɛ̃pydɑ̃s] *nf* impudence.

impudent, e [ɛ̃pydɑ̃, -ɑ̃t] *adj* impudent.

impudeur [ɛ̃pydœʀ] *nf* shamelessness.

impudique [ɛ̃pydik] *adj* shameless.

impuissance [ɛ̃pɥisɑ̃s] *nf* helplessness; ineffectualness; impotence.

impuissant, e [ɛ̃pɥisɑ̃, -ɑ̃t] *adj* helpless; (*sans effet*) ineffectual; (*sexuellement*) impotent ♦ *nm* impotent man; ~ **à faire qch** powerless to do sth.

impulsif, ive [ɛ̃pylsif, -iv] *adj* impulsive.

impulsion [ɛ̃pylsjɔ̃] *nf* (*ÉLEC, instinct*) impulse; (*élan, influence*) impetus.

impulsivement [ɛ̃pylsivmɑ̃] *adv* impulsively.

impulsivité [ɛ̃pylsivite] *nf* impulsiveness.

impunément [ɛ̃pynemɑ̃] *adv* with impunity.

impuni, e [ɛ̃pyni] *adj* unpunished.

impunité [ɛ̃pynite] *nf* impunity.

impur, e [ɛ̃pyʀ] *adj* impure.

impureté [ɛ̃pyʀte] *nf* impurity.

imputable [ɛ̃pytabl(ə)] *adj* (*attribuable*): ~ **à** imputable to, ascribable to; (*COMM: somme*): ~ **sur** chargeable to.

imputation [ɛ̃pytasjɔ̃] *nf* imputation, charge.

imputer [ɛ̃pyte] *vt* (*attribuer*): ~ **qch à** to ascribe *ou* impute sth to; (*COMM*): ~ **qch à** *ou* **sur** to charge sth to.

imputrescible [ɛ̃pytʀesibl(ə)] *adj* rotproof.

in [in] *adj inv* in, trendy.

INA [ina] *sigle m* (= *Institut national de l'audio-visuel*) *library of television archives*.

inabordable [inabɔʀdabl(ə)] *adj* (*lieu*) inaccessible; (*cher*) prohibitive.

inaccentué, e [inaksɑ̃tɥe] *adj* (*LING*) unstressed.

inacceptable [inaksɛptabl(ə)] *adj* unacceptable.

inaccessible [inaksesibl(ə)] *adj* inaccessible; (*objectif*) unattainable; (*insensible*): ~ **à** impervious to.

inaccoutumé, e [inakutyme] *adj* unaccustomed.

inachevé, e [inaʃve] *adj* unfinished.

inactif, ive [inaktif, -iv] *adj* inactive, idle.

inaction [inaksjɔ̃] *nf* inactivity.

inactivité [inaktivite] *nf* (*ADMIN*): **en** ~ out of active service.

inadaptation [inadaptasjɔ̃] *nf* (*PSYCH*) maladjustment.

inadapté, e [inadapte] *adj* (*PSYCH: adulte, enfant*) maladjusted ♦ *nm/f* (*péj: adulte: asocial*) misfit; ~ **à** not adapted to, unsuited to.

inadéquat, e [inadekwa, wat] *adj* inadequate.

inadéquation [inadekwɑsjɔ̃] *nf* inadequacy.

inadmissible [inadmisibl(ə)] *adj* inadmissible.

inadvertance [inadvɛrtɑ̃s]: **par** ~ *adv* inadvertently.

inaliénable [inaljenabl(ə)] *adj* inalienable.

inaltérable [inaltɛrabl(ə)] *adj* (*matière*) stable; (*fig*) unchanging; ~ **à** unaffected by; **couleur** ~ (**au lavage/à la lumière**) fast colour/fade-resistant colour.

inamovible [inamɔvibl(ə)] *adj* fixed; (*JUR*) irremovable.

inanimé, e [inanime] *adj* (*matière*) inanimate; (*évanoui*) unconscious; (*sans vie*) lifeless.

inanité [inanite] *nf* futility.

inanition [inanisjɔ̃] *nf*: **tomber d'**~ to faint with hunger (and exhaustion).

inaperçu, e [inapɛrsy] *adj*: **passer** ~ to go unnoticed.

inappétence [inapetɑ̃s] *nf* lack of appetite.

inapplicable [inaplikabl(ə)] *adj* inapplicable.

inapplication [inaplikɑsjɔ̃] *nf* lack of application.

inappliqué, e [inaplike] *adj* lacking in application.

inappréciable [inapresjabl(ə)] *adj* (*service*) invaluable; (*différence, nuance*) inappreciable.

inapte [inapt(ə)] *adj*: ~ **à** incapable of; (*MIL*) unfit for.

inaptitude [inaptityd] *nf* inaptitude; unfitness.

inarticulé, e [inartikyle] *adj* inarticulate.

inassimilable [inasimilabl(ə)] *adj* that cannot be assimilated.

inassouvi, e [inasuvi] *adj* unsatisfied, unfulfilled.

inattaquable [inatakabl(ə)] *adj* (*MIL*) unassailable; (*texte, preuve*) irrefutable.

inattendu, e [inatɑ̃dy] *adj* unexpected ♦ *nm*: **l'**~ the unexpected.

inattentif, ive [inatɑ̃tif, -iv] *adj* inattentive; ~ **à** (*dangers, détails*) heedless of.

inattention [inatɑ̃sjɔ̃] *nf* inattention; (*inadvertance*): **une minute d'**~ a minute of inattention, a minute's carelessness; **par** ~ inadvertently; **faute d'**~ careless mistake.

inaudible [inodibl(ə)] *adj* inaudible.

inaugural, e, aux [inɔgyral, -o] *adj* (*cérémonie*) inaugural, opening; (*vol, voyage*) maiden.

inauguration [inɔgyrɑsjɔ̃] *nf* unveiling; opening; **discours/cérémonie d'**~ inaugural speech/ceremony.

inaugurer [inɔgyre] *vt* (*monument*) to unveil; (*exposition, usine*) to open; (*fig*) to inaugurate.

inauthenticité [inɔtɑ̃tisite] *nf* inauthenticity.

inavouable [inavwabl(ə)] *adj* undisclosable;

(*honteux*) shameful.

inavoué, e [inavwe] *adj* unavowed.

INC *sigle m* (= *Institut national de la consommation*) *consumer research organization.*

inca [ɛ̃ka] *adj inv* Inca ♦ *nm/f*: **I**~ Inca.

incalculable [ɛ̃kalkylabl(ə)] *adj* incalculable; **un nombre** ~ **de** countless numbers of.

incandescence [ɛ̃kɑ̃desɑ̃s] *nf* incandescence; **en** ~ incandescent, white-hot; **porter à** ~ to heat white-hot; **lampe/manchon à** ~ incandescent lamp/(gas) mantle.

incandescent, e [ɛ̃kɑ̃desɑ̃, -ɑ̃t] *adj* incandescent, white-hot.

incantation [ɛ̃kɑ̃tɑsjɔ̃] *nf* incantation.

incantatoire [ɛ̃kɑ̃tatwar] *adj*: **formule** ~ incantation.

incapable [ɛ̃kapabl(ə)] *adj* incapable; ~ **de faire** incapable of doing; (*empêché*) unable to do.

incapacitant, e [ɛ̃kapasitɑ̃, -ɑ̃t] *adj* (*MIL*) incapacitating.

incapacité [ɛ̃kapasite] *nf* incapability; (*JUR*) incapacity; **être dans l'**~ **de faire** to be unable to do; ~ **permanente/de travail** permanent/industrial disablement; ~ **électorale** ineligibility to vote.

incarcération [ɛ̃karserɑsjɔ̃] *nf* incarceration.

incarcérer [ɛ̃karsere] *vt* to incarcerate.

incarnat, e [ɛ̃karna, -at] *adj* (*rosy*) pink.

incarnation [ɛ̃karnɑsjɔ̃] *nf* incarnation.

incarné, e [ɛ̃karne] *adj* incarnate; (*ongle*) ingrown.

incarner [ɛ̃karne] *vt* to embody, personify; (*THÉÂT*) to play; (*REL*) to incarnate; **s'**~ **dans** (*REL*) to be incarnate in.

incartade [ɛ̃kartad] *nf* prank, escapade.

incassable [ɛ̃kasabl(ə)] *adj* unbreakable.

incendiaire [ɛ̃sɑ̃djɛr] *adj* incendiary; (*fig: discours*) inflammatory ♦ *nm/f* fire-raiser, arsonist.

incendie [ɛ̃sɑ̃di] *nm* fire; ~ **criminel** arson *no pl*; ~ **de forêt** forest fire.

incendier [ɛ̃sɑ̃dje] *vt* (*mettre le feu à*) to set fire to, set alight; (*brûler complètement*) to burn down.

incertain, e [ɛ̃sɛrtɛ̃, -ɛn] *adj* uncertain; (*temps*) uncertain, unsettled; (*imprécis: contours*) indistinct, blurred.

incertitude [ɛ̃sɛrtityd] *nf* uncertainty.

incessamment [ɛ̃sesamɑ̃] *adv* very shortly.

incessant, e [ɛ̃sesɑ̃, -ɑ̃t] *adj* incessant, unceasing.

incessible [ɛ̃sesibl(ə)] *adj* (*JUR*) non-transferable.

inceste [ɛ̃sɛst(ə)] *nm* incest.

incestueux, euse [ɛ̃sɛstɥø, -øz] *adj* incestuous.

inchangé, e [ɛ̃ʃɑ̃ʒe] *adj* unchanged, unaltered.

inchantable [ɛ̃ʃɑ̃tabl(ə)] *adj* unsingable.

inchauffable [ɛ̃ʃofabl(ə)] *adj* impossible

to heat.

incidemment [ɛ̃sidamɑ̃] *adv* in passing.

incidence [ɛ̃sidɑ̃s] *nf* (*effet, influence*) effect; (*PHYSIQUE*) incidence.

incident [ɛ̃sidɑ̃] *nm* incident; ~ **de frontière** border incident; ~ **de parcours** minor hitch *ou* setback; ~ **technique** technical difficulties *pl*, technical hitch.

incinérateur [ɛ̃sineʀatœʀ] *nm* incinerator.

incinération [ɛ̃sineʀasjɔ̃] *nf* (*d'ordures*) incineration; (*crémation*) cremation.

incinérer [ɛ̃sineʀe] *vt* (*ordures*) to incinerate; (*mort*) to cremate.

incise [ɛ̃siz] *nf* (*LING*) interpolated clause.

inciser [ɛ̃size] *vt* to make an incision in; (*abcès*) to lance.

incisif, ive [ɛ̃sizif, -iv] *adj* incisive, cutting ♦ *nf* incisor.

incision [ɛ̃sizjɔ̃] *nf* incision; (*d'un abcès*) lancing.

incitation [ɛ̃sitasjɔ̃] *nf* (*encouragement*) incentive; (*provocation*) incitement.

inciter [ɛ̃site] *vt*: ~ **qn à (faire) qch** to prompt *ou* encourage sb to do sth; (*à la révolte etc*) to incite sb to do sth.

incivil, e [ɛ̃sivil] *adj* uncivil.

incivilité [ɛ̃sivilite] *nf* incivility.

inclinable [ɛ̃klinabl(ə)] *adj* (*dossier etc*) tilting; **siège à dossier** ~ reclining seat.

inclinaison [ɛ̃klinezɔ̃] *nf* (*déclivité: d'une route etc*) incline; (*: d'un toit*) slope; (*état penché: d'un mur*) lean; (*: de la tête*) tilt; (*: d'un navire*) list.

inclination [ɛ̃klinasjɔ̃] *nf* (*penchant*) inclination, tendency; **montrer de l'~ pour les sciences** *etc* to show an inclination for the sciences *etc*; ~**s égoïstes/altruistes** egoistic/altruistic tendencies; ~ **de (la) tête** nod (of the head); ~ **(de buste)** bow.

incliner [ɛ̃kline] *vt* (*bouteille*) to tilt; (*tête*) to incline; (*inciter*): ~ **qn à qch/à faire** to encourage sb towards sth/to do ♦ *vi*: ~ **à qch/à faire** (*tendre à, pencher pour*) to incline towards sth/doing, tend towards sth/to do; **s'~** (*route*) to slope; (*toit*) to be sloping; **s'~ (devant)** to bow (before).

inclure [ɛ̃klyʀ] *vt* to include; (*joindre à un envoi*) to enclose; **jusqu'au 10 mars inclus** until 10th March inclusive.

inclus, e [ɛ̃kly, -yz] *pp de* **inclure** ♦ *adj* (*joint à un envoi*) enclosed; (*compris: frais, dépense*) included; (*MATH: ensemble*): ~ **dans** included in; **jusqu'au troisième chapitre** ~ up to and including the third chapter.

inclusion [ɛ̃klyzjɔ̃] *nf* (*voir inclure*) inclusion; enclosing.

inclusivement [ɛ̃klyzivmɑ̃] *adv* inclusively.

inclut [ɛ̃kly] *vb voir* **inclure**.

incoercible [ɛ̃kɔɛʀsibl(ə)] *adj* uncontrollable.

incognito [ɛ̃kɔɲito] *adv* incognito ♦ *nm*: **garder l'~** to remain incognito.

incohérence [ɛ̃kɔeʀɑ̃s] *nf* inconsistency; incoherence.

incohérent, e [ɛ̃kɔeʀɑ̃, -ɑ̃t] *adj* inconsistent; incoherent.

incollable [ɛ̃kɔlabl(ə)] *adj* (*riz*) that does not stick; (*fam: personne*): **il est** ~ he's got all the answers.

incolore [ɛ̃kɔlɔʀ] *adj* colourless.

incomber [ɛ̃kɔbe]: ~ **à** *vt* (*suj: devoirs, responsabilité*) to rest *ou* be incumbent upon; (*: frais, travail*) to be the responsibility of.

incombustible [ɛ̃kɔbystibl(ə)] *adj* incombustible.

incommensurable [ɛ̃kɔmɑ̃syʀabl(ə)] *adj* immeasurable.

incommodant, e [ɛ̃kɔmɔdɑ̃, -ɑ̃t] *adj* (*bruit*) annoying; (*chaleur*) uncomfortable.

incommode [ɛ̃kɔmɔd] *adj* inconvenient; (*posture, siège*) uncomfortable.

incommodément [ɛ̃kɔmɔdemɑ̃] *adv* (*installé, assis*) uncomfortably; (*logé, situé*) inconveniently.

incommoder [ɛ̃kɔmɔde] *vt*: ~ **qn** to bother *ou* inconvenience sb; (*embarrasser*) to make sb feel uncomfortable *ou* ill at ease.

incommodité [ɛ̃kɔmɔdite] *nf* inconvenience.

incommunicable [ɛ̃kɔmynikabl(ə)] *adj* (*JUR: droits, privilèges*) non-transferable; (*pensée*) incommunicable.

incomparable [ɛ̃kɔparabl(ə)] *adj* not comparable; (*inégalable*) incomparable, matchless.

incomparablement [ɛ̃kɔparabləmɑ̃] *adv* incomparably.

incompatibilité [ɛ̃kɔpatibilite] *nf* incompatibility; ~ **d'humeur** (mutual) incompatibility.

incompatible [ɛ̃kɔpatibl(ə)] *adj* incompatible.

incompétence [ɛ̃kɔpetɑ̃s] *nf* lack of expertise; incompetence.

incompétent, e [ɛ̃kɔpetɑ̃, -ɑ̃t] *adj* (*ignorant*) inexpert; (*incapable*) incompetent, not competent.

incomplet, ète [ɛ̃kɔplɛ, -ɛt] *adj* incomplete.

incomplètement [ɛ̃kɔplɛtmɑ̃] *adv* not completely, incompletely.

incompréhensible [ɛ̃kɔpʀeɑ̃sibl(ə)] *adj* incomprehensible.

incompréhensif, ive [ɛ̃kɔpʀeɑ̃sif, -iv] *adj* lacking in understanding, unsympathetic.

incompréhension [ɛ̃kɔpʀeɑ̃sjɔ̃] *nf* lack of understanding.

incompressible [ɛ̃kɔpʀesibl(ə)] *adj* (*PHYSIQUE*) incompressible; (*fig: dépenses*) that cannot be reduced; (*JUR: peine*) irreducible.

incompris, e [ɛ̃kɔpʀi, -iz] *adj* misunderstood.

inconcevable [ɛ̃kɔsvabl(ə)] *adj* (*conduite etc*) inconceivable; (*mystère*) incredible.

inconciliable [ɛ̃kɔsiljabl(ə)] *adj* irreconcilable.

inconditionnel, le [ɛ̃kɔdisjɔnɛl] *adj* unconditional; (*partisan*) unquestioning ♦ *nm/f* (*partisan*) unquestioning supporter.

inconditionnellement [ɛ̃kɔdisjɔnɛlmɑ̃] *adv*

unconditionally.

inconduite [ɛ̃kɔ̃dɥit] *nf* bad *ou* unsuitable behaviour *no pl.*

inconfort [ɛ̃kɔ̃fɔʀ] *nm* lack of comfort, discomfort.

inconfortable [ɛ̃kɔ̃fɔʀtabl(ə)] *adj* uncomfortable.

inconfortablement [ɛ̃kɔ̃fɔʀtabləmɑ̃] *adv* uncomfortably.

incongru, e [ɛ̃kɔ̃gʀy] *adj* unseemly; *(remarque)* ill-chosen, incongruous.

incongruité [ɛ̃kɔ̃gʀyite] *nf* unseemliness; incongruity; *(parole incongrue)* ill-chosen remark.

inconnu, e [ɛ̃kɔny] *adj* unknown; *(sentiment, plaisir)* new, strange ♦ *nm/f* stranger; unknown person *(ou* artist *etc)* ♦ *nm*: **l'**~ the unknown ♦ *nf (MATH)* unknown; *(fig)* unknown factor.

inconsciemment [ɛ̃kɔ̃sjamɑ̃] *adv* unconsciously.

inconscience [ɛ̃kɔ̃sjɑ̃s] *nf* unconsciousness; recklessness.

inconscient, e [ɛ̃kɔ̃sjɑ̃, -ɑ̃t] *adj* unconscious; *(irréfléchi)* reckless ♦ *nm (PSYCH)*: **l'**~ the subconscious, the unconscious; ~ **de** unaware of.

inconséquence [ɛ̃kɔ̃sekɑ̃s] *nf* inconsistency; thoughtlessness; *(action, parole)* thoughtless thing to do *(ou* say).

inconséquent, e [ɛ̃kɔ̃sekɑ̃, -ɑ̃t] *adj (illogique)* inconsistent; *(irréfléchi)* thoughtless.

inconsidéré, e [ɛ̃kɔ̃sideʀe] *adj* ill-considered.

inconsidérément [ɛ̃kɔ̃sideʀemɑ̃] *adv* thoughtlessly.

inconsistant, e [ɛ̃kɔ̃sistɑ̃, -ɑ̃t] *adj* flimsy, weak; *(crème etc)* runny.

inconsolable [ɛ̃kɔ̃sɔlabl(ə)] *adj* inconsolable.

inconstance [ɛ̃kɔ̃stɑ̃s] *nf* inconstancy, fickleness.

inconstant, e [ɛ̃kɔ̃stɑ̃, -ɑ̃t] *adj* inconstant, fickle.

inconstitutionnel, le [ɛ̃kɔ̃stitysjɔnɛl] *adj* unconstitutional.

incontestable [ɛ̃kɔ̃tɛstabl(ə)] *adj* unquestionable, indisputable.

incontestablement [ɛ̃kɔ̃tɛstabləmɑ̃] *adv* unquestionably, indisputably.

incontesté, e [ɛ̃kɔ̃tɛste] *adj* undisputed.

incontinence [ɛ̃kɔ̃tinɑ̃s] *nf (MÉD)* incontinence.

incontinent, e [ɛ̃kɔ̃tinɑ̃, -ɑ̃t] *adj (MÉD)* incontinent ♦ *adv (tout de suite)* forthwith.

incontournable [ɛ̃kɔ̃tuʀnabl(ə)] *adj* unavoidable.

incontrôlable [ɛ̃kɔ̃tʀolabl(ə)] *adj* unverifiable.

incontrôlé, e [ɛ̃kɔ̃tʀole] *adj* uncontrolled.

inconvenance [ɛ̃kɔ̃vnɑ̃s] *nf (parole, action)* impropriety.

inconvenant, e [ɛ̃kɔ̃vnɑ̃, -ɑ̃t] *adj* unseemly, improper.

inconvénient [ɛ̃kɔ̃venjɑ̃] *nm (d'une situation,*

d'un projet) disadvantage, drawback; *(d'un remède, changement etc)* risk, inconvenience; **si vous n'y voyez pas d'**~ if you have no objections; **y a-t-il un** ~ **à ...?** *(risque)* isn't there a risk in ...?; *(objection)* is there any objection to ...?

inconvertible [ɛ̃kɔ̃vɛʀtibl(ə)] *adj* inconvertible.

incorporation [ɛ̃kɔʀpɔʀasjɔ̃] *nf (MIL)* call-up.

incorporé, e [ɛ̃kɔʀpɔʀe] *adj (micro etc)* built-in.

incorporel, le [ɛ̃kɔʀpɔʀɛl] *adj (JUR)*: **biens** ~**s** intangible property.

incorporer [ɛ̃kɔʀpɔʀe] *vt*: ~ **(à)** to mix in (with); *(paragraphe etc)*: ~ **(dans)** to incorporate (in); *(territoire, immigrants)*: ~ **(dans)** to incorporate (into); *(MIL: appeler)* to recruit, call up; *(: affecter)*: ~ **qn dans** to enlist sb into.

incorrect, e [ɛ̃kɔʀɛkt] *adj (impropre, inconvenant)* improper; *(défectueux)* faulty; *(inexact)* incorrect; *(impoli)* impolite; *(déloyal)* underhand.

incorrectement [ɛ̃kɔʀɛktəmɑ̃] *adv* improperly; faultily; incorrectly; impolitely; in an underhand way.

incorrection [ɛ̃kɔʀɛksjɔ̃] *nf* impropriety; incorrectness; underhand nature; *(terme impropre)* impropriety; *(action, remarque)* improper behaviour *(ou* remark.

incorrigible [ɛ̃kɔʀiʒibl(ə)] *adj* incorrigible.

incorruptible [ɛ̃kɔʀyptibl(ə)] *adj* incorruptible.

incrédibilité [ɛ̃kʀedibilite] *nf* incredibility.

incrédule [ɛ̃kʀedyl] *adj* incredulous; *(REL)* unbelieving.

incrédulité [ɛ̃kʀedylite] *nf* incredulity; **avec** ~ incredulously.

increvable [ɛ̃kʀəvabl(ə)] *adj (pneu)* puncture-proof; *(fam)* tireless.

incriminer [ɛ̃kʀimine] *vt (personne)* to incriminate; *(action, conduite)* to bring under attack; *(bonne foi, honnêteté)* to call into question; **livre/article incriminé** offending book/article.

incrochetable [ɛ̃kʀɔʃtabl(ə)] *adj (serrure)* that can't be picked, burglarproof.

incroyable [ɛ̃kʀwajabl(ə)] *adj* incredible, unbelievable.

incroyablement [ɛ̃kʀwajabləmɑ̃] *adv* incredibly, unbelievably.

incroyant, e [ɛ̃kʀwajɑ̃, -ɑ̃t] *nm/f* non-believer.

incrustation [ɛ̃kʀystasjɔ̃] *nf* inlaying *no pl*; inlay; *(dans une chaudière etc)* fur *no pl*, scale *no pl.*

incruster [ɛ̃kʀyste] *vt (ART)*: ~ **qch dans/qch de** to inlay sth into/sth with; *(radiateur etc)* to coat with scale *ou* fur; **s'**~ *vi (invité)* to take root; *(radiateur etc)* to become coated with fur *ou* scale; **s'**~ **dans** *(suj: corps étranger, caillou)* to become embedded in.

incubateur [ɛ̃kybatœʀ] *nm* incubator.

incubation [ɛ̃kybɑsjɔ̃] nf incubation.
inculpation [ɛ̃kylpɑsjɔ̃] nf charging no pl;
charge; **sous l'~ de** on a charge of.
inculpé, e [ɛ̃kylpe] nm/f accused.
inculper [ɛ̃kylpe] vt: ~ **(de)** to charge (with).
inculquer [ɛ̃kylke] vt: ~ **qch à** to inculcate sth
in, instil sth into.
inculte [ɛ̃kylt(ə)] adj uncultivated; (esprit,
peuple) uncultured; (barbe) unkempt.
incultivable [ɛ̃kyltivabl(ə)] adj (terrain)
unworkable.
inculture [ɛ̃kyltyʀ] nf lack of education.
incurable [ɛ̃kyʀabl(ə)] adj incurable.
incurie [ɛ̃kyʀi] nf carelessness.
incursion [ɛ̃kyʀsjɔ̃] nf incursion, foray.
incurvé, e [ɛ̃kyʀve] adj curved.
incurver [ɛ̃kyʀve] vt (barre de fer) to bend into
a curve; **s'~** vi (planche, route) to bend.
Inde [ɛ̃d] nf: **l'~** India.
indécemment [ɛ̃desamɑ̃] adv indecently.
indécence [ɛ̃desɑ̃s] nf indecency; (propos,
acte) indecent remark (ou act etc).
indécent, e [ɛ̃desɑ̃, -ɑ̃t] adj indecent.
indéchiffrable [ɛ̃deʃifʀabl(ə)] adj
indecipherable.
indéchirable [ɛ̃deʃiʀabl(ə)] adj tearproof.
indécis, e [ɛ̃desi, -iz] adj indecisive; (perplexe)
undecided.
indécision [ɛ̃desizjɔ̃] nf indecision,
indecisiveness.
indéclinable [ɛ̃deklinabl(ə)] adj (LING: mot)
indeclinable.
indécomposable [ɛ̃dekɔ̃pozabl(ə)] adj that
cannot be broken down.
indécrottable [ɛ̃dekʀɔtabl(ə)] adj (fam)
hopeless.
indéfectible [ɛ̃defɛktibl(ə)] adj (attachement)
indestructible.
indéfendable [ɛ̃defɑ̃dabl(ə)] adj indefensible.
indéfini, e [ɛ̃defini] adj (imprécis, incertain)
undefined; (illimité, LING) indefinite.
indéfiniment [ɛ̃definimɑ̃] adv indefinitely.
indéfinissable [ɛ̃definisabl(ə)] adj indefinable.
indéformable [ɛ̃defɔʀmabl(ə)] adj that keeps
its shape.
indélébile [ɛ̃delebil] adj indelible.
indélicat, e [ɛ̃delika, -at] adj tactless;
(malhonnête) dishonest.
indélicatesse [ɛ̃delikatɛs] nf tactlessness;
dishonesty.
indémaillable [ɛ̃demajabl(ə)] adj run-resist.
indemne [ɛ̃dɛmn(ə)] adj unharmed.
indemnisable [ɛ̃dɛmnizabl(ə)] adj entitled to
compensation.
indemnisation [ɛ̃dɛmnizasjɔ̃] nf (somme)
indemnity, compensation.
indemniser [ɛ̃dɛmnize] vt: ~ **qn (de)** to
compensate sb (for); **se faire** ~ to get
compensation.
indemnité [ɛ̃dɛmnite] nf (dédommagement)
compensation no pl; (allocation) allowance; ~
de licenciement redundancy payment; ~ **de**

logement housing allowance; ~
parlementaire ≈ M.P.'s (BRIT) ou
Congressman's (US) salary.
indémontable [ɛ̃demɔ̃tabl(ə)] adj (meuble etc)
that cannot be dismantled, in one piece.
indéniable [ɛ̃denjabl(ə)] adj undeniable,
indisputable.
indéniablement [ɛ̃denjabləmɑ̃] adv
undeniably.
indépendamment [ɛ̃depɑ̃damɑ̃] adv
independently; ~ **de** independently of;
(abstraction faite de) irrespective of; (en plus
de) over and above.
indépendance [ɛ̃depɑ̃dɑ̃s] nf independence; ~
matérielle financial independence.
indépendant, e [ɛ̃depɑ̃dɑ̃, -ɑ̃t] adj
independent; ~ **de** independent of; **chambre**
~**e** room with private entrance; **travailleur**
~ self-employed worker.
indépendantiste [ɛ̃depɑ̃dɑ̃tist(ə)] adj, nm/f
separatist.
indéracinable [ɛ̃deʀasinabl(ə)] adj (fig:
croyance etc) ineradicable.
indéréglable [ɛ̃deʀeglabl(ə)] adj which will not
break down.
indescriptible [ɛ̃dɛskʀiptibl(ə)] adj
indescribable.
indésirable [ɛ̃dezirabl(ə)] adj undesirable.
indestructible [ɛ̃dɛstʀyktibl(ə)] adj
indestructible; (marque, impression)
indelible.
indéterminable [ɛ̃detɛʀminabl(ə)] adj
indeterminable.
indétermination [ɛ̃detɛʀminasjɔ̃] nf
indecision, indecisiveness.
indéterminé, e [ɛ̃detɛʀmine] adj unspecified;
indeterminate; indeterminable.
index [ɛ̃dɛks] nm (doigt) index finger; (d'un
livre etc) index; **mettre à l'~** to blacklist.
indexation [ɛ̃dɛksɑsjɔ̃] nf indexing.
indexé, e [ɛ̃dɛkse] adj (ÉCON): ~ **(sur)** index-
linked (to).
indexer [ɛ̃dɛkse] vt (salaire, emprunt): ~ **(sur)**
to index (on).
indicateur [ɛ̃dikatœʀ] nm (POLICE) informer;
(livre) guide; (: liste) directory; (TECH) gauge;
indicator; (ÉCON) indicator ♦ adj: **poteau** ~
signpost; **tableau** ~ indicator (board); ~ **des
chemins de fer** railway timetable; ~ **de
direction** (AUTO) indicator; ~ **immobilier**
property gazette; ~ **de niveau** level, gauge;
~ **de pression** pressure gauge; ~ **de rues**
street directory; ~ **de vitesse** speedometer.
indicatif, ive [ɛ̃dikatif, -iv] adj: **à titre** ~ for
(your) information ♦ nm (LING) indicative;
(d'une émission) theme ou signature tune;
(TÉL) dialling code; ~ **d'appel** (RADIO) call
sign.
indication [ɛ̃dikɑsjɔ̃] nf indication;
(renseignement) information no pl; ~**s** nfpl
(directives) instructions; ~ **d'origine** (COMM)
place of origin.

indice [ɛ̃dis] *nm* (*marque, signe*) indication, sign; (*POLICE: lors d'une enquête*) clue; (*JUR: présomption*) piece of evidence; (*SCIENCE, ÉCON, TECH*) index; (*ADMIN*) grading; rating; ~ **du coût de la vie** cost-of-living index; ~ **inférieur** subscript; ~ **d'octane** octane rating; ~ **des prix** price index; ~ **de traitement** salary grading.

indicible [ɛ̃disibl(ə)] *adj* inexpressible.

indien, ne [ɛ̃djɛ̃, -ɛn] *adj* Indian ♦ *nm/f*: **I~, ne** (*d'Amérique*) (American *ou* Red) Indian; (*d'Inde*) Indian.

indifféremment [ɛ̃diferamɑ̃] *adv* (*sans distinction*) equally; indiscriminately.

indifférence [ɛ̃diferɑ̃s] *nf* indifference.

indifférencié, e [ɛ̃diferɑ̃sje] *adj* undifferentiated.

indifférent, e [ɛ̃diferɑ̃, -ɑ̃t] *adj* (*peu intéressé*) indifferent; ~ **à** (*insensible à*) indifferent to, unconcerned about; (*peu intéressant pour*) indifferent to; immaterial to; **ça m'est ~ (que ...)** it doesn't matter to me (**whether ...**).

indifférer [ɛ̃difere] *vt*: **cela m'indiffère** I'm indifferent about it.

indigence [ɛ̃diʒɑ̃s] *nf* poverty; **être dans l'~** to be destitute.

indigène [ɛ̃diʒɛn] *adj* native, indigenous; (*de la région*) local ♦ *nm/f* native.

indigent, e [ɛ̃diʒɑ̃, -ɑ̃t] *adj* destitute, poverty-stricken; (*fig*) poor.

indigeste [ɛ̃diʒɛst(ə)] *adj* indigestible.

indigestion [ɛ̃diʒɛstjɔ̃] *nf* indigestion *no pl*; **avoir une ~** to have indigestion.

indignation [ɛ̃diɲasjɔ̃] *nf* indignation; **avec ~** indignantly.

indigne [ɛ̃diɲ] *adj*: ~ **(de)** unworthy (of).

indigné, e [ɛ̃diɲe] *adj* indignant.

indignement [ɛ̃diɲmɑ̃] *adv* shamefully.

indigner [ɛ̃diɲe] *vt* to make indignant; **s'~ (de/contre)** to be (*ou* become) indignant (at).

indignité [ɛ̃diɲite] *nf* unworthiness *no pl*; (*acte*) shameful act.

indigo [ɛ̃digo] *nm* indigo.

indiqué, e [ɛ̃dike] *adj* (*date, lieu*) given, appointed; (*adéquat*) appropriate, suitable; (*conseillé*) advisable; (*remède, traitement*) appropriate.

indiquer [ɛ̃dike] *vt* (*désigner*): ~ **qch/qn à qn** to point sth/sb out to sb; (*suj: pendule, aiguille*) to show; (*suj: étiquette, plan*) to show, indicate; (*faire connaître: médecin, restaurant*): ~ **qch/qn à qn** to tell sb of sth/sb; (*renseigner sur*) to point out, tell; (*déterminer: date, lieu*) to give, state; (*dénoter*) to indicate, point to; ~ **du doigt** to point out; ~ **de la main** to indicate with one's hand; ~ **du regard** to glance towards *ou* in the direction of; **pourriez-vous m'~ les toilettes/l'heure?** could you direct me to the toilets/tell me the time?

indirect, e [ɛ̃dirɛkt] *adj* indirect.

indirectement [ɛ̃dirɛktəmɑ̃] *adv* indirectly; (*apprendre*) in a roundabout way.

indiscernable [ɛ̃disɛrnabl(ə)] *adj* indiscernable.

indiscipline [ɛ̃disiplin] *nf* lack of discipline.

indiscipliné, e [ɛ̃disipline] *adj* undisciplined; (*fig*) unmanageable.

indiscret, ète [ɛ̃diskrɛ, -ɛt] *adj* indiscreet.

indiscrétion [ɛ̃diskresjɔ̃] *nf* indiscretion; **sans ~, ...** without wishing to be indiscreet, ...

indiscutable [ɛ̃diskytabl(ə)] *adj* indisputable.

indiscutablement [ɛ̃diskytabləmɑ̃] *adv* indisputably.

indiscuté, e [ɛ̃dispyte] *adj* (*incontesté: droit, chef*) undisputed.

indispensable [ɛ̃dispɑ̃sabl(ə)] *adj* indispensable, essential; ~ **à qn/pour faire qch** essential for sb/to do sth.

indisponibilité [ɛ̃disponibilite] *nf* unavailability.

indisponible [ɛ̃disponibl(ə)] *adj* unavailable.

indisposé, e [ɛ̃dispoze] *adj* indisposed, unwell.

indisposer [ɛ̃dispoze] *vt* (*incommoder*) to upset; (*déplaire à*) to antagonize.

indisposition [ɛ̃dispozisjɔ̃] *nf* (*slight*) illness, indisposition.

indissociable [ɛ̃disɔsjabl(ə)] *adj* indissociable.

indissoluble [ɛ̃disɔlybl(ə)] *adj* indissoluble.

indissolublement [ɛ̃disɔlybləmɑ̃] *adv* indissolubly.

indistinct, e [ɛ̃distɛ̃, -ɛ̃kt(ə)] *adj* indistinct.

indistinctement [ɛ̃distɛ̃ktəmɑ̃] *adv* (*voir, prononcer*) indistinctly; (*sans distinction*) without distinction, indiscriminately.

individu [ɛ̃dividy] *nm* individual.

individualiser [ɛ̃dividɥalize] *vt* to individualize; (*personnaliser*) to tailor to individual requirements; **s'~** to develop one's own identity.

individualisme [ɛ̃dividɥalism(ə)] *nm* individualism.

individualiste [ɛ̃dividɥalist(ə)] *nm/f* individualist.

individualité [ɛ̃dividɥalite] *nf* individuality.

individuel, le [ɛ̃dividɥɛl] *adj* (*gén*) individual; (*opinion, livret, contrôle, avantages*) personal; **chambre ~le** single room; **maison ~le** detached house; **propriété ~le** personal *ou* private property.

individuellement [ɛ̃dividɥɛlmɑ̃] *adv* individually.

indivis, e [ɛ̃divi, -iz] *adj* (*JUR: bien, propriété, succession*) indivisible; (: *cohéritiers, propriétaires*) joint.

indivisible [ɛ̃divizibl(ə)] *adj* indivisible.

Indochine [ɛ̃dɔʃin] *nf*: **l'~** Indochina.

indochinois, e [ɛ̃dɔʃinwa, -waz] *adj* Indo-chinese.

indocile [ɛ̃dɔsil] *adj* unruly.

indo-européen, ne [ɛ̃dɔørɔpeɛ̃, -ɛn] *adj* Indo-

European ♦ *nm* (*LING*) Indo-European.
indolence [ɛ̃dɔlɑ̃s] *nf* indolence.
indolent, e [ɛ̃dɔlɑ̃, -ɑ̃t] *adj* indolent.
indolore [ɛ̃dɔlɔʀ] *adj* painless.
indomptable [ɛ̃dɔ̃tabl(ə)] *adj* untameable; (*fig*) invincible, indomitable.
indompté, e [ɛ̃dɔ̃te] *adj* (*cheval*) unbroken.
Indonésie [ɛ̃dɔnezi] *nf*: l'~ Indonesia.
indonésien, ne [ɛ̃dɔnezjɛ̃, -ɛn] *adj* Indonesian ♦ *nm/f*: l~, **ne** Indonesian.
indu, e [ɛ̃dy] *adj*: **à des heures ~es** at an ungodly hour.
indubitable [ɛ̃dybitabl(ə)] *adj* indubitable.
indubitablement [ɛ̃dybitabləmɑ̃] *adv* indubitably.
induction [ɛ̃dyksjɔ̃] *nf* induction.
induire [ɛ̃dɥiʀ] *vt*: ~ **qch de** to induce sth from; ~ **qn en erreur** to lead sb astray, mislead sb.
indulgence [ɛ̃dylʒɑ̃s] *nf* indulgence; leniency; **avec** ~ indulgently; leniently.
indulgent, e [ɛ̃dylʒɑ̃, -ɑ̃t] *adj* (*parent, regard*) indulgent; (*juge, examinateur*) lenient.
indûment [ɛ̃dymɑ̃] *adv* without due cause; (*illégitimement*) wrongfully.
industrialisation [ɛ̃dystʀijalizɑsjɔ̃] *nf* industrialization.
industrialiser [ɛ̃dystʀijalize] *vt* to industrialize; **s'**~ to become industrialized.
industrie [ɛ̃dystʀi] *nf* industry; ~ **automobile/textile** car/textile industry; ~ **du spectacle** entertainment business.
industriel, le [ɛ̃dystʀijɛl] *adj* industrial; (*produit industriellement: pain etc*) mass-produced, factory-produced ♦ *nm* industrialist; (*fabricant*) manufacturer.
industriellement [ɛ̃dystʀijɛlmɑ̃] *adv* industrially.
industrieux, euse [ɛ̃dystʀijø, -øz] *adj* industrious.
inébranlable [inebʀɑ̃labl(ə)] *adj* (*masse, colonne*) solid; (*personne, certitude, foi*) steadfast, unwavering.
inédit, e [inedi, -it] *adj* (*correspondance etc*) (hitherto) unpublished; (*spectacle, moyen*) novel, original.
ineffable [inefabl(ə)] *adj* inexpressible, ineffable.
ineffaçable [inefasabl(ə)] *adj* indelible.
inefficace [inefikas] *adj* (*remède, moyen*) ineffective; (*machine, employé*) inefficient.
inefficacité [inefikasite] *nf* ineffectiveness; inefficiency.
inégal, e, aux [inegal, -o] *adj* unequal; (*irrégulier*) uneven.
inégalable [inegalabl(e)] *adj* matchless.
inégalé, e [inegale] *adj* unmatched, unequalled.
inégalement [inegalmɑ̃] *adv* unequally.
inégalité [inegalite] *nf* inequality; unevenness *no pl*; ~ **de 2 hauteurs** difference *ou* disparity between 2 heights; ~**s de terrain**

uneven ground.
inélégance [inelegɑ̃s] *nf* inelegance.
inélégant, e [inelegɑ̃, -ɑ̃t] *adj* inelegant; (*indélicat*) discourteous.
inéligible [ineliʒibl(ə)] *adj* ineligible.
inéluctable [inelyktabl(ə)] *adj* inescapable.
inéluctablement [inelyktabləmɑ̃] *adv* inescapably.
inemployable [inɑ̃plwajabl(ə)] *adj* unusable.
inemployé, e [inɑ̃plwaje] *adj* unused.
inénarrable [inenaʀabl(ə)] *adj* hilarious.
inepte [inɛpt(ə)] *adj* inept.
ineptie [inɛpsi] *nf* ineptitude; (*propos*) nonsense *no pl*.
inépuisable [inepɥizabl(ə)] *adj* inexhaustible.
inéquitable [inekitabl(ə)] *adj* inequitable.
inerte [inɛʀt(ə)] *adj* lifeless; (*apathique*) passive, inert; (*PHYSIQUE, CHIMIE*) inert.
inertie [inɛʀsi] *nf* inertia.
inescompté, e [inɛskɔ̃te] *adj* unexpected, unhoped-for.
inespéré, e [inɛspeʀe] *adj* unhoped-for, unexpected.
inesthétique [inɛstetik] *adj* unsightly.
inestimable [inɛstimabl(e)] *adj* priceless; (*fig: bienfait*) invaluable.
inévitable [inevitabl(ə)] *adj* unavoidable; (*fatal, habituel*) inevitable.
inévitablement [inevitabləmɑ̃] *adv* inevitably.
inexact, e [inɛgzakt] *adj* inaccurate, inexact; (*non ponctuel*) unpunctual.
inexactement [inɛgzaktəmɑ̃] *adv* inaccurately.
inexactitude [inɛgzaktityd] *nf* inaccuracy.
inexcusable [inɛkskyzabl(ə)] *adj* inexcusable, unforgivable.
inexécutable [inɛgzekytabl(ə)] *adj* impracticable, unworkable; (*MUS*) unplayable.
inexistant, e [inɛgzistɑ̃, -ɑ̃t] *adj* non-existent.
inexorable [inɛgzɔʀabl(ə)] *adj* inexorable; (*personne: dur*): ~ **(à)** unmoved (by).
inexorablement [inɛgzɔʀabləmɑ̃] *adv* inexorably.
inexpérience [inɛkspeʀjɑ̃s] *nf* inexperience, lack of experience.
inexpérimenté, e [inɛkspeʀimɑ̃te] *adj* inexperienced; (*arme, procédé*) untested.
inexplicable [inɛksplikabl(ə)] *adj* inexplicable.
inexplicablement [inɛksplikabləmɑ̃] *adv* inexplicably.
inexpliqué, e [inɛksplike] *adj* unexplained.
inexploitable [inɛksplwatabl(ə)] *adj* (*gisement, richesse*) unexploitable; (*données, renseignements*) unusable.
inexploité, e [inɛksplwate] *adj* unexploited, untapped.
inexploré, e [inɛksplɔʀe] *adj* unexplored.
inexpressif, ive [inɛkspʀesif, -iv] *adj* inexpressive; (*regard etc*) expressionless.
inexpressivité [inɛkspʀesivite] *nf* expressionlessness.

inexprimable [inɛksprimabl(ə)] *adj* inexpressible.

inexprimé, e [inɛksprime] *adj* unspoken, unexpressed.

inexpugnable [inɛkspygnabl(ə)] *adj* impregnable.

inextensible [inɛkstɑ̃sibl(ə)] *adj* (*tissu*) non-stretch.

in extenso [inɛkstɛ̃so] *adv* in full.

inextinguible [inɛkstɛ̃gibl(ə)] *adj* (*soif*) unquenchable; (*rire*) uncontrollable.

in extremis [inɛkstremis] *adv* at the last minute ♦ *adj* last-minute; (*testament*) death bed *cpd*.

inextricable [inɛkstrikabl(ə)] *adj* inextricable.

inextricablement [inɛkstrikabləmɑ̃] *adv* inextricably.

infaillibilité [ɛ̃fajibilite] *nf* infallibility.

infaillible [ɛ̃fajibl(ə)] *adj* infallible; (*instinct*) infallible, unerring.

infailliblement [ɛ̃fajibləmɑ̃] *adv* (*certainement*) without fail.

infaisable [ɛ̃fəzabl(ə)] *adj* impossible, impractical.

infamant, e [ɛ̃famɑ̃, -ɑ̃t] *adj* libellous, defamatory.

infâme [ɛ̃fɑm] *adj* vile.

infamie [ɛ̃fami] *nf* infamy.

infanterie [ɛ̃fɑ̃tri] *nf* infantry.

infanticide [ɛ̃fɑ̃tisid] *nm/f* child-murderer/eress ♦ *nm* (*meurtre*) infanticide.

infantile [ɛ̃fɑ̃til] *adj* (*MÉD*) infantile, child *cpd*; (*péj: ton, réaction*) infantile, childish.

infantilisme [ɛ̃fɑ̃tilism(ə)] *nm* infantilism.

infarctus [ɛ̃farktys] *nm*: ~ **(du myocarde)** coronary (thrombosis).

infatigable [ɛ̃fatigabl(ə)] *adj* tireless, indefatigable.

infatigablement [ɛ̃fatigabləmɑ̃] *adv* tirelessly, indefatigably.

infatué, e [ɛ̃fatɥe] *adj* conceited; ~ **de** full of.

infécond, e [ɛ̃fekɔ̃, -ɔ̃d] *adj* infertile, barren.

infect, e [ɛ̃fɛkt] *adj* vile, foul; (*repas, vin*) revolting, foul.

infecter [ɛ̃fɛkte] *vt* (*atmosphère, eau*) to contaminate; (*MÉD*) to infect; **s'**~ to become infected *ou* septic.

infectieux, euse [ɛ̃fɛksjø, -øz] *adj* infectious.

infection [ɛ̃fɛksjɔ̃] *nf* infection.

inféoder [ɛ̃feɔde] *vt*: **s'**~ **à** to pledge allegiance to.

inférer [ɛ̃fere] *vt*: ~ **qch de** to infer sth from.

inférieur, e [ɛ̃ferjœr] *adj* lower; (*en qualité, intelligence*) inferior ♦ *nm/f* inferior; ~ **à** (*somme, quantité*) less *ou* smaller than; (*moins bon que*) inferior to; (*tâche: pas à la hauteur de*) unequal to.

infériorité [ɛ̃ferjɔrite] *nf* inferiority; ~ **en nombre** inferiority in numbers.

infernal, e, aux [ɛ̃fɛrnal, -o] *adj* (*chaleur, rythme*) infernal; (*méchanceté, complot*) diabolical.

infester [ɛ̃fɛste] *vt* to infest; **infesté de moustiques** infested with mosquitoes, mosquito-ridden.

infidèle [ɛ̃fidɛl] *adj* unfaithful; (*REL*) infidel.

infidélité [ɛ̃fidelite] *nf* unfaithfulness *no pl*.

infiltration [ɛ̃filtrasjɔ̃] *nf* infiltration.

infiltrer [ɛ̃filtre]: **s'**~ *vi*: **s'**~ **dans** to penetrate into; (*liquide*) to seep into; (*fig: noyauter*) to infiltrate.

infime [ɛ̃fim] *adj* minute, tiny; (*inférieur*) lowly.

infini, e [ɛ̃fini] *adj* infinite ♦ *nm* infinity; **à l'**~ (*MATH*) to infinity; (*discourir*) ad infinitum, endlessly; (*agrandir, varier*) infinitely; (*à perte de vue*) endlessly (into the distance).

infiniment [ɛ̃finimɑ̃] *adv* infinitely; ~ **grand/petit** (*MATH*) infinitely great/infinitesimal.

infinité [ɛ̃finite] *nf*: **une** ~ **de** an infinite number of.

infinitésimal, e, aux [ɛ̃finitezimal, -o] *adj* infinitesimal.

infinitif, ive [ɛ̃finitif, -iv] *adj, nm* infinitive.

infirme [ɛ̃firm(ə)] *adj* disabled ♦ *nm/f* disabled person; ~ **mental** mentally-handicapped person; ~ **moteur** spastic; ~ **de guerre** war cripple; ~ **du travail** industrially disabled person.

infirmer [ɛ̃firme] *vt* to invalidate.

infirmerie [ɛ̃firməri] *nf* sick bay.

infirmier, ière [ɛ̃firmje, -jɛr] *nm/f* nurse ♦ *adj*: **élève** ~ student nurse; **infirmière chef** sister; **infirmière diplômée** registered nurse; **infirmière visiteuse** visiting nurse, ≈ district nurse (*BRIT*).

infirmité [ɛ̃firmite] *nf* disability.

inflammable [ɛ̃flamabl(ə)] *adj* (in)flammable.

inflammation [ɛ̃flamasjɔ̃] *nf* inflammation.

inflammatoire [ɛ̃flamatwar] *adj* (*MÉD*) inflammatory.

inflation [ɛ̃flɑsjɔ̃] *nf* inflation; ~ **rampante/galopante** creeping/galloping inflation.

inflationniste [ɛ̃flɑsjɔnist(ə)] *adj* inflationist.

infléchir [ɛ̃fleʃir] *vt* (*fig: politique*) to reorientate, redirect; **s'**~ *vi* (*poutre, tringle*) to bend, sag.

inflexibilité [ɛ̃flɛksibilite] *nf* inflexibility.

inflexible [ɛ̃flɛksibl(ə)] *adj* inflexible.

inflexion [ɛ̃flɛksjɔ̃] *nf* inflexion; ~ **de la tête** slight nod (of the head).

infliger [ɛ̃fliʒe] *vt*: ~ **qch (à qn)** to inflict sth (on sb); (*amende, sanction*) to impose sth (on sb).

influençable [ɛ̃flyɑ̃sabl(ə)] *adj* easily influenced.

influence [ɛ̃flyɑ̃s] *nf* influence; (*d'un médicament*) effect.

influencer [ɛ̃flyɑ̃se] *vt* to influence.

influent, e [ɛ̃flyɑ̃, -ɑ̃t] *adj* influential.

influer [ɛ̃flye]: ~ **sur** *vt* to have an influence upon.

influx [ɛ̃fly] *nm*: ~ **nerveux** (nervous) impulse.

infographie [ɛ̃fɔgrafi] *nf* computer

graphics *sg*.

informateur, trice [ɛfɔʀmatœʀ, -tʀis] *nm/f*
informant.

informaticien, ne [ɛfɔʀmatisjɛ̃, -ɛn] *nm/f*
computer scientist.

informatif, ive [ɛfɔʀmatif, -iv] *adj*
informative.

information [ɛfɔʀmasjɔ̃] *nf* (*renseignement*)
piece of information; (*PRESSE, TV: nouvelle*)
item of news; (*diffusion de renseignements,
INFORM*) information; (*JUR*) inquiry,
investigation; ~**s** *nfpl* (*TV*) news *sg*; **voyage
d'**~ fact-finding trip; **agence d'**~ news
agency; **journal d'**~ quality (*BRIT*) *ou* serious
newspaper.

informatique [ɛfɔʀmatik] *nf* (*technique*) data
processing; (*science*) computer science ♦ *adj*
computer *cpd*.

informatisation [ɛfɔʀmatizasjɔ̃] *nf*
computerization.

informatiser [ɛfɔʀmatize] *vt* to computerize.

informe [ɛfɔʀm(ə)] *adj* shapeless.

informé, e [ɛfɔʀme] *adj*: **jusqu'à plus ample** ~
until further information is available.

informel, le [ɛfɔʀmɛl] *adj* informal.

informer [ɛfɔʀme] *vt*: ~ **qn (de)** to inform sb
(of) ♦ *vi* (*JUR*): ~ **contre qn/sur qch** to
initiate inquiries about sb/sth; **s'**~ **(sur)** to
inform o.s. (about); **s'**~ **(de qch/si)** to
inquire *ou* find out (about sth/whether *ou*
if).

informulé, e [ɛfɔʀmyle] *adj* unformulated.

infortune [ɛfɔʀtyn] *nf* misfortune.

infos [ɛfo] *nfpl* (= *informations*) news.

infraction [ɛfʀaksjɔ̃] *nf* offence; ~ **à** violation
ou breach of; **être en** ~ to be in breach of
the law.

infranchissable [ɛfʀɑ̃ʃisabl(ə)] *adj*
impassable; (*fig*) insuperable.

infrarouge [ɛfʀaʀuʒ] *adj, nm* infrared.

infrason [ɛfʀasɔ̃] *nm* infrasonic vibration.

infrastructure [ɛfʀastʀyktyʀ] *nf* (*d'une route
etc*) substructure; (*AVIAT, MIL*) ground
installations *pl*; (*touristique etc*) facilities.

infréquentable [ɛfʀekɑ̃tabl(ə)] *adj* not to be
associated with.

infroissable [ɛfʀwasabl(ə)] *adj* crease-
resistant.

infructueux, euse [ɛfʀyktɥø, -øz] *adj*
fruitless, unfruitful.

infus [ɛfy, -yz] *adj*: **avoir la science** ~**e** to
have innate knowledge.

infuser [ɛfyze] *vt* (*aussi:* **faire** ~: *thé*) to brew;
(*: tisane*) to infuse ♦ *vi* to brew; to infuse;
laisser ~ (to leave) to brew.

infusion [ɛfyzjɔ̃] *nf* (*tisane*) infusion, herb tea.

ingambe [ɛ̃gɑ̃b] *adj* spry, nimble.

ingénier [ɛ̃ʒenje]: **s'**~ *vi*: **s'**~ **à faire** to strive
to do.

ingénierie [ɛ̃ʒeniʀi] *nf* engineering.

ingénieur [ɛ̃ʒenjœʀ] *nm* engineer; ~
agronome/chimiste agricultural/chemical

engineer; ~ **conseil** consulting engineer; ~
du son sound engineer.

ingénieusement [ɛ̃ʒenjøzmɑ̃] *adv*
ingeniously.

ingénieux, euse [ɛ̃ʒenjø, -øz] *adj* ingenious,
clever.

ingéniosité [ɛ̃ʒenjozite] *nf* ingenuity.

ingénu, e [ɛ̃ʒeny] *adj* ingenuous, artless ♦ *nf*
(*THÉÂT*) ingénue.

ingénuité [ɛ̃ʒenɥite] *nf* ingenuousness.

ingénument [ɛ̃ʒenymɑ̃] *adv* ingenuously.

ingérence [ɛ̃ʒeʀɑ̃s] *nf* interference.

ingérer [ɛ̃ʒeʀe]: **s'**~ *vi*: **s'**~ **dans** to interfere
in.

ingouvernable [ɛ̃guvɛʀnabl(ə)] *adj*
ungovernable.

ingrat, e [ɛ̃gʀa, -at] *adj* (*personne*) ungrateful;
(*sol*) poor; (*travail, sujet*) arid, thankless;
(*visage*) unprepossessing.

ingratitude [ɛ̃gʀatityd] *nf* ingratitude.

ingrédient [ɛ̃gʀedjɑ̃] *nm* ingredient.

inguérissable [ɛ̃geʀisabl(ə)] *adj* incurable.

ingurgiter [ɛ̃gyʀʒite] *vt* to swallow; **faire** ~
qch à qn to make sb swallow sth; (*fig:
connaissances*) to force sth into sb.

inhabile [inabil] *adj* clumsy; (*fig*) inept.

inhabitable [inabitabl(ə)] *adj* uninhabitable.

inhabité, e [inabite] *adj* (*régions*) uninhabited;
(*maison*) unoccupied.

inhabituel, le [inabitɥɛl] *adj* unusual.

inhalateur [inalatœʀ] *nm* inhaler; ~ **d'oxygène**
oxygen mask.

inhalation [inalɑsjɔ̃] *nf* (*MÉD*) inhalation; **faire
des** ~**s** to use an inhalation bath.

inhaler [inale] *vt* to inhale.

inhérent, e [ineʀɑ̃, -ɑ̃t] *adj*: ~ **à** inherent in.

inhiber [inibe] *vt* to inhibit.

inhibition [inibisjɔ̃] *nf* inhibition.

inhospitalier, ière [inɔspitalje, -jɛʀ] *adj*
inhospitable.

inhumain, e [inymɛ̃, -ɛn] *adj* inhuman.

inhumation [inymɑsjɔ̃] *nf* interment, burial.

inhumer [inyme] *vt* to inter, bury.

inimaginable [inimaʒinabl(ə)] *adj*
unimaginable.

inimitable [inimitabl(ə)] *adj* inimitable.

inimitié [inimitje] *nf* enmity.

ininflammable [inɛ̃flamabl(ə)] *adj* nonflammable.

inintelligent, e [inɛ̃teliʒɑ̃, -ɑ̃t] *adj*
unintelligent.

inintelligible [inɛ̃teliʒibl(ə)] *adj* unintelligible.

inintelligiblement [inɛ̃teliʒibləmɑ̃] *adv*
unintelligibly.

inintéressant, e [inɛ̃teʀesɑ̃, -ɑ̃t] *adj*
uninteresting.

ininterrompu, e [inɛ̃teʀɔ̃py] *adj* (*file, série*)
unbroken; (*flot, vacarme*) uninterrupted,
non-stop; (*effort*) unremitting, continuous.

iniquité [inikite] *nf* iniquity.

initial, e, aux [inisjal, -o] *adj, nf* initial; ~**es** *nfpl*
initials.

initialement [inisjalmɑ̃] _adv_ initially.
initialiser [inisjalize] _vt_ to initialize.
initiateur, trice [inisjatœʀ, -tʀis] _nm/f_ initiator; (_d'une mode, technique_) innovator, pioneer.
initiation [inisjɑsjɔ̃] _nf_ initiation.
initiatique [inisjatik] _adj_ (_rites, épreuves_) initiatory.
initiative [inisjativ] _nf_ initiative; **prendre l'~ de qch/de faire** to take the initiative for sth/of doing; **avoir de l'~** to have initiative, show enterprise; **esprit/qualités d'~** spirit/ qualities of initiative; **à** _ou_ **sur l'~ de qn** on sb's initiative; **de sa propre ~** on one's own initiative.
initié, e [inisje] _adj_ initiated ♦ _nm/f_ initiate.
initier [inisje] _vt_ to initiate; **~ qn à** to initiate sb into; (_faire découvrir: art, jeu_) to introduce sb to; **s'~ à** (_métier, profession, technique_) to become initiated into.
injectable [ɛ̃ʒɛktabl(ə)] _adj_ injectable.
injecté, e [ɛ̃ʒɛkte] _adj_: **yeux ~s de sang** bloodshot eyes.
injecter [ɛ̃ʒɛkte] _vt_ to inject.
injection [ɛ̃ʒɛksjɔ̃] _nf_ injection; **à ~** (_AUTO_) fuel injection _cpd_.
injonction [ɛ̃ʒɔ̃ksjɔ̃] _nf_ injunction, order; **~ de payer** (_JUR_) order to pay.
injouable [ɛ̃ʒwabl(ə)] _adj_ unplayable.
injure [ɛ̃ʒyʀ] _nf_ insult, abuse _no pl_.
injurier [ɛ̃ʒyʀje] _vt_ to insult, abuse.
injurieux, euse [ɛ̃ʒyʀjø, -øz] _adj_ abusive, insulting.
injuste [ɛ̃ʒyst(ə)] _adj_ unjust, unfair.
injustement [ɛ̃ʒystəmɑ̃] _adv_ unjustly, unfairly.
injustice [ɛ̃ʒystis] _nf_ injustice.
injustifiable [ɛ̃ʒystifjabl(ə)] _adj_ unjustifiable.
injustifié, e [ɛ̃ʒystifje] _adj_ unjustified, unwarranted.
inlassable [ɛ̃lɑsabl(ə)] _adj_ tireless, indefatigable.
inlassablement [ɛ̃lɑsabləmɑ̃] _adv_ tirelessly.
inné, e [ine] _adj_ innate, inborn.
innocemment [inɔsamɑ̃] _adv_ innocently.
innocence [inɔsɑ̃s] _nf_ innocence.
innocent, e [inɔsɑ̃, -ɑ̃t] _adj_ innocent ♦ _nm/f_ innocent person; **faire l'~** to play _ou_ come the innocent.
innocenter [inɔsɑ̃te] _vt_ to clear, prove innocent.
innocuité [inɔkɥite] _nf_ innocuousness.
innombrable [inɔ̃bʀabl(ə)] _adj_ innumerable.
innommable [inɔmabl(ə)] _adj_ unspeakable.
innovateur, trice [inɔvatœʀ, -tʀis] _adj_ innovatory.
innovation [inɔvɑsjɔ̃] _nf_ innovation.
innover [inɔve] _vi_: **~ en matière d'art** to break new ground in the field of art.
inobservance [inɔpsɛʀvɑ̃s] _nf_ non-observance.
inobservation [inɔpsɛʀvɑsjɔ̃] _nf_ non-observation, inobservance.

inoccupé, e [inɔkype] _adj_ unoccupied.
inoculer [inɔkyle] _vt_: **~ qch à qn** (_volontairement_) to inoculate sb with sth; (_accidentellement_) to infect sb with sth; **~ qn contre** to inoculate sb against.
inodore [inɔdɔʀ] _adj_ (_gaz_) odourless; (_fleur_) scentless.
inoffensif, ive [inɔfɑ̃sif, -iv] _adj_ harmless, innocuous.
inondable [inɔ̃dabl(ə)] _adj_ (_zone etc_) liable to flooding.
inondation [inɔ̃dɑsjɔ̃] _nf_ flooding _no pl_; (_torrent eau_) flood.
inonder [inɔ̃de] _vt_ to flood; (_fig_) to inundate, overrun; **~ de** (_fig_) to flood _ou_ swamp with.
inopérable [inɔpeʀabl(ə)] _adj_ inoperable.
inopérant, e [inɔpeʀɑ̃, -ɑ̃t] _adj_ inoperative, ineffective.
inopiné, e [inɔpine] _adj_ unexpected, sudden.
inopinément [inɔpinemɑ̃] _adv_ unexpectedly.
inopportun, e [inɔpɔʀtœ̃, -yn] _adj_ ill-timed, untimely; inappropriate; (_moment_) inopportune.
inorganisation [inɔʀganizɑsjɔ̃] _nf_ lack of organization.
inorganisé, e [inɔʀganize] _adj_ (_travailleurs_) non-organized.
inoubliable [inublijabl(ə)] _adj_ unforgettable.
inouï, e [inwi] _adj_ unheard-of, extraordinary.
inox [inɔks] _adj_, _nm_ (= inoxydable) stainless (steel).
inoxydable [inɔksidabl(ə)] _adj_ stainless; (_couverts_) stainless steel _cpd_.
inqualifiable [ɛ̃kalifjabl(ə)] _adj_ unspeakable.
inquiet, ète [ɛ̃kjɛ, -ɛt] _adj_ (_par nature_) anxious; (_momentanément_) worried; **~ de qch/au sujet de qn** worried about sth/sb.
inquiétant, e [ɛ̃kjetɑ̃, -ɑ̃t] _adj_ worrying, disturbing.
inquiéter [ɛ̃kjete] _vt_ to worry, disturb; (_harceler_) to harass; **s'~** to worry, become anxious; **s'~ de** to worry about; (_s'enquérir de_) to inquire about.
inquiétude [ɛ̃kjetyd] _nf_ anxiety; **donner de l'~** _ou_ **des ~s à** to worry; **avoir de l'~** _ou_ **des ~s au sujet de** to feel anxious _ou_ worried about.
inquisiteur, trice [ɛ̃kizitœʀ, -tʀis] _adj_ (_regards, questions_) inquisitive, prying.
inquisition [ɛ̃kizisjɔ̃] _nf_ inquisition.
INR _sigle m_ = _Institut national (belge) de radiodiffusion_.
INRA [inʀa] _sigle m_ = _Institut national de la recherche agronomique_.
inracontable [ɛ̃ʀakɔ̃tabl(ə)] _adj_ (_trop osé_) unrepeatable; (_trop compliqué_): **l'histoire est ~** the story is too complicated to relate.
insaisissable [ɛ̃sezisabl(ə)] _adj_ elusive.
insalubre [ɛ̃salybʀ(ə)] _adj_ unhealthy, insalubrious.
insalubrité [ɛ̃salybʀite] _nf_ unhealthiness, insalubrity.

insanité [ɛ̃sanite] *nf* madness *no pl*, insanity *no pl*.
insatiable [ɛ̃sasjabl(ə)] *adj* insatiable.
insatisfaction [ɛ̃satisfaksjɔ̃] *nf* dissatisfaction.
insatisfait, e [ɛ̃satisfɛ, -ɛt] *adj* (*non comblé*) unsatisfied; (*: passion, envie*) unfulfilled; (*mécontent*) dissatisfied.
inscription [ɛ̃skripsjɔ̃] *nf* (*sur un mur, écriteau etc*) inscription; (*à une institution: voir s'inscrire*) enrolment; registration.
inscrire [ɛ̃skrir] *vt* (*marquer: sur son calepin etc*) to note *ou* write down; (*: sur un mur, une affiche etc*) to write; (*: dans la pierre, le métal*) to inscribe; (*mettre: sur une liste, un budget etc*) to put down; (*enrôler: soldat*) to enlist; ~ **qn à** (*club, école etc*) to enrol sb at; **s'~** (*pour une excursion etc*) to put one's name down; **s'~** (**à**) (*club, parti*) to join; (*université*) to register *ou* enrol (at); (*examen, concours*) to register *ou* enter (for); **s'~ dans** (*se situer: négociations etc*) to come within the scope of; **s'~ en faux contre** to deny (strongly); (*JUR*) to challenge.
inscrit, e [ɛ̃skri, it] *pp de* **inscrire** ♦ *adj* (*étudiant, électeur etc*) registered.
insécable [ɛ̃sekabl(ə)] *adj* (*INFORM*) indivisible.
insecte [ɛ̃sɛkt(ə)] *nm* insect.
insecticide [ɛ̃sɛktisid] *nm* insecticide.
insécurité [ɛ̃sekyrite] *nf* insecurity, lack of security.
INSEE [inse] *sigle m* (= *Institut national de la statistique et des études économiques*) *national institute of statistical and economic information.*
insémination [ɛ̃seminasjɔ̃] *nf* insemination.
insensé, e [ɛ̃sɑ̃se] *adj* insane, mad.
insensibiliser [ɛ̃sɑ̃sibilize] *vt* to anaesthetize; (*à une allergie*) to desensitize; ~ **à qch** (*fig*) to cause to become insensitive to sth.
insensibilité [ɛ̃sɑ̃sibilite] *nf* insensitivity.
insensible [ɛ̃sɑ̃sibl(ə)] *adj* (*nerf, membre*) numb; (*dur, indifférent*) insensitive; (*imperceptible*) imperceptible.
insensiblement [ɛ̃sɑ̃sibləmɑ̃] *adv* (*doucement, peu à peu*) imperceptibly.
inséparable [ɛ̃separabl(ə)] *adj*: ~ (**de**) inseparable (from) ♦ *nmpl*: ~**s** (*oiseaux*) lovebirds.
insérer [ɛ̃sere] *vt* to insert; **s'~ dans** to fit into; (*fig*) to come within.
INSERM [ɛ̃sɛrm] *sigle m* (= *Institut national de la santé et de la recherche médicale*) *national institute for medical research.*
insert [ɛ̃sɛr] *nm* enclosed fireplace burning solid fuel.
insertion [ɛ̃sɛrsjɔ̃] *nf* (*d'une personne*) integration.
insidieusement [ɛ̃sidjøzmɑ̃] *adv* insidiously.
insidieux, euse [ɛ̃sidjø, -øz] *adj* insidious.
insigne [ɛ̃siɲ] *nm* (*d'un parti, club*) badge ♦ *adj* distinguished; ~**s** *nmpl* (*d'une fonction*)

insignia *pl*.
insignifiant, e [ɛ̃siɲifjɑ̃, -ɑ̃t] *adj* insignificant; (*somme, affaire, détail*) trivial, insignificant.
insinuant, e [ɛ̃sinɥɑ̃, -ɑ̃t] *adj* ingratiating.
insinuation [ɛ̃sinɥasjɔ̃] *nf* innuendo, insinuation.
insinuer [ɛ̃sinɥe] *vt* to insinuate, imply; **s'~ dans** to seep into; (*fig*) to worm one's way into, creep into.
insipide [ɛ̃sipid] *adj* insipid.
insistance [ɛ̃sistɑ̃s] *nf* insistence; **avec** ~ insistently.
insistant, e [ɛ̃sistɑ̃, -ɑ̃t] *adj* insistent.
insister [ɛ̃siste] *vi* to insist; (*s'obstiner*) to keep on; ~ **sur** (*détail, note*) to stress; ~ **pour qch/ pour faire qch** to be insistent about sth/ about doing sth.
insociable [ɛ̃sɔsjabl(ə)] *adj* unsociable.
insolation [ɛ̃sɔlasjɔ̃] *nf* (*MÉD*) sunstroke *no pl*; (*ensoleillement*) period of sunshine.
insolence [ɛ̃sɔlɑ̃s] *nf* insolence *no pl*; **avec** ~ insolently.
insolent, e [ɛ̃sɔlɑ̃, -ɑ̃t] *adj* insolent.
insolite [ɛ̃sɔlit] *adj* strange, unusual.
insoluble [ɛ̃sɔlybl(ə)] *adj* insoluble.
insolvable [ɛ̃sɔlvabl(ə)] *adj* insolvent.
insomniaque [ɛ̃sɔmnjak] *adj*, *nm/f* insomniac.
insomnie [ɛ̃sɔmni] *nf* insomnia *no pl*, sleeplessness *no pl*; **avoir des** ~**s** to suffer from insomnia.
insondable [ɛ̃sɔ̃dabl(ə)] *adj* unfathomable.
insonore [ɛ̃sɔnɔr] *adj* soundproof.
insonorisation [ɛ̃sɔnɔrizasjɔ̃] *nf* sound-proofing.
insonoriser [ɛ̃sɔnɔrize] *vt* to soundproof.
insouciance [ɛ̃susjɑ̃s] *nf* carefree attitude; heedless attitude.
insouciant, e [ɛ̃susjɑ̃, -ɑ̃t] *adj* carefree; (*imprévoyant*) heedless.
insoumis, e [ɛ̃sumi, -iz] *adj* (*caractère, enfant*) rebellious, refractory; (*contrée, tribu*) unsubdued; (*MIL: soldat*) absent without leave ♦ *nm* (*MIL: soldat*) absentee.
insoumission [ɛ̃sumisjɔ̃] *nf* rebelliousness; (*MIL*) absence without leave.
insoupçonnable [ɛ̃supsɔnabl(ə)] *adj* above suspicion.
insoupçonné, e [ɛ̃supsɔne] *adj* unsuspected.
insoutenable [ɛ̃sutnabl(ə)] *adj* (*argument*) untenable; (*chaleur*) unbearable.
inspecter [ɛ̃spɛkte] *vt* to inspect.
inspecteur, trice [ɛ̃spɛktœr, -tris] *nm/f* inspector; (*des assurances*) assessor; ~ **d'Académie** (regional) director of education; ~ (**de l'enseignement**) **primaire** primary school inspector; ~ **des finances** ≈ tax inspector (*BRIT*), ≈ Internal Revenue Service agent (*US*); ~ (**de police**) (police) inspector.
inspection [ɛ̃spɛksjɔ̃] *nf* inspection.
inspirateur, trice [ɛ̃spiratœr, -tris] *nm/f* (*instigateur*) instigator; (*animateur*) inspirer.

inspiration [ɛ̃spiʀɑsjɔ̃] *nf* inspiration; breathing in *no pl*; (*idée*) flash of inspiration, brainwave; **sous l'~ de** prompted by.

inspiré, e [ɛ̃spiʀe] *adj*: **être bien/mal ~ de faire qch** to be well-advised/ill-advised to do sth.

inspirer [ɛ̃spiʀe] *vt* (*gén*) to inspire ♦ *vi* (*aspirer*) to breathe in; **s'~ de** (*suj: artiste*) to draw one's inspiration from; (*suj: tableau*) to be inspired by; **~ qch à qn** (*œuvre, project, action*) to inspire sb with sth; (*dégoût, crainte, horreur*) to fill sb with sth; **ça ne m'inspire pas** I'm not keen on the idea.

instabilité [ɛ̃stabilite] *nf* instability.

instable [ɛ̃stabl(ə)] *adj* (*meuble, équilibre*) unsteady; (*population, temps*) unsettled; (*paix, régime, caractère*) unstable.

installateur [ɛ̃stalatœʀ] *nm* fitter.

installation [ɛ̃stalɑsjɔ̃] *nf* installation; putting in *ou* up; fitting out; settling in; (*appareils etc*) fittings *pl*, installations *pl*; **~s** *nfpl* installations; (*industrielles*) plant *sg*; (*de loisirs*) facilities.

installé, e [ɛ̃stale] *adj*: **bien/mal ~** well/poorly equipped; (*personne*) well/not very well set up *ou* organized.

installer [ɛ̃stale] *vt* (*loger*): **~ qn** to get sb settled, install sb; (*asseoir, coucher*) to settle (down); (*placer*) to put, place; (*meuble*) to put in; (*rideau, étagère, tente*) to put up; (*gaz, électricité etc*) to put in, install; (*appartement*) to fit out; (*aménager*): **~ une salle de bains dans une pièce** to fit out a room with a bathroom suite; **s'~** (*s'établir: artisan, dentiste etc*) to set o.s. up; (*se loger*): **s'~ à l'hôtel/chez qn** to move into a hotel/in with sb; (*emménager*) to settle in; (*sur un siège, à un emplacement*) to settle (down); (*fig: maladie, grève*) to take a firm hold *ou* grip.

instamment [ɛ̃stamɑ̃] *adv* urgently.

instance [ɛ̃stɑ̃s] *nf* (*JUR: procédure*) (legal) proceedings *pl*; (*ADMIN: autorité*) authority; **~s** *nfpl* (*prières*) entreaties; **affaire en ~** matter pending; **courrier en ~** mail ready for posting; **être en ~ de divorce** to be awaiting a divorce; **train en ~ de départ** train on the point of departure; **tribunal de première ~** court of first instance; **en seconde ~** on appeal.

instant [ɛ̃stɑ̃] *nm* moment, instant; **dans un ~** in a moment; **à l'~** this instant; **je l'ai vu à l'~** I've just this minute seen him, I saw him a moment ago; **à l'~** (**même**) **où** at the (very) moment that *ou* when, (just) as; **à chaque ~, à tout ~** at any moment; constantly; **pour l'~** for the moment, for the time being; **par ~s** at times; **de tous les ~s** perpetual; **dès l'~ où** *ou* **que ...** from the moment when ..., since that moment when ....

instantané, e [ɛ̃stɑ̃tane] *adj* (*lait, café*) instant; (*explosion, mort*) instantaneous ♦ *nm* snapshot.

instantanément [ɛ̃stɑ̃tanemɑ̃] *adv* instantaneously.

instar [ɛ̃staʀ]: **à l'~ de** *prép* following the example of, like.

instaurer [ɛ̃stɔʀe] *vt* to institute; **s'~** *vi* to set o.s. up; (*collaboration etc*) to be established.

instigateur, trice [ɛ̃stigatœʀ, -tʀis] *nm/f* instigator.

instigation [ɛ̃stigɑsjɔ̃] *nf*: **à l'~ de qn** at sb's instigation.

instiller [ɛ̃stile] *vt* to instil, apply.

instinct [ɛ̃stɛ̃] *nm* instinct; **d'~** (*spontanément*) instinctively; **~ grégaire** herd instinct; **~ de conservation** instinct of self-preservation.

instinctif, ive [ɛ̃stɛ̃ktif, -iv] *adj* instinctive.

instinctivement [ɛ̃stɛ̃ktivmɑ̃] *adv* instinctively.

instituer [ɛ̃stitɥe] *vt* to institute, set up; **s'~ défenseur d'une cause** to set o.s up as defender of a cause.

institut [ɛ̃stity] *nm* institute; **~ de beauté** beauty salon; **~ médico-légal** mortuary; **I~ universitaire de technologie (IUT)** technical college.

instituteur, trice [ɛ̃stitytœʀ, -tʀis] *nm/f* (primary (*BRIT*) *ou* grade (*US*)) school) teacher.

institution [ɛ̃stitysjɔ̃] *nf* institution; (*collège*) private school.

institutionnaliser [ɛ̃stitysjɔnalize] *vt* to institutionalize.

instructeur, trice [ɛ̃stʀyktœʀ, -tʀis] *adj* (*MIL*): **sergent ~** drill sergeant; (*JUR*): **juge ~** examining (*BRIT*) *ou* committing (*US*) magistrate ♦ *nm/f* instructor.

instructif, ive [ɛ̃stʀyktif, -iv] *adj* instructive.

instruction [ɛ̃stʀyksjɔ̃] *nf* (*enseignement, savoir*) education; (*JUR*) (preliminary) investigation and hearing; (*directive*) instruction; (*ADMIN: document*) directive; **~s** *nfpl* instructions; (*mode d'emploi*) directions, instructions; **~ civique** civics *sg*; **~ primaire/publique** primary/public education; **~ religieuse** religious instruction; **~ professionnelle** vocational training.

instruire [ɛ̃stʀɥiʀ] *vt* (*élèves*) to teach; (*recrues*) to train; (*JUR: affaire*) to conduct the investigation for; **s'~** to educate o.s.; **s'~ auprès de qn de qch** (*s'informer*) to find sth out from sb; **~ qn de qch** (*informer*) to inform *ou* advise sb of sth; **~ contre qn** (*JUR*) to investigate sb.

instruit, e [ɛ̃stʀɥi, -it] *pp de* **instruire** ♦ *adj* educated.

instrument [ɛ̃stʀymɑ̃] *nm* instrument; **~ à cordes/vent** stringed/wind instrument; **~ de mesure** measuring instrument; **~ de musique** musical instrument; **~ de travail** (working) tool.

instrumental, e, aux [ɛ̃stʀymɑ̃tal, -o] *adj* instrumental.

instrumentation [ɛ̃stʀymɑ̃tasjɔ̃] *nf*
instrumentation.
instrumentiste [ɛ̃stʀymɑ̃tist(ə)] *nm/f*
instrumentalist.
insu [ɛ̃sy] *nm*: **à l'~ de qn** without sb knowing.
insubmersible [ɛ̃sybmɛʀsibl(ə)] *adj*
unsinkable.
insubordination [ɛ̃sybɔʀdinasjɔ̃] *nf*
rebelliousness; (*MIL*) insubordination.
insubordonné, e [ɛ̃sybɔʀdɔne] *adj*
insubordinate.
insuccès [ɛ̃syksɛ] *nm* failure.
insuffisamment [ɛ̃syfizamɑ̃] *adv*
insufficiently.
insuffisance [ɛ̃syfizɑ̃s] *nf* insufficiency;
inadequacy; **~s** *nfpl* (*lacunes*) inadequacies;
~ cardiaque cardiac insufficiency *no pl*; **~
hépatique** liver deficiency.
insuffisant, e [ɛ̃syfizɑ̃, -ɑ̃t] *adj* insufficient;
(*élève, travail*) inadequate.
insuffler [ɛ̃syfle] *vt*: **~ qch dans** to blow sth
into; **~ qch à qn** to inspire sb with sth.
insulaire [ɛ̃sylɛʀ] *adj* island *cpd*; (*attitude*)
insular.
insularité [ɛ̃sylaʀite] *nf* insularity.
insuline [ɛ̃sylin] *nf* insulin.
insultant, e [ɛ̃syltɑ̃, -ɑ̃t] *adj* insulting.
insulte [ɛ̃sylt(ə)] *nf* insult.
insulter [ɛ̃sylte] *vt* to insult.
insupportable [ɛ̃sypɔʀtabl(ə)] *adj* unbearable.
insurgé, e [ɛ̃syʀʒe] *adj, nm/f* insurgent, rebel.
insurger [ɛ̃syʀʒe]: **s'~** *vi*: **s'~ (contre)** to rise
up *ou* rebel (against).
insurmontable [ɛ̃syʀmɔ̃tabl(ə)] *adj* (*difficulté*)
insuperable; (*aversion*) unconquerable.
insurpassable [ɛ̃syʀpasabl(ə)] *adj*
unsurpassable, unsurpassed.
insurrection [ɛ̃syʀɛksjɔ̃] *nf* insurrection,
revolt.
insurrectionnel, le [ɛ̃syʀɛksjɔnɛl] *adj*
insurrectionary.
intact, e [ɛ̃takt] *adj* intact.
intangible [ɛ̃tɑ̃ʒibl(ə)] *adj* intangible; (*principe*)
inviolable.
intarissable [ɛ̃taʀisabl(ə)] *adj* inexhaustible.
intégral, e, aux [ɛ̃tegʀal, -o] *adj* complete ♦ *nf*
(*MATH*) integral; (*œuvres complètes*)
complete works.
intégralement [ɛ̃tegʀalmɑ̃] *adv* in full, fully.
intégralité [ɛ̃tegʀalite] *nf* (*d'une somme, d'un
revenu*) whole (*ou* full) amount; **dans son ~**
in its entirety.
intégrant, e [ɛ̃tegʀɑ̃, -ɑ̃t] *adj*: **faire partie ~e
de** to be an integral part of, be part and
parcel of.
intégration [ɛ̃tegʀasjɔ̃] *nf* integration.
intégrationniste [ɛ̃tegʀasjɔnist(ə)] *adj, nm/f*
integrationist.
intègre [ɛ̃tegʀ(ə)] *adj* perfectly honest,
upright.
intégré, e [ɛ̃tegʀe] *adj*: **circuit ~** integrated
circuit.

intégrer [ɛ̃tegʀe] *vt*: **~ qch à** *ou* **dans** to
integrate sth into; **s'~ à** *ou* **dans** to become
integrated into.
intégrisme [ɛ̃tegʀism(ə)] *nm* fundamentalism.
intégriste [ɛ̃tegʀist(ə)] *adj, nm/f*
fundamentalist.
intégrité [ɛ̃tegʀite] *nf* integrity.
intellect [ɛ̃telɛkt] *nm* intellect.
intellectualisme [ɛ̃telɛktɥalism(ə)] *nm*
intellectualism.
intellectuel, le [ɛ̃telɛktɥɛl] *adj, nm/f*
intellectual; (*péj*) highbrow.
intellectuellement [ɛ̃telɛktɥɛlmɑ̃] *adv*
intellectually.
intelligemment [ɛ̃teliʒamɑ̃] *adv* intelligently.
intelligence [ɛ̃teliʒɑ̃s] *nf* intelligence;
(*compréhension*): **l'~ de** the understanding
of; (*complicité*): **regard d'~** glance of
complicity, meaningful *ou* knowing look;
(*accord*): **vivre en bonne ~ avec qn** to be on
good terms with sb; **~s** *nfpl* (*MIL, fig*) secret
contacts; **être d'~** to have an
understanding; **~ artificielle** artificial
intelligence (A.I.).
intelligent, e [ɛ̃teliʒɑ̃, -ɑ̃t] *adj* intelligent; (*capable*): **~ en affaires** competent in business.
intelligentsia [ɛ̃telidʒɛnsja] *nf* intelligentsia.
intelligible [ɛ̃teliʒibl(ə)] *adj* intelligible.
intello [ɛ̃telo] *adj, nm/f* (*fam*) highbrow.
intempérance [ɛ̃tɑ̃peʀɑ̃s] *nf* overindulgence
no pl; intemperance *no pl*.
intempérant, e [ɛ̃tɑ̃peʀɑ̃, -ɑ̃t] *adj*
overindulgent; (*moralement*) intemperate.
intempéries [ɛ̃tɑ̃peʀi] *nfpl* bad weather *sg*.
intempestif, ive [ɛ̃tɑ̃pɛstif, -iv] *adj* untimely.
intenable [ɛ̃tnabl(ə)] *adj* unbearable.
intendance [ɛ̃tɑ̃dɑ̃s] *nf* (*MIL*) supply corps;
(*: bureau*) supplies office; (*SCOL*) bursar's
office.
intendant, e [ɛ̃tɑ̃dɑ̃, -ɑ̃t] *nm/f* (*MIL*)
quartermaster; (*SCOL*) bursar; (*d'une
propriété*) steward.
intense [ɛ̃tɑ̃s] *adj* intense.
intensément [ɛ̃tɑ̃semɑ̃] *adv* intensely.
intensif, ive [ɛ̃tɑ̃sif, -iv] *adj* intensive; **cours ~**
crash course; **~ en main-d'œuvre** labour-
intensive; **~ en capital** capital-intensive.
intensification [ɛ̃tɑ̃sifikasjɔ̃] *nf*
intensification.
intensifier [ɛ̃tɑ̃sifje] *vt*, **s'~** *vi* to intensify.
intensité [ɛ̃tɑ̃site] *nf* intensity.
intensivement [ɛ̃tɑ̃sivmɑ̃] *adv* intensively.
intenter [ɛ̃tɑ̃te] *vt*: **~ un procès contre** *ou* **à qn**
to start proceedings against sb.
intention [ɛ̃tɑ̃sjɔ̃] *nf* intention; (*JUR*) intent;
avoir l'~ de faire to intend to do, have the
intention of doing; **dans l'~ de faire qch**
with a view to doing sth; **à l'~ de** *prép* for;
(*renseignement*) for the benefit *ou*
information of; (*film, ouvrage*) aimed at; **à
cette ~** with this aim in view; **sans ~**
unintentionally; **faire qch sans mauvaise ~**

to do sth without ill intent; **agir dans une bonne** ~ to act with good intentions.

intentionné, e [ɛ̃tɑ̃sjɔne] *adj:* **bien** ~ well-meaning *ou* -intentioned; **mal** ~ ill-intentioned.

intentionnel, le [ɛ̃tɑ̃sjɔnɛl] *adj* intentional, deliberate.

intentionnellement [ɛ̃tɑ̃sjɔnɛlmɑ̃] *adv* intentionally, deliberately.

inter [ɛ̃tɛʀ] *nm* (*TÉL:* = *interurbain*) long-distance call service; (*SPORT*): ~ **gauche/ droit** inside-left/-right.

interactif, ive [ɛ̃tɛʀaktif, -iv] *adj* (*aussi INFORM*) interactive.

interaction [ɛ̃tɛʀaksjɔ̃] *nf* interaction.

interarmées [ɛ̃tɛʀaʀme] *adj inv* inter-army, combined.

interbancaire [ɛ̃tɛʀbɑ̃kɛʀ] *adj* interbank.

intercalaire [ɛ̃tɛʀkalɛʀ] *adj, nm:* **(feuillet)** ~ insert; **(fiche)** ~ divider.

intercaler [ɛ̃tɛʀkale] *vt* to insert; **s'**~ **entre** to come in between; to slip in between.

intercéder [ɛ̃tɛʀsede] *vi:* ~ **(pour qn)** to intercede (on behalf of sb).

intercepter [ɛ̃tɛʀsɛpte] *vt* to intercept; (*lumière, chaleur*) to cut off.

intercepteur [ɛ̃tɛʀsɛptœʀ] *nm* (*AVIAT*) interceptor.

interception [ɛ̃tɛʀsɛpsjɔ̃] *nf* interception; **avion d'**~ interceptor.

intercession [ɛ̃tɛʀsesjɔ̃] *nf* intercession.

interchangeable [ɛ̃tɛʀʃɑ̃ʒabl(ə)] *adj* interchangeable.

interclasse [ɛ̃tɛʀklɑs] *nm* (*SCOL*) break (between classes).

interclubs [ɛ̃tɛʀklœb] *adj inv* interclub.

intercommunal, e, aux [ɛ̃tɛʀkɔmynal, -o] *adj* intervillage, intercommunity.

intercommunautaire [ɛ̃tɛʀkɔmynotɛʀ] *adj* intercommunity.

interconnexion [ɛ̃tɛʀkɔnɛksjɔ̃] *nf* (*INFORM*) networking.

intercontinental, e, aux [ɛ̃tɛʀkɔ̃tinɑ̃tal, -o] *adj* intercontinental.

intercostal, e, aux [ɛ̃tɛʀkɔstal, -o] *adj* intercostal, between the ribs.

interdépartemental, e, aux [ɛ̃tɛʀdepaʀtəmɑ̃tal, -o] *adj* interdepartmental.

interdépendance [ɛ̃tɛʀdepɑ̃dɑ̃s] *nf* interdependence.

interdépendant, e [ɛ̃tɛʀdepɑ̃dɑ̃, -ɑ̃t] *adj* interdependent.

interdiction [ɛ̃tɛʀdiksjɔ̃] *nf* ban; ~ **de faire qch** ban on doing sth; ~ **de séjour** (*JUR*) *order banning ex-prisoner from frequenting specified places.*

interdire [ɛ̃tɛʀdiʀ] *vt* to forbid; (*ADMIN: stationnement, meeting, passage*) to ban, prohibit; (*: journal, livre*) to ban; ~ **qch à qn** to forbid sb sth; ~ **à qn de faire** to forbid sb to do, prohibit sb from doing; (*suj: empêchement*) to prevent *ou* preclude sb

from doing; **s'**~ **qch** (*éviter*) to refrain *ou* abstain from sth; (*se refuser*): **il s'interdit d'y penser** he doesn't allow himself to think about it.

interdisciplinaire [ɛ̃tɛʀdisiplinɛʀ] *adj* interdisciplinary.

interdit, e [ɛ̃tɛʀdi, -it] *pp de* **interdire** ♦ *adj* (*stupéfait*) taken aback; (*défendu*) forbidden, prohibited ♦ *nm* interdict, prohibition; **film** ~ **aux moins de 18/13 ans** ≈ 18-/PG-rated film; **sens** ~ one way; **stationnement** ~ no parking; ~ **de chéquier** having cheque book facilities suspended; ~ **de séjour** subject to an *interdiction de séjour*.

intéressant, e [ɛ̃teʀesɑ̃, -ɑ̃t] *adj* interesting; **faire l'**~ to draw attention to o.s.

intéressé, e [ɛ̃teʀese] *adj* (*parties*) involved, concerned; (*amitié, motifs*) self-interested ♦ *nm:* **l'**~ the interested party; **les** ~**s** those concerned *ou* involved.

intéressement [ɛ̃teʀesmɑ̃] *nm* (*COMM*) profit-sharing.

intéresser [ɛ̃teʀese] *vt* to interest; (*toucher*) to be of interest *ou* concern to; (*ADMIN: concerner*) to affect, concern; (*COMM: travailleur*) to give a share in the profits to; (*: partenaire*) to interest (in the business); **s'**~ **à** to take an interest in, be interested in; ~ **qn à qch** to get sb interested in sth.

intérêt [ɛ̃teʀe] *nm* (*aussi COMM*) interest; (*égoïsme*) self-interest; **porter de l'**~ **à qn** to take an interest in sb; **agir par** ~ to act out of self-interest; **avoir des** ~**s dans** (*COMM*) to have a financial interest *ou* a stake in; **avoir** ~ **à faire** to do well to do; **il y a** ~ **à ...** it would be a good thing to ...; ~ **composé** compound interest.

interface [ɛ̃tɛʀfas] *nf* (*INFORM*) interface.

interférence [ɛ̃tɛʀfeʀɑ̃s] *nf* interference.

interférer [ɛ̃tɛʀfeʀe] *vi:* ~ **(avec)** to interfere (with).

intergouvernemental, e, aux [ɛ̃tɛʀguvɛʀnəmɑ̃tal, -o] *adj* intergovernmental.

intérieur, e [ɛ̃teʀjœʀ] *adj* (*mur, escalier, poche*) inside; (*commerce, politique*) domestic; (*cour, calme, vie*) inner; (*navigation*) inland ♦ *nm* (*d'une maison, d'un récipient etc*) inside; (*d'un pays, aussi: décor, mobilier*) interior; (*POL*): **l'I**~ (the Department of) the Interior, ≈ the Home Office (*BRIT*); **à l'**~ **(de)** inside; (*fig*) within; **de l'**~ (*fig*) from the inside; **en** ~ (*CINÉ*) in the studio; **vêtement d'**~ indoor garment.

intérieurement [ɛ̃teʀjœʀmɑ̃] *adv* inwardly.

intérim [ɛ̃teʀim] *nm* interim period; **assurer l'**~ **(de)** to deputize (for); **par** ~ *adj* interim ♦ *adv* in a temporary capacity.

intérimaire [ɛ̃teʀimɛʀ] *adj* temporary, interim ♦ *nm/f* (*secrétaire etc*) temporary, temp (*BRIT*); (*suppléant*) deputy.

intérioriser [ɛ̃teʀjɔʀize] *vt* to internalize.

interjection [ɛ̃tɛʀʒɛksjɔ̃] *nf* interjection.

interjeter [ɛ̃tɛʀʒəte] *vt* (*JUR*): ~ **appel** to lodge an appeal.

interligne [ɛ̃tɛʀliɲ] *nm* inter-line space ♦ *nf* (*TYPO*) lead, leading; **simple/double** ~ single/double spacing.

interlocuteur, trice [ɛ̃tɛʀlɔkytœʀ, -tʀis] *nm/f* speaker; (*POL*): ~ **valable** valid representative; **son** ~ the person he *ou* she was speaking to.

interlope [ɛ̃tɛʀlɔp] *adj* illicit; (*milieu, bar*) shady.

interloquer [ɛ̃tɛʀlɔke] *vt* to take aback.

interlude [ɛ̃tɛʀlyd] *nm* interlude.

intermède [ɛ̃tɛʀmɛd] *nm* interlude.

intermédiaire [ɛ̃tɛʀmedjɛʀ] *adj* intermediate; middle; half-way ♦ *nm/f* intermediary; (*COMM*) middleman; **sans** ~ directly; **par l'**~ **de** through.

interminable [ɛ̃tɛʀminabl(ə)] *adj* never-ending.

interminablement [ɛ̃tɛʀminabləmɑ̃] *adv* interminably.

interministériel, le [ɛ̃tɛʀministeʀjɛl] *adj*: **comité** ~ interdepartmental committee.

intermittence [ɛ̃tɛʀmitɑ̃s] *nf*: **par** ~ intermittently, sporadically.

intermittent, e [ɛ̃tɛʀmitɑ̃, -ɑ̃t] *adj* intermittent, sporadic.

internat [ɛ̃tɛʀna] *nm* (*SCOL*) boarding school.

international, e, aux [ɛ̃tɛʀnasjɔnal, -o] *adj*, *nm/f* international.

internationalisation [ɛ̃tɛʀnasjɔnalizasjɔ̃] *nf* internationalization.

internationaliser [ɛ̃tɛʀnasjɔnalize] *vt* to internationalize.

internationalisme [ɛ̃tɛʀnasjɔnalism(ə)] *nm* internationalism.

interne [ɛ̃tɛʀn(ə)] *adj* internal ♦ *nm/f* (*SCOL*) boarder; (*MÉD*) houseman (*BRIT*), intern (*US*).

internement [ɛ̃tɛʀnəmɑ̃] *nm* (*POL*) internment; (*MÉD*) confinement.

interner [ɛ̃tɛʀne] *vt* (*POL*) to intern; (*MÉD*) to confine to a mental institution.

interparlementaire [ɛ̃tɛʀpaʀləmɑ̃tɛʀ] *adj* interparliamentary.

interpellation [ɛ̃tɛʀpelasjɔ̃] *nf* interpellation; (*POL*) question.

interpeller [ɛ̃tɛʀpele] *vt* (*appeler*) to call out to; (*apostropher*) to shout at; (*POLICE*) to take in for questioning; (*POL*) to question; **s'**~ to exchange insults.

interphone [ɛ̃tɛʀfɔn] *nm* intercom.

interplanétaire [ɛ̃tɛʀplanetɛʀ] *adj* interplanetary.

Interpol [ɛ̃tɛʀpɔl] *sigle m* Interpol.

interpoler [ɛ̃tɛʀpɔle] *vt* to interpolate.

interposer [ɛ̃tɛʀpoze] *vt* to interpose; **s'**~ *vi* to intervene; **par personnes interposées** through a third party.

interprétariat [ɛ̃tɛʀpʀetaʀja] *nm* interpreting.

interprétation [ɛ̃tɛʀpʀetasjɔ̃] *nf* interpretation.

interprète [ɛ̃tɛʀpʀɛt] *nm/f* interpreter; (*porte-parole*) spokesman.

interpréter [ɛ̃tɛʀpʀete] *vt* to interpret.

interprofessionnel, le [ɛ̃tɛʀpʀofesjɔnɛl] *adj* interprofessional.

interrogateur, trice [ɛ̃teʀɔgatœʀ, -tʀis] *adj* questioning, inquiring ♦ *nm/f* (*SCOL*) (oral) examiner.

interrogatif, ive [ɛ̃teʀɔgatif, -iv] *adj* (*LING*) interrogative.

interrogation [ɛ̃teʀɔgasjɔ̃] *nf* question; (*SCOL*) (written *ou* oral) test.

interrogatoire [ɛ̃teʀɔgatwaʀ] *nm* (*POLICE*) questioning *no pl*; (*JUR*) cross-examination, interrogation.

interroger [ɛ̃teʀɔʒe] *vt* to question; (*INFORM*) to interrogate; (*SCOL: candidat*) to test; ~ **qn (sur qch)** to question sb (about sth); ~ **qn du regard** to look questioningly at sb, give sb a questioning look; **s'**~ **sur qch** to ask o.s. about sth, ponder (about) sth.

interrompre [ɛ̃teʀɔ̃pʀ(ə)] *vt* (*gén*) to interrupt; (*travail, voyage*) to break off, interrupt; **s'**~ to break off.

interrupteur [ɛ̃teʀyptœʀ] *nm* switch; ~ **à bascule** (*INFORM*) toggle switch.

interruption [ɛ̃teʀypsjɔ̃] *nf* interruption; **sans** ~ without a break; ~ **de grossesse** termination of pregnancy; ~ **volontaire de grossesse** voluntary termination of pregnancy, abortion.

interscolaire [ɛ̃tɛʀskɔlɛʀ] *adj* interschool(s).

intersection [ɛ̃tɛʀsɛksjɔ̃] *nf* intersection.

intersidéral, e, aux [ɛ̃tɛʀsideʀal, -o] *adj* intersidereal, interstellar.

interstice [ɛ̃tɛʀstis] *nm* crack, slit.

intersyndical, e, aux [ɛ̃tɛʀsɛ̃dikal, -o] *adj* interunion.

interurbain [ɛ̃tɛʀyʀbɛ̃] (*TÉL*) *nm* long-distance call service ♦ *adj* long-distance.

intervalle [ɛ̃tɛʀval] *nm* (*espace*) space; (*de temps*) interval; **dans l'**~ in the meantime; **à 2 mois d'**~ after a space of 2 months; **à** ~**s rapprochés** at close intervals; **par** ~**s** at intervals.

intervenant, e [ɛ̃tɛʀvənɑ̃, -ɑ̃t] *vb voir* **intervenir** ♦ *nm/f* speaker (*at conference*).

intervenir [ɛ̃tɛʀvəniʀ] *vi* (*gén*) to intervene; (*survenir*) to take place; (*faire une conférence*) to give a talk *ou* lecture; ~ **auprès de/en faveur de qn** to intervene with/on behalf of sb; **la police a dû** ~ police had to step in *ou* intervene; **les médecins ont dû** ~ the doctors had to operate.

intervention [ɛ̃tɛʀvɑ̃sjɔ̃] *nf* intervention; (*conférence*) talk, paper; ~ (**chirurgicale**) operation.

interventionnisme [ɛ̃tɛʀvɑ̃sjɔnism(ə)] *nm* interventionism.

interventionniste [ɛ̃tɛʀvɑ̃sjɔnist(ə)] *adj* interventionist.

intervenu, e [ɛ̃tɛʀv(ə)ny] *pp de* **intervenir.**
intervertible [ɛ̃tɛʀvɛʀtibl(ə)] *adj*
interchangeable.
intervertir [ɛ̃tɛʀvɛʀtiʀ] *vt* to invert (the order
of), reverse.
interviendrai [ɛ̃tɛʀvjɛ̃dʀe], **interviens**
[ɛ̃tɛʀvjɛ̃] *etc vb voir* **intervenir.**
interview [ɛ̃tɛʀvju] *nf* interview.
interviewer [ɛ̃tɛʀvjuve] *vt* to interview ♦ *nm*
[ɛ̃tɛʀvjuvœʀ] (*journaliste*) interviewer.
intervins [ɛ̃tɛʀvɛ̃] *etc vb voir* **intervenir.**
intestat [ɛ̃tɛsta] *adj* (*JUR*): **décéder** ~ to die
intestate.
intestin, e [ɛ̃tɛstɛ̃, -in] *adj* internal ♦ *nm*
intestine; ~ **grêle** small intestine.
intestinal, e, aux [ɛ̃tɛstinal, -o] *adj* intestinal.
intime [ɛ̃tim] *adj* intimate; (*vie, journal*)
private; (*convictions*) inmost; (*dîner,
cérémonie*) held among friends, quiet
♦ *nm/f* close friend.
intimement [ɛ̃timmɑ̃] *adv* (*profondément*)
deeply, firmly; (*étroitement*) intimately.
intimer [ɛ̃time] *vt* (*JUR*) to notify; ~ **à qn
l'ordre de faire** to order sb to do.
intimidant, e [ɛ̃timidɑ̃, -ɑ̃t] *adj* intimidating.
intimidation [ɛ̃timidɑsjɔ̃] *nf* intimidation;
manœuvres d'~ (*action*) acts of
intimidation; (*stratégie*) intimidatory tactics.
intimider [ɛ̃timide] *vt* to intimidate.
intimité [ɛ̃timite] *nf* intimacy; (*vie privée*)
privacy; private life; **dans l'**~ in private;
(*sans formalités*) with only a few friends,
quietly.
intitulé [ɛ̃tityle] *nm* title.
intituler [ɛ̃tityle] *vt*: **comment a-t-il intitulé
son livre?** what title did he give his book?;
s'~ to be entitled; (*personne*) to call o.s.
intolérable [ɛ̃tɔleʀabl(ə)] *adj* intolerable.
intolérance [ɛ̃tɔleʀɑ̃s] *nf* intolerance; ~ **aux
antibiotiques** intolerance to antibiotics.
intolérant, e [ɛ̃tɔleʀɑ̃, -ɑ̃t] *adj* intolerant.
intonation [ɛ̃tɔnasjɔ̃] *nf* intonation.
intouchable [ɛ̃tuʃabl(ə)] *adj* (*fig*) above the
law, sacrosanct; (*REL*) untouchable.
intoxication [ɛ̃tɔksikasjɔ̃] *nf* poisoning *no pl*;
(*toxicomanie*) drug addiction; (*fig*)
brainwashing; ~ **alimentaire** food
poisoning.
intoxiqué, e [ɛ̃tɔksike] *nm/f* addict.
intoxiquer [ɛ̃tɔksike] *vt* to poison; (*fig*) to
brainwash; **s'**~ to poison o.s.
intradermique [ɛ̃tʀadɛʀmik] *adj, nf*: **(injection)**
~ intradermal *ou* intracutaneous injection.
intraduisible [ɛ̃tʀadɥizibl(ə)] *adj*
untranslatable; (*fig*) inexpressible.
intraitable [ɛ̃tʀɛtabl(ə)] *adj* inflexible,
uncompromising.
intramusculaire [ɛ̃tʀamyskylɛʀ] *adj, nf*:
(injection) ~ intramuscular injection.
intransigeance [ɛ̃tʀɑ̃ziʒɑ̃s] *nf* intransigence.
intransigeant, e [ɛ̃tʀɑ̃ziʒɑ̃, -ɑ̃t] *adj*
intransigent; (*morale, passion*)

uncompromising.
intransitif, ive [ɛ̃tʀɑ̃zitif, -iv] *adj* (*LING*)
intransitive.
intransportable [ɛ̃tʀɑ̃spɔʀtabl(ə)] *adj* (*blessé*)
unable to travel.
intraveineux, euse [ɛ̃tʀavɛnø, -øz] *adj*
intravenous.
intrépide [ɛ̃tʀepid] *adj* dauntless, intrepid.
intrépidité [ɛ̃tʀepidite] *nf* dauntlessness.
intrigant, e [ɛ̃tʀigɑ̃, -ɑ̃t] *nm/f* schemer.
intrigue [ɛ̃tʀig] *nf* intrigue; (*scénario*) plot.
intriguer [ɛ̃tʀige] *vi* to scheme ♦ *vt* to puzzle,
intrigue.
intrinsèque [ɛ̃tʀɛ̃sɛk] *adj* intrinsic.
introductif, ive [ɛ̃tʀɔdyktif, -iv] *adj*
introductory.
introduction [ɛ̃tʀɔdyksjɔ̃] *nf* introduction;
paroles/chapitre d'~ introductory words/
chapter; **lettre/mot d'**~ letter/note of
introduction.
introduire [ɛ̃tʀɔdɥiʀ] *vt* to introduce; (*visiteur*)
to show in; (*aiguille, clef*): ~ **qch dans** to
insert *ou* introduce sth into; (*personne*): ~ **à
qch** to introduce to sth; (: *présenter*): ~ **qn à
qn/dans un club** to introduce sb to sb/to a
club; (*INFORM*) to input, enter; **s'**~
(*techniques, usages*) to be introduced; **s'**~
dans to gain entry into; to get o.s. accepted
into; (*eau, fumée*) to get into; ~ **au clavier** to
key in.
introduit, e [ɛ̃tʀɔdɥi, -it] *pp de* **introduire** ♦ *adj*:
bien ~ (*personne*) well-received.
introniser [ɛ̃tʀɔnize] *vt* to enthrone.
introspection [ɛ̃tʀɔspɛksjɔ̃] *nf* introspection.
introuvable [ɛ̃tʀuvabl(ə)] *adj* which cannot be
found; (*COMM*) unobtainable.
introverti, e [ɛ̃tʀɔvɛʀti] *nm/f* introvert.
intrus, e [ɛ̃tʀy, -yz] *nm/f* intruder.
intrusion [ɛ̃tʀyzjɔ̃] *nf* intrusion; (*ingérence*)
interference.
intuitif, ive [ɛ̃tɥitif, -iv] *adj* intuitive.
intuition [ɛ̃tɥisjɔ̃] *nf* intuition; **avoir une** ~ to
have a feeling; **avoir l'**~ **de qch** to have an
intuition of sth; **avoir de l'**~ to have
intuition.
intuitivement [ɛ̃tɥitivmɑ̃] *adv* intuitively.
inusable [inyzabl(ə)] *adj* hard-wearing.
inusité, e [inyzite] *adj* rarely used.
inutile [inytil] *adj* useless; (*superflu*)
unnecessary.
inutilement [inytilmɑ̃] *adv* needlessly.
inutilisable [inytilizabl(ə)] *adj* unusable.
inutilisé, e [inytilize] *adj* unused.
inutilité [inytilite] *nf* uselessness.
invaincu, e [ɛ̃vɛ̃ky] *adj* unbeaten; (*armée,
peuple*) unconquered.
invalide [ɛ̃valid] *adj* disabled ♦ *nm/f*: ~ **de
guerre** disabled ex-serviceman; ~ **du travail**
industrially disabled person.
invalider [ɛ̃valide] *vt* to invalidate.
invalidité [ɛ̃validite] *nf* disability.
invariable [ɛ̃vaʀjabl(ə)] *adj* invariable.

invariablement – irons

invariablement [ɛ̃vaʀjabləmɑ̃] *adv* invariably.
invasion [ɛ̃vazjɔ̃] *nf* invasion.
invective [ɛ̃vɛktiv] *nf* invective.
invectiver [ɛ̃vɛktive] *vt* to hurl abuse at ♦ *vi:* ~ **contre** to rail against.
invendable [ɛ̃vɑ̃dabl(ə)] *adj* unsaleable, unmarketable.
invendu, e [ɛ̃vɑ̃dy] *adj* unsold ♦ *nm* return; ~**s** *nmpl* unsold goods.
inventaire [ɛ̃vɑ̃tɛʀ] *nm* inventory; (*COMM: liste*) stocklist; (*: opération*) stocktaking *no pl*; (*fig*) survey; **faire un** ~ to make an inventory; (*COMM*) to take stock; **faire** *ou* **procéder à l'**~ to take stock.
inventer [ɛ̃vɑ̃te] *vt* to invent; (*subterfuge*) to devise, invent; (*histoire, excuse*) to make up, invent; ~ **de faire** to hit on the idea of doing.
inventeur, trice [ɛ̃vɑ̃tœʀ, -tʀis] *nm/f* inventor.
inventif, ive [ɛ̃vɑ̃tif, -iv] *adj* inventive.
invention [ɛ̃vɑ̃sjɔ̃] *nf* invention; (*imagination, inspiration*) inventiveness.
inventivité [ɛ̃vɑ̃tivite] *nf* inventiveness.
inventorier [ɛ̃vɑ̃tɔʀje] *vt* to make an inventory of.
invérifiable [ɛ̃veʀifjabl(ə)] *adj* unverifiable.
inverse [ɛ̃vɛʀs(ə)] *adj* (*ordre*) reverse; (*sens*) opposite; (*rapport*) inverse ♦ *nm* reverse; inverse; **en proportion** ~ in inverse proportion; **dans le sens** ~ **des aiguilles d'une montre** anti-clockwise; **en sens** ~ in (*ou* from) the opposite direction; **à l'**~ conversely.
inversement [ɛ̃vɛʀsəmɑ̃] *adv* conversely.
inverser [ɛ̃vɛʀse] *vt* to reverse, invert; (*ÉLEC*) to reverse.
inversion [ɛ̃vɛʀsjɔ̃] *nf* reversal; inversion.
invertébré, e [ɛ̃vɛʀtebʀe] *adj, nm* invertebrate.
inverti, e [ɛ̃vɛʀti] *nm/f* homosexual.
investigation [ɛ̃vɛstigasjɔ̃] *nf* investigation, inquiry.
investir [ɛ̃vɛstiʀ] *vt* to invest; **s'**~ *vi* (*PSYCH*) to involve o.s.; ~ **qn de** to vest *ou* invest sb with.
investissement [ɛ̃vɛstismɑ̃] *nm* investment; (*PSYCH*) involvement.
investisseur [ɛ̃vɛstisœʀ] *nm* investor.
investiture [ɛ̃vɛstityʀ] *nf* investiture; (*à une élection*) nomination.
invétéré, e [ɛ̃veteʀe] *adj* (*habitude*) ingrained; (*bavard, buveur*) inveterate.
invincible [ɛ̃vɛ̃sibl(ə)] *adj* invincible, unconquerable.
invinciblement [ɛ̃vɛ̃sibləmɑ̃] *adv* (*fig*) invincibly.
inviolabilité [ɛ̃vjɔlabilite] *nf:* ~ **parlementaire** parliamentary immunity.
inviolable [ɛ̃vjɔlabl(ə)] *adj* inviolable.
invisible [ɛ̃vizibl(ə)] *adj* invisible; (*fig: personne*) not available.
invitation [ɛ̃vitasjɔ̃] *nf* invitation; **à/sur l'**~ **de qn** at/on sb's invitation; **carte/lettre d'**~

invitation card/letter.
invite [ɛ̃vit] *nf* invitation.
invité, e [ɛ̃vite] *nm/f* guest.
inviter [ɛ̃vite] *vt* to invite; ~ **qn à faire qch** to invite sb to do sth; (*suj: chose*) to induce *ou* tempt sb to do sth.
invivable [ɛ̃vivabl(ə)] *adj* unbearable, impossible.
involontaire [ɛ̃vɔlɔ̃tɛʀ] *adj* (*mouvement*) involuntary; (*insulte*) unintentional; (*complice*) unwitting.
involontairement [ɛ̃vɔlɔ̃tɛʀmɑ̃] *adv* involuntarily.
invoquer [ɛ̃vɔke] *vt* (*Dieu, muse*) to call upon, invoke; (*prétexte*) to put forward (as an excuse); (*témoignage*) to call upon; (*loi, texte*) to refer to; ~ **la clémence de qn** to beg sb *ou* appeal to sb for clemency.
invraisemblable [ɛ̃vʀɛsɑ̃blabl(ə)] *adj* unlikely, improbable; (*bizarre*) incredible.
invraisemblance [ɛ̃vʀɛsɑ̃blɑ̃s] *nf* unlikelihood *no pl*, improbability.
invulnérable [ɛ̃vylneʀabl(ə)] *adj* invulnerable.
iode [jɔd] *nm* iodine.
iodé, e [jɔde] *adj* iodized.
ion [jɔ̃] *nm* ion.
ionique [jɔnik] *adj* (*ARCHIT*) Ionic; (*SCIENCE*) ionic.
ioniseur [jɔnizœʀ] *nm* ionizer.
iota [jɔta] *nm:* **sans changer un** ~ without changing one iota *ou* the tiniest bit.
IPC *sigle m* (= *Indice des prix à la consommation*) CPI.
IR. *abr* = **infrarouge**.
IRA *sigle f* (= *Irish Republican Army*) IRA.
irai [iʀe] *etc vb voir* **aller**.
Irak [iʀak] *nm:* **l'**~ Iraq *ou* Irak.
irakien, ne [iʀakjɛ̃, -ɛn] *adj* Iraqi ♦ *nm/f:* **I**~, **ne** Iraqi.
Iran [iʀɑ̃] *nm:* **l'**~ Iran.
iranien, ne [iʀanjɛ̃, -ɛn] *adj* Iranian ♦ *nm* (*LING*) Iranian ♦ *nm/f:* **I**~, **ne** Iranian.
Iraq [iʀak] = **Irak**.
iraquien, ne [iʀakjɛ̃, -ɛn] = **irakien, ne**.
irascible [iʀasibl(ə)] *adj* short-tempered, irascible.
irions [iʀjɔ̃] *etc vb voir* **aller**.
iris [iʀis] *nm* iris.
irisé, e [iʀize] *adj* iridescent.
irlandais, e [iʀlɑ̃dɛ, -ɛz] *adj, nm* (*LING*) Irish ♦ *nm/f:* **I**~, **e** Irishman/woman; **les I**~ the Irish.
Irlande [iʀlɑ̃d] *nf:* **l'**~ (*pays*) Ireland; (*état*) the Irish Republic, the Republic of Ireland, Eire; ~ **du Nord** Northern Ireland, Ulster; ~ **du Sud** Southern Ireland, Irish Republic, Eire; **la mer d'**~ the Irish Sea.
ironie [iʀɔni] *nf* irony.
ironique [iʀɔnik] *adj* ironical.
ironiquement [iʀɔnikmɑ̃] *adv* ironically.
ironiser [iʀɔnize] *vi* to be ironical.
irons [iʀɔ̃] *etc vb voir* **aller**.

IRPP *sigle m* (= *impôt sur le revenu des personnes physiques*) income tax.
irradiation [iʀadjɑsjɔ̃] *nf* irradiation.
irradier [iʀadje] *vi* to radiate ♦ *vt* to irradiate.
irraisonné, e [iʀɛzɔne] *adj* irrational, unreasoned.
irrationnel, le [iʀasjɔnɛl] *adj* irrational.
irrattrapable [iʀatʀapabl(ə)] *adj* (*retard*) that cannot be made up; (*bévue*) that cannot be made good.
irréalisable [iʀealizabl(ə)] *adj* unrealizable; (*projet*) impracticable.
irréalisme [iʀealism(ə)] *nm* lack of realism.
irréaliste [iʀealist(ə)] *adj* unrealistic.
irréalité [iʀealite] *nf* unreality.
irrecevable [iʀsəvabl(ə)] *adj* unacceptable.
irréconciliable [iʀekɔ̃siljabl(ə)] *adj* irreconcilable.
irrécouvrable [iʀekuvʀabl(ə)] *adj* irrecoverable.
irrécupérable [iʀekypeʀabl(ə)] *adj* unreclaimable, beyond repair; (*personne*) beyond redemption *ou* recall.
irrécusable [iʀekyzabl(ə)] *adj* (*témoignage*) unimpeachable; (*preuve*) incontestable, indisputable.
irréductible [iʀedyktibl(ə)] *adj* indomitable, implacable; (*MATH: fraction, équation*) irreducible.
irréductiblement [iʀedyktibləmɑ̃] *adv* implacably.
irréel, le [iʀeɛl] *adj* unreal.
irréfléchi, e [iʀefleʃi] *adj* thoughtless.
irréfutable [iʀefytabl(ə)] *adj* irrefutable.
irréfutablement [iʀefytabləmɑ̃] *adv* irrefutably.
irrégularité [iʀegylaʀite] *nf* irregularity; unevenness *no pl*.
irrégulier, ière [iʀegylje, -jɛʀ] *adj* irregular; (*surface, rythme, écriture*) uneven, irregular; (*élève, athlète*) erratic.
irrégulièrement [iʀegyljɛʀmɑ̃] *adv* irregularly.
irrémédiable [iʀemedjabl(ə)] *adj* irreparable.
irrémédiablement [iʀemedjabləmɑ̃] *adv* irreparably.
irremplaçable [iʀɑ̃plasabl(ə)] *adj* irreplaceable.
irréparable [iʀepaʀabl(ə)] *adj* beyond repair, irreparable; (*fig*) irreparable.
irrépréhensible [iʀepʀeɑ̃sibl(ə)] *adj* irreprehensible.
irrépressible [iʀepʀesibl(ə)] *adj* irrepressible.
irréprochable [iʀepʀɔʃabl(ə)] *adj* irreproachable, beyond reproach; (*tenue, toilette*) impeccable.
irrésistible [iʀezistibl(ə)] *adj* irresistible; (*preuve, logique*) compelling.
irrésistiblement [iʀezistibləmɑ̃] *adv* irresistibly.
irrésolu, e [iʀezɔly] *adj* irresolute.
irrésolution [iʀezɔlysjɔ̃] *nf* irresoluteness.

irrespectueux, euse [iʀɛspɛktɥø, -øz] *adj* disrespectful.
irrespirable [iʀɛspiʀabl(ə)] *adj* unbreathable; (*fig*) oppressive, stifling.
irresponsabilité [iʀɛspɔ̃sabilite] *nf* irresponsibility.
irresponsable [iʀɛspɔ̃sabl(ə)] *adj* irresponsible.
irrévérencieux, euse [iʀeveʀɑ̃sjø, -øz] *adj* irreverent.
irréversible [iʀevɛʀsibl(ə)] *adj* irreversible.
irréversiblement [iʀevɛʀsibləmɑ̃] *adv* irreversibly.
irrévocable [iʀevɔkabl(ə)] *adj* irrevocable.
irrévocablement [iʀevɔkabləmɑ̃] *adv* irrevocably.
irrigation [iʀigɑsjɔ̃] *nf* irrigation.
irriguer [iʀige] *vt* to irrigate.
irritabilité [iʀitabilite] *nf* irritability.
irritable [iʀitabl(ə)] *adj* irritable.
irritant, e [iʀitɑ̃, -ɑ̃t] *adj* irritating; (*MÉD*) irritant.
irritation [iʀitɑsjɔ̃] *nf* irritation.
irrité, e [iʀite] *adj* irritated.
irriter [iʀite] *vt* (*agacer*) to irritate, annoy; (*MÉD: enflammer*) to irritate; **s'~ contre qn/de qch** to get annoyed *ou* irritated with sb/at sth.
irruption [iʀypsjɔ̃] *nf* irruption *no pl*; **faire ~ dans** to burst into.
ISBN *sigle m* (= *International Standard Book Number*) ISBN.
Islam [islam] *nm* Islam.
islamique [islamik] *adj* Islamic.
islamiste [islamist(ə)] *adj*, *nm/f* Islamic.
islandais, e [islɑ̃dɛ, -ɛz] *adj* Icelandic ♦ *nm* (*LING*) Icelandic ♦ *nm/f*: **I~, e** Icelander.
Islande [islɑ̃d] *nf*: **l'~** Iceland.
ISMH *sigle m* (= *Inventaire supplémentaire des monuments historiques*): **monument inscrit à l'~** ≈ listed building.
isocèle [izɔsɛl] *adj* isoceles.
isolant, e [izɔlɑ̃, -ɑ̃t] *adj* insulating; (*insonorisant*) soundproofing ♦ *nm* insulator.
isolateur [izɔlatœʀ] *nm* (*ÉLEC*) insulator.
isolation [izɔlasjɔ̃] *nf* insulation; **~ acoustique/thermique** sound/thermal insulation.
isolationnisme [izɔlɑsjɔnism(ə)] *nm* isolationism.
isolé, e [izɔle] *adj* isolated; (*ÉLEC*) insulated.
isolement [izɔlmɑ̃] *nm* isolation; solitary confinement.
isolément [izɔlemɑ̃] *adv* in isolation.
isoler [izɔle] *vt* to isolate; (*prisonnier*) to put in solitary confinement; (*ville*) to cut off, isolate; (*ÉLEC*) to insulate.
isoloir [izɔlwaʀ] *nm* polling booth.
isorel [izɔʀɛl] *nm* ® hardboard.
isotherme [izɔtɛʀm(ə)] *adj* (*camion*) refrigerated.
Israël [isʀaɛl] *nm*: **l'~** Israel.

israélien, ne [israeljɛ̃, -ɛn] *adj* Israeli ♦ *nm/f*: I~, **ne** Israeli.

israélite [israelit] *adj* Jewish; (*dans l'Ancien Testament*) Israelite ♦ *nm/f*: I~ Jew/Jewess; Israelite.

issu, e [isy] *adj*: ~ **de** descended from; (*fig*) stemming from ♦ *nf* (*ouverture, sortie*) exit; (*solution*) way out, solution; (*dénouement*) outcome; **à l'~e de** at the conclusion *ou* close of; **rue sans ~e** dead end, no through road (*BRIT*), no outlet (*US*); ~**e de secours** emergency exit.

Istamboul *ou* **Istanbul** [istãbul] *n* Istanbul.

isthme [ism(ə)] *nm* isthmus.

Italie [itali] *nf*: **l'~** Italy.

italien, ne [italjɛ̃, -ɛn] *adj* Italian ♦ *nm* (*LING*) Italian ♦ *nm/f*: I~, **ne** Italian.

italique [italik] *nm*: **en ~(s)** in italics.

item [itɛm] *nm* item; (*question*) question, test.

itinéraire [itinerɛr] *nm* itinerary, route.

itinérant, e [itinerã, -ãt] *adj* itinerant, travelling.

ITP *sigle m* (= *ingénieur des travaux publics*) civil engineer.

IUT *sigle m* = **Institut universitaire de technologie.**

IVG *sigle f* (= *interruption volontaire de grossesse*) abortion.

ivoire [ivwar] *nm* ivory.

ivoirien, ne [ivwarjɛ̃, -ɛn] *adj* of *ou* from the Ivory Coast.

ivraie [ivrɛ] *nf*: **séparer l'~ du bon grain** (*fig*) to separate the wheat from the chaff.

ivre [ivr(ə)] *adj* drunk; ~ **de** (*colère*) wild with; (*bonheur*) drunk *ou* intoxicated with; ~ **mort** dead drunk.

ivresse [ivrɛs] *nf* drunkenness; (*euphorie*) intoxication.

ivrogne [ivrɔɲ] *nm/f* drunkard.

J j

J, j [ʒi] *nm inv* J, j ♦ *abr* (= *jour*): **jour ~** D-day; (= *Joule*) J; **J comme Joseph** J for Jack (*BRIT*) *ou* Jig (*US*).

j' [ʒ] *pron voir* **je.**

jabot [ʒabo] *nm* (*ZOOL*) crop; (*de vêtement*) jabot.

JAC [ʒak] *sigle f* (= *Jeunesse agricole catholique*) *youth organization.*

jacasser [ʒakase] *vi* to chatter.

jachère [ʒaʃɛr] *nf*: **(être) en ~** (to lie) fallow.

jacinthe [ʒasɛ̃t] *nf* hyacinth; ~ **des bois** bluebell.

jack [dʒak] *nm* jack plug.

jacquard [ʒakar] *adj inv* Fair Isle.

jacquerie [ʒakri] *nf* riot.

jade [ʒad] *nm* jade.

jadis [ʒadis] *adv* in times past, formerly.

jaguar [ʒagwar] *nm* (*ZOOL*) jaguar.

jaillir [ʒajir] *vi* (*liquide*) to spurt out, gush out; (*lumière*) to flood out; (*fig*) to rear up; to burst out.

jaillissement [ʒajismã] *nm* spurt, gush.

jais [ʒɛ] *nm* jet; (**d'un noir**) **de ~** jet-black.

jalon [ʒalɔ̃] *nm* range pole; (*fig*) milestone; **poser des ~s** (*fig*) to pave the way.

jalonner [ʒalone] *vt* to mark out; (*fig*) to mark, punctuate.

jalousement [ʒaluzmã] *adv* jealously.

jalouser [ʒaluze] *vt* to be jealous of.

jalousie [ʒaluzi] *nf* jealousy; (*store*) (venetian) blind.

jaloux, ouse [ʒalu, -uz] *adj* jealous; **être ~ de qn/qch** to be jealous of sb/sth.

jamaïquain, e [ʒamaikɛ̃, -ɛn] *adj* Jamaican.

Jamaïque [ʒamaik] *nf*: **la ~** Jamaica.

jamais [ʒamɛ] *adv* never; (*sans négation*) ever; **ne ... ~** never; ~ **de la vie!** never!; **si ~ ...** if ever ...; **à (tout) ~, pour ~** for ever, for ever and ever.

jambage [ʒãbaʒ] *nm* (*de lettre*) downstroke; (*de porte*) jamb.

jambe [ʒãb] *nf* leg; **à toutes ~s** as fast as one's legs can carry one.

jambières [ʒãbjɛr] *nfpl* legwarmers; (*SPORT*) shin pads.

jambon [ʒãbɔ̃] *nm* ham.

jambonneau, x [ʒãbɔno] *nm* knuckle of ham.

jante [ʒãt] *nf* (wheel) rim.

janvier [ʒãvje] *nm* January; *voir aussi* **juillet.**

Japon [ʒapɔ̃] *nm*: **le ~** Japan.

japonais, e [ʒapɔnɛ, -ɛz] *adj* Japanese ♦ *nm* (*LING*) Japanese ♦ *nm/f*: J~, **e** Japanese.

japonaiserie [ʒapɔnɛzri] *nf* (*bibelot*) Japanese curio.

jappement [ʒapmã] *nm* yap, yelp.

japper [ʒape] *vi* to yap, yelp.

jaquette [ʒakɛt] *nf* (*de cérémonie*) morning coat; (*de femme*) jacket; (*de livre*) dust cover, (dust) jacket.

jardin [ʒardɛ̃] *nm* garden; ~ **d'acclimatation** zoological gardens *pl*; ~ **botanique** botanical gardens *pl*; ~ **d'enfants** nursery school; ~ **potager** vegetable garden; ~ **public** (public) park, public gardens *pl*; ~**s suspendus** hanging gardens.

jardinage [ʒardinaʒ] *nm* gardening.

jardiner [ʒardine] *vi* to garden, do some gardening.

jardinet [ʒardinɛ] *nm* little garden.

jardinier, ière [ʒardinje, -jɛr] *nm/f* gardener ♦ *nf* (*de fenêtre*) window box; **jardinière d'enfants** nursery school teacher; **jardinière (de légumes)** (*CULIN*) mixed vegetables.

jargon [ʒargɔ̃] *nm* (*charabia*) gibberish; (*publicitaire, scientifique etc*) jargon.

jarre [ʒaʀ] *nf* (earthenware) jar.
jarret [ʒaʀɛ] *nm* back of knee; (*CULIN*) knuckle, shin.
jarretelle [ʒaʀtɛl] *nf* suspender (*BRIT*), garter (*US*).
jarretière [ʒaʀtjɛʀ] *nf* garter.
jars [ʒaʀ] *nm* (*ZOOL*) gander.
jaser [ʒɑze] *vi* to chatter, prattle; (*indiscrètement*) to gossip.
jasmin [ʒasmɛ̃] *nm* jasmin.
jaspe [ʒasp(ə)] *nm* jasper.
jaspé, e [ʒaspe] *adj* marbled, mottled.
jatte [ʒat] *nf* basin, bowl.
jauge [ʒoʒ] *nf* (*capacité*) capacity, tonnage; (*instrument*) gauge; **~ (de niveau) d'huile** dipstick.
jauger [ʒoʒe] *vt* to gauge the capacity of; (*fig*) to size up; **~ 3 000 tonneaux** to measure 3,000 tons.
jaunâtre [ʒonɑtʀ(ə)] *adj* (*couleur, teint*) yellowish.
jaune [ʒon] *adj, nm* yellow ♦ *nm/f* Asiatic; (*briseur de grève*) blackleg ♦ *adv* (*fam*): **rire ~** to laugh on the other side of one's face; **~ d'œuf** (egg) yolk.
jaunir [ʒoniʀ] *vi, vt* to turn yellow.
jaunisse [ʒonis] *nf* jaundice.
Java [ʒava] *nf* Java.
java [ʒava] *nf* (*fam*): **faire la ~** to live it up, have a real party.
javanais, e [ʒavanɛ, -ɛz] *adj* Javanese.
Javel [ʒavɛl] *nf voir* **eau**.
javelliser [ʒavelize] *vt* (*eau*) to chlorinate.
javelot [ʒavlo] *nm* javelin; (*SPORT*): **faire du ~** to throw the javelin.
jazz [dʒaz] *nm* jazz.
J.-C. *abr* = **Jésus-Christ**.
JCR *sigle f* (= *Jeunesse communiste révolutionnaire*) *communist youth movement*.
je, j' [ʒ(ə)] *pron* I.
jean [dʒin] *nm* jeans *pl*.
jeannette [ʒanɛt] *nf* (*planchette*) sleeveboard; (*petite fille scout*) Brownie.
JEC [ʒɛk] *sigle f* (= *Jeunesse étudiante chrétienne*) *youth organization*.
jeep [(d)ʒip] *nf* ® (*AUTO*) jeep ®.
jérémiades [ʒeʀemjad] *nfpl* moaning *sg*.
jerrycan [ʒeʀikan] *nm* jerrycan.
Jersey [ʒɛʀzɛ] *nf* Jersey.
jersey [ʒɛʀzɛ] *nm* jersey; (*TRICOT*): **pointe de ~** stocking stitch.
jersiais, e [ʒɛʀzjɛ, -ɛz] *adj* Jersey *cpd*, of *ou* from Jersey.
Jérusalem [ʒeʀyzalɛm] *n* Jerusalem.
jésuite [ʒezɥit] *nm* Jesuit.
Jésus-Christ [ʒezykʀi(st)] *n* Jesus Christ; **600 avant/après ~** *ou* **J.-C.** 600 B.C./A.D.
jet¹ [ʒɛ] *nm* (*lancer*) throwing *no pl*, throw; (*jaillissement*) jet; spurt; (*de tuyau*) nozzle; (*fig*): **premier ~** (*ébauche*) rough outline; **arroser au ~** to hose; **d'un (seul) ~** (*d'un seul*

coup) at (*ou* in) one go; **du premier ~** at the first attempt *ou* shot; **~ d'eau** spray; (*fontaine*) fountain.
jet² [dʒɛt] *nm* (*avion*) jet.
jetable [ʒətabl(ə)] *adj* disposable.
jeté [ʒəte] *nm* (*TRICOT*): **un ~** make one; **~ de table** (table) runner; **~ de lit** bedspread.
jetée [ʒəte] *nf* jetty; pier.
jeter [ʒəte] *vt* (*gén*) to throw; (*se défaire de*) to throw away *ou* out; (*son, lueur etc*) to give out; **~ qch à qn** to throw sth to sb; (*de façon agressive*) to throw sth at sb; (*NAVIG*): **~ l'ancre** to cast anchor; **~ un coup d'œil (à)** to take a look (at); **~ les bras en avant/la tête en arrière** to throw one's arms forward/one's head back(ward); **~ l'effroi parmi** to spread fear among; **~ un sort à qn** to cast a spell on sb; **~ qn dans la misère** to reduce sb to poverty; **~ qn dehors/en prison** to throw sb out/into prison; **~ l'éponge** (*fig*) to throw in the towel; **~ des fleurs à qn** (*fig*) to say lovely things to sb; **~ la pierre à qn** (*accuser, blâmer*) to accuse sb; **se ~ sur** to throw o.s. onto; **se ~ dans** (*suj: fleuve*) to flow into; **se ~ par la fenêtre** to throw o.s. out of the window; **se ~ à l'eau** (*fig*) to take the plunge.
jeton [ʒətɔ̃] *nm* (*au jeu*) counter; (*de téléphone*) token; **~s de présence** (director's) fees.
jette [ʒɛt] *etc vb voir* **jeter**.
jeu, x [ʒø] *nm* (*divertissement, TECH: d'une pièce*) play; (*défini par des règles, TENNIS: partie, FOOTBALL etc: façon de jouer*) game; (*THÉÂT etc*) acting; (*fonctionnement*) working, interplay; (*série d'objets, jouet*) set; (*CARTES*) hand; (*au casino*): **le ~** gambling; **cacher son ~** (*fig*) to keep one's cards hidden, conceal one's hand; **c'est un ~ d'enfant!** (*fig*) it's child's play!; **en ~** at stake; at work; (*FOOTBALL*) in play; **remettre en ~** to throw in; **entrer/mettre en ~** to come/bring into play; **par ~** (*pour s'amuser*) for fun; **d'entrée de ~** (*tout de suite, dès le début*) from the outset; **entrer dans le ~/le ~ de qn** (*fig*) to play the game/sb's game; **jouer gros ~** to play for high stakes; **se piquer/se prendre au ~** to get excited over/get caught up in *ou* involved in the game; **~ de boules** game of bowls; (*endroit*) bowling pitch; (*boules*) set of bowls; **~ de cartes** card game; (*paquet*) pack of cards; **~ de construction** building set; **~ d'échecs** chess set; **~ d'écritures** (*COMM*) paper transaction; **~ de hasard** game of chance; **~ de mots** pun; **le ~ de l'oie** snakes and ladders *sg*; **~ d'orgue(s)** organ stop; **~ de patience** puzzle; **~ de physionomie** facial expressions *pl*; **~ de société** parlour game; **~ vidéo** computer game; **~x de lumière** lighting effects; **J~x olympiques (JO)** Olympic Games.
jeu-concours, *pl* **jeux-concours** [ʒøkɔ̃kuʀ] *nm* competition.

jeudi [ʒødi] *nm* Thursday; ~ **saint** Maundy Thursday; *voir aussi* **lundi**.

jeun [ʒœn]: **à** ~ *adv* on an empty stomach.

jeune [ʒœn] *adj* young ♦ *adv*: **faire/s'habiller** ~ to look/dress young; **les** ~**s** young people, the young; ~ **fille** *nf* girl; ~ **homme** *nm* young man; ~ **loup** *nm* (*POL, ÉCON*) young go-getter; ~ **premier** leading man; ~**s gens** *nmpl* young people; ~**s mariés** *nmpl* newly weds.

jeûne [ʒøn] *nm* fast.

jeûner [ʒøne] *vt* to fast, go without food.

jeunesse [ʒœnɛs] *nf* youth; (*aspect*) youthfulness; (*jeunes*) young people *pl*, youth.

jf *sigle f* = **jeune fille**.

jh *sigle m* = **jeune homme**.

JI *sigle m* = **juge d'instruction**.

jiu-jitsu [ʒyʒitsy] *nm inv* (*SPORT*) jujitsu.

JMF *sigle f* (= *Jeunesses musicales de France*) *association to promote music among the young*.

JO *sigle m* = **Journal officiel** ♦ *sigle mpl* = **Jeux olympiques**.

joaillerie [ʒɔajʀi] *nf* jewel trade; jewellery (*BRIT*), jewelry (*US*).

joaillier, ière [ʒɔaje, -jɛR] *nm/f* jeweller (*BRIT*), jeweler (*US*).

job [dʒɔb] *nm* job.

jobard [ʒɔbaR] *nm* (*péj*) sucker, mug.

JOC [ʒɔk] *sigle f* (= *Jeunesse ouvrière chrétienne*) *youth organization*.

jockey [ʒɔkɛ] *nm* jockey.

jodler [ʒɔdle] *vi* to yodel.

jogging [dʒɔgiŋ] *nm* tracksuit (*BRIT*), sweatsuit (*US*); **faire du** ~ to jog, go jogging.

joie [ʒwa] *nf* joy.

joignais [ʒwaɲɛ] *etc vb voir* **joindre**.

joindre [ʒwɛ̃dR(ə)] *vt* to join; (*à une lettre*): ~ **qch à** to enclose sth with; (*contacter*) to contact, get in touch with; ~ **les mains/talons** to put one's hands/heels together; ~ **les deux bouts** (*fig: du mois*) to make ends meet; **se** ~ (*mains etc*) to come together; **se** ~ **à qn** to join sb; **se** ~ **à qch** to join in sth.

joint, e [ʒwɛ̃, -ɛ̃t] *pp de* **joindre** ♦ *adj*: ~ **(à)** (*lettre, paquet*) attached (to), enclosed (with); **pièce** ~**e** enclosure ♦ *nm* joint; (*ligne*) join; (*de ciment etc*) pointing *no pl*; **chercher/trouver le** ~ (*fig*) to look for/come up with the answer; ~ **de cardan** cardan joint; ~ **de culasse** cylinder head gasket; ~ **de robinet** washer; ~ **universel** universal joint.

jointure [ʒwɛ̃tyR] *nf* (*ANAT: articulation*) joint; (*TECH: assemblage*) joint; (: *ligne*) join.

joker [ʒɔkɛR] *nm* (*CARTES*) joker.

joli, e [ʒɔli] *adj* pretty, attractive; **une** ~**e somme/situation** a nice little sum/situation; **un** ~ **gâchis** *etc* a nice mess *etc*; **c'est du** ~! that's very nice!; **tout ça, c'est bien** ~ **mais** ... that's all very well but ....

joliment [ʒɔlimɑ̃] *adv* prettily, attractively; (*fam: très*) pretty.

jonc [ʒɔ̃] *nm* (*bul*)rush; (*bague, bracelet*) band.

joncher [ʒɔ̃ʃe] *vt* (*suj: choses*) to be strewed on; **jonché de** strewn with.

jonction [ʒɔ̃ksjɔ̃] *nf* joining; (**point de**) ~ (*de routes*) junction; (*de fleuves*) confluence; **opérer une** ~ (*MIL etc*) to rendez-vous.

jongler [ʒɔ̃gle] *vi* to juggle; (*fig*): ~ **avec** to juggle with, play with.

jongleur, euse [ʒɔ̃glœR, -øz] *nm/f* juggler.

jonquille [ʒɔ̃kij] *nf* daffodil.

Jordanie [ʒɔRdani] *nf*: **la** ~ Jordan.

jordanien, ne [ʒɔRdanjɛ̃, -ɛn] *adj* Jordanian ♦ *nm/f*: **J**~, **ne** Jordanian.

jouable [ʒwabl(ə)] *adj* playable.

joue [ʒu] *nf* cheek; **mettre en** ~ to take aim at.

jouer [ʒwe] *vt* (*partie, carte, coup, MUS: morceau*) to play; (*somme d'argent, réputation*) to stake, wager; (*pièce, rôle*) to perform; (*film*) to show; (*simuler: sentiment*) to affect, feign ♦ *vi* to play; (*THÉÂT, CINÉ*) to act, perform; (*bois, porte: se voiler*) to warp; (*clef, pièce: avoir du jeu*) to be loose; (*entrer ou être en jeu*) to come into play, come into it; ~ **sur** (*miser*) to gamble on; ~ **de** (*MUS*) to play; ~ **du couteau/des coudes** to use knives/one's elbows; ~ **à** (*jeu, sport, roulette*) to play; ~ **au héros** to act *ou* play the hero; ~ **avec** (*risquer*) to gamble with; **se** ~ **de** (*difficultés*) to make light of; **se** ~ **de qn** to deceive *ou* dupe sb; ~ **un tour à qn** to play a trick on sb; ~ **la comédie** (*fig*) to put on an act, put it on; ~ **aux courses** to back horses, bet on horses; ~ **à la baisse/hausse** (*BOURSE*) to play for a fall/rise; ~ **serré** to play a close game; ~ **de malchance** to be dogged with ill-luck; ~ **sur les mots** to play with words; **à toi/nous de** ~ it's your/our go *ou* turn.

jouet [ʒwɛ] *nm* toy; **être le** ~ **de** (*illusion etc*) to be the victim of.

joueur, euse [ʒwœR, -øz] *nm/f* player ♦ *adj* (*enfant, chat*) playful; **être beau/mauvais** ~ to be a good/bad loser.

joufflu, e [ʒufly] *adj* chubby(-cheeked).

joug [ʒu] *nm* yoke.

jouir [ʒwiR]: ~ **de** *vt* to enjoy.

jouissance [ʒwisɑ̃s] *nf* pleasure; (*JUR*) use.

jouisseur, euse [ʒwisœR, -øz] *nm/f* sensualist.

joujou [ʒuʒu] *nm* (*fam*) toy.

jour [ʒuR] *nm* day; (*opposé à la nuit*) day, daytime; (*clarté*) daylight; (*fig: aspect*): **sous un** ~ **favourable/nouveau** in a favourable/new light; (*ouverture*) opening; (*COUTURE*) openwork *no pl*; **au** ~ **le** ~ from day to day; **de nos** ~**s** these days, nowadays; **tous les** ~**s** every day; **de** ~ **en** ~ day by day; **d'un** ~ **à l'autre** from one day to the next; **du** ~ **au lendemain** overnight; **il fait** ~ it's daylight; **en plein** ~ in broad daylight; **au** ~ in daylight; **au petit** ~ at daybreak; **au grand** ~ (*fig*) in the open; **mettre au** ~ to uncover, disclose; **être à** ~ to be up to date; **mettre à**

~ to bring up to date, update; **mise à** ~ updating; **donner le** ~ **à** to give birth to; **voir le** ~ to be born; **se faire** ~ (*fig*) to become clear; ~ **férié** public holiday; **le** ~ **J** D-day.

Jourdain [ʒuʀdɛ̃] *nm*: **le** ~ the (River) Jordan.

journal, aux [ʒuʀnal, -o] *nm* (news)paper; (*personnel*) journal, diary; ~ **de bord** log; ~ **de mode** fashion magazine; **le J**~ **officiel (de la République française) (JO)** *bulletin giving details of laws and official announcements*; ~ **parlé/télévisé** radio/television news *sg*.

journalier, ière [ʒuʀnalje, -jɛʀ] *adj* daily; (*banal*) everyday ♦ *nm* day labourer.

journalisme [ʒuʀnalism(ə)] *nm* journalism.

journaliste [ʒuʀnalist(ə)] *nm/f* journalist.

journalistique [ʒuʀnalistik] *adj* journalistic.

journée [ʒuʀne] *nf* day; **la** ~ **continue** the 9 to 5 working day (*with short lunch break*).

journellement [ʒuʀnɛlmɑ̃] *adv* (*tous les jours*) daily; (*souvent*) every day.

joute [ʒut] *nf* (*tournoi*) duel; (*verbale*) duel, battle of words.

jouvence [ʒuvɑ̃s] *nf*: **bain de** ~ rejuvenating experience.

jouxter [ʒukste] *vt* to adjoin.

jovial [ʒɔvjal] *adj* jovial, jolly.

jovialité [ʒɔvjalite] *nf* joviality.

joyau, x [ʒwajo] *nm* gem, jewel.

joyeusement [ʒwajøzmɑ̃] *adv* joyfully, gladly.

joyeux, euse [ʒwajø, -øz] *adj* joyful, merry; ~ **Noël!** merry *ou* happy Christmas!; ~ **anniversaire!** many happy returns!

JT *sigle m* = **journal télévisé**.

jubilation [ʒybilɑsjɔ̃] *nf* jubilation.

jubilé [ʒybile] *nm* jubilee.

jubiler [ʒybile] *vi* to be jubilant, exult.

jucher [ʒyʃe] *vt*: ~ **qch sur** to perch sth (up)on ♦ *vi* (*oiseau*): ~ **sur** to perch (up)on; **se** ~ **sur** to perch o.s. (up)on.

judaïque [ʒydaik] *adj* (*loi*) Judaic; (*religion*) Jewish.

judaïsme [ʒydaism(ə)] *nm* Judaism.

judas [ʒyda] *nm* (*trou*) spy-hole.

Judée [ʒyde] *nf*: **la** ~ Jud(a)ea.

judéo- [ʒydeɔ] *préfixe* Judeo-.

judéo-allemand, e [ʒydeɔalmɑ̃, -ɑ̃d] *adj, nm* Yiddish.

judéo-chrétien, ne [ʒydeɔkʀetjɛ̃, -ɛn] *adj* Judeo-Christian.

judiciaire [ʒydisjɛʀ] *adj* judicial.

judicieusement [ʒydisjøzmɑ̃] *adv* judiciously.

judicieux, euse [ʒydisjø, -øz] *adj* judicious.

judo [ʒydo] *nm* judo.

judoka [ʒydɔka] *nm/f* judoka.

juge [ʒyʒ] *nm* judge; ~ **des enfants** children's judge, ≈ juvenile magistrate; ~ **d'instruction** examining (*BRIT*) *ou* committing (*US*) magistrate; ~ **de paix** justice of the peace; ~ **de touche** linesman.

jugé [ʒyʒe]: **au** ~ *adv* by guesswork.

jugement [ʒyʒmɑ̃] *nm* judgment; (*JUR*: *au pénal*) sentence; (: *au civil*) decision; ~ **de valeur** value judgment.

jugeote [ʒyʒɔt] *nf* (*fam*) gumption.

juger [ʒyʒe] *vt* to judge ♦ *nm*: **au** ~ by guesswork; ~ **qn/qch satisfaisant** to consider sb/sth (to be) satisfactory; ~ **que** to think *ou* consider that; ~ **bon de faire** to consider it a good idea to do, see fit to do; ~ **de** *vt* to judge; **jugez de ma surprise** imagine my surprise.

jugulaire [ʒygylɛʀ] *adj* jugular ♦ *nf* (*MIL*) chinstrap.

juguler [ʒygyle] *vt* (*maladie*) to halt; (*révolte*) to suppress, put down; (*inflation etc*) to control, curb.

juif, ive [ʒɥif, -iv] *adj* Jewish ♦ *nm/f*: **J**~, **ive** Jew/Jewess *ou* Jewish woman.

juillet [ʒɥijɛ] *nm* July; **le premier** ~ the first of July (*BRIT*), July first (*US*); **le deux/onze** ~ the second/eleventh of July, July second/eleventh; **il est venu le 5** ~ he came on 5th July *ou* July 5th; **en** ~ in July; **début/fin** ~ at the beginning/end of July.

In France, le 14 juillet is a national holiday commemorating the storming of the Bastille during the French Revolution. Throughout the country there are celebrations, parades, music, dancing and firework displays. In Paris, there is a military parade, along the Champs-Élysées, attended by the President.

---

juin [ʒɥɛ̃] *nm* June; *voir aussi* **juillet**.

juive [ʒɥiv] *voir* **juif**.

jumeau, elle, x [ʒymo, -ɛl] *adj, nm/f* twin; **maisons jumelles** semidetached houses.

jumelage [ʒymlaʒ] *nm* twinning.

jumeler [ʒymle] *vt* to twin; **roues jumelées** double wheels; **billets de loterie jumelés** double series lottery tickets; **pari jumelé** double bet.

jumelle [ʒymɛl] *adj f*, *nf voir* **jumeau** ♦ *vb voir* **jumeler**.

jumelles [ʒymɛl] *nfpl* binoculars.

jument [ʒymɑ̃] *nf* mare.

jungle [ʒɔ̃gl(ə)] *nf* jungle.

junior [ʒynjɔʀ] *adj* junior.

junte [ʒœ̃t] *nf* junta.

jupe [ʒyp] *nf* skirt.

jupe-culotte, *pl* **jupes-culottes** [ʒypkylɔt] *nf* divided skirt, culotte(s).

jupette [ʒypɛt] *nf* short skirt.

jupon [ʒypɔ̃] *nm* waist slip *ou* petticoat.

Jura [ʒyʀa] *nm*: **le** ~ the Jura (Mountains).

jurassien, ne [ʒyʀasjɛ̃, -ɛn] *adj* of *ou* from the Jura Mountains.

juré, e [ʒyʀe] *nm/f* juror ♦ *adj*: **ennemi** ~ sworn *ou* avowed enemy.

jurer [ʒyʀe] *vt* (*obéissance etc*) to swear, vow ♦ *vi* (*dire des jurons*) to swear, curse; (*dissoner*): ~ (**avec**) to clash (with); (*s'engager*): ~ **de faire/que** to swear *ou* vow to do/that; (*affirmer*): ~ **que** to swear *ou* vouch that; ~ **de qch** (*s'en porter garant*) to swear to sth; **ils ne jurent que par lui** they swear by him; **je vous jure!** honestly!

juridiction [ʒyʀidiksjɔ̃] *nf* jurisdiction; (*tribunal, tribunaux*) court(s) of law.

juridique [ʒyʀidik] *adj* legal.

juridiquement [ʒyʀidikmɑ̃] *adv* (*devant la justice*) juridically; (*du point de vue du droit*) legally.

jurisconsulte [ʒyʀikɔ̃sylt(ə)] *nm* jurisconsult.

jurisprudence [ʒyʀispʀydɑ̃s] *nf* (*JUR: décisions*) (legal) precedents; (*principes juridiques*) jurisprudence; **faire** ~ (*faire autorité*) to set a precedent.

juriste [ʒyʀist(ə)] *nm/f* jurist; lawyer.

juron [ʒyʀɔ̃] *nm* curse, swearword.

jury [ʒyʀi] *nm* (*JUR*) jury; (*SCOL*) board (of examiners), jury.

jus [ʒy] *nm* juice; (*de viande*) gravy, (meat) juice; ~ **de fruits** fruit juice; ~ **de raisin/ tomates** grape/tomato juice.

jusant [ʒyzɑ̃] *nm* ebb (tide).

jusqu'au-boutiste [ʒyskobutist(ə)] *nm/f* extremist, hardliner.

jusque [ʒysk(ə)]: **jusqu'à** *prép* (*endroit*) as far as, (up) to; (*moment*) until, till; (*limite*) up to; ~ **sur/dans** up to, as far as; (*y compris*) even on/in; **jusque vers** until about; **jusqu'à ce que** *conj* until; **jusque-là** (*temps*) until then; (*espace*) up to there; **jusqu'ici** (*temps*) until now; (*espace*) up to here; **jusqu'à présent** until now, so far.

justaucorps [ʒystokɔʀ] *nm inv* (*DANSE, SPORT*) leotard.

juste [ʒyst(ə)] *adj* (*équitable*) just, fair; (*légitime*) just, justified; (*exact, vrai*) right; (*étroit, insuffisant*) tight ♦ *adv* right; tight; (*chanter*) in tune; (*seulement*) just; ~ **assez/ au-dessus** just enough/above; **pouvoir tout** ~ **faire** to be only just able to do; **au** ~ exactly, actually; **comme de** ~ of course, naturally; **le** ~ **milieu** the happy medium; **à** ~ **titre** rightfully.

justement [ʒystəmɑ̃] *adv* rightly; justly; (*précisément*): **c'est** ~ **ce qu'il fallait faire** that's just *ou* precisely what needed doing.

justesse [ʒystɛs] *nf* (*précision*) accuracy; (*d'une remarque*) aptness; (*d'une opinion*) soundness; **de** ~ just, by a narrow margin.

justice [ʒystis] *nf* (*équité*) fairness, justice; (*ADMIN*) justice; **rendre la** ~ to dispense justice; **traduire en** ~ to bring before the courts; **obtenir** ~ to obtain justice; **rendre** ~ **à qn** to do sb justice; **se faire** ~ to take the law into one's own hands; (*se suicider*) to take one's life.

justiciable [ʒystisjabl(ə)] *adj*: ~ **de** (*JUR*) answerable to.

justicier, ière [ʒystisje, -jɛʀ] *nm/f* judge, righter of wrongs.

justifiable [ʒystifjabl(ə)] *adj* justifiable.

justificatif, ive [ʒystifikatif, -iv] *adj* (*document etc*) supporting ♦ *nm* supporting proof.

justification [ʒystifikasjɔ̃] *nf* justification.

justifier [ʒystifje] *vt* to justify; ~ **de** *vt* to prove; **non justifié** unjustified; **justifié à droite/gauche** ranged right/left.

jute [ʒyt] *nm* jute.

juteux, euse [ʒytø, -øz] *adj* juicy.

juvénile [ʒyvenil] *adj* young, youthful.

juxtaposer [ʒykstapoze] *vt* to juxtapose.

juxtaposition [ʒykstapozisjɔ̃] *nf* juxtaposition.

Kk

K, k [ka] *nm inv* K, k ♦ *abr* (= *kilo*) kg; (= *kilooctet*) K; **K comme Kléber** K for King.

Kaboul, Kabul [kabul] *n* Kabul.

kabyle [kabil] *adj* Kabyle ♦ *nm* (*LING*) Kabyle ♦ *nm/f*: **K~** Kabyle.

Kabylie [kabili] *nf*: **la** ~ Kabylia.

kafkaïen, ne [kafkajɛ̃, -ɛn] *adj* Kafkaesque.

kaki [kaki] *adj inv* khaki.

Kalahari [kalaaʀi] *n*: **désert de** ~ Kalahari Desert.

kaléidoscope [kaleidɔskɔp] *nm* kaleidoscope.

Kampala [kɑ̃pala] *n* Kampala.

Kampuchéa [kɑ̃putʃea] *nm*: **le** ~ **(démocratique)** (the People's Republic of) Kampuchea.

kangourou [kɑ̃guʀu] *nm* kangaroo.

kaolin [kaɔlɛ̃] *nm* kaolin.

kapok [kapɔk] *nm* kapok.

karaoke [kaʀaoke] *nm* karaoke.

karaté [kaʀate] *nm* karate.

kart [kaʀt] *nm* go-cart.

karting [kaʀtiŋ] *nm* go-carting, karting.

kascher [kaʃɛʀ] *adj inv* kosher.

kayac, kayak [kajak] *nm* kayak.

Kazakhstan [kazakstɑ̃] *nm* Kazakhstan.

Kenya [kenja] *nm*: **le** ~ Kenya.

kenyan, e [kenjɑ̃, -an] *adj* Kenyan ♦ *nm/f*: **K~, ne** Kenyan.

képi [kepi] *nm* kepi.

Kerguelen [kɛʀgelɛn]: **les (îles)** ~ Kerguelen.

kermesse [kɛʀmɛs] *nf* bazaar, (charity) fête; village fair.

kérosène [keʀozɛn] *nm* jet fuel; rocket fuel.

kg *abr* (= *kilogramme*) kg.

KGB *sigle m* KGB.

khmer, ère [kmɛʀ] *adj* Khmer ♦ *nm* (*LING*) Khmer.

khôl [kol] *nm* khol.

kibboutz [kibuts] *nm* kibbutz.

kidnapper [kidnape] *vt* to kidnap.

kidnappeur, euse [kidnapœʀ, -øz] *nm/f*

kidnapper.
kidnapping [kidnapiŋ] *nm* kidnapping.
Kilimandjaro [kilimɑ̃dʒaʀo] *nm*: **le ~** Mount Kilimanjaro.
kilo [kilo] *nm* kilo.
kilogramme [kilɔgʀam] *nm* kilogramme (*BRIT*), kilogram (*US*).
kilométrage [kilɔmetʀaʒ] *nm* number of kilometres travelled, ≈ mileage.
kilomètre [kilɔmetʀ(ə)] *nm* kilometre (*BRIT*), kilometer (*US*); **~s-heure** kilometres per hour.
kilométrique [kilɔmetʀik] *adj* (*distance*) in kilometres; **compteur ~** ≈ mileage indicator.
kilooctet [kilɔɔktɛ] *nm* kilobyte.
kilowatt [kilɔwat] *nm* kilowatt.
kinésithérapeute [kineziteʀapøt] *nm/f* physiotherapist.
kinésithérapie [kineziteʀapi] *nf* physiotherapy.
kiosque [kjɔsk(ə)] *nm* kiosk, stall; (*TÉL etc*) *telephone and/or videotext information service.*
Kirghizistan [kiʀgizistɑ̃] *nm* Kirghizia.
kirsch [kiʀʃ] *nm* kirsch.
kitchenette [kitʃ(ə)nɛt] *nf* kitchenette.
kiwi [kiwi] *nm* (*ZOOL*) kiwi; (*BOT*) kiwi (fruit).
klaxon [klaksɔn] *nm* horn.
klaxonner [klaksɔne] *vi*, *vt* to hoot (*BRIT*), honk (one's horn) (*US*).
kleptomane [klɛptɔman] *nm/f* kleptomaniac.
km *abr* (= *kilomètre*) km.
km/h *abr* (= *kilomètres/heure*) km/h.
knock-out [nɔkawt] *nm* knock-out.
Ko *abr* (*INFORM*: = *kilooctet*) K.
K.-O. [kao] *adj inv* (knocked) out, out for the count.
koala [kɔala] *nm* koala (bear).
kolkhoze [kɔlkoz] *nm* kolkhoz.
Koweit *ou* **Kuweit** [kɔwɛt] *nm*: **le ~** Kuwait, Koweit.
koweitien, ne [kɔwɛtjɛ̃, -ɛn] *adj* Kuwaiti ♦ *nm/f*: **K~, ne** Kuwaiti.
krach [kʀak] *nm* (*ÉCON*) crash.
kraft [kʀaft] *nm* brown *ou* kraft paper.
Kremlin [kʀɛmlɛ̃] *nm*: **le ~** the Kremlin.
Kuala Lumpur [kwalalympuʀ] *n* Kuala Lumpur.
kurde [kyʀd(ə)] *adj* Kurdish ♦ *nm* (*LING*) Kurdish ♦ *nm/f*: **K~** Kurd.
Kurdistan [kyʀdistɑ̃] *nm*: **le ~** Kurdistan.
Kuweit [kɔwɛt] = **Koweit**.
kW *abr* (= *kilowatt*) kW.
kW/h *abr* (= *kilowatt/heure*) kW/h.
kyrielle [kiʀjɛl] *nf*: **une ~ de** a stream of.
kyste [kist(ə)] *nm* cyst.

L l

L, l [ɛl] *nm inv* L, l ♦ *abr* (= *litre*) l; (*SCOL*): **L ès L** = **Licence ès Lettres**; **L en D** = **Licence en Droit**; **L comme Louis** L for Lucy (*BRIT*) *ou* Love (*US*).
l' [l] *dét voir* **le**.
la [la] *dét*, *pron voir* **le** ♦ *nm* (*MUS*) A; (*en chantant la gamme*) la.
là [la] *adv* (*voir aussi* **-ci**, **celui**) there; (*ici*) here; (*dans le temps*) then; **est-ce que Catherine est ~?** is Catherine there (*ou* here)?; **c'est ~ que** this is where; **~ où** where; **de ~** (*fig*) hence; **par ~** (*fig*) by that; **tout est ~** (*fig*) that's what it's all about.
là-bas [laba] *adv* there.
label [labɛl] *nm* stamp, seal.
labeur [labœʀ] *nm* toil *no pl*, toiling *no pl*.
labo [labo] *nm* (= *laboratoire*) lab.
laborantin, e [labɔʀɑ̃tɛ̃, -in] *nm/f* laboratory assistant.
laboratoire [labɔʀatwaʀ] *nm* laboratory; **~ de langues/d'analyses** language/(medical) analysis laboratory.
laborieux, euse [labɔʀjø, -øz] *adj* (*tâche*) laborious; **classes ~euses** working classes.
laborieusement [labɔʀjøzmɑ̃] *adv* laboriously.
labour [labuʀ] *nm* ploughing *no pl* (*BRIT*), plowing *no pl* (*US*); **~s** *nmpl* (*champs*) ploughed fields; **cheval de ~** plough- *ou* cart-horse; **bœuf de ~** ox (*pl* oxen).
labourage [labuʀaʒ] *nm* ploughing (*BRIT*), plowing (*US*).
labourer [labuʀe] *vt* to plough (*BRIT*), plow (*US*); (*fig*) to make deep gashes *ou* furrows in.
laboureur [labuʀœʀ] *nm* ploughman (*BRIT*), plowman (*US*).
labrador [labʀadɔʀ] *nm* (*chien*) labrador; (*GÉO*): **le L~** Labrador.
labyrinthe [labiʀɛ̃t] *nm* labyrinth, maze.
lac [lak] *nm* lake; **le ~ Léman** Lake Geneva; **les Grands L~s** the Great Lakes; *voir aussi* **lacs**.
lacer [lase] *vt* to lace *ou* do up.
lacérer [laseʀe] *vt* to tear to shreds.
lacet [lasɛ] *nm* (*de chaussure*) lace; (*de route*) sharp bend; (*piège*) snare; **chaussures à ~s** lace-up *ou* lacing shoes.
lâche [lɑʃ] *adj* (*poltron*) cowardly; (*desserré*) loose, slack; (*morale, mœurs*) lax ♦ *nm/f* coward.
lâchement [lɑʃmɑ̃] *adv* (*par peur*) like a coward; (*par bassesse*) despicably.

lâcher [lɑʃe] *nm* (*de ballons, oiseaux*) release ♦ *vt* to let go of; (*ce qui tombe, abandonner*) to drop; (*oiseau, animal: libérer*) to release, set free; (*fig: mot, remarque*) to let slip, come out with; (*SPORT: distancer*) to leave behind ♦ *vi* (*fil, amarres*) to break, give way; (*freins*) to fail; ~ **les amarres** (*NAVIG*) to cast off (the moorings); ~ **prise** to let go.

lâcheté [lɑʃte] *nf* cowardice; (*bassesse*) lowness.

lacis [lasi] *nm* (*de ruelles*) maze.

laconique [lakɔnik] *adj* laconic.

laconiquement [lakɔnikmɑ̃] *adv* laconically.

lacrymal, e, aux [lakʀimal, -o] *adj* (*canal, glande*) tear *cpd*.

lacrymogène [lakʀimɔʒɛn] *adj*: **grenade/gaz** ~ tear gas grenade/tear gas.

lacs [lɑ] *nm* (*piège*) snare.

lactation [laktasjɔ̃] *nf* lactation.

lacté, e [lakte] *adj* milk *cpd*.

lactique [laktik] *adj*: **acide/ferment** ~ lactic acid/ferment.

lactose [laktoz] *nm* lactose, milk sugar.

lacune [lakyn] *nf* gap.

lacustre [lakystʀ(ə)] *adj* lake *cpd*, lakeside *cpd*.

lad [lad] *nm* stable-lad.

là-dedans [ladədɑ̃] *adv* inside (there), in it; (*fig*) in that.

là-dehors [ladəɔʀ] *adv* out there.

là-derrière [ladɛʀjɛʀ] *adv* behind there; (*fig*) behind that.

là-dessous [ladsu] *adv* underneath, under there; (*fig*) behind that.

là-dessus [ladsy] *adv* on there; (*fig*) at that point; (*: à ce sujet*) about that.

là-devant [ladvɑ̃] *adv* there (in front).

ladite [ladit] *dét voir* **ledit**.

ladre [lɑdʀ(ə)] *adj* miserly.

lagon [lagɔ̃] *nm* lagoon.

Lagos [lagɔs] *n* Lagos.

lagune [lagyn] *nf* lagoon.

là-haut [lao] *adv* up there.

laïc [laik] *adj, nm/f* = **laïque**.

laïciser [laisize] *vt* to secularize.

laïcité [laisite] *nf* secularity, secularism.

laid, e [lɛ, lɛd] *adj* ugly; (*fig: acte*) mean, cheap.

laideron [lɛdʀɔ̃] *nm* ugly girl.

laideur [lɛdœʀ] *nf* ugliness *no pl*; meanness *no pl*.

laie [lɛ] *nf* wild sow.

lainage [lɛnaʒ] *nm* woollen garment; (*étoffe*) woollen material.

laine [lɛn] *nf* wool; ~ **peignée** worsted (wool); ~ **à tricoter** knitting wool; ~ **de verre** glass wool; ~ **vierge** new wool.

laineux, euse [lɛnø, -øz] *adj* woolly.

lainier, ière [lɛnje, -jɛʀ] *adj* (*industrie etc*) woollen.

laïque [laik] *adj* lay, civil; (*SCOL*) state *cpd* (*as opposed to private and Roman Catholic*) ♦ *nm/f* layman/woman.

laisse [lɛs] *nf* (*de chien*) lead, leash; **tenir en** ~ to keep on a lead *ou* leash.

laissé-pour-compte, laissée-, laissés- [lesepuʀkɔ̃t] *adj* (*COMM*) unsold; (*: refusé*) returned ♦ *nm/f* (*fig*) reject; **les laissés-pour-compte de la reprise économique** those who are left out of the economic upturn.

laisser [lese] *vt* to leave ♦ *vb aux*: ~ **qn faire** to let sb do; **se** ~ **exploiter** to let o.s. be exploited; **se** ~ **aller** to let o.s. go; ~ **qn tranquille** to let *ou* leave sb alone; **laisse-toi faire** let me (*ou* him) do it; **rien ne laisse penser que ...** there is no reason to think that ...; **cela ne laisse pas de surprendre** nonetheless it is surprising.

laisser-aller [leseale] *nm* carelessness, slovenliness.

laisser-faire [lesefɛʀ] *nm* laissez-faire.

laissez-passer [lesepase] *nm inv* pass.

lait [lɛ] *nm* milk; **frère/sœur de** ~ foster brother/sister; ~ **écrémé/concentré/ condensé** skimmed/concentrated/evaporated milk; ~ **en poudre** powdered milk, milk powder; ~ **de chèvre/vache** goat's/cow's milk; ~ **maternel** mother's milk; ~ **démaquillant/de beauté** cleansing/beauty lotion.

laitage [lɛtaʒ] *nm* milk product.

laiterie [lɛtʀi] *nf* dairy.

laiteux, euse [lɛtø, -øz] *adj* milky.

laitier, ière [lɛtje, -jɛʀ] *adj* dairy ♦ *nm/f* milkman/dairywoman.

laiton [lɛtɔ̃] *nm* brass.

laitue [lɛty] *nf* lettuce.

laïus [lajys] *nm* (*péj*) spiel.

lama [lama] *nm* llama.

lambeau, x [lɑ̃bo] *nm* scrap; **en** ~**x** in tatters, tattered.

lambin, e [lɑ̃bɛ̃, -in] *adj* (*péj*) slow.

lambiner [lɑ̃bine] *vi* (*péj*) to dawdle.

lambris [lɑ̃bʀi] *nm* panelling *no pl*.

lambrissé, e [lɑ̃bʀise] *adj* panelled.

lame [lam] *nf* blade; (*vague*) wave; (*lamelle*) strip; ~ **de fond** ground swell *no pl*; ~ **de rasoir** razor blade.

lamé [lame] *nm* lamé.

lamelle [lamɛl] *nf* (*lame*) small blade; (*morceau*) sliver; (*de champignon*) gill; **couper en** ~**s** to slice thinly.

lamentable [lamɑ̃tabl(ə)] *adj* (*déplorable*) appalling; (*pitoyable*) pitiful.

lamentablement [lamɑ̃tabləmɑ̃] *adv* (*échouer*) miserably; (*se conduire*) appallingly.

lamentation [lamɑ̃tasjɔ̃] *nf* wailing *no pl*, lamentation; moaning *no pl*.

lamenter [lamɑ̃te]: **se** ~ *vi*: **se** ~ (**sur**) to moan (over).

laminage [laminaʒ] *nm* lamination.

laminer [lamine] *vt* to laminate; (*fig: écraser*) to wipe out.

laminoir [laminwaʀ] *nm* rolling mill; **passer au** ~ (*fig*) to go (*ou* put) through the mill.

lampadaire [lɑ̃padɛʀ] *nm* (*de salon*) standard

lamp; (*dans la rue*) street lamp.

lampe [lɑ̃p(ə)] *nf* lamp; (*TECH*) valve; ~ **à alcool** spirit lamp; ~ **à bronzer** sunlamp; ~ **de poche** torch (*BRIT*), flashlight (*US*); ~ **à souder** blowlamp; ~ **témoin** warning light.

lampée [lɑ̃pe] *nf* gulp, swig.

lampe-tempête, *pl* **lampes-tempête** [lɑ̃ptɑ̃pɛt] *nf* storm lantern.

lampion [lɑ̃pjɔ̃] *nm* Chinese lantern.

lampiste [lɑ̃pist(ə)] *nm* light (maintenance) man; (*fig*) underling.

lamproie [lɑ̃pʀwa] *nf* lamprey.

lance [lɑ̃s] *nf* spear; ~ **d'arrosage** garden hose; ~ **à eau** water hose; ~ **d'incendie** fire hose.

lancée [lɑ̃se] *nf*: **être/continuer sur sa** ~ to be under way/keep going.

lance-flammes [lɑ̃sflam] *nm inv* flamethrower.

lance-fusées [lɑ̃sfyze] *nm inv* rocket launcher.

lance-grenades [lɑ̃sgʀənad] *nm inv* grenade launcher.

lancement [lɑ̃smɑ̃] *nm* launching *no pl*, launch; **offre de** ~ introductory offer.

lance-missiles [lɑ̃smisil] *nm inv* missile launcher.

lance-pierres [lɑ̃spjɛʀ] *nm inv* catapult.

lancer [lɑ̃se] *nm* (*SPORT*) throwing *no pl*, throw; (*PÊCHE*) rod and reel fishing ♦ *vt* to throw; (*émettre, projeter*) to throw out, send out; (*produit, fusée, bateau, artiste*) to launch; (*injure*) to hurl, fling; (*proclamation, mandat d'arrêt*) to issue; (*emprunt*) to float; (*moteur*) to send roaring away; ~ **qch à qn** to throw sth to sb; (*de façon agressive*) to throw sth at sb; ~ **un cri** *ou* **un appel** to shout *ou* call out; **se** ~ *vi* (*prendre de l'élan*) to build up speed; (*se précipiter*): **se** ~ **sur** *ou* **contre** to rush at; **se** ~ **dans** (*discussion*) to launch into; (*aventure*) to embark on; (*les affaires, la politique*) to go into; ~ **du poids** *nm* putting the shot.

lance-roquettes [lɑ̃sʀɔkɛt] *nm inv* rocket launcher.

lance-torpilles [lɑ̃stɔʀpij] *nm inv* torpedo tube.

lanceur, euse [lɑ̃sœʀ, -øz] *nm/f* bowler; (*BASEBALL*) pitcher ♦ *nm* (*ESPACE*) launcher.

lancinant, e [lɑ̃sinɑ̃, -ɑ̃t] *adj* (*regrets etc*) haunting; (*douleur*) shooting.

lanciner [lɑ̃sine] *vi* to throb; (*fig*) to nag.

landais, e [lɑ̃dɛ, -ɛz] *adj* of *ou* from the Landes.

landau [lɑ̃do] *nm* pram (*BRIT*), baby carriage (*US*).

lande [lɑ̃d] *nf* moor.

Landes [lɑ̃d] *nfpl*: **les** ~ the Landes.

langage [lɑ̃gaʒ] *nm* language; ~ **d'assemblage** (*INFORM*) assembly language; ~ **du corps** body language; ~ **évolué/machine** (*INFORM*) high-level/machine language; ~ **de programmation** (*INFORM*) programming language.

lange [lɑ̃ʒ] *nm* flannel blanket; ~**s** *nmpl* swaddling clothes.

langer [lɑ̃ʒe] *vt* to change (the nappy (*BRIT*) *ou* diaper (*US*) of); **table à** ~ changing table.

langoureux, euse [lɑ̃guʀø, -øz] *adj* languorous.

langoureusement [lɑ̃guʀøzmɑ̃] *adv* languorously.

langouste [lɑ̃gust(ə)] *nf* crayfish *inv*.

langoustine [lɑ̃gustin] *nf* Dublin Bay prawn.

langue [lɑ̃g] *nf* (*ANAT, CULIN*) tongue; (*LING*) language; (*bande*): ~ **de terre** spit of land; **tirer la** ~ (**à**) to stick out one's tongue (at); **donner sa** ~ **au chat** to give up, give in; **de** ~ **française** French-speaking; ~ **de bois** officialese; ~ **maternelle** native language, mother tongue; ~ **verte** slang; ~ **vivante** modern language.

langue-de-chat [lɑ̃gdəʃa] *nf* finger biscuit.

languedocien, ne [lɑ̃gdɔsjɛ̃, -ɛn] *adj* of *ou* from the Languedoc.

languette [lɑ̃gɛt] *nf* tongue.

langueur [lɑ̃gœʀ] *nf* languidness.

languir [lɑ̃giʀ] *vi* to languish; (*conversation*) to flag; **se** ~ *vi* to be languishing; **faire** ~ **qn** to keep sb waiting.

languissant, e [lɑ̃gisɑ̃, -ɑ̃t] *adj* languid.

lanière [lanjɛʀ] *nf* (*de fouet*) lash; (*de valise, bretelle*) strap.

lanoline [lanɔlin] *nf* lanolin.

lanterne [lɑ̃tɛʀn(ə)] *nf* (*portable*) lantern; (*électrique*) light, lamp; (*de voiture*) (side)light; ~ **rouge** (*fig*) tail-ender; ~ **vénitienne** Chinese lantern.

lanterneau, x [lɑ̃tɛʀno] *nm* skylight.

lanterner [lɑ̃tɛʀne] *vi*: **faire** ~ **qn** to keep sb hanging around.

Laos [laɔs] *nm*: **le** ~ Laos.

laotien, ne [laɔsjɛ̃, -ɛn] *adj* Laotian.

lapalissade [lapalisad] *nf* statement of the obvious.

La Paz [lapaz] *n* La Paz.

laper [lape] *vt* to lap up.

lapereau, x [lapʀo] *nm* young rabbit.

lapidaire [lapidɛʀ] *adj* stone *cpd*; (*fig*) terse.

lapider [lapide] *vt* to stone.

lapin [lapɛ̃] *nm* rabbit; (*fourrure*) cony; **coup du** ~ rabbit punch; **poser un** ~ **à qn** to stand sb up; ~ **de garenne** wild rabbit.

lapis(-lazuli) [lapis(lazyli)] *nm inv* lapis lazuli.

lapon, e [lapɔ̃, -ɔn] *adj* Lapp, Lappish ♦ *nm* (*LING*) Lapp, Lappish ♦ *nm/f*: **L~, e** Lapp, Laplander.

Laponie [laponi] *nf*: **la** ~ Lapland.

laps [laps] *nm*: ~ **de temps** space of time, time *no pl*.

lapsus [lapsys] *nm* slip.

laquais [lakɛ] *nm* lackey.

laque [lak] *nf* lacquer; (*brute*) shellac; (*pour cheveux*) hair spray ♦ *nm* lacquer; piece of lacquer ware.

laqué, e [lake] *adj* lacquered.

laquelle [lakɛl] *pron voir* **lequel**.

larbin [laʀbɛ̃] *nm* (*péj*) flunkey.

larcin [laʀsɛ̃] *nm* theft.

lard [laʀ] *nm* (*graisse*) fat; (*bacon*) (streaky) bacon.

larder [laʀde] *vt* (*CULIN*) to lard.

lardon [laʀdɔ̃] *nm* (*CULIN*) piece of chopped bacon; (*fam: enfant*) kid.

large [laʀʒ(ə)] *adj* wide; broad; (*fig*) generous ♦ *adv*: **calculer/voir** ~ to allow extra/think big ♦ *nm* (*largeur*): **5 m de** ~ 5 m wide *ou* in width; (*mer*): **le** ~ the open sea; **en** ~ *adv* sideways; **au** ~ **de** off; ~ **d'esprit** broadminded; **ne pas en mener** ~ to have one's heart in one's boots.

largement [laʀʒəmɑ̃] *adv* widely; (*de loin*) greatly; (*amplement, au minimum*) easily; (*sans compter: donner etc*) generously.

largesse [laʀʒɛs] *nf* generosity; ~**s** *nfpl* liberalities.

largeur [laʀʒœʀ] *nf* (*qu'on mesure*) width; (*impression visuelle*) wideness, width; breadth; broadness.

larguer [laʀge] *vt* to drop; (*fam: se débarrasser de*) to get rid of; ~ **les amarres** to cast off (the moorings).

larme [laʀm(ə)] *nf* tear; (*fig*): **une** ~ **de** a drop of; **en** ~**s** in tears; **pleurer à chaudes** ~**s** to cry one's eyes out, cry bitterly.

larmoyant, e [laʀmwajɑ̃, -ɑ̃t] *adj* tearful.

larmoyer [laʀmwaje] *vi* (*yeux*) to water; (*se plaindre*) to whimper.

larron [laʀɔ̃] *nm* thief (*pl* thieves).

larve [laʀv(ə)] *nf* (*ZOOL*) larva (*pl* -ae); (*fig*) worm.

larvé, e [laʀve] *adj* (*fig*) latent.

laryngite [laʀɛ̃ʒit] *nf* laryngitis.

laryngologiste [laʀɛ̃gɔlɔʒist(ə)] *nm/f* throat specialist.

larynx [laʀɛ̃ks] *nm* larynx.

las, lasse [lɑ, lɑs] *adj* weary.

lasagne [lazaɲ] *nf* lasagne.

lascar [laskaʀ] *nm* character; (*malin*) rogue.

lascif, ive [lasif, -iv] *adj* lascivious.

laser [lazɛʀ] *nm*: (**rayon**) ~ laser (beam); **chaîne** *ou* **platine** ~ compact disc (player); **disque** ~ compact disc.

lassant, e [lɑsɑ̃, -ɑ̃t] *adj* tiresome, wearisome.

lasse [lɑs] *adj f voir* **las**.

lasser [lɑse] *vt* to weary, tire; **se** ~ **de** to grow weary *ou* tired of.

lassitude [lɑsityd] *nf* lassitude, weariness.

lasso [laso] *nm* lasso; **prendre au** ~ to lasso.

latent, e [latɑ̃, -ɑ̃t] *adj* latent.

latéral, e, aux [lateʀal, -o] *adj* side *cpd*, lateral.

latéralement [lateʀalmɑ̃] *adv* edgeways; (*arriver, souffler*) from the side.

latex [latɛks] *nm inv* latex.

latin, e [latɛ̃, -in] *adj* Latin ♦ *nm* (*LING*) Latin ♦ *nm/f*: **L**~, **e** Latin; **j'y perds mon** ~ it's all Greek to me.

latiniste [latinist(ə)] *nm/f* Latin scholar (*ou* student).

latino-américain, e [latinɔameʀikɛ̃, -ɛn] *adj* Latin-American.

latitude [latityd] *nf* latitude; (*fig*): **avoir la** ~ **de faire** to be left free *ou* be at liberty to do; **à 48° de** ~ **Nord** at latitude 48° North; **sous toutes les** ~**s** (*fig*) world-wide, throughout the world.

latrines [latʀin] *nfpl* latrines.

latte [lat] *nf* lath, slat; (*de plancher*) board.

lattis [lati] *nm* lathwork.

laudanum [lodanɔm] *nm* laudanum.

laudatif, ive [lodatif, -iv] *adj* laudatory.

lauréat, e [lɔʀea, -at] *nm/f* winner.

laurier [lɔʀje] *nm* (*BOT*) laurel; (*CULIN*) bay leaves *pl*; ~**s** *nmpl* (*fig*) laurels.

laurier-rose, *pl* **lauriers-rose** [lɔʀjeʀoz] *nm* oleander.

laurier-tin, *pl* **lauriers-tins** [lɔʀjetɛ̃] *nm* laurustinus.

lavable [lavabl(ə)] *adj* washable.

lavabo [lavabo] *nm* washbasin; ~**s** *nmpl* toilet *sg*.

lavage [lavaʒ] *nm* washing *no pl*, wash; ~ **d'estomac/d'intestin** stomach/intestinal wash; ~ **de cerveau** brainwashing *no pl*.

lavande [lavɑ̃d] *nf* lavender.

lavandière [lavɑ̃djɛʀ] *nf* washerwoman.

lave [lav] *nf* lava *no pl*.

lave-glace [lavglas] *nm* (*AUTO*) windscreen (*BRIT*) *ou* windshield (*US*) washer.

lave-linge [lavlɛ̃ʒ] *nm inv* washing machine.

lavement [lavmɑ̃] *nm* (*MÉD*) enema.

laver [lave] *vt* to wash; (*tache*) to wash off; (*fig: affront*) to avenge; **se** ~ to have a wash, wash; **se** ~ **les mains/dents** to wash one's hands/clean one's teeth; ~ **la vaisselle/le linge** to wash the dishes/clothes; ~ **qn de** (*accusation*) to clear sb of.

laverie [lavʀi] *nf*: ~ (**automatique**) launderette.

lavette [lavɛt] *nf* (*chiffon*) dish cloth; (*brosse*) dish mop; (*fam: homme*) wimp, drip.

laveur, euse [lavœʀ, -øz] *nm/f* cleaner.

lave-vaisselle [lavvɛsɛl] *nm inv* dishwasher.

lavis [lavi] *nm* (*technique*) washing; (*dessin*) wash drawing.

lavoir [lavwaʀ] *nm* wash house; (*bac*) washtub.

laxatif, ive [laksatif, -iv] *adj, nm* laxative.

laxisme [laksism(ə)] *nm* laxity.

laxiste [laksist(ə)] *adj* lax.

layette [lɛjɛt] *nf* layette.

layon [lɛjɔ̃] *nm* trail.

lazaret [lazaʀɛ] *nm* quarantine area.

lazzi [ladzi] *nm* gibe.

LCR *sigle f* (= *Ligue communiste révolutionnaire*) political party.

═══════════════════════════════ *MOT-CLÉ*

le (l'), la [l(ə)] (*pl* **les**) *art déf* **1** the; ~ **livre/la pomme/l'arbre** the book/the apple/the tree; **les étudiants** the students

2 (*noms abstraits*): ~ **courage/l'amour/la**

jeunesse courage/love/youth
3 (_indiquant la possession_): **se casser la jambe** _etc_ to break one's leg _etc_; **levez la main** put your hand up; **avoir les yeux gris/ ~ nez rouge** to have grey eyes/a red nose
4 (_temps_): **le matin/soir** in the morning/ evening; mornings/evenings; **~ jeudi** _etc_ (_d'habitude_) on Thursdays _etc_; (_ce jeudi-là etc_) on (the) Thursday; **nous venons ~ 3 décembre** (_parlé_) we're coming on the 3rd of December _ou_ on December the 3rd; (_écrit_) we're coming (on) 3rd _ou_ 3 December
5 (_distribution, évaluation_) a, an; **10 F ~ mètre/kilo** 10 F a _ou_ per metre/kilo; **~ tiers/quart de** a third/quarter of
♦ _pron_ **1** (_personne: mâle_) him; (: _femelle_) her; (: _pluriel_) them; **je ~/la/les vois** I can see him/her/them
2 (_animal, chose: singulier_) it; (: _pluriel_) them; **je ~** (_ou_ **la**) **vois** I can see it; **je les vois** I can see them
3 (_remplaçant une phrase_): **je ne ~ savais pas** I didn't know (about it); **il était riche et ne l'est plus** he was once rich but no longer is.

lé [le] _nm_ (_de tissu_) width; (_de papier peint_) strip, length.
leader [lidœʀ] _nm_ leader.
leadership [lidœʀʃip] _nm_ (POL) leadership.
leasing [liziŋ] _nm_ leasing.
lèche-bottes [lɛʃbɔt] _nm inv_ bootlicker.
lèchefrite [lɛʃfʀit] _nf_ dripping pan _ou_ tray.
lécher [leʃe] _vt_ to lick; (_laper: lait, eau_) to lick _ou_ lap up; (_finir, polir_) to over-refine; **~ les vitrines** to go window-shopping; **se ~ les doigts/lèvres** to lick one's fingers/lips.
lèche-vitrines [lɛʃvitʀin] _nm inv_: **faire du ~** to go window-shopping.
leçon [ləsɔ̃] _nf_ lesson; **faire la ~** to teach; **faire la ~ à** (_fig_) to give a lecture to; **~s de conduite** driving lessons; **~s particulières** private lessons _ou_ tuition _sg_ (BRIT).
lecteur, trice [lɛktœʀ, -tʀis] _nm/f_ reader; (_d'université_) (foreign language) assistant (BRIT), (foreign) teaching assistant (US)
♦ _nm_ (TECH): **~ de cassettes** cassette player; (INFORM): **~ de disquette(s)** _ou_ **de disque** disk drive; **~ compact-disc** _ou_ **CD** compact disc (player).
lectorat [lɛktɔʀa] _nm_ (foreign language _ou_ teaching) assistantship.
lecture [lɛktyʀ] _nf_ reading.
LED [lɛd] _sigle f_ (= _light emitting diode_) LED; **affichage ~** LED display.
ledit [lədi], **ladite** [ladit], _mpl_ **lesdits** [ledi], _fpl_ **lesdites** [ledit] _dét_ the aforesaid.
légal, e, aux [legal, -o] _adj_ legal.
légalement [legalmɑ̃] _adv_ legally.
légalisation [legalizasjɔ̃] _nf_ legalization.
légaliser [legalize] _vt_ to legalize.
légalité [legalite] _nf_ legality, lawfulness; **être dans/sortir de la ~** to be within/step outside

the law.
légat [lega] _nm_ (REL) legate.
légataire [legatɛʀ] _nm_ legatee.
légendaire [leʒɑ̃dɛʀ] _adj_ legendary.
légende [leʒɑ̃d] _nf_ (_mythe_) legend; (_de carte, plan_) key, legend; (_de dessin_) caption, legend.
léger, ère [leʒe, -ɛʀ] _adj_ light; (_bruit, retard_) slight; (_boisson, parfum_) weak; (_couche, étoffe_) thin; (_superficiel_) thoughtless; (_volage_) free and easy; flighty; (_peu sérieux_) lightweight; **blessé ~** slightly injured person; **à la légère** _adv_ (_parler, agir_) rashly, thoughtlessly.
légèrement [leʒɛʀmɑ̃] _adv_ lightly; thoughtlessly, rashly; **~ plus grand** slightly bigger.
légèreté [leʒɛʀte] _nf_ lightness; thoughtlessness.
légiférer [leʒifeʀe] _vi_ to legislate.
légion [leʒjɔ̃] _nf_ legion; **la L~ étrangère** the Foreign Legion; **la L~ d'honneur** the Legion of Honour.

Created by Napoleon in 1802 to reward service to the state, **la Légion d'honneur** is a prestigious French order headed by the President of the Republic, the Grand Maître. Members receive a nominal tax-free payment each year.

---

légionnaire [leʒjɔnɛʀ] _nm_ (MIL) legionnaire; (_de la Légion d'honneur_) holder of the Legion of Honour.
législateur [leʒislatœʀ] _nm_ legislator, lawmaker.
législatif, ive [leʒislatif, -iv] _adj_ legislative; **législatives** _nfpl_ general election _sg_.
législation [leʒislasjɔ̃] _nf_ legislation.
législature [leʒislatyʀ] _nf_ legislature; (_période_) term (of office).
légiste [leʒist(ə)] _nm_ jurist ♦ _adj_: **médecin ~** forensic scientist (BRIT), medical examiner (US).
légitime [leʒitim] _adj_ (JUR) lawful, legitimate; (_enfant_) legitimate; (_fig_) rightful, legitimate; **en état de ~ défense** in self-defence.
légitimement [leʒitimmɑ̃] _adv_ lawfully; legitimately; rightfully.
légitimer [leʒitime] _vt_ (_enfant_) to legitimize; (_justifier: conduite etc_) to justify.
légitimité [leʒitimite] _nf_ (JUR) legitimacy.
legs [lɛg] _nm_ legacy.
léguer [lege] _vt_: **~ qch à qn** (JUR) to bequeath sth to sb; (_fig_) to hand sth down _ou_ pass sth on to sb.
légume [legym] _nm_ vegetable; **~s verts** green vegetables; **~s secs** pulses.
légumier [legymje] _nm_ vegetable dish.
leitmotiv [lejtmɔtiv] _nm_ leitmotiv, leitmotif.
Léman [lemɑ̃] _nm voir_ **lac**.
lendemain [lɑ̃dmɛ̃] _nm_: **le ~** the next _ou_ following day; **le ~ matin/soir** the next _ou_

following morning/evening; **le ~ de** the day after; **au ~ de** in the days following; in the wake of; **penser au ~** to think of the future; **sans ~** short-lived; **de beaux ~s** bright prospects; **des ~s qui chantent** a rosy future.

lénifiant, e [lenifjã, -ãt] *adj* soothing.

léniniste [leninist(ə)] *adj, nm/f* Leninist.

lent, e [lã, lãt] *adj* slow.

lente [lãt] *nf* nit.

lentement [lãtmã] *adv* slowly.

lenteur [lãtœʀ] *nf* slowness *no pl*; ~s *nfpl* (*actions, décisions lentes*) slowness *sg*.

lentille [lãtij] *nf* (*OPTIQUE*) lens *sg*; (*BOT*) lentil; **~ d'eau** duckweed; **~s de contact** contact lenses.

léonin, e [leɔnɛ̃, -in] *adj* (*fig: contrat etc*) one-sided.

léopard [leɔpaʀ] *nm* leopard.

LEP [lɛp] *sigle m* (= *lycée d'enseignement professionnel*) *secondary school for vocational training, pre-1986.*

lèpre [lɛpʀ(ə)] *nf* leprosy.

lépreux, euse [lepʀø, -øz] *nm/f* leper ♦ *adj* (*fig*) flaking, peeling.

━━━━━━━━━━━━ *MOT-CLÉ*

lequel, laquelle [ləkɛl, lakɛl] (*mpl* **lesquels,** *fpl* **lesquelles;** *à + lequel =* **auquel,** *de + lequel =* **duquel**) *pron* **1** (*interrogatif*) which, which one

2 (*relatif: personne: sujet*) who; (: *objet, après préposition*) whom; (*sujet: possessif*) whose; (: *chose*) which; **je l'ai proposé au directeur, ~ est d'accord** I suggested it to the director, who agrees; **la femme à laquelle j'ai acheté mon chien** the woman from whom I bought my dog; **le pont sur ~ nous sommes passés** the bridge (over) which we crossed; **un homme sur la compétence duquel on peut compter** a man whose competence one can count on

♦ *adj:* **auquel cas** in which case.

━━━━━━━━━━━━

les [le] *dét voir* **le.**

lesbienne [lɛsbjɛn] *nf* lesbian.

lesdits [ledi], **lesdites** [ledit] *dét voir* **ledit.**

lèse-majesté [lɛzmaʒɛste] *nf inv:* **crime de ~** crime of lese-majesty.

léser [leze] *vt* to wrong; (*MÉD*) to injure.

lésiner [lezine] *vt:* **~ (sur)** to skimp (on).

lésion [lezjɔ̃] *nf* lesion, damage *no pl*; **~s cérébrales** brain damage.

Lesotho [lezɔto] *nm:* **le ~** Lesotho.

lesquels, lesquelles [lekɛl] *pron voir* **lequel.**

lessivable [lesivabl(ə)] *adj* washable.

lessive [lesiv] *nf* (*poudre*) washing powder; (*linge*) washing *no pl*, wash; (*opération*) washing *no pl*; **faire la ~** to do the washing.

lessivé, e [lesive] *adj* (*fam*) washed out.

lessiver [lesive] *vt* to wash.

lessiveuse [lesivøz] *nf* (*récipient*) (laundry) boiler.

lessiviel [lesivjɛl] *adj* detergent.

lest [lɛst] *nm* ballast; **jeter** *ou* **lâcher du ~** (*fig*) to make concessions.

leste [lɛst(ə)] *adj* (*personne, mouvement*) sprightly, nimble; (*désinvolte: manières*) offhand; (*osé: plaisanterie*) risqué.

lestement [lɛstəmã] *adv* nimbly.

lester [lɛste] *vt* to ballast.

letchi [lɛtʃi] *nm* = litchi.

léthargie [letaʀʒi] *nf* lethargy.

léthargique [letaʀʒik] *adj* lethargic.

letton, ne [lɛtɔ̃, -ɔn] *adj* Latvian, Lett.

Lettonie [lɛtɔni] *nf:* **la ~** Latvia.

lettre [lɛtʀ(ə)] *nf* letter; **~s** *nfpl* (*étude, culture*) literature *sg*; (*SCOL*) arts (subjects); **à la ~** (*au sens propre*) literally; (*ponctuellement*) to the letter; **en ~s majuscules** *ou* **capitales** in capital letters, in capitals; **en toutes ~s** in words, in full; **~ de change** bill of exchange; **~ piégée** letter bomb; **~ de voiture (aérienne)** (air) waybill, (air) bill of lading; **~s de noblesse** pedigree.

lettré, e [letʀe] *adj* well-read, scholarly.

lettre-transfert, *pl* **lettres-transferts** [letʀatʀãsfɛʀ] *nf* (pressure) transfer.

leu [lø] *voir* **queue.**

leucémie [løsemi] *nf* leukaemia.

━━━━━━━━━━━━ *MOT-CLÉ*

leur [lœʀ] *adj possessif* their; **~ maison** their house; **~s amis** their friends; **à ~ approche** as they came near; **à ~ vue** at the sight of them

♦ *pron* **1** (*objet indirect*) (to) them; **je ~ ai dit la vérité** I told them the truth; **je le ~ ai donné** I gave it to them, I gave them it

2 (*possessif*): **le(la) ~, les ~s** theirs.

━━━━━━━━━━━━

leurre [lœʀ] *nm* (*appât*) lure; (*fig*) delusion; (: *piège*) snare.

leurrer [lœʀe] *vt* to delude, deceive.

levain [ləvɛ̃] *nm* leaven; **sans ~** unleavened.

levant, e [ləvã, -ãt] *adj:* **soleil ~** rising sun ♦ *nm:* **le L~** the Levant; **au soleil ~** at sunrise.

levantin, e [ləvãtɛ̃, -in] *adj* Levantine ♦ *nm/f:* **L~, e** Levantine.

levé, e [ləve] *adj:* **être ~** to be up ♦ *nm:* **~ de terrain** land survey; **à mains ~es** (*vote*) by a show of hands; **au pied ~** at a moment's notice.

levée [ləve] *nf* (*POSTES*) collection; (*CARTES*) trick; **~ de boucliers** general outcry; **~ du corps** collection of the body from house of the deceased, before funeral; **~ d'écrou** release from custody; **~ de terre** levee; **~ de troupes** levy.

lever [ləve] *vt* (*vitre, bras etc*) to raise; (*soulever de terre, supprimer: interdiction, siège*) to lift; (: *difficulté*) to remove; (*séance*) to close; (*impôts, armée*) to levy; (*CHASSE: lièvre*) to start; (: *perdrix*) to flush; (*fam: fille*) to pick up ♦ *vi* (*CULIN*) to rise ♦ *nm:* **au ~ on getting up; se ~** *vi* to get up; (*soleil*) to rise; (*jour*) to break; (*brouillard*) to lift; **ça va se ~** the weather will clear; **~ du jour** daybreak; **~ du rideau** (*THÉÂT*) curtain; **~ de rideau** (*pièce*) curtain raiser; **~ de soleil** sunrise.

lève-tard [lɛvtaʀ] *nm/f inv* late riser.

lève-tôt [lɛvto] *nm/f inv* early riser, early bird.

levier [ləvje] *nm* lever; **faire ~ sur** to lever up (*ou* off); **~ de changement de vitesse** gear lever.

lévitation [levitɑsjɔ̃] *nf* levitation.

levraut [ləvʀo] *nm* (*ZOOL*) leveret.

lèvre [lɛvʀ(ə)] *nf* lip; **~s** *nfpl* (*d'une plaie*) edges; **petites/grandes ~s** labia minora/majora; **du bout des ~s** half-heartedly.

lévrier [levʀije] *nm* greyhound.

levure [ləvyʀ] *nf* yeast; **~ chimique** baking powder.

lexical, e, aux [lɛksikal, -o] *adj* lexical.

lexicographe [lɛksikɔgʀaf] *nm/f* lexicographer.

lexicographie [lɛksikɔgʀafi] *nf* lexicography, dictionary writing.

lexicologie [lɛksikɔlɔʒi] *nf* lexicology.

lexique [lɛksik] *nm* vocabulary, lexicon; (*glossaire*) vocabulary.

lézard [lezaʀ] *nm* lizard; (*peau*) lizardskin.

lézarde [lezaʀd(ə)] *nf* crack.

lézarder [lezaʀde]: **se ~** *vi* to crack.

liaison [ljɛzɔ̃] *nf* (*rapport*) connection, link; (*RAIL, AVIAT etc*) link; (*relation: d'amitié*) friendship; (: *d'affaires*) relationship; (: *amoureuse*) affair; (*CULIN, PHONÉTIQUE*) liaison; **entrer/être en ~ avec** to get/be in contact with; **~ radio** radio contact; **~ (de transmission de données)** (*INFORM*) data link.

liane [ljan] *nf* creeper.

liant, e [ljɑ̃, -ɑ̃t] *adj* sociable.

liasse [ljas] *nf* wad, bundle.

Liban [libɑ̃] *nm:* **le ~** (the) Lebanon.

libanais, e [libanɛ, -ɛz] *adj* Lebanese ♦ *nm/f:* **L~, e** Lebanese.

libations [libɑsjɔ̃] *nfpl* libations.

libelle [libɛl] *nm* lampoon.

libellé [libele] *nm* wording.

libeller [libele] *vt* (*chèque, mandat*): **~ (au nom de)** to make out (to); (*lettre*) to word.

libellule [libelyl] *nf* dragonfly.

libéral, e, aux [libeʀal, -o] *adj, nm/f* liberal; **les professions ~es** the professions.

libéralement [libeʀalmɑ̃] *adv* liberally.

libéralisation [libeʀalizɑsjɔ̃] *nf* liberalization; **~ du commerce** easing of trade restrictions.

libéraliser [libeʀalize] *vt* to liberalize.

libéralisme [libeʀalism(ə)] *nm* liberalism.

libéralité [libeʀalite] *nf* liberality *no pl*, generosity *no pl*.

libérateur, trice [libeʀatœʀ, -tʀis] *adj*

liberating ♦ *nm/f* liberator.

libération [libeʀɑsjɔ̃] *nf* liberation, freeing; release; discharge; **~ conditionnelle** release on parole.

libéré, e [libeʀe] *adj* liberated; **~ de** freed from; **être ~ sous caution/sur parole** to be released on bail/on parole.

libérer [libeʀe] *vt* (*délivrer*) to free, liberate; (: *moralement, PSYCH*) to liberate; (*relâcher: prisonnier*) to release; (: *soldat*) to discharge; (*dégager: gaz, cran d'arrêt*) to release; (*ÉCON: échanges commerciaux*) to ease restrictions on; **se ~** (*de rendez-vous*) to try and be free, get out of previous engagements; **~ qn de** (*liens, dette*) to free sb from; (*promesse*) to release sb from.

Libéria [libeʀja] *nm:* **le ~** Liberia.

libérien, ne [libeʀjɛ̃, -ɛn] *adj* Liberian ♦ *nm/f:* **L~, ne** Liberian.

libéro [libeʀo] *nm* (*FOOTBALL*) sweeper.

libertaire [libeʀtɛʀ] *adj* libertarian.

liberté [libeʀte] *nf* freedom; (*loisir*) free time; **~s** *nfpl* (*privautés*) liberties; **mettre/être en ~** to set/be free; **en ~ provisoire/surveillée/ conditionnelle** on bail/probation/parole; **~ d'association** right of association; **~ de conscience** freedom of conscience; **~ du culte** freedom of worship; **~ d'esprit** independence of mind; **~ d'opinion** freedom of thought; **~ de la presse** freedom of the press; **~ de réunion** right to hold meetings; **~ syndicale** union rights *pl*; **~s individuelles** personal freedom *sg*; **~s publiques** civil rights.

libertin, e [libɛʀtɛ̃, -in] *adj* libertine, licentious.

libertinage [libɛʀtinaʒ] *nm* licentiousness.

libidineux, euse [libidinø, -øz] *adj* libidinous, lustful.

libido [libido] *nf* libido.

libraire [libʀɛʀ] *nm/f* bookseller.

libraire-éditeur, *pl* **libraires-éditeurs** [libʀɛʀeditœʀ] *nm* publisher and bookseller.

librairie [libʀeʀi] *nf* bookshop.

librairie-papeterie, *pl* **librairies-papeteries** [libʀeʀipapetʀi] bookseller's and stationer's.

libre [libʀ(ə)] *adj* free; (*route*) clear; (*place etc*) vacant, free; (*fig: propos, manières*) open; (*SCOL*) private and Roman Catholic (*as opposed to "laïque"*); **de ~** (*place*) free; **~ de qch/de faire** free from sth/to do; **vente ~** (*COMM*) unrestricted sale; **~ arbitre** free will; **~ concurrence** free-market economy; **~ entreprise** free enterprise.

libre-échange [libʀeʃɑ̃ʒ] *nm* free trade.

librement [libʀəmɑ̃] *adv* freely.

libre-penseur, euse [libʀəpɑ̃sœʀ, -øz] *nm/f* free thinker.

libre-service [libʀəsɛʀvis] *nm inv* (*magasin*) self-service store; (*restaurant*) self-service restaurant.

librettiste [libʀetist(ə)] *nm/f* librettist.

Libye [libi] *nf*: **la ~** Libya.
libyen, ne [libjɛ̃, -ɛn] *adj* Libyan ♦ *nm/f*: **L~, ne** Libyan.
lice [lis] *nf*: **entrer en ~** (*fig*) to enter the lists.
licence [lisɑ̃s] *nf* (*permis*) permit; (*diplôme*) (first) degree; (*liberté*) liberty; (*poétique, orthographique*) licence (*BRIT*), license (*US*); (*des mœurs*) licentiousness; **~ ès lettres/en droit** arts/law degree.

After gaining their **DEUG**, *French university students take their* **licence** *after a third year of study. It is roughly equivalent to a Bachelor's Degree in Britain.*

---

licencié, e [lisɑ̃sje] *nm/f* (*SCOL*): **~ ès lettres/en droit** ≈ Bachelor of Arts/Law arts/law graduate; (*SPORT*) permit-holder.
licenciement [lisɑ̃simɑ̃] *nm* dismissal; redundancy; laying off *no pl*.
licencier [lisɑ̃sje] *vt* (*renvoyer*) to dismiss; (*débaucher*) to make redundant; to lay off.
licencieux, euse [lisɑ̃sjø, -øz] *adj* licentious.
lichen [likɛn] *nm* lichen.
licite [lisit] *adj* lawful.
licorne [likɔrn(ə)] *nf* unicorn.
licou [liku] *nm* halter.
lie [li] *nf* dregs *pl*, sediment.
lié, e [lje] *adj*: **très ~ avec** (*fig*) very friendly with *ou* close to; **~ par** (*serment, promesse*) bound by; **avoir partie ~e (avec qn)** to be involved (with sb).
Liechtenstein [liʃtɛnʃtajn] *nm*: **le ~** Liechtenstein.
lie-de-vin [lidvɛ̃] *adj inv* wine(-coloured).
liège [ljɛʒ] *nm* cork.
liégeois, e [ljeʒwa, -waz] *adj* of *ou* from Liège ♦ *nm/f*: **L~, e** inhabitant *ou* native of Liège; **café/chocolat ~** coffee/chocolate ice cream topped with whipped cream.
lien [ljɛ̃] *nm* (*corde, fig: affectif, culturel*) bond; (*rapport*) link, connection; (*analogie*) link; **~ de parenté** family tie.
lier [lje] *vt* (*attacher*) to tie up; (*joindre*) to link up; (*fig: unir, engager*) to bind; (*CULIN*) to thicken; **~ qch à** (*attacher*) to tie sth to; (*associer*) to link sth to; **~ amitié/conversation (avec)** to strike up a friendship/conversation (with); **se ~ avec** to make friends with.
lierre [ljɛr] *nm* ivy.
liesse [ljɛs] *nf*: **être en ~** to be jubilant.
lieu, x [ljø] *nm* place; **~x** *nmpl* (*locaux*) premises; (*endroit: d'un accident etc*) scene *sg*; **en ~ sûr** in a safe place; **en haut ~** in high places; **vider** *ou* **quitter les ~x** to leave the premises; **arriver/être sur les ~x** to arrive/be on the scene; **en premier ~** in the first place; **en dernier ~** lastly; **avoir ~** to take place; **avoir ~ de faire** to have grounds *ou* good reason for doing; **tenir ~ de** to take the place of; (*servir de*) to serve as; **donner**

~ à to give rise to, give cause for; **au ~ de** instead of; **au ~ qu'il y aille** instead of him going; **~ commun** commonplace; **~ géométrique** locus; **~ de naissance** place of birth; **~ de rendez-vous** venue, meeting place.
lieu-dit, *pl* **lieux-dits** [ljødi] *nm* locality.
lieue [ljø] *nf* league.
lieutenant [ljøtnɑ̃] *nm* lieutenant; **~ de vaisseau** (*NAVIG*) lieutenant.
lieutenant-colonel, *pl* **lieutenants-colonels** [ljøtnɑ̃kɔlɔnɛl] *nm* (*armée de terre*) lieutenant colonel; (*armée de l'air*) wing commander (*BRIT*), lieutenant colonel (*US*).
lièvre [ljɛvr(ə)] *nm* hare; (*coureur*) pacemaker; **lever un ~** (*fig*) to bring up a prickly subject.
liftier, ière [liftje, -jɛr] lift (*BRIT*) *ou* elevator (*US*) attendant.
lifting [liftiŋ] *nm* face lift.
ligament [ligamɑ̃] *nm* ligament.
ligature [ligatyr] *nf* ligature.
lige [liʒ] *adj*: **homme ~** (*péj*) henchman.
ligne [liɲ] *nf* (*gén*) line; (*TRANSPORTS: liaison*) service; (*: trajet*) route; (*silhouette*): **garder la ~** to keep one's figure; **en ~** (*INFORM*) on line; **en ~ droite** as the crow flies; **"à la ~"** "new paragraph"; **entrer en ~ de compte** to be taken into account; to come into it; **~ de but/médiane** goal/halfway line; **~ d'arrivée/de départ** finishing/starting line; **~ de conduite** course of action; **~ directrice** guiding line; **~ d'horizon** skyline; **~ de mire** line of sight; **~ de touche** touchline.
ligné, e [liɲe] *adj*: **papier ~** ruled paper ♦ *nf* (*race, famille*) line, lineage; (*postérité*) descendants *pl*.
ligneux, euse [liɲø, -øz] *adj* ligneous, woody.
lignite [liɲit] *nm* lignite.
ligoter [ligɔte] *vt* to tie up.
ligue [lig] *nf* league.
liguer [lige]: **se ~** *vi* to form a league; **se ~ contre** (*fig*) to combine against.
lilas [lila] *nm* lilac.
lillois, e [lilwa, -waz] *adj* of *ou* from Lille.
Lima [lima] *n* Lima.
limace [limas] *nf* slug.
limaille [limaj] *nf*: **~ de fer** iron filings *pl*.
limande [limɑ̃d] *nf* dab.
limande-sole [limɑ̃dsɔl] *nf* lemon sole.
limbes [lɛ̃b] *nmpl* limbo *sg*; **être dans les ~** (*fig: projet etc*) to be up in the air.
lime [lim] *nf* (*TECH*) file; (*BOT*) lime; **~ à ongles** nail file.
limer [lime] *vt* (*bois, métal*) to file (down); (*ongles*) to file; (*fig: prix*) to pare down.
limier [limje] *nm* (*ZOOL*) bloodhound; (*détective*) sleuth.
liminaire [liminɛr] *adj* (*propos*) introductory.
limitatif, ive [limitatif, -iv] *adj* restrictive.
limitation [limitasjɔ̃] *nf* limitation, restriction; **sans ~ de temps** with no time limit; **~ des**

naissances birth control; ~ **de vitesse** speed limit.

limite [limit] *nf* (*de terrain*) boundary; (*partie ou point extrême*) limit; **dans la ~ de** within the limits of; **à la ~** (*au pire*) if the worst comes (*ou* came) to the worst; **sans ~s** (*bêtise, richesse, pouvoir*) limitless, boundless; **vitesse/charge ~** maximum speed/load; **cas ~** borderline case; **date ~** deadline; **date ~ de vente/consommation** sell-by/best-before date; **prix ~** upper price limit; **~ d'âge** maximum age, age limit.

limiter [limite] *vt* (*restreindre*) to limit, restrict; (*délimiter*) to border, form the boundary of; **se ~** (**à qch/à faire**) (*personne*) to limit *ou* confine o.s. (to sth/to doing sth); **se ~ à** (*chose*) to be limited to.

limitrophe [limitʀɔf] *adj* border *cpd*; **~ de** bordering on.

limogeage [limɔʒaʒ] *nm* dismissal.

limoger [limɔʒe] *vt* to dismiss.

limon [limɔ̃] *nm* silt.

limonade [limɔnad] *nf* lemonade.

limonadier, ière [limɔnadje, -jɛʀ] *nm/f* (*commerçant*) café owner; (*fabricant de limonade*) soft drinks manufacturer.

limoneux, euse [limɔnø, -øz] *adj* muddy.

limousin, e [limuzɛ̃, -in] *adj of ou* from Limousin ♦ *nm* (*région*): **le L~** the Limousin ♦ *nf* limousine.

limpide [lɛ̃pid] *adj* limpid.

lin [lɛ̃] *nm* (BOT) flax; (*tissu, toile*) linen.

linceul [lɛ̃sœl] *nm* shroud.

linéaire [lineɛʀ] *adj* linear ♦ *nm*: **~ (de vente)** shelves *pl*.

linéament [lineamɑ̃] *nm* outline.

linge [lɛ̃ʒ] *nm* (*serviettes etc*) linen; (*pièce de tissu*) cloth; (*aussi*: **~ de corps**) underwear; (*aussi*: **~ de toilette**) towel; (*lessive*) washing; **~ sale** dirty linen.

lingère [lɛ̃ʒɛʀ] *nf* linen maid.

lingerie [lɛ̃ʒʀi] *nf* lingerie, underwear.

lingot [lɛ̃go] *nm* ingot.

linguiste [lɛ̃gɥist(ə)] *nm/f* linguist.

linguistique [lɛ̃gɥistik] *adj* linguistic ♦ *nf* linguistics *sg*.

lino(léum) [linɔ(leɔm)] *nm* lino(leum).

linotte [linɔt] *nf*: **tête de ~** bird brain.

linteau, x [lɛ̃to] *nm* lintel.

lion, ne [ljɔ̃, ljɔn] *nm/f* lion/lioness; (*signe*): **le L~** Leo, the Lion; **être du L~** to be Leo; **~ de mer** sealion.

lionceau, x [ljɔ̃so] *nm* lion cub.

liposuccion [liposyksjɔ̃] *nf* liposuction.

lippu, e [lipy] *adj* thick-lipped.

liquéfier [likefje] *vt* to liquefy; **se ~** *vi* (*gaz etc*) to liquefy; (*fig: personne*) to succumb.

liqueur [likœʀ] *nf* liqueur.

liquidateur, trice [likidatœʀ, -tʀis] *nm/f* (JUR) receiver; **~ judiciaire** official liquidator.

liquidation [likidasjɔ̃] *nf* liquidation; (COMM) clearance (sale); **~ judiciaire** compulsory

liquidation.

liquide [likid] *adj* liquid ♦ *nm* liquid; (COMM): **en ~** in ready money *ou* cash.

liquider [likide] *vt* (*société, biens, témoin gênant*) to liquidate; (*compte, problème*) to settle; (COMM: *articles*) to clear, sell off.

liquidités [likidite] *nfpl* (COMM) liquid assets.

liquoreux, euse [likɔʀø, -øz] *adj* syrupy.

lire [liʀ] *nf* (*monnaie*) lira ♦ *vt, vi* to read; **~ qch à qn** to read sth (out) to sb.

lis *vb* [li] *voir* **lire** ♦ *nm* [lis] = **lys**.

lisais [lizɛ] *etc vb voir* **lire**.

Lisbonne [lizbɔn] *n* Lisbon.

lise [liz] *etc vb voir* **lire**.

liseré [lizʀe] *nm* border, edging.

liseron [lizʀɔ̃] *nm* bindweed.

liseuse [lizøz] *nf* book-cover; (*veste*) bedjacket.

lisible [lizibl(ə)] *adj* legible; (*digne d'être lu*) readable.

lisiblement [lizibləmɑ̃] *adv* legibly.

lisière [lizjɛʀ] *nf* (*de forêt*) edge; (*de tissu*) selvage.

lisons [lizɔ̃] *vb voir* **lire**.

lisse [lis] *adj* smooth.

lisser [lise] *vt* to smooth.

listage [listaʒ] *nm* (INFORM) listing.

liste [list(ə)] *nf* list; (INFORM) listing; **faire la ~ de** to list, make out a list of; **~ d'attente** waiting list; **~ civile** civil list; **~ électorale** electoral roll; **~ de mariage** wedding (present) list; **~ noire** hit list.

lister [liste] *vt* (*aussi* INFORM) to list; **~ la mémoire** to dump.

listéria [listeʀja] *nf* listeria.

listing [listiŋ] *nm* (INFORM) listing; **qualité ~** draft quality.

lit [li] *nm* (*gén*) bed; **faire son ~** to make one's bed; **aller/se mettre au ~** to go to/get into bed; **prendre le ~** to take to one's bed; **d'un premier ~** (JUR) of a first marriage; **~ de camp** campbed (BRIT), cot (US); **~ d'enfant** cot (BRIT), crib (US).

litanie [litani] *nf* litany.

lit-cage, *pl* **lits-cages** [likaʒ] *nm* folding bed.

litchi [litʃi] *nm* lychee.

literie [litʀi] *nf* bedding; (*linge*) bedding, bedclothes *pl*.

litière [litjɛʀ] *nf* litter.

litige [litiʒ] *nm* dispute; **en ~** in contention.

litigieux, euse [litiʒjø, -øz] *adj* litigious, contentious.

litote [litɔt] *nf* understatement.

litre [litʀ(ə)] *nm* litre; (*récipient*) litre measure.

littéraire [liteʀɛʀ] *adj* literary.

littéral, e, aux [liteʀal, -o] *adj* literal.

littéralement [liteʀalmɑ̃] *adv* literally.

littérature [liteʀatyʀ] *nf* literature.

littoral, e, aux [litɔʀal, -o] *adj* coastal ♦ *nm* coast.

Lituanie [lityani] *nf*: **la** ~ Lithuania.
lituanien, ne [lityanjɛ̃, -ɛn] *adj* Lithuanian
♦ *nm* (*LING*) Lithuanian ♦ *nm/f*: **L~, ne**
Lithuanian.
liturgie [lityʀʒi] *nf* liturgy.
liturgique [lityʀʒik] *adj* liturgical.
livide [livid] *adj* livid, pallid.
living(-room) [liviŋ(ʀum)] *nm* living room.
livrable [livʀabl(ə)] *adj* (*COMM*) that can be
delivered.
livraison [livʀɛzɔ̃] *nf* delivery; ~ **à domicile**
home delivery (service).
livre [livʀ(ə)] *nm* book; (*imprimerie etc*): **le** ~ the
book industry ♦ *nf* (*poids, monnaie*) pound;
traduire qch à ~ **ouvert** to translate sth off
the cuff *ou* at sight; ~ **blanc** official report
(*prepared by independent body, following war,
natural disaster etc*); ~ **de bord** (*NAVIG*)
logbook; ~ **de comptes** account(s) book; ~
de cuisine cookery book (*BRIT*), cookbook; ~
de messe mass *ou* prayer book; ~ **d'or**
visitors' book; ~ **de poche** paperback (*cheap
and pocket size*); ~ **verte** green pound.
livré, e [livʀe] *nf* livery ♦ *adj*: ~ **à** (*l'anarchie
etc*) given over to; ~ **à soi-même** left to
oneself *ou* one's own devices.
livrer [livʀe] *vt* (*COMM*) to deliver; (*otage,
coupable*) to hand over; (*secret, information*)
to give away; **se** ~ **à** (*se confier*) to confide
in; (*se rendre*) to give o.s. up to;
(*s'abandonner à: débauche etc*) to give o.s. up
ou over to; (*faire: pratiques, actes*) to indulge
in; (*travail*) to be engaged in, engage in;
(: *sport*) to practise; (: *enquête*) to carry out;
~ **bataille** to give battle.
livresque [livʀɛsk(ə)] *adj* (*péj*) bookish.
livret [livʀɛ] *nm* booklet; (*d'opéra*) libretto (*pl -
s*); ~ **de caisse d'épargne** (savings) bank-
book; ~ **de famille** (official) family record
book; ~ **scolaire** (school) report book.
livreur, euse [livʀœʀ, -øz] *nm/f* delivery boy
ou man/girl *ou* woman.
LO *sigle f* (= *Lutte ouvrière*) *political party*.
lob [lɔb] *nm* lob.
lobe [lɔb] *nm*: ~ **de l'oreille** ear lobe.
lobé, e [lɔbe] *adj* (*ARCHIT*) foiled.
lober [lɔbe] *vt* to lob.
local, e, aux [lɔkal, -o] *adj* local ♦ *nm* (*salle*)
premises *pl* ♦ *nmpl* premises.
localement [lɔkalmɑ̃] *adv* locally.
localisé, e [lɔkalize] *adj* localized.
localiser [lɔkalize] *vt* (*repérer*) to locate, place;
(*limiter*) to localize, confine.
localité [lɔkalite] *nf* locality.
locataire [lɔkatɛʀ] *nm/f* tenant; (*de chambre*)
lodger.
locatif, ive [lɔkatif, -iv] *adj* (*charges,
réparations*) incumbent upon the tenant;
(*valeur*) rental; (*immeuble*) with rented flats,
used as a letting *ou* rental (*US*) concern.
location [lɔkasjɔ̃] *nf* (*par le locataire*) renting;
(*par l'usager: de voiture etc*) hiring (*BRIT*),

renting (*US*); (*par le propriétaire*) renting out,
letting; hiring out (*BRIT*); (*de billets, places*)
booking; (*bureau*) booking office; "~ **de
voitures**" "car hire (*BRIT*) *ou* rental (*US*)".
location-vente [lɔkasjɔ̃vɑ̃t] *nf* form of hire
purchase (*BRIT*) *ou* instalment plan (*US*).
lock-out [lɔkawt] *nm inv* lockout.
locomoteur, trice [lɔkɔmɔtœʀ, -tʀis] *adj, nf*
locomotive.
locomotion [lɔkɔmɔsjɔ̃] *nf* locomotion.
locomotive [lɔkɔmɔtiv] *nf* locomotive, engine;
(*fig*) pacesetter, pacemaker.
locuteur, trice [lɔkytœʀ, -tʀis] *nm/f* (*LING*)
speaker.
locution [lɔkysjɔ̃] *nf* phrase.
loden [lɔdɛn] *nm* loden.
lofer [lɔfe] *vi* (*NAVIG*) to luff.
logarithme [lɔgaʀitm(ə)] *nm* logarithm.
loge [lɔʒ] *nf* (*THÉÂT: d'artiste*) dressing room;
(: *de spectateurs*) box; (*de concierge, franc-
maçon*) lodge.
logeable [lɔʒabl(ə)] *adj* habitable; (*spacieux*)
roomy.
logement [lɔʒmɑ̃] *nm* flat (*BRIT*), apartment
(*US*); accommodation *no pl* (*BRIT*),
accommodations *pl* (*US*); **le** ~ housing;
chercher un ~ to look for a flat *ou*
apartment, look for accommodation(s);
construire des ~**s bon marché** to build
cheap housing *sg*; **crise du** ~ housing
shortage; ~ **de fonction** (*ADMIN*) company
flat *ou* apartment, accommodation(s)
provided with one's job.
loger [lɔʒe] *vt* to accommodate ♦ *vi* to live; **se**
~: **trouver à se** ~ to find accommodation; **se**
~ **dans** (*suj: balle, flèche*) to lodge itself in.
logeur, euse [lɔʒœʀ, -øz] *nm/f* landlord/
landlady.
loggia [lɔdʒja] *nf* loggia.
logiciel [lɔʒisjɛl] *nm* software.
logicien, ne [lɔʒisjɛ̃, -ɛn] *nm/f* logician.
logique [lɔʒik] *adj* logical ♦ *nf* logic; **c'est** ~ it
stands to reason.
logiquement [lɔʒikmɑ̃] *adv* logically.
logis [lɔʒi] *nm* home; abode, dwelling.
logisticien, ne [lɔʒistisjɛ̃, -ɛn] *nm/f* logistician.
logistique [lɔʒistik] *nf* logistics *sg* ♦ *adj*
logistic.
logo [lɔgo], **logotype** [lɔgɔtip] *nm* logo.
loi [lwa] *nf* law; **faire la** ~ to lay down the law;
les ~**s de la mode** (*fig*) the dictates of
fashion; **proposition de** ~ (private
member's) bill; **projet de** ~ (government)
bill.
loi-cadre, *pl* **lois-cadres** [lwakadʀ(ə)] *nf* (*POL*)
blueprint law.
loin [lwɛ̃] *adv* far; (*dans le temps: futur*) a long
way off; (: *passé*) a long time ago; **plus** ~
further; **moins** ~ (**que**) not as far (as); ~ **de**
far from; **pas** ~ **de 1 000 F** not far off 1000
F; **au** ~ far off; **de** ~ *adv* from a distance;
(*fig: de beaucoup*) by far; **il vient de** ~ he's

come a long way; he comes from a long way away; **de ~ en ~** here and there; (*de temps en temps*) (every) now and then; **~ de là** (*au contraire*) far from it.

lointain, e [lwɛ̃tɛ̃, -ɛn] *adj* faraway, distant; (*dans le futur, passé*) distant, far-off; (*cause, parent*) remote, distant ♦ *nm*: **dans le ~** in the distance.

loi-programme, *pl* **lois-programmes** [lwapʀɔɡʀam] *nf* (*POL*) act providing framework for government programme.

loir [lwaʀ] *nm* dormouse (*pl* -mice).

Loire [lwaʀ] *nf*: **la ~** the Loire.

loisible [lwazibl(ə)] *adj*: **il vous est ~ de …** you are free to ….

loisir [lwaziʀ] *nm*: **heures de ~** spare time; **~s** *nmpl* leisure *sg*; (*activités*) leisure activities; **avoir le ~ de faire** to have the time *ou* opportunity to do; (**tout**) **à ~** (*en prenant son temps*) at leisure; (*autant qu'on le désire*) at one's pleasure.

lombaire [lɔ̃bɛʀ] *adj* lumbar.

lombalgie [lɔ̃balʒi] *nf* back pain.

lombard, e [lɔ̃baʀ, -aʀd(ə)] *adj* Lombard.

Lombardie [lɔ̃baʀdi] *nf*: **la ~** Lombardy.

londonien, ne [lɔ̃dɔnjɛ̃, -ɛn] *adj* London *cpd*, of London ♦ *nm/f*: **L~, ne** Londoner.

Londres [lɔ̃dʀ(ə)] *n* London.

long, longue [lɔ̃, lɔ̃ɡ] *adj* long ♦ *adv*: **en savoir ~** to know a great deal ♦ *nm*: **de 3 m de ~** 3 m long, 3 m in length ♦ *nf*: **à la longue** in the end; **faire ~ feu** to fizzle out; **ne pas faire ~ feu** not to last long; **au ~ cours** (*NAVIG*) ocean *cpd*, ocean-going; **de longue date** *adj* long-standing; **longue durée** *adj* long-term; **de longue haleine** *adj* long-term; **être ~ à faire** to take a long time to do; **en ~** *adv* lengthwise, lengthways; (**tout**) **le ~ de** (all) along; **tout au ~ de** (*année, vie*) throughout; **de ~ en large** (*marcher*) to and fro, up and down; **en ~ et en large** (*fig*) in every detail.

longanimité [lɔ̃ɡanimite] *nf* forbearance.

long-courrier [lɔ̃kuʀje] *nm* (*AVIAT*) long-haul aircraft.

longe [lɔ̃ʒ] *nf* (*corde: pour attacher*) tether; (*pour mener*) lead; (*CULIN*) loin.

longer [lɔ̃ʒe] *vt* to go (*ou* walk *ou* drive) along(side); (*suj: mur, route*) to border.

longévité [lɔ̃ʒevite] *nf* longevity.

longiligne [lɔ̃ʒilin] *adj* long-limbed.

longitude [lɔ̃ʒityd] *nf* longitude; **à 45° de ~ ouest** at 45° longitude west.

longitudinal, e, aux [lɔ̃ʒitydinal, -o] *adj* longitudinal, lengthways; (*entaille, vallée*) running lengthways.

longtemps [lɔ̃tɑ̃] *adv* (for) a long time, (for) long; **ça ne va pas durer ~** it won't last long; **avant ~** before long; **pour/pendant ~** for a long time; **je n'en ai pas pour ~** I shan't be long; **mettre ~ à faire** to take a long time to do; **il en a pour ~** he'll be a long time; **il y a ~ que je travaille** I have been working (for)

a long time; **il n'y a pas ~ que je l'ai rencontré** it's not long since I met him.

longue [lɔ̃ɡ] *adj f voir* **long**.

longuement [lɔ̃ɡmɑ̃] *adv* (*longtemps: parler, regarder*) for a long time; (*en détail: expliquer, raconter*) at length.

longueur [lɔ̃ɡœʀ] *nf* length; **~s** *nfpl* (*fig: d'un film etc*) tedious parts; **sur une ~ de 10 km** for *ou* over 10 km; **en ~** *adv* lengthwise, lengthways; **tirer en ~** to drag on; **à ~ de journée** all day long; **d'une ~** (*gagner*) by a length; **~ d'onde** wavelength.

longue-vue [lɔ̃ɡvy] *nf* telescope.

looping [lupiŋ] *nm* (*AVIAT*): **faire des ~s** to loop the loop.

lopin [lɔpɛ̃] *nm*: **~ de terre** patch of land.

loquace [lɔkas] *adj* talkative, loquacious.

loque [lɔk] *nf* (*personne*) wreck; **~s** *nfpl* (*habits*) rags; **être** *ou* **tomber en ~s** to be in rags.

loquet [lɔkɛ] *nm* latch.

lorgner [lɔʀɲe] *vt* to eye; (*convoiter*) to have one's eye on.

lorgnette [lɔʀɲɛt] *nf* opera glasses *pl*.

lorgnon [lɔʀɲɔ̃] *nm* (*face-à-main*) lorgnette; (*pince-nez*) pince-nez.

loriot [lɔʀjo] *nm* (*golden*) oriole.

lorrain, e [lɔʀɛ̃, -ɛn] *adj* of *ou* from Lorraine; **quiche ~e** quiche lorraine.

lors [lɔʀ]: **~ de** *prép* (*au moment de*) at the time of; (*pendant*) during; **~ même que** even though.

lorsque [lɔʀsk(ə)] *conj* when, as.

losange [lɔzɑ̃ʒ] *nm* diamond; (*GÉOM*) lozenge; **en ~** diamond-shaped.

lot [lo] *nm* (*part*) share; (*de loterie*) prize; (*fig: destin*) fate, lot; (*COMM, INFORM*) batch; **~ de consolation** consolation prize.

loterie [lɔtʀi] *nf* lottery; (*tombola*) raffle; **L~ nationale** (*formerly*) French national lottery.

loti, e [lɔti] *adj*: **bien/mal ~** well-/badly off, lucky/unlucky.

lotion [losjɔ̃] *nf* lotion; **~ après rasage** after-shave (lotion); **~ capillaire** hair lotion.

lotir [lɔtiʀ] *vt* (*terrain: diviser*) to divide into plots; (*: vendre*) to sell by lots.

lotissement [lɔtismɑ̃] *nm* (*groupe de maisons, d'immeubles*) housing development; (*parcelle*) (building) plot, lot.

loto [lɔto] *nm* lotto.

Le Loto *is a state-run national lottery with large cash prizes. Participants select 7 numbers out of 49. There is a sliding scale of winnings: all 7 numbers correct wins the top prize, 6 correct wins a smaller sum and so on. The draw is televised twice weekly.*

---

lotte [lɔt] *nf* (*ZOOL: de rivière*) burbot; (*: de mer*) monkfish.

louable [lwabl(ə)] *adj* (*appartement, garage*) rentable; (*action, personne*) praiseworthy, commendable.

louage [lwaʒ] *nm*: **voiture de** ~ hired (*BRIT*) *ou* rented (*US*) car; (*à louer*) hire (*BRIT*) *ou* rental (*US*) car.

louange [lwɑ̃ʒ] *nf*: **à la** ~ **de** in praise of; ~**s** *nfpl* praise *sg*.

loubar(d) [lubaʀ] *nm* (*fam*) lout.

louche [luʃ] *adj* shady, fishy, dubious ♦ *nf* ladle.

loucher [luʃe] *vi* to squint; (*fig*): ~ **sur** to have one's (beady) eye on.

louer [lwe] *vt* (*maison: suj: propriétaire*) to let, rent (out); (*: locataire*) to rent; (*voiture etc*) to hire out (*BRIT*), rent (out); to hire (*BRIT*), rent; (*réserver*) to book; (*faire l'éloge de*) to praise; **"à** ~**"** "to let" (*BRIT*), "for rent" (*US*); ~ **qn de** to praise sb for; **se** ~ **de** to congratulate o.s. on.

loufoque [lufɔk] *adj* (*fam*) crazy, zany.

loukoum [lukum] *nm* Turkish delight.

loulou [lulu] *nm* (*chien*) spitz; ~ **de Poméranie** Pomeranian (dog).

loup [lu] *nm* wolf (*pl* wolves); (*poisson*) bass; (*masque*) (eye) mask; **jeune** ~ young go-getter; ~ **de mer** (*marin*) old seadog.

loupe [lup] *nf* magnifying glass; ~ **de noyer** burr walnut; **à la** ~ (*fig*) in minute detail.

louper [lupe] *vt* (*fam: manquer*) to miss; (*: gâcher*) to mess up, bungle.

lourd, e [luʀ, luʀd(ə)] *adj* heavy; (*chaleur, temps*) sultry; (*fig: personne, style*) heavy-handed ♦ *adv*: **peser** ~ to be heavy; ~ **de** (*menaces*) charged with; (*conséquences*) fraught with; **artillerie/industrie** ~**e** heavy artillery/industry.

lourdaud, e [luʀdo, -od] *adj* oafish.

lourdement [luʀdəmɑ̃] *adv* heavily; **se tromper** ~ to make a big mistake.

lourdeur [luʀdœʀ] *nf* heaviness; ~ **d'estomac** indigestion *no pl*.

loustic [lustik] *nm* (*fam péj*) joker.

loutre [lutʀ(ə)] *nf* otter; (*fourrure*) otter skin.

louve [luv] *nf* she-wolf.

louveteau, x [luvto] *nm* (*ZOOL*) wolf-cub; (*scout*) cub (scout).

louvoyer [luvwaje] *vi* (*NAVIG*) to tack; (*fig*) to hedge, evade the issue.

lover [lɔve]: **se** ~ *vi* to coil up.

loyal, e, aux [lwajal, -o] *adj* (*fidèle*) loyal, faithful; (*fair-play*) fair.

loyalement [lwajalmɑ̃] *adv* loyally, faithfully; fairly.

loyalisme [lwajalism(ə)] *nm* loyalty.

loyauté [lwajote] *nf* loyalty, faithfulness; fairness.

loyer [lwaje] *nm* rent; ~ **de l'argent** interest rate.

LP *sigle m* (= *lycée professionnel*) *secondary school for vocational training.*

LPO *sigle f* (= *Ligue pour la protection des oiseaux*) *bird protection society.*

LSD *sigle m* (= *Lyserg Säure Diäthylamid*) LSD.

lu, e [ly] *pp de* **lire**.

lubie [lybi] *nf* whim, craze.

lubricité [lybʀisite] *nf* lust.

lubrifiant [lybʀifjɑ̃] *nm* lubricant.

lubrifier [lybʀifje] *vt* to lubricate.

lubrique [lybʀik] *adj* lecherous.

lucarne [lykaʀn(ə)] *nf* skylight.

lucide [lysid] *adj* (*conscient*) lucid, conscious; (*perspicace*) clear-headed.

lucidité [lysidite] *nf* lucidity.

luciole [lysjɔl] *nf* firefly.

lucratif, ive [lykʀatif, -iv] *adj* lucrative; profitable; **à but non** ~ non profit-making.

ludique [lydik] *adj* play *cpd*, playing.

ludothèque [lydɔtɛk] *nf* toy library.

luette [lɥɛt] *nf* uvula.

lueur [lɥœʀ] *nf* (*chatoyante*) glimmer *no pl*; (*métallique, mouillée*) gleam *no pl*; (*rougeoyante, chaude*) glow *no pl*; (*pâle*) (faint) light; (*fig*) spark; (*: d'espérance*) glimmer, gleam.

luge [lyʒ] *nf* sledge (*BRIT*), sled (*US*); **faire de la** ~ to sledge (*BRIT*), sled (*US*), toboggan.

lugubre [lygybʀ(ə)] *adj* gloomy; dismal.

════════════════════════════ *MOT-CLÉ*

lui [lɥi] *pp de* **luire**
  ♦ *pron* **1** (*objet indirect: mâle*) (to) him; (*: femelle*) (to) her; (*: chose, animal*) (to) it; **je** ~ **ai parlé** I have spoken to him (*ou* to her); **il** ~ **a offert un cadeau** he gave him (*ou* her) a present; **je le** ~ **ai donné** I gave it to him (*ou* her)
  2 (*après préposition, comparatif: personne*) him; (*: chose, animal*) it; **elle est contente de** ~ she is pleased with him; **je la connais mieux que** ~ I know her better than he does; I know her better than him; **cette voiture est à** ~ this car belongs to him, this is HIS car
  3 (*sujet, forme emphatique*) he; ~, **il est à Paris** HE is in Paris; **c'est** ~ **qui l'a fait** HE did it.

lui-même [lɥimɛm] *pron* (*personne*) himself; (*chose*) itself.

luire [lɥiʀ] *vi* (*gén*) to shine, gleam; (*surface mouillée*) to glisten; (*reflets chauds, cuivrés*) to glow.

luisant, e [lɥizɑ̃, -ɑ̃t] *vb voir* **luire** ♦ *adj* shining, gleaming.

lumbago [lɔ̃bago] *nm* lumbago.

lumière [lymjɛʀ] *nf* light; ~**s** *nfpl* (*d'une personne*) knowledge *sg*, wisdom *sg*; **à la** ~ **de** by the light of; (*fig: événements*) in the light of; **fais de la** ~ let's have some light, give us some light; **faire (toute) la** ~ **sur** (*fig*) to clarify (completely); **mettre en** ~ (*fig*) to highlight; ~ **du jour/soleil** day/sunlight.

luminaire [lyminɛʀ] *nm* lamp, light.

lumineux, euse [lyminø, -øz] *adj* (*émettant de la lumière*) luminous; (*éclairé*) illuminated; (*ciel, journée, couleur*) bright; (*relatif à la*

lumière: rayon etc) of light, light *cpd*; (*fig: regard*) radiant.
luminosité [lyminɔzite] *nf* (*TECH*) luminosity.
lump [lœp] *nm*: **œufs de** ~ lump-fish roe.
lunaire [lynɛʀ] *adj* lunar, moon *cpd*.
lunatique [lynatik] *adj* whimsical, temperamental.
lunch [lœntʃ] *nm* (*réception*) buffet lunch.
lundi [lœdi] *nm* Monday; **on est** ~ it's Monday; **le** ~ **20 août** Monday 20th August; **il est venu** ~ he came on Monday; **le(s)** ~**(s)** on Mondays; **à** ~! see you (on) Monday!; ~ **de Pâques** Easter Monday; ~ **de Pentecôte** Whit Monday (*BRIT*).
lune [lyn] *nf* moon; **pleine/nouvelle** ~ full/new moon; **être dans la** ~ (*distrait*) to have one's head in the clouds; ~ **de miel** honeymoon.
luné, e [lyne] *adj*: **bien/mal** ~ in a good/bad mood.
lunette [lynɛt] *nf*: ~**s** *nfpl* glasses, spectacles; (*protectrices*) goggles; ~ **d'approche** telescope; ~ **arrière** (*AUTO*) rear window; ~**s noires** dark glasses; ~**s de soleil** sunglasses.
lurent [lyʀ] *vb voir* **lire**.
lurette [lyʀɛt] *nf*: **il y a belle** ~ ages ago.
luron, ne [lyʀɔ̃, -ɔn] *nm/f* lad/lass; **joyeux** *ou* **gai** ~ gay dog.
lus [ly] *etc vb voir* **lire**.
lustre [lystʀ(ə)] *nm* (*de plafond*) chandelier; (*fig: éclat*) lustre.
lustrer [lystʀe] *vt*: ~ **qch** (*faire briller*) to make sth shine; (*user*) to make sth shiny.
lut [ly] *vb voir* **lire**.
luth [lyt] *nm* lute.
luthier [lytje] *nm* (stringed-)instrument maker.
lutin [lytɛ̃] *nm* imp, goblin.
lutrin [lytʀɛ̃] *nm* lectern.
lutte [lyt] *nf* (*conflit*) struggle; (*SPORT*): **la** ~ wrestling; **de haute** ~ after a hard-fought struggle; ~ **des classes** class struggle; ~ **libre** (*SPORT*) all-in wrestling.
lutter [lyte] *vi* to fight, struggle; (*SPORT*) to wrestle.
lutteur, euse [lytœʀ, -øz] *nm/f* (*SPORT*) wrestler; (*fig*) battler, fighter.
luxation [lyksasjɔ̃] *nf* dislocation.
luxe [lyks(ə)] *nm* luxury; **un** ~ **de** (*détails, précautions*) a wealth of; **de** ~ *adj* luxury *cpd*.
Luxembourg [lyksɑ̃buʀ] *nm*: **le** ~ Luxembourg.
luxembourgeois, e [lyksɑ̃buʀʒwa, -waz] *adj* of *ou* from Luxembourg ♦ *nm/f*: **L**~, **e** inhabitant *ou* native of Luxembourg.
luxer [lykse] *vt*: **se** ~ **l'épaule** to dislocate one's shoulder.
luxueusement [lyksyøzmɑ̃] *adv* luxuriously.
luxueux, euse [lyksyø, -øz] *adj* luxurious.
luxure [lyksyʀ] *nf* lust.
luxuriant, e [lyksyʀjɑ̃, -ɑ̃t] *adj* luxuriant, lush.
luzerne [lyzɛʀn(ə)] *nf* lucerne, alfalfa.
lycée [lise] *nm* (state) secondary (*BRIT*) *ou*

high (*US*) school; ~ **technique** technical secondary *ou* high school.

French pupils spend the last three years of their secondary education at a *lycée*, where they sit their **baccalauréat** before leaving school or going on to higher education. There are various types of *lycée*, including the "*lycées d'enseignement technologique*" providing technical courses and the "*lycées d'enseignement professionnel*" providing vocational courses. Some *lycées*, particularly those with a wide catchment area or those providing specialist courses, have boarding facilities; *see also* **école maternelle/primaire**, **collège**.

lycéen, ne [liseɛ̃, -ɛn] *nm/f* secondary school pupil.
Lycra [likʀa] *nm* ® Lycra ®.
lymphatique [lɛ̃fatik] *adj* (*fig*) lethargic, sluggish.
lymphe [lɛ̃f] *nf* lymph.
lyncher [lɛ̃ʃe] *vt* to lynch.
lynx [lɛ̃ks] *nm* lynx.
Lyon [ljɔ̃] *n* Lyons.
lyonnais, e [ljɔnɛ, -ɛz] *adj* of *ou* from Lyons; (*CULIN*) Lyonnaise.
lyophilisé, e [ljɔfilize] *adj* freeze-dried.
lyre [liʀ] *nf* lyre.
lyrique [liʀik] *adj* lyrical; (*OPÉRA*) lyric; **artiste** ~ opera singer; **comédie** ~ comic opera; **théâtre** ~ opera house (*for light opera*).
lyrisme [liʀism(ə)] *nm* lyricism.
lys [lis] *nm* lily.

M m

M, m [ɛm] *nm inv* M, m ♦ *abr* = **majeur, masculin, mètre, Monsieur**; (= *million*) M; **M comme Marcel** M for Mike.
m' [m] *pron voir* **me**.
MA *sigle m* = **maître auxiliaire**.
ma [ma] *dét voir* **mon**.
maboul, e [mabul] *adj* (*fam*) loony.
macabre [makabʀ(ə)] *adj* macabre, gruesome.
macadam [makadam] *nm* tarmac (*BRIT*), asphalt.
Macao [makao] *nf* Macao.
macaron [makaʀɔ̃] *nm* (*gâteau*) macaroon; (*insigne*) (round) badge.
macaroni(s) [makaʀɔni] *nm(pl)* macaroni *sg*; ~ **au fromage** *ou* **au gratin** macaroni cheese (*BRIT*), macaroni and cheese (*US*).
Macédoine [masedwan] *nf* Macedonia.

macédoine [masedwan] *nf*: ~ **de fruits** fruit salad; ~ **de légumes** mixed vegetables *pl*.

macédonien, ne [masedɔnjɛ̃, -ɛn] *adj* Macedonian ♦ *nm/f*: **M~, ne** Macedonian.

macérer [maseʀe] *vi, vt* to macerate; (*dans du vinaigre*) to pickle.

mâchefer [mɑʃfɛʀ] *nm* clinker, cinders *pl*.

mâcher [mɑʃe] *vt* to chew; **ne pas ~ ses mots** not to mince one's words; ~ **le travail à qn** (*fig*) to spoonfeed sb, do half sb's work for him.

machiavélique [makjavelik] *adj* Machiavellian.

machin [maʃɛ̃] *nm* (*fam*) thingamajig, thing; (*personne*): **M~** what's-his(*ou*-her)-name.

machinal, e, aux [maʃinal, -o] *adj* mechanical, automatic.

machination [maʃinasjɔ̃] *nf* scheming, frame-up.

machine [maʃin] *nf* machine; (*locomotive; de navire etc*) engine; (*fig: rouages*) machinery; (*fam: personne*): **M~** what's-her-name; **faire** ~ **arrière** (*NAVIG*) to go astern; (*fig*) to back-pedal; ~ **à laver/coudre/tricoter** washing/sewing/knitting machine; ~ **à écrire** typewriter; ~ **à sous** fruit machine; ~ **à vapeur** steam engine.

machine-outil, *pl* **machines-outils** [maʃinuti] *nf* machine tool.

machinerie [maʃinʀi] *nf* machinery, plant; (*d'un navire*) engine room.

machinisme [maʃinism(ə)] *nm* mechanization.

machiniste [maʃinist(ə)] *nm* (*THÉÂT*) scene shifter; (*de bus, métro*) driver.

mâchoire [mɑʃwaʀ] *nf* jaw; ~ **de frein** brake shoe.

mâchonner [mɑʃɔne] *vt* to chew (at).

mâcon [mɑkɔ̃] *nm* Mâcon wine.

maçon [masɔ̃] *nm* bricklayer; (*constructeur*) builder.

maçonner [masɔne] *vt* (*revêtir*) to face, render (with cement); (*boucher*) to brick up.

maçonnerie [masɔnʀi] *nf* (*murs: de brique*) brickwork; (*: de pierre*) masonry, stonework; (*activité*) bricklaying; building; ~ **de béton** concrete.

maçonnique [masɔnik] *adj* masonic.

macramé [makʀame] *nm* macramé.

macrobiotique [makʀɔbjɔtik] *adj* macrobiotic.

macrocosme [makʀɔkɔsm(ə)] *nm* macrocosm.

macro-économie [makʀɔekɔnɔmi] *nf* macroeconomics *sg*.

macrophotographie [makʀɔfɔtɔgʀafi] *nf* macrophotography.

maculer [makyle] *vt* to stain; (*TYPO*) to mackle.

Madagascar [madagaskaʀ] *nf* Madagascar.

Madame [madam], *pl* **Mesdames** [medam] *nf*: ~ **X** Mrs X; **occupez-vous de** ~/**Monsieur/Mademoiselle** please serve this lady/gentleman/(young) lady; **bonjour** ~/

Monsieur/Mademoiselle good morning; (*ton déférent*) good morning Madam/Sir/Madam; (*le nom est connu*) good morning Mrs X/Mr X/Miss X; ~/**Monsieur/Mademoiselle!** (*pour appeler*) excuse me!; (*ton déférent*) Madam/Sir/Miss!; ~/**Monsieur/Mademoiselle** (*sur lettre*) Dear Madam/Sir/Madam; **chère** ~/**cher Monsieur/chère Mademoiselle** Dear Mrs X/Mr X/Miss X; ~ **la Directrice** the director; the manageress; the headteacher; **Mesdames** Ladies.

Madeleine [madlɛn]: **îles de la** ~ *nfpl* Magdalen Islands.

madeleine [madlɛn] *nf* madeleine, ≈ sponge finger cake.

Madelinot, e [madlino, -ɔt] *nm/f* inhabitant *ou* native of the Magdalen Islands.

Mademoiselle [madmwazɛl], *pl* **Mesdemoiselles** [medmwazɛl] *nf* Miss; *voir aussi* **Madame**.

Madère [madɛʀ] *nf* Madeira ♦ *nm*: **m~** Madeira (wine).

madone [madɔn] *nf* madonna.

madré, e [madʀe] *adj* crafty, wily.

Madrid [madʀid] *n* Madrid.

madrier [madʀije] *nm* beam.

madrigal, aux [madʀigal, -o] *nm* madrigal.

madrilène [madʀilɛn] *adj* of *ou* from Madrid.

maestria [maɛstʀija] *nf* (*masterly*) skill.

maestro [maɛstʀo] *nm* maestro.

maf(f)ia [mafja] *nf* Maf(f)ia.

magasin [magazɛ̃] *nm* (*boutique*) shop; (*entrepôt*) warehouse; (*d'arme, appareil-photo*) magazine; **en** ~ (*COMM*) in stock; **faire les** ~**s** to go (a)round the shops, do the shops; ~ **d'alimentation** grocer's shop (*BRIT*), grocery store (*US*).

magasinier [magazinje] *nm* warehouseman.

magazine [magazin] *nm* magazine.

mage [maʒ] *nm*: **les Rois M~s** the Magi, the (Three) Wise Men.

Maghreb [magʀɛb] *nm*: **le** ~ the Maghreb, North(-West) Africa.

maghrébin, e [magʀebɛ̃, -in] *adj* of *ou* from the Maghreb ♦ *nm/f*: **M~, e** North African, Maghrebi.

magicien, ne [maʒisjɛ̃, -ɛn] *nm/f* magician.

magie [maʒi] *nf* magic; ~ **noire** black magic.

magique [maʒik] *adj* (*occulte*) magic; (*fig*) magical.

magistral, e, aux [maʒistʀal, -o] *adj* (*œuvre, adresse*) masterly; (*ton*) authoritative; (*gifle etc*) sound, resounding; (*ex cathedra*): **enseignement** ~ lecturing, lectures *pl*; **cours** ~ lecture.

magistrat [maʒistʀa] *nm* magistrate.

magistrature [maʒistʀatyʀ] *nf* magistracy, magistrature; ~ **assise** judges *pl*, bench; ~ **debout** state prosecutors *pl*.

magma [magma] *nm* (*GÉO*) magma; (*fig*) jumble.

magnanerie [maɲanʀi] *nf* silk farm.

magnanime [maɲanim] *adj* magnanimous.
magnanimité [maɲanimite] *nf* magnanimity.
magnat [magna] *nm* tycoon, magnate; ~ **de la presse** press baron.
magner [maɲe]: **se** ~ *vi* (*fam*) to get a move on.
magnésie [maɲezi] *nf* magnesia.
magnésium [maɲezjɔm] *nm* magnesium.
magnétique [maɲetik] *adj* magnetic.
magnétiser [maɲetize] *vt* to magnetize; (*fig*) to mesmerize, hypnotize.
magnétiseur, euse [maɲetizœʀ, -øz] *nm/f* hypnotist.
magnétisme [maɲetism(ə)] *nm* magnetism.
magnéto [maɲeto] *nm* (= *magnétocassette*) cassette deck; (= *magnétophone*) tape recorder.
magnétocassette [maɲetɔkasɛt] *nm* cassette deck.
magnétophone [maɲetɔfɔn] *nm* tape recorder; ~ **à cassettes** cassette recorder.
magnétoscope [maɲetɔskɔp] *nm*: ~ **(à cassette)** video (recorder).
magnificence [maɲifisɑ̃s] *nf* (*faste*) magnificence, splendour (*BRIT*), splendor (*US*); (*générosité, prodigalité*) munificence, lavishness.
magnifier [maɲifje] *vt* (*glorifier*) to glorify; (*idéaliser*) to idealize.
magnifique [maɲifik] *adj* magnificent.
magnifiquement [maɲifikmɑ̃] *adv* magnificently.
magnolia [maɲɔlja] *nm* magnolia.
magnum [magnɔm] *nm* magnum.
magot [mago] *nm* (*argent*) pile (of money); (*économies*) nest egg.
magouille [maguj] *nf* (*fam*) scheming.
mahométan, e [maɔmetɑ̃, -an] *adj* Mohammedan, Mahometan.
mai [mɛ] *nm* May; *voir aussi* **juillet**.

Le premier mai *is a public holiday in France commemorating demonstrations by the unions in the United States in 1886 to secure the eight-hour working day. It is traditional in France to exchange and wear sprigs of lily of the valley.*
Le 8 mai *is a public holiday in France commemorating the surrender of the German army to Eisenhower on May 7, 1945. There are parades of ex-servicemen in most towns. The social upheavals of May and June 1968, marked by student demonstrations, workers' strikes and general rioting, are generally referred to as "les événements de* mai 68". *De Gaulle's government survived the onslaught, but reforms in education and a move towards decentralization ensued.*

---

maigre [mɛgʀ(ə)] *adj* (very) thin, skinny; (*viande*) lean; (*fromage*) low-fat; (*végétation*) thin, sparse; (*fig*) poor, meagre, skimpy

♦ *adv*: **faire** ~ not to eat meat; **jours** ~**s** days of abstinence, fish days.
maigrelet, te [mɛgʀəlɛ, -ɛt] *adj* skinny, scrawny.
maigreur [mɛgʀœʀ] *nf* thinness.
maigrichon, ne [megʀiʃɔ̃, -ɔn] *adj* = **maigrelet, te**.
maigrir [megʀiʀ] *vi* to get thinner, lose weight ♦ *vt*: ~ **qn** (*suj: vêtement*) to make sb look slim(mer).
mailing [mɛliŋ] *nm* direct mail *no pl*; **un** ~ a mailshot.
maille [maj] *nf* (*boucle*) stitch; (*ouverture*) hole (in the mesh); **avoir** ~ **à partir avec qn** to have a brush with sb; ~ **à l'endroit/à l'envers** knit one/purl one; (*boucle*) plain/purl stitch.
maillechort [majʃɔʀ] *nm* nickel silver.
maillet [majɛ] *nm* mallet.
maillon [majɔ̃] *nm* link.
maillot [majo] *nm* (*aussi*: ~ **de corps**) vest; (*de danseur*) leotard; (*de sportif*) jersey; ~ **de bain** bathing costume (*BRIT*), swimsuit; (*d'homme*) bathing trunks *pl*; ~ **une pièce** one-piece swimsuit; ~ **deux pièces** two-piece swimsuit, bikini.
main [mɛ̃] *nf* hand; **la** ~ **dans la** ~ hand in hand; **à deux** ~**s** with both hands; **à une** ~ with one hand; **à la** ~ (*tenir, avoir*) in one's hand; (*faire, tricoter etc*) by hand; **donner la** ~ to hold hands; **donner** *ou* **tendre la** ~ **à qn** to hold out one's hand to sb; **se serrer la** ~ to shake hands; **serrer la** ~ **à qn** to shake hands with sb; **sous la** ~ to *ou* at hand; **haut les** ~**s!** hands up!; **à** ~ **levée** (*ART*) freehand; **à** ~**s levées** (*voter*) with a show of hands; **attaque à** ~ **armée** armed attack; **à** ~ **droite/gauche** to the right/left; **à remettre en** ~**s propres** to be delivered personally; **de première** ~ (*renseignement*) first-hand; (*COMM: voiture etc*) with only one previous owner; **faire** ~ **basse sur** to help o.s. to; **mettre la dernière** ~ **à** to put the finishing touches to; **mettre la** ~ **à la pâte** (*fig*) to lend a hand; **prendre qch en** ~ (*fig*) to take sth in hand; **avoir/passer la** ~ (*CARTES*) to lead/hand over the lead; **s'en laver les** ~**s** (*fig*) to wash one's hands of it; **se faire/perdre la** ~ to get one's hand in/lose one's touch; **avoir qch bien en** ~ to have got the hang of sth; **en un tour de** ~ (*fig*) in the twinkling of an eye; ~ **courante** handrail.
mainate [mɛnat] *nm* myna(h) bird.
main-d'œuvre [mɛ̃dœvʀ(ə)] *nf* manpower, labour (*BRIT*), labor (*US*).
main-forte [mɛ̃fɔʀt(ə)] *nf*: **prêter** ~ **à qn** to come to sb's assistance.
mainmise [mɛ̃miz] *nf* seizure; (*fig*): **avoir la** ~ **sur** to have a complete hold on.
maint, e [mɛ̃, mɛ̃t] *adj* many a; ~**s** many; **à** ~**es reprises** time and (time) again.
maintenance [mɛ̃tnɑ̃s] *nf* maintenance.

maintenant [mɛ̃tnɑ̃] adv now; (actuellement) nowadays.
maintenir [mɛ̃tniʀ] vt (retenir, soutenir) to support; (contenir: foule etc) to keep in check, hold back; (conserver) to maintain, uphold; (affirmer) to maintain; se ~ vi (paix, temps) to hold; (préjugé) to persist; (malade) to remain stable.
maintien [mɛ̃tjɛ̃] nm maintaining, upholding; (attitude) bearing; ~ **de l'ordre** maintenance of law and order.
maintiendrai [mɛ̃tjɛ̃dʀe], **maintiens** [mɛ̃tjɛ̃] etc vb voir **maintenir**.
maire [mɛʀ] nm mayor.
mairie [meʀi] nf (endroit) town hall; (administration) town council.
mais [mɛ] conj but; ~ **non**! of course not!; ~ **enfin** but after all; (indignation) look here!; ~ **encore**? is that all?
maïs [mais] nm maize (BRIT), corn (US).
maison [mɛzɔ̃] nf (bâtiment) house; (chez-soi) home; (COMM) firm; (famille): **ami de la ~ friend of the family** ♦ adj inv (CULIN) home-made; (: au restaurant) made by the chef; (COMM) in-house, own; (fam) first-rate; **à la ~** at home; (direction) home; ~ **d'arrêt** (short-stay) prison; ~ **de campagne** country cottage; ~ **centrale** prison; ~ **close** brothel; ~ **de correction** ≈ remand home (BRIT), ≈ reformatory (US); ~ **de la culture** ≈ arts centre; ~ **des jeunes** ≈ youth club; ~ **mère** parent company; ~ **de passe** = ~ **close**; ~ **de repos** convalescent home; ~ **de retraite** old people's home; ~ **de santé** mental home.

> Maisons des jeunes et de la culture are centres for young people which combine the functions of youth club and community arts centre. They organize a wide range of sporting and cultural activities (theatre, music, exhibitions), and are also engaged in welfare work. The centres are, in part, publicly financed.

Maison-Blanche [mɛzɔ̃blɑ̃ʃ] nf: **la ~** the White House.
maisonnée [mɛzɔne] nf household, family.
maisonnette [mɛzɔnɛt] nf small house, cottage.
maître, esse [mɛtʀ(ə), mɛtʀɛs] nm/f master/mistress; (SCOL) teacher, schoolmaster/mistress ♦ nm (peintre etc) master; (titre): **M~ (Me) Maître**, term of address for lawyers etc ♦ nf (amante) mistress ♦ adj (principal, essentiel) main; **maison de ~** family seat; **être ~ de** (soi-même, situation) to be in control of; **se rendre ~ de** (pays, ville) to gain control of; (situation, incendie) to bring under control; **être passé ~ dans l'art de** to be a (past) master in the art of; **une maîtresse femme** a forceful woman; ~ **d'armes** fencing master; ~ **auxiliaire (MA)**

(SCOL) temporary teacher; ~ **chanteur** blackmailer; ~ **de chapelle** choirmaster; ~ **de conférences** ≈ senior lecturer (BRIT), ≈ assistant professor (US); ~**/maîtresse d'école** teacher, schoolmaster/mistress; ~ **d'hôtel** (domestique) butler; (d'hôtel) head waiter; ~ **de maison** host; ~ **nageur** lifeguard; ~ **d'œuvre** (CONSTR) project manager; ~ **d'ouvrage** (CONSTR) client; ~ **à penser** intellectual leader; ~ **queux** chef; **maîtresse de maison** hostess; (ménagère) housewife (pl -wives).
maître-assistant, e, pl **maîtres-assistants, es** [mɛtʀasistɑ̃, -ɑ̃t] nm/f ≈ lecturer.
maître-autel, pl **maîtres-autels** [mɛtʀotɛl] nm high altar.
maîtrise [mɛtʀiz] nf (aussi: ~ **de soi**) self-control, self-possession; (habileté) skill, mastery; (suprématie) mastery, command; (diplôme) ≈ master's degree; (chefs d'équipe) supervisory staff.

> The **maîtrise** is a French university degree awarded following two years successful study after the **DEUG**. Students wishing to undertake research or take the **agrégation** must have a maîtrise.

maîtriser [mɛtʀize] vt (cheval, incendie) to (bring under) control; (sujet) to master; (émotion) to control; se ~ to control o.s.
majesté [maʒɛste] nf majesty.
majestueux, euse [maʒɛstɥø, -øz] adj majestic.
majeur, e [maʒœʀ] adj (important) major; (JUR) of age; (fig) adult ♦ nm/f (JUR) person who has come of age ou attained his (ou her) majority ♦ nm (doigt) middle finger; **en ~e partie** for the most part; **la ~e partie de** the major part of.
major [maʒɔʀ] nm adjutant; (SCOL): ~ **de la promotion** first in one's year.
majoration [maʒɔʀɑsjɔ̃] nf increase.
majordome [maʒɔʀdɔm] nm major-domo.
majorer [maʒɔʀe] vt to increase.
majorette [maʒɔʀɛt] nf majorette.
majoritaire [maʒɔʀitɛʀ] adj majority cpd; **système/scrutin** ~ majority system/ballot.
majorité [maʒɔʀite] nf (gén) majority; (parti) party in power; **en ~** (composé etc) mainly.
Majorque [maʒɔʀk(ə)] nf Majorca.
majorquin, e [maʒɔʀkɛ̃, -in] adj Majorcan ♦ nm/f: **M~, e** Majorcan.
majuscule [maʒyskyl] adj, nf: **(lettre)** ~ capital (letter).
MAL [mal] sigle f (= Maison d'animation et des loisirs) cultural centre.
mal, maux [mal, mo] nm (opposé au bien) evil; (tort, dommage) harm; (douleur physique) pain, ache; (maladie) illness, sickness no pl; (difficulté, peine) trouble; (souffrance morale) pain ♦ adv badly ♦ adj: **c'est ~ (de faire)** it's

bad *ou* wrong (to do); **être** ~ to be uncomfortable; **être** ~ **avec qn** to be on bad terms with sb; **être au plus** ~ (*malade*) to be very bad; (*brouillé*) to be at daggers drawn; **il comprend** ~ he has difficulty in understanding; **il a** ~ **compris** he misunderstood; ~ **tourner** to go wrong; **dire/penser du** ~ **de** to speak/think ill of; **ne vouloir de** ~ **à personne** to wish nobody any ill; **il n'a rien fait de** ~ he has done nothing wrong; **avoir du** ~ **à faire qch** to have trouble doing sth; **se donner du** ~ **pour faire qch** to go to a lot of trouble to do sth; **ne voir aucun** ~ **à** to see no harm in, see nothing wrong in; **craignant** ~ **faire** fearing he *etc* was doing the wrong thing; **sans penser** *ou* **songer à** ~ without meaning any harm; **faire du** ~ **à qn** to hurt sb; to harm sb; **se faire** ~ to hurt o.s.; **se faire** ~ **au pied** to hurt one's foot; **ça fait** ~ it hurts; **j'ai** ~ **(ici)** it hurts (here); **j'ai** ~ **au dos** my back aches, I've got a pain in my back; **avoir** ~ **à la tête/à la gorge/aux dents** to have a headache/a sore throat/toothache; **avoir le** ~ **de l'air** to be airsick; **avoir le** ~ **du pays** to be homesick; ~ **de mer** seasickness; ~ **de la route** carsickness; ~ **en point** *adj inv* in a bad state; **maux de ventre** stomach ache *sg*; *voir* **cœur.**

Malabar [malabaʀ] *nm*: **le** ~, **la côte de** ~ the Malabar (Coast).

malabar [malabaʀ] *nm* (*fam*) muscle man.

malade [malad] *adj* ill, sick; (*poitrine, jambe*) bad; (*plante*) diseased; (*fig: entreprise, monde*) ailing ♦ *nm/f* invalid, sick person; (*à l'hôpital etc*) patient; **tomber** ~ to fall ill; **être** ~ **du cœur** to have heart trouble *ou* a bad heart; **grand** ~ seriously ill person; ~ **mental** mentally sick *ou* ill person.

maladie [maladi] *nf* (*spécifique*) disease, illness; (*mauvaise santé*) illness, sickness; (*fig: manie*) mania; **être rongé par la** ~ to be wasting away (through illness); ~ **d'Alzheimer** Alzheimer's disease; ~ **de peau** skin disease.

maladif, ive [maladif, -iv] *adj* sickly; (*curiosité, besoin*) pathological.

maladresse [maladʀɛs] *nf* clumsiness *no pl*; (*gaffe*) blunder.

maladroit, e [maladʀwa, -wat] *adj* clumsy.

maladroitement [maladʀwatmɑ̃] *adv* clumsily.

mal-aimé, e [maleme] *nm/f* unpopular person; (*de la scène politique, de la société*) persona non grata; **le** ~ **du bureau** the unpopular one in the office.

malais, e [malɛ, -ɛz] *adj* Malay, Malayan ♦ *nm* (*LING*) Malay ♦ *nm/f*: **M**~, **e** Malay, Malayan.

malaise [malɛz] *nm* (*MÉD*) feeling of faintness; feeling of discomfort; (*fig*) uneasiness, malaise; **avoir un** ~ to feel faint *ou* dizzy.

malaisé, e [maleze] *adj* difficult.

Malaisie [malɛzi] *nf*: **la** ~ Malaya, West Malaysia; **la péninsule de** ~ the Malay Peninsula.

malappris, e [malapʀi, -iz] *nm/f* ill-mannered *ou* boorish person.

malaria [malaʀja] *nf* malaria.

malavisé, e [malavize] *adj* ill-advised, unwise.

Malawi [malawi] *nm*: **le** ~ Malawi.

malaxer [malakse] *vt* (*pétrir*) to knead; (*mêler*) to mix.

Malaysia [malɛzja] *nf*: **la** ~ Malaysia.

malchance [malʃɑ̃s] *nf* misfortune, ill luck *no pl*; **par** ~ unfortunately; **quelle** ~! what bad luck!

malchanceux, euse [malʃɑ̃sø, -øz] *adj* unlucky.

malcommode [malkɔmɔd] *adj* impractical, inconvenient.

Maldives [maldiv] *nfpl*: **les** ~ the Maldive Islands.

maldonne [maldɔn] *nf* (*CARTES*) misdeal; **il y a** ~ (*fig*) there's been a misunderstanding.

mâle [mɑl] *adj* (*aussi ÉLEC, TECH*) male; (*viril: voix, traits*) manly ♦ *nm* male.

malédiction [malediksjɔ̃] *nf* curse.

maléfice [malefis] *nm* evil spell.

maléfique [malefik] *adj* evil, baleful.

malencontreusement [malɑ̃kɔ̃tʀøzmɑ̃] *adv* (*arriver*) at the wrong moment; (*rappeler, mentionner*) inopportunely.

malencontreux, euse [malɑ̃kɔ̃tʀø, -øz] *adj* unfortunate, untoward.

malentendant, e [malɑ̃tɑ̃dɑ̃, -ɑ̃t] *nm/f*: **les** ~**s** the hard of hearing.

malentendu [malɑ̃tɑ̃dy] *nm* misunderstanding.

malfaçon [malfasɔ̃] *nf* fault.

malfaisant, e [malfəzɑ̃, -ɑ̃t] *adj* evil, harmful.

malfaiteur [malfɛtœʀ] *nm* lawbreaker, criminal; (*voleur*) thief (*pl* thieves).

malfamé, e [malfame] *adj* disreputable, of ill repute.

malfrat [malfʀa] *nm* villain, crook.

malgache [malgaʃ] *adj* Malagasy, Madagascan ♦ *nm* (*LING*) Malagasy ♦ *nm/f*: **M**~ Malagasy, Madagascan.

malgré [malgʀe] *prép* in spite of, despite; ~ **tout** *adv* in spite of everything.

malhabile [malabil] *adj* clumsy.

malheur [malœʀ] *nm* (*situation*) adversity, misfortune; (*événement*) misfortune; (*: plus fort*) disaster, tragedy; **par** ~ unfortunately; **quel** ~! what a shame *ou* pity!; **faire un** ~ (*fam: un éclat*) to do something desperate; (*: avoir du succès*) to be a smash hit.

malheureusement [malœʀøzmɑ̃] *adv* unfortunately.

malheureux, euse [malœʀø, -øz] *adj* (*triste*) unhappy, miserable; (*infortuné, regrettable*) unfortunate; (*malchanceux*) unlucky; (*insignifiant*) wretched ♦ *nm/f* (*infortuné, misérable*) poor soul; (*indigent, miséreux*) unfortunate creature; **les** ~ the destitute; **avoir la main malheureuse** (*au jeu*) to be unlucky; (*tout casser*) to be ham-fisted.

malhonnête [malɔnɛt] *adj* dishonest; (*impoli*) rude.

malhonnêtement [malɔnɛtmɑ̃] *adv* dishonestly.

malhonnêteté [malɔnɛtte] *nf* dishonesty; rudeness *no pl*.

Mali [mali] *nm*: **le ~** Mali.

malice [malis] *nf* mischievousness; (*méchanceté*): **par ~** out of malice *ou* spite; **sans ~** guileless.

malicieusement [malisjøzmɑ̃] *adv* mischievously.

malicieux, euse [malisjø, -øz] *adj* mischievous.

malien, ne [maljɛ̃, -ɛn] *adj* Malian.

malignité [maliɲite] *nf* (*d'une tumeur, d'un mal*) malignancy.

malin, igne [malɛ̃, -iɲ] *adj* (*futé: f gén*: **maline**) smart, shrewd; (*: sourire*) knowing; (*MÉD, influence*) malignant; **faire le ~** to show off; **éprouver un ~ plaisir à** to take malicious pleasure in.

malingre [malɛ̃gʀ(ə)] *adj* puny.

malintentionné, e [malɛ̃tɑ̃sjɔne] *adj* ill-intentioned, malicious.

malle [mal] *nf* trunk; (*AUTO*): **~ (arrière)** boot (*BRIT*), trunk (*US*).

malléable [maleabl(ə)] *adj* malleable.

malle-poste, *pl* **malles-poste** [malpɔst(ə)] *nf* mail coach.

mallette [malɛt] *nf* (*valise*) (small) suitcase; (*aussi*: **~ de voyage**) overnight case; (*pour documents*) attaché case.

malmener [malməne] *vt* to manhandle; (*fig*) to give a rough ride to.

malnutrition [malnytʀisjɔ̃] *nf* malnutrition.

malodorant, e [malɔdɔʀɑ̃, -ɑ̃t] *adj* foul-smelling.

malotru [malɔtʀy] *nm* lout, boor.

malouin, e [malwɛ̃, -in] *adj* of *ou* from Saint Malo.

Malouines [malwin] *nfpl*: **les ~** the Falklands, the Falkland Islands.

malpoli, e [malpɔli] *nm/f* rude individual.

malpropre [malpʀɔpʀ(ə)] *adj* (*personne, vêtement*) dirty; (*travail*) slovenly; (*histoire, plaisanterie*) unsavoury (*BRIT*), unsavory (*US*), smutty; (*malhonnête*) dishonest.

malpropreté [malpʀɔpʀəte] *nf* dirtiness.

malsain, e [malsɛ̃, -ɛn] *adj* unhealthy.

malséant, e [malseɑ̃, -ɑ̃t] *adj* unseemly, unbecoming.

malsonnant, e [malsɔnɑ̃, -ɑ̃t] *adj* offensive.

malt [malt] *nm* malt; **pur ~** (*whisky*) malt (whisky).

maltais, e [maltɛ, -ɛz] *adj* Maltese.

Malte [malt(ə)] *nf* Malta.

malté, e [malte] *adj* (*lait etc*) malted.

maltraiter [maltʀete] *vt* (*brutaliser*) to manhandle, ill-treat; (*critiquer, éreinter*) to

slate (*BRIT*), roast.

malus [malys] *nm* (*ASSURANCES*) car insurance weighting, penalty.

malveillance [malvɛjɑ̃s] *nf* (*animosité*) ill will; (*intention de nuire*) malevolence; (*JUR*) malicious intent *no pl*.

malveillant, e [malvɛjɑ̃, -ɑ̃t] *adj* malevolent, malicious.

malvenu, e [malvəny] *adj*: **être ~ de** *ou* **à faire qch** not to be in a position to do sth.

malversation [malvɛʀsɑsjɔ̃] *nf* embezzlement, misappropriation (of funds).

maman [mamɑ̃] *nf* mum(my) (*BRIT*), mom (*US*).

mamelle [mamɛl] *nf* teat.

mamelon [mamlɔ̃] *nm* (*ANAT*) nipple; (*colline*) knoll, hillock.

mamie [mami] *nf* (*fam*) granny.

mammifère [mamifɛʀ] *nm* mammal.

mammouth [mamut] *nm* mammoth.

manager [manadʒɛʀ] *nm* (*SPORT*) manager; (*COMM*): **~ commercial** commercial director.

manceau, elle, x [mɑ̃so, -ɛl] *adj* of *ou* from Le Mans.

manche [mɑ̃ʃ] *nf* (*de vêtement*) sleeve; (*d'un jeu, tournoi*) round; (*GÉO*): **la M~** the (English) Channel ♦ *nm* (*d'outil, casserole*) handle; (*de pelle, pioche etc*) shaft; (*de violon, guitare*) neck; (*fam*) clumsy oaf; **faire la ~** to pass the hat; **~ à air** *nf* (*AVIAT*) wind-sock; **~ à balai** *nm* broomstick; (*AVIAT, INFORM*) joystick.

manchette [mɑ̃ʃɛt] *nf* (*de chemise*) cuff; (*coup*) forearm blow; (*titre*) headline.

manchon [mɑ̃ʃɔ̃] *nm* (*de fourrure*) muff; **~ à incandescence** incandescent (gas) mantle.

manchot [mɑ̃ʃo] *nm* one-armed man; armless man; (*ZOOL*) penguin.

mandarine [mɑ̃daʀin] *nf* mandarin (orange), tangerine.

mandat [mɑ̃da] *nm* (*postal*) postal *ou* money order; (*d'un député etc*) mandate; (*procuration*) power of attorney, proxy; (*POLICE*) warrant; **~ d'amener** summons *sg*; **~ d'arrêt** warrant for arrest; **~ de dépôt** committal order; **~ de perquisition** (*POLICE*) search warrant.

mandataire [mɑ̃datɛʀ] *nm/f* (*représentant, délégué*) representative; (*JUR*) proxy.

mandat-carte, *pl* **mandats-cartes** [mɑ̃dakaʀt(ə)] *nm* money order (*in postcard form*).

mandater [mɑ̃date] *vt* (*personne*) to appoint; (*POL: député*) to elect.

mandat-lettre, *pl* **mandats-lettres** [mɑ̃dalɛtʀ(ə)] *nm* money order (*with space for correspondence*).

mandchou, e [mɑ̃tʃu] *adj* Manchu, Manchurian ♦ *nm* (*LING*) Manchu ♦ *nm/f*: **M~, e** Manchu.

Mandchourie [mɑ̃tʃuʀi] *nf*: **la ~** Manchuria.

mander [mɑ̃de] *vt* to summon.
mandibule [mɑ̃dibyl] *nf* mandible.
mandoline [mɑ̃dɔlin] *nf* mandolin(e).
manège [manɛʒ] *nm* riding school; (*à la foire*) roundabout (*BRIT*), merry-go-round; (*fig*) game, ploy; **faire un tour de** ~ to go for a ride on a *ou* the roundabout *etc*; ~ **(de chevaux de bois)** roundabout (*BRIT*), merry-go-round.
manette [manɛt] *nf* lever, tap; ~ **de jeu** (*INFORM*) joystick.
manganèse [mɑ̃ganɛz] *nm* manganese.
mangeable [mɑ̃ʒabl(ə)] *adj* edible, eatable.
mangeaille [mɑ̃ʒaj] *nf* (*péj*) grub.
mangeoire [mɑ̃ʒwaʀ] *nf* trough, manger.
manger [mɑ̃ʒe] *vt* to eat; (*ronger: suj: rouille etc*) to eat into *ou* away; (*utiliser, consommer*) to eat up ♦ *vi* to eat.
mange-tout [mɑ̃ʒtu] *nm inv* mange-tout.
mangeur, euse [mɑ̃ʒœʀ, -øz] *nm/f* eater.
mangouste [mɑ̃gust(ə)] *nf* mongoose.
mangue [mɑ̃g] *nf* mango.
maniabilité [manjabilite] *nf* (*d'un outil*) handiness; (*d'un véhicule, voilier*) manoeuvrability.
maniable [manjabl(ə)] *adj* (*outil*) handy; (*voiture, voilier*) easy to handle, manoeuvrable (*BRIT*), maneuverable (*US*); (*fig: personne*) easily influenced, manipulable.
maniaque [manjak] *adj* (*pointilleux, méticuleux*) finicky, fussy; (*atteint de manie*) suffering from a mania ♦ *nm/f* maniac.
manie [mani] *nf* mania; (*tic*) odd habit.
maniement [manimɑ̃] *nm* handling; ~ **d'armes** arms drill.
manier [manje] *vt* to handle; **se** ~ *vi* (*fam*) to get a move on.
manière [manjɛʀ] *nf* (*façon*) way, manner; (*genre, style*) style; ~**s** *nfpl* (*attitude*) manners; (*chichis*) fuss *sg*; **de** ~ **à** so as to; **de telle** ~ **que** in such a way that; **de cette** ~ in this way *ou* manner; **d'une** ~ **générale** generally speaking, as a general rule; **de toute** ~ in any case; **d'une certaine** ~ in a (certain) way; **faire des** ~**s** to put on airs; **employer la** ~ **forte** to use strong-arm tactics; **adverbe de** ~ adverb of manner.
maniéré, e [manjeʀe] *adj* affected.
manif [manif] *nf* (= *manifestation*) demo (*pl* -s).
manifestant, e [manifɛstɑ̃, -ɑ̃t] *nm/f* demonstrator.
manifestation [manifɛstɑsjɔ̃] *nf* (*de joie, mécontentement*) expression, demonstration; (*symptôme*) outward sign; (*fête etc*) event; (*POL*) demonstration.
manifeste [manifɛst(ə)] *adj* obvious, evident ♦ *nm* manifesto (*pl* -s).
manifestement [manifɛstəmɑ̃] *adv* obviously.
manifester [manifɛste] *vt* (*volonté, intentions*) to show, indicate; (*joie, peur*) to express, show ♦ *vi* (*POL*) to demonstrate; **se** ~ *vi*

(*émotion*) to show *ou* express itself; (*difficultés*) to arise; (*symptômes*) to appear; (*témoin etc*) to come forward.
manigance [manigɑ̃s] *nf* scheme.
manigancer [manigɑ̃se] *vt* to plot, devise.
Manille [manij] *n* Manila.
manioc [manjɔk] *nm* cassava, manioc.
manipulateur, trice [manipylatœʀ, -tʀis] *adj* (*technicien*) technician, operator; (*prestidigitateur*) conjurer; (*péj*) manipulator.
manipulation [manipylɑsjɔ̃] *nf* handling; manipulation.
manipuler [manipyle] *vt* to handle; (*fig*) to manipulate.
manivelle [manivɛl] *nf* crank.
manne [man] *nf* (*REL*) manna; (*fig*) godsend.
mannequin [mankɛ̃] *nm* (*COUTURE*) dummy; (*MODE*) model.
manœuvrable [manœvʀabl(ə)] *adj* (*bateau, véhicule*) manoeuvrable (*BRIT*), maneuverable (*US*).
manœuvre [manœvʀ(ə)] *nf* (*gén*) manoeuvre (*BRIT*), maneuver (*US*) ♦ *nm* (*ouvrier*) labourer (*BRIT*), laborer (*US*).
manœuvrer [manœvʀe] *vt* to manoeuvre (*BRIT*), maneuver (*US*); (*levier, machine*) to operate; (*personne*) to manipulate ♦ *vi* to manoeuvre *ou* maneuver.
manoir [manwaʀ] *nm* manor *ou* country house.
manomètre [manɔmɛtʀ(ə)] *nm* gauge, manometer.
manquant, e [mɑ̃kɑ̃, -ɑ̃t] *adj* missing.
manque [mɑ̃k] *nm* (*insuffisance*): ~ **de** lack of; (*vide*) emptiness, gap; (*MÉD*) withdrawal; ~**s** *nmpl* (*lacunes*) faults, defects; **par** ~ **de** for want of; ~ **à gagner** loss of profit *ou* earnings.
manqué, e [mɑ̃ke] *adj* failed; **garçon** ~ tomboy.
manquement [mɑ̃kmɑ̃] *nm*: ~ **à** (*discipline, règle*) breach of.
manquer [mɑ̃ke] *vi* (*faire défaut*) to be lacking; (*être absent*) to be missing; (*échouer*) to fail ♦ *vt* to miss ♦ *vb impers*: **il (nous) manque encore 100 F** we are still 100 F short; **il manque des pages (au livre)** there are some pages missing *ou* some pages are missing (from the book); **l'argent qui leur manque** the money they need *ou* are short of; **le pied/la voix lui manqua** he missed his footing/his voice failed him; ~ **à qn** (*absent etc*): **il/cela me manque** I miss him/that; ~ **à** *vt* (*règles etc*) to be in breach of, fail to observe; ~ **de** *vt* to lack; (*COMM*) to be out of (stock of); **ne pas** ~ **de faire: il n'a pas manqué de le dire** he certainly said it; ~ **(de) faire: il a manqué (de) se tuer** he very nearly got killed; **il ne manquerait plus qu'il fasse** all we need now is for him to do; **je n'y manquerai pas** leave it to me, I'll definitely do it.
mansarde [mɑ̃saʀd(ə)] *nf* attic.

mansardé, e [mɑ̃saʀde] adj attic cpd.
mansuétude [mɑ̃sɥetyd] nf leniency.
mante [mɑ̃t] nf: ~ **religieuse** praying mantis.
manteau, x [mɑ̃to] nm coat; ~ **de cheminée** mantelpiece; **sous le** ~ (fig) under cover.
mantille [mɑ̃tij] nf mantilla.
Mantoue [mɑ̃tu] n Mantua.
manucure [manykyʀ] nf manicurist.
manuel, le [manɥɛl] adj manual ♦ nm/f manually gifted pupil etc (as opposed to intellectually gifted) ♦ nm (ouvrage) manual, handbook.
manuellement [manɥɛlmɑ̃] adv manually.
manufacture [manyfaktyʀ] nf (établissement) factory; (fabrication) manufacture.
manufacturé, e [manyfaktyʀe] adj manufactured.
manufacturier, ière [manyfaktyʀje, -jɛʀ] nm/f factory owner.
manuscrit, e [manyskʀi, -it] adj handwritten ♦ nm manuscript.
manutention [manytɑ̃sjɔ̃] nf (COMM) handling; (local) storehouse.
manutentionnaire [manytɑ̃sjɔnɛʀ] nm/f warehouseman/woman, packer.
manutentionner [manytɑ̃sjɔne] vt to handle.
MAP sigle f (PHOTO: = mise au point) focusing.
mappemonde [mapmɔ̃d] nf (plane) map of the world; (sphère) globe.
maquereau, x [makʀo] nm mackerel inv; (fam: proxénète) pimp.
maquerelle [makʀɛl] nf (fam) madam.
maquette [makɛt] nf (d'un décor, bâtiment, véhicule) (scale) model; (TYPO) mockup; (: d'une page illustrée, affiche) paste-up; (: prêt à la réproduction) artwork.
maquignon [makiɲɔ̃] nm horse-dealer.
maquillage [makijaʒ] nm making up; faking; (produits) make-up.
maquiller [makije] vt (personne, visage) to make up; (truquer: passeport, statistique) to fake; (: voiture volée) to do over (respray etc); **se** ~ to make o.s. up.
maquilleur, euse [makijœʀ, -øz] nm/f make-up artist.
maquis [maki] nm (GÉO) scrub; (fig) tangle; (MIL) maquis, underground fighting no pl.
maquisard, e [makizaʀ, -aʀd(ə)] nm/f maquis, member of the Resistance.
marabout [maʀabu] nm (ZOOL) marabou(t).
maraîcher, ère [maʀeʃe, maʀeʃɛʀ] adj: **cultures maraîchères** market gardening sg ♦ nm/f market gardener.
marais [maʀɛ] nm marsh, swamp; ~ **salant** saltworks.
marasme [maʀasm(ə)] nm (POL, ÉCON) stagnation, sluggishness; (accablement) dejection, depression.
marathon [maʀatɔ̃] nm marathon.
marâtre [maʀɑtʀ(ə)] nf cruel mother.
maraude [maʀod] nf pilfering, thieving (of poultry, crops); (dans un verger) scrumping;

(vagabondage) prowling; **en** ~ on the prowl; (taxi) cruising.
maraudeur, euse [maʀodœʀ, -øz] nm/f marauder; prowler.
marbre [maʀbʀ(ə)] nm (pierre, statue) marble; (d'une table, commode) marble top; (TYPO) stone, bed; **rester de** ~ to remain stonily indifferent.
marbrer [maʀbʀe] vt to mottle, blotch; (TECH: papier) to marble.
marbrerie [maʀbʀəʀi] nf (atelier) marble mason's workshop; (industrie) marble industry.
marbrier [maʀbʀije] nm monumental mason.
marbrière [maʀbʀijɛʀ] nf marble quarry.
marbrures [maʀbʀyʀ] nfpl blotches pl; (TECH) marbling sg.
marc [maʀ] nm (de raisin, pommes) marc; ~ **de café** coffee grounds pl ou dregs pl.
marcassin [maʀkasɛ̃] nm young wild boar.
marchand, e [maʀʃɑ̃, -ɑ̃d] nm/f shopkeeper, tradesman/woman; (au marché) stallholder; (spécifique): ~ **de cycles/tapis** bicycle/carpet dealer; ~ **de charbon/vins** coal/wine merchant ♦ adj: **prix/valeur** ~**(e)** market price/value; **qualité** ~**e** standard quality; ~ **en gros/au détail** wholesaler/retailer; ~ **de biens** real estate agent; ~ **de canons** (péj) arms dealer; ~ **de couleurs** ironmonger (BRIT), hardware dealer (US); ~**/e de fruits** fruiterer (BRIT), fruit seller (US); ~**/e de journaux** newsagent; ~**/e de légumes** greengrocer (BRIT), produce dealer (US); ~**/e de poisson** fishmonger (BRIT), fish seller (US); ~**/e de(s) quatre-saisons** costermonger (BRIT), street vendor (selling fresh fruit and vegetables); ~ **de sable** (fig) sandman; ~ **de tableaux** art dealer.
marchandage [maʀʃɑ̃daʒ] nm bargaining; (péj: électoral) bargaining, manoeuvring.
marchander [maʀʃɑ̃de] vt (article) to bargain ou haggle over; (éloges) to be sparing with ♦ vi to bargain, haggle.
marchandisage [maʀʃɑ̃dizaʒ] nm merchandizing.
marchandise [maʀʃɑ̃diz] nf goods pl, merchandise no pl.
marche [maʀʃ(ə)] nf (d'escalier) step; (activité) walking; (promenade, trajet, allure) walk; (démarche) walk, gait; (MIL etc, MUS) march; (fonctionnement) running; (progression) progress; course; **à une heure de** ~ an hour's walk (away); **ouvrir/fermer la** ~ to lead the way/bring up the rear; **dans le sens de la** ~ (RAIL) facing the engine; **en** ~ (monter etc) while the vehicle is moving ou in motion; **mettre en** ~ to start; **remettre qch en** ~ to set ou start sth going again; **se mettre en** ~ (personne) to get moving; (machine) to start; ~ **arrière** (AUTO) reverse (gear); **faire** ~ **arrière** (AUTO) to reverse; (fig) to backtrack, back-pedal; ~ **à suivre**

(correct) procedure; (*sur notice*) (step by step) instructions *pl*.

marché [maʀʃe] *nm* (*lieu, COMM, ÉCON*) market; (*ville*) trading centre; (*transaction*) bargain, deal; **par-dessus le ~** into the bargain; **faire son ~** to do one's shopping; **mettre le ~ en main à qn** to tell sb to take it or leave it; **~ au comptant** (*BOURSE*) spot market; **M~ commun** Common Market; **~ aux fleurs** flower market; **~ noir** black market; **faire du ~ noir** to buy and sell on the black market; **~ aux puces** flea market; **~ à terme** (*BOURSE*) forward market; **~ du travail** labour market.

marchepied [maʀʃəpje] *nm* (*RAIL*) step; (*AUTO*) running board; (*fig*) stepping stone.

marcher [maʀʃe] *vi* to walk; (*MIL*) to march; (*aller: voiture, train, affaires*) to go; (*prospérer*) to go well; (*fonctionner*) to work, run; (*fam*) to go along, agree; (: *croire naïvement*) to be taken in; **~ sur** to walk on; (*mettre le pied sur*) to step on *ou* in; (*MIL*) to march upon; **~ dans** (*herbe etc*) to walk in *ou* on; (*flaque*) to step in; **faire ~ qn** (*pour rire*) to pull sb's leg; (*pour tromper*) to lead sb up the garden path.

marcheur, euse [maʀʃœʀ, -øz] *nm/f* walker.

marcotter [maʀkɔte] *vt* to layer.

mardi [maʀdi] *nm* Tuesday; **M~ gras** Shrove Tuesday; *voir aussi* **lundi**.

mare [maʀ] *nf* pond; **~ de sang** pool of blood.

marécage [maʀekaʒ] *nm* marsh, swamp.

marécageux, euse [maʀekaʒø, -øz] *adj* marshy, swampy.

maréchal, aux [maʀeʃal, -o] *nm* marshal; **~ des logis** (*MIL*) sergeant.

maréchal-ferrant, *pl* **maréchaux-ferrants** [maʀeʃalfɛʀɑ̃, maʀeʃo-] *nm* blacksmith, farrier (*BRIT*).

maréchaussée [maʀeʃose] *nf* (*humoristique: gendarmes*) constabulary (*BRIT*), police.

marée [maʀe] *nf* tide; (*poissons*) fresh (sea) fish; **~ haute/basse** high/low tide; **~ montante/descendante** rising/ebb tide; **~ noire** oil slick.

marelle [maʀɛl] *nf*: **(jouer à) la ~** (to play) hopscotch.

marémotrice [maʀemɔtʀis] *adj f* tidal.

mareyeur, euse [maʀejœʀ, -øz] *nm/f* wholesale (sea) fish merchant.

margarine [maʀgaʀin] *nf* margarine.

marge [maʀʒ(ə)] *nf* margin; **en ~** in the margin; **en ~ de** (*fig*) on the fringe of; (*en dehors de*) cut off from; (*qui se rapporte à*) connected with; **~ bénéficiaire** profit margin, mark-up; **~ de sécurité** safety margin.

margelle [maʀʒɛl] *nf* coping.

margeur [maʀʒœʀ] *nm* margin stop.

marginal, e, aux [maʀʒinal, -o] *adj* marginal ♦ *nm/f* dropout.

marguerite [maʀgəʀit] *nf* marguerite, (oxeye) daisy; (*INFORM*) daisy wheel.

marguillier [maʀgije] *nm* churchwarden.

mari [maʀi] *nm* husband.

mariage [maʀjaʒ] *nm* (*union, état, fig*) marriage; (*noce*) wedding; **~ civil/religieux** registry office (*BRIT*) *ou* civil/church wedding; **un ~ de raison/d'amour** a marriage of convenience/a love match; **~ blanc** unconsummated marriage; **~ en blanc** white wedding.

marié, e [maʀje] *adj* married ♦ *nm/f* (bride)groom/bride; **les ♦ ~s** the bride and groom; **les (jeunes) ~s** the newly-weds.

marier [maʀje] *vt* to marry; (*fig*) to blend; **se ~ (avec)** to marry, get married (to); (*fig*) to blend (with).

marijuana [maʀiʒwana] *nf* marijuana.

marin, e [maʀɛ̃, -in] *adj* sea *cpd*, marine ♦ *nm* sailor ♦ *nf* navy; (*ART*) seascape; (*couleur*) navy (blue); **avoir le pied ~** to be a good sailor; (*garder son équilibre*) to have one's sea legs; **~e de guerre** navy; **~e marchande** merchant navy; **~e à voiles** sailing ships *pl*.

marina [maʀina] *nf* marina.

marinade [maʀinad] *nf* marinade.

marine [maʀin] *adj f, nf voir* **marin** ♦ *adj inv* navy (blue) ♦ *nm* (*MIL*) marine.

mariner [maʀine] *vi, vt* to marinate, marinade.

marinier [maʀinje] *nm* bargee.

marinière [maʀinjɛʀ] *nf* (*blouse*) smock ♦ *adj inv*: **moules ~** (*CULIN*) mussels in white wine.

marionnette [maʀjɔnɛt] *nf* puppet.

marital, e, aux [maʀital, -o] *adj*: **autorisation ~e** husband's permission.

maritalement [maʀitalmɑ̃] *adv*: **vivre ~** to live together (as husband and wife).

maritime [maʀitim] *adj* sea *cpd*, maritime; (*ville*) coastal, seaside; (*droit*) shipping, maritime.

marjolaine [maʀʒɔlɛn] *nf* marjoram.

mark [maʀk] *nm* (*monnaie*) mark.

marketing [maʀkɔtiŋ] *nm* (*COMM*) marketing.

marmaille [maʀmɑj] *nf* (*péj*) (gang of) brats *pl*.

marmelade [maʀməlad] *nf* (*compote*) stewed fruit, compote; **~ d'oranges** (orange) marmalade; **en ~** (*fig*) crushed (to a pulp).

marmite [maʀmit] *nf* (cooking-)pot.

marmiton [maʀmitɔ̃] *nm* kitchen boy.

marmonner [maʀmɔne] *vt, vi* to mumble, mutter.

marmot [maʀmo] *nm* (*fam*) brat.

marmotte [maʀmɔt] *nf* marmot.

marmotter [maʀmɔte] *vt* (*prière*) to mumble, mutter.

marne [maʀn(ə)] *nf* (*GÉO*) marl.

Maroc [maʀɔk] *nm*: **le ~** Morocco.

marocain, e [maʀɔkɛ̃, -ɛn] *adj* Moroccan ♦ *nm/f*: **M~, e** Moroccan.

maroquin [maʀɔkɛ̃] *nm* (*peau*) morocco (leather); (*fig*) (minister's) portfolio.

maroquinerie [maʀɔkinʀi] *nf* (*industrie*) leather craft; (*commerce*) leather shop;

(*articles*) fine leather goods *pl*.

maroquinier [maʀɔkinje] *nm* (*fabricant*) leather craftsman; (*marchand*) leather dealer.

marotte [maʀɔt] *nf* fad.

marquant, e [maʀkɑ̃, -ɑ̃t] *adj* outstanding.

marque [maʀk(ə)] *nf* mark; (*SPORT, JEU*: *décompte des points*) score; (*COMM*: *de produits*) brand, make; (: *de disques*) label; (*insigne: d'une fonction*) badge; (*fig*): ~ **d'affection** token of affection; ~ **de joie** sign of joy; **à vos ~s!** (*SPORT*) on your marks!; **de** ~ *adj* (*COMM*) brand-name *cpd*; proprietary; (*fig*) high-class; (: *personnage, hôte*) distinguished; **produit de** ~ (*COMM*) quality product; ~ **déposée** registered trademark; ~ **de fabrique** trademark.

marqué, e [maʀke] *adj* marked.

marquer [maʀke] *vt* to mark; (*inscrire*) to write down; (*bétail*) to brand; (*SPORT: but etc*) to score; (: *joueur*) to mark; (*accentuer: taille etc*) to emphasize; (*manifester: refus, intérêt*) to show ♦ *vi* (*événement, personnalité*) to stand out, be outstanding; (*SPORT*) to score; ~ **qn de son influence/empreinte** to have an influence/leave its impression on sb; ~ **un temps d'arrêt** to pause momentarily; ~ **le pas** (*fig*) to mark time; **il a marqué ce jour-là d'une pierre blanche** that was a red-letter day for him; ~ **les points** (*tenir la marque*) to keep the score.

marqueté, e [maʀkəte] *adj* inlaid.

marqueterie [maʀkətʀi] *nf* inlaid work, marquetry.

marqueur, euse [maʀkœʀ, -øz] *nm/f* (*SPORT*: *de but*) scorer ♦ *nm* (*crayon feutre*) marker pen.

marquis, e [maʀki, -iz] *nm/f* marquis *ou* marquess/marchioness ♦ *nf* (*auvent*) glass canopy *ou* awning.

Marquises [maʀkiz] *nfpl*: **les (îles)** ~ the Marquesas Islands.

marraine [maʀɛn] *nf* godmother; (*d'un navire, d'une rose etc*) namer.

Marrakech [maʀakɛʃ] *n* Marrakech *ou* Marrakesh.

marrant, e [maʀɑ̃, -ɑ̃t] *adj* (*fam*) funny.

marre [maʀ] *adv* (*fam*): **en avoir** ~ **de** to be fed up with.

marrer [maʀe]: **se** ~ *vi* (*fam*) to have a (good) laugh.

marron, ne [maʀɔ̃, -ɔn] *nm* (*fruit*) chestnut ♦ *adj inv* brown ♦ *adj* (*péj*) crooked; (: *faux*) bogus; ~**s glacés** marrons glacés.

marronnier [maʀɔnje] *nm* chestnut (tree).

Mars [maʀs] *nm ou f* Mars.

mars [maʀs] *nm* March; *voir aussi* **juillet**.

marseillais, e [maʀsɛjɛ, -ɛz] *adj* of *ou* from Marseilles ♦ *nf*: **la M~e** the French national anthem.

La Marseillaise *has been France's national anthem since 1879. The words of the "Chant de guerre de l'armée du Rhin", as the song was originally called, were written to an anonymous tune by the army captain Rouget de Lisle in 1792. Adopted as a marching song by the battalion of Marseille, it was finally popularized as the Marseillaise.*

Marseille [maʀsɛj] *n* Marseilles.

marsouin [maʀswɛ̃] *nm* porpoise.

marsupiaux [maʀsypjo] *nmpl* marsupials.

marteau, x [maʀto] *nm* hammer; (*de porte*) knocker; ~ **pneumatique** pneumatic drill.

marteau-pilon, *pl* **marteaux-pilons** [maʀtopilɔ̃] *nm* power hammer.

marteau-piqueur, *pl* **marteaux-piqueurs** [maʀtopikœʀ] *nm* pneumatic drill.

martel [maʀtɛl] *nm*: **se mettre** ~ **en tête** to worry o.s.

martèlement [maʀtɛlmɑ̃] *nm* hammering.

marteler [maʀtəle] *vt* to hammer; (*mots, phrases*) to rap out.

martial, e, aux [maʀsjal, -o] *adj* martial; **cour** ~**e** court-martial.

martien, ne [maʀsjɛ̃, -ɛn] *adj* Martian, of *ou* from Mars.

martinet [maʀtinɛ] *nm* (*fouet*) small whip; (*ZOOL*) swift.

martingale [maʀtɛ̃gal] *nf* (*COUTURE*) half-belt; (*JEU*) winning formula.

martiniquais, e [maʀtinikɛ, -ɛz] *adj* of *ou* from Martinique.

Martinique [maʀtinik] *nf*: **la** ~ Martinique.

martin-pêcheur, *pl* **martins-pêcheurs** [maʀtɛ̃peʃœʀ] *nm* kingfisher.

martre [maʀtʀ(ə)] *nf* marten; ~ **zibeline** sable.

martyr, e [maʀtiʀ] *nm/f* martyr ♦ *adj* martyred; **enfants** ~**s** battered children.

martyre [maʀtiʀ] *nm* martyrdom; (*fig: sens affaibli*) agony, torture; **souffrir le** ~ to suffer agonies.

martyriser [maʀtiʀize] *vt* (*REL*) to martyr; (*fig*) to bully; (: *enfant*) to batter.

marxisme [maʀksism(ə)] *nm* Marxism.

marxiste [maʀksist(ə)] *adj, nm/f* Marxist.

mas [mɑ(s)] *nm traditional house or farm in Provence*.

mascara [maskaʀa] *nm* mascara.

mascarade [maskaʀad] *nf* masquerade.

mascotte [maskɔt] *nf* mascot.

masculin, e [maskylɛ̃, -in] *adj* masculine; (*sexe, population*) male; (*équipe, vêtements*) men's; (*viril*) manly ♦ *nm* masculine.

masochisme [mazɔfism(ə)] *nm* masochism.

masochiste [mazɔfist(ə)] *adj* masochistic ♦ *nm/f* masochist.

masque [mask(ə)] *nm* mask; ~ **de beauté** face pack; ~ **à gaz** gas mask; ~ **de plongée** diving mask.

masqué, e [maske] *adj* masked.

masquer [maske] *vt* (*cacher: porte, goût*) to hide, conceal; (*dissimuler: vérité, projet*) to mask, obscure.

massacrant, e [masakʀɑ̃, -ɑ̃t] *adj*: **humeur ~e** foul temper.

massacre [masakʀ(ə)] *nm* massacre, slaughter; **jeu de ~** (*fig*) wholesale slaughter.

massacrer [masakʀe] *vt* to massacre, slaughter; (*fig: adversaire*) to slaughter; (*: texte etc*) to murder.

massage [masaʒ] *nm* massage.

masse [mas] *nf* mass; (*péj*): **la ~** the masses *pl*; (*ÉLEC*) earth; (*maillet*) sledgehammer; **~s** *nfpl* masses; **une ~ de, des ~s de** (*fam*) masses *ou* loads of; **en ~** *adv* (*en bloc*) in bulk; (*en foule*) en masse ♦ *adj* (*exécutions, production*) mass *cpd*; **~ monétaire** (*ÉCON*) money supply; **~ salariale** (*COMM*) wage(s) bill.

massepain [maspɛ̃] *nm* marzipan.

masser [mase] *vt* (*assembler*) to gather; (*pétrir*) to massage; **se ~** *vi* to gather.

masseur, euse [masœʀ, -øz] *nm/f* (*personne*) masseur/masseuse ♦ *nm* (*appareil*) massager.

massicot [masiko] *nm* (*TYPO*) guillotine.

massif, ive [masif, -iv] *adj* (*porte*) solid, massive; (*visage*) heavy, large; (*bois, or*) solid; (*dose*) massive; (*déportations etc*) mass *cpd* ♦ *nm* (*montagneux*) massif; (*de fleurs*) clump, bank.

massivement [masivmɑ̃] *adv* (*répondre*) en masse; (*administrer, injecter*) in massive doses.

mass media [masmedja] *nmpl* mass media.

massue [masy] *nf* club, bludgeon ♦ *adj inv*: **argument ~** sledgehammer argument.

mastectomie [mastɛktɔmi] *nf* mastectomy.

mastic [mastik] *nm* (*pour vitres*) putty; (*pour fentes*) filler.

masticage [mastikaʒ] *nm* (*d'une fente*) filling; (*d'une vitre*) puttying.

mastication [mastikɑsjɔ̃] *nf* chewing, mastication.

mastiquer [mastike] *vt* (*aliment*) to chew, masticate; (*fente*) to fill; (*vitre*) to putty.

mastoc [mastɔk] *adj inv* hefty.

mastodonte [mastɔdɔ̃t] *nm* monster (*fig*).

masturbation [mastyʀbɑsjɔ̃] *nf* masturbation.

masturber [mastyʀbe] *vt*: **se ~** to masturbate.

m'as-tu-vu [matyvy] *nm/f inv* show-off.

masure [mazyʀ] *nf* tumbledown cottage.

mat, e [mat] *adj* (*couleur, métal*) mat(t); (*bruit, son*) dull ♦ *adj inv* (*ÉCHECS*): **être ~** to be checkmate.

mât [mɑ] *nm* (*NAVIG*) mast; (*poteau*) pole, post.

matamore [matamɔʀ] *nm* braggart, blusterer.

match [matʃ] *nm* match; **~ nul** draw, tie (*US*); **faire ~ nul** to draw (*BRIT*), tie (*US*); **~ aller** first leg; **~ retour** second leg, return match.

matelas [matla] *nm* mattress; **~ pneumatique** air bed *ou* mattress; **~ à ressorts** spring *ou* interior-sprung mattress.

matelasser [matlase] *vt* to pad.

matelot [matlo] *nm* sailor, seaman.

mater [mate] *vt* (*personne*) to bring to heel, subdue; (*révolte*) to put down; (*fam*) to watch, look at.

matérialisation [mateʀjalizɑsjɔ̃] *nf* materialization.

matérialiser [mateʀjalize]: **se ~** *vi* to materialize.

matérialisme [mateʀjalism(ə)] *nm* materialism.

matérialiste [mateʀjalist(ə)] *adj* materialistic ♦ *nm/f* materialist.

matériau, x [mateʀjo] *nm* material; **~x** *nmpl* material(s); **~x de construction** building materials.

matériel, le [mateʀjɛl] *adj* material; (*organisation, aide, obstacle*) practical; (*fig: péj: personne*) materialistic ♦ *nm* equipment *no pl*; (*de camping etc*) gear *no pl*; **il n'a pas le temps ~ de le faire** he doesn't have the time (needed) to do it; **~ d'exploitation** (*COMM*) plant; **~ roulant** rolling stock.

matériellement [mateʀjɛlmɑ̃] *adv* (*financièrement*) materially; **~ à l'aise** comfortably off; **je n'en ai ~ pas le temps** I simply do not have the time.

maternel, le [matɛʀnɛl] *adj* (*amour, geste*) motherly, maternal; (*grand-père, oncle*) maternal ♦ *nf* (*aussi*: **école ~le**) (state) nursery school.

materner [matɛʀne] *vt* (*personne*) to mother.

maternisé, e [matɛʀnize] *adj*: **lait ~** (*infant*) formula.

maternité [matɛʀnite] *nf* (*établissement*) maternity hospital; (*état de mère*) motherhood, maternity; (*grossesse*) pregnancy.

math [mat] *nfpl* maths (*BRIT*), math (*US*).

mathématicien, ne [matematisjɛ̃, -ɛn] *nm/f* mathematician.

mathématique [matematik] *adj* mathematical.

mathématiques [matematik] *nfpl* mathematics *sg*.

matheux, euse [matø, -øz] *nm/f* (*fam*) maths (*BRIT*) *ou* math (*US*) student; (*fort en math*) mathematical genius.

maths [mat] *nfpl* maths (*BRIT*), math (*US*).

matière [matjɛʀ] *nf* (*PHYSIQUE*) matter; (*COMM, TECH*) material, matter *no pl*; (*fig: d'un livre etc*) subject matter; (*SCOL*) subject; **en ~ de** as regards; **donner ~ à** to give cause to; **~ grise** grey matter; **~ plastique** plastic; **~s fécales** faeces; **~s grasses** fat (content) *sg*; **~s premières** raw materials.

MATIF [matif] *sigle m* (= *Marché à terme des instruments financiers*) *body which regulates the activities of the French Stock Exchange.*

> L'hôtel **Matignon** *is the Paris office and residence of the French Prime Minister. By extension, the term "Matignon" is often used to refer to the Prime Minister or his staff.*

matin [matɛ̃] *nm, adv* morning; **le ~** (*pendant le ~*) in the morning; **demain ~** tomorrow morning; **le lendemain ~** (the) next morning; **du ~ au soir** from morning till night; **une heure du ~** one o'clock in the morning; **de grand** *ou* **bon ~** early in the morning.

matinal, e, aux [matinal, -o] *adj* (*toilette, gymnastique*) morning *cpd*; (*de bonne heure*) early; **être ~** (*personne*) to be up early; (*: habituellement*) to be an early riser.

mâtiné, e [matine] *adj* crossbred, mixed race *cpd*.

matinée [matine] *nf* morning; (*spectacle*) matinée, afternoon performance.

matois, e [matwa, -waz] *adj* wily.

matou [matu] *nm* tom(cat).

matraquage [matʀakaʒ] *nm* beating up; **~ publicitaire** plug, plugging.

matraque [matʀak] *nf* (*de malfaiteur*) cosh (*BRIT*), club; (*de policier*) truncheon (*BRIT*), billy (*US*).

matraquer [matʀake] *vt* to beat up (with a truncheon *ou* billy); to cosh (*BRIT*), club; (*fig: touristes etc*) to rip off; (*: disque*) to plug.

matriarcal, e, aux [matʀijaʀkal, -o] *adj* matriarchal.

matrice [matʀis] *nf* (*ANAT*) womb; (*TECH*) mould; (*MATH etc*) matrix.

matricule [matʀikyl] *nf* (*aussi:* **registre ~**) roll, register ♦ *nm* (*aussi:* **numéro ~:** *MIL*) regimental number; (*: ADMIN*) reference number.

matrimonial, e, aux [matʀimɔnjal, -o] *adj* marital, marriage *cpd*.

matrone [matʀɔn] *nf* matron.

mâture [matyʀ] *nf* masts *pl*.

maturité [matyʀite] *nf* maturity; (*d'un fruit*) ripeness, maturity.

maudire [modiʀ] *vt* to curse.

maudit, e [modi, -it] *adj* (*fam: satané*) blasted, confounded.

maugréer [mogʀee] *vi* to grumble.

mauresque [mɔʀɛsk(ə)] *adj* Moorish.

Maurice [mɔʀis] *nf*: **(l'île) ~** Mauritius.

mauricien, ne [mɔʀisjɛ̃, -ɛn] *adj* Mauritian.

Mauritanie [mɔʀitani] *nf*: **la ~** Mauritania.

mauritanien, ne [mɔʀitanjɛ̃, -ɛn] *adj* Mauritanian.

mausolée [mozɔle] *nm* mausoleum.

maussade [mosad] *adj* (*air, personne*) sullen; (*ciel, temps*) dismal.

mauvais, e [movɛ, -ɛz] *adj* bad; (*faux*): **le ~ numéro/moment** the wrong number/moment; (*méchant, malveillant*) malicious, spiteful ♦ *nm*: **le ~** the bad side ♦ *adv*: **il fait ~**

the weather is bad; **sentir ~** to have a nasty smell, smell bad *ou* nasty; **la mer est ~e** the sea is rough; **~ coucheur** awkward customer; **~ coup** (*fig*) criminal venture; **~ garçon** tough; **~ pas** tight spot; **~ plaisant** hoaxer; **~ traitements** ill treatment *sg*; **~e herbe** weed; **~e langue** gossip, scandalmonger (*BRIT*); **~e passe** difficult situation; (*période*) bad patch; **~e tête** rebellious *ou* headstrong customer.

mauve [mov] *adj* (*couleur*) mauve ♦ *nf* (*BOT*) mallow.

mauviette [movjɛt] *nf* (*péj*) weakling.

maux [mo] *nmpl voir* **mal.**

max. *abr* (= *maximum*) max.

maximal, e, aux [maksimal, -o] *adj* maximal.

maxime [maksim] *nf* maxim.

maximum [maksimɔm] *adj, nm* maximum; **atteindre un/son ~** to reach a/his peak; **au ~** *adv* (*le plus possible*) to the full; as much as one can; (*tout au plus*) at the (very) most *ou* maximum.

Mayence [majɑ̃s] *n* Mainz.

mayonnaise [majɔnɛz] *nf* mayonnaise.

Mayotte [majɔt] *nf* Mayotte.

mazout [mazut] *nm* (fuel) oil; **chaudière/poêle à ~** oil-fired boiler/stove.

mazouté, e [mazute] *adj* oil-polluted.

MDM *sigle mpl* (= *Médecins du Monde*) *medical association for aid to Third World countries.*

Me *abr* = **Maître.**

me, m' [m(ə)] *pron* me; (*réfléchi*) myself.

méandres [meɑ̃dʀ(ə)] *nmpl* meanderings.

mec [mɛk] *nm* (*fam*) guy, bloke (*BRIT*).

mécanicien, ne [mekanisjɛ̃, -ɛn] *nm/f* mechanic; (*RAIL*) (train *ou* engine) driver; **~ navigant** *ou* **de bord** (*AVIAT*) flight engineer.

mécanicien-dentiste [mekanisjɛ̃dɑ̃tist(ə)], **mécanicienne-dentiste** [mekanisjɛn-] (*pl* **~s-~s**) *nm/f* dental technician.

mécanique [mekanik] *adj* mechanical ♦ *nf* (*science*) mechanics *sg*; (*technologie*) mechanical engineering; (*mécanisme*) mechanism; engineering; works *pl*; **ennui ~** engine trouble *no pl*; **s'y connaître en ~** to be mechanically minded; **~ hydraulique** hydraulics *sg*; **~ ondulatoire** wave mechanics *sg*.

mécaniquement [mekanikmɑ̃] *adv* mechanically.

mécanisation [mekanizasjɔ̃] *nf* mechanization.

mécaniser [mekanize] *vt* to mechanize.

mécanisme [mekanism(ə)] *nm* mechanism; **~ des taux de change** exchange rate mechanism.

mécano [mekano] *nm* (*fam*) mechanic.

mécanographie [mekanɔgʀafi] *nf* (mechanical) data processing.

mécène [mesɛn] *nm* patron.

méchamment [meʃamɑ̃] *adv* nastily,

maliciously, spitefully; viciously.
méchanceté [meʃɑ̃ste] *nf* (*d'une personne,
d'une parole*) nastiness, maliciousness,
spitefulness; (*parole, action*) nasty *ou*
spiteful *ou* malicious remark (*ou* action).
méchant, e [meʃɑ̃, -ɑ̃t] *adj* nasty, malicious,
spiteful; (*enfant: pas sage*) naughty; (*animal*)
vicious; (*avant le nom: valeur péjorative*)
nasty; miserable; (: *intensive*) terrific.
mèche [mɛʃ] *nf* (*de lampe, bougie*) wick; (*d'un
explosif*) fuse; (*MÉD*) pack, dressing; (*de
vilebrequin, perceuse*) bit; (*de dentiste*) drill;
(*de fouet*) lash; (*de cheveux*) lock; **se faire
faire des** ~**s** (*chez le coiffeur*) to have one's
hair streaked, have highlights put in one's
hair; **vendre la** ~ to give the game away; **de**
~ **avec** in league with.
méchoui [meʃwi] *nm whole sheep barbecue.*
mécompte [mekɔ̃t] *nm* (*erreur*) miscalculation; (*déception*) disappointment.
méconnais [mekɔnɛ] *etc vb voir* **méconnaître.**
méconnaissable [mekɔnɛsabl(ə)] *adj*
unrecognizable.
méconnaissais [mekɔnɛsɛ] *etc vb voir*
méconnaître.
méconnaissance [mekɔnɛsɑ̃s] *nf* ignorance.
méconnaître [mekɔnɛtʀ(ə)] *vt* (*ignorer*) to be
unaware of; (*mésestimer*) to misjudge.
méconnu, e [mekɔny] *pp de* **méconnaître** ♦ *adj*
(*génie etc*) unrecognized.
mécontent, e [mekɔ̃tɑ̃, -ɑ̃t] *adj*: ~ **(de)**
(*insatisfait*) discontented *ou* dissatisfied *ou*
displeased (with); (*contrarié*) annoyed (at)
♦ *nm/f* malcontent, dissatisfied person.
mécontentement [mekɔ̃tɑ̃tmɑ̃] *nm*
dissatisfaction, discontent, displeasure;
annoyance.
mécontenter [mekɔ̃tɑ̃te] *vt* to displease.
Mecque [mɛk] *nf*: **la** ~ Mecca.
mécréant, e [mekʀeɑ̃, -ɑ̃t] *adj* (*peuple*) infidel;
(*personne*) atheistic.
méd. *abr* = **médecin.**
médaille [medaj] *nf* medal.
médaillé, e [medaje] *nm/f* (*SPORT*) medal-
holder.
médaillon [medajɔ̃] *nm* (*portrait*) medallion;
(*bijou*) locket; (*CULIN*) médaillon; **en** ~ *adj*
(*carte etc*) inset.
médecin [medsɛ̃] *nm* doctor; ~ **du bord**
(*NAVIG*) ship's doctor; ~ **généraliste** general
practitioner, GP; ~ **légiste** forensic
scientist (*BRIT*), medical examiner (*US*); ~
traitant family doctor, GP.
médecine [medsin] *nf* medicine; ~ **générale**
general medicine; ~ **infantile** paediatrics *sg*
(*BRIT*), pediatrics *sg* (*US*); ~ **légale** forensic
medicine; ~ **préventive** preventive
medicine; ~ **du travail** occupational *ou*
industrial medicine; ~**s parallèles** *ou* **douces**
alternative medicine.
médian, e [medjɑ̃, -an] *adj* median.
médias [medja] *nmpl*: **les** ~ the media.

médiateur, trice [medjatœʀ, -tʀis] *nm/f* (*voir
médiation*) mediator; arbitrator.
médiathèque [medjatɛk] *nf* media library.
médiation [medjasjɔ̃] *nf* mediation; (*dans
conflit social etc*) arbitration.
médiatique [medjatik] *adj* media *cpd*.
médiatisé, e [medjatize] *adj* reported in the
media; **ce procès a été très** ~ (*péj*) this trial
was turned into a media event.
médiator [medjatɔʀ] *nm* plectrum.
médical, e, aux [medikal, -o] *adj* medical;
visiteur *ou* **délégué** ~ medical rep *ou*
representative.
médicalement [medikalmɑ̃] *adv* medically.
médicament [medikamɑ̃] *nm* medicine, drug.
médicamenteux, euse [medikamɑ̃tø, -øz] *adj*
medicinal.
médication [medikasjɔ̃] *nf* medication.
médicinal, e, aux [medisinal, -o] *adj*
medicinal.
médico-légal, e, aux [medikɔlegal, -o] *adj*
forensic.
médico-social, e, aux [medikɔsɔsjal, -o] *adj*:
assistance ~**e** medical and social
assistance.
médiéval, e, aux [medjeval, -o] *adj* medieval.
médiocre [medjɔkʀ(ə)] *adj* mediocre, poor.
médiocrité [medjɔkʀite] *nf* mediocrity.
médire [medir] *vi*: ~ **de** to speak ill of.
médisance [medizɑ̃s] *nf* scandalmongering *no
pl* (*BRIT*), mud-slinging *no pl*; (*propos*) piece of
scandal *ou* malicious gossip.
médisant, e [medizɑ̃, -ɑ̃t] *vb voir* **médire** ♦ *adj*
slanderous, malicious.
médit, e [medi, -it] *pp de* **médire.**
méditatif, ive [meditatif, -iv] *adj* thoughtful.
méditation [meditasjɔ̃] *nf* meditation.
méditer [medite] *vt* (*approfondir*) to meditate
on, ponder (over); (*combiner*) to meditate
♦ *vi* to meditate; ~ **de faire** to contemplate
doing, plan to do.
Méditerranée [meditɛrane] *nf*: **la (mer)** ~ the
Mediterranean (Sea).
méditerranéen, ne [meditɛraneɛ̃, -ɛn] *adj*
Mediterranean ♦ *nm/f*: **M**~, **ne**
Mediterranean.
médium [medjɔm] *nm* medium (*spiritualist*).
médius [medjys] *nm* middle finger.
méduse [medyz] *nf* jellyfish.
méduser [medyze] *vt* to dumbfound.
meeting [mitiŋ] *nm* (*POL, SPORT*) rally,
meeting; ~ **d'aviation** air show.
méfait [mefɛ] *nm* (*faute*) misdemeanour,
wrongdoing; ~**s** *nmpl* (*ravages*) ravages.
méfiance [mefjɑ̃s] *nf* mistrust, distrust.
méfiant, e [mefjɑ̃, -ɑ̃t] *adj* mistrustful,
distrustful.
méfier [mefje]: **se** ~ *vi* to be wary; (*faire
attention*) to be careful; **se** ~ **de** *vt* to
mistrust, distrust, be wary of; to be careful
about.
mégalomane [megalɔman] *adj* megalomaniac.

mégalomanie [megalɔmani] *nf* megalomania.
mégalopole [megalɔpɔl] *nf* megalopolis.
méga-octet [megaɔktɛ] *nm* megabyte.
mégarde [megaʀd(ə)] *nf*: **par ~** accidentally; (*par erreur*) by mistake.
mégatonne [megatɔn] *nf* megaton.
mégère [meʒɛʀ] *nf* (*péj: femme*) shrew.
mégot [mego] *nm* cigarette end *ou* butt.
mégoter [megote] *vi* to nitpick.
meilleur, e [mɛjœʀ] *adj, adv* better; (*valeur superlative*) best ♦ *nm*: **le ~** (*celui qui ...*) the best (one); (*ce qui ...*) the best ♦ *nf*: **la ~e** the best (one); **le ~ des deux** the better of the two; **de ~e heure** earlier; **~ marché** cheaper.
méjuger [meʒyʒe] *vt* to misjudge.
mélancolie [melɑ̃kɔli] *nf* melancholy, gloom.
mélancolique [melɑ̃kɔlik] *adj* melancholy, gloomy.
Mélanésie [melanezi] *nf*: **la ~** Melanesia.
mélange [melɑ̃ʒ] *nm* (*opération*) mixing; blending; (*résultat*) mixture; blend; **sans ~** unadulterated.
mélanger [melɑ̃ʒe] *vt* (*substances*) to mix; (*vins, couleurs*) to blend; (*mettre en désordre, confondre*) to mix up, muddle (up); **se ~** (*liquides, couleurs*) to blend, mix.
mélanine [melanin] *nf* melanin.
mélasse [melas] *nf* treacle, molasses *sg*.
mêlée [mele] *nf* (*bataille, cohue*) mêlée, scramble; (*lutte, conflit*) tussle, scuffle; (*RUGBY*) scrum(mage).
mêler [mele] *vt* (*substances, odeurs, races*) to mix; (*embrouiller*) to muddle (up), mix up; **se ~ to** mix; (*se joindre, s'allier*) to mingle; **se à** (*suj: personne*) to join; **to** mix with; (*: odeurs etc*) to mingle with; **se ~ de** (*suj: personne*) to meddle with, interfere in; **mêle-toi de tes affaires!** mind your own business!; **~ à** *ou* **avec** *ou* **de** to mix with; to mingle with; **~ qn à** (*affaire*) to get sb mixed up *ou* involved in.
mélo [melo] *nm, adj* = **mélodrame, mélodramatique.**
mélodie [melɔdi] *nf* melody.
mélodieux, euse [melɔdjø, -øz] *adj* melodious, tuneful.
mélodique [melɔdik] *adj* melodic.
mélodramatique [melɔdʀamatik] *adj* melodramatic.
mélodrame [melɔdʀam] *nm* melodrama.
mélomane [melɔman] *nm/f* music lover.
melon [məlɔ̃] *nm* (*BOT*) (honeydew) melon; (*aussi:* **chapeau ~**) bowler (hat); **~ d'eau** watermelon.
mélopée [melɔpe] *nf* monotonous chant.
membrane [mɑ̃bʀan] *nf* membrane.
membre [mɑ̃bʀ(ə)] *nm* (*ANAT*) limb; (*personne, pays, élément*) member ♦ *adj* member; **être ~ de** to be a member of; **~** (*viril*) (male) organ.
mémé [meme] *nf* (*fam*) granny; (*: vieille femme*) old dear.

═══════════════ **MOT-CLÉ**

même [mɛm] *adj* **1** (*avant le nom*) same; **en ~ temps** at the same time; **ils ont les ~s goûts** they have the same *ou* similar tastes
2 (*après le nom: renforcement*): **il est la loyauté ~** he is loyalty itself; **ce sont ses paroles/celles-là ~** they are his very words/ the very ones
♦ *pron*: **le(la) ~** the same one
♦ *adv* **1** (*renforcement*): **il n'a ~ pas pleuré** he didn't even cry; **~ lui l'a dit** even HE said it; **ici ~** at this very place; **~ si** even if
2: **à ~**: **à ~ la bouteille** straight from the bottle; **à ~ la peau** next to the skin; **être à ~ de faire** to be in a position to do, be able to do; **mettre qn à ~ de faire** to enable sb to do
3: **de ~**: likewise; **faire de ~** to do likewise *ou* the same; **lui de ~** so does (*ou* did *ou* is) he; **de ~ que** just as; **il en va de ~ pour** the same goes for.

mémento [memɛ̃to] *nm* (*agenda*) appointments diary; (*ouvrage*) summary.
mémoire [memwaʀ] *nf* memory ♦ *nm* (*ADMIN, JUR*) memorandum (*pl* -a); (*SCOL*) dissertation, paper; **avoir la ~ des visages/ chiffres** to have a (good) memory for faces/ figures; **n'avoir aucune ~** to have a terrible memory; **avoir de la ~** to have a good memory; **à la ~ de** to the *ou* in memory of; **pour ~** *adv* for the record; **de ~** *adv* from memory; **de ~ d'homme** in living memory; **mettre en ~** (*INFORM*) to store; **~ morte** ROM; **~ rémanente** *ou* **non volatile** non-volatile memory; **~ vive** RAM.
mémoires [memwaʀ] *nmpl* memoirs.
mémorable [memɔʀabl(ə)] *adj* memorable.
mémorandum [memɔʀɑ̃dɔm] *nm* memorandum (*pl* -a); (*carnet*) notebook.
mémorial, aux [memɔʀjal, -o] *nm* memorial.
mémoriser [memɔʀize] *vt* to memorize; (*INFORM*) to store.
menaçant, e [mənasɑ̃, -ɑ̃t] *adj* threatening, menacing.
menace [mənas] *nf* threat; **~ en l'air** empty threat.
menacer [mənase] *vt* to threaten; **~ qn de qch/de faire qch** to threaten sb with sth/to do sth.
ménage [menaʒ] *nm* (*travail*) housekeeping, housework; (*couple*) (married) couple; (*famille, ADMIN*) household; **faire le ~** to do the housework; **faire des ~s** to work as a cleaner (*in people's homes*); **monter son ~** to set up house; **se mettre en ~** (*avec*) to set up house (with); **heureux en ~** happily married; **faire bon ~ avec** to get on well with; **~ de poupée** doll's kitchen set; **~ à trois** love triangle.
ménagement [menaʒmɑ̃] *nm* care and attention; **~s** *nmpl* (*égards*) consideration *sg*,

attention *sg*.

ménager [menaʒe] *vt* (*traiter avec mesure*) to handle with tact; to treat considerately; (*utiliser*) to use with care; (*: avec économie*) to use sparingly; (*prendre soin de*) to take (great) care of, look after; (*organiser*) to arrange; (*installer*) to put in; to make; **se ~** to look after o.s.; **~ qch à qn** (*réserver*) to have sth in store for sb.

ménager, ère [menaʒe, -ɛʀ] *adj* household *cpd*, domestic ♦ *nf* (*femme*) housewife (*pl* -wives); (*couverts*) canteen (of cutlery).

ménagerie [menaʒʀi] *nf* menagerie.

mendiant, e [mãdjã, -ãt] *nm/f* beggar.

mendicité [mãdisite] *nf* begging.

mendier [mãdje] *vi* to beg ♦ *vt* to beg (for); (*fig: éloges, compliments*) to fish for.

menées [məne] *nfpl* intrigues, manœuvres (*BRIT*), maneuvers (*US*); (*COMM*) activities.

mener [məne] *vt* to lead; (*enquête*) to conduct; (*affaires*) to manage, conduct, run ♦ *vi*: **~ (à la marque)** to lead, be in the lead; **~ à/dans** (*emmener*) to take to/into; **~ qch à bonne fin** *ou* **à terme** *ou* **à bien** to see sth through (to a successful conclusion), complete sth successfully.

meneur, euse [mənœʀ, -øz] *nm/f* leader; (*péj: agitateur*) ringleader; **~ d'hommes** born leader; **~ de jeu** host, quizmaster (*BRIT*).

menhir [meniʀ] *nm* standing stone.

méningite [menɛ̃ʒit] *nf* meningitis *no pl*.

ménisque [menisk] *nm* (*ANAT*) meniscus.

ménopause [menopoz] *nf* menopause.

menotte [mənɔt] *nf* (*langage enfantin*) handie; **~s** *nfpl* handcuffs; **passer les ~s à** to handcuff.

mens [mã] *vb voir* **mentir**.

mensonge [mãsɔ̃ʒ] *nm*: **le ~** lying *no pl*; **un ~** a lie.

mensonger, ère [mãsɔ̃ʒe, -ɛʀ] *adj* false.

menstruation [mãstʀyasjɔ̃] *nf* menstruation.

menstruel, le [mãstʀyɛl] *adj* menstrual.

mensualiser [mãsyalize] *vt* to pay monthly.

mensualité [mãsyalite] *nf* (*somme payée*) monthly payment; (*somme perçue*) monthly salary.

mensuel, le [mãsyɛl] *adj* monthly ♦ *nm/f* (*employé*) employee paid monthly ♦ *nm* (*PRESSE*) monthly.

mensuellement [mãsyɛlmã] *adv* monthly.

mensurations [mãsyʀasjɔ̃] *nfpl* measurements.

mentais [mãtɛ] *etc vb voir* **mentir**.

mental, e, aux [mãtal, -o] *adj* mental.

mentalement [mãtalmã] *adv* in one's head, mentally.

mentalité [mãtalite] *nf* mentality.

menteur, euse [mãtœʀ, -øz] *nm/f* liar.

menthe [mãt] *nf* mint; **~ (à l'eau)** peppermint cordial.

mentholé, e [mãtɔle] *adj* menthol *cpd*, mentholated.

mention [mãsjɔ̃] *nf* (*note*) note, comment; (*SCOL*): **~ (très) bien/passable** (*very*) good/ satisfactory pass; **faire ~ de** to mention; **"rayer la ~ inutile"** "delete as appropriate".

mentionner [mãsjɔne] *vt* to mention.

mentir [mãtiʀ] *vi* to lie.

menton [mãtɔ̃] *nm* chin.

mentonnière [mãtɔnjɛʀ] *nf* chin strap.

menu, e [məny] *adj* (*mince*) thin; (*petit*) tiny; (*frais, difficulté*) minor ♦ *adv* (*couper, hacher*) very fine ♦ *nm* menu; **par le ~** (*raconter*) in minute detail; **~ touristique** popular *ou* tourist menu; **~e monnaie** small change.

menuet [mənyɛ] *nm* minuet.

menuiserie [mənyizʀi] *nf* (*travail*) joinery, carpentry; (*d'amateur*) woodwork; (*local*) joiner's workshop; (*ouvrages*) woodwork *no pl*.

menuisier [mənyizje] *nm* joiner, carpenter.

méprendre [mepʀãdʀ(ə)]: **se ~** *vi*: **se ~ sur** to be mistaken about.

mépris, e [mepʀi, -iz] *pp de* **méprendre** ♦ *nm* (*dédain*) contempt, scorn; (*indifférence*): **le ~ de** contempt *ou* disregard for; **au ~ de** regardless of, in defiance of.

méprisable [mepʀizabl(ə)] *adj* contemptible, despicable.

méprisant, e [mepʀizã, -ãt] *adj* contemptuous, scornful.

méprise [mepʀiz] *nf* mistake, error; (*malentendu*) misunderstanding.

mépriser [mepʀize] *vt* to scorn, despise; (*gloire, danger*) to scorn, spurn.

mer [mɛʀ] *nf* sea; (*marée*) tide; **~ fermée** inland sea; **en ~** at sea; **prendre la ~** to put out to sea; **en haute** *ou* **pleine ~** off shore, on the open sea; **la ~ Adriatique** the Adriatic (Sea); **la ~ des Antilles** *ou* **des Caraïbes** the Caribbean (Sea); **la ~ Baltique** the Baltic (Sea); **la ~ Caspienne** the Caspian Sea; **la ~ de Corail** the Coral Sea; **la ~ Égée** the Aegean (Sea); **la ~ Ionienne** the Ionian Sea; **la ~ Morte** the Dead Sea; **la ~ Noire** the Black Sea; **la ~ du Nord** the North Sea; **la ~ Rouge** the Red Sea; **la ~ des Sargasses** the Sargasso Sea, the Sargasso Sea; **les ~s du Sud** the South Seas; **la ~ Tyrrhénienne** the Tyrrhenian Sea.

mercantile [mɛʀkãtil] *adj* (*péj*) mercenary.

mercantilisme [mɛʀkãtilism(ə)] *nm* (*esprit mercantile*) mercenary attitude.

mercenaire [mɛʀsənɛʀ] *nm* mercenary.

mercerie [mɛʀsəʀi] *nf* (*COUTURE*) haberdashery (*BRIT*), notions *pl* (*US*); (*boutique*) haberdasher's shop (*BRIT*), notions store (*US*).

merci [mɛʀsi] *excl* thank you ♦ *nf*: **à la ~ de qn/qch** at sb's mercy/the mercy of sth; **~ beaucoup** thank you very much; **~ de** *ou* **pour** thank you for; **sans ~** *adj* merciless ♦ *adv* mercilessly.

mercier, ière [mɛʀsje, -jɛʀ] *nm/f* haberdasher.

mercredi [mɛʀkʀədi] nm Wednesday; ~ **des Cendres** Ash Wednesday; voir aussi **lundi**.

mercure [mɛʀkyʀ] nm mercury.

merde [mɛʀd(ə)] (fam!) nf shit (!) ♦ excl (bloody) hell (!).

merdeux, euse [mɛʀdø, -øz] nm/f (fam!) little bugger (BRIT !), little devil.

mère [mɛʀ] nf mother ♦ adj inv mother cpd; ~ **célibataire** single parent, unmarried mother.

merguez [mɛʀgɛz] nf spicy North African sausage.

méridien [meʀidjɛ̃] nm meridian.

méridional, e, aux [meʀidjɔnal, -o] adj southern; (du midi de la France) Southern (French) ♦ nm/f Southerner.

meringue [məʀɛ̃g] nf meringue.

mérinos [meʀinos] nm merino.

merisier [məʀizje] nm wild cherry (tree).

méritant, e [meʀitɑ̃, -ɑ̃t] adj deserving.

mérite [meʀit] nm merit; **le ~ (de ceci) lui revient** the credit (for this) is his.

mériter [meʀite] vt to deserve; ~ **de réussir** to deserve to succeed; **il mérite qu'on fasse ...** he deserves people to do ....

méritocratie [meʀitɔkʀasi] nf meritocracy.

méritoire [meʀitwaʀ] adj praiseworthy, commendable.

merlan [mɛʀlɑ̃] nm whiting.

merle [mɛʀl(ə)] nm blackbird.

mérou [meʀu] nm grouper (fish).

merveille [mɛʀvɛj] nf marvel, wonder; **faire ~ ou des ~s** to work wonders; **à ~** perfectly, wonderfully.

merveilleux, euse [mɛʀvɛjø, -øz] adj marvellous, wonderful.

mes [me] dét voir **mon**.

mésalliance [mezaljɑ̃s] nf misalliance, mismatch.

mésallier [mezalje]: **se ~** vi to marry beneath (ou above) o.s.

mésange [mezɑ̃ʒ] nf tit(mouse) (pl -mice); ~ **bleue** bluetit.

mésaventure [mezavɑ̃tyʀ] nf misadventure, misfortune.

Mesdames [medam] nfpl voir **Madame**.

Mesdemoiselles [medmwazɛl] nfpl voir **Mademoiselle**.

mésentente [mezɑ̃tɑ̃t] nf dissension, disagreement.

mésestimer [mezɛstime] vt to underestimate, underrate.

Mésopotamie [mezɔpɔtami] nf: **la ~** Mesopotamia.

mésopotamien, ne [mezɔpɔtamjɛ̃, -ɛn] adj Mesopotamian.

mesquin, e [mɛskɛ̃, -in] adj mean, petty.

mesquinerie [mɛskinʀi] nf meanness no pl, pettiness no pl.

mess [mɛs] nm mess.

message [mesaʒ] nm message; ~ **d'erreur** (INFORM) error message; ~ **(de guidage)** (INFORM) prompt; ~ **publicitaire** ad, advertisement; ~ **téléphoné** telegram dictated by telephone.

messager, ère [mesaʒe, -ɛʀ] nm/f messenger.

messagerie [mesaʒʀi] nf: ~ **(électronique)** (electronic) bulletin board; ~ **rose** lonely hearts and contact service on videotext; **~s aériennes/ maritimes** air freight/shipping service sg; **~s de presse** press distribution service.

messe [mɛs] nf mass; **aller à la ~** to go to mass; ~ **de minuit** midnight mass; **faire des ~s basses** (fig, péj) to mutter.

messie [mesi] nm: **le M~** the Messiah.

Messieurs [mesjø] nmpl voir **Monsieur**.

mesure [məzyʀ] nf (évaluation, dimension) measurement; (étalon, récipient, contenu) measure; (MUS: cadence) time, tempo; (: division) bar; (retenue) moderation; (disposition) measure, step; **unité/système de ~** unit/system of measurement; **sur ~** (costume) made-to-measure; (fig) personally adapted; **à la ~ de** (fig: personne) worthy of; (chambre etc) on the same scale as; **dans la ~ où** insofar as, inasmuch as; **dans une certaine ~** to some ou a certain extent; **à ~ que** as; **en ~** (MUS) in time ou tempo; **être en ~ de** to be in a position to; **dépasser la ~** (fig) to overstep the mark.

mesuré, e [məzyʀe] adj (ton, effort) measured; (personne) restrained.

mesurer [məzyʀe] vt to measure; (juger) to weigh up, assess; (limiter) to limit, ration; (modérer) to moderate; (proportionner): ~ **qch à** to match sth to, gear sth to; **se ~ avec** to have a confrontation with; to tackle; **il mesure 1 m 80** he's 1 m 80 tall.

met [mɛ] vb voir **mettre**.

métabolisme [metabɔlism(ə)] nm metabolism.

métairie [meteʀi] nf smallholding.

métal, aux [metal, -o] nm metal.

métalangue [metalɑ̃g] nm metalanguage.

métallique [metalik] adj metallic.

métallisé, e [metalize] adj metallic.

métallurgie [metalyʀʒi] nf metallurgy.

métallurgique [metalyʀʒik] adj steel cpd, metal cpd.

métallurgiste [metalyʀʒist(ə)] nm/f (ouvrier) steel ou metal worker; (industriel) metallurgist.

métamorphose [metamɔʀfoz] nf metamorphosis (pl -oses).

métamorphoser [metamɔʀfoze] vt to transform.

métaphore [metafɔʀ] nf metaphor.

métaphorique [metafɔʀik] adj metaphorical, figurative.

métaphoriquement [metafɔʀikmɑ̃] adv metaphorically.

métaphysique [metafizik] nf metaphysics sg ♦ adj metaphysical.

métapsychique [metapsiʃik] adj psychic,

parapsychological.

métayer, ère [meteje, metɛjɛʀ] *nm/f* (tenant) farmer.

météo [meteo] *nf* (*bulletin*) (weather) forecast; (*service*) ≈ Met Office (*BRIT*), ≈ National Weather Service (*US*).

météore [meteɔʀ] *nm* meteor.

météorite [meteɔʀit] *nm ou f* meteorite.

météorologie [meteɔʀɔlɔʒi] *nf* (*étude*) meteorology; (*service*) ≈ Meteorological Office (*BRIT*), ≈ National Weather Service (*US*).

météorologique [meteɔʀɔlɔʒik] *adj* meteorological, weather *cpd*.

météorologue [meteɔʀɔlɔg] *nm/f*, **météorologiste** [meteɔʀɔlɔʒist(ə)] *nm/f* meteorologist, weather forecaster.

métèque [metɛk] *nm* (*péj*) wop (*!*).

méthane [metan] *nm* methane.

méthanier [metanje] *nm* (*bateau*) (liquefied) gas carrier *ou* tanker.

méthode [metɔd] *nf* method; (*livre, ouvrage*) manual, tutor.

méthodique [metɔdik] *adj* methodical.

méthodiquement [metɔdikmã] *adv* methodically.

méthodiste [metɔdist(ə)] *adj, nm/f* (*REL*) Methodist.

méthylène [metilɛn] *nm*: **bleu de ~** *nm* methylene blue.

méticuleux, euse [metikylø, -øz] *adj* meticulous.

métier [metje] *nm* (*profession: gén*) job; (: *manuel*) trade; (: *artisanal*) craft; (*technique, expérience*) (acquired) skill *ou* technique; (*aussi*: **~ à tisser**) (weaving) loom; **être du ~** to be in the trade *ou* profession.

métis, se [metis] *adj, nm/f* half-caste, half-breed.

métisser [metise] *vt* to cross(breed).

métrage [metʀaʒ] *nm* (*de tissu*) length; (*CINÉ*) footage, length; **long/moyen/court ~** feature *ou* full-length/medium-length/short film.

mètre [mɛtʀ(ə)] *nm* metre (*BRIT*), meter (*US*); (*règle*) (metre *ou* meter) rule; (*ruban*) tape measure; **~ carré/cube** square/cubic metre *ou* meter.

métrer [metʀe] *vt* (*TECH*) to measure (in metres *ou* meters); (*CONSTR*) to survey.

métreur, euse [metʀœʀ, -øz] *nm/f*: **~ (vérificateur), métreuse (vérificatrice)** (quantity) surveyor.

métrique [metʀik] *adj* metric ♦ *nf* metrics *sg*.

métro [metʀo] *nm* underground (*BRIT*), subway (*US*).

métronome [metʀɔnɔm] *nm* metronome.

métropole [metʀɔpɔl] *nf* (*capitale*) metropolis; (*pays*) home country.

métropolitain, e [metʀɔpɔlitɛ̃, -ɛn] *adj* metropolitan.

mets [mɛ] *nm* dish ♦ *vb voir* **mettre**.

mettable [mɛtabl(ə)] *adj* fit to be worn, decent.

metteur [mɛtœʀ] *nm*: **~ en scène** (*THÉÂT*) producer; (*CINÉ*) director; **~ en ondes** (*RADIO*) producer.

=== *MOT-CLÉ*

mettre [mɛtʀ(ə)] *vt* **1** (*placer*) to put; **~ en bouteille/en sac** to bottle/put in bags *ou* sacks; **~ qch à la poste** to post sth (*BRIT*), mail sth; **~ en examen (pour)** to charge (with) (*BRIT*), indict (for) (*US*); **~ une note gaie/amusante** to inject a cheerful/an amusing note; **~ qn debout/assis** to help sb up *ou* to their feet/help sb to sit down

2 (*vêtements: revêtir*) to put on; (: *porter*) to wear; **mets ton gilet** put your cardigan on; **je ne mets plus mon manteau** I no longer wear my coat

3 (*faire fonctionner: chauffage, électricité*) to put on; (: *reveil, minuteur*) to set; (*installer: gaz, eau*) to put in, lay on; **~ en marche** to start up

4 (*consacrer*): **~ du temps/2 heures à faire qch** to take time/2 hours to do sth *ou* over sth; **y ~ du sien** to pull one's weight

5 (*noter, écrire*) to say, put (down); **qu'est-ce qu'il a mis sur la carte?** what did he say *ou* write on the card?; **mettez au pluriel** ... put ... into the plural

6 (*supposer*): **mettons que** ... let's suppose *ou* say that ...

7 (*faire +vb*): **faire ~ le gaz/l'électricité** to have gas/electricity put in *ou* installed

se ~ *vi* **1** (*se placer*): **vous pouvez vous ~ là** you can sit (*ou* stand) there; **où ça se met?** where does it go?; **se ~ au lit** to get into bed; **se ~ au piano** to sit down at the piano; **se ~ à l'eau** to get into the water; **se ~ de l'encre sur les doigts** to get ink on one's fingers

2 (*s'habiller*): **se ~ en maillot de bain** to get into *ou* put on a swimsuit; **n'avoir rien à se ~** to have nothing to wear

3 (*dans rapports*): **se ~ bien/mal avec qn** to get on the right/wrong side of sb; **se ~ qn à dos** to get on sb's bad side; **se ~ avec qn** (*prendre parti*) to side with sb; (*faire équipe*) to team up with sb; (*en ménage*) to move in with sb

4: **se ~ à** to begin, start; **se ~ à faire** to begin *ou* start doing *ou* to do; **se ~ au piano** to start learning the piano; **se ~ au régime** to go on a diet; **se ~ au travail/à l'étude** to get down to work/one's studies; **il est temps de s'y ~** it's time we got down to it *ou* got on with it.

==========

meublant, e [mœblã, -ãt] *adj* (*tissus etc*) effective (in the room).

meuble [mœbl(ə)] *nm* (*objet*) piece of furniture; (*ameublement*) furniture *no pl* ♦ *adj* (*terre*) loose, friable; (*JUR*): **biens ~s** movables.

meublé [mœble] *nm* (*pièce*) furnished room; (*appartement*) furnished flat (*BRIT*) *ou* apartment (*US*).

meubler [mœble] *vt* to furnish; (*fig*): ~ **qch (de)** to fill sth (with); **se ~** to furnish one's house.

meugler [møgle] *vi* to low, moo.

meule [møl] *nf* (*à broyer*) millstone; (*à aiguiser*) grindstone; (*à polir*) buffwheel; (*de foin, blé*) stack; (*de fromage*) round.

meunerie [mønʀi] *nf* (*industrie*) flour trade; (*métier*) milling.

meunier, ière [mønje, -jɛʀ] *nm* miller ♦ *nf* miller's wife ♦ *adj f* (*CULIN*) meunière.

meurs [mœʀ] *etc vb voir* **mourir.**

meurtre [mœʀtʀ(ə)] *nm* murder.

meurtrier, ière [mœʀtʀije, -jɛʀ] *adj* (*arme, épidémie, combat*) deadly; (*accident*) fatal; (*carrefour, route*) lethal; (*fureur, instincts*) murderous ♦ *nm/f* murderer/murderess ♦ *nf* (*ouverture*) loophole.

meurtrir [mœʀtʀiʀ] *vt* to bruise; (*fig*) to wound.

meurtrissure [mœʀtʀisyʀ] *nf* bruise; (*fig*) scar.

meus [mœ] *etc vb voir* **mouvoir.**

Meuse [møz] *nf*: **la ~** the Meuse.

meute [møt] *nf* pack.

meuve [mœv] *etc vb voir* **mouvoir.**

mévente [mevɑ̃t] *nf* slump (in sales).

mexicain, e [mɛksikɛ̃, -ɛn] *adj* Mexican ♦ *nm/f*: **M~, e** Mexican.

Mexico [mɛksiko] *n* Mexico City.

Mexique [mɛksik] *nm*: **le ~** Mexico.

MF *sigle mpl = millions de francs* ♦ *sigle f* (*RADIO*: = *modulation de fréquence*) FM.

Mgr *abr =* **Monseigneur.**

mi [mi] *nm* (*MUS*) E; (*en chantant la gamme*) mi.

mi... [mi] *préfixe* half(-); mid-; **à la ~-janvier** in mid-January; **~-bureau, ~-chambre** half office, half bedroom; **à ~-jambes/-corps** (up *ou* down) to the knees/waist; **à ~-hauteur/-pente** halfway up (*ou* down)/up (*ou* down) the hill.

miaou [mjau] *nm* miaow.

miaulement [mjolmɑ̃] *nm* (*cri*) miaow; (*continu*) miaowing *no pl*.

miauler [mjole] *vi* to miaow.

mi-bas [miba] *nm inv* knee-length sock.

mica [mika] *nm* mica.

mi-carême [mikaʀɛm] *nf*: **la ~** the third Thursday in Lent.

miche [miʃ] *nf* round *ou* cob loaf.

mi-chemin [miʃmɛ̃]: **à ~** *adv* halfway, midway.

mi-clos, e [miklo, -kloz] *adj* half-closed.

micmac [mikmak] *nm* (*péj*) carry-on.

mi-côte [mikot]: **à ~** *adv* halfway up (*ou* down) the hill.

mi-course [mikuʀs]: **à ~** *adv* halfway through the race.

micro [mikʀo] *nm* mike, microphone; (*INFORM*) micro; **~ cravate** lapel mike.

microbe [mikʀɔb] *nm* germ, microbe.

microbiologie [mikʀɔbjɔlɔʒi] *nf* microbiology.

microchirurgie [mikʀɔʃiʀyʀʒi] *nf* microsurgery.

microclimat [mikʀoklima] *nm* microclimate.

microcosme [mikʀɔkɔsm(ə)] *nm* microcosm.

micro-édition [mikʀɔedisjɔ̃] *nf* desk-top publishing.

micro-électronique [mikʀɔelɛktʀɔnik] *nf* microelectronics *sg*.

microfiche [mikʀɔfiʃ] *nf* microfiche.

microfilm [mikʀɔfilm] *nm* microfilm.

micro-onde [mikʀɔɔ̃d] *nf*: **four à ~s** microwave oven.

micro-ordinateur [mikʀɔɔʀdinatœʀ] *nm* microcomputer.

micro-organisme [mikʀoɔʀganism(ə)] *nm* micro-organism.

microphone [mikʀɔfɔn] *nm* microphone.

microplaquette [mikʀɔplakɛt] *nf* microchip.

microprocesseur [mikʀɔpʀɔsɛsœʀ] *nm* microprocessor.

microscope [mikʀoskɔp] *nm* microscope; **au ~** under *ou* through the microscope.

microscopique [mikʀɔskɔpik] *adj* microscopic.

microsillon [mikʀɔsijɔ̃] *nm* long-playing record.

MIDEM [midɛm] *sigle m* (= *Marché international du disque et de l'édition musicale*) music industry trade fair.

midi [midi] *nm* (*milieu du jour*) midday, noon; (*moment du déjeuner*) lunchtime; (*sud*) south; (: *de la France*): **le M~** the South (of France), the Midi; **à ~** at 12 (o'clock) *ou* midday *ou* noon; **tous les ~s** every lunchtime; **le repas de ~** lunch; **en plein ~** (right) in the middle of the day; (*sud*) facing south.

midinette [midinɛt] *nf* silly young townie.

mie [mi] *nf* inside (of the loaf).

miel [mjɛl] *nm* honey; **être tout ~** (*fig*) to be all sweetness and light.

mielleux, euse [mjɛlø, -øz] *adj* (*péj*) sugary, honeyed.

mien, ne [mjɛ̃, mjɛn] *adj, pron*: **le (la) ~(ne), les ~s** mine; **les ~s** (*ma famille*) my family.

miette [mjɛt] *nf* (*de pain, gâteau*) crumb; (*fig: de la conversation etc*) scrap; **en ~s** (*fig*) in pieces *ou* bits.

═══════════════════ *MOT-CLÉ*

mieux [mjø] *adv* **1** (*d'une meilleure façon*): ~ **(que)** better (than); **elle travaille/mange ~** she works/eats better; **aimer ~** to prefer; **j'attendais ~ de vous** I expected better of you; **elle va ~** she is better; **de ~ en ~** better and better

2 (*de la meilleure façon*) best; **ce que je sais**

le ~ what I know best; **les livres les ~ faits**
the best made books
3 (*intensif*): **vous feriez ~ de faire ...** you
would be better to do ...; **crier à qui ~ ~ to**
try to shout each other down
♦ *adj* **1** (*plus à l'aise, en meilleure forme*)
better; **se sentir ~** to feel better
2 (*plus satisfaisant*) better; **c'est ~ ainsi** it's
better like this; **c'est le ~ des deux** it's the
better of the two; **le(la) ~, les ~** the best;
demandez-lui, c'est le ~ ask him, it's the
best thing
3 (*plus joli*) better-looking; (*plus gentil*)
nicer; **il est ~ que son frère** (*plus beau*) he's
better-looking than his brother; (*plus gentil*)
he's nicer than his brother; **il est ~ sans
moustache** he looks better without a
moustache
4: **au ~** at best; **au ~ avec** on the best of
terms with; **pour le ~** for the best; **qui ~ est**
even better, better still
♦ *nm* **1** (*progrès*) improvement
2: **de mon/ton ~** as best I/you can (*ou*
could); **faire de son ~** to do one's best; **du ~
qu'il peut** the best he can; **faute de ~** for
want of anything better, failing anything
better.

mieux-être [mjøzɛtʀ(ə)] *nm* greater well-
being; (*financier*) improved standard of
living.
mièvre [mjɛvʀ(ə)] *adj* sickly sentimental.
mignon, ne [miɲɔ̃, -ɔn] *adj* sweet, cute.
migraine [migʀɛn] *nf* headache; migraine.
migrant, e [migʀɑ̃, -ɑ̃t] *adj, nm/f* migrant.
migrateur, trice [migʀatœʀ, -tʀis] *adj*
migratory.
migration [migʀasjɔ̃] *nf* migration.
mijaurée [miʒɔʀe] *nf* pretentious (young)
madam.
mijoter [miʒɔte] *vt* to simmer; (*préparer avec
soin*) to cook lovingly; (*affaire, projet*) to plot,
cook up ♦ *vi* to simmer.
mil [mil] *num* = **mille.**
Milan [milɑ̃] *n* Milan.
milanais, e [milanɛ, -ɛz] *adj* Milanese.
mildiou [mildju] *nm* mildew.
milice [milis] *nf* militia.
milicien, ne [milisjɛ̃, -ɛn] *nm/f* militiaman/
woman.
milieu, x [miljø] *nm* (*centre*) middle; (*fig*)
middle course *ou* way; (*aussi*: **juste ~**)
happy medium; (*BIO, GÉO*) environment;
(*entourage social*) milieu; (*familial*)
background; circle; (*pègre*): **le ~** the
underworld; **au ~ de** in the middle of; **au
beau** *ou* **en plein ~ (de)** right in the middle
(of); **~ de terrain** (*FOOTBALL: joueur*) midfield
player; (: *joueurs*) midfield.
militaire [militɛʀ] *adj* military ♦ *nm*
serviceman; **service ~** military service.
militant, e [militɑ̃, -ɑ̃t] *adj, nm/f* militant.

militantisme [militɑ̃tism(ə)] *nm* militancy.
militariser [militaʀize] *vt* to militarize.
militarisme [militaʀism(ə)] *nm* (*péj*)
militarism.
militer [milite] *vi* to be a militant; **~ pour/
contre** to militate in favour of/against.
milk-shake [milkʃɛk] *nm* milk shake.
mille [mil] *num* a *ou* one thousand ♦ *nm*
(*mesure*): **~ (marin)** nautical mile; **mettre
dans le ~** to hit the bull's-eye; (*fig*) to be
bang on (target).
millefeuille [milfœj] *nm* cream *ou* vanilla
slice.
millénaire [milenɛʀ] *nm* millennium ♦ *adj*
thousand-year-old; (*fig*) ancient.
mille-pattes [milpat] *nm inv* centipede.
millésime [milezim] *nm* year.
millésimé, e [milezime] *adj* vintage *cpd*.
millet [mijɛ] *nm* millet.
milliard [miljaʀ] *nm* milliard, thousand
million (*BRIT*), billion (*US*).
milliardaire [miljaʀdɛʀ] *nm/f* multimillionaire
(*BRIT*), billionaire (*US*).
millième [miljɛm] *num* thousandth.
millier [milje] *nm* thousand; **un ~ (de)** a
thousand or so, about a thousand; **par ~s** in
(their) thousands, by the thousand.
milligramme [miligʀam] *nm* milligramme
(*BRIT*), milligram (*US*).
millimètre [milimɛtʀ(ə)] *nm* millimetre (*BRIT*),
millimeter (*US*).
millimétré, e [milimetʀe] *adj*: **papier ~** graph
paper.
million [miljɔ̃] *nm* million; **deux ~s de** two
million; **riche à ~s** worth millions.
millionième [miljɔnjɛm] *num* millionth.
millionnaire [miljɔnɛʀ] *nm/f* millionaire.
mi-lourd [miluʀ] *adj m, nm* light heavyweight.
mime [mim] *nm/f* (*acteur*) mime(r); (*imitateur*)
mimic ♦ *nm* (*art*) mime, miming.
mimer [mime] *vt* to mime; (*singer*) to mimic,
take off.
mimétisme [mimetism(ə)] *nm* (*BIO*) mimicry.
mimique [mimik] *nf* (funny) face; (*signes*)
gesticulations *pl*, sign language *no pl*.
mimosa [mimoza] *nm* mimosa.
mi-moyen [mimwajɛ̃] *adj m, nm* welterweight.
MIN *sigle m* (= *Marché d'intérêt national*)
*wholesale market for fruit, vegetables and
agricultural produce.*
min. *abr* (= *minimum*) min.
minable [minabl(ə)] *adj* (*personne*) shabby
(-looking); (*travail*) pathetic.
minaret [minaʀɛ] *nm* minaret.
minauder [minode] *vi* to mince, simper.
minauderies [minodʀi] *nfpl* simperings.
mince [mɛ̃s] *adj* thin; (*personne, taille*) slim,
slender; (*fig: profit, connaissance*) slight,
small; (: *prétexte*) weak ♦ *excl*: **~ (alors)!** darn
it!
minceur [mɛ̃sœʀ] *nf* thinness; slimness,
slenderness.

mincir [mɛ̃siʀ] *vi* to get slimmer *ou* thinner.

mine [min] *nf* (*physionomie*) expression, look; (*extérieur*) exterior, appearance; (*de crayon*) lead; (*gisement, exploitation, explosif*) mine; ~**s** *nfpl* (*péj*) simpering airs; **les M~s** (*ADMIN*) *the national mining and geological service*; *the government vehicle testing department*; **avoir bonne** ~ (*personne*) to look well; (*ironique*) to look an utter idiot; **avoir mauvaise** ~ to look unwell *ou* poorly; **faire** ~ **de faire** to make a pretence of doing; to make as if to do; **ne pas payer de** ~ to be not much to look at; ~ **de rien** *adv* with a casual air; although you wouldn't think so; ~ **de charbon** coalmine; ~ **à ciel ouvert** opencast (*BRIT*) *ou* open-air (*US*) mine.

miner [mine] *vt* (*saper*) to undermine, erode; (*MIL*) to mine.

minerai [minʀɛ] *nm* ore.

minéral, e, aux [mineʀal, -o] *adj* mineral; (*CHIMIE*) inorganic ♦ *nm* mineral.

minéralier [mineʀalje] *nm* (*bateau*) ore tanker.

minéralisé, e [mineʀalize] *adj* mineralized.

minéralogie [mineʀalɔʒi] *nf* mineralogy.

minéralogique [mineʀalɔʒik] *adj* mineralogical; **plaque** ~ number (*BRIT*) *ou* license (*US*) plate; **numéro** ~ registration (*BRIT*) *ou* license (*US*) number.

minet, te [minɛ, -ɛt] *nm/f* (*chat*) pussy-cat; (*péj*) young trendy.

mineur, e [minœʀ] *adj* minor ♦ *nm/f* (*JUR*) minor ♦ *nm* (*travailleur*) miner; (*MIL*) sapper; ~ **de fond** face worker.

miniature [minjatyʀ] *adj, nf* miniature.

miniaturisation [minjatyʀizasjɔ̃] *nf* miniaturization.

miniaturiser [minjatyʀize] *vt* to miniaturize.

minibus [minibys] *nm* minibus.

mini-cassette [minikasɛt] *nf* cassette (recorder).

minichaîne [miniʃɛn] *nf* mini system.

minier, ière [minje, -jɛʀ] *adj* mining.

mini-jupe [miniʒyp] *nf* mini-skirt.

minimal, e, aux [minimal, -o] *adj* minimum.

minimaliste [minimalist(ə)] *adj* (*ART*) minimalist.

minime [minim] *adj* minor, minimal ♦ *nm/f* (*SPORT*) junior.

minimiser [minimize] *vt* to minimize; (*fig*) to play down.

minimum [minimɔm] *adj, nm* minimum; **au** ~ at the very least; ~ **vital** (*salaire*) living wage; (*niveau de vie*) subsistance level.

mini-ordinateur [miniɔʀdinatœʀ] *nm* minicomputer.

ministère [ministɛʀ] *nm* (*cabinet*) government; (*département*) ministry (*BRIT*), department; (*REL*) ministry; ~ **public** (*JUR*) Prosecution, State Prosecutor.

ministériel, le [ministeʀjɛl] *adj* government *cpd*; ministerial, departmental; (*partisan*) pro-government.

ministrable [ministʀabl(ə)] *adj* (*POL*): **il est** ~ he's a potential minister.

ministre [ministʀ(ə)] *nm* minister (*BRIT*), secretary; (*REL*) minister; ~ **d'État** senior minister *ou* secretary.

Minitel [minitɛl] *nm* ® *videotext terminal and service.*

Minitel *is a personal computer terminal supplied free of charge by France-Télécom to telephone subscribers. It serves as a computerized telephone directory as well as giving access to a wide variety of services, including information on train timetables, the stock market and situations vacant. Services are accessed by dialling the relevant number on the telephone, and services used are included in the subscriber's phone bill.*

---

minium [minjɔm] *nm* red lead paint.

minois [minwa] *nm* little face.

minorer [minɔʀe] *vt* to cut, reduce.

minoritaire [minɔʀitɛʀ] *adj* minority *cpd*.

minorité [minɔʀite] *nf* minority; **être en** ~ to be in the *ou* a minority; **mettre en** ~ (*POL*) to defeat.

Minorque [minɔʀk] *nf* Minorca.

minorquin, e [minɔʀkɛ̃, -in] *adj* Minorcan.

minoterie [minɔtʀi] *nf* flour-mill.

minuit [minɥi] *nm* midnight.

minuscule [minyskyl] *adj* minute, tiny ♦ *nf*: (**lettre**) ~ small letter.

minutage [minytaʒ] *nm* timing.

minute [minyt] *nf* minute; (*JUR: original*) minute, draft ♦ *excl* just a minute!, hang on!; **à la** ~ (*présent*) (just) this instant; (*passé*) there and then; **entrecôte** *ou* **steak** ~ minute steak.

minuter [minyte] *vt* to time.

minuterie [minytʀi] *nf* time switch.

minuteur [minytœʀ] *nm* timer.

minutie [minysi] *nf* meticulousness; minute detail; **avec** ~ meticulously; in minute detail.

minutieusement [minysjøzmɑ̃] *adv* (*organiser, travailler*) meticulously; (*examiner*) minutely.

minutieux, euse [minysjø, -øz] *adj* (*personne*) meticulous; (*inspection*) minutely detailed; (*travail*) requiring painstaking attention to detail.

mioche [mjɔʃ] *nm* (*fam*) nipper, brat.

mirabelle [miʀabɛl] *nf* (*fruit*) (cherry) plum; (*eau-de-vie*) plum brandy.

miracle [miʀakl(ə)] *nm* miracle.

miraculé, e [miʀakyle] *adj* who has been miraculously cured (*ou* rescued).

miraculeux, euse [miʀakylø, -øz] *adj* miraculous.

mirador [miʀadɔʀ] *nm* (*MIL*) watchtower.

mirage [miʀaʒ] *nm* mirage.

mire [miʀ] *nf* (*d'un fusil*) sight; (*TV*) test card; **point de** ~ target; (*fig*) focal point; **ligne de**

~ line of sight.

mirent [miʀ] *vb voir* **mettre**.

mirer [miʀe] *vt* (œufs) to candle; **se** ~ *vi*: **se** ~ **dans** (suj: personne) to gaze at one's reflection in; (: chose) to be mirrored in.

mirifique [miʀifik] *adj* wonderful.

mirobolant, e [miʀɔbɔlɑ̃, -ɑ̃t] *adj* fantastic.

miroir [miʀwaʀ] *nm* mirror.

miroiter [miʀwate] *vi* to sparkle, shimmer; **faire** ~ **qch à qn** to paint sth in glowing colours for sb, dangle sth in front of sb's eyes.

miroiterie [miʀwatʀi] *nf* (usine) mirror factory; (magasin) mirror dealer's (shop).

Mis *abr* = **marquis**.

mis, e [mi, miz] *pp de* **mettre** ♦ *adj* (couvert, table) set, laid; (personne): **bien** ~ well dressed ♦ *nf* (argent: au jeu) stake; (tenue) clothing; attire; **être de** ~**e** to be acceptable *ou* in season; ~**e en bouteilles** bottling; ~**e en examen** charging, indictment; ~**e à feu** blast-off; ~**e de fonds** capital outlay; ~**e à jour** updating; ~**e à mort** kill; ~**e à pied** (d'un employé) suspension; lay-off; ~**e sur pied** (d'une affaire, entreprise) setting up; ~**e en plis** set; ~**e au point** (PHOTO) focusing; (fig) clarification; ~**e à prix** reserve (BRIT) *ou* upset price; ~**e en scène** production.

misaine [mizɛn] *nf*: **mât de** ~ foremast.

misanthrope [mizɑ̃tʀɔp] *nm/f* misanthropist.

Mise *abr* = **marquise**.

mise [miz] *adj f, nf voir* **mis**.

miser [mize] *vt* (enjeu) to stake, bet; ~ **sur** *vt* (cheval, numéro) to bet on; (fig) to bank *ou* count on.

misérable [mizeʀabl(ə)] *adj* (lamentable, malheureux) pitiful, wretched; (pauvre) poverty-stricken; (insignifiant, mesquin) miserable ♦ *nm/f* wretch; (miséreux) poor wretch.

misère [mizɛʀ] *nf* (pauvreté) (extreme) poverty, destitution; ~**s** *nfpl* (malheurs) woes, miseries; (ennuis) little troubles; **être dans la** ~ to be destitute *ou* poverty-stricken; **salaire de** ~ starvation wage; **faire des** ~**s à qn** to torment sb; ~ **noire** utter destitution, abject poverty.

miséreux, euse [mizeʀø, -øz] *adj* poverty-stricken ♦ *nm/f* down-and-out.

miséricorde [mizeʀikɔʀd(ə)] *nf* mercy, forgiveness.

miséricordieux, euse [mizeʀikɔʀdjø, -øz] *adj* merciful, forgiving.

misogyne [mizɔʒin] *adj* misogynous ♦ *nm/f* misogynist.

missel [misɛl] *nm* missal.

missile [misil] *nm* missile.

mission [misjɔ̃] *nf* mission; **partir en** ~ (ADMIN, POL) to go on an assignment.

missionnaire [misjɔnɛʀ] *nm/f* missionary.

missive [misiv] *nf* missive.

mistral [mistʀal] *nm* mistral (wind).

mit [mi] *vb voir* **mettre**.

mitaine [mitɛn] *nf* mitt(en).

mite [mit] *nf* clothes moth.

mité, e [mite] *adj* moth-eaten.

mi-temps [mitɑ̃] *nf inv* (SPORT: période) half (pl halves); (: pause) half-time; **à** ~ *adj, adv* part-time.

miteux, euse [mitø, -øz] *adj* seedy, shabby.

mitigé, e [mitiʒe] *adj* (conviction, ardeur) lukewarm; (sentiments) mixed.

mitonner [mitɔne] *vt* (préparer) to cook with loving care; (fig) to cook up quietly.

mitoyen, ne [mitwajɛ̃, -ɛn] *adj* common, party *cpd*; **maisons** ~**nes** semi-detached houses; (plus de deux) terraced (BRIT) *ou* row (US) houses.

mitraille [mitʀaj] *nf* (balles de fonte) grapeshot; (décharge d'obus) shellfire.

mitrailler [mitʀaje] *vt* to machine-gun; (fig: photographier) to snap away at; ~ **qn de** to pelt *ou* bombard sb with.

mitraillette [mitʀajɛt] *nf* submachine gun.

mitrailleur [mitʀajœʀ] *nm* machine gunner ♦ *adj m*: **fusil** ~ machine gun.

mitrailleuse [mitʀajøz] *nf* machine gun.

mitre [mitʀ(ə)] *nf* mitre.

mitron [mitʀɔ̃] *nm* baker's boy.

mi-voix [mivwa]: **à** ~ *adv* in a low *ou* hushed voice.

mixage [miksaʒ] *nm* (CINÉ) (sound) mixing.

mixer, mixeur [miksœʀ] *nm* (CULIN) (food) mixer.

mixité [miksite] *nf* (SCOL) coeducation.

mixte [mikst(ə)] *adj* (gén) mixed; (SCOL) mixed, coeducational; **à usage** ~ dual-purpose; **cuisinière** ~ combined gas and electric cooker; **équipe** ~ combined team.

mixture [mikstyʀ] *nf* mixture; (fig) concoction.

MJC *sigle f* (= maison des jeunes et de la culture) community arts centre and youth club.

ml *abr* (= millilitre) ml.

MLF *sigle m* (= Mouvement de libération de la femme) Women's Movement.

Mlle, *pl* **Mlles** *abr* = **Mademoiselle**.

MM *abr* = **Messieurs**; *voir* **Monsieur**.

Mme, *pl* **Mmes** *abr* = **Madame**.

mn. *abr* (= minute) min.

mnémotechnique [mnemɔtɛknik] *adj* mnemonic.

MNS *sigle m* (= maître nageur sauveteur) ≈ lifeguard.

MO *sigle f* (= main-d'œuvre) labour costs (on invoices).

Mo *abr* = **méga-octet**, **métro**.

mobile [mɔbil] *adj* mobile; (amovible) loose, removable; (pièce de machine) moving; (élément de meuble etc) movable ♦ *nm* (motif) motive; (œuvre d'art) mobile; (PHYSIQUE) moving object *ou* body.

mobilier, ière [mɔbilje, -jɛʀ] *adj* (JUR) personal ♦ *nm* (meubles) furniture; **valeurs**

mobilières transferable securities; **vente mobilière** sale of personal property ou chattels.

mobilisation [mɔbilizasjɔ̃] nf mobilization.

mobiliser [mɔbilize] vt (MIL, gén) to mobilize.

mobilité [mɔbilite] nf mobility.

mobylette [mɔbilɛt] nf ® moped.

mocassin [mɔkasɛ̃] nm moccasin.

moche [mɔʃ] adj (fam: laid) ugly; (: mauvais, méprisable) rotten.

modalité [mɔdalite] nf form, mode; **~s** nfpl (d'un accord etc) clauses, terms; **~s de paiement** methods of payment.

mode [mɔd] nf fashion; (commerce) fashion trade ou industry ♦ nm (manière) form, mode, method; (LING) mood; (INFORM, MUS) mode; **travailler dans la ~** to be in the fashion business; **à la ~** fashionable, in fashion; **~ dialogué** (INFORM) interactive ou conversational mode; **~ d'emploi** directions pl (for use); **~ de vie** way of life.

modelage [mɔdlaʒ] nm modelling.

modelé [mɔdle] nm (GÉO) relief; (du corps etc) contours pl.

modèle [mɔdɛl] adj model ♦ nm model; (qui pose: de peintre) sitter; (type) type; (gabarit, patron) pattern; **~ courant** ou **de série** (COMM) production model; **~ déposé** registered design; **~ réduit** small-scale model.

modeler [mɔdle] vt (ART) to model, mould; (suj: vêtement, érosion) to mould, shape; **~ qch sur/d'après** to model sth on.

modélisation [mɔdelizasjɔ̃] nf (MATH) modelling.

modéliste [mɔdelist(ə)] nm/f (COUTURE) designer; (de modèles réduits) model maker.

modem [mɔdɛm] nm modem.

Modène [mɔdɛn] n Modena.

modérateur, trice [mɔderatœr, -tris] adj moderating ♦ nm/f moderator.

modération [mɔderasjɔ̃] nf moderation; **~ de peine** reduction of sentence.

modéré, e [mɔdere] adj, nm/f moderate.

modérément [mɔderemɑ̃] adv moderately, in moderation.

modérer [mɔdere] vt to moderate; **se ~** vi to restrain o.s.

moderne [mɔdɛrn(ə)] adj modern ♦ nm (ART) modern style; (ameublement) modern furniture.

modernisation [mɔdɛrnizasjɔ̃] nf modernization.

moderniser [mɔdɛrnize] vt to modernize.

modernisme [mɔdɛrnism(ə)] nm modernism.

modernité [mɔdɛrnite] nf modernity.

modeste [mɔdɛst(ə)] adj modest; (origine) humble, lowly.

modestement [mɔdɛstəmɑ̃] adv modestly.

modestie [mɔdɛsti] nf modesty; **fausse ~** false modesty.

modicité [mɔdisite] nf: **la ~ des prix** etc the low prices etc.

modificatif, ive [mɔdifikatif, -iv] adj modifying.

modification [mɔdifikasjɔ̃] nf modification.

modifier [mɔdifje] vt to modify, alter; (LING) to modify; **se ~** vi to alter.

modique [mɔdik] adj (salaire, somme) modest.

modiste [mɔdist(ə)] nf milliner.

modulaire [mɔdylɛr] adj modular.

modulation [mɔdylasjɔ̃] nf modulation; **~ de fréquence (FM** ou **MF)** frequency modulation (FM).

module [mɔdyl] nm module.

moduler [mɔdyle] vt to modulate; (air) to warble.

moelle [mwal] nf marrow; (fig) pith, core; **~ épinière** spinal chord.

moelleux, euse [mwalø, -øz] adj soft; (au goût, à l'ouïe) mellow; (gracieux, souple) smooth.

moellon [mwalɔ̃] nm rubble stone.

mœurs [mœr] nfpl (conduite) morals; (manières) manners; (pratiques sociales) habits; (mode de vie) life style sg; (d'une espèce animale) behaviour sg (BRIT), behavior sg (US); **femme de mauvaises ~** loose woman; **passer dans les ~** to become the custom; **contraire aux bonnes ~** contrary to proprieties.

mohair [mɔɛr] nm mohair.

moi [mwa] pron me; (emphatique): **~, je** ... for my part, I ..., I myself ... ♦ nm inv (PSYCH) ego, self; **à ~!** (à l'aide) help (me)!

moignon [mwaɲɔ̃] nm stump.

moi-même [mwamɛm] pron myself; (emphatique) I myself.

moindre [mwɛ̃dr(ə)] adj lesser; lower; **le(la) ~, les ~s** the least; the slightest; **le(la) ~ de** the least of; **c'est la ~ des choses** it's nothing at all.

moindrement [mwɛ̃drəmɑ̃] adv: **pas le ~** not in the least.

moine [mwan] nm monk, friar.

moineau, x [mwano] nm sparrow.

═══════════════════════════════ MOT-CLÉ

moins [mwɛ̃] adv **1** (comparatif): **~ (que)** less (than); **~ grand que** less tall than, not as tall as; **il a 3 ans de ~ que moi** he's 3 years younger than me; **il est ~ intelligent que moi** he's not as clever as me, he's less clever than me; **~ je travaille, mieux je me porte** the less I work, the better I feel
2 (superlatif): **le ~** (the) least; **c'est ce que j'aime le ~** it's what I like (the) least; **le(la) ~ doué(e)** the least gifted; **au ~, du ~** at least; **pour le ~** at the very least
3: **~ de** (quantité) less (than); (nombre) fewer (than); **~ de sable/d'eau** less sand/ water; **~ de livres/gens** fewer books/people; **~ de 2 ans** less than 2 years; **~ de midi** not yet midday
4: **de ~, en ~**: **100 F/3 jours de ~** 100 F/3

days less; **3 livres en** ~ 3 books fewer; 3 books too few; **de l'argent en** ~ less money; **le soleil en** ~ but for the sun, minus the sun; **de** ~ **en** ~ less and less; **en** ~ **de deux** in a flash *ou* a trice
5: à ~ **de, à** ~ **que** unless; **à** ~ **de faire** unless we do (*ou* he does *etc*); **à** ~ **que tu ne fasses** unless you do; **à** ~ **d'un accident** barring any accident
♦ *prép*: **4** ~ **2** 4 minus 2; **10 heures** ~ **5** 5 to 10; **il fait** ~ **5** it's 5 (degrees) below (freezing), it's minus 5; **il est** ~ **5** it's 5 to
♦ *nm* (*signe*) minus sign.

moins-value [mwɛ̃valy] *nf* (*ÉCON, COMM*) depreciation.
moire [mwaʀ] *nf* moiré.
moiré, e [mwaʀe] *adj* (*tissu, papier*) moiré, watered; (*reflets*) shimmering.
mois [mwa] *nm* month; (*salaire, somme dû*) (monthly) pay *ou* salary; **treizième** ~, **double** ~ extra month's salary.
moïse [mɔiz] *nm* Moses basket.
moisi, e [mwazi] *adj* mouldy (*BRIT*), moldy (*US*), mildewed ♦ *nm* mould, mold, mildew; **odeur de** ~ musty smell.
moisir [mwaziʀ] *vi* to go mouldy (*BRIT*) *ou* moldy (*US*); (*fig*) to rot; (*personne*) to hang about ♦ *vt* to make mouldy *ou* moldy.
moisissure [mwazisyʀ] *nf* mould *no pl* (*BRIT*), mold *no pl* (*US*).
moisson [mwasɔ̃] *nf* harvest; (*époque*) harvest (time); (*fig*): **faire une** ~ **de** to gather a wealth of.
moissonner [mwasɔne] *vt* to harvest, reap; (*fig*) to collect.
moissonneur, euse [mwasɔnœʀ, -øz] *nm/f* harvester, reaper ♦ *nf* (*machine*) harvester.
moissonneuse-batteuse, *pl* **moissonneuses-batteuses**
[mwasɔnøzbatøz] *nf* combine harvester.
moite [mwat] *adj* (*peau, mains*) sweaty, sticky; (*atmosphère*) muggy.
moitié [mwatje] *nf* half (*pl* halves); (*épouse*): **sa** ~ his better half; **la** ~ half; **la** ~ **de** half (of), half the amount (*ou* number) of; **la** ~ **du temps/des gens** half the time/the people; **à la** ~ **de** halfway through; ~ **moins grand** half as tall; ~ **plus long** half as long again, longer by half; **à** ~ half (*avant le verbe*), half- (*avant l'adjectif*); **à** ~ **prix** (at) half price, half-price; **de** ~ by half; ~ ~ half-and-half.
moka [mɔka] *nm* (*café*) mocha coffee; (*gâteau*) mocha cake.
mol [mɔl] *adj m voir* **mou.**
molaire [mɔlɛʀ] *nf* molar.
moldave [mɔldav] *adj* Moldavian.
Moldavie [mɔldavi] *nf*: **la** ~ Moldavia.
môle [mol] *nm* jetty.
moléculaire [mɔlekylɛʀ] *adj* molecular.
molécule [mɔlekyl] *nf* molecule.
moleskine [mɔlɛskin] *nf* imitation leather.

molester [mɔlɛste] *vt* to manhandle, maul (about).
molette [mɔlɛt] *nf* toothed *ou* cutting wheel.
mollasse [mɔlas] *adj* (*péj: sans énergie*) sluggish; (*: flasque*) flabby.
molle [mɔl] *adj f voir* **mou.**
mollement [mɔlmɑ̃] *adv* softly; (*péj*) sluggishly; (*protester*) feebly.
mollesse [mɔlɛs] *nf* (*voir mou*) softness; flabbiness; limpness; sluggishness; feebleness.
mollet [mɔlɛ] *nm* calf (*pl* calves) ♦ *adj m*: **œuf** ~ soft-boiled egg.
molletière [mɔltjɛʀ] *adj f*: **bande** ~ puttee.
molleton [mɔltɔ̃] *nm* (*TEXTILES*) felt.
molletonné, e [mɔltɔne] *adj* (*gants etc*) fleece-lined.
mollir [mɔliʀ] *vi* (*jambes*) to give way; (*NAVIG: vent*) to drop, die down; (*fig: personne*) to relent; (*: courage*) to fail, flag.
mollusque [mɔlysk(ə)] *nm* (*ZOOL*) mollusc; (*fig: personne*) lazy lump.
molosse [mɔlɔs] *nm* big ferocious dog.
môme [mom] *nm/f* (*fam: enfant*) brat; (*: fille*) bird (*BRIT*), chick.
moment [mɔmɑ̃] *nm* moment; (*occasion*): **profiter du** ~ to take (advantage of) the opportunity; **ce n'est pas le** ~ this is not the right time; **à un certain** ~ at some point; **à un** ~ **donné** at a certain point; **à quel** ~? when exactly?; **au même** ~ at the same time; (*instant*) at the same moment; **pour un bon** ~ for a good while; **pour le** ~ for the moment, for the time being; **au** ~ **de** at the time of; **au** ~ **où** as; at a time when; **à tout** ~ at any time *ou* moment; (*continuellement*) constantly, continually; **en ce** ~ at the moment; (*aujourd'hui*) at present; **sur le** ~ at the time; **par** ~s now and then, at times; **d'un** ~ **à l'autre** any time (now); **du** ~ **où** *ou* **que** seeing that, since; **n'avoir pas un** ~ **à soi** not to have a minute to oneself.
momentané, e [mɔmɑ̃tane] *adj* temporary, momentary.
momentanément [mɔmɑ̃tanemɑ̃] *adv* for a moment, for a while.
momie [mɔmi] *nf* mummy.
mon [mɔ̃], **ma** [ma], *pl* **mes** [me] *dét* my.
monacal, e, aux [mɔnakal, -o] *adj* monastic.
Monaco [mɔnako] *nm*: **le** ~ Monaco.
monarchie [mɔnaʀʃi] *nf* monarchy.
monarchiste [mɔnaʀʃist(ə)] *adj, nm/f* monarchist.
monarque [mɔnaʀk(ə)] *nm* monarch.
monastère [mɔnastɛʀ] *nm* monastery.
monastique [mɔnastik] *adj* monastic.
monceau, x [mɔ̃so] *nm* heap.
mondain, e [mɔ̃dɛ̃, -ɛn] *adj* (*soirée, vie*) society *cpd*; (*obligations*) social; (*peintre, écrivain*) fashionable; (*personne*) society *cpd* ♦ *nm/f* society man/woman, socialite ♦ *nf*: **la M**~**e**, **la police** ~**e** ≈ the vice squad.

mondanités [mɔ̃danite] *nfpl* (*vie mondaine*) society life *sg*; (*paroles*) (society) small talk *sg*; (*PRESSE*) (society) gossip column *sg*.

monde [mɔ̃d] *nm* world; (*personnes mondaines*): **le ~** (high) society; (*milieu*): **être du même ~** to move in the same circles; (*gens*): **il y a du ~** (*beaucoup de gens*) there are a lot of people; (*quelques personnes*) there are some people; **y a-t-il du ~ dans le salon?** is there anybody in the lounge?; **beaucoup/peu de ~** many/few people; **le meilleur** *etc* **du ~** the best *etc* in the world *ou* on earth; **mettre au ~** to bring into the world; **pas le moins du ~** not in the least; **se faire un ~ de qch** to make a great deal of fuss about sth; **tour du ~** round-the-world trip; **homme/femme du ~** society man/woman.

mondial, e, aux [mɔ̃djal, -o] *adj* (*population*) world *cpd*; (*influence*) world-wide.

mondialement [mɔ̃djalmɑ̃] *adv* throughout the world.

mondialisation [mɔ̃djalizasjɔ̃] *nf* (*d'une technique*) global application; (*d'un conflit*) global spread.

mondovision [mɔ̃dɔvizjɔ̃] *nf* (world coverage by) satellite television.

monégasque [mɔnegask(ə)] *adj* Monegasque, of *ou* from Monaco ♦ *nm/f*: **M~** Monegasque.

monétaire [mɔnetɛʀ] *adj* monetary.

monétarisme [mɔnetaʀism(ə)] *nm* monetarism.

monétique [mɔnetik] *nf* electronic money.

mongol, e [mɔ̃gɔl] *adj* Mongol, Mongolian ♦ *nm* (*LING*) Mongolian ♦ *nm/f*: **M~, e** (*MÉD*) Mongol, Mongoloid; (*de la Mongolie*) Mongolian.

Mongolie [mɔ̃gɔli] *nf*: **la ~** Mongolia.

mongolien, ne [mɔ̃gɔljɛ̃, -ɛn] *adj, nm/f* mongol.

mongolisme [mɔ̃gɔlism(ə)] *nm* mongolism, Down's syndrome.

moniteur, trice [mɔnitœʀ, -tʀis] *nm/f* (*SPORT*) instructor/instructress; (*de colonie de vacances*) supervisor ♦ *nm* (*écran*) monitor; **~ cardiaque** cardiac monitor; **~ d'auto-école** driving instructor.

monitorage [mɔnitɔʀaʒ] *nm* monitoring.

monitorat [mɔnitɔʀa] *nm* (*formation*) instructor's training (course); (*fonction*) instructorship.

monnaie [mɔnɛ] *nf* (*pièce*) coin; (*ÉCON, gén: moyen d'échange*) currency; (*petites pièces*): **avoir de la ~** to have (some) change; **faire de la ~** to get (some) change; **avoir/faire la ~ de 20 F** to have change of/get change for 20 F; **faire** *ou* **donner à qn la ~ de 20 F** to give sb change for 20 F, change 20 F for sb; **rendre à qn la ~ (sur 20 F)** to give sb the change (from *ou* out of 20 F); **servir de ~ d'échange** (*fig*) to be used as a bargaining counter *ou* as bargaining counters; **payer en ~ de singe** to fob (sb) off with empty

promises; **c'est ~ courante** it's a common occurrence; **~ légale** legal tender.

monnayable [mɔnɛjabl(ə)] *adj* (*vendable*) convertible into cash; **mes services sont ~s** my services are worth money.

monnayer [mɔnɛje] *vt* to convert into cash; (*talent*) to capitalize on.

monnayeur [mɔnɛjœʀ] *nm voir* **faux**.

mono [mɔno] *nf* (= *monophonie*) mono ♦ *nm* (= *monoski*) monoski.

monochrome [mɔnɔkʀom] *adj* monochrome.

monocle [mɔnɔkl(ə)] *nm* monocle, eyeglass.

monocoque [mɔnɔkɔk] *adj* (*voiture*) monocoque ♦ *nm* (*voilier*) monohull.

monocorde [mɔnɔkɔʀd(ə)] *adj* monotonous.

monoculture [mɔnɔkyltyʀ] *nf* single-crop farming, monoculture.

monogamie [mɔnɔgami] *nf* monogamy.

monogramme [mɔnɔgʀam] *nm* monogram.

monokini [mɔnɔkini] *nm* one-piece bikini, bikini pants *pl*.

monolingue [mɔnɔlɛ̃g] *adj* monolingual.

monolithique [mɔnɔlitik] *adj* (*lit, fig*) monolithic.

monologue [mɔnɔlɔg] *nm* monologue, soliloquy; **~ intérieur** stream of consciousness.

monologuer [mɔnɔlɔge] *vi* to soliloquize.

monôme [mɔnom] *nm* (*MATH*) monomial; (*d'étudiants*) students' rag procession.

monoparental, e, aux [mɔnɔpaʀɑ̃tal, -o] *adj*: **famille ~e** single-parent *ou* one-parent family.

monophasé, e [mɔnɔfaze] *adj* single-phase *cpd*.

monophonie [mɔnɔfɔni] *nf* monophony.

monoplace [mɔnɔplas] *adj, nm, nf* single-seater, one-seater.

monoplan [mɔnɔplɑ̃] *nm* monoplane.

monopole [mɔnɔpɔl] *nm* monopoly.

monopolisation [mɔnɔpɔlizasjɔ̃] *nf* monopolization.

monopoliser [mɔnɔpɔlize] *vt* to monopolize.

monorail [mɔnɔʀaj] *nm* monorail; monorail train.

monoski [mɔnɔski] *nm* monoski.

monosyllabe [mɔnɔsilab] *nm* monosyllable, word of one syllable.

monosyllabique [mɔnɔsilabik] *adj* monosyllabic.

monotone [mɔnɔtɔn] *adj* monotonous.

monotonie [mɔnɔtɔni] *nf* monotony.

monseigneur [mɔ̃sɛɲœʀ] *nm* (*archevêque, évêque*) Your (*ou* His) Grace; (*cardinal*) Your (*ou* His) Eminence; **Mgr Thomas** Bishop Thomas; Cardinal Thomas.

Monsieur [məsjø] *pl* **Messieurs** [mesjø] *titre* Mr ['mɪstə*] ♦ *nm* (*homme quelconque*): **un/le m~** a/the gentleman; *voir aussi* **Madame**.

monstre [mɔ̃stʀ(ə)] *nm* monster ♦ *adj* (*fam: effet, publicité*) massive; **un travail ~** a fantastic amount of work; an enormous job;

~ **sacré** superstar.

monstrueux, euse [mɔ̃stʀyø, -øz] *adj* monstrous.

monstruosité [mɔ̃stʀyozite] *nf* monstrosity.

mont [mɔ̃] *nm*: **par ~s et par vaux** up hill and down dale; **le M~ Blanc** Mont Blanc; ~ **de Vénus** mons veneris.

montage [mɔ̃taʒ] *nm* putting up; (*d'un bijou*) mounting, setting; (*d'une machine etc*) assembly; (*PHOTO*) photomontage; (*CINÉ*) editing; ~ **sonore** sound editing.

montagnard, e [mɔ̃taɲaʀ, -aʀd(ə)] *adj* mountain *cpd* ♦ *nm/f* mountain-dweller.

montagne [mɔ̃taɲ] *nf* (*cime*) mountain; (*région*): **la** ~ the mountains *pl*; **la haute** ~ the high mountains; **les ~s Rocheuses** the Rocky Mountains, the Rockies; **~s russes** big dipper *sg*, switchback *sg*.

montagneux, euse [mɔ̃taɲø, -øz] *adj* mountainous; hilly.

montant, e [mɔ̃tɑ̃, -ɑ̃t] *adj* (*mouvement, marée*) rising; (*chemin*) uphill; (*robe, corsage*) high-necked ♦ *nm* (*somme, total*) (sum) total, (total) amount; (*de fenêtre*) upright; (*de lit*) post.

mont-de-piété, *pl* **monts-de-piété** [mɔ̃dpjete] *nm* pawnshop.

monte [mɔ̃t] *nf* (*accouplement*): **la** ~ stud; (*d'un jockey*) seat.

monté, e [mɔ̃te] *adj*: **être** ~ **contre qn** to be angry with sb; (*fourni, équipé*): ~ **en** equipped with.

monte-charge [mɔ̃tʃaʀʒ(ə)] *nm inv* goods lift, hoist.

montée [mɔ̃te] *nf* rising, rise; (*escalade*) ascent, climb; (*chemin*) way up; (*côte*) hill; **au milieu de la** ~ halfway up; **le moteur chauffe dans les ~s** the engine overheats going uphill.

monte-plats [mɔ̃tpla] *nm inv* service lift.

monter [mɔ̃te] *vt* (*escalier, côte*) to go (*ou* come) up; (*valise, paquet*) to take (*ou* bring) up; (*cheval*) to mount; (*femelle*) to cover, serve; (*tente, échafaudage*) to put up; (*machine*) to assemble; (*bijou*) to mount, set; (*COUTURE*) to sew on; (: *manche*) to set in; (*CINÉ*) to edit; (*THÉÂT*) to put on, stage; (*société, coup etc*) to set up; (*fournir, équiper*) to equip ♦ *vi* to go (*ou* come) up; (*avion, voiture*) to climb, go up; (*chemin, niveau, température, voix, prix*) to go up, rise; (*brouillard, bruit*) to rise, come up; (*passager*) to get on; (*à cheval*): ~ **bien/mal** to ride well/badly; ~ **à cheval/bicyclette** to get on *ou* mount a horse/bicycle; (*faire du cheval etc*) to ride (a horse); to (ride a) bicycle; ~ **à pied/en voiture** to walk/drive up, go up on foot/by car; ~ **dans le train/l'avion** to get into the train/plane, board the train/plane; ~ **sur** to climb up onto; ~ **sur** *ou* **à un arbre/une échelle** to climb (up) a tree/ladder; ~ **à bord** to (get on) board; ~ **à la tête de qn** to

go to sb's head; ~ **sur les planches** to go on the stage; ~ **en grade** to be promoted; **se** ~ (*s'équiper*) to equip o.s., get kitted out (*BRIT*); **se** ~ **à** (*frais etc*) to add up to, come to; ~ **qn contre qn** to set sb against sb; ~ **la tête à qn** to give sb ideas.

monteur, euse [mɔ̃tœʀ, -øz] *nm/f* (*TECH*) fitter; (*CINÉ*) (film) editor.

monticule [mɔ̃tikyl] *nm* mound.

montmartrois, e [mɔ̃maʀtʀwa, -waz] *adj* of *ou* from Montmartre.

montre [mɔ̃tʀ(ə)] *nf* watch; (*ostentation*): **pour la** ~ for show; ~ **en main** exactly, to the minute; **faire** ~ **de** to show, display; **contre la** ~ (*SPORT*) against the clock; ~ **de plongée** diver's watch.

Montréal [mɔ̃real] *n* Montreal.

montréalais, e [mɔ̃realɛ, -ɛz] *adj* of *ou* from Montreal ♦ *nm/f*: **M~, e** Montrealer.

montre-bracelet, *pl* **montres-bracelets** [mɔ̃tʀəbʀaslɛ] *nf* wrist watch.

montrer [mɔ̃tʀe] *vt* to show; **se** ~ to appear; ~ **qch à qn** to show sb sth; ~ **qch du doigt** to point to sth, point one's finger at sth; **se** ~ **intelligent** to prove (to be) intelligent.

montreur, euse [mɔ̃tʀœʀ, -øz] *nm/f*: ~ **de marionnettes** puppeteer.

monture [mɔ̃tyʀ] *nf* (*bête*) mount; (*d'une bague*) setting; (*de lunettes*) frame.

monument [mɔnymɑ̃] *nm* monument; ~ **aux morts** war memorial.

monumental, e, aux [mɔnymɑ̃tal, -o] *adj* monumental.

moquer [mɔke]: **se** ~ **de** *vt* to make fun of, laugh at; (*fam: se désintéresser de*) not to care about; (*tromper*): **se** ~ **de qn** to take sb for a ride.

moquerie [mɔkʀi] *nf* mockery *no pl*.

moquette [mɔkɛt] *nf* fitted carpet, wall-to-wall carpeting *no pl*.

moquetter [mɔkete] *vt* to carpet.

moqueur, euse [mɔkœʀ, -øz] *adj* mocking.

moral, e, aux [mɔʀal, -o] *adj* moral ♦ *nm* morale ♦ *nf* (*conduite*) morals *pl*; (*règles*) moral code, ethic; (*valeurs*) moral standards *pl*, morality; (*science*) ethics *sg*, moral philosophy; (*conclusion: d'une fable etc*) moral; **au** ~, **sur le plan** ~ morally; **avoir le** ~ **à zéro** to be really down; **faire la ~e à qn** to lecture, preach at.

moralement [mɔʀalmɑ̃] *adv* morally.

moralisateur, trice [mɔʀalizatœʀ, -tʀis] *adj* moralizing, sanctimonious ♦ *nm/f* moralizer.

moraliser [mɔʀalize] *vt* (*sermonner*) to lecture, preach at.

moraliste [mɔʀalist(ə)] *nm/f* moralist ♦ *adj* moralistic.

moralité [mɔʀalite] *nf* (*d'une action, attitude*) morality; (*conduite*) morals *pl*; (*conclusion, enseignement*) moral.

moratoire [mɔʀatwaʀ] *adj m*: **intérêts ~s** (*ÉCON*) interest on arrears.

morave [mɔʀav] *adj* Moravian.

Moravie [mɔʀavi] *nf*: **la** ~ Moravia.

morbide [mɔʀbid] *adj* morbid.

morceau, x [mɔʀso] *nm* piece, bit; (*d'une œuvre*) passage, extract; (*MUS*) piece; (*CULIN*: *de viande*) cut; **mettre en** ~**x** to pull to pieces *ou* bits.

morceler [mɔʀsəle] *vt* to break up, divide up.

morcellement [mɔʀsɛlmɑ̃] *nm* breaking up.

mordant, e [mɔʀdɑ̃, -ɑ̃t] *adj* scathing, cutting; (*froid*) biting ♦ *nm* (*dynamisme, énergie*) spirit; (*fougue*) bite, punch.

mordicus [mɔʀdikys] *adv* (*fam*) obstinately, stubbornly.

mordiller [mɔʀdije] *vt* to nibble at, chew at.

mordoré, e [mɔʀdɔʀe] *adj* lustrous bronze.

mordre [mɔʀdʀ(ə)] *vt* to bite; (*suj: lime, vis*) to bite into ♦ *vi* (*poisson*) to bite; ~ **dans** to bite into; ~ **sur** (*fig*) to go over into, overlap into; ~ **à qch** (*comprendre, aimer*) to take to; ~ **à l'hameçon** to bite, rise to the bait.

mordu, e [mɔʀdy] *pp de* **mordre** ♦ *adj* (*amoureux*) smitten ♦ *nm/f*: **un** ~ **du jazz/de la voile** a jazz/sailing fanatic *ou* buff.

morfondre [mɔʀfɔ̃dʀ(ə)]: **se** ~ *vi* to mope.

morgue [mɔʀg(ə)] *nf* (*arrogance*) haughtiness; (*lieu: de la police*) morgue; (: *à l'hôpital*) mortuary.

moribond, e [mɔʀibɔ̃, -ɔ̃d] *adj* dying, moribund.

morille [mɔʀij] *nf* morel (*mushroom*).

mormon, e [mɔʀmɔ̃, -ɔn] *adj, nm/f* Mormon.

morne [mɔʀn(ə)] *adj* (*personne, visage*) glum, gloomy; (*temps, vie*) dismal, dreary.

morose [mɔʀoz] *adj* sullen, morose; (*marché*) sluggish.

morphine [mɔʀfin] *nf* morphine.

morphinomane [mɔʀfinɔman] *nm/f* morphine addict.

morphologie [mɔʀfɔlɔʒi] *nf* morphology.

morphologique [mɔʀfɔlɔʒik] *adj* morphological.

mors [mɔʀ] *nm* bit.

morse [mɔʀs(ə)] *nm* (*ZOOL*) walrus; (*TÉL*) Morse (code).

morsure [mɔʀsyʀ] *nf* bite.

mort¹ [mɔʀ] *nf* death; **se donner la** ~ to take one's own life; **de** ~ (*silence, pâleur*) deathly; **blessé à** ~ fatally wounded *ou* injured; **à la vie, à la** ~ for better, for worse; ~ **clinique** brain death; ~ **subite du nourrisson**, ~ **au berceau** cot death.

mort², e [mɔʀ, mɔʀt(ə)] *pp de* **mourir** ♦ *adj* dead ♦ *nm/f* (*défunt*) dead man/woman; (*victime*): **il y a eu plusieurs** ~**s** several people were killed, there were several killed ♦ *nm* (*CARTES*) dummy; ~ **ou vif** dead or alive; ~ **de peur/fatigue** frightened to death/dead tired; ~**s et blessés** casualties; **faire le** ~ to play dead; (*fig*) to lie low.

mortadelle [mɔʀtadɛl] *nf* mortadella (*type of luncheon meat*).

mortalité [mɔʀtalite] *nf* mortality, death rate.

mort-aux-rats [mɔʀtoʀa] *nf inv* rat poison.

mortel, le [mɔʀtɛl] *adj* (*poison etc*) deadly, lethal; (*accident, blessure*) fatal; (*REL, danger, frayeur*) mortal; (*fig: froid*) deathly; (: *ennui, soirée*) deadly (boring) ♦ *nm/f* mortal.

mortellement [mɔʀtɛlmɑ̃] *adv* (*blessé etc*) fatally, mortally; (*pâle etc*) deathly; (*fig: ennuyeux etc*) deadly.

morte-saison, *pl* **mortes-saisons** [mɔʀtəsɛzɔ̃] *nf* slack *ou* off season.

mortier [mɔʀtje] *nm* (*gén*) mortar.

mortifier [mɔʀtifje] *vt* to mortify.

mort-né, e [mɔʀne] *adj* (*enfant*) stillborn; (*fig*) abortive.

mortuaire [mɔʀtɥɛʀ] *adj* funeral *cpd*; **avis** ~**s** death announcements, intimations; **chapelle** ~ mortuary chapel; **couronne** ~ (funeral) wreath; **domicile** ~ house of the deceased; **drap** ~ pall.

morue [mɔʀy] *nf* (*ZOOL*) cod *inv*; (*CULIN*: *salée*) salt-cod.

morutier [mɔʀytje] *nm* (*pêcheur*) cod fisherman; (*bateau*) cod fishing boat.

morvandeau, elle, x [mɔʀvɑ̃do, -ɛl] *adj* of *ou* from the Morvan region.

morveux, euse [mɔʀvø, -øz] *adj* (*fam*) snotty-nosed.

mosaïque [mɔzaik] *nf* (*ART*) mosaic; (*fig*) patchwork.

Moscou [mɔsku] *n* Moscow.

moscovite [mɔskɔvit] *adj* of *ou* from Moscow, Moscow *cpd* ♦ *nm/f*: **M**~ Muscovite.

mosquée [mɔske] *nf* mosque.

mot [mo] *nm* word; (*message*) line, note; (*bon mot etc*) saying; **le** ~ **de la fin** the last word; ~ **à** ~ *adj, adv* word for word; ~ **pour** ~ word for word, verbatim; **sur** *ou* **à ces** ~**s** with these words; **en un** ~ in a word; **à** ~**s couverts** in veiled terms; **prendre qn au** ~ to take sb at his word; **se donner le** ~ to send the word round; **avoir son** ~ **à dire** to have a say; ~ **d'ordre** watchword; ~ **de passe** password; ~**s croisés** crossword (puzzle) *sg*.

motard [mɔtaʀ] *nm* biker; (*policier*) motorcycle cop.

motel [mɔtɛl] *nm* motel.

moteur, trice [mɔtœʀ, -tʀis] *adj* (*ANAT, PHYSIOL*) motor; (*TECH*) driving; (*AUTO*): **à 4 roues motrices** 4-wheel drive ♦ *nm* engine, motor; (*fig*) mover, mainspring; **à** ~ power-driven, motor *cpd*; ~ **à deux temps** two-stroke engine; ~ **à explosion** internal combustion engine; ~ **à réaction** jet engine; ~ **thermique** heat engine.

motif [mɔtif] *nm* (*cause*) motive; (*décoratif*) design, pattern, motif; (*d'un tableau*) subject, motif; (*MUS*) figure, motif; ~**s** *nmpl* (*JUR*) grounds *pl*; **sans** ~ *adj* groundless.

motion [mosjɔ̃] *nf* motion; ~ **de censure** motion of censure, vote of no confidence.

motivation [mɔtivasjɔ̃] *nf* motivation.

motivé, e [mɔtive] _adj (acte)_ justified;
(personne) motivated.

motiver [mɔtive] _vt (justifier)_ to justify,
account for; _(ADMIN, JUR, PSYCH)_ to
motivate.

moto [mɔto] _nf_ (motor)bike; ~ **verte** _ou_ **de
trial** trail _(BRIT) ou_ dirt _(US)_ bike.

moto-cross [mɔtɔkʀɔs] _nm_ motocross.

motoculteur [mɔtɔkyltœʀ] _nm_ (motorized)
cultivator.

motocyclette [mɔtɔsiklɛt] _nf_ motorbike,
motorcycle.

motocyclisme [mɔtɔsiklism(ə)] _nm_
motorcycle racing.

motocycliste [mɔtɔsiklist(ə)] _nm/f_
motorcyclist.

motoneige [mɔtɔnɛʒ] _nf_ snow bike.

motorisé, e [mɔtɔʀize] _adj (troupe)_ motorized;
(personne) having one's own transport.

motrice [mɔtʀis] _adj f voir_ **moteur**.

motte [mɔt] _nf:_ ~ **de terre** lump of earth, clod
(of earth); ~ **de gazon** turf, sod; ~ **de beurre**
lump of butter.

motus [mɔtys] _excl:_ ~ **(et bouche cousue)!**
mum's the word!

mou (mol), molle [mu, mɔl] _adj_ soft; _(péj:
visage, traits)_ flabby; _(: geste)_ limp;
(: personne) sluggish; _(: résistance,
protestations)_ feeble ♦ _nm (homme mou)_
wimp; _(abats)_ lights _pl_, lungs _pl_; _(de la corde)_:
avoir du ~ to be slack; **donner du** ~ to
slacken, loosen; **avoir les jambes molles** to
be weak at the knees.

mouchard, e [muʃaʀ, -aʀd(ə)] _nm/f (péj: SCOL)_
sneak; _(: POLICE)_ stool pigeon, grass _(BRIT)_
♦ _nm (appareil)_ control device; _(: de camion)_
tachograph.

mouche [muʃ] _nf_ fly; _(ESCRIME)_ button; _(de
taffetas)_ patch; **prendre la** ~ to go into a
huff; **faire** ~ to score a bull's-eye.

moucher [muʃe] _vt (enfant)_ to blow the nose
of; _(chandelle)_ to snuff (out); **se** ~ to blow
one's nose.

moucheron [muʃʀɔ̃] _nm_ midge.

moucheté, e [muʃte] _adj (cheval)_ dappled;
(laine) flecked; _(ESCRIME)_ buttoned.

mouchoir [muʃwaʀ] _nm_ handkerchief, hanky;
~ **en papier** tissue, paper hanky.

moudre [mudʀ(ə)] _vt_ to grind.

moue [mu] _nf_ pout; **faire la** ~ to pout; _(fig)_ to
pull a face.

mouette [mwɛt] _nf_ (sea)gull.

mouf(f)ette [mufɛt] _nf_ skunk.

moufle [mufl(ə)] _nf (gant)_ mitt(en); _(TECH)_
pulley block.

mouflon [muflɔ̃] _nm_ mouf(f)lon.

mouillage [mujaʒ] _nm (NAVIG: lieu)_ anchorage,
moorings _pl_.

mouillé, e [muje] _adj_ wet.

mouiller [muje] _vt (humecter)_ to wet, moisten;
(tremper): ~ **qn/qch** to make sb/sth wet;
(CULIN: ragoût) to add stock _ou_ wine to;

(couper, diluer) to water down; _(mine etc)_ to
lay ♦ _vi (NAVIG)_ to lie _ou_ be at anchor; **se** ~
to get wet; _(fam)_ to commit o.s.; to get (o.s.)
involved; ~ **l'ancre** to drop _ou_ cast anchor.

mouillette [mujɛt] _nf_ (bread) finger.

mouillure [mujyʀ] _nf_ wet _no pl_; _(tache)_ wet
patch.

moulage [mulaʒ] _nm_ moulding _(BRIT)_, molding
_(US)_; casting; _(objet)_ cast.

moulais [mulɛ] _etc vb voir_ **moudre**.

moulant, e [mulɑ̃, -ɑ̃t] _adj_ figure-hugging.

moule [mul] _vb voir_ **moudre** ♦ _nf (mollusque)_
mussel ♦ _nm (creux, CULIN)_ mould _(BRIT)_,
mold _(US)_; _(modèle plein)_ cast; ~ **à gâteau** _nm_
cake tin _(BRIT) ou_ pan _(US)_; ~ **à gaufre** _nm_
waffle iron; ~ **à tarte** _nm_ pie _ou_ flan dish.

moulent [mul] _vb voir_ **moudre, mouler**.

mouler [mule] _vt (brique)_ to mould _(BRIT)_,
mold _(US)_; _(statue)_ to cast; _(visage, bas-relief)_
to make a cast of; _(lettre)_ to shape with care;
(suj: vêtement) to hug, fit closely round; ~
qch sur _(fig)_ to model sth on.

moulin [mulɛ̃] _nm_ mill; _(fam)_ engine; ~ **à café**
coffee mill; ~ **à eau** watermill; ~ **à
légumes** (vegetable) shredder; ~ **à paroles**
(fig) chatterbox; ~ **à poivre** pepper mill; ~ **à
prières** prayer wheel; ~ **à vent** windmill.

mouliner [muline] _vt_ to shred.

moulinet [mulinɛ] _nm (de treuil)_ winch; _(de
canne à pêche)_ reel; _(mouvement)_: **faire des**
~**s avec qch** to whirl sth around.

moulinette [mulinɛt] _nf_ ® (vegetable)
shredder.

moulons [mulɔ̃] _etc vb voir_ **moudre**.

moulu, e [muly] _pp de_ **moudre** ♦ _adj (café)_
ground.

moulure [mulyʀ] _nf (ornement)_ moulding
(BRIT), molding _(US)_.

mourant, e [muʀɑ̃, -ɑ̃t] _vb voir_ **mourir** ♦ _adj_
dying ♦ _nm/f_ dying man/woman.

mourir [muʀiʀ] _vi_ to die; _(civilisation)_ to die
out; ~ **assassiné** to be murdered; ~ **de
froid/faim/vieillesse** to die of exposure/
hunger/old age; ~ **de faim/d'ennui** _(fig)_ to be
starving/be bored to death; ~ **d'envie de
faire** to be dying to do; **s'ennuyer à** ~ to be
bored to death.

mousquetaire [muskətɛʀ] _nm_ musketeer.

mousqueton [muskətɔ̃] _nm (fusil)_ carbine;
(anneau) snap-link, karabiner.

moussant, e [musɑ̃, -ɑ̃t] _adj_ foaming; **bain** ~
foam _ou_ bubble bath, bath foam.

mousse [mus] _nf (BOT)_ moss; _(écume: sur eau,
bière)_ froth, foam; _(: shampooing)_ lather; _(de
champagne)_ bubbles _pl_; _(CULIN)_ mousse; _(en
caoutchouc etc)_ foam ♦ _nm (NAVIG)_ ship's boy;
bain de ~ bubble bath; **bas** ~ stretch
stockings; **balle** ~ rubber ball; ~ **carbonique**
(fire-fighting) foam; ~ **de nylon** nylon foam;
(tissu) stretch nylon; ~ **à raser** shaving
foam.

mousseline [muslin] _nf (TEXTILES)_ muslin;

chiffon; **pommes** ~ (CULIN) creamed potatoes.
mousser [muse] vi to foam; to lather.
mousseux, euse [musø, -øz] adj (chocolat) frothy; (eau) foamy, frothy; (vin) sparkling ♦ nm: (**vin**) ~ sparkling wine.
mousson [musɔ̃] nf monsoon.
moussu, e [musy] adj mossy.
moustache [mustaʃ] nf moustache; ~s nfpl (d'animal) whiskers pl.
moustachu, e [mustaʃy] adj wearing a moustache.
moustiquaire [mustikɛʀ] nf (rideau) mosquito net; (chassis) mosquito screen.
moustique [mustik] nm mosquito.
moutarde [mutaʀd(ə)] nf mustard ♦ adj inv mustard(-coloured).
moutardier [mutaʀdje] nm mustard jar.
mouton [mutɔ̃] nm (ZOOL, péj) sheep inv; (peau) sheepskin; (CULIN) mutton.
mouture [mutyʀ] nf grinding; (péj) rehash.
mouvant, e [muvɑ̃, -ɑ̃t] adj unsettled; changing; shifting.
mouvement [muvmɑ̃] nm (gén, aussi: mécanisme) movement; (ligne courbe) contours pl; (fig: tumulte, agitation) activity, bustle; (: impulsion) impulse; reaction; (geste) gesture; (MUS: rythme) tempo (pl -s ou tempi); **en** ~ in motion; on the move; **mettre qch en** ~ to set sth in motion, set sth going; ~ **d'humeur** fit ou burst of temper; ~ **d'opinion** trend of (public) opinion; **le** ~ **perpétuel** perpetual motion.
mouvementé, e [muvmɑ̃te] adj (vie, poursuite) eventful; (réunion) turbulent.
mouvoir [muvwaʀ] vt (levier, membre) to move; (machine) to drive; **se** ~ to move.
moyen, ne [mwajɛ̃, -ɛn] adj average; (tailles, prix) medium; (de grandeur moyenne) medium-sized ♦ nm (façon) means sg, way ♦ nf average; (STATISTIQUE) mean; (SCOL: à l'examen) pass mark; (AUTO) average speed; ~s nmpl (capacités) means; **au** ~ **de** by means of; **y a-t-il** ~ **de** ...? is it possible to ...?, can one ...?; **par quel** ~? how?, which way?, by which means?; **par tous les** ~s by every possible means, every possible way; **avec les** ~s **du bord** (fig) with what's available ou what comes to hand; **employer les grands** ~s to resort to drastic measures; **par ses propres** ~s all by oneself; **en** ~**ne** on (an) average; **faire la** ~**ne** to work out the average; ~ **de locomotion/d'expression** means of transport/expression; ~ **âge** Middle Ages; ~ **de transport** means of transport; ~**ne d'âge** average age; ~**ne entreprise** (COMM) medium-sized firm.
moyenâgeux, euse [mwajɛnaʒø, -øz] adj medieval.
moyen-courrier [mwajɛ̃kuʀje] nm (AVIAT) medium-haul aircraft.
moyennant [mwajɛnɑ̃] prép (somme) for;

(service, conditions) in return for; (travail, effort) with.
moyennement [mwajɛnmɑ̃] adv fairly, moderately; (faire qch) fairly ou moderately well.
Moyen-Orient [mwajɛnɔʀjɑ̃] nm: **le** ~ the Middle East.
moyeu, x [mwajø] nm hub.
mozambicain, e [mɔzɑ̃bikɛ̃, -ɛn] adj Mozambican.
Mozambique [mɔzɑ̃bik] nm: **le** ~ Mozambique.
MRAP sigle m = Mouvement contre le racisme, l'antisémitisme et pour la paix.
MRG sigle m (= Mouvement des radicaux de gauche) political party.
MRP sigle m (= Mouvement républicain populaire) political party.
ms abr (= manuscrit) MS., ms.
MST sigle f (= maladie sexuellement transmissible) STD (= sexually transmitted disease).
mû, mue [my] pp de **mouvoir**.
mucosité [mykozite] nf mucus no pl.
mucus [mykys] nm mucus no pl.
mue [my] pp de **mouvoir** ♦ nf moulting (BRIT), molting (US); sloughing; breaking of the voice.
muer [mɥe] vi (oiseau, mammifère) to moult (BRIT), molt (US); (serpent) to slough; (jeune garçon): **il mue** his voice is breaking; **se** ~ **en** to transform into.
muet, te [mɥe, -ɛt] adj dumb; (fig): ~ **d'admiration** etc speechless with admiration etc; (joie, douleur, CINÉ) silent; (LING: lettre) silent, mute; (carte) blank ♦ nm/f mute ♦ nm: **le** ~ (CINÉ) the silent cinema ou movies (esp US).
mufle [myfl(ə)] nm muzzle; (goujat) boor ♦ adj boorish.
mugir [myʒiʀ] vi (bœuf) to bellow; (vache) to low, moo; (fig) to howl.
mugissement [myʒismɑ̃] nm (voir mugir) bellowing; lowing, mooing; howling.
muguet [mygɛ] nm (BOT) lily of the valley; (MÉD) thrush.
mulâtre, tresse [mylɑtʀ(ə), -tʀɛs] nm/f mulatto.
mule [myl] nf (ZOOL) (she-)mule.
mules [myl] nfpl (pantoufles) mules.
mulet [mylɛ] nm (ZOOL) (he-)mule; (poisson) mullet.
muletier, ière [myltje, -jɛʀ] adj: **sentier** ou **chemin** ~ mule track.
mulot [mylo] nm fieldmouse (pl -mice).
multicolore [myltikɔlɔʀ] adj multicoloured (BRIT), multicolored (US).
multicoque [myltikɔk] nm multihull.
multidisciplinaire [myltidisiplinɛʀ] adj multidisciplinary.
multiforme [myltifɔʀm(ə)] adj many-sided.
multilatéral, e, aux [myltilateʀal, -o] adj

multilateral.

multimilliardaire [myltimiljaʀdɛʀ], **multimillionnaire** [myltimiljɔnɛʀ] *adj, nm/f* multimillionaire.

multinational, e, aux [myltinasjɔnal, -o] *adj, nf* multinational.

multiple [myltipl(ə)] *adj* multiple, numerous; (*varié*) many, manifold ♦ *nm* (*MATH*) multiple.

multiplex [myltiplɛks] *nm* (*RADIO*) live link-up.

multiplicateur [myltiplikatœʀ] *nm* multiplier.

multiplication [myltiplikasjɔ̃] *nf* multiplication.

multiplicité [myltiplisite] *nf* multiplicity.

multiplier [myltiplije] *vt* to multiply; **se ~** *vi* to multiply; (*fig: personne*) to be everywhere at once.

multiprogrammation [myltipʀɔgramasjɔ̃] *nf* (*INFORM*) multiprogramming.

multipropriété [myltipʀɔprijete] *nf* timesharing *no pl*.

multirisque [myltiʀisk] *adj*: **assurance ~** multiple-risk insurance.

multisalles [myltisal] *adj*: (**cinéma**) **~** multiplex (cinema).

multitraitement [myltitʀɛtmɑ̃] *nm* (*INFORM*) multiprocessing.

multitude [myltityd] *nf* multitude; mass; **une ~ de** a vast number of, a multitude of.

Munich [mynik] *n* Munich.

munichois, e [mynikwa, -waz] *adj* of *ou* from Munich.

municipal, e, aux [mynisipal, -o] *adj* municipal; town *cpd*.

municipalité [mynisipalite] *nf* (*corps municipal*) town council, corporation; (*commune*) town, municipality.

munificence [mynifisɑ̃s] *nf* munificence.

munir [myniʀ] *vt*: **~ qn/qch de** to equip sb/sth with; **se ~ de** to provide o.s. with.

munitions [mynisjɔ̃] *nfpl* ammunition *sg*.

muqueuse [mykøz] *nf* mucous membrane.

mur [myʀ] *nm* wall; (*fig*) stone *ou* brick wall; **faire le ~** (*interne, soldat*) to jump the wall; **~ du son** sound barrier.

mûr, e [myʀ] *adj* ripe; (*personne*) mature ♦ *nf* (*de la ronce*) blackberry; (*du mûrier*) mulberry.

muraille [myʀaj] *nf* (high) wall.

mural, e, aux [myʀal, -o] *adj* wall *cpd* ♦ *nm* (*ART*) mural.

mûre [myʀ] *nf voir* **mûr**.

mûrement [myʀmɑ̃] *adv*: **ayant ~ réfléchi** having given the matter much thought.

murène [myʀɛn] *nf* moray (eel).

murer [myʀe] *vt* (*enclos*) to wall (in); (*porte, issue*) to wall up; (*personne*) to wall up *ou* in.

muret [myʀɛ] *nm* low wall.

mûrier [myʀje] *nm* mulberry tree; (*ronce*) blackberry bush.

mûrir [myʀiʀ] *vi* (*fruit, blé*) to ripen; (*abcès, furoncle*) to come to a head; (*fig: idée,*

personne) to mature; (*projet*) to develop ♦ *vt* (*fruit, blé*) to ripen; (*personne*) to (make) mature; (*pensée, projet*) to nurture.

murmure [myʀmyʀ] *nm* murmur; **~s** *nmpl* (*plaintes*) murmurings, mutterings.

murmurer [myʀmyʀe] *vi* to murmur; (*se plaindre*) to mutter, grumble.

mus [my] *etc vb voir* **mouvoir**.

musaraigne [myzaʀɛɲ] *nf* shrew.

musarder [myzaʀde] *vi* to idle (about); (*en marchant*) to dawdle (along).

musc [mysk] *nm* musk.

muscade [myskad] *nf* (*aussi*: **noix ~**) nutmeg.

muscat [myska] *nm* (*raisin*) muscat grape; (*vin*) muscatel (wine).

muscle [myskl(ə)] *nm* muscle.

musclé, e [myskle] *adj* (*personne, corps*) muscular; (*fig: politique, régime etc*) strong-arm *cpd*.

muscler [myskle] *vt* to develop the muscles of.

musculaire [myskylɛʀ] *adj* muscular.

musculation [myskylasjɔ̃] *nf*: **exercices de ~** muscle-developing exercises.

musculature [myskylatyʀ] *nf* muscle structure, muscles *pl*, musculature.

muse [myz] *nf* muse.

museau, x [myzo] *nm* muzzle.

musée [myze] *nm* museum; (*de peinture*) art gallery.

museler [myzle] *vt* to muzzle.

muselière [myzəljɛʀ] *nf* muzzle.

musette [myzɛt] *nf* (*sac*) lunchbag ♦ *adj inv* (*orchestre etc*) accordion *cpd*.

muséum [myzeɔm] *nm* museum.

musical, e, aux [myzikal, -o] *adj* musical.

music-hall [myzikol] *nm* variety theatre; (*genre*) variety.

musicien, ne [myzisjɛ̃, -ɛn] *adj* musical ♦ *nm/f* musician.

musique [myzik] *nf* music; (*fanfare*) band; **faire de la ~** to make music; (*jouer d'un instrument*) to play an instrument; **~ de chambre** chamber music; **~ de fond** background music.

musqué, e [myske] *adj* musky.

must [mœst] *nm* must.

musulman, e [myzylmɑ̃, -an] *adj, nm/f* Moslem, Muslim.

mutant, e [mytɑ̃, -ɑ̃t] *nm/f* mutant.

mutation [mytasjɔ̃] *nf* (*ADMIN*) transfer; (*BIO*) mutation.

muter [myte] *vt* (*ADMIN*) to transfer.

mutilation [mytilasjɔ̃] *nf* mutilation.

mutilé, e [mytile] *nm/f* disabled person (*through loss of limbs*); **~ de guerre** disabled ex-serviceman; **grand ~** severely disabled person.

mutiler [mytile] *vt* to mutilate, maim; (*fig*) to mutilate, deface.

mutin, e [mytɛ̃, -in] *adj* (*enfant, air, ton*) mischievous, impish ♦ *nm/f* (*MIL, NAVIG*) mutineer.

mutiner [mytine]: **se** ~ *vi* to mutiny.

mutinerie [mytinʀi] *nf* mutiny.

mutisme [mytism(ə)] *nm* silence.

mutualiste [mytɥalist(ə)] *adj*: **société** ~ mutual benefit society, ≈ Friendly Society.

mutualité [mytɥalite] *nf (assurance)* mutual (benefit) insurance scheme.

mutuel, le [mytɥɛl] *adj* mutual ♦ *nf* mutual benefit society.

mutuellement [mytɥɛlmɑ̃] *adv* each other, one another.

Myanmar [mjanmaʀ] *nm* Myanmar.

myocarde [mjɔkaʀd(ə)] *nm voir* **infarctus.**

myope [mjɔp] *adj* short-sighted.

myopie [mjɔpi] *nf* short-sightedness, myopia.

myosotis [mjozɔtis] *nm* forget-me-not.

myriade [miʀjad] *nf* myriad.

myrtille [miʀtij] *nf* bilberry *(BRIT)*, blueberry *(US)*, whortleberry.

mystère [mistɛʀ] *nm* mystery.

mystérieusement [misteʀjøzmɑ̃] *adv* mysteriously.

mystérieux, euse [misteʀjø, -øz] *adj* mysterious.

mysticisme [mistisism(ə)] *nm* mysticism.

mystificateur, trice [mistifikatœʀ, -tʀis] *nm/f* hoaxer, practical joker.

mystification [mistifikasjɔ̃] *nf (tromperie, mensonge)* hoax; *(mythe)* mystification.

mystifier [mistifje] *vt* to fool, take in; *(tromper)* to mystify.

mystique [mistik] *adj* mystic, mystical ♦ *nm/f* mystic.

mythe [mit] *nm* myth.

mythifier [mitifje] *vt* to turn into a myth, mythologize.

mythique [mitik] *adj* mythical.

mythologie [mitɔlɔʒi] *nf* mythology.

mythologique [mitɔlɔʒik] *adj* mythological.

mythomane [mitɔman] *adj, nm/f* mythomaniac.

N n

N, n [ɛn] *nm inv* N, n ♦ *abr* (= *nord*) N; **N comme Nicolas** N for Nelly *(BRIT)* ou Nan *(US)*.

n' [n] *adv voir* **ne.**

nabot [nabo] *nm* dwarf.

nacelle [nasɛl] *nf (de ballon)* basket.

nacre [nakʀ(ə)] *nf* mother of pearl.

nacré, e [nakʀe] *adj* pearly.

nage [naʒ] *nf* swimming; *(manière)* style of swimming, stroke; **traverser/s'éloigner à la** ~ to swim across/away; **en** ~ bathed in

perspiration; ~ **indienne** sidestroke; ~ **libre** freestyle; ~ **papillon** butterfly.

nageoire [naʒwaʀ] *nf* fin.

nager [naʒe] *vi* to swim; *(fig: ne rien comprendre)* to be all at sea; ~ **dans** to be swimming in; *(vêtements)* to be lost in; ~ **dans le bonheur** to be overjoyed.

nageur, euse [naʒœʀ, -øz] *nm/f* swimmer.

naguère [nagɛʀ] *adv (il y a peu de temps)* not long ago; *(autrefois)* formerly.

naïf, ïve [naif, naiv] *adj* naïve.

nain, e [nɛ̃, nɛn] *adj, nm/f* dwarf.

Nairobi [naiʀɔbi] *n* Nairobi.

nais [nɛ], **naissais** [nɛsɛ] *etc vb voir* **naître.**

naissance [nɛsɑ̃s] *nf* birth; **donner** ~ **à** to give birth to; *(fig)* to give rise to; **prendre** ~ to originate; **aveugle de** ~ born blind; **Français de** ~ French by birth; **à la** ~ **des cheveux** at the roots of the hair; **lieu de** ~ place of birth.

naissant, e [nɛsɑ̃, -ɑ̃t] *vb voir* **naître** ♦ *adj* budding, incipient; *(jour)* dawning.

naît [nɛ] *vb voir* **naître.**

naître [nɛtʀ(ə)] *vi* to be born; *(conflit, complications)*: ~ **de** to arise from, be born out of; ~ **à** *(amour, poésie)* to awaken to; **il est né en 1960** he was born in 1960; **il naît plus de filles que de garçons** there are more girls born than boys; **faire** ~ *(fig)* to give rise to, arouse.

naïvement [naivmɑ̃] *adv* naïvely.

naïveté [naivte] *nf* naïvety.

Namibie [namibi] *nf*: **la** ~ Namibia.

nana [nana] *nf (fam: fille)* bird *(BRIT)*, chick.

nancéien, ne [nɑ̃sejɛ̃, -ɛn] *adj* of ou from Nancy.

nantais, e [nɑ̃tɛ, -ɛz] *adj* of ou from Nantes.

nantir [nɑ̃tiʀ] *vt*: ~ **qn de** to provide sb with; **les nantis** *(péj)* the well-to-do.

NAP *sigle a* (= *Neuilly Auteuil Passy*) ≈ preppy, ≈ Sloane Ranger *cpd (BRIT)*.

napalm [napalm] *nm* napalm.

naphtaline [naftalin] *nf*: **boules de** ~ mothballs.

Naples [napl(ə)] *n* Naples.

napolitain, e [napɔlitɛ̃, -ɛn] *adj* Neapolitan; **tranche** ~**e** Neapolitan ice cream.

nappe [nap] *nf* tablecloth; *(fig)* sheet; layer; ~ **de mazout** oil slick; ~ **(phréatique)** water table.

napper [nape] *vt*: ~ **qch de** to coat sth with.

napperon [napʀɔ̃] *nm* table-mat; ~ **individuel** place mat.

naquis [naki] *etc vb voir* **naître.**

narcisse [naʀsis] *nm* narcissus.

narcissique [naʀsisik] *adj* narcissistic.

narcissisme [naʀsisism(ə)] *nm* narcissism.

narcodollars [naʀkodɔlaʀ] *nmpl* drug money *no pl.*

narcotique [naʀkɔtik] *adj, nm* narcotic.

narguer [naʀge] *vt* to taunt.

narine [naʀin] *nf* nostril.

narquois, e [naʀkwa, -waz] *adj* derisive, mocking.

narrateur, trice [naʀatœʀ, -tʀis] *nm/f* narrator.

narration [naʀɑsjɔ̃] *nf* narration, narrative; (*SCOL*) essay.

narrer [naʀe] *vt* to tell the story of, recount.

NASA [nasa] *sigle f* (= *National Aeronautics and Space Administration*) NASA.

nasal, e, aux [nazal, -o] *adj* nasal.

naseau, x [nazo] *nm* nostril.

nasillard, e [nazijaʀ, -aʀd(ə)] *adj* nasal.

nasiller [nazije] *vi* to speak with a (nasal) twang.

Nassau [naso] *n* Nassau.

nasse [nas] *nf* fish-trap.

natal, e [natal] *adj* native.

nataliste [natalist(ə)] *adj* supporting a rising birth rate.

natalité [natalite] *nf* birth rate.

natation [natɑsjɔ̃] *nf* swimming; **faire de la** ~ to go swimming (*regularly*); ~ **synchronisée** synchronized swimming.

natif, ive [natif, -iv] *adj* native.

nation [nɑsjɔ̃] *nf* nation; **les N~s unies (NU)** the United Nations (UN).

national, e, aux [nasjɔnal, -o] *adj* national ♦ *nf*: (**route**) ~**e** ≈ A road (*BRIT*), ≈ state highway (*US*); **obsèques** ~**es** state funeral.

nationalisation [nasjɔnalizasjɔ̃] *nf* nationalization.

nationaliser [nasjɔnalize] *vt* to nationalize.

nationalisme [nasjɔnalism(ə)] *nm* nationalism.

nationaliste [nasjɔnalist(ə)] *adj, nm/f* nationalist.

nationalité [nasjɔnalite] *nf* nationality; **de** ~ **française** of French nationality.

natte [nat] *nf* (*tapis*) mat; (*cheveux*) plait.

natter [nate] *vt* (*cheveux*) to plait.

naturalisation [natyʀalizɑsjɔ̃] *nf* naturalization.

naturaliser [natyʀalize] *vt* to naturalize; (*empailler*) to stuff.

naturaliste [natyʀalist(ə)] *nm/f* naturalist; (*empailleur*) taxidermist.

nature [natyʀ] *nf* nature ♦ *adj, adv* (*CULIN*) plain, without seasoning or sweetening; (*café, thé: sans lait*) black; (*: sans sucre*) without sugar; **payer en** ~ to pay in kind; **peint d'après** ~ painted from life; **être de** ~ **à faire qch** (*propre à*) to be the sort of thing (*ou* person) to do sth; ~ **morte** still-life.

naturel, le [natyʀɛl] *adj* (*gén, aussi: enfant*) natural ♦ *nm* naturalness; (*caractère*) disposition, nature; (*autochtone*) native; **au** ~ (*CULIN*) in water; in its own juices.

naturellement [natyʀɛlmɑ̃] *adv* naturally; (*bien sûr*) of course.

naturisme [natyʀism(ə)] *nm* naturism.

naturiste [natyʀist(ə)] *nm/f* naturist.

naufrage [nofʀaʒ] *nm* (ship)wreck; (*fig*) wreck; **faire** ~ to be shipwrecked.

naufragé, e [nofʀaʒe] *nm/f* shipwreck victim, castaway.

Nauru [noʀy] *nm* Nauru.

nauséabond, e [nozeabɔ̃, -ɔ̃d] *adj* foul, nauseous.

nausée [noze] *nf* nausea; **avoir la** ~ to feel sick; **avoir des** ~**s** to have waves of nausea, feel nauseous *ou* sick.

nautique [notik] *adj* nautical, water *cpd*; **sports** ~**s** water sports.

nautisme [notism(ə)] *nm* water sports *pl*.

naval, e [naval] *adj* naval.

navarrais, e [navaʀɛ, -ɛz] *adj* Navarrian.

navet [navɛ] *nm* turnip; (*péj*) third-rate film.

navette [navɛt] *nf* shuttle; (*en car etc*) shuttle (service); **faire la** ~ (**entre**) to go to and fro (between), shuttle (between); ~ **spatiale** space shuttle.

navigabilité [navigabilite] *nf* (*d'un navire*) seaworthiness; (*d'un avion*) airworthiness.

navigable [navigabl(ə)] *adj* navigable.

navigant, e [navigɑ̃, -ɑ̃t] *adj* (*AVIAT: personnel*) flying ♦ *nm/f*: **les** ~**s** the flying staff *ou* personnel.

navigateur [navigatœʀ] *nm* (*NAVIG*) seafarer, sailor; (*AVIAT*) navigator.

navigation [navigɑsjɔ̃] *nf* navigation, sailing; (*COMM*) shipping; **compagnie de** ~ shipping company; ~ **spatiale** space navigation.

naviguer [navige] *vi* to navigate, sail.

navire [naviʀ] *nm* ship; ~ **de guerre** warship; ~ **marchand** merchantman.

navire-citerne, *pl* **navires-citernes** [naviʀsitɛʀn(ə)] *nm* tanker.

navire-hôpital, *pl* **navires-hôpitaux** [naviʀɔpital, -to] *nm* hospital ship.

navrant, e [navʀɑ̃, -ɑ̃t] *adj* (*affligeant*) upsetting; (*consternant*) annoying.

navrer [navʀe] *vt* to upset, distress; **je suis navré (de/de faire/que)** I'm so sorry (for/for doing/that).

nazaréen, ne [nazaʀeɛ̃, -ɛn] *adj* Nazarene.

Nazareth [nazaʀɛt] *n* Nazareth.

NB *abr* (= *nota bene*) NB.

nbr. *abr* = **nombreux**.

nbses *abr* = **nombreuses**.

n.c. *abr* = *non communiqué, non coté*.

ND *sigle f* = *Notre Dame*.

n.d. *abr* = *non daté, non disponible*.

NDA *sigle f* = *note de l'auteur*.

NDE *sigle f* = *note de l'éditeur*.

NDLR *sigle f* = *note de la rédaction*.

ne, n' [n(ə)] *adv voir* **pas, plus, jamais** *etc*; (*explétif*) *non traduit*.

né, e [ne] *pp de* **naître**; ~ **en 1960** born in 1960; ~**e Scott** née Scott; ~(**e) de ... et de ...** son/ daughter of ... and of ...; ~ **d'une mère française** having a French mother; ~ **pour commander** born to lead ♦ *adj*: **un comédien** ~ a born comedian.

néanmoins [neɑ̃mwɛ̃] *adv* nevertheless, yet.

néant [neɑ̃] *nm* nothingness; **réduire à** ~ to bring to nought; (*espoir*) to dash.

nébuleux, euse [nebylø, -øz] adj (ciel) cloudy; (fig) nebulous ♦ nf (ASTRONOMIE) nebula.

nébuliser [nebylize] vt (liquide) to spray.

nébulosité [nebylozite] nf cloud cover; ~ variable cloudy in places.

nécessaire [nesesɛʀ] adj necessary ♦ nm necessary; (sac) kit; **faire le** ~ to do the necessary; **n'emporter que le strict** ~ to take only what is strictly necessary; ~ **de couture** sewing kit; ~ **de toilette** toilet bag; ~ **de voyage** overnight bag.

nécessairement [nesesɛʀmɑ̃] adv necessarily.

nécessité [nesesite] nf necessity; **se trouver dans la** ~ **de faire qch** to find it necessary to do sth; **par** ~ out of necessity.

nécessiter [nesesite] vt to require.

nécessiteux, euse [nesesitø, -øz] adj needy.

nec plus ultra [nekplysyltʀa] nm: **le** ~ **de** the last word in.

nécrologie [nekʀɔlɔʒi] nf obituary.

nécrologique [nekʀɔlɔʒik] adj: **article** ~ obituary; **rubrique** ~ obituary column.

nécromancie [nekʀɔmɑ̃si] nf necromancy.

nécromancien, ne [nekʀɔmɑ̃sjɛ̃, -ɛn] nm/f necromancer.

nécrose [nekʀoz] nf necrosis.

nectar [nɛktaʀ] nm nectar.

nectarine [nɛktaʀin] nf nectarine.

néerlandais, e [neɛʀlɑ̃dɛ, -ɛz] adj Dutch, of the Netherlands ♦ nm (LING) Dutch ♦ nm/f: **N~, e** Dutchman/woman; **les N~** the Dutch.

nef [nɛf] nf (d'église) nave.

néfaste [nefast(ə)] adj baneful; ill-fated.

négatif, ive [negatif, iv] adj negative ♦ nm (PHOTO) negative.

négation [negasjɔ̃] nf denial; (LING) negation.

négativement [negativmɑ̃] adv: **répondre** ~ to give a negative response.

négligé, e [negliʒe] adj (en désordre) slovenly ♦ nm (tenue) negligee.

négligeable [negliʒabl(ə)] adj insignificant, negligible.

négligemment [negliʒamɑ̃] adv carelessly.

négligence [negliʒɑ̃s] nf carelessness no pl; (faute) careless omission.

négligent, e [negliʒɑ̃, -ɑ̃t] adj careless; (JUR etc) negligent.

négliger [negliʒe] vt (épouse, jardin) to neglect; (tenue) to be careless about; (avis, précautions) to disregard, overlook; ~ **de faire** to fail to do, not bother to do; **se** ~ to neglect o.s.

négoce [negɔs] nm trade.

négociable [negɔsjabl(ə)] adj negotiable.

négociant [negɔsjɑ̃] nm merchant.

négociateur [negɔsjatœʀ] nm negotiator.

négociation [negɔsjasjɔ̃] nf negotiation; ~**s collectives** collective bargaining sg.

négocier [negɔsje] vi, vt to negotiate.

nègre [nɛgʀ(ə)] nm (péj) Negro; (péj: écrivain) ghost writer ♦ adj Negro.

négresse [negʀɛs] nf (péj) Negress.

négrier [negʀije] nm (fig) slave driver.

négroïde [negʀɔid] adj negroid.

neige [nɛʒ] nf snow; **battre les œufs en** ~ (CULIN) to whip ou beat the egg whites until stiff; ~ **carbonique** dry ice; ~ **fondue** (par terre) slush; (qui tombe) sleet; ~ **poudreuse** powder snow.

neiger [neʒe] vi to snow.

neigeux, euse [nɛʒø, -øz] adj snowy, snow-covered.

nénuphar [nenyfaʀ] nm water-lily.

néo-calédonien, ne [neɔkaledɔnjɛ̃, -ɛn] adj New Caledonian ♦ nm/f: **N~, ne** native of New Caledonia.

néocapitalisme [neokapitalism(ə)] nm neocapitalism.

néo-colonialisme [neokɔlɔnjalism(ə)] nm neocolonialism.

néologisme [neɔlɔʒism(ə)] nm neologism.

néon [neɔ̃] nm neon.

néo-natal, e [neɔnatal] adj neonatal.

néophyte [neɔfit] nm/f novice.

néo-zélandais, e [neɔzelɑ̃dɛ, -ɛz] adj New Zealand cpd ♦ nm/f: **N~, e** New Zealander.

Népal [nepal] nm: **le** ~ Nepal.

népalais, e [nepalɛ, -ɛz] adj Nepalese, Nepali ♦ nm (LING) Nepalese, Nepali ♦ nm/f: **N~, e** Nepalese, Nepali.

néphrétique [nefʀetik] adj (MÉD: colique) nephritic.

néphrite [nefʀit] nf (MÉD) nephritis.

népotisme [nepɔtism(ə)] nm nepotism.

nerf [nɛʀ] nm nerve; (fig) spirit; (: forces) stamina; ~**s** nmpl nerves; **être** ou **vivre sur les** ~**s** to live on one's nerves; **être à bout de** ~**s** to be at the end of one's tether; **passer ses** ~**s sur qn** to take it out on sb.

nerveusement [nɛʀvøzmɑ̃] adv nervously.

nerveux, euse [nɛʀvø, -øz] adj nervous; (cheval) highly-strung; (voiture) nippy, responsive; (tendineux) sinewy.

nervosité [nɛʀvozite] nf nervousness; (émotivité) excitability.

nervure [nɛʀvyʀ] nf (de feuille) vein; (ARCHIT, TECH) rib.

n'est-ce pas [nɛspɑ] adv isn't it?, won't you? etc, selon le verbe qui précède; **c'est bon,** ~**?** it's good, isn't it?; **il a peur,** ~**?** he's afraid, isn't he?; ~ **que c'est bon?** don't you think it's good?; **lui,** ~, **il peut se le permettre** he, of course, can afford to do that, can't he?

net, nette [nɛt] adj (sans équivoque, distinct) clear; (photo) sharp; (évident) definite; (propre) neat, clean; (COMM: prix, salaire, poids) net ♦ adv (refuser) flatly ♦ nm: **mettre au** ~ to copy out; **s'arrêter** ~ to stop dead; **la lame a cassé** ~ the blade snapped clean through; **faire place nette** to make a clean sweep; ~ **d'impôt** tax free.

nettement [nɛtmɑ̃] adv (distinctement) clearly; (évidemment) definitely; (avec comparatif, superlatif): ~ **mieux** definitely ou clearly

better.
netteté [nɛtte] *nf* clearness.
nettoie [nɛtwa] *etc vb voir* **nettoyer**.
nettoiement [nɛtwamɑ̃] *nm* (*ADMIN*) cleaning; **service du** ~ refuse collection.
nettoierai [nɛtwaʀe] *etc vb voir* **nettoyer**.
nettoyage [nɛtwajaʒ] *nm* cleaning; ~ **à sec** dry cleaning.
nettoyant [nɛtwajɑ̃] *nm* (*produit*) cleaning agent.
nettoyer [nɛtwaje] *vt* to clean; (*fig*) to clean out.
neuf [nœf] *num* nine.
neuf, neuve [nœf, nœv] *adj* new ♦ *nm*: **repeindre à** ~ to redecorate; **remettre à** ~ to do up (as good as new), refurbish; **n'acheter que du** ~ to buy everything new; **quoi de** ~? what's new?
neurasthénique [nøʀastenik] *adj* neurasthenic.
neurochirurgie [nøʀoʃiʀyʀʒi] *nf* neurosurgery.
neurochirurgien [nøʀoʃiʀyʀʒjɛ̃] *nm* neurosurgeon.
neuroleptique [nøʀɔlɛptik] *adj* neuroleptic.
neurologie [nøʀɔlɔʒi] *nf* neurology.
neurologique [nøʀɔlɔʒik] *adj* neurological.
neurologue [nøʀɔlɔg] *nm/f* neurologist.
neurone [nøʀɔn] *nm* neuron(e).
neuropsychiatre [nøʀopsikjatʀ(ə)] *nm/f* neuropsychiatrist.
neutralisation [nøtʀalizasjɔ̃] *nf* neutralization.
neutraliser [nøtʀalize] *vt* to neutralize.
neutralisme [nøtʀalism(ə)] *nm* neutralism.
neutraliste [nøtʀalist(ə)] *adj* neutralist.
neutralité [nøtʀalite] *nf* neutrality.
neutre [nøtʀ(ə)] *adj, nm* (*aussi LING*) neutral.
neutron [nøtʀɔ̃] *nm* neutron.
neuve [nœv] *adj f voir* **neuf**.
neuvième [nœvjɛm] *num* ninth.
névé [neve] *nm* permanent snowpatch.
neveu, x [nəvø] *nm* nephew.
névralgie [nevʀalʒi] *nf* neuralgia.
névralgique [nevʀalʒik] *adj* (*fig: sensible*) sensitive; **centre** ~ nerve centre.
névrite [nevʀit] *nf* neuritis.
névrose [nevʀoz] *nf* neurosis.
névrosé, e [nevʀoze] *adj, nm/f* neurotic.
névrotique [nevʀɔtik] *adj* neurotic.
New York [njujɔʀk] *n* New York.
new-yorkais, e [njujɔʀkɛ, -ɛz] *adj* of *ou* from New York, New York *cpd* ♦ *nm/f*: **New-Yorkais, e** New Yorker.
nez [ne] *nm* nose; **rire au** ~ **de qn** to laugh in sb's face; **avoir du** ~ to have flair; **avoir le** ~ **fin** to have foresight; ~ **à** ~ **avec** face to face with; **à vue de** ~ roughly.
NF *sigle mpl = nouveaux francs* ♦ *sigle f* (*INDUSTRIE: = norme française*) industrial standard.
ni [ni] *conj*: ~ **l'un** ~ **l'autre ne sont** *ou* **n'est**

neither one nor the other is; **il n'a rien dit** ~ **fait** he hasn't said or done anything.
Niagara [njagaʀa] *nm*: **les chutes du** ~ the Niagara Falls.
niais, e [njɛ, -ɛz] *adj* silly, thick.
niaiserie [njɛzʀi] *nf* gullibility; (*action, propos, futilité*) silliness.
Nicaragua [nikaʀagwa] *nm*: **le** ~ Nicaragua.
nicaraguayen, ne [nikaʀagwajɛ̃, -ɛn] *adj* Nicaraguan ♦ *nm/f*: **N~, ne** Nicaraguan.
Nice [nis] *n* Nice.
niche [niʃ] *nf* (*du chien*) kennel; (*de mur*) recess, niche; (*farce*) trick.
nichée [niʃe] *nf* brood, nest.
nicher [niʃe] *vi* to nest; **se** ~ **dans** (*personne: se blottir*) to snuggle into; (*: se cacher*) to hide in; (*objet*) to lodge itself in.
nichon [niʃɔ̃] *nm* (*fam*) boob, tit.
nickel [nikɛl] *nm* nickel.
niçois, e [niswa, -waz] *adj* of *ou* from Nice; (*CULIN*) Nicoise.
Nicosie [nikɔsi] *n* Nicosia.
nicotine [nikɔtin] *nf* nicotine.
nid [ni] *nm* nest; (*fig: repaire etc*) den, lair; ~ **d'abeilles** (*COUTURE, TEXTILE*) honeycomb stitch; ~ **de poule** pothole.
nièce [njɛs] *nf* niece.
nième [ɛnjɛm] *adj*: **la** ~ **fois** the nth *ou* umpteenth time.
nier [nje] *vt* to deny.
nigaud, e [nigo, -od] *nm/f* booby, fool.
Niger [niʒɛʀ] *nm*: **le** ~ Niger; (*fleuve*) the Niger.
Nigéria [niʒeʀja] *nm ou nf* Nigeria.
nigérian, e [niʒeʀjɑ̃, -an] *adj* Nigerian ♦ *nm/f*: **N~, e** Nigerian.
nigérien, ne [niʒeʀjɛ̃, -ɛn] *adj* of *ou* from Niger.
night-club [najtklœb] *nm* nightclub.
nihilisme [niilism(ə)] *nm* nihilism.
nihiliste [niilist(ə)] *adj* nihilist, nihilistic.
Nil [nil] *nm*: **le** ~ the Nile.
n'importe [nɛ̃pɔʀt(ə)] *adv*: ~! no matter!; ~ **qui/quoi/où** anybody/anything/anywhere; ~ **quoi!** (*fam: désapprobation*) what rubbish!; ~ **quand** any time; ~ **quel/quelle** any; ~ **lequel/laquelle** any (one); ~ **comment** (*sans soin*) carelessly; ~ **comment, il part ce soir** he's leaving tonight in any case.
nippes [nip] *nfpl* (*fam*) togs.
nippon, e *ou* **ne** [nipɔ̃, -ɔn] *adj* Japanese.
nique [nik] *nf*: **faire la** ~ **à** to thumb one's nose at (*fig*).
nitouche [nituʃ] *nf* (*péj*): **c'est une sainte** ~ she looks as if butter wouldn't melt in her mouth.
nitrate [nitʀat] *nm* nitrate.
nitrique [nitʀik] *adj*: **acide** ~ nitric acid.
nitroglycérine [nitʀogliseʀin] *nf* nitroglycerin(e).
niveau, x [nivo] *nm* level; (*des élèves, études*) standard; **au** ~ **de** at the level of; (*personne*)

on a level with; **de ~ (avec)** level (with); **le ~ de la mer** sea level; **~ (à bulle)** spirit level; **~ (d'eau)** water level; **~ de vie** standard of living.

niveler [nivle] *vt* to level.

niveleuse [nivløz] *nf* (*TECH*) grader.

nivellement [nivɛlmɑ̃] *nm* levelling.

nivernais, e [nivɛrnɛ, -ɛz] *adj* of *ou* from Nevers (and region) ♦ *nm/f*: **N~, e** inhabitant *ou* native of Nevers (and region).

NL *sigle f* = **nouvelle lune**.

NN *abr* (= **nouvelle norme**) *revised standard of hotel classification.*

n° *abr* (= **numéro**) no.

nobiliaire [nɔbiljɛr] *adj f voir* **particule**.

noble [nɔbl(ə)] *adj* noble; (*de qualité: métal etc*) precious ♦ *nm/f* noble(man/woman).

noblesse [nɔblɛs] *nf* (*classe sociale*) nobility; (*d'une action etc*) nobleness.

noce [nɔs] *nf* wedding; (*gens*) wedding party (*ou* guests *pl*); **il l'a épousée en secondes ~s** she was his second wife; **faire la ~** (*fam*) to go on a binge; **~s d'or/d'argent/de diamant** golden/silver/diamond wedding.

noceur [nɔsœr] *nm* (*fam*): **c'est un sacré ~** he's a real party animal.

nocif, ive [nɔsif, -iv] *adj* harmful, noxious.

noctambule [nɔktɑ̃byl] *nm* night-bird.

nocturne [nɔktyrn(ə)] *adj* nocturnal ♦ *nf* (*SPORT*) floodlit fixture; (*d'un magasin*) late opening.

Noël [nɔɛl] *nm* Christmas; **la (fête de) ~** Christmas time.

nœud [nø] *nm* (*de corde, du bois, NAVIG*) knot; (*ruban*) bow, bend, tie; (: *d'une question*) crux; (*THÉÂT etc*): **le ~ de l'action** the web of events; **~ coulant** noose; **~ gordien** Gordian knot; **~ papillon** bow tie.

noie [nwa] *etc vb voir* **noyer**.

noir, e [nwar] *adj* black; (*obscur, sombre*) dark ♦ *nm/f* black man/woman, Negro/Negro woman ♦ *nm*: **dans le ~** in the dark ♦ *nf* (*MUS*) crotchet (*BRIT*), quarter note (*US*); **il fait ~** it is dark; **au ~** *adv* (*acheter, vendre*) on the black market; **travail au ~** moonlighting.

noirâtre [nwarɑtr(ə)] *adj* (*teinte*) blackish.

noirceur [nwarsœr] *nf* blackness; darkness.

noircir [nwarsir] *vt, vi* to blacken.

noise [nwaz] *nf*: **chercher ~ à** to try and pick a quarrel with.

noisetier [nwaztje] *nm* hazel (tree).

noisette [nwazɛt] *nf* hazelnut; (*morceau: de beurre etc*) small knob ♦ *adj* (*yeux*) hazel.

noix [nwa] *nf* walnut; (*fam*) twit; (*CULIN*): **une ~ de beurre** a knob of butter; **à la ~** (*fam*) worthless; **~ de cajou** cashew nut; **~ de coco** coconut; **~ muscade** nutmeg; **~ de veau** (*CULIN*) round fillet of veal.

nom [nɔ̃] *nm* name; (*LING*) noun; **connaître qn de ~** to know sb by name; **au ~ de** in the name of; **~ d'une pipe** *ou* **d'un chien!** (*fam*) for goodness' sake!; **~ de Dieu!** (*fam!*)

bloody hell! (*BRIT*), my God!; **~ commun/ propre** common/proper noun; **~ composé** (*LING*) compound noun; **~ déposé** trade name; **~ d'emprunt** assumed name; **~ de famille** surname; **~ de fichier** file name; **~ de jeune fille** maiden name.

nomade [nɔmad] *adj* nomadic ♦ *nm/f* nomad.

nombre [nɔ̃br(ə)] *nm* number; **venir en ~** to come in large numbers; **depuis ~ d'années** for many years; **ils sont au ~ de 3** there are 3 of them; **au ~ de mes amis** among my friends; **sans ~** countless; **(bon) ~ de** (*beaucoup, plusieurs*) a (large) number of; **~ premier/entier** prime/whole number.

nombreux, euse [nɔ̃brø, -øz] *adj* many, numerous; (*avec nom sg: foule etc*) large; **peu ~** few; small; **de ~ cas** many cases.

nombril [nɔ̃bri] *nm* navel.

nomenclature [nɔmɑ̃klatyr] *nf* wordlist; list of items.

nominal, e, aux [nɔminal, -o] *adj* nominal; (*appel, liste*) of names.

nominatif, ive [nɔminatif, -iv] *nm* (*LING*) nominative ♦ *adj*: **liste ~ive** list of names; **carte ~ive** calling card; **titre ~** registered name.

nomination [nɔminasjɔ̃] *nf* nomination.

nommément [nɔmemɑ̃] *adv* (*désigner*) by name.

nommer [nɔme] *vt* (*baptiser*) to name, give a name to; (*qualifier*) to call; (*mentionner*) to name, give the name of; (*élire*) to appoint, nominate; **se ~**: **il se nomme Pascal** his name's Pascal, he's called Pascal.

non [nɔ̃] *adv* (*réponse*) no; (*suivi d'un adjectif, adverbe*) not; **Paul est venu, ~?** Paul came, didn't he?; **répondre** *ou* **dire que ~** to say no; **~ pas que** not that; **~ plus: moi ~ plus** neither do I, I don't either; **je préférerais que ~** I would prefer not; **il se trouve que ~** perhaps not; **je pense que ~** I don't think so; **~ mais!** well really!; **~ mais des fois!** you must be joking!; **~ alcoolisé** non-alcoholic; **~ loin/seulement** not far/only.

nonagénaire [nɔnaʒenɛr] *nm/f* nonagenarian.

non-agression [nɔnagresjɔ̃] *nf*: **pacte de ~** non-aggression pact.

non aligné, e [nɔnaliɲe] *adj* (*POL*) non-aligned.

nonante [nɔnɑ̃t] *num* (*Belgique, Suisse*) ninety.

non-assistance [nɔnasistɑ̃s] *nf* (*JUR*): **~ à personne en danger** *failure to render assistance to a person in danger.*

nonce [nɔ̃s] *nm* (*REL*) nuncio.

nonchalamment [nɔ̃ʃalamɑ̃] *adv* nonchalantly.

nonchalance [nɔ̃ʃalɑ̃s] *nf* nonchalance, casualness.

nonchalant, e [nɔ̃ʃalɑ̃, -ɑ̃t] *adj* nonchalant, casual.

non-conformisme [nɔ̃kɔ̃fɔrmism(ə)] *nm* nonconformism.

non-conformiste [nɔ̃kɔ̃fɔrmist(ə)] *adj, nm/f*

non-conformist.
non-conformité [nɔ̃kɔ̃fɔrmite] *nf*
nonconformity.
non-croyant, e [nɔ̃krwajɑ̃, -ɑ̃t] *nm/f* (*REL*)
non-believer.
non(-)engagé, e [nɔnɑ̃gaʒe] *adj* non-aligned.
non-fumeur [nɔ̃fymœr] *nm* non-smoker.
non-ingérence [nɔnɛ̃ʒerɑ̃s] *nf* non-
interference.
non-initié, e [nɔ̃ninisje] *nm/f* lay person; **les**
~s the uninitiated.
non-inscrit, e [nɔnɛ̃skri, -it] *nm/f* (*POL*: *député*)
independent.
non-intervention [nɔnɛ̃tɛrvɑ̃sjɔ̃] *nf* non-
intervention.
non-lieu [nɔ̃ljø] *nm*: **il y a eu ~** the case was
dismissed.
nonne [nɔn] *nf* nun.
nonobstant [nɔnɔpstɑ̃] *prép* notwithstanding.
non-paiement [nɔ̃pemɑ̃] *nm* non-payment.
non-prolifération [nɔ̃proliferasjɔ̃] *nf* non-
proliferation.
non-résident [nɔ̃residɑ̃] *nm* (*ÉCON*) non-
resident.
non-retour [nɔ̃rətur] *nm*: **point de ~** point of
no return.
non-sens [nɔ̃sɑ̃s] *nm* absurdity.
non-spécialiste [nɔ̃spesjalist(ə)] *nm/f* non-
specialist.
non-stop [nɔnstɔp] *adj inv* nonstop.
non-syndiqué, e [nɔ̃sɛ̃dike] *nm/f* non-union
member.
non-violence [nɔ̃vjɔlɑ̃s] *nf* nonviolence.
non-violent, e [nɔ̃vjɔlɑ̃, -ɑ̃t] *adj* non-violent.
nord [nɔr] *nm* North ♦ *adj* northern; north; **au**
~ (*situation*) in the north; (*direction*) to the
north; **au ~ de** north of, to the north of;
perdre le ~ to lose the place (*fig*).
nord-africain, e [nɔrafrikɛ̃, -ɛn] *adj* North-
African ♦ *nm/f*: **Nord-Africain, e** North
African.
nord-américain, e [nɔramerikɛ̃, -ɛn] *adj*
North American ♦ *nm/f*: **Nord-Américain, e**
North American.
nord-coréen, ne [nɔrkɔreɛ̃, -ɛn] *adj* North
Korean ♦ *nm/f*: **Nord-Coréen, ne** North
Korean.
nord-est [nɔrɛst] *nm* North-East.
nordique [nɔrdik] *adj* (*pays, race*) Nordic;
(*langues*) Scandinavian, Nordic ♦ *nm/f*: **N~**
Scandinavian.
nord-ouest [nɔrwɛst] *nm* North-West.
nord-vietnamien, ne [nɔrvjɛtnamjɛ̃, -ɛn] *adj*
North Vietnamese ♦ *nm/f*: **Nord-Vietnamien,**
ne North Vietnamese.
normal, e, aux [nɔrmal, -o] *adj* normal ♦ *nf*: **la**
~e the norm, the average.
normalement [nɔrmalmɑ̃] *adv* (*en général*)
normally; (*comme prévu*): **~, il le fera demain**
he should be doing it tomorrow, he's
supposed to do it tomorrow.
normalien, ne [nɔrmaljɛ̃, -ɛn] *nm/f* student of

École normale supérieure.
normalisation [nɔrmalizasjɔ̃] *nf*
standardization; normalization.
normaliser [nɔrmalize] *vt* (*COMM, TECH*) to
standardize; (*POL*) to normalize.
normand, e [nɔrmɑ̃, -ɑ̃d] *adj* (*de Normandie*)
Norman ♦ *nm/f*: **N~, e** (*de Normandie*)
Norman.
Normandie [nɔrmɑ̃di] *nf*: **la ~** Normandy.
norme [nɔrm(ə)] *nf* norm; (*TECH*) standard.
Norvège [nɔrvɛʒ] *nf*: **la ~** Norway.
norvégien, ne [nɔrveʒjɛ̃, -ɛn] *adj* Norwegian
♦ *nm* (*LING*) Norwegian ♦ *nm/f*: **N~, ne**
Norwegian.
nos [no] *dét voir* **notre**.
nostalgie [nɔstalʒi] *nf* nostalgia.
nostalgique [nɔstalʒik] *adj* nostalgic.
notabilité [nɔtabilite] *nf* notability.
notable [nɔtabl(ə)] *adj* notable, noteworthy;
(*marqué*) noticeable, marked ♦ *nm*
prominent citizen.
notablement [nɔtabləmɑ̃] *adv* notably;
(*sensiblement*) noticeably.
notaire [nɔtɛr] *nm* notary; solicitor.
notamment [nɔtamɑ̃] *adv* in particular,
among others.
notariat [nɔtarja] *nm* profession of notary (*ou*
solicitor).
notarié, e [nɔtarje] *adj*: **acte ~** deed drawn up
by a notary (*ou* solicitor).
notation [nɔtasjɔ̃] *nf* notation.
note [nɔt] *nf* (*écrite, MUS*) note; (*SCOL*) mark
(*BRIT*), grade; (*facture*) bill; **prendre des ~s** to
take notes; **prendre ~ de** to note; (*par écrit*)
to note, write down; **dans la ~** exactly right;
forcer la ~ to exaggerate; **une ~ de**
tristesse/de gaieté a sad/happy note; **~ de**
service memorandum.
noté, e [nɔte] *adj*: **être bien/mal ~** (*employé*
etc) to have a good/bad record.
noter [nɔte] *vt* (*écrire*) to write down, note;
(*remarquer*) to note, notice; (*SCOL, ADMIN*:
donner une appréciation) to mark, give a
grade to; **notez bien que ...** (please) note
that ....
notice [nɔtis] *nf* summary, short article;
(*brochure*): **~ explicative** explanatory leaflet,
instruction booklet.
notification [nɔtifikasjɔ̃] *nf* notification.
notifier [nɔtifje] *vt*: **~ qch à qn** to notify sb of
sth, notify sth to sb.
notion [nɔsjɔ̃] *nf* notion, idea; **~s** *nfpl*
(*rudiments*) rudiments.
notoire [nɔtwar] *adj* widely known; (*en mal*)
notorious; **le fait est ~** the fact is common
knowledge.
notoriété [nɔtɔrjete] *nf*: **c'est de ~ publique**
it's common knowledge.
notre, nos [nɔtr(ə), no] *dét* our.
nôtre [notr(ə)] *adj* ours ♦ *pron*: **le/la ~** ours; **les**
~s ours; (*alliés etc*) our own people; **soyez**
des ~s join us.

nouba [nuba] *nf (fam)*: **faire la** ~ to live it up.
nouer [nwe] *vt* to tie, knot; *(fig: alliance etc)* to strike up; ~ **la conversation** to start a conversation; **se** ~ *vi*: **c'est là où l'intrigue se noue** it's at that point that the strands of the plot come together; **ma gorge se noua** a lump came to my throat.
noueux, euse [nwø, -øz] *adj* gnarled.
nougat [nuga] *nm* nougat.
nougatine [nugatin] *nf kind of nougat.*
nouille [nuj] *nf (pâtes)*: ~**s** noodles; pasta *sg*; *(fam)* noodle *(BRIT)*, fathead.
nounou [nunu] *nf nanny.*
nounours [nunuʀs] *nm* teddy (bear).
nourri, e [nuʀi] *adj (feu etc)* sustained.
nourrice [nuʀis] *nf ≈* baby-minder; *(autrefois)* wet-nurse.
nourrir [nuʀiʀ] *vt* to feed; *(fig: espoir)* to harbour, nurse; **logé nourri** with board and lodging; ~ **au sein** to breast-feed; **se** ~ **de légumes/rêves** to live on vegetables/dreams.
nourrissant, e [nuʀisɑ̃, -ɑ̃t] *adj* nourishing, nutritious.
nourrisson [nuʀisɔ̃] *nm* (unweaned) infant.
nourriture [nuʀityʀ] *nf food.*
nous [nu] *pron (sujet)* we; *(objet)* us.
nous-mêmes [numɛm] *pron* ourselves.
nouveau (nouvel), elle, x [nuvo, -ɛl] *adj* new; *(original)* novel ♦ *nm/f* new pupil *(ou* employee) ♦ *nm*: **il y a du** ~ there's something new ♦ *nf (piece of) news sg*; *(LITTÉRATURE)* short story; **nouvelles** *nfpl (PRESSE, TV)* news; **de** ~, **à** ~ again; **je suis sans nouvelles de lui** I haven't heard from him; **Nouvel An** New Year; ~ **riche** nouveau riche; ~ **venu, nouvelle venue** newcomer; ~**x mariés** newly-weds; **nouvelle vague** new wave.
nouveau-né, e [nuvone] *nm/f newborn (baby).*
nouveauté [nuvote] *nf novelty; (chose nouvelle)* innovation, something new; *(COMM)* new film *(ou* book *ou* creation *etc).*
nouvel *adj m,* **nouvelle** *adj f, nf* [nuvɛl] *voir* **nouveau.**
Nouvelle-Angleterre [nuvɛlɑ̃glətɛʀ] *nf*: **la** ~ New England.
Nouvelle-Calédonie [nuvɛlkaledɔni] *nf*: **la** ~ New Caledonia.
Nouvelle-Écosse [nuvɛlekɔs] *nf*: **la** ~ Nova Scotia.
Nouvelle-Galles du Sud [nuvɛlgaldysyd] *nf*: **la** ~ New South Wales.
Nouvelle-Guinée [nuvɛlgine] *nf*: **la** ~ New Guinea.
nouvellement [nuvɛlmɑ̃] *adv (arrivé etc)* recently, newly.
Nouvelle-Orléans [nuvɛlɔʀleɑ̃] *nf*: **la** ~ New Orleans.
Nouvelles-Hébrides [nuvɛlsebʀid] *nfpl*: **les** ~ the New Hebrides.
Nouvelle-Zélande [nuvɛlzelɑ̃d] *nf*: **la** ~ New

Zealand.
nouvelliste [nuvelist(ə)] *nm/f editor ou* writer of short stories.
novateur, trice [nɔvatœʀ, -tʀis] *adj* innovative ♦ *nm/f* innovator.
novembre [nɔvɑ̃bʀ(ə)] *nm* November; *voir aussi* **juillet.**

Le 11 novembre *is a public holiday in France commemorating the signing of the armistice, near Compiègne, at the end of World War I.*

---

novice [nɔvis] *adj* inexperienced ♦ *nm/f* novice.
noviciat [nɔvisja] *nm (REL)* noviciate.
noyade [nwajad] *nf drowning no pl.*
noyau, x [nwajo] *nm (de fruit)* stone; *(BIO, PHYSIQUE)* nucleus; *(ÉLEC, GÉO, fig: centre)* core; *(fig: d'artistes etc)* group; *(: de résistants etc)* cell.
noyautage [nwajotaʒ] *nm (POL)* infiltration.
noyauter [nwajote] *vt (POL)* to infiltrate.
noyé, e [nwaje] *nm/f drowning (ou* drowned) man/woman ♦ *adj (fig: dépassé)* out of one's depth.
noyer [nwaje] *nm* walnut (tree); *(bois)* walnut ♦ *vt* to drown; *(fig)* to flood; to submerge; *(AUTO: moteur)* to flood; **se** ~ to be drowned, drown; *(suicide)* to drown o.s; ~ **son chagrin** to drown one's sorrows; ~ **le poisson** to duck the issue.
NSP *sigle m (REL) = Notre Saint Père; (dans les sondages: = ne sais pas)* don't know.
NT *sigle m (= Nouveau Testament)* NT.
NU *sigle fpl (= Nations unies)* UN.
nu, e [ny] *adj* naked; *(membres)* naked, bare; *(chambre, fil, plaine)* bare ♦ *nm (ART)* nude; **le** ~ **intégral** total nudity; **à mains** ~**es** with one's bare hands; **se mettre** ~ to strip; **mettre à** ~ to bare.
nuage [nɥaʒ] *nm* cloud; **être dans les** ~**s** *(distrait)* to have one's head in the clouds; ~ **de lait** drop of milk.
nuageux, euse [nɥaʒø, -øz] *adj* cloudy.
nuance [nɥɑ̃s] *nf (de couleur, sens)* shade; **il y a une** ~ **(entre)** there's a slight difference (between); **une** ~ **de tristesse** a tinge of sadness.
nuancé, e [nɥɑ̃se] *adj (opinion)* finely-shaded, subtly differing; **être** ~ **dans ses opinions** to have finely-shaded opinions.
nuancer [nɥɑ̃se] *vt (pensée, opinion)* to qualify.
nubile [nybil] *adj* nubile.
nucléaire [nykleɛʀ] *adj* nuclear ♦ *nm* nuclear power.
nudisme [nydism(ə)] *nm* nudism.
nudiste [nydist(ə)] *adj, nm/f* nudist.
nudité [nydite] *nf (voir nu)* nudity, nakedness; bareness.
nuée [nɥe] *nf*: **une** ~ **de** a cloud *ou* host *ou* swarm of.
nues [ny] *nfpl*: **tomber des** ~ to be taken aback; **porter qn aux** ~ to praise sb to

the skies.

nui [nɥi] *pp de* **nuire.**

nuire [nɥiʀ] *vi* to be harmful; ~ **à** to harm, do damage to.

nuisance [nɥizɑ̃s] *nf* nuisance; ~**s** *nfpl* pollution *sg.*

nuisible [nɥizibl(ə)] *adj* harmful; (*animal*) ~ pest.

nuisis [nɥizi] *etc vb voir* **nuire.**

nuit [nɥi] *nf* night; **payer sa** ~ to pay for one's overnight accommodation; **il fait** ~ it's dark; **cette** ~ (*hier*) last night; (*aujourd'hui*) tonight; **de** ~ (*vol, service*) night *cpd;* ~ **blanche** sleepless night; ~ **de noces** wedding night; ~ **de Noël** Christmas Eve.

nuitamment [nɥitamɑ̃] *adv* by night.

nuitées [nɥite] *nfpl* overnight stays, beds occupied (*in statistics*).

nul, nulle [nyl] *adj* (*aucun*) no; (*minime*) nil, non-existent; (*non valable*) null; (*péj*) useless, hopeless ♦ *pron* none, no one; **résultat** ~, **match** ~ draw; **nulle part** *adv* nowhere.

nullement [nylmɑ̃] *adv* by no means.

nullité [nylite] *nf* nullity; (*péj*) hopelessness; (*: personne*) hopeless individual, nonentity.

numéraire [nymeʀɛʀ] *nm* cash; metal currency.

numéral, e, aux [nymeʀal, -o] *adj* numeral.

numérateur [nymeʀatœʀ] *nm* numerator.

numération [nymeʀasjɔ̃] *nf:* ~ **décimale/ binaire** decimal/binary notation; ~ **globulaire** blood count.

numérique [nymeʀik] *adj* numerical; (*INFORM*) digital.

numériquement [nymeʀikmɑ̃] *adv* numerically.

numériser [nymeʀize] *vt* (*INFORM*) to digitize.

numéro [nymeʀo] *nm* number; (*spectacle*) act, turn; **faire** *ou* **composer un** ~ to dial a number; ~ **d'identification personnel** personal identification number (PIN); ~ **d'immatriculation** *ou* **minéralogique** *ou* **de police** registration (*BRIT*) *ou* license (*US*) number; ~ **de téléphone** (tele)phone number; ~ **vert** ≈ Freefone ® number (*BRIT*), ≈ toll-free number (*US*).

numérotage [nymeʀotaʒ] *nm* numbering.

numérotation [nymeʀotasjɔ̃] *nf* numeration.

numéroter [nymeʀote] *vt* to number.

numerus clausus [nymeʀysklozys] *nm inv* restriction *ou* limitation of numbers.

numismate [nymismat] *nm/f* numismatist, coin collector.

nu-pieds [nypje] *nm inv* sandal ♦ *adj inv* barefoot.

nuptial, e, aux [nypsjal, -o] *adj* nuptial; wedding *cpd.*

nuptialité [nypsjalite] *nf:* **taux de** ~ marriage rate.

nuque [nyk] *nf* nape of the neck.

nu-tête [nytɛt] *adj inv* bareheaded.

nutritif, ive [nytʀitif, -iv] *adj* nutritional; (*aliment*) nutritious, nourishing.

nutrition [nytʀisjɔ̃] *nf* nutrition.

nutritionnel, le [nytʀisjɔnɛl] *adj* nutritional.

nutritionniste [nytʀisjɔnist(ə)] *nm/f* nutritionist.

nylon [nilɔ̃] *nm* nylon.

nymphomane [nɛ̃fɔman] *adj, nf* nymphomaniac.

O o

O, o [o] *nm inv* O, o ♦ *abr* (= *ouest*) W; **O comme Oscar** ≈ O for Oliver (*BRIT*) *ou* Oboe (*US*).

OAS *sigle f* (= *Organisation de l'armée secrète*) *organization opposed to Algerian independence (1961-63).*

oasis [ɔazis] *nf ou m* oasis (*pl* oases).

obédience [ɔbedjɑ̃s] *nf* allegiance.

obéir [ɔbeiʀ] *vi* to obey; ~ **à** to obey; (*suj: moteur, véhicule*) to respond to.

obéissance [ɔbeisɑ̃s] *nf* obedience.

obéissant, e [ɔbeisɑ̃, -ɑ̃t] *adj* obedient.

obélisque [ɔbelisk(ə)] *nm* obelisk.

obèse [ɔbɛz] *adj* obese.

obésité [ɔbezite] *nf* obesity.

objecter [ɔbʒɛkte] *vt* (*prétexter*) to plead, put forward as an excuse; ~ **qch à** (*argument*) to put forward sth against; ~ (**à qn**) **que** to object (to sb) that.

objecteur [ɔbʒɛktœʀ] *nm:* ~ **de conscience** conscientious objector.

objectif, ive [ɔbʒɛktif, -iv] *adj* objective ♦ *nm* (*OPTIQUE, PHOTO*) lens *sg;* (*MIL, fig*) objective; ~ **grand angulaire/à focale variable** wide-angle/zoom lens.

objection [ɔbʒɛksjɔ̃] *nf* objection; ~ **de conscience** conscientious objection.

objectivement [ɔbʒɛktivmɑ̃] *adv* objectively.

objectivité [ɔbʒɛktivite] *nf* objectivity.

objet [ɔbʒɛ] *nm* (*chose*) object; (*d'une discussion, recherche*) subject; **être** *ou* **faire l'~ de** (*discussion*) to be the subject of; (*soins*) to be given *ou* shown; **sans** ~ *adj* purposeless; (*sans fondement*) groundless; ~ **d'art** objet d'art; ~**s personnels** personal items; ~**s de toilette** toiletries; ~**s trouvés** lost property *sg* (*BRIT*), lost-and-found *sg* (*US*).

objurgations [ɔbʒyʀgasjɔ̃] *nfpl* objurgations; (*prières*) entreaties.

obligataire [ɔbligatɛʀ] *adj* bond *cpd* ♦ *nm/f* bondholder, debenture holder.

obligation [ɔbligasjɔ̃] *nf* obligation; (*gén pl: devoir*) duty; (*COMM*) bond, debenture; **sans**

~ **d'achat** with no obligation (to buy); **être dans l'**~ **de faire** to be obliged to do; **avoir l'**~ **de faire** to be under an obligation to do; ~**s familiales** family obligations *ou* responsibilities; ~**s militaires** military obligations *ou* duties.

obligatoire [ɔbligatwaʀ] *adj* compulsory, obligatory.

obligatoirement [ɔbligatwaʀmɑ̃] *adv* compulsorily; (*fatalement*) necessarily.

obligé, e [ɔbliʒe] *adj* (*redevable*): **être très ~ à qn** to be most obliged to sb; (*contraint*): **je suis (bien) ~ (de le faire)** I have to (do it); (*nécessaire: conséquence*) necessary; **c'est ~!** it's inevitable!

obligeamment [ɔbliʒamɑ̃] *adv* obligingly.

obligeance [ɔbliʒɑ̃s] *nf*: **avoir l'**~ **de** to be kind *ou* good enough to.

obligeant, e [ɔbliʒɑ̃, -ɑ̃t] *adj* obliging; kind.

obliger [ɔbliʒe] *vt* (*contraindre*): ~ **qn à faire** to force *ou* oblige sb to do; (*JUR: engager*) to bind; (*rendre service à*) to oblige.

oblique [ɔblik] *adj* oblique; **regard** ~ sidelong glance; **en** ~ *adv* diagonally.

obliquer [ɔblike] *vi*: ~ **vers** to turn off towards.

oblitération [ɔbliteʀasjɔ̃] *nf* cancelling *no pl*, cancellation; obstruction.

oblitérer [ɔbliteʀe] *vt* (*timbre-poste*) to cancel; (*MÉD: canal, vaisseau*) to obstruct.

oblong, oblongue [ɔblɔ̃, ɔblɔ̃g] *adj* oblong.

obnubiler [ɔbnybile] *vt* to obsess.

obole [ɔbɔl] *nf* offering.

obscène [ɔpsɛn] *adj* obscene.

obscénité [ɔpsenite] *nf* obscenity.

obscur, e [ɔpskyʀ] *adj* (*sombre*) dark; (*fig: raisons*) obscure; (: *sentiment, malaise*) vague; (: *personne, vie*) humble, lowly.

obscurcir [ɔpskyʀsiʀ] *vt* to darken; (*fig*) to obscure; **s'**~ *vi* to grow dark.

obscurité [ɔpskyʀite] *nf* darkness; **dans l'**~ in the dark, in darkness; (*anonymat, médiocrité*) in obscurity.

obsédant, e [ɔpsedɑ̃, -ɑ̃t] *adj* obsessive.

obsédé, e [ɔpsede] *nm/f* fanatic; ~**(e) sexuel(le)** sex maniac.

obséder [ɔpsede] *vt* to obsess, haunt.

obsèques [ɔpsɛk] *nfpl* funeral *sg*.

obséquieux, euse [ɔpsekjø, -øz] *adj* obsequious.

observance [ɔpsɛʀvɑ̃s] *nf* observance.

observateur, trice [ɔpsɛʀvatœʀ, -tʀis] *adj* observant, perceptive ♦ *nm/f* observer.

observation [ɔpsɛʀvasjɔ̃] *nf* observation; (*d'un règlement etc*) observance; (*commentaire*) observation, remark; (*reproche*) reproof; **en** ~ (*MÉD*) under observation.

observatoire [ɔpsɛʀvatwaʀ] *nm* observatory; (*lieu élevé*) observation post, vantage point.

observer [ɔpsɛʀve] *vt* (*regarder*) to observe, watch; (*examiner*) to examine;

(*scientifiquement, aussi: règlement, jeûne etc*) to observe; (*surveiller*) to watch; (*remarquer*) to observe, notice; **faire** ~ **qch à qn** (*dire*) to point out sth to sb; **s'**~ (*se surveiller*) to keep a check on o.s.

obsession [ɔpsesjɔ̃] *nf* obsession; **avoir l'**~ **de** to have an obsession with.

obsessionnel, le [ɔpsesjɔnɛl] *adj* obsessive.

obsolescent, e [ɔpsɔlesɑ̃, -ɑ̃t] *adj* obsolescent.

obstacle [ɔpstakl(ə)] *nm* obstacle; (*ÉQUITATION*) jump, hurdle; **faire** ~ **à** (*lumière*) to block out; (*projet*) to hinder, put obstacles in the path of; ~**s antichars** tank defences.

obstétricien, ne [ɔpstetʀisjɛ̃, -ɛn] *nm/f* obstetrician.

obstétrique [ɔpstetʀik] *nf* obstetrics *sg*.

obstination [ɔpstinasjɔ̃] *nf* obstinacy.

obstiné, e [ɔpstine] *adj* obstinate.

obstinément [ɔpstinemɑ̃] *adv* obstinately.

obstiner [ɔpstine]: **s'**~ *vi* to insist, dig one's heels in; **s'**~ **à faire** to persist (obstinately) in doing; **s'**~ **sur qch** to keep working at sth, labour away at sth.

obstruction [ɔpstʀyksjɔ̃] *nf* obstruction, blockage; (*sport*) obstruction; **faire de l'**~ (*fig*) to be obstructive.

obstruer [ɔpstʀye] *vt* to block, obstruct; **s'**~ *vi* to become blocked.

obtempérer [ɔptɑ̃peʀe] *vi* to obey; ~ **à** to obey, comply with.

obtenir [ɔptəniʀ] *vt* to obtain, get; (*total*) to arrive at, reach; (*résultat*) to achieve, obtain; ~ **de pouvoir faire** to obtain permission to do; ~ **qch à qn** to obtain sth for sb; ~ **de qn qu'il fasse** to get sb to agree to do(ing).

obtention [ɔptɑ̃sjɔ̃] *nf* obtaining.

obtenu, e [ɔpt(ə)ny] *pp de* **obtenir**.

obtiendrai [ɔptjɛ̃dʀe], **obtiens** [ɔptjɛ̃], **obtint** [ɔptɛ̃] *etc vb voir* **obtenir**.

obturateur [ɔptyʀatœʀ] *nm* (*PHOTO*) shutter; ~ **à rideau** focal plane shutter.

obturation [ɔptyʀasjɔ̃] *nf* closing (up); ~ (*dentaire*) filling; **vitesse d'**~ (*PHOTO*) shutter speed.

obturer [ɔptyʀe] *vt* to close (up); (*dent*) to fill.

obtus, e [ɔpty, -yz] *adj* obtuse.

obus [ɔby] *nm* shell; ~ **explosif** high-explosive shell; ~ **incendiaire** incendiary device, fire bomb.

obvier [ɔbvje]: ~ **à** *vt* to obviate.

OC *sigle fpl* (= *ondes courtes*) SW.

occasion [ɔkazjɔ̃] *nf* (*aubaine, possibilité*) opportunity; (*circonstance*) occasion; (*COMM: article non neuf*) secondhand buy; (: *acquisition avantageuse*) bargain; **à plusieurs** ~**s** on several occasions; **à la première** ~ at the first *ou* earliest opportunity; **avoir l'**~ **de faire** to have the opportunity to do; **être l'**~ **de** to occasion, give rise to; **à l'**~ *adv* sometimes, on occasions; (*un jour*) some time; **à l'**~ **de** on the occasion of; **d'**~ *adj, adv* secondhand.

occasionnel, le [ɔkazjɔnɛl] *adj* (*fortuit*) chance *cpd*; (*non régulier*) occasional; (*: travail*) casual.

occasionner [ɔkazjɔne] *vt* to cause, bring about; ~ **qch à qn** to cause sb sth.

occident [ɔksidã] *nm*: **l'O**~ the West.

occidental, e, aux [ɔksidãtal, -o] *adj* western; (*POL*) Western ♦ *nm/f* Westerner.

occidentaliser [ɔksidãtalize] *vt* (*coutumes, mœurs*) to westernize.

occiput [ɔksipyt] *nm* back of the head, occiput.

occire [ɔksiʀ] *vt* to slay.

occitan, e [ɔksitã, -an] *adj* of the langue d'oc, of Provençal French.

occlusion [ɔklyzjɔ̃] *nf*: ~ **intestinale** obstruction of the bowel.

occulte [ɔkylt(ə)] *adj* occult, supernatural.

occulter [ɔkylte] *vt* (*fig*) to overshadow.

occupant, e [ɔkypã, -ãt] *adj* occupying ♦ *nm/f* (*d'un appartement*) occupier, occupant; (*d'un véhicule*) occupant ♦ *nm* (*MIL*) occupying forces *pl*; (*POL: d'usine etc*) occupier.

occupation [ɔkypasjɔ̃] *nf* occupation; **l'O**~ the Occupation (of France).

occupationnel, le [ɔkypasjɔnɛl] *adj*: **thérapie** ~**le** occupational therapy.

occupé, e [ɔkype] *adj* (*MIL, POL*) occupied; (*personne: affairé, pris*) busy; (*esprit: absorbé*) occupied; (*place, sièges*) taken; (*toilettes, ligne*) engaged.

occuper [ɔkype] *vt* to occupy; (*poste, fonction*) to hold; (*main-d'œuvre*) to employ; **s'**~ (**à qch**) to occupy o.s. *ou* keep o.s. busy (with sth); **s'**~ **de** (*être responsable de*) to take charge of; (*se charger de: affaire*) to take charge of, deal with; (*: clients etc*) to attend to; (*s'intéresser à, pratiquer: politique etc*) to be involved in; **ça occupe trop de place** it takes up too much room.

occurrence [ɔkyʀãs] *nf*: **en l'**~ in this case.

OCDE *sigle f* (= *Organisation de coopération et de développement économique*) OECD.

océan [ɔseã] *nm* ocean; **l'**~ **Indien** the Indian Ocean.

Océanie [ɔseani] *nf*: **l'**~ Oceania, South Sea Islands.

océanique [ɔseanik] *adj* oceanic.

océanographe [ɔseanɔgʀaf] *nm/f* oceanographer.

océanographie [ɔseanɔgʀafi] *nf* oceanography.

océanologie [ɔseanɔlɔʒi] *nf* oceanology.

ocelot [ɔslo] *nm* (*ZOOL*) ocelot; (*fourrure*) ocelot fur.

ocre [ɔkʀ(ə)] *adj inv* ochre.

octane [ɔktan] *nm* octane.

octante [ɔktãt] *num* (*Belgique, Suisse*) eighty.

octave [ɔktav] *nf* octave.

octet [ɔktɛ] *nm* byte.

octobre [ɔktɔbʀ(ə)] *nm* October; *voir aussi* juillet.

octogénaire [ɔktɔʒenɛʀ] *adj, nm/f* octogenarian.

octogonal, e, aux [ɔktɔgonal, -o] *adj* octagonal.

octogone [ɔktɔgon] *nm* octagon.

octroi [ɔktʀwa] *nm* granting.

octroyer [ɔktʀwaje] *vt*: ~ **qch à qn** to grant sth to sb, grant sb sth.

oculaire [ɔkylɛʀ] *adj* ocular, eye *cpd* ♦ *nm* (*de microscope*) eyepiece.

oculiste [ɔkylist(ə)] *nm/f* eye specialist, oculist.

ode [ɔd] *nf* ode.

odeur [ɔdœʀ] *nf* smell.

odieusement [ɔdjøzmã] *adv* odiously.

odieux, euse [ɔdjø, -øz] *adj* odious, hateful.

odontologie [ɔdɔ̃tɔlɔʒi] *nf* odontology.

odorant, e [ɔdɔʀã, -ãt] *adj* sweet-smelling, fragrant.

odorat [ɔdɔʀa] *nm* (sense of) smell; **avoir l'**~ **fin** to have a keen sense of smell.

odoriférant, e [ɔdɔʀifeʀã, -ãt] *adj* sweet-smelling, fragrant.

odyssée [ɔdise] *nf* odyssey.

OEA *sigle f* (= *Organisation des États américains*) OAS.

œcuménique [ekymenik] *adj* ecumenical.

œdème [edɛm] *nm* oedema (*BRIT*), edema (*US*).

œil [œj], *pl* **yeux** [jø] *nm* eye; **avoir un** ~ **poché** *ou* **au beurre noir** to have a black eye; **à l'**~ (*fam*) for free; **à l'**~ **nu** with the naked eye; **tenir qn à l'**~ to keep an eye *ou* a watch on sb; **avoir l'**~ **à** to keep an eye on; **faire de l'**~ **à qn** to make eyes at sb; **voir qch d'un bon/mauvais** ~ to view sth in a favourable/an unfavourable light; **à l'**~ **vif** with a lively expression; **à mes/ses yeux** in my/his eyes; **de ses propres yeux** with his own eyes; **fermer les yeux (sur)** (*fig*) to turn a blind eye (to); **les yeux fermés** (*aussi fig*) with one's eyes shut; **fermer l'**~ to get a moment's sleep; ~ **pour** ~, **dent pour dent** an eye for an eye, a tooth for a tooth; **pour les beaux yeux de qn** (*fig*) for love of sb; ~ **de verre** glass eye.

œil-de-bœuf, *pl* **œils-de-bœuf** [œjdəbœf] *nm* bull's-eye (window).

œillade [œjad] *nf*: **lancer une** ~ **à qn** to wink at sb, give sb a wink; **faire des** ~**s à** to make eyes at.

œillères [œjɛʀ] *nfpl* blinkers (*BRIT*), blinders (*US*); **avoir des** ~ (*fig*) to be blinkered, wear blinders.

œillet [œjɛ] *nm* (*BOT*) carnation; (*trou*) eyelet.

œnologue [enɔlɔg] *nm/f* wine expert.

œsophage [ezɔfaʒ] *nm* oesophagus (*BRIT*), esophagus (*US*).

œstrogène [ɛstʀɔʒɛn] *adj* oestrogen (*BRIT*), estrogen (*US*).

œuf [œf, *pl* ø] *nm* egg; **étouffer dans l'**~ to nip

in the bud; ~ **à la coque/dur/mollet** boiled/
hard-boiled/soft-boiled egg; ~ **au plat/poché**
fried/poached egg; ~**s brouillés** scrambled
eggs; ~ **de Pâques** Easter egg; ~ **à repriser**
darning egg.

œuvre [œvʀ(ə)] nf (tâche) task, undertaking;
(ouvrage achevé, livre, tableau etc) work;
(ensemble de la production artistique) works
pl; (organisation charitable) charity ♦ nm (d'un
artiste) works pl; (CONSTR): **le gros ~** the
shell; ~**s** nfpl (actes) deeds, works; **être/se
mettre à l'~** to be at/get (down) to work;
mettre en ~ (moyens) to make use of; (plan,
loi, projet etc) to implement; ~ **d'art** work of
art; **bonnes ~s** good works ou deeds; ~**s de
bienfaisance** charitable works.

OFCE sigle m (= Observatoire français des
conjonctures économiques) economic
research institute.

offensant, e [ɔfɑ̃sɑ̃, -ɑ̃t] adj offensive,
insulting.

offense [ɔfɑ̃s] nf (affront) insult; (REL: péché)
transgression, trespass.

offenser [ɔfɑ̃se] vt to offend, hurt; (principes,
Dieu) to offend against; **s'~ de** to take
offence (BRIT) ou offense (US) at.

offensif, ive [ɔfɑ̃sif, -iv] adj (armes, guerre)
offensive ♦ nf offensive; (fig: du froid, de
l'hiver) onslaught; **passer à l'offensive** to go
into the attack ou offensive.

offert, e [ɔfɛʀ, -ɛʀt(ə)] pp de **offrir**.

offertoire [ɔfɛʀtwaʀ] nm offertory.

office [ɔfis] nm (charge) office; (agence)
bureau, agency; (REL) service ♦ nm ou nf
(pièce) pantry; **faire ~ de** to act as; to do
duty as; **d'~** adv automatically; **bons ~s**
(POL) good offices; ~ **du tourisme** tourist
bureau.

officialiser [ɔfisjalize] vt to make official.

officiel, le [ɔfisjɛl] adj, nm/f official.

officiellement [ɔfisjɛlmɑ̃] adv officially.

officier [ɔfisje] nm officer ♦ vi (REL) to
officiate; ~ **de l'état-civil** registrar; ~
ministériel member of the legal profession;
~ **de police** ≈ police officer.

officieusement [ɔfisjøzmɑ̃] adv unofficially.

officieux, euse [ɔfisjø, -øz] adj unofficial.

officinal, e, aux [ɔfisinal, -o] adj: **plantes ~es**
medicinal plants.

officine [ɔfisin] nf (de pharmacie) dispensary;
(ADMIN: pharmacie) pharmacy; (gén péj:
bureau) agency, office.

offrais [ɔfʀɛ] etc vb voir **offrir**.

offrande [ɔfʀɑ̃d] nf offering.

offrant [ɔfʀɑ̃] nm: **au plus ~** to the highest
bidder.

offre [ɔfʀ(ə)] vb voir **offrir** ♦ nf offer; (aux
enchères) bid; (ADMIN: soumission) tender;
(ÉCON): **l'~** supply; ~ **d'emploi** job
advertised; **"~s d'emploi"** "situations
vacant"; ~ **publique d'achat (OPA)** takeover
bid; ~**s de service** offer of service.

offrir [ɔfʀiʀ] vt: ~ **(à qn)** to offer (to sb); (faire
cadeau) to give to (sb); **s'~** vi (se présenter:
occasion, paysage) to present itself ♦ vt (se
payer: vacances, voiture) to treat o.s. to; ~ **(à
qn) de faire qch** to offer to do sth (for sb); ~
à boire à qn to offer sb a drink; **s'~ à faire
qch** to offer ou volunteer to do sth; **s'~
comme guide/en otage** to offer one's
services as (a) guide/offer o.s. as (a)
hostage; **s'~ aux regards** (suj: personne) to
expose o.s. to the public gaze.

offset [ɔfsɛt] nm offset (printing).

offusquer [ɔfyske] vt to offend; **s'~ de** to take
offence (BRIT) ou offense (US) at, be
offended by.

ogive [ɔʒiv] nf (ARCHIT) diagonal rib; (d'obus,
de missile) nose cone; **voûte en ~** rib vault;
arc en ~ lancet arch; ~ **nucléaire** nuclear
warhead.

ogre [ɔgʀ(ə)] nm ogre.

oh [o] excl oh!; ~ **la la!** oh (dear)!; **pousser des
~! et des ah!** to gasp with admiration.

oie [wa] nf (ZOOL) goose (pl geese); ~ **blanche**
(fig) young innocent.

oignon [ɔɲɔ̃] nm (CULIN) onion; (de tulipe etc:
bulbe) bulb; (MÉD) bunion; **ce ne sont pas tes
~s** (fam) that's none of your business.

oindre [wɛ̃dʀ(ə)] vt to anoint.

oiseau, x [wazo] nm bird; ~ **de proie** bird of
prey.

oiseau-mouche, pl **oiseaux-mouches**
[wazomuʃ] nm hummingbird.

oiseleur [wazlœʀ] nm bird-catcher.

oiselier, ière [wazəlje, -jɛʀ] nm/f bird-seller.

oisellerie [wazɛlʀi] nf bird shop.

oiseux, euse [wazø, -øz] adj pointless, idle;
(sans valeur, importance) trivial.

oisif, ive [wazif, -iv] adj idle ♦ nm/f (péj) man/
lady of leisure.

oisillon [wazijɔ̃] nm little ou baby bird.

oisiveté [wazivte] nf idleness.

OIT sigle f (= Organisation internationale du
travail) ILO.

OK [ɔke] excl OK!, all right!

OL sigle fpl (= ondes longues) LW.

oléagineux, euse [ɔleaʒinø, -øz] adj
oleaginous, oil-producing.

oléiculture [ɔleikyltyʀ] nm olive growing.

oléoduc [ɔleɔdyk] nm (oil) pipeline.

olfactif, ive [ɔlfaktif, -iv] adj olfactory.

olibrius [ɔlibʀijys] nm oddball.

oligarchie [ɔligaʀʃi] nf oligarchy.

oligo-élément [ɔligɔelemɑ̃] nm trace element.

oligopole [ɔligɔpɔl] nm oligopoly.

olivâtre [ɔlivɑtʀ(ə)] adj olive-greenish; (teint)
sallow.

olive [ɔliv] nf (BOT) olive ♦ adj inv olive
(-green).

oliveraie [ɔlivʀɛ] nf olive grove.

olivier [ɔlivje] nm olive (tree); (bois) olive
(wood).

olographe [ɔlɔgʀaf] adj: **testament ~** will

written, dated and signed by the testator.

OLP *sigle f* (= *Organisation de libération de la Palestine*) PLO.

olympiade [ɔlɛ̃pjad] *nf* (*période*) Olympiad; **les ~s** (*jeux*) the Olympiad *sg*.

olympien, ne [ɔlɛ̃pjɛ̃, -ɛn] *adj* Olympian, of Olympian aloofness.

olympique [ɔlɛ̃pik] *adj* Olympic.

OM *sigle fpl* (= *ondes moyennes*) MW.

Oman [ɔman] *nm*: **l'~, le sultanat d'~** (the Sultanate of) Oman.

ombilical, e, aux [ɔ̃bilikal, -o] *adj* umbilical.

ombrage [ɔ̃bʀaʒ] *nm* (*ombre*) (leafy) shade; (*fig*): **prendre ~ de** to take umbrage at; **faire** *ou* **porter ~ à qn** to offend sb.

ombragé, e [ɔ̃bʀaʒe] *adj* shaded, shady.

ombrageux, euse [ɔ̃bʀaʒø, -øz] *adj* (*cheval*) skittish, nervous; (*personne*) touchy, easily offended.

ombre [ɔ̃bʀ(ə)] *nf* (*espace non ensoleillé*) shade; (*ombre portée, tache*) shadow; **à l'~** in the shade; (*fam: en prison*) behind bars; **à l'~ de** in the shade of; (*tout près de, fig*) in the shadow of; **tu me fais de l'~** you're in my light; **ça nous donne de l'~** it gives us (some) shade; **il n'y a pas l'~ d'un doute** there's not the shadow of a doubt; **dans l'~** in the shade; **vivre dans l'~** (*fig*) to live in obscurity; **laisser dans l'~** (*fig*) to leave in the dark; **~ à paupières** eyeshadow; **~ portée** shadow; **~s chinoises** (*spectacle*) shadow show *sg*.

ombrelle [ɔ̃bʀɛl] *nf* parasol, sunshade.

ombrer [ɔ̃bʀe] *vt* to shade.

omelette [ɔmlɛt] *nf* omelette; **~ baveuse** runny omelette; **~ au fromage/au jambon** cheese/ham omelette; **~ aux herbes** omelette with herbs; **~ norvégienne** baked Alaska.

omettre [ɔmɛtʀ(ə)] *vt* to omit, leave out; **~ de faire** to fail *ou* omit to do.

omis, e [ɔmi, -iz] *pp de* **omettre**.

omission [ɔmisjɔ̃] *nf* omission.

omnibus [ɔmnibys] *nm* slow *ou* stopping train.

omnipotent, e [ɔmnipɔtɑ̃, -ɑ̃t] *adj* omnipotent.

omnipraticien, ne [ɔmnipʀatisjɛ̃, -ɛn] *nm/f* (*MÉD*) general practitioner.

omniprésent, e [ɔmnipʀezɑ̃, -ɑ̃t] *adj* omnipresent.

omniscient, e [ɔmnisjɑ̃, -ɑ̃t] *adj* omniscient.

omnisports [ɔmnispɔʀ] *adj inv* (*club*) general sports *cpd*; (*salle*) multi-purpose *cpd*; (*terrain*) all-purpose *cpd*.

omnium [ɔmnjɔm] *nm* (*COMM*) corporation; (*CYCLISME*) omnium; (*COURSES*) open handicap.

omnivore [ɔmnivɔʀ] *adj* omnivorous.

omoplate [ɔmɔplat] *nf* shoulder blade.

OMS *sigle f* (= *Organisation mondiale de la santé*) WHO.

MOT-CLÉ

on [ɔ̃] *pron* **1** (*indéterminé*) you, one; **~ peut le faire ainsi** you *ou* one can do it like this, it can be done like this; **~ dit que ...** they say that ..., it is said that ...

2 (*quelqu'un*): **~ les a attaqués** they were attacked; **~ vous demande au téléphone** there's a phone call for you, you're wanted on the phone; **~ frappe à la porte** someone's knocking at the door

3 (*nous*) we; **~ va y aller demain** we're going tomorrow

4 (*les gens*) they; **autrefois, ~ croyait ...** they used to believe ...

5: **~ ne peut plus** *adv*: **~ ne peut plus stupide** as stupid as can be.

---

once [ɔ̃s] *nf*: **une ~ de** an ounce of.

oncle [ɔ̃kl(ə)] *nm* uncle.

onction [ɔ̃ksjɔ̃] *nf voir* **extrême-onction**.

onctueux, euse [ɔ̃ktɥø, -øz] *adj* creamy, smooth; (*fig*) smooth, unctuous.

onde [ɔ̃d] *nf* (*PHYSIQUE*) wave; **sur l'~** on the waters; **sur les ~s** on the radio; **mettre en ~s** to produce for the radio; **~ de choc** shock wave; **~s courtes (OC)** short wave *sg*; **petites ~s (PO), ~s moyennes (OM)** medium wave *sg*; **grandes ~s (GO), ~s longues (OL)** long wave *sg*; **~s sonores** sound waves.

ondée [ɔ̃de] *nf* shower.

on-dit [ɔ̃di] *nm inv* rumour.

ondoyer [ɔ̃dwaje] *vi* to ripple, wave ♦ *vt* (*REL*) to baptize (*in an emergency*).

ondulant, e [ɔ̃dylɑ̃, -ɑ̃t] *adj* (*démarche*) swaying; (*ligne*) undulating.

ondulation [ɔ̃dylasjɔ̃] *nf* undulation; wave.

ondulé, e [ɔ̃dyle] *adj* undulating; wavy.

onduler [ɔ̃dyle] *vi* to undulate; (*cheveux*) to wave.

onéreux, euse [ɔneʀø, -øz] *adj* costly; **à titre ~** in return for payment.

ONF *sigle m* (= *Office national des forêts*) ≈ Forestry Commission (*BRIT*), ≈ National Forest Service (*US*).

ongle [ɔ̃gl(ə)] *nm* (*ANAT*) nail; **manger** *ou* **ronger ses ~s** to bite one's nails; **se faire les ~s** to do one's nails.

onglet [ɔ̃glɛ] *nm* (*rainure*) (thumbnail) groove; (*bande de papier*) tab.

onguent [ɔ̃gɑ̃] *nm* ointment.

onirique [ɔniʀik] *adj* dreamlike, dream *cpd*.

onirisme [ɔniʀism(ə)] *nm* dreams *pl*.

onomatopée [ɔnɔmatɔpe] *nf* onomatopoeia.

ont [ɔ̃] *vb voir* **avoir**.

ontarien, ne [ɔ̃taʀjɛ̃, -ɛn] *adj* Ontarian.

ONU [ɔny] *sigle f* (= *Organisation des Nations unies*) UN(O).

onusien, ne [ɔnyzjɛ̃, -ɛn] *adj* of the UN(O), of the United Nations (Organization).

onyx [ɔniks] *nm* onyx.

onze [ɔ̃z] *num* eleven.

onzième [ɔ̃zjɛm] *num* eleventh.
op [ɔp] *nf* (= *opération*): **salle d'~** (operating) theatre.
OPA *sigle f* = **offre publique d'achat.**
opacité [ɔpasite] *nf* opaqueness.
opale [ɔpal] *nf* opal.
opalescent, e [ɔpalesɑ̃, -ɑ̃t] *adj* opalescent.
opalin, e [ɔpalɛ̃, -in] *adj*, *nf* opaline.
opaque [ɔpak] *adj* (*vitre, verre*) opaque; (*brouillard, nuit*) impenetrable.
OPE *sigle f* (= *offre publique d'échange*) take-over bid where bidder offers shares in his company in exchange for shares in target company.
OPEP [ɔpɛp] *sigle f* (= *Organisation des pays exportateurs de pétrole*) OPEC.
opéra [ɔpeʀa] *nm* opera; (*édifice*) opera house.
opérable [ɔpeʀabl(ə)] *adj* operable.
opéra-comique, *pl* **opéras-comiques** [ɔpeʀakɔmik] *nm* light opera, opéra comique.
opérant, e [ɔpeʀɑ̃, -ɑ̃t] *adj* (*mesure*) effective.
opérateur, trice [ɔpeʀatœʀ, -tʀis] *nm/f* operator; ~ **(de prise de vues)** cameraman.
opération [ɔpeʀasjɔ̃] *nf* operation; (*COMM*) dealing; **salle/table d'~** operating theatre/table; ~ **de sauvetage** rescue operation; ~ **à cœur ouvert** open-heart surgery *no pl*.
opérationnel, le [ɔpeʀasjɔnɛl] *adj* operational.
opératoire [ɔpeʀatwaʀ] *adj* (*manœuvre, méthode*) operating; (*choc etc*) post-operative.
opéré, e [ɔpeʀe] *nm/f* post-operative patient.
opérer [ɔpeʀe] *vt* (*MÉD*) to operate on; (*faire, exécuter*) to carry out, make ♦ *vi* (*remède: faire effet*) to act, work; (*procéder*) to proceed; (*MÉD*) to operate; **s'~** *vi* (*avoir lieu*) to occur, take place; **se faire ~** to have an operation; **se faire ~ des amygdales/du cœur** to have one's tonsils out/have a heart operation.
opérette [ɔpeʀɛt] *nf* operetta, light opera.
ophtalmique [ɔftalmik] *adj* ophthalmic.
ophtalmologie [ɔftalmɔlɔʒi] *nf* ophthalmology.
ophtalmologue [ɔftalmɔlɔg] *nm/f* ophthalmologist.
opiacé, e [ɔpjase] *adj* opiate.
opiner [ɔpine] *vi*: ~ **de la tête** to nod assent ♦ *vt*: ~ **à** to consent to.
opiniâtre [ɔpinjɑtʀ(ə)] *adj* stubborn.
opiniâtreté [ɔpinjɑtʀəte] *nf* stubbornness.
opinion [ɔpinjɔ̃] *nf* opinion; **l'~ (publique)** public opinion; **avoir bonne/mauvaise ~ de** to have a high/low opinion of.
opiomane [ɔpjɔman] *nm/f* opium addict.
opium [ɔpjɔm] *nm* opium.
OPJ *sigle m* (= *officier de police judiciaire*) ≈ DC (= *Detective Constable*).
opportun, e [ɔpɔʀtœ̃, -yn] *adj* timely, opportune; **en temps ~** at the appropriate time.

opportunément [ɔpɔʀtynemɑ̃] *adv* opportunely.
opportunisme [ɔpɔʀtynism(ə)] *nm* opportunism.
opportuniste [ɔpɔʀtynist(ə)] *adj*, *nm/f* opportunist.
opportunité [ɔpɔʀtynite] *nf* timeliness, opportuneness.
opposant, e [ɔpozɑ̃, -ɑ̃t] *adj* opposing ♦ *nm/f* opponent.
opposé, e [ɔpoze] *adj* (*direction, rive*) opposite; (*faction*) opposing; (*couleurs*) contrasting; (*opinions, intérêts*) conflicting; (*contre*): ~ **à** opposed to, against ♦ *nm*: **l'~** the other *ou* opposite side (*ou* direction); (*contraire*) the opposite; **être ~ à** to be opposed to; **à l'~** (*fig*) on the other hand; **à l'~ de** on the other *ou* opposite side from; (*fig*) contrary to, unlike.
opposer [ɔpoze] *vt* (*meubles, objets*) to place opposite each other; (*personnes, armées, équipes*) to oppose; (*couleurs, termes, tons*) to contrast; (*comparer: livres, avantages*) to contrast; ~ **qch à** (*comme obstacle, défense*) to set sth against; (*comme objection*) to put sth forward against; (*en contraste*) to set sth opposite; to match sth with; **s'~** (*sens réciproque*) to conflict; to clash; to face each other; to contrast; **s'~ à** (*interdire, empêcher*) to oppose; (*tenir tête à*) to rebel against; **sa religion s'y oppose** it's against his religion; **s'~ à ce que qn fasse** to be opposed to sb's doing.
opposition [ɔpozisjɔ̃] *nf* opposition; **par ~** in contrast; **par ~ à** as opposed to, in contrast with; **entrer en ~ avec** to come into conflict with; **être en ~ avec** (*idées, conduite*) to be at variance with; **faire ~ à un chèque** to stop a cheque.
oppressant, e [ɔpʀesɑ̃, -ɑ̃t] *adj* oppressive.
oppresser [ɔpʀese] *vt* to oppress; **se sentir oppressé** to feel breathless.
oppresseur [ɔpʀesœʀ] *nm* oppressor.
oppressif, ive [ɔpʀesif, -iv] *adj* oppressive.
oppression [ɔpʀesjɔ̃] *nf* oppression; (*malaise*) feeling of suffocation.
opprimer [ɔpʀime] *vt* (*asservir: peuple, faibles*) to oppress; (*étouffer: liberté, opinion*) to suppress, stifle; (*suj: chaleur etc*) to suffocate, oppress.
opprobre [ɔpʀɔbʀ(ə)] *nm* disgrace.
opter [ɔpte] *vi*: ~ **pour** to opt for; ~ **entre** to choose between.
opticien, ne [ɔptisjɛ̃, -ɛn] *nm/f* optician.
optimal, e, aux [ɔptimal, -o] *adj* optimal.
optimisation [ɔptimizasjɔ̃] *nf* optimization.
optimiser [ɔptimize] *vt* to optimize.
optimisme [ɔptimism(ə)] *nm* optimism.
optimiste [ɔptimist(ə)] *adj* optimistic ♦ *nm/f* optimist.
optimum [ɔptimɔm] *adj*, *nm* optimum.
option [ɔpsjɔ̃] *nf* option; (*AUTO: supplément*)

optional extra; **matière à** ~ (*SCOL*) optional subject (*BRIT*), elective (*US*); **prendre une** ~ **sur** to take (out) an option on; ~ **par défaut** (*INFORM*) default (option).

optionnel, le [ɔpsjɔnɛl] *adj* optional.

optique [ɔptik] *adj* (*nerf*) optic; (*verres*) optical ♦ *nf* (*PHOTO: lentilles etc*) optics *pl*; (*science, industrie*) optics *sg*; (*fig: manière de voir*) perspective.

opulence [ɔpylɑ̃s] *nf* wealth, opulence.

opulent, e [ɔpylɑ̃, -ɑ̃t] *adj* wealthy, opulent; (*formes, poitrine*) ample, generous.

OPV *sigle f* (= *offre publique de vente*) public offer of sale.

or [ɔʀ] *nm* gold ♦ *conj* now, but; **d'**~ (*fig*) golden; **en** ~ gold *cpd*; (*occasion*) golden; **un mari/enfant en** ~ a treasure; **une affaire en** ~ (*achat*) a real bargain; (*commerce*) a gold mine; **plaqué** ~ gold-plated; ~ **noir** black gold.

oracle [ɔʀakl(ə)] *nm* oracle.

orage [ɔʀaʒ] *nm* (thunder)storm.

orageux, euse [ɔʀaʒø, -øz] *adj* stormy.

oraison [ɔʀɛzɔ̃] *nf* orison, prayer; ~ **funèbre** funeral oration.

oral, e, aux [ɔʀal, -o] *adj* (*déposition, promesse*) oral, verbal; (*MÉD*): **par voie** ~**e** by mouth, orally ♦ *nm* (*SCOL*) oral.

oralement [ɔʀalmɑ̃] *adv* orally.

orange [ɔʀɑ̃ʒ] *adj inv, nf* orange; ~ **sanguine** blood orange; ~ **pressée** freshly-squeezed orange juice.

orangé, e [ɔʀɑ̃ʒe] *adj* orangey, orange-coloured.

orangeade [ɔʀɑ̃ʒad] *nf* orangeade.

oranger [ɔʀɑ̃ʒe] *nm* orange tree.

orangeraie [ɔʀɑ̃ʒʀɛ] *nf* orange grove.

orangerie [ɔʀɑ̃ʒʀi] *nf* orangery.

orang-outan(g) [ɔʀɑ̃utɑ̃] *nm* orang-utan.

orateur [ɔʀatœʀ] *nm* speaker; orator.

oratoire [ɔʀatwaʀ] *nm* (*lieu, chapelle*) oratory; (*au bord du chemin*) wayside shrine ♦ *adj* oratorical.

oratorio [ɔʀatɔʀjo] *nm* oratorio.

orbital, e, aux [ɔʀbital, -o] *adj* orbital; **station** ~**e** space station.

orbite [ɔʀbit] *nf* (*ANAT*) (eye-)socket; (*PHYSIQUE*) orbit; **mettre sur** ~ to put into orbit; (*fig*) to launch; **dans l'**~ **de** (*fig*) within the sphere of influence of.

Orcades [ɔʀkad] *nfpl*: **les** ~ the Orkneys, the Orkney Islands.

orchestral, e, aux [ɔʀkɛstʀal, -o] *adj* orchestral.

orchestrateur, trice [ɔʀkɛstʀatœʀ, -tʀis] *nm/f* orchestrator.

orchestration [ɔʀkɛstʀasjɔ̃] *nf* orchestration.

orchestre [ɔʀkɛstʀ(ə)] *nm* orchestra; (*de jazz, danse*) band; (*places*) stalls *pl* (*BRIT*), orchestra (*US*).

orchestrer [ɔʀkɛstʀe] *vt* (*MUS*) to orchestrate; (*fig*) to mount, stage-manage.

orchidée [ɔʀkide] *nf* orchid.

ordinaire [ɔʀdinɛʀ] *adj* ordinary; (*coutumier: maladresse etc*) usual; (*de tous les jours*) everyday; (*modèle, qualité*) standard ♦ *nm* ordinary; (*menus*) everyday fare ♦ *nf* (*essence*) ≈ two-star (petrol) (*BRIT*), ≈ regular (gas) (*US*); **d'**~ usually, normally; **à l'**~ usually, ordinarily.

ordinairement [ɔʀdinɛʀmɑ̃] *adv* ordinarily, usually.

ordinal, e, aux [ɔʀdinal, -o] *adj* ordinal.

ordinateur [ɔʀdinatœʀ] *nm* computer; **mettre sur** ~ to computerize, put on computer; ~ **de bureau** desktop computer; ~ **domestique** home computer; ~ **individuel** *ou* **personnel** personal computer; ~ **portatif** laptop (computer).

ordination [ɔʀdinasjɔ̃] *nf* ordination.

ordonnance [ɔʀdɔnɑ̃s] *nf* organization; (*groupement, disposition*) layout; (*MÉD*) prescription; (*JUR*) order; (*MIL*) orderly, batman (*BRIT*); **d'**~ (*MIL*) regulation *cpd*; **officier d'**~ aide-de-camp.

ordonnateur, trice [ɔʀdɔnatœʀ, -tʀis] *nm/f* (*d'une cérémonie, fête*) organizer; ~ **des pompes funèbres** funeral director.

ordonné, e [ɔʀdɔne] *adj* tidy, orderly; (*MATH*) ordered ♦ *nf* (*MATH*) Y-axis, ordinate.

ordonner [ɔʀdɔne] *vt* (*agencer*) to organize, arrange; (*: meubles, appartement*) to lay out, arrange; (*donner un ordre*): ~ **à qn de faire** to order sb to do; (*MATH*) to (arrange in) order; (*REL*) to ordain; (*MÉD*) to prescribe; (*JUR*) to order; **s'**~ (*faits*) to organize themselves.

ordre [ɔʀdʀ(ə)] *nm* (*gén*) order; (*propreté et soin*) orderliness, tidiness; (*association professionnelle, honorifique*) association; (*COMM*): **à l'**~ **de** payable to; (*nature*): **d'**~ **pratique** of a practical nature; ~**s** *nmpl* (*REL*) holy orders; **avoir de l'**~ to be tidy *ou* orderly; **mettre en** ~ to tidy (up), put in order; **mettre bon** ~ **à** to put to rights, sort out; **procéder par** ~ to take things one at a time; **être aux** ~**s de qn/sous les** ~**s de qn** to be at sb's disposal/under sb's command; **rappeler qn à l'**~ to call sb to order; **jusqu'à nouvel** ~ until further notice; **dans le même** ~ **d'idées** in this connection; **par** ~ **d'entrée en scène** in order of appearance; **un** ~ **de grandeur** some idea of the size (*ou* amount); **de premier** ~ first-rate; **de grève** strike call; ~ **du jour** (*d'une réunion*) agenda; (*MIL*) order of the day; **à l'**~ **du jour** on the agenda; (*fig*) topical; (*MIL: citer*) in dispatches; ~ **de mission** (*MIL*) orders *pl*; ~ **public** law and order; ~ **de route** marching orders *pl*.

ordure [ɔʀdyʀ] *nf* filth *no pl*; (*propos, écrit*) obscenity, (piece of) filth; ~**s** *nfpl* (*balayures, déchets*) rubbish *sg*, refuse *sg*; ~**s ménagères** household refuse.

ordurier, ière [ɔʀdyʀje, -jɛʀ] *adj* lewd, filthy.

oreille [ɔʀɛj] nf (ANAT) ear; (de marmite, tasse) handle; (TECH: d'un écrou) wing; **avoir de l'**~ to have a good ear (for music); **avoir l'**~ **fine** to have good ou sharp ears; **l'**~ **basse** crestfallen, dejected; **se faire tirer l'**~ **de** to take a lot of persuading; **dire qch à l'**~ **de qn** to have a word in sb's ear (about sth).

oreiller [ɔʀeje] nm pillow.

oreillette [ɔʀɛjɛt] nf (ANAT) auricle.

oreillons [ɔʀɛjɔ̃] nmpl mumps sg.

ores [ɔʀ]: **d'**~ **et déjà** adv already.

orfèvre [ɔʀfɛvʀ(ə)] nm goldsmith; silversmith.

orfèvrerie [ɔʀfɛvʀəʀi] nf (art, métier) goldsmith's (ou silversmith's) trade; (ouvrage) (silver ou gold) plate.

orfraie [ɔʀfʀɛ] nm white-tailed eagle; **pousser des cris d'**~ to yell at the top of one's voice.

organe [ɔʀgan] nm organ; (véhicule, instrument) instrument; (voix) voice; (porte-parole) representative, mouthpiece; ~**s de commande** (TECH) controls; ~**s de transmission** (TECH) transmission system sg.

organigramme [ɔʀganigʀam] nm (hiérarchique, structurel) organization chart; (des opérations) flow chart.

organique [ɔʀganik] adj organic.

organisateur, trice [ɔʀganizatœʀ, -tʀis] nm/f organizer.

organisation [ɔʀganizɑsjɔ̃] nf organization; **O**~ **des Nations unies (ONU)** United Nations (Organization) (UN, UNO); **O**~ **mondiale de la santé (OMS)** World Health Organization (WHO); **O**~ **du traité de l'Atlantique Nord (OTAN)** North Atlantic Treaty Organization (NATO).

organisationnel, le [ɔʀganizasjɔnɛl] adj organizational.

organiser [ɔʀganize] vt to organize; (mettre sur pied: service etc) to set up; **s'**~ to get organized.

organisme [ɔʀganism(ə)] nm (BIO) organism; (corps humain) body; (ADMIN, POL etc) body, organism.

organiste [ɔʀganist(ə)] nm/f organist.

orgasme [ɔʀgasm(ə)] nm orgasm, climax.

orge [ɔʀʒ(ə)] nf barley.

orgeat [ɔʀʒa] nm: **sirop d'**~ barley water.

orgelet [ɔʀʒəlɛ] nm sty(e).

orgie [ɔʀʒi] nf orgy.

orgue [ɔʀg(ə)] nm organ; ~**s** nfpl organ sg; ~ **de Barbarie** barrel ou street organ.

orgueil [ɔʀgœj] nm pride.

orgueilleux, euse [ɔʀgœjø, -øz] adj proud.

Orient [ɔʀjɑ̃] nm: **l'**~ the East, the Orient.

orientable [ɔʀjɑ̃tabl(ə)] adj (phare, lampe etc) adjustable.

oriental, e, aux [ɔʀjɑ̃tal, -o] adj oriental, eastern; (frontière) eastern ♦ nm/f: **O**~, **e** Oriental.

orientation [ɔʀjɑ̃tɑsjɔ̃] nf positioning; adjustment; orientation; direction; (d'une maison etc) aspect; (d'un journal) leanings pl;

avoir le sens de l'~ to have a (good) sense of direction; **course d'**~ orienteering exercise; ~ **professionnelle** careers advice ou guidance; (service) careers advisory service.

orienté, e [ɔʀjɑ̃te] adj (fig: article, journal) slanted; **bien/mal** ~ (appartement) well/badly positioned; ~ **au sud** facing south, with a southern aspect.

orienter [ɔʀjɑ̃te] vt (situer) to position; (placer, disposer: pièce mobile) to adjust, position; (tourner) to direct, turn; (voyageur, touriste, recherches) to direct; (fig: élève) to orientate; **s'**~ (se repérer) to find one's bearings; **s'**~ **vers** (fig) to turn towards.

orienteur, euse [ɔʀjɑ̃tœʀ, -øz] nm/f (SCOL) careers adviser.

orifice [ɔʀifis] nm opening, orifice.

oriflamme [ɔʀiflam] nf banner, standard.

origan [ɔʀigɑ̃] nm oregano.

originaire [ɔʀiʒinɛʀ] adj original; **être** ~ **de** (pays, lieu) to be a native of; (provenir de) to originate from; to be native to.

original, e, aux [ɔʀiʒinal, -o] adj original; (bizarre) eccentric ♦ nm/f (fam: excentrique) eccentric; (: fantaisiste) joker ♦ nm (document etc, ART) original; (dactylographie) top copy.

originalité [ɔʀiʒinalite] nf (d'un nouveau modèle) originality no pl; (excentricité, bizarrerie) eccentricity.

origine [ɔʀiʒin] nf origin; (d'un message, appel téléphonique) source; (d'une révolution, réussite) root; ~**s** nfpl (d'une personne) origins; **d'**~ of origin; (pneus etc) original; (bureau postal) dispatching; **d'**~ **française** of French origin; **dès l'**~ from the outset; **à l'**~ originally; **avoir son** ~ **dans** to have its origins in, originate in.

originel, le [ɔʀiʒinɛl] adj original.

originellement [ɔʀiʒinɛlmɑ̃] adv (à l'origine) originally; (dès l'origine) from the beginning.

oripeaux [ɔʀipo] nmpl rags.

ORL sigle f (= oto-rhino-laryngologie) ENT ♦ sigle m/f (= oto-rhino-laryngologiste) ENT specialist; **être en** ~ (malade) to be in the ENT hospital ou department.

orme [ɔʀm(ə)] nm elm.

orné, e [ɔʀne] adj ornate; ~ **de** adorned ou decorated with.

ornement [ɔʀnəmɑ̃] nm ornament; (fig) embellishment, adornment; ~**s sacerdotaux** vestments.

ornemental, e, aux [ɔʀnəmɑ̃tal, -o] adj ornamental.

ornementer [ɔʀnəmɑ̃te] vt to ornament.

orner [ɔʀne] vt to decorate, adorn; ~ **qch de** to decorate sth with.

ornière [ɔʀnjɛʀ] nf rut; (fig): **sortir de l'**~ (routine) to get out of the rut; (impasse) to get out of a spot.

ornithologie [ɔʀnitɔlɔʒi] nf

ornithology.
ornithologue [ɔʀnitɔlɔg] *nm/f* ornithologist; ~
amateur birdwatcher.
orphelin, e [ɔʀfəlɛ̃, -in] *adj* orphan(ed) ♦ *nm/f*
orphan; ~ **de père/mère** fatherless/
motherless.
orphelinat [ɔʀfəlina] *nm* orphanage.
ORSEC [ɔʀsɛk] *sigle f* (= *Organisation des
secours*): **le plan** ~ *disaster contingency
plan*.
ORSECRAD [ɔʀsɛkʀad] *sigle m* = ORSEC *en cas
d'accident nucléaire*.
orteil [ɔʀtɛj] *nm* toe; **gros** ~ big toe.
ORTF *sigle m* (= *Office de radio-diffusion
télévision française*) *(former) French
broadcasting corporation*.
orthodontiste [ɔʀtɔdɔ̃tist(ə)] *nm/f*
orthodontist.
orthodoxe [ɔʀtɔdɔks(ə)] *adj* orthodox.
orthodoxie [ɔʀtɔdɔksi] *nf* orthodoxy.
orthogénie [ɔʀtɔʒeni] *nf* family planning.
orthographe [ɔʀtɔgʀaf] *nf* spelling.
orthographier [ɔʀtɔgʀafje] *vt* to spell; **mal
orthographié** misspelt.
orthopédie [ɔʀtɔpedi] *nf* orthopaedics *sg*
(*BRIT*), orthopedics *sg* (*US*).
orthopédique [ɔʀtɔpedik] *adj* orthopaedic
(*BRIT*), orthopedic (*US*).
orthopédiste [ɔʀtɔpedist(ə)] *nm/f* orthopaedic
(*BRIT*) *ou* orthopedic (*US*) specialist.
orthophonie [ɔʀtɔfɔni] *nf* (*MÉD*) speech
therapy; (*LING*) correct pronunciation.
orthophoniste [ɔʀtɔfɔnist(ə)] *nm/f* speech
therapist.
ortie [ɔʀti] *nf* (stinging) nettle; ~ **blanche**
white dead-nettle.
OS *sigle m* = **ouvrier spécialisé**.
os [ɔs, *pl* o] *nm* bone; **sans** ~ (*BOUCHERIE*) off
the bone, boned; ~ **à moelle** marrowbone.
oscillation [ɔsilasjɔ̃] *nf* oscillation; ~**s** *nfpl* (*fig*)
fluctuations.
osciller [ɔsile] *vi* (*pendule*) to swing; (*au vent
etc*) to rock; (*TECH*) to oscillate; (*fig*): ~ **entre**
to waver *ou* fluctuate between.
osé, e [oze] *adj* daring, bold.
oseille [ozɛj] *nf* sorrel.
oser [oze] *vi, vt* to dare; ~ **faire** to dare (to) do.
osier [ozje] *nm* (*BOT*) willow; **d'**~, **en** ~
wicker(work) *cpd*.
Oslo [ɔslo] *n* Oslo.
osmose [ɔsmoz] *nf* osmosis.
ossature [ɔsatyʀ] *nf* (*ANAT: squelette*) frame,
skeletal structure; (*: du visage*) bone
structure; (*fig*) framework.
osselet [ɔslɛ] *nm* (*ANAT*) ossicle; **jouer aux** ~**s**
to play jacks.
ossements [ɔsmɑ̃] *nmpl* bones.
osseux, euse [ɔsø, -øz] *adj* bony; (*tissu,
maladie, greffe*) bone *cpd*.
ossifier [ɔsifje]: **s'**~ *vi* to ossify.
ossuaire [ɔsɥɛʀ] *nm* ossuary.
Ostende [ɔstɑ̃d] *n* Ostend.

ostensible [ɔstɑ̃sibl(ə)] *adj* conspicuous.
ostensiblement [ɔstɑ̃sibləmɑ̃] *adv*
conspicuously.
ostensoir [ɔstɑ̃swaʀ] *nm* monstrance.
ostentation [ɔstɑ̃tasjɔ̃] *nf* ostentation; **faire** ~
de to parade, make a display of.
ostentatoir [ɔstɑ̃tatwaʀ] *adj* ostentatious.
ostracisme [ɔstʀasism(ə)] *nm* ostracism;
frapper d'~ to ostracize.
ostréicole [ɔstʀeikɔl] *adj* oyster *cpd*.
ostréiculture [ɔstʀeikyltyʀ] *nf* oyster-
farming.
otage [ɔtaʒ] *nm* hostage; **prendre qn comme** ~
to take sb hostage.
OTAN [ɔtɑ̃] *sigle f* (= *Organisation du traité de
l'Atlantique Nord*) NATO.
otarie [ɔtaʀi] *nf* sea-lion.
OTASE [ɔtaz] *sigle f* (= *Organisation du traité de
l'Asie du Sud-Est*) SEATO (= *Southeast Asia
Treaty Organization*).
ôter [ote] *vt* to remove; (*soustraire*) to take
away; ~ **qch à qn** to take sth (away) from
sb; ~ **qch de** to remove sth from; **6 ôté de
10 égale 4** 6 from 10 equals *ou* is 4.
otite [ɔtit] *nf* ear infection.
oto-rhino(-laryngologiste) [ɔtɔʀinɔ(-
laʀɛ̃gɔlɔʒist(ə))] *nm/f* ear, nose and throat
specialist.
ottomane [ɔtɔman] *nf* ottoman.
ou [u] *conj* or; ~ ... ~ either ... or; ~ **bien** or
(else).

═══════════════════════════════ *MOT-CLÉ*

où [u] *pron relatif* **1** (*position, situation*) where,
that (*souvent omis*); **la chambre** ~ **il était** the
room (that) he was in, the room where he
was; **la ville** ~ **je l'ai rencontré** the town
where I met him; **la pièce d'**~ **il est sorti** the
room he came out of; **le village d'**~ **je viens**
the village I come from; **les villes par** ~ **il
est passé** the towns he went through
2 (*temps, état*) that (*souvent omis*); **le jour** ~
il est parti the day (that) he left; **au prix** ~
c'est at the price it is
♦ *adv* **1** (*interrogation*) where; ~ **est-il/va-t-il?**
where is he/is he going?; **par** ~**?** which
way?; **d'**~ **vient que ...?** how come ...?
2 (*position*) where; **je sais** ~ **il est** I know
where he is; ~ **que l'on aille** wherever you
go.

═══════════════════════════════════════

OUA *sigle f* (= *Organisation de l'unité africaine*)
OAU (= *Organization of African Unity*).
ouais [wɛ] *excl* yeah.
ouate [wat] *nf* cotton wool (*BRIT*), cotton (*US*);
(*bourre*) padding, wadding; ~ **(hydrophile)**
cotton wool (*BRIT*), (absorbent) cotton (*US*).
ouaté, e [wate] *adj* cotton-wool; (*doublé*)
padded; (*fig: atmosphère*) cocoon-like; (*: pas,
bruit*) muffled.
oubli [ubli] *nm* (*acte*): **l'**~ **de** forgetting;
(*étourderie*) forgetfulness *no pl*; (*négligence*)

omission, oversight; (*absence de souvenirs*) oblivion; ~ **de soi** self-effacement, self-negation.

oublier [ublije] *vt* (*gén*) to forget; (*ne pas voir: erreurs etc*) to miss; (*ne pas mettre: virgule, nom*) to leave out, forget; (*laisser quelque part: chapeau etc*) to leave behind; **s'** ~ to forget o.s; (*enfant, animal*) to have an accident (*euphemism*); ~ **l'heure** to forget (about) the time.

oubliettes [ublijɛt] *nfpl* dungeon *sg*; **(jeter) aux** ~ (*fig*) (to put) completely out of mind.

oublieux, euse [ublijø, -øz] *adj* forgetful.

oued [wɛd] *nm* wadi.

ouest [wɛst] *nm* west ♦ *adj inv* west; (*région*) western; **à l'**~ in the west; (to the) west, westwards; **à l'**~ **de** (to the) west of; **vent d'**~ westerly wind.

ouest-allemand, e [wɛstalmɑ̃, -ɑ̃d] *adj* West German.

ouf [uf] *excl* phew!

Ouganda [ugɑ̃da] *nm*: **l'**~ Uganda.

ougandais, e [ugɑ̃dɛ, -ɛz] *adj* Ugandan.

oui [wi] *adv* yes; **répondre (par)** ~ to answer yes; **mais** ~, **bien sûr** yes, of course; **je pense que** ~ I think so; **pour un** ~ **ou pour un non** for no apparent reason.

ouï-dire [widiR]: **par** ~ *adv* by hearsay.

ouïe [wi] *nf* hearing; ~**s** *nfpl* (*de poisson*) gills; (*de violon*) sound-hole *sg*.

ouïr [wiR] *vt* to hear; **avoir ouï dire que** to have heard it said that.

ouistiti [wistiti] *nm* marmoset.

ouragan [uRagɑ̃] *nm* hurricane; (*fig*) storm.

Oural [uRal] *nm*: **l'**~ (*fleuve*) the Ural; (*aussi*: **les monts** ~) the Urals, the Ural Mountains.

ouralo-altaïque [uRaloaltaik] *adj*, *nm* Ural-Altaic.

ourdir [uRdiR] *vt* (*complot*) to hatch.

ourdou [uRdu] *adj inv* Urdu ♦ *nm* (*LING*) Urdu.

ourlé, e [uRle] *adj* hemmed; (*fig*) rimmed.

ourler [uRle] *vt* to hem.

ourlet [uRlɛ] *nm* hem; (*de l'oreille*) rim; **faire un** ~ **à** to hem.

ours [uRs] *nm* bear; ~ **brun/blanc** brown/polar bear; ~ **marin** fur seal; ~ **mal léché** uncouth fellow; ~ **(en peluche)** teddy (bear).

ourse [uRs(ə)] *nf* (*ZOOL*) she-bear; **la Grande/Petite O**~ the Great/Little Bear, Ursa Major/Minor.

oursin [uRsɛ̃] *nm* sea urchin.

ourson [uRsɔ̃] *nm* (bear-)cub.

ouste [ust(ə)] *excl* hop it!

outil [uti] *nm* tool.

outillage [utijaʒ] *nm* set of tools; (*d'atelier*) equipment *no pl*.

outiller [utije] *vt* (*ouvrier, usine*) to equip.

outrage [utRaʒ] *nm* insult; **faire subir les derniers** ~**s à** (*femme*) to ravish; ~ **aux bonnes mœurs** (*JUR*) outrage to public decency; ~ **à magistrat** (*JUR*) contempt of court; ~ **à la pudeur** (*JUR*) indecent

behaviour *no pl*.

outragé, e [utRaʒe] *adj* offended; outraged.

outrageant, e [utRaʒɑ̃, -ɑ̃t] *adj* offensive.

outrager [utRaʒe] *vt* to offend gravely; (*fig: contrevenir à*) to outrage, insult.

outrageusement [utRaʒøzmɑ̃] *adv* outrageously.

outrance [utRɑ̃s] *nf* excessiveness *no pl*, excess; **à** ~ *adv* excessively, to excess.

outrancier, ière [utRɑ̃sje, -jɛR] *adj* extreme.

outre [utR(ə)] *nf* goatskin, water skin ♦ *prép* besides ♦ *adv*: **passer** ~ to carry on regardless; **passer** ~ **à** to disregard, take no notice of; **en** ~ besides, moreover; ~ **que** apart from the fact that; ~ **mesure** immoderately; unduly.

outré, e [utRe] *adj* (*flatterie, éloge*) excessive, exaggerated; (*indigné, scandalisé*) outraged.

outre-Atlantique [utRatlɑ̃tik] *adv* across the Atlantic.

outrecuidance [utRəkɥidɑ̃s] *nf* presumptuousness *no pl*.

outre-Manche [utRəmɑ̃ʃ] *adv* across the Channel.

outremer [utRəmɛR] *adj inv* ultramarine.

outre-mer [utRəmɛR] *adv* overseas; **d'**~ overseas.

outrepasser [utRəpase] *vt* to go beyond, exceed.

outrer [utRe] *vt* (*pensée, attitude*) to exaggerate; (*indigner: personne*) to outrage.

outre-Rhin [utRəRɛ̃] *adv* across the Rhine, in Germany.

outsider [awtsajdœR] *nm* outsider.

ouvert, e [uvɛR, -ɛRt(ə)] *pp de* **ouvrir** ♦ *adj* open; (*robinet, gaz etc*) on; **à bras** ~**s** with open arms.

ouvertement [uvɛRtəmɑ̃] *adv* openly.

ouverture [uvɛRtyR] *nf* opening; (*MUS*) overture; (*POL*): **l'**~ the widening of the political spectrum; (*PHOTO*): ~ **(du diaphragme)** aperture; ~**s** *nfpl* (*propositions*) overtures; ~ **d'esprit** open-mindedness; **heures d'**~ (*COMM*) opening hours; **jours d'**~ (*COMM*) days of opening.

ouvrable [uvRabl(ə)] *adj*: **jour** ~ working day, weekday; **heures** ~**s** business hours.

ouvrage [uvRaʒ] *nm* (*tâche, de tricot etc, MIL*) work *no pl*; (*objet: COUTURE, ART*) (piece of) work; (*texte, livre*) work; **panier** *ou* **corbeille à** ~ work basket; ~ **d'art** (*GÉNIE CIVIL*) bridge or tunnel etc.

ouvragé, e [uvRaʒe] *adj* finely embroidered (*ou* worked *ou* carved).

ouvrant, e [uvRɑ̃, -ɑ̃t] *vb voir* **ouvrir** ♦ *adj*: **toit** ~ sunroof.

ouvré, e [uvRe] *adj* finely-worked; **jour** ~ working day.

ouvre-boîte(s) [uvRəbwat] *nm inv* tin (*BRIT*) *ou* can opener.

ouvre-bouteille(s) [uvRəbutɛj] *nm inv* bottle-opener.

ouvreuse [uvʀøz] *nf* usherette.

ouvrier, ière [uvʀije, -jɛʀ] *nm/f* worker ♦ *nf* (*ZOOL*) worker (bee) ♦ *adj* working-class; (*problèmes, conflit*) industrial, labour *cpd* (*BRIT*), labor *cpd* (*US*); (*revendications*) workers'; **classe ouvrière** working class; ~ **agricole** farmworker; ~ **qualifié** skilled worker; ~ **spécialisé (OS)** semiskilled worker; ~ **d'usine** factory worker.

ouvrir [uvʀiʀ] *vt* (*gén*) to open; (*brèche, passage*) to open up; (*commencer l'exploitation de, créer*) to open (up); (*eau, électricité, chauffage, robinet*) to turn on; (*MÉD: abcès*) to open up, cut open ♦ *vi* to open; to open up; (*CARTES*): ~ **à trèfle** to open in clubs; **s'**~ *vi* to open; **s'**~ **à** (*art etc*) to open one's mind to; **s'**~ **à qn (de qch)** to open one's heart to sb (about sth); **s'**~ **les veines** to slash *ou* cut one's wrists; ~ **sur** to open onto; ~ **l'appétit à qn** to whet sb's appetite; ~ **des horizons** to open up new horizons; ~ **l'esprit** to broaden one's horizons; ~ **une session** (*INFORM*) to log in.

ouvroir [uvʀwaʀ] *nm* workroom, sewing room.

ovaire [ɔvɛʀ] *nm* ovary.

ovale [ɔval] *adj* oval.

ovation [ɔvasjɔ̃] *nf* ovation.

ovationner [ɔvasjɔne] *vt*: ~ **qn** to give sb an ovation.

ovin, e [ɔvɛ̃, -in] *adj* ovine.

OVNI [ɔvni] *sigle m* (= *objet volant non identifié*) UFO.

ovoïde [ɔvɔid] *adj* egg-shaped.

ovulation [ɔvylasjɔ̃] *nf* (*PHYSIOL*) ovulation.

ovule [ɔvyl] *nm* (*PHYSIOL*) ovum (*pl* ova); (*MÉD*) pessary.

oxfordien, ne [ɔksfɔʀdjɛ̃, -ɛn] *adj* Oxonian ♦ *nm/f*: **O**~, **ne** Oxonian.

oxydable [ɔksidabl(ə)] *adj* liable to rust.

oxyde [ɔksid] *nm* oxide; ~ **de carbone** carbon monoxide.

oxyder [ɔkside]: **s'**~ *vi* to become oxidized.

oxygène [ɔksiʒɛn] *nm* oxygen; (*fig*): **cure d'**~ fresh air cure.

oxygéné, e [ɔksiʒene] *adj*: **eau** ~**e** hydrogen peroxide; **cheveux** ~**s** bleached hair.

ozone [ozɔn] *nm* ozone; **trou dans la couche d'**~ ozone hole.

P p

P, p [pe] *nm inv* P, p ♦ *abr* (= *Père*) Fr; (= *page*) p; **P comme Pierre** P for Peter.

PA *sigle fpl* = **petites annonces**.

PAC *sigle f* (= *Politique agricole commune*) CAP.

pacage [pakaʒ] *nm* grazing, pasture.

pace-maker [pɛsmɛkœʀ] *nm* pacemaker.

pachyderme [paʃidɛʀm(ə)] *nm* pachyderm; elephant.

pacificateur, trice [pasifikatœʀ, -tʀis] *adj* pacificatory.

pacification [pasifikasjɔ̃] *nf* pacification.

pacifier [pasifje] *vt* to pacify.

pacifique [pasifik] *adj* (*personne*) peaceable; (*intentions, coexistence*) peaceful ♦ *nm*: **le P**~, **l'océan P**~ the Pacific (Ocean).

pacifiquement [pasifikmɑ̃] *adv* peaceably; peacefully.

pacifisme [pasifism(ə)] *nm* pacifism.

pacifiste [pasifist(ə)] *nm/f* pacifist.

pack [pak] *nm* pack.

pacotille [pakɔtij] *nf* (*péj*) cheap goods *pl*; **de** ~ cheap.

pacte [pakt(ə)] *nm* pact, treaty.

pactiser [paktize] *vi*: ~ **avec** to come to terms with.

pactole [paktɔl] *nm* gold mine (*fig*).

paddock [padɔk] *nm* paddock.

Padoue [padu] *n* Padua.

PAF *sigle f* (= *Police de l'air et des frontières*) *police authority responsible for civil aviation, border control etc* ♦ *sigle m* (= *paysage audiovisuel français*) *French broadcasting scene.*

pagaie [pagɛ] *nf* paddle.

pagaille [pagaj] *nf* mess, shambles *sg*; **il y en a en** ~ there are loads *ou* heaps of them.

paganisme [paganism(ə)] *nm* paganism.

pagayer [pageje] *vi* to paddle.

page [paʒ] *nf* page; (*passage: d'un roman*) passage ♦ *nm* page (boy); **mettre en** ~**s** to make up (into pages); **mise en** ~ layout; **à la** ~ (*fig*) up-to-date; ~ **blanche** blank page; ~ **de garde** endpaper.

page-écran, *pl* **pages-écrans** [paʒekʀɑ̃] *nf* (*INFORM*) screen page.

pagination [paʒinasjɔ̃] *nf* pagination.

paginer [paʒine] *vt* to paginate.

pagne [paɲ] *nm* loincloth.

pagode [pagɔd] *nf* pagoda.

paie [pɛ] *nf* = **paye**.

paiement [pɛmɑ̃] *nm* = **payement**.

païen, ne [pajɛ̃, -ɛn] *adj, nm/f* pagan, heathen.

paillard, e [pajaʀ, -aʀd(ə)] *adj* bawdy.
paillasse [pajas] *nf* (*matelas*) straw mattress; (*d'un évier*) draining board.
paillasson [pajasɔ̃] *nm* doormat.
paille [paj] *nf* straw; (*défaut*) flaw; **être sur la ~** to be ruined; **~ de fer** steel wool.
paillé, e [paje] *adj* with a straw seat.
pailleté, e [pajte] *adj* sequined.
paillette [pajɛt] *nf* speck, flake; **~s** *nfpl* (*décoratives*) sequins, spangles; **lessive en ~s** soapflakes *pl*.
pain [pɛ̃] *nm* (*substance*) bread; (*unité*) loaf (*pl* loaves) (of bread); (*morceau*): **~ de cire** *etc* bar of wax *etc*; (*CULIN*): **~ de poisson/légumes** fish/vegetable loaf; **petit ~** (bread) roll; **~ bis/complet** brown/wholemeal (*BRIT*) *ou* wholewheat (*US*) bread; **~ de campagne** farmhouse bread; **~ d'épice** ≈ gingerbread; **~ grillé** toast; **~ de mie** sandwich loaf; **~ perdu** French toast; **~ de seigle** rye bread; **~ de sucre** sugar loaf.
pair, e [pɛʀ] *adj* (*nombre*) even ♦ *nm* peer; **aller de ~ (avec)** to go hand in hand *ou* together (with); **au ~** (*FINANCE*) at par; **valeur au ~** par value; **jeune fille au ~** au pair.
paire [pɛʀ] *nf* pair; **une ~ de lunettes/tenailles** a pair of glasses/pincers; **faire la ~: les deux font la ~** they are two of a kind.
pais [pɛ] *vb voir* **paître**.
paisible [pezibl(ə)] *adj* peaceful, quiet.
paisiblement [pezibləmɑ̃] *adv* peacefully, quietly.
paître [pɛtʀ(ə)] *vi* to graze.
paix [pɛ] *nf* peace; (*fig*) peacefulness, peace; **faire la ~ avec** to make peace with; **avoir la ~** to have peace (and quiet).
Pakistan [pakistɑ̃] *nm*: **le ~** Pakistan.
pakistanais, e [pakistanɛ, -ez] *adj* Pakistani.
PAL *sigle m* (= *Phase Alternation Line*) PAL.
palabrer [palabʀe] *vi* to argue endlessly.
palabres [palabʀ(ə)] *nfpl ou mpl* endless discussions.
palace [palas] *nm* luxury hotel.
palais [palɛ] *nm* palace; (*ANAT*) palate; **le P~ Bourbon** *the seat of the French National Assembly*; **le P~ de l'Élysée** the Élysée Palace; **~ des expositions** exhibition centre; **le P~ de Justice** the Law Courts *pl*.
palan [palɑ̃] *nm* hoist.
Palatin [palatɛ̃]: **le (mont) ~** the Palatine (Hill).
pale [pal] *nf* (*d'hélice, de rame*) blade; (*de roue*) paddle.
pâle [pal] *adj* pale; (*fig*): **une ~ imitation** a pale imitation; **bleu ~** pale blue; **~ de colère** white *ou* pale with anger.
palefrenier [palfʀənje] *nm* groom (*for horses*).
paléontologie [paleɔ̃tɔlɔʒi] *nf* paleontology.
paléontologiste [paleɔ̃tɔlɔʒist(ə)], **paléontologue** [paleɔ̃tɔlɔg] *nm/f* paleontologist.
Palerme [palɛʀm(ə)] *n* Palermo.

Palestine [palɛstin] *nf*: **la ~** Palestine.
palestinien, ne [palɛstinjɛ̃, -ɛn] *adj* Palestinian ♦ *nm/f*: **P~, ne** Palestinian.
palet [palɛ] *nm* disc; (*HOCKEY*) puck.
paletot [palto] *nm* (short) coat.
palette [palɛt] *nf* palette; (*produits*) range.
palétuvier [paletyvje] *nm* mangrove.
pâleur [palœʀ] *nf* paleness.
palier [palje] *nm* (*d'escalier*) landing; (*fig*) level, plateau; (: *phase stable*) levelling (*BRIT*) *ou* leveling (*US*) off, new level; (*TECH*) bearing; **nos voisins de ~** our neighbo(u)rs across the landing (*BRIT*) *ou* the hall (*US*); **en ~** *adv* level; **par ~s** in stages.
palière [paljɛʀ] *adj f* landing *cpd*.
pâlir [paliʀ] *vi* to turn *ou* go pale; (*couleur*) to fade; **faire ~ qn** (*de jalousie*) to make sb green (with envy).
palissade [palisad] *nf* fence.
palissandre [palisɑ̃dʀ(ə)] *nm* rosewood.
palliatif [paljatif] *nm* palliative; (*expédient*) stopgap measure.
pallier [palje] *vt*, **~ à** *vt* to offset, make up for.
palmarès [palmaʀɛs] *nm* record (of achievements); (*SCOL*) prize list; (*SPORT*) list of winners.
palme [palm(ə)] *nf* (*BOT*) palm leaf (*pl* leaves); (*symbole*) palm; (*de plongeur*) flipper; **~s (académiques)** *decoration for services to education*.
palmé, e [palme] *adj* (*pattes*) webbed.
palmeraie [palməʀɛ] *nf* palm grove.
palmier [palmje] *nm* palm tree.
palmipède [palmipɛd] *nm* palmiped, webfooted bird.
palois, e [palwa, -waz] *adj* of *ou* from Pau ♦ *nm/f*: **P~, e** inhabitant *ou* native of Pau.
palombe [palɔ̃b] *nf* woodpigeon, ringdove.
pâlot, te [palo, -ɔt] *adj* pale, peaky.
palourde [paluʀd(ə)] *nf* clam.
palpable [palpabl(ə)] *adj* tangible, palpable.
palper [palpe] *vt* to feel, finger.
palpitant, e [palpitɑ̃, -ɑ̃t] *adj* thrilling, gripping.
palpitation [palpitasjɔ̃] *nf* palpitation.
palpiter [palpite] *vi* (*cœur, pouls*) to beat; (: *plus fort*) to pound, throb; (*narines, chair*) to quiver.
paludisme [palydism(ə)] *nm* malaria.
palustre [palystʀ(ə)] *adj* (*coquillage etc*) marsh *cpd*; (*fièvre*) malarial.
pâmer [pame]: **se ~** *vi* to swoon; (*fig*): **se ~ devant** to go into raptures over.
pâmoison [pamwazɔ̃] *nf*: **tomber en ~** to swoon.
pampa [pɑ̃pa] *nf* pampas *pl*.
pamphlet [pɑ̃flɛ] *nm* lampoon, satirical tract.
pamphlétaire [pɑ̃fletɛʀ] *nm/f* lampoonist.
pamplemousse [pɑ̃pləmus] *nm* grapefruit.
pan [pɑ̃] *nm* section, piece; (*côté: d'un prisme, d'une tour*) side, face ♦ *excl* bang!; **~ de chemise** shirt tail; **~ de mur** section of wall.

panacée [panase] _nf_ panacea.

panachage [panaʃaʒ] _nm_ blend, mix; (_POL_) voting for candidates from different parties instead of for the set list of one party.

panache [panaʃ] _nm_ plume; (_fig_) spirit, panache.

panaché, e [panaʃe] _adj_: œillet ~ variegated carnation; **glace** ~**e** mixed ice cream; **salade** ~**e** mixed salad; **bière** ~**e** shandy.

panais [panɛ] _nm_ parsnip.

Panama [panama] _nm_: **le** ~ Panama.

panaméen, ne [panameɛ̃, -ɛn] _adj_ Panamanian ♦ _nm/f_: P~, **ne** Panamanian.

panaris [panaʀi] _nm_ whitlow.

pancarte [pɑ̃kaʀt(ə)] _nf_ sign, notice; (_dans un défilé_) placard.

pancréas [pɑ̃kʀeas] _nm_ pancreas.

panda [pɑ̃da] _nm_ panda.

pané, e [pane] _adj_ fried in breadcrumbs.

panégyrique [paneʒiʀik] _nm_: **faire le** ~ **de qn** to extol sb's merits _ou_ virtues.

panier [panje] _nm_ basket; (_à diapositives_) magazine; **mettre au** ~ to chuck away; ~ **de crabes**: **c'est un** ~ **de crabes** (_fig_) they're constantly at one another's throats; ~ **percé** (_fig_) spendthrift; ~ **à provisions** shopping basket; ~ **à salade** (_CULIN_) salad shaker; (_POLICE_) paddy wagon, police van.

panier-repas, _pl_ **paniers-repas** [panjeʀ(ə)pɑ] _nm_ packed lunch.

panification [panifikasjɔ̃] _nf_ bread-making.

panique [panik] _adj_ panicky ♦ _nf_ panic.

paniquer [panike] _vi_ to panic.

panne [pan] _nf_ (_d'un mécanisme, moteur_) breakdown; **être/tomber en** ~ to have broken down/break down; **être en** ~ **d'essence** _ou_ **en** ~ **sèche** to have run out of petrol (_BRIT_) _ou_ gas (_US_); **mettre en** ~ (_NAVIG_) to bring to; ~ **d'électricité** _ou_ **de courant** power _ou_ electrical failure.

panneau, x [pano] _nm_ (_écriteau_) sign, notice; (_de boiserie, de tapisserie etc_) panel; **tomber dans le** ~ (_fig_) to walk into the trap; ~ **d'affichage** notice (_BRIT_) _ou_ bulletin (_US_) board; ~ **électoral** board for election poster; ~ **indicateur** signpost; ~ **publicitaire** hoarding (_BRIT_), billboard (_US_); ~ **de signalisation** roadsign; ~ **solaire** solar panel.

panneau-réclame, _pl_ **panneaux-réclame** [panoʀeklam] _nm_ hoarding (_BRIT_), billboard (_US_).

panonceau, x [panɔ̃so] _nm_ (_de magasin etc_) sign; (_de médecin etc_) plaque.

panoplie [panɔpli] _nf_ (_jouet_) outfit; (_d'armes_) display; (_fig_) array.

panorama [panɔʀama] _nm_ (_vue_) all-round view, panorama; (_peinture_) panorama; (_fig: étude complète_) complete overview.

panoramique [panɔʀamik] _adj_ panoramic; (_carrosserie_) with panoramic windows ♦ _nm_ (_CINÉ, TV_) panoramic shot.

panse [pɑ̃s] _nf_ paunch.

pansement [pɑ̃smɑ̃] _nm_ dressing, bandage; ~ **adhésif** sticking plaster (_BRIT_), bandaid ® (_US_).

panser [pɑ̃se] _vt_ (_plaie_) to dress, bandage; (_bras_) to put a dressing on, bandage; (_cheval_) to groom.

pantalon [pɑ̃talɔ̃] _nm_ (_aussi:_ ~**s, paire de** ~**s**) trousers _pl_ (_BRIT_), pants _pl_ (_US_), pair of trousers _ou_ pants; ~ **de ski** ski pants _pl_.

pantalonnade [pɑ̃talɔnad] _nf_ slapstick (comedy).

pantelant, e [pɑ̃tlɑ̃, -ɑ̃t] _adj_ gasping for breath, panting.

panthère [pɑ̃tɛʀ] _nf_ panther.

pantin [pɑ̃tɛ̃] _nm_ (_jouet_) jumping jack; (_péj: personne_) puppet.

pantois [pɑ̃twa] _adj m_: **rester** ~ to be flabbergasted.

pantomime [pɑ̃tɔmim] _nf_ mime; (_pièce_) mime show; (_péj_) fuss, carry-on.

pantouflard, e [pɑ̃tuflaʀ, -aʀd(ə)] _adj_ (_péj_) stay-at-home.

pantoufle [pɑ̃tufl(ə)] _nf_ slipper.

panure [panyʀ] _nf_ breadcrumbs _pl_.

PAO _sigle f_ (= _publication assistée par ordinateur_) desk-top publishing.

paon [pɑ̃] _nm_ peacock.

papa [papa] _nm_ dad(dy).

papauté [papote] _nf_ papacy.

papaye [papaj] _nf_ pawpaw.

pape [pap] _nm_ pope.

paperasse [papʀas] _nf_ (_péj_) bumf _no pl_, papers _pl_; forms _pl_.

paperasserie [papʀasʀi] _nf_ (_péj_) red tape _no pl_; paperwork _no pl_.

papeterie [papetʀi] _nf_ (_fabrication du papier_) paper-making (industry); (_usine_) paper mill; (_magasin_) stationer's (shop) (_BRIT_); (_articles_) stationery.

papetier, ière [paptje, -jɛʀ] _nm/f_ paper-maker; stationer.

papetier-libraire, _pl_ **papetiers-libraires** [paptjelibʀɛʀ] _nm_ bookseller and stationer.

papier [papje] _nm_ paper; (_feuille_) sheet _ou_ piece of paper; (_article_) article; (_écrit officiel_) document; ~**s** _nmpl_ (_aussi:_ ~**s d'identité**) (identity) papers; **sur le** ~ (_théoriquement_) on paper; **noircir du** ~ to write page after page; ~ **couché/glacé** art/glazed paper; ~ **(d')aluminium** aluminium (_BRIT_) _ou_ aluminum (_US_) foil, tinfoil; ~ **d'Arménie** incense paper; ~ **bible** India _ou_ bible paper; ~ **de brouillon** rough _ou_ scrap paper; ~ **bulle** manil(l)a paper; ~ **buvard** blotting paper; ~ **calque** tracing paper; ~ **carbone** carbon paper; ~ **collant** Sellotape ® (_BRIT_), Scotch ® (_US_) _ou_ sticky tape; ~ **en continu** continuous stationery; ~ **à dessin** drawing paper; ~ **d'emballage** wrapping paper; ~ **gommé** gummed paper; ~ **hygiénique** toilet paper; ~ **journal** newsprint; (_pour emballer_) newspaper; ~ **à lettres** writing paper,

papier-filtre – parallélépipède

notepaper; ~ **mâché** papier-mâché; ~ **machine** typing paper; ~ **peint** wallpaper; ~ **pelure** India paper; ~ **à pliage accordéon** fanfold paper; ~ **de soie** tissue paper; ~ **thermique** thermal paper; ~ **de tournesol** litmus paper; ~ **de verre** sandpaper.

papier-filtre, *pl* **papiers-filtres** [papjefiltʀ(ə)] *nm* filter paper.

papier-monnaie, *pl* **papiers-monnaies** [papjemɔnɛ] *nm* paper money.

papille [papij] *nf*: ~**s gustatives** taste buds.

papillon [papijɔ̃] *nm* butterfly; (*fam: contravention*) (parking) ticket; (*TECH: écrou*) wing *ou* butterfly nut; ~ **de nuit** moth.

papillonner [papijɔne] *vi* to flit from one thing (*ou* person) to another.

papillote [papijɔt] *nf* (*pour cheveux*) curlpaper; (*de gigot*) (paper) frill.

papilloter [papijɔte] *vi* (*yeux*) to blink; (*paupières*) to flutter; (*lumière*) to flicker.

papotage [papɔtaʒ] *nm* chitchat.

papoter [papɔte] *vi* to chatter.

papou, e [papu] *adj* Papuan.

Papouasie-Nouvelle-Guinée [papwazi-nuvɛlgine] *nf*: **la** ~ Papua-New-Guinea.

paprika [papʀika] *nm* paprika.

papyrus [papiʀys] *nm* papyrus.

pâque [pɑk] *nf*: **la** ~ Passover; *voir aussi* **Pâques.**

paquebot [pakbo] *nm* liner.

pâquerette [pɑkʀɛt] *nf* daisy.

Pâques [pɑk] *nm,* *nfpl* Easter; **faire ses** ~ to do one's Easter duties; **l'île de** ~ Easter Island.

paquet [pakɛ] *nm* packet; (*colis*) parcel; (*ballot*) bundle; (*dans négociations*) package (deal); (*fig: tas*): ~ **de** pile *ou* heap of; ~**s** *nmpl* (*bagages*) bags; **mettre le** ~ (*fam*) to give one's all; ~ **de mer** big wave.

paquetage [paktaʒ] *nm* (*MIL*) kit, pack.

paquet-cadeau, *pl* **paquets-cadeaux** [pakɛkado] *nm* gift-wrapped parcel.

par [paʀ] *prép* by; **finir** *etc* ~ to end *etc* with; ~ **amour** out of love; **passer** ~ **Lyon/la côte** to go via *ou* through Lyons/along by the coast; ~ **la fenêtre** (*jeter, regarder*) out of the window; **3** ~ **jour/personne** 3 a *ou* per day/head; **deux** ~ **deux** two at a time; (*marcher etc*) in twos; **où?** which way?; ~ **ici** this way; (*dans le coin*) round here; ~**-ci, ~-là** here and there.

para [paʀa] *nm* (= *parachutiste*) para.

parabole [paʀabɔl] *nf* (*REL*) parable; (*GÉOM*) parabola.

parabolique [paʀabɔlik] *adj* parabolic; **antenne** ~ satellite dish.

parachever [paʀaʃve] *vt* to perfect.

parachutage [paʀaʃytaʒ] *nm* (*de soldats, vivres*) parachuting-in; **nous sommes contre le** ~ **d'un candidat parisien dans notre circonscription** (*POL, fig*) we are against a Parisian candidate being landed on us.

parachute [paʀaʃyt] *nm* parachute.

parachuter [paʀaʃyte] *vt* (*soldat etc*) to parachute; (*fig*) to pitchfork; **il a été parachuté à la tête de l'entreprise** he was brought in from outside as head of the company.

parachutisme [paʀaʃytism(ə)] *nm* parachuting.

parachutiste [paʀaʃytist(ə)] *nm/f* parachutist; (*MIL*) paratrooper.

parade [paʀad] *nf* (*spectacle, défilé*) parade; (*ESCRIME, BOXE*) parry; (*ostentation*): **faire** ~ **de** to display, show off; (*défense, riposte*): **trouver la** ~ **à une attaque** to find the answer to an attack; **de** ~ *adj* ceremonial; (*superficiel*) superficial, outward.

parader [paʀade] *vi* to swagger (around), show off.

paradis [paʀadi] *nm* heaven, paradise; **P~ terrestre** (*REL*) Garden of Eden; (*fig*) heaven on earth.

paradisiaque [paʀadizjak] *adj* heavenly, divine.

paradoxal, e, aux [paʀadɔksal, -o] *adj* paradoxical.

paradoxalement [paʀadɔksalmɑ̃] *adv* paradoxically.

paradoxe [paʀadɔks(ə)] *nm* paradox.

parafe [paʀaf] *nm,* **parafer** [paʀafe] *vt* = **paraphe, parapher.**

paraffine [paʀafin] *nf* paraffin; paraffin wax.

paraffiné, e [paʀafine] *adj*: **papier** ~ wax(ed) paper.

parafoudre [paʀafudʀ(ə)] *nm* (*ÉLEC*) lightning conductor.

parages [paʀaʒ] *nmpl* (*NAVIG*) waters; **dans les** ~ (**de**) in the area *ou* vicinity (of).

paragraphe [paʀagʀaf] *nm* paragraph.

Paraguay [paʀagwɛ] *nm*: **le** ~ Paraguay.

paraguayen, ne [paʀagwajɛ̃, -ɛn] *adj* Paraguayan ♦ *nm/f*: **P~, ne** Paraguayan.

paraître [paʀɛtʀ(ə)] *vb avec attribut* to seem, look, appear ♦ *vi* to appear; (*être visible*) to show; (*PRESSE, ÉDITION*) to be published, come out, appear; (*briller*) to show off; **laisser** ~ **qch** to let (sth) show ♦ *vb impers*: **il paraît que** it seems *ou* appears that; **il me paraît que** it seems to me that; **il paraît absurde de** it seems absurd to; **il ne paraît pas son âge** he doesn't look his age; ~ **en justice** to appear before the court(s); ~ **en scène/en public/à l'écran** to appear on stage/in public/on the screen.

parallèle [paʀalɛl] *adj* parallel; (*police, marché*) unofficial; (*société, énergie*) alternative ♦ *nm* (*comparaison*): **faire un** ~ **entre** to draw a parallel between; (*GÉO*) parallel ♦ *nf* parallel (line); **en** ~ in parallel; **mettre en** ~ (*choses opposées*) to compare; (*choses semblables*) to parallel.

parallèlement [paʀalɛlmɑ̃] *adv* in parallel; (*fig: en même temps*) at the same time.

parallélépipède [paʀalelepipɛd] *nm*

parallelepiped.
parallélisme [paralelism(ə)] *nm* parallelism; (*AUTO*) wheel alignment.
parallélogramme [paralelɔgram] *nm* parallelogram.
paralyser [paralize] *vt* to paralyze.
paralysie [paralizi] *nf* paralysis.
paralytique [paralitik] *adj*, *nm/f* paralytic.
paramédical, e, aux [paramedikal, -o] *adj* paramedical.
paramètre [parametR(ə)] *nm* parameter.
paramilitaire [paramilitɛR] *adj* paramilitary.
paranoïa [paranɔja] *nf* paranoia.
paranoïaque [paranɔjak] *nm/f* paranoiac.
paranormal, e, aux [paranɔrmal, -o] *adj* paranormal.
parapet [parapɛ] *nm* parapet.
paraphe [paraf] *nm* (*trait*) flourish; (*signature*) initials *pl*; signature.
parapher [parafe] *vt* to initial; to sign.
paraphrase [parafRaz] *nf* paraphrase.
paraphraser [parafRaze] *vt* to paraphrase.
paraplégie [paraple3i] *nf* paraplegia.
paraplégique [paraple3ik] *adj*, *nm/f* paraplegic.
parapluie [paraplɥi] *nm* umbrella; ~ **atomique** *ou* **nucléaire** nuclear umbrella; ~ **pliant** telescopic umbrella.
parapsychique [parapsiʃik] *adj* parapsychological.
parapsychologie [parapsikɔlɔ3i] *nf* parapsychology.
parapublic, ique [parapyblik] *adj partly state-controlled*.
parascolaire [paraskɔlɛR] *adj* extracurricular.
parasitaire [parazitɛR] *adj* parasitic(al).
parasite [parazit] *nm* parasite ♦ *adj* (*BOT*, *BIO*) parasitic(al); ~s *nmpl* (*TÉL*) interference *sg*.
parasitisme [parazitism(ə)] *nm* parasitism.
parasol [parasɔl] *nm* parasol, sunshade.
paratonnerre [paratɔnɛR] *nm* lightning conductor.
paravent [paravɑ̃] *nm* folding screen; (*fig*) screen.
parc [park] *nm* (public) park, gardens *pl*; (*de château etc*) grounds *pl*; (*pour le bétail*) pen, enclosure; (*d'enfant*) playpen; (*MIL*: *entrepôt*) depot; (*ensemble d'unités*) stock; (*de voitures etc*) fleet; ~ **d'attractions** amusement park; ~ **automobile** (*d'un pays*) number of cars on the roads; ~ **à huîtres** oyster bed; ~ **à thème** theme park; ~ **national** national park; ~ **naturel** nature reserve; ~ **de stationnement** car park; ~ **zoologique** zoological gardens *pl*.
parcelle [parsɛl] *nf* fragment, scrap; (*de terrain*) plot, parcel.
parcelliser [parselize] *vt* to divide *ou* split up.
parce que [parsk(ə)] *conj* because.
parchemin [parʃəmɛ̃] *nm* parchment.
parcheminé, e [parʃəmine] *adj* wrinkled; (*papier*) with a parchment finish.

parcimonie [parsimɔni] *nf* parsimony, parsimoniousness.
parcimonieux, euse [parsimɔnjø, -øz] *adj* parsimonious, miserly.
parc(o)mètre [park(ɔ)mɛtR(ə)] *nm* parking meter.
parcotrain [parkɔtRɛ̃] *nm* station car park (*BRIT*) *ou* parking lot (*US*), park-and-ride car park (*BRIT*).
parcourir [parkuRiR] *vt* (*trajet, distance*) to cover; (*article, livre*) to skim *ou* glance through; (*lieu*) to go all over, travel up and down; (*suj: frisson, vibration*) to run through; ~ **des yeux** to run one's eye over.
parcours [parkuR] *vb voir* **parcourir** ♦ *nm* (*trajet*) journey; (*itinéraire*) route; (*SPORT: terrain*) course; (*: tour*) round; run; lap; ~ **du combattant** assault course.
parcouru, e [parkuRy] *pp de* **parcourir**.
par-delà [pardəla] *prép* beyond.
par-dessous [pardəsu] *prép, adv* under(neath).
pardessus [pardəsy] *nm* overcoat.
par-dessus [pardəsy] *prép* over (the top of) ♦ *adv* over (the top); ~ **le marché** on top of it all.
par-devant [pardəvɑ̃] *prép* in the presence of, before ♦ *adv* at the front; round the front.
pardon [pardɔ̃] *nm* forgiveness *no pl* ♦ *excl* (*excuses*) (I'm) sorry; (*pour interpeller etc*) excuse me; (*demander de répéter*) (I beg your) pardon? (*BRIT*), pardon me? (*US*).
pardonnable [pardɔnabl(ə)] *adj* forgivable, excusable.
pardonner [pardɔne] *vt* to forgive; ~ **qch à qn** to forgive sb for sth; **qui ne pardonne pas** (*maladie, erreur*) fatal.
paré, e [pare] *adj* ready, prepared.
pare-balles [parbal] *adj inv* bulletproof.
pare-boue [parbu] *nm inv* mudflap.
pare-brise [parbriz] *nm inv* windscreen (*BRIT*), windshield (*US*).
pare-chocs [parʃɔk] *nm inv* bumper (*BRIT*), fender (*US*).
pare-étincelles [paretɛ̃sɛl] *nm inv* fireguard.
pare-feu [parfø] *nm inv* firebreak ♦ *adj inv*: **portes** ~ fire (resistant) doors.
pareil, le [parɛj] *adj* (*identique*) the same, alike; (*similaire*) similar; (*tel*): **un courage/livre** ~ such courage/a book, courage/a book like this; **de** ~**s livres** such books ♦ *adv*: **habillés** ~ dressed the same (way), dressed alike; **faire** ~ to do the same (thing); **j'en veux un** ~ I'd like one just like it; **rien de** ~ no (*ou* any) such thing, nothing (*ou* anything) like it; **ses** ~**s** one's fellow men; one's peers; **ne pas avoir son (sa)** ~**(le)** to be second to none; ~ **à** the same as; similar to; **sans** ~ unparalleled, unequalled; **c'est du** ~ **au même** it comes to the same thing, it's six (of one) and half-a-dozen (of the other); **en** ~ **cas** in such a case; **rendre la** ~**le à qn** to pay sb back in his own coin.

pareillement [paʀɛjmɑ̃] *adv* the same, alike; in such a way; (*également*) likewise.

parement [paʀmɑ̃] *nm* (*CONSTR, revers d'un col, d'une manche*) facing; (*REL*): ~ **d'autel** antependium.

parent, e [paʀɑ̃, -ɑ̃t] *nm/f*: **un/une ~/e** a relative *ou* relation ♦ *adj*: **être ~ de** to be related to; ~**s** *nmpl* (*père et mère*) parents; (*famille, proches*) relatives, relations; ~ **unique** lone parent; ~**s par alliance** relatives *ou* relations by marriage; ~**s en ligne directe** blood relations.

parental, e, aux [paʀɑ̃tal, -o] *adj* parental.

parenté [paʀɑ̃te] *nf* (*lien*) relationship; (*personnes*) relatives *pl*, relations *pl*.

parenthèse [paʀɑ̃tɛz] *nf* (*ponctuation*) bracket, parenthesis; (*MATH*) bracket; (*digression*) parenthesis, digression; **ouvrir/fermer la ~** to open/close the brackets; **entre ~s** in brackets; (*fig*) incidentally.

parer [paʀe] *vt* to adorn; (*CULIN*) to dress, trim; (*éviter*) to ward off; **~ à** (*danger*) to ward off; (*inconvénient*) to deal with; **se ~ de** (*fig: qualité, titre*) to assume; **~ à toute éventualité** to be ready for every eventuality; **~ au plus pressé** to attend to what's most urgent.

pare-soleil [paʀsɔlɛj] *nm inv* sun visor.

paresse [paʀɛs] *nf* laziness.

paresser [paʀese] *vi* to laze around.

paresseusement [paʀɛsøzmɑ̃] *adv* lazily; sluggishly.

paresseux, euse [paʀesø, -øz] *adj* lazy; (*fig*) slow, sluggish ♦ *nm* (*ZOOL*) sloth.

parfaire [paʀfɛʀ] *vt* to perfect, complete.

parfait, e [paʀfɛ, -ɛt] *pp de* **parfaire** ♦ *adj* perfect ♦ *nm* (*LING*) perfect (tense); (*CULIN*) parfait ♦ *excl* fine, excellent.

parfaitement [paʀfɛtmɑ̃] *adv* perfectly ♦ *excl* (most) certainly.

parfaites [paʀfɛt], **parfasse** [paʀfas], **parferai** [paʀfʀe] *etc vb voir* **parfaire**.

parfois [paʀfwa] *adv* sometimes.

parfum [paʀfœ̃] *nm* (*produit*) perfume, scent; (*odeur: de fleur*) scent, fragrance; (*: de tabac, vin*) aroma; (*goût: de glace, milk-shake*) flavour (*BRIT*), flavor (*US*).

parfumé, e [paʀfyme] *adj* (*fleur, fruit*) fragrant; (*papier à lettres etc*) scented; (*femme*) wearing perfume *ou* scent, perfumed; (*aromatisé*): **~ au café** coffee-flavoured (*BRIT*) *ou* -flavored (*US*).

parfumer [paʀfyme] *vt* (*suj: odeur, bouquet*) to perfume; (*mouchoir*) to put scent *ou* perfume on; (*crème, gâteau*) to flavour (*BRIT*), flavor (*US*); **se ~** to put on (some) perfume *ou* scent; (*d'habitude*) to use perfume *ou* scent.

parfumerie [paʀfymʀi] *nf* (*commerce*) perfumery; (*produits*) perfumes *pl*; (*boutique*) perfume shop (*BRIT*) *ou* store (*US*).

pari [paʀi] *nm* bet, wager; (*SPORT*) bet; ~ **mutuel urbain (PMU)** *system of betting on horses*.

paria [paʀja] *nm* outcast.

parier [paʀje] *vt* to bet; **j'aurais parié que si/non** I'd have said that (*ou* you *etc*) would/wouldn't.

parieur [paʀjœʀ] *nm* (*turfiste etc*) punter.

Paris [paʀi] *n* Paris.

parisien, ne [paʀizjɛ̃, -ɛn] *adj* Parisian; (*GÉO, ADMIN*) Paris *cpd* ♦ *nm/f*: **P~, ne** Parisian.

paritaire [paʀitɛʀ] *adj*: **commission ~** joint commission.

parité [paʀite] *nf* parity; ~ **de change** (*ÉCON*) exchange parity.

parjure [paʀʒyʀ] *nm* (*faux serment*) false oath, perjury; (*violation de serment*) breach of oath, perjury ♦ *nm/f* perjurer.

parjurer [paʀʒyʀe]: **se ~** *vi* to perjure o.s.

parka [paʀka] *nf* parka.

parking [paʀkiŋ] *nm* (*lieu*) car park (*BRIT*), parking lot (*US*).

parlant, e [paʀlɑ̃, -ɑ̃t] *adj* (*fig*) graphic, vivid; (*: comparaison, preuve*) eloquent; (*CINÉ*) talking ♦ *adv*: **généralement ~** generally speaking.

parlé, e [paʀle] *adj*: **langue ~e** spoken language.

parlement [paʀləmɑ̃] *nm* parliament; **le P~ européen** the European Parliament.

parlementaire [paʀləmɑ̃tɛʀ] *adj* parliamentary ♦ *nm/f* (*député*) ≈ Member of Parliament (*BRIT*) *ou* Congress (*US*); parliamentarian; (*négociateur*) negotiator, mediator.

parlementarisme [paʀləmɑ̃taʀism(ə)] *nm* parliamentary government.

parlementer [paʀləmɑ̃te] *vi* (*ennemis*) to negotiate, parley; (*s'entretenir, discuter*) to argue at length, have lengthy talks.

parler [paʀle] *nm* speech; dialect ♦ *vi* to speak, talk; (*avouer*) to talk; **~ (à qn) de** to talk *ou* speak (to sb) about; **~ pour qn** (*intercéder*) to speak for sb; **~ en l'air** to say the first thing that comes into one's head; **~ le/en français** to speak French/in French; **~ affaires** to talk business; **~ en dormant/du nez** to talk in one's sleep/through one's nose; **sans ~ de** (*fig*) not to mention, to say nothing of; **tu parles!** you must be joking!; **n'en parlons plus!** let's forget it!

parleur [paʀlœʀ] *nm*: **beau ~** fine talker.

parloir [paʀlwaʀ] *nm* (*d'une prison, d'un hôpital*) visiting room; (*REL*) parlour (*BRIT*), parlor (*US*).

parlote [paʀlɔt] *nf* chitchat.

Parme [paʀm(ə)] *n* Parma.

parme [paʀm(ə)] *adj* violet (blue).

parmesan [paʀməzɑ̃] *nm* Parmesan (cheese).

parmi [paʀmi] *prép* among(st).

parodie [paʀɔdi] *nf* parody.

parodier [paʀɔdje] *vt* (*œuvre, auteur*) to

parody.

paroi [paʁwa] *nf* wall; (*cloison*) partition; ~ **rocheuse** rock face.

paroisse [paʁwas] *nf* parish.

paroissial, e, aux [paʁwasjal, -o] *adj* parish *cpd*.

paroissien, ne [paʁwasjɛ̃, -ɛn] *nm/f* parishioner ♦ *nm* prayer book.

parole [paʁɔl] *nf* (*faculté*): **la** ~ speech; (*mot, promesse*) word; (*REL*): **la bonne** ~ the word of God; ~**s** *nfpl* (*MUS*) words, lyrics; **tenir** ~ to keep one's word; **avoir la** ~ to have the floor; **n'avoir qu'une** ~ to be true to one's word; **donner la** ~ **à qn** to hand over to sb; **prendre la** ~ to speak; **demander la** ~ to ask for permission to speak; **perdre la** ~ to lose the power of speech; (*fig*) to lose one's tongue; **je le crois sur** ~ I'll take his word for it, I'll take him at his word; **temps de** ~ (*TV, RADIO etc*) discussion time; **ma** ~! my word!, good heavens!; ~ **d'honneur** word of honour (*BRIT*) *ou* honor (*US*).

parolier, ière [paʁɔlje, -jɛʁ] *nm/f* lyricist; (*OPÉRA*) librettist.

paroxysme [paʁɔksism(ə)] *nm* height, paroxysm.

parpaing [paʁpɛ̃] *nm* bond-stone, parpen.

parquer [paʁke] *vt* (*voiture, matériel*) to park; (*bestiaux*) to pen (in *ou* up); (*prisonniers*) to pack in.

parquet [paʁkɛ] *nm* (*parquet*) floor; (*JUR: bureau*) public prosecutor's office; **le** ~ (**général**) (*magistrats*) ≈ the Bench.

parqueter [paʁkəte] *vt* to lay a parquet floor in.

parrain [paʁɛ̃] *nm* godfather; (*d'un navire*) namer; (*d'un nouvel adhérent*) sponsor, proposer.

parrainage [paʁenaʒ] *nm* sponsorship.

parrainer [paʁene] *vt* (*nouvel adhérent*) to sponsor, propose; (*entreprise*) to promote, sponsor.

parricide [paʁisid] *nm*, *nf* parricide.

pars [paʁ] *vb voir* **partir**.

parsemer [paʁsəme] *vt* (*suj: feuilles, papiers*) to be scattered over; ~ **qch de** to scatter sth with.

parsi, e [paʁsi] *adj* Parsee.

part [paʁ] *vb voir* **partir** ♦ *nf* (*qui revient à qn*) share; (*fraction, partie*) part; (*de gâteau, fromage*) portion; (*FINANCE*) (non-voting) share; **prendre** ~ **à** (*débat etc*) to take part in; (*soucis, douleur de qn*) to share in; **faire** ~ **de qch à qn** to announce sth to sb, inform sb of sth; **pour ma** ~ as for me, as far as I'm concerned; **à** ~ **entière** *adj* full; **de la** ~ **de** (*au nom de*) on behalf of; (*donné par*) from; **c'est de la** ~ **de qui?** (*au téléphone*) who's calling *ou* speaking (please)?; **de toute(s)** ~**(s)** from all sides *ou* quarters; **de** ~ **et d'autre** on both sides, on either side; **de** ~ **en** ~ right through; **d'une** ~ ... **d'autre** ~ on the one hand ... on the other hand; **nulle/ autre/quelque** ~ nowhere/elsewhere/ somewhere; **à** ~ *adv* separately; (*de côté*) aside ♦ *prép* apart from, except for ♦ *adj* exceptional, special; **pour une large** *ou* **bonne** ~ to a great extent; **prendre qch en bonne/mauvaise** ~ to take sth well/badly; **faire la** ~ **des choses** to make allowances; **faire la** ~ **du feu** (*fig*) to cut one's losses; **faire la** ~ **(trop) belle à qn** to give sb more than his (*ou* her) share.

part. *abr* = **particulier**.

partage [paʁtaʒ] *nm* (*voir partager*) sharing (out) *no pl*, share-out; sharing; dividing up; (*POL: de suffrages*) share; **recevoir qch en** ~ to receive sth as one's share (*ou* lot); **sans** ~ undivided.

partagé, e [paʁtaʒe] *adj* (*opinions etc*) divided; (*amour*) shared; **temps** ~ (*INFORM*) time sharing; **être** ~ **entre** to be shared between; **être** ~ **sur** to be divided about.

partager [paʁtaʒe] *vt* to share; (*distribuer, répartir*) to share (out); (*morceler, diviser*) to divide (up); **se** ~ *vt* (*héritage etc*) to share between themselves (*ou* ourselves *etc*).

partance [paʁtɑ̃s]: **en** ~ *adv* outbound, due to leave; **en** ~ **pour** (bound) for.

partant, e [paʁtɑ̃, -ɑ̃t] *vb voir* **partir** ♦ *adj*: **être** ~ **pour qch** (*d'accord pour*) to be quite ready for sth ♦ *nm* (*SPORT*) starter; (*HIPPISME*) runner.

partenaire [paʁtənɛʁ] *nm/f* partner; ~**s sociaux** management and workforce.

parterre [paʁtɛʁ] *nm* (*de fleurs*) (flower) bed, border; (*THÉÂT*) stalls *pl*.

parti [paʁti] *nm* (*POL*) party; (*décision*) course of action; (*personne à marier*) match; **tirer** ~ **de** to take advantage of, turn to good account; **prendre le** ~ **de faire** to make up one's mind to do, resolve to do; **prendre le** ~ **de qn** to stand up for sb, side with sb; **prendre** ~ (**pour/contre**) to take sides *ou* a stand (for/against); **prendre son** ~ **de** to come to terms with; ~ **pris** bias.

partial, e, aux [paʁsjal, -o] *adj* biased, partial.

partialement [paʁsjalmɑ̃] *adv* in a biased way.

partialité [paʁsjalite] *nf* bias, partiality.

participant, e [paʁtisipɑ̃, -ɑ̃t] *nm/f* participant; (*à un concours*) entrant; (*d'une société*) member.

participation [paʁtisipasjɔ̃] *nf* participation; sharing; (*COMM*) interest; **la** ~ **aux bénéfices** profit-sharing; **la** ~ **ouvrière** worker participation; **"avec la** ~ **de ..."** "featuring ...".

participe [paʁtisip] *nm* participle; ~ **passé/ présent** past/present participle.

participer [paʁtisipe]: ~ **à** *vt* (*course, réunion*) to take part in; (*profits etc*) to share in; (*frais etc*) to contribute to; (*entreprise: financièrement*) to cooperate in; (*chagrin, succès de qn*) to share (in); ~ **de** *vt* to partake of.

particulariser [paʀtikylaʀize] *vt*: **se ~** to mark o.s. (*ou* itself) out.

particularisme [paʀtikylaʀism(ə)] *nm* sense of identity.

particularité [paʀtikylaʀite] *nf* particularity; (*distinctive*) characteristic, feature.

particule [paʀtikyl] *nf* particle; **~ (nobiliaire)** nobiliary particle.

particulier, ière [paʀtikylje, -jɛʀ] *adj* (*personnel, privé*) private; (*spécial*) special, particular; (*caractéristique*) characteristic, distinctive; (*spécifique*) particular ♦ *nm* (*individu: ADMIN*) private individual; "**~ vend ...**" (*COMM*) "for sale privately ...", "for sale by owner ..." (*US*); **~ à** peculiar to; **en ~** *adv* (*surtout*) in particular, particularly; (*à part*) separately; (*en privé*) in private.

particulièrement [paʀtikyljɛʀmɑ̃] *adv* particularly.

partie [paʀti] *nf* (*gén*) part; (*profession, spécialité*) field, subject; (*JUR etc: protagonistes*) party; (*de cartes, tennis etc*) game; (*fig: lutte, combat*) struggle, fight; **une ~ de campagne/de pêche** an outing in the country/a fishing party *ou* trip; **en ~** *adv* partly, in part; **faire ~ de** to belong to; (*suj: chose*) to be part of; **prendre qn à ~** to take sb to task; (*malmener*) to set on sb; **en grande ~** largely, in the main; **ce n'est que ~ remise** it will be for another time *ou* the next time; **avoir ~ liée avec qn** to be in league with sb; **~ civile** (*JUR*) *party claiming damages in a criminal case*.

partiel, le [paʀsjɛl] *adj* partial ♦ *nm* (*SCOL*) class exam.

partiellement [paʀsjɛlmɑ̃] *adv* partially, partly.

partir [paʀtiʀ] *vi* (*gén*) to go; (*quitter*) to go, leave; (*s'éloigner*) to go (*ou* drive *etc*) away *ou* off; (*moteur*) to start; (*pétard*) to go off; (*bouchon*) to come out; (*bouton*) to come off; **~ de** (*lieu: quitter*) to leave; (*: commencer à*) to start from; (*date*) to run *ou* start from; **~ pour/à** (*lieu, pays etc*) to leave for/go off to; **à ~ de** from.

partisan, e [paʀtizɑ̃, -an] *nm/f* partisan; (*d'un parti, régime etc*) supporter ♦ *adj* (*lutte, querelle*) partisan, one-sided; **être ~ de qch/faire** to be in favour (*BRIT*) *ou* favor (*US*) of sth/doing.

partitif, ive [paʀtitif, -iv] *adj*: **article ~** partitive article.

partition [paʀtisjɔ̃] *nf* (*MUS*) score.

partout [paʀtu] *adv* everywhere; **~ où il allait** everywhere *ou* wherever he went; **trente ~** (*TENNIS*) thirty all.

paru [paʀy] *pp de* **paraître**.

parure [paʀyʀ] *nf* (*bijoux etc*) finery *no pl*; jewellery *no pl* (*BRIT*), jewelry *no pl* (*US*); (*assortiment*) set.

parus [paʀy] *etc vb voir* **paraître**.

parution [paʀysjɔ̃] *nf* publication, appearance.

parvenir [paʀvəniʀ]: **~ à** *vt* (*atteindre*) to reach; (*obtenir, arriver à*) to attain; (*réussir*): **~ à faire** to manage to do, succeed in doing; **faire ~ qch à qn** to have sth sent to sb.

parvenu, e [paʀvəny] *pp de* **parvenir** ♦ *nm/f* (*péj*) parvenu, upstart.

parviendrai [paʀvjɛ̃dʀe], **parviens** [paʀvjɛ̃] *etc voir* **parvenir**.

parvis [paʀvi] *nm* square (*in front of a church*).

══════════════════════════════ *MOT-CLÉ*

pas¹ [pɑ] *adv* **1** (*en corrélation avec ne, non etc*) not; **il ne pleure ~** (*habituellement*) he does not *ou* doesn't cry; (*maintenant*) he's not *ou* isn't crying; **je ne mange ~ de viande** I don't *ou* do not eat meat; **il n'a ~ pleuré/ne pleurera ~** he did not *ou* didn't/will not *ou* won't cry; **ils n'ont ~ de voiture/d'enfants** they haven't got a car/any children, they have no car/children; **il m'a dit de ne ~ le faire** he told me not to do it; **non ~ que ...** not that ...

2 (*employé sans ne etc*): **~ moi** not me, not I, I don't (*ou* can't *etc*); **elle travaille, (mais) lui ~ ou ~ lui** she works but he doesn't *ou* does not; **une pomme ~ mûre** an apple which isn't ripe; **~ plus tard qu'hier** only yesterday; **~ du tout** not at all; **~ de sucre, merci** no sugar, thanks; **ceci est à vous ou ~?** is this yours or not?, is this yours or isn't it?

3: **~ mal** (*joli: personne, maison*) not bad; **~ mal fait** not badly done *ou* made; **comment ça va? — ~ mal** how are things? — not bad; **~ mal de** quite a lot of.

──────────────────────────────

pas² [pɑ] *nm* (*allure, mesure*) pace; (*démarche*) tread; (*enjambée, DANSE, fig: étape*) step; (*bruit*) (foot)step; (*trace*) footprint; (*allure*) pace; (*d'un cheval*) walk; (*mesure*) pace; (*TECH: de vis, d'écrou*) thread; **~ à ~** step by step; **au ~** at walking pace; **de ce ~** (*à l'instant même*) straightaway, at once; **marcher à grands ~** to stride along; **mettre qn au ~** to bring sb to heel; **au ~ de gymnastique/de course** at a jog trot/at a run; **à ~ de loup** stealthily; **faire les cent ~** to pace up and down; **faire les premiers ~** to make the first move; **retourner** *ou* **revenir sur ses ~** to retrace one's steps; **se tirer d'un mauvais ~** to get o.s. out of a tight spot; **sur le ~ de la porte** on the doorstep; **le ~ de Calais** (*détroit*) the Straits *pl* of Dover; **~ de porte** (*fig*) key money.

pascal, e, aux [paskal, -o] *adj* Easter *cpd*.

passable [pɑsabl(ə)] *adj* passable, tolerable.

passablement [pɑsabləmɑ̃] *adv* (*pas trop mal*) reasonably well; (*beaucoup*) quite a lot.

passade [pɑsad] *nf* passing fancy, whim.

passage [pɑsaʒ] *nm* (*fait de passer*) *voir* **passer**;

(lieu, prix de la traversée, extrait de livre etc) passage; *(chemin)* way; *(itinéraire)*: **sur le ~ du cortège** along the route of the procession; **"laissez/n'obstruez pas le ~"** "keep clear/do not obstruct"; **au ~** *(en passant)* as I *(ou* he etc*)* went by; **de ~** *(touristes)* passing through; *(amants etc)* casual; **~ clouté** pedestrian crossing; **"~ interdit"** "no entry"; **~ à niveau** level *(BRIT) ou* grade *(US)* crossing; **"~ protégé"** right of way over secondary road(s) on your right; **~ souterrain** subway *(BRIT)*, underpass; **~ à tabac** beating-up; **~ à vide** *(fig)* bad patch.

passager, ère [pɑsaʒe, -ɛR] *adj* passing; *(hôte)* short-stay *cpd; (oiseau)* migratory ♦ *nm/f* passenger; **~ clandestin** stowaway.

passagèrement [pɑsaʒɛRmɑ̃] *adv* temporarily, for a short time.

passant, e [pɑsɑ̃, -ɑ̃t] *adj (rue, endroit)* busy ♦ *nm/f* passer-by ♦ *nm (pour ceinture etc)* loop; **en ~**: **remarquer qch en ~** to notice sth in passing.

passation [pɑsasjɔ̃] *nf (JUR: d'un acte)* signing; **~ des pouvoirs** transfer *ou* handover of power.

passe [pɑs] *nf (SPORT, magnétique)* pass; *(NAVIG)* channel ♦ *nm (passe-partout)* master *ou* skeleton key; **être en ~ de faire** to be on the way to doing; **être dans une bonne/mauvaise ~** *(fig)* to be going through a good/bad patch; **~ d'armes** *(fig)* heated exchange.

passé, e [pɑse] *adj (événement, temps)* past; *(couleur, tapisserie)* faded; *(précédent)*: **dimanche ~** last Sunday ♦ *prép* after ♦ *nm* past; *(LING)* past (tense); **il est ~ midi** *ou* **midi ~** it's gone *(BRIT) ou* past twelve; **~ de mode** out of fashion; **~ composé** perfect (tense); **~ simple** past historic.

passe-droit [pɑsdRwa] *nm* special privilege.

passéiste [pɑseist(ə)] *adj* backward-looking.

passementerie [pɑsmɑ̃tRi] *nf* trimmings *pl.*

passe-montagne [pɑsmɔ̃taɲ] *nm* balaclava.

passe-partout [pɑspartu] *nm inv* master *ou* skeleton key ♦ *adj inv* all-purpose.

passe-passe [pɑspɑs] *nm*: **tour de ~** trick, sleight of hand *no pl.*

passe-plat [pɑspla] *nm* serving hatch.

passeport [pɑspɔR] *nm* passport.

passer [pɑse] *vi (se rendre, aller)* to go; *(voiture, piétons: défiler)* to pass (by), go by; *(faire une halte rapide: facteur, laitier etc)* to come, call; *(: pour rendre visite)* to call *ou* drop in; *(courant, air, lumière, franchir un obstacle etc)* to get through; *(accusé, projet de loi)*: **~ devant** to come before; *(film, émission)* to be on; *(temps, jours)* to pass, go by; *(liquide, café)* to go through; *(être digéré, avalé)* to go down; *(couleur, papier)* to fade; *(mode)* to be out; *(douleur)* to pass, go away; *(CARTES)* to pass; *(SCOL)* to go up (to the next class); *(devenir)*: **~ président** to be appointed *ou*

become president ♦ *vt (frontière, rivière etc)* to cross; *(douane)* to go through; *(examen)* to sit, take; *(visite médicale etc)* to have; *(journée, temps)* to spend; *(donner)*: **~ qch à qn** to pass sth to sb; to give sb sth; *(transmettre)*: **~ qch à qn** to pass sth on to sb; *(enfiler: vêtement)* to slip on; *(faire entrer, mettre)*: **(faire) ~ qch dans/par** to get sth into/through; *(café)* to pour the water on; *(thé, soupe)* to strain; *(film, pièce)* to show, put on; *(disque)* to play, put on; *(marché, accord)* to agree on; *(tolérer)*: **~ qch à qn** to let sb get away with sth; **se ~** *vi (avoir lieu: scène, action)* to take place; *(se dérouler: entretien etc)* to go; *(arriver)*: **que s'est-il passé?** what happened?; *(s'écouler: semaine etc)* to pass, go by; **se ~ de** *vt* to go *ou* do without; **se ~ les mains sous l'eau/de l'eau sur le visage** to put one's hands under the tap/run water over one's face; **en passant** in passing; **~ par** to go through; **passez devant/par ici** go in front/this way; **~ sur** *vt (faute, détail inutile)* to pass over; **~ dans les mœurs/l'usage** to become the custom/normal usage; **~ avant qch/qn** *(fig)* to come before sth/sb; **laisser ~** *(air, lumière, personne)* to let through; *(occasion)* to let slip, miss; *(erreur)* to overlook; **faire ~** *(message)* to get over *ou* across; **faire ~ à qn le goût de qch** to cure sb of his *(ou* her) taste for sth; **~ à la radio/fouille** to be X-rayed/searched; **~ à la radio/télévision** to be on the radio/on television; **~ à table** to sit down to eat; **~ au salon** to go into the sitting room; **~ à l'opposition** to go over to the opposition; **~ aux aveux** to confess, make a confession; **~ à l'action** to go into action; **~ pour riche** to be taken for a rich man; **il passait pour avoir** he was said to have; **faire ~ qn/qch pour** to make sb/sth out to be; **passe encore de le penser, mais de le dire!** it's one thing to think it, but to say it!; **passons!** let's say no more (about it); **et j'en passe!** and that's not all!; **~ en seconde, ~ la seconde** *(AUTO)* to change into second; **~ qch en fraude** to smuggle sth in *(ou* out); **~ la main par la portière** to stick one's hand out of the door; **~ le balai/l'aspirateur** to sweep up/hoover; **~ commande/la parole à qn** to hand over to sb; **je vous passe M X** *(je vous mets en communication avec lui)* I'm putting you through to Mr X; *(je lui passe l'appareil)* here is Mr X, I'll hand you over to Mr X; **~ prendre** to (come and) collect.

passereau, x [pɑsRo] *nm* sparrow.

passerelle [pɑsRɛl] *nf* footbridge; *(de navire, avion)* gangway; *(NAVIG)*: **~ (de commandement)** bridge.

passe-temps [pɑstɑ̃] *nm inv* pastime.

passette [pɑsɛt] *nf* (tea-)strainer.

passeur, euse [pɑsœR, -øz] *nm/f* smuggler.

passible [pasibl(ə)] *adj*: **~ de** liable to.

passif, ive [pasif, -iv] adj passive ♦ nm (LING) passive; (COMM) liabilities pl.

passion [pasjɔ̃] nf passion; **avoir la ~ de** to have a passion for; **fruit de la ~** passion fruit.

passionnant, e [pasjɔnɑ̃, -ɑ̃t] adj fascinating.

passionné, e [pasjɔne] adj (personne, tempérament) passionate; (description) impassioned ♦ nm/f: **c'est un ~ d'échecs** he's a chess fanatic; **être ~ de** ou **pour qch** to have a passion for sth.

passionnel, le [pasjɔnɛl] adj of passion.

passionnément [pasjɔnemɑ̃] adv passionately.

passionner [pasjɔne] vt (personne) to fascinate, grip; (débat, discussion) to inflame; **se ~ pour** to take an avid interest in; to have a passion for.

passivement [pasivmɑ̃] adv passively.

passivité [pasivite] nf passivity, passiveness.

passoire [paswaʀ] nf sieve; (à légumes) colander; (à thé) strainer.

pastel [pastɛl] nm, adj inv (ART) pastel.

pastèque [pastɛk] nf watermelon.

pasteur [pastœʀ] nm (protestant) minister, pastor.

pasteurisation [pastœʀizasjɔ̃] nf pasteurization.

pasteuriser [pastœʀize] vt to pasteurize.

pastiche [pastiʃ] nm pastiche.

pastille [pastij] nf (à sucer) lozenge, pastille; (de papier etc) (small) disc; **~s pour la toux** cough drops ou lozenges.

pastis [pastis] nm anise-flavoured alcoholic drink.

pastoral, e, aux [pastɔʀal, -o] adj pastoral.

patagon, ne [patagɔ̃, -ɔn] adj Patagonian.

Patagonie [patagɔni] nf: **la ~** Patagonia.

patate [patat] nf spud; **~ douce** sweet potato.

pataud, e [pato, -od] adj lumbering.

patauger [patoʒe] vi (pour s'amuser) to splash about; (avec effort) to wade about; (fig) to flounder; **~ dans** (en marchant) to wade through.

patch [patʃ] nm nicotine patch.

patchouli [patʃuli] nm patchouli.

patchwork [patʃwœʀk] nm patchwork.

pâte [pat] nf (à tarte) pastry; (à pain) dough; (à frire) batter; (substance molle) paste; cream; **~s** nfpl (macaroni etc) pasta sg; **fromage à ~ dure/molle** hard/soft cheese; **~ d'amandes** almond paste; **~ brisée** shortcrust (BRIT) ou pie crust (US) pastry; **~ à choux/feuilletée** choux/puff ou flaky (BRIT) pastry; **~ de fruits** crystallized fruit no pl; **~ à modeler** modelling clay, Plasticine ® (BRIT); **~ à papier** paper pulp.

pâté [pate] nm (charcuterie: terrine) pâté; (tache) ink blot; (de sable) sandpie; **~ (en croûte)** ≈ meat pie; **~ de foie** liver pâté; **~ de maisons** block (of houses).

pâtée [pate] nf mash, feed.

patelin [patlɛ̃] nm little place.

patente [patɑ̃t] nf (COMM) trading licence (BRIT) ou license (US).

patenté, e [patɑ̃te] adj (COMM) licensed; (fig: attitré) registered, (officially) recognized.

patère [patɛʀ] nf (coat-)peg.

paternalisme [patɛʀnalism(ə)] nm paternalism.

paternaliste [patɛʀnalist(ə)] adj paternalistic.

paternel, le [patɛʀnɛl] adj (amour, soins) fatherly; (ligne, autorité) paternal.

paternité [patɛʀnite] nf paternity, fatherhood.

pâteux, euse [patø, -øz] adj thick; pasty; **avoir la bouche** ou **langue pâteuse** to have a furred (BRIT) ou coated tongue.

pathétique [patetik] adj pathetic, moving.

pathologie [patɔlɔʒi] nf pathology.

pathologique [patɔlɔʒik] adj pathological.

patibulaire [patibylɛʀ] adj sinister.

patiemment [pasjamɑ̃] adv patiently.

patience [pasjɑ̃s] nf patience; **être à bout de ~** to have run out of patience; **perdre/ prendre ~** to lose (one's)/have patience.

patient, e [pasjɑ̃, -ɑ̃t] adj, nm/f patient.

patienter [pasjɑ̃te] vi to wait.

patin [patɛ̃] nm skate; (sport) skating; (de traîneau, luge) runner; (pièce de tissu) cloth pad (used as slippers to protect polished floor); **~ (de frein)** brake block; **~s (à glace)** (ice) skates; **~s à roulettes** roller skates.

patinage [patinaʒ] nm skating; **~ artistique/de vitesse** figure/speed skating.

patine [patin] nf sheen.

patiner [patine] vi to skate; (embrayage) to slip; (roue, voiture) to spin; **se ~** vi (meuble, cuir) to acquire a sheen, become polished.

patineur, euse [patinœʀ, -øz] nm/f skater.

patinoire [patinwaʀ] nf skating rink, (ice) rink.

patio [patjo] nm patio.

pâtir [patiʀ]: **~ de** vt to suffer because of.

pâtisserie [patisʀi] nf (boutique) cake shop; (métier) confectionery; (à la maison) pastry- ou cake-making, baking; **~s** nfpl (gâteaux) pastries, cakes.

pâtissier, ière [patisje, -jɛʀ] nm/f pastrycook; confectioner.

patois [patwa] nm dialect, patois.

patriarche [patʀijaʀʃ(ə)] nm patriarch.

patrie [patʀi] nf homeland.

patrimoine [patʀimwan] nm inheritance, patrimony; (culture) heritage; **~ génétique** ou **héréditaire** genetic inheritance.

patriote [patʀijɔt] adj patriotic ♦ nm/f patriot.

patriotique [patʀijɔtik] adj patriotic.

patriotisme [patʀijɔtism(ə)] nm patriotism.

patron, ne [patʀɔ̃, -ɔn] nm/f (chef) boss, manager/eress; (propriétaire) owner, proprietor/tress; (employeur) employer; (MÉD) ≈ senior consultant; (REL) patron saint ♦ nm (COUTURE) pattern; **~ de thèse** supervisor (of postgraduate thesis).

patronage [patʀɔnaʒ] *nm* patronage; (*organisation, club*) (parish) youth club; (parish) children's club.

patronal, e, aux [patʀɔnal, -o] *adj* (*syndicat, intérêts*) employers'.

patronat [patʀɔna] *nm* employers *pl.*

patronner [patʀɔne] *vt* to sponsor, support.

patronnesse [patʀɔnɛs] *adj f*: **dame ~** patroness.

patronyme [patʀɔnim] *nm* name.

patronymique [patʀɔnimik] *adj*: **nom ~** patronymic (name).

patrouille [patʀuj] *nf* patrol.

patrouiller [patʀuje] *vi* to patrol, be on patrol.

patrouilleur [patʀujœʀ] *nm* (*AVIAT*) scout (plane); (*NAVIG*) patrol boat.

patte [pat] *nf* (*jambe*) leg; (*pied: de chien, chat*) paw; (*: d'oiseau*) foot; (*languette*) strap; (*: de poche*) flap; (*favoris*): **~s (de lapin)** (short) sideburns; **à ~s d'éléphant** *adj* (*pantalon*) flared; **~s de mouche** (*fig*) spidery scrawl *sg*; **~s d'oie** (*fig*) crow's feet.

pattemouille [patmuj] *nf* damp cloth (*for ironing*).

pâturage [pɑtyʀaʒ] *nm* pasture.

pâture [pɑtyʀ] *nf* food.

paume [pom] *nf* palm.

paumé, e [pome] *nm/f* (*fam*) drop-out.

paumer [pome] *vt* (*fam*) to lose.

paupérisation [popeʀizasjɔ̃] *nf* pauperization.

paupérisme [popeʀism(ə)] *nm* pauperism.

paupière [popjɛʀ] *nf* eyelid.

paupiette [popjɛt] *nf*: **~s de veau** veal olives.

pause [poz] *nf* (*arrêt*) break; (*en parlant, MUS*) pause.

pause-café, *pl* **pauses-café** [pozkafe] *nf* coffee-break.

pauvre [povʀ(ə)] *adj* poor ♦ *nm/f* poor man/woman; **les ~s** the poor; **~ en calcium** low in calcium.

pauvrement [povʀəmɑ̃] *adv* poorly.

pauvreté [povʀəte] *nf* (*état*) poverty.

pavage [pavaʒ] *nm* paving; cobbles *pl.*

pavaner [pavane]: **se ~** *vi* to strut about.

pavé, e [pave] *adj* (*cour*) paved; (*rue*) cobbled ♦ *nm* (*bloc*) paving stone; cobblestone; (*pavage*) paving; (*bifteck*) slab of steak; (*fam: livre*) hefty tome; **être sur le ~** (*sans domicile*) to be on the streets; (*sans emploi*) to be out of a job; **~ numérique** (*INFORM*) keypad.

pavillon [pavijɔ̃] *nm* (*de banlieue*) small (detached) house; (*kiosque*) lodge; pavilion; (*d'hôpital*) ward; (*MUS: de cor etc*) bell; (*ANAT: de l'oreille*) pavilion, pinna; (*NAVIG*) flag; **~ de complaisance** flag of convenience.

pavoiser [pavwaze] *vt* to deck with flags ♦ *vi* to put out flags; (*fig*) to rejoice, exult.

pavot [pavo] *nm* poppy.

payable [pɛjabl(ə)] *adj* payable.

payant, e [pɛjɑ̃, -ɑ̃t] *adj* (*spectateurs etc*) paying; (*billet*) that you pay for, to be paid

for; (*fig: entreprise*) profitable; **c'est ~** you have to pay, there is a charge.

paye [pɛj] *nf* pay, wages *pl.*

payement [pɛjmɑ̃] *nm* payment.

payer [peje] *vt* (*créancier, employé, loyer*) to pay; (*achat, réparations, fig: faute*) to pay for ♦ *vi* to pay; (*métier*) to pay, be well-paid; (*effort, tactique etc*) to pay off; **il me l'a fait ~ 10 F** he charged me 10 F for it; **~ qn de** (*ses efforts, peines*) to reward sb for; **~ qch à qn** to buy sth for sb, buy sb sth; **ils nous ont payé le voyage** they paid for our trip; **~ de sa personne** to give of oneself; **~ d'audace** to act with great daring; **~ cher qch** to pay dear(ly) for sth; **cela ne paie pas de mine** it doesn't look much; **se ~ qch** to buy o.s. sth; **se ~ de mots** to shoot one's mouth off; **se ~ la tête de qn** to take the mickey out of sb (*BRIT*), make a fool of sb; (*duper*) to take sb for a ride.

payeur, euse [pɛjœʀ, -øz] *adj* (*organisme, bureau*) payments *cpd* ♦ *nm/f* payer.

pays [pei] *nm* (*territoire, habitants*) country, land; (*région*) region; (*village*) village; **du ~** *adj* local; **le ~ de Galles** Wales.

paysage [peizaʒ] *nm* landscape.

paysager, ère [peizaʒe, -ɛʀ] *adj* (*jardin, parc*) landscaped.

paysagiste [peizaʒist(ə)] *nm/f* (*de jardin*) landscape gardener; (*ART*) landscapist, landscape painter.

paysan, ne [peizɑ̃, -an] *nm/f* countryman/woman; farmer; (*péj*) peasant ♦ *adj* country *cpd*, farming; farmers'.

paysannat [peizana] *nm* peasantry.

Pays-Bas [peiba] *nmpl*: **les ~** the Netherlands.

PC *sigle m* (*POL*) = **parti communiste**; (*INFORM*: = *personal computer*) PC; (= *prêt conventionné*) type of loan for house purchase; (*CONSTR*) = **permis de construire**; (*MIL*) = **poste de commandement**.

pcc *abr* (= *pour copie conforme*) c.c.

Pce *abr* = **prince**.

Pcesse *abr* = **princesse**.

PCV *abr* (= *percevoir*) *voir* **communication**.

p de p *abr* = **pas de porte**.

PDG *sigle m* = **président directeur général**.

p.ê. *abr* = **peut-être**.

PEA *sigle m* (= *plan d'épargne en actions*) building society savings plan.

péage [peaʒ] *nm* toll; (*endroit*) tollgate; **pont à ~** toll bridge.

peau, x [po] *nf* skin; (*cuir*): **gants de ~** leather gloves; **être bien/mal dans sa ~** to be at ease/odds with oneself; **se mettre dans la ~ de qn** to put o.s. in sb's place *ou* shoes; **faire ~ neuve** (*se renouveler*) to change one's image; **~ de chamois** (*chiffon*) chamois leather, shammy; **~ d'orange** orange peel.

peaufiner [pofine] *vt* to polish (up).

Peau-Rouge [poʀuʒ] *nm/f* Red Indian, red skin.

peccadille [pekadij] *nf* trifle, peccadillo.

péché [peʃe] *nm* sin; ~ **mignon** weakness.

pêche [pɛʃ] *nf* (*sport, activité*) fishing; (*poissons pêchés*) catch; (*fruit*) peach; **aller à la** ~ to go fishing; **avoir la** ~ (*fam*) to be on (top) form; ~ **à la ligne** (*en rivière*) angling; ~ **sous-marine** deep-sea fishing.

pêche-abricot, *pl* **pêches-abricots** [pɛʃabʀiko] *nf* yellow peach.

pécher [peʃe] *vi* (*REL*) to sin; (*fig: personne*) to err; (*: chose*) to be flawed; ~ **contre la bienséance** to break the rules of good behaviour.

pêcher [peʃe] *nm* peach tree ♦ *vi* to go fishing; (*en rivière*) to go angling ♦ *vt* (*attraper*) to catch, land; (*chercher*) to fish for; ~ **au chalut** to trawl.

pécheur, eresse [peʃœʀ, peʃʀɛs] *nm/f* sinner.

pêcheur [pɛʃœʀ] *nm* (*voir pêcher*) fisherman; angler; ~ **de perles** pearl diver.

pectine [pɛktin] *nf* pectin.

pectoral, e, aux [pɛktɔʀal, -o] *adj* (*ANAT*) pectoral; (*sirop*) throat *cpd*, cough *cpd* ♦ *nmpl* pectoral muscles.

pécule [pekyl] *nm* savings *pl*, nest egg; (*d'un détenu*) earnings *pl* (*paid on release*).

pécuniaire [pekynjɛʀ] *adj* financial.

pédagogie [pedagɔʒi] *nf* educational methods *pl*, pedagogy.

pédagogique [pedagɔʒik] *adj* educational; **formation** ~ teacher training.

pédagogue [pedagɔg] *nm/f* teacher; education(al)ist.

pédale [pedal] *nf* pedal; **mettre la** ~ **douce** to soft-pedal.

pédaler [pedale] *vi* to pedal.

pédalier [pedalje] *nm* pedal and gear mechanism.

pédalo [pedalo] *nm* pedalo, pedal-boat.

pédant, e [pedɑ̃, -ɑ̃t] *adj* (*péj*) pedantic ♦ *nm/f* pedant.

pédantisme [pedɑ̃tism(ə)] *nm* pedantry.

pédéraste [pedeʀast(ə)] *nm* homosexual, pederast.

pédérastie [pedeʀasti] *nf* homosexuality, pederasty.

pédestre [pedɛstʀ(ə)] *adj*: **tourisme** ~ hiking; **randonnée** ~ (*activité*) rambling; (*excursion*) ramble.

pédiatre [pedjatʀ(ə)] *nm/f* paediatrician (*BRIT*), pediatrician *ou* pediatrist (*US*), child specialist.

pédiatrie [pedjatʀi] *nf* paediatrics *sg* (*BRIT*), pediatrics *sg* (*US*).

pédicure [pedikyʀ] *nm/f* chiropodist.

pedigree [pedigʀe] *nm* pedigree.

peeling [piliŋ] *nm* exfoliation treatment.

PEEP *sigle f* = Fédération des parents d'élèves de l'enseignement public.

pègre [pɛgʀ(ə)] *nf* underworld.

peignais [peɲɛ] *etc vb voir* **peindre.**

peigne [peɲ] *vb voir* **peindre, peigner** ♦ *nm* comb.

peigné, e [peɲe] *adj*: **laine** ~**e** wool worsted; combed wool.

peigner [peɲe] *vt* to comb (the hair of); **se** ~ to comb one's hair.

peignez [peɲe] *etc vb voir* **peindre.**

peignoir [peɲwaʀ] *nm* dressing gown; ~ **de bain** bathrobe; ~ **de plage** beach robe.

peignons [peɲɔ̃] *vb voir* **peindre.**

peinard, e [penaʀ, -aʀd(ə)] *adj* (*emploi*) cushy (*BRIT*), easy; (*personne*): **on est** ~ **ici** we're left in peace here.

peindre [pɛ̃dʀ(ə)] *vt* to paint; (*fig*) to portray, depict.

peine [pɛn] *nf* (*affliction*) sorrow, sadness *no pl*; (*mal, effort*) trouble *no pl*, effort; (*difficulté*) difficulty; (*punition, châtiment*) punishment; (*JUR*) sentence; **faire de la** ~ **à qn** to distress *ou* upset sb; **prendre la** ~ **de faire** to go to the trouble of doing; **se donner de la** ~ to make an effort; **ce n'est pas la** ~ **de faire** there's no point in doing, it's not worth doing; **ce n'est pas la** ~ **que vous fassiez** there's no point (in) you doing; **avoir de la** ~ **à faire** to have difficulty doing; **donnez-vous** *ou* **veuillez-vous donner la** ~ **d'entrer** please do come in; **c'est** ~ **perdue** it's a waste of time (and effort); **à** ~ *adv* scarcely, hardly, barely; **à** ~ ... **que** hardly ... than; **c'est à** ~ **si** ... it's (*ou* it was) a job to ...; **sous** ~: **sous** ~ **d'être puni** for fear of being punished; **défense d'afficher sous** ~ **d'amende** billposters will be fined; ~ **capitale** capital punishment; ~ **de mort** death sentence *ou* penalty.

peiner [pene] *vi* to work hard; to struggle; (*moteur, voiture*) to labour (*BRIT*), labor (*US*) ♦ *vt* to grieve, sadden.

peint, e [pɛ̃, pɛ̃t] *pp de* **peindre.**

peintre [pɛ̃tʀ(ə)] *nm* painter; ~ **en bâtiment** house painter, painter and decorator; ~ **d'enseignes** signwriter.

peinture [pɛ̃tyʀ] *nf* painting; (*couche de couleur, couleur*) paint; (*surfaces peintes: aussi:* ~**s**) paintwork; **je ne peux pas le voir en** ~ I can't stand the sight of him; ~ **mate/ brillante** matt/gloss paint; "~ **fraîche**" "wet paint".

péjoratif, ive [peʒɔʀatif, -iv] *adj* pejorative, derogatory.

Pékin [pekɛ̃] *n* Peking.

pékinois, e [pekinwa, -waz] *adj* Peking(g)ese ♦ *nm* (*chien*) peke, pekin(g)ese; (*LING*) Mandarin, Pekin(g)ese ♦ *nm/f*: **P**~, **e** Pekin(g)ese.

PEL *sigle m* (= plan d'épargne logement) *savings scheme providing lower-interest mortgages.*

pelade [pəlad] *nf* alopecia.

pelage [pəlaʒ] *nm* coat, fur.

pelé, e [pəle] *adj* (*chien*) hairless; (*vêtement*) threadbare; (*terrain*) bare.

pêle-mêle [pɛlmɛl] *adv* higgledy-piggledy.

peler [pəle] *vt, vi* to peel.

pèlerin [pɛlʀɛ̃] *nm* pilgrim.

pèlerinage [pɛlʀinaʒ] *nm* (*voyage*) pilgrimage; (*lieu*) place of pilgrimage, shrine.

pèlerine [pɛlʀin] *nf* cape.

pélican [pelikɑ̃] *nm* pelican.

pelisse [pəlis] *nf* fur-lined cloak.

pelle [pɛl] *nf* shovel; (*d'enfant, de terrassier*) spade; ~ **à gâteau** cake slice; ~ **mécanique** mechanical digger.

pelletée [pɛlte] *nf* shovelful; spadeful.

pelleter [pɛlte] *vt* to shovel (up).

pelleteuse [pɛltøz] *nf* mechanical digger, excavator.

pelletier [pɛltje] *nm* furrier.

pellicule [pelikyl] *nf* film; ~**s** *nfpl* (*MÉD*) dandruff *sg*.

Péloponnèse [pelɔpɔnɛz] *nm*: **le** ~ the Peloponnese.

pelote [pəlɔt] *nf* (*de fil, laine*) ball; (*d'épingles*) pin cushion; ~ **basque** pelota.

peloter [pəlɔte] *vt* (*fam*) to feel (up); **se** ~ to pet.

peloton [pəlɔtɔ̃] *nm* (*groupe: personnes*) group; (: *pompiers, gendarmes*) squad; (: *SPORT*) pack; (*de laine*) ball; ~ **d'exécution** firing squad.

pelotonner [pəlɔtɔne]: **se** ~ *vi* to curl (o.s.) up.

pelouse [pəluz] *nf* lawn; (*HIPPISME*) *spectating area inside racetrack*.

peluche [pəlyʃ] *nf* (bit of) fluff; **animal en** ~ soft toy, fluffy animal.

pelucher [p(ə)lyʃe] *vi* to become fluffy, fluff up.

pelucheux, euse [p(ə)lyʃø, -øz] *adj* fluffy.

pelure [pəlyʀ] *nf* peeling, peel *no pl*; ~ **d'oignon** onion skin.

pénal, e, aux [penal, -o] *adj* penal.

pénalisation [penalizɑsjɔ̃] *nf* (*SPORT*) sanction, penalty.

pénaliser [penalize] *vt* to penalize.

pénalité [penalite] *nf* penalty.

penalty, ies [penalti, -z] *nm* (*SPORT*) penalty (kick).

pénard, e [penaʀ, -aʀd(ə)] *adj* = **peinard**.

pénates [penat] *nmpl*: **regagner ses** ~ to return to the bosom of one's family.

penaud, e [pəno, -od] *adj* sheepish, contrite.

penchant [pɑ̃ʃɑ̃] *nm*: **un** ~ **à faire/à qch** a tendency to do/to sth; **un** ~ **pour qch** a liking *ou* fondness for sth.

penché, e [pɑ̃ʃe] *adj* slanting.

pencher [pɑ̃ʃe] *vi* to tilt, lean over ♦ *vt* to tilt; **se** ~ *vi* to lean over; (*se baisser*) to bend down; **se** ~ **sur** to bend over; (*fig: problème*) to look into; **se** ~ **au dehors** to lean out; ~ **pour** to be inclined to favour (*BRIT*) *ou* favor (*US*).

pendable [pɑ̃dabl(ə)] *adj*: **tour** ~ rotten trick; **c'est un cas** ~! he (*ou* she) deserves to be shot!

pendaison [pɑ̃dɛzɔ̃] *nf* hanging.

pendant, e [pɑ̃dɑ̃, -ɑ̃t] *adj* hanging (out); (*ADMIN, JUR*) pending ♦ *nm* counterpart; matching piece ♦ *prép* during; **faire** ~ **à** to match; to be the counterpart of; ~ **que** while; ~**s d'oreilles** drop *ou* pendant earrings.

pendeloque [pɑ̃dlɔk] *nf* pendant.

pendentif [pɑ̃dɑ̃tif] *nm* pendant.

penderie [pɑ̃dʀi] *nf* wardrobe; (*placard*) walk-in cupboard.

pendiller [pɑ̃dije] *vi* to flap (about).

pendre [pɑ̃dʀ(ə)] *vt, vi* to hang; **se** ~ **(à)** (*se suicider*) to hang o.s. (on); **se** ~ **à** (*se suspendre*) to hang from; ~ **à** to hang (down) from; ~ **qch à** (*mur*) to hang sth (up) on; (*plafond*) to hang sth (up) from.

pendu, e [pɑ̃dy] *pp de* **pendre** ♦ *nm/f* hanged man (*ou* woman).

pendulaire [pɑ̃dylɛʀ] *adj* pendular, of a pendulum.

pendule [pɑ̃dyl] *nf* clock ♦ *nm* pendulum.

pendulette [pɑ̃dylɛt] *nf* small clock.

pêne [pɛn] *nm* bolt.

pénétrant, e [penetʀɑ̃, -ɑ̃t] *adj* (*air, froid*) biting; (*pluie*) that soaks right through you; (*fig: odeur*) noticeable; (*œil, regard*) piercing; (*clairvoyant, perspicace*) perceptive ♦ *nf* (*route*) expressway.

pénétration [penetʀɑsjɔ̃] *nf* (*fig: d'idées etc*) penetration; (*perspicacité*) perception.

pénétré, e [penetʀe] *adj* (*air, ton*) earnest; **être** ~ **de soi-même/son importance** to be full of oneself/one's own importance.

pénétrer [penetʀe] *vi* to come *ou* get in ♦ *vt* to penetrate; ~ **dans** to enter; (*suj: froid, projectile*) to penetrate; (: *air, eau*) to come into, get into; (*mystère, secret*) to fathom; **se** ~ **de qch** to get sth firmly set in one's mind.

pénible [penibl(ə)] *adj* (*astreignant*) hard; (*affligeant*) painful; (*personne, caractère*) tiresome; **il m'est** ~ **de** ... I'm sorry to ....

péniblement [penibləmɑ̃] *adv* with difficulty.

péniche [peniʃ] *nf* barge; ~ **de débarquement** landing craft *inv*.

pénicilline [penisilin] *nf* penicillin.

péninsulaire [penɛ̃sylɛʀ] *adj* peninsular.

péninsule [penɛ̃syl] *nf* peninsula.

pénis [penis] *nm* penis.

pénitence [penitɑ̃s] *nf* (*repentir*) penitence; (*peine*) penance; (*punition, châtiment*) punishment; **mettre un enfant en** ~ ≈ to make a child stand in the corner; **faire** ~ to do a penance.

pénitencier [penitɑ̃sje] *nm* prison, penitentiary (*US*).

pénitent, e [penitɑ̃, -ɑ̃t] *adj* penitent.

pénitentiaire [penitɑ̃sjɛʀ] *adj* prison *cpd*, penitentiary (*US*).

pénombre [penɔ̃bʀ(ə)] *nf* half-light.

pensable [pɑ̃sabl(ə)] *adj*: **ce n'est pas** ~ it's unthinkable.

pensant, e [pɑ̃sɑ̃, -ɑ̃t] *adj*: **bien ~** right-thinking.

pense-bête [pɑ̃sbɛt] *nm* aide-mémoire, mnemonic device.

pensée [pɑ̃se] *nf* thought; (*démarche, doctrine*) thinking *no pl*; (*BOT*) pansy; **se représenter qch par la ~** to conjure up a mental picture of sth; **en ~** in one's mind.

penser [pɑ̃se] *vi* to think ♦ *vt* to think; (*concevoir: problème, machine*) to think out; **~ à** to think of; (*songer à: ami, vacances*) to think of *ou* about; (*réfléchir à: problème, offre*): **~ à qch** to think about sth, think sth over; **~ à faire qch** to think of doing sth; **~ faire qch** to be thinking of doing sth, intend to do sth; **faire ~ à** to remind one of; **n'y pensons plus** let's forget it; **vous n'y pensez pas!** don't let it bother you!; **sans ~ à mal** without meaning any harm; **je le pense aussi** I think so too; **je pense que oui/non** I think so/don't think so.

penseur [pɑ̃sœʀ] *nm* thinker; **libre ~** free-thinker.

pensif, ive [pɑ̃sif, -iv] *adj* pensive, thoughtful.

pension [pɑ̃sjɔ̃] *nf* (*allocation*) pension; (*prix du logement*) board and lodging, bed and board; (*maison particulière*) boarding house; (*hôtel*) guesthouse, hotel; (*école*) boarding school; **prendre ~ chez** to take board and lodging at; **prendre qn en ~** to take sb (in) as a lodger; **mettre en ~** to send to boarding school; **~ alimentaire** (*d'étudiant*) living allowance; (*de divorcée*) maintenance allowance; alimony; **~ complète** full board; **~ de famille** boarding house, guesthouse; **~ de guerre/d'invalidité** war/disablement pension.

pensionnaire [pɑ̃sjɔnɛʀ] *nm/f* boarder; guest.

pensionnat [pɑ̃sjɔna] *nm* boarding school.

pensionné, e [pɑ̃sjɔne] *nm/f* pensioner.

pensivement [pɑ̃sivmɑ̃] *adv* pensively, thoughtfully.

pensum [pɛ̃sɔm] *nm* (*SCOL*) punishment exercise; (*fig*) chore.

pentagone [pɛ̃tagɔn] *nm* pentagon; **le P~** the Pentagon.

pentathlon [pɛ̃tatlɔ̃] *nm* pentathlon.

pente [pɑ̃t] *nf* slope; **en ~** adj sloping.

Pentecôte [pɑ̃tkot] *nf*: **la ~** Whitsun (*BRIT*), Pentecost; (*dimanche*) Whitsunday (*BRIT*); **lundi de ~** Whit Monday (*BRIT*).

pénurie [penyʀi] *nf* shortage; **~ de main-d'œuvre** undermanning.

PEP [pɛp] *sigle m* (= *plan d'épargne populaire*) individual savings plan.

pépé [pepe] *nm* (*fam*) grandad.

pépère [pepɛʀ] *adj* (*fam*) cushy (*fam*), quiet ♦ *nm* (*fam*) grandad.

pépier [pepje] *vi* to chirp, tweet.

pépin [pepɛ̃] *nm* (*BOT: graine*) pip; (*fam: ennui*) snag, hitch; (: *parapluie*) brolly (*BRIT*), umbrella.

pépinière [pepinjɛʀ] *nf* nursery; (*fig*) nest, breeding-ground.

pépiniériste [pepinjeʀist(ə)] *nm* nurseryman.

pépite [pepit] *nf* nugget.

PEPS *abr* (= *premier entré premier sorti*) first in first out.

PER [pɛʀ] *sigle m* (= *plan d'épargne retraite*) type of personal pension plan.

perçant, e [pɛʀsɑ̃, -ɑ̃t] *adj* (*vue, regard, yeux*) sharp, keen; (*cri, voix*) piercing, shrill.

percée [pɛʀse] *nf* (*trouée*) opening; (*MIL, COMM, fig*) breakthrough; (*SPORT*) break.

perce-neige [pɛʀsənɛʒ] *nm ou f inv* snowdrop.

perce-oreille [pɛʀsɔʀɛj] *nm* earwig.

percepteur [pɛʀsɛptœʀ] *nm* tax collector.

perceptible [pɛʀsɛptibl(ə)] *adj* (*son, différence*) perceptible; (*impôt*) payable, collectable.

perception [pɛʀsɛpsjɔ̃] *nf* perception; (*d'impôts etc*) collection; (*bureau*) tax (collector's) office.

percer [pɛʀse] *vt* to pierce; (*ouverture etc*) to make; (*mystère, énigme*) to penetrate ♦ *vi* to come through; (*réussir*) to break through; **~ une dent** to cut a tooth.

perceuse [pɛʀsøz] *nf* drill; **~ à percussion** hammer drill.

percevable [pɛʀsəvabl(ə)] *adj* collectable, payable.

percevoir [pɛʀsəvwaʀ] *vt* (*distinguer*) to perceive, detect; (*taxe, impôt*) to collect; (*revenu, indemnité*) to receive.

perche [pɛʀʃ(ə)] *nf* (*ZOOL*) perch; (*bâton*) pole; **~ à son** (sound) boom.

percher [pɛʀʃe] *vt*: **~ qch sur** to perch sth on ♦ *vi*, **se ~** *vi* (*oiseau*) to perch.

perchiste [pɛʀʃist(ə)] *nm/f* (*SPORT*) pole vaulter; (*TV etc*) boom operator.

perchoir [pɛʀʃwaʀ] *nm* perch; (*fig*) *presidency of the French National Assembly*.

perclus, e [pɛʀkly, -yz] *adj*: **~ de** (*rhumatismes*) crippled with.

perçois [pɛʀswa] *etc vb voir* **percevoir**.

percolateur [pɛʀkɔlatœʀ] *nm* percolator.

perçu, e [pɛʀsy] *pp de* **percevoir**.

percussion [pɛʀkysjɔ̃] *nf* percussion.

percussionniste [pɛʀkysjɔnist(ə)] *nm/f* percussionist.

percutant, e [pɛʀkytɑ̃, -ɑ̃t] *adj* (*article etc*) resounding, forceful.

percuter [pɛʀkyte] *vt* to strike; (*suj: véhicule*) to crash into ♦ *vi*: **~ contre** to crash into.

percuteur [pɛʀkytœʀ] *nm* firing pin, hammer.

perdant, e [pɛʀdɑ̃, -ɑ̃t] *nm/f* loser ♦ *adj* losing.

perdition [pɛʀdisjɔ̃] *nf* (*morale*) ruin; **en ~** (*NAVIG*) in distress; **lieu de ~** den of vice.

perdre [pɛʀdʀ(ə)] *vt* to lose; (*gaspiller: temps, argent*) to waste; (: *occasion*) to waste, miss; (*personne: moralement etc*) to ruin ♦ *vi* to lose; (*sur une vente etc*) to lose out; (*récipient*) to leak; **se ~** *vi* (*s'égarer*) to get lost, lose one's way; (*fig: se gâter*) to go to waste; (*disparaître*) to disappear, vanish; **il ne perd**

rien pour attendre it can wait, it'll keep.
perdreau, x [pɛʀdʀo] *nm* (young) partridge.
perdrix [pɛʀdʀi] *nf* partridge.
perdu, e [pɛʀdy] *pp de* **perdre** ♦ *adj* (*enfant, cause, objet*) lost; (*isolé*) out-of-the-way; (*COMM: emballage*) non-returnable; (*récolte etc*) ruined; (*malade*): **il est ~** there's no hope left for him; **à vos moments ~s** in your spare time.
père [pɛʀ] *nm* father; **~s** *nmpl* (*ancêtres*) forefathers; **de ~ en fils** from father to son; **~ de famille** father; family man; **mon ~** (*REL*) Father; **le ~ Noël** Father Christmas.
pérégrinations [peʀegʀinɑsjɔ̃] *nfpl* travels.
péremption [peʀɑ̃psjɔ̃] *nf*: **date de ~** expiry date.
péremptoire [peʀɑ̃ptwaʀ] *adj* peremptory.
pérennité [peʀenite] *nf* durability, lasting quality.
péréquation [peʀekwɑsjɔ̃] *nf* (*des salaires*) realignment; (*des prix, impôts*) equalization.
perfectible [pɛʀfɛktibl(ə)] *adj* perfectible.
perfection [pɛʀfɛksjɔ̃] *nf* perfection; **à la ~** *adv* to perfection.
perfectionné, e [pɛʀfɛksjɔne] *adj* sophisticated.
perfectionnement [pɛʀfɛksjɔnmɑ̃] *nm* improvement.
perfectionner [pɛʀfɛksjɔne] *vt* to improve, perfect; **se ~ en anglais** to improve one's English.
perfectionniste [pɛʀfɛksjɔnist(ə)] *nm/f* perfectionist.
perfide [pɛʀfid] *adj* perfidious, treacherous.
perfidie [pɛʀfidi] *nf* treachery.
perforant, e [pɛʀfɔʀɑ̃, -ɑ̃t] *adj* (*balle*) armour-piercing (*BRIT*), armor-piercing (*US*).
perforateur, trice [pɛʀfɔʀatœʀ, -tʀis] *nm/f* punch-card operator ♦ *nm* (*perceuse*) borer; drill ♦ *nf* (*perceuse*) borer; drill; (*pour cartes*) card-punch; (*de bureau*) punch.
perforation [pɛʀfɔʀɑsjɔ̃] *nf* perforation; punching; (*trou*) hole.
perforatrice [pɛʀfɔʀatʀis] *nf voir* **perforateur**.
perforé, e [pɛʀfɔʀe] *adj*: **bande ~** punched tape; **carte ~** punch card.
perforer [pɛʀfɔʀe] *vt* to perforate, punch a hole (*ou* holes) in; (*ticket, bande, carte*) to punch.
perforeuse [pɛʀfɔʀøz] *nf* (*machine*) (card) punch; (*personne*) card punch operator.
performance [pɛʀfɔʀmɑ̃s] *nf* performance.
performant, e [pɛʀfɔʀmɑ̃, -ɑ̃t] *adj* (*ÉCON: produit, entreprise*) high-return *cpd*; (*TECH: appareil, machine*) high-performance *cpd*.
perfusion [pɛʀfyzjɔ̃] *nf* perfusion; **faire une ~ à qn** to put sb on a drip.
péricliter [peʀiklite] *vi* to go downhill.
péridurale [peʀidyʀal] *nf* epidural.
périgourdin, e [peʀiguʀdɛ̃, -in] *adj* of *ou* from the Perigord.
péril [peʀil] *nm* peril; **au ~ de sa vie** at the risk

of his life; **à ses risques et ~s** at his (*ou* her) own risk.
périlleux, euse [peʀijø, -øz] *adj* perilous.
périmé, e [peʀime] *adj* (out)dated; (*ADMIN*) out-of-date, expired.
périmètre [peʀimɛtʀ(ə)] *nm* perimeter.
périnatal, e [peʀinatal] *adj* perinatal.
période [peʀjɔd] *nf* period.
périodique [peʀjɔdik] *adj* (*phases*) periodic; (*publication*) periodical; (*MATH: fraction*) recurring ♦ *nm* periodical; **garniture** *ou* **serviette ~** sanitary towel (*BRIT*) *ou* napkin (*US*).
périodiquement [peʀjɔdikmɑ̃] *adv* periodically.
péripéties [peʀipesi] *nfpl* events, episodes.
périphérie [peʀifeʀi] *nf* periphery; (*d'une ville*) outskirts *pl*.
périphérique [peʀifeʀik] *adj* (*quartiers*) outlying; (*ANAT, TECH*) peripheral; (*station de radio*) operating from a neighbouring country ♦ *nm* (*INFORM*) peripheral; (*AUTO*): **(boulevard) ~** ring road (*BRIT*), circular route (*US*).
périphrase [peʀifʀɑz] *nf* circumlocution.
périple [peʀipl(ə)] *nm* journey.
périr [peʀiʀ] *vi* to die, perish.
périscolaire [peʀiskɔlɛʀ] *adj* extracurricular.
périscope [peʀiskɔp] *nm* periscope.
périssable [peʀisabl(ə)] *adj* perishable.
péristyle [peʀistil] *nm* peristyle.
péritonite [peʀitɔnit] *nf* peritonitis.
perle [pɛʀl(ə)] *nf* pearl; (*de plastique, métal, sueur*) bead; (*personne, chose*) gem, treasure; (*erreur*) gem, howler.
perlé, e [pɛʀle] *adj* (*rire*) rippling, tinkling; (*travail*) exquisite; (*orge*) pearl *cpd*; **grève ~e** go-slow, selective strike (action).
perler [pɛʀle] *vi* to form in droplets.
perlier, ière [pɛʀlje, -jɛʀ] *adj* pearl *cpd*.
permanence [pɛʀmanɑ̃s] *nf* permanence; (*local*) (duty) office; strike headquarters; (*service des urgences*) emergency service; (*SCOL*) study room; **assurer une ~** (*service public, bureaux*) to operate *ou* maintain a basic service; **être de ~** to be on call *ou* duty; **en ~** *adv* (*toujours*) permanently; (*continûment*) continuously.
permanent, e [pɛʀmanɑ̃, -ɑ̃t] *adj* permanent; (*spectacle*) continuous; (*armée, comité*) standing ♦ *nf* perm ♦ *nm/f* (*d'un syndicat, parti*) paid official.
perméable [pɛʀmeabl(ə)] *adj* (*terrain*) permeable; **~ à** (*fig*) receptive *ou* open to.
permettre [pɛʀmɛtʀ(ə)] *vt* to allow, permit; **~ à qn de faire/qch** to allow sb to do/sth; **se ~ de faire qch** to take the liberty of doing sth; **permettez!** excuse me!
permis, e [pɛʀmi, -iz] *pp de* **permettre** ♦ *nm* permit, licence (*BRIT*), license (*US*); **~ de chasse** hunting permit; **~ (de conduire)** (driving) licence (*BRIT*), (driver's) license

(*US*); ~ **de construire** planning permission
(*BRIT*), building permit (*US*); ~ **d'inhumer**
burial certificate; ~ **poids lourds** ≈ HGV
(driving) licence (*BRIT*), ≈ class E (driver's)
license (*US*); ~ **de séjour** residence permit;
~ **de travail** work permit.
permissif, ive [pɛʀmisif, -iv] *adj* permissive.
permission [pɛʀmisjɔ̃] *nf* permission; (*MIL*)
leave; (: *papier*) pass; **en** ~ on leave; **avoir la**
~ **de faire** to have permission to do, be
allowed to do.
permissionnaire [pɛʀmisjɔnɛʀ] *nm* soldier on
leave.
permutable [pɛʀmytabl(ə)] *adj* which can be
changed *ou* switched around.
permuter [pɛʀmyte] *vt* to change around,
permutate ♦ *vi* to change, swap.
pernicieux, euse [pɛʀnisjø, -øz] *adj*
pernicious.
péroné [peʀɔne] *nm* fibula.
pérorer [peʀɔʀe] *vi* to hold forth.
Pérou [peʀu] *nm*: **le** ~ Peru.
perpendiculaire [pɛʀpɑ̃dikylɛʀ] *adj, nf*
perpendicular.
perpendiculairement [pɛʀpɑ̃dikylɛʀmɑ̃] *adv*
perpendicularly.
perpète [pɛʀpɛt] *nf*: **à** ~ (*fam*: *loin*) miles
away; (: *longtemps*) forever.
perpétrer [pɛʀpetʀe] *vt* to perpetrate.
perpétuel, le [pɛʀpetɥɛl] *adj* perpetual;
(*ADMIN etc*) permanent; for life.
perpétuellement [pɛʀpetɥɛlmɑ̃] *adv*
perpetually, constantly.
perpétuer [pɛʀpetɥe] *vt* to perpetuate; **se** ~
(*usage, injustice*) to be perpetuated; (*espèces*)
to survive.
perpétuité [pɛʀpetɥite] *nf*: **à** ~ *adj, adv* for life;
être condamné à ~ to be sentenced to life
imprisonment, receive a life sentence.
perplexe [pɛʀplɛks(ə)] *adj* perplexed, puzzled.
perplexité [pɛʀplɛksite] *nf* perplexity.
perquisition [pɛʀkizisjɔ̃] *nf* (police) search.
perquisitionner [pɛʀkizisjɔne] *vi* to carry out
a search.
perron [pɛʀɔ̃] *nm* steps *pl* (*in front of mansion
etc*).
perroquet [pɛʀɔkɛ] *nm* parrot.
perruche [peʀyʃ] *nf* budgerigar (*BRIT*), budgie
(*BRIT*), parakeet (*US*).
perruque [peʀyk] *nf* wig.
persan, e [pɛʀsɑ̃, -an] *adj* Persian ♦ *nm* (*LING*)
Persian.
perse [pɛʀs(ə)] *adj* Persian ♦ *nm* (*LING*) Persian
♦ *nm/f*: **P**~ Persian ♦ *nf*: **la P**~ Persia.
persécuter [pɛʀsekyte] *vt* to persecute.
persécution [pɛʀsekysjɔ̃] *nf* persecution.
persévérance [pɛʀseveʀɑ̃s] *nf* perseverance.
persévérant, e [pɛʀseveʀɑ̃, -ɑ̃t] *adj*
persevering.
persévérer [pɛʀseveʀe] *vi* to persevere; ~ **à**
croire que to continue to believe that.
persiennes [pɛʀsjɛn] *nfpl* (slatted) shutters.

persiflage [pɛʀsiflaʒ] *nm* mockery *no pl*.
persifleur, euse [pɛʀsiflœʀ, -øz] *adj* mocking.
persil [pɛʀsi] *nm* parsley.
persillé, e [pɛʀsije] *adj* (sprinkled) with
parsley; (*fromage*) veined; (*viande*) marbled,
with fat running through.
Persique [pɛʀsik] *adj*: **le golfe** ~ the (Persian)
Gulf.
persistance [pɛʀsistɑ̃s] *nf* persistence.
persistant, e [pɛʀsistɑ̃, -ɑ̃t] *adj* persistent;
(*feuilles*) evergreen; **à feuillage** ~
evergreen.
persister [pɛʀsiste] *vi* to persist; ~ **à faire qch**
to persist in doing sth.
personnage [pɛʀsɔnaʒ] *nm* (*notable*)
personality; figure; (*individu*) character,
individual; (*THÉÂT*) character; (*PEINTURE*)
figure.
personnaliser [pɛʀsɔnalize] *vt* to personalize;
(*appartement*) to give a personal touch to.
personnalité [pɛʀsɔnalite] *nf* personality;
(*personnage*) prominent figure.
personne [pɛʀsɔn] *nf* person ♦ *pron* nobody, no
one; (*quelqu'un*) anybody, anyone; ~**s** *nfpl*
people *pl*; **il n'y a** ~ there's nobody in *ou*
there, there isn't anybody in *ou* there; **10 F**
par ~ 10 F per person *ou* a head; **en** ~
personally, in person; ~ **âgée** elderly
person; ~ **à charge** (*JUR*) dependent; ~
morale *ou* **civile** (*JUR*) legal entity.
personnel, le [pɛʀsɔnɛl] *adj* personal; (*égoïste*:
personne) selfish, self-centred; (*idée,*
opinion): **j'ai des idées** ~**les à ce sujet** I have
my own ideas about that ♦ *nm* personnel,
staff; **service du** ~ personnel department.
personnellement [pɛʀsɔnɛlmɑ̃] *adv*
personally.
personnification [pɛʀsɔnifikasjɔ̃] *nf*
personification; **c'est la** ~ **de la cruauté** he's
cruelty personified.
personnifier [pɛʀsɔnifje] *vt* to personify; to
typify; **c'est l'honnêteté personnifiée** he (*ou*
she *etc*) is honesty personified.
perspective [pɛʀspɛktiv] *nf* (*ART*) perspective;
(*vue, coup d'œil*) view; (*point de vue*)
viewpoint, angle; (*chose escomptée,*
envisagée) prospect; **en** ~ in prospect.
perspicace [pɛʀspikas] *adj* clear-sighted,
gifted with (*ou* showing) insight.
perspicacité [pɛʀspikasite] *nf* insight,
perspicacity.
persuader [pɛʀsɥade] *vt*: ~ **qn (de/de faire)** to
persuade sb (of/to do); **j'en suis persuadé**
I'm quite sure *ou* convinced (of it).
persuasif, ive [pɛʀsɥazif, -iv] *adj* persuasive.
persuasion [pɛʀsɥazjɔ̃] *nf* persuasion.
perte [pɛʀt(ə)] *nf* loss; (*de temps*) waste; (*fig*:
morale) ruin; ~**s** *nfpl* losses; **à** ~ (*COMM*) at a
loss; **à** ~ **de vue** as far as the eye can (*ou*
could) see; (*fig*) interminably; **en pure** ~ for
absolutely nothing; **courir à sa** ~ to be on
the road to ruin; **être en** ~ **de vitesse** (*fig*) to

be losing momentum; **avec ~ et fracas** forcibly; **~ de chaleur** heat loss; **~ sèche** dead loss; **~s blanches** (vaginal) discharge *sg.*

pertinemment [pɛʀtinamɑ̃] *adv* to the point; (*savoir*) perfectly well, full well.

pertinence [pɛʀtinɑ̃s] *nf* pertinence, relevance; discernment.

pertinent, e [pɛʀtinɑ̃, -ɑ̃t] *adj* (*remarque*) apt, pertinent, relevant; (*analyse*) discerning, judicious.

perturbateur, trice [pɛʀtyʀbatœʀ, -tʀis] *adj* disruptive.

perturbation [pɛʀtyʀbasjɔ̃] *nf* (*dans un service public*) disruption; (*agitation, trouble*) perturbation; **~ (atmosphérique)** atmospheric disturbance.

perturber [pɛʀtyʀbe] *vt* to disrupt; (*PSYCH*) to perturb, disturb.

péruvien, ne [peʀyvjɛ̃, -ɛn] *adj* Peruvian ♦ *nm/f*: **P~, ne** Peruvian.

pervenche [pɛʀvɑ̃ʃ] *nf* periwinkle; (*fam*) traffic warden (*BRIT*), meter maid (*US*).

pervers, e [pɛʀvɛʀ, -ɛʀs(ə)] *adj* perverted, depraved; (*malfaisant*) perverse.

perversion [pɛʀvɛʀsjɔ̃] *nf* perversion.

perversité [pɛʀvɛʀsite] *nf* depravity; perversity.

perverti, e [pɛʀvɛʀti] *nm/f* pervert.

pervertir [pɛʀvɛʀtiʀ] *vt* to pervert.

pesage [pəzaʒ] *nm* weighing; (*HIPPISME: action*) weigh-in; (*: salle*) weighing room; (*: enceinte*) enclosure.

pesamment [pəzamɑ̃] *adv* heavily.

pesant, e [pəzɑ̃, -ɑ̃t] *adj* heavy; (*fig*) burdensome ♦ *nm*: **valoir son ~ de** to be worth one's weight in.

pesanteur [pəzɑ̃tœʀ] *nf* gravity.

pèse-bébé [pɛzbebe] *nm* (baby) scales *pl.*

pesée [pəze] *nf* weighing; (*BOXE*) weigh-in; (*pression*) pressure.

pèse-lettre [pɛzlɛtʀ(ə)] *nm* letter scales *pl.*

pèse-personne [pɛzpɛʀsɔn] *nm* (bathroom) scales *pl.*

peser [pəze] *vt*, *vb avec attribut* to weigh; (*considérer, comparer*) to weigh up ♦ *vi* to be heavy; (*fig*) to carry weight; **~ sur** (*levier, bouton*) to press, push; (*fig: accabler*) to lie heavy on; (*: influencer*) to influence; **~ à qn** to weigh heavy on sb.

pessaire [pesɛʀ] *nm* pessary.

pessimisme [pesimism(ə)] *nm* pessimism.

pessimiste [pesimist(ə)] *adj* pessimistic ♦ *nm/f* pessimist.

peste [pɛst(ə)] *nf* plague; (*fig*) pest, nuisance.

pester [pɛste] *vi*: **~ contre** to curse.

pesticide [pɛstisid] *nm* pesticide.

pestiféré, e [pɛstifeʀe] *nm/f* plague victim.

pestilentiel, le [pɛstilɑ̃sjɛl] *adj* foul.

pet [pɛ] *nm* (*fam!*) fart (*!*).

pétale [petal] *nm* petal.

pétanque [petɑ̃k] *nf* type of bowls.

Pétanque *is a version of the game of* **boules***, played on a variety of hard surfaces. Standing with their feet together, players throw steel bowls towards a wooden jack. Pétanque originated in the south of France and is still very much associated with that area.*

---

pétarade [petaʀad] *nf* backfiring *no pl.*

pétarader [petaʀade] *vi* to backfire.

pétard [petaʀ] *nm* (*feu d'artifice*) banger (*BRIT*), firecracker; (*de cotillon*) cracker; (*RAIL*) detonator.

pet-de-nonne, *pl* **pets-de-nonne** [pednɔn] *nm* ≈ choux bun.

péter [pete] *vi* (*fam: casser, sauter*) to burst; to bust; (*fam!*) to fart (*!*).

pète-sec [pɛtsɛk] *adj inv* abrupt, sharp (-tongued).

pétillant, e [petijɑ̃, -ɑ̃t] *adj* sparkling.

pétiller [petije] *vi* (*flamme, bois*) to crackle; (*mousse, champagne*) to bubble; (*pierre, métal*) to glisten; (*yeux*) to sparkle; (*fig*): **~ d'esprit** to sparkle with wit.

petit, e [pəti, -it] *adj* (*gén*) small; (*main, objet, colline, en âge: enfant*) small, little; (*mince, fin: personne, taille, pluie*) slight; (*voyage*) short, little; (*bruit etc*) faint, slight; (*mesquin*) mean; (*peu important*) minor ♦ *nm/f* (*petit enfant*) little one, child ♦ *nmpl* (*d'un animal*) young *pl*; **faire des ~s** to have kittens (*ou* puppies *etc*); **en ~** in miniature; **mon ~** son; little one; **ma ~e** dear; little one; **pauvre ~** poor little thing; **la classe des ~s** the infant class; **pour ~s et grands** for children and adults; **les tout-~s** the little ones, the tiny tots; **~ à ~** bit by bit, gradually; **~(e) ami/e** boyfriend/girlfriend; **les ~es annonces** the small ads; **~ déjeuner** breakfast; **~ doigt** little finger; **le ~ écran** the small screen; **~ four** petit four; **~ pain** (bread) roll; **~e monnaie** small change; **~e vérole** smallpox; **~s pois** petit pois *pl*, garden peas; **~es gens** people of modest means.

petit-beurre, *pl* **petits-beurre** [pətibœʀ] *nm* sweet butter biscuit (*BRIT*) *ou* cookie (*US*).

petit(e)-bourgeois(e), *pl* **petit(e)s-bourgeois(es)** [pəti(t)buʀʒwa(z)] *adj* (*péj*) petit-bourgeois, middle-class.

petite-fille, *pl* **petites-filles** [pətitfij] *nf* granddaughter.

petitement [pətitmɑ̃] *adv* poorly; meanly; **être logé ~** to be in cramped accommodation.

petitesse [pətitɛs] *nf* smallness; (*d'un salaire, de revenus*) modestness; (*mesquinerie*) meanness.

petit-fils, *pl* **petits-fils** [pətifis] *nm* grandson.

pétition [petisjɔ̃] *nf* petition; **faire signer une ~** to get up a petition.

pétitionnaire [petisjɔnɛʀ] *nm/f* petitioner.

pétitionner [petisjɔne] *vt* to petition.

petit-lait, *pl* **petits-laits** [pətilɛ] *nm* whey *no pl.*

petit-nègre [pətinɛgʀ(ə)] *nm* (*péj*) pidgin French.

petits-enfants [pətizɑ̃fɑ̃] *nmpl* grandchildren.

petit-suisse, *pl* **petits-suisses** [pətisɥis] *nm small individual pot of cream cheese.*

pétoche [petɔʃ] *nf* (*fam*): **avoir la** ~ to be scared out of one's wits.

pétri, e [petʀi] *adj*: ~ **d'orgueil** filled with pride.

pétrifier [petʀifje] *vt* to petrify; (*fig*) to paralyze, transfix.

pétrin [petʀɛ̃] *nm* kneading-trough; (*fig*): **dans le** ~ in a jam *ou* fix.

pétrir [petʀiʀ] *vt* to knead.

pétrochimie [petʀɔʃimi] *nf* petrochemistry.

pétrochimique [petʀɔʃimik] *adj* petrochemical.

pétrodollar [petʀodɔlaʀ] *nm* petrodollar.

pétrole [petʀɔl] *nm* oil; (*aussi*: ~ **lampant**) paraffin (*BRIT*), kerosene (*US*).

pétrolier, ière [petʀɔlje, -jɛʀ] *adj* oil *cpd*; (*pays*) oil-producing ♦ *nm* (*navire*) oil tanker; (*financier*) oilman; (*technicien*) petroleum engineer.

pétrolifère [petʀɔlifɛʀ] *adj* oil(-bearing).

P et T *sigle fpl* = postes et télécommunications.

pétulant, e [petylɑ̃, -ɑ̃t] *adj* exuberant.

pétunia [petynja] *nm* petunia.

=================================== *MOT-CLÉ*

peu [pø] *adv* **1** (*modifiant verbe, adjectif, adverbe*): **il boit** ~ he doesn't drink (very) much; **il est** ~ **bavard** he's not very talkative; ~ **avant/après** shortly before/ afterwards; **pour** ~ **qu'il fasse** if he should do, if by any chance he does
2 (*modifiant nom*): ~ **de**: ~ **de gens/d'arbres** few *ou* not (very) many people/trees; **il a** ~ **d'espoir** he hasn't (got) much hope, he has little hope; **pour** ~ **de temps for** (only) a short while; **à** ~ **de frais** for very little cost
3: ~ **à** ~ little by little; **à** ~ **près** just about, more or less; **à** ~ **près 10 kg/10 F** approximately 10 kg/10 F
♦ *nm* **1**: **le** ~ **de gens qui** the few people who; **le** ~ **de sable qui** what little sand, the little sand which
2: **un** ~ a little; **un petit** ~ a little bit; **un** ~ **d'espoir** a little hope; **elle est un** ~ **bavarde** she's rather talkative; **un** ~ **plus/moins de** slightly more/less (*ou* fewer) than; **pour un** ~ **il** ..., **un** ~ **plus et il** ... he very nearly *ou* all but ...; **essayez un** ~! have a go!, just try it!
♦ *pron*: ~ **le savent** few know (it); **avant** ~ **sous** ~ shortly, before long; **depuis** ~ for a short *ou* little while; (*au passé*) a short *ou* little while ago; **de** ~ (only) just; **c'est** ~ **de chose** it's nothing; **il est de** ~ **mon cadet** he's just a little *ou* bit younger than me.

peuplade [pœplad] *nf* (*horde, tribu*) tribe, people.

peuple [pœpl(ə)] *nm* people; (*masse indifférenciée*): **un** ~ **de vacanciers** a crowd of holiday-makers; **il y a du** ~ there are a lot of people.

peuplé, e [pœple] *adj*: **très/peu** ~ densely/ sparsely populated.

peupler [pœple] *vt* (*pays, région*) to populate; (*étang*) to stock; (*suj: hommes, poissons*) to inhabit; (*fig: imagination, rêves*) to fill; **se** ~ *vi* (*ville, région*) to become populated; (*fig: s'animer*) to fill (up), be filled.

peuplier [pøplije] *nm* poplar (tree).

peur [pœʀ] *nf* fear; **avoir** ~ (**de/de faire/que**) to be frightened *ou* afraid (of/of doing/that); **prendre** ~ to take fright; **faire** ~ **à** to frighten; **de** ~ **de/que** for fear of/that; **j'ai** ~ **qu'il ne soit trop tard** I'm afraid it might be too late; **j'ai** ~ **qu'il (ne) vienne (pas)** I'm afraid he may (not) come.

peureux, euse [pœrø, -øz] *adj* fearful, timorous.

peut [pø] *vb voir* **pouvoir**.

peut-être [pøtɛtʀ(ə)] *adv* perhaps, maybe; ~ **que** perhaps, maybe; ~ **bien qu'il fera/est** he may well do/be.

peuvent [pœv], **peux** [pø] *etc vb voir* **pouvoir**.

p. ex. *abr* (= *par exemple*) e.g.

phalange [falɑ̃ʒ] *nf* (*ANAT*) phalanx (*pl* phalanges); (*MIL, fig*) phalanx (*pl* -es).

phallique [falik] *adj* phallic.

phallocrate [falɔkʀat] *nm* male chauvinist.

phallocratie [falɔkʀasi] *nf* male chauvinism.

phallus [falys] *nm* phallus.

pharaon [faʀaɔ̃] *nm* Pharaoh.

phare [faʀ] *nm* (*en mer*) lighthouse; (*d'aéroport*) beacon; (*de véhicule*) headlight, headlamp (*BRIT*) ♦ *adj*: **produit** ~ leading product; **se mettre en** ~**s, mettre ses** ~**s** to put on one's headlights; ~**s de recul** reversing (*BRIT*) *ou* back-up (*US*) lights.

pharmaceutique [faʀmasøtik] *adj* pharmaceutic(al).

pharmacie [faʀmasi] *nf* (*science*) pharmacology; (*magasin*) chemist's (*BRIT*), pharmacy; (*officine*) dispensary; (*produits*) pharmaceuticals *pl*; (*armoire*) medicine chest *ou* cupboard, first-aid cupboard.

pharmacien, ne [faʀmasjɛ̃, -ɛn] *nm/f* pharmacist, chemist (*BRIT*).

pharmacologie [faʀmakɔlɔʒi] *nf* pharmacology.

pharyngite [faʀɛ̃ʒit] *nf* pharyngitis *no pl*.

pharynx [faʀɛ̃ks] *nm* pharynx.

phase [faz] *nf* phase.

phénoménal, e, aux [fenɔmenal, -o] *adj* phenomenal.

phénomène [fenɔmɛn] *nm* phenomenon (*pl* -a); (*monstre*) freak.

philanthrope [filɑ̃tʀɔp] *nm/f* philanthropist.

philanthropie [filɑ̃tʀɔpi] *nf* philanthropy.

philanthropique [filɑ̃tʀɔpik] *adj*

philanthropic.
philatélie [filateli] *nf* philately, stamp collecting.
philatélique [filatelik] *adj* philatelic.
philatéliste [filatelist(ə)] *nm/f* philatelist, stamp collector.
philharmonique [filaʀmɔnik] *adj* philharmonic.
philippin, e [filipɛ̃, -in] *adj* Filipino.
Philippines [filipin] *nfpl*: **les ~** the Philippines.
philistin [filistɛ̃] *nm* philistine.
philo [filo] *nf* (*fam*: = *philosophie*) philosophy.
philosophe [filɔzɔf] *nm/f* philosopher ♦ *adj* philosophical.
philosopher [filɔzɔfe] *vi* to philosophize.
philosophie [filɔzɔfi] *nf* philosophy.
philosophique [filɔzɔfik] *adj* philosophical.
philosophiquement [filɔzɔfikmɑ̃] *adv* philosophically.
philtre [filtʀ(ə)] *nm* philtre, love potion.
phlébite [flebit] *nf* phlebitis.
phlébologue [flebɔlɔg] *nm/f* vein specialist.
phobie [fɔbi] *nf* phobia.
phonétique [fɔnetik] *adj* phonetic ♦ *nf* phonetics *sg*.
phonétiquement [fɔnetikmɑ̃] *adv* phonetically.
phonographe [fɔnɔgʀaf] *nm* (wind-up) gramophone.
phoque [fɔk] *nm* seal; (*fourrure*) sealskin.
phosphate [fɔsfat] *nm* phosphate.
phosphaté, e [fɔsfate] *adj* phosphate-enriched.
phosphore [fɔsfɔʀ] *nm* phosphorus.
phosphoré, e [fɔsfɔʀe] *adj* phosphorous.
phosphorescent, e [fɔsfɔʀesɑ̃, -ɑ̃t] *adj* luminous.
phosphorique [fɔsfɔʀik] *adj*: **acide ~** phosphoric acid.
photo [fɔto] *nf* (= *photographie*) photo ♦ *adj*: **appareil/pellicule ~** camera/film; **en ~** in *ou* on a photo; **prendre en ~** to take a photo of; **aimer la/faire de la ~** to like taking/take photos; **~ en couleurs** colour photo; **~ d'identité** passport photo.
photo... [fɔto] *préfixe* photo....
photocopie [fɔtɔkɔpi] *nf* (*procédé*) photocopying; (*document*) photocopy.
photocopier [fɔtɔkɔpje] *vt* to photocopy.
photocopieur [fɔtɔkɔpjœʀ] *nm*, **photocopieuse** [fɔtɔkɔpjøz] *nf* (photo)copier.
photo-électrique [fɔtɔelɛktʀik] *adj* photo-electric.
photo-finish, *pl* **photos-finish** [fɔtofiniʃ] *nf* (*appareil*) photo finish camera; (*photo*) photo finish picture; **il y a eu ~ pour la troisième place** there was a photo finish for third place.
photogénique [fɔtɔʒenik] *adj* photogenic.
photographe [fɔtɔgʀaf] *nm/f* photographer.
photographie [fɔtɔgʀafi] *nf* (*procédé,*

technique) photography; (*cliché*) photograph; **faire de la ~** to have photography as a hobby; (*comme métier*) to be a photographer.
photographier [fɔtɔgʀafje] *vt* to photograph, take.
photographique [fɔtɔgʀafik] *adj* photographic.
photogravure [fɔtɔgʀavyʀ] *nf* photoengraving.
photomaton [fɔtɔmatɔ̃] *nm* photo-booth, photomat.
photomontage [fɔtɔmɔ̃taʒ] *nm* photomontage.
photo-robot [fɔtɔʀɔbo] *nf* Identikit ® (picture).
photosensible [fɔtɔsɑ̃sibl(ə)] *adj* photosensitive.
photostat [fɔtɔsta] *nm* photostat.
phrase [fʀɑz] *nf* (*LING*) sentence; (*propos, MUS*) phrase; **~s** *nfpl* (*péj*) flowery language *sg*.
phraséologie [fʀazeɔlɔʒi] *nf* phraseology; (*rhétorique*) flowery language.
phraseur, euse [fʀazœʀ, -øz] *nm/f*: **c'est un ~** he uses such flowery language.
phrygien, ne [fʀiʒjɛ̃, -ɛn] *adj*: **bonnet ~** Phrygian cap.
phtisie [ftizi] *nf* consumption.
phylloxéra [filɔkseʀa] *nm* phylloxera.
physicien, ne [fizisjɛ̃, -ɛn] *nm/f* physicist.
physiologie [fizjɔlɔʒi] *nf* physiology.
physiologique [fizjɔlɔʒik] *adj* physiological.
physiologiquement [fizjɔlɔʒikmɑ̃] *adv* physiologically.
physionomie [fizjɔnɔmi] *nf* face; (*d'un paysage etc*) physiognomy.
physionomiste [fizjɔnɔmist(ə)] *nm/f* good judge of faces; person who has a good memory for faces.
physiothérapie [fizjɔteʀapi] *nf* natural medicine, alternative medicine.
physique [fizik] *adj* physical ♦ *nm* physique ♦ *nf* physics *sg*; **au ~** physically.
physiquement [fizikmɑ̃] *adv* physically.
phytothérapie [fitɔteʀapi] *nf* herbal medicine.
p.i. *abr* = **par intérim**; *voir* **intérim**.
piaffer [pjafe] *vi* to stamp.
piaillement [pjajmɑ̃] *nm* squawking *no pl*.
piailler [pjaje] *vi* to squawk.
pianiste [pjanist(ə)] *nm/f* pianist.
piano [pjano] *nm* piano; **~ à queue** grand piano.
pianoter [pjanɔte] *vi* to tinkle away (at the piano); (*tapoter*): **~ sur** to drum one's fingers on.
piaule [pjol] *nf* (*fam*) pad.
piauler [pjole] *vi* (*enfant*) to whimper; (*oiseau*) to cheep.
PIB *sigle m* (= *produit intérieur brut*) GDP.
pic [pik] *nm* (*instrument*) pick(axe); (*montagne*)

peak; (*ZOOL*) woodpecker; **à** ~ *adv*
vertically; (*fig*) just at the right time; **couler
à** ~ (*bateau*) to go straight down; ~ **à glace**
ice pick.
picard, e [pikaʀ, -aʀd(ə)] *adj* of *ou* from
Picardy.
Picardie [pikaʀdi] *nf*: **la** ~ Picardy.
picaresque [pikaʀɛsk(ə)] *adj* picaresque.
piccolo [pikɔlo] *nm* piccolo.
pichenette [piʃnɛt] *nf* flick.
pichet [piʃɛ] *nm* jug.
pickpocket [pikpɔkɛt] *nm* pickpocket.
pick-up [pikœp] *nm inv* record player.
picorer [pikɔʀe] *vt* to peck.
picot [piko] *nm* sprocket; **entraînement par
roue à** ~**s** sprocket feed.
picotement [pikɔtmɑ̃] *nm* smarting *no pl*,
prickling *no pl*.
picoter [pikɔte] *vt* (*suj: oiseau*) to peck ♦ *vi*
(*irriter*) to smart, prickle.
pictural, e, aux [piktyʀal, -o] *adj* pictorial.
pie [pi] *nf* magpie; (*fig*) chatterbox ♦ *adj inv*:
cheval ~ piebald; **vache** ~ black and white
cow.
pièce [pjɛs] *nf* (*d'un logement*) room; (*THÉÂT*)
play; (*de mécanisme, machine*) part; (*de
monnaie*) coin; (*COUTURE*) patch; (*document*)
document; (*de drap, fragment, d'une
collection*) piece; (*de bétail*) head; **mettre en**
~**s** to smash to pieces; **dix francs** ~ ten
francs each; **vendre à la** ~ to sell separately
ou individually; **travailler/payer à la** ~ to do
piecework/pay piece rate; **de toutes** ~**s**:
c'est inventé de toutes ~**s** it's a complete
fabrication; **un maillot une** ~ a one-piece
swimsuit; **un deux-**~**s cuisine** a two-
room(ed) flat (*BRIT*) *ou* apartment (*US*) with
kitchen; **tout d'une** ~ (*personne: franc*) blunt;
(*: sans souplesse*) inflexible; ~ **à conviction**
exhibit; ~ **d'eau** ornamental lake *ou* pond;
~ **d'identité: avez-vous une** ~ **d'identité?**
have you got any (means of) identification?;
~ **montée** tiered cake; ~ **de rechange** spare
(part); ~ **de résistance** pièce de résistance;
(*plat*) main dish; ~**s détachées** spares,
(spare) parts; **en** ~**s détachées** (*à monter*) in
kit form; ~**s justificatives** supporting
documents.
pied [pje] *nm* foot (*pl* feet); (*de verre*) stem; (*de
table*) leg; (*de lampe*) base; (*plante*) plant; ~**s
nus** barefoot; **à** ~ on foot; **à** ~ **sec** without
getting one's feet wet; **à** ~ **d'œuvre** ready to
start (work); **au** ~ **de la lettre** literally; **au** ~
levé at a moment's notice; **de** ~ **en cap** from
head to foot; **en** ~ (*portrait*) full-length; **avoir**
~ to be able to touch the bottom, not to be
out of one's depth; **avoir le** ~ **marin** to be a
good sailor; **perdre** ~ to lose one's footing;
(*fig*) to get out of one's depth; **sur** ~ (*AGR*)
on the stalk, uncut; (*debout, rétabli*) about
and about; **mettre sur** ~ (*entreprise*) to set up;
mettre à ~ to suspend; to lay off; **mettre qn**

au ~ **du mur** to get sb with his (*ou* her) back
to the wall; **sur le** ~ **de guerre** ready for
action; **sur un** ~ **d'égalité** on an equal
footing; **sur** ~ **d'intervention** on stand-by;
faire du ~ **à qn** (*prévenir*) to give sb a
(warning) kick; (*galamment*) to play footsie
with sb; **mettre les** ~**s quelque part** to set
foot somewhere; **faire des** ~**s et des mains**
(*fig*) to move heaven and earth, pull out all
the stops; **c'est le** ~! (*fam*) it's terrific!; **se
lever du bon** ~/**du** ~ **gauche** to get out of
bed on the right/wrong side; ~ **de lit**
footboard; ~ **de nez: faire un** ~ **de nez à** to
thumb one's nose at; ~ **de vigne** vine.
pied-à-terre [pjetatɛʀ] *nm inv* pied-à-terre.
pied-bot, *pl* **pieds-bots** [pjebo] *nm* person
with a club foot.
pied-de-biche, *pl* **pieds-de-biche** [pjedbiʃ]
nm claw; (*COUTURE*) presser foot.
pied-de-poule [pjedpul] *adj inv* hound's-tooth.
piédestal, aux [pjedɛstal, -o] *nm* pedestal.
pied-noir, *pl* **pieds-noirs** [pjenwaʀ] *nm*
Algerian-born Frenchman.
piège [pjɛʒ] *nm* trap; **prendre au** ~ to trap.
piéger [pjeʒe] *vt* (*animal, fig*) to trap; (*avec une
bombe*) to booby-trap; **lettre/voiture piégée**
letter-/car-bomb.
pierraille [pjɛʀɑj] *nf* loose stones *pl*.
pierre [pjɛʀ] *nf* stone; **première** ~ (*d'un édifice*)
foundation stone; **mur de** ~**s sèches**
drystone wall; **faire d'une** ~ **deux coups** to
kill two birds with one stone; ~ **à briquet**
flint; ~ **fine** semiprecious stone; ~ **ponce**
pumice stone; ~ **de taille** freestone *no pl*; ~
tombale tombstone, gravestone; ~ **de
touche** touchstone.
pierreries [pjɛʀʀi] *nfpl* gems, precious stones.
pierreux, euse [pjɛʀø, -øz] *adj* stony.
piété [pjete] *nf* piety.
piétinement [pjetinmɑ̃] *nm* stamping *no pl*.
piétiner [pjetine] *vi* (*trépigner*) to stamp (one's
foot); (*marquer le pas*) to stand about; (*fig*) to
be at a standstill ♦ *vt* to trample on.
piéton, ne [pjetɔ̃, -ɔn] *nm/f* pedestrian ♦ *adj*
pedestrian *cpd*.
piétonnier, ière [pjetɔnje, -jɛʀ] *adj*
pedestrian *cpd*.
piètre [pjɛtʀ(ə)] *adj* poor, mediocre.
pieu, x [pjø] *nm* (*piquet*) post; (*pointu*) stake;
(*fam: lit*) bed.
pieusement [pjøzmɑ̃] *adv* piously.
pieuvre [pjœvʀ(ə)] *nf* octopus.
pieux, euse [pjø, -øz] *adj* pious.
pif [pif] *nm* (*fam*) conk (*BRIT*), beak; **au** ~ = **au
pifomètre.**
piffer [pife] *vt* (*fam*): **je ne peux pas le** ~ I can't
stand him.
pifomètre [pifɔmɛtʀ(ə)] *nm* (*fam*): **choisir** *etc*
au ~ to follow one's nose when choosing
etc.
pige [piʒ] *nf* piecework rate.
pigeon [piʒɔ̃] *nm* pigeon; ~ **voyageur** homing

pigeon.

pigeonnant, e [piʒɔnɑ̃, -ɑ̃t] *adj* full, well-developed.

pigeonneau, x [piʒɔno] *nm* young pigeon.

pigeonnier [piʒɔnje] *nm* pigeon loft, dovecot(e).

piger [piʒe] *vi (fam)* to get it ♦ *vt (fam)* to get, understand.

pigiste [piʒist(ə)] *nm/f (typographe)* typesetter on piecework; *(journaliste)* freelance journalist *(paid by the line)*.

pigment [pigmɑ̃] *nm* pigment.

pignon [piɲɔ̃] *nm (de mur)* gable; *(d'engrenage)* cog(wheel), gearwheel; *(graine)* pine kernel; **avoir ~ sur rue** *(fig)* to have a prosperous business.

pile [pil] *nf (tas, pilier)* pile; *(ÉLEC)* battery ♦ *adj*: **le côté ~** tails ♦ *adv (net, brusquement)* dead; *(à temps, à point nommé)* just at the right time; **à deux heures ~** at two on the dot; **jouer à ~ ou face** to toss up (for it); **~ ou face?** heads or tails?

piler [pile] *vt* to crush, pound.

pileux, euse [pilø, -øz] *adj*: **système ~** (body) hair.

pilier [pilje] *nm (colonne, support)* pillar; *(personne)* mainstay; *(RUGBY)* prop (forward).

pillage [pijaʒ] *nm* pillaging, plundering, looting.

pillard, e [pijaR, -aRd(ə)] *nm/f* looter; plunderer.

piller [pije] *vt* to pillage, plunder, loot.

pilleur, euse [pijœR, -øz] *nm/f* looter.

pilon [pilɔ̃] *nm (instrument)* pestle; *(de volaille)* drumstick; **mettre un livre au ~** to pulp a book.

pilonner [pilɔne] *vt* to pound.

pilori [pilɔRi] *nm*: **mettre** *ou* **clouer au ~** to pillory.

pilotage [pilɔtaʒ] *nm* piloting; flying; **~ automatique** automatic piloting; **~ sans visibilité** blind flying.

pilote [pilɔt] *nm* pilot; *(de char, voiture)* driver ♦ *adj* pilot *cpd*; **usine/ferme ~** experimental factory/farm; **~ de chasse/d'essai/de ligne** fighter/test/airline pilot; **~ de course** racing driver.

piloter [pilɔte] *vt (navire)* to pilot; *(avion)* to fly; *(automobile)* to drive; *(fig)*: **~ qn** to guide sb round; **piloté par menu** *(INFORM)* menu-driven.

pilotis [pilɔti] *nm* pile; stilt.

pilule [pilyl] *nf* pill; **prendre la ~** to be on the pill; **~ du lendemain** morning-after pill.

pimbêche [pɛ̃bɛʃ] *nf (péj)* stuck-up girl.

piment [pimɑ̃] *nm (BOT)* pepper, capsicum; *(fig)* spice, piquancy; **~ rouge** *(CULIN)* chilli.

pimenté, e [pimɑ̃te] *adj* hot and spicy.

pimenter [pimɑ̃te] *vt (plat)* to season (with peppers *ou* chillis); *(fig)* to add *ou* give spice to.

pimpant, e [pɛ̃pɑ̃, -ɑ̃t] *adj* spruce.

pin [pɛ̃] *nm* pine (tree); *(bois)* pine(wood).

pinacle [pinakl(ə)] *nm*: **porter qn au ~** *(fig)* to praise sb to the skies.

pinard [pinaR] *nm (fam)* (cheap) wine, plonk *(BRIT)*.

pince [pɛ̃s] *nf (outil)* pliers *pl*; *(de homard, crabe)* pincer, claw; *(COUTURE: pli)* dart; **~ à sucre/glace** sugar/ice tongs *pl*; **~ à épiler** tweezers *pl*; **~ à linge** clothes peg *(BRIT)* *ou* pin *(US)*; **~ universelle** (universal) pliers *pl*; **~s de cycliste** bicycle clips.

pincé, e [pɛ̃se] *adj (air)* stiff; *(mince: bouche)* pinched ♦ *nf*: **une ~e de** a pinch of.

pinceau, x [pɛ̃so] *nm* (paint)brush.

pincement [pɛ̃smɑ̃] *nm*: **~ au cœur** twinge of regret.

pince-monseigneur, *pl* **pinces-monseigneur** [pɛ̃smɔ̃sɛɲœR] *nf* crowbar.

pince-nez [pɛ̃sne] *nm inv* pince-nez.

pincer [pɛ̃se] *vt* to pinch; *(MUS: cordes)* to pluck; *(COUTURE)* to dart, put darts in; *(fam)* to nab; **se ~ le doigt** to squeeze *ou* nip one's finger; **se ~ le nez** to hold one's nose.

pince-sans-rire [pɛ̃ssɑ̃RiR] *adj inv* deadpan.

pincettes [pɛ̃sɛt] *nfpl* tweezers; *(pour le feu)* (fire) tongs.

pinçon [pɛ̃sɔ̃] *nm* pinch mark.

pinède [pinɛd] *nf* pinewood, pine forest.

pingouin [pɛ̃gwɛ̃] *nm* penguin.

ping-pong [piŋpɔ̃g] *nm* table tennis.

pingre [pɛ̃gR(ə)] *adj* niggardly.

pinson [pɛ̃sɔ̃] *nm* chaffinch.

pintade [pɛ̃tad] *nf* guinea-fowl.

pin up [pinœp] *nf inv* pin-up (girl).

pioche [pjɔʃ] *nf* pickaxe.

piocher [pjɔʃe] *vt* to dig up (with a pickaxe); *(fam)* to swot *(BRIT)* *ou* grind *(US)* at; **~ dans** to dig into.

piolet [pjɔlɛ] *nm* ice axe.

pion, ne [pjɔ̃, pjɔn] *nm/f (SCOL: péj)* student paid to supervise schoolchildren ♦ *nm (ÉCHECS)* pawn; *(DAMES)* piece, draught *(BRIT)*, checker *(US)*.

pionnier [pjɔnje] *nm* pioneer.

pipe [pip] *nf* pipe; **fumer la** *ou* **une ~** to smoke a pipe; **~ de bruyère** briar pipe.

pipeau, x [pipo] *nm* (reed-)pipe.

pipe-line [piplin] *nm* pipeline.

piper [pipe] *vt (dé)* to load; *(carte)* to mark; **sans ~ mot** *(fam)* without a squeak; **les dés sont pipés** *(fig)* the dice are loaded.

pipette [pipɛt] *nf* pipette.

pipi [pipi] *nm (fam)*: **faire ~** to have a wee.

piquant, e [pikɑ̃, -ɑ̃t] *adj (barbe, rosier etc)* prickly; *(saveur, sauce)* hot, pungent; *(fig: description, style)* racy; *(: mordant, caustique)* biting ♦ *nm (épine)* thorn, prickle; *(de hérisson)* quill, spine; *(fig)* spiciness, spice.

pique [pik] *nf (arme)* pike; *(fig)*: **envoyer** *ou* **lancer des ~s à qn** to make cutting remarks to sb ♦ *nm (CARTES: couleur)* spades *pl*;

(: *carte*) spade.

piqué, e [pike] *adj* (*COUTURE*) (machine-) stitched; quilted; (*livre, glace*) mildewed; (*vin*) sour; (*MUS: note*) staccato; (*fam: personne*) nuts ♦ *nm* (*AVIAT*) dive; (*TEXTILE*) piqué.

pique-assiette [pikasjɛt] *nm/f inv* (*péj*) scrounger, sponger.

pique-fleurs [pikflœʀ] *nm inv* flower holder.

pique-nique [piknik] *nm* picnic.

pique-niquer [piknike] *vi* to (have a) picnic.

pique-niqueur, euse [piknikœʀ, -øz] *nm/f* picnicker.

piquer [pike] *vt* (*percer*) to prick; (*planter*): ~ **qch dans** to stick sth into; (*fixer*): ~ **qch à** *ou* **sur** to pin sth onto; (*MÉD*) to give an injection to; (: *animal blessé etc*) to put to sleep; (*suj: insecte, fumée, ortie*) to sting; (: *poivre*) to burn; (: *froid*) to bite; (*COUTURE*) to machine (stitch); (*intérêt etc*) to arouse; (*fam: prendre*) to pick up; (: *voler*) to pinch; (: *arrêter*) to nab ♦ *vi* (*oiseau, avion*) to go into a dive; (*saveur*) to be pungent; to be sour; **se** ~ (*avec une aiguille*) to prick o.s.; (*se faire une piqûre*) to inject o.s.; (*se vexer*) to get annoyed; **se** ~ **de faire** to pride o.s. on doing; ~ **sur** to swoop down on; to head straight for; ~ **du nez** (*avion*) to go into a nose-dive; ~ **une tête** (*plonger*) to dive headfirst; ~ **un galop/un cent mètres** to break into a gallop/put on a sprint; ~ **une crise** to throw a fit; ~ **au vif** (*fig*) to sting.

piquet [pikɛ] *nm* (*pieu*) post, stake; (*de tente*) peg; **mettre un élève au** ~ to make a pupil stand in the corner; ~ **de grève** (strike) picket; ~ **d'incendie** fire-fighting squad.

piqueté, e [pikte] *adj*: ~ **de** dotted with.

piquette [pikɛt] *nf* (*fam*) cheap wine, plonk (*BRIT*).

piqûre [pikyʀ] *nf* (*d'épingle*) prick; (*d'ortie*) sting; (*de moustique*) bite; (*MÉD*) injection, shot (*US*); (*COUTURE*) (straight) stitch; straight stitching; (*de ver*) hole; (*tache*) (spot of) mildew; **faire une** ~ **à qn** to give sb an injection.

piranha [piʀana] *nm* piranha.

piratage [piʀataʒ] *nm* piracy.

pirate [piʀat] *adj* pirate *cpd* ♦ *nm* pirate; (*fig: escroc*) crook, shark; ~ **de l'air** hijacker.

pirater [piʀate] *vt* to pirate.

piraterie [piʀatʀi] *nf* (act of) piracy; ~ **aérienne** hijacking.

pire [piʀ] *adj* (*comparatif*) worse; (*superlatif*): **le (la)** ~ ... the worst ... ♦ *nm*: **le** ~ **(de)** the worst (of).

Pirée [piʀe] *n* Piraeus.

pirogue [piʀog] *nf* dugout (canoe).

pirouette [piʀwɛt] *nf* pirouette; (*fig: volte-face*) about-turn.

pis [pi] *nm* (*de vache*) udder; (*pire*): **le** ~ the worst ♦ *adj, adv* worse; **qui** ~ **est** what is worse; **au** ~ **aller** if the worst comes to the

worst, at worst.

pis-aller [pizale] *nm inv* stopgap.

pisciculture [pisikyltyʀ] *nf* fish farming.

piscine [pisin] *nf* (swimming) pool; ~ **couverte** indoor (swimming) pool.

Pise [piz] *n* Pisa.

pissenlit [pisāli] *nm* dandelion.

pisser [pise] *vi* (*fam!*) to pee.

pissotière [pisɔtjɛʀ] *nf* (*fam*) public urinal.

pistache [pistaʃ] *nf* pistachio (nut).

pistard [pistaʀ] *nm* (*CYCLISME*) track cyclist.

piste [pist(ə)] *nf* (*d'un animal, sentier*) track, trail; (*indice*) lead; (*de stade, de magnétophone, INFORM*) track; (*de cirque*) ring; (*de danse*) floor; (*de patinage*) rink; (*de ski*) run; (*AVIAT*) runway; ~ **cavalière** bridle path; ~ **cyclable** cycle track, bikeway (*US*); ~ **sonore** sound track.

pister [piste] *vt* to track, trail.

pisteur [pistœʀ] *nm* (*SKI*) member of the ski patrol.

pistil [pistil] *nm* pistil.

pistolet [pistɔlɛ] *nm* (*arme*) pistol, gun; (*à peinture*) spray gun; ~ **à bouchon/air comprimé** popgun/airgun; ~ **à eau** water pistol.

pistolet-mitrailleur, *pl* **pistolets-mitrailleurs** [pistɔlɛmitʀajœʀ] *nm* submachine gun.

piston [pistɔ̃] *nm* (*TECH*) piston; (*MUS*) valve; (*fig: appui*) string-pulling.

pistonner [pistɔne] *vt* (*candidat*) to pull strings for.

pitance [pitɑ̃s] *nf* (*péj*) (means of) sustenance.

piteusement [pitøzmɑ̃] *adv* (*échouer*) miserably.

piteux, euse [pitø, -øz] *adj* pitiful, sorry (*avant le nom*); **en** ~ **état** in a sorry state.

pitié [pitje] *nf* pity; **sans** ~ *adj* pitiless, merciless; **faire** ~ to inspire pity; **il me fait** ~ I pity him, I feel sorry for him; **avoir** ~ **de** (*compassion*) to pity, feel sorry for; (*merci*) to have pity *ou* mercy on; **par** ~! for pity's sake!

piton [pitɔ̃] *nm* (*clou*) peg, bolt; ~ **rocheux** rocky outcrop.

pitoyable [pitwajabl(ə)] *adj* pitiful.

pitre [pitʀ(ə)] *nm* clown.

pitrerie [pitʀəʀi] *nf* tomfoolery *no pl*.

pittoresque [pitɔʀɛsk(ə)] *adj* picturesque; (*expression, détail*) colourful (*BRIT*), colorful (*US*).

pivert [pivɛʀ] *nm* green woodpecker.

pivoine [pivwan] *nf* peony.

pivot [pivo] *nm* pivot; (*d'une dent*) post.

pivoter [pivɔte] *vi* (*fauteuil*) to swivel; (*porte*) to revolve; ~ **sur ses talons** to swing round.

pixel [piksɛl] *nm* pixel.

pizza [pidza] *nf* pizza.

PJ *sigle f* = **police judiciaire** ♦ *sigle fpl* (= *pièces jointes*) encl.

PL *sigle m* (*AUTO*) = **poids lourd**.

Pl. *abr* = **place.**

placage [plakaʒ] *nm* (*bois*) veneer.

placard [plakaʀ] *nm* (*armoire*) cupboard; (*affiche*) poster, notice; (*TYPO*) galley; ~ **publicitaire** display advertisement.

placarder [plakaʀde] *vt* (*affiche*) to put up; (*mur*) to stick posters on.

place [plas] *nf* (*emplacement, situation, classement*) place; (*de ville, village*) square; (*ÉCON*): ~ **financière/boursière** money/stock market; (*espace libre*) room, space; (*de parking*) space; (*siège: de train, cinéma, voiture*) seat; (*prix: au cinéma etc*) price; (: *dans un bus, taxi*) fare; (*emploi*) job; **en** ~ (*mettre*) in its place; **de** ~ **en** ~, **par** ~**s** here and there, in places; **sur** ~ on the spot; **faire** ~ **à** to give way to; **faire de la** ~ **à** to make room for; **ça prend de la** ~ it takes up a lot of room *ou* space; **prendre** ~ to take one's place; **remettre qn à sa** ~ to put sb in his (*ou* her) place; **ne pas rester** *ou* **tenir en** ~ to be always on the go; **à la** ~ **de** in place of, instead of; **une quatre** ~**s** (*AUTO*) a four-seater; **il y a 20** ~**s assises/debout** there are 20 seats/there is standing room for 20; ~ **forte** fortified town; ~ **d'honneur** place (*ou* seat) of honour (*BRIT*) *ou* honor (*US*).

placé, e [plase] *adj* (*HIPPISME*) placed; **haut** ~ (*fig*) high-ranking; **être bien/mal** ~ to be well/badly placed; (*spectateur*) to have a good/bad seat; **être bien/mal** ~ **pour faire** to be in/not to be in a position to do.

placebo [plasebo] *nm* placebo.

placement [plasmã] *nm* placing; (*FINANCE*) investment; **agence** *ou* **bureau de** ~ employment agency.

placenta [plasɛ̃ta] *nm* placenta.

placer [plase] *vt* to place, put; (*convive, spectateur*) to seat; (*capital, argent*) to place, invest; (*dans la conversation*) to put *ou* get in; ~ **qn chez** to get sb a job at (*ou* with); **se** ~ **au premier rang** to go and stand (*ou* sit) in the first row.

placide [plasid] *adj* placid.

placidité [plasidite] *nf* placidity.

placier, ière [plasje, -jɛʀ] *nm/f* commercial rep(resentative), salesman/woman.

Placoplâtre [plakoplatʀ] *nm* ® plasterboard.

plafond [plafɔ̃] *nm* ceiling.

plafonner [plafɔne] *vt* (*pièce*) to put a ceiling (up) in ♦ *vi* to reach one's (*ou* a) ceiling.

plafonnier [plafɔnje] *nm* ceiling light; (*AUTO*) interior light.

plage [plaʒ] *nf* beach; (*station*) (seaside) resort; (*fig*) band, bracket; (*de disque*) track, band; ~ **arrière** (*AUTO*) parcel *ou* back shelf.

plagiaire [plaʒjɛʀ] *nm/f* plagiarist.

plagiat [plaʒja] *nm* plagiarism.

plagier [plaʒje] *vt* to plagiarize.

plagiste [plaʒist(ə)] *nm/f* beach attendant.

plaid [plɛd] *nm* (tartan) car rug, lap robe (*US*).

plaidant, e [plɛdɑ̃, -ɑ̃t] *adj* litigant.

plaider [plede] *vi* (*avocat*) to plead; (*plaignant*) to go to court, litigate ♦ *vt* to plead; ~ **pour** (*fig*) to speak for.

plaideur, euse [plɛdœʀ, -øz] *nm/f* litigant.

plaidoirie [plɛdwaʀi] *nf* (*JUR*) speech for the defence (*BRIT*) *ou* defense (*US*).

plaidoyer [plɛdwaje] *nm* (*JUR*) speech for the defence (*BRIT*) *ou* defense (*US*); (*fig*) plea.

plaie [plɛ] *nf* wound.

plaignant, e [plɛɲɑ̃, -ɑ̃t] *vb voir* **plaindre** ♦ *nm/f* plaintiff.

plaindre [plɛ̃dʀ(ə)] *vt* to pity, feel sorry for; **se** ~ *vi* (*gémir*) to moan; (*protester, rouspéter*): **se** ~ (**à qn**) (**de**) to complain (to sb) (about); (*souffrir*): **se** ~ **de** to complain of.

plaine [plɛn] *nf* plain.

plain-pied [plɛ̃pje]: **de** ~ *adv* at street-level; (*fig*) straight; **de** ~ (**avec**) on the same level (as).

plaint, e [plɛ̃, -ɛ̃t] *pp de* **plaindre** ♦ *nf* (*gémissement*) moan, groan; (*doléance*) complaint; **porter** ~**e** to lodge a complaint.

plaintif, ive [plɛ̃tif, -iv] *adj* plaintive.

plaire [plɛʀ] *vi* to be a success, be successful; **to please;** ~ **à: cela me plaît** I like it; **essayer de** ~ **à qn** (*en étant serviable etc*) to try and please sb; **elle plaît aux hommes** she's a success with men, men like her; **se** ~ **quelque part** to like being somewhere, like it somewhere; **se** ~ **à faire** to take pleasure in doing; **ce qu'il vous plaira** what(ever) you like *ou* wish; **s'il vous plaît** please.

plaisamment [plɛzamɑ̃] *adv* pleasantly.

plaisance [plɛzɑ̃s] *nf* (*aussi:* **navigation de** ~) (pleasure) sailing, yachting.

plaisancier [plɛzɑ̃sje] *nm* amateur sailor, yachting enthusiast.

plaisant, e [plɛzɑ̃, -ɑ̃t] *adj* pleasant; (*histoire, anecdote*) amusing.

plaisanter [plɛzɑ̃te] *vi* to joke ♦ *vt* (*personne*) to tease, make fun of; **pour** ~ for a joke; **on ne plaisante pas avec cela** that's no joking matter; **tu plaisantes!** you're joking *ou* kidding!

plaisanterie [plɛzɑ̃tʀi] *nf* joke; joking *no pl*.

plaisantin [plɛzɑ̃tɛ̃] *nm* joker; (*fumiste*) fly-by-night.

plaise [plɛz] *etc vb voir* **plaire.**

plaisir [plɛziʀ] *nm* pleasure; **faire** ~ **à qn** (*délibérément*) to be nice to sb, please sb; (*suj: cadeau, nouvelle etc*): **ceci me fait** ~ I'm delighted *ou* very pleased with this; **prendre** ~ **à/à faire** to take pleasure in/in doing; **j'ai le** ~ **de** ... it is with great pleasure that I ...; **M. et Mme X ont le** ~ **de vous faire part de** ... M. and Mme X are pleased to announce ...; **se faire un** ~ **de faire qch** to be (only too) pleased to do sth; **faites-moi le** ~ **de** ... would you mind ..., would you be kind enough to ...; **à** ~ freely; for the sake of it; **au** ~ (**de vous revoir**) (I hope to) see you again; **pour le** *ou* **pour son** *ou* **par** ~ for pleasure.

plaît [plɛ] *vb voir* **plaire**.

plan, e [plɑ̃, -an] *adj* flat ♦ *nm* plan; (*GÉOM*) plane; (*fig*) level, plane; (*CINÉ*) shot; **au premier/second** ~ in the foreground/middle distance; **à l'arrière** ~ in the background; **mettre qch au premier** ~ (*fig*) to consider sth to be of primary importance; **sur le** ~ **sexuel** sexually, as far as sex is concerned; **laisser/rester en** ~ to abandon/be abandoned; ~ **d'action** plan of action; ~ **directeur** (*ÉCON*) master plan; ~ **d'eau** lake; pond; ~ **de travail** work-top, work surface; ~ **de vol** (*AVIAT*) flight plan.

planche [plɑ̃ʃ] *nf* (*pièce de bois*) plank, (wooden) board; (*illustration*) plate; (*de salades, radis, poireaux*) bed; (*d'un plongeoir*) (diving) board; **les** ~**s** (*THÉÂT*) the boards; **en** ~**s** *adj* wooden; **faire la** ~ (*dans l'eau*) to float on one's back; **avoir du pain sur la** ~ to have one's work cut out; ~ **à découper** chopping board; ~ **à dessin** drawing board; ~ **à pain** breadboard; ~ **à repasser** ironing board; ~ (**à roulettes**) (*planche*) skateboard; (*sport*) skateboarding; ~ **de salut** (*fig*) sheet anchor; ~ **à voile** (*planche*) windsurfer, sailboard; (*sport*) windsurfing.

plancher [plɑ̃ʃe] *nm* floor; (*planches*) floorboards *pl*; (*fig*) minimum level ♦ *vi* to work hard.

planchiste [plɑ̃ʃist(ə)] *nm/f* windsurfer.

plancton [plɑ̃ktɔ̃] *nm* plankton.

planer [plane] *vi* (*oiseau, avion*) to glide; (*fumée, vapeur*) to float, hover; (*drogué*) to be (on a) high; ~ **sur** (*fig*) to hang over; to hover above.

planétaire [planetɛʀ] *adj* planetary.

planétarium [planetaʀjɔm] *nm* planetarium.

planète [planɛt] *nf* planet.

planeur [planœʀ] *nm* glider.

planification [planifikasjɔ̃] *nf* (economic) planning.

planifier [planifje] *vt* to plan.

planisphère [planisfɛʀ] *nm* planisphere.

planning [planiŋ] *nm* programme (*BRIT*), program (*US*), schedule; ~ **familial** family planning.

planque [plɑ̃k] *nf* (*fam: combine, filon*) cushy (*BRIT*) *ou* easy number; (: *cachette*) hideout.

planquer [plɑ̃ke] *vt* (*fam*) to hide (away), stash away; **se** ~ to hide.

plant [plɑ̃] *nm* seedling, young plant.

plantaire [plɑ̃tɛʀ] *adj voir* **voûte**.

plantation [plɑ̃tasjɔ̃] *nf* planting; (*de fleurs, légumes*) bed; (*exploitation*) plantation.

plante [plɑ̃t] *nf* plant; ~ **d'appartement** house *ou* pot plant; ~ **du pied** sole (of the foot); ~ **verte** house plant.

planter [plɑ̃te] *vt* (*plante*) to plant; (*enfoncer*) to hammer *ou* drive in; (*tente*) to put up, pitch; (*drapeau, échelle, décors*) to put up; (*fam: mettre*) to dump; (: *abandonner*): ~ **là** to

ditch; **se** ~ *vi* (*fam: se tromper*) to get it wrong; ~ **qch dans** to hammer *ou* drive sth into; to stick sth into; **se** ~ **dans** to sink into; to get stuck in; **se** ~ **devant** to plant o.s. in front of.

planteur [plɑ̃tœʀ] *nm* planter.

planton [plɑ̃tɔ̃] *nm* orderly.

plantureux, euse [plɑ̃tyʀø, -øz] *adj* (*repas*) copious, lavish; (*femme*) buxom.

plaquage [plakaʒ] *nm* (*RUGBY*) tackle.

plaque [plak] *nf* plate; (*de verre*) sheet; (*de verglas, d'eczéma*) patch; (*dentaire*) plaque; (*avec inscription*) plaque; ~ (**minéralogique** *ou* **de police** *ou* **d'immatriculation**) number (*BRIT*) *ou* license (*US*) plate; ~ **de beurre** slab of butter; ~ **chauffante** hotplate; ~ **de chocolat** bar of chocolate; ~ **de cuisson** hob; ~ **d'identité** identity disc; ~ **tournante** (*fig*) centre (*BRIT*), center (*US*).

plaqué, e [plake] *adj*: ~ **or/argent** gold-/silver-plated ♦ *nm*: ~ **or/argent** gold/silver plate; ~ **acajou** with a mahogany veneer.

plaquer [plake] *vt* (*bijou*) to plate; (*bois*) to veneer; (*aplatir*): ~ **qch sur/contre** to make sth stick *ou* cling to; (*RUGBY*) to bring down; (*fam: laisser tomber*) to drop, ditch; **se** ~ **contre** to flatten o.s. against; ~ **qn contre** to pin sb to.

plaquette [plakɛt] *nf* tablet; (*de chocolat*) bar; (*de beurre*) slab, packet; (*livre*) small volume; (*MÉD: de pilules, gélules*) pack, packet; (*INFORM*) circuit board; ~ **de frein** (*AUTO*) brake pad.

plasma [plasma] *nm* plasma.

plastic [plastik] *nm* plastic explosive.

plastifié, e [plastifje] *adj* plastic-coated.

plastifier [plastifje] *vt* (*document, photo*) to laminate.

plastiquage [plastikaʒ] *nm* bombing, bomb attack.

plastique [plastik] *adj* plastic ♦ *nm* plastic ♦ *nf* plastic arts *pl*; (*d'une statue*) modelling.

plastiquer [plastike] *vt* to blow up.

plastiqueur [plastikœʀ] *nm* terrorist (*planting a plastic bomb*).

plastron [plastʀɔ̃] *nm* shirt front.

plastronner [plastʀɔne] *vi* to swagger.

plat, e [pla, -at] *adj* flat; (*fade: vin*) flat-tasting, insipid; (*personne, livre*) dull ♦ *nm* (*récipient, CULIN*) dish; (*d'un repas*): **le premier** ~ the first course; (*partie plate*): **le** ~ **de la main** the flat of the hand; (: *d'une route*) flat (part); **à** ~ **ventre** *adv* face down; (*tomber*) flat on one's face; **à** ~ *adj* (*pneu, batterie*) flat; (*fam: fatigué*) dead beat, tired out; ~ **cuisiné** pre-cooked meal (*ou* dish); ~ **du jour** dish of the day; ~ **de résistance** main course; ~**s préparés** convenience food(s).

platane [platan] *nm* plane tree.

plateau, x [plato] *nm* (*support*) tray; (*d'une table*) top; (*d'une balance*) pan; (*GÉO*) plateau; (*de tourne-disques*) turntable; (*CINÉ*) set; (*TV*):

nous avons 2 journalistes sur le ~ ce soir we have 2 journalists with us tonight; **~ à fromages** cheeseboard.

plateau-repas, *pl* **plateaux-repas** [platoʀəpa] *nm* tray meal, TV dinner (*US*).

plate-bande, *pl* **plates-bandes** [platbɑ̃d] *nf* flower bed.

platée [plate] *nf* dish(ful).

plate-forme, *pl* **plates-formes** [platfɔʀm(ə)] *nf* platform; **~ de forage/pétrolière** drilling/ oil rig.

platine [platin] *nm* platinum ♦ *nf* (*d'un tourne-disque*) turntable; **~ disque/cassette** record/cassette deck; **~ laser** *ou* **compact-disc** compact disc (player).

platitude [platityd] *nf* platitude.

platonique [platɔnik] *adj* platonic.

plâtras [platʀa] *nm* rubble *no pl.*

plâtre [platʀ(ə)] *nm* (*matériau*) plaster; (*statue*) plaster statue; (*MÉD*) (plaster) cast; **~s** *nmpl* plasterwork *sg*; **avoir un bras dans le ~** to have an arm in plaster.

plâtrer [platʀe] *vt* to plaster; (*MÉD*) to set *ou* put in a (plaster) cast.

plâtrier [platʀije] *nm* plasterer.

plausible [plozibl(ə)] *adj* plausible.

play-back [plɛbak] *nm* miming.

play-boy [plɛbɔj] *nm* playboy.

plébiscite [plebisit] *nm* plebiscite.

plébisciter [plebisite] *vt* (*approuver*) to give overwhelming support to; (*élire*) to elect by an overwhelming majority.

plectre [plɛktʀ(ə)] *nm* plectrum.

plein, e [plɛ̃, -ɛn] *adj* full; (*porte, roue*) solid; (*chienne, jument*) big (with young) ♦ *nm:* **faire le ~ (d'essence)** to fill up (with petrol (*BRIT*) *ou* gas (*US*)) ♦ *prép:* **avoir de l'argent ~ les poches** to have loads of money; **~ de** full of; **avoir les mains ~es** to have one's hands full; **à ~es mains** (*ramasser*) in handfuls; (*empoigner*) firmly; **à ~ régime** at maximum revs; (*fig*) at full speed; **à ~ temps** full-time; **en ~ air** in the open air; **jeux en ~ air** outdoor games; **en ~e mer** on the open sea; **en ~ soleil** in direct sunlight; **en ~e nuit/rue** in the middle of the night/street; **en ~ milieu** right in the middle; **en ~ jour** in broad daylight; **les ~s** the downstrokes (*in handwriting*); **faire le ~ des voix** to get the maximum number of votes possible; **en ~ sur** right on; **en avoir ~ le dos** (*fam*) to have had it up to here.

pleinement [plɛnmɑ̃] *adv* fully; to the full.

plein-emploi [plɛnɑ̃plwa] *nm* full employment.

plénière [plenjɛʀ] *adj f:* **assemblée ~** plenary assembly.

plénipotentiaire [plenipɔtɑ̃sjɛʀ] *nm* plenipotentiary.

plénitude [plenityd] *nf* fullness.

pléthore [pletɔʀ] *nf:* **~ de** overabundance *ou* plethora of.

pléthorique [pletɔʀik] *adj* (*classes*) overcrowded; (*documentation*) excessive.

pleurer [plœʀe] *vi* to cry; (*yeux*) to water ♦ *vt* to mourn (for); **~ sur** *vt* to lament (over), bemoan; **~ de rire** to laugh till one cries.

pleurésie [plœʀezi] *nf* pleurisy.

pleureuse [plœʀøz] *nf* professional mourner.

pleurnicher [plœʀniʃe] *vi* to snivel, whine.

pleurs [plœʀ] *nmpl:* **en ~** in tears.

pleut [plø] *vb voir* **pleuvoir**.

pleutre [pløtʀ(ə)] *adj* cowardly.

pleuvait [pløvɛ] *etc vb voir* **pleuvoir**.

pleuviner [pløvine] *vb impers* to drizzle.

pleuvoir [pløvwaʀ] *vb impers* to rain ♦ *vi* (*fig*): **~ (sur)** to shower down (upon), be showered upon; **il pleut** it's raining; **il pleut des cordes** *ou* **à verse** *ou* **à torrents** it's pouring (down), it's raining cats and dogs.

pleuvra [pløvʀa] *etc vb voir* **pleuvoir**.

plexiglas [plɛksiglas] *nm* ® Plexiglas ® (*US*).

pli [pli] *nm* fold; (*de jupe*) pleat; (*de pantalon*) crease; (*aussi:* **faux ~**) crease; (*enveloppe*) envelope; (*lettre*) letter; (*CARTES*) trick; **prendre le ~ de faire** to get into the habit of doing; **ça ne fait pas un ~!** don't you worry!; **~ d'aisance** inverted pleat.

pliable [plijabl(ə)] *adj* pliable, flexible.

pliage [plijaʒ] *nm* (*ART*) origami.

pliant, e [plijɑ̃, -ɑ̃t] *adj* folding ♦ *nm* folding stool, campstool.

plier [plije] *vt* to fold; (*pour ranger*) to fold up; (*table pliante*) to fold down; (*genou, bras*) to bend ♦ *vi* to bend; (*fig*) to yield; **se ~ à** to submit to; **~ bagages** (*fig*) to pack up (and go).

plinthe [plɛ̃t] *nf* skirting board.

plissé, e [plise] *adj* (*jupe, robe*) pleated; (*peau*) wrinkled; (*GÉO*) folded ♦ *nm* (*COUTURE*) pleats *pl.*

plissement [plismɑ̃] *nm* (*GÉO*) fold.

plisser [plise] *vt* (*chiffonner: papier, étoffe*) to crease; (*rider: front*) to furrow, wrinkle; (*: bouche*) to pucker; (*jupe*) to put pleats in; **se ~** *vi* (*vêtement, étoffe*) to crease.

pliure [plijyʀ] *nf* (*du bras, genou*) bend; (*d'un ourlet*) fold.

plomb [plɔ̃] *nm* (*métal*) lead; (*d'une cartouche*) (lead) shot; (*PÊCHE*) sinker; (*sceau*) (lead) seal; (*ÉLEC*) fuse; **de ~** (*soleil*) blazing; **sans ~** (*essence*) unleaded; **sommeil de ~** heavy *ou* very deep sleep; **mettre à ~** to plumb.

plombage [plɔ̃baʒ] *nm* (*de dent*) filling.

plomber [plɔ̃be] *vt* (*canne, ligne*) to weight (with lead); (*colis, wagon*) to put a lead seal on; (*TECH: mur*) to plumb; (*dent*) to fill (*BRIT*), stop (*US*); (*INFORM*) to protect.

plomberie [plɔ̃bʀi] *nf* plumbing.

plombier [plɔ̃bje] *nm* plumber.

plonge [plɔ̃ʒ] *nf:* **faire la ~** to be a washer-up (*BRIT*) *ou* dishwasher (*person*).

plongeant, e [plɔ̃ʒɑ̃, -ɑ̃t] *adj* (*vue*) from above; (*tir, décolleté*) plunging.

plongée [plɔ̃ʒe] *nf* (*SPORT*) diving *no pl*; (: *sans scaphandre*) skin diving; (*de sous-marin*) submersion, dive; **en** ~ (*sous-marin*) submerged; (*prise de vue*) high angle.

plongeoir [plɔ̃ʒwaʀ] *nm* diving board.

plongeon [plɔ̃ʒɔ̃] *nm* dive.

plonger [plɔ̃ʒe] *vi* to dive ♦ *vt*: ~ **qch dans** to plunge sth into; ~ **dans un sommeil profond** to sink straight into a deep sleep; ~ **qn dans l'embarras** to throw sb into a state of confusion.

plongeur, euse [plɔ̃ʒœʀ, -øz] *nm/f* diver; (*de café*) washer-up (*BRIT*), dishwasher (*person*).

plot [plo] *nm* (*ÉLEC*) contact.

ploutocratie [plutɔkʀasi] *nf* plutocracy.

ploutocratique [plutɔkʀatik] *adj* plutocratic.

ployer [plwaje] *vt* to bend ♦ *vi* to bend; (*plancher*) to sag.

plu [ply] *pp de* **plaire, pleuvoir**.

pluie [plɥi] *nf* rain; (*averse, ondée*): **une** ~ **brève** a shower; (*fig*): ~ **de** shower of; **une** ~ **fine** fine rain; **retomber en** ~ to shower down; **sous la** ~ in the rain.

plumage [plymaʒ] *nm* plumage *no pl*, feathers *pl*.

plume [plym] *nf* feather; (*pour écrire*) (pen) nib; (*fig*) pen; **dessin à la** ~ pen and ink drawing.

plumeau, x [plymo] *nm* feather duster.

plumer [plyme] *vt* to pluck.

plumet [plymɛ] *nm* plume.

plumier [plymje] *nm* pencil box.

plupart [plypaʀ]: **la** ~ *pron* the majority, most (of them); **la** ~ **des** most, the majority of; **la** ~ **du temps/d'entre nous** most of the time/ of us; **pour la** ~ *adv* for the most part, mostly.

pluralisme [plyʀalism(ə)] *nm* pluralism.

pluralité [plyʀalite] *nf* plurality.

pluridisciplinaire [plyʀidisiplinɛʀ] *adj* multidisciplinary.

pluriel [plyʀjɛl] *nm* plural; **au** ~ in the plural.

plus¹ [ply] *vb voir* **plaire**.

═══════════════════════ *MOT-CLÉ*

plus² [ply] *adv* **1** (*forme négative*): **ne ...** ~ no more, no longer; **je n'ai** ~ **d'argent** I've got no more money *ou* no money left; **il ne travaille** ~ he's no longer working, he doesn't work any more

2 [ply, plyz +*voyelle*] (*comparatif*) more, ...+er; (*superlatif*): **le** ~ the most, the ...+est; ~ **grand/intelligent (que)** bigger/more intelligent (than); **le** ~ **grand/intelligent** the biggest/most intelligent; **tout au** ~ at the very most

3 [plys] (*davantage*) more; **il travaille** ~ **(que)** he works more (than); ~ **il travaille,** ~ **il est heureux** the more he works, the happier he is; ~ **de pain** more bread; ~ **de 10 personnes/3 heures/4 kilos** more than *ou* over 10 people/3 hours/4 kilos; **3 heures de** ~ **que** 3 hours more than; ~ **de minuit** after *ou* past midnight; **de** ~ what's more, moreover; **il a 3 ans de** ~ **que moi** he's 3 years older than me; **3 kilos en** ~ 3 kilos more; **en** ~ **de** in addition to; **de** ~ **en** ~ more and more; **en** ~ **de cela** ... what is more ...; ~ **ou moins** more or less; **ni** ~ **ni moins** no more, no less; **sans** ~ (but) no more than that, (but) that's all; **qui** ~ **est** what is more

♦ *prép* [plys]: **4** ~ **2** 4 plus 2.

plusieurs [plyzjœʀ] *dét, pron* several; **ils sont** ~ there are several of them.

plus-que-parfait [plyskəpaʀfɛ] *nm* pluperfect, past perfect.

plus-value [plyvaly] *nf* (*d'un bien*) appreciation; (*bénéfice*) capital gain; (*budgétaire*) surplus.

plut [ply] *vb voir* **plaire, pleuvoir**.

plutonium [plytɔnjɔm] *nm* plutonium.

plutôt [plyto] *adv* rather; **je ferais** ~ **ceci** I'd rather *ou* sooner do this; **fais** ~ **comme ça** try this way instead, you'd better try this way; ~ **que (de) faire** rather than *ou* instead of doing.

pluvial, e, aux [plyvjal, -o] *adj* (*eaux*) rain *cpd*.

pluvieux, euse [plyvjø, -øz] *adj* rainy, wet.

pluviosité [plyvjozite] *nf* rainfall.

PM *sigle f* = *Police militaire*.

p.m. *abr* (= *pour mémoire*) for the record.

PME *sigle fpl* = *petites et moyennes entreprises*.

PMI *sigle fpl* = *petites et moyennes industries* ♦ *sigle f* = **protection maternelle et infantile**.

PMU *sigle m* = *pari mutuel urbain*; (*café*) betting agency.

─────────────────────────────

*The PMU is a government-regulated network of horse-race betting counters run from bars displaying the PMU sign. Punters buy fixed-price tickets predicting winners or finishing positions. The traditional bet is the **tiercé**, a triple forecast, although other multiple forecasts (**quarté** etc) are becoming increasingly popular.*

─────────────────────────────

PNB *sigle m* (= *produit national brut*) GNP.

pneu [pnø] *nm* (*de roue*) tyre (*BRIT*), tire (*US*); (*message*) letter sent by pneumatic tube.

pneumatique [pnømatik] *adj* pneumatic; (*gonflable*) inflatable ♦ *nm* tyre (*BRIT*), tire (*US*).

pneumonie [pnømɔni] *nf* pneumonia.

PO *sigle fpl* (= *petites ondes*) MW.

po [po] *abr voir* **science**.

Pô [po] *nm*: **le** ~ the Po.

p.o. *abr* (= *par ordre*) p.p. (*on letters etc*).

poche [pɔʃ] *nf* pocket; (*déformation*): **faire une/des** ~**(s)** to bag; (*sous les yeux*) bag, pouch; (*ZOOL*) pouch ♦ *nm* (= *livre de* ~) (pocket-size) paperback; **de** ~ pocket *cpd*; **en être de sa** ~ to be out of pocket; **c'est**

dans la ~ it's in the bag.
poché, e [pɔʃe] *adj*: **œuf ~** poached egg; **œil ~**
black eye.
pocher [pɔʃe] *vt* (*CULIN*) to poach; (*ART*) to
sketch ♦ *vi* (*vêtement*) to bag.
poche-revolver, *pl* **poches-revolver**
[pɔʃRəvɔlvɛR] *nf* hip pocket.
pochette [pɔʃɛt] *nf* (*de timbres*) wallet,
envelope; (*d'aiguilles etc*) case; (*sac: de
femme*) clutch bag, purse; (*: d'homme*) bag;
(*sur veston*) breast pocket; (*mouchoir*) breast
pocket handkerchief; ~ **d'allumettes** book
of matches; ~ **de disque** record sleeve; ~
surprise lucky bag.
pochoir [pɔʃwaR] *nm* (*ART: cache*) stencil;
(*: tampon*) transfer.
podium [pɔdjɔm] *nm* podium (*pl* -ia).
poêle [pwal] *nm* stove ♦ *nf*: ~ (**à frire**) frying
pan.
poêlon [pwalɔ̃] *nm* casserole.
poème [pɔɛm] *nm* poem.
poésie [pɔezi] *nf* (*poème*) poem; (*art*): **la** ~
poetry.
poète [pɔɛt] *nm* poet; (*fig*) dreamer ♦ *adj*
poetic.
poétique [pɔetik] *adj* poetic.
pognon [pɔɲɔ̃] *nm* (*fam: argent*) dough.
poids [pwa] *nm* weight; (*SPORT*) shot; **vendre
au ~** to sell by weight; **de ~** *adj* (*argument
etc*) weighty; **prendre du ~** to put on weight;
faire le ~ (*fig*) to measure up; ~ **plume/
mouche/coq/moyen** (*BOXE*) feather/fly/
bantam/ middleweight; ~ **et haltères** *nmpl*
weight lifting *sg*; ~ **lourd** (*BOXE*)
heavyweight; (*camion: aussi*: **PL**) (big) lorry
(*BRIT*), truck (*US*); (*: ADMIN*) large goods
vehicle (*BRIT*), truck (*US*); ~ **mort** dead
weight; ~ **utile** net weight.
poignant, e [pwaɲɑ̃, -ɑ̃t] *adj* poignant,
harrowing.
poignard [pwaɲaR] *nm* dagger.
poignarder [pwaɲaRde] *vt* to stab, knife.
poigne [pwaɲ] *nf* grip; (*fig*) firm-handedness;
à ~ firm-handed.
poignée [pwaɲe] *nf* (*de sel etc, fig*) handful; (*de
couvercle, porte*) handle; ~ **de main**
handshake.
poignet [pwaɲɛ] *nm* (*ANAT*) wrist; (*de chemise*)
cuff.
poil [pwal] *nm* (*ANAT*) hair; (*de pinceau, brosse*)
bristle; (*de tapis, tissu*) strand; (*pelage*) coat;
(*ensemble des poils*): **avoir du ~ sur la
poitrine** to have hair(s) on one's chest, have
a hairy chest; **à ~** *adj* (*fam*) starkers; **au ~**
adj (*fam*) hunky-dory; **de tout ~** of all kinds;
être de bon/mauvais ~ to be in a good/bad
mood; ~ **à gratter** itching powder.
poilu, e [pwaly] *adj* hairy.
poinçon [pwɛ̃sɔ̃] *nm* awl; bodkin; (*marque*)
hallmark.
poinçonner [pwɛ̃sɔne] *vt* (*marchandise*) to
stamp; (*bijou etc*) to hallmark; (*billet, ticket*)

to clip, punch.
poinçonneuse [pwɛ̃sɔnøz] *nf* (*outil*) punch.
poindre [pwɛ̃dR(ə)] *vi* (*fleur*) to come up;
(*aube*) to break; (*jour*) to dawn.
poing [pwɛ̃] *nm* fist; **dormir à ~s fermés** to
sleep soundly.
point [pwɛ̃] *vb voir* **poindre** ♦ *nm* (*marque, signe*)
dot; (*: de ponctuation*) full stop, period (*US*);
(*moment, de score etc, fig: question*) point;
(*endroit*) spot; (*COUTURE, TRICOT*) stitch ♦ *adv*
= **pas**; **ne** ... ~ not (at all); **faire le** ~ (*NAVIG*)
to take a bearing; (*fig*) to take stock (of the
situation); **faire le** ~ **sur** to review; **en tout** ~
in every respect; **sur le** ~ **de faire** (just)
about to do; **au** ~ **que, à tel** ~ **que** so much
so that; **mettre au** ~ (*mécanisme, procédé*) to
develop; (*appareil-photo*) to focus; (*affaire*) to
settle; **à** ~ (*CULIN*) just right; (*: viande*)
medium; **à** ~ (**nommé**) just at the right
time; ~ **de croix/tige/chaînette** (*COUTURE*)
cross/stem/chain stitch; ~ **mousse/jersey**
(*TRICOT*) garter/stocking stitch; ~ **de
départ/d'arrivée/d'arrêt** departure/arrival/
stopping point; ~ **chaud** (*MIL, POL*) hot spot;
~ **de chute** landing place; (*fig*) stopping-off
point; ~ (**de côté**) stitch (*pain*); ~ **culminant**
summit; (*fig*) height, climax; ~ **d'eau** spring;
water point; ~ **d'exclamation** exclamation
mark; ~ **faible** weak spot; ~ **final** full stop,
period (*US*); ~ **d'interrogation** question
mark; ~ **mort** (*FINANCE*) break-even point;
au ~ **mort** (*AUTO*) in neutral; (*affaire,
entreprise*) at a standstill; ~ **noir** (*sur le
visage*) blackhead; (*AUTO*) accident black
spot; ~ **de non-retour** point of no return; ~
de repère landmark; (*dans le temps*) point of
reference; ~ **de vente** retail outlet; ~ **de
vue** viewpoint; (*fig: opinion*) point of view;
du ~ **de vue de** from the point of view of;
~**s cardinaux** points of the compass,
cardinal points; ~**s de suspension**
suspension points.
pointage [pwɛ̃taʒ] *nm* ticking off; checking
in.
pointe [pwɛ̃t] *nf* point; (*de la côte*) headland;
(*allusion*) dig; sally; (*fig*): **une ~ d'ail/
d'accent** a touch *ou* hint of garlic/of an
accent; ~**s** *nfpl* (*DANSE*) points, point shoes;
être à la ~ de (*fig*) to be in the forefront of;
faire *ou* **pousser une ~ jusqu'à** ... to press on
as far as ...; **sur la ~ des pieds** on tiptoe; **en
~** *adv* (*tailler*) into a point ♦ *adj* pointed,
tapered; **de ~** *adj* (*technique etc*) leading;
(*vitesse*) maximum, top; **heures/jours de ~**
peak hours/days; **faire du 180 en ~** (*AUTO*) to
have a top *ou* maximum speed of 180; **faire
des ~s** (*DANSE*) to dance on points; ~
d'asperge asparagus tip; ~ **de courant** surge
(of current); ~ **de tension** (*INFORM*) spike; ~
de vitesse burst of speed.
pointer [pwɛ̃te] *vt* (*cocher*) to tick off;
(*employés etc*) to check in; (*diriger: canon,*

longue-vue, doigt]: ~ **vers qch** to point at sth; (*MUS: note*) to dot ♦ *vi* (*employé*) to clock in; (*pousses*) to come through; (*jour*) to break; ~ **les oreilles** (*chien*) to prick up its ears.

pointeur, euse [pwɛ̃tœʀ, -øz] *nm/f* time-keeper ♦ *nf* timeclock.

pointillé [pwɛ̃tije] *nm* (*trait*) dotted line; (*ART*) stippling *no pl.*

pointilleux, euse [pwɛ̃tijø, -øz] *adj* particular, pernickety.

pointu, e [pwɛ̃ty] *adj* pointed; (*clou*) sharp; (*voix*) shrill; (*analyse*) precise.

pointure [pwɛ̃tyʀ] *nf* size.

point-virgule, *pl* **points-virgules** [pwɛ̃viʀgyl] *nm* semi-colon.

poire [pwaʀ] *nf* pear; (*fam: péj*) mug; ~ **électrique** (*pear-shaped*) switch; ~ **à injections** syringe.

poireau, x [pwaʀo] *nm* leek.

poireauter [pwaʀote] *vi* (*fam*) to hang about (waiting).

poirier [pwaʀje] *nm* pear tree; (*GYMNASTIQUE*): **faire le** ~ to do a headstand.

pois [pwa] *nm* (*BOT*) pea; (*sur une étoffe*) dot, spot; **à** ~ (*cravate etc*) spotted, polka-dot *cpd*; ~ **chiche** chickpea; ~ **de senteur** sweet pea; ~ **cassés** split peas.

poison [pwazɔ̃] *nm* poison.

poisse [pwas] *nf* rotten luck.

poisser [pwase] *vt* to make sticky.

poisseux, euse [pwasø, -øz] *adj* sticky.

poisson [pwasɔ̃] *nm* fish *gén inv*; **les P~s** (*signe*) Pisces, the Fish; **être des P~s** to be Pisces; **pêcher** *ou* **prendre du** ~ *ou* **des ~s** to fish; ~ **d'avril** April fool; (*blague*) April fool's day trick; ~ **rouge** goldfish.

> *The traditional prank in France on April 1 involves placing a cut-out paper fish, known as a* **poisson d'avril**, *on the back of one's victim, without being caught.*

poisson-chat, *pl* **poissons-chats** [pwasɔ̃ʃa] *nm* catfish.

poissonnerie [pwasɔnʀi] *nf* fishmonger's (*BRIT*), fish store (*US*).

poissonneux, euse [pwasɔnø, -øz] *adj* abounding in fish.

poissonnier, ière [pwasɔnje, -jɛʀ] *nm/f* fishmonger (*BRIT*), fish merchant (*US*) ♦ *nf* (*ustensile*) fish kettle.

poisson-scie, *pl* **poissons-scies** [pwasɔ̃si] *nm* sawfish.

poitevin, e [pwatvɛ̃, -in] *adj* (*région*) of *ou* from Poitou; (*ville*) of *ou* from Poitiers.

poitrail [pwatʀaj] *nm* (*d'un cheval etc*) breast.

poitrine [pwatʀin] *nf* (*ANAT*) chest; (*seins*) bust, bosom; (*CULIN*) breast; ~ **de bœuf** brisket.

poivre [pwavʀ(ə)] *nm* pepper; ~ **en grains/ moulu** whole/ground pepper; ~ **de cayenne** cayenne (pepper); ~ **et sel** *adj* (*cheveux*) pepper-and-salt.

poivré, e [pwavʀe] *adj* peppery.

poivrer [pwavʀe] *vt* to pepper.

poivrier [pwavʀije] *nm* (*BOT*) pepper plant.

poivrière [pwavʀijɛʀ] *nf* pepperpot, pepper shaker (*US*).

poivron [pwavʀɔ̃] *nm* pepper, capsicum; ~ **vert/rouge** green/red pepper.

poix [pwa] *nf* pitch (*tar*).

poker [pɔkɛʀ] *nm*: **le** ~ poker; **partie de** ~ (*fig*) gamble; ~ **d'as** four aces.

polaire [pɔlɛʀ] *adj* polar.

polarisation [pɔlaʀizasjɔ̃] *nf* (*PHYSIQUE, ÉLEC*) polarization; (*fig*) focusing.

polariser [pɔlaʀize] *vt* to polarize; (*fig: attirer*) to attract; (*: réunir, concentrer*) to focus; **être polarisé sur** (*personne*) to be completely bound up with *ou* absorbed by.

pôle [pol] *nm* (*GÉO, ÉLEC*) pole; **le** ~ **Nord/Sud** the North/South Pole; ~ **d'attraction** (*fig*) centre of attraction.

polémique [pɔlemik] *adj* controversial, polemic(al) ♦ *nf* controversy.

polémiquer [pɔlemike] *vi* to be involved in controversy.

polémiste [pɔlemist(ə)] *nm/f* polemist, polemicist.

poli, e [pɔli] *adj* polite; (*lisse*) smooth; polished.

police [pɔlis] *nf* police; (*discipline*): **assurer la** ~ **de** *ou* **dans** to keep order in; **peine de simple** ~ sentence given by a magistrate's *ou* police court; ~ (**d'assurance**) (insurance) policy; ~ (**de caractères**) (*TYPO, INFORM*) typeface; ~ **judiciaire (PJ)** ≈ Criminal Investigation Department (CID) (*BRIT*), ≈ Federal Bureau of Investigation (FBI) (*US*); ~ **des mœurs** ≈ vice squad; ~ **secours** ≈ emergency services *pl.*

polichinelle [pɔliʃinɛl] *nm* Punch; (*péj*) buffoon; **secret de** ~ open secret.

policier, ière [pɔlisje, -jɛʀ] *adj* police *cpd* ♦ *nm* policeman; (*aussi:* **roman** ~) detective novel.

policlinique [pɔliklinik] *nf* ≈ outpatients *sg* (clinic).

poliment [pɔlimɑ̃] *adv* politely.

polio(myélite) [pɔljo(mjelit)] *nf* polio(myelitis).

polio(myélitique) [pɔljo(mjelitik)] *nm/f* polio patient *ou* case.

polir [pɔliʀ] *vt* to polish.

polisson, ne [pɔlisɔ̃, -ɔn] *adj* naughty.

politesse [pɔlitɛs] *nf* politeness; ~**s** *nfpl* (exchange of) courtesies; **rendre une** ~ **à qn** to return sb's favour (*BRIT*) *ou* favor (*US*).

politicard [pɔlitikaʀ] *nm* (*péj*) politico, political schemer.

politicien, ne [pɔlitisjɛ̃, -ɛn] *adj* political ♦ *nm/f* politician.

politique [pɔlitik] *adj* political ♦ *nf* (*science, activité*) politics *sg*; (*principes, tactique*) policy, policies *pl* ♦ *nm* (*politicien*) politician; ~ **étrangère/intérieure** foreign/domestic policy.

politique-fiction [pɔlitikfiksjɔ̃] *nf* political fiction.

politiquement [pɔlitikmɑ̃] *adv* politically.

politisation [pɔlitizɑsjɔ̃] *nf* politicization.

politiser [pɔlitize] *vt* to politicize; ~ **qn** to make sb politically aware.

pollen [pɔlɛn] *nm* pollen.

polluant, e [pɔlɥɑ̃, -ɑ̃t] *adj* polluting ♦ *nm* polluting agent, pollutant.

polluer [pɔlɥe] *vt* to pollute.

pollueur, euse [pɔlɥœʀ, -øz] *nm/f* polluter.

pollution [pɔlysjɔ̃] *nf* pollution.

polo [pɔlo] *nm* (*sport*) polo; (*tricot*) polo shirt.

Pologne [pɔlɔɲ] *nf*: **la** ~ Poland.

polonais, e [pɔlɔnɛ, -ɛz] *adj* Polish ♦ *nm* (*LING*) Polish ♦ *nm/f*: **P~, e** Pole.

poltron, ne [pɔltʀɔ̃, -ɔn] *adj* cowardly.

poly... [pɔli] *préfixe* poly....

polyamide [pɔliamid] *nf* polyamide.

polychrome [pɔlikʀom] *adj* polychrome, polychromatic.

polyclinique [pɔliklinik] *nf* (*private*) clinic (*treating different illnesses*).

polycopie [pɔlikɔpi] *nf* (*procédé*) duplicating; (*reproduction*) duplicated copy.

polycopié, e [pɔlikɔpje] *adj* duplicated ♦ *nm* handout, duplicated notes *pl*.

polycopier [pɔlikɔpje] *vt* to duplicate.

polyculture [pɔlikyltyʀ] *nf* mixed farming.

polyester [pɔliɛstɛʀ] *nm* polyester.

polyéthylène [pɔlietilɛn] *nm* polyethylene.

polygame [pɔligam] *adj* polygamous.

polygamie [pɔligami] *nf* polygamy.

polyglotte [pɔliglɔt] *adj* polyglot.

polygone [pɔligɔn] *nm* polygon.

Polynésie [pɔlinezi] *nf*: **la** ~ Polynesia; **la** ~ **française** French Polynesia.

polynésien, ne [pɔlinezjɛ̃, -ɛn] *adj* Polynesian.

polynôme [pɔlinom] *nm* polynomial.

polype [pɔlip] *nm* polyp.

polystyrène [pɔlistiʀɛn] *nm* polystyrene.

polytechnicien, ne [pɔliteknisjɛ̃, -ɛn] *nm/f* student or former student of the *École polytechnique*.

Polytechnique [pɔliteknik] *nf*: (**École**) **p~** *prestigious military academy producing high-ranking officers and engineers.*

polyvalent, e [pɔlivalɑ̃, -ɑ̃t] *adj* (*vaccin*) polyvalent; (*personne*) versatile; (*salle*) multi-purpose ♦ *nm* ≈ tax inspector.

pomélo [pɔmelo] *nm* pomelo, grapefruit.

Poméranie [pɔmeʀani] *nf*: **la** ~ Pomerania.

pommade [pɔmad] *nf* ointment, cream.

pomme [pɔm] *nf* (*BOT*) apple; (*boule décorative*) knob; (*pomme de terre*): **steak ~s** (**frites**) steak and chips (*BRIT*) *ou* (French) fries (*US*); **tomber dans les ~s** (*fam*) to pass out; ~ **d'Adam** Adam's apple; **~s allumettes** French fries (*thin-cut*); ~ **d'arrosoir**

(sprinkler) rose; ~ **de pin** pine *ou* fir cone; ~ **de terre** potato; **~s vapeur** boiled potatoes.

pommé, e [pɔme] *adj* (*chou etc*) firm, with a firm heart.

pommeau, x [pɔmo] *nm* (*boule*) knob; (*de selle*) pommel.

pommelé, e [pɔmle] *adj*: **gris** ~ dapple grey.

pommette [pɔmɛt] *nf* cheekbone.

pommier [pɔmje] *nm* apple tree.

pompe [pɔ̃p] *nf* pump; (*faste*) pomp (and ceremony); ~ **de bicyclette** bicycle pump; ~ **à eau/essence** water/petrol pump; ~ **à huile** oil pump; ~ **à incendie** fire engine (*apparatus*); **~s funèbres** undertaker's *sg*, funeral parlour *sg* (*BRIT*), mortician's *sg* (*US*).

Pompéi [pɔ̃pei] *n* Pompeii.

pompéien, ne [pɔ̃pejɛ̃, -ɛn] *adj* Pompeiian.

pomper [pɔ̃pe] *vt* to pump; (*évacuer*) to pump out; (*aspirer*) to pump up; (*absorber*) to soak up ♦ *vi* to pump.

pompeusement [pɔ̃pøzmɑ̃] *adv* pompously.

pompeux, euse [pɔ̃pø, -øz] *adj* pompous.

pompier [pɔ̃pje] *nm* fireman ♦ *adj m* (*style*) pretentious, pompous.

pompiste [pɔ̃pist(ə)] *nm/f* petrol (*BRIT*) *ou* gas (*US*) pump attendant.

pompon [pɔ̃pɔ̃] *nm* pompom, bobble.

pomponner [pɔ̃pɔne] *vt* to titivate (*BRIT*), dress up.

ponce [pɔ̃s] *nf*: **pierre** ~ pumice stone.

poncer [pɔ̃se] *vt* to sand (down).

ponceuse [pɔ̃søz] *nf* sander.

poncif [pɔ̃sif] *nm* cliché.

ponction [pɔ̃ksjɔ̃] *nf* (*d'argent etc*) withdrawal; ~ **lombaire** lumbar puncture.

ponctualité [pɔ̃ktɥalite] *nf* punctuality.

ponctuation [pɔ̃ktɥasjɔ̃] *nf* punctuation.

ponctuel, le [pɔ̃ktɥɛl] *adj* (*à l'heure, aussi TECH*) punctual; (*fig: opération etc*) one-off, single; (*scrupuleux*) punctilious, meticulous.

ponctuellement [pɔ̃ktɥɛlmɑ̃] *adv* punctually; punctiliously, meticulously.

ponctuer [pɔ̃ktɥe] *vt* to punctuate; (*MUS*) to phrase.

pondéré, e [pɔ̃deʀe] *adj* level-headed, composed.

pondérer [pɔ̃deʀe] *vt* to balance.

pondeuse [pɔ̃døz] *nf* layer, laying hen.

pondre [pɔ̃dʀ(ə)] *vt* to lay; (*fig*) to produce ♦ *vi* to lay.

poney [pɔnɛ] *nm* pony.

pongiste [pɔ̃ʒist(ə)] *nm/f* table tennis player.

pont [pɔ̃] *nm* bridge; (*AUTO*): ~ **arrière/avant** rear/front axle; (*NAVIG*) deck; **faire le** ~ to take the extra day off; **faire un** ~ **d'or à qn** to offer sb a fortune to take a job; ~ **aérien** airlift; ~ **basculant** bascule bridge; ~ **d'envol** flight deck; ~ **élévateur** hydraulic ramp; ~ **de graissage** ramp (*in garage*); ~ **à péage** tollbridge; ~ **roulant** travelling crane; ~ **suspendu** suspension bridge; ~

tournant swing bridge; **P~s et Chaussées** highways department.

---

*The expression "**faire le pont**" refers to the practice of taking a Monday or Friday off to make a long weekend if a public holiday falls on a Tuesday or Thursday. The French commonly take an extra day off to give four consecutive days holiday at l'**Ascension**, l'**Assomption** and le **14 juillet**.*

---

ponte [pɔ̃t] *nf* laying; (*œufs pondus*) clutch
♦ *nm* (*fam*) big shot.
pontife [pɔ̃tif] *nm* pontiff.
pontifier [pɔ̃tifje] *vi* to pontificate.
pont-levis, *pl* **ponts-levis** [pɔ̃lvi] *nm* drawbridge.
ponton [pɔ̃tɔ̃] *nm* pontoon (*on water*).
pop [pɔp] *adj inv* pop ♦ *nm*: **le ~** pop (music).
pop-corn [pɔpkɔrn] *nm* popcorn.
popeline [pɔplin] *nf* poplin.
populace [pɔpylas] *nf* (*péj*) rabble.
populaire [pɔpylɛʀ] *adj* popular; (*manifestation*) mass *cpd*, of the people; (*milieux, clientèle*) working-class; (*LING: mot etc*) used by the lower classes (of society).
populariser [pɔpylaʀize] *vt* to popularize.
popularité [pɔpylaʀite] *nf* popularity.
population [pɔpylasjɔ̃] *nf* population; **~ active/agricole** working/farming population.
populeux, euse [pɔpylø, -øz] *adj* densely populated.
porc [pɔʀ] *nm* (*ZOOL*) pig; (*CULIN*) pork; (*peau*) pigskin.
porcelaine [pɔʀsəlɛn] *nf* (*substance*) porcelain, china; (*objet*) piece of china(ware).
porcelet [pɔʀsəlɛ] *nm* piglet.
porc-épic, *pl* **porcs-épics** [pɔʀkepik] *nm* porcupine.
porche [pɔʀʃ(ə)] *nm* porch.
porcher, ère [pɔʀʃe, -ɛʀ] *nm/f* pig-keeper.
porcherie [pɔʀʃəʀi] *nf* pigsty.
porcin, e [pɔʀsɛ̃, -in] *adj* (*race*) porcine; (*élevage*) pig *cpd*; (*fig*) piglike.
pore [pɔʀ] *nm* pore.
poreux, euse [pɔʀø, -øz] *adj* porous.
porno [pɔʀno] *adj* porno ♦ *nm* porn.
pornographie [pɔʀnɔgʀafi] *nf* pornography.
pornographique [pɔʀnɔgʀafik] *adj* pornographic.
port [pɔʀ] *nm* (*NAVIG*) harbour (*BRIT*), harbor (*US*), port; (*ville, aussi INFORM*) port; (*de l'uniforme etc*) wearing; (*pour lettre*) postage; (*pour colis, aussi: posture*) carriage; **~ de commerce/de pêche** commercial/fishing port; **arriver à bon ~** to arrive safe and sound; **~ d'arme** (*JUR*) carrying of a firearm; **~ d'attache** (*NAVIG*) port of registry; (*fig*) home base; **~ d'escale** port of call; **~ franc** free port.
portable [pɔʀtabl(ə)] *adj* (*vêtement*) wearable; (*portatif*) transportable.

portail [pɔʀtaj] *nm* gate; (*de cathédrale*) portal.
portant, e [pɔʀtɑ̃, -ɑ̃t] *adj* (*murs*) structural, supporting; (*roues*) running; **bien/mal ~** in good/poor health.
portatif, ive [pɔʀtatif, -iv] *adj* portable.
porte [pɔʀt(ə)] *nf* door; (*de ville, forteresse, SKI*) gate; **mettre à la ~** to throw out; **prendre la ~** to leave, go away; **à ma/sa ~** (*tout près*) on my/his (*ou* her) doorstep; **~ (d'embarquement)** (*AVIAT*) (departure) gate; **~ d'entrée** front door; **~ à ~** *nm* door-to-door selling; **~ de secours** emergency exit; **~ de service** service entrance.
porté, e [pɔʀte] *adj*: **être ~ à faire qch** to be apt to do sth, tend to do sth; **être ~ sur qch** to be partial to sth.
porte-à-faux [pɔʀtafo] *nm*: **en ~** cantilevered; (*fig*) in an awkward position.
porte-aiguilles [pɔʀtegɥij] *nm inv* needle case.
porte-avions [pɔʀtavjɔ̃] *nm inv* aircraft carrier.
porte-bagages [pɔʀtbagaʒ] *nm inv* luggage rack (*ou* basket *etc*).
porte-bébé [pɔʀtbebe] *nm* baby sling *ou* carrier.
porte-bonheur [pɔʀtbɔnœʀ] *nm inv* lucky charm.
porte-bouteilles [pɔʀtbutej] *nm inv* bottle carrier; (*à casiers*) wine rack.
porte-cartes [pɔʀtəkaʀt(ə)] *nm inv* (*de cartes d'identité*) card holder; (*de cartes géographiques*) map wallet.
porte-cigarettes [pɔʀtsigaʀɛt] *nm inv* cigarette case.
porte-clefs [pɔʀtəkle] *nm inv* key ring.
porte-conteneurs [pɔʀtəkɔ̃tnœʀ] *nm inv* container ship.
porte-couteau, x [pɔʀtkuto] *nm* knife rest.
porte-crayon [pɔʀtkʀejɔ̃] *nm* pencil holder.
porte-documents [pɔʀtdɔkymɑ̃] *nm inv* attaché *ou* document case.
porte-drapeau, x [pɔʀtdʀapo] *nm* standard bearer.
portée [pɔʀte] *nf* (*d'une arme*) range; (*fig: importance*) impact, import; (*: capacités*) scope, capability; (*de chatte etc*) litter; (*MUS*) stave, staff (*pl* staves); **à/hors de ~ (de)** within/out of reach (of); **à ~ de (la) main** within (arm's) reach; **à ~ de voix** within earshot; **à la ~ de qn** (*fig*) at sb's level, within sb's capabilities; **à la ~ de toutes les bourses** to suit every pocket, within everyone's means.
portefaix [pɔʀtəfɛ] *nm inv* porter.
porte-fenêtre, *pl* **portes-fenêtres** [pɔʀtfənɛtʀ(ə)] *nf* French window.
portefeuille [pɔʀtəfœj] *nm* wallet; (*POL, BOURSE*) portfolio; **faire un lit en ~** to make an apple-pie bed.
porte-jarretelles [pɔʀtʒaʀtɛl] *nm inv* suspender belt (*BRIT*), garter belt (*US*).
porte-jupe [pɔʀtəʒyp] *nm* skirt hanger.

portemanteau, x [pɔʀtmɑ̃to] *nm* coat rack.
porte-mine [pɔʀtəmin] *nm* propelling (*BRIT*)
ou mechanical (*US*) pencil.
porte-monnaie [pɔʀtmɔnɛ] *nm inv* purse.
porte-parapluies [pɔʀtparaplɥi] *nm inv*
umbrella stand.
porte-parole [pɔʀtparɔl] *nm inv* spokesperson.
porte-plume [pɔʀtəplym] *nm inv* penholder.
porter [pɔʀte] *vt* (*charge ou sac etc, aussi:
fœtus*) to carry; (*sur soi: vêtement, barbe,
bague*) to wear; (*fig: responsabilité etc*) to
bear, carry; (*inscription, marque, titre,
patronyme, suj: arbre: fruits, fleurs*) to bear;
(*jugement*) to pass; (*apporter*): ~ **qch quelque
part/à qn** to take sth somewhere/to sb;
(*inscrire*): ~ **qch sur** to put sth down on; to
enter sth in ♦ *vi* (*voix, regard, canon*) to carry;
(*coup, argument*) to hit home; **se ~** *vi* (*se
sentir*): **se ~ bien/mal** to be well/unwell;
(*aller*): **se ~ vers** to go towards; ~ **sur** (*peser*)
to rest on; (*accent*) to fall on; (*conférence etc*)
to concern; (*heurter*) to strike; **être porté à
faire** to be apt *ou* inclined to do; **elle portait
le nom de Rosalie** she was called Rosalie; ~
qn au pouvoir to bring sb to power; ~
bonheur à qn to bring sb luck; ~ **qn à croire**
to lead sb to believe; ~ **son âge** to look
one's age; ~ **un toast** to drink a toast; ~ **de
l'argent au crédit d'un compte** to credit an
account with some money; **se ~ partie civile**
*to associate in a court action with the
public prosecutor*; **se ~ garant de qch** to
guarantee sth, vouch for sth; **se ~ candidat
à la députation** ≈ to stand for Parliament
(*BRIT*), ≈ run for Congress (*US*); **se faire ~
malade** to report sick; ~ **la main à son
chapeau** to raise one's hand to one's hat; ~
son effort sur to direct one's efforts
towards; ~ **un fait à la connaissance de qn**
to bring a fact to sb's attention *ou* notice.
porte-savon [pɔʀtsavɔ̃] *nm* soap dish.
porte-serviettes [pɔʀtsɛʀvjɛt] *nm inv* towel
rail.
portes-ouvertes [pɔʀtuvɛʀt(ə)] *adj inv*:
journée ~ open day.
porteur, euse [pɔʀtœʀ, -øz] *adj* (*COMM*)
strong, promising; (*nouvelle, chèque etc*):
être ~ de to be the bearer of ♦ *nm/f* (*de
messages*) bearer ♦ *nm* (*de bagages*) porter;
(*COMM: de chèque*) bearer; (*: d'actions*)
holder; (**avion**) **gros ~** wide-bodied aircraft,
jumbo (jet).
porte-voix [pɔʀtəvwa] *nm inv* megaphone,
loudhailer (*BRIT*).
portier [pɔʀtje] *nm* doorman,
commissionnaire (*BRIT*).
portière [pɔʀtjɛʀ] *nf* door.
portillon [pɔʀtijɔ̃] *nm* gate.
portion [pɔʀsjɔ̃] *nf* (*part*) portion, share;
(*partie*) portion, section.
portique [pɔʀtik] *nm* (*GYMNASTIQUE*)
crossbar; (*ARCHIT*) portico; (*RAIL*) gantry.

porto [pɔʀto] *nm* port (wine).
portoricain, e [pɔʀtɔʀikɛ̃, -ɛn] *adj* Puerto
Rican.
Porto Rico [pɔʀtɔʀiko] *nf* Puerto Rico.
portrait [pɔʀtʀɛ] *nm* portrait; (*photographie*)
photograph; (*fig*): **elle est le ~ de sa mère**
she's the image of her mother.
portraitiste [pɔʀtʀetist(ə)] *nm/f* portrait
painter.
portrait-robot [pɔʀtʀeʀɔbo] *nm* Identikit ® *ou*
Photo-fit ® (*BRIT*) picture.
portuaire [pɔʀtɥeʀ] *adj* port *cpd*, harbour *cpd*
(*BRIT*), harbor *cpd* (*US*).
portugais, e [pɔʀtygɛ, -ɛz] *adj* Portuguese
♦ *nm* (*LING*) Portuguese ♦ *nm/f*: **P~, e**
Portuguese.
Portugal [pɔʀtygal] *nm*: **le ~** Portugal.
POS *sigle m* (= *plan d'occupation des sols*)
zoning ordinances *ou* regulations.
pose [poz] *nf* (*de moquette*) laying; (*de rideaux,
papier peint*) hanging; (*attitude, d'un modèle*)
pose; (*PHOTO*) exposure.
posé, e [poze] *adj* calm, unruffled.
posément [pozemɑ̃] *adv* calmly.
posemètre [pozmɛtʀ(ə)] *nm* exposure meter.
poser [poze] *vt* (*déposer*): ~ **qch (sur)/qn à** to
put sth down (on)/drop sb at; (*placer*): ~ **qch
sur/quelque part** to put sth on/somewhere;
(*installer: moquette, carrelage*) to lay; (*rideaux,
papier peint*) to hang; (*MATH: chiffre*) to put
(down); (*question*) to ask; (*principe,
conditions*) to lay *ou* set down; (*problème*) to
formulate; (*difficulté*) to pose; (*personne:
mettre en valeur*) to give standing to ♦ *vi*
(*modèle*) to pose; to sit; **se ~** (*oiseau, avion*)
to land; (*question*) to arise; **se ~ en** to pass
o.s. off as, pose as; ~ **son** *ou* **un regard sur
qn/qch** to turn one's gaze on sb/sth; ~ **sa
candidature** to apply; (*POL*) to put o.s. up for
election.
poseur, euse [pozœʀ, -øz] *nm/f* (*péj*) show-off,
poseur; ~ **de parquets/ carrelages** floor/tile
layer.
positif, ive [pozitif, -iv] *adj* positive.
position [pozisjɔ̃] *nf* position; **prendre ~** (*fig*)
to take a stand.
positionner [pozisjɔne] *vt* to position; (*compte
en banque*) to calculate the balance of.
positivement [pozitivmɑ̃] *adv* positively.
posologie [pozɔlɔʒi] *nf* directions *pl* for use,
dosage.
possédant, e [posedɑ̃, -ɑ̃t] *adj* (*classe*) wealthy
♦ *nm/f*: **les ~s** the haves, the wealthy.
possédé, e [posede] *nm/f* person possessed.
posséder [posede] *vt* to own, possess; (*qualité,
talent*) to have, possess; (*bien connaître:
métier, langue*) to have mastered, have a
thorough knowledge of; (*sexuellement, aussi:
suj: colère etc*) to possess; (*fam: duper*) to take
in.
possesseur [posesœʀ] *nm* owner.
possessif, ive [posesif, -iv] *adj, nm* (*aussi LING*)

possessive.

possession [pɔsesjɔ̃] nf ownership no pl; possession; **être/entrer en ~ de qch** to be in/take possession of sth.

possibilité [pɔsibilite] nf possibility; **~s** nfpl (moyens) means; (potentiel) potential sg; **avoir la ~ de faire** to be in a position to do; to have the opportunity to do.

possible [pɔsibl(ə)] adj possible; (projet, entreprise) feasible ♦ nm: **faire son ~** to do all one can, do one's utmost; **(ce n'est) pas ~!** impossible!; **le plus/moins de livres ~** as many/few books as possible; **dès que ~** as soon as possible; **gentil** etc **au ~** as nice etc as it is possible to be.

postal, e, aux [pɔstal, -o] adj postal, post office cpd; **sac ~** mailbag, postbag.

postdater [pɔstdate] vt to postdate.

poste [pɔst(ə)] nf (service) post, postal service; (administration, bureau) post office ♦ nm (fonction, MIL) post; (TÉL) extension; (de radio etc) set; (de budget) item; **~s** nfpl post office sg; **P~s télécommunications et télédiffusion (PTT)** postal and telecommunications service; **agent** ou **employé des ~s** post office worker; **mettre à la ~** to post; **~ de commandement (PC)** nm (MIL etc) headquarters; **~ de contrôle** nm checkpoint; **~ de douane** nm customs post; **~ émetteur** nm transmitting set; **~ d'essence** nm filling station; **~ d'incendie** nm fire point; **~ de péage** nm tollgate; **~ de pilotage** nm cockpit; **~ (de police)** nm police station; **~ de radio** nm radio set; **~ restante (PR)** nf poste restante (BRIT), general delivery (US); **~ de secours** nm first-aid post; **~ de télévision** nm television set; **~ de travail** nm work station.

poster vt [pɔste] to post ♦ nm [pɔstɛʀ] poster; **se ~** to position o.s.

postérieur, e [pɔsteʀjœʀ] adj (date) later; (partie) back ♦ nm (fam) behind.

postérieurement [pɔsteʀjœʀmɑ̃] adv later, subsequently; **~ à** after.

posteriori [pɔsteʀjɔʀi]: **a ~** adv with hindsight, a posteriori.

postérité [pɔsteʀite] nf posterity.

postface [pɔstfas] nf appendix.

posthume [pɔstym] adj posthumous.

postiche [pɔstiʃ] adj false ♦ nm hairpiece.

postier, ière [pɔstje, -jɛʀ] nm/f post office worker.

postillon [pɔstijɔ̃] nm: **envoyer des ~s** to splutter.

postillonner [pɔstijɔne] vi to splutter.

post-natal, e [pɔstnatal] adj postnatal.

postopératoire [pɔstɔpeʀatwaʀ] adj post-operative.

postscolaire [pɔstskɔlɛʀ] adj further, continuing.

post-scriptum [pɔstskʀiptɔm] nm inv postscript.

postsynchronisation [pɔstsɛ̃kʀɔnizasjɔ̃] nf dubbing.

postsynchroniser [pɔstsɛ̃kʀɔnize] vt to dub.

postulant, e [pɔstylɑ̃, -ɑ̃t] nm/f (candidat) applicant; (REL) postulant.

postulat [pɔstyla] nm postulate.

postuler [pɔstyle] vt (emploi) to apply for, put in for.

posture [pɔstyʀ] nf posture, position; (fig) position.

pot [po] nm jar, pot; (en plastique, carton) carton; (en métal) tin; (fam): **avoir du ~** to be lucky; **boire** ou **prendre un ~** (fam) to have a drink; **découvrir le ~ aux roses** to find out what's been going on; **~ catalytique** catalytic converter; **~ (de chambre)** (chamber)pot; **~ d'échappement** exhaust pipe; **~ de fleurs** plant pot, flowerpot; (plante) pot plant; **~ à tabac** tobacco jar.

potable [pɔtabl(ə)] adj (fig: boisson) drinkable; (: travail, devoir) decent; **eau (non) ~** (not) drinking water.

potache [pɔtaʃ] nm schoolboy.

potage [pɔtaʒ] nm soup.

potager, ère [pɔtaʒe, -ɛʀ] adj (plante) edible, vegetable cpd; **(jardin) ~** kitchen ou vegetable garden.

potasse [pɔtas] nf potassium hydroxide; (engrais) potash.

potasser [pɔtase] vt (fam) to swot up (BRIT), cram.

potassium [pɔtasjɔm] nm potassium.

pot-au-feu [pɔtofø] nm inv (beef) stew; (viande) stewing beef ♦ adj (fam: personne) stay-at-home.

pot-de-vin, pl **pots-de-vin** [podvɛ̃] nm bribe.

pote [pɔt] nm (fam) mate (BRIT), pal.

poteau, x [pɔto] nm post; **~ de départ/arrivée** starting/finishing post; **~ (d'exécution)** execution post, stake; **~ indicateur** signpost; **~ télégraphique** telegraph pole; **~x (de but)** goal-posts.

potée [pɔte] nf hotpot (of pork and cabbage).

potelé, e [pɔtle] adj plump, chubby.

potence [pɔtɑ̃s] nf gallows sg; **en ~** T-shaped.

potentat [pɔtɑ̃ta] nm potentate; (fig: péj) despot.

potentiel, le [pɔtɑ̃sjɛl] adj, nm potential.

potentiellement [pɔtɑ̃sjɛlmɑ̃] adv potentially.

poterie [pɔtʀi] nf (fabrication) pottery; (objet) piece of pottery.

potiche [pɔtiʃ] nf large vase.

potier [pɔtje] nm potter.

potins [pɔtɛ̃] nmpl gossip sg.

potion [pɔsjɔ̃] nf potion.

potiron [pɔtiʀɔ̃] nm pumpkin.

pot-pourri, pl **pots-pourris** [popuʀi] nm (MUS) potpourri, medley.

pou, x [pu] nm louse (pl lice).

pouah [pwa] excl ugh!, yuk!

poubelle [pubɛl] nf (dust)bin.

pouce [pus] nm thumb; **se tourner** ou **se rouler les ~s** (fig) to twiddle one's thumbs; **manger**

sur le ~ to eat on the run, snatch something to eat.

poudre [pudʀ(ə)] *nf* powder; (*fard*) (face) powder; (*explosif*) gunpowder; **en ~: café en ~** instant coffee; **savon en ~** soap powder; **lait en ~** dried *ou* powdered milk; **~ à canon** gunpowder; **~ à éternuer** sneezing powder; **~ à récurer** scouring powder; **~ de riz** face powder.

poudrer [pudʀe] *vt* to powder.

poudrerie [pudʀəʀi] *nf* gunpowder factory.

poudreux, euse [pudʀø, -øz] *adj* dusty; (*neige*) powdery, powder *cpd*.

poudrier [pudʀije] *nm* (powder) compact.

poudrière [pudʀijɛʀ] *nf* (powder) magazine; (*fig*) powder keg.

poudroyer [pudʀwaje] *vi* to rise in clouds *ou* a flurry.

pouf [puf] *nm* pouffe.

pouffer [pufe] *vi:* **~ (de rire)** to snigger; to giggle.

pouffiasse [pufjas] *nf* (*fam*) fat cow; (*prostituée*) tart.

pouilleux, euse [pujø, -øz] *adj* flea-ridden; (*fig*) seedy.

poulailler [pulaje] *nm* henhouse; (*THÉÂT*): **le ~** the gods *sg*.

poulain [pulɛ̃] *nm* foal; (*fig*) protégé.

poularde [pulaʀd(ə)] *nf* fatted chicken.

poule [pul] *nf* (*ZOOL*) hen; (*CULIN*) (boiling) fowl; (*SPORT*) (round-robin) tournament; (*RUGBY*) group; (*fam*) bird (*BRIT*), chick, broad (*US*); (*prostituée*) tart; **~ d'eau** moorhen; **~ mouillée** coward; **~ pondeuse** laying hen, layer; **~ au riz** chicken and rice.

poulet [pulɛ] *nm* chicken; (*fam*) cop.

poulette [pulɛt] *nf* (*jeune poule*) pullet.

pouliche [puliʃ] *nf* filly.

poulie [puli] *nf* pulley.

poulpe [pulp(ə)] *nm* octopus.

pouls [pu] *nm* pulse (*ANAT*); **prendre le ~ de qn** to feel sb's pulse.

poumon [pumɔ̃] *nm* lung; **~ d'acier** *ou* **artificiel** iron *ou* artificial lung.

poupe [pup] *nf* stern; **en ~** astern.

poupée [pupe] *nf* doll; **jouer à la ~** to play with one's doll (*ou* dolls); **de ~** (*très petit*): **jardin de ~** doll's garden, pocket-handkerchief-sized garden.

poupin, e [pupɛ̃, -in] *adj* chubby.

poupon [pupɔ̃] *nm* babe-in-arms.

pouponner [pupɔne] *vi* to fuss (around).

pouponnière [pupɔnjɛʀ] *nf* crèche, day nursery.

pour [puʀ] *prép* for ♦ *nm:* **le ~ et le contre** the pros and cons; **~ faire** (so as) to do, in order to do; **~ avoir fait** for having done; **~ que** so that, in order that; **~ moi** (*à mon avis, pour ma part*) for my part, personally; **~ riche qu'il soit** rich though he may be; **~ 100 francs d'essence** 100 francs' worth of petrol; **~ cent** per cent; **~ ce qui est de** as

for; **y être ~ quelque chose** to have something to do with it.

pourboire [puʀbwaʀ] *nm* tip.

pourcentage [puʀsɑ̃taʒ] *nm* percentage; **travailler au ~** to work on commission.

pourchasser [puʀʃase] *vt* to pursue.

pourfendeur [puʀfɑ̃dœʀ] *nm* sworn opponent.

pourfendre [puʀfɑ̃dʀ(ə)] *vt* to assail.

pourlécher [puʀleʃe]: **se ~** *vi* to lick one's lips.

pourparlers [puʀpaʀle] *nmpl* talks, negotiations; **être en ~ avec** to be having talks with.

pourpre [puʀpʀ(ə)] *adj* crimson.

pourquoi [puʀkwa] *adv, conj* why ♦ *nm inv:* **le ~ (de)** the reason (for).

pourrai [puʀe] *etc vb voir* **pouvoir**.

pourri, e [puʀi] *adj* rotten; (*roche, pierre*) crumbling; (*temps, climat*) filthy, foul ♦ *nm:* **sentir le ~** to smell rotten.

pourrir [puʀiʀ] *vi* to rot; (*fruit*) to go rotten *ou* bad; (*fig: situation*) to deteriorate ♦ *vt* to rot; (*fig: corrompre: personne*) to corrupt; (*: gâter: enfant*) to spoil thoroughly.

pourrissement [puʀismɑ̃] *nm* deterioration.

pourriture [puʀityʀ] *nf* rot.

pourrons [puʀɔ̃] *etc vb voir* **pouvoir**.

poursuis [puʀsɥi] *etc vb voir* **poursuivre**.

poursuite [puʀsɥit] *nf* pursuit, chase; **~s** *nfpl* (*JUR*) legal proceedings; **(course) ~** track race; (*fig*) chase.

poursuivant, e [puʀsɥivɑ̃, -ɑ̃t] *vb voir* **poursuivre** ♦ *nm/f* pursuer; (*JUR*) plaintiff.

poursuivre [puʀsɥivʀ(ə)] *vt* to pursue, chase (after); (*relancer*) to hound, harry; (*obséder*) to haunt; (*JUR*) to bring proceedings against, prosecute; (*: au civil*) to sue; (*but*) to strive towards; (*voyage, études*) to carry on with, continue ♦ *vi* to carry on, go on; **se ~** *vi* to go on, continue.

pourtant [puʀtɑ̃] *adv* yet; **mais ~** but nevertheless, but even so; **c'est ~ facile** (and) yet it's easy.

pourtour [puʀtuʀ] *nm* perimeter.

pourvoi [puʀvwa] *nm* appeal.

pourvoir [puʀvwaʀ] *nm* (*COMM*) supply ♦ *vt:* **~ qch/qn de** to equip sth/sb with ♦ *vi:* **~ à** to provide for; (*emploi*) to fill; **se ~** (*JUR*): **se ~ en cassation** to take one's case to the Court of Appeal.

pourvoyeur, euse [puʀvwajœʀ, -øz] *nm/f* supplier.

pourvu, e [puʀvy] *pp de* **pourvoir** ♦ *adj:* **~ de** equipped with; **~ que** *conj* (*si*) provided that, so long as; (*espérons que*) let's hope (that).

pousse [pus] *nf* growth; (*bourgeon*) shoot.

poussé, e [puse] *adj* sophisticated, advanced; (*moteur*) souped-up.

pousse-café [puskafe] *nm inv* (after-dinner) liqueur.

poussée [puse] *nf* thrust; (*coup*) push; (*MÉD*) eruption; (*fig*) upsurge.

pousse-pousse [puspus] *nm inv* rickshaw.
pousser [puse] *vt* to push; *(inciter)*: ~ **qn à** to
urge *ou* press sb to + *infinitif*; *(acculer)*: ~ **qn à**
to drive sb to; *(moteur, voiture)* to drive
hard; *(émettre: cri etc)* to give; *(stimuler)* to
urge on; to drive hard; *(poursuivre)* to carry
on ♦ *vi* to push; *(croître)* to grow; *(aller)*: ~
plus loin to push on a bit further; **se** ~ *vi* to
move over; **faire** ~ *(plante)* to grow; ~ **le**
dévouement *etc* **jusqu'à** ... to take devotion
etc as far as ....
poussette [puset] *nf (voiture d'enfant)*
pushchair *(BRIT)*, stroller *(US)*.
poussette-canne, *pl* **poussettes-cannes**
[pusetkan] *nf* baby buggy *(BRIT)*, (folding)
stroller *(US)*.
poussier [pusje] *nm* coaldust.
poussière [pusjɛʀ] *nf* dust; *(grain)* speck of
dust; **et des** ~**s** *(fig)* and a bit; ~ **de charbon**
coaldust.
poussiéreux, euse [pusjeʀø, -øz] *adj* dusty.
poussif, ive [pusif, -iv] *adj* wheezy, wheezing.
poussin [pusɛ̃] *nm* chick.
poussoir [puswaʀ] *nm* button.
poutre [putʀ(ə)] *nf* beam; *(en fer, ciment armé)*
girder; ~**s apparentes** exposed beams.
poutrelle [putʀɛl] *nf (petite poutre)* small
beam; *(barre d'acier)* girder.

=============================== *MOT-CLÉ*

pouvoir [puvwaʀ] *nm* power; *(POL: dirigeants)*:
le ~ those in power; **les** ~**s publics** the
authorities; **avoir** ~ **de faire** *(autorisation)* to
have (the) authority to do; *(droit)* to have
the right to do; ~ **absolu** absolute power; ~
absorbant absorbency; ~ **d'achat**
purchasing power; ~ **calorifique** calorific
value
♦ *vb semi-aux* **1** *(être en état de)* can, be able to;
je ne peux pas le réparer I can't *ou* I am not
able to repair it; **déçu de ne pas** ~ **le faire**
disappointed not to be able to do it
2 *(avoir la permission)* can, may, be allowed
to; **vous pouvez aller au cinéma** you can *ou*
may go to the pictures
3 *(probabilité, hypothèse)* may, might, could;
il a pu avoir un accident he may *ou* might he
could have had an accident; **il aurait pu le**
dire! he might *ou* could have said (so)!
4 *(expressions)*: **tu ne peux pas savoir!** you
have no idea!; **tu peux le dire!** you can say
that again!
♦ *vb impers* may, might, could; **il peut arriver**
que it may *ou* might *ou* could happen that; **il**
pourrait pleuvoir it might rain
♦ *vt* **1** can, be able to; **j'ai fait tout ce que j'ai**
pu I did all I could; **je n'en peux plus**
(épuisé) I'm exhausted; *(à bout)* I can't take
any more
2 *(vb +adj ou adv comparatif)*: **je me porte on**
ne peut mieux I'm absolutely fine, I couldn't
be better; **elle est on ne peut plus gentille**

she couldn't be nicer, she's as nice as can
be
se ~ *vi*: **il se peut que** it may *ou* might be
that; **cela se pourrait** that's quite possible.

PP *sigle f* (= *préventive de la pellagre: vitamine*)
niacin ♦ *abr* (= *pages*) pp.
p.p. *abr* (= *par procuration*) p.p.
p.p.c.m. *sigle m* (*MATH: = plus petit commun*
multiple) LCM (= *lowest common*
multiple).
PQ *sigle f* (*Canada: = province de Québec*) PQ.
PR *sigle m* = *parti républicain* ♦ *sigle f* = **poste**
restante.
pr *abr* = **pour**.
pragmatique [pʀagmatik] *adj* pragmatic.
pragmatisme [pʀagmatism(ə)] *nm*
pragmatism.
Prague [pʀag] *n* Prague.
prairie [pʀeʀi] *nf* meadow.
praline [pʀalin] *nf (bonbon)* sugared almond;
(au chocolat) praline.
praliné, e [pʀaline] *adj (amande)* sugared;
(chocolat, glace) praline *cpd*.
praticable [pʀatikabl(ə)] *adj (route etc)*
passable, practicable; *(projet)* practicable.
praticien, ne [pʀatisjɛ̃, -ɛn] *nm/f* practitioner.
pratiquant, e [pʀatikɑ̃, -ɑ̃t] *adj* practising
(BRIT), practicing *(US)*.
pratique [pʀatik] *nf* practice ♦ *adj* practical;
(commode: horaire etc) convenient; *(: outil)*
handy, useful; **dans la** ~ in (actual)
practice; **mettre en** ~ to put into practice.
pratiquement [pʀatikmɑ̃] *adv (dans la*
pratique) in practice; *(pour ainsi dire)*
practically, virtually.
pratiquer [pʀatike] *vt* to practise *(BRIT)*,
practice *(US)*; *(SPORT etc)* to go (in for),
play; *(appliquer: méthode, théorie)* to apply;
(intervention, opération) to carry out;
(ouverture, abri) to make ♦ *vi (REL)* to be a
churchgoer.
pré [pʀe] *nm* meadow.
préalable [pʀealabl(ə)] *adj* preliminary;
condition ~ **(de)** precondition (for),
prerequisite (for); **sans avis** ~ without prior
ou previous notice; **au** ~ first, beforehand.
préalablement [pʀealabləmɑ̃] *adv* first,
beforehand.
Préalpes [pʀealp(ə)] *nfpl*: **les** ~ the Pre-Alps.
préalpin, e [pʀealpɛ̃, -in] *adj* of the Pre-Alps.
préambule [pʀeɑ̃byl] *nm* preamble; *(fig)*
prelude; **sans** ~ straight away.
préau, x [pʀeo] *nm (d'une cour d'école)*
covered playground; *(d'un monastère, d'une*
prison) inner courtyard.
préavis [pʀeavi] *nm* notice; ~ **de congé** notice;
communication avec ~ *(TÉL)* personal *ou*
person-to-person call.
prébende [pʀebɑ̃d] *nf (péj)* remuneration.
précaire [pʀekɛʀ] *adj* precarious.
précaution [pʀekosjɔ̃] *nf* precaution; **avec** ~

cautiously; **prendre des** *ou* **ses** ~**s** to take
precautions; **par** ~ as a precaution; **pour
plus de** ~ to be on the safe side; ~**s
oratoires** carefully phrased remarks.

précautionneux, euse [pʀekosjɔnø, -øz] *adj*
cautious, careful.

précédemment [pʀesedamɑ̃] *adv* before,
previously.

précédent, e [pʀesedɑ̃, -ɑ̃t] *adj* previous ♦ *nm*
precedent; **sans** ~ unprecedented; **le jour** ~
the day before, the previous day.

précéder [pʀesede] *vt* to precede; (*marcher ou
rouler devant*) to be in front of; (*arriver avant*)
to get ahead of.

précepte [pʀesɛpt(ə)] *nm* precept.

précepteur, trice [pʀesɛptœʀ, -tʀis] *nm/f*
(*private*) tutor.

préchauffer [pʀeʃofe] *vt* to preheat.

prêcher [pʀeʃe] *vt*, *vi* to preach.

prêcheur, euse [pʀɛʃœʀ, -øz] *adj* moralizing
♦ *nm/f* (*REL*) preacher; (*fig*) moralizer.

précieusement [pʀesjøzmɑ̃] *adv* (*avec soin*)
carefully; (*avec préciosité*) preciously.

précieux, euse [pʀesjø, -øz] *adj* precious;
(*collaborateur, conseils*) invaluable; (*style,
écrivain*) précieux, precious.

préciosité [pʀesjozite] *nf* preciosity,
preciousness.

précipice [pʀesipis] *nm* drop, chasm; (*fig*)
abyss; **au bord du** ~ at the edge of the
precipice.

précipitamment [pʀesipitamɑ̃] *adv* hurriedly,
hastily.

précipitation [pʀesipitɑsjɔ̃] *nf* (*hâte*) haste; ~**s
(atmosphériques)** *nfpl* precipitation *sg*.

précipité, e [pʀesipite] *adj* (*respiration*) fast;
(*pas*) hurried; (*départ*) hasty.

précipiter [pʀesipite] *vt* (*faire tomber*): ~ **qn/
qch du haut de** to throw *ou* hurl sb/sth off
ou from; (*hâter: marche*) to quicken; (*: départ*)
to hasten; **se** ~ *vi* (*événements*) to move
faster; (*respiration*) to speed up; **se** ~ **sur/
vers** to rush at/towards; **se** ~ **au-devant de
qn** to throw o.s. before sb.

précis, e [pʀesi, -iz] *adj* precise; (*tir, mesures*)
accurate, precise ♦ *nm* handbook.

précisément [pʀesizemɑ̃] *adv* precisely; **ma
vie n'est pas** ~ **distrayante** my life is not
exactly entertaining.

préciser [pʀesize] *vt* (*expliquer*) to be more
specific about, clarify; (*spécifier*) to state,
specify; **se** ~ *vi* to become clear(er).

précision [pʀesizjɔ̃] *nf* precision; accuracy;
(*détail*) point *ou* detail (*made clear or to be
clarified*); ~**s** *nfpl* further details.

précoce [pʀekɔs] *adj* early; (*enfant*)
precocious; (*calvitie*) premature.

précocité [pʀekɔsite] *nf* earliness;
precociousness.

préconçu, e [pʀekɔ̃sy] *adj* preconceived.

préconiser [pʀekɔnize] *vt* to advocate.

précontraint, e [pʀekɔ̃tʀɛ̃, -ɛ̃t] *adj*: **béton** ~

prestressed concrete.

précuit, e [pʀekɥi, -it] *adj* precooked.

précurseur [pʀekyʀsœʀ] *adj m* precursory
♦ *nm* forerunner, precursor.

prédateur [pʀedatœʀ] *nm* predator.

prédécesseur [pʀedesesœʀ] *nm* predecessor.

prédécoupé, e [pʀedekupe] *adj* pre-cut.

prédestiner [pʀedɛstine] *vt*: ~ **qn à qch/à faire**
to predestine sb for sth/to do.

prédicateur [pʀedikatœʀ] *nm* preacher.

prédiction [pʀediksjɔ̃] *nf* prediction.

prédilection [pʀedilɛksjɔ̃] *nf*: **avoir une** ~ **pour**
to be partial to; **de** ~ favourite (*BRIT*),
favorite (*US*).

prédire [pʀediʀ] *vt* to predict.

prédisposer [pʀedispoze] *vt*: ~ **qn à qch/à
faire** to predispose sb to sth/to do.

prédisposition [pʀedispozisjɔ̃] *nf*
predisposition.

prédit, e [pʀedi, -it] *pp de* **prédire**.

prédominance [pʀedɔminɑ̃s] *nf*
predominance.

prédominant, e [pʀedɔminɑ̃, -ɑ̃t] *adj*
predominant; prevailing.

prédominer [pʀedɔmine] *vi* to predominate;
(*avis*) to prevail.

pré-électoral, e, aux [pʀeelɛktɔʀal, -o] *adj*
pre-election *cpd*.

pré-emballé, e [pʀeɑ̃bale] *adj* pre-packed.

prééminent, e [pʀeeminɑ̃, -ɑ̃t] *adj* pre-
eminent.

préemption [pʀeɑ̃psjɔ̃] *nf*: **droit de** ~ (*JUR*)
pre-emptive right.

pré-encollé, e [pʀeɑ̃kɔle] *adj* pre-pasted.

préétabli, e [pʀeetabli] *adj* pre-established.

préexistant, e [pʀeɛgzistɑ̃, -ɑ̃t] *adj* pre-
existing.

préfabriqué, e [pʀefabʀike] *adj* prefabricated;
(*péj: sourire*) artificial ♦ *nm* prefabricated
material.

préface [pʀefas] *nf* preface.

préfacer [pʀefase] *vt* to write a preface for.

préfectoral, e, aux [pʀefɛktɔʀal, -o] *adj*
prefectorial.

préfecture [pʀefɛktyʀ] *nf* prefecture; ~ **de
police** police headquarters.

> The **préfecture** *is the administrative
> headquarters of the* **département**. *The* **préfet**,
> *a senior civil servant appointed by the
> government, is responsible for executing
> government decisions. France's 22 regions,
> each comprising a number of départements,
> also have a préfet, the préfet de région.*

préférable [pʀefeʀabl(ə)] *adj* preferable.

préféré, e [pʀefeʀe] *adj*, *nm/f* favourite (*BRIT*),
favorite (*US*).

préférence [pʀefeʀɑ̃s] *nf* preference; **de** ~
preferably; **de** *ou* **par** ~ **à** in preference to,
rather than; **donner la** ~ **à qn** to give
preference to sb; **par ordre de** ~ in order of

preference; **obtenir la ~ sur** to have preference over.

préférentiel, le [pʀefeʀɑ̃sjɛl] *adj* preferential.

préférer [pʀefeʀe] *vt*: **~ qn/qch (à)** to prefer sb/sth (to), like sb/sth better (than); **~ faire** to prefer to do; **je préférerais du thé** I would rather have tea, I'd prefer tea.

préfet [pʀefɛ] *nm* prefect; **~ de police** ≈ Chief Constable (*BRIT*), ≈ Police Commissioner (*US*).

préfigurer [pʀefigyʀe] *vt* to prefigure.

préfixe [pʀefiks(ə)] *nm* prefix.

préhistoire [pʀeistwaʀ] *nf* prehistory.

préhistorique [pʀeistɔʀik] *adj* prehistoric.

préjudice [pʀeʒydis] *nm* (*matériel*) loss; (*moral*) harm *no pl*; **porter ~ à** to harm, be detrimental to; **au ~ de** at the expense of.

préjudiciable [pʀeʒydisjabl(ə)] *adj*: **~ à** prejudicial *ou* harmful to.

préjugé [pʀeʒyʒe] *nm* prejudice; **avoir un ~ contre** to be prejudiced *ou* biased against; **bénéficier d'un ~ favorable** to be viewed favourably.

préjuger [pʀeʒyʒe]: **~ de** *vt* to prejudge.

prélasser [pʀelɑse]: **se ~** *vi* to lounge.

prélat [pʀela] *nm* prelate.

prélavage [pʀelavaʒ] *nm* pre-wash.

prélèvement [pʀelɛvmɑ̃] *nm* deduction; withdrawal; **faire un ~ de sang** to take a blood sample.

prélever [pʀelve] *vt* (*échantillon*) to take; (*argent*): **~ (sur)** to deduct (from); (*: sur son compte*): **~ (sur)** to withdraw (from).

préliminaire [pʀeliminɛʀ] *adj* preliminary; **~s** *nmpl* preliminaries; (*négociations*) preliminary talks.

prélude [pʀelyd] *nm* prelude; (*avant le concert*) warm-up.

prématuré, e [pʀematyʀe] *adj* premature; (*retraite*) early ♦ *nm* premature baby.

prématurément [pʀematyʀemɑ̃] *adv* prematurely.

préméditation [pʀemeditasjɔ̃] *nf*: **avec ~** *adj* premeditated ♦ *adv* with intent.

préméditer [pʀemedite] *vt* to premeditate, plan.

prémices [pʀemis] *nfpl* beginnings.

premier, ière [pʀəmje, -jɛʀ] *adj* first; (*branche, marche, grade*) bottom; (*fig: fondamental*) basic; prime; (*en importance*) first, foremost ♦ *nm* (*~ étage*) first (*BRIT*) *ou* second (*US*) floor ♦ *nf* (*AUTO*) first (gear); (*RAIL, AVIAT etc*) first class; (*SCOL: classe*) penultimate school year (age 16-17); (*THÉÂT*) first night; (*CINÉ*) première; (*exploit*) first; **au ~ abord** at first sight; **au** *ou* **du ~ coup** at the first attempt *ou* go; **de ~ ordre** first-class, first-rate; **de première qualité, de ~ choix** best *ou* top quality; **de première importance** of the highest importance; **de première nécessité** absolutely essential; **le ~ venu** the first person to come along; **jeune ~** leading man;

le ~ de l'an New Year's Day; **enfant du ~ lit** child of a first marriage; **en ~ lieu** in the first place; **~ âge** (*d'un enfant*) the first 3 months (of life); **P~ Ministre** Prime Minister.

premièrement [pʀəmjɛʀmɑ̃] *adv* firstly.

première-née, *pl* **premières-nées** [pʀəmjɛʀne] *nf* first-born.

premier-né, *pl* **premiers-nés** [pʀəmjene] *nm* first-born.

prémisse [pʀemis] *nf* premise.

prémolaire [pʀemɔlɛʀ] *nf* premolar.

prémonition [pʀemɔnisjɔ̃] *nf* premonition.

prémonitoire [pʀemɔnitwaʀ] *adj* premonitory.

prémunir [pʀemyniʀ]: **se ~** *vi*: **se ~ contre** to protect o.s. from, guard against.

prenant, e [pʀənɑ̃, -ɑ̃t] *vb voir* **prendre** ♦ *adj* absorbing, engrossing.

prénatal, e [pʀenatal] *adj* (*MÉD*) antenatal; (*allocation*) maternity *cpd*.

prendre [pʀɑ̃dʀ(ə)] *vt* to take; (*ôter*): **~ qch à** to take sth from; (*aller chercher*) to get, fetch; (*se procurer*) to get; (*réserver: place*) to book; (*acquérir: du poids, de la valeur*) to put on, gain; (*malfaiteur, poisson*) to catch; (*passager*) to pick up; (*personnel, aussi: couleur, goût*) to take on; (*locataire*) to take in; (*traiter: enfant, problème*) to handle; (*voix, ton*) to put on; (*prélever: pourcentage, argent*) to take off; (*coincer*): **se ~ les doigts dans** to get one's fingers caught in ♦ *vi* (*liquide, ciment*) to set; (*greffe, vaccin*) to take; (*mensonge*) to be successful; (*feu: foyer*) to go; (*: incendie*) to start; (*allumette*) to light; (*se diriger*): **~ à gauche** to turn (to the) left; **~ son origine** *ou* **sa source** (*mot, rivière*) to have its source; **~ qn pour** to take sb for; **se ~ pour** to think one is; **~ sur soi de faire qch** to take it upon o.s. to do sth; **~ qn en sympathie/horreur** to get to like/loathe sb; **à tout ~** all things considered; **s'en ~ à** (*agresser*) to set about; (*passer sa colère sur*) to take it out on; (*critiquer*) to attack; (*remettre en question*) to challenge; **~ d'amitié/d'affection pour** to befriend/become fond of; **s'y ~** (*procéder*) to set about it; **s'y ~ à l'avance** to see to it in advance; **s'y ~ à deux fois** to try twice, make two attempts.

preneur [pʀənœʀ] *nm*: **être ~** to be willing to buy; **trouver ~** to find a buyer.

prénom [pʀenɔ̃] *nm* first name.

prénommer [pʀenɔme] *vt*: **elle se prénomme Claude** her (first) name is Claude.

prénuptial, e, aux [pʀenypsjal, -o] *adj* premarital.

préoccupant, e [pʀeɔkypɑ̃, -ɑ̃t] *adj* worrying.

préoccupation [pʀeɔkypasjɔ̃] *nf* (*souci*) concern; (*idée fixe*) preoccupation.

préoccupé, e [pʀeɔkype] *adj* concerned; preoccupied.

préoccuper [pʀeɔkype] *vt* (*tourmenter, tracasser*) to concern; (*absorber, obséder*) to preoccupy; **se ~ de qch** to be concerned about sth; to show concern about sth.

préparateur, trice [pʀepaʀatœʀ, -tʀis] *nm/f* assistant.

préparatifs [pʀepaʀatif] *nmpl* preparations.

préparation [pʀepaʀasjɔ̃] *nf* preparation; (*SCOL*) piece of homework.

préparatoire [pʀepaʀatwaʀ] *adj* preparatory.

préparer [pʀepaʀe] *vt* to prepare; (*café, repas*) to make; (*examen*) to prepare for; (*voyage, entreprise*) to plan; **se ~** *vi* (*orage, tragédie*) to brew, be in the air; **se ~ (à qch/à faire)** to prepare (o.s.) *ou* get ready (for sth/to do); **~ qch à qn** (*surprise etc*) to have sth in store for sb; **~ qn à qch** (*nouvelle etc*) to prepare sb for sth.

prépondérance [pʀepɔ̃deʀɑ̃s] *nf*: **~ (sur)** predominance (over).

prépondérant, e [pʀepɔ̃deʀɑ̃, -ɑ̃t] *adj* major, dominating; **voix ~e** casting vote.

préposé, e [pʀepoze] *adj*: **~ à** in charge of ♦ *nm/f* (*gén: employé*) employee; (*ADMIN: facteur*) postman/woman (*BRIT*), mailman/woman (*US*); (*de la douane etc*) official; (*de vestiaire*) attendant.

préposer [pʀepoze] *vt*: **~ qn à qch** to appoint sb to sth.

préposition [pʀepozisjɔ̃] *nf* preposition.

prérentrée [pʀeʀɑ̃tʀe] *nf* in-service training period before start of school term.

préretraite [pʀeʀətʀɛt] *nf* early retirement.

prérogative [pʀeʀɔgativ] *nf* prerogative.

près [pʀɛ] *adv* near, close; **~ de** *prép* near (to), close to; (*environ*) nearly, almost; **de ~** *adv* closely; **à 5 kg ~** to within about 5 kg; **à cela ~ que** apart from the fact that; **je ne suis pas ~ de lui pardonner** I'm nowhere near ready to forgive him; **on n'est pas à un jour ~** one day (either way) won't make any difference, we're not going to quibble over the odd day.

présage [pʀezaʒ] *nm* omen.

présager [pʀezaʒe] *vt* (*prévoir*) to foresee; (*annoncer*) to portend.

pré-salé, pl prés-salés [pʀesale] *nm* (*CULIN*) salt-meadow lamb.

presbyte [pʀɛsbit] *adj* long-sighted (*BRIT*), far-sighted (*US*).

presbytère [pʀɛsbitɛʀ] *nm* presbytery.

presbytérien, ne [pʀɛsbiteʀjɛ̃, -ɛn] *adj, nm/f* Presbyterian.

presbytie [pʀɛsbisi] *nf* long-sightedness (*BRIT*), far-sightedness (*US*).

prescience [pʀesjɑ̃s] *nf* prescience, foresight.

préscolaire [pʀeskɔlɛʀ] *adj* preschool *cpd*.

prescription [pʀɛskʀipsjɔ̃] *nf* (*instruction*) order, instruction; (*MÉD, JUR*) prescription.

prescrire [pʀɛskʀiʀ] *vt* to prescribe; **se ~** *vi* (*JUR*) to lapse.

prescrit, e [pʀɛskʀi, -it] *pp de* **prescrire** ♦ *adj* (*date etc*) stipulated.

préséance [pʀeseɑ̃s] *nf* precedence *no pl*.

présélection [pʀeselɛksjɔ̃] *nf* (*de candidats*) short-listing; **effectuer une ~** to draw up a shortlist.

présélectionner [pʀeselɛksjɔne] *vt* to preselect; (*dispositif*) to preset; (*candidats*) to make an initial selection from among, short-list (*BRIT*).

présence [pʀezɑ̃s] *nf* presence; (*au bureau etc*) attendance; **en ~** face to face; **en ~ de** in (the) presence of; (*fig*) in the face of; **faire acte de ~** to put in a token appearance; **~ d'esprit** presence of mind.

présent, e [pʀezɑ̃, -ɑ̃t] *adj, nm* present; (*ADMIN, COMM*): **la ~e lettre/loi** this letter/law ♦ *nm/f*: **les ~s** (*personnes*) those present ♦ *nf* (*COMM: lettre*): **la ~e** this letter; **à ~** now, at present; **dès à ~** here and now; **jusqu'à ~** up till now, until now; **à ~ que** now that.

présentable [pʀezɑ̃tabl(ə)] *adj* presentable.

présentateur, trice [pʀezɑ̃tatœʀ, -tʀis] *nm/f* presenter.

présentation [pʀezɑ̃tasjɔ̃] *nf* presentation; introduction; (*allure*) appearance.

présenter [pʀezɑ̃te] *vt* to present; (*invité, candidat*) to introduce; (*félicitations, condoléances*) to offer; (*montrer: billet, pièce d'identité*) to show, produce; (*faire inscrire: candidat*) to put forward; (*soumettre*) to submit ♦ *vi*: **~ mal/bien** to have an unattractive/a pleasing appearance; **se ~** *vi* (*sur convocation*) to report, come; (*se faire connaître*) to come forward; (*à une élection*) to stand; (*occasion*) to arise; **se ~ à un examen** to sit an exam; **se ~ bien/mal** to look good/not too good.

présentoir [pʀezɑ̃twaʀ] *nm* (*étagère*) display shelf (*pl* shelves); (*vitrine*) showcase; (*étal*) display stand.

préservatif [pʀezɛʀvatif] *nm* condom, sheath.

préservation [pʀezɛʀvasjɔ̃] *nf* protection, preservation.

préserver [pʀezɛʀve] *vt*: **~ de** (*protéger*) to protect from; (*sauver*) to save from.

présidence [pʀezidɑ̃s] *nf* presidency; chairmanship.

président [pʀezidɑ̃] *nm* (*POL*) president; (*d'une assemblée, COMM*) chairman; **~ directeur général (PDG)** chairman and managing director (*BRIT*), chairman and president (*US*); **~ du jury** (*JUR*) foreman of the jury; (*d'examen*) chief examiner.

présidente [pʀezidɑ̃t] *nf* president; (*femme du président*) president's wife; (*d'une réunion*) chairwoman.

présidentiable [pʀezidɑ̃sjabl(ə)] *adj, nm/f* potential president.

présidentiel, le [pʀezidɑ̃sjɛl] *adj* presidential; **~les** *nfpl* presidential election(s).

présider [pʀezide] *vt* to preside over; (*dîner*) to be the guest of honour (*BRIT*) *ou* honor (*US*) at; **~ à** *vt* to direct; to govern.

présomption [pʀezɔ̃psjɔ̃] *nf* presumption.

présomptueux, euse [prezɔ̃ptɥø, -øz] *adj* presumptuous.

presque [prɛsk(ə)] *adv* almost, nearly; ~ **rien** hardly anything; ~ **pas** hardly (at all); ~ **pas de** hardly any; **personne, ou** ~ next to nobody, hardly anyone; **la** ~ **totalité (de)** almost *ou* nearly all.

presqu'île [prɛskil] *nf* peninsula.

pressant, e [prɛsɑ̃, -ɑ̃t] *adj* urgent; (*personne*) insistent; **se faire** ~ to become insistent.

presse [prɛs] *nf* press; (*affluence*): **heures de** ~ busy times; **sous** ~ gone to press; **mettre sous** ~ to send to press; **avoir une bonne/ mauvaise** ~ to have a good/bad press; ~ **féminine** women's magazines *pl*; ~ **d'information** quality newspapers *pl*.

pressé, e [prese] *adj* in a hurry; (*air*) hurried; (*besogne*) urgent ♦ *nm*: **aller au plus** ~ to see to first things first; **être** ~ **de faire qch** to be in a hurry to do sth; **orange** ~**e** freshly squeezed orange juice.

presse-citron [prɛsitrɔ̃] *nm inv* lemon squeezer.

presse-fruits [prɛsfrɥi] *nm inv* lemon squeezer.

pressentiment [prɛsɑ̃timɑ̃] *nm* foreboding, premonition.

pressentir [prɛsɑ̃tir] *vt* to sense; (*prendre contact avec*) to approach.

presse-papiers [prɛspapje] *nm inv* paperweight.

presse-purée [prɛspyre] *nm inv* potato masher.

presser [prese] *vt* (*fruit, éponge*) to squeeze; (*interrupteur, bouton*) to press, push; (*allure, affaire*) to speed up; (*débiteur etc*) to press; (*inciter*): ~ **qn de faire** to urge *ou* press sb to do ♦ *vi* to be urgent; **se** ~ (*se hâter*) to hurry (up); (*se grouper*) to crowd; **rien ne presse** there's no hurry; **se** ~ **contre qn** to squeeze up against sb; ~ **le pas** to quicken one's step; ~ **qn entre ses bras** to squeeze sb tight.

pressing [presiŋ] *nm* (*repassage*) steampressing; (*magasin*) dry-cleaner's.

pression [prɛsjɔ̃] *nf* pressure; (*bouton*) press stud (*BRIT*), snap fastener; **faire** ~ **sur** to put pressure on; **sous** ~ pressurized, under pressure; (*fig*) keyed up; ~ **artérielle** blood pressure.

pressoir [prɛswar] *nm* (wine *ou* oil *etc*) press.

pressurer [presyre] *vt* (*fig*) to squeeze.

pressurisé, e [presyrize] *adj* pressurized.

prestance [prɛstɑ̃s] *nf* presence, imposing bearing.

prestataire [prɛstatɛr] *nm/f* person receiving benefits; (*COMM*): ~ **de services** provider of services.

prestation [prɛstasjɔ̃] *nf* (*allocation*) benefit; (*d'une assurance*) cover *no pl*; (*d'une entreprise*) service provided; (*d'un joueur, artiste*) performance; ~ **de serment** taking the oath; ~ **de service** provision of a service; ~**s familiales** ≈ child benefit.

preste [prɛst(ə)] *adj* nimble.

prestement [prɛstəmɑ̃] *adv* nimbly.

prestidigitateur, trice [prɛstidiʒitatœr, -tris] *nm/f* conjurer.

prestidigitation [prɛstidiʒitasjɔ̃] *nf* conjuring.

prestige [prɛstiʒ] *nm* prestige.

prestigieux, euse [prɛstiʒjø, -øz] *adj* prestigious.

présumer [prezyme] *vt*: ~ **que** to presume *ou* assume that; ~ **de** to overrate; ~ **qn coupable** to presume sb guilty.

présupposé [presypoze] *nm* presupposition.

présupposer [presypoze] *vt* to presuppose.

présupposition [presypozisjɔ̃] *nf* presupposition.

présure [prezyr] *nf* rennet.

prêt, e [prɛ, prɛt] *adj* ready ♦ *nm* lending *no pl*; (*somme prêtée*) loan; ~ **à faire** ready to do; ~ **à tout** ready for anything; ~ **sur gages** pawnbroking *no pl*.

prêt-à-porter, *pl* **prêts-à-porter** [prɛtaporte] *nm* ready-to-wear *ou* off-the-peg (*BRIT*) clothes *pl*.

prétendant [pretɑ̃dɑ̃] *nm* pretender; (*d'une femme*) suitor.

prétendre [pretɑ̃dr(ə)] *vt* (*affirmer*): ~ **que** to claim that; (*avoir l'intention de*): ~ **faire qch** to mean *ou* intend to do sth; ~ **à** *vt* (*droit, titre*) to lay claim to.

prétendu, e [pretɑ̃dy] *adj* (*supposé*) so-called.

prétendument [pretɑ̃dymɑ̃] *adv* allegedly.

prête-nom [prɛtnɔ̃] *nm* (*péj*) figurehead; (*COMM etc*) dummy.

prétentieux, euse [pretɑ̃sjø, -øz] *adj* pretentious.

prétention [pretɑ̃sjɔ̃] *nf* pretentiousness; (*exigence, ambition*) claim; **sans** ~ unpretentious.

prêter [prete] *vt* (*livres, argent*): ~ **qch (à)** to lend sth (to); (*supposer*): ~ **à qn** (*caractère, propos*) to attribute to sb ♦ *vi* (*aussi*: **se** ~: *tissu, cuir*) to give; ~ **à** (*commentaires etc*) to be open to, give rise to; **se** ~ **à** to lend o.s. (*ou* itself) to; (*manigances etc*) to go along with; ~ **assistance à** to give help to; ~ **attention** to pay attention; ~ **serment** to take the oath; ~ **l'oreille** to listen.

prêteur, euse [pretœr, -øz] *nm/f* moneylender; ~ **sur gages** pawnbroker.

prétexte [pretɛkst(ə)] *nm* pretext, excuse; **sous aucun** ~ on no account; **sous (le)** ~ **que/de** on the pretext that/of.

prétexter [pretɛkste] *vt* to give as a pretext *ou* an excuse.

prêtre [prɛtr(ə)] *nm* priest.

prêtre-ouvrier, *pl* **prêtres-ouvriers** [prɛtruvrije] *nm* worker-priest.

prêtrise [prɛtriz] *nf* priesthood.

preuve [prœv] *nf* proof; (*indice*) proof, evidence *no pl*; **jusqu'à** ~ **du contraire** until proved otherwise; **faire ~ de** to show; **faire ses ~s** to prove o.s. (*ou* itself); **~ matérielle** material evidence.

prévaloir [pʀevalwaʀ] *vi* to prevail; **se ~ de** *vt* to take advantage of; (*tirer vanité de*) to pride o.s. on.

prévarication [pʀevaʀikɑsjɔ̃] *nf* maladministration.

prévaut [pʀevo] *etc vb voir* **prévaloir**.

prévenances [pʀevnɑ̃s] *nfpl* thoughtfulness *sg*, kindness *sg*.

prévenant, e [pʀevnɑ̃, -ɑ̃t] *adj* thoughtful, kind.

prévenir [pʀevniʀ] *vt* (*avertir*): **~ qn (de)** to warn sb (about); (*informer*): **~ qn (de)** to tell *ou* inform sb (about); (*éviter*) to avoid, prevent; (*anticiper*) to anticipate; (*influencer*): **~ qn contre** to prejudice sb against.

préventif, ive [pʀevɑ̃tif, -iv] *adj* preventive.

prévention [pʀevɑ̃sjɔ̃] *nf* prevention; (*préjugé*) prejudice; (*JUR*) custody, detention; **~ routière** road safety.

prévenu, e [pʀevny] *nm/f* (*JUR*) defendant, accused.

prévisible [pʀevizibl(ə)] *adj* foreseeable.

prévision [pʀevizjɔ̃] *nf*: **~s** predictions; (*météorologiques, économiques*) forecast *sg*; **en ~ de** in anticipation of; **~s météorologiques** *ou* **du temps** weather forecast *sg*.

prévisionnel, le [pʀevizjɔnɛl] *adj* concerned with future requirements.

prévit [pʀevi] *etc vb voir* **prévoir**.

prévoir [pʀevwaʀ] *vt* (*deviner*) to foresee; (*s'attendre à*) to expect, reckon on; (*prévenir*) to anticipate; (*organiser*) to plan; (*préparer, réserver*) to allow; **prévu pour 4 personnes** designed for 4 people; **prévu pour 10 h** scheduled for 10 o'clock.

prévoyance [pʀevwajɑ̃s] *nf* foresight; **société/caisse de ~** provident society/ contingency fund.

prévoyant, e [pʀevwajɑ̃, -ɑ̃t] *vb voir* **prévoir** ♦ *adj* gifted with (*ou* showing) foresight, far-sighted.

prévu, e [pʀevy] *pp de* **prévoir**.

prier [pʀije] *vi* to pray ♦ *vt* (*Dieu*) to pray to; (*implorer*) to beg; (*demander*): **~ qn de faire** to ask sb to do; (*inviter*): **~ qn à dîner** to invite sb to dinner; **se faire ~** to need coaxing *ou* persuading; **je vous en prie** (*allez-y*) please do; (*de rien*) don't mention it; **je vous prie de faire** please (would you) do.

prière [pʀijɛʀ] *nf* prayer; (*demande instante*) plea, entreaty; **"~ de faire ..."** "please do ...".

primaire [pʀimɛʀ] *adj* primary; (*péj: personne*) simple-minded; (: *idées*) simplistic ♦ *nm* (*SCOL*) primary education.

primauté [pʀimote] *nf* (*fig*) primacy.

prime [pʀim] *nf* (*bonification*) bonus; (*subside*) allowance; (*COMM: cadeau*) free gift; (*ASSURANCES, BOURSE*) premium ♦ *adj*: **de ~ abord** at first glance; **~ de risque** danger money *no pl*; **~ de transport** travel allowance.

primer [pʀime] *vt* (*l'emporter sur*) to prevail over; (*récompenser*) to award a prize to ♦ *vi* to dominate, prevail.

primesautier, ière [pʀimsotje, -jɛʀ] *adj* impulsive.

primeur [pʀimœʀ] *nf*: **avoir la ~ de** to be the first to hear (*ou* see *etc*); **~s** *nfpl* (*fruits, légumes*) early fruits and vegetables; **marchand de ~** greengrocer (*BRIT*), produce dealer (*US*).

primevère [pʀimvɛʀ] *nf* primrose.

primitif, ive [pʀimitif, -iv] *adj* primitive; (*originel*) original ♦ *nm/f* primitive.

primo [pʀimo] *adv* first (of all), firstly.

primordial, e, aux [pʀimɔʀdjal, -o] *adj* essential, primordial.

prince [pʀɛ̃s] *nm* prince; **~ charmant** Prince Charming; **~ de Galles** *nm inv* (*tissu*) check cloth; **~ héritier** crown prince.

princesse [pʀɛ̃sɛs] *nf* princess.

princier, ière [pʀɛ̃sje, -jɛʀ] *adj* princely.

principal, e, aux [pʀɛ̃sipal, -o] *adj* principal, main ♦ *nm* (*SCOL*) head(teacher) (*BRIT*), principal (*US*); (*essentiel*) main thing ♦ *nf* (*LING*): (**proposition**) **~e** main clause.

principalement [pʀɛ̃sipalmɑ̃] *adv* principally, mainly.

principauté [pʀɛ̃sipote] *nf* principality.

principe [pʀɛ̃sip] *nm* principle; **partir du ~ que** to work on the principle *ou* assumption that; **pour le ~** on principle, for the sake of it; **de ~** *adj* (*hostilité*) automatic; (*accord*) in principle; **par ~** on principle; **en ~** (*habituellement*) as a rule; (*théoriquement*) in principle.

printanier, ière [pʀɛ̃tanje, -jɛʀ] *adj* spring *cpd*; spring-like.

printemps [pʀɛ̃tɑ̃] *nm* spring; **au ~** in spring.

priori [pʀijɔʀi]: **a ~** *adv* at first glance; initially; a priori.

prioritaire [pʀijɔʀitɛʀ] *adj* having priority; (*AUTO*) having right of way; (*INFORM*) foreground.

priorité [pʀijɔʀite] *nf* (*AUTO*): **avoir la ~ (sur)** to have right of way (over); **~ à droite** right of way to vehicles coming from the right; **en ~** as a (matter of) priority.

pris, e [pʀi, pʀiz] *pp de* **prendre** ♦ *adj* (*place*) taken; (*billets*) sold; (*journée, mains*) full; (*personne*) busy; (*crème, ciment*) set; (*MÉD: enflammé*): **avoir le nez/la gorge ~(e)** to have a stuffy nose/a bad throat; (*saisi*): **être ~ de peur/de fatigue** to be stricken with fear/ overcome with fatigue.

prise [pʀiz] *nf* (*d'une ville*) capture; (*PÊCHE, CHASSE*) catch; (*de judo ou catch, point d'appui ou pour empoigner*) hold; (*ÉLEC: fiche*) plug; (: *femelle*) socket; (: *au mur*) point; **en ~**

(*AUTO*) in gear; **être aux ~s avec** to be grappling with; to be battling with; **lâcher ~** to let go; **donner ~ à** (*fig*) to give rise to; **avoir ~ sur qn** to have a hold over sb; **~ en charge** (*taxe*) pick-up charge; (*par la sécurité sociale*) *undertaking to reimburse costs;* **~ de contact** initial meeting, first contact; **~ de courant** power point; **~ d'eau** water (supply) point; tap; **~ multiple** adaptor; **~ d'otages** hostage-taking; **~ à partie** (*JUR*) *action against a judge;* **~ de sang** blood test; **~ de son** sound recording; **~ de tabac** pinch of snuff; **~ de terre** earth; **~ de vue** (*photo*) shot; (*action*): **~ de vue(s)** filming, shooting.

priser [pRize] *vt* (*tabac, héroïne*) to take; (*estimer*) to prize, value ♦ *vi* to take snuff.

prisme [pRism(ə)] *nm* prism.

prison [pRizɔ̃] *nf* prison; **aller/être en ~** to go to/be in prison *ou* jail; **faire de la ~** to serve time; **être condamné à 5 ans de ~** to be sentenced to 5 years' imprisonment *ou* 5 years in prison.

prisonnier, ière [pRizɔnje, -jɛR] *nm/f* prisoner ♦ *adj* captive; **faire qn ~** to take sb prisoner.

prit [pRi] *vb voir* **prendre**.

privatif, ive [pRivatif, -iv] *adj* (*jardin etc*) private; (*peine*) which deprives one of one's liberties.

privations [pRivasjɔ̃] *nfpl* privations, hardships.

privatisation [pRivatizasjɔ̃] *nf* privatization.

privatiser [pRivatize] *vt* to privatize.

privautés [pRivote] *nfpl* liberties.

privé, e [pRive] *adj* private; (*dépourvu*): **~ de** without, lacking; **en ~, dans le ~** in private.

priver [pRive] *vt*: **~ qn de** to deprive sb of; **se ~ de** to go without *ou* do without; **ne pas se ~ de faire** not to refrain from doing.

privilège [pRivilɛʒ] *nm* privilege.

privilégié, e [pRivileʒje] *adj* privileged.

privilégier [pRivileʒje] *vt* to favour (*BRIT*), favor (*US*).

prix [pRi] *nm* (*valeur*) price; (*récompense, SCOL*) prize; **mettre à ~** to set a reserve (*BRIT*) *ou* upset (*US*) price on; **au ~ fort** at a very high price; **acheter qch à ~ d'or** to pay a (small) fortune for sth; **hors de ~** exorbitantly priced; **à aucun ~** not at any price; **à tout ~** at all costs; **grand ~** (*SPORT*) Grand Prix; **~ d'achat/de vente/de revient** purchasing/selling/cost price; **~ conseillé** manufacturer's recommended price (MRP).

pro [pRo] *nm* (= *professionnel*) pro.

probabilité [pRobabilite] *nf* probability; **selon toute ~** in all probability.

probable [pRobabl(ə)] *adj* likely, probable.

probablement [pRobabləmɑ̃] *adv* probably.

probant, e [pRobɑ̃, -ɑ̃t] *adj* convincing.

probatoire [pRobatwaR] *adj* (*examen, test*) preliminary; (*stage*) probationary, trial *cpd.*

probité [pRobite] *nf* integrity, probity.

problématique [pRoblematik] *adj* problematic(al) ♦ *nf* problematics *sg;* (*problème*) problem.

problème [pRoblɛm] *nm* problem.

procédé [pRosede] *nm* (*méthode*) process; (*comportement*) behaviour *no pl* (*BRIT*), behavior *no pl* (*US*).

procéder [pRosede] *vi* to proceed; to behave; **~ à** *vt* to carry out.

procédure [pRosedyR] *nf* (*ADMIN, JUR*) procedure.

procès [pRosɛ] *nm* (*JUR*) trial; (*: poursuites*) proceedings *pl;* **être en ~ avec** to be involved in a lawsuit with; **faire le ~ de qn/ qch** (*fig*) to put sb/sth on trial; **sans autre forme de ~** without further ado.

processeur [pRosesœR] *nm* processor.

procession [pRosesjɔ̃] *nf* procession.

processus [pRosesys] *nm* process.

procès-verbal, aux [pRosɛvɛRbal, -o] *nm* (*constat*) statement; (*aussi: PV*): **avoir un ~** to get a parking ticket; to be booked; (*de réunion*) minutes *pl.*

prochain, e [pRoʃɛ̃, -ɛn] *adj* next; (*proche*) impending; near ♦ *nm* fellow man; **la ~e fois/semaine ~e** next time/week; **à la ~e!** (*fam*), **à la ~e fois** see you!, till the next time!; **un ~ jour** (some day) soon.

prochainement [pRoʃɛnmɑ̃] *adv* soon, shortly.

proche [pRoʃ] *adj* nearby; (*dans le temps*) imminent; close at hand; (*parent, ami*) close; **~s** *nmpl* (*parents*) close relatives, next of kin; (*amis*): **l'un de ses ~s** one of those close to him (*ou* her); **être ~ (de)** to be near, be close (to); **de ~ en ~** gradually.

Proche-Orient [pRoʃɔRjɑ̃] *nm*: **le ~** the Near East.

proclamation [pRoklamasjɔ̃] *nf* proclamation.

proclamer [pRoklame] *vt* to proclaim; (*résultat d'un examen*) to announce.

procréer [pRokRee] *vt* to procreate.

procuration [pRokyRasjɔ̃] *nf* proxy; power of attorney; **voter par ~** to vote by proxy.

procurer [pRokyRe] *vt* (*fournir*): **~ qch à qn** to get *ou* obtain sth for sb; (*causer: plaisir etc*): **~ qch à qn** to bring *ou* give sb sth; **se ~** *vt* to get.

procureur [pRokyRœR] *nm* public prosecutor; **~ général** public prosecutor (*in appeal court*).

prodigalité [pRodigalite] *nf* (*générosité*) generosity; (*extravagance*) extravagance, wastefulness.

prodige [pRodiʒ] *nm* (*miracle, merveille*) marvel, wonder; (*personne*) prodigy.

prodigieusement [pRodiʒjøzmɑ̃] *adv* tremendously.

prodigieux, euse [pRodiʒjø, -øz] *adj* prodigious; phenomenal.

prodigue [pRodig] *adj* (*généreux*) generous; (*dépensier*) extravagant, wasteful; **fils ~**

prodigal son.

prodiguer [pʀɔdige] *vt* (*argent, biens*) to be lavish with; (*soins, attentions*): ~ **qch à qn** to lavish sth on sb.

producteur, trice [pʀɔdyktœʀ, -tʀis] *adj*: ~ **de blé** wheat-producing; (*CINÉ*): **société productrice** film *ou* movie company ♦ *nm/f* producer.

productif, ive [pʀɔdyktif, -iv] *adj* productive.

production [pʀɔdyksjɔ̃] *nf* (*gén*) production; (*rendement*) output; (*produits*) products *pl*, goods *pl*; (*œuvres*): **la ~ dramatique du XVIIe siècle** the plays of the 17th century.

productivité [pʀɔdyktivite] *nf* productivity.

produire [pʀɔdɥiʀ] *vt, vi* to produce; **se ~** *vi* (*acteur*) to perform, appear; (*événement*) to happen, occur.

produit, e [pʀɔdɥi, -it] *pp de* **produire** ♦ *nm* (*gén*) product; ~ **d'entretien** cleaning product; ~ **national brut (PNB)** gross national product (GNP); ~ **net** net profit; ~ **pour la vaisselle** washing-up (*BRIT*) *ou* dish-washing (*US*) liquid; ~ **des ventes** income from sales; ~**s agricoles** farm produce *sg*; ~**s alimentaires** foodstuffs; ~**s de beauté** beauty products, cosmetics.

proéminent, e [pʀɔeminɑ̃, -ɑ̃t] *adj* prominent.

prof [pʀɔf] *nm* (*fam: = professeur*) teacher; professor; lecturer.

prof. [pʀɔf] *abr = professeur, professionnel*.

profane [pʀɔfan] *adj* (*REL*) secular; (*ignorant, non initié*) uninitiated ♦ *nm/f* layman.

profaner [pʀɔfane] *vt* to desecrate; (*fig: sentiment*) to defile; (*: talent*) to debase.

proférer [pʀɔfeʀe] *vt* to utter.

professer [pʀɔfese] *vt* to profess.

professeur [pʀɔfesœʀ] *nm* teacher; (*titulaire d'une chaire*) professor; ~ **(de faculté)** (university) lecturer.

profession [pʀɔfesjɔ̃] *nf* (*libérale*) profession; (*gén*) occupation; **faire ~ de** (*opinion, religion*) to profess; **de ~** by profession; "**sans ~**" "unemployed"; (*femme mariée*) "housewife".

professionnel, le [pʀɔfesjɔnɛl] *adj* professional ♦ *nm/f* professional; (*ouvrier qualifié*) skilled worker.

professoral, e, aux [pʀɔfesɔʀal, -o] *adj* professorial; **le corps ~** the teaching profession.

professorat [pʀɔfesɔʀa] *nm*: **le ~** the teaching profession.

profil [pʀɔfil] *nm* profile; (*d'une voiture*) line, contour; **de ~** in profile.

profilé, e [pʀɔfile] *adj* shaped; (*aile etc*) streamlined.

profiler [pʀɔfile] *vt* to streamline; **se ~** *vi* (*arbre, tour*) to stand out, be silhouetted.

profit [pʀɔfi] *nm* (*avantage*) benefit, advantage; (*COMM, FINANCE*) profit; **au ~ de** in aid of; **tirer** *ou* **retirer ~ de** to profit from; **mettre à ~** to take advantage of; to turn to good

account; ~**s et pertes** (*COMM*) profit and loss(es).

profitable [pʀɔfitabl(ə)] *adj* beneficial; profitable.

profiter [pʀɔfite] *vi*: ~ **de** to take advantage of; to make the most of; ~ **de ce que** ... to take advantage of the fact that ...; ~ **à** to be of benefit to, benefit; to be profitable to.

profiteur, euse [pʀɔfitœʀ, -øz] *nm/f* (*péj*) profiteer.

profond, e [pʀɔfɔ̃, -ɔ̃d] *adj* deep; (*méditation, mépris*) profound; **au plus ~ de** in the depths of, at the (very) bottom of; **la France ~e** the heartlands of France.

profondément [pʀɔfɔ̃demɑ̃] *adv* deeply; profoundly.

profondeur [pʀɔfɔ̃dœʀ] *nf* depth.

profusément [pʀɔfyzemɑ̃] *adv* profusely.

profusion [pʀɔfyzjɔ̃] *nf* profusion; **à ~** in plenty.

progéniture [pʀɔʒenityʀ] *nf* offspring *inv*.

progiciel [pʀɔʒisjɛl] *nm* (*INFORM*) (software) package; ~ **d'application** applications package, applications software *no pl*.

progouvernemental, e, aux [pʀɔguvɛʀnəmɑ̃tal, -o] *adj* pro-government *cpd*.

programmable [pʀɔgʀamabl(ə)] *adj* programmable.

programmateur, trice [pʀɔgʀamatœʀ, -tʀis] *nm/f* (*CINÉ, TV*) programme (*BRIT*) *ou* program (*US*) planner ♦ *nm* (*de machine à laver etc*) timer.

programmation [pʀɔgʀamɑsjɔ̃] *nf* programming.

programme [pʀɔgʀam] *nm* programme (*BRIT*), program (*US*); (*TV, RADIO*) program(me)s *pl*; (*SCOL*) syllabus, curriculum; (*INFORM*) program; **au ~ de ce soir** (*TV*) among tonight's program(me)s.

programmé, e [pʀɔgʀame] *adj*: **enseignement ~** programmed learning.

programmer [pʀɔgʀame] *vt* (*TV, RADIO*) to put on, show; (*organiser, prévoir*) to schedule; (*INFORM*) to program.

programmeur, euse [pʀɔgʀamœʀ, -øz] *nm/f* (computer) programmer.

progrès [pʀɔgʀɛ] *nm* progress *no pl*; **faire des/être en ~** to make/be making progress.

progresser [pʀɔgʀese] *vi* to progress; (*troupes etc*) to make headway *ou* progress.

progressif, ive [pʀɔgʀesif, -iv] *adj* progressive.

progression [pʀɔgʀesjɔ̃] *nf* progression; (*d'une troupe etc*) advance, progress.

progressiste [pʀɔgʀesist(ə)] *adj* progressive.

progressivement [pʀɔgʀesivmɑ̃] *adv* progressively.

prohiber [pʀɔibe] *vt* to prohibit, ban.

prohibitif, ive [pʀɔibitif, -iv] *adj* prohibitive.

prohibition [pʀɔibisjɔ̃] *nf* ban, prohibition; (*HIST*) Prohibition.

proie [pʀwa] *nf* prey *no pl*; **être la ~ de** to fall prey to; **être en ~ à** (*doutes, sentiment*) to be prey to; (*douleur, mal*) to be suffering.

projecteur [pʀɔʒɛktœʀ] *nm* projector; (*de théâtre, cirque*) spotlight.

projectile [pʀɔʒɛktil] *nm* missile; (*d'arme*) projectile, bullet (*ou* shell *etc*).

projection [pʀɔʒɛksjɔ̃] *nf* projection; showing; **conférence avec ~s** lecture with slides (*ou* a film).

projectionniste [pʀɔʒɛksjɔnist(ə)] *nm/f* (*CINÉ*) projectionist.

projet [pʀɔʒɛ] *nm* plan; (*ébauche*) draft; **faire des ~s** to make plans; **~ de loi** bill.

projeter [pʀɔʒte] *vt* (*envisager*) to plan; (*film, photos*) to project; (*passer*) to show; (*ombre, lueur*) to throw, cast, project; (*jeter*) to throw up (*ou* off *ou* out); **~ de faire qch** to plan to do sth.

prolétaire [pʀɔletɛʀ] *adj, nm/f* proletarian.

prolétariat [pʀɔletaʀja] *nm* proletariat.

prolétarien, -ne [pʀɔletaʀjɛ̃, -ɛn] *adj* proletarian.

prolifération [pʀɔlifeʀasjɔ̃] *nf* proliferation.

proliférer [pʀɔlifeʀe] *vi* to proliferate.

prolifique [pʀɔlifik] *adj* prolific.

prolixe [pʀɔliks(ə)] *adj* verbose.

prolo [pʀɔlo] *nm/f* (*fam: = prolétaire*) prole (*péj*).

prologue [pʀɔlɔg] *nm* prologue.

prolongateur [pʀɔlɔ̃gatœʀ] *nm* (*ÉLEC*) extension cable.

prolongation [pʀɔlɔ̃gasjɔ̃] *nf* prolongation; extension; **~s** *nfpl* (*FOOTBALL*) extra time *sg*.

prolongement [pʀɔlɔ̃ʒmã] *nm* extension; **~s** *nmpl* (*fig*) repercussions, effects; **dans le ~ de** running on from.

prolonger [pʀɔlɔ̃ʒe] *vt* (*débat, séjour*) to prolong; (*délai, billet, rue*) to extend; (*suj: chose*) to be a continuation *ou* an extension of; **se ~** *vi* to go on.

promenade [pʀɔmnad] *nf* walk (*ou* drive *ou* ride); **faire une ~** to go for a walk; **une ~ (à pied)/en voiture/à vélo** a walk/drive/ (bicycle) ride.

promener [pʀɔmne] *vt* (*personne, chien*) to take out for a walk; (*fig*) to carry around; to trail round; (*doigts, regard*): **~ qch sur** to run sth over; **se ~** *vi* (*à pied*) to go for (*ou* be out for) a walk; (*en voiture*) to go for (*ou* be out for) a drive; (*fig*): **se ~ sur** to wander over.

promeneur, euse [pʀɔmnœʀ, -øz] *nm/f* walker, stroller.

promenoir [pʀɔmənwaʀ] *nm* gallery, (covered) walkway.

promesse [pʀɔmɛs] *nf* promise; **~ d'achat** commitment to buy.

prometteur, euse [pʀɔmɛtœʀ, -øz] *adj* promising.

promettre [pʀɔmɛtʀ(ə)] *vt* to promise ♦ *vi* (*récolte, arbre*) to look promising; (*enfant, musicien*) to be promising; **se ~ de faire** to resolve *ou* mean to do; **~ à qn de faire** to promise sb that one will do.

promeus [pʀɔmø] *etc vb voir* **promouvoir**.

promis, e [pʀɔmi, -iz] *pp de* **promettre** ♦ *adj*: **être ~ à qch** (*destiné*) to be destined for sth.

promiscuité [pʀɔmiskɥite] *nf* crowding; lack of privacy.

promit [pʀɔmi] *vb voir* **promettre**.

promontoire [pʀɔmɔ̃twaʀ] *nm* headland.

promoteur, trice [pʀɔmɔtœʀ, -tʀis] *nm/f* (*instigateur*) instigator, promoter; **~ (immobilier)** property developer (*BRIT*), real estate promoter (*US*).

promotion [pʀɔmɔsjɔ̃] *nf* (*avancement*) promotion; (*SCOL*) year (*BRIT*), class; **en ~** (*COMM*) on promotion, on (special) offer.

promotionnel, le [pʀɔmɔsjɔnɛl] *adj* (*article*) on promotion, on (special) offer; (*vente*) promotional.

promouvoir [pʀɔmuvwaʀ] *vt* to promote.

prompt, e [pʀɔ̃, pʀɔ̃t] *adj* swift, rapid; (*intervention, changement*) sudden; **~ à faire qch** quick to do sth.

promptement [pʀɔ̃ptəmã] *adv* swiftly.

prompteur [pʀɔ̃tœʀ] *nm* ® Autocue ® (*BRIT*), Teleprompter ® (*US*).

promptitude [pʀɔ̃tityd] *nf* swiftness, rapidity.

promu, e [pʀɔmy] *pp de* **promouvoir**.

promulguer [pʀɔmylge] *vt* to promulgate.

prôner [pʀone] *vt* (*louer*) to laud, extol; (*préconiser*) to advocate, commend.

pronom [pʀɔnɔ̃] *nm* pronoun.

pronominal, e, aux [pʀɔnɔminal, -o] *adj* pronominal; (*verbe*) reflexive, pronominal.

prononcé, e [pʀɔnɔ̃se] *adj* pronounced, marked.

prononcer [pʀɔnɔ̃se] *vt* (*son, mot, jugement*) to pronounce; (*dire*) to utter; (*allocution*) to deliver ♦ *vi* (*JUR*) to deliver *ou* give a verdict; **~ bien/mal** to have a good/poor pronunciation; **se ~** *vi* to reach a decision, give a verdict; **se ~ sur** to give an opinion on; **se ~ contre** to come down against; **ça se prononce comment?** how do you pronounce this?

prononciation [pʀɔnɔ̃sjasjɔ̃] *nf* pronunciation.

pronostic [pʀɔnɔstik] *nm* (*MÉD*) prognosis (*pl* -oses); (*fig: aussi*: **~s**) forecast.

pronostiquer [pʀɔnɔstike] *vt* (*MÉD*) to prognosticate; (*annoncer, prévoir*) to forecast, foretell.

pronostiqueur, euse [pʀɔnɔstikœʀ, -øz] *nm/f* forecaster.

propagande [pʀɔpagãd] *nf* propaganda; **faire de la ~ pour qch** to plug *ou* push sth.

propagandiste [pʀɔpagãdist(ə)] *nm/f* propagandist.

propagation [pʀɔpagasjɔ̃] *nf* propagation.

propager [pʀɔpaʒe] *vt* to spread; **se ~** *vi* to spread; (*PHYSIQUE*) to be propagated.

propane [pʀɔpan] *nm* propane.

propension [prɔpɑ̃sjɔ̃] _nf:_ ~ **à (faire) qch** propensity to (do) sth.

prophète [prɔfɛt], **prophétesse** [prɔfetɛs] _nm/f_ prophet(ess).

prophétie [prɔfesi] _nf_ prophecy.

prophétique [prɔfetik] _adj_ prophetic.

prophétiser [prɔfetize] _vt_ to prophesy.

prophylactique [prɔfilaktik] _adj_ prophylactic.

propice [prɔpis] _adj_ favourable (_BRIT_), favorable (_US_).

proportion [prɔpɔʀsjɔ̃] _nf_ proportion; **il n'y a aucune** ~ **entre le prix demandé et le prix réel** the asking price bears no relation to the real price; **à** ~ **de** proportionally to, in proportion to; **en** ~ **(de)** in proportion (to); **hors de** ~ out of proportion; **toute(s)** ~**(s) gardée(s)** making due allowance(s).

proportionné, e [prɔpɔʀsjɔne] _adj:_ **bien** ~ well-proportioned; ~ **à** proportionate to.

proportionnel, le [prɔpɔʀsjɔnɛl] _adj_ proportional; ~ **à** proportional to ♦ _nf_ proportional representation.

proportionnellement [prɔpɔʀsjɔnɛlmɑ̃] _adv_ proportionally, proportionately.

proportionner [prɔpɔʀsjɔne] _vt:_ ~ **qch à** to proportion _ou_ adjust sth to.

propos [prɔpo] _nm_ (_paroles_) talk _no pl_, remark; (_intention, but_) intention, aim; (_sujet_): **à quel** ~**?** what about?; **à** ~ **de** about, regarding; **à tout** ~ for no reason at all; **à ce** ~ on that subject, in this connection; **à** ~ _adv_ by the way; (_opportunément_) (just) at the right moment; **hors de** ~, **mal à** ~ _adv_ at the wrong moment.

proposer [prɔpoze] _vt_ (_suggérer_): ~ **qch (à qn)/de faire** to suggest sth (to sb)/doing, propose sth (to sb)/to do; (_offrir_): ~ **qch à qn/de faire** to offer sb sth/to do; (_candidat_) to nominate, put forward; (_loi, motion_) to propose; **se** ~ **(pour faire)** to offer one's services (to do); **se** ~ **de faire** to intend _ou_ propose to do.

proposition [prɔpozisjɔ̃] _nf_ suggestion; proposal; offer; (_LING_) clause; **sur la** ~ **de** at the suggestion of; ~ **de loi** private bill.

propre [prɔpʀ(ə)] _adj_ clean; (_net_) neat, tidy; (_qui ne salit pas: chien, chat_) house-trained; (: _enfant_) toilet-trained; (_fig: honnête_) honest; (_possessif_) own; (_sens_) literal; (_particulier_): ~ **à** peculiar to, characteristic of; (_approprié_): ~ **à** suitable _ou_ appropriate for; (_de nature à_): ~ **à faire** likely to do, that will do ♦ _nm:_ **recopier au** ~ to make a fair copy of; (_particularité_): **le** ~ **de** the peculiarity of, the distinctive feature of; **au** ~ (_LING_) literally; **appartenir à qn en** ~ to belong to sb (exclusively); ~ **à rien** _nm/f_ (_péj_) good-for-nothing.

proprement [prɔpʀəmɑ̃] _adv_ cleanly; neatly, tidily; **à** ~ **parler** strictly speaking; **le village** ~ **dit** the actual village, the village itself.

propret, te [prɔpʀɛ, -ɛt] _adj_ neat and tidy, spick-and-span.

propreté [prɔpʀəte] _nf_ cleanliness, cleanness, neatness, tidiness.

propriétaire [prɔpʀijetɛʀ] _nm/f_ owner; (_d'hôtel etc_) proprietor/tress, owner; (_pour le locataire_) landlord/lady; ~ **(immobilier)** house-owner; householder; ~ **récoltant** grower; ~ **(terrien)** landowner.

propriété [prɔpʀijete] _nf_ (_droit_) ownership; (_objet, immeuble etc_) property _gén no pl_; (_villa_) residence, property; (_terres_) property _gén no pl_, land _gén no pl_; (_qualité, CHIMIE, MATH_) property; (_correction_) appropriateness, suitability; ~ **artistique et littéraire** artistic and literary copyright; ~ **industrielle** patent rights _pl_.

propulser [prɔpylse] _vt_ (_missile_) to propel; (_projeter_) to hurl, fling.

propulsion [prɔpylsjɔ̃] _nf_ propulsion.

prorata [prɔʀata] _nm inv:_ **au** ~ **de** in proportion to, on the basis of.

prorogation [prɔʀɔgasjɔ̃] _nf_ deferment; extension; adjournment.

proroger [prɔʀɔʒe] _vt_ to put back, defer; (_prolonger_) to extend; (_assemblée_) to adjourn, prorogue.

prosaïque [prɔzaik] _adj_ mundane, prosaic.

proscription [prɔskʀipsjɔ̃] _nf_ banishment; (_interdiction_) banning; prohibition.

proscrire [prɔskʀiʀ] _vt_ (_bannir_) to banish; (_interdire_) to ban, prohibit.

prose [pʀoz] _nf_ prose (_style_).

prosélyte [prɔzelit] _nm/f_ proselyte, convert.

prospecter [prɔspɛkte] _vt_ to prospect; (_COMM_) to canvass.

prospecteur-placier, _pl_ **prospecteurs-placiers** [prɔspɛktœʀplasje] _nm_ placement officer.

prospectif, ive [prɔspɛktif, -iv] _adj_ prospective.

prospectus [prɔspɛktys] _nm_ (_feuille_) leaflet; (_dépliant_) brochure, leaflet.

prospère [prɔspɛʀ] _adj_ prosperous; (_santé, entreprise_) thriving, flourishing.

prospérer [prɔspeʀe] _vi_ to thrive.

prospérité [prɔspeʀite] _nf_ prosperity.

prostate [prɔstat] _nf_ prostate (gland).

prosterner [prɔstɛʀne]: **se** ~ _vi_ to bow low, prostrate o.s.

prostituée [prɔstitɥe] _nf_ prostitute.

prostitution [prɔstitysjɔ̃] _nf_ prostitution.

prostré, e [prɔstʀe] _adj_ prostrate.

protagoniste [prɔtagɔnist(ə)] _nm_ protagonist.

protecteur, trice [prɔtɛktœʀ, -tʀis] _adj_ protective; (_air, ton: péj_) patronizing ♦ _nm/f_ (_défenseur_) protector; (_des arts_) patron.

protection [prɔtɛksjɔ̃] _nf_ protection; (_d'un personnage influent: aide_) patronage; **écran de** ~ protective screen; ~ **civile** state-financed civilian rescue service; ~ **maternelle et infantile (PMI)** social service concerned with child welfare.

protectionnisme [pʀɔtɛksjɔnism(ə)] nm protectionism.

protectionniste [pʀɔtɛksjɔnist(ə)] adj protectionist.

protégé, e [pʀɔteʒe] nm/f protégé/e.

protège-cahier [pʀɔtɛʒkaje] nm exercise book cover.

protéger [pʀɔteʒe] vt to protect; (aider, patronner: personne, arts) to be a patron of; (: carrière) to further; **se ~ de/contre** to protect o.s. from.

protéine [pʀɔtein] nf protein.

protestant, e [pʀɔtɛstɑ̃, -ɑ̃t] adj, nm/f Protestant.

protestantisme [pʀɔtɛstɑ̃tism(ə)] nm Protestantism.

protestataire [pʀɔtɛstatɛʀ] nm/f protestor.

protestation [pʀɔtɛstɑsjɔ̃] nf (plainte) protest; (déclaration) protestation, profession.

protester [pʀɔtɛste] vi: **~ (contre)** to protest (against ou about); **~ de** (son innocence, sa loyauté) to protest.

prothèse [pʀɔtɛz] nf artificial limb, prosthesis (pl -ses); **~ dentaire** (appareil) denture; (science) dental engineering.

protocolaire [pʀɔtɔkɔlɛʀ] adj formal; (questions, règles) of protocol.

protocole [pʀɔtɔkɔl] nm protocol; (fig) etiquette; **~ d'accord** draft treaty; **~ opératoire** (MÉD) operating procedure.

prototype [pʀɔtɔtip] nm prototype.

protubérance [pʀɔtybeʀɑ̃s] nf bulge, protuberance.

protubérant, e [pʀɔtybeʀɑ̃, -ɑ̃t] adj protruding, bulging, protuberant.

proue [pʀu] nf bow(s pl), prow.

prouesse [pʀuɛs] nf feat.

prouver [pʀuve] vt to prove.

provenance [pʀɔvnɑ̃s] nf origin; (de mot, coutume) source; **avion en ~ de** plane (arriving) from.

provençal, e, aux [pʀɔvɑ̃sal, -o] adj Provençal ♦ nm (LING) Provençal.

Provence [pʀɔvɑ̃s] nf: **la ~** Provence.

provenir [pʀɔvniʀ]: **~ de** vt to come from; (résulter de) to be due to, be the result of.

proverbe [pʀɔvɛʀb(ə)] nm proverb.

proverbial, e, aux [pʀɔvɛʀbjal, -o] adj proverbial.

providence [pʀɔvidɑ̃s] nf: **la ~** providence.

providentiel, le [pʀɔvidɑ̃sjɛl] adj providential.

province [pʀɔvɛ̃s] nf province.

provincial, e, aux [pʀɔvɛ̃sjal, -o] adj, nm/f provincial.

proviseur [pʀɔvizœʀ] nm ≈ head(teacher) (BRIT), ≈ principal (US).

provision [pʀɔvizjɔ̃] nf (réserve) stock, supply; (avance: à un avocat, avoué) retainer, retaining fee; (COMM) funds pl (in account); reserve; **~s** nfpl (vivres) provisions, food no pl; **faire ~ de** to stock up with; **placard** ou **armoire à ~s** food cupboard.

provisoire [pʀɔvizwaʀ] adj temporary; (JUR) provisional; **mise en liberté ~** release on bail.

provisoirement [pʀɔvizwaʀmɑ̃] adv temporarily, for the time being.

provocant, e [pʀɔvɔkɑ̃, -ɑ̃t] adj provocative.

provocateur, trice [pʀɔvɔkatœʀ, -tʀis] adj provocative ♦ nm (meneur) agitator.

provocation [pʀɔvɔkasjɔ̃] nf provocation.

provoquer [pʀɔvɔke] vt (défier) to provoke; (causer) to cause, bring about; (: curiosité) to arouse, give rise to; (: aveux) to prompt, elicit; (inciter): **~ qn à** to incite sb to.

prox. abr = **proximité**.

proxénète [pʀɔksenɛt] nm procurer.

proxénétisme [pʀɔksenetism(ə)] nm procuring.

proximité [pʀɔksimite] nf nearness, closeness, proximity; (dans le temps) imminence, closeness; **à ~** near ou close by; **à ~ de** near (to), close to.

prude [pʀyd] adj prudish.

prudemment [pʀydamɑ̃] adv (voir prudent) carefully; cautiously; prudently; wisely, sensibly.

prudence [pʀydɑ̃s] nf carefulness; caution; prudence; **avec ~** carefully; cautiously; wisely; **par (mesure de) ~** as a precaution.

prudent, e [pʀydɑ̃, -ɑ̃t] adj (pas téméraire) careful, cautious, prudent; (: en général) safety-conscious; (sage, conseillé) wise, sensible; (réservé) cautious; **ce n'est pas ~** it's risky; it's not sensible; **soyez ~** take care, be careful.

prune [pʀyn] nf plum.

pruneau, x [pʀyno] nm prune.

prunelle [pʀynɛl] nf pupil; (œil) eye; (BOT) sloe; (eau de vie) sloe gin.

prunier [pʀynje] nm plum tree.

Prusse [pʀys] nf: **la ~** Prussia.

PS sigle m = **parti socialiste**; (= post-scriptum) PS.

psalmodier [psalmɔdje] vt to chant; (fig) to drone out.

psaume [psom] nm psalm.

pseudonyme [psødɔnim] nm (gén) fictitious name; (d'écrivain) pseudonym, pen name; (de comédien) stage name.

PSIG sigle m (= Peloton de surveillance et d'intervention de gendarmerie) type of police commando squad.

PSU sigle m = **parti socialiste unifié**.

psy [psi] nm/f (fam, péj: = psychiatre, psychologue) shrink.

psychanalyse [psikanaliz] nf psychoanalysis.

psychanalyser [psikanalize] vt to psychoanalyze; **se faire ~** to undergo (psycho)analysis.

psychanalyste [psikanalist(ə)] nm/f psychoanalyst.

psychanalytique [psikanalitik] adj psychoanalytical.

psychédélique [psikedelik] adj psychedelic.

psychiatre [psikjatʀ(ə)] *nm/f* psychiatrist.
psychiatrie [psikjatʀi] *nf* psychiatry.
psychiatrique [psikjatʀik] *adj* psychiatric; (*hôpital*) mental, psychiatric.
psychique [psiʃik] *adj* psychological.
psychisme [psiʃism(ə)] *nm* psyche.
psychologie [psikɔlɔʒi] *nf* psychology.
psychologique [psikɔlɔʒik] *adj* psychological.
psychologiquement [psikɔlɔʒikmɑ̃] *adv* psychologically.
psychologue [psikɔlɔg] *nm/f* psychologist; **être ~** (*fig*) to be a good psychologist.
psychomoteur, trice [psikɔmɔtœʀ, -tʀis] *adj* psychomotor.
psychopathe [psikɔpat] *nm/f* psychopath.
psychopédagogie [psikɔpedagɔʒi] *nf* educational psychology.
psychose [psikoz] *nf* (*MÉD*) psychosis (*pl* -ses); (*obsession, idée fixe*) obsessive fear.
psychosomatique [psikɔsɔmatik] *adj* psychosomatic.
psychothérapie [psikɔteʀapi] *nf* psychotherapy.
psychotique [psikɔtik] *adj* psychotic.
PTCA *sigle m = poids total en charge autorisé.*
Pte *abr* = **Porte.**
pte *abr* (= *pointe*) pt.
PTMA *sigle m* (= *poids total maximum autorisé*) maximum loaded weight.
PTT *sigle fpl voir* **poste.**
pu [py] *pp de* **pouvoir.**
puanteur [pɥɑ̃tœʀ] *nf* stink, stench.
pub [pyb] *nf* (*fam*: = *publicité*): **la ~** advertising.
pubère [pybɛʀ] *adj* pubescent.
puberté [pybɛʀte] *nf* puberty.
pubis [pybis] *nm* (*bas-ventre*) pubes *pl*; (*os*) pubis.
public, ique [pyblik] *adj* public; (*école, instruction*) state *cpd*; (*scrutin*) open ♦ *nm* public; (*assistance*) audience; **en ~** in public; **le grand ~** the general public.
publication [pyblikasjɔ̃] *nf* publication.
publiciste [pyblisist(ə)] *nm/f* adman.
publicitaire [pyblisitɛʀ] *adj* advertising *cpd*; (*film, voiture*) publicity *cpd*; (*vente*) promotional ♦ *nm* adman; **rédacteur ~** copywriter.
publicité [pyblisite] *nf* (*méthode, profession*) advertising; (*annonce*) advertisement; (*révélations*) publicity.
publier [pyblije] *vt* to publish; (*nouvelle*) to publicize, make public.
publipostage [pyblipɔstaʒ] *nm* mailshot, (mass) mailing.
publique [pyblik] *adj f voir* **public.**
publiquement [pyblikmɑ̃] *adv* publicly.
puce [pys] *nf* flea; (*INFORM*) chip; (*marché aux*) **~s** flea market *sg*; **mettre la ~ à l'oreille de qn** to give sb something to think about.
puceau, x [pyso] *adj m*: **être ~** to be a virgin.
pucelle [pysɛl] *adj f*: **être ~** to be a virgin.

puceron [pysʀɔ̃] *nm* aphid.
pudeur [pydœʀ] *nf* modesty.
pudibond, e [pydibɔ̃, -ɔ̃d] *adj* prudish.
pudique [pydik] *adj* (*chaste*) modest; (*discret*) discreet.
pudiquement [pydikmɑ̃] *adv* modestly.
puer [pɥe] (*péj*) *vi* to stink ♦ *vt* to stink of, reek of.
puéricultrice [pɥeʀikyltʀis] *nf* ≈ nursery nurse.
puériculture [pɥeʀikyltyʀ] *nf* infant care.
puéril, e [pɥeʀil] *adj* childish.
puérilement [pɥeʀilmɑ̃] *adv* childishly.
puérilité [pɥeʀilite] *nf* childishness; (*acte, idée*) childish thing.
pugilat [pyʒila] *nm* (*fist*) fight.
puis [pɥi] *vb voir* **pouvoir** ♦ *adv* (*ensuite*) then; (*dans une énumération*) next; (*en outre*): **et ~** and (then); **et ~ (après ou quoi)?** so (what)?
puisard [pɥizaʀ] *nm* (*égout*) cesspool.
puiser [pɥize] *vt*: **~ (dans)** to draw (from); **~ dans qch** to dip into sth.
puisque [pɥisk(ə)] *conj* since; (*valeur intensive*): **~ je te le dis!** I'm telling you!
puissamment [pɥisamɑ̃] *adv* powerfully.
puissance [pɥisɑ̃s] *nf* power; **en ~** *adj* potential; **2 (à la) ~ 5** 2 to the power (of) 5.
puissant, e [pɥisɑ̃, -ɑ̃t] *adj* powerful.
puisse [pɥis] *etc vb voir* **pouvoir.**
puits [pɥi] *nm* well; **~ artésien** artesian well; **~ de mine** mine shaft; **~ de science** fount of knowledge.
pull(-over) [pyl(ɔvœʀ)] *nm* sweater, jumper (*BRIT*).
pulluler [pylyle] *vi* to swarm; (*fig: erreurs*) to abound, proliferate.
pulmonaire [pylmɔnɛʀ] *adj* lung *cpd*; (*artère*) pulmonary.
pulpe [pylp(ə)] *nf* pulp.
pulsation [pylsasjɔ̃] *nf* (*MÉD*) beat.
pulsé [pylse] *adj m*: **chauffage à air ~** warm air heating.
pulsion [pylsjɔ̃] *nf* (*PSYCH*) drive, urge.
pulvérisateur [pylveʀizatœʀ] *nm* spray.
pulvérisation [pylveʀizasjɔ̃] *nf* spraying.
pulvériser [pylveʀize] *vt* (*solide*) to pulverize; (*liquide*) to spray; (*fig: anéantir: adversaire*) to pulverize; (: *record*) to smash, shatter; (: *argument*) to demolish.
puma [pyma] *nm* puma, cougar.
punaise [pynɛz] *nf* (*ZOOL*) bug; (*clou*) drawing pin (*BRIT*), thumb tack (*US*).
punch [pɔ̃ʃ] *nm* (*boisson*) punch; [pœnʃ] (*BOXE*) punching ability; (*fig*) punch.
punching-ball [pœnʃiŋbol] *nm* punchball.
punir [pyniʀ] *vt* to punish; **~ qn de qch** to punish sb for sth.
punitif, ive [pynitif, -iv] *adj* punitive.
punition [pynisjɔ̃] *nf* punishment.
pupille [pypij] *nf* (*ANAT*) pupil ♦ *nm/f* (*enfant*) ward; **~ de l'État** child in care; **~ de la Nation** war orphan.

pupitre [pypitR(ə)] *nm* (*SCOL*) desk; (*REL*) lectern; (*de chef d'orchestre*) rostrum; (*INFORM*) console; ~ **de commande** control panel.

pupitreur, euse [pypitRœR, -øz] *nm/f* (*INFORM*) (computer) operator, keyboarder.

pur, e [pyR] *adj* pure; (*vin*) undiluted; (*whisky*) neat; (*intentions*) honourable (*BRIT*), honorable (*US*) ♦ *nm* (*personne*) hard-liner; **en ~e perte** fruitlessly, to no avail.

purée [pyRe] *nf*: ~ **(de pommes de terre)** ≈ mashed potatoes *pl*; ~ **de marrons** chestnut purée; ~ **de pois** (*fig*) peasoup(er).

purement [pyRmɑ̃] *adv* purely.

pureté [pyRte] *nf* purity.

purgatif [pyRgatif] *nm* purgative, purge.

purgatoire [pyRgatwaR] *nm* purgatory.

purge [pyRʒ(ə)] *nf* (*POL*) purge; (*MÉD*) purging *no pl*; purge.

purger [pyRʒe] *vt* (*radiateur*) to flush (out), drain; (*circuit hydraulique*) to bleed; (*MÉD, POL*) to purge; (*JUR: peine*) to serve.

purification [pyRifikasjɔ̃] *nf* (*de l'eau*) purification; ~ **ethnique** ethnic cleansing.

purifier [pyRifje] *vt* to purify; (*TECH: métal*) to refine.

purin [pyRɛ̃] *nm* liquid manure.

puriste [pyRist(ə)] *nm/f* purist.

puritain, e [pyRitɛ̃, -ɛn] *adj, nm/f* Puritan.

puritanisme [pyRitanism(ə)] *nm* Puritanism.

pur-sang [pyRsɑ̃] *nm inv* thoroughbred, pure-bred.

purulent, e [pyRylɑ̃, -ɑ̃t] *adj* purulent.

pus [py] *vb voir* **pouvoir** ♦ *nm* pus.

pusillanime [pyzilanim] *adj* fainthearted.

pustule [pystyl] *nf* pustule.

putain [pytɛ̃] *nf* (*fam!*) whore (*!*); **ce/cette ~ de ...** this bloody (*BRIT*) *ou* goddamn (*US*) ... (*!*).

putois [pytwa] *nm* polecat; **crier comme un ~** to yell one's head off.

putréfaction [pytRefaksjɔ̃] *nf* putrefaction.

putréfier [pytRefje] *vt*, **se ~** *vi* to putrefy, rot.

putride [pytRid] *adj* putrid.

putsch [putʃ] *nm* (*POL*) putsch.

puzzle [pœzl(ə)] *nm* jigsaw (puzzle).

PV *sigle m* = **procès-verbal**.

PVC *sigle f* (= *polychlorure de vinyle*) PVC.

PVD *sigle mpl* (= *pays en voie de développement*) developing countries.

Px *abr* = **prix**.

pygmée [pigme] *nm* pygmy.

pyjama [piʒama] *nm* pyjamas *pl*, pair of pyjamas.

pylône [pilon] *nm* pylon.

pyramide [piRamid] *nf* pyramid.

pyrénéen, ne [piReneɛ̃, -ɛn] *adj* Pyrenean.

Pyrénées [piRene] *nfpl*: **les ~** the Pyrenees.

pyrex [piRɛks] *nm* ® Pyrex ®.

pyrogravure [piRɔgRavyR] *nf* poker-work.

pyromane [piRɔman] *nm/f* arsonist.

python [pitɔ̃] *nm* python.

Q q

Q, q [ky] *nm inv* Q, q ♦ *abr* (= *quintal*) q; **Q comme Quintal** Q for Queen.

Qatar [kataR] *nm*: **le ~** Qatar.

qcm *sigle m* (= *questionnaire à choix multiple*) multiple choice question paper.

QG *sigle m* (= *quartier général*) HQ.

QHS *sigle m* (= *quartier de haute sécurité*) high-security wing *ou* prison.

QI *sigle m* (= *quotient intellectuel*) IQ.

qqch. *abr* = *quelque chose*) sth.

qqe(s) *abr* = **quelque(s)**.

qqn *abr* (= *quelqu'un*) sb, s.o.

quadragénaire [kadRaʒenɛR] *nm/f* (*de quarante ans*) forty-year-old; (*de quarante à cinquante ans*) man/woman in his/her forties.

quadrangulaire [kwadRɑ̃gylɛR] *adj* quadrangular.

quadrature [kwadRatyR] *nf*: **c'est la ~ du cercle** it's like trying to square the circle.

quadrichromie [kwadRikRɔmi] *nf* four-colour (*BRIT*) *ou* -color (*US*) printing.

quadrilatère [k(w)adRilatɛR] *nm* (*GÉOM, MIL*) quadrilateral; (*terrain*) four-sided area.

quadrillage [kadRijaʒ] *nm* (*lignes etc*) square pattern, criss-cross pattern.

quadrillé, e [kadRije] *adj* (*papier*) squared.

quadriller [kadRije] *vt* (*papier*) to mark out in squares; (*POLICE: ville, région etc*) to keep under tight control, be positioned throughout.

quadrimoteur [k(w)adRimɔtœR] *nm* four-engined plane.

quadripartite [kwadRipaRtit] *adj* (*entre pays*) four-power; (*entre partis*) four-party.

quadriphonie [kadRifɔni] *nf* quadraphony.

quadriréacteur [k(w)adRiReaktœR] *nm* four-engined jet.

quadrupède [k(w)adRypɛd] *nm* quadruped.

quadruple [k(w)adRypl(ə)] *nm*: **le ~ de** four times as much as.

quadrupler [k(w)adRyple] *vt, vi* to quadruple, increase fourfold.

quadruplés, ées [k(w)adRyple] *nm/fpl* quadruplets, quads.

quai [ke] *nm* (*de port*) quay; (*de gare*) platform; (*de cours d'eau, canal*) embankment; **être à ~** (*navire*) to be alongside; (*train*) to be in the station; **le Q~ d'Orsay** *offices of the French Ministry for Foreign Affairs*; **le Q~ des Orfèvres** *central police headquarters*.

qualifiable [kalifjabl(ə)] *adj*: **ce n'est pas ~** it defies description.

qualificatif, ive [kalifikatif, -iv] *adj* (*LING*) qualifying ♦ *nm* (*terme*) term; (*LING*) qualifier.

qualification [kalifikɑsjɔ̃] *nf* qualification.

qualifier [kalifje] *vt* to qualify; (*appeler*): ~ **qch/qn de** to describe sth/sb as; **se** ~ *vi* (*SPORT*) to qualify; **être qualifié pour** to be qualified for.

qualitatif, ive [kalitatif, -iv] *adj* qualitative.

qualité [kalite] *nf* quality; (*titre, fonction*) position; **en** ~ **de** in one's capacity as; **ès** ~**s** in an official capacity; **avoir** ~ **pour** to have authority to; **de** ~ *adj* quality *cpd*; **rapport** ~-**prix** value (for money).

quand [kɑ̃] *conj, adv* when; ~ **je serai riche** when I'm rich; ~ **même** (*cependant, pourtant*) nevertheless; (*tout de même*) all the same; really; ~ **bien même** even though.

quant [kɑ̃]: ~ **à** *prép* (*pour ce qui est de*) as for, as to; (*au sujet de*) regarding.

quant-à-soi [kɑ̃taswa] *nm*: **rester sur son** ~ to remain aloof.

quantième [kɑ̃tjɛm] *nm* date, day (of the month).

quantifiable [kɑ̃tifjabl(ə)] *adj* quantifiable.

quantifier [kɑ̃tifje] *vt* to quantify.

quantitatif, ive [kɑ̃titatif, -iv] *adj* quantitative.

quantitativement [kɑ̃titativmɑ̃] *adv* quantitatively.

quantité [kɑ̃tite] *nf* quantity, amount; (*SCIENCE*) quantity; (*grand nombre*): **une** *ou* **des** ~**(s)** de a great deal of; a lot of; **en grande** ~ in large quantities; **en** ~**s industrielles** in vast amounts; **du travail en** ~ a great deal of work; ~ **de** many.

quarantaine [kaʀɑ̃tɛn] *nf* (*isolement*) quarantine; (*âge*): **avoir la** ~ to be around forty; (*nombre*): **une** ~ (**de**) forty or so, about forty; **mettre en** ~ to put into quarantine; (*fig*) to send to Coventry (*BRIT*), ostracize.

quarante [kaʀɑ̃t] *num* forty.

quarantième [kaʀɑ̃tjɛm] *num* fortieth.

quark [kwaʀk] *nm* quark.

quart [kaʀ] *nm* (*fraction*) quarter; (*surveillance*) watch; (*partie*): **un** ~ **de poulet/fromage** a chicken quarter/a quarter of a cheese; **un** ~ **de beurre** a quarter kilo of butter, ≈ a half pound of butter; **un** ~ **de vin** a quarter litre of wine; **une livre un** ~ *ou* **et** ~ one and a quarter pounds; **le** ~ **de** a quarter of; ~ **d'heure** quarter of an hour; **2 h et** *ou* **un** ~ (a) quarter past 2, (a) quarter after 2 (*US*); **il est le** ~ it's (a) quarter past *ou* after (*US*); **une heure moins le** ~ (a) quarter to one, (a) quarter of one (*US*); **il est moins le** ~ it's (a) quarter to; **être de/prendre le** ~ to keep/take the watch; ~ **de tour** quarter turn; **au** ~ **de tour** (*fig*) straight off; ~**s de finale** (*SPORT*) quarter finals.

quarté [kaʀte] *nm* (*COURSES*) system of forecast betting giving first four horses.

quarteron [kaʀtəʀɔ̃] *nm* (*péj*) small bunch, handful.

quartette [kwaʀtɛt] *nm* quartet(te).

quartier [kaʀtje] *nm* (*de ville*) district, area; (*de bœuf, de la lune*) quarter; (*de fruit, fromage*) piece; ~**s** *nmpl* (*MIL, BLASON*) quarters; **cinéma/salle de** ~ local cinema/hall; **avoir** ~ **libre** to be free; (*MIL*) to have leave from barracks; **ne pas faire de** ~ to spare no one, give no quarter; ~ **commerçant/résidentiel** shopping/residential area; ~ **général** (**QG**) headquarters (HQ).

quartier-maître [kaʀtjemɛtʀ(ə)] *nm* ≈ leading seaman.

quartz [kwaʀts] *nm* quartz.

quasi [kazi] *adv* almost, nearly ♦ *préfixe*: ~-**certitude** near certainty.

quasiment [kazimɑ̃] *adv* almost, very nearly.

quaternaire [kwatɛʀnɛʀ] *adj* (*GÉO*) Quaternary.

quatorze [katɔʀz(ə)] *num* fourteen.

quatorzième [katɔʀzjɛm] *num* fourteenth.

quatrain [katʀɛ̃] *nm* quatrain.

quatre [katʀ(ə)] *num* four; **à** ~ **pattes** on all fours; **tiré à** ~ **épingles** dressed up to the nines; **faire les** ~ **cent coups** to be a bit wild; **se mettre en** ~ **pour qn** to go out of one's way for sb; ~ **à** ~ (*monter, descendre*) four at a time; **à** ~ **mains** (*jouer*) four-handed.

quatre-vingt-dix [katʀəvɛ̃dis] *num* ninety.

quatre-vingts [katʀəvɛ̃] *num* eighty.

quatrième [katʀijɛm] *num* fourth.

quatuor [kwatɥɔʀ] *nm* quartet(te).

=== *MOT-CLÉ*

que [kə] *conj* **1** (*introduisant complétive*) that; **il sait** ~ **tu es là** he knows (that) you're here; **je veux** ~ **tu acceptes** I want you to accept; **il a dit** ~ **oui** he said he would (*ou* it was *etc*)

2 (*reprise d'autres conjonctions*): **quand il rentrera et qu'il aura mangé** when he gets back and (when) he has eaten; **si vous y allez ou** ~ **vous** ... if you go there or if you ...

3 (*en tête de phrase: hypothèse, souhait etc*): **qu'il le veuille ou non** whether he likes it or not; **qu'il fasse ce qu'il voudra!** let him do as he pleases!

4 (*but*): **tenez-le qu'il ne tombe pas** hold it so (that) it doesn't fall

5 (*après comparatif*) than; as; *voir aussi* **plus**; **aussi**; **autant** *etc*

6 (*seulement*): **ne** ... ~ only; **il ne boit** ~ **de l'eau** he only drinks water

7 (*temps*): **elle venait à peine de sortir qu'il se mit à pleuvoir** she had just gone out when it started to rain, no sooner had she gone out than it started to rain; **il y a 4 ans qu'il est parti** it is 4 years since he left, he left 4 years ago

◆ adv (exclamation): **qu'il** ou **qu'est-ce qu'il est bête/court vite!** he's so silly!/he runs so fast!; ~ **de livres!** what a lot of books!

◆ pron **1** (relatif: personne) whom; (: chose) that, which; **l'homme** ~ **je vois** the man (whom) I see; **le livre** ~ **tu vois** the book (that ou which) you see; **un jour** ~ **j'étais** ... a day when I was ...

2 (interrogatif) what; ~ **fais-tu?, qu'est-ce** ~ **tu fais?** what are you doing?; **qu'est-ce** ~ **c'est?** what is it?, what's that?; ~ **faire?** what can one do?; ~ **préfères-tu, celui-ci** ou **celui-là?** which (one) do you prefer, this one or that one?

Québec [kebɛk] n (ville) Quebec ◆ nm: **le** ~ Quebec (Province).

québécois, e [kebekwa, -waz] adj Quebec cpd ◆ nm (LING) Quebec French ◆ nm/f: **Q**~, **e** Quebecois, Quebec(k)er.

================= MOT-CLÉ

quel, quelle [kɛl] adj **1** (interrogatif: personne) who; (: chose) what; which; ~ **est cet homme?** who is this man?; ~ **est ce livre?** what is this book?; ~ **livre/homme?** what book/man?; (parmi un certain choix) which book/man?; ~**s acteurs préférez-vous?** which actors do you prefer?; **dans** ~**s pays êtes-vous allé** which ou what countries did you go to?

2 (exclamatif): **quelle surprise/coïncidence!** what a surprise/coincidence!

3: **quel(le) que soit coupable** whoever is guilty; ~ **que soit votre avis** whatever your opinion (may be).

quelconque [kɛlkɔ̃k] adj (médiocre) indifferent, poor; (sans attrait) ordinary, plain; (indéfini): **un ami/prétexte** ~ some friend/pretext or other; **un livre** ~ **suffira** any book will do; **pour une raison** ~ for some reason (or other).

================= MOT-CLÉ

quelque [kɛlkə] adj **1** some; a few; (tournure interrogative) any; ~ **espoir** some hope; **il a** ~**s amis** he has a few ou some friends; **a-t-il** ~**s amis?** has he any friends?; **les** ~**s livres qui** the few books which; **20 kg et** ~**(s)** a bit over 20 kg; **il habite à** ~ **distance d'ici** he lives some distance ou way (away) from here

2: ~ ... **que** whatever, whichever; ~ **livre qu'il choisisse** whatever (ou whichever) book he chooses; **par** ~ **temps qu'il fasse** whatever the weather

3: ~ **chose** something; (tournure interrogative) anything; ~ **chose d'autre** something else; anything else; **y être pour** ~ **chose** to have something to do with it; **faire** ~ **chose à qn** to have an effect on sb, do

something to sb; ~ **part** somewhere; anywhere; **en** ~ **sorte** as it were

◆ adv **1** (environ): ~ **100 mètres** some 100 metres

2: ~ **peu** rather, somewhat.

quelquefois [kɛlkəfwa] adv sometimes.

quelques-uns, -unes [kɛlkəzœ̃, -yn] pron some, a few; ~ **des lecteurs** some of the readers.

quelqu'un [kɛlkœ̃] pron someone, somebody, tournure interrogative ou négative + anyone ou anybody; ~ **d'autre** someone ou somebody else; anybody else.

quémander [kemɑ̃de] vt to beg for.

qu'en dira-t-on [kɑ̃diʀatɔ̃] nm inv: **le** ~ gossip, what people say.

quenelle [kənɛl] nf quenelle.

quenouille [kənuj] nf distaff.

querelle [kəʀɛl] nf quarrel; **chercher** ~ **à qn** to pick a quarrel with sb.

quereller [kəʀele]: **se** ~ vi to quarrel.

querelleur, euse [kəʀɛlœʀ, -øz] adj quarrelsome.

qu'est-ce que (ou **qui**) [kɛskə(ki)] voir **que**, **qui**.

question [kɛstjɔ̃] nf (gén) question; (fig) matter; issue; **il a été** ~ **de** we (ou they) spoke about; **il est** ~ **de les emprisonner** there's talk of them being jailed; **c'est une** ~ **de temps** it's a matter ou question of time; **de quoi est-il** ~? what is it about?; **il n'en est pas** ~ there's no question of it; **en** ~ in question; **hors de** ~ out of the question; **je ne me suis jamais posé la** ~ I've never thought about it; **(re)mettre en** ~ (autorité, science) to question; **poser la** ~ **de confiance** (POL) to ask for a vote of confidence; ~ **piège** (d'apparence facile) trick question; (pour nuire) loaded question; ~ **subsidiaire** tiebreaker.

questionnaire [kɛstjɔnɛʀ] nm questionnaire.

questionner [kɛstjɔne] vt to question.

quête [kɛt] nf (collecte) collection; (recherche) quest, search; **faire la** ~ (à l'église) to take the collection; (artiste) to pass the hat round; **se mettre en** ~ **de qch** to go in search of sth.

quêter [kete] vi (à l'église) to take the collection; (dans la rue) to collect money (for charity) ◆ vt to seek.

quetsche [kwɛtʃ(ə)] nf damson.

queue [kø] nf tail; (fig: du classement) bottom; (: de poêle) handle; (: de fruit, feuille) stalk; (: de train, colonne, file) rear; (file: de personnes) queue (BRIT), line (US); **en** ~ **(de train)** at the rear (of the train); **faire la** ~ to queue (up) (BRIT), line up (US); **se mettre à la** ~ to join the queue ou line; **histoire sans ni tête** cock and bull story; **à la** ~ **leu leu** in single file; (fig) one after the other; ~ **de cheval** ponytail; ~ **de poisson: faire une** ~

de poisson à qn (*AUTO*) to cut in front of sb; **finir en** ~ **de poisson** (*film*) to come to an abrupt end.

queue-de-pie, *pl* **queues-de-pie** [kødpi] *nf* (*habit*) tails *pl*, tail coat.

queux [kø] *adj m voir* **maître.**

qui [ki] *pron* (*personne*) who, *prép* + whom; (*chose, animal*) which, that; (*interrogatif indirect: sujet*): **je me demande** ~ **est là?** I wonder who is there?; (: *objet*): **elle ne sait à** ~ **se plaindre** she doesn't know who to complain to *ou* to whom to complain; **qu'est-ce** ~ **est sur la table?** what is on the table?; **à** ~ **est ce sac?** whose bag is this?; **à** ~ **parlais-tu?** who were you talking to?, to whom were you talking?; **chez** ~ **allez-vous?** whose house are you going to?; **amenez** ~ **vous voulez** bring who(ever) you like; ~ **est-ce** ~ **...?** who?; ~ **est-ce que ...?** who?; whom?; ~ **que ce soit** whoever it may be.

quiche [kiʃ] *nf* quiche; ~ **lorraine** quiche Lorraine.

quiconque [kikɔ̃k] *pron* (*celui qui*) whoever, anyone who; (*n'importe qui, personne*) anyone, anybody.

quidam [kɥidam] *nm* (*hum*) fellow.

quiétude [kjetyd] *nf* (*d'un lieu*) quiet, tranquillity; (*d'une personne*) peace (of mind), serenity; **en toute** ~ in complete peace; (*mentale*) with complete peace of mind.

quignon [kiɲɔ̃] *nm*: ~ **de pain** (*croûton*) crust of bread; (*morceau*) hunk of bread.

quille [kij] *nf* ninepin, skittle (*BRIT*); (*NAVIG: d'un bateau*) keel; (**jeu de**) ~**s** ninepins *sg*, skittles *sg* (*BRIT*).

quincaillerie [kɛ̃kajʀi] *nf* (*ustensiles, métier*) hardware, ironmongery (*BRIT*); (*magasin*) hardware shop *ou* store (*US*), ironmonger's (*BRIT*).

quincaillier, ière [kɛ̃kaje, -jɛʀ] *nm/f* hardware dealer, ironmonger (*BRIT*).

quinconce [kɛ̃kɔ̃s] *nm*: **en** ~ in staggered rows.

quinine [kinin] *nf* quinine.

quinquagénaire [kɛ̃kaʒenɛʀ] *nm/f* (*de cinquante ans*) fifty-year old; (*de cinquante à soixante ans*) man/woman in his/her fifties.

quinquennal, e, aux [kɛ̃kenal, -o] *adj* five-year, quinquennial.

quintal, aux [kɛ̃tal, -o] *nm* quintal (*100 kg*).

quinte [kɛ̃t] *nf*: ~ (**de toux**) coughing fit.

quintessence [kɛ̃tesɑ̃s] *nf* quintessence, very essence.

quintette [kɛ̃tɛt] *nm* quintet(te).

quintuple [kɛ̃typl(ə)] *nm*: **le** ~ **de** five times as much as.

quintupler [kɛ̃typle] *vt, vi* to increase fivefold.

quintuplés, ées [kɛ̃typle] *nm/fpl* quintuplets, quins.

quinzaine [kɛ̃zɛn] *nf*: **une** ~ (**de**) about fifteen, fifteen or so; **une** ~ (**de jours**) (*deux*

semaines) a fortnight (*BRIT*), two weeks; ~ **publicitaire** *ou* **commerciale** (two-week) sale.

quinze [kɛ̃z] *num* fifteen; **demain en** ~ a fortnight (*BRIT*) *ou* two weeks tomorrow; **dans** ~ **jours** in a fortnight('s time) (*BRIT*), in two weeks(' time).

quinzième [kɛ̃zjɛm] *num* fifteenth.

quiproquo [kipʀɔko] *nm* (*méprise sur une personne*) mistake; (*malentendu sur un sujet*) misunderstanding; (*THÉÂT*) (case of) mistaken identity.

Quito [kito] *n* Quito.

quittance [kitɑ̃s] *nf* (*reçu*) receipt; (*facture*) bill.

quitte [kit] *adj*: **être** ~ **envers qn** to be no longer in sb's debt; (*fig*) to be quits with sb; **être** ~ **de** (*obligation*) to be clear of; **en être** ~ **à bon compte** to have got off lightly; ~ **à faire** even if it means doing; ~ **ou double** (*jeu*) double or quits; (*fig*): **c'est du** ~ **ou double** it's a big risk.

quitter [kite] *vt* to leave; (*espoir, illusion*) to give up; (*vêtement*) to take off; **se** ~ (*couples, interlocuteurs*) to part; **ne quittez pas** (*au téléphone*) hold the line; **ne pas** ~ **qn d'une semelle** to stick to sb like glue.

quitus [kitys] *nm* final discharge; **donner** ~ **à** to discharge.

qui-vive [kiviv] *nm inv*: **être sur le** ~ to be on the alert.

quoi [kwa] *pron* (*interrogatif*) what; ~ **de neuf** *ou* **de nouveau?** what's new *ou* the news?; **as-tu de** ~ **écrire?** have you anything to write with?; **il n'a pas de** ~ **se l'acheter** he can't afford it, he hasn't got the money to buy it; **il y a de** ~ **être fier** that's something to be proud of; **"il n'y a pas de** ~**"** "(please) don't mention it", "not at all"; ~ **qu'il arrive** whatever happens; ~ **qu'il en soit** be that as it may; ~ **que ce soit** anything at all; **en** ~ **puis-je vous aider?** how can I help you?; **à** ~ **bon?** what's the use *ou* point?; **et puis** ~ **encore!** what(ever) next!; ~ **faire?** what's to be done?; **sans** ~ (*ou sinon*) otherwise.

quoique [kwak(ə)] *conj* (al)though.

quolibet [kɔlibɛ] *nm* gibe, jeer.

quorum [kɔʀɔm] *nm* quorum.

quota [kwɔta] *nm* quota.

quote-part [kɔtpaʀ] *nf* share.

quotidien, ne [kɔtidjɛ̃, -ɛn] *adj* (*journalier*) daily; (*banal*) ordinary, everyday ♦ *nm* (*journal*) daily (paper); (*vie quotidienne*) daily life, day-to-day existence; **les grands** ~**s** the big (national) dailies.

quotidiennement [kɔtidjɛnmɑ̃] *adv* daily, every day.

quotient [kɔsjɑ̃] *nm* (*MATH*) quotient; ~ **intellectuel (QI)** intelligence quotient (IQ).

quotité [kɔtite] *nf* (*FINANCE*) quota.

R r

R, r [ɛʀ] *nm inv* R, r ♦ *abr* = **route, rue; R comme Raoul** R for Robert (*BRIT*) *ou* Roger (*US*).

rab [ʀab] (*fam*), **rabiot** [ʀabjo] *nm* extra, more.

rabâcher [ʀabaʃe] *vi* to harp on ♦ *vt* keep on repeating.

rabais [ʀabɛ] *nm* reduction, discount; **au ~** at a reduction *ou* discount.

rabaisser [ʀabese] *vt* (*rabattre*) to reduce; (*dénigrer*) to belittle.

rabane [ʀaban] *nf* raffia (matting).

Rabat [ʀaba(t)] *n* Rabat.

rabat [ʀaba] *vb voir* **rabattre** ♦ *nm* flap.

rabat-joie [ʀabaʒwa] *nm/f inv* killjoy (*BRIT*), spoilsport.

rabatteur, euse [ʀabatœʀ, -øz] *nm/f* (*de gibier*) beater; (*péj*) tout.

rabattre [ʀabatʀ(ə)] *vt* (*couvercle, siège*) to pull down; (*col*) to turn down; (*couture*) to stitch down; (*gibier*) to drive; (*somme d'un prix*) to deduct, take off; (*orgueil, prétentions*) to humble; (*TRICOT*) to decrease; **se ~** *vi* (*bords, couvercle*) to fall shut; (*véhicule, coureur*) to cut in; **se ~ sur** (*accepter*) to fall back on.

rabattu, e [ʀabaty] *pp de* **rabattre** ♦ *adj* turned down.

rabbin [ʀabɛ̃] *nm* rabbi.

rabique [ʀabik] *adj* rabies *cpd*.

râble [ʀɑbl(ə)] *nm* back; (*CULIN*) saddle.

râblé, e [ʀɑble] *adj* broad-backed, stocky.

rabot [ʀabo] *nm* plane.

raboter [ʀabɔte] *vt* to plane (down).

raboteux, euse [ʀabɔtø, -øz] *adj* uneven, rough.

rabougri, e [ʀabugʀi] *adj* stunted.

rabrouer [ʀabʀue] *vt* to snub, rebuff.

racaille [ʀakaj] *nf* (*péj*) rabble, riffraff.

raccommodage [ʀakɔmɔdaʒ] *nm* mending *no pl*, repairing *no pl*; darning *no pl*.

raccommoder [ʀakɔmɔde] *vt* to mend, repair; (*chaussette etc*) to darn; (*fam: réconcilier: amis, ménage*) to bring together again; **se ~ (avec)** (*fam*) to patch it up (with).

raccompagner [ʀakɔ̃paɲe] *vt* to take *ou* see back.

raccord [ʀakɔʀ] *nm* link; **~ de maçonnerie** pointing *no pl*; **~ de peinture** join; touch-up.

raccordement [ʀakɔʀdəmɑ̃] *nm* joining up; connection.

raccorder [ʀakɔʀde] *vt* to join (up), link up; (*suj: pont etc*) to connect, link; **se ~ à** to join up with; (*fig: se rattacher à*) to tie in with; **~ au réseau du téléphone** to connect to the telephone service.

raccourci [ʀakuʀsi] *nm* short cut; **en ~** in brief.

raccourcir [ʀakuʀsiʀ] *vt* to shorten ♦ *vi* (*vêtement*) to shrink.

raccroc [ʀakʀo]: **par ~** *adv* by chance.

raccrocher [ʀakʀɔʃe] *vt* (*tableau, vêtement*) to hang back up; (*récepteur*) to put down; (*fig: affaire*) to save ♦ *vi* (*TÉL*) to hang up, ring off; **se ~ à** *vt* to cling to, hang on to; **ne raccrochez pas** (*TÉL*) hold on, don't hang up.

race [ʀas] *nf* race; (*d'animaux, fig: espèce*) breed; (*ascendance, origine*) stock, race; **de ~** *adj* purebred, pedigree.

racé, e [ʀase] *adj* thoroughbred.

rachat [ʀaʃa] *nm* buying; buying back; redemption; atonement.

racheter [ʀaʃte] *vt* (*article perdu*) to buy another; (*davantage*): **~ du lait/3 œufs** to buy more milk/another 3 eggs *ou* 3 more eggs; (*après avoir vendu*) to buy back; (*d'occasion*) to buy; (*COMM: part, firme*) to buy up; (: *pension, rente*) to redeem; (*REL: pécheur*) to redeem; (: *péché*) to atone for, expiate; (*mauvaise conduite, oubli, défaut*) to make up for; **se ~** (*REL*) to redeem o.s.; (*gén*) to make amends, make up for it.

rachidien, ne [ʀaʃidjɛ̃, -ɛn] *adj* rachidian, of the spine.

rachitique [ʀaʃitik] *adj* suffering from rickets; (*fig*) scraggy, scrawny.

rachitisme [ʀaʃitism(ə)] *nm* rickets *sg*.

racial, e, aux [ʀasjal, -o] *adj* racial.

racine [ʀasin] *nf* root; (*fig: attache*) roots *pl*; **~ carrée/cubique** square/cube root; **prendre ~** (*fig*) to take root; to put down roots.

racisme [ʀasism(ə)] *nm* racism, racialism.

raciste [ʀasist(ə)] *adj, nm/f* racist, racialist.

racket [ʀakɛt] *nm* racketeering *no pl*.

racketteur [ʀakɛtœʀ] *nm* racketeer.

raclée [ʀɑkle] *nf* (*fam*) hiding, thrashing.

raclement [ʀɑkləmɑ̃] *nm* (*bruit*) scraping (noise).

racler [ʀɑkle] *vt* (*os, plat*) to scrape; (*tache, boue*) to scrape off; (*fig: instrument*) to scrape on; (*suj: chose: frotter contre*) to scrape (against).

raclette [ʀɑklɛt] *nf* (*CULIN*) raclette (*Swiss cheese dish*).

racloir [ʀɑklwaʀ] *nm* (*outil*) scraper.

racolage [ʀakɔlaʒ] *nm* soliciting; touting.

racoler [ʀakɔle] *vt* (*attirer: suj: prostituée*) to solicit; (: *parti, marchand*) to tout for; (*attraper*) to pick up.

racoleur, euse [ʀakɔlœʀ, -øz] *adj* (*péj: publicité*) cheap and alluring ♦ *nm* (*péj: de clients etc*) tout ♦ *nf* streetwalker.

racontars [ʀakɔ̃taʀ] *nmpl* stories, gossip *sg*.

raconter [ʀakɔ̃te] *vt*: **~ (à qn)** (*décrire*) to relate (to sb), tell (sb) about; (*dire*) to tell (sb).

racorni, e [ʀakɔʀni] *adj* hard(ened).

racornir [ʀakɔʀniʀ] *vt* to harden.
radar [ʀadaʀ] *nm* radar; **système** ~ radar system; **écran** ~ radar screen.
rade [ʀad] *nf* (natural) harbour; **en** ~ **de Toulon** in Toulon harbour; **rester en** ~ *(fig)* to be left stranded.
radeau, x [ʀado] *nm* raft; ~ **de sauvetage** life raft.
radial, e, aux [ʀadjal, -o] *adj* radial; **pneu à carcasse** ~**e** radial tyre.
radiant, e [ʀadjɑ̃, -ɑ̃t] *adj* radiant.
radiateur [ʀadjatœʀ] *nm* radiator, heater; *(AUTO)* radiator; ~ **électrique/à gaz** electric/gas heater *ou* fire.
radiation [ʀadjasjɔ̃] *nf (d'un nom etc)* striking off *no pl*; *(PHYSIQUE)* radiation.
radical, e, aux [ʀadikal, -o] *adj* radical ♦ *nm* *(LING)* stem; *(MATH)* root sign; *(POL)* radical.
radicalement [ʀadikalmɑ̃] *adv* radically, completely.
radicaliser [ʀadikalize] *vt (durcir: opinions etc)* to harden; **se** ~ *vi (mouvement etc)* to become more radical.
radicalisme [ʀadikalism(ə)] *nm (POL)* radicalism.
radier [ʀadje] *vt* to strike off.
radiesthésie [ʀadjɛstezi] *nf* divination (by radiation).
radiesthésiste [ʀadjɛstezist(ə)] *nm/f* diviner.
radieux, euse [ʀadjø, -øz] *adj (visage, personne)* radiant; *(journée, soleil)* brilliant, glorious.
radin, e [ʀadɛ̃, -in] *adj (fam)* stingy.
radio [ʀadjo] *nf* radio; *(MÉD)* X-ray ♦ *nm (personne)* radio operator; **à la** ~ on the radio; **avoir la** ~ to have a radio; **passer à la** ~ to be on the radio; **se faire faire une** ~**/une** ~ **des poumons** to have an X-ray/a chest X-ray.
radio... [ʀadjo] *préfixe* radio....
radioactif, ive [ʀadjoaktif, -iv] *adj* radioactive.
radioactivité [ʀadjoaktivite] *nf* radioactivity.
radioamateur [ʀadjoamatœʀ] *nm* (radio) ham.
radiobalise [ʀadjobaliz] *nf* radio beacon.
radiocassette [ʀadjokasɛt] *nf* cassette radio.
radiodiffuser [ʀadjodifyze] *vt* to broadcast.
radiodiffusion [ʀadjodifyzjɔ̃] *nf* (radio) broadcasting.
radioélectrique [ʀadjoelɛktʀik] *adj* radio *cpd*.
radiogoniomètre [ʀadjogonjomɛtʀ(ə)] *nm* direction finder, radiogoniometer.
radiographie [ʀadjogʀafi] *nf* radiography; *(photo)* X-ray photograph, radiograph.
radiographier [ʀadjogʀafje] *vt* to X-ray; **se faire** ~ to have an X-ray.
radioguidage [ʀadjogidaʒ] *nm (NAVIG, AVIAT)* radio control; *(AUTO)* (broadcast of) traffic information.
radioguider [ʀadjogide] *vt (NAVIG, AVIAT)* to guide by radio, control by radio.
radiologie [ʀadjolɔʒi] *nf* radiology.
radiologique [ʀadjolɔʒik] *adj* radiological.

radiologue [ʀadjolɔg] *nm/f* radiologist.
radionavigant [ʀadjonavigɑ̃] *nm* radio officer.
radiophare [ʀadjofaʀ] *nm* radio beacon.
radiophonique [ʀadjofɔnik] *adj*: **programme/émission/jeu** ~ radio programme/broadcast/game.
radioreportage [ʀadjoʀəpɔʀtaʒ] *nm* radio report.
radio(-)réveil [ʀadjoʀevɛj] *nm* clock radio.
radioscopie [ʀadjoskɔpi] *nf* radioscopy.
radio-taxi [ʀadjotaksi] *nm* radiotaxi.
radiotélégraphie [ʀadjotelegʀafi] *nf* radiotelegraphy.
radiotéléphone [ʀadjotelefɔn] *nm* radiotelephone.
radiotélescope [ʀadjotelɛskɔp] *nm* radiotelescope.
radiotélévisé, e [ʀadjotelevize] *adj* broadcast on radio and television.
radiothérapie [ʀadjoteʀapi] *nf* radiotherapy.
radis [ʀadi] *nm* radish; ~ **noir** horseradish *no pl*.
radium [ʀadjɔm] *nm* radium.
radoter [ʀadote] *vi* to ramble on.
radoub [ʀadu] *nm*: **bassin** *ou* **cale de** ~ dry dock.
radouber [ʀadube] *vt* to repair, refit.
radoucir [ʀadusiʀ]: **se** ~ *vi (se réchauffer)* to become milder; *(se calmer)* to calm down; to soften.
radoucissement [ʀadusismɑ̃] *nm* milder period, better weather.
rafale [ʀafal] *nf (vent)* gust (of wind); *(de balles, d'applaudissements)* burst; ~ **de mitrailleuse** burst of machine-gun fire.
raffermir [ʀafɛʀmiʀ] *vt*, **se** ~ *vi (tissus, muscle)* to firm up; *(fig)* to strengthen.
raffermissement [ʀafɛʀmismɑ̃] *nm (fig)* strengthening.
raffinage [ʀafinaʒ] *nm* refining.
raffiné, e [ʀafine] *adj* refined.
raffinement [ʀafinmɑ̃] *nm* refinement.
raffiner [ʀafine] *vt* to refine.
raffinerie [ʀafinʀi] *nf* refinery.
raffoler [ʀafɔle]: ~ **de** *vt* to be very keen on.
raffut [ʀafy] *nm (fam)* row, racket.
rafiot [ʀafjo] *nm* tub.
rafistoler [ʀafistɔle] *vt (fam)* to patch up.
rafle [ʀafl(ə)] *nf (de police)* roundup, raid.
rafler [ʀafle] *vt (fam)* to swipe, nick.
rafraîchir [ʀafʀeʃiʀ] *vt (atmosphère, température)* to cool (down); *(aussi: mettre à* ~*)* to chill; *(suj: air, eau)* to freshen up; *(: boisson)* to refresh; *(fig: rénover)* to brighten up ♦ *vi*: **mettre du vin/une boisson à** ~ to chill wine/a drink; **se** ~ *vi* to grow cooler; to freshen up; *(personne: en buvant etc)* to refresh o.s; ~ **la mémoire** *ou* **les idées à qn** to refresh sb's memory.
rafraîchissant, e [ʀafʀeʃisɑ̃, -ɑ̃t] *adj* refreshing.
rafraîchissement [ʀafʀeʃismɑ̃] *nm* cooling;

(*boisson*) cool drink; ~**s** *nmpl* (*boissons, fruits etc*) refreshments.

ragaillardir [ʀagajaʀdiʀ] *vt* (*fam*) to perk *ou* buck up.

rage [ʀaʒ] *nf* (*MÉD*): **la** ~ rabies; (*fureur*) rage, fury; **faire** ~ to rage; ~ **de dents** (raging) toothache.

rager [ʀaʒe] *vi* to fume (with rage); **faire** ~ **qn** to enrage sb, get sb mad.

rageur, euse [ʀaʒœʀ, -øz] *adj* snarling; ill-tempered.

raglan [ʀaglɑ̃] *adj inv* raglan.

ragot [ʀago] *nm* (*fam*) malicious gossip *no pl*.

ragoût [ʀagu] *nm* (*plat*) stew.

ragoûtant, e [ʀagutɑ̃, -ɑ̃t] *adj*: **peu** ~ unpalatable.

rai [ʀɛ] *nm*: **un** ~ **de soleil/lumière** a shaft of sunshine/light.

raid [ʀɛd] *nm* (*MIL*) raid; (*attaque aérienne*) air raid; (*SPORT*) long-distance trek.

raide [ʀɛd] *adj* (*tendu*) taut, tight; (*escarpé*) steep; (*droit: cheveux*) straight; (*ankylosé, dur, guindé*) stiff; (*fam: cher*) steep, stiff; (: *sans argent*) flat broke; (*osé, licencieux*) daring ♦ *adv* (*en pente*) steeply; ~ **mort** stone dead.

raideur [ʀɛdœʀ] *nf* steepness; stiffness.

raidir [ʀɛdiʀ] *vt* (*muscles*) to stiffen; (*câble*) to pull taut, tighten; **se** ~ *vi* to stiffen; to become taut; (*personne: se crisper*) to tense up; (: *devenir intransigeant*) to harden.

raidissement [ʀɛdismɑ̃] *nm* stiffening; tightening; hardening.

raie [ʀɛ] *nf* (*ZOOL*) skate, ray; (*rayure*) stripe; (*des cheveux*) parting.

raifort [ʀɛfɔʀ] *nm* horseradish.

rail [ʀɑj] *nm* (*barre d'acier*) rail; (*chemins de fer*) railways *pl* (*BRIT*), railroads *pl* (*US*); **les** ~**s** (*la voie ferrée*) the rails, the track *sg*; **par** ~ by rail; ~ **conducteur** live *ou* conductor rail.

railler [ʀɑje] *vt* to scoff at, jeer at.

raillerie [ʀɑjʀi] *nf* mockery.

railleur, euse [ʀɑjœʀ, -øz] *adj* mocking.

rail-route [ʀɑjʀut] *nm* road-rail.

rainurage [ʀenyʀaʒ] *nm* (*AUTO*) uneven road surface.

rainure [ʀenyʀ] *nf* groove; slot.

rais [ʀɛ] *nm inv* = **rai**.

raisin [ʀɛzɛ̃] *nm* (*aussi*: ~**s**) grapes *pl*; (*variété*): ~ **blanc/noir** white (*ou* green)/black grape; ~ **muscat** muscat grape; ~**s secs** raisins.

raison [ʀɛzɔ̃] *nf* reason; **avoir** ~ to be right; **donner** ~ **à qn** (*personne*) to agree with sb; (*fait*) to prove sb right; **avoir** ~ **de qn/qch** to get the better of sb/sth; **se faire une** ~ to learn to live with it; **perdre la** ~ to become insane; (*fig*) to take leave of one's senses; **recouvrer la** ~ to come to one's senses; **ramener qn à la** ~ to make sb see sense; **demander** ~ **à qn de** (*affront etc*) to demand satisfaction from sb for; **entendre** ~ to listen to reason, see reason; **plus que de** ~ too much, more than is reasonable; ~ **de**

plus all the more reason; **à plus forte** ~ all the more so; **en** ~ **de** (*à cause de*) because of; (*à proportion de*) in proportion to; **à** ~ **de** at the rate of; ~ **d'État** reason of state; ~ **d'être** raison d'être; ~ **sociale** corporate name.

raisonnable [ʀɛzɔnabl(ə)] *adj* reasonable, sensible.

raisonnablement [ʀɛzɔnabləmɑ̃] *adv* reasonably.

raisonné, e [ʀɛzɔne] *adj* reasoned.

raisonnement [ʀɛzɔnmɑ̃] *nm* reasoning; arguing; argument.

raisonner [ʀɛzɔne] *vi* (*penser*) to reason; (*argumenter, discuter*) to argue ♦ *vt* (*personne*) to reason with; (*attitude: justifier*) to reason out; **se** ~ to reason with oneself.

raisonneur, euse [ʀɛzɔnœʀ, -øz] *adj* (*péj*) quibbling.

rajeunir [ʀaʒœniʀ] *vt* (*suj: coiffure, robe*): ~ **qn** to make sb look younger; (*suj: cure etc*) to rejuvenate; (*fig: rafraîchir*) to brighten up; (: *moderniser*) to give a new look to; (: *en recrutant*) to inject new blood into ♦ *vi* (*personne*) to become (*ou* look) younger; (*entreprise, quartier*) to be modernized.

rajout [ʀaʒu] *nm* addition.

rajouter [ʀaʒute] *vt* (*commentaire*) to add; ~ **du sel/un œuf** to add some more salt/ another egg; ~ **que** to add that; **en** ~ to lay it on thick.

rajustement [ʀaʒystəmɑ̃] *nm* adjustment.

rajuster [ʀaʒyste] *vt* (*vêtement*) to straighten, tidy; (*salaires*) to adjust; (*machine*) to readjust; **se** ~ to tidy *ou* straighten o.s. up.

râle [ʀɑl] *nm* groan; ~ **d'agonie** death rattle.

ralenti [ʀalɑ̃ti] *nm*: **au** ~ (*CINÉ*) in slow motion; (*fig*) at a slower pace; **tourner au** ~ (*AUTO*) to tick over, idle.

ralentir [ʀalɑ̃tiʀ] *vt*, *vi*, **se** ~ *vi* to slow down.

ralentissement [ʀalɑ̃tismɑ̃] *nm* slowing down.

râler [ʀɑle] *vi* to groan; (*fam*) to grouse, moan (and groan).

ralliement [ʀalimɑ̃] *nm* (*rassemblement*) rallying; (*adhésion: à une cause, une opinion*) winning over; **point/signe de** ~ rallying point/sign.

rallier [ʀalje] *vt* (*rassembler*) to rally; (*rejoindre*) to rejoin; (*gagner à sa cause*) to win over; **se** ~ **à** (*avis*) to come over *ou* round to.

rallonge [ʀalɔ̃ʒ] *nf* (*de table*) (extra) leaf (*pl* leaves); (*argent etc*) extra *no pl*; (*ÉLEC*) extension (cable *ou* flex); (*fig: de crédit etc*) extension.

rallonger [ʀalɔ̃ʒe] *vt* to lengthen.

rallumer [ʀalyme] *vt* to light up again, relight; (*fig*) to revive; **se** ~ *vi* (*lumière*) to come on again.

rallye [ʀali] *nm* rally; (*POL*) march.

ramages [ʀamaʒ] *nmpl* (*dessin*) leaf pattern *sg*; (*chants*) songs.

ramassage [ramɑsaʒ] *nm*: ~ **scolaire** school bus service.

ramassé, e [ramɑse] *adj* (*trapu*) squat, stocky; (*concis: expression etc*) compact.

ramasse-miettes [ramɑsmjɛt] *nm inv* tabletidy.

ramasse-monnaie [ramɑsmɔnɛ] *nm inv* change-tray.

ramasser [ramɑse] *vt* (*objet tombé ou par terre, fam*) to pick up; (*recueillir*) to collect; (*récolter*) to gather; (: *pommes de terre*) to lift; **se** ~ *vi* (*sur soi-même*) to huddle up; to crouch.

ramasseur, euse [ramɑsœr, -øz] *nm/f*: ~ **de balles** ballboy/girl.

ramassis [ramɑsi] *nm* (*péj: de gens*) bunch; (: *de choses*) jumble.

rambarde [rɑ̃bard(ə)] *nf* guardrail.

rame [ram] *nf* (*aviron*) oar; (*de métro*) train; (*de papier*) ream; ~ **de haricots** bean support; **faire force de** ~**s** to row hard.

rameau, x [ramo] *nm* (small) branch; (*fig*) branch; **les R~x** (*REL*) Palm Sunday *sg*.

ramener [ramne] *vt* to bring back; (*reconduire*) to take back; (*rabattre: couverture, visière*): ~ **qch sur** to pull sth back over; ~ **qch à** (*réduire à, aussi MATH*) to reduce sth to; ~ **qn à la vie/raison** to bring sb back to life/bring sb to his (*ou* her) senses; **se** ~ *vi* (*fam*) to roll *ou* turn up; **se** ~ **à** (*se réduire à*) to come *ou* boil down to.

ramequin [ramkɛ̃] *nm* ramekin.

ramer [rame] *vi* to row.

rameur, euse [ramœr, -øz] *nm/f* rower.

rameuter [ramøte] *vt* to gather together.

ramier [ramje] *nm*: (**pigeon**) ~ woodpigeon.

ramification [ramifikɑsjɔ̃] *nf* ramification.

ramifier [ramifje]: **se** ~ *vi* (*tige, secte, réseau*): **se** ~ (**en**) to branch out (into); (*veines, nerfs*) to ramify.

ramolli, e [ramɔli] *adj* soft.

ramollir [ramɔlir] *vt* to soften; **se** ~ *vi* (*os, tissus*) to get (*ou* go) soft; (*beurre, asphalte*) to soften.

ramonage [ramɔnaʒ] *nm* (chimney-) sweeping.

ramoner [ramɔne] *vt* (*cheminée*) to sweep; (*pipe*) to clean.

ramoneur [ramɔnœr] *nm* (chimney) sweep.

rampe [rɑ̃p] *nf* (*d'escalier*) banister(s *pl*); (*dans un garage, d'un terrain*) ramp; (*THÉÂT*): **la** ~ the footlights *pl*; (*lampes: lumineuse, de balisage*) floodlights *pl*; **passer la** ~ (*toucher le public*) to get across to the audience; ~ **de lancement** launching pad.

ramper [rɑ̃pe] *vi* (*reptile, animal*) to crawl; (*plante*) to creep.

rancard [rɑ̃kar] *nm* (*fam*) date; tip.

rancart [rɑ̃kar] *nm*: **mettre au** ~ (*article, projet*) to scrap; (*personne*) to put on the scrapheap.

rance [rɑ̃s] *adj* rancid.

rancir [rɑ̃sir] *vi* to go off, go rancid.

rancœur [rɑ̃kœr] *nf* rancour (*BRIT*), rancor (*US*), resentment.

rançon [rɑ̃sɔ̃] *nf* ransom; (*fig*): **la** ~ **du succès** *etc* the price of success *etc*.

rançonner [rɑ̃sɔne] *vt* to hold to ransom.

rancune [rɑ̃kyn] *nf* grudge, rancour (*BRIT*), rancor (*US*); **garder** ~ **à qn (de qch)** to bear sb a grudge (for sth); **sans** ~! no hard feelings!

rancunier, ière [rɑ̃kynje, -jɛr] *adj* vindictive, spiteful.

randonnée [rɑ̃dɔne] *nf* ride; (*à pied*) walk, ramble; hike, hiking *no pl*.

randonneur, euse [rɑ̃dɔnœr, -øz] *nm/f* hiker.

rang [rɑ̃] *nm* (*rangée*) row; (*de perles*) row, string, rope; (*grade, condition sociale, classement*) rank; ~**s** *nmpl* (*MIL*) ranks; **se mettre en** ~**s/sur un** ~ to get into *ou* form rows/a line; **sur 3** ~**s** (lined up) 3 deep; **se mettre en** ~**s par 4** to form fours *ou* rows of 4; **se mettre sur les** ~**s** (*fig*) to get into the running; **au premier** ~ in the first row; (*fig*) ranking first; **rentrer dans le** ~ to get into line; **au** ~ **de** (*au nombre de*) among (the ranks of); **avoir** ~ **de** to hold the rank of.

rangé, e [rɑ̃ʒe] *adj* (*sérieux*) orderly, steady.

rangée [rɑ̃ʒe] *nf* row.

rangement [rɑ̃ʒmɑ̃] *nm* tidying-up, putting-away; **faire des** ~**s** to tidy up.

ranger [rɑ̃ʒe] *vt* (*classer, grouper*) to order, arrange; (*mettre à sa place*) to put away; (*voiture dans la rue*) to park; (*mettre de l'ordre dans*) to tidy up; (*arranger, disposer: en cercle etc*) to arrange; (*fig: classer*): ~ **qn/qch parmi** to rank sb/sth among; **se** ~ *vi* (*se placer, se disposer: autour d'une table etc*) to take one's place, sit round; (*véhicule, conducteur: s'écarter*) to pull over; (: *s'arrêter*) to pull in; (*piéton*) to step aside; (*s'assagir*) to settle down; **se** ~ **à** (*avis*) to come round to, fall in with.

ranimer [ranime] *vt* (*personne évanouie*) to bring round; (*revigorer: forces, courage*) to restore; (*réconforter: troupes etc*) to kindle new life in; (*douleur, souvenir*) to revive; (*feu*) to rekindle.

rapace [rapas] *nm* bird of prey ♦ *adj* (*péj*) rapacious, grasping; ~ **diurne/nocturne** diurnal/nocturnal bird of prey.

rapatrié, e [rapatrije] *nm/f* repatriate (*esp French North African settler*).

rapatriement [rapatrimɑ̃] *nm* repatriation.

rapatrier [rapatrije] *vt* to repatriate; (*capitaux*) to bring (back) into the country.

râpe [rɑp] *nf* (*CULIN*) grater; (*à bois*) rasp.

râpé, e [rɑpe] *adj* (*tissu*) threadbare; (*CULIN*) grated.

râper [rɑpe] *vt* (*CULIN*) to grate; (*gratter, râcler*) to rasp.

rapetasser [raptase] *vt* (*fam*) to patch up.

rapetisser [raptise] *vt*: ~ **qch** to shorten sth; to make sth look smaller ♦ *vi*, **se** ~ *vi* to

shrink.
râpeux, euse [Rɑpø, -øz] *adj* rough.
raphia [Rafja] *nm* raffia.
rapide [Rapid] *adj* fast; (*prompt*) quick;
(*intelligence*) quick ♦ *nm* express (train); (*de cours d'eau*) rapid.
rapidement [Rapidmɑ̃] *adv* fast; quickly.
rapidité [Rapidite] *nf* speed; quickness.
rapiécer [Rapjese] *vt* to patch.
rappel [Rapɛl] *nm* (*d'un ambassadeur, MIL*)
recall; (*THÉÂT*) curtain call; (*MÉD: vaccination*) booster; (*ADMIN: de salaire*) back
pay *no pl*; (*d'une aventure, d'un nom*)
reminder; (*de limitation de vitesse: sur écriteau*) speed limit sign (*reminder*); (*TECH*)
return; (*NAVIG*) sitting out; (*ALPINISME: aussi:*
~ **de corde**) abseiling *no pl*, roping down *no pl*; abseil; ~ **à l'ordre** call to order.
rappeler [Raple] *vt* (*pour faire revenir, retéléphoner*) to call back; (*ambassadeur, MIL,
INFORM*) to recall; (*acteur*) to call back (onto
the stage); (*faire se souvenir*): ~ **qch à qn** to
remind sb of sth; **se** ~ *vt* (*se souvenir de*) to
remember, recall; ~ **qn à la vie** to bring sb
back to life; ~ **qn à la décence** to recall sb
to a sense of decency; **ça rappelle la
Provence** it's reminiscent of Provence, it
reminds you of Provence; **se** ~ **que...** to
remember that....
rappelle [Rapɛl] *etc vb voir* **rappeler.**
rappliquer [Raplike] *vi* (*fam*) to turn up.
rapport [Rapɔʀ] *nm* (*compte rendu*) report;
(*profit*) yield, return; revenue; (*lien, analogie*)
relationship; (*corrélation*) connection;
(*proportion: MATH, TECH*) ratio (*pl* -s); ~**s** *nmpl*
(*entre personnes, pays*) relations; **avoir** ~ **à**
to have something to do with, concern; **être
en** ~ **avec** (*idée de corrélation*) to be related
to; **être/se mettre en** ~ **avec qn** to be/get in
touch with sb; **par** ~ **à** (*comparé à*) in
relation to; (*à propos de*) with regard to;
sous le ~ **de** from the point of view of; **sous
tous (les)** ~**s** in all respects; ~**s (sexuels)**
(sexual) intercourse *sg*; ~ **qualité-prix** value
(for money).
rapporté, e [Rapɔʀte] *adj*: **pièce** ~**e** (*COUTURE*)
patch.
rapporter [Rapɔʀte] *vt* (*rendre, ramener*) to
bring back; (*apporter davantage*) to bring
more; (*COUTURE*) to sew on; (*suj:
investissement*) to yield; (*: activité*) to bring
in; (*relater*) to report; (*JUR: annuler*) to
revoke ♦ *vi* (*investissement*) to give a good
return *ou* profit; (*activité*) to be very
profitable; (*péj: moucharder*) to tell; ~ **qch à**
(*fig: rattacher*) to relate sth to; **se** ~ **à**
(*correspondre à*) to relate to; **s'en** ~ **à** to rely
on.
rapporteur, euse [Rapɔʀtœʀ, -øz] *nm/f* (*de
procès, commission*) reporter; (*péj*) telltale
♦ *nm* (*GÉOM*) protractor.
rapproché, e [Raprɔʃe] *adj* (*proche*) near,

close at hand; ~**s** (*l'un de l'autre*) at close
intervals.
rapprochement [Raprɔʃmɑ̃] *nm* (*réconciliation:
de nations, familles*) reconciliation; (*analogie,
rapport*) parallel.
rapprocher [Raprɔʃe] *vt* (*chaise d'une table*): ~
qch (de) to bring sth closer (to); (*deux
objets*) to bring closer together; (*réunir*) to
bring together; (*comparer*) to establish a
parallel between; **se** ~ *vi* to draw closer *ou*
nearer; (*fig: familles, pays*) to come together;
to come closer together; **se** ~ **de** to come
closer to; (*présenter une analogie avec*) to be
close to.
rapt [Rapt] *nm* abduction.
raquette [Rakɛt] *nf* (*de tennis*) racket; (*de
ping-pong*) bat; (*à neige*) snowshoe.
rare [RaR] *adj* rare; (*main-d'œuvre, denrées*)
scarce; (*cheveux, herbe*) sparse; **il est** ~ **que**
it's rare that, it's unusual that; **se faire** ~ to
become scarce; (*fig: personne*) to make
oneself scarce.
raréfaction [Rarefaksjɔ̃] *nf* scarcity; (*de l'air*)
rarefaction.
raréfier [Rarefje]: **se** ~ *vi* to grow scarce; (*air*)
to rarefy.
rarement [RaRmɑ̃] *adv* rarely, seldom.
rareté [RaRte] *nf* (*voir rare*) rarity; scarcity.
rarissime [Rarisim] *adj* extremely rare.
RAS *abr* = **rien à signaler.**
ras, e [Rɑ, Rɑz] *adj* (*tête, cheveux*) close-
cropped; (*poil, herbe*) short; (*mesure, cuillère*)
level ♦ *adv* short; **faire table** ~**e** to make a
clean sweep; **en** ~**e campagne** in open
country; **à** ~ **bords** to the brim; **au** ~ **de**
level with; **en avoir** ~ **le bol** (*fam*) to be fed
up; ~ **du cou** *adj* (*pull, robe*) crew-neck.
rasade [Rɑzad] *nf* glassful.
rasant, e [Rɑzɑ̃, ɑ̃t] *adj* (*MIL: balle, tir*) grazing;
(*fam*) boring.
rascasse [Raskas] *nf* (*ZOOL*) scorpion fish.
rasé, e [Rɑze] *adj*: ~ **de frais** freshly shaven; ~
de près close-shaven.
rase-mottes [Rɑzmɔt] *nm inv*: **faire du** ~ to
hedgehop; **vol en** ~ hedgehopping.
raser [Rɑze] *vt* (*barbe, cheveux*) to shave off;
(*menton, personne*) to shave; (*fam: ennuyer*)
to bore; (*démolir*) to raze (to the ground);
(*frôler*) to graze, skim; **se** ~ to shave; (*fam*)
to be bored (to tears).
rasoir [Rɑzwaʀ] *nm* razor; ~ **électrique**
electric shaver *ou* razor; ~ **mécanique** *ou*
de sûreté safety razor.
rassasier [Rasazje] *vt* to satisfy; **être rassasié**
(*dégoûté*) to be sated; to have had more than
enough.
rassemblement [Rasɑ̃bləmɑ̃] *nm* (*groupe*)
gathering; (*POL*) union; association; (*MIL*): **le**
~ **parade.**
rassembler [Rasɑ̃ble] *vt* (*réunir*) to assemble,
gather; (*regrouper, amasser*) to gather
together, collect; **se** ~ *vi* to gather; ~ **ses**

idées/ses esprits/son courage to collect one's thoughts/gather one's wits/screw up one's courage.
rasseoir [Raswar]: **se ~** *vi* to sit down again.
rasséréner [Raserene] *vt*: **se ~** *vi* to recover one's serenity.
rassir [Rasir] *vi* to go stale.
rassis, e [Rasi, -iz] *adj* (*pain*) stale.
rassurant, e [Rasyrɑ̃, -ɑ̃t] *adj* (*nouvelles etc*) reassuring.
rassuré, e [Rasyre] *adj*: **ne pas être très ~** to be rather ill at ease.
rassurer [Rasyre] *vt* to reassure; **se ~** to be reassured; **rassure-toi** don't worry.
rat [Ra] *nm* rat; **~ d'hôtel** hotel thief (*pl* thieves); **~ musqué** muskrat.
ratatiné, e [Ratatine] *adj* shrivelled (up), wrinkled.
ratatiner [Ratatine] *vt* to shrivel; (*peau*) to wrinkle; **se ~** *vi* to shrivel; to become wrinkled.
ratatouille [Ratatuj] *nf* (*CULIN*) ratatouille.
rate [Rat] *nf* female rat; (*ANAT*) spleen.
raté, e [Rate] *adj* (*tentative*) unsuccessful, failed ♦ *nm/f* failure ♦ *nm* misfiring *no pl.*
râteau, x [Rɑto] *nm* rake.
râtelier [Rɑtəlje] *nm* rack; (*fam*) false teeth *pl.*
rater [Rate] *vi* (*ne pas partir: coup de feu*) to fail to go off; (*affaire, projet etc*) to go wrong, fail ♦ *vt* (*cible, train, occasion*) to miss; (*démonstration, plat*) to spoil; (*examen*) to fail; **~ son coup** to fail, not to bring it off.
raticide [Ratisid] *nm* rat poison.
ratification [Ratifikɑsjɔ̃] *nf* ratification.
ratifier [Ratifje] *vt* to ratify.
ratio [Rasjo] *nm* ratio (*pl* -s).
ration [Rɑsjɔ̃] *nf* ration; (*fig*) share; **~ alimentaire** food intake.
rationalisation [Rasjɔnalizɑsjɔ̃] *nf* rationalization.
rationaliser [Rasjɔnalize] *vt* to rationalize.
rationnel, le [Rasjɔnɛl] *adj* rational.
rationnellement [Rasjɔnɛlmɑ̃] *adv* rationally.
rationnement [Rasjɔnmɑ̃] *nm* rationing; **ticket de ~** ration coupon.
rationner [Rasjɔne] *vt* to ration; (*personne*) to put on rations; **se ~** to ration o.s.
ratisser [Ratise] *vt* (*allée*) to rake; (*feuilles*) to rake up; (*suj: armée, police*) to comb; **~ large** to cast one's nets wide.
raton [Ratɔ̃] *nm*: **~ laveur** raccoon.
RATP *sigle f* (= *Régie autonome des transports parisiens*) *Paris transport authority.*
rattacher [Rataʃe] *vt* (*animal, cheveux*) to tie up again; (*incorporer: ADMIN etc*): **~ qch à** to join sth to, unite sth with; (*fig: relier*): **~ qch à** to link sth with, relate sth to; (*: lier*): **~ qn à** to bind *ou* tie sb to; **se ~ à** (*fig: avoir un lien avec*) to be linked (*ou* connected) with.
rattrapage [Ratrapaʒ] *nm* (*SCOL*) remedial classes *pl*; (*ÉCON*) catching up.
rattraper [Ratrape] *vt* (*fugitif*) to recapture;

(*retenir, empêcher de tomber*) to catch (hold of); (*atteindre, rejoindre*) to catch up with; (*réparer: imprudence, erreur*) to make up for; **se ~** *vi* (*regagner: du temps*) to make up for lost time; (*: de l'argent etc*) to make good one's losses; (*réparer une gaffe etc*) to make up for it; **se ~ (à)** (*se raccrocher*) to stop o.s. falling (by catching hold of); **~ son retard/le temps perdu** to make up (for) lost time.
rature [Ratyr] *nf* deletion, erasure.
raturer [Ratyre] *vt* to cross out, delete, erase.
rauque [Rok] *adj* raucous; hoarse.
ravagé, e [Ravaʒe] *adj* (*visage*) harrowed.
ravager [Ravaʒe] *vt* to devastate, ravage.
ravages [Ravaʒ] *nmpl* ravages; **faire des ~** to wreak havoc; (*fig: séducteur*) to break hearts.
ravalement [Ravalmɑ̃] *nm* restoration.
ravaler [Ravale] *vt* (*mur, façade*) to restore; (*déprécier*) to lower; (*avaler de nouveau*) to swallow again; **~ sa colère/son dégoût** to stifle one's anger/distaste.
ravaudage [Ravodaʒ] *nm* repairing, mending.
ravauder [Ravode] *vt* to repair, mend.
rave [Rav] *nf* (*BOT*) rape.
R avec AR *abr* (= *recommandé avec accusé de réception*) recorded delivery.
ravi, e [Ravi] *adj* delighted; **être ~ de/que** to be delighted with/that.
ravier [Ravje] *nm* hors d'œuvre dish.
ravigote [Ravigɔt] *adj*: **sauce ~** oil and vinegar dressing with shallots.
ravigoter [Ravigɔte] *vt* (*fam*) to buck up.
ravin [Ravɛ̃] *nm* gully, ravine.
raviner [Ravine] *vt* to furrow, gully.
ravioli [Ravjɔli] *nmpl* ravioli -s.
ravir [Ravir] *vt* (*enchanter*) to delight; (*enlever*) **~ qch à qn** to rob sb of sth; **à ~** *adv* delightfully, beautifully; **être beau à ~** to be ravishingly beautiful.
raviser [Ravize]: **se ~** *vi* to change one's mind.
ravissant, e [Ravisɑ̃, -ɑ̃t] *adj* delightful.
ravissement [Ravismɑ̃] *nm* (*enchantement, délice*) rapture.
ravisseur, euse [Ravisœr, -øz] *nm/f* abductor, kidnapper.
ravitaillement [Ravitajmɑ̃] *nm* resupplying; refuelling; (*provisions*) supplies *pl*; **aller au ~** to go for fresh supplies; **~ en vol** (*AVIAT*) in-flight refuelling.
ravitailler [Ravitaje] *vt* to resupply; (*véhicule*) to refuel; **se ~** *vi* to get fresh supplies.
raviver [Ravive] *vt* (*feu, douleur*) to revive; (*couleurs*) to brighten up.
ravoir [Ravwar] *vt* to get back.
rayé, e [Reje] *adj* (*à rayures*) striped; (*éraflé*) scratched.
rayer [Reje] *vt* (*érafler*) to scratch; (*barrer*) to cross *ou* score out; (*d'une liste: radier*) to cross *ou* strike off.
rayon [Rɛjɔ̃] *nm* (*de soleil etc*) ray; (*GÉOM*) radius; (*de roue*) spoke; (*étagère*) shelf (*pl*

shelves); (*de grand magasin*) department; (*fig: domaine*) responsibility, concern; (*de ruche*) (honey)comb; **dans un ~ de** within a radius of; **~s** *nmpl* (*radiothérapie*) radiation; **~ d'action** range; **~ de braquage** (*AUTO*) turning circle; **~ laser** laser beam; **~ de soleil** sunbeam, ray of sunshine; **~s X** X-rays.

rayonnage [Rɛjɔnaʒ] *nm* set of shelves.

rayonnant, e [Rɛjɔnɑ̃, -ɑ̃t] *adj* radiant.

rayonne [Rɛjɔn] *nf* rayon.

rayonnement [Rɛjɔnmɑ̃] *nm* radiation; (*fig: éclat*) radiance; (: *influence*) influence.

rayonner [Rɛjɔne] *vi* (*chaleur, énergie*) to radiate; (*fig: émotion*) to shine forth; (: *visage*) to be radiant; (*avenues, axes etc*) to radiate; (*touriste*) to go touring (*from one base*).

rayure [Rejyr] *nf* (*motif*) stripe; (*éraflure*) scratch; (*rainure, d'un fusil*) groove; **à ~s** striped.

raz-de-marée [Rɑdmare] *nm inv* tidal wave.

razzia [Razja] *nf* raid, foray.

RBE *sigle m* (= *revenu brut d'exploitation*) gross profit (*of a farm*).

R-D *sigle f* (= *Recherche-Développement*) R & D.

RDA *sigle f* (= *République démocratique allemande*) GDR.

RDB *sigle m* (*STATISTIQUES*: = *revenu disponible brut*) total income (*of a family etc*).

rdc *abr* = **rez-de-chaussée**.

ré [Re] *nm* (*MUS*) D; (*en chantant la gamme*) re.

réabonnement [Reabɔnmɑ̃] *nm* renewal of subscription.

réabonner [Reabɔne] *vt*: **~ qn à** to renew sb's subscription to; **se ~ (à)** to renew one's subscription (to).

réac [Reak] *adj, nm/f* (*fam*: = *réactionnaire*) reactionary.

réacteur [Reaktœr] *nm* jet engine; **~ nucléaire** nuclear reactor.

réactif [Reaktif] *nm* reagent.

réaction [Reaksjɔ̃] *nf* reaction; **par ~** jet-propelled; **avion/moteur à ~** jet (plane)/jet engine; **~ en chaîne** chain reaction.

réactionnaire [Reaksjɔnɛr] *adj, nm/f* reactionary.

réactualiser [Reaktɥalize] *vt* to update, bring up to date.

réadaptation [Readaptasjɔ̃] *nf* readjustment; rehabilitation.

réadapter [Readapte] *vt* to readjust; (*MÉD*) to rehabilitate; **se ~ (à)** to readjust (to).

réaffirmer [Reafirme] *vt* to reaffirm, reassert.

réagir [Reaʒir] *vi* to react.

réajuster [Reaʒyste] *vt* = **rajuster**.

réalisable [Realizabl(ə)] *adj* (*projet, plan*) feasible; (*COMM*: *valeur*) realizable.

réalisateur, trice [Realizatœr, -tris] *nm/f* (*TV, CINÉ*) director.

réalisation [Realizasjɔ̃] *nf* carrying out; realization; fulfilment; achievement;

production; (*œuvre*) production, work; (*création*) creation.

réaliser [Realize] *vt* (*projet, opération*) to carry out, realize; (*rêve, souhait*) to realize, fulfil; (*exploit*) to achieve; (*achat, vente*) to make; (*film*) to produce; (*se rendre compte de, COMM: bien, capital*) to realize; **se ~** *vi* to be realized.

réalisme [Realism(ə)] *nm* realism.

réaliste [Realist(ə)] *adj* realistic; (*peintre, roman*) realist ♦ *nm/f* realist.

réalité [Realite] *nf* reality; **en ~** in (actual) fact; **dans la ~** in reality; **~ virtuelle** virtual reality.

réanimation [Reanimasjɔ̃] *nf* resuscitation; **service de ~** intensive care unit.

réanimer [Reanime] *vt* (*MÉD*) to resuscitate.

réapparaître [Reaparɛtr(ə)] *vi* to reappear.

réapparition [Reaparisjɔ̃] *nf* reappearance.

réapprovisionner [Reaprɔvizjɔne] *vt* (*magasin*) to restock; **se ~ (en)** to restock (with).

réarmement [Rearməmɑ̃] *nm* rearmament.

réarmer [Rearme] *vt* (*arme*) to reload ♦ *vi* (*état*) to rearm.

réassortiment [Reasɔrtimɑ̃] *nm* (*COMM*) restocking.

réassortir [Reasɔrtir] *vt* to match up.

réassurance [Reasyrɑ̃s] *nf* reinsurance.

réassurer [Reasyre] *vt* to reinsure.

réassureur [Reasyrœr] *nm* reinsurer.

rebaptiser [Rəbatize] *vt* (*rue*) to rename.

rébarbatif, ive [Rebarbatif, -iv] *adj* forbidding; (*style*) off-putting (*BRIT*), crabbed.

rebattre [Rəbatr(ə)] *vt*: **~ les oreilles à qn de qch** to keep harping on to sb about sth.

rebattu, e [Rəbaty] *pp de* **rebattre** ♦ *adj* hackneyed.

rebelle [Rəbɛl] *nm/f* rebel ♦ *adj* (*troupes*) rebel; (*enfant*) rebellious; (*mèche etc*) unruly; **~ à qch** unamenable to sth; **~ à faire** unwilling to do.

rebeller [Rəbele]: **se ~** *vi* to rebel.

rébellion [Rebeljɔ̃] *nf* rebellion; (*rebelles*) rebel forces *pl*.

rebiffer [Rəbife]: **se ~** *vr* to fight back.

reboisement [Rəbwazmɑ̃] *nm* reafforestation.

reboiser [Rəbwaze] *vt* to replant with trees, reafforest.

rebond [Rəbɔ̃] *nm* (*voir rebondir*) bounce; rebound.

rebondi, e [Rəbɔ̃di] *adj* (*ventre*) rounded; (*joues*) chubby, well-rounded.

rebondir [Rəbɔ̃dir] *vi* (*ballon: au sol*) to bounce; (: *contre un mur*) to rebound; (*fig: procès, action, conversation*) to get moving again, be suddenly revived.

rebondissement [Rəbɔ̃dismɑ̃] *nm* new development.

rebord [Rəbɔr] *nm* edge.

reboucher [Rəbuʃe] *vt* (*flacon*) to put the

stopper (*ou* top) back on, recork; (*trou*) to stop up.

rebours [RəbuR]: **à** ~ *adv* the wrong way.

rebouteux, euse [Rəbutø, -øz] *nm/f* (*péj*) bonesetter.

reboutonner [Rəbutɔne] *vt* (*vêtement*) to button up (again).

rebrousse-poil [RəbRuspwal]: **à** ~ *adv* the wrong way.

rebrousser [RəbRuse] *vt* (*cheveux, poils*) to brush back, brush up; ~ **chemin** to turn back.

rebuffade [Rəbyfad] *nf* rebuff.

rébus [Rebys] *nm inv* (*jeu d'esprit*) rebus; (*fig*) puzzle.

rebut [Rəby] *nm*: **mettre au** ~ to scrap, discard.

rebutant, e [Rəbytɑ̃, -ɑ̃t] *adj* (*travail, démarche*) off-putting, disagreeable.

rebuter [Rəbyte] *vt* to put off.

récalcitrant, e [RekalsitRɑ̃, -ɑ̃t] *adj* refractory, recalcitrant.

recaler [Rəkale] *vt* (*SCOL*) to fail.

récapitulatif, ive [Rekapitylatif, -iv] *adj* (*liste, tableau*) summary *cpd*, that sums up.

récapituler [Rekapityle] *vt* to recapitulate; (*résumer*) to sum up.

recel [Rəsɛl] *nm* receiving (stolen goods).

receler [Rəsəle] *vt* (*produit d'un vol*) to receive; (*malfaiteur*) to harbour; (*fig*) to conceal.

receleur, euse [RəsəlœR, -øz] *nm/f* receiver.

récemment [Resamɑ̃] *adv* recently.

recensement [Rəsɑ̃smɑ̃] *nm* census; inventory.

recenser [Rəsɑ̃se] *vt* (*population*) to take a census of; (*inventorier*) to make an inventory of; (*dénombrer*) to list.

récent, e [Resɑ̃, -ɑ̃t] *adj* recent.

recentrer [Rəsɑ̃tRe] *vt* (*POL*) to move towards the centre.

récépissé [Resepise] *nm* receipt.

réceptacle [Reseptakl(ə)] *nm* (*où les choses aboutissent*) recipient; (*où les choses sont stockées*) repository; (*BOT*) receptacle.

récepteur, trice [ReseptœR, -tris] *adj* receiving ♦ *nm* receiver; ~ **(de papier)** (*INFORM*) stacker; ~ **(de radio)** radio set *ou* receiver.

réceptif, ive [Reseptif, -iv] *adj*: ~ **(à)** receptive (to).

réception [Resepsjɔ̃] *nf* receiving *no pl*; (*d'une marchandise, commande*) receipt; (*accueil*) reception, welcome; (*bureau*) reception (desk); (*réunion mondaine*) reception, party; (*pièces*) reception rooms *pl*; (*SPORT: après un saut*) landing; (*du ballon*) catching *no pl*; **jour/heures de** ~ day/hours for receiving visitors (*ou* students *etc*).

réceptionnaire [ResepsjɔnɛR] *nm/f* receiving clerk.

réceptionner [Resepsjɔne] *vt* (*COMM*) to take delivery of; (*SPORT: ballon*) to catch (and control).

réceptionniste [Resepsjɔnist(ə)] *nm/f* receptionist.

réceptivité [Reseptivite] *nf* (*à une influence*) receptiveness; (*à une maladie*) susceptibility.

récessif, ive [Resesif, -iv] *adj* (*BIOL*) recessive.

récession [Resesjɔ̃] *nf* recession.

recette [Rəsɛt] *nf* (*CULIN*) recipe; (*fig*) formula, recipe; (*COMM*) takings *pl*; (*ADMIN: bureau*) tax *ou* revenue office; ~**s** *nfpl* (*COMM: rentrées*) receipts; **faire** ~ (*spectacle, exposition*) to be a winner.

receveur, euse [RəsəvœR, -øz] *nm/f* (*des contributions*) tax collector; (*des postes*) postmaster/mistress; (*d'autobus*) conductor/conductress; (*MÉD: de sang, organe*) recipient.

recevoir [RəsəvwaR] *vt* to receive; (*lettre, prime*) to receive, get; (*client, patient, représentant*) to see; (*jour, soleil: suj: pièce*) to get; (*SCOL: candidat*) to pass ♦ *vi* to receive visitors; to give parties; to see patients *etc*; **se** ~ *vi* (*athlète*) to land; ~ **qn à dîner** to invite sb to dinner; **il reçoit de 8 à 10** he's at home from 8 to 10, he will see visitors from 8 to 10; (*docteur, dentiste etc*) he sees patients from 8 to 10; **être reçu** (*à un examen*) to pass; **être bien/mal reçu** to be well/badly received.

rechange [Rəʃɑ̃ʒ]: **de** ~ *adj* (*pièces, roue*) spare; (*fig: solution*) alternative; **des vêtements de** ~ a change of clothes.

rechaper [Rəʃape] *vt* to remould (*BRIT*), remold (*US*), retread.

réchapper [Reʃape]: ~ **de** *ou* **à** *vt* (*accident, maladie*) to come through; **va-t-il en** ~? is he going to get over it?, is he going to come through (it)?

recharge [RəʃaRʒ(ə)] *nf* refill.

rechargeable [RəʃaRʒabl(ə)] *adj* refillable; rechargeable.

recharger [RəʃaRʒe] *vt* (*camion, fusil, appareil-photo*) to reload; (*briquet, stylo*) to refill; (*batterie*) to recharge.

réchaud [Reʃo] *nm* (portable) stove; plate-warmer.

réchauffé [Reʃofe] *nm* (*nourriture*) reheated food; (*fig*) stale news (*ou* joke *etc*).

réchauffement [Reʃofmɑ̃] *nm* warming (up); **le** ~ **de la planète** global warming.

réchauffer [Reʃofe] *vt* (*plat*) to reheat; (*mains, personne*) to warm; **se** ~ *vi* to get warmer; **se** ~ **les doigts** to warm (up) one's fingers.

rêche [Rɛʃ] *adj* rough.

recherche [RəʃɛRʃ(ə)] *nf* (*action*): **la** ~ **de** the search for; (*raffinement*) affectedness, studied elegance; (*scientifique etc*): **la** ~ research; ~**s** *nfpl* (*de la police*) investigations; (*scientifiques*) research *sg*; **être/se mettre à la** ~ **de** to be/go in search of.

recherché, e [RəʃɛRʃe] *adj* (*rare, demandé*) much sought-after; (*entouré: acteur, femme*) in demand; (*raffiné*) studied, affected.

rechercher [RəʃɛRʃe] *vt* (*objet égaré, personne*) to look for, search for; (*témoins, coupable, main-d'œuvre*) to look for; (*causes d'un phénomène, nouveau procédé*) to try to find; (*bonheur etc, l'amitié de qn*) to seek; "~ **et remplacer**" (*INFORM*) "search and replace".

rechigner [Rəʃiɲe] *vi*: ~ (**à**) to balk (at).

rechute [Rəʃyt] *nf* (*MÉD*) relapse; (*dans le péché, le vice*) lapse; **faire une** ~ to have a relapse.

rechuter [Rəʃyte] *vi* (*MÉD*) to relapse.

récidive [Residiv] *nf* (*JUR*) second (*ou* subsequent) offence; (*fig*) repetition; (*MÉD*) recurrence.

récidiver [Residive] *vi* to commit a second (*ou* subsequent) offence; (*fig*) to do it again.

récidiviste [Residivist(ə)] *nm/f* second (*ou* habitual) offender, recidivist.

récif [Resif] *nm* reef.

récipiendaire [Resipjɑ̃dɛR] *nm* recipient (*of diploma etc*); (*d'une societé*) newly elected member.

récipient [Resipjɑ̃] *nm* container.

réciproque [ResipRɔk] *adj* reciprocal ♦ *nf*: **la** ~ (*l'inverse*) the converse.

réciproquement [ResipRɔkmɑ̃] *adv* reciprocally; **et** ~ and vice versa.

récit [Resi] *nm* (*action de narrer*) telling; (*conte, histoire*) story.

récital [Resital] *nm* recital.

récitant, e [Resitɑ̃, -ɑ̃t] *nm/f* narrator.

récitation [Resitasjɔ̃] *nf* recitation.

réciter [Resite] *vt* to recite.

réclamation [Reklamasjɔ̃] *nf* complaint; ~**s** *nfpl* (*bureau*) complaints department *sg*.

réclame [Reklam] *nf*: **la** ~ advertising; **une** ~ an ad(vertisement), an advert (*BRIT*); **faire de la** ~ (**pour qch/qn**) to advertise (sth/sb); **article en** ~ special offer.

réclamer [Reklame] *vt* (*aide, nourriture etc*) to ask for; (*revendiquer: dû, part, indemnité*) to claim, demand; (*nécessiter*) to demand, require ♦ *vi* to complain; **se** ~ **de** to give as one's authority; to claim filiation with.

reclassement [Rəklɑsmɑ̃] *nm* reclassifying; regrading; rehabilitation.

reclasser [Rəklɑse] *vt* (*fiches, dossiers*) to reclassify; (*fig: fonctionnaire etc*) to regrade; (*: ouvrier licencié*) to place, rehabilitate.

reclus, e [Rəkly, -yz] *nm/f* recluse.

réclusion [Reklyzjɔ̃] *nf* imprisonment; ~ **à perpétuité** life imprisonment.

recoiffer [Rəkwafe] *vt*: ~ **un enfant** to do a child's hair again; **se** ~ to do one's hair again.

recoin [Rəkwɛ̃] *nm* nook, corner; (*fig*) hidden recess.

reçois [Rəswa] *etc vb voir* **recevoir**.

reçoive [Rəswav] *etc vb voir* **recevoir**.

recoller [Rəkɔle] *vt* (*enveloppe*) to stick back down.

récolte [Rekɔlt(ə)] *nf* harvesting, gathering; (*produits*) harvest, crop; (*fig*) crop, collection; (*: d'observations*) findings.

récolter [Rekɔlte] *vt* to harvest, gather (in); (*fig*) to get.

recommandable [Rəkɔmɑ̃dabl(ə)] *adj* commendable; **peu** ~ not very commendable.

recommandation [Rəkɔmɑ̃dasjɔ̃] *nf* recommendation.

recommandé [Rəkɔmɑ̃de] *nm* (*méthode etc*) recommended; (*POSTES*): **en** ~ by registered mail.

recommander [Rəkɔmɑ̃de] *vt* to recommend; (*suj: qualités etc*) to commend; (*POSTES*) to register; ~ **qch à qn** to recommend sth to sb; ~ **à qn de faire** to recommend sb to do; ~ **qn auprès de qn** *ou* **à qn** to recommend sb to sb; **il est recommandé de faire** ... it is recommended that one does ...; **se** ~ **à qn** to commend o.s. to sb; **se** ~ **de qn** to give sb's name as a reference.

recommencer [Rəkɔmɑ̃se] *vt* (*reprendre: lutte, séance*) to resume, start again; (*refaire: travail, explications*) to start afresh, start (over) again; (*récidiver: erreur*) to make again ♦ *vi* to start again; (*récidiver*) to do it again; ~ **à faire** to start doing again; **ne recommence pas!** don't do that again!

récompense [Rekɔ̃pɑ̃s] *nf* reward; (*prix*) award; **recevoir qch en** ~ to get sth as a reward, be rewarded with sth.

récompenser [Rekɔ̃pɑ̃se] *vt*: ~ **qn** (**de** *ou* **pour**) to reward sb (for).

réconciliation [Rekɔ̃siljasjɔ̃] *nf* reconciliation.

réconcilier [Rekɔ̃silje] *vt* to reconcile; ~ **qn avec qn** to reconcile sb with sb; ~ **qn avec qch** to reconcile sb to sth; **se** ~ (**avec**) to be reconciled (with).

reconductible [Rəkɔ̃dyktibl(ə)] *adj* (*JUR: contrat, bail*) renewable.

reconduction [Rəkɔ̃dyksjɔ̃] *nf* renewal; (*POL: d'une politique*) continuation.

reconduire [Rəkɔ̃dɥiR] *vt* (*raccompagner*) to take *ou* see back; (*: à la porte*) to show out; (*: à son domicile*) to see home, take home; (*JUR, POL: renouveler*) to renew.

réconfort [Rekɔ̃fɔR] *nm* comfort.

réconfortant, e [Rekɔ̃fɔRtɑ̃, -ɑ̃t] *adj* (*idée, paroles*) comforting; (*boisson*) fortifying.

réconforter [Rekɔ̃fɔRte] *vt* (*consoler*) to comfort; (*revigorer*) to fortify.

reconnais [R(ə)kɔnɛ] *etc vb voir* **reconnaître**.

reconnaissable [Rəkɔnɛsabl(ə)] *adj* recognizable.

reconnaissais [R(ə)kɔnɛsɛ] *etc vb voir* **reconnaître**.

reconnaissance [Rəkɔnɛsɑ̃s] *nf* recognition; acknowledgement; (*gratitude*) gratitude, gratefulness; (*MIL*) reconnaissance, recce; **en** ~ (*MIL*) on reconnaissance; ~ **de dette** acknowledgement of a debt, IOU.

reconnaissant, e [ʀəkɔnɛsɑ̃, -ɑ̃t] *vb voir*
reconnaître ♦ *adj* grateful; **je vous serais ~
de bien vouloir** I should be most grateful if
you would (kindly).

reconnaître [ʀəkɔnɛtʀ(ə)] *vt* to recognize;
(*MIL: lieu*) to reconnoitre; (*JUR: enfant, dette,
droit*) to acknowledge; **~ que** to admit *ou*
acknowledge that; **~ qn/qch à** (*l'identifier
grâce à*) to recognize sb/sth by; **~ à qn: je lui
reconnais certaines qualités** I recognize
certain qualities in him; **se ~ quelque part**
(*s'y retrouver*) to find one's way around (a
place).

reconnu, e [ʀ(ə)kɔny] *pp de* **reconnaître ♦** *adj*
(*indiscuté, connu*) recognized.

reconquérir [ʀəkɔ̃keʀiʀ] *vt* (*aussi fig*) to
reconquer, recapture; (*sa dignité etc*) to
recover.

reconquête [ʀəkɔ̃kɛt] *nf* recapture; recovery.

reconsidérer [ʀəkɔ̃sideʀe] *vt* to reconsider.

reconstituant, e [ʀəkɔ̃stitɥɑ̃, -ɑ̃t] *adj* (*régime*)
strength-building ♦ *nm* tonic, pick-me-up.

reconstituer [ʀəkɔ̃stitɥe] *vt* (*monument ancien*)
to recreate, build a replica of; (*fresque, vase
brisé*) to piece together, reconstitute;
(*événement, accident*) to reconstruct;
(*fortune, patrimoine*) to rebuild; (*BIO: tissus
etc*) to regenerate.

reconstitution [ʀəkɔ̃stitysjɔ̃] *nf* (*d'un accident
etc*) reconstruction.

reconstruction [ʀəkɔ̃stʀyksjɔ̃] *nf* rebuilding,
reconstruction.

reconstruire [ʀəkɔ̃stʀɥiʀ] *vt* to rebuild,
reconstruct.

reconversion [ʀəkɔ̃vɛʀsjɔ̃] *nf* (*du personnel*)
redeployment.

reconvertir [ʀəkɔ̃vɛʀtiʀ] *vt* (*usine*) to
reconvert; (*personnel, troupes etc*) to
redeploy; **se ~ dans** (*un métier, une branche*)
to move into, be redeployed into.

recopier [ʀəkɔpje] *vt* (*transcrire*) to copy out
again, write out again; (*mettre au propre:
devoir*) to make a clean *ou* fair copy of.

record [ʀəkɔʀ] *nm, adj* record; **~ du monde**
world record.

recoucher [ʀəkuʃe] *vt* (*enfant*) to put back to
bed.

recoudre [ʀəkudʀ(ə)] *vt* (*bouton*) to sew back
on; (*plaie, incision*) to sew (back) up, stitch
up.

recoupement [ʀəkupmɑ̃] *nm:* **faire un ~** *ou*
des ~s to cross-check; **par ~** by cross-
checking.

recouper [ʀəkupe] *vt* (*tranche*) to cut again;
(*vêtement*) to recut ♦ *vi* (*CARTES*) to cut
again; **se ~** *vi* (*témoignages*) to tie *ou* match
up.

recourais [ʀəkuʀɛ] *etc vb voir* **recourir**.

recourbé, e [ʀəkuʀbe] *adj* curved; hooked;
bent.

recourber [ʀəkuʀbe] *vt* (*branche, tige de métal*)
to bend.

recourir [ʀəkuʀiʀ] *vi* (*courir de nouveau*) to run
again; (*refaire une course*) to race again; **~ à**
vt (*ami, agence*) to turn *ou* appeal to; (*force,
ruse, emprunt*) to resort to, have recourse to.

recours [ʀəkuʀ] *vb voir* **recourir ♦** *nm* (*JUR*)
appeal; **avoir ~ à = recourir à; en dernier ~**
as a last resort; **sans ~** final; with no way
out; **~ en grâce** plea for clemency (*ou*
pardon).

recouru, e [ʀəkuʀy] *pp de* **recourir**.

recousu, e [ʀəkuzy] *pp de* **recoudre**.

recouvert, e [ʀəkuvɛʀ, -ɛʀt(ə)] *pp de* **recouvrir**.

recouvrable [ʀəkuvʀabl(ə)] *adj* (*somme*)
recoverable.

recouvrais [ʀəkuvʀɛ] *etc vb voir* **recouvrer,
recouvrir**.

recouvrement [ʀəkuvʀəmɑ̃] *nm* recovery.

recouvrer [ʀəkuvʀe] *vt* (*vue, santé etc*) to
recover, regain; (*impôts*) to collect;
(*créance*) to recover.

recouvrir [ʀəkuvʀiʀ] *vt* (*couvrir à nouveau*) to
re-cover; (*couvrir entièrement, aussi fig*) to
cover; (*cacher, masquer*) to conceal, hide; **se
~** (*se superposer*) to overlap.

recracher [ʀəkʀaʃe] *vt* to spit out.

récréatif, ive [ʀekʀeatif, -iv] *adj* of
entertainment; recreational.

récréation [ʀekʀeasjɔ̃] *nf* recreation,
entertainment; (*SCOL*) break.

recréer [ʀəkʀee] *vt* to recreate.

récrier [ʀekʀije]: **se ~** *vi* to exclaim.

récriminations [ʀekʀiminasjɔ̃] *nfpl*
remonstrations, complaints.

récriminer [ʀekʀimine] *vi:* **~ contre qn/qch** to
remonstrate against sb/sth.

recroqueviller [ʀəkʀɔkvije]: **se ~** *vi* (*feuilles*)
to curl *ou* shrivel up; (*personne*) to huddle
up.

recru, e [ʀəkʀy] *adj:* **~ de fatigue** exhausted
♦ *nf* recruit.

recrudescence [ʀəkʀydesɑ̃s] *nf* fresh
outbreak.

recrutement [ʀəkʀytmɑ̃] *nm* recruiting,
recruitment.

recruter [ʀəkʀyte] *vt* to recruit.

rectal, e, aux [ʀɛktal, -o] *adj:* **par voie ~e**
rectally.

rectangle [ʀɛktɑ̃gl(ə)] *nm* rectangle; **~ blanc**
(*TV*) "adults only" symbol.

rectangulaire [ʀɛktɑ̃gylɛʀ] *adj* rectangular.

recteur [ʀɛktœʀ] *nm* ≈ (regional) director of
education (*BRIT*), ≈ state superintendent of
education (*US*).

rectificatif, ive [ʀɛktifikatif, -iv] *adj* corrected
♦ *nm* correction.

rectification [ʀɛktifikasjɔ̃] *nf* correction.

rectifier [ʀɛktifje] *vt* (*tracé, virage*) to
straighten; (*calcul, adresse*) to correct;
(*erreur, faute*) to rectify, put right.

rectiligne [ʀɛktiliɲ] *adj* straight; (*GÉOM*)
rectilinear.

rectitude [ʀɛktityd] *nf* rectitude, uprightness.

recto [rɛkto] nm front (of a sheet of paper).

rectorat [rɛktɔra] nm (fonction) position of recteur; (bureau) recteur's office; see also **recteur**.

rectum [rɛktɔm] nm rectum.

reçu, e [rəsy] pp de **recevoir** ♦ adj (admis, consacré) accepted ♦ nm (COMM) receipt.

recueil [rəkœj] nm collection.

recueillement [rəkœjmɑ̃] nm meditation, contemplation.

recueilli, e [rəkœji] adj contemplative.

recueillir [rəkœjir] vt to collect; (voix, suffrages) to win; (accueillir: réfugiés, chat) to take in; **se** ~ vi to gather one's thoughts; to meditate.

recuire [rəkɥir] vi: **faire** ~ to recook.

recul [rəkyl] nm retreat; recession; decline; (d'arme à feu) recoil, kick; **avoir un mouvement de** ~ to recoil, start back; **prendre du** ~ to stand back; **avec le** ~ with the passing of time, in retrospect.

reculade [rəkylad] nf (péj) climb-down.

reculé, e [rəkyle] adj remote.

reculer [rəkyle] vi to move back, back away; (AUTO) to reverse, back (up); (fig: civilisation, épidémie) to (be on the) decline; (: se dérober) to shrink back ♦ vt to move back; to reverse, back (up); (fig: possibilités, limites) to extend; (: date, décision) to postpone; ~ **devant** (danger, difficulté) to shrink from; ~ **pour mieux sauter** (fig) to postpone the evil day.

reculons [rəkylɔ̃]: **à** ~ adv backwards.

récupérable [rekyperabl(ə)] adj (créance) recoverable; (heures) which can be made up; (ferraille) salvageable.

récupération [rekyperasjɔ̃] nf (de vieux métaux etc) salvage, reprocessing; (POL) bringing into line.

récupérer [rekypere] vt (rentrer en possession de) to recover, get back; (: forces) to recover; (déchets etc) to salvage (for reprocessing); (remplacer: journée, heures de travail) to make up; (délinquant etc) to rehabilitate; (POL) to bring into line ♦ vi to recover.

récurer [rekyre] vt to scour; **poudre à** ~ scouring powder.

reçus [rəsy] etc vb voir **recevoir**.

récusable [rekyzabl(ə)] adj (témoin) challengeable; (témoignage) impugnable.

récuser [rekyze] vt to challenge; **se** ~ to decline to give an opinion.

recyclage [rəsiklaʒ] nm reorientation; retraining; recycling; **cours de** ~ retraining course.

recycler [rəsikle] vt (SCOL) to reorientate; (employés) to retrain; (matériau) to recycle; **se** ~ to retrain; to go on a retraining course.

rédacteur, trice [redaktœr, -tris] nm/f (journaliste) writer; subeditor; (d'ouvrage de référence) editor, compiler; ~ **en chef** chief editor; ~ **publicitaire** copywriter.

rédaction [redaksjɔ̃] nf writing; (rédacteurs) editorial staff; (bureau) editorial office(s); (SCOL: devoir) essay, composition.

reddition [redisjɔ̃] nf surrender.

redéfinir [rədefinir] vt to redefine.

redemander [rədmɑ̃de] vt (renseignement) to ask again for; (nourriture): ~ **de** to ask for more (ou another); (objet prêté): ~ **qch** to ask for sth back.

redémarrer [rədemare] vi (véhicule) to start again, get going again; (fig: industrie etc) to get going again.

rédemption [redɑ̃psjɔ̃] nf redemption.

redéploiement [rədeplwamɑ̃] nm redeployment.

redescendre [rədesɑ̃dR(ə)] vi (à nouveau) to go back down; (après la montée) to go down (again) ♦ vt (pente etc) to go down.

redevable [rədvabl(ə)] adj: **être** ~ **de qch à qn** (somme) to owe sb sth; (fig) to be indebted to sb for sth.

redevance [rədvɑ̃s] nf (TÉL) rental charge; (TV) licence (BRIT) ou license (US) fee.

redevenir [rədvənir] vi to become again.

rédhibitoire [redibitwar] adj: **vice** ~ (JUR) latent defect in merchandise that renders the sales contract void; (fig: défaut) crippling.

rediffuser [rədifyze] vt (RADIO, TV) to repeat, broadcast again.

rediffusion [rədifyzjɔ̃] nf repeat (programme).

rédiger [rediʒe] vt to write; (contrat) to draw up.

redire [rədir] vt to repeat; **trouver à** ~ **à** to find fault with.

redistribuer [rədistribɥe] vt (cartes etc) to deal again; (richesses, tâches, revenus) to redistribute.

redite [rədit] nf (needless) repetition.

redondance [rədɔ̃dɑ̃s] nf redundancy.

redonner [rədɔne] vt (restituer) to give back, return; (du courage, des forces) to restore.

redoublé, e [rəduble] adj: **à coups** ~**s** even harder, twice as hard.

redoubler [rəduble] vi (tempête, violence) to intensify, get even stronger ou fiercer etc; (SCOL) to repeat a year ♦ vt (SCOL: classe) to repeat; (LING: lettre) to double; ~ **de** vt to be twice as + adjectif; **le vent redouble de violence** the wind is blowing twice as hard.

redoutable [rədutabl(ə)] adj formidable, fearsome.

redouter [rədute] vt to fear; (appréhender) to dread; ~ **de faire** to dread doing.

redoux [rədu] nm milder spell.

redressement [rədrɛsmɑ̃] nm (de l'économie etc) putting right; **maison de** ~ reformatory; ~ **fiscal** repayment of back taxes.

redresser [RədRese] _vt_ (_arbre, mât_) to set upright, right; (_pièce tordue_) to straighten out; (_AVIAT, AUTO_) to straighten up; (_situation, économie_) to put right; **se ~** _vi_ (_objet penché_) to right itself; to straighten up; (_personne_) to sit (_ou_ stand) up; to sit (_ou_ stand) up straight; (_fig: pays, situation_) to recover; **~ (les roues)** (_AUTO_) to straighten up.

redresseur [RədRɛsœR] _nm_: **~ de torts** righter of wrongs.

réducteur, trice [RedyktœR, -tRis] _adj_ simplistic.

réduction [Redyksjɔ̃] _nf_ reduction; **en ~** _adv_ in miniature, scaled-down.

réduire [Redɥiʀ] _vt_ (_gén, aussi CULIN, MATH_) to reduce; (_prix, dépenses_) to cut, reduce; (_carte_) to scale down, reduce; (_MÉD: fracture_) to set; **~ qn/qch à** to reduce sb/sth to; **se ~ à** (_revenir à_) to boil down to; **se ~ en** (_se transformer en_) to be reduced to; **en être réduit à** to be reduced to.

réduit, e [Redɥi, -it] _pp de_ **réduire** ♦ _adj_ (_prix, tarif, échelle_) reduced; (_mécanisme_) scaled-down; (_vitesse_) reduced ♦ _nm_ tiny room; recess.

rééchelonner [Reeʃlɔne] _vt_ to reschedule.

rééditer [Reedite] _vt_ to republish.

réédition [Reedisjɔ̃] _nf_ new edition.

rééducation [Reedykɑsjɔ̃] _nf_ (_d'un membre_) re-education; (_de délinquants, d'un blessé_) rehabilitation; **~ de la parole** speech therapy; **centre de ~** physiotherapy _ou_ physical therapy (_US_) centre.

rééduquer [Reedyke] _vt_ to reeducate; to rehabilitate.

réel, le [Reɛl] _adj_ real ♦ _nm_: **le ~** reality.

réélection [Reelɛksjɔ̃] _nf_ re-election.

rééligible [Reeliʒibl(ə)] _adj_ re-eligible.

réélire [Reeliʀ] _vt_ to re-elect.

réellement [Reɛlmɑ̃] _adv_ really.

réembaucher [Reɑ̃boʃe] _vt_ to take on again.

réemploi [Reɑ̃plwa] _nm_ = **remploi**.

réemployer [Reɑ̃plwaje] _vt_ (_méthode, produit_) to re-use; (_argent_) to reinvest; (_personnel, employé_) to re-employ.

rééquilibrer [Reekilibʀe] _vt_ (_budget_) to balance (again).

réescompte [Reɛskɔ̃t] _nm_ rediscount.

réessayer [Reeseje] _vt_ to try on again.

réévaluation [Reevalɥɑsjɔ̃] _nf_ revaluation.

réévaluer [Reevalɥe] _vt_ to revalue.

réexaminer [Reɛgzamine] _vt_ to re-examine.

réexpédier [Reɛkspedje] _vt_ (_à l'envoyeur_) to return, send back; (_au destinataire_) to send on, forward.

réexporter [Reɛkspɔʀte] _vt_ to re-export.

réf. _abr_ (= _référence(s)_): **V/~** Your ref.

refaire [RəfɛR] _vt_ (_faire de nouveau, recommencer_) to do again; (_réparer, restaurer_) to do up; **se ~** _vi_ (_en argent_) to make up one's losses; **se ~ une santé** to recuperate; **se ~ à**

qch (_se réhabituer à_) to get used to sth again

refasse [Rəfas] _etc vb voir_ **refaire**.

réfection [Refɛksjɔ̃] _nf_ repair; **en ~** under repair.

réfectoire [RefɛktwaR] _nm_ refectory.

referai [R(ə)fʀe] _etc vb voir_ **refaire**.

référé [Refere] _nm_ (_JUR_) emergency interim proceedings _ou_ ruling.

référence [Referɑ̃s] _nf_ reference; **~s** _nfpl_ (_recommandations_) reference _sg_; **faire ~ à** to refer to; **ouvrage de ~** reference work; **ce n'est pas une ~** (_fig_) that's no recommendation.

référendum [Referɑ̃dɔm] _nm_ referendum.

référer [Refere]: **se ~ à** _vt_ to refer to; **en ~ à qn** to refer the matter to sb.

refermer [RəfɛRme] _vt_ to close again, shut again.

refiler [Rəfile] _vt_ (_fam_): **~ qch à qn** to palm (_BRIT_) _ou_ fob sth off on sb; to pass sth on to sb.

refit [Rəfi] _etc vb voir_ **refaire**.

réfléchi, e [Refleʃi] _adj_ (_caractère_) thoughtful; (_action_) well-thought-out; (_LING_) reflexive.

réfléchir [RefleʃiR] _vt_ to reflect ♦ _vi_ to think; **~ à** _ou_ **sur** to think about; **c'est tout réfléchi** my mind's made up.

réflecteur [ReflɛktœR] _nm_ (_AUTO_) reflector.

reflet [Rəflɛ] _nm_ reflection; (_sur l'eau etc_) sheer _no pl_, glint; **~s** _nmpl_ gleam _sg_.

refléter [Rəflete] _vt_ to reflect; **se ~** _vi_ to be reflected.

réflex [Reflɛks] _adj inv_ (_PHOTO_) reflex.

réflexe [Reflɛks(ə)] _adj, nm_ reflex; **~ conditionné** conditioned reflex.

réflexion [Reflɛksjɔ̃] _nf_ (_de la lumière etc, pensée_) reflection; (_fait de penser_) thought; (_remarque_) remark; **~s** _nfpl_ (_méditations_) thought _sg_, reflection _sg_; **sans ~** without thinking; **~ faite, à la ~, après ~** on reflection; **délai de ~** cooling-off period; **groupe de ~** think tank.

refluer [Rəflye] _vi_ to flow back; (_foule_) to surge back.

reflux [Rəfly] _nm_ (_de la mer_) ebb; (_fig_) backward surge.

refondre [Rəfɔ̃dʀ(ə)] _vt_ (_texte_) to recast.

refont [R(ə)fɔ̃] _vb voir_ **refaire**.

reformater [RəfɔRmate] _vt_ to reformat.

réformateur, trice [RefɔRmatœR, -tRis] _nm/f_ reformer ♦ _adj_ (_mesures_) reforming.

Réformation [RefɔRmɑsjɔ̃] _nf_: **la ~** the Reformation.

réforme [Refɔʀm(ə)] _nf_ reform; (_MIL_) declaration of unfitness for service; discharge (_on health grounds_); (_REL_): **la R~** the Reformation.

réformé, e [RefɔRme] _adj, nm/f_ (_REL_) Protestant.

reformer [RəfɔRme] _vt_, **se ~** _vi_ to reform; **~ les rangs** (_MIL_) to fall in again.

réformer [RefɔRme] _vt_ to reform; (_MIL: recrue_)

to declare unfit for service; (: *soldat*) to discharge, invalid out; (*matériel*) to scrap.

réformisme [ʀefɔʀmism(ə)] *nm* reformism, policy of reform.

réformiste [ʀefɔʀmist(ə)] *adj*, *nmf* (*POL*) reformist.

refoulé, e [ʀəfule] *adj* (*PSYCH*) repressed.

refoulement [ʀəfulmɑ̃] *nm* (*d'une armée*) driving back; (*PSYCH*) repression.

refouler [ʀəfule] *vt* (*envahisseurs*) to drive back, repulse; (*liquide*) to force back; (*fig*) to suppress; (*PSYCH*) to repress.

réfractaire [ʀefʀaktɛʀ] *adj* (*minerai*) refractory; (*brique*) fire *cpd*; (*maladie*) which is resistant to treatment; (*prêtre*) non-juring; **soldat** ~ draft evader; **être** ~ **à** to resist.

réfracter [ʀefʀakte] *vt* to refract.

réfraction [ʀefʀaksjɔ̃] *nf* refraction.

refrain [ʀəfʀɛ̃] *nm* (*MUS*) refrain, chorus; (*air, fig*) tune.

refréner, réfréner [ʀəfʀene, ʀefʀene] *vt* to curb, check.

réfrigérant, e [ʀefʀiʒeʀɑ̃, -ɑ̃t] *adj* refrigerant, cooling.

réfrigérateur [ʀefʀiʒeʀatœʀ] *nm* refrigerator; ~**-congélateur** fridge-freezer.

réfrigération [ʀefʀiʒeʀasjɔ̃] *nf* refrigeration.

réfrigéré, e [ʀefʀiʒeʀe] *adj* (*camion, wagon*) refrigerated.

réfrigérer [ʀefʀiʒeʀe] *vt* to refrigerate; (*fam: glacer, aussi fig*) to cool.

refroidir [ʀəfʀwadiʀ] *vt* to cool; (*fig*) to have a cooling effect on ♦ *vi* to cool (down); **se** ~ *vi* (*prendre froid*) to catch a chill; (*temps*) to get cooler *ou* colder; (*fig*) to cool (off).

refroidissement [ʀəfʀwadismɑ̃] *nm* cooling; (*grippe etc*) chill.

refuge [ʀəfyʒ] *nm* refuge; (*pour piétons*) (traffic) island; **demander** ~ **à qn** to ask sb for refuge.

réfugié, e [ʀefyʒje] *adj*, *nmf* refugee.

réfugier [ʀefyʒje]: **se** ~ *vi* to take refuge.

refus [ʀəfy] *nm* refusal; **ce n'est pas de** ~ I won't say no, it's very welcome.

refuser [ʀəfyze] *vt* to refuse; (*SCOL: candidat*) to fail ♦ *vi* to refuse; ~ **qch à qn/de faire** to refuse sb sth/to do; ~ **du monde** to have to turn people away; **se** ~ **à qch** *ou* **à faire qch** to refuse to do sth; **il ne se refuse rien** he doesn't stint himself; **se** ~ **à qn** to refuse sb.

réfutable [ʀefytabl(ə)] *adj* refutable.

réfuter [ʀefyte] *vt* to refute.

regagner [ʀəɡaɲe] *vt* (*argent, faveur*) to win back; (*lieu*) to get back to; ~ **le temps perdu** to make up (for) lost time; ~ **du terrain** to regain ground.

regain [ʀəɡɛ̃] *nm* (*herbe*) second crop of hay; (*renouveau*): **un** ~ **de** renewed + *nom*.

régal [ʀeɡal] *nm* treat; **un** ~ **pour les yeux** a pleasure *ou* delight to look at.

régalade [ʀeɡalad] *adv*: **à la** ~ from the bottle (held away from the lips).

régaler [ʀeɡale] *vt*: ~ **qn** to treat sb to a delicious meal; ~ **qn de** to treat sb to; **se** ~ *vi* to have a delicious meal; (*fig*) to enjoy o.s.

regard [ʀəɡaʀ] *nm* (*coup d'œil*) look, glance; (*expression*) look (in one's eye); **parcourir/menacer du** ~ to cast an eye over/look threateningly at; **au** ~ **de** (*loi, morale*) from the point of view of; **en** ~ (*vis à vis*) opposite; **en** ~ **de** in comparison with.

regardant, e [ʀəɡaʀdɑ̃, -ɑ̃t] *adj*: **très/peu** ~ **(sur)** quite fussy/very free (about); (*économe*) very tight-fisted/quite generous (with).

regarder [ʀəɡaʀde] *vt* (*examiner, observer, lire*) to look at; (*film, télévision, match*) to watch; (*envisager: situation, avenir*) to view; (*considérer: son intérêt etc*) to be concerned with; (*être orienté vers*): ~ **(vers)** to face; (*concerner*) to concern ♦ *vi* to look; ~ **à** *vt* (*dépense, qualité, détails*) to be fussy with *ou* over; ~ **à faire** to hesitate to do; **dépenser sans** ~ to spend freely; ~ **qn/qch comme** to regard sb/sth as; ~ **(qch) dans le dictionnaire/l'annuaire** to look (sth up) in the dictionary/directory; ~ **par la fenêtre** to look out of the window; **cela me regarde** it concerns me, it's my business.

régate(s) [ʀeɡat] *nf(pl)* regatta.

régénérer [ʀeʒeneʀe] *vt* to regenerate; (*fig*) to revive.

régent [ʀeʒɑ̃] *nm* regent.

régenter [ʀeʒɑ̃te] *vt* to rule over; to dictate to.

régie [ʀeʒi] *nf* (*COMM, INDUSTRIE*) state-owned company; (*THÉÂT, CINÉ*) production; (*RADIO, TV*) control room; **la** ~ **de l'État** state control.

regimber [ʀəʒɛ̃be] *vi* to balk, jib.

régime [ʀeʒim] *nm* (*POL, GÉO*) régime; (*ADMIN: carcéral, fiscal etc*) system; (*MÉD*) diet; (*TECH*) (engine) speed; (*fig*) rate, pace; (*de bananes, dattes*) bunch; **se mettre au/suivre un** ~ to go on/be on a diet; ~ **sans sel** salt-free diet; **à bas/haut** ~ (*AUTO*) at low/high revs; **à plein** ~ flat out, at full speed; ~ **matrimonial** marriage settlement.

régiment [ʀeʒimɑ̃] *nm* (*MIL: unité*) regiment; (*fig: fam*): **un** ~ **de** an army of; **un copain de** ~ a pal from military service *ou* (one's) army days.

région [ʀeʒjɔ̃] *nf* region; **la** ~ **parisienne** the Paris area.

régional, e, aux [ʀeʒjɔnal, -o] *adj* regional.

régionalisation [ʀeʒjɔnalizasjɔ̃] *nf* regionalization.

régionalisme [ʀeʒjɔnalism(ə)] *nm* regionalism.

régir [ʀeʒiʀ] *vt* to govern.

régisseur [ʀeʒisœʀ] *nm* (*d'un domaine*) steward; (*CINÉ, TV*) assistant director; (*THÉÂT*) stage manager.

registre [ʀəʒistʀ(ə)] *nm* (*livre*) register;

logbook; ledger; (*MUS, LING*) register; (*d'orgue*) stop; ~ **de comptabilité** ledger; ~ **de l'état civil** register of births, marriages and deaths.

réglable [ʀeglabl(ə)] *adj* (*siège, flamme etc*) adjustable; (*achat*) payable.

réglage [ʀeglaʒ] *nm* (*d'une machine*) adjustment; (*d'un moteur*) tuning.

règle [ʀɛgl(ə)] *nf* (*instrument*) ruler; (*loi, prescription*) rule; ~**s** *nfpl* (*PHYSIOL*) period *sg*; **avoir pour** ~ **de** to make it a rule that *ou* to; **en** ~ (*papiers d'identité*) in order; **être/se mettre en** ~ to be/put o.s. straight with the authorities; **en** ~ **générale** as a (general) rule; **être la** ~ to be the rule; **être de** ~ to be usual; ~ **à calcul** slide rule; ~ **de trois** (*MATH*) rule of three.

réglé, e [ʀegle] *adj* well-ordered; stable, steady; (*papier*) ruled; (*arrangé*) settled; (*femme*): **bien** ~**e** whose periods are regular.

règlement [ʀɛgləmɑ̃] *nm* settling; (*paiement*) settlement; (*arrêté*) regulation; (*règles, statuts*) regulations *pl*, rules *pl*; ~ **à la commande** cash with order; ~ **de compte(s)** settling of scores; ~ **en espèces/par chèque** payment in cash/by cheque; ~ **intérieur** (*SCOL*) school rules *pl*; (*ADMIN*) by-laws *pl*; ~ **judiciaire** compulsory liquidation.

réglementaire [ʀɛgləmɑ̃tɛʀ] *adj* conforming to the regulations; (*tenue, uniforme*) regulation *cpd*.

réglementation [ʀɛgləmɑ̃tasjɔ̃] *nf* regulation, control; (*règlements*) regulations *pl*.

réglementer [ʀɛgləmɑ̃te] *vt* to regulate, control.

régler [ʀegle] *vt* (*mécanisme, machine*) to regulate, adjust; (*moteur*) to tune; (*thermostat etc*) to set, adjust; (*emploi du temps etc*) to organize, plan; (*question, conflit, facture, dette*) to settle; (*fournisseur*) to settle up with, pay; (*papier*) to rule; ~ **qch sur** to model sth on; ~ **son compte à qn** to sort sb out, settle sb; ~ **un compte avec qn** to settle a score with sb.

réglisse [ʀeglis] *nf ou m* liquorice; **bâton de** ~ liquorice stick.

règne [ʀɛɲ] *nm* (*d'un roi etc, fig*) reign; (*BIO*): **le** ~ **végétal/animal** the vegetable/animal kingdom.

régner [ʀeɲe] *vi* (*roi*) to rule, reign; (*fig*) to reign.

regonfler [ʀ(ə)gɔ̃fle] *vt* (*ballon, pneu*) to reinflate, blow up again.

regorger [ʀəgɔʀʒe] *vi* to overflow; ~ **de** to overflow with, be bursting with.

régresser [ʀegʀese] *vi* (*phénomène*) to decline; (*enfant, malade*) to regress.

régressif, ive [ʀegʀesif, -iv] *adj* regressive.

régression [ʀegʀesjɔ̃] *nf* decline; regression; **être en** ~ to be on the decline.

regret [ʀəgʀɛ] *nm* regret; **à** ~ with regret;

avec ~ regretfully; **être au** ~ **de devoir/ne pas pouvoir faire** to regret to have to/that one is unable to do; **j'ai le** ~ **de vous informer que** ... I regret to inform you that ....

regrettable [ʀəgʀɛtabl(ə)] *adj* regrettable.

regretter [ʀəgʀete] *vt* to regret; (*personne*) to miss; ~ **d'avoir fait** to regret doing; ~ **que** to regret that, be sorry that; **non, je regrette** no, I'm sorry.

regroupement [ʀ(ə)gʀupmɑ̃] *nm* grouping together; (*groupe*) group.

regrouper [ʀəgʀupe] *vt* (*grouper*) to group together; (*contenir*) to include, comprise; **se** ~ *vi* to gather (together).

régularisation [ʀegylaʀizasjɔ̃] *nf* (*de papiers, passeport*) putting in order; (*de sa situation: par le mariage*) regularization; (*d'un mécanisme*) regulation.

régulariser [ʀegylaʀize] *vt* (*fonctionnement, trafic*) to regulate; (*passeport, papiers*) to put in order; (*sa situation*) to straighten out, regularize.

régularité [ʀegylaʀite] *nf* regularity.

régulateur, trice [ʀegylatœʀ, -tʀis] *adj* regulating ♦ *nm* (*TECH*): ~ **de vitesse/de température** speed/temperature regulator.

régulation [ʀegylasjɔ̃] *nf* (*du trafic*) regulation; ~ **des naissances** birth control.

régulier, ière [ʀegylje, -jɛʀ] *adj* (*gén*) regular; (*vitesse, qualité*) steady; (*répartition, pression, paysage*) even; (*TRANSPORTS: ligne, service*) scheduled, regular; (*légal, réglementaire*) lawful, in order; (*fam: correct*) straight, on the level.

régulièrement [ʀegyljɛʀmɑ̃] *adv* regularly; steadily; evenly; normally.

régurgiter [ʀegyʀʒite] *vt* to regurgitate.

réhabiliter [ʀeabilite] *vt* to rehabilitate; (*fig*) to restore to favour (*BRIT*) *ou* favor (*US*).

réhabituer [ʀeabitɥe] *vt*: **se** ~ **à qch/à faire qch** to get used to sth again/to doing sth again.

rehausser [ʀəose] *vt* to heighten, raise; (*fig*) to set off, enhance.

réimporter [ʀeɛ̃pɔʀte] *vt* to reimport.

réimposer [ʀeɛ̃poze] *vt* (*FINANCE*) to reimpose; to tax again.

réimpression [ʀeɛ̃pʀesjɔ̃] *nf* reprinting; (*ouvrage*) reprint.

réimprimer [ʀeɛ̃pʀime] *vt* to reprint.

Reims [ʀis] *n* Rheims.

rein [ʀɛ̃] *nm* kidney; ~**s** *nmpl* (*dos*) back *sg*; **avoir mal aux** ~**s** to have backache; ~ **artificiel** kidney machine.

réincarnation [ʀeɛ̃kaʀnasjɔ̃] *nf* reincarnation.

réincarner [ʀeɛ̃kaʀne]: **se** ~ *vr* to be reincarnated.

reine [ʀɛn] *nf* queen.

reine-claude [ʀɛnklod] *nf* greengage.

reinette [ʀɛnɛt] *nf* rennet, pippin.

réinitialisation [ʀeinisjalizasjɔ̃] *nf* (*INFORM*)

reset.

réinsérer [ʀeɛ̃seʀe] *vt* (*délinquant, handicapé etc*) to rehabilitate.

réinsertion [ʀeɛ̃sɛʀsjɔ̃] *nf* rehabilitation.

réintégrer [ʀeɛ̃tegʀe] *vt* (*lieu*) to return to; (*fonctionnaire*) to reinstate.

réitérer [ʀeiteʀe] *vt* to repeat, reiterate.

rejaillir [ʀəʒajiʀ] *vi* to splash up; ~ **sur** to splash up onto; (*fig*) to rebound on; to fall upon.

rejet [ʀəʒɛ] *nm* (*action, aussi MÉD*) rejection; (*POÉSIE*) enjambement, rejet; (*BOT*) shoot.

rejeter [ʀəʒte] *vt* (*relancer*) to throw back; (*vomir*) to bring *ou* throw up; (*écarter*) to reject; (*déverser*) to throw out, discharge; (*reporter*): ~ **un mot à la fin d'une phrase** to transpose a word to the end of a sentence; **se ~ sur qch** (*accepter faute de mieux*) to fall back on sth; ~ **la tête/les épaules en arrière** to throw one's head/pull one's shoulders back; ~ **la responsabilité de qch sur qn** to lay the responsibility for sth at sb's door.

rejeton [ʀəʒtɔ̃] *nm* offspring.

rejette [ʀ(ə)ʒɛt] *etc vb voir* **rejeter**.

rejoignais [ʀ(ə)ʒwaɲɛ] *etc vb voir* **rejoindre**.

rejoindre [ʀəʒwɛ̃dʀ(ə)] *vt* (*famille, régiment*) to rejoin, return to; (*lieu*) to get (back) to; (*suj: route etc*) to meet, join; (*rattraper*) to catch up (with); **se ~** *vi* to meet; **je te rejoins au café** I'll see *ou* meet you at the café.

réjoui, e [ʀeʒwi] *adj* joyous.

réjouir [ʀeʒwiʀ] *vt* to delight; **se ~** *vi* to be delighted; **se ~ de qch/de faire** to be delighted about sth/to do; **se ~ que** to be delighted that.

réjouissances [ʀeʒwisɑ̃s] *nfpl* (*joie*) rejoicing *sg*; (*fête*) festivities, merry-making *sg*.

réjouissant, e [ʀeʒwisɑ̃, -ɑ̃t] *adj* heartening, delightful.

relâche [ʀəlɑʃ]: **faire ~** *vi* (*navire*) to put into port; (*CINÉ*) to be closed; **c'est le jour de ~** (*CINÉ*) it's closed today; **sans ~** *adv* without respite *ou* a break.

relâché, e [ʀəlɑʃe] *adj* loose, lax.

relâchement [ʀəlɑʃmɑ̃] *nm* (*d'un prisonnier*) release; (*de la discipline, musculaire*) relaxation.

relâcher [ʀəlɑʃe] *vt* (*ressort, prisonnier*) to release; (*étreinte, cordes*) to loosen; (*discipline*) to relax ♦ *vi* (*NAVIG*) to put into port; **se ~** *vi* to loosen; (*discipline*) to become slack *ou* lax; (*élève etc*) to slacken off.

relais [ʀəlɛ] *nm* (*SPORT*): **(course de)** ~ relay (race); (*RADIO, TV*) relay; (*intermédiaire*) go-between; **équipe de** ~ shift team; (*SPORT*) relay team; **prendre le** ~ **(de)** to take over (from); ~ **de poste** post house, coaching inn; ~ **routier** ≈ transport café (*BRIT*), ≈ truck stop (*US*).

relance [ʀəlɑ̃s] *nf* boosting, revival; (*ÉCON*) reflation.

relancer [ʀəlɑ̃se] *vt* (*balle*) to throw back

(again); (*moteur*) to restart; (*fig*) to boost, revive; (*personne*): ~ **qn** to pester sb; to get on to sb again.

relater [ʀəlate] *vt* to relate, recount.

relatif, ive [ʀəlatif, -iv] *adj* relative.

relation [ʀəlasjɔ̃] *nf* (*récit*) account, report; (*rapport*) relation(ship); ~**s** *nfpl* (*rapports*) relations; relationship; (*connaissances*) connections; **être/entrer en ~(s) avec** to be in contact *ou* be dealing/get in contact with; **mettre qn en ~(s) avec** to put sb in touch with; ~**s internationales** international relations; ~**s publiques (RP)** public relations (PR); ~**s (sexuelles)** sexual relations, (sexual) intercourse *sg*.

relativement [ʀəlativmɑ̃] *adv* relatively; ~ **à** in relation to.

relativiser [ʀəlativize] *vt* to see in relation to; to put into context.

relativité [ʀəlativite] *nf* relativity.

relax [ʀəlaks] *adj inv*, **relaxe** [ʀəlaks(ə)] *adj* relaxed, informal, casual; easy-going; **(fauteuil-)** ~ *nm* reclining chair.

relaxant, e [ʀəlaksɑ̃, -ɑ̃t] *adj* (*cure, médicament*) relaxant; (*ambiance*) relaxing.

relaxation [ʀ(ə)laksɑsjɔ̃] *nf* relaxation.

relaxer [ʀəlakse] *vt* to relax; (*JUR*) to discharge; **se ~** *vi* to relax.

relayer [ʀəleje] *vt* (*collaborateur, coureur etc*) to relieve, take over from; (*RADIO, TV*) to relay; **se ~** (*dans une activité*) to take it in turns.

relecture [ʀ(ə)lɛktyʀ] *nf* rereading.

relégation [ʀəlegɑsjɔ̃] *nf* (*SPORT*) relegation.

reléguer [ʀəlege] *vt* to relegate; ~ **au second plan** to push into the background.

relent(s) [ʀəlɑ̃] *nm(pl)* stench *sg*.

relevé, e [ʀəlve] *adj* (*bord de chapeau*) turned-up; (*manches*) rolled-up; (*fig: style*) elevated; (: *sauce*) highly-seasoned ♦ *nm* (*lecture*) reading; (*de cotes*) plotting; (*liste*) statement; list; (*facture*) account; ~ **de compte** bank statement; ~ **d'identité bancaire (RIB)** (bank) account number.

relève [ʀəlɛv] *nf* relief; (*équipe*) relief team (*ou* troops *pl*); **prendre la** ~ to take over.

relèvement [ʀəlɛvmɑ̃] *nm* (*d'un taux, niveau*) raising.

relever [ʀəlve] *vt* (*statue, meuble*) to stand up again; (*personne tombée*) to help up; (*vitre, plafond, niveau de vie*) to raise; (*pays, économie, entreprise*) to put back on its feet; (*col*) to turn up; (*style, conversation*) to elevate; (*plat, sauce*) to season; (*sentinelle, équipe*) to relieve; (*souligner: fautes, points*) to pick out; (*constater: traces etc*) to find, pick up; (*répliquer à: remarque*) to react to, reply to; (: *défi*) to accept, take up; (*noter: adresse etc*) to take down, note; (: *plan*) to sketch; (: *cotes etc*) to plot; (*compteur*) to read; (*ramasser: cahiers, copies*) to collect, take in ♦ *vi* (*jupe, bord*) to ride up; ~ **de** *vt* (*maladie*) to be recovering from; (*être du ressort de*) to be a matter for; (*ADMIN*: *dépendre de*) to come under; (*fig*) to pertain to; **se ~** *vi* (*se remettre debout*) to get up; (*fig*): **se ~** (**de**) to recover (from); **~ qn de** (*vœux*) to release sb from; (*fonctions*) to relieve sb of; **~ la tête** to look up; to hold up one's head.

relief [Rəljɛf] *nm* relief; (*de pneu*) tread pattern; **~s** *nmpl* (*restes*) remains; **en ~** in relief; (*photographie*) three-dimensional; **mettre en ~** (*fig*) to bring out, highlight.

relier [Rəlje] *vt* to link up; (*livre*) to bind; **~ qch à** to link sth to; **livre relié cuir** leather-bound book.

relieur, euse [RəljœR, -øz] *nm/f* (book)binder.

religieusement [R(ə)liʒjøzmɑ̃] *adv* religiously; (*enterré, mariés*) in church; **vivre ~** to lead a religious life.

religieux, euse [Rəliʒjø, -øz] *adj* religious ♦ *nm* monk ♦ *nf* nun; (*gâteau*) cream bun.

religion [Rəliʒjɔ̃] *nf* religion; (*piété, dévotion*) faith; **entrer en ~** to take one's vows.

reliquaire [RəlikɛR] *nm* reliquary.

reliquat [Rəlika] *nm* (*d'une somme*) balance; (*JUR*: *de succession*) residue.

relique [Rəlik] *nf* relic.

relire [RəliR] *vt* (*à nouveau*) to reread, read again; (*vérifier*) to read over; **se ~** to read through what one has written.

reliure [RəljyR] *nf* binding; (*art, métier*): **la ~** book-binding.

reloger [R(ə)lɔʒe] *vt* (*locataires, sinistrés*) to rehouse.

relu, e [Rəly] *pp de* **relire**.

reluire [RəlɥiR] *vi* to gleam.

reluisant, e [Rəlɥizɑ̃, -ɑ̃t] *vb voir* **reluire** ♦ *adj* gleaming; **peu ~** (*fig*) unattractive; unsavoury (*BRIT*), unsavory (*US*).

reluquer [R(ə)lyke] *vt* (*fam*) to eye (up), ogle.

remâcher [Rəmɑʃe] *vt* to chew *ou* ruminate over.

remailler [Rəmɑje] *vt* (*tricot*) to darn; (*filet*) to mend.

remaniement [Rəmanimɑ̃] *nm*: **~ ministériel** Cabinet reshuffle.

remanier [Rəmanje] *vt* to reshape, recast; (*POL*) to reshuffle.

remarier [R(ə)marje]: **se ~** *vi* to remarry, get married again.

remarquable [Rəmarkabl(ə)] *adj* remarkable.

remarquablement [R(ə)markabləmɑ̃] *adv* remarkably.

remarque [Rəmark(ə)] *nf* remark; (*écrite*) note.

remarquer [Rəmarke] *vt* (*voir*) to notice; (*dire*): **~ que** to remark that; **se ~** to be noticeable; **se faire ~** to draw attention to o.s.; **faire ~ (à qn) que** to point out (to sb) that; **faire ~ qch (à qn)** to point sth out (to sb); **remarquez, ...** mark you, ..., mind you, ...

remballer [Rɑ̃bale] *vt* to wrap up (again); (*dans un carton*) to pack up (again).

rembarrer [Rɑ̃baRe] *vt*: **~ qn** (*repousser*) to rebuff sb; (*remettre à sa place*) to put sb in

his (*ou* her) place.

remblai [Rɑ̃blɛ] *nm* embankment.

remblayer [Rɑ̃bleje] *vt* to bank up; (*fossé*) to fill in.

rembobiner [Rɑ̃bɔbine] *vt* to rewind.

rembourrage [Rɑ̃buRaʒ] *nm* stuffing; padding.

rembourré, e [Rɑ̃buRe] *adj* padded.

rembourrer [Rɑ̃buRe] *vt* to stuff; (*dossier, vêtement, souliers*) to pad.

remboursable [Rɑ̃buRsabl(ə)] *adj* repayable.

remboursement [Rɑ̃buRsəmɑ̃] *nm* repayment; **envoi contre ~** cash on delivery.

rembourser [Rɑ̃buRse] *vt* to pay back, repay.

rembrunir [Rɑ̃bRyniR]: **se ~** *vi* to grow sombre (*BRIT*) *ou* somber (*US*).

remède [Rəmɛd] *nm* (*médicament*) medicine; (*traitement, fig*) remedy, cure; **trouver un ~ à** (*MÉD, fig*) to find a cure for.

remédier [Rəmedje]: **~ à** *vt* to remedy.

remembrement [Rəmɑ̃bRəmɑ̃] *nm* (*AGR*) regrouping of lands.

remémorer [Rəmemɔre]: **se ~** *vt* to recall, recollect.

remerciements [RəmɛRsimɑ̃] *nmpl* thanks; (**avec**) **tous mes ~** (with) grateful *ou* many thanks.

remercier [RəmɛRsje] *vt* to thank; (*congédier*) to dismiss; **~ qn de/d'avoir fait** to thank sb for/for having done; **non, je vous remercie** no thank you.

remettre [Rəmɛtʀ(ə)] *vt* (*vêtement*): **~ qch** to put sth back on, put sth on again; (*replacer*): **~ qch quelque part** to put sth back somewhere; (*ajouter*): **~ du sel/un sucre** to add more salt/another lump of sugar; (*rétablir: personne*): **~ qn** to set sb back on his (*ou* her) feet; (*rendre, restituer*): **~ qch à qn** to give sth back to sb, return sth to sb; (*donner, confier: paquet, argent*): **~ qch à qn** to hand sth over to sb, deliver sth to sb; (*prix, décoration*): **~ qch à qn** to present sb with sth; (*ajourner*): **~ qch (à)** to postpone sth *ou* put sth off (until); **se ~** *vi* to get better, recover; **se ~ de** to recover from, get over; **s'en ~ à** to leave it (up) to; **se ~ à faire/qch** to start doing/sth again; **~ une pendule à l'heure** to put a clock right; **~ un moteur/ une machine en marche** to get an engine/a machine going again; **~ en état/en ordre** to repair/sort out; **~ en cause/question** to challenge/question again; **~ sa démission** to hand in one's notice; **~ qch à neuf** to make sth as good as new; **~ qn à sa place** (*fig*) to put sb in his (*ou* her) place.

réminiscence [Reminisɑ̃s] *nf* reminiscence.

remis, e [Rəmi, -iz] *pp de* **remettre** ♦ *nf* delivery; presentation; (*rabais*) discount; (*local*) shed; **~ en marche/en ordre** starting up again/sorting out; **~ en cause/question** calling into question/challenging; **~ de fonds** remittance; **~ en jeu** (*FOOTBALL*) throw-in; **~ à neuf** restoration; **~ de peine**

remission of sentence.

remiser [Rəmize] vt to put away.

rémission [Remisjɔ̃]: **sans** ~ adj irremediable ♦ adv unremittingly.

remodeler [Rəmɔdle] vt to remodel; (fig: restructurer) to restructure.

rémois, e [Remwa, -waz] adj of ou from Rheims ♦ nm/f: **R~, e** inhabitant ou native of Rheims.

remontant [Rəmɔ̃tɑ̃] nm tonic, pick-me-up.

remontée [Rəmɔ̃te] nf rising; ascent; ~s **mécaniques** (SKI) ski lifts, ski tows.

remonte-pente [Rəmɔ̃tpɑ̃t] nm ski lift, (ski) tow.

remonter [Rəmɔ̃te] vi (à nouveau) to go back up; (sur un cheval) to remount; (après une descente) to go up (again); (dans une voiture) to get back in; (jupe) to ride up ♦ vt (pente) to go up; (fleuve) to sail (ou swim etc) up; (manches, pantalon) to roll up; (col) to turn up; (niveau, limite) to raise; (fig: personne) to buck up; (moteur, meuble) to put back together, reassemble; (garde-robe etc) to renew, replenish; (montre, mécanisme) to wind up; ~ **le moral à qn** to raise sb's spirits; ~ **à** (dater de) to date ou go back to; ~ **en voiture** to get back into the car.

remontoir [Rəmɔ̃twaR] nm winding mechanism, winder.

remontrance [Rəmɔ̃tRɑ̃s] nf reproof, reprimand.

remontrer [Rəmɔ̃tRe] vt (montrer de nouveau): ~ **qch (à qn)** to show sth again (to sb); (fig): **en** ~ **à** to prove one's superiority over.

remords [RəmɔR] nm remorse no pl; **avoir des** ~ to feel remorse, be conscience-stricken.

remorque [RəmɔRk(ə)] nf trailer; **prendre/être en** ~ to tow/be on tow; **être à la** ~ (fig) to tag along (behind).

remorquer [RəmɔRke] vt to tow.

remorqueur [RəmɔRkœR] nm tug(boat).

rémoulade [Remulad] nf dressing with mustard and herbs.

rémouleur [Remulœr] nm (knife- ou scissor-) grinder.

remous [Rəmu] nm (d'un navire) (back)wash no pl; (de rivière) swirl, eddy ♦ nmpl (fig) stir sg.

rempailler [Rɑ̃paje] vt to reseat (with straw).

rempart [Rɑ̃paR] nm rampart; **faire à qn un** ~ **de son corps** to shield sb with one's (own) body.

rempiler [Rɑ̃pile] vt (dossiers, livres etc) to pile up again ♦ vi (MIL: fam) to join up again.

remplaçant, e [Rɑ̃plasɑ̃, -ɑ̃t] nm/f replacement, substitute, stand-in; (THÉÂT) understudy; (SCOL) supply (BRIT) ou substitute (US) teacher.

remplacement [Rɑ̃plasmɑ̃] nm replacement; (job) replacement work no pl; (suppléance: SCOL) supply (BRIT) ou substitute (US) teacher; **assurer le** ~ **de qn** (suj: remplaçant) to stand in ou substitute for sb; **faire des** ~s

(professeur) to do supply ou substitute teaching; (médecin) to do locum work.

remplacer [Rɑ̃plase] vt to replace; (prendre temporairement la place de) to stand in for; (tenir lieu de) to take the place of, act as a substitute for; ~ **qch/qn par** to replace sth/sb with.

rempli, e [Rɑ̃pli] adj (emploi du temps) full, busy; ~ **de** full of, filled with.

remplir [Rɑ̃pliR] vt to fill (up); (questionnaire) to fill out ou up; (obligations, fonction, condition) to fulfil; **se** ~ vi to fill up; ~ **qch de** to fill sth with.

remplissage [Rɑ̃plisaʒ] nm (fig: péj) padding.

remploi [Rɑ̃plwa] nm re-use.

rempocher [Rɑ̃pɔʃe] vt to put back into one's pocket.

remporter [Rɑ̃pɔRte] vt (marchandise) to take away; (fig) to win, achieve.

rempoter [Rɑ̃pɔte] vt to repot.

remuant, e [Rəmɥɑ̃, -ɑ̃t] adj restless.

remue-ménage [Rəmymenaʒ] nm inv commotion.

remuer [Rəmɥe] vt to move; (café, sauce) to stir ♦ vi to move; (fig: opposants) to show signs of unrest; **se** ~ vi to move; (se démener) to stir o.s.; (fam) to get a move on.

rémunérateur, trice [RemyneRatœR, -tRis] adj remunerative, lucrative.

rémunération [RemyneRasjɔ̃] nf remuneration.

rémunérer [RemyneRe] vt to remunerate, pay.

renâcler [Rənɑkle] vi to snort; (fig) to grumble, balk.

renaissance [Rənɛsɑ̃s] nf rebirth, revival; **la R~** the Renaissance.

renaître [RənɛtR(ə)] vi to be revived; ~ **à la vie** to take on a new lease of life; ~ **à l'espoir** to find fresh hope.

rénal, e, aux [Renal, -o] adj renal, kidney cpd.

renard [RənaR] nm fox.

renardeau [RənaRdo] nm fox cub.

rencard [Rɑ̃kaR] nm = **rancard**.

rencart [Rɑ̃kaR] nm = **rancart**.

renchérir [Rɑ̃ʃeRiR] vi to become more expensive; (fig): ~ **(sur)** to add something (to).

renchérissement [Rɑ̃ʃeRismɑ̃] nm increase (in the cost ou price of).

rencontre [Rɑ̃kɔ̃tR(ə)] nf (de cours d'eau) confluence; (véhicules) collision; (entrevue, congrès, match etc) meeting; (imprévue) encounter; **faire la** ~ **de qn** to meet sb; **aller à la** ~ **de qn** to go and meet sb; **amours de** ~ casual love affairs.

rencontrer [Rɑ̃kɔ̃tRe] vt to meet; (mot, expression) to come across; (difficultés) to meet with; **se** ~ to meet; (véhicules) to collide.

rendement [Rɑ̃dmɑ̃] nm (d'un travailleur, d'une machine) output; (d'une culture) yield; (d'un investissement) return; **à plein** ~ at full capacity.

rendez-vous [ʀɑ̃devu] *nm* (*rencontre*)
appointment; (: *d'amoureux*) date; (*lieu*)
meeting place; **donner ~ à qn** to arrange to
meet sb; **recevoir sur ~** to have an
appointment system; **fixer un ~ à qn** to give
sb an appointment; **avoir/prendre ~ (avec)**
to have/make an appointment (with);
prendre ~ chez le médecin to make an
appointment with the doctor; **~ spatial** *ou*
orbital docking (in space).

rendormir [ʀɑ̃dɔʀmiʀ]: **se ~** *vr* to go back to
sleep.

rendre [ʀɑ̃dʀ(ə)] *vt* (*livre, argent etc*) to give
back, return; (*otages, visite, politesse,* JUR:
verdict) to return; (*honneurs*) to pay; (*sang,
aliments*) to bring up; (*sons: suj: instrument*)
to produce, make; (*exprimer, traduire*) to
render; (*jugement*) to pronounce, render;
(*faire devenir*): **~ qn célèbre/qch possible** to
make sb famous/sth possible; **se ~** *vi*
(*capituler*) to surrender, give o.s. up; (*aller*):
se ~ quelque part to go somewhere; **se ~ à**
(*arguments etc*) to bow to; (*ordres*) to comply
with; **se ~ compte de qch** to realize sth; **~ la
vue/la santé à qn** to restore sb's sight/
health; **~ la liberté à qn** to set sb free; **~ la
monnaie** to give change; **se ~
insupportable/malade** to become
unbearable/make o.s. ill.

rendu, e [ʀɑ̃dy] *pp de* **rendre** ♦ *adj* (*fatigué*)
exhausted.

renégat, e [ʀənega, -at] *nm/f* renegade.

renégocier [ʀənegɔsje] *vt* to renegociate.

rênes [ʀɛn] *nfpl* reins.

renfermé, e [ʀɑ̃fɛʀme] *adj* (*fig*) withdrawn
♦ *nm*: **sentir le ~** to smell stuffy.

renfermer [ʀɑ̃fɛʀme] *vt* to contain; **se ~ (sur
soi-même)** to withdraw into o.s.

renfiler [ʀɑ̃file] *vt* (*collier*) to rethread; (*pull*) to
slip on.

renflé, e [ʀɑ̃fle] *adj* bulging, bulbous.

renflement [ʀɑ̃fləmɑ̃] *nm* bulge.

renflouer [ʀɑ̃flue] *vt* to refloat; (*fig*) to set
back on its (*ou* his/her *etc*) feet (again).

renfoncement [ʀɑ̃fɔ̃smɑ̃] *nm* recess.

renforcer [ʀɑ̃fɔʀse] *vt* to reinforce; **~ qn dans
ses opinions** to confirm sb's opinion.

renfort [ʀɑ̃fɔʀ]: **~s** *nmpl* reinforcements; **en ~**
as a back-up; **à grand ~ de** with a great
deal of.

renfrogné, e [ʀɑ̃fʀɔɲe] *adj* sullen, scowling.

renfrogner [ʀɑ̃fʀɔɲe]: **se ~** *vi* to scowl.

rengager [ʀɑ̃gaʒe] *vt* (*personnel*) to take on
again; **se ~** (MIL) to re-enlist.

rengaine [ʀɑ̃gɛn] *nf* (*péj*) old tune.

rengainer [ʀɑ̃gene] *vt* (*revolver*) to put back in
its holster; (*épée*) to sheathe; (*fam:
compliment, discours*) to save, withhold.

rengorger [ʀɑ̃gɔʀʒe]: **se ~** *vi* (*fig*) to puff o.s.
up.

renier [ʀənje] *vt* (*parents*) to disown,

repudiate; (*engagements*) to go back on; (*foi*)
to renounce.

renifler [ʀənifle] *vi* to sniff ♦ *vt* (*tabac*) to sniff
up; (*odeur*) to sniff.

rennais, e [ʀɛnɛ, -ɛz] *adj* of *ou* from Rennes
♦ *nm/f*: **R~, e** inhabitant *ou* native of Rennes.

renne [ʀɛn] *nm* reindeer *inv*.

renom [ʀənɔ̃] *nm* reputation; (*célébrité*)
renown; **vin de grand ~** celebrated *ou*
highly renowned wine.

renommé, e [ʀ(ə)nɔme] *adj* celebrated,
renowned ♦ *nf* fame.

renoncement [ʀənɔ̃smɑ̃] *nm* abnegation,
renunciation.

renoncer [ʀənɔ̃se] *vi*: **~ à** *vt* to give up; **~ à
faire** to give up the idea of doing; **j'y
renonce!** I give up!

renouer [ʀənwe] *vt* (*cravate etc*) to retie; (*fig:
conversation, liaison*) to renew, resume; **~
avec** (*tradition*) to revive; (*habitude*) to take
up again; **~ avec qn** to take up with sb
again.

renouveau, x [ʀənuvo] *nm* revival; **~ de
succès** renewed success.

renouvelable [ʀ(ə)nuvlabl(ə)] *adj* (*contrat, bail*)
renewable; (*expérience*) which can be
renewed.

renouveler [ʀənuvle] *vt* to renew; (*exploit,
méfait*) to repeat; **se ~** *vi* (*incident*) to recur,
happen again, be repeated; (*cellules etc*) to
be renewed *ou* replaced; (*artiste, écrivain*) to
try something new.

renouvellement [ʀ(ə)nuvɛlmɑ̃] *nm* renewal;
recurrence.

rénovation [ʀenɔvasjɔ̃] *nf* renovation;
restoration; reform(ing); redevelopment.

rénover [ʀenɔve] *vt* (*immeuble*) to renovate,
do up; (*meuble*) to restore; (*enseignement*) to
reform; (*quartier*) to redevelop.

renseignement [ʀɑ̃sɛɲmɑ̃] *nm* information *no
pl*, piece of information; (MIL) intelligence *no
pl*; **prendre des ~s sur** to make inquiries
about, ask for information about; (**guichet
des**) **~s** information desk; (**service des**) **~s**
(TÉL) directory inquiries (BRIT), information
(US); **service/agent de ~s** (MIL) intelligence
service/agent; **les ~s généraux** ≈ the secret
police.

renseigner [ʀɑ̃seɲe] *vt*: **~ qn (sur)** to give
information to sb (about); **se ~** *vi* to ask for
information, make inquiries.

rentabiliser [ʀɑ̃tabilize] *vt* (*capitaux,
production*) to make profitable.

rentabilité [ʀɑ̃tabilite] *nf* profitability; cost-
effectiveness; (*d'un investissement*) return;
seuil de ~ break-even point.

rentable [ʀɑ̃tabl(ə)] *adj* profitable; cost-
effective.

rente [ʀɑ̃t] *nf* income; (*pension*) pension; (*titre*)
government stock *ou* bond; **~ viagère** life
annuity.

rentier, ière [ʀɑ̃tje, -jɛʀ] *nm/f* person of

private *ou* independent means.

rentrée [ʀɑ̃tʀe] *nf*: ~ **(d'argent)** cash *no pl* coming in; **la** ~ **(des classes)** the start of the new school year; **la** ~ **(parlementaire)** the reopening *ou* reassembly of parliament; **faire sa** ~ (*artiste, acteur*) to make a comeback.

> La rentrée (des classes) *in September each year is more than going back to school for children and teachers. It is also the time when political and social life begin again after the long summer break, and it thus marks an important point in the French year.*

rentrer [ʀɑ̃tʀe] *vi* (*entrer de nouveau*) to go (*ou* come) back in; (*entrer*) to go (*ou* come) in; (*revenir chez soi*) to go (*ou* come) (back) home; (*air, clou: pénétrer*) to go in; (*revenu, argent*) to come in ♦ *vt* (*foins*) to bring in; (*véhicule*) to put away; (*chemise dans pantalon etc*) to tuck in; (*griffes*) to draw in; (*train d'atterrissage*) to raise; (*fig: larmes, colère etc*) to hold back; ~ **le ventre** to pull in one's stomach; ~ **dans** to go (*ou* come) back into; to go (*ou* come) into; (*famille, patrie*) to go back *ou* return to; (*heurter*) to crash into; (*appartenir à*) to be included in; (*: catégorie etc*) to fall into; ~ **dans l'ordre** to get back to normal; ~ **dans ses frais** to recover one's expenses (*ou* initial outlay).

enverrai [ɑ̃vɛʀe] *etc vb voir* **renvoyer**.

enversant, e [ɑ̃vɛʀsɑ̃, -ɑ̃t] *adj* amazing, astounding.

enverse [ɑ̃vɛʀs(ə)]: **à la** ~ *adv* backwards.

enversé, e [ɑ̃vɛʀse] *adj* (*écriture*) backhand; (*image*) reversed; (*stupéfait*) staggered.

enversement [ɑ̃vɛʀsəmɑ̃] *nm* (*d'un régime, des traditions*) overthrow; ~ **de la situation** reversal of the situation.

enverser [ɑ̃vɛʀse] *vt* (*faire tomber: chaise, verre*) to knock over, overturn; (*piéton*) to knock down; (*liquide, contenu*) to spill, upset; (*retourner: verre, image*) to turn upside down, invert; (*: ordre des mots etc*) to reverse; (*fig: gouvernement etc*) to overthrow; (*stupéfier*) to bowl over, stagger; **se** ~ *vi* to fall over; to overturn; to spill; **se** ~ **(en arrière)** to lean back; ~ **la tête/le corps (en arrière)** to tip one's head back/throw oneself back; ~ **la vapeur** (*fig*) to change course.

envoi [ɑ̃vwa] *nm* dismissal; return; reflection; postponement; (*référence*) cross-reference; (*éructation*) belch.

envoyer [ɑ̃vwaje] *vt* to send back; (*congédier*) to dismiss; (*TENNIS*) to return; (*lumière*) to reflect; (*son*) to echo; (*ajourner*): ~ **qch (à)** to put sth off *ou* postpone sth (until); ~ **qch à qn** (*rendre*) to return sth to sb; ~ **qn à** (*fig*) to refer sb to.

éorganisation [ʀeɔʀganizasjɔ̃] *nf* reorganization.

réorganiser [ʀeɔʀganize] *vt* to reorganize.

réorienter [ʀeɔʀjɑ̃te] *vt* to reorient(ate), redirect.

réouverture [ʀeuvɛʀtyʀ] *nf* reopening.

repaire [ʀəpɛʀ] *nm* den.

repaître [ʀəpɛtʀ(ə)] *vt* to feast; to feed; **se** ~ **de** *vt* (*animal*) to feed on; (*fig*) to wallow *ou* revel in.

répandre [ʀepɑ̃dʀ(ə)] *vt* (*renverser*) to spill; (*étaler, diffuser*) to spread; (*lumière*) to shed; (*chaleur, odeur*) to give off; **se** ~ *vi* to spill; to spread; **se** ~ **en** (*injures etc*) to pour out.

répandu, e [ʀepɑ̃dy] *pp de* **répandre** ♦ *adj* (*opinion, usage*) widespread.

réparable [ʀepaʀabl(ə)] *adj* (*montre etc*) repairable; (*perte etc*) which can be made up for.

reparaître [ʀəpaʀɛtʀ(ə)] *vi* to reappear.

réparateur, trice [ʀepaʀatœʀ, -tʀis] *nm/f* repairer.

réparation [ʀepaʀasjɔ̃] *nf* repairing *no pl*, repair; **en** ~ (*machine etc*) under repair; **demander à qn** ~ **de** (*offense etc*) to ask sb to make amends for.

réparer [ʀepaʀe] *vt* to repair; (*fig: offense*) to make up for, atone for; (*: oubli, erreur*) to put right.

reparler [ʀəpaʀle] *vi*: ~ **de qn/qch** to talk about sb/sth again; ~ **à qn** to speak to sb again.

repars [ʀəpaʀ] *etc vb voir* **repartir**.

repartie [ʀəpaʀti] *nf* retort; **avoir de la** ~ to be quick at repartee.

repartir [ʀəpaʀtiʀ] *vi* to set off again; to leave again; (*fig*) to get going again, pick up again; ~ **à zéro** to start from scratch (again).

répartir [ʀepaʀtiʀ] *vt* (*pour attribuer*) to share out; (*pour disperser, disposer*) to divide up; (*poids, chaleur*) to distribute; (*étaler: dans le temps*): ~ **sur** to spread over; (*classer, diviser*): ~ **en** to divide into, split up into; **se** ~ *vt* (*travail, rôles*) to share out between themselves.

répartition [ʀepaʀtisjɔ̃] *nf* sharing out; dividing up; distribution.

repas [ʀəpa] *nm* meal; **à l'heure des** ~ at mealtimes.

repassage [ʀəpasaʒ] *nm* ironing.

repasser [ʀəpase] *vi* to come (*ou* go) back ♦ *vt* (*vêtement, tissu*) to iron; (*examen*) to retake, resit; (*film*) to show again; (*lame*) to sharpen; (*leçon, rôle: revoir*) to go over (again); (*plat, pain*): ~ **qch à qn** to pass sth back to sb.

repasseuse [ʀəpasøz] *nf* (*machine*) ironing machine.

repayer [ʀəpeje] *vt* to pay again.

repêchage [ʀəpɛʃaʒ] *nm* (*SCOL*): **question de** ~ question to give candidates a second chance.

repêcher [ʀəpeʃe] *vt* (*noyé*) to recover the

body of, fish out; (_fam: candidat_) to pass (_by inflating marks_); to give a second chance to.

repeindre [Rəpɛ̃dR(ə)] _vt_ to repaint.

repentir [Rəpɑ̃tiR] _nm_ repentance; **se ~** _vi_: **se ~ (de)** to repent (of).

répercussions [RepɛRkysjɔ̃] _nfpl_ repercussions.

répercuter [RepɛRkyte] _vt_ (_réfléchir, renvoyer: son, voix_) to reflect; (_faire transmettre: consignes, charges etc_) to pass on; **se ~** _vi_ (_bruit_) to reverberate; (_fig_): **se ~ sur** to have repercussions on.

repère [RəpɛR] _nm_ mark; (_monument etc_) landmark; **(point de) ~** point of reference.

repérer [Rəpere] _vt_ (_erreur, connaissance_) to spot; (_abri, ennemi_) to locate; **se ~** _vi_ to get one's bearings; **se faire ~** to be spotted.

répertoire [RepɛRtwaR] _nm_ (_liste_) (alphabetical) list; (_carnet_) index notebook; (_INFORM_) directory; (_de carnet_) thumb index; (_indicateur_) directory, index; (_d'un théâtre, artiste_) repertoire.

répertorier [RepɛRtɔRje] _vt_ to itemize, list.

répéter [Repete] _vt_ to repeat; (_préparer: leçon: aussi vi_) to learn, go over; (_THÉÂT_) to rehearse; **se ~** (_redire_) to repeat o.s.; (_se reproduire_) to be repeated, recur.

répéteur [Repetœʀ] _nm_ (_TÉL_) repeater.

répétitif, ive [Repetitif, -iv] _adj_ repetitive.

répétition [Repetisjɔ̃] _nf_ repetition; (_THÉÂT_) rehearsal; **~s** _nfpl_ (_leçons_) private coaching _sg_; **armes à ~** repeater weapons; **~ générale** final dress rehearsal.

repeupler [Rəpœple] _vt_ to repopulate; (_forêt, rivière_) to restock.

repiquage [Rəpikaʒ] _nm_ pricking out, planting out; re-recording.

repiquer [Rəpike] _vt_ (_plants_) to prick out, plant out; (_enregistrement_) to re-record.

répit [Repi] _nm_ respite; **sans ~** without letting up.

replacer [Rəplase] _vt_ to replace, put back.

replanter [Rəplɑ̃te] _vt_ to replant.

replat [Rəpla] _nm_ ledge.

replâtrer [RəplɑtRe] _vt_ (_mur_) to replaster; (_fig_) to patch up.

replet, ète [Rəplɛ, -ɛt] _adj_ chubby, fat.

repli [Rəpli] _nm_ (_d'une étoffe_) fold; (_MIL, fig_) withdrawal.

replier [Rəplije] _vt_ (_rabattre_) to fold down _ou_ over; **se ~** _vi_ (_troupes, armée_) to withdraw, fall back; **se ~ sur soi-même** to withdraw into oneself.

réplique [Replik] _nf_ (_repartie, fig_) reply; (_objection_) retort; (_THÉÂT_) line; (_copie_) replica; **donner la ~ à** to play opposite; **sans ~** _adj_ no-nonsense; irrefutable.

répliquer [Replike] _vi_ to reply; (_avec impertinence_) to answer back; (_riposter_) to retaliate.

replonger [Rəplɔ̃ʒe] _vt_: **~ qch dans** to plunge sth back into; **se ~ dans** (_journal etc_) to

immerse o.s. in again.

répondant, e [Repɔ̃dɑ̃, -ɑ̃t] _nm/f_ (_garant_) guarantor, surety.

répondeur [Repɔ̃dœR] _nm_: **~ (automatique)** (_TÉL_) (telephone) answering machine.

répondre [Repɔ̃dR(ə)] _vi_ to answer, reply; (_freins, mécanisme_) to respond; **~ à** _vt_ to reply to, answer; (_avec impertinence_): **~ à qn** to answer sb back; (_invitation, convocation_) to reply to; (_affection, salut_) to return; (_provocation, suj: mécanisme_) to respond to; (_correspondre à: besoin_) to answer; (: _conditions_) to meet; (: _description_) to match; **~ que** to answer _ou_ reply that; **~ de** to answer for.

réponse [Repɔ̃s] _nf_ answer, reply; **avec ~ payée** (_POSTES_) reply-paid, post-paid (_US_); **avoir ~ à tout** to have an answer for everything; **en ~ à** in reply to; **carte-/ bulletin-~** reply card/slip.

report [RəpɔR] _nm_ postponement; transfer; **~ d'incorporation** (_MIL_) deferment.

reportage [RəpɔRtaʒ] _nm_ (_bref_) report; (_écrit: documentaire_) story; article; (_en direct_) commentary; (_genre, activité_): **le ~** reporting.

reporter _nm_ [RəpɔRtɛR] reporter ♦ _vt_ [RəpɔRte] (_total_): **~ qch sur** to carry sth forward _ou_ over to; (_ajourner_): **~ qch (à)** to postpone sth (until); (_transférer_): **~ qch sur** to transfer sth to; **se ~ à** (_époque_) to think back to; (_document_) to refer to.

repos [Rəpo] _nm_ rest; (_fig_) peace (and quiet); (_mental_) peace of mind; (_MIL_): **~!** (stand) at ease!; **en ~** at rest; **au ~** at rest; (_soldat_) at ease; **de tout ~** safe.

reposant, e [R(ə)pozɑ̃, -ɑ̃t] _adj_ restful; (_sommeil_) refreshing.

repose [Rəpoz] _nf_ refitting.

reposé, e [Rəpoze] _adj_ fresh, rested; **à tête ~e** in a leisurely way, taking time to think.

repose-pied [Rəpozpje] _nm inv_ footrest.

reposer [Rəpoze] _vt_ (_verre, livre_) to put down; (_rideaux, carreaux_) to put back; (_délasser_) to rest; (_problème_) to reformulate ♦ _vi_ (_liquide, pâte_) to settle, rest; (_personne_): **ici repose ...** here lies ...; **~ sur** to be built on; (_fig_) to rest on; **se ~** _vi_ to rest; **se ~ sur qn** to rely on sb.

repoussant, e [Rəpusɑ̃, -ɑ̃t] _adj_ repulsive.

repoussé, e [Rəpuse] _adj_ (_cuir_) embossed (by hand).

repousser [Rəpuse] _vi_ to grow again ♦ _vt_ to repel, repulse; (_offre_) to turn down, reject; (_tiroir, personne_) to push back; (_différer_) to put back.

répréhensible [RepReɑ̃sibl(ə)] _adj_ reprehensible.

reprendre [RəpRɑ̃dR(ə)] _vt_ (_prisonnier, ville_) to recapture; (_objet prêté, donné_) to take back; (_chercher_): **je viendrai te ~ à 4 h** I'll come and fetch you _ou_ I'll come back for you at 4; (_se resservir de_): **~ du pain/un œuf** to take (*ou* eat) more bread/another egg; (*COMM: article usagé*) to take back; to take in part exchange; (*firme, entreprise*) to take over; (*travail, promenade*) to resume; (*emprunter: argument, idée*) to take up, use; (*refaire: article etc*) to go over again; (*jupe etc*) to alter; (*émission, pièce*) to put on again; (*réprimander*) to tell off; (*corriger*) to correct ♦ *vi* (*classes, pluie*) to start (up) again; (*activités, travaux, combats*) to resume, start (up) again; (*affaires, industrie*) to pick up; (*dire*): **reprit-il** he went on; **se** ~ (*se ressaisir*) to recover, pull o.s. together; **s'y** ~ to make another attempt; ~ **des forces** to recover one's strength; ~ **courage** to take new heart; ~ **ses habitudes/sa liberté** to get back into one's old habits/regain one's freedom; ~ **la route** to resume one's journey, set off again; ~ **connaissance** to come to, regain consciousness; ~ **haleine** *ou* **son souffle** to get one's breath back; ~ **la parole** to speak again.

repreneur [RəpRənœR] *nm* company fixer *ou* doctor.

reprenne [RəpREn] *etc vb voir* **reprendre**.

représailles [RəpRezɑj] *nfpl* reprisals, retaliation *sg*.

représentant, e [RəpRezɑ̃tɑ̃, -ɑ̃t] *nm/f* representative.

représentatif, ive [RəpRezɑ̃tatif, -iv] *adj* representative.

représentation [RəpRezɑ̃tɑsjɔ̃] *nf* representation; performing; (*symbole, image*) representation; (*spectacle*) performance; (*COMM*): **la** ~ commercial travelling; sales representation; **frais de** ~ (*d'un diplomate*) entertainment allowance.

représenter [RəpRezɑ̃te] *vt* to represent; (*donner: pièce, opéra*) to perform; **se** ~ *vt* (*se figurer*) to imagine; to visualize ♦ *vi*: **se** ~ **à** (*POL*) to stand *ou* run again at; (*SCOL*) to resit.

répressif, ive [RepResif, -iv] *adj* repressive.

répression [RepResjɔ̃] *nf* (*voir réprimer*) suppression; repression; (*POL*): **la** ~ repression; **mesures de** ~ repressive measures.

réprimande [RepRimɑ̃d] *nf* reprimand, rebuke.

réprimander [RepRimɑ̃de] *vt* to reprimand, rebuke.

réprimer [RepRime] *vt* (*émotions*) to suppress; (*peuple etc*) repress.

repris, e [Rəpri, -iz] *pp de* **reprendre** ♦ *nm*: ~ **de justice** ex-prisoner, ex-convict.

reprise [RəpRiz] *nf* (*recommencement*) resumption; (*économique*) recovery; (*TV*) repeat; (*CINÉ*) rerun; (*BOXE etc*) round; (*AUTO*) acceleration *no pl*; (*COMM*) trade-in, part exchange; (*de location*) *sum asked for any extras or improvements made to the property*; (*raccommodage*) darn; mend; **la** ~

des hostilités the resumption of hostilities; **à plusieurs** ~**s** on several occasions, several times.

repriser [RəpRize] *vt* to darn; to mend; **aiguille/coton à** ~ darning needle/thread.

réprobateur, trice [RepRɔbatœR, -tRis] *adj* reproving.

réprobation [RepRɔbɑsjɔ̃] *nf* reprobation.

reproche [RəpRɔʃ] *nm* (*remontrance*) reproach; **ton/air de** ~ reproachful tone/look; **faire des** ~**s à qn** to reproach sb; **faire** ~ **à qn de qch** to reproach sb for sth; **sans** ~**(s)** beyond *ou* above reproach.

reprocher [RəpRɔʃe] *vt*: ~ **qch à qn** to reproach *ou* blame sb for sth; ~ **qch à** (*machine, théorie*) to have sth against; **se** ~ **qch/d'avoir fait qch** to blame o.s. for sth/for doing sth.

reproducteur, trice [RəpRɔdyktœR, -tRis] *adj* reproductive.

reproduction [RəpRɔdyksjɔ̃] *nf* reproduction; ~ **interdite** all rights (of reproduction) reserved.

reproduire [RəpRɔdɥiR] *vt* to reproduce; **se** ~ *vi* (*BIO*) to reproduce; (*recommencer*) to recur, re-occur.

reprographie [RəpRɔgRafi] *nf* (photo)copying.

réprouvé, e [RepRuve] *nm/f* reprobate.

réprouver [RepRuve] *vt* to reprove.

reptation [REptɑsjɔ̃] *nf* crawling.

reptile [REptil] *nm* reptile.

repu, e [Rəpy] *pp de* **repaître** ♦ *adj* satisfied, sated.

républicain, e [Repyblikɛ̃, -ɛn] *adj, nm/f* republican.

république [Repyblik] *nf* republic; R~ **arabe du Yémen** Yemen Arab Republic; R~ **Centrafricaine** Central African Republic; R~ **de Corée** South Korea; R~ **démocratique allemande (RDA)** German Democratic Republic (GDR); R~ **dominicaine** Dominican Republic; R~ **fédérale d'Allemagne (RFA)** Federal Republic of Germany (FRG); R~ **d'Irlande** Irish Republic, Eire; R~ **populaire de Chine** People's Republic of China; R~ **populaire démocratique de Corée** Democratic People's Republic of Korea; R~ **populaire du Yémen** People's Democratic Republic of Yemen.

répudier [Repydje] *vt* (*femme*) to repudiate; (*doctrine*) to renounce.

répugnance [Repyɲɑ̃s] *nf* repugnance, loathing; **avoir** *ou* **éprouver de la** ~ **pour** (*médicament, comportement, travail etc*) to have an aversion to; **avoir** *ou* **éprouver de la** ~ **à faire qch** to be reluctant to do sth.

répugnant, e [Repyɲɑ̃, -ɑ̃t] *adj* repulsive, loathsome.

répugner [Repyɲe] *vi*: ~ **à qn** to repel *ou* disgust sb; ~ **à faire** to be loath *ou* reluctant to do.

répulsion [Repylsjɔ̃] *nf* repulsion.

réputation [Repytasjɔ̃] *nf* reputation; **avoir la ~ d'être** ... to have a reputation for being ...; **connaître qn/qch de ~** to know sb/sth by repute; **de ~ mondiale** world-renowned.

réputé, e [Repyte] *adj* renowned; **être ~ pour** to have a reputation for, be renowned for.

requérir [RəkeRiR] *vt (nécessiter)* to require, call for; *(au nom de la loi)* to call upon; *(JUR: peine)* to call for, demand.

requête [Rəkɛt] *nf* request, petition; *(JUR)* petition.

requiem [Rekɥijɛm] *nm* requiem.

requiers [RəkjɛR] *etc vb voir* **requérir**.

requin [Rəkɛ̃] *nm* shark.

requinquer [Rəkɛ̃ke] *vt* to set up, pep up.

requis, e [Rəki, -iz] *pp de* **requérir** ♦ *adj* required.

réquisition [Rekizisjɔ̃] *nf* requisition.

réquisitionner [Rekizisjɔne] *vt* to requisition.

réquisitoire [RekizitwaR] *nm (JUR)* closing speech for the prosecution; *(fig):* **~ contre** indictment of.

RER *sigle m* (= *Réseau express régional)* Greater Paris high speed train service.

rescapé, e [Rɛskape] *nm/f* survivor.

rescousse [Rɛskus] *nf:* **aller à la ~ de qn** to go to sb's aid *ou* rescue; **appeler qn à la ~** to call on sb for help.

réseau, x [Rezo] *nm* network.

réséda [Rezeda] *nm (BOT)* reseda, mignonette.

réservation [RezɛRvasjɔ̃] *nf* reservation; booking.

réserve [RezɛRv(ə)] *nf (retenue)* reserve; *(entrepôt)* storeroom; *(restriction, aussi: d'Indiens)* reservation; *(de pêche, chasse)* preserve; *(restrictions):* **faire des ~s** to have reservations; **officier de ~** reserve officer; **sous toutes ~s** with all reserve; *(dire)* with reservations; **sous ~ de** subject to; **sans ~** *adv* unreservedly; **en ~** in reserve; **de ~** *(provisions etc)* in reserve.

réservé, e [RezɛRve] *adj (discret)* reserved; *(chasse, pêche)* private; **~ à ou pour** reserved for.

réserver [RezɛRve] *vt (gén)* to reserve; *(chambre, billet etc)* to book, reserve; *(mettre de côté, garder):* **~ qch pour ou à** to keep *ou* save sth for; **~ qch à qn** to reserve *(ou* book) sth for sb; *(fig: destiner)* to have sth in store for sb; **se ~ le droit de faire** to reserve the right to do.

réserviste [RezɛRvist(ə)] *nm* reservist.

réservoir [RezɛRvwaR] *nm* tank.

résidence [Rezidɑ̃s] *nf* residence; **~ principale/secondaire** main/second home; **~ universitaire** hall of residence; **(en) ~ surveillée** (under) house arrest.

résident, e [Rezidɑ̃, -ɑ̃t] *nm/f (ressortissant)* foreign resident; *(d'un immeuble)* resident ♦ *adj (INFORM)* resident.

résidentiel, le [Rezidɑ̃sjɛl] *adj* residential.

résider [Rezide] *vi:* **~ à ou dans ou en** to reside in; **~ dans** *(fig)* to lie in.

résidu [Rezidy] *nm* residue *no pl.*

résiduel, le [Rezidɥɛl] *adj* residual.

résignation [Reziɲasjɔ̃] *nf* resignation.

résigné, e [Reziɲe] *adj* resigned.

résigner [Reziɲe] *vt* to relinquish, resign; **se ~** *vi:* **se ~ (à qch/à faire)** to resign o.s. (to sth/to doing).

résiliable [Reziljabl(ə)] *adj* which can be terminated.

résilier [Rezilje] *vt* to terminate.

résille [Rezij] *nf* (hair)net.

résine [Rezin] *nf* resin.

résiné, e [Rezine] *adj:* **vin ~** retsina.

résineux, euse [Rezinø, -øz] *adj* resinous ♦ *nm* coniferous tree.

résistance [Rezistɑ̃s] *nf* resistance; *(de réchaud, bouilloire: fil)* element.

résistant, e [Rezistɑ̃, -ɑ̃t] *adj (personne)* robust, tough; *(matériau)* strong, hard-wearing ♦ *nm/f (patriote)* Resistance worker *ou* fighter.

résister [Reziste] *vi* to resist; **~ à** *vt (assaut, tentation)* to resist; *(effort, souffrance)* to withstand; *(suj: matériau, plante)* to stand up to, withstand; *(personne: désobéir à)* to stand up to, oppose.

résolu, e [Rezɔly] *pp de* **résoudre** ♦ *adj (ferme)* resolute; **être ~ à qch/faire** to be set upon sth/doing.

résolument [Rezɔlymɑ̃] *adv* resolutely, steadfastly; **~ contre qch** firmly against sth.

résolution [Rezɔlysjɔ̃] *nf* solving; *(fermeté, décision, INFORM)* resolution; **prendre la ~ de** to make a resolution to.

résolvais [Rezɔlvɛ] *etc vb voir* **résoudre**.

résonance [Rezɔnɑ̃s] *nf* resonance.

résonner [Rezɔne] *vi (cloche, pas)* to reverberate, resound; *(salle)* to be resonant; **~ de** to resound with.

résorber [RezɔRbe]: **se ~** *vi (MÉD)* to be resorbed; *(fig)* to be absorbed.

résoudre [RezudR(ə)] *vt* to solve; **~ qn à faire qch** to get sb to make up his *(ou* her) mind to do sth; **~ de faire** to resolve to do; **se ~ à faire** to bring o.s. to do.

respect [Rɛspɛ] *nm* respect; **tenir en ~** to keep at bay.

respectabilité [Rɛspɛktabilite] *nf* respectability.

respectable [Rɛspɛktabl(ə)] *adj* respectable.

respecter [Rɛspɛkte] *vt* to respect; **faire ~** to enforce; **le lexicographe qui se respecte** *(fig)* any self-respecting lexicographer.

respectif, ive [Rɛspɛktif, -iv] *adj* respective.

respectivement [Rɛspɛktivmɑ̃] *adv* respectively.

respectueusement [Rɛspɛktɥøzmɑ̃] *adv* respectfully.

respectueux, euse [Rɛspɛktɥø, -øz] *adj* respectful; **~ de** respectful of.

respirable [ʀɛspiʀabl(ə)] *adj*: **peu ~** unbreathable.

respiration [ʀɛspiʀɑsjɔ̃] *nf* breathing *no pl*; **faire une ~ complète** to breathe in and out; **retenir sa ~** to hold one's breath; **~ artificielle** artificial respiration.

respiratoire [ʀɛspiʀatwaʀ] *adj* respiratory.

respirer [ʀɛspiʀe] *vi* to breathe; (*fig: se reposer*) to get one's breath, have a break; (*: être soulagé*) to breathe again ♦ *vt* to breathe (in), inhale; (*manifester: santé, calme etc*) to exude.

resplendir [ʀɛsplɑ̃diʀ] *vi* to shine; (*fig*): **~ (de)** to be radiant (with).

resplendissant, e [ʀɛsplɑ̃disɑ̃, -ɑ̃t] *adj* radiant.

responsabilité [ʀɛspɔ̃sabilite] *nf* responsibility; (*légale*) liability; **refuser la ~ de** to deny responsibility (*ou* liability) for; **prendre ses ~s** to assume responsibility for one's actions; **~ civile** civil liability; **~ pénale/morale/collective** criminal/moral/collective responsibility.

responsable [ʀɛspɔ̃sabl(ə)] *adj* responsible ♦ *nm/f* (*du ravitaillement etc*) person in charge; (*de parti, syndicat*) official; **~ de** responsible for; (*légalement: de dégâts etc*) liable for; (*chargé de*) in charge of, responsible for.

esquiller [ʀɛskije] *vi* (*au cinéma, au stade*) to get in on the sly; (*dans le train*) to fiddle a free ride.

esquilleur, euse [ʀɛskijœʀ, -øz] *nm/f* (*qui n'est pas invité*) gatecrasher; (*qui ne paie pas*) fare dodger.

essac [ʀəsak] *nm* backwash.

essaisir [ʀəseziʀ]: **se ~** *vi* to regain one's self-control; (*équipe sportive*) to rally.

essasser [ʀəsase] *vt* (*remâcher*) to keep turning over; (*redire*) to keep trotting out.

essemblance [ʀəsɑ̃blɑ̃s] *nf* (*visuelle*) resemblance, similarity, likeness; (*: ART*) likeness; (*analogie, trait commun*) similarity.

essemblant, e [ʀəsɑ̃blɑ̃, -ɑ̃t] *adj* (*portrait*) lifelike, true to life.

essembler [ʀəsɑ̃ble]: **~ à** *vt* to be like, resemble; (*visuellement*) to look like; **se ~** to be (*ou* look) alike.

essemeler [ʀəsəmle] *vt* to (re)sole.

essens [ʀ(ə)sɑ̃] *etc vb voir* **ressentir**.

essentiment [ʀəsɑ̃timɑ̃] *nm* resentment.

essentir [ʀəsɑ̃tiʀ] *vt* to feel; **se ~ de** to feel (*ou* show) the effects of.

esserre [ʀəsɛʀ] *nf* shed.

esserrement [ʀ(ə)sɛʀmɑ̃] *nm* narrowing; strengthening; (*goulet*) narrow part.

esserrer [ʀəseʀe] *vt* (*pores*) to close; (*nœud, boulon*) to tighten (up); (*fig: liens*) to strengthen; **se ~** *vi* (*route, vallée*) to narrow; (*liens*) to strengthen; **se ~ (autour de)** to draw closer (around); to close in (on).

essers [ʀ(ə)sɛʀ] *etc vb voir* **resservir**.

esservir [ʀəsɛʀviʀ] *vi* to do *ou* serve again

♦ *vt*: **~ qch (à qn)** to serve sth up again (to sb); **~ de qch (à qn)** to give (sb) a second helping of sth; **~ qn (d'un plat)** to give sb a second helping (of a dish); **se ~ de** (*plat*) to take a second helping of; (*outil etc*) to use again.

ressort [ʀəsɔʀ] *vb voir* **ressortir** ♦ *nm* (*pièce*) spring; (*force morale*) spirit; (*recours*): **en dernier ~** as a last resort; (*compétence*): **être du ~ de** to fall within the competence of.

ressortir [ʀəsɔʀtiʀ] *vi* to go (*ou* come) out (again); (*contraster*) to stand out; **~ de** (*résulter de*): **il ressort de ceci que** it emerges from this that; **~ à** (*JUR*) to come under the jurisdiction of; (*ADMIN*) to be the concern of; **faire ~** (*fig: souligner*) to bring out.

ressortissant, e [ʀəsɔʀtisɑ̃, -ɑ̃t] *nm/f* national.

ressouder [ʀəsude] *vt* to solder together again.

ressource [ʀəsuʀs(ə)] *nf*: **avoir la ~ de** to have the possibility of; **~s** *nfpl* resources; (*fig*) possibilities; **leur seule ~ était de** the only course open to them was to; **~s d'énergie** energy resources.

ressusciter [ʀesysite] *vt* to resuscitate, restore to life; (*fig*) to revive, bring back ♦ *vi* to rise (from the dead); (*fig: pays*) to come back to life.

restant, e [ʀɛstɑ̃, -ɑ̃t] *adj* remaining ♦ *nm*: **le ~ (de)** the remainder (of); **un ~ de** (*de trop*) some leftover; (*fig: vestige*) a remnant *ou* last trace of.

restaurant [ʀɛstɔʀɑ̃] *nm* restaurant; **manger au ~** to eat out; **~ d'entreprise** staff canteen *ou* cafeteria (*US*); **~ universitaire (RU)** university refectory *ou* cafeteria (*US*).

restaurateur, trice [ʀɛstɔʀatœʀ, -tʀis] *nm/f* restaurant owner, restaurateur; (*de tableaux*) restorer.

restauration [ʀɛstɔʀɑsjɔ̃] *nf* restoration; (*hôtellerie*) catering; **~ rapide** fast food.

restaurer [ʀɛstɔʀe] *vt* to restore; **se ~** *vi* to have something to eat.

restauroute [ʀɛstɔʀut] *nm* = **restoroute**.

reste [ʀɛst(ə)] *nm* (*restant*): **le ~ (de)** the rest (of); (*de trop*): **un ~ (de)** some leftover; (*vestige*): **un ~ de** a remnant *ou* last trace of; (*MATH*) remainder; **~s** *nmpl* leftovers; (*d'une cité etc, dépouille mortelle*) remains; **avoir du temps de ~** to have time to spare; **ne voulant pas être en ~** not wishing to be outdone; **partir sans attendre** *ou* **demander son ~** (*fig*) to leave without waiting to hear more; **du ~, au ~** *adv* besides, moreover; **pour le reste, quant au ~** *adv* as for the rest.

rester [ʀɛste] *vi* (*dans un lieu, un état, une position*) to stay, remain; (*subsister*) to remain, be left; (*durer*) to last, live on ♦ *vb impers*: **il reste du pain/2 œufs** there's some bread/there are 2 eggs left (over); **il reste du temps/10 minutes** there's some time/there are 10 minutes left; **il me reste assez**

de temps I have enough time left; **voilà tout ce qui (me) reste** that's all I've got left; **ce qui reste à faire** what remains to be done; **ce qui me reste à faire** what remains for me to do; **(il) reste à savoir/établir si** ... it remains to be seen/established if *ou* whether ...; **il n'en reste pas moins que** ... the fact remains that ..., it's nevertheless a fact that ...; **en ~ à** (*stade, menaces*) to go no further than, only go as far as; **restons-en là** let's leave it at that; **~ sur une impression** to retain an impression; **y ~**: **il a failli y ~** he nearly met his end.

restituer [ʀɛstitɥe] *vt* (*objet, somme*): **~ qch (à qn)** to return *ou* restore sth (to sb); (*énergie*) to release; (*son*) to reproduce.

restitution [ʀɛstitysjɔ̃] *nf* restoration.

restoroute [ʀɛstɔʀut] *nm* motorway (*BRIT*) *ou* highway (*US*) restaurant.

restreindre [ʀɛstʀɛ̃dʀ(ə)] *vt* to restrict, limit; **se ~** (*dans ses dépenses etc*) to cut down; (*champ de recherches*) to narrow.

restreint, e [ʀɛstʀɛ̃, -ɛ̃t] *pp de* **restreindre** ♦ *adj* restricted, limited.

restrictif, ive [ʀɛstʀiktif, -iv] *adj* restrictive, limiting.

restriction [ʀɛstʀiksjɔ̃] *nf* restriction; (*condition*) qualification; **~s** *nfpl* (*mentales*) reservations; **sans ~** *adv* unreservedly.

restructuration [ʀəstʀyktyʀasjɔ̃] *nf* restructuring.

restructurer [ʀəstʀyktyʀe] *vt* to restructure.

résultante [ʀezyltɑ̃t] *nf* (*conséquence*) result, consequence.

résultat [ʀezylta] *nm* result; (*conséquence*) outcome *no pl*, result; (*d'élection etc*) results *pl*; **~s** *nmpl* (*d'une enquête*) findings; **~s sportifs** sports results.

résulter [ʀezylte]: **~ de** *vt* to result from, be the result of; **il résulte de ceci que** ... the result of this is that ....

résumé [ʀezyme] *nm* summary, résumé; **faire le ~ de** to summarize; **en ~** *adv* in brief; (*pour conclure*) to sum up.

résumer [ʀezyme] *vt* (*texte*) to summarize; (*récapituler*) to sum up; (*fig*) to epitomize, typify; **~ vi** (*personne*) to sum up (one's ideas); **se ~ à** to come down to.

resurgir [ʀəsyʀʒiʀ] *vi* to reappear, re-emerge.

résurrection [ʀezyʀɛksjɔ̃] *nf* resurrection; (*fig*) revival.

rétablir [ʀetabliʀ] *vt* to restore, re-establish; (*personne: suj: traitement*): **~ qn** to restore sb to health, help sb recover; (*ADMIN*): **~ qn dans son emploi/ses droits** to reinstate sb in his post/restore sb's rights; **se ~** *vi* (*guérir*) to recover; (*silence, calme*) to return, be restored; (*GYM etc*): **se ~ (sur)** to pull o.s. up (onto).

rétablissement [ʀetablismɑ̃] *nm* restoring; recovery; pull-up.

rétamer [ʀetame] *vt* to re-coat, re-tin.

rétameur [ʀetamœʀ] *nm* tinker.

retaper [ʀətape] *vt* (*maison, voiture etc*) to do up; (*fam: revigorer*) to buck up; (*redactylographier*) to retype.

retard [ʀətaʀ] *nm* (*d'une personne attendue*) lateness *no pl*; (*sur l'horaire, un programme, une échéance*) delay; (*fig: scolaire, mental etc*) backwardness; **être en ~** (*pays*) to be backward; (*dans paiement, travail*) to be behind; **en ~ (de 2 heures)** (2 hours) late; **avoir un ~ de 2 km** (*SPORT*) to be 2 km behind; **rattraper son ~** to catch up; **avoir du ~** to be late; (*sur un programme*) to be behind (schedule); **prendre du ~** (*train, avion*) to be delayed; (*montre*) to lose (time); **sans ~** *adv* without delay; **~ à l'allumage** (*AUTO*) retarded spark; **~ scolaire** backwardness at school.

retardataire [ʀətaʀdatɛʀ] *adj* late; (*enfant, idées*) backward ♦ *nm/f* latecomer; backward child.

retardé, e [ʀətaʀde] *adj* backward.

retardement [ʀətaʀdəmɑ̃]: **à ~** *adj* delayed action *cpd*; **bombe à ~** time bomb.

retarder [ʀətaʀde] *vt* (*sur un horaire*): **~ qn (d'une heure)** to delay sb (an hour); (*sur un programme*): **~ qn (de 3 mois)** to set sb back *ou* delay sb (3 months); (*départ, date*): **~ qch (de 2 jours)** to put sth back (2 days), delay sth (for *ou* by 2 days); (*horloge*) to put back ♦ *vi* (*montre*) to be slow; (: *habituellement*) to lose (time); **je retarde (d'une heure)** I'm (an hour) slow.

retendre [ʀətɑ̃dʀ(ə)] *vt* (*câble etc*) to stretch again; (*MUS: cordes*) to retighten.

retenir [ʀətniʀ] *vt* (*garder, retarder*) to keep, detain; (*maintenir: objet qui glisse, fig: colère, larmes, rire*) to hold back; (: *objet suspendu*) to hold; (: *chaleur, odeur*) to retain; (*fig: empêcher d'agir*): **~ qn (de faire)** to hold sb back (from doing); (*se rappeler*) to retain; (*réserver*) to reserve; (*accepter*) to accept; (*prélever*): **~ qch (sur)** to deduct sth (from); **se ~** (*euphémisme*) to hold on; (*se raccrocher*): **se ~ à** to hold onto; (*se contenir*): **se ~ de faire** to restrain o.s. from doing; **~ son souffle** *ou* **haleine** to hold one's breath; **~ qn à dîner** to ask sb to stay for dinner; **je pose 3 et je retiens 2** put down 3 and carry 2.

rétention [ʀetɑ̃sjɔ̃] *nf*: **~ d'urine** urine retention.

retentir [ʀətɑ̃tiʀ] *vi* to ring out; (*salle*): **~ de** to ring *ou* resound with; **~ sur** *vt* (*fig*) to have an effect upon.

retentissant, e [ʀətɑ̃tisɑ̃, -ɑ̃t] *adj* resounding; (*fig*) impact-making.

retentissement [ʀətɑ̃tismɑ̃] *nm* (*retombées*) repercussions *pl*; effect, impact.

retenu, e [ʀətny] *pp de* **retenir** ♦ *adj* (*place*) reserved; (*personne: empêché*) held up; (*propos: contenu, discret*) restrained ♦ *nf* (*prélèvement*) deduction; (*MATH*) number to carry over; (*SCOL*) detention; (*modération*) (self-)restraint; (*réserve*) reserve, reticence; (*AUTO*) tailback.

réticence [ʀetisɑ̃s] *nf* reticence *no pl*, reluctance *no pl*; **sans ~** without hesitation.

réticent, e [ʀetisɑ̃, -ɑ̃t] *adj* reticent, reluctant.

retiendrai [ʀətjɛ̃dʀe], **retiens** [ʀətjɛ̃] *etc vb voir* **retenir**.

rétif, ive [ʀetif, -iv] *adj* restive.

rétine [ʀetin] *nf* retina.

retint [ʀətɛ̃] *etc vb voir* **retenir**.

retiré, e [ʀətiʀe] *adj* (*solitaire*) secluded; (*éloigné*) remote.

retirer [ʀətiʀe] *vt* to withdraw; (*vêtement, lunettes*) to take off, remove; (*enlever*): **~ qch à qn** to take sth from sb; (*extraire*): **~ qn/qch de** to take sb away from/sth out of, remove sb/sth from; (*reprendre: bagages, billets*) to collect, pick up; **~ des avantages de** to derive advantages from; **se ~** *vi* (*partir, reculer*) to withdraw; (*prendre sa retraite*) to retire; **se ~ de** to withdraw from; to retire from.

retombées [ʀətɔ̃be] *nfpl* (*radioactives*) fallout *sg*; (*fig*) fallout; spin-offs.

retomber [ʀətɔ̃be] *vi* (*à nouveau*) to fall again; (*rechuter*): **~ malade/dans l'erreur** to fall ill again/fall back into error; (*atterrir: après un saut etc*) to land; (*tomber, redescendre*) to fall back; (*pendre*) to fall, hang (down); (*échoir*): **~ sur qn** to fall on sb.

retordre [ʀətɔʀdʀ(ə)] *vt*: **donner du fil à ~ à qn** to make life difficult for sb.

rétorquer [ʀetɔʀke] *vt*: **~ (à qn) que** to retort (to sb) that.

retors, e [ʀətɔʀ, -ɔʀs(ə)] *adj* wily.

rétorsion [ʀetɔʀsjɔ̃] *nf*: **mesures de ~** reprisals.

retouche [ʀətuʃ] *nf* touching up *no pl*; alteration; **faire une ~** *ou* **des ~s à** to touch up.

retoucher [ʀətuʃe] *vt* (*photographie, tableau*) to touch up; (*texte, vêtement*) to alter.

retour [ʀətuʀ] *nm* return; **au ~** (*en arrivant*) when we (*ou* they *etc*) get (*ou* got) back; (*en route*) on the way back; **pendant le ~** on the way *ou* journey back; **à mon/ton ~** on my/your return; **au ~ de** on the return of (*en*); **être de ~ (de)** to be back (from); **de ~ à .../chez moi** back at .../back home; **en ~** *adv* in return; **par ~ du courrier** by return of post; **par un juste ~ des choses** by a favourable twist of fate; **match ~** return match; **~ en arrière** (*CINÉ*) flashback; (*mesure*) backward step; **~ de bâton** kickback; **~ du chariot** carriage return; **~ à l'envoyeur** (*POSTES*) return to sender; **~ de flamme** backfire; **~ (automatique) à la ligne** (*INFORM*) wordwrap; **~ de manivelle** (*fig*) backfire; **~ offensif** renewed attack; **~ aux sources** (*fig*) return to basics.

retournement [ʀətuʀnəmɑ̃] *nm* (*d'une*

personne: revirement) turning (round); **~ de la situation** reversal of the situation.

retourner [ʀətuʀne] *vt* (*dans l'autre sens: matelas, crêpe*) to turn (over); (*: caisse*) to turn upside down; (*: sac, vêtement*) to turn inside out; (*fig: argument*) to turn back; (*en remuant: terre, sol, foin*) to turn over; (*émouvoir: personne*) to shake; (*renvoyer, restituer*): **~ qch à qn** to return sth to sb ♦ *vi* (*aller, revenir*): **~ quelque part/à** to go back *ou* return somewhere/to; **~ à** (*état, activité*) to return to, go back to; **se ~** *vi* to turn over; (*tourner la tête*) to turn round; **s'en ~** to go back; **se ~ contre** (*fig*) to turn against; **savoir de quoi il retourne** to know what it is all about; **~ sa veste** (*fig*) to turn one's coat; **~ en arrière** *ou* **sur ses pas** to turn back, retrace one's steps; **~ aux sources** to go back to basics.

retracer [ʀətʀase] *vt* to relate, recount.

rétracter [ʀetʀakte] *vt*, **se ~** *vi* to retract.

retraduire [ʀətʀadɥiʀ] *vt* to translate again; (*dans la langue de départ*) to translate back.

retrait [ʀətʀɛ] *nm* (*voir retirer*) withdrawal; collection; (*voir se retirer*) withdrawal; (*rétrécissement*) shrinkage; **en ~** *adj* set back; **écrire en ~** to indent; **~ du permis (de conduire)** disqualification from driving (*BRIT*), revocation of driver's license (*US*).

retraite [ʀətʀɛt] *nf* (*d'une armée, REL, refuge*) retreat; (*d'un employé*) retirement; (*revenu*) (retirement) pension; **être/mettre à la ~** to be retired/pension off *ou* retire; **prendre sa ~** to retire; **~ anticipée** early retirement; **~ aux flambeaux** torchlight tattoo.

retraité, e [ʀətʀete] *adj* retired ♦ *nm/f* (old age) pensioner.

retraitement [ʀətʀɛtmɑ̃] *nm* reprocessing.

retraiter [ʀətʀete] *vt* to reprocess.

retranchement [ʀətʀɑ̃ʃmɑ̃] *nm* entrenchment; **poursuivre qn dans ses derniers ~s** to drive sb into a corner.

retrancher [ʀətʀɑ̃ʃe] *vt* (*passage, détails*) to take out, remove; (*nombre, somme*): **~ qch de** to take *ou* deduct sth from; (*couper*) to cut off; **se ~ derrière/dans** to entrench o.s. behind/in; (*fig*) to take refuge behind/in.

retranscrire [ʀətʀɑ̃skʀiʀ] *vt* to retranscribe.

retransmettre [ʀətʀɑ̃smɛtʀ(ə)] *vt* (*RADIO*) to broadcast, relay; (*TV*) to show.

retransmission [ʀətʀɑ̃smisjɔ̃] *nf* broadcast; showing.

retravailler [ʀətʀavaje] *vi* to start work again ♦ *vt* to work on again.

retraverser [ʀətʀavɛʀse] *vt* (*dans l'autre sens*) to cross back over.

rétréci, e [ʀetʀesi] *adj* (*idées, esprit*) narrow.

rétrécir [ʀetʀesiʀ] *vt* (*vêtement*) to take in ♦ *vi* to shrink; **se ~** *vi* to narrow.

rétrécissement [ʀetʀesismɑ̃] *nm* narrowing.

retremper [ʀətʀɑ̃pe] *vt*: **se ~ dans** (*fig*) to reimmerse o.s. in.

rétribuer [ʀetʀibɥe] *vt* (*travail*) to pay for; (*personne*) to pay.

rétribution [ʀetʀibysjɔ̃] *nf* payment.

rétro [ʀetʀo] *adj inv* old-style ♦ *nm* (= *rétroviseur*) (rear-view) mirror; **la mode** ~ the nostalgia vogue.

rétroactif, ive [ʀetʀoaktif, -iv] *adj* retroactive.

rétrocéder [ʀetʀosede] *vt* to retrocede.

rétrocession [ʀetʀosesjɔ̃] *nf* retrocession.

rétrofusée [ʀetʀofyze] *nf* retrorocket.

rétrograde [ʀetʀoɡʀad] *adj* reactionary, backward-looking.

rétrograder [ʀetʀoɡʀade] *vi* (*élève*) to fall back; (*économie*) to regress; (*AUTO*) to change down.

rétroprojecteur [ʀetʀopʀoʒɛktœʀ] *nm* overhead projector.

rétrospectif, ive [ʀetʀospɛktif, -iv] *adj*, *nf* retrospective.

rétrospectivement [ʀetʀospɛktivmɑ̃] *adv* in retrospect.

retroussé, e [ʀətʀuse] *adj*: **nez** ~ turned-up nose.

retrousser [ʀətʀuse] *vt* to roll up; (*fig: nez*) to wrinkle; (*: lèvres*) to curl up.

retrouvailles [ʀətʀuvaj] *nfpl* reunion *sg*.

retrouver [ʀətʀuve] *vt* (*fugitif, objet perdu*) to find; (*occasion*) to find again; (*calme, santé*) to regain; (*reconnaître: expression, style*) to recognize; (*revoir*) to see again; (*rejoindre*) to meet (again), join; **se** ~ *vi* to meet; (*s'orienter*) to find one's way; **se** ~ **quelque part** to find o.s. somewhere; to end up somewhere; **se** ~ **seul/sans argent** to find o.s. alone/with no money; **se** ~ **dans** (*calculs, dossiers, désordre*) to make sense of; **s'y** ~ (*rentrer dans ses frais*) to break even.

rétroviseur [ʀetʀovizœʀ] *nm* (rear-view) mirror.

réunifier [ʀeynifje] *vt* to reunify.

Réunion [ʀeynjɔ̃] *nf*: **la** ~, **l'île de la** ~ Reunion.

réunion [ʀeynjɔ̃] *nf* bringing together; joining; (*séance*) meeting.

réunionnais, e [ʀeynjɔnɛ, -ɛz] *adj* of *ou* from Reunion.

réunir [ʀeyniʀ] *vt* (*convoquer*) to call together; (*rassembler*) to gather together; (*cumuler*) to combine; (*rapprocher*) to bring together (again), reunite; (*rattacher*) to join (together); **se** ~ *vi* (*se rencontrer*) to meet; (*s'allier*) to unite.

réussi, e [ʀeysi] *adj* successful.

réussir [ʀeysiʀ] *vi* to succeed, be successful; (*à un examen*) to pass; (*plante, culture*) to thrive, do well ♦ *vt* to make a success of; to bring off; ~ **à faire** to succeed in doing; ~ **à qn** to go right for sb; (*aliment*) to agree with sb; **le travail/le mariage lui réussit** work/married life agrees with him.

réussite [ʀeysit] *nf* success; (*CARTES*) patience.

réutiliser [ʀeytilize] *vt* to re-use.

revaloir [ʀəvalwaʀ] *vt*: **je vous revaudrai cela** I'll repay you some day; (*en mal*) I'll pay you back for this.

revalorisation [ʀəvalɔʀizɑsjɔ̃] *nf* revaluation; raising.

revaloriser [ʀəvalɔʀize] *vt* (*monnaie*) to revalue; (*salaires, pensions*) to raise the level of; (*institution, tradition*) to reassert the value of.

revanche [ʀəvɑ̃ʃ] *nf* revenge; **prendre sa** ~ **(sur)** to take one's revenge (on); **en** ~ (*par contre*) on the other hand; (*en compensation*) in return.

rêvasser [ʀɛvase] *vi* to daydream.

rêve [ʀɛv] *nm* dream; (*activité psychique*): **le** ~ dreaming; **paysage/silence de** ~ dreamlike landscape/silence; ~ **éveillé** daydreaming *no pl*, daydream.

rêvé, e [ʀeve] *adj* (*endroit, mari etc*) ideal.

revêche [ʀəvɛʃ] *adj* surly, sour-tempered.

réveil [ʀevɛj] *nm* (*d'un dormeur*) waking up *no pl*; (*fig*) awakening; (*pendule*) alarm (clock); **au** ~ when I (*ou* you *etc*) wake (*ou* woke) up, on waking (up); **sonner le** ~ (*MIL*) to sound the reveille.

réveille-matin [ʀevɛjmatɛ̃] *nm inv* alarm clock.

réveiller [ʀeveje] *vt* (*personne*) to wake up; (*fig*) to awaken, revive; **se** ~ *vi* to wake up; (*fig*) to be revived, reawaken.

réveillon [ʀevɛjɔ̃] *nm* Christmas Eve; (*de la Saint-Sylvestre*) New Year's Eve; Christmas Eve (*ou* New Year's Eve) party *ou* dinner.

réveillonner [ʀevɛjɔne] *vi* to celebrate Christmas Eve (*ou* New Year's Eve).

révélateur, trice [ʀevelatœʀ, -tʀis] *adj*: ~ **(de qch)** revealing (sth) ♦ *nm* (*PHOTO*) developer.

révélation [ʀevelɑsjɔ̃] *nf* revelation.

révéler [ʀevele] *vt* (*gén*) to reveal; (*divulguer*) to disclose, reveal; (*dénoter*) to reveal, show; (*faire connaître au public*): ~ **qn/qch** to make sb/sth widely known, bring sb/sth to the public's notice; **se** ~ *vi* to be revealed, reveal itself ♦ *vb avec attribut*: **se** ~ **facile/faux** to prove (to be) easy/false; **se** ~ **cruel/un allié sûr** to show o.s. to be cruel/a trustworthy ally.

revenant, e [ʀəvnɑ̃, -ɑ̃t] *nm/f* ghost.

revendeur, euse [ʀəvɑ̃dœʀ, -øz] *nm/f* (*détaillant*) retailer; (*d'occasions*) secondhand dealer.

revendicatif, ive [ʀəvɑ̃dikatif, -iv] *adj* (*mouvement*) of protest.

revendication [ʀəvɑ̃dikasjɔ̃] *nf* claim, demand; **journée de** ~ day of action (in support of one's claims).

revendiquer [ʀəvɑ̃dike] *vt* to claim, demand; (*responsabilité*) to claim ♦ *vi* to agitate in favour of one's claims.

revendre [ʀəvɑ̃dʀ(ə)] *vt* (*d'occasion*) to resell; (*détailler*) to sell; (*vendre davantage de*): ~ **du**

sucre/un foulard/deux bagues to sell more sugar/another scarf/another two rings; **à ~** *adv* (*en abondance*) to spare.

revenir [ʀəvniʀ] *vi* to come back; (*CULIN*): **faire ~** to brown; (*coûter*): **~ cher/à 100 F (à qn)** to cost (sb) a lot/100 F; **~ à** (*études, projet*) to return to, go back to; (*équivaloir à*) to amount to; **~ à qn** (*rumeur, nouvelle*) to get back to sb, reach sb's ears; (*part, honneur*) to go to sb, be sb's; (*souvenir, nom*) to come back to sb; **~ de** (*fig: maladie, étonnement*) to recover from; **~ sur** (*question, sujet*) to go back over; (*engagement*) to go back on; **~ à la charge** to return to the attack; **~ à soi** to come round; **n'en pas ~: je n'en reviens pas** I can't get over it; **~ sur ses pas** to retrace one's steps; **cela revient à dire que/au même** it amounts to saying that/to the same thing; **~ de loin** (*fig*) to have been at death's door.

revente [ʀəvɑ̃t] *nf* resale.

revenu, e [ʀəvny] *pp de* **revenir** ♦ *nm* income; (*de l'État*) revenue; (*d'un capital*) yield; **~s** *nmpl* income *sg*; **~ national brut** gross national income.

revenu, e [ʀəvny] *pp de* **revenir**.

rêver [ʀeve] *vi, vt* to dream; (*rêvasser*) to (day)dream; **~ de** (*voir en rêve*) to dream of *ou* about; **~ de qch/de faire** to dream of sth/of doing; **~ à** to dream of.

réverbération [ʀevɛʀbeʀɑsjɔ̃] *nf* reflection.

réverbère [ʀevɛʀbɛʀ] *nm* street lamp *ou* light.

réverbérer [ʀevɛʀbeʀe] *vt* to reflect.

reverdir [ʀəvɛʀdiʀ] *vi* (*arbre etc*) to turn green again.

révérence [ʀeveʀɑ̃s] *nf* (*vénération*) reverence; (*salut: d'homme*) bow; (*: de femme*) curtsey.

révérencieux, euse [ʀeveʀɑ̃sjø, -øz] *adj* reverent.

révérend, e [ʀeveʀɑ̃, -ɑ̃d] *adj*: **le ~ père Pascal** the Reverend Father Pascal.

révérer [ʀeveʀe] *vt* to revere.

rêverie [ʀɛvʀi] *nf* daydreaming *no pl*, daydream.

reverrai [ʀəveʀe] *etc vb voir* **revoir**.

revers [ʀəvɛʀ] *nm* (*de feuille, main*) back; (*d'étoffe*) wrong side; (*de pièce, médaille*) back, reverse; (*TENNIS, PING-PONG*) backhand; (*de veston*) lapel; (*de pantalon*) turn-up; (*fig: échec*) setback; **~ de fortune** reverse of fortune; **d'un ~ de main** with the back of one's hand; **le ~ de la médaille** (*fig*) the other side of the coin; **prendre à ~** (*MIL*) to take from the rear.

reverser [ʀəvɛʀse] *vt* (*reporter: somme etc*): **~ sur** to put back into; (*liquide*): **~ (dans)** to pour some more (into).

réversible [ʀevɛʀsibl(ə)] *adj* reversible.

revêtement [ʀəvɛtmɑ̃] *nm* (*de paroi*) facing; (*des sols*) flooring; (*de chaussée*) surface; (*de tuyau etc: enduit*) coating.

revêtir [ʀəvetiʀ] *vt* (*habit*) to don, put on; (*fig*) to take on; **~ qn de** to dress sb in; (*fig*) to

endow *ou* invest sb with; **~ qch de** to cover sth with; (*fig*) to cloak sth in; **~ d'un visa** to append a visa to.

rêveur, euse [ʀɛvœʀ, -øz] *adj* dreamy ♦ *nm/f* dreamer.

reviendrai [ʀəvjɛ̃dʀe] *etc vb voir* **revenir**.

revienne [ʀəvjɛn] *etc vb voir* **revenir**.

revient [ʀəvjɛ̃] *vb voir* **revenir** ♦ *nm*: **prix de ~** cost price.

revigorer [ʀəvigɔʀe] *vt* to invigorate, revive, buck up.

revint [ʀəvɛ̃] *etc vb voir* **revenir**.

revirement [ʀəviʀmɑ̃] *nm* change of mind; (*d'une situation*) reversal.

revis [ʀəvi] *etc vb voir* **revoir**.

révisable [ʀevizabl(ə)] *adj* (*procès, taux etc*) reviewable, subject to review.

réviser [ʀevize] *vt* (*texte, SCOL: matière*) to revise; (*comptes*) to audit; (*machine, installation, moteur*) to overhaul, service; (*JUR: procès*) to review.

révision [ʀevizjɔ̃] *nf* revision; auditing *no pl*; overhaul, servicing *no pl*; review; **conseil de ~** (*MIL*) recruiting board; **faire ses ~s** (*SCOL*) to do one's revision (*BRIT*), revise (*BRIT*), review (*US*); **la ~ des 10 000 km** (*AUTO*) the 10,000 km service.

révisionnisme [ʀevizjɔnism(ə)] *nm* revisionism.

revisser [ʀəvise] *vt* to screw back again.

revit [ʀəvi] *vb voir* **revoir**.

revitaliser [ʀəvitalize] *vt* to revitalize.

revivifier [ʀəvivifje] *vt* to revitalize.

revivre [ʀəvivʀ(ə)] *vi* (*reprendre des forces*) to come alive again; (*traditions*) to be revived ♦ *vt* (*épreuve, moment*) to relive; **faire ~** (*mode, institution, usage*) to bring back to life.

révocable [ʀevɔkabl(ə)] *adj* (*délégué*) dismissible; (*contrat*) revocable.

révocation [ʀevɔkɑsjɔ̃] *nf* dismissal; revocation.

revoir [ʀəvwaʀ] *vt* to see again; (*réviser*) to revise (*BRIT*), review (*US*) ♦ *nm*: **au ~** goodbye; **dire au ~ à qn** to say goodbye to sb; **se ~** (*amis*) to meet (again), see each other again.

révoltant, e [ʀevɔltɑ̃, -ɑ̃t] *adj* revolting.

révolte [ʀevɔlt(ə)] *nf* rebellion, revolt.

révolter [ʀevɔlte] *vt* to revolt, outrage; **se ~** *vi*: **se ~ (contre)** to rebel (against); **se ~ (à)** to be outraged (by).

révolu, e [ʀevɔly] *adj* past; (*ADMIN*): **âgé de 18 ans ~s** over 18 years of age; **après 3 ans ~s** when 3 full years have passed.

révolution [ʀevɔlysjɔ̃] *nf* revolution; **être en ~** (*pays etc*) to be in revolt; **la ~ industrielle** the industrial revolution.

révolutionnaire [ʀevɔlysjɔnɛʀ] *adj, nm/f* revolutionary.

révolutionner [ʀevɔlysjɔne] *vt* to revolutionize; (*fig*) to stir up.

revolver [RɛvɔlvɛR] _nm_ gun; (_à barillet_) revolver.

révoquer [Revɔke] _vt_ (_fonctionnaire_) to dismiss, remove from office; (_arrêt, contrat_) to revoke.

revoyais [Rǝvwajɛ] _etc vb voir_ **revoir**.

revu, e [Rǝvy] _pp de_ **revoir** ♦ _nf_ (_inventaire, examen_) review; (MIL: _défilé_) review, march past; (: _inspection_) inspection, review; (_périodique_) review, magazine; (_pièce satirique_) revue; (_de music-hall_) variety show; **passer en** ~ to review, inspect; (_fig_) to review; ~ **de (la) presse** press review.

révulsé, e [Revylse] _adj_ (_yeux_) rolled upwards; (_visage_) contorted.

Reykjavik [Rekjavik] _n_ Reykjavik.

rez-de-chaussée [Redʃose] _nm inv_ ground floor.

rez-de-jardin [RedʒaRdɛ̃] _nm inv_ garden level.

RF _sigle f_ = _République française_.

RFA _sigle f_ (= _République fédérale d'Allemagne_) FRG.

RFO _sigle f_ (= _Radio-Télévision Française d'Outre-mer_) _French overseas broadcasting service_.

RG _sigle mpl_ (= _renseignements généraux_) _security section of the police force_.

rhabiller [Rabije] _vt_: **se** ~ to get dressed again, put one's clothes on again.

rhapsodie [Rapsɔdi] _nf_ rhapsody.

rhénan, e [Renɑ̃, -an] _adj_ Rhine _cpd_, of the Rhine.

Rhénanie [Renani] _nf_: **la** ~ the Rhineland.

rhéostat [Reɔsta] _nm_ rheostat.

rhésus [Rezys] _adj, nm_ rhesus; ~ **positif/ négatif** rhesus positive/negative.

rhétorique [RetɔRik] _nf_ rhetoric ♦ _adj_ rhetorical.

rhéto-roman, e [RetɔRɔmɑ̃, -an] _adj_ Rhaeto-Romanic.

Rhin [Rɛ̃] _nm_: **le** ~ the Rhine.

rhinite [Rinit] _nf_ rhinitis.

rhinocéros [RinɔseRɔs] _nm_ rhinoceros.

rhinopharyngite [RinɔfaRɛ̃ʒit] _nf_ throat infection.

rhodanien, ne [Rɔdanjɛ̃, -ɛn] _adj_ Rhône _cpd_, of the Rhône.

Rhodes [Rɔd] _n_: (**l'île de**) ~ (the island of) Rhodes.

Rhodésie [Rɔdezi] _nf_: **la** ~ Rhodesia.

rhodésien, ne [Rɔdezjɛ̃, -ɛn] _adj_ Rhodesian.

rhododendron [RɔdɔdɛdRɔ̃] _nm_ rhodo-dendron.

Rhône [Ron] _nm_: **le** ~ the Rhône.

rhubarbe [RybaRb(ǝ)] _nf_ rhubarb.

rhum [Rɔm] _nm_ rum.

rhumatisant, e [Rymatizɑ̃, -ɑ̃t] _adj, nm/f_ rheumatic.

rhumatismal, e, aux [Rymatismal, -o] _adj_ rheumatic.

rhumatisme [Rymatism(ǝ)] _nm_ rheumatism _no pl_.

rhumatologie [Rymatɔlɔʒi] _nf_ rheumatology.

rhumatologue [Rymatɔlɔg] _nm/f_ rheuma-tologist.

rhume [Rym] _nm_ cold; ~ **de cerveau** head cold; **le** ~ **des foins** hay fever.

rhumerie [RɔmRi] _nf_ (_distillerie_) rum distillery.

RI _sigle m_ (MIL) = _régiment d'infanterie_ ♦ _sigle mpl_ (= _Républicains indépendants_) _political party_.

ri [Ri] _pp de_ **rire**.

riant, e [Rjɑ̃, -ɑ̃t] _vb voir_ **rire** ♦ _adj_ smiling, cheerful; (_campagne, paysage_) pleasant.

RIB _sigle m_ = **relevé d'identité bancaire**.

ribambelle [Ribɑ̃bɛl] _nf_: **une** ~ **de** a herd _ou_ swarm of.

ricain, e [Rikɛ̃, -ɛn] _adj_ (_fam_) Yank, Yankee.

ricanement [Rikanmɑ̃] _nm_ snigger; giggle.

ricaner [Rikane] _vi_ (_avec méchanceté_) to snigger; (_bêtement, avec gêne_) to giggle.

riche [Riʃ] _adj_ (_gén_) rich; (_personne, pays_) rich, wealthy; ~ **en** rich in; ~ **de** full of; rich in.

richement [Riʃmɑ̃] _adv_ richly.

richesse [Riʃɛs] _nf_ wealth; (_fig_) richness; ~**s** _nfpl_ wealth _sg_; treasures; ~ **en vitamines** high vitamin content.

richissime [Riʃisim] _adj_ extremely rich _ou_ wealthy.

ricin [Risɛ̃] _nm_: **huile de** ~ castor oil.

ricocher [Rikɔʃe] _vi_: ~ (**sur**) to rebound (off); (_sur l'eau_) to bounce (on _ou_ off); **faire** ~ (_galet_) to skim.

ricochet [Rikɔʃɛ] _nm_ rebound; bounce; **faire** ~ to rebound, bounce; (_fig_) to rebound; **faire des** ~**s** to skip stones; **par** ~ _adv_ on the rebound; (_fig_) as an indirect result.

rictus [Riktys] _nm_ grin; (_snarling_) grimace.

ride [Rid] _nf_ wrinkle; (_fig_) ripple.

ridé, e [Ride] _adj_ wrinkled.

rideau, x [Rido] _nm_ curtain; **tirer/ouvrir les** ~**x** to draw/open the curtains; ~ **de fer** metal shutter; (POL): **le** ~ **de fer** the Iron Curtain.

ridelle [Ridɛl] _nf_ slatted side (_of truck_).

rider [Ride] _vt_ to wrinkle; (_fig_) to ripple, ruffle the surface of; **se** ~ _vi_ to become wrinkled.

ridicule [Ridikyl] _adj_ ridiculous ♦ _nm_ ridiculousness _no pl_; **le** ~ ridicule; (_travers: gén pl_) absurdities _pl_; **tourner en** ~ to ridicule.

ridiculement [Ridikylmɑ̃] _adv_ ridiculously.

ridiculiser [Ridikylize] _vt_ to ridicule; **se** ~ to make a fool of o.s.

ridule [Ridyl] _nf_ (_euph: ride_) little wrinkle.

rie [Ri] _etc vb voir_ **rire**.

════════════════════════ _MOT-CLÉ_

rien [Rjɛ̃] _pron_ **1**: (**ne**) ... ~ nothing; _tournure negative_ + anything; **qu'est-ce que vous avez?** - ~ what have you got? — nothing; **il n'a** ~ **dit/fait** he said/did nothing; he hasn't said/ done anything; **il n'a** ~ (_n'est pas blessé_) he's all right; **ça ne fait** ~ it doesn't matter; **il n'y est pour** ~ he's got nothing to do with it **2** (_quelque chose_): **a-t-il jamais** ~ **fait pour**

nous? has he ever done anything for us?
3: ~ **de:** ~ **d'intéressant** nothing interesting;
p **d'autre** nothing else; ~ **du tout** nothing at
all; **il n'a ~ d'un champion** he's no
champion, there's nothing of the champion
about him
4: ~ **que** just, only; nothing but; ~ **que pour
lui faire plaisir** only *ou* just to please him; ~
que la vérité nothing but the truth; ~ **que
cela** that alone
♦ *excl:* **de ~!** not at all!, don't mention it!; **il
n'en est ~!** nothing of the sort!; ~ **à faire!**
it's no good!, it's no use!
♦ *nm:* **un petit ~** (*cadeau*) a little something;
des ~s trivia *pl*; **un ~ de** a hint of; **en un ~
de temps** in no time at all; **avoir peur d'un ~**
to be frightened of the slightest thing.

rieur, euse [ʀjœʀ, -øz] *adj* cheerful.
rigide [ʀiʒid] *adj* stiff; (*fig*) rigid; (*moralement*)
strict.
rigidité [ʀiʒidite] *nf* stiffness; **la ~ cadavérique**
rigor mortis.
rigolade [ʀiɡɔlad] *nf:* **la ~** fun; (*fig*): **c'est de la
~** it's a big farce; (*c'est facile*) it's a cinch.
rigole [ʀiɡɔl] *nf* (*conduit*) channel; (*filet d'eau*)
rivulet.
rigoler [ʀiɡɔle] *vi* (*rire*) to laugh; (*s'amuser*) to
have (some) fun; (*plaisanter*) to be joking *ou*
kidding.
rigolo, ote [ʀiɡɔlo, -ɔt] *adj* (*fam*) funny ♦ *nm/f*
comic; (*péj*) fraud, phoney.
rigorisme [ʀiɡɔʀism(ə)] *nm* (moral) rigorism.
rigoriste [ʀiɡɔʀist(ə)] *adj* rigorist.
rigoureusement [ʀiɡuʀøzmɑ̃] *adv* rigorously;
~ **vrai/interdit** strictly true/forbidden.
rigoureux, euse [ʀiɡuʀø, -øz] *adj* (*morale*)
rigorous, strict; (*personne*) stern, strict;
(*climat, châtiment*) rigorous, harsh, severe;
(*interdiction, neutralité*) strict; (*preuves,
analyse, méthode*) rigorous.
rigueur [ʀiɡœʀ] *nf* rigour (*BRIT*), rigor (*US*);
strictness; harshness; **"tenue de soirée de
~"** "evening dress (to be worn)"; **être de ~**
to be the usual thing, be the rule; **à la ~** at
a pinch; possibly; **tenir ~ à qn de qch** to
hold sth against sb.
riions [ʀijɔ̃] *etc vb voir* **rire.**
rillettes [ʀijɛt] *nfpl* ≈ potted meat *sg.*
rime [ʀim] *nf* rhyme; **n'avoir ni ~ ni raison** to
have neither rhyme nor reason.
rimer [ʀime] *vi:* ~ **(avec)** to rhyme (with); **ne ~
à rien** not to make sense.
Rimmel [ʀimɛl] *nm* ® mascara.
rinçage [ʀɛ̃saʒ] *nm* rinsing (out); (*opération*)
rinse.
rince-doigts [ʀɛ̃sdwa] *nm inv* finger-bowl.
rincer [ʀɛ̃se] *vt* to rinse; (*récipient*) to rinse
out; **se ~ la bouche** to rinse out one's
mouth.
ring [ʀiŋ] *nm* (boxing) ring; **monter sur le ~**
(*aussi fig*) to enter the ring; (*: faire carrière de*

boxeur) to take up boxing.
ringard, e [ʀɛ̃ɡaʀ, -aʀd(ə)] *adj* (*péj*) old-
fashioned.
Rio de Janeiro [ʀiodʒaneʀ(o)] *n* Rio de
Janeiro.
rions [ʀjɔ̃] *vb voir* **rire.**
ripaille [ʀipaj] *nf:* **faire ~** to feast.
riper [ʀipe] *vi* to slip, slide.
ripoliné, e [ʀipoline] *adj* enamel-painted.
riposte [ʀipɔst(ə)] *nf* retort, riposte; (*fig*)
counter-attack, reprisal.
riposter [ʀipɔste] *vi* to retaliate ♦ *vt:* ~ **que** to
retort that; ~ **à** *vt* to counter; to reply to.
rire [ʀiʀ] *vi* to laugh; (*se divertir*) to have fun;
(*plaisanter*) to joke ♦ *nm* laugh; **le ~** laughter;
~ **de** *vt* to laugh at; **se ~ de** to make light of;
tu veux ~! you must be joking!; ~ **aux
éclats/aux larmes** to roar with laughter/
laugh until one cries; ~ **jaune** to force
oneself to laugh; ~ **sous cape** to laugh up
one's sleeve; ~ **au nez de qn** to laugh in sb's
face; **pour ~** (*pas sérieusement*) for a joke *ou*
a laugh.
ris [ʀi] *vb voir* **rire** ♦ *nm:* ~ **de veau** (calf)
sweetbread.
risée [ʀize] *nf:* **être la ~ de** to be the laughing
stock of.
risette [ʀizɛt] *nf:* **faire ~ (à)** to give a nice
little smile (to).
risible [ʀizibl(ə)] *adj* laughable, ridiculous.
risque [ʀisk(ə)] *nm* risk; **l'attrait du ~** the lure
of danger; **prendre des ~s** to take risks; **à
ses ~s et périls** at his own risk; **au ~ de** at
the risk of; ~ **d'incendie** fire risk; ~ **calculé**
calculated risk.
risqué, e [ʀiske] *adj* risky; (*plaisanterie*)
risqué, daring.
risquer [ʀiske] *vt* to risk; (*allusion, question*) to
venture, hazard; **tu risques qu'on te renvoie**
you risk being dismissed; **ça ne risque rien**
it's quite safe; ~ **de: il risque de se tuer** he
could die *ou* risks getting himself killed; **il
a risqué de se tuer** he almost got himself
killed; **ce qui risque de se produire** what
might *ou* could well happen; **il ne risque pas
de recommencer** there's no chance of him
doing that again; **se ~ dans** (*s'aventurer*) to
venture into; **se ~ à faire** (*tenter*) to venture
ou dare to do; ~ **le tout pour le tout** to risk
the lot.
risque-tout [ʀiskatu] *nm/f inv* daredevil.
rissoler [ʀisɔle] *vi, vt:* **(faire) ~** to brown.
ristourne [ʀistuʀn(ə)] *nf* rebate; discount.
rit [ʀi] *etc vb voir* **rire.**
rite [ʀit] *nm* rite; (*fig*) ritual; ~**s d'initiation**
initiation rites.
ritournelle [ʀituʀnɛl] *nf* (*fig*) tune; **c'est
toujours la même ~** (*fam*) it's always the
same old story.
rituel, le [ʀitɥɛl] *adj, nm* ritual.
rituellement [ʀitɥɛlmɑ̃] *adv* religiously.
riv. *abr* (= *rivière*) R.

rivage [ʁivaʒ] *nm* shore.

rival, e, aux [ʁival, -o] *adj, nm/f* rival; **sans** ~ *adj* unrivalled.

rivaliser [ʁivalize] *vi*: ~ **avec** to rival, vie with; (*être comparable*) to hold its own against, compare with; ~ **avec qn de** (*élégance etc*) to vie with *ou* rival sb in.

rivalité [ʁivalite] *nf* rivalry.

rive [ʁiv] *nf* shore; (*de fleuve*) bank.

river [ʁive] *vt* (*clou, pointe*) to clinch; (*plaques*) to rivet together; **être rivé sur/à** to be riveted on/to.

riverain, e [ʁivʁɛ̃, -ɛn] *adj* riverside *cpd*; lakeside *cpd*; roadside *cpd* ♦ *nm/f* riverside (*ou* lakeside) resident; local *ou* roadside resident.

rivet [ʁivɛ] *nm* rivet.

riveter [ʁivte] *vt* to rivet (together).

Riviera [ʁivjɛʁa] *nf*: **la** ~ **(italienne)** the Italian Riviera.

rivière [ʁivjɛʁ] *nf* river; ~ **de diamants** diamond rivière.

rixe [ʁiks(ə)] *nf* brawl, scuffle.

Riyad [ʁijad] *n* Riyadh.

riz [ʁi] *nm* rice; ~ **au lait** ≈ rice pudding.

rizière [ʁizjɛʁ] *nf* paddy field.

RMC *sigle f* = Radio Monte Carlo.

RMI *sigle m* (= *revenu minimum d'insertion*) ≈ income support (*BRIT*), ≈ welfare (*US*).

RN *sigle f* = **route nationale**.

robe [ʁɔb] *nf* dress; (*de juge, d'ecclésiastique*) robe; (*de professeur*) gown; (*pelage*) coat; ~ **de soirée/de mariée** evening/wedding dress; ~ **de baptême** christening robe; ~ **de chambre** dressing gown; ~ **de grossesse** maternity dress.

robinet [ʁɔbinɛ] *nm* tap, faucet (*US*); ~ **du gaz** gas tap; ~ **mélangeur** mixer tap.

robinetterie [ʁɔbinɛtʁi] *nf* taps *pl*, plumbing.

roboratif, ive [ʁɔbɔʁatif, -iv] *adj* bracing, invigorating.

robot [ʁɔbo] *nm* robot; ~ **de cuisine** food processor.

robotique [ʁɔbɔtik] *nf* robotics *sg*.

robotiser [ʁɔbɔtize] *vt* (*personne, travailleur*) to turn into a robot; (*monde, vie*) to automate.

robuste [ʁɔbyst(ə)] *adj* robust, sturdy.

robustesse [ʁɔbystɛs] *nf* robustness, sturdiness.

roc [ʁɔk] *nm* rock.

rocade [ʁɔkad] *nf* (*AUTO*) bypass.

rocaille [ʁɔkaj] *nf* (*pierres*) loose stones *pl*; (*terrain*) rocky *ou* stony ground; (*jardin*) rockery, rock garden ♦ *adj* (*style*) rocaille.

rocailleux, euse [ʁɔkajø, -øz] *adj* rocky, stony; (*voix*) harsh.

rocambolesque [ʁɔkãbɔlɛsk(ə)] *adj* fantastic, incredible.

roche [ʁɔʃ] *nf* rock.

rocher [ʁɔʃe] *nm* rock; (*ANAT*) petrosal bone.

rochet [ʁɔʃɛ] *nm*: **roue à** ~ ratchet wheel.

rocheux, euse [ʁɔʃø, -øz] *adj* rocky; **les**

(montagnes) Rocheuses the Rockies, the Rocky Mountains.

rock (and roll) [ʁɔk(ɛnʁɔl)] *nm* (*musique*) rock(-'n'-roll); (*danse*) rock.

rocker [ʁɔkœʁ] *nm* (*chanteur*) rock musician; (*adepte*) rock fan.

rocking-chair [ʁɔkiŋ(t)ʃɛʁ] *nm* rocking chair.

rococo [ʁɔkɔko] *nm* rococo ♦ *adj* rococo.

rodage [ʁɔdaʒ] *nm* running in (*BRIT*), breaking in (*US*); **en** ~ (*AUTO*) running *ou* breaking in.

rodé, e [ʁɔde] *adj* run in (*BRIT*), broken in (*US*); (*personne*): ~ **à qch** having got the hang of sth.

rodéo [ʁɔdeo] *nm* rodeo (*pl* -s).

roder [ʁɔde] *vt* (*moteur, voiture*) to run in (*BRIT*), break in (*US*); ~ **un spectacle/service** to iron out the initial problems of a show/service.

rôder [ʁode] *vi* to roam *ou* wander about; (*de façon suspecte*) to lurk (about *ou* around).

rôdeur, euse [ʁodœʁ, -øz] *nm/f* prowler.

rodomontades [ʁɔdɔmɔ̃tad] *nfpl* bragging *sg*; sabre rattling *sg*.

rogatoire [ʁɔgatwaʁ] *adj*: **commission** ~ letters rogatory.

rogne [ʁɔɲ] *nf*: **être en** ~ to be mad *ou* in a temper; **se mettre en** ~ to get mad *ou* in a temper.

rogner [ʁɔɲe] *vt* to trim; (*fig*) to whittle down; ~ **sur** (*fig*) to cut down *ou* back on.

rognons [ʁɔɲɔ̃] *nmpl* kidneys.

rognures [ʁɔɲyʁ] *nfpl* trimmings.

rogue [ʁɔg] *adj* arrogant.

roi [ʁwa] *nm* king; **les R**~**s mages** the Three Wise Men, the Magi; **le jour** *ou* **la fête des R**~**s, les R**~**s** Twelfth Night.

La fête des Rois *is celebrated on January 6. Figurines representing the magi are traditionally added to the Christmas crib and people eat* la galette des Rois, *a plain, flat cake in which a porcelain charm (*la fève*) is hidden. Whoever finds the charm is king or queen for the day and chooses a partner.*

---

roitelet [ʁwatlɛ] *nm* wren; (*péj*) kinglet.

rôle [ʁol] *nm* role; (*contribution*) part.

rollmops [ʁɔlmɔps] *nm* rollmop.

romain, e [ʁɔmɛ̃, -ɛn] *adj* Roman ♦ *nm/f*: **R**~**, e** Roman ♦ *nf* (*CULIN*) cos (lettuce).

roman, e [ʁɔmã, -an] *adj* (*ARCHIT*) Romanesque; (*LING*) Romance *cpd*, Romanic ♦ *nm* novel; ~ **policier** detective novel; ~ **d'espionnage** spy novel *ou* story; ~ **noir** thriller.

romance [ʁɔmãs] *nf* ballad.

romancer [ʁɔmãse] *vt* to romanticize.

romanche [ʁɔmãʃ] *adj, nm* Romansh.

romancier, ière [ʁɔmãsje, -jɛʁ] *nm/f* novelist.

romand, e [ʁɔmã, -ãd] *adj* of *ou* from French-speaking Switzerland ♦ *nm/f*: **R**~**, e** French-speaking Swiss.

romanesque [ʀɔmanɛsk(ə)] adj (*fantastique*) fantastic; storybook cpd; (*sentimental*) romantic; (LITTÉRATURE) novelistic.

roman-feuilleton, pl **romans-feuilletons** [ʀɔmɑ̃fœjtɔ̃] nm serialized novel.

roman-fleuve, pl **romans-fleuves** [ʀɔmɑ̃flœv] nm saga, roman-fleuve.

romanichel, le [ʀɔmaniʃɛl] nm/f gipsy.

roman-photo, pl **romans-photos** [ʀɔmɑ̃fɔto] nm (romantic) picture story.

romantique [ʀɔmɑ̃tik] adj romantic.

romantisme [ʀɔmɑ̃tism(ə)] nm romanticism.

romarin [ʀɔmaʀɛ̃] nm rosemary.

rombière [ʀɔ̃bjɛʀ] nf (péj) old bag.

Rome [ʀɔm] n Rome.

rompre [ʀɔ̃pʀ(ə)] vt to break; (*entretien, fiançailles*) to break off ♦ vi (*fiancés*) to break it off; **se** ~ vi to break; (MÉD) to burst, rupture; **se** ~ **les os** ou **le cou** to break one's neck; ~ **avec** to break with; **à tout** ~ adv wildly; **applaudir à tout** ~ to bring down the house, applaud wildly; ~ **la glace** (*fig*) to break the ice; **rompez (les rangs)!** (MIL) dismiss!, fall out!

rompu, e [ʀɔ̃py] pp de **rompre** ♦ adj (*fourbu*) exhausted, worn out; ~ **à** with wide experience of; inured to.

romsteck [ʀɔ̃mstɛk] nm rump steak no pl.

ronce [ʀɔ̃s] nf (BOT) bramble branch; (MENUISERIE): ~ **de noyer** burr walnut; ~**s** nf pl brambles, thorns.

ronchonner [ʀɔ̃ʃɔne] vi (fam) to grouse, grouch.

rond, e [ʀɔ̃, ʀɔ̃d] adj round; (*joues, mollets*) well-rounded; (fam: *ivre*) tight; (*sincère, décidé*): **être** ~ **en affaires** to be on the level in business, do an honest deal ♦ nm (*cercle*) ring; (fam: *sou*): **je n'ai plus un** ~ I haven't a penny left ♦ nf (*gén: de surveillance*) rounds pl, patrol; (*danse*) round (dance); (MUS) semibreve (BRIT), whole note (US) ♦ adv: **tourner** ~ (*moteur*) to run smoothly; **ça ne tourne pas** ~ (*fig*) there's something not quite right about it; **pour faire un compte** ~ to make (it) a round figure, to round (it) off; **avoir le dos** ~ to be round-shouldered; **en** ~ (*s'asseoir, danser*) in a ring; **à la** ~**e** (*alentour*): **à 10 km à la** ~**e** for 10 km round; (*à chacun son tour*): **passer qch à la** ~**e** to pass sth (a)round, to hand sth round; **faire des** ~**s de jambe** to bow and scrape; ~ **de serviette** napkin ring.

rond-de-cuir, pl **ronds-de-cuir** [ʀɔ̃dkɥiʀ] nm (péj) penpusher.

rondelet, te [ʀɔ̃dlɛ, -ɛt] adj plump; (*fig: somme*) tidy; (: *bourse*) well-lined, fat.

rondelle [ʀɔ̃dɛl] nf (TECH) washer; (*tranche*) slice, round.

rondement [ʀɔ̃dmɑ̃] adv (*avec décision*) briskly; (*loyalement*) frankly.

rondeur [ʀɔ̃dœʀ] nf (*d'un bras, des formes*) plumpness; (*bonhomie*) friendly straight-forwardness; ~**s** nf pl (*d'une femme*) curves.

rondin [ʀɔ̃dɛ̃] nm log.

rond-point, pl **ronds-points** [ʀɔ̃pwɛ̃] nm roundabout (BRIT), traffic circle (US).

ronéotyper [ʀɔneɔtipe] vt to duplicate, roneo.

ronflant, e [ʀɔ̃flɑ̃, -ɑ̃t] adj (péj) high-flown, grand.

ronflement [ʀɔ̃fləmɑ̃] nm snore, snoring no pl.

ronfler [ʀɔ̃fle] vi to snore; (*moteur, poêle*) to hum; (: *plus fort*) to roar.

ronger [ʀɔ̃ʒe] vt to gnaw (at); (*suj: vers, rouille*) to eat into; ~ **son frein** to champ (at) the bit (*fig*); **se** ~ **de souci, se** ~ **les sangs** to worry o.s. sick, fret; **se** ~ **les ongles** to bite one's nails.

rongeur, euse [ʀɔ̃ʒœʀ, -øz] nm/f rodent.

ronronnement [ʀɔ̃ʀɔnmɑ̃] nm purring; (*bruit*) purr.

ronronner [ʀɔ̃ʀɔne] vi to purr.

roque [ʀɔk] nm (ÉCHECS) castling.

roquefort [ʀɔkfɔʀ] nm Roquefort.

roquer [ʀɔke] vi to castle.

roquet [ʀɔkɛ] nm nasty little lap-dog.

roquette [ʀɔkɛt] nf rocket; ~ **antichar** antitank rocket.

rosace [ʀozas] nf (*vitrail*) rose window, rosace; (*motif: de plafond etc*) rose.

rosaire [ʀozɛʀ] nm rosary.

rosbif [ʀɔsbif] nm: **du** ~ roasting beef; (*cuit*) roast beef; **un** ~ a joint of (roasting) beef.

rose [ʀoz] nf rose; (*vitrail*) rose window ♦ adj pink; ~ **bonbon** adj inv candy pink; ~ **des vents** compass card.

rosé, e [ʀoze] adj pinkish; (*vin*) ~ rosé (wine).

roseau, x [ʀozo] nm reed.

rosée [ʀoze] adj f voir **rosé** ♦ nf: **goutte de** ~ dewdrop.

roseraie [ʀozʀɛ] nf rose garden; (*plantation*) rose nursery.

rosette [ʀozɛt] nf rosette (gen of the Légion d'honneur).

rosier [ʀozje] nm rosebush, rose tree.

rosir [ʀoziʀ] vi to go pink.

rosse [ʀɔs] nf (péj: *cheval*) nag ♦ adj nasty, vicious.

rosser [ʀɔse] vt (fam) to thrash.

rossignol [ʀɔsiɲɔl] nm (ZOOL) nightingale; (*crochet*) picklock.

rot [ʀo] nm belch; (*de bébé*) burp.

rotatif, ive [ʀɔtatif, -iv] adj rotary ♦ nf rotary press.

rotation [ʀɔtasjɔ̃] nf rotation; (*fig*) rotation, swap-around; (*renouvellement*) turnover; **par** ~ on a rota (BRIT) ou rotation (US) basis; ~ **des cultures** rotation of crops; ~ **des stocks** stock turnover.

rotatoire [ʀɔtatwaʀ] adj: **mouvement** ~ rotary movement.

roter [ʀɔte] vi (fam) to burp, belch.

rôti [ʀoti] nm: **du** ~ roasting meat; (*cuit*) roast meat; **un** ~ **de bœuf/porc** a joint of (roasting) beef/pork.

rotin [ʀɔtɛ̃] nm rattan (cane); **fauteuil en** ~

cane (arm)chair.

rôtir [ʀotiʀ] *vt* (*aussi:* **faire** ~) to roast ♦ *vi* to roast; **se** ~ **au soleil** to bask in the sun.

rôtisserie [ʀotisʀi] *nf* (*restaurant*) steakhouse; (*comptoir, magasin*) roast meat counter (*ou* shop).

rôtissoire [ʀotiswaʀ] *nf* (roasting) spit.

rotonde [ʀotɔ̃d] *nf* (*ARCHIT*) rotunda; (*RAIL*) engine shed.

rotondité [ʀotɔ̃dite] *nf* roundness.

rotor [ʀotɔʀ] *nm* rotor.

Rotterdam [ʀotɛʀdam] *n* Rotterdam.

rotule [ʀotyl] *nf* kneecap, patella.

roturier, ière [ʀotyʀje, -jɛʀ] *nm/f* commoner.

rouage [ʀwaʒ] *nm* cog(wheel), gearwheel; (*de montre*) part; (*fig*) cog; ~**s** *nmpl* (*fig*) internal structure *sg*.

Rouanda [ʀwɑ̃da] *nm*: **le** ~ Rwanda.

roubaisien, ne [ʀubɛzjɛ̃, -ɛn] *adj* of *ou* from Roubaix.

roublard, e [ʀublaʀ, -aʀd(ə)] *adj* (*péj*) crafty, wily.

rouble [ʀubl(ə)] *nm* rouble.

roucoulement [ʀukulmɑ̃] *nm* (*de pigeons, fig*) coo, cooing.

roucouler [ʀukule] *vi* to coo; (*fig: péj*) to warble; (*: amoureux*) to bill and coo.

roue [ʀu] *nf* wheel; **faire la** ~ (*paon*) to spread *ou* fan its tail; (*GYM*) to do a cartwheel; **descendre en** ~ **libre** to freewheel *ou* coast down; **pousser à la** ~ to put one's shoulder to the wheel; **grande** ~ (*à la foire*) big wheel; ~ **à aubes** paddle wheel; ~ **dentée** cogwheel; ~ **de secours** spare wheel.

roué, e [ʀwe] *adj* wily.

rouennais, e [ʀwanɛ, -ɛz] *adj* of *ou* from Rouen.

rouer [ʀwe] *vt*: ~ **qn de coups** to give sb a thrashing.

rouet [ʀwɛ] *nm* spinning wheel.

rouge [ʀuʒ] *adj, nm/f* red ♦ *nm* red; (*fard*) rouge; **(vin)** ~ red wine; **passer au** ~ (*signal*) to go red; (*automobiliste*) to go through a red light; **porter au** ~ (*métal*) to make red hot; **sur la liste** ~ (*TÉL*) ex-directory (*BRIT*), unlisted (*US*); ~ **de honte/colère** red with shame/anger; **se fâcher tout/voir** ~ to blow one's top/see red; ~ **(à lèvres)** lipstick.

rougeâtre [ʀuʒɑtʀ(ə)] *adj* reddish.

rougeaud, e [ʀuʒo, -od] *adj* (*teint*) red; (*personne*) red-faced.

rouge-gorge [ʀuʒgɔʀʒ(ə)] *nm* robin (redbreast).

rougeoiement [ʀuʒwamɑ̃] *nm* reddish glow.

rougeole [ʀuʒɔl] *nf* measles *sg*.

rougeoyant, e [ʀuʒwajɑ̃, -ɑ̃t] *adj* (*ciel, braises*) glowing; (*aube, reflets*) glowing red.

rougeoyer [ʀuʒwaje] *vi* to glow red.

rouget [ʀuʒɛ] *nm* mullet.

rougeur [ʀuʒœʀ] *nf* redness; (*du visage*) red face; ~**s** *nfpl* (*MÉD*) red blotches.

rougir [ʀuʒiʀ] *vi* (*de honte, timidité*) to blush,

flush; (*de plaisir, colère*) to flush; (*fraise, tomate*) to go *inv* turn red; (*ciel*) to redden.

rouille [ʀuj] *adj inv* rust-coloured, rusty ♦ *nf* rust; (*CULIN*) spicy (Provençal) sauce served with fish dishes.

rouillé, e [ʀuje] *adj* rusty.

rouiller [ʀuje] *vt* to rust ♦ *vi* to rust, go rusty; **se** ~ *vi* to rust; (*fig: mentalement*) to become rusty; (*: physiquement*) to grow stiff.

roulade [ʀulad] *nf* (*GYM*) roll; (*CULIN*) rolled meat *no pl*; (*MUS*) roulade, run.

roulage [ʀulaʒ] *nm* (*transport*) haulage.

roulant, e [ʀulɑ̃, -ɑ̃t] *adj* (*meuble*) on wheels; (*surface, trottoir*) moving; **matériel** ~ (*RAIL*) rolling stock; **personnel** ~ (*RAIL*) train crews *pl*.

roulé, e [ʀule] *adj*: **bien** ~**e** (*fam: femme*) shapely, curvy.

rouleau, x [ʀulo] *nm* (*de papier, tissu, pièces de monnaie, SPORT*) roll; (*de machine à écrire*) roller, platen; (*à mise en plis, à peinture, vague*) roller; **être au bout du** ~ (*fig*) to be at the end of the line; ~ **compresseur** steamroller; ~ **à pâtisserie** rolling pin; ~ **de pellicule** roll of film.

roulé-boulé, *pl* **roulés-boulés** [ʀulebule] (*SPORT*) roll.

roulement [ʀulmɑ̃] *nm* (*bruit*) rumbling *no pl*, rumble; (*rotation*) rotation; turnover; (*: de capitaux*) circulation; **par** ~ on a rota (*BRIT*) *ou* rotation (*US*) basis; ~ **(à billes)** ball bearings *pl*; ~ **de tambour** drum roll; ~ **d'yeux** roll(ing) of the eyes.

rouler [ʀule] *vt* to roll; (*papier, tapis*) to roll up; (*CULIN: pâte*) to roll out; (*fam*) to do, con ♦ *vi* (*bille, boule*) to roll; (*voiture, train*) to go, run; (*automobiliste*) to drive; (*cycliste*) to ride; (*bateau*) to roll; (*tonnerre*) to rumble, roll; (*dégringoler*): ~ **en bas de** to roll down; ~ **sur** (*suj: conversation*) to turn on; **se** ~ **dans** (*boue*) to roll in; (*couverture*) to roll o.s. (up) in; ~ **dans la farine** (*fam*) to con; ~ **les épaules/hanches** to sway one's shoulders/ wiggle one's hips; ~ **les "r"** to roll one's r's; ~ **sur l'or** to be rolling in money, be rolling in it; ~ **(sa bosse)** to go places.

roulette [ʀulɛt] *nf* (*de table, fauteuil*) castor; (*de pâtissier*) pastry wheel; (*jeu*): **la** ~ roulette; **à** ~**s** on castors; **la** ~ **russe** Russian roulette.

roulis [ʀuli] *nm* roll(ing).

roulotte [ʀulɔt] *nf* caravan.

roumain, e [ʀumɛ̃, -ɛn] *adj* Rumanian, Romanian ♦ *nm* (*LING*) Rumanian, Romanian ♦ *nm/f*: **R~, e** Rumanian, Romanian.

Roumanie [ʀumani] *nf*: **la** ~ Rumania, Romania.

roupiller [ʀupije] *vi* (*fam*) to sleep.

rouquin, e [ʀukɛ̃, -in] *nm/f* (*péj*) redhead.

rouspéter [ʀuspete] *vi* (*fam*) to moan, grouse.

rousse [ʀus] *adj f voir* **roux**.

rousseur [ʀusœʀ] *nf*: **tache de** ~ freckle.

roussi [ʀusi] *nm*: **ça sent le** ~ there's a smell

of burning; (*fig*) I can smell trouble.

roussir [ʀusiʀ] *vt* to scorch ♦ *vi* (*feuilles*) to go *ou* turn brown; (*CULIN*): **faire ~** to brown.

routage [ʀutaʒ] *nm* (collective) mailing.

routard, e [ʀutaʀ, -aʀd(ə)] *nm/f* traveller.

route [ʀut] *nf* road; (*fig: chemin*) way; (*itinéraire, parcours*) route; (*fig: voie*) road, path; **par (la) ~** by road; **il y a 3 heures de ~** it's a 3-hour ride *ou* drive; **en ~** *adv* on the way; **en ~!** let's go!; **en cours de ~** en route; **mettre en ~** to start up; **se mettre en ~** to set off; **faire ~ vers** to head towards; **faire fausse ~** (*fig*) to be on the wrong track; **~ nationale (RN)** ≈ A-road (*BRIT*), ≈ state highway (*US*).

routier, ière [ʀutje, -jɛʀ] *adj* road *cpd* ♦ *nm* (*camionneur*) (long-distance) lorry (*BRIT*) *ou* truck driver; (*restaurant*) ≈ transport café (*BRIT*), ≈ truck stop (*US*); (*scout*) ≈ rover; (*cycliste*) road racer ♦ *nf* (*voiture*) touring car; **vieux ~** old stager; **carte routière** road map.

routine [ʀutin] *nf* routine; **visite/contrôle de ~** routine visit/check.

routinier, ière [ʀutinje, -jɛʀ] *adj* (*péj: travail*) humdrum, routine; (*: personne*) addicted to routine.

rouvert, e [ʀuvɛʀ, -ɛʀt(ə)] *pp de* **rouvrir**.

rouvrir [ʀuvʀiʀ] *vt, vi* to reopen, open again; **se ~** *vi* (*blessure*) to open up again.

roux, rousse [ʀu, ʀus] *adj* red; (*personne*) red-haired ♦ *nm/f* redhead ♦ *nm* (*CULIN*) roux.

royal, e, aux [ʀwajal, -o] *adj* royal; (*fig*) fit for a king, princely; blissful; thorough.

royalement [ʀwajalmɑ̃] *adv* royally.

royaliste [ʀwajalist(ə)] *adj, nm/f* royalist.

royaume [ʀwajom] *nm* kingdom; (*fig*) realm; **le ~ des cieux** the kingdom of heaven.

Royaume-Uni [ʀwajomyni] *nm*: **le ~** the United Kingdom.

royauté [ʀwajote] *nf* (*dignité*) kingship; (*régime*) monarchy.

RP *sigle f* (= *recette principale*) ≈ main post office; = *région parisienne* ♦ *sigle fpl* (= *relations publiques*) PR.

RPR *sigle m* (= *Rassemblement pour la République*) political party.

R.S.V.P. *abr* (= *répondez s'il vous plaît*) R.S.V.P.

RTB *sigle f* = *Radio-Télévision belge*.

Rte *abr* = **route**.

RTL *sigle f* = *Radio-Télévision Luxembourg*.

RTVE *sigle f* = *Radio-Télévision espagnole*.

RU [ʀy] *sigle m* = **restaurant universitaire**.

ruade [ʀɥad] *nf* kick.

Ruanda [ʀwɑ̃da] *nm*: **le ~** Rwanda.

ruban [ʀybɑ̃] *nm* (*gén*) ribbon; (*pour ourlet, couture*) binding; (*de téléscripteur etc*) tape; (*d'acier*) strip; **~ adhésif** adhesive tape; **~ carbone** carbon ribbon.

rubéole [ʀybeɔl] *nf* German measles *sg*, rubella.

rubicond, e [ʀybikɔ̃, -ɔ̃d] *adj* rubicund, ruddy.

rubis [ʀybi] *nm* ruby; (*HORLOGERIE*) jewel; **payer ~ sur l'ongle** to pay cash on the nail.

rubrique [ʀybʀik] *nf* (*titre, catégorie*) heading, rubric; (*PRESSE: article*) column.

ruche [ʀyʃ] *nf* hive.

rucher [ʀyʃe] *nm* apiary.

rude [ʀyd] *adj* (*barbe, toile*) rough; (*métier, tâche*) hard, tough; (*climat*) severe, harsh; (*bourru*) harsh, rough; (*fruste*) rugged, tough; (*fam*) jolly good; **être mis à ~ épreuve** to be put through the mill.

rudement [ʀydmɑ̃] *adv* (*tomber, frapper*) hard; (*traiter, reprocher*) harshly; (*fam: très*) terribly; (*: beaucoup*) terribly hard.

rudesse [ʀydɛs] *nf* roughness; toughness; severity; harshness.

rudimentaire [ʀydimɑ̃tɛʀ] *adj* rudimentary, basic.

rudiments [ʀydimɑ̃] *nmpl* rudiments; basic knowledge *sg*; basic principles.

rudoyer [ʀydwaje] *vt* to treat harshly.

rue [ʀy] *nf* street; **être/jeter qn à la ~** to be on the streets/throw sb out onto the street.

ruée [ʀɥe] *nf* rush; **la ~ vers l'or** the gold rush.

ruelle [ʀɥɛl] *nf* alley(way).

ruer [ʀɥe] *vi* (*cheval*) to kick out; **se ~** *vi*: **se ~ sur** to pounce on; **se ~ vers/dans/hors de** to rush *ou* dash towards/into/out of; **~ dans les brancards** to become rebellious.

rugby [ʀygbi] *nm* rugby (football); **~ à treize/quinze** rugby league/union.

rugir [ʀyʒiʀ] *vi* to roar.

rugissement [ʀyʒismɑ̃] *nm* roar, roaring *no pl*.

rugosité [ʀygozite] *nf* roughness; (*aspérité*) rough patch.

rugueux, euse [ʀygø, -øz] *adj* rough.

ruine [ʀɥin] *nf* ruin; **~s** *nfpl* ruins; **tomber en ~** to fall into ruin(s).

ruiner [ʀɥine] *vt* to ruin.

ruineux, euse [ʀɥinø, -øz] *adj* terribly expensive to buy (*ou* run), ruinous; extravagant.

ruisseau, x [ʀɥiso] *nm* stream, brook; (*caniveau*) gutter; (*fig*): **~x de larmes/sang** floods of tears/streams of blood.

ruisselant, e [ʀɥislɑ̃, -ɑ̃t] *adj* streaming.

ruisseler [ʀɥisle] *vi* to stream; **~ (d'eau)** to be streaming (with water); **~ de lumière** to stream with light.

ruissellement [ʀɥisɛlmɑ̃] *nm* streaming; **~ de lumière** stream of light.

rumeur [ʀymœʀ] *nf* (*bruit confus*) rumbling; hubbub *no pl*; (*protestation*) murmur(ing); (*nouvelle*) rumour (*BRIT*), rumor (*US*).

ruminer [ʀymine] *vt* (*herbe*) to ruminate; (*fig*) to ruminate on *ou* over, chew over ♦ *vi* (*vache*) to chew the cud, ruminate.

rumsteck [ʀɔ̃mstɛk] *nm* = **romsteck**.

rupestre [ʀypɛstʀ(ə)] *adj* (*plante*) rock *cpd*; (*art*) wall *cpd*.

rupture [ʀyptyʀ] *nf* (*de câble, digue*) breaking; (*de tendon*) rupture, tearing; (*de négociations* *etc*) breakdown; (*de contrat*) breach; (*séparation, désunion*) break-up, split; **en ~ de ban** at odds with authority; **en ~ de stock** (*COMM*) out of stock.

rural, e, aux [ʀyʀal, -o] *adj* rural, country *cpd* ♦ *nmpl*: **les ruraux** country people.

ruse [ʀyz] *nf*: **la ~** cunning, craftiness; trickery; **une ~** a trick, a ruse; **par ~** by trickery.

rusé, e [ʀyze] *adj* cunning, crafty.

russe [ʀys] *adj* Russian ♦ *nm* (*LING*) Russian ♦ *nm/f*: **R~** Russian.

Russie [ʀysi] *nf*: **la ~** Russia; **la ~ blanche** White Russia; **la ~ soviétique** Soviet Russia.

rustine [ʀystin] *nf* repair patch (*for bicycle inner tube*).

rustique [ʀystik] *adj* rustic; (*plante*) hardy.

rustre [ʀystʀ(ə)] *nm* boor.

rut [ʀyt] *nm*: **être en ~** (*animal domestique*) to be in *ou* on heat; (*animal sauvage*) to be rutting.

rutabaga [ʀytabaga] *nm* swede.

rutilant, e [ʀytilɑ̃, -ɑ̃t] *adj* gleaming.

RV *sigle m* = **rendez-vous**.

Rwanda [ʀwɑ̃da] *nm*: **le ~** Rwanda.

rythme [ʀitm(ə)] *nm* rhythm; (*vitesse*) rate; (*: de la vie*) pace, tempo; **au ~ de 10 par jour** at the rate of 10 a day.

rythmé, e [ʀitme] *adj* rhythmic(al).

rythmer [ʀitme] *vt* to give rhythm to.

rythmique [ʀitmik] *adj* rhythmic(al) ♦ *nf* rhythmics *sg*.

S s

S, s [ɛs] *nm inv* S, s ♦ *abr* (= *sud*) S; (= *seconde*) sec; (= *siècle*) c., century; **S comme Suzanne** S for Sugar.

s' [s] *pron voir* **se**.

s/ *abr* = **sur**.

SA *sigle f* = **société anonyme**; (= *Son Altesse*) HH.

sa [sa] *dét voir* **son**.

sabbatique [sabatik] *adj*: **année ~** sabbatical year.

sable [sabl(ə)] *nm* sand; **~s mouvants** quicksand(s).

sablé [sable] *adj* (*allée*) sandy ♦ *nm* shortbread biscuit; **pâte ~e** (*CULIN*) shortbread dough.

sabler [sable] *vt* to sand; (*contre le verglas*) to grit; **~ le champagne** to drink champagne.

sableux, euse [sablø, -øz] *adj* sandy.

sablier [sablije] *nm* hourglass; (*de cuisine*) egg timer.

sablière [sablijɛʀ] *nf* sand quarry.

sablonneux, euse [sablɔnø, -øz] *adj* sandy.

saborder [sabɔʀde] *vt* (*navire*) to scuttle; (*fig*) to wind up, shut down.

sabot [sabo] *nm* clog; (*de cheval, bœuf*) hoof; **~ (de Denver)** (wheel) clamp; **~ de frein** brake shoe.

sabotage [sabɔtaʒ] *nm* sabotage.

saboter [sabɔte] *vt* (*travail, morceau de musique*) to botch, make a mess of; (*machine, installation, négociation etc*) to sabotage.

saboteur, euse [sabɔtœʀ, -øz] *nm/f* saboteur.

sabre [sɑbʀ(ə)] *nm* sabre; **le ~** (*fig*) the sword, the army.

sabrer [sɑbʀe] *vt* to cut down.

SAC [sak] *sigle m* (= *Service d'action civile*) *former Gaullist parapolice*.

sac [sak] *nm* bag; (*à charbon etc*) sack; (*pillage*) sack(ing); **mettre à ~** to sack; **~ à provisions/de voyage** shopping/travelling bag; **~ de couchage** sleeping bag; **~ à dos** rucksack; **~ à main** handbag; **~ de plage** beach bag.

saccade [sakad] *nf* jerk; **par ~s** jerkily; haltingly.

saccadé, e [sakade] *adj* jerky.

saccage [sakaʒ] *nm* havoc.

saccager [sakaʒe] *vt* (*piller*) to sack, lay waste to; (*dévaster*) to create havoc in, wreck.

saccharine [sakaʀin] *nf* saccharin(e).

saccharose [sakaʀoz] *nm* sucrose.

SACEM [sasɛm] *sigle f* (= *Société des auteurs, compositeurs et éditeurs de musique*) *body responsible for collecting and distributing royalties*.

sacerdoce [sasɛʀdɔs] *nm* priesthood; (*fig*) calling, vocation.

sacerdotal, e, aux [sasɛʀdɔtal, -o] *adj* priestly, sacerdotal.

sachant [saʃɑ̃] *etc vb voir* **savoir**.

sache [saʃ] *etc vb voir* **savoir**.

sachet [saʃɛ] *nm* (small) bag; (*de lavande, poudre, shampooing*) sachet; **thé en ~s** tea bags; **~ de thé** tea bag.

sacoche [sakɔʃ] *nf* (*gén*) bag; (*de bicyclette*) saddlebag; (*du facteur*) (post-)bag; (*d'outils*) toolbag.

sacquer [sake] *vt* (*fam: candidat, employé*) to sack; (*: réprimander, mal noter*) to plough.

sacraliser [sakʀalize] *vt* to make sacred.

sacre [sakʀ(ə)] *nm* coronation; consecration.

sacré, e [sakʀe] *adj* sacred; (*fam: satané*) blasted; (*: fameux*): **un ~ ...** a heck of a ...; (*ANAT*) sacral.

sacrement [sakʀəmɑ̃] *nm* sacrament; **les derniers ~s** the last rites.

sacrer [sakʀe] *vt* (*roi*) to crown; (*évêque*) to consecrate ♦ *vi* to curse, swear.

sacrifice [sakʀifis] *nm* sacrifice; **faire le ~ de** to sacrifice.

sacrificiel, le [sakʀifisjɛl] *adj* sacrificial.

sacrifier [sakʀifje] *vt* to sacrifice; **~ à** *vt* to

conform to; **se** ~ to sacrifice o.s.; **articles sacrifiés** (*COMM*) items sold at rock-bottom *ou* give-away prices.

sacrilège [sakʀilɛʒ] *nm* sacrilege ♦ *adj* sacrilegious.

sacristain [sakʀistɛ̃] *nm* sexton; sacristan.

sacristie [sakʀisti] *nf* sacristy; (*culte protestant*) vestry.

sacro-saint, e [sakʀosɛ̃, -ɛ̃t] *adj* sacrosanct.

sadique [sadik] *adj* sadistic ♦ *nm/f* sadist.

sadisme [sadism(ə)] *nm* sadism.

sadomasochisme [sadɔmazɔʃism(ə)] *nm* sadomasochism.

sadomasochiste [sadɔmazɔʃist(ə)] *nm/f* sadomasochist.

safari [safaʀi] *nm* safari; **faire un** ~ to go on safari.

safari-photo [safaʀifɔto] *nm* photographic safari.

SAFER [safɛʀ] *sigle f* (= *Société d'aménagement foncier et d'établissement rural*) *organization with the right to buy land in order to retain it for agricultural use.*

safran [safʀɑ̃] *nm* saffron.

saga [saga] *nf* saga.

sagace [sagas] *adj* sagacious, shrewd.

sagacité [sagasite] *nf* sagacity, shrewdness.

sagaie [sagɛ] *nf* assegai.

sage [saʒ] *adj* wise; (*enfant*) good ♦ *nm* wise man; sage.

sage-femme [saʒfam] *nf* midwife (*pl* -wives).

sagement [saʒmɑ̃] *adv* (*raisonnablement*) wisely, sensibly; (*tranquillement*) quietly.

sagesse [saʒɛs] *nf* wisdom.

Sagittaire [saʒitɛʀ] *nm:* **le** ~ Sagittarius, the Archer; **être du** ~ to be Sagittarius.

Sahara [saaʀa] *nm:* **le** ~ the Sahara (Desert); **le** ~ **occidental** (*pays*) Western Sahara.

saharien, ne [saaʀjɛ̃, -ɛn] *adj* Saharan ♦ *nf* safari jacket.

Sahel [saɛl] *nm:* **le** ~ the Sahel.

sahélien, ne [saeljɛ̃, -ɛn] *adj* Sahelian.

saignant, e [sɛɲɑ̃, -ɑ̃t] *adj* (*viande*) rare; (*blessure, plaie*) bleeding.

saignée [seɲe] *nf* (*MÉD*) bleeding *no pl*, bloodletting *no pl*; (*ANAT*): **la** ~ **du bras** the bend of the arm; (*fig: MIL*) heavy losses *pl*; (*: prélèvement*) savage cut.

saignement [sɛɲmɑ̃] *nm* bleeding; ~ **de nez** nosebleed.

saigner [seɲe] *vi* to bleed ♦ *vt* to bleed; (*animal*) to bleed to death; ~ **qn à blanc** (*fig*) to bleed sb white; ~ **du nez** to have a nosebleed.

Saigon [sajgɔ̃] *n* Saigon.

saillant, e [sajɑ̃, -ɑ̃t] *adj* (*pommettes, menton*) prominent; (*corniche etc*) projecting; (*fig*) salient, outstanding.

saillie [saji] *nf* (*sur un mur etc*) projection; (*trait d'esprit*) witticism; (*accouplement*) covering, serving; **faire** ~ to project, stick out; **en** ~, **formant** ~ projecting, overhanging.

saillir [sajiʀ] *vi* to project, stick out; (*veine, muscle*) to bulge ♦ *vt* (*ÉLEVAGE*) to cover, serve.

sain, e [sɛ̃, sɛn] *adj* healthy; (*dents, constitution*) healthy, sound; (*lectures*) wholesome; ~ **et sauf** safe and sound, unharmed; ~ **d'esprit** sound in mind, sane.

saindoux [sɛ̃du] *nm* lard.

sainement [sɛnmɑ̃] *adv* (*vivre*) healthily; (*raisonner*) soundly.

saint, e [sɛ̃, sɛ̃t] *adj* holy; (*fig*) saintly ♦ *nm/f* saint; **le S~ Esprit** the Holy Spirit *ou* Ghost; **la S~e Vierge** the Blessed Virgin.

saint-bernard [sɛ̃bɛʀnaʀ] *nm inv* (*chien*) St Bernard.

Sainte-Hélène [sɛ̃telɛn] *nf* St Helena.

Sainte-Lucie [sɛ̃tlysi] *nf* Saint Lucia.

Saint-Esprit [sɛ̃tɛspʀi] *nm:* **le** ~ the Holy Spirit *ou* Ghost.

sainteté [sɛ̃te] *nf* holiness; saintliness.

Saint-Laurent [sɛ̃lɔʀɑ̃] *nm:* **le** ~ the St Lawrence.

Saint-Marin [sɛ̃maʀɛ̃] *nm:* **le** ~ San Marino.

Saint-Père [sɛ̃pɛʀ] *nm:* **le** ~ the Holy Father, the Pontiff.

Saint-Pierre [sɛ̃pjɛʀ] *nm* Saint Peter; (*église*) Saint Peter's.

Saint-Pierre-et-Miquelon [sɛ̃pjɛʀemiklɔ̃] *nm* Saint Pierre and Miquelon.

Saint-Siège [sɛ̃sjɛʒ] *nm:* **le** ~ the Holy See.

Saint-Sylvestre [sɛ̃silvɛstʀ(ə)] *nf:* **la** ~ New Year's Eve.

Saint-Thomas [sɛ̃tɔma] *nf* Saint Thomas.

Saint-Vincent et les Grenadines [sɛ̃vɛ̃sɑ̃elegʀənadin] *nm* St Vincent and the Grenadines.

sais [sɛ] *etc vb voir* **savoir.**

saisie [sezi] *nf* seizure; **à la** ~ (*texte*) being keyed; ~ (**de données**) (data) capture.

saisine [sezin] *nf* (*JUR*) submission of a case to the court.

saisir [seziʀ] *vt* to take hold of, grab; (*fig: occasion*) to seize; (*comprendre*) to grasp; (*entendre*) to get, catch; (*suj: émotions*) to take hold of, come over; (*INFORM*) to capture, keyboard; (*CULIN*) to fry quickly; (*JUR: biens, publication*) to seize; (*: juridiction*): ~ **un tribunal d'une affaire** to submit *ou* refer a case to a court; **se** ~ **de** *vt* to seize; **être saisi** (*frappé de*) to be overcome.

saisissant, e [sezisɑ̃, -ɑ̃t] *adj* startling, striking; (*froid*) biting.

saisissement [sezismɑ̃] *nm:* **muet/figé de** ~ speechless/frozen with emotion.

saison [sɛzɔ̃] *nf* season; **la belle/mauvaise** ~ the summer/winter months; **être de** ~ to be in season; **en/hors** ~ in/out of season; **haute/basse/morte** ~ high/low/slack season; **la** ~ **des pluies/des amours** the rainy/mating season.

saisonnier, ière [sɛzɔnje, -jɛʀ] *adj* seasonal ♦ *nm* (*travailleur*) seasonal worker; (*vacancier*) seasonal holidaymaker.

sait [sɛ] *vb voir* **savoir.**

salace [salas] *adj* salacious.

salade [salad] *nf* (*BOT*) lettuce *etc* (*generic term*); (*CULIN*) (green) salad; (*fam*) tangle, muddle; ~**s** *nfpl* (*fam*): **raconter des** ~**s** to tell tales (*fam*); **haricots en** ~ bean salad; ~ **de concombres** cucumber salad; ~ **de fruits** fruit salad; ~ **niçoise** salade niçoise; ~ **russe** Russian salad.

saladier [saladje] *nm* (salad) bowl.

salaire [salɛR] *nm* (*annuel, mensuel*) salary; (*hebdomadaire, journalier*) pay, wages *pl*; (*fig*) reward; ~ **de base** basic salary (*ou* wage); ~ **de misère** starvation wage; ~ **minimum interprofessionnel de croissance (SMIC)** *index-linked guaranteed minimum wage.*

salaison [salɛzɔ̃] *nf* salting; ~**s** *nfpl* salt meat *sg.*

salamandre [salamɑ̃dR(ə)] *nf* salamander.

salami [salami] *nm* salami *no pl*, salami sausage.

salant [salɑ̃] *adj m*: **marais** ~ salt pan.

salarial, e, aux [salaRjal, -o] *adj* salary *cpd*, wage(s) *cpd*.

salariat [salaRja] *nm* salaried staff.

salarié, e [salaRje] *adj* salaried; wage-earning ♦ *nm/f* salaried employee; wage-earner.

salaud [salo] *nm* (*fam!*) sod (*!*), bastard (*!*).

sale [sal] *adj* dirty; (*fig: avant le nom*) nasty.

salé, e [sale] *adj* (*liquide, saveur*) salty; (*CULIN*) salted, salt *cpd*; (*fig*) spicy, juicy; (*: note, facture*) steep, stiff ♦ *nm* (*porc salé*) salt pork; **petit** ~ ≈ boiling bacon.

salement [salmɑ̃] *adv* (*manger etc*) dirtily, messily.

saler [sale] *vt* to salt.

saleté [salte] *nf* (*état*) dirtiness; (*crasse*) dirt, filth; (*tache etc*) dirt *no pl*, something dirty, dirty mark; (*fig: tour*) filthy trick; (*: chose sans valeur*) rubbish *no pl*; (*: obscénité*) filth *no pl*; (*: microbe etc*) bug; **vivre dans la** ~ to live in squalor.

salière [saljɛR] *nf* saltcellar.

saligaud [saligo] *nm* (*fam!*) bastard (*!*), sod (*!*).

salin, e [salɛ̃, -in] *adj* saline ♦ *nf* saltworks *sg.*

salinité [salinite] *nf* salinity, salt-content.

salir [saliR] *vt* to (make) dirty; (*fig*) to soil the reputation of; **se** ~ to get dirty.

salissant, e [salisɑ̃, -ɑ̃t] *adj* (*tissu*) which shows the dirt; (*métier*) dirty, messy.

salissure [salisyR] *nf* dirt *no pl*; (*tache*) dirty mark.

salive [saliv] *nf* saliva.

saliver [salive] *vi* to salivate.

salle [sal] *nf* room; (*d'hôpital*) ward; (*de restaurant*) dining room; (*d'un cinéma*) auditorium; (*: public*) audience; **faire** ~ **comble** to have a full house; ~ **d'armes** (*pour l'escrime*) arms room; ~ **d'attente** waiting room; ~ **de bain(s)** bathroom; ~ **de bal** ballroom; ~ **de cinéma** cinema; ~ **de**

classe classroom; ~ **commune** (*d'hôpital*) ward; ~ **de concert** concert hall; ~ **de consultation** consulting room (*BRIT*), office (*US*); ~ **de danse** dance hall; ~ **de douches** shower-room; ~ **d'eau** shower-room; ~ **d'embarquement** (*à l'aéroport*) departure lounge; ~ **d'exposition** showroom; ~ **de jeux** games room; playroom; ~ **des machines** engine room; ~ **à manger** dining room; (*mobilier*) dining room suite; ~ **obscure** cinema (*BRIT*), movie theater (*US*); ~ **d'opération** (*d'hôpital*) operating theatre; ~ **de projection** film theatre; ~ **de séjour** living room; ~ **de spectacle** theatre; cinema; ~ **des ventes** saleroom.

salmonellose [salmɔneloz] *nf* (*MÉD*) salmonella poisoning.

Salomon [salɔmɔ̃]: **les îles** ~ the Solomon Islands.

salon [salɔ̃] *nm* lounge, sitting room; (*mobilier*) lounge suite; (*exposition*) exhibition, show; (*mondain, littéraire*) salon; ~ **de coiffure** hairdressing salon; ~ **de thé** tearoom.

salopard [salɔpaR] *nm* (*fam!*) bastard (*!*).

salope [salɔp] *nf* (*fam!*) bitch (*!*).

saloper [salɔpe] *vt* (*fam!*) to muck up, mess up.

saloperie [salɔpRi] *nf* (*fam!*) filth *no pl*; dirty trick; rubbish *no pl.*

salopette [salɔpɛt] *nf* dungarees *pl*; (*d'ouvrier*) overall(s).

salpêtre [salpɛtR(ə)] *nm* saltpetre.

salsifis [salsifi] *nm* salsify, oyster plant.

SALT [salt] *sigle* (= *Strategic Arms Limitation Talks ou Treaty*) SALT.

saltimbanque [saltɛ̃bɑ̃k] *nm/f* (travelling) acrobat.

salubre [salybR(ə)] *adj* healthy, salubrious.

salubrité [salybRite] *nf* healthiness, salubrity; ~ **publique** public health.

saluer [salɥe] *vt* (*pour dire bonjour, fig*) to greet; (*pour dire au revoir*) to take one's leave; (*MIL*) to salute.

salut [saly] *nm* (*sauvegarde*) safety; (*REL*) salvation; (*geste*) wave; (*parole*) greeting; (*MIL*) salute ♦ *excl* (*fam: pour dire bonjour*) hi (there); (*: pour dire au revoir*) see you!, bye!; (*style relevé*) (all) hail.

salutaire [salytɛR] *adj* (*remède*) beneficial; (*conseils*) salutary.

salutations [salytɑsjɔ̃] *nfpl* greetings; **recevez mes** ~ **distinguées** *ou* **respectueuses** yours faithfully.

salutiste [salytist(ə)] *nm/f* Salvationist.

Salvador [salvadɔR] *nm*: **le** ~ El Salvador.

salve [salv(ə)] *nf* salvo; volley of shots; ~ **d'applaudissements** burst of applause.

Samarie [samaRi] *nf*: **la** ~ Samaria.

samaritain [samaRitɛ̃] *nm*: **le bon S**~ the Good Samaritan.

samedi [samdi] *nm* Saturday; *voir aussi* **lundi.**

Samoa [samɔa] *nfpl*: **les (îles)** ~ Samoa, the

Samoa Islands.
SAMU [samy] *sigle m* (= *service d'assistance médicale d'urgence*) ≈ ambulance (service) (*BRIT*), ≈ paramedics (*US*).
sanatorium [sanatɔʀjɔm] *nm* sanatorium (*pl* -a).
sanctifier [sãktifje] *vt* to sanctify.
sanction [sãksjɔ̃] *nf* sanction; (*fig*) penalty; **prendre des ~s contre** to impose sanctions on.
sanctionner [sãksjɔne] *vt* (*loi, usage*) to sanction; (*punir*) to punish.
sanctuaire [sãktɥɛʀ] *nm* sanctuary.
sandale [sãdal] *nf* sandal.
sandalette [sãdalɛt] *nf* sandal.
sandow [sãdo] *nm* ® luggage elastic.
sandwich [sãdwitʃ] *nm* sandwich; **pris en ~** sandwiched.
sang [sã] *nm* blood; **en ~** covered in blood; **jusqu'au ~** (*mordre, pincer*) till the blood comes; **se faire du mauvais ~** to fret, get in a state.
sang-froid [sãfʀwa] *nm* calm, sangfroid; **garder/perdre/reprendre son ~** to keep/lose/regain one's cool; **de ~** in cold blood.
sanglant, e [sãglã, -ãt] *adj* bloody, covered in blood; (*combat*) bloody; (*fig: reproche, affront*) cruel.
sangle [sãgl(ə)] *nf* strap; **~s** *nfpl* (*pour lit etc*) webbing *sg*.
sangler [sãgle] *vt* to strap up; (*animal*) to girth.
sanglier [sãglije] *nm* (wild) boar.
sanglot [sãglo] *nm* sob.
sangloter [sãglɔte] *vi* to sob.
sangsue [sãsy] *nf* leech.
sanguin, e [sãgɛ̃, -in] *adj* blood *cpd*; (*fig*) fiery ♦ *nf* blood orange; (*ART*) red pencil drawing.
sanguinaire [sãginɛʀ] *adj* (*animal, personne*) bloodthirsty; (*lutte*) bloody.
sanguinolent, e [sãginɔlã, -ãt] *adj* streaked with blood.
Sanisette [sanizɛt] *nf* ® coin-operated public lavatory.
sanitaire [sanitɛʀ] *adj* health *cpd*; **~s** *nmpl* (*salle de bain et w.-c.*) bathroom *sg*; **installation/appareil ~** bathroom equipment/appliance.
sans [sã] *prép* without; **~ qu'il s'en aperçoive** without him *ou* his noticing; **~ scrupules** unscrupulous; **~ manches** sleeveless.
sans-abri [sãzabʀi] *nmpl* homeless.
sans-emploi [sãzãplwa] *nmpl* jobless.
sans-façon [sãfasɔ̃] *adj inv* fuss-free; free and easy.
sans-gêne [sãʒɛn] *adj inv* inconsiderate ♦ *nm inv* (*attitude*) lack of consideration.
sans-logis [sãlɔʒi] *nmpl* homeless.
sans-souci [sãsusi] *adj inv* carefree.
sans-travail [sãtʀavaj] *nmpl* unemployed, jobless.
santal [sãtal] *nm* sandal(wood).
santé [sãte] *nf* health; **avoir une ~ de fer** to be

bursting with health; **être en bonne ~** to be in good health, be healthy; **boire à la ~ de qn** to drink (to) sb's health; **"à la ~ de"** "here's to"; **à ta** *ou* **votre ~!** cheers!; **service de ~** (*dans un port etc*) quarantine service; **la ~ publique** public health.
Santiago (du Chili) [sãtjago(dyʃili)] *n* Santiago (de Chile).
santon [sãtɔ̃] *nm ornamental figure at a Christmas crib.*
saoudien, ne [saudjɛ̃, -ɛn] *adj* Saudi (Arabian) ♦ *nm/f*: **S~, ne** Saudi (Arabian).
saoul, e [su, sul] *adj* = **soûl, e.**
sape [sap] *nf*: **travail de ~** (*MIL*) sap; (*fig*) insidious undermining process *ou* work; **~s** *nfpl* (*fam*) gear *sg*, togs.
saper [sape] *vt* to undermine, sap; **se ~** *vi* (*fam*) to dress.
sapeur [sapœʀ] *nm* sapper.
sapeur-pompier [sapœʀpɔ̃pje] *nm* fireman.
saphir [safiʀ] *nm* sapphire; (*d'électrophone*) needle, sapphire.
sapin [sapɛ̃] *nm* fir (tree); (*bois*) fir; **~ de Noël** Christmas tree.
sapinière [sapinjɛʀ] *nf* fir plantation *ou* forest.
SAR *sigle f* (= *Son Altesse Royale*) HRH.
sarabande [saʀabãd] *nf* saraband; (*fig*) hullabaloo; whirl.
sarbacane [saʀbakan] *nf* blowpipe, blowgun; (*jouet*) peashooter.
sarcasme [saʀkasm(ə)] *nm* sarcasm *no pl*; (*propos*) piece of sarcasm.
sarcastique [saʀkastik] *adj* sarcastic.
sarcastiquement [saʀkastikmã] *adv* sarcastically.
sarclage [saʀklaʒ] *nm* weeding.
sarcler [saʀkle] *vt* to weed.
sarcloir [saʀklwaʀ] *nm* (weeding) hoe, spud.
sarcophage [saʀkɔfaʒ] *nm* sarcophagus (*pl* -i).
Sardaigne [saʀdɛɲ] *nf*: **la ~** Sardinia.
sarde [saʀd(ə)] *adj* Sardinian.
sardine [saʀdin] *nf* sardine; **~s à l'huile** sardines in oil.
sardinerie [saʀdinʀi] *nf* sardine cannery.
sardinier, ière [saʀdinje, -jɛʀ] *adj* (*pêche, industrie*) sardine *cpd* ♦ *nm* (*bateau*) sardine boat.
sardonique [saʀdɔnik] *adj* sardonic.
sari [saʀi] *nm* sari.
SARL [saʀl] *sigle f* = **société à responsabilité limitée.**
sarment [saʀmã] *nm*: **~ (de vigne)** vine shoot.
sarrasin [saʀazɛ̃] *nm* buckwheat.
sarrau [saʀo] *nm* smock.
Sarre [saʀ] *nf*: **la ~** the Saar.
sarriette [saʀjɛt] *nf* savory.
sarrois, e [saʀwa, -waz] *adj* Saar *cpd* ♦ *nm/f*: **S~, e** inhabitant *ou* native of the Saar.
sas [sas] *nm* (*de sous-marin, d'engin spatial*) airlock; (*d'écluse*) lock.
satané, e [satane] *adj* confounded.
satanique [satanik] *adj* satanic, fiendish.

satelliser [satelize] *vt* (*fusée*) to put into orbit; (*fig: pays*) to make into a satellite.

satellite [satelit] *nm* satellite; **pays** ~ satellite country.

satellite-espion, *pl* **satellites-espions** [satelitεspjɔ̃] *nm* spy satellite.

satellite-observatoire, *pl* **satellites-observatoires** [satelitɔpsεrvatwar] *nm* observation satellite.

satellite-relais, *pl* **satellites-relais** [satelitRəlε] *nm* (*TV*) relay satellite.

satiété [sasjete]: **à** ~ *adv* to satiety *ou* satiation; (*répéter*) ad nauseam.

satin [satɛ̃] *nm* satin.

satiné, e [satine] *adj* satiny; (*peau*) satin-smooth.

satinette [satinεt] *nf* satinet, sateen.

satire [satiR] *nf* satire; **faire la** ~ to satirize.

satirique [satiRik] *adj* satirical.

satiriser [satiRize] *vt* to satirize.

satiriste [satiRist(ə)] *nm/f* satirist.

satisfaction [satisfaksjɔ̃] *nf* satisfaction; **à ma grande** ~ to my great satisfaction; **obtenir** ~ to obtain *ou* get satisfaction; **donner** ~ (**à**) to give satisfaction (to).

satisfaire [satisfεR] *vt* to satisfy; **se** ~ **de** to be satisfied *ou* content with; ~ **à** *vt* (*engagement*) to fulfil; (*revendications, conditions*) to satisfy, meet.

satisfaisant, e [satisfəzɑ̃, -ɑ̃t] *vb voir* **satisfaire** ♦ *adj* satisfactory; (*qui fait plaisir*) satisfying.

satisfait, e [satisfε, -εt] *pp de* **satisfaire** ♦ *adj* satisfied; ~ **de** happy *ou* satisfied with.

satisfasse [satisfas], **satisferai** [satisfRe] *etc vb voir* **satisfaire.**

saturation [satyRasjɔ̃] *nf* saturation; **arriver à** ~ to reach saturation point.

saturer [satyRe] *vt* to saturate; ~ **qn/qch de** to saturate sb/sth with.

saturnisme [satyRnism(ə)] *nm* (*MÉD*) lead poisoning.

satyre [satiR] *nm* satyr; (*péj*) lecher.

sauce [sos] *nf* sauce; (*avec un rôti*) gravy; **en** ~ in a sauce; ~ **blanche** white sauce; ~ **chasseur** sauce chasseur; ~ **tomate** tomato sauce.

saucer [sose] *vt* (*assiette*) to soak up the sauce from.

saucière [sosjεR] *nf* sauceboat; gravy boat.

saucisse [sosis] *nf* sausage.

saucisson [sosisɔ̃] *nm* (slicing) sausage; ~ **à l'ail** garlic sausage.

saucissonner [sosisɔne] *vt* to cut up, slice ♦ *vi* to picnic.

sauf [sof] *prép* except; ~ **si** (*à moins que*) unless; ~ **avis contraire** unless you hear to the contrary; ~ **empêchement** barring (any) problems; ~ **erreur** if I'm not mistaken; ~ **imprévu** unless anything unforeseen arises, barring accidents.

sauf, sauve [sof, sov] *adj* unharmed, unhurt; (*fig: honneur*) intact, saved; **laisser la vie**

sauve à qn to spare sb's life.

sauf-conduit [sofkɔ̃dɥi] *nm* safe-conduct.

sauge [soʒ] *nf* sage.

saugrenu, e [sogRəny] *adj* preposterous, ludicrous.

saule [sol] *nm* willow (tree); ~ **pleureur** weeping willow.

saumâtre [somɑtR(ə)] *adj* briny; (*désagréable: plaisanterie*) unsavoury (*BRIT*), unsavory (*US*).

saumon [somɔ̃] *nm* salmon *inv* ♦ *adj inv* salmon (pink).

saumoné, e [somɔne] *adj*: **truite** ~**e** salmon trout.

saumure [somyR] *nf* brine.

sauna [sona] *nm* sauna.

saupoudrer [sopudRe] *vt*: ~ **qch de** to sprinkle sth with.

saupoudreuse [sopudRøz] *nf* dredger.

saur [sɔR] *adj m*: **hareng** ~ smoked *ou* red herring, kipper.

saurai [sɔRe] *etc vb voir* **savoir.**

saut [so] *nm* jump; (*discipline sportive*) jumping; **faire un** ~ to (make a) jump *ou* leap; **faire un** ~ **chez qn** to pop over to sb's (place); **au** ~ **du lit** on getting out of bed; **en hauteur/longueur** high/long jump; ~ **à la corde** skipping; ~ **de page** (*INFORM*) page break; ~ **en parachute** parachuting *no pl*; ~ **à la perche** pole vaulting; ~ **à l'élastique** bungee jumping; ~ **périlleux** somersault.

saute [sot] *nf*: ~ **de vent/température** sudden change of wind direction/in the temperature; **avoir des** ~**s d'humeur** to have sudden changes of mood.

sauté, e [sote] *adj* (*CULIN*) sauté ♦ *nm*: ~ **de veau** sauté of veal.

saute-mouton [sotmutɔ̃] *nm*: **jouer à** ~ to play leapfrog.

sauter [sote] *vi* to jump, leap; (*exploser*) to blow up, explode; (*: fusibles*) to blow; (*se rompre*) to snap, burst; (*se détacher*) to pop out (*ou* off) ♦ *vt* to jump (over), leap (over); (*fig: omettre*) to skip, miss (out); **faire** ~ to blow up; to burst open; (*CULIN*) to sauté; ~ **à pieds joints/à cloche-pied** to make a standing jump/to hop; ~ **en parachute** to make a parachute jump; ~ **à la corde** to skip; ~ **de joie** to jump for joy; ~ **de colère** to be hopping with rage *ou* hopping mad; ~ **au cou de qn** to fly into sb's arms; ~ **aux yeux** to be quite obvious; ~ **au plafond** (*fig*) to hit the roof.

sauterelle [sotRεl] *nf* grasshopper.

sauterie [sotRi] *nf* party, hop.

sauteur, euse [sotœR, -øz] *nm/f* (*athlète*) jumper ♦ *nf* (*casserole*) shallow pan, frying pan; ~ **à la perche** pole vaulter; ~ **à skis** skijumper.

sautillement [sotijmɑ̃] *nm* hopping; skipping.

sautiller [sotije] *vi* to hop; to skip.

sautoir [sotwaR] *nm* chain; (*SPORT*:

emplacement) jumping pit; ~ **(de perles)** string of pearls.

sauvage [sovaʒ] *adj (gén)* wild; *(peuplade)* savage; *(farouche)* unsociable; *(barbare)* wild, savage; *(non officiel)* unauthorized, unofficial ♦ *nm/f* savage; *(timide)* unsociable type, recluse.

sauvagement [sovaʒmã] *adv* savagely.

sauvageon, ne [sovaʒɔ̃, -ɔn] *nm/f* little savage.

sauvagerie [sovaʒʀi] *nf* wildness; savagery; unsociability.

sauve [sov] *adj f voir* **sauf**.

sauvegarde [sovgaʀd(ə)] *nf* safeguard; **sous la ~ de** under the protection of; **disquette/ fichier de ~** (*INFORM*) backup disk/file.

sauvegarder [sovgaʀde] *vt* to safeguard; (*INFORM: enregistrer*) to save; (*: copier*) to back up.

sauve-qui-peut [sovkipø] *nm inv* stampede, mad rush ♦ *excl* run for your life!

sauver [sove] *vt* to save; *(porter secours à)* to rescue; *(récupérer)* to salvage, rescue; **se ~** *vi (s'enfuir)* to run away; *(fam: partir)* to be off; ~ **qn de** to save sb from; ~ **la vie à qn** to save sb's life; ~ **les apparences** to keep up appearances.

sauvetage [sovtaʒ] *nm* rescue; ~ **en montagne** mountain rescue; **ceinture de ~** lifebelt (*BRIT*), life preserver (*US*); **brassière** *ou* **gilet de ~** lifejacket (*BRIT*), life preserver (*US*).

sauveteur [sovtœʀ] *nm* rescuer.

sauvette [sovɛt]: **à la ~** *adv (vendre)* without authorization; *(se marier etc)* hastily, hurriedly; **vente à la ~** (unauthorized) street trading, (street) peddling.

sauveur [sovœʀ] *nm* saviour (*BRIT*), savior (*US*).

SAV *sigle m* = **service après vente**.

savais [save] *etc vb voir* **savoir**.

savamment [savamã] *adv (avec érudition)* learnedly; *(habilement)* skilfully, cleverly.

savane [savan] *nf* savannah.

savant, e [savã, -ãt] *adj* scholarly, learned; *(calé)* clever ♦ *nm* scientist; **animal ~** performing animal.

savate [savat] *nf* worn-out shoe; (*SPORT*) French boxing.

saveur [savœʀ] *nf* flavour (*BRIT*), flavor (*US*); *(fig)* savour (*BRIT*), savor (*US*).

Savoie [savwa] *nf*: **la ~** Savoy.

savoir [savwaʀ] *vt* to know; *(être capable de)*: **il sait nager** he knows how to swim, he can swim ♦ *nm* knowledge; **se ~** *(être connu)* to be known; **se ~ malade/incurable** to know that one is ill/incurably ill; **il est petit: tu ne peux pas ~!** you won't believe how small he is!; **vous n'êtes pas sans ~ que** you are not *ou* will not be unaware of the fact that; **je crois ~ que** ... I believe that ..., I think I know that ...; **je n'en sais rien** I (really) don't know; **à ~ (que)** that is, namely; **faire ~ qch à qn** to inform sb about sth, let sb know sth; **pas que je sache** not as far as I know; **sans le ~** *adv* unknowingly, unwittingly; **en ~ long** to know a lot.

savoir-faire [savwaʀfɛʀ] *nm inv* savoir-faire, know-how.

savoir-vivre [savwaʀvivʀ(ə)] *nm inv*: **le ~** savoir-faire, good manners *pl*.

savon [savɔ̃] *nm (produit)* soap; *(morceau)* bar *ou* tablet of soap; *(fam)*: **passer un ~ à qn** to give sb a good dressing-down.

savonner [savɔne] *vt* to soap.

savonnerie [savɔnʀi] *nf* soap factory.

savonnette [savɔnɛt] *nf* bar *ou* tablet of soap.

savonneux, euse [savɔnø, -øz] *adj* soapy.

savons [savɔ̃] *vb voir* **savoir**.

savourer [savuʀe] *vt* to savour (*BRIT*), savor (*US*).

savoureux, euse [savuʀø, -øz] *adj* tasty; *(fig)* spicy, juicy.

savoyard, e [savwajaʀ, -aʀd(ə)] *adj* Savoyard.

Saxe [saks(ə)] *nf*: **la ~** Saxony.

saxo(phone) [saksɔ(fɔn)] *nm* sax(ophone).

saxophoniste [saksɔfɔnist(ə)] *nm/f* saxophonist, sax(ophone) player.

saynète [sɛnɛt] *nf* playlet.

SBB *sigle f (= Schweizerische Bundesbahn)* Swiss federal railways.

sbire [sbiʀ] *nm (péj)* henchman.

sc. *abr* = **scène**.

s/c *abr (= sous couvert de)* ≈ c/o.

scabreux, euse [skabʀø, -øz] *adj* risky; *(indécent)* improper, shocking.

scalpel [skalpɛl] *nm* scalpel.

scalper [skalpe] *vt* to scalp.

scampi [skãpi] *nmpl* scampi.

scandale [skãdal] *nm* scandal; *(tapage)*: **faire du ~** to make a scene, create a disturbance; **faire ~** to scandalize people; **au grand ~ de** ... to the great indignation of ....

scandaleusement [skãdaløzmã] *adv* scandalously, outrageously.

scandaleux, euse [skãdalø, -øz] *adj* scandalous, outrageous.

scandaliser [skãdalize] *vt* to scandalize; **se ~ (de)** to be scandalized (by).

scander [skãde] *vt (vers)* to scan; *(mots, syllabes)* to stress separately; *(slogans)* to chant.

scandinave [skãdinav] *adj* Scandinavian ♦ *nm/f*: **S~** Scandinavian.

Scandinavie [skãdinavi] *nf*: **la ~** Scandinavia.

scanner [skanɛʀ] *nm (MÉD)* scanner.

scanographie [skanɔgʀafi] *nf (MÉD)* scanning; *(image)* scan.

scaphandre [skafãdʀ(ə)] *nm (de plongeur)* diving suit; *(de cosmonaute)* space-suit; ~ **autonome** aqualung.

scaphandrier [skafãdʀije] *nm* diver.

scarabée [skaʀabe] *nm* beetle.

scarlatine [skaʀlatin] *nf* scarlet fever.

scarole [skaʀɔl] *nf* endive.
scatologique [skatɔlɔʒik] *adj* scatological,
lavatorial.
sceau, x [so] *nm* seal; (*fig*) stamp, mark; **sous
le ~ du secret** under the seal of secrecy.
scélérat, e [seleʀa, -at] *nm/f* villain,
blackguard ♦ *adj* villainous, blackguardly.
sceller [sele] *vt* to seal.
scellés [sele] *nmpl* seals.
scénario [senaʀjo] *nm* (*CINÉ*) screenplay,
script; (: *idée, plan*) scenario; (*fig*) pattern;
scenario.
scénariste [senaʀist(ə)] *nm/f* scriptwriter.
scène [sɛn] *nf* (*gén*) scene; (*estrade, fig: théâtre*)
stage; **entrer en ~** to come on stage; **mettre
en ~** (*THÉÂT*) to stage; (*CINÉ*) to direct; (*fig*)
to present, introduce; **sur le devant de la ~**
(*en pleine actualité*) in the forefront; **porter à
la ~** to adapt for the stage; **faire une ~ (à
qn)** to make a scene (with sb); **~ de ménage**
domestic fight *ou* scene.
scénique [senik] *adj* (*effets*) theatrical; (*art*)
scenic.
scepticisme [sɛptisism(ə)] *nm* scepticism.
sceptique [sɛptik] *adj* sceptical ♦ *nm/f* sceptic.
sceptre [sɛptʀ(ə)] *nm* sceptre.
schéma [ʃema] *nm* (*diagramme*) diagram,
sketch; (*fig*) outline.
schématique [ʃematik] *adj* diagrammatic(al),
schematic; (*fig*) oversimplified.
schématiquement [ʃematikmɑ̃] *adv*
schematically, diagrammatically.
schématisation [ʃematizasjɔ̃] *nf*
schematization; oversimplification.
schématiser [ʃematize] *vt* to schematize; to
(over)simplify.
schismatique [ʃismatik] *adj* schismatic.
schisme [ʃism(ə)] *nm* schism; rift, split.
schiste [ʃist(ə)] *nm* schist.
schizophrène [skizɔfʀɛn] *nm/f* schizophrenic.
schizophrénie [skizɔfʀeni] *nf* schizophrenia.
sciatique [sjatik] *adj:* **nerf ~** sciatic nerve ♦ *nf*
sciatica.
scie [si] *nf* saw; (*fam: rengaine*) catch-tune;
(: *personne*) bore; **~ à bois** wood saw; **~
circulaire** circular saw; **~ à découper**
fretsaw; **~ à métaux** hacksaw; **~ sauteuse**
jigsaw.
sciemment [sjamɑ̃] *adv* knowingly, wittingly.
science [sjɑ̃s] *nf* science; (*savoir*) knowledge;
(*savoir-faire*) art, skill; **~s humaines/sociales**
social sciences; **~s naturelles** natural
science *sg*, biology *sg*; **~s po** political
studies.
science-fiction [sjɑ̃sfiksjɔ̃] *nf* science fiction.
scientifique [sjɑ̃tifik] *adj* scientific ♦ *nm/f*
(*savant*) scientist; (*étudiant*) science student.
scientifiquement [sjɑ̃tifikmɑ̃] *adv*
scientifically.
scier [sje] *vt* to saw; (*retrancher*) to saw off.
scierie [siʀi] *nf* sawmill.
scieur [sjœʀ] *nm:* **~ de long** pit sawyer.

Scilly [sili]: **les îles ~** the Scilly Isles, the
Scillies, the Isles of Scilly.
scinder [sɛ̃de] *vt,* **se ~** *vi* to split (up).
scintillant, e [sɛ̃tijɑ̃, -ɑ̃t] *adj* sparkling.
scintillement [sɛ̃tijmɑ̃] *nm* sparkling *no pl.*
scintiller [sɛ̃tije] *vi* to sparkle.
scission [sisjɔ̃] *nf* split.
sciure [sjyʀ] *nf:* **~ (de bois)** sawdust.
sclérose [skleʀoz] *nf* sclerosis; (*fig*)
ossification; **~ en plaques (SEP)** multiple
sclerosis (MS).
sclérosé, e [skleʀoze] *adj* sclerosed, sclerotic;
ossified.
scléroser [skleʀoze]: **se ~** *vi* to become
sclerosed; (*fig*) to become ossified.
scolaire [skɔlɛʀ] *adj* school *cpd*; (*péj*)
schoolish; **l'année ~** the school year; (*à
l'université*) the academic year; **en âge ~** of
school age.
scolarisation [skɔlaʀizasjɔ̃] *nf* (*d'un enfant*)
schooling; **la ~ d'une région** the provision
of schooling in a region; **le taux de ~** the
proportion of children in full-time
education.
scolariser [skɔlaʀize] *vt* to provide with
schooling (*ou* schools).
scolarité [skɔlaʀite] *nf* schooling; **frais de ~**
school fees (*BRIT*), tuition (*US*).
scolastique [skɔlastik] *adj* (*péj*) scholastic.
scoliose [skɔljoz] *nf* curvature of the spine,
scoliosis.
scoop [skup] *nm* (*PRESSE*) scoop, exclusive.
scooter [skutœʀ] *nm* (motor) scooter.
scorbut [skɔʀbyt] *nm* scurvy.
score [skɔʀ] *nm* score; (*électoral etc*) result.
scories [skɔʀi] *nfpl* scoria *pl.*
scorpion [skɔʀpjɔ̃] *nm* (*signe*): **le S~** Scorpio,
the Scorpion; **être du S~** to be Scorpio.
scotch [skɔtʃ] *nm* (*whisky*) scotch, whisky;
(*adhésif*) Sellotape ® (*BRIT*), Scotch tape ®
(*US*).
scotcher [skɔtʃe] *vt* to sellotape ® (*BRIT*),
scotchtape ® (*US*).
scout, e [skut] *adj, nm* scout.
scoutisme [skutism(ə)] *nm* (boy) scout
movement; (*activités*) scouting.
scribe [skʀib] *nm* scribe; (*péj*) penpusher.
scribouillard [skʀibujaʀ] *nm* penpusher.
script [skʀipt(ə)] *nm* printing; (*CINÉ*) (shooting)
script.
scripte [skʀipt(ə)] *nf* continuity girl.
script-girl [skʀiptgœʀl] *nf* continuity girl.
scriptural, e, aux [skʀiptyʀal, -o] *adj:*
monnaie ~e bank money.
scrupule [skʀypyl] *nm* scruple; **être sans ~s** to
be unscrupulous; **se faire un ~ de qch** to
have scruples *ou* qualms about doing sth.
scrupuleusement [skʀypyløzmɑ̃] *adv*
scrupulously.
scrupuleux, euse [skʀypylø, -øz] *adj*
scrupulous.
scrutateur, trice [skʀytatœʀ, -tʀis] *adj*

searching ♦ nm/f scrutineer.

scruter [skʀyte] vt to search, scrutinize; (l'obscurité) to peer into; (motifs, comportement) to examine, scrutinize.

scrutin [skʀytɛ̃] nm (vote) ballot; (ensemble des opérations) poll; ~ **proportionnel/majoritaire** election on a proportional/majority basis; ~ **à deux tours** poll with two ballots ou rounds; ~ **de liste** list system.

sculpter [skylte] vt to sculpt; (suj: érosion) to carve.

sculpteur [skyltœʀ] nm sculptor.

sculptural, e, aux [skyltyʀal, -o] adj sculptural; (fig) statuesque.

sculpture [skyltyʀ] nf sculpture; ~ **sur bois** wood carving.

sdb. abr = **salle de bain**.

S.D.F. sigle m (= sans domicile fixe) homeless person; **les** ~ the homeless.

SDN sigle f (= Société des Nations) League of Nations.

SE sigle f (= Son Excellence) HE.

═══════════════ MOT-CLÉ

se (s') [s(ə)] pron **1** (emploi réfléchi) oneself; (: masc) himself; (: fém) herself; (: sujet non humain) itself; (: pl) themselves; **se voir comme l'on est** to see o.s. as one is
2 (réciproque) one another, each other; **ils s'aiment** they love one another ou each other
3 (passif): **cela se répare facilement** it is easily repaired
4 (possessif): **se casser la jambe/laver les mains** to break one's leg/wash one's hands.

séance [seɑ̃s] nf (d'assemblée, récréative) meeting, session; (de tribunal) sitting, session; (musicale, CINÉ, THÉÂT) performance; **ouvrir/lever la** ~ to open/close the meeting; ~ **tenante** forthwith.

séant, e [seɑ̃, -ɑ̃t] adj seemly, fitting ♦ nm posterior.

seau, x [so] nm bucket, pail; ~ **à glace** ice bucket.

sébum [sebɔm] nm sebum.

sec, sèche [sɛk, sɛʃ] adj dry; (raisins, figues) dried; (cœur, personne: insensible) hard, cold; (maigre, décharné) spare, lean; (réponse, ton) sharp, curt; (démarrage) sharp, sudden ♦ nm: **tenir au** ~ to keep in a dry place ♦ adv hard; (démarrer) sharply; **boire** ~ to be a heavy drinker; **je le bois** ~ I drink it straight ou neat; **à pied** ~ without getting one's feet wet; **à** ~ adj dried up; (à court d'argent) broke.

SECAM [sekam] sigle m (= procédé séquentiel à mémoire) SECAM.

sécante [sekɑ̃t] nf secant.

sécateur [sekatœʀ] nm secateurs pl (BRIT), shears pl, pair of secateurs ou shears.

sécession [sesesjɔ̃] nf: **faire** ~ to secede; **la**

guerre de S~ the American Civil War.

séchage [seʃaʒ] nm drying; (de bois) seasoning.

sèche [sɛʃ] adj f voir **sec** ♦ nf (fam) cigarette, fag (BRIT).

sèche-cheveux [sɛʃʃəvø] nm inv hair-drier.

sèche-linge [sɛʃlɛ̃ʒ] nm inv drying cabinet.

sèche-mains [sɛʃmɛ̃] nm inv hand drier.

sèchement [sɛʃmɑ̃] adv (frapper etc) sharply; (répliquer etc) drily, sharply.

sécher [seʃe] vt to dry; (dessécher: peau, blé) to dry (out); (: étang) to dry up; (bois) to season; (fam: classe, cours) to skip, miss ♦ vi to dry; to dry out; to dry up; (fam: candidat) to be stumped; **se** ~ (après le bain) to dry o.s.

sécheresse [sɛʃʀɛs] nf dryness; (absence de pluie) drought.

séchoir [seʃwaʀ] nm drier.

second, e [səgɔ̃, -ɔ̃d] adj second ♦ nm (assistant) second in command; (étage) second floor (BRIT), third floor (US); (NAVIG) first mate ♦ nf second; (SCOL) ≈ fifth form (BRIT), ≈ tenth grade (US); **en** ~ (en second rang) in second place; **voyager en** ~**e** to travel second-class; **doué de** ~**e vue** having (the gift of) second sight; **trouver son** ~ **souffle** (SPORT, fig) to get one's second wind; **être dans un état** ~ to be in a daze (ou trance); **de** ~**e main** second-hand.

secondaire [səgɔ̃dɛʀ] adj secondary.

seconder [səgɔ̃de] vt to assist; (favoriser) to back.

secouer [səkwe] vt to shake; (passagers) to rock; (traumatiser) to shake (up); **se** ~ (chien) to shake itself; (fam: se démener) to shake o.s. up; ~ **la poussière d'un tapis** to shake the dust off a carpet; ~ **la tête** to shake one's head.

secourable [səkuʀabl(ə)] adj helpful.

secourir [səkuʀiʀ] vt (aller sauver) to (go and) rescue; (prodiguer des soins à) to help, assist; (venir en aide à) to assist, aid.

secourisme [səkuʀism(ə)] nm (premiers soins) first aid; (sauvetage) life saving.

secouriste [səkuʀist(ə)] nm/f first-aid worker.

secourons [səkuʀɔ̃] etc vb voir **secourir**.

secours [səkuʀ] vb voir **secourir** ♦ nm help, aid, assistance ♦ nmpl aid sg; **cela lui a été d'un grand** ~ this was a great help to him; **au** ~! help!; **appeler au** ~ to shout ou call for help; **appeler qn à son** ~ to call sb to one's assistance; **porter** ~ **à qn** to give sb assistance, help sb; **les premiers** ~ first aid sg; **le** ~ **en montagne** mountain rescue.

secouru, e [səkuʀy] pp de **secourir**.

secousse [səkus] nf jolt, bump; (électrique) shock; (fig: psychologique) jolt, shock; ~ **sismique** ou **tellurique** earth tremor.

secret, ète [səkʀɛ, -ɛt] adj secret; (fig: renfermé) reticent, reserved ♦ nm secret; (discrétion absolue): **le** ~ secrecy; **en** ~ in secret, secretly; **au** ~ in solitary confinement; ~ **de fabrication** trade secret; ~ **professionnel** professional secrecy.

secrétaire [səkʀetɛʀ] *nm/f* secretary ♦ *nm* (*meuble*) writing desk, secretaire; ~ **d'ambassade** embassy secretary; ~ **de direction** private *ou* personal secretary; ~ **d'État** ≈ junior minister; ~ **général (SG)** Secretary-General; (*COMM*) company secretary; ~ **de mairie** town clerk; ~ **médicale** medical secretary; ~ **de rédaction** sub-editor.

secrétariat [s(ə)kʀetaʀja] *nm* (*profession*) secretarial work; (*bureau: d'entreprise, d'école*) (secretary's) office; (: *d'organisation internationale*) secretariat; (*POL etc: fonction*) secretaryship, office of Secretary.

secrètement [səkʀɛtmã] *adv* secretly.

sécréter [sekʀete] *vt* to secrete.

sécrétion [sekʀesjɔ̃] *nf* secretion.

sectaire [sɛktɛʀ] *adj* sectarian, bigoted.

sectarisme [sɛktaʀism(ə)] *nm* sectarianism.

secte [sɛkt(ə)] *nf* sect.

secteur [sɛktœʀ] *nm* sector; (*ADMIN*) district; (*ÉLEC*): **branché sur le** ~ plugged into the mains (supply); **fonctionne sur pile et** ~ battery or mains operated; **le** ~ **privé/public** (*ÉCON*) the private/public sector; **le** ~ **primaire/tertiaire** the primary/tertiary sector.

section [sɛksjɔ̃] *nf* section; (*de parcours d'autobus*) fare stage; (*MIL: unité*) platoon; ~ **rythmique** rhythm section.

sectionner [sɛksjɔne] *vt* to sever; **se** ~ *vi* to be severed.

sectionneur [sɛksjɔnœʀ] *nm* (*ÉLEC*) isolation switch.

sectoriel, le [sɛktɔʀjɛl] *adj* sector-based.

sectorisation [sɛktɔʀizasjɔ̃] *nf* division into sectors.

sectoriser [sɛktɔʀize] *vt* to divide into sectors.

sécu [seky] *nf* (*fam: = sécurité sociale*) ≈ dole (*BRIT*), ≈ Welfare (*US*).

séculaire [sekylɛʀ] *adj* secular; (*très vieux*) age-old.

séculariser [sekylaʀize] *vt* to secularize.

séculier, ière [sekylje, -jɛʀ] *adj* secular.

sécurisant, e [sekyʀizã, -ãt] *adj* secure, giving a sense of security.

sécuriser [sekyʀize] *vt* to give a sense of security to.

sécurité [sekyʀite] *nf* security; (*absence de danger*) safety; **impression de** ~ sense of security; **la** ~ **internationale** international security; **système de** ~ security (*ou* safety) system; **être en** ~ to be safe; **la** ~ **de l'emploi** job security; **la** ~ **routière** road safety; **la** ~ **sociale** ≈ (the) Social Security (*BRIT*), ≈ (the) Welfare (*US*).

sédatif, ive [sedatif, -iv] *adj, nm* sedative.

sédentaire [sedãtɛʀ] *adj* sedentary.

sédiment [sedimã] *nm* sediment; ~**s** *nmpl*

(*alluvions*) sediment *sg*.

sédimentaire [sedimãtɛʀ] *adj* sedimentary.

sédimentation [sedimãtasjɔ̃] *nf* sedimentation.

séditieux, euse [sedisjø, -øz] *adj* insurgent; seditious.

sédition [sedisjɔ̃] *nf* insurrection; sedition.

séducteur, trice [sedyktœʀ, -tʀis] *adj* seductive ♦ *nm/f* seducer/seductress.

séduction [sedyksjɔ̃] *nf* seduction; (*charme, attrait*) appeal, charm.

séduire [seduiʀ] *vt* to charm; (*femme: abuser de*) to seduce; (*suj: chose*) to appeal to.

séduisant, e [seduizã, -ãt] *vb voir* **séduire** ♦ *adj* (*femme*) seductive; (*homme, offre*) very attractive.

séduit, e [sedui, -it] *pp de* **séduire**.

segment [sɛgmã] *nm* segment; (*AUTO*): ~ **(de piston)** piston ring; ~ **de frein** brake shoe.

segmenter [sɛgmãte] *vt*, **se** ~ *vi* to segment.

ségrégation [segʀegasjɔ̃] *nf* segregation.

ségrégationnisme [segʀegasjɔnism(ə)] *nm* segregationism.

ségrégationniste [segʀegasjɔnist(ə)] *adj* segregationist.

seiche [sɛʃ] *nf* cuttlefish.

séide [seid] *nm* (*péj*) henchman.

seigle [sɛgl(ə)] *nm* rye.

seigneur [sɛɲœʀ] *nm* lord; **le S**~ the Lord.

seigneurial, e, aux [sɛɲœʀjal, -o] *adj* lordly, stately.

sein [sɛ̃] *nm* breast; (*entrailles*) womb; **au** ~ **de** *prép* (*équipe, institution*) within; (*flots, bonheur*) in the midst of; **donner le** ~ **à** (*bébé*) to feed (at the breast); to breast-feed; **nourrir au** ~ to breast-feed.

Seine [sɛn] *nf*: **la** ~ the Seine.

séisme [seism(ə)] *nm* earthquake.

séismique *etc* [seismik] *voir* **sismique** *etc*.

SEITA [seita] *sigle f* = *Société d'exploitation industrielle des tabacs et allumettes*.

seize [sɛz] *num* sixteen.

seizième [sɛzjɛm] *num* sixteenth.

séjour [seʒuʀ] *nm* stay; (*pièce*) living room.

séjourner [seʒuʀne] *vi* to stay.

sel [sɛl] *nm* salt; (*fig*) wit; spice; ~ **de cuisine/ de table** cooking/table salt; ~ **gemme** rock salt; ~**s de bain** bathsalts.

sélect, e [selɛkt] *adj* select.

sélectif, ive [selɛktif, -iv] *adj* selective.

sélection [selɛksjɔ̃] *nf* selection; **faire/opérer une** ~ **parmi** to make a selection from among; **épreuve de** ~ (*SPORT*) trial (for selection); ~ **naturelle** natural selection; ~ **professionnelle** professional recruitment.

sélectionné, e [selɛksjɔne] *adj* (*joueur*) selected; (*produit*) specially selected.

sélectionner [selɛksjɔne] *vt* to select.

sélectionneur, euse [selɛksjɔnœʀ, -øz] *nm/f* selector.

sélectivement [selɛktivmã] *adv* selectively.

sélectivité [selɛktivite] *nf* selectivity.

sélénologie [selenɔlɔʒi] *nf* study of the moon, selenology.

self [sɛlf] *nm* (*fam*) self-service.

self-service [sɛlfsɛrvis] *adj* self-service ♦ *nm* self-service (restaurant); (*magasin*) self-service shop.

selle [sɛl] *nf* saddle; ~**s** *nfpl* (*MÉD*) stools; **aller à la ~** (*MÉD*) to have a bowel movement; **se mettre en ~** to mount, get into the saddle.

seller [sele] *vt* to saddle.

sellette [sɛlɛt] *nf*: **être sur la ~** to be on the carpet (*fig*).

sellier [selje] *nm* saddler.

selon [səlɔ̃] *prép* according to; (*en se conformant à*) in accordance with; ~ **moi** as I see it; ~ **que** according to, depending on whether.

SEm *sigle f* (= *Son Éminence*) HE.

semailles [səmɑj] *nfpl* sowing *sg*.

semaine [səmɛn] *nf* week; (*salaire*) week's wages *ou* pay, weekly wages *ou* pay; **en ~** during the week, on weekdays; **à la petite ~** from day to day; **la ~ sainte** Holy Week.

semainier [səmɛnje] *nm* (*bracelet*) bracelet made up of seven bands; (*calendrier*) desk diary; (*meuble*) chest of (seven) drawers.

sémantique [semɑ̃tik] *adj* semantic ♦ *nf* semantics *sg*.

sémaphore [semafɔr] *nm* (*RAIL*) semaphore signal.

semblable [sɑ̃blabl(ə)] *adj* similar; (*de ce genre*): **de ~s mésaventures** such mishaps ♦ *nm* fellow creature *ou* man; ~ **à** similar to, like.

semblant [sɑ̃blɑ̃] *nm*: **un ~ de vérité** a semblance of truth; **faire ~ (de faire)** to pretend (to do).

sembler [sɑ̃ble] *vb avec attribut* to seem ♦ *vb impers*: **il semble (bien) que/inutile de** it (really) seems *ou* appears that/useless to; **il me semble (bien) que** it (really) seems to me that, I (really) think (that); **il me semble le connaître** I think *ou* I've a feeling I know him; ~ **être** to seem to be; **comme bon lui semble** as he sees fit; **me semble-t-il, à ce qu'il me semble** it seems to me, to my mind.

semelle [səmɛl] *nf* sole; (*intérieure*) insole, inner sole; **battre la ~** to stamp one's feet (to keep them warm); (*fig*) to hang around (waiting); ~**s compensées** platform soles.

semence [səmɑ̃s] *nf* (*graine*) seed; (*clou*) tack.

semer [səme] *vt* to sow; (*fig: éparpiller*) to scatter; (*confusion*) to spread; (: *poursuivants*) to lose, shake off; ~ **la discorde/terreur parmi** to sow discord/terror among; **semé de** (*difficultés*) riddled with.

semestre [səmɛstr(ə)] *nm* half-year; (*SCOL*) semester.

semestriel, le [səmɛstrijɛl] *adj* half-yearly; semestral.

semeur, euse [səmœr, -øz] *nm/f* sower.

semi-automatique [səmiɔtɔmatik] *adj* semiautomatic.

semiconducteur [səmikɔ̃dyktœr] *nm* (*INFORM*) semiconductor.

semi-conserve [səmikɔ̃sɛrv(ə)] *nf* semi-perishable foodstuff.

semi-fini [səmifini] *adj m* (*produit*) semi-finished.

semi-liberté [səmilibɛrte] *nf* (*JUR*) partial release from prison (*in order to follow a profession or undergo medical treatment*).

sémillant, e [semijɑ̃, -ɑ̃t] *adj* vivacious; dashing.

séminaire [seminɛr] *nm* seminar; (*REL*) seminary.

séminariste [seminarist(ə)] *nm* seminarist.

sémiologie [semjɔlɔʒi] *nf* semiology.

semi-public, ique [səmipyblik] *adj* (*JUR*) semipublic.

semi-remorque [səmirəmɔrk(ə)] *nf* trailer ♦ *nm* articulated lorry (*BRIT*), semi(trailer) (*US*).

semis [səmi] *nm* (*terrain*) seedbed, seed plot; (*plante*) seedling.

sémite [semit] *adj* Semitic.

sémitique [semitik] *adj* Semitic.

semoir [səmwar] *nm* seed-bag; seeder.

semonce [səmɔ̃s] *nf*: **un coup de ~** a shot across the bows.

semoule [səmul] *nf* semolina; ~ **de riz** ground rice.

sempiternel, le [sɛ̃pitɛrnɛl] *adj* eternal, never-ending.

sénat [sena] *nm* senate.

The **Sénat** *is the upper house of the French parliament, sitting in the Palais du Luxembourg in Paris. One third of* **sénateurs** *are elected for a nine-year term every three years by an electoral college consisting of* **députés** *and other elected representatives. The Sénat has a wide range of powers but is overridden by the* **Assemblée nationale** *in cases of disagreement.*

---

sénateur [senatœr] *nm* senator.

sénatorial, e, aux [senatɔrjal, -o] *adj* senatorial, Senate *cpd*.

Sénégal [senegal] *nm*: **le ~** Senegal.

sénégalais, e [senegalɛ, -ɛz] *adj* Senegalese.

sénevé [sɛnve] *nm* (*BOT*) mustard; (*graine*) mustard seed.

sénile [senil] *adj* senile.

sénilité [senilite] *nf* senility.

senior [senjɔr] *nm/f* (*SPORT*) senior.

sens [sɑ̃] *vb voir* **sentir** ♦ *nm* [sɑ̃s] (*PHYSIOL, instinct*) sense; (*signification*) meaning, sense; (*direction*) direction, way ♦ *nmpl* (*sensualité*) senses; **reprendre ses ~** to regain consciousness; **avoir le ~ des affaires/de la mesure** to have business sense/a sense of moderation; **ça n'a pas de ~** that doesn't make (any) sense; **en dépit du bon ~**

contrary to all good sense; **tomber sous le ~** to stand to reason, be perfectly obvious; **en un ~, dans un ~** in a way; **en ce ~ que** in the sense that; **à mon ~** to my mind; **dans le ~ des aiguilles d'une montre** clockwise; **dans le ~ de la longueur/largeur** lengthways/widthways; **dans le mauvais ~** the wrong way; in the wrong direction; **bon ~** good sense; **~ commun** common sense; **~ dessus dessous** upside down; **~ interdit, ~ unique** one-way street.

sensass [sɑ̃sas] *adj (fam)* fantastic.

sensation [sɑ̃sasjɔ̃] *nf* sensation; **faire ~** to cause a sensation, create a stir; **à ~** *(péj)* sensational.

sensationnel, le [sɑ̃sasjɔnɛl] *adj* sensational.

sensé, e [sɑ̃se] *adj* sensible.

sensibilisation [sɑ̃sibilizasjɔ̃] *nf* consciousness-raising: **une campagne de ~ de l'opinion** a campaign to raise public awareness.

sensibiliser [sɑ̃sibilize] *vt* to sensitize; **~ qn (à)** to make sb sensitive (to).

sensibilité [sɑ̃sibilite] *nf* sensitivity; *(affectivité, émotivité)* sensitivity, sensibility.

sensible [sɑ̃sibl(ə)] *adj* sensitive; *(aux sens)* perceptible; *(appréciable: différence, progrès)* appreciable, noticeable; **~ à** sensitive to.

sensiblement [sɑ̃sibləmɑ̃] *adv (notablement)* appreciably, noticeably; *(à peu près)*: **ils ont ~ le même poids** they weigh approximately the same.

sensiblerie [sɑ̃sibləʀi] *nf* sentimentality; squeamishness.

sensitif, ive [sɑ̃sitif, -iv] *adj (nerf)* sensory; *(personne)* oversensitive.

sensoriel, le [sɑ̃sɔʀjɛl] *adj* sensory, sensorial.

sensualité [sɑ̃sɥalite] *nf* sensuality, sensuousness.

sensuel, le [sɑ̃sɥɛl] *adj* sensual; sensuous.

sent [sɑ̃] *vb voir* **sentir.**

sente [sɑ̃t] *nf* path.

sentence [sɑ̃tɑ̃s] *nf (jugement)* sentence; *(adage)* maxim.

sentencieusement [sɑ̃tɑ̃sjøzmɑ̃] *adv* sententiously.

sentencieux, euse [sɑ̃tɑ̃sjø, -øz] *adj* sententious.

senteur [sɑ̃tœʀ] *nf* scent, perfume.

senti, e [sɑ̃ti] *adj*: **bien ~** *(mots etc)* well-chosen.

sentier [sɑ̃tje] *nm* path.

sentiment [sɑ̃timɑ̃] *nm* feeling; *(conscience, impression)*: **avoir le ~ de/que** to be aware of/have the feeling that; **recevez mes ~s respectueux** yours faithfully; **faire du ~** *(péj)* to be sentimental; **si vous me prenez par les ~s** if you appeal to my feelings.

sentimental, e, aux [sɑ̃timɑ̃tal, -o] *adj* sentimental; *(vie, aventure)* love *cpd.*

sentimentalisme [sɑ̃timɑ̃talism(ə)] *nm* sentimentalism.

sentimentalité [sɑ̃timɑ̃talite] *nf* sentimentality.

sentinelle [sɑ̃tinɛl] *nf* sentry; **en ~** standing guard; *(soldat: en faction)* on sentry duty.

sentir [sɑ̃tiʀ] *vt (par l'odorat)* to smell; *(par le goût)* to taste; *(au toucher, fig)* to feel; *(répandre une odeur de)* to smell of; *(: ressemblance)* to smell like; *(avoir la saveur de)* to taste of; to taste like; *(fig: dénoter, annoncer)* to be indicative of; to smack of; to foreshadow ♦ *vi* to smell; **~ mauvais** to smell bad; **se ~ bien** to feel good; **se ~ mal** *(être indisposé)* to feel unwell *ou* ill; **se ~ le courage/la force de faire** to feel brave/strong enough to do; **ne plus se ~ de joie** to be beside o.s. with joy; **il ne peut pas le ~** *(fam)* he can't stand him.

seoir [swaʀ]: **~ à** *vt* to become, befit; **comme il (leur) sied** as it is fitting (to them).

Seoul [seul] *n* Seoul.

SEP *sigle f* (= *sclérose en plaques*) MS.

séparation [sepaʀasjɔ̃] *nf* separation; *(cloison)* division, partition; **~ de biens** division of property *(in marriage settlement)*; **~ de corps** legal separation.

séparatisme [sepaʀatism(ə)] *nm* separatism.

séparatiste [sepaʀatist(ə)] *adj, nm/f (POL)* separatist.

séparé, e [sepaʀe] *adj (appartements, pouvoirs)* separate; *(époux)* separated; **~ de** separate from; separated from.

séparément [sepaʀemɑ̃] *adv* separately.

séparer [sepaʀe] *vt (gén)* to separate; *(suj: divergences etc)* to divide; to drive apart; *(: différences, obstacles)* to stand between; *(détacher)*: **~ qch de** to pull sth (off) from; *(dissocier)* to distinguish between; *(diviser)*: **~ qch par** to divide sth (up) with; **~ une pièce en deux** to divide a room into two; **se ~** *(époux)* to separate, part; *(prendre congé: amis etc)* to part, leave each other; *(adversaires)* to separate; *(se diviser: route, tige etc)* to divide; *(se détacher)*: **se ~ (de)** to split off (from); to come off; **se ~ de** *(époux)* to separate *ou* part from; *(employé, objet personnel)* to part with.

sépia [sepja] *nf* sepia.

sept [sɛt] *num* seven.

septante [sɛptɑ̃t] *num (Belgique, Suisse)* seventy.

septembre [sɛptɑ̃bʀ(ə)] *nm* September; *voir aussi* **juillet.**

septennal, e, aux [sɛptenal, -o] *adj* seven-year; *(festival)* seven-year, septennial.

septennat [sɛptena] *nm* seven-year term (of office); seven-year reign.

septentrional, e, aux [sɛptɑ̃tʀijɔnal, -o] *adj* northern.

septicémie [sɛptisemi] *nf* blood poisoning, septicaemia.

septième [sɛtjɛm] *num* seventh; **être au ~ ciel** to be on cloud nine.

septique [sɛptik] *adj*: **fosse ~** septic tank.

septuagénaire [sɛptɥaʒenɛʀ] *adj, nm/f* septuagenarian.
sépulcral, e, aux [sepylkʀal, -o] *adj* (*voix*) sepulchral.
sépulcre [sepylkʀ(ə)] *nm* sepulchre.
sépulture [sepyltyʀ] *nf* burial; (*tombeau*) burial place, grave.
séquelles [sekɛl] *nfpl* after-effects; (*fig*) aftermath *sg*; consequences.
séquence [sekɑ̃s] *nf* sequence.
séquentiel, le [sekɑ̃sjɛl] *adj* sequential.
séquestration [sekɛstʀasjɔ̃] *nf* illegal confinement; impounding.
séquestre [sekɛstʀ(ə)] *nm* impoundment; **mettre sous** ~ to impound.
séquestrer [sekɛstʀe] *vt* (*personne*) to confine illegally; (*biens*) to impound.
serai [səʀe] *etc vb voir* **être**.
sérail [seʀaj] *nm* seraglio; harem; **rentrer au** ~ to return to the fold.
serbe [sɛʀb(ə)] *adj* Serbian ♦ *nm* (*LING*) Serbian ♦ *nm/f:* **S~** Serb.
Serbie [sɛʀbi] *nf:* **la** ~ Serbia.
serbo-croate [sɛʀbokʀɔat] *adj* Serbo-Croat, Serbo-Croatian ♦ *nm* (*LING*) Serbo-Croat.
serein, e [səʀɛ̃, -ɛn] *adj* serene; (*jugement*) dispassionate.
sereinement [səʀɛnmɑ̃] *adv* serenely.
sérénade [seʀenad] *nf* serenade; (*fam*) hullabaloo.
sérénité [seʀenite] *nf* serenity.
serez [səʀe] *vb voir* **être**.
serf, serve [sɛʀ, sɛʀv(ə)] *nm/f* serf.
serfouette [sɛʀfwɛt] *nf* weeding hoe.
serge [sɛʀʒ(ə)] *nf* serge.
sergent [sɛʀʒɑ̃] *nm* sergeant.
sergent-chef [sɛʀʒɑ̃ʃɛf] *nm* staff sergeant.
sergent-major [sɛʀʒɑ̃maʒɔʀ] *nm* ≈ quartermaster sergeant.
sériciculture [seʀisikyltyʀ] *nf* silkworm breeding, sericulture.
série [seʀi] *nf* (*de questions, d'accidents, TV*) series *inv*; (*de clés, casseroles, outils*) set; (*catégorie: SPORT*) rank; class; **en** ~ in quick succession; (*COMM*) mass *cpd*; **de** ~ *adj* standard; **hors** ~ (*COMM*) custom-built; (*fig*) outstanding; **imprimante** ~ (*INFORM*) serial printer; **soldes de fin de** ~**s** end of line special offers; ~ **noire** *nm* (crime) thriller ♦ *nf* (*suite de malheurs*) run of bad luck.
sérier [seʀje] *vt* to classify, sort out.
sérieusement [seʀjøzmɑ̃] *adv* seriously; reliably; responsibly; **il parle** ~ he's serious, he means it; **~?** are you serious?, do you mean it?
sérieux, euse [seʀjø, -øz] *adj* serious; (*élève, employé*) reliable, responsible; (*client, maison*) reliable, dependable; (*offre, proposition*) genuine, serious; (*grave, sévère*) serious, solemn; (*maladie, situation*) serious, grave; (*important*) considerable ♦ *nm* seriousness; reliability; **ce n'est pas** ~

(*raisonnable*) that's not on; **garder son** ~ to keep a straight face; **manquer de** ~ not to be very responsible (*ou* reliable); **prendre qch/qn au** ~ to take sth/sb seriously.
sérigraphie [seʀigʀafi] *nf* silk screen printing.
serin [səʀɛ̃] *nm* canary.
seriner [səʀine] *vt:* ~ **qch à qn** to drum sth into sb.
seringue [səʀɛ̃g] *nf* syringe.
serions [səʀjɔ̃] *etc vb voir* **être**.
serment [sɛʀmɑ̃] *nm* (*juré*) oath; (*promesse*) pledge, vow; **prêter** ~ to take the *ou* an oath; **faire le** ~ **de** to take a vow to, swear to; **sous** ~ on *ou* under oath.
sermon [sɛʀmɔ̃] *nm* sermon; (*péj*) sermon, lecture.
sermonner [sɛʀmɔne] *vt* to lecture.
SERNAM [sɛʀnam] *sigle m* (= *Service national de messageries*) rail delivery service.
sérologie [seʀɔlɔʒi] *nf* serology.
séronégatif, ive [seʀonegatif, -iv] *adj* HIV negative.
séropositif, ive [seʀopozitif, -iv] *adj* HIV positive.
serpe [sɛʀp(ə)] *nf* billhook.
serpent [sɛʀpɑ̃] *nm* snake; ~ **à sonnettes** rattlesnake; ~ **monétaire (européen)** (European) monetary snake.
serpenter [sɛʀpɑ̃te] *vi* to wind.
serpentin [sɛʀpɑ̃tɛ̃] *nm* (*tube*) coil; (*ruban*) streamer.
serpillière [sɛʀpijɛʀ] *nf* floorcloth.
serrage [seʀaʒ] *nm* tightening; **collier de** ~ clamp.
serre [sɛʀ] *nf* (*AGR*) greenhouse; ~ **chaude** hothouse; ~ **froide** unheated greenhouse.
serré, e [seʀe] *adj* (*tissu*) closely woven; (*réseau*) dense; (*écriture*) close; (*habits*) tight; (*fig: lutte, match*) tight, close-fought; (*passagers etc*) (tightly) packed; (*café*) strong ♦ *adv:* **jouer** ~ to play it close, play a close game; **écrire** ~ to write a cramped hand; **avoir la gorge** ~**e** to have a lump in one's throat.
serre-livres [sɛʀlivʀ(ə)] *nm inv* book ends *pl*.
serrement [sɛʀmɑ̃] *nm:* ~ **de main** handshake; ~ **de cœur** pang of anguish.
serrer [seʀe] *vt* (*tenir*) to grip *ou* hold tight; (*comprimer, coincer*) to squeeze; (*poings, mâchoires*) to clench; (*suj: vêtement*) to be too tight for; to fit tightly; (*rapprocher*) to close up, move closer together; (*ceinture, nœud, frein, vis*) to tighten ♦ *vi:* ~ **à droite** to keep to the right; to move into the right-hand lane; **se** ~ (*se rapprocher*) to squeeze up; **se** ~ **contre qn** to huddle up to sb; **se** ~ **les coudes** to stick together, back one another up; **se** ~ **la ceinture** to tighten one's belt; ~ **la main à qn** to shake sb's hand; ~ **qn dans ses bras** to hug sb, clasp sb in one's arms; ~ **la gorge à qn** (*suj: chagrin*) to bring a lump to sb's throat; ~ **les dents** to clench *ou* grit

one's teeth; ~ **qn de près** to follow close
behind sb; ~ **le trottoir** to hug the kerb; ~ **sa
droite** to keep well to the right; ~ **la vis à qn**
to crack down harder on sb; ~ **les rangs** to
close ranks.

serres [sɛʀ] *nfpl (griffes)* claws, talons.

serre-tête [sɛʀtɛt] *nm inv (bandeau)* headband;
(bonnet) skullcap.

serrure [seʀyʀ] *nf* lock.

serrurerie [seʀyʀʀi] *nf (métier)* locksmith's
trade; *(ferronnerie)* ironwork; ~ **d'art**
ornamental ironwork.

serrurier [seʀyʀje] *nm* locksmith.

sers, sert [sɛʀ] *vb voir* **servir**.

sertir [sɛʀtiʀ] *vt (pierre)* to set; *(pièces
métalliques)* to crimp.

sérum [seʀɔm] *nm* serum; ~ **antivenimeux**
snakebite serum; ~ **sanguin** (blood) serum;
~ **de vérité** truth drug.

servage [sɛʀvaʒ] *nm* serfdom.

servant [sɛʀvɑ̃] *nm* server.

servante [sɛʀvɑ̃t] *nf* (maid)servant.

serve [sɛʀv] *nf voir* **serf** ♦ *vb voir* **servir**.

serveur, euse [sɛʀvœʀ, -øz] *nm/f* waiter/
waitress ♦ *adj*: **centre** ~ *(INFORM)* service
centre.

servi, e [sɛʀvi] *adj*: **être bien** ~ to get a large
helping *(ou* helpings); **vous êtes** ~? are you
being served?

serviable [sɛʀvjabl(ə)] *adj* obliging, willing to
help.

service [sɛʀvis] *nm (gén)* service; *(série
de repas)*: **premier** ~ first sitting;
(pourboire) service (charge); *(assortiment
de vaisselle)* set, service; *(linge de table)*
set; *(bureau: de la vente etc)* department,
section; *(travail)*: **pendant le** ~ on duty; ~**s**
nmpl (travail, ÉCON) services, inclusive/
exclusive of service; **faire le** ~ to serve;
être en ~ **chez qn** *(domestique)* to be in
sb's service; **être au** ~ **de** *(patron,
patrie)* to be in the service of; **être au** ~
de qn *(collaborateur, voiture)* to be at sb's
service; **porte de** ~ tradesman's
entrance; **rendre** ~ **à** to help; **il aime rendre**
~ he likes to help; **rendre un** ~ **à qn** to
do sb a favour; **heures de** ~ hours of
duty; **être de** ~ to be on duty; **reprendre
du** ~ to get back into action; **avoir 25
ans de** ~ to have completed 25 years'
service; **être/mettre en** ~ to be in/put
into service *ou* operation; **hors** ~ not
in use; out of order; ~ **à thé/café** tea/
coffee set *ou* service; ~ **après vente (SAV)**
after-sales service; **en** ~ **commandé**
on an official assignment; ~ **funèbre**
funeral service; ~ **militaire** military
service; ~ **d'ordre** police *(ou* stewards) in
charge of maintaining order; ~**s publics**
public services, (public) utilities; ~**s
secrets** secret service *sg*; ~**s sociaux** social
services.

> French men over eighteen years of age are
> required to do ten months' **service militaire** *if*
> *passed fit. The call-up can be delayed if the
> conscript is a full-time student in higher
> education. Conscientious objectors are
> required to do two years' public service. Since
> 1970, women have been able to do military
> service, though few do.*

serviette [sɛʀvjɛt] *nf (de table)* (table) napkin,
serviette; *(de toilette)* towel; *(porte-
documents)* briefcase; ~ **éponge** terry
towel; ~ **hygiénique** sanitary towel.

servile [sɛʀvil] *adj* servile.

servir [sɛʀviʀ] *vt (gén)* to serve; *(dîneur: au
restaurant)* to wait on; *(client: au magasin)* to
serve, attend to; *(fig: aider)*: ~ **qn** to aid sb;
to serve sb's interests; to stand sb in good
stead; *(COMM: rente)* to pay ♦ *vi (TENNIS)* to
serve; *(CARTES)* to deal; *(être militaire)* to
serve; ~ **qch à qn** to serve sb with sth, help
sb to sth; **qu'est-ce que je vous sers?** what
can I get you?; **se** ~ *(prendre d'un plat)* to
help o.s.; *(s'approvisionner)*: **se** ~ **chez** to
shop at; **se** ~ **de** *(plat)* to help o.s. to; *(voiture,
outil, relations)* to use; ~ **à qn** *(diplôme, livre)*
to be of use to sb; **ça m'a servi pour faire** it
was useful to me when I did; I used it to do;
~ **à qch/à faire** *(outil etc)* to be used for
sth/for doing; **ça peut** ~ it may come in
handy; **ça peut encore** ~ it can still be used
(ou of use); **à quoi cela sert-il (de faire)?**
what's the use (of doing)?; **cela ne sert à
rien** it's no use; ~ **(à qn) de ...** to serve as ...
(for sb); ~ **à dîner (à qn)** to serve dinner (to sb).

serviteur [sɛʀvitœʀ] *nm* servant.

servitude [sɛʀvityd] *nf* servitude; *(fig)*
constraint; *(JUR)* easement.

servofrein [sɛʀvɔfʀɛ̃] *nm* servo(-assisted)
brake.

servomécanisme [sɛʀvɔmekanism(ə)] *nm*
servo system.

ses [se] *dét voir* **son**.

sésame [sezam] *nm (BOT)* sesame; *(graine)*
sesame seed.

session [sesjɔ̃] *nf* session.

set [sɛt] *nm* set; *(napperon)* placemat; ~ **de
table** set of placemats.

seuil [sœj] *nm* doorstep; *(fig)* threshold; **sur
le** ~ **de sa maison** in the doorway of his
house, on his doorstep; **au** ~ **de** *(fig)* on the
threshold *ou* brink *ou* edge of; ~ **de
rentabilité** *(COMM)* breakeven point.

seul, e [sœl] *adj (sans compagnie)* alone; *(avec
nuance affective: isolé)* lonely; *(unique)*: **un** ~
livre only one book, a single book; **le** ~ **livre**
the only book; ~ **ce livre, ce livre** ~ this book
alone, only this book; **d'un** ~ **coup**
(soudainement) all at once; *(à la fois)* at one
blow ♦ *adv (vivre)* alone, on one's own; **parler
tout** ~ to talk to oneself; **faire qch (tout)** ~

to do sth (all) on one's own *ou* (all) by oneself ♦ *nm, nf*: **il en reste un(e) ~(e)** there's only one left; **pas un(e) ~(e)** not a single; **à lui (tout) ~** single-handed, on his own; **~ à ~** in private.

seulement [sœlmɑ̃] *adv* (*pas davantage*): **~ 5, 5 ~** only 5; (*exclusivement*): **~ eux** only them, them alone; (*pas avant*): **~ hier/à 10h** only yesterday/at 10 o'clock; (*mais, toutefois*): **il consent, ~ il demande des garanties** he agrees, only he wants guarantees; **non ~ ... mais aussi** *ou* **encore** not only ... but also.

sève [sɛv] *nf* sap.

sévère [sevɛʀ] *adj* severe.

sévèrement [sevɛʀmɑ̃] *adv* severely.

sévérité [severite] *nf* severity.

sévices [sevis] *nmpl* (physical) cruelty *sg*, ill treatment *sg*.

Séville [sevil] *n* Seville.

sévir [seviʀ] *vi* (*punir*) to use harsh measures, crack down; (*suj: fléau*) to rage, be rampant; **~ contre** (*abus*) to deal ruthlessly with, crack down on.

sevrage [səvʀaʒ] *nm* weaning; deprivation; (*d'un toxicomane*) withdrawal.

sevrer [səvʀe] *vt* to wean; (*fig*): **~ qn de** to deprive sb of.

sexagénaire [sɛgzaʒenɛʀ] *adj, nm/f* sexagenarian.

SExc *sigle f* (= *Son Excellence*) HE.

sexe [sɛks(ə)] *nm* sex; (*organe mâle*) member.

sexisme [sɛksism(ə)] *nm* sexism.

sexiste [sɛksist(ə)] *adj, nm* sexist.

sexologie [sɛksɔlɔʒi] *nf* sexology.

sexologue [sɛksɔlɔg] *nm/f* sexologist, sex specialist.

sextant [sɛkstɑ̃] *nm* sextant.

sexualité [sɛksɥalite] *nf* sexuality.

sexué, e [sɛksɥe] *adj* sexual.

sexuel, le [sɛksɥɛl] *adj* sexual; **acte ~** sex act.

sexuellement [sɛksɥɛlmɑ̃] *adv* sexually.

seyait [sɛjɛ] *vb voir* **seoir**.

seyant, e [sɛjɑ̃, -ɑ̃t] *vb voir* **seoir** ♦ *adj* becoming.

Seychelles [seʃɛl] *nfpl*: **les ~** the Seychelles.

SFIO *sigle f* (= *Section française de l'internationale ouvrière*) *former name of French Socialist Party*.

SG *sigle m* = **secrétaire général**.

SGEN *sigle m* (= *Syndicat général de l'éducation nationale*) *trades union*.

shaker [ʃɛkœʀ] *nm* (cocktail) shaker.

shampooiner [ʃɑ̃pwine] *vt* to shampoo.

shampooineur, euse [ʃɑ̃pwinœʀ, -øz] *nm/f* (*personne*) junior (*who does the shampooing*).

shampooing [ʃɑ̃pwɛ̃] *nm* shampoo; **se faire un ~** to shampoo one's hair; **~ colorant** (colour) rinse; **~ traitant** medicated shampoo.

Shetland [ʃɛtlɑ̃d] *n*: **les îles ~** the Shetland Islands, Shetland.

shoot [ʃut] *nm* (FOOTBALL) shot.

shooter [ʃute] *vi* (FOOTBALL) to shoot; **se ~**

(*drogué*) to mainline.

shopping [ʃɔpiŋ] *nm*: **faire du ~** to go shopping.

short [ʃɔʀt] *nm* (pair of) shorts *pl*.

SI *sigle m* = **syndicat d'initiative**.

=========================== *MOT-CLÉ*

si [si] *nm* (MUS) B; (*en chantant la gamme*) ti
♦ *adv* **1** (*oui*) yes; **"Paul n'est pas venu" — "~!"** "Paul hasn't come" — "Yes he has!"; **je vous assure que ~** I assure you he did/ she is *etc*

2 (*tellement*) so; **~ gentil/rapidement** so kind/fast; **(tant et) ~ bien que** so much so that; **~ rapide qu'il soit** however fast he may be

♦ *conj* if; **~ tu veux** if you want; **je me demande ~** I wonder if *ou* whether; **~ j'étais toi** if I were you; **~ seulement** if only; **~ ce n'est que** apart from; **une des plus belles, ~ ce n'est la plus belle** one of the most beautiful, if not THE most beautiful; **s'il est aimable, eux par contre ...** while *ou* whereas he's nice, they (on the other hand) ...

siamois, e [sjamwa, -waz] *adj* Siamese; **frères/sœurs ~(es)** Siamese twins.

Sibérie [sibeʀi] *nf*: **la ~** Siberia.

sibérien, ne [sibeʀjɛ̃, -ɛn] *adj* Siberian ♦ *nm/f*: **S~, ne** Siberian.

sibyllin, e [sibilɛ̃, -in] *adj* sibylline.

SICAV [sikav] *sigle f* (= *société d'investissement à capital variable*) open-ended investment trust; share in such a trust.

Sicile [sisil] *nf*: **la ~** Sicily.

sicilien, ne [sisiljɛ̃, -ɛn] *adj* Sicilian.

SIDA, sida [sida] *nm* (= *syndrome immuno-déficitaire acquis*) AIDS *sg*.

sidéral, e, aux [sideʀal, -o] *adj* sideral.

sidérant, e [sideʀɑ̃, -ɑ̃t] *adj* staggering.

sidéré, e [sidere] *adj* staggered.

sidérurgie [sideʀyʀʒi] *nf* steel industry.

sidérurgique [sideʀyʀʒik] *adj* steel *cpd*.

sidérurgiste [sideʀyʀʒist(ə)] *nm/f* steel worker.

siècle [sjɛkl(ə)] *nm* century; (*époque*): **le ~ des lumières/de l'atome** the age of enlighten-ment/atomic age; (REL): **le ~** the world.

sied [sje] *vb voir* **seoir**.

siège [sjɛʒ] *nm* seat; (*d'entreprise*) head office; (*d'organisation*) headquarters *pl*; (MIL) siege; **lever le ~** to raise the siege; **mettre le ~ devant** to besiege; **présentation par le ~** (MÉD) breech presentation; **~ avant/arrière** (AUTO) front/back seat; **~ baquet** bucket seat; **~ social** registered office.

siéger [sjeʒe] *vi* (*assemblée, tribunal*) to sit; (*résider, se trouver*) to lie, be located.

sien, ne [sjɛ̃, sjɛn] *pron*: **le(la) ~(ne), les ~s(~nes)** *m* his; *f* hers; *non humain* its; **y mettre du ~** to pull one's weight; **faire des**

~nes (*fam*) to be up to one's (usual) tricks; **les ~s** (*sa famille*) one's family.

siérait [sjɛrɛ] *etc vb voir* **seoir**.

Sierra Leone [sjɛraleɔne] *nf*: **la ~** Sierra Leone.

sieste [sjɛst(ə)] *nf* (afternoon) snooze *ou* nap, siesta; **faire la ~** to have a snooze *ou* nap.

sieur [sjœr] *nm*: **le ~ Thomas** Mr Thomas; (*en plaisantant*) Master Thomas.

sifflant, e [siflɑ̃, -ɑ̃t] *adj* (*bruit*) whistling; (*toux*) wheezing; (**consonne**) **~e** sibilant.

sifflement [sifləmɑ̃] *nm* whistle, whistling *no pl*; wheezing *no pl*; hissing *no pl*.

siffler [sifle] *vi* (*gén*) to whistle; (*avec un sifflet*) to blow (on) one's whistle; (*en respirant*) to wheeze; (*serpent, vapeur*) to hiss ♦ *vt* (*chanson*) to whistle; (*chien etc*) to whistle for; (*fille*) to whistle at; (*pièce, orateur*) to hiss, boo; (*faute*) to blow one's whistle at; (*fin du match, départ*) to blow one's whistle for; (*fam: verre, bouteille*) to guzzle, knock back (BRIT).

sifflet [siflɛ] *nm* whistle; **~s** *nmpl* (*de mécontentement*) whistles, boos; **coup de ~** whistle.

siffloter [siflɔte] *vi*, *vt* to whistle.

sigle [sigl(ə)] *nm* acronym, (set of) initials *pl*.

signal, aux [siɲal, -o] *nm* (*signe convenu, appareil*) signal; (*indice, écriteau*) sign; **donner le ~ de** to give the signal for; **~ d'alarme** alarm signal; **~ d'alerte/de détresse** warning/distress signal; **~ horaire** time signal; **~ optique/sonore** warning light/sound; visual/acoustic signal; **signaux (lumineux)** (AUTO) traffic signals; **signaux routiers** road signs; (*lumineux*) traffic lights.

signalement [siɲalmɑ̃] *nm* description, particulars *pl*.

signaler [siɲale] *vt* to indicate; to announce; to report; (*être l'indice de*) to indicate; (*faire remarquer*): **~ qch à qn/à qn que** to point out sth to sb/to sb that; (*appeler l'attention sur*): **~ qn à la police** to bring sb to the notice of the police; **se ~ par** to distinguish o.s. by; **se ~ à l'attention de qn** to attract sb's attention.

signalétique [siɲaletik] *adj*: **fiche ~** identification sheet.

signalisation [siɲalizasjɔ̃] *nf* signalling, signposting; signals *pl*; roadsigns *pl*; **panneau de ~** roadsign.

signaliser [siɲalize] *vt* to put up roadsigns on; to put signals on.

signataire [siɲatɛr] *nm/f* signatory.

signature [siɲatyr] *nf* signature; (*action*) signing.

signe [siɲ] *nm* sign; (TYPO) mark; **ne pas donner ~ de vie** to give no sign of life; **c'est bon ~** it's a good sign; **c'est ~ que** it's a sign that; **faire un ~ de la main/tête** to give a sign with one's hand/shake one's head; **faire ~ à qn** (*fig*) to get in touch with sb; **faire ~ à qn d'entrer** to motion (to) sb to come in; **en**

~ de as a sign *ou* mark of; **le ~ de la croix** the sign of the Cross; **~ de ponctuation** punctuation mark; **~ du zodiaque** sign of the zodiac; **~s particuliers** distinguishing marks.

signer [siɲe] *vt* to sign; **se ~** *vi* to cross o.s.

signet [siɲɛ] *nm* bookmark.

significatif, ive [siɲifikatif, -iv] *adj* significant.

signification [siɲifikasjɔ̃] *nf* meaning.

signifier [siɲifje] *vt* (*vouloir dire*) to mean, signify; (*faire connaître*): **~ qch (à qn)** to make sth known (to sb); (JUR): **~ qch à qn** to serve notice of sth on sb.

silence [silɑ̃s] *nm* silence; (MUS) rest; **garder le ~ (sur qch)** to keep silent (about sth), say nothing (about sth); **passer sous ~** to pass over (in silence); **réduire au ~** to silence.

silencieusement [silɑ̃sjøzmɑ̃] *adv* silently.

silencieux, euse [silɑ̃sjø, -øz] *adj* quiet, silent ♦ *nm* silencer (BRIT), muffler (US).

silex [silɛks] *nm* flint.

silhouette [silwɛt] *nf* outline, silhouette; (*lignes, contour*) outline; (*figure*) figure.

silice [silis] *nf* silica.

siliceux, euse [silisø, -øz] *adj* (*terrain*) chalky.

silicium [silisjɔm] *nm* silicon; **plaquette de ~** silicon chip.

silicone [silikon] *nf* silicone.

silicose [silikoz] *nf* silicosis, dust disease.

sillage [sijaʒ] *nm* wake; (*fig*) trail; **dans le ~ de** (*fig*) in the wake of.

sillon [sijɔ̃] *nm* (*d'un champ*) furrow; (*de disque*) groove.

sillonner [sijone] *vt* (*creuser*) to furrow; (*traverser*) to cross, criss-cross.

silo [silo] *nm* silo.

simagrées [simagre] *nfpl* fuss *sg*; airs and graces.

simiesque [simjɛsk(ə)] *adj* monkey-like, ape-like.

similaire [similɛr] *adj* similar.

similarité [similarite] *nf* similarity.

simili [simili] *nm* imitation; (TYPO) half-tone ♦ *nf* half-tone engraving.

simili... [simili] *préfixe* imitation *cpd*, artificial.

similicuir [similikɥir] *nm* imitation leather.

similigravure [similigravyr] *nf* half-tone engraving.

similitude [similityd] *nf* similarity.

simple [sɛ̃pl(ə)] *adj* (*gén*) simple; (*non multiple*) single; **~s** *nmpl* (MÉD) medicinal plants; **~ messieurs** *nm* (TENNIS) men's singles *sg*; **un ~ particulier** an ordinary citizen; **une ~ formalité** a mere formality; **cela varie du ~ au double** it can double, it can double the price *etc*; **dans le plus ~ appareil** in one's birthday suit; **~ course** *adj* single; **~ d'esprit** *nm/f* simpleton; **~ soldat** private.

simplement [sɛ̃pləmɑ̃] *adv* simply.

simplet, te [sɛ̃plɛ, -ɛt] *adj* (*personne*) simple-minded.

simplicité [sɛ̃plisite] *nf* simplicity; **en toute ~**

quite simply.
simplification [sɛ̃plifikɑsjɔ̃] *nf* simplification.
simplifier [sɛ̃plifje] *vt* to simplify.
simpliste [sɛ̃plist(ə)] *adj* simplistic.
simulacre [simylakʀ(ə)] *nm* enactment; (*péj*):
un ~ de a pretence of, a sham.
simulateur, trice [simylatœʀ, -tʀis] *nm/f*
shammer, pretender; (*qui se prétend malade*)
malingerer ♦ *nm:* ~ **de vol** flight simulator.
simulation [simylɑsjɔ̃] *nf* shamming,
simulation; malingering.
simuler [simyle] *vt* to sham, simulate.
simultané, e [simyltane] *adj* simultaneous.
simultanéité [simyltaneite] *nf* simultaneity.
simultanément [simyltanemɑ̃] *adv*
simultaneously.
Sinaï [sinai] *nm:* **le** ~ Sinai.
sinapisme [sinapism(ə)] *nm* (*MÉD*) mustard
poultice.
sincère [sɛ̃sɛʀ] *adj* sincere; genuine; heartfelt;
mes ~**s condoléances** my deepest
sympathy.
sincèrement [sɛ̃sɛʀmɑ̃] *adv* sincerely,
genuinely.
sincérité [sɛ̃seʀite] *nf* sincerity; **en toute** ~ in
all sincerity.
sinécure [sinekyʀ] *nf* sinecure.
sine die [sinedje] *adv* sine die, indefinitely.
sine qua non [sinekwanɔn] *adj:* **condition** ~
indispensable condition.
Singapour [sɛ̃gapuʀ] *nm:* **le** ~ Singapore.
singe [sɛ̃ʒ] *nm* monkey; (*de grande taille*) ape.
singer [sɛ̃ʒe] *vt* to ape, mimic.
singeries [sɛ̃ʒʀi] *nfpl* antics; (*simagrées*) airs
and graces.
singulariser [sɛ̃gylaʀize] *vt* to mark out; **se** ~
to call attention to o.s.
singularité [sɛ̃gylaʀite] *nf* peculiarity.
singulier, ière [sɛ̃gylje, -jɛʀ] *adj* remarkable,
singular; (*LING*) singular ♦ *nm* singular.
singulièrement [sɛ̃gyljɛʀmɑ̃] *adv* singularly,
remarkably.
sinistre [sinistʀ(ə)] *adj* sinister; (*intensif*): **un** ~
imbécile an incredible idiot ♦ *nm* (*incendie*)
blaze; (*catastrophe*) disaster; (*ASSURANCES*)
damage (*giving rise to a claim*).
sinistré, e [sinistʀe] *adj* disaster-stricken
♦ *nm/f* disaster victim.
sinistrose [sinistʀoz] *nf* pessimism.
sino... [sino] *préfixe:* ~**-indien** Sino-Indian,
Chinese-Indian.
sinon [sinɔ̃] *conj* (*autrement, sans quoi*)
otherwise, or else; (*sauf*) except, other than;
(*si ce n'est*) if not.
sinueux, euse [sinɥø, -øz] *adj* winding; (*fig*)
tortuous.
sinuosités [sinɥozite] *nfpl* winding *sg*, curves.
sinus [sinys] *nm* (*ANAT*) sinus; (*GÉOM*) sine.
sinusite [sinyzit] *nf* sinusitis, sinus infection.
sinusoïdal, e, aux [sinyzɔidal, -o] *adj*
sinusoidal.
sinusoïde [sinyzɔid] *nf* sinusoid.

sionisme [sjɔnism(ə)] *nm* Zionism.
sioniste [sjɔnist(ə)] *adj, nm/f* Zionist.
siphon [sifɔ̃] *nm* (*tube, d'eau gazeuse*) siphon;
(*d'évier etc*) U-bend.
siphonner [sifɔne] *vt* to siphon.
sire [siʀ] *nm* (*titre*): **S**~ Sire; **un triste** ~ an
unsavoury individual.
sirène [siʀɛn] *nf* siren; ~ **d'alarme** fire alarm;
(*pendant la guerre*) air-raid siren.
sirop [siʀo] *nm* (*à diluer: de fruit etc*) syrup,
cordial (*BRIT*); (*boisson*) fruit drink;
(*pharmaceutique*) syrup, mixture; ~ **de**
menthe mint syrup *ou* cordial; ~ **contre la**
toux cough syrup *ou* mixture.
siroter [siʀote] *vt* to sip.
sirupeux, euse [siʀypø, -øz] *adj* syrupy.
sis, e [si, siz] *adj:* ~ **rue de la Paix** located in
the rue de la Paix.
sisal [sizal] *nm* (*BOT*) sisal.
sismique [sismik] *adj* seismic.
sismographe [sismɔgʀaf] *nm* seismograph.
sismologie [sismɔlɔʒi] *nf* seismology.
site [sit] *nm* (*paysage, environnement*) setting;
(*d'une ville etc: emplacement*) site; ~
(**pittoresque**) beauty spot; ~**s touristiques**
places of interest; ~**s naturels/historiques**
natural/historic sites.
sitôt [sito] *adv:* ~ **parti** as soon as he *etc* had
left; ~ **après** straight after; **pas de** ~ not for
a long time; ~ (**après**) **que** as soon as.
situation [sitɥɑsjɔ̃] *nf* (*gén*) situation; (*d'un*
édifice, d'une ville) situation, position;
(*emplacement*) location; **être en** ~ **de faire**
qch to be in a position to do sth; ~ **de famille**
marital status.
situé, e [sitɥe] *adj:* **bien** ~ well situated, in a
good location; ~ **à/près de** situated at/near.
situer [sitɥe] *vt* to site, situate; (*en pensée*) to
set, place; **se** ~ *vi:* **se** ~ **à/près de** to be
situated at/near.
SIVOM [sivɔm] *sigle m* (= *Syndicat inter-*
communal à vocation multiple) *association of*
"*communes*".
six [sis] *num* six.
sixième [sizjɛm] *num* sixth.
skaï [skaj] *nm* ® ≈ Leatherette ®.
skate(-board) [sket(bɔʀd)] *nm* (*sport*)
skateboarding; (*planche*) skateboard.
sketch [skɛtʃ] *nm* (variety) sketch.
ski [ski] *nm* (*objet*) ski; (*sport*) skiing; **faire du**
~ to ski; ~ **alpin** Alpine skiing; ~ **court**
short ski; ~ **évolutif** short ski method; ~ **de**
fond cross-country skiing; ~ **nautique**
water-skiing; ~ **de piste** downhill skiing; ~
de randonnée cross-country skiing.
ski-bob [skibɔb] *nm* skibob.
skier [skje] *vi* to ski.
skieur, euse [skjœʀ, -øz] *nm/f* skier.
skif(f) [skif] *nm* skiff.
slalom [slalɔm] *nm* slalom; **faire du** ~ **entre** to
slalom between; ~ **géant/spécial** giant/
special slalom.

slalomer [slalɔme] *vi* (*entre des obstacles*) to weave in and out; (*SKI*) to slalom.

slalomeur, euse [slalɔmœʀ, -øz] *nm/f* (*SKI*) slalom skier.

slave [slav] *adj* Slav(onic), Slavic ♦ *nm* (*LING*) Slavonic ♦ *nm/f*: **S~** Slav.

slip [slip] *nm* (*sous-vêtement*) underpants *pl*, pants *pl* (*BRIT*), briefs *pl*; (*de bain: d'homme*) (bathing *ou* swimming) trunks *pl*; (: *du bikini*) (bikini) briefs *pl ou* bottoms *pl*.

slogan [slɔgɑ̃] *nm* slogan.

slovaque [slɔvak] *adj* Slovak ♦ *nm* (*LING*) Slovak ♦ *nm/f*: **S~** Slovak.

Slovaquie [slɔvaki] *nf*: **la ~** Slovakia.

slovène [slɔvɛn] *adj* Slovene ♦ *nm* (*LING*) Slovene ♦ *nm/f*: **S~** Slovene.

Slovénie [slɔveni] *nf*: **la ~** Slovenia.

slow [slo] *nm* (*danse*) slow number.

SM *sigle f* (= *Sa Majesté*) HM.

SMAG [smag] *sigle m* = *salaire minimum agricole garanti.*

smasher [smaʃe] *vi* to smash the ball ♦ *vt* (*balle*) to smash.

SME *sigle m* (= *Système monétaire européen*) EMS.

SMIC [smik] *sigle m* = **salaire minimum interprofessionnel de croissance**.

> *In France, the **SMIC** is the minimum hourly rate below which it is illegal to pay workers over the age of eighteen. The SMIC is index-linked and is raised each time the cost of living rises by 2%.*

smicard, e [smikaʀ, -aʀd(ə)] *nm/f* minimum wage earner.

smocks [smɔk] *nmpl* (*COUTURE*) smocking *no pl.*

smoking [smɔkiŋ] *nm* dinner *ou* evening suit.

SMUR [smyʀ] *sigle m* (= *service médical d'urgence et de réanimation*) specialist mobile emergency unit.

snack [snak] *nm* snack bar.

SNC *abr* = *service non compris.*

SNCB *sigle f* (= *Société nationale des chemins de fer belges*) Belgian railways.

SNCF *sigle f* (= *Société nationale des chemins de fer français*) French railways.

SNES [snɛs] *sigle m* (= *Syndicat national de l'enseignement secondaire*) secondary teachers' union.

SNE-sup [ɛsɛnəsyp] *sigle m* (= *Syndicat national de l'enseignement supérieur*) university teachers' union.

SNI *sigle m* (= *Syndicat national des instituteurs*) primary teachers' union.

SNJ *sigle m* (= *Syndicat national des journalistes*) journalists' union.

snob [snɔb] *adj* snobbish ♦ *nm/f* snob.

snober [snɔbe] *vt*: **~ qn** to give sb the cold shoulder, treat sb with disdain.

snobinard, e [snɔbinaʀ, -aʀd(ə)] *nm/f* snooty *ou* stuck-up person.

snobisme [snɔbism(ə)] *nm* snobbery.

SNSM *sigle f* (= *Société nationale de sauvetage en mer*) national sea-rescue association.

s.o. *abr* (= *sans objet*) no longer applicable.

sobre [sɔbʀ(ə)] *adj* temperate, abstemious; (*élégance, style*) restrained, sober; **~ de** (*gestes, compliments*) sparing of.

sobrement [sɔbʀəmɑ̃] *adv* in moderation, abstemiously; soberly.

sobriété [sɔbʀijete] *nf* temperance, abstemiousness; sobriety.

sobriquet [sɔbʀikɛ] *nm* nickname.

soc [sɔk] *nm* ploughshare.

sociabilité [sɔsjabilite] *nf* sociability.

sociable [sɔsjabl(ə)] *adj* sociable.

social, e, aux [sɔsjal, -o] *adj* social.

socialement [sɔsjalmɑ̃] *adv* socially.

socialisant, e [sɔsjalizɑ̃, -ɑ̃t] *adj* with socialist tendencies.

socialisation [sɔsjalizasjɔ̃] *nf* socialisation.

socialiser [sɔsjalize] *vt* to socialize.

socialisme [sɔsjalism(ə)] *nm* socialism.

socialiste [sɔsjalist(ə)] *adj, nm/f* socialist.

sociétaire [sɔsjetɛʀ] *nm/f* member.

société [sɔsjete] *nf* society; (*d'abeilles, de fourmis*) colony; (*sportive*) club; (*COMM*) company; **la bonne ~** polite society; **se plaire dans la ~** to enjoy the society of; **l'archipel de la S~** the Society Islands; **la ~ d'abondance/de consommation** the affluent/consumer society; **~ par actions** joint stock company; **~ anonyme (SA)** ≈ limited company (Ltd) (*BRIT*), ≈ incorporated company (Inc.) (*US*); **~ d'investissement à capital variable (SICAV)** ≈ investment trust (*BRIT*), ≈ mutual fund (*US*); **~ à responsabilité limitée (SARL)** *type of limited liability company (with non-negotiable shares)*; **~ savante** learned society; **~ de services** service company.

socioculturel, le [sɔsjokyltyʀɛl] *adj* sociocultural.

socio-économique [sɔsjoekɔnɔmik] *adj* socioeconomic.

socio-éducatif, -ive [sɔsjoedykatif, -iv] *adj* socioeducational.

sociolinguistique [sɔsjolɛ̃ɡɥistik] *adj* sociolinguistic.

sociologie [sɔsjɔlɔʒi] *nf* sociology.

sociologique [sɔsjɔlɔʒik] *adj* sociological.

sociologue [sɔsjɔlɔg] *nm/f* sociologist.

socio-professionnel, le [sɔsjopʀɔfɛsjɔnɛl] *adj* socioprofessional.

socle [sɔkl(ə)] *nm* (*de colonne, statue*) plinth, pedestal; (*de lampe*) base.

socquette [sɔkɛt] *nf* ankle sock.

soda [sɔda] *nm* (*boisson*) fizzy drink, soda (*US*).

sodium [sɔdjɔm] *nm* sodium.

sodomie [sɔdɔmi] *nf* sodomy; buggery.

sodomiser [sɔdɔmize] *vt* to sodomize; to

bugger.

sœur [sœʀ] *nf* sister; (*religieuse*) nun, sister; ~ **Élisabeth** (*REL*) Sister Elizabeth; ~ **de lait** foster sister.

sofa [sɔfa] *nm* sofa.

Sofia [sɔfja] *n* Sofia.

SOFRES [sɔfʀɛs] *sigle f* (= *Société française d'enquête par sondage*) *company which conducts opinion polls.*

soi [swa] *pron* oneself; **cela va de** ~ that *ou* it goes without saying, it stands to reason.

soi-disant [swadizɑ̃] *adj inv* so-called ♦ *adv* supposedly.

soie [swa] *nf* silk; (*de porc, sanglier: poil*) bristle.

soient [swa] *vb voir* **être**.

soierie [swaʀi] *nf* (*industrie*) silk trade; (*tissu*) silk.

soif [swaf] *nf* thirst; (*fig*): ~ **de** thirst *ou* craving for; **avoir** ~ to be thirsty; **donner** ~ **à qn** to make sb thirsty.

soigné, e [swaɲe] *adj* (*tenue*) well-groomed, neat; (*travail*) careful, meticulous; (*fam*) whopping; stiff.

soigner [swaɲe] *vt* (*malade, maladie: suj: docteur*) to treat; (: *suj: infirmière, mère*) to nurse, look after; (*blessé*) to tend; (*travail, détails*) to take care over; (*jardin, chevelure, invités*) to look after.

soigneur [swaɲœʀ] *nm* (*CYCLISME, FOOTBALL*) trainer; (*BOXE*) second.

soigneusement [swaɲøzmɑ̃] *adv* carefully.

soigneux, euse [swaɲø, -øz] *adj* (*propre*) tidy, neat; (*méticuleux*) painstaking, careful; ~ **de** careful with.

soi-même [swamɛm] *pron* oneself.

soin [swɛ̃] *nm* (*application*) care; (*propreté, ordre*) tidiness, neatness; (*responsabilité*): **le** ~ **de qch** the care of sth; ~**s** *nmpl* (*à un malade, blessé*) treatment *sg*, medical attention *sg*; (*attentions, prévenance*) care and attention *sg*; (*hygiène*) care *sg*; ~**s de la chevelure/de beauté** hair/beauty care; ~**s du corps/ménage** care of one's body/the home; **avoir** *ou* **prendre** ~ **de** to take care of, look after; **avoir** *ou* **prendre** ~ **de faire** to take care to do; **sans** ~ *adj* careless; untidy; **les premiers** ~**s** first aid *sg*; **aux bons** ~**s de** c/o, care of; **être aux petits** ~**s pour qn** to wait on sb hand and foot, see to sb's every need; **confier qn aux** ~**s de qn** to hand sb over to sb's care.

soir [swaʀ] *nm, adv* evening; **le** ~ in the evening(s); **ce** ~ this evening, tonight; **à ce** ~! see you this evening (*ou* tonight)!; **la veille au** ~ the previous evening; **sept/dix heures du** ~ seven in the evening/ten at night; **le repas/journal du** ~ the evening meal/newspaper; **dimanche** ~ Sunday evening; **hier** ~ yesterday evening; **demain** ~ tomorrow evening, tomorrow night.

soirée [swaʀe] *nf* evening; (*réception*) party;

donner en ~ (*film, pièce*) to give an evening performance of.

soit [swa] *vb voir* **être** ♦ *conj* (*à savoir*) namely, to wit; (*ou*): ~ ... ~ either ... or ♦ *adv* so be it, very well; ~ **un triangle ABC** let ABC be a triangle; ~ **que** ... ~ **que** *ou* **ou que** whether ... or whether.

soixantaine [swasɑ̃tɛn] *nf*: **une** ~ (**de**) sixty or so, about sixty; **avoir la** ~ to be around sixty.

soixante [swasɑ̃t] *num* sixty.

soixante-dix [swasɑ̃tdis] *num* seventy.

soixante-dixième [swasɑ̃tdizjɛm] *num* seventieth.

soixante-huitard, e [swazɑ̃tɥitaʀ, -aʀd(ə)] *adj* relating to the demonstrations of May 1968 ♦ *nm/f* participant in the demonstrations of May 1968.

soixantième [swasɑ̃tjɛm] *num* sixtieth.

soja [sɔʒa] *nm* soya; (*graines*) soya beans *pl*; **germes de** ~ beansprouts.

sol [sɔl] *nm* ground; (*de logement*) floor; (*revêtement*) flooring *no pl*; (*territoire, AGR, GÉO*) soil; (*MUS*) G; (: *en chantant la gamme*) so(h).

solaire [sɔlɛʀ] *adj* solar, sun *cpd*.

solarium [sɔlaʀjɔm] *nm* solarium.

soldat [sɔlda] *nm* soldier; **S~ inconnu** Unknown Warrior *ou* Soldier; ~ **de plomb** tin *ou* toy soldier.

solde [sɔld(ə)] *nf* pay ♦ *nm* (*COMM*) balance; ~**s** *nmpl ou nfpl* (*COMM*) sales; (*articles*) sale goods; **à la** ~ **de qn** (*péj*) in sb's pay; ~ **créditeur/débiteur** credit/debit balance; ~ **à payer** balance outstanding; **en** ~ at sale price; **aux** ~**s** at the sales.

solder [sɔlde] *vt* (*compte*) to settle; (*marchandise*) to sell at sale price, sell off; **se** ~ **par** (*fig*) to end in; **article soldé (à) 10 F** item reduced to 10 F.

soldeur, euse [sɔldœʀ, -øz] *nm/f* (*COMM*) discounter.

sole [sɔl] *nf* sole *inv* (*fish*).

soleil [sɔlɛj] *nm* sun; (*lumière*) sun(light); (*temps ensoleillé*) sun(shine); (*feu d'artifice*) Catherine wheel; (*ACROBATIE*) grand circle; (*BOT*) sunflower; **il y a** *ou* **il fait du** ~ it's sunny; **au** ~ in the sun; **en plein** ~ in full sun; **le** ~ **levant/couchant** the rising/setting sun; **le** ~ **de minuit** the midnight sun.

solennel, le [sɔlanɛl] *adj* solemn; ceremonial.

solennellement [sɔlanɛlmɑ̃] *adv* solemnly.

solenniser [sɔlanize] *vt* to solemnize.

solennité [sɔlanite] *nf* (*d'une fête*) solemnity; ~**s** *nfpl* (*formalités*) formalities.

solénoïde [sɔlenɔid] *nm* (*ÉLEC*) solenoid.

solfège [sɔlfɛʒ] *nm* rudiments *pl* of music; (*exercices*) ear training *no pl*.

solfier [sɔlfje] *vt*: ~ **un morceau** to sing a piece using the sol-fa.

soli [sɔli] *pl de* **solo**.

solidaire [sɔlidɛʀ] *adj* (*personnes*) who stand

together, who show solidarity; (*pièces mécaniques*) interdependent; (*JUR*: *engagement*) binding on all parties; (*: débiteurs*) jointly liable; **être ~ de** (*collègues*) to stand by; (*mécanisme*) to be bound up with, be dependent on.

solidairement [sɔlidɛʀmɑ̃] *adv* jointly.

solidariser [sɔlidaʀize]: **se ~ avec** *vt* to show solidarity with.

solidarité [sɔlidaʀite] *nf* (*entre personnes*) solidarity; (*de mécanisme, phénomènes*) interdependence; **par ~ (avec)** (*cesser le travail etc*) in sympathy (with).

solide [sɔlid] *adj* solid; (*mur, maison, meuble*) solid, sturdy; (*connaissances, argument*) sound; (*personne*) robust, sturdy; (*estomac*) strong ♦ *nm* solid; **avoir les reins ~s** (*fig*) to be in a good financial position; to have sound financial backing.

solidement [sɔlidmɑ̃] *adv* solidly; (*fermement*) firmly.

solidifier [sɔlidifje] *vt*, **se ~** *vi* to solidify.

solidité [sɔlidite] *nf* solidity; sturdiness.

soliloque [sɔlilɔk] *nm* soliloquy.

soliste [sɔlist(ə)] *nm/f* soloist.

solitaire [sɔlitɛʀ] *adj* (*sans compagnie*) solitary, lonely; (*isolé*) solitary, isolated, lone; (*lieu*) lonely ♦ *nm/f* recluse; loner ♦ *nm* (*diamant, jeu*) solitaire.

solitude [sɔlityd] *nf* loneliness; (*paix*) solitude.

solive [sɔliv] *nf* joist.

sollicitations [sɔlisitasjɔ̃] *nfpl* (*requêtes*) entreaties, appeals; (*attractions*) enticements; (*TECH*) stress *sg*.

solliciter [sɔlisite] *vt* (*personne*) to appeal to; (*emploi, faveur*) to seek; (*moteur*) to prompt; (*suj: occupations, attractions etc*): **~ qn** to appeal to sb's curiosity *etc*; to entice sb; to make demands on sb's time; **~ qn de faire** to appeal to sb *ou* request sb to do.

sollicitude [sɔlisityd] *nf* concern.

solo [sɔlo] *nm*, *pl* **soli** [sɔli] (*MUS*) solo (*pl* -s *ou* soli).

sol-sol [sɔlsɔl] *adj inv* surface-to-surface.

solstice [sɔlstis] *nm* solstice; **~ d'hiver/d'été** winter/summer solstice.

solubilisé, e [sɔlybilize] *adj* soluble.

solubilité [sɔlybilite] *nf* solubility.

soluble [sɔlybl(ə)] *adj* (*sucre, cachet*) soluble; (*problème etc*) soluble, solvable.

soluté [sɔlyte] *nm* solution.

solution [sɔlysjɔ̃] *nf* solution; **~ de continuité** gap, break; **~ de facilité** easy way out.

solutionner [sɔlysjɔne] *vt* to solve, find a solution for.

solvabilité [sɔlvabilite] *nf* solvency.

solvable [sɔlvabl(ə)] *adj* solvent.

solvant [sɔlvɑ̃] *nm* solvent.

Somalie [sɔmali] *nf*: **la ~** Somalia.

somalien, ne [sɔmaljɛ̃, -ɛn] *adj* Somalian.

Somaliland [sɔmalilɑ̃d] *nm* Somaliland.

somatique [sɔmatik] *adj* somatic.

sombre [sɔ̃bʀ(ə)] *adj* dark; (*fig*) sombre, gloomy; (*sinistre*) awful, dreadful.

sombrer [sɔ̃bʀe] *vi* (*bateau*) to sink, go down; **~ corps et biens** to go down with all hands; **~ dans** (*misère, désespoir*) to sink into.

sommaire [sɔmɛʀ] *adj* (*simple*) basic; (*expéditif*) summary ♦ *nm* summary; **faire le ~ de** to make a summary of, summarize; **exécution ~** summary execution.

sommairement [sɔmɛʀmɑ̃] *adv* basically; summarily.

sommation [sɔmasjɔ̃] *nf* (*JUR*) summons *sg*; (*avant de faire feu*) warning.

somme [sɔm] *nf* (*MATH*) sum; (*fig*) amount; (*argent*) sum, amount ♦ *nm*: **faire un ~** to have a (short) nap; **faire la ~ de** to add up; **en ~, ~ toute** *adv* all in all.

sommeil [sɔmɛj] *nm* sleep; **avoir ~** to be sleepy; **avoir le ~ léger** to be a light sleeper; **en ~** (*fig*) dormant.

sommeiller [sɔmeje] *vi* to doze; (*fig*) to lie dormant.

sommelier [sɔməlje] *nm* wine waiter.

sommer [sɔme] *vt*: **~ qn de faire** to command *ou* order sb to do; (*JUR*) to summon sb to do.

sommes [sɔm] *vb voir* **être**; *voir aussi* **somme**.

sommet [sɔmɛ] *nm* top; (*d'une montagne*) summit, top; (*fig: de la perfection, gloire*) height; (*GÉOM: d'angle*) vertex (*pl* vertices); (*conférence*) summit (conference).

sommier [sɔmje] *nm* bed base, bedspring (*US*); (*ADMIN: registre*) register; **~ à ressorts** (interior sprung) divan base (*BRIT*), box spring (*US*); **~ à lattes** slatted bed base.

sommité [sɔmite] *nf* prominent person, leading light.

somnambule [sɔmnɑ̃byl] *nm/f* sleepwalker.

somnambulisme [sɔmnɑ̃bylism(ə)] *nm* sleepwalking.

somnifère [sɔmnifɛʀ] *nm* sleeping drug; (*comprimé*) sleeping pill *ou* tablet.

somnolence [sɔmnɔlɑ̃s] *nf* drowsiness.

somnolent, e [sɔmnɔlɑ̃, -ɑ̃t] *adj* sleepy, drowsy.

somnoler [sɔmnɔle] *vi* to doze.

somptuaire [sɔ̃ptɥɛʀ] *adj*: **lois ~s** sumptuary laws; **dépenses ~s** extravagant expenditure *sg*.

somptueusement [sɔ̃ptɥøzmɑ̃] *adv* sumptuously.

somptueux, euse [sɔ̃ptɥø, -øz] *adj* sumptuous; (*cadeau*) lavish.

somptuosité [sɔ̃ptɥozite] *nf* sumptuousness; (*d'un cadeau*) lavishness.

son [sɔ̃], **sa** [sa], *pl* **ses** [se] *dét* (*antécédent humain mâle*) his; (*: femelle*) her; (*: valeur indéfinie*) one's, his/her; (*: non humain*) its; *voir note sous* **il**.

son [sɔ̃] *nm* sound; (*de blé etc*) bran; **~ et lumière** *adj inv* son et lumière.

sonar [sɔnaʀ] *nm* (*NAVIG*) sonar.

sonate [sɔnat] *nf* sonata.

sondage [sɔ̃daʒ] *nm* (*de terrain*) boring, drilling; (*mer, atmosphère*) sounding; probe; (*enquête*) survey, sounding out of opinion; ~ (*d'opinion*) (opinion) poll.

sonde [sɔ̃d] *nf* (*NAVIG*) lead *ou* sounding line; (*MÉTÉOROLOGIE*) sonde; (*MÉD*) probe; catheter; (*d'alimentation*) feeding tube; (*TECH*) borer, driller; (*de forage, sondage*) drill; (*pour fouiller etc*) probe; ~ **à avalanche** pole (*for probing snow and locating victims*); ~ **spatiale** probe.

sonder [sɔ̃de] *vt* (*NAVIG*) to sound; (*atmosphère, plaie, bagages etc*) to probe; (*TECH*) to bore, drill; (*fig: personne*) to sound out; (: *opinion*) to probe; ~ **le terrain** (*fig*) to see how the land lies.

songe [sɔ̃ʒ] *nm* dream.

songer [sɔ̃ʒe] *vi* to dream; ~ **à** (*rêver à*) to muse over, think over; (*penser à*) to think of; (*envisager*) to contemplate, think of, consider; ~ **que** to consider that; to think that.

songerie [sɔ̃ʒʀi] *nf* reverie.

songeur, euse [sɔ̃ʒœʀ, -øz] *adj* pensive; **ça me laisse** ~ that makes me wonder.

sonnailles [sɔnaj] *nfpl* jingle of bells.

sonnant, e [sɔnɑ̃, -ɑ̃t] *adj*: **en espèces ~es et trébuchantes** in coin of the realm; **à 8 heures ~es** on the stroke of 8.

sonné, e [sɔne] *adj* (*fam*) cracked; (*passé*): **il est midi** ~ it's gone twelve; **il a quarante ans bien** ~s he's well into his forties.

sonner [sɔne] *vi* (*retentir*) to ring; (*donner une impression*) to sound ♦ *vt* (*cloche*) to ring; (*glas, tocsin*) to sound; (*portier, infirmière*) to ring for; (*messe*) to ring the bell for; (*fam: suj: choc, coup*) to knock out; ~ **du clairon** to sound the bugle; ~ **bien/mal/creux** to sound good/bad/hollow; ~ **faux** (*instrument*) to sound out of tune; (*rire*) to ring false; ~ **les heures** to strike the hours; **minuit vient de** ~ midnight has just struck; ~ **chez qn** to ring sb's doorbell, ring at sb's door.

sonnerie [sɔnʀi] *nf* (*son*) ringing; (*sonnette*) bell; (*mécanisme d'horloge*) striking mechanism; ~ **d'alarme** alarm bell; ~ **de clairon** bugle call.

sonnet [sɔnɛ] *nm* sonnet.

sonnette [sɔnɛt] *nf* bell; ~ **d'alarme** alarm bell; ~ **de nuit** night-bell.

sono [sɔno] *nf* (= *sonorisation*) PA (system); (*d'une discothèque*) sound system.

sonore [sɔnɔʀ] *adj* (*voix*) sonorous, ringing; (*salle, métal*) resonant; (*ondes, film, signal*) sound *cpd*; (*LING*) voiced; **effets ~s** sound effects.

sonorisation [sɔnɔʀizasjɔ̃] *nf* (*installations*) public address system; (*d'une discothèque*) sound system.

sonoriser [sɔnɔʀize] *vt* (*film, spectacle*) to add the sound track to; (*salle*) to fit with a public address system.

sonorité [sɔnɔʀite] *nf* (*de piano, violon*) tone; (*de voix, mot*) sonority; (*d'une salle*) resonance; acoustics *pl*.

sonothèque [sɔnɔtɛk] *nf* sound library.

sont [sɔ̃] *vb voir* **être**.

sophisme [sɔfism(ə)] *nm* sophism.

sophiste [sɔfist(ə)] *nm/f* sophist.

sophistication [sɔfistikasjɔ̃] *nf* sophistication.

sophistiqué, e [sɔfistike] *adj* sophisticated.

soporifique [sɔpɔʀifik] *adj* soporific.

soprano [sɔpʀano] *nm/f* soprano (*pl* -s).

sorbet [sɔʀbɛ] *nm* water ice, sorbet.

sorbetière [sɔʀbɔtjɛʀ] *nf* ice-cream maker.

sorbier [sɔʀbje] *nm* service tree.

sorcellerie [sɔʀsɛlʀi] *nf* witchcraft *no pl*, sorcery *no pl*.

sorcier, ière [sɔʀsje, -jɛʀ] *nm/f* sorcerer/witch *ou* sorceress ♦ *adj*: **ce n'est pas** ~ (*fam*) it's as easy as pie.

sordide [sɔʀdid] *adj* sordid; squalid.

Sorlingues [sɔʀlɛ̃g] *nfpl*: **les (îles)** ~ the Scilly Isles, the Isles of Scilly, the Scillies.

sornettes [sɔʀnɛt] *nfpl* twaddle *sg*.

sort [sɔʀ] *vb voir* **sortir** ♦ *nm* (*fortune, destinée*) fate; (*condition, situation*) lot; (*magique*): **jeter un** ~ to cast a spell; **un coup du** ~ a blow dealt by fate; **le** ~ **en est jeté** the die is cast; **tirer au** ~ to draw lots; **tirer qch au** ~ to draw lots for sth.

sortable [sɔʀtabl(ə)] *adj*: **il n'est pas** ~ you can't take him anywhere.

sortant, e [sɔʀtɑ̃, -ɑ̃t] *vb voir* **sortir** ♦ *adj* (*numéro*) which comes up (*in a draw etc*); (*député, président*) outgoing.

sorte [sɔʀt(ə)] *vb voir* **sortir** ♦ *nf* sort, kind; **de la** ~ *adv* in that way; **en quelque** ~ in a way; **de** ~ **à** so as to, in order to; **de (telle)** ~ **que, en** ~ **que** (*de manière que*) so that; (*si bien que*) so much so that; **faire en** ~ **que** to see to it that.

sortie [sɔʀti] *nf* (*issue*) way out, exit; (*MIL*) sortie; (*fig: verbale*) outburst, sally; (: *parole incongrue*) odd remark; (*d'un gaz, de l'eau*) outlet; (*promenade*) outing; (*le soir: au restaurant etc*) night out; (*de produits*) export; (*de capitaux*) outflow; (*COMM: somme*): ~**s** items of expenditure; outgoings *sans sg*; (*INFORM*) output; (*d'imprimante*) printout; **à sa** ~ as he went out *ou* left; **à la** ~ **de l'école/l'usine** (*moment*) after school/work; when school/the factory comes out; (*lieu*) at the school/factory gates; **à la** ~ **de ce nouveau modèle** when this new model comes out (*ou* came out), when they bring (*ou* brought) out this new model; ~ **de bain** (*vêtement*) bathrobe; "~ **de camions**" "vehicle exit"; ~ **papier** hard copy; ~ **de secours** emergency exit.

sortilège [sɔʀtilɛʒ] *nm* (magic) spell.

sortir [sɔʀtiʀ] *vi* (*gén*) to come out; (*partir, se promener, aller au spectacle etc*) to go out; (*bourgeon, plante, numéro gagnant*) to come up ♦ *vt* (*gén*) to take out; (*produit, ouvrage, modèle*) to bring out; (*boniments, incongruités*) to come out with; (*INFORM*) to output; (: *sur papier*) to print out; (*fam: expulser*) to throw out ♦ *nm*: **au ~ de l'hiver/ l'enfance** as winter/childhood nears its end; **~ qch de** to take sth out of; **~ qn d'embarras** to get sb out of trouble; **~ de** (*gén*) to leave; (*endroit*) to go (*ou* come) out of, leave; (*rainure etc*) to get out of; (*maladie*) to get over; (*époque*) to get through; (*cadre, compétence*) to be outside; (*provenir de: famille etc*) to come from; **~ de table** to leave the table; **~ du système** (*INFORM*) to log out; **~ de ses gonds** (*fig*) to fly off the handle; **se ~ de** (*affaire, situation*) to get out of; **s'en ~** (*malade*) to pull through; (*d'une difficulté etc*) to come through all right; to get through; be able to manage.

SOS *sigle m* mayday, SOS.

sosie [sɔzi] *nm* double.

sot, sotte [so, sɔt] *adj* silly, foolish ♦ *nm/f* fool.

sottement [sɔtmɑ̃] *adv* foolishly.

sottise [sɔtiz] *nf* silliness *no pl*, foolishness *no pl*; (*propos, acte*) silly *ou* foolish thing (to do *ou* say).

sou [su] *nm*: **près de ses ~s** tight-fisted; **sans le ~** penniless; **~ à ~** penny by penny; **pas un ~ de bon sens** not a scrap *ou* an ounce of good sense; **de quatre ~s** worthless.

souahéli, e [swaeli] *adj* Swahili ♦ *nm* (*LING*) Swahili.

soubassement [subasmɑ̃] *nm* base.

soubresaut [subʀəso] *nm* (*de peur etc*) start; (*cahot: d'un véhicule*) jolt.

soubrette [subʀɛt] *nf* soubrette, maidservant.

souche [suʃ] *nf* (*d'arbre*) stump; (*de carnet*) counterfoil (*BRIT*), stub; **dormir comme une ~** to sleep like a log; **de vieille ~** of old stock.

souci [susi] *nm* (*inquiétude*) worry; (*préoccupation*) concern; (*BOT*) marigold; **se faire du ~** to worry; **avoir (le) ~ de** to have concern for; **par ~ de** for the sake of, out of concern for.

soucier [susje]: **se ~ de** *vt* to care about.

soucieux, euse [susjø, -øz] *adj* concerned, worried; **~ de** concerned about; **peu ~ de/ que** caring little about/whether.

soucoupe [sukup] *nf* saucer; **~ volante** flying saucer.

soudain, e [sudɛ̃, -ɛn] *adj* (*douleur, mort*) sudden ♦ *adv* suddenly, all of a sudden.

soudainement [sudɛnmɑ̃] *adv* suddenly.

soudaineté [sudɛnte] *nf* suddenness.

Soudan [sudɑ̃] *nm*: **le ~** the Sudan.

soudanais, e [sudanɛ, -ɛz] *adj* Sudanese.

soude [sud] *nf* soda.

soudé, e [sude] *adj* (*fig: pétales, organes*) joined (together).

souder [sude] *vt* (*avec fil à souder*) to solder; (*par soudure autogène*) to weld; (*fig*) to bind

ou knit together; to fuse (together); **se ~** *vi* (*os*) to knit (together).

soudeur, euse [sudœʀ, -øz] *nm/f* (*ouvrier*) welder.

soudoyer [sudwaje] *vt* (*péj*) to bribe, buy over.

soudure [sudyʀ] *nf* soldering; welding; (*joint*) soldered joint; weld; **faire la ~** (*COMM*) to fill a gap; (*fig: assurer une transition*) to bridge the gap.

souffert, e [sufɛʀ, -ɛʀt(ə)] *pp de* **souffrir**.

soufflage [suflaʒ] *nm* (*du verre*) glass-blowing.

souffle [sufl(ə)] *nm* (*en expirant*) breath; (*en soufflant*) puff, blow; (*respiration*) breathing; (*d'explosion, de ventilateur*) blast; (*du vent*) blowing; (*fig*) inspiration; **retenir son ~** to hold one's breath; **avoir du/manquer de ~** to have a lot of puff/be short of breath; **être à bout de ~** to be out of breath; **avoir le ~ court** to be short-winded; **un ~ d'air** *ou* **de vent** a breath of air, a puff of wind; **~ au cœur** (*MÉD*) heart murmur.

soufflé, e [sufle] *adj* (*CULIN*) soufflé; (*fam: ahuri, stupéfié*) staggered ♦ *nm* (*CULIN*) soufflé.

souffler [sufle] *vi* (*gén*) to blow; (*haleter*) to puff (and blow) ♦ *vt* (*feu, bougie*) to blow out; (*chasser: poussière etc*) to blow away; (*TECH: verre*) to blow; (*suj: explosion*) to destroy (with its blast); (*dire*): **~ qch à qn** to whisper sth to sb; (*fam: voler*): **~ qch à qn** to pinch sth from sb; **~ son rôle à qn** to prompt sb; **ne pas ~ mot** not to breathe a word; **laisser ~ qn** (*fig*) to give sb a breather.

soufflet [suflɛ] *nm* (*instrument*) bellows *pl*; (*entre wagons*) vestibule; (*COUTURE*) gusset; (*gifle*) slap (in the face).

souffleur, euse [suflœʀ, -øz] *nm/f* (*THÉÂT*) prompter; (*TECH*) glass-blower.

souffrance [sufʀɑ̃s] *nf* suffering; **en ~** (*marchandise*) awaiting delivery; (*affaire*) pending.

souffrant, e [sufʀɑ̃, -ɑ̃t] *adj* unwell.

souffre-douleur [sufʀədulœʀ] *nm inv* whipping boy (*BRIT*), butt, underdog.

souffreteux, euse [sufʀətø, -øz] *adj* sickly.

souffrir [sufʀiʀ] *vi* to suffer; (*éprouver des douleurs*) to be in pain ♦ *vt* to suffer, endure; (*supporter*) to bear, stand; (*admettre: exception etc*) to allow *ou* admit of; **~ de** (*maladie, froid*) to suffer from; **~ des dents** to have trouble with one's teeth; **ne pas pouvoir ~ qch/que** ... not to be able to endure *ou* bear sth/that ...; **faire ~ qn** (*suj: personne*) to make sb suffer; (: *dents, blessure etc*) to hurt sb.

soufre [sufʀ(ə)] *nm* sulphur (*BRIT*), sulfur (*US*).

soufrer [sufʀe] *vt* (*vignes*) to treat with sulphur *ou* sulfur.

souhait [swɛ] *nm* wish; **tous nos ~s de** good wishes *ou* our best wishes for; **riche** *etc* **à ~** as rich *etc* as one could wish; **à vos ~s!**

bless you!

souhaitable [swɛtabl(ə)] *adj* desirable.

souhaiter [swete] *vt* to wish for; ~ **le bonjour à qn** to bid sb good day; ~ **la bonne année à qn** to wish sb a happy New Year; **il est à** ~ **que** it is to be hoped that.

souiller [suje] *vt* to dirty, soil; (*fig*) to sully, tarnish.

souillure [sujyʀ] *nf* stain.

soûl, e [su, sul] *adj* drunk; (*fig*): ~ **de musique/plaisirs** drunk with music/pleasure ♦ *nm*: **tout son** ~ to one's heart's content.

soulagement [sulaʒmɑ̃] *nm* relief.

soulager [sulaʒe] *vt* to relieve; ~ **qn de** to relieve sb of.

soûler [sule] *vt*: ~ **qn** to get sb drunk; (*suj: boisson*) to make sb drunk; (*fig*) to make sb's head spin *ou* reel; **se** ~ to get drunk; **se** ~ **de** (*fig*) to intoxicate o.s. with.

soûlerie [sulʀi] *nf* (*péj*) drunken binge.

soulèvement [sulɛvmɑ̃] *nm* uprising; (*GÉO*) upthrust.

soulever [sulve] *vt* to lift; (*vagues, poussière*) to send up; (*peuple*) to stir up (to revolt); (*enthousiasme*) to arouse; (*question, débat, protestations, difficultés*) to raise; **se** ~ *vi* (*peuple*) to rise up; (*personne couchée*) to lift o.s. up; (*couvercle etc*) to lift; **cela me soulève le cœur** it makes me feel sick.

soulier [sulje] *nm* shoe; ~**s bas** low-heeled shoes; ~**s plats/à talons** flat/heeled shoes.

souligner [suliɲe] *vt* to underline; (*fig*) to emphasize, stress.

soumettre [sumɛtʀ] *vt* (*pays*) to subject, subjugate; (*rebelles*) to put down, subdue; ~ **qn/qch à** to subject sb/sth to; ~ **qch à qn** (*projet etc*) to submit sth to sb; **se** ~ (**à**) (*se rendre, obéir*) to submit (to); **se** ~ **à** (*formalités etc*) to submit to; (*régime etc*) to submit o.s. to.

soumis, e [sumi, -iz] *pp de* **soumettre** ♦ *adj* submissive; **revenus** ~ **à l'impôt** taxable income.

soumission [sumisjɔ̃] *nf* (*voir se soumettre*) submission; (*docilité*) submissiveness; (*COMM*) tender.

soumissionner [sumisjɔne] *vt* (*COMM: travaux*) to bid for, tender for.

soupape [supap] *nf* valve; ~ **de sûreté** safety valve.

soupçon [supsɔ̃] *nm* suspicion; (*petite quantité*): **un** ~ **de** a hint *ou* touch of; **avoir** ~ **de** to suspect; **au dessus de tout** ~ above (all) suspicion.

soupçonner [supsɔne] *vt* to suspect; ~ **qn de qch/d'être** to suspect sb of sth/of being.

soupçonneux, euse [supsɔnø, -øz] *adj* suspicious.

soupe [sup] *nf* soup; ~ **au lait** *adj inv* quick-tempered; ~ **à l'oignon/de poisson** onion/fish soup; ~ **populaire** soup kitchen.

soupente [supɑ̃t] *nf* (*mansarde*) attic; (*placard*)

cupboard (*BRIT*) *ou* closet (*US*) under the stairs.

souper [supe] *vi* to have supper ♦ *nm* supper; **avoir soupé de** (*fam*) to be sick and tired of.

soupeser [supəze] *vt* to weigh in one's hand(s), feel the weight of; (*fig*) to weigh up.

soupière [supjɛʀ] *nf* (soup) tureen.

soupir [supiʀ] *nm* sigh; (*MUS*) crotchet rest (*BRIT*), quarter note rest (*US*); **rendre le dernier** ~ to breathe one's last.

soupirail, aux [supiʀaj, -o] *nm* (small) basement window.

soupirant [supiʀɑ̃] *nm* (*péj*) suitor, wooer.

soupirer [supiʀe] *vi* to sigh; ~ **après qch** to yearn for sth.

souple [supl(ə)] *adj* supple; (*col*) soft; (*fig: règlement, caractère*) flexible; (: *démarche, taille*) lithe, supple; **disque(tte)** ~ (*INFORM*) floppy disk, diskette.

souplesse [suplɛs] *nf* suppleness; flexibility.

source [suʀs(ə)] *nf* (*point d'eau*) spring; (*d'un cours d'eau, fig*) source; **prendre sa** ~ **à/dans** (*suj: cours d'eau*) to have its source at/in; **tenir qch de bonne** ~/**de** ~ **sûre** to have sth on good authority/from a reliable source; ~ **thermale/d'eau minérale** hot *ou* thermal/mineral spring.

sourcier, ière [suʀsje, -jɛʀ] *nm* water diviner.

sourcil [suʀsij] *nm* (eye)brow.

sourcilière [suʀsiljɛʀ] *adj f voir* **arcade**.

sourciller [suʀsije] *vi*: **sans** ~ without turning a hair *ou* batting an eyelid.

sourcilleux, euse [suʀsijø, -øz] *adj* (*hautain, sévère*) haughty, supercilious; (*pointilleux*) finicky, pernickety.

sourd, e [suʀ, suʀd(ə)] *adj* deaf; (*bruit, voix*) muffled; (*couleur*) muted; (*douleur*) dull; (*lutte*) silent, hidden; (*LING*) voiceless ♦ *nm/f* deaf person; **être** ~ **à** to be deaf to.

sourdement [suʀdəmɑ̃] *adv* (*avec un bruit sourd*) dully; (*secrètement*) silently.

sourdine [suʀdin] *nf* (*MUS*) mute; **en** ~ *adv* softly, quietly; **mettre une** ~ **à** (*fig*) to tone down.

sourd-muet, sourde-muette [suʀmyɛ, suʀdmyɛt] *adj* deaf-and-dumb ♦ *nm/f* deaf-mute.

sourdre [suʀdʀ(ə)] *vi* (*eau*) to spring up; (*fig*) to rise.

souriant, e [suʀjɑ̃, -ɑ̃t] *vb voir* **sourire** ♦ *adj* cheerful.

souricière [suʀisjɛʀ] *nf* mousetrap; (*fig*) trap.

sourie [suʀi] *etc vb voir* **sourire**.

sourire [suʀiʀ] *nm* smile ♦ *vi* to smile; ~ **à qn** to smile at sb; (*fig*) to appeal to sb; (: *chance*) to smile on sb; **faire un** ~ **à qn** to give sb a smile; **garder le** ~ to keep smiling.

souris [suʀi] *nf* mouse (*pl* mice); (*INFORM*) mouse.

sournois, e [suʀnwa, -waz] *adj* deceitful, underhand.

sournoisement [suʀnwazmɑ̃] _adv_ deceitfully.
sournoiserie [suʀnwazʀi] _nf_ deceitfulness, underhandedness.
sous [su] _prép (gén)_ under; ~ **la pluie/le soleil** in the rain/sunshine; ~ **mes yeux** before my eyes; ~ **terre** _adj, adv_ underground; ~ **vide** _adj, adv_ vacuum-packed; ~ **l'influence/l'action de** under the influence of/by the action of; ~ **antibiotiques/perfusion** on antibiotics/a drip; ~ **cet angle/ce rapport** from this angle/in this respect; ~ **peu** _adv_ shortly, before long.
sous... [su, suz + _vowel_] _préfixe_ sub-; under....
sous-alimentation [suzalimɑ̃tasjɔ̃] _nf_ undernourishment.
sous-alimenté, e [suzalimɑ̃te] _adj_ undernourished.
sous-bois [subwa] _nm inv_ undergrowth.
sous-catégorie [sukategɔʀi] _nf_ subcategory.
sous-chef [suʃɛf] _nm_ deputy chief, second in command; ~ **de bureau** deputy head clerk.
sous-comité [sukɔmite] _nm_ subcommittee.
sous-commission [sukɔmisjɔ̃] _nf_ subcommittee.
sous-continent [sukɔ̃tinɑ̃] _nm_ subcontinent.
sous-couche [sukuʃ] _nf (de peinture)_ undercoat.
souscripteur, trice [suskʀiptœʀ, -tʀis] _nm/f_ subscriber.
souscription [suskʀipsjɔ̃] _nf_ subscription; **offert en** ~ available on subscription.
souscrire [suskʀiʀ]: ~ **à** _vt_ to subscribe to.
sous-cutané, e [sukytane] _adj_ subcutaneous.
sous-développé, e [sudevlɔpe] _adj_ underdeveloped.
sous-développement [sudevlɔpmɑ̃] _nm_ underdevelopment.
sous-directeur, trice [sudiʀɛktœʀ, -tʀis] _nm/f_ assistant manager/manageress, submanager/manageress.
sous-emploi [suzɑ̃plwa] _nm_ underemployment.
sous-employé, e [suzɑ̃plwaje] _adj_ underemployed.
sous-ensemble [suzɑ̃sɑ̃bl(ə)] _nm_ subset.
sous-entendre [suzɑ̃tɑ̃dʀ(ə)] _vt_ to imply, infer.
sous-entendu, e [suzɑ̃tɑ̃dy] _adj_ implied; _(LING)_ understood ♦ _nm_ innuendo, insinuation.
sous-équipé, e [suzekipe] _adj_ underequipped; ~ **en infrastructures industrielles** _(ÉCON: pays, région)_ with an insufficient industrial infrastructure.
sous-estimer [suzɛstime] _vt_ to underestimate.
sous-exploiter [suzɛksplwate] _vt_ to underexploit.
sous-exposer [suzɛkspoze] _vt_ to underexpose.
sous-fifre [sufifʀ(ə)] _nm (péj)_ underling.
sous-groupe [sugʀup] _nm_ subgroup.

sous-homme [suzɔm] _nm_ sub-human.
sous-jacent, e [suʒasɑ̃, -ɑ̃t] _adj_ underlying.
sous-lieutenant [suljøtnɑ̃] _nm_ sub-lieutenant.
sous-locataire [sulɔkatɛʀ] _nm/f_ subtenant.
sous-location [sulɔkasjɔ̃] _nf_ subletting.
sous-louer [sulwe] _vt_ to sublet.
sous-main [sumɛ̃] _nm inv_ desk blotter; **en** ~ _adv_ secretly.
sous-marin, e [sumaʀɛ̃, -in] _adj (flore, volcan)_ submarine; _(navigation, pêche, explosif)_ underwater ♦ _nm_ submarine.
sous-médicalisé, e [sumedikalize] _adj_ lacking adequate medical care.
sous-nappe [sunap] _nf_ undercloth.
sous-officier [suzɔfisje] _nm_ ≈ non-commissioned officer (NCO).
sous-ordre [suzɔʀdʀ(ə)] _nm_ subordinate; **créancier en** ~ creditor's creditor.
sous-payé, e [supeje] _adj_ underpaid.
sous-préfecture [supʀefɛktyʀ] _nf_ subprefecture.
sous-préfet [supʀefɛ] _nm_ sub-prefect.
sous-production [supʀɔdyksjɔ̃] _nf_ underproduction.
sous-produit [supʀɔdɥi] _nm_ by-product; _(fig: péj)_ pale imitation.
sous-programme [supʀɔgʀam] _nm (INFORM)_ subroutine.
sous-pull [supul] _nm_ thin poloneck sweater.
sous-secrétaire [susəkʀetɛʀ] _nm:_ ~ **d'État** Under-Secretary of State.
soussigné, e [susiɲe] _adj:_ **je** ~ I the undersigned.
sous-sol [susɔl] _nm_ basement; _(GÉO)_ subsoil.
sous-tasse [sutas] _nf_ saucer.
sous-tendre [sutɑ̃dʀ(ə)] _vt_ to underlie.
sous-titre [sutitʀ(ə)] _nm_ subtitle.
sous-titré, e [sutitʀe] _adj_ with subtitles.
soustraction [sustʀaksjɔ̃] _nf_ subtraction.
soustraire [sustʀɛʀ] _vt_ to subtract, take away; _(dérober):_ ~ **qch à qn** to remove sth from sb; ~ **qn à** _(danger)_ to shield sb from; **se** ~ **à** _(autorité, obligation, devoir)_ to elude, escape from.
sous-traitance [sutʀɛtɑ̃s(ə)] _nf_ subcontracting.
sous-traitant [sutʀɛtɑ̃] _nm_ subcontractor.
sous-traiter [sutʀete] _vt, vi_ to subcontract.
soustrayais [sustʀɛjɛ] _etc vb voir_ **soustraire**.
sous-verre [suvɛʀ] _nm inv_ glass mount.
sous-vêtement [suvɛtmɑ̃] _nm_ undergarment, item of underwear; ~**s** _nmpl_ underwear _sg_.
soutane [sutan] _nf_ cassock, soutane.
soute [sut] _nf_ hold; ~ **à bagages** baggage hold.
soutenable [sutnabl(ə)] _adj (opinion)_ tenable, defensible.
soutenance [sutnɑ̃s] _nf:_ ~ **de thèse** ≈ viva (voce).
soutènement [sutɛnmɑ̃] _nm:_ **mur de** ~ retaining wall.
souteneur [sutnœʀ] _nm_ procurer.

soutenir [sutniʀ] *vt* to support; (*assaut, choc, regard*) to stand up to, withstand; (*intérêt, effort*) to keep up; (*assurer*): ~ **que** to maintain that; **se** ~ (*dans l'eau etc*) to hold o.s. up; (*être soutenable: point de vue*) to be tenable; (*s'aider mutuellement*) to stand by each other; ~ **la comparaison avec** to bear *ou* stand comparison with; ~ **le regard de qn** to be able to look sb in the face.

soutenu, e [sutny] *pp de* **soutenir** ♦ *adj* (*efforts*) sustained, unflagging; (*style*) elevated; (*couleur*) strong.

souterrain, e [sutɛʀɛ, -ɛn] *adj* underground; (*fig*) subterranean ♦ *nm* underground passage.

soutien [sutjɛ̃] *nm* support; **apporter son** ~ **à** to lend one's support to; ~ **de famille** breadwinner.

soutiendrai [sutjɛ̃dʀe] *etc vb voir* **soutenir**.

soutien-gorge, *pl* **soutiens-gorge** [sutjɛ̃gɔʀʒ(ə)] *nm* bra; (*de maillot de bain*) top.

soutiens [sutjɛ̃], **soutint** [sutɛ̃] *etc vb voir* **soutenir**.

soutirer [sutiʀe] *vt*: ~ **qch à qn** to squeeze *ou* get sth out of sb.

souvenance [suvnɑ̃s] *nf*: **avoir** ~ **de** to recollect.

souvenir [suvniʀ] *nm* (*réminiscence*) memory; (*cadeau*) souvenir, keepsake; (*de voyage*) souvenir ♦ *vb*: **se** ~ **de** *vt* to remember; **se** ~ **que** to remember that; **garder le** ~ **de** to retain the memory of; **en** ~ **de** in memory *ou* remembrance of; **avec mes affectueux/meilleurs** ~**s**, ... with love from, .../ regards, ...

souvent [suvɑ̃] *adv* often; **peu** ~ seldom, infrequently; **le plus** ~ more often than not, most often.

souvenu, e [suvəny] *pp de* **se souvenir**.

souverain, e [suvʀɛ̃, -ɛn] *adj* sovereign; (*fig: mépris*) supreme ♦ *nm/f* sovereign, monarch.

souverainement [suvʀɛnmɑ̃] *adv* (*sans appel*) with sovereign power; (*extrêmement*) supremely, intensely.

souveraineté [suvʀɛnte] *nf* sovereignty.

souviendrai [suvjɛ̃dʀe], **souviens** [suvjɛ̃], **souvint** [suvɛ̃] *etc vb voir* **se souvenir**.

soviétique [sɔvjetik] *adj* Soviet ♦ *nm/f*: **S**~ Soviet citizen.

soviétiser [sɔvjetize] *vt* to sovietize.

soviétologue [sɔvjetɔlɔg] *nm/f* Kremlinologist.

soyeux, euse [swajø, -øz] *adj* silky.

soyez [swaje] *etc vb voir* **être**.

SPA *sigle f* (= *Société protectrice des animaux*) ≈ RSPCA (*BRIT*), ≈ SPCA (*US*).

spacieux, euse [spasjø, -øz] *adj* spacious; roomy.

spaciosité [spasjozite] *nf* spaciousness.

spaghettis [spageti] *nmpl* spaghetti *sg*.

sparadrap [spaʀadʀa] *nm* adhesive *ou* sticking (*BRIT*) plaster, bandaid ® (*US*).

Sparte [spaʀt(ə)] *nf* Sparta.

spartiate [spaʀsjat] *adj* Spartan; ~**s** *nfpl* (*sandales*) Roman sandals.

spasme [spazm(ə)] *nm* spasm.

spasmodique [spazmɔdik] *adj* spasmodic.

spatial, e, aux [spasjal, -o] *adj* (*AVIAT*) space *cpd*; (*PSYCH*) spatial.

spatule [spatyl] *nf* (*ustensile*) slice; spatula; (*bout*) tip.

speaker, ine [spikœʀ, -kʀin] *nm/f* announcer.

spécial, e, aux [spesjal, -o] *adj* special; (*bizarre*) peculiar.

spécialement [spesjalmɑ̃] *adv* especially, particularly; (*tout exprès*) specially; **pas** ~ not particularly.

spécialisation [spesjalizasjɔ̃] *nf* specialization.

spécialisé, e [spesjalize] *adj* specialised; **ordinateur** ~ dedicated computer.

spécialiser [spesjalize]: **se** ~ *vi* to specialize.

spécialiste [spesjalist(ə)] *nm/f* specialist.

spécialité [spesjalite] *nf* speciality; (*SCOL*) special field; ~ **pharmaceutique** patent medicine.

spécieux, euse [spesjø, -øz] *adj* specious.

spécification [spesifikasjɔ̃] *nf* specification.

spécificité [spesifisite] *nf* specificity.

spécifier [spesifje] *vt* to specify, state.

spécifique [spesifik] *adj* specific.

spécifiquement [spesifikmɑ̃] *adv* (*typiquement*) typically; (*tout exprès*) specifically.

spécimen [spesimɛn] *nm* specimen; (*revue etc*) specimen *ou* sample copy.

spectacle [spɛktakl(ə)] *nm* (*tableau, scène*) sight; (*représentation*) show; (*industrie*) show business, entertainment; **se donner en** ~ (*péj*) to make a spectacle *ou* an exhibition of o.s; **pièce/revue à grand** ~ spectacular (play/revue); **au** ~ **de ...** at the sight of ....

spectaculaire [spɛktakylɛʀ] *adj* spectacular.

spectateur, trice [spɛktatœʀ, -tʀis] *nm/f* (*CINÉ etc*) member of the audience; (*SPORT*) spectator; (*d'un événement*) onlooker, witness.

spectre [spɛktʀ(ə)] *nm* (*fantôme, fig*) spectre; (*PHYSIQUE*) spectrum (*pl* -a); ~ **solaire** solar spectrum.

spéculateur, trice [spekylatœʀ, -tʀis] *nm/f* speculator.

spéculatif, ive [spekylatif, -iv] *adj* speculative.

spéculation [spekylasjɔ̃] *nf* speculation.

spéculer [spekyle] *vi* to speculate; ~ **sur** (*COMM*) to speculate in; (*réfléchir*) to speculate on; (*tabler sur*) to bank *ou* rely on.

spéléologie [speleɔlɔʒi] *nf* (*étude*) speleology; (*activité*) potholing.

spéléologue [speleɔlɔg] *nm/f* speleologist; potholer.

spermatozoïde [spɛʀmatozɔid] *nm* sperm, spermatozoon (*pl* -zoa).

sperme [spɛʀm(ə)] *nm* semen, sperm.
spermicide [spɛʀmisid] *adj*, *nm* spermicide.
sphère [sfɛʀ] *nf* sphere.
sphérique [sferik] *adj* spherical.
sphincter [sfɛ̃ktɛʀ] *nm* sphincter.
sphinx [sfɛ̃ks] *nm inv* sphinx; (*ZOOL*) hawkmoth.
spiral, aux [spiʀal, -o] *nm* hairspring.
spirale [spiʀal] *nf* spiral; **en ~** in a spiral.
spire [spiʀ] *nf* (*d'une spirale*) turn; (*d'une coquille*) whorl.
spiritisme [spiʀitism(ə)] *nm* spiritualism, spiritism.
spirituel, le [spiʀitɥɛl] *adj* spiritual; (*fin, piquant*) witty; **musique ~le** sacred music; **concert ~** concert of sacred music.
spirituellement [spiʀitɥɛlmɑ̃] *adv* spiritually; wittily.
spiritueux [spiʀitɥø] *nm* spirit.
splendeur [splɑ̃dœʀ] *nf* splendour (*BRIT*), splendor (*US*).
splendide [splɑ̃did] *adj* splendid, magnificent.
spolier [spɔlje] *vt*: **~ qn (de)** to despoil sb (of).
spongieux, euse [spɔ̃ʒjø, -øz] *adj* spongy.
sponsor [spɔ̃sɔʀ] *nm* sponsor.
sponsoriser [spɔ̃sɔʀize] *vt* to sponsor.
spontané, e [spɔ̃tane] *adj* spontaneous.
spontanéité [spɔ̃taneite] *nf* spontaneity.
spontanément [spɔ̃tanemɑ̃] *adv* spontaneously.
sporadique [spɔʀadik] *adj* sporadic.
sporadiquement [spɔʀadikmɑ̃] *adv* sporadically.
sport [spɔʀ] *nm* sport ♦ *adj inv* (*vêtement*) casual; (*fair-play*) sporting; **faire du ~** to do sport; **~ individuel/d'équipe** individual/team sport; **~ de combat** combative sport; **~s d'hiver** winter sports.
sportif, ive [spɔʀtif, -iv] *adj* (*journal, association, épreuve*) sports *cpd*; (*allure, démarche*) athletic; (*attitude, esprit*) sporting; **les résultats ~s** the sports results.
sportivement [spɔʀtivmɑ̃] *adv* sportingly.
sportivité [spɔʀtivite] *nf* sportsmanship.
spot [spɔt] *nm* (*lampe*) spot(light); (*annonce*): **~ (publicitaire)** commercial (break).
spray [spʀɛ] *nm* spray, aerosol.
sprint [spʀint] *nm* sprint; **piquer un ~** to put on a (final) spurt.
sprinter *nm* [spʀintœʀ] sprinter ♦ *vi* [spʀinte] to sprint.
squale [skwal] *nm* (*type of*) shark.
square [skwaʀ] *nm* public garden(s).
squash [skwaʃ] *nm* squash.
squat [skwat] *nm* (*lieu*) squat.
squatter *nm* [skwatœʀ] squatter ♦ *vt* [skwate] to squat.
squelette [skəlɛt] *nm* skeleton.
squelettique [skəletik] *adj* scrawny; (*fig*) skimpy.
Sri Lanka [sʀilɑ̃ka] *nm* Sri Lanka.
sri-lankais, e [sʀilɑ̃kɛ, -ɛz] *adj* Sri-Lankan.

SS *sigle f* = **sécurité sociale**; (= *Sa Sainteté*) HH.
ss *abr* = **sous**.
S/S *sigle m* (= *steamship*) SS.
SSR *sigle f* (= *Société suisse romande*) the Swiss French-language broadcasting company.
stabilisateur, trice [stabilizatœʀ, -tʀis] *adj* stabilizing ♦ *nm* stabilizer; (*véhicule*) anti-roll device; (*avion*) tailplane.
stabiliser [stabilize] *vt* to stabilize; (*terrain*) to consolidate.
stabilité [stabilite] *nf* stability.
stable [stabl(ə)] *adj* stable, steady.
stade [stad] *nm* (*SPORT*) stadium; (*phase, niveau*) stage.
stage [staʒ] *nm* training period; training course; (*d'avocat stagiaire*) articles *pl*.
stagiaire [staʒjɛʀ] *nm/f*, *adj* trainee (*cpd*).
stagnant, e [stagnɑ̃, -ɑ̃t] *adj* stagnant.
stagnation [stagnasjɔ̃] *nf* stagnation.
stagner [stagne] *vi* to stagnate.
stalactite [stalaktit] *nf* stalactite.
stalagmite [stalagmit] *nf* stalagmite.
stalle [stal] *nf* stall, box.
stand [stɑ̃d] *nm* (*d'exposition*) stand; (*de foire*) stall; **~ de tir** (*à la foire, SPORT*) shooting range; **~ de ravitaillement** pit.
standard [stɑ̃daʀ] *adj inv* standard ♦ *nm* (*type, norme*) standard; (*téléphonique*) switchboard.
standardisation [stɑ̃daʀdizasjɔ̃] *nf* standardization.
standardiser [stɑ̃daʀdize] *vt* to standardize.
standardiste [stɑ̃daʀdist(ə)] *nm/f* switchboard operator.
standing [stɑ̃diŋ] *nm* standing; **immeuble de grand ~** block of luxury flats (*BRIT*), condo(minium) (*US*).
star [staʀ] *nf* star.
starlette [staʀlɛt] *nf* starlet.
starter [staʀtɛʀ] *nm* (*AUTO*) choke; (*SPORT: personne*) starter; **mettre le ~** to pull out the choke.
station [stasjɔ̃] *nf* station; (*de bus*) stop; (*de villégiature*) resort; (*posture*): **la ~ debout** standing, an upright posture; **~ balnéaire** seaside resort; **~ de graissage** lubrication bay; **~ de lavage** carwash; **~ de ski** ski resort; **~ de sports d'hiver** winter sports resort; **~ de taxis** taxi rank (*BRIT*) *ou* stand (*US*); **~ thermale** thermal spa; **~ de travail** workstation.
stationnaire [stasjɔnɛʀ] *adj* stationary.
stationnement [stasjɔnmɑ̃] *nm* parking; **zone de ~ interdit** no parking area; **~ alterné** parking on alternate sides.
stationner [stasjɔne] *vi* to park.
station-service [stasjɔ̃sɛʀvis] *nf* service station.
statique [statik] *adj* static.
statisticien, ne [statistisjɛ̃, -ɛn] *nm/f* statistician.
statistique [statistik] *nf* (*science*) statistics *sg*;

(*rapport, étude*) statistic ♦ *adj* statistical; **~s**
nfpl (*données*) statistics *pl*.

statistiquement [statistikmɑ̃] *adv*
statistically.

statue [staty] *nf* statue.

statuer [statɥe] *vi*: **~ sur** to rule on, give a
ruling on.

statuette [statɥɛt] *nf* statuette.

statu quo [statykwo] *nm* status quo.

stature [statyʀ] *nf* stature; **de haute ~** of
great stature.

statut [staty] *nm* status; **~s** *nmpl* (*JUR, ADMIN*)
statutes.

statutaire [statytɛʀ] *adj* statutory.

St(e) *abr* (= *Saint(e)*) St.

Sté *abr* (= *société*) soc.

steak [stɛk] *nm* steak.

stèle [stɛl] *nf* stela, stele.

stellaire [stelɛʀ] *adj* stellar.

stencil [stɛnsil] *nm* stencil.

sténodactylo [stenɔdaktilo] *nm/f* shorthand
typist (*BRIT*), stenographer (*US*).

sténodactylographie [stenɔdaktilɔgʀafi] *nf*
shorthand typing (*BRIT*), stenography (*US*).

sténo(graphe) [stenɔ(gʀaf)] *nm/f* shorthand
typist (*BRIT*), stenographer (*US*).

sténo(graphie) [stenɔ(gʀafi)] *nf* shorthand;
prendre en ~ to take down in shorthand.

sténographier [stenɔgʀafje] *vt* to take down
in shorthand.

sténographique [stenɔgʀafik] *adj* shorthand
cpd.

stentor [stɑ̃tɔʀ] *nm*: **voix de ~** stentorian
voice.

step [stɛp] *nm* ® step aerobics *sg* ®, step
Reebok ®.

stéphanois, e [stefanwa, -waz] *adj* of *ou* from
Saint-Étienne.

steppe [stɛp] *nf* steppe.

stère [stɛʀ] *nm* stere.

stéréo(phonie) [steʀeɔ(fɔni)] *nf*
stereo(phony); **émission en ~** stereo
broadcast.

stéréo(phonique) [steʀeɔ(fɔnik)] *adj*
stereo(phonic).

stéréoscope [steʀeɔskɔp] *nm* stereoscope.

stéréoscopique [steʀeɔskɔpik] *adj*
stereoscopic.

stéréotype [steʀeɔtip] *nm* stereotype.

stéréotypé, e [steʀeɔtipe] *adj* stereotyped.

stérile [steʀil] *adj* sterile; (*terre*) barren; (*fig*)
fruitless, futile.

stérilement [steʀilmɑ̃] *adv* fruitlessly.

stérilet [steʀilɛ] *nm* coil, loop.

stérilisateur [steʀilizatœʀ] *nm* sterilizer.

stérilisation [steʀilizasjɔ̃] *nf* sterilization.

stériliser [steʀilize] *vt* to sterilize.

stérilité [steʀilite] *nf* sterility.

sternum [stɛʀnɔm] *nm* breastbone, sternum.

stéthoscope [stetɔskɔp] *nm* stethoscope.

stick [stik] *nm* stick.

stigmates [stigmat] *nmpl* scars, marks; (*REL*)

stigmata *pl*.

stigmatiser [stigmatize] *vt* to denounce,
stigmatize.

stimulant, e [stimylɑ̃, -ɑ̃t] *adj* stimulating
♦ *nm* (*MÉD*) stimulant; (*fig*) stimulus (*pl* -i),
incentive.

stimulateur [stimylatœʀ] *nm*: **~ cardiaque**
pacemaker.

stimulation [stimylasjɔ̃] *nf* stimulation.

stimuler [stimyle] *vt* to stimulate.

stimulus, i [stimylys, -i] *nm* stimulus (*pl* -i).

stipulation [stipylasjɔ̃] *nf* stipulation.

stipuler [stipyle] *vt* to stipulate, specify.

stock [stɔk] *nm* stock; **en ~** in stock.

stockage [stɔkaʒ] *nm* stocking; storage.

stocker [stɔke] *vt* to stock; (*déchets*) to store.

Stockholm [stɔkɔlm] *n* Stockholm.

stockiste [stɔkist(ə)] *nm* stockist.

stoïcisme [stɔisism(ə)] *nm* stoicism.

stoïque [stɔik] *adj* stoic, stoical.

stoïquement [stɔikmɑ̃] *adv* stoically.

stomacal, e, aux [stɔmakal, -o] *adj* gastric,
stomach *cpd*.

stomatologie [stɔmatɔlɔʒi] *nf* stomatology.

stomatologue [stɔmatɔlɔg] *nm/f*
stomatologist.

stop [stɔp] *nm* (*AUTO: écriteau*) stop sign;
(*: signal*) brake-light; (*dans un télégramme*)
stop ♦ *excl* stop!

stoppage [stɔpaʒ] *nm* invisible mending.

stopper [stɔpe] *vt* to stop, halt; (*COUTURE*) to
mend ♦ *vi* to stop, halt.

store [stɔʀ] *nm* blind; (*de magasin*) shade,
awning.

strabisme [stʀabism(ə)] *nm* squint(ing).

strangulation [stʀɑ̃gylasjɔ̃] *nf* strangulation.

strapontin [stʀapɔ̃tɛ̃] *nm* jump *ou* foldaway
seat.

Strasbourg [stʀazbuʀ] *n* Strasbourg.

strass [stʀas] *nm* paste, strass.

stratagème [stʀataʒɛm] *nm* stratagem.

strate [stʀat] *nf* (*GÉO*) stratum, layer.

stratège [stʀatɛʒ] *nm* strategist.

stratégie [stʀateʒi] *nf* strategy.

stratégique [stʀateʒik] *adj* strategic.

stratégiquement [stʀateʒikmɑ̃] *adv*
strategically.

stratifié, e [stʀatifje] *adj* (*GÉO*) stratified;
(*TECH*) laminated.

stratosphère [stʀatɔsfɛʀ] *nf* stratosphere.

stress [stʀɛs] *nm inv* stress.

stressant, e [stʀɛsɑ̃, -ɑ̃t] *adj* stressful.

stresser [stʀɛse] *vt* to stress, cause stress in.

strict, e [stʀikt(ə)] *adj* strict; (*tenue, décor*)
severe, plain; **son droit le plus ~** his most
basic right; **dans la plus ~e intimité** strictly
in private; **le ~ nécessaire/minimum** the
bare essentials/minimum.

strictement [stʀiktəmɑ̃] *adv* strictly; plainly.

strident, e [stʀidɑ̃, -ɑ̃t] *adj* shrill, strident.

stridulations [stʀidylasjɔ̃] *nfpl* stridulations,
chirrings.

strie [stʀi] *nf* streak; (*ANAT, GÉO*) stria (*pl* -ae).
strier [stʀije] *vt* to streak; to striate.
strip-tease [stʀiptiz] *nm* striptease.
strip-teaseuse [stʀiptizøz] *nf* stripper, striptease artist.
striures [stʀijyʀ] *nfpl* streaking *sg.*
stroboscope [stʀɔbɔskɔp] *nm* strobe (light).
strophe [stʀɔf] *nf* verse, stanza.
structure [stʀyktyʀ] *nf* structure; ~s **d'accueil/touristiques** reception/tourist facilities.
structurer [stʀyktyʀe] *vt* to structure.
strychnine [stʀiknin] *nf* strychnine.
stuc [styk] *nm* stucco.
studieusement [stydjøzmɑ̃] *adv* studiously.
studieux, euse [stydjø, -øz] *adj* (*élève*) studious; (*vacances*) study *cpd.*
studio [stydjo] *nm* (*logement*) studio flat (*BRIT*) *ou* apartment (*US*); (*d'artiste, TV etc*) studio (*pl* -s).
stupéfaction [stypefaksjɔ̃] *nf* stupefaction, astonishment.
stupéfait, e [stypefɛ, -ɛt] *adj* astonished.
stupéfiant, e [stypefjɑ̃, -ɑ̃t] *adj* stunning, astonishing ♦ *nm* (*MÉD*) drug, narcotic.
stupéfier [stypefje] *vt* to stupefy; (*étonner*) to stun, astonish.
stupeur [stypœʀ] *nf* (*inertie, insensibilité*) stupor; (*étonnement*) astonishment, amazement.
stupide [stypid] *adj* stupid; (*hébété*) stunned.
stupidement [stypidmɑ̃] *adv* stupidly.
stupidité [stypidite] *nf* stupidity *no pl*; (*propos, action*) stupid thing (to say *ou* do).
stups [styp] *nmpl* (= *stupéfiants*): **brigade des** ~ narcotics bureau *ou* squad.
style [stil] *nm* style; **meuble/robe de** ~ piece of period furniture/period dress; ~ **de vie** lifestyle.
stylé, e [stile] *adj* well-trained.
stylet [stilɛ] *nm* (*poignard*) stiletto; (*CHIRURGIE*) stylet.
stylisé, e [stilize] *adj* stylized.
styliste [stilist(ə)] *nm/f* designer; stylist.
stylistique [stilistik] *nf* stylistics *sg* ♦ *adj* stylistic.
stylo [stilo] *nm*: ~ (**à encre**) (fountain) pen; ~ (**à) bille** ballpoint pen.
stylo-feutre [stiloføtʀ(ə)] *nm* felt-tip pen.
su, e [sy] *pp de* **savoir** ♦ *nm*: **au** ~ **de** with the knowledge of.
suaire [sɥɛʀ] *nm* shroud.
suant, e [sɥɑ̃, -ɑ̃t] *adj* sweaty.
suave [sɥav] *adj* (*odeur*) sweet; (*voix*) suave, smooth; (*coloris*) soft, mellow.
subalterne [sybaltɛʀn(ə)] *adj* (*employé, officier*) junior; (*rôle*) subordinate, subsidiary ♦ *nm/f* subordinate, inferior.
subconscient [sypkɔ̃sjɑ̃] *nm* subconscious.
subdiviser [sybdivize] *vt* to subdivide.
subdivision [sybdivizjɔ̃] *nf* subdivision.
subir [sybiʀ] *vt* (*affront, dégâts, mauvais*

traitements) to suffer; (*influence, charme*) to be under, be subjected to; (*traitement, opération, châtiment*) to undergo; (*personne*) to suffer, be subjected to.
subit, e [sybi, -it] *adj* sudden.
subitement [sybitmɑ̃] *adv* suddenly, all of a sudden.
subjectif, ive [syb3ɛktif, -iv] *adj* subjective.
subjectivement [syb3ɛktivmɑ̃] *adv* subjectively.
subjectivité [syb3ɛktivite] *nf* subjectivity.
subjonctif [syb3ɔ̃ktif] *nm* subjunctive.
subjuguer [syb3yge] *vt* to subjugate.
sublime [syblim] *adj* sublime.
sublimer [syblime] *vt* to sublimate.
submergé, e [sybmɛʀ3e] *adj* submerged; (*fig*): ~ **de** snowed under with; overwhelmed with.
submerger [sybmɛʀ3e] *vt* to submerge; (*suj: foule*) to engulf; (*fig*) to overwhelm.
submersible [sybmɛʀsibl(ə)] *nm* submarine.
subordination [sybɔʀdinasjɔ̃] *nf* subordination.
subordonné, e [sybɔʀdɔne] *adj, nm/f* subordinate; ~ **à** (*personne*) subordinate to; (*résultats etc*) subject to, depending on.
subordonner [sybɔʀdɔne] *vt*: ~ **qn/qch à** to subordinate sb/sth to.
subornation [sybɔʀnasjɔ̃] *nf* bribing.
suborner [sybɔʀne] *vt* to bribe.
subrepticement [sybʀɛptismɑ̃] *adv* surreptitiously.
subroger [sybʀɔ3e] *vt* (*JUR*) to subrogate.
subside [sypsid] *nm* grant.
subsidiaire [sypsidjɛʀ] *adj* subsidiary; **question** ~ deciding question.
subsistance [sybzistɑ̃s] *nf* subsistence; **pourvoir à la** ~ **de qn** to keep sb, provide for sb's subsistence *ou* keep.
subsister [sybziste] *vi* (*rester*) to remain, subsist; (*vivre*) to live; (*survivre*) to live on.
subsonique [sybsɔnik] *adj* subsonic.
substance [sypstɑ̃s] *nf* substance; **en** ~ in substance.
substantiel, le [sypstɑ̃sjɛl] *adj* substantial.
substantif [sypstɑ̃tif] *nm* noun, substantive.
substantiver [sypstɑ̃tive] *vt* to nominalize.
substituer [sypstitɥe] *vt*: ~ **qn/qch à** to substitute sb/sth for; **se** ~ **à qn** (*représenter*) to substitute for sb; (*évincer*) to substitute o.s. for sb.
substitut [sypstity] *nm* (*JUR*) deputy public prosecutor; (*succédané*) substitute.
substitution [sypstitysjɔ̃] *nf* substitution.
subterfuge [syptɛʀfy3] *nm* subterfuge.
subtil, e [syptil] *adj* subtle.
subtilement [syptilmɑ̃] *adv* subtly.
subtiliser [syptilize] *vt*: ~ **qch (à qn)** to spirit sth away (from sb).
subtilité [syptilite] *nf* subtlety.
subtropical, e, aux [sybtʀɔpikal, -o] *adj* subtropical.

suburbain, e [sybyʀbɛ̃, -ɛn] *adj* suburban.
subvenir [sybvəniʀ]: ~ **à** *vt* to meet.
subvention [sybvɑ̃sjɔ̃] *nf* subsidy, grant.
subventionner [sybvɑ̃sjɔne] *vt* to subsidize.
subversif, ive [sybvɛʀsif, -iv] *adj* subversive.
subversion [sybvɛʀsjɔ̃] *nf* subversion.
suc [syk] *nm* (*BOT*) sap; (*de viande, fruit*) juice;
~**s gastriques** gastric juices.
succédané [syksedane] *nm* substitute.
succéder [syksede]: ~ **à** *vt* (*directeur, roi etc*) to
succeed; (*venir après: dans une série*) to
follow, succeed; **se** ~ *vi* (*accidents, années*) to
follow one another.
succès [syksɛ] *nm* success; **avec** ~
successfully; **sans** ~ unsuccessfully; **avoir
du** ~ to be a success, be successful; **à** ~
successful; **livre à** ~ bestseller; ~ **de
librairie** bestseller; ~ (**féminins**) conquests.
successeur [syksesœʀ] *nm* successor.
successif, ive [syksesif, -iv] *adj* successive.
succession [syksesjɔ̃] *nf* (*série, POL*)
succession; (*JUR: patrimoine*) estate,
inheritance; **prendre la** ~ **de** (*directeur*) to
succeed, take over from; (*entreprise*) to take
over.
successivement [syksesivmɑ̃] *adv*
successively.
succinct, e [syksɛ̃, -ɛ̃t] *adj* succinct.
succinctement [syksɛ̃tmɑ̃] *adv* succinctly.
succion [syksjɔ̃] *nf*: **bruit de** ~ sucking noise.
succomber [sykɔ̃be] *vi* to die, succumb; (*fig*):
~ **à** to give way to, succumb to.
succulent, e [sykylɑ̃, -ɑ̃t] *adj* succulent.
succursale [sykyʀsal] *nf* branch; **magasin à**
~**s multiples** chain *ou* multiple store.
sucer [syse] *vt* to suck.
sucette [sysɛt] *nf* (*bonbon*) lollipop; (*de bébé*)
dummy (*BRIT*), pacifier (*US*), comforter (*US*).
suçoter [sysɔte] *vt* to suck.
sucre [sykʀ(ə)] *nm* (*substance*) sugar;
(*morceau*) lump of sugar, sugar lump *ou*
cube; ~ **de canne/betterave** cane/beet
sugar; ~ **en morceaux/cristallisé/en poudre**
lump *ou* cube/granulated/caster sugar; ~
glace icing sugar; ~ **d'orge** barley sugar.
sucré, e [sykʀe] *adj* (*produit alimentaire*)
sweetened; (*au goût*) sweet; (*péj*) sugary,
honeyed.
sucrer [sykʀe] *vt* (*thé, café*) to sweeten, put
sugar in; ~ **qn** to put sugar in sb's tea (*ou*
coffee *etc*); **se** ~ to help o.s. to sugar, have
some sugar; (*fam*) to line one's pocket(s).
sucrerie [sykʀəʀi] *nf* (*usine*) sugar refinery;
~**s** *nfpl* (*bonbons*) sweets, sweet things.
sucrier, ière [sykʀije, -jɛʀ] *adj* (*industrie*)
sugar *cpd*; (*région*) sugar-producing ♦ *nm*
(*fabricant*) sugar producer; (*récipient*) sugar
bowl *ou* basin.
sud [syd] *nm*: **le** ~ the south ♦ *adj inv* south;
(*côte*) south, southern; **au** ~ (*situation*) in the
south; (*direction*) to the south; **au** ~ **de** (to
the) south of.

sud-africain, e [sydafʀikɛ̃, -ɛn] *adj* South
African ♦ *nm/f*: **Sud-Africain, e** South
African.
sud-américain, e [sydameʀikɛ̃, -ɛn] *adj* South
American ♦ *nm/f*: **Sud-Américain, e** South
American.
sudation [sydasjɔ̃] *nf* sweating, sudation.
sud-coréen, ne [sydkɔʀeɛ̃, -ɛn] *adj* South
Korean ♦ *nm/f*: **Sud-Coréen, ne** South
Korean.
sud-est [sydɛst] *nm, adj inv* south-east.
sud-ouest [sydwɛst] *nm, adj inv* south-west.
sud-vietnamien, ne [sydvjɛtnamjɛ̃, -ɛn] *adj*
South Vietnamese ♦ *nm/f*: **Sud-Vietnamien,
ne** South Vietnamese.
Suède [sɥɛd] *nf*: **la** ~ Sweden.
suédois, e [sɥedwa, -waz] *adj* Swedish ♦ *nm*
(*LING*) Swedish ♦ *nm/f*: **S~, e** Swede.
suer [sɥe] *vi* to sweat; (*suinter*) to ooze ♦ *vt* (*fig*)
to exude; ~ **à grosses gouttes** to sweat
profusely.
sueur [sɥœʀ] *nf* sweat; **en** ~ sweating, in a
sweat; **avoir des** ~**s froides** to be in a cold
sweat.
suffire [syfiʀ] *vi* (*être assez*): ~ (**à qn/pour
qch/pour faire**) to be enough *ou* sufficient
(for sb/for sth/to do); (*satisfaire*): **cela lui
suffit** he's content with this, this is enough
for him; **se** ~ *vi* to be self-sufficient; **cela
suffit pour les irriter/qu'ils se fâchent** it's
enough to annoy them/for them to get
angry; **il suffit d'une négligence/qu'on
oublie pour que** ... it only takes one act of
carelessness/one only needs to forget for
...; **ça suffit!** that's enough!, that'll do!
suffisamment [syfizamɑ̃] *adv* sufficiently,
enough; ~ **de** sufficient, enough.
suffisance [syfizɑ̃s] *nf* (*vanité*) self-
importance, bumptiousness; (*quantité*): **en** ~
in plenty.
suffisant, e [syfizɑ̃, -ɑ̃t] *adj* (*temps, ressources*)
sufficient; (*résultats*) satisfactory; (*vaniteux*)
self-important, bumptious.
suffisons [syfizɔ̃] *etc vb voir* **suffire**.
suffixe [syfiks(ə)] *nm* suffix.
suffocant, e [syfɔkɑ̃, -ɑ̃t] *adj* (*étouffant*)
suffocating; (*stupéfiant*) staggering.
suffocation [syfɔkasjɔ̃] *nf* suffocation.
suffoquer [syfɔke] *vt* to choke, suffocate;
(*stupéfier*) to stagger, astound ♦ *vi* to choke,
suffocate; ~ **de colère/d'indignation** to
choke with anger/indignation.
suffrage [syfʀaʒ] *nm* (*POL: voix*) vote;
(: *méthode*): ~ **universel/direct/indirect**
universal/direct/indirect suffrage; (*du
public etc*) approval *no pl*; ~**s exprimés** valid
votes.
suggérer [syɡʒeʀe] *vt* to suggest; ~ **que/de
faire** to suggest that/doing.
suggestif, ive [syɡʒɛstif, -iv] *adj* suggestive.
suggestion [syɡʒɛstjɔ̃] *nf* suggestion.
suggestivité [syɡʒɛstivite] *nf* suggestiveness,

suggestive nature.

suicidaire [sɥisidɛʀ] *adj* suicidal.

suicide [sɥisid] *nm* suicide ♦ *adj*: **opération ~** suicide mission.

suicidé, e [sɥiside] *nm/f* suicide.

suicider [sɥiside]: **se ~** *vi* to commit suicide.

suie [sɥi] *nf* soot.

suif [sɥif] *nm* tallow.

suinter [sɥɛ̃te] *vi* to ooze.

suis [sɥi] *vb voir* **être, suivre.**

suisse [sɥis] *adj* Swiss ♦ *nm* (*bedeau*) ≈ verger ♦ *nm/f*: **S~** Swiss *pl inv* ♦ *nf*: **la S~** Switzerland; **la S~ romande/allemande** French-speaking/German-speaking Switzerland; **~ romand** Swiss French.

suisse-allemand, e [sɥisalmɑ̃, -ɑ̃d] *adj*, *nm/f* Swiss German.

Suissesse [sɥisɛs] *nf* Swiss (woman *ou* girl).

suit [sɥi] *vb voir* **suivre.**

suite [sɥit] *nf* (*continuation: d'énumération etc*) rest, remainder; (*: de feuilleton*) continuation; (*: second film etc sur le même thème*) sequel; (*série: de maisons, succès*): **une ~ de** a series *ou* succession of; (*MATH*) series *sg*; (*conséquence*) result; (*ordre, liaison logique*) coherence; (*appartement, MUS*) suite; (*escorte*) retinue, suite; **~s** *nfpl* (*d'une maladie etc*) effects; **prendre la ~ de** (*directeur etc*) to succeed, take over from; **donner ~ à** (*requête, projet*) to follow up; **faire ~ à** to follow; (**faisant**) **~ à votre lettre du** further to your letter of the; **sans ~** *adj* incoherent, disjointed ♦ *adv* incoherently, disjointedly; **de ~** *adv* (*d'affilée*) in succession; (*immédiatement*) at once; **par la ~** afterwards, subsequently; **à la ~** *adv* one after the other; **à la ~ de** (*derrière*) behind; (*en conséquence de*) following; **par ~ de** owing to, as a result of; **avoir de la ~ dans les idées** to show great singleness of purpose; **attendre la ~ des événements** to (wait and see) what happens.

suivant, e [sɥivɑ̃, -ɑ̃t] *vb voir* **suivre** ♦ *adj* next, following; (*ci-après*) **l'exercice ~** the following exercise ♦ *prép* (*selon*) according to; **~ que** according to whether; **au ~!** next!

suive [sɥiv] *etc vb voir* **suivre.**

suiveur [sɥivœʀ] *nm* (*CYCLISME*) (official) follower; (*péj*) (camp) follower.

suivi, e [sɥivi] *pp de* **suivre** ♦ *adj* (*régulier*) regular; (*COMM: article*) in general production; (*cohérent*) consistent; coherent ♦ *nm* follow-up; **très/peu ~** (*cours*) well-/poorly-attended; (*mode*) widely/not widely adopted; (*feuilleton etc*) widely/not widely followed.

suivre [sɥivʀ(ə)] *vt* (*gén*) to follow; (*SCOL: cours*) to attend; (*: leçon*) to follow, attend to; (*: programme*) to keep up with; (*COMM: article*) to continue to stock ♦ *vi* to follow; (*élève: écouter*) to attend, pay attention to; (*: assimiler le programme*) to keep up, follow;

se ~ (*accidents, personnes, voitures etc*) to follow one after the other; (*raisonnement*) to be coherent; **~ des yeux** to follow with one's eyes; **faire ~** (*lettre*) to forward; **~ son cours** (*suj: enquête etc*) to run *ou* take its course; **"à ~"** "to be continued".

sujet, te [syʒɛ, -ɛt] *adj*: **être ~ à** (*accidents*) to be prone to; (*vertige etc*) to be liable *ou* subject to ♦ *nm/f* (*d'un souverain*) subject ♦ *nm* subject; **un ~ de dispute/discorde/mécontentement** a cause for argument/dissension/dissatisfaction; **c'est à quel ~?** what is it about?; **avoir ~ de se plaindre** to have cause for complaint; **au ~ de** *prép* about; **~ à caution** *adj* questionable; **~ de conversation** topic *ou* subject of conversation; **~ d'examen** (*SCOL*) examination question; examination paper; **~ d'expérience** (*BIO etc*) experimental subject.

sujétion [syʒesjɔ̃] *nf* subjection; (*fig*) constraint.

sulfater [sylfate] *vt* to spray with copper sulphate.

sulfureux, euse [sylfyʀø, -øz] *adj* sulphurous (*BRIT*), sulfurous (*US*).

sulfurique [sylfyʀik] *adj*: **acide ~** sulphuric (*BRIT*) *ou* sulfuric (*US*) acid.

sulfurisé, e [sylfyʀize] *adj*: **papier ~** greaseproof (*BRIT*) *ou* wax (*US*) paper.

Sumatra [symatʀa] *nf* Sumatra.

summum [sɔmɔm] *nm*: **le ~ de** the height of.

sumo [symo] *nm inv* sumo (wrestling).

super [sypɛʀ] *adj inv* great, fantastic ♦ *nm* (= *supercarburant*) ≈ 4-star (*BRIT*), ≈ premium (*US*).

superbe [sypɛʀb(ə)] *adj* magnificent, superb ♦ *nf* arrogance.

superbement [sypɛʀbəmɑ̃] *adv* superbly.

supercarburant [sypɛʀkaʀbyʀɑ̃] *nm* ≈ 4-star petrol (*BRIT*), ≈ premium gas (*US*).

supercherie [sypɛʀʃəʀi] *nf* trick, trickery *no pl*; (*fraude*) fraud.

supérette [sypeʀɛt] *nf* minimarket.

superfétatoire [sypɛʀfetatwaʀ] *adj* superfluous.

superficie [sypɛʀfisi] *nf* (*surface*) area; (*fig*) surface.

superficiel, le [sypɛʀfisjɛl] *adj* superficial.

superficiellement [sypɛʀfisjɛlmɑ̃] *adv* superficially.

superflu, e [sypɛʀfly] *adj* superfluous ♦ *nm*: **le ~** the superfluous.

superforme [sypɛʀfɔʀm(ə)] *nf* (*fam*) top form, excellent shape.

super-grand [sypɛʀgʀɑ̃] *nm* superpower.

super-huit [sypɛʀɥit] *adj*: **camera/film ~** super-eight camera/film.

supérieur, e [sypeʀjœʀ] *adj* (*lèvre, étages, classes*) upper; (*plus élevé: température, niveau*): **~ (à)** higher (than); (*meilleur: qualité, produit*): **~ (à)** superior (to); (*excellent,*

hautain) superior ♦ *nm/f* superior; **Mère ~e**
Mother Superior; **à l'étage ~** on the next
floor up; **~ en nombre** superior in number.
supérieurement [sypeʀjœʀmɑ̃] *adv*
exceptionally well, exceptionally + *adj*.
supériorité [sypeʀjɔʀite] *nf* superiority.
superlatif [sypeʀlatif] *nm* superlative.
supermarché [sypeʀmaʀʃe] *nm* supermarket.
supernova [sypeʀnɔva] *nf* supernova.
superposable [sypeʀpozabl(ə)] *adj* (*figures*)
that may be superimposed; (*lits*) stackable.
superposer [sypeʀpoze] *vt* to superpose;
(*meubles, caisses*) to stack; (*faire chevaucher*)
to superimpose; **se ~** (*images, souvenirs*) to
be superimposed; **lits superposés** bunk
beds.
superposition [sypeʀpozisjɔ̃] *nf*
superposition; superimposition.
superpréfet [sypeʀpʀefɛ] *nm* prefect in
charge of a region.
superproduction [sypeʀpʀɔdyksjɔ̃] *nf* (*film*)
spectacular.
superpuissance [sypeʀpɥisɑ̃s] *nf*
superpower.
supersonique [sypeʀsɔnik] *adj* supersonic.
superstitieux, euse [sypeʀstisjø, -øz] *adj*
superstitious.
superstition [sypeʀstisjɔ̃] *nf* superstition.
superstructure [sypeʀstʀyktyʀ] *nf*
superstructure.
supertanker [sypeʀtɑ̃kœʀ] *nm* supertanker.
superviser [sypeʀvize] *vt* to supervise.
supervision [sypeʀvizjɔ̃] *nf* supervision.
suppl. *abr* = **supplément**.
supplanter [syplɑ̃te] *vt* to supplant.
suppléance [sypleɑ̃s] *nf* (*poste*) supply post
(*BRIT*), substitute teacher's post (*US*).
suppléant, e [sypleɑ̃, -ɑ̃t] *adj* (*juge,
fonctionnaire*) deputy *cpd*; (*professeur*) supply
cpd (*BRIT*), substitute *cpd* (*US*) ♦ *nm/f* deputy;
supply *ou* substitute teacher; **médecin ~**
locum.
suppléer [syplee] *vt* (*ajouter: mot manquant etc*)
to supply, provide; (*compenser: lacune*) to fill
in; (: *défaut*) to make up for; (*remplacer:
professeur*) to stand in for; (: *juge*) to
deputize for; **~ à** *vt* to make up for; to
substitute for.
supplément [syplemɑ̃] *nm* supplement; **un ~
de travail** extra *ou* additional work; **un ~ de
frites** *etc* an extra portion of chips *etc*; **un ~
de 100 F** a supplement of 100 F, an
additional 100 F; **ceci est en ~** (*au menu etc*)
this is extra, there is an extra charge for
this; **~ d'information** additional
information.
supplémentaire [syplemɑ̃tɛʀ] *adj* additional,
further; (*train, bus*) relief *cpd*, extra.
supplétif, ive [sypletif, -iv] *adj* (*MIL*) auxiliary.
suppliant, e [syplijɑ̃, -ɑ̃t] *adj* imploring.
supplication [syplikasjɔ̃] *nf* (*REL*)
supplication; **~s** *nfpl* (*adjurations*) pleas,

entreaties.
supplice [syplis] *nm* (*peine corporelle*) torture
no pl; form of torture; (*douleur physique,
morale*) torture, agony; **être au ~** to be in
agony.
supplier [syplije] *vt* to implore, beseech.
supplique [syplik] *nf* petition.
support [sypɔʀ] *nm* support; (*pour livre, outils*)
stand; **~ audio-visuel** audio-visual aid; **~
publicitaire** advertising medium.
supportable [sypɔʀtabl(ə)] *adj* (*douleur,
température*) bearable; (*procédé, conduite*)
tolerable.
supporter *nm* [sypɔʀtɛʀ] supporter, fan ♦ *vt*
[sypɔʀte] (*poids, poussée, SPORT: concurrent,
équipe*) to support; (*conséquences, épreuve*)
to bear, endure; (*défauts, personne*) to
tolerate, put up with; (*suj: chose: chaleur etc*)
to withstand; (*suj: personne: chaleur, vin*) to
take.
supposé, e [sypoze] *adj* (*nombre*) estimated;
(*auteur*) supposed.
supposer [sypoze] *vt* to suppose; (*impliquer*)
to presuppose; **en supposant** *ou* **à ~ que**
supposing (that).
supposition [sypozisjɔ̃] *nf* supposition.
suppositoire [sypozitwaʀ] *nm* suppository.
suppôt [sypo] *nm* (*péj*) henchman.
suppression [sypʀesjɔ̃] *nf* (*voir supprimer*)
removal; deletion; cancellation;
suppression.
supprimer [sypʀime] *vt* (*cloison, cause, anxiété*)
to remove; (*clause, mot*) to delete; (*congés,
service d'autobus etc*) to cancel; (*publication,
article*) to suppress; (*emplois, privilèges,
témoin gênant*) to do away with; **~ qch à qn**
to deprive sb of sth.
suppurer [sypyʀe] *vi* to suppurate.
supputations [sypytɑsjɔ̃] *nfpl* calculations,
reckonings.
supputer [sypyte] *vt* to calculate, reckon.
supranational, e, aux [sypʀanasjɔnal, -o] *adj*
supranational.
suprématie [sypʀemasi] *nf* supremacy.
suprême [sypʀɛm] *adj* supreme.
suprêmement [sypʀɛmmɑ̃] *adv* supremely.

════════════════════════ *MOT-CLÉ*

sur [syʀ] *prép* **1** (*position*) on; (*pardessus*) over;
(*au-dessus*) above; **pose-le ~ la table** put it
on the table; **je n'ai pas d'argent ~ moi** I
haven't any money on me
2 (*direction*) towards; **en allant ~ Paris** going
towards Paris; **~ votre droite** on *ou* to your
right
3 (*à propos de*) on, about; **un livre/une
conférence ~ Balzac** a book/lecture on *ou*
about Balzac
4 (*proportion, mesures*) out of; by; **un ~ 10**
one in 10; (*SCOL*) one out of 10; **~ 20, 2 sont
venus** out of 20, 2 came; **4 m ~ 2** 4 m by 2;
avoir accident ~ accident to have one

accident after another
5 (*cause*): ~ **sa recommandation** on *ou* at
his recommendation; ~ **son invitation** at his
invitation
sur ce *adv* whereupon; ~ **ce, il faut que je
vous quitte** and now I must leave you.

sur, e [syʀ] *adj* sour.
sûr, e [syʀ] *adj* sure, certain; (*digne de
confiance*) reliable; (*sans danger*) safe; **peu ~**
unreliable; ~ **de qch** sure *ou* certain of sth;
être ~ de qn to be sure of sb; ~ **et certain**
absolutely certain; ~ **de soi** self-assured,
self-confident; **le plus ~ est de** the safest
thing is to.
surabondance [syʀabɔ̃dɑ̃s] *nf*
overabundance.
surabondant, e [syʀabɔ̃dɑ̃, -ɑ̃t] *adj*
overabundant.
surabonder [syʀabɔ̃de] *vi* to be overabundant;
~ **de** to abound with, have an
overabundance of.
suractivité [syʀaktivite] *nf* hyperactivity.
suraigu, ë [syʀegy] *adj* very shrill.
surajouter [syʀaʒute] *vt:* ~ **qch à** to add sth
to.
suralimentation [syʀalimɑ̃tɑsjɔ̃] *nf*
overfeeding; (*TECH: d'un moteur*)
supercharging.
suralimenté, e [syʀalimɑ̃te] *adj* (*personne*)
overfed; (*moteur*) supercharged.
suranné, e [syʀane] *adj* outdated, outmoded.
surarmement [syʀaʀməmɑ̃] *nm* (*excess*)
stockpiling of arms (*ou* weapons).
surbaissé, e [syʀbese] *adj* lowered, low.
surcapacité [syʀkapasite] *nf* overcapacity.
surcharge [syʀʃaʀʒ(ə)] *nf* (*de passagers,
marchandises*) excess load; (*de détails,
d'ornements*) overabundance, excess;
(*correction*) alteration; (*POSTES*) surcharge;
prendre des passagers en ~ to take on
excess *ou* extra passengers; ~ **de bagages**
excess luggage; ~ **de travail** extra work.
surchargé, e [syʀʃaʀʒe] *adj* (*décoration, style*)
over-elaborate, overfussy; (*voiture, emploi
du temps*) overloaded.
surcharger [syʀʃaʀʒe] *vt* to overload; (*timbre-
poste*) to surcharge; (*décoration*) to overdo.
surchauffe [syʀʃof] *nf* overheating.
surchauffé, e [syʀʃofe] *adj* overheated; (*fig:
imagination*) overactive.
surchoix [syʀʃwa] *adj inv* top-quality.
surclasser [syʀklɑse] *vt* to outclass.
surconsommation [syʀkɔ̃sɔmɑsjɔ̃] *nf* (*ÉCON*)
overconsumption.
surcoté, e [syʀkɔte] *adj* overpriced.
surcouper [syʀkupe] *vt* to overtrump.
surcroît [syʀkʀwa] *nm:* **un ~ de** additional
+ *nom*; **par** *ou* **de ~** moreover; **en ~** in
addition.
surdi-mutité [syʀdimytite] *nf:* **atteint de ~**
deaf and dumb.

surdité [syʀdite] *nf* deafness; **atteint de ~
totale** profoundly deaf.
surdoué, e [syʀdwe] *adj* gifted.
sureau, x [syʀo] *nm* elder (tree).
sureffectif [syʀefɛktif] *nm* overmanning.
surélever [syʀelve] *vt* to raise, heighten.
sûrement [syʀmɑ̃] *adv* reliably; safely,
securely; (*certainement*) certainly; ~ **pas**
certainly not.
suremploi [syʀɑ̃plwa] *nm* (*ÉCON*)
overemployment.
surenchère [syʀɑ̃ʃɛʀ] *nf* (*aux enchères*)
higher bid; (*sur prix fixe*) overbid; (*fig*)
overstatement; outbidding tactics *pl*; ~ **de
violence** build-up of violence; ~ **électorale**
political (*ou* electoral) one-upmanship.
surenchérir [syʀɑ̃ʃeʀiʀ] *vi* to bid higher; to
raise one's bid; (*fig*) to try and outbid each
other.
surendettement [syʀɑ̃dɛtmɑ̃] *nm* excessive
debt.
surent [syʀ] *vb voir* **savoir**.
surentraîné, e [syʀɑ̃tʀene] *adj* overtrained.
suréquipé, e [syʀekipe] *adj* overequipped.
surestimer [syʀɛstime] *vt* (*tableau*) to
overvalue; (*possibilité, personne*) to
overestimate.
sûreté [syʀte] *nf* (*voir sûr*) reliability; safety;
(*JUR*) guaranty; surety; **mettre en ~** to put
in a safe place; **pour plus de ~** as an extra
precaution; to be on the safe side; **la ~ de
l'État** State security; **la S~ (nationale)**
*division of the Ministère de l'Intérieur
heading all police forces except the
gendarmerie and the Paris préfecture de
police.*
surexcité, e [syʀɛksite] *adj* overexcited.
surexciter [syʀɛksite] *vt* (*personne*) to
overexcite; **cela surexcite ma curiosité** it
really rouses my curiosity.
surexploiter [syʀɛksplwate] *vt* to overexploit.
surexposer [syʀɛkspoze] *vt* to overexpose.
surf [sœʀf] *nm* surfing; **faire du ~** to go
surfing.
surface [syʀfas] *nf* surface; (*superficie*)
surface area; **faire ~** to surface; **en ~** *adv*
near the surface; (*fig*) superficially; **la pièce
fait 100 m² de ~** the room has a surface
area of 100m²; ~ **de réparation** (*SPORT*)
penalty area; ~ **porteuse** *ou* **de sustentation**
(*AVIAT*) aerofoil.
surfait, e [syʀfɛ, -ɛt] *adj* overrated.
surfeur, euse [sœʀfœʀ, -øz] *nm/f* surfer.
surfiler [syʀfile] *vt* (*COUTURE*) to oversew.
surfin, e [syʀfɛ̃, -in] *adj* superfine.
surgélateur [syʀʒelatœʀ] *nm* deep freeze.
surgélation [syʀʒelasjɔ̃] *nf* deep-freezing.
surgelé, e [syʀʒəle] *adj* (deep-)frozen.
surgeler [syʀʒəle] *vt* to (deep-)freeze.
surgir [syʀʒiʀ] *vi* (*personne, véhicule*) to appear
suddenly; (*jaillir*) to shoot up; (*montagne etc*)
to rise up, loom up; (*fig: problème, conflit*) to

arise.

surhomme [syʀɔm] *nm* superman.

surhumain, e [syʀymɛ̃, -ɛn] *adj* superhuman.

surimposer [syʀɛ̃poze] *vt* to overtax.

surimpression [syʀɛ̃pʀesjɔ̃] *nf* (*PHOTO*) double exposure; **en** ~ superimposed.

surimprimer [syʀɛ̃pʀime] *vt* to overstrike, overprint.

Surinam [syʀinam] *nm*: **le** ~ Surinam.

surinfection [syʀɛ̃fɛksjɔ̃] *nf* (*MÉD*) secondary infection.

surjet [syʀʒɛ] *nm* (*COUTURE*) overcast seam.

sur-le-champ [syʀləʃɑ̃] *adv* immediately.

surlendemain [syʀlɑ̃dmɛ̃] *nm*: **le** ~ (**soir**) two days later (in the evening); **le** ~ **de** two days after.

surligneur [syʀliɲœʀ] *nm* (*feutre*) highlighter (pen).

surmenage [syʀmənaʒ] *nm* overwork; **le** ~ **intellectuel** mental fatigue.

surmené, e [syʀməne] *adj* overworked.

surmener [syʀməne] *vt*, **se** ~ *vi* to overwork.

surmonter [syʀmɔ̃te] *vt* (*suj: coupole etc*) to surmount, top; (*vaincre*) to overcome, surmount.

surmultiplié, e [syʀmyltiplije] *adj*, *nf*: (**vitesse**) ~**e** overdrive.

surnager [syʀnaʒe] *vi* to float.

surnaturel, le [syʀnatyʀɛl] *adj*, *nm* supernatural.

surnom [syʀnɔ̃] *nm* nickname.

surnombre [syʀnɔ̃bʀ(ə)] *nm*: **être en** ~ to be too many (*ou* one too many).

surnommer [syʀnɔme] *vt* to nickname.

surnuméraire [syʀnymeʀɛʀ] *nm/f* supernumerary.

suroît [syʀwa] *nm* sou'wester.

surpasser [syʀpase] *vt* to surpass; **se** ~ to surpass o.s., excel o.s.

surpayer [syʀpeje] *vt* (*personne*) to overpay; (*article etc*) to pay too much for.

surpeuplé, e [syʀpœple] *adj* overpopulated.

surpeuplement [syʀpœpləmɑ̃] *nm* overpopulation.

surpiquer [syʀpike] *vt* (*COUTURE*) to overstitch.

surpiqûre [syʀpikyʀ] *nf* (*COUTURE*) overstitching.

surplace [syʀplas] *nm*: **faire du** ~ to mark time.

surplis [syʀpli] *nm* surplice.

surplomb [syʀplɔ̃] *nm* overhang; **en** ~ overhanging.

surplomber [syʀplɔ̃be] *vi* to be overhanging ♦ *vt* to overhang; (*dominer*) to tower above.

surplus [syʀply] *nm* (*COMM*) surplus; (*reste*): ~ **de bois** wood left over; **au** ~ moreover; ~ **américains** American army surplus *sg*.

surpopulation [syʀpɔpylasjɔ̃] *nf* overpopulation.

surprenant, e [syʀpʀənɑ̃, -ɑ̃t] *vb voir* **surprendre** ♦ *adj* amazing.

surprendre [syʀpʀɑ̃dʀ(ə)] *vt* (*étonner, prendre à l'improviste*) to amaze, surprise; (*secret*) to discover; (*tomber sur: intrus etc*) to catch; (*fig*) to detect; to chance *ou* happen upon; (*clin d'œil*) to intercept; (*conversation*) to overhear; (*suj: orage, nuit etc*) to catch out, take by surprise; ~ **la vigilance/bonne foi de qn** to catch sb out/betray sb's good faith; **se** ~ **à faire** to catch *ou* find o.s. doing.

surprime [syʀpʀim] *nf* additional premium.

surpris, e [syʀpʀi, -iz] *pp de* **surprendre** ♦ *adj*: ~ (**de/que**) amazed *ou* surprised (at/that).

surprise [syʀpʀiz] *nf* surprise; **faire une** ~ **à qn** to give sb a surprise; **voyage sans** ~**s** uneventful journey; **par** ~ *adv* by surprise.

surprise-partie [syʀpʀizpaʀti] *nf* party.

surprit [syʀpʀi] *vb voir* **surprendre**.

surproduction [syʀpʀɔdyksjɔ̃] *nf* overproduction.

surréaliste [syʀʀealist(ə)] *adj*, *nm/f* surrealist.

sursaut [syʀso] *nm* start, jump; ~ **de** (*énergie, indignation*) sudden fit *ou* burst of; **en** ~ *adv* with a start.

sursauter [syʀsote] *vi* to (give a) start, jump.

surseoir [syʀswaʀ]: ~ **à** *vt* to defer; (*JUR*) to stay.

sursis [syʀsi] *nm* (*JUR: gén*) suspended sentence; (*à l'exécution capitale, aussi fig*) reprieve; (*MIL*): ~ (**d'appel** *ou* **d'incorporation**) deferment; **condamné à 5 mois (de prison) avec** ~ given a 5-month suspended (prison) sentence.

sursitaire [syʀsitɛʀ] *nm* (*MIL*) deferred conscript.

sursois [syʀswa], **sursoyais** [syʀswaje] *etc vb voir* **surseoir**.

surtaxe [syʀtaks(ə)] *nf* surcharge.

surtension [syʀtɑ̃sjɔ̃] *nf* (*ÉLEC*) overvoltage.

surtout [syʀtu] *adv* (*avant tout, d'abord*) above all; (*spécialement, particulièrement*) especially; **il aime le sport,** ~ **le football** he likes sport, especially football; **cet été, il a** ~ **fait de la pêche** this summer he went fishing more than anything (else); ~ **pas d'histoires!** no fuss now!; ~, **ne dites rien!** whatever you do - don't say anything!; ~ **pas!** certainly *ou* definitely not!; ~ **que** ... especially as ....

survécu, e [syʀveky] *pp de* **survivre**.

surveillance [syʀvejɑ̃s] *nf* watch; (*POLICE, MIL*) surveillance; **sous** ~ **médicale** under medical supervision; **la** ~ **du territoire** internal security; *voir aussi* DST.

surveillant, e [syʀvejɑ̃, -ɑ̃t] *nm/f* (*de prison*) warder; (*SCOL*) monitor; (*de travaux*) supervisor, overseer.

surveiller [syʀveje] *vt* (*enfant, élèves, bagages*) to watch, keep an eye on; (*malade*) to watch over; (*prisonnier, suspect*) to keep (a) watch on; (*territoire, bâtiment*) to (keep) watch over; (*travaux, cuisson*) to supervise; (*SCOL: examen*) to invigilate; **se** ~ to keep a check *ou* watch on o.s.; ~ **son langage/sa ligne** to watch one's language/figure.

survenir [syʀvəniʀ] *vi* (*incident, retards*) to occur, arise; (*événement*) to take place; (*personne*) to appear, arrive.

survenu, e [syʀv(ə)ny] *pp de* **survenir**.

survêt(ement) [syʀvɛt(mã)] *nm* tracksuit (*BRIT*), sweat suit (*US*).

survie [syʀvi] *nf* survival; (*REL*) afterlife; **équipement de** ~ survival equipment; **une** ~ **de quelques mois** a few more months of life.

surviens [syʀvjɛ̃], **survint** [syʀvɛ̃] *etc vb voir* **survenir**.

survit [syʀvi] *etc vb voir* **survivre**.

survitrage [syʀvitʀaʒ] *nm* double-glazing.

survivance [syʀvivãs] *nf* relic.

survivant, e [syʀvivã, -ãt] *vb voir* **survivre** ♦ *nm/f* survivor.

survivre [syʀvivʀ(ə)] *vi* to survive; ~ **à** *vt* (*accident etc*) to survive; (*personne*) to outlive; **la victime a peu de chance de** ~ the victim has little hope of survival.

survol [syʀvɔl] *nm* flying over.

survoler [syʀvɔle] *vt* to fly over; (*fig: livre*) to skim through; (: *question, problèmes*) to skim over.

survolté, e [syʀvɔlte] *adj* (*ÉLEC*) stepped up, boosted; (*fig*) worked up.

sus [sy(s)]: **en** ~ **de** *prép* in addition to, over and above; **en** ~ *adv* in addition; ~ **à** *excl*: ~ **au tyran!** at the tyrant! ♦ *vb* [sy] *voir* **savoir**.

susceptibilité [syseptibilite] *nf* sensitivity *no pl*.

susceptible [syseptibl(ə)] *adj* touchy, sensitive; ~ **d'amélioration** *ou* **d'être amélioré** that can be improved, open to improvement; ~ **de faire** (*capacité*) able to do; (*probabilité*) liable to do.

susciter [sysite] *vt* (*admiration*) to arouse; (*obstacles, ennuis*): ~ (**à qn**) to create (for sb).

susdit, e [sysdi, -dit] *adj* foresaid.

susmentionné, e [sysmãsjɔne] *adj* above-mentioned.

susnommé, e [sysnɔme] *adj* above-named.

suspect, e [syspɛ(kt), -ɛkt(ə)] *adj* suspicious; (*témoignage, opinions, vin etc*) suspect ♦ *nm/f* suspect; **peu** ~ **de** most unlikely to be suspected of.

suspecter [syspɛkte] *vt* to suspect; (*honnêteté de qn*) to question, have one's suspicions about; ~ **qn d'être/d'avoir fait qch** to suspect sb of being/having done sth.

suspendre [syspãdʀ(ə)] *vt* (*accrocher: vêtement*): ~ **qch (à)** to hang sth up (on); (*fixer: lustre etc*): ~ **qch à** to hang sth from; (*interrompre, démettre*) to suspend; (*remettre*) to defer; **se** ~ **à** to hang from.

suspendu, e [syspãdy] *pp de* **suspendre** ♦ *adj* (*accroché*): ~ **à** hanging on (*ou* from); (*perché*): ~ **au-dessus de** suspended over;

(*AUTO*): **bien/mal** ~ with good/poor suspension; **être** ~ **aux lèvres de qn** to hang upon sb's every word.

suspens [syspã]: **en** ~ *adv* (*affaire*) in abeyance; **tenir en** ~ to keep in suspense.

suspense [syspãs] *nm* suspense.

suspension [syspãsjɔ̃] *nf* suspension; deferment; (*AUTO*) suspension; (*lustre*) pendant light fitting; **en** ~ in suspension, suspended; ~ **d'audience** adjournment.

suspicieux, euse [syspisjø, -øz] *adj* suspicious.

suspicion [syspisjɔ̃] *nf* suspicion.

sustentation [systãtasjɔ̃] *nf* (*AVIAT*) lift; **base** *ou* **polygone de** ~ support polygon.

sustenter [systãte]: **se** ~ *vi* to take sustenance.

susurrer [sysyʀe] *vt* to whisper.

sut [sy] *vb voir* **savoir**.

suture [sytyʀ] *nf*: **point de** ~ stitch.

suturer [sytyʀe] *vt* to stitch up, suture.

suzeraineté [syzʀɛnte] *nf* suzerainty.

svelte [svɛlt(ə)] *adj* slender, svelte.

SVP *sigle* (= *s'il vous plaît*) please.

Swaziland [swazilãd] *nm*: **le** ~ Swaziland.

syllabe [silab] *nf* syllable.

sylphide [silfid] *nf* (*fig*): **sa taille de** ~ her sylph-like figure.

sylvestre [silvɛstʀ(ə)] *adj*: **pin** ~ Scots pine, Scotch fir.

sylvicole [silvikɔl] *adj* forestry *cpd*.

sylviculteur [silvikyltœʀ] *nm* forester.

sylviculture [silvikyltyʀ] *nf* forestry, sylviculture.

symbole [sɛ̃bɔl] *nm* symbol; ~ **graphique** (*INFORM*) icon.

symbolique [sɛ̃bɔlik] *adj* symbolic; (*geste, offrande*) token *cpd*; (*salaire, dommages-intérêts*) nominal.

symboliquement [sɛ̃bɔlikmã] *adv* symbolically.

symboliser [sɛ̃bɔlize] *vt* to symbolize.

symétrie [simetʀi] *nf* symmetry.

symétrique [simetʀik] *adj* symmetrical.

symétriquement [simetʀikmã] *adv* symmetrically.

sympa [sɛ̃pa] *adj inv* (= *sympathique*) nice; friendly; good.

sympathie [sɛ̃pati] *nf* (*inclination*) liking; (*affinité*) fellow feeling; (*condoléances*) sympathy; **accueillir avec** ~ (*projet*) to receive favourably; **avoir de la** ~ **pour qn** to like sb, have a liking for sb; **témoignages de** ~ expressions of sympathy; **croyez à toute ma** ~ you have my deepest sympathy.

sympathique [sɛ̃patik] *adj* (*personne, figure*) nice, friendly, likeable; (*geste*) friendly; (*livre*) good; (*déjeuner*) nice; (*réunion, endroit*) pleasant, nice.

sympathisant, e [sɛ̃patizã, -ãt] *nm/f* sympathizer.

sympathiser [sɛ̃patize] *vi* (*voisins etc*:

s'entendre) to get on (BRIT) ou along (US)
(well); (: se fréquenter) to socialize, see each
other; ~ **avec** to get on ou along (well) with;
to see, socialize with.

symphonie [sɛ̃fɔni] nf symphony.

symphonique [sɛ̃fɔnik] adj (orchestre, concert)
symphony cpd; (musique) symphonic.

symposium [sɛ̃pozjɔm] nm symposium.

symptomatique [sɛ̃ptɔmatik] adj
symptomatic.

symptôme [sɛ̃ptom] nm symptom.

synagogue [sinagɔg] nf synagogue.

synchrone [sɛ̃kRɔn] adj synchronous.

synchronique [sɛ̃kRɔnik] adj: **tableau** ~
synchronic table of events.

synchronisation [sɛ̃kRɔnizɑsjɔ̃] nf
synchronization.

synchronisé, e [sɛ̃kRɔnize] adj synchronized.

synchroniser [sɛ̃kRɔnize] vt to synchronize.

syncope [sɛ̃kɔp] nf (MÉD) blackout; (MUS)
syncopation; **tomber en** ~ to faint, pass out.

syncopé, e [sɛ̃kɔpe] adj syncopated.

syndic [sɛ̃dik] nm managing agent.

syndical, e, aux [sɛ̃dikal, -o] adj (trade-)union
cpd; **centrale** ~**e** group of affiliated trade
unions.

syndicalisme [sɛ̃dikalism(ə)] nm (mouvement)
trade unionism; (activités) union(ist)
activities pl.

syndicaliste [sɛ̃dikalist(ə)] nm/f trade unionist.

syndicat [sɛ̃dika] nm (d'ouvriers, employés)
(trade(s)) union; (autre association d'intérêts)
union, association; ~ **d'initiative (SI)** tourist
office ou bureau; ~ **patronal** employers'
syndicate, federation of employers; ~ **de**
propriétaires association of property owners.

syndiqué, e [sɛ̃dike] adj belonging to a
(trade) union; **non** ~ non-union.

syndiquer [sɛ̃dike]: **se** ~ vi to form a trade
union; (adhérer) to join a trade union.

syndrome [sɛ̃dRom] nm syndrome; ~
prémenstruel premenstrual syndrome
(PMS).

synergie [sinɛRʒi] nf synergy.

synode [sinɔd] nm synod.

synonyme [sinɔnim] adj synonymous ♦ nm
synonym; ~ **de** synonymous with.

synopsis [sinɔpsis] nm ou nf synopsis.

synoptique [sinɔptik] adj: **tableau** ~ synoptic
table.

synovie [sinɔvi] nf synovia; **épanchement de**
~ water on the knee.

syntaxe [sɛ̃taks(ə)] nf syntax.

synthèse [sɛ̃tɛz] nf synthesis (pl -es); **faire la**
~ **de** to synthesize.

synthétique [sɛ̃tetik] adj synthetic.

synthétiser [sɛ̃tetize] vt to synthesize.

synthétiseur [sɛ̃tetizœR] nm (MUS)
synthesizer.

syphilis [sifilis] nf syphilis.

Syrie [siRi] nf: **la** ~ Syria.

syrien, ne [siRjɛ̃, -ɛn] adj Syrian ♦ nm/f: **S~, ne**
Syrian.

systématique [sistematik] adj systematic.

systématiquement [sistematikmɑ̃] adv
systematically.

systématiser [sistematize] vt to systematize.

système [sistɛm] nm system; **le** ~ **D**
resourcefulness; ~ **décimal** decimal
system; ~ **expert** expert system; ~
d'exploitation à disques (INFORM) disk
operating system; ~ **immunitaire** immune
system; ~ **métrique** metric system; ~
solaire solar system.

Tt

T, t [te] nm inv T, t ♦ abr (= tonne) t; **T comme**
Thérèse T for Tommy.

t' [t(ə)] pron voir **te**.

ta [ta] dét voir **ton**.

tabac [taba] nm tobacco; (aussi: **débit** ou
bureau de ~) tobacconist's (shop) ♦ adj inv:
(couleur) ~ buff, tobacco cpd; **passer qn à** ~
to beat sb up; **faire un** ~ (fam) to be a big
hit; ~ **blond/brun** light/dark tobacco; ~ **gris**
shag; ~ **à priser** snuff.

tabagie [tabaʒi] nf smoke den.

tabagisme [tabaʒism(ə)] nm nicotine
addiction; ~ **passif** passive smoking.

tabasser [tabase] vt to beat up.

tabatière [tabatjɛR] nf snuffbox.

tabernacle [tabɛRnakl(ə)] nm tabernacle.

table [tabl(ə)] nf table; **avoir une bonne** ~ to
keep a good table; **à** ~! dinner etc is ready!;
se mettre à ~ to sit down to eat; (fig: fam) to
come clean; **mettre** ou **dresser/desservir la**
~ to lay ou set/clear the table; **faire** ~ **rase**
de to make a clean sweep of; ~ **basse**
coffee table; ~ **de cuisson** (à l'électricité)
hotplate; (au gaz) gas ring; ~ **d'écoute**
wire-tapping set; ~ **d'harmonie** sounding
board; ~ **d'hôte** set menu; ~ **de lecture**
turntable; ~ **des matières** (table of)
contents pl; ~ **de multiplication**
multiplication table; ~ **des négociations**
negotiating table; ~ **de nuit** ou **de chevet**
bedside table; ~ **ronde** (débat) round table;
~ **roulante** (tea) trolley; ~ **de toilette**
washstand; ~ **traçante** (INFORM) plotter.

tableau, x [tablo] nm (ART) painting;
(reproduction, fig) picture; (panneau) board;
(schéma) table, chart; ~ **d'affichage** notice
board; ~ **de bord** dashboard; (AVIAT)
instrument panel; ~ **de chasse** tally; ~ **de**
contrôle console, control panel; ~ **de maître**
masterpiece; ~ **noir** blackboard.

tablée [table] *nf* (*personnes*) table.
tabler [table] *vi*: ~ **sur** to count *ou* bank on.
tablette [tablɛt] *nf* (*planche*) shelf (*pl* shelves);
~ **de chocolat** bar of chocolate.
tableur [tablœR] *nm* (*INFORM*) spreadsheet.
tablier [tablije] *nm* apron; (*de pont*) roadway;
(*de cheminée*) (flue-)shutter.
tabou, e [tabu] *adj, nm* taboo.
tabouret [taburɛ] *nm* stool.
tabulateur [tabylatœR] *nm* (*TECH*) tabulator.
TAC *sigle m* (= *train autos-couchettes*) car-
sleeper train, ≈ Motorail ® (*BRIT*).
tac [tak] *nm*: **du** ~ **au** ~ **tit for tat**.
tache [taʃ] *nf* (*saleté*) stain, mark; (*ART, de
couleur, lumière*) spot; splash, patch; **faire** ~
d'huile to spread, gain ground; ~ **de
rousseur** *ou* **de son** freckle; ~ **de vin** (*sur la
peau*) strawberry mark.
tâche [taʃ] *nf* task; **travailler à la** ~ to do
piecework.
tacher [taʃe] *vt* to stain, mark; (*fig*) to sully,
stain; **se** ~ *vi* (*fruits*) to become marked.
tâcher [taʃe] *vi*: ~ **de faire** to try to do,
endeavour (*BRIT*) *ou* endeavor (*US*) to do.
tâcheron [taʃRɔ̃] *nm* (*fig*) drudge.
tacheté, e [taʃte] *adj*: ~ **de** speckled *ou*
spotted with.
tachisme [taʃism(ə)] *nm* (*PEINTURE*) tachisme.
tachygraphe [takigRaf] *nm* tachograph.
tachymètre [takimɛtR(ə)] *nm* tachometer.
tacite [tasit] *adj* tacit.
tacitement [tasitmã] *adv* tacitly.
taciturne [tasityRn(ə)] *adj* taciturn.
tacot [tako] *nm* (*péj: voiture*) banger (*BRIT*),
clunker (*US*).
tact [takt] *nm* tact; **avoir du** ~ to be tactful,
have tact.
tacticien, ne [taktisjɛ̃, -ɛn] *nm/f* tactician.
tactile [taktil] *adj* tactile.
tactique [taktik] *adj* tactical ♦ *nf* (*technique*)
tactics *sg*; (*plan*) tactic.
Tadjikistan [tadʒikistã] *nm* Tajikistan.
taffetas [tafta] *nm* taffeta.
Tage [taʒ] *nm*: **le** ~ the (river) Tagus.
Tahiti [taiti] *nf* Tahiti.
tahitien, ne [taisjɛ̃, -ɛn] *adj* Tahitian.
taie [tɛ] *nf*: ~ (**d'oreiller**) pillowslip,
pillowcase.
taillader [tajade] *vt* to gash.
taille [taj] *nf* cutting; pruning; (*milieu du
corps*) waist; (*hauteur*) height; (*grandeur*)
size; **de** ~ **à faire** capable of doing; **de** ~ *adj*
sizeable; **quelle** ~ **faites- vous?** what size
are you?
taillé, e [taje] *adj* (*moustache, ongles, arbre*)
trimmed; ~ **pour** (*fait pour, apte à*) cut out
for; tailor-made for; ~ **en pointe** sharpened
to a point.
taille-crayon(s) [tajkRɛjɔ̃] *nm inv* pencil
sharpener.
tailler [taje] *vt* (*pierre, diamant*) to cut; (*arbre,
plante*) to prune; (*vêtement*) to cut out;

(*crayon*) to sharpen; **se** ~ *vt* (*ongles, barbe*) to
trim, cut; (*fig: réputation*) to gain, win ♦ *vi*
(*fam: s'enfuir*) to beat it; ~ **dans** (*chair, bois*)
to cut into; ~ **grand/petit** to be on the
large/small side.
tailleur [tajœR] *nm* (*couturier*) tailor;
(*vêtement*) suit, costume; **en** ~ (*assis*) cross-
legged; ~ **de diamants** diamond-cutter.
tailleur-pantalon [tajœRpãtalɔ̃] *nm* trouser
(*BRIT*) *ou* pant(s) suit.
taillis [taji] *nm* copse.
tain [tɛ̃] *nm* silvering; **glace sans** ~ two-way
mirror.
taire [tɛR] *vt* to keep to o.s., conceal ♦ *vi*: **faire**
~ **qn** to make sb be quiet; (*fig*) to silence sb;
se ~ *vi* (*s'arrêter de parler*) to fall silent, stop
talking; (*ne pas parler*) to be silent *ou* quiet;
(*s'abstenir de s'exprimer*) to keep quiet; (*bruit,
voix*) to disappear; **tais-toi!**, **taisez-vous!** be
quiet!
Taiwan [tajwan] *nf* Taiwan.
talc [talk] *nm* talc, talcum powder.
talé, e [tale] *adj* (*fruit*) bruised.
talent [talã] *nm* talent; **avoir du** ~ to be
talented, have talent.
talentueux, euse [talãtɥø, -øz] *adj* talented.
talion [taljɔ̃] *nm*: **la loi du** ~ an eye for an eye.
talisman [talismã] *nm* talisman.
talkie-walkie [tɔkiwɔki] *nm* walkie-talkie.
taloche [talɔʃ] *nf* (*fam: claque*) slap; (*TECH*)
plaster float.
talon [talɔ̃] *nm* heel; (*de chèque, billet*) stub,
counterfoil (*BRIT*); ~**s plats/aiguilles** flat/
stiletto heels; **être sur les** ~**s de qn** to be on
sb's heels; **tourner les** ~**s** to turn on one's
heel; **montrer les** ~**s** (*fig*) to show a clean
pair of heels.
talonner [talɔne] *vt* to follow hard behind;
(*fig*) to hound; (*RUGBY*) to heel.
talonnette [talɔnɛt] *nf* (*de chaussure*)
heelpiece; (*de pantalon*) stirrup.
talquer [talke] *vt* to put talc(um powder) on.
talus [taly] *nm* embankment; ~ **de remblai/
déblai** embankment/excavation slope.
tamarin [tamaRɛ̃] *nm* (*BOT*) tamarind.
tambour [tãbuR] *nm* (*MUS, aussi TECH*) drum;
(*musicien*) drummer; (*porte*) revolving
door(s *pl*); **sans** ~ **ni trompette**
unobtrusively.
tambourin [tãbuRɛ̃] *nm* tambourine.
tambouriner [tãbuRine] *vi*: ~ **contre** to drum
against *ou* on.
tambour-major, *pl* **tambours-majors**
[tãbuRmaʒɔR] *nm* drum major.
tamis [tami] *nm* sieve.
Tamise [tamiz] *nf*: **la** ~ the Thames.
tamisé, e [tamize] *adj* (*fig*) subdued, soft.
tamiser [tamize] *vt* to sieve, sift.
tampon [tãpɔ̃] *nm* (*de coton, d'ouate*) pad;
(*aussi*: ~ **hygiénique** *ou* **périodique**) tampon;
(*amortisseur, INFORM: aussi*: **mémoire** ~)
buffer; (*bouchon*) plug, stopper; (*cachet,*

timbre) stamp; (*CHIMIE*) buffer; ~ **buvard** blotter; ~ **encreur** inking pad; ~ **(à récurer)** scouring pad.

tamponné, e [tɑ̃pɔne] *adj*: **solution** ~**e** buffer solution.

tamponner [tɑ̃pɔne] *vt* (*timbres*) to stamp; (*heurter*) to crash *ou* ram into; (*essuyer*) to mop up; **se** ~ (*voitures*) to crash (into each other).

tamponneuse [tɑ̃pɔnøz] *adj f*: **autos** ~**s** dodgems, bumper cars.

tam-tam [tamtam] *nm* tomtom.

tancer [tɑ̃se] *vt* to scold.

tanche [tɑ̃ʃ] *nf* tench.

tandem [tɑ̃dɛm] *nm* tandem; (*fig*) duo, pair.

tandis [tɑ̃di]: ~ **que** *conj* while.

tangage [tɑ̃gaʒ] *nm* pitching (and tossing).

tangent, e [tɑ̃ʒɑ̃, -ɑ̃t] *adj* (*MATH*): ~ **à** tangential to; (*fam: de justesse*) close ♦ *nf* (*MATH*) tangent.

Tanger [tɑ̃ʒe] *n* Tangier.

tangible [tɑ̃ʒibl(ə)] *adj* tangible, concrete.

tango [tɑ̃go] *nm* (*MUS*) tango ♦ *adj inv* (*couleur*) dark orange.

tanguer [tɑ̃ge] *vi* to pitch (and toss).

tanière [tanjɛʀ] *nf* lair, den.

tanin [tanɛ̃] *nm* tannin.

tank [tɑ̃k] *nm* tank.

tanker [tɑ̃kɛʀ] *nm* tanker.

tanné, e [tane] *adj* weather-beaten.

tanner [tane] *vt* to tan.

tannerie [tanʀi] *nf* tannery.

tanneur [tanœʀ] *nm* tanner.

tant [tɑ̃] *adv* so much; ~ **de** (*sable, eau*) so much; (*gens, livres*) so many; ~ **que** *conj* as long as; ~ **que** (*comparatif*) as much as; ~ **mieux** that's great; so much the better; ~ **mieux pour lui** good for him; ~ **pis** too bad; **un** ~ **soit peu** (*un peu*) a little bit; (*même un peu*) (even) remotely; ~ **bien que mal** as well as can be expected; ~ **s'en faut** far from it, not by a long way.

tante [tɑ̃t] *nf* aunt.

tantinet [tɑ̃tinɛ]: **un** ~ *adv* a tiny bit.

tantôt [tɑ̃to] *adv* (*parfois*): ~ ... ~ now ... now; (*cet après-midi*) this afternoon.

Tanzanie [tɑ̃zani] *nf*: **la** ~ Tanzania.

tanzanien, ne [tɑ̃zanjɛ̃, -ɛn] *adj* Tanzanian.

TAO *sigle f* (= *traduction assistée par ordinateur*) MAT (= *machine-aided translation*).

taon [tɑ̃] *nm* horsefly, gadfly.

tapage [tapaʒ] *nm* uproar, din; (*fig*) fuss, row; ~ **nocturne** (*JUR*) disturbance of the peace (*at night*).

tapageur, euse [tapaʒœʀ, -øz] *adj* (*bruyant*: *enfants etc*) noisy; (*toilette*) loud, flashy; (*publicité*) obtrusive.

tape [tap] *nf* slap.

tape-à-l'œil [tapalœj] *adj inv* flashy, showy.

taper [tape] *vt* (*personne*) to clout; (*porte*) to bang, slam; (*dactylographier*) to type (out); (*INFORM*) to key(board); (*fam: emprunter*): ~

qn de 10 F to touch sb for 10 F, cadge 10 F off sb ♦ *vi* (*soleil*) to beat down; **se** ~ *vt* (*fam: travail*) to get landed with; (: *boire, manger*) to down; ~ **sur qn** to thump sb; (*fig*) to run sb down; ~ **sur qch** (*clou etc*) to hit sth; (*table etc*) to bang on sth; ~ à (*porte etc*) to knock on; ~ **dans** (*se servir*) to dig into; ~ **des mains/pieds** to clap one's hands/stamp one's feet; ~ **(à la machine)** to type.

tapi, e [tapi] *adj*: ~ **dans/derrière** (*blotti*) crouching *ou* cowering in/behind; (*caché*) hidden away in/behind.

tapinois [tapinwa]: **en** ~ *adv* stealthily.

tapioca [tapjɔka] *nm* tapioca.

tapir [tapiʀ]: **se** ~ *vi* to hide away.

tapis [tapi] *nm* carpet; (*de table*) cloth; **mettre sur le** ~ (*fig*) to bring up for discussion; **aller au** ~ (*BOXE*) to go down; **envoyer au** ~ (*BOXE*) to floor; ~ **roulant** conveyor belt; ~ **de sol** (*de tente*) groundsheet.

tapis-brosse [tapibʀɔs] *nm* doormat.

tapisser [tapise] *vt* (*avec du papier peint*) to paper; (*recouvrir*): ~ **qch (de)** to cover sth (with).

tapisserie [tapisʀi] *nf* (*tenture, broderie*) tapestry; (: *travail*) tapestry-making; (: *ouvrage*) tapestry work; (*papier peint*) wallpaper; (*fig*): **faire** ~ to sit out, be a wallflower.

tapissier, ière [tapisje, -jɛʀ] *nm/f*: ~**(-décorateur)** upholsterer (and decorator).

tapoter [tapɔte] *vt* to pat, tap.

taquet [takɛ] *nm* (*cale*) wedge; (*cheville*) peg.

taquin, e [takɛ̃, -in] *adj* teasing.

taquiner [takine] *vt* to tease.

taquinerie [takinʀi] *nf* teasing *no pl*.

tarabiscoté, e [taʀabiskɔte] *adj* over-ornate, fussy.

tarabuster [taʀabyste] *vt* to bother, worry.

tarama [taʀama] *nm* (*CULIN*) taramasalata.

tarauder [taʀode] *vt* (*TECH*) to tap; to thread; (*fig*) to pierce.

tard [taʀ] *adv* late; **au plus** ~ at the latest; **plus** ~ later (on) ♦ *nm*: **sur le** ~ (*à une heure avancée*) late in the day; (*vers la fin de la vie*) late in life.

tarder [taʀde] *vi* (*chose*) to be a long time coming; (*personne*): ~ **à faire** to delay doing; **il me tarde d'être** I am longing to be; **sans (plus)** ~ without (further) delay.

tardif, ive [taʀdif, -iv] *adj* (*heure, repas, fruit*) late; (*talent, goût*) late in developing.

tardivement [taʀdivmɑ̃] *adv* late.

tare [taʀ] *nf* (*COMM*) tare; (*fig*) defect; taint, blemish.

targette [taʀʒɛt] *nf* (*verrou*) bolt.

targuer [taʀge]: **se** ~ **de** *vt* to boast about.

tarif [taʀif] *nm* (*liste*) price list, tariff (*BRIT*); (*barème*) rate, rates *pl*, tariff (*BRIT*); (: *de taxis etc*) fares *pl*; **voyager à plein** ~**/à** réduit to travel at full/reduced fare.

tarifaire [taʀifɛʀ] *adj* (*voir tarif*) relating to

price lists *etc*.
tarifé, e [taʀife] *adj*: ~ **10 F** priced at 10 F.
tarifer [taʀife] *vt* to fix the price *ou* rate for.
tarification [taʀifikasjɔ̃] *nf fixing of a price scale*.
tarir [taʀiʀ] *vi* to dry up, run dry ♦ *vt* to dry up.
tarot(s) [taʀo] *nm(pl)* tarot cards.
tartare [taʀtaʀ] *adj* (*CULIN*) tartar(e).
tarte [taʀt(ə)] *nf* tart; ~ **aux pommes/à la crème** apple/custard tart.
tartelette [taʀtəlɛt] *nf* tartlet.
tartine [taʀtin] *nf* slice of bread (and butter (*ou* jam)); ~ **de miel** slice of bread and honey; ~ **beurrée** slice of bread and butter.
tartiner [taʀtine] *vt* to spread; **fromage à** ~ cheese spread.
tartre [taʀtʀ(ə)] *nm* (*des dents*) tartar; (*de chaudière*) fur, scale.
tas [tɑ] *nm* heap, pile; (*fig*): **un** ~ **de** heaps of, lots of; **en** ~ in a heap *ou* pile; **dans le** ~ (*fig*) in the crowd; among them; **formé sur le** ~ trained on the job.
Tasmanie [tasmani] *nf*: **la** ~ Tasmania.
tasmanien, ne [tasmanjɛ̃, -ɛn] *adj* Tasmanian.
tasse [tɑs] *nf* cup; **boire la** ~ (*en se baignant*) to swallow a mouthful; ~ **à café/thé** coffee/teacup.
tassé, e [tɑse] *adj*: **bien** ~ (*café etc*) strong.
tasseau, x [tɑso] *nm* length of wood.
tassement [tɑsmɑ̃] *nm* (*de vertèbres*) compression; (*ÉCON, POL: ralentissement*) fall-off, slowdown; (*BOURSE*) dullness.
tasser [tɑse] *vt* (*terre, neige*) to pack down; (*entasser*): ~ **qch dans** to cram sth into; (*INFORM*) to pack; **se** ~ *vi* (*terrain*) to settle; (*personne: avec l'âge*) to shrink; (*fig*) to sort itself out, settle down.
tâter [tɑte] *vt* to feel; (*fig*) to sound out; ~ **de** (*prison etc*) to have a taste of; **se** ~ (*hésiter*) to be in two minds; ~ **le terrain** (*fig*) to test the ground.
tatillon, ne [tatijɔ̃, -ɔn] *adj* pernickety.
tâtonnement [tɑtɔnmɑ̃] *nm*: **par** ~**s** (*fig*) by trial and error.
tâtonner [tɑtɔne] *vi* to grope one's way along; (*fig*) to grope around (in the dark).
tâtons [tɑtɔ̃]: **à** ~ *adv*: **chercher/avancer à** ~ to grope around for/grope one's way forward.
tatouage [tatwaʒ] *nm* tattooing; (*dessin*) tattoo.
tatouer [tatwe] *vt* to tattoo.
taudis [todi] *nm* hovel, slum.
taule [tol] *nf* (*fam*) nick (*BRIT*), jail.
taupe [top] *nf* mole; (*peau*) moleskin.
taupinière [topinjɛʀ] *nf* molehill.
taureau, x [tɔʀo] *nm* bull; (*signe*): **le T**~ Taurus, the Bull; **être du T**~ to be Taurus.
taurillon [tɔʀijɔ̃] *nm* bull-calf.
tauromachie [tɔʀɔmaʃi] *nf* bullfighting.
taux [to] *nm* rate; (*d'alcool*) level; ~

d'escompte discount rate; ~ **d'intérêt** interest rate; ~ **de mortalité** mortality rate.
tavelé, e [tavle] *adj* marked.
taverne [tavɛʀn(ə)] *nf* inn, tavern.
taxable [taksabl(ə)] *adj* taxable.
taxation [taksasjɔ̃] *nf* taxation; (*TÉL*) charges *pl*.
taxe [taks(ə)] *nf* tax; (*douanière*) duty; **toutes** ~**s comprises (TTC)** inclusive of tax; ~ **de base** (*TÉL*) unit charge; ~ **de séjour** tourist tax; ~ **à** *ou* **sur la valeur ajoutée (TVA)** value added tax (VAT).
taxer [takse] *vt* (*personne*) to tax; (*produit*) to put a tax on, tax; (*fig*): ~ **qn de** (*qualifier de*) to call sb + *attribut*; (*accuser de*) to accuse sb of, tax sb with.
taxi [taksi] *nm* taxi.
taxidermie [taksidɛʀmi] *nf* taxidermy.
taxidermiste [taksidɛʀmist(ə)] *nm/f* taxidermist.
taximètre [taksimɛtʀ(ə)] *nm* (taxi)meter.
taxiphone [taksifɔn] *nm* pay phone.
TB *abr* = **très bien, très bon**.
tbe *abr* (= **très bon état**) VGC, vgc.
TCA *sigle f* (= **taxe sur le chiffre d'affaires**) tax on turnover.
TCF *sigle m* (= *Touring Club de France*) ≈ AA *ou* RAC (*BRIT*), ≈ AAA (*US*).
Tchad [tʃad] *nm*: **le** ~ Chad.
tchadien, ne [tʃadjɛ̃, -ɛn] *adj* Chad(ian), of *ou* from Chad.
tchao [tʃao] *excl* (*fam*) bye(-bye)!
tchécoslovaque [tʃekɔslɔvak] *adj* Czechoslovak(ian) ♦ *nm/f*: **T**~ Czechoslovak(ian).
Tchécoslovaquie [tʃekɔslɔvaki] *nf*: **la** ~ Czechoslovakia.
tchèque [tʃɛk] *adj* Czech ♦ *nm* (*LING*) Czech ♦ *nm/f*: **T**~ Czech.
TCS *sigle m* (= *Touring Club de Suisse*) ≈ AA *ou* RAC (*BRIT*), ≈ AAA (*US*).
TD *sigle mpl* = **travaux dirigés**.
TDF *sigle f* (= *Télévision de France*) French broadcasting authority.
te, t' [t(ə)] *pron* you; (*réfléchi*) yourself.
té [te] *nm* T-square.
technicien, ne [tɛknisjɛ̃, -ɛn] *nm/f* technician.
technicité [tɛknisite] *nf* technical nature.
technico-commercial, e, aux [tɛknikokɔmɛʀsjal, -o] *adj*: **agent** ~ sales technician.
technique [tɛknik] *adj* technical ♦ *nf* technique.
techniquement [tɛknikmɑ̃] *adv* technically.
techno [tɛkno] *nf* (*MUS*) techno.
technocrate [tɛknɔkʀat] *nm/f* technocrat.
technocratie [tɛknɔkʀasi] *nf* technocracy.
technologie [tɛknɔlɔʒi] *nf* technology.
technologique [tɛknɔlɔʒik] *adj* technological.
technologue [tɛknɔlɔg] *nm/f* technologist.
teck [tɛk] *nm* teak.
teckel [tekɛl] *nm* dachshund.

TEE *sigle m* = *Trans-Europ-Express*.
tee-shirt [tiʃœrt] *nm* T-shirt, tee-shirt.
Téhéran [teerã] *n* Teheran.
teigne [tɛɲ] *vb voir* **teindre ♦** *nf* (*ZOOL*) moth;
(*MÉD*) ringworm.
teigneux, euse [tɛɲø, -øz] *adj* (*péj*) nasty,
scabby.
teindre [tɛ̃dʀ(ə)] *vt* to dye; **se ~ (les cheveux)**
to dye one's hair.
teint, e [tɛ̃, tɛ̃t] *pp de* **teindre ♦** *adj* dyed **♦** *nm*
(*du visage: permanent*) complexion,
colouring (*BRIT*), coloring (*US*); (*momentané*)
colour (*BRIT*), color (*US*), **♦** *nf* shade, colour,
color; (*fig: petite dose*): **une ~e de** a hint of;
grand ~ *adj inv* colourfast; **bon ~** *adj inv*
(*couleur*) fast; (*tissu*) colourfast; (*personne*)
staunch, firm.
teinté, e [tɛ̃te] *adj* (*verres*) tinted; (*bois*)
stained; **~ acajou** mahogany-stained; **~ de**
(*fig*) tinged with.
teinter [tɛ̃te] *vt* to tint; (*bois*) to stain; (*fig:
d'ironie etc*) to tinge.
teinture [tɛ̃tyʀ] *nf* dyeing; (*substance*) dye;
(*MÉD*): **~ d'iode** tincture of iodine.
teinturerie [tɛ̃tyʀʀi] *nf* dry cleaner's.
teinturier, ière [tɛ̃tyʀje, -jɛʀ] *nm/f* dry
cleaner.
tel, telle [tɛl] *adj* (*pareil*) such; (*comme*): **~
un/des ...** like a/like ...; (*indéfini*) such-and-
such a, a given; (*intensif*): **un ~/de ~s ...**
such (a)/such ...; **rien de ~** nothing like it, no
such thing; **~ que** *conj* like, such as; **~ quel**
as it is *ou* stands (*ou* was *etc*).
tél. *abr* = *téléphone*.
Tel Aviv [tɛlaviv] *n* Tel Aviv.
télé [tele] *nf* (= *télévision*) TV, telly (*BRIT*); **à la**
~ on TV *ou* telly.
télébenne [teleben] *nm*, *nf* telecabine,
gondola.
télécabine [telekabin] *nm*, *nf* telecabine,
gondola.
télécarte [telekart(ə)] *nf* phonecard.
télécharger [teleʃaʀʒe] *vt* (*INFORM*) to
download.
TELECOM [telekɔm] *abr*
(= *Télécommunications*) ≈ Telecom.
télécommande [telekɔmɑ̃d] *nf* remote
control.
télécommander [telekɔmɑ̃de] *vt* to operate
by remote control, radio-control.
télécommunications [telekɔmynikɑsjɔ̃] *nfpl*
telecommunications.
télécopie [telekɔpi] *nf* fax, telefax.
télécopieur [telekɔpjœʀ] *nm* fax (machine).
télédétection [teledetɛksjɔ̃] *nf* remote
sensing.
télédiffuser [teledifyze] *vt* to broadcast (on
television).
télédiffusion [teledifyzjɔ̃] *nf* television
broadcasting.
télédistribution [teledistʀibysjɔ̃] *nf* cable TV.
téléenseignement [teleɑ̃sɛɲmɑ̃] *nm* distance

teaching (*ou* learning).
téléférique [teleferik] *nm* = **téléphérique**.
téléfilm [telefilm] *nm* film made for TV, TV
film.
télégramme [telegram] *nm* telegram.
télégraphe [telegraf] *nm* telegraph.
télégraphie [telegrafi] *nf* telegraphy.
télégraphier [telegrafje] *vt* to telegraph,
cable.
télégraphique [telegrafik] *adj* telegraph *cpd*,
telegraphic; (*fig*) telegraphic.
télégraphiste [telegrafist(ə)] *nm/f*
telegraphist.
téléguider [telegide] *vt* to operate by remote
control, radio-control.
téléinformatique [teleɛ̃fɔrmatik] *nf* remote
access computing.
téléjournal, aux [teleʒurnal, -o] *nm* television
news magazine programme.
télématique [telematik] *nf* telematics *sg* **♦** *adj*
telematic.
téléobjectif [teleɔbʒɛktif] *nm* telephoto lens
sg.
télépathie [telepati] *nf* telepathy.
téléphérique [teleferik] *nm* cable-car.
téléphone [telefɔn] *nm* telephone; **avoir le ~**
to be on the (tele)phone; **au ~** on the phone;
les T~s the (tele)phone service *sg*; **~ arabe**
bush telegraph; **~ à carte (magnétique)**
cardphone; **~ cellulaire** cellphone, cellular
phone; **~ manuel** manually-operated
telephone system; **~ rouge** hotline.
téléphoner [telefɔne] *vt* to telephone **♦** *vi* to
telephone; to make a phone call; **~ à** to
phone up, ring up, call up.
téléphonie [telefɔni] *nf* telephony.
téléphonique [telefɔnik] *adj* telephone *cpd*,
phone *cpd*; **cabine ~** call box (*BRIT*),
(tele)phone box (*BRIT*) *ou* booth;
conversation/appel ~ (tele)phone
conversation/call.
téléphoniste [telefɔnist(ə)] *nm/f* telephonist,
telephone operator; (*d'entreprise*)
switchboard operator.
téléport [telepɔr] *nm* teleport.
téléprospection [teleprɔspɛksjɔ̃] *nf* telephone
selling.
télescopage [telɛskɔpaʒ] *nm* crash.
télescope [telɛskɔp] *nm* telescope.
télescoper [telɛskɔpe] *vt* to smash up; **se ~**
(*véhicules*) to collide, crash into each other.
télescopique [telɛskɔpik] *adj* telescopic.
téléscripteur [teleskriptœr] *nm* teleprinter.
télésiège [telesjɛʒ] *nm* chairlift.
téléski [teleski] *nm* ski-tow; **~ à archets** T-bar
tow; **~ à perche** button lift.
téléspectateur, trice [telespɛktatœr, -tris]
nm/f (television) viewer.
télétexte [teletɛkst] *nm* ® Teletext ®.
téléthon [teletɔ̃] *nm* telethon.
télétraitement [teletrɛtmɑ̃] *nm* remote
processing.

télétransmission [teletʀɑ̃smisjɔ̃] *nf* remote transmission.

télétype [teletip] *nm* teleprinter.

télévente [televɑ̃t] *nf* telesales.

téléviser [televize] *vt* to televise.

téléviseur [televizœʀ] *nm* television set.

télévision [televizjɔ̃] *nf* television; **(poste de)** ~ television (set); **avoir la** ~ to have a television; **à la** ~ on television; ~ **par câble/ satellite** cable/satellite television.

télex [telɛks] *nm* telex.

télexer [telɛkse] *vt* to telex.

télexiste [telɛksist(ə)] *nm/f* telex operator.

telle [tɛl] *adj f voir* **tel**.

tellement [tɛlmɑ̃] *adv* (*tant*) so much; (*si*) so; ~ **plus grand (que)** so much bigger (than); ~ **de** (*sable, eau*) so much; (*gens, livres*) so many; **il s'est endormi** ~ **il était fatigué** he was so tired (that) he fell asleep; **pas** ~ not really; **pas** ~ **fort/lentement** not (all) that strong/slowly; **il ne mange pas** ~ he doesn't eat (all that) much.

tellurique [telyʀik] *adj*: **secousse** ~ earth tremor.

téméraire [temeʀɛʀ] *adj* reckless, rash.

témérité [temeʀite] *nf* recklessness, rashness.

témoignage [temwaɲaʒ] *nm* (*JUR: déclaration*) testimony *no pl*, evidence *no pl*; (: *faits*) evidence *no pl*; (*gén: rapport, récit*) account; (*fig: d'affection etc*) token, mark; expression.

témoigner [temwaɲe] *vt* (*manifester: intérêt, gratitude*) to show ♦ *vi* (*JUR*) to testify, give evidence; ~ **que** to testify that; (*fig: démontrer*) to reveal that, testify to the fact that; ~ **de** *vt* (*confirmer*) to bear witness to, testify to.

témoin [temwɛ̃] *nm* witness; (*fig*) testimony; (*SPORT*) baton; (*CONSTR*) telltale ♦ *adj* control *cpd*, test *cpd* ♦ *adv*: ~ **le fait que ...** (as) witness the fact that ...; **appartement-**~ show flat (*BRIT*), model apartment (*US*); **être** ~ **de** (*voir*) to witness; **prendre à** ~ to call to witness; ~ **à charge** witness for the prosecution; **T**~ **de Jéhovah** Jehovah's Witness; ~ **de moralité** character reference; ~ **oculaire** eyewitness.

tempe [tɑ̃p] *nf* (*ANAT*) temple.

tempérament [tɑ̃peʀamɑ̃] *nm* temperament, disposition; (*santé*) constitution; **à** ~ (*vente*) on deferred (payment) terms; (*achat*) by instalments, hire purchase *cpd*; **avoir du** ~ to be hot-blooded.

tempérance [tɑ̃peʀɑ̃s] *nf* temperance; **société de** ~ temperance society.

tempérant, e [tɑ̃peʀɑ̃, -ɑ̃t] *adj* temperate.

température [tɑ̃peʀatyʀ] *nf* temperature; **prendre la** ~ **de** to take the temperature of; (*fig*) to gauge the feeling of; **avoir** *ou* **faire de la** ~ to be running *ou* have a temperature.

tempéré, e [tɑ̃peʀe] *adj* temperate.

tempérer [tɑ̃peʀe] *vt* to temper.

tempête [tɑ̃pɛt] *nf* storm; ~ **de sable/neige** sand/snowstorm; **vent de** ~ gale.

tempêter [tɑ̃pete] *vi* to rant and rave.

temple [tɑ̃pl(ə)] *nm* temple; (*protestant*) church.

tempo [tɛmpo] *nm* tempo (*pl* -s).

temporaire [tɑ̃pɔʀɛʀ] *adj* temporary.

temporairement [tɑ̃pɔʀɛʀmɑ̃] *adv* temporarily.

temporel, le [tɑ̃pɔʀɛl] *adj* temporal.

temporisateur, trice [tɑ̃pɔʀizatœʀ, -tʀis] *adj* temporizing, delaying.

temporisation [tɑ̃pɔʀizasjɔ̃] *nf* temporizing, playing for time.

temporiser [tɑ̃pɔʀize] *vi* to temporize, play for time.

temps [tɑ̃] *nm* (*atmosphérique*) weather; (*durée*) time; (*époque*) time, times *pl*; (*LING*) tense; (*MUS*) beat; (*TECH*) stroke; **les** ~ **changent/sont durs** times are changing/ hard; **il fait beau/mauvais** ~ the weather is fine/bad; **avoir le** ~/**tout le** ~/**juste le** ~ to have time/plenty of time/just enough time; **avoir fait son** ~ (*fig*) to have had its (*ou* his *etc*) day; **en** ~ **de paix/guerre** in peacetime/ wartime; **en** ~ **utile** *ou* **voulu** in due time *ou* course; **de** ~ **en** ~, **de** ~ **à autre** from time to time, now and again; **en même** ~ at the same time; **à** ~ (*partir, arriver*) in time; **à plein/mi-**~ *adv, adj* full-/part-time; **à** ~ **partiel** *adv, adj* part-time; **dans le** ~ at one time; **de tout** ~ always; **du** ~ **que** at the time when, in the days when; **dans le** *ou* **du** *ou* **au** ~ **où** at the time when; **pendant ce** ~ in the meantime; ~ **d'accès** (*INFORM*) access time; ~ **d'arrêt** pause, halt; ~ **mort** (*SPORT*) stoppage (time); (*COMM*) slack period; ~ **partagé** (*INFORM*) time-sharing; ~ **réel** (*INFORM*) real time.

tenable [tənabl(ə)] *adj* bearable.

tenace [tənas] *adj* tenacious, persistent.

ténacité [tenasite] *nf* tenacity, persistence.

tenailler [tənaje] *vt* (*fig*) to torment, torture.

tenailles [tənaj] *nfpl* pincers.

tenais [t(ə)nɛ] *etc vb voir* **tenir**.

tenancier, ière [tənɑ̃sje, -jɛʀ] *nm/f* (*d'hôtel, de bistro*) manager/manageress.

tenant, e [tənɑ̃, -ɑ̃t] *adj f voir* **séance** ♦ *nm/f* (*SPORT*): ~ **du titre** title-holder ♦ *nm*: **d'un seul** ~ in one piece; **les** ~**s et les aboutissants** (*fig*) the ins and outs.

tendance [tɑ̃dɑ̃s] *nf* (*opinions*) leanings *pl*, sympathies *pl*; (*inclination*) tendency; (*évolution*) trend; ~ **à la hausse/baisse** upward/downward trend; **avoir** ~ **à** to have a tendency to, tend to.

tendancieux, euse [tɑ̃dɑ̃sjø, -øz] *adj* tendentious.

tendeur [tɑ̃dœʀ] *nm* (*de vélo*) chain-adjuster; (*de câble*) wire-strainer; (*de tente*) runner; (*attache*) elastic strap.

tendinite [tɑ̃dinit] *nf* tendinitis, tendonitis.

tendon [tɑ̃dɔ̃] *nm* tendon, sinew; ~ **d'Achille**

Achilles' tendon.

tendre [tādʀ(ə)] adj (viande, légumes) tender; (bois, roche, couleur) soft; (affectueux) tender, loving ♦ vt (élastique, peau) to stretch, draw tight; (muscle) to tense; (donner): ~ **qch à qn** to hold sth out to sb; to offer sb sth; (fig: piège) to set, lay; (tapisserie): **tendu de soie** hung with silk, with silk hangings; **se** ~ vi (corde) to tighten; (relations) to become strained; ~ **à qch/à faire** to tend towards sth/to do; ~ **l'oreille** to prick up one's ears; ~ **la main/le bras** to hold out one's hand/stretch out one's arm; ~ **la perche à qn** (fig) to throw sb a line.

tendrement [tādʀəmā] adv tenderly, lovingly.

tendresse [tādʀɛs] nf tenderness; ~s nfpl (caresses etc) tenderness no pl, caresses.

tendu, e [tādy] pp de **tendre** ♦ adj tight; tensed; strained.

ténèbres [tenɛbʀ(ə)] nfpl darkness sg.

ténébreux, euse [tenebʀø, -øz] adj obscure, mysterious; (personne) saturnine.

Ténérife [teneʀif] nf Tenerife.

teneur [tənœʀ] nf content, substance; (d'une lettre) terms pl, content; ~ **en cuivre** copper content.

ténia [tenja] nm tapeworm.

tenir [təniʀ] vt to hold; (magasin, hôtel) to run; (promesse) to keep ♦ vi to hold; (neige, gel) to last; (survivre) to survive; **se** ~ vi (avoir lieu) to be held, take place; (être: personne) to stand; **se** ~ **droit** to stand up (ou sit up) straight; **bien se** ~ to behave well; **se** ~ **à qch** to hold on to sth; **s'en** ~ **à qch** to confine o.s. to sth; to stick to sth; ~ **à** vt to be attached to, care about (ou for); (avoir pour cause) to be due to, stem from; ~ **à faire** to want to do, be keen to do; ~ **à ce que qn fasse qch** to be anxious that sb should do sth; ~ **de** vt to partake of; (ressembler à) to take after; **ça ne tient qu'à lui** it is entirely up to him; ~ **qn pour** to take sb for; ~ **qch de qn** (histoire) to have heard ou learnt sth from sb; (qualité, défaut) to have inherited ou got sth from sb; ~ **les comptes** to keep the books; ~ **un rôle** to play a part; ~ **de la place** to take up space ou room; ~ **l'alcool** to be able to hold a drink; ~ **le coup** to hold out; ~ **bon** to stand ou hold fast; ~ **3 jours/2 mois** (résister) to hold out ou last 3 days/2 months; ~ **au chaud/à l'abri** to keep hot/under shelter ou cover; ~ **prêt** to have ready; ~ **sa langue** (fig) to hold one's tongue; **tiens (ou tenez), voilà le stylo** there's the pen!; **tiens, Alain!** look, here's Alain!; **tiens?** (surprise) really?; **tiens-toi bien!** (pour informer) brace yourself!, take a deep breath!

tennis [tenis] nm tennis; (aussi: **court de** ~) tennis court ♦ nmpl ou fpl (aussi: **chaussures de** ~) tennis ou gym shoes; ~ **de table** table tennis.

tennisman [tenisman] nm tennis player.

ténor [tenɔʀ] nm tenor.

tension [tāsjɔ̃] nf tension; (fig: des relations, de la situation) tension; (: concentration, effort) strain; (MÉD) blood pressure; **faire** ou **avoir de la** ~ to have high blood pressure; ~ **nerveuse/raciale** nervous/racial tension.

tentaculaire [tātakylɛʀ] adj (fig) sprawling.

tentacule [tātakyl] nm tentacle.

tentant, e [tātā, -āt] adj tempting.

tentateur, trice [tātatœʀ, -tʀis] adj tempting ♦ nm (REL) tempter.

tentation [tātasjɔ̃] nf temptation.

tentative [tātativ] nf attempt, bid; ~ **d'évasion** escape bid; ~ **de suicide** suicide attempt.

tente [tāt] nf tent; ~ **à oxygène** oxygen tent.

tenter [tāte] vt (éprouver, attirer) to tempt; (essayer): ~ **qch/de faire** to attempt ou try sth/to do; **être tenté de** to be tempted to; ~ **sa chance** to try one's luck.

tenture [tātyʀ] nf hanging.

tenu, e [təny] pp de **tenir** ♦ adj (maison, comptes): **bien** ~ well-kept; (obligé): ~ **de faire** under an obligation to do ♦ nf (action de tenir) running; keeping; holding; (vêtements) clothes pl, gear; (allure) dress no pl, appearance; (comportement) manners pl, behaviour (BRIT), behavior (US); **être en** ~**e** to be dressed (up); **se mettre en** ~**e** to dress (up); **en grande** ~**e** in full dress; **en petite** ~**e** scantily dressed ou clad; **avoir de la** ~**e** to have good manners; (journal) to have a high standard; ~**e de combat** combat gear ou dress; ~**e de pompier** fireman's uniform; ~**e de route** (AUTO) road-holding; ~**e de soirée** evening dress; ~**e de sport/voyage** sports/travelling clothes pl ou gear no pl.

ténu, e [təny] adj (indice, nuance) tenuous, subtle; (fil, objet) fine; (voix) thin.

ter [tɛʀ] adj: **16** ~ **16b** ou **B**.

térébenthine [teʀebātin] nf: **(essence de)** ~ (oil of) turpentine.

tergal [tɛʀgal] nm ® Terylene ®.

tergiversations [tɛʀʒivɛʀsasjɔ̃] nfpl shilly-shallying no pl.

tergiverser [tɛʀʒivɛʀse] vi to shilly-shally.

terme [tɛʀm(ə)] nm term; (fin) end; **être en bons/mauvais** ~**s avec qn** to be on good/bad terms with sb; **vente/achat à** ~ (COMM) forward sale/purchase; **au** ~ **de** at the end of; **en d'autres** ~**s** in other words; **moyen** ~ (solution intermédiaire) middle course; **à court/long** ~ adj short-/long-term ou -range ♦ adv in the short/long term; **à** ~ adj (MÉD) full-term ♦ adv sooner or later, eventually; (MÉD) at term; **avant** ~ (MÉD) adj premature ♦ adv prematurely; **mettre un** ~ **à** to put an end ou a stop to; **toucher à son** ~ to be nearing its end.

terminaison [tɛʀminɛzɔ̃] nf (LING) ending.

terminal, e, aux [tɛʀminal, -o] adj (partie,

phase) final; (*MÉD*) terminal ♦ *nm* terminal ♦ *nf* (*SCOL*) ≈ sixth form *ou* year (*BRIT*), ≈ twelfth grade (*US*).

terminer [tɛʀmine] *vt* to end; (*travail, repas*) to finish; **se** ~ *vi* to end; **se** ~ **par** to end with.

terminologie [tɛʀminɔlɔʒi] *nf* terminology.

terminus [tɛʀminys] *nm* terminus (*pl* -i); ~**!** all change!

termite [tɛʀmit] *nm* termite, white ant.

termitière [tɛʀmitjɛʀ] *nf* ant-hill.

ternaire [tɛʀnɛʀ] *adj* compound.

terne [tɛʀn(ə)] *adj* dull.

ternir [tɛʀniʀ] *vt* to dull; (*fig*) to sully, tarnish; **se** ~ *vi* to become dull.

terrain [tɛʀɛ̃] *nm* (*sol, fig*) ground; (*COMM*) land *no pl*, plot (of land); (*: à bâtir*) site; **sur le** ~ (*fig*) on the field; ~ **de football/rugby** football/rugby pitch (*BRIT*) *ou* field (*US*); ~ **d'atterrissage** landing strip; ~ **d'aviation** airfield; ~ **de camping** campsite; **un** ~ **d'entente** an area of agreement; ~ **de golf** golf course; ~ **de jeu** playground; (*SPORT*) games field; ~ **de sport** sports ground; ~ **vague** waste ground *no pl*.

terrasse [tɛʀas] *nf* terrace; (*de café*) pavement area, terrasse; **à la** ~ (*café*) outside.

terrassement [tɛʀasmɑ̃] *nm* earth-moving, earthworks *pl*; embankment.

terrasser [tɛʀase] *vt* (*adversaire*) to floor, bring down; (*suj: maladie etc*) to lay low.

terrassier [tɛʀasje] *nm* navvy, roadworker.

terre [tɛʀ] *nf* (*gén, aussi ÉLEC*) earth; (*substance*) soil, earth; (*opposé à mer*) land *no pl*; (*contrée*) land; ~**s** *nfpl* (*terrains*) lands, land *sg*; **travail de la** ~ work on the land; **en** ~ (*pipe, poterie*) clay *cpd*; **mettre en** ~ (*plante etc*) to plant; (*personne: enterrer*) to bury; **à** *ou* **par** ~ (*mettre, être*) on the ground (*ou* floor); (*jeter, tomber*) to the ground, down; ~ **à** ~ *adj inv* down-to-earth, matter-of-fact; **la T**~ **Adélie** Adélie Coast *ou* Land; ~ **de bruyère** (heath-)peat; ~ **cuite** earthenware; terracotta; **la** ~ **ferme** dry land, terra firma; **la T**~ **de feu** Tierra del Fuego; ~ **glaise** clay; **la T**~ **promise** the Promised Land; **la T**~ **Sainte** the Holy Land.

terreau [tɛʀo] *nm* compost.

Terre-Neuve [tɛʀnœv] *nf*: **la** ~ (*aussi*: **l'île de** ~) Newfoundland.

terre-plein [tɛʀplɛ̃] *nm* platform.

terrer [tɛʀe]: **se** ~ *vi* to hide away; to go to ground.

terrestre [tɛʀɛstʀ(ə)] *adj* (*surface*) earth's, of the earth; (*BOT, ZOOL, MIL*) land *cpd*; (*REL*) earthly, worldly.

terreur [tɛʀœʀ] *nf* terror *no pl*, fear.

terreux, euse [tɛʀø, -øz] *adj* muddy; (*goût*) earthy.

terrible [tɛʀibl(ə)] *adj* terrible, dreadful; (*fam: fantastique*) terrific.

terriblement [tɛʀibləmɑ̃] *adv* (*très*) terribly, awfully.

terrien, ne [tɛʀjɛ̃, -ɛn] *adj*: **propriétaire** ~ landowner ♦ *nm/f* countryman/woman, man/ woman of the soil; (*non martien etc*) earthling; (*non marin*) landsman.

terrier [tɛʀje] *nm* burrow, hole; (*chien*) terrier.

terrifiant, e [tɛʀifjɑ̃, -ɑ̃t] *adj* (*effrayant*) terrifying; (*extraordinaire*) terrible, awful.

terrifier [tɛʀifje] *vt* to terrify.

terril [tɛʀil] *nm* slag heap.

terrine [tɛʀin] *nf* (*récipient*) terrine; (*CULIN*) pâté.

territoire [tɛʀitwaʀ] *nm* territory; **T**~ **des Afars et des Issas** French Territory of Afars and Issas.

territorial, e, aux [tɛʀitɔʀjal, -o] *adj* territorial; **eaux** ~**es** territorial waters; **armée** ~**e** regional defence force, ≈ Territorial Army (*BRIT*); **collectivités** ~**es** local and regional authorities.

terroir [tɛʀwaʀ] *nm* (*AGR*) soil; (*région*) region; **accent du** ~ country *ou* rural accent.

terroriser [tɛʀɔʀize] *vt* to terrorize.

terrorisme [tɛʀɔʀism(ə)] *nm* terrorism.

terroriste [tɛʀɔʀist(ə)] *nm/f* terrorist.

tertiaire [tɛʀsjɛʀ] *adj* tertiary ♦ *nm* (*ÉCON*) tertiary sector, service industries *pl*.

tertiarisation [tɛʀsjaʀizasjɔ̃] *nf* expansion or development of the service sector.

tertre [tɛʀtʀ(ə)] *nm* hillock, mound.

tes [te] *dét voir* **ton**.

tesson [tesɔ̃] *nm*: ~ **de bouteille** piece of broken bottle.

test [tɛst] *nm* test; ~ **de grossesse** pregnancy test.

testament [tɛstamɑ̃] *nm* (*JUR*) will; (*fig*) legacy; (*REL*): **T**~ Testament; **faire son** ~ to make one's will.

testamentaire [tɛstamɑ̃tɛʀ] *adj* of a will.

tester [tɛste] *vt* to test.

testicule [tɛstikyl] *nm* testicle.

tétanie [tetani] *nf* tetany.

tétanos [tetanos] *nm* tetanus.

têtard [tɛtaʀ] *nm* tadpole.

tête [tɛt] *nf* head; (*cheveux*) hair *no pl*; (*visage*) face; (*longueur*): **gagner d'une (courte)** ~ to win by a (short) head; (*FOOTBALL*) header; **de** ~ *adj* (*wagon etc*) front *cpd*; (*concurrent*) leading ♦ *adv* (*calculer*) in one's head, mentally; **par** ~ (*par personne*) per head; **se mettre en** ~ **que** to get it into one's head that; **se mettre en** ~ **de faire** to take it into one's head to do; **prendre la** ~ **de qch** to take the lead in sth; **perdre la** ~ (*fig: s'affoler*) to lose one's head; (*: devenir fou*) to go off one's head; **ça ne va pas, la** ~**?** (*fam*) are you crazy?; **tenir** ~ **à qn** to stand up to *ou* defy sb; **la** ~ **en bas** with one's head down; **la** ~ **la première** (*tomber*) headfirst; **la** ~ **basse** hanging one's head; **avoir la** ~ **dure** (*fig*) to be thickheaded; **faire une** ~ (*FOOTBALL*) to head the ball; **faire la** ~ (*fig*) to sulk; **en** ~ (*SPORT*) in the lead; at the front *ou* head; **de**

la ~ **aux pieds** from head to toe; ~ **d'affiche**
(*THÉÂT etc*) top of the bill; ~ **de bétail** head
inv of cattle; ~ **brulée** desperado; ~
chercheuse homing device; ~
d'enregistrement recording head; ~
d'impression printhead; ~ **de lecture**
(playback) head; ~ **de ligne** (*TRANSPORTS*)
start of the line; ~ **de liste** (*POL*) chief
candidate; ~ **de mort** skull and crossbones;
~ **de pont** (*MIL*) bridge- *ou* beachhead; ~ **de**
série (*TENNIS*) seeded player, seed; ~ **de**
Turc (*fig*) whipping boy (*BRIT*), butt; ~ **de**
veau (*CULIN*) calf's head.

tête-à-queue [tɛtakø] *nm inv*: **faire un** ~ to
spin round.

tête-à-tête [tɛtatɛt] *nm inv* tête-à-tête;
(*service*) breakfast set for two; **en** ~ in
private, alone together.

tête-bêche [tɛtbɛʃ] *adv* head to tail.

tétée [tete] *nf* (*action*) sucking; (*repas*) feed.

téter [tete] *vt*: ~ **(sa mère)** to suck at one's
mother's breast, feed.

tétine [tetin] *nf* teat; (*sucette*) dummy (*BRIT*),
pacifier (*US*).

téton [tetɔ̃] *nm* breast.

têtu, e [tety] *adj* stubborn, pigheaded.

texte [tɛkst(ə)] *nm* text; (*SCOL: d'un devoir*)
subject, topic; **apprendre son** ~ (*THÉÂT*) to
learn one's lines; **un** ~ **de loi** the wording of
a law.

textile [tɛkstil] *adj* textile *cpd* ♦ *nm* textile;
(*industrie*) textile industry.

textuel, le [tɛkstɥɛl] *adj* literal, word for
word.

textuellement [tɛkstɥɛlmɑ̃] *adv* literally.

texture [tɛkstyʀ] *nf* texture; (*fig: d'un texte,*
livre) feel.

TF1 *sigle f* (= *Télévision française 1*) TV channel.

TG *sigle f* = **Trésorerie générale**.

TGI *sigle m* = **tribunal de grande instance**.

TGV *sigle m* = **train à grande vitesse**.

thaï, e [tai] *adj* Thai ♦ *nm* (*LING*) Thai.

thaïlandais, e [tailɑ̃dɛ, -ɛz] *adj* Thai.

Thaïlande [tailɑ̃d] *nf*: **la** ~ Thailand.

thalassothérapie [talasoteʀapi] *nf* sea-water
therapy.

thé [te] *nm* tea; (*réunion*) tea party; **prendre le**
~ to have tea; ~ **au lait/citron** tea with
milk/lemon.

théâtral, e, aux [teatʀal, -o] *adj* theatrical.

théâtre [teatʀ(ə)] *nm* theatre; (*techniques,*
genre) drama, theatre; (*activité*) stage,
theatre; (*œuvres*) plays *pl*, dramatic works
pl; (*fig: lieu*): **le** ~ **de** the scene of;
histrionics *pl*, playacting; **faire du** ~ (*en*
professionnel) to be on the stage; (*en*
amateur) to do some acting; ~ **filmé** filmed
stage productions *pl*.

thébain, e [tebɛ̃, -ɛn] *adj* Theban.

Thèbes [tɛb] *n* Thebes.

théière [tejɛʀ] *nf* teapot.

théine [tein] *nf* theine.

théisme [teism(ə)] *nm* theism.

thématique [tematik] *adj* thematic.

thème [tɛm] *nm* theme; (*SCOL: traduction*)
prose (composition); ~ **astral** birth chart.

théocratie [teɔkʀasi] *nf* theocracy.

théologie [teɔlɔʒi] *nf* theology.

théologien, ne [teɔlɔʒjɛ̃, -ɛn] *nm* theologian.

théologique [teɔlɔʒik] *adj* theological.

théorème [teɔʀɛm] *nm* theorem.

théoricien, ne [teɔʀisjɛ̃, -ɛn] *nm/f*
theoretician, theorist.

théorie [teɔʀi] *nf* theory; **en** ~ in theory.

théorique [teɔʀik] *adj* theoretical.

théoriquement [teɔʀikmɑ̃] *adv* theoretically.

théoriser [teɔʀize] *vi* to theorize.

thérapeutique [teʀapøtik] *adj* therapeutic ♦ *nf*
(*MÉD: branche*) therapeutics *sg*; (*: traitement*)
therapy.

thérapie [teʀapi] *nf* therapy; ~ **de groupe**
group therapy.

thermal, e, aux [tɛʀmal, -o] *adj* thermal;
station ~**e** spa; **cure** ~**e** water cure.

thermes [tɛʀm(ə)] *nmpl* thermal baths;
(*romains*) thermae *pl*.

thermique [tɛʀmik] *adj* (*énergie*) thermic;
(*unité*) thermal.

thermodynamique [tɛʀmɔdinamik] *nf*
thermodynamics *sg*.

thermoélectrique [tɛʀmoelɛktʀik] *adj*
thermoelectric.

thermomètre [tɛʀmɔmɛtʀ(ə)] *nm*
thermometer.

thermonucléaire [tɛʀmɔnykleɛʀ] *adj*
thermonuclear.

thermos [tɛʀmos] *nm ou nf* ®: (**bouteille**) ~
vacuum *ou* Thermos ® flask (*BRIT*) *ou* bottle
(*US*).

thermostat [tɛʀmɔsta] *nm* thermostat.

thésauriser [tezoʀize] *vi* to hoard money.

thèse [tɛz] *nf* thesis (*pl* theses).

Thessalie [tesali] *nf*: **la** ~ Thessaly.

thessalien, ne [tesaljɛ̃, -ɛn] *adj* Thessalian.

thibaude [tibod] *nf* carpet underlay.

thon [tɔ̃] *nm* tuna (fish).

thonier [tɔnje] *nm* tuna boat.

thoracique [tɔʀasik] *adj* thoracic.

thorax [tɔʀaks] *nm* thorax.

thrombose [tʀɔ̃boz] *nf* thrombosis.

thym [tɛ̃] *nm* thyme.

thyroïde [tiʀɔid] *nf* thyroid (gland).

TI *sigle m* = **tribunal d'instance**.

tiare [tjaʀ] *nf* tiara.

Tibet [tibɛ] *nm*: **le** ~ Tibet.

tibétain, e [tibetɛ̃, -ɛn] *adj* Tibetan.

tibia [tibja] *nm* shin; (*os*) shinbone, tibia.

Tibre [tibʀ(ə)] *nm*: **le** ~ the Tiber.

tic [tik] *nm* tic, (nervous) twitch; (*de langage*
etc) mannerism.

ticket [tikɛ] *nm* ticket; ~ **de caisse** till receipt;
~ **modérateur** *patient's contribution*
towards medical costs; ~ **de quai** platform
ticket; ~ **repas** luncheon voucher.

tic-tac [tiktak] *nm inv* tick-tock.
tictaquer [tiktake] *vi* to tick (away).
tiède [tjɛd] *adj* (*bière etc*) lukewarm; (*thé, café etc*) tepid; (*bain, accueil, sentiment*) lukewarm; (*vent, air*) mild, warm ♦ *adv*: **boire** ~ to drink things lukewarm.
tièdement [tjɛdmɑ̃] *adv* coolly, half-heartedly.
tiédeur [tjedœR] *nf* lukewarmness; (*du vent, de l'air*) mildness.
tiédir [tjediR] *vi* (*se réchauffer*) to grow warmer; (*refroidir*) to cool.
tien, tienne [tjɛ̃, tjɛn] *pron*: **le** ~ (**la tienne**), **les** ~**s** (**tiennes**) yours; **à la tienne!** cheers!
tiendrai [tjɛ̃dRe] *etc vb voir* **tenir**.
tienne [tjɛn] *vb voir* **tenir** ♦ *pron voir* **tien**.
tiens [tjɛ̃] *vb, excl voir* **tenir**.
tierce [tjɛRS(ə)] *adj f, nf voir* **tiers**.
tiercé [tjɛRSe] *nm system of forecast betting giving first three horses.*
tiers, tierce [tjɛR, tjɛRS(ə)] *adj* third ♦ *nm* (*JUR*) third party; (*fraction*) third ♦ *nf* (*MUS*) third; (*CARTES*) tierce; **une tierce personne** a third party; **assurance au** ~ third-party insurance; **le** ~ **monde** the third world; ~ **payant** *direct payment by insurers of medical expenses*; ~ **provisionnel** *interim payment of tax.*
tiersmondisme [tjɛRmɔ̃dism(ə)] *nm* support for the Third World.
TIG *sigle m* = **travail d'intérêt général**.
tige [tiʒ] *nf* stem; (*baguette*) rod.
tignasse [tiɲas] *nf* (*péj*) shock *ou* mop of hair.
Tigre [tigR(ə)] *nm*: **le** ~ the Tigris.
tigre [tigR(ə)] *nm* tiger.
tigré, e [tigRe] *adj* (*rayé*) striped; (*tacheté*) spotted.
tigresse [tigRɛs] *nf* tigress.
tilleul [tijœl] *nm* lime (tree), linden (tree); (*boisson*) lime(-blossom) tea.
tilt [tilt(ə)] *nm*: **faire** ~ (*fig: échouer*) to miss the target; (: *inspirer*) to ring a bell.
timbale [tɛ̃bal] *nf* (*metal*) tumbler; ~**s** *nfpl* (*MUS*) timpani, kettledrums.
timbrage [tɛ̃bRaʒ] *nm*: **dispensé de** ~ post(age) paid.
timbre [tɛ̃bR(ə)] *nm* (*tampon*) stamp; (*aussi*: ~-**poste**) (postage) stamp; (*cachet de la poste*) postmark; (*sonnette*) bell; (*MUS: de voix, instrument*) timbre, tone; ~ **anti-tabac** nicotine patch; ~ **dateur** date stamp.
timbré, e [tɛ̃bRe] *adj* (*enveloppe*) stamped; (*voix*) resonant; (*fam: fou*) cracked, nuts.
timbrer [tɛ̃bRe] *vt* to stamp.
timide [timid] *adj* (*emprunté*) shy, timid; (*timoré*) timid, timorous.
timidement [timidmɑ̃] *adv* shyly; timidly.
timidité [timidite] *nf* shyness; timidity.
timonerie [timɔnRi] *nf* wheelhouse.
timonier [timɔnje] *nm* helmsman.
timoré, e [timɔRe] *adj* timorous.
tint [tɛ̃] *etc vb voir* **tenir**.

tintamarre [tɛ̃tamaR] *nm* din, uproar.
tintement [tɛ̃tmɑ̃] *nm* ringing, chiming; ~**s d'oreilles** ringing in the ears.
tinter [tɛ̃te] *vi* to ring, chime; (*argent, clefs*) to jingle.
Tipp-Ex [tipɛks] *nm* ® Tipp-Ex ®.
tique [tik] *nf* tick (*insect*).
tiquer [tike] *vi* (*personne*) to make a face.
TIR *sigle mpl* (= *Transports internationaux routiers*) TIR.
tir [tiR] *nm* (*sport*) shooting; (*fait ou manière de tirer*) firing *no pl*; (*FOOTBALL*) shot; (*stand*) shooting gallery; ~ **d'obus/de mitraillette** shell/machine gun fire; ~ **à l'arc** archery; ~ **de barrage** barrage fire; ~ **au fusil** (rifle) shooting; ~ **au pigeon** (*d'argile*) clay pigeon shooting.
tirade [tiRad] *nf* tirade.
tirage [tiRaʒ] *nm* (*action*) printing; (*PHOTO*) print; (*INFORM*) printout; (*de journal*) circulation; (*de livre*) (print-)run; edition; (*de cheminée*) draught (*BRIT*), draft (*US*); (*de loterie*) draw; (*fig: désaccord*) friction; ~ **au sort** drawing lots.
tiraillement [tiRajmɑ̃] *nm* (*douleur*) sharp pain; (*fig: doutes*) agony *no pl* of indecision; (*conflits*) friction *no pl*.
tirailler [tiRaje] *vt* to pull at, tug at; (*fig*) to gnaw at ♦ *vi* to fire at random.
tirailleur [tiRajœR] *nm* skirmisher.
tirant [tiRɑ̃] *nm*: ~ **d'eau** draught (*BRIT*), draft (*US*).
tire [tiR] *nf*: **vol à la** ~ pickpocketing.
tiré [tiRe] *adj* (*visage, traits*) drawn ♦ *nm* (*COMM*) drawee; ~ **par les cheveux** far-fetched; ~ **à part** off-print.
tire-au-flanc [tiRoflɑ̃] *nm inv* (*péj*) skiver.
tire-bouchon [tiRbuʃɔ̃] *nm* corkscrew.
tire-bouchonner [tiRbuʃɔne] *vt* to twirl.
tire-d'aile [tiRdɛl]: **à** ~ *adv* swiftly.
tire-fesses [tiRfɛs] *nm inv* ski-tow.
tire-lait [tiRlɛ] *nm inv* breast-pump.
tire-larigot [tiRlaRigo]: **à** ~ *adv* as much as one likes, to one's heart's content.
tirelire [tiRliR] *nf* moneybox.
tirer [tiRe] *vt* (*gén*) to pull; (*extraire*): ~ **qch de** to take *ou* pull sth out of; to get sth out of; to extract sth from; (*tracer: ligne, trait*) to draw, trace; (*fermer: volet, porte, trappe*) to pull to, close; (: *rideau*) to draw; (*choisir: carte, conclusion, aussi COMM: chèque*) to draw; (*en faisant feu: balle, coup*) to fire; (: *animal*) to shoot; (*journal, livre, photo*) to print; (*FOOTBALL: corner etc*) to take ♦ *vi* (*faire feu*) to fire; (*faire du tir, FOOTBALL*) to shoot; (*cheminée*) to draw; **se** ~ *vi* (*fam*) to push off; **s'en** ~ to pull through; ~ **sur** (*corde, poignée*) to pull on *ou* at; (*faire feu sur*) to shoot *ou* fire at; (*pipe*) to draw on; (*fig: avoisiner*) to verge *ou* border on; ~ **6 mètres** (*NAVIG*) to draw 6 metres of water; ~ **son nom de** to take *ou* get its name from; ~ **la langue** to stick out

one's tongue; ~ **qn de** (*embarras etc*) to help *ou* get sb out of; ~ **à l'arc/la carabine** to shoot with a bow and arrow/with a rifle; ~ **en longueur** to drag on; ~ **à sa fin** to be drawing to an end; ~ **les cartes** to read *ou* tell the cards.

tiret [tiʀɛ] *nm* dash; (*en fin de ligne*) hyphen.

tireur, euse [tiʀœʀ, -øz] *nm/f* gunman; (*COMM*) drawer; **bon** ~ good shot; ~ **d'élite** marksman; ~ **de cartes** fortuneteller.

tiroir [tiʀwaʀ] *nm* drawer.

tiroir-caisse [tiʀwaʀkɛs] *nm* till.

tisane [tizan] *nf* herb tea.

tison [tizɔ̃] *nm* brand.

tisonner [tizɔne] *vt* to poke.

tisonnier [tizɔnje] *nm* poker.

tissage [tisaʒ] *nm* weaving *no pl*.

tisser [tise] *vt* to weave.

tisserand, e [tisʀɑ̃, -ɑ̃d] *nm/f* weaver.

tissu [tisy] *nm* fabric, material, cloth *no pl*; (*fig*) fabric; (*ANAT, BIO*) tissue; ~ **de mensonges** web of lies.

tissu, e [tisy] *adj*: ~ **de** woven through with.

tissu-éponge [tisyepɔ̃ʒ] *nm* (terry) towelling *no pl*.

titane [titan] *nm* titanium.

titanesque [titanɛsk(ə)] *adj* titanic.

titiller [titile] *vt* to titillate.

titrage [titʀaʒ] *nm* (*d'un film*) titling; (*d'un alcool*) determination of alcohol content.

titre [titʀ(ə)] *nm* (*gén*) title; (*de journal*) headline; (*diplôme*) qualification; (*COMM*) security; (*CHIMIE*) titre; **en** ~ (*champion, responsable*) official, recognized; **à juste** ~ with just cause, rightly; **à quel** ~? on what grounds?; **à aucun** ~ on no account; **au même** ~ **(que)** in the same way (as); **au** ~ **de la coopération** *etc* in the name of cooperation *etc*; **à** ~ **d'exemple** as an *ou* by way of an example; **à** ~ **exceptionnel** exceptionally; **à** ~ **d'information** for (your) information; **à** ~ **gracieux** free of charge; **à** ~ **d'essai** on a trial basis; **à** ~ **privé** in a private capacity; ~ **courant** running head; ~ **de propriété** title deed; ~ **de transport** ticket.

titré, e [titʀe] *adj* (*livre, film*) entitled; (*personne*) titled.

titrer [titʀe] *vt* (*CHIMIE*) to titrate; to assay; (*PRESSE*) to run as a headline; (*suj: vin*): ~ **10°** to be 10° proof.

titubant, e [titybɑ̃, -ɑ̃t] *adj* staggering, reeling.

tituber [titybe] *vi* to stagger *ou* reel (along).

titulaire [titylɛʀ] *adj* (*ADMIN*) appointed, with tenure ♦ *nm* (*ADMIN*) incumbent; **être** ~ **de** to hold.

titularisation [titylaʀizɑsjɔ̃] *nf* granting of tenure.

titulariser [titylaʀize] *vt* to give tenure to.

TNP *sigle m* = *Théâtre national populaire*.

TNT *sigle m* (= *Trinitrotoluène*) TNT.

toast [tost] *nm* slice *ou* piece of toast; (*de bienvenue*) (welcoming) toast; **porter un** ~ **à qn** to propose *ou* drink a toast to sb.

toboggan [tɔbɔgɑ̃] *nm* toboggan; (*jeu*) slide; (*AUTO*) flyover (*BRIT*), overpass (*US*); ~ **de secours** (*AVIAT*) escape chute.

toc [tɔk] *nm*: **en** ~ imitation *cpd*.

tocsin [tɔksɛ̃] *nm* alarm (bell).

toge [tɔʒ] *nf* toga; (*de juge*) gown.

Togo [tɔgo] *nm*: **le** ~ Togo.

togolais, e [tɔgɔlɛ, -ɛz] *adj* Togolese.

tohu-bohu [tɔybɔy] *nm* (*désordre*) confusion; (*tumulte*) commotion.

toi [twa] *pron* you; ~, **tu l'as fait?** did YOU do it?

toile [twal] *nf* (*matériau*) cloth *no pl*; (*bâche*) piece of canvas; (*tableau*) canvas; **grosse** ~ canvas; **tisser sa** ~ (*araignée*) to spin its web; ~ **d'araignée** spider's web; (*au plafond etc: à enlever*) cobweb; ~ **cirée** oilcloth; ~ **émeri** emery cloth; ~ **de fond** (*fig*) backdrop; ~ **de jute** hessian; ~ **de lin** linen; ~ **de tente** canvas.

toilettage [twalɛtaʒ] *nm* grooming *no pl*; (*d'un texte*) tidying up.

toilette [twalɛt] *nf* wash; (*s'habiller et se préparer*) getting ready, washing and dressing; (*habits*) outfit; dress *no pl*; ~**s** *nfpl* toilet *sg*; **les** ~**s des dames/messieurs** the ladies'/gents' (toilets) (*BRIT*), the ladies'/mens' (rest)room (*US*); **faire sa** ~ to have a wash, get washed; **faire la** ~ **de** (*animal*) to groom; (*voiture etc*) to clean, wash; (*texte*) to tidy up; **articles de** ~ toiletries; ~ **intime** personal hygiene.

toi-même [twamɛm] *pron* yourself.

toise [twaz] *nf*: **passer à la** ~ to have one's height measured.

toiser [twaze] *vt* to eye up and down.

toison [twazɔ̃] *nf* (*de mouton*) fleece; (*cheveux*) mane.

toit [twa] *nm* roof; ~ **ouvrant** sun roof.

toiture [twatyʀ] *nf* roof.

Tokyo [tɔkjo] *n* Tokyo.

tôle [tol] *nf* sheet metal *no pl*; (*plaque*) steel (*ou* iron) sheet; ~**s** *nfpl* (*carrosserie*) bodywork *sg* (*BRIT*), body *sg*; panels; ~ **d'acier** sheet steel *no pl*; ~ **ondulée** corrugated iron.

Tolède [tɔlɛd] *n* Toledo.

tolérable [tɔleʀabl(ə)] *adj* tolerable, bearable.

tolérance [tɔleʀɑ̃s] *nf* tolerance; (*hors taxe*) allowance.

tolérant, e [tɔleʀɑ̃, -ɑ̃t] *adj* tolerant.

tolérer [tɔleʀe] *vt* to tolerate; (*ADMIN: hors taxe etc*) to allow.

tôlerie [tolʀi] *nf* sheet metal manufacture; (*atelier*) sheet metal workshop; (*ensemble des tôles*) panels *pl*.

tollé [tɔle] *nm*: **un** ~ **(de protestations)** a general outcry.

TOM [*parfois*: tɔm] *sigle m(pl)* = *territoire(s) d'outre-mer*.

tomate [tɔmat] *nf* tomato.
tombal, e [tɔ̃bal] *adj*: **pierre ~e** tombstone, gravestone.
tombant, e [tɔ̃bɑ̃, -ɑ̃t] *adj* (*fig*) drooping, sloping.
tombe [tɔ̃b] *nf* (*sépulture*) grave; (*avec monument*) tomb.
tombeau, x [tɔ̃bo] *nm* tomb; **à ~ ouvert** at breakneck speed.
tombée [tɔ̃be] *nf*: **à la ~ du jour** *ou* **de la nuit** at the close of day, at nightfall.
tomber [tɔ̃be] *vi* to fall ♦ *vt*: **~ la veste** to slip off one's jacket; **laisser ~** to drop; **~ sur** *vt* (*rencontrer*) to come across; (*attaquer*) to set about; **~ de fatigue/sommeil** to drop from exhaustion/be falling asleep on one's feet; **~ à l'eau** (*fig: projet etc*) to fall through; **~ en panne** to break down; **~ juste** (*opération, calcul*) to come out right; **~ en ruine** to fall into ruins; **ça tombe bien/mal** (*fig*) that's come at the right/wrong time; **il est bien/mal tombé** (*fig*) he's been lucky/unlucky.
tombereau, x [tɔ̃bʀo] *nm* tipcart.
tombeur [tɔ̃bœʀ] *nm* (*péj*) Casanova.
tombola [tɔ̃bɔla] *nf* tombola.
Tombouctou [tɔ̃buktu] *n* Timbuktu.
tome [tɔm] *nm* volume.
tommette [tɔmɛt] *nf* hexagonal floor tile.
ton, ta, *pl* **tes** [tɔ̃, ta, te] *dét* your.
ton [tɔ̃] *nm* (*gén*) tone; (*MUS*) key; (*couleur*) shade, tone; (*de la voix: hauteur*) pitch; **donner le ~** to set the tone; **élever** *ou* **hausser le ~** to raise one's voice; **de bon ~** in good taste; **si vous le prenez sur ce ~** if you're going to take it like that; **~ sur ~** in matching shades.
tonal, e [tɔnal] *adj* tonal.
tonalité [tɔnalite] *nf* (*au téléphone*) dialling tone; (*MUS*) tonality; (: *ton*) key; (*fig*) tone.
tondeuse [tɔ̃døz] *nf* (*à gazon*) (lawn)mower; (*du coiffeur*) clippers *pl*; (*pour la tonte*) shears *pl*.
tondre [tɔ̃dʀ(ə)] *vt* (*pelouse, herbe*) to mow; (*haie*) to cut, clip; (*mouton, toison*) to shear; (*cheveux*) to crop.
tondu, e [tɔ̃dy] *pp de* **tondre** ♦ *adj* (*cheveux*) cropped; (*mouton, crâne*) shorn.
Tonga [tɔ̃ga]: **les îles ~** Tonga.
tonicité [tɔnisite] *nf* (*MÉD: des tissus*) tone; (*fig: de l'air, la mer*) bracing effect.
tonifiant, e [tɔnifjɑ̃, -ɑ̃t] *adj* invigorating, revivifying.
tonifier [tɔnifje] *vt* (*air, eau*) to invigorate; (*peau, organisme*) to tone up.
tonique [tɔnik] *adj* fortifying; (*personne*) dynamic ♦ *nm, nf* tonic.
tonitruant, e [tɔnitʀyɑ̃, -ɑ̃t] *adj*: **voix ~e** thundering voice.
Tonkin [tɔ̃kɛ̃] *nm*: **le ~** Tonkin, Tongking.
tonkinois, e [tɔ̃kinwa, -waz] *adj* Tonkinese.
tonnage [tɔnaʒ] *nm* tonnage.
tonnant, e [tɔnɑ̃, -ɑ̃t] *adj* thunderous.

tonne [tɔn] *nf* metric ton, tonne.
tonneau, x [tɔno] *nm* (*à vin, cidre*) barrel; (*NAVIG*) ton; **faire des ~x** (*voiture, avion*) to roll over.
tonnelet [tɔnlɛ] *nm* keg.
tonnelier [tɔnəlje] *nm* cooper.
tonnelle [tɔnɛl] *nf* bower, arbour (*BRIT*), arbor (*US*).
tonner [tɔne] *vi* to thunder; (*parler avec véhémence*): **~ contre qn/qch** to inveigh against sb/sth; **il tonne** it is thundering, there's some thunder.
tonnerre [tɔnɛʀ] *nm* thunder; **coup de ~** (*fig*) thunderbolt, bolt from the blue; **un ~ d'applaudissements** thunderous applause; **du ~** *adj* (*fam*) terrific.
tonsure [tɔ̃syʀ] *nf* bald patch; (*de moine*) tonsure.
tonte [tɔ̃t] *nf* shearing.
tonus [tɔnys] *nm* (*des muscles*) tone; (*d'une personne*) dynamism.
top [tɔp] *nm*: **au 3ème ~** at the 3rd stroke ♦ *adj*: **~ secret** top secret ♦ *excl* go!
topaze [tɔpaz] *nf* topaz.
toper [tɔpe] *vi*: **tope-/topez-là** it's a deal!, you're on!
topinambour [tɔpinɑ̃buʀ] *nm* Jerusalem artichoke.
topo [tɔpo] *nm* (*discours, exposé*) talk; (*fam*) spiel.
topographie [tɔpɔgʀafi] *nf* topography.
topographique [tɔpɔgʀafik] *adj* topographical.
toponymie [tɔpɔnimi] *nf* study of place names, toponymy.
toquade [tɔkad] *nf* fad, craze.
toque [tɔk] *nf* (*de fourrure*) fur hat; **~ de jockey/juge** jockey's/judge's cap; **~ de cuisinier** chef's hat.
toqué, e [tɔke] *adj* (*fam*) touched, cracked.
torche [tɔʀʃ(ə)] *nf* torch; **se mettre en ~** (*parachute*) to candle.
torcher [tɔʀʃe] *vt* (*fam*) to wipe.
torchère [tɔʀʃɛʀ] *nf* flare.
torchon [tɔʀʃɔ̃] *nm* cloth, duster; (*à vaisselle*) tea towel *ou* cloth.
tordre [tɔʀdʀ(ə)] *vt* (*chiffon*) to wring; (*barre, fig: visage*) to twist; **se ~** *vi* (*barre*) to bend; (*roue*) to twist, buckle; (*ver, serpent*) to writhe; **se ~ le pied/bras** to twist one's foot/arm; **se ~ de douleur/rire** to writhe in pain/be doubled up with laughter.
tordu, e [tɔʀdy] *pp de* **tordre** ♦ *adj* (*fig*) warped, twisted.
torero [tɔʀeʀo] *nm* bullfighter.
tornade [tɔʀnad] *nf* tornado.
toron [tɔʀɔ̃] *nm* strand (of rope).
Toronto [tɔʀɔ̃to] *n* Toronto.
torontois, e [tɔʀɔ̃twa, -waz] *adj* Torontonian ♦ *nm/f*: **T~, e** Torontonian.
torpeur [tɔʀpœʀ] *nf* torpor, drowsiness.
torpille [tɔʀpij] *nf* torpedo.

torpiller [tɔʀpije] vt to torpedo.
torpilleur [tɔʀpijœʀ] nm torpedo boat.
torréfaction [tɔʀefaksjɔ̃] nf roasting.
torréfier [tɔʀefje] vt to roast.
torrent [tɔʀɑ̃] nm torrent, mountain stream; (fig): un ~ de a torrent ou flood of; il pleut à ~s the rain is lashing down.
torrentiel, le [tɔʀɑ̃sjɛl] adj torrential.
torride [tɔʀid] adj torrid.
tors, torse ou **torte** [tɔʀ, tɔʀs(ə) ou tɔʀt(ə)] adj twisted.
torsade [tɔʀsad] nf twist; (ARCHIT) cable moulding (BRIT) ou molding (US).
torsader [tɔʀsade] vt to twist.
torse [tɔʀs(ə)] nm torso; (poitrine) chest.
torsion [tɔʀsjɔ̃] nf (action) twisting; (TECH, PHYSIQUE) torsion.
tort [tɔʀ] nm (défaut) fault; (préjudice) wrong no pl; ~s nmpl (JUR) fault sg; avoir ~ to be wrong; être dans son ~ to be in the wrong; donner ~ à qn to lay the blame on sb; (fig) to prove sb wrong; causer du ~ à to harm; to be harmful ou detrimental to; en ~ in the wrong, at fault; à ~ wrongly; à ~ ou à raison rightly or wrongly; à ~ et à travers wildly.
torte [tɔʀt(ə)] adj f voir **tors**.
torticolis [tɔʀtikɔli] nm stiff neck.
tortiller [tɔʀtije] vt (corde, mouchoir) to twist; (doigts) to twiddle; se ~ vi to wriggle, squirm.
tortionnaire [tɔʀsjɔnɛʀ] nm torturer.
tortue [tɔʀty] nf tortoise; (fig) slowcoach (BRIT), slowpoke (US).
tortueux, euse [tɔʀtɥø, -øz] adj (rue) twisting; (fig) tortuous.
torture [tɔʀtyʀ] nf torture.
torturer [tɔʀtyʀe] vt to torture; (fig) to torment.
torve [tɔʀv(ə)] adj: regard ~ menacing ou grim look.
toscan, e [tɔskɑ̃, -an] adj Tuscan.
Toscane [tɔskan] nf: la ~ Tuscany.
tôt [to] adv early; ~ ou tard sooner or later; si ~ so early; (déjà) so soon; au plus ~ at the earliest, as soon as possible; plus ~ earlier; il eut ~ fait de faire ... he soon did ....
total, e, aux [tɔtal, -o] adj, nm total; au ~ in total ou all; (fig) all in all; faire le ~ to work out the total.
totalement [tɔtalmɑ̃] adv totally, completely.
totalisateur [tɔtalizatœʀ] nm adding machine.
totaliser [tɔtalize] vt to total (up).
totalitaire [tɔtalitɛʀ] adj totalitarian.
totalitarisme [tɔtalitaʀism(ə)] nm totalitarianism.
totalité [tɔtalite] nf: la ~ de: la ~ des élèves all (of) the pupils; la ~ de la population/classe the whole population/class; en ~ entirely.
totem [tɔtɛm] nm totem.
toubib [tubib] nm (fam) doctor.
touchant, e [tuʃɑ̃, -ɑ̃t] adj touching.

touche [tuʃ] nf (de piano, de machine à écrire) key; (de violon) fingerboard; (de télécommande etc) key, button; (PEINTURE etc) stroke, touch; (fig: de couleur, nostalgie) touch, hint; (RUGBY) line-out; (FOOTBALL: aussi: remise en ~) throw-in; (aussi: ligne de ~) touch-line; (ESCRIME) hit; en ~ in (ou into) touch; avoir une drôle de ~ to look a sight; ~ de commande/de fonction/de retour (INFORM) control/function/return key; ~ à effleurement ou sensitive touch-sensitive control ou key.
touche-à-tout [tuʃatu] nm inv (péj: gén: enfant) meddler; (: fig: inventeur etc) dabbler.
toucher [tuʃe] nm touch ♦ vt to touch; (palper) to feel; (atteindre: d'un coup de feu etc) to hit; (affecter) to touch, affect; (concerner) to concern, affect; (contacter) to reach, contact; (recevoir: récompense) to receive, get; (: salaire) to draw, get; (chèque) to cash; (aborder: problème, sujet) to touch on; au ~ to the touch; by the feel; se ~ (être en contact) to touch; ~ à to touch; (modifier) to touch, tamper ou meddle with; (traiter de, concerner) to have to do with, concern; je vais lui en ~ un mot I'll have a word with him about it; ~ au but (fig) to near one's goal; ~ à sa fin to be drawing to a close.
touffe [tuf] nf tuft.
touffu, e [tufy] adj thick, dense; (fig) complex, involved.
toujours [tuʒuʀ] adv always; (encore) still; (constamment) forever; depuis ~ always; essaie ~ (you can) try anyway; pour ~ forever; ~ est-il que the fact remains that; ~ plus more and more.
toulonnais, e [tulɔnɛ, -ɛz] of ou from Toulon.
toulousain, e [tuluzɛ̃, -ɛn] adj of ou from Toulouse.
toupet [tupɛ] nm quiff (BRIT), tuft; (fam) nerve, cheek (BRIT).
toupie [tupi] nf (spinning) top.
tour [tuʀ] nf tower; (immeuble) high-rise block (BRIT) ou building (US), tower block (BRIT); (ÉCHECS) castle, rook ♦ nm (excursion: à pied) stroll, walk; (: en voiture etc) run, ride; (: plus long) trip; (SPORT: aussi: ~ de piste) lap; (d'être servi ou de jouer etc, tournure, de vis ou clef) turn; (de roue etc) revolution; (circonférence): de 3 m de ~ 3 m round, with a circumference ou girth of 3 m; (POL: aussi: ~ de scrutin) ballot; (ruse, de prestidigitation, de cartes) trick; (de potier) wheel; (à bois, métaux) lathe; faire le ~ de to go (a)round; (à pied) to walk (a)round; (fig) to review; faire le ~ de l'Europe to tour Europe; faire un ~ to go for a walk; (en voiture etc) to go for a ride; faire 2 ~s to go (a)round twice; (hélice etc) to turn ou revolve twice; fermer à double ~ vi to double-lock the door; c'est au ~ de Renée it's Renée's turn; à ~ de rôle, ~ à ~ in turn; à ~ de bras with all one's

strength; (*fig*) non-stop, relentlessly; ~ **de taille/tête** waist/head measurement; ~ **de chant** song recital; ~ **de contrôle** *nf* control tower; ~ **de garde** spell of duty; ~ **d'horizon** (*fig*) general survey; ~ **de lit** valance; ~ **de main** dexterity, knack; **en un** ~ **de main** (as) quick as a flash; ~ **de passe-passe** trick, sleight of hand; ~ **de reins** sprained back.

The **Tour de France** *is an annual road race for professional cyclists taking about three weeks to complete in daily stages or "étapes" of approximately 110 miles over terrain of varying difficulty. The leading cyclist wears a yellow jersey, the* **maillot jaune**. *There are a number of time trials. The route varies and is not usually confined only to France, but the race always ends in Paris.*

tourangeau, elle, x [tuʀɑ̃ʒo, -ɛl] *adj* (*de la région*) of *ou* from Touraine; (*de la ville*) of *ou* from Tours.
tourbe [tuʀb(ə)] *nf* peat.
tourbière [tuʀbjɛʀ] *nf* peat-bog.
tourbillon [tuʀbijɔ̃] *nm* whirlwind; (*d'eau*) whirlpool; (*fig*) whirl, swirl.
tourbillonner [tuʀbijɔne] *vi* to whirl, swirl; (*objet, personne*) to whirl *ou* twirl round.
tourelle [tuʀɛl] *nf* turret.
tourisme [tuʀism(ə)] *nm* tourism; **agence de** ~ tourist agency; **avion/voiture de** ~ private plane/car; **faire du** ~ to do some sightseeing, go touring.
touriste [tuʀist(ə)] *nm/f* tourist.
touristique [tuʀistik] *adj* tourist *cpd*; (*région*) touristic (*péj*), with tourist appeal.
tourment [tuʀmɑ̃] *nm* torment.
tourmente [tuʀmɑ̃t] *nf* storm.
tourmenté, e [tuʀmɑ̃te] *adj* tormented, tortured; (*mer, période*) turbulent, tempestuous.
tourmenter [tuʀmɑ̃te] *vt* to torment; **se** ~ *vi* to fret, worry o.s.
tournage [tuʀnaʒ] *nm* (*d'un film*) shooting.
tournant, e [tuʀnɑ̃, -ɑ̃t] *adj* (*feu, scène*) revolving; (*chemin*) winding; (*escalier*) spiral *cpd*; (*mouvement*) circling ♦ *nm* (*de route*) bend (*BRIT*), curve (*US*); (*fig*) turning point; *voir* **plaque**, **grève**.
tourné, e [tuʀne] *adj* (*lait, vin*) sour, off; (*MENUISERIE: bois*) turned; (*fig: compliment*) well-phrased; **bien** ~ (*personne*) shapely; **mal** ~ (*lettre*) badly expressed; **avoir l'esprit mal** ~ to have a dirty mind.
tournebroche [tuʀnəbʀɔʃ] *nm* roasting spit.
tourne-disque [tuʀnədisk(ə)] *nm* record player.
tournedos [tuʀnədo] *nm* tournedos.
tournée [tuʀne] *nf* (*du facteur etc*) round; (*d'artiste, politicien*) tour; (*au café*) round (of drinks); ~ **électorale/musicale** election/concert tour; **faire la** ~ **de** to go (a)round.

tournemain [tuʀnəmɛ̃]: **en un** ~ *adv* in a flash.
tourner [tuʀne] *vt* to turn; (*sauce, mélange*) to stir; (*contourner*) to get (a)round; (*CINÉ*) to shoot; to make ♦ *vi* to turn; (*moteur*) to run; (*compteur*) to tick away; (*lait etc*) to turn (sour); (*fig: chance, vie*) to turn out; **se** ~ *vi* to turn (a)round; **se** ~ **vers** to turn to; to turn towards; **bien** ~ to turn out well; ~ **autour de** to go (a)round; (*planète*) to revolve (a)round; (*péj*) to hang (a)round; ~ **autour du pot** (*fig*) to go (a)round in circles; ~ **à/en** to turn into; ~ **à la pluie/au rouge** to turn rainy/red; ~ **en ridicule** to ridicule; ~ **le dos à** (*mouvement*) to turn one's back on; (*position*) to have one's back to; ~ **court** to come to a sudden end; **se** ~ **les pouces** to twiddle one's thumbs; ~ **la tête** to look away; ~ **la tête à qn** (*fig*) to go to sb's head; ~ **de l'œil** to pass out; ~ **la page** (*fig*) to turn the page.
tournesol [tuʀnəsɔl] *nm* sunflower.
tourneur [tuʀnœʀ] *nm* turner; lathe-operator.
tournevis [tuʀnəvis] *nm* screwdriver.
tourniquer [tuʀnike] *vi* to go (a)round in circles.
tourniquet [tuʀnikɛ] *nm* (*pour arroser*) sprinkler; (*portillon*) turnstile; (*présentoir*) revolving stand, spinner; (*CHIRURGIE*) tourniquet.
tournis [tuʀni] *nm*: **avoir/donner le** ~ to feel/make dizzy.
tournoi [tuʀnwa] *nm* tournament.
tournoyer [tuʀnwaje] *vi* (*oiseau*) to wheel (a)round; (*fumée*) to swirl (a)round.
tournure [tuʀnyʀ] *nf* (*LING: syntaxe*) turn of phrase; form; (: *d'une phrase*) phrasing; (*évolution*): **la** ~ **de qch** the way sth is developing; (*aspect*): **la** ~ **de** the look of; **la** ~ **des événements** the turn of events; **prendre** ~ to take shape; ~ **d'esprit** turn *ou* cast of mind.
tour-opérateur [tuʀɔpeʀatœʀ] *nm* tour operator.
tourte [tuʀt(ə)] *nf* pie.
tourteau, x [tuʀto] *nm* (*AGR*) oilcake, cattle-cake; (*ZOOL*) edible crab.
tourtereaux [tuʀtəʀo] *nmpl* lovebirds.
tourterelle [tuʀtəʀɛl] *nf* turtledove.
tourtière [tuʀtjɛʀ] *nf* pie dish *ou* plate.
tous *dét* [tu] , *pron* [tus] *voir* **tout**.
Toussaint [tusɛ̃] *nf*: **la** ~ All Saints' Day.

La **Toussaint**, *November 1, is a public holiday in France. People traditionally visit the graves of friends and relatives to lay wreaths of heather and chrysanthemums.*

tousser [tuse] *vi* to cough.
toussoter [tusɔte] *vi* to have a slight cough; to cough a little; (*pour avertir*) to give a slight cough.

===================== MOT-CLÉ =====================

tout, e [tu, tut] (*mpl* **tous**, *fpl* **toutes**) *adj* **1** (*avec article singulier*) all; ~ **le lait** all the milk; ~**e la nuit** all night, the whole night; ~ **le livre** the whole book; ~ **un pain** a whole loaf; ~ **le temps** all the time, the whole time; **c'est ~ le contraire** it's quite the opposite; **c'est ~e une affaire** *ou* **histoire** it's quite a business, it's a whole rigmarole

2 (*avec article pluriel*) every; all; **tous les livres** all the books; ~**es les nuits** every night; ~**es les fois** every time; ~**es les trois/deux semaines** every third/other *ou* second week, every three/two weeks; **tous les deux** both *ou* each of us (*ou* them *ou* you); ~**es les trois** all three of us (*ou* them *ou* you)

3 (*sans article*): **à** ~ **âge** at any age; **pour** ~**e nourriture, il avait** ... his only food was ...; **de tous côtés, de** ~**es parts** from everywhere, from every side

♦ *pron* everything, all; **il a** ~ **fait** he's done everything; **je les vois tous** I can see them all *ou* all of them; **nous y sommes tous allés** all of us went, we all went; **c'est** ~ that's all; **en** ~ in all; **en** ~ **et pour** ~ all in all; ~ **ce qu'il sait** all he knows; **c'était** ~ **ce qu'il y a de chic** it was the last word *ou* the ultimate in chic

♦ *nm* whole; **le** ~ all of it (*ou* them); **le** ~ **est de ...** the main thing is to ...; **pas du** ~ not at all; **elle a** ~ **d'une mère/d'une intrigante** she's a real *ou* true mother/schemer; **du** ~ **au** ~ utterly

♦ *adv* **1** (*très, complètement*) very; ~ **près** *ou* **à côté** very near; **le** ~ **premier** the very first; ~ **seul** all alone; **il était** ~ **rouge** he was really *ou* all red; **parler** ~ **bas** to speak very quietly; **le livre** ~ **entier** the whole book; ~ **en haut** right at the top; ~ **droit** straight ahead

2: ~ **en** while; ~ **en travaillant** while working, as he *etc* works

3: ~ **d'abord** first of all; ~ **à coup** suddenly; ~ **à fait** absolutely; ~ **à l'heure** a short while ago; (*futur*) in a short while, shortly; **à** ~ **à l'heure!** see you later!; **il répondit** ~ **court que non** he just answered no (and that was all); ~ **de même** all the same; ~ **le monde** everybody; ~ **ou rien** all or nothing; ~ **simplement** quite simply; ~ **de suite** immediately, straight away

♦ *excl*: ~ **à fait!** exactly!

tout-à-l'égout [tutalegu] *nm inv* mains drainage.
toutefois [tutfwa] *adv* however.
toutou [tutu] *nm* (*fam*) doggie.
tout-petit [tup(ə)ti] *nm* toddler.
tout-puissant, toute-puissante [tupɥisɑ̃, tutpɥisɑ̃t] *adj* all-powerful, omnipotent.

tout-venant [tuvnɑ̃] *nm*: **le** ~ everyday stuff.
toux [tu] *nf* cough.
toxémie [tɔksemi] *nf* toxaemia (*BRIT*), toxemia (*US*).
toxicité [tɔksisite] *nf* toxicity.
toxicologie [tɔksikɔlɔʒi] *nf* toxicology.
toxicomane [tɔksikɔman] *nm/f* drug addict.
toxicomanie [tɔksikɔmani] *nf* drug addiction.
toxine [tɔksin] *nf* toxin.
toxique [tɔksik] *adj* toxic, poisonous.
toxoplasmose [tɔksoplasmoz] *nf* toxoplasmosis.
TP *sigle mpl* = **travaux pratiques, travaux publics** ♦ *sigle m* = **trésor public**.
TPG *sigle m* = **Trésorier-payeur général**.
tps *abr* = **temps**.
trac [tʀak] *nm* nerves *pl*; (*THÉÂT*) stage fright; **avoir le** ~ to get an attack of nerves; to have stage fright; **tout à** ~ all of a sudden.
traçant, e [tʀasɑ̃, -ɑ̃t] *adj*: **table** ~**e** (*INFORM*) (graph) plotter.
tracas [tʀaka] *nm* bother *no pl*, worry *no pl*.
tracasser [tʀakase] *vt* to worry, bother; (*harceler*) to harass; **se** ~ *vi* to worry o.s., fret.
tracasserie [tʀakasʀi] *nf* annoyance *no pl*; harassment *no pl*.
tracassier, ière [tʀakasje, -jɛʀ] *adj* irksome.
trace [tʀas] *nf* (*empreintes*) tracks *pl*; (*marques, aussi fig*) mark; (*restes, vestige*) trace; (*indice*) sign; **suivre à la** ~ to track; ~**s de pas** footprints.
tracé [tʀase] *nm* (*contour*) line; (*plan*) layout.
tracer [tʀase] *vt* to draw; (*mot*) to trace; (*piste*) to open up; (*fig: chemin*) to show.
traceur [tʀasœʀ] *nm* (*INFORM*) plotter.
trachée(-artère) [tʀaʃe(aʀtɛʀ)] *nf* windpipe, trachea.
trachéite [tʀakeit] *nf* tracheitis.
tract [tʀakt] *nm* tract, pamphlet; (*publicitaire*) handout.
tractations [tʀaktasjɔ̃] *nfpl* dealings, bargaining *sg*.
tracter [tʀakte] *vt* to tow.
tracteur [tʀaktœʀ] *nm* tractor.
traction [tʀaksjɔ̃] *nf* traction; (*GYM*) pull-up; ~ **avant/arrière** front-wheel/rear-wheel drive; ~ **électrique** electric(al) traction *ou* haulage.
trad. *abr* (= *traduit*) translated; (= *traduction*) translation; (= *traducteur*) translator.
tradition [tʀadisjɔ̃] *nf* tradition.
traditionalisme [tʀadisjɔnalism(ə)] *nm* traditionalism.
traditionaliste [tʀadisjɔnalist(ə)] *adj, nm/f* traditionalist.
traditionnel, le [tʀadisjɔnɛl] *adj* traditional.
traditionnellement [tʀadisjɔnɛlmɑ̃] *adv* traditionally.
traducteur, trice [tʀadyktœʀ, -tʀis] *nm/f* translator.
traduction [tʀadyksjɔ̃] *nf* translation.

traduire [tʀadɥiʀ] *vt* to translate; (*exprimer*) to render, convey; **se ~ par** to find expression in; **~ en français** to translate into French; **~ en justice** to bring before the courts.

traduis [tʀadɥi] *etc vb voir* **traduire**.

traduisible [tʀadɥizibl(ə)] *adj* translatable.

traduit, e [tʀadɥi, -it] *pp de* **traduire**.

trafic [tʀafik] *nm* traffic; **~ d'armes** arms dealing; **~ de drogue** drug peddling.

trafiquant, e [tʀafikɑ̃, -ɑ̃t] *nm/f* trafficker; dealer.

trafiquer [tʀafike] *vt* (*péj*) to doctor, tamper with ♦ *vi* to traffic, be engaged in trafficking.

tragédie [tʀaʒedi] *nf* tragedy.

tragédien, ne [tʀaʒedjɛ̃, -ɛn] *nm/f* tragedian/ tragedienne.

tragi-comique [tʀaʒikɔmik] *adj* tragi-comic.

tragique [tʀaʒik] *adj* tragic ♦ *nm*: **prendre qch au ~** to make a tragedy out of sth.

tragiquement [tʀaʒikmɑ̃] *adv* tragically.

trahir [tʀaiʀ] *vt* to betray; (*fig*) to give away, reveal; **se ~** to betray o.s., give o.s. away.

trahison [tʀaizɔ̃] *nf* betrayal; (*JUR*) treason.

traie [tʀɛ] *etc vb voir* **traire**.

train [tʀɛ̃] *nm* (*RAIL*) train; (*allure*) pace; (*fig: ensemble*) set; **être en ~ de faire qch** to be doing sth; **mettre qch en ~** to get sth under way; **mettre qn en ~** to put sb in good spirits; **se mettre en ~** (*commencer*) to get started; (*faire de la gymnastique*) to warm up; **se sentir en ~** to feel in good form; **aller bon ~** to make good progress; **~ avant/arrière** front-wheel/rear-wheel axle unit; **~ à grande vitesse (TGV)** high-speed train; **~ d'atterrissage** undercarriage; **~ autos-couchettes** car-sleeper train; **~ électrique** (*jouet*) (electric) train set; **~ de pneus** set of tyres *ou* tires; **~ de vie** style of living.

traînailler [tʀɛnaje] *vi* = **traînasser**.

traînant, e [tʀɛnɑ̃, -ɑ̃t] *adj* (*voix, ton*) drawling.

traînard, e [tʀɛnaʀ, -aʀd(ə)] *nm/f* (*péj*) slowcoach (*BRIT*), slowpoke (*US*).

traînasser [tʀɛnase] *vi* to dawdle.

traîne [tʀɛn] *nf* (*de robe*) train; **être à la ~** to be in tow; (*en arrière*) to lag behind; (*en désordre*) to be lying around.

traîneau, x [tʀɛno] *nm* sleigh, sledge.

traînée [tʀɛne] *nf* streak, trail; (*péj*) slut.

traîner [tʀɛne] *vt* (*remorque*) to pull; (*enfant, chien*) to drag *ou* trail along; (*maladie*): **il traine un rhume depuis l'hiver** he has a cold which has been dragging on since winter ♦ *vi* (*être en désordre*) to lie around; (*marcher lentement*) to dawdle (along); (*vagabonder*) to hang about; (*agir lentement*) to idle about; (*durer*) to drag on; **se ~** *vi* (*ramper*) to crawl along; (*marcher avec difficulté*) to drag o.s. along; (*durer*) to drag on; **se ~ par terre** to crawl (on the ground); **~ qn au cinéma** to drag sb to the cinema; **~ les pieds** to drag one's feet; **~ par terre** to trail on the ground; **~ en longueur** to drag out.

training [tʀɛniŋ] *nm* (*pull*) tracksuit top; (*chaussure*) trainer (*BRIT*), sneaker (*US*).

train-train [tʀɛ̃tʀɛ̃] *nm* humdrum routine.

traire [tʀɛʀ] *vt* to milk.

trait, e [tʀɛ, -ɛt] *pp de* **traire** ♦ *nm* (*ligne*) line; (*de dessin*) stroke; (*caractéristique*) feature, trait; (*flèche*) dart, arrow; shaft; **~s** *nmpl* (*du visage*) features; **d'un ~** (*boire*) in one gulp; **de ~** *adj* (*animal*) draught (*BRIT*), draft (*US*); **avoir ~ à** to concern; **~ pour ~** line for line; **~ de caractère** characteristic, trait; **~ d'esprit** flash of wit; **~ de génie** brainwave; **~ d'union** hyphen; (*fig*) link.

traitable [tʀɛtabl(ə)] *adj* (*personne*) accommodating; (*sujet*) manageable.

traitant, e [tʀɛtɑ̃, -ɑ̃t] *adj*: **votre médecin ~** your usual *ou* family doctor; **shampooing ~** medicated shampoo; **crème ~e** conditioning cream, conditioner.

traite [tʀɛt] *nf* (*COMM*) draft; (*AGR*) milking; (*trajet*) stretch; **d'une (seule) ~** without stopping (once); **la ~ des noirs** the slave trade; **la ~ des blanches** the white slave trade.

traité [tʀɛte] *nm* treaty.

traitement [tʀɛtmɑ̃] *nm* treatment; processing; (*salaire*) salary; **suivre un ~** to undergo treatment; **mauvais ~** ill-treatment; **~ de données** *ou* **de l'information** (*INFORM*) data processing; **~ hormono-supplétif** hormone replacement therapy; **~ par lots** (*INFORM*) batch processing; **~ de texte** (*INFORM*) word processing.

traiter [tʀɛte] *vt* (*gén*) to treat; (*TECH: matériaux*) to process, treat; (*INFORM*) to process; (*affaire*) to deal with, handle; (*qualifier*): **~ qn d'idiot** to call sb a fool ♦ *vi* to deal; **~ de** *vt* to deal with; **bien/mal ~** to treat well/ill-treat.

traiteur [tʀɛtœʀ] *nm* caterer.

traître, esse [tʀɛtʀ(ə), -tʀɛs] *adj* (*dangereux*) treacherous ♦ *nm* traitor; **prendre qn en ~** to make an insidious attack on sb.

traîtrise [tʀɛtʀiz] *nf* treachery.

trajectoire [tʀaʒɛktwaʀ] *nf* trajectory, path.

trajet [tʀaʒɛ] *nm* journey; (*itinéraire*) route; (*fig*) path, course.

tralala [tʀalala] *nm* (*péj*) fuss.

tram [tʀam] *nm* tram (*BRIT*), streetcar (*US*).

trame [tʀam] *nf* (*de tissu*) weft; (*fig*) framework; texture; (*TYPO*) screen.

tramer [tʀame] *vt* to plot, hatch.

trampoline [tʀɑ̃pɔlin], **trampolino** [tʀɑ̃pɔlino] *nm* trampoline; (*SPORT*) trampolining.

tramway [tʀamwɛ] *nm* tram(way); (*voiture*) tram(car) (*BRIT*), streetcar (*US*).

tranchant, e [tʀɑ̃ʃɑ̃, -ɑ̃t] *adj* sharp; (*fig: personne*) peremptory; (*: couleurs*) striking ♦ *nm* (*d'un couteau*) cutting edge; (*de la main*) edge; **à double ~** (*argument, procédé*) double-edged.

tranche [tʀɑ̃ʃ] nf (morceau) slice; (arête) edge; (partie) section; (série) block; (d'impôts, revenus etc) bracket; (loterie) issue; ~ **d'âge** age bracket; ~ **(de silicium)** wafer.

tranché, e [tʀɑ̃ʃe] adj (couleurs) distinct, sharply contrasted; (opinions) clear-cut, definite ♦ nf trench.

trancher [tʀɑ̃ʃe] vt to cut, sever; (fig: résoudre) to settle ♦ vi to be decisive; (entre deux choses) to settle the argument; ~ **avec** to contrast sharply with.

tranchet [tʀɑ̃ʃɛ] nm knife.

tranchoir [tʀɑ̃ʃwaʀ] nm chopper.

tranquille [tʀɑ̃kil] adj calm, quiet; (enfant, élève) quiet; (rassuré) easy in one's mind, with one's mind at rest; **se tenir** ~ (enfant) to be quiet; **avoir la conscience** ~ to have an easy conscience; **laisse-moi/laisse-ça** ~ leave me/it alone.

tranquillement [tʀɑ̃kilmɑ̃] adv calmly.

tranquillisant, e [tʀɑ̃kilizɑ̃, -ɑ̃t] adj (nouvelle) reassuring ♦ nm tranquillizer.

tranquilliser [tʀɑ̃kilize] vt to reassure; **se** ~ to calm (o.s.) down.

tranquillité [tʀɑ̃kilite] nf quietness; peace (and quiet); **en toute** ~ with complete peace of mind; ~ **d'esprit** peace of mind.

transaction [tʀɑ̃zaksjɔ̃] nf (COMM) transaction, deal.

transafricain, e [tʀɑ̃safʀikɛ̃, -ɛn] adj transafrican.

transalpin, e [tʀɑ̃zalpɛ̃, -in] adj transalpine.

transaméricain, e [tʀɑ̃zameʀikɛ̃, -ɛn] adj transamerican.

transat [tʀɑ̃zat] nm deckchair ♦ nf = course transatlantique.

transatlantique [tʀɑ̃zatlɑ̃tik] adj transatlantic ♦ nm transatlantic liner.

transborder [tʀɑ̃sbɔʀde] vt to tran(s)ship.

transcendant, e [tʀɑ̃sɑ̃dɑ̃, -ɑ̃t] adj (PHILOSOPHIE, MATH) transcendental; (supérieur) transcendent.

transcodeur [tʀɑ̃skɔdœʀ] nm compiler.

transcontinental, e, aux [tʀɑ̃skɔ̃tinɑtal, -o] adj transcontinental.

transcription [tʀɑ̃skʀipsjɔ̃] nf transcription.

transcrire [tʀɑ̃skʀiʀ] vt to transcribe.

transe [tʀɑ̃s] nf: **entrer en** ~ to go into a trance; ~**s** nfpl agony sg.

transférable [tʀɑ̃sfeʀabl(ə)] adj transferable.

transfèrement [tʀɑ̃sfɛʀmɑ̃] nm transfer.

transférer [tʀɑ̃sfeʀe] vt to transfer.

transfert [tʀɑ̃sfɛʀ] nm transfer.

transfiguration [tʀɑ̃sfigyʀasjɔ̃] nf transformation, transfiguration.

transfigurer [tʀɑ̃sfigyʀe] vt to transform.

transfo [tʀɑ̃sfo] nm (= transformateur) transformer.

transformable [tʀɑ̃sfɔʀmabl(ə)] adj convertible.

transformateur [tʀɑ̃sfɔʀmatœʀ] nm transformer.

transformation [tʀɑ̃sfɔʀmasjɔ̃] nf transformation; (RUGBY) conversion; **industries de** ~ processing industries.

transformer [tʀɑ̃sfɔʀme] vt to transform, alter ("alter" implique un changement moins radical); (matière première, appartement, RUGBY) to convert; ~ **en** to transform into; to turn into; to convert into; **se** ~ vi to be transformed; to alter.

transfuge [tʀɑ̃sfyʒ] nm renegade.

transfuser [tʀɑ̃sfyze] vt to transfuse.

transfusion [tʀɑ̃sfyzjɔ̃] nf: ~ **sanguine** blood transfusion.

transgresser [tʀɑ̃sgʀese] vt to contravene, disobey.

transhumance [tʀɑ̃zymɑ̃s] nf transhumance, seasonal move to new pastures.

transi, e [tʀɑ̃zi] adj numb (with cold), chilled to the bone.

transiger [tʀɑ̃ziʒe] vi to compromise, come to an agreement; ~ **sur** ou **avec qch** to compromise on sth.

transistor [tʀɑ̃zistɔʀ] nm transistor.

transistorisé, e [tʀɑ̃zistɔʀize] adj transistorized.

transit [tʀɑ̃zit] nm transit; **de** ~ transit cpd; **en** ~ in transit.

transitaire [tʀɑ̃zitɛʀ] nm/f forwarding agent.

transiter [tʀɑ̃zite] vi to pass in transit.

transitif, ive [tʀɑ̃zitif, -iv] adj transitive.

transition [tʀɑ̃zisjɔ̃] nf transition; **de** ~ transitional.

transitoire [tʀɑ̃zitwaʀ] adj (mesure, gouvernement) transitional, provisional; (fugitif) transient.

translucide [tʀɑ̃slysid] adj translucent.

transmet [tʀɑ̃smɛ] etc vb voir **transmettre**.

transmettais [tʀɑ̃smɛtɛ] etc vb voir **transmettre**.

transmetteur [tʀɑ̃smɛtœʀ] nm transmitter.

transmettre [tʀɑ̃smɛtʀ(ə)] vt (passer): ~ **qch à qn** to pass sth on to sb; (TECH, TÉL, MÉD) to transmit; (TV, RADIO: retransmettre) to broadcast.

transmis, e [tʀɑ̃smi, -iz] pp de **transmettre**.

transmissible [tʀɑ̃smisibl(ə)] adj transmissible.

transmission [tʀɑ̃smisjɔ̃] nf transmission, passing on; (AUTO) transmission; ~**s** nfpl (MIL) ≈ signals corps sg; ~ **de données** (INFORM) data transmission; ~ **de pensée** thought transmission.

transocéanien, ne [tʀɑ̃zɔseanjɛ̃, -ɛn] adj, **transocéanique** [tʀɑ̃zɔseanik] adj transoceanic.

transparaître [tʀɑ̃spaʀɛtʀ(ə)] vi to show (through).

transparence [tʀɑ̃spaʀɑ̃s] nf transparence; **par** ~ (regarder) against the light; (voir) showing through.

transparent, e [tʀɑ̃spaʀɑ̃, -ɑ̃t] adj

transparent.

transpercer [tʀɑ̃spɛʀse] *vt* to go through, pierce.

transpiration [tʀɑ̃spiʀasjɔ̃] *nf* perspiration.

transpirer [tʀɑ̃spiʀe] *vi* to perspire; (*information, nouvelle*) to come to light.

transplant [tʀɑ̃splɑ̃] *nm* transplant.

transplantation [tʀɑ̃splɑ̃tɑsjɔ̃] *nf* transplant.

transplanter [tʀɑ̃splɑ̃te] *vt* (*MÉD, BOT*) to transplant; (*personne*) to uproot, move.

transport [tʀɑ̃spɔʀ] *nm* transport; (*émotions*): ~ **de colère** fit of rage; ~ **de joie** transport of delight; ~ **de voyageurs/marchandises** passenger/goods transportation; ~**s en commun** public transport *sg*; ~**s routiers** haulage (*BRIT*), trucking (*US*).

transportable [tʀɑ̃spɔʀtabl(ə)] *adj* (*marchandises*) transportable; (*malade*) fit (enough) to be moved.

transporter [tʀɑ̃spɔʀte] *vt* to carry, move; (*COMM*) to transport, convey; (*fig*): ~ **qn (de joie)** to send sb into raptures; **se** ~ **quelque part** (*fig*) to let one's imagination carry one away (somewhere); ~ **qn à l'hôpital** to take sb to hospital.

transporteur [tʀɑ̃spɔʀtœʀ] *nm* haulage contractor (*BRIT*), trucker (*US*).

transposer [tʀɑ̃spoze] *vt* to transpose.

transposition [tʀɑ̃spozisjɔ̃] *nf* transposition.

transrhénan, e [tʀɑ̃sʀenɑ̃, -an] *adj* transrhenane.

transsaharien, ne [tʀɑ̃ssaaʀjɛ̃, -ɛn] *adj* trans-Saharan.

transsexuel, le [tʀɑ̃ssɛksɥɛl] *adj, nm/f* transsexual.

transsibérien, ne [tʀɑ̃ssibeʀjɛ̃, -ɛn] *adj* trans-Siberian.

transvaser [tʀɑ̃svaze] *vt* to decant.

transversal, e, aux [tʀɑ̃svɛʀsal, -o] *adj* transverse, cross(-); (*route etc*) cross-country; (*mur, chemin, rue*) running at right angles; (*AUTO*): **axe** ~ main cross-country road (*BRIT*) *ou* highway (*US*).

transversalement [tʀɑ̃svɛʀsalmɑ̃] *adv* crosswise.

trapèze [tʀapɛz] *nm* (*GÉOM*) trapezium; (*au cirque*) trapeze.

trapéziste [tʀapezist(ə)] *nm/f* trapeze artist.

trappe [tʀap] *nf* (*de cave, grenier*) trap door; (*piège*) trap.

trappeur [tʀapœʀ] *nm* trapper, fur trader.

trapu, e [tʀapy] *adj* squat, stocky.

traquenard [tʀaknaʀ] *nm* trap.

traquer [tʀake] *vt* to track down; (*harceler*) to hound.

traumatisant, e [tʀomatizɑ̃, -ɑ̃t] *adj* traumatic.

traumatiser [tʀomatize] *vt* to traumatize.

traumatisme [tʀomatism(ə)] *nm* traumatism; ~ **crânien** cranial traumatism.

traumatologie [tʀomatɔlɔʒi] *nf branch of medicine concerned with accidents.*

travail, aux [tʀavaj, -o] *nm* (*gén*) work; (*tâche,* métier) work *no pl*, job; (*ÉCON, MÉD*) labour (*BRIT*), labor (*US*); (*INFORM*) job ♦ *nmpl* (*de réparation, agricoles etc*) work *sg*; (*sur route*) roadworks; (*de construction*) building (work) *sg*; **être/entrer en** ~ (*MÉD*) to be in/start labour; **être sans** ~ (*employé*) to be out of work, be unemployed; ~ **d'intérêt général (TIG)** ≈ community service; ~ **(au) noir** moonlighting; ~ **posté** shiftwork; **travaux des champs** farmwork *sg*; **travaux dirigés (TD)** (*SCOL*) supervised practical work *sg*; **travaux forcés** hard labour *sg*; **travaux manuels** (*SCOL*) handicrafts; **travaux ménagers** housework *sg*; **travaux pratiques (TP)** (*gén*) practical work; (*en laboratoire*) lab work (*BRIT*), lab (*US*); **travaux publics (TP)** ≈ public works *sg*.

travaillé, e [tʀavaje] *adj* (*style*) polished.

travailler [tʀavaje] *vi* to work; (*bois*) to warp ♦ *vt* (*bois, métal*) to work; (*pâte*) to knead; (*objet d'art, discipline, fig: influencer*) to work on; **cela le travaille** it is on his mind; ~ **la terre** to work the land; ~ **son piano** to do one's piano practice; ~ **à** to work on; (*fig: contribuer à*) to work towards; ~ **à faire** to endeavour (*BRIT*) *ou* endeavor (*US*) to do.

travailleur, euse [tʀavajœʀ, -øz] *adj* hard-working ♦ *nm/f* worker; ~ **de force** labourer (*BRIT*), laborer (*US*); ~ **intellectuel** non-manual worker; ~ **social** social worker; **travailleuse familiale** home help.

travailliste [tʀavajist(ə)] *adj* ≈ Labour *cpd* ♦ *nm/f* member of the Labour party.

travée [tʀave] *nf* row; (*ARCHIT*) bay; span.

traveller's (chèque) [tʀavlœʀs(ʃɛk)] *nm* traveller's cheque.

travelling [tʀavliŋ] *nm* (*chariot*) dolly; (*technique*) tracking; ~ **optique** zoom shots *pl*.

travelo [tʀavlo] *nm* (*fam*) (drag) queen.

travers [tʀavɛʀ] *nm* fault, failing; **en** ~ **(de)** across; **au** ~ **(de)** through; **de** ~ *adj* askew ♦ *adv* sideways; (*fig*) the wrong way; **à** ~ through; **regarder de** ~ (*fig*) to look askance at.

traverse [tʀavɛʀs(ə)] *nf* (*de voie ferrée*) sleeper; **chemin de** ~ shortcut.

traversée [tʀavɛʀse] *nf* crossing.

traverser [tʀavɛʀse] *vt* (*gén*) to cross; (*ville, tunnel, aussi: percer, fig*) to go through; (*suj: ligne, trait*) to run across.

traversin [tʀavɛʀsɛ̃] *nm* bolster.

travesti [tʀavɛsti] *nm* (*costume*) fancy dress; (*artiste de cabaret*) female impersonator, drag artist; (*pervers*) transvestite.

travestir [tʀavɛstiʀ] *vt* (*vérité*) to misrepresent; **se** ~ (*se costumer*) to dress up; (*artiste*) to put on drag; (*PSYCH*) to dress as a woman.

trayais [tʀɛjɛ] *etc vb voir* **traire**.

trayeuse [tʀɛjøz] *nf* milking machine.

trébucher [tʀebyʃe] *vi*: ~ **(sur)** to stumble

(over), trip (over).

trèfle [tʀɛfl(ə)] nm (BOT) clover; (CARTES: couleur) clubs pl; (: carte) club; ~ **à quatre feuilles** four-leaf clover.

treillage [tʀɛjaʒ] nm lattice work.

treille [tʀɛj] nf (tonnelle) vine arbour (BRIT) ou arbor (US); (vigne) climbing vine.

treillis [tʀɛji] nm (métallique) wire-mesh; (toile) canvas; (uniforme) battle-dress.

treize [tʀɛz] num thirteen.

treizième [tʀɛzjɛm] num thirteenth.

> **Le treizième mois** is an end-of-year bonus corresponding roughly to one month's salary. For many employees it is a standard part of their salary package.

tréma [tʀema] nm diaeresis.

tremblant, e [tʀɑ̃blɑ̃, -ɑ̃t] adj trembling, shaking.

tremble [tʀɑ̃bl(ə)] nm (BOT) aspen.

tremblé, e [tʀɑ̃ble] adj shaky.

tremblement [tʀɑ̃bləmɑ̃] nm trembling no pl, shaking no pl, shivering no pl; ~ **de terre** earthquake.

trembler [tʀɑ̃ble] vi to tremble, shake; ~ **de** (froid, fièvre) to shiver ou tremble with; (peur) to shake ou tremble with; ~ **pour qn** to fear for sb.

tremblotant, e [tʀɑ̃blɔtɑ̃, -ɑ̃t] adj trembling.

trembloter [tʀɑ̃blɔte] vi to tremble ou shake slightly.

trémolo [tʀemɔlo] nm (d'un instrument) tremolo; (de la voix) quaver.

trémousser [tʀemuse]: **se** ~ vi to jig about, wriggle about.

trempe [tʀɑ̃p] nf (fig): **de cette/sa** ~ of this/his calibre (BRIT) ou caliber (US).

trempé, e [tʀɑ̃pe] adj soaking (wet), drenched; (TECH): **acier** ~ tempered steel.

tremper [tʀɑ̃pe] vt to soak, drench; (aussi: **faire** ~, **mettre à** ~) to soak; (plonger): ~ **qch dans** to dip sth in(to) ♦ vi to soak; (fig): ~ **dans** to be involved ou have a hand in; **se** ~ vi to have a quick dip; **se faire** ~ to get soaked ou drenched.

trempette [tʀɑ̃pɛt] nf: **faire** ~ to go paddling.

tremplin [tʀɑ̃plɛ̃] nm springboard; (SKI) ski jump.

trentaine [tʀɑ̃tɛn] nf (âge): **avoir la** ~ to be around thirty; **une** ~ **(de)** thirty or so, about thirty.

trente [tʀɑ̃t] num thirty; **voir** ~**-six chandelles** (fig) to see stars; **être/se mettre sur son** ~ **et un** to be/get dressed to kill; ~**-trois tours** nm long-playing record, LP.

trentième [tʀɑ̃tjɛm] num thirtieth.

trépanation [tʀepanasjɔ̃] nf trepan.

trépaner [tʀepane] vt to trepan, trephine.

trépasser [tʀepase] vi to pass away.

trépidant, e [tʀepidɑ̃, -ɑ̃t] adj (fig: rythme) pulsating; (: vie) hectic.

trépidation [tʀepidasjɔ̃] nf (d'une machine, d'un moteur) vibration; (fig: de la vie) whirl.

trépider [tʀepide] vi to vibrate.

trépied [tʀepje] nm (d'appareil) tripod; (meuble) trivet.

trépignement [tʀepiɲmɑ̃] nm stamping (of feet).

trépigner [tʀepiɲe] vi to stamp (one's feet).

très [tʀɛ] adv very; much + pp, highly + pp; ~ **beau/bien** very beautiful/well; ~ **critiqué** much criticized; ~ **industrialisé** highly industrialized; **j'ai** ~ **faim** I'm very hungry.

trésor [tʀezɔʀ] nm treasure; (ADMIN) finances pl; (d'un organisation) funds pl; ~ **(public) (TP)** public revenue; (service) public revenue office.

trésorerie [tʀezɔʀʀi] nf (fonds) funds pl; (gestion) accounts pl; (bureaux) accounts department; (poste) treasurership; **difficultés de** ~ cash problems, shortage of cash ou funds; ~ **générale (TG)** local government finance office.

trésorier, ière [tʀezɔʀje, -jɛʀ] nm/f treasurer.

Trésorier-payeur [tʀezɔʀjepɛjœʀ] nm: ~ **général (TPG)** paymaster.

tressaillement [tʀesajmɑ̃] nm shiver, shudder; quiver.

tressaillir [tʀesajiʀ] vi (de peur etc) to shiver, shudder; (de joie) to quiver.

tressauter [tʀesote] vi to start, jump.

tresse [tʀɛs] nf (de cheveux) braid, plait; (cordon, galon) braid.

tresser [tʀese] vt (cheveux) to braid, plait; (fil, jonc) to plait; (corbeille) to weave; (corde) to twist.

tréteau, x [tʀeto] nm trestle; **les** ~**x** (fig: THÉÂT) the boards.

treuil [tʀœj] nm winch.

trêve [tʀɛv] nf (MIL, POL) truce; (fig) respite; **sans** ~ unremittingly; ~ **de ...** enough of this ...; **les États de la T**~ the Trucial States.

tri [tʀi] nm (voir trier) sorting (out) no pl; selection; screening; (INFORM) sort; (POSTES: action) sorting; (: bureau) sorting office.

triage [tʀijaʒ] nm (RAIL) shunting; (gare) marshalling yard.

trial [tʀijal] nm (SPORT) scrambling.

triangle [tʀijɑ̃gl(ə)] nm triangle; **isocèle/ équilatéral** isoceles/equilateral triangle; ~ **rectangle** right-angled triangle.

triangulaire [tʀijɑ̃gylɛʀ] adj triangular.

triathlon [tʀi(j)atlɔ̃] nm triathlon.

tribal, e, aux [tʀibal, -o] adj tribal.

tribord [tʀibɔʀ] nm: **à** ~ to starboard, on the starboard side.

tribu [tʀiby] nf tribe.

tribulations [tʀibylasjɔ̃] nfpl tribulations, trials.

tribunal, aux [tʀibynal, -o] nm (JUR) court; (MIL) tribunal; ~ **de police/pour enfants** police/juvenile court; ~ **d'instance (TI)** ≈ magistrates' court (BRIT), ≈ district court

(*US*); ~ **de grande instance (TGI)** ≈ High Court (*BRIT*), ≈ Supreme Court (*US*).

tribune [tʀibyn] *nf* (*estrade*) platform, rostrum; (*débat*) forum; (*d'église, de tribunal*) gallery; (*de stade*) stand; ~ **libre** (*PRESSE*) opinion column.

tribut [tʀiby] *nm* tribute.

tributaire [tʀibytɛʀ] *adj*: **être** ~ **de** to be dependent on; (*GÉO*) to be a tributary of.

tricentenaire [tʀisɑ̃tnɛʀ] *nm* tercentenary, tricentennial.

tricher [tʀiʃe] *vi* to cheat.

tricherie [tʀiʃʀi] *nf* cheating *no pl*.

tricheur, euse [tʀiʃœʀ, -øz] *nm/f* cheat.

trichromie [tʀikʀɔmi] *nf* three-colour (*BRIT*) *ou* -color (*US*) printing.

tricolore [tʀikɔlɔʀ] *adj* three-coloured (*BRIT*), three-colored (*US*); (*français: drapeau*) red, white and blue; (: *équipe etc*) French.

tricot [tʀiko] *nm* (*technique, ouvrage*) knitting *no pl*; (*tissu*) knitted fabric; (*vêtement*) jersey, sweater; ~ **de corps** vest (*BRIT*), undershirt (*US*).

tricoter [tʀikɔte] *vt* to knit; **machine/aiguille à** ~ knitting machine/needle (*BRIT*) *ou* pin (*US*).

trictrac [tʀiktʀak] *nm* backgammon.

tricycle [tʀisikl(ə)] *nm* tricycle.

tridimensionnel, le [tʀidimɑ̃sjɔnɛl] *adj* three-dimensional.

triennal, e, aux [tʀiɛnal, -o] *adj* (*prix, foire, élection*) three-yearly; (*charge, mandat, plan*) three-year.

trier [tʀije] *vt* (*classer*) to sort (out); (*choisir*) to select; (*visiteurs*) to screen; (*POSTES, INFORM*) to sort.

trieur, euse [tʀijœʀ, -øz] *nm/f* sorter.

trigonométrie [tʀigɔnɔmetʀi] *nf* trigonometry.

trigonométrique [tʀigɔnɔmetʀik] *adj* trigonometric.

trilingue [tʀilɛ̃g] *adj* trilingual.

trilogie [tʀilɔʒi] *nf* trilogy.

trimaran [tʀimaʀɑ̃] *nm* trimaran.

trimbaler [tʀɛ̃bale] *vt* to cart around, trail along.

trimer [tʀime] *vi* to slave away.

trimestre [tʀimɛstʀ(ə)] *nm* (*SCOL*) term; (*COMM*) quarter.

trimestriel, le [tʀimɛstʀijɛl] *adj* quarterly; (*SCOL*) end-of-term.

trimoteur [tʀimɔtœʀ] *nm* three-engined aircraft.

tringle [tʀɛ̃gl(ə)] *nf* rod.

Trinité [tʀinite] *nf* Trinity.

Trinité et Tobago [tʀiniteetɔbago] *nf* Trinidad and Tobago.

trinquer [tʀɛ̃ke] *vi* to clink glasses; (*fam*) to cop it; ~ **à qch/la santé de qn** to drink to sth/sb.

trio [tʀijo] *nm* trio.

triolet [tʀijɔlɛ] *nm* (*MUS*) triplet.

triomphal, e, aux [tʀijɔ̃fal, -o] *adj* triumphant, triumphal.

triomphalement [tʀijɔ̃falmɑ̃] *adv* triumphantly.

triomphant, e [tʀijɔ̃fɑ̃, -ɑ̃t] *adj* triumphant.

triomphateur, trice [tʀijɔ̃fatœʀ, -tʀis] *nm/f* (triumphant) victor.

triomphe [tʀijɔ̃f] *nm* triumph; **être reçu/porté en** ~ to be given a triumphant welcome/be carried shoulder-high in triumph.

triompher [tʀijɔ̃fe] *vi* to triumph; ~ **de** to triumph over, overcome.

triparti, e [tʀipaʀti] *adj* (*aussi*: **tripartite**: *réunion, assemblée*) tripartite, three-party.

triperie [tʀipʀi] *nf* tripe shop.

tripes [tʀip] *nfpl* (*CULIN*) tripe *sg*; (*fam*) guts.

triplace [tʀiplas] *adj* three-seater *cpd*.

triple [tʀipl(ə)] *adj* (*à trois élements*) triple; (*trois fois plus grand*) treble ♦ *nm*: **le** ~ **(de)** (*comparaison*) three times as much (as); **en** ~ **exemplaire** in triplicate; ~ **saut** (*SPORT*) triple jump.

triplé [tʀiple] *nm* hat-trick (*BRIT*), triple success.

triplement [tʀipləmɑ̃] *adv* (*à un degré triple*) three times over; (*de trois façons*) in three ways; (*pour trois raisons*) on three counts ♦ *nm* trebling, threefold increase.

tripler [tʀiple] *vi, vt* to triple, treble, increase threefold.

triplés, ées [tʀiple] *nm/fpl* triplets.

Tripoli [tʀipɔli] *n* Tripoli.

triporteur [tʀipɔʀtœʀ] *nm* delivery tricycle.

tripot [tʀipo] *nm* (*péj*) dive.

tripotage [tʀipɔtaʒ] *nm* (*péj*) jiggery-pokery.

tripoter [tʀipɔte] *vt* to fiddle with, finger ♦ *vi* (*fam*) to rummage about.

trique [tʀik] *nf* cudgel.

trisannuel, le [tʀizanɥɛl] *adj* triennial.

trisomie [tʀizɔmi] *nf* Down's syndrome.

triste [tʀist(ə)] *adj* sad; (*péj*): ~ **personnage/ affaire** sorry individual/affair; **c'est pas** ~! (*fam*) it's something else!

tristement [tʀistəmɑ̃] *adv* sadly.

tristesse [tʀistɛs] *nf* sadness.

triton [tʀitɔ̃] *nm* triton.

triturer [tʀityʀe] *vt* (*pâte*) to knead; (*objets*) to manipulate.

trivial, e, aux [tʀivjal, -o] *adj* coarse, crude; (*commun*) mundane.

trivialité [tʀivjalite] *nf* coarseness, crudeness; mundaneness.

troc [tʀɔk] *nm* (*ÉCON*) barter; (*transaction*) exchange, swap.

troène [tʀɔɛn] *nm* privet.

troglodyte [tʀɔglɔdit] *nm/f* cave dweller, troglodyte.

trognon [tʀɔɲɔ̃] *nm* (*de fruit*) core; (*de légume*) stalk.

trois [tʀwa] *num* three.

trois-huit [tʀwaɥit] *nmpl*: **faire les** ~ to work eight-hour shifts (round the clock).

troisième [tʀwazjɛm] num third; **le ~ âge** the years of retirement.

troisièmement [tʀwazjɛmmɑ̃] adv thirdly.

trois-quarts [tʀwakaʀ] nmpl: **les ~ de** three-quarters of.

trolleybus [tʀɔlɛbys] nm trolley bus.

trombe [tʀɔ̃b] nf waterspout; **des ~s d'eau** a downpour; **en ~** (arriver, passer) like a whirlwind.

trombone [tʀɔ̃bɔn] nm (MUS) trombone; (de bureau) paper clip; **~ à coulisse** slide trombone.

tromboniste [tʀɔ̃bɔnist(ə)] nm/f trombonist.

trompe [tʀɔ̃p] nf (d'éléphant) trunk; (MUS) trumpet, horn; **~ d'Eustache** Eustachian tube; **~s utérines** Fallopian tubes.

trompe-l'œil [tʀɔ̃plœj] nm: **en ~** in trompe-l'œil style.

tromper [tʀɔ̃pe] vt to deceive; (fig: espoir, attente) to disappoint; (vigilance, poursuivants) to elude; **se ~** vi to make a mistake, be mistaken; **se ~ de voiture/jour** to take the wrong car/get the day wrong; **se ~ de 3 cm/20 F** to be out by 3 cm/20 F.

tromperie [tʀɔ̃pʀi] nf deception, trickery no pl.

trompette [tʀɔ̃pɛt] nf trumpet; **en ~** (nez) turned-up.

trompettiste [tʀɔ̃petist(ə)] nm/f trumpet player.

trompeur, euse [tʀɔ̃pœʀ, -øz] adj deceptive, misleading.

tronc [tʀɔ̃] nm (BOT, ANAT) trunk; (d'église) collection box; **~ d'arbre** tree trunk; **~ commun** (SCOL) common-core syllabus; **~ de cône** truncated cone.

tronche [tʀɔ̃ʃ] nf (fam) mug, face.

tronçon [tʀɔ̃sɔ̃] nm section.

tronçonner [tʀɔ̃sɔne] vt (arbre) to saw up; (pierre) to cut up.

tronçonneuse [tʀɔ̃sɔnøz] nf chain saw.

trône [tʀon] nm throne; **monter sur le ~** to ascend the throne.

trôner [tʀone] vi (fig) to have (ou take) pride of place (BRIT), have the place of honour (BRIT) ou honor (US).

tronquer [tʀɔ̃ke] vt to truncate; (fig) to curtail.

trop [tʀo] adv vb + too much; too + adjectif, adverbe; **~ (nombreux)** too many; **~ peu (nombreux)** too few; **~ (souvent)** too often; **~ (longtemps)** (for) too long; **~ de** (nombre) too many; (quantité) too much; **de ~, en ~:** **des livres en ~** a few books too many, a few extra books; **du lait en ~** too much milk; **3 livres/5 F de ~** 3 books too many/5 F too much.

trophée [tʀofe] nm trophy.

tropical, e, aux [tʀɔpikal, -o] adj tropical.

tropique [tʀɔpik] nm tropic; **~s** nmpl tropics; **~ du Cancer/Capricorne** Tropic of Cancer/Capricorn.

trop-plein [tʀɔplɛ̃] nm (tuyau) overflow ou outlet (pipe); (liquide) overflow.

troquer [tʀɔke] vt: **~ qch contre** to barter ou trade sth for; (fig) to swap sth for.

trot [tʀo] nm trot; **aller au ~** to trot along; **partir au ~** to set off at a trot.

trotter [tʀɔte] vi to trot; (fig) to scamper along (ou about).

trotteuse [tʀɔtøz] nf (de montre) second hand.

trottiner [tʀɔtine] vi (fig) to scamper along (ou about).

trottinette [tʀɔtinɛt] nf (child's) scooter.

trottoir [tʀɔtwaʀ] nm pavement (BRIT), sidewalk (US); **faire le ~** (péj) to walk the streets; **~ roulant** moving pavement (BRIT) ou walkway.

trou [tʀu] nm hole; (fig) gap; (COMM) deficit; **~ d'aération** (air) vent; **~ d'air** air pocket; **~ de mémoire** blank, lapse of memory; **~ noir** black hole; **~ de la serrure** keyhole.

troublant, e [tʀublɑ̃, -ɑ̃t] adj disturbing.

trouble [tʀubl(ə)] adj (liquide) cloudy; (image, mémoire) indistinct, hazy; (affaire) shady, murky ♦ adv indistinctly ♦ nm (désarroi) distress, agitation; (émoi sensuel) turmoil, agitation; (embarras) confusion; (zizanie) unrest, discord; **~s** nmpl (POL) disturbances, troubles, unrest sg; (MÉD) trouble sg, disorders; **~s de la personnalité** personality problems; **~s de la vision** eye trouble.

trouble-fête [tʀublfɛt] nm/f inv spoilsport.

troubler [tʀuble] vt (embarrasser) to confuse, disconcert; (émouvoir) to agitate; to disturb; to perturb; (perturber: ordre etc) to disrupt, disturb; (liquide) to make cloudy; **se ~** vi (personne) to become flustered ou confused; **~ l'ordre public** to cause a breach of the peace.

troué, e [tʀue] adj with a hole (ou holes) in it ♦ nf gap; (MIL) breach.

trouer [tʀue] vt to make a hole (ou holes) in; (fig) to pierce.

trouille [tʀuj] nf (fam): **avoir la ~** to be scared stiff, be scared out of one's wits.

troupe [tʀup] nf (MIL) troop; (groupe) troop, group; **la ~** (MIL: l'armée) the army; (: les simples soldats) the troops pl; **~ (de théâtre)** (theatrical) company; **~s de choc** shock troops.

troupeau, x [tʀupo] nm (de moutons) flock; (de vaches) herd.

trousse [tʀus] nf case, kit; (d'écolier) pencil case; (de docteur) instrument case; **aux ~s de** (fig) on the heels ou tail of; **~ à outils** toolkit; **~ de toilette** toilet ou sponge (BRIT) bag.

trousseau, x [tʀuso] nm (de mariée) trousseau; **~ de clefs** bunch of keys.

trouvaille [tʀuvaj] nf find; (fig: idée, expression etc) brainwave.

trouvé, e [tʀuve] adj: **tout ~** ready-made.

trouver [tʀuve] vt to find; (rendre visite): **aller/venir ~ qn** to go/come and see sb; **je trouve**

que I find *ou* think that; ~ **à boire/critiquer** to find something to drink/criticize; ~ **asile/refuge** to find refuge/shelter; **se ~** *vi* (*être*) to be; (*être soudain*) to find o.s.; **se ~ être/avoir** to happen to be/have; **il se trouve que** it happens that, it turns out that; **se ~ bien** to feel well; **se ~ mal** to pass out.

truand [tʀyɑ̃] *nm* villain, crook.

truander [tʀyɑ̃de] *vi* (*fam*) to cheat, do.

trublion [tʀyblijɔ̃] *nm* troublemaker.

truc [tʀyk] *nm* (*astuce*) way, device; (*de cinéma, prestidigitateur*) trick effect; (*chose*) thing; (*machin*) thingumajig, whatsit (*BRIT*); **avoir le ~** to have the knack; **c'est pas son** (*ou* **mon** *etc*) ~ (*fam*) it's not really his (*ou* my *etc*) thing.

truchement [tʀyʃmɑ̃] *nm*: **par le ~ de qn** through (the intervention of) sb.

trucider [tʀyside] *vt* (*fam*) to do in, bump off.

truculence [tʀykylɑ̃s] *nf* colourfulness (*BRIT*), colorfulness (*US*).

truculent, e [tʀykylɑ̃, -ɑ̃t] *adj* colourful (*BRIT*), colorful (*US*).

truelle [tʀyɛl] *nf* trowel.

truffe [tʀyf] *nf* truffle; (*nez*) nose.

truffer [tʀyfe] *vt* (*CULIN*) to garnish with truffles; **truffé de** (*fig: citations*) peppered with; (*: pièges*) bristling with.

truie [tʀyi] *nf* sow.

truite [tʀyit] *nf* trout *inv*.

truquage [tʀykaʒ] *nm* fixing; (*CINÉ*) special effects *pl*.

truquer [tʀyke] *vt* (*élections, serrure, dés*) to fix; (*CINÉ*) to use special effects in.

trust [tʀœst] *nm* (*COMM*) trust.

truster [tʀœste] *vt* (*COMM*) to monopolize.

ts *abr* = **tous**.

tsar [dzaʀ] *nm* tsar.

tsé-tsé [tsetse] *nf*: **mouche ~** tsetse fly.

TSF *sigle f* (= *télégraphie sans fil*) wireless.

tsigane [tsigan] *adj, nm/f* = **tzigane**.

TSVP *abr* (= *tournez s'il vous plaît*) PTO.

tt *abr* = **tout**.

TT(A) *sigle m* (= *transit temporaire (autorisé)*) vehicle registration for cars etc bought in France for export tax-free by non-residents.

TTC *abr* = **toutes taxes comprises**.

ttes *abr* = **toutes**.

TU *sigle m* = *temps universel*.

tu [ty] *pron* you ♦ *nm*: **employer le ~** to use the "tu" form.

tu, e [ty] *pp de* **taire**.

tuant, e [tɥɑ̃, -ɑ̃t] *adj* (*épuisant*) killing; (*énervant*) infuriating.

tuba [tyba] *nm* (*MUS*) tuba; (*SPORT*) snorkel.

tubage [tybaʒ] *nm* (*MÉD*) intubation.

tube [tyb] *nm* tube; (*de canalisation, métallique etc*) pipe; (*chanson, disque*) hit song *ou* record; ~ **digestif** alimentary canal, digestive tract; ~ **à essai** test tube.

tuberculeux, euse [tybɛʀkylø, -øz] *adj* tubercular ♦ *nm/f* tuberculosis *ou* TB patient.

tuberculose [tybɛʀkyloz] *nf* tuberculosis, TB.

tubulaire [tybylɛʀ] *adj* tubular.

tubulure [tybylyʀ] *nf* pipe; piping *no pl*; (*AUTO*): ~ **d'échappement/d'admission** exhaust/inlet manifold.

TUC [tyk] *sigle m* (= *travail d'utilité collective*) community work scheme for the young unemployed.

tuciste [tysist(ə)] *nm/f* young person on a community work scheme.

tué, e [tɥe] *nm/f*: **5 ~s** 5 killed *ou* dead.

tue-mouche [tymyʃ] *adj*: **papier ~(s)** flypaper.

tuer [tɥe] *vt* to kill; **se ~** (*se suicider*) to kill o.s.; (*dans un accident*) to be killed; **se ~ au travail** (*fig*) to work o.s. to death.

tuerie [tyʀi] *nf* slaughter *no pl*, massacre.

tue-tête [tytɛt]: **à ~** *adv* at the top of one's voice.

tueur [tɥœʀ] *nm* killer; ~ **à gages** hired killer.

tuile [tɥil] *nf* tile; (*fam*) spot of bad luck, blow.

tulipe [tylip] *nf* tulip.

tulle [tyl] *nm* tulle.

tuméfié, e [tymefje] *adj* puffy, swollen.

tumeur [tymœʀ] *nf* growth, tumour (*BRIT*), tumor (*US*).

tumulte [tymylt(ə)] *nm* commotion, hubbub.

tumultueux, euse [tymyltɥø, -øz] *adj* stormy, turbulent.

tuner [tynɛʀ] *nm* tuner.

tungstène [tœ̃kstɛn] *nm* tungsten.

tunique [tynik] *nf* tunic; (*de femme*) smock, tunic.

Tunis [tynis] *n* Tunis.

Tunisie [tynizi] *nf*: **la ~** Tunisia.

tunisien, ne [tynizjɛ̃, -ɛn] *adj* Tunisian ♦ *nm/f*: **T~, ne** Tunisian.

tunisois, e [tynizwa, -waz] *adj* of *ou* from Tunis.

tunnel [tynɛl] *nm* tunnel; **le ~ sous la Manche** the Channel Tunnel, the Chunnel.

TUP *sigle m* (= *titre universel de paiement*) ≈ payment slip.

turban [tyʀbɑ̃] *nm* turban.

turbin [tyʀbɛ̃] *nm* (*fam*) work *no pl*.

turbine [tyʀbin] *nf* turbine.

turbo [tyʀbo] *nm* turbo; **un moteur ~** a turbo (-charged) engine.

turbomoteur [tyʀbomotœʀ] *nm* turbo (-boosted) engine.

turbopropulseur [tyʀbopʀopylsœʀ] *nm* turboprop.

turboréacteur [tyʀboʀeaktœʀ] *nm* turbojet.

turbot [tyʀbo] *nm* turbot.

turbotrain [tyʀbotʀɛ̃] *nm* turbotrain.

turbulences [tyʀbylɑ̃s] *nfpl* (*AVIAT*) turbulence *sg*.

turbulent, e [tyʀbylɑ̃, -ɑ̃t] *adj* boisterous, unruly.

turc, turque [tyʀk(ə)] *adj* Turkish; (*w.-c.*) seatless ♦ *nm* (*LING*) Turkish ♦ *nm/f*: **T~, Turque** Turk/Turkish woman; **à la turque**

adv (*assis*) cross-legged.
urf [tyʀf] *nm* racing.
urfiste [tyʀfist(ə)] *nm/f* racegoer.
Turks et Caïques *ou* **Caicos** [tyʀkekaik(ɔs)] *nfpl* Turks and Caicos Islands.
urpitude [tyʀpityd] *nf* base act, baseness *no pl*.
urque [tyʀk(ə)] *adj f, nf voir* **turc**.
Turquie [tyʀki] *nf*: **la ~** Turkey.
urquoise [tyʀkwaz] *nf, adj inv* turquoise.
ut [ty] *etc vb voir* **taire**.
utelle [tytɛl] *nf* (*JUR*) guardianship; (*POL*) trusteeship; **sous la ~ de** (*fig*) under the supervision of.
uteur, trice [tytœʀ, -tʀis] *nm/f* (*JUR*) guardian; (*de plante*) stake, support.
utoiement [tytwamɑ̃] *nm* use of familiar "tu" form.
utoyer [tytwaje] *vt*: **~ qn** to address sb as "tu".
utti quanti [tutikwɑ̃ti] *nmpl*: **et ~** and all the rest (of them).
utu [tyty] *nm* (*DANSE*) tutu.
Tuvalu [tyvaly] *nm*: **le ~** Tuvalu.
uyau, x [tɥijo] *nm* pipe; (*flexible*) tube; (*fam: conseil*) tip; (: *mise au courant*) gen *no pl*; **~ d'arrosage** hosepipe; **~ d'échappement** exhaust pipe; **~ d'incendie** fire hose.
uyauté, e [tɥijote] *adj* fluted.
uyauterie [tɥijotʀi] *nf* piping *no pl*.
uyère [tɥijɛʀ] *nf* nozzle.
TV [teve] *nf* TV, telly (*BRIT*).
TVA *sigle f* = **taxe à** *ou* **sur la valeur ajoutée**.
weed [twid] *nm* tweed.
ympan [tɛ̃pɑ̃] *nm* (*ANAT*) eardrum.
ype [tip] *nm* type; (*personne, chose: représentant*) classic example, epitome; (*fam*) chap, guy ♦ *adj* typical, standard; **avoir le ~ nordique** to be Nordic-looking.
ypé, e [tipe] *adj* ethnic (*euph*).
yphoïde [tifɔid] *nf* typhoid (fever).
yphon [tifɔ̃] *nm* typhoon.
yphus [tifys] *nm* typhus (fever).
ypique [tipik] *adj* typical.
ypiquement [tipikmɑ̃] *adv* typically.
ypographe [tipɔgʀaf] *nm/f* typographer.
ypographie [tipɔgʀafi] *nf* typography; (*procédé*) letterpress (printing).
ypographique [tipɔgʀafik] *adj* typographical; letterpress *cpd*.
ypologie [tipɔlɔʒi] *nf* typology.
yran [tiʀɑ̃] *nm* tyrant.
yrannie [tiʀani] *nf* tyranny.
yrannique [tiʀanik] *adj* tyrannical.
yranniser [tiʀanize] *vt* to tyrannize.
Tyrol [tiʀɔl] *nm*: **le ~** the Tyrol.
yrolien, ne [tiʀɔljɛ̃, -ɛn] *adj* Tyrolean.
zar [dzaʀ] *nm* = **tsar**.
zigane [dzigan] *adj* gipsy, tzigane ♦ *nm/f* (Hungarian) gipsy, Tzigane.

U u

U, u [y] *nm inv* U, u ♦ *abr* (= *unité*) 10,000 *francs*; **maison à vendre 50 U** house for sale: 500,000 francs; **U comme Ursule** U for Uncle.
ubiquité [ybikɥite] *nf*: **avoir le don d'~** to be everywhere at once, be ubiquitous.
UDF *sigle f* (= *Union pour la démocratie française*) *political party*.
UE *sigle f* (= *Union européenne*) EU.
UEFA [yefa] *sigle f* (= *Union of European Football Associations*) UEFA.
UEM *sigle f* (= *Union économique et monétaire*) EMU.
UER *sigle f* (= *unité d'enseignement et de recherche*) old title of UFR; (= *Union européenne de radiodiffusion*) EBU (= *European Broadcasting Union*).
UFC *sigle f* (= *Union fédérale des consommateurs*) *national consumer group*.
UFR *sigle f* (= *unité de formation et de recherche*) ≈ university department.
UHF *sigle f* (= *ultra-haute fréquence*) UHF.
UHT *sigle* (= *ultra-haute température*) UHT.
UIT *sigle f* (= *Union internationale des télécommunications*) ITU (= *International Telecommunications Union*).
UJP *sigle f* (= *Union des jeunes pour le progrès*) *political party*.
Ukraine [ykʀɛn] *nf*: **l'~** the Ukraine.
ukrainien, ne [ykʀɛnjɛ̃, -ɛn] *adj* Ukrainian ♦ *nm* (*LING*) Ukrainian ♦ *nm/f*: **U~, ne** Ukrainian.
ulcère [ylsɛʀ] *nm* ulcer; **~ à l'estomac** stomach ulcer.
ulcérer [ylseʀe] *vt* (*MÉD*) to ulcerate; (*fig*) to sicken, appal.
ulcéreux, euse [ylseʀø, -øz] *adj* (*plaie, lésion*) ulcerous; (*membre*) ulcerated.
ULM *sigle m* (= *ultra léger motorisé*) microlight.
ultérieur, e [ylteʀjœʀ] *adj* later, subsequent; **remis à une date ~e** postponed to a later date.
ultérieurement [ylteʀjœʀmɑ̃] *adv* later.
ultimatum [yltimatɔm] *nm* ultimatum.
ultime [yltim] *adj* final.
ultra... [yltʀa] *préfixe* ultra....
ultramoderne [yltʀamɔdɛʀn(ə)] *adj* ultra-modern.
ultra-rapide [yltʀaʀapid] *adj* ultra-fast.
ultra-sensible [yltʀasɑ̃sibl(ə)] *adj* (*PHOTO*) high-speed.
ultra(-)son [yltʀasɔ̃] *nm* ultrasound *no pl*; **~s**

nmpl ultrasonics.

ultra(-)violet, te [yltravjɔlɛ, -ɛt] *adj*
ultraviolet ♦ *nm*: **les ~s** ultraviolet rays.

ululer [ylyle] *vi* = **hululer**.

UME *sigle f* (= *Union monétaire européenne*)
EMU.

════════════════════════ *MOT-CLÉ*

un, une [œ̃, yn] *art indéf* a; (*devant voyelle*) an;
~ **garçon/vieillard** a boy/an old man; **une**
fille a girl
♦ *pron* one; **l'~ des meilleurs** one of the best;
l'~ ..., l'autre (the) one ..., the other; **les ~s**
..., les autres some ..., others; **l'~ et l'autre**
both (of them); **l'~ ou l'autre** either (of
them); **l'~ l'autre, les ~s les autres** each
other, one another; **pas ~ seul** not a single
one; ~ **par** ~ one by one
♦ *num* one; **une pomme seulement** one apple
only
♦ *nf*: **la une** (*PRESSE*) the front page.

unanime [ynanim] *adj* unanimous; **ils sont ~s**
(à penser que) they are unanimous (in
thinking that).

unanimement [ynanimmɑ̃] *adv* (*par tous*)
unanimously; (*d'un commun accord*) with
one accord.

unanimité [ynanimite] *nf* unanimity; **à l'~**
unanimously; **faire l'~** to be approved
unanimously.

UNEF [ynef] *sigle f* = *Union nationale des*
étudiants de France.

UNESCO [ynɛsko] *sigle f* (= *United Nations*
Educational, Scientific and Cultural
Organization) UNESCO.

Unetelle [yntɛl] *nf voir* **Untel**.

UNI *sigle f* = *Union nationale interuniversitaire*.

uni, e [yni] *adj* (*ton, tissu*) plain; (*surface*)
smooth, even; (*famille*) close(-knit); (*pays*)
united.

UNICEF [ynisɛf] *sigle m ou f* (= *United Nations*
International Children's Emergency Fund)
UNICEF.

unidirectionnel, le [ynidirɛksjɔnɛl] *adj*
unidirectional, one-way.

unième [ynjɛm] *num*: **vingt/trente et** ~
twenty-/thirty-first; **cent** ~ (one) hundred
and first.

unificateur, trice [ynifikatœr, -tris] *adj*
unifying.

unification [ynifikɑsjɔ̃] *nf* uniting; unification;
standardization.

unifier [ynifje] *vt* to unite, unify; (*systèmes*) to
standardize, unify; **s'~** to become united.

uniforme [ynifɔrm(ə)] *adj* (*mouvement*)
regular, uniform; (*surface, ton*) even;
(*objets, maisons*) uniform; (*fig: vie, conduite*)
unchanging ♦ *nm* uniform; **être sous l'~**
(*MIL*) to be serving.

uniformément [ynifɔrmemɑ̃] *adv* uniformly.

uniformisation [ynifɔrmizɑsjɔ̃] *nf*
standardization.

uniformiser [ynifɔrmize] *vt* to make uniform;
(*systèmes*) to standardize.

uniformité [ynifɔrmite] *nf* regularity;
uniformity; evenness.

unijambiste [yniʒɑ̃bist(ə)] *nm/f* one-legged
man/woman.

unilatéral, e, aux [ynilateral, -o] *adj*
unilateral; **stationnement** ~ parking on one
side only.

unilatéralement [ynilateralmɑ̃] *adv*
unilaterally.

uninominal, e, aux [yninɔminal, -o] *adj*
uncontested.

union [ynjɔ̃] *nf* union; ~ **conjugale** union of
marriage; ~ **de consommateurs** consumers'
association; ~ **libre** free love; **l'U~ des**
Républiques socialistes soviétiques (URSS)
the Union of Soviet Socialist Republics
(USSR); **l'U~ soviétique** the Soviet Union.

unique [ynik] *adj* (*seul*) only; (*le même*): **un**
prix/système ~ a single price/system;
(*exceptionnel*) unique; **ménage à salaire** ~
one-salary family; **route à voie** ~ single-
lane road; **fils/fille** ~ only son/daughter,
only child; ~ **en France** the only one of its
kind in France.

uniquement [ynikmɑ̃] *adv* only, solely; (*juste*)
only, merely.

unir [ynir] *vt* (*nations*) to unite; (*éléments,*
couleurs) to combine; (*en mariage*) to unite,
join together; ~ **qch à** to unite sth with; to
combine sth with; **s'~** to unite; (*en mariage*)
to be joined together; **s'~ à** *ou* **avec** to unite
with.

unisexe [ynisɛks] *adj* unisex.

unisson [ynisɔ̃]: **à l'~** *adv* in unison.

unitaire [ynitɛr] *adj* unitary; (*POL*) unitarian;
prix ~ unit price.

unité [ynite] *nf* (*harmonie, cohésion*) unity;
(*COMM, MIL, de mesure, MATH*) unit; ~
centrale (de traitement) central processing
unit (CPU); ~ **de valeur (UV)** (university)
course, credit.

univers [yniver] *nm* universe.

universalisation [yniversalizɑsjɔ̃] *nf*
universalization.

universaliser [yniversalize] *vt* to universalize.

universalité [yniversalite] *nf* universality.

universel, le [yniversɛl] *adj* universal; (*esprit*)
all-embracing.

universellement [yniversɛlmɑ̃] *adv*
universally.

universitaire [yniversitɛr] *adj* university *cpd*;
(*diplôme, études*) academic, university *cpd*
♦ *nm/f* academic.

université [yniversite] *nf* university.

univoque [ynivɔk] *adj* unambiguous; (*MATH*)
one-to-one.

UNR *sigle f* (= *Union pour la nouvelle république*)
former political party.

UNSS *sigle f* = *Union nationale de sport scolaire*.

Untel, Unetelle [œ̃tɛl, yntɛl] *nm/f*: **Monsieur ~** Mr so-and-so.
uranium [yranjɔm] *nm* uranium.
urbain, e [yrbɛ̃, -ɛn] *adj* urban, city *cpd*, town *cpd*; *(poli)* urbane.
urbanisation [yrbanizasjɔ̃] *nf* urbanization.
urbaniser [yrbanize] *vt* to urbanize.
urbanisme [yrbanism(ə)] *nm* town planning.
urbaniste [yrbanist(ə)] *nm/f* town planner.
urbanité [yrbanite] *nf* urbanity.
urée [yre] *nf* urea.
urémie [yremi] *nf* uraemia *(BRIT)*, uremia *(US)*.
urgence [yrʒɑ̃s] *nf* urgency; *(MÉD etc)* emergency; **d'~** *adj* emergency *cpd* ♦ *adv* as a matter of urgency; **en cas d'~** in case of emergency; **service des ~s** emergency service.
urgent, e [yrʒɑ̃, -ɑ̃t] *adj* urgent.
urinaire [yrinɛr] *adj* urinary.
urinal, aux [yrinal, -o] *nm* (bed) urinal.
urine [yrin] *nf* urine.
uriner [yrine] *vi* to urinate.
urinoir [yrinwar] *nm* (public) urinal.
urne [yrn(ə)] *nf* (*électorale)* ballot box; (*vase)* urn; **aller aux ~s** (*voter)* to go to the polls.
urologie [yrɔlɔʒi] *nf* urology.
URSS [*parfois*: yrs] *sigle f* (= *Union des Républiques Socialistes Soviétiques)* USSR.
URSSAF [yrsaf] *sigle f* (= *Union pour le recouvrement de la sécurité sociale et des allocations familiales) administrative body responsible for social security funds and payments.*
urticaire [yrtikɛr] *nf* nettle rash, urticaria.
Uruguay [yrygwɛ] *nm*: **l'~** Uruguay.
uruguayen, ne [yrygwajɛ̃, -ɛn] *adj* Uruguayan ♦ *nm/f*: **U~, ne** Uruguayan.
us [ys] *nmpl*: **~ et coutumes** (habits and) customs.
US(A) *sigle mpl* (= *United States (of America))* US(A).
usage [yzaʒ] *nm* (*emploi, utilisation)* use; (*coutume)* custom; (*éducation)* (good) manners *pl*, (good) breeding; (*LING)*: **l'~** usage; **faire ~ de** (*pouvoir, droit)* to exercise; **avoir l'~ de** to have the use of; **à l'~** *adv* with use; **à l'~ de** (*pour)* for (use of); **en ~** in use; **hors d'~** out of service; **à ~ interne** to be taken; **à ~ externe** for external use only.
usagé, e [yzaʒe] *adj* (*usé)* worn; (*d'occasion)* used.
usager, ère [yzaʒe, -ɛr] *nm/f* user.
usé, e [yze] *adj* worn (down *ou* out *ou* away); ruined; (*banal)* hackneyed.
user [yze] *vt* (*outil)* to wear down; (*vêtement)* to wear out; (*matière)* to wear away; (*consommer: charbon etc)* to use; (*fig: santé)* to ruin; (: *personne)* to wear out; **s'~** *vi* to wear; to wear out; (*fig)* to decline; **s'~ à la tâche** to wear o.s. out with work; **~ de** *vt* (*moyen, procédé)* to use, employ; (*droit)* to

exercise.
usine [yzin] *nf* factory; **~ atomique** nuclear power plant; **~ à gaz** gasworks *sg*; **~ marémotrice** tidal power station.
usiner [yzine] *vt* (*TECH)* to machine; (*fabriquer)* to manufacture.
usité, e [yzite] *adj* in common use, common; **peu ~** rarely used.
ustensile [ystɑ̃sil] *nm* implement; **~ de cuisine** kitchen utensil.
usuel, le [yzɥɛl] *adj* everyday, common.
usufruit [yzyfrɥi] *nm* usufruct.
usuraire [yzyrɛr] *adj* usurious.
usure [yzyr] *nf* wear; worn state; (*de l'usurier)* usury; **avoir qn à l'~** to wear sb down; **~ normale** fair wear and tear.
usurier, ière [yzyrje, -jɛr] *nm/f* usurer.
usurpateur, trice [yzyrpatœr, -tris] *nm/f* usurper.
usurpation [yzyrpasjɔ̃] *nf* usurpation.
usurper [yzyrpe] *vt* to usurp.
ut [yt] *nm* (*MUS)* C.
UTA *sigle f* = *Union des transporteurs aériens.*
utérin, e [yterɛ̃, -in] *adj* uterine.
utérus [yterys] *nm* uterus, womb.
utile [ytil] *adj* useful; **~ à qn/qch** of use to sb/ sth.
utilement [ytilmɑ̃] *adv* usefully.
utilisable [ytilizabl(ə)] *adj* usable.
utilisateur, trice [ytilizatœr, -tris] *nm/f* user.
utilisation [ytilizasjɔ̃] *nf* use.
utiliser [ytilize] *vt* to use.
utilitaire [ytilitɛr] *adj* utilitarian; (*objets)* practical ♦ *nm* (*INFORM)* utility.
utilité [ytilite] *nf* usefulness *no pl*; use; **jouer les ~s** (*THÉÂT)* to play bit parts; **reconnu d'~ publique** state-approved; **c'est d'une grande ~** it's extremely useful; **il n'y a aucune ~ à ...** there's no use in ....
utopie [ytɔpi] *nf* (*idée, conception)* utopian idea *ou* view; (*société etc idéale)* utopia.
utopique [ytɔpik] *adj* utopian.
utopiste [ytɔpist(ə)] *nm/f* utopian.
UV *sigle f* (*SCOL)* = *unité de valeur.*
uvule [yvyl] *nf* uvula.

V v

V, v [ve] *nm inv* V, v ♦ *abr* (= *voir, verset)* v.; (= *vers: de poésie)* l.; (: *en direction de)* toward(s); **V comme Victor** V for Victor; **en ~ V-shaped; encolure en ~** V-neck; **décolleté en ~** plunging neckline.
va [va] *vb voir* **aller**.
vacance [vakɑ̃s] *nf* (*ADMIN)* vacancy; **~s** *nfpl*

holiday(s *pl*) (*BRIT*), vacation *sg* (*US*); **les grandes ~s** the summer holidays *ou* vacation; **prendre des/ses ~s** to take a holiday *ou* vacation/one's holiday(s) *ou* vacation; **aller en ~s** to go on holiday *ou* vacation.

vacancier, ière [vakɑ̃sje, -jɛʀ] *nm/f* holidaymaker (*BRIT*), vacationer (*US*).

vacant, e [vakɑ̃, -ɑ̃t] *adj* vacant.

vacarme [vakaʀm(ə)] *nm* row, din.

vacataire [vakatɛʀ] *nm/f* temporary (employee); (*enseignement*) supply (*BRIT*) *ou* substitute (*US*) teacher; (*UNIVERSITÉ*) part-time temporary lecturer.

vaccin [vaksɛ̃] *nm* vaccine; (*opération*) vaccination.

vaccination [vaksinɑsjɔ̃] *nf* vaccination.

vacciner [vaksine] *vt* to vaccinate; (*fig*) to make immune; **être vacciné** (*fig*) to be immune.

vache [vaʃ] *nf* (*ZOOL*) cow; (*cuir*) cowhide ♦ *adj* (*fam*) rotten, mean; **~ à eau** (canvas) water bag; (**manger de la**) **~ enragée** (to go through) hard times; **~ à lait** (*péj*) mug, sucker; **~ laitière** dairy cow; **période des ~s maigres** lean times *pl*, lean period.

vachement [vaʃmɑ̃] *adv* (*fam*) damned, fantastically.

vacher, ère [vaʃe, -ɛʀ] *nm/f* cowherd.

vacherie [vaʃʀi] *nf* (*fam*) meanness *no pl*; (*action*) dirty trick; (*propos*) nasty remark.

vacherin [vaʃʀɛ̃] *nm* (*fromage*) vacherin cheese; (*gâteau*): **~ glacé** vacherin (*type of cream gâteau*).

vachette [vaʃɛt] *nf* calfskin.

vacillant, e [vasijɑ̃, -ɑ̃t] *adj* wobbly; flickering; failing, faltering.

vaciller [vasije] *vi* to sway, wobble; (*bougie, lumière*) to flicker; (*fig*) to be failing, falter; **~ dans ses réponses** to falter in one's replies; **~ dans ses résolutions** to waver in one's resolutions.

vacuité [vakɥite] *nf* emptiness, vacuity.

vade-mecum [vademekɔm] *nm inv* pocketbook.

vadrouille [vadʀuj] *nf*: **être/partir en ~** to be on/go for a wander.

vadrouiller [vadʀuje] *vi* to wander around *ou* about.

va-et-vient [vaevjɛ̃] *nm inv* (*de pièce mobile*) to and fro (*ou* up and down) movement; (*de personnes, véhicules*) comings and goings *pl*, to-ings and fro-ings *pl*; (*ÉLEC*) two-way switch.

vagabond, e [vagabɔ̃, -ɔ̃d] *adj* wandering; (*imagination*) roaming, roving ♦ *nm* (*rôdeur*) tramp, vagrant; (*voyageur*) wanderer.

vagabondage [vagabɔ̃daʒ] *nm* roaming, wandering; (*JUR*) vagrancy.

vagabonder [vagabɔ̃de] *vi* to roam, wander.

vagin [vaʒɛ̃] *nm* vagina.

vaginal, e, aux [vaʒinal, -o] *adj* vaginal.

vagissement [vaʒismɑ̃] *nm* cry (*of newborn baby*).

vague [vag] *nf* wave ♦ *adj* vague; (*regard*) faraway; (*manteau, robe*) loose(-fitting); (*quelconque*): **un ~ bureau/cousin** some office/cousin or other ♦ *nm*: **être dans le ~** to be rather in the dark; **rester dans le ~** to keep things rather vague; **regarder dans le ~** to gaze into space; **~ à l'âme** *nm* vague melancholy; **~ d'assaut** *nf* (*MIL*) wave of assault; **~ de chaleur** *nf* heatwave; **~ de fond** *nf* ground swell; **~ de froid** *nf* cold spell.

vaguelette [vaglɛt] *nf* ripple.

vaguement [vagmɑ̃] *adv* vaguely.

vaillamment [vajamɑ̃] *adv* bravely, gallantly.

vaillant, e [vajɑ̃, -ɑ̃t] *adj* (*courageux*) brave, gallant; (*robuste*) vigorous, hale and hearty; **n'avoir plus un sou ~** to be penniless.

vaille [vaj] *vb voir* **valoir**.

vain, e [vɛ̃, vɛn] *adj* vain; **en ~** *adv* in vain.

vaincre [vɛ̃kʀ(ə)] *vt* to defeat; (*fig*) to conquer, overcome.

vaincu, e [vɛ̃ky] *pp de* **vaincre** ♦ *nm/f* defeated party.

vainement [vɛnmɑ̃] *adv* vainly.

vainquais [vɛ̃kɛ] *etc vb voir* **vaincre**.

vainqueur [vɛ̃kœʀ] *nm* victor; (*SPORT*) winner ♦ *adj m* victorious.

vais [vɛ] *vb voir* **aller**.

vaisseau, x [vɛso] *nm* (*ANAT*) vessel; (*NAVIG*) ship, vessel; **~ spatial** spaceship.

vaisselier [vɛsəlje] *nm* dresser.

vaisselle [vɛsɛl] *nf* (*service*) crockery; (*plats etc à laver*) (dirty) dishes *pl*; **faire la ~** to do the washing-up (*BRIT*) *ou* the dishes.

val, vaux *ou* **vals** [val, vo] *nm* valley.

valable [valabl(ə)] *adj* valid; (*acceptable*) decent, worthwhile.

valablement [valabləmɑ̃] *adv* legitimately; (*de façon satisfaisante*) satisfactorily.

Valence [valɑ̃s] *n* (*en Espagne*) Valencia; (*en France*) Valence.

valent [val] *etc vb voir* **valoir**.

valet [valɛ] *nm* valet; (*péj*) lackey; (*CARTES*) jack, knave (*BRIT*); **~ de chambre** manservant, valet; **~ de ferme** farmhand; **~ de pied** footman.

valeur [valœʀ] *nf* (*gén*) value; (*mérite*) worth, merit; (*COMM*: *titre*) security; **mettre en ~** (*bien*) to exploit; (*terrain, région*) to develop; (*fig*) to highlight; to show off to advantage; **avoir de la ~** to be valuable; **prendre de la ~** to go up *ou* gain in value; **sans ~** worthless; **~ absolue** absolute value; **~ d'échange** exchange value; **~ nominale** face value; **~s mobilières** transferable securities.

valeureux, euse [valœʀø, -øz] *adj* valorous.

validation [validɑsjɔ̃] *nf* validation.

valide [valid] *adj* (*en bonne santé*) fit, well; (*indemne*) able-bodied, fit; (*valable*) valid.

valider [valide] *vt* to validate.

validité [validite] *nf* validity.

valions [valjɔ̃] *etc vb voir* **valoir**.

valise [valiz] *nf* (suit)case; **faire sa ~** to pack one's (suit)case; **la ~ (diplomatique)** the diplomatic bag.

vallée [vale] *nf* valley.

vallon [valɔ̃] *nm* small valley.

vallonné, e [valɔne] *adj* undulating.

vallonnement [valɔnmɑ̃] *nm* undulation.

valoir [valwaʀ] *vi* (*être valable*) to hold, apply ♦ *vt* (*prix, valeur, effort*) to be worth; (*causer*): **~ qch à qn** to earn sb sth; **se ~** to be of equal merit; (*péj*) to be two of a kind; **faire ~** (*droits, prérogatives*) to assert; (*domaine, capitaux*) to exploit; **faire ~ que** to point out that; **se faire ~** to make the most of o.s.; **à ~** on account; **à ~ sur** to be deducted from; **vaille que vaille** somehow or other; **ça ne me dit rien qui vaille** I don't like the look of it at all; **ce climat ne me vaut rien** this climate doesn't suit me; **la peine** to be worth the trouble, be worth it; **~ mieux: il vaut mieux se taire** it's better to say nothing; **il vaut mieux que je fasse/comme ceci** it's better if I do/like this; **ça ne vaut rien** it's worthless; **que vaut ce candidat?** how good is this applicant?

valorisation [valɔʀizɑsjɔ̃] *nf* (economic) development; increased standing.

valoriser [valɔʀize] *vt* (*ÉCON*) to develop (the economy of); (*produit*) to increase the value of; (*PSYCH*) to increase the standing of; (*fig*) to highlight, bring out.

valse [vals(ə)] *nf* waltz; **c'est la ~ des étiquettes** the prices don't stay the same from one moment to the next.

valser [valse] *vi* to waltz; (*fig*): **aller ~** to go flying.

valu, e [valy] *pp de* **valoir**.

valve [valv(ə)] *nf* valve.

vamp [vɑp] *nf* vamp.

vampire [vɑpiʀ] *nm* vampire.

van [vɑ̃] *nm* horse box (*BRIT*) *ou* trailer (*US*).

vandale [vɑdal] *nm/f* vandal.

vandalisme [vɑdalism(ə)] *nm* vandalism.

vanille [vanij] *nf* vanilla; **glace à la ~** vanilla ice cream.

vanillé, e [vanije] *adj* vanilla *cpd*.

vanité [vanite] *nf* vanity.

vaniteux, euse [vanitø, -øz] *adj* vain, conceited.

vanity-case [vaniti(e)kɛz] *nm* vanity case.

vanne [van] *nf* gate; (*fam: remarque*) dig, (nasty) crack; **lancer une ~ à qn** to have a go at sb (*BRIT*), knock sb.

vanneau, x [vano] *nm* lapwing.

vanner [vane] *vt* to winnow.

vannerie [vanʀi] *nf* basketwork.

vantail, aux [vɑtaj, -o] *nm* door, leaf (*pl* leaves).

vantard, e [vɑtaʀ, -aʀd(ə)] *adj* boastful.

vantardise [vɑtaʀdiz] *nf* boastfulness *no pl*; boast.

vanter [vɑte] *vt* to speak highly of, vaunt; **se ~** *vi* to boast, brag; **se ~ de** to pride o.s. on; (*péj*) to boast of.

Vanuatu [vanwatu] *nm*: **le ~** Vanuatu.

va-nu-pieds [vanypje] *nm/f inv* tramp, beggar.

vapeur [vapœʀ] *nf* steam; (*émanation*) vapour (*BRIT*), vapor (*US*), fumes *pl*; (*brouillard, buée*) haze; **~s** *nfpl* (*bouffées*) vapours, vapors; **à ~** steam-powered, steam *cpd*; **à toute ~** full steam ahead; (*fig*) at full tilt; **renverser la ~** to reverse engines; (*fig*) to backtrack, backpedal; **cuit à la ~** steamed.

vapocuiseur [vapɔkyizœʀ] *nm* pressure cooker.

vaporeux, euse [vapɔʀø, -øz] *adj* (*flou*) hazy, misty; (*léger*) filmy, gossamer *cpd*.

vaporisateur [vapɔʀizatœʀ] *nm* spray.

vaporiser [vapɔʀize] *vt* (*CHIMIE*) to vaporize; (*parfum etc*) to spray.

vaquer [vake] *vi* (*ADMIN*) to be on vacation; **~ à ses occupations** to attend to one's affairs, go about one's business.

varappe [vaʀap] *nf* rock climbing.

varappeur, euse [vaʀapœʀ, -øz] *nm/f* (rock) climber.

varech [vaʀɛk] *nm* wrack, varec.

vareuse [vaʀøz] *nf* (*blouson*) pea jacket; (*d'uniforme*) tunic.

variable [vaʀjabl(ə)] *adj* variable; (*temps, humeur*) changeable; (*TECH: à plusieurs positions etc*) adaptable; (*LING*) inflectional; (*divers: résultats*) varied, various ♦ *nf* (*INFORM, MATH*) variable.

variante [vaʀjɑt] *nf* variant.

variation [vaʀjɑsjɔ̃] *nf* variation; changing *no pl*, change; (*MUS*) variation.

varice [vaʀis] *nf* varicose vein.

varicelle [vaʀisɛl] *nf* chickenpox.

varié, e [vaʀje] *adj* varied; (*divers*) various; **hors-d'œuvre ~s** selection of hors d'œuvres.

varier [vaʀje] *vi* to vary; (*temps, humeur*) to change ♦ *vt* to vary.

variété [vaʀjete] *nf* variety; **spectacle de ~s** variety show.

variole [vaʀjɔl] *nf* smallpox.

variqueux, euse [vaʀikø, -øz] *adj* varicose.

Varsovie [vaʀsɔvi] *n* Warsaw.

vas [va] *vb voir* **aller**; **~-y!** [vazi] go on!

vasculaire [vaskylɛʀ] *adj* vascular.

vase [vɑz] *nm* vase ♦ *nf* silt, mud; **en ~ clos** in isolation; **~ de nuit** chamberpot; **~s communicants** communicating vessels.

vasectomie [vazɛktɔmi] *nf* vasectomy.

vaseline [vazlin] *nf* Vaseline ®.

vaseux, euse [vɑzø, -øz] *adj* silty, muddy; (*fig: confus*) woolly, hazy; (*: fatigué*) peaky; (*: étourdi*) woozy.

vasistas [vazistɑs] *nm* fanlight.

vasque [vask(ə)] *nf* (*bassin*) basin; (*coupe*) bowl.

vassal, e, aux [vasal, -o] *nm/f* vassal.

vaste [vast(ə)] *adj* vast, immense.
Vatican [vatikã] *nm*: **le ~** the Vatican.
vaticiner [vatisine] *vi* (*péj*) to make pompous predictions.
va-tout [vatu] *nm*: **jouer son ~** to stake one's all.
vaudeville [vodvil] *nm* vaudeville, light comedy.
vaudrai [vodʀe] *etc vb voir* **valoir**.
vau-l'eau [volo]: **à ~** *adv* with the current; **s'en aller à ~** (*fig: projets*) to be adrift.
vaurien, ne [voʀjɛ̃, -ɛn] *nm/f* good-for-nothing, guttersnipe.
vaut [vo] *vb voir* **valoir**.
vautour [votuʀ] *nm* vulture.
vautrer [votʀe]: **se ~** *vi*: **se ~ dans** to wallow in; **se ~ sur** to sprawl on.
vaux [vo] *pl de* **val ♦** *vb voir* **valoir**.
va-vite [vavit]: **à la ~** *adv* in a rush.
vd *abr* = **vend**.
VDQS *abr* (= *vin délimité de qualité supérieure*) *label guaranteeing quality of wine.*

VDQS, *on a bottle of French wine, indicates that it contains high-quality wine from an approved regional vineyard. It is the second highest French wine classification after* **AOC** *and is followed by* **vin de pays**. *Unlike the previous categories,* **vin de table** *or* **vin ordinaire** *is table wine of unspecified origin, often blended.*

---

vds *abr* = **vends**.
veau, x [vo] *nm* (*ZOOL*) calf (*pl* calves); (*CULIN*) veal; (*peau*) calfskin; **tuer le ~ gras** to kill the fatted calf.
vecteur [vɛktœʀ] *nm* vector; (*MIL, BIO*) carrier.
vécu, e [veky] *pp de* **vivre ♦** *adj* (*aventure*) real(-life).
vedettariat [vədɛtaʀja] *nm* stardom; (*attitude*) acting like a star.
vedette [vədɛt] *nf* (*artiste etc*) star; (*canot*) patrol boat; launch; **avoir la ~** to top the bill, get star billing; **mettre qn en ~** (*CINÉ etc*) to give sb the starring role; (*fig*) to push sb into the limelight; **voler la ~ à qn** to steal the show from sb.
végétal, e, aux [veʒetal, -o] *adj* vegetable **♦** *nm* vegetable, plant.
végétalien, ne [veʒetaljɛ̃, -ɛn] *adj, nm/f* vegan.
végétalisme [veʒetalism(ə)] *nm* veganism.
végétarien, ne [veʒetaʀjɛ̃, -ɛn] *adj, nm/f* vegetarian.
végétarisme [veʒetaʀism(ə)] *nm* vegetarianism.
végétatif, ive [veʒetatif, -iv] *adj*: **une vie ~ive** a vegetable existence.
végétation [veʒetasjɔ̃] *nf* vegetation; **~s** *nfpl* (*MÉD*) adenoids.
végéter [veʒete] *vi* (*fig*) to vegetate; to stagnate.
véhémence [veemãs] *nf* vehemence.

véhément, e [veemã, -ãt] *adj* vehement.
véhicule [veikyl] *nm* vehicle; **~ utilitaire** commercial vehicle.
véhiculer [veikyle] *vt* (*personnes, marchandises*) to transport, convey; (*fig: idées, substances*) to convey, serve as a vehicle for.
veille [vɛj] *nf* (*garde*) watch; (*PSYCH*) wakefulness; (*jour*): **la ~** the day before, the previous day; **la ~ au soir** the previous evening; **la ~ de** the day before; **à la ~ de** on the eve of; **l'état de ~** the waking state.
veillée [veje] *nf* (*soirée*) evening; (*réunion*) evening gathering; **~ d'armes** night before combat; (*fig*) vigil; **~ (mortuaire)** watch.
veiller [veje] *vi* (*rester debout*) to stay *ou* sit up; (*ne pas dormir*) to be awake; (*être de garde*) to be on watch; (*être vigilant*) to be watchful **♦** *vt* (*malade, mort*) to watch over, sit up with; **~ à** *vt* to attend to, see to; **~ à ce que** to make sure that, see to it that; **~ sur** *vt* to keep a watch *ou* an eye on.
veilleur [vejœʀ] *nm*: **~ de nuit** night watchman.
veilleuse [vejøz] *nf* (*lampe*) night light; (*AUTO*) sidelight; (*flamme*) pilot light; **en ~** *adj* (*lampe*) dimmed; (*fig: affaire*) shelved, set aside.
veinard, e [vɛnaʀ, -aʀd(ə)] *nm/f* (*fam*) lucky devil.
veine [vɛn] *nf* (*ANAT, du bois etc*) vein; (*filon*) vein, seam; (*fam: chance*): **avoir de la ~** to be lucky; (*inspiration*) inspiration.
veiné, e [vene] *adj* veined; (*bois*) grained.
veineux, euse [venø, -øz] *adj* venous.
Velcro [vɛlkʀo] *nm* ® Velcro ®.
vêler [vele] *vi* to calve.
vélin [velɛ̃] *nm*: **(papier) ~** vellum (paper).
véliplanchiste [veliplãʃist(ə)] *nm/f* windsurfer.
velléitaire [veleitɛʀ] *adj* irresolute, indecisive.
velléités [veleite] *nfpl* vague impulses.
vélo [velo] *nm* bike, cycle; **faire du ~** to go cycling.
véloce [velɔs] *adj* swift.
vélocité [velɔsite] *nf* (*MUS*) nimbleness, swiftness; (*vitesse*) velocity.
vélodrome [velɔdʀɔm] *nm* velodrome.
vélomoteur [velɔmɔtœʀ] *nm* moped.
véloski [veloski] *nm* skibob.
velours [vəluʀ] *nm* velvet; **~ côtelé** corduroy.
velouté, e [vəlute] *adj* (*au toucher*) velvety; (*à la vue*) soft, mellow; (*au goût*) smooth, mellow **♦** *nm*: **~ d'asperges/de tomates** cream of asparagus/tomato soup.
velouteux, euse [vəlutø, -øz] *adj* velvety.
velu, e [vəly] *adj* hairy.
venais [vənɛ] *etc vb voir* **venir**.
venaison [vənɛzɔ̃] *nf* venison.
vénal, e, aux [venal, -o] *adj* venal.
vénalité [venalite] *nf* venality.
venant [vənã]: **à tout ~** *adv* to all and sundry.
vendable [vãdabl(ə)] *adj* saleable, marketable.

vendange [vãdãʒ] *nf (opération, période: aussi:* ~**s**) grape harvest; (*raisins*) grape crop, grapes *pl.*

vendanger [vãdãʒe] *vi* to harvest the grapes.

vendangeur, euse [vãdãʒœR, -øz] *nm/f* grape-picker.

vendéen, ne [vãdeẽ, -ɛn] *adj* of *ou* from the Vendée.

vendeur, euse [vãdœR, -øz] *nm/f (de magasin)* shop *ou* sales assistant (*BRIT*), sales clerk (*US*); (*COMM*) salesman/woman ♦ *nm (JUR)* vendor, seller; ~ **de journaux** newspaper seller.

vendre [vãdR(ə)] *vt* to sell; ~ **qch à qn** to sell sb sth; **cela se vend à la douzaine** these are sold by the dozen; **cela se vend bien** it's selling well; **"à ~"** "for sale".

vendredi [vãdRədi] *nm* Friday; **V**~ **saint** Good Friday; *voir aussi* **lundi**.

vendu, e [vãdy] *pp de* **vendre** ♦ *adj (péj)* corrupt.

venelle [vənɛl] *nf* alley.

vénéneux, euse [venenø, -øz] *adj* poisonous.

vénérable [veneRabl(ə)] *adj* venerable.

vénération [veneRasjɔ̃] *nf* veneration.

vénérer [veneRe] *vt* to venerate.

vénerie [vɛnRi] *nf* hunting.

vénérien, ne [venerjẽ, -ɛn] *adj* venereal.

Venezuela [venezɥɛla] *nm:* **le** ~ Venezuela.

vénézuélien, ne [venezɥeljẽ, -ɛn] *adj* Venezuelan ♦ *nm/f:* **V**~, **ne** Venezuelan.

vengeance [vãʒãs] *nf* vengeance *no pl,* revenge *no pl;* (*acte*) act of vengeance *ou* revenge.

venger [vãʒe] *vt* to avenge; **se** ~ *vi* to avenge o.s.; (*par rancune*) to take revenge; **se** ~ **de qch** to avenge o.s. for sth; to take one's revenge for sth; **se** ~ **de qn** to take revenge on sb; **se** ~ **sur** to wreak vengeance upon; to take revenge on *ou* through; to take it out on.

vengeur, eresse [vãʒœR, -ʒRɛs] *adj* vengeful ♦ *nm/f* avenger.

véniel, le [venjɛl] *adj* venial.

venimeux, euse [vənimø, -øz] *adj* poisonous, venomous; (*fig: haineux*) venomous, vicious.

venin [vənẽ] *nm* venom, poison; (*fig*) venom.

venir [vəniR] *vi* to come; ~ **de** to come from; ~ **de faire: je viens d'y aller/de le voir** I've just been there/seen him; **s'il vient à pleuvoir** if it should rain, if it happens to rain; **en** ~ **à faire: j'en viens à croire que** I am coming to believe that; **où veux-tu en** ~? what are you getting at?; **il en est venu à mendier** he has been reduced to begging; **en** ~ **aux mains** to come to blows; **les années/générations à** ~ the years/generations to come; **il me vient une idée** an idea has just occurred to me; **il me vient des soupçons** I'm beginning to be suspicious; **je te vois** ~ I know what you're after; **faire** ~ (*docteur, plombier*) to call (out); **d'où vient que ...?** how is it that ...?; ~ **au**

monde to come into the world.

Venise [vəniz] *n* Venice.

vénitien, ne [venisjẽ, -ɛn] *adj* Venetian.

vent [vã] *nm* wind; **il y a du** ~ it's windy; **c'est du** ~ it's all hot air; **au** ~ to windward; **sous le** ~ to leeward; **avoir le** ~ **debout/arrière** to head into the wind/have the wind astern; **dans le** ~ (*fam*) trendy; **prendre le** ~ (*fig*) to see which way the wind blows; **avoir** ~ **de** to get wind of; **contre** ~**s et marées** come hell or high water.

vente [vãt] *nf* sale; **la** ~ (*activité*) selling; (*secteur*) sales *pl;* **mettre en** ~ to put on sale; (*objets personnels*) to put up for sale; ~ **de charité** jumble (*BRIT*) *ou* rummage (*US*) sale; ~ **par correspondance (VPC)** mail-order selling; ~ **aux enchères** auction sale.

venté, e [vãte] *adj* windswept, windy.

venter [vãte] *vb impers:* **il vente** the wind is blowing.

venteux, euse [vãtø, -øz] *adj* windswept, windy.

ventilateur [vãtilatœR] *nm* fan.

ventilation [vãtilasjɔ̃] *nf* ventilation.

ventiler [vãtile] *vt* to ventilate; (*total, statistiques*) to break down.

ventouse [vãtuz] *nf (ampoule)* cupping glass; (*de caoutchouc*) suction pad; (*ZOOL*) sucker.

ventre [vãtR(ə)] *nm (ANAT)* stomach; (*fig*) belly; **prendre du** ~ to be getting a paunch; **avoir mal au** ~ to have (a) stomach ache.

ventricule [vãtRikyl] *nm* ventricle.

ventriloque [vãtRilɔk] *nm/f* ventriloquist.

ventripotent, e [vãtRipɔtã, -ãt] *adj* potbellied.

ventru, e [vãtRy] *adj* potbellied.

venu, e [vəny] *pp de* **venir** ♦ *adj:* **être mal** ~ **à** *ou* **de faire** to have no grounds for doing, be in no position to do; **mal** ~ ill-timed, unwelcome; **bien** ~ timely, welcome ♦ *nf* coming.

vêpres [vɛpR(ə)] *nfpl* vespers.

ver [vɛR] *nm voir aussi* **vers**; worm; (*des fruits etc*) maggot; (*du bois*) woodworm *no pl;* ~ **blanc** May beetle grub; ~ **luisant** glow-worm; ~ **à soie** silkworm; ~ **solitaire** tapeworm; ~ **de terre** earthworm.

véracité [veRasite] *nf* veracity.

véranda [veRãda] *nf* veranda(h).

verbal, e, aux [vɛRbal, -o] *adj* verbal.

verbalement [vɛRbalmã] *adv* verbally.

verbaliser [vɛRbalize] *vi (POLICE)* to book *ou* report an offender; (*PSYCH*) to verbalize.

verbe [vɛRb(ə)] *nm (LING)* verb; (*voix*): **avoir le** ~ **sonore** to have a sonorous tone (of voice); (*expression*): **la magie du** ~ the magic of language *ou* the word; (*REL*): **le V**~ the Word.

verbeux, euse [vɛRbø, -øz] *adj* verbose, wordy.

verbiage [vɛRbjaʒ] *nm* verbiage.

verbosité [vɛRbozite] *nf* verbosity.

verdâtre [vɛRdɑtR(ə)] *adj* greenish.

verdeur [vɛʀdœʀ] *nf* (*vigueur*) vigour (*BRIT*), vigor (*US*), vitality; (*crudité*) forthrightness; (*défaut de maturité*) tartness, sharpness.

verdict [vɛʀdik(t)] *nm* verdict.

verdir [vɛʀdiʀ] *vi*, *vt* to turn green.

verdoyant, e [vɛʀdwajɑ̃, -ɑ̃t] *adj* green, verdant.

verdure [vɛʀdyʀ] *nf* (*arbres, feuillages*) greenery; (*légumes verts*) green vegetables *pl*, greens *pl*.

véreux, euse [veʀø, -øz] *adj* worm-eaten; (*malhonnête*) shady, corrupt.

verge [vɛʀʒ(ə)] *nf* (*ANAT*) penis; (*baguette*) stick, cane.

verger [vɛʀʒe] *nm* orchard.

vergeture [vɛʀʒətyʀ] *nf gén pl* stretch mark.

verglacé, e [vɛʀglase] *adj* icy, iced-over.

verglas [vɛʀgla] *nm* (black) ice.

vergogne [vɛʀgɔɲ]: **sans ~** *adv* shamelessly.

véridique [veʀidik] *adj* truthful.

verificateur, trice [veʀifikatœʀ, -tʀis] *nm/f* controller, checker ♦ *nf* (*machine*) verifier; **~ des comptes** (*FINANCE*) auditor.

vérification [veʀifikasjɔ̃] *nf* checking *no pl*, check; **~ d'identité** identity check.

vérifier [veʀifje] *vt* to check; (*corroborer*) to confirm, bear out; (*INFORM*) to verify; **se ~** *vi* to be confirmed *ou* verified.

vérin [veʀɛ̃] *nm* jack.

véritable [veʀitabl(ə)] *adj* real; (*ami, amour*) true; **un ~ désastre** an absolute disaster; **que le ~ X sorte du rang!** ≈ will the real X (please) stand up!

véritablement [veʀitabləmɑ̃] *adv* (*effectivement*) really; (*absolument*) absolutely.

vérité [veʀite] *nf* truth; (*d'un portrait*) lifelikeness; (*sincérité*) truthfulness, sincerity; **en ~, à la ~** to tell the truth.

verlan [vɛʀlɑ̃] *nm* (back) slang.

Verlan *is a form of slang popularized in the fifties by Auguste Le Breton. It consists in inverting the syllables of words, verlan itself coming from* l'envers *(à l'envers = back to front). Typical examples are* féca *(café),* ripou *(pourri),* meuf *(femme),* beur *(Arabe).*

---

vermeil, le [vɛʀmɛj] *adj* bright red, ruby red ♦ *nm* (*substance*) vermeil.

vermicelles [vɛʀmisɛl] *nmpl* vermicelli *sg*.

vermifuge [vɛʀmifyʒ] *nm*: **poudre ~** worm powder.

vermillon [vɛʀmijɔ̃] *adj inv* vermilion, scarlet.

vermine [vɛʀmin] *nf* vermin *pl*.

vermoulu, e [vɛʀmuly] *adj* worm-eaten, with woodworm.

vermout(h) [vɛʀmut] *nm* vermouth.

verni, e [vɛʀni] *adj* varnished; glazed; (*fam*) lucky; **cuir ~** patent leather; **souliers ~s** patent (leather) shoes.

vernir [vɛʀniʀ] *vt* (*bois, tableau, ongles*) to varnish; (*poterie*) to glaze.

vernis [vɛʀni] *nm* (*enduit*) varnish; glaze; (*fig*) veneer; **~ à ongles** nail varnish (*BRIT*) *ou* polish.

vernissage [vɛʀnisaʒ] *nm* varnishing; glazing; (*d'une exposition*) preview.

vernisser [vɛʀnise] *vt* to glaze.

vérole [veʀɔl] *nf* (*variole*) smallpox; (*fam: syphilis*) pox.

Vérone [veʀɔn] *n* Verona.

verrai [veʀe] *etc vb voir* **voir**.

verre [vɛʀ] *nm* glass; (*de lunettes*) lens *sg*; **~s** *nmpl* (*lunettes*) glasses; **boire** *ou* **prendre un ~** to have a drink; **~ à vin/à liqueur** wine/liqueur glass; **~ à dents** tooth mug; **~ dépoli** frosted glass; **~ de lampe** lamp glass *ou* chimney; **~ de montre** watch glass; **~ à pied** stemmed glass; **~s de contact** contact lenses; **~s fumés** tinted lenses.

verrerie [vɛʀʀi] *nf* (*fabrique*) glassworks *sg*; (*activité*) glass-making, glass-working; (*objets*) glassware.

verrier [vɛʀje] *nm* glass-blower.

verrière [vɛʀjɛʀ] *nf* (*grand vitrage*) window; (*toit vitré*) glass roof.

verrons [vɛʀɔ̃] *etc vb voir* **voir**.

verroterie [vɛʀɔtʀi] *nf* glass beads *pl*, glass jewellery (*BRIT*) *ou* jewelry (*US*).

verrou [vɛʀu] *nm* (*targette*) bolt; (*fig*) constriction; **mettre le ~** to bolt the door; **mettre qn sous les ~s** to put sb behind bars.

verrouillage [vɛʀujaʒ] *nm* (*dispositif*) locking mechanism; (*AUTO*): **~ central** *ou* **centralisé** central locking.

verrouiller [vɛʀuje] *vt* to bolt; to lock; (*MIL: brèche*) to close.

verrue [vɛʀy] *nf* wart; (*plantaire*) verruca; (*fig*) eyesore.

vers [vɛʀ] *nm* line ♦ *nmpl* (*poésie*) verse *sg* ♦ *prép* (*en direction de*) toward(s); (*près de*) around (about); (*temporel*) about, around.

versant [vɛʀsɑ̃] *nm* slopes *pl*, side.

versatile [vɛʀsatil] *adj* fickle, changeable.

verse [vɛʀs(ə)]: **à ~** *adv*: **il pleut à ~** it's pouring (with rain).

versé, e [vɛʀse] *adj*: **être ~ dans** (*science*) to be (well-)versed in.

Verseau [vɛʀso] *nm*: **le ~** Aquarius, the water-carrier; **être du ~** to be Aquarius.

versement [vɛʀsəmɑ̃] *nm* payment; (*sur un compte*) deposit, remittance; **en 3 ~s** in 3 instalments.

verser [vɛʀse] *vt* (*liquide, grains*) to pour; (*larmes, sang*) to shed; (*argent*) to pay; (*soldat: affecter*): **~ qn dans** to assign sb to ♦ *vi* (*véhicule*) to overturn; (*fig*): **~ dans** to lapse into; **~ à un compte** to pay into an account.

verset [vɛʀsɛ] *nm* verse; versicle.

verseur [vɛʀsœʀ] *adj m voir* **bec, bouchon**.

versification [vɛʀsifikasjɔ̃] *nf* versification.

versifier [vɛʀsifje] *vt* to put into verse ♦ *vi* to

versify, write verse.

version [vɛʀsjɔ̃] nf version; (SCOL) translation (into the mother tongue); **film en ~ originale** film in the original language.

verso [vɛʀso] nm back; **voir au ~** see over(leaf).

vert, e [vɛʀ, vɛʀt(ə)] adj green; (vin) young; (vigoureux) sprightly; (cru) forthright ♦ nm green; **dire des ~es (et des pas mûres)** to say some pretty spicy things; **il en a vu des ~es** he's seen a thing or two; **~ bouteille** adj inv bottle-green; **~ d'eau** adj inv sea-green; **~ pomme** adj inv apple-green.

vert-de-gris [vɛʀdəgʀi] nm verdigris ♦ adj inv grey(ish)-green.

vertébral, e, aux [vɛʀtebʀal, -o] adj back cpd; voir **colonne**.

vertèbre [vɛʀtɛbʀ(ə)] nf vertebra (pl -ae).

vertébré, e [vɛʀtebʀe] adj, nm vertebrate.

vertement [vɛʀtəmɑ̃] adv (réprimander) sharply.

vertical, e, aux [vɛʀtikal, -o] adj, nf vertical; **à la ~e** adv vertically.

verticalement [vɛʀtikalmɑ̃] adv vertically.

verticalité [vɛʀtikalite] nf verticalness, verticality.

vertige [vɛʀtiʒ] nm (peur du vide) vertigo; (étourdissement) dizzy spell; (fig) fever; **ça me donne le ~** it makes me dizzy; (fig) it makes my head spin ou reel.

vertigineux, euse [vɛʀtiʒinø, -øz] adj (hausse, vitesse) breathtaking; (altitude, gorge) breathtakingly high (ou deep).

vertu [vɛʀty] nf virtue; **une ~** a saint, a paragon of virtue; **avoir la ~ de faire** to have the virtue of doing; **en ~ de** prép in accordance with.

vertueusement [vɛʀtɥøzmɑ̃] adv virtuously.

vertueux, euse [vɛʀtɥø, -øz] adj virtuous.

verve [vɛʀv(ə)] nf witty eloquence; **être en ~** to be in brilliant form.

verveine [vɛʀvɛn] nf (BOT) verbena, vervain; (infusion) verbena tea.

vésicule [vezikyl] nf vesicle; **~ biliaire** gall-bladder.

vespasienne [vɛspazjɛn] nf urinal.

vespéral, e, aux [vɛspeʀal, -o] adj vespertine, evening cpd.

vessie [vesi] nf bladder.

veste [vɛst(ə)] nf jacket; **~ droite/croisée** single-/double-breasted jacket; **retourner sa ~** (fig) to change one's colours.

vestiaire [vɛstjɛʀ] nm (au théâtre etc) cloakroom; (de stade etc) changing-room (BRIT), locker-room (US); (métallique): **(armoire) ~** locker.

vestibule [vɛstibyl] nm hall.

vestige [vɛstiʒ] nm (objet) relic; (fragment) trace; (fig) remnant, vestige; **~s** nmpl (d'une ville) remains; (d'une civilisation, du passé) remnants, relics.

vestimentaire [vɛstimɑ̃tɛʀ] adj (dépenses) clothing; (détail) of dress; (élégance) sartorial.

veston [vɛstɔ̃] nm jacket.

Vésuve [vezyv] nm: **le ~** Vesuvius.

vêtais [vɛtɛ] etc vb voir **vêtir**.

vêtement [vɛtmɑ̃] nm garment, item of clothing; (COMM): **le ~** the clothing industry; **~s** nmpl clothes; **~s de sport** sportswear sg, sports clothes.

vétéran [veteʀɑ̃] nm veteran.

vétérinaire [veteʀinɛʀ] adj veterinary ♦ nm/f vet, veterinary surgeon (BRIT), veterinarian (US).

vétille [vetij] nf trifle, triviality.

vétilleux, euse [vetijø, -øz] adj punctilious.

vêtir [vetiʀ] vt to clothe, dress; **se ~** to dress (o.s.).

vêtit [veti] etc vb voir **vêtir**.

vétiver [vetivɛʀ] nm (BOT) vetiver.

veto [veto] nm veto; **droit de ~** right of veto; **mettre ou opposer un ~ à** to veto.

vêtu, e [vɛty] pp de **vêtir** ♦ adj: **~ de** dressed in, wearing; **chaudement ~** warmly dressed.

vétuste [vetyst(ə)] adj ancient, timeworn.

vétusté [vetyste] nf age, delapidation.

veuf, veuve [vœf, vœv] adj widowed ♦ nm widower ♦ nf widow.

veuille [vœj], **veuillez** [vœje] etc vb voir **vouloir**.

veule [vøl] adj spineless.

veulent [vœl] etc vb voir **vouloir**.

veulerie [vølʀi] nf spinelessness.

veut [vø] vb voir **vouloir**.

veuvage [vœvaʒ] nm widowhood.

veuve [vœv] adj f, nf voir **veuf**.

veux [vø] vb voir **vouloir**.

vexant, e [vɛksɑ̃, -ɑ̃t] adj (contrariant) annoying; (blessant) upsetting.

vexations [vɛksasjɔ̃] nfpl humiliations.

vexatoire [vɛksatwaʀ] adj: **mesures ~s** harassment sg.

vexer [vɛkse] vt to hurt, upset; **se ~** vi to be hurt, get upset.

VF sigle f (CINÉ) = version française.

VHF sigle f (= Very High Frequency) VHF.

via [vja] prép via.

viabiliser [vjabilize] vt to provide with services (water etc).

viabilité [vjabilite] nf viability; (d'un chemin) practicability.

viable [vjabl(ə)] adj viable.

viaduc [vjadyk] nm viaduct.

viager, ère [vjaʒe, -ɛʀ] adj: **rente ~ère** life annuity ♦ nm: **mettre en ~** to sell in return for a life annuity.

viande [vjɑ̃d] nf meat.

viatique [vjatik] nm (REL) viaticum; (fig) provisions pl ou money for the journey.

vibrant, e [vibʀɑ̃, -ɑ̃t] adj vibrating; (voix) vibrant; (émouvant) emotive.

vibraphone [vibʀafɔn] nm vibraphone, vibes pl.

vibraphoniste [vibʀafɔnist(ə)] *nm/f* vibraphone player.

vibration [vibʀɑsjɔ̃] *nf* vibration.

vibratoire [vibʀatwaʀ] *adj* vibratory.

vibrer [vibʀe] *vi* to vibrate; (*son, voix*) to be vibrant; (*fig*) to be stirred by; **faire ~** to (cause to) vibrate; to stir, thrill.

vibromasseur [vibʀɔmasœʀ] *nm* vibrator.

vicaire [vikɛʀ] *nm* curate.

vice... [vis] *préfixe* vice-.

vice [vis] *nm* vice; (*défaut*) fault; **~ caché** (*COMM*) latent *ou* inherent defect; **~ de forme** legal flaw *ou* irregularity.

vice-consul [viskɔ̃syl] *nm* vice-consul.

vice-présidence [vispʀezidɑ̃s] *nf* (*d'un pays*) vice-presidency; (*d'une société*) vice-presidency, vice-chairmanship (*BRIT*).

vice-président, e [vispʀezidɑ̃, -ɑ̃t] *nm/f* vice-president; vice-chairman.

vice-roi [visʀwa] *nm* viceroy.

vice-versa [visevɛʀsa] *adv* vice versa.

vichy [viʃi] *nm* (*toile*) gingham; (*eau*) Vichy water; **carottes V~** boiled carrots.

vichyssois, e [viʃiswa, -waz] *adj* of *ou* from Vichy, Vichy *cpd* ♦ *nf* (*soupe*) vichyssoise (soup), *cream of leek and potato soup* ♦ *nm/f*: **V~, e** native *ou* inhabitant of Vichy.

vicié, e [visje] *adj* (*air*) polluted, tainted; (*JUR*) invalidated.

vicier [visje] *vt* (*JUR*) to invalidate.

vicieux, euse [visjø, -øz] *adj* (*pervers*) dirty (-minded); (*méchant*) nasty; (*fautif*) incorrect, wrong.

vicinal, e, aux [visinal, -o] *adj*: **chemin ~** byroad, byway.

vicissitudes [visisityd] *nfpl* (trials and) tribulations.

vicomte [vikɔ̃t] *nm* viscount.

vicomtesse [vikɔ̃tɛs] *nf* viscountess.

victime [viktim] *nf* victim; (*d'accident*) casualty; **être (la) ~ de** to be the victim of; **être ~ d'une attaque/d'un accident** to suffer a stroke/be involved in an accident.

victoire [viktwaʀ] *nf* victory.

victorieusement [viktɔʀjøzmɑ̃] *adv* triumphantly, victoriously.

victorieux, euse [viktɔʀjø, -øz] *adj* victorious; (*sourire, attitude*) triumphant.

victuailles [viktɥɑj] *nfpl* provisions.

vidange [vidɑ̃ʒ] *nf* (*d'un fossé, réservoir*) emptying; (*AUTO*) oil change; (*de lavabo: bonde*) waste outlet; **~s** *nfpl* (*matières*) sewage *sg*; **faire la ~** (*AUTO*) to change the oil, do an oil change; **tuyau de ~** drainage pipe.

vidanger [vidɑ̃ʒe] *vt* to empty; **faire ~ la voiture** to have the oil changed in one's car.

vide [vid] *adj* empty ♦ *nm* (*PHYSIQUE*) vacuum; (*espace*) (empty) space, gap; (*sous soi: dans une falaise etc*) drop; (*futilité, néant*) void; **~ de** empty of; (*de sens etc*) devoid of; **sous ~** *adv* in a vacuum; **emballé sous ~** vacuum-packed; **regarder dans le ~** to stare into space; **avoir peur du ~** to be afraid of heights; **parler dans le ~** to waste one's breath; **faire le ~** (*dans son esprit*) to make one's mind go blank; **faire le ~ autour de qn** to isolate sb; **à ~** *adv* (*sans occupants*) empty; (*sans charge*) unladen; (*TECH*) without gripping *ou* being in gear.

vidé, e [vide] *adj* (*épuisé*) done in, all in.

vidéo [video] *nf, adj inv* video; **~ inverse** reverse video.

vidéocassette [videokasɛt] *nf* video cassette.

vidéoclub [videoklœb] *nm* video club.

vidéodisque [videodisk] *nm* videodisc.

vide-ordures [vidɔʀdyʀ] *nm inv* (rubbish) chute.

vidéotex [videotɛks] *nm* ® teletext.

vide-poches [vidpɔʃ] *nm inv* tidy; (*AUTO*) glove compartment.

vide-pomme [vidpɔm] *nm inv* apple-corer.

vider [vide] *vt* to empty; (*CULIN: volaille, poisson*) to gut, clean out; (*régler: querelle*) to settle; (*fatiguer*) to wear out; (*fam: expulser*) to throw out, chuck out; **se ~** *vi* to empty; **~ les lieux** to quit *ou* vacate the premises.

videur [vidœʀ] *nm* (*de boîte de nuit*) bouncer.

vie [vi] *nf* life (*pl* lives); **être en ~** to be alive; **sans ~** lifeless; **à ~** for life; **membre à ~** life member; **dans la ~ courante** in everyday life; **avoir la ~ dure** to have nine lives; to die hard; **mener la ~ dure à qn** to make life a misery for sb.

vieil [vjɛj] *adj m voir* **vieux**.

vieillard [vjɛjaʀ] *nm* old man; **les ~s** old people, the elderly.

vieille [vjɛj] *adj f, nf voir* **vieux**.

vieilleries [vjɛjʀi] *nfpl* old things *ou* stuff *sg*.

vieillesse [vjɛjɛs] *nf* old age; (*vieillards*): **la ~** the old *pl*, the elderly *pl*.

vieilli, e [vjeji] *adj* (*marqué par l'âge*) aged; (*suranné*) dated.

vieillir [vjejiʀ] *vi* (*prendre de l'âge*) to grow old; (*population, vin*) to age; (*doctrine, auteur*) to become dated ♦ *vt* to age; **il a beaucoup vieilli** he has aged a lot; **se ~** to make o.s. older.

vieillissement [vjejismɑ̃] *nm* growing old; ageing.

vieillot, te [vjɛjo, -ɔt] *adj* antiquated, quaint.

vielle [vjɛl] *nf* hurdy-gurdy.

viendrai [vjɛ̃dʀe] *etc vb voir* **venir**.

Vienne [vjɛn] *n* (*en Autriche*) Vienna.

vienne [vjɛn], **viens** [vjɛ̃] *etc vb voir* **venir**.

viennois, e [vjɛnwa, -waz] *adj* Viennese.

vierge [vjɛʀʒ(ə)] *adj* virgin; (*film*) blank; (*page*) clean, blank; (*jeune fille*): **être ~** to be a virgin ♦ *nf* virgin; (*signe*): **la V~** Virgo, the Virgin; **être de la V~** to be Virgo; **~ de** (*sans*) free from, unsullied by.

Viêt-nam, Vietnam [vjɛtnam] *nm*: **le ~** Vietnam; **le ~ du Nord/du Sud** North/South Vietnam.

vietnamien, ne [vjɛtnamjɛ̃, -ɛn] *adj*
Vietnamese ♦ *nm* (*LING*) Vietnamese ♦ *nm/f*:
V~, ne Vietnamese; V~, ne du Nord/Sud
North/South Vietnamese.

vieux (vieil), vieille [vjø, vjɛj] *adj* old ♦ *nm/f*
old man/woman ♦ *nmpl*: **les** ~ the old, old
people; (*fam*: parents) the old folk *ou* ones;
un petit ~ a little old man; **mon ~/ma vieille**
(*fam*) old man/girl; **pauvre** ~ poor old soul;
prendre un coup de ~ to put years on; **se**
faire ~ to make o.s. look older; **un** ~ **de la**
vieille one of the old brigade; ~ **garçon** *nm*
bachelor; ~ **jeu** *adj inv* old-fashioned; ~ **rose**
adj inv old rose; **vieil or** *adj inv* old gold; **vieille**
fille *nf* spinster.

vif, vive [vif, viv] *adj* (*animé*) lively; (*alerte*)
sharp, quick; (*brusque*) sharp, brusque;
(*aigu*) sharp; (*lumière, couleur*) brilliant; (*air*)
crisp; (*vent, émotion*) keen; (*froid*) bitter;
(*fort: regret, déception*) great, deep; (*vivant*):
brûlé ~ burnt alive; **eau vive** running water;
de vive voix personally; **piquer qn au** ~ to
cut sb to the quick; **tailler dans le** ~ to cut
into the living flesh; **à** ~ (*plaie*) open; **avoir**
les nerfs à ~ to be on edge; **sur le** ~ (*ART*)
from life; **entrer dans le** ~ **du sujet** to get to
the very heart of the matter.

vif-argent [vifaʁʒɑ̃] *nm inv* quicksilver.

vigie [viʒi] *nf* (*matelot*) look-out; (*poste*) look-
out post, crow's nest.

vigilance [viʒilɑ̃s] *nf* vigilance.

vigilant, e [viʒilɑ̃, -ɑ̃t] *adj* vigilant.

vigile [viʒil] *nm* (*veilleur de nuit*) (night)
watchman; (*police privée*) vigilante.

vigne [viɲ] *nf* (*plante*) vine; (*plantation*)
vineyard; ~ **vierge** Virginia creeper.

vigneron [viɲʁɔ̃] *nm* wine grower.

vignette [viɲɛt] *nf* (*motif*) vignette; (*de*
marque) manufacturer's label *ou* seal; (*petite*
illustration) (small) illustration; (*ADMIN*)
≈ (road) tax disc (*BRIT*), ≈ license plate
sticker (*US*); (: *sur médicament*) price label
(*on medicines for reimbursement by Social*
Security).

vignoble [viɲɔbl(ə)] *nm* (*plantation*) vineyard;
(*vignes d'une région*) vineyards *pl*.

vigoureusement [viguʁøzmɑ̃] *adv* vigorously.

vigoureux, euse [viguʁø, -øz] *adj* vigorous,
robust.

vigueur [vigœʁ] *nf* vigour (*BRIT*), vigor (*US*);
être/entrer en ~ to be in/come into force; **en**
~ current.

vil, e [vil] *adj* vile, base; **à** ~ **prix** at a very low
price.

vilain, e [vilɛ̃, -ɛn] *adj* (*laid*) ugly; (*affaire,*
blessure) nasty; (*pas sage: enfant*) naughty
♦ *nm* (*paysan*) villein, villain; **ça va tourner**
au ~ things are going to turn nasty; ~ **mot**
bad word.

vilainement [vilɛnmɑ̃] *adv* badly.

vilebrequin [vilbʁəkɛ̃] *nm* (*outil*) (bit-)brace;
(*AUTO*) crankshaft.

vilenie [vilni] *nf* vileness *no pl*, baseness *no pl*.

vilipender [vilipɑ̃de] *vt* to revile, vilify.

villa [vila] *nf* (detached) house.

village [vilaʒ] *nm* village; ~ **de toile** tent
village; ~ **de vacances** holiday village.

villageois, e [vilaʒwa, -waz] *adj* village *cpd*
♦ *nm/f* villager.

ville [vil] *nf* town; (*importante*) city;
(*administration*): **la** ~ ≈ the Corporation;
≈ the (town) council; **aller en** ~ to go to
town; **habiter en** ~ to live in town; ~
nouvelle new town.

ville-champignon, *pl* **villes-champignons**
[vilʃɑ̃piɲɔ̃] *nf* boom town.

ville-dortoir, *pl* **villes-dortoirs** [vildɔʁtwaʁ]
nf dormitory town.

villégiature [vileʒjatyʁ] *nf* (*séjour*) holiday;
(*lieu*) (holiday) resort.

vin [vɛ̃] *nm* wine; **avoir le** ~ **gai/triste** to get
happy/miserable after a few drinks; ~
blanc/rosé/rouge white/rosé/red wine; ~
d'honneur reception (*with wine and snacks*);
~ **de messe** altar wine; ~ **ordinaire** *ou* **de**
table table wine; ~ **de pays** local wine; *voir*
aussi AOC; VDQS.

vinaigre [vinɛgʁ(ə)] *nm* vinegar; **tourner au** ~
(*fig*) to turn sour; ~ **de vin/d'alcool** wine/
spirit vinegar.

vinaigrette [vinɛgʁɛt] *nf* vinaigrette, French
dressing.

vinaigrier [vinɛgʁije] *nm* (*fabricant*) vinegar-
maker; (*flacon*) vinegar cruet *ou* bottle.

vinasse [vinas] *nf* (*péj*) cheap wine, plonk
(*BRIT*).

vindicatif, ive [vɛ̃dikatif, -iv] *adj* vindictive.

vindicte [vɛ̃dikt(ə)] *nf*: **désigner qn à la** ~
publique to expose sb to public
condemnation.

vineux, euse [vinø, -øz] *adj* win(e)y.

vingt [vɛ̃, vɛ̃t + *vowel and in 22, 23 etc*] *num*
twenty; ~**-quatre heures sur** ~**-quatre**
twenty-four hours a day, round the clock.

vingtaine [vɛ̃tɛn] *nf*: **une** ~ **(de)** around
twenty, twenty or so.

vingtième [vɛ̃tjɛm] *num* twentieth.

vinicole [vinikɔl] *adj* (*production*) wine *cpd*;
(*région*) wine-growing.

vinification [vinifikasjɔ̃] *nf* wine-making, wine
production; (*des sucres*) vinification.

vinyle [vinil] *nm* vinyl.

viol [vjɔl] *nm* (*d'une femme*) rape; (*d'un lieu*
sacré) violation.

violacé, e [vjɔlase] *adj* purplish, mauvish.

violation [vjɔlasjɔ̃] *nf* desecration; violation;
(*d'un droit*) breach.

violemment [vjɔlamɑ̃] *adv* violently.

violence [vjɔlɑ̃s] *nf* violence; ~**s** *nfpl* acts of
violence; **faire** ~ **à qn** to do violence to sb;
se faire ~ to force o.s.

violent, e [vjɔlɑ̃, -ɑ̃t] *adj* violent; (*remède*)
drastic; (*besoin, désir*) intense, urgent.

violenter [vjɔlɑ̃te] *vt* to assault (sexually).

violer [vjɔle] *vt* (*femme*) to rape; (*sépulture*) to desecrate, violate; (*loi, traité*) to violate.

violet, te [vjɔlε, -εt] *adj, nm* purple, mauve ♦ *nf* (*fleur*) violet.

violeur [vjɔlœʀ] *nm* rapist.

violine [vjɔlin] *nf* deep purple.

violon [vjɔlɔ̃] *nm* violin; (*dans la musique folklorique etc*) fiddle; (*fam: prison*) lock-up; **premier** ~ first violin; ~ **d'Ingres** (artistic) hobby.

violoncelle [vjɔlɔ̃sεl] *nm* cello.

violoncelliste [vjɔlɔ̃selist(ə)] *nm/f* cellist.

violoniste [vjɔlɔnist(ə)] *nm/f* violinist, violin-player; (*folklorique etc*) fiddler.

VIP *sigle m* (= *Very Important Person*) VIP.

vipère [vipεʀ] *nf* viper, adder.

virage [viʀaʒ] *nm* (*d'un véhicule*) turn; (*d'une route, piste*) bend; (*CHIMIE*) change in colour (*BRIT*) *ou* color (*US*); (*de cuti-réaction*) positive reaction; (*PHOTO*) toning; (*fig: POL*) about-turn; **prendre un** ~ to go into a bend, take a bend; ~ **sans visibilité** blind bend.

viral, e, aux [viʀal, -o] *adj* viral.

virée [viʀe] *nf* (*courte*) run; (: *à pied*) walk; (*longue*) trip; hike, walking tour.

virement [viʀmɑ̃] *nm* (*COMM*) transfer; ~ **bancaire** (bank) credit transfer, ≈ (bank) giro transfer (*BRIT*); ~ **postal** Post office credit transfer, ≈ Girobank ® transfer (*BRIT*).

virent [viʀ] *vb voir* **voir**.

virer [viʀe] *vt* (*COMM*): ~ **qch (sur)** to transfer sth (into); (*PHOTO*) to tone; (*fam: renvoyer*) to sack, boot out ♦ *vi* to turn; (*CHIMIE*) to change colour (*BRIT*) *ou* color (*US*); (*cuti-réaction*) to come up positive; (*PHOTO*) to tone; ~ **au bleu** to turn blue; ~ **de bord** to tack; (*fig*) to change tack; ~ **sur l'aile** to bank.

virevolte [viʀvɔlt(ə)] *nf* twirl; (*d'avis, d'opinion*) about-turn.

virevolter [viʀvɔlte] *vi* to twirl around.

virginal, e, aux [viʀʒinal, -o] *adj* virginal.

virginité [viʀʒinite] *nf* virginity; (*fig*) purity.

virgule [viʀgyl] *nf* comma; (*MATH*) point; **4** ~ **2** 4 point 2; ~ **flottante** floating decimal.

viril, e [viʀil] *adj* (*propre à l'homme*) masculine; (*énergique, courageux*) manly, virile.

viriliser [viʀilize] *vt* to make (more) manly *ou* masculine.

virilité [viʀilite] *nf* (*attributs masculins*) masculinity; (*fermeté, courage*) manliness; (*sexuelle*) virility.

virologie [viʀɔlɔʒi] *nf* virology.

virtualité [viʀtɥalite] *nf* virtuality; potentiality.

virtuel, le [viʀtɥεl] *adj* potential; (*théorique*) virtual.

virtuellement [viʀtɥεlmɑ̃] *adj* potentially; (*presque*) virtually.

virtuose [viʀtɥoz] *nm/f* (*MUS*) virtuoso; (*gén*) master.

virtuosité [viʀtɥozite] *nf* virtuosity; masterliness, masterful skills *pl*.

virulence [viʀylɑ̃s] *nf* virulence.

virulent, e [viʀylɑ̃, -ɑ̃t] *adj* virulent.

virus [viʀys] *nm* virus.

vis *vb voir* **voir, vivre** ♦ *nf* [vis] screw; ~ **à tête plate/ronde** flat-headed/round-headed screw; ~ **platinées** (*AUTO*) (contact) points; ~ **sans fin** worm, endless screw.

visa [viza] *nm* (*sceau*) stamp; (*validation de passeport*) visa; ~ **de censure** (censor's) certificate.

visage [vizaʒ] *nm* face; **à** ~ **découvert** (*franchement*) openly.

visagiste [vizaʒist(ə)] *nm/f* beautician.

vis-à-vis [vizavi] *adv* face to face ♦ *nm* person opposite; house *etc* opposite; ~ **de** *prép* opposite; (*fig*) towards, vis-à-vis; **en** ~ facing *ou* opposite each other; **sans** ~ (*immeuble*) with an open outlook.

viscéral, e, aux [viseʀal, -o] *adj* (*fig*) deep-seated, deep-rooted.

viscères [visεʀ] *nmpl* intestines, entrails.

viscose [viskoz] *nf* viscose.

viscosité [viskozite] *nf* viscosity.

visée [vize] *nf* (*avec une arme*) aiming; (*ARPENTAGE*) sighting; ~**s** *nfpl* (*intentions*) designs; **avoir des** ~**s sur qn/qch** to have designs on sb/sth.

viser [vize] *vi* to aim ♦ *vt* to aim at; (*concerner*) to be aimed *ou* directed at; (*apposer un visa sur*) to stamp, visa; ~ **à qch/faire** to aim at sth/at doing *ou* to do.

viseur [vizœʀ] *nm* (*d'arme*) sights *pl*; (*PHOTO*) viewfinder.

visibilité [vizibilite] *nf* visibility; **sans** ~ (*pilotage, virage*) blind *cpd*.

visible [vizibl(ə)] *adj* visible; (*disponible*): **est-il** ~**?** can he see me?, will he see visitors?

visiblement [vizibləmɑ̃] *adv* visibly, obviously.

visière [vizjεʀ] *nf* (*de casquette*) peak; (*qui s'attache*) eyeshade.

vision [vizjɔ̃] *nf* vision; (*sens*) (eye)sight, vision; (*fait de voir*): **la** ~ **de** the sight of; **première** ~ (*CINÉ*) first showing.

visionnaire [vizjɔnεʀ] *adj, nm/f* visionary.

visionner [vizjɔne] *vt* to view.

visionneuse [vizjɔnøz] *nf* viewer.

visiophone [vizjɔfɔn] *nm* videophone.

visite [vizit] *nf* visit; (*visiteur*) visitor; (*touristique: d'un musée etc*) tour; (*COMM: de représentant*) call; (*expertise, d'inspection*) inspection; (*médicale, à domicile*) visit, call; **la** ~ (*MÉD*) medical examination; (*MIL: d'entrée*) medicals *pl*; (: *quotidienne*) sick parade; **faire une** ~ **à qn** to call on sb, pay sb a visit; **rendre** ~ **à qn** to visit sb, pay sb a visit; **être en** ~ (**chez qn**) to be visiting (sb); **heures de** ~ (*hôpital, prison*) visiting hours; **le droit de** ~ (*JUR: aux enfants*) right of access, access; ~ **de douane** customs inspection *ou* examination.

visiter [vizite] *vt* to visit; (*musée, ville*) to visit, go round.

visiteur, euse [vizitœr, -øz] *nm/f* visitor; ~ **des douanes** customs inspector; ~ **médical** medical rep(resentative); ~ **de prison** prison visitor.

vison [vizɔ̃] *nm* mink.

visqueux, euse [viskø, -øz] *adj* viscous; (*péj*) gooey; (: *manières*) slimy.

visser [vise] *vt*: ~ **qch** (*fixer, serrer*) to screw sth on.

visu [vizy]: **de** ~ *adv* with one's own eyes.

visualisation [vizɥalizɑsjɔ̃] *nf* (*INFORM*) display; **écran de** ~ visual display unit (VDU).

visualiser [vizɥalize] *vt* to visualize; (*INFORM*) to display, bring up on screen.

visuel, le [vizɥɛl] *adj* visual ♦ *nm* (visual) display; (*INFORM*) visual display unit (VDU).

visuellement [vizɥɛlmɑ̃] *adv* visually.

vit [vi] *vb voir* **vivre, voir**.

vital, e, aux [vital, -o] *adj* vital.

vitalité [vitalite] *nf* vitality.

vitamine [vitamin] *nf* vitamin.

vitaminé, e [vitamine] *adj* with (added) vitamins.

vitaminique [vitaminik] *adj* vitamin *cpd*.

vite [vit] *adv* (*rapidement*) quickly, fast; (*sans délai*) quickly; soon; **faire** ~ (*agir rapidement*) to act fast; (*se dépêcher*) to be quick; **ce sera** ~ **fini** this will soon be finished; **viens** ~ come quick(ly).

vitesse [vitɛs] *nf* speed; (*AUTO: dispositif*) gear; **faire de la** ~ to drive fast *ou* at speed; **prendre qn de** ~ to outstrip sb, get ahead of sb; **prendre de la** ~ to pick up *ou* gather speed; **à toute** ~ at full *ou* top speed; **en perte de** ~ (*avion*) losing lift; (*fig*) losing momentum; **changer de** ~ (*AUTO*) to change gear; ~ **acquise** momentum; ~ **de croisière** cruising speed; ~ **de pointe** top speed; ~ **du son** speed of sound.

viticole [vitikɔl] *adj* (*industrie*) wine *cpd*; (*région*) wine-growing.

viticulteur [vitikyltœr] *nm* wine grower.

viticulture [vitikyltyr] *nf* wine growing.

vitrage [vitraʒ] *nm* (*cloison*) glass partition; (*toit*) glass roof; (*rideau*) net curtain.

vitrail, aux [vitraj, -o] *nm* stained-glass window.

vitre [vitr(ə)] *nf* (window) pane; (*de portière, voiture*) window.

vitré, e [vitre] *adj* glass *cpd*.

vitrer [vitre] *vt* to glaze.

vitreux, euse [vitrø, -øz] *adj* vitreous; (*terne*) glassy.

vitrier [vitrije] *nm* glazier.

vitrifier [vitrifje] *vt* to vitrify; (*parquet*) to glaze.

vitrine [vitrin] *nf* (*devanture*) (shop) window; (*étalage*) display; (*petite armoire*) display cabinet; **en** ~ in the window, on display; ~ **publicitaire** display case, showcase.

vitriol [vitrijɔl] *nm* vitriol; **au** ~ (*fig*) vitriolic.

vitupérations [vityperɑsjɔ̃] *nfpl* invective *sg*.

vitupérer [vitypere] *vi* to rant and rave; ~ **contre** to rail against.

vivable [vivabl(ə)] *adj* (*personne*) livable-with; (*endroit*) fit to live in.

vivace *adj* [vivas] (*arbre, plante*) hardy; (*fig*) enduring ♦ *adv* [vivatʃe] (*MUS*) vivace.

vivacité [vivasite] *nf* (*voir vif*) liveliness, vivacity; sharpness; brilliance.

vivant, e [vivɑ̃, -ɑ̃t] *vb voir* **vivre** ♦ *adj* (*qui vit*) living, alive; (*animé*) lively; (*preuve, exemple*) living; (*langue*) modern ♦ *nm*: **du** ~ **de qn** in sb's lifetime; **les** ~**s et les morts** the living and the dead.

vivarium [vivarjɔm] *nm* vivarium.

vivats [viva] *nmpl* cheers.

vive [viv] *adj f voir* **vif** ♦ *vb voir* **vivre** ♦ *excl*: ~ **le roi!** long live the king!; ~ **les vacances!** hurrah for the holidays!

vivement [vivmɑ̃] *adv* vivaciously; sharply ♦ *excl*: ~ **les vacances!** I can't wait for the holidays!, roll on the holidays!

viveur [vivœr] *nm* (*péj*) high liver, pleasure-seeker.

vivier [vivje] *nm* (*au restaurant etc*) fish tank; (*étang*) fishpond.

vivifiant, e [vivifjɑ̃, -ɑ̃t] *adj* invigorating.

vivifier [vivifje] *vt* to invigorate; (*fig: souvenirs, sentiments*) to liven up, enliven.

vivipare [vivipar] *adj* viviparous.

vivisection [viviseksjɔ̃] *nf* vivisection.

vivoter [vivɔte] *vi* (*personne*) to scrape a living, get by; (*fig: affaire etc*) to struggle along.

vivre [vivr(ə)] *vi*, *vt* to live ♦ *nm*: **le** ~ **et le logement** board and lodging ♦ ~**s** *nmpl* provisions, food supplies; **il vit encore** he is still alive; **se laisser** ~ to take life as it comes; **ne plus** ~ (*être anxieux*) to live on one's nerves; **il a vécu** (*eu une vie aventureuse*) he has seen life; **ce régime a vécu** this regime has had its day; **être facile à** ~ to be easy to get on with; **faire** ~ **qn** (*pourvoir à sa subsistance*) to provide (a living) for sb; ~ **mal** (*chichement*) to have a meagre existence; ~ **de** (*salaire etc*) to live on.

vivrier, ière [vivrije, -jɛr] *adj* food-producing *cpd*.

vlan [vlɑ̃] *excl* wham!, bang!

VO *sigle f* (*CINÉ*: = *version originale*): **voir un film en** ~ to see a film in its original language.

v⁰ *abr* = **verso**.

vocable [vɔkabl(ə)] *nm* term.

vocabulaire [vɔkabylɛr] *nm* vocabulary.

vocal, e, aux [vɔkal, -o] *adj* vocal.

vocalique [vɔkalik] *adj* vocalic, vowel *cpd*.

vocalise [vɔkaliz] *nf* singing exercise.

vocaliser [vɔkalize] *vi* (*LING*) to vocalize;

(*MUS*) to do one's singing exercises.

vocation [vɔkɑsjɔ̃] *nf* vocation, calling; **avoir la ~** to have a vocation.

vociférations [vɔsiferɑsjɔ̃] *nfpl* cries of rage, screams.

vociférer [vɔsifere] *vi, vt* to scream.

vodka [vɔdka] *nf* vodka.

vœu, x [vø] *nm* wish; (*à Dieu*) vow; **faire ~ de** to take a vow of; **avec tous nos ~x** with every good wish *ou* our best wishes; **~x de bonheur** best wishes for your future happiness; **~x de bonne année** best wishes for the New Year.

vogue [vɔg] *nf* fashion, vogue; **en ~** in fashion, in vogue.

voguer [vɔge] *vi* to sail.

voici [vwasi] *prép* (*pour introduire, désigner*) here is + *sg*, here are + *pl*; **et ~ que** ... and now it (*ou* he) ...; **il est parti ~ 3 ans** he left 3 years ago; **~ une semaine que je l'ai vue** it's a week since I've seen her; **me ~** here I am; *voir aussi* **voilà**.

voie [vwa] *vb voir* **voir** ♦ *nf* way; (*RAIL*) track, line; (*AUTO*) lane; **par ~ buccale** *ou* **orale** orally; **par ~ rectale** rectally; **suivre la ~ hiérarchique** to go through official channels; **ouvrir/montrer la ~** to open up/show the way; **être en bonne ~** to be shaping *ou* going well; **mettre qn sur la ~** to put sb on the right track; **être en ~ d'achèvement/de rénovation** to be nearing completion/in the process of renovation; **à ~ étroite** narrow-gauge; **à ~ unique** single-track; **route à 2/3 ~s** 2-/3-lane road; **par la ~ aérienne/maritime** by air/sea; **~ d'eau** (*NAVIG*) leak; **~ express** expressway; **~ de fait** (*JUR*) assault (and battery); **~ ferrée** track; railway line (*BRIT*), railroad (*US*); **par ~ ferrée** by rail, by railroad; **~ de garage** (*RAIL*) siding; **la ~ lactée** the Milky Way; **~ navigable** waterway; **~ prioritaire** (*AUTO*) road with right of way; **~ privée** private road; **la ~ publique** the public highway.

voilà [vwala] *prép* (*en désignant*) there is + *sg*, there are + *pl*; **les ~** *ou* **voici** here *ou* there they are; **en ~** *ou* **voici un** here's one, there's one; **~** *ou* **voici deux ans** two years ago; **~** *ou* **voici deux ans que** it's two years since; **et ~!** there we are!; **~ tout** that's all; **"~** *ou* **voici"** (*en offrant etc*) "there *ou* here you are".

voilage [vwalaʒ] *nm* (*rideau*) net curtain; (*tissu*) net.

voile [vwal] *nm* veil; (*tissu léger*) net ♦ *nf* sail; (*sport*) sailing; **prendre le ~** to take the veil; **mettre à la ~** to make way under sail; **~ du palais** *nm* soft palate, velum; **~ au poumon** *nm* shadow on the lung.

voiler [vwale] *vt* to veil; (*PHOTO*) to fog; (*fausser: roue*) to buckle; (: *bois*) to warp; **se ~** *vi* (*lune, regard*) to mist over; (*ciel*) to grow hazy; (*voix*) to become husky; (*roue, disque*)

to buckle; (*planche*) to warp; **se ~ la face** to hide one's face.

voilette [vwalɛt] *nf* (hat) veil.

voilier [vwalje] *nm* sailing ship; (*de plaisance*) sailing boat.

voilure [vwalyʀ] *nf* (*de voilier*) sails *pl*; (*d'avion*) aerofoils *pl* (*BRIT*), airfoils *pl* (*US*); (*de parachute*) canopy.

voir [vwaʀ] *vi, vt* to see; **se ~**: **se ~ critiquer/transformer** to be criticized/transformed; **cela se voit** (*cela arrive*) it happens; (*c'est visible*) that's obvious, it shows; **~ à faire qch** to see to it that sth is done; **~ loin** (*fig*) to be far-sighted; **~ venir** (*fig*) to wait and see; **faire ~ qch à qn** to show sb sth; **en faire ~ à qn** (*fig*) to give sb a hard time; **ne pas pouvoir ~ qn** (*fig*) not to be able to stand sb; **regardez ~** just look; **montrez ~** show (me); **dites ~** tell me; **voyons!** let's see now; (*indignation etc*) come (along) now!; **c'est à ~!** we'll see!; **c'est ce qu'on va ~!** we'll see about that!; **avoir quelque chose à ~ avec** to have something to do with; **ça n'a rien à ~ avec lui** that has nothing to do with him.

voire [vwaʀ] *adv* indeed; nay; or even.

voirie [vwaʀi] *nf* highway maintenance; (*administration*) highways department; (*enlèvement des ordures*) refuse (*BRIT*) *ou* garbage (*US*) collection.

vois [vwa] *vb voir* **voir**.

voisin, e [vwazɛ̃, -in] *adj* (*proche*) neighbouring (*BRIT*), neighboring (*US*); (*contigu*) next; (*ressemblant*) connected ♦ *nm/f* neighbo(u)r; (*de table, de dortoir etc*) person next to me (*ou* him *etc*); **~ de palier** neighbo(u)r across the landing (*BRIT*) *ou* hall (*US*).

voisinage [vwazinaʒ] *nm* (*proximité*) proximity; (*environs*) vicinity; (*quartier, voisins*) neighbourhood (*BRIT*), neighborhood (*US*); **relations de bon ~** neighbo(u)rly terms.

voisiner [vwazine] *vi*: **~ avec** to be side by side with.

voit [vwa] *vb voir* **voir**.

voiture [vwatyʀ] *nf* car; (*wagon*) coach, carriage; **en ~!** all aboard!; **~ à bras** handcart; **~ d'enfant** pram (*BRIT*), baby carriage (*US*); **~ d'infirme** invalid carriage; **~ de sport** sports car.

voiture-lit, *pl* **voitures-lits** [vwatyʀli] *nf* sleeper.

voiture-restaurant, *pl* **voitures-restaurants** [vwatyʀʀɛstɔʀɑ̃] *nf* dining car.

voix [vwa] *nf* voice; (*POL*) vote; **la ~ de la conscience/raison** the voice of conscience/reason; **à haute ~** aloud; **à ~ basse** in a low voice; **faire la grosse ~** to speak gruffly; **avoir de la ~** to have a good voice; **rester sans ~** to be speechless; **~ de basse/ténor** *etc* bass/tenor *etc* voice; **à 2/4 ~** (*MUS*) in 2/4 parts; **avoir ~ au chapitre** to have a say in the matter; **mettre aux** ~ to put to the vote; ~ **off** voice-over.

vol [vɔl] nm (mode de locomotion) flying; (trajet, voyage, groupe d'oiseaux) flight; (mode d'appropriation) theft, stealing; (larcin) theft; **à** ~ **d'oiseau** as the crow flies; **au** ~: **attraper qch au** ~ to catch sth as it flies past; **saisir une remarque au** ~ to pick up a passing remark; **prendre son** ~ to take flight; **de haut** ~ (fig) of the highest order; **en** ~ in flight; ~ **avec effraction** breaking and entering no pl, break-in; ~ **à l'étalage** shoplifting no pl; ~ **libre** hang-gliding; ~ **à main armée** armed robbery; ~ **de nuit** night flight; ~ **plané** (AVIAT) glide, gliding no pl; ~ **à la tire** pickpocketing no pl; ~ **à voile** gliding.

vol. abr (= volume) vol.

volage [vɔlaʒ] adj fickle.

volaille [vɔlɑj] nf (oiseaux) poultry pl; (viande) poultry no pl; (oiseau) fowl.

volailler [vɔlɑje] nm poulterer.

volant, e [vɔlɑ̃, -ɑ̃t] adj voir **feuille** etc ♦ nm (d'automobile) (steering) wheel; (de commande) wheel; (objet lancé) shuttlecock; (jeu) battledore and shuttlecock; (bande de tissu) flounce; (feuillet détachable) tear-off portion; **le personnel** ~, **les** ~**s** (AVIAT) the flight staff; ~ **de sécurité** (fig) reserve, margin, safeguard.

volatil, e [vɔlatil] adj volatile.

volatile [vɔlatil] nm (volaille) bird; (tout oiseau) winged creature.

volatiliser [vɔlatilize]: **se** ~ vi (CHIMIE) to volatilize; (fig) to vanish into thin air.

vol-au-vent [vɔlovɑ̃] nm inv vol-au-vent.

volcan [vɔlkɑ̃] nm volcano; (fig: personne) hothead.

volcanique [vɔlkanik] adj volcanic; (fig: tempérament) volatile.

volcanologie [vɔlkanɔlɔʒi] nf vulcanology.

volcanologue [vɔlkanɔlɔg] nm/f vulcanologist.

volée [vɔle] nf (groupe d'oiseaux) flight, flock; (TENNIS) volley; ~ **de coups/de flèches** volley of blows/arrows; **à la** ~: **rattraper à la** ~ to catch in midair; **lancer à la** ~ to fling about; **semer à la** ~ (to sow) broadcast; **à toute** ~ (sonner les cloches) vigorously; (lancer un projectile) with full force; **de haute** ~ (fig) of the highest order.

voler [vɔle] vi (avion, oiseau, fig) to fly; (voleur) to steal ♦ vt (objet) to steal; (personne) to rob; ~ **en éclats** to smash to smithereens; ~ **de ses propres ailes** (fig) to stand on one's own two feet; ~ **au vent** to fly in the wind; ~ **qch à qn** to steal sth from sb.

volet [vɔlɛ] nm (de fenêtre) shutter; (AVIAT) flap; (de feuillet, document) section; (fig: d'un plan) facet; **trié sur le** ~ hand-picked.

voleter [vɔlte] vi to flutter (about).

voleur, euse [vɔlœʁ, -øz] nm/f thief (pl thieves) ♦ adj thieving.

volière [vɔljɛʁ] nf aviary.

volley(-ball) [vɔlɛ(bɔl)] nm volleyball.

volleyeur, euse [vɔlɛjœʁ, -øz] nm/f volleyball player.

volontaire [vɔlɔ̃tɛʁ] adj (acte, activité) voluntary; (délibéré) deliberate; (caractère, personne: décidé) self-willed ♦ nm/f volunteer.

volontairement [vɔlɔ̃tɛʁmɑ̃] adv voluntarily; deliberately.

volontariat [vɔlɔ̃taʁja] nm voluntary service.

volontarisme [vɔlɔ̃taʁism(ə)] nm voluntarism.

volontariste [vɔlɔ̃taʁist(ə)] adj, nm/f voluntarist.

volonté [vɔlɔ̃te] nf (faculté de vouloir) will; (énergie, fermeté) will(power); (souhait, désir) wish; **se servir/boire à** ~ to take/drink as much as one likes; **bonne** ~ goodwill, willingness; **mauvaise** ~ lack of goodwill, unwillingness.

volontiers [vɔlɔ̃tje] adv (de bonne grâce) willingly; (avec plaisir) willingly, gladly; (habituellement, souvent) readily, willingly; "~" "with pleasure", "I'd be glad to".

volt [vɔlt] nm volt.

voltage [vɔltaʒ] nm voltage.

volte-face [vɔltəfas] nf inv about-turn; (fig) about-turn, U-turn; **faire** ~ to do an about-turn; to do a U-turn.

voltige [vɔltiʒ] nf (ÉQUITATION) trick riding; (au cirque) acrobatics sg; (AVIAT) (aerial) acrobatics sg; **numéro de haute** ~ acrobatic act.

voltiger [vɔltiʒe] vi to flutter (about).

voltigeur [vɔltiʒœʁ] nm (au cirque) acrobat; (MIL) light infantryman.

voltmètre [vɔltmɛtʁ(ə)] nm voltmeter.

volubile [vɔlybil] adj voluble.

volubilis [vɔlybilis] nm convolvulus.

volume [vɔlym] nm volume; (GÉOM: solide) solid.

volumineux, euse [vɔlyminø, -øz] adj voluminous, bulky.

volupté [vɔlypte] nf sensual delight ou pleasure.

voluptueusement [vɔlyptɥøzmɑ̃] adv voluptuously.

voluptueux, euse [vɔlyptɥø, -øz] adj voluptuous.

volute [vɔlyt] nf (ARCHIT) volute; ~ **de fumée** curl of smoke.

vomi [vɔmi] nm vomit.

vomir [vɔmiʁ] vi to vomit, be sick ♦ vt to vomit, bring up; (fig) to belch out, spew out; (exécrer) to loathe, abhor.

vomissement [vɔmismɑ̃] nm (action) vomiting no pl; **des** ~**s** vomit sg.

vomissure [vɔmisyʁ] nf vomit no pl.

vomitif [vɔmitif] nm emetic.

vont [vɔ̃] vb voir **aller**.

vorace [vɔʁas] adj voracious.

voracement [vɔʁasmɑ̃] adv voraciously.

voracité [vɔʁasite] nf voracity.

vos [vo] *dét voir* **votre.**

Vosges [voʒ] *nfpl:* **les ~** the Vosges.

vosgien, ne [voʒjɛ̃, -ɛn] *adj* of *ou* from the Vosges ♦ *nm/f* inhabitant *ou* native of the Vosges.

VOST *sigle f (CINÉ:* = version originale sous-titrée) sub-titled version.

votant, e [vɔtɑ̃, -ɑ̃t] *nm/f* voter.

vote [vɔt] *nm* vote; **~ par correspondance/ procuration** postal/proxy vote; **~ à main levée** vote by show of hands; **~ secret, ~ à bulletins secrets** secret ballot.

voter [vɔte] *vi* to vote ♦ *vt (loi, décision)* to vote for.

votre [vɔtʀ(ə)], *pl* **vos** [vo] *dét* your.

vôtre [votʀ(ə)] *pron:* **le ~, la ~, les ~s** yours; **les ~s** *(fig)* your family *ou* folks; **à la ~** *(toast)* your (good) health!

voudrai [vudʀe] *etc vb voir* **vouloir.**

voué, e [vwe] *adj:* **~ à** doomed to, destined for.

vouer [vwe] *vt:* **~ qch à** *(Dieu/un saint)* to dedicate sth to; **~ sa vie/son temps à** *(étude, cause etc)* to devote one's life/time to; **~ une haine/amitié éternelle à qn** to vow undying hatred/friendship to sb.

════════════════════════════ *MOT-CLÉ*

vouloir [vulwaʀ] *nm:* **le bon ~ de qn** sb's goodwill; sb's pleasure

♦ *vt* **1** *(exiger, désirer)* to want; **~ faire/que qn fasse** to want to do/sb to do; **voulez-vous du thé?** would you like *ou* do you want some tea?; **~ qch à qn** to wish sth for sb; **que me veut-il?** what does he want with me?; **que veux-tu que je te dise?** what do you want me to say?; **sans le ~** *(involontairement)* without meaning to, unintentionally; **je voudrais ceci/faire** I would *ou* I'd like this/to do; **le hasard a voulu que ...** as fate would have it, ...; **la tradition veut que ...** tradition demands that ...; **... qui se veut moderne** ... which purports to be modern

2 *(consentir)*: **je veux bien** *(bonne volonté)* I'll be happy to; *(concession)* fair enough, that's fine; **oui, si on veut** *(en quelque sorte)* yes, if you like; **comme tu veux** as you wish; *(en quelque sorte)* if you like; **veuillez attendre** please wait; **veuillez agréer ...** *(formule épistolaire)* yours faithfully

3: **en ~** *(être ambitieux)* to be out to win; **en ~ à qn** to bear sb a grudge; **je lui en veux d'avoir fait ça** I resent his having done that; **s'en ~ (de)** to be annoyed with o.s. (for); **il en veut à mon argent** he's after my money

4: **~ de** to want; **la compagnie ne veut plus de lui** the firm doesn't want him any more; **elle ne veut pas de son aide** she doesn't want his help

5: **~ dire** to mean.

voulu, e [vuly] *pp de* **vouloir** ♦ *adj (requis)* required, requisite; *(délibéré)* deliberate, intentional.

voulus [vuly] *etc vb voir* **vouloir.**

vous [vu] *pron* you; *(objet indirect)* (to) you; *(réfléchi)* yourself *(pl* yourselves); *(réciproque)* each other ♦ *nm:* **employer le ~** *(vouvoyer)* to use the "vous" form; **~-même** yourself; **~-mêmes** yourselves.

voûte [vut] *nf* vault; **la ~ céleste** the vault of heaven; **~ du palais** *(ANAT)* roof of the mouth; **~ plantaire** arch (of the foot).

voûté, e [vute] *adj* vaulted, arched; *(dos, personne)* bent, stooped.

voûter [vute] *vt (ARCHIT)* to arch, vault; **se ~** *vi (dos, personne)* to become stooped.

vouvoiement [vuvwamɑ̃] *nm* use of formal "vous" form.

vouvoyer [vuvwaje] *vt:* **~ qn** to address sb as "vous".

voyage [vwajaʒ] *nm* journey, trip; *(fait de voyager)*: **le ~** travel(ling); **partir/être en ~** to go off/be away on a journey *ou* trip; **faire un ~** to go on *ou* make a trip *ou* journey; **faire bon ~** to have a good journey; **les gens du ~** travelling people; **~ d'agrément/ d'affaires** pleasure/business trip; **~ de noces** honeymoon; **~ organisé** package tour.

voyager [vwajaʒe] *vi* to travel.

voyageur, euse [vwajaʒœʀ, -øz] *nm/f* traveller; *(passager)* passenger ♦ *adj (tempérament)* nomadic, wayfaring; **~ (de commerce)** commercial traveller.

voyagiste [vwajaʒist(ə)] *nm* tour operator.

voyais [vwajɛ] *etc vb voir* **voir.**

voyance [vwajɑ̃s] *nf* clairvoyance.

voyant, e [vwajɑ̃, -ɑ̃t] *adj (couleur)* loud, gaudy ♦ *nm/f (personne qui voit)* sighted person ♦ *nm (signal)* (warning) light ♦ *nf* clairvoyant.

voyelle [vwajɛl] *nf* vowel.

voyeur, euse [vwajœʀ, -øz] *nm/f* voyeur; peeping Tom.

voyeurisme [vwajœʀism(ə)] *nm* voyeurism.

voyons [vwajɔ̃] *etc vb voir* **voir.**

voyou [vwaju] *nm* lout, hoodlum; *(enfant)* guttersnipe.

VPC *sigle f (= vente par correspondance)* mail order selling.

vrac [vʀak]: **en ~** *adv* higgledy-piggledy; *(COMM)* in bulk.

vrai, e [vʀɛ] *adj (véridique: récit, faits)* true; *(non factice, authentique)* real ♦ *nm:* **le ~** the truth; **à ~ dire** to tell the truth; **il est ~ que** it is true that; **être dans le ~** to be right.

vraiment [vʀɛmɑ̃] *adv* really.

vraisemblable [vʀɛsɑ̃blabl(ə)] *adj (plausible)* likely, plausible; *(probable)* likely, probable.

vraisemblablement [vʀɛsɑ̃blabləmɑ̃] *adv* in all likelihood, very likely.

vraisemblance [vʀɛsɑ̃blɑ̃s] *nf* likelihood, plausibility; *(romanesque)* verisimilitude;

selon toute ~ in all likelihood.
vraquier [vʀakje] *nm* freighter.
vrille [vʀij] *nf* (*de plante*) tendril; (*outil*) gimlet; (*spirale*) spiral; (*AVIAT*) spin.
vriller [vʀije] *vt* to bore into, pierce.
vrombir [vʀɔ̃biʀ] *vi* to hum.
vrombissant, e [vʀɔ̃bisɑ̃, -ɑ̃t] *adj* humming.
vrombissement [vʀɔ̃bismɑ̃] *nm* hum(ming).
VRP *sigle m* (= *voyageur, représentant, placier*) (sales) rep.
VTT *sigle m* (= *vélo tout-terrain*) mountain bike.
vu [vy] *prép* (*en raison de*) in view of; ~ **que** in view of the fact that.
vu, e [vy] *pp de* **voir** ♦ *adj*: **bien/mal** ~ (*personne*) well/poorly thought of; (*conduite*) good/bad form ♦ *nm*: **au** ~ **et au su de tous** openly and publicly; **ni** ~ **ni connu** what the eye doesn't see ...!, no one will be any the wiser; **c'est tout** ~ it's a foregone conclusion.
vue [vy] *nf* (*fait de voir*): **la** ~ **de** the sight of; (*sens, faculté*) (eye)sight; (*panorama, image, photo*) view; (*spectacle*) sight; ~**s** *nfpl* (*idées*) views; (*dessein*) designs; **perdre la** ~ to lose one's (eye)sight; **perdre de** ~ to lose sight of; **à la** ~ **de tous** in full view of everybody; **hors de** ~ out of sight; **à première** ~ at first sight; **connaître de** ~ to know by sight; **à** ~ (*COMM*) at sight; **tirer à** ~ to shoot on sight; **à** ~ **d'œil** *adv* visibly; (*à première vue*) at a quick glance; **avoir** ~ **sur** to have a view of; **en** ~ (*visible*) in sight; (*COMM*) in the public eye; **avoir qch en** ~ (*intentions*) to have one's sights on sth; **en** ~ **de faire** with the intention of doing, with a view to doing; ~ **d'ensemble** overall view; ~ **de l'esprit** theoretical view.
vulcanisation [vylkanizɑsjɔ̃] *nf* vulcanization.
vulcaniser [vylkanize] *vt* to vulcanize.
vulcanologie [vylkanɔlɔʒi] *nf* = **volcanologie**.
vulcanologue [vylkanɔlɔg] *nm/f* = **volcanologue**.
vulgaire [vylgɛʀ] *adj* (*grossier*) vulgar, coarse; (*trivial*) commonplace, mundane; (*péj: quelconque*): **de** ~**s touristes/chaises de cuisine** common tourists/kitchen chairs; (*BOT, ZOOL: non latin*) common.
vulgairement [vylgɛʀmɑ̃] *adv* vulgarly, coarsely; (*communément*) commonly.
vulgarisation [vylgaʀizɑsjɔ̃] *nf*: **ouvrage de** ~ popularizing work, popularization.
vulgariser [vylgaʀize] *vt* to popularize.
vulgarité [vylgaʀite] *nf* vulgarity, coarseness.
vulnérabilité [vylneʀabilite] *nf* vulnerability.
vulnérable [vylneʀabl(ə)] *adj* vulnerable.
vulve [vylv(ə)] *nf* vulva.
vumètre [vymɛtʀ(ə)] *nm* recording level gauge.
Vve *abr* = **veuve**.
VVF *sigle m* (= *village vacances famille*) state-subsidized holiday village.
vx *abr* = **vieux**.

W w

W, w [dubləve] *nm inv* W, w ♦ *abr* (= *watt*) W; **W comme William** W for William.
wagon [vagɔ̃] *nm* (*de voyageurs*) carriage; (*de marchandises*) truck, wagon.
wagon-citerne, *pl* **wagons-citernes** [vagɔ̃sitɛʀn(ə)] *nm* tanker.
wagon-lit, *pl* **wagons-lits** [vagɔ̃li] *nm* sleeper, sleeping car.
wagonnet [vagɔnɛ] *nm* small truck.
wagon-poste, *pl* **wagons-postes** [vagɔ̃pɔst(ə)] *nm* mail van.
wagon-restaurant, *pl* **wagons-restaurants** [vagɔ̃ʀɛstɔʀɑ̃] *nm* restaurant *ou* dining car.
Walkman [wɔkman] *nm* ® Walkman ®, personal stereo.
Wallis et Futuna [walisefytyna]: **les îles** ~ the Wallis and Futuna Islands.
wallon, ne [walɔ̃, -ɔn] *adj* Walloon ♦ *nm* (*LING*) Walloon ♦ *nm/f*: **W~, ne** Walloon.
Wallonie [walɔni] *nf*: **la** ~ French-speaking (part of) Belgium.
water-polo [watɛʀpolo] *nm* water polo.
waters [watɛʀ] *nmpl* toilet *sg*, loo *sg* (*BRIT*).
watt [wat] *nm* watt.
w.-c. [vese] *nmpl* toilet *sg*, lavatory *sg*.
week-end [wikɛnd] *nm* weekend.
western [wɛstɛʀn] *nm* western.
Westphalie [vɛsfali] *nf*: **la** ~ Westphalia.
whisky, *pl* **whiskies** [wiski] *nm* whisky.
white-spirit [wajtspiʀit] *nm* white spirit.
Winchester [wintʃɛstɛʀ]: **disque** ~ Winchester disk.
wok [wɔk] *nm* wok.

X x

X, x [iks] *nm inv* X, x ♦ *sigle m* = (**École**) **polytechnique**; **plainte contre X** (*JUR*) action against person or persons unknown; **X comme Xavier** X for Xmas.
xénophobe [gzenɔfɔb] *adj* xenophobic ♦ *nm/f* xenophobe.
xénophobie [gzenɔfɔbi] *nf* xenophobia.
xérès [gzeʀɛs] *nm* sherry.

xylographie [ksilɔgʀafi] *nf* xylography; (*image*) xylograph.
xylophone [ksilɔfɔn] *nm* xylophone.

Y y

Y, y [igʀɛk] *nm inv* Y, y; **Y comme Yvonne** Y for Yellow (*BRIT*) *ou* Yoke (*US*).
y [i] *adv* (*à cet endroit*) there; (*dessus*) on it (*ou* them); (*dedans*) in it (*ou* them) ♦ *pron* (*about ou* on *ou* of) it : *vérifier la syntaxe du verbe employé*; **j'~ pense** I'm thinking about it; *voir aussi* **aller**, **avoir**.
yacht [jɔt] *nm* yacht.
yaourt [jauʀt] *nm* yoghurt.
yaourtière [jauʀtjɛʀ] *nf* yoghurt-maker.
Yémen [jemɛn] *nm*: **le ~** Yemen.
yéménite [jemenit] *adj* Yemini.
yeux [jø] *pl de* **œil**.
yoga [jɔga] *nm* yoga.
yoghourt [jɔguʀt] *nm* = **yaourt**.
yole [jɔl] *nf* skiff.
yougoslave [jugɔslav] *adj* Yugoslav(ian) ♦ *nm/f*: **Y~** Yugoslav(ian).
Yougoslavie [jugɔslavi] *nf*: **la ~** Yugoslavia.
youyou [juju] *nm* dinghy.
yo-yo [jojo] *nm inv* yo-yo.
yucca [juka] *nm* yucca (tree *ou* plant).

Z z

Z, z [zɛd] *nm inv* Z, z; **Z comme Zoé** Z for Zebra.
ZAC [zak] *sigle f* (= *zone d'aménagement concerté*) urban development zone.
ZAD [zad] *sigle f* (= *zone d'aménagement différé*) future development zone.
Zaïre [zaiʀ] *nm*: **le ~** Zaïre.
zaïrois, e [zaiʀwa, -waz] *adj* Zaïrese.
Zambèze [zãbɛz] *nm*: **le ~** the Zambezi.
Zambie [zãbi] *nf*: **la ~** Zambia.
zambien, ne [zãbjɛ̃, -ɛn] *adj* Zambian.
zapping [zapiŋ] *nm*: **faire du ~** to flick through the channels.
zèbre [zɛbʀ(ə)] *nm* (*ZOOL*) zebra.
zébré, e [zebʀe] *adj* striped, streaked.
zébrure [zebʀyʀ] *nf* stripe, streak.

zélateur, trice [zelatœʀ, -tʀis] *nm/f* partisan, zealot.
zèle [zɛl] *nm* diligence, assiduousness; **faire du ~** (*péj*) to be over-zealous.
zélé, e [zele] *adj* zealous.
zénith [zenit] *nm* zenith.
ZEP [zɛp] *sigle f* (= *zone d'éducation prioritaire*) *area targeted for special help in education.*
zéro [zeʀo] *nm* zero, nought (*BRIT*); **au-dessous de ~** below zero (Centigrade), below freezing; **partir de ~** to start from scratch; **réduire à ~** to reduce to nothing; **trois (buts) à ~ 3** (goals) to nil.
zeste [zɛst(ə)] *nm* peel, zest; **un ~ de citron** a piece of lemon peel.
zézaiement [zezɛmã] *nm* lisp.
zézayer [zezeje] *vi* to have a lisp.
ZI *sigle f* = **zone industrielle**.
zibeline [ziblin] *nf* sable.
ZIF [zif] *sigle f* (= *zone d'intervention foncière*) intervention zone.
zigouiller [ziguje] *vt* (*fam*) to do in.
zigzag [zigzag] *nm* zigzag.
zigzaguer [zigzage] *vi* to zigzag (along).
Zimbabwe [zimbabwe] *nm*: **le ~** Zimbabwe.
zimbabwéen, ne [zimbabweɛ̃, -ɛn] *adj* Zimbabwean.
zinc [zɛ̃g] *nm* (*CHIMIE*) zinc; (*comptoir*) bar, counter.
zinguer [zɛ̃ge] *vt* to cover with zinc.
zircon [ziʀkɔ̃] *nm* zircon.
zizanie [zizani] *nf*: **semer la ~** to stir up ill-feeling.
zizi [zizi] *nm* (*fam*) willy (*BRIT*), peter (*US*).
zodiacal, e, aux [zɔdjakal, -o] *adj* (*signe*) of the zodiac.
zodiaque [zɔdjak] *nm* zodiac.
zona [zona] *nm* shingles *sg*.
zonage [zonaʒ] *nm* (*ADMIN*) zoning.
zonard, e [zonaʀ, -aʀd] *nm/f* (*fam*) (young) hooligan *ou* thug.
zone [zon] *nf* zone, area; (*INFORM*) field; (*quartiers*): **la ~** the slum belt; **de seconde ~** (*fig*) second-rate; **~ d'action** (*MIL*) sphere of activity; **~ bleue** ≈ restricted parking area; **~ d'extension** *ou* **d'urbanisation** urban development area; **~ franche** free zone; **~ industrielle (ZI)** industrial estate; **~ résidentielle** residential area; **~ tampon** buffer zone.
zoner [zone] *vi* (*fam*) to hang around.
zoo [zoo] *nm* zoo.
zoologie [zɔɔlɔʒi] *nf* zoology.
zoologique [zɔɔlɔʒik] *adj* zoological.
zoologiste [zɔɔlɔʒist(ə)] *nm/f* zoologist.
zoom [zum] *nm* (*PHOTO*) zoom (lens).
ZUP [zyp] *sigle f* (= *zone à urbaniser en priorité*) = **ZAC**.
Zurich [zyʀik] *n* Zürich.
zut [zyt] *excl* dash (it)! (*BRIT*), nuts! (*US*).

English-French

Anglais-Français

A a

A, a [eɪ] *n* (*letter*) A, a *m*; (*SCOL: mark*) A; (*MUS*): **A** la *m*; **A for Andrew**, (*US*) **A for Able** A comme Anatole; **A road** *n* (*BRIT AUT*) route nationale; **A shares** *npl* (*BRIT STOCK EXCHANGE*) actions *fpl* prioritaires.

a [eɪ, ə] (*before vowel or silent h:* **an**) *indef art* **1** un(e); ~ **book** un livre; **an apple** une pomme; **she's** ~ **doctor** elle est médecin
2 (*instead of the number "one"*) un(e); ~ **year ago** il y a un an; ~ **hundred/thousand** *etc* **pounds** cent/mille *etc* livres
3 (*in expressing ratios, prices etc*): **3** ~ **day/ week** 3 par jour/semaine; **10 km an hour** 10 km à l'heure; **30p** ~ **kilo** 30p le kilo.

a. *abbr* = **acre**.

AA *n abbr* (*BRIT:* = *Automobile Association*) ≈ ACF *m*; (*US:* = *Associate in/of Arts*) diplôme universitaire; (= *Alcoholics Anonymous*) AA; (= *anti-aircraft*) AA.

AAA *n abbr* (= *American Automobile Association*) ≈ ACF *m*; (*BRIT*) = *Amateur Athletics Association*.

A & R *n abbr* (*MUS:* = *artists and repertoire*): ~ **man** découvreur *m* de talent.

AAUP *n abbr* (= *American Association of University Professors*) syndicat universitaire.

AB *abbr* (*BRIT*) = **able-bodied seaman**; (*Canada*) = *Alberta*.

aback [ə'bæk] *adv*: **to be taken** ~ être décontenancé(e).

abacus, *pl* **abaci** ['æbəkəs, -saɪ] *n* boulier *m*.

abandon [ə'bændən] *vt* abandonner ♦ *n* abandon *m*; **to** ~ **ship** évacuer le navire.

abandoned [ə'bændənd] *adj* (*child, house etc*) abandonné(e); (*unrestrained*) sans retenue.

abase [ə'beɪs] *vt*: **to** ~ **o.s. (so far as to do)** s'abaisser (à faire).

abashed [ə'bæʃt] *adj* confus(e), embarrassé(e).

abate [ə'beɪt] *vi* s'apaiser, se calmer.

abatement [ə'beɪtmənt] *n*: **noise** ~ lutte *f* contre le bruit.

abattoir ['æbətwɑː*] *n* (*BRIT*) abattoir *m*.

abbey ['æbɪ] *n* abbaye *f*.

abbot ['æbət] *n* père supérieur.

abbreviate [ə'briːvɪeɪt] *vt* abréger.

abbreviation [əbriːvɪ'eɪʃən] *n* abréviation *f*.

ABC *n abbr* (= *American Broadcasting Company*) chaîne de télévision.

abdicate ['æbdɪkeɪt] *vt*, *vi* abdiquer.

abdication [æbdɪ'keɪʃən] *n* abdication *f*.

abdomen ['æbdəmən] *n* abdomen *m*.

abdominal [æb'dɔmɪnl] *adj* abdominal(e).

abduct [æb'dʌkt] *vt* enlever.

abduction [æb'dʌkʃən] *n* enlèvement *m*.

Aberdonian [æbə'dəunɪən] *adj* d'Aberdeen ♦ *n* habitant/e d'Aberdeen; natif/ive d'Aberdeen.

aberration [æbə'reɪʃən] *n* anomalie *f*; **in a moment of mental** ~ dans un moment d'égarement.

abet [ə'bɛt] *vt see* **aid**.

abeyance [ə'beɪəns] *n*: **in** ~ (*law*) en désuétude; (*matter*) en suspens.

abhor [əb'hɔː*] *vt* abhorrer, exécrer.

abhorrent [əb'hɔrənt] *adj* odieux(euse), exécrable.

abide [ə'baɪd] *vt* souffrir, supporter.
▶**abide by** *vt fus* observer, respecter.

abiding [ə'baɪdɪŋ] *adj* (*memory etc*) durable.

ability [ə'bɪlɪtɪ] *n* compétence *f*; capacité *f*; (*skill*) talent *m*; **to the best of my** ~ de mon mieux.

abject ['æbdʒɛkt] *adj* (*poverty*) sordide; (*coward*) méprisable; **an** ~ **apology** les excuses les plus plates.

ablaze [ə'bleɪz] *adj* en feu, en flammes; ~ **with light** resplendissant de lumière.

able ['eɪbl] *adj* compétent(e); **to be** ~ **to do sth** pouvoir faire qch, être capable de faire qch.

able-bodied ['eɪbl'bɔdɪd] *adj* robuste; ~
seaman (*BRIT*) matelot breveté.
ably ['eɪblɪ] *adv* avec compétence *or* talent,
habilement.
ABM *n abbr* = anti-ballistic missile.
abnormal [æb'nɔ:məl] *adj* anormal(e).
abnormality [æbnɔ:'mælɪtɪ] *n* (*condition*)
caractère anormal; (*instance*) anomalie *f*.
aboard [ə'bɔ:d] *adv* à bord ♦ *prep* à bord de;
(*train*) dans.
abode [ə'bəud] *n* (*old*) demeure *f*; (*LAW*): **of no
fixed** ~ sans domicile fixe.
abolish [ə'bɔlɪʃ] *vt* abolir.
abolition [æbə'lɪʃən] *n* abolition *f*.
abominable [ə'bɔmɪnəbl] *adj* abominable.
aborigine [æbə'rɪdʒɪnɪ] *n* aborigène *m/f*.
abort [ə'bɔ:t] *vt* (*MED, fig*) faire avorter;
(*COMPUT*) abandonner.
abortion [ə'bɔ:ʃən] *n* avortement *m*; **to have
an** ~ se faire avorter.
abortionist [ə'bɔ:ʃənɪst] *n* avorteur/euse.
abortive [ə'bɔ:tɪv] *adj* manqué(e).
abound [ə'baund] *vi* abonder; **to** ~ **in** abonder
en, regorger de.

================= *KEYWORD*

about [ə'baut] *adv* **1** (*approximately*) environ, à
peu près; ~ **a hundred/thousand** *etc*
environ cent/mille *etc*, une centaine/un
millier *etc*; **it takes** ~ **10 hours** ça prend
environ *or* à peu près 10 heures; **at** ~ **2
o'clock** vers 2 heures; **I've just** ~ **finished**
j'ai presque fini
2 (*referring to place*) çà et là, de côté et
d'autre; **to run** ~ courir çà et là; **to walk** ~
se promener, aller et venir; **is Paul** ~? (*BRIT*)
est-ce que Paul est là?; **it's** ~ **here** c'est par
ici, c'est dans les parages; **they left all their
things lying** ~ ils ont laissé traîner toutes
leurs affaires
3: **to be** ~ **to do sth** être sur le point de
faire qch; **I'm not** ~ **to do all that for
nothing** (*col*) je ne vais quand même pas
faire tout ça pour rien
4 (*opposite*): **it's the other way** ~ (*BRIT*) c'est
l'inverse
♦ *prep* **1** (*relating to*) au sujet de, à propos de;
a book ~ **London** un livre sur Londres;
what is it ~? de quoi s'agit-il?; **we talked** ~
it nous en avons parlé; **do something** ~ **it!**
faites quelque chose!; **what** *or* **how** ~ **doing
this?** et si nous faisions ceci?
2 (*referring to place*) dans; **to walk** ~ **the
town** se promener dans la ville.

about face, about turn *n* (*MIL*) demi-tour *m*;
(*fig*) volte-face *f*.
above [ə'bʌv] *adv* au-dessus ♦ *prep* au-dessus
de; **mentioned** ~ mentionné ci-dessus;
costing ~ **£10** coûtant plus de 10 livres; ~
all par-dessus tout, surtout.
aboveboard [ə'bʌv'bɔ:d] *adj* franc(franche),

loyal(e); honnête.
abrasion [ə'breɪʒən] *n* frottement *m*; (*on skin*)
écorchure *f*.
abrasive [ə'breɪzɪv] *adj* abrasif(ive); (*fig*)
caustique, agressif(ive).
abreast [ə'brɛst] *adv* de front; **to keep** ~ **of** se
tenir au courant de.
abridge [ə'brɪdʒ] *vt* abréger.
abroad [ə'brɔ:d] *adv* à l'étranger; **there is a
rumour** ~ **that** ... (*fig*) le bruit court que ....
abrupt [ə'brʌpt] *adj* (*steep, blunt*) abrupt(e);
(*sudden, gruff*) brusque.
abscess ['æbsɪs] *n* abcès *m*.
abscond [əb'skɔnd] *vi* disparaître, s'enfuir.
absence ['æbsəns] *n* absence *f*; **in the** ~ **of**
(*person*) en l'absence de; (*thing*) faute de.
absent ['æbsənt] *adj* absent(e); ~ **without
leave (AWOL)** (*MIL*) en absence irrégulière.
absentee [æbsən'ti:] *n* absent/e.
absenteeism [æbsən'ti:ɪzəm] *n* absentéisme
m.
absent-minded ['æbsənt'maɪndɪd] *adj*
distrait(e).
absent-mindedness ['æbsənt'maɪndɪdnɪs] *n*
distraction *f*.
absolute ['æbsəlu:t] *adj* absolu(e).
absolutely [æbsə'lu:tlɪ] *adv* absolument.
absolve [əb'zɔlv] *vt*: **to** ~ **sb (from)** (*sin etc*)
absoudre qn (de); **to** ~ **sb from** (*oath*) délier
qn de.
absorb [əb'zɔ:b] *vt* absorber; **to be** ~**ed in a
book** être plongé(e) dans un livre.
absorbent [əb'zɔ:bənt] *adj* absorbant(e).
absorbent cotton *n* (*US*) coton *m* hydrophile.
absorbing [əb'zɔ:bɪŋ] *adj* absorbant(e); (*book,
film etc*) captivant(e).
absorption [əb'sɔ:pʃən] *n* absorption *f*.
abstain [əb'steɪn] *vi*: **to** ~ **(from)** s'abstenir
(de).
abstemious [əb'sti:mɪəs] *adj* sobre, frugal(e).
abstention [əb'stɛnʃən] *n* abstention *f*.
abstinence ['æbstɪnəns] *n* abstinence *f*.
abstract *adj, n* ['æbstrækt] *adj* abstrait(e) ♦ *n*
(*summary*) résumé *m* ♦ *vt* [æb'strækt]
extraire.
absurd [əb'sə:d] *adj* absurde.
absurdity [əb'sə:dɪtɪ] *n* absurdité *f*.
ABTA ['æbtə] *n abbr* = Association of British
Travel Agents.
Abu Dhabi ['æbu:'dɑ:bɪ] *n* Ab(o)u Dhabî *m*.
abundance [ə'bʌndəns] *n* abondance *f*.
abundant [ə'bʌndənt] *adj* abondant(e).
abuse *n* [ə'bju:s] insultes *fpl*, injures *fpl*; (*of
power etc*) abus *m* ♦ *vt* [ə'bju:z] abuser de; **to
be open to** ~ se prêter à des abus.
abusive [ə'bju:sɪv] *adj* grossier(ière),
injurieux(euse).
abysmal [ə'bɪzməl] *adj* exécrable; (*ignorance
etc*) sans bornes.
abyss [ə'bɪs] *n* abîme *m*, gouffre *m*.
AC *n abbr* (*US*) = athletic club.
a/c *abbr* (*BANKING etc*) = account, account

current.

academic [ækə'dɛmɪk] *adj* universitaire; (*pej: issue*) oiseux(euse), purement théorique ♦ *n* universitaire *m/f*; ~ **freedom** liberté *f* académique.

academic year *n* année *f* universitaire.

academy [ə'kædəmɪ] *n* (*learned body*) académie *f*; (*school*) collège *m*; **military/ naval** ~ école militaire/navale; ~ **of music** conservatoire *m*.

ACAS ['eɪkæs] *n abbr* (*BRIT*: = *Advisory, Conciliation and Arbitration Service*) *organisme de conciliation et d'arbitrage des conflits du travail.*

accede [æk'siːd] *vi*: **to** ~ **to** (*request, throne*) accéder à.

accelerate [æk'sɛləreɪt] *vt, vi* accélérer.

acceleration [æksɛlə'reɪʃən] *n* accélération *f*.

accelerator [æk'sɛləreɪtə*] *n* accélérateur *m*.

accent ['æksɛnt] *n* accent *m*.

accentuate [æk'sɛntjueɪt] *vt* (*syllable*) accentuer; (*need, difference etc*) souligner.

accept [ək'sɛpt] *vt* accepter.

acceptable [ək'sɛptəbl] *adj* acceptable.

acceptance [ək'sɛptəns] *n* acceptation *f*; **to meet with general** ~ être favorablement accueilli par tous.

access ['æksɛs] *n* accès *m* ♦ *vt* (*COMPUT*) accéder à; **to have** ~ **to** (*information, library etc*) avoir accès à, pouvoir utiliser *or* consulter; (*person*) avoir accès auprès de; **the burglars gained** ~ **through a window** les cambrioleurs sont entrés par une fenêtre.

accessible [æk'sɛsəbl] *adj* accessible.

accession [æk'sɛʃən] *n* accession *f*; (*of king*) avènement *m*; (*to library*) acquisition *f*.

accessory [æk'sɛsərɪ] *n* accessoire *m*; **toilet accessories** (*BRIT*) articles *mpl* de toilette.

access road *n* voie *f* d'accès; (*to motorway*) bretelle *f* de raccordement.

access time *n* (*COMPUT*) temps *m* d'accès.

accident ['æksɪdənt] *n* accident *m*; (*chance*) hasard *m*; **to meet with** *or* **to have an** ~ avoir un accident; ~**s at work** accidents du travail; **by** ~ par hasard; (*not deliberately*) accidentellement.

accidental [æksɪ'dɛntl] *adj* accidentel(le).

accidentally [æksɪ'dɛntəlɪ] *adv* accidentellement.

accident insurance *n* assurance *f* accident.

accident-prone ['æksɪdənt'prəun] *adj* sujet(te) aux accidents.

acclaim [ə'kleɪm] *vt* acclamer ♦ *n* acclamation *f*.

acclamation [æklə'meɪʃən] *n* (*approval*) acclamation *f*; (*applause*) ovation *f*.

acclimatize [ə'klaɪmətaɪz], (*US*) **acclimate** [ə'klaɪmət] *vt*: **to become** ~**d** s'acclimater.

accolade ['ækəleɪd] *n* accolade *f*; (*fig*) marque *f* d'honneur.

accommodate [ə'kɔmədeɪt] *vt* loger, recevoir; (*oblige, help*) obliger; (*adapt*): **to** ~ **one's plans to** adapter ses projets à; **this car** ~**s 4 people comfortably** on tient confortablement à 4 dans cette voiture.

accommodating [ə'kɔmədeɪtɪŋ] *adj* obligeant(e), arrangeant(e).

accommodation, (*US*) **accommodations** [əkɔmə'deɪʃən(z)] *n(pl)* logement *m*; **he's found** ~ il a trouvé à se loger; **"~ to let"** (*BRIT*) "appartement (*or* studio *etc*) à louer"; **they have** ~ **for 500** ils peuvent recevoir 500 personnes, il y a de la place pour 500 personnes; **the hall has seating** ~ **for 600** (*BRIT*) la salle contient 600 places assises.

accompaniment [ə'kʌmpənɪmənt] *n* accompagnement *m*.

accompanist [ə'kʌmpənɪst] *n* accompagnateur/trice.

accompany [ə'kʌmpənɪ] *vt* accompagner.

accomplice [ə'kʌmplɪs] *n* complice *m/f*.

accomplish [ə'kʌmplɪʃ] *vt* accomplir.

accomplished [ə'kʌmplɪʃt] *adj* accompli(e).

accomplishment [ə'kʌmplɪʃmənt] *n* accomplissement *m*; (*achievement*) réussite *f*; ~**s** *npl* (*skills*) talents *mpl*.

accord [ə'kɔːd] *n* accord *m* ♦ *vt* accorder; **of his own** ~ de son plein gré; **with one** ~ d'un commun accord.

accordance [ə'kɔːdəns] *n*: **in** ~ **with** conformément à.

according [ə'kɔːdɪŋ]: ~ **to** *prep* selon; ~ **to plan** comme prévu.

accordingly [ə'kɔːdɪŋlɪ] *adv* en conséquence.

accordion [ə'kɔːdɪən] *n* accordéon *m*.

accost [ə'kɔst] *vt* accoster, aborder.

account [ə'kaunt] *n* (*COMM*) compte *m*; (*report*) compte rendu, récit *m*; ~**s** *npl* (*BOOK-KEEPING*) comptabilité *f*, comptes; **"~ payee only"** (*BRIT*) "chèque non endossable"; **to keep an** ~ **of** noter; **to bring sb to** ~ **for sth/ for having done sth** amener qn à rendre compte de qch/d'avoir fait qch; **by all** ~**s** au dire de tous; **of little** ~ de peu d'importance; **to pay £5 on** ~ verser un acompte de 5 livres; **to buy sth on** ~ acheter qch à crédit; **on no** ~ en aucun cas; **on** ~ **of** à cause de; **to take into** ~, **take** ~ **of** tenir compte de.

►**account for** *vt fus* expliquer, rendre compte de; **all the children were** ~**ed for** aucun enfant ne manquait; **4 people are still not** ~**ed for** on n'a toujours pas retrouvé 4 personnes.

accountability [əkauntə'bɪlɪtɪ] *n* responsabilité *f*; (*financial, political*) transparence *f*.

accountable [ə'kauntəbl] *adj*: ~ **(for)** responsable (de).

accountancy [ə'kauntənsɪ] *n* comptabilité *f*.

accountant [ə'kauntənt] *n* comptable *m/f*.

accounting [ə'kauntɪŋ] *n* comptabilité *f*.

accounting period *n* exercice financier, période *f* comptable.

account number *n* numéro *m* de compte.

account payable *n* compte *m* fournisseurs.

account receivable *n* compte *m* clients.
accredited [əˈkrɛdɪtɪd] *adj (person)*
accrédité(e).
accretion [əˈkriːʃən] *n* accroissement *m*.
accrue [əˈkruː] *vi* s'accroître; *(mount up)*
s'accumuler; **to ~ to** s'ajouter à; **~d interest**
intérêt couru.
accumulate [əˈkjuːmjuleɪt] *vt* accumuler,
amasser ♦ *vi* s'accumuler, s'amasser.
accumulation [əkjuːmjuˈleɪʃən] *n*
accumulation *f*.
accuracy [ˈækjurəsɪ] *n* exactitude *f*, précision
f.
accurate [ˈækjurɪt] *adj* exact(e), précis(e).
accurately [ˈækjurɪtlɪ] *adv* avec précision.
accusation [ækjuˈzeɪʃən] *n* accusation *f*.
accusative [əˈkjuːzətɪv] *n (LING)* accusatif *m*.
accuse [əˈkjuːz] *vt* accuser.
accused [əˈkjuːzd] *n* accusé/e.
accuser [əˈkjuːzə*] *n* accusateur/trice.
accustom [əˈkʌstəm] *vt* accoutumer,
habituer; **to ~ o.s. to sth** s'habituer à qch.
accustomed [əˈkʌstəmd] *adj (usual)*
habituel(le); **~ to** habitué(e) *or*
accoutumé(e) à.
AC/DC *abbr* = **alternating current/direct**
current.
ACE [eɪs] *n abbr* = **American Council on**
Education.
ace [eɪs] *n* as *m*; **within an ~ of** *(BRIT)* à deux
doigts *or* un cheveu de.
acerbic [əˈsəːbɪk] *adj (also fig)* acerbe.
acetate [ˈæsɪteɪt] *n* acétate *m*.
ache [eɪk] *n* mal *m*, douleur *f* ♦ *vi (be sore)*
faire mal, être douloureux(euse); *(yearn)*: **to**
~ to do sth mourir d'envie de faire qch; **I've**
got stomach ~ *or* *(US)* **a stomach ~** j'ai mal
à l'estomac; **my head ~s** j'ai mal à la tête;
I'm aching all over j'ai mal partout.
achieve [əˈtʃiːv] *vt (aim)* atteindre; *(victory,*
success) remporter, obtenir; *(task)*
accomplir.
achievement [əˈtʃiːvmənt] *n* exploit *m*,
réussite *f*; *(of aims)* réalisation *f*.
Achilles heel [əˈkɪliːz-] *n* talon *m* d'Achille.
acid [ˈæsɪd] *adj*, *n* acide *(m)*.
acidity [əˈsɪdɪtɪ] *n* acidité *f*.
acid rain *n* pluies *fpl* acides.
acid test *n (fig)* épreuve décisive.
acknowledge [əkˈnɔlɪdʒ] *vt (also:* **~ receipt of**)
accuser réception de; *(fact)* reconnaître.
acknowledgement [əkˈnɔlɪdʒmənt] *n* accusé
m de réception; **~s** *(in book)* remerciements
mpl.
ACLU *n abbr* (= *American Civil Liberties Union*)
ligue des droits de l'homme.
acme [ˈækmɪ] *n* point culminant.
acne [ˈæknɪ] *n* acné *m*.
acorn [ˈeɪkɔːn] *n* gland *m*.
acoustic [əˈkuːstɪk] *adj* acoustique.
acoustic coupler *n (COMPUT)* coupleur *m*
acoustique.

acoustics [əˈkuːstɪks] *n*, *npl* acoustique *f*.
acquaint [əˈkweɪnt] *vt*: **to ~ sb with sth**
mettre qn au courant de qch; **to be ~ed**
with *(person)* connaître; *(fact)* savoir.
acquaintance [əˈkweɪntəns] *n* connaissance *f*;
to make sb's ~ faire la connaissance de qn.
acquiesce [ækwɪˈɛs] *vi (agree)*: **to ~ (in)**
acquiescer (à).
acquire [əˈkwaɪə*] *vt* acquérir.
acquired [əˈkwaɪəd] *adj* acquis(e); **an ~ taste**
un goût acquis.
acquisition [ækwɪˈzɪʃən] *n* acquisition *f*.
acquisitive [əˈkwɪzɪtɪv] *adj* qui a l'instinct de
possession *or* le goût de la propriété.
acquit [əˈkwɪt] *vt* acquitter; **to ~ o.s. well** s'en
tirer très honorablement.
acquittal [əˈkwɪtl] *n* acquittement *m*.
acre [ˈeɪkə*] *n* acre *f* (= 4047 m^2).
acreage [ˈeɪkərɪdʒ] *n* superficie *f*.
acrid [ˈækrɪd] *adj (smell)* âcre; *(fig)*
mordant(e).
acrimonious [ækrɪˈməunɪəs] *adj*
acrimonieux(euse), aigre.
acrobat [ˈækrəbæt] *n* acrobate *m/f*.
acrobatic [ækrəˈbætɪk] *adj* acrobatique.
acrobatics [ækrəˈbætɪks] *n*, *npl* acrobatie *f*.
Acropolis [əˈkrɔpəlɪs] *n*: **the ~** l'Acropole *f*.
across [əˈkrɔs] *prep (on the other side)* de
l'autre côté de; *(crosswise)* en travers de
♦ *adv* de l'autre côté; en travers; **to walk ~**
(the road) traverser (la route); **to take sb ~**
the road faire traverser la route à qn; **a**
road ~ the wood une route qui traverse le
bois; **the lake is 12 km ~** le lac fait 12 km de
large; **~ from** en face de; **to get sth ~ (to sb)**
faire comprendre qch (à qn).
acrylic [əˈkrɪlɪk] *adj*, *n* acrylique *(m)*.
ACT *n abbr* (= *American College Test*) *examen*
de fin d'études secondaires.
act [ækt] *n* acte *m*, action *f*; *(THEAT: part of play)*
acte; *(: of performer)*·numéro *m*; *(LAW)* loi *f*
♦ *vi* agir; *(THEAT)* jouer; *(pretend)* jouer la
comédie ♦ *vt (role)* jouer, tenir; **~ of God**
(LAW) catastrophe naturelle; **to catch sb in**
the ~ prendre qn sur le fait *or* en flagrant
délit; **it's only an ~** c'est du cinéma; **to ~**
Hamlet *(BRIT)* tenir *or* jouer le rôle
d'Hamlet; **to ~ the fool** *(BRIT)* faire l'idiot;
to ~ as servir de; **it ~s as a deterrent** cela a
un effet dissuasif; **~ing in my capacity as**
chairman, I ... en ma qualité de président,
je ....
▶**act on** *vt*: **to ~ on sth** agir sur la base de
qch.
▶**act out** *vt (event)* raconter en mimant;
(fantasies) réaliser.
acting [ˈæktɪŋ] *adj* suppléant(e), par intérim
♦ *n (of actor)* jeu *m*; *(activity)*: **to do some ~**
faire du théâtre *(or* du cinéma); **he is the ~**
manager il remplace (provisoirement) le
directeur.
action [ˈækʃən] *n* action *f*; *(MIL)* combat(s)

m(pl); (*LAW*) procès *m*, action en justice; **to bring an ~ against sb** (*LAW*) poursuivre qn en justice, intenter un procès contre qn; **killed in ~** (*MIL*) tué au champ d'honneur; **out of ~** hors de combat; (*machine etc*) hors d'usage; **to take ~** agir, prendre des mesures; **to put a plan into ~** mettre un projet à exécution.

action replay *n* (*BRIT TV*) retour *m* sur une séquence.

activate ['æktɪveɪt] *vt* (*mechanism*) actionner, faire fonctionner; (*CHEM, PHYSICS*) activer.

active ['æktɪv] *adj* actif(ive); (*volcano*) en activité; **to play an ~ part in** jouer un rôle actif dans.

active duty (AD) *n* (*US MIL*) campagne *f*.

actively ['æktɪvlɪ] *adv* activement.

active partner *n* (*COMM*) associé/e.

active service *n* (*BRIT MIL*) campagne *f*.

activist ['æktɪvɪst] *n* activiste *m/f*.

activity [æk'tɪvɪtɪ] *n* activité *f*.

actor ['æktə*] *n* acteur *m*.

actress ['æktrɪs] *n* actrice *f*.

actual ['æktjuəl] *adj* réel(le), véritable.

actually ['æktjuəlɪ] *adv* réellement, véritablement; (*in fact*) en fait.

actuary ['æktjuərɪ] *n* actuaire *m*.

actuate ['æktjueɪt] *vt* déclencher, actionner.

acuity [ə'kjuːɪtɪ] *n* acuité *f*.

acumen ['ækjumən] *n* perspicacité *f*; **business ~** sens *m* des affaires.

acupuncture ['ækjupʌŋktʃə*] *n* acupuncture *f*.

acute [ə'kjuːt] *adj* aigu(ë); (*mind, observer*) pénétrant(e).

AD *adv abbr* (= *Anno Domini*) ap. J.-C. ♦ *n abbr* (*US MIL*) = **active duty.**

ad [æd] *n abbr* = **advertisement.**

adamant ['ædəmənt] *adj* inflexible.

Adam's apple ['ædəmz-] *n* pomme *f* d'Adam.

adapt [ə'dæpt] *vt* adapter ♦ *vi*: **to ~ (to)** s'adapter (à).

adaptability [ədæptə'bɪlɪtɪ] *n* faculté *f* d'adaptation.

adaptable [ə'dæptəbl] *adj* (*device*) adaptable; (*person*) qui s'adapte facilement.

adaptation [ædæp'teɪʃən] *n* adaptation *f*.

adapter [ə'dæptə*] *n* (*ELEC*) adapteur *m*.

ADC *n abbr* (*MIL*) = **aide-de-camp**; (*US*: = *Aid to Dependent Children*) *aide pour enfants assistés.*

add [æd] *vt* ajouter; (*figures*) additionner ♦ *vi*: **to ~ to** (*increase*) ajouter à, accroître.

▶**add on** *vt* ajouter.

▶**add up** *vt* (*figures*) additionner ♦ *vi* (*fig*): **it doesn't ~ up** cela ne rime à rien; **it doesn't ~ up to much** ça n'est pas grand'chose.

adder ['ædə*] *n* vipère *f*.

addict ['ædɪkt] *n* toxicomane *m/f*; (*fig*) fanatique *m/f*; **heroin ~** héroïnomane *m/f*; **drug ~** drogué/e *m/f*.

addicted [ə'dɪktɪd] *adj*: **to be ~ to** (*drink etc*) être adonné(e) à; (*fig: football etc*) être un(e) fanatique de.

addiction [ə'dɪkʃən] *n* (*MED*) dépendance *f*.

adding machine ['ædɪŋ-] *n* machine *f* à calculer.

Addis Ababa ['ædɪs'æbəbə] *n* Addis Abeba, Addis Ababa.

addition [ə'dɪʃən] *n* addition *f*; **in ~** de plus, de surcroît; **in ~ to** en plus de.

additional [ə'dɪʃənl] *adj* supplémentaire.

additive ['ædɪtɪv] *n* additif *m*.

addled ['ædld] *adj* (*BRIT: egg*) pourri(e).

address [ə'drɛs] *n* adresse *f*; (*talk*) discours *m*, allocution *f* ♦ *vt* adresser; (*speak to*) s'adresser à; **form of ~** titre *m*; **what form of ~ do you use for ...?** comment s'adresse-t-on à ...?; **to ~ (o.s. to)** sth (*problem, issue*) aborder qch; **absolute/relative ~** (*COMPUT*) adresse absolue/relative.

address book *n* carnet *m* d'adresses.

addressee [ædrɛ'siː] *n* destinataire *m/f*.

Aden ['eɪdən] *n*: **Gulf of ~** Golfe *m* d'Aden.

adenoids ['ædɪnɔɪdz] *npl* végétations *fpl*.

adept ['ædɛpt] *adj*: **~ at** expert(e) à *or* en.

adequate ['ædɪkwɪt] *adj* (*enough*) suffisant(e); **to feel ~ to the task** se sentir à la hauteur de la tâche.

adequately ['ædɪkwɪtlɪ] *adv* de façon adéquate.

adhere [əd'hɪə*] *vi*: **to ~ to** adhérer à; (*fig: rule, decision*) se tenir à.

adhesion [əd'hiːʒən] *n* adhésion *f*.

adhesive [əd'hiːzɪv] *adj* adhésif(ive) ♦ *n* adhésif *m*; **~ tape** (*BRIT*) ruban adhésif; (*US*) sparadrap *m*.

ad hoc [æd'hɔk] *adj* (*decision*) de circonstance; (*committee*) ad hoc.

ad infinitum ['ædɪnfɪ'naɪtəm] *adv* à l'infini.

adjacent [ə'dʒeɪsənt] *adj* adjacent(e), contigu(ë); **~ to** adjacent à.

adjective ['ædʒɛktɪv] *n* adjectif *m*.

adjoin [ə'dʒɔɪn] *vt* jouxter.

adjoining [ə'dʒɔɪnɪŋ] *adj* voisin(e), adjacent(e), attenant(e) ♦ *prep* voisin de, adjacent à.

adjourn [ə'dʒəːn] *vt* ajourner ♦ *vi* suspendre la séance; lever la séance; clore la session; (*go*) se retirer; **to ~ a meeting till the following week** reporter une réunion à la semaine suivante; **they ~ed to the pub** (*BRIT col*) ils ont filé au pub.

adjournment [ə'dʒəːnmənt] *n* (*period*) ajournement *m*.

Adjt *abbr* (*MIL*: = *adjutant*) Adj.

adjudicate [ə'dʒuːdɪkeɪt] *vt* (*contest*) juger; (*claim*) statuer (sur) ♦ *vi* se prononcer.

adjudication [ədʒuːdɪ'keɪʃən] *n* (*LAW*) jugement *m*.

adjust [ə'dʒʌst] *vt* ajuster, régler; rajuster ♦ *vi*: **to ~ (to)** s'adapter (à).

adjustable [ə'dʒʌstəbl] *adj* réglable.

adjuster [ə'dʒʌstə*] *n see* **loss.**

adjustment [ə'dʒʌstmənt] *n* ajustage *m*,

réglage *m*; (*of prices, wages*) rajustement *m*; (*of person*) adaptation *f*.

adjutant ['ædʒətənt] *n* adjudant *m*.

ad-lib [æd'lɪb] *vt, vi* improviser ♦ *n* improvisation *f* ♦ *adv*: **ad lib** à volonté, à discrétion.

adman ['ædmæn] *n* (*col*) publicitaire *m*.

admin ['ædmɪn] *n abbr* (*col*) = **administration**.

administer [əd'mɪnɪstə*] *vt* administrer; (*justice*) rendre.

administration [ədmɪnɪs'treɪʃən] *n* administration *f*; **the A~** (*US*) le gouvernement.

administrative [əd'mɪnɪstrətɪv] *adj* administratif(ive).

administrator [əd'mɪnɪstreɪtə*] *n* administrateur/trice.

admirable ['ædmərəbl] *adj* admirable.

admiral ['ædmərəl] *n* amiral *m*.

Admiralty ['ædmərəltɪ] *n* (*BRIT: also*: ~ **Board**) ministère *m* de la Marine.

admiration [ædmə'reɪʃən] *n* admiration *f*.

admire [əd'maɪə*] *vt* admirer.

admirer [əd'maɪərə*] *n* admirateur/trice.

admiring [əd'maɪərɪŋ] *adj* admiratif(ive).

admissible [əd'mɪsəbl] *adj* acceptable, admissible; (*evidence*) recevable.

admission [əd'mɪʃən] *n* admission *f*; (*to exhibition, night club etc*) entrée *f*; (*confession*) aveu *m*; "~ **free**", "**free** ~" "entrée libre"; **by his own** ~ de son propre aveu.

admit [əd'mɪt] *vt* laisser entrer; admettre; (*agree*) reconnaître, admettre; "**children not ~ted**" "entrée interdite aux enfants"; **this ticket ~s two** ce billet est valable pour deux personnes; **I must** ~ **that** ... je dois admettre *or* reconnaître que ....

▶**admit of** *vt fus* admettre, permettre.

▶**admit to** *vt fus* reconnaître, avouer.

admittance [əd'mɪtəns] *n* admission *f*, (droit *m* d')entrée *f*; "**no** ~" "défense d'entrer".

admittedly [əd'mɪtɪdlɪ] *adv* il faut en convenir.

admonish [əd'mɔnɪʃ] *vt* donner un avertissement à; réprimander.

ad nauseam [æd'nɔːsɪæm] *adv* à satiété.

ado [ə'duː] *n*: **without (any) more** ~ sans plus de cérémonies.

adolescence [ædəu'lɛsns] *n* adolescence *f*.

adolescent [ædəu'lɛsnt] *adj, n* adolescent(e).

adopt [ə'dɔpt] *vt* adopter.

adopted [ə'dɔptɪd] *adj* adoptif(ive), adopté(e).

adoption [ə'dɔpʃən] *n* adoption *f*.

adore [ə'dɔː*] *vt* adorer.

adoring [ə'dɔːrɪŋ] *adj*: **his** ~ **wife** sa femme qui est en adoration devant lui.

adoringly [ə'dɔːrɪŋlɪ] *adv* avec adoration.

adorn [ə'dɔːn] *vt* orner.

adornment [ə'dɔːnmənt] *n* ornement *m*.

ADP *n abbr* = **automatic data processing**.

adrenalin [ə'drɛnəlɪn] *n* adrénaline *f*; **to get the** ~ **going** faire monter le taux

d'adrénaline.

Adriatic (Sea) [eɪdrɪ'ætɪk-] *n* Adriatique *f*.

adrift [ə'drɪft] *adv* à la dérive; **to come** ~ (*boat*) aller à la dérive; (*wire, rope, fastening etc*) se défaire.

adroit [ə'drɔɪt] *adj* adroit(e), habile.

ADT *abbr* (*US*: = *Atlantic Daylight Time*) *heure d'été de New York*.

adult ['ædʌlt] *n* adulte *m/f*.

adult education *n* éducation *f* des adultes.

adulterate [ə'dʌltəreɪt] *vt* frelater, falsifier.

adulterer [ə'dʌltərə*] *n* homme *m* adultère.

adulteress [ə'dʌltərɪs] *n* femme *f* adultère.

adultery [ə'dʌltərɪ] *n* adultère *m*.

adulthood ['ædʌlthud] *n* âge *m* adulte.

advance [əd'vɑːns] *n* avance *f* ♦ *vt* avancer ♦ *vi* s'avancer; **in** ~ en avance, d'avance; **to make** ~**s to sb** (*gen*) faire des propositions à qn; (*amorously*) faire des avances à qn.

advanced [əd'vɑːnst] *adj* avancé(e); (*SCOL: studies*) supérieur(e); ~ **in years** d'un âge avancé.

advancement [əd'vɑːnsmənt] *n* avancement *m*.

advance notice *n* préavis *m*.

advantage [əd'vɑːntɪdʒ] *n* (*also TENNIS*) avantage *m*; **to take** ~ **of** profiter de; **it's to our** ~ c'est notre intérêt; **it's to our** ~ **to** ... nous avons intérêt à ....

advantageous [ædvən'teɪdʒəs] *adj* avantageux(euse).

advent ['ædvənt] *n* avènement *m*, venue *f*; **A~** (*REL*) avent *m*.

Advent calendar *n* calendrier *m* de l'avent.

adventure [əd'vɛntʃə*] *n* aventure *f*.

adventure playground *n* aire *f* de jeux.

adventurous [əd'vɛntʃərəs] *adj* aventureux(euse).

adverb ['ædvəːb] *n* adverbe *m*.

adversary ['ædvəsərɪ] *n* adversaire *m/f*.

adverse ['ædvəːs] *adj* contraire, adverse; ~ **to** hostile à; **in** ~ **circumstances** dans l'adversité.

adversity [əd'vəːsɪtɪ] *n* adversité *f*.

advert ['ædvəːt] *n abbr* (*BRIT*) = **advertisement**.

advertise ['ædvətaɪz] *vi(vt)* faire de la publicité *or* de la réclame (pour); (*in classified ads etc*) mettre une annonce (pour vendre); **to** ~ **for** (*staff*) recruter par (voie d')annonce.

advertisement [əd'vəːtɪsmənt] *n* (*COMM*) réclame *f*, publicité *f*; (*in classified ads etc*) annonce *f*.

advertiser ['ædvətaɪzə*] *n* annonceur *m*.

advertising ['ædvətaɪzɪŋ] *n* publicité *f*.

advertising agency *n* agence *f* de publicité.

advertising campaign *n* campagne *f* de publicité.

advice [əd'vaɪs] *n* conseils *mpl*; (*notification*) avis *m*; **piece of** ~ conseil; **to ask (sb) for** ~ demander conseil (à qn); **to take legal** ~ consulter un avocat.

advice note n (BRIT) avis m d'expédition.
advisable [əd'vaɪzəbl] adj recommandable, indiqué(e).
advise [əd'vaɪz] vt conseiller; **to ~ sb of sth** aviser or informer qn de qch; **to ~ sb against sth** déconseiller qch à qn; **to ~ sb against doing sth** conseiller à qn de ne pas faire qch; **you would be well/ill ~d to go** vous feriez mieux d'y aller/de ne pas y aller, vous auriez intérêt à y aller/à ne pas y aller.
advisedly [əd'vaɪzɪdlɪ] adv (deliberately) délibérément.
adviser [əd'vaɪzə*] n conseiller/ère.
advisory [əd'vaɪzərɪ] adj consultatif(ive); **in an ~ capacity** à titre consultatif.
advocate n ['ædvəkɪt] (upholder) défenseur m, avocat/e ♦ vt ['ædvəkeɪt] recommander, prôner; **to be an ~ of** être partisan/e de.
advt. abbr = **advertisement**.
AEA n abbr (BRIT: = Atomic Energy Authority) ≈ AEN f (= Agence pour l'énergie nucléaire).
AEC n abbr (US: = Atomic Energy Commission) CEA m (= Commissariat à l'énergie atomique).
AEEU n abbr (BRIT: = Amalgamated Engineering and Electrical Union) syndicat de techniciens et d'électriciens.
Aegean (Sea) [iː'dʒiːən-] n mer f Égée.
aegis ['iːdʒɪs] n: **under the ~ of** sous l'égide de.
aeon ['iːən] n éternité f.
aerial ['ɛərɪəl] n antenne f ♦ adj aérien(ne).
aerie ['ɛərɪ] n (US) aire f.
aerobatics ['ɛərəu'bætɪks] npl acrobaties aériennes.
aerobics [ɛə'rəubɪks] n aérobic m.
aerodrome ['ɛərədrəum] n (BRIT) aérodrome m.
aerodynamic ['ɛərəudaɪ'næmɪk] adj aérodynamique.
aeronautics [ɛərə'nɔːtɪks] n aéronautique f.
aeroplane ['ɛərəpleɪn] n (BRIT) avion m.
aerosol ['ɛərəsɔl] n aérosol m.
aerospace industry ['ɛərəuspeɪs-] n (industrie) aérospatiale f.
aesthetic [ɪs'θɛtɪk] adj esthétique.
afar [ə'faː*] adv: **from ~** de loin.
AFB n abbr (US) = **Air Force Base**.
AFDC n abbr (US: = Aid to Families with Dependent Children) aide pour enfants assistés.
affable ['æfəbl] adj affable.
affair [ə'fɛə*] n affaire f; (also: **love ~**) liaison f; aventure f; **~s** (business) affaires.
affect [ə'fɛkt] vt affecter.
affectation [æfɛk'teɪʃən] n affectation f.
affected [ə'fɛktɪd] adj affecté(e).
affection [ə'fɛkʃən] n affection f.
affectionate [ə'fɛkʃənɪt] adj affectueux(euse).
affectionately [ə'fɛkʃənɪtlɪ] adv affectueusement.
affidavit [æfɪ'deɪvɪt] n (LAW) déclaration

écrite sous serment.
affiliated [ə'fɪlɪeɪtɪd] adj affilié(e); **~ company** filiale f.
affinity [ə'fɪnɪtɪ] n affinité f.
affirm [ə'fəːm] vt affirmer.
affirmation [æfə'meɪʃən] n affirmation f, assertion f.
affirmative [ə'fəːmətɪv] adj affirmatif(ive) ♦ n: **in the ~** dans or par l'affirmative.
affix [ə'fɪks] vt apposer, ajouter.
afflict [ə'flɪkt] vt affliger.
affliction [ə'flɪkʃən] n affliction f.
affluence ['æfluəns] n aisance f, opulence f.
affluent ['æfluənt] adj opulent(e); (person) dans l'aisance, riche; **the ~ society** la société d'abondance.
afford [ə'fɔːd] vt (goods etc) avoir les moyens d'acheter or d'entretenir; (behaviour) se permettre; (provide) fournir, procurer; **can we ~ a car?** avons-nous de quoi acheter or les moyens d'acheter une voiture?; **I can't ~ the time** je n'ai vraiment pas le temps.
affordable [ə'fɔːdəbl] adj abordable.
affray [ə'freɪ] n (BRIT LAW) échauffourée f, rixe f.
affront [ə'frʌnt] n affront m.
affronted [ə'frʌntɪd] adj insulté(e).
Afghan ['æfgæn] adj afghan(e) ♦ n Afghan/e.
Afghanistan [æf'gænɪstæn] n Afghanistan m.
afield [ə'fiːld] adv: **far ~** loin.
AFL-CIO n abbr (= American Federation of Labor and Congress of Industrial Organizations) confédération syndicale.
afloat [ə'fləut] adj à flot ♦ adv: **to stay ~** surnager; **to keep/get a business ~** maintenir à flot/lancer une affaire.
afoot [ə'fut] adv: **there is something ~** il se prépare quelque chose.
aforementioned [ə'fɔːmɛnʃənd] adj, **aforesaid** [ə'fɔːsɛd] adj susdit(e), susmentionné(e).
afraid [ə'freɪd] adj effrayé(e); **to be ~ of** or **to** avoir peur de; **I am ~ that** je crains que + sub; **I'm ~ so/not** oui/non, malheureusement.
afresh [ə'frɛʃ] adv de nouveau.
Africa ['æfrɪkə] n Afrique f.
African ['æfrɪkən] adj africain(e) ♦ n Africain/e.
Afrikaans [æfrɪ'kɑːns] n afrikaans m.
Afrikaner [æfrɪ'kɑːnə*] n Afrikaner m/f.
Afro-American ['æfrəu'mɛrɪkən] adj afro-américain(e).
AFT n abbr (= American Federation of Teachers) syndicat enseignant.
aft [ɑːft] adv à l'arrière, vers l'arrière.
after ['ɑːftə*] prep, adv après ♦ conj après que, après avoir or être + pp; **~ dinner** après (le) dîner; **the day ~ tomorrow** après demain; **quarter ~ two** (US) deux heures et quart; **what/who are you ~?** que/qui cherchez-vous?; **the police are ~ him** la police est à ses trousses; **~ you!** après vous!; **~ all**

après tout.

afterbirth ['ɑ:ftəbə:θ] *n* placenta *m*.

aftercare ['ɑ:ftəkɛə*] *n* (*BRIT MED*) post-cure *f*.

after-effects ['ɑ:ftərɪfɛkts] *npl* répercussions *fpl*; (*of illness*) séquelles *fpl*, suites *fpl*.

afterlife ['ɑ:ftəlaif] *n* vie future.

aftermath ['ɑ:ftəmɑ:θ] *n* conséquences *fpl*; **in the ~ of** dans les mois *or* années *etc* qui suivirent, au lendemain de.

afternoon ['ɑ:ftə'nu:n] *n* après-midi *m or f*; **good ~!** bonjour!; (*goodbye*) au revoir!

afters ['ɑ:ftəz] *n* (*BRIT col: dessert*) dessert *m*.

after-sales service [ɑ:ftə'seɪlz-] *n* service *m* après-vente, SAV *m*.

after-shave (lotion) ['ɑ:ftəʃeɪv-] *n* lotion *f* après-rasage.

aftershock ['ɑ:ftəʃɔk] *n* réplique *f* (sismique).

aftertaste ['ɑ:ftəteɪst] *n* arrière-goût *m*.

afterthought ['ɑ:ftəθɔ:t] *n*: **I had an ~** il m'est venu une idée après coup.

afterwards ['ɑ:ftəwədz] *adv* après.

again [ə'gɛn] *adv* de nouveau, encore une fois; **to begin/see ~** recommencer/revoir; **not ~ ...** ne ... plus; ~ **and ~** à plusieurs reprises; **he's opened it ~** il l'a rouvert, il l'a de nouveau *or* l'a encore ouvert; **now and ~** de temps à autre.

against [ə'gɛnst] *prep* contre; ~ **a blue background** sur un fond bleu; (**as**) ~ (*BRIT*) contre.

age [eɪdʒ] *n* âge *m* ♦ *vt, vi* vieillir; **what ~ is he?** quel âge a-t-il?; **he is 20 years of ~** il a 20 ans; **under ~** mineur(e); **to come of ~** atteindre sa majorité; **it's been ~s since** ça fait une éternité que ... ne ..

aged ['eɪdʒd] *adj* âgé(e); ~ **10** âgé de 10 ans; **the ~** ['eɪdʒɪd] *npl* les personnes âgées.

age group *n* tranche *f* d'âge; **the 40 to 50 ~** la tranche d'âge des 40 à 50 ans.

ageing ['eɪdʒɪŋ] *adj* vieillissant(e).

ageless ['eɪdʒlɪs] *adj* sans âge.

age limit *n* limite *f* d'âge.

agency ['eɪdʒənsɪ] *n* agence *f*; **through** *or* **by the ~ of** par l'entremise *or* l'action de.

agenda [ə'dʒɛndə] *n* ordre *m* du jour; **on the ~** à l'ordre du jour.

agent ['eɪdʒənt] *n* agent *m*.

aggravate ['ægrəveɪt] *vt* aggraver; (*annoy*) exaspérer, agacer.

aggravation [ægrə'veɪʃən] *n* agacements *mpl*.

aggregate ['ægrɪgɪt] *n* ensemble *m*, total *m*; **on ~** (*SPORT*) au total des points.

aggression [ə'grɛʃən] *n* agression *f*.

aggressive [ə'grɛsɪv] *adj* agressif(ive).

aggressiveness [ə'grɛsɪvnɪs] *n* agressivité *f*.

aggressor [ə'grɛsə*] *n* agresseur *m*.

aggrieved [ə'gri:vd] *adj* chagriné(e), affligé(e).

aggro ['ægrəʊ] *n* (*col: physical*) grabuge *m*; (*: hassle*) embêtements *mpl*.

aghast [ə'gɑ:st] *adj* consterné(e), atterré(e).

agile ['ædʒaɪl] *adj* agile.

agility [ə'dʒɪlɪtɪ] *n* agilité *f*, souplesse *f*.

agitate ['ædʒɪteɪt] *vt* rendre inquiet(ète) *or* agité(e) ♦ *vi* faire de l'agitation (politique); **to ~ for** faire campagne pour.

agitator ['ædʒɪteɪtə*] *n* agitateur/trice (politique).

AGM *n abbr* = **annual general meeting**.

ago [ə'gəʊ] *adv*: **2 days ~** il y a 2 jours; **not long ~** il n'y a pas longtemps; **as long ~ as 1960** déjà en 1960; **how long ~?** il y a combien de temps (de cela)?

agog [ə'gɔg] *adj*: (**all**) ~ en émoi.

agonize ['ægənaɪz] *vi*: **he ~d over the problem** ce problème lui a causé bien du tourment.

agonizing ['ægənaɪzɪŋ] *adj* angoissant(e); (*cry*) déchirant(e).

agony ['ægənɪ] *n* grande souffrance *or* angoisse; **to be in ~** souffrir le martyre.

agony aunt *n* (*BRIT col*) journaliste qui tient la rubrique du courrier du cœur.

agony column *n* courrier *m* du cœur.

agree [ə'gri:] *vt* (*price*) convenir de ♦ *vi*: **to ~ (with)** (*person*) être d'accord (avec); (*statements etc*) concorder (avec); (*LING*) s'accorder (avec); **to ~ to do** accepter de *or* consentir à faire; **to ~ to sth** consentir à qch; **to ~ that** (*admit*) convenir *or* reconnaître que; **it was ~d that ...** il a été convenu que ...; **they ~ on this** ils sont d'accord sur ce point; **they ~d on going/a price** ils se mirent d'accord pour y aller/sur un prix; **garlic doesn't ~ with me** je ne supporte pas l'ail.

agreeable [ə'gri:əbl] *adj* (*pleasant*) agréable; (*willing*) consentant(e), d'accord; **are you ~ to this?** est-ce que vous êtes d'accord?

agreed [ə'gri:d] *adj* (*time, place*) convenu(e); **to be ~** être d'accord.

agreement [ə'gri:mənt] *n* accord *m*; **in ~** d'accord; **by mutual ~** d'un commun accord.

agricultural [ægrɪ'kʌltʃərəl] *adj* agricole.

agriculture ['ægrɪkʌltʃə*] *n* agriculture *f*.

aground [ə'graund] *adv*: **to run ~** s'échouer.

ahead [ə'hɛd] *adv* en avant; devant; **go right** *or* **straight ~** allez tout droit; **go ~!** (*fig*) allez-y!; ~ **of** devant; (*fig: schedule etc*) en avance sur; ~ **of time** en avance; **they were (right)** ~ **of us** ils nous précédaient (de peu), ils étaient (juste) devant nous.

AI *n abbr* = **Amnesty International**; (*COMPUT*) = **artificial intelligence**.

AIB *n abbr* (*BRIT*: = *Accident Investigation Bureau*) commission d'enquête sur les accidents.

AID *n abbr* (= *artificial insemination by donor*) IAD *f*; (*US*: = *Agency for International Development*) agence pour le développement international.

aid [eɪd] *n* aide *f* ♦ *vt* aider; **with the ~ of** avec l'aide de; **in ~ of** en faveur de; **to ~ and abet** (*LAW*) se faire le complice de.

aide [eɪd] *n* (*person*) assistant/e.

AIDS [eɪdz] *n abbr* (= *acquired immune* (*or immuno-*)*deficiency syndrome*) SIDA *m*.
AIH *n abbr* (= *artificial insemination by husband*) IAC *f*.
ailment ['eɪlmənt] *n* affection *f*.
aim [eɪm] *n* but *m* ♦ *vt*: **to ~ sth at** (*gun, camera*) braquer *or* pointer qch sur, diriger qch contre; (*missile*) pointer qch vers *or* sur; (*remark, blow*) destiner *or* adresser qch à ♦ *vi* (*also*: **to take ~**) viser; **to ~ at** viser; (*fig*) viser (à); avoir pour but *or* ambition; **to ~ to do** avoir l'intention de faire.
aimless ['eɪmlɪs] *adj* sans but.
aimlessly ['eɪmlɪslɪ] *adv* sans but.
ain't [eɪnt] (*col*) = **am not, aren't, isn't**.
air [ɛə*] *n* air *m* ♦ *vt* aérer; (*idea, grievance, views*) mettre sur le tapis; (*knowledge*) faire étalage de ♦ *cpd* (*currents, attack etc*) aérien(ne); **by ~** par avion; **to be on the ~** (*RADIO, TV: programme*) être diffusé(e); (: *station*) émettre.
air bag *n* airbag *m*.
air base *n* base aérienne.
airbed ['ɛəbɛd] *n* (*BRIT*) matelas *m* pneumatique.
airborne ['ɛəbɔːn] *adj* (*plane*) en vol; (*troops*) aeroporté(e); (*particles*) dans l'air; **as soon as the plane was ~** dès que l'avion eut décollé.
air cargo *n* fret aérien.
air-conditioned ['ɛəkən'dɪʃənd] *adj* climatisé(e), à air conditionné.
air conditioning [-kən'dɪʃnɪŋ] *n* climatisation *f*.
air-cooled ['ɛəkuːld] *adj* à refroidissement à air.
aircraft ['ɛəkrɑːft] *n* (*pl inv*) avion *m*.
aircraft carrier *n* porte-avions *m inv*.
air cushion *n* coussin *m* d'air.
airdrome ['ɛədrəum] *n* (*US*) aérodrome *m*.
airfield ['ɛəfiːld] *n* terrain *m* d'aviation.
Air Force *n* Armée *f* de l'air.
air freight *n* fret aérien.
airgun ['ɛəgʌn] *n* fusil *m* à air comprimé.
air hostess *n* (*BRIT*) hôtesse *f* de l'air.
airily ['ɛərɪlɪ] *adv* d'un air dégagé.
airing ['ɛərɪŋ] *n*: **to give an ~ to** aérer; (*fig: ideas, views etc*) mettre sur le tapis.
air letter *n* (*BRIT*) aérogramme *m*.
airlift ['ɛəlɪft] *n* pont aérien.
airline ['ɛəlaɪn] *n* ligne aérienne, compagnie aérienne.
airliner ['ɛəlaɪnə*] *n* avion *m* de ligne.
airlock ['ɛəlɔk] *n* sas *m*.
airmail ['ɛəmeɪl] *n*: **by ~** par avion.
air mattress *n* matelas *m* pneumatique.
airplane ['ɛəpleɪn] *n* (*US*) avion *m*.
air pocket *n* trou *m* d'air.
airport ['ɛəpɔːt] *n* aéroport *m*.
air raid *n* attaque aérienne.
air rifle *n* carabine *f* à air comprimé.
airsick ['ɛəsɪk] *adj*: **to be ~** avoir le mal de l'air.

airspeed ['ɛəspiːd] *n* vitesse relative.
airstrip ['ɛəstrɪp] *n* terrain *m* d'atterrissage.
air terminal *n* aérogare *f*.
airtight ['ɛətaɪt] *adj* hermétique.
air time *n* (*RADIO, TV*) temps *m* d'antenne.
air traffic control *n* contrôle *m* de la navigation aérienne.
air traffic controller *n* aiguilleur *m* du ciel.
airway ['ɛəweɪ] *n* (*AVIAT*) voie aérienne; **~s** (*ANAT*) voies aériennes.
airy ['ɛərɪ] *adj* bien aéré(e); (*manners*) dégagé(e).
aisle [aɪl] *n* (*of church*) allée centrale; nef latérale; (*in theatre*) allée *f*; (*on plane*) couloir *m*.
ajar [ə'dʒɑː*] *adj* entrouvert(e).
AK *abbr* (*US*) = **Alaska**.
aka *abbr* (= *also known as*) alias.
akin [ə'kɪn] *adj*: **~ to** semblable à, du même ordre que.
AL *abbr* (*US*) = **Alabama**.
ALA *n abbr* = *American Library Association*.
Ala. *abbr* (*US*) = **Alabama**.
alacrity [ə'lækrɪtɪ] *n*: **with ~** avec empressement, promptement.
alarm [ə'lɑːm] *n* alarme *f* ♦ *vt* alarmer.
alarm clock *n* réveille-matin *m inv*, réveil *m*.
alarmed [ə'lɑːmd] *adj* (*frightened*) alarmé(e); (*protected by an alarm*) protégé(e) par un système d'alarme; **to become ~** prendre peur.
alarming [ə'lɑːmɪŋ] *adj* alarmant(e).
alarmingly [ə'lɑːmɪŋlɪ] *adv* d'une manière alarmante; **~ close** dangereusement proche; **~ quickly** à une vitesse inquiétante.
alarmist [ə'lɑːmɪst] *n* alarmiste *m/f*.
alas [ə'læs] *excl* hélas.
Alas. *abbr* (*US*) = **Alaska**.
Alaska [ə'læskə] *n* Alaska *m*.
Albania [æl'beɪnɪə] *n* Albanie *f*.
Albanian [æl'beɪnɪən] *adj* albanais(e) ♦ *n* Albanais/e; (*LING*) albanais *m*.
albatross ['ælbətrɔs] *n* albatros *m*.
albeit [ɔːl'biːɪt] *conj* bien que + *sub*, encore que + *sub*.
album ['ælbəm] *n* album *m*.
albumen ['ælbjumɪn] *n* albumine *f*; (*of egg*) albumen *m*.
alchemy ['ælkɪmɪ] *n* alchimie *f*.
alcohol ['ælkəhɔl] *n* alcool *m*.
alcohol-free ['ælkəhɔlfriː] *adj* sans alcool.
alcoholic [ælkə'hɔlɪk] *adj, n* alcoolique (*m/f*).
alcoholism ['ælkəhɔlɪzəm] *n* alcoolisme *m*.
alcove ['ælkəuv] *n* alcôve *f*.
Ald. *abbr* = **alderman**.
alderman ['ɔːldəmən] *n* conseiller municipal (*en Angleterre*).
ale [eɪl] *n* bière *f*.
alert [ə'lɔːt] *adj* alerte, vif(vive); (*watchful*) vigilant(e) ♦ *n* alerte *f* ♦ *vt*: **to ~ sb (to sth)** attirer l'attention de qn (sur qch); **to ~ sb**

to the dangers of sth avertir qn des dangers de qch; **on the ~** sur le qui-vive; (*MIL*) en état d'alerte.

Aleutian Islands [ə'lu:ʃən-] *npl* îles Aléoutiennes.

A levels *npl* ≈ baccalauréat *msg*.

Alexandria [ælɪg'zɑ:ndrɪə] *n* Alexandrie.

alfresco [æl'freskəu] *adj, adv* en plein air.

algebra ['ældʒɪbrə] *n* algèbre *m*.

Algeria [æl'dʒɪərɪə] *n* Algérie *f*.

Algerian [æl'dʒɪərɪən] *adj* algérien(ne) ♦ *n* Algérien/ne.

Algiers [æl'dʒɪəz] *n* Alger.

algorithm ['ælgərɪðm] *n* algorithme *m*.

alias ['eɪlɪəs] *adv* alias ♦ *n* faux nom, nom d'emprunt.

alibi ['ælɪbaɪ] *n* alibi *m*.

alien ['eɪlɪən] *n* étranger/ère ♦ *adj*: ~ **(to)** étranger(ère) (à).

alienate ['eɪlɪəneɪt] *vt* aliéner; (*subj: person*) s'aliéner.

alienation [eɪlɪə'neɪʃən] *n* aliénation *f*.

alight [ə'laɪt] *adj, adv* en feu ♦ *vi* mettre pied à terre; (*passenger*) descendre; (*bird*) se poser.

align [ə'laɪn] *vt* aligner.

alignment [ə'laɪnmənt] *n* alignement *m*; **it's out of ~ (with)** ce n'est pas aligné (avec).

alike [ə'laɪk] *adj* semblable, pareil(le) ♦ *adv* de même; **to look ~** se ressembler.

alimony ['ælɪmənɪ] *n* (*payment*) pension *f* alimentaire.

alive [ə'laɪv] *adj* vivant(e); (*active*) plein(e) de vie; ~ **with** grouillant(e) de; ~ **to** sensible à.

alkali ['ælkəlaɪ] *n* alcali *m*.

═══════════════════════════ *KEYWORD*

all [ɔ:l] *adj* (*singular*) tout(e); (*plural*) tous(toutes); ~ **day** tout le jour; ~ **night** toute la nuit; ~ **men** tous les hommes; ~ **five** tous les cinq; ~ **the food** toute la nourriture; ~ **the books** tous les livres; ~ **the time** tout le temps; ~ **his life** toute sa vie ♦ *pron* **1** tout; **I ate it ~, I ate ~ of it** j'ai tout mangé; ~ **of us went** nous y sommes tous allés; ~ **of the boys went** tous les garçons y sont allés; **is that ~?** c'est tout?; (*in shop*) ce sera tout?

2 (*in phrases*): **above ~** surtout, par-dessus tout; **after ~** après tout; **at ~: not at ~** (*in answer to question*) pas du tout; (*in answer to thanks*) je vous en prie!; **I'm not at ~ tired** je ne suis pas du tout fatigué(e); **anything at ~ will do** n'importe quoi fera l'affaire; ~ **in ~** tout bien considéré, en fin de compte ♦ *adv*: ~ **alone** tout(e) seul(e); **it's not as hard as ~ that** ce n'est pas si difficile que ça; ~ **the more/the better** d'autant plus/mieux; ~ **but** presque, pratiquement; **to be ~ in** (*BRIT col*) être complètement à plat; ~ **out** *adv* à fond; **the score is 2 ~** le score est de 2 partout.

all-around [ɔ:lə'raund] *adj* (*US*) = **all-round**.

allay [ə'leɪ] *vt* (*fears*) apaiser, calmer.

all clear *n* (*also fig*) fin *f* d'alerte.

allegation [ælɪ'geɪʃən] *n* allégation *f*.

allege [ə'lɛdʒ] *vt* alléguer, prétendre; **he is ~d to have said** il aurait dit.

alleged [ə'lɛdʒd] *adj* prétendu(e).

allegedly [ə'lɛdʒɪdlɪ] *adv* à ce que l'on prétend, paraît-il.

allegiance [ə'li:dʒəns] *n* fidélité *f*, obéissance *f*.

allegory ['ælɪgərɪ] *n* allégorie *f*.

all-embracing ['ɔ:lɪm'breɪsɪŋ] *adj* universel(le).

allergic [ə'lə:dʒɪk] *adj*: ~ **to** allergique à.

allergy ['ælədʒɪ] *n* allergie *f*.

alleviate [ə'li:vɪeɪt] *vt* soulager, adoucir.

alley ['ælɪ] *n* ruelle *f*; (*in garden*) allée *f*.

alleyway ['ælɪweɪ] *n* ruelle *f*.

alliance [ə'laɪəns] *n* alliance *f*.

allied ['ælaɪd] *adj* allié(e).

alligator ['ælɪgeɪtə*] *n* alligator *m*.

all-important ['ɔ:lɪm'pɔ:tənt] *adj* capital(e), crucial(e).

all-in ['ɔ:lɪn] *adj, adv* (*BRIT: charge*) tout compris.

all-in wrestling *n* (*BRIT*) catch *m*.

alliteration [əlɪtə'reɪʃən] *n* allitération *f*.

all-night ['ɔ:l'naɪt] *adj* ouvert(e) *or* qui dure toute la nuit.

allocate ['æləkeɪt] *vt* (*share out*) répartir, distribuer; (*duties*): **to ~ sth to** assigner *or* attribuer qch à; (*sum, time*): **to ~ sth to** allouer qch à; **to ~ sth for** affecter qch à.

allocation [æləu'keɪʃən] *n* (*see vb*) répartition *f*; attribution *f*; allocation *f*; affectation *f*; (*money*) crédit(s) *m(pl)*, somme(s) allouée(s).

allot [ə'lɔt] *vt* (*share out*) répartir, distribuer; (*time*): **to ~ sth to** allouer qch à; (*duties*): **to ~ sth to** assigner qch à; **in the ~ted time** dans le temps imparti.

allotment [ə'lɔtmənt] *n* (*share*) part *f*; (*garden*) lopin *m* de terre (*loué à la municipalité*).

all-out ['ɔ:laut] *adj* (*effort etc*) total(e).

allow [ə'lau] *vt* (*practice, behaviour*) permettre, autoriser; (*sum to spend etc*) accorder, allouer; (*sum, time estimated*) compter, prévoir; (*concede*): **to ~ that** convenir que; **to ~ sb to do** permettre à qn de faire, autoriser qn à faire; **he is ~ed to ...** on lui permet de ...; **smoking is not ~ed** il est interdit de fumer; **we must ~ 3 days for the journey** il faut compter 3 jours pour le voyage.

▶ **allow for** *vt fus* tenir compte de.

allowance [ə'lauəns] *n* (*money received*) allocation *f*; (: *from parent etc*) subside *m*; (: *for expenses*) indemnité *f*; (*TAX*) somme *f* déductible du revenu imposable, abattement *m*; **to make ~s for** tenir compte de.

alloy ['ælɔɪ] *n* alliage *m*.

all right *adv* (*feel, work*) bien; (*as answer*) d'accord.

all-round ['ɔːl'raund] adj compétent(e) dans tous les domaines; (athlete etc) complet(ète).

all-rounder [ɔːl'raundə*] n (BRIT): **to be a good ~** être doué(e) en tout.

allspice ['ɔːlspaɪs] n poivre m de la Jamaïque.

all-time ['ɔːl'taɪm] adj (record) sans précédent, absolu(e).

allude [ə'luːd] vi: **to ~ to** faire allusion à.

alluring [ə'ljuərɪŋ] adj séduisant(e), alléchant(e).

allusion [ə'luːʒən] n allusion f.

alluvium [ə'luːvɪəm] n alluvions fpl.

ally n ['ælaɪ] allié m ♦ vt [ə'laɪ]: **to ~ o.s. with** s'allier avec.

almighty [ɔːl'maɪtɪ] adj tout-puissant.

almond ['ɑːmənd] n amande f.

almost ['ɔːlməust] adv presque; **he ~ fell** il a failli tomber.

alms [ɑːmz] n aumône(s) f(pl).

aloft [ə'lɔft] adv en haut, en l'air; (NAUT) dans la mâture.

alone [ə'ləun] adj, adv seul(e); **to leave sb ~** laisser qn tranquille; **to leave sth ~** ne pas toucher à qch; **let ~ ... sans parler de ...;** encore moins ....

along [ə'lɔŋ] prep le long de ♦ adv: **is he coming ~?** vient-il avec nous?; **he was hopping/limping ~** il venait or avançait en sautillant/boitant; **~ with** avec, en plus de; (person) en compagnie de.

alongside [ə'lɔŋ'saɪd] prep le long de; au côté de ♦ adv bord à bord; côte à côte; **we brought our boat ~** (of a pier, shore etc) nous avons accosté.

aloof [ə'luːf] adj, adv à distance, à l'écart; **to stand ~** se tenir à l'écart or à distance.

aloofness [ə'luːfnɪs] n réserve (hautaine), attitude distante.

aloud [ə'laud] adv à haute voix.

alphabet ['ælfəbɛt] n alphabet m.

alphabetical [ælfə'bɛtɪkl] adj alphabétique; **in ~ order** par ordre alphabétique.

alphanumeric [ælfənjuː'mɛrɪk] adj alphanumérique.

alpine ['ælpaɪn] adj alpin(e), alpestre; **~ hut** cabane f or refuge m de montagne; **~ pasture** pâturage m (de montagne); **~ skiing** ski alpin.

Alps [ælps] npl: **the ~** les Alpes fpl.

already [ɔːl'rɛdɪ] adv déjà.

alright ['ɔːl'raɪt] adv (BRIT) = **all right**.

Alsace ['ælsæs] n Alsace f.

Alsatian [æl'seɪʃən] adj alsacien(ne), d'Alsace ♦ n Alsacien/ne; (BRIT: dog) berger allemand.

also ['ɔːlsəu] adv aussi.

Alta. abbr (Canada) = Alberta.

altar ['ɔltə*] n autel m.

alter ['ɔltə*] vt, vi changer, modifier.

alteration [ɔltə'reɪʃən] n changement m, modification f; **~s** (SEWING) retouches fpl; (ARCHIT) modifications fpl; **timetable subject to ~** horaires sujets à modifications.

altercation [ɔltə'keɪʃən] n altercation f.

alternate adj [ɔl'təːnɪt] alterné(e), alternant(e), alternatif(ive) ♦ vi ['ɔltəːneɪt] alterner; **on ~ days** un jour sur deux, tous les deux jours.

alternately [ɔl'təːnɪtlɪ] adv alternativement, en alternant.

alternating ['ɔltəːneɪtɪŋ] adj (current) alternatif(ive).

alternative [ɔl'təːnətɪv] adj (solutions) interchangeable, possible; (solution) autre, de remplacement; (energy) doux(douce); (society) parallèle ♦ n (choice) alternative f; (other possibility) autre possibilité f.

alternatively [ɔl'təːnətɪvlɪ] adv: **~ one could** une autre or l'autre solution serait de.

alternative medicine n médecines fpl parallèles or douces.

alternator ['ɔltəːneɪtə*] n (AUT) alternateur m.

although [ɔːl'ðəu] conj bien que + sub.

altitude ['æltɪtjuːd] n altitude f.

alto ['æltəu] n (female) contralto m; (male) haute-contre f.

altogether [ɔːltə'gɛðə*] adv entièrement, tout à fait; (on the whole) tout compte fait; (in all) en tout; **how much is that ~?** ça fait combien en tout?

altruism ['æltruɪzəm] n altruisme m.

altruistic [æltru'ɪstɪk] adj altruiste.

aluminium [ælju'mɪnɪəm], (US) **aluminum** [ə'luːmɪnəm] n aluminium m.

alumna, pl alumnae [ə'lʌmnə, -niː] n (US: SCOL) ancienne élève; (: UNIVERSITY) ancienne étudiante.

alumnus, pl alumni [ə'lʌmnəs, -naɪ] n (US: SCOL) ancien élève; (:UNIVERSITY) ancien étudiant.

always ['ɔːlweɪz] adv toujours.

Alzheimer's disease ['æltshaɪməz-] n maladie f d'Alzheimer.

AM abbr = amplitude modulation.

am [æm] vb see **be**.

a.m. adv abbr (= ante meridiem) du matin.

AMA n abbr = American Medical Association.

amalgam [ə'mælgəm] n amalgame m.

amalgamate [ə'mælgəmeɪt] vt, vi fusionner.

amalgamation [əmælgə'meɪʃən] n fusion f; (COMM) fusionnement m.

amass [ə'mæs] vt amasser.

amateur ['æmətə*] n amateur m ♦ adj (SPORT) amateur inv; **~ dramatics** le théâtre amateur.

amateurish ['æmətərɪʃ] adj (pej) d'amateur, un peu amateur.

amaze [ə'meɪz] vt surprendre, étonner; **to be ~d (at)** être surpris or étonné (de).

amazement [ə'meɪzmənt] n surprise f, étonnement m.

amazing [ə'meɪzɪŋ] adj étonnant(e), incroyable; (bargain, offer) exceptionnel(le).

amazingly [ə'meɪzɪŋlɪ] adv incroyablement.

Amazon ['æməzən] n (GEO, MYTHOLOGY)

Amazone *f* ♦ *cpd* amazonien(ne), de l'Amazone; **the ~ basin** le bassin de l'Amazone; **the ~ jungle** la forêt amazonienne.

Amazonian [æmə'zəʊnɪən] *adj* amazonien(ne).

ambassador [æm'bæsədə*] *n* ambassadeur *m*.

amber ['æmbə*] *n* ambre *m*; **at ~** (*BRIT AUT*) à l'orange.

ambidextrous [æmbɪ'dɛkstrəs] *adj* ambidextre.

ambience ['æmbɪəns] *n* ambiance *f*.

ambiguity [æmbɪ'gjuɪtɪ] *n* ambiguïté *f*.

ambiguous [æm'bɪgjuəs] *adj* ambigu(ë).

ambition [æm'bɪʃən] *n* ambition *f*.

ambitious [æm'bɪʃəs] *adj* ambitieux(euse).

ambivalent [æm'bɪvələnt] *adj* (*attitude*) ambivalent(e).

amble ['æmbl] *vi* (*also*: **to ~ along**) aller d'un pas tranquille.

ambulance ['æmbjuləns] *n* ambulance *f*.

ambush ['æmbʊʃ] *n* embuscade *f* ♦ *vt* tendre une embuscade à.

ameba [ə'miːbə] *n* (*US*) = **amoeba**.

ameliorate [ə'miːlɪəreɪt] *vt* améliorer.

amen ['ɑː'mɛn] *excl* amen.

amenable [ə'miːnəbl] *adj*: **~ to** (*advice etc*) disposé(e) à écouter *or* suivre; **~ to the law** responsable devant la loi.

amend [ə'mɛnd] *vt* (*law*) amender; (*text*) corriger; (*habits*) réformer ♦ *vi* s'amender, se corriger; **to make ~s** réparer ses torts, faire amende honorable.

amendment [ə'mɛndmənt] *n* (*to law*) amendement *m*; (*to text*) correction *f*.

amenities [ə'miːnɪtɪz] *npl* aménagements *mpl*, équipements *mpl*.

amenity [ə'miːnɪtɪ] *n* charme *m*, agrément *m*.

America [ə'mɛrɪkə] *n* Amérique *f*.

American [ə'mɛrɪkən] *adj* américain(e) ♦ *n* Américain/e.

americanize [ə'mɛrɪkənaɪz] *vt* américaniser.

amethyst ['æmɪθɪst] *n* améthyste *f*.

Amex ['æmɛks] *n abbr* = American Stock Exchange.

amiable ['eɪmɪəbl] *adj* aimable, affable.

amicable ['æmɪkəbl] *adj* amical(e).

amicably ['æmɪkəblɪ] *adv* amicalement.

amid(st) [ə'mɪd(st)] *prep* parmi, au milieu de.

amiss [ə'mɪs] *adj*, *adv*: **there's something ~** il y a quelque chose qui ne va pas *or* qui cloche; **to take sth ~** prendre qch mal *or* de travers.

ammo ['æməʊ] *n abbr* (*col*) = **ammunition**.

ammonia [ə'məʊnɪə] *n* (*gas*) ammoniac *m*; (*liquid*) ammoniaque *f*.

ammunition [æmju'nɪʃən] *n* munitions *fpl*; (*fig*) arguments *mpl*.

ammunition dump *n* dépôt *m* de munitions.

amnesia [æm'niːzɪə] *n* amnésie *f*.

amnesty ['æmnɪstɪ] *n* amnistie *f*; **to grant an ~** to accorder une amnistie à.

Amnesty International *n* Amnesty International.

amoeba, (*US*) **ameba** [ə'miːbə] *n* amibe *f*.

amok [ə'mɔk] *adv*: **to run ~** être pris(e) d'un accès de folie furieuse.

among(st) [ə'mʌŋ(st)] *prep* parmi, entre.

amoral [æ'mɔrəl] *adj* amoral(e).

amorous ['æmərəs] *adj* amoureux(euse).

amorphous [ə'mɔːfəs] *adj* amorphe.

amortization [əmɔːtaɪ'zeɪʃən] *n* (*COMM*) amortissement *m*.

amount [ə'maʊnt] *n* (*sum of money*) somme *f*; (*total*) montant *m*; (*quantity*) quantité *f*, nombre *m* ♦ *vi*: **to ~ to** (*total*) s'élever à; (*be same as*) équivaloir à, revenir à; **this ~s to a refusal** cela équivaut à un refus; **the total ~** (*of money*) le montant total.

amp(ere) ['æmp(ɛə*)] *n* ampère *m*; **a 13 amp plug** une fiche de 13 A.

ampersand ['æmpəsænd] *n* signe &, "et" commercial.

amphetamine [æm'fɛtəmiːn] *n* amphétamine *f*.

amphibian [æm'fɪbɪən] *n* batracien *m*.

amphibious [æm'fɪbɪəs] *adj* amphibie.

amphitheatre, (*US*) **amphitheater** ['æmfɪθɪətə*] *n* amphithéâtre *m*.

ample ['æmpl] *adj* ample; spacieux(euse); (*enough*): **this is ~** c'est largement suffisant; **to have ~ time/room** avoir bien assez de temps/place, avoir largement le temps/la place.

amplifier ['æmplɪfaɪə*] *n* amplificateur *m*.

amplify ['æmplɪfaɪ] *vt* amplifier.

amply ['æmplɪ] *adv* amplement, largement.

ampoule, (*US*) **ampule** ['æmpuːl] *n* (*MED*) ampoule *f*.

amputate ['æmpjuteɪt] *vt* amputer.

amputee [æmpju'tiː] *n* amputé/e.

Amsterdam ['æmstədæm] *n* Amsterdam.

amt *abbr* = **amount**.

amuck [ə'mʌk] *adv* = **amok**.

amuse [ə'mjuːz] *vt* amuser; **to ~ o.s. with sth/by doing sth** se divertir avec qch/à faire qch; **to be ~d at** être amusé par; **he was not ~d** il n'a pas apprécié.

amusement [ə'mjuːzmənt] *n* amusement *m*.

amusement arcade *n* salle *f* de jeu.

amusement park *n* parc *m* d'attractions.

amusing [ə'mjuːzɪŋ] *adj* amusant(e), divertissant(e).

an [æn, ən, n] *indef art see* **a**.

ANA *n abbr* = American Newspaper Association; American Nurses Association.

anachronism [ə'nækrənɪzəm] *n* anachronisme *m*.

anaemia [ə'niːmɪə] *n* anémie *f*.

anaemic [ə'niːmɪk] *adj* anémique.

anaesthetic [ænɪs'θɛtɪk] *adj*, *n* anesthésique (*m*); **under the ~** sous anesthésie; **local/general ~** anesthésie locale/générale.

anaesthetist [æ'niːsθɪtɪst] *n* anesthésiste *m/f*.

anagram ['ænəgræm] *n* anagramme *m*.

nal ['eɪnl] *adj* anal(e).

nalgesic [ænæl'dʒiːsɪk] *adj, n* analgésique *(m)*.

nalogous [ə'næləgəs] *adj*: ~ **(to** *or* **with)** analogue (à).

nalog(ue) ['ænələg] *adj (watch, computer)* analogique.

nalogy [ə'nælədʒɪ] *n* analogie *f*; **to draw an ~ between** établir une analogie entre.

nalyse ['ænəlaɪz] *vt (BRIT)* analyser.

nalysis, *pl* **analyses** [ə'næləsɪs, -siːz] *n* analyse *f*; **in the last ~** en dernière analyse.

nalyst ['ænəlɪst] *n (political ~ etc)* analyste *m/f*; *(US)* psychanalyste *m/f*.

nalytic(al) [ænə'lɪtɪk(əl)] *adj* analytique.

nalyze ['ænəlaɪz] *vt (US)* = **analyse**.

narchic [æ'nɑːkɪk] *adj* anarchique.

narchist ['ænəkɪst] *adj, n* anarchiste *(m/f)*.

narchy ['ænəkɪ] *n* anarchie *f*.

nathema [ə'næθɪmə] *n*: **it is ~ to him** il a cela en abomination.

natomical [ænə'tɔmɪkəl] *adj* anatomique.

natomy [ə'nætəmɪ] *n* anatomie *f*.

NC *n abbr (= African National Congress)* ANC *m*.

ncestor ['ænsɪstə*] *n* ancêtre *m*, aïeul *m*.

ncestral [æn'sɛstrəl] *adj* ancestral(e).

ncestry ['ænsɪstrɪ] *n* ancêtres *mpl*; ascendance *f*.

nchor ['æŋkə*] *n* ancre *f* ♦ *vi (also:* **to drop ~)** jeter l'ancre, mouiller ♦ *vt* mettre à l'ancre.

nchorage ['æŋkərɪdʒ] *n* mouillage *m*, ancrage *m*.

nchor man, anchor woman *n (TV, RADIO)* présentateur/trice.

nchovy ['æntʃəvɪ] *n* anchois *m*.

ncient ['eɪnʃənt] *adj* ancien(ne), antique; *(fig)* d'un âge vénérable, antique; **~ monument** monument *m* historique.

ncillary [æn'sɪlərɪ] *adj* auxiliaire.

nd [ænd] *conj* et; **~ so on** et ainsi de suite; **try ~ come** tâchez de venir; **come ~ sit here** venez vous asseoir ici; **better ~ better** de mieux en mieux; **more ~ more** de plus en plus.

ndes ['ændiːz] *npl*: **the ~** les Andes *fpl*.

necdote ['ænɪkdəut] *n* anecdote *f*.

nemia [ə'niːmɪə] *n* = **anaemia**.

nemic [ə'niːmɪk] *adj* = **anaemic**.

nemone [ə'nɛmənɪ] *n (BOT)* anémone *f*; **sea ~** anémone de mer.

nesthesiologist [ænɪsθiːzɪ'ɔlədʒɪst] *n (US)* anesthésiste *m/f*.

nesthetic [ænɪs'θetɪk] *adj, n* = **anaesthetic**.

nesthetist [æ'niːsθɪtɪst] *n* = **anaesthetist**.

new [ə'njuː] *adv* à nouveau.

ngel ['eɪndʒəl] *n* ange *m*.

ngel dust *n* poussière *f* d'ange.

nger ['æŋgə*] *n* colère *f* ♦ *vt* mettre en colère, irriter.

ngina [æn'dʒaɪnə] *n* angine *f* de poitrine.

ngle ['æŋgl] *n* angle *m* ♦ *vi*: **to ~ for** *(trout)* pêcher; *(compliments)* chercher, quêter;

from their ~ de leur point de vue.

angler ['æŋglə*] *n* pêcheur/euse à la ligne.

Anglican ['æŋglɪkən] *adj, n* anglican(e).

anglicize ['æŋglɪsaɪz] *vt* angliciser.

angling ['æŋglɪŋ] *n* pêche *f* à la ligne.

Anglo- ['æŋgləu] *prefix* anglo(-).

Anglo-French ['æŋgləu'frɛntʃ] *adj* anglo-français(e).

Anglo-Saxon ['æŋgləu'sæksən] *adj, n* anglo-saxon(ne).

Angola [æŋ'gəulə] *n* Angola *m*.

Angolan [æŋ'gəulən] *adj* angolais(e) ♦ *n* Angolais/e.

angrily ['æŋgrɪlɪ] *adv* avec colère.

angry ['æŋgrɪ] *adj* en colère, furieux(euse); **to be ~ with sb/at sth** être furieux contre qn/ de qch; **to get ~** se fâcher, se mettre en colère; **to make sb ~** mettre qn en colère.

anguish ['æŋgwɪʃ] *n* angoisse *f*.

anguished ['æŋgwɪʃt] *adj (mentally)* angoissé(e); *(physically)* plein(e) de souffrance.

angular ['æŋgjulə*] *adj* anguleux(euse).

animal ['ænɪməl] *n* animal *m* ♦ *adj* animal(e).

animal rights *npl* droits *mpl* de l'animal.

animate *vt* ['ænɪmeɪt] animer ♦ *adj* ['ænɪmɪt] animé(e), vivant(e).

animated ['ænɪmeɪtɪd] *adj* animé(e).

animation [ænɪ'meɪʃən] *n (of person)* entrain *m*; *(of street, CINE)* animation *f*.

animosity [ænɪ'mɔsɪtɪ] *n* animosité *f*.

aniseed ['ænɪsiːd] *n* anis *m*.

Ankara ['æŋkərə] *n* Ankara.

ankle ['æŋkl] *n* cheville *f*.

ankle socks *npl* socquettes *fpl*.

annex *n* ['ænɛks] *(also: BRIT:* **annexe)** annexe *f* ♦ *vt* [ə'nɛks] annexer.

annexation [ænɛks'eɪʃən] *n* annexion *f*.

annihilate [ə'naɪəleɪt] *vt* annihiler, anéantir.

annihilation [ənaɪə'leɪʃən] *n* anéantissement *m*.

anniversary [ænɪ'vəːsərɪ] *n* anniversaire *m*.

anniversary dinner *n* dîner commémoratif *or* anniversaire.

annotate ['ænəuteɪt] *vt* annoter.

announce [ə'nauns] *vt* annoncer; *(birth, death)* faire part de; **he ~d that he wasn't going** il a déclaré qu'il n'irait pas.

announcement [ə'naunsmənt] *n* annonce *f*; *(for births etc: in newspaper)* avis *m* de faire-part; *(: letter, card)* faire-part *m*; **I'd like to make an ~** j'ai une communication à faire.

announcer [ə'naunsə*] *n (RADIO, TV: between programmes)* speaker/ine; *(: in a programme)* présentateur/trice.

annoy [ə'nɔɪ] *vt* agacer, ennuyer, contrarier; **to be ~ed (at sth/with sb)** être en colère *or* irrité (contre qch/qn); **don't get ~ed!** ne vous fâchez pas!

annoyance [ə'nɔɪəns] *n* mécontentement *m*, contrariété *f*.

annoying [ə'nɔɪɪŋ] *adj* ennuyeux(euse),

agaçant(e), contrariant(e).
annual ['ænjuəl] *adj* annuel(le) ♦ *n* (*BOT*)
plante annuelle; (*book*) album *m*.
annual general meeting (AGM) *n* (*BRIT*)
assemblée générale annuelle (AGA).
annually ['ænjuəlɪ] *adv* annuellement.
annual report *n* rapport annuel.
annuity [ə'njuːɪtɪ] *n* rente *f*; **life** ~ rente
viagère.
annul [ə'nʌl] *vt* annuler; (*law*) abroger.
annulment [ə'nʌlmənt] *n* (*see vb*) annulation *f*;
abrogation *f*.
annum ['ænəm] *n see* **per annum**.
Annunciation [ənʌnsɪ'eɪʃən] *n* Annonciation *f*.
anode ['ænəud] *n* anode *f*.
anoint [ə'nɔɪnt] *vt* oindre.
anomalous [ə'nɔmələs] *adj* anormal(e).
anomaly [ə'nɔmælɪ] *n* anomalie *f*.
anon. [ə'nɔn] *abbr* = **anonymous**.
anonymity [ænə'nɪmɪtɪ] *n* anonymat *m*.
anonymous [ə'nɔnɪməs] *adj* anonyme; **to**
remain ~ garder l'anonymat.
anorak ['ænəræk] *n* anorak *m*.
anorexia [ænə'rɛksɪə] *n* (*also:* ~ **nervosa**)
anorexie *f*.
anorexic [ænə'rɛksɪk] *adj, n* anorexique (*m/f*).
another [ə'nʌðə*] *adj*: ~ **book** (*one more*) un
autre livre, encore un livre, un livre de
plus; (*a different one*) un autre livre; ~ **drink?**
encore un verre?; **in** ~ **5 years** dans 5 ans
♦ *pron* un(e) autre, encore un(e), un(e) de
plus; *see also* **one**.
ANSI ['ænsɪ] *n abbr* (= *American National
Standards Institution*) ANSI *m* (*Institut
américain de normalisation*).
answer ['ɑːnsə*] *n* réponse *f*; (*to problem*)
solution *f* ♦ *vi* répondre ♦ *vt* (*reply to*)
répondre à; (*problem*) résoudre; (*prayer*)
exaucer; **to** ~ **the phone** répondre (au
téléphone); **in** ~ **to your letter** suite à *or* en
réponse à votre lettre; **to** ~ **the bell** *or* **the**
door aller *or* venir ouvrir (la porte).
▶**answer back** *vi* répondre, répliquer.
▶**answer for** *vt fus* répondre de, se porter
garant de; (*crime, one's actions*) répondre de.
▶**answer to** *vt fus* (*description*) répondre *or*
correspondre à.
answerable ['ɑːnsərəbl] *adj*: ~ **(to sb/for sth)**
responsable (devant qn/de qch); **I am** ~ **to**
no-one je n'ai de comptes à rendre à
personne.
answering machine ['ɑːnsərɪŋ-] *n* répondeur
m.
ant [ænt] *n* fourmi *f*.
ANTA *n abbr* = *American National Theater and
Academy.*
antagonism [æn'tægənɪzəm] *n* antagonisme
m.
antagonist [æn'tægənɪst] *n* antagoniste *m/f*,
adversaire *m/f*.
antagonistic [æntægə'nɪstɪk] *adj* (*attitude,
feelings*) hostile.

antagonize [æn'tægənaɪz] *vt* éveiller
l'hostilité de, contrarier.
Antarctic [ænt'ɑːktɪk] *adj* antarctique,
austral(e) ♦ *n*: **the** ~ l'Antarctique *m*.
Antarctica [ænt'ɑːktɪkə] *n* Antarctique *m*,
Terres Australes.
Antarctic Circle *n* cercle *m* Antarctique.
Antarctic Ocean *n* océan *m* Antarctique *or*
Austral.
ante ['æntɪ] *n*: **to up the** ~ faire monter les
enjeux.
ante... ['æntɪ] *prefix* anté..., anti..., pré....
anteater ['æntiːtə*] *n* fourmilier *m*, tamanoir
m.
antecedent [æntɪ'siːdənt] *n* antécédent *m*.
antechamber ['æntɪtʃeɪmbə*] *n* antichambre
f.
antelope ['æntɪləup] *n* antilope *f*.
antenatal ['æntɪ'neɪtl] *adj* prénatal(e).
antenatal clinic *n* service *m* de consultation
prénatale.
antenna, *pl* ~**e** [æn'tɛnə, -niː] *n* antenne *f*.
anthem ['ænθəm] *n* motet *m*; **national** ~
hymne national.
ant-hill ['ænthɪl] *n* fourmilière *f*.
anthology [æn'θɔlədʒɪ] *n* anthologie *f*.
anthropologist [ænθrə'pɔlədʒɪst] *n*
anthropologue *m/f*.
anthropology [ænθrə'pɔlədʒɪ] *n* anthropologie
f.
anti- ['æntɪ] *prefix* anti-.
anti-aircraft ['æntɪ'ɛəkrɑːft] *adj*
antiaérien(ne).
anti-aircraft defence *n* défense *f* contre
avions, DCA *f*.
antiballistic [æntɪbə'lɪstɪk] *adj* antibalistique
antibiotic ['æntɪbaɪ'ɔtɪk] *adj, n* antibiotique
(*m*).
antibody ['æntɪbɔdɪ] *n* anticorps *m*.
anticipate [æn'tɪsɪpeɪt] *vt* s'attendre à,
prévoir; (*wishes, request*) aller au devant de,
devancer; **this is worse than I** ~**d** c'est pire
que je ne pensais; **as** ~**d** comme prévu.
anticipation [æntɪsɪ'peɪʃən] *n* attente *f*;
thanking you in ~ en vous remerciant
d'avance, avec mes remerciements
anticipés.
anticlimax ['æntɪ'klaɪmæks] *n réalisation
décevante d'un événement que l'on
escomptait important, intéressant etc.*
anticlockwise ['æntɪ'klɔkwaɪz] *adj* dans le
sens inverse des aiguilles d'une montre.
antics ['æntɪks] *npl* singeries *fpl*.
anticyclone ['æntɪ'saɪkləun] *n* anticyclone *m*.
antidote ['æntɪdəut] *n* antidote *m*,
contrepoison *m*.
antifreeze ['æntɪfriːz] *n* antigel *m*.
antihistamine [æntɪ'hɪstəmɪn] *n*
antihistaminique *m*.
Antilles [æn'tɪliːz] *npl*: **the** ~ les Antilles *fpl*.
antipathy [æn'tɪpəθɪ] *n* antipathie *f*.
antiperspirant [æntɪ'pəːspɪrənt] *n* déodorant

m anti-transpiration.

Antipodean [æntɪpə'diːən] *adj* australien(ne) et néozélandais(e), d'Australie et de Nouvelle-Zélande.

Antipodes [æn'tɪpədiːz] *npl*: **the** ~ l'Australie *f* et la Nouvelle-Zélande.

antiquarian [æntɪ'kwɛərɪən] *adj*: ~ **bookshop** librairie *f* d'ouvrages anciens ♦ *n* expert *m* en objets *or* livres anciens; amateur *m* d'antiquités.

antiquated ['æntɪkweɪtɪd] *adj* vieilli(e), suranné(e), vieillot(te).

antique [æn'tiːk] *n* objet *m* d'art ancien, meuble ancien *or* d'époque, antiquité *f* ♦ *adj* ancien(ne); (*pre-mediaeval*) antique.

antique dealer *n* antiquaire *m/f*.

antique shop *n* magasin *m* d'antiquités.

antiquity [æn'tɪkwɪtɪ] *n* antiquité *f*.

anti-Semitic ['æntɪsɪ'mɪtɪk] *adj* antisémite.

anti-Semitism ['æntɪ'semɪtɪzəm] *n* antisémitisme *m*.

antiseptic [æntɪ'septɪk] *adj, n* antiseptique (*m*).

antisocial ['æntɪ'səuʃəl] *adj* peu liant(e), sauvage, insociable; (*against society*) antisocial(e).

antitank [æntɪ'tæŋk] *adj* antichar.

antithesis, *pl* **antitheses** [æn'tɪθɪsɪs, -siːz] *n* antithèse *f*.

antitrust [æntɪ'trʌst] *adj*: ~ **legislation** loi *f* anti-trust.

antlers ['æntləz] *npl* bois *mpl*, ramure *f*.

Antwerp ['æntwəːp] *n* Anvers.

anus ['eɪnəs] *n* anus *m*.

anvil ['ænvɪl] *n* enclume *f*.

anxiety [æŋ'zaɪətɪ] *n* anxiété *f*; (*keenness*): ~ **to do** grand désir *or* impatience *f* de faire.

anxious ['æŋkʃəs] *adj* anxieux(euse), (très) inquiet(ète); (*keen*): ~ **to do/that** qui tient beaucoup à faire/à ce que; impatient(e) de faire/que; **I'm very** ~ **about you** je me fais beaucoup de souci pour toi.

anxiously ['æŋkʃəslɪ] *adv* anxieusement.

═══════════════════════ *KEYWORD*

any ['enɪ] *adj* **1** (*in questions etc: singular*) du, de l', de la; (*in questions etc: plural*) des; **have you** ~ **butter/children/ink?** avez-vous du beurre/des enfants/de l'encre?

2 (*with negative*) de, d'; **I haven't** ~ **money/ books** je n'ai pas d'argent/de livres; **without** ~ **difficulty** sans la moindre difficulté

3 (*no matter which*) n'importe quel(le), quelconque; (*each and every*) tout(e), chaque; **choose** ~ **book you like** vous pouvez choisir n'importe quel livre

4 (*in phrases*): **in** ~ **case** de toute façon; ~ **day now** d'un jour à l'autre; **at** ~ **moment** à tout moment, d'un instant à l'autre; **at** ~ **rate** en tout cas

♦ *pron* **1** (*in questions etc*) en; **have you got** ~? est-ce que vous en avez?; **can** ~ **of you sing?** est-ce que parmi vous il y en a qui

chantent?

2 (*with negative*) en; **I haven't** ~ **(of them)** je n'en ai pas, je n'en ai aucun

3 (*no matter which one(s)*) n'importe lequel (*or* laquelle); (*anybody*) n'importe qui; **take** ~ **of those books (you like)** vous pouvez prendre n'importe lequel de ces livres

♦ *adv* **1** (*in questions etc*): **do you want** ~ **more soup/sandwiches?** voulez-vous encore de la soupe/des sandwichs?; **are you feeling** ~ **better?** est-ce que vous vous sentez mieux?

2 (*with negative*): **I can't hear him** ~ **more** je ne l'entends plus; **don't wait** ~ **longer** n'attendez pas plus longtemps.

─────────────────────────

anybody ['enɪbɔdɪ] *pron* n'importe qui; (*in interrogative sentences*) quelqu'un; (*in negative sentences*): **I don't see** ~ je ne vois personne.

anyhow ['enɪhau] *adv* quoi qu'il en soit; (*haphazardly*) n'importe comment; **I shall go** ~ j'irai de toute façon.

anyone ['enɪwʌn] = **anybody**.

anyplace ['enɪpleɪs] *adv* (*US*) = **anywhere**.

anything ['enɪθɪŋ] *pron* n'importe quoi; (*in interrogative sentences*) quelque chose; (*in negative sentences*): **I don't want** ~ je ne veux rien; ~ **else?** (*in shop*) et avec ça?; **it can cost** ~ **between £15 and £20** (*BRIT*) ça peut coûter dans les 15 à 20 livres.

anytime ['enɪtaɪm] *adv* n'importe quand.

anyway ['enɪweɪ] *adv* de toute façon.

anywhere ['enɪwɛə*] *adv* n'importe où; (*in interrogative sentences*) quelque part; (*in negative sentences*): **I don't see him** ~ je ne le vois nulle part; ~ **in the world** n'importe où dans le monde.

Anzac ['ænzæk] *n abbr* (= *Australia-New Zealand Army Corps*) soldat du corps ANZAC.

┌─────────────────────────────────┐
Anzac Day est le 25 avril, jour férié en Australie et en Nouvelle-Zélande commémorant le débarquement des soldats du corps **ANZAC** à Gallipoli en 1915, pendant la Première Guerre mondiale. Ce fut la plus célèbre des campagnes du corps **ANZAC**.
└─────────────────────────────────┘

apart [ə'paːt] *adv* (*to one side*) à part; de côté; à l'écart; (*separately*) séparément; **10 miles/a long way** ~ à 10 milles/très éloignés l'un de l'autre; **they are living** ~ ils sont séparés; ~ **from** *prep* à part, excepté.

apartheid [ə'paːteɪt] *n* apartheid *m*.

apartment [ə'paːtmənt] *n* (*US*) appartement *m*, logement *m*.

apartment building *n* (*US*) immeuble *m*; maison divisée en appartements.

apathetic [æpə'θetɪk] *adj* apathique, indifférent(e).

apathy ['æpəθɪ] *n* apathie *f*, indifférence *f*.

APB *n abbr* (*US*: = *all points bulletin*) *expression* *de la police signifiant "découvrir et appréhender le suspect".*

ape [eɪp] n (grand) singe ♦ vt singer.

Apennines ['æpənaɪnz] npl: **the ~** les Apennins mpl.

apéritif [ə'pɛrɪtiːf] n apéritif m.

aperture ['æpətʃjuə*] n orifice m, ouverture f; (PHOT) ouverture (du diaphragme).

APEX ['eɪpɛks] n abbr (AVIAT: = advance purchase excursion) APEX m.

apex ['eɪpɛks] n sommet m.

aphid ['eɪfɪd] n puceron m.

aphrodisiac [æfrəu'dɪzɪæk] adj, n aphrodisiaque (m).

API n abbr = American Press Institute.

apiece [ə'piːs] adv (for each person) chacun(e), par tête; (for each item) chacun(e), (la) pièce.

aplomb [ə'plɔm] n sang-froid m, assurance f.

APO n abbr (US: = Army Post Office) service postal de l'armée.

apocalypse [ə'pɔkəlɪps] n apocalypse f.

apolitical [eɪpə'lɪtɪkl] adj apolitique.

apologetic [əpɔlə'dʒɛtɪk] adj (tone, letter) d'excuse; **to be very ~ about** s'excuser vivement de.

apologetically [əpɔlə'dʒɛtɪkəlɪ] adv (say) en s'excusant.

apologize [ə'pɔlədʒaɪz] vi: **to ~ (for sth to sb)** s'excuser (de qch auprès de qn), présenter des excuses (à qn pour qch).

apology [ə'pɔlədʒɪ] n excuses fpl; **to send one's apologies** envoyer une lettre or un mot d'excuse, s'excuser (de ne pas pouvoir venir); **please accept my apologies** vous voudrez bien m'excuser.

apoplectic [æpə'plɛktɪk] adj (MED) apoplectique; (col): **~ with rage** fou(folle) de rage.

apoplexy ['æpəplɛksɪ] n apoplexie f.

apostle [ə'pɔsl] n apôtre m.

apostrophe [ə'pɔstrəfɪ] n apostrophe f.

appal [ə'pɔːl] vt consterner, atterrer; horrifier.

Appalachian Mountains [æpə'leɪʃən-] npl: **the ~** les (monts mpl) Appalaches mpl.

appalling [ə'pɔːlɪŋ] adj épouvantable; (stupidity) consternant(e); **she's an ~ cook** c'est une très mauvaise cuisinière.

apparatus [æpə'reɪtəs] n appareil m, dispositif m; (in gymnasium) agrès mpl.

apparel [ə'pærl] n (US) habillement m, confection f.

apparent [ə'pærənt] adj apparent(e); **it is ~ that** il est évident que.

apparently [ə'pærəntlɪ] adv apparemment.

apparition [æpə'rɪʃən] n apparition f.

appeal [ə'piːl] vi (LAW) faire ou interjeter appel ♦ n (LAW) appel m; (request) appel; prière f, (charm) attrait m, charme m; **to ~ for** demander (instamment); implorer; **to ~ to** (subj: person) faire appel à; (subj: thing) plaire à; **to ~ to sb for mercy** implorer la pitié de qn, prier ou adjurer qn d'avoir pitié; **it doesn't ~ to me** cela ne m'attire pas; **right of ~** droit m de recours.

appealing [ə'piːlɪŋ] adj (nice) attrayant(e); (touching) attendrissant(e).

appear [ə'pɪə*] vi apparaître, se montrer; (LAW) comparaître; (publication) paraître, sortir, être publié(e); (seem) paraître, sembler; **it would ~ that** il semble que; **to ~ in Hamlet** jouer dans Hamlet; **to ~ on TV** passer à la télé.

appearance [ə'pɪərəns] n apparition f; parution f; (look, aspect) apparence f, aspect m; **to put in** ou **make an ~** faire acte de présence; (THEAT): **by order of ~** par ordre d'entrée en scène; **to keep up ~s** sauver les apparences; **to all ~s** selon toute apparence.

appease [ə'piːz] vt apaiser, calmer.

appeasement [ə'piːzmənt] n (POL) apaisement m.

appellate court [ə'pɛlɪt-] n (US) cour f d'appel.

append [ə'pɛnd] vt (COMPUT) ajouter (à la fin d'un fichier).

appendage [ə'pɛndɪdʒ] n appendice m.

appendicitis [əpɛndɪ'saɪtɪs] n appendicite f.

appendix, pl **appendices** [ə'pɛndɪks, -siːz] n appendice m; **to have one's ~ out** se faire opérer de l'appendicite.

appetite ['æpɪtaɪt] n appétit m; **that walk has given me an ~** cette promenade m'a ouvert l'appétit.

appetizer ['æpɪtaɪzə*] n (food) amuse-gueule m; (drink) apéritif m.

appetizing ['æpɪtaɪzɪŋ] adj appétissant(e).

applaud [ə'plɔːd] vt, vi applaudir.

applause [ə'plɔːz] n applaudissements mpl.

apple ['æpl] n pomme f; (also: **~ tree**) pommier m; **it's the ~ of my eye** j'y tiens comme à la prunelle de mes yeux.

apple turnover n chausson m aux pommes.

appliance [ə'plaɪəns] n appareil m; **electrical ~s** l'électroménager m.

applicable [ə'plɪkəbl] adj applicable; **the law is ~ from January** la loi entre en vigueur au mois de janvier; **to be ~ to** valoir pour.

applicant ['æplɪkənt] n: **~ (for)** (ADMIN: for benefit etc) demandeur/euse (de); (for post) candidat/e (à).

application [æplɪ'keɪʃən] n application f; (for a job, a grant etc) demande f; candidature f; **on ~** sur demande.

application form n formulaire m de demande.

application program n (COMPUT) programme m d'application.

applications package n (COMPUT) progiciel m d'application.

applied [ə'plaɪd] adj appliqué(e); **~ arts** npl arts décoratifs.

apply [ə'plaɪ] *vt*: **to ~ (to)** (*paint, ointment*) appliquer (sur); (*theory, technique*) appliquer (à) ♦ *vi*: **to ~ to** (*ask*) s'adresser à; (*be suitable for, relevant to*) s'appliquer à, être valable pour; **to ~ (for)** (*permit, grant*) faire une demande (en vue d'obtenir); (*job*) poser sa candidature (pour), faire une demande d'emploi (concernant); **to ~ the brakes** actionner les freins, freiner; **to ~ o.s. to** s'appliquer à.

appoint [ə'pɔɪnt] *vt* nommer, engager; (*date, place*) fixer, désigner.

appointee [əpɔɪn'tiː] *n* personne nommée; candidat retenu.

appointment [ə'pɔɪntmənt] *n* (*to post*) nomination *f*; (*arrangement to meet*) rendez-vous *m*; **to make an ~ (with)** prendre rendez-vous (avec); **"~s (vacant)"** (*PRESS*) "offres d'emploi"; **by ~** sur rendez-vous.

apportion [ə'pɔːʃən] *vt* (*share out*) répartir, distribuer; **to ~ sth to sb** attribuer *or* assigner *or* allouer qch à qn.

appraisal [ə'preɪzl] *n* évaluation *f*.

appraise [ə'preɪz] *vt* (*value*) estimer; (*situation etc*) évaluer.

appreciable [ə'priːʃəbl] *adj* appréciable.

appreciably [ə'priːʃəblɪ] *adv* sensiblement, de façon appréciable.

appreciate [ə'priːʃɪeɪt] *vt* (*like*) apprécier, faire cas de; (*be grateful for*) être reconnaissant(e) de; (*assess*) évaluer; (*be aware of*) comprendre, se rendre compte de ♦ *vi* (*FINANCE*) prendre de la valeur; **I ~ your help** je vous remercie pour votre aide.

appreciation [əpriːʃɪ'eɪʃən] *n* appréciation *f*; (*gratitude*) reconnaissance *f*; (*FINANCE*) hausse *f*, valorisation *f*.

appreciative [ə'priːʃɪətɪv] *adj* (*person*) sensible; (*comment*) élogieux(euse).

apprehend [æprɪ'hɛnd] *vt* appréhender, arrêter; (*understand*) comprendre.

apprehension [æprɪ'hɛnʃən] *n* appréhension *f*, inquiétude *f*.

apprehensive [æprɪ'hɛnsɪv] *adj* inquiet(ète), appréhensif(ive).

apprentice [ə'prɛntɪs] *n* apprenti *m* ♦ *vt*: **to be ~d to** être en apprentissage chez.

apprenticeship [ə'prɛntɪʃɪp] *n* apprentissage *m*; **to serve one's ~** faire son apprentissage.

appro. ['æprəu] *abbr* (*BRIT COMM: col*) = **approval**.

approach [ə'prəutʃ] *vi* approcher ♦ *vt* (*come near*) approcher de; (*ask, apply to*) s'adresser à; (*subject, passer-by*) aborder ♦ *n* approche *f*, accès *m*, abord *m*; démarche *f* (*auprès de qn*); démarche (*intellectuelle*); **to ~ sb about sth** aller *or* venir voir qn pour qch.

approachable [ə'prəutʃəbl] *adj* accessible.

approach road *n* voie *f* d'accès.

approbation [æprə'beɪʃən] *n* approbation *f*.

appropriate *vt* [ə'prəuprɪeɪt] (*take*) s'approprier; (*allot*): **to ~ sth for** affecter qch à ♦ *adj* [ə'prəuprɪɪt] qui convient, approprié(e); (*timely*) opportun(e); **~ for** *or* **to** approprié à; **it would not be ~ for me to comment** il ne me serait pas approprié de commenter.

appropriately [ə'prəuprɪɪtlɪ] *adv* pertinemment, avec à-propos.

appropriation [əprəuprɪ'eɪʃən] *n* dotation *f*, affectation *f*.

approval [ə'pruːvəl] *n* approbation *f*; **to meet with sb's ~** (*proposal etc*) recueillir l'assentiment de qn; **on ~** (*COMM*) à l'examen.

approve [ə'pruːv] *vt* approuver.

▶**approve of** *vt fus* approuver.

approved school [ə'pruːvd-] *n* (*BRIT*) centre *m* d'éducation surveillée.

approvingly [ə'pruːvɪŋlɪ] *adv* d'un air approbateur.

approx. *abbr* (= *approximately*) env.

approximate *adj* [ə'prɒksɪmɪt] approximatif(ive) ♦ *vt* [ə'prɒksɪmeɪt] se rapprocher de; être proche de.

approximation [ə'prɒksɪ'meɪʃən] *n* approximation *f*.

Apr. *abbr* = **April**.

apr *n abbr* (= *annual percentage rate*) taux (d'intérêt) annuel.

apricot ['eɪprɪkɒt] *n* abricot *m*.

April ['eɪprəl] *n* avril *m*; **~ fool!** poisson d'avril!; *for phrases see also* **July**.

April Fool's Day *n* le premier avril.

April Fool's Day est le 1er avril, à l'occasion duquel on fait des farces de toutes sortes. Les victimes de ces farces sont les "*April fools*". Les médias britanniques se prennent aussi au jeu, diffusant de fausses nouvelles, comme la découverte d'îles de la taille de l'Irlande, ou faisant des reportages bidon, montrant par exemple la culture d'arbres à spaghettis en Italie.

---

apron ['eɪprən] *n* tablier *m*; (*AVIAT*) aire *f* de stationnement.

apse [æps] *n* (*ARCHIT*) abside *f*.

APT *n abbr* (*BRIT*: = *advanced passenger train*) ≈ TGV *m*.

Apt. *abbr* (= *apartment*) appt.

apt [æpt] *adj* (*suitable*) approprié(e); (*able*): **~ (at)** doué(e) (pour); apte (à); (*likely*): **~ to do** susceptible de faire; ayant tendance à faire.

aptitude ['æptɪtjuːd] *n* aptitude *f*.

aptitude test *n* test *m* d'aptitude.

aptly ['æptlɪ] *adv* (*fort*) à propos.

aqualung ['ækwəlʌŋ] *n* scaphandre *m* autonome.

aquarium [ə'kwɛərɪəm] *n* aquarium *m*.

Aquarius [ə'kwɛərɪəs] *n* le Verseau; **to be ~** être du Verseau.

aquatic [ə'kwætɪk] *adj* aquatique; (*sport*)

nautique.
aqueduct ['ækwɪdʌkt] *n* aqueduc *m*.
AR *abbr* (*US*) = Arkansas.
ARA *n abbr* (*BRIT*) = *Associate of the Royal Academy.*
Arab ['ærəb] *n* Arabe *m/f* ♦ *adj* arabe.
Arabia [ə'reɪbɪə] *n* Arabie *f*.
Arabian [ə'reɪbɪən] *adj* arabe.
Arabian Desert *n* désert *m* d'Arabie.
Arabian Sea *n* mer *f* d'Arabie.
Arabic ['ærəbɪk] *adj*, *n* arabe *(m)*.
Arabic numerals *npl* chiffres *mpl* arabes.
arable ['ærəbl] *adj* arable.
ARAM *n abbr* (*BRIT*) = *Associate of the Royal Academy of Music.*
arbiter ['ɑːbɪtə*] *n* arbitre *m*.
arbitrary ['ɑːbɪtrərɪ] *adj* arbitraire.
arbitrate ['ɑːbɪtreɪt] *vi* arbitrer; trancher.
arbitration [ɑːbɪ'treɪʃən] *n* arbitrage *m*; **the dispute went to** ~ le litige a été soumis à arbitrage.
arbitrator ['ɑːbɪtreɪtə*] *n* arbitre *m*, médiateur/trice.
ARC *n abbr* = *American Red Cross.*
arc [ɑːk] *n* arc *m*.
arcade [ɑː'keɪd] *n* arcade *f*; (*passage with shops*) passage *m*, galerie *f*.
arch [ɑːtʃ] *n* arche *f*; (*of foot*) cambrure *f*, voûte *f* plantaire ♦ *vt* arquer, cambrer ♦ *adj* malicieux(euse) ♦ *prefix*: ~(-) achevé(e); par excellence; **pointed** ~ ogive *f*.
archaeological [ɑːkɪə'lɒdʒɪkl] *adj* archéologique.
archaeologist [ɑːkɪ'ɒlədʒɪst] *n* archéologue *m/f*.
archaeology [ɑːkɪ'ɒlədʒɪ] *n* archéologie *f*.
archaic [ɑː'keɪɪk] *adj* archaïque.
archangel ['ɑːkeɪndʒəl] *n* archange *m*.
archbishop [ɑːtʃ'bɪʃəp] *n* archevêque *m*.
archenemy [ɑːtʃ'enɪmɪ] *n* ennemi *m* de toujours *or* par excellence.
archeology [ɑːkɪ'ɒlədʒɪ] *etc* (*US*) = **archaeology** *etc*.
archer ['ɑːtʃə*] *n* archer *m*.
archery ['ɑːtʃərɪ] *n* tir *m* à l'arc.
archetypal ['ɑːkɪtaɪpəl] *adj* archétype.
archetype ['ɑːkɪtaɪp] *n* prototype *m*, archétype *m*.
archipelago [ɑːkɪ'pelɪgəʊ] *n* archipel *m*.
architect ['ɑːkɪtekt] *n* architecte *m*.
architectural [ɑːkɪ'tektʃərəl] *adj* architectural(e).
architecture ['ɑːkɪtektʃə*] *n* architecture *f*.
archive ['ɑːkaɪv] *n* (*often pl*) archives *fpl*.
archive file *n* (*COMPUT*) fichier *m* d'archives.
archives ['ɑːkaɪvz] *npl* archives *fpl*.
archivist ['ɑːkɪvɪst] *n* archiviste *m/f*.
archway ['ɑːtʃweɪ] *n* voûte *f*, porche voûté *or* cintré.
ARCM *n abbr* (*BRIT*) = *Associate of the Royal College of Music.*
Arctic ['ɑːktɪk] *adj* arctique ♦ *n*: **the** ~

l'Arctique *m*.
Arctic Circle *n* cercle *m* Arctique.
Arctic Ocean *n* océan *m* Arctique.
ARD *n abbr* (*US MED*) = *acute respiratory disease*
ardent ['ɑːdənt] *adj* fervent(e).
ardour, (*US*) **ardor** ['ɑːdə*] *n* ardeur *f*.
arduous ['ɑːdjuəs] *adj* ardu(e).
are [ɑː*] *vb see* **be**.
area ['ɛərɪə] *n* (*GEOM*) superficie *f*; (*zone*) région *f*; (*: smaller*) secteur *m*; **dining** ~ coin *m* salle à manger; **the London** ~ la région Londonienne.
area code *n* (*TEL*) indicatif *m* de zone.
arena [ə'riːnə] *n* arène *f*.
aren't [ɑːnt] = **are not**.
Argentina [ɑːdʒən'tiːnə] *n* Argentine *f*.
Argentinian [ɑːdʒən'tɪnɪən] *adj* argentin(e) ♦ *n* Argentin/e.
arguable ['ɑːgjuəbl] *adj* discutable, contestable; **it is** ~ **whether** on peut se demander si.
arguably ['ɑːgjuəblɪ] *adv*: **it is** ~ ... on peut soutenir que c'est ....
argue ['ɑːgjuː] *vi* (*quarrel*) se disputer; (*reason*) argumenter ♦ *vt* (*debate: case, matter*) débattre; **to** ~ **about sth (with sb)** se disputer (avec qn) au sujet de qch; **to** ~ **that** objecter *or* alléguer que, donner comme argument que.
argument ['ɑːgjumənt] *n* (*reasons*) argument *m*; (*quarrel*) dispute *f*, discussion *f*; (*debate*) discussion, controverse *f*; ~ **for/against** argument pour/contre.
argumentative [ɑːgju'mentətɪv] *adj* ergoteur(euse), raisonneur(euse).
aria ['ɑːrɪə] *n* aria *f*.
ARIBA [ə'riːbə] *n abbr* (*BRIT*) = *Associate of the Royal Institute of British Architects.*
arid ['ærɪd] *adj* aride.
aridity [ə'rɪdɪtɪ] *n* aridité *f*.
Aries ['ɛərɪz] *n* le Bélier; **to be** ~ être du Bélier.
arise, *pt* **arose**, *pp* **arisen** [ə'raɪz, ə'rəʊz, ə'rɪzn] *vi* survenir, se présenter; **to** ~ **from** résulter de; **should the need** ~ en cas de besoin.
aristocracy [ærɪs'tɒkrəsɪ] *n* aristocratie *f*.
aristocrat ['ærɪstəkræt] *n* aristocrate *m/f*.
aristocratic [ærɪstə'krætɪk] *adj* aristocratique.
arithmetic [ə'rɪθmətɪk] *n* arithmétique *f*.
arithmetical [ærɪθ'metɪkl] *adj* arithmétique.
Ariz. *abbr* (*US*) = Arizona.
ark [ɑːk] *n*: **Noah's A**~ l'Arche *f* de Noé.
Ark. *abbr* (*US*) = Arkansas.
arm [ɑːm] *n* bras *m* ♦ *vt* armer; ~ **in** ~ bras dessus bras dessous.
armaments ['ɑːməmənts] *npl* (*weapons*) armement *m*.
armband ['ɑːmbænd] *n* brassard *m*.
armchair ['ɑːmtʃɛə*] *n* fauteuil *m*.
armed [ɑːmd] *adj* armé(e); **the** ~ **forces** les forces armées.

armed robbery n vol m à main armée.

Armenia [ɑːˈmiːnɪə] n Arménie f.

Armenian [ɑːˈmiːnɪən] adj arménien(ne) ♦ n Arménien/ne; (LING) arménien m.

armful [ˈɑːmful] n brassée f.

armistice [ˈɑːmɪstɪs] n armistice m.

armour, (US) **armor** [ˈɑːmə*] n armure f; (also: ~-plating) blindage m; (MIL: tanks) blindés mpl.

armo(u)red car [ˈɑːməd-] n véhicule blindé.

armo(u)ry [ˈɑːmərɪ] n arsenal m.

armpit [ˈɑːmpɪt] n aisselle f.

armrest [ˈɑːmrɛst] n accoudoir m.

arms [ɑːmz] npl (weapons, HERALDRY) armes fpl.

arms control n contrôle m des armements.

arms race n course f aux armements.

army [ˈɑːmɪ] n armée f.

aroma [əˈrəumə] n arôme m.

aromatherapy [ərəuməˈθɛrəpɪ] n aromathérapie f.

aromatic [ærəˈmætɪk] adj aromatique.

arose [əˈrəuz] pt of **arise**.

around [əˈraund] adv (tout) autour; (nearby) dans les parages ♦ prep autour de; (fig: about) environ; vers; **is he ~?** est-il dans les parages or là?

arousal [əˈrauzəl] n (sexual) excitation sexuelle, éveil m.

arouse [əˈrauz] vt (sleeper) éveiller; (curiosity, passions) éveiller, susciter; exciter.

arpeggio [ɑːˈpɛdʒɪəu] n arpège m.

arrange [əˈreɪndʒ] vt arranger; (programme) arrêter, convenir de ♦ vi: **we have ~d for a car to pick you up** nous avons prévu qu'une voiture vienne vous prendre; **it was ~d that** ... il a été convenu que ..., il a été décidé que ...; **to ~ to do sth** prévoir de faire qch.

arrangement [əˈreɪndʒmənt] n arrangement m; (plans etc): **~s** dispositions fpl; **to come to an ~ (with sb)** se mettre d'accord (avec qn); **home deliveries by ~** livraison à domicile sur demande; **I'll make ~s for you to be met** je vous enverrai chercher.

arrant [ˈærənt] adj: **he's talking ~ nonsense** il raconte vraiment n'importe quoi.

array [əˈreɪ] n (of objects) déploiement m, étalage m; (MATH, COMPUT) tableau m.

arrears [əˈrɪəz] npl arriéré m; **to be in ~ with one's rent** devoir un arriéré de loyer, être en retard pour le paiement de son loyer.

arrest [əˈrɛst] vt arrêter; (sb's attention) retenir, attirer ♦ n arrestation f; **under ~** en état d'arrestation.

arresting [əˈrɛstɪŋ] adj (fig: beauty) saisissante(e); (: charm, candour) désarmant(e).

arrival [əˈraɪvl] n arrivée f; (COMM) arrivage m; (person) arrivant/e; **new ~** nouveau venu/nouvelle venue.

arrive [əˈraɪv] vi arriver.

▶**arrive at** vt fus (fig) parvenir à.

arrogance [ˈærəgəns] n arrogance f.

arrogant [ˈærəgənt] adj arrogant(e).

arrow [ˈærəu] n flèche f.

arse [ɑːs] n (BRIT col!) cul m (!).

arsenal [ˈɑːsɪnl] n arsenal m.

arsenic [ˈɑːsnɪk] n arsenic m.

arson [ˈɑːsn] n incendie criminel.

art [ɑːt] n art m; (craft) métier m; **work of ~** œuvre f d'art.

artefact [ˈɑːtɪfækt] n objet fabriqué.

arterial [ɑːˈtɪərɪəl] adj (ANAT) artériel(le); (road etc) à grande circulation.

artery [ˈɑːtərɪ] n artère f.

artful [ˈɑːtful] adj rusé(e).

art gallery n musée m d'art; (small and private) galerie f de peinture.

arthritis [ɑːˈθraɪtɪs] n arthrite f.

artichoke [ˈɑːtɪtʃəuk] n artichaut m; **Jerusalem ~** topinambour m.

article [ˈɑːtɪkl] n article m; (BRIT LAW: training): **~s** npl ≈ stage m; **~s of clothing** vêtements mpl.

articles of association npl (COMM) statuts mpl d'une société.

articulate adj [ɑːˈtɪkjulɪt] (person) qui s'exprime clairement et aisément; (speech) bien articulé(e), prononcé(e) clairement ♦ vi [ɑːˈtɪkjuleɪt] articuler, parler distinctement.

articulated lorry [ɑːˈtɪkjuleɪtɪd-] n (BRIT) (camion m) semi-remorque m.

artifact [ˈɑːtɪfækt] n (US) objet fabriqué.

artifice [ˈɑːtɪfɪs] n ruse f.

artificial [ɑːtɪˈfɪʃəl] adj artificiel(le).

artificial insemination [-ɪnsɛmɪˈneɪʃən] n insémination artificielle.

artificial intelligence (A.I.) n intelligence artificielle (IA).

artificial respiration n respiration artificielle.

artillery [ɑːˈtɪlərɪ] n artillerie f.

artisan [ˈɑːtɪzæn] n artisan/e.

artist [ˈɑːtɪst] n artiste m/f.

artistic [ɑːˈtɪstɪk] adj artistique.

artistry [ˈɑːtɪstrɪ] n art m, talent m.

artless [ˈɑːtlɪs] adj naïf(naïve), simple, ingénu(e).

arts [ɑːts] npl (SCOL) lettres fpl.

art school n ≈ école f des beaux-arts.

artwork [ˈɑːtwəːk] n maquette f (prête pour la photogravure).

ARV n abbr (= American Revised Version) traduction américaine de la Bible.

AS n abbr (US SCOL: = Associate in/of Science) diplôme universitaire ♦ abbr (US) = American Samoa.

──────── KEYWORD

as [æz] conj **1** (time: moment) comme, alors que; à mesure que; (: duration) tandis que; **he came in ~ I was leaving** il est arrivé comme je partais; **~ the years went by** à

mesure que les années passaient; ~ **from tomorrow** à partir de demain
2 (*in comparisons*): ~ **big** ~ aussi grand que; **twice** ~ **big** ~ deux fois plus grand que; **big** ~ **it is** si grand que ce soit; **much** ~ **I like them, I** ... je les aime bien, mais je ...; ~ **much** *or* **many** ~ autant que; ~ **much money/many books** autant d'argent/de livres que; ~ **soon** ~ dès que
3 (*since, because*) comme, puisque; ~ **he had to be home by 10** ... comme il *or* puisqu'il devait être de retour avant 10 h ...
4 (*referring to manner, way*) comme; **do** ~ **you wish** faites comme vous voudrez
5 (*concerning*): ~ **for** *or* **to that** quant à cela, pour ce qui est de cela
6: ~ **for** *or* **though** comme si; **he looked** ~ **if he was ill** il avait l'air d'être malade; *see also* **long**; **such**; **well**
♦ *prep* (*in the capacity of*) en tant que, en qualité de; **he works** ~ **a driver** il travaille comme chauffeur; ~ **chairman of the company, he** ... en tant que président de la compagnie, il ...; **dressed up** ~ **a cowboy** déguisé en cowboy; **he gave me it** ~ **a present** il me l'a offert, il m'en a fait cadeau.

ASA *n abbr* (= *American Standards Association*) *association de normalisation.*
a.s.a.p. *abbr* = **as soon as possible.**
asbestos [æz'bɛstəs] *n* asbeste *m*, amiante *m*.
ascend [ə'sɛnd] *vt* gravir.
ascendancy [ə'sɛndənsɪ] *n* ascendant *m*.
ascendant [ə'sɛndənt] *n*: **to be in the** ~ monter.
ascension [ə'sɛnʃən] *n*: **the A**~ (*REL*) l'Ascension *f*.
Ascension Island *n* île *f* de l'Ascension.
ascent [ə'sɛnt] *n* ascension *f*.
ascertain [æsə'teɪn] *vt* s'assurer de, vérifier; établir.
ascetic [ə'sɛtɪk] *adj* ascétique.
asceticism [ə'sɛtɪsɪzəm] *n* ascétisme *m*.
ASCII ['æskiː] *n abbr* (= *American Standard Code for Information Interchange*) ASCII.
ascribe [ə'skraɪb] *vt*: **to** ~ **sth to** attribuer qch à; (*blame*) imputer qch à.
ASCU *n abbr* (*US*) = *Association of State Colleges and Universities.*
ASE *n abbr* = *American Stock Exchange.*
ASH [æʃ] *n abbr* (*BRIT*: = *Action on Smoking and Health*) *ligue anti-tabac.*
ash [æʃ] *n* (*dust*) cendre *f*; (*also*: ~ **tree**) frêne *m*.
ashamed [ə'ʃeɪmd] *adj* honteux(euse), confus(e); **to be** ~ **of** avoir honte de; **to be** ~ (**of o.s.**) **for having done** avoir honte d'avoir fait.
ashen ['æʃən] *adj* (*pale*) cendreux(euse), blême.
ashore [ə'ʃɔː*] *adv* à terre; **to go** ~ aller à terre, débarquer.
ashtray ['æʃtreɪ] *n* cendrier *m*.
Ash Wednesday *n* mercredi *m* des Cendres.
Asia ['eɪʃə] *n* Asie *f*.
Asia Minor *n* Asie Mineure.
Asian ['eɪʃən] *n* Asiatique *m/f* ♦ *adj* asiatique.
Asiatic [eɪsɪ'ætɪk] *adj* asiatique.
aside [ə'saɪd] *adv* de côté; à l'écart ♦ *n* aparté *m*; ~ **from** *prep* à part, excepté.
ask [ɑːsk] *vt* demander; (*invite*) inviter; **to** ~ **sb sth/to do sth** demander à qn qch/de faire qch; **to** ~ **sb the time** demander l'heure à qn; **to** ~ **sb about sth** questionner qn au sujet de qch; se renseigner auprès de qn au sujet de qch; **to** ~ **about the price** s'informer du prix, se renseigner au sujet du prix; **to** ~ **(sb) a question** poser une question (à qn); **to** ~ **sb out to dinner** inviter qn au restaurant.
▶**ask after** *vt fus* demander des nouvelles de.
▶**ask for** *vt fus* demander; **it's just** ~**ing for trouble** *or* **for it** ce serait chercher des ennuis.
askance [ə'skɑːns] *adv*: **to look** ~ **at sb** regarder qn de travers *or* d'un œil désapprobateur.
askew [ə'skjuː] *adv* de travers, de guinguois.
asking price ['ɑːskɪŋ-] *n* prix demandé.
asleep [ə'sliːp] *adj* endormi(e); **to be** ~ dormir, être endormi; **to fall** ~ s'endormir.
ASLEF ['æzlɛf] *n abbr* (*BRIT*: = *Associated Society of Locomotive Engineers and Firemen*) *syndicat de cheminots.*
asp [æsp] *n* aspic *m*.
asparagus [əs'pærəgəs] *n* asperges *fpl*.
asparagus tips *npl* pointes *fpl* d'asperges.
ASPCA *n abbr* (= *American Society for the Prevention of Cruelty to Animals*) ≈ SPA *f*.
aspect ['æspɛkt] *n* aspect *m*; (*direction in which a building etc faces*) orientation *f*, exposition *f*.
aspersions [əs'pəːʃənz] *npl*: **to cast** ~ **on** dénigrer.
asphalt ['æsfælt] *n* asphalte *m*.
asphyxiate [æs'fɪksɪeɪt] *vt* asphyxier.
asphyxiation [æsfɪksɪ'eɪʃən] *n* asphyxie *f*.
aspirate *vt* ['æspəreɪt] aspirer ♦ *adj* ['æspərɪt] aspiré(e).
aspiration [æspə'reɪʃən] *n* aspiration *f*.
aspire [əs'paɪə*] *vi*: **to** ~ **to** aspirer à.
aspirin ['æsprɪn] *n* aspirine *f*.
aspiring [əs'paɪərɪŋ] *adj* (*artist, writer*) en herbe; (*manager*) potentiel(le).
ass [æs] *n* âne *m*; (*col*) imbécile *m/f*; (*US col!*) cul *m* (*!*).
assail [ə'seɪl] *vt* assaillir.
assailant [ə'seɪlənt] *n* agresseur *m*; assaillant *m*.
assassin [ə'sæsɪn] *n* assassin *m*.
assassinate [ə'sæsɪneɪt] *vt* assassiner.
assassination [əsæsɪ'neɪʃən] *n* assassinat *m*.

assault [ə'sɔːlt] n (MIL) assaut m; (gen: attack) agression f; (LAW): ~ **(and battery)** voies fpl de fait, coups mpl et blessures fpl ♦ vt attaquer; (sexually) violenter.

assemble [ə'sɛmbl] vt assembler ♦ vi s'assembler, se rassembler.

assembly [ə'sɛmblɪ] n (meeting) rassemblement m; (construction) assemblage m.

assembly language n (COMPUT) langage m d'assemblage.

assembly line n chaîne f de montage.

assent [ə'sɛnt] n assentiment m, consentement m ♦ vi: **to** ~ **(to sth)** donner son assentiment (à qch), consentir (à qch).

assert [ə'sɜːt] vt affirmer, déclarer; établir; **to** ~ **o.s.** s'imposer.

assertion [ə'sɜːʃən] n assertion f, affirmation f.

assertive [ə'sɜːtɪv] adj assuré(e); péremptoire.

assess [ə'sɛs] vt évaluer, estimer; (tax, damages) établir or fixer le montant de; (property etc: for tax) calculer la valeur imposable de.

assessment [ə'sɛsmənt] n évaluation f, estimation f; (judgment): ~ **(of)** jugement m or opinion f (sur).

assessor [ə'sɛsə*] n expert m (en matière d'impôt et d'assurance).

asset ['æsɛt] n avantage m, atout m; (person) atout; ~**s** npl (COMM) capital m; avoir(s) m(pl); actif m.

asset-stripping ['æsɛt'strɪpɪŋ] n (COMM) récupération f (et démantèlement m) d'une entreprise en difficulté.

assiduous [ə'sɪdjuəs] adj assidu(e).

assign [ə'saɪn] vt (date) fixer, arrêter; (task): **to** ~ **sth to** assigner qch à; (resources): **to** ~ **sth to** affecter qch à; (cause, meaning): **to** ~ **sth to** attribuer qch à.

assignment [ə'saɪnmənt] n tâche f, mission f.

assimilate [ə'sɪmɪleɪt] vt assimiler.

assimilation [əsɪmɪ'leɪʃən] n assimilation f.

assist [ə'sɪst] vt aider, assister; (injured person etc) secourir.

assistance [ə'sɪstəns] n aide f, assistance f; secours mpl.

assistant [ə'sɪstənt] n assistant/e, adjoint/e; (BRIT: also: **shop** ~) vendeur/euse.

assistant manager n sous-directeur m.

assizes [ə'saɪzɪz] npl assises fpl.

associate adj, n [ə'səuʃiɪt] associé(e) ♦ vb [ə'səuʃieɪt] vt associer ♦ vi: **to** ~ **with sb** fréquenter qn; ~ **director** directeur adjoint; ~**d company** société affiliée.

association [əsəusɪ'eɪʃən] n association f; in ~ **with** en collaboration avec.

association football n (BRIT) football m.

assorted [ə'sɔːtɪd] adj assorti(e); in ~ **sizes** en plusieurs tailles.

assortment [ə'sɔːtmənt] n assortiment m.

Asst. abbr = **assistant**.

assuage [ə'sweɪdʒ] vt (grief, pain) soulager; (thirst, appetite) assouvir.

assume [ə'sjuːm] vt supposer; (responsibilities etc) assumer; (attitude, name) prendre, adopter.

assumed name [ə'sjuːmd-] n nom m d'emprunt.

assumption [ə'sʌmpʃən] n supposition f, hypothèse f; **on the** ~ **that** dans l'hypothèse où; (on condition that) à condition que.

assurance [ə'ʃuərəns] n assurance f; **I can give you no** ~**s** je ne peux rien vous garantir.

assure [ə'ʃuə*] vt assurer.

assured [ə'ʃuəd] adj assuré(e).

AST abbr (US: = Atlantic Standard Time) heure d'hiver de New York.

asterisk ['æstərɪsk] n astérisque m.

astern [ə'stɜːn] adv à l'arrière.

asteroid ['æstərɔɪd] n astéroïde m.

asthma ['æsmə] n asthme m.

asthmatic [æs'mætɪk] adj, n asthmatique (m/f).

astigmatism [ə'stɪgmətɪzəm] n astigmatisme m.

astir [ə'stɜː*] adv en émoi.

astonish [ə'stɔnɪʃ] vt étonner, stupéfier.

astonishing [ə'stɔnɪʃɪŋ] adj étonnant(e), stupéfiant(e); **I find it** ~ **that** ... je trouve incroyable que ....

astonishingly [ə'stɔnɪʃɪŋlɪ] adv incroyablement.

astonishment [ə'stɔnɪʃmənt] n (grand) étonnement m, stupéfaction f.

astound [ə'staund] vt stupéfier, sidérer.

astray [ə'streɪ] adv: **to go** ~ s'égarer; (fig) quitter le droit chemin; **to go** ~ **in one's calculations** faire fausse route dans ses calculs.

astride [ə'straɪd] adv à cheval ♦ prep à cheval sur.

astringent [əs'trɪndʒənt] adj astringent(e) ♦ n astringent m.

astrologer [əs'trɔlədʒə*] n astrologue m.

astrology [əs'trɔlədʒɪ] n astrologie f.

astronaut ['æstrənɔːt] n astronaute m/f.

astronomer [əs'trɔnəmə*] n astronome m.

astronomical [æstrə'nɔmɪkl] adj astronomique.

astronomy [əs'trɔnəmɪ] n astronomie f.

astrophysics ['æstrəu'fɪzɪks] n astrophysique f.

astute [əs'tjuːt] adj astucieux(euse), malin(igne).

asunder [ə'sʌndə*] adv: **to tear** ~ déchirer.

ASV n abbr (= American Standard Version) traduction de la Bible.

asylum [ə'saɪləm] n asile m; **to seek political** ~ demander l'asile politique.

asymmetric(al) [eɪsɪ'mɛtrɪk(l)] adj asymétrique.

=========================== *KEYWORD*

at [æt] *prep* **1** (*referring to position, direction*) à;
~ **the top** au sommet; ~ **home/school** à la
maison *or* chez soi/à l'école; ~ **the baker's** à
la boulangerie, chez le boulanger; **to look** ~
sth regarder qch
2 (*referring to time*): ~ **4 o'clock** à 4 heures;
~ **Christmas** à Noël; ~ **night** la nuit; ~ **times**
par moments, parfois
3 (*referring to rates, speed etc*) à; ~ **£1 a kilo**
une livre le kilo; **two** ~ **a time** deux à la
fois; ~ **50 km/h** à 50 km/h; ~ **full speed** à
toute vitesse
4 (*referring to manner*): ~ **a stroke** d'un seul
coup; ~ **peace** en paix
5 (*referring to activity*): **to be** ~ **work** être à
l'œuvre, travailler; **to play** ~ **cowboys** jouer
aux cowboys; **to be good** ~ **sth** être bon en
qch
6 (*referring to cause*): **shocked/surprised/**
annoyed ~ **sth** choqué par/étonné de/agacé
par qch; **I went** ~ **his suggestion** j'y suis
allé sur son conseil.

ate [eɪt] *pt of* **eat**.
atheism ['eɪθɪɪzəm] *n* athéisme *m*.
atheist ['eɪθɪɪst] *n* athée *m/f*.
Athenian [ə'θiːnɪən] *adj* athénien(ne) ♦ *n*
Athénien/ne.
Athens ['æθɪnz] *n* Athènes.
athlete ['æθliːt] *n* athlète *m/f*.
athletic [æθ'lɛtɪk] *adj* athlétique.
athletics [æθ'lɛtɪks] *n* athlétisme *m*.
Atlantic [ət'læntɪk] *adj* atlantique ♦ *n*: **the** ~
(Ocean) l'Atlantique *m*, l'océan *m*
Atlantique.
atlas ['ætləs] *n* atlas *m*.
Atlas Mountains *npl*: **the** ~ les monts *mpl* de
l'Atlas, l'Atlas *m*.
ATM *abbr* (= *Automated Telling Machine*)
guichet *m* automatique.
atmosphere ['ætməsfɪə*] *n* atmosphère *f*; (*air*)
air *m*.
atmospheric [ætməs'fɛrɪk] *adj*
atmosphérique.
atmospherics [ætməs'fɛrɪks] *n* (*RADIO*)
parasites *mpl*.
atoll ['ætɔl] *n* atoll *m*.
atom ['ætəm] *n* atome *m*.
atomic [ə'tɔmɪk] *adj* atomique.
atom(ic) bomb *n* bombe *f* atomique.
atomizer ['ætəmaɪzə*] *n* atomiseur *m*.
atone [ə'təun] *vi*: **to** ~ **for** expier, racheter.
atonement [ə'təunmənt] *n* expiation *f*.
A to Z *n* ® guide *m* A à Z; (*map*) plan *m* des
rues.
ATP *n abbr* (= *Association of Tennis*
Professionals) ATP *f* (= *Association des*
tennismen professionnels).
atrocious [ə'trəuʃəs] *adj* (*very bad*) atroce,
exécrable.

atrocity [ə'trɔsɪtɪ] *n* atrocité *f*.
atrophy ['ætrəfɪ] *n* atrophie *f* ♦ *vt* atrophier
♦ *vi* s'atrophier.
attach [ə'tætʃ] *vt* (*gen*) attacher; (*document,*
letter) joindre; (*employee, troops*) affecter; **to**
be ~**ed to sb/sth** (*to like*) être attaché à qn/
qch; **the** ~**ed letter** la lettre ci-jointe.
attaché [ə'tæʃeɪ] *n* attaché *m*.
attaché case *n* mallette *f*, attaché-case *m*.
attachment [ə'tætʃmənt] *n* (*tool*) accessoire
m; (*love*): ~ **(to)** affection *f* (pour),
attachement *m* (à).
attack [ə'tæk] *vt* attaquer; (*task etc*) s'attaquer
à ♦ *n* attaque *f*; (*also:* **heart** ~) crise *f*
cardiaque.
attacker [ə'tækə*] *n* attaquant *m*; agresseur *m*.
attain [ə'teɪn] *vt* (*also:* **to** ~ **to**) parvenir à,
atteindre; acquérir.
attainments [ə'teɪnmənts] *npl* connaissances
fpl, résultats *mpl*.
attempt [ə'tɛmpt] *n* tentative *f* ♦ *vt* essayer,
tenter; ~**ed theft** *etc* (*LAW*) tentative de vol
etc; **to make an** ~ **on sb's life** attenter à la
vie de qn; **he made no** ~ **to help** il n'a rien
fait pour m'aider (*or* l'aider *etc*).
attend [ə'tɛnd] *vt* (*course*) suivre; (*meeting,*
talk) assister à; (*school, church*) aller à,
fréquenter; (*patient*) soigner, s'occuper de;
to ~ **(up)on** servir; être au service de.
▶**attend to** *vt fus* (*needs, affairs etc*) s'occuper
de; (*customer*) s'occuper de, servir.
attendance [ə'tɛndəns] *n* (*being present*)
présence *f*; (*people present*) assistance *f*.
attendant [ə'tɛndənt] *n* employé/e; gardien/
ne ♦ *adj* concomitant(e), qui accompagne *or*
s'ensuit.
attention [ə'tɛnʃən] *n* attention *f*; ~**s**
attentions *fpl*, prévenances *fpl*; ~! (*MIL*)
garde-à-vous!; **at** ~ (*MIL*) au garde-à-vous;
for the ~ **of** (*ADMIN*) à l'attention de; **it has**
come to my ~ **that** ... je constate que ....
attentive [ə'tɛntɪv] *adj* attentif(ive); (*kind*)
prévenant(e).
attentively [ə'tɛntɪvlɪ] *adv* attentivement,
avec attention.
attenuate [ə'tɛnjueɪt] *vt* atténuer ♦ *vi*
s'atténuer.
attest [ə'tɛst] *vi*: **to** ~ **to** témoigner de,
attester (de).
attic ['ætɪk] *n* grenier *m*, combles *mpl*.
attire [ə'taɪə*] *n* habit *m*, atours *mpl*.
attitude ['ætɪtjuːd] *n* (*behaviour*) attitude *f*,
manière *f*; (*posture*) pose *f*, attitude *f*; (*view*):
~ **(to)** attitude (envers).
attorney [ə'təːnɪ] *n* (*US: lawyer*) avocat *m*;
(*having proxy*) mandataire *m*; **power of** ~
procuration *f*.
Attorney General *n* (*BRIT*) ≈ procureur
général; (*US*) ≈ garde *m* des Sceaux,
ministre *m* de la Justice.
attract [ə'trækt] *vt* attirer.
attraction [ə'trækʃən] *n* (*gen pl: pleasant*

things) attraction f, attrait m; (PHYSICS)
attraction; (fig: towards sth) attirance f.
attractive [ə'træktɪv] adj séduisant(e),
attrayant(e).
attribute n ['ætrɪbjuːt] attribut m ♦ vt
[ə'trɪbjuːt]: **to ~ sth to** attribuer qch à.
attrition [ə'trɪʃən] n: **war of ~** guerre f
d'usure.
Atty. Gen. abbr = **Attorney General.**
ATV n abbr (= all terrain vehicle) véhicule m
tout-terrain.
atypical [eɪ'tɪpɪkl] adj atypique.
aubergine ['əʊbəʒiːn] n aubergine f.
auburn ['ɔːbən] adj auburn inv, châtain roux
inv.
auction ['ɔːkʃən] n (also: **sale by ~**) vente f
aux enchères ♦ vt (also: **to sell by ~**) vendre
aux enchères; (also: **to put up for ~**) mettre
aux enchères.
auctioneer [ɔːkʃə'nɪə*] n commissaire-
priseur m.
auction room n salle f des ventes.
audacious [ɔː'deɪʃəs] adj impudent(e);
audacieux(euse), intrépide.
audacity [ɔː'dæsɪtɪ] n impudence f; audace f.
audible ['ɔːdɪbl] adj audible.
audience ['ɔːdɪəns] n (people) assistance f,
auditoire m; auditeurs mpl; spectateurs mpl;
(interview) audience f.
audiotypist ['ɔːdɪəʊtaɪpɪst] n audiotypiste m/f.
audiovisual [ɔːdɪəʊ'vɪzjuəl] adj audio-
visuel(le); **~ aids** supports or moyens
audiovisuels.
audit ['ɔːdɪt] n vérification f des comptes,
apurement m ♦ vt vérifier, apurer.
audition [ɔː'dɪʃən] n audition f ♦ vi
auditionner.
auditor ['ɔːdɪtə*] n vérificateur m des
comptes.
auditorium [ɔːdɪ'tɔːrɪəm] n auditorium m,
salle f de concert or de spectacle.
Aug. abbr = **August.**
augment [ɔːg'ment] vt, vi augmenter.
augur ['ɔːgə*] vt (be a sign of) présager,
annoncer ♦ vi: **it ~s well** c'est bon signe or
de bon augure, cela s'annonce bien.
August ['ɔːgəst] n août m; for phrases see also
July.
august [ɔː'gʌst] adj majestueux(euse),
imposant(e).
aunt [ɑːnt] n tante f.
auntie, aunty ['ɑːntɪ] n diminutive of **aunt.**
au pair ['əʊ'pɛə*] n (also: **~ girl**) jeune fille f au
pair.
aura ['ɔːrə] n atmosphère f.
auspices ['ɔːspɪsɪz] npl: **under the ~ of** sous
les auspices de.
auspicious [ɔːs'pɪʃəs] adj de bon augure,
propice.
austere [ɔs'tɪə*] adj austère.
austerity [ɔs'tɛrɪtɪ] n austérité f.
Australasia [ɔːstrə'leɪzɪə] n Australasie f.

Australia [ɔs'treɪlɪə] n Australie f.
Australian [ɔs'treɪlɪən] adj australien(ne) ♦ n
Australien/ne.
Austria ['ɔstrɪə] n Autriche f.
Austrian ['ɔstrɪən] adj autrichien(ne) ♦ n
Autrichien/ne.
AUT n abbr (BRIT: = Association of University
Teachers) syndicat universitaire.
authentic [ɔː'θentɪk] adj authentique.
authenticate [ɔː'θentɪkeɪt] vt établir
l'authenticité de.
authenticity [ɔːθen'tɪsɪtɪ] n authenticité f.
author ['ɔːθə*] n auteur m.
authoritarian [ɔːθɔrɪ'tɛərɪən] adj autoritaire.
authoritative [ɔː'θɔrɪtətɪv] adj (account) digne
de foi; (study, treatise) qui fait autorité;
(manner) autoritaire.
authority [ɔː'θɔrɪtɪ] n autorité f; (permission)
autorisation (formelle); **the authorities** les
autorités, l'administration f; **to have ~ to do
sth** être habilité à faire qch.
authorization [ɔːθəraɪ'zeɪʃən] n autorisation f.
authorize ['ɔːθəraɪz] vt autoriser.
authorized capital ['ɔːθəraɪzd-] n (COMM)
capital social.
authorship ['ɔːθəʃɪp] n paternité f (littéraire
etc).
autistic [ɔː'tɪstɪk] adj autistique.
auto ['ɔːtəu] n (US) auto f, voiture f.
autobiography [ɔːtəbaɪ'ɔgrəfɪ] n
autobiographie f.
autocratic [ɔːtə'krætɪk] adj autocratique.
Autocue ['ɔːtəukjuː] n ® (télé)prompteur m.
autograph ['ɔːtəgrɑːf] n autographe m ♦ vt
signer, dédicacer.
autoimmune [ɔːtəuɪ'mjuːn] adj auto-immune.
automat ['ɔːtəmæt] n (vending machine)
distributeur m (automatique); (US: place)
cafétéria f avec distributeurs automatiques.
automated ['ɔːtəmeɪtɪd] adj automatisé(e).
automatic [ɔːtə'mætɪk] adj automatique ♦ n
(gun) automatique m; (washing machine)
lave-linge m automatique; (BRIT AUT) voiture
f à transmission automatique.
automatically [ɔːtə'mætɪklɪ] adv
automatiquement.
automatic data processing (ADP) n
traitement m automatique des données.
automation [ɔːtə'meɪʃən] n automatisation f.
automaton, pl **automata** [ɔː'tɔmətən, -tə] n
automate m.
automobile ['ɔːtəməbiːl] n (US) automobile f.
autonomous [ɔː'tɔnəməs] adj autonome.
autonomy [ɔː'tɔnəmɪ] n autonomie f.
autopsy ['ɔːtɔpsɪ] n autopsie f.
autumn ['ɔːtəm] n automne m.
auxiliary [ɔːg'zɪlɪərɪ] adj, n auxiliaire (m/f).
AV n abbr (= Authorized Version) traduction
anglaise de la Bible ♦ abbr = **audiovisual.**
Av. abbr (= avenue) Av.
avail [ə'veɪl] vt: **to ~ o.s. of** user de; profiter
de ♦ n: **to no ~** sans résultat, en vain, en

pure perte.

availability [əveɪlə'bɪlɪtɪ] *n* disponibilité *f*.

available [ə'veɪləbl] *adj* disponible; **every ~ means** tous les moyens possibles *or* à sa (*or* notre *etc*) disposition; **is the manager ~?** est-ce que le directeur peut (me) recevoir?; (*on phone*) pourrais-je parler au directeur?; **to make sth ~ to sb** mettre qch à la disposition de qn.

avalanche ['ævəlɑːnʃ] *n* avalanche *f*.

avant-garde ['ævɑ̃'gɑːd] *adj* d'avant-garde.

avaricious [ævə'rɪʃəs] *adj* âpre au gain.

avdp. *abbr* = *avoirdupoids*.

Ave. *abbr* (= *avenue*) Av.

avenge [ə'vendʒ] *vt* venger.

avenue ['ævənjuː] *n* avenue *f*.

average ['ævərɪdʒ] *n* moyenne *f* ♦ *adj* moyen(ne) ♦ *vt* (*a certain figure*) atteindre *or* faire *etc* en moyenne; **on ~** en moyenne; **above/below (the) ~** au-dessus/en-dessous de la moyenne.

▶**average out** *vi*: **to ~ out at** représenter en moyenne, donner une moyenne de.

averse [ə'vɜːs] *adj*: **to be ~ to sth/doing** éprouver une forte répugnance envers qch/à faire; **I wouldn't be ~ to a drink** un petit verre ne serait pas de refus, je ne dirais pas non à un petit verre.

aversion [ə'vɜːʃən] *n* aversion *f*, répugnance *f*.

avert [ə'vɜːt] *vt* prévenir, écarter; (*one's eyes*) détourner.

aviary ['eɪvɪərɪ] *n* volière *f*.

aviation [eɪvɪ'eɪʃən] *n* aviation *f*.

avid ['ævɪd] *adj* avide.

avidly ['ævɪdlɪ] *adv* avidement, avec avidité.

avocado [ævə'kɑːdəʊ] *n* (*also*: *BRIT*: **~ pear**) avocat *m*.

avoid [ə'vɔɪd] *vt* éviter.

avoidable [ə'vɔɪdəbl] *adj* évitable.

avoidance [ə'vɔɪdəns] *n le fait d'éviter*.

avowed [ə'vaʊd] *adj* déclaré(e).

AVP *n abbr* (*US*) = *assistant vice-president*.

AWACS ['eɪwæks] *n abbr* (= *airborne warning and control system*) AWACS (*système aéroporté d'alerte et de contrôle*).

await [ə'weɪt] *vt* attendre; **~ing attention/ delivery** (*COMM*) en souffrance; **long ~ed** tant attendu(e).

awake [ə'weɪk] *adj* éveillé(e); (*fig*) en éveil ♦ *vb* (*pt* **awoke** [ə'wəʊk], *pp* **awoken** [ə'wəʊkən], **awaked**) *vt* éveiller ♦ *vi* s'éveiller; **~ to** conscient de; **he was still ~** il ne dormait pas encore.

awakening [ə'weɪknɪŋ] *n* réveil *m*.

award [ə'wɔːd] *n* récompense *f*, prix *m* ♦ *vt* (*prize*) décerner; (*LAW: damages*) accorder.

aware [ə'wɛə*] *adj*: **~ of** (*conscious*) conscient(e) de; (*informed*) au courant de; **to become ~ of** avoir conscience de, prendre conscience de; se rendre compte de; **politically/socially ~** sensibilisé(e) aux *or* ayant pris conscience des problèmes

politiques/sociaux; **I am fully ~ that** je me rends parfaitement compte que.

awareness [ə'wɛənɪs] *n* conscience *f*, connaissance *f*; **to develop people's ~ (of)** sensibiliser le public (à).

awash [ə'wɔʃ] *adj* recouvert(e) (d'eau); **~ with** inondé(e) de.

away [ə'weɪ] *adj*, *adv* (au) loin; absent(e); **two kilometres ~** à (une distance de) deux kilomètres, à deux kilomètres de distance; **two hours ~ by car** à deux heures de voiture *or* de route; **the holiday was two weeks ~** il restait deux semaines jusqu'aux vacances; **~ from** loin de; **he's ~ for a week** il est parti (pour) une semaine; **he's ~ in Milan** il est (parti) à Milan; **to take ~** *vt* emporter; **to pedal/work/laugh** *etc* **~** *la particule indique la constance et l'énergie de l'action*: il pédalait *etc* tant qu'il pouvait; **to fade/ wither** *etc* **~** *la particule renforce l'idée de la disparition, l'éloignement*.

away game *n* (*SPORT*) match *m* à l'extérieur.

awe [ɔː] *n* respect mêlé de crainte, effroi mêlé d'admiration.

awe-inspiring ['ɔːɪnspaɪərɪŋ], **awesome** ['ɔːsəm] *adj* impressionnant(e).

awestruck ['ɔːstrʌk] *adj* frappé(e) d'effroi.

awful ['ɔːfəl] *adj* affreux(euse); **an ~ lot of** énormément de.

awfully ['ɔːfəlɪ] *adv* (*very*) terriblement, vraiment.

awhile [ə'waɪl] *adv* un moment, quelque temps.

awkward ['ɔːkwəd] *adj* (*clumsy*) gauche, maladroit(e); (*inconvenient*) malaisé(e), d'emploi malaisé, peu pratique; (*embarrassing*) gênant(e),

awkwardness ['ɔːkwədnɪs] *n* (*embarrassment*) gêne *f*.

awl [ɔːl] *n* alêne *f*.

awning ['ɔːnɪŋ] *n* (*of tent*) auvent *m*; (*of shop*) store *m*; (*of hotel etc*) marquise *f* (de toile).

awoke [ə'wəʊk] *pt of* **awake**.

awoken [ə'wəʊkən] *pp of* **awake**.

AWOL ['eɪwɔl] *abbr* (*MIL*) = **absent without leave.**

awry [ə'raɪ] *adv*, *adj* de travers; **to go ~** mal tourner.

axe, (*US*) **ax** [æks] *n* hache *f* ♦ *vt* (*employee*) renvoyer; (*project etc*) abandonner; (*jobs*) supprimer; **to have an ~ to grind** (*fig*) prêcher pour son saint.

axes ['æksiːz] *npl of* **axis.**

axiom ['æksɪəm] *n* axiome *m*.

axiomatic [æksɪəu'mætɪk] *adj* axiomatique.

axis, *pl* **axes** ['æksɪs, -siːz] *n* axe *m*.

axle ['æksl] *n* (*also*: **~-tree**) essieu *m*.

ay(e) [aɪ] *excl* (*yes*) oui ♦ *n*: **the ~s** les oui.

AYH *n abbr* = *American Youth Hostels.*

AZ *abbr* (*US*) = *Arizona.*

azalea [ə'zeɪlɪə] *n* azalée *f*.

Azerbaijan [æzəbaɪ'dʒɑːn] *n* Azerbaïdjan *m*.

Azerbaijani, Azeri [æzəbaɪ'dʒɑːnɪ, ə'zɛərɪ] *adj* azerbaïdjanais(e) ♦ *n* Azerbaïdjanais/e.
Azores [ə'zɔːz] *npl*: **the ~** les Açores *fpl*.
AZT *n abbr* (= *azidothymidine*) AZT *f*.
Aztec ['æztɛk] *adj* aztèque ♦ *n* Aztèque *m/f*.
azure ['eɪʒə*] *adj* azuré(e).

B b

B, b [biː] *n* (*letter*) B, b *m*; (*SCOL: mark*) B; (*MUS*): **B** si *m*; **B for Benjamin**, (*US*) **B for Baker** B comme Berthe; **B road** *n* (*BRIT AUT*) route départementale.
b. *abbr* = **born**.
BA *n abbr* = *British Academy*; (*SCOL*) = **Bachelor of Arts**.
babble ['bæbl] *vi* babiller ♦ *n* babillage *m*.
baboon [bə'buːn] *n* babouin *m*.
baby ['beɪbɪ] *n* bébé *m*.
baby carriage *n* (*US*) voiture *f* d'enfant.
baby grand *n* (*also*: **~ piano**) (piano *m*) demi-queue *m*.
babyhood ['beɪbɪhud] *n* petite enfance.
babyish ['beɪbɪɪʃ] *adj* enfantin(e), de bébé.
baby-minder ['beɪbɪmaɪndə*] *n* (*BRIT*) gardienne *f* (d'enfants).
baby-sit ['beɪbɪsɪt] *vi* garder les enfants.
baby-sitter ['beɪbɪsɪtə*] *n* baby-sitter *m/f*.
bachelor ['bætʃələ*] *n* célibataire *m*; **B~ of Arts/Science (BA/BSc)** ≈ licencié/e ès *or* en lettres/sciences; **B~ of Arts/Science degree (BA/BSc)** *n* ≈ licence *f* ès *or* en lettres/sciences.

Un **Bachelor's degree** *est un diplôme accordé après trois ou quatre années d'université. Les Bachelor's degrees les plus courants sont le* **BA** *(Bachelor of Arts), le* **BSc** *(Bachelor of Science), le* **BEd** *(Bachelor of Education) et le* **LLB** *(Bachelor of Laws).*

bachelorhood ['bætʃələhud] *n* célibat *m*.
bachelor party *n* (*US*) enterrement *m* de vie de garçon.
back [bæk] *n* (*of person, horse*) dos *m*; (*of hand*) dos, revers *m*; (*of house*) derrière *m*; (*of car, train*) arrière *m*; (*of chair*) dossier *m*; (*of page*) verso *m*; (*FOOTBALL*) arrière *m*; **to have one's ~ to the wall** (*fig*) être au pied du mur; **to break the ~ of a job** (*BRIT*) faire le gros d'un travail; **~ to front** à l'envers ♦ *vt* (*financially*) soutenir (financièrement); (*candidate: also*: **~ up**) soutenir, appuyer; (*horse: at races*) parier *or* miser sur; (*car*) (faire) reculer ♦ *vi* reculer; (*car etc*) faire marche arrière ♦ *adj* (*in compounds*) de derrière, à l'arrière; **~**

seats/wheels (*AUT*) sièges *mpl*/roues *fpl* arrière; **~ payments/rent** arriéré *m* de paiements/loyer; **~ garden/room** jardin/pièce sur l'arrière; **to take a ~ seat** (*fig*) se contenter d'un second rôle, être relégué(e) au second plan ♦ *adv* (*not forward*) en arrière; (*returned*): **he's ~** il est rentré, il est de retour; **when will you be ~?** quand seras-tu de retour?; **he ran ~** il est revenu en courant; (*restitution*): **throw the ball ~** renvoie la balle; **can I have it ~?** puis-je le ravoir?, peux-tu me le rendre?; (*again*): **he called ~** il a rappelé.
backbench ['bæk'bɛntʃ] *n* (*BRIT*) banc des députés sans portefeuille.
► **back down** *vi* rabattre de ses prétentions.
► **back on to** *vt fus*: **the house ~s on to the golf course** la maison donne derrière sur le terrain de golf.
► **back out** *vi* (*of promise*) se dédire.
► **back up** *vt* (*COMPUT*) faire une copie de sauvegarde de.
backache ['bækeɪk] *n* maux *mpl* de reins.

Le terme **back benches** *désigne les bancs les plus éloignés de l'allée centrale de la Chambre des communes. Les députés qui occupent ces bancs sont les "backbenchers" et ils n'ont pas de portefeuille ministériel.*

backbiting ['bækbaɪtɪŋ] *n* médisance(s) *f(pl)*.
backbone ['bækbəun] *n* colonne vertébrale, épine dorsale; **he's the ~ of the organization** c'est sur lui que repose l'organisation.
backchat ['bæktʃæt] *n* (*BRIT col*) impertinences *fpl*.
back-cloth ['bækklɔθ] *n* (*BRIT*) toile *f* de fond.
backcomb ['bækkəum] *vt* (*BRIT*) crêper.
backdate [bæk'deɪt] *vt* (*letter*) antidater; **~d pay rise** augmentation *f* avec effet rétroactif.
backdrop ['bækdrɔp] *n* = **backcloth**.
backer ['bækə*] *n* partisan *m*; (*COMM*) commanditaire *m*.
backfire [bæk'faɪə*] *vi* (*AUT*) pétarader; (*plans*) mal tourner.
backgammon ['bækgæmən] *n* trictrac *m*.
background ['bækgraund] *n* arrière-plan *m*; (*of events*) situation *f*, conjoncture *f*; (*basic knowledge*) éléments *mpl* de base; (*experience*) formation *f* ♦ *cpd* (*noise, music*) de fond; **~ reading** lecture(s) générale(s) (sur un sujet); **family ~** milieu familial.
backhand ['bækhænd] *n* (*TENNIS: also*: **~ stroke**) revers *m*.
backhanded ['bæk'hændɪd] *adj* (*fig*) déloyal(e); équivoque.
backhander ['bæk'hændə*] *n* (*BRIT: bribe*) pot-de-vin *m*.
backing ['bækɪŋ] *n* (*fig*) soutien *m*, appui *m*; (*COMM*) soutien (financier); (*MUS*) accompagnement *m*.
backlash ['bæklæʃ] *n* contre-coup *m*,

répercussion *f*.

backlog ['bæklɔg] *n*: ~ **of work** travail *m* en retard.

back number *n* (*of magazine etc*) vieux numéro.

backpack ['bækpæk] *n* sac *m* à dos.

backpacker ['bækpækə*] *n* randonneur/euse.

back pay *n* rappel *m* de salaire.

backpedal ['bækpɛdl] *vi* (*fig*) faire marche arrière.

backseat driver ['bæksiːt-] *n passager qui donne des conseils au conducteur*.

backside ['bæksaɪd] *n* (*col*) derrière *m*, postérieur *m*.

backslash ['bækslæʃ] *n* barre oblique inversée.

backslide ['bækslaɪd] *vi* retomber dans l'erreur.

backspace ['bækspeɪs] *vi* (*in typing*) appuyer sur la touche retour.

backstage [bæk'steɪdʒ] *adv* dans les coulisses.

back-street ['bækstriːt] *adj* (*abortion*) clandestin(e); ~ **abortionist** avorteur/euse (*clandestin*).

backstroke ['bækstrəuk] *n* dos crawlé.

backtrack ['bæktræk] *vi* (*fig*) = **backpedal**.

backup ['bækʌp] *adj* (*train, plane*) supplémentaire, de réserve; (*COMPUT*) de sauvegarde ♦ *n* (*support*) appui *m*, soutien *m*; (*COMPUT: also:* ~ **file**) sauvegarde *f*.

backward ['bækwəd] *adj* (*movement*) en arrière; (*measure*) rétrograde; (*person, country*) arriéré(e); attardé(e); (*shy*) hésitant(e); ~ **and forward movement** mouvement de va-et-vient.

backwards ['bækwədz] *adv* (*move, go*) en arrière; (*read a list*) à l'envers, à rebours; (*fall*) à la renverse; (*walk*) à reculons; (*in time*) en arrière, vers le passé; **to know sth** ~ *or* (*US*) ~ **and forwards** (*col*) connaître qch sur le bout des doigts.

backwater ['bækwɔːtə*] *n* (*fig*) coin reculé; bled perdu.

back yard *n* arrière-cour *f*.

bacon ['beɪkən] *n* bacon *m*, lard *m*.

bacteria [bæk'tɪərɪə] *npl* bactéries *fpl*.

bacteriology [bæktɪərɪ'ɔlədʒɪ] *n* bactériologie *f*.

bad [bæd] *adj* mauvais(e); (*child*) vilain(e); (*meat, food*) gâté(e), avarié(e); **his** ~ **leg** sa jambe malade; **to go** ~ (*meat, food*) se gâter; (*milk*) tourner; **to have a** ~ **time of it** traverser une mauvaise passe; **I feel** ~ **about it** (*guilty*) j'ai un peu mauvaise conscience; ~ **debt** créance douteuse; **in** ~ **faith** de mauvaise foi.

baddie, baddy ['bædɪ] *n* (*col: CINE etc*) méchant *m*.

bade [bæd] *pt of* **bid**.

badge [bædʒ] *n* insigne *m*; (*of policeman*) plaque *f*; (*stick-on, sew-on*) badge *m*.

badger ['bædʒə*] *n* blaireau *m* ♦ *vt* harceler.

badly ['bædlɪ] *adv* (*work, dress etc*) mal; ~ **wounded** grièvement blessé; **he needs it** ~ il en a absolument besoin; **things are going** ~ les choses vont mal; ~ **off** *adj, adv* dans la gêne.

bad-mannered ['bæd'mænəd] *adj* mal élevé(e).

badminton ['bædmɪntən] *n* badminton *m*.

bad-mouth ['bæd'mauθ] *vt* (*US col: take*) débiner.

bad-tempered ['bæd'tɛmpəd] *adj* (*by nature*) ayant mauvais caractère; (*on one occasion*) de mauvaise humeur.

baffle ['bæfl] *vt* (*puzzle*) déconcerter.

baffling ['bæflɪŋ] *adj* déroutant(e), déconcertant(e).

bag [bæg] *n* sac *m*; (*of hunter*) gibecière *f*, chasse *f* ♦ *vt* (*col: take*) empocher; s'approprier; (*TECH*) mettre en sacs; ~**s of** (*col: lots of*) des masses de; **to pack one's** ~**s** faire ses valises *or* bagages; ~**s under the eyes** poches *fpl* sous les yeux.

bagful ['bægful] *n* plein sac.

baggage ['bægɪdʒ] *n* bagages *mpl*.

baggage claim *n* (*at airport*) livraison *f* des bagages.

baggy ['bægɪ] *adj* avachi(e), qui fait des poches.

Baghdad [bæg'dæd] *n* Baghdâd, Bagdad.

bag lady *n* (*col*) clocharde *f*.

bagpipes ['bægpaɪps] *npl* cornemuse *f*.

bag-snatcher ['bægsnætʃə*] *n* (*BRIT*) voleur *m* à l'arraché.

bag-snatching ['bægsnætʃɪŋ] *n* (*BRIT*) vol *m* à l'arraché.

Bahamas [bə'hɑːməz] *npl*: **the** ~ les Bahamas *fpl*.

Bahrain [bɑː'reɪn] *n* Bahreïn *m*.

bail [beɪl] *n* caution *f* ♦ *vt* (*prisoner: also:* **grant** ~ **to**) mettre en liberté sous caution; (*boat: also:* ~ **out**) écoper; **to be released on** ~ être libéré(e) sous caution; *see* **bale**.

▶**bail out** *vt* (*prisoner*) payer la caution de.

bailiff ['beɪlɪf] *n* huissier *m*.

bait [beɪt] *n* appât *m* ♦ *vt* appâter; (*fig*) tourmenter.

bake [beɪk] *vt* (faire) cuire au four ♦ *vi* (*bread etc*) cuire (au four); (*make cakes etc*) faire de la pâtisserie.

baked beans [beɪkt-] *npl* haricots blancs à la sauce tomate.

baker ['beɪkə*] *n* boulanger *m*.

bakery ['beɪkərɪ] *n* boulangerie *f*; boulangerie industrielle.

baking ['beɪkɪŋ] *n* cuisson *f*.

baking powder *n* levure *f* (chimique).

baking tin *n* (*for cake*) moule *m* à gâteaux; (*for meat*) plat *m* pour le four.

baking tray *n* plaque *f* à gâteaux.

balaclava [bælə'klɑːvə] *n* (*also:* ~ **helmet**) passe-montagne *m*.

balance ['bæləns] *n* équilibre *m*; (*COMM: sum*) solde *m*; (*scales*) balance *f* ♦ *vt* mettre *or*

faire tenir en équilibre; (*pros and cons*) peser; (*budget*) équilibrer; (*account*) balancer; (*compensate*) compenser, contrebalancer; ~ **of trade/payments** balance commerciale/des comptes *or* paiements; ~ **carried forward** solde *m* à reporter; ~ **brought forward** solde reporté; **to** ~ **the books** arrêter les comptes, dresser le bilan.
balanced ['bælənst] *adj* (*personality, diet*) équilibré(e).
balance sheet *n* bilan *m*.
balcony ['bælkənɪ] *n* balcon *m*.
bald [bɔːld] *adj* chauve; (*tyre*) lisse.
baldness ['bɔːldnɪs] *n* calvitie *f*.
bale [beɪl] *n* balle *f*, ballot *m*.
▶**bale out** *vi* (*of a plane*) sauter en parachute ♦ *vt* (*NAUT: water, boat*) écoper.
Balearic Islands [bælɪ'ærɪk-] *npl:* **the** ~ les (îles *fpl*) Baléares *fpl*.
baleful ['beɪlful] *adj* funeste, maléfique.
balk [bɔːk] *vi:* **to** ~ **(at)** (*person*) regimber (contre); (*horse*) se dérober (devant).
Balkan ['bɔːlkən] *adj* balkanique ♦ *n:* **the** ~**s** les Balkans *mpl*.
ball [bɔːl] *n* boule *f*; (*football*) ballon *m*; (*for tennis, golf*) balle *f*; (*dance*) bal *m*; **to play** ~ **(with sb)** jouer au ballon (*or* à la balle) (avec qn); (*fig*) coopérer (avec qn); **to be on the** ~ (*fig: competent*) être à la hauteur; (: *alert*) être éveillé(e), être vif(vive); **to start the** ~ **rolling** (*fig*) commencer; **the** ~ **is in their court** (*fig*) la balle est dans leur camp.
ballad ['bæləd] *n* ballade *f*.
ballast ['bæləst] *n* lest *m*.
ball bearing *n* roulement *m* à billes.
ball cock *n* robinet *m* à flotteur.
ballerina [bælə'riːnə] *n* ballerine *f*.
ballet ['bæleɪ] *n* ballet *m*; (*art*) danse *f* (classique).
ballet dancer *n* danseur/euse de ballet.
ballistic [bə'lɪstɪk] *adj* balistique.
ballistics [bə'lɪstɪks] *n* balistique *f*.
balloon [bə'luːn] *n* ballon *m*; (*in comic strip*) bulle *f* ♦ *vi* gonfler.
balloonist [bə'luːnɪst] *n* aéronaute *m/f*.
ballot ['bælət] *n* scrutin *m*.
ballot box *n* urne (électorale).
ballot paper *n* bulletin *m* de vote.
ballpark ['bɔːlpɑːk] *n* (*US*) stade *m* de baseball.
ballpark figure *n* (*col*) chiffre approximatif.
ball-point pen ['bɔːlpɔɪnt-] *n* stylo *m* à bille.
ballroom ['bɔːlrum] *n* salle *f* de bal.
balls [bɔːlz] *npl* (*col!*) couilles *fpl* (*!*).
balm [bɑːm] *n* baume *m*.
balmy ['bɑːmɪ] *adj* (*breeze, air*) doux(douce); (*BRIT col*) = **barmy**.
BALPA ['bælpə] *n abbr* (= *British Airline Pilots' Association*) syndicat *des* pilotes de ligne.
balsam ['bɔːlsəm] *n* baume *m*.
balsa (wood) ['bɔːlsə-] *n* balsa *m*.

Baltic ['bɔːltɪk] *adj, n:* **the** ~ **(Sea)** la (mer) Baltique.
balustrade [bæləs'treɪd] *n* balustrade *f*.
bamboo [bæm'buː] *n* bambou *m*.
bamboozle [bæm'buːzl] *vt* (*col*) embobiner.
ban [bæn] *n* interdiction *f* ♦ *vt* interdire; **he was** ~**ned from driving** (*BRIT*) on lui a retiré le permis (de conduire).
banal [bə'nɑːl] *adj* banal(e).
banana [bə'nɑːnə] *n* banane *f*.
band [bænd] *n* bande *f*; (*at a dance*) orchestre *m*; (*MIL*) musique *f*, fanfare *f*.
▶**band together** *vi* se liguer.
B & B *n abbr* = **bed and breakfast**.
bandage ['bændɪdʒ] *n* bandage *m*, pansement *m* ♦ *vt* (*wound, leg*) mettre un pansement *or* un bandage sur; (*person*) mettre un pansement *or* un bandage à.
Band-Aid ['bændeɪd] *n* ® (*US*) pansement adhésif.
bandit ['bændɪt] *n* bandit *m*.
bandstand ['bændstænd] *n* kiosque *m* (à musique).
bandwagon ['bændwægən] *n:* **to jump on the** ~ (*fig*) monter dans *or* prendre le train en marche.
bandy ['bændɪ] *vt* (*jokes, insults*) échanger.
▶**bandy about** *vt* employer à tout bout de champ *or* à tort et à travers.
bandy-legged ['bændɪ'lɛgɪd] *adj* aux jambes arquées.
bane [beɪn] *n:* **it** (*or* **he** *etc*) **is the** ~ **of my life** c'est (*or* il est *etc*) le drame de ma vie.
bang [bæŋ] *n* détonation *f*; (*of door*) claquement *m*; (*blow*) coup (violent) ♦ *vt* frapper (violemment); (*door*) claquer ♦ *vi* détoner; claquer ♦ *adv:* **to be** ~ **on time** (*BRIT col*) être à l'heure pile; **to** ~ **at the door** cogner à la porte; **to** ~ **into sth** se cogner contre qch.
banger ['bæŋə*] *n* (*BRIT: car. also:* **old** ~) (vieux) tacot; (*BRIT col: sausage*) saucisse *f*; (*firework*) pétard *m*.
Bangkok [bæŋ'kɔk] *n* Bangkok.
Bangladesh [bæŋglə'dɛʃ] *n* Bangladesh *m*.
bangle ['bæŋgl] *n* bracelet *m*.
bangs [bæŋz] *npl* (*US: fringe*) frange *f*.
banish ['bænɪʃ] *vt* bannir.
banister(s) ['bænɪstə(z)] *n(pl)* rampe *f* (d'escalier).
banjo, ~**es** *or* ~**s** ['bændʒəu] *n* banjo *m*.
bank [bæŋk] *n* banque *f*; (*of river, lake*) bord *m*, rive *f*; (*of earth*) talus *m*, remblai *m* ♦ *vi* (*AVIAT*) virer sur l'aile; (*COMM*): **they** ~ **with Pitt's** leur banque *or* banquier est Pitt's.
▶**bank on** *vt fus* miser *or* tabler sur.
bank account *n* compte *m* en banque.
bank balance *n* solde *m* bancaire.
bank card *n* = **banker's card**.
bank charges *npl* (*BRIT*) frais *mpl* de banque.
bank draft *n* traite *f* bancaire.
banker ['bæŋkə*] *n* banquier *m*; ~**'s card** (*BRIT*)

carte *f* d'identité bancaire; ~'s **order** (*BRIT*) ordre *m* de virement.
bank giro *n* paiement *m* par virement.
bank holiday *n* (*BRIT*) jour férié (*où les banques sont fermées*).

Un **bank holiday** *en Grande-Bretagne est un lundi férié et donc l'occasion d'un week-end prolongé. La circulation sur les routes et le trafic dans les gares et les aéroports augmentent considérablement à ces périodes. Les principaux* **bank holidays**, *à part Pâques et Noël, ont lieu au mois de mai et fin août.*

---

banking ['bæŋkɪŋ] *n* opérations *fpl* bancaires; profession *f* de banquier.
banking hours *npl* heures *fpl* d'ouverture des banques.
bank loan *n* prêt *m* bancaire.
bank manager *n* directeur *m* d'agence (bancaire).
banknote ['bæŋknəut] *n* billet *m* de banque.
bank rate *n* taux *m* de l'escompte.
bankrupt ['bæŋkrʌpt] *n* failli/e ♦ *adj* en faillite; **to go** ~ faire faillite.
bankruptcy ['bæŋkrʌptsɪ] *n* faillite *f*.
bank statement *n* relevé *m* de compte.
banner ['bænə*] *n* bannière *f*.
bannister(s) ['bænɪstə(z)] *n(pl)* = **banister(s)**.
banns [bænz] *npl* bans *mpl* (de mariage).
banquet ['bæŋkwɪt] *n* banquet *m*, festin *m*.
bantam-weight ['bæntəmweɪt] *n* poids *m* coq *inv*.
banter ['bæntə*] *n* badinage *m*.
BAOR *n abbr* (= *British Army of the Rhine*) forces britanniques en Allemagne.
baptism ['bæptɪzəm] *n* baptême *m*.
Baptist ['bæptɪst] *n* baptiste *m/f*.
baptize [bæp'taɪz] *vt* baptiser.
bar [bɑ:*] *n* barre *f*; (*of window etc*) barreau *m*; (*of chocolate*) tablette *f*, plaque *f*; (*fig*) obstacle *m*; mesure *f* d'exclusion; (*pub*) bar *m*; (*counter: in pub*) comptoir *m*, bar; (*MUS*) mesure *f* ♦ *vt* (*road*) barrer; (*window*) munir de barreaux; (*person*) exclure; (*activity*) interdire; ~ **of soap** savonnette *f*; **behind** ~s (*prisoner*) derrière les barreaux; **the B**~ (*LAW*) le barreau; ~ **none** sans exception.
Barbados [bɑ:'beɪdɔs] *n* Barbade *f*.
barbaric [bɑ:'bærɪk] *adj* barbare.
barbarous ['bɑ:bərəs] *adj* barbare, cruel(le).
barbecue ['bɑ:bɪkju:] *n* barbecue *m*.
barbed wire ['bɑ:bd-] *n* fil *m* de fer barbelé.
barber ['bɑ:bə*] *n* coiffeur *m* (pour hommes).
barbiturate [bɑ:'bɪtjurɪt] *n* barbiturique *m*.
Barcelona [bɑ:sə'ləunə] *n* Barcelone *f*.
bar chart *n* diagramme *m* en bâtons.
bar code *n* code *m* à barres.
bare [bɛə*] *adj* nu(e) ♦ *vt* mettre à nu, dénuder; (*teeth*) montrer; **the** ~ **essentials** le strict nécessaire.
bareback ['bɛəbæk] *adv* à cru, sans selle.

barefaced ['bɛəfeɪst] *adj* impudent(e), effronté(e).
barefoot ['bɛəfut] *adj, adv* nu-pieds, (les) pieds nus.
bareheaded [bɛə'hɛdɪd] *adj, adv* nu-tête, (la) tête nue.
barely ['bɛəlɪ] *adv* à peine.
Barents Sea ['bærənts-] *n*: **the** ~ la mer de Barents.
bargain ['bɑ:gɪn] *n* (*transaction*) marché *m*; (*good buy*) affaire *f*, occasion *f* ♦ *vi* (*haggle*) marchander; (*trade*) négocier, traiter; **into the** ~ par-dessus le marché.
▶**bargain for** *vi* (*col*): **he got more than he** ~**ed for!** il en a eu pour son argent!
bargaining ['bɑ:gənɪŋ] *n* marchandage *m*; négociations *fpl*.
bargaining position *n*: **to be in a weak/ strong** ~ être en mauvaise/bonne position pour négocier.
barge [bɑ:dʒ] *n* péniche *f*.
▶**barge in** *vi* (*walk in*) faire irruption; (*interrupt talk*) intervenir mal à propos.
▶**barge into** *vt fus* rentrer dans.
baritone ['bærɪtəun] *n* baryton *m*.
barium meal ['bɛərɪəm-] *n* (bouillie *f* de) sulfate *m* de baryum.
bark [bɑ:k] *n* (*of tree*) écorce *f*; (*of dog*) aboiement *m* ♦ *vi* aboyer.
barley ['bɑ:lɪ] *n* orge *f*.
barley sugar *n* sucre *m* d'orge.
barmaid ['bɑ:meɪd] *n* serveuse *f* (*de bar*), barmaid *f*.
barman ['bɑ:mən] *n* serveur *m* (*de bar*), barman *m*.
barmy ['bɑ:mɪ] *adj* (*BRIT col*) timbré(e), cinglé(e).
barn [bɑ:n] *n* grange *f*.
barnacle ['bɑ:nəkl] *n* anatife *m*, bernache *f*.
barn owl *n* chouette-effraie *f*, chat-huant *m*.
barometer [bə'rɔmɪtə*] *n* baromètre *m*.
baron ['bærən] *n* baron *m*; **the press/oil** ~s les magnats *mpl or* barons *mpl* de la presse/du pétrole.
baroness ['bærənɪs] *n* baronne *f*.
barrack ['bærək] *vt* (*BRIT*) chahuter.
barracking ['bærəkɪŋ] *n* (*BRIT*): **to give sb a** ~ chahuter qn.
barracks ['bærəks] *npl* caserne *f*.
barrage ['bærɑ:ʒ] *n* (*MIL*) tir *m* de barrage; (*dam*) barrage *m*; **a** ~ **of questions** un feu roulant de questions.
barrel ['bærəl] *n* tonneau *m*; (*of gun*) canon *m*.
barrel organ *n* orgue *m* de Barbarie.
barren ['bærən] *adj* stérile; (*hills*) aride.
barricade [bærɪ'keɪd] *n* barricade *f* ♦ *vt* barricader.
barrier ['bærɪə*] *n* barrière *f*; (*BRIT: also:* **crash** ~) rail *m* de sécurité.
barrier cream *n* (*BRIT*) crème protectrice.
barring ['bɑ:rɪŋ] *prep* sauf.
barrister ['bærɪstə*] *n* (*BRIT*) avocat (plaidant).

*En Angleterre, un **barrister**, que l'on appelle également "barrister-at-law", est un avocat qui représente ses clients devant la cour et plaide pour eux. Le client doit d'abord passer par l'intermédiaire d'un **solicitor**. On obtient le diplôme de barrister après avoir fait des études dans l'une des Inns of Court, les quatre écoles de droit londoniennes.*

barrow ['bærəu] *n* (*cart*) charrette *f* à bras.
barstool ['bɑːstuːl] *n* tabouret *m* de bar.
Bart. *abbr* (*BRIT*) = baronet.
bartender ['bɑːtɛndə*] *n* (*US*) serveur *m* (*de bar*), barman *m*.
barter ['bɑːtə*] *n* échange *m*, troc *m* ♦ *vt*: to ~ sth for échanger qch contre.
base [beɪs] *n* base *f* ♦ *vt* (*troops*): to be ~d at être basé(e) à; (*opinion, belief*): to ~ sth on baser *or* fonder qch sur ♦ *adj* vil(e), bas(se); **coffee-~d** à base de café; **a Paris-~d firm** une maison opérant de Paris *or* dont le siège est à Paris; **I'm ~d in London** je suis basé(e) à Londres.
baseball ['beɪsbɔːl] *n* base-ball *m*.
baseboard ['beɪsbɔːd] *n* (*US*) plinthe *f*.
base camp *n* camp *m* de base.
Basel [bɑːl] *n* = Basle.
baseline ['beɪslaɪn] *n* (*TENNIS*) ligne *f* de fond.
basement ['beɪsmənt] *n* sous-sol *m*.
base rate *n* taux *m* de base.
bases ['beɪsiːz] *npl of* **basis**; ['beɪsɪz] *npl of* **base**.
bash [bæʃ] *vt* (*col*) frapper, cogner ♦ *n*: **I'll have a ~ (at it)** (*BRIT col*) je vais essayer un coup; **~ed in** *adj* enfoncé(e), défoncé(e).
▶**bash up** *vt* (*col: car*) bousiller; (*: BRIT: person*) tabasser.
bashful ['bæʃful] *adj* timide; modeste.
bashing ['bæʃɪŋ] *n* (*col*) raclée *f*; **Paki-~** ≈ ratonnade *f*; **queer-~** chasse *f* aux pédés.
BASIC ['beɪsɪk] *n* (*COMPUT*) BASIC *m*.
basic ['beɪsɪk] *adj* (*precautions, rules*) élémentaire; (*principles, research*) fondamental(e); (*vocabulary, salary*) de base; réduit(e) au minimum, rudimentaire.
basically ['beɪsɪklɪ] *adv* (*really*) en fait; (*essentially*) fondamentalement.
basic rate *n* (*of tax*) première tranche d'imposition.
basil ['bæzl] *n* basilic *m*.
basin ['beɪsn] *n* (*vessel, also GEO*) cuvette *f*, bassin *m*; (*BRIT: for food*) bol *m*; (*: bigger*) saladier *m*; (*also: wash~*) lavabo *m*.
basis *pl* **bases** ['beɪsɪs, -siːz] *n* base *f*; **on the ~ of what you've said** d'après *or* compte tenu de ce que vous dites.
bask [bɑːsk] *vi*: to ~ in the sun se chauffer au soleil.
basket ['bɑːskɪt] *n* corbeille *f*; (*with handle*) panier *m*.
basketball ['bɑːskɪtbɔːl] *n* basket-ball *m*.
basketball player *n* basketteur/euse.

Basle [bɑːl] *n* Bâle.
basmati rice [bəz'mætɪ-] *n* riz *m* basmati.
Basque [bæsk] *adj* basque ♦ *n* Basque *m/f*.
bass [beɪs] *n* (*MUS*) basse *f*.
bass clef *n* clé *f* de fa.
bassoon [bə'suːn] *n* basson *m*.
bastard ['bɑːstəd] *n* enfant naturel(le), bâtard/e; (*col!*) salaud *m* (*!*).
baste [beɪst] *vt* (*CULIN*) arroser; (*SEWING*) bâtir, faufiler.
bastion ['bæstɪən] *n* bastion *m*.
bat [bæt] *n* chauve-souris *f*; (*for baseball etc*) batte *f*; (*BRIT: for table tennis*) raquette *f* ♦ *vt*: **he didn't ~ an eyelid** il n'a pas sourcillé *or* bronché; **off one's own ~** de sa propre initiative.
batch [bætʃ] *n* (*of bread*) fournée *f*; (*of papers*) liasse *f*; (*of applicants, letters*) paquet *m*; (*of work*) monceau *m*; (*of goods*) lot *m*.
batch processing *n* (*COMPUT*) traitement *m* par lot.
bated ['beɪtɪd] *adj*: **with ~ breath** en retenant son souffle.
bath [bɑːθ, *pl* bɑːðz] *n* bain *m*; (*bathtub*) baignoire *f* ♦ *vt* baigner, donner un bain à; **to have a ~** prendre un bain; *see also* **baths**.
Bath chair *n* (*BRIT*) fauteuil roulant.
bathe [beɪð] *vi* se baigner ♦ *vt* baigner; (*wound etc*) laver.
bather ['beɪðə*] *n* baigneur/euse.
bathing ['beɪðɪŋ] *n* baignade *f*.
bathing cap *n* bonnet *m* de bain.
bathing costume, (*US*) **bathing suit** *n* maillot *m* (de bain).
bathmat ['bɑːθmæt] *n* tapis *m* de bain.
bathrobe ['bɑːθrəub] *n* peignoir *m* de bain.
bathroom ['bɑːθrum] *n* salle *f* de bains.
baths [bɑːðz] *npl* établissement *m* de bains(-douches).
bath towel *n* serviette *f* de bain.
bathtub ['bɑːθtʌb] *n* baignoire *f*.
batman ['bætmən] *n* (*BRIT MIL*) ordonnance *f*.
baton ['bætən] *n* bâton *m*; (*MUS*) baguette *f*; (*club*) matraque *f*.
battalion [bə'tælɪən] *n* bataillon *m*.
batten ['bætn] *n* (*CARPENTRY*) latte *f*; (*NAUT: on sail*) latte de voile.
▶**batten down** *vt* (*NAUT*): **to ~ down the hatches** fermer les écoutilles.
batter ['bætə*] *vt* battre ♦ *n* pâte *f* à frire.
battered ['bætəd] *adj* (*hat, pan*) cabossé(e); **~ wife/child** épouse/enfant maltraité(e) *or* martyr(e).
battering ram ['bætərɪŋ-] *n* bélier *m* (*fig*).
battery ['bætərɪ] *n* batterie *f*; (*of torch*) pile *f*.
battery charger *n* chargeur *m*.
battery farming *n* élevage *m* en batterie.
battle ['bætl] *n* bataille *f*, combat *m* ♦ *vi* se battre, lutter; **that's half the ~** (*fig*) c'est déjà bien; **it's a** *or* **we're fighting a losing ~** (*fig*) c'est perdu d'avance, c'est peine perdue.

battle dress *n* tenue *f* de campagne *or* d'assaut.
battlefield ['bætlfiːld] *n* champ *m* de bataille.
battlements ['bætlmənts] *npl* remparts *mpl*.
battleship ['bætlʃɪp] *n* cuirassé *m*.
batty ['bætɪ] *adj* (*col*: *person*) toqué(e); (: *idea, behaviour*) loufoque.
bauble ['bɔːbl] *n* babiole *f*.
baud [bɔːd] *n* (*COMPUT*) baud *m*.
baud rate *n* (*COMPUT*) vitesse *f* de transmission.
baulk [bɔːlk] *vi* = **balk**.
bauxite ['bɔːksaɪt] *n* bauxite *f*.
Bavaria [bə'vɛərɪə] *n* Bavière *f*.
Bavarian [bə'vɛərɪən] *adj* bavarois(e) ♦ *n* Bavarois/e.
bawdy ['bɔːdɪ] *adj* paillard(e).
bawl [bɔːl] *vi* hurler, brailler.
bay [beɪ] *n* (*of sea*) baie *f*; (*BRIT*: *for parking*) place *f* de stationnement; (: *for loading*) aire *f* de chargement; (*horse*) bai/e *m/f*; **to hold sb at** ~ tenir qn à distance *or* en échec.
bay leaf *n* laurier *m*.
bayonet ['beɪənɪt] *n* baïonnette *f*.
bay tree *n* laurier *m*.
bay window *n* baie vitrée.
bazaar [bə'zɑː*] *n* bazar *m*; vente *f* de charité.
bazooka [bə'zuːkə] *n* bazooka *m*.
BB *n abbr* (*BRIT*: = *Boys' Brigade*) *mouvement de garçons.*
BBB *n abbr* (*US*: = *Better Business Bureau*) *organisme de défense du consommateur.*
BBC *n abbr* (= *British Broadcasting Corporation*) *office de la radiodiffusion et télévision britannique.*

> *La **BBC** est un organisme centralisé dont les membres, nommés par l'État, gèrent les chaînes de télévision publiques (BBC1, qui présente des émissions d'intérêt général, et BBC2, qui est plutôt orientée vers les émissions plus culturelles) et les stations de radio publiques (5 au niveau national, et 37 à l'échelle locale). Bien que non contrôlée par l'État, la BBC est responsable devant le* **parliament** *quant au contenu des émissions qu'elle diffuse. Par ailleurs, la BBC offre un service mondial de diffusion d'émissions, en anglais et dans 35 autres langues, appelé BBC World Service. La BBC est financée par la redevance télévision et par l'exportation d'émissions.*

BC *adv abbr* (= *before Christ*) av. J.-C. ♦ *abbr* (*Canada*) = *British Columbia.*
BCG *n abbr* (= *Bacillus Calmette-Guérin*) BCG *m*.
BD *n abbr* (= *Bachelor of Divinity*) *diplôme universitaire.*
B/D *abbr* = **bank draft**.
BDS *n abbr* (= *Bachelor of Dental Surgery*) *diplôme universitaire.*

══════════════════ *KEYWORD*

be [biː] (*pt* **was, were,** *pp* **been**) *aux vb* **1** (*with present participle: forming continuous tenses*): **what are you doing?** que faites-vous?; **they're coming tomorrow** ils viennent demain; **I've been waiting for you for 2 hours** je t'attends depuis 2 heures
2 (*with pp: forming passives*) être; **to** ~ **killed** être tué(e); **he was nowhere to** ~ **seen** on ne le voyait nulle part
3 (*in tag questions*): **it was fun, wasn't it?** c'était drôle, n'est-ce pas?; **she's back, is she?** elle est rentrée, n'est-ce pas *or* alors?
4 (*+to +infinitive*): **the house is to** ~ **sold** la maison doit être vendue; **he's not to open it** il ne doit pas l'ouvrir; **am I to understand that ...?** dois-je comprendre que ...?; **he was to have come yesterday** il devait venir hier
5 (*possibility, supposition*): **if I were you, I ...** à votre place, je ..., si j'étais vous, je ...
♦ *vb + complement* **1** (*gen*) être; **I'm English** je suis anglais(e); **I'm tired** je suis fatigué(e); **I'm hot/cold** j'ai chaud/froid; **he's a doctor** il est médecin; **2 and 2 are 4** 2 et 2 font 4
2 (*of health*) aller; **how are you?** comment allez-vous?; **he's fine now** il va bien maintenant; **he's very ill** il est très malade
3 (*of age*) avoir; **how old are you?** quel âge avez-vous?; **I'm sixteen (years old)** j'ai seize ans
4 (*cost*) coûter; **how much was the meal?** combien a coûté le repas?; **that'll** ~ **£5, please** ça fera 5 livres, s'il vous plaît
♦ *vi* **1** (*exist, occur etc*) être, exister; **the prettiest girl that ever was** la fille la plus jolie qui ait jamais existé; ~ **that as it may** quoi qu'il en soit; **so** ~ **it** soit
2 (*referring to place*) être, se trouver; **I won't** ~ **here tomorrow** je ne serai pas là demain; **Edinburgh is in Scotland** Édimbourg est *or* se trouve en Écosse
3 (*referring to movement*) aller; **where have you been?** où êtes-vous allé(s)?
♦ *impers vb* **1** (*referring to time, distance*) être; **it's 5 o'clock** il est 5 heures; **it's the 28th of April** c'est le 28 avril; **it's 10 km to the village** le village est à 10 km
2 (*referring to the weather*) faire; **it's too hot/cold** il fait trop chaud/froid; **it's windy** il y a du vent
3 (*emphatic*): **it's me/the postman** c'est moi/le facteur.

B/E *abbr* = **bill of exchange**.
beach [biːtʃ] *n* plage *f* ♦ *vt* échouer.
beachcomber ['biːtʃkəumə*] *n* ramasseur *m* d'épaves; (*fig*) glandeur *m*.
beachwear ['biːtʃwɛə*] *n* tenues *fpl* de plage.
beacon ['biːkən] *n* (*lighthouse*) fanal *m*; (*marker*) balise *f*; (*also*: **radio** ~) radiophare *m*.

bead [bi:d] n perle f; (of dew, sweat) goutte f; ~s (necklace) collier m.

beady ['bi:dɪ] adj: ~ **eyes** yeux mpl de fouine.

beagle [bi:gl] n beagle m.

beak [bi:k] n bec m.

beaker ['bi:kə*] n gobelet m.

beam [bi:m] n poutre f; (of light) rayon m; (RADIO) faisceau m radio ♦ vi rayonner; **to drive on full** or **main** or (US) **high** ~ **rouler en pleins phares.**

beaming ['bi:mɪŋ] adj (sun, smile) radieux(euse).

bean [bi:n] n haricot m; (of coffee) grain m.

beanpole ['bi:npəul] n (col) perche f.

bean sprouts npl pousses fpl (de soja).

bear [bɛə*] n ours m; (STOCK EXCHANGE) baissier m ♦ vb (pt bore, pp borne [bɔː*, bɔːn]) vt porter; (endure) supporter; (traces, signs) porter; (COMM: interest) rapporter ♦ vi: **to ~ right/left** obliquer à droite/gauche, se diriger vers la droite/gauche; **to ~ the responsibility of** assumer la responsabilité de; **to ~ comparison with** soutenir la comparaison avec; **I can't ~ him** je ne peux pas le supporter or souffrir; **to bring pressure to ~ on sb** faire pression sur qn.

▶**bear out** vt (theory, suspicion) confirmer.

▶**bear up** vi supporter, tenir le coup; **he bore up well** il a tenu le coup.

▶**bear with** vt fus (sb's moods, temper) supporter; ~ **with me a minute** un moment, s'il vous plaît.

bearable ['bɛərəbl] adj supportable.

beard [bɪəd] n barbe f.

bearded ['bɪədɪd] adj barbu(e).

bearer ['bɛərə*] n porteur m; (of passport etc) titulaire m/f.

bearing ['bɛərɪŋ] n maintien m, allure f; (connection) rapport m; (TECH): (ball) ~s npl roulement m (à billes); **to take a** ~ faire le point; **to find one's ~s** s'orienter.

beast [bi:st] n bête f; (col): **he's a** ~ c'est une brute.

beastly ['bi:stlɪ] adj infect(e).

beat [bi:t] n battement m; (MUS) temps m, mesure f; (of policeman) ronde f ♦ vt (pt beat, pp beaten) battre; **off the** ~**en track** hors des chemins or sentiers battus; **to ~ about the bush** tourner autour du pot; **to ~ time** battre la mesure; **that ~s everything!** c'est le comble!

▶**beat down** vt (door) enfoncer; (price) faire baisser; (seller) faire descendre ♦ vi (rain) tambouriner; (sun) taper.

▶**beat off** vt repousser.

▶**beat up** vt (eggs) battre; (col: person) tabasser.

beater ['bi:tə*] n (for eggs, cream) fouet m, batteur m.

beating ['bi:tɪŋ] n raclée f.

beat-up ['bi:t'ʌp] adj (col) déglingué(e).

beautician [bju:'tɪʃən] n esthéticien/ne.

beautiful ['bju:tɪful] adj beau(belle).

beautifully ['bju:tɪflɪ] adv admirablement.

beautify ['bju:tɪfaɪ] vt embellir.

beauty ['bju:tɪ] n beauté f; **the** ~ **of it is that ...** le plus beau, c'est que ....

beauty contest n concours m de beauté.

beauty queen n reine f de beauté.

beauty salon n institut m de beauté.

beauty sleep n: **I'm going to bed, I need my** ~ je vais me coucher, j'ai besoin de faire un gros dodo.

beauty spot n grain m de beauté; (BRIT TOURISM) site naturel (d'une grande beauté).

beaver ['bi:və*] n castor m.

becalmed [bɪ'kɑ:md] adj immobilisé(e) par le calme plat.

became [bɪ'keɪm] pt of **become**.

because [bɪ'kɔz] conj parce que; ~ **of** prep à cause de.

beck [bɛk] n: **to be at sb's** ~ **and call** être à l'entière disposition de qn.

beckon ['bɛkən] vt (also: ~ **to**) faire signe (de venir) à.

become [bɪ'kʌm] vt (irreg: like come) devenir; **to ~ fat/thin** grossir/maigrir; **to ~ angry** se mettre en colère; **it became known that** on apprit que; **what has ~ of him?** qu'est-il devenu?

becoming [bɪ'kʌmɪŋ] adj (behaviour) convenable, bienséant(e); (clothes) seyant(e).

BECTU ['bɛktu] n abbr (BRIT) = Broadcasting, Entertainment, Cinematographic and Theatre Union.

BEd n abbr (= Bachelor of Education) diplôme d'aptitude à l'enseignement.

bed [bɛd] n lit m; (of flowers) parterre m; (of coal, clay) couche f; (of sea, lake) fond m; **to go to** ~ aller se coucher.

▶**bed down** vi se coucher.

bed and breakfast (B & B) n (terms) chambre et petit déjeuner; (place) ≈ chambre f d'hôte.

Un **bed and breakfast** *est une petite pension dans une maison particulière ou une ferme où l'on peut louer une chambre avec petit déjeuner compris pour un prix modique par rapport à ce que l'on paierait dans un hôtel. Ces établissements sont communément appelés B & B, et sont signalés par une pancarte dans le jardin ou au-dessus de la porte.*

---

bedbug ['bɛdbʌg] n punaise f.

bedclothes ['bɛdkləuðz] npl couvertures fpl et draps mpl.

bedcover ['bɛdkʌvə*] n couvre-lit m, dessus-de-lit m.

bedding ['bɛdɪŋ] n literie f.

bedevil [bɪ'dɛvl] vt (harass) harceler; **to be**

~**led by** être victime de.
bedfellow ['bɛdfɛləu] n: **they are strange ~s**
(*fig*) ça fait un drôle de mélange.
bedlam ['bɛdləm] n chahut m, cirque m.
bedpan ['bɛdpæn] n bassin m (hygiénique).
bedpost ['bɛdpəust] n colonne f de lit.
bedraggled [bɪ'drægld] adj dépenaillé(e), les
vêtements en désordre.
bedridden ['bɛdrɪdn] adj cloué(e) au lit.
bedrock ['bɛdrɔk] n (*fig*) principes essentiels
or de base, essentiel m; (*GEO*) roche f en
place, socle m.
bedroom ['bɛdrum] n chambre f (à coucher).
Beds abbr (*BRIT*) = Bedfordshire.
bed settee n canapé-lit m.
bedside ['bɛdsaɪd] n: **at sb's ~** au chevet de
qn ♦ cpd (book, lamp) de chevet.
bedsit(ter) ['bɛdsɪt(ə*)] n (*BRIT*) chambre
meublée, studio m.
bedspread ['bɛdsprɛd] n couvre-lit m,
dessus-de-lit m.
bedtime ['bɛdtaɪm] n: **it's ~** c'est l'heure de
se coucher.
bee [biː] n abeille f; **to have a ~ in one's
bonnet (about sth)** être obnubilé(e) (par
qch).
beech [biːtʃ] n hêtre m.
beef [biːf] n bœuf m.
▶**beef up** vt (col: support) renforcer;
(: essay) étoffer.
beefburger ['biːfbəːgə*] n hamburger m.
beefeater ['biːfiːtə*] n hallebardier m (de la
tour de Londres).
beehive ['biːhaɪv] n ruche f.
bee-keeping ['biːkiːpɪŋ] n apiculture f.
beeline ['biːlaɪn] n: **to make a ~ for** se diriger
tout droit vers.
been [biːn] pp of **be**.
beep [biːp] n bip m.
beeper ['biːpə*] n (pager) bip m.
beer [bɪə*] n bière f.
beer belly n (col) bedaine f (de buveur de
bière).
beer can n canette f de bière.
beetle ['biːtl] n scarabée m, coléoptère m.
beetroot ['biːtruːt] n (*BRIT*) betterave f.
befall [bɪ'fɔːl] vt, vi (irreg: like **fall**) advenir (à).
befit [bɪ'fɪt] vt seoir à.
before [bɪ'fɔː*] prep (of time) avant; (of space)
devant ♦ conj avant que + sub; avant de
♦ adv avant; ~ **going** avant de partir; ~ **she
goes** avant qu'elle (ne) parte; **the week ~** la
semaine précédente or d'avant; **I've seen it
~** je l'ai déjà vu; **I've never seen it ~** c'est
la première fois que je le vois.
beforehand [bɪ'fɔːhænd] adv au préalable, à
l'avance.
befriend [bɪ'frɛnd] vt venir en aide à; traiter
en ami.
befuddled [bɪ'fʌdld] adj: **to be ~** avoir les
idées brouillées.
beg [bɛg] vi mendier ♦ vt mendier; (favour)

quémander, solliciter; (entreat) supplier; **I ~
your pardon** (apologising) excusez-moi; (: not
hearing) pardon?; **that ~s the question of** ...
cela soulève la question de ..., cela suppose
réglée la question de ....
began [bɪ'gæn] pt of **begin**.
beggar ['bɛgə*] n (also: ~**man**, ~**woman**)
mendiant/e.
begin, pt **began**, pp **begun** [bɪ'gɪn, -'gæn,
-'gʌn] vt, vi commencer; **to ~ doing** or **to do
sth** commencer à faire qch; ~**ning (from)
Monday** à partir de lundi; **I can't ~ to thank
you** je ne saurais vous remercier; **to ~ with**
d'abord, pour commencer.
beginner [bɪ'gɪnə*] n débutant/e.
beginning [bɪ'gɪnɪŋ] n commencement m,
début m; **right from the ~** dès le début.
begrudge [bɪ'grʌdʒ] vt: **to ~ sb sth** envier qch
à qn; donner qch à contrecœur or à regret à
qn.
beguile [bɪ'gaɪl] vt (enchant) enjôler.
beguiling [bɪ'gaɪlɪŋ] adj (charming)
séduisant(e), enchanteur(eresse).
begun [bɪ'gʌn] pp of **begin**.
behalf [bɪ'hɑːf] n: **on ~ of**, (*US*) **in ~ of** de la
part de; au nom de; pour le compte de.
behave [bɪ'heɪv] vi se conduire, se comporter;
(well: also: ~ **o.s.**) se conduire bien or
comme il faut.
behaviour, (*US*) **behavior** [bɪ'heɪvjə*] n
comportement m, conduite f.
behead [bɪ'hɛd] vt décapiter.
beheld [bɪ'hɛld] pt, pp of **behold**.
behind [bɪ'haɪnd] prep derrière; (time) en
retard sur ♦ adv derrière; en retard ♦ n
derrière m; ~ **the scenes** dans les coulisses;
to leave sth ~ (forget) oublier de prendre
qch; **to be ~ (schedule) with sth** être en
retard dans qch.
behold [bɪ'həuld] vt (irreg: like **hold**)
apercevoir, voir.
beige [beɪʒ] adj beige.
being ['biːɪŋ] n être m; **to come into ~**
prendre naissance.
Beirut [beɪ'ruːt] n Beyrouth.
Belarus [bɛlə'rus] n Bélarus f.
Belarussian [bɛlə'rʌʃən] adj biélorusse ♦ n
Biélorusse m/f; (*LING*) biélorusse m.
belated [bɪ'leɪtɪd] adj tardif(ive).
belch [bɛltʃ] vi avoir un renvoi, roter ♦ vt
(also: ~ **out**: smoke etc) vomir, cracher.
beleaguered [bɪ'liːgɪd] adj (city) assiégé(e);
(army) cerné(e); (fig) sollicité(e) de toutes
parts.
Belfast ['bɛlfɑːst] n Belfast.
belfry ['bɛlfrɪ] n beffroi m.
Belgian ['bɛldʒən] adj belge, de Belgique ♦ n
Belge m/f.
Belgium ['bɛldʒəm] n Belgique f.
Belgrade [bɛl'greɪd] n Belgrade.
belie [bɪ'laɪ] vt démentir; (give false impression
of) occulter.

belief [bɪ'liːf] n (opinion) conviction f; (trust, faith) foi f; (acceptance as true) croyance f; **it's beyond ~** c'est incroyable; **in the ~ that** dans l'idée que.

believable [bɪ'liːvəbl] adj croyable.

believe [bɪ'liːv] vt, vi croire, estimer; **to ~ in** (God) croire en; (ghosts, method) croire à; **I don't ~ in corporal punishment** je ne suis pas partisan des châtiments corporels; **he is ~d to be abroad** il serait à l'étranger.

believer [bɪ'liːvə*] n (in idea, activity): **~ in** partisan/e de; (REL) croyant/e.

belittle [bɪ'lɪtl] vt déprécier, rabaisser.

Belize [bɛ'liːz] n Bélize m.

bell [bɛl] n cloche f; (small) clochette f, grelot m; (on door) sonnette f; (electric) sonnerie f; **that rings a ~** (fig) cela me rappelle qch.

bell-bottoms ['bɛlbɔtəmz] npl pantalon m à pattes d'éléphant.

bellboy ['bɛlbɔɪ], (US) **bellhop** ['bɛlhɔp] n groom m, chasseur m.

belligerent [bɪ'lɪdʒərənt] adj (at war) belligérant(e); (fig) agressif(ive).

bellow ['bɛləu] vi mugir; beugler ♦ vt (orders) hurler.

bellows ['bɛləuz] npl soufflet m.

bell push n (BRIT) bouton m de sonnette.

belly ['bɛlɪ] n ventre m.

bellyache ['bɛlɪeɪk] (col) n colique f ♦ vi ronchonner.

bellybutton ['bɛlɪbʌtn] n nombril m.

bellyful ['bɛlɪful] n (col): **I've had a ~** j'en ai ras le bol.

belong [bɪ'lɔŋ] vi: **to ~ to** appartenir à; (club etc) faire partie de; **this book ~s here** ce livre va ici, la place de ce livre est ici.

belongings [bɪ'lɔŋɪŋz] npl affaires fpl, possessions fpl; **personal ~** effets personnels.

Belorussia [bɛlə'rʌʃə] n Biélorussie f.

Belorussian [bɛlə'rʌʃən] adj, n = **Belarussian**.

beloved [bɪ'lʌvɪd] adj (bien-)aimé(e), chéri(e) ♦ n bien-aimé/e.

below [bɪ'ləu] prep sous, au-dessous de ♦ adv en dessous; en contre-bas; **see ~** voir plus bas or plus loin or ci-dessous; **temperatures ~ normal** températures inférieures à la normale.

belt [bɛlt] n ceinture f; (TECH) courroie f ♦ vt (thrash) donner une raclée à ♦ vi (BRIT col) filer (à toutes jambes); **industrial ~** zone industrielle.

▶**belt out** vt (song) chanter à tue-tête or à pleins poumons.

▶**belt up** vi (BRIT col) la boucler.

beltway ['bɛltweɪ] n (US AUT) route f de ceinture; (: motorway) périphérique m.

bemoan [bɪ'məun] vt se lamenter sur.

bemused [bɪ'mjuːzd] adj médusé(e).

bench [bɛntʃ] n banc m; (in workshop) établi m; **the B~** (LAW) la magistrature, la Cour.

bench mark n repère m.

bend [bɛnd] vb (pt, pp **bent** [bɛnt]) vt courber; (leg, arm) plier ♦ vi se courber ♦ n (BRIT: in road) virage m, tournant m; (in pipe, river) coude m.

▶**bend down** vi se baisser.

▶**bend over** vi se pencher.

bends [bɛndz] npl (MED) maladie f des caissons.

beneath [bɪ'niːθ] prep sous, au-dessous de; (unworthy of) indigne de ♦ adv dessous, au-dessous, en bas.

benefactor ['bɛnɪfæktə*] n bienfaiteur m.

benefactress ['bɛnɪfæktrɪs] n bienfaitrice f.

beneficial [bɛnɪ'fɪʃəl] adj: **~ (to)** salutaire (pour), bénéfique (à).

beneficiary [bɛnɪ'fɪʃərɪ] n (LAW) bénéficiaire m/f.

benefit ['bɛnɪfɪt] n avantage m, profit m; (allowance of money) allocation f ♦ vt faire du bien à, profiter à ♦ vi: **he'll ~ from it** cela lui fera du bien, il y gagnera or s'en trouvera bien.

benefit performance n représentation f or gala m de bienfaisance.

Benelux ['bɛnɪlʌks] n Bénélux m.

benevolent [bɪ'nɛvələnt] adj bienveillant(e).

BEng n abbr (= Bachelor of Engineering) diplôme universitaire.

benign [bɪ'naɪn] adj (person, smile) bienveillant(e), affable; (MED) bénin(igne).

bent [bɛnt] pt, pp of **bend** ♦ n inclination f, penchant m ♦ adj (wire, pipe) coudé(e); (col: dishonest) véreux(euse); **to be ~ on** être résolu(e) à.

bequeath [bɪ'kwiːð] vt léguer.

bequest [bɪ'kwɛst] n legs m.

bereaved [bɪ'riːvd] n: **the ~** la famille du disparu ♦ adj endeuillé(e).

bereavement [bɪ'riːvmənt] n deuil m.

beret ['bɛreɪ] n béret m.

Bering Sea ['bɛrɪŋ-] n: **the ~** la mer de Béring.

berk [bəːk] n (BRIT col) andouille m/f.

Berks abbr (BRIT) = Berkshire.

Berlin [bəː'lɪn] n Berlin; **East/West ~** Berlin Est/Ouest.

berm [bəːm] n (US AUT) accotement m.

Bermuda [bəː'mjuːdə] n Bermudes fpl.

Bermuda shorts npl bermuda m.

Bern [bəːn] n Berne.

berry ['bɛrɪ] n baie f.

berserk [bə'səːk] adj: **to go ~** être pris(e) d'une rage incontrôlable; se déchaîner.

berth [bəːθ] n (bed) couchette f; (for ship) poste m d'amarrage, mouillage m ♦ vi (in harbour) venir à quai; (at anchor) mouiller; **to give sb a wide ~** (fig) éviter qn.

beseech, pt, pp **besought** [bɪ'siːtʃ, -'sɔːt] vt implorer, supplier.

beset, pt, pp **beset** [bɪ'sɛt] vt assaillir ♦ adj: **~ with** semé(e) de.

besetting [bɪ'sɛtɪŋ] adj: **his ~ sin** son vice, son

gros défaut.

beside [bɪ'saɪd] *prep* à côté de; (*compared with*) par rapport à; **that's ~ the point** ça n'a rien à voir; **to be ~ o.s. (with anger)** être hors de soi.

besides [bɪ'saɪdz] *adv* en outre, de plus ♦ *prep* en plus de; (*except*) excepté.

besiege [bɪ'siːdʒ] *vt* (*town*) assiéger; (*fig*) assaillir.

besotted [bɪ'sɔtɪd] *adj* (*BRIT*): **~ with** entiché(e) de.

besought [bɪ'sɔːt] *pt, pp of* **beseech**.

bespectacled [bɪ'spɛktɪkld] *adj* à lunettes.

bespoke [bɪ'spəuk] *adj* (*BRIT: garment*) fait(e) sur mesure; **~ tailor** tailleur *m* à façon.

best [bɛst] *adj* meilleur(e) ♦ *adv* le mieux; **the ~ part of** (*quantity*) le plus clair de, la plus grande partie de; **at ~** au mieux; **to make the ~ of sth** s'accommoder de qch (du mieux que l'on peut); **to do one's ~** faire de son mieux; **to the ~ of my knowledge** pour autant que je sache; **to the ~ of my ability** du mieux que je pourrai; **he's not exactly patient at the ~ of times** il n'est jamais spécialement patient; **the ~ thing to do is ...** le mieux, c'est de ....

best man *n* garçon *m* d'honneur.

bestow [bɪ'stəu] *vt* accorder; (*title*) conférer.

bestseller ['bɛst'sɛlə*] *n* bestseller *m*, succès *m* de librairie.

bet [bɛt] *n* pari *m* ♦ *vt, vi* (*pt, pp* **bet** *or* **betted**) parier; **it's a safe ~** (*fig*) il y a de fortes chances.

Bethlehem ['bɛθlɪhɛm] *n* Bethléem.

betray [bɪ'treɪ] *vt* trahir.

betrayal [bɪ'treɪəl] *n* trahison *f*.

better ['bɛtə*] *adj* meilleur(e) ♦ *adv* mieux ♦ *vt* améliorer ♦ *n*: **to get the ~ of** triompher de, l'emporter sur; **a change for the ~** une amélioration; **I had ~ go** il faut que je m'en aille; **you had ~ do it** vous feriez mieux de le faire; **he thought ~ of it** il s'est ravisé; **to get ~** aller mieux; s'améliorer; **that's ~!** c'est mieux!; **~ off** *adj* plus à l'aise financièrement; (*fig*): **you'd be ~ off this way** vous vous en trouveriez mieux ainsi, ce serait mieux *or* plus pratique ainsi.

betting ['bɛtɪŋ] *n* paris *mpl*.

betting shop *n* (*BRIT*) bureau *m* de paris.

between [bɪ'twiːn] *prep* entre ♦ *adv* (*also*: **in ~**) au milieu, dans l'intervalle; **the road ~ here and London** la route d'ici à Londres; **we only had 5 ~ us** nous n'en avions que 5 en tout.

bevel ['bɛvəl] *n* (*also*: **~ edge**) biseau *m*.

beverage ['bɛvərɪdʒ] *n* boisson *f* (*gén sans alcool*).

bevy ['bɛvɪ] *n*: **a ~ of** un essaim *or* une volée de.

bewail [bɪ'weɪl] *vt* se lamenter sur.

beware [bɪ'wɛə*] *vt, vi*: **to ~ (of)** prendre garde (à).

bewildered [bɪ'wɪldəd] *adj* dérouté(e),

ahuri(e).

bewildering [bɪ'wɪldrɪŋ] *adj* déroutant(e), ahurissant(e).

bewitching [bɪ'wɪtʃɪŋ] *adj* enchanteur(teresse).

beyond [bɪ'jɔnd] *prep* (*in space*) au-delà de; (*exceeding*) au-dessus de ♦ *adv* au-delà; **~ doubt** hors de doute; **~ repair** irréparable.

b/f *abbr* = brought forward.

BFPO *n abbr* (= *British Forces Post Office*) *service postal de l'armée.*

bhp *n abbr* (*AUT*: = *brake horsepower*) puissance *f* aux freins.

bi... [baɪ] *prefix* bi....

biannual [baɪ'ænjuəl] *adj* semestriel(le).

bias ['baɪəs] *n* (*prejudice*) préjugé *m*, parti pris; (*preference*) prévention *f*.

bias(s)ed ['baɪəst] *adj* partial(e), montrant un parti pris; **to be ~ against** avoir un préjugé contre.

biathlon [baɪ'æθlən] *n* biathlon *m*.

bib [bɪb] *n* bavoir *m*, bavette *f*.

Bible ['baɪbl] *n* Bible *f*.

Bible Belt *n* (*US*): **the ~** *les États du Sud profondément protestants.*

bibliography [bɪblɪ'ɔgrəfɪ] *n* bibliographie *f*.

bicarbonate of soda [baɪ'kɑːbənɪt-] *n* bicarbonate *m* de soude.

bicentenary [baɪsɛn'tiːnərɪ] *n*, **bicentennial** [baɪsɛn'tɛnɪəl] *n* bicentenaire *m*.

biceps ['baɪsɛps] *n* biceps *m*.

bicker ['bɪkə*] *vi* se chamailler.

bicycle ['baɪsɪkl] *n* bicyclette *f*.

bicycle path *n*, **bicycle track** *n* piste *f* cyclable.

bicycle pump *n* pompe *f* à vélo.

bid [bɪd] *n* offre *f*; (*at auction*) enchère *f*; (*attempt*) tentative *f* ♦ *vb* (*pt* **bid** *or* **bade** [bæd], *pp* **bid** *or* **bidden** ['bɪdn]) *vi* faire une enchère *or* offre ♦ *vt* faire une enchère *or* offre de; **to ~ sb good day** souhaiter le bonjour à qn.

bidder ['bɪdə*] *n*: **the highest ~** le plus offrant.

bidding ['bɪdɪŋ] *n* enchères *fpl*.

bide [baɪd] *vt*: **to ~ one's time** attendre son heure.

bidet ['biːdeɪ] *n* bidet *m*.

bidirectional ['baɪdɪ'rɛkʃənl] *adj* bidirectionnel(le).

biennial [baɪ'ɛnɪəl] *adj* biennal(e), bisannuel(le) ♦ *n* biennale *f*; (*plant*) plante bisannuelle.

bier [bɪə*] *n* bière *f* (*cercueil*).

bifocals [baɪ'fəuklz] *npl* lunettes *fpl* à double foyer.

big [bɪg] *adj* (*in height: person, building, tree*) grand(e); (*in bulk, amount: person, parcel, book*) gros(se); **to do things in a ~ way** faire les choses en grand.

bigamy ['bɪgəmɪ] *n* bigamie *f*.

big dipper [-'dɪpə*] *n* montagnes *fpl* russes.

big end n (AUT) tête f de bielle.
biggish ['bɪgɪʃ] adj (see big) assez grand(e); assez gros(se).
bigheaded ['bɪg'hɛdɪd] adj prétentieux(euse).
big-hearted ['bɪg'hɑːtɪd] adj au grand cœur.
bigot ['bɪgət] n fanatique m/f, sectaire m/f.
bigoted ['bɪgətɪd] adj fanatique, sectaire.
bigotry ['bɪgətrɪ] n fanatisme m, sectarisme m.
big toe n gros orteil.
big top n grand chapiteau.
big wheel n (at fair) grande roue.
bigwig ['bɪgwɪg] n (col) grosse légume, huile f.
bike [baɪk] n vélo m, bécane f.
bikini [bɪ'kiːnɪ] n bikini m.
bilateral [baɪ'lætərl] adj bilatéral(e).
bile [baɪl] n bile f.
bilingual [baɪ'lɪŋgwəl] adj bilingue.
bilious ['bɪlɪəs] adj bilieux(euse); (fig) maussade, irritable.
bill [bɪl] n note f, facture f; (POL) projet m de loi; (US: banknote) billet m (de banque); (in restaurant) addition f, note f; (notice) affiche f; (THEAT): **on the ~** à l'affiche; (of bird) bec m ♦ vt (item) facturer; (customer) remettre la facture à; **may I have the ~ please?** (est-ce que je peux avoir) l'addition, s'il vous plaît?; **"stick** or **post no ~s"** "défense d'afficher"; **to fit** or **fill the ~** (fig) faire l'affaire; **~ of exchange** lettre f de change; **~ of lading** connaissement m; **~ of sale** contrat m de vente.
billboard ['bɪlbɔːd] n panneau m d'affichage.
billet ['bɪlɪt] n cantonnement m (chez l'habitant) ♦ vt (troops) cantonner.
billfold ['bɪlfəuld] n (US) portefeuille m.
billiards ['bɪljədz] n (jeu f de) billard m.
billion ['bɪljən] n (BRIT) billion m (million de millions); (US) milliard m.
billow ['bɪləu] n nuage m ♦ vi (smoke) s'élever en nuage; (sail) se gonfler.
billy goat ['bɪlɪgəut] n bouc m.
bimbo ['bɪmbəu] n (col) ravissante idiote f.
bin [bɪn] n boîte f; (BRIT: also: **dust~**, **litter~**) poubelle f; (for coal) coffre m.
binary ['baɪnərɪ] adj binaire.
bind, pt, pp **bound** [baɪnd, baund] vt attacher; (book) relier; (oblige) obliger, contraindre.
▶**bind over** vt (LAW) mettre en liberté conditionnelle.
▶**bind up** vt (wound) panser; **to be bound up in** (work, research etc) être complètement absorbé par, être accroché par; **to be bound up with** (person) être accroché à.
binder ['baɪndə*] n (file) classeur m.
binding ['baɪndɪŋ] n (of book) reliure f ♦ adj (contract) qui constitue une obligation.
binge [bɪndʒ] n (col): **to go on a ~** faire la bringue.
bingo ['bɪŋgəu] n sorte de jeu de loto pratiqué dans des établissements publics.

bin liner n sac m poubelle.
binoculars [bɪ'nɒkjuləz] npl jumelles fpl.
biochemistry [baɪə'kemɪstrɪ] n biochimie f.
biodegradable ['baɪəudɪ'greɪdəbl] adj biodégradable.
biodiversity ['baɪəudaɪ'vəːsɪtɪ] n biodiversité f.
biofuel ['baɪəufjuəl] n combustible m organique.
biographer [baɪ'ɒgrəfə*] n biographe m/f.
biographic(al) [baɪə'græfɪk(l)] adj biographique.
biography [baɪ'ɒgrəfɪ] n biographie f.
biological [baɪə'lɒdʒɪkl] adj biologique.
biological clock n horloge f physiologique.
biologist [baɪ'ɒlədʒɪst] n biologiste m/f.
biology [baɪ'ɒlədʒɪ] n biologie f.
biophysics ['baɪəu'fɪzɪks] n biophysique f.
biopic ['baɪəupɪk] n film m biographique.
biopsy ['baɪɒpsɪ] n biopsie f.
biosphere ['baɪəsfɪə*] n biosphère f.
biotechnology ['baɪəutek'nɒlədʒɪ] n biotechnologie f.
birch [bəːtʃ] n bouleau m.
bird [bəːd] n oiseau m; (BRIT col: girl) nana f.
bird of prey n oiseau m de proie.
bird's-eye view ['bəːdzaɪ-] n vue f à vol d'oiseau; (fig) vue d'ensemble or générale.
bird watcher [-wɔtʃə*] n ornithologue m/f amateur.
Biro ['baɪərəu] n ® stylo m à bille.
birth [bəːθ] n naissance f; **to give ~ to** donner naissance à, mettre au monde; (animal) mettre bas.
birth certificate n acte m de naissance.
birth control n limitation f des naissances; méthode(s) contraceptive(s).
birthday ['bəːθdeɪ] n anniversaire m.
birthmark ['bəːθmɑːk] n envie f, tache f de vin.
birthplace ['bəːθpleɪs] n lieu m de naissance.
birth rate n (taux m de) natalité f.
Biscay ['bɪskeɪ] n: **the Bay of ~** le golfe de Gascogne.
biscuit ['bɪskɪt] n (BRIT) biscuit m; (US) petit pain au lait.
bisect [baɪ'sɛkt] vt couper or diviser en deux.
bisexual ['baɪ'sɛksjuəl] adj, n bisexuel(le).
bishop ['bɪʃəp] n évêque m; (CHESS) fou m.
bistro ['biːstrəu] n petit restaurant m, bistrot m.
bit [bɪt] pt of **bite** ♦ n morceau m; (of tool) mèche f; (of horse) mors m; (COMPUT) bit m, élément m binaire; **a ~ of** un peu de; **a ~ mad/dangerous** un peu fou/risqué; **~ by ~** petit à petit; **to come to ~s** (break) tomber en morceaux, se déglinguer; **bring all your ~s and pieces** apporte toutes tes affaires; **to do one's ~** y mettre du sien.
bitch [bɪtʃ] n (dog) chienne f; (col!) salope f (!), garce f.
bite [baɪt] vt, vi (pt **bit** [bɪt], pp **bitten** ['bɪtn]) mordre ♦ n morsure f; (insect ~) piqûre f;

(*mouthful*) bouchée *f*; **let's have a ~ (to eat)** mangeons un morceau; **to ~ one's nails** se ronger les ongles.

biting ['baɪtɪŋ] *adj* mordant(e).

bit part *n* (*THEAT*) petit rôle.

bitten ['bɪtn] *pp of* **bite**.

bitter ['bɪtə*] *adj* amer(ère); (*criticism*) cinglant(e); (*icy: weather, wind*) glacial(e) ♦ *n* (*BRIT: beer*) bière *f* (*à forte teneur en houblon*); **to the ~ end** jusqu'au bout.

bitterly ['bɪtəlɪ] *adv* (*complain, weep*) amèrement; (*oppose, criticise*) durement, âprement; (*jealous, disappointed*) horriblement; **it's ~ cold** il fait un froid de loup.

bitterness ['bɪtənɪs] *n* amertume *f*; goût amer.

bittersweet ['bɪtəswiːt] *adj* aigre-doux(douce).

bitty ['bɪtɪ] *adj* (*BRIT col*) décousu(e).

bitumen ['bɪtjumɪn] *n* bitume *m*.

bivouac ['bɪvuæk] *n* bivouac *m*.

bizarre [bɪ'zɑː*] *adj* bizarre.

bk *abbr* = **bank, book**.

BL *n abbr* (= *Bachelor of Law(s), Bachelor of Letters*) diplôme universitaire; (*US*: = *Bachelor of Literature*) diplôme universitaire.

bl *abbr* = **bill of lading**.

blab [blæb] *vi* jaser, trop parler ♦ *vt* (*also: ~ out*) laisser échapper, aller raconter.

black [blæk] *adj* noir(e) ♦ *n* (*colour*) noir *m*; (*person*): **B~** noir/e ♦ *vt* (*shoes*) cirer; (*BRIT INDUSTRY*) boycotter; **to give sb a ~ eye** pocher l'œil à qn, faire un œil au beurre noir à qn; **~ coffee** café noir; **there it is in ~ and white** (*fig*) c'est écrit noir sur blanc; **to be in the ~** (*in credit*) avoir un compte créditeur; **~ and blue** *adj* couvert(e) de bleus.

▶**black out** *vi* (*faint*) s'évanouir.

black belt *n* (*JUDO etc*) ceinture noire; **he's a ~** il est ceinture noire.

blackberry ['blækbərɪ] *n* mûre *f*.

blackbird ['blækbəːd] *n* merle *m*.

blackboard ['blækbɔːd] *n* tableau noir.

black box *n* (*AVIAT*) boîte noire.

Black Country *n* (*BRIT*): **the ~** le Pays Noir (*dans les Midlands*).

blackcurrant ['blæk'kʌrənt] *n* cassis *m*.

black economy *n* (*BRIT*) travail *m* au noir.

blacken ['blækn] *vt* noircir.

Black Forest *n*: **the ~** la Forêt Noire.

blackhead ['blækhɛd] *n* point noir.

black hole *n* (*ASTRONOMY*) trou noir.

black ice *n* verglas *m*.

blackjack ['blækdʒæk] *n* (*CARDS*) vingt-et-un *m*; (*US: truncheon*) matraque *f*.

blackleg ['blækleg] *n* (*BRIT*) briseur *m* de grève, jaune *m*.

blacklist ['blæklɪst] *n* liste noire ♦ *vt* mettre sur la liste noire.

blackmail ['blækmeɪl] *n* chantage *m* ♦ *vt* faire chanter, soumettre au chantage.

blackmailer ['blækmeɪlə*] *n* maître-chanteur *m*.

black market *n* marché noir.

blackout ['blækaut] *n* panne *f* d'électricité; (*in wartime*) black-out *m*; (*TV*) interruption *f* d'émission; (*fainting*) syncope *f*.

black pepper *n* poivre noir.

Black Sea *n*: **the ~** la mer Noire.

black sheep *n* brebis galeuse.

blacksmith ['blæksmɪθ] *n* forgeron *m*.

black spot *n* (*AUT*) point noir.

bladder ['blædə*] *n* vessie *f*.

blade [bleɪd] *n* lame *f*; (*of oar*) plat *m*; **~ of grass** brin *m* d'herbe.

blame [bleɪm] *n* faute *f*, blâme *m* ♦ *vt*: **to ~ sb/ sth for sth** attribuer à qn/qch la responsabilité de qch; reprocher qch à qn/ qch; **who's to ~?** qui est le fautif *or* coupable *or* responsable?; **I'm not to ~** ce n'est pas ma faute.

blameless ['bleɪmlɪs] *adj* irréprochable.

blanch [blɑːntʃ] *vi* (*person, face*) blêmir ♦ *vt* (*CULIN*) blanchir.

bland [blænd] *adj* affable; (*taste*) doux(douce), fade.

blank [blæŋk] *adj* blanc(blanche); (*look*) sans expression, dénué(e) d'expression ♦ *n* espace *m* vide, blanc *m*; (*cartridge*) cartouche *f* à blanc; **we drew a ~** (*fig*) nous n'avons abouti à rien.

blank cheque, (*US*) **blank check** *n* chèque *m* en blanc; **to give sb a ~ to do ...** (*fig*) donner carte blanche à qn pour faire ....

blanket ['blæŋkɪt] *n* couverture *f* ♦ *adj* (*statement, agreement*) global(e), de portée générale; **to give ~ cover** (*subj: insurance policy*) couvrir tous les risques.

blare [blɛə*] *vi* (*brass band, horns, radio*) beugler.

blarney ['blɑːnɪ] *n* boniment *m*.

blasé ['blɑːzeɪ] *adj* blasé(e).

blasphemous ['blæsfɪməs] *adj* (*words*) blasphématoire; (*person*) blasphémateur(trice).

blasphemy ['blæsfɪmɪ] *n* blasphème *m*.

blast [blɑːst] *n* explosion *f*; (*shock wave*) souffle *m*; (*of air, steam*) bouffée *f* ♦ *vt* faire sauter *or* exploser ♦ *excl* (*BRIT col*) zut!; **(at) full ~** (*play music etc*) à plein volume.

▶**blast off** *vi* (*SPACE*) décoller.

blast-off ['blɑːstɔf] *n* (*SPACE*) lancement *m*.

blatant ['bleɪtənt] *adj* flagrant(e), criant(e).

blatantly ['bleɪtəntlɪ] *adv* (*lie*) ouvertement; **it's ~ obvious** c'est l'évidence même.

blaze [bleɪz] *n* (*fire*) incendie *m*; (*flames: of fire, sun etc*) embrasement *m*; (*: in hearth*) flamme *f*, flambée *f*; (*fig*) flamboiement *m* ♦ *vi* (*fire*) flamber; (*fig*) flamboyer, resplendir ♦ *vt*: **to ~ a trail** (*fig*) montrer la voie; **in a ~ of publicity** à grand renfort de publicité.

blazer ['bleɪzə*] *n* blazer *m*.

bleach [bliːtʃ] *n* (*also:* **household** ~) eau *f* de Javel ♦ *vt* (*linen*) blanchir.

bleached [bliːtʃt] *adj* (*hair*) oxygéné(e), décoloré(e).

bleachers ['bliːtʃəz] *npl* (*US SPORT*) gradins *mpl* (*en plein soleil*).

bleak [bliːk] *adj* morne, désolé(e); (*weather*) triste, maussade; (*smile*) lugubre; (*prospect, future*) morose.

bleary-eyed ['blɪərɪ'aɪd] *adj* aux yeux pleins de sommeil.

bleat [bliːt] *n* bêlement *m* ♦ *vi* bêler.

bleed, *pt, pp* **bled** [bliːd, blɛd] *vt* saigner; (*brakes, radiator*) purger ♦ *vi* saigner; **my nose is** ~**ing** je saigne du nez.

bleep [bliːp] *n* (*RADIO, TV*) top *m*; (*of pocket device*) bip *m* ♦ *vi* émettre des signaux ♦ *vt* (*doctor etc*) appeler (*au moyen d'un bip*).

bleeper ['bliːpə*] *n* (*of doctor etc*) bip *m*.

blemish ['blɛmɪʃ] *n* défaut *m*; (*on reputation*) tache *f*.

blend [blɛnd] *n* mélange *m* ♦ *vt* mélanger ♦ *vi* (*colours etc*) se mélanger, se fondre, s'allier.

blender ['blɛndə*] *n* (*CULIN*) mixeur *m*.

bless, *pt, pp* **blessed** *or* **blest** [blɛs, blɛst] *vt* bénir; **to be** ~**ed with** avoir le bonheur de jouir de *or* d'avoir.

blessed ['blɛsɪd] *adj* (*REL: holy*) béni(e); (*happy*) bienheureux(euse); **it rains every** ~ **day** il ne se passe pas de jour sans qu'il ne pleuve.

blessing ['blɛsɪŋ] *n* bénédiction *f*; bienfait *m*; **to count one's** ~**s** s'estimer heureux; **it was a** ~ **in disguise** c'est un bien pour un mal.

blew [bluː] *pt of* **blow**.

blight [blaɪt] *n* (*of plants*) rouille *f* ♦ *vt* (*hopes etc*) anéantir, briser.

blimey ['blaɪmɪ] *excl* (*BRIT col*) mince alors!

blind [blaɪnd] *adj* aveugle ♦ *n* (*for window*) store *m* ♦ *vt* aveugler; **to turn a** ~ **eye (on** *or* **to)** fermer les yeux (sur).

blind alley *n* impasse *f*.

blind corner *n* (*BRIT*) virage *m* sans visibilité.

blind date *n* rendez-vous galant (avec un(e) inconnu(e)).

blindfold ['blaɪndfəʊld] *n* bandeau *m* ♦ *adj, adv* les yeux bandés ♦ *vt* bander les yeux à.

blindly ['blaɪndlɪ] *adv* aveuglément.

blindness ['blaɪndnɪs] *n* cécité *f*; (*fig*) aveuglement *m*.

blind spot *n* (*AUT etc*) angle *m* aveugle; (*fig*) angle mort.

blink [blɪŋk] *vi* cligner des yeux; (*light*) clignoter ♦ *n*: **the TV's on the** ~ (*col*) la télé ne va pas tarder à nous lâcher.

blinkers ['blɪŋkəz] *npl* œillères *fpl*.

blinking ['blɪŋkɪŋ] *adj* (*BRIT col*): **this** ~ ... ce fichu *or* sacré ....

blip [blɪp] *n* (*on radar etc*) spot *m*; (*on graph*) petite aberration; (*fig*) petite anomalie (*passagère*).

bliss [blɪs] *n* félicité *f*, bonheur *m* sans mélange.

blissful ['blɪsfʊl] *adj* (*event, day*) merveilleux(euse); (*smile*) de bonheur; **a** ~ **sigh** un soupir d'aise; **in** ~ **ignorance** dans une ignorance béate.

blissfully ['blɪsfʊlɪ] *adv* (*smile*) béatement; (*happy*) merveilleusement.

blister ['blɪstə*] *n* (*on skin*) ampoule *f*, cloque *f*; (*on paintwork*) boursouflure *f* ♦ *vi* (*paint*) se boursoufler, se cloquer.

blithely ['blaɪðlɪ] *adv* (*unconcernedly*) tranquillement; (*joyfully*) gaiement.

blithering ['blɪðərɪŋ] *adj* (*col*): **this** ~ **idiot** cet espèce d'idiot.

BLit(t) *n abbr* (= *Bachelor of Literature*) diplôme universitaire.

blitz [blɪts] *n* bombardement (aérien); **to have a** ~ **on sth** (*fig*) s'attaquer à qch.

blizzard ['blɪzəd] *n* blizzard *m*, tempête *f* de neige.

BLM *n abbr* (*US:* = *Bureau of Land Management*) ≈ les domaines.

bloated ['bləʊtɪd] *adj* (*face*) bouffi(e); (*stomach*) gonflé(e).

blob [blɔb] *n* (*drop*) goutte *f*; (*stain, spot*) tache *f*.

bloc [blɔk] *n* (*POL*) bloc *m*.

block [blɔk] *n* bloc *m*; (*in pipes*) obstruction *f*; (*toy*) cube *m*; (*of buildings*) pâté *m* (de maisons) ♦ *vt* bloquer; (*COMPUT*) grouper; ~ **of flats** (*BRIT*) immeuble (locatif); **3** ~**s from here** à trois rues d'ici; **mental** ~ blocage *m*; ~ **and tackle** (*TECH*) palan *m*.

▶**block up** *vt* boucher.

blockade [blɔ'keɪd] *n* blocus *m* ♦ *vt* faire le blocus de.

blockage ['blɔkɪdʒ] *n* obstruction *f*.

block booking *n* réservation *f* en bloc.

blockbuster ['blɔkbʌstə*] *n* (*film, book*) grand succès.

block capitals *npl* majuscules *fpl* d'imprimerie.

blockhead ['blɔkhɛd] *n* imbécile *m/f*.

block letters *npl* majuscules *fpl*.

block release *n* (*BRIT*) congé *m* de formation.

block vote *n* (*BRIT*) vote *m* de délégation.

bloke [bləʊk] *n* (*BRIT col*) type *m*.

blonde [blɔnd] *adj, n* blond(e).

blood [blʌd] *n* sang *m*.

blood bank *n* banque *f* du sang.

blood count *n* numération *f* globulaire.

bloodcurdling ['blʌdkəːdlɪŋ] *adj* à vous glacer le sang.

blood donor *n* donneur/euse de sang.

blood group *n* groupe sanguin.

bloodhound ['blʌdhaʊnd] *n* limier *m*.

bloodless ['blʌdlɪs] *adj* (*victory*) sans effusion de sang; (*pale*) anémié(e).

bloodletting ['blʌdlɛtɪŋ] *n* (*MED*) saignée *f*; (*fig*) effusion *f* de sang, représailles *fpl*.

blood poisoning *n* empoisonnement *m* du sang.

blood pressure n tension (artérielle); **to have high/low** ~ faire de l'hypertension/ l'hypotension.

bloodshed ['blʌdʃɛd] n effusion f de sang, carnage m.

bloodshot ['blʌdʃɔt] adj: ~ **eyes** yeux injectés de sang.

bloodstained ['blʌdsteɪnd] adj taché(e) de sang.

bloodstream ['blʌdstri:m] n sang m, système sanguin.

blood test n analyse f de sang.

bloodthirsty ['blʌdθə:stɪ] adj sanguinaire.

blood transfusion n transfusion f de sang.

blood type n groupe sanguin.

blood vessel n vaisseau sanguin.

bloody ['blʌdɪ] adj sanglant(e); (BRIT col!): **this** ~ ... ce foutu ..., ce putain de ... (!); ~ **strong/good** (col!) vachement or sacrément fort/bon.

bloody-minded ['blʌdɪ'maɪndɪd] adj (BRIT col) contrariant(e), obstiné(e).

bloom [blu:m] n fleur f; (fig) épanouissement m ♦ vi être en fleur; (fig) s'épanouir; être florissant(e).

blooming ['blu:mɪŋ] adj (col): **this** ~ ... ce fichu or sacré ....

blossom ['blɔsəm] n fleur(s) f(pl) ♦ vi être en fleurs; (fig) s'épanouir; **to** ~ **into** (fig) devenir.

blot [blɔt] n tache f ♦ vt tacher; (ink) sécher; **to be a** ~ **on the landscape** gâcher le paysage; **to** ~ **one's copy book** (fig) faire un impair.

► **blot out** vt (memories) effacer; (view) cacher, masquer; (nation, city) annihiler.

blotchy ['blɔtʃɪ] adj (complexion) couvert(e) de marbrures.

blotter ['blɔtə*] n, **blotting paper** ['blɔtɪŋ-] n buvard m.

blotto ['blɔtəu] adj (col) bourré(e).

blouse [blauz] n (feminine garment) chemisier m, corsage m.

blow [bləu] n coup m ♦ vb (pt **blew**, pp **blown** [blu:, bləun]) vi souffler ♦ vt (glass) souffler; (fuse) faire sauter; **to** ~ **one's nose** se moucher; **to** ~ **a whistle** siffler; **to come to** ~**s** en venir aux coups.

► **blow away** vi s'envoler ♦ vt chasser, faire s'envoler.

► **blow down** vt faire tomber, renverser.

► **blow off** vi s'envoler ♦ vt (hat) emporter; (ship): **to** ~ **off course** faire dévier.

► **blow out** vi (tyre) éclater; (fuse) sauter.

► **blow over** vi s'apaiser.

► **blow up** vi exploser, sauter ♦ vt faire sauter; (tyre) gonfler; (PHOT) agrandir.

blow-dry ['bləudraɪ] n (hairstyle) brushing m ♦ vt faire un brushing à.

blowlamp ['bləulæmp] n (BRIT) chalumeau m.

blow-out ['bləuaut] n (of tyre) éclatement m; (BRIT col: big meal) gueuleton m.

blowtorch ['bləutɔ:tʃ] n chalumeau m.

blowzy ['blauzɪ] adj (BRIT) peu soigné(e).

BLS n abbr (US) = Bureau of Labor Statistics.

blubber ['blʌbə*] n blanc m de baleine ♦ vi (pej) pleurer comme un veau.

bludgeon ['blʌdʒən] n gourdin m, trique f.

blue [blu:] adj bleu(e); ~ **film/joke** film m/ histoire f pornographique; **(only) once in a** ~ **moon** tous les trente-six du mois; **out of the** ~ (fig) à l'improviste, sans qu'on si attende.

blue baby n enfant bleu(e).

bluebell ['blu:bɛl] n jacinthe f des bois.

blueberry ['blu:bərɪ] n myrtille f, airelle f.

bluebottle ['blu:bɔtl] n mouche f à viande.

blue cheese n (fromage) bleu m.

blue-chip ['blu:tʃɪp] adj: ~ **investment** investissement m de premier ordre.

blue-collar worker ['blu:kɔlə*-] n ouvrier/ ère, col bleu.

blue jeans npl blue-jeans mpl.

blueprint ['blu:prɪnt] n bleu m; (fig) projet m, plan directeur.

blues [blu:z] npl: **the** ~ (MUS) le blues; **to have the** ~ (col: feeling) avoir le cafard.

bluff [blʌf] vi bluffer ♦ n bluff m; (cliff) promontoire m, falaise f ♦ adj (person) bourru(e), brusque; **to call sb's** ~ mettre qn au défi d'exécuter ses menaces.

blunder ['blʌndə*] n gaffe f, bévue f ♦ vi faire une gaffe or une bévue; **to** ~ **into sb/sth** buter contre qn/qch.

blunt [blʌnt] adj émoussé(e), peu tranchant(e); (pencil) mal taillé(e); (person) brusque, ne mâchant pas ses mots ♦ vt émousser; ~ **instrument** (LAW) instrument contondant.

bluntly ['blʌntlɪ] adv carrément, sans prendre de gants.

bluntness ['blʌntnɪs] n (of person) brusquerie f, franchise brutale.

blur [blə:*] n tache or masse floue or confuse ♦ vt brouiller, rendre flou(e).

blurb [blə:b] n (for book) texte m de présentation; (pej) baratin m.

blurred [blə:d] adj flou(e).

blurt [blə:t]: **to** ~ **out** vt (reveal) lâcher; (say) balbutier, dire d'une voix entrecoupée.

blush [blʌʃ] vi rougir ♦ n rougeur f.

blusher ['blʌʃə*] n rouge m à joues.

bluster ['blʌstə*] n paroles fpl en l'air; (boasting) fanfaronnades fpl; (threats) menaces fpl en l'air ♦ vi parler en l'air; fanfaronner.

blustering ['blʌstərɪŋ] adj fanfaron(ne).

blustery ['blʌstərɪ] adj (weather) à bourrasques.

Blvd abbr (= boulevard) Bd.

BM n abbr = British Museum; (SCOL: = Bachelor of Medicine) diplôme universitaire.

BMA n abbr = British Medical Association.

BMJ n abbr = British Medical Journal.

BMus n abbr (= Bachelor of Music) diplôme universitaire.

BMX *n abbr* (= *bicycle motorcross*) BMX *m*.
BO *n abbr* (*col*: = *body odour*) odeurs
corporelles; (*US*) = **box office**.
boar [bɔː*] *n* sanglier *m*.
board [bɔːd] *n* planche *f*; (*on wall*) panneau *m*;
(*for chess etc*) plateau *m*; (*committee*) conseil
m, comité *m*; (*in firm*) conseil
d'administration; (*NAUT, AVIAT*): **on** ~ à bord
♦ *vt* (*ship*) monter à bord de; (*train*) monter
dans; **full** ~ (*BRIT*) pension complète; **half** ~
(*BRIT*) demi-pension *f*; ~ **and lodging** *n*
chambre *f* avec pension; **with** ~ **and lodging**
logé nourri; **above** ~ (*fig*) régulier(ère);
across the ~ (*fig: ad*) systématiquement;
(*: a*) de portée générale; **to go by the** ~ être
abandonné(e); (*be unimportant*) compter
pour rien, n'avoir aucune importance.
▶**board up** *vt* (*door*) condamner (*au moyen de
planches, de tôle*).
boarder ['bɔːdə*] *n* pensionnaire *m/f*; (*SCOL*)
interne *m/f*, pensionnaire.
board game *n* jeu *m* de société.
boarding card ['bɔːdɪŋ-] *n* (*AVIAT, NAUT*) carte
f d'embarquement.
boarding house ['bɔːdɪŋ-] *n* pension *f*.
boarding party ['bɔːdɪŋ-] *n* section *f*
d'abordage.
boarding pass ['bɔːdɪŋ-] *n* (*BRIT*) = **boarding
card**.
boarding school ['bɔːdɪŋ-] *n* internat *m*,
pensionnat *m*.
board meeting *n* réunion *f* du conseil
d'administration.
board room *n* salle *f* du conseil
d'administration.
boardwalk ['bɔːdwɔːk] *n* (*US*) cheminement *m*
en planches.
boast [bəust] *vi*: **to** ~ **(about** *or* **of)** se vanter
(de) ♦ *vt* s'enorgueillir de ♦ *n* vantardise *f*;
sujet *m* d'orgueil *or* de fierté.
boastful ['bəustful] *adj* vantard(e).
boastfulness ['bəustfulnɪs] *n* vantardise *f*.
boat [bəut] *n* bateau *m*; (*small*) canot *m*;
barque *f*; **to go by** ~ aller en bateau; **to be in
the same** ~ (*fig*) être logé à la même
enseigne.
boater ['bəutə*] *n* (*hat*) canotier *m*.
boating ['bəutɪŋ] *n* canotage *m*.
boat people *npl* boat people *mpl*.
boatswain ['bəusn] *n* maître *m* d'équipage.
bob [bɔb] *vi* (*boat, cork on water: also*: ~ **up and
down**) danser, se balancer ♦ *n* (*BRIT col*)
= **shilling**.
▶**bob up** *vi* surgir *or* apparaître
brusquement.
bobbin ['bɔbɪn] *n* bobine *f*; (*of sewing machine*)
navette *f*.
bobby ['bɔbɪ] *n* (*BRIT col*) ≈ agent *m* (de
police).
bobby pin *n* (*US*) pince *f* à cheveux.
bobsleigh ['bɔbsleɪ] *n* bob *m*.
bode [bəud] *vi*: **to** ~ **well/ill (for)** être de bon/

mauvais augure (pour).
bodice ['bɔdɪs] *n* corsage *m*.
bodily ['bɔdɪlɪ] *adj* corporel(le); (*pain, comfort*)
physique; (*needs*) matériel(le) ♦ *adv* (*carry,
lift*) dans ses bras.
body ['bɔdɪ] *n* corps *m*; (*of car*) carrosserie *f*;
(*of plane*) fuselage *m*; (*also*: ~ **stocking**) body
m, justaucorps *m*; (*fig: society*) organe *m*,
organisme *m*; (*: quantity*) ensemble *m*, masse
f; (*of wine*) corps *m*; **ruling** ~ organe directeur;
in a ~ en masse, ensemble; (*speak*) comme
un seul et même homme.
body blow *n* (*fig*) coup dur, choc *m*.
body-building ['bɔdɪbɪldɪŋ] *n* body-building
m, culturisme *m*.
bodyguard ['bɔdɪgɑːd] *n* garde *m* du corps.
body language *n* langage *m* du corps.
body repairs *npl* travaux *mpl* de carrosserie.
body search *n* fouille *f* (corporelle); **to carry
out a** ~ **on sb** fouiller qn; **to submit to** *or*
undergo a ~ se faire fouiller.
bodywork ['bɔdɪwɜːk] *n* carrosserie *f*.
boffin ['bɔfɪn] *n* (*BRIT*) savant *m*.
bog [bɔg] *n* tourbière *f* ♦ *vt*: **to get** ~**ged down
(in)** (*fig*) s'enliser (dans).
boggle ['bɔgl] *vi*: **the mind** ~**s** c'est
incroyable, on en reste sidéré.
bogie ['bəugɪ] *n* bogie *m*.
Bogotá [bəugə'tɑː] *n* Bogotá.
bogus ['bəugəs] *adj* bidon *inv*; fantôme.
Bohemia [bəu'hiːmɪə] *n* Bohême *f*.
Bohemian [bəu'hiːmɪən] *adj* bohémien(ne) ♦ *n*
Bohémien/ne; (*gipsy: also*: **b**~) bohémien/ne.
boil [bɔɪl] *vt* (faire) bouillir ♦ *vi* bouillir ♦ *n*
(*MED*) furoncle *m*; **to come to the** *or* (*US*) **a** ~
bouillir; **to bring to the** *or* (*US*) **a** ~ porter à
ébullition; ~**ed egg** œuf *m* à la coque; ~**ed
potatoes** pommes *fpl* à l'anglaise *or* à l'eau.
▶**boil down** *vi* (*fig*): **to** ~ **down** to se réduire
or ramener à.
▶**boil over** *vi* déborder.
boiler ['bɔɪlə*] *n* chaudière *f*.
boiler suit *n* (*BRIT*) bleu *m* de travail,
combinaison *f*.
boiling ['bɔɪlɪŋ] *adj*: **I'm** ~ **(hot)** (*col*) je crève
de chaud.
boiling point *n* point *m* d'ébullition.
boil-in-the-bag [bɔɪlɪnðə'bæg] *adj* (*rice etc*) en
sachet cuisson.
boisterous ['bɔɪstərəs] *adj* bruyant(e),
tapageur(euse).
bold [bəuld] *adj* hardi(e), audacieux(euse);
(*pej*) effronté(e); (*outline, colour*)
franc(franche), tranché(e), marqué(e).
boldness ['bəuldnɪs] *n* hardiesse *f*, audace *f*;
aplomb *m*, effronterie *f*.
bold type *n* (*TYP*) caractères *mpl* gras.
Bolivia [bə'lɪvɪə] *n* Bolivie *f*.
Bolivian [bə'lɪvɪən] *adj* bolivien(ne) ♦ *n*
Bolivien/ne.
bollard ['bɔləd] *n* (*NAUT*) bitte *f* d'amarrage;
(*BRIT AUT*) borne lumineuse *or* de

signalisation.
bolshy ['bɔlʃɪ] *adj* râleur(euse); **to be in a ~ mood** être peu coopératif(ive).
bolster ['bəulstə*] *n* traversin *m*.
▶**bolster up** *vt* soutenir.
bolt [bəult] *n* verrou *m*; (*with nut*) boulon *m* ♦ *adv*: ~ **upright** droit(e) comme un piquet ♦ *vt* verrouiller; (*food*) engloutir ♦ *vi* se sauver, filer (comme une flèche); **a ~ from the blue** (*fig*) un coup de tonnerre dans un ciel bleu.
bomb [bɔm] *n* bombe *f* ♦ *vt* bombarder.
bombard [bɔm'bɑːd] *vt* bombarder.
bombardment [bɔm'bɑːdmənt] *n* bombardement *m*.
bombastic [bɔm'bæstɪk] *adj* grandiloquent(e), pompeux(euse).
bomb disposal *n*: ~ **unit** section *f* de déminage; ~ **expert** artificier *m*.
bomber ['bɔmə*] *n* caporal *m* d'artillerie; (*AVIAT*) bombardier *m*; (*terrorist*) poseur de bombes.
bombing ['bɔmɪŋ] *n* bombardement *m*.
bomb scare *n* alerte *f* à la bombe.
bombshell ['bɔmʃɛl] *n* obus *m*; (*fig*) bombe *f*.
bomb site *n* zone *f* de bombardement.
bona fide ['bəunə'faɪdɪ] *adj* de bonne foi; (*offer*) sérieux(euse).
bonanza [bə'nænzə] *n* filon *m*.
bond [bɔnd] *n* lien *m*; (*binding promise*) engagement *m*, obligation *f*; (*FINANCE*) obligation; **in ~** (*of goods*) en entrepôt.
bondage ['bɔndɪdʒ] *n* esclavage *m*.
bonded warehouse ['bɔndɪd-] *n* entrepôt *m* sous douanes.
bone [bəun] *n* os *m*; (*of fish*) arête *f* ♦ *vt* désosser; ôter les arêtes de.
bone china *n* porcelaine *f* tendre.
bone-dry ['bəun'draɪ] *adj* absolument sec(sèche).
bone idle *adj* fainéant(e).
bone marrow *n* moelle osseuse.
boner ['bəunə*] *n* (*US*) gaffe *f*, bourde *f*.
bonfire ['bɔnfaɪə*] *n* feu *m* (de joie); (*for rubbish*) feu.
bonk [bɔŋk] (*col!*) *vt* s'envoyer (!), sauter (!) ♦ *vi* s'envoyer en l'air (!).
bonkers ['bɔŋkəz] *adj* (*BRIT col*) cinglé(e), dingue.
Bonn [bɔn] *n* Bonn.
bonnet ['bɔnɪt] *n* bonnet *m*; (*BRIT: of car*) capot *m*.
bonny ['bɔnɪ] *adj* (*Scottish*) joli(e).
bonus ['bəunəs] *n* prime *f*, gratification *f*; (*on wages*) prime.
bony ['bəunɪ] *adj* (*arm, face, MED: tissue*) osseux(euse); (*thin: person*) squelettique; (*meat*) plein(e) d'os; (*fish*) plein d'arêtes.
boo [buː] *excl* hou!, peuh! ♦ *vt* huer ♦ *n* huée *f*.
boob [buːb] *n* (*col: breast*) nichon *m*; (: *BRIT: mistake*) gaffe *f*.
booby prize ['buːbɪ-] *n* timbale *f* (*ironique*).

booby trap ['buːbɪ-] *n* guet-apens *m*.
booby-trapped ['buːbɪtræpt] *adj* piégé(e).
book [buk] *n* livre *m*; (*of stamps etc*) carnet *m*; (*COMM*): ~**s** comptes *mpl*, comptabilité *f* ♦ *vt* (*ticket*) prendre; (*seat, room*) réserver; (*driver*) dresser un procès-verbal à; (*football player*) prendre le nom de, donner un carton à; **to keep the ~s** tenir la comptabilité; **by the ~** à la lettre, selon les règles; **to throw the ~ at sb** passer un savon à qn.
▶**book in** *vi* (*BRIT: at hotel*) prendre sa chambre.
▶**book up** *vt* réserver; **all seats are ~ed up** tout est pris, c'est complet; **the hotel is ~ed up** l'hôtel est complet.
bookable ['bukəbl] *adj*: **seats are ~** on peut réserver ses places.
bookcase ['bukkeɪs] *n* bibliothèque *f* (*meuble*).
book ends *npl* serre-livres *m inv*.
booking ['bukɪŋ] *n* (*BRIT*) réservation *f*.
booking office *n* (*BRIT*) bureau *m* de location.
book-keeping ['buk'kiːpɪŋ] *n* comptabilité *f*.
booklet ['buklɪt] *n* brochure *f*.
bookmaker ['bukmeɪkə*] *n* bookmaker *m*.
bookseller ['bukselə*] *n* libraire *m/f*.
bookshelf ['bukʃelf] *n* (*single*) étagère *f* (à livres); **bookshelves** rayons *mpl* (de bibliothèque).
bookshop ['bukʃɔp] *n* librairie *f*.
bookstall ['bukstɔːl] *n* kiosque *m* à journaux.
bookstore ['bukstɔː*] *n* = **bookshop**.
book token *n* bon-cadeau *m* (pour un livre).
book value *n* valeur *f* comptable.
bookworm ['bukwəːm] *n* dévoreur/euse de livres.
boom [buːm] *n* (*noise*) grondement *m*; (*busy period*) boom *m*, vague *f* de prospérité ♦ *vi* gronder; prospérer.
boomerang ['buːməræŋ] *n* boomerang *m*.
boom town *n* ville *f* en plein essor.
boon [buːn] *n* bénédiction *f*, grand avantage *m*.
boorish ['buərɪʃ] *adj* grossier(ère), rustre.
boost [buːst] *n* stimulant *m*, remontant *m* ♦ *vt* stimuler; **to give a ~ to sb's spirits** *or* **to sb** remonter le moral à qn.
booster ['buːstə*] *n* (*TV*) amplificateur *m* (de signal); (*ELEC*) survolteur *m*; (*also*: ~ **rocket**) booster *m*; (*MED: vaccine*) rappel *m*.
booster seat *n* (*AUT: for children*) siège *m* rehausseur.
boot [buːt] *n* botte *f*; (*for hiking*) chaussure *f* (de marche); (*for football etc*) soulier *m*; (*ankle* ~) bottine *f*; (*BRIT: of car*) coffre *m* ♦ *vt* (*COMPUT*) lancer, mettre en route; **to ~** (*in addition*) par-dessus le marché, en plus; **to give sb the ~** (*col*) flanquer qn dehors, virer qn.
booth [buːð] *n* (*at fair*) baraque (foraine); (*of cinema, telephone etc*) cabine *f*; (*also*: **voting** ~) isoloir *m*.
bootleg ['buːtlɛg] *adj* de contrebande; ~ **record** enregistrement *m* pirate.

booty ['buːtɪ] n butin m.
booze [buːz] (col) n boissons fpl alcooliques, alcool m ♦ vi boire, picoler.
boozer ['buːzə*] n (col: person): **he's a** ~ il picole pas mal; (BRIT col: pub) pub m.
border ['bɔːdə*] n bordure f; bord m; (of a country) frontière f; **the B**~ la frontière entre l'Écosse et l'Angleterre; **the B**~s la région frontière entre l'Écosse et l'Angleterre.
▶**border on** vt fus être voisin(e) de, toucher à.
borderline ['bɔːdəlaɪn] n (fig) ligne f de démarcation ♦ adj: ~ **case** cas m limite.
bore [bɔː*] pt of **bear** ♦ vt (hole) percer; (person) ennuyer, raser ♦ n (person) raseur/euse; (of gun) calibre m; **he's** ~**d to tears** or ~**d to death** or ~**d stiff** il s'ennuie à mourir.
boredom ['bɔːdəm] n ennui m.
boring ['bɔːrɪŋ] adj ennuyeux(euse).
born [bɔːn] adj: **to be** ~ naître; **I was** ~ **in 1960** je suis né en 1960; ~ **blind** aveugle de naissance; **a** ~ **comedian** un comédien-né.
born-again [bɔːnə'gɛn] adj: ~ **Christian** ≈ évangeliste m/f.
borne [bɔːn] pp of **bear**.
Borneo ['bɔːnɪəu] n Bornéo f.
borough ['bʌrə] n municipalité f.
borrow ['bɔrəu] vt: **to** ~ **sth (from sb)** emprunter qch (à qn); **may I** ~ **your car?** est-ce que je peux vous emprunter votre voiture?
borrower ['bɔrəuə*] n emprunteur/euse.
borrowing ['bɔrəuɪŋ] n emprunt(s) m(pl).
borstal ['bɔːstl] n (BRIT) ≈ maison f de correction.
Bosnia ['bɔznɪə] n Bosnie f.
Bosnia-Herzegovina ['bɔːsnɪəherzə'gəuviːnə] n (also: **Bosnia-Hercegovina**) Bosnie-Herzégovine f.
Bosnian ['bɔznɪən] adj bosniaque, bosnien(ne) ♦ n Bosniaque m/f, Bosnien/ne.
bosom ['buzəm] n poitrine f; (fig) sein m.
bosom friend n ami/e intime.
boss [bɔs] n patron/ne ♦ vt (also: ~ **about**, ~ **around**) mener à la baguette.
bossy ['bɔsɪ] adj autoritaire.
bosun ['bəusn] n maître m d'équipage.
botanical [bə'tænɪkl] adj botanique.
botanist ['bɔtənɪst] n botaniste m/f.
botany ['bɔtənɪ] n botanique f.
botch [bɔtʃ] vt (also: ~ **up**) saboter, bâcler.
both [bəuθ] adj les deux, l'un(e) et l'autre ♦ pron: ~ **(of them)** les deux, tous(toutes) (les) deux, l'un(e) et l'autre; ~ **of us went**, **we** ~ **went** nous y sommes allés tous les deux ♦ adv: **they sell** ~ **the fabric and the finished curtains** ils vendent (et) le tissu et les rideaux (finis), ils vendent à la fois le tissu et les rideaux (finis).
bother ['bɔðə*] vt (worry) tracasser; (needle, bait) importuner, ennuyer; (disturb) déranger ♦ vi (also: ~ **o.s.**) se tracasser, se

faire du souci ♦ n: **it is a** ~ **to have to do** c'est vraiment ennuyeux d'avoir à faire ♦ excl zut!; **to** ~ **doing** prendre la peine de faire; **I'm sorry to** ~ **you** excusez-moi de vous déranger; **please don't** ~ ne vous dérangez pas; **don't** ~ ce n'est pas la peine; **it's no** ~ aucun problème.
Botswana [bɔt'swɑːnə] n Botswana m.
bottle ['bɔtl] n bouteille f; (baby's) biberon m; (of perfume, medicine) flacon m ♦ vt mettre en bouteille(s); ~ **of wine/milk** bouteille de vin/lait; **wine/milk** ~ bouteille à vin/lait.
▶**bottle up** vt refouler, contenir.
bottle bank n conteneur m (de bouteilles).
bottleneck ['bɔtlnɛk] n (in traffic) bouchon m; (in production) goulet m d'étranglement.
bottle-opener ['bɔtləupnə*] n ouvre-bouteille m.
bottom ['bɔtəm] n (of container, sea etc) fond m; (buttocks) derrière m; (of page, list) bas m; (of chair) siège m; (of mountain, tree, hill) pied m ♦ adj du fond; du bas; **to get to the** ~ **of sth** (fig) découvrir le fin fond de qch.
bottomless ['bɔtəmlɪs] adj sans fond, insondable.
bottom line n: **the** ~ **is that ...** l'essentiel, c'est que ....
botulism ['bɔtjulɪzəm] n botulisme m.
bough [bau] n branche f, rameau m.
bought [bɔːt] pt, pp of **buy**.
boulder ['bəuldə*] n gros rocher (gén lisse, arrondi).
bounce [bauns] vi (ball) rebondir; (cheque) être refusé (étant sans provision); (also: **to** ~ **forward/out** etc) bondir, s'élancer ♦ vt faire rebondir ♦ n (rebound) rebond m; **he's got plenty of** ~ (fig) il est plein d'entrain or d'allant.
bouncer ['baunsə*] n (col) videur m.
bouncy castle ['baunsɪ-] n ® château m gonflable.
bound [baund] pt, pp of **bind** ♦ n (gen pl) limite f; (leap) bond m ♦ vt (leap) bondir; (limit) borner ♦ adj: **to be** ~ **to do sth** (obliged) être obligé(e) or avoir obligation de faire qch; **he's** ~ **to fail** (likely) il est sûr d'échouer, son échec est inévitable or assuré; ~ **for** à destination de; **out of** ~**s** dont l'accès est interdit.
boundary ['baundrɪ] n frontière f.
boundless ['baundlɪs] adj illimité(e), sans bornes.
bountiful ['bauntɪful] adj (person) généreux(euse); (God) bienfaiteur(trice); (supply) ample.
bounty ['bauntɪ] n (generosity) générosité f.
bouquet ['bukeɪ] n bouquet m.
bourbon ['buəbən] n (US: also: ~ **whiskey**) bourbon m.
bourgeois ['buəʒwɑː] adj, n bourgeois(e).
bout [baut] n période f; (of malaria etc) accès m, crise f, attaque f; (BOXING etc) combat m,

match *m*.
boutique [buː'tiːk] *n* boutique *f*.
bow¹ [bəu] *n* nœud *m*; (*weapon*) arc *m*; (*MUS*) archet *m*.
bow² [bau] *n* (*with body*) révérence *f*, inclination *f* (du buste *or* corps); (*NAUT: also:* ~**s**) proue *f* ♦ *vi* faire une révérence, s'incliner; (*yield*): **to** ~ **to** *or* **before** s'incliner devant, se soumettre à; **to** ~ **to the inevitable** accepter l'inévitable *or* l'inéluctable.
bowels [bauəlz] *npl* intestins *mpl*; (*fig*) entrailles *fpl*.
bowl [bəul] *n* (*for eating*) bol *m*; (*for washing*) cuvette *f*; (*ball*) boule *f*; (*of pipe*) fourneau *m* ♦ *vi* (*CRICKET*) lancer (la balle).
▶**bowl over** *vt* (*fig*) renverser.
bow-legged ['bəu'lɛgɪd] *adj* aux jambes arquées.
bowler ['bəulə*] *n* joueur *m* de boules; (*CRICKET*) lanceur *m* (de la balle); (*BRIT: also:* ~ **hat**) (chapeau *m*) melon *m*.
bowling ['bəulɪŋ] *n* (*game*) jeu *m* de boules; jeu de quilles.
bowling alley *n* bowling *m*.
bowling green *n* terrain *m* de boules (*gazonné et carré*).
bowls [bəulz] *n* (*jeu m de*) boules *fpl*.
bow tie [bəu-] *n* nœud *m* papillon.
box [bɔks] *n* boîte *f*; (*also:* **cardboard** ~) carton *m*; (*crate*) caisse *f*; (*THEAT*) loge *f*; (*BRIT AUT*) intersection *f* (*matérialisée par des marques au sol*) ♦ *vt* mettre en boîte; (*SPORT*) boxer avec ♦ *vi* boxer, faire de la boxe.
boxcar ['bɔkskɑː*] *n* (*US RAIL*) wagon *m* (de marchandises) couvert.
boxer ['bɔksə*] *n* (*person*) boxeur *m*; (*dog*) boxer *m*.
boxing ['bɔksɪŋ] *n* (*sport*) boxe *f*.
Boxing Day *n* (*BRIT*) le lendemain de Noël.

Boxing Day *est le lendemain de Noël, férié en Grande-Bretagne. Si Noël tombe un samedi, le jour férié est reculé jusqu'au lundi suivant. Ce nom vient d'une coutume du XIXe siècle qui consistait à donner des cadeaux de Noël (dans des boîtes) à ses employés etc le 26 décembre.*

---

boxing gloves *npl* gants *mpl* de boxe.
boxing ring *n* ring *m*.
box number *n* (*for advertisements*) numéro *m* d'annonce.
box office *n* bureau *m* de location.
box room *n* débarras *m*; chambrette *f*.
boy [bɔɪ] *n* garçon *m*.
boycott ['bɔɪkɔt] *n* boycottage *m* ♦ *vt* boycotter.
boyfriend ['bɔɪfrɛnd] *n* (petit) ami.
boyish ['bɔɪɪʃ] *adj* d'enfant, de garçon.
Bp *abbr* = **bishop**.

BR *abbr* = **British Rail**.
Br. *abbr* (*REL*) = **brother**.
bra [brɑː] *n* soutien-gorge *m*.
brace [breɪs] *n* attache *f*, agrafe *f*; (*on teeth*) appareil *m* (dentaire); (*tool*) vilbrequin *m*; (*TYP: also:* ~ **bracket**) accolade *f* ♦ *vt* consolider, soutenir; **to** ~ **o.s.** (*fig*) se préparer mentalement.
bracelet ['breɪslɪt] *n* bracelet *m*.
braces ['breɪsɪz] *npl* (*BRIT*) bretelles *fpl*.
bracing ['breɪsɪŋ] *adj* tonifiant(e), tonique.
bracken ['brækən] *n* fougère *f*.
bracket ['brækɪt] *n* (*TECH*) tasseau *m*, support *m*; (*group*) classe *f*, tranche *f*; (*also:* **brace** ~) accolade *f*; (*also:* **round** ~) parenthèse *f*; (*also:* **square** ~) crochet *m* ♦ *vt* mettre entre parenthèses; (*fig: also:* ~ **together**) regrouper; **income** ~ tranche *f* des revenus; **in** ~**s** entre parenthèses (*or* crochets).
brackish ['brækɪʃ] *adj* (*water*) saumâtre.
brag [bræg] *vi* se vanter.
braid [breɪd] *n* (*trimming*) galon *m*; (*of hair*) tresse *f*, natte *f*.
Braille [breɪl] *n* braille *m*.
brain [breɪn] *n* cerveau *m*; ~**s** *npl* cervelle *f*; **he's got** ~**s** il est intelligent.
brainchild ['breɪntʃaɪld] *n* trouvaille (personnelle), invention *f*.
braindead ['breɪndɛd] *adj* (*MED*) dans un coma dépassé; (*col*) demeuré(e).
brainless ['breɪnlɪs] *adj* sans cervelle, stupide.
brainstorm ['breɪnstɔːm] *n* (*fig*) moment *m* d'égarement; (*US: brainwave*) idée *f* de génie.
brainwash ['breɪnwɔʃ] *vt* faire subir un lavage de cerveau à.
brainwave ['breɪnweɪv] *n* idée *f* de génie.
brainy ['breɪnɪ] *adj* intelligent(e), doué(e).
braise [breɪz] *vt* braiser.
brake [breɪk] *n* (*on vehicle*) frein *m* ♦ *vt, vi* freiner.
brake light *n* feu *m* de stop.
brake pedal *n* pédale *f* de frein.
bramble ['bræmbl] *n* ronces *fpl*; (*fruit*) mûre *f*.
bran [bræn] *n* son *m*.
branch [brɑːntʃ] *n* branche *f*; (*COMM*) succursale *f*; (*: bank*) agence *f*; (*of association*) section locale ♦ *vi* bifurquer.
▶**branch out** *vi* diversifier ses activités; **to** ~ **out into** étendre ses activités à.
branch line *n* (*RAIL*) bifurcation *f*, embranchement *m*.
branch manager *n* directeur/trice de succursale (*or* d'agence).
brand [brænd] *n* marque (commerciale) ♦ *vt* (*cattle*) marquer (au fer rouge); (*fig: pej*): **to** ~ **sb a communist** *etc* traiter *or* qualifier qn de communiste *etc*.
brandish ['brændɪʃ] *vt* brandir.
brand name *n* nom *m* de marque.
brand-new ['brænd'njuː] *adj* tout(e) neuf(neuve), flambant neuf(neuve).
brandy ['brændɪ] *n* cognac *m*, fine *f*.

brash [bræʃ] *adj* effronté(e).
Brasilia [brə'zɪlɪə] *n* Brasilia.
brass [brɑːs] *n* cuivre *m* (jaune), laiton *m*; **the ~** (*MUS*) les cuivres.
brass band *n* fanfare *f*.
brassiere ['bræsɪə*] *n* soutien-gorge *m*.
brass tacks *npl*: **to get down to ~** en venir au fait.
brat [bræt] *n* (*pej*) mioche *m/f*, môme *m/f*.
bravado [brə'vɑːdəu] *n* bravade *f*.
brave [breɪv] *adj* courageux(euse), brave ♦ *n* guerrier indien ♦ *vt* braver, affronter.
bravery ['breɪvərɪ] *n* bravoure *f*, courage *m*.
bravo [brɑː'vəu] *excl* bravo!
brawl [brɔːl] *n* rixe *f*, bagarre *f* ♦ *vi* se bagarrer.
brawn [brɔːn] *n* muscle *m*; (*meat*) fromage *m* de tête.
brawny ['brɔːnɪ] *adj* musclé(e), costaud(e).
bray [breɪ] *n* braiement *m* ♦ *vi* braire.
brazen ['breɪzn] *adj* impudent(e), effronté(e) ♦ *vt*: **to ~ it out** payer d'effronterie, crâner.
brazier ['breɪzɪə*] *n* brasero *m*.
Brazil [brə'zɪl] *n* Brésil *m*.
Brazilian [brə'zɪljən] *adj* brésilien(ne) ♦ *n* Brésilien/ne.
Brazil nut *n* noix *f* du Brésil.
breach [briːtʃ] *vt* ouvrir une brèche dans ♦ *n* (*gap*) brèche *f*; (*estrangement*) brouille *f*; (*breaking*): **~ of contract** rupture *f* de contrat; **~ of the peace** attentat *m* à l'ordre public; **~ of trust** abus *m* de confiance.
bread [bred] *n* pain *m*; (*col: money*) fric *m*; **~ and butter** *n* tartines (beurrées) *f*; (*fig*) subsistance *f*; **to earn one's daily ~** gagner son pain; **to know which side one's ~ is buttered (on)** savoir où est son avantage *or* intérêt.
breadbin ['bredbɪn] *n* (*BRIT*) boîte *f* *or* huche *f* à pain.
breadboard ['bredbɔːd] *n* planche *f* à pain; (*COMPUT*) montage expérimental.
breadbox ['bredbɔks] *n* (*US*) boîte *f* *or* huche *f* à pain.
breadcrumbs ['bredkrʌmz] *npl* miettes *fpl* de pain; (*CULIN*) chapelure *f*, panure *f*.
breadline ['bredlaɪn] *n*: **to be on the ~** être sans le sou *or* dans l'indigence.
breadth [bretθ] *n* largeur *f*.
breadwinner ['bredwɪnə*] *n* soutien *m* de famille.
break [breɪk] *vb* (*pt* **broke** [brəuk], *pp* **broken** ['brəukən]) *vt* casser, briser; (*promise*) rompre; (*law*) violer ♦ *vi* casser, se briser; (*weather*) tourner ♦ *n* (*gap*) brèche *f*; (*fracture*) cassure *f*; (*rest*) interruption *f*, arrêt *m*; (*: short*) pause *f*; (*: at school*) récréation *f*; (*chance*) chance *f*, occasion *f* favorable; **to ~ one's leg** *etc* se casser la jambe *etc*; **to ~ a record** battre un record; **to ~ the news to sb** annoncer la nouvelle à qn; **to ~ with sb** rompre avec qn; **to ~ even**

vi rentrer dans ses frais; **to ~ free** *or* **loose** *vi* se dégager, s'échapper; **to take a ~** (*few minutes*) faire une pause, s'arrêter cinq minutes; (*holiday*) prendre un peu de repos; **without a ~** sans interruption, sans arrêt.
▶**break down** *vt* (*door etc*) enfoncer; (*resistance*) venir à bout de; (*figures, data*) décomposer, analyser ♦ *vi* s'effondrer; (*MED*) faire une dépression (nerveuse); (*AUT*) tomber en panne.
▶**break in** *vt* (*horse etc*) dresser ♦ *vi* (*burglar*) entrer par effraction.
▶**break into** *vt fus* (*house*) s'introduire *or* pénétrer par effraction dans.
▶**break off** *vi* (*speaker*) s'interrompre; (*branch*) se rompre ♦ *vt* (*talks, engagement*) rompre.
▶**break open** *vt* (*door etc*) forcer, fracturer.
▶**break out** *vi* éclater, se déclarer; **to ~ out in spots** se couvrir de boutons.
▶**break through** *vi*: **the sun broke through** le soleil a fait son apparition ♦ *vt fus* (*defences, barrier*) franchir; (*crowd*) se frayer un passage à travers.
▶**break up** *vi* (*partnership*) cesser, prendre fin; (*marriage*) se briser; (*friends*) se séparer ♦ *vt* fracasser, casser; (*fight etc*) interrompre, faire cesser; (*marriage*) désunir.
breakable ['breɪkəbl] *adj* cassable, fragile ♦ *n*: **~s** objets *mpl* fragiles.
breakage ['breɪkɪdʒ] *n* casse *f*; **to pay for ~s** payer la casse.
breakaway ['breɪkəweɪ] *adj* (*group etc*) dissident(e).
breakdown ['breɪkdaun] *n* (*AUT*) panne *f*; (*in communications*) rupture *f*; (*MED: also*: **nervous ~**) dépression (nerveuse); (*of figures*) ventilation *f*, répartition *f*.
breakdown service *n* (*BRIT*) service *m* de dépannage.
breakdown van *n* (*BRIT*) dépanneuse *f*.
breaker ['breɪkə*] *n* brisant *m*.
breakeven ['breɪk'iːvn] *cpd*: **~ chart** graphique *m* de rentabilité; **~ point** seuil *m* de rentabilité.
breakfast ['brekfəst] *n* petit déjeuner *m*.
breakfast cereal *n* céréales *fpl*.
break-in ['breɪkɪn] *n* cambriolage *m*.
breaking point ['breɪkɪŋ-] *n* limites *fpl*.
breakthrough ['breɪkθruː] *n* percée *f*.
break-up ['breɪkʌp] *n* (*of partnership, marriage*) rupture *f*.
break-up value *n* (*COMM*) valeur *f* de liquidation.
breakwater ['breɪkwɔːtə*] *n* brise-lames *m inv*, digue *f*.
breast [brest] *n* (*of woman*) sein *m*; (*chest*) poitrine *f*.
breast-feed ['brestfiːd] *vt, vi* (*irreg: like* **feed**) allaiter.
breast pocket *n* poche *f* (de) poitrine.

breaststroke ['brɛststrəuk] *n* brasse *f*.
breath [brɛθ] *n* haleine *f*, souffle *m*; **to go out for a ~ of air** sortir prendre l'air; **out of ~** à bout de souffle, essoufflé(e).
breathalyse ['brɛəəlaɪz] *vt* faire subir l'alcootest à.
Breathalyser ['brɛθəlaɪzə*] *n* ® alcootest *m*.
breathe [briːð] *vt, vi* respirer; **I won't ~ a word about it** je n'en soufflerai pas mot, je n'en dirai rien à personne.
▶**breathe in** *vi* inspirer ♦ *vt* aspirer.
▶**breathe out** *vt, vi* expirer.
breather ['briːðə*] *n* moment *m* de repos *or* de répit.
breathing ['briːðɪŋ] *n* respiration *f*.
breathing space *n* (*fig*) (moment *m* de) répit *m*.
breathless ['brɛθlɪs] *adj* essoufflé(e), haletant(e); oppressé(e); **~ with excitement** le souffle coupé par l'émotion.
breath-taking ['brɛθteɪkɪŋ] *adj* stupéfiant(e), à vous couper le souffle.
breath test *n* alcootest *m*.
-bred [brɛd] *suffix*: **well/ill~** bien/mal élevé(e).
breed [briːd] (*pt, pp* **bred** [brɛd]) *vt* élever, faire l'élevage de; (*fig: hate, suspicion*) engendrer ♦ *vi* se reproduire ♦ *n* race *f*, variété *f*.
breeder ['briːdə*] *n* (*person*) éleveur *m*; (*PHYSICS: also: ~* **reactor**) (réacteur *m*) surrégénérateur *m*.
breeding ['briːdɪŋ] *n* reproduction *f*; élevage *m*; (*upbringing*) éducation *f*.
breeze [briːz] *n* brise *f*.
breezeblock ['briːzblɔk] *n* (*BRIT*) parpaing *m*.
breezy ['briːzɪ] *adj* frais(fraîche); aéré(e); désinvolte, jovial(e).
Breton ['brɛtən] *adj* breton(ne) ♦ *n* Breton/ne; (*LING*) breton *m*.
brevity ['brɛvɪtɪ] *n* brièveté *f*.
brew [bruː] *vt* (*tea*) faire infuser; (*beer*) brasser; (*plot*) tramer, préparer ♦ *vi* (*tea*) infuser; (*beer*) fermenter; (*fig*) se préparer, couver.
brewer ['bruːə*] *n* brasseur *m*.
brewery ['bruːərɪ] *n* brasserie *f* (fabrique).
briar ['braɪə*] *n* (*thorny bush*) ronces *fpl*; (*wild rose*) églantine *f*.
bribe [braɪb] *n* pot-de-vin *m* ♦ *vt* acheter; soudoyer; **to ~ sb to do sth** soudoyer qn pour qu'il fasse qch.
bribery ['braɪbərɪ] *n* corruption *f*.
bric-a-brac ['brɪkəbræk] *n* bric-à-brac *m*.
brick [brɪk] *n* brique *f*.
bricklayer ['brɪkleɪə*] *n* maçon *m*.
brickwork ['brɪkwəːk] *n* briquetage *m*, maçonnerie *f*.
brickworks ['brɪkwəːks] *n* briqueterie *f*.
bridal ['braɪdl] *adj* nuptial(e); **~ party** noce *f*.
bride [braɪd] *n* mariée *f*, épouse *f*.
bridegroom ['braɪdgruːm] *n* marié *m*, époux *m*.

bridesmaid ['braɪdzmeɪd] *n* demoiselle *f* d'honneur.
bridge [brɪdʒ] *n* pont *m*; (*NAUT*) passerelle *f* (de commandement); (*of nose*) arête *f*; (*CARDS, DENTISTRY*) bridge *m* ♦ *vt* (*river*) construire un pont sur; (*gap*) combler.
bridging loan ['brɪdʒɪŋ-] *n* (*BRIT*) prêt *m* relais.
bridle ['braɪdl] *n* bride *f* ♦ *vt* refréner, mettre la bride à; (*horse*) brider.
bridle path *n* piste *or* allée cavalière.
brief [briːf] *adj* bref(brève) ♦ *n* (*LAW*) dossier *m*, cause *f* ♦ *vt* (*MIL etc*) donner des instructions à; **in ~ ...** (en) bref ...; **to ~ sb (about sth)** mettre qn au courant (de qch).
briefcase ['briːfkeɪs] *n* serviette *f*; porte-documents *m inv*.
briefing ['briːfɪŋ] *n* instructions *fpl*.
briefly ['briːflɪ] *adv* brièvement; (*visit*) en coup de vent; **to glimpse ~** entrevoir.
briefness ['briːfnɪs] *n* brièveté *f*.
briefs [briːfs] *npl* slip *m*.
Brig. *abbr* = **brigadier**.
brigade [brɪ'geɪd] *n* (*MIL*) brigade *f*.
brigadier [brɪgə'dɪə*] *n* brigadier général.
bright [braɪt] *adj* brillant(e); (*room, weather*) clair(e); (*person*) intelligent(e), doué(e); (*colour*) vif(vive); **to look on the ~ side** regarder le bon côté des choses.
brighten ['braɪtn] (*also: ~* **up**) *vt* (*room*) éclaircir; égayer ♦ *vi* s'éclaircir; (*person*) retrouver un peu de sa gaieté.
brightly ['braɪtlɪ] *adv* brillamment.
brill [brɪl] *adj* (*BRIT col*) super *inv*.
brilliance ['brɪljəns] *n* éclat *m*; (*fig: of person*) brio *m*.
brilliant ['brɪljənt] *adj* brillant(e).
brim [brɪm] *n* bord *m*.
brimful ['brɪm'ful] *adj* plein(e) à ras bord; (*fig*) débordant(e).
brine [braɪn] *n* eau salée; (*CULIN*) saumure *f*.
bring, *pt, pp* **brought** [brɪŋ, brɔːt] *vt* (*thing*) apporter; (*person*) amener; **to ~ sth to an end** mettre fin à qch; **I can't ~ myself to fire him** je ne peux me résoudre à le mettre à la porte.
▶**bring about** *vt* provoquer, entraîner.
▶**bring back** *vt* rapporter; (*person*) ramener.
▶**bring down** *vt* (*lower*) abaisser; (*shoot down*) abattre; (*government*) faire s'effondrer.
▶**bring forward** *vt* avancer; (*BOOK-KEEPING*) reporter.
▶**bring in** *vt* (*person*) faire entrer; (*object*) rentrer; (*POL: legislation*) introduire; (*LAW: verdict*) rendre; (*produce: income*) rapporter.
▶**bring off** *vt* (*task, plan*) réussir, mener à bien; (*deal*) mener à bien.
▶**bring out** *vt* (*meaning*) faire ressortir, mettre en relief; (*new product, book*) sortir.
▶**bring round , bring to** *vt* (*unconscious person*) ranimer.

▶**bring up** vt élever; (question) soulever; (food: vomit) vomir, rendre.

brink [brɪŋk] n bord m; **on the ~ of doing** sur le point de faire, à deux doigts de faire; **she was on the ~ of tears** elle était au bord des larmes.

brisk [brɪsk] adj vif(vive); (abrupt) brusque; (trade etc) actif(ive); **to go for a ~ walk** se promener d'un bon pas; **business is ~** les affaires marchent (bien).

bristle ['brɪsl] n poil m ♦ vi se hérisser; **bristling with** hérissé(e) de.

bristly ['brɪslɪ] adj (beard, hair) hérissé(e); **your chin's all ~** ton menton gratte.

Brit [brɪt] n abbr (col: = British person) Britannique m/f.

Britain ['brɪtən] n (also: Great ~) la Grande-Bretagne; **in ~** en Grande-Bretagne.

British ['brɪtɪʃ] adj britannique; **the ~** npl les Britanniques mpl; **the ~ Isles** les îles fpl Britanniques.

British Rail (BR) n compagnie ferroviaire britannique, ≈ SNCF f.

British Summer Time n heure f d'été britannique.

Briton ['brɪtən] n Britannique m/f.

Brittany ['brɪtənɪ] n Bretagne f.

brittle ['brɪtl] adj cassant(e), fragile.

Bro. abbr (REL) = brother.

broach [brəʊtʃ] vt (subject) aborder.

broad [brɔːd] adj large; (distinction) général(e); (accent) prononcé(e) ♦ n (US col) nana f; **~ hint** allusion transparente; **in ~ daylight** en plein jour; **the ~ outlines** les grandes lignes.

broad bean n fève f.

broadcast ['brɔːdkɑːst] n émission f ♦ vb (pt, pp **broadcast**) vt radiodiffuser; téléviser ♦ vi émettre.

broadcaster ['brɔːdkɑːstə*] n personnalité f de la radio or de la télévision.

broadcasting ['brɔːdkɑːstɪŋ] n radiodiffusion f; télévision f.

broadcasting station n station f de radio (or de télévision).

broaden ['brɔːdn] vt élargir ♦ vi s'élargir.

broadly ['brɔːdlɪ] adv en gros, généralement.

broad-minded ['brɔːd'maɪndɪd] adj large d'esprit.

broadsheet ['brɔːdʃiːt] n (BRIT) journal m grand format.

broccoli ['brɒkəlɪ] n brocoli m.

brochure ['brəʊʃjʊə*] n prospectus m, dépliant m.

brogue ['brəʊg] n (accent) accent régional; (shoe) (sorte de) chaussure basse de cuir épais.

broil [brɔɪl] vt rôtir.

broiler ['brɔɪlə*] n (fowl) poulet m (à rôtir).

broke [brəʊk] pt of **break** ♦ adj (col) fauché(e); **to go ~** (business) faire faillite.

broken ['brəʊkn] pp of **break** ♦ adj (stick, leg etc)

cassé(e); (promise, vow) rompu(e); **a ~ marriage** un couple dissocié; **a ~ home** un foyer désuni; **in ~ French/English** dans un français/anglais approximatif or hésitant.

broken-down ['brəʊkn'daʊn] adj (car) en panne; (machine) fichu(e); (house) en ruines.

broken-hearted ['brəʊkn'hɑːtɪd] adj (ayant) le cœur brisé.

broker ['brəʊkə*] n courtier m.

brokerage ['brəʊkrɪdʒ] n courtage m.

brolly ['brɒlɪ] n (BRIT col) pépin m, parapluie m.

bronchitis [brɒŋ'kaɪtɪs] n bronchite f.

bronze [brɒnz] n bronze m.

bronzed ['brɒnzd] adj bronzé(e), hâlé(e).

brooch [brəʊtʃ] n broche f.

brood [bruːd] n couvée f ♦ vi (hen, storm) couver; (person) méditer (sombrement), ruminer.

broody ['bruːdɪ] adj (fig) taciturne, mélancolique.

brook [brʊk] n ruisseau m.

broom [brum] n balai m.

broomstick ['brumstɪk] n manche m à balai.

Bros. abbr (COMM: = brothers) Frères.

broth [brɒθ] n bouillon m de viande et de légumes.

brothel ['brɒθl] n maison close, bordel m.

brother ['brʌðə*] n frère m.

brotherhood ['brʌðəhud] n fraternité f.

brother-in-law ['brʌðərɪn'lɔː*] n beau-frère m.

brotherly ['brʌðəlɪ] adj fraternel(le).

brought [brɔːt] pt, pp of **bring**.

brow [braʊ] n front m; (rare: gen: **eye~**) sourcil m; (of hill) sommet m.

browbeat ['braʊbiːt] vt intimider, brusquer.

brown [braʊn] adj brun(e), marron inv; (hair) châtain inv; (rice, bread, flour) complet(ète) ♦ n (colour) brun m, marron m ♦ vt brunir; (CULIN) faire dorer, faire roussir; **to go ~** (person) bronzer; (leaves) jaunir.

brownie ['braʊnɪ] n jeannette f, éclaireuse (cadette).

brown paper n papier m d'emballage, papier kraft.

brown sugar n cassonade f.

browse [braʊz] vi (among books) bouquiner, feuilleter les livres; (animal) paître; **to ~ through a book** feuilleter un livre.

bruise [bruːz] n bleu m, ecchymose f, contusion f ♦ vt contusionner, meurtrir ♦ vi (fruit) se taler, se meurtrir; **to ~ one's arm** se faire un bleu au bras.

Brum [brʌm] n abbr, **Brummagem** ['brʌmədʒəm] n (col) = Birmingham.

Brummie ['brʌmɪ] n (col) habitant/e de Birmingham; natif/ive de Birmingham.

brunch [brʌntʃ] n brunch m.

brunette [bruː'nɛt] n (femme) brune.

brunt [brʌnt] n: **the ~ of** (attack, criticism etc) le plus gros de.

brush [brʌʃ] n brosse f; (quarrel) accrochage m, prise f de bec ♦ vt brosser; (also: ~ **past**, ~

against) effleurer, frôler; **to have a ~ with sb** s'accrocher avec qn; **to have a ~ with the police** avoir maille à partir avec la police.

▶**brush aside** *vt* écarter, balayer.

▶**brush up** *vt* (*knowledge*) rafraîchir, réviser.

brushed [brʌʃt] *adj* (*TECH: steel, chrome etc*) brossé(e); (*nylon, denim etc*) gratté(e).

brush-off ['brʌʃɔf] *n* (*col*): **to give sb the ~** envoyer qn promener.

brushwood ['brʌʃwud] *n* broussailles *fpl*, taillis *m*.

brusque [bruːsk] *adj* (*person, manner*) brusque, cassant(e); (*tone*) sec(sèche), cassant(e).

Brussels ['brʌslz] *n* Bruxelles.

Brussels sprout *n* chou *m* de Bruxelles.

brutal ['bruːtl] *adj* brutal(e).

brutality [bruː'tælɪtɪ] *n* brutalité *f*.

brutalize ['bruːtəlaɪz] *vt* (*harden*) rendre brutal(e); (*ill-treat*) brutaliser.

brute [bruːt] *n* brute *f* ♦ *adj*: **by ~ force** par la force.

brutish ['bruːtɪʃ] *adj* grossier(ère), brutal(e).

BS *n abbr* (*US: = Bachelor of Science*) diplôme *universitaire*.

bs *abbr* = **bill of sale**.

BSA *n abbr* = Boy Scouts of America.

BSc *n abbr* = Bachelor of Science.

BSE *n abbr* (= *bovine spongiform encephalopathy*) ESB *f*, BSE *f*.

BSI *n abbr* (= *British Standards Institution*) association de normalisation.

BST *abbr* (= *British Summer Time*) heure *f* d'été.

Bt. *abbr* (*BRIT*) = baronet.

btu *n abbr* (= *British thermal unit*) btu (= *1054,2 joules*).

bubble ['bʌbl] *n* bulle *f* ♦ *vi* bouillonner, faire des bulles; (*sparkle, fig*) pétiller.

bubble bath *n* bain moussant.

bubblejet printer ['bʌbldʒet-] *n* imprimante *f* à bulle d'encre.

bubbly ['bʌblɪ] *adj* (*drink*) pétillant(e); (*person*) plein(e) de vitalité ♦ *n* (*col*) champ *m*.

Bucharest [buːkə'rest] *n* Bucarest.

buck [bʌk] *n* mâle *m* (*d'un lapin, lièvre, daim etc*); (*US col*) dollar *m* ♦ *vi* ruer, lancer une ruade; **to pass the ~ (to sb)** se décharger de la responsabilité (sur qn).

▶**buck up** *vi* (*cheer up*) reprendre du poil de la bête, se remonter ♦ *vt*: **to ~ one's ideas up** se reprendre.

bucket ['bʌkɪt] *n* seau *m* ♦ *vi* (*BRIT col*): **the rain is ~ing (down)** il pleut à verse.

> Buckingham Palace *est la résidence officielle londonienne du souverain britannique depuis 1762. Construit en 1703, il fut à l'origine le palais du duc de Buckingham. Il a été partiellement reconstruit au début du siècle.*

buckle ['bʌkl] *n* boucle *f* ♦ *vt* boucler, attacher; (*warp*) tordre, gauchir; (*: wheel*) voiler.

▶**buckle down** *vi* s'y mettre.

Bucks [bʌks] *abbr* (*BRIT*) = Buckinghamshire.

bud [bʌd] *n* bourgeon *m*; (*of flower*) bouton *m* ♦ *vi* bourgeonner; (*flower*) éclore.

Budapest [bjuːdə'pest] *n* Budapest.

Buddha ['budə] *n* Bouddha *m*.

Buddhism ['budɪzəm] *n* bouddhisme *m*.

Buddhist ['budɪst] *adj* bouddhiste ♦ *n* Bouddhiste *m/f*.

budding ['bʌdɪŋ] *adj* (*flower*) en bouton; (*poet etc*) en herbe; (*passion etc*) naissant(e).

buddy ['bʌdɪ] *n* (*US*) copain *m*.

budge [bʌdʒ] *vt* faire bouger ♦ *vi* bouger.

budgerigar ['bʌdʒərɪgaː*] *n* perruche *f*.

budget ['bʌdʒɪt] *n* budget *m* ♦ *vi*: **to ~ for sth** inscrire qch au budget; **I'm on a tight ~** je dois faire attention à mon budget.

budgie ['bʌdʒɪ] *n* = **budgerigar**.

Buenos Aires ['bweɪnɔs'aɪrɪz] *n* Buenos Aires.

buff [bʌf] *adj* (*couleur f*) chamois *m* ♦ *n* (*enthusiast*) mordu(e).

buffalo, *pl* ~ *or* ~**es** ['bʌfələu] *n* buffle *m*; (*US*) bison *m*.

buffer ['bʌfə*] *n* tampon *m*; (*COMPUT*) mémoire *f* tampon.

buffering ['bʌfərɪŋ] *n* (*COMPUT*) mise *f* en mémoire tampon.

buffer state *n* état *m* tampon.

buffer zone *n* zone *f* tampon.

buffet *n* ['bufeɪ] (*food, BRIT: bar*) buffet *m* ♦ *vt* ['bʌfɪt] gifler, frapper; secouer, ébranler.

buffet car *n* (*BRIT RAIL*) voiture-bar *f*.

buffet lunch *n* lunch *m*.

buffoon [bə'fuːn] *n* buffon *m*, pitre *m*.

bug [bʌg] *n* (*insect*) punaise *f*; (*: gen*) insecte *m*, bestiole *f*; (*fig: germ*) virus *m*, microbe *m*; (*spy device*) dispositif *m* d'écoute (électronique), micro clandestin; (*COMPUT: of program*) erreur *f*; (*: of equipment*) défaut *m* ♦ *vt* (*room*) poser des micros dans; (*col: annoy*) embêter; **I've got the travel ~** (*fig*) j'ai le virus du voyage.

bugbear ['bʌgbɛə*] *n* cauchemar *m*, bête noire.

bugger ['bʌgə*] (*col!*) *n* salaud *m* (*!*); connard *m* (*!*) ♦ *vb*: **~ off!** tire-toi! (*!*); **~ (it)!** merde! (*!*).

bugle ['bjuːgl] *n* clairon *m*.

build [bɪld] *n* (*of person*) carrure *f*, charpente *f* ♦ *vt* (*pt, pp* **built** [bɪlt]) construire, bâtir.

▶**build on** *vt fus* (*fig*) tirer parti de, partir de.

▶**build up** *vt* accumuler, amasser; (*business*) développer; (*reputation*) bâtir; (*increase: production*) développer, accroître.

builder ['bɪldə*] *n* entrepreneur *m*.

building ['bɪldɪŋ] *n* construction *f*; (*structure*) bâtiment *m*, construction; (*: residential, offices*) immeuble *m*.

building contractor *n* entrepreneur *m* (en bâtiment).

building industry *n* (industrie *f* du) bâtiment *m*.

building site n chantier m (de construction).
building society n (BRIT) société f de crédit immobilier.

Une **building society** est une mutuelle dont les épargnants et emprunteurs sont les propriétaires. Ces mutuelles offrent deux services principaux: on peut y avoir un compte d'épargne duquel on peut retirer son argent sur demande ou moyennant un court préavis; et on peut également y faire des emprunts à long terme, par exemple pour acheter une maison. Les building societies ont eu jusqu'en 1985 le quasi-monopole des comptes d'épargne et des prêts immobiliers, mais les banques ont maintenant une part importante de ce marché.

---

building trade n = building industry.
build-up ['bɪldʌp] n (of gas etc) accumulation f; (publicity): **to give sb/sth a good** ~ faire de la pub pour qn/qch.
built [bɪlt] pt, pp of build.
built-in ['bɪlt'ɪn] adj (cupboard) encastré(e); (device) incorporé(e); intégré(e).
built-up area ['bɪltʌp-] n agglomération (urbaine); zone urbanisée.
bulb [bʌlb] n (BOT) bulbe m, oignon m; (ELEC) ampoule f.
bulbous ['bʌlbəs] adj bulbeux(euse).
Bulgaria [bʌl'gɛərɪə] n Bulgarie f.
Bulgarian [bʌl'gɛərɪən] adj bulgare ♦ n Bulgare m/f; (LING) bulgare m.
bulge [bʌldʒ] n renflement m, gonflement m; (in birth rate, sales) brusque augmentation f ♦ vi faire saillie; présenter un renflement; **to be bulging with** être plein(e) à craquer de.
bulimia [bə'lɪmɪə] n boulimie f.
bulk [bʌlk] n masse f, volume m; **in** ~ (COMM) en gros, en vrac; **the** ~ **of** la plus grande or grosse partie de.
bulk buying [-'baɪɪŋ] n achat m en gros.
bulk carrier n cargo m.
bulkhead ['bʌlkhɛd] n cloison f (étanche).
bulky ['bʌlkɪ] adj volumineux(euse), encombrant(e).
bull [bul] n taureau m; (STOCK EXCHANGE) haussier m; (REL) bulle f.
bulldog ['buldɔg] n bouledogue m.
bulldoze ['buldəuz] vt passer or raser au bulldozer; **I was** ~**d into doing it** (fig: col) on m'a forcé la main.
bulldozer ['buldəuzə*] n bulldozer m.
bullet ['bulɪt] n balle f (de fusil etc).
bulletin ['bulɪtɪn] n bulletin m, communiqué m.
bulletin board n (COMPUT) messagerie f (électronique).
bulletproof ['bulɪtpru:f] adj à l'épreuve des balles; ~ **vest** gilet m pare-balles.
bullfight ['bulfaɪt] n corrida f, course f de taureaux.
bullfighter ['bulfaɪtə*] n torero m.

bullfighting ['bulfaɪtɪŋ] n tauromachie f.
bullion ['buljən] n or m or argent m en lingots.
bullock ['bulək] n bœuf m.
bullring ['bulrɪŋ] n arène f.
bull's-eye ['bulzaɪ] n centre m (de la cible).
bullshit ['bulʃɪt] (col!) n connerie(s) f(pl) (!) ♦ vt raconter des conneries à (!) ♦ vi déconner (!).
bully ['bulɪ] n brute f, tyran m ♦ vt tyranniser, rudoyer; (frighten) intimider.
bullying ['bulɪŋ] n brimades fpl.
bum [bʌm] n (col: backside) derrière m; (: tramp) vagabond/e, traîne-savates m/f inv; (: idler) glandeur m.
▶**bum around** vi (col) vagabonder.
bumblebee ['bʌmblbi:] n bourdon m.
bumf [bʌmf] n (col: forms etc) paperasses fpl.
bump [bʌmp] n (blow) coup m, choc m; (jolt) cahot m; (on road etc, on head) bosse f ♦ vt heurter, cogner; (car) emboutir.
▶**bump along** vi avancer en cahotant.
▶**bump into** vt fus rentrer dans, tamponner; (col: meet) tomber sur.
bumper ['bʌmpə*] n pare-chocs m inv ♦ adj: ~ **crop/harvest** récolte/moisson exceptionnelle.
bumper cars npl (US) autos tamponneuses.
bumph [bʌmf] n = bumf.
bumptious ['bʌmpʃəs] adj suffisant(e), prétentieux(euse).
bumpy ['bʌmpɪ] adj cahoteux(euse); **it was a** ~ **flight/ride** on a été secoués dans l'avion/la voiture.
bun [bʌn] n petit pain au lait; (of hair) chignon m.
bunch [bʌntʃ] n (of flowers) bouquet m; (of keys) trousseau m; (of bananas) régime m; (of people) groupe m; ~ **of grapes** grappe f de raisin.
bundle ['bʌndl] n paquet m ♦ vt (also: ~ up) faire un paquet de; (put): **to** ~ **sth/sb into** fourrer or enfourner qch/qn dans.
▶**bundle off** vt (person) faire sortir (en toute hâte); expédier.
▶**bundle out** vt éjecter, sortir (sans ménagements).
bun fight n (BRIT col) réception f; (tea party) thé m.
bung [bʌŋ] n bonde f, bouchon m ♦ vt (BRIT: throw: also: ~ **into**) flanquer; (also: ~ **up**: pipe, hole) boucher; **my nose is** ~**ed up** j'ai le nez bouché.
bungalow ['bʌŋgələu] n bungalow m.
bungee jumping ['bʌndʒiː'dʒʌmpɪŋ] n saut m à l'élastique.
bungle ['bʌŋgl] vt bâcler, gâcher.
bunion ['bʌnjən] n oignon m (au pied).
bunk [bʌŋk] n couchette f; (BRIT col): **to do a** ~ mettre les bouts or les voiles.
▶**bunk off** vi (BRIT col: SCOL) sécher (les cours); **I'll** ~ **off at 3 o'clock this afternoon** je vais mettre les bouts or les voiles à 3

heures cet après-midi.

bunk beds *npl* lits superposés.

bunker ['bʌŋkə*] *n* (*coal store*) soute *f* à charbon; (*MIL, GOLF*) bunker *m*.

bunny ['bʌnɪ] *n* (*also*: ~ **rabbit**) Jeannot *m* lapin.

bunny girl *n* (*BRIT*) hôtesse de cabaret.

bunny hill *n* (*US SKI*) piste *f* pour débutants.

bunting ['bʌntɪŋ] *n* pavoisement *m*, drapeaux *mpl*.

buoy [bɔɪ] *n* bouée *f*.

▶**buoy up** *vt* faire flotter; (*fig*) soutenir, épauler.

buoyancy ['bɔɪənsɪ] *n* (*of ship*) flottabilité *f*.

buoyant ['bɔɪənt] *adj* (*ship*) flottable; (*carefree*) gai(e), plein(e) d'entrain; (*COMM: market*) actif(ive); (*: prices, currency*) soutenu(e).

burden ['bə:dn] *n* fardeau *m*, charge *f* ♦ *vt* charger; (*oppress*) accabler, surcharger; **to be a ~ to sb** être un fardeau pour qn.

bureau, *pl* ~**x** ['bjuərəu, -z] *n* (*BRIT: writing desk*) bureau *m*, secrétaire *m*; (*US: chest of drawers*) commode *f*; (*office*) bureau, office *m*.

bureaucracy [bjuə'rɔkrəsɪ] *n* bureaucratie *f*.

bureaucrat ['bjuərəkræt] *n* bureaucrate *m/f*, rond-de-cuir *m*.

bureaucratic [bjuərə'krætɪk] *adj* bureaucratique.

burgeon ['bə:dʒən] *vi* (*fig*) être en expansion rapide.

burger ['bə:gə*] *n* hamburger *m*.

burglar ['bə:glə*] *n* cambrioleur *m*.

burglar alarm *n* sonnerie *f* d'alarme.

burglarize ['bə:glərAɪz] *vt* (*US*) cambrioler.

burglary ['bə:glərɪ] *n* cambriolage *m*.

burgle ['bə:gl] *vt* cambrioler.

Burgundy ['bə:gəndɪ] *n* Bourgogne *f*.

burial ['bɛrɪəl] *n* enterrement *m*.

burial ground *n* cimetière *m*.

burlesque [bə:'lɛsk] *n* caricature *f*, parodie *f*.

burly ['bə:lɪ] *adj* de forte carrure, costaud(e).

Burma ['bə:mə] *n* Birmanie *f*; *see also* **Myanmar**.

Burmese [bə:'mi:z] *adj* birman(e), de Birmanie ♦ *n* (*pl inv*) Birman/e; (*LING*) birman *m*.

burn [bə:n] *vt, vi* (*pt, pp* **burned** *or* **burnt** [bə:nt]) brûler ♦ *n* brûlure *f*; **the cigarette ~t a hole in her dress** la cigarette a fait un trou dans sa robe; **I've ~t myself!** je me suis brûlé(e)!

▶**burn down** *vt* incendier, détruire par le feu.

▶**burn out** *vt* (*subj: writer etc*): **to ~ o.s. out** s'user (à force de travailler).

burner ['bə:nə*] *n* brûleur *m*.

burning ['bə:nɪŋ] *adj* (*building, forest*) en flammes; (*issue, question*) brûlant(e).

burnish ['bə:nɪʃ] *vt* polir.

burnt [bə:nt] *pt, pp of* **burn**.

burnt sugar *n* (*BRIT*) caramel *m*.

burp [bə:p] (*col*) *n* rot *m* ♦ *vi* roter.

burrow ['bʌrəu] *n* terrier *m* ♦ *vt* creuser.

bursar ['bə:sə*] *n* économe *m/f*; (*BRIT: student*) boursier/ère.

bursary ['bə:sərɪ] *n* (*BRIT*) bourse *f* (d'études).

burst [bə:st] *vb* (*pt, pp* **burst**) *vt* faire éclater ♦ *vi* éclater ♦ *n* explosion *f*; (*also*: ~ **pipe**) fuite *f* (*due à une rupture*); ~ **of energy** déploiement soudain d'énergie, activité soudaine; ~ **of laughter** éclat *m* de rire; **a ~ of applause** une salve d'applaudissement; **a ~ of speed** une pointe de vitesse; ~ **blood vessel** rupture *f* de vaisseau sanguin; **the river has ~ its banks** le cours d'eau est sorti de son lit; **to ~ into flames** s'enflammer soudainement; **to ~ out laughing** éclater de rire; **to ~ into tears** fondre en larmes; **to ~ open** *vi* s'ouvrir violemment *or* soudainement; **to be ~ing with** être plein(e) (à craquer) de; regorger de.

▶**burst into** *vt fus* (*room etc*) faire irruption dans.

▶**burst out of** *vt fus* sortir précipitamment de.

bury ['bɛrɪ] *vt* enterrer; **to ~ one's face in one's hands** se couvrir le visage de ses mains; **to ~ one's head in the sand** (*fig*) pratiquer la politique de l'autruche; **to ~ the hatchet** (*fig*) enterrer la hache de guerre.

bus, ~**es** [bʌs, 'bʌsɪz] *n* autobus *m*.

busboy ['bʌsbɔɪ] *n* (*US*) aide-serveur *m*.

bush [buʃ] *n* buisson *m*; (*scrub land*) brousse *f*.

bushed [buʃt] *adj* (*col*) crevé(e), claqué(e).

bushel ['buʃl] *n* boisseau *m*.

bushfire ['buʃfAɪə*] *n* feu *m* de brousse.

bushy ['buʃɪ] *adj* broussailleux(euse), touffu(e).

busily ['bɪzɪlɪ] *adv*: **to be ~ doing sth** s'affairer à faire qch.

business ['bɪznɪs] *n* (*matter, firm*) affaire *f*; (*trading*) affaires *fpl*; (*job, duty*) travail *m*; **to be away on ~** être en déplacement d'affaires; **I'm here on ~** je suis là pour affaires; **he's in the insurance/transport ~** il est dans les assurances/les transports; **to do ~ with sb** traiter avec qn; **it's none of my ~** cela ne me regarde pas, ce ne sont pas mes affaires; **he means** ~ il ne plaisante pas, il est sérieux.

business address n adresse professionnelle or au bureau.

business card n carte f de visite (professionnelle).

businesslike ['bɪznɪslaɪk] adj sérieux(euse); efficace.

businessman ['bɪznɪsmən] n homme d'affaires.

business trip n voyage m d'affaires.

businesswoman ['bɪznɪswumən] n femme f d'affaires.

busker ['bʌskə*] n (BRIT) artiste ambulant(e).

bus lane n (BRIT) voie réservée aux autobus.

bus shelter n abribus m.

bus station n gare routière.

bus stop n arrêt m d'autobus.

bust [bʌst] n buste m ♦ adj (col: broken) fichu(e), fini(e) ♦ vt (col: POLICE: arrest) pincer; **to go** ~ faire faillite.

bustle ['bʌsl] n remue-ménage m, affairement m ♦ vi s'affairer, se démener.

bustling ['bʌslɪŋ] adj (person) affairé(e); (town) très animé(e).

bust-up ['bʌstʌp] n (BRIT col) engueulade f.

busty ['bʌstɪ] adj (col) à la poitrine plantureuse.

busy ['bɪzɪ] adj occupé(e); (shop, street) très fréquenté(e); (US: telephone, line) occupé ♦ vt: **to** ~ **o.s.** s'occuper; **he's a** ~ **man** (normally) c'est un homme très pris; (temporarily) il est très pris.

busybody ['bɪzɪbɔdɪ] n mouche f du coche, âme f charitable.

busy signal n (US) tonalité f occupé.

but [bʌt] conj mais; **I'd love to come,** ~ **I'm busy** j'aimerais venir mais je suis occupé ♦ prep (apart from, except) sauf, excepté; **nothing** ~ rien d'autre que; **we've had nothing** ~ **trouble** nous n'avons eu que des ennuis; **no-one** ~ **him can do it** lui seul peut le faire; ~ **for you/your help** sans toi/ton aide; **anything** ~ **that** tout sauf or excepté ça, tout mais pas ça; **the last** ~ **one** (BRIT) l'avant-dernier(ère)
♦ adv (just, only) ne ... que; **she's** ~ **a child** elle n'est qu'une enfant; **had I** ~ **known** si seulement j'avais su; **all** ~ **finished** pratiquement terminé; **anything** ~ **finished** tout sauf fini, très loin d'être fini.

butane ['bju:teɪn] n (also: ~ **gas**) butane m.

butch [butʃ] adj (col: man) costaud, viril; (: woman) costaude, masculine.

butcher ['butʃə*] n boucher m ♦ vt massacrer; (cattle etc for meat) tuer; ~'**s (shop)** boucherie f.

butler ['bʌtlə*] n maître m d'hôtel.

butt [bʌt] n (cask) gros tonneau; (thick end)

(gros) bout; (of gun) crosse f; (of cigarette) mégot m; (BRIT fig: target) cible f ♦ vt donner un coup de tête à.

▶**butt in** vi (interrupt) interrompre.

butter ['bʌtə*] n beurre m ♦ vt beurrer.

buttercup ['bʌtəkʌp] n bouton m d'or.

butter dish n beurrier m.

butterfingers ['bʌtəfɪŋgəz] n (col) maladroit/e.

butterfly ['bʌtəflaɪ] n papillon m; (SWIMMING: also: ~ **stroke**) brasse f papillon.

buttocks ['bʌtəks] npl fesses fpl.

button ['bʌtn] n bouton m ♦ vt (also: ~ **up**) boutonner ♦ vi se boutonner.

buttonhole ['bʌtnhəul] n boutonnière f ♦ vt accrocher, arrêter, retenir.

buttress ['bʌtrɪs] n contrefort m.

buxom ['bʌksəm] adj aux formes avantageuses or épanouies, bien galbé(e).

buy [baɪ] vb (pt, pp **bought** [bɔːt]) vt acheter; (COMM: company) (r)acheter ♦ n: **that was a good/bad** ~ c'était un bon/mauvais achat; **to** ~ **sb sth/sth from sb** acheter qch à qn; **to** ~ **sb a drink** offrir un verre or à boire à qn.

▶**buy back** vt racheter.

▶**buy in** vt (BRIT: goods) acheter, faire venir.

▶**buy into** vt fus (BRIT COMM) acheter des actions de.

▶**buy off** vt (bribe) acheter.

▶**buy out** vt (partner) désintéresser; (business) racheter.

▶**buy up** vt acheter en bloc, rafler.

buyer ['baɪə*] n acheteur/euse; ~'**s market** marché m favorable aux acheteurs.

buy-out ['baɪaut] n (COMM) rachat m (d'entreprise).

buzz [bʌz] n bourdonnement m; (col: phone call) coup m de fil ♦ vi bourdonner ♦ vt (call on intercom) appeler; (with buzzer) sonner; (AVIAT: plane, building) raser; **my head is** ~**ing** j'ai la tête qui bourdonne.

▶**buzz off** vi (col) s'en aller, ficher le camp.

buzzard ['bʌzəd] n buse f.

buzzer ['bʌzə*] n timbre m électrique.

buzz word n (col) mot m à la mode or dans le vent.

by [baɪ] prep **1** (referring to cause, agent) par, de; **killed** ~ **lightning** tué par la foudre; **surrounded** ~ **a fence** entouré d'une barrière; **a painting** ~ **Picasso** un tableau de Picasso

2 (referring to method, manner, means): ~ **bus/car** en autobus/voiture; ~ **train** par le or en train; **to pay** ~ **cheque** payer par chèque; ~ **saving hard, he ...** à force d'économiser, il ...

3 (via, through) par; **we came** ~ **Dover** nous sommes venus par Douvres

4 (close to, past) à côté de; **the house** ~ **the school** la maison à côté de l'école; **a holiday**

~ **the sea** des vacances au bord de la mer; **she sat** ~ **his bed** elle était assise à son chevet; **she went** ~ **me** elle est passée à côté de moi; **I go** ~ **the post office every day** je passe devant la poste tous les jours
5 (*with time: not later than*) avant; (: *during*): ~ **daylight** à la lumière du jour; ~ **night** la nuit, de nuit; ~ **4 o'clock** avant 4 heures; ~ **this time tomorrow** d'ici demain à la même heure; ~ **the time I got here it was too late** lorsque je suis arrivé il était déjà trop tard
6 (*amount*) à; ~ **the kilo/metre** au kilo/au mètre; **paid** ~ **the hour** payé à l'heure; **to increase** *etc* ~ **the hour** augmenter *etc* d'heure en heure
7 (*MATH, measure*): **to divide/multiply** ~ **3** diviser/multiplier par 3; **a room 3 metres** ~ **4** une pièce de 3 mètres sur 4; **it's broader** ~ **a metre** c'est plus large d'un mètre; **the bullet missed him** ~ **inches** la balle est passée à quelques centimètres de lui; **one** ~ **one** un à un; **little** ~ **little** petit à petit, peu à peu
8 (*according to*) d'après, selon; **it's 3 o'clock** ~ **my watch** il est 3 heures à ma montre; **it's all right** ~ **me** je n'ai rien contre
9: (all) ~ **oneself** *etc* tout(e) seul(e)
10: ~ **the way** au fait, à propos
♦ *adv* **1** *see* **go; pass** *etc*
2: ~ **and** ~ un peu plus tard, bientôt; ~ **and large** dans l'ensemble.

bye(-bye) ['baɪ('baɪ)] *excl* au revoir!, salut!
by(e)-law ['baɪlɔː] *n* arrêté municipal.
by-election ['baɪɪlekʃən] *n* (*BRIT*) élection (législative) partielle.
Byelorussia [bjɛləʊ'rʌʃə] *n* Biélorussie *f*.
Byelorussian [bjɛləʊ'rʌʃən] *adj, n* = **Belorussian**.
bygone ['baɪɡɒn] *adj* passé(e) ♦ *n*: **let** ~**s be** ~**s** passons l'éponge, oublions le passé.
bypass ['baɪpɑːs] *n* (*route f de*) contournement *m*; (*MED*) pontage *m* ♦ *vt* éviter.
by-product ['baɪprɒdʌkt] *n* sous-produit *m*, dérivé *m*; (*fig*) conséquence *f* secondaire, retombée *f*.
byre ['baɪə*] *n* (*BRIT*) étable *f* (à vaches).
bystander ['baɪstændə*] *n* spectateur/trice, badaud/e.
byte [baɪt] *n* (*COMPUT*) octet *m*.
byway ['baɪweɪ] *n* chemin détourné.
byword ['baɪwəːd] *n*: **to be a** ~ **for** être synonyme de (*fig*).
by-your-leave ['baɪjɔː'liːv] *n*: **without so much as a** ~ sans même demander la permission.

Cc

C, c [siː] *n* (*letter*) C, c *m*; (*SCOL: mark*) C; (*MUS*): C do *m*; **C for Charlie** C comme Célestin.
C *abbr* (= *Celsius, centigrade*) C.
c *abbr* (= *century*) s.; (= *circa*) v.; (*US etc*) = **cent(s)**.
CA *n abbr* = **Central America**; (*BRIT*) = **chartered accountant** ♦ *abbr* (*US*) = **California**.
ca. *abbr* (= *circa*) v.
c/a *abbr* = **capital account, credit account, current account**.
CAA *n abbr* (*BRIT*: = *Civil Aviation Authority*, *US*: = *Civil Aeronautics Authority*) direction de l'aviation civile.
CAB *n abbr* (*BRIT*) = **Citizens' Advice Bureau**.
cab [kæb] *n* taxi *m*; (*of train, truck*) cabine *f*; (*horse-drawn*) fiacre *m*.
cabaret ['kæbəreɪ] *n* attractions *fpl*, spectacle *m* de cabaret.
cabbage ['kæbɪdʒ] *n* chou *m*.
cabbie, cabby ['kæbɪ] *n* (*col*), **cab driver** *n* taxi *m*, chauffeur *m* de taxi.
cabin ['kæbɪn] *n* cabane *f*, hutte *f*; (*on ship*) cabine *f*.
cabin cruiser *n* yacht *m* (à moteur).
cabinet ['kæbɪnɪt] *n* (*POL*) cabinet *m*; (*furniture*) petit meuble à tiroirs et rayons; (*also*: **display** ~) vitrine *f*, petite armoire vitrée.
cabinet-maker ['kæbɪnɪt'meɪkə*] *n* ébéniste *m*.
cabinet minister *n* ministre *m* (*membre du cabinet*).
cable ['keɪbl] *n* câble *m* ♦ *vt* câbler, télégraphier.
cable-car ['keɪblkɑː*] *n* téléphérique *m*.
cablegram ['keɪblɡræm] *n* câblogramme *m*.
cable railway *n* (*BRIT*) funiculaire *m*.
cable television *n* télévision *f* par câble.
cache [kæʃ] *n* cachette *f*; **a** ~ **of food** *etc* un dépôt secret de provisions *etc*, une cachette contenant des provisions *etc*.
cackle ['kækl] *vi* caqueter.
cactus, *pl* **cacti** ['kæktəs, -taɪ] *n* cactus *m*.
CAD *n abbr* (= *computer-aided design*) CAO *f*.
caddie ['kædɪ] *n* caddie *m*.
cadet [kə'dɛt] *n* (*MIL*) élève *m* officier; **police** ~ élève agent de police.
cadge [kædʒ] *vt* (*col*) se faire donner; **to** ~ **a meal (off sb)** se faire inviter à manger (par qn).
cadger ['kædʒə*] *n* pique-assiette *m/f inv*, tapeur/euse.
cadre ['kædrɪ] *n* cadre *m*.

Caesarean, (US) **Cesarean** [siː'zɛərɪən] adj: ~ (**section**) césarienne f.
CAF abbr (BRIT: = cost and freight) C et F.
café ['kæfeɪ] n ≈ café(-restaurant) m (sans alcool).
cafeteria [kæfɪ'tɪərɪə] n cafeteria f.
caffein(e) ['kæfiːn] n caféine f.
cage [keɪdʒ] n cage f ♦ vt mettre en cage.
cagey ['keɪdʒɪ] adj (col) réticent(e); méfiant(e).
cagoule [kə'guːl] n K-way m ®.
cahoots [kə'huːts] n: **to be in** ~ (**with**) être de mèche (avec).
CAI n abbr (= computer-aided instruction) EAO m.
Cairo ['kaɪərəu] n le Caire.
cajole [kə'dʒəul] vt couvrir de flatteries or de gentillesses.
cake [keɪk] n gâteau m; ~ **of soap** savonnette f; **it's a piece of** ~ (col) c'est un jeu d'enfant; **he wants to have his** ~ **and eat it (too)** (fig) il veut tout avoir.
caked [keɪkt] adj: ~ **with** raidi(e) par, couvert(e) d'une croûte de.
cake shop n pâtisserie f.
Cal. abbr (US) = California.
calamitous [kə'læmɪtəs] adj catastrophique, désastreux(euse).
calamity [kə'læmɪtɪ] n calamité f, désastre m.
calcium ['kælsɪəm] n calcium m.
calculate ['kælkjuleɪt] vt calculer; (estimate: chances, effect) évaluer.
▶**calculate on** vt fus: **to** ~ **on sth/on doing sth** compter sur qch/faire qch.
calculated ['kælkjuleɪtɪd] adj (insult, action) délibéré(e); **a** ~ **risk** un risque pris en toute connaissance de cause.
calculating ['kælkjuleɪtɪŋ] adj calculateur(trice).
calculation [kælkju'leɪʃən] n calcul m.
calculator ['kælkjuleɪtə*] n machine f à calculer, calculatrice f.
calculus ['kælkjuləs] n analyse f (mathématique), calcul infinitésimal; **integral/differential** ~ calcul intégral/différentiel.
calendar ['kæləndə*] n calendrier m.
calendar month n mois m (de calendrier).
calendar year n année civile.
calf, pl **calves** [kaːf, kaːvz] n (of cow) veau m; (of other animals) petit m; (also: ~**skin**) veau m, vachette f; (ANAT) mollet m.
caliber ['kælɪbə*] n (US) = **calibre**.
calibrate ['kælɪbreɪt] vt (gun etc) calibrer; (scale of measuring instrument) étalonner.
calibre, (US) **caliber** ['kælɪbə*] n calibre m.
calico ['kælɪkəu] n (BRIT) calicot m; (US) indienne f.
Calif. abbr (US) = California.
California [kælɪ'fɔːnɪə] n Californie f.
calipers ['kælɪpəz] npl (US) = **calipers**.
call [kɔːl] vt (gen, also TEL) appeler; (announce:

flight) annoncer; (meeting) convoquer; (strike) lancer ♦ vi appeler; (visit: also: ~ **in**, ~ **round**): **to** ~ (**for**) passer (prendre) ♦ n (shout) appel m, cri m; (summons: for flight etc, fig: lure) appel; (visit) visite f; (also: **telephone** ~) coup m de téléphone; communication f; **to be on** ~ être de permanence; **she's** ~**ed Suzanne** elle s'appelle Suzanne; **who is** ~**ing?** (TEL) qui est à l'appareil?; **London** ~**ing** (RADIO) ici Londres; **please give me a** ~ **at 7** appelez-moi à 7 heures; **to make a** ~ téléphoner, passer un coup de fil; **to pay a** ~ **on sb** rendre visite à qn, passer voir qn; **there's not much** ~ **for these items** ces articles ne sont pas très demandés.
▶**call at** vt fus (subj: ship) faire escale à; (: train) s'arrêter à.
▶**call back** vi (return) repasser; (TEL) rappeler ♦ vt (TEL) rappeler.
▶**call for** vt fus demander.
▶**call in** vt (doctor, expert, police) appeler, faire venir.
▶**call off** vt annuler; **the strike was** ~**ed off** l'ordre de grève a été rapporté.
▶**call on** vt fus (visit) rendre visite à, passer voir; (request): **to** ~ **on sb to do** inviter qn à faire.
▶**call out** vi pousser un cri or des cris ♦ vt (doctor, police, troops) appeler.
▶**call up** vt (MIL) appeler, mobiliser.
Callanetics [kælə'nɛtɪks] n ® stretching m.
callbox ['kɔːlbɔks] n (BRIT) cabine f téléphonique.
caller ['kɔːlə*] n personne f qui appelle; visiteur m; **hold the line,** ~! (TEL) ne quittez pas, Monsieur (or Madame)!
call girl n call-girl f.
call-in ['kɔːlɪn] n (US RADIO, TV) programme m à ligne ouverte.
calling ['kɔːlɪŋ] n vocation f; (trade, occupation) état m.
calling card n (US) carte f de visite.
callipers, (US) **calipers** ['kælɪpəz] npl (MATH) compas m; (MED) appareil m orthopédique; gouttière f; étrier m.
callous ['kæləs] adj dur(e), insensible.
callousness ['kæləsnɪs] n dureté f, manque m de cœur, insensibilité f.
callow ['kæləu] adj sans expérience (de la vie).
calm [kaːm] adj calme ♦ n calme m ♦ vt calmer, apaiser.
▶**calm down** vi se calmer, s'apaiser ♦ vt calmer, apaiser.
calmly ['kaːmlɪ] adv calmement, avec calme.
calmness ['kaːmnɪs] n calme m.
Calor gas ['kælə*-] n ® (BRIT) butane m, butagaz m ®.
calorie ['kælərɪ] n calorie f; **low** ~ **product** produit m pauvre en calories.
calve [kaːv] vi vêler, mettre bas.

calves [kɑːvz] *npl of* calf.
CAM *n abbr* (= *computer-aided manufacturing*) FAO *f*.
camber ['kæmbə*] *n* (*of road*) bombement *m*.
Cambodia [kæm'bəʊdjə] *n* Cambodge *m*.
Cambodian [kæm'bəʊdɪən] *adj* cambodgien(ne) ♦ *n* Cambodgien/ne.
Cambs *abbr* (*BRIT*) = Cambridgeshire.
camcorder ['kæmkɔːdə*] *n* caméscope *m*.
came [keɪm] *pt of* come.
camel ['kæməl] *n* chameau *m*.
cameo ['kæmɪəʊ] *n* camée *m*.
camera ['kæmərə] *n* appareil-photo *m*; (*CINE, TV*) caméra *f*; **35mm ~** appareil 24 x 36 *or* petit format; **in ~** à huis clos, en privé.
cameraman ['kæmərəmæn] *n* caméraman *m*.
Cameroon, Cameroun [kæmə'ruːn] *n* Cameroun *m*.
camouflage ['kæməflɑːʒ] *n* camouflage *m* ♦ *vt* camoufler.
camp [kæmp] *n* camp *m* ♦ *vi* camper; **to go ~ing** faire du camping.
campaign [kæm'peɪn] *n* (*MIL, POL etc*) campagne *f* ♦ *vi* (*also fig*) faire campagne; **to ~ for/against** militer pour/contre.
campaigner [kæm'peɪnə*] *n*: **~ for** partisan/e de; **~ against** opposant/e à.
campbed ['kæmp'bɛd] *n* (*BRIT*) lit *m* de camp.
camper ['kæmpə*] *n* campeur/euse.
camping ['kæmpɪŋ] *n* camping *m*.
camp(ing) site *n* (terrain *m* de) camping *m*.
campus ['kæmpəs] *n* campus *m*.
camshaft ['kæmʃɑːft] *n* arbre *m* à came.
can¹ [kæn] *aux vb see keyword* ♦ *n* (*of milk, oil, water*) bidon *m*; (*tin*) boîte *f* (de conserve) ♦ *vt* mettre en conserve; **a ~ of beer** une canette de bière; **he had to carry the ~** (*BRIT col*) on lui a fait porter le chapeau.

═══════════════════════ *KEYWORD*

can² [kæn] (*negative* **cannot, can't**; *conditional and pt* **could**) *aux vb* **1** (*be able to*) pouvoir; **you ~ do it if you try** vous pouvez le faire si vous essayez; **I ~'t hear you** je ne t'entends pas
2 (*know how to*) savoir; **I ~ swim/play tennis/drive** je sais nager/jouer au tennis/conduire; **~ you speak French?** parlez-vous français?
3 (*may*) pouvoir; **~ I use your phone?** puis-je me servir de votre téléphone?
4 (*expressing disbelief, puzzlement etc*): **it ~'t be true!** ce n'est pas possible!; **what CAN he want?** qu'est-ce qu'il peut bien vouloir?
5 (*expressing possibility, suggestion etc*): **he could be in the library** il est peut-être dans la bibliothèque; **she could have been delayed** il se peut qu'elle ait été retardée; **they could have forgotten** ils ont pu oublier.

Canada ['kænədə] *n* Canada *m*.
Canadian [kə'neɪdɪən] *adj* canadien(ne) ♦ *n* Canadien/ne.
canal [kə'næl] *n* canal *m*.
canary [kə'nɛərɪ] *n* canari *m*, serin *m*.
Canary Islands, Canaries [kə'nɛərɪz] *npl*: **the ~** les (îles *fpl*) Canaries *fpl*.
Canberra ['kænbərə] *n* Canberra *m*.
cancel ['kænsəl] *vt* annuler; (*train*) supprimer; (*party, appointment*) décommander; (*cross out*) barrer, rayer; (*stamp*) oblitérer; (*cheque*) faire opposition à.
▶**cancel out** *vt* annuler; **they ~ each other out** ils s'annulent.
cancellation [kænsə'leɪʃən] *n* annulation *f*; suppression *f*; oblitération *f*; (*TOURISM*) réservation annulée, client *etc* qui s'est décommandé.
cancer ['kænsə*] *n* cancer *m*; **C~** (*sign*) le Cancer; **to be C~** être du Cancer.
cancerous ['kænsrəs] *adj* cancéreux(euse).
cancer patient *n* cancéreux/euse.
cancer research *n* recherche *f* contre le cancer.
C and F *abbr* (*BRIT*: = *cost and freight*) C et F.
candid ['kændɪd] *adj* (très) franc(franche), sincère.
candidacy ['kændɪdəsɪ] *n* candidature *f*.
candidate ['kændɪdeɪt] *n* candidat/e.
candidature ['kændɪdətʃə*] *n* (*BRIT*) = **candidacy**.
candied ['kændɪd] *adj* confit(e); **~ apple** (*US*) pomme caramélisée.
candle ['kændl] *n* bougie *f*; (*of tallow*) chandelle *f*; (*in church*) cierge *m*.
candlelight ['kændllaɪt] *n*: **by ~** à la lumière d'une bougie; (*dinner*) aux chandelles.
candlestick ['kændlstɪk] *n* (*also*: **candle holder**) bougeoir *m*; (*bigger, ornate*) chandelier *m*.
candour, (*US*) **candor** ['kændə*] *n* (grande) franchise *or* sincérité.
C & W *n abbr* = **country and western (music)**.
candy ['kændɪ] *n* sucre candi; (*US*) bonbon *m*.
candy-floss ['kændɪflɔs] *n* (*BRIT*) barbe *f* à papa.
candy store *n* (*US*) confiserie *f*.
cane [keɪn] *n* canne *f*; (*for baskets, chairs etc*) rotin *m* ♦ *vt* (*BRIT SCOL*) administrer des coups de bâton à.
canine ['kænaɪn] *adj* canin(e).
canister ['kænɪstə*] *n* boîte *f* (*gén en métal*).
cannabis ['kænəbɪs] *n* (*drug*) cannabis *m*; (*also*: **~ plant**) chanvre indien.
canned ['kænd] *adj* (*food*) en boîte, en conserve; (*col*: *music*) enregistré(e); (*BRIT col*: *drunk*) bourré(e); (*US col*: *worker*) mis(e) à la porte.
cannibal ['kænɪbəl] *n* cannibale *m/f*, anthropophage *m/f*.
cannibalism ['kænɪbəlɪzəm] *n* cannibalisme *m*, anthropophagie *f*.
cannon, *pl* **~** *or* **~s** ['kænən] *n* (*gun*) canon *m*.
cannonball ['kænənbɔːl] *n* boulet *m* de canon.
cannon fodder *n* chair *f* à canon.

cannot ['kænɔt] = **can not**.
canny ['kænɪ] adj madré(e), finaud(e).
canoe [kə'nu:] n pirogue f; (SPORT) canoë m.
canoeing [kə'nu:ɪŋ] n (sport) canoë m.
canoeist [kə'nu:ɪst] n canoéiste m/f.
canon ['kænən] n (clergyman) chanoine m; (standard) canon m.
canonize ['kænənaɪz] vt canoniser.
can opener [-'əupnə*] n ouvre-boîte m.
canopy ['kænəpɪ] n baldaquin m; dais m.
cant [kænt] n jargon m ♦ vt, vi pencher.
can't [kænt] = **can not**.
Cantab. abbr (BRIT: = cantabrigiensis) of Cambridge.
cantankerous [kæn'tæŋkərəs] adj querelleur(euse), acariâtre.
canteen [kæn'ti:n] n cantine f; (BRIT: of cutlery) ménagère f.
canter ['kæntə*] n petit galop ♦ vi aller au petit galop.
cantilever ['kæntɪli:və*] n porte-à-faux m inv.
canvas ['kænvəs] n (gen) toile f; **under ~** (camping) sous la tente; (NAUT) toutes voiles dehors.
canvass ['kænvəs] vt (POL: district) faire la tournée électorale dans; (: person) solliciter le suffrage de; (COMM: district) prospecter; (citizens, opinions) sonder.
canvasser ['kænvəsə*] n (POL) agent électoral; (COMM) démarcheur m.
canvassing ['kænvəsɪŋ] n (POL) prospection électorale, démarchage électoral; (COMM) démarchage, prospection.
canyon ['kænjən] n cañon m, gorge (profonde).
CAP n abbr (= Common Agricultural Policy) PAC f.
cap [kæp] n casquette f; (for swimming) bonnet m de bain; (of pen) capuchon m; (of bottle) capsule f; (BRIT: contraceptive: also: **Dutch ~**) diaphragme m; (: FOOTBALL) sélection f pour l'équipe nationale ♦ vt capsuler; (outdo) surpasser; **~ped with** coiffé(e) de; **and to ~ it all, he ...** (BRIT) pour couronner le tout, il ....
capability [keɪpə'bɪlɪtɪ] n aptitude f, capacité f.
capable ['keɪpəbl] adj capable; **~ of** (interpretation etc) susceptible de.
capacious [kə'peɪʃəs] adj vaste.
capacity [kə'pæsɪtɪ] n (of container) capacité f, contenance f; (ability) aptitude f; **filled to ~** plein(e); **in his ~ as** en sa qualité de; **this work is beyond my ~** ce travail dépasse mes capacités; **in an advisory ~** à titre consultatif; **to work at full ~** travailler à plein rendement.
cape [keɪp] n (garment) cape f; (GEO) cap m.
Cape of Good Hope n cap m de Bonne Espérance.
caper ['keɪpə*] n (CULIN: also: **~s**) câpre f.
Cape Town n Le Cap.
capita ['kæpɪtə] see **per capita**.

capital ['kæpɪtl] n (also: **~ city**) capitale f; (money) capital m; (also: **~ letter**) majuscule f.
capital account n balance f des capitaux; (of country) compte capital.
capital allowance n provision f pour amortissement.
capital assets npl immobilisations fpl.
capital expenditure n dépenses fpl d'équipement.
capital gains tax n impôt m sur les plus-values.
capital goods n biens mpl d'équipement.
capital-intensive ['kæpɪtlɪn'tɛnsɪv] adj à forte proportion de capitaux.
capitalism ['kæpɪtəlɪzəm] n capitalisme m.
capitalist ['kæpɪtəlɪst] adj, n capitaliste (m/f).
capitalize ['kæpɪtəlaɪz] vt (provide with capital) financer.
▶**capitalize on** vt fus (fig) profiter de.
capital punishment n peine capitale.
capital transfer tax n (BRIT) impôt m sur le transfert de propriété.
Capitol ['kæpɪtl] n: **the ~** le Capitole.

Le **Capitol** est le siège du **Congress**, à Washington. Il est situé sur Capitol Hill.

---

capitulate [kə'pɪtjuleɪt] vi capituler.
capitulation [kəpɪtju'leɪʃən] n capitulation f.
capricious [kə'prɪʃəs] adj capricieux(euse), fantasque.
Capricorn ['kæprɪkɔ:n] n le Capricorne; **to be ~** être du Capricorne.
caps [kæps] abbr = **capital letters**.
capsize [kæp'saɪz] vt faire chavirer ♦ vi chavirer.
capstan ['kæpstən] n cabestan m.
capsule ['kæpsju:l] n capsule f.
Capt. abbr (= captain) Cne.
captain ['kæptɪn] n capitaine m ♦ vt commander, être le capitaine de.
caption ['kæpʃən] n légende f.
captivate ['kæptɪveɪt] vt captiver, fasciner.
captive ['kæptɪv] adj, n captif(ive).
captivity [kæp'tɪvɪtɪ] n captivité f.
captor ['kæptə*] n (unlawful) ravisseur m; (lawful): **his ~s** les gens (or ceux etc) qui l'ont arrêté.
capture ['kæptʃə*] vt capturer, prendre; (attention) capter ♦ n capture f.
car [kɑ:*] n voiture f, auto f; (US RAIL) wagon m, voiture; **by ~** en voiture.
Caracas [kə'rækəs] n Caracas.
carafe [kə'ræf] n carafe f.
carafe wine n (in restaurant) ≈ vin ouvert.
caramel ['kærəməl] n caramel m.
carat ['kærət] n carat m; **18 ~ gold** or m à 18 carats.
caravan ['kærəvæn] n caravane f.
caravan site n (BRIT) camping m pour caravanes.

caraway ['kærəweɪ] *n*: ~ **seed** graine *f* de cumin, cumin *m*.

carbohydrates [kɑːbəu'haɪdreɪts] *npl* (*foods*) aliments *mpl* riches en hydrate de carbone.

carbolic acid [kɑː'bɒlɪk-] *n* phénol *m*.

car bomb *n* voiture piégée.

carbon ['kɑːbən] *n* carbone *m*.

carbonated ['kɑːbəneɪtɪd] *adj* (*drink*) gazeux(euse).

carbon copy *n* carbone *m*.

carbon dioxide *n* gas *m* carbonique, dioxyde *m* de carbone.

carbon paper *n* papier *m* carbone.

carbon ribbon *n* ruban *m* carbone.

car boot sale *n marché aux puces où des particuliers vendent des objets entreposés dans le coffre de leur voiture.*

carburettor, (*US*) **carburetor** [kɑːbju'rɛtə*] *n* carburateur *m*.

carcass ['kɑːkəs] *n* carcasse *f*.

carcinogenic [kɑːsɪnə'dʒɛnɪk] *adj* cancérigène.

card [kɑːd] *n* carte *f*; (*membership ~*) carte d'adhérent; **to play ~s** jouer aux cartes.

cardamom ['kɑːdəməm] *n* cardamome *f*.

cardboard ['kɑːdbɔːd] *n* carton *m*.

cardboard box *n* (boîte *f* en) carton *m*.

cardboard city *n endroit de la ville où dorment les SDF dans des boîtes en carton.*

card-carrying member ['kɑːdkærɪɪŋ-] *n* membre actif.

card game *n* jeu *m* de cartes.

cardiac ['kɑːdɪæk] *adj* cardiaque.

cardigan ['kɑːdɪgən] *n* cardigan *m*.

cardinal ['kɑːdɪnl] *adj* cardinal(e) ♦ *n* cardinal *m*.

card index *n* fichier *m* (alphabétique).

cardphone ['kɑːdfəun] *n* téléphone *m* à carte (magnétique).

cardsharp ['kɑːdʃɑːp] *n* tricheur/euse professionnel(le).

card vote *n* (*BRIT*) vote *m* de délégués.

CARE [kɛə*] *n abbr* (= *Cooperative for American Relief Everywhere*) association charitable.

care [kɛə*] *n* soin *m*, attention *f*; (*worry*) souci *m* ♦ *vi*: **to ~ about** se soucier de, s'intéresser à; **in sb's ~** à la garde de qn, confié à qn; **~ of (c/o)** (*on letter*) aux bons soins de; **"with ~"** "fragile"; **to take ~ (to do)** faire attention (à faire); **to take ~ of** *vt* s'occuper de, prendre soin de; (*details, arrangements*) s'occuper de; **the child has been taken into ~** l'enfant a été placé en institution; **would you ~ to/for ...?** voulez-vous ...?; **I wouldn't ~ to do it** je n'aimerais pas le faire; **I don't ~** ça m'est bien égal, peu m'importe; **I couldn't ~ less** cela m'est complètement égal, je m'en fiche complètement.

▶**care for** *vt fus* s'occuper de; (*like*) aimer.

careen [kə'riːn] *vi* (*ship*) donner de la bande ♦ *vt* caréner, mettre en carène.

career [kə'rɪə*] *n* carrière *f* ♦ *vi* (*also*: ~ **along**) aller à toute allure.

career girl *n* jeune fille *f* (*or* femme *f*) qui veut faire carrière.

careers officer *n* conseiller/ère d'orientation (professionnelle).

carefree ['kɛəfriː] *adj* sans souci, insouciant(e).

careful ['kɛəful] *adj* soigneux(euse); (*cautious*) prudent(e); **(be) ~!** (fais) attention!; **to be ~ with one's money** regarder à la dépense.

carefully ['kɛəfəlɪ] *adv* avec soin, soigneusement; prudemment.

careless ['kɛəlɪs] *adj* négligent(e); (*heedless*) insouciant(e).

carelessly ['kɛəlɪslɪ] *adv* négligemment; avec insouciance.

carelessness ['kɛəlɪsnɪs] *n* manque *m* de soin, négligence *f*; insouciance *f*.

carer ['kɛərə*] *n personne qui s'occupe d'un proche qui est malade.*

caress [kə'rɛs] *n* caresse *f* ♦ *vt* caresser.

caretaker ['kɛəteɪkə*] *n* gardien/ne, concierge *m/f*.

caretaker government *n* (*BRIT*) gouvernement *m* intérimaire.

car-ferry ['kɑːfɛrɪ] *n* (*on sea*) ferry(-boat) *m*; (*on river*) bac *m*.

cargo, *pl* ~**es** ['kɑːgəu] *n* cargaison *f*, chargement *m*.

cargo boat *n* cargo *m*.

cargo plane *n* avion-cargo *m*.

car hire *n* (*BRIT*) location *f* de voitures.

Caribbean [kærɪ'biːən] *adj* des Caraïbes; **the ~ (Sea)** la mer des Antilles *or* des Caraïbes.

caricature ['kærɪkətjuə*] *n* caricature *f*.

caring ['kɛərɪŋ] *adj* (*person*) bienveillant(e); (*society, organization*) humanitaire.

carnage ['kɑːnɪdʒ] *n* carnage *m*.

carnal ['kɑːnl] *adj* charnel(le).

carnation [kɑː'neɪʃən] *n* œillet *m*.

carnival ['kɑːnɪvl] *n* (*public celebration*) carnaval *m*; (*US: funfair*) fête foraine.

carnivorous [kɑː'nɪvərəs] *adj* carnivore, carnassier(ière).

carol ['kærəl] *n*: **(Christmas) ~** chant *m* de Noël.

carouse [kə'rauz] *vi* faire la bringue.

carousel [kærə'sɛl] *n* (*US*) manège *m*.

carp [kɑːp] *n* (*fish*) carpe *f*.

▶**carp at** *vt fus* critiquer.

car park *n* parking *m*, parc *m* de stationnement.

carpenter ['kɑːpɪntə*] *n* charpentier *m*.

carpentry ['kɑːpɪntrɪ] *n* charpenterie *f*, métier *m* de charpentier; (*woodwork: at school etc*) menuiserie *f*.

carpet ['kɑːpɪt] *n* tapis *m* ♦ *vt* recouvrir (d'un tapis); **fitted ~** (*BRIT*) moquette *f*.

carpet bombing *n* bombardement intensif.

carpet slippers *npl* pantoufles *fpl*.

carpet sweeper [-'swiːpə*] *n* balai *m* mécanique.

car phone n téléphone m de voiture.
car rental n (*US*) location f de voitures.
carriage ['kærɪdʒ] n voiture f; (*of goods*) transport m; (*: cost*) port m; (*of typewriter*) chariot m; (*bearing*) maintien m, port m; ~ **forward** port dû; ~ **free** franco de port; ~ **paid** (en) port payé.
carriage return n retour m à la ligne.
carriageway ['kærɪdʒweɪ] n (*BRIT: part of road*) chaussée f.
carrier ['kærɪə*] n transporteur m, camionneur m; (*MED*) porteur/euse; (*NAUT*) porte-avions m inv.
carrier bag n (*BRIT*) sac m en papier or en plastique.
carrier pigeon n pigeon voyageur.
carrion ['kærɪən] n charogne f.
carrot ['kærət] n carotte f.
carry ['kærɪ] vt (*subj: person*) porter; (*: vehicle*) transporter; (*a motion, bill*) voter, adopter; (*MATH: figure*) retenir; (*COMM: interest*) rapporter; (*involve: responsibilities etc*) comporter, impliquer ♦ vi (*sound*) porter; **to be carried away** (*fig*) s'emballer, s'enthousiasmer; **this loan carries 10% interest** ce prêt est à 10% (d'intérêt).
► **carry forward** vt (*gen, BOOK-KEEPING*) reporter.
► **carry on** vi (*continue*): **to ~ on with sth/ doing** continuer qch/à faire; (*col: make a fuss*) faire des histoires ♦ vt entretenir, poursuivre.
► **carry out** vt (*orders*) exécuter; (*investigation*) effectuer; (*idea, threat*) mettre à exécution.
carrycot ['kærɪkɒt] n (*BRIT*) porte-bébé m.
carry-on ['kærɪ'ɒn] n (*col: fuss*) histoires fpl; (*: annoying behaviour*) cirque m, cinéma m.
cart [kɑːt] n charrette f ♦ vt transporter.
carte blanche ['kɑːt'blɒnʃ] n: **to give sb ~** donner carte blanche à qn.
cartel [kɑː'tɛl] n (*COMM*) cartel m.
cartilage ['kɑːtɪlɪdʒ] n cartilage m.
cartographer [kɑː'tɒgrəfə*] n cartographe m/f.
cartography [kɑː'tɒgrəfɪ] n cartographie f.
carton ['kɑːtən] n (*box*) carton m; (*of yogurt*) pot m (en carton); (*of cigarettes*) cartouche f.
cartoon [kɑː'tuːn] n (*PRESS*) dessin m (humoristique); (*satirical*) caricature f; (*comic strip*) bande dessinée; (*CINE*) dessin animé.
cartoonist [kɑː'tuːnɪst] n dessinateur/trice humoristique; caricaturiste m/f; auteur m de dessins animés; auteur de bandes dessinées.
cartridge ['kɑːtrɪdʒ] n (*for gun, pen*) cartouche f; (*for camera*) chargeur m; (*music tape*) cassette f; (*of record player*) cellule f.
cartwheel ['kɑːtwiːl] n roue f; **to turn a ~** faire la roue.
carve [kɑːv] vt (*meat: also: ~ up*) découper; (*wood, stone*) tailler, sculpter.
carving ['kɑːvɪŋ] n (*in wood etc*) sculpture f.

carving knife n couteau m à découper.
car wash n station f de lavage (de voitures).
Casablanca [kæsə'blæŋkə] n Casablanca.
cascade [kæs'keɪd] n cascade f ♦ vi tomber en cascade.
case [keɪs] n cas m; (*LAW*) affaire f, procès m; (*box*) caisse f, boîte f, étui m; (*BRIT: also: suit~*) valise f; (*TYP*): **lower/upper ~** minuscule f/majuscule f; **to have a good ~** avoir de bons arguments; **there's a strong ~ for reform** il y aurait lieu d'engager une réforme; **in ~ of** en cas de; **in ~ he** au cas où il; **just in ~** à tout hasard.
case history n (*MED*) dossier médical, antécédents médicaux.
case study n étude f de cas.
cash [kæʃ] n argent m; (*COMM*) argent liquide, numéraire m; liquidités fpl; (*: in payment*) argent comptant, espèces fpl ♦ vt encaisser; **to pay (in) ~** payer (en argent) comptant or en espèces; ~ **with order/on delivery** (*COMM*) payable or paiement à la commande/livraison; **to be short of ~** être à court d'argent.
► **cash in** vt (*insurance policy etc*) toucher.
► **cash in on** vt fus profiter de.
cash account n compte m caisse.
cash and carry n libre-service m de gros, cash and carry m inv.
cashbook ['kæʃbuk] n livre m de caisse.
cash box n caisse f.
cash card n carte de retrait or accréditive.
cash desk n (*BRIT*) caisse f.
cash discount n escompte m de caisse (pour paiement au comptant), remise f au comptant.
cash dispenser n distributeur m automatique de billets.
cashew [kæ'ʃuː] n (*also:* ~ **nut**) noix f de cajou.
cash flow n cash-flow m, marge brute d'autofinancement.
cashier [kæ'ʃɪə*] n caissier/ère ♦ vt (*MIL*) destituer, casser.
cashmere ['kæʃmɪə*] n cachemire m.
cash payment n paiement comptant, versement m en espèces.
cash price n prix comptant.
cash register n caisse enregistreuse.
cash sale n vente f au comptant.
casing ['keɪsɪŋ] n revêtement (protecteur), enveloppe (protectrice).
casino [kə'siːnəu] n casino m.
cask [kɑːsk] n tonneau m.
casket ['kɑːskɪt] n coffret m; (*US: coffin*) cercueil m.
Caspian Sea ['kæspɪən-] n: **the ~** la mer Caspienne.
casserole ['kæsərəul] n cocotte f; (*food*) ragoût m (en cocotte).
cassette [kæ'sɛt] n cassette f, musicassette f.
cassette deck n platine f cassette.

cassette player n lecteur m de cassettes.
cassette recorder n magnétophone m à cassettes.
cast [kɑːst] vb (pt, pp **cast**) vt (throw) jeter; (shed) perdre; se dépouiller de; (metal) couler, fondre; (THEAT): **to ~ sb as Hamlet** attribuer à qn le rôle d'Hamlet ♦ n (THEAT) distribution f; (mould) moule m; (also: **plaster ~**) plâtre m; **to ~ one's vote** voter, exprimer son suffrage.
▶**cast aside** vt (reject) rejeter.
▶**cast off** vi (NAUT) larguer les amarres; (KNITTING) arrêter les mailles ♦ vt (KNITTING) arrêter.
▶**cast on** (KNITTING) vt monter ♦ vi monter les mailles.
castanets [kæstə'nɛts] npl castagnettes fpl.
castaway ['kɑːstəweɪ] n naufragé/e.
caste [kɑːst] n caste f, classe sociale.
caster sugar ['kɑːstə-] n (BRIT) sucre m semoule.
casting vote ['kɑːstɪŋ-] n (BRIT) voix prépondérante (pour départager).
cast iron n fonte f ♦ adj: **cast-iron** (fig: will) de fer; (: alibi) en béton.
castle ['kɑːsl] n château-fort m; (manor) château m.
cast-offs ['kɑːstɔfs] npl vêtements mpl dont on ne veut plus.
castor ['kɑːstə*] n (wheel) roulette f.
castor oil n huile f de ricin.
castrate [kæs'treɪt] vt châtrer.
casual ['kæʒjul] adj (by chance) de hasard, fait(e) au hasard, fortuit(e); (irregular: work etc) temporaire; (unconcerned) désinvolte; ~ **wear** vêtements mpl sport inv.
casual labour n main-d'œuvre f temporaire.
casually ['kæʒjuli] adv avec désinvolture, négligemment; (by chance) fortuitement.
casualty ['kæʒjultɪ] n accidenté/e, blessé/e; (dead) victime f, mort/e; **heavy casualties** lourdes pertes.
casualty ward n (BRIT) service m des urgences.
cat [kæt] n chat m.
catacombs ['kætəkuːmz] npl catacombes fpl.
catalogue, (US) **catalog** ['kætəlɔg] n catalogue m ♦ vt cataloguer.
catalyst ['kætəlɪst] n catalyseur m.
catalytic converter [kætə'lɪtɪkkən'vəːtə*] n pot m catalytique.
catapult ['kætəpʌlt] n lance-pierres m inv, fronde m; (HISTORY) catapulte f.
cataract ['kætərækt] n (also MED) cataracte f.
catarrh [kə'tɑː*] n rhume m chronique, catarrhe f.
catastrophe [kə'tæstrəfɪ] n catastrophe f.
catastrophic [kætə'strɔfɪk] adj catastrophique.
catcall ['kætkɔːl] n (at meeting etc) sifflet m.
catch [kætʃ] vb (pt, pp **caught** [kɔːt]) vt (ball, train, thief, cold) attraper; (person: by surprise)

prendre, surprendre; (understand) saisir; (get entangled) accrocher ♦ vi (fire) prendre; (get entangled) s'accrocher ♦ n (fish etc caught) prise f; (thief etc caught) capture f; (trick) attrape f; (TECH) loquet m; cliquet m; **to ~ sb's attention** or **eye** attirer l'attention de qn; **to ~ fire** prendre feu; **to ~ sight of** apercevoir.
▶**catch on** vi (become popular) prendre; (understand): **to ~ on (to sth)** saisir (qch).
▶**catch out** vt (BRIT fig: with trick question) prendre en défaut.
▶**catch up** vi se rattraper, combler son retard ♦ vt (also: ~ **up with**) rattraper.
catching ['kætʃɪŋ] adj (MED) contagieux(euse)
catchment area ['kætʃmənt-] n (BRIT SCOL) aire f de recrutement; (GEO) bassin m hydrographique.
catch phrase n slogan m; expression toute faite.
catch-22 ['kætʃtwentɪ'tuː] n: **it's a ~ situation** c'est (une situation) sans issue.
catchy ['kætʃɪ] adj (tune) facile à retenir.
catechism ['kætɪkɪzəm] n catéchisme m.
categoric(al) [kætɪ'gɔrɪk(l)] adj catégorique.
categorize ['kætɪgəraɪz] vt classer par catégories.
category ['kætɪgərɪ] n catégorie f.
cater ['keɪtə*] vi (provide food): **to ~ (for)** préparer des repas (pour), se charger de la restauration (pour).
▶**cater for** vt fus (BRIT: needs) satisfaire, pourvoir à; (: readers, consumers) s'adresser à, pourvoir aux besoins de.
caterer ['keɪtərə*] n traiteur m; fournisseur m.
catering ['keɪtərɪŋ] n restauration f; approvisionnement m, ravitaillement m.
caterpillar ['kætəpɪlə*] n chenille f ♦ cpd (vehicle) à chenille; ~ **track** n chenille f.
cat flap n chatière f.
cathedral [kə'θiːdrəl] n cathédrale f.
cathode ['kæθəud] n cathode f.
cathode ray tube n tube m cathodique.
catholic ['kæθəlɪk] adj éclectique; universel(le); libéral(e); **C~** adj, n (REL) catholique (m/f).
cat's-eye ['kæts'aɪ] n (BRIT AUT) (clou m à) catadioptre m.
catsup ['kætsəp] n (US) ketchup m.
cattle ['kætl] npl bétail m, bestiaux mpl.
catty ['kætɪ] adj méchant(e).
catwalk ['kætwɔːk] n passerelle f; (for models) podium m (de défilé de mode).
Caucasian [kɔː'keɪzɪən] adj, n caucasien(ne).
Caucasus ['kɔːkəsəs] n Caucase m.
caucus ['kɔːkəs] n (US POL) comité électoral (pour désigner des candidats); (BRIT POL: group) comité local (d'un parti politique).

_Un_ **caucus** _aux États-Unis est une réunion restreinte des principaux dirigeants d'un parti politique, précédant souvent une assemblée_ *générale, dans le but de choisir des candidats ou de définir une ligne d'action. Par extension, ce terme désigne également l'état-major d'un parti politique.*

caught [kɔːt] *pt, pp of* **catch**.
cauliflower ['kɒlɪflauə*] *n* chou-fleur *m*.
cause [kɔːz] *n* cause *f* ♦ *vt* causer; **there is no ~ for concern** il n'y a pas lieu de s'inquiéter; **to ~ sth to be done** faire faire qch; **to ~ sb to do sth** faire faire qch à qn.
causeway ['kɔːzweɪ] *n* chaussée (surélevée).
caustic ['kɔːstɪk] *adj* caustique.
caution ['kɔːʃən] *n* prudence *f*; (*warning*) avertissement *m* ♦ *vt* avertir, donner un avertissement à.
cautious ['kɔːʃəs] *adj* prudent(e).
cautiously ['kɔːʃəslɪ] *adv* prudemment, avec prudence.
cautiousness ['kɔːʃəsnɪs] *n* prudence *f*.
cavalier [kævə'lɪə*] *adj* cavalier(ère), désinvolte ♦ *n* (*knight*) cavalier *m*.
cavalry ['kævəlrɪ] *n* cavalerie *f*.
cave [keɪv] *n* caverne *f*, grotte *f* ♦ *vi*: **to go caving** faire de la spéléo(logie).
▶**cave in** *vi* (*roof etc*) s'effondrer.
caveman ['keɪvmæn] *n* homme *m* des cavernes.
cavern ['kævən] *n* caverne *f*.
caviar(e) ['kævɪɑː*] *n* caviar *m*.
cavity ['kævɪtɪ] *n* cavité *f*.
cavity wall insulation *n* isolation *f* des murs creux.
cavort [kə'vɔːt] *vi* cabrioler, faire des cabrioles.
cayenne [keɪ'ɛn] *n* (*also*: ~ **pepper**) poivre *m* de cayenne.
CB *n abbr* (= *Citizens' Band (Radio)*) CB *f*; (*BRIT*: = *Companion of (the Order of) the Bath*) *titre honorifique*.
CBC *n abbr* (= *Canadian Broadcasting Corporation*) *organisme de radiodiffusion*.
CBE *n abbr* (= *Companion of (the Order of) the British Empire*) *titre honorifique*.
CBI *n abbr* (= *Confederation of British Industry*) ≈ CNPF *m* (= *Conseil national du patronat français*).
CBS *n abbr* (*US*: = *Columbia Broadcasting System*) *chaîne de télévision*.
CC *abbr* (*BRIT*) = *county council*.
cc *abbr* (= *cubic centimetre*) cm³; (*on letter etc*) = *carbon copy*.
CCA *n abbr* (*US*: = *Circuit Court of Appeals*) *cour d'appel itinérante*.
CCU *n abbr* (*US*: = *coronary care unit*) unité *f* de soins cardiologiques.
CD *n abbr* (= *compact disc*) CD *m*; (*MIL*: = *Civil Defence (Corps)* (*BRIT*), *Civil Defense* (*US*) ♦ *abbr* (*BRIT*: = *Corps Diplomatique*) CD.
CDC *n abbr* (*US*) = *center for disease control*.
CD-I *n abbr* ® (= *Compact Disc Interactive*) CD-I *m*, disque compact interactif.

CD player *n* platine *f* laser.
Cdr. *abbr* (= *commander*) Cdt.
CD-ROM [siːdiː'rɒm] *n abbr* (= *compact disc read-only memory*) CD-ROM *m inv*.
CDT *abbr* (*US*: = *Central Daylight Time*) *heure d'été du centre*.
CDW *n abbr* = **collision damage waiver**.
cease [siːs] *vt, vi* cesser.
ceasefire ['siːsfaɪə*] *n* cessez-le-feu *m*.
ceaseless ['siːslɪs] *adj* incessant(e), continuel(le).
CED *n abbr* (*US*) = *Committee for Economic Development*.
cedar ['siːdə*] *n* cèdre *m*.
cede [siːd] *vt* céder.
cedilla [sɪ'dɪlə] *n* cédille *f*.
CEEB *n abbr* (*US*: = *College Entrance Examination Board*) *commission d'admission dans l'enseignement supérieur*.
ceilidh ['keɪlɪ] *n* bal *m* folklorique écossais *or* irlandais.
ceiling ['siːlɪŋ] *n* (*also fig*) plafond *m*.
celebrate ['sɛlɪbreɪt] *vt, vi* célébrer.
celebrated ['sɛlɪbreɪtɪd] *adj* célèbre.
celebration [sɛlɪ'breɪʃən] *n* célébration *f*.
celebrity [sɪ'lɛbrɪtɪ] *n* célébrité *f*.
celeriac [sə'lɛrɪæk] *n* céleri(-rave) *m*.
celery ['sɛlərɪ] *n* céleri *m* (en branches).
celestial [sɪ'lɛstɪəl] *adj* céleste.
celibacy ['sɛlɪbəsɪ] *n* célibat *m*.
cell [sɛl] *n* (*gen*) cellule *f*; (*ELEC*) élément *m* (*de pile*).
cellar ['sɛlə*] *n* cave *f*.
'cellist ['tʃɛlɪst] *n* violoncelliste *m/f*.
'cello ['tʃɛləu] *n* violoncelle *m*.
cellophane ['sɛləfeɪn] *n* ® cellophane *f* ®.
cellphone ['sɛlfəun] *n* téléphone *m* cellulaire.
cellular ['sɛljulə*] *adj* cellulaire.
Celluloid ['sɛljulɔɪd] *n* ® celluloïd *m* ®.
cellulose ['sɛljuləus] *n* cellulose *f*.
Celsius ['sɛlsɪəs] *adj* Celsius *inv*.
Celt [kɛlt, sɛlt] *n* Celte *m/f*.
Celtic ['kɛltɪk, 'sɛltɪk] *adj* celte, celtique ♦ *n* (*LING*) celtique *m*.
cement [sə'mɛnt] *n* ciment *m* ♦ *vt* cimenter.
cement mixer *n* bétonnière *f*.
cemetery ['sɛmɪtrɪ] *n* cimetière *m*.
cenotaph ['sɛnətɑːf] *n* cénotaphe *m*.
censor ['sɛnsə*] *n* censeur *m* ♦ *vt* censurer.
censorship ['sɛnsəʃɪp] *n* censure *f*.
censure ['sɛnʃə*] *vt* blâmer, critiquer.
census ['sɛnsəs] *n* recensement *m*.
cent [sɛnt] *n* (*US*: *coin*) cent *m* (= *1:100 du dollar*); *see also* **per**.
centenary [sɛn'tiːnərɪ], **centennial** [sɛn'tɛnɪəl] *n* centenaire *m*.
center ['sɛntə*] *n, vt* (*US*) = **centre**.
centigrade ['sɛntɪgreɪd] *adj* centigrade.
centilitre, (*US*) **centiliter** ['sɛntɪliːtə*] *n* centilitre *m*.
centimetre, (*US*) **centimeter** ['sɛntɪmiːtə*] *n*

centimètre *m*.
centipede ['sɛntɪpiːd] *n* mille-pattes *m inv*.
central ['sɛntrəl] *adj* central(e).
Central African Republic *n* République Centrafricaine.
Central America *n* Amérique centrale.
central heating *n* chauffage central.
centralize ['sɛntrəlaɪz] *vt* centraliser.
central processing unit (CPU) *n* (*COMPUT*) unité centrale (de traitement).
central reservation *n* (*BRIT AUT*) terre-plein central.
centre, (*US*) **center** ['sɛntə*] *n* centre *m* ♦ *vt* centrer; (*PHOT*) cadrer; (*concentrate*): **to ~ (on)** centrer (sur).
centrefold, (*US*) **centerfold** ['sɛntəfəʊld] *n* (*PRESS*) pages centrales détachables (*avec photo de pin up*).
centre-forward ['sɛntə'fɔːwəd] *n* (*SPORT*) avant-centre *m*.
centre-half ['sɛntə'hɑːf] *n* (*SPORT*) demi-centre *m*.
centrepiece, (*US*) **centerpiece** ['sɛntəpiːs] *n* milieu *m* de table; (*fig*) pièce maîtresse.
centre spread *n* (*BRIT*) publicité *f* en double page.
centre-stage [sɛntə'steɪdʒ] *n*: **to take ~** occuper le centre de la scène.
centrifugal [sɛn'trɪfjʊɡl] *adj* centrifuge.
centrifuge ['sɛntrɪfjuːʒ] *n* centrifugeuse *f*.
century ['sɛntjʊrɪ] *n* siècle *m*; **in the twentieth ~** au vingtième siècle.
CEO *n abbr* (*US*) = **chief executive officer**.
ceramic [sɪ'ræmɪk] *adj* céramique.
cereal ['siːrɪəl] *n* céréale *f*.
cerebral ['sɛrɪbrəl] *adj* cérébral(e).
ceremonial [sɛrɪ'məʊnɪəl] *n* cérémonial *m*; (*rite*) rituel *m*.
ceremony ['sɛrɪmənɪ] *n* cérémonie *f*; **to stand on ~** faire des façons.
cert [səːt] *n* (*BRIT col*): **it's a dead ~** ça ne fait pas un pli.
certain ['səːtən] *adj* certain(e); **to make ~ of** s'assurer de; **for ~** certainement, sûrement.
certainly ['səːtənlɪ] *adv* certainement.
certainty ['səːtəntɪ] *n* certitude *f*.
certificate [sə'tɪfɪkɪt] *n* certificat *m*.
certified letter ['səːtɪfaɪd-] *n* (*US*) lettre recommandée.
certified public accountant (CPA) ['səːtɪfaɪd-] *n* (*US*) expert-comptable *m*.
certify ['səːtɪfaɪ] *vt* certifier ♦ *vi*: **to ~ to** attester.
cervical ['səːvɪkl] *adj*: **~ cancer** cancer *m* du col de l'utérus; **~ smear** frottis vaginal.
cervix ['səːvɪks] *n* col *m* de l'utérus.
Cesarean [siː'zɛərɪən] *adj*, *n* (*US*) = **Caesarean**.
cessation [sə'seɪʃən] *n* cessation *f*, arrêt *m*.
cesspit ['sɛspɪt] *n* fosse *f* d'aisance.
CET *abbr* (= *Central European Time*) *heure d'Europe centrale*.
Ceylon [sɪ'lɒn] *n* Ceylan *m*.

cf. *abbr* (= *compare*) cf., voir.
c/f *abbr* (*COMM*) = *carried forward*.
CFC *n abbr* (= *chlorofluorocarbon*) CFC *m*.
CG *n abbr* (*US*) = **coastguard**.
cg *abbr* (= *centigram*) cg.
CH *n abbr* (*BRIT*: = *Companion of Honour*) *titre honorifique*.
ch *abbr* (*BRIT*: = *central heating*) c.c.
ch. *abbr* (= *chapter*) chap.
Chad [tʃæd] *n* Tchad *m*.
chafe [tʃeɪf] *vt* irriter, frotter contre ♦ *vi* (*fig*): **to ~ against** se rebiffer contre, regimber contre.
chaffinch ['tʃæfɪntʃ] *n* pinson *m*.
chagrin ['ʃæɡrɪn] *n* contrariété *f*, déception *f*.
chain [tʃeɪn] *n* (*gen*) chaîne *f* ♦ *vt* (*also*: **~ up**) enchaîner, attacher (avec une chaîne).
chain reaction *n* réaction *f* en chaîne.
chain-smoke ['tʃeɪnsməʊk] *vi* fumer cigarette sur cigarette.
chain store *n* magasin *m* à succursales multiples.
chair [tʃɛə*] *n* chaise *f*; (*armchair*) fauteuil *m*; (*of university*) chaire *f* ♦ *vt* (*meeting*) présider the **~** (*US*: *electric ~*) la chaise électrique.
chairlift ['tʃɛəlɪft] *n* télésiège *m*.
chairman ['tʃɛəmən] *n* président *m*.
chairperson ['tʃɛəpəːsn] *n* président/e.
chairwoman ['tʃɛəwumən] *n* présidente *f*.
chalet ['ʃæleɪ] *n* chalet *m*.
chalice ['tʃælɪs] *n* calice *m*.
chalk [tʃɔːk] *n* craie *f*.
► chalk up *vt* écrire à la craie; (*fig: success etc*) remporter.
challenge ['tʃælɪndʒ] *n* défi *m* ♦ *vt* défier; (*statement, right*) mettre en question, contester; **to ~ sb to a fight/game** inviter qn à se battre/à jouer (*sous forme d'un défi*); **to ~ sb to do something** mettre qn au défi de faire.
challenger ['tʃælɪndʒə*] *n* (*SPORT*) challenger *m*.
challenging ['tʃælɪndʒɪŋ] *adj* de défi, provocateur(trice).
chamber ['tʃeɪmbə*] *n* chambre *f*; **~ of commerce** chambre de commerce.
chambermaid ['tʃeɪmbəmeɪd] *n* femme *f* de chambre.
chamber music *n* musique *f* de chambre.
chamberpot ['tʃeɪmbəpɒt] *n* pot *m* de chambre.
chameleon [kə'miːlɪən] *n* caméléon *m*.
chamois ['ʃæmwɑː] *n* chamois *m*.
chamois leather ['ʃæmɪ-] *n* peau *f* de chamois.
champagne [ʃæm'peɪn] *n* champagne *m*.
champers ['ʃæmpəz] *n* (*col*) champ *m*.
champion ['tʃæmpɪən] *n* (*also of cause*) champion/ne ♦ *vt* défendre.
championship ['tʃæmpɪənʃɪp] *n* championnat *m*.
chance [tʃɑːns] *n* hasard *m*; (*opportunity*) occasion *f*, possibilité *f*; (*hope, likelihood*)

chance *f* ♦ *vt* (*risk*): **to ~ it** risquer (le coup), essayer; (*happen*): **to ~ to do** faire par hasard ♦ *adj* fortuit(e), de hasard; **there is little ~ of his coming** il est peu probable *or* il y a peu de chances qu'il vienne; **to take a ~** prendre un risque; **it's the ~ of a lifetime** c'est une occasion unique; **by ~** par hasard.
▶**chance (up)on** *vt fus* (*person*) tomber sur, rencontrer par hasard; (*thing*) trouver par hasard.

chancel ['tʃɑːnsəl] *n* chœur *m*.

chancellor ['tʃɑːnsələ*] *n* chancelier *m*; **C~ of the Exchequer** (*BRIT*) chancelier de l'Échiquier.

chandelier [ʃændəˈliə*] *n* lustre *m*.

change [tʃeɪndʒ] *vt* (*alter, replace, COMM: money*) changer; (*switch, substitute: gear, hands, trains, clothes, one's name etc*) changer de; (*transform*): **to ~ sb into** changer *or* transformer qn en ♦ *vi* (*gen*) changer; (*change clothes*) se changer; (*be transformed*): **to ~ into** se changer *or* transformer en ♦ *n* changement *m*; (*money*) monnaie *f*; **to ~ one's mind** changer d'avis; **she ~d into an old skirt** elle (s'est changée et) a enfilé une vieille jupe; **a ~ of clothes** des vêtements de rechange; **for a ~** pour changer; **small ~** petite monnaie; **to give sb ~ for** *or* **of £10** faire à qn la monnaie de 10 livres.

changeable ['tʃeɪndʒəbl] *adj* (*weather*) variable; (*person*) d'humeur changeante.

change machine *n* distributeur *m* de monnaie.

changeover ['tʃeɪndʒəuvə*] *n* (*to new system*) changement *m*, passage *m*.

changing ['tʃeɪndʒɪŋ] *adj* changeant(e).

changing room *n* (*BRIT: in shop*) salon *m* d'essayage; (*: SPORT*) vestiaire *m*.

channel ['tʃænl] *n* (*TV*) chaîne *f*; (*waveband, groove, fig: medium*) canal *m*; (*of river, sea*) chenal *m* ♦ *vt* canaliser; (*fig: interest, energies*): **to ~ into** diriger vers; **through the usual ~s** en suivant la filière habituelle; **green/red ~** (*CUSTOMS*) couloir *m or* sortie *f* "rien à déclarer"/"marchandises à déclarer"; **the (English) C~** la Manche.

Channel Islands *npl*: **the ~** les îles de la Manche, les îles anglo-normandes.

Channel Tunnel *n*: **the ~** le tunnel sous la Manche.

chant [tʃɑːnt] *n* chant *m*; mélopée *f*; psalmodie *f* ♦ *vt* chanter, scander; psalmodier.

chaos ['keɪɔs] *n* chaos *m*.

chaos theory *n* théorie *f* du chaos.

chaotic [keɪˈɔtɪk] *adj* chaotique.

chap [tʃæp] *n* (*BRIT col: man*) type *m*; (*term of address*): **old ~** mon vieux ♦ *vt* (*skin*) gercer, crevasser.

chapel ['tʃæpl] *n* chapelle *f*.

chaperon ['ʃæpərəun] *n* chaperon *m* ♦ *vt* chaperonner.

chaplain ['tʃæplɪn] *n* aumônier *m*.

chapter ['tʃæptə*] *n* chapitre *m*.

char [tʃɑː*] *vt* (*burn*) carboniser ♦ *vi* (*BRIT: cleaner*) faire des ménages ♦ *n* (*BRIT*) = **charlady**.

character ['kærɪktə*] *n* caractère *m*; (*in novel, film*) personnage *m*; (*eccentric*) numéro *m*, phénomène *m*; **a person of good ~** une personne bien.

character code *n* (*COMPUT*) code *m* de caractère.

characteristic ['kærɪktəˈrɪstɪk] *adj, n* caractéristique (*f*).

characterize ['kærɪktəraɪz] *vt* caractériser; **to ~ (as)** définir (comme).

charade [ʃəˈrɑːd] *n* charade *f*.

charcoal ['tʃɑːkəul] *n* charbon *m* de bois.

charge [tʃɑːdʒ] *n* accusation *f*; (*LAW*) inculpation *f*; (*cost*) prix (demandé); (*of gun, battery, MIL: attack*) charge *f* ♦ *vt* (*LAW*): **to ~ sb (with)** inculper qn (de); (*gun, battery, MIL: enemy*) charger; (*customer, sum*) faire payer ♦ *vi* (*gen with: up, along etc*) foncer; **~s** *npl*: **bank/labour ~s** frais *mpl* de banque/main-d'œuvre; **to ~ in/out** entrer/sortir en trombe; **to ~ down/up** dévaler/grimper à toute allure; **is there a ~?** doit-on payer?; **there's no ~** c'est gratuit, on ne fait pas payer; **extra ~** supplément *m*; **to take ~ of** se charger de; **to be in ~ of** être responsable de, s'occuper de; **to have ~ of sb** avoir la charge de qn; **they ~d us £10 for the meal** ils nous ont fait payer le repas 10 livres, ils nous ont compté 10 livres pour le repas; **how much do you ~ for this repair?** combien demandez-vous pour cette réparation?; **to ~ an expense (up) to sb** mettre une dépense sur le compte de qn; **~ it to my account** facturez-le sur mon compte.

charge account *n* compte *m* client.

charge card *n* carte *f* de client (*émise par un grand magasin*).

chargehand ['tʃɑːdʒhænd] *n* (*BRIT*) chef *m* d'équipe.

charger ['tʃɑːdʒə*] *n* (*also: battery ~*) chargeur *m*; (*old: warhorse*) cheval *m* de bataille.

charitable ['tʃærɪtəbl] *adj* charitable.

charity ['tʃærɪtɪ] *n* charité *f*; (*organization*) institution *f* charitable *or* de bienfaisance, œuvre *f* (de charité).

charlady ['tʃɑːleɪdɪ] *n* (*BRIT*) femme *f* de ménage.

charm [tʃɑːm] *n* charme *m* ♦ *vt* charmer, enchanter.

charm bracelet *n* bracelet *m* à breloques.

charming ['tʃɑːmɪŋ] *adj* charmant(e).

chart [tʃɑːt] *n* tableau *m*, diagramme *m*; graphique *m*; (*map*) carte marine; (*weather ~*) carte *f* du temps ♦ *vt* dresser *or* établir la carte de; (*sales, progress*) établir la courbe de; **to be in the ~s** (*record, pop group*) figurer au hit-parade.

charter ['tʃɑːtə*] vt (plane) affréter ♦ n (document) charte f; **on** ~ (plane) affrété(e).

chartered accountant (CA) ['tʃɑːtəd-] n (BRIT) expert-comptable m.

charter flight n charter m.

charwoman ['tʃɑːwumən] n = **charlady**.

chase [tʃeɪs] vt poursuivre, pourchasser ♦ n poursuite f, chasse f.

►**chase down** vt (US) = chase up.

►**chase up** vt (BRIT: person) relancer; (: information) rechercher.

chasm ['kæzəm] n gouffre m, abîme m.

chassis ['ʃæsɪ] n châssis m.

chastened ['tʃeɪsnd] adj assagi(e), rappelé(e) à la raison.

chastening ['tʃeɪsnɪŋ] adj qui fait réfléchir.

chastise [tʃæs'taɪz] vt punir, châtier; corriger.

chastity ['tʃæstɪtɪ] n chasteté f.

chat [tʃæt] vi (also: **have a** ~) bavarder, causer ♦ n conversation f.

►**chat up** vt (BRIT col: girl) baratiner.

chatline ['tʃætlaɪn] n numéro téléphonique qui permet de bavarder avec plusieurs personnes en même temps.

chat show n (BRIT) entretien télévisé.

chattel ['tʃætl] see **goods**.

chatter ['tʃætə*] vi (person) bavarder, papoter ♦ n bavardage m, papotage m; **my teeth are** ~**ing** je claque des dents.

chatterbox ['tʃætəbɔks] n moulin m à paroles, babillard/e.

chattering classes ['tʃætərɪŋ-] npl: **the** ~ (col, pej) les intellos mpl.

chatty ['tʃætɪ] adj (style) familier(ière); (person) enclin(e) à bavarder or au papotage.

chauffeur ['ʃəufə*] n chauffeur m (de maître).

chauvinism ['ʃəuvɪnɪzəm] n (also: **male** ~) phallocratie f, machisme m; (nationalism) chauvinisme m.

chauvinist ['ʃəuvɪnɪst] n (also: **male** ~) phallocrate m, macho m; (nationalist) chauvin/e.

ChE abbr = chemical engineer.

cheap [tʃiːp] adj bon marché inv, pas cher(chère); (reduced: ticket) à prix réduit; (: fare) réduit(e); (joke) facile, d'un goût douteux; (poor quality) à bon marché, de qualité médiocre ♦ adv à bon marché, pour pas cher; ~**er** adj moins cher(chère).

cheapen ['tʃiːpn] vt rabaisser, déprécier.

cheaply ['tʃiːplɪ] adv à bon marché, à bon compte.

cheat [tʃiːt] vi tricher; (in exam) copier ♦ vt tromper, duper; (rob) escroquer ♦ n tricheur/euse; escroc m; (trick) duperie f, tromperie f; **to** ~ **on sb** (col: husband, wife etc) tromper qn.

cheating ['tʃiːtɪŋ] n tricherie f.

check [tʃek] vt vérifier; (passport, ticket)

contrôler; (halt) enrayer; (restrain) maîtriser ♦ vi (official etc) se renseigner ♦ n vérification f; contrôle m; (curb) frein m; (bill) addition f; (pattern: gen pl) carreaux mpl (US) = **cheque** ♦ adj (also: ~ed: pattern, cloth) à carreaux; **to** ~ **with sb** demander à qn; **to keep a** ~ **on sb/sth** surveiller qn/qch.

►**check in** vi (in hotel) remplir sa fiche (d'hôtel); (at airport) se présenter à l'enregistrement ♦ vt (luggage) (faire) enregistrer.

►**check off** vt cocher.

►**check out** vi (in hotel) régler sa note ♦ vt (luggage) retirer; (investigate: story) vérifier; (person) prendre des renseignements sur.

►**check up** vi: **to** ~ **up (on sth)** vérifier (qch); **to** ~ **up on sb** se renseigner sur le compte de qn.

checkered ['tʃekəd] adj (US) = **chequered**.

checkers ['tʃekəz] n (US) jeu m de dames.

check guarantee card n (US) carte f (d'identité) bancaire.

check-in ['tʃekin] n (also: ~ desk: at airport) enregistrement m.

checking account ['tʃekiŋ-] n (US) compte courant.

checklist ['tʃeklɪst] n liste f de contrôle.

checkmate ['tʃekmeɪt] n échec et mat m.

checkout ['tʃekaut] n (in supermarket) caisse f.

checkpoint ['tʃekpɔɪnt] n contrôle m.

checkup ['tʃekʌp] n (MED) examen médical, check-up m.

cheek [tʃiːk] n joue f; (impudence) toupet m, culot m.

cheekbone ['tʃiːkbəun] n pommette f.

cheeky ['tʃiːkɪ] adj effronté(e), culotté(e).

cheep [tʃiːp] n (of bird) piaulement m ♦ vi piauler.

cheer [tʃɪə*] vt acclamer, applaudir; (gladden) réjouir, réconforter ♦ vi applaudir ♦ n (gen pl) acclamations fpl, applaudissements mpl; bravos mpl, hourras mpl; ~**s!** (à votre) santé

►**cheer on** vt encourager (par des cris etc).

►**cheer up** vi se dérider, reprendre courage ♦ vt remonter le moral à or de, dérider, égayer.

cheerful ['tʃɪəful] adj gai(e), joyeux(euse).

cheerfulness ['tʃɪəfulnɪs] n gaieté f, bonne humeur.

cheerio [tʃɪərɪ'əu] excl (BRIT) salut!, au revoir!

cheerleader ['tʃɪəliːdə*] n membre d'un groupe de majorettes qui chantent et dansent pour soutenir leur équipe pendant les matchs de football américain.

cheerless ['tʃɪəlɪs] adj sombre, triste.

cheese [tʃiːz] n fromage m.

cheeseboard ['tʃiːzbɔːd] n plateau m à fromages; (with cheese on it) plateau m de fromages.

cheeseburger ['tʃiːzbəːgə*] n cheeseburger m.

cheesecake ['tʃiːzkeɪk] n tarte f au fromage.

:heetah ['tʃiːtə] n guépard m.
:hef [ʃɛf] n chef (cuisinier).
:hemical ['kɛmɪkl] adj chimique ♦ n produit m chimique.
:hemist ['kɛmɪst] n (BRIT: pharmacist) pharmacien/ne; (scientist) chimiste m/f; ~'s (shop) n (BRIT) pharmacie f.
:hemistry ['kɛmɪstrɪ] n chimie f.
:hemotherapy [kiːməu'θerəpɪ] n chimiothérapie f.
:heque, (US) **check** [tʃɛk] n chèque m; **to pay by** ~ payer par chèque.
:hequebook, (US) **(check)checkbook** ['tʃɛkbuk] n chéquier m, carnet m de chèques.
:heque card n (BRIT) carte f (d'identité) bancaire.
:hequered, (US) **checkered** ['tʃɛkəd] adj (fig) varié(e).
:herish ['tʃerɪʃ] vt chérir; (hope etc) entretenir.
:heroot [ʃə'ruːt] n cigare m de Manille.
:herry ['tʃerɪ] n cerise f.
:hes abbr (BRIT) = Cheshire.
:hess [tʃes] n échecs mpl.
:hessboard ['tʃesbɔːd] n échiquier m.
:hessman ['tʃesmən] n pièce f (de jeu d'échecs).
:hessplayer ['tʃespleɪə*] n joueur/euse d'échecs.
:hest [tʃest] n poitrine f; (box) coffre m, caisse f; **to get sth off one's** ~ (col) vider son sac; ~ **of drawers** n commode f.
:hest measurement n tour m de poitrine.
:hestnut ['tʃesnʌt] n châtaigne f; (also: ~ **tree**) châtaignier m; (colour) châtain m ♦ adj (hair) châtain inv; (horse) alezan.
:hesty ['tʃestɪ] adj (cough) de poitrine.
:hew [tʃuː] vt mâcher.
:hewing gum ['tʃuːɪŋ-] n chewing-gum m.
:hic [ʃiːk] adj chic inv, élégant(e).
:hick [tʃɪk] n poussin m; (US col) pépée f.
:hicken ['tʃɪkɪn] n poulet m; (col: coward) poule mouillée.
:hicken out vi (col) se dégonfler.
:hicken feed n (fig) broutilles fpl, bagatelle f.
:hickenpox ['tʃɪkɪnpɔks] n varicelle f.
:hickpea ['tʃɪkpiː] n pois m chiche.
:hicory ['tʃɪkərɪ] n (for coffee) chicorée f; (salad) endive f.
:hide [tʃaɪd] vt réprimander, gronder.
:hief [tʃiːf] n chef m ♦ adj principal(e); **C**~ **of Staff** (MIL) chef d'État-major.
:hief constable n (BRIT) ≈ préfet m de police.
:hief executive, (US) **chief executive officer** n directeur général.
:hiefly ['tʃiːflɪ] adv principalement, surtout.
:hiffon ['ʃɪfɔn] n mousseline f de soie.
:hilblain ['tʃɪlbleɪn] n engelure f.
:hild, pl ~**ren** [tʃaɪld, 'tʃɪldrən] n enfant m/f.
:hild benefit n (BRIT) ≈ allocations familiales.

childbirth ['tʃaɪldbəːθ] n accouchement m.
childhood ['tʃaɪldhud] n enfance f.
childish ['tʃaɪldɪʃ] adj puéril(e), enfantin(e).
childless ['tʃaɪldlɪs] adj sans enfants.
childlike ['tʃaɪldlaɪk] adj innocent(e), pur(e).
child minder n (BRIT) garde f d'enfants.
child prodigy n enfant m/f prodige.
children ['tʃɪldrən] npl of **child**.
children's home ['tʃɪldrənz-] n ≈ foyer m d'accueil (pour enfants).
Chile ['tʃɪlɪ] n Chili m.
Chilean ['tʃɪlɪən] adj chilien(ne) ♦ n Chilien/ne.
chill [tʃɪl] n froid m; (MED) refroidissement m, coup m de froid ♦ adj froid(e), glacial(e) ♦ vt faire frissonner; refroidir; (CULIN) mettre au frais, rafraîchir; **"serve ~ed"** "à servir frais".
▶**chill out** vi (col: esp US) se relaxer.
chilli, (US) **chili** ['tʃɪlɪ] n piment m (rouge).
chilling ['tʃɪlɪŋ] adj (wind) frais(fraîche), froid(e); (look, smile) glacé(e); (thought) qui donne le frisson.
chilly ['tʃɪlɪ] adj froid(e), glacé(e); (sensitive to cold) frileux(euse); **to feel** ~ avoir froid.
chime [tʃaɪm] n carillon m ♦ vi carillonner, sonner.
chimney ['tʃɪmnɪ] n cheminée f.
chimney sweep n ramonneur m.
chimpanzee [tʃɪmpæn'ziː] n chimpanzé m.
chin [tʃɪn] n menton m.
China ['tʃaɪnə] n Chine f.
china ['tʃaɪnə] n porcelaine f; (vaisselle f en) porcelaine.
Chinese [tʃaɪ'niːz] adj chinois(e) ♦ n (pl inv) Chinois/e; (LING) chinois m.
chink [tʃɪŋk] n (opening) fente f, fissure f; (noise) tintement m.
chinwag ['tʃɪnwæg] n (BRIT col): **to have a** ~ tailler une bavette.
chip [tʃɪp] n (gen pl: CULIN) frite f; (: US: also: **potato** ~) chip m; (of wood) copeau m; (of glass, stone) éclat m; (also: **micro**~) puce f; (in gambling) fiche f ♦ vt (cup, plate) ébrécher; **when the** ~**s are down** (fig) au moment critique.
▶**chip in** vi (col) mettre son grain de sel.
chipboard ['tʃɪpbɔːd] n aggloméré m, panneau m de particules.
chipmunk ['tʃɪpmʌŋk] n suisse m (animal).
chippings ['tʃɪpɪŋz] npl: **loose** ~ gravillons mpl.
chip shop n (BRIT) friterie f.

---

*Un **chip shop**, que l'on appelle également un "fish-and-chip shop", est un magasin où l'on vend des plats à emporter. Les chip shops sont d'ailleurs à l'origine des **takeaways**. On y achète en particulier du poisson frit et des frites, mais on y trouve également des plats traditionnels britanniques (steak pies, saucisses, etc). Tous les plats étaient à l'origine emballés dans du papier journal.*

*Dans certains de ces magasins, on peut
s'asseoir pour consommer sur place.*

chiropodist [kɪ'rɔpədɪst] n (BRIT) pédicure m/f.
chiropody [kɪ'rɔpədɪ] n (BRIT) pédicurie f.
chirp [tʃəːp] n pépiement m, gazouillis m; (of crickets) stridulation f ♦ vi pépier, gazouiller; chanter, striduler.
chirpy ['tʃəːpɪ] adj (col) plein(e) d'entrain, tout guilleret(te).
chisel ['tʃɪzl] n ciseau m.
chit [tʃɪt] n mot m, note f.
chitchat ['tʃɪttʃæt] n bavardage m, papotage m.
chivalrous ['ʃɪvəlrəs] adj chevaleresque.
chivalry ['ʃɪvəlrɪ] n chevalerie f; esprit m chevaleresque.
chives [tʃaɪvz] npl ciboulette f, civette f.
chloride ['klɔːraɪd] n chlorure m.
chlorinate ['klɔrɪneɪt] vt chlorer.
chlorine ['klɔːriːn] n chlore m.
chock [tʃɔk] n cale f.
chock-a-block ['tʃɔkə'blɔk], **chock-full** [tʃɔk'ful] adj plein(e) à craquer.
chocolate ['tʃɔklɪt] n chocolat m.
choice [tʃɔɪs] n choix m ♦ adj de choix; **by** or **from** ~ par choix; **a wide** ~ un grand choix.
choir ['kwaɪə*] n chœur m, chorale f.
choirboy ['kwaɪəbɔɪ] n jeune choriste m, petit chanteur.
choke [tʃəuk] vi étouffer ♦ vt étrangler; étouffer; (block) boucher, obstruer ♦ n (AUT) starter m.
cholera ['kɔlərə] n choléra m.
cholesterol [kə'lɛstərɔl] n cholestérol m.
choose, pt **chose**, pp **chosen** [tʃuːz, tʃəuz, 'tʃəuzn] vt choisir ♦ vi: **to** ~ **between** choisir entre; **to** ~ **from** choisir parmi; **to** ~ **to do** décider de faire, juger bon de faire.
choosy ['tʃuːzɪ] adj: **(to be)** ~ (faire le) difficile.
chop [tʃɔp] vt (wood) couper (à la hache); (CULIN: also: ~ **up**) couper (fin), émincer, hacher (en morceaux) ♦ n coup m (de hache, du tranchant de la main); (CULIN) côtelette f; **to get the** ~ (BRIT col: project) tomber à l'eau; (: person: be sacked) se faire renvoyer.
▶**chop down** vt (tree) abattre.
chopper ['tʃɔpə*] n (helicopter) hélicoptère m, hélico m.
choppy ['tʃɔpɪ] adj (sea) un peu agité(e).
chops [tʃɔps] npl (jaws) mâchoires fpl; babines fpl.
chopsticks ['tʃɔpstɪks] npl baguettes fpl.
choral ['kɔːrəl] adj choral(e), chanté(e) en chœur.
chord [kɔːd] n (MUS) accord m.
chore [tʃɔː*] n travail m de routine; **household** ~**s** travaux mpl du ménage.
choreographer [kɔrɪ'ɔgrəfə*] n chorégraphe m/f.
choreography [kɔrɪ'ɔgrəfɪ] n chorégraphie f.

chorister ['kɔrɪstə*] n choriste m/f.
chortle ['tʃɔːtl] vi glousser.
chorus ['kɔːrəs] n chœur m; (repeated part of song, also fig) refrain m.
chose [tʃəuz] pt of **choose**.
chosen ['tʃəuzn] pp of **choose**.
chow [tʃau] n (dog) chow-chow m.
chowder ['tʃaudə*] n soupe f de poisson.
Christ [kraɪst] n Christ m.
christen ['krɪsn] vt baptiser.
christening ['krɪsnɪŋ] n baptême m.
Christian ['krɪstɪən] adj, n chrétien(ne).
Christianity [krɪstɪ'ænɪtɪ] n christianisme m.
Christian name n prénom m.
Christmas ['krɪsməs] n Noël m or f; **happy** or **merry** ~! joyeux Noël!
Christmas card n carte f de Noël.
Christmas Day n le jour de Noël.
Christmas Eve n la veille de Noël; la nuit de Noël.
Christmas Island n île f Christmas.
Christmas tree n arbre m de Noël.
chrome [krəum] n = **chromium**.
chromium ['krəumɪəm] n chrome m; (also: ~ **plating**) chromage m.
chromosome ['krəuməsəum] n chromosome m.
chronic ['krɔnɪk] adj chronique; (fig: liar, smoker) invétéré(e).
chronicle ['krɔnɪkl] n chronique f.
chronological [krɔnə'lɔdʒɪkl] adj chronologique.
chrysanthemum [krɪ'sænθəməm] n chrysanthème m.
chubby ['tʃʌbɪ] adj potelé(e), rondelet(te).
chuck [tʃʌk] vt lancer, jeter; **to** ~ (**up** or **in**) v (BRIT: job) lâcher; (: person) plaquer.
▶**chuck out** vt flanquer dehors or à la porte.
chuckle ['tʃʌkl] vi glousser.
chuffed [tʃʌft] adj (BRIT col): **to be** ~ **about s1** être content(e) de qch.
chug [tʃʌg] vi faire teuf-teuf; souffler.
chum [tʃʌm] n copain/copine.
chump ['tʃʌmp] n (col) imbécile m/f, crétin/e.
chunk [tʃʌŋk] n gros morceau; (of bread) quignon m.
chunky ['tʃʌŋkɪ] adj (furniture etc) massif(ive) (person) trapu(e); (knitwear) en grosse laine
Chunnel ['tʃʌnəl] n = **Channel Tunnel**.
church [tʃəːtʃ] n église f; **the C**~ **of England** l'Église anglicane.
churchyard ['tʃəːtʃjɑːd] n cimetière m.
churlish ['tʃəːlɪʃ] adj grossier(ère); hargneux(euse).
churn [tʃəːn] n (for butter) baratte f; (for transport: also: **milk** ~) (grand) bidon à lait.
▶**churn out** vt débiter.
chute [ʃuːt] n glissoire f; (also: **rubbish** ~) vide-ordures m inv; (BRIT: children's slide) toboggan m.
chutney ['tʃʌtnɪ] n chutney m.
CIA n abbr (US: = Central Intelligence Agency)

CIA *f*.
CID *n abbr* (*BRIT*: = *Criminal Investigation Department*) ≈ P.J. *f* (= *police judiciaire*).
cider ['saɪdə*] *n* cidre *m*.
CIF *abbr* (= *cost, insurance and freight*) CAF.
cigar [sɪ'gɑ:*] *n* cigare *m*.
cigarette [sɪgə'ret] *n* cigarette *f*.
cigarette case *n* étui *m* à cigarettes.
cigarette end *n* mégot *m*.
cigarette holder *n* fume-cigarettes *m inv*.
C-in-C *abbr* = **commander-in-chief**.
cinch [sɪntʃ] *n* (*col*): **it's a ~** c'est du gâteau, c'est l'enfance de l'art.
cinder ['sɪndə*] *n* cendre *f*.
Cinderella [sɪndə'rɛlə] *n* Cendrillon.
cine-camera ['sɪnɪ'kæmərə] *n* (*BRIT*) caméra *f*.
cine-film ['sɪnɪfɪlm] *n* (*BRIT*) film *m*.
cinema ['sɪnəmə] *n* cinéma *m*.
cine-projector ['sɪnɪprə'dʒɛktə*] *n* (*BRIT*) projecteur *m* de cinéma.
cinnamon ['sɪnəmən] *n* cannelle *f*.
cipher ['saɪfə*] *n* code secret; (*fig: faceless employee etc*) numéro *m*; **in ~** codé(e).
circa ['sɜ:kə] *prep* circa, environ.
circle ['sɜ:kl] *n* cercle *m*; (*in cinema*) balcon *m* ♦ *vi* faire *or* décrire des cercles ♦ *vt* (*surround*) entourer, encercler; (*move round*) faire le tour de, tourner autour de.
circuit ['sɜ:kɪt] *n* circuit *m*.
circuit board *n* plaquette *f*.
circuitous [sɜ:'kjuɪtəs] *adj* indirect(e), qui fait un détour.
circular ['sɜ:kjulə*] *adj* circulaire ♦ *n* circulaire *f*; (*as advertisement*) prospectus *m*.
circulate ['sɜ:kjuleɪt] *vi* circuler ♦ *vt* faire circuler.
circulation [sɜ:kju'leɪʃən] *n* circulation *f*; (*of newspaper*) tirage *m*.
circumcise ['sɜ:kəmsaɪz] *vt* circoncire.
circumference [sə'kʌmfərəns] *n* circonférence *f*.
circumflex ['sɜ:kəmflɛks] *n* (*also: ~ accent*) accent *m* circonflexe.
circumscribe ['sɜ:kəmskraɪb] *vt* circonscrire.
circumspect ['sɜ:kəmspɛkt] *adj* circonspect(e).
circumstances ['sɜ:kəmstənsɪz] *npl* circonstances *fpl*; (*financial condition*) moyens *mpl*, situation financière; **in the ~** dans ces conditions; **under no ~** en aucun cas, sous aucun prétexte.
circumstantial [sɜ:kəm'stænʃl] *adj* (*report, statement*) circonstancié(e); **~ evidence** preuve indirecte.
circumvent [sɜ:kəm'vɛnt] *vt* (*rule etc*) tourner.
circus ['sɜ:kəs] *n* cirque *m*; (*also:* **C~:** *in place names*) place *f*.
cirrhosis [sɪ'rəusɪs] *n* (*also: ~ of the liver*) cirrhose *f* (du foie).
CIS *n abbr* (= *Commonwealth of Independent States*) CEI *f*.
cissy ['sɪsɪ] *n* = **sissy**.

cistern ['sɪstən] *n* réservoir *m* (d'eau); (*in toilet*) réservoir de la chasse d'eau.
citation [saɪ'teɪʃən] *n* citation *f*; (*US*) P.-V. *m*.
cite [saɪt] *vt* citer.
citizen ['sɪtɪzn] *n* (*POL*) citoyen/ne; (*resident*): **the ~s of this town** les habitants de cette ville.
Citizens' Advice Bureau ['sɪtɪznz-] *n* (*BRIT*) ≈ Bureau *m* d'aide sociale.
citizenship ['sɪtɪznʃɪp] *n* citoyenneté *f*.
citric ['sɪtrɪk] *adj*: **~ acid** acide *m* citrique.
citrus fruit ['sɪtrəs-] *n* agrume *m*.
city ['sɪtɪ] *n* ville *f*, cité *f*; **the C~** la Cité de Londres (*centre des affaires*).
city centre *n* centre ville *m*.
City Hall *n* (*US*) ≈ hôtel *m* de ville.
City Technology College *n* (*BRIT*) établissement *m* d'enseignement technologique (*situé dans un quartier défavorisé*).
civic ['sɪvɪk] *adj* civique.
civic centre *n* (*BRIT*) centre administratif (municipal).
civil ['sɪvɪl] *adj* civil(e); (*polite*) poli(e), civil(e).
civil disobedience *n* désobéissance civile.
civil engineer *n* ingénieur civil.
civil engineering *n* génie civil, travaux publics.
civilian [sɪ'vɪlɪən] *adj, n* civil(e).
civilization [sɪvɪlaɪ'zeɪʃən] *n* civilisation *f*.
civilized ['sɪvɪlaɪzd] *adj* civilisé(e); (*fig*) où règnent les bonnes manières, empreint(e) d'une courtoisie de bon ton.
civil law *n* code civil; (*study*) droit civil.
civil liberties *npl* libertés *fpl* civiques.
civil rights *npl* droits *mpl* civiques.
civil servant *n* fonctionnaire *m/f*.
Civil Service *n* fonction publique, administration *f*.
civil war *n* guerre civile.
civvies ['sɪvɪz] *npl*: **in ~** (*col*) en civil.
cl *abbr* (= *centilitre*) cl.
clad [klæd] *adj*: **~ (in)** habillé(e) de, vêtu(e) de.
claim [kleɪm] *vt* (*rights etc*) revendiquer; (*compensation*) réclamer; **to ~ that/to be** prétendre que/être ♦ *vi* (*for insurance*) faire une déclaration de sinistre ♦ *n* revendication *f*; prétention *f*; (*right*) droit *m*; (*for expenses*) note *f* de frais; (**insurance**) **~** demande *f* d'indemnisation, déclaration *f* de sinistre; **to put in a ~ for** (*pay rise etc*) demander.
claimant ['kleɪmənt] *n* (*ADMIN, LAW*) requérant/e.
claim form *n* (*gen*) formulaire *m* de demande.
clairvoyant [klɛə'vɔɪənt] *n* voyant/e, extra-lucide *m/f*.
clam [klæm] *n* palourde *f*.
▶**clam up** *vi* (*col*) la boucler.
clamber ['klæmbə*] *vi* grimper, se hisser.
clammy ['klæmɪ] *adj* humide et froid(e) (au

toucher), moite.

clamour, (*US*) **clamor** ['klæmə*] *n* (*noise*)
clameurs *fpl*; (*protest*) protestations
bruyantes ♦ *vi*: **to ~ for sth** réclamer qch à
grands cris.

clamp [klæmp] *n* étau *m* à main; agrafe *f*,
crampon *m* ♦ *vt* serrer; cramponner.

▶**clamp down on** *vt fus* sévir contre,
prendre des mesures draconiennes à
l'égard de.

clampdown ['klæmpdaun] *n*: **there has been a
~ on** ... des mesures énergiques ont été
prises contre ....

clan [klæn] *n* clan *m*.

clandestine [klæn'dɛstɪn] *adj* clandestin(e).

clang [klæŋ] *n* bruit *m or* fracas *m* métallique
♦ *vi* émettre un bruit *or* fracas métallique.

clanger ['klæŋə*] *n*: **to drop a ~** (*BRIT col*) faire
une boulette.

clansman ['klænzmən] *n* membre *m* d'un clan
(écossais).

clap [klæp] *vi* applaudir ♦ *vt*: **to ~** (**one's
hands**) battre des mains ♦ *n* claquement *m*;
tape *f*; **a ~ of thunder** un coup de tonnerre.

clapping ['klæpɪŋ] *n* applaudissements *mpl*.

claptrap ['klæptræp] *n* (*col*) baratin *m*.

claret ['klærət] *n* (vin *m* de) bordeaux *m*
(rouge).

clarification [klærɪfɪ'keɪʃən] *n* (*fig*)
clarification *f*, éclaircissement *m*.

clarify ['klærɪfaɪ] *vt* clarifier.

clarinet [klærɪ'nɛt] *n* clarinette *f*.

clarity ['klærɪtɪ] *n* clarté *f*.

clash [klæʃ] *n* (*sound*) choc *m*, fracas *m*; (*with
police*) affrontement *m*; (*fig*) conflit *m* ♦ *vi* se
heurter; être *or* entrer en conflit; (*dates,
events*) tomber en même temps.

clasp [klɑːsp] *n* fermoir *m* ♦ *vt* serrer,
étreindre.

class [klɑːs] *n* (*gen*) classe *f*; (*group, category*)
catégorie *f* ♦ *vt* classer, classifier.

class-conscious ['klɑːs'kɔnʃəs] *adj*
conscient(e) de son appartenance sociale.

class consciousness *n* conscience *f* de
classe.

classic ['klæsɪk] *adj* classique ♦ *n* (*author*)
classique *m*; (*race etc*) classique *f*.

classical ['klæsɪkl] *adj* classique.

classics ['klæsɪks] *npl* (*SCOL*) lettres *fpl*
classiques.

classification [klæsɪfɪ'keɪʃən] *n* classification
f.

classified ['klæsɪfaɪd] *adj* (*information*)
secret(ète); **~ ads** petites annonces.

classify ['klæsɪfaɪ] *vt* classifier, classer.

classless society ['klɑːslɪs-] *n* société *f* sans
classes.

classmate ['klɑːsmeɪt] *n* camarade *m/f* de
classe.

classroom ['klɑːsrum] *n* (salle *f* de) classe *f*.

clatter ['klætə*] *n* cliquetis *m* ♦ *vi* cliqueter.

clause [klɔːz] *n* clause *f*; (*LING*) proposition *f*.

claustrophobia [klɔːstrə'fəubɪə] *n*
claustrophobie *f*.

claustrophobic [klɔːstrə'fəubɪk] *adj* (*person*)
claustrophobe; (*place*) claustrophobique.

claw [klɔː] *n* griffe *f*; (*of bird of prey*) serre *f*;
(*of lobster*) pince *f* ♦ *vt* griffer; déchirer.

clay [kleɪ] *n* argile *f*.

clean [kliːn] *adj* propre; (*clear, smooth*) net(te)
♦ *vt* nettoyer ♦ *adv*: **he ~ forgot** il a
complètement oublié; **to come ~** (*col: admit
guilt*) se mettre à table; **to ~ one's teeth**
(*BRIT*) se laver les dents; **~ driving licence** *or*
(*US*) **record** permis où n'est portée aucune
indication de contravention.

▶**clean off** *vt* enlever.

▶**clean out** *vt* nettoyer (à fond).

▶**clean up** *vt* nettoyer; (*fig*) remettre de
l'ordre dans ♦ *vi* (*fig: make profit*): **to ~ up on**
faire son beurre avec.

clean-cut ['kliːn'kʌt] *adj* (*man*) soigné;
(*situation etc*) bien délimité(e), net(te),
clair(e).

cleaner ['kliːnə*] *n* (*person*) nettoyeur/euse,
femme *f* de ménage; (*also:* **dry ~er**)
teinturier/ière; (*product*) détachant *m*.

cleaning ['kliːnɪŋ] *n* nettoyage *m*.

cleaning lady *n* femme *f* de ménage.

cleanliness ['klɛnlɪnɪs] *n* propreté *f*.

cleanly ['kliːnlɪ] *adv* proprement; nettement.

cleanse [klɛnz] *vt* nettoyer; purifier.

cleanser ['klɛnzə*] *n* détergent *m*; (*for face*)
démaquillant *m*.

clean-shaven ['kliːn'ʃeɪvn] *adj* rasé(e) de
près.

cleansing department ['klɛnzɪŋ-] *n* (*BRIT*)
service *m* de voirie.

clean sweep *n*: **to make a ~** (*SPORT*) rafler
tous les prix.

clean-up ['kliːnʌp] *n* nettoyage *m*.

clear [klɪə*] *adj* clair(e); (*road, way*) libre,
dégagé(e); (*profit, majority*) net(te) ♦ *vt*
dégager, déblayer, débarrasser; (*room etc:
of people*) faire évacuer; (*woodland*)
défricher; (*cheque*) compenser; (*COMM:
goods*) liquider; (*LAW: suspect*) innocenter;
(*obstacle*) franchir *or* sauter sans heurter
♦ *vi* (*weather*) s'éclaircir; (*fog*) se dissiper
♦ *adv*: **~ of** à distance de, à l'écart de ♦ *n*: **to
be in the ~** (*out of debt*) être dégagé(e) de
toute dette; (*out of suspicion*) être lavé(e) de
tout soupçon; (*out of danger*) être hors de
danger; **to ~ the table** débarrasser la table,
desservir; **to ~ one's throat** s'éclaircir la
gorge; **to ~ a profit** faire un bénéfice net; **to
make o.s. ~** se faire bien comprendre; **to
make it ~ to sb that** ... bien faire
comprendre à qn que ...; **I have a ~ day
tomorrow** (*BRIT*) je n'ai rien de prévu
demain; **to keep ~ of sb/sth** éviter qn/qch.

▶**clear off** *vi* (*col: leave*) dégager.

▶**clear up** *vi* s'éclaircir, se dissiper ♦ *vt*
ranger, mettre en ordre; (*mystery*) éclaircir.

résoudre.
clearance ['klɪərəns] n (removal) déblayage m; (free space) dégagement m; (permission) autorisation f.
clearance sale n (COMM) liquidation f.
clear-cut ['klɪə'kʌt] adj précis(e), nettement défini(e).
clearing ['klɪərɪŋ] n (in forest) clairière f; (BRIT BANKING) compensation f, clearing m.
clearing bank n (BRIT) banque f qui appartient à une chambre de compensation.
clearly ['klɪəlɪ] adv clairement; (obviously) de toute évidence.
clearway ['klɪəweɪ] n (BRIT) route f à stationnement interdit.
cleavage ['kliːvɪdʒ] n (of dress) décolleté m.
cleaver ['kliːvə*] n fendoir m, couperet m.
clef [klɛf] n (MUS) clé f.
cleft [klɛft] n (in rock) crevasse f, fissure f.
clemency ['klɛmənsɪ] n clémence f.
clement ['klɛmənt] adj (weather) clément(e).
clench [klɛntʃ] vt serrer.
clergy ['kləːdʒɪ] n clergé m.
clergyman ['kləːdʒɪmən] n ecclésiastique m.
clerical ['klɛrɪkl] adj de bureau, d'employé de bureau; (REL) clérical(e), du clergé.
clerk [klɑːk, (US) kləːrk] n employé/e de bureau; (US: salesman/woman) vendeur/euse; **C~ of Court** (LAW) greffier m (du tribunal).
clever ['klɛvə*] adj (mentally) intelligent(e); (deft, crafty) habile, adroit(e); (device, arrangement) ingénieux(euse), astucieux(euse).
cleverly ['klɛvəlɪ] adv (skilfully) habilement; (craftily) astucieusement.
clew [kluː] n (US) = **clue**.
cliché ['kliːʃeɪ] n cliché m.
click [klɪk] vi faire un bruit sec or un déclic ♦ vt: **to ~ one's tongue** faire claquer sa langue; **to ~ one's heels** claquer des talons.
client ['klaɪənt] n client/e.
clientele [kliːɑːn'tɛl] n clientèle f.
cliff [klɪf] n falaise f.
cliffhanger ['klɪfhæŋə*] n (TV, fig) histoire pleine de suspense.
climactic [klaɪ'mæktɪk] adj à son point culminant, culminant(e).
climate ['klaɪmɪt] n climat m.
climax ['klaɪmæks] n apogée m, point culminant; (sexual) orgasme m.
climb [klaɪm] vi grimper, monter; (plane) prendre de l'altitude ♦ vt gravir, escalader, monter sur ♦ n montée f, escalade f; **to ~ over a wall** passer par dessus un mur.
▶**climb down** vi (re)descendre; (BRIT fig) rabattre de ses prétentions.
climbdown ['klaɪmdaun] n (BRIT) reculade f.
climber ['klaɪmə*] n (also: **rock ~**) grimpeur/euse, varappeur/euse.
climbing ['klaɪmɪŋ] n (also: **rock ~**) escalade f, varappe f.

clinch [klɪntʃ] vt (deal) conclure, sceller.
clincher ['klɪntʃə*] n: **that was the ~** c'est ce qui a fait pencher la balance.
cling [klɪŋ], pt, pp **clung** [klʌŋ, klʌŋ] vi: **to ~ (to)** se cramponner (à), s'accrocher (à); (of clothes) coller (à).
clingfilm ['klɪŋfɪlm] n film m alimentaire.
clinic ['klɪnɪk] n clinique f; centre médical; (session: MED) consultation(s) f(pl), séance(s) f(pl); (: SPORT) séance(s) de perfectionnement.
clinical ['klɪnɪkl] adj clinique; (fig) froid(e).
clink [klɪŋk] vi tinter, cliqueter.
clip [klɪp] n (for hair) barrette f; (also: **paper ~**) trombone m; (BRIT: also: **bulldog ~**) pince f de bureau; (holding hose etc) collier m or bague f (métallique) de serrage ♦ vt (also: **~ together**: papers) attacher; (hair, nails) couper; (hedge) tailler.
clippers ['klɪpəz] npl tondeuse f; (also: **nail ~**) coupe-ongles m inv.
clipping ['klɪpɪŋ] n (from newspaper) coupure f de journal.
clique [kliːk] n clique f, coterie f.
cloak [kləuk] n grande cape.
cloakroom ['kləukrum] n (for coats etc) vestiaire m; (BRIT: W.C.) toilettes fpl.
clock [klɔk] n (large) horloge f; (small) pendule f; **round the ~** (work etc) vingt-quatre heures sur vingt-quatre; **to sleep round the ~** or **the ~ round** faire le tour du cadran; **30,000 on the ~** (BRIT AUT) 30 000 milles au compteur; **to work against the ~** faire la course contre la montre.
▶**clock in**, **clock on** vi (BRIT) pointer (en arrivant).
▶**clock off**, **clock out** vi (BRIT) pointer (en partant).
▶**clock up** vt (miles, hours etc) faire.
clockwise ['klɔkwaɪz] adv dans le sens des aiguilles d'une montre.
clockwork ['klɔkwəːk] n mouvement m (d'horlogerie); rouages mpl, mécanisme m ♦ adj (toy, train) mécanique.
clog [klɔg] n sabot m ♦ vt boucher, encrasser ♦ vi se boucher, s'encrasser.
cloister ['klɔɪstə*] n cloître m.
clone [kləun] n clone m.
close adj, adv and derivatives [kləus] adj (near): **~ (to)** près (de), proche (de); (writing, texture) serré(e); (watch) étroit(e), strict(e); (examination) attentif(ive), minutieux(euse); (weather) lourd(e), étouffant(e); (room) mal aéré(e) ♦ adv près, de près, à proximité; **~ to** prep près de; **~ by**, **~ at hand** adj, adv tout(e) près; **how ~ is Edinburgh to Glasgow?** combien de kilomètres y-a-t-il entre Édimbourg et Glasgow?; **a ~ friend** un ami intime; **to have a ~ shave** (fig) l'échapper belle; **at ~ quarters** tout près, à côté ♦ vb and derivatives [kləuz] vt fermer; (bargain, deal) conclure ♦ vi (shop etc) fermer; (lid, door etc) se fermer;

(_end_) se terminer, se conclure ♦ _n_ (_end_) conclusion _f_; **to bring sth to a ~** mettre fin à qch.

►**close down** _vt, vi_ fermer (_définitivement_).

►**close in** _vi_ (_hunters_) approcher; (_night, fog_) tomber; **the days are closing in** les jours raccourcissent; **to ~ in on sb** cerner qn.

►**close off** _vt_ (_area_) boucler.

closed [kləuzd] _adj_ (_shop etc_) fermé(e); (_road_) fermé à la circulation.

closed-circuit ['kləuzd'sə:kɪt] _adj_: **~ television** télévision _f_ en circuit fermé.

closed shop _n_ organisation _f_ qui n'admet que des travailleurs syndiqués.

close-knit ['kləus'nɪt] _adj_ (_family, community_) très uni(e).

closely ['kləuslɪ] _adv_ (_examine, watch_) de près; **we are ~ related** nous sommes proches parents; **a ~ guarded secret** un secret bien gardé.

close season [kləus-] _n_ (_BRIT: HUNTING_) fermeture _f_ de la chasse/pêche; (: _FOOTBALL_) trêve _f_.

closet ['klɔzɪt] _n_ (_cupboard_) placard _m_, réduit _m_.

close-up ['kləusʌp] _n_ gros plan.

closing ['kləuzɪŋ] _adj_ (_stages, remarks_) final(e); **~ price** (_STOCK EXCHANGE_) cours _m_ de clôture; **~ time** heure _f_ de fermeture.

closure ['kləuʒə*] _n_ fermeture _f_.

clot [klɔt] _n_ (_gen: blood ~_) caillot _m_; (_col: person_) ballot _m_ ♦ _vi_ (_blood_) former des caillots; (: _external bleeding_) se coaguler.

cloth [klɔθ] _n_ (_material_) tissu _m_, étoffe _f_; (_BRIT: also: tea~_) torchon _m_; lavette _f_; (_also: table~_) nappe _f_.

clothe [kləuð] _vt_ habiller, vêtir.

clothes [kləuðz] _npl_ vêtements _mpl_, habits _mpl_; **to put one's ~ on** s'habiller; **to take one's ~ off** enlever ses vêtements.

clothes brush _n_ brosse _f_ à habits.

clothes line _n_ corde _f_ (à linge).

clothes peg, (_US_) **clothes pin** _n_ pince _f_ à linge.

clothing ['kləuðɪŋ] _n_ = **clothes.**

clotted cream ['klɔtɪd-] _n_ (_BRIT_) crème caillée.

cloud [klaud] _n_ nuage _m_ ♦ _vt_ (_liquid_) troubler; **to ~ the issue** brouiller les cartes; **every ~ has a silver lining** (_proverb_) à quelque chose malheur est bon (_proverbe_).

►**cloud over** _vi_ se couvrir; (_fig_) s'assombrir.

cloudburst ['klaudbə:st] _n_ violente averse.

cloud-cuckoo-land ['klaud'kuku:'lænd] _n_ (_BRIT_) monde _m_ imaginaire.

cloudy ['klaudɪ] _adj_ nuageux(euse), couvert(e); (_liquid_) trouble.

clout [klaut] _n_ (_blow_) taloche _f_; (_fig_) pouvoir _m_ ♦ _vt_ flanquer une taloche à.

clove [kləuv] _n_ clou _m_ de girofle; **~ of garlic** gousse _f_ d'ail.

clover ['kləuvə*] _n_ trèfle _m_.

cloverleaf ['kləuvəli:f] _n_ feuille _f_ de trèfle; (_AUT_) croisement _m_ en trèfle.

clown [klaun] _n_ clown _m_ ♦ _vi_ (_also: ~ about, ~ around_) faire le clown.

cloying ['klɔɪɪŋ] _adj_ (_taste, smell_) écœurant(e).

club [klʌb] _n_ (_society_) club _m_; (_weapon_) massue _f_, matraque _f_; (_also: golf ~_) club ♦ _vt_ matraquer ♦ _vi_: **to ~ together** s'associer; **~s** _npl_ (_CARDS_) trèfle _m_.

club car _n_ (_US RAIL_) wagon-restaurant _m_.

club class _n_ (_AVIAT_) classe _f_ club.

clubhouse ['klʌbhaus] _n_ pavillon _m_.

club soda _n_ (_US_) eau _f_ de seltz.

cluck [klʌk] _vi_ glousser.

clue [klu:] _n_ indice _m_; (_in crosswords_) définition _f_; **I haven't a ~** je n'en ai pas la moindre idée.

clued up, (_US_) **clued in** [klu:d-] _adj_ (_col_) (vachement) calé(e).

clump [klʌmp] _n_: **~ of trees** bouquet _m_ d'arbres.

clumsy ['klʌmzɪ] _adj_ (_person_) gauche, maladroit(e); (_object_) malcommode, peu maniable.

clung [klʌŋ] _pt, pp_ of **cling.**

cluster ['klʌstə*] _n_ (petit) groupe ♦ _vi_ se rassembler.

clutch [klʌtʃ] _n_ (_grip, grasp_) étreinte _f_, prise _f_; (_AUT_) embrayage _m_ ♦ _vt_ agripper, serrer fort; **to ~ at** se cramponner à.

clutter ['klʌtə*] _vt_ (_also: ~ up_) encombrer ♦ _n_ désordre _m_, fouillis _m_.

CM _abbr_ (_US POST_) = _North Marianna Islands._

cm _abbr_ (= _centimetre_) cm.

CNAA _n abbr_ (_BRIT_) := _Council for National Academic Awards_) organisme non universitaire délivrant des diplômes.

CND _n abbr_ = _Campaign for Nuclear Disarmament._

CO _n abbr_ (= _commanding officer_) Cdt; (_BRIT_) = _Commonwealth Office_ ♦ _abbr_ (_US_) = _Colorado_

Co. _abbr_ = _company, county._

c/o _abbr_ (= _care of_) c/o, aux bons soins de.

coach [kəutʃ] _n_ (_bus_) autocar _m_; (_horse-drawn_) diligence _f_; (_of train_) voiture _f_, wagon _m_; (_SPORT: trainer_) entraîneur/euse; (_school: tutor_) répétiteur/trice ♦ _vt_ entraîner; donner des leçons particulières à.

coach trip _n_ excursion _f_ en car.

coagulate [kəu'ægjuleɪt] _vt_ coaguler ♦ _vi_ se coaguler.

coal [kəul] _n_ charbon _m_.

coal face _n_ front _m_ de taille.

coalfield ['kəulfi:ld] _n_ bassin houiller.

coalition [kəuə'lɪʃən] _n_ coalition _f_.

coalman ['kəulmən] _n_ charbonnier _m_, marchand _m_ de charbon.

coal mine _n_ mine _f_ de charbon.

coal miner _n_ mineur _m_.

coal mining _n_ extraction _f_ du charbon.

coarse [kɔ:s] _adj_ grossier(ère), rude; (_vulgar_) vulgaire.

coast [kəust] *n* côte *f* ♦ *vi* (*with cycle etc*) descendre en roue libre.
coastal ['kəustl] *adj* côtier(ère).
coaster ['kəustə*] *n* (*NAUT*) caboteur *m*; (*for glass*) dessous *m* de verre.
coastguard ['kəustgɑːd] *n* garde-côte *m*.
coastline ['kəustlaɪn] *n* côte *f*, littoral *m*.
coat [kəut] *n* manteau *m*; (*of animal*) pelage *m*, poil *m*; (*of paint*) couche *f* ♦ *vt* couvrir, enduire; ~ **of arms** *n* blason *m*, armoiries *fpl*.
coat hanger *n* cintre *m*.
coating ['kəutɪŋ] *n* couche *f*, enduit *m*.
co-author ['kəu'ɔːθə*] *n* co-auteur *m*.
coax [kəuks] *vt* persuader par des cajoleries.
cob [kɔb] *n see* **corn**.
cobbler ['kɔblə*] *n* cordonnier *m*.
cobbles, cobblestones ['kɔblz, 'kɔblstəunz] *npl* pavés (ronds).
COBOL ['kəubɔl] *n* COBOL *m*.
cobra ['kəubrə] *n* cobra *m*.
cobweb ['kɔbwɛb] *n* toile *f* d'araignée.
cocaine [kə'keɪn] *n* cocaïne *f*.
cock [kɔk] *n* (*rooster*) coq *m*; (*male bird*) mâle *m* ♦ *vt* (*gun*) armer; **to ~ one's ears** (*fig*) dresser l'oreille.
cock-a-hoop [kɔkə'huːp] *adj* jubilant(e).
cockerel ['kɔkərl] *n* jeune coq *m*.
cock-eyed ['kɔkaɪd] *adj* (*fig*) de travers; qui louche; qui ne tient pas debout (*fig*).
cockle ['kɔkl] *n* coque *f*.
cockney ['kɔknɪ] *n* cockney *m/f* (*habitant des quartiers populaires de l'East End de Londres*), ≈ faubourien/ne.
cockpit ['kɔkpɪt] *n* (*in aircraft*) poste *m* de pilotage, cockpit *m*.
cockroach ['kɔkrəutʃ] *n* cafard *m*, cancrelat *m*.
cocktail ['kɔkteɪl] *n* cocktail *m*; **prawn ~**, (*US*) **shrimp ~** cocktail de crevettes.
cocktail cabinet *n* (meuble-)bar *m*.
cocktail party *n* cocktail *m*.
cocktail shaker [-'ʃeɪkə*] *n* shaker *m*.
cocky ['kɔkɪ] *adj* trop sûr(e) de soi.
cocoa ['kəukəu] *n* cacao *m*.
coconut ['kəukənʌt] *n* noix *f* de coco.
cocoon [kə'kuːn] *n* cocon *m*.
COD *abbr* = **cash on delivery, collect on delivery** (*US*).
cod [kɔd] *n* morue (fraîche), cabillaud *m*.
code [kəud] *n* code *m*; ~ **of behaviour** règles *fpl* de conduite; ~ **of practice** déontologie *f*.
codeine ['kəudiːn] *n* codéine *f*.
codger ['kɔdʒə*] *n*: **an old ~** (*BRIT col*) un drôle de vieux bonhomme.
codicil ['kɔdɪsɪl] *n* codicille *m*.
codify ['kəudɪfaɪ] *vt* codifier.
cod-liver oil ['kɔdlɪvər-] *n* huile *f* de foie de morue.
co-driver ['kəu'draɪvə*] *n* (*in race*) copilote *m*; (*of lorry*) deuxième chauffeur *m*.
co-ed ['kəu'ɛd] *adj abbr* = **coeducational** ♦ *n abbr* (*US: female student*) étudiante d'une

université mixte; (*BRIT: school*) école *f* mixte.
coeducational ['kəuɛdju'keɪʃənl] *adj* mixte.
coerce [kəu'əːs] *vt* contraindre.
coercion [kəu'əːʃən] *n* contrainte *f*.
coexistence ['kəuɪg'zɪstəns] *n* coexistence *f*.
C. of C. *n abbr* = **chamber of commerce**.
C of E *abbr* = **Church of England**.
coffee ['kɔfɪ] *n* café *m*; **white ~**, (*US*) ~ **with cream** (café-)crème *m*.
coffee bar *n* (*BRIT*) café *m*.
coffee bean *n* grain *m* de café.
coffee break *n* pause-café *f*.
coffeecake ['kɔfɪkeɪk] *n* (*US*) ≈ petit pain aux raisins.
coffee cup *n* tasse *f* à café.
coffeepot ['kɔfɪpɔt] *n* cafetière *f*.
coffee table *n* (petite) table basse.
coffin ['kɔfɪn] *n* cercueil *m*.
C of I *abbr* = **Church of Ireland**.
C of S *abbr* = **Church of Scotland**.
cog [kɔg] *n* dent *f* (d'engrenage).
cogent ['kəudʒənt] *adj* puissant(e), convaincant(e).
cognac ['kɔnjæk] *n* cognac *m*.
cogwheel ['kɔgwiːl] *n* roue dentée.
cohabit [kəu'hæbɪt] *vi* (*formal*): **to ~ (with sb)** cohabiter (avec qn).
coherent [kəu'hɪərənt] *adj* cohérent(e).
cohesion [kəu'hiːʒən] *n* cohésion *f*.
cohesive [kəu'hiːsɪv] *adj* (*fig*) cohésif(ive).
COI *n abbr* (*BRIT*: = *Central Office of Information*) service d'information gouvernementale.
coil [kɔɪl] *n* rouleau *m*, bobine *f*; (*one loop*) anneau *m*, spire *f*; (*of smoke*) volute *f*; (*contraceptive*) stérilet *m* ♦ *vt* enrouler.
coin [kɔɪn] *n* pièce *f* de monnaie ♦ *vt* (*word*) inventer.
coinage ['kɔɪnɪdʒ] *n* monnaie *f*, système *m* monétaire.
coin-box ['kɔɪnbɔks] *n* (*BRIT*) cabine *f* téléphonique.
coincide [kəuɪn'saɪd] *vi* coïncider.
coincidence [kəu'ɪnsɪdəns] *n* coïncidence *f*.
coin-operated ['kɔɪn'ɔpəreɪtɪd] *adj* (*machine, launderette*) automatique.
Coke [kəuk] *n* ® coca *m*.
coke [kəuk] *n* coke *m*.
Col. *abbr* (= *colonel*) Col; (*US*) = *Colorado*.
COLA *n abbr* (*US*: = *cost-of-living adjustment*) réajustement (des salaires, indemnités etc) en fonction du coût de la vie.
colander ['kɔləndə*] *n* passoire *f* (à légumes).
cold [kəuld] *adj* froid(e) ♦ *n* froid *m*; (*MED*) rhume *m*; **it's ~** il fait froid; **to be ~** avoir froid; **to catch ~** prendre *or* attraper froid; **to catch a ~** s'enrhumer, attraper un rhume; **in ~ blood** de sang-froid; **to have ~ feet** avoir froid aux pieds; (*fig*) avoir la frousse *or* la trouille; **to give sb the ~ shoulder** battre froid à qn.
cold-blooded ['kəuld'blʌdɪd] *adj* (*ZOOL*) à sang froid.

cold cream n crème f de soins.
coldly ['kəʊldlɪ] adv froidement.
cold sore n bouton m de fièvre.
cold sweat n: **to be in a ~ (about sth)** avoir des sueurs froides (au sujet de qch).
cold turkey n (col) manque m; **to go ~** être en manque.
Cold War n: **the ~** la guerre froide.
coleslaw ['kəʊlslɔː] n sorte de salade de chou cru.
colic ['kɒlɪk] n colique(s) f(pl).
colicky ['kɒlɪkɪ] adj qui souffre de coliques.
collaborate [kə'læbəreɪt] vi collaborer.
collaboration [kəlæbə'reɪʃən] n collaboration f.
collaborator [kə'læbəreɪtə*] n collaborateur/trice.
collage [kɔ'lɑːʒ] n (ART) collage m.
collagen ['kɒlədʒən] n collagène m.
collapse [kə'læps] vi s'effondrer, s'écrouler ♦ n effondrement m, écroulement m; (of government) chute f.
collapsible [kə'læpsəbl] adj pliant(e); télescopique.
collar ['kɒlə*] n (of coat, shirt) col m; (for dog) collier m; (TECH) collier, bague f ♦ vt (col: person) pincer.
collarbone ['kɒləbəʊn] n clavicule f.
collate [kɔ'leɪt] vt collationner.
collateral [kə'lætərl] n nantissement m.
collation [kə'leɪʃən] n collation f.
colleague ['kɒliːg] n collègue m/f.
collect [kə'lɛkt] vt rassembler; (pick up) ramasser; (as a hobby) collectionner; (BRIT: call for) (passer) prendre; (mail) faire la levée de, ramasser; (money owed) encaisser; (donations, subscriptions) recueillir ♦ vi (people) se rassembler; (dust, dirt) s'amasser; **to ~ one's thoughts** réfléchir, réunir ses idées; **~ on delivery (COD)** (US COMM) payable or paiement à la livraison; **to call ~** (US TEL) téléphoner en PCV.
collected [kə'lɛktɪd] adj: **~ works** œuvres complètes.
collection [kə'lɛkʃən] n collection f; (of mail) levée f; (for money) collecte f, quête f.
collective [kə'lɛktɪv] adj collectif(ive) ♦ n collectif m.
collective bargaining n convention collective.
collector [kə'lɛktə*] n collectionneur m; (of taxes) percepteur m; (of rent, cash) encaisseur m; **~'s item** or **piece** pièce f de collection.
college ['kɒlɪdʒ] n collège m; (of technology, agriculture etc) institut m; **to go to ~** faire des études supérieures; **~ of education** ≈ école normale.
collide [kə'laɪd] vi: **to ~ (with)** entrer en collision (avec).
collie ['kɒlɪ] n (dog) colley m.

colliery ['kɒlɪərɪ] n (BRIT) mine f de charbon, houillère f.
collision [kə'lɪʒən] n collision f, heurt m; **to be on a ~ course** aller droit à la collision; (fig) aller vers l'affrontement.
collision damage waiver n (INSURANCE) rachat m de franchise.
colloquial [kə'ləʊkwɪəl] adj familier(ère).
collusion [kə'luːʒən] n collusion f; **in ~ with** en complicité avec.
Colo. abbr (US) = Colorado.
cologne [kə'ləʊn] n (also: **eau de ~**) eau f de cologne.
Colombia [kə'lɒmbɪə] n Colombie f.
Colombian [kə'lɒmbɪən] adj colombien(ne)
♦ n Colombien/ne.
colon ['kəʊlən] n (sign) deux-points mpl; (MED) côlon m.
colonel ['kɜːnl] n colonel m.
colonial [kə'ləʊnɪəl] adj colonial(e).
colonize ['kɒlənaɪz] vt coloniser.
colony ['kɒlənɪ] n colonie f.
color etc ['kʌlə*] (US) = **colour** etc.
Colorado beetle [kɒlə'rɑːdəʊ-] n doryphore m.
colossal [kə'lɒsl] adj colossal(e).
colour, (US) **color** ['kʌlə*] n couleur f ♦ vt colorer; peindre; (with crayons) colorier; (news) fausser, exagérer ♦ vi rougir ♦ cpd (film, photograph, television) en couleur; **~s** npl (of party, club) couleurs fpl.
colo(u)r bar n discrimination raciale (dans un établissement etc).
colo(u)r-blind ['kʌləblaɪnd] adj daltonien(ne).
colo(u)red ['kʌləd] adj coloré(e); (photo) couleur.
colo(u)rful ['kʌləful] adj coloré(e), vif(vive); (personality) pittoresque, haut(e) en couleurs.
colo(u)ring ['kʌlərɪŋ] n colorant m; (complexion) teint m.
colo(u)r scheme n combinaison f de(s) couleur(s).
colour supplement n (BRIT PRESS) supplément m magazine.
colt [kəʊlt] n poulain m.
column ['kɒləm] n colonne f; (fashion ~, sports ~ etc) rubrique f; **the editorial ~** l'éditorial m.
columnist ['kɒləmnɪst] n rédacteur/trice d'une rubrique.
coma ['kəʊmə] n coma m.
comb [kəʊm] n peigne m ♦ vt (hair) peigner; (area) ratisser, passer au peigne fin.
combat ['kɒmbæt] n combat m ♦ vt combattre, lutter contre.
combination [kɒmbɪ'neɪʃən] n (gen) combinaison f.
combination lock n serrure f à combinaison.
combine vb [kəm'baɪn] vt combiner; (one quality with another): **to ~ sth with sth** joindre qch à qch, allier qch à qch ♦ vi s'associer; (CHEM) se combiner ♦ n

['kɔmbaɪn] association f; (ECON) trust m; **a ~d effort** un effort conjugué.

combine (harvester) n moissonneuse-batteuse(-lieuse) f.

combo ['kɔmbəʊ] n (JAZZ etc) groupe m de musiciens.

combustible [kəm'bʌstɪbl] adj combustible.

combustion [kəm'bʌstʃən] n combustion f.

come, pt **came**, pp **come** [kʌm, keɪm] vi venir; (col: sexually) jouir; **~ with me** suivez-moi; **we've just ~ from Paris** nous arrivons de Paris; ... **what might ~ of it** ... ce qui pourrait en résulter, ... ce qui pourrait advenir or se produire; **to ~ into sight** or **view** apparaître; **to ~ to** (decision etc) parvenir or arriver à; **to ~ undone/loose** se défaire/desserrer; **coming!** j'arrive!; **if it ~s to it** s'il le faut, dans le pire des cas.

come about vi se produire, arriver.

come across vt fus rencontrer par hasard, tomber sur ♦ vi: **to ~ across well/badly** faire une bonne/mauvaise impression.

come along vi (pupil, work) faire des progrès, avancer; **~ along!** viens!; allons!, allez!

come apart vi s'en aller en morceaux; se détacher.

come away vi partir, s'en aller; (become detached) se détacher.

come back vi revenir; (reply): **can I ~ back to you on that one?** est-ce qu'on peut revenir là-dessus plus tard?

come by vt fus (acquire) obtenir, se procurer.

come down vi descendre; (prices) baisser; (buildings) s'écrouler; (: be demolished) être démoli(e).

come forward vi s'avancer; (make o.s. known) se présenter, s'annoncer.

come from vt fus venir de; (place) venir de, être originaire de.

come in vi entrer.

come in for vt fus (criticism etc) être l'objet de.

come into vt fus (money) hériter de.

come off vi (button) se détacher; (stain) s'enlever; (attempt) réussir.

come on vi (lights, electricity) s'allumer; (central heating) se mettre en marche; (pupil, work, project) faire des progrès, avancer; **~ on!** viens!; allons!, allez!

come out vi sortir; (book) paraître; (strike) cesser le travail, se mettre en grève.

come over vt fus: **I don't know what's ~ over him!** je ne sais pas ce qui lui a pris!

come round vi (after faint, operation) revenir à soi, reprendre connaissance.

come through vi (survive) s'en sortir; (telephone call): **the call came through** l'appel est bien parvenu.

come to vi revenir à soi ♦ vt (add up to: amount): **how much does it ~ to?** ça fait combien?

▶**come under** vt fus (heading) se trouver sous; (influence) subir.

▶**come up** vi monter.

▶**come up against** vt fus (resistance, difficulties) rencontrer.

▶**come up to** vt fus arriver à; **the film didn't ~ up to our expectations** le film nous a déçu.

▶**come up with** vt fus: **he came up with an idea** il a eu une idée, il a proposé quelque chose.

▶**come upon** vt fus tomber sur.

comeback ['kʌmbæk] n (reaction) réaction f; (response) réponse f; (THEAT etc) rentrée f.

Comecon ['kɔmɪkɔn] n abbr (= Council for Mutual Economic Aid) COMECON m.

comedian [kə'miːdɪən] n (in music hall etc) comique m; (THEAT) comédien m.

comedienne [kəmiːdɪ'ɛn] n comique f.

comedown ['kʌmdaʊn] n déchéance f.

comedy ['kɔmɪdɪ] n comédie f.

comet ['kɔmɪt] n comète f.

comeuppance [kʌm'ʌpəns] n: **to get one's ~** recevoir ce qu'on mérite.

comfort ['kʌmfət] n confort m, bien-être m; (solace) consolation f, réconfort m ♦ vt consoler, réconforter.

comfortable ['kʌmfətəbl] adj confortable; **I don't feel very ~ about it** cela m'inquiète un peu.

comfortably ['kʌmfətəblɪ] adv (sit) confortablement; (live) à l'aise.

comforter ['kʌmfətə*] n (US) édredon m.

comforts ['kʌmfəts] npl aises fpl.

comfort station n (US) toilettes fpl.

comic ['kɔmɪk] adj comique ♦ n comique m; (magazine) illustré m.

comical ['kɔmɪkl] adj amusant(e).

comic strip n bande dessinée.

coming ['kʌmɪŋ] n arrivée f ♦ adj (next) prochain(e); (future) à venir; **in the ~ weeks** dans les prochaines semaines.

coming(s) and going(s) n(pl) va-et-vient m inv.

Comintern ['kɔmɪntəːn] n Comintern m.

comma ['kɔmə] n virgule f.

command [kə'mɑːnd] n ordre m, commandement m; (MIL: authority) commandement m; (mastery) maîtrise f; (COMPUT) commande f ♦ vt (troops) commander; (be able to get) (pouvoir) disposer de, avoir à sa disposition; (deserve) avoir droit à; **to ~ sb to do** donner l'ordre or commander à qn de faire; **to have/take ~ of** avoir/prendre le commandement de; **to have at one's ~** (money, resources etc) disposer de.

command economy n économie planifiée.

commandeer [kɔmən'dɪə*] vt réquisitionner (par la force).

commander [kə'mɑːndə*] n chef m; (MIL)

commandant *m*.

commander-in-chief [kə'mɑːndərɪn'tʃiːf] *n* (*MIL*) commandant *m* en chef.

commanding [kə'mɑːndɪŋ] *adj* (*appearance*) imposant(e); (*voice, tone*) autoritaire; (*lead, position*) dominant(e).

commanding officer *n* commandant *m*.

commandment [kə'mɑːndmənt] *n* (*REL*) commandement *m*.

command module *n* (*SPACE*) module *m* de commande.

commando [kə'mɑːndəu] *n* commando *m*; membre *m* d'un commando.

commemorate [kə'mɛmərɛit] *vt* commémorer.

commemoration [kəmɛmə'reɪʃən] *n* commémoration *f*.

commemorative [kə'mɛmərətɪv] *adj* commémoratif(ive).

commence [kə'mɛns] *vt, vi* commencer.

commend [kə'mɛnd] *vt* louer; recommander.

commendable [kə'mɛndəbl] *adj* louable.

commendation [kɔmɛn'deɪʃən] *n* éloge *m*; recommandation *f*.

commensurate [kə'mɛnʃərɪt] *adj*: ~ **with/to** en rapport avec/selon.

comment ['kɔmɛnt] *n* commentaire *m* ♦ *vi* faire des remarques *or* commentaires; **to ~ on** faire des remarques sur; **to ~ that** faire remarquer que; "**no ~**" "je n'ai rien à déclarer".

commentary ['kɔməntəri] *n* commentaire *m*; (*SPORT*) reportage *m* (en direct).

commentator ['kɔmənteɪtə*] *n* commentateur *m*; (*SPORT*) reporter *m*.

commerce ['kɔmɔːs] *n* commerce *m*.

commercial [kə'mɔːʃəl] *adj* commercial(e) ♦ *n* (*RADIO, TV*) annonce *f* publicitaire, spot *m* (publicitaire).

commercial bank *n* banque *f* d'affaires.

commercial break *n* (*RADIO, TV*) spot *m* (publicitaire).

commercial college *n* école *f* de commerce.

commercialism [kə'mɔːʃəlɪzəm] *n* mercantilisme *m*.

commercial television *n* publicité *f* à la télévision; chaînes privées (financées par la publicité).

commercial traveller *n* voyageur *m* de commerce.

commercial vehicle *n* véhicule *m* utilitaire.

commiserate [kə'mɪzərɛit] *vi*: **to ~ with sb** témoigner de la sympathie pour qn.

commission [kə'mɪʃən] *n* (*committee; fee: also for salesman*) commission *f*; (*order for work of art etc*) commande *f* ♦ *vt* (*MIL*) nommer (à un commandement); (*work of art*) commander, charger un artiste de l'exécution de; **out of ~** (*NAUT*) hors de service; (*machine*) hors service; **I get 10% ~** je reçois une commission de 10%; **~ of inquiry** (*BRIT*) commission d'enquête.

commissionaire [kəmɪʃə'nɛə*] *n* (*BRIT: at shop, cinema etc*) portier *m* (en uniforme).

commissioner [kə'mɪʃənə*] *n* membre *m* d'une commission; (*POLICE*) préfet *m* (de police).

commit [kə'mɪt] *vt* (*act*) commettre; (*to sb's care*) confier (à); **to ~ o.s. (to do)** s'engager (à faire); **to ~ suicide** se suicider; **to ~ to writing** coucher par écrit; **to ~ sb for trial** traduire qn en justice.

commitment [kə'mɪtmənt] *n* engagement *m*; (*obligation*) responsabilité(s) *f(pl)*.

committed [kə'mɪtɪd] *adj* (*writer, politician etc*) engagé(e).

committee [kə'mɪti] *n* comité *m*; commission *f*; **to be on a ~** siéger dans un comité (*or* une commission).

committee meeting *n* réunion *f* de comité *or* commission.

commodity [kə'mɔdɪti] *n* produit *m*, marchandise *f*, article *m*; (*food*) denrée *f*.

commodity exchange *n* bourse *f* de marchandises.

common ['kɔmən] *adj* (*gen, also pej*) commun(e); (*usual*) courant(e) ♦ *n* terrain communal; **in ~** en commun; **in ~ use** d'un usage courant; **it's ~ knowledge that** il est bien connu *or* notoire que; **to the ~ good** pour le bien de tous, dans l'intérêt général.

common cold *n*: **the ~** le rhume.

common denominator *n* dénominateur commun.

commoner ['kɔmənə*] *n* roturier/ière *m*.

common ground *n* (*fig*) terrain *m* d'entente.

common land *n* terrain communal.

common law *n* droit coutumier.

common-law ['kɔmənlɔː] *adj*: ~ **wife** épouse de facto.

commonly ['kɔmənli] *adv* communément, généralement; couramment.

Common Market *n* Marché commun.

commonplace ['kɔmənpleɪs] *adj* banal(e), ordinaire.

commonroom ['kɔmənrum] *n* salle commune; (*SCOL*) salle des professeurs.

Commons ['kɔmənz] *npl* (*BRIT POL*): **the (House of) ~** la chambre des Communes.

common sense *n* bon sens.

Commonwealth ['kɔmənwɛlθ] *n*: **the ~** le Commonwealth.

> Le **Commonwealth** regroupe 50 États indépendants et plusieurs territoires qui reconnaissent tous le souverain britannique comme chef de cette association.

commotion [kə'məuʃən] *n* désordre *m*, tumulte *m*.

communal ['kɔmjuːnl] *adj* (*life*) communautaire; (*for common use*) commun(e).

commune *n* ['kɔmjuːn] (*group*) communauté

♦ vi [kə'mjuːn]: **to ~ with** converser intimement avec; communier avec.

communicate [kə'mjuːnɪkeɪt] vt communiquer, transmettre ♦ vi: **to ~ (with)** communiquer (avec).

communication [kəmjuːnɪ'keɪʃən] n communication f.

communication cord n (BRIT) sonnette f d'alarme.

communications network n réseau m de communications.

communications satellite n satellite m de télécommunications.

communicative [kə'mjuːnɪkətɪv] adj communicatif(ive).

communion [kə'mjuːnɪən] n (also: **Holy C~**) communion f.

communiqué [kə'mjuːnɪkeɪ] n communiqué m.

communism ['kɔmjunɪzəm] n communisme m.

communist ['kɔmjunɪst] adj, n communiste (m/f).

community [kə'mjuːnɪtɪ] n communauté f.

community centre n foyer socio-éducatif, centre m de loisirs.

community chest n (US) fonds commun.

community health centre n centre médico-social.

community service n ≈ travail m d'intérêt général, TIG m.

community spirit n solidarité f.

commutation ticket [kɔmju'teɪʃən-] n (US) carte f d'abonnement.

commute [kə'mjuːt] vi faire le trajet journalier (de son domicile à un lieu de travail assez éloigné) ♦ vt (LAW) commuer; (MATH: terms etc) opérer la commutation de.

commuter [kə'mjuːtə*] n banlieusard/e (qui ... see vi).

compact adj [kəm'pækt] compact(e) ♦ n ['kɔmpækt] contrat m, entente f; (also: **powder ~**) poudrier m.

compact disc n disque compact.

compact disc player n lecteur m de disques compacts.

companion [kəm'pænjən] n compagnon/compagne.

companionship [kəm'pænjənʃɪp] n camaraderie f.

companionway [kəm'pænjənweɪ] n (NAUT) escalier m des cabines.

company ['kʌmpənɪ] n (also COMM, MIL, THEAT) compagnie f; **he's good ~** il est d'une compagnie agréable; **we have ~** nous avons de la visite; **to keep sb ~** tenir compagnie à qn; **to part ~ with** se séparer de; **Smith and C~** Smith et Compagnie.

company car n voiture f de fonction.

company director n administrateur/trice.

company secretary n (BRIT COMM) secrétaire général (d'une société).

comparable ['kɔmpərəbl] adj comparable.

comparative [kəm'pærətɪv] adj comparatif(ive); (relative) relatif(ive).

comparatively [kəm'pærətɪvlɪ] adv (relatively) relativement.

compare [kəm'pɛə*] vt: **to ~ sth/sb with/to** comparer qch/qn avec or et/à ♦ vi: **to ~ (with)** se comparer (à); être comparable (à); **how do the prices ~?** comment sont les prix?, est-ce que les prix sont comparables?; **~d with** or **to** par rapport à.

comparison [kəm'pærɪsn] n comparaison f; **in ~ (with)** en comparaison (de).

compartment [kəm'pɑːtmənt] n (also RAIL) compartiment m.

compass ['kʌmpəs] n boussole f; **within the ~ of** dans les limites de.

compasses ['kʌmpəsɪz] npl compas m.

compassion [kəm'pæʃən] n compassion f, humanité f.

compassionate [kəm'pæʃənɪt] adj accessible à la compassion, au cœur charitable et bienveillant; **on ~ grounds** pour raisons personnelles or de famille.

compassionate leave n congé exceptionnel (pour raisons de famille).

compatibility [kəmpætɪ'bɪlɪtɪ] n compatibilité f.

compatible [kəm'pætɪbl] adj compatible.

compel [kəm'pɛl] vt contraindre, obliger.

compelling [kəm'pɛlɪŋ] adj (fig: argument) irrésistible.

compendium [kəm'pɛndɪəm] n (summary) abrégé m.

compensate ['kɔmpənseɪt] vt indemniser, dédommager ♦ vi: **to ~ for** compenser.

compensation [kɔmpən'seɪʃən] n compensation f; (money) dédommagement m, indemnité f.

compere ['kɔmpɛə*] n présentateur/trice, animateur/trice.

compete [kəm'piːt] vi (take part) concourir; (vie): **to ~ (with)** rivaliser (avec), faire concurrence (à).

competence ['kɔmpɪtəns] n compétence f, aptitude f.

competent ['kɔmpɪtənt] adj compétent(e), capable.

competing [kəm'piːtɪŋ] adj (ideas, theories) opposé(e); (companies) concurrent(e).

competition [kɔmpɪ'tɪʃən] n compétition f, concours m; (ECON) concurrence f; **in ~ with** en concurrence avec.

competitive [kəm'pɛtɪtɪv] adj (ECON) concurrentiel(le); (sports) de compétition.

competitive examination n concours m.

competitor [kəm'pɛtɪtə*] n concurrent/e.

compile [kəm'paɪl] vt compiler.

complacency [kəm'pleɪsnsɪ] n contentement m de soi, autosatisfaction f.

complacent [kəm'pleɪsnt] adj (trop) content(e) de soi.

complain [kəm'pleɪn] *vi*: **to ~ (about)** se plaindre (de); (*in shop etc*) réclamer (au sujet de).
▶**complain of** *vt fus* (*MED*) se plaindre de.
complaint [kəm'pleɪnt] *n* plainte *f*; (*in shop etc*) réclamation *f*; (*MED*) affection *f*.
complement ['kɔmplɪmənt] *n* complément *m*; (*esp of ship's crew etc*) effectif complet ♦ *vt* compléter.
complementary [kɔmplɪ'mɛntərɪ] *adj* complémentaire.
complete [kəm'pliːt] *adj* complet(ète) ♦ *vt* achever, parachever; (*a form*) remplir.
completely [kəm'pliːtlɪ] *adv* complètement.
completion [kəm'pliːʃən] *n* achèvement *m*; **to be nearing ~** être presque terminé; **on ~ of contract** dès signature du contrat.
complex ['kɔmplɛks] *adj* complexe ♦ *n* (*PSYCH, buildings etc*) complexe *m*.
complexion [kəm'plɛkʃən] *n* (*of face*) teint *m*; (*of event etc*) aspect *m*, caractère *m*.
complexity [kəm'plɛksɪtɪ] *n* complexité *f*.
compliance [kəm'plaɪəns] *n* (*submission*) docilité *f*; (*agreement*): **~ with** le fait de se conformer à; **in ~ with** en conformité avec, conformément à.
compliant [kəm'plaɪənt] *adj* docile, très accommodant(e).
complicate ['kɔmplɪkeɪt] *vt* compliquer.
complicated ['kɔmplɪkeɪtɪd] *adj* compliqué(e).
complication [kɔmplɪ'keɪʃən] *n* complication *f*.
complicity [kəm'plɪsɪtɪ] *n* complicité *f*.
compliment *n* ['kɔmplɪmənt] compliment *m* ♦ *vt* ['kɔmplɪmɛnt] complimenter; **~s** *npl* compliments *mpl*, hommages *mpl*; vœux *mpl*; **to pay sb a ~** faire *or* adresser un compliment à qn; **to ~ sb (on sth/on doing sth)** féliciter qn (pour qch/de faire qch).
complimentary [kɔmplɪ'mɛntərɪ] *adj* flatteur(euse); (*free*) à titre gracieux.
complimentary ticket *n* billet *m* de faveur.
compliments slip *n* fiche *f* de transmission.
comply [kəm'plaɪ] *vi*: **to ~ with** se soumettre à, se conformer à.
component [kəm'pəunənt] *adj* composant(e), constituant(e) ♦ *n* composant *m*, élément *m*.
compose [kəm'pəuz] *vt* composer; **to ~ o.s.** se calmer, se maîtriser; prendre une contenance.
composed [kəm'pəuzd] *adj* calme, posé(e).
composer [kəm'pəuzə*] *n* (*MUS*) compositeur *m*.
composite ['kɔmpəzɪt] *adj* composite; (*BOT, MATH*) composé(e).
composition [kɔmpə'zɪʃən] *n* composition *f*.
compost ['kɔmpɔst] *n* compost *m*.
composure [kəm'pəuʒə*] *n* calme *m*, maîtrise *f* de soi.
compound ['kɔmpaund] *n* (*CHEM, LING*) composé *m*; (*enclosure*) enclos *m*, enceinte *f* ♦ *adj* composé(e) ♦ *vt* [kɔm'paund] (*fig:*

problem etc) aggraver.
compound fracture *n* fracture compliquée.
compound interest *n* intérêt composé.
comprehend [kɔmprɪ'hɛnd] *vt* comprendre.
comprehension [kɔmprɪ'hɛnʃən] *n* compréhension *f*.
comprehensive [kɔmprɪ'hɛnsɪv] *adj* (très) complet(ète).
comprehensive insurance policy *n* assurance *f* tous risques.
comprehensive (school) *n* (*BRIT*) école secondaire non sélective avec libre circulation d'une section à l'autre, ≈ CES *m*.
compress *vt* [kəm'prɛs] comprimer ♦ *n* ['kɔmprɛs] (*MED*) compresse *f*.
compression [kəm'prɛʃən] *n* compression *f*.
comprise [kəm'praɪz] *vt* (*also*: **be ~d of**) comprendre.
compromise ['kɔmprəmaɪz] *n* compromis *m* ♦ *vt* compromettre ♦ *vi* transiger, accepter un compromis ♦ *cpd* (*decision, solution*) de compromis.
compulsion [kəm'pʌlʃən] *n* contrainte *f*, force *f*; **under ~** sous la contrainte.
compulsive [kəm'pʌlsɪv] *adj* (*PSYCH*) compulsif(ive); **he's a ~ smoker** c'est un fumeur invétéré.
compulsory [kəm'pʌlsərɪ] *adj* obligatoire.
compulsory purchase *n* expropriation *f*.
compunction [kəm'pʌŋkʃən] *n* scrupule *m*; **to have no ~ about doing sth** n'avoir aucun scrupule à faire qch.
computer [kəm'pjuːtə*] *n* ordinateur *m*; (*mechanical*) calculatrice *f*.
computer game *n* jeu *m* vidéo.
computerize [kəm'pjuːtəraɪz] *vt* traiter *or* automatiser par ordinateur.
computer language *n* langage *m* machine *o* informatique.
computer literate *adj* initié(e) à l'informatique.
computer peripheral *n* périphérique *m*.
computer program *n* programme *m* informatique.
computer programmer *n* programmeur/ euse.
computer programming *n* programmation *f*.
computer science *n* informatique *f*.
computer scientist *n* informaticien/ne.
computing [kəm'pjuːtɪŋ] *n* informatique *f*.
comrade ['kɔmrɪd] *n* camarade *m/f*.
comradeship ['kɔmrɪdʃɪp] *n* camaraderie *f*.
comsat ['kɔmsæt] *n abbr* = **communications satellite**.
con [kɔn] *vt* duper; escroquer ♦ *n* escroquerie *f*; **to ~ sb into doing sth** tromper qn pour lu faire faire qch.
concave ['kɔn'keɪv] *adj* concave.
conceal [kən'siːl] *vt* cacher, dissimuler.
concede [kən'siːd] *vt* concéder ♦ *vi* céder.

conceit [kən'si:t] n vanité f, suffisance f, prétention f.

conceited [kən'si:tɪd] adj vaniteux(euse), suffisant(e).

conceivable [kən'si:vəbl] adj concevable, imaginable; **it is ~ that** il est concevable que.

conceivably [kən'si:vəblɪ] adv: **he may ~ be right** il n'est pas impossible qu'il ait raison.

conceive [kən'si:v] vt concevoir ♦ vi: **to ~ of sth/of doing sth** imaginer qch/de faire qch.

concentrate ['kɔnsəntreɪt] vi se concentrer ♦ vt concentrer.

concentration [kɔnsən'treɪʃən] n concentration f.

concentration camp n camp m de concentration.

concentric [kɔn'sɛntrɪk] adj concentrique.

concept ['kɔnsɛpt] n concept m.

conception [kən'sɛpʃən] n conception f; (idea) idée f.

concern [kən'sə:n] n affaire f; (COMM) entreprise f, firme f; (anxiety) inquiétude f, souci m ♦ vt concerner; **to be ~ed (about)** s'inquiéter (de), être inquiet(ète) (au sujet de); **"to whom it may ~"** "à qui de droit"; **as far as I am ~ed** en ce qui me concerne; **to be ~ed with** (person: involved with) s'occuper de; **the department ~ed** (under discussion) le service en question; (involved) le service concerné.

concerning [kən'sə:nɪŋ] prep en ce qui concerne, à propos de.

concert ['kɔnsət] n concert m; **in ~** à l'unisson, en chœur; ensemble.

concerted [kən'sə:tɪd] adj concerté(e).

concert hall n salle f de concert.

concertina [kɔnsə'ti:nə] n concertina m ♦ vi se télescoper, se caramboler.

concerto [kən'tʃə:təu] n concerto m.

concession [kən'sɛʃən] n concession f.

concessionaire [kənsɛʃə'nɛə*] n concessionnaire m/f.

concessionary [kən'sɛʃənrɪ] adj (ticket, fare) à tarif réduit.

conciliation [kənsɪlɪ'eɪʃən] n conciliation f, apaisement m.

conciliatory [kən'sɪlɪətrɪ] adj conciliateur(trice); conciliant(e).

concise [kən'saɪs] adj concis(e).

conclave ['kɔnkleɪv] n assemblée secrète; (REL) conclave m.

conclude [kən'klu:d] vt conclure ♦ vi (speaker) conclure; (events): **to ~ (with)** se terminer (par).

concluding [kən'klu:dɪŋ] adj (remarks etc) final(e).

conclusion [kən'klu:ʒən] n conclusion f; **to come to the ~ that** (en) conclure que.

conclusive [kən'klu:sɪv] adj concluant(e), définitif(ive).

concoct [kən'kɔkt] vt confectionner, composer.

concoction [kən'kɔkʃən] n (food, drink) mélange m.

concord ['kɔŋkɔ:d] n (harmony) harmonie f; (treaty) accord m.

concourse ['kɔŋkɔ:s] n (hall) hall m, salle f des pas perdus; (crowd) affluence f; multitude f.

concrete ['kɔŋkri:t] n béton m ♦ adj concret(ète); (CONSTR) en béton.

concrete mixer n bétonnière f.

concur [kən'kə:*] vi être d'accord.

concurrently [kən'kʌrntlɪ] adv simultanément.

concussion [kən'kʌʃən] n (MED) commotion (cérébrale).

condemn [kən'dɛm] vt condamner.

condemnation [kɔndɛm'neɪʃən] n condamnation f.

condensation [kɔndɛn'seɪʃən] n condensation f.

condense [kən'dɛns] vi se condenser ♦ vt condenser.

condensed milk [kən'dɛnst-] n lait concentré (sucré).

condescend [kɔndɪ'sɛnd] vi condescendre, s'abaisser; **to ~ to do sth** daigner faire qch.

condescending [kɔndɪ'sɛndɪŋ] adj condescendant(e).

condition [kən'dɪʃən] n condition f; (disease) maladie f ♦ vt déterminer, conditionner; **in good/poor ~** en bon/mauvais état; **a heart ~** une maladie cardiaque; **weather ~s** conditions fpl météorologiques; **on ~ that** à condition que + sub, à condition de.

conditional [kən'dɪʃənl] adj conditionnel(le); **to be ~ upon** dépendre de.

conditioner [kən'dɪʃənə*] n (for hair) baume démêlant.

condo ['kɔndəu] n abbr (US col) = **condominium**.

condolences [kən'dəulənsɪz] npl condoléances fpl.

condom ['kɔndəm] n préservatif m.

condominium [kɔndə'mɪnɪəm] n (US: building) immeuble m (en copropriété); (: rooms) appartement m (dans un immeuble en copropriété).

condone [kən'dəun] vt fermer les yeux sur, approuver (tacitement).

conducive [kən'dju:sɪv] adj: **~ to** favorable à, qui contribue à.

conduct n ['kɔndʌkt] conduite f ♦ vt [kən'dʌkt] conduire; (manage) mener, diriger; (MUS) diriger; **to ~ o.s.** se conduire, se comporter.

conducted tour [kən'dʌktɪd-] n voyage organisé; (of building) visite guidée.

conductor [kən'dʌktə*] n (of orchestra) chef m d'orchestre; (on bus) receveur m; (US: on train) chef m de train; (ELEC) conducteur m.

conductress [kən'dʌktrɪs] n (on bus) receveuse f.

conduit ['kɔndɪt] n conduit m, tuyau m; tube m.

cone [kəun] n cône m; (for ice-cream) cornet m; (BOT) pomme f de pin, cône.

confectioner [kən'fɛkʃənə*] n (of cakes) pâtissier/ière; (of sweets) confiseur/euse; ~'s (shop) confiserie(-pâtisserie) f.

confectionery [kən'fɛkʃənrɪ] n (cakes) pâtisserie f; (sweets) confiserie f.

confederate [kən'fɛdrɪt] adj confédéré(e) ♦ n (pej) acolyte m; (US HISTORY) confédéré/e.

confederation [kənfɛdə'reɪʃən] n confédération f.

confer [kən'fəː*] vt: to ~ sth on conférer qch à ♦ vi conférer, s'entretenir; to ~ (with sb about sth) s'entretenir (de qch avec qn).

conference ['kɔnfərns] n conférence f; to be in ~ être en réunion or en conférence.

conference room n salle f de conférence.

confess [kən'fɛs] vt confesser, avouer ♦ vi se confesser.

confession [kən'fɛʃən] n confession f.

confessional [kən'fɛʃənl] n confessional m.

confessor [kən'fɛsə*] n confesseur m.

confetti [kən'fɛtɪ] n confettis mpl.

confide [kən'faɪd] vi: to ~ in s'ouvrir à, se confier à.

confidence ['kɔnfɪdns] n confiance f; (also: self-~) assurance f, confiance en soi; (secret) confidence f; to have (every) ~ that être certain que; motion of no ~ motion f de censure; to tell sb sth in strict ~ dire qch à qn en toute confidence.

confidence trick n escroquerie f.

confident ['kɔnfɪdənt] adj sûr(e), assuré(e).

confidential [kɔnfɪ'dɛnʃəl] adj confidentiel(le); (secretary) particulier(ère).

confidentiality ['kɔnfɪdɛnʃɪ'ælɪtɪ] n confidentialité f.

configuration [kən'fɪgju'reɪʃən] n (also COMPUT) configuration f.

confine [kən'faɪn] vt limiter, borner; (shut up) confiner, enfermer; to ~ o.s. to doing sth/to sth se contenter de faire qch/se limiter à qch.

confined [kən'faɪnd] adj (space) restreint(e), réduit(e).

confinement [kən'faɪnmənt] n emprisonnement m, détention f; (MIL) consigne f (au quartier); (MED) accouchement m.

confines ['kɔnfaɪnz] npl confins mpl, bornes fpl.

confirm [kən'fəːm] vt (report, REL) confirmer; (appointment) ratifier.

confirmation [kɔnfə'meɪʃən] n confirmation f; ratification f.

confirmed [kən'fəːmd] adj invétéré(e), incorrigible.

confiscate ['kɔnfɪskeɪt] vt confisquer.

confiscation [kɔnfɪs'keɪʃən] n confiscation f.

conflagration [kɔnflə'greɪʃən] n incendie m; (fig) conflagration f.

conflict n ['kɔnflɪkt] conflit m, lutte f ♦ vi [kən'flɪkt] être or entrer en conflit; (opinions) s'opposer, se heurter.

conflicting [kən'flɪktɪŋ] adj contradictoire.

conform [kən'fɔːm] vi: to ~ (to) se conformer (à).

conformist [kən'fɔːmɪst] n conformiste m/f.

confound [kən'faund] vt confondre; (amaze) rendre perplexe.

confounded [kən'faundɪd] adj maudit(e), sacré(e).

confront [kən'frʌnt] vt confronter, mettre en présence; (enemy, danger) affronter, faire face à.

confrontation [kɔnfrən'teɪʃən] n confrontation f.

confrontational [kɔnfrən'teɪʃənl] adj conflictuel(le).

confuse [kən'fjuːz] vt embrouiller; (one thing with another) confondre.

confused [kən'fjuːzd] adj (person) dérouté(e), désorienté(e); (situation) embrouillé(e).

confusing [kən'fjuːzɪŋ] adj peu clair(e), déroutant(e).

confusion [kən'fjuːʒən] n confusion f.

congeal [kən'dʒiːl] vi (oil) se figer; (blood) se coaguler.

congenial [kən'dʒiːnɪəl] adj sympathique, agréable.

congenital [kən'dʒɛnɪtl] adj congénital(e).

conger eel ['kɔŋgər-] n congre m.

congested [kən'dʒɛstɪd] adj (MED) congestionné(e); (fig) surpeuplé(e); congestionné; bloqué(e); (telephone lines) encombré(e).

congestion [kən'dʒɛstʃən] n congestion f; (fig) encombrement m.

conglomerate [kən'glɔmərɪt] n (COMM) conglomérat m.

conglomeration [kənglɔmə'reɪʃən] n groupement m; agglomération f.

Congo ['kɔŋgəu] n (state) (république f du) Congo.

congratulate [kən'grætjuleɪt] vt: to ~ sb (on) féliciter qn (de).

congratulations [kəngrætju'leɪʃənz] npl: ~ (on) félicitations fpl (pour) ♦ excl: ~! (toutes mes) félicitations!

congregate ['kɔŋgrɪgeɪt] vi se rassembler, se réunir.

congregation [kɔŋgrɪ'geɪʃən] n assemblée f (des fidèles).

congress ['kɔŋgrɛs] n congrès m.

Le **Congress** est le parlement des États-Unis. Il comprend la **House of Representatives** et le **Senate**. Représentants et sénateurs sont élus au suffrage universel direct. Le Congrès se réunit au **Capitol**, à Washington.

congressman ['kɔŋgrɛsmən], **congress-woman** ['kɔŋgrɛswumən] n (US) membre m du Congrès.

conical ['kɔnɪkl] *adj* (de forme) conique.
conifer ['kɔnɪfə*] *n* conifère *m*.
coniferous [kə'nɪfərəs] *adj* (*forest*) de conifères.
conjecture [kən'dʒɛktʃə*] *n* conjecture *f* ♦ *vt*, *vi* conjecturer.
conjugal ['kɔndʒugl] *adj* conjugal(e).
conjugate ['kɔndʒugeɪt] *vt* conjuguer.
conjugation [kɔndʒə'geɪʃən] *n* conjugaison *f*.
conjunction [kən'dʒʌŋkʃən] *n* conjonction *f*; **in ~ with** (conjointement) avec.
conjunctivitis [kəndʒʌŋktɪ'vaɪtɪs] *n* conjonctivite *f*.
conjure ['kʌndʒə*] *vt* faire apparaître (par la prestidigitation); [kən'dʒuə*] conjurer, supplier ♦ *vi* faire des tours de passe-passe.
▶**conjure up** *vt* (*ghost, spirit*) faire apparaître; (*memories*) évoquer.
conjurer ['kʌndʒərə*] *n* prestidigitateur *m*, illusionniste *m/f*.
conjuring trick ['kʌndʒərɪŋ-] *n* tour *m* de prestidigitation.
conker ['kɔŋkə*] *n* (*BRIT*) marron *m* (d'Inde).
conk out [kɔŋk-] *vi* (*col*) tomber *or* rester en panne.
conman ['kɔnmæn] *n* escroc *m*.
Conn. *abbr* (*US*) = Connecticut.
connect [kə'nɛkt] *vt* joindre, relier; (*ELEC*) connecter; (*fig*) établir un rapport entre, faire un rapprochement entre ♦ *vi* (*train*): **to ~ with** assurer la correspondance avec; **to be ~ed with** avoir un rapport avec; (*have dealings with*) avoir des rapports avec, être en relation avec; **I am trying to ~ you** (*TEL*) j'essaie d'obtenir votre communication.
connection [kə'nɛkʃən] *n* relation *f*, lien *m*; (*ELEC*) connexion *f*; (*TEL*) communication *f*; (*train etc*) correspondance *f*; **in ~ with** à propos de; **what is the ~ between them?** quel est le lien entre eux?; **business ~s** relations d'affaires; **to miss/get one's ~** (*train etc*) rater/avoir sa correspondance.
connexion [kə'nɛkʃən] *n* (*BRIT*) = **connection**.
conning tower ['kɔnɪŋ-] *n* kiosque *m* (de sous-marin).
connive [kə'naɪv] *vi*: **to ~ at** se faire le complice de.
connoisseur [kɔnɪ'sə:*] *n* connaisseur *m*.
connotation [kɔnə'teɪʃən] *n* connotation *f*, implication *f*.
connubial [kə'nju:bɪəl] *adj* conjugal(e).
conquer ['kɔŋkə*] *vt* conquérir; (*feelings*) vaincre, surmonter.
conqueror ['kɔŋkərə*] *n* conquérant *m*, vainqueur *m*.
conquest ['kɔŋkwɛst] *n* conquête *f*.
cons [kɔnz] *npl see* **pro**, **convenience**.
conscience ['kɔnʃəns] *n* conscience *f*; **in all ~** en conscience.
conscientious [kɔnʃɪ'ɛnʃəs] *adj* consciencieux(euse); (*scruple, objection*) de conscience.

conscientious objector *n* objecteur *m* de conscience.
conscious ['kɔnʃəs] *adj* conscient(e); (*deliberate: insult, error*) délibéré(e); **to become ~ of sth/that** prendre conscience de qch/que.
consciousness ['kɔnʃəsnɪs] *n* conscience *f*; (*MED*) connaissance *f*; **to lose/regain ~** perdre/reprendre connaissance.
conscript ['kɔnskrɪpt] *n* conscrit *m*.
conscription [kən'skrɪpʃən] *n* conscription *f*.
consecrate ['kɔnsɪkreɪt] *vt* consacrer.
consecutive [kən'sɛkjutɪv] *adj* consécutif(ive); **on three ~ occasions** trois fois de suite.
consensus [kən'sɛnsəs] *n* consensus *m*; **the ~ (of opinion)** le consensus (d'opinion).
consent [kən'sɛnt] *n* consentement *m* ♦ *vi*: **to ~ (to)** consentir (à); **age of ~** âge nubile (légal); **by common ~** d'un commun accord.
consenting adults [kən'sɛntɪŋ-] *npl* personnes consentantes.
consequence ['kɔnsɪkwəns] *n* suites *fpl*, conséquence *f*; importance *f*; **in ~** en conséquence, par conséquent.
consequently ['kɔnsɪkwəntlɪ] *adv* par conséquent, donc.
conservation [kɔnsə'veɪʃən] *n* préservation *f*, protection *f*; (*also*: **nature ~**) défense *f* de l'environnement; **energy ~** économies *fpl* d'énergie.
conservationist [kɔnsə'veɪʃnɪst] *n* protecteur/trice de la nature.
conservative [kən'sə:vətɪv] *adj* conservateur(trice); (*cautious*) prudent(e); **C~** *adj*, *n* (*BRIT POL*) conservateur(trice); **the C~ Party** le parti conservateur.
conservatory [kən'sə:vətrɪ] *n* (*greenhouse*) serre *f*.
conserve [kən'sə:v] *vt* conserver, préserver; (*supplies, energy*) économiser ♦ *n* confiture *f*, conserve *f* (de fruits).
consider [kən'sɪdə*] *vt* considérer, réfléchir à; (*take into account*) penser à, prendre en considération; (*regard, judge*) considérer, estimer; **to ~ doing sth** envisager de faire qch; **~ yourself lucky** estimez-vous heureux; **all things ~ed** (toute) réflexion faite.
considerable [kən'sɪdərəbl] *adj* considérable.
considerably [kən'sɪdərəblɪ] *adv* nettement.
considerate [kən'sɪdərɪt] *adj* prévenant(e), plein(e) d'égards.
consideration [kənsɪdə'reɪʃən] *n* considération *f*; (*reward*) rétribution *f*, rémunération *f*; **out of ~ for** par égard pour; **under ~** à l'étude; **my first ~ is my family** ma famille passe avant tout le reste.
considered [kən'sɪdəd] *adj*: **it is my ~ opinion that ...** après avoir mûrement réfléchi, je pense que ....
considering [kən'sɪdərɪŋ] *prep*: **~ (that)** étant donné (que).

consign [kən'saɪn] *vt* expédier, livrer.
consignee [kɔnsaɪ'niː] *n* destinataire *m/f*.
consignment [kən'saɪnmənt] *n* arrivage *m*, envoi *m*.
consignment note *n* (*COMM*) bordereau *m* d'expédition.
consignor [kən'saɪnə*] *n* expéditeur/trice.
consist [kən'sɪst] *vi*: ~ of consister en, se composer de.
consistency [kən'sɪstənsɪ] *n* consistance *f*; (*fig*) cohérence *f*.
consistent [kən'sɪstənt] *adj* logique, cohérent(e); ~ with compatible avec, en accord avec.
consolation [kɔnsə'leɪʃən] *n* consolation *f*.
console *vt* [kən'səul] consoler ♦ *n* ['kɔnsəul] console *f*.
consolidate [kən'sɔlɪdeɪt] *vt* consolider.
consols ['kɔnsɔlz] *npl* (*BRIT STOCK EXCHANGE*) rente *f* d'État.
consommé [kən'sɔmeɪ] *n* consommé *m*.
consonant ['kɔnsənənt] *n* consonne *f*.
consort *n* ['kɔnsɔːt] époux/épouse; **prince** ~ prince *m* consort ♦ *vi* [kən'sɔːt] (*often pej*): **to** ~ **with sb** frayer avec qn.
consortium [kən'sɔːtɪəm] *n* consortium *m*, comptoir *m*.
conspicuous [kən'spɪkjuəs] *adj* voyant(e), qui attire la vue *or* l'attention; **to make o.s.** ~ se faire remarquer.
conspiracy [kən'spɪrəsɪ] *n* conspiration *f*, complot *m*.
conspiratorial [kən'spɪrə'tɔːrɪəl] *adj* (*behaviour*) de conspirateur; (*glance*) conspirateur(trice).
conspire [kən'spaɪə*] *vi* conspirer, comploter.
constable ['kʌnstəbl] *n* (*BRIT*) ≈ agent *m* de police, gendarme *m*.
constabulary [kən'stæbjulərɪ] *n* ≈ police *f*, gendarmerie *f*.
constant ['kɔnstənt] *adj* constant(e); incessant(e).
constantly ['kɔnstəntlɪ] *adv* constamment, sans cesse.
constellation [kɔnstə'leɪʃən] *n* constellation *f*.
consternation [kɔnstə'neɪʃən] *n* consternation *f*.
constipated ['kɔnstɪpeɪtɪd] *adj* constipé(e).
constipation [kɔnstɪ'peɪʃən] *n* constipation *f*.
constituency [kən'stɪtjuənsɪ] *n* circonscription électorale; (*people*) électorat *m*.

Une **constituency** *est à la fois une région qui élit un député au parlement et l'ensemble des électeurs dans cette région. En Grande-Bretagne, les députés font régulièrement des "permanences" dans leur circonscription électorale lors desquelles les électeurs peuvent venir les voir pour parler de leurs problèmes de logement etc.*

---

constituency party *n* section locale (d'un parti).
constituent [kən'stɪtjuənt] *n* électeur/trice; (*part*) élément constitutif, composant *m*.
constitute ['kɔnstɪtjuːt] *vt* constituer.
constitution [kɔnstɪ'tjuːʃən] *n* constitution *f*.
constitutional [kɔnstɪ'tjuːʃənl] *adj* constitutionnel(le).
constitutional monarchy *n* monarchie constitutionnelle.
constrain [kən'streɪn] *vt* contraindre, forcer.
constrained [kən'streɪnd] *adj* contraint(e), gêné(e).
constraint [kən'streɪnt] *n* contrainte *f*; (*embarrassment*) gêne *f*.
constrict [kən'strɪkt] *vt* rétrécir, resserrer; gêner, limiter.
construct [kən'strʌkt] *vt* construire.
construction [kən'strʌkʃən] *n* construction *f*; (*fig: interpretation*) interprétation *f*; **under** ~ (*building etc*) en construction.
construction industry *n* (industrie *f* du) bâtiment.
constructive [kən'strʌktɪv] *adj* constructif(ive).
construe [kən'struː] *vt* analyser, expliquer.
consul ['kɔnsl] *n* consul *m*.
consulate ['kɔnsjulɪt] *n* consulat *m*.
consult [kən'sʌlt] *vt* consulter; **to** ~ **sb (about sth)** consulter qn (à propos de qch).
consultancy [kən'sʌltənsɪ] *n* service *m* de conseils.
consultancy fee *n* honoraires *mpl* d'expert.
consultant [kən'sʌltənt] *n* (*MED*) médecin consultant; (*other specialist*) consultant *m*, (expert-)conseil *m* ♦ *cpd*: ~ **engineer** *n* ingénieur-conseil *m*; ~ **paediatrician** *n* pédiatre *m*; **legal/management** ~ conseiller *m* juridique/en gestion.
consultation [kɔnsəl'teɪʃən] *n* consultation *f*; **in** ~ **with** en consultation avec.
consultative [kən'sʌltətɪv] *adj* consultatif(ive).
consulting room [kən'sʌltɪŋ-] *n* (*BRIT*) cabinet *m* de consultation.
consume [kən'sjuːm] *vt* consommer.
consumer [kən'sjuːmə*] *n* consommateur/trice; (*of electricity, gas etc*) usager *m*.
consumer credit *n* crédit *m* aux consommateurs.
consumer durables *npl* biens *mpl* de consommation durables.
consumer goods *npl* biens *mpl* de consommation.
consumerism [kən'sjuːmərɪzəm] *n* (*consumer protection*) défense *f* du consommateur; (*ECON*) consumérisme *m*.
consumer society *n* société *f* de consommation.
consumer watchdog *n* organisme *m* pour la défense des consommateurs.
consummate ['kɔnsʌmeɪt] *vt* consommer.

consumption [kən'sʌmpʃən] n consommation f; (MED) consomption f (pulmonaire); **not fit for human** ~ non comestible.

cont. abbr = **continued.**

contact ['kɔntækt] n contact m; (person) connaissance f, relation f ♦ vt se mettre en contact or en rapport avec; **to be in** ~ **with sb/sth** être en contact avec qn/qch; **business** ~**s** relations fpl d'affaires, contacts mpl.

contact lenses npl verres mpl de contact.

contagious [kən'teɪdʒəs] adj contagieux(euse).

contain [kən'teɪn] vt contenir; **to** ~ **o.s.** se contenir, se maîtriser.

container [kən'teɪnə*] n récipient m; (for shipping etc) conteneur m.

containerize [kən'teɪnəraɪz] vt conteneuriser.

container ship n porte-conteneurs m inv.

contaminate [kən'tæmɪneɪt] vt contaminer.

contamination [kəntæmɪ'neɪʃən] n contamination f.

cont'd abbr = **continued.**

contemplate ['kɔntəmpleɪt] vt contempler; (consider) envisager.

contemplation [kɔntəm'pleɪʃən] n contemplation f.

contemporary [kən'tɛmpərərɪ] adj contemporain(e); (design, wallpaper) moderne ♦ n contemporain/e.

contempt [kən'tɛmpt] n mépris m, dédain m; ~ **of court** (LAW) outrage m à l'autorité de la justice.

contemptible [kən'tɛmptəbl] adj méprisable, vil(e).

contemptuous [kən'tɛmptjuəs] adj dédaigneux(euse), méprisant(e).

contend [kən'tɛnd] vt: **to** ~ **that** soutenir or prétendre que ♦ vi: **to** ~ **with** (compete) lutter avec; **to have to** ~ **with** (be faced with) avoir affaire à, être aux prises avec.

contender [kən'tɛndə*] n prétendant/e; candidat/e.

content [kən'tɛnt] adj content(e), satisfait(e) ♦ vt contenter, satisfaire ♦ n ['kɔntɛnt] contenu m; teneur f; ~**s** npl contenu m; **(table of)** ~**s** table f des matières; **to be** ~ **with** se contenter de; **to** ~ **o.s. with sth/with doing sth** se contenter de qch/de faire qch.

contented [kən'tɛntɪd] adj content(e), satisfait(e).

contentedly [kən'tɛntɪdlɪ] adv avec un sentiment de (profonde) satisfaction.

contention [kən'tɛnʃən] n dispute f, contestation f; (argument) assertion f, affirmation f; **bone of** ~ sujet m de discorde.

contentious [kən'tɛnʃəs] adj querelleur(euse), litigieux(euse).

contentment [kən'tɛntmənt] n contentement m, satisfaction f.

contest n ['kɔntɛst] combat m, lutte f; (competition) concours m ♦ vt [kən'tɛst]

contester, discuter; (compete for) disputer; (LAW) attaquer.

contestant [kən'tɛstənt] n concurrent/e; (in fight) adversaire m/f.

context ['kɔntɛkst] n contexte m; **in/out of** ~ dans le/hors contexte.

continent ['kɔntɪnənt] n continent m; **the C**~ (BRIT) l'Europe continentale; **on the C**~ en Europe (continentale).

continental [kɔntɪ'nɛntl] adj continental(e) ♦ n (BRIT) Européen/ne (continental(e)).

continental breakfast n café (or thé) complet.

continental quilt n (BRIT) couette f.

contingency [kən'tɪndʒənsɪ] n éventualité f, événement imprévu.

contingency plan n plan m d'urgence.

contingent [kən'tɪndʒənt] adj contingent(e) ♦ n contingent m; **to be** ~ **upon** dépendre de.

continual [kən'tɪnjuəl] adj continuel(le).

continually [kən'tɪnjuəlɪ] adv continuellement, sans cesse.

continuation [kəntɪnju'eɪʃən] n continuation f; (after interruption) reprise f; (of story) suite f.

continue [kən'tɪnju:] vi continuer ♦ vt continuer; (start again) reprendre; **to be** ~**d** (story) à suivre; ~**d on page 10** suite page 10.

continuing education [kən'tɪnjuɪŋ-] n formation permanente or continue.

continuity [kɔntɪ'nju:ɪtɪ] n continuité f; (CINE) script m.

continuity girl n (CINE) script-girl f.

continuous [kən'tɪnjuəs] adj continu(e), permanent(e); ~ **performance** (CINE) séance permanente; ~ **stationery** (COMPUT) papier m en continu.

continuously [kən'tɪnjuəslɪ] adv (repeatedly) continuellement; (uninterruptedly) sans interruption.

contort [kən'tɔːt] vt tordre, crisper.

contortion [kən'tɔːʃən] n crispation f, torsion f; (of acrobat) contorsion f.

contortionist [kən'tɔːʃənɪst] n contorsionniste m/f.

contour ['kɔntuə*] n contour m, profil m; (also: ~ **line**) courbe f de niveau.

contraband ['kɔntrəbænd] n contrebande f ♦ adj de contrebande.

contraception [kɔntrə'sɛpʃən] n contraception f.

contraceptive [kɔntrə'sɛptɪv] adj contraceptif(ive), anticonceptionnel(le) ♦ n contraceptif m.

contract n ['kɔntrækt] contrat m ♦ cpd ['kɔntrækt] (price, date) contractuel(le); (work) à forfait ♦ vb [kən'trækt] vi (become smaller) se contracter, se resserrer; (COMM): **to** ~ **to do sth** s'engager (par contrat) à faire qch ♦ vt contracter; ~ **of employment/service** contrat de travail/de service.

▶**contract in** *vi* s'engager (par contrat); (*BRIT ADMIN*) s'affilier au régime de retraite complémentaire.

▶**contract out** *vi* se dégager; (*BRIT ADMIN*) opter pour la non-affiliation au régime de retraite complémentaire.

contraction [kən'trækʃən] *n* contraction *f*; (*LING*) forme contractée.

contractor [kən'træktə*] *n* entrepreneur *m*.

contractual [kən'træktʃuəl] *adj* contractuel(le).

contradict [kɔntrə'dıkt] *vt* contredire; (*be contrary to*) démentir, être en contradiction avec.

contradiction [kɔntrə'dıkʃən] *n* contradiction *f*; **to be in ~ with** contredire, être en contradiction avec.

contradictory [kɔntrə'dıktərı] *adj* contradictoire.

contralto [kən'træltəu] *n* contralto *m*.

contraption [kən'træpʃən] *n* (*pej*) machin *m*, truc *m*.

contrary[1] ['kɔntrərı] *adj* contraire, opposé(e) ♦ *n* contraire *m*; **on the ~** au contraire; **unless you hear to the ~** sauf avis contraire; **~ to what we thought** contrairement à ce que nous pensions.

contrary[2] [kən'trɛərı] *adj* (*perverse*) contrariant(e), entêté(e).

contrast *n* ['kɔntrɑːst] contraste *m* ♦ *vt* [kən'trɑːst] mettre en contraste, contraster; **in ~ to** *or* **with** contrairement à, par opposition à.

contrasting [kən'trɑːstıŋ] *adj* opposé(e), contrasté(e).

contravene [kɔntrə'viːn] *vt* enfreindre, violer, contrevenir à.

contravention [kɔntrə'vɛnʃən] *n*: **~ (of)** infraction *f* (à).

contribute [kən'trıbjuːt] *vi* contribuer ♦ *vt*: **to ~ £10/an article to** donner 10 livres/un article à; **to ~ to** (*gen*) contribuer à; (*newspaper*) collaborer à; (*discussion*) prendre part à.

contribution [kɔntrı'bjuːʃən] *n* contribution *f*.

contributor [kən'trıbjutə*] *n* (*to newspaper*) collaborateur/trice.

contributory [kən'trıbjutərı] *adj* (*cause*) annexe; **it was a ~ factor in ...** ce facteur a contribué à ....

contributory pension scheme *n* (*BRIT*) régime *m* de retraite salariale.

contrite ['kɔntraıt] *adj* contrit(e).

contrivance [kən'traıvəns] *n* (*scheme*) machination *f*, combinaison *f*; (*device*) appareil *m*, dispositif *m*.

contrive [kən'traıv] *vt* combiner, inventer ♦ *vi*: **to ~ to do** s'arranger pour faire, trouver le moyen de faire.

control [kən'trəul] *vt* maîtriser; (*check*) contrôler ♦ *n* maîtrise *f*; **~s** *npl* commandes *fpl*; **to take ~ of** se rendre maître de; (*COMM*)

acquérir une participation majoritaire dans; **to be in ~ of** être maître de, maîtriser; (*in charge of*) être responsable de; **to ~ o.s.** se contrôler; **everything is under ~** j'ai (*or* il a *etc*) la situation en main; **the car went out of ~** j'ai (*or* il a *etc*) perdu le contrôle du véhicule; **beyond our ~** indépendant(e) de notre volonté.

control key *n* (*COMPUT*) touche *f* de commande.

controller [kən'trəulə*] *n* contrôleur *m*.

controlling interest [kən'trəulıŋ-] *n* (*COMM*) participation *f* majoritaire.

control panel *n* (*on aircraft, ship, TV etc*) tableau *m* de commandes.

control point *n* (poste *m* de) contrôle *m*.

control room *n* (*NAUT, MIL*) salle *f* des commandes; (*RADIO, TV*) régie *f*.

control tower *n* (*AVIAT*) tour *f* de contrôle.

control unit *n* (*COMPUT*) unité *f* de contrôle.

controversial [kɔntrə'vəːʃl] *adj* discutable, controversé(e).

controversy ['kɔntrəvəːsı] *n* controverse *f*, polémique *f*.

conurbation [kɔnə'beıʃən] *n* conurbation *f*.

convalesce [kɔnvə'lɛs] *vi* relever de maladie, se remettre (d'une maladie).

convalescence [kɔnvə'lɛsns] *n* convalescence *f*.

convalescent [kɔnvə'lɛsnt] *adj, n* convalescent(e).

convector [kən'vɛktə*] *n* radiateur *m* à convection, appareil *m* de chauffage par convection.

convene [kən'viːn] *vt* convoquer, assembler ♦ *vi* se réunir, s'assembler.

convener [kən'viːnə*] *n* organisateur *m*.

convenience [kən'viːnıəns] *n* commodité *f*; **at your ~** quand *or* comme cela vous convient; **at your earliest ~** (*COMM*) dans les meilleurs délais, le plus tôt possible; **all modern ~s**, (*BRIT*) **all mod cons** avec tout le confort moderne, tout confort.

convenience foods *npl* plats cuisinés.

convenient [kən'viːnıənt] *adj* commode; **if it is ~ to you** si cela vous convient, si cela ne vous dérange pas.

conveniently [kən'viːnıəntlı] *adv* (*happen*) à pic; (*situated*) commodément.

convent ['kɔnvənt] *n* couvent *m*.

convention [kən'vɛnʃən] *n* convention *f*.

conventional [kən'vɛnʃənl] *adj* conventionnel(le).

convent school *n* couvent *m*.

converge [kən'vəːdʒ] *vi* converger.

conversant [kən'vəːsnt] *adj*: **to be ~ with** s'y connaître en; être au courant de.

conversation [kɔnvə'seıʃən] *n* conversation *f*.

conversational [kɔnvə'seıʃənl] *adj* de la conversation; (*COMPUT*) conversationnel(le).

conversationalist [kɔnvə'seıʃnəlıst] *n*

brillant(e) causeur/euse.
converse n ['kɒnvɜːs] contraire m, inverse m
♦ vi [kən'vɜːs]: **to ~ (with sb about sth)**
s'entretenir (avec qn de qch).
conversely [kɒn'vɜːslɪ] adv inversement,
réciproquement.
conversion [kən'vɜːʃən] n conversion f; (BRIT:
of house) transformation f, aménagement m.
conversion table n table f de conversion.
convert vt [kən'vɜːt] (REL, COMM) convertir;
(alter) transformer, aménager; (RUGBY)
transformer ♦ n ['kɒnvɜːt] converti/e.
convertible [kən'vɜːtəbl] adj convertible ♦ n
(voiture f) décapotable f.
convex ['kɒn'vɛks] adj convexe.
convey [kən'veɪ] vt transporter; (thanks)
transmettre; (idea) communiquer.
conveyance [kən'veɪəns] n (of goods)
transport m de marchandises; (vehicle)
moyen m de transport.
conveyancing [kən'veɪənsɪŋ] n (LAW)
rédaction f des actes de cession de
propriété.
conveyor belt [kən'veɪə*-] n convoyeur m,
tapis roulant.
convict vt [kən'vɪkt] déclarer (or reconnaître)
coupable ♦ n ['kɒnvɪkt] forçat m, convict m.
conviction [kən'vɪkʃən] n condamnation f;
(belief) conviction f.
convince [kən'vɪns] vt convaincre, persuader;
to ~ sb (of sth/that) persuader qn (de qch/
que).
convincing [kən'vɪnsɪŋ] adj persuasif(ive),
convaincant(e).
convincingly [kən'vɪnsɪŋlɪ] adv de façon
convaincante.
convivial [kən'vɪvɪəl] adj joyeux(euse),
plein(e) d'entrain.
convoluted ['kɒnvəluːtɪd] adj (shape)
tarabiscoté(e); (argument) compliqué(e).
convoy ['kɒnvɔɪ] n convoi m.
convulse [kən'vʌls] vt ébranler; **to be ~d with
laughter** se tordre de rire.
convulsion [kən'vʌlʃən] n convulsion f.
coo [kuː] vi roucouler.
cook [kuk] vt (faire) cuire ♦ vi cuire; (person)
faire la cuisine ♦ n cuisinier/ière.
▶**cook up** vt (col: excuse, story) inventer.
cookbook ['kukbuk] n livre m de cuisine.
cooker ['kukə*] n cuisinière f.
cookery ['kukərɪ] n cuisine f.
cookery book n (BRIT) = **cookbook**.
cookie ['kukɪ] n (US) biscuit m, petit gâteau
sec.
cooking ['kukɪŋ] n cuisine f ♦ cpd (apples,
chocolate) à cuire; (utensils, salt) de cuisine.
cookout ['kukaut] n (US) barbecue m.
cool [kuːl] adj frais(fraîche); (not afraid)
calme; (unfriendly) froid(e); (impertinent)
effronté(e) ♦ vt, vi rafraîchir, refroidir; **it's
~ (weather)** il fait frais; **to keep sth ~** or **in a
~ place** garder or conserver qch au frais.

▶**cool down** vi refroidir; (fig: person,
situation) se calmer.
coolant ['kuːlənt] n liquide m de
refroidissement.
cool box, (US) **cooler** ['kuːlə*] n boîte f
isotherme.
cooling ['kuːlɪŋ] adj (breeze) rafraîchissant(e).
cooling tower n refroidisseur m.
coolly ['kuːlɪ] adv (calmly) calmement;
(audaciously) sans se gêner;
(unenthusiastically) froidement.
coolness ['kuːlnɪs] n fraîcheur f; sang-froid m,
calme m; froideur f.
coop [kuːp] n poulailler m ♦ vt: **to ~ up** (fig)
cloîtrer, enfermer.
co-op ['kəuɒp] n abbr (= cooperative (society))
coop f.
cooperate [kəu'ɒpəreɪt] vi coopérer,
collaborer.
cooperation [kəuɒpə'reɪʃən] n coopération f,
collaboration f.
cooperative [kəu'ɒpərətɪv] adj coopératif(ive)
♦ n coopérative f.
coopt [kəu'ɒpt] vt: **to ~ sb onto a committee**
coopter qn pour faire partie d'un comité.
coordinate vt [kəu'ɔːdɪneɪt] coordonner ♦ n
[kəu'ɔːdɪnət] (MATH) coordonnée f; **~s** npl
(clothes) ensemble m, coordonnés mpl.
coordination [kəuɔːdɪ'neɪʃən] n coordination
f.
coot [kuːt] n foulque f.
co-ownership ['kəu'əunəʃɪp] n copropriété f.
cop [kɒp] n (col) flic m.
cope [kəup] vi s'en sortir, tenir le coup; **to ~
with** faire face à; (take care of) s'occuper de.
Copenhagen ['kəupn'heɪgən] n Copenhague.
copier ['kɒpɪə*] n (also: photo~) copieur m.
co-pilot ['kəu'paɪlət] n copilote m.
copious ['kəupɪəs] adj copieux(euse),
abondant(e).
copper ['kɒpə*] n cuivre m; (col: policeman)
flic m; **~s** npl petite monnaie.
coppice ['kɒpɪs], **copse** [kɒps] n taillis m.
copulate ['kɒpjuleɪt] vi copuler.
copy ['kɒpɪ] n copie f; (book etc) exemplaire m;
(material: for printing) copie ♦ vt copier;
(imitate) imiter; **rough ~** (gen) premier jet;
(SCOL) brouillon m; **fair ~** version définitive;
propre m; **to make good ~** (PRESS) faire un
bon sujet d'article.
▶**copy out** vt copier.
copycat ['kɒpɪkæt] n (pej) copieur/euse.
copyright ['kɒpɪraɪt] n droit m d'auteur,
copyright m; **~ reserved** tous droits (de
reproduction) réservés.
copy typist n dactylo m/f.
copywriter ['kɒpɪraɪtə*] n rédacteur/trice
publicitaire.
coral ['kɒrəl] n corail m.
coral reef n récif m de corail.
Coral Sea n: **the ~** la mer de Corail.
cord [kɔːd] n corde f; (fabric) velours côtelé;

whipcord *m*; corde *f*; (*ELEC*) cordon *m*
(d'alimentation), fil *m* (électrique); ~s *npl*
(*trousers*) pantalon *m* de velours côtelé.
cordial ['kɔ:dɪəl] *adj* cordial(e),
chaleureux(euse) ♦ *n* sirop *m*; cordial *m*.
cordless ['kɔ:dlɪs] *adj* sans fil.
cordon ['kɔ:dn] *n* cordon *m*.
▶**cordon off** *vt* (*area*) interdire l'accès à;
(*crowd*) tenir à l'écart.
corduroy ['kɔ:dərɔɪ] *n* velours côtelé.
CORE [kɔ:*] *n abbr* (*US*) = *Congress of Racial
Equality*.
core [kɔ:*] *n* (*of fruit*) trognon *m*, cœur *m*;
(*TECH: also of earth*) noyau *m*; (*of nuclear
reactor, fig: of problem etc*) cœur ♦ *vt* enlever
le trognon *or* le cœur de; **rotten to the** ~
complètement pourri.
Corfu [kɔ:'fu:] *n* Corfou.
coriander [kɔrɪ'ændə*] *n* coriandre *f*.
cork [kɔ:k] *n* liège *m*; (*of bottle*) bouchon *m*.
corkage ['kɔ:kɪdʒ] *n droit payé par le client
qui apporte sa propre bouteille de vin*.
corked [kɔ:kt], (*US*) **corky** ['kɔ:kɪ] *adj* (*wine*)
qui sent le bouchon.
corkscrew ['kɔ:kskru:] *n* tire-bouchon *m*.
cormorant ['kɔ:mərnt] *n* cormoran *m*.
Corn *abbr* (*BRIT*) = *Cornwall*.
corn [kɔ:n] *n* (*BRIT: wheat*) blé *m*; (*US: maize*)
maïs *m*; (*on foot*) cor *m*; ~ **on the cob** (*CULIN*)
épi *m* de maïs au naturel.
cornea ['kɔ:nɪə] *n* cornée *f*.
corned beef ['kɔ:nd-] *n* corned-beef *m*.
corner ['kɔ:nə*] *n* coin *m*; (*AUT*) tournant *m*,
virage *m*; (*FOOTBALL: also*: ~ **kick**) corner *m*
♦ *vt* acculer, mettre au pied du mur;
coincer; (*COMM: market*) accaparer ♦ *vi*
prendre un virage; **to cut** ~**s** (*fig*) prendre
des raccourcis.
corner flag *n* (*FOOTBALL*) piquet *m* de coin.
corner kick *n* (*FOOTBALL*) corner *m*.
cornerstone ['kɔ:nəstəun] *n* pierre *f*
angulaire.
cornet ['kɔ:nɪt] *n* (*MUS*) cornet *m* à pistons;
(*BRIT: of ice-cream*) cornet (de glace).
cornflakes ['kɔ:nfleɪks] *npl* cornflakes *mpl*.
cornflour ['kɔ:nflauə*] *n* (*BRIT*) farine *f* de
maïs, maïzena *f* ®.
cornice ['kɔ:nɪs] *n* corniche *f*.
Cornish ['kɔ:nɪʃ] *adj* de Cornouailles,
cornouaillais(e).
corn oil *n* huile *f* de maïs.
cornstarch ['kɔ:nstɑ:tʃ] *n* (*US*) farine *f* de
maïs, maïzena *f* ®.
cornucopia [kɔ:nju'kəupɪə] *n* corne *f*
d'abondance.
Cornwall ['kɔ:nwəl] *n* Cornouailles *f*.
corny ['kɔ:nɪ] *adj* (*col*) rebattu(e), galvaudé(e).
corollary [kə'rɔlərɪ] *n* corollaire *m*.
coronary ['kɔrənərɪ] *n*: ~ **(thrombosis)**
infarctus *m* (du myocarde), thrombose *f*
coronaire.
coronation [kɔrə'neɪʃən] *n* couronnement *m*.

coroner ['kɔrənə*] *n* coroner *m*.
coronet ['kɔrənɪt] *n* couronne *f*.
Corp. *abbr* = *corporation*.
corporal ['kɔ:pərl] *n* caporal *m*, brigadier *m*
♦ *adj*: ~ **punishment** châtiment corporel.
corporate ['kɔ:pərɪt] *adj* en commun; (*COMM*)
constitué(e) (en corporation).
corporate hospitality *n arrangement selon
lequel une entreprise offre des places de
théâtre, concert etc à ses clients*.
corporate identity, corporate image *n* (*of
organization*) image *f* de l'entreprise.
corporation [kɔ:pə'reɪʃən] *n* (*of town*)
municipalité *f*, conseil municipal; (*COMM*)
société *f*.
corporation tax *n* ≈ impôt *m* sur les
bénéfices.
corps [kɔ:*], *pl* **corps** [kɔ:z] *n* corps *m*; **the
press** ~ la presse.
corpse [kɔ:ps] *n* cadavre *m*.
corpuscle ['kɔ:pʌsl] *n* corpuscule *m*.
corral [kə'rɑ:l] *n* corral *m*.
correct [kə'rɛkt] *adj* (*accurate*) correct(e),
exact(e); (*proper*) correct, convenable ♦ *vt*
corriger; **you are** ~ vous avez raison.
correction [kə'rɛkʃən] *n* correction *f*.
correlate ['kɔrɪleɪt] *vt* mettre en corrélation
♦ *vi*: **to** ~ **with** correspondre à.
correlation [kɔrɪ'leɪʃən] *n* corrélation *f*.
correspond [kɔrɪs'pɔnd] *vi* correspondre.
correspondence [kɔrɪs'pɔndəns] *n*
correspondance *f*.
correspondence course *n* cours *m* par
correspondance.
correspondent [kɔrɪs'pɔndənt] *n*
correspondant/e.
corridor ['kɔrɪdɔ:*] *n* couloir *m*, corridor *m*.
corroborate [kə'rɔbəreɪt] *vt* corroborer,
confirmer.
corrode [kə'rəud] *vt* corroder, ronger ♦ *vi* se
corroder.
corrosion [kə'rəuʒən] *n* corrosion *f*.
corrosive [kə'rəuzɪv] *adj* corrosif(ive).
corrugated ['kɔrəgeɪtɪd] *adj* plissé(e);
ondulé(e).
corrugated iron *n* tôle ondulée.
corrupt [kə'rʌpt] *adj* corrompu(e) ♦ *vt*
corrompre; (*data*) altérer; ~ **practices**
(*dishonesty, bribery*) malversation *f*.
corruption [kə'rʌpʃən] *n* corruption *f*;
altération *f* (de données).
corset ['kɔ:sɪt] *n* corset *m*.
Corsica ['kɔ:sɪkə] *n* Corse *f*.
Corsican ['kɔ:sɪkən] *adj* corse ♦ *n* Corse *m/f*.
cortège [kɔ:'teɪʒ] *n* cortège *m* (*gén funèbre*).
cortisone ['kɔ:tɪzəun] *n* cortisone *f*.
coruscating ['kɔrəskeɪtɪŋ] *adj* scintillant(e).
c.o.s. *abbr* (= *cash on shipment*) paiement *m* à
l'expédition.
cosh [kɔʃ] *n* (*BRIT*) matraque *f*.
cosignatory ['kəu'sɪgnətərɪ] *n* cosignataire
m/f.

cosiness ['kəʊzɪnɪs] n atmosphère douillette, confort m.

cos lettuce ['kɔs-] n (laitue f) romaine f.

cosmetic [kɔz'mɛtɪk] n produit m de beauté, cosmétique m ♦ adj (preparation) cosmétique; (surgery) esthétique; (fig: reforms) symbolique, superficiel(le).

cosmic ['kɔzmɪk] adj cosmique.

cosmonaut ['kɔzmənɔːt] n cosmonaute m/f.

cosmopolitan [kɔzmə'pɔlɪtn] adj cosmopolite.

cosmos ['kɔzmɔs] n cosmos m.

cosset ['kɔsɪt] vt choyer, dorloter.

cost [kɔst] n coût m ♦ vb (pt, pp cost) vi coûter ♦ vt établir or calculer le prix de revient de; ~s npl (LAW) dépens mpl; **how much does it ~?** combien ça coûte?; **it ~s £5/too much** cela coûte 5 livres/trop cher; **what will it ~ to have it repaired?** combien cela coûtera de le faire réparer?; **it ~ him his life/job** ça lui a coûté la vie/son emploi; **the ~ of living** le coût de la vie; **at all ~s** coûte que coûte, à tout prix.

cost accountant n analyste m/f de coûts.

co-star ['kəʊstɑː*] n partenaire m/f.

Costa Rica ['kɔstə'riːkə] n Costa Rica m.

cost centre n centre m de coût.

cost control n contrôle m des coûts.

cost-effective ['kɔstɪ'fɛktɪv] adj rentable.

cost-effectiveness ['kɔstɪ'fɛktɪvnɪs] n rentabilité f.

costing ['kɔstɪŋ] n calcul m du prix de revient.

costly ['kɔstlɪ] adj coûteux(euse).

cost-of-living ['kɔstəv'lɪvɪŋ] adj: ~ **allowance** indemnité f de vie chère; ~ **index** indice m du coût de la vie.

cost price n (BRIT) prix coûtant or de revient.

costume ['kɔstjuːm] n costume m; (lady's suit) tailleur m; (BRIT: also: **swimming** ~) maillot m (de bain).

costume jewellery n bijoux mpl de fantaisie.

cosy, (US) **cozy** ['kəʊzɪ] adj (bed) douillet(te); (scarf, gloves) bien chaud(e); (atmosphere) chaleureux(euse); (room) mignon(ne).

cot [kɔt] n (BRIT: child's) lit m d'enfant, petit lit; (US: campbed) lit de camp.

cot death n mort subite du nourrisson.

Cotswolds ['kɔtswəʊldz] npl: **the** ~ région de collines du Gloucestershire.

cottage ['kɔtɪdʒ] n petite maison (à la campagne), cottage m.

cottage cheese n fromage blanc (maigre).

cottage industry n industrie familiale or artisanale.

cottage pie n ≈ hachis m Parmentier.

cotton ['kɔtn] n coton m; ~ **dress** etc robe etc en or de coton.

►**cotton on** vi (col): **to** ~ **on (to sth)** piger (qch).

cotton wool n (BRIT) ouate f, coton m hydrophile.

couch [kaʊtʃ] n canapé m; divan m; (doctor's) table f d'examen; (psychiatrist's) divan ♦ vt formuler, exprimer.

couchette [kuː'ʃɛt] n couchette f.

couch potato n (col) mollasson/ne (qui passe son temps devant la télé).

cough [kɔf] vi tousser ♦ n toux f.

cough drop n pastille f pour or contre la toux.

cough mixture, cough syrup n sirop m pour la toux.

could [kʊd] pt of **can**.

couldn't ['kʊdnt] = **could not**.

council ['kaʊnsl] n conseil m; **city** or **town** ~ conseil municipal; **C**~ **of Europe** Conseil de l'Europe.

council estate n (BRIT) (quartier m or zone f de) logements loués à/par la municipalité.

council house n (BRIT) maison f (à loyer modéré) louée par la municipalité.

councillor ['kaʊnslə*] n conseiller/ère.

council tax n (BRIT) impôts locaux.

counsel ['kaʊnsl] n consultation f, délibération f; (person) avocat/e ♦ vt: **to** ~ **sth/sb to do sth** conseiller qch/à qn de faire qch; ~ **for the defence/the prosecution** (avocat de la) défense/avocat du ministère public.

counsellor, (US) **counselor** ['kaʊnslə*] n conseiller/ère; (US LAW) avocat m.

count [kaʊnt] vt, vi compter ♦ n compte m; (nobleman) comte m; **to** ~ (**up**) **to 10** compter jusqu'à 10; **to keep** ~ **of sth** tenir le compte de qch; **not** ~**ing the children** sans compter les enfants; **10** ~**ing him** 10 avec lui, 10 en le comptant; **to** ~ **the cost of** établir le coût de; **it** ~**s for very little** cela n'a pas beaucoup d'importance; ~ **yourself lucky** estimez-vous heureux.

►**count on** vt fus compter sur; **to** ~ **on doing sth** compter faire qch.

►**count up** vt compter, additionner.

countdown ['kaʊntdaʊn] n compte m à rebours.

countenance ['kaʊntɪnəns] n expression f ♦ vt approuver.

counter ['kaʊntə*] n comptoir m; (in post office, bank) guichet m; (in game) jeton m ♦ vt aller à l'encontre de, opposer; (blow) parer ♦ adv: ~ **to** à l'encontre de; contrairement à; **to buy under the** ~ (fig) acheter sous le manteau or en sous-main; **to** ~ **sth with sth/by doing sth** contrer or riposter à qch par qch/en faisant qch.

counteract ['kaʊntər'ækt] vt neutraliser, contrebalancer.

counterattack ['kaʊntərə'tæk] n contre-attaque f ♦ vi contre-attaquer.

counterbalance ['kaʊntə'bæləns] vt contrebalancer, faire contrepoids à.

counter-clockwise ['kaʊntə'klɔkwaɪz] adv en sens inverse des aiguilles d'une montre.

counter-espionage ['kaʊntər'ɛspɪənɑːʒ] n

contre-espionnage *m*.

counterfeit ['kauntəfɪt] *n* faux *m*, contrefaçon *f* ♦ *vt* contrefaire ♦ *adj* faux(fausse).

counterfoil ['kauntəfɔɪl] *n* talon *m*, souche *f*.

counterintelligence ['kauntərɪn'tɛlɪdʒəns] *n* contre-espionnage *m*.

countermand ['kauntəmɑːnd] *vt* annuler.

countermeasure ['kauntəmɛʒə*] *n* contre-mesure *f*.

counteroffensive ['kauntərə'fɛnsɪv] *n* contre-offensive *f*.

counterpane ['kauntəpeɪn] *n* dessus-de-lit *m*.

counterpart ['kauntəpɑːt] *n* (*of document etc*) double *m*; (*of person*) homologue *m/f*.

counterproductive ['kauntəprə'dʌktɪv] *adj* contre-productif(ive).

counterproposal ['kauntəprə'pəuzl] *n* contre-proposition *f*.

countersign ['kauntəsaɪn] *vt* contresigner.

countersink ['kauntəsɪŋk] *vt* (*hole*) fraiser.

countess ['kauntɪs] *n* comtesse *f*.

countless ['kauntlɪs] *adj* innombrable.

countrified ['kʌntrɪfaɪd] *adj* rustique, à l'air campagnard.

country ['kʌntrɪ] *n* pays *m*; (*native land*) patrie *f*; (*as opposed to town*) campagne *f*; (*region*) région *f*, pays; **in the ~** à la campagne; **mountainous ~** pays de montagne, région montagneuse.

country and western (music) *n* musique *f* country.

country dancing *n* (*BRIT*) danse *f* folklorique.

country house *n* manoir *m*, (petit) château.

countryman ['kʌntrɪmən] *n* (*national*) compatriote *m*; (*rural*) habitant *m* de la campagne, campagnard *m*.

countryside ['kʌntrɪsaɪd] *n* campagne *f*.

countrywide ['kʌntrɪ'waɪd] *adj* s'étendant à l'ensemble du pays; (*problem*) à l'échelle nationale ♦ *adv* à travers *or* dans tout le pays.

county ['kauntɪ] *n* comté *m*.

county council *n* (*BRIT*) ≈ conseil régional.

county town *n* (*BRIT*) chef-lieu *m*.

coup, ~s [kuː, -z] *n* beau coup; (*also:* **~ d'état**) coup d'État.

coupé [kuː'peɪ] *n* (*AUT*) coupé *m*.

couple ['kʌpl] *n* couple *m* ♦ *vt* (*carriages*) atteler; (*TECH*) coupler; (*ideas, names*) associer; **a ~ of** deux; (*a few*) deux ou trois.

couplet ['kʌplɪt] *n* distique *m*.

coupling ['kʌplɪŋ] *n* (*RAIL*) attelage *m*.

coupon ['kuːpɔn] *n* (*voucher*) bon-prime *m*, bon-réclame *m*; (*detachable form*) coupon *m* détachable, coupon-réponse *m*; (*FINANCE*) coupon.

courage ['kʌrɪdʒ] *n* courage *m*.

courageous [kə'reɪdʒəs] *adj* courageux(euse).

courgette [kuə'ʒɛt] *n* (*BRIT*) courgette *f*.

courier ['kurɪə*] *n* messager *m*, courrier *m*; (*for tourists*) accompagnateur/trice.

course [kɔːs] *n* cours *m*; (*of ship*) route *f*; (*for golf*) terrain *m*; (*part of meal*) plat *m*; **first ~** entrée *f*; **of ~** *adv* bien sûr; **(no) of ~ not!** bien sûr que non!, évidemment que non!; **in the ~ of the next few days** au cours des prochains jours; **in due ~** en temps utile *or* voulu; **~ (of action)** parti *m*, ligne *f* de conduite; **the best ~ would be to ...** le mieux serait de ...; **we have no other ~ but to ...** nous n'avons pas d'autre solution que de ...; **~ of lectures** série *f* de conférences; **~ of treatment** (*MED*) traitement *m*.

court [kɔːt] *n* cour *f*; (*LAW*) cour, tribunal *m*; (*TENNIS*) court *m* ♦ *vt* (*woman*) courtiser, faire la cour à; (*fig: favour, popularity*) rechercher; (*: death, disaster*) courir après, flirter avec; **out of ~** (*LAW: settle*) à l'amiable; **to take to ~** actionner *or* poursuivre en justice; **~ of appeal** cour d'appel.

courteous ['kəːtɪəs] *adj* courtois(e), poli(e).

courtesan [kɔːtɪ'zæn] *n* courtisane *f*.

courtesy ['kəːtəsɪ] *n* courtoisie *f*, politesse *f*; **by ~ of** avec l'aimable autorisation de.

courtesy light *n* (*AUT*) plafonnier *m*.

court-house ['kɔːthaus] *n* (*US*) palais *m* de justice.

courtier ['kɔːtɪə*] *n* courtisan *m*, dame *f* de cour.

court martial, *pl* **courts martial** *n* cour martiale, conseil *m* de guerre.

courtroom ['kɔːtrum] *n* salle *f* de tribunal.

court shoe *n* escarpin *m*.

courtyard ['kɔːtjɑːd] *n* cour *f*.

cousin ['kʌzn] *n* cousin/e.

cove [kəuv] *n* petite baie, anse *f*.

covenant ['kʌvənənt] *n* contrat *m*, engagement *m* ♦ *vt*: **to ~ £200 per year to a charity** s'engager à verser 200 livres par an à une œuvre de bienfaisance.

Coventry ['kɔvəntrɪ] *n*: **to send sb to ~** (*fig*) mettre qn en quarantaine.

cover ['kʌvə*] *vt* couvrir; (*PRESS: report on*) faire un reportage sur ♦ *n* (*for bed, of book, COMM*) couverture *f*; (*of pan*) couvercle *m*; (*over furniture*) housse *f*; (*shelter*) abri *m*; **to take ~** se mettre à l'abri; **under ~** à l'abri; **under ~ of darkness** à la faveur de la nuit; **under separate ~** (*COMM*) sous pli séparé; **£10 will ~ everything** 10 livres suffiront (pour tout payer).

▶**cover up** *vt* (*person, object*): **to ~ up (with)** couvrir (de); (*fig: truth, facts*) occulter; **to ~ up for sb** (*fig*) couvrir qn.

coverage ['kʌvərɪdʒ] *n* (*in media*) reportage *m*, (*INSURANCE*) couverture *f*.

cover charge *n* couvert *m* (*supplément à payer*).

covering ['kʌvərɪŋ] *n* couverture *f*, enveloppe *f*.

covering letter, (*US*) **cover letter** *n* lettre explicative.

cover note *n* (*INSURANCE*) police *f* provisoire.

cover price n prix m de l'exemplaire.
covert ['kʌvət] adj (threat) voilé(e), caché(e); (attack) indirect(e); (glance) furtif(ive).
cover-up ['kʌvərʌp] n tentative f pour étouffer une affaire.
covet ['kʌvɪt] vt convoiter.
cow [kau] n vache f ♦ cpd femelle ♦ vt effrayer, intimider.
coward ['kauəd] n lâche m/f.
cowardice ['kauədɪs] n lâcheté f.
cowardly ['kauədlɪ] adj lâche.
cowboy ['kaubɔɪ] n cow-boy m.
cower ['kauə*] vi se recroqueviller; trembler.
cowshed ['kauʃɛd] n étable f.
cowslip ['kauslɪp] n (BOT) (fleur f de) coucou m.
coxswain ['kɔksn] n (abbr: cox) barreur m; (of ship) patron m.
coy [kɔɪ] adj faussement effarouché(e) or timide.
coyote [kɔɪ'əutɪ] n coyote m.
cozy ['kəuzɪ] adj (US) = cosy.
CP n abbr (= Communist Party) PC m.
cp. abbr (= compare) cf.
c/p abbr (BRIT) = carriage paid.
CPA n abbr (US) = certified public accountant.
CPI n abbr (= Consumer Price Index) IPC m.
Cpl. abbr (= corporal) C/C.
CP/M n abbr (= Central Program for Microprocessors) CP/M m.
c.p.s. abbr (= characters per second) caractères/seconde.
CPSA n abbr (BRIT: = Civil and Public Services Association) syndicat de la fonction publique.
CPU n abbr = central processing unit.
cr. abbr = credit; creditor.
crab [kræb] n crabe m.
crab apple n pomme f sauvage.
crack [kræk] n fente f, fissure f; (in bone, dish, glass) fêlure f; (in wall) lézarde f; (noise) craquement m, coup (sec); (joke) plaisanterie f; (col: attempt): **to have a ~ (at sth)** essayer (qch); (DRUGS) crack m ♦ vt fendre, fissurer; fêler; lézarder; (whip) faire claquer; (nut) casser; (solve) résoudre, trouver la clef de; déchiffrer ♦ cpd (athlete) de première classe, d'élite; **to ~ jokes** (col) raconter des blagues; **to get ~ing** (col) s'y mettre, se magner.
►**crack down on** vt fus (crime) sévir contre, réprimer; (spending) mettre un frein à.
►**crack up** vi être au bout de son rouleau, flancher.
crackdown ['krækdaun] n: ~ **(on)** (on crime) répression f (de); (on spending) restrictions fpl (de).
cracked [krækt] adj (col) toqué(e), timbré(e).
cracker ['krækə*] n pétard m; (biscuit) biscuit (salé), craquelin m; **a ~ of a ...** (BRIT col) un(e) ... formidable; **he's ~s** (BRIT col) il est cinglé.

crackle ['krækl] vi crépiter, grésiller.
crackling ['kræklɪŋ] n crépitement m, grésillement m; (on radio, telephone) grésillement, friture f; (of pork) couenne f.
crackpot ['krækpɔt] n (col) tordu/e.
cradle ['kreɪdl] n berceau m ♦ vt (child) bercer; (object) tenir dans ses bras.
craft [krɑːft] n métier (artisanal); (cunning) ruse f, astuce f; (boat) embarcation f, barque f.
craftsman ['krɑːftsmən] n artisan m, ouvrier (qualifié).
craftsmanship ['krɑːftsmənʃɪp] n métier m, habileté f.
crafty ['krɑːftɪ] adj rusé(e), malin(igne), astucieux(euse).
crag [kræg] n rocher escarpé.
craggy ['krægɪ] adj escarpé(e), rocheux(euse).
cram [kræm] vt (fill): **to ~ sth with** bourrer qch de; (put): **to ~ sth into** fourrer qch dans.
cramming ['kræmɪŋ] n (for exams) bachotage m.
cramp [kræmp] n crampe f ♦ vt gêner, entraver.
cramped [kræmpt] adj à l'étroit, très serré(e).
crampon ['kræmpən] n crampon m.
cranberry ['krænbərɪ] n canneberge f.
crane [kreɪn] n grue f ♦ vt, vi: **to ~ forward, to ~ one's neck** allonger le cou.
cranium, pl **crania** ['kreɪnɪəm, 'kreɪnɪə] n boîte crânienne.
crank [kræŋk] n manivelle f; (person) excentrique m/f.
crankshaft ['kræŋkʃɑːft] n vilebrequin m.
cranky ['kræŋkɪ] adj excentrique, loufoque; (bad-tempered) grincheux(euse), revêche.
cranny ['krænɪ] n see **nook**.
crap [kræp] n (col!) conneries fpl (!); **to have a ~** chier (!).
crappy ['kræpɪ] adj (col) merdique (!).
crash [kræʃ] n fracas m; (of car, plane) collision f; (of business) faillite f; (STOCK EXCHANGE) krach m ♦ vt (plane) écraser ♦ vi (plane) s'écraser; (two cars) se percuter, s'emboutir; (fig) s'effondrer; **to ~ into** se jeter or se fracasser contre; **he ~ed the car into a wall** il s'est écrasé contre un mur avec sa voiture.
crash barrier n (BRIT AUT) rail m de securité.
crash course n cours intensif.
crash helmet n casque (protecteur).
crash landing n atterrissage forcé or en catastrophe.
crass [kræs] adj grossier(ière), crasse.
crate [kreɪt] n cageot m.
crater ['kreɪtə*] n cratère m.
cravat [krə'væt] n foulard m (noué autour du cou).
crave [kreɪv] vt, vi: **to ~ for** désirer violemment, avoir un besoin physiologique de, avoir une envie irrésistible de.

craving ['kreɪvɪŋ] *n*: ~ **(for)** (*for food, cigarettes etc*) envie *f* irrésistible (de).

crawl [krɔːl] *vi* ramper; (*vehicle*) avancer au pas ♦ *n* (*SWIMMING*) crawl *m*; **to ~ on one's hands and knees** aller à quatre pattes; **to ~ to sb** (*col*) faire de la lèche à qn.

crawler lane ['krɔːlə-] *n* (*BRIT AUT*) file *f or* voie *f* pour véhicules lents.

crayfish ['kreɪfɪʃ] *n* (*pl inv*) (*freshwater*) écrevisse *f*; (*saltwater*) langoustine *f*.

crayon ['kreɪən] *n* crayon *m* (de couleur).

craze [kreɪz] *n* engouement *m*.

crazed [kreɪzd] *adj* (*look, person*) affolé(e); (*pottery, glaze*) craquelé(e).

crazy ['kreɪzɪ] *adj* fou(folle); **to go ~** devenir fou; **to be ~ about sb** (*col*) aimer qn à la folie; **he's ~ about skiing** (*col*) c'est un fana(tique) de ski.

crazy paving *n* (*BRIT*) dallage irrégulier (en pierres plates).

creak [kriːk] *vi* (*hinge*) grincer; (*floor, shoes*) craquer.

cream [kriːm] *n* crème *f* ♦ *adj* (*colour*) crème *inv*; **whipped ~** crème fouettée.

►**cream off** *vt* (*fig*) prélever.

cream cake *n* (petit) gâteau à la crème.

cream cheese *n* fromage *m* à la crème, fromage blanc.

creamery ['kriːmərɪ] *n* (*shop*) crémerie *f*; (*factory*) laiterie *f*.

creamy ['kriːmɪ] *adj* crémeux(euse).

crease [kriːs] *n* pli *m* ♦ *vt* froisser, chiffonner ♦ *vi* se froisser, se chiffonner.

crease-resistant ['kriːsrɪzɪstənt] *adj* infroissable.

create [kriː'eɪt] *vt* créer; (*impression, fuss*) faire.

creation [kriː'eɪʃən] *n* création *f*.

creative [kriː'eɪtɪv] *adj* créateur(trice).

creativity [kriːeɪ'tɪvɪtɪ] *n* créativité *f*.

creator [kriː'eɪtə*] *n* créateur/trice.

creature ['kriːtʃə*] *n* créature *f*.

creature comforts *npl* petit confort.

crèche [krɛʃ] *n* garderie *f*, crèche *f*.

credence ['kriːdns] *n* croyance *f*, foi *f*.

credentials [krɪ'denʃlz] *npl* (*papers*) références *fpl*; (*letters of reference*) pièces justificatives.

credibility [kredɪ'bɪlɪtɪ] *n* crédibilité *f*.

credible ['kredɪbl] *adj* digne de foi, crédible.

credit ['kredɪt] *n* crédit *m*; (*SCOL*) unité *f* de valeur ♦ *vt* (*COMM*) créditer; (*believe: also*: **give ~ to**) ajouter foi à, croire; **to ~ sb with** (*fig*) prêter or attribuer à qn; **to ~ £5 to sb** créditer (le compte de) qn de 5 livres; **to be in ~** (*person, bank account*) être créditeur(trice); **on ~** à crédit; **to one's ~** à son honneur; **to be in one's asset**; **to take the ~ for** s'attribuer le mérite de; **it does him ~** cela lui fait honneur.

creditable ['kredɪtəbl] *adj* honorable, estimable.

credit account *n* compte *m* client.

credit agency *n* (*BRIT*) agence *f* de renseignements commerciaux.

credit balance *n* solde créditeur.

credit bureau *n* (*US*) agence *f* de renseignements commerciaux.

credit card *n* carte *f* de crédit.

credit control *n* suivi *m* des factures.

credit facilities *npl* facilités *fpl* de paiement.

credit limit *n* limite *f* de crédit.

credit note *n* (*BRIT*) avoir *m*.

creditor ['kredɪtə*] *n* créancier/ière.

credits ['kredɪts] *npl* (*CINE*) générique *m*.

credit transfer *n* virement *m*.

creditworthy ['kredɪtwəːðɪ] *adj* solvable.

credulity [krɪ'djuːlɪtɪ] *n* crédulité *f*.

creed [kriːd] *n* croyance *f*; credo *m*, principes *mpl*.

creek [kriːk] *n* crique *f*, anse *f*; (*US*) ruisseau *m*, petit cours d'eau.

creel ['kriːl] *n* panier *m* de pêche; (*also*: **lobster ~**) panier à homards.

creep, *pt, pp* **crept** [kriːp, krept] *vi* ramper; (*fig*) se faufiler, se glisser; (*plant*) grimper ♦ *n* (*col*) saligaud *m*; **he's a ~** c'est un type puant; **it gives me the ~s** cela me fait froid dans le dos; **to ~ up on sb** s'approcher furtivement de qn.

creeper ['kriːpə*] *n* plante grimpante.

creepers ['kriːpəz] *npl* (*US: for baby*) barboteuse *f*.

creepy ['kriːpɪ] *adj* (*frightening*) qui fait frissonner, qui donne la chair de poule.

creepy-crawly ['kriːpɪ'krɔːlɪ] *n* (*col*) bestiole *f*.

cremate [krɪ'meɪt] *vt* incinérer.

cremation [krɪ'meɪʃən] *n* incinération *f*.

crematorium, *pl* **crematoria** [kremə'tɔːrɪəm, -'tɔːrɪə] *n* four *m* crématoire.

creosote ['krɪəsəut] *n* créosote *f*.

crepe [kreɪp] *n* crêpe *m*.

crepe bandage *n* (*BRIT*) bande *f* Velpeau ®.

crepe paper *n* papier *m* crépon.

crepe sole *n* semelle *f* de crêpe.

crept [krept] *pt, pp of* **creep**.

crescendo [krɪ'ʃendəu] *n* crescendo *m*.

crescent ['kresnt] *n* croissant *m*; (*street*) rue *f* (en arc de cercle).

cress [kres] *n* cresson *m*.

crest [krest] *n* crête *f*; (*of helmet*) cimier *m*; (*of coat of arms*) timbre *m*.

crestfallen ['krestfɔːlən] *adj* déconfit(e), découragé(e).

Crete ['kriːt] *n* Crète *f*.

crevasse [krɪ'væs] *n* crevasse *f*.

crevice ['krevɪs] *n* fissure *f*, lézarde *f*, fente *f*.

crew [kruː] *n* équipage *m*; (*CINE*) équipe *f* (de tournage); (*gang*) bande *f*.

crew-cut ['kruːkʌt] *n*: **to have a ~** avoir les cheveux en brosse.

crew-neck ['kruːnek] *n* col ras.

crib [krɪb] *n* lit *m* d'enfant ♦ *vt* (*col*) copier.

cribbage ['krɪbɪdʒ] *n* sorte *de* jeu de cartes.

crick [krɪk] n crampe f; ~ **in the neck** torticolis m.
cricket ['krɪkɪt] n (insect) grillon m, cri-cri m inv; (game) cricket m.
cricketer ['krɪkɪtə*] n joueur m de cricket.
crime [kraɪm] n crime m; **minor** ~ délit m or infraction f mineure).
crime wave n poussée f de la criminalité.
criminal ['krɪmɪnl] adj, n criminel(le).
crimp [krɪmp] vt friser, frisotter.
crimson ['krɪmzn] adj cramoisi(e).
cringe [krɪndʒ] vi avoir un mouvement de recul; (fig) s'humilier, ramper.
crinkle ['krɪŋkl] vt froisser, chiffonner.
cripple ['krɪpl] n boiteux/euse, infirme m/f ♦ vt estropier, paralyser; (ship, plane) immobiliser; (production, exports) paralyser; ~**d with rheumatism** perclus(e) de rhumatismes.
crippling ['krɪplɪŋ] adj (disease) handicapant(e); (taxation, debts) écrasant(e).
crisis, pl **crises** ['kraɪsɪs, -siːz] n crise f.
crisp [krɪsp] adj croquant(e); (fig) vif(vive); brusque.
crisps [krɪsps] npl (BRIT) (pommes) chips fpl.
crisscross ['krɪskrɒs] adj entrecroisé(e), en croisillons ♦ vt sillonner; ~ **pattern** croisillons mpl.
criterion, pl **criteria** [kraɪ'tɪərɪən, -'tɪərɪə] n critère m.
critic ['krɪtɪk] n critique m/f.
critical ['krɪtɪkl] adj critique; **to be** ~ **of sb/sth** critiquer qn/qch.
critically ['krɪtɪklɪ] adv (examine) d'un œil critique; (speak) sévèrement; ~ **ill** gravement malade.
criticism ['krɪtɪsɪzəm] n critique f.
criticize ['krɪtɪsaɪz] vt critiquer.
croak [krəuk] vi (frog) coasser; (raven) croasser.
Croat ['krəuæt] adj, n = **Croatian**.
Croatia [krəu'eɪʃə] n Croatie f.
Croatian [krəu'eɪʃən] adj croate ♦ n Croate m/f; (LING) croate m.
crochet ['krəuʃeɪ] n travail m au crochet.
crock [krɒk] n cruche f; (col: also: **old** ~) épave f.
crockery ['krɒkərɪ] n vaisselle f.
crocodile ['krɒkədaɪl] n crocodile m.
crocus ['krəukəs] n crocus m.
croft [krɒft] n (BRIT) petite ferme.
crofter ['krɒftə*] n (BRIT) fermier m.
crone [krəun] n vieille bique, (vieille) sorcière.
crony ['krəunɪ] n copain/copine.
crook [kruk] n escroc m; (of shepherd) houlette f.
crooked ['krukɪd] adj courbé(e), tordu(e); (action) malhonnête.
crop [krɒp] n (produce) culture f; (amount produced) récolte f; (riding ~) cravache f; (of bird) jabot m ♦ vt (hair) tondre; (subj: animals: grass) brouter.
▶**crop up** vi surgir, se présenter, survenir.
cropper ['krɒpə*] n: **to come a** ~ (col) faire la culbute, s'étaler.
crop spraying [-spreɪŋ] n pulvérisation f des cultures.
croquet ['krəukeɪ] n croquet m.
croquette [krə'kɛt] n croquette f.
cross [krɒs] n croix f; (BIOL) croisement m ♦ vt (street etc) traverser; (arms, legs, BIOL) croiser; (cheque) barrer; (thwart: person, plan) contrarier ♦ vi: **the boat** ~**es from ... to ...** le bateau fait la traversée de ... à ... ♦ adj en colère, fâché(e); **to** ~ **o.s.** se signer, faire le signe de (la) croix; **we have a** ~**ed line** (BRIT: on telephone) il y a des interférences; **they've got their lines** ~**ed** (fig) il y a un malentendu entre eux; **to be/get** ~ **with sb** (about sth) être en colère/se fâcher contre qn (à propos de qch).
▶**cross out** vt barrer, biffer.
▶**cross over** vi traverser.
crossbar ['krɒsbɑː*] n barre transversale.
crossbow ['krɒsbəu] n arbalète f.
crossbreed ['krɒsbriːd] n hybride m, métis/se.
cross-Channel ferry ['krɒs'tʃænl-] n ferry m qui fait la traversée de la Manche.
cross-check ['krɒstʃɛk] n recoupement m ♦ vi vérifier par recoupement.
cross-country (race) ['krɒs'kʌntrɪ-] n cross(-country) m.
cross-dressing [krɒs'drɛsɪŋ] n travestisme m.
cross-examination ['krɒsɪgzæmɪ'neɪʃən] n (LAW) examen m contradictoire (d'un témoin).
cross-examine ['krɒsɪg'zæmɪn] vt (LAW) faire subir un examen contradictoire à.
cross-eyed ['krɒsaɪd] adj qui louche.
crossfire ['krɒsfaɪə*] n feux croisés.
crossing ['krɒsɪŋ] n croisement m, carrefour m; (sea passage) traversée f; (also: **pedestrian** ~) passage clouté.
crossing point n poste frontalier.
cross-purposes ['krɒs'pəːpəsɪz] npl: **to be at** ~ **with sb** comprendre qn de travers; **we're (talking) at** ~ on ne parle pas de la même chose.
cross-question ['krɒs'kwɛstʃən] vt faire subir un interrogatoire à.
cross-reference ['krɒs'rɛfrəns] n renvoi m, référence f.
crossroads ['krɒsrəudz] n carrefour m.
cross section n (BIOL) coupe transversale; (in population) échantillon m.
crosswalk ['krɒswɔːk] n (US) passage clouté.
crosswind ['krɒswɪnd] n vent m de travers.
crosswise ['krɒswaɪz] adv en travers.
crossword ['krɒswəːd] n mots mpl croisés.
crotch [krɒtʃ] n (of garment) entre-jambes m inv.
crotchet ['krɒtʃɪt] n (MUS) noire f.
crotchety ['krɒtʃɪtɪ] adj (person) grognon(ne),

grincheux(euse).

crouch [krautʃ] *vi* s'accroupir; se tapir; se ramasser.

croup [kru:p] *n* (*MED*) croup *m*.

crouton ['kru:tɔn] *n* croûton *m*.

crow [krəu] *n* (*bird*) corneille *f*; (*of cock*) chant *m* du coq, cocorico *m* ♦ *vi* (*cock*) chanter; (*fig*) pavoiser, chanter victoire.

crowbar ['krəubɑ:ʳ] *n* levier *m*.

crowd [kraud] *n* foule *f* ♦ *vt* bourrer, remplir ♦ *vi* affluer, s'attrouper, s'entasser; ~**s of people** une foule de gens.

crowded ['kraudɪd] *adj* bondé(e), plein(e); ~ **with** plein de.

crowd scene *n* (*CINE, THEAT*) scène *f* de foule.

crown [kraun] *n* couronne *f*; (*of head*) sommet *m* de la tête, calotte crânienne; (*of hat*) fond *m*; (*of hill*) sommet *m* ♦ *vt* (*also tooth*) couronner.

crown court *n* (*BRIT*) ≈ Cour *f* d'assises.

En Angleterre et au Pays de Galles, une **crown court** *est une cour de justice où sont jugées les affaires très graves, telles que le meurtre, l'homicide, le viol et le vol, en présence d'un jury. Tous les crimes et délits, quel que soit leur degré de gravité, doivent d'abord passer devant une* **magistrates' court.** *Il existe environ 90 crown courts.*

---

crowning ['kraunɪŋ] *adj* (*achievement, glory*) suprême.

crown jewels *npl* joyaux *mpl* de la Couronne.

crown prince *n* prince héritier.

crow's-feet ['krəuzfi:t] *npl* pattes *fpl* d'oie (*fig*).

crow's-nest ['krəuznest] *n* (*on sailing-ship*) nid *m* de pie.

crucial ['kru:ʃl] *adj* crucial(e), décisif(ive); ~ **to** essentiel(le) à.

crucifix ['kru:sɪfɪks] *n* crucifix *m*.

crucifixion [kru:sɪ'fɪkʃən] *n* crucifiement *m*, crucifixion *f*.

crucify ['kru:sɪfaɪ] *vt* crucifier, mettre en croix; (*fig*) crucifier.

crude [kru:d] *adj* (*materials*) brut(e); non raffiné(e); (*basic*) rudimentaire, sommaire; (*vulgar*) cru(e), grossier(ière).

crude (oil) *n* (pétrole) brut *m*.

cruel ['kruəl] *adj* cruel(le).

cruelty ['kruəltɪ] *n* cruauté *f*.

cruet ['kru:ɪt] *n* huilier *m*; vinaigrier *m*.

cruise [kru:z] *n* croisière *f* ♦ *vi* (*ship*) croiser; (*car*) rouler; (*aircraft*) voler; (*taxi*) être en maraude.

cruise missile *n* missile *m* de croisière.

cruiser ['kru:zəʳ] *n* croiseur *m*.

cruising speed ['kru:zɪŋ-] *n* vitesse *f* de croisière.

crumb [krʌm] *n* miette *f*.

crumble ['krʌmbl] *vt* émietter ♦ *vi* s'émietter; (*plaster etc*) s'effriter; (*land, earth*) s'ébouler;

(*building*) s'écrouler, crouler; (*fig*) s'effondrer.

crumbly ['krʌmblɪ] *adj* friable.

crummy ['krʌmɪ] *adj* (*col*) minable; (: *unwell*) mal fichu(e), patraque.

crumpet ['krʌmpɪt] *n* petite crêpe (épaisse).

crumple ['krʌmpl] *vt* froisser, friper.

crunch [krʌntʃ] *vt* croquer; (*underfoot*) faire craquer, écraser; faire crisser ♦ *n* (*fig*) instant *m or* moment *m* critique, moment de vérité.

crunchy ['krʌntʃɪ] *adj* croquant(e), croustillant(e).

crusade [kru:'seɪd] *n* croisade *f* ♦ *vi* (*fig*): **to ~ for/against** partir en croisade pour/contre.

crusader [kru:'seɪdəʳ] *n* croisé *m*; (*fig*): ~ (**for**) champion *m* (de).

crush [krʌʃ] *n* foule *f*, cohue *f*; (*love*): **to have a ~ on sb** avoir le béguin pour qn; (*drink*): **lemon** ~ citron pressé ♦ *vt* écraser; (*crumple*) froisser; (*grind, break up: garlic, ice*) piler; (: *grapes*) presser.

crush barrier *n* (*BRIT*) barrière *f* de sécurité.

crushing ['krʌʃɪŋ] *adj* écrasant(e).

crust [krʌst] *n* croûte *f*.

crustacean [krʌs'teɪʃən] *n* crustacé *m*.

crusty ['krʌstɪ] *adj* (*bread*) croustillant(e); (*col: person*) revêche, bourru(e); (: *remark*) irrité(e).

crutch [krʌtʃ] *n* béquille *f*; (*TECH*) support *m*; (*also: crotch*) entrejambe *m*.

crux [krʌks] *n* point crucial.

cry [kraɪ] *vi* pleurer; (*shout: also:* ~ **out**) crier ♦ *n* cri *m*; **what are you ~ing about?** pourquoi pleures-tu?; **to ~ for help** appeler à l'aide; **she had a good** ~ elle a pleuré un bon coup; **it's a far ~ from ...** (*fig*) on est loin de ....

▶**cry off** *vi* se dédire; se décommander.

crying ['kraɪɪŋ] *adj* (*fig*) criant(e), flagrant(e).

crypt [krɪpt] *n* crypte *f*.

cryptic ['krɪptɪk] *adj* énigmatique.

crystal ['krɪstl] *n* cristal *m*.

crystal-clear ['krɪstl'klɪəʳ] *adj* clair(e) comme de l'eau de roche.

crystallize ['krɪstəlaɪz] *vt* cristalliser ♦ *vi* (se) cristalliser; ~**d fruits** (*BRIT*) fruits confits.

CSA *n abbr* = *Confederate States of America;* (*BRIT*: = *Child Support Agency*) organisme pour la protection des enfants de parents séparés, qui contrôle le versement des pensions alimentaires.

CSC *n abbr* (= *Civil Service Commission*) commission de recrutement des fonctionnaires.

CSE *n abbr* (*BRIT*: = *Certificate of Secondary Education*) ≈ BEPC *m*.

CS gas *n* (*BRIT*) gaz *m* C.S.

CST *abbr* (*US*: = *Central Standard Time*) fuseau horaire.

CT *abbr* (*US*) = *Connecticut.*

ct *abbr* = **carat.**

CTC n abbr (BRIT) = **city technology college**.
CT scanner n abbr (MED: = computerized tomography scanner) scanner m, tomodensitomètre m.
cu. abbr = **cubic**.
cub [kʌb] n petit m (d'un animal); (also: ~ **scout**) louveteau m.
Cuba ['kju:bə] n Cuba m.
Cuban ['kju:bən] adj cubain(e) ♦ n Cubain/e.
cubbyhole ['kʌbɪhəʊl] n cagibi m.
cube [kju:b] n cube m ♦ vt (MATH) élever au cube.
cube root n racine f cubique.
cubic ['kju:bɪk] adj cubique; ~ **metre** etc mètre m etc cube; ~ **capacity** (AUT) cylindrée f.
cubicle ['kju:bɪkl] n box m, cabine f.
cuckoo ['kuku:] n coucou m.
cuckoo clock n (pendule f à) coucou m.
cucumber ['kju:kʌmbə*] n concombre m.
cud [kʌd] n: **to chew the** ~ ruminer.
cuddle ['kʌdl] vt câliner, caresser ♦ vi se blottir l'un contre l'autre.
cuddly ['kʌdlɪ] adj câlin(e).
cudgel ['kʌdʒl] n gourdin m ♦ vt: **to** ~ **one's brains** se creuser la tête.
cue [kju:] n queue f de billard; (THEAT etc) signal m.
cuff [kʌf] n (of shirt, coat etc) poignet m, manchette f; (US: on trousers) revers m; (blow) gifle f ♦ vt gifler; **off the** ~ adv de chic, à l'improviste.
cufflink ['kʌflɪŋk] n bouton m de manchette.
cu. in. abbr = cubic inches.
cuisine [kwɪ'zi:n] n cuisine f, art m culinaire.
cul-de-sac ['kʌldəsæk] n cul-de-sac m, impasse f.
culinary ['kʌlɪnərɪ] adj culinaire.
cull [kʌl] vt sélectionner; (kill selectively) pratiquer l'abattage sélectif de.
culminate ['kʌlmɪneɪt] vi: **to** ~ **in** finir or se terminer par; (lead to) mener à.
culmination [kʌlmɪ'neɪʃən] n point culminant.
culottes [kju:'lɒts] npl jupe-culotte f.
culpable ['kʌlpəbl] adj coupable.
culprit ['kʌlprɪt] n coupable m/f.
cult [kʌlt] n culte m.
cult figure n idole f.
cultivate ['kʌltɪveɪt] vt (also fig) cultiver.
cultivation [kʌltɪ'veɪʃən] n culture f.
cultural ['kʌltʃərəl] adj culturel(le).
culture ['kʌltʃə*] n (also fig) culture f.
cultured ['kʌltʃəd] adj cultivé(e) (fig).
cumbersome ['kʌmbəsəm] adj encombrant(e), embarrassant(e).
cumin ['kʌmɪn] n (spice) cumin m.
cumulative ['kju:mjulətɪv] adj cumulatif(ive).
cunning ['kʌnɪŋ] n ruse f, astuce f ♦ adj rusé(e), malin(igne); (clever: device, idea) astucieux(euse).
cunt [kʌnt] n (col!) chatte f (!); (insult) salaud m (!), salope f (!).

cup [kʌp] n tasse f; (prize, event) coupe f; (of bra) bonnet m; **a** ~ **of tea** une tasse de thé.
cupboard ['kʌbəd] n placard m.
cup final n (BRIT FOOTBALL) finale f de la coupe.
Cupid ['kju:pɪd] n Cupidon m; (figurine) amour m.
cupidity [kju:'pɪdɪtɪ] n cupidité f.
cupola ['kju:pələ] n coupole f.
cuppa ['kʌpə] n (BRIT col) tasse f de thé.
cup-tie ['kʌptaɪ] n (BRIT FOOTBALL) match m de coupe.
curable ['kjuərəbl] adj guérissable, curable.
curate ['kjuərɪt] n vicaire m.
curator [kjuə'reɪtə*] n conservateur m (d'un musée etc).
curb [kə:b] vt refréner, mettre un frein à; (expenditure) limiter, juguler ♦ n frein m (fig); (US) = **kerb**.
curd cheese n ≈ fromage blanc.
curdle ['kə:dl] vi (se) cailler.
curds [kə:dz] npl lait caillé.
cure [kjuə*] vt guérir; (CULIN) saler; fumer; sécher ♦ n remède m; **to be** ~**d of sth** être guéri de qch.
cure-all ['kjuərɔ:l] n (also fig) panacée f.
curfew ['kə:fju:] n couvre-feu m.
curio ['kjuərɪəu] n bibelot m, curiosité f.
curiosity [kjuərɪ'ɔsɪtɪ] n curiosité f.
curious ['kjuərɪəs] adj curieux(euse); **I'm** ~ **about him** il m'intrigue.
curiously ['kjuərɪəslɪ] adv curieusement; (inquisitively) avec curiosité; ~ **enough,** ... bizarrement, ...
curl [kə:l] n boucle f (de cheveux); (of smoke etc) volute f ♦ vt, vi boucler; (tightly) friser.
▶**curl up** vi s'enrouler; se pelotonner.
curler ['kə:lə*] n bigoudi m, rouleau m; (SPORT) joueur/euse de curling.
curlew ['kə:lu:] n courlis m.
curling ['kə:lɪŋ] n (sport) curling m.
curling tongs, (US) **curling irons** npl fer m à friser.
curly ['kə:lɪ] adj bouclé(e); (tightly curled) frisé(e).
currant ['kʌrnt] n raisin m de Corinthe, raisin sec.
currency ['kʌrnsɪ] n monnaie f; **foreign** ~ devises étrangères, monnaie étrangère; **to gain** ~ (fig) s'accréditer.
current ['kʌrnt] n courant m ♦ adj courant(e); (tendency, price, event) actuel(le); **direct/ alternating** ~ (ELEC) courant continu/ alternatif; **the** ~ **issue of a magazine** le dernier numéro d'un magazine; **in** ~ **use** d'usage courant.
current account n (BRIT) compte courant.
current affairs npl (questions fpl d')actualité f.
current assets npl (COMM) actif m disponible.
current liabilities npl (COMM) passif m exigible.

currently ['kʌrntlɪ] *adv* actuellement.
curriculum, *pl* ~**s** *or* **curricula** [kə'rɪkjuləm, -lə] *n* programme *m* d'études.
curriculum vitae (CV) [-'viːtaɪ] *n* curriculum vitae (CV) *m*.
curry ['kʌrɪ] *n* curry *m* ♦ *vt*: **to ~ favour with** chercher à gagner la faveur *or* à s'attirer les bonnes grâces de; **chicken ~** curry de poulet, poulet *m* au curry.
curry powder *n* poudre *f* de curry.
curse [kəːs] *vi* jurer, blasphémer ♦ *vt* maudire ♦ *n* malédiction *f*; fléau *m*; (*swearword*) juron *m*.
cursor ['kəːsə*] *n* (*COMPUT*) curseur *m*.
cursory ['kəːsərɪ] *adj* superficiel(le), hâtif(ive).
curt [kəːt] *adj* brusque, sec(sèche).
curtail [kəː'teɪl] *vt* (*visit etc*) écourter; (*expenses etc*) réduire.
curtain ['kəːtn] *n* rideau *m*; **to draw the ~s** (*together*) fermer *or* tirer les rideaux; (*apart*) ouvrir les rideaux.
curtain call *n* (*THEAT*) rappel *m*.
curts(e)y ['kəːtsɪ] *n* révérence *f* ♦ *vi* faire une révérence.
curvature ['kəːvətʃə*] *n* courbure *f*.
curve [kəːv] *n* courbe *f*; (*in the road*) tournant *m*, virage *m* ♦ *vt* courber ♦ *vi* se courber; (*road*) faire une courbe.
curved [kəːvd] *adj* courbe.
cushion ['kuʃən] *n* coussin *m* ♦ *vt* (*seat*) rembourrer; (*shock*) amortir.
cushy ['kuʃɪ] *adj* (*col*): **a ~ job** un boulot de tout repos; **to have a ~ time** se la couler douce.
custard ['kʌstəd] *n* (*for pouring*) crème anglaise.
custard powder *n* (*BRIT*) ≈ crème pâtissière instantanée.
custodial sentence [kʌs'təudɪəl-] *n* peine *f* de prison.
custodian [kʌs'təudɪən] *n* gardien/ne; (*of collection etc*) conservateur/trice.
custody ['kʌstədɪ] *n* (*of child*) garde *f*; (*for offenders*) détention préventive; **to take sb into ~** placer qn en détention préventive; **in the ~ of** sous la garde de.
custom ['kʌstəm] *n* coutume *f*, usage *m*; (*LAW*) droit coutumier, coutume; (*COMM*) clientèle *f*.
customary ['kʌstəmərɪ] *adj* habituel(le); **it is ~ to do it** l'usage veut qu'on le fasse.
custom-built ['kʌstəm'bɪlt] *adj see* **custom-made.**
customer ['kʌstəmə*] *n* client/e; **he's an awkward ~** (*col*) ce n'est pas quelqu'un de facile.
customer profile *n* profil *m* du client.
customized ['kʌstəmaɪzd] *adj* personnalisé(e).
custom-made ['kʌstəm'meɪd] *adj* (*clothes*) fait(e) sur mesure; (*other goods: also:* **custom-built**) hors série, fait(e) sur commande.
customs ['kʌstəmz] *npl* douane *f*; **to go through (the) ~** passer la douane.
Customs and Excise *n* (*BRIT*) administration *f* des douanes.
customs officer *n* douanier *m*.
cut [kʌt] *vb* (*pt, pp* **cut**) *vt* couper; (*meat*) découper; (*shape, make*) tailler; couper; creuser; graver; (*reduce*) réduire; (*col: lecture, appointment*) manquer ♦ *vi* couper; (*intersect*) se couper ♦ *n* (*gen*) coupure *f*; (*of clothes*) coupe *f*; (*of jewel*) taille *f*; (*in salary etc*) réduction *f*; (*of meat*) morceau *m*; **cold ~s** *npl* (*US*) viandes froides; **to ~ teeth** (*baby*) faire ses dents; **to ~ a tooth** percer une dent; **to ~ one's finger** se couper le doigt; **to get one's hair ~** se faire couper les cheveux; **to ~ sth short** couper court à qch; **to ~ sb dead** ignorer (complètement) qn.
▶**cut back** *vt* (*plants*) tailler; (*production, expenditure*) réduire.
▶**cut down** *vt* (*tree*) abattre; (*reduce*) réduire; **to ~ sb down to size** (*fig*) remettre qn à sa place.
▶**cut down on** *vt fus* réduire.
▶**cut in** *vi* (*interrupt: conversation*): **to ~ in (on)** couper la parole (à); (*AUT*) faire une queue de poisson.
▶**cut off** *vt* couper; (*fig*) isoler; **we've been ~ off** (*TEL*) nous avons été coupés.
▶**cut out** *vt* (*picture etc*) découper; (*remove*) ôter; supprimer.
▶**cut up** *vt* découper.
cut-and-dried ['kʌtən'draɪd] *adj* (*also:* **cut-and-dry**) tout(e) fait(e), tout(e) décidé(e).
cutaway ['kʌtəweɪ] *adj, n*: ~ (**drawing**) écorché *m*.
cutback ['kʌtbæk] *n* réduction *f*.
cute [kjuːt] *adj* mignon(ne), adorable; (*clever*) rusé(e), astucieux(euse).
cut glass *n* cristal taillé.
cuticle ['kjuːtɪkl] *n* (*on nail*): ~ **remover** repousse-peaux *m inv*.
cutlery ['kʌtlərɪ] *n* couverts *mpl*; (*trade*) coutellerie *f*.
cutlet ['kʌtlɪt] *n* côtelette *f*.
cutoff ['kʌtɔf] *n* (*also:* ~ **point**) seuil-limite *m*.
cutoff switch *n* interrupteur *m*.
cutout ['kʌtaut] *n* coupe-circuit *m inv*; (*paper figure*) découpage *m*.
cut-price ['kʌt'praɪs], (*US*) **cut-rate** ['kʌt'reɪt] *adj* au rabais, à prix réduit.
cutthroat ['kʌtθrəut] *n* assassin *m* ♦ *adj*: ~ **competition** concurrence *f* sauvage.
cutting ['kʌtɪŋ] *adj* tranchant(e), coupant(e); (*fig*) cinglant(e), mordant(e) ♦ *n* (*BRIT: from newspaper*) coupure *f* (de journal); (: *RAIL*) tranchée *f*; (*CINE*) montage *m*.
cutting edge *n* (*of knife*) tranchant *m*; **on** *or* **at the ~ of** à la pointe de.
cuttlefish ['kʌtlfɪʃ] *n* seiche *f*.
cut-up ['kʌtʌp] *adj* affecté(e), démoralisé(e).

CV *n abbr* = **curriculum vitae**.
cwo *abbr* (*COMM*) = **cash with order**.
cwt. *abbr* = **hundredweight**.
cyanide ['saɪənaɪd] *n* cyanure *m*.
cybernetics [saɪbə'nɛtɪks] *n* cybernétique *f*.
cyclamen ['sɪkləmən] *n* cyclamen *m*.
cycle ['saɪkl] *n* cycle *m* ♦ *vi* faire de la bicyclette.
cycle race *n* course *f* cycliste.
cycle rack *n* râtelier *m* à bicyclette.
cycling ['saɪklɪŋ] *n* cyclisme *m*; **to go on a ~ holiday** (*BRIT*) faire du cyclotourisme.
cyclist ['saɪklɪst] *n* cycliste *m/f*.
cyclone ['saɪkləun] *n* cyclone *m*.
cygnet ['sɪgnɪt] *n* jeune cygne *m*.
cylinder ['sɪlɪndə*] *n* cylindre *m*.
cylinder block *n* bloc-cylindres *m*.
cylinder capacity *n* cylindrée *f*.
cylinder head *n* culasse *f*.
cylinder-head gasket ['sɪlɪndəhɛd-] *n* joint *m* de culasse.
cymbals ['sɪmblz] *npl* cymbales *fpl*.
cynic ['sɪnɪk] *n* cynique *m/f*.
cynical ['sɪnɪkl] *adj* cynique.
cynicism ['sɪnɪsɪzəm] *n* cynisme *m*.
CYO *n abbr* (*US*: = *Catholic Youth Organization*) ≈ JC *f*.
cypress ['saɪprɪs] *n* cyprès *m*.
Cypriot ['sɪprɪət] *adj* cypriote, chypriote ♦ *n* Cypriote *m/f*, Chypriote *m/f*.
Cyprus ['saɪprəs] *n* Chypre *f*.
cyst [sɪst] *n* kyste *m*.
cystitis [sɪs'taɪtɪs] *n* cystite *f*.
CZ *n abbr* (*US*: = *Central Zone*) zone du canal de Panama.
czar [zɑː*] *n* tsar *m*.
Czech [tʃɛk] *adj* tchèque ♦ *n* Tchèque *m/f*; (*LING*) tchèque *m*; **the ~ Republic** la République tchèque.
Czechoslovak [tʃɛkə'sləuvæk] *adj*, *n* = **Czechoslovakian**.
Czechoslovakia [tʃɛkəslə'vækɪə] *n* Tchécoslovaquie *f*.
Czechoslovakian [tʃɛkəslə'vækɪən] *adj* tchécoslovaque ♦ *n* Tchécoslovaque *m/f*.

D d

D, d [diː] *n* (*letter*) D, d *m*; (*MUS*): **D** ré *m*; **D for David**, (*US*) **D for Dog** D comme Désirée.
D *abbr* (*US POL*) = **democrat(ic)**.
d *abbr* (*BRIT*: *old*) = **penny**.
d. *abbr* = **died**.
DA *n abbr* (*US*) = **district attorney**.
dab [dæb] *vt* (*eyes, wound*) tamponner; (*paint, cream*) appliquer (par petites touches *or* rapidement); **a ~ of paint** un petit coup de peinture.
dabble ['dæbl] *vi*: **to ~ in** faire *or* se mêler *or* s'occuper un peu de.
Dacca ['dækə] *n* Dacca.
dachshund ['dækshund] *n* teckel *m*.
dad, daddy [dæd, 'dædɪ] *n* papa *m*.
daddy-long-legs [dædɪ'lɔŋlɛgz] *n* tipule *f*; faucheux *m*.
daffodil ['dæfədɪl] *n* jonquille *f*.
daft [dɑːft] *adj* (*col*) idiot(e), stupide; **to be ~ about** être toqué(e) *or* mordu(e) de.
dagger ['dægə*] *n* poignard *m*; **to be at ~s drawn with sb** être à couteaux tirés avec qn; **to look ~s at sb** foudroyer qn du regard.
dahlia ['deɪljə] *n* dahlia *m*.
daily ['deɪlɪ] *adj* quotidien(ne), journalier(ière) ♦ *n* quotidien *m*; (*BRIT*: *servant*) femme *f* de ménage (*à la journée*) ♦ *adv* tous les jours; **twice ~** deux fois par jour.
dainty ['deɪntɪ] *adj* délicat(e), mignon(ne).
dairy ['dɛərɪ] *n* (*shop*) crémerie *f*, laiterie *f*; (*on farm*) laiterie ♦ *adj* laitier(ière).
dairy cow *n* vache laitière.
dairy farm *n* exploitation *f* pratiquant l'élevage laitier.
dairy produce *n* produits laitiers.
dais ['deɪɪs] *n* estrade *f*.
daisy ['deɪzɪ] *n* pâquerette *f*.
daisy wheel *n* (*on printer*) marguerite *f*.
daisy-wheel printer ['deɪzɪwiːl-] *n* imprimante *f* à marguerite.
Dakar ['dækə] *n* Dakar.
dale [deɪl] *n* vallon *m*.
dally ['dælɪ] *vi* musarder, flâner.
dalmatian [dæl'meɪʃən] *n* (*dog*) dalmatien/ne.
dam [dæm] *n* barrage *m*; (*reservoir*) réservoir *m*, lac *m* de retenue ♦ *vt* endiguer.
damage ['dæmɪdʒ] *n* dégâts *mpl*, dommages *mpl*; (*fig*) tort *m* ♦ *vt* endommager, abîmer; (*fig*) faire du tort à; **~ to property** dégâts matériels.
damages ['dæmɪdʒɪz] *npl* (*LAW*) dommages-intérêts *mpl*; **to pay £5000 in ~** payer 5000 livres de dommages-intérêts.
damaging ['dæmɪdʒɪŋ] *adj*: **~ (to)** préjudiciable (à), nuisible (à).
Damascus [də'mɑːskəs] *n* Damas.
dame [deɪm] *n* (*title*) titre porté par une *femme décorée de l'ordre de l'Empire Britannique ou d'un ordre de chevalerie*; *titre porté par la femme ou la veuve d'un chevalier ou baronnet*; (*US col*) nana *f*; (*THEAT*) vieille dame (*rôle comique joué par un homme*).
damn [dæm] *vt* condamner; (*curse*) maudire ♦ *n* (*col*): **I don't give a ~** je m'en fous ♦ *adj* (*col*): **this ~ ...** ce sacré *or* foutu ...; **~ (it)!** zut!

damnable ['dæmnəbl] *adj* (*col: behaviour*) odieux(euse), détestable; (: *weather*) épouvantable, abominable.

damnation [dæm'neɪʃən] *n* (*REL*) damnation *f* ♦ *excl* (*col*) malédiction!, merde!

damning ['dæmɪŋ] *adj* (*evidence*) accablant(e).

damp [dæmp] *adj* humide ♦ *n* humidité *f* ♦ *vt* (*also: ~en: cloth, rag*) humecter; (: *enthusiasm etc*) refroidir.

dampcourse ['dæmpkɔːs] *n* couche isolante (contre l'humidité).

damper ['dæmpə*] *n* (*MUS*) étouffoir *m*; (*of fire*) registre *m*; **to put a ~ on** (*fig: atmosphere, enthusiasm*) refroidir.

dampness ['dæmpnɪs] *n* humidité *f*.

damson ['dæmzən] *n* prune *f* de Damas.

dance [dɑːns] *n* danse *f*; (*ball*) bal *m* ♦ *vi* danser; **to ~ about** sautiller, gambader.

dance hall *n* salle *f* de bal, dancing *m*.

dancer ['dɑːnsə*] *n* danseur/euse.

dancing ['dɑːnsɪŋ] *n* danse *f*.

D and C *n abbr* (*MED: = dilation and curettage*) curetage *m*.

dandelion ['dændɪlaɪən] *n* pissenlit *m*.

dandruff ['dændrəf] *n* pellicules *fpl*.

dandy ['dændɪ] *n* dandy *m*, élégant *m* ♦ *adj* (*US col*) fantastique, super.

Dane [deɪn] *n* Danois/e.

danger ['deɪndʒə*] *n* danger *m*; **there is a ~ of fire** il y a (un) risque d'incendie; **in ~** en danger; **he was in ~ of falling** il risquait de tomber; **out of ~** hors de danger.

danger list *n* (*MED*): **on the ~** dans un état critique.

danger money *n* (*BRIT*) prime *f* de risque.

dangerous ['deɪndʒrəs] *adj* dangereux(euse).

dangerously ['deɪndʒrəslɪ] *adv* dangereusement; **~ ill** très gravement malade, en danger de mort.

danger zone *n* zone dangereuse.

dangle ['dæŋgl] *vt* balancer; (*fig*) faire miroiter ♦ *vi* pendre, se balancer.

Danish ['deɪnɪʃ] *adj* danois(e) ♦ *n* (*LING*) danois *m*.

Danish pastry *n* feuilleté *m* (*recouvert d'un glaçage et fourré aux fruits etc*).

dank [dæŋk] *adj* froid(e) et humide.

Danube ['dænjuːb] *n*: **the ~** le Danube.

dapper ['dæpə*] *adj* pimpant(e).

Dardanelles [dɑːdə'nɛlz] *npl* Dardanelles *fpl*.

dare [dɛə*] *vt*: **to ~ sb to do** défier qn *or* mettre qn au défi de faire ♦ *vi*: **to ~ (to) do sth** oser faire qch; **I ~n't tell him** (*BRIT*) je n'ose pas le lui dire; **I ~ say he'll turn up** il est probable qu'il viendra.

daredevil ['dɛədɛvl] *n* casse-cou *m inv*.

Dar-es-Salaam [dɑːrɛssə'lɑːm] *n* Dar-es-Salaam, Dar-es-Salam.

daring ['dɛərɪŋ] *adj* hardi(e), audacieux(euse) ♦ *n* audace *f*, hardiesse *f*.

dark [dɑːk] *adj* (*night, room*) obscur(e), sombre; (*colour, complexion*) foncé(e), sombre; (*fig*) sombre ♦ *n*: **in the ~** dans le noir; **in the ~ about** (*fig*) ignorant tout de; **after ~** après la tombée de la nuit; **it is/is getting ~** il fait nuit/commence à faire nuit.

darken [dɑːkn] *vt* obscurcir, assombrir ♦ *vi* s'obscurcir, s'assombrir.

dark glasses *npl* lunettes noires.

dark horse *n* (*fig*): **he's a ~** on ne sait pas grand-chose de lui.

darkly ['dɑːklɪ] *adv* (*gloomily*) mélancoliquement; (*in a sinister way*) lugubrement.

darkness ['dɑːknɪs] *n* obscurité *f*.

darkroom ['dɑːkrum] *n* chambre noire.

darling ['dɑːlɪŋ] *adj*, *n* chéri(e).

darn [dɑːn] *vt* repriser.

dart [dɑːt] *n* fléchette *f* ♦ *vi*: **to ~ towards** (*also: make a ~ towards*) se précipiter *or* s'élancer vers; **to ~ away/along** partir/passer comme une flèche.

dartboard ['dɑːtbɔːd] *n* cible *f* (de jeu de fléchettes).

darts [dɑːts] *n* jeu *m* de fléchettes.

dash [dæʃ] *n* (*sign*) tiret *m*; (*small quantity*) goutte *f*, larme *f* ♦ *vt* (*missile*) jeter *or* lancer violemment; (*hopes*) anéantir ♦ *vi*: **to ~ towards** (*also: make a ~ towards*) se précipiter *or* se ruer vers; **a ~ of soda** un peu d'eau gazeuse.

▶**dash away** *vi* partir à toute allure.

dashboard ['dæʃbɔːd] *n* (*AUT*) tableau *m* de bord.

dashing ['dæʃɪŋ] *adj* fringant(e).

dastardly ['dæstədlɪ] *adj* lâche.

DAT *n abbr* (= *digital audio tape*) cassette *f* audio digitale.

data ['deɪtə] *npl* données *fpl*.

database ['deɪtəbeɪs] *n* base *f* de données.

data capture *n* saisie *f* de données.

data processing *n* traitement *m* (électronique) de l'information.

data transmission *n* transmission *f* de données.

date [deɪt] *n* date *f*; (*appointment*) rendez-vous *m*; (*fruit*) datte *f* ♦ *vt* dater; (*col: girl etc*) sortir avec; **what's the ~ today?** quelle date sommes-nous aujourd'hui?; **~ of birth** date de naissance; **closing ~** date de clôture; **to ~ adv** à ce jour; **out of ~** périmé(e); **up to ~** à la page; mis(e) à jour; moderne; **to bring up to ~** (*correspondence, information*) mettre à jour; (*method*) moderniser; (*person*) mettre au courant; **letter ~d 5th July** *or* (*US*) **July 5th** lettre (datée) du 5 juillet.

dated ['deɪtɪd] *adj* démodé(e).

dateline ['deɪtlaɪn] *n* ligne *f* de changement de date.

date rape *n* viol *m* (*à l'issue d'un rendez-vous galant*).

date stamp *n* timbre-dateur *m*.

daub [dɔːb] *vt* barbouiller.

daughter ['dɔːtə*] *n* fille *f*.

daughter-in-law ['dɔːtərɪnlɔː] n belle-fille f, bru f.
daunt [dɔːnt] vt intimider, décourager.
daunting ['dɔːntɪŋ] adj décourageant(e), intimidant(e).
dauntless ['dɔːntlɪs] adj intrépide.
dawdle ['dɔːdl] vi traîner, lambiner; **to ~ over one's work** traînasser or lambiner sur son travail.
dawn [dɔːn] n aube f, aurore f ♦ vi (day) se lever, poindre; (fig) naître, se faire jour; **at ~** à l'aube; **from ~ to dusk** du matin au soir; **it ~ed on him that ...** il lui vint à l'esprit que ....
dawn chorus n (BRIT) chant m des oiseaux à l'aube.
day [deɪ] n jour m; (as duration) journée f; (period of time, age) époque f, temps m; **the ~ before** la veille, le jour précédent; **the ~ after, the following ~** le lendemain, le jour suivant; **the ~ before yesterday** avant-hier; **the ~ after tomorrow** après-demain; **(on) the ~ that ...** le jour où ...; **~ by ~** jour après jour; **by ~** de jour; **paid by the ~** payé(e) à la journée; **these ~s, in the present ~** de nos jours, à l'heure actuelle.
daybook ['deɪbuk] n (BRIT) main courante, brouillard m, journal m.
day boy n (SCOL) externe m.
daybreak ['deɪbreɪk] n point m du jour.
daycare centre ['deɪkɛə-] n garderie f.
daydream ['deɪdriːm] n rêverie f ♦ vi rêver (tout éveillé).
day girl n (SCOL) externe f.
daylight ['deɪlaɪt] n (lumière f du) jour m.
daylight robbery n: **it's ~** (fig, col) c'est du vol caractérisé or manifeste.
daylight saving time n (US) heure f d'été.
day release n: **to be on ~** avoir une journée de congé pour formation professionnelle.
day return (ticket) n (BRIT) billet m d'aller-retour (valable pour la journée).
day shift n équipe f de jour.
daytime ['deɪtaɪm] n jour m, journée f.
day-to-day ['deɪtə'deɪ] adj (routine, expenses) journalier(ière); **on a ~ basis** au jour le jour.
day trip n excursion f (d'une journée).
day tripper n excursionniste m/f.
daze [deɪz] vt (subj: drug) hébéter; (: blow) étourdir ♦ n: **in a ~** hébété(e); étourdi(e).
dazzle ['dæzl] vt éblouir, aveugler.
dazzling ['dæzlɪŋ] adj (light) aveuglant(e), éblouissant(e); (fig) éblouissant(e).
DC abbr (ELEC) = direct current; (US) = District of Columbia.
DCC n abbr ® (= digital compact cassette) DCC ®.
DD n abbr (= Doctor of Divinity) titre universitaire.
dd. abbr (COMM) = delivered.
D/D abbr = direct debit.

D-day ['diːdeɪ] n le jour J.
DDS n abbr (US: = Doctor of Dental Science, Doctor of Dental Surgery) titres universitaires.
DDT n abbr (= dichlorodiphenyl trichloroethane) DDT m.
DE abbr (US) = Delaware.
DEA n abbr (US: = Drug Enforcement Administration) ≈ brigade f des stupéfiants.
deacon ['diːkən] n diacre m.
dead [dɛd] adj mort(e); (numb) engourdi(e), insensible ♦ adv absolument, complètement; **the ~** npl les morts; **he was shot ~** il a été tué d'un coup de revolver; **~ on time** à l'heure pile; **~ tired** éreinté(e), complètement fourbu(e); **to stop ~** s'arrêter pile or net; **the line has gone ~** (TEL) on n'entend plus rien.
dead beat adj (col) claqué(e), crevé(e).
deaden [dɛdn] vt (blow, sound) amortir; (make numb) endormir, rendre insensible.
dead end n impasse f.
dead-end ['dɛdɛnd] adj: **a ~ job** un emploi or poste sans avenir.
dead heat n (SPORT): **to finish in a ~** terminer ex aequo.
dead-letter office [dɛd'lɛtər-] n ≈ centre m de recherche du courrier.
deadline ['dɛdlaɪn] n date f or heure f limite; **to work to a ~** avoir des délais stricts à respecter.
deadlock ['dɛdlɔk] n impasse f (fig).
dead loss n (col): **to be a ~** (person) n'être bon(bonne) à rien; (thing) ne rien valoir.
deadly ['dɛdlɪ] adj mortel(le); (weapon) meurtrier(ière); **~ dull** ennuyeux(euse) à mourir, mortellement ennuyeux.
deadpan ['dɛdpæn] adj impassible; (humour) pince-sans-rire inv.
Dead Sea n: **the ~** la mer Morte.
dead season n (TOURISM) morte saison.
deaf [dɛf] adj sourd(e); **to turn a ~ ear to sth** faire la sourde oreille à qch.
deaf-aid ['dɛfeɪd] n (BRIT) appareil auditif.
deaf-and-dumb ['dɛfən'dʌm] adj sourd(e)-muet(te); **~ alphabet** alphabet m des sourds-muets.
deafen ['dɛfn] vt rendre sourd(e); (fig) assourdir.
deafening ['dɛfnɪŋ] adj assourdissant(e).
deaf-mute ['dɛfmjuːt] n sourd/e-muet/te.
deafness ['dɛfnɪs] n surdité f.
deal [diːl] n affaire f, marché m ♦ vt (pt, pp **dealt** [dɛlt]) (blow) porter; (cards) donner, distribuer; **to strike a ~ with sb** faire or conclure un marché avec qn; **it's a ~!** (col) marché conclu!, tope-là!, topez-là!; **he got a bad ~ from them** ils ont mal agi envers lui; **he got a fair ~ from them** ils ont agi loyalement envers lui; **a good ~** (a lot) beaucoup; **a good ~ of, a great ~ of** beaucoup de, énormément de.

▶**deal in** *vt fus* (*COMM*) faire le commerce de, être dans le commerce de.

▶**deal with** *vt fus* (*COMM*) traiter avec; (*handle*) s'occuper *or* se charger de; (*be about: book etc*) traiter de.

dealer ['di:lə*] *n* marchand *m*.

dealership ['di:ləʃɪp] *n* concession *f*.

dealings ['di:lɪŋz] *npl* (*in goods, shares*) opérations *fpl*, transactions *fpl*; (*relations*) relations *fpl*, rapports *mpl*.

dealt [dɛlt] *pt, pp of* **deal**.

dean [di:n] *n* (*REL, BRIT SCOL*) doyen *m*; (*US SCOL*) conseiller/ère (principal(e)) d'éducation.

dear [dɪə*] *adj* cher(chère); (*expensive*) cher, coûteux(euse) ♦ *n*: **my ~** mon cher/ma chère; **~ me!** mon Dieu!; **D~ Sir/Madam** (*in letter*) Monsieur/Madame; **D~ Mr/Mrs X** Cher Monsieur/Chère Madame X.

dearly ['dɪəlɪ] *adv* (*love*) tendrement; (*pay*) cher.

dearth [də:θ] *n* disette *f*, pénurie *f*.

death [dɛθ] *n* mort *f*; (*ADMIN*) décès *m*.

deathbed ['dɛθbɛd] *n* lit *m* de mort.

death certificate *n* acte *m* de décès.

death duties *npl* (*BRIT*) droits *mpl* de succession.

deathly ['dɛθlɪ] *adj* de mort ♦ *adv* comme la mort.

death penalty *n* peine *f* de mort.

death rate *n* taux *m* de mortalité.

death row [-'rəu] *n* (*US*) quartier *m* des condamnés à mort; **to be on ~** être condamné à la peine de mort.

death sentence *n* condamnation *f* à mort.

death squad *n* escadron *m* de la mort.

deathtrap ['dɛθtræp] *n* endroit (*or* véhicule *etc*) dangereux.

deb [dɛb] *n abbr* (*col*) = **debutante**.

debar [dɪ'bɑ:*] *vt*: **to ~ sb from a club** *etc* exclure qn d'un club *etc*; **to ~ sb from doing** interdire à qn de faire.

debase [dɪ'beɪs] *vt* (*currency*) déprécier, dévaloriser; (*person*) abaisser, avilir.

debatable [dɪ'beɪtəbl] *adj* discutable, contestable; **it is ~ whether ...** il est douteux que ....

debate [dɪ'beɪt] *n* discussion *f*, débat *m* ♦ *vt* discuter, débattre ♦ *vi* (*consider*): **to ~ whether** se demander si.

debauchery [dɪ'bɔ:tʃərɪ] *n* débauche *f*.

debenture [dɪ'bɛntʃə*] *n* (*COMM*) obligation *f*.

debilitate [dɪ'bɪlɪteɪt] *vt* débiliter.

debit ['dɛbɪt] *n* débit *m* ♦ *vt*: **to ~ a sum to sb** *or* **to sb's account** porter une somme au débit de qn, débiter qn d'une somme.

debit balance *n* solde débiteur.

debit note *n* note *f* de débit.

debrief [di:'bri:f] *vt* demander un compte rendu de fin de mission à.

debriefing [di:'bri:fɪŋ] *n* compte rendu *m*.

debris ['dɛbri:] *n* débris *mpl*, décombres *mpl*.

debt [dɛt] *n* dette *f*; **to be in ~** avoir des dettes, être endetté(e); **bad ~** créance *f* irrécouvrable.

debt collector *n* agent *m* de recouvrements.

debtor ['dɛtə*] *n* débiteur/trice.

debug ['di:'bʌg] *vt* (*COMPUT*) déverminer.

debunk [di:'bʌŋk] *vt* (*theory, claim*) montrer le ridicule de.

debut ['deɪbju:] *n* début(s) *m(pl)*.

debutante ['dɛbjutænt] *n* débutante *f*.

Dec. *abbr* (= *December*) déc.

decade ['dɛkeɪd] *n* décennie *f*, décade *f*.

decadence ['dɛkədəns] *n* décadence *f*.

decadent ['dɛkədənt] *adj* décadent(e).

de-caff ['di:kæf] *n* (*col*) déca *m*.

decaffeinated [dɪ'kæfɪneɪtɪd] *adj* décaféiné(e).

decamp [dɪ'kæmp] *vi* (*col*) décamper, filer.

decant [dɪ'kænt] *vt* (*wine*) décanter.

decanter [dɪ'kæntə*] *n* carafe *f*.

decarbonize [di:'kɑ:bənaɪz] *vt* (*AUT*) décalaminer.

decathlon [dɪ'kæθlən] *n* décathlon *m*.

decay [dɪ'keɪ] *n* décomposition *f*, pourrissement *m*; (*fig*) déclin *m*, délabrement *m*; (*also*: **tooth ~**) carie *f* (dentaire) ♦ *vi* (*rot*) se décomposer, pourrir; (*fig*) se délabrer; décliner; se détériorer.

decease [dɪ'si:s] *n* décès *m*.

deceased [dɪ'si:st] *n*: **the ~** le/la défunt/e.

deceit [dɪ'si:t] *n* tromperie *f*, supercherie *f*.

deceitful [dɪ'si:tful] *adj* trompeur(euse).

deceive [dɪ'si:v] *vt* tromper; **to ~ o.s.** s'abuser.

decelerate [di:'sɛləreɪt] *vt, vi* ralentir.

December [dɪ'sɛmbə*] *n* décembre *m*; *for phrases see also* **July**.

decency ['di:sənsɪ] *n* décence *f*.

decent ['di:sənt] *adj* décent(e), convenable; **they were very ~ about it** ils se sont montrés très chics.

decently ['di:səntlɪ] *adv* (*respectably*) décemment, convenablement; (*kindly*) décemment.

decentralization [di:sɛntrəlaɪ'zeɪʃən] *n* décentralisation *f*.

decentralize [di:'sɛntrəlaɪz] *vt* décentraliser.

deception [dɪ'sɛpʃən] *n* tromperie *f*.

deceptive [dɪ'sɛptɪv] *adj* trompeur(euse).

decibel ['dɛsɪbɛl] *n* décibel *m*.

decide [dɪ'saɪd] *vt* (*person*) décider; (*question, argument*) trancher, régler ♦ *vi* se décider, décider; **to ~ to do/that** décider de faire/que; **to ~ on** décider, se décider pour; **to ~ on doing** décider de faire; **to ~ against doing** décider de ne pas faire.

decided [dɪ'saɪdɪd] *adj* (*resolute*) résolu(e), décidé(e); (*clear, definite*) net(te), marqué(e).

decidedly [dɪ'saɪdɪdlɪ] *adv* résolument; incontestablement, nettement.

deciding [dɪ'saɪdɪŋ] *adj* décisif(ive).

deciduous [dɪ'sɪdjuəs] *adj* à feuilles caduques.

decimal ['dɛsɪməl] adj décimal(e) ♦ n décimale f; **to three ~ places** (jusqu')à la troisième décimale.

decimalize ['dɛsɪməlaɪz] vt (BRIT) décimaliser.

decimal point n ≈ virgule f.

decimate ['dɛsɪmeɪt] vt décimer.

decipher [dɪ'saɪfə*] vt déchiffrer.

decision [dɪ'sɪʒən] n décision f; **to make a ~** prendre une décision.

decisive [dɪ'saɪsɪv] adj décisif(ive); (influence) décisif, déterminant(e); (manner, person) décidé(e), catégorique; (reply) ferme, catégorique.

deck [dɛk] n (NAUT) pont m; (of bus): **top ~** impériale f; (of cards) jeu m; **to go up on ~** monter sur le pont; **below ~** dans l'entrepont; **record/cassette ~** platine-disques/-cassettes f.

deckchair ['dɛktʃeə*] n chaise longue.

deck hand n matelot m.

declaration [dɛklə'reɪʃən] n déclaration f.

declare [dɪ'klɛə*] vt déclarer.

declassify [di:'klæsɪfaɪ] vt rendre accessible au public or à tous.

decline [dɪ'klaɪn] n (decay) déclin m; (lessening) baisse f ♦ vt refuser, décliner ♦ vi décliner; être en baisse, baisser; **~ in living standards** baisse du niveau de vie; **to ~ to do sth** refuser (poliment) de faire qch.

declutch ['di:'klʌtʃ] vi (BRIT) débrayer.

decode ['di:'kəud] vt décoder.

decoder [di:'kəudə*] n (COMPUT, TV) décodeur m.

decompose [di:kəm'pəuz] vi se décomposer.

decomposition [di:kɔmpə'zɪʃən] n décomposition f.

decompression [di:kəm'prɛʃən] n décompression f.

decompression chamber n caisson m de décompression.

decongestant [di:kən'dʒɛstənt] n décongestif m.

decontaminate [di:kən'tæmɪneɪt] vt décontaminer.

decontrol [di:kən'trəul] vt (prices etc) libérer.

décor ['deɪkɔ:*] n décor m.

decorate ['dɛkəreɪt] vt (adorn, give a medal to) décorer; (paint and paper) peindre et tapisser.

decoration [dɛkə'reɪʃən] n (medal etc, adornment) décoration f.

decorative ['dɛkərətɪv] adj décoratif(ive).

decorator ['dɛkəreɪtə*] n peintre m en bâtiment.

decorum [dɪ'kɔ:rəm] n décorum m, bienséance f.

decoy ['di:kɔɪ] n piège m; **they used him as a ~ for the enemy** ils se sont servis de lui pour attirer l'ennemi.

decrease n ['di:kri:s] diminution f ♦ vt, vi [di:'kri:s] diminuer; **to be on the ~** diminuer, être en diminution.

decreasing [di:'kri:sɪŋ] adj en voie de diminution.

decree [dɪ'kri:] n (POL, REL) décret m; (LAW) arrêt m, jugement m ♦ vt: **to ~ (that)** décréter (que), ordonner (que); **~ absolute** jugement définitif (de divorce); **~ nisi** jugement provisoire de divorce.

decrepit [dɪ'krɛpɪt] adj (person) décrépit(e); (building) délabré(e).

decry [dɪ'kraɪ] vt condamner ouvertement, déplorer; (disparage) dénigrer, décrier.

dedicate ['dɛdɪkeɪt] vt consacrer; (book etc) dédier.

dedicated ['dɛdɪkeɪtɪd] adj (person) dévoué(e); (COMPUT) spécialisé(e), dédié(e); **~ word processor** station f de traitement de texte.

dedication [dɛdɪ'keɪʃən] n (devotion) dévouement m; (in book) dédicace f.

deduce [dɪ'dju:s] vt déduire, conclure.

deduct [dɪ'dʌkt] vt: **to ~ sth (from)** déduire qch (de), retrancher qch (de); (from wage etc) prélever qch (sur), retenir qch (sur).

deduction [dɪ'dʌkʃən] n (deducting) déduction f; (from wage etc) prélèvement m, retenue f; (deducing) déduction, conclusion f.

deed [di:d] n action f, acte m; (LAW) acte notarié, contrat m; **~ of covenant** (acte m de) donation f.

deem [di:m] vt (formal) juger, estimer; **to ~ it wise to do** juger bon de faire.

deep [di:p] adj (water, sigh, sorrow, thoughts) profond(e); (voice) grave ♦ adv: **~ in snow** recouvert(e) d'une épaisse couche de neige; **spectators stood 20 ~** il y avait 20 rangs de spectateurs; **knee-~ in water** dans l'eau jusqu'aux genoux; **4 metres ~** de 4 mètres de profondeur; **he took a ~ breath** il inspira profondément, il prit son souffle.

deepen [di:pn] vt (hole) approfondir ♦ vi s'approfondir; (darkness) s'épaissir.

deep-freeze ['di:p'fri:z] n congélateur m ♦ vt surgeler.

deep-fry ['di:p'fraɪ] vt faire frire (dans une friteuse).

deeply ['di:plɪ] adv profondément; (dig) en profondeur; (regret, interest) vivement.

deep-rooted ['di:p'ru:tɪd] adj (prejudice) profondément enraciné(e); (affection) profond(e); (habit) invétéré(e).

deep-sea ['di:p'si:] adj: **~ diver** plongeur sous-marin; **~ diving** plongée sous-marine; **~ fishing** pêche hauturière.

deep-seated ['di:p'si:tɪd] adj (beliefs) profondément enraciné(e).

deep-set ['di:psɛt] adj (eyes) enfoncé(e).

deer [dɪə*] n (pl inv): **the ~** les cervidés mpl (ZOOL); **(red) ~** cerf m; **(fallow) ~** daim m; **(roe) ~** chevreuil m.

deerskin ['dɪəskɪn] n peau f de daim.

deerstalker ['dɪəstɔ:kə*] n (person) chasseur m de cerf; (hat) casquette f à la Sherlock Holmes.

deface [dɪ'feɪs] *vt* dégrader; barbouiller; rendre illisible.

defamation [dɛfə'meɪʃən] *n* diffamation *f*.

defamatory [dɪ'fæmətrɪ] *adj* diffamatoire, diffamant(e).

default [dɪ'fɔːlt] *vi* (*LAW*) faire défaut; (*gen*) manquer à ses engagements ♦ *n* (*COMPUT: also:* ~ **value**) valeur *f* par défaut; **by** ~ (*LAW*) par défaut, par contumace; (*SPORT*) par forfait; **to** ~ **on a debt** ne pas s'acquitter d'une dette.

defaulter [dɪ'fɔːltə*] *n* (*on debt*) débiteur défaillant.

default option *n* (*COMPUT*) option *f* par défaut.

defeat [dɪ'fiːt] *n* défaite *f* ♦ *vt* (*team, opponents*) battre; (*fig: plans, efforts*) faire échouer.

defeatism [dɪ'fiːtɪzəm] *n* défaitisme *m*.

defeatist [dɪ'fiːtɪst] *adj, n* défaitiste (*m/f*).

defecate ['dɛfəkeɪt] *vi* déféquer.

defect *n* ['diːfɛkt] défaut *m* ♦ *vi* [dɪ'fɛkt]: **to** ~ **to the enemy/the West** passer à l'ennemi/l'Ouest; **physical** ~ malformation *f*, vice *m* de conformation; **mental** ~ anomalie *or* déficience mentale.

defective [dɪ'fɛktɪv] *adj* défectueux(euse).

defector [dɪ'fɛktə*] *n* transfuge *m/f*.

defence, (*US*) **defense** [dɪ'fɛns] *n* défense *f*; **in** ~ **of** pour défendre; **witness for the** ~ témoin *m* à décharge; **the Ministry of D**~, (*US*) **the Department of Defense** le ministère de la Défense nationale.

defenceless [dɪ'fɛnslɪs] *adj* sans défense.

defend [dɪ'fɛnd] *vt* défendre; (*decision, action, opinion*) justifier, défendre.

defendant [dɪ'fɛndənt] *n* défendeur/deresse; (*in criminal case*) accusé/e, prévenu/e.

defender [dɪ'fɛndə*] *n* défenseur *m*.

defending champion [dɪ'fɛndɪŋ-] *n* (*SPORT*) champion/ne en titre.

defending counsel [dɪ'fɛndɪŋ-] *n* (*LAW*) avocat *m* de la défense.

defense [dɪ'fɛns] *n* (*US*) = **defence**.

defensive [dɪ'fɛnsɪv] *adj* défensif(ive) ♦ *n* défensive *f*; **on the** ~ sur la défensive.

defer [dɪ'fə:*] *vt* (*postpone*) différer, ajourner ♦ *vi* (*submit*): **to** ~ **to sb/sth** déférer à qn/qch, s'en remettre à qn/qch.

deference ['dɛfərəns] *n* déférence *f*, égards *mpl*; **out of** *or* **in** ~ **to** par déférence *or* égards pour.

defiance [dɪ'faɪəns] *n* défi *m*; **in** ~ **of** au mépris de.

defiant [dɪ'faɪənt] *adj* provocant(e), de défi.

defiantly [dɪ'faɪəntlɪ] *adv* d'un air (*or* d'un ton) de défi.

deficiency [dɪ'fɪʃənsɪ] *n* insuffisance *f*, déficience *f*; carence *f*; (*COMM*) déficit *m*, découvert *m*.

deficiency disease *n* maladie *f* de carence.

deficient [dɪ'fɪʃənt] *adj* insuffisant(e); défectueux(euse); déficient(e); **to be** ~ **in** manquer de.

deficit ['dɛfɪsɪt] *n* déficit *m*.

defile [dɪ'faɪl] *vt* souiller ♦ *vi* défiler ♦ *n* ['diːfaɪl] défilé *m*.

define [dɪ'faɪn] *vt* définir.

definite ['dɛfɪnɪt] *adj* (*fixed*) défini(e), (bien) déterminé(e); (*clear, obvious*) net(te), manifeste; (*LING*) défini(e); **he was** ~ **about it** il a été catégorique; il était sûr de son fait.

definitely ['dɛfɪnɪtlɪ] *adv* sans aucun doute.

definition [dɛfɪ'nɪʃən] *n* définition *f*.

definitive [dɪ'fɪnɪtɪv] *adj* définitif(ive).

deflate [diː'fleɪt] *vt* dégonfler; (*pompous person*) rabattre le caquet à; (*ECON*) provoquer la déflation de; (: *prices*) faire tomber *or* baisser.

deflation [diː'fleɪʃən] *n* (*ECON*) déflation *f*.

deflationary [diː'fleɪʃənrɪ] *adj* (*ECON*) déflationniste.

deflect [dɪ'flɛkt] *vt* détourner, faire dévier.

defog ['diː'fɒg] *vt* (*US AUT*) désembuer.

defogger ['diː'fɒgə*] *n* (*US AUT*) dispositif *m* anti-buée *inv*.

deform [dɪ'fɔːm] *vt* déformer.

deformed [dɪ'fɔːmd] *adj* difforme.

deformity [dɪ'fɔːmɪtɪ] *n* difformité *f*.

defraud [dɪ'frɔːd] *vt* frauder; **to** ~ **sb of sth** soutirer qch malhonnêtement à qn; escroquer qch à qn; frustrer qn de qch.

defray [dɪ'freɪ] *vt*: **to** ~ **sb's expenses** défrayer qn (de ses frais), rembourser *or* payer à qn ses frais.

defrost [diː'frɒst] *vt* (*fridge*) dégivrer; (*frozen food*) décongeler.

deft [dɛft] *adj* adroit(e), preste.

defunct [dɪ'fʌŋkt] *adj* défunt(e).

defuse [diː'fjuːz] *vt* désamorcer.

defy [dɪ'faɪ] *vt* défier; (*efforts etc*) résister à.

degenerate *vi* [dɪ'dʒɛnəreɪt] dégénérer ♦ *adj* [dɪ'dʒɛnərɪt] dégénéré(e).

degradation [dɛgrə'deɪʃən] *n* dégradation *f*.

degrade [dɪ'greɪd] *vt* dégrader.

degrading [dɪ'greɪdɪŋ] *adj* dégradant(e).

degree [dɪ'griː] *n* degré *m*; (*SCOL*) diplôme *m* (universitaire); **10** ~**s below (zero)** 10 degrés au-dessous de zéro; **a (first)** ~ **in maths** (*BRIT*) une licence en maths; **a considerable** ~ **of risk** un considérable facteur *or* élément de risque; **by** ~**s** (*gradually*) par degrés; **to some** ~, **to a certain** ~ jusqu'à un certain point, dans une certaine mesure.

dehydrated [diːhaɪ'dreɪtɪd] *adj* déshydraté(e); (*milk, eggs*) en poudre.

dehydration [diːhaɪ'dreɪʃən] *n* déshydratation *f*.

de-ice ['diː'aɪs] *vt* (*windscreen*) dégivrer.

de-icer ['diː'aɪsə*] *n* dégivreur *m*.

deign [deɪn] *vi*: **to** ~ **to do** daigner faire.

deity ['diːɪtɪ] *n* divinité *f*; dieu *m*, déesse *f*.

déjà vu [deɪʒɑː'vuː] *n*: **I had a sense of** ~ j'ai

eu une impression de déjà-vu.

dejected [dɪ'dʒɛktɪd] adj abattu(e), déprimé(e).

dejection [dɪ'dʒɛkʃən] n abattement m, découragement m.

Del. abbr (US) = Delaware.

del. abbr = delete.

delay [dɪ'leɪ] vt (journey, operation) retarder, différer; (travellers, trains) retarder; (payment) différer ♦ vi s'attarder ♦ n délai m, retard m; **without ~** sans délai, sans tarder.

delayed-action [dɪ'leɪd'ækʃən] adj à retardement.

delectable [dɪ'lɛktəbl] adj délicieux(euse).

delegate n ['dɛlɪgɪt] vt déléguée/e ♦ vt ['dɛlɪgeɪt] déléguer; **to ~ sth to sb/sb to do sth** déléguer qch à qn/qn pour faire qch.

delegation [dɛlɪ'geɪʃən] n délégation f.

delete [dɪ'liːt] vt rayer, supprimer; (COMPUT) effacer.

Delhi ['dɛlɪ] n Delhi.

deli ['dɛlɪ] n épicerie fine.

deliberate adj [dɪ'lɪbərɪt] (intentional) délibéré(e); (slow) mesuré(e) ♦ vi [dɪ'lɪbəreɪt] délibérer, réfléchir.

deliberately [dɪ'lɪbərɪtlɪ] adv (on purpose) exprès, délibérément.

deliberation [dɪlɪbə'reɪʃən] n délibération f, réflexion f; (gen pl: discussion) délibérations, débats mpl.

delicacy ['dɛlɪkəsɪ] n délicatesse f; (choice food) mets fin or délicat, friandise f.

delicate ['dɛlɪkɪt] adj délicat(e).

delicately ['dɛlɪkɪtlɪ] adv délicatement; (act, express) avec délicatesse, avec tact.

delicatessen [dɛlɪkə'tɛsn] n épicerie fine.

delicious [dɪ'lɪʃəs] adj délicieux(euse), exquis(e).

delight [dɪ'laɪt] n (grande) joie, grand plaisir ♦ vt enchanter; **a ~ to the eyes** un régal or plaisir pour les yeux; **to take ~ in** prendre grand plaisir à; **to be the ~ of** faire les délices or la joie de.

delighted [dɪ'laɪtɪd] adj: **~ (at** or **with sth)** ravi(e) (de qch); **to be ~ to do sth/that** être enchanté(e) or ravi(e) de faire qch/que; **I'd be ~** j'en serais enchanté or ravi.

delightful [dɪ'laɪtful] adj (person, child) absolument charmant(e), adorable; (evening, view) merveilleux(euse); (meal) délicieux(euse).

delimit [diː'lɪmɪt] vt délimiter.

delineate [dɪ'lɪnɪeɪt] vt tracer, esquisser; (fig) dépeindre, décrire.

delinquency [dɪ'lɪŋkwənsɪ] n délinquance f.

delinquent [dɪ'lɪŋkwənt] adj, n délinquant(e).

delirious [dɪ'lɪrɪəs] adj (MED, fig) délirant(e); **to be ~** délirer.

delirium [dɪ'lɪrɪəm] n délire m.

deliver [dɪ'lɪvə*] vt (mail) distribuer; (goods) livrer; (message) remettre; (speech) prononcer; (warning, ultimatum) lancer;

(free) délivrer; (MED) accoucher; **to ~ the goods** (fig) tenir ses promesses.

deliverance [dɪ'lɪvrəns] n délivrance f, libération f.

delivery [dɪ'lɪvərɪ] n (of mail) distribution f; (of goods) livraison f; (of speaker) élocution f; (MED) accouchement m; **to take ~ of** prendre livraison de.

delivery note n bon m de livraison.

delivery van, (US) **delivery truck** n fourgonnette f or camionnette f de livraison.

delouse ['diː'laus] vt épouiller, débarrasser de sa (or leur etc) vermine.

delta ['dɛltə] n delta m.

delude [dɪ'luːd] vt tromper, leurrer; **to ~ o.s.** se leurrer, se faire des illusions.

deluge ['dɛljuːdʒ] n déluge m ♦ vt (fig): **to ~ (with)** inonder (de).

delusion [dɪ'luːʒən] n illusion f; **to have ~s of grandeur** être un peu mégalomane.

de luxe [də'lʌks] adj de luxe.

delve [dɛlv] vi: **to ~ into** fouiller dans.

Dem. abbr (US POL) = **democrat(ic).**

demagogue ['dɛməgɔg] n démagogue m/f.

demand [dɪ'mɑːnd] vt réclamer, exiger; (need) exiger, requérir ♦ n exigence f; (claim) revendication f; (ECON) demande f; **to ~ sth (from** or **of sb)** exiger qch (de qn), réclamer qch (à qn); **in ~** demandé(e), recherché(e); **on ~** sur demande.

demanding [dɪ'mɑːndɪŋ] adj (person) exigeant(e); (work) astreignant(e).

demarcation [diːmɑː'keɪʃən] n démarcation f.

demarcation dispute n (INDUSTRY) conflit m d'attributions.

demean [dɪ'miːn] vt: **to ~ o.s.** s'abaisser.

demeanour, (US) **demeanor** [dɪ'miːnə*] n comportement m; maintien m.

demented [dɪ'mɛntɪd] adj dément(e), fou(folle).

demilitarized zone [diː'mɪlɪtəraɪzd-] n zone démilitarisée.

demise [dɪ'maɪz] n décès m.

demist [diː'mɪst] vt (BRIT AUT) désembuer.

demister [diː'mɪstə*] n (BRIT AUT) dispositif m anti-buée inv.

demo ['dɛməu] n abbr (col: = demonstration) manif f.

demobilize [diː'məubɪlaɪz] vt démobiliser.

democracy [dɪ'mɔkrəsɪ] n démocratie f.

democrat ['dɛməkræt] n démocrate m/f.

democratic [dɛmə'krætɪk] adj démocratique; **the D~ Party** (US) le parti démocrate.

demography [dɪ'mɔgrəfɪ] n démographie f.

demolish [dɪ'mɔlɪʃ] vt démolir.

demolition [dɛmə'lɪʃən] n démolition f.

demon ['diːmən] n démon m ♦ cpd: **a ~ squash player** un crack en squash; **a ~ driver** un fou du volant.

demonstrate ['dɛmənstreɪt] vt démontrer, prouver ♦ vi: **to ~ (for/against)** manifester (en faveur de/contre).

demonstration [dɛmən'streɪʃən] *n*
démonstration *f*; (*POL etc*) manifestation *f*;
to hold a ~ (*POL etc*) organiser une
manifestation, manifester.

demonstrative [dɪ'mɒnstrətɪv] *adj*
démonstratif(ive).

demonstrator ['dɛmənstreɪtə*] *n* (*POL etc*)
manifestant/e; (*COMM: sales person*)
vendeur/euse; (*: car, computer etc*) modèle *m*
de démonstration.

demoralize [dɪ'mɒrəlaɪz] *vt* démoraliser.

demote [dɪ'məut] *vt* rétrograder.

demotion [dɪ'məuʃən] *n* rétrogradation *f*.

demur [dɪ'mə:*] *vi*: **to ~ (at sth)** hésiter
(devant qch); (*object*) élever des objections
(contre qch) ♦ **to ~ without** ~ sans hésiter;
sans faire de difficultés.

demure [dɪ'mjuə*] *adj* sage, réservé(e); d'une
modestie affectée.

demurrage [dɪ'mʌrɪdʒ] *n* droits *mpl* de
magasinage; surestarie *f*.

den [dɛn] *n* tanière *f*, antre *m*.

denationalization [di:næʃnəlaɪ'zeɪʃən] *n*
dénationalisation *f*.

denationalize [di:'næʃnəlaɪz] *vt*
dénationaliser.

denial [dɪ'naɪəl] *n* (*of accusation*) démenti *m*;
(*of rights, guilt, truth*) dénégation *f*.

denier ['dɛnɪə*] *n* denier *m*; **15 ~ stockings**
bas de 15 deniers.

denigrate ['dɛnɪgreɪt] *vt* dénigrer.

denim ['dɛnɪm] *n* coton émerisé.

denim jacket *n* veste *f* en jean.

denims ['dɛnɪmz] *npl* (blue-)jeans *mpl*.

denizen ['dɛnɪzn] *n* (*inhabitant*) habitant/e;
(*foreigner*) étranger/ère.

Denmark ['dɛnmɑ:k] *n* Danemark *m*.

denomination [dɪnɒmɪ'neɪʃən] *n* (*money*)
valeur *f*; (*REL*) confession *f*; culte *m*.

denominator [dɪ'nɒmɪneɪtə*] *n* dénominateur
m.

denote [dɪ'nəut] *vt* dénoter.

denounce [dɪ'nauns] *vt* dénoncer.

dense [dɛns] *adj* dense; (*col: stupid*) obtus(e),
dur(e) *or* lent(e) à la comprenette.

densely ['dɛnslɪ] *adv*: **~ wooded** couvert(e)
d'épaisses forêts; **~ populated** à forte
densité (de population), très peuplé(e).

density ['dɛnsɪtɪ] *n* densité *f*; **single/double ~
disk** (*COMPUT*) disquette *f* (à) simple/double
densité.

dent [dɛnt] *n* bosse *f* ♦ *vt* (*also*: **make a ~ in**)
cabosser; **to make a ~ in** (*fig*) entamer.

dental ['dɛntl] *adj* dentaire.

dental floss [-flɒs] *n* fil *m* dentaire.

dental surgeon *n* (chirurgien/ne) dentiste.

dentifrice ['dɛntɪfrɪs] *n* dentifrice *m*.

dentist ['dɛntɪst] *n* dentiste *m/f*; **~'s surgery**
(*BRIT*) cabinet *m* de dentiste.

dentistry ['dɛntɪstrɪ] *n* art *m* dentaire.

denture(s) ['dɛntʃə(z)] *n(pl)* dentier *m*.

denunciation [dɪnʌnsɪ'eɪʃən] *n* dénonciation *f*.

deny [dɪ'naɪ] *vt* nier; (*refuse*) refuser; (*disown*)
renier; **he denies having said it** il nie l'avoir
dit.

deodorant [di:'əudərənt] *n* désodorisant *m*,
déodorant *m*.

depart [dɪ'pɑ:t] *vi* partir; **to ~ from** (*leave*)
quitter, partir de; (*fig: differ from*) s'écarter
de.

departed [dɪ'pɑ:tɪd] *adj* (*dead*) défunt(e); **the
(dear) ~** le défunt/la défunte/les défunts.

department [dɪ'pɑ:tmənt] *n* (*COMM*) rayon *m*;
(*SCOL*) section *f*; (*POL*) ministère *m*,
département *m*; **that's not my ~** (*fig*) ce
n'est pas mon domaine *or* ma compétence,
ce n'est pas mon rayon; **D~ of State** (*US*)
Département d'État.

departmental [di:pɑ:t'mɛntl] *adj* d'une *or* de
la section; d'un *or* du ministère, d'un *or* du
département; **~ manager** chef *m* de service;
(*in shop*) chef *m* de rayon.

department store *n* grand magasin.

departure [dɪ'pɑ:tʃə*] *n* départ *m*; (*fig*): **~
from** écart *m* par rapport à; **a new ~** une
nouvelle voie.

departure lounge *n* salle *f* de départ.

depend [dɪ'pɛnd] *vi*: **to ~ (up)on** dépendre de;
(*rely on*) compter sur; (*financially*) dépendre
(financièrement) de, être à la charge de; **it
~s** cela dépend; **~ing on the result** ... selon
le résultat ....

dependable [dɪ'pɛndəbl] *adj* sûr(e), digne de
confiance.

dependant [dɪ'pɛndənt] *n* personne *f* à
charge.

dependence [dɪ'pɛndəns] *n* dépendance *f*.

dependent [dɪ'pɛndənt] *adj*: **to be ~ (on)**
dépendre (de) ♦ *n* = **dependant**.

depict [dɪ'pɪkt] *vt* (*in picture*) représenter; (*in
words*) (dé)peindre, décrire.

depilatory [dɪ'pɪlətrɪ] *n* (*also*: **~ cream**)
dépilatoire *m*, crème *f* à épiler.

depleted [dɪ'pli:tɪd] *adj* (considérablement)
réduit(e) *or* diminué(e).

deplorable [dɪ'plɔ:rəbl] *adj* déplorable,
lamentable.

deplore [dɪ'plɔ:*] *vt* déplorer.

deploy [dɪ'plɔɪ] *vt* déployer.

depopulate [di:'pɒpjuleɪt] *vt* dépeupler.

depopulation ['di:pɒpju'leɪʃən] *n*
dépopulation *f*, dépeuplement *m*.

deport [dɪ'pɔ:t] *vt* déporter, expulser.

deportation [di:pɔ:'teɪʃən] *n* déportation *f*,
expulsion *f*.

deportation order *n* arrêté *m* d'expulsion.

deportee [di:pɔ:'ti:] *n* déporté/e.

deportment [dɪ'pɔ:tmənt] *n* maintien *m*, tenue
f.

depose [dɪ'pəuz] *vt* déposer.

deposit [dɪ'pɒzɪt] *n* (*CHEM, COMM, GEO*) dépôt
m; (*of ore, oil*) gisement *m*; (*part payment*)
arrhes *fpl*, acompte *m*; (*on bottle etc*) consigne *f*; (*for hired goods etc*) cautionnement

m, garantie *f* ♦ *vt* déposer; (*valuables*) mettre *or* laisser en dépôt; **to put down a ~ of £50** verser 50 livres d'arrhes *or* d'acompte; laisser 50 livres en garantie.

deposit account *n* compte *m* de dépôt.

depositor [dɪ'pɒzɪtə*] *n* déposant/e.

depository [dɪ'pɒzɪtərɪ] *n* (*person*) dépositaire *m/f*; (*place*) dépôt *m*.

depot ['dɛpəʊ] *n* dépôt *m*.

depraved [dɪ'preɪvd] *adj* dépravé(e), perverti(e).

depravity [dɪ'prævɪtɪ] *n* dépravation *f*.

deprecate ['dɛprɪkeɪt] *vt* désapprouver.

deprecating ['dɛprɪkeɪtɪŋ] *adj* (*disapproving*) désapprobateur(trice); (*apologetic*): **a ~ smile** un sourire d'excuse.

depreciate [dɪ'priːʃɪeɪt] *vt* déprécier ♦ *vi* se déprécier, se dévaloriser.

depreciation [dɪpriːʃɪ'eɪʃən] *n* dépréciation *f*.

depress [dɪ'prɛs] *vt* déprimer; (*press down*) appuyer sur, abaisser.

depressant [dɪ'prɛsnt] *n* (*MED*) dépresseur *m*.

depressed [dɪ'prɛst] *adj* (*person*) déprimé(e), abattu(e); (*area*) en déclin, touché(e) par le sous-emploi; (*COMM: market, trade*) maussade; **to get ~** se démoraliser, se laisser abattre.

depressing [dɪ'prɛsɪŋ] *adj* déprimant(e).

depression [dɪ'prɛʃən] *n* (*also ECON*) dépression *f*.

deprivation [dɛprɪ'veɪʃən] *n* privation *f*; (*loss*) perte *f*.

deprive [dɪ'praɪv] *vt*: **to ~ sb of** priver qn de; enlever à qn.

deprived [dɪ'praɪvd] *adj* déshérité(e).

dept. *abbr* (= *department*) dép., dépt.

depth [dɛpθ] *n* profondeur *f*; **in the ~s of** au fond de; au cœur de; au plus profond de; **at a ~ of 3 metres** à 3 mètres de profondeur; **to be out of one's ~** (*BRIT: swimmer*) ne plus avoir pied; (*fig*) être dépassé(e), nager; **to study sth in ~** étudier qch en profondeur.

depth charge *n* grenade sous-marine.

deputation [dɛpju'teɪʃən] *n* députation *f*, délégation *f*.

deputize ['dɛpjutaɪz] *vi*: **to ~ for** assurer l'intérim de.

deputy ['dɛpjutɪ] *n* (*replacement*) suppléant/e, intérimaire *m/f*; (*second in command*) adjoint/e ♦ *adj*: **~ chairman** vice-président *m*; **~ head** (*SCOL*) directeur/trice adjoint(e), sous-directeur/trice; **~ leader** (*BRIT POL*) vice-président/e, secrétaire adjoint(e).

derail [dɪ'reɪl] *vt* faire dérailler; **to be ~ed** dérailler.

derailment [dɪ'reɪlmənt] *n* déraillement *m*.

deranged [dɪ'reɪndʒd] *adj*: **to be (mentally) ~** avoir le cerveau dérangé.

derby ['dɜːrbɪ] *n* (*US*) (chapeau *m*) melon *m*.

Derbys *abbr* (*BRIT*) = *Derbyshire*.

deregulate [dɪ'rɛgjuleɪt] *vt* libérer, dérégler.

deregulation [dɪrɛgju'leɪʃən] *n* libération *f*,

dérèglement *m*.

derelict ['dɛrɪlɪkt] *adj* abandonné(e), à l'abandon.

deride [dɪ'raɪd] *vt* railler.

derision [dɪ'rɪʒən] *n* dérision *f*.

derisive [dɪ'raɪsɪv] *adj* moqueur(euse), railleur(euse).

derisory [dɪ'raɪsərɪ] *adj* (*sum*) dérisoire; (*smile, person*) moqueur(euse), railleur(euse).

derivation [dɛrɪ'veɪʃən] *n* dérivation *f*.

derivative [dɪ'rɪvətɪv] *n* dérivé *m* ♦ *adj* dérivé(e).

derive [dɪ'raɪv] *vt*: **to ~ sth from** tirer qch de; trouver qch dans ♦ *vi*: **to ~ from** provenir de, dériver de.

dermatitis [dəːmə'taɪtɪs] *n* dermatite *f*.

dermatology [dəːmə'tɒlədʒɪ] *n* dermatologie *f*.

derogatory [dɪ'rɒgətərɪ] *adj* désobligeant(e); péjoratif(ive).

derrick ['dɛrɪk] *n* mât *m* de charge; derrick *m*.

derv [dəːv] *n* (*BRIT*) gas-oil *m*, diesel *m*.

DES *n abbr* (*BRIT*: = *Department of Education and Science*) ministère de l'éducation nationale et des sciences.

desalination [diːsælɪ'neɪʃən] *n* dessalement *m*, dessalage *m*.

descend [dɪ'sɛnd] *vt*, *vi* descendre; **to ~ from** descendre de, être issu(e) de; **in ~ing order of importance** par ordre d'importance décroissante.

▶**descend on** *vt fus* (*subj: enemy, angry person*) tomber *or* sauter sur; (: *misfortune*) s'abattre sur; (: *gloom, silence*) envahir; **visitors ~ed (up)on us** des gens sont arrivés chez nous à l'improviste.

descendant [dɪ'sɛndənt] *n* descendant/e.

descent [dɪ'sɛnt] *n* descente *f*; (*origin*) origine *f*.

describe [dɪs'kraɪb] *vt* décrire.

description [dɪs'krɪpʃən] *n* description *f*; (*sort*) sorte *f*, espèce *f*; **of every ~** de toutes sortes.

descriptive [dɪs'krɪptɪv] *adj* descriptif(ive).

desecrate ['dɛsɪkreɪt] *vt* profaner.

desert *n* ['dɛzət] désert *m* ♦ *vb* [dɪ'zəːt] *vt* déserter, abandonner ♦ *vi* (*MIL*) déserter.

deserter [dɪ'zəːtə*] *n* déserteur *m*.

desertion [dɪ'zəːʃən] *n* désertion *f*.

desert island *n* île déserte.

deserts [dɪ'zəːts] *npl*: **to get one's just ~** n'avoir que ce qu'on mérite.

deserve [dɪ'zəːv] *vt* mériter.

deservedly [dɪ'zəːvɪdlɪ] *adv* à juste titre, à bon droit.

deserving [dɪ'zəːvɪŋ] *adj* (*person*) méritant(e); (*action, cause*) méritoire.

desiccated ['dɛsɪkeɪtɪd] *adj* séché(e).

design [dɪ'zaɪn] *n* (*sketch*) plan *m*, dessin *m*; (*layout, shape*) conception *f*, ligne *f*; (*pattern*) dessin, motif(s) *m(pl)*; (*of dress, car*) modèle *m*; (*art*) design *m*, stylisme *m*; (*intention*) dessein *m* ♦ *vt* dessiner; (*plan*) concevoir; **to**

have ~**s on** avoir des visées sur; **well-**~**ed**
adj bien conçu(e); **industrial** ~ esthétique
industrielle.
designate *vt* ['dɛzɪgneɪt] désigner ♦ *adj*
['dɛzɪgnɪt] désigné(e).
designation [dɛzɪg'neɪʃən] *n* désignation *f*.
designer [dɪ'zaɪnə*] *n* (*ARCHIT, ART*)
dessinateur/trice; (*INDUSTRY*) concepteur *m*,
designer *m*; (*FASHION*) modéliste *m/f*.
desirability [dɪzaɪərə'bɪlɪtɪ] *n* avantage *m*;
attrait *m*.
desirable [dɪ'zaɪərəbl] *adj* désirable; **it is** ~
that il est souhaitable que.
desire [dɪ'zaɪə*] *n* désir *m* ♦ *vt* désirer, vouloir;
to ~ **to do sth/that** désirer faire qch/que.
desirous [dɪ'zaɪərəs] *adj*: ~ **of** désireux(euse)
de.
desk [dɛsk] *n* (*in office*) bureau *m*; (*for pupil*)
pupitre *m*; (*BRIT: in shop, restaurant*) caisse *f*;
(*in hotel, at airport*) réception *f*.
desktop computer ['dɛsktɒp-] *n* ordinateur *m*
de bureau *or* de table.
desktop publishing ['dɛsktɒp-] *n* publication
assistée par ordinateur, PAO *f*.
desolate ['dɛsəlɪt] *adj* désolé(e).
desolation [dɛsə'leɪʃən] *n* désolation *f*.
despair [dɪs'pɛə*] *n* désespoir *m* ♦ *vi*: **to** ~ **of**
désespérer de; **to be in** ~ être au désespoir.
despatch [dɪs'pætʃ] *n, vt* = **dispatch**.
desperate ['dɛspərɪt] *adj* désespéré(e);
(*fugitive*) prêt(e) à tout; (*measures*)
désespéré, extrême; **we are getting**
~ nous commençons à désespérer.
desperately ['dɛspərɪtlɪ] *adv* désespérément;
(*very*) terriblement, extrêmement; ~ **ill** très
gravement malade.
desperation [dɛspə'reɪʃən] *n* désespoir *m*; **in** ~
en désespoir de cause.
despicable [dɪs'pɪkəbl] *adj* méprisable.
despise [dɪs'paɪz] *vt* mépriser, dédaigner.
despite [dɪs'paɪt] *prep* malgré, en dépit de.
despondent [dɪs'pɒndənt] *adj* découragé(e),
abattu(e).
despot ['dɛspɒt] *n* despote *m/f*.
dessert [dɪ'zɜːt] *n* dessert *m*.
dessertspoon [dɪ'zɜːtspuːn] *n* cuiller *f* à
dessert.
destabilize [diː'steɪbɪlaɪz] *vt* déstabiliser.
destination [dɛstɪ'neɪʃən] *n* destination *f*.
destine ['dɛstɪn] *vt* destiner.
destined ['dɛstɪnd] *adj*: **to be** ~ **to do sth** être
destiné(e) à faire qch; ~ **for London** à
destination de Londres.
destiny ['dɛstɪnɪ] *n* destinée *f*, destin *m*.
destitute ['dɛstɪtjuːt] *adj* indigent(e), dans le
dénuement; ~ **of** dépourvu(e) *or* dénué(e)
de.
destroy [dɪs'trɔɪ] *vt* détruire.
destroyer [dɪs'trɔɪə*] *n* (*NAUT*) contre-
torpilleur *m*.
destruction [dɪs'trʌkʃən] *n* destruction *f*.
destructive [dɪs'trʌktɪv] *adj*

destructeur(trice).
desultory ['dɛsəltərɪ] *adj* (*reading,
conversation*) décousu(e); (*contact*)
irrégulier(ière).
detach [dɪ'tætʃ] *vt* détacher.
detachable [dɪ'tætʃəbl] *adj* amovible,
détachable.
detached [dɪ'tætʃt] *adj* (*attitude*) détaché(e).
detached house *n* pavillon *m*, maison(nette)
(individuelle).
detachment [dɪ'tætʃmənt] *n* (*MIL*)
détachement *m*; (*fig*) détachement,
indifférence *f*.
detail ['diːteɪl] *n* détail *m*; (*MIL*) détachement *m*
♦ *vt* raconter en détail, énumérer; (*MIL*): **to**
~ **sb (for)** affecter qn (à), détacher qn
(pour); **in** ~ en détail; **to go into** ~**(s)** entrer
dans les détails.
detailed ['diːteɪld] *adj* détaillé(e).
detain [dɪ'teɪn] *vt* retenir; (*in captivity*) détenir;
(*in hospital*) hospitaliser.
detainee [diːteɪ'niː] *n* détenu/e.
detect [dɪ'tɛkt] *vt* déceler, percevoir; (*MED,
POLICE*) dépister; (*MIL, RADAR, TECH*)
détecter.
detection [dɪ'tɛkʃən] *n* découverte *f*; (*MED,
POLICE*) dépistage *m*; (*MIL, RADAR, TECH*)
détection *f*; **to escape** ~ échapper aux
recherches, éviter d'être découvert(e);
(*mistake*) passer inaperçu(e); **crime** ~ le
dépistage des criminels.
detective [dɪ'tɛktɪv] *n* agent *m* de la sûreté,
policier *m*; **private** ~ détective privé.
detective story *n* roman policier.
detector [dɪ'tɛktə*] *n* détecteur *m*.
détente [deɪ'taːnt] *n* détente *f*.
detention [dɪ'tɛnʃən] *n* détention *f*; (*SCOL*)
retenue *f*, consigne *f*.
deter [dɪ'tɜː*] *vt* dissuader.
detergent [dɪ'tɜːdʒənt] *n* détersif *m*,
détergent *m*.
deteriorate [dɪ'tɪərɪəreɪt] *vi* se détériorer, se
dégrader.
deterioration [dɪtɪərɪə'reɪʃən] *n* détérioration
f.
determination [dɪtɜːmɪ'neɪʃən] *n*
détermination *f*.
determine [dɪ'tɜːmɪn] *vt* déterminer; **to** ~ **to
do** résoudre de faire, se déterminer à faire.
determined [dɪ'tɜːmɪnd] *adj* (*person*)
déterminé(e), décidé(e); (*quantity*)
déterminé, établi(e); (*effort*) très gros(se).
deterrence [dɪ'tɛrns] *n* dissuasion *f*.
deterrent [dɪ'tɛrənt] *n* effet *m* de dissuasion;
force *f* de dissuasion; **to act as a** ~ avoir un
effet dissuasif.
detest [dɪ'tɛst] *vt* détester, avoir horreur de.
detestable [dɪ'tɛstəbl] *adj* détestable,
odieux(euse).
detonate ['dɛtəneɪt] *vi* exploser ♦ *vt* faire
exploser *or* détoner.
detonator ['dɛtəneɪtə*] *n* détonateur *m*.

detour ['di:tuə*] n détour m; (US AUT: diversion) déviation f.

detract [dɪ'trækt] vt: **to ~ from** (quality, pleasure) diminuer; (reputation) porter atteinte à.

detractor [dɪ'træktə*] n détracteur/trice.

detriment ['dɛtrɪmənt] n: **to the ~ of** au détriment de, au préjudice de; **without ~ to** sans porter atteinte or préjudice à, sans conséquences fâcheuses pour.

detrimental [dɛtrɪ'mɛntl] adj: **~ to** préjudiciable or nuisible à.

deuce [dju:s] n (TENNIS) égalité f.

devaluation [dɪvælju'eɪʃən] n dévaluation f.

devalue ['di:'vælju:] vt dévaluer.

devastate ['dɛvəsteɪt] vt dévaster; **he was ~d by the news** cette nouvelle lui a porté un coup terrible.

devastating ['dɛvəsteɪtɪŋ] adj dévastateur(trice).

devastation [dɛvəs'teɪʃən] n dévastation f.

develop [dɪ'vɛləp] vt (gen) développer; (habit) contracter; (resources) mettre en valeur, exploiter; (land) aménager ♦ vi se développer; (situation, disease: evolve) évoluer; (facts, symptoms: appear) se manifester, se produire; **to ~ a taste for sth** prendre goût à qch; **to ~ into** devenir.

developer [dɪ'vɛləpə*] n (PHOT) révélateur m; (of land) promoteur m; (also: **property ~**) promoteur immobilier.

developing country [dɪ'vɛləpɪŋ-] n pays m en voie de développement.

development [dɪ'vɛləpmənt] n développement m; (of affair, case) rebondissement m, fait(s) nouveau(x).

development area n zone f à urbaniser.

deviate ['di:vɪeɪt] vi: **to ~ (from)** dévier (de).

deviation [di:vɪ'eɪʃən] n déviation f.

device [dɪ'vaɪs] n (scheme) moyen m, expédient m; (apparatus) engin m, dispositif m; **explosive ~** engin explosif.

devil ['dɛvl] n diable m; démon m.

devilish ['dɛvlɪʃ] adj diabolique.

devil-may-care ['dɛvlmeɪ'kɛə*] adj je-m'en-foutiste.

devil's advocate n: **to play ~** se faire avocat du diable.

devious ['di:vɪəs] adj (means) détourné(e); (person) sournois(e), dissimulé(e).

devise [dɪ'vaɪz] vt imaginer, concevoir.

devoid [dɪ'vɔɪd] adj: **~ of** dépourvu(e) de, dénué(e) de.

devolution [di:və'lu:ʃən] n (POL) décentralisation f.

devolve [dɪ'vɔlv] vi: **to ~ (up)on** retomber sur.

devote [dɪ'vəut] vt: **to ~ sth to** consacrer qch à.

devoted [dɪ'vəutɪd] adj dévoué(e); **to be ~ to** être dévoué(e) or très attaché(e) à; (subj: book etc) être consacré(e) à.

devotee [dɛvəu'ti:] n (REL) adepte m/f; (MUS, SPORT) fervent/e.

devotion [dɪ'vəuʃən] n dévouement m, attachement m; (REL) dévotion f, piété f.

devour [dɪ'vauə*] vt dévorer.

devout [dɪ'vaut] adj pieux(euse), dévot(e).

dew [dju:] n rosée f.

dexterity [dɛks'tɛrɪtɪ] n dextérité f, adresse f.

dext(e)rous ['dɛkstrəs] adj adroit(e).

dg abbr (= decigram) dg.

diabetes [daɪə'bi:ti:z] n diabète m.

diabetic [daɪə'bɛtɪk] n diabétique m/f ♦ adj (person) diabétique; (chocolate, jam) pour diabétiques.

diabolical [daɪə'bɔlɪkl] adj diabolique; (col: dreadful) infernal(e), atroce.

diaeresis [daɪ'ɛrɪsɪs] n tréma m.

diagnose [daɪəg'nəuz] vt diagnostiquer.

diagnosis, pl diagnoses [daɪəg'nəusɪs, -si:z] n diagnostic m.

diagonal [daɪ'ægənl] adj diagonal(e) ♦ n diagonale f.

diagram ['daɪəgræm] n diagramme m, schéma m.

dial ['daɪəl] n cadran m ♦ vt (number) faire, composer; **to ~ a wrong number** faire un faux numéro; **can I ~ London direct?** puis-je or est-ce-que je peux avoir Londres par l'automatique?

dial. abbr = dialect.

dialect ['daɪəlɛkt] n dialecte m.

dialling code ['daɪəlɪŋ-], (US) **dial code** n indicatif m (téléphonique).

dialling tone ['daɪəlɪŋ-], (US) **dial tone** n tonalité f.

dialogue ['daɪəlɔg] n dialogue m.

dialysis [daɪ'ælɪsɪs] n dialyse f.

diameter [daɪ'æmɪtə*] n diamètre m.

diametrically [daɪə'mɛtrɪklɪ] adv: **~ opposed (to)** diamétralement opposé(e) (à).

diamond ['daɪəmənd] n diamant m; (shape) losange m; **~s** npl (CARDS) carreau m.

diamond ring n bague f de diamant(s).

diaper ['daɪəpə*] n (US) couche f.

diaphragm ['daɪəfræm] n diaphragme m.

diarrhoea, (US) **diarrhea** [daɪə'ri:ə] n diarrhée f.

diary ['daɪərɪ] n (daily account) journal m; (book) agenda m; **to keep a ~** tenir un journal.

diatribe ['daɪətraɪb] n diatribe f.

dice [daɪs] n (pl inv) dé m ♦ vt (CULIN) couper en dés or en cubes.

dicey ['daɪsɪ] adj (col): **it's a bit ~** c'est un peu risqué.

dichotomy [daɪ'kɔtəmɪ] n dichotomie f.

dickhead ['dɪkhɛd] n (BRIT col!) tête f de nœud f.

Dictaphone ['dɪktəfəun] n ® Dictaphone m ®.

dictate vt [dɪk'teɪt] dicter ♦ vi: **to ~ to** (person)

imposer sa volonté à, régenter; **I won't be ~d to** je n'ai d'ordres à recevoir de personne ♦ *n* ['dɪkteɪt] injonction *f*.

dictation [dɪk'teɪʃən] *n* dictée *f*; **at ~ speed** à une vitesse de dictée.

dictator [dɪk'teɪtə*] *n* dictateur *m*.

dictatorship [dɪk'teɪtəʃɪp] *n* dictature *f*.

diction ['dɪkʃən] *n* diction *f*, élocution *f*.

dictionary ['dɪkʃənrɪ] *n* dictionnaire *m*.

did [dɪd] *pt of* **do**.

didactic [daɪ'dæktɪk] *adj* didactique.

didn't [dɪdnt] = **did not**.

die [daɪ] *n* (*pl:* **dice**) dé *m*; (*pl:* **dies**) coin *m*; matrice *f*, étampe *f* ♦ *vi:* **to ~ (of** *or* **from)** mourir (de); **to be dying for sth** avoir une envie folle de qch; **to be dying to do sth** mourir d'envie de faire qch.

▶**die away** *vi* s'éteindre.

▶**die down** *vi* se calmer, s'apaiser.

▶**die out** *vi* disparaître, s'éteindre.

diehard ['daɪhɑːd] *n* réactionnaire *m/f*, jusqu'au-boutiste *m/f*.

diesel ['diːzl] *n* diesel *m*.

diesel engine *n* moteur *m* diesel.

diesel fuel, diesel oil *n* carburant *m* diesel.

diet ['daɪət] *n* alimentation *f*; (*restricted food*) régime *m* ♦ *vi* (*also:* **be on a ~**) suivre un régime; **to live on a ~ of** se nourrir de.

dietician [daɪə'tɪʃən] *n* diététicien/ne.

differ ['dɪfə*] *vi:* **to ~ from sth** être différent(e) de; différer de; **to ~ from sb over sth** ne pas être d'accord avec qn au sujet de qch.

difference ['dɪfrəns] *n* différence *f*; (*quarrel*) différend *m*, désaccord *m*; **it makes no ~ to me** cela m'est égal, cela m'est indifférent; **to settle one's ~s** résoudre la situation.

different ['dɪfrənt] *adj* différent(e).

differential [dɪfə'renʃəl] *n* (*AUT, wages*) différentiel *m*.

differentiate [dɪfə'renʃɪeɪt] *vt* différencier ♦ *vi* se différencier; **to ~ between** faire une différence entre.

differently ['dɪfrəntlɪ] *adv* différemment.

difficult ['dɪfɪkəlt] *adj* difficile; **~ to understand** difficile à comprendre.

difficulty ['dɪfɪkəltɪ] *n* difficulté *f*; **to have difficulties with** avoir des ennuis *or* problèmes avec; **to be in ~** avoir des difficultés, avoir des problèmes.

diffidence ['dɪfɪdəns] *n* manque *m* de confiance en soi, manque d'assurance.

diffident ['dɪfɪdənt] *adj* qui manque de confiance *or* d'assurance, peu sûr(e) de soi.

diffuse *adj* [dɪ'fjuːs] diffus(e) ♦ *vt* [dɪ'fjuːz] diffuser, répandre.

dig [dɪg] *vt* (*pt, pp* **dug** [dʌg]) (*hole*) creuser; (*garden*) bêcher ♦ *n* (*prod*) coup *m* de coude; (*fig*) coup de griffe *or* de patte; (*ARCHAEOLOGY*) fouille *f*; **to ~ into** (*snow, soil*) creuser; **to ~ into one's pockets for sth**

fouiller dans ses poches pour chercher *or* prendre qch; **to ~ one's nails into** enfoncer ses ongles dans.

▶**dig in** *vi* (*also:* **~ o.s. in:** *MIL*) se retrancher; (: *fig*) tenir bon, se braquer; (*col: eat*) attaquer (un repas *or* un plat *etc*) ♦ *vt* (*compost*) bien mélanger à la bêche; (*knife, claw*) enfoncer; **to ~ in one's heels** (*fig*) se braquer, se buter.

▶**dig out** *vt* (*survivors, car from snow*) sortir *or* dégager (à coups de pelles *or* pioches).

▶**dig up** *vt* déterrer.

digest *vt* [daɪ'dʒest] digérer ♦ *n* ['daɪdʒest] sommaire *m*, résumé *m*.

digestible [dɪ'dʒestəbl] *adj* digestible.

digestion [dɪ'dʒestʃən] *n* digestion *f*.

digestive [dɪ'dʒestɪv] *adj* digestif(ive).

digit ['dɪdʒɪt] *n* chiffre *m* (*de 0 à 9*); (*finger*) doigt *m*.

digital ['dɪdʒɪtl] *adj* digital(e); (*watch*) à affichage numérique *or* digital.

digital compact cassette *n* cassette *f* numérique.

dignified ['dɪgnɪfaɪd] *adj* digne.

dignitary ['dɪgnɪtərɪ] *n* dignitaire *m*.

dignity ['dɪgnɪtɪ] *n* dignité *f*.

digress [daɪ'gres] *vi:* **to ~ from** s'écarter de, s'éloigner de.

digression [daɪ'greʃən] *n* digression *f*.

digs [dɪgz] *npl* (*BRIT col*) piaule *f*, chambre meublée.

dilapidated [dɪ'læpɪdeɪtɪd] *adj* délabré(e).

dilate [daɪ'leɪt] *vt* dilater ♦ *vi* se dilater.

dilatory ['dɪlətərɪ] *adj* dilatoire.

dilemma [daɪ'lemə] *n* dilemme *m*; **to be in a ~** être pris dans un dilemme.

diligent ['dɪlɪdʒənt] *adj* appliqué(e), assidu(e).

dill [dɪl] *n* aneth *m*.

dilly-dally ['dɪlɪ'dælɪ] *vi* hésiter, tergiverser; traînasser, lambiner.

dilute [daɪ'luːt] *vt* diluer ♦ *adj* dilué(e).

dim [dɪm] *adj* (*light, eyesight*) faible; (*memory, outline*) vague, indécis(e); (*stupid*) borné(e), obtus(e) ♦ *vt* (*light*) réduire, baisser; (*US AUT*) mettre en code, baisser; **to take a ~ view of sth** voir qch d'un mauvais œil.

dime [daɪm] *n* (*US*) = 10 cents.

dimension [daɪ'menʃən] *n* dimension *f*.

-dimensional [dɪ'menʃənl] *adj suffix:* **two~** à deux dimensions.

diminish [dɪ'mɪnɪʃ] *vt, vi* diminuer.

diminished [dɪ'mɪnɪʃt] *adj:* **~ responsibility** (*LAW*) responsabilité atténuée.

diminutive [dɪ'mɪnjutɪv] *adj* minuscule, tout(e) petit(e) ♦ *n* (*LING*) diminutif *m*.

dimly ['dɪmlɪ] *adv* faiblement; vaguement.

dimmer ['dɪmə*] *n* (*also:* **~ switch**) variateur *m*; **~s** *npl* (*US AUT:* dipped headlights) phares *mpl* code *inv*; (: *parking lights*) feux *mpl* de position.

dimple ['dɪmpl] *n* fossette *f*.

dim-witted ['dɪm'wɪtɪd] *adj* (*col*) stupide,

borné(e).

din [dɪn] n vacarme m ♦ vt: **to ~ sth into sb** (col) enfoncer qch dans la tête or la caboche de qn.

dine [daɪn] vi dîner.

diner ['daɪnə*] n (person) dîneur/euse; (RAIL) = **dining car**; (US: eating place) petit restaurant.

dinghy ['dɪŋgɪ] n youyou m; (inflatable) canot m pneumatique; (also: **sailing ~**) voilier m, dériveur m.

dingy ['dɪndʒɪ] adj miteux(euse), minable.

dining car ['daɪnɪŋ-] n voiture-restaurant f, wagon-restaurant m.

dining room ['daɪnɪŋ-] n salle f à manger.

dinner ['dɪnə*] n dîner m; (public) banquet m; **~'s ready!** à table!

dinner jacket n smoking m.

dinner party n dîner m.

dinner time n heure f du dîner.

dinosaur ['daɪnəsɔː*] n dinosaure m.

dint [dɪnt] n: **by ~ of (doing) sth** à force de (faire) qch.

diocese ['daɪəsɪs] n diocèse m.

dioxide [daɪˈɔksaɪd] n dioxyde m.

Dip. abbr (BRIT) = **diploma**.

dip [dɪp] n déclivité f; (in sea) baignade f, bain m ♦ vt tremper, plonger; (BRIT AUT: lights) mettre en code, baisser ♦ vi plonger.

diphtheria [dɪfˈθɪərɪə] n diphtérie f.

diphthong ['dɪfθɔŋ] n diphtongue f.

diploma [dɪˈpləʊmə] n diplôme m.

diplomacy [dɪˈpləʊməsɪ] n diplomatie f.

diplomat ['dɪpləmæt] n diplomate m.

diplomatic [dɪpləˈmætɪk] adj diplomatique; **to break off ~ relations (with)** rompre les relations diplomatiques (avec).

diplomatic corps n corps m diplomatique.

diplomatic immunity n immunité f diplomatique.

dipstick ['dɪpstɪk] n (AUT) jauge f de niveau d'huile.

dipswitch ['dɪpswɪtʃ] n (BRIT AUT) commutateur m de code.

dire [daɪə*] adj extrême, affreux(euse).

direct [daɪˈrɛkt] adj direct(e); (manner, person) direct, franc(franche) ♦ vt diriger, orienter; **can you ~ me to ...?** pouvez-vous m'indiquer le chemin de ...?; **to ~ sb to do sth** ordonner à qn de faire qch.

direct cost n (COMM) coût m variable.

direct current n (ELEC) courant continu.

direct debit n (BANKING) prélèvement m automatique.

direct dialling n (TEL) automatique m.

direct hit n (MIL) coup m au but, touché m.

direction [dɪˈrɛkʃən] n direction f; (THEAT) mise f en scène; (CINE, TV) réalisation f; **~s** npl (instructions: to a place) indications fpl; **~s for use** mode m d'emploi; **to ask for ~s** demander sa route or son chemin; **sense of ~** sens m de l'orientation; **in the ~ of** dans la direction de, vers.

directive [dɪˈrɛktɪv] n directive f; **a government ~** une directive du gouvernement.

direct labour n main-d'œuvre directe; employés municipaux.

directly [dɪˈrɛktlɪ] adv (in straight line) directement, tout droit; (at once) tout de suite, immédiatement.

direct mail n vente f par publicité directe.

direct mailshot n (BRIT) publicité postale.

directness [daɪˈrɛktnɪs] n (of person, speech) franchise f.

director [dɪˈrɛktə*] n directeur m; (board member) administrateur m; (THEAT) metteur m en scène; (CINE, TV) réalisateur/trice; **D~ of Public Prosecutions** (BRIT) ≈ procureur général.

directory [dɪˈrɛktərɪ] n annuaire m; (also: **street ~**) indicateur m de rues; (also: **trade ~**) annuaire du commerce; (COMPUT) répertoire m.

directory enquiries, (US) **directory assistance** n (TEL: service) renseignements mpl.

dirt [dəːt] n saleté f; (mud) boue f; **to treat sb like ~** traiter qn comme un chien.

dirt-cheap ['dəːtˈtʃiːp] adj (ne) coûtant presque rien.

dirt road n chemin non macadamisé or non revêtu.

dirty ['dəːtɪ] adj sale ♦ vt salir; **~ story** histoire cochonne; **~ trick** coup tordu.

disability [dɪsəˈbɪlɪtɪ] n invalidité f, infirmité f.

disability allowance n allocation f d'invalidité or d'infirmité.

disable [dɪsˈeɪbl] vt (subj: illness, accident) rendre or laisser infirme; (tank, gun) mettre hors d'action.

disabled [dɪsˈeɪbld] adj infirme, invalide; (maimed) mutilé(e); (through illness, old age) impotent(e).

disadvantage [dɪsədˈvɑːntɪdʒ] n désavantage m, inconvénient m.

disadvantaged [dɪsədˈvɑːntɪdʒd] adj (person) désavantagé(e).

disadvantageous [dɪsædvɑːnˈteɪdʒəs] adj désavantageux(euse).

disaffected [dɪsəˈfɛktɪd] adj: **~ (to or towards)** mécontent(e) (de).

disaffection [dɪsəˈfɛkʃən] n désaffection f, mécontentement m.

disagree [dɪsəˈgriː] vi (differ) ne pas concorder; (be against, think otherwise): **to ~ (with)** ne pas être d'accord (avec); **garlic ~s with me** l'ail ne me convient pas, je ne supporte pas l'ail.

disagreeable [dɪsəˈgriːəbl] adj désagréable.

disagreement [dɪsəˈgriːmənt] n désaccord m, différend m.

disallow ['dɪsəˈlaʊ] vt rejeter, désavouer; (BRIT FOOTBALL: goal) refuser.

disappear [dısə'pıə*] *vi* disparaître.
disappearance [dısə'pıərəns] *n* disparition *f*.
disappoint [dısə'pɔınt] *vt* décevoir.
disappointed [dısə'pɔıntıd] *adj* déçu(e).
disappointing [dısə'pɔıntıŋ] *adj* décevant(e).
disappointment [dısə'pɔıntmənt] *n* déception *f*.
disapproval [dısə'pru:vəl] *n* désapprobation *f*.
disapprove [dısə'pru:v] *vi*: **to ~ of** désapprouver.
disapproving [dısə'pru:vıŋ] *adj* désapprobateur(trice), de désapprobation.
disarm [dıs'ɑ:m] *vt* désarmer.
disarmament [dıs'ɑ:məmənt] *n* désarmement *m*.
disarming [dıs'ɑ:mıŋ] *adj* (*smile*) désarmant(e).
disarray [dısə'reı] *n* désordre *m*, confusion *f*; **in ~** (*troops*) en déroute; (*thoughts*) embrouillé(e); (*clothes*) en désordre; **to throw into ~** semer la confusion *or* le désordre dans (*or* parmi).
disaster [dı'zɑ:stə*] *n* catastrophe *f*, désastre *m*.
disastrous [dı'zɑ:strəs] *adj* désastreux(euse).
disband [dıs'bænd] *vt* démobiliser; disperser ♦ *vi* se séparer; se disperser.
disbelief ['dısbə'li:f] *n* incrédulité *f*; **in ~** avec incrédulité.
disbelieve ['dısbə'li:v] *vt* (*person*) ne pas croire; (*story*) mettre en doute; **I don't ~ you** je veux bien vous croire.
disc [dısk] *n* disque *m*.
disc. *abbr* (*COMM*) = **discount**.
discard [dıs'kɑ:d] *vt* (*old things*) se défaire de, mettre au rencart *or* au rebut; (*fig*) écarter, renoncer à.
disc brake *n* frein *m* à disque.
discern [dı'sə:n] *vt* discerner, distinguer.
discernible [dı'sə:nəbl] *adj* discernable, perceptible; (*object*) visible.
discerning [dı'sə:nıŋ] *adj* judicieux(euse), perspicace.
discharge *vt* [dıs'tʃɑ:dʒ] (*duties*) s'acquitter de; (*settle: debt*) s'acquitter de, régler; (*waste etc*) déverser; décharger; (*ELEC, MED*) émettre; (*patient*) renvoyer (chez lui); (*employee, soldier*) congédier, licencier; (*defendant*) relaxer, élargir ♦ *n* ['dıstʃɑ:dʒ] (*ELEC, MED etc*) émission *f*; (*also:* **vaginal ~**) pertes blanches; (*dismissal*) renvoi *m*; licenciement *m*; élargissement *m*; **to ~ one's gun** faire feu; **~d bankrupt** failli/e réhabilité(e).
disciple [dı'saıpl] *n* disciple *m*.
disciplinary ['dısıplınərı] *adj* disciplinaire; **to take ~ action against sb** prendre des mesures disciplinaires à l'encontre de qn.
discipline ['dısıplın] *n* discipline *f* ♦ *vt* discipliner; (*punish*) punir; **to ~ o.s. to do sth** s'imposer *or* s'astreindre à une discipline pour faire qch.

disc jockey (DJ) *n* disque-jockey *m* (DJ).
disclaim [dıs'kleım] *vt* désavouer, dénier.
disclaimer [dıs'kleımə*] *n* démenti *m*, dénégation *f*; **to issue a ~** publier un démenti.
disclose [dıs'kləuz] *vt* révéler, divulguer.
disclosure [dıs'kləuʒə*] *n* révélation *f*, divulgation *f*.
disco ['dıskəu] *n abbr* = **discothèque**.
discolour, (*US*) **discolor** [dıs'kʌlə*] *vt* décolorer; (*sth white*) jaunir ♦ *vi* se décolorer; jaunir.
discolo(u)ration [dıskʌlə'reıʃən] *n* décoloration *f*; jaunissement *m*.
discolo(u)red [dıs'kʌləd] *adj* décoloré(e); jauni(e).
discomfort [dıs'kʌmfət] *n* malaise *m*, gêne *f*; (*lack of comfort*) manque *m* de confort.
disconcert [dıskən'sə:t] *vt* déconcerter, décontenancer.
disconnect [dıskə'nekt] *vt* détacher; (*ELEC, RADIO*) débrancher; (*gas, water*) couper.
disconnected [dıskə'nektıd] *adj* (*speech, thoughts*) décousu(e), peu cohérent(e).
disconsolate [dıs'kɔnsəlıt] *adj* inconsolable.
discontent [dıskən'tent] *n* mécontentement *m*.
discontented [dıskən'tentıd] *adj* mécontent(e).
discontinue [dıskən'tınju:] *vt* cesser, interrompre; "**~d**" (*COMM*) "fin de série".
discord ['dıskɔ:d] *n* discorde *f*, dissension *f*; (*MUS*) dissonance *f*.
discordant [dıs'kɔ:dənt] *adj* discordant(e), dissonant(e).
discotheque ['dıskəutek] *n* discothèque *f*.
discount *n* ['dıskaunt] remise *f*, rabais *m* ♦ *vt* [dıs'kaunt] (*report etc*) ne pas tenir compte de; **to give sb a ~ on sth** faire une remise *or* un rabais à qn sur qch; **~ for cash** escompte *f* au comptant; **at a ~** avec une remise *or* réduction, au rabais.
discount house *n* (*FINANCE*) banque *f* d'escompte; (*COMM: also:* **discount store**) magasin *m* de discount.
discount rate *n* taux *m* de remise.
discourage [dıs'kʌrıdʒ] *vt* décourager; (*dissuade, deter*) dissuader, décourager.
discouragement [dıs'kʌrıdʒmənt] *n* (*depression*) découragement *m*; **to act as a ~ to sb** dissuader qn.
discouraging [dıs'kʌrıdʒıŋ] *adj* décourageant(e).
discourteous [dıs'kə:tıəs] *adj* incivil(e), discourtois(e).
discover [dıs'kʌvə*] *vt* découvrir.
discovery [dıs'kʌvərı] *n* découverte *f*.
discredit [dıs'kredıt] *vt* mettre en doute; discréditer ♦ *n* discrédit *m*.
discreet [dı'skri:t] *adj* discret(ète).
discreetly [dı'skri:tlı] *adv* discrètement.
discrepancy [dı'skrepənsı] *n* divergence *f*,

contradiction *f.*

discretion [dɪ'skreʃən] *n* discrétion *f*; **use your own** ~ à vous de juger.

discretionary [dɪ'skreʃənrɪ] *adj* (*powers*) discrétionnaire.

discriminate [dɪ'skrɪmɪneɪt] *vi*: **to** ~ **between** établir une distinction entre, faire la différence entre; **to** ~ **against** pratiquer une discrimination contre.

discriminating [dɪ'skrɪmɪneɪtɪŋ] *adj* qui a du discernement.

discrimination [dɪskrɪmɪ'neɪʃən] *n* discrimination *f*; (*judgment*) discernement *m*; **racial/sexual** ~ discrimination raciale/ sexuelle.

discus ['dɪskəs] *n* disque *m.*

discuss [dɪ'skʌs] *vt* discuter de; (*debate*) discuter.

discussion [dɪ'skʌʃən] *n* discussion *f*; **under** ~ en discussion.

disdain [dɪs'deɪn] *n* dédain *m.*

disease [dɪ'ziːz] *n* maladie *f.*

diseased [dɪ'ziːzd] *adj* malade.

disembark [dɪsɪm'baːk] *vt, vi* débarquer.

disembarkation [dɪsɛmbaː'keɪʃən] *n* débarquement *m.*

disembodied ['dɪsɪm'bɔdɪd] *adj* désincarné(e).

disembowel ['dɪsɪm'bauəl] *vt* éviscérer, étriper.

disenchanted ['dɪsɪn'tʃɑːntɪd] *adj*: ~ **(with)** désenchanté(e) (de), désabusé(e) (de).

disenfranchise ['dɪsɪn'fræntʃaɪz] *vt* priver du droit de vote; (*COMM*) retirer la franchise à.

disengage [dɪsɪn'geɪdʒ] *vt* dégager; (*TECH*) déclencher; **to** ~ **the clutch** (*AUT*) débrayer.

disentangle [dɪsɪn'tæŋgl] *vt* démêler.

disfavour, (*US*) **disfavor** [dɪs'feɪvə*] *n* défaveur *f*; disgrâce *f.*

disfigure [dɪs'fɪgə*] *vt* défigurer.

disgorge [dɪs'gɔːdʒ] *vt* déverser.

disgrace [dɪs'greɪs] *n* honte *f*; (*disfavour*) disgrâce *f* ♦ *vt* déshonorer, couvrir de honte.

disgraceful [dɪs'greɪsful] *adj* scandaleux(euse), honteux(euse).

disgruntled [dɪs'grʌntld] *adj* mécontent(e).

disguise [dɪs'gaɪz] *n* déguisement *m* ♦ *vt* déguiser; (*voice*) déguiser, contrefaire; (*feelings etc*) masquer, dissimuler; **in** ~ déguisé(e); **to** ~ **o.s. as** se déguiser en; **there's no disguising the fact that ...** on ne peut se dissimuler que ....

disgust [dɪs'gʌst] *n* dégoût *m*, aversion *f* ♦ *vt* dégoûter, écœurer.

disgusting [dɪs'gʌstɪŋ] *adj* dégoûtant(e), révoltant(e).

dish [dɪʃ] *n* plat *m*; **to do** *or* **wash the** ~**es** faire la vaisselle.

▶**dish out** *vt* distribuer.

▶**dish up** *vt* servir; (*facts, statistics*) sortir, débiter.

dishcloth ['dɪʃklɔθ] *n* (*for drying*) torchon *m*;

(*for washing*) lavette *f.*

dishearten [dɪs'haːtn] *vt* décourager.

dishevelled, (*US*) **disheveled** [dɪ'ʃevəld] *adj* ébouriffé(e); décoiffé(e); débraillé(e).

dishonest [dɪs'ɔnɪst] *adj* malhonnête.

dishonesty [dɪs'ɔnɪstɪ] *n* malhonnêteté *f.*

dishonour, (*US*) **dishonor** [dɪs'ɔnə*] *n* déshonneur *m.*

dishono(u)rable [dɪs'ɔnərəbl] *adj* déshonorant(e).

dish soap *n* (*US*) produit *m* pour la vaisselle.

dishtowel ['dɪʃtauəl] *n* torchon *m* (à vaisselle).

dishwasher ['dɪʃwɔʃə*] *n* lave-vaisselle *m*; (*person*) plongeur/euse.

dishy ['dɪʃɪ] *adj* (*BRIT col*) séduisant(e), sexy *inv.*

disillusion [dɪsɪ'luːʒən] *vt* désabuser, désenchanter ♦ *n* désenchantement *m*; **to become** ~**ed (with)** perdre ses illusions (en ce qui concerne).

disillusionment [dɪsɪ'luːʒənmənt] *n* désillusionnement *m*, désillusion *f.*

disincentive [dɪsɪn'sɛntɪv] *n*: **it's a** ~ c'est démotivant; **to be a** ~ **to sb** démotiver qn.

disinclined ['dɪsɪn'klaɪnd] *adj*: **to be** ~ **to do sth** être peu disposé(e) *or* peu enclin(e) à faire qch.

disinfect [dɪsɪn'fɛkt] *vt* désinfecter.

disinfectant [dɪsɪn'fɛktənt] *n* désinfectant *m.*

disinflation [dɪsɪn'fleɪʃən] *n* désinflation *f.*

disinformation [dɪsɪnfə'meɪʃən] *n* désinformation *f.*

disinherit [dɪsɪn'hɛrɪt] *vt* déshériter.

disintegrate [dɪs'ɪntɪgreɪt] *vi* se désintégrer.

disinterested [dɪs'ɪntrəstɪd] *adj* désintéressé(e).

disjointed [dɪs'dʒɔɪntɪd] *adj* décousu(e), incohérent(e).

disk [dɪsk] *n* (*COMPUT*) disquette *f*; **single-/ double-sided** ~ disquette une face/double face.

disk drive *n* lecteur *m* de disquette.

diskette [dɪs'kɛt] *n* (*COMPUT*) disquette *f.*

disk operating system (DOS) *n* système *m* d'exploitation à disques (DOS).

dislike [dɪs'laɪk] *n* aversion *f*, antipathie *f* ♦ *vt* ne pas aimer; **to take a** ~ **to sb/sth** prendre qn/qch en grippe; **I** ~ **the idea** l'idée me déplaît.

dislocate ['dɪsləkeɪt] *vt* disloquer, déboîter; (*services etc*) désorganiser; **he has** ~**d his shoulder** il s'est disloqué l'épaule.

dislodge [dɪs'lɔdʒ] *vt* déplacer, faire bouger; (*enemy*) déloger.

disloyal [dɪs'lɔɪəl] *adj* déloyal(e).

dismal ['dɪzml] *adj* lugubre, maussade.

dismantle [dɪs'mæntl] *vt* démonter; (*fort, warship*) démanteler.

dismast [dɪs'maːst] *vt* démâter.

dismay [dɪs'meɪ] *n* consternation *f* ♦ *vt* consterner; **much to my** ~ à ma grande consternation, à ma grande inquiétude.

dismiss [dɪsˈmɪs] *vt* congédier, renvoyer; (*idea*) écarter; (*LAW*) rejeter ♦ *vi* (*MIL*) rompre les rangs.

dismissal [dɪsˈmɪsl] *n* renvoi *m*.

dismount [dɪsˈmaʊnt] *vi* mettre pied à terre.

disobedience [dɪsəˈbiːdɪəns] *n* désobéissance *f*.

disobedient [dɪsəˈbiːdɪənt] *adj* désobéissant(e), indiscipliné(e).

disobey [dɪsəˈbeɪ] *vt* désobéir à; (*rule*) transgresser, enfreindre.

disorder [dɪsˈɔːdə*] *n* désordre *m*; (*rioting*) désordres *mpl*; (*MED*) troubles *mpl*.

disorderly [dɪsˈɔːdəlɪ] *adj* (*room*) en désordre; (*behaviour, retreat, crowd*) désordonné(e).

disorderly conduct *n* (*LAW*) conduite *f* contraire aux bonnes mœurs.

disorganized [dɪsˈɔːgənaɪzd] *adj* désorganisé(e).

disorientated [dɪsˈɔːrɪɛnteɪtɪd] *adj* désorienté(e).

disown [dɪsˈəʊn] *vt* renier.

disparaging [dɪsˈpærɪdʒɪŋ] *adj* désobligeant(e); **to be ~ about sb/sth** faire des remarques désobligeantes sur qn/qch.

disparate ['dɪspərɪt] *adj* disparate.

disparity [dɪsˈpærɪtɪ] *n* disparité *f*.

dispassionate [dɪsˈpæʃənət] *adj* calme, froid(e); impartial(e), objectif(ive).

dispatch [dɪsˈpætʃ] *vt* expédier, envoyer; (*deal with: business*) régler, en finir avec ♦ *n* envoi *m*, expédition *f*; (*MIL, PRESS*) dépêche *f*.

dispatch department *n* service *m* des expéditions.

dispatch rider *n* (*MIL*) estafette *f*.

dispel [dɪsˈpɛl] *vt* dissiper, chasser.

dispensary [dɪsˈpɛnsərɪ] *n* pharmacie *f*; (*in chemist's*) officine *f*.

dispense [dɪsˈpɛns] *vt* distribuer, administrer; (*medicine*) préparer (et vendre); **to ~ sb from** dispenser qn de.
▶**dispense with** *vt fus* se passer de; (*make unnecessary*) rendre superflu(e).

dispenser [dɪsˈpɛnsə*] *n* (*device*) distributeur *m*.

dispensing chemist [dɪsˈpɛnsɪŋ-] *n* (*BRIT*) pharmacie *f*.

dispersal [dɪsˈpəːsl] *n* dispersion *f*; (*ADMIN*) déconcentration *f*.

disperse [dɪsˈpəːs] *vt* disperser; (*knowledge*) disséminer ♦ *vi* se disperser.

dispirited [dɪsˈpɪrɪtɪd] *adj* découragé(e), déprimé(e).

displace [dɪsˈpleɪs] *vt* déplacer.

displaced person [dɪsˈpleɪst-] *n* (*POL*) personne déplacée.

displacement [dɪsˈpleɪsmənt] *n* déplacement *m*.

display [dɪsˈpleɪ] *n* (*of goods*) étalage *m*; affichage *m*; (*computer ~: information*) visualisation *f*; (*: device*) visuel *m*; (*of feeling*)

manifestation *f*; (*pej*) ostentation *f*; (*show, spectacle*) spectacle *m*; (*military ~*) parade *f* militaire ♦ *vt* montrer; (*goods*) mettre à l'étalage, exposer; (*results, departure times*) afficher; (*pej*) faire étalage de; **on ~** (*exhibits*) exposé(e), exhibé(e); (*goods*) à l'étalage.

display advertising *n* publicité rédactionnelle.

displease [dɪsˈpliːz] *vt* mécontenter, contrarier; **~d with** mécontent(e) de.

displeasure [dɪsˈplɛʒə*] *n* mécontentement *m*.

disposable [dɪsˈpəʊzəbl] *adj* (*pack etc*) jetable; (*income*) disponible; **~ nappy** (*BRIT*) couche *f* à jeter, couche-culotte *f*.

disposal [dɪsˈpəʊzl] *n* (*availability, arrangement*) disposition *f*; (*of property etc: by selling*) vente *f*; (*: by giving away*) cession *f*; (*of rubbish*) évacuation *f*, destruction *f*; **at one's ~** à sa disposition; **to put sth at sb's ~** mettre qch à la disposition de qn.

dispose [dɪsˈpəʊz] *vt* disposer.
▶**dispose of** *vt fus* (*time, money*) disposer de; (*unwanted goods*) se débarrasser de, se défaire de; (*COMM: stock*) écouler, vendre; (*problem*) expédier.

disposed [dɪsˈpəʊzd] *adj*: **~ to do** disposé(e) à faire.

disposition [dɪspəˈzɪʃən] *n* disposition *f*; (*temperament*) naturel *m*.

dispossess ['dɪspəˈzɛs] *vt*: **to ~ sb (of)** déposséder qn (de).

disproportion [dɪsprəˈpɔːʃən] *n* disproportion *f*.

disproportionate [dɪsprəˈpɔːʃənət] *adj* disproportionné(e).

disprove [dɪsˈpruːv] *vt* réfuter.

dispute [dɪsˈpjuːt] *n* discussion *f*; (*also: industrial ~*) conflit *m* ♦ *vt* contester; (*matter*) discuter; (*victory*) disputer; **to be in** *or* **under ~** (*matter*) être en discussion; (*territory*) être contesté(e).

disqualification [dɪskwɔlɪfɪˈkeɪʃən] *n* disqualification *f*; **~ (from driving)** (*BRIT*) retrait *m* du permis (de conduire).

disqualify [dɪsˈkwɔlɪfaɪ] *vt* (*SPORT*) disqualifier; **to ~ sb for sth/from doing** (*status, situation*) rendre qn inapte à qch/à faire; (*authority*) signifier à qn l'interdiction de faire; **to ~ sb (from driving)** (*BRIT*) retirer à qn son permis (de conduire).

disquiet [dɪsˈkwaɪət] *n* inquiétude *f*, trouble *m*.

disquieting [dɪsˈkwaɪətɪŋ] *adj* inquiétant(e), alarmant(e).

disregard [dɪsrɪˈgɑːd] *vt* ne pas tenir compte de ♦ *n* (*indifference*): **~ (for)** (*feelings*) indifférence *f* (pour), insensibilité *f* (à); (*danger, money*) mépris *m* (pour).

disrepair ['dɪsrɪˈpɛə*] *n* mauvais état; **to fall into ~** (*building*) tomber en ruine; (*street*) se dégrader.

disreputable [dɪsˈrɛpjutəbl] *adj* (*person*) de

mauvaise réputation, peu recommandable; (*behaviour*) déshonorant(e); (*area*) mal famé(e), louche.

disrepute ['dɪsrɪ'pjuːt] *n* déshonneur *m*, discrédit *m*; **to bring into** ~ faire tomber dans le discrédit.

disrespectful [dɪsrɪ'spɛktful] *adj* irrespectueux(euse).

disrupt [dɪs'rʌpt] *vt* (*plans, meeting, lesson*) perturber, déranger.

disruption [dɪs'rʌpʃən] *n* perturbation *f*, dérangement *m*.

disruptive [dɪs'rʌptɪv] *adj* perturbateur-(trice).

dissatisfaction [dɪssætɪs'fækʃən] *n* mécontentement *m*, insatisfaction *f*.

dissatisfied [dɪs'sætɪsfaɪd] *adj*: ~ **(with)** mécontent(e) *or* insatisfait(e) (de).

dissect [dɪ'sɛkt] *vt* disséquer; (*fig*) disséquer, éplucher.

disseminate [dɪ'sɛmɪneɪt] *vt* disséminer.

dissent [dɪ'sɛnt] *n* dissentiment *m*, différence *f* d'opinion.

dissenter [dɪ'sɛntə*] *n* (*REL, POL etc*) dissident/e.

dissertation [dɪsə'teɪʃən] *n* (*SCOL*) mémoire *m*.

disservice [dɪs'səːvɪs] *n*: **to do sb a** ~ rendre un mauvais service à qn; desservir qn.

dissident ['dɪsɪdnt] *adj, n* dissident(e).

dissimilar [dɪ'sɪmɪlə*] *adj*: ~ **(to)** dissemblable (à), différent(e) (de).

dissipate ['dɪsɪpeɪt] *vt* dissiper; (*energy, efforts*) disperser.

dissipated ['dɪsɪpeɪtɪd] *adj* dissolu(e); débauché(e).

dissociate [dɪ'səuʃɪeɪt] *vt* dissocier; **to** ~ **o.s. from** se désolidariser de.

dissolute ['dɪsəluːt] *adj* débauché(e), dissolu(e).

dissolution [dɪsə'luːʃən] *n* dissolution *f*.

dissolve [dɪ'zɒlv] *vt* dissoudre ♦ *vi* se dissoudre, fondre; (*fig*) disparaître.

dissuade [dɪ'sweɪd] *vt*: **to** ~ **sb (from)** dissuader qn (de).

distaff ['dɪstɑːf] *n*: ~ **side** côté maternel.

distance ['dɪstns] *n* distance *f*; **what's the** ~ **to London?** à quelle distance se trouve Londres?; **it's within walking** ~ on peut y aller à pied; **in the** ~ au loin.

distant ['dɪstnt] *adj* lointain(e), éloigné(e); (*manner*) distant(e), froid(e).

distaste [dɪs'teɪst] *n* dégoût *m*.

distasteful [dɪs'teɪstful] *adj* déplaisant(e), désagréable.

Dist. Atty. *abbr* (*US*) = **district attorney**.

distemper [dɪs'tɛmpə*] *n* (*paint*) détrempe *f*, badigeon *m*; (*of dogs*) maladie *f* de Carré.

distended [dɪs'tɛndɪd] *adj* (*stomach*) dilaté(e).

distil, (*US*) **distill** [dɪs'tɪl] *vt* distiller.

distillery [dɪs'tɪlərɪ] *n* distillerie *f*.

distinct [dɪs'tɪŋkt] *adj* distinct(e); (*preference,*

progress) marqué(e); **as** ~ **from** par opposition à, en contraste avec.

distinction [dɪs'tɪŋkʃən] *n* distinction *f*; (*in exam*) mention *f* très bien; **to draw a** ~ **between** faire une distinction entre; **a writer of** ~ un écrivain réputé.

distinctive [dɪs'tɪŋktɪv] *adj* distinctif(ive).

distinctly [dɪs'tɪŋktlɪ] *adv* distinctement; (*specify*) expressément.

distinguish [dɪs'tɪŋgwɪʃ] *vt* distinguer ♦ *vi*: **to** ~ **between** (*concepts*) distinguer entre, faire une distinction entre; **to** ~ **o.s.** se distinguer.

distinguished [dɪs'tɪŋgwɪʃt] *adj* (*eminent, refined*) distingué(e); (*career*) remarquable, brillant(e).

distinguishing [dɪs'tɪŋgwɪʃɪŋ] *adj* (*feature*) distinctif(ive), caractéristique.

distort [dɪs'tɔːt] *vt* déformer.

distortion [dɪs'tɔːʃən] *n* déformation *f*.

distract [dɪs'trækt] *vt* distraire, déranger.

distracted [dɪs'træktɪd] *adj* (*look etc*) éperdu(e), égaré(e).

distraction [dɪs'trækʃən] *n* distraction *f*, dérangement *m*; **to drive sb to** ~ rendre qn fou(folle).

distraught [dɪs'trɔːt] *adj* éperdu(e).

distress [dɪs'trɛs] *n* détresse *f*; (*pain*) douleur *f* ♦ *vt* affliger; **in** ~ (*ship*) en perdition; (*plane*) en détresse; ~**ed area** (*BRIT*) zone sinistrée.

distressing [dɪs'trɛsɪŋ] *adj* douloureux(euse), pénible, affligeant(e).

distress signal *n* signal *m* de détresse.

distribute [dɪs'trɪbjuːt] *vt* distribuer.

distribution [dɪstrɪ'bjuːʃən] *n* distribution *f*.

distribution cost *n* coût *m* de distribution.

distributor [dɪs'trɪbjutə*] *n* (*gen, TECH*) distributeur *m*; (*COMM*) concessionnaire *m/f*.

district ['dɪstrɪkt] *n* (*of country*) région *f*; (*of town*) quartier *m*; (*ADMIN*) district *m*.

district attorney *n* (*US*) ≈ procureur *m* de la République.

district council *n* (*BRIT*) ≈ conseil municipal.

> *En Grande-Bretagne, un* **district council** *est une administration locale qui gère un* **district***. Les conseillers ("***councillors***") sont élus au niveau local, en général tous les 4 ans. Le district council est financé par des impôts locaux et par des subventions du gouvernement.*

district nurse *n* (*BRIT*) infirmière visiteuse.

distrust [dɪs'trʌst] *n* méfiance *f*, doute *m* ♦ *vt* se méfier de.

distrustful [dɪs'trʌstful] *adj* méfiant(e).

disturb [dɪs'təːb] *vt* troubler; (*inconvenience*) déranger; **sorry to** ~ **you** excusez-moi de vous déranger.

disturbance [dɪs'təːbəns] *n* dérangement *m*; (*political etc*) troubles *mpl*; (*by drunks etc*) tapage *m*; **to cause a** ~ troubler l'ordre public; ~ **of the peace** (*LAW*) tapage injurieux *or* nocturne.

disturbed [dɪs'tə:bd] *adj* agité(e), troublé(e);
 to be mentally/emotionally ~ avoir des
 problèmes psychologiques/affectifs.

disturbing [dɪs'tə:bɪŋ] *adj* troublant(e),
 inquiétant(e).

disuse [dɪs'ju:s] *n:* **to fall into ~** tomber en
 désuétude.

disused [dɪs'ju:zd] *adj* désaffecté(e).

ditch [dɪtʃ] *n* fossé *m* ♦ *vt* (*col*) abandonner.

dither ['dɪðə*] *vi* hésiter.

ditto ['dɪtəu] *adv* idem.

divan [dɪ'væn] *n* divan *m*.

divan bed *n* divan-lit *m*.

dive [daɪv] *n* plongeon *m*; (*of submarine*)
 plongée *f*; (*AVIAT*) piqué *m*; (*pej: café, bar etc*)
 bouge *m* ♦ *vi* plonger.

diver ['daɪvə*] *n* plongeur *m*.

diverge [daɪ'və:dʒ] *vi* diverger.

divergent [daɪ'də:dʒənt] *adj* divergent(e).

diverse [daɪ'və:s] *adj* divers(e).

diversification [daɪvə:sɪfɪ'keɪʃən] *n*
 diversification *f*.

diversify [daɪ'və:sɪfaɪ] *vt* diversifier.

diversion [daɪ'və:ʃən] *n* (*BRIT AUT*) déviation *f*;
 (*distraction, MIL*) diversion *f*.

diversionary tactics [daɪ'və:ʃənrɪ-] *npl*
 tactique *fsg* de diversion.

diversity [daɪ'və:sɪtɪ] *n* diversité *f*, variété *f*.

divert [daɪ'və:t] *vt* (*BRIT: traffic*) dévier; (*plane*)
 dérouter; (*train, river*) détourner; (*amuse*)
 divertir.

divest [daɪ'vɛst] *vt:* **to ~ sb of** dépouiller qn
 de.

divide [dɪ'vaɪd] *vt* diviser; (*separate*) séparer
 ♦ *vi* se diviser; **to ~ (between** *or* **among)**
 répartir *or* diviser (entre); **40 ~d by 5** 40
 divisé par 5.

▶**divide out** *vt:* **to ~ out (between** *or* **among)**
 distribuer *or* répartir (entre).

divided [dɪ'vaɪdɪd] *adj* (*fig: country, couple*)
 désuni(e); (*opinions*) partagé(e).

divided skirt *n* jupe-culotte *f*.

dividend ['dɪvɪdɛnd] *n* dividende *m*.

dividend cover *n* rapport *m* dividendes-
 résultat.

dividers [dɪ'vaɪdəz] *npl* compas *m* à pointes
 sèches; (*between pages*) feuillets *mpl*
 intercalaires.

divine [dɪ'vaɪn] *adj* divin(e) ♦ *vt* (*future*)
 prédire; (*truth*) deviner, entrevoir; (*water,
 metal*) détecter la présence de (*par
 l'intermédiaire de la radiesthésie*).

diving ['daɪvɪŋ] *n* plongée (sous-marine).

diving board *n* plongeoir *m*.

diving suit *n* scaphandre *m*.

divinity [dɪ'vɪnɪtɪ] *n* divinité *f*; (*as study*)
 théologie *f*.

division [dɪ'vɪʒən] *n* (*also BRIT FOOTBALL*)
 division *f*; (*separation*) séparation *f*; (*BRIT
 POL*) vote *m*; **~ of labour** division du travail.

divisive [dɪ'vaɪsɪv] *adj* qui entraîne la division,

qui crée des dissensions.

divorce [dɪ'vɔ:s] *n* divorce *m* ♦ *vt* divorcer
 d'avec.

divorced [dɪ'vɔ:st] *adj* divorcé(e).

divorcee [dɪvɔ:'si:] *n* divorcé/e.

divot ['dɪvət] *n* (*GOLF*) motte *f* de gazon.

divulge [daɪ'vʌldʒ] *vt* divulguer, révéler.

DIY *adj, n abbr* (*BRIT*) = **do-it-yourself**.

dizziness ['dɪzɪnɪs] *n* vertige *m*,
 étourdissement *m*.

dizzy ['dɪzɪ] *adj* (*height*) vertigineux(euse); **to
 make sb ~** donner le vertige à qn; **I feel ~**
 la tête me tourne, j'ai la tête qui tourne.

DJ *n abbr* = **disc jockey**.

d.j. *n abbr* = **dinner jacket**.

Djakarta [dʒə'kɑːtə] *n* Djakarta.

DJIA *n abbr* (*US STOCK EXCHANGE*) = Dow-Jones
 Industrial Average.

dl *abbr* (= decilitre) dl.

DLit(t) *n abbr* (= Doctor of Literature, Doctor of
 Letters) *titre universitaire*.

DLO *n abbr* = **dead-letter office**.

dm *abbr* (= decimetre) dm.

DMus *n abbr* (= Doctor of Music) *titre
 universitaire*.

DMZ *n abbr* = **demilitarized zone**.

DNA *n abbr* (= deoxyribonucleic acid) ADN *m*.

do *abbr* (= ditto) d⁰.

════════════════════════════════ *KEYWORD*

do [du:] (*pt* **did**, *pp* **done**) *n* (*inf: party etc*) soirée
 f, fête *f*; (: *formal gathering*) réception *f*
 ♦ *vb* **1** (*in negative constructions*) *non traduit*; **I
 ~n't understand** je ne comprends pas
 2 (*to form questions*) *non traduit*; **didn't you
 know?** vous ne le saviez pas?; **why didn't
 you come?** pourquoi n'êtes-vous pas venu?
 3 (*for emphasis, in polite expressions*): **she
 does seem rather late** je trouve qu'elle est
 bien en retard; **~ sit down/help yourself**
 asseyez-vous/servez-vous je vous en prie; **I
 DO wish I could go** j'aimerais tant y aller;
 but I DO like it! mais si, je l'aime!
 4 (*used to avoid repeating vb*): **she swims
 better than I ~** elle nage mieux que moi; **~
 you agree? — yes, I ~/no, I ~n't** vous êtes
 d'accord? — oui/non; **she lives in Glasgow
 — so ~ I** elle habite Glasgow — moi aussi;
 who broke it? — I did qui l'a cassé? — c'est
 moi
 5 (*in question tags*): **he laughed, didn't he?** il
 a ri, n'est-ce pas?; **I ~n't know him, ~ I?** je
 ne le connais pas, je crois
 ♦ *vt* (*gen: carry out, perform etc*) faire; (*visit:
 city, museum*) faire, visiter; **what are you
 ~ing tonight?** qu'est-ce que vous faites ce
 soir?; **what did he ~ with the cat?** qu'a t'il
 fait du chat?; **to ~ the cooking/washing-up**
 faire la cuisine/la vaisselle; **to ~ one's
 teeth/hair/nails** se brosser les dents/se
 coiffer/se faire les ongles; **the car was ~ing
 100** la voiture faisait du 100 (à l'heure)

♦ *vi* **1** (*act, behave*) faire; ~ **as I** ~ faites comme moi
2 (*get on, fare*) marcher; **the firm is ~ing well** l'entreprise marche bien; **how ~ you ~?** comment allez-vous?; (*on being introduced*) enchanté(e)!
3 (*suit*) aller; **will it ~?** est-ce que ça ira?
4 (*be sufficient*) suffire, aller; **will £10 ~?** est-ce que 10 livres suffiront?; **that'll ~!** ça suffit, ça ira; **that'll ~!** (*in annoyance*) ça va *or* suffit comme ça!; **to make ~ (with)** se contenter (de)
►**do away with** *vt fus* abolir; (*kill*) supprimer
►**do for** *vt fus* (*BRIT col: clean for*) faire le ménage chez
►**do up** *vt* (*laces, dress*) attacher; (*buttons*) boutonner; (*zip*) fermer; (*renovate: room*) refaire; (*: house*) remettre à neuf; **to ~ o.s. up** se faire beau(belle)
►**do with** *vt fus* (*need*): **I could ~ with a drink/some help** quelque chose à boire/un peu d'aide ne serait pas de refus; **it could ~ with a wash** ça ne lui ferait pas de mal d'être lavé; (*be connected*): **that has nothing to ~ with you** cela ne vous concerne pas; **I won't have anything to ~ with it** je ne veux pas m'en mêler; **what has that got to ~ with it?** quel rapport y-a-t-il?, qu'est-ce que cela vient faire là-dedans?
►**do without** *vi* s'en passer ♦ *vt fus* se passer de.

DOA *abbr* (= *dead on arrival*) décédé(e) à l'admission.
d.o.b. *abbr* = **date of birth**.
doc [dɔk] *n* (*col*) toubib *m*.
docile ['dəusaɪl] *adj* docile.
dock [dɔk] *n* dock *m*; (*wharf*) quai *m*; (*LAW*) banc *m* des accusés ♦ *vi* se mettre à quai ♦ *vt*: **they ~ed a third of his wages** ils lui ont retenu *or* décompté un tiers de son salaire.
dock dues *npl* droits *mpl* de bassin.
docker ['dɔkə*] *n* docker *m*.
docket ['dɔkɪt] *n* bordereau *m*; (*on parcel etc*) étiquette *f or* fiche *f* (*décrivant le contenu d'un paquet etc*).
dockyard ['dɔkjɑːd] *n* chantier *m* de construction navale.
doctor ['dɔktə*] *n* médecin *m*, docteur *m*; (*PhD etc*) docteur ♦ *vt* (*cat*) couper; (*interfere with: food*) altérer; (*: drink*) frelater; (*: text, document*) arranger; **~'s office** (*US*) cabinet *m* de consultation; **D~ of Philosophy (PhD)** doctorat *m*; titulaire *m/f* d'un doctorat.
doctorate ['dɔktərɪt] *n* doctorat *m*.

*Le **doctorate** est le diplôme universitaire le plus prestigieux. Il est le résultat d'au minimum trois années de recherche et est accordé après soutenance d'une thèse devant un jury. Le doctorat le plus courant est le PhD (Doctor of Philosophy), accordé en lettres, en*

*sciences et en ingénierie, bien qu'il existe également d'autres doctorats spécialisés (en musique, en droit, etc); voir **Bachelor's degree**, **Master's degree***

doctrine ['dɔktrɪn] *n* doctrine *f*.
docudrama ['dɔkjudrɑːmə] *n* (*TV*) docudrame *m*.
document *n* ['dɔkjumənt] document *m* ♦ *vt* ['dɔkjumɛnt] documenter.
documentary [dɔkju'mɛntərɪ] *adj, n* documentaire (*m*).
documentation [dɔkjumən'teɪʃən] *n* documentation *f*.
DOD *n abbr* (*US*) = **Department of Defense**.
doddering ['dɔdərɪŋ] *adj* (*senile*) gâteux(euse).
doddery ['dɔdərɪ] *adj* branlant(e).
doddle ['dɔdl] *n*: **it's a ~** (*col*) c'est simple comme bonjour, c'est du gâteau.
Dodecanese (Islands) [dəudɪkə'niːz-] *n(pl)* Dodécanèse *m*.
dodge [dɔdʒ] *n* truc *m*; combine *f* ♦ *vt* esquiver, éviter ♦ *vi* faire un saut de côté; (*SPORT*) faire une esquive; **to ~ out of the way** s'esquiver; **to ~ through the traffic** se faufiler *or* faire de savantes manœuvres entre les voitures.
dodgems ['dɔdʒəmz] *npl* (*BRIT*) autos tamponneuses.
dodgy ['dɔdʒɪ] *adj* (*col: uncertain*) douteux(euse); (*: shady*) louche.
DOE *n abbr* (*BRIT*) = *Department of the Environment*; (*US*) = *Department of Energy*.
doe [dəu] *n* (*deer*) biche *f*; (*rabbit*) lapine *f*.
does [dʌz] *see* **do**.
doesn't ['dʌznt] = **does not**.
dog [dɔg] *n* chien/ne ♦ *vt* (*follow closely*) suivre de près, ne pas lâcher d'une semelle; (*fig: memory etc*) poursuivre, harceler; **to go to the ~s** (*nation etc*) aller à vau-l'eau.
dog biscuits *npl* biscuits *mpl* pour chien.
dog collar *n* collier *m* de chien; (*fig*) faux-col *m* d'ecclésiastique.
dog-eared ['dɔgɪəd] *adj* corné(e).
dog food *n* nourriture *f* pour les chiens *or* le chien.
dogged ['dɔgɪd] *adj* obstiné(e), opiniâtre.
doggy ['dɔgɪ] *n* (*col*) toutou *m*.
doggy bag *n* petit sac pour emporter les restes.
dogma ['dɔgmə] *n* dogme *m*.
dogmatic [dɔg'mætɪk] *adj* dogmatique.
do-gooder [duː'gudə*] *n* (*pej*) faiseur/euse de bonnes œuvres.
dogsbody ['dɔgzbɔdɪ] *n* (*BRIT*) bonne *f* à tout faire, tâcheron *m*.
doily ['dɔɪlɪ] *n* dessus *m* d'assiette.
doing ['duɪŋ] *n*: **this is your ~** c'est votre travail, c'est vous qui avez fait ça.
doings ['duɪŋz] *npl* activités *fpl*.
do-it-yourself ['duːɪtjɔː'sɛlf] *n* bricolage *m*.
doldrums ['dɔldrəmz] *npl*: **to be in the ~** avoir

le cafard; être dans le marasme.
dole [dəul] *n* (*BRIT: payment*) allocation *f* de chômage; **on the ~** au chômage.
▶**dole out** *vt* donner au compte-goutte.
doleful ['dəulful] *adj* triste, lugubre.
doll [dɔl] *n* poupée *f*.
▶**doll up** *vt*: **to ~ o.s. up** se faire beau(belle).
dollar ['dɔlə*] *n* dollar *m*.
dollop ['dɔləp] *n* (*of butter, cheese*) bon morceau; (*of cream*) bonne cuillerée.
dolly ['dɔlɪ] *n* poupée *f*.
dolphin ['dɔlfɪn] *n* dauphin *m*.
domain [də'meɪn] *n* (*also fig*) domaine *m*.
dome [dəum] *n* dôme *m*.
domestic [də'mɛstɪk] *adj* (*duty, happiness*) familial(e); (*policy, affairs, flights*) intérieur(e); (*news*) national(e); (*animal*) domestique.
domesticated [də'mɛstɪkeɪtɪd] *adj* domestiqué(e); (*pej*) d'intérieur; **he's very ~** il participe volontiers aux tâches ménagères; question ménage, il est très organisé.
domesticity [dəumɛs'tɪsɪtɪ] *n* vie *f* de famille.
domestic servant *n* domestique *m/f*.
domicile ['dɔmɪsaɪl] *n* domicile *m*.
dominant ['dɔmɪnənt] *adj* dominant(e).
dominate ['dɔmɪneɪt] *vt* dominer.
domination [dɔmɪ'neɪʃən] *n* domination *f*.
domineering [dɔmɪ'nɪərɪŋ] *adj* dominateur(trice), autoritaire.
Dominican Republic [də'mɪnɪkən-] *n* République Dominicaine.
dominion [də'mɪnɪən] *n* domination *f*; territoire *m*; dominion *m*.
domino, ~**es** ['dɔmɪnəu] *n* domino *m*; ~**es** *n* (*game*) dominos *mpl*.
don [dɔn] *n* (*BRIT*) professeur *m* d'université ♦ *vt* revêtir.
donate [də'neɪt] *vt* faire don de, donner.
donation [də'neɪʃən] *n* donation *f*, don *m*.
done [dʌn] *pp of* **do**.
donkey ['dɔŋkɪ] *n* âne *m*.
donkey-work ['dɔŋkɪwə:k] *n* (*BRIT col*) le gros du travail, le plus dur (du travail).
donor ['dəunə*] *n* (*of blood etc*) donneur/euse; (*to charity*) donateur/trice.
donor card *n* carte *f* de don d'organes.
don't [dəunt] = **do not**.
doodle ['du:dl] *n* griffonnage *m*, gribouillage *m* ♦ *vi* griffonner, gribouiller.
doom [du:m] *n* (*fate*) destin *m*; (*ruin*) ruine *f* ♦ *vt*: **to be ~ed (to failure)** être voué(e) à l'échec.
doomsday ['du:mzdeɪ] *n* le Jugement dernier.
door [dɔ:*] *n* porte *f*; (*of vehicle*) portière *f*, porte; **to go from ~ to ~** aller de porte en porte.
doorbell ['dɔ:bɛl] *n* sonnette *f*.
door handle *n* poignée *f* de porte.
doorman ['dɔ:mən] *n* (*in hotel*) portier *m*; (*in*

block of flats) concierge *m*.
doormat ['dɔ:mæt] *n* paillasson *m*.
doorpost ['dɔ:pəust] *n* montant *m* de porte.
doorstep ['dɔ:stɛp] *n* pas *m* de (la) porte, seuil *m*.
door-to-door ['dɔ:tə'dɔ:*] *adj*: ~ **selling** vente *f* à domicile.
doorway ['dɔ:weɪ] *n* (embrasure *f* de) porte *f*.
dope [dəup] *n* (*col*) drogue *f*; (: *information*) tuyaux *mpl*, rancards *mpl* ♦ *vt* (*horse etc*) doper.
dopey ['dəupɪ] *adj* (*col*) à moitié endormi(e).
dormant ['dɔ:mənt] *adj* assoupi(e), en veilleuse; (*rule, law*) inappliqué(e).
dormer ['dɔ:mə*] *n* (*also:* ~ **window**) lucarne *f*.
dormice ['dɔ:maɪs] *npl of* **dormouse**.
dormitory ['dɔ:mɪtrɪ] *n* dortoir *m*; (*US: hall of residence*) foyer *m* d'étudiants.
dormouse, *pl* **dormice** ['dɔ:maus, -maɪs] *n* loir *m*.
Dors *abbr* (*BRIT*) = **Dorset**.
DOS [dɔs] *n abbr* = **disk operating system**.
dosage ['dəusɪdʒ] *n* dose *f*; dosage *m*; (*on label*) posologie *f*.
dose [dəus] *n* dose *f*; (*BRIT: bout*) attaque *f* ♦ *vt*: **to ~ o.s.** se bourrer de médicaments; **a ~ of flu** une belle or bonne grippe.
dosser ['dɔsə*] *n* (*BRIT col*) clochard/e.
doss house ['dɔs-] *n* (*BRIT*) asile *m* de nuit.
dossier ['dɔsɪeɪ] *n* dossier *m*.
DOT *n abbr* (*US*) = Department of Transportation.
dot [dɔt] *n* point *m* ♦ *vt*: ~**ted with** parsemé(e) de; **on the ~** à l'heure tapante.
dot command *n* (*COMPUT*) commande précédée d'un point.
dote [dəut]: **to ~ on** *vt fus* être fou(folle) de.
dot-matrix printer [dɔt'meɪtrɪks-] *n* imprimante matricielle.
dotted line ['dɔtɪd-] *n* ligne pointillée; (*AUT*) ligne discontinue; **to sign on the ~** signer à l'endroit indiqué or sur la ligne pointillée; (*fig*) donner son consentement.
dotty ['dɔtɪ] *adj* (*col*) loufoque, farfelu(e).
double ['dʌbl] *adj* double ♦ *adv* (*fold*) en deux; (*twice*): **to cost ~ (sth)** coûter le double (de qch) *or* deux fois plus (que qch) ♦ *n* double *m*; (*CINE*) doublure *f* ♦ *vt* doubler; (*fold*) plier en deux ♦ *vi* doubler; (*have two uses*): **to ~ as** servir aussi de; ~ **five two six (5526)** (*BRIT TEL*) cinquante-cinq - vingt-six; **it's spelt with a ~ "l"** ça s'écrit avec deux "l"; **on the ~,** (*BRIT*) **at the ~** au pas de course.
▶**double back** *vi* (*person*) revenir sur ses pas.
▶**double up** *vi* (*bend over*) se courber, se plier; (*share room*) partager la chambre.
double bass *n* contrebasse *f*.
double bed *n* grand lit.
double-breasted ['dʌbl'brɛstɪd] *adj* croisé(e).
double-check ['dʌbl'tʃɛk] *vt, vi* revérifier.
double-clutch ['dʌbl'klʌtʃ] *vi* (*US*) faire un

double débrayage.

double cream n (BRIT) crème fraîche épaisse.

doublecross ['dʌbl'krɔs] vt doubler, trahir.

doubledecker ['dʌbl'dɛkə*] n autobus m à impériale.

double declutch vi (BRIT) faire un double débrayage.

double exposure n (PHOT) surimpression f.

double glazing n (BRIT) double vitrage m.

double-page ['dʌblpeɪdʒ] adj: ~ **spread** publicité f en double page.

double parking n stationnement m en double file.

double room n chambre f pour deux.

doubles ['dʌblz] n (TENNIS) double m.

double whammy [-'wæmɪ] n (col) double contretemps m.

doubly ['dʌblɪ] adv doublement, deux fois plus.

doubt [daut] n doute m ♦ vt douter de; **without (a)** ~ sans aucun doute; **beyond** ~ adv indubitablement ♦ adj indubitable; **to** ~ **that** douter que; **I** ~ **it very much** j'en doute fort.

doubtful ['dautful] adj douteux(euse); (person) incertain(e); **to be** ~ **about sth** avoir des doutes sur qch, ne pas être convaincu de qch; **I'm a bit** ~ je n'en suis pas certain or sûr.

doubtless ['dautlɪs] adv sans doute, sûrement.

dough [dəu] n pâte f; (col: money) fric m, pognon m.

doughnut ['dəunʌt] n beignet m.

dour [duə*] adj austère.

douse [dauz] vt (with water) tremper, inonder; (flames) éteindre.

dove [dʌv] n colombe f.

Dover ['dəuvə*] n Douvres f.

dovetail ['dʌvteɪl] n: ~ **joint** assemblage m à queue d'aronde ♦ vi (fig) concorder.

dowager ['dauədʒə*] n douairière f.

dowdy ['daudɪ] adj démodé(e); mal fagoté(e).

Dow-Jones average ['dau'dʒəunz-] n (US) indice m Dow-Jones.

down [daun] n (fluff) duvet m; (hill) colline (dénudée) ♦ adv en bas ♦ prep en bas de ♦ vt (enemy) abattre; (col: drink) siffler; ~ **there** là-bas (en bas), là au fond; ~ **here** ici en bas; **the price of meat is** ~ le prix de la viande a baissé; **I've got it** ~ **in my diary** c'est inscrit dans mon agenda; **to pay £2** ~ verser 2 livres d'arrhes or en acompte; **England is two goals** ~ l'Angleterre a deux buts de retard; **to** ~ **tools** (BRIT) cesser le travail; ~ **with X!** à bas X!

down-and-out ['daunəndaut] n (tramp) clochard/e.

down-at-heel ['daunət'hi:l] adj (fig) miteux(euse).

downbeat ['daunbi:t] n (MUS) temps frappé ♦ adj sombre, négatif(ive).

downcast ['daunkɑ:st] adj démoralisé(e).

downer ['daunə*] n (col: drug) tranquillisant m; **to be on a** ~ (depressed) flipper.

downfall ['daunfɔ:l] n chute f; ruine f.

downgrade ['daungreɪd] vt déclasser.

downhearted ['daun'hɑ:tɪd] adj découragé(e).

downhill ['daun'hɪl] adv (face, look) en aval, vers l'aval; (roll, go) vers le bas, en bas ♦ n (SKI: also: ~ **race**) descente f; **to go** ~ descendre; (business) péricliter, aller à vau-l'eau.

Downing Street ['daunɪŋ-] n (BRIT): **10** ~ résidence du Premier ministre.

> **Downing Street** est une rue de Westminster (à Londres) où se trouve la résidence officielle du Premier ministre (numéro 10) et celle du ministre des Finances (numéro 11). Le nom "**Downing Street**" est souvent utilisé pour désigner le gouvernement britannique.

download ['daunləud] vt télécharger.

down-market ['daun'mɑ:kɪt] adj (product) bas de gamme inv.

down payment n acompte m.

downplay ['daunpleɪ] vt (US) minimiser (l'importance de).

downpour ['daunpɔ:*] n pluie torrentielle, déluge m.

downright ['daunraɪt] adj franc(franche); (refusal) catégorique.

Downs [daunz] npl (BRIT): **the** ~ collines crayeuses du sud-est de l'Angleterre.

downsize [daun'saɪz] vt réduire l'effectif de.

Down's syndrome [daunz-] n mongolisme m, trisomie f; **a** ~ **baby** un bébé mongolien or trisomique.

downstairs ['daun'stɛəz] adv (on or to ground floor) au rez-de-chaussée; (on or to floor below) à l'étage inférieur; **to come** ~, **to go** ~ descendre (l'escalier).

downstream ['daunstri:m] adv en aval.

downtime ['dauntaɪm] n (of machine etc) temps mort; (of person) temps d'arrêt.

down-to-earth ['dauntu'ə:θ] adj terre à terre inv.

downtown ['daun'taun] adv en ville ♦ adj (US): ~ **Chicago** le centre commerçant de Chicago.

downtrodden ['dauntrɔdn] adj opprimé(e).

down under adv en Australie (or Nouvelle Zélande).

downward ['daunwəd] adj vers le bas; **a** ~ **trend** une tendance à la baisse, une diminution progressive.

downward(s) ['daunwəd(z)] adv vers le bas.

dowry ['dauri] n dot f.

doz. abbr (= dozen) douz.

doze [dəuz] vi sommeiller.

▶**doze off** vi s'assoupir.

dozen ['dʌzn] n douzaine f; **a** ~ **books** une douzaine de livres; **80p a** ~ 80p la douzaine; ~**s of times** des centaines de fois.

DPh, DPhil *n abbr* (= *Doctor of Philosophy*) *titre universitaire.*
DPP *n abbr* (*BRIT*) = **Director of Public Prosecutions.**
DPT *n abbr* (*MED*: = *diphtheria, pertussis, tetanus*) DCT *m.*
DPW *n abbr* (*US*) = *Department of Public Works.*
Dr *abbr* (= *doctor*) Dr.
Dr. *abbr* (= *doctor*) Dr; (*in street names*) = **drive.**
dr *abbr* (*COMM*) = **debtor.**
drab [dræb] *adj* terne, morne.
draft [drɑːft] *n* brouillon *m*; (*of contract, document*) version *f* préliminaire; (*COMM*) traite *f*; (*US MIL*) contingent *m*; (: *call-up*) conscription *f* ♦ *vt* faire le brouillon de; (*document, report*) rédiger une version préliminaire de; *see also* **draught.**
drag [dræg] *vt* traîner; (*river*) draguer ♦ *vi* traîner ♦ *n* (*AVIAT, NAUT*) résistance *f*; (*col: person*) raseur/euse; (: *task etc*) corvée *f*; (*women's clothing*): **in ~** (en) travesti.
▶**drag away** *vt*: **to ~ away (from)** arracher *or* emmener de force (de).
▶**drag on** *vi* s'éterniser.
dragnet ['drægnɛt] *n* drège *f*; (*fig*) piège *m*, filets *mpl.*
dragon ['drægn] *n* dragon *m.*
dragonfly ['drægənflaɪ] *n* libellule *f.*
dragoon [drə'guːn] *n* (*cavalryman*) dragon *m* ♦ *vt*: **to ~ sb into doing sth** (*BRIT*) forcer qn à faire qch.
drain [dreɪn] *n* égout *m*; (*on resources*) saignée *f* ♦ *vt* (*land, marshes*) drainer, assécher; (*vegetables*) égoutter; (*reservoir etc*) vider ♦ *vi* (*water*) s'écouler; **to feel ~ed (of energy** *or* **emotion)** être miné(e).
drainage ['dreɪnɪdʒ] *n* système *m* d'égouts.
draining board ['dreɪnɪŋ-], (*US*) **drainboard** ['dreɪnbɔːd] *n* égouttoir *m.*
drainpipe ['dreɪnpaɪp] *n* tuyau *m* d'écoulement.
drake [dreɪk] *n* canard *m* (mâle).
dram [dræm] *n* petit verre.
drama ['drɑːmə] *n* (*art*) théâtre *m*, art *m* dramatique; (*play*) pièce *f*; (*event*) drame *m.*
dramatic [drə'mætɪk] *adj* (*THEAT*) dramatique; (*impressive*) spectaculaire.
dramatically [drə'mætɪklɪ] *adv* de façon spectaculaire.
dramatist ['dræmətɪst] *n* auteur *m* dramatique.
dramatize ['dræmətaɪz] *vt* (*events etc*) dramatiser; (*adapt*) adapter pour la télévision (*or* pour l'écran).
drank [dræŋk] *pt of* **drink.**
drape [dreɪp] *vt* draper.
draper ['dreɪpə*] *n* (*BRIT*) marchand/e de nouveautés.
drapes [dreɪps] *npl* (*US*) rideaux *mpl.*
drastic ['dræstɪk] *adj* (*measures*) d'urgence, énergique; (*change*) radical(e).
drastically ['dræstɪklɪ] *adv* radicalement.

draught, (*US*) **draft** [drɑːft] *n* courant *m* d'air; (*of chimney*) tirage *m*; (*NAUT*) tirant *m* d'eau; **on ~** (*beer*) à la pression.
draught beer *n* bière *f* (à la) pression.
draughtboard ['drɑːftbɔːd] *n* (*BRIT*) damier *m.*
draughts [drɑːfts] *n* (*BRIT*) (jeu *m* de) dames *fpl.*
draughtsman, (*US*) **draftsman** ['drɑːftsmən] *n* dessinateur/trice (industriel(le)).
draughtsmanship, (*US*) **draftsmanship** ['drɑːftsmənʃɪp] *n* (*technique*) dessin industriel; (*art*) graphisme *m.*
draw [drɔː] *vb* (*pt* **drew**, *pp* **drawn** [druː, drɔːn]) *vt* tirer; (*attract*) attirer; (*picture*) dessiner; (*line, circle*) tracer; (*money*) retirer; (*comparison, distinction*): **to ~ (between)** faire (entre) ♦ *vi* (*SPORT*) faire match nul ♦ *n* match nul; (*lottery*) loterie *f*; (: *picking of ticket*) tirage *m* au sort; **to ~ to a close** toucher à *or* tirer à sa fin; **to ~ near** *vi* s'approcher; approcher.
▶**draw back** *vi* (*move back*): **to ~ back (from)** reculer (de).
▶**draw in** *vi* (*BRIT: car*) s'arrêter le long du trottoir; (: *train*) entrer en gare *or* dans la station.
▶**draw on** *vt* (*resources*) faire appel à; (*imagination, person*) avoir recours à, faire appel à.
▶**draw out** *vi* (*lengthen*) s'allonger ♦ *vt* (*money*) retirer.
▶**draw up** *vi* (*stop*) s'arrêter ♦ *vt* (*document*) établir, dresser; (*plans*) formuler, dessiner.
drawback ['drɔːbæk] *n* inconvénient *m*, désavantage *m.*
drawbridge ['drɔːbrɪdʒ] *n* pont-levis *m.*
drawee [drɔː'iː] *n* tiré *m.*
drawer [drɔː*] *n* tiroir *m*; ['drɔːə*] (*of cheque*) tireur *m.*
drawing ['drɔːɪŋ] *n* dessin *m.*
drawing board *n* planche *f* à dessin.
drawing pin *n* (*BRIT*) punaise *f.*
drawing room *n* salon *m.*
drawl [drɔːl] *n* accent traînant.
drawn [drɔːn] *pp of* **draw** ♦ *adj* (*haggard*) tiré(e), crispé(e).
drawstring ['drɔːstrɪŋ] *n* cordon *m.*
dread [drɛd] *n* épouvante *f*, effroi *m* ♦ *vt* redouter, appréhender.
dreadful ['drɛdful] *adj* épouvantable, affreux(euse).
dream [driːm] *n* rêve *m* ♦ *vt, vi* (*pt, pp* **dreamed** *or* **dreamt** [drɛmt]) rêver; **to have a ~ about sb/sth** rêver à qn/qch; **sweet ~s!** faites de beaux rêves!
▶**dream up** *vt* inventer.
dreamer ['driːmə*] *n* rêveur/euse.
dream world *n* monde *m* imaginaire.
dreamy ['driːmɪ] *adj* (*absent-minded*) rêveur(euse).
dreary ['drɪərɪ] *adj* triste; monotone.
dredge [drɛdʒ] *vt* draguer.

▶**dredge up** vt draguer; (fig: unpleasant facts) (faire) ressortir.

dredger ['drɛdʒə*] n (ship) dragueur m; (machine) drague f; (BRIT: also: **sugar** ~) saupoudreuse f.

dregs [drɛgz] npl lie f.

drench [drɛntʃ] vt tremper; ~**ed to the skin** trempé(e) jusqu'aux os.

dress [drɛs] n robe f; (clothing) habillement m, tenue f ♦ vt habiller; (wound) panser; (food) préparer ♦ vi: **she** ~**es very well** elle s'habille très bien; **to** ~ **o.s., to get** ~**ed** s'habiller; **to** ~ **a shop window** faire l'étalage or la vitrine.

▶**dress up** vi s'habiller; (in fancy dress) se déguiser.

dress circle n premier balcon.

dress designer n modéliste m/f, dessinateur/ trice de mode.

dresser ['drɛsə*] n (THEAT) habilleur/euse; (also: **window** ~) étalagiste m/f; (furniture) vaisselier m.

dressing ['drɛsɪŋ] n (MED) pansement m; (CULIN) sauce f, assaisonnement m.

dressing gown n (BRIT) robe f de chambre.

dressing room n (THEAT) loge f; (SPORT) vestiaire m.

dressing table n coiffeuse f.

dressmaker ['drɛsmeɪkə*] n couturière f.

dressmaking ['drɛsmeɪkɪŋ] n couture f; travaux mpl de couture.

dress rehearsal n (répétition f) générale f.

dress shirt n chemise f à plastron.

dressy ['drɛsɪ] adj (col: clothes) (qui fait) habillé(e).

drew [dru:] pt of **draw**.

dribble ['drɪbl] vi tomber goutte à goutte; (baby) baver ♦ vt (ball) dribbler.

dried [draɪd] adj (fruit, beans) sec(sèche); (eggs, milk) en poudre.

drier ['draɪə*] n = **dryer**.

drift [drɪft] n (of current etc) force f; direction f; (of sand etc) amoncellement m; (of snow) rafale f; coulée f; (: on ground) congère f; (general meaning) sens général ♦ vi (boat) aller à la dérive, dériver; (sand, snow) s'amonceler, s'entasser; **to let things** ~ laisser les choses aller à la dérive; **to** ~ **apart** (friends, lovers) s'éloigner l'un de l'autre; **I get** or **catch your** ~ je vois en gros ce que vous voulez dire.

drifter ['drɪftə*] n personne f sans but dans la vie.

driftwood ['drɪftwud] n bois flotté.

drill [drɪl] n perceuse f; (bit) foret m; (of dentist) roulette f, fraise f; (MIL) exercice m ♦ vt percer; (soldiers) faire faire l'exercice à; (pupils: in grammar) faire faire des exercices à ♦ vi (for oil) faire un or des forage(s).

drilling ['drɪlɪŋ] n (for oil) forage m.

drilling rig n (on land) tour f (de forage), derrick m; (at sea) plate-forme f de forage.

drily ['draɪlɪ] adv = **dryly**.

drink [drɪŋk] n boisson f ♦ vt, vi (pt **drank**, pp **drunk** [dræŋk, drʌŋk]) boire; **to have a** ~ boire quelque chose, boire un verre; **a** ~ **of water** un verre d'eau; **would you like something to** ~? aimeriez-vous boire quelque chose?; **we had** ~**s before lunch** on a pris l'apéritif.

▶**drink in** vt (fresh air) inspirer profondément; (story) avaler, ne pas perdre une miette de; (sight) se remplir la vue de.

drinkable ['drɪŋkəbl] adj (not dangerous) potable; (palatable) buvable.

drink-driving ['drɪŋk'draɪvɪŋ] n conduite f en état d'ivresse.

drinker ['drɪŋkə*] n buveur/euse.

drinking ['drɪŋkɪŋ] n (drunkenness) boisson f, alcoolisme m.

drinking fountain n (in park etc) fontaine publique; (in building) jet m d'eau potable.

drinking water n eau f potable.

drip [drɪp] n goutte f; (sound: of water etc) bruit m de l'eau qui tombe goutte à goutte; (MED) goutte-à-goutte m inv, perfusion f; (col: person) lavette f, nouille f ♦ vi tomber goutte à goutte; (washing) s'égoutter; (wall) suinter.

drip-dry ['drɪp'draɪ] adj (shirt) sans repassage.

drip-feed ['drɪpfiːd] vt alimenter au goutte-à-goutte or par perfusion.

dripping ['drɪpɪŋ] n graisse f de rôti ♦ adj: ~ **wet** trempé(e).

drive [draɪv] n promenade f or trajet m en voiture; (also: ~**way**) allée f; (energy) dynamisme m, énergie f; (PSYCH) besoin m; pulsion f; (campaign) effort (concerté); campagne f; (SPORT) drive m; (TECH) entraînement m; traction f; transmission f; (COMPUT: also: **disk** ~) lecteur m de disquette ♦ vb (pt **drove**, pp **driven** [drəuv, 'drɪvn]) vt conduire; (nail) enfoncer; (push) chasser, pousser; (TECH: motor) actionner; entraîner ♦ vi (be at the wheel) conduire; (travel by car) aller en voiture; **to go for a** ~ aller faire une promenade en voiture; **it's 3 hours'** ~ **from London** Londres est à 3 heures de route; **left-/right-hand** ~ (AUT) conduite f à gauche/droite; **front-/rear-wheel** ~ (AUT) traction f avant/arrière; **to** ~ **sb to (do) sth** pousser or conduire qn à (faire) qch; **to** ~ **sb mad** rendre qn fou(folle).

▶**drive at** vt fus (fig: intend, mean) vouloir dire, en venir à.

▶**drive on** vi poursuivre sa route, continuer; (after stopping) reprendre sa route, repartir ♦ vt (incite, encourage) inciter.

drive-by ['draɪvbaɪ] n (also: ~ **shooting**) (tentative d')assassinat par coups de feu tirés d'une voiture.

drive-in ['draɪvɪn] adj, n (esp US) drive-in (m).

drive-in window n (US) guichet-auto m.

drivel ['drɪvl] n (col) idioties fpl, imbécillités fpl.

driven ['drɪvn] *pp of* **drive**.
driver ['draɪvə*] *n* conducteur/trice; (*of taxi, bus*) chauffeur *m*.
driver's license *n* (*US*) permis *m* de conduire.
driveway ['draɪvweɪ] *n* allée *f*.
driving ['draɪvɪŋ] *adj*: ~ **rain** *n* pluie battante ♦ *n* conduite *f*.
driving force *n* locomotive *f*, élément *m* dynamique.
driving instructor *n* moniteur *m* d'auto-école.
driving lesson *n* leçon *f* de conduite.
driving licence *n* (*BRIT*) permis *m* de conduire.
driving school *n* auto-école *f*.
driving test *n* examen *m* du permis de conduire.
drizzle ['drɪzl] *n* bruine *f*, crachin *m* ♦ *vi* bruiner.
droll [drəul] *adj* drôle.
dromedary ['drɔmədərɪ] *n* dromadaire *m*.
drone [drəun] *vi* (*bee*) bourdonner; (*engine etc*) ronronner; (*also*: ~ **on**) parler d'une voix monocorde ♦ *n* bourdonnement *m*; ronronnement *m*; (*male bee*) faux-bourdon *m*.
drool [druːl] *vi* baver; **to** ~ **over sb/sth** (*fig*) baver d'admiration *or* être en extase devant qn/qch.
droop [druːp] *vi* s'affaisser; tomber.
drop [drɔp] *n* goutte *f*; (*fall: also in price*) baisse *f*; (*: in salary*) réduction *f*, (*also*: **parachute** ~) saut *m*; (*of cliff*) dénivellation *f*, à-pic *m* ♦ *vt* laisser tomber; (*voice, eyes, price*) baisser; (*set down from car*) déposer ♦ *vi* (*wind, temperature, price, voice*) tomber; (*numbers, attendance*) diminuer; ~**s** *npl* (*MED*) gouttes; **cough** ~**s** pastilles *fpl* pour la toux; **a** ~ **of 10%** une baisse (*or* réduction) de 10%; **to** ~ **anchor** jeter l'ancre; **to** ~ **sb a line** mettre un mot à qn.
▶**drop in** *vi* (*col: visit*): **to** ~ **in (on)** faire un saut (chez), passer (chez).
▶**drop off** *vi* (*sleep*) s'assoupir ♦ *vt*: **to** ~ **sb off** déposer qn.
▶**drop out** *vi* (*withdraw*) se retirer; (*student etc*) abandonner, décrocher.
droplet ['drɔplɪt] *n* gouttelette *f*.
dropout ['drɔpaut] *n* (*from society*) marginal/e; (*from university*) drop-out *m/f*, dropé/e.
dropper ['drɔpə*] *n* (*MED etc*) compte-gouttes *m inv*.
droppings ['drɔpɪŋz] *npl* crottes *fpl*.
dross [drɔs] *n* déchets *mpl*; rebut *m*.
drought [draut] *n* sécheresse *f*.
drove [drəuv] *pt of* **drive** ♦ *n*: ~**s of people** une foule de gens.
drown [draun] *vt* noyer; (*also*: ~ **out**: *sound*) couvrir, étouffer ♦ *vi* se noyer.
drowse [drauz] *vi* somnoler.
drowsy ['drauzɪ] *adj* somnolent(e).
drudge [drʌdʒ] *n* bête *f* de somme (*fig*).

drudgery ['drʌdʒərɪ] *n* corvée *f*.
drug [drʌg] *n* médicament *m*; (*narcotic*) drogue *f* ♦ *vt* droguer; **he's on** ~**s** il se drogue; (*MED*) il est sous médication.
drug addict *n* toxicomane *m/f*.
druggist ['drʌgɪst] *n* (*US*) pharmacien/ne-droguiste.
drug peddler *n* revendeur/euse de drogue.
drugstore ['drʌgstɔː*] *n* (*US*) pharmacie-droguerie *f*, drugstore *m*.
drum [drʌm] *n* tambour *m*; (*for oil, petrol*) bidon *m* ♦ *vt*: **to** ~ **one's fingers on the table** pianoter *or* tambouriner sur la table; ~**s** *npl* (*MUS*) batterie *f*.
▶**drum up** *vt* (*enthusiasm, support*) susciter, rallier.
drummer ['drʌmə*] *n* (joueur *m* de) tambour *m*.
drum roll *n* roulement *m* de tambour.
drumstick ['drʌmstɪk] *n* (*MUS*) baguette *f* de tambour; (*of chicken*) pilon *m*.
drunk [drʌŋk] *pp of* **drink** ♦ *adj* ivre, soûl(e) ♦ *n* soûlard/e; homme/femme soûl(e); **to get** ~ s'enivrer, se soûler.
drunkard ['drʌŋkəd] *n* ivrogne *m/f*.
drunken ['drʌŋkən] *adj* ivre, soûl(e); (*habitual*) ivrogne, d'ivrogne; ~ **driving** conduite *f* en état d'ivresse.
drunkenness ['drʌŋkənnɪs] *n* ivresse *f*; ivrognerie *f*.
dry [draɪ] *adj* sec(sèche); (*day*) sans pluie; (*humour*) pince-sans-rire; (*uninteresting*) aride, rébarbatif(ive) ♦ *vt* sécher; (*clothes*) faire sécher ♦ *vi* sécher; **on** ~ **land** sur la terre ferme; **to** ~ **one's hands/hair/eyes** se sécher les mains/les cheveux/les yeux.
▶**dry up** *vi* (*also fig: source of supply, imagination*) se tarir; (*: speaker*) sécher, rester sec.
dry-clean ['draɪ'kliːn] *vt* nettoyer à sec.
dry-cleaner ['draɪ'kliːnə*] *n* teinturier *m*.
dry-cleaner's ['draɪ'kliːnəz] *n* teinturerie *f*.
dry-cleaning ['draɪ'kliːnɪŋ] *n* nettoyage *m* à sec.
dry dock *n* (*NAUT*) cale sèche, bassin *m* de radoub.
dryer ['draɪə*] *n* séchoir *m*; (*spin-*~) essoreuse *f*.
dry goods *npl* (*COMM*) textiles *mpl*, mercerie *f*.
dry goods store *n* (*US*) magasin *m* de nouveautés.
dry ice *n* neige *f* carbonique.
dryly ['draɪlɪ] *adv* sèchement, d'un ton sec.
dryness ['draɪnɪs] *n* sécheresse *f*.
dry rot *n* pourriture sèche (*du bois*).
dry run *n* (*fig*) essai *m*.
dry ski slope *n* piste (de ski) artificielle.
DSc *n abbr* (= *Doctor of Science*) *titre universitaire*.
DSS *n abbr* (*BRIT*) = *Department of Social Security*.
DST *abbr* (*US*: = *Daylight Saving Time*) *heure d'été*.

DT n abbr (COMPUT) = **data transmission**.
DTI n abbr (BRIT) = Department of Trade and
Industry.
DTP n abbr = **desktop publishing**.
DT's [di:'ti:z] n abbr (col: = delirium tremens)
delirium tremens m.
dual ['djuəl] adj double.
dual carriageway n (BRIT) route f à quatre
voies.
dual-control ['djuəlkən'trəul] adj à doubles
commandes.
dual nationality n double nationalité f.
dual-purpose ['djuəl'pə:pəs] adj à double
emploi.
dubbed [dʌbd] adj (CINE) doublé(e);
(nicknamed) surnommé(e).
dubious ['dju:biəs] adj hésitant(e),
incertain(e); (reputation, company)
douteux(euse); **I'm very ~ about it** j'ai des
doutes sur la question, je n'en suis pas sûr
du tout.
Dublin ['dʌblin] n Dublin.
Dubliner ['dʌblinə*] n habitant/e de Dublin;
originaire m/f de Dublin.
duchess ['dʌtʃis] n duchesse f.
duck [dʌk] n canard m ♦ vi se baisser
vivement, baisser subitement la tête ♦ vt
plonger dans l'eau.
duckling ['dʌklıŋ] n caneton m.
duct [dʌkt] n conduite f, canalisation f; (ANAT)
conduit m.
dud [dʌd] n (shell) obus non éclaté; (object,
tool): **it's a ~** c'est de la camelote, ça ne
marche pas ♦ adj (BRIT: cheque) sans
provision; (: note, coin) faux(fausse).
due [dju:] adj dû(due); (expected) attendu(e);
(fitting) qui convient ♦ n dû m ♦ adv: ~ **north**
droit vers le nord; ~**s** npl (for club, union)
cotisation f; (in harbour) droits mpl (de port);
in ~ course en temps utile or voulu; (in the
end) finalement; ~ **to** dû à; causé par; **the
rent is ~ on the 30th** il faut payer le loyer le
30; **the train is ~ at 8** le train est attendu à
8 h; **she is ~ back tomorrow** elle doit
rentrer demain; **I am ~ 6 days' leave** j'ai
droit à 6 jours de congé.
due date n date f d'échéance.
duel ['djuəl] n duel m.
duet [dju:'et] n duo m.
duff [dʌf] adj (BRIT col) nullard(e), nul(le).
duffelbag, duffle bag ['dʌflbæg] n sac marin.
duffelcoat, duffle coat ['dʌflkəut] n duffel-
coat m.
duffer ['dʌfə*] n (col) nullard/e.
dug [dʌg] pt, pp of **dig**.
dugout ['dʌgaut] n (SPORT) banc m de touche.
duke [dju:k] n duc m.
dull [dʌl] adj (boring) ennuyeux(euse); (slow)
borné(e); (lacklustre) morne, terne; (sound,
pain) sourd(e); (weather, day) gris(e),
maussade; (blade) émoussé(e) ♦ vt (pain,
grief) atténuer; (mind, senses) engourdir.

duly ['dju:li] adv (on time) en temps voulu; (as
expected) comme il se doit.
dumb [dʌm] adj muet(te); (stupid) bête; **to be
struck ~** (fig) rester abasourdi(e), être
sidéré(e).
dumbbell ['dʌmbel] n (SPORT) haltère m.
dumbfounded [dʌm'faundid] adj sidéré(e).
dummy ['dʌmi] n (tailor's model) mannequin
m; (SPORT) feinte f; (BRIT: for baby) tétine f
♦ adj faux(fausse), factice.
dummy run n essai m.
dump [dʌmp] n tas m d'ordures; (place)
décharge (publique); (MIL) dépôt m;
(COMPUT) listage m (de la mémoire) ♦ vt (put
down) déposer; déverser; (get rid of) se
débarrasser de; (COMPUT) lister; (COMM:
goods) vendre à perte (sur le marché
extérieur); **to be (down) in the ~s** (col) avoir
le cafard, broyer du noir.
dumping ['dʌmpiŋ] n (ECON) dumping m; (of
rubbish): **"no ~"** "décharge interdite".
dumpling ['dʌmpliŋ] n boulette f (de pâte).
dumpy ['dʌmpi] adj courtaud(e), boulot(te).
dunce [dʌns] n âne m, cancre m.
dune [dju:n] n dune f.
dung [dʌŋ] n fumier m.
dungarees [dʌŋɡə'ri:z] npl bleu(s) m(pl); (for
child, woman) salopette f.
dungeon ['dʌndʒən] n cachot m.
dunk [dʌŋk] vt tremper.
Dunkirk [dʌn'kə:k] n Dunkerque.
duo ['dju:əu] n (gen, MUS) duo m.
duodenal [dju:əu'di:nl] adj duodénal(e); ~
ulcer ulcère m du duodénum.
dupe [dju:p] n dupe f ♦ vt duper, tromper.
duplex ['dju:pleks] n (US: also: ~ **apartment**)
duplex m.
duplicate n ['dju:plikət] double m, copie
exacte; (copy of letter etc) duplicata m ♦ adj
(copy) en double ♦ vt ['dju:plikeit] faire un
double de; (on machine) polycopier; **in ~** en
deux exemplaires, en double; ~ **key** double
m de la (or d'une) clé.
duplicating machine ['dju:plikeitiŋ-],
duplicator ['dju:plikeitə*] n duplicateur m.
duplicity [dju:'plisiti] n duplicité f, fausseté f.
Dur abbr (BRIT) = Durham.
durability [djuərə'biliti] n solidité f; durabilité
f.
durable ['djuərəbl] adj durable; (clothes, metal)
résistant(e), solide.
duration [djuə'reiʃən] n durée f.
duress [djuə'res] n: **under ~** sous la
contrainte.
Durex ['djuəreks] n ® (BRIT) préservatif
(masculin).
during ['djuəriŋ] prep pendant, au cours de.
dusk [dʌsk] n crépuscule m.
dusky ['dʌski] adj sombre.
dust [dʌst] n poussière f ♦ vt (furniture)
essuyer, épousseter; (cake etc): **to ~ with**
saupoudrer de.

▶**dust off** *vt* (*also fig*) dépoussiérer.
dustbin ['dʌstbɪn] *n* (*BRIT*) poubelle *f*.
duster ['dʌstə*] *n* chiffon *m*.
dust jacket *n* jacquette *f*.
dustman ['dʌstmən] *n* (*BRIT*) boueux *m*, éboueur *m*.
dustpan ['dʌstpæn] *n* pelle *f* à poussière.
dusty ['dʌstɪ] *adj* poussiéreux(euse).
Dutch [dʌtʃ] *adj* hollandais(e), néerlandais(e) ♦ *n* (*LING*) hollandais *m*, néerlandais *m* ♦ *adv*: **to go** ~ *or* **d**~ partager les frais; **the** ~ *npl* les Hollandais, les Néerlandais.
Dutch auction *n* enchères *fpl* à la baisse.
Dutchman ['dʌtʃmən], **Dutchwoman** ['dʌtʃwumən] *n* Hollandais/e.
dutiable ['djuːtɪəbl] *adj* taxable; soumis(e) à des droits de douane.
dutiful ['djuːtɪful] *adj* (*child*) respectueux(euse); (*husband, wife*) plein(e) d'égards, prévenant(e); (*employee*) consciencieux(euse).
duty ['djuːtɪ] *n* devoir *m*; (*tax*) droit *m*, taxe *f*; **duties** *npl* fonctions *fpl*; **to make it one's** ~ **to do sth** se faire un devoir de faire qch; **to pay** ~ **on sth** payer un droit *or* une taxe sur qch; **on** ~ de service; (*at night etc*) de garde; **off** ~ libre, pas de service *or* de garde.
duty-free ['djuːtɪ'friː] *adj* exempté(e) de douane, hors-taxe; ~ **shop** boutique *f* hors-taxe.
duty officer *n* (*MIL etc*) officier *m* de permanence.
duvet ['duːveɪ] *n* (*BRIT*) couette *f*.
DV *abbr* (= *Deo volente*) si Dieu le veut.
DVLA *n abbr* (*BRIT*: = *Driver and Vehicle Licensing Agency*) *service qui délivre les cartes grises et les permis de conduire*.
DVM *n abbr* (*US*: = *Doctor of Veterinary Medicine*) *titre universitaire*.
dwarf [dwɔːf] *n* nain/e ♦ *vt* écraser.
dwell, *pt, pp* **dwelt** [dwel, dwelt] *vi* demeurer.
▶**dwell on** *vt fus* s'étendre sur.
dweller ['dwelə*] *n* habitant/e.
dwelling ['dwelɪŋ] *n* habitation *f*, demeure *f*.
dwindle ['dwɪndl] *vi* diminuer, décroître.
dwindling ['dwɪndlɪŋ] *adj* décroissant(e), en diminution.
dye [daɪ] *n* teinture *f* ♦ *vt* teindre; **hair** ~ teinture pour les cheveux.
dyestuffs ['daɪstʌfs] *npl* colorants *mpl*.
dying ['daɪɪŋ] *adj* mourant(e), agonisant(e).
dyke [daɪk] *n* (*embankment*) digue *f*.
dynamic [daɪ'næmɪk] *adj* dynamique.
dynamics [daɪ'næmɪks] *n or npl* dynamique *f*.
dynamite ['daɪnəmaɪt] *n* dynamite *f* ♦ *vt* dynamiter, faire sauter à la dynamite.
dynamo ['daɪnəməu] *n* dynamo *f*.
dynasty ['dɪnəstɪ] *n* dynastie *f*.
dysentery ['dɪsntrɪ] *n* dysenterie *f*.
dyslexia [dɪs'leksɪə] *n* dyslexie *f*.
dyslexic [dɪs'leksɪk] *adj, n* dyslexique *m/f*.
dyspepsia [dɪs'pepsɪə] *n* dyspepsie *f*.

dystrophy ['dɪstrəfɪ] *n* dystrophie *f*; **muscular** ~ dystrophie musculaire.

E e

E, e [iː] *n* (*letter*) E, e *m*; (*MUS*): **E** mi *m*; **E for Edward**, (*US*) **E for Easy** E comme Eugène.
E *abbr* (= *east*) E ♦ *n abbr* (*DRUGS*) = **ecstasy**.
E111 ['iːwʌnɪ'levn] *n abbr* (*also*: **form** ~) formulaire *m* E111.
ea. *abbr* = **each**.
E.A. *n abbr* (*US*: = *educational age*) *niveau scolaire*.
each [iːtʃ] *adj* chaque ♦ *pron* chacun(e); ~ **one** chacun(e); ~ **other** se (*or* nous *etc*); **they hate** ~ **other** ils se détestent (mutuellement); **you are jealous of** ~ **other** vous êtes jaloux l'un de l'autre; ~ **day** chaque jour, tous les jours; **they have 2 books** ~ ils ont 2 livres chacun; **they cost £5** ~ ils coûtent 5 livres (la) pièce; ~ **of us** chacun(e) de nous.
eager ['iːgə*] *adj* impatient(e); avide; ardent(e), passionné(e); (*keen: pupil*) plein(e) d'enthousiasme, qui se passionne pour les études; **to be** ~ **to do sth** être impatient de faire qch, brûler de faire qch; **you are jealous of** ~ **other** *(désir vivement faire qch; to be ~ for)* désirer vivement faire qch; **to be** ~ **for** désirer vivement, être avide de.
eagle ['iːgl] *n* aigle *m*.
E and OE *abbr* = **errors and omissions excepted**.
ear [ɪə*] *n* oreille *f*; (*of corn*) épi *m*; **up to one's** ~**s in debt** endetté(e) jusqu'au cou.
earache ['ɪəreɪk] *n* douleurs *fpl* aux oreilles.
eardrum ['ɪədrʌm] *n* tympan *m*.
earful ['ɪəful] *n* (*col*): **to give sb an** ~ passer un savon à qn.
earl [əːl] *n* comte *m*.
earlier ['əːlɪə*] *adj* (*date etc*) plus rapproché(e); (*edition etc*) plus ancien(ne), antérieur(e) ♦ *adv* plus tôt.
early ['əːlɪ] *adv* tôt, de bonne heure; (*ahead of time*) en avance ♦ *adj* précoce; qui se manifeste (*or* se fait) tôt *or* de bonne heure; (*Christians, settlers*) premier(ière); **have an** ~ **night/start** couchez-vous/partez tôt *or* de bonne heure; **take the** ~ **train** prenez le premier train; **in the** ~ *or* ~ **in the spring/19th century** au début *or* commencement du printemps/19ème siècle; **you're** ~! tu es en avance!; ~ **in the morning** tôt le matin; **she's in her** ~ **forties** elle a un peu plus de quarante ans *or* de la quarantaine; **at your earliest convenience** (*COMM*) dans les meilleurs délais.

early retirement n retraite anticipée.
early warning system n système m de première alerte.
earmark ['iəmɑːk] vt: **to ~ sth for** réserver or destiner qch à.
earn [əːn] vt gagner; (COMM: yield) rapporter; **to ~ one's living** gagner sa vie; **this ~ed him much praise, he ~ed much praise for this** ceci lui a valu de nombreux éloges; **he's ~ed his rest/reward** il mérite or a bien mérité or a bien gagné son repos/sa récompense.
earned income [əːnd-] n revenu m du travail.
earnest ['əːnɪst] adj sérieux(euse) ♦ n (also: ~ **money**) acompte m, arrhes fpl; **in ~** adv sérieusement, pour de bon.
earnings ['əːnɪŋz] npl salaire m; gains mpl; (of company etc) profits mpl, bénéfices mpl.
ear, nose and throat specialist n oto-rhino-laryngologiste m/f.
earphones ['iəfəunz] npl écouteurs mpl.
earplugs ['iəplʌgz] npl boules fpl Quiès ®; (to keep out water) protège-tympans mpl.
earring ['iərɪŋ] n boucle f d'oreille.
earshot ['iəʃɔt] n: **out of/within ~** hors de portée/à portée de voix.
earth [əːθ] n (gen, also BRIT ELEC) terre f; (of fox etc) terrier m ♦ vt (BRIT ELEC) relier à la terre.
earthenware ['əːθnwεə*] n poterie f; faïence f ♦ adj de or en faïence.
earthly ['əːθlɪ] adj terrestre; **~ paradise** paradis m terrestre; **there is no ~ reason to think** ... il n'y a absolument aucune raison or pas la moindre raison de penser ....
earthquake ['əːθkweɪk] n tremblement m de terre, séisme m.
earth-shattering ['əːθʃætərɪŋ] adj stupéfiant(e).
earth tremor n secousse f sismique.
earthworks ['əːθwəːks] npl travaux mpl de terrassement.
earthworm ['əːθwəːm] n ver m de terre.
earthy ['əːθɪ] adj (fig) terre à terre inv; truculent(e).
earwax ['iəwæks] n cérumen m.
earwig ['iəwɪg] n perce-oreille m.
ease [iːz] n facilité f, aisance f ♦ vt (soothe) calmer; (loosen) relâcher, détendre; (help pass): **to ~ sth in/out** faire pénétrer/sortir qch délicatement or avec douceur; faciliter la pénétration/la sortie de qch ♦ vi (situation) se détendre; **with ~** sans difficulté, aisément; **life of ~** vie oisive; **at ~** à l'aise; (MIL) au repos.
►**ease off, ease up** vi diminuer; (slow down) ralentir; (relax) se détendre.
easel ['iːzl] n chevalet m.
easily ['iːzɪlɪ] adv facilement.
easiness ['iːsɪnɪs] n facilité f; (of manner) aisance f; nonchalance f.
east [iːst] n est m ♦ adj d'est ♦ adv à l'est, vers

l'est; **the E~** l'Orient m; (POL) les pays mpl de l'Est.
Easter ['iːstə*] n Pâques fpl ♦ adj (holidays) de Pâques, pascal(e).
Easter egg n œuf m de Pâques.
Easter Island n île f de Pâques.
easterly ['iːstəlɪ] adj d'est.
Easter Monday n le lundi de Pâques.
eastern ['iːstən] adj de l'est, oriental(e); **E~ Europe** l'Europe de l'Est; **the E~ bloc** (POL) les pays mpl de l'est.
Easter Sunday n le dimanche de Pâques.
East Germany n (formerly) Allemagne f de l'Est.
eastward(s) ['iːstwəd(z)] adv vers l'est, à l'est.
easy ['iːzɪ] adj facile; (manner) aisé(e) ♦ adv: **to take it** or **things ~** ne pas se fatiguer; (not worry) ne pas (trop) s'en faire; **payment on ~ terms** (COMM) facilités fpl de paiement; **that's easier said than done** c'est plus facile à dire qu'à faire, c'est vite dit; **I'm ~** (col) ça m'est égal.
easy chair n fauteuil m.
easy-going ['iːzɪ'gəuɪŋ] adj accommodant(e), facile à vivre.
easy touch n (col): **he's an ~** c'est une bonne poire.
eat, pt **ate**, pp **eaten** [iːt, eɪt, 'iːtn] vt, vi manger.
►**eat away** vt (subj: sea) saper, éroder; (: acid) ronger, corroder.
►**eat away at, eat into** vt fus ronger, attaquer.
►**eat out** vi manger au restaurant.
►**eat up** vt (food) finir (de manger); **it ~s up electricity** ça bouffe du courant, ça consomme beaucoup d'électricité.
eatable ['iːtəbl] adj mangeable; (safe to eat) comestible.
eau de Cologne ['əudəkə'ləun] n eau f de Cologne.
eaves [iːvz] npl avant-toit m.
eavesdrop ['iːvzdrɔp] vi: **to ~ (on)** écouter de façon indiscrète.
ebb [εb] n reflux m ♦ vi refluer; (fig: also: ~ **away**) décliner; **the ~ and flow** le flux et le reflux; **to be at a low ~** (fig) être bien bas(se), ne pas aller bien fort.
ebb tide n marée descendante, reflux m.
ebony ['εbənɪ] n ébène f.
ebullient [ɪ'bʌlɪənt] adj exubérant(e).
EC n abbr (= European Community) CE f (= Communauté européenne).
eccentric [ɪk'sεntrɪk] adj, n excentrique (m/f).
ecclesiastic(al) [ɪkliːzɪ'æstɪk(l)] adj ecclésiastique.
ECG n abbr = **electrocardiogram**.
ECGD n abbr (= Export Credits Guarantee Department) service de garantie financière à l'exportation.
echo, **~es** ['εkəu] n écho m ♦ vt répéter; faire

chorus avec ♦ vi résonner; faire écho.

éclair ['eɪklɛə*] n éclair m (CULIN).

eclipse [ɪ'klɪps] n éclipse f ♦ vt éclipser.

ECM n abbr (US) = European Common Market.

eco- ['i:kəu] prefix éco-.

eco-friendly [i:kəu'frɛndlɪ] adj non nuisible à or qui ne nuit pas à l'environnement.

ecological [i:kə'lɔdʒɪkəl] adj écologique.

ecologist [ɪ'kɔlədʒɪst] n écologiste m/f.

ecology [ɪ'kɔlədʒɪ] n écologie f.

economic [i:kə'nɔmɪk] adj économique; (profitable) rentable.

economical [i:kə'nɔmɪkl] adj économique; (person) économe.

economically [i:kə'nɔmɪklɪ] adv économiquement.

economics [i:kə'nɔmɪks] n économie f politique ♦ npl côté m or aspect m économique.

economist [ɪ'kɔnəmɪst] n économiste m/f.

economize [ɪ'kɔnəmaɪz] vi économiser, faire des économies.

economy [ɪ'kɔnəmɪ] n économie f; **economies of scale** économies d'échelle.

economy class n (AVIAT etc) classe f touriste.

economy size n taille f économique.

ecosystem ['i:kəusɪstəm] n écosystème m.

eco-tourism [i:kəu'tuərɪzəm] n écotourisme m.

ECSC n abbr (= European Coal & Steel Community) CECA f (= Communauté européenne du charbon et de l'acier).

ecstasy ['ɛkstəsɪ] n extase f; (DRUGS) ecstasy m; **to go into ecstasies over** s'extasier sur.

ecstatic [ɛks'tætɪk] adj extatique, en extase.

ECT n abbr = electroconvulsive therapy.

ECU, ecu ['eɪkju:] n abbr (= European Currency Unit) ECU m, écu m.

Ecuador ['ɛkwədɔ:*] n Équateur m.

ecumenical [i:kju'mɛnɪkl] adj œcuménique.

eczema ['ɛksɪmə] n eczéma m.

eddy ['ɛdɪ] n tourbillon m.

edge [ɛdʒ] n bord m; (of knife etc) tranchant m, fil m ♦ vt border ♦ vi: **to ~ forward** avancer petit à petit; **to ~ away from** s'éloigner furtivement de; **on ~** (fig) = edgy; **to have the ~ on** (fig) l'emporter (de justesse) sur, être légèrement meilleur que.

edgeways ['ɛdʒweɪz] adv latéralement; **he couldn't get a word in ~** il ne pouvait pas placer un mot.

edging ['ɛdʒɪŋ] n bordure f.

edgy ['ɛdʒɪ] adj crispé(e), tendu(e).

edible ['ɛdɪbl] adj comestible; (meal) mangeable.

edict ['i:dɪkt] n décret m.

edifice ['ɛdɪfɪs] n édifice m.

edifying ['ɛdɪfaɪɪŋ] adj édifiant(e).

Edinburgh ['ɛdɪnbərə] n Édimbourg.

edit ['ɛdɪt] vt éditer; (magazine) diriger; (newspaper) être le rédacteur or la rédactrice en chef de.

edition [ɪ'dɪʃən] n édition f.

editor ['ɛdɪtə*] n (in newspaper) rédacteur/trice; rédacteur/trice en chef; (of sb's work) éditeur/trice; (also: **film ~**) monteur/euse.

editorial [ɛdɪ'tɔ:rɪəl] adj de la rédaction, éditorial(e) ♦ n éditorial m; **the ~ staff** la rédaction.

EDP n abbr = electronic data processing.

EDT abbr (US: = Eastern Daylight Time) heure d'été de New York.

educate ['ɛdjukeɪt] vt instruire; éduquer; **~d at ...** qui a fait ses études à ....

educated guess ['ɛdjukeɪtɪd-] n supposition éclairée.

education [ɛdju'keɪʃən] n éducation f; (schooling) enseignement m, instruction f; (at university: subject etc) pédagogie f; **primary** or (US) **elementary/secondary ~** instruction f primaire/secondaire.

educational [ɛdju'keɪʃənl] adj pédagogique; scolaire; (useful) instructif(ive); (games, toys) éducatif(ive); **~ technology** technologie f de l'enseignement.

Edwardian [ɛd'wɔ:dɪən] adj de l'époque du roi Édouard VII, des années 1900.

EE abbr = electrical engineer.

EEC n abbr (= European Economic Community) C.E.E. f (= Communauté économique européenne).

EEG n abbr = electroencephalogram.

eel [i:l] n anguille f.

EENT n abbr (US MED) = eye, ear, nose and throat.

EEOC n abbr (US) = Equal Employment Opportunity Commission.

eerie ['ɪərɪ] adj inquiétant(e), spectral(e), surnaturel(le).

EET abbr (= Eastern European Time) HEO (= heure d'Europe orientale).

effect [ɪ'fɛkt] n effet m ♦ vt effectuer; **to take ~** (LAW) entrer en vigueur, prendre effet; (drug) agir, faire son effet; **to put into ~** (plan) mettre en application or à exécution; **to have an ~ on sb/sth** avoir or produire un effet sur qn/qch; **in ~** en fait; **his letter is to the ~ that ...** sa lettre nous apprend que ....

effective [ɪ'fɛktɪv] adj efficace; (striking: display, outfit) frappant(e), qui produit or fait de l'effet; **to become ~** (LAW) entrer en vigueur, prendre effet; **~ date** date f d'effet or d'entrée en vigueur.

effectively [ɪ'fɛktɪvlɪ] adv efficacement; (strikingly) d'une manière frappante, avec beaucoup d'effet; (in reality) effectivement, en fait.

effectiveness [ɪ'fɛktɪvnɪs] n efficacité f.

effects [ɪ'fɛkts] npl (THEAT) effets mpl; (property) affaires fpl.

effeminate [ɪ'fɛmɪnɪt] adj efféminé(e).

effervescent [ɛfə'vɛsnt] adj effervescent(e).

efficacy ['ɛfɪkəsɪ] n efficacité f.

efficiency [ɪ'fɪʃənsɪ] n efficacité f; rendement

m.

efficiency apartment n (US) studio m avec coin cuisine.

efficient [ɪ'fɪʃənt] adj efficace; (machine, car) d'un bon rendement.

efficiently [ɪ'fɪʃəntlɪ] adv efficacement.

effigy ['ɛfɪdʒɪ] n effigie f.

effluent ['ɛfluənt] n effluent m.

effort ['ɛfət] n effort m; **to make an ~ to do sth** faire or fournir un effort pour faire qch.

effortless ['ɛfətlɪs] adj sans effort, aisé(e).

effrontery [ɪ'frʌntərɪ] n effronterie f.

effusive [ɪ'fjuːsɪv] adj (person) expansif(ive); (welcome) chaleureux(euse).

EFL n abbr (SCOL) = English as a Foreign Language.

EFTA ['ɛftə] n abbr (= European Free Trade Association) AELE f (= Association européenne de libre-échange).

e.g. adv abbr (= exempli gratia) par exemple, p. ex.

egalitarian [ɪgælɪ'tɛərɪən] adj égalitaire.

egg [ɛg] n œuf m.

egg on vt pousser.

eggcup ['ɛgkʌp] n coquetier m.

eggplant ['ɛgplɑːnt] n aubergine f.

eggshell ['ɛgʃɛl] n coquille f d'œuf ♦ adj (colour) blanc cassé inv.

egg-timer ['ɛgtaɪmə*] n sablier m.

egg white n blanc m d'œuf.

egg yolk n jaune m d'œuf.

ego ['iːgəu] n moi m.

egoism ['ɛgəuɪzəm] n égoïsme m.

egoist ['ɛgəuɪst] n égoïste m/f.

egotism ['ɛgəutɪzəm] n égotisme m.

egotist ['ɛgəutɪst] n égocentrique m/f.

ego trip n: **to be on an ~** être en plein délire d'autosatisfaction.

Egypt ['iːdʒɪpt] n Égypte f.

Egyptian [ɪ'dʒɪpʃən] adj égyptien(ne) ♦ n Egyptien/ne.

eiderdown ['aɪdədaun] n édredon m.

eight [eɪt] num huit.

eighteen [eɪ'tiːn] num dix-huit.

eighth [eɪtθ] num huitième.

eighty ['eɪtɪ] num quatre-vingt(s).

Eire ['ɛərə] n République f d'Irlande.

EIS n abbr (= Educational Institute of Scotland) syndicat enseignant.

either ['aɪðə*] adj l'un ou l'autre; (both, each) chaque; **on ~ side** de chaque côté ♦ pron: **~ (of them)** l'un ou l'autre; **I don't like ~** je n'aime ni l'un ni l'autre ♦ adv non plus; **no, I don't ~** moi non plus ♦ conj: **~ good or bad** ou bon ou mauvais, soit bon soit mauvais; **I haven't seen ~ one or the other** je n'ai vu ni l'un ni l'autre.

ejaculation [ɪdʒækju'leɪʃən] n (PHYSIOL) éjaculation f.

eject [ɪ'dʒɛkt] vt expulser; éjecter ♦ vi (pilot) s'éjecter.

ejector seat [ɪ'dʒɛktə-] n siège m éjectable.

eke [iːk]: **to ~ out** vt faire durer; augmenter.

EKG n abbr (US) = **electrocardiogram**.

el [ɛl] n abbr (US col) = **elevated railroad**.

elaborate adj [ɪ'læbərɪt] compliqué(e), recherché(e), minutieux(euse) ♦ vb [ɪ'læbəreɪt] vt élaborer ♦ vi entrer dans les détails.

elapse [ɪ'læps] vi s'écouler, passer.

elastic [ɪ'læstɪk] adj, n élastique (m).

elastic band n (BRIT) élastique m.

elasticity [ɪlæs'tɪsɪtɪ] n élasticité f.

elated [ɪ'leɪtɪd] adj transporté(e) de joie.

elation [ɪ'leɪʃən] n (grande) joie, allégresse f.

elbow ['ɛlbəu] n coude m ♦ vt: **to ~ one's way through the crowd** se frayer un passage à travers la foule (en jouant des coudes).

elbow grease n: **to use a bit of ~** mettre de l'huile de coude.

elder ['ɛldə*] adj aîné(e) ♦ n (tree) sureau m; **one's ~s** ses aînés.

elderly ['ɛldəlɪ] adj âgé(e) ♦ npl: **the ~** les personnes âgées.

elder statesman n vétéran m de la politique.

eldest ['ɛldɪst] adj, n: **the ~ (child)** l'aîné(e) (des enfants).

elect [ɪ'lɛkt] vt élire; (choose): **to ~ to do** choisir de faire ♦ adj: **the president ~** le président désigné.

election [ɪ'lɛkʃən] n élection f; **to hold an ~** procéder à une élection.

election campaign n campagne électorale.

electioneering [ɪlɛkʃə'nɪərɪŋ] n propagande électorale, manœuvres électorales.

elector [ɪ'lɛktə*] n électeur/trice.

electoral [ɪ'lɛktərəl] adj électoral(e).

electoral college n collège électoral.

electoral roll n (BRIT) liste électorale.

electorate [ɪ'lɛktərɪt] n électorat m.

electric [ɪ'lɛktrɪk] adj électrique.

electrical [ɪ'lɛktrɪkl] adj électrique.

electrical engineer n ingénieur électricien.

electrical failure n panne d'électricité or de courant.

electric blanket n couverture chauffante.

electric chair n chaise f électrique.

electric cooker n cuisinière f électrique.

electric current n courant m électrique.

electric fire n (BRIT) radiateur m électrique.

electrician [ɪlɛk'trɪʃən] n électricien m.

electricity [ɪlɛk'trɪsɪtɪ] n électricité f; **to switch on/off the ~** rétablir/couper le courant.

electricity board n (BRIT) ≈ agence régionale de l'E.D.F.

electric light n lumière f électrique.

electric shock n choc m or décharge f électrique.

electrify [ɪ'lɛktrɪfaɪ] vt (RAIL) électrifier; (audience) électriser.

electro... [ɪ'lɛktrəu] prefix électro....

electrocardiogram (ECG) [ɪ'lɛktrə

'kɑːdɪəgræm] n électrocardiogramme m (ECG).
electro-convulsive therapy [ɪ'lɛktrə kən'vʌlsɪv-] n électrochocs mpl.
electrocute [ɪ'lɛktrəkjuːt] vt électrocuter.
electrode [ɪ'lɛktrəud] n électrode f.
electroencephalogram (EEG) [ɪ'lɛktrəu ɛn'sɛfələgræm] n électroencéphalogramme m (EEG).
electrolysis [ɪlɛk'trɔlɪsɪs] n électrolyse f.
electromagnetic [ɪ'lɛktrəmæg'nɛtɪk] adj électromagnétique.
electron [ɪ'lɛktrɔn] n électron m.
electronic [ɪlɛk'trɔnɪk] adj électronique.
electronic data processing (EDP) n traitement m électronique des données.
electronic mail n courrier m électronique.
electronics [ɪlɛk'trɔnɪks] n électronique f.
electronics engineer n électronicien/ne.
electron microscope n microscope m électronique.
electroplated [ɪ'lɛktrə'pleɪtɪd] adj plaqué(e) or doré(e) or argenté(e) par galvanoplastie.
electrotherapy [ɪ'lɛktrə'θɛrəpɪ] n électrothérapie f.
elegance ['ɛlɪgəns] n élégance f.
elegant ['ɛlɪgənt] adj élégant(e).
element ['ɛlɪmənt] n (gen) élément m; (of heater, kettle etc) résistance f.
elementary [ɛlɪ'mɛntərɪ] adj élémentaire; (school, education) primaire.

Aux États-Unis et au Canada, une **elementary school** *(également appelée "grade school" ou "grammar school" aux États-Unis) est une école publique où les enfants passent les six à huit premières années de leur scolarité.*

---

elephant ['ɛlɪfənt] n éléphant m.
elevate ['ɛlɪveɪt] vt élever.
elevated railroad ['ɛlɪveɪtɪd-] n (US) métro aérien.
elevation [ɛlɪ'veɪʃən] n élévation f; (height) altitude f.
elevator ['ɛlɪveɪtə*] n élévateur m, monte-charge m inv; (US: lift) ascenseur m.
eleven [ɪ'lɛvn] num onze.
elevenses [ɪ'lɛvnzɪz] npl (BRIT) ≈ pause-café f.
eleventh [ɪ'lɛvnθ] adj onzième; **at the ~ hour** (fig) à la dernière minute.
elf, pl **elves** [ɛlf, ɛlvz] n lutin m.
elicit [ɪ'lɪsɪt] vt: **to ~ (from)** obtenir (de); tirer (de).
eligible ['ɛlɪdʒəbl] adj éligible; (for membership) admissible; **~ for a pension** ayant droit à la retraite.
eliminate [ɪ'lɪmɪneɪt] vt éliminer.
elimination [ɪlɪmɪ'neɪʃən] n élimination f; **by process of ~** par élimination.
élite [eɪ'liːt] n élite f.
élitist [eɪ'liːtɪst] adj (pej) élitiste.

elixir [ɪ'lɪksə*] n élixir m.
Elizabethan [ɪlɪzə'biːθən] adj élisabéthain(e).
ellipse [ɪ'lɪps] n ellipse f.
elliptical [ɪ'lɪptɪkl] adj elliptique.
elm [ɛlm] n orme m.
elocution [ɛlə'kjuːʃən] n élocution f.
elongated ['iːlɔŋgeɪtɪd] adj étiré(e), allongé(e).
elope [ɪ'ləup] vi (lovers) s'enfuir (ensemble).
elopement [ɪ'ləupmənt] n fugue amoureuse.
eloquence ['ɛləkwəns] n éloquence f.
eloquent ['ɛləkwənt] adj éloquent(e).
else [ɛls] adv d'autre; **something ~** quelque chose d'autre, autre chose; **somewhere ~** ailleurs, autre part; **everywhere ~** partout ailleurs; **everyone ~** tous les autres; **nothing ~** rien d'autre; **is there anything ~ I can do?** est-ce que je peux faire quelque chose d'autre?; **where ~?** à quel autre endroit?; **little ~** pas grand-chose d'autre.
elsewhere [ɛls'wɛə*] adv ailleurs, autre part.
ELT n abbr (SCOL) = English Language Teaching.
elucidate [ɪ'luːsɪdeɪt] vt élucider.
elude [ɪ'luːd] vt échapper à; (question) éluder.
elusive [ɪ'luːsɪv] adj insaisissable; (answer) évasif(ive).
elves [ɛlvz] npl of **elf**.
emaciated [ɪ'meɪsɪeɪtɪd] adj émacié(e), décharné(e).
E-mail, e-mail ['iːmeɪl] n abbr (= electronic mail) courrier m électronique ♦ vt: **to ~ sb** envoyer un message électronique à qn.
emanate ['ɛməneɪt] vi: **to ~ from** émaner de.
emancipate [ɪ'mænsɪpeɪt] vt émanciper.
emancipation [ɪmænsɪ'peɪʃən] n émancipation f.
emasculate [ɪ'mæskjuleɪt] vt émasculer.
embalm [ɪm'bɑːm] vt embaumer.
embankment [ɪm'bæŋkmənt] n (of road, railway) remblai m, talus m; (riverside) berge f, quai m; (dyke) digue f.
embargo, **~es** [ɪm'bɑːgəu] n (COMM, NAUT) embargo m ♦ vt frapper d'embargo, mettre l'embargo sur; **to put an ~ on sth** mettre l'embargo sur qch.
embark [ɪm'bɑːk] vi: **to ~ (on)** (s')embarquer (à bord de or sur) ♦ vt embarquer; **to ~ on** (journey etc) commencer, entreprendre; (fig) se lancer or s'embarquer dans.
embarkation [ɛmbɑː'keɪʃən] n embarquement m.
embarkation card n carte f d'embarquement.
embarrass [ɪm'bærəs] vt embarrasser, gêner; **to be ~ed** être gêné(e).
embarrassing [ɪm'bærəsɪŋ] adj gênant(e), embarrassant(e).
embarrassment [ɪm'bærəsmənt] n embarras m, gêne f.
embassy ['ɛmbəsɪ] n ambassade f; **the French E~** l'ambassade de France.
embed [ɪm'bɛd] vt enfoncer; sceller.

embellish [ɪm'bɛlɪʃ] vt embellir; enjoliver.

embers ['ɛmbəz] npl braise f.

embezzle [ɪm'bɛzl] vt détourner.

embezzlement [ɪm'bɛzlmənt] n détournement m (de fonds).

embezzler [ɪm'bɛzlə*] n escroc m.

embitter [ɪm'bɪtə*] vt aigrir; envenimer.

emblem ['ɛmbləm] n emblème m.

embodiment [ɪm'bɒdɪmənt] n personification f, incarnation f.

embody [ɪm'bɒdɪ] vt (features) réunir, comprendre; (ideas) formuler, exprimer.

embolden [ɪm'bəuldn] vt enhardir.

embolism ['ɛmbəlɪzəm] n embolie f.

embossed [ɪm'bɒst] adj repoussé(e); gaufré(e); ~ **with** où figure(nt) en relief.

embrace [ɪm'breɪs] vt embrasser, étreindre; (include) embrasser, couvrir, comprendre ♦ vi s'embrasser, s'étreindre ♦ n étreinte f.

embroider [ɪm'brɔɪdə*] vt broder; (fig: story) enjoliver.

embroidery [ɪm'brɔɪdərɪ] n broderie f.

embroil [ɪm'brɔɪl] vt: **to become** ~**ed** (**in sth**) se retrouver mêlé(e) (à qch), se laisser entraîner (dans qch).

embryo ['ɛmbrɪəu] n (also fig) embryon m.

emcee [ɛm'siː] n maître m de cérémonie.

emend [ɪ'mɛnd] vt (text) corriger.

emerald ['ɛmərəld] n émeraude f.

emerge [ɪ'məːdʒ] vi apparaître, surgir; **it** ~**s that** (BRIT) il ressort que.

emergence [ɪ'məːdʒəns] n apparition f; (of nation) naissance f.

emergency [ɪ'məːdʒənsɪ] n urgence f; **in an** ~ en cas d'urgence; **state of** ~ état m d'urgence.

emergency exit n sortie f de secours.

emergency landing n atterrissage forcé.

emergency lane n (US AUT) accotement stabilisé.

emergency road service n (US) service m de dépannage.

emergency service n service m d'urgence.

emergency stop n (BRIT AUT) arrêt m d'urgence.

emergent [ɪ'məːdʒənt] adj: ~ **nation** pays m en voie de développement.

emery board ['ɛmərɪ-] n lime f à ongles (en carton émerisé).

emery paper ['ɛmərɪ-] n papier m (d')émeri.

emetic [ɪ'mɛtɪk] n vomitif m, émétique m.

emigrant ['ɛmɪgrənt] n émigrant/e.

emigrate ['ɛmɪgreɪt] vi émigrer.

emigration [ɛmɪ'greɪʃən] n émigration f.

émigré ['ɛmɪgreɪ] n émigré/e.

eminence ['ɛmɪnəns] n éminence f.

eminent ['ɛmɪnənt] adj éminent(e).

eminently ['ɛmɪnəntlɪ] adv éminemment, admirablement.

emission [ɪ'mɪʃən] n émission f.

emit [ɪ'mɪt] vt émettre.

emolument [ɪ'mɒljumənt] n (often pl: formal) émoluments mpl; (fee) honoraires mpl; (salary) traitement m.

emotion [ɪ'məuʃən] n sentiment m; (as opposed to reason) émotion f, sentiments.

emotional [ɪ'məuʃənl] adj (person) émotif(ive), très sensible; (scene) émouvant(e); (tone, speech) qui fait appel aux sentiments.

emotionally [ɪ'məuʃnəlɪ] adv (behave) émotivement; (be involved) affectivement; (speak) avec émotion; ~ **disturbed** qui souffre de troubles de l'affectivité.

emotive [ɪ'məutɪv] adj émotif(ive); ~ **power** capacité f d'émouvoir or de toucher.

empathy ['ɛmpəθɪ] n communion f d'idées or de sentiments; empathie f; **to feel** ~ **with sb** se mettre à la place de qn.

emperor ['ɛmpərə*] n empereur m.

emphasis, pl **-ases** ['ɛmfəsɪs, -siːz] n accent m; force f, insistance f; **to lay** or **place** ~ **on sth** (fig) mettre l'accent sur, insister sur; **the** ~ **is on reading** la lecture tient une place primordiale, on accorde une importance particulière à la lecture.

emphasize ['ɛmfəsaɪz] vt (syllable, word, point) appuyer or insister sur; (feature) souligner, accentuer.

emphatic [ɛm'fætɪk] adj (strong) énergique, vigoureux(euse); (unambiguous, clear) catégorique.

emphatically [ɛm'fætɪklɪ] adv avec vigueur or énergie; catégoriquement.

empire ['ɛmpaɪə*] n empire m.

empirical [ɛm'pɪrɪkl] adj empirique.

employ [ɪm'plɔɪ] vt employer; **he's** ~**ed in a bank** il est employé de banque, il travaille dans une banque.

employee [ɪmplɔɪ'iː] n employé/e.

employer [ɪm'plɔɪə*] n employeur/euse.

employment [ɪm'plɔɪmənt] n emploi m; **to find** ~ trouver un emploi or du travail; **without** ~ au chômage, sans emploi; **place of** ~ lieu m de travail.

employment agency n agence f or bureau m de placement.

employment exchange n (BRIT) agence f pour l'emploi.

empower [ɪm'pauə*] vt: **to** ~ **sb to do** autoriser or habiliter qn à faire.

empress ['ɛmprɪs] n impératrice f.

emptiness ['ɛmptɪnɪs] n vide m.

empty ['ɛmptɪ] adj vide; (street, area) désert(e); (threat, promise) en l'air, vain(e) ♦ n (bottle) bouteille f vide ♦ vt vider ♦ vi se vider; (liquid) s'écouler; **on an** ~ **stomach** à jeun; **to** ~ **into** (river) se jeter dans, se déverser dans.

empty-handed ['ɛmptɪ'hændɪd] adj les mains vides.

empty-headed ['ɛmptɪ'hɛdɪd] adj écervelé(e), qui n'a rien dans la tête.

EMS n abbr (= European Monetary System) SME

m.

EMT *n abbr = emergency medical technician.*

EMU *n abbr (= European Monetary Union)* UME *f.*

emulate ['ɛmjuleɪt] *vt* rivaliser avec, imiter.

emulsion [ɪ'mʌlʃən] *n* émulsion *f*; *(also: ~ paint)* peinture mate.

enable [ɪ'neɪbl] *vt*: **to ~ sb to do** permettre à qn de faire, donner à qn la possibilité de faire.

enact [ɪ'nækt] *vt (LAW)* promulguer; *(play, scene)* jouer, représenter.

enamel [ɪ'næməl] *n* émail *m.*

enamel paint *n* peinture émaillée.

enamoured [ɪ'næməd] *adj*: **~ of** amoureux(euse) de; *(idea)* enchanté(e) par.

encampment [ɪn'kæmpmənt] *n* campement *m.*

encased [ɪn'keɪst] *adj*: **~ in** enfermé(e) dans, recouvert(e) de.

enchant [ɪn'tʃɑːnt] *vt* enchanter.

enchanting [ɪn'tʃɑːntɪŋ] *adj* ravissant(e), enchanteur(eresse).

encircle [ɪn'səːkl] *vt* entourer, encercler.

enc(l). *abbr (on letters etc: = enclosed, enclosure)* PJ.

enclose [ɪn'kləuz] *vt (land)* clôturer; *(letter etc)*: **to ~ (with)** joindre (à); **please find ~d** veuillez trouver ci-joint.

enclosure [ɪn'kləuʒə*] *n* enceinte *f*; *(in letter etc)* annexe *f.*

encoder [ɪn'kəudə*] *n (COMPUT)* encodeur *m.*

encompass [ɪn'kʌmpəs] *vt* encercler, entourer; *(include)* contenir, inclure.

encore [ɔŋ'kɔː*] *excl, n* bis *(m).*

encounter [ɪn'kauntə*] *n* rencontre *f* ♦ *vt* rencontrer.

encourage [ɪn'kʌrɪdʒ] *vt* encourager; *(industry, growth)* favoriser; **to ~ sb to do sth** encourager qn à faire qch.

encouragement [ɪn'kʌrɪdʒmənt] *n* encouragement *m.*

encouraging [ɪn'kʌrɪdʒɪŋ] *adj* encourageant(e).

encroach [ɪn'krəutʃ] *vi*: **to ~ (up)on** empiéter sur.

encrust [ɪn'krʌst] *vt* encroûter; *(with jewels etc)* incruster.

encrusted [ɪn'krʌstɪd] *adj*: **~ (with)** incrusté(e) (de).

encumber [ɪn'kʌmbə*] *vt*: **to be ~ed with** *(luggage)* être encombré(e) de; *(debts)* être grevé(e) de.

encyclop(a)edia [ɛnsaɪkləu'piːdɪə] *n* encyclopédie *f.*

end [ɛnd] *n (gen, also: aim)* fin *f*; *(of table, street, line, rope etc)* bout *m*, extrémité *f*; *(of pointed object)* pointe *f*; *(of town)* bout ♦ *vt* terminer; *(also:* **bring to an ~**, **put an ~ to**) mettre fin à ♦ *vi* se terminer, finir; **from ~ to ~** d'un bout à l'autre; **to come to an ~** prendre fin; **to be at an ~** être fini(e), être terminé(e); **in the ~** finalement; **on ~** *(object)* debout, dressé(e);

to stand on ~ *(hair)* se dresser sur la tête; **for 5 hours on ~** durant 5 heures d'affilée *or* de suite; **for hours on ~** pendant des heures (et des heures); **at the ~ of the day** *(BRIT fig)* en fin de compte; **to this ~**, **with this ~ in view** à cette fin, dans ce but.

▶**end up** *vi*: **to ~ up in** finir *or* se terminer par; *(place)* finir *or* aboutir à.

endanger [ɪn'deɪndʒə*] *vt* mettre en danger; **an ~ed species** une espèce en voie de disparition.

endear [ɪn'dɪə*] *vt*: **to ~ o.s. to sb** se faire aimer de qn.

endearing [ɪn'dɪərɪŋ] *adj* attachant(e).

endearment [ɪn'dɪəmənt] *n*: **to whisper ~s** murmurer des mots *or* choses tendres; **term of ~** terme *m* d'affection.

endeavour, *(US)* **endeavor** [ɪn'dɛvə*] *n* tentative *f*, effort *m* ♦ *vi*: **to ~ to do** tenter *or* s'efforcer de faire.

endemic [ɛn'dɛmɪk] *adj* endémique.

ending ['ɛndɪŋ] *n* dénouement *m*, conclusion *f*; *(LING)* terminaison *f.*

endive ['ɛndaɪv] *n (curly)* chicorée *f*; *(smooth, flat)* endive *f.*

endless ['ɛndlɪs] *adj* sans fin, interminable; *(patience, resources)* inépuisable, sans limites; *(possibilities)* illimité(e).

endorse [ɪn'dɔːs] *vt (cheque)* endosser; *(approve)* appuyer, approuver, sanctionner.

endorsee [ɪndɔː'siː] *n* bénéficiaire *m/f*, endossataire *m/f.*

endorsement [ɪn'dɔːsmənt] *n (approval)* caution *f*, aval *m*; *(signature)* endossement *m*; *(BRIT: on driving licence)* contravention *f (portée au permis de conduire).*

endorser [ɪn'dɔːsə*] *n* avaliste *m*, endosseur *m.*

endow [ɪn'dau] *vt (provide with money)* faire une donation à, doter; *(equip)*: **to ~ with** gratifier de, doter de.

endowment [ɪn'daumənt] *n* dotation *f.*

endowment mortgage *n* hypothèque liée à une assurance-vie.

endowment policy *n* assurance *f* à capital différé.

end product *n (INDUSTRY)* produit fini; *(fig)* résultat *m*, aboutissement *m.*

end result *n* résultat final.

endurable [ɪn'djuərəbl] *adj* supportable.

endurance [ɪn'djuərəns] *n* endurance *f*, résistance *f*; patience *f.*

endurance test *n* test *m* d'endurance.

endure [ɪn'djuə*] *vt* supporter, endurer ♦ *vi* durer.

end user *n (COMPUT)* utilisateur final.

enema ['ɛnɪmə] *n (MED)* lavement *m.*

enemy ['ɛnəmɪ] *adj*, *n* ennemi(e); **to make an ~ of sb** se faire un(e) ennemi(e) de qn, se mettre qn à dos.

energetic [ɛnə'dʒɛtɪk] *adj* énergique; *(activity)* très actif(ive), qui fait se dépenser (physiquement).

energy [ˈɛnədʒɪ] n énergie f; **Department of E~** ministère m de l'Énergie.

energy crisis n crise f de l'énergie.

energy-saving [ˈɛnədʒɪˈseɪvɪŋ] adj (policy) d'économie d'énergie; (device) qui permet de réaliser des économies d'énergie.

enervating [ˈɛnəveɪtɪŋ] adj débilitant(e), affaiblissant(e).

enforce [ɪnˈfɔːs] vt (LAW) appliquer, faire respecter.

enforced [ɪnˈfɔːst] adj forcé(e).

enfranchise [ɪnˈfræntʃaɪz] vt accorder le droit de vote à; (set free) affranchir.

engage [ɪnˈɡeɪdʒ] vt engager; (MIL) engager le combat avec; (lawyer) prendre ♦ vi (TECH) s'enclencher, s'engrener; **to ~ in** se lancer dans; **to ~ sb in conversation** engager la conversation avec qn.

engaged [ɪnˈɡeɪdʒd] adj (BRIT: busy, in use) occupé(e); (betrothed) fiancé(e); **to get ~** se fiancer; **he is ~ in research/a survey** il fait de la recherche/une enquête.

engaged tone n (BRIT TEL) tonalité f occupé inv.

engagement [ɪnˈɡeɪdʒmənt] n obligation f, engagement m; (appointment) rendez-vous m inv; (to marry) fiançailles fpl; (MIL) combat m; **I have a previous ~** j'ai déjà un rendez-vous, je suis déjà prise(e).

engagement ring n bague f de fiançailles.

engaging [ɪnˈɡeɪdʒɪŋ] adj engageant(e), attirant(e).

engender [ɪnˈdʒɛndə*] vt produire, causer.

engine [ˈɛndʒɪn] n (AUT) moteur m; (RAIL) locomotive f.

engine driver n (BRIT: of train) mécanicien m.

engineer [ɛndʒɪˈnɪə*] n ingénieur m; (BRIT: for domestic appliances) réparateur m; (US RAIL) mécanicien m; **civil/mechanical ~** ingénieur des Travaux Publics or des Ponts et Chaussées/mécanicien.

engineering [ɛndʒɪˈnɪərɪŋ] n engineering m, ingénierie f; (of bridges, ships) génie m; (of machine) mécanique f ♦ cpd: **~ works** or **factory** atelier m de construction mécanique.

engine failure n panne f.

engine trouble n ennuis mpl mécaniques.

England [ˈɪŋɡlənd] n Angleterre f.

English [ˈɪŋɡlɪʃ] adj anglais(e) ♦ n (LING) anglais m; **the ~** npl les Anglais; **an ~ speaker** un anglophone.

English Channel n: **the ~** la Manche.

Englishman [ˈɪŋɡlɪʃmən], **Englishwoman** [ˈɪŋɡlɪʃwumən] n Anglais/e.

English-speaking [ˈɪŋɡlɪʃˈspiːkɪŋ] adj qui parle anglais; anglophone.

engrave [ɪnˈɡreɪv] vt graver.

engraving [ɪnˈɡreɪvɪŋ] n gravure f.

engrossed [ɪnˈɡrəust] adj: **~ in** absorbé(e)

par, plongé(e) dans.

engulf [ɪnˈɡʌlf] vt engloutir.

enhance [ɪnˈhɑːns] vt rehausser, mettre en valeur; (position) améliorer; (reputation) accroître.

enigma [ɪˈnɪɡmə] n énigme f.

enigmatic [ɛnɪɡˈmætɪk] adj énigmatique.

enjoy [ɪnˈdʒɔɪ] vt aimer, prendre plaisir à; (have benefit of: health, fortune) jouir de; (: success) connaître; **to ~ o.s.** s'amuser.

enjoyable [ɪnˈdʒɔɪəbl] adj agréable.

enjoyment [ɪnˈdʒɔɪmənt] n plaisir m.

enlarge [ɪnˈlɑːdʒ] vt accroître; (PHOT) agrandir ♦ vi: **to ~ on** (subject) s'étendre sur.

enlarged [ɪnˈlɑːdʒd] adj (edition) augmenté(e); (MED: organ, gland) anormalement gros(se), hypertrophié(e).

enlargement [ɪnˈlɑːdʒmənt] n (PHOT) agrandissement m.

enlighten [ɪnˈlaɪtn] vt éclairer.

enlightened [ɪnˈlaɪtnd] adj éclairé(e).

enlightening [ɪnˈlaɪtnɪŋ] adj instructif(ive), révélateur(trice).

enlightenment [ɪnˈlaɪtnmənt] n édification f; éclaircissements mpl; (HISTORY): **the E~** ≈ le Siècle des lumières.

enlist [ɪnˈlɪst] vt recruter; (support) s'assurer ♦ vi s'engager; **~ed man** (US MIL) simple soldat m.

enliven [ɪnˈlaɪvn] vt animer, égayer.

enmity [ˈɛnmɪtɪ] n inimitié f.

ennoble [ɪˈnəubl] vt (with title) anoblir.

enormity [ɪˈnɔːmɪtɪ] n énormité f.

enormous [ɪˈnɔːməs] adj énorme.

enormously [ɪˈnɔːməslɪ] adv (increase) dans des proportions énormes; (rich) extrêmement.

enough [ɪˈnʌf] adj, n: **~ time/books** assez or suffisamment de temps/livres ♦ adv: **big ~** assez or suffisamment grand; **have you got ~?** (en) avez-vous assez?; **will 5 be ~?** est-ce que 5 suffiront?, est-ce qu'il y en aura assez avec 5?; **that's ~!** ça suffit!, assez!; **that's ~, thanks** cela suffit or c'est assez, merci; **I've had ~!** je n'en peux plus!; **he has not worked ~** il n'a pas assez or suffisamment travaillé, il n'a pas travaillé assez or suffisamment; **~! assez!**, ça suffit!; **it's hot ~ (as it is)!** il fait assez chaud comme ça!; **he was kind ~ to lend me the money** il a eu la gentillesse de me prêter l'argent; **... which, funnily ~ ...** qui, chose curieuse.

enquire [ɪnˈkwaɪə*] vt, vi = **inquire**.

enrage [ɪnˈreɪdʒ] vt mettre en fureur or en rage, rendre furieux(euse).

enrich [ɪnˈrɪtʃ] vt enrichir.

enrol, (US) **enroll** [ɪnˈrəul] vt inscrire ♦ vi s'inscrire.

enrol(l)ment [ɪnˈrəulmənt] n inscription f.

en route [ɒnˈruːt] adv en route, en chemin; **~ for** or **to** en route vers, à destination de.

ensconced [ɪn'skɔnst] *adj*: ~ **in** bien calé(e) dans.

enshrine [ɪn'ʃraɪn] *vt* (*fig*) préserver.

ensign *n* (*NAUT*) ['ɛnsən] enseigne *f*, pavillon *m*; (*MIL*) ['ɛnsaɪn] porte-étendard *m*.

enslave [ɪn'sleɪv] *vt* asservir.

ensue [ɪn'sjuː] *vi* s'ensuivre, résulter.

ensure [ɪn'ʃuə*] *vt* assurer, garantir; **to ~ that** s'assurer que.

ENT *n abbr* (= *Ear, Nose and Throat*) ORL *f*.

entail [ɪn'teɪl] *vt* entraîner, nécessiter.

entangle [ɪn'tæŋgl] *vt* emmêler, embrouiller; **to become ~d in sth** (*fig*) se laisser entraîner *or* empêtrer dans qch.

enter ['ɛntə*] *vt* (*room*) entrer dans, pénétrer dans; (*club, army*) entrer à; (*profession*) embrasser; (*competition*) s'inscrire à *or* pour; (*sb for a competition*) (faire) inscrire; (*write down*) inscrire, noter; (*COMPUT*) entrer, introduire ♦ *vi* entrer.

▶**enter for** *vt fus* s'inscrire à, se présenter pour *or* à.

▶**enter into** *vt fus* (*explanation*) se lancer dans; (*negotiations*) entamer; (*debate*) prendre part à; (*agreement*) conclure.

▶**enter up** *vt* inscrire.

▶**enter (up)on** *vt fus* commencer.

enteritis [ɛntə'raɪtɪs] *n* entérite *f*.

enterprise ['ɛntəpraɪz] *n* (*company, undertaking*) entreprise *f*; (*initiative*) (esprit *m* d')initiative *f*.

enterprising ['ɛntəpraɪzɪŋ] *adj* entreprenant(e), dynamique.

entertain [ɛntə'teɪn] *vt* amuser, distraire; (*invite*) recevoir (à dîner); (*idea, plan*) envisager.

entertainer [ɛntə'teɪnə*] *n* artiste *m/f* de variétés.

entertaining [ɛntə'teɪnɪŋ] *adj* amusant(e), distrayant(e) ♦ *n*: **to do a lot of ~** beaucoup recevoir.

entertainment [ɛntə'teɪnmənt] *n* (*amusement*) distraction *f*, divertissement *m*, amusement *m*; (*show*) spectacle *m*.

entertainment allowance *n* frais *mpl* de représentation.

enthral [ɪn'θrɔːl] *vt* captiver, passionner.

enthralling [ɪn'θrɔːlɪŋ] *adj* captivant(e); enchanteur(eresse).

enthuse [ɪn'θuːz] *vi*: **to ~ about** *or* **over** parler avec enthousiasme de.

enthusiasm [ɪn'θuːzɪæzəm] *n* enthousiasme *m*.

enthusiast [ɪn'θuːzɪæst] *n* enthousiaste *m/f*; **a jazz** *etc* ~ un fervent *or* passionné du jazz *etc*.

enthusiastic [ɪnθuːzɪ'æstɪk] *adj* enthousiaste; **to be ~ about** être enthousiasmé(e) par.

entice [ɪn'taɪs] *vt* attirer, séduire.

enticing [ɪn'taɪsɪŋ] *adj* (*person, offer*) séduisant(e); (*food*) alléchant(e).

entire [ɪn'taɪə*] *adj* (tout) entier(ère).

entirely [ɪn'taɪəlɪ] *adv* entièrement, complètement.

entirety [ɪn'taɪərətɪ] *n*: **in its ~** dans sa totalité.

entitle [ɪn'taɪtl] *vt* (*allow*): **to ~ sb to do** donner (le) droit à qn de faire; **to ~ sb to sth** donner droit à qch à qn.

entitled [ɪn'taɪtld] *adj* (*book*) intitulé(e); **to be ~ to sth/to do sth** avoir droit à qch/le droit de faire qch.

entity ['ɛntɪtɪ] *n* entité *f*.

entrails ['ɛntreɪlz] *npl* entrailles *fpl*.

entrance *n* ['ɛntrns] entrée *f* ♦ *vt* [ɪn'trɑːns] enchanter, ravir; **to gain ~ to** (*university etc*) être admis à.

entrance examination *n* examen *m* d'entrée *or* d'admission.

entrance fee *n* droit *m* d'inscription; (*to museum etc*) prix *m* d'entrée.

entrance ramp *n* (*US AUT*) bretelle *f* d'accès.

entrancing [ɪn'trɑːnsɪŋ] *adj* enchanteur(teresse), ravissant(e).

entrant ['ɛntrnt] *n* (*in race etc*) participant/e, concurrent/e; (*BRIT: in exam*) candidat/e.

entreat [ɛn'triːt] *vt* supplier.

entreaty [ɛn'triːtɪ] *n* supplication *f*, prière *f*.

entrée ['ɔntreɪ] *n* (*CULIN*) entrée *f*.

entrenched [ɛn'trɛntʃt] *adj* retranché(e).

entrepreneur ['ɔntrəprə'nə:*] *n* entrepreneur *m*.

entrepreneurial ['ɔntrəprə'nə:rɪəl] *adj* animé(e) d'un esprit d'entreprise.

entrust [ɪn'trʌst] *vt*: **to ~ sth to** confier qch à.

entry ['ɛntrɪ] *n* entrée *f*; (*in register, diary*) inscription *f*; (*in ledger*) écriture *f*; **"no ~"** "défense d'entrer", "entrée interdite"; (*AUT*) "sens interdit"; **single/double ~ book-keeping** comptabilité *f* en partie simple/double.

entry form *n* feuille *f* d'inscription.

entry phone *n* (*BRIT*) interphone *m* (*à l'entrée d'un immeuble*).

entwine [ɪn'twaɪn] *vt* entrelacer.

E-number ['iːnʌmbə*] *n* additif *m* (alimentaire).

enumerate [ɪ'njuːməreɪt] *vt* énumérer.

enunciate [ɪ'nʌnsɪeɪt] *vt* énoncer; prononcer.

envelop [ɪn'vɛləp] *vt* envelopper.

envelope ['ɛnvələup] *n* enveloppe *f*.

enviable ['ɛnvɪəbl] *adj* enviable.

envious ['ɛnvɪəs] *adj* envieux(euse).

environment [ɪn'vaɪrnmənt] *n* milieu *m*; environnement *m*; **Department of the E~** (*BRIT*) ministère *m* de l'équipement et de l'aménagement du territoire.

environmental [ɪnvaɪrn'mɛntl] *adj* écologique, relatif(ive) à l'environnement; **~ studies** (*in school etc*) écologie *f*.

environmentalist [ɪnvaɪrn'mɛntlɪst] *n* écologiste *m/f*.

environmentally [ɪnvaɪrn'mɛntlɪ] *adv*: **~ sound/friendly** qui ne nuit pas à l'environnement.

Environmental Protection Agency (EPA) n (US) ≈ ministère m de l'Environnement.

envisage [ɪn'vɪzɪdʒ] vt envisager; prévoir.

envision [ɪn'vɪʒən] vt envisager, concevoir.

envoy ['ɛnvɔɪ] n envoyé/e.

envy ['ɛnvɪ] n envie f ♦ vt envier; **to ~ sb sth** envier qch à qn.

enzyme ['ɛnzaɪm] n enzyme m.

EPA n abbr (US) = **Environmental Protection Agency**.

ephemeral [ɪ'fɛmərl] adj éphémère.

epic ['ɛpɪk] n épopée f ♦ adj épique.

epicentre, (US) epicenter ['ɛpɪsɛntə*] n épicentre m.

epidemic [ɛpɪ'dɛmɪk] n épidémie f.

epilepsy ['ɛpɪlɛpsɪ] n épilepsie f.

epileptic [ɛpɪ'lɛptɪk] adj, n épileptique (m/f).

epilogue ['ɛpɪlɔg] n épilogue m.

episcopal [ɪ'pɪskəpl] adj épiscopal(e).

episode ['ɛpɪsəud] n épisode m.

epistle [ɪ'pɪsl] n épître f.

epitaph ['ɛpɪtɑːf] n épitaphe f.

epithet ['ɛpɪθɛt] n épithète f.

epitome [ɪ'pɪtəmɪ] n (fig) quintessence f, type m.

epitomize [ɪ'pɪtəmaɪz] vt (fig) illustrer, incarner.

epoch ['iːpɔk] n époque f, ère f.

epoch-making ['iːpɔkmeɪkɪŋ] adj qui fait époque.

eponymous [ɪ'pɔnɪməs] adj de ce or du même nom, éponyme.

equable ['ɛkwəbl] adj égal(e); de tempérament égal.

equal ['iːkwl] adj égal(e) ♦ n égal/e ♦ vt égaler; **~ to** (task) à la hauteur de; **~ to doing** de taille à or capable de faire.

equality [iː'kwɔlɪtɪ] n égalité f.

equalize ['iːkwəlaɪz] vt, vi égaliser.

equalizer ['iːkwəlaɪzə*] n but égalisateur.

equally ['iːkwəlɪ] adv également; (just as) tout aussi; **they are ~ clever** ils sont tout aussi intelligents.

Equal Opportunities Commission, (US) Equal Employment Opportunity Commission n commission pour la non discrimination dans l'emploi.

equal(s) sign n signe m d'égalité.

equanimity [ɛkwə'nɪmɪtɪ] n égalité f d'humeur.

equate [ɪ'kweɪt] vt: **to ~ sth with** comparer qch à; assimiler qch à; **to ~ sth to** mettre qch en équation avec; égaler qch à.

equation [ɪ'kweɪʃən] n (MATH) équation f.

equator [ɪ'kweɪtə*] n équateur m.

equatorial [ɛkwə'tɔːrɪəl] adj équatorial(e).

Equatorial Guinea n Guinée équatoriale.

equestrian [ɪ'kwɛstrɪən] adj équestre ♦ n écuyer/ère, cavalier/ère.

equilibrium [iːkwɪ'lɪbrɪəm] n équilibre m.

equinox ['iːkwɪnɔks] n équinoxe m.

equip [ɪ'kwɪp] vt équiper; **to ~ sb/sth with** équiper or munir qn/qch de; **he is well ~ped for the job** il a les compétences or les qualités requises pour ce travail.

equipment [ɪ'kwɪpmənt] n équipement m; (electrical etc) appareillage m, installation f.

equitable ['ɛkwɪtəbl] adj équitable.

equities ['ɛkwɪtɪz] npl (BRIT COMM) actions cotées en Bourse.

equity ['ɛkwɪtɪ] n équité f.

equity capital n capitaux mpl propres.

equivalent [ɪ'kwɪvəlnt] adj équivalent(e) ♦ n équivalent m; **to be ~ to** équivaloir à, être équivalent(e) à.

equivocal [ɪ'kwɪvəkl] adj équivoque; (open to suspicion) douteux(euse).

equivocate [ɪ'kwɪvəkeɪt] vi user de faux-fuyants; éviter de répondre.

equivocation [ɪkwɪvə'keɪʃən] n équivoque f.

ER abbr (BRIT: = Elizabeth Regina) la reine Élisabeth.

ERA n abbr (US POL: = Equal Rights Amendment) amendement sur l'égalité des droits des femmes.

era ['ɪərə] n ère f, époque f.

eradicate [ɪ'rædɪkeɪt] vt éliminer.

erase [ɪ'reɪz] vt effacer.

eraser [ɪ'reɪzə*] n gomme f.

erect [ɪ'rɛkt] adj droit(e) ♦ vt construire; (monument) ériger, élever; (tent etc) dresser.

erection [ɪ'rɛkʃən] n (PHYSIOL) érection f; (of building) construction f; (of machinery etc) installation f.

ergonomics [əːgə'nɔmɪks] n ergonomie f.

ERISA n abbr (US: = Employee Retirement Income Security Act) loi sur les pensions de retraite.

Eritrea [ɛrɪ'treɪə] n Érythrée f.

ERM n abbr (= Exchange Rate Mechanism) mécanisme m des taux de change.

ermine ['əːmɪn] n hermine f.

ERNIE ['əːnɪ] n abbr (BRIT: = Electronic Random Number Indicator Equipment) ordinateur servant au tirage des bons à lots gagnants.

erode [ɪ'rəud] vt éroder; (metal) ronger.

erogenous zone [ɪ'rɔdʒənəs-] n zone f érogène.

erosion [ɪ'rəuʒən] n érosion f.

erotic [ɪ'rɔtɪk] adj érotique.

eroticism [ɪ'rɔtɪsɪzəm] n érotisme m.

err [əː*] vi se tromper; (REL) pécher.

errand ['ɛrnd] n course f, commission f; **to run ~s** faire des courses; **~ of mercy** mission f de charité, acte m charitable.

errand boy n garçon m de courses.

erratic [ɪ'rætɪk] adj irrégulier(ière); inconstant(e).

erroneous [ɪ'rəunɪəs] adj erroné(e).

error ['ɛrə*] n erreur f; **typing/spelling ~** faute f de frappe/d'orthographe; **in ~** par erreur, par méprise; **~s and omissions excepted** sauf erreur ou omission.

error message n (*COMPUT*) message m
d'erreur.

erstwhile ['ə:stwaɪl] adj précédent(e),
d'autrefois.

erudite ['ɛrjudaɪt] adj savant(e).

erupt [ɪ'rʌpt] vi entrer en éruption; (*fig*)
éclater, exploser.

eruption [ɪ'rʌpʃən] n éruption f; (*of anger,
violence*) explosion f.

ESA n abbr (= European Space Agency) ASE f
(= Agence spatiale européenne).

escalate ['ɛskəleɪt] vi s'intensifier; (*costs*)
monter en flèche.

escalation [ɛskə'leɪʃən] n escalade f.

escalation clause n clause f d'indexation.

escalator ['ɛskəleɪtə*] n escalier roulant.

escapade [ɛskə'peɪd] n fredaine f; équipée f.

escape [ɪ'skeɪp] n évasion f, fuite f; (*of gas etc*)
fuite; (*: TECH*) échappement m ♦ vi
s'échapper, fuir; (*from jail*) s'évader; (*fig*)
s'en tirer, en réchapper; (*leak*) fuir;
s'échapper ♦ vt échapper à; **to ~ from**
(*person*) échapper à; (*place*) s'échapper de;
(*fig*) fuir; **to ~ to** (*another place*) fuir à,
s'enfuir à; **to ~ to safety** se réfugier dans or
gagner un endroit sûr; **to ~ notice** passer
inaperçu(e).

escape artist n virtuose m/f de l'évasion.

escape clause n clause f dérogatoire.

escapee [ɪskeɪ'pi:] n évadé/e.

escape key n (*COMPUT*) touche f
d'échappement.

escape route n (*from fire*) issue f de secours;
(*of prisoners etc*) voie empruntée pour
s'échapper.

escapism [ɪ'skeɪpɪzəm] n évasion f (*fig*).

escapist [ɪ'skeɪpɪst] adj (*literature*) d'évasion
♦ n personne f qui se réfugie hors de la
réalité.

escapologist [ɛskə'pɔlədʒɪst] n (*BRIT*) = **escape
artist**.

escarpment [ɪs'kɑ:pmənt] n escarpement m.

eschew [ɪs'tʃu:] vt éviter.

escort vt [ɪ'skɔ:t] escorter ♦ n [ɛskɔ:t] escorte
f; (*to dance etc*): **her ~** son compagnon or
cavalier; **his ~** sa compagne.

escort agency n bureau m d'hôtesses.

Eskimo ['ɛskɪməu] adj esquimau(de), eskimo
♦ n Esquimau/de; (*LING*) esquimau m.

ESL n abbr (*SCOL*) = English as a Second
Language.

esophagus [i:'sɔfəgəs] n (*US*) = **oesophagus**.

esoteric [ɛsə'tɛrɪk] adj ésotérique.

ESP n abbr (= extrasensory perception); (*SCOL*) =
English for Special Purposes.

esp. abbr = **especially**.

especially [ɪ'spɛʃlɪ] adv (*specifically*)
spécialement, exprès; (*more than usually*)
particulièrement; (*above all*)
particulièrement, surtout.

espionage ['ɛspɪənɑ:ʒ] n espionnage m.

esplanade [ɛsplə'neɪd] n esplanade f.

espouse [ɪ'spauz] vt épouser, embrasser.

Esquire [ɪ'skwaɪə*] n (*BRIT*: abbr **Esq.**): **J.
Brown, ~** Monsieur J. Brown.

essay ['ɛseɪ] n (*SCOL*) dissertation f;
(*LITERATURE*) essai m; (*attempt*) tentative f.

essence ['ɛsns] n essence f; **in ~** en
substance; **speed is of the ~** l'essentiel,
c'est la rapidité.

essential [ɪ'sɛnʃl] adj essentiel(le); (*basic*)
fondamental(e) ♦ n élément essentiel; **it is ~
that** il est essentiel or primordial que.

essentially [ɪ'sɛnʃlɪ] adv essentiellement.

EST abbr (*US*: = Eastern Standard Time) heure
d'hiver de New York.

est. abbr = established, estimate(d).

establish [ɪ'stæblɪʃ] vt établir; (*business*)
fonder, créer; (*one's power etc*) asseoir,
affermir.

establishment [ɪ'stæblɪʃmənt] n
établissement m; création f; (*institution*)
établissement m; **the E~** les pouvoirs établis;
l'ordre établi.

estate [ɪ'steɪt] n (*land*) domaine m, propriété f;
(*LAW*) biens mpl, succession f; (*BRIT*: also:
housing ~) lotissement m.

estate agency n (*BRIT*) agence immobilière.

estate agent n (*BRIT*) agent immobilier.

estate car n (*BRIT*) break m.

esteem [ɪ'sti:m] n estime f ♦ vt estimer;
apprécier; **to hold sb in high ~** tenir qn en
haute estime.

esthetic [ɪs'θɛtɪk] adj (*US*) = **aesthetic**.

estimate n ['ɛstɪmət] estimation f; (*COMM*)
devis m ♦ vb ['ɛstɪmeɪt] vt estimer ♦ vi (*BRIT
COMM*): **to ~ for** estimer, faire une
estimation de; (*bid for*) faire un devis pour;
to give sb an ~ of faire or donner un devis à
qn pour; **at a rough ~** approximativement.

estimation [ɛstɪ'meɪʃən] n opinion f; estime f;
in my ~ à mon avis, selon moi.

Estonia [ɛ'stəunɪə] n Estonie f.

Estonian [ɛ'stəunɪən] adj estonien(ne) ♦ n
Estonien/ne; (*LING*) estonien m.

estranged [ɪs'treɪndʒd] adj (*couple*) séparé(e);
(*husband, wife*) dont on s'est séparé(e).

estrangement [ɪs'treɪndʒmənt] n (*from wife,
family*) séparation f.

estrogen ['i:strəudʒən] n (*US*) = **oestrogen**.

estuary ['ɛstjuərɪ] n estuaire m.

ET n abbr (*BRIT*: = Employment Training)
formation professionnelle pour les
demandeurs d'emploi ♦ abbr (*US*: = Eastern
Time) heure de New York.

ETA n abbr (= estimated time of arrival) HPA f
(= heure probable d'arrivée).

et al. abbr (= et alii: and others) et coll.

etc. abbr (= et cetera) etc.

etch [ɛtʃ] vt graver à l'eau forte.

etching ['ɛtʃɪŋ] n eau-forte f.

ETD n abbr (= estimated time of departure) HPD
f (= heure probable de départ).

eternal [ɪ'tə:nl] adj éternel(le).

eternity [ɪ'tə:nɪtɪ] *n* éternité *f*.
ether ['i:θə*] *n* éther *m*.
ethereal [ɪ'θɪərɪəl] *adj* éthéré(e).
ethical ['εθɪkl] *adj* moral(e).
ethics ['εθɪks] *n* éthique *f* ♦ *npl* moralité *f*.
Ethiopia [i:θɪ'əupɪə] *n* Éthiopie *f*.
Ethiopian [i:θɪ'əupɪən] *adj* éthiopien(ne) ♦ *n* Éthiopien/ne.
ethnic ['εθnɪk] *adj* ethnique; (*clothes, food*) folklorique, exotique; *propre aux minorités ethniques non-occidentales.*
ethnic cleansing [-'klεnzɪŋ] *n* purification *f* ethnique.
ethnology [εθ'nɔlədʒɪ] *n* ethnologie *f*.
ethos ['i:θɔs] *n* (système *m* de) valeurs *fpl*.
etiquette ['εtɪkεt] *n* convenances *fpl*, étiquette *f*.
ETV *n abbr* (*US*: = *Educational Television*) télévision scolaire.
etymology [εtɪ'mɔlədʒɪ] *n* étymologie *f*.
EU *n abbr* (= *European Union*) UE *f*.
eucalyptus [ju:kə'lɪptəs] *n* eucalyptus *m*.
eulogy ['ju:lədʒɪ] *n* éloge *m*.
euphemism ['ju:fəmɪzəm] *n* euphémisme *m*.
euphemistic [ju:fə'mɪstɪk] *adj* euphémique.
euphoria [ju:'fɔ:rɪə] *n* euphorie *f*.
Eurasia [juə'reɪʃə] *n* Eurasie *f*.
Eurasian [juə'reɪʃən] *adj* eurasien(ne); (*continent*) eurasiatique ♦ *n* Eurasien/ne.
Euratom [juə'rætəm] *n abbr* (= *European Atomic Energy Community*) EURATOM *f*.
Euro- ['juərəu] *prefix* euro-.
Eurocheque ['juərəutʃεk] *n* eurochèque *m*.
Eurocrat ['juərəukræt] *n* eurocrate *m/f*.
Eurodollar ['juərəudɔlə*] *n* eurodollar *m*.
Europe ['juərəp] *n* Europe *f*.
European [juərə'pi:ən] *adj* européen(ne) ♦ *n* Européen/ne.
European Court of Justice *n* Cour *f* de Justice de la CEE.
Euro-sceptic ['juərəuskεptɪk] *n* eurosceptique *m/f*.
euthanasia [ju:θə'neɪzɪə] *n* euthanasie *f*.
evacuate [ɪ'vækjueɪt] *vt* évacuer.
evacuation [ɪvækju'eɪʃən] *n* évacuation *f*.
evacuee [ɪvækju'i:] *n* évacué/e.
evade [ɪ'veɪd] *vt* échapper à; (*question etc*) éluder; (*duties*) se dérober à.
evaluate [ɪ'væljueɪt] *vt* évaluer.
evangelist [ɪ'vændʒəlɪst] *n* évangéliste *m*.
evangelize [ɪ'vændʒəlaɪz] *vt* évangéliser, prêcher l'Évangile à.
evaporate [ɪ'væpəreɪt] *vi* s'évaporer ♦ *vt* faire évaporer.
evaporated milk [ɪ'væpəreɪtɪd-] *n* lait condensé (non sucré).
evaporation [ɪvæpə'reɪʃən] *n* évaporation *f*.
evasion [ɪ'veɪʒən] *n* dérobade *f*; (*excuse*) faux-fuyant *m*.
evasive [ɪ'veɪsɪv] *adj* évasif(ive).
eve [i:v] *n*: **on the ~ of** à la veille de.
even ['i:vn] *adj* régulier(ière), égal(e);

(*number*) pair(e) ♦ *adv* même; **~ if** même si + *indicative*; **~ though** quand (bien) même + *conditional*, alors même que + *conditional*; **~ more** encore plus; **~ faster** encore plus vite; **~ so** quand même; **not ~** pas même; **to break ~** s'y retrouver, équilibrer ses comptes; **to get ~ with sb** prendre sa revanche sur qn.
►**even out** *vi* s'égaliser.
even-handed [i:vn'hændɪd] *adj* équitable.
evening ['i:vnɪŋ] *n* soir *m*; (*as duration, event*) soirée *f*; **in the ~** le soir; **this ~** ce soir; **tomorrow/yesterday ~** demain/hier soir.
evening class *n* cours *m* du soir.
evening dress *n* (*man's*) habit *m* de soirée, smoking *m*; (*woman's*) robe *f* de soirée.
evenly ['i:vnlɪ] *adv* uniformément, également; (*space*) régulièrement.
evensong ['i:vnsɔŋ] *n* office *m* du soir.
event [ɪ'vεnt] *n* événement *m*; (*SPORT*) épreuve *f*; **in the course of ~s** par la suite; **in the ~ of** en cas de; **in the ~** en réalité, en fait; **at all ~s** (*BRIT*), **in any ~** en tout cas, de toute manière.
eventful [ɪ'vεntful] *adj* mouvementé(e).
eventing [ɪ'vεntɪŋ] *n* (*HORSE-RIDING*) concours complet (équitation).
eventual [ɪ'vεntʃuəl] *adj* final(e).
eventuality [ɪvεntʃu'ælɪtɪ] *n* possibilité *f*, éventualité *f*.
eventually [ɪ'vεntʃuəlɪ] *adv* finalement.
ever ['εvə*] *adv* jamais; (*at all times*) toujours; **the best ~** le meilleur qu'on ait jamais vu; **did you ~ meet him?** est-ce qu'il vous est arrivé de le rencontrer?; **have you ~ been there?** y êtes-vous déjà allé?; **for ~** pour toujours; **hardly ~** ne ... presque jamais; **~ since** *adv* depuis ♦ *conj* depuis que; **~ so pretty** si joli; **thank you ~ so much** merci mille fois;
Everest ['εvərɪst] *n* (*also*: **Mount ~**) le mont Everest, l'Everest *m*.
evergreen ['εvəgri:n] *n* arbre *m* à feuilles persistantes.
everlasting [εvə'lɑ:stɪŋ] *adj* éternel(le).
every ['εvrɪ] *adj* chaque; **~ day** tous les jours, chaque jour; **~ other/third day** tous les deux/trois jours; **~ other car** une voiture sur deux; **~ now and then** de temps en temps; **I have ~ confidence in him** j'ai entièrement *or* pleinement confiance en lui.
everybody ['εvrɪbɔdɪ] *pron* tout le monde, tous *pl*; **~ knows about it** tout le monde le sait; **~ else** tous les autres.
everyday ['εvrɪdeɪ] *adj* (*expression*) courant(e), d'usage courant; (*use*) courant; (*occurrence, experience*) de tous les jours, ordinaire.
everyone ['εvrɪwʌn] = **everybody**.
everything ['εvrɪθɪŋ] *pron* tout; **~ is ready** tout est prêt; **he did ~ possible** il a fait tout son possible.

everywhere ['ɛvrɪweə*] *adv* partout; ~ **you go you meet ...** où qu'on aille, on rencontre ....
evict [ɪ'vɪkt] *vt* expulser.
eviction [ɪ'vɪkʃən] *n* expulsion *f*.
eviction notice *n* préavis *m* d'expulsion.
evidence ['ɛvɪdns] *n* (*proof*) preuve(s) *f(pl)*; (*of witness*) témoignage *m*; (*sign*): **to show ~ of** donner des signes de; **to give ~** témoigner, déposer; **in ~** (*obvious*) en évidence; en vue.
evident ['ɛvɪdnt] *adj* évident(e).
evidently ['ɛvɪdntlɪ] *adv* de toute évidence.
evil ['iːvl] *adj* mauvais(e) ♦ *n* mal *m*.
evince [ɪ'vɪns] *vt* manifester.
evocative [ɪ'vɔkətɪv] *adj* évocateur(trice).
evoke [ɪ'vəuk] *vt* évoquer; (*admiration*) susciter.
evolution [iːvə'luːʃən] *n* évolution *f*.
evolve [ɪ'vɔlv] *vt* élaborer ♦ *vi* évoluer, se transformer.
ewe [juː] *n* brebis *f*.
ewer ['juːə*] *n* broc *m*.
ex- [ɛks] *prefix* (*former: husband, president etc*) ex-; (*out of*): **the price ~ works** le prix départ usine.
exacerbate [ɛks'æsəbeɪt] *vt* (*pain*) exacerber, accentuer; (*fig*) aggraver.
exact [ɪg'zækt] *adj* exact(e) ♦ *vt*: **to ~ sth (from)** extorquer qch (à); exiger qch (de).
exacting [ɪg'zæktɪŋ] *adj* exigeant(e); (*work*) fatigant(e).
exactitude [ɪg'zæktɪtjuːd] *n* exactitude *f*, précision *f*.
exactly [ɪg'zæktlɪ] *adv* exactement; ~! parfaitement!, précisément!
exaggerate [ɪg'zædʒəreɪt] *vt*, *vi* exagérer.
exaggeration [ɪgzædʒə'reɪʃən] *n* exagération *f*.
exalted [ɪg'zɔːltɪd] *adj* (*rank*) élevé(e); (*person*) haut placé(e); (*person*) exalté(e).
exam [ɪg'zæm] *n abbr* (*SCOL*) = **examination**.
examination [ɪgzæmɪ'neɪʃən] *n* (*SCOL, MED*) examen *m*; **to take** *or* (*BRIT*) **sit an ~** passer un examen; **the matter is under ~** la question est à l'examen.
examine [ɪg'zæmɪn] *vt* (*gen*) examiner; (*SCOL, LAW: person*) interroger; (*inspect: machine, premises*) inspecter; (*passport*) contrôler; (*luggage*) fouiller.
examiner [ɪg'zæmɪnə*] *n* examinateur/trice.
example [ɪg'zɑːmpl] *n* exemple *m*; **for ~** par exemple; **to set a good/bad** ~ donner le bon/mauvais exemple.
exasperate [ɪg'zɑːspəreɪt] *vt* exaspérer, agacer.
exasperation [ɪgzɑːspə'reɪʃən] *n* exaspération *f*, irritation *f*.
excavate ['ɛkskəveɪt] *vt* excaver; (*object*) mettre au jour.
excavation [ɛkskə'veɪʃən] *n* excavation *f*.
excavator ['ɛkskəveɪtə*] *n* excavateur *m*, excavatrice *f*.
exceed [ɪk'siːd] *vt* dépasser; (*one's powers*) outrepasser.

exceedingly [ɪk'siːdɪŋlɪ] *adv* excessivement.
excel [ɪk'sɛl] *vi* exceller ♦ *vt* surpasser; **to ~ o.s.** (*BRIT*) se surpasser.
excellence ['ɛksələns] *n* excellence *f*.
Excellency ['ɛksələnsɪ] *n*: **His ~ son** Excellence *f*.
excellent ['ɛksələnt] *adj* excellent(e).
except [ɪk'sɛpt] *prep* (*also*: ~ **for**, ~**ing**) sauf, excepté, à l'exception de ♦ *vt* excepter; ~ **if/when** sauf si/quand; ~ **that** excepté que, si ce n'est que.
exception [ɪk'sɛpʃən] *n* exception *f*; **to take ~ to** s'offusquer de; **with the ~ of** à l'exception de.
exceptional [ɪk'sɛpʃənl] *adj* exceptionnel(le).
excerpt ['ɛksəːpt] *n* extrait *m*.
excess [ɪk'sɛs] *n* excès *m*; **in ~ of** plus de.
excess baggage *n* excédent *m* de bagages.
excess fare *n* supplément *m*.
excessive [ɪk'sɛsɪv] *adj* excessif(ive).
excess supply *n* suroffre *f*, offre *f* excédentaire.
exchange [ɪks'tʃeɪndʒ] *n* échange *m*; (*also*: **telephone ~**) central *m* ♦ *vt*: **to ~ (for)** échanger (contre); **in ~ for** en échange de; **foreign ~** (*COMM*) change *m*.
exchange control *n* contrôle *m* des changes.
exchange market *n* marché *m* des changes.
exchange rate *n* taux *m* de change.
exchequer [ɪks'tʃɛkə*] *n* (*BRIT*) Échiquier *m*, ≈ ministère *m* des Finances.
excisable [ɪk'saɪzəbl] *adj* taxable.
excise *n* ['ɛksaɪz] taxe *f* ♦ *vt* [ɛk'saɪz] exciser.
excise duties *npl* impôts indirects.
excitable [ɪk'saɪtəbl] *adj* excitable, nerveux(euse).
excite [ɪk'saɪt] *vt* exciter; **to get ~d** s'exciter.
excitement [ɪk'saɪtmənt] *n* excitation *f*.
exciting [ɪk'saɪtɪŋ] *adj* passionnant(e).
excl. *abbr* = **excluding, exclusive (of)**.
exclaim [ɪk'skleɪm] *vi* s'exclamer.
exclamation [ɛksklə'meɪʃən] *n* exclamation *f*.
exclamation mark *n* point *m* d'exclamation.
exclude [ɪk'skluːd] *vt* exclure.
excluding [ɪk'skluːdɪŋ] *prep*: ~ **VAT** la TVA non comprise.
exclusion [ɪk'skluːʒən] *n* exclusion *f*; **to the ~ of** à l'exclusion de.
exclusion clause *n* clause *f* d'exclusion.
exclusion zone *n* zone interdite.
exclusive [ɪk'skluːsɪv] *adj* exclusif(ive); (*club, district*) sélect(e); (*item of news*) en exclusivité ♦ *adv* (*COMM*) exclusivement, non inclus; ~ **of VAT** TVA non comprise; ~ **of postage** (les) frais de poste non compris; **from 1st to 15th March** ~ du 1er au 15 mars exclusivement *or* exclu; ~ **rights** (*COMM*) exclusivité *f*.
exclusively [ɪk'skluːsɪvlɪ] *adv* exclusivement.
excommunicate [ɛkskə'mjuːnɪkeɪt] *vt* excommunier.

xcrement ['ɛkskrəmənt] n excrément m.
xcruciating [ɪk'skruːʃɪeɪtɪŋ] adj atroce,
déchirant(e).
xcursion [ɪk'skəːʃən] n excursion f.
xcursion ticket n billet m tarif excursion.
xcusable [ɪk'skjuːzəbl] adj excusable.
xcuse n [ɪk'skjuːs] excuse f ♦ vt [ɪk'skjuːz]
excuser; (justify) excuser, justifier; **to ~ sb
from** (activity) dispenser qn de; **~ me!**
excusez-moi!, pardon!; **now if you will ~
me, ...** maintenant, si vous (le) permettez ...;
to make ~s for sb trouver des excuses à qn;
to ~ o.s. for sth/for doing sth s'excuser de/
d'avoir fait qch.
x-directory ['ɛksdɪ'rɛktərɪ] adj (BRIT): **~
(phone) number** numéro m (de téléphone)
sur la liste rouge.
xcute ['ɛksɪkjuːt] vt exécuter.
xecution [ɛksɪ'kjuːʃən] n exécution f.
xecutioner [ɛksɪ'kjuːʃnə*] n bourreau m.
xecutive [ɪg'zɛkjutɪv] n (COMM) cadre m;
(POL) exécutif m ♦ adj exécutif(ive);
(position, job) de cadre; (secretary) de
direction; (offices) de la direction; (car,
plane) de fonction.
xecutive director n administrateur/trice.
xecutor [ɪg'zɛkjutə*] n exécuteur/trice
testamentaire.
xemplary [ɪg'zɛmpləri] adj exemplaire.
xemplify [ɪg'zɛmplɪfaɪ] vt illustrer.
xempt [ɪg'zɛmpt] adj: **~ from** exempté(e) or
dispensé(e) de ♦ vt: **to ~ sb from** exempter
or dispenser qn de.
xemption [ɪg'zɛmpʃən] n exemption f,
dispense f.
xercise ['ɛksəsaɪz] n exercice m ♦ vt exercer;
(patience etc) faire preuve de; (dog)
promener ♦ vi (also: **to take ~**) prendre de
l'exercice.
xercise bike n vélo m d'appartement.
xercise book n cahier m.
xert [ɪg'zəːt] vt exercer, employer; (strength,
force) employer; **to ~ o.s.** se dépenser.
xertion [ɪg'zəːʃən] n effort m.
x gratia ['ɛks'greɪʃə] adj: **~ payment**
gratification f.
xhale [ɛks'heɪl] vt expirer; exhaler ♦ vi
expirer.
xhaust [ɪg'zɔːst] n (also: **~ fumes**) gaz mpl
d'échappement; (also: **~ pipe**) tuyau m
d'échappement ♦ vt épuiser; **to ~ o.s.**
s'épuiser.
xhausted [ɪg'zɔːstɪd] adj épuisé(e).
xhausting [ɪg'zɔːstɪŋ] adj épuisant(e).
xhaustion [ɪg'zɔːstʃən] n épuisement m;
nervous ~ fatigue nerveuse.
xhaustive [ɪg'zɔːstɪv] adj très complet(ète).
xhibit [ɪg'zɪbɪt] n (ART) pièce f or objet m
exposé(e); (LAW) pièce à conviction ♦ vt
exposer; (courage, skill) faire preuve de.
xhibition [ɛksɪ'bɪʃən] n exposition f; **~ of
temper** manifestation f de colère.

exhibitionist [ɛksɪ'bɪʃənɪst] n exhibitionniste
m/f.
exhibitor [ɪg'zɪbɪtə*] n exposant/e.
exhilarating [ɪg'zɪləreɪtɪŋ] adj grisant(e);
stimulant(e).
exhilaration [ɪgzɪlə'reɪʃən] n euphorie f,
ivresse f.
exhort [ɪg'zɔːt] vt exhorter.
exile ['ɛksaɪl] n exil m; (person) exilé/e ♦ vt
exiler; **in ~** en exil.
exist [ɪg'zɪst] vi exister.
existence [ɪg'zɪstəns] n existence f; **to be in ~**
exister.
existentialism [ɛgzɪs'tɛnʃlɪzəm] n
existentialisme m.
existing [ɪg'zɪstɪŋ] adj (laws) existant(e);
(system, regime) actuel(le).
exit ['ɛksɪt] n sortie f ♦ vi (COMPUT, THEAT)
sortir.
exit poll n sondage m (fait à la sortie de
l'isoloir).
exit ramp n (US AUT) bretelle f d'accès.
exit visa n visa m de sortie.
exodus ['ɛksədəs] n exode m.
ex officio ['ɛksə'fɪʃɪəu] adj, adv d'office, de
droit.
exonerate [ɪg'zɒnəreɪt] vt: **to ~ from**
disculper de.
exorbitant [ɪg'zɔːbɪtnt] adj (price)
exorbitant(e), excessif(ive); (demands)
exorbitant, démesuré(e).
exorcize ['ɛksɔːsaɪz] vt exorciser.
exotic [ɪg'zɒtɪk] adj exotique.
expand [ɪk'spænd] vt (area) agrandir;
(quantity) accroître; (influence etc) étendre
♦ vi (population, production) s'accroître;
(trade, influence etc) se développer,
s'étendre; (gas, metal) se dilater; **to ~ on**
(notes, story etc) développer.
expanse [ɪk'spæns] n étendue f.
expansion [ɪk'spænʃən] n (see expand)
développement m; accroissement m;
extension f; dilatation f.
expansionism [ɪk'spænʃənɪzəm] n
expansionnisme m.
expansionist [ɪk'spænʃənɪst] adj
expansionniste.
expatriate n [ɛks'pætrɪət] expatrié/e ♦ vt
[ɛks'pætrɪeɪt] expatrier, exiler.
expect [ɪk'spɛkt] vt (anticipate) s'attendre à,
s'attendre à ce que + sub; (count on) compter
sur, escompter; (hope for) espérer; (require)
demander, exiger; (suppose) supposer;
(await, also baby) attendre ♦ vi: **to be ~ing**
être enceinte; **to ~ sb to do** (anticipate)
s'attendre à ce que qn fasse; (demand)
attendre de qn qu'il fasse; **to ~ to do sth**
penser or compter faire qch, s'attendre à
faire qch; **as ~ed** comme prévu; **I ~ so** je
crois que oui, je crois bien.
expectancy [ɪks'pɛktənsɪ] n attente f; **life ~**
espérance f de vie.

expectant [ɪk'spɛktənt] *adj* qui attend (quelque chose); ~ **mother** future maman.
expectantly [ɪk'spɛktəntlɪ] *adv* (*look, listen*) avec l'air d'attendre quelque chose.
expectation [ɛkspɛk'teɪʃən] *n* attente *f*, prévisions *fpl*; espérance(s) *f(pl)*; **in ~ of** dans l'attente de, en prévision de; **against** *or* **contrary to all ~(s)** contre toute attente, contrairement à ce qu'on attendait; **to come** *or* **live up to sb's ~s** répondre à l'attente *or* aux espérances de qn.
expedience, expediency [ɪk'spiːdɪəns, ɪk'spiːdɪənsɪ] *n* opportunité *f*; convenance *f* (du moment); **for the sake of** ~ parce que c'est (*or* c'était) plus simple *or* plus commode.
expedient [ɪk'spiːdɪənt] *adj* indiqué(e), opportun(e); commode ♦ *n* expédient *m*.
expedite ['ɛkspədaɪt] *vt* hâter; expédier.
expedition [ɛkspə'dɪʃən] *n* expédition *f*.
expeditionary force [ɛkspə'dɪʃənrɪ-] *n* corps *m* expéditionnaire.
expeditious [ɛkspə'dɪʃəs] *adj* expéditif(ive), prompt(e).
expel [ɪk'spɛl] *vt* chasser, expulser; (*SCOL*) renvoyer, exclure.
expend [ɪk'spɛnd] *vt* consacrer; (*use up*) dépenser.
expendable [ɪk'spɛndəbl] *adj* remplaçable.
expenditure [ɪk'spɛndɪtʃə*] *n* dépense *f*; dépenses *fpl*.
expense [ɪk'spɛns] *n* (*cost*) coût *m*; (*spending*) dépense *f*, frais *mpl*; ~**s** *npl* frais *mpl*; dépenses; **to go to the ~ of** faire la dépense de; **at great/little ~** à grands/peu de frais; **at the ~ of** aux frais de; (*fig*) aux dépens de.
expense account *n* (note *f* de) frais *mpl*.
expensive [ɪk'spɛnsɪv] *adj* cher(chère), coûteux(euse); **to be ~** coûter cher; ~ **tastes** goûts *mpl* de luxe.
experience [ɪk'spɪərɪəns] *n* expérience *f* ♦ *vt* connaître; éprouver; **to know by ~** savoir par expérience.
experienced [ɪk'spɪərɪənst] *adj* expérimenté(e).
experiment [ɪk'spɛrɪmənt] *n* expérience *f* ♦ *vi* faire une expérience; **to ~ with** expérimenter; **to perform** *or* **carry out an ~** faire une expérience; **as an ~** à titre d'expérience.
experimental [ɪkspɛrɪ'mɛntl] *adj* expérimental(e).
expert ['ɛkspəːt] *adj* expert(e) ♦ *n* expert *m*; ~ **in** *or* **at doing sth** spécialiste de qch; **an ~ on sth** un spécialiste de qch; ~ **witness** (*LAW*) expert *m*.
expertise [ɛkspəː'tiːz] *n* (grande) compétence.
expire [ɪk'spaɪə*] *vi* expirer.
expiry [ɪk'spaɪərɪ] *n* expiration *f*.
explain [ɪk'spleɪn] *vt* expliquer.
▶**explain away** *vt* justifier, excuser.

explanation [ɛksplə'neɪʃən] *n* explication *f*; **to find an ~ for sth** trouver une explication à qch.
explanatory [ɪk'splænətrɪ] *adj* explicatif(ive).
expletive [ɪk'spliːtɪv] *n* juron *m*.
explicit [ɪk'splɪsɪt] *adj* explicite; (*definite*) formel(le).
explode [ɪk'spləud] *vi* exploser ♦ *vt* faire exploser; (*fig: theory*) démolir; **to ~ a myth** détruire un mythe.
exploit *n* ['ɛksplɔɪt] exploit *m* ♦ *vt* [ɪk'splɔɪt] exploiter.
exploitation [ɛksplɔɪ'teɪʃən] *n* exploitation *f*.
exploration [ɛksplə'reɪʃən] *n* exploration *f*.
exploratory [ɪk'splɔrətrɪ] *adj* (*fig: talks*) préliminaire; ~ **operation** (*MED*) intervention *f* (à visée) exploratrice.
explore [ɪk'splɔː*] *vt* explorer; (*possibilities*) étudier, examiner.
explorer [ɪk'splɔːrə*] *n* explorateur/trice.
explosion [ɪk'spləuʒən] *n* explosion *f*.
explosive [ɪk'spləusɪv] *adj* explosif(ive) ♦ *n* explosif *m*.
exponent [ɪk'spəunənt] *n* (*of school of thought etc*) interprète *m*, représentant *m*; (*MATH*) exposant *m*.
export *vt* [ɛk'spɔːt] exporter ♦ *n* ['ɛkspɔːt] exportation *f* ♦ *cpd* d'exportation.
exportation [ɛkspɔː'teɪʃən] *n* exportation *f*.
exporter [ɛk'spɔːtə*] *n* exportateur *m*.
export licence *n* licence *f* d'exportation.
expose [ɪk'spəuz] *vt* exposer; (*unmask*) démasquer, dévoiler; **to ~ o.s.** (*LAW*) commettre un outrage à la pudeur.
exposed [ɪk'spəuzd] *adj* (*land, house*) exposé(e); (*ELEC: wire*) à nu; (*pipe, beam*) apparent(e).
exposition [ɛkspə'zɪʃən] *n* exposition *f*.
exposure [ɪk'spəuʒə*] *n* exposition *f*; (*PHOT*) (temps *m* de) pose; (*: shot*) pose; **suffering from ~** (*MED*) souffrant des effets du froid et de l'épuisement; **to die of ~** (*MED*) mouri de froid.
exposure meter *n* posemètre *m*.
expound [ɪk'spaund] *vt* exposer, expliquer.
express [ɪk'sprɛs] *adj* (*definite*) formel(le), exprès(esse); (*BRIT: letter etc*) exprès *inv* ♦ *n* (*train*) rapide *m* ♦ *adv* (*send*) exprès ♦ *vt* exprimer; **to ~ o.s.** s'exprimer.
expression [ɪk'sprɛʃən] *n* expression *f*.
expressionism [ɪk'sprɛʃənɪzəm] *n* expressionnisme *m*.
expressive [ɪk'sprɛsɪv] *adj* expressif(ive).
expressly [ɪk'sprɛslɪ] *adv* expressément, formellement.
expressway [ɪk'sprɛsweɪ] *n* (*US*) voie *f* express (à plusieurs files).
expropriate [ɛks'prəuprɪeɪt] *vt* exproprier.
expulsion [ɪk'spʌlʃən] *n* expulsion *f*; renvoi *m*
exquisite [ɛk'skwɪzɪt] *adj* exquis(e).
ex-serviceman ['ɛks'səːvɪsmən] *n* ancien combattant.

ext. abbr (TEL) = **extension**.

extemporize [ɪk'stɛmpəraɪz] vi improviser.

extend [ɪk'stɛnd] vt (visit, street) prolonger; (deadline) reporter, remettre; (building) agrandir; (offer) présenter, offrir; (COMM: credit) accorder ♦ vi (land) s'étendre.

extension [ɪk'stɛnʃən] n (see extend) prolongation f; agrandissement m; (building) annexe f; (to wire, table) rallonge f; (telephone: in offices) poste m; (: in private house) téléphone m supplémentaire; **~ 3718** (TEL) poste 3718.

extension cable n (ELEC) rallonge f.

extensive [ɪk'stɛnsɪv] adj étendu(e), vaste; (damage, alterations) considérable; (inquiries) approfondi(e); (use) largement répandu(e).

extensively [ɪk'stɛnsɪvlɪ] adv (altered, damaged etc) considérablement; **he's travelled ~** il a beaucoup voyagé.

extent [ɪk'stɛnt] n étendue f; (degree: of damage, loss) importance f; **to some ~** dans une certaine mesure; **to a certain ~** dans une certaine mesure, jusqu'à un certain point; **to a large ~** en grande partie; **to what ~?** dans quelle mesure?, jusqu'à quel point?; **to such an ~ that ...** à tel point que ....

extenuating [ɪk'stɛnjueɪtɪŋ] adj: **~ circumstances** circonstances atténuantes.

exterior [ɛk'stɪərɪə*] adj extérieur(e), du dehors ♦ n extérieur m; dehors m.

exterminate [ɪk'stɜːmɪneɪt] vt exterminer.

extermination [ɪkstəːmɪ'neɪʃən] n extermination f.

external [ɛk'stəːnl] adj externe ♦ n: **the ~s** les apparences fpl; **for ~ use only** (MED) à usage externe.

externally [ɛk'stəːnəlɪ] adv extérieurement.

extinct [ɪk'stɪŋkt] adj éteint(e).

extinction [ɪk'stɪŋkʃən] n extinction f.

extinguish [ɪk'stɪŋgwɪʃ] vt éteindre.

extinguisher [ɪk'stɪŋgwɪʃə*] n extincteur m.

extol, (US) **extoll** [ɪk'stəul] vt (merits) chanter, prôner; (person) chanter les louanges de.

extort [ɪk'stɔːt] vt: **to ~ sth (from)** extorquer qch (à).

extortion [ɪk'stɔːʃən] n extorsion f.

extortionate [ɪk'stɔːʃnɪt] adj exorbitant(e).

extra ['ɛkstrə] adj supplémentaire, de plus ♦ adv (in addition) en plus ♦ n supplément m; (THEAT) figurant/e; **wine will cost ~** le vin sera en supplément; **~ large sizes** très grandes tailles.

extra... ['ɛkstrə] prefix extra....

extract vt [ɪk'strækt] extraire; (tooth) arracher; (money, promise) soutirer ♦ n ['ɛkstrækt] extrait m.

extraction [ɪk'strækʃən] n (also descent) extraction f.

extractor fan [ɪk'stræktə-] n exhausteur m, ventilateur m extracteur.

extracurricular ['ɛkstrəkə'rɪkjulə*] adj (SCOL) parascolaire.

extradite ['ɛkstrədaɪt] vt extrader.

extradition [ɛkstrə'dɪʃən] n extradition f.

extramarital ['ɛkstrə'mærɪtl] adj extraconjugal(e).

extramural ['ɛkstrə'mjuərl] adj hors-faculté inv.

extraneous [ɛk'streɪnɪəs] adj: **~ to** étranger(ère) à.

extraordinary [ɪk'strɔːdnrɪ] adj extraordinaire; **the ~ thing is that ...** le plus étrange or étonnant c'est que ....

extraordinary general meeting n assemblée générale extraordinaire.

extrapolation [ɛkstræpə'leɪʃən] n extrapolation f.

extrasensory perception (ESP) ['ɛkstrə'sɛnsərɪ-] n perception extra-sensorielle.

extra time n (FOOTBALL) prolongations fpl.

extravagance [ɪk'strævəgəns] n (excessive spending) prodigalités fpl; (thing bought) folie f, dépense excessive or exagérée.

extravagant [ɪk'strævəgənt] adj extravagant(e); (in spending: person) prodigue, dépensier(ière); (: tastes) dispendieux(euse).

extreme [ɪk'striːm] adj, n extrême (m); **the ~ left/right** (POL) l'extrême gauche f/droite f; **~s of temperature** différences fpl extrêmes de température.

extremely [ɪk'striːmlɪ] adv extrêmement.

extremist [ɪk'striːmɪst] adj, n extrémiste (m/f).

extremity [ɪk'strɛmɪtɪ] n extrémité f.

extricate ['ɛkstrɪkeɪt] vt: **to ~ sth (from)** dégager qch (de).

extrovert ['ɛkstrəvəːt] n extraverti/e.

exuberance [ɪg'zjuːbərns] n exubérance f.

exuberant [ɪg'zjuːbərnt] adj exubérant(e).

exude [ɪg'zjuːd] vt exsuder; (fig) respirer; **the charm etc he ~s** le charme etc qui émane de lui.

exult [ɪg'zʌlt] vi exulter, jubiler.

exultant [ɪg'zʌltənt] adj (shout, expression) de triomphe; **to be ~** jubiler, triompher.

exultation [ɛgzʌl'teɪʃən] n exultation f, jubilation f.

eye [aɪ] n œil m (pl yeux); (of needle) trou m, chas m ♦ vt examiner; **as far as the ~ can see** à perte de vue; **to keep an ~ on** surveiller; **to have an ~ for sth** avoir l'œil pour qch; **in the public ~** en vue; **with an ~ to doing sth** (BRIT) en vue de faire qch; **there's more to this than meets the ~** ce n'est pas aussi simple que cela paraît.

eyeball ['aɪbɔːl] n globe m oculaire.

eyebath ['aɪbɑːθ] n (BRIT) œillère f (pour bains d'œil).

eyebrow ['aɪbrau] n sourcil m.

eyebrow pencil n crayon m à sourcils.

eye-catching ['aɪkætʃɪŋ] adj voyant(e), accrocheur(euse).

eye cup *n* (*US*) = **eyebath**.
eyedrops ['aɪdrɒps] *npl* gouttes *fpl* pour les yeux.
eyeful ['aɪful] *n*: **to get an ~ (of sth)** se rincer l'œil (en voyant qch).
eyeglass ['aɪglɑːs] *n* monocle *m*.
eyelash ['aɪlæʃ] *n* cil *m*.
eyelet ['aɪlɪt] *n* œillet *m*.
eye-level ['aɪlɛvl] *adj* en hauteur.
eyelid ['aɪlɪd] *n* paupière *f*.
eyeliner ['aɪlaɪnə*] *n* eye-liner *m*.
eye-opener ['aɪəupnə*] *n* révélation *f*.
eyeshadow ['aɪʃædəu] *n* ombre *f* à paupières.
eyesight ['aɪsaɪt] *n* vue *f*.
eyesore ['aɪsɔː*] *n* horreur *f*, chose *f* qui dépare or enlaidit.
eyestrain ['aɪstreɪn] *adj*: **to get ~** se fatiguer la vue *or* les yeux.
eyetooth, *pl* **-teeth** ['aɪtuːθ, -tiːθ] *n* canine supérieure; **to give one's eyeteeth for sth/to do sth** (*fig*) donner n'importe quoi pour qch/pour faire qch.
eyewash ['aɪwɒʃ] *n* bain *m* d'œil; (*fig*) frime *f*.
eye witness *n* témoin *m* oculaire.
eyrie ['ɪərɪ] *n* aire *f*.

Ff

F, f [ɛf] *n* (*letter*) F, f *m*; (*MUS*): **F** fa *m*; **F for Frederick**, (*US*) **F for Fox** F comme François.
F *abbr* (= *Fahrenheit*) F.
FA *n abbr* (*BRIT*: = *Football Association*) *fédération de football*.
FAA *n abbr* (*US*) = *Federal Aviation Administration*.
fable ['feɪbl] *n* fable *f*.
fabric ['fæbrɪk] *n* tissu *m* ♦ *cpd*: **~ ribbon** *n* (*for typewriter*) ruban *m* (en) tissu.
fabricate ['fæbrɪkeɪt] *vt* fabriquer, inventer.
fabrication [fæbrɪ'keɪʃən] *n* fabrication *f*, invention *f*.
fabulous ['fæbjuləs] *adj* fabuleux(euse); (*col*: *super*) formidable, sensationnel(le).
façade [fə'sɑːd] *n* façade *f*.
face [feɪs] *n* visage *m*, figure *f*; expression *f*; grimace *f*; (*of clock*) cadran *m*; (*of building*) façade *f*; (*side, surface*) face *f* ♦ *vt* faire face à; (*facts etc*) accepter; **~ down** (*person*) à plat ventre; (*card*) face en dessous; **to lose/save ~** perdre/sauver la face; **to pull a ~** faire une grimace; **in the ~ of** (*difficulties etc*) face à, devant; **on the ~ of it** à première vue.
►**face up to** *vt fus* faire face à, affronter.
face cloth *n* (*BRIT*) gant *m* de toilette.

face cream *n* crème *f* pour le visage.
face lift *n* lifting *m*; (*of façade etc*) ravalement *m*, retapage *m*.
face powder *n* poudre *f* (pour le visage).
face-saving ['feɪsseɪvɪŋ] *adj* qui sauve la face.
facet ['fæsɪt] *n* facette *f*.
facetious [fə'siːʃəs] *adj* facétieux(euse).
face-to-face ['feɪstə'feɪs] *adv* face à face.
face value ['feɪs'væljuː] *n* (*of coin*) valeur nominale; **to take sth at ~** (*fig*) prendre qch pour argent comptant.
facia ['feɪʃə] *n* = **fascia**.
facial ['feɪʃl] *adj* facial(e) ♦ *n* soin complet du visage.
facile ['fæsaɪl] *adj* facile.
facilitate [fə'sɪlɪteɪt] *vt* faciliter.
facility [fə'sɪlɪtɪ] *n* facilité *f*; **facilities** *npl* installations *fpl*, équipement *m*; **credit facilities** facilités de paiement.
facing ['feɪsɪŋ] *prep* face à, en face de ♦ *n* (*of wall etc*) revêtement *m*; (*SEWING*) revers *m*.
facsimile [fæk'sɪmɪlɪ] *n* (*exact replica*) facsimilé *m*; (*also*: **~ machine**) télécopieur *m*; (*transmitted document*) télécopie *f*.
fact [fækt] *n* fait *m*; **in ~** en fait; **to know for a ~ that ...** savoir pertinemment que ....
fact-finding ['fæktfaɪndɪŋ] *adj*: **a ~ tour** *or* **mission** une mission d'enquête.
faction ['fækʃən] *n* faction *f*.
factional ['fækʃənl] *adj* de factions.
factor ['fæktə*] *n* facteur *m*; (*COMM*) factor *m*, société *f* d'affacturage; (*: agent*) dépositaire *m/f* ♦ *vi* faire du factoring; **safety ~** facteur de sécurité.
factory ['fæktərɪ] *n* usine *f*, fabrique *f*.
factory farming *n* (*BRIT*) élevage industriel.
factory floor *n*: **the ~** (*workers*) les ouvriers *mpl*; (*workshop*) l'usine *f*; **on the ~** dans les ateliers.
factory ship *n* navire-usine *m*.
factual ['fæktjuəl] *adj* basé(e) sur les faits.
faculty ['fækəltɪ] *n* faculté *f*; (*US: teaching staff*) corps enseignant.
fad [fæd] *n* (*col*) manie *f*; engouement *m*.
fade [feɪd] *vi* se décolorer, passer; (*light, sound, hope*) s'affaiblir, disparaître; (*flower*) se faner.
►**fade in** *vt* (*picture*) ouvrir en fondu; (*sound*) monter progressivement.
►**fade out** *vt* (*picture*) fermer en fondu; (*sound*) baisser progressivement.
faeces, (*US*) **feces** ['fiːsiːz] *npl* fèces *fpl*.
fag [fæg] *n* (*BRIT col: cigarette*) sèche *f*; (*: chore*): **what a ~!** quelle corvée!; (*US col: homosexual*) pédé *m*.
fag end *n* (*BRIT col*) mégot *m*.
fagged out *adj* (*BRIT col*) crevé(e).
fail [feɪl] *vt* (*exam*) échouer à; (*candidate*) recaler; (*subj: courage, memory*) faire défaut à ♦ *vi* échouer; (*supplies*) manquer; (*eyesight, health, light: also*: **be ~ing**) baisser, s'affaiblir; (*brakes*) lâcher; **to ~ to do sth**

(*neglect*) négliger de *or* ne pas faire qch; (*be unable*) ne pas arriver *or* parvenir à faire qch; **without** ~ à coup sûr; sans faute.

ailing ['feɪlɪŋ] *n* défaut *m* ♦ *prep* faute de; ~ **that** à défaut, sinon.

ailsafe ['feɪlseɪf] *adj* (*device etc*) à sûreté intégrée.

ailure ['feɪljə*] *n* échec *m*; (*person*) raté/e; (*mechanical etc*) défaillance *f*; **his** ~ **to turn up** le fait de n'être pas venu *or* qu'il ne soit pas venu.

aint [feɪnt] *adj* faible; (*recollection*) vague; (*mark*) à peine visible; (*smell, breeze, trace*) léger(ère) ♦ *n* évanouissement *m* ♦ *vi* s'évanouir; **to feel** ~ défaillir.

aintest ['feɪntɪst] *adj*: **I haven't the** ~ **idea** je n'en ai pas la moindre idée.

aint-hearted ['feɪnt'hɑːtɪd] *adj* pusillanime.

aintly ['feɪntlɪ] *adv* faiblement; vaguement.

aintness ['feɪntnɪs] *n* faiblesse *f*.

air [fɛə*] *adj* équitable, juste; (*reasonable*) correct(e), honnête; (*hair*) blond(e); (*skin, complexion*) pâle, blanc, blanche); (*weather*) beau(belle); (*good enough*) assez bon(ne) ♦ *adv*: **to play** ~ jouer franc jeu ♦ *n* foire *f*; (*BRIT: funfair*) fête (foraine); (*also*: **trade** ~) foire(-exposition) commerciale; **it's not** ~! ce n'est pas juste!; **a** ~ **amount of** une quantité considérable de.

air copy *n* copie *f* au propre; corrigé *m*.

air game *n*: **to be** ~ **(for)** être une cible légitime (pour).

airground ['fɛəgraʊnd] *n* champ *m* de foire.

air-haired [fɛə'hɛəd] *adj* (*person*) aux cheveux clairs, blond(e).

airly ['fɛəlɪ] *adv* équitablement; (*quite*) assez; **I'm** ~ **sure** j'en suis quasiment *or* presque sûr.

airness ['fɛənɪs] *n* (*of trial etc*) justice *f*, équité *f*; (*of person*) sens *m* de la justice; **in all** ~ en toute justice.

air play *n* fair play *m*.

airy ['fɛərɪ] *n* fée *f*.

airy godmother *n* bonne fée.

airy lights *npl* (*BRIT*) guirlande *f* électrique.

airy tale *n* conte *m* de fées.

aith [feɪθ] *n* foi *f*; (*trust*) confiance *f*; (*sect*) culte *m*, religion *f*; **to have** ~ **in sb/sth** avoir confiance en qn/qch.

aithful ['feɪθful] *adj* fidèle.

aithfully ['feɪθfəlɪ] *adv* fidèlement; **yours** ~ (*BRIT: in letters*) veuillez agréer l'expression de mes salutations les plus distinguées.

aith healer [-hiːlə*] *n* guérisseur/euse.

ake [feɪk] *n* (*painting etc*) faux *m*; (*photo*) trucage *m*; (*person*) imposteur *m* ♦ *adj* faux(fausse) ♦ *vt* (*emotions*) simuler; (*photo*) truquer; (*story*) fabriquer; **his illness is a** ~ sa maladie est une comédie *or* de la simulation.

alcon ['fɔːkən] *n* faucon *m*.

Falkland Islands ['fɔːlklənd-] *npl*: **the** ~ les Malouines *fpl*, les îles *fpl* Falkland.

fall [fɔːl] *n* chute *f*; (*decrease*) baisse *f*; (*US: autumn*) automne *m* ♦ *vi* (*pt* **fell**, *pp* **fallen** [fɛl, 'fɔːlən]) tomber; ~**s** *npl* (*waterfall*) chute *f* d'eau, cascade *f*; **to** ~ **flat** *vi* (*on one's face*) tomber de tout son long, s'étaler; (*joke*) tomber à plat; (*plan*) échouer; **to** ~ **short of** (*sb's expectations*) ne pas répondre à; **a** ~ **of snow** (*BRIT*) une chute de neige.

▶**fall apart** *vi* tomber en morceaux; (*col: emotionally*) craquer.

▶**fall back** *vi* reculer, se retirer.

▶**fall back on** *vt fus* se rabattre sur; **to have something to** ~ **back on** (*money etc*) avoir quelque chose en réserve; (*job etc*) avoir une solution de rechange.

▶**fall behind** *vi* prendre du retard.

▶**fall down** *vi* (*person*) tomber; (*building, hopes*) s'effondrer, s'écrouler.

▶**fall for** *vt fus* (*trick*) se laisser prendre à; (*person*) tomber amoureux(euse) de.

▶**fall in** *vi* s'effondrer; (*MIL*) se mettre en rangs.

▶**fall in with** *vt fus* (*sb's plans etc*) accepter.

▶**fall off** *vi* tomber; (*diminish*) baisser, diminuer.

▶**fall out** *vi* (*friends etc*) se brouiller.

▶**fall over** *vi* tomber (par terre).

▶**fall through** *vi* (*plan, project*) tomber à l'eau.

fallacy ['fæləsɪ] *n* erreur *f*, illusion *f*.

fallback ['fɔːlbæk] *adj*: ~ **position** position *f* de repli.

fallen ['fɔːlən] *pp of* **fall**.

fallible ['fæləbl] *adj* faillible.

fallopian tube [fə'ləʊpɪən-] *n* (*ANAT*) trompe *f* de Fallope.

fallout ['fɔːlaʊt] *n* retombées (radioactives).

fallout shelter *n* abri *m* anti-atomique.

fallow ['fæləʊ] *adj* en jachère; en friche.

false [fɔːls] *adj* faux(fausse); **under** ~ **pretences** sous un faux prétexte.

false alarm *n* fausse alerte.

falsehood ['fɔːlshʊd] *n* mensonge *m*.

falsely ['fɔːlslɪ] *adv* (*accuse*) à tort.

false teeth *npl* (*BRIT*) fausses dents.

falsify ['fɔːlsɪfaɪ] *vt* falsifier; (*accounts*) maquiller.

falter ['fɔːltə*] *vi* chanceler, vaciller.

fame [feɪm] *n* renommée *f*, renom *m*.

familiar [fə'mɪlɪə*] *adj* familier(ière); **to be** ~ **with sth** connaître qch; **to make o.s.** ~ **with sth** se familiariser avec qch; **to be on** ~ **terms with sb** bien connaître qn.

familiarity [fəmɪlɪ'ærɪtɪ] *n* familiarité *f*.

familiarize [fə'mɪlɪəraɪz] *vt* familiariser.

family ['fæmɪlɪ] *n* famille *f*.

family allowance *n* (*BRIT*) allocations familiales.

family business *n* entreprise familiale.

family credit *n* (*BRIT*) complément familial.

family doctor *n* médecin *m* de famille.

family life *n* vie *f* de famille.

family man n père m de famille.
family planning clinic n centre m de planning familial.
family tree n arbre m généalogique.
famine ['fæmɪn] n famine f.
famished ['fæmɪʃt] adj affamé(e); **I'm ~!** (col) je meurs de faim!
famous ['feɪməs] adj célèbre.
famously ['feɪməslɪ] adv (get on) fameusement, à merveille.
fan [fæn] n (folding) éventail m; (ELEC) ventilateur m; (person) fan m, admirateur/trice; (: SPORT) supporter m/f ♦ vt éventer; (fire, quarrel) attiser.
▶**fan out** vi se déployer (en éventail).
fanatic [fə'nætɪk] n fanatique m/f.
fanatical [fə'nætɪkl] adj fanatique.
fan belt n courroie f de ventilateur.
fancied ['fænsɪd] adj imaginaire.
fanciful ['fænsɪful] adj fantaisiste.
fan club n fan-club m.
fancy ['fænsɪ] n fantaisie f, envie f; imagination f ♦ cpd (de) fantaisie inv ♦ vt (feel like, want) avoir envie de; (imagine) imaginer; **to take a ~ to** se prendre d'affection pour; s'enticher de; **it took** or **caught my ~** ça m'a plu; **when the ~ takes him** quand ça lui prend; **to ~ that** ... se figurer or s'imaginer que ...; **he fancies her** elle lui plaît.
fancy dress n déguisement m, travesti m.
fancy-dress ball [fænsɪ'drɛs-] n bal masqué or costumé.
fancy goods npl articles mpl (de) fantaisie.
fanfare ['fænfɛə*] n fanfare f (musique).
fanfold paper ['fænfəuld-] n papier m à pliage accordéon.
fang [fæŋ] n croc m; (of snake) crochet m.
fan heater n (BRIT) radiateur soufflant.
fanlight ['fænlaɪt] n imposte f.
fanny ['fænɪ] n (BRIT col!) chatte f (!); (US col) cul m (!).
fantasize ['fæntəsaɪz] vi fantasmer.
fantastic [fæn'tæstɪk] adj fantastique.
fantasy ['fæntəsɪ] n imagination f, fantaisie f; fantasme m.
fanzine ['fænziːn] n fanzine m.
FAO n abbr (= Food and Agriculture Organization) FAO f.
FAQ abbr (= free alongside quay) FLQ.
far [fɑː*] adj: **the ~ side/end** l'autre côté/bout; **the ~ left/right** (POL) l'extrême gauche f/droite f ♦ adv loin; **is it ~ to London?** est-ce qu'on est loin de Londres?; **it's not ~ (from here)** ce n'est pas loin (d'ici); **~ away, ~ off** au loin, dans le lointain; **~ better** beaucoup mieux; **~ from** loin de; **by ~** de loin, de beaucoup; **as ~ back as the 13th century** dès le 13e siècle; **go as ~ as the farm** allez jusqu'à la ferme; **as ~ as I know** pour autant que je sache; **as ~ as possible** dans la mesure du possible; **how ~ have you got**

with your work? où en êtes-vous dans votre travail?
faraway ['fɑːrəweɪ] adj lointain(e); (look) absent(e).
farce [fɑːs] n farce f.
farcical ['fɑːsɪkl] adj grotesque.
fare [fɛə*] n (on trains, buses) prix m du billet; (in taxi) prix de la course; (passenger in taxi) client m; (food) table f, chère f ♦ vi se débrouiller.
Far East n: **the ~** l'Extrême-Orient m.
farewell [fɛə'wɛl] excl, n adieu (m) ♦ cpd (party etc) d'adieux.
far-fetched ['fɑː'fɛtʃt] adj exagéré(e), poussé(e).
farm [fɑːm] n ferme f ♦ vt cultiver.
▶**farm out** vt (work etc) distribuer.
farmer ['fɑːmə*] n fermier/ière; cultivateur/trice.
farmhand ['fɑːmhænd] n ouvrier/ière agricole.
farmhouse ['fɑːmhaus] n (maison f de) ferme f.
farming ['fɑːmɪŋ] n agriculture f; **intensive ~** culture intensive; **sheep ~** élevage m du mouton.
farm labourer n = **farmhand**.
farmland ['fɑːmlænd] n terres cultivées or arables.
farm produce n produits mpl agricoles.
farm worker n = **farmhand**.
farmyard ['fɑːmjɑːd] n cour f de ferme.
Faroe Islands ['fɛərəu-] npl, **Faroes** ['fɛərəuz] npl: **the ~** les îles fpl Féroé or Faeroe.
far-reaching ['fɑː'riːtʃɪŋ] adj d'une grande portée.
far-sighted ['fɑː'saɪtɪd] adj presbyte; (fig) prévoyant(e), qui voit loin.
fart [fɑːt] (col!) n pet m ♦ vi péter.
farther ['fɑːðə*] adv plus loin ♦ adj plus eloigné(e), plus lointain(e).
farthest ['fɑːðɪst] superlative of **far**.
FAS abbr (BRIT: = free alongside ship) FLB.
fascia ['feɪʃə] n (AUT) (garniture f du) tableau m de bord.
fascinate ['fæsɪneɪt] vt fasciner, captiver.
fascinating ['fæsɪneɪtɪŋ] adj fascinant(e).
fascination [fæsɪ'neɪʃən] n fascination f.
fascism ['fæʃɪzəm] n fascisme m.
fascist ['fæʃɪst] adj, n fasciste (m/f).
fashion ['fæʃən] n mode f; (manner) façon f, manière f ♦ vt façonner; **in ~** à la mode; **out of ~** démodé(e); **in the Greek ~** à la grecque; **after a ~** (finish, manage etc) tant bien que mal.
fashionable ['fæʃnəbl] adj à la mode.
fashion designer n (grand(e)) couturier/ière.
fashion show n défilé m de mannequins or de mode.
fast [fɑːst] adj rapide; (clock): **to be ~** avancer; (dye, colour) grand or bon teint inv ♦ adv vite,

rapidement; (*stuck, held*) solidement ♦ *n*
jeûne *m* ♦ *vi* jeûner; **my watch is 5 minutes**
~ **ma montre avance de 5 minutes; ~ asleep**
profondément endormi; **as ~ as I can** aussi
vite que je peux; **to make a boat ~** (*BRIT*)
amarrer un bateau.

fasten ['fɑːsn] *vt* attacher, fixer; (*coat*)
attacher, fermer ♦ *vi* se fermer, s'attacher.
▶**fasten (up)on** *vt fus* (*idea*) se cramponner à.

fastener ['fɑːsnə*], **fastening** ['fɑːsnɪŋ] *n*
fermeture *f*, attache *f*; (*BRIT*: *zip* ~)
fermeture éclair *inv* ® *or* à glissière.

fast food *n* fast food *m*, restauration *f* rapide.

fastidious [fæs'tɪdɪəs] *adj* exigeant(e),
difficile.

fast lane *n* (*AUT*: *in Britain*) voie *f* de droite.

fat [fæt] *adj* gros(se) ♦ *n* graisse *f*; (*on meat*)
gras *m*; **to live off the ~ of the land** vivre
grassement.

fatal ['feɪtl] *adj* fatal(e); (*leading to death*)
mortel(le).

fatalism ['feɪtlɪzəm] *n* fatalisme *m*.

fatality [fə'tælɪtɪ] *n* (*road death etc*) victime *f*,
décès *m*.

fatally ['feɪtəlɪ] *adv* fatalement; mortellement.

fate [feɪt] *n* destin *m*; (*of person*) sort *m*; **to
meet one's ~** trouver la mort.

fated ['feɪtɪd] *adj* (*person*) condamné(e);
(*project*) voué(e) à l'échec.

fateful ['feɪtful] *adj* fatidique.

fat-free ['fæt'friː] *adj* sans matières grasses.

father ['fɑːðə*] *n* père *m*.

Father Christmas *n* le Père Noël.

fatherhood ['fɑːðəhud] *n* paternité *f*.

father-in-law ['fɑːðərənlɔː] *n* beau-père *m*.

fatherland ['fɑːðəlænd] *n* (*mère f*) patrie *f*.

fatherly ['fɑːðəlɪ] *adj* paternel(le).

fathom ['fæðəm] *n* brasse *f* (= 1828 mm) ♦ *vt*
(*mystery*) sonder, pénétrer.

fatigue [fə'tiːg] *n* fatigue *f*; (*MIL*) corvée *f*;
metal ~ fatigue du métal.

fatness ['fætnɪs] *n* corpulence *f*, grosseur *f*.

fatten ['fætn] *vt*, *vi* engraisser; **chocolate is
~ing** le chocolat fait grossir.

fatty ['fætɪ] *adj* (*food*) gras(se) ♦ *n* (*col*) gros/
grosse.

fatuous ['fætjuəs] *adj* stupide.

faucet ['fɔːsɪt] *n* (*US*) robinet *m*.

fault [fɔːlt] *n* faute *f*; (*defect*) défaut *m*; (*GEO*)
faille *f* ♦ *vt* trouver des défauts à, prendre
en défaut; **it's my ~** c'est de ma faute; **to
find ~ with** trouver à redire *or* à critiquer
à; **at ~** fautif(ive), coupable; **to a ~** à
l'excès.

faultless ['fɔːltlɪs] *adj* impeccable;
irréprochable.

faulty ['fɔːltɪ] *adj* défectueux(euse).

fauna ['fɔːnə] *n* faune *f*.

faux pas ['fəu'pɑː] *n* impair *m*, bévue *f*, gaffe
f.

favour, (*US*) **favor** ['feɪvə*] *n* faveur *f*; (*help*)
service *m* ♦ *vt* (*proposition*) être en faveur

de; (*pupil etc*) favoriser; (*team, horse*) donner
gagnant; **to do sb a ~** rendre un service à
qn; **in ~ of** en faveur de; **to be in ~ of sth/of
doing sth** être partisan de qch/de faire qch;
to find ~ with sb trouver grâce aux yeux de
qn.

favo(u)rable ['feɪvrəbl] *adj* favorable; (*price*)
avantageux(euse).

favo(u)rably ['feɪvrəblɪ] *adv* favorablement.

favo(u)rite ['feɪvrɪt] *adj*, *n* favori(te).

favo(u)ritism ['feɪvrɪtɪzəm] *n* favoritisme *m*.

fawn [fɔːn] *n* faon *m* ♦ *adj* (*also*: ~**-coloured**)
fauve ♦ *vi*: **to ~ (up)on** flatter servilement.

fax [fæks] *n* (*document*) télécopie *f*; (*machine*)
télécopieur *m* ♦ *vt* envoyer par télécopie.

FBI *n abbr* (*US*: = *Federal Bureau of Investigation*)
FBI *m*.

FCC *n abbr* (*US*) = *Federal Communications
Commission*.

FCO *n abbr* (*BRIT*: = *Foreign and Commonwealth
Office*) ministère des Affaires étrangères et
du Commonwealth.

FD *n abbr* (*US*) = **fire department**.

FDA *n abbr* (*US*: = *Food and Drug Administration*)
office de contrôle des produits
pharmaceutiques et alimentaires.

FE *n abbr* = **further education**.

fear [fɪə*] *n* crainte *f*, peur *f* ♦ *vt* craindre ♦ *vi*:
to ~ for craindre pour; **to ~ that** craindre
que; ~ **of heights** vertige *m*; **for ~ of** de peur
que + *sub or* de + *infinitive*.

fearful ['fɪəful] *adj* craintif(ive); (*sight, noise*)
affreux(euse), épouvantable; **to be ~ of**
avoir peur de, craindre.

fearfully ['fɪəfəlɪ] *adv* (*timidly*) craintivement;
(*col*: *very*) affreusement.

fearless ['fɪəlɪs] *adj* intrépide, sans peur.

fearsome ['fɪəsəm] *adj* (*opponent*) redoutable;
(*sight*) épouvantable.

feasibility [fiːzə'bɪlɪtɪ] *n* (*of plan*) possibilité *f*
de réalisation, faisabilité *f*.

feasibility study *n* étude *f* de faisabilité.

feasible ['fiːzəbl] *adj* faisable, réalisable.

feast [fiːst] *n* festin *m*, banquet *m*; (*REL*: *also*: ~
day) fête *f* ♦ *vi* festoyer; **to ~ on** se régaler
de.

feat [fiːt] *n* exploit *m*, prouesse *f*.

feather ['fɛðə*] *n* plume *f* ♦ *vt*: **to ~ one's nest**
(*fig*) faire sa pelote ♦ *cpd* (*bed etc*) de
plumes.

feather-weight ['fɛðəweɪt] *n* poids *m* plume
inv.

feature ['fiːtʃə*] *n* caractéristique *f*; (*article*)
chronique *f*, rubrique *f* ♦ *vt* (*subj*: *film*) avoir
pour vedette(s) ♦ *vi* figurer (en bonne
place); ~**s** *npl* (*of face*) traits *mpl*; **a (special)
~ on sth/sb** un reportage sur qch/qn; **it ~d
prominently in ...** cela a figuré en bonne
place sur *or* dans ....

feature film *n* long métrage.

featureless ['fiːtʃəlɪs] *adj* anonyme, sans
traits distinctifs.

Feb. *abbr* (= *February*) fév.
February ['fɛbruərɪ] *n* février *m*; *for phrases see also July.*
feces ['fiːsiːz] *npl* (*US*) = **faeces**.
feckless ['fɛklɪs] *adj* inepte.
Fed *abbr* (*US*) = **federal; federation**.
fed [fɛd] *pt, pp of* **feed; to be ~ up** en avoir marre *or* plein le dos.
Fed. [fɛd] *n abbr* (*US col*) = **Federal Reserve Board**.
federal ['fɛdərəl] *adj* fédéral(e).
Federal Reserve Board *n* (*US*) *organe de contrôle de la banque centrale américaine.*
Federal Trade Commission (FTC) *n* (*US*) *organisme de protection contre les pratiques commerciales abusives.*
federation [fɛdə'reɪʃən] *n* fédération *f*.
fee [fiː] *n* rémunération *f*; (*of doctor, lawyer*) honoraires *mpl*; (*of school, college etc*) frais *mpl* de scolarité; (*for examination*) droits *mpl*; **entrance/membership ~** droit d'entrée/d'inscription; **for a small ~** pour une somme modique.
feeble ['fiːbl] *adj* faible.
feeble-minded ['fiːbl'maɪndɪd] *adj* faible d'esprit.
feed [fiːd] *n* (*of baby*) tétée *f*; (*of animal*) fourrage *m*; pâture *f*; (*on printer*) mécanisme *m* d'alimentation ♦ *vt* (*pt, pp* **fed** [fɛd]) nourrir; (*horse etc*) donner à manger à; (*machine*) alimenter; (*data etc*): **to ~ sth into** fournir qch à, introduire qch dans.
▶**feed back** *vt* (*results*) donner en retour.
▶**feed on** *vt fus* se nourrir de.
feedback ['fiːdbæk] *n* feed-back *m*; (*from person*) réactions *fpl*.
feeder ['fiːdə*] *n* (*bib*) bavette *f*.
feeding bottle ['fiːdɪŋ-] *n* (*BRIT*) biberon *m*.
feel [fiːl] *n* sensation *f* ♦ *vt* (*pt, pp* **felt** [fɛlt]) (*touch*) toucher; tâter, palper; (*cold, pain*) sentir; (*grief, anger*) ressentir, éprouver; (*think, believe*): **to ~ (that)** trouver que; **I ~ that you ought to do it** il me semble que vous devriez le faire; **to ~ hungry/cold** avoir faim/froid; **to ~ lonely/better** se sentir seul/mieux; **I don't ~ well** je ne me sens pas bien; **to ~ sorry for** avoir pitié de; **it ~s soft** c'est doux au toucher; **it ~s colder here** je trouve qu'il fait plus froid ici; **it ~s like velvet** on dirait du velours, ça ressemble au velours; **to ~ like** (*want*) avoir envie de; **to ~ about** *or* **around** fouiller, tâtonner; **to get the ~ of sth** (*fig*) s'habituer à qch.
feeler ['fiːlə*] *n* (*of insect*) antenne *f*; (*fig*): **to put out a ~** *or* **~s** tâter le terrain.
feeling ['fiːlɪŋ] *n* sensation *f*, sentiment *m*; (*impression*) sentiment; **to hurt sb's ~s** froisser qn; **~s ran high about it** cela a déchaîné les passions; **what are your ~s about the matter?** quel est votre sentiment sur cette question?; **my ~ is that ...** j'estime

que ...; **I have a ~ that** ... j'ai l'impression que ....
fee-paying school ['fiːpeɪɪŋ-] *n* établissement (d'enseignement) privé.
feet [fiːt] *npl of* **foot**.
feign [feɪn] *vt* feindre, simuler.
felicitous [fɪ'lɪsɪtəs] *adj* heureux(euse).
fell [fɛl] *pt of* **fall** ♦ *vt* (*tree*) abattre ♦ *n* (*BRIT: mountain*) montagne *f*; (: *moorland*): **the ~s** la lande ♦ *adj*: **with one ~ blow** d'un seul coup.
fellow ['fɛləu] *n* type *m*; (*comrade*) compagnon *m*; (*of learned society*) membre *m*; (*of university*) universitaire *m/f* (*membre du conseil*) ♦ *cpd*: **their ~ prisoners/students** leurs camarades prisonniers/étudiants; **his ~ workers** ses collègues *mpl* (de travail).
fellow citizen *n* concitoyen/ne.
fellow countryman *n* compatriote *m*.
fellow feeling *n* sympathie *f*.
fellow men *npl* semblables *mpl*.
fellowship ['fɛləuʃɪp] *n* (*society*) association *f*; (*comradeship*) amitié *f*, camaraderie *f*; (*SCOL*) *sorte de bourse universitaire.*
fellow traveller *n* compagnon/compagne de route; (*POL*) communisant/e.
fell-walking ['fɛlwɔːkɪŋ] *n* (*BRIT*) randonnée *f* en montagne.
felon ['fɛlən] *n* (*LAW*) criminel/le.
felony ['fɛlənɪ] *n* (*LAW*) crime *m*, forfait *m*.
felt [fɛlt] *pt, pp of* **feel** ♦ *n* feutre *m*.
felt-tip pen ['fɛlttɪp-] *n* stylo-feutre *m*.
female ['fiːmeɪl] *n* (*ZOOL*) femelle *f*; (*pej: woman*) bonne femme ♦ *adj* (*BIOL, ELEC*) femelle; (*sex, character*) féminin(e); (*vote etc*) des femmes; (*child etc*) du sexe féminin; **male and ~ students** étudiants et étudiantes.
female impersonator *n* (*THEAT*) travesti *m*.
feminine ['fɛmɪnɪn] *adj* féminin(e) ♦ *n* féminin *m*.
femininity [fɛmɪ'nɪnɪtɪ] *n* féminité *f*.
feminism ['fɛmɪnɪzəm] *n* féminisme *m*.
feminist ['fɛmɪnɪst] *n* féministe *m/f*.
fen [fɛn] *n* (*BRIT*): **the F~s** les plaines *fpl* du Norfolk (*anciennement marécageuses*).
fence [fɛns] *n* barrière *f*; (*SPORT*) obstacle *m*; (*col: person*) receleur/euse ♦ *vt* (*also: ~ in*) clôturer ♦ *vi* faire de l'escrime; **to sit on the ~** (*fig*) ne pas se mouiller.
fencing ['fɛnsɪŋ] *n* (*sport*) escrime *m*.
fend [fɛnd] *vi*: **to ~ for o.s.** se débrouiller (tout seul).
▶**fend off** *vt* (*attack etc*) parer.
fender ['fɛndə*] *n* (*of fireplace*) garde-feu *m inv*; (*on boat*) défense *f*; (*US: of car*) aile *f*.
fennel ['fɛnl] *n* fenouil *m*.
ferment *vi* [fə'mɛnt] fermenter ♦ *n* ['fəːmɛnt] agitation *f*, effervescence *f*.
fermentation [fəːmɛn'teɪʃən] *n* fermentation *f*.
fern [fəːn] *n* fougère *f*.
ferocious [fə'rəuʃəs] *adj* féroce.

ferocity [fə'rɔsɪtɪ] n férocité f.

ferret ['fɛrɪt] n furet m.

▶**ferret about, ferret around** vi fureter.

▶**ferret out** vt dénicher.

ferry ['fɛrɪ] n (small) bac m; (large: also: ~**boat**) ferry(-boat m) m ♦ vt transporter; **to ~ sth/ sb across** or **over** faire traverser qch/qn.

ferryman ['fɛrɪmən] n passeur m.

fertile ['fə:taɪl] adj fertile; (BIOL) fécond(e); ~ **period** période f de fécondité.

fertility [fə'tɪlɪtɪ] n fertilité f; fécondité f.

fertility drug n médicament m contre la stérilité.

fertilize ['fə:tɪlaɪz] vt fertiliser; féconder.

fertilizer ['fə:tɪlaɪzə*] n engrais m.

fervent ['fə:vənt] adj fervent(e), ardent(e).

fervour, (US) **fervor** ['fə:və*] n ferveur f.

fester ['fɛstə*] vi suppurer.

festival ['fɛstɪvəl] n (REL) fête f; (ART, MUS) festival m.

festive ['fɛstɪv] adj de fête; **the ~ season** (BRIT: Christmas) la période des fêtes.

festivities [fɛs'tɪvɪtɪz] npl réjouissances fpl.

festoon [fɛs'tu:n] vt: **to ~ with** orner de.

fetch [fɛtʃ] vt aller chercher; (BRIT: sell for) se vendre; **how much did it ~?** ça a atteint quel prix?

▶**fetch up** vi (BRIT) se retrouver.

fetching ['fɛtʃɪŋ] adj charmant(e).

fête [feɪt] n fête f, kermesse f.

fetid ['fɛtɪd] adj fétide.

fetish ['fɛtɪʃ] n fétiche m.

fetter ['fɛtə*] vt entraver.

fetters ['fɛtəz] npl chaînes fpl.

fettle ['fɛtl] n (BRIT): **in fine ~** en bonne forme.

fetus ['fi:təs] n (US) = **foetus**.

feud [fju:d] n dispute f, dissension f ♦ vi se disputer, se quereller; **a family ~** une querelle de famille.

feudal ['fju:dl] adj féodal(e).

feudalism ['fju:dlɪzəm] n féodalité f.

fever ['fi:və*] n fièvre f; **he has a ~** il a de la fièvre.

feverish ['fi:vərɪʃ] adj fiévreux(euse), fébrile.

few [fju:] adj peu de ♦ pron: ~ **succeed** il y en a peu qui réussissent, (bien) peu réussissent; **they were ~** ils étaient peu (nombreux), il y en avait peu; **a ~** ... quelques ...; **I know a ~** j'en connais quelques-uns; **quite a ~** ... un certain nombre de ..., pas mal de ...; **in the next ~ days** dans les jours qui viennent; **in the past ~ days** ces derniers jours; **every ~ days/months** tous les deux ou trois jours/ mois; **a ~ more** ... encore quelques ..., quelques ... de plus.

fewer ['fju:ə*] adj moins de ♦ pron moins; **they are ~ now** il y en a moins maintenant, ils sont moins (nombreux) maintenant.

fewest ['fju:ɪst] adj le moins nombreux.

FFA n abbr = Future Farmers of America.

FH abbr (BRIT) = **fire hydrant**.

FHA n abbr (US: = Federal Housing Administration) office fédéral du logement.

fiancé [fɪ'ɑ̃:ŋseɪ] n fiancé m.

fiancée [fɪ'ɑ̃:ŋseɪ] n fiancée f.

fiasco [fɪ'æskəu] n fiasco m.

fib [fɪb] n bobard m.

fibre, (US) **fiber** ['faɪbə*] n fibre f.

fibreboard, (US) **fiberboard** ['faɪbəbɔ:d] n panneau m de fibres.

fibre-glass, (US) **fiber-glass** ['faɪbəglɑ:s] n fibre de verre.

fibrositis [faɪbrə'saɪtɪs] n aponévrosite f.

FICA n abbr (US) = Federal Insurance Contributions Act.

fickle ['fɪkl] adj inconstant(e), volage, capricieux(euse).

fiction ['fɪkʃən] n romans mpl, littérature f romanesque; (invention) fiction f.

fictional ['fɪkʃənl] adj fictif(ive).

fictionalize ['fɪkʃnəlaɪz] vt romancer.

fictitious [fɪk'tɪʃəs] adj fictif(ive), imaginaire.

fiddle ['fɪdl] n (MUS) violon m; (cheating) combine f; escroquerie f ♦ vt (BRIT: accounts) falsifier, maquiller; **tax ~** fraude fiscale, combine f pour échapper au fisc; **to work a ~** traficoter.

▶**fiddle with** vt fus tripoter.

fiddler ['fɪdlə*] n violoniste m/f.

fiddly ['fɪdlɪ] adj (task) minutieux(euse).

fidelity [fɪ'dɛlɪtɪ] n fidélité f.

fidget ['fɪdʒɪt] vi se trémousser, remuer.

fidgety ['fɪdʒɪtɪ] adj agité(e), qui a la bougeotte.

fiduciary [fɪ'dju:ʃɪərɪ] n agent m fiduciaire.

field [fi:ld] n champ m; (fig) domaine m, champ; (SPORT: ground) terrain m; (COMPUT) champ, zone f; **to lead the ~** (SPORT, COMM) dominer; **the children had a ~ day** (fig) c'était un grand jour pour les enfants.

field glasses npl jumelles fpl.

field hospital n antenne chirurgicale.

field marshal n maréchal m.

fieldwork ['fi:ldwə:k] n travaux mpl pratiques (or recherches fpl) sur le terrain.

fiend [fi:nd] n démon m.

fiendish ['fi:ndɪʃ] adj diabolique.

fierce [fɪəs] adj (look) féroce, sauvage; (wind, attack) (très) violent(e); (fighting, enemy) acharné(e).

fiery ['faɪərɪ] adj ardent(e), brûlant(e); fougueux(euse).

FIFA ['fi:fə] n abbr (= Fédération internationale de Football Association) FIFA f.

fifteen [fɪf'ti:n] num quinze.

fifth [fɪfθ] num cinquième.

fiftieth ['fɪftɪɪθ] num cinquantième.

fifty ['fɪftɪ] num cinquante.

fifty-fifty ['fɪftɪ'fɪftɪ] adv: **to share ~ with sb** partager moitié-moitié avec qn ♦ adj: **to have a ~ chance (of success)** avoir une chance sur deux (de réussir).

fig [fɪg] n figue f.

fight [faɪt] n bagarre f; (MIL) combat m;

(*against cancer etc*) lutte *f* ♦ *vb* (*pt, pp* **fought** [fɔːt]) *vt* se battre contre; (*cancer, alcoholism*) combattre, lutter contre; (*LAW: case*) défendre ♦ *vi* se battre; (*fig*): **to ~ (for/ against**) lutter (pour/contre).

fighter ['faɪtə*] *n* lutteur *m* (*fig*); (*plane*) chasseur *m*.

fighter pilot *n* pilote *m* de chasse.

fighting ['faɪtɪŋ] *n* combats *mpl*; (*brawls*) bagarres *fpl*.

figment ['fɪgmənt] *n*: **a ~ of the imagination** une invention.

figurative ['fɪgjurətɪv] *adj* figuré(e).

figure ['fɪgə*] *n* (*DRAWING, GEOM*) figure *f*; (*number, cipher*) chiffre *m*; (*body, outline*) silhouette *f*, ligne *f*, formes *fpl*; (*person*) personnage *m* ♦ *vt* (*US*) supposer ♦ *vi* (*appear*) figurer; (*US: make sense*) s'expliquer; **public ~** personnalité *f*; **~ of speech** figure *f* de rhétorique.

▶**figure on** *vt fus* (*US*): **to ~ on doing** compter faire.

▶**figure out** *vt* arriver à comprendre; calculer.

figurehead ['fɪgəhɛd] *n* (*NAUT*) figure *f* de proue; (*pej*) prête-nom *m*.

figure skating *n* figures imposées (*en patinage*); patinage *m* artistique.

Fiji (Islands) ['fiːdʒiː-] *n(pl)* (îles *fpl*) Fi(d)ji *fpl*.

filament ['fɪləmənt] *n* filament *m*.

filch [fɪltʃ] *vt* (*col: steal*) voler, chiper.

file [faɪl] *n* (*tool*) lime *f*; (*dossier*) dossier *m*; (*folder*) dossier, chemise *f*; (*: binder*) classeur *m*; (*COMPUT*) fichier *m*; (*row*) file *f* ♦ *vt* (*nails, wood*) limer; (*papers*) classer; (*LAW: claim*) faire enregistrer; déposer ♦ *vi*: **to ~ in/out** entrer/sortir l'un derrière l'autre; **to ~ past** défiler devant; **to ~ a suit against sb** (*LAW*) intenter un procès à qn.

file name *n* (*COMPUT*) nom *m* de fichier.

filibuster ['fɪlɪbʌstə*] *n* (*esp US POL*) *n* (*also:* **~er**) obstructionniste *m/f* ♦ *vi* faire de l'obstructionnisme.

filing ['faɪlɪŋ] *n* (*travaux mpl de*) classement *m*; **~s** *npl* limaille *f*.

filing cabinet *n* classeur *m* (*meuble*).

filing clerk *n* documentaliste *m/f*.

Filipino [fɪlɪ'piːnəu] *n* (*person*) Philippin/e; (*LING*) tagalog *m*.

fill [fɪl] *vt* remplir; (*vacancy*) pourvoir à ♦ *n*: **to eat one's ~** manger à sa faim.

▶**fill in** *vt* (*hole*) boucher; (*form*) remplir; (*details, report*) compléter.

▶**fill out** *vt* (*form, receipt*) remplir.

▶**fill up** *vt* remplir ♦ *vi* (*AUT*) faire le plein; **~ it up, please** (*AUT*) le plein, s'il vous plaît.

fillet ['fɪlɪt] *n* filet *m* ♦ *vt* préparer en filets.

fillet steak *n* filet *m* de bœuf, tournedos *m*.

filling ['fɪlɪŋ] *n* (*CULIN*) garniture *f*, farce *f*; (*for tooth*) plombage *m*.

filling station *n* station *f* d'essence.

fillip ['fɪlɪp] *n* coup *m* de fouet (*fig*).

filly ['fɪlɪ] *n* pouliche *f*.

film [fɪlm] *n* film *m*; (*PHOT*) pellicule *f*, film *m* ♦ *vt* (*scene*) filmer.

film star *n* vedette *f* de cinéma.

filmstrip ['fɪlmstrɪp] *n* (film *m* pour) projection *f* fixe.

film studio *n* studio *m* (de cinéma).

Filofax ['faɪləufæks] *n* ® Filofax *m* ®.

filter ['fɪltə*] *n* filtre *m* ♦ *vt* filtrer.

filter coffee *n* café *m* filtre.

filter lane *n* (*BRIT AUT*) voie *f* de sortie.

filter tip *n* bout *m* filtre.

filth [fɪlθ] *n* saleté *f*.

filthy ['fɪlθɪ] *adj* sale, dégoûtant(e); (*language*) ordurier(ière), grossier(ière).

fin [fɪn] *n* (*of fish*) nageoire *f*.

final ['faɪnl] *adj* final(e), dernier(ière); (*decision, answer*) définitif(ive) ♦ *n* (*SPORT*) finale *f*; **~s** *npl* (*SCOL*) examens *mpl* de dernière année; **~ demand** (*on invoice etc*) dernier rappel.

finale [fɪ'nɑːlɪ] *n* finale *m*.

finalist ['faɪnəlɪst] *n* (*SPORT*) finaliste *m/f*.

finalize ['faɪnəlaɪz] *vt* mettre au point.

finally ['faɪnəlɪ] *adv* (*lastly*) en dernier lieu; (*eventually*) enfin, finalement; (*irrevocably*) définitivement.

finance [faɪ'næns] *n* finance *f* ♦ *vt* financer; **~s** *npl* finances *fpl*.

financial [faɪ'nænʃəl] *adj* financier(ière); **~ statement** bilan *m*, exercice financier.

financially [faɪ'nænʃəlɪ] *adv* financièrement.

financial year *n* année *f* budgétaire.

financier [faɪ'nænsɪə*] *n* financier *m*.

find [faɪnd] *vt* (*pt, pp* **found** [faund]) trouver; (*lost object*) retrouver ♦ *n* trouvaille *f*, découverte *f*; **to ~ sb guilty** (*LAW*) déclarer qn coupable; **to ~ (some) difficulty in doing sth** avoir du mal à faire qch.

▶**find out** *vt* se renseigner sur; (*truth, secret*) découvrir; (*person*) démasquer ♦ *vi*: **to ~ out about** se renseigner sur; (*by chance*) apprendre.

findings ['faɪndɪŋz] *npl* (*LAW*) conclusions *fpl*, verdict *m*; (*of report*) constatations *fpl*.

fine [faɪn] *adj* beau(belle); excellent(e); (*subtle, not coarse*) fin(e) ♦ *adv* (*well*) très bien; (*small*) fin, finement ♦ *n* (*LAW*) amende *f*; contravention *f* ♦ *vt* (*LAW*) condamner à une amende; donner une contravention à; **he's ~** il va bien; **the weather is ~** il fait beau; **you're doing ~** c'est bien, vous vous débrouillez bien; **to cut it ~** calculer un peu juste.

fine arts *npl* beaux-arts *mpl*.

fine print *n*: **the ~** ce qui est imprimé en tout petit.

finery ['faɪnərɪ] *n* parure *f*.

finesse [fɪ'nɛs] *n* finesse *f*, élégance *f*.

fine-tooth comb ['faɪntuː-θ-] *n*: **to go through sth with a ~** (*fig*) passer qch au peigne fin *or* au crible.

finger ['fɪŋgə*] n doigt m ♦ vt palper, toucher.
fingernail ['fɪŋgəneɪl] n ongle m (de la main).
fingerprint ['fɪŋgəprɪnt] n empreinte digitale ♦ vt (person) prendre les empreintes digitales de.
fingerstall ['fɪŋgəstɔːl] n doigtier m.
fingertip ['fɪŋgətɪp] n bout m du doigt; (fig): **to have sth at one's ~s** avoir qch à sa disposition; (knowledge) savoir qch sur le bout du doigt.
finicky ['fɪnɪkɪ] adj tatillon(ne), méticuleux(euse); minutieux(euse).
finish ['fɪnɪʃ] n fin f; (SPORT) arrivée f; (polish etc) finition f ♦ vt finir, terminer ♦ vi finir, se terminer; (session) s'achever; **to ~ doing sth** finir de faire qch; **to ~ third** arriver or terminer troisième.
▶**finish off** vt finir, terminer; (kill) achever.
▶**finish up** vi, vt finir.
finished product ['fɪnɪʃt-] n produit fini.
finishing line ['fɪnɪʃɪŋ-] n ligne f d'arrivée.
finishing school ['fɪnɪʃɪŋ-] n institution privée (pour jeunes filles).
finite ['faɪnaɪt] adj fini(e); (verb) conjugué(e).
Finland ['fɪnlənd] n Finlande f.
Finn [fɪn] n Finnois/e; Finlandais/e.
Finnish ['fɪnɪʃ] adj finnois(e); finlandais(e) ♦ n (LING) finnois m.
fiord [fjɔːd] n fjord m.
fir [fəː*] n sapin m.
fire ['faɪə*] n feu m; incendie m ♦ vt (discharge): **to ~ a gun** tirer un coup de feu; (fig) enflammer, animer; (dismiss) mettre à la porte, renvoyer ♦ vi tirer, faire feu ♦ cpd: ~ **hazard, ~ risk: that's a ~ hazard** or **risk** cela présente un risque d'incendie; **on ~** en feu; **to set ~ to sth, set sth on ~** mettre le feu à qch; **insured against ~** assuré contre l'incendie.
fire alarm n avertisseur m d'incendie.
firearm ['faɪərɑːm] n arme f à feu.
fire brigade n (BRIT) (régiment m de sapeurs-)pompiers mpl.
fire chief n (US) = **fire master**.
fire department n (US) = **fire brigade**.
fire door n porte f coupe-feu.
fire engine n pompe f à incendie.
fire escape n escalier m de secours.
fire extinguisher n extincteur m.
fireguard ['faɪəgɑːd] n (BRIT) garde-feu m inv.
fire insurance n assurance f incendie.
fireman ['faɪəmən] n pompier m.
fire master n (BRIT) capitaine m des pompiers.
fireplace ['faɪəpleɪs] n cheminée f.
fireproof ['faɪəpruːf] adj ignifuge.
fire regulations npl consignes fpl en cas d'incendie.
fire screen n (decorative) écran m de cheminée; (for protection) garde-feu m inv.
fireside ['faɪəsaɪd] n foyer m, coin m du feu.
fire station n caserne f de pompiers.

firewood ['faɪəwud] n bois m de chauffage.
firework ['faɪəwəːk] n feu m d'artifice; ~**s** npl (display) feu(x) d'artifice.
firing ['faɪərɪŋ] n (MIL) feu m, tir m.
firing squad n peloton m d'exécution.
firm [fəːm] adj ferme ♦ n compagnie f, firme f.
firmly ['fəːmlɪ] adv fermement.
firmness ['fəːmnɪs] n fermeté f.
first [fəːst] adj premier(ière) ♦ adv (before others) le premier, la première; (before other things) en premier, d'abord; (when listing reasons etc) en premier lieu, premièrement ♦ n (person: in race) premier/ière; (BRIT SCOL) mention f très bien; (AUT) première f; **the ~ of January** le premier janvier; **at ~** au commencement, au début; ~ **of all** tout d'abord, pour commencer; **in the ~ instance** en premier lieu; **I'll do it ~ thing tomorrow** je le ferai tout de suite demain matin.
first aid n premiers secours or soins.
first-aid kit [fəːst'eɪd-] n trousse f à pharmacie.
first-class ['fəːst'klɑːs] adj de première classe.
first-class mail n courrier m rapide.
first-hand ['fəːst'hænd] adj de première main.
first lady n (US) femme f du président.
firstly ['fəːstlɪ] adv premièrement, en premier lieu.
first name n prénom m.
first night n (THEAT) première f.
first-rate ['fəːst'reɪt] adj excellent(e).
first-time buyer ['fəːsttaɪm-] n personne achetant une maison ou un appartement pour la première fois.
fir tree n sapin m.
FIS n abbr (BRIT: = Family Income Supplement) complément familial.
fiscal ['fɪskl] adj fiscal(e); ~ **year** exercice financier.
fish [fɪʃ] n (pl inv) poisson m; poissons mpl ♦ vt, vi pêcher; **to ~ a river** pêcher dans une rivière; **to go ~ing** aller à la pêche.
fisherman ['fɪʃəmən] n pêcheur m.
fishery ['fɪʃərɪ] n pêcherie f.
fish factory n (BRIT) conserverie f de poissons.
fish farm n établissement m piscicole.
fish fingers npl (BRIT) bâtonnets de poisson (congelés).
fish hook n hameçon m.
fishing boat ['fɪʃɪŋ-] n barque f de pêche.
fishing industry ['fɪʃɪŋ-] n industrie f de la pêche.
fishing line ['fɪʃɪŋ-] n ligne f (de pêche).
fishing rod ['fɪʃɪŋ-] n canne f à pêche.
fishing tackle ['fɪʃɪŋ-] n attirail m de pêche.
fish market n marché m au poisson.
fishmonger ['fɪʃmʌŋgə*] n marchand m de poisson; ~'**s (shop)** poissonnerie f.
fish slice n (BRIT) pelle f à poisson.
fish sticks npl (US) = **fish fingers**.
fishy ['fɪʃɪ] adj (fig) suspect(e), louche.

fission ['fɪʃən] *n* fission *f*; **atomic** *or* **nuclear** ~ fission nucléaire.

fissure ['fɪʃə*] *n* fissure *f*.

fist [fɪst] *n* poing *m*.

fistfight ['fɪstfaɪt] *n* pugilat *m*, bagarre *f* (à coups de poing).

fit [fɪt] *adj* (MED, SPORT) en (bonne) forme; (*proper*) convenable; approprié(e) ♦ *vt* (*subj: clothes*) aller à; (*adjust*) ajuster; (*put in, attach*) installer, poser; adapter; (*equip*) équiper, garnir, munir ♦ *vi* (*clothes*) aller; (*parts*) s'adapter; (*in space, gap*) entrer, s'adapter ♦ *n* (MED) accès *m*, crise *f*; (*of coughing*) quinte *f*; ~ **to** en état de; ~ **for** digne de; apte à; **to keep** ~ se maintenir en forme; **this dress is a tight/good** ~ cette robe est un peu juste/(me) va très bien; **a** ~ **of anger** un accès de colère; **to have a** ~ (MED) faire *or* avoir une crise; (*col*) piquer une crise; **by** ~**s and starts** par à-coups.

▶**fit in** *vi* s'accorder; (*person*) s'adapter.

▶**fit out** *vt* (BRIT: *also*: **fit up**) équiper.

fitful ['fɪtful] *adj* intermittent(e).

fitment ['fɪtmənt] *n* meuble encastré, élément *m*.

fitness ['fɪtnɪs] *n* (MED) forme *f* physique; (*of remark*) à-propos *m*, justesse *f*.

fitted kitchen ['fɪtɪd-] *n* (BRIT) cuisine équipée.

fitter ['fɪtə*] *n* monteur *m*; (DRESSMAKING) essayeur/euse.

fitting ['fɪtɪŋ] *adj* approprié(e) ♦ *n* (*of dress*) essayage *m*; (*of piece of equipment*) pose *f*, installation *f*.

fitting room *n* (*in shop*) cabine *f* d'essayage.

fittings ['fɪtɪŋz] *npl* installations *fpl*.

five [faɪv] *num* cinq.

five-day week ['faɪvdeɪ-] *n* semaine *f* de cinq jours.

fiver ['faɪvə*] *n* (*col*: BRIT) billet *m* de cinq livres; (: US) billet de cinq dollars.

fix [fɪks] *vt* fixer; (*sort out*) arranger; (*mend*) réparer; (*make ready: meal, drink*) préparer; (*col*: *game etc*) truquer ♦ *n*: **to be in a** ~ être dans le pétrin.

▶**fix up** *vt* (*meeting*) arranger; **to** ~ **sb up with sth** faire avoir qch à qn.

fixation [fɪk'seɪʃən] *n* (PSYCH) fixation *f*; (*fig*) obsession *f*.

fixed [fɪkst] *adj* (*prices etc*) fixe; **there's a** ~ **charge** il y a un prix forfaitaire; **how are you** ~ **for money?** (*col*) question fric, ça va?

fixed assets *npl* immobilisations *fpl*.

fixture ['fɪkstʃə*] *n* installation *f* (fixe); (SPORT) rencontre *f* (au programme).

fizz [fɪz] *vi* pétiller.

fizzle ['fɪzl] *vi* pétiller.

▶**fizzle out** *vi* rater.

fizzy ['fɪzɪ] *adj* pétillant(e); gazeux(euse).

fjord [fjɔːd] *n* = **fiord**.

FL, Fla. *abbr* (US) = *Florida*.

flabbergasted ['flæbəgɑːstɪd] *adj* sidéré(e),

ahuri(e).

flabby ['flæbɪ] *adj* mou(molle).

flag [flæg] *n* drapeau *m*; (*also*: ~**stone**) dalle *f* ♦ *vi* faiblir; fléchir; ~ **of convenience** pavillon *m* de complaisance.

▶**flag down** *vt* héler, faire signe (de s'arrêter) à.

flagon ['flægən] *n* bonbonne *f*.

flagpole ['flægpəul] *n* mât *m*.

flagrant ['fleɪgrənt] *adj* flagrant(e).

flag stop *n* (US: *for bus*) arrêt facultatif.

flair [flɛə*] *n* flair *m*.

flak [flæk] *n* (MIL) tir antiaérien; (*col*: *criticism*) critiques *fpl*.

flake [fleɪk] *n* (*of rust, paint*) écaille *f*; (*of snow, soap powder*) flocon *m* ♦ *vi* (*also*: ~ **off**) s'écailler.

flaky ['fleɪkɪ] *adj* (*paintwork*) écaillé(e); (*skin*) desquamé(e); (*pastry*) feuilleté(e).

flamboyant [flæm'bɔɪənt] *adj* flamboyant(e), éclatant(e); (*person*) haut(e) en couleur.

flame [fleɪm] *n* flamme *f*.

flamingo [flə'mɪŋgəu] *n* flamant *m* (rose).

flammable ['flæməbl] *adj* inflammable.

flan [flæn] *n* (BRIT) tarte *f*.

Flanders ['flɑːndəz] *n* Flandre(s) *f(pl)*.

flange [flændʒ] *n* boudin *m*; collerette *f*.

flank [flæŋk] *n* flanc *m* ♦ *vt* flanquer.

flannel ['flænl] *n* (BRIT: *also*: **face** ~) gant *m* de toilette; (*fabric*) flanelle *f*; (BRIT *col*) baratin *m*; ~**s** *npl* pantalon *m* de flanelle.

flap [flæp] *n* (*of pocket, envelope*) rabat *m* ♦ *vt* (*wings*) battre (de) ♦ *vi* (*sail, flag*) claquer; (*col*: *also*: **be in a** ~) paniquer.

flapjack ['flæpdʒæk] *n* (US: *pancake*) ≈ crêpe *f*; (BRIT: *biscuit*) galette *f*.

flare [flɛə*] *n* fusée éclairante; (*in skirt etc*) évasement *m*.

▶**flare up** *vi* s'embraser; (*fig*: *person*) se mettre en colère, s'emporter; (: *revolt*) éclater.

flared ['flɛəd] *adj* (*trousers*) à jambes évasées; (*skirt*) évasé(e).

flash [flæʃ] *n* éclair *m*; (*also*: **news** ~) flash *m* (d'information); (PHOT) flash ♦ *vt* (*switch on*) allumer (brièvement); (*direct*): **to** ~ **sth at** braquer qch sur; (*flaunt*) étaler, exhiber; (*send: message*) câbler ♦ *vi* briller; jeter des éclairs; (*light on ambulance etc*) clignoter; **in a** ~ en un clin d'œil; **to** ~ **one's headlights** faire un appel de phares; **he** ~**ed by** *or* **past** il passa (devant nous) comme un éclair.

flashback ['flæʃbæk] *n* flashback *m*, retour *m* en arrière.

flashbulb ['flæʃbʌlb] *n* ampoule *f* de flash.

flash card *n* (SCOL) carte *f* (*support visuel*).

flashcube ['flæʃkjuːb] *n* cube-flash *m*.

flasher ['flæʃə*] *n* (AUT) clignotant *m*.

flashlight ['flæʃlaɪt] *n* lampe *f* de poche.

flashpoint ['flæʃpɔɪnt] *n* point *m* d'ignition; (*fig*): **to be at** ~ être sur le point d'exploser.

flashy ['flæʃɪ] *adj* (*pej*) tape-à-l'œil *inv*,

tapageur(euse).

flask [flɑːsk] n flacon m, bouteille f; (CHEM) ballon m; (also: **vacuum ~**) bouteille f thermos ®.

flat [flæt] adj plat(e); (tyre) dégonflé(e), à plat; (denial) catégorique; (MUS) bémolisé(e); (: voice) faux(fausse) ♦ n (BRIT: rooms) appartement m; (AUT) crevaison f, pneu crevé; (MUS) bémol m; **~ out** (work) sans relâche; (race) à fond; **~ rate of pay** (COMM) (salaire m) fixe.

flat-footed ['flæt'futɪd] adj: **to be ~** avoir les pieds plats.

flatly ['flætlɪ] adv catégoriquement.

flatmate ['flætmeɪt] n (BRIT): **he's my ~** il partage l'appartement avec moi.

flatness ['flætnɪs] n (of land) absence f de relief, aspect plat.

flat-screen ['flætskriːn] adj à écran plat.

flatten ['flætn] vt (also: **~ out**) aplatir; (house, city) raser.

flatter ['flætə*] vt flatter.

flatterer ['flætərə*] n flatteur m.

flattering ['flætərɪŋ] adj flatteur(euse); (clothes etc) seyant(e).

flattery ['flætərɪ] n flatterie f.

flatulence ['flætjuləns] n flatulence f.

flaunt [flɔːnt] vt faire étalage de.

flavour, (US) **flavor** ['fleɪvə*] n goût m, saveur f; (of ice cream etc) parfum m ♦ vt parfumer, aromatiser; **vanilla-~ed** à l'arôme de vanille, vanillé(e); **to give** or **add ~ to** donner du goût à, relever.

flavo(u)ring ['fleɪvərɪŋ] n arôme m (synthétique).

flaw [flɔː] n défaut m.

flawless ['flɔːlɪs] adj sans défaut.

flax [flæks] n lin m.

flaxen ['flæksən] adj blond(e).

flea [fliː] n puce f.

flea market n marché m aux puces.

fleck [flɛk] n (of dust) particule f; (of mud, paint, colour) tacheture f, moucheture f ♦ vt tacher, éclabousser; **brown ~ed with white** brun moucheté de blanc.

fledg(e)ling ['flɛdʒlɪŋ] n oisillon m.

flee, pt, pp **fled** [fliː, flɛd] vt fuir, s'enfuir de ♦ vi fuir, s'enfuir.

fleece [fliːs] n toison f ♦ vt (col) voler, filouter.

fleecy ['fliːsɪ] adj (blanket) moelleux(euse); (cloud) floconneux(euse).

fleet [fliːt] n flotte f; (of lorries, cars etc) parc m; convoi m.

fleeting ['fliːtɪŋ] adj fugace, fugitif(ive); (visit) très bref(brève).

Flemish ['flɛmɪʃ] adj flamand(e) ♦ n (LING) flamand m; **the ~** npl les Flamands.

flesh [flɛʃ] n chair f.

flesh wound [-wuːnd] n blessure superficielle.

flew [fluː] pt of **fly**.

flex [flɛks] n fil m or câble m électrique

(souple) ♦ vt fléchir; (muscles) tendre.

flexibility [flɛksɪ'bɪlɪtɪ] n flexibilité f.

flexible ['flɛksəbl] adj flexible; (person, schedule) souple.

flexitime ['flɛksɪtaɪm] n horaire m variable or à la carte.

flick [flɪk] n petite tape; chiquenaude f; sursaut m.

▶**flick through** vt fus feuilleter.

flicker ['flɪkə*] vi vaciller ♦ n vacillement m; **a ~ of light** une brève lueur.

flick knife n (BRIT) couteau m à cran d'arrêt.

flicks [flɪks] npl (col) ciné m.

flier ['flaɪə*] n aviateur m.

flight [flaɪt] n vol m; (escape) fuite f; (also: **~ of steps**) escalier m; **to take ~** prendre la fuite; **to put to ~** mettre en fuite.

flight attendant n (US) steward m, hôtesse f de l'air.

flight crew n équipage m.

flight deck n (AVIAT) poste m de pilotage; (NAUT) pont m d'envol.

flight path n trajectoire f (de vol).

flight recorder n enregistreur m de vol.

flimsy ['flɪmzɪ] adj (partition, fabric) peu solide, mince; (excuse) pauvre, mince.

flinch [flɪntʃ] vi tressaillir; **to ~ from** se dérober à, reculer devant.

fling [flɪŋ] vt (pt, pp flung [flʌŋ]) jeter, lancer ♦ n (love affair) brève liaison, passade f.

flint [flɪnt] n silex m; (in lighter) pierre f (à briquet).

flip [flɪp] n chiquenaude f ♦ vt donner une chiquenaude à; (US: pancake) faire sauter ♦ vi: **to ~ for sth** (US) jouer qch à pile ou face.

▶**flip through** vt fus feuilleter.

flippant ['flɪpənt] adj désinvolte, irrévérencieux(euse).

flipper ['flɪpə*] n (of animal) nageoire f; (for swimmer) palme f.

flip side n (of record) deuxième face f.

flirt [fləːt] vi flirter ♦ n flirteuse f.

flirtation [fləː'teɪʃən] n flirt m.

flit [flɪt] vi voleter.

float [fləut] n flotteur m; (in procession) char m; (sum of money) réserve f ♦ vi flotter; (bather) flotter, faire la planche ♦ vt faire flotter; (loan, business, idea) lancer.

floating ['fləutɪŋ] adj flottant(e); **~ vote** voix flottante; **~ voter** électeur indécis.

flock [flɔk] n troupeau m; (of birds) vol m; (of people) foule f.

floe [fləu] n (also: **ice ~**) iceberg m.

flog [flɔg] vt fouetter.

flood [flʌd] n inondation f; (of words, tears etc) flot m, torrent m ♦ vt inonder; (AUT: carburettor) noyer; **to ~ the market** (COMM) inonder le marché; **in ~** en crue.

flooding ['flʌdɪŋ] n inondation f.

floodlight ['flʌdlaɪt] n projecteur m ♦ vt éclairer aux projecteurs, illuminer.

floodlit ['flʌdlɪt] *pt, pp of* **floodlight ♦** *adj* illuminé(e).

flood tide *n* marée montante.

floodwater ['flʌdwɔːtə*] *n* eau *f* de la crue.

floor [flɔː*] *n* sol *m*; (*storey*) étage *m*; (*of sea, valley*) fond *m*; (*fig: at meeting*): **the ~** l'assemblée *f*, les membres *mpl* de l'assemblée **♦** *vt* terrasser; (*baffle*) désorienter; **on the ~** par terre; **ground ~**, (*US*) **first ~** rez-de-chaussée *m*; **first ~**, (*US*) **second ~** premier étage; **top ~** dernier étage; **to have the ~** (*speaker*) avoir la parole.

floorboard ['flɔːbɔːd] *n* planche *f* (*du plancher*).

flooring ['flɔːrɪŋ] *n* sol *m*; (*wooden*) plancher *m*; (*material to make floor*) matériau(x) *m(pl)* pour planchers; (*covering*) revêtement *m* de sol.

floor lamp *n* (*US*) lampadaire *m*.

floor show *n* spectacle *m* de variétés.

floorwalker ['flɔːwɔːkə*] *n* (*esp US*) surveillant *m* (de grand magasin).

flop [flɔp] *n* fiasco *m* **♦** *vi* (*fail*) faire fiasco.

floppy ['flɔpɪ] *adj* lâche, flottant(e); **~ hat** chapeau *m* à bords flottants.

floppy disk *n* disquette *f*, disque *m* souple.

flora ['flɔːrə] *n* flore *f*.

floral ['flɔːrl] *adj* floral(e).

Florence ['flɔrəns] *n* Florence.

florid ['flɔrɪd] *adj* (*complexion*) fleuri(e); (*style*) plein(e) de fioritures.

florist ['flɔrɪst] *n* fleuriste *m/f*; **~'s (shop)** magasin *m or* boutique *f* de fleuriste.

flotation [fləʊ'teɪʃən] *n* (*of shares*) émission *f*; (*of company*) lancement *m* (en Bourse).

flounce [flaʊns] *n* volant *m*.

▶**flounce out** *vi* sortir dans un mouvement d'humeur.

flounder ['flaʊndə*] *n* (*ZOOL*) flet *m* **♦** *vi* patauger.

flour ['flaʊə*] *n* farine *f*.

flourish ['flʌrɪʃ] *vi* prospérer **♦** *vt* brandir **♦** *n* fioriture *f*; (*of trumpets*) fanfare *f*.

flourishing ['flʌrɪʃɪŋ] *adj* prospère, florissant(e).

flout [flaʊt] *vt* se moquer de, faire fi de.

flow [fləʊ] *n* (*of water, traffic etc*) écoulement *m*; (*tide, influx*) flux *m*; (*of orders, letters etc*) flot *m*; (*of blood, ELEC*) circulation *f*; (*of river*) courant *m* **♦** *vi* couler; (*traffic*) s'écouler; (*robes, hair*) flotter.

flow chart, flow diagram *n* organigramme *m*.

flower ['flaʊə*] *n* fleur *f* **♦** *vi* fleurir; **in ~** en fleur.

flower bed *n* plate-bande *f*.

flowerpot ['flaʊəpɔt] *n* pot *m* (à fleurs).

flowery ['flaʊərɪ] *adj* fleuri(e).

flown [fləʊn] *pp of* **fly**.

flu [fluː] *n* grippe *f*.

fluctuate ['flʌktjueɪt] *vi* varier, fluctuer.

fluctuation [flʌktju'eɪʃən] *n* fluctuation *f*, variation *f*.

flue [fluː] *n* conduit *m*.

fluency ['fluːənsɪ] *n* facilité *f*, aisance *f*.

fluent ['fluːənt] *adj* (*speech, style*) coulant(e), aisé(e); **he's a ~ speaker/reader** il s'exprime/lit avec aisance *or* facilité; **he speaks ~ French, he's ~ in French** il parle le français couramment.

fluently ['fluːəntlɪ] *adv* couramment; avec aisance *or* facilité.

fluff [flʌf] *n* duvet *m*; peluche *f*.

fluffy ['flʌfɪ] *adj* duveteux(euse); pelucheux(euse); **~ toy** jouet *m* en peluche.

fluid ['fluːɪd] *n* fluide *m*; (*in diet*) liquide *m* **♦** *adj* fluide.

fluid ounce *n* (*BRIT*) = 0.028 l; 0.05 pints.

fluke [fluːk] *n* (*col*) coup *m* de veine.

flummox ['flʌməks] *vt* dérouter, déconcerter.

flung [flʌŋ] *pt, pp of* **fling**.

flunky ['flʌŋkɪ] *n* larbin *m*.

fluorescent [fluə'rɛsnt] *adj* fluorescent(e).

fluoride ['fluəraɪd] *n* fluor *m*.

fluorine ['fluəriːn] *n* fluor *m*.

flurry ['flʌrɪ] *n* (*of snow*) rafale *f*, bourrasque *f*; **~ of activity/excitement** affairement *m/* excitation *f* soudain(e).

flush [flʌʃ] *n* rougeur *f*; (*fig*) éclat *m*; afflux *m* **♦** *vt* nettoyer à grande eau; (*also:* **~ out**) débusquer **♦** *vi* rougir **♦** *adj* (*col*) en fonds; (*level*): **~ with** au ras de, de niveau avec; **to ~ the toilet** tirer la chasse (d'eau); **hot ~es** (*MED*) bouffées *fpl* de chaleur.

flushed ['flʌʃt] *adj* (tout(e)) rouge.

fluster ['flʌstə*] *n* agitation *f*, trouble *m*.

flustered ['flʌstəd] *adj* énervé(e).

flute [fluːt] *n* flûte *f*.

fluted ['fluːtɪd] *adj* cannelé(e).

flutter ['flʌtə*] *n* agitation *f*; (*of wings*) battement *m* **♦** *vi* battre des ailes, voleter; (*person*) aller et venir dans une grande agitation.

flux [flʌks] *n*: **in a state of ~** fluctuant sans cesse.

fly [flaɪ] *n* (*insect*) mouche *f*; (*on trousers: also*: **flies**) braguette *f* **♦** *vb* (*pt* **flew**, *pp* **flown** [fluː, fləʊn]) *vt* (*plane*) piloter; (*passengers, cargo*) transporter (par avion); (*distances*) parcourir **♦** *vi* voler; (*passengers*) aller en avion; (*escape*) s'enfuir, fuir; (*flag*) se déployer; **to ~ open** s'ouvrir brusquement; **to ~ off the handle** s'énerver, s'emporter.

▶**fly away** *vi* s'envoler.

▶**fly in** *vi* (*plane*) atterrir; (*person*): **he flew in yesterday** il est arrivé hier (par avion).

▶**fly off** *vi* s'envoler.

▶**fly out** *vi* (*see* **fly in**) s'envoler; partir (par avion).

fly-fishing ['flaɪfɪʃɪŋ] *n* pêche *f* à la mouche.

flying ['flaɪɪŋ] *n* (*activity*) aviation *f* **♦** *adj*: **~ visit** visite *f* éclair *inv*; **with ~ colours** haut la main; **he doesn't like ~** il n'aime pas voyager en avion.

flying buttress n arc-boutant m.

flying picket n piquet m de grève volant.

flying saucer n soucoupe volante.

flying squad n (POLICE) brigade volante.

flying start n: **to get off to a ~** faire un excellent départ.

flyleaf ['flaɪliːf] n page f de garde.

flyover ['flaɪəuvə*] n (BRIT: overpass) saut-de-mouton m, pont autoroutier.

flypast ['flaɪpɑːst] n défilé aérien.

flysheet ['flaɪʃiːt] n (for tent) double toit m.

flyweight ['flaɪweɪt] n (SPORT) poids m mouche.

flywheel ['flaɪwiːl] n volant m (de commande).

FM abbr (BRIT MIL) = **field marshal**; (RADIO) = **frequency modulation**.

FMB n abbr (US) = Federal Maritime Board.

FMCS n abbr (US: = Federal Mediation and Conciliation Services) organisme de conciliation en cas de conflits du travail.

FO n abbr (BRIT) = **Foreign Office**.

foal [fəul] n poulain m.

foam [fəum] n écume f; (on beer) mousse f; (also: **plastic ~**) mousse cellulaire or de plastique ♦ vi écumer; (soapy water) mousser.

foam rubber n caoutchouc m mousse.

FOB abbr (= free on board) fob.

fob [fɔb] n (also: **watch ~**) chaîne f, ruban m ♦ vt: **to ~ sb off with** refiler à qn; se débarrasser de qn avec.

foc abbr (BRIT) = **free of charge**.

focal ['fəukl] adj (also fig) focal(e).

focal point n foyer m; (fig) centre m de l'attention, point focal.

focus ['fəukəs] n (pl: **~es**) foyer m; (of interest) centre m ♦ vt (field glasses etc) mettre au point; (light rays) faire converger ♦ vi: **to ~ (on)** (with camera) régler la mise au point (sur); (person) fixer son regard (sur); **in ~** au point; **out of ~** pas au point.

fodder ['fɔdə*] n fourrage m.

FOE n abbr (= Friends of the Earth) AT mpl (= Amis de la Terre); (US: = Fraternal Order of Eagles) organisation charitable.

foe [fəu] n ennemi m.

foetus, (US) fetus ['fiːtəs] n fœtus m.

fog [fɔg] n brouillard m.

fogbound ['fɔgbaund] adj bloqué(e) par le brouillard.

foggy ['fɔgɪ] adj: **it's ~** il y a du brouillard.

fog lamp, (US) fog light n (AUT) phare m anti-brouillard.

foible ['fɔɪbl] n faiblesse f.

foil [fɔɪl] vt déjouer, contrecarrer ♦ n feuille f de métal; (kitchen ~) papier m d'alu(minium); (FENCING) fleuret m; **to act as a ~ to** (fig) servir de repoussoir or de faire-valoir à.

foist [fɔɪst] vt: **to ~ sth on sb** imposer qch à qn.

fold [fəuld] n (bend, crease) pli m; (AGR) parc m

à moutons; (fig) bercail m ♦ vt plier; **to ~ one's arms** croiser les bras.

▶**fold up** vi (map etc) se plier, se replier; (business) fermer boutique ♦ vt (map etc) plier, replier.

folder ['fəuldə*] n (for papers) chemise f; (: binder) classeur m; (brochure) dépliant m.

folding ['fəuldɪŋ] adj (chair, bed) pliant(e).

foliage ['fəulɪɪdʒ] n feuillage m.

folk [fəuk] npl gens mpl ♦ cpd folklorique; **~s** npl famille f, parents mpl.

folklore ['fəuklɔː*] n folklore m.

folksong ['fəuksɔŋ] n chanson f folklorique; (contemporary) chanson folk inv.

follow ['fɔləu] vt suivre ♦ vi suivre; (result) s'ensuivre; **to ~ sb's advice** suivre les conseils de qn; **I don't quite ~ you** je ne vous suis plus; **to ~ in sb's footsteps** emboîter le pas à qn; (fig) suivre les traces de qn; **it ~s that ...** de ce fait, il s'ensuit que ...; **he ~ed suit** il fit de même.

▶**follow out** vt (idea, plan) poursuivre, mener à terme.

▶**follow through** vt = **follow out**.

▶**follow up** vt (victory) tirer parti de; (letter, offer) donner suite à; (case) suivre.

follower ['fɔləuə*] n disciple m/f, partisan/e.

following ['fɔləuɪŋ] adj suivant(e) ♦ n partisans mpl, disciples mpl.

follow-up ['fɔləuʌp] n suite f; suivi m.

folly ['fɔlɪ] n inconscience f; sottise f; (building) folie f.

fond [fɔnd] adj (memory, look) tendre, affectueux(euse); **to be ~ of** aimer beaucoup.

fondle ['fɔndl] vt caresser.

fondly ['fɔndlɪ] adv (lovingly) tendrement; (naïvely) naïvement.

fondness ['fɔndnɪs] n (for things) attachement m; (for people) sentiments affectueux; **a special ~ for** une prédilection pour.

font [fɔnt] n (REL) fonts baptismaux; (TYP) police f de caractères.

food [fuːd] n nourriture f.

food chain n chaîne f alimentaire.

food mixer n mixeur m.

food poisoning n intoxication f alimentaire.

food processor n robot m de cuisine.

food stamp n (US) bon m de nourriture (pour indigents).

foodstuffs ['fuːdstʌfs] npl denrées fpl alimentaires.

fool [fuːl] n idiot/e; (HISTORY: of king) bouffon m, fou m; (CULIN) purée f de fruits à la crème ♦ vt berner, duper ♦ vi (also: **~ around**) faire l'idiot or l'imbécile; **to make a ~ of sb** (ridicule) ridiculiser qn; (trick) avoir or duper qn; **to make a ~ of o.s.** se couvrir de ridicule; **you can't ~ me** vous (ne) me la ferez pas, on (ne) me la fait pas.

▶**fool about, fool around** vi (pej: waste time) traînailler, glandouiller; (: behave foolishly) faire l'imbécile.

foolhardy ['fuːlhɑːdɪ] *adj* téméraire, imprudent(e).

foolish ['fuːlɪʃ] *adj* idiot(e), stupide; (*rash*) imprudent(e).

foolishly ['fuːlɪʃlɪ] *adv* stupidement.

foolishness ['fuːlɪʃnɪs] *n* idiotie *f*, stupidité *f*.

foolproof ['fuːlpruːf] *adj* (*plan etc*) infaillible.

foolscap ['fuːlskæp] *n* ≈ papier *m* ministre.

foot [fut] *n* (*pl*: **feet** [fiːt]) pied *m*; (*measure*) pied (= 304 mm; 12 inches); (*of animal*) patte *f* ♦ *vt* (*bill*) casquer, payer; **on** ~ à pied; **to find one's feet** (*fig*) s'acclimater; **to put one's** ~ **down** (*AUT*) appuyer sur le champignon; (*say no*) s'imposer.

footage ['futɪdʒ] *n* (*CINE: length*) ≈ métrage *m*; (*: material*) séquences *fpl*.

foot and mouth (disease) *n* fièvre aphteuse.

football ['futbɔːl] *n* ballon *m* (de football); (*sport: BRIT*) football *m*; (*: US*) football américain.

footballer ['futbɔːlə*] *n* (*BRIT*) = **football player**.

football game *n* match *m* de football.

football ground *n* terrain *m* de football.

football match *n* (*BRIT*) match *m* de foot(ball).

football player *n* footballeur *m*, joueur *m* de football.

Les **football pools** *- ou plus familièrement les* "**pools**" *- consistent à parier sur les résultats des matches de football qui se jouent tous les samedis. L'expression consacrée en anglais est* "*to do the pools*". *Les parieurs envoient à l'avance les fiches qu'ils ont complétées à l'organisme qui gère les paris et ils attendent 17 h le samedi que les résultats soient annoncés. Les sommes gagnées se comptent parfois en milliers (ou même en millions) de livres sterling.*

---

footbrake ['futbreɪk] *n* frein *m* à pied.

footbridge ['futbrɪdʒ] *n* passerelle *f*.

foothills ['futhɪlz] *npl* contreforts *mpl*.

foothold ['futhəuld] *n* prise *f* (de pied).

footing ['futɪŋ] *n* (*fig*) position *f*; **to lose one's** ~ perdre pied; **on an equal** ~ sur pied d'égalité.

footlights ['futlaɪts] *npl* rampe *f*.

footman ['futmən] *n* laquais *m*.

footnote ['futnəut] *n* note *f* (en bas de page).

footpath ['futpɑːθ] *n* sentier *m*; (*in street*) trottoir *m*.

footprint ['futprɪnt] *n* trace *f* (de pied).

footrest ['futrɛst] *n* marchepied *m*.

footsie ['futsɪ] *n* (*col*): **to play** ~ **with sb** faire du pied à qn.

footsore ['futsɔː*] *adj*: **to be** ~ avoir mal aux pieds.

footstep ['futstɛp] *n* pas *m*.

footwear ['futwɛə*] *n* chaussure(s) *f(pl)* (*terme générique en anglais*).

FOR *abbr* (= *free on rail*) franco wagon.

========================= *KEYWORD*

for [fɔː*] *prep* **1** (*indicating destination, intention, purpose*) pour; **the train** ~ **London** le train pour *or* (à destination) de Londres; **he went** ~ **the paper** il est allé chercher le journal; **it's time** ~ **lunch** c'est l'heure du déjeuner; **what's it** ~? ça sert à quoi?; **what** ~? (*why*) pourquoi?; (*to what end*) pour quoi faire?, à quoi bon?; ~ **sale** à vendre

2 (*on behalf of, representing*) pour; **the MP** ~ **Hove** le député de Hove; **to work** ~ **sb/sth** travailler pour qn/qch; **G** ~ **George** G comme Georges

3 (*because of*) pour; ~ **this reason** pour cette raison; ~ **fear of being criticized** de peur d'être critiqué

4 (*with regard to*) pour; **it's cold** ~ **July** il fait froid pour juillet; **a gift** ~ **languages** un don pour les langues

5 (*in exchange for*): **I sold it** ~ **£5** je l'ai vendu 5 livres; **to pay 50 pence** ~ **a ticket** payer 50 pence un billet

6 (*in favour of*) pour; **are you** ~ **or against us?** êtes-vous pour ou contre nous?

7 (*referring to distance*) pendant, sur; **there are roadworks** ~ **5 km** il y a des travaux sur *or* pendant 5 km; **we walked** ~ **miles** nous avons marché pendant des kilomètres

8 (*referring to time*) pendant; depuis; pour; **he was away** ~ **2 years** il a été absent pendant 2 ans; **she will be away** ~ **a month** elle sera absente (pendant) un mois; **I have known her** ~ **years** je la connais depuis des années; **can you do it** ~ **tomorrow?** est-ce que tu peux le faire pour demain?

9 (*with infinitive clauses*): **it is not** ~ **me to decide** ce n'est pas à moi de décider; **it would be best** ~ **you to leave** le mieux serait que vous partiez; **there is still time** ~ **you to do it** vous avez encore le temps de le faire; ~ **this to be possible** ... pour que cela soit possible ...

10 (*in spite of*): ~ **all that** malgré cela, néanmoins; ~ **all his work/efforts** malgré tout son travail/tous ses efforts; ~ **all his complaints, he's very fond of her** il a beau se plaindre, il l'aime beaucoup

♦ *conj* (*since, as: rather formal*) car.

---

forage ['fɔrɪdʒ] *n* fourrage *m* ♦ *vi* fourrager, fouiller.

forage cap *n* calot *m*.

foray ['fɔreɪ] *n* incursion *f*.

forbad(e) [fə'bæd] *pt of* **forbid**.

forbearing [fɔː'bɛərɪŋ] *adj* patient(e), tolérant(e).

forbid, *pt* **forbad(e)**, *pp* **forbidden** [fə'bɪd,

-'bæd, -'bidn] *vt* défendre, interdire; **to ~ sb to do** défendre *or* interdire à qn de faire.
forbidden [fə'bidn] *adj* défendu(e).
forbidding [fə'bidiŋ] *adj* d'aspect *or* d'allure sévère *or* sombre.
force [fɔːs] *n* force *f* ♦ *vt* forcer; **the F~s** *npl* (*BRIT*) l'armée *f*; **to ~ sb to do sth** forcer qn à faire qch; **in ~** en force; **to come into ~** entrer en vigueur; **a ~ 5 wind** un vent de force 5; **the sales ~** (*COMM*) la force de vente; **to join ~s** unir ses forces.
►**force back** *vt* (*crowd, enemy*) repousser; (*tears*) refouler.
►**force down** *vt* (*food*) se forcer à manger.
forced [fɔːst] *adj* forcé(e).
force-feed ['fɔːsfiːd] *vt* nourrir de force.
forceful ['fɔːsful] *adj* énergique, volontaire.
forcemeat ['fɔːsmiːt] *n* (*BRIT CULIN*) farce *f*.
forceps ['fɔːseps] *npl* forceps *m*.
forcibly ['fɔːsəbli] *adv* par la force, de force; (*vigorously*) énergiquement.
ford [fɔːd] *n* gué *m* ♦ *vt* passer à gué.
fore [fɔː*] *n*: **to the ~** en évidence.
forearm ['fɔːrɑːm] *n* avant-bras *m inv*.
forebear ['fɔːbɛə*] *n* ancêtre *m*.
foreboding [fɔː'bəudiŋ] *n* pressentiment *m* (néfaste).
forecast ['fɔːkɑːst] *n* prévision *f*; (*also: weather ~*) prévisions météorologiques, météo *f* ♦ *vt* (*irreg: like* **cast**) prévoir.
foreclose [fɔː'kləuz] *vt* (*LAW: also: ~ on*) saisir.
foreclosure [fɔː'kləuʒə*] *n* saisie *f* du bien hypothéqué.
forecourt ['fɔːkɔːt] *n* (*of garage*) devant *m*.
forefathers ['fɔːfɑːðəz] *npl* ancêtres *mpl*.
forefinger ['fɔːfiŋgə*] *n* index *m*.
forefront ['fɔːfrʌnt] *n*: **in the ~ of** au premier rang *or* plan de.
forego, *pt* **forewent**, *pp* **foregone** [fɔː'gəu, -'went, -'gɔn] *vt* renoncer à.
foregoing ['fɔːgəuiŋ] *adj* susmentionné(e) ♦ *n*: **the ~** ce qui précède.
foregone ['fɔːgɔn] *adj*: **it's a ~ conclusion** c'est à prévoir, c'est couru d'avance.
foreground ['fɔːgraund] *n* premier plan ♦ *cpd* (*COMPUT*) prioritaire.
forehand ['fɔːhænd] *n* (*TENNIS*) coup droit.
forehead ['fɔrid] *n* front *m*.
foreign ['fɔrin] *adj* étranger(ère); (*trade*) extérieur(e).
foreign body *n* corps étranger.
foreign currency *n* devises étrangères.
foreigner ['fɔrinə*] *n* étranger/ère.
foreign exchange *n* (*system*) change *m*; (*money*) devises *fpl*.
foreign exchange market *n* marché *m* des devises.
foreign exchange rate *n* cours *m* des devises.
foreign investment *n* investissement *m* à l'étranger.
foreign Office *n* (*BRIT*) ministère *m* des Affaires étrangères.

foreign secretary *n* (*BRIT*) ministre *m* des Affaires étrangères.
foreleg ['fɔːlɛg] *n* patte *f* de devant; jambe antérieure.
foreman ['fɔːmən] *n* contremaître *m*; (*LAW: of jury*) président *m* (du jury).
foremost ['fɔːməust] *adj* le(la) plus en vue; premier(ière) ♦ *adv*: **first and ~** avant tout, tout d'abord.
forename ['fɔːneim] *n* prénom *m*.
forensic [fə'rensik] *adj*: **~ medicine** médecine légale; **~ expert** expert *m* de la police, expert légiste.
foreplay ['fɔːplei] *n* stimulation *f* érotique, prélude *m*.
forerunner ['fɔːrʌnə*] *n* précurseur *m*.
foresee, *pt* **foresaw**, *pp* **foreseen** [fɔː'siː, -'sɔː, -'siːn] *vt* prévoir.
foreseeable [fɔː'siːəbl] *adj* prévisible.
foreshadow [fɔː'ʃædəu] *vt* présager, annoncer, laisser prévoir.
foreshorten [fɔː'ʃɔːtn] *vt* (*figure, scene*) réduire, faire en raccourci.
foresight ['fɔːsait] *n* prévoyance *f*.
foreskin ['fɔːskin] *n* (*ANAT*) prépuce *m*.
forest ['fɔrist] *n* forêt *f*.
forestall [fɔː'stɔːl] *vt* devancer.
forestry ['fɔristri] *n* sylviculture *f*.
foretaste ['fɔːteist] *n* avant-goût *m*.
foretell, *pt, pp* **foretold** [fɔː'tɛl, -'təuld] *vt* prédire.
forethought ['fɔːθɔːt] *n* prévoyance *f*.
forever [fə'rɛvə*] *adv* pour toujours; (*fig*) continuellement.
forewarn [fɔː'wɔːn] *vt* avertir.
forewent [fɔː'wɛnt] *pt of* **forego**.
foreword ['fɔːwəːd] *n* avant-propos *m inv*.
forfeit ['fɔːfit] *n* prix *m*, rançon *f* ♦ *vt* perdre; (*one's life, health*) payer de.
forgave [fə'geiv] *pt of* **forgive**.
forge [fɔːdʒ] *n* forge *f* ♦ *vt* (*signature*) contrefaire; (*wrought iron*) forger; **to ~ documents/a will** fabriquer de faux papiers/un faux testament; **to ~ money** (*BRIT*) fabriquer de la fausse monnaie.
►**forge ahead** *vi* pousser de l'avant, prendre de l'avance.
forger ['fɔːdʒə*] *n* faussaire *m*.
forgery ['fɔːdʒəri] *n* faux *m*, contrefaçon *f*.
forget, *pt* **forgot**, *pp* **forgotten** [fə'gɛt, -'gɔt, -'gɔtn] *vt, vi* oublier.
forgetful [fə'gɛtful] *adj* distrait(e), étourdi(e); **~ of** oublieux(euse) de.
forgetfulness [fə'gɛtfulnis] *n* tendance *f* aux oublis; (*oblivion*) oubli *m*.
forget-me-not [fə'gɛtminɔt] *n* myosotis *m*.
forgive, *pt* **forgave**, *pp* **forgiven** [fə'giv, -'geiv, -'givn] *vt* pardonner; **to ~ sb for sth/ for doing sth** pardonner qch à qn/à qn de faire qch.
forgiveness [fə'givnis] *n* pardon *m*.

forgiving [fə'gɪvɪŋ] *adj* indulgent(e).
forgo, *pt* **forwent,** *pp* **forgone** [fɔː'gəu, -'wɛnt, -'gɒn] *vt* = **forego.**
forgot [fə'gɒt] *pt of* **forget.**
forgotten [fə'gɒtn] *pp of* **forget.**
fork [fɔːk] *n* (*for eating*) fourchette *f;* (*for gardening*) fourche *f;* (*of roads*) bifurcation *f;* (*of railways*) embranchement *m* ♦ *vi* (*road*) bifurquer.
▶**fork out** (*col: pay*) *vt* allonger, se fendre de ♦ *vi* casquer.
forked [fɔːkt] *adj* (*lightning*) en zigzags, ramifié(e).
fork-lift truck [ˈfɔːklɪft-] *n* chariot élévateur.
forlorn [fə'lɔːn] *adj* abandonné(e), délaissé(e); (*hope, attempt*) désespéré(e).
form [fɔːm] *n* forme *f;* (*SCOL*) classe *f;* (*questionnaire*) formulaire *m* ♦ *vt* former; **in the ~ of** sous forme de; **to ~ part of sth** faire partie de qch; **to be in good ~** (*SPORT, fig*) être en forme; **in top ~** en pleine forme.
formal ['fɔːməl] *adj* (*offer, receipt*) en bonne et due forme; (*person*) cérémonieux(euse), à cheval sur les convenances; (*occasion, dinner*) officiel(le); (*ART, PHILOSOPHY*) formel(le); ~ **dress** tenue *f* de cérémonie; (*evening dress*) tenue de soirée.
formality [fɔː'mælɪtɪ] *n* formalité *f;* cérémonie(s) *f(pl).*
formalize ['fɔːməlaɪz] *vt* officialiser.
formally ['fɔːməlɪ] *adv* officiellement; formellement; cérémonieusement.
format ['fɔːmæt] *n* format *m* ♦ *vt* (*COMPUT*) formater.
formation [fɔː'meɪʃən] *n* formation *f.*
formative ['fɔːmətɪv] *adj:* ~ **years** années *fpl* d'apprentissage (*fig*) *or* de formation (*d'un enfant, d'un adolescent*).
former ['fɔːmə*] *adj* ancien(ne) (*before n*), précédent(e); **the ~ ... the latter** le premier ... le second, celui-là ... celui-ci; **the ~ president** l'ex-président; **the ~ Yugoslavia/ Soviet Union** l'ex Yougoslavie/Union Soviétique.
formerly ['fɔːməlɪ] *adv* autrefois.
form feed *n* (*on printer*) alimentation *f* en feuilles.
formidable ['fɔːmɪdəbl] *adj* redoutable.
formula ['fɔːmjulə] *n* formule *f;* **F~ One** (*AUT*) Formule un.
formulate ['fɔːmjuleɪt] *vt* formuler.
fornicate ['fɔːnɪkeɪt] *vi* forniquer.
forsake, *pt* **forsook,** *pp* **forsaken** [fə'seɪk, -'suk, -'seɪkən] *vt* abandonner.
fort [fɔːt] *n* fort *m;* **to hold the ~** (*fig*) assurer la permanence.
forte ['fɔːtɪ] *n* (point) fort *m.*
forth [fɔːθ] *adv* en avant; **to go back and ~** aller et venir; **and so ~** et ainsi de suite.
forthcoming [fɔːθ'kʌmɪŋ] *adj* qui va paraître *or* avoir lieu prochainement; (*character*) ouvert(e), communicatif(ive).

forthright ['fɔːθraɪt] *adj* franc(franche), direct(e).
forthwith ['fɔːθ'wɪθ] *adv* sur le champ.
fortieth ['fɔːtɪɪθ] *num* quarantième.
fortification [fɔːtɪfɪ'keɪʃən] *n* fortification *f.*
fortified wine ['fɔːtɪfaɪd-] *n* vin liquoreux *or* de liqueur.
fortify ['fɔːtɪfaɪ] *vt* fortifier.
fortitude ['fɔːtɪtjuːd] *n* courage *m,* force *f* d'âme.
fortnight ['fɔːtnaɪt] *n* (*BRIT*) quinzaine *f,* quinze jours *mpl;* **it's a ~ since ...** il y a quinze jours que ....
fortnightly ['fɔːtnaɪtlɪ] *adj* bimensuel(le) ♦ *adv* tous les quinze jours.
FORTRAN ['fɔːtræn] *n* FORTRAN *m.*
fortress ['fɔːtrɪs] *n* forteresse *f.*
fortuitous [fɔː'tjuːɪtəs] *adj* fortuit(e).
fortunate ['fɔːtʃənɪt] *adj:* **to be ~** avoir de la chance; **it is ~ that** c'est une chance que, il est heureux que.
fortunately ['fɔːtʃənɪtlɪ] *adv* heureusement, par bonheur.
fortune ['fɔːtʃən] *n* chance *f;* (*wealth*) fortune *f;* **to make a ~** faire fortune.
fortuneteller ['fɔːtʃəntɛlə*] *n* diseuse *f* de bonne aventure.
forty ['fɔːtɪ] *num* quarante.
forum ['fɔːrəm] *n* forum *m,* tribune *f.*
forward ['fɔːwəd] *adj* (*movement, position*) en avant, vers l'avant; (*not shy*) effronté(e); (*COMM: delivery, sales, exchange*) à terme ♦ *adv* en avant ♦ *n* (*SPORT*) avant *m* ♦ *vt* (*letter*) faire suivre; (*parcel, goods*) expédier; (*fig*) promouvoir, contribuer au développement *or* à l'avancement de; **to move ~** avancer; **"please ~"** "prière de faire suivre"; ~ **planning** planification *f* à long terme.
forwards ['fɔːwədz] *adv* en avant.
forwent [fɔː'wɛnt] *pt of* **forgo.**
fossil ['fɒsl] *adj, n* fossile (*m*); ~ **fuel** combustible *m* fossile.
foster ['fɒstə*] *vt* encourager, favoriser.
foster brother *n* frère adoptif; frère de lait.
foster child *n* enfant adopté.
foster mother *n* mère adoptive; mère nourricière.
fought [fɔːt] *pt, pp of* **fight.**
foul [faul] *adj* (*weather, smell, food*) infect(e); (*language*) ordurier(ière); (*deed*) infâme ♦ *n* (*FOOTBALL*) faute *f* ♦ *vt* salir, encrasser; (*football player*) commettre une faute sur; (*entangle: anchor, propeller*) emmêler.
foul play *n* (*SPORT*) jeu déloyal; ~ **is not suspected** la mort (*or* l'incendie *etc*) n'a pas de causes suspectes, on écarte l'hypothèse d'un meurtre (*or* d'un acte criminel).
found [faund] *pt, pp of* **find** ♦ *vt* (*establish*) fonder.
foundation [faun'deɪʃən] *n* (*act*) fondation *f;* (*base*) fondement *m;* (*also:* ~ **cream**) fond *m* de teint; ~**s** *npl* (*of building*) fondations *fpl;* **to**

lay the ~s (*fig*) poser les fondements.
foundation stone *n* première pierre.
founder ['faundə*] *n* fondateur *m* ♦ *vi* couler, sombrer.
founding ['faundɪŋ] *adj:* ~ **fathers** (*esp US*) pères *mpl* fondateurs; ~ **member** membre *m* fondateur.
foundry ['faundrɪ] *n* fonderie *f*.
fount [faunt] *n* source *f*; (*TYP*) fonte *f*.
fountain ['fauntɪn] *n* fontaine *f*.
fountain pen *n* stylo *m* (à encre).
four [fɔ:*] *num* quatre; **on all ~s** à quatre pattes.
four-letter word ['fɔ:lɛtə-] *n* obscénité *f*, gros mot.
four-poster ['fɔ:'pəustə*] *n* (*also:* ~ **bed**) lit *m* à baldaquin.
foursome ['fɔ:səm] *n* partie *f* à quatre; sortie *f* à quatre.
fourteen ['fɔ:'ti:n] *num* quatorze.
fourth ['fɔ:θ] *num* quatrième ♦ *n* (*AUT:* also: ~ **gear**) quatrième *f*.
four-wheel drive ['fɔ:wi:l-] *n* (*AUT*): **with** ~ à quatre roues motrices.
fowl [faul] *n* volaille *f*.
fox [fɔks] *n* renard *m* ♦ *vt* mystifier.
fox fur *n* renard *m*.
foxglove ['fɔksglʌv] *n* (*BOT*) digitale *f*.
fox-hunting ['fɔkshʌntɪŋ] *n* chasse *f* au renard.
foyer ['fɔiei] *n* vestibule *m*; (*THEAT*) foyer *m*.
FP *n abbr* (*BRIT*) = former pupil; (*US*) = fireplug.
FPA *n abbr* (*BRIT*) = Family Planning Association.
Fr. *abbr* (= father: *REL*) P; (= friar) F.
fr. *abbr* (= franc) F.
fracas ['fræka:] *n* bagarre *f*.
fraction ['frækʃən] *n* fraction *f*.
fractionally ['frækʃnəlɪ] *adv:* ~ **smaller** *etc* un poil plus petit *etc*.
fractious ['frækʃəs] *adj* grincheux(euse).
fracture ['fræktʃə*] *n* fracture *f* ♦ *vt* fracturer.
fragile ['frædʒaɪl] *adj* fragile.
fragment ['frægmənt] *n* fragment *m*.
fragmentary ['frægməntərɪ] *adj* fragmentaire.
fragrance ['freigrəns] *n* parfum *m*.
fragrant ['freigrənt] *adj* parfumé(e), odorant(e).
frail [freil] *adj* fragile, délicat(e).
frame [freim] *n* (*of building*) charpente *f*; (*of human, animal*) charpente, ossature *f*; (*of picture*) cadre *m*; (*of door, window*) encadrement *m*, chambranle *m*; (*of spectacles: also:* ~**s**) monture *f* ♦ *vt* encadrer; (*theory, plan*) construire, élaborer; **to** ~ **sb** (*col*) monter un coup contre qn; ~ **of mind** disposition *f* d'esprit.
framework ['freimwə:k] *n* structure *f*.
France [fra:ns] *n* la France; **in** ~ en France.
franchise ['fræntʃaɪz] *n* (*POL*) droit *m* de vote; (*COMM*) franchise *f*.
franchisee [fræntʃaɪ'zi:] *n* franchisé *m*.
franchiser ['fræntʃaɪzə*] *n* franchiseur *m*.

frank [fræŋk] *adj* franc(franche) ♦ *vt* (*letter*) affranchir.
Frankfurt ['fræŋkfə:t] *n* Francfort.
franking machine ['fræŋkɪŋ-] *n* machine *f* à affranchir.
frankly ['fræŋklɪ] *adv* franchement.
frankness ['fræŋknɪs] *n* franchise *f*.
frantic ['fræntɪk] *adj* frénétique; (*desperate: need, desire*) effréné(e); (*person*) hors de soi.
frantically ['fræntɪklɪ] *adv* frénétiquement.
fraternal [frə'tə:nl] *adj* fraternel(le).
fraternity [frə'tə:nɪtɪ] *n* (*club*) communauté *f*, confrérie *f*; (*spirit*) fraternité *f*.
fraternize ['frætənaɪz] *vi* fraterniser.
fraud [frɔ:d] *n* supercherie *f*, fraude *f*, tromperie *f*; (*person*) imposteur *m*.
fraudulent ['frɔ:djulənt] *adj* frauduleux(euse).
fraught [frɔ:t] *adj* (*tense: person*) très tendu(e); (*: situation*) pénible; ~ **with** (*difficulties etc*) chargé(e) de, plein(e) de.
fray [frei] *n* bagarre *f*; (*MIL*) combat *m* ♦ *vt* effilocher ♦ *vi* s'effilocher; **tempers were** ~**ed** les gens commençaient à s'énerver; **her nerves were** ~**ed** elle était à bout de nerfs.
FRB *n abbr* (*US*) = **Federal Reserve Board.**
FRCM *n abbr* (*BRIT*) = *Fellow of the Royal College of Music.*
FRCO *n abbr* (*BRIT*) = *Fellow of the Royal College of Organists.*
FRCP *n abbr* (*BRIT*) = *Fellow of the Royal College of Physicians.*
FRCS *n abbr* (*BRIT*) = *Fellow of the Royal College of Surgeons.*
freak [fri:k] *n* (*also cpd*) phénomène *m*, créature ou événement exceptionnel par sa rareté, son caractère d'anomalie; (*pej: fanatic*): **health** ~ fana *m/f* or obsédé/e de l'alimentation saine (*or* de la forme physique).
▶**freak out** *vi* (*col: drop out*) se marginaliser; (*: on drugs*) se défoncer.
freakish ['fri:kɪʃ] *adj* insolite; anormal(e).
freckle ['frɛkl] *n* tache *f* de rousseur.
free [fri:] *adj* libre; (*gratis*) gratuit(e); (*liberal*) généreux(euse), large ♦ *vt* (*prisoner etc*) libérer; (*jammed object or person*) dégager; **to give sb a** ~ **hand** donner carte blanche à qn; ~ **and easy** sans façon, décontracté(e); **admission** ~ entrée libre; ~ **(of charge)** *adv* gratuitement.
freebie ['fri:bɪ] *n* (*col*): **it's a** ~ c'est gratuit.
freedom ['fri:dəm] *n* liberté *f*.
freedom fighter *n* combattant *m* de la liberté.
free enterprise *n* libre entreprise *f*.
Freefone ['fri:fəun] *n* ® numéro vert.
free-for-all ['fri:fərɔ:l] *n* mêlée générale *f*.
free gift *n* prime *f*.
freehold ['fri:həuld] *n* propriété foncière libre.
free kick *n* (*SPORT*) coup franc.

freelance ['friːlɑːns] *adj* (*journalist etc*) indépendant(e); (*work*) à la pige, à la tâche.
freeloader ['friːləʊdə*] *n* (*pej*) parasite *m*.
freely ['friːlɪ] *adv* librement; (*liberally*) libéralement.
free-market economy [friː'mɑːkɪt-] *n* économie *f* de marché.
freemason ['friːmeɪsn] *n* franc-maçon *m*.
freemasonry ['friːmeɪsnrɪ] *n* franc-maçonnerie *f*.
freepost ['friːpəʊst] *n* franchise postale.
free-range ['friː'reɪndʒ] *adj* (*eggs*) de ferme.
free sample *n* échantillon gratuit.
free speech *n* liberté *f* d'expression.
free trade *n* libre-échange *m*.
freeway ['friːweɪ] *n* (*US*) autoroute *f*.
freewheel [friː'wiːl] *vi* descendre en roue libre.
freewheeling [friː'wiːlɪŋ] *adj* indépendant(e), libre.
free will *n* libre arbitre *m*; **of one's own ~** de son plein gré.
freeze [friːz] *vb* (*pt* **froze**, *pp* **frozen** [frəʊz, 'frəʊzn]) *vi* geler ♦ *vt* geler; (*food*) congeler; (*prices, salaries*) bloquer, geler ♦ *n* gel *m*; blocage *m*.
▶**freeze over** *vi* (*river*) geler; (*windscreen*) se couvrir de givre *or* de glace.
▶**freeze up** *vi* geler.
freeze-dried ['friːzdraɪd] *adj* lyophilisé(e).
freezer ['friːzə*] *n* congélateur *m*.
freezing ['friːzɪŋ] *adj*: **~ (cold)** (*room etc*) glacial(e); (*person, hands*) gelé(e), glacé(e) ♦ *n*: **3 degrees below ~** 3 degrés au-dessous de zéro.
freezing point *n* point *m* de congélation.
freight [freɪt] *n* (*goods*) fret *m*, cargaison *f*; (*money charged*) fret, prix *m* du transport; **~ forward** port dû; **~ inward** port payé par le destinataire.
freighter ['freɪtə*] *n* (*NAUT*) cargo *m*.
freight forwarder [-fɔːwədə*] *n* transitaire *m*.
freight train *n* (*US*) train *m* de marchandises.
French [frɛntʃ] *adj* français(e) ♦ *n* (*LING*) français *m*; **the ~** *npl* les Français.
French bean *n* (*BRIT*) haricot vert.
French bread *n* pain *m* (*français*).
French Canadian *adj* canadien(ne) français(e) ♦ *n* Canadien/ne français(e).
French dressing *n* (*CULIN*) vinaigrette *f*.
French fried potatoes, (*US*) **French fries** *npl* (pommes de terre *fpl*) frites *fpl*.
French Guiana [-gaɪ'ænə] *n* Guyane française.
French loaf *n* ≈ pain *m*, ≈ parisien *m*.
Frenchman ['frɛntʃmən] *n* Français *m*.
French Riviera *n*: **the ~** la Côte d'Azur.
French stick *n* ≈ baguette *f*.
French window *n* porte-fenêtre *f*.
Frenchwoman ['frɛntʃwʊmən] *n* Française *f*.
frenetic [frə'nɛtɪk] *adj* frénétique.
frenzy ['frɛnzɪ] *n* frénésie *f*.

frequency ['friːkwənsɪ] *n* fréquence *f*.
frequency modulation (FM) *n* modulation *f* de fréquence (FM, MF).
frequent *adj* ['friːkwənt] fréquent(e) ♦ *vt* [frɪ'kwɛnt] fréquenter.
frequently ['friːkwəntlɪ] *adv* fréquemment.
fresco ['frɛskəʊ] *n* fresque *f*.
fresh [frɛʃ] *adj* frais(fraîche); (*new*) nouveau(nouvelle); (*cheeky*) familier(ière), culotté(e); **to make a ~ start** prendre un nouveau départ.
freshen ['frɛʃən] *vi* (*wind, air*) fraîchir.
▶**freshen up** *vi* faire un brin de toilette.
freshener ['frɛʃnə*] *n*: **skin ~** astringent *m*; **air ~** désodorisant *m*.
fresher ['frɛʃə*] *n* (*BRIT SCOL: col*) = **freshman**.
freshly ['frɛʃlɪ] *adv* nouvellement, récemment.
freshman ['frɛʃmən] *n* (*SCOL*) bizuth *m*, étudiant/e de première année.
freshness ['frɛʃnɪs] *n* fraîcheur *f*.
freshwater ['frɛʃwɔːtə*] *adj* (*fish*) d'eau douce.
fret [frɛt] *vi* s'agiter, se tracasser.
fretful ['frɛtful] *adj* (*child*) grincheux(euse).
Freudian ['frɔɪdɪən] *adj* freudien(ne); **~ slip** lapsus *m*.
FRG *n abbr* (= *Federal Republic of Germany*) RFA *f*.
Fri. *abbr* (= *Friday*) ve.
friar ['fraɪə*] *n* moine *m*, frère *m*.
friction ['frɪkʃən] *n* friction *f*, frottement *m*.
friction feed *n* (*on printer*) entraînement *m* par friction.
Friday ['fraɪdɪ] *n* vendredi *m*; *for phrases see also* **Tuesday.**
fridge [frɪdʒ] *n* (*BRIT*) frigo *m*, frigidaire *m* ®.
fridge-freezer ['frɪdʒ'friːzə*] *n* réfrigérateur-congélateur *m*.
fried [fraɪd] *pt, pp of* **fry** ♦ *adj* frit(e); **~ egg** œuf *m* sur le plat.
friend [frɛnd] *n* ami/e; **to make ~s with** se lier (d'amitié) avec.
friendliness ['frɛndlɪnɪs] *n* attitude amicale.
friendly ['frɛndlɪ] *adj* amical(e); (*kind*) sympathique, gentil(le); (*POL: country, government*) ami(e) ♦ *n* (*also:* **~ match**) match amical; **to be ~ with** être ami(e) avec; **to be ~ to** être bien disposé(e) à l'égard de.
friendly fire *n*: **they were killed by ~** ils sont morts sous les tirs de leur propre camp.
friendly society *n* société *f* mutualiste.
friendship ['frɛndʃɪp] *n* amitié *f*.
frieze [friːz] *n* frise *f*, bordure *f*.
frigate ['frɪgɪt] *n* (*NAUT: modern*) frégate *f*.
fright [fraɪt] *n* peur *f*, effroi *m*; **to take ~** prendre peur, s'effrayer; **she looks a ~** elle a l'air d'un épouvantail.
frighten ['fraɪtn] *vt* effrayer, faire peur à.
▶**frighten away, frighten off** *vt* (*birds, children etc*) faire fuir, effaroucher.
frightened ['fraɪtnd] *adj*: **to be ~ (of)** avoir

peur (de).
frightening ['fraɪtnɪŋ] adj effrayant(e).
frightful ['fraɪtful] adj affreux(euse).
frightfully ['fraɪtfəlɪ] adv affreusement.
frigid ['frɪdʒɪd] adj (woman) frigide.
frigidity [frɪ'dʒɪdɪtɪ] n frigidité f.
frill [frɪl] n (of dress) volant m; (of shirt) jabot m;
without ~s (fig) sans manières.
frilly ['frɪlɪ] adj à fanfreluches.
fringe [frɪndʒ] n frange f; (edge: of forest etc)
bordure f; (fig): **on the ~** en marge.
fringe benefits npl avantages sociaux or en
nature.
fringe theatre n théâtre m d'avant-garde.
Frisbee ['frɪzbɪ] n ® Frisbee m ®.
frisk [frɪsk] vt fouiller.
frisky ['frɪskɪ] adj vif(vive), sémillant(e).
fritter ['frɪtə*] n beignet m.
▶**fritter away** vt gaspiller.
frivolity [frɪ'vɔlɪtɪ] n frivolité f.
frivolous ['frɪvələs] adj frivole.
frizzy ['frɪzɪ] adj crépu(e).
fro [frəʊ] see **to**.
frock [frɔk] n robe f.
frog [frɔg] n grenouille f; **to have a ~ in one's
throat** avoir un chat dans la gorge.
frogman ['frɔgmən] n homme-grenouille m.
frogmarch ['frɔgmɑːtʃ] vt: **to ~ sb in/
out** faire entrer/sortir qn de force.
frolic ['frɔlɪk] n ébats mpl ♦ vi folâtrer,
batifoler.

================= *KEYWORD*

from [frɔm] prep **1** (indicating starting place,
origin etc) de; **where do you come ~?, where
are you ~?** d'où venez-vous?; **where has he
come ~?** d'où arrive-t-il?; **~ London to Paris**
de Londres à Paris; **a letter/telephone call ~
my sister** une lettre/un appel de ma sœur;
to drink ~ the bottle boire à (même) la
bouteille
2 (indicating time) (à partir) de; **~ one
o'clock to or until or till two** d'une heure à
deux heures; **~ January (on)** à partir de
janvier
3 (indicating distance) de; **the hotel is one
kilometre ~ the beach** l'hôtel est à un
kilomètre de la plage
4 (indicating price, number etc) de; **the
interest rate was increased ~ 9% to 10%** le
taux d'intérêt a augmenté de 9 à 10%
5 (indicating difference) de; **he can't tell red ~
green** il ne peut pas distinguer le rouge du
vert
6 (because of, on the basis of): **~ what he
says** d'après ce qu'il dit; **weak ~ hunger**
affaibli par la faim.

frond [frɔnd] n fronde f.
front [frʌnt] n (of house, dress) devant m; (of
coach, train) avant m; (of book) couverture f;
(promenade: also: **sea ~**) bord m de mer;
(MIL, POL, METEOROLOGY) front m; (fig:
appearances) contenance f, façade f ♦ adj de
devant; premier(ière) ♦ vi: **to ~ onto sth**
donner sur qch; **in ~ (of)** devant.
frontage ['frʌntɪdʒ] n façade f; (of shop)
devanture f.
frontal ['frʌntl] adj frontal(e).

> Le **front bench** est le banc du gouvernement,
> placé à la droite du **Speaker**, ou celui du
> cabinet fantôme, placé à sa gauche. Ils se font
> face dans l'enceinte de la Chambre des
> communes. Par extension, **front bench**
> désigne les dirigeants des groupes
> parlementaires de la majorité et de
> l'opposition, qui sont appelés "frontbenchers"
> par opposition aux autres députés qui sont
> appelés "backbenchers".

front desk n (US: in hotel, at doctor's)
réception f.
front door n porte f d'entrée; (of car) portière
f avant.
frontier ['frʌntɪə*] n frontière f.
frontispiece ['frʌntɪspiːs] n frontispice m.
front page n première page.
front room n (BRIT) pièce f de devant, salon
m.
front runner n (fig) favori/te.
front-wheel drive ['frʌntwiːl-] n traction f
avant.
frost [frɔst] n gel m, gelée f; (also: **hoar~**)
givre m.
frostbite ['frɔstbaɪt] n gelures fpl.
frosted ['frɔstɪd] adj (glass) dépoli(e); (esp US:
cake) glacé(e).
frosting ['frɔstɪŋ] n (esp US: on cake) glaçage
m.
frosty ['frɔstɪ] adj (window) couvert(e) de
givre; (welcome) glacial(e).
froth [frɔθ] n mousse f; écume f.
frown [fraun] n froncement m de sourcils ♦ vi
froncer les sourcils.
▶**frown on** vt (fig) désapprouver.
froze [frəʊz] pt of **freeze**.
frozen ['frəʊzn] pp of **freeze** ♦ adj (food)
congelé(e); (COMM: assets) gelé(e).
FRS n abbr (BRIT: = Fellow of the Royal Society)
membre de l'Académie des sciences; (US: =
Federal Reserve System) banque centrale
américaine.
frugal ['fruːgl] adj frugal(e).
fruit [fruːt] n (pl inv) fruit m.
fruiterer ['fruːtərə*] n fruitier m, marchand/e
de fruits; **~'s (shop)** fruiterie f.
fruit fly n mouche f du vinaigre, drosophile f.
fruitful ['fruːtful] adj fructueux(euse); (plant,
soil) fécond(e).
fruition [fruː'ɪʃən] n: **to come to ~** se réaliser.
fruit juice n jus m de fruit.
fruitless ['fruːtlɪs] adj (fig) vain(e),
infructueux(euse).

fruit machine *n* (*BRIT*) machine *f* à sous.
fruit salad *n* salade *f* de fruits.
frump [frʌmp] *n* mocheté *f*.
frustrate [frʌsˈtreɪt] *vt* frustrer; (*plot, plans*) faire échouer.
frustrated [frʌsˈtreɪtɪd] *adj* frustré(e).
frustrating [frʌsˈtreɪtɪŋ] *adj* (*job*) frustrant(e); (*day*) démoralisant(e).
frustration [frʌsˈtreɪʃən] *n* frustration *f*.
fry, *pt, pp* **fried** [fraɪ, -d] *vt* (faire) frire; **the small ~** le menu fretin.
frying pan [ˈfraɪɪŋ-] *n* poêle *f* (à frire).
FT *n abbr* (*BRIT*: = Financial Times) journal financier.
ft. *abbr* = **foot, feet**.
FTC *n abbr* (*US*) = **Federal Trade Commission**.
FTSE 100 (Share) Index *n abbr* (= Financial Times Stock Exchange 100 (Share) Index) indice *m* Footsie des cent grandes valeurs.
fuchsia [ˈfjuːʃə] *n* fuchsia *m*.
fuck [fʌk] *vt, vi* (*col!*) baiser (*!*); **~ off!** fous le camp! (*!*).
fuddled [ˈfʌdld] *adj* (*muddled*) embrouillé(e), confus(e).
fuddy-duddy [ˈfʌdɪdʌdɪ] *adj* (*pej*) vieux jeu *inv*, ringard(e).
fudge [fʌdʒ] *n* (*CULIN*) sorte de confiserie à base de sucre, de beurre et de lait ♦ *vt* (*issue, problem*) esquiver.
fuel [fjuəl] *n* (*for heating*) combustible *m*; (*for propelling*) carburant *m*.
fuel oil *n* mazout *m*.
fuel pump *n* (*AUT*) pompe *f* d'alimentation.
fuel tank *n* cuve *f* à mazout, citerne *f*, (*in vehicle*) réservoir *m* de or à carburant.
fug [fʌg] *n* (*BRIT*) puanteur *f*, odeur *f* de renfermé.
fugitive [ˈfjuːdʒɪtɪv] *n* fugitif/ive.
fulfil, (*US*) **fulfill** [fulˈfɪl] *vt* (*function*) remplir; (*order*) exécuter; (*wish, desire*) satisfaire, réaliser.
fulfilled [fulˈfɪld] *adj* (*person*) comblé(e), épanoui(e).
fulfil(l)ment [fulˈfɪlmənt] *n* (*of wishes*) réalisation *f*.
full [ful] *adj* plein(e); (*details, information*) complet(ète); (*price*) fort(e), normal(e); (*skirt*) ample, large ♦ *adv*: **to know ~ well that** savoir fort bien que; **~ (up)** (*hotel etc*) complet(ète); **I'm ~ (up)** j'ai bien mangé; **~ employment/fare** plein emploi/tarif; **a ~ two hours** deux bonnes heures; **at ~ speed** à toute vitesse; **in ~** (*reproduce, quote, pay*) intégralement; (*write name etc*) en toutes lettres.
fullback [ˈfulbæk] *n* (*RUGBY, FOOTBALL*) arrière *m*.
full-blooded [ˈfulˈblʌdɪd] *adj* (*vigorous*) vigoureux(euse).
full-cream [ˈfulˈkriːm] *adj*: **~ milk** (*BRIT*) lait entier.
full-grown [ˈfulˈgrəun] *adj* arrivé(e) à maturité, adulte.
full-length [ˈfulˈleŋθ] *adj* (*portrait*) en pied; **~ film** long métrage.
full moon *n* pleine lune.
full-scale [ˈfulskeɪl] *adj* (*model*) grandeur nature *inv*; (*search, retreat*) complet(ète), total(e).
full-sized [ˈfulˈsaɪzd] *adj* (*portrait etc*) grandeur nature *inv*.
full stop *n* point *m*.
full-time [ˈfulˈtaɪm] *adj* (*work*) à plein temps ♦ *n* (*SPORT*) fin *f* du match.
fully [ˈfulɪ] *adv* entièrement, complètement; (*at least*): **~ as big** au moins aussi grand.
fully-fledged [ˈfulɪˈfledʒd] *adj* (*teacher, barrister*) diplômé(e); (*citizen, member*) à part entière.
fulsome [ˈfulsəm] *adj* (*pej: praise*) excessif(ive); (: *manner*) exagéré(e).
fumble [ˈfʌmbl] *vi* fouiller, tâtonner ♦ *vt* (*ball*) mal réceptionner, cafouiller.
▶**fumble with** *vt fus* tripoter.
fume [fjuːm] *vi* rager; **~s** *npl* vapeurs *fpl*, émanations *fpl*, gaz *mpl*.
fumigate [ˈfjuːmɪgeɪt] *vt* désinfecter (par fumigation).
fun [fʌn] *n* amusement *m*, divertissement *m*; **to have ~** s'amuser; **for ~** pour rire; **it's not much ~** ce n'est pas très drôle *or* amusant; **to make ~ of** se moquer de.
function [ˈfʌŋkʃən] *n* fonction *f*; (*reception, dinner*) cérémonie *f*, soirée officielle ♦ *vi* fonctionner; **to ~ as** faire office de.
functional [ˈfʌŋkʃənl] *adj* fonctionnel(le).
function key *n* (*COMPUT*) touche *f* de fonction.
fund [fʌnd] *n* caisse *f*, fonds *m*; (*source, store*) source *f*, mine *f*; **~s** *npl* fonds *mpl*.
fundamental [fʌndəˈmentl] *adj* fondamental(e); **~s** *npl* principes *mpl* de base.
fundamentalism [fʌndəˈmentəlɪzəm] *n* intégrisme *m*.
fundamentalist [fʌndəˈmentəlɪst] *n* intégriste *m/f*.
fundamentally [fʌndəˈmentəlɪ] *adv* fondamentalement.
funding [ˈfʌndɪŋ] *n* financement *m*.
fund-raising [ˈfʌndreɪzɪŋ] *n* collecte *f* de fonds.
funeral [ˈfjuːnərəl] *n* enterrement *m*, obsèques *fpl* (*more formal occasion*).
funeral director *n* entrepreneur *m* des pompes funèbres.
funeral parlour *n* dépôt *m* mortuaire.
funeral service *n* service *m* funèbre.
funereal [fjuːˈnɪərɪəl] *adj* lugubre, funèbre.
fun fair *n* (*BRIT*) fête (foraine).
fungus, *pl* **fungi** [ˈfʌŋgəs, -gaɪ] *n* champignon *m*; (*mould*) moisissure *f*.
funicular [fjuːˈnɪkjulə*] *n* (*also:* **~ railway**) funiculaire *m*.

ınky ['fʌŋkɪ] adj (music) funky inv; (col: excellent) super inv.

ınnel ['fʌnl] n entonnoir m; (of ship) cheminée f.

ınnily ['fʌnɪlɪ] adv (see funny) drôlement; curieusement.

ınny ['fʌnɪ] adj amusant(e), drôle; (strange) curieux(euse), bizarre.

ınny bone n endroit sensible du coude.

ın run n course f de fond (pour amateurs).

ır [fəː*] n fourrure f; (BRIT: in kettle etc) (dépôt m de) tartre m.

ır coat n manteau m de fourrure.

ırious ['fjuərɪəs] adj furieux(euse); (effort) acharné(e); **to be ~ with sb** être dans une fureur noire contre qn.

ıriously ['fjuərɪəslɪ] adv furieusement; avec acharnement.

ırl [fəːl] vt rouler; (NAUT) ferler.

ırlong ['fəːlɔŋ] n = 201.17 m (terme d'hippisme).

ırlough ['fəːləu] n permission f, congé m.

ırnace ['fəːnɪs] n fourneau m.

ırnish ['fəːnɪʃ] vt meubler; (supply) fournir; **~ed flat** or (US) **apartment** meublé m.

ırnishings ['fəːnɪʃɪŋz] npl mobilier m, articles mpl d'ameublement.

ırniture ['fəːnɪtʃə*] n meubles mpl, mobilier m; **piece of ~** meuble m.

ırniture polish n encaustique f.

ırore [fjuə'rɔːrɪ] n (protests) protestations fpl.

ırrier ['fʌrɪə*] n fourreur m.

ırrow ['fʌrəu] n sillon m.

ırry ['fəːrɪ] adj (animal) à fourrure; (toy) en peluche.

ırther ['fəːðə*] adj supplémentaire, autre; nouveau(nouvelle) ♦ adv plus loin; (more) davantage; (moreover) de plus ♦ vt faire avancer or progresser, promouvoir; **how much ~ is it?** quelle distance or combien reste-t-il à parcourir?; **until ~ notice** jusqu'à nouvel ordre or avis; **~ to your letter of ...** (COMM) suite à votre lettre du ....

ırther education n enseignement m postscolaire (recyclage, formation professionnelle).

ırthermore [fəːðə'mɔː*] adv de plus, en outre.

ırthermost ['fəːðəməust] adj le(la) plus éloigné(e).

ırthest ['fəːðɪst] superlative of **far**.

ırtive ['fəːtɪv] adj furtif(ive).

ırtively ['fəːtɪvlɪ] adv furtivement.

ıry ['fjuərɪ] n fureur f.

ıse, (US) **fuze** [fjuːz] n fusible m; (for bomb etc) amorce f, détonateur m ♦ vt, vi (metal) fondre; (fig) fusionner; (ELEC): **to ~ the lights** faire sauter les fusibles or les plombs; **a ~ has blown** un fusible a sauté.

ıse box n boîte f à fusibles.

ıselage ['fjuːzəlɑːʒ] n fuselage m.

ıse wire n fusible m.

ısillade [fjuːzɪ'leɪd] n fusillade f; (fig) feu

roulant.

fusion ['fjuːʒən] n fusion f.

fuss [fʌs] n (anxiety, excitement) chichis mpl, façons fpl; (commotion) tapage m; (complaining, trouble) histoire(s) f(pl) ♦ vi faire des histoires ♦ vt (person) embêter; **to make a ~** faire des façons (or des histoires); **to make a ~ of sb** dorloter qn.

▶**fuss over** vt fus (person) dorloter.

fusspot ['fʌspɔt] n (col): **don't be such a ~!** ne fais pas tant d'histoires!

fussy ['fʌsɪ] adj (person) tatillon(ne), difficile; chichiteux(euse); (dress, style) tarabiscoté(e); **I'm not ~** (col) ça m'est égal.

fusty ['fʌstɪ] adj (old-fashioned) vieillot(te); (smell) de renfermé or moisi.

futile ['fjuːtaɪl] adj futile.

futility [fjuː'tɪlɪtɪ] n futilité f.

futon ['fuːtɔn] n futon m.

future ['fjuːtʃə*] adj futur(e) ♦ n avenir m; (LING) futur m; **in (the) ~** à l'avenir; **in the near/immediate ~** dans un avenir proche/immédiat.

futures ['fjuːtʃəz] npl (COMM) opérations fpl à terme.

futuristic [fjuːtʃə'rɪstɪk] adj futuriste.

fuze [fjuːz] n, vt, vi (US) = **fuse**.

fuzzy ['fʌzɪ] adj (PHOT) flou(e); (hair) crépu(e).

fwd. abbr = **forward**.

fwy abbr (US) = **freeway**.

FY abbr = **fiscal year**.

FYI abbr = **for your information**.

G g

G, g [dʒiː] n (letter) G, g m; (MUS): **G** sol m; **G for George** G comme Gaston.

G n abbr (BRIT SCOL: = good) b (= bien); (US CINE: = general (audience)) ≈ tous publics; **G7** (POL) G7 m.

g abbr (= gram, gravity) g.

GA abbr (US) = **Georgia**.

gab [gæb] n (col): **to have the gift of the ~** avoir la langue bien pendue.

gabble ['gæbl] vi bredouiller; jacasser.

gaberdine [gæbə'diːn] n gabardine f.

gable ['geɪbl] n pignon m.

Gabon [gə'bɔn] n Gabon m.

gad about ['gædə'baut] vi (col) se balader.

gadget ['gædʒɪt] n gadget m.

Gaelic ['geɪlɪk] adj, n gaélique (m).

gaffe [gæf] n gaffe f.

gaffer ['gæfə*] n (BRIT: foreman) contremaître m; (BRIT col: boss) patron m.

gag [gæg] n bâillon m; (joke) gag m ♦ vt

(*prisoner etc*) bâillonner ♦ *vi* (*choke*) étouffer.

gaga ['gɑːgɑː] *adj*: **to go ~** devenir gaga *or* gâteux(euse).

gaiety ['geɪɪtɪ] *n* gaieté *f*.

gaily ['geɪlɪ] *adv* gaiement.

gain [geɪn] *n* gain *m*, profit *m* ♦ *vt* gagner ♦ *vi* (*watch*) avancer; **to ~ in/by** gagner en/à; **to ~ 3lbs (in weight)** prendre 3 livres; **to ~ ground** gagner du terrain.

▶**gain (up)on** *vt fus* rattraper.

gainful ['geɪnful] *adj* profitable, lucratif(ive).

gainfully ['geɪnfəlɪ] *adv*: **to be ~ employed** avoir un emploi rémunéré.

gainsay [geɪn'seɪ] *vt* (*irreg: like* **say**) contredire; nier.

gait [geɪt] *n* démarche *f*.

gal. *abbr* = **gallon**.

gala ['gɑːlə] *n* gala *m*; **swimming ~** grand concours de natation.

Galápagos (Islands) [gə'læpəgəs-] *npl*: **the ~** les (îles *fpl*) Galapagos *fpl*.

galaxy ['gæləksɪ] *n* galaxie *f*.

gale [geɪl] *n* coup *m* de vent; **~ force 10** vent *m* de force 10.

gall [gɔːl] *n* (*ANAT*) bile *f*; (*fig*) effronterie *f* ♦ *vt* ulcérer, irriter.

gall. *abbr* = **gallon**.

gallant ['gælənt] *adj* vaillant(e), brave; (*towards ladies*) empressé(e), galant(e).

gallantry ['gæləntrɪ] *n* bravoure *f*, vaillance *f*; empressement *m*, galanterie *f*.

gall-bladder ['gɔːlblædə*] *n* vésicule *f* biliaire.

galleon ['gælɪən] *n* galion *m*.

gallery ['gælərɪ] *n* galerie *f*; (*for spectators*) tribune *f*; (: *in theatre*) dernier balcon; (*also*: **art ~**) musée *m*; (: *private*) galerie.

galley ['gælɪ] *n* (*ship's kitchen*) cambuse *f*; (*ship*) galère *f*; (*also*: **~ proof**) placard *m*, galée *f*.

Gallic ['gælɪk] *adj* (*of Gaul*) gaulois(e); (*French*) français(e).

galling ['gɔːlɪŋ] *adj* irritant(e).

gallon ['gælən] *n* gallon *m* (= *8 pints; BRIT* = 4.543 l; *US* = 3.785 l).

gallop ['gæləp] *n* galop *m* ♦ *vi* galoper; **~ing inflation** inflation galopante.

gallows ['gæləuz] *n* potence *f*.

gallstone ['gɔːlstəun] *n* calcul *m* (biliaire).

Gallup Poll ['gæləp-] *n* sondage *m* Gallup.

galore [gə'lɔː*] *adv* en abondance, à gogo.

galvanize ['gælvənaɪz] *vt* galvaniser; (*fig*): **to ~ sb into action** galvaniser qn.

Gambia ['gæmbɪə] *n* Gambie *f*.

gambit ['gæmbɪt] *n* (*fig*): **(opening) ~** manœuvre *f* stratégique.

gamble ['gæmbl] *n* pari *m*, risque calculé ♦ *vt*, *vi* jouer; **to ~ on the Stock Exchange** jouer en *or* à la Bourse; **to ~ on** (*fig*) miser sur.

gambler ['gæmblə*] *n* joueur *m*.

gambling ['gæmblɪŋ] *n* jeu *m*.

gambol ['gæmbl] *vi* gambader.

game [geɪm] *n* jeu *m*; (*event*) match *m*;

(*HUNTING*) gibier *m* ♦ *adj* brave; (*ready*): **to be ~ (for sth/to do)** être prêt(e) (à qch/à faire), se sentir de taille (à faire); **a ~ of football/ tennis** une partie de football/tennis; **~s** (*SCOL*) sport *m*; **big ~** gros gibier.

game bird *n* gibier *m* à plume.

gamekeeper ['geɪmkiːpə*] *n* garde-chasse *m*.

gamely ['geɪmlɪ] *adv* vaillamment.

game reserve *n* réserve animalière.

games console ['geɪmz-] *n* console *f* de jeux vidéo.

gameshow ['geɪmʃəu] *n* jeu télévisé.

gamesmanship ['geɪmzmənʃɪp] *n* roublardis *f*.

gaming ['geɪmɪŋ] *n* jeu *m*, jeux *mpl* d'argent.

gammon ['gæmən] *n* (*bacon*) quartier *m* de lard fumé; (*ham*) jambon fumé.

gamut ['gæmət] *n* gamme *f*.

gang [gæŋ] *n* bande *f*, groupe *m*.

▶**gang up** *vi*: **to ~ up on sb** se liguer contre qn.

Ganges ['gændʒiːz] *n*: **the ~** le Gange.

gangland ['gæŋlænd] *adj*: **~ killer** tueur professionnel du milieu; **~ boss** chef *m* de gang.

gangling ['gæŋglɪŋ], **gangly** ['gæŋglɪ] *adj* dégingandé(e).

gangplank ['gæŋplæŋk] *n* passerelle *f*.

gangrene ['gæŋgriːn] *n* gangrène *f*.

gangster ['gæŋstə*] *n* gangster *m*, bandit *m*.

gangway ['gæŋweɪ] *n* passerelle *f*; (*BRIT: of bus*) couloir central.

gantry ['gæntrɪ] *n* portique *m*; (*for rocket*) tou *f* de lancement.

GAO *n abbr* (*US*: = *General Accounting Office*) ≈ Cour *f* des comptes.

gaol [dʒeɪl] *n*, *vt* (*BRIT*) = **jail**.

gap [gæp] *n* trou *m*; (*in time*) intervalle *m*; (*fig*) lacune *f*; vide *m*.

gape [geɪp] *vi* être *or* rester bouche bée.

gaping ['geɪpɪŋ] *adj* (*hole*) béant(e).

garage ['gærɑːʒ] *n* garage *m*.

garb [gɑːb] *n* tenue *f*, costume *m*.

garbage ['gɑːbɪdʒ] *n* ordures *fpl*, détritus *mpl*; (*fig: col*) conneries *fpl*.

garbage can *n* (*US*) poubelle *f*, boîte *f* à ordures.

garbage collector *n* (*US*) éboueur *m*.

garbage disposal (unit) *n* broyeur *m* d'ordures.

garbage truck *n* (*US*) camion *m* (du ramassage) des ordures, benne *f* à ordures

garbled ['gɑːbld] *adj* déformé(e); faussé(e).

garden ['gɑːdn] *n* jardin *m* ♦ *vi* jardiner; **~s** *n* (*public*) jardin public; (*private*) parc *m*.

garden centre *n* garden-centre *m*, pépinière *f*.

garden city *n* (*BRIT*) cité-jardin *f*.

gardener ['gɑːdnə*] *n* jardinier *m*.

gardening ['gɑːdnɪŋ] *n* jardinage *m*.

gargle ['gɑːgl] *vi* se gargariser ♦ *n* gargarism *m*.

gargoyle ['gɑːgɔɪl] n gargouille f.
garish ['gɛərɪʃ] adj criard(e), voyant(e).
garland ['gɑːlənd] n guirlande f, couronne f.
garlic ['gɑːlɪk] n ail m.
garment ['gɑːmənt] n vêtement m.
garner ['gɑːnə*] vt engranger, amasser.
garnish ['gɑːnɪʃ] vt garnir.
garret ['gærɪt] n mansarde f.
garrison ['gærɪsn] n garnison f ♦ vt mettre en garnison, stationner.
garrulous ['gærjuləs] adj volubile, loquace.
garter ['gɑːtə*] n jarretière f; (US: suspender) jarretelle f.
garter belt n (US) porte-jarretelles m inv.
gas [gæs] n gaz m; (used as anaesthetic): **to be given** ~ se faire endormir; (US: gasoline) essence f ♦ vt asphyxier; (MIL) gazer.
Gascony ['gæskənɪ] n Gascogne f.
gas cooker n (BRIT) cuisinière f à gaz.
gas cylinder n bouteille f de gaz.
gaseous ['gæsɪəs] adj gazeux(euse).
gas fire n (BRIT) radiateur m à gaz.
gas-fired ['gæsfaɪəd] adj au gaz.
gash [gæʃ] n entaille f; (on face) balafre f ♦ vt taillader; balafrer.
gasket ['gæskɪt] n (AUT) joint m de culasse.
gas mask n masque m à gaz.
gas meter n compteur m à gaz.
gasoline ['gæsəliːn] n (US) essence f.
gasp [gɑːsp] vi haleter; (fig) avoir le souffle coupé.
gasp out vt (say) dire dans un souffle or d'une voix entrecoupée.
gas ring n brûleur m.
gas station n (US) station-service f.
gas stove n réchaud m à gaz; (cooker) cuisinière f à gaz.
gassy ['gæsɪ] adj gazeux(euse).
gas tank n (US AUT) réservoir m d'essence.
gas tap n bouton m (de cuisinière à gaz); (on pipe) robinet m à gaz.
gastric ['gæstrɪk] adj gastrique.
gastric ulcer n ulcère m de l'estomac.
gastroenteritis ['gæstrəuɛntə'raɪtɪs] n gastroentérite f.
gastronomy [gæs'trɔnəmɪ] n gastronomie f.
gasworks ['gæswəːks] n, npl usine f à gaz.
gate [geɪt] n (of garden) portail m; (of farm, at level crossing) barrière f; (of building, town, at airport) porte f; (of lock) vanne f.
gâteau, pl ~x ['gætəu, -z] n gros gâteau à la crème.
gatecrash ['geɪtkræʃ] vt s'introduire sans invitation dans.
gatecrasher ['geɪtkræʃə*] n intrus/e.
gatehouse ['geɪthaus] n loge f.
gateway ['geɪtweɪ] n porte f.
gather ['gæðə*] vt (flowers, fruit) cueillir; (pick up) ramasser; (assemble) rassembler, réunir; recueillir; (understand) comprendre ♦ vi (assemble) se rassembler; (dust) s'amasser; (clouds) s'amonceler; **to** ~

(from/that) conclure or déduire (de/que); **as far as I can** ~ d'après ce que je comprends; **to** ~ **speed** prendre de la vitesse.
gathering ['gæðərɪŋ] n rassemblement m.
GATT [gæt] n abbr (= General Agreement on Tariffs and Trade) GATT m.
gauche [gəuʃ] adj gauche, maladroit(e).
gaudy ['gɔːdɪ] adj voyant(e).
gauge [geɪdʒ] n (standard measure) calibre m; (RAIL) écartement m; (instrument) jauge f ♦ vt jauger; (fig: sb's capabilities, character) juger de; **to** ~ **the right moment** calculer le moment propice; **petrol** ~, (US) **gas** ~ jauge d'essence.
Gaul [gɔːl] n (country) Gaule f; (person) Gaulois/e.
gaunt [gɔːnt] adj décharné(e); (grim, desolate) désolé(e).
gauntlet ['gɔːntlɪt] n (fig): **to throw down the** ~ jeter le gant; **to run the** ~ **through an angry crowd** se frayer un passage à travers une foule hostile or entre deux haies de manifestants etc hostiles.
gauze [gɔːz] n gaze f.
gave [geɪv] pt of **give**.
gavel ['gævl] n marteau m.
gawky ['gɔːkɪ] adj dégingandé(e), godiche.
gawp [gɔːp] vi: **to** ~ **at** regarder bouche bée.
gay [geɪ] adj (homosexual) homosexuel(le); (slightly old-fashioned: cheerful) gai(e), réjoui(e); (colour) gai, vif(vive).
gaze [geɪz] n regard m fixe ♦ vi: **to** ~ **at** vt fixer du regard.
gazelle [gə'zɛl] n gazelle f.
gazette [gə'zɛt] n (newspaper) gazette f; (official publication) journal officiel.
gazetteer [gæzə'tɪə*] n dictionnaire m géographique.
gazump [gə'zʌmp] vi (BRIT) revenir sur une promesse de vente pour accepter un prix plus élevé.
gazumping [gə'zʌmpɪŋ] n le fait de revenir sur une promesse de vente pour accepter un prix plus élevé.
GB abbr = **Great Britain**.
GBH n abbr (BRIT LAW: col) = **grievous bodily harm**.
GC n abbr (BRIT: = George Cross) distinction honorifique.
GCE n abbr (BRIT) = General Certificate of Education.
GCHQ n abbr (BRIT: = Government Communications Headquarters) centre d'interception des télécommunications étrangères.
GCSE n abbr (BRIT: = General Certificate of Secondary Education) examen passé à l'âge de 16 ans sanctionnant les connaissances de l'élève; **she's got eight** ~**s** elle a réussi dans huit matières aux épreuves du GCSE.
Gdns. abbr = gardens.
GDP n abbr = **gross domestic product**.

GDR *n abbr* (*old*: = *German Democratic Republic*) RDA *f*.

gear [gɪə*] *n* matériel *m*, équipement *m*; (*TECH*) engrenage *m*; (*AUT*) vitesse *f* ♦ *vt* (*fig*: *adapt*) adapter; **top** *or* (*US*) **high/low/bottom** ~ quatrième (*or* cinquième)/deuxième/ première vitesse; **in** ~ en prise; **out of** ~ au point mort; **our service is** ~**ed to meet the needs of the disabled** notre service répond de façon spécifique aux besoins des handicapés.

▶**gear up** *vi*: **to** ~ **up (to do)** se préparer (à faire).

gear box *n* boîte *f* de vitesse.

gear lever, (*US*) **gear shift** *n* levier *m* de vitesse.

GED *n abbr* (*US SCOL*) = *general educational development*.

geese [giːs] *npl of* **goose**.

geezer ['giːzə*] *n* (*BRIT col*) mec *m*.

Geiger counter ['gaɪgə-] *n* compteur *m* Geiger.

gel [dʒɛl] *n* gelée *f*; (*CHEMISTRY*) colloïde *m*.

gelatin(e) ['dʒɛləti:n] *n* gélatine *f*.

gelignite ['dʒɛlɪgnaɪt] *n* plastic *m*.

gem [dʒɛm] *n* pierre précieuse.

Gemini ['dʒɛmɪnaɪ] *n* les Gémeaux *mpl*; **to be** ~ être des Gémeaux.

gen [dʒɛn] *n* (*BRIT col*): **to give sb the** ~ **on sth** mettre qn au courant de qch.

Gen. *abbr* (*MIL*: = *general*) Gal.

gen. *abbr* (= *general, generally*) gén.

gender ['dʒɛndə*] *n* genre *m*.

gene [dʒi:n] *n* (*BIOL*) gène *m*.

genealogy [dʒiːnɪˈælədʒɪ] *n* généalogie *f*.

general ['dʒɛnərl] *n* général *m* ♦ *adj* général(e); **in** ~ en général; **the** ~ **public** le grand public; ~ **audit** (*COMM*) vérification annuelle.

general anaesthetic *n* anesthésie générale.

general election *n* élection(s) législative(s).

generalization ['dʒɛnrəlaɪˈzeɪʃən] *n* généralisation *f*.

generalize ['dʒɛnrəlaɪz] *vi* généraliser.

generally ['dʒɛnrəlɪ] *adv* généralement.

general manager *n* directeur général.

general practitioner (GP) *n* généraliste *m/f*; **who's your GP?** qui est votre médecin traitant?

general strike *n* grève générale.

generate ['dʒɛnəreɪt] *vt* engendrer; (*electricity*) produire.

generation [dʒɛnəˈreɪʃən] *n* génération *f*; (*of electricity etc*) production *f*.

generator ['dʒɛnəreɪtə*] *n* générateur *m*.

generic [dʒɪˈnɛrɪk] *adj* générique.

generosity [dʒɛnəˈrɒsɪtɪ] *n* générosité *f*.

generous ['dʒɛnərəs] *adj* généreux(euse); (*copious*) copieux(euse).

genesis ['dʒɛnɪsɪs] *n* genèse *f*.

genetic [dʒɪˈnɛtɪk] *adj* génétique.

genetic engineering *n* génie *m* génétique.

genetic fingerprinting [-ˈfɪŋɡəprɪntɪŋ] *n* système *m* d'empreinte génétique.

genetics [dʒɪˈnɛtɪks] *n* génétique *f*.

Geneva [dʒɪˈniːvə] *n* Genève; **Lake** ~ le lac Léman.

genial ['dʒiːnɪəl] *adj* cordial(e), chaleureux(euse); (*climate*) clément(e).

genitals ['dʒɛnɪtlz] *npl* organes génitaux.

genitive ['dʒɛnɪtɪv] *n* génitif *m*.

genius ['dʒiːnɪəs] *n* génie *m*.

Genoa ['dʒɛnəuə] *n* Gênes.

genocide ['dʒɛnəusaɪd] *n* génocide *m*.

gent [dʒɛnt] *n abbr* (*BRIT col*) = **gentleman**.

genteel [dʒɛnˈtiːl] *adj* de bon ton, distingué(e)

gentle ['dʒɛntl] *adj* doux(douce).

gentleman ['dʒɛntlmən] *n* monsieur *m*; (*well-bred man*) gentleman *m*; ~**'s agreement** gentleman's agreement *m*.

gentlemanly ['dʒɛntlmənlɪ] *adj* bien élevé(e).

gentleness ['dʒɛntlnɪs] *n* douceur *f*.

gently ['dʒɛntlɪ] *adv* doucement.

gentry ['dʒɛntrɪ] *n* petite noblesse.

gents [dʒɛnts] *n* W.-C. *mpl* (pour hommes).

genuine ['dʒɛnjuɪn] *adj* véritable, authentique; (*person, emotion*) sincère.

genuinely ['dʒɛnjuɪnlɪ] *adv* sincèrement, vraiment.

geographer [dʒɪˈɒgrəfə*] *n* géographe *m/f*.

geographic(al) [dʒɪəˈgræfɪk(l)] *adj* géographique.

geography [dʒɪˈɒgrəfɪ] *n* géographie *f*.

geological [dʒɪəˈlɒdʒɪkl] *adj* géologique.

geologist [dʒɪˈɒlədʒɪst] *n* géologue *m/f*.

geology [dʒɪˈɒlədʒɪ] *n* géologie *f*.

geometric(al) [dʒɪəˈmɛtrɪk(l)] *adj* géométrique.

geometry [dʒɪˈɒmətrɪ] *n* géométrie *f*.

Geordie ['dʒɔːdɪ] *n* (*col*) habitant/e de Tyneside; originaire *m/f* de Tyneside.

Georgia ['dʒɔːdʒə] *n* Géorgie *f*.

Georgian ['dʒɔːdʒən] *adj* (*GEO*) géorgien(ne) ♦ *n* Géorgien/ne; (*LING*) géorgien *m*.

geranium [dʒɪˈreɪnɪəm] *n* géranium *m*.

geriatric [dʒɛrɪˈætrɪk] *adj* gériatrique.

germ [dʒəːm] *n* (*MED*) microbe *m*; (*BIO, fig*) germe *m*.

German ['dʒəːmən] *adj* allemand(e) ♦ *n* Allemand/e; (*LING*) allemand *m*.

germane [dʒəːˈmeɪn] *adj* (*formal*): ~ **(to)** se rapportant (à).

German measles *n* rubéole *f*.

Germany ['dʒəːmənɪ] *n* Allemagne *f*.

germination [dʒəːmɪˈneɪʃən] *n* germination *f*.

germ warfare *n* guerre *f* bactériologique.

gerrymandering ['dʒɛrɪmændərɪŋ] *n* tripotag *m* du découpage électoral.

gestation [dʒɛsˈteɪʃən] *n* gestation *f*.

gesticulate [dʒɛsˈtɪkjuleɪt] *vi* gesticuler.

gesture ['dʒɛstjə*] *n* geste *m*; **as a** ~ **of friendship** en témoignage d'amitié.

=== KEYWORD

get [gɛt] (*pt, pp* **got**, *pp* **gotten** (*US*)) *vi* **1**
(*become, be*) devenir; **to ~ old/tired** devenir
vieux/fatigué, vieillir/se fatiguer; **to ~**
drunk s'enivrer; **to ~ ready/washed/shaved**
etc se préparer/laver/raser *etc*; **to ~ killed**
se faire tuer; **when do I ~ paid?** quand est-
ce que je serai payé?; **it's ~ting late** il se
fait tard
2 (*go*): **to ~ to/from** aller à/de; **to ~ home**
rentrer chez soi; **how did you ~ here?**
comment es-tu arrivé ici?; **he got across the**
bridge/under the fence il a traversé le pont/
est passé au-dessous de la barrière
3 (*begin*) commencer *or* se mettre à; **I'm**
~ting to like him je commence à
l'apprécier; **let's ~ going** *or* **started** allons-y
4 (*modal aux vb*): **you've got to do it** il faut
que vous le fassiez; **I've got to tell the police**
je dois le dire à la police
♦ *vt* **1**: **to ~ sth done** (*do*) faire qch; (*have*
done) faire faire qch; **to ~ sth/sb ready**
préparer qch/qn; **to ~ one's hair cut** se faire
couper les cheveux; **to ~ sb to do sth** faire
faire qch à qn; **to ~ sb drunk** enivrer qn
2 (*obtain: money, permission, results*) obtenir,
avoir; (*find: job, flat*) trouver; (*fetch: person,*
doctor, object) aller chercher; **to ~ sth for sb**
procurer qch à qn; **~ me Mr Jones, please**
(*on phone*) passez-moi Mr Jones, s'il vous
plaît; **can I ~ you a drink?** est-ce que je peux
vous servir à boire?
3 (*receive: present, letter*) recevoir, avoir;
(*acquire: reputation*) avoir; (*: prize*) obtenir;
what did you ~ for your birthday? qu'est-ce
que tu as eu pour ton anniversaire?
4 (*catch*) prendre, saisir, attraper; (*hit:*
target etc) atteindre; **to ~ sb by the arm/**
throat prendre *or* saisir *or* attraper qn par
le bras/à la gorge; **~ him!** arrête-le!; **he**
really ~s me! il me porte sur les nerfs!; **do you**
think we'll ~ it through the door? on arrivera à le
faire passer par la porte?; **I'll ~ you there**
somehow je me débrouillerai pour t'y
emmener
6 (*catch, take: plane, bus etc*) prendre
7 (*understand*) comprendre, saisir; (*hear*)
entendre; **I've got it!** j'ai compris!; **I didn't ~**
your name je n'ai pas entendu votre nom
8 (*have, possess*): **to have got** avoir; **how**
many have you got? vous en avez combien?
get about *vi* se déplacer; (*news*) se
répandre
get across *vt*: **to ~ across (to)** (*message,*
meaning) faire passer à ♦ *vi*: **to ~ across to**
(*subj: speaker*) se faire comprendre (par)
get along *vi* (*agree*) s'entendre; (*depart*) s'en
aller; (*manage*) = **get by**
get at *vt fus* (*attack*) s'en prendre à; (*reach*)
attraper, atteindre; **what are you ~ting at?**
à quoi voulez-vous en venir?
▶**get away** *vi* partir, s'en aller; (*escape*)
s'échapper
▶**get away with** *vt fus* en être quitte pour; se
faire passer *or* pardonner
▶**get back** *vi* (*return*) rentrer ♦ *vt* récupérer,
recouvrer; **to ~ back to** (*start again*)
retourner *or* revenir à; (*contact again*)
recontacter
▶**get back at** *vt fus* (*col*): **to ~ back at sb**
rendre la monnaie de sa pièce à qn
▶**get by** *vi* (*pass*) passer; (*manage*) se
débrouiller; **I can ~ by in Dutch** je me
débrouille en hollandais
▶**get down** *vi, vt fus* descendre ♦ *vt* descendre;
(*depress*) déprimer
▶**get down to** *vt fus* (*work*) se mettre à
(faire); **to ~ down to business** passer aux
choses sérieuses
▶**get in** *vi* entrer; (*arrive home*) rentrer; (*train*)
arriver ♦ *vt* (*bring in: harvest*) rentrer; (*: coal*)
faire rentrer; (*: supplies*) faire des
provisions de
▶**get into** *vt fus* entrer dans; (*car, train etc*)
monter dans; (*clothes*) mettre, enfiler,
endosser; **to ~ into bed/a rage** se mettre au
lit/en colère
▶**get off** *vi* (*from train etc*) descendre; (*depart:*
person, car) s'en aller; (*escape*) s'en tirer ♦ *vt*
(*remove: clothes, stain*) enlever; (*send off*)
expédier; (*have as leave: day, time*): **we got 2**
days off nous avons eu 2 jours de congé ♦ *vt*
fus (*train, bus*) descendre de; **to ~ off to a**
good start (*fig*) prendre un bon départ
▶**get on** *vi* (*at exam etc*) se débrouiller;
(*agree*): **to ~ on (with)** s'entendre (avec);
how are you ~ting on? comment ça va? ♦ *vt*
fus monter dans; (*horse*) monter sur
▶**get on to** *vt fus* (*BRIT: deal with: problem*)
s'occuper de; (*contact: person*) contacter
▶**get out** *vi* sortir; (*of vehicle*) descendre;
(*news etc*) s'ébruiter ♦ *vt* sortir
▶**get out of** *vt fus* sortir de; (*duty etc*)
échapper à, se soustraire à
▶**get over** *vt fus* (*illness*) se remettre de ♦ *vt*
(*communicate: idea etc*) communiquer;
(*finish*): **let's ~ it over (with)** finissons-en
▶**get round** *vi*: **to ~ round to doing sth** se
mettre (finalement) à faire qch ♦ *vt fus*
contourner; (*fig: person*) entortiller
▶**get through** *vi* (*TEL*) avoir la
communication; **to ~ through to sb**
atteindre qn ♦ *vt fus* (*finish: work, book*) finir,
terminer
▶**get together** *vi* se réunir ♦ *vt* rassembler
▶**get up** *vi* (*rise*) se lever ♦ *vt fus* monter
▶**get up to** *vt fus* (*reach*) arriver à; (*prank etc*)
faire.

getaway ['gɛtəweɪ] *n* fuite *f*.
getaway car *n* voiture prévue pour prendre
la fuite.

get-together |'gɛttəgɛðə*| n petite réunion, petite fête.

get-up |'gɛtʌp| n (col: outfit) accoutrement m.

get-well card |gɛt'wɛl-| n carte f de vœux de bon rétablissement.

geyser |'giːzə*| n chauffe-eau m inv; (GEO) geyser m.

Ghana |'gɑːnə| n Ghana m.

Ghanaian |gɑː'neɪən| adj ghanéen(ne) ♦ n Ghanéen/ne.

ghastly |'gɑːstlɪ| adj atroce, horrible; (pale) livide, blême.

gherkin |'gɜːkɪn| n cornichon m.

ghetto |'gɛtəʊ| n ghetto m.

ghetto blaster |-blɑːstə*| n (col) gros radiocassette.

ghost |gəʊst| n fantôme m, revenant m ♦ vt (sb else's book) écrire.

ghostly |'gəʊstlɪ| adj fantomatique.

ghostwriter |'gəʊstraɪtə*| n nègre m (fig).

ghoul |guːl| n (ghost) vampire m.

ghoulish |'guːlɪʃ| adj (tastes etc) morbide.

GHQ n abbr (MIL: = general headquarters) GQG m.

GI n abbr (US col: = government issue) soldat de l'armée américaine, GI m.

giant |'dʒaɪənt| n géant/e ♦ adj géant(e), énorme; ~ (size) packet paquet géant.

giant killer n (SPORT) équipe inconnue qui remporte un match contre une équipe renommée.

gibber |'dʒɪbə*| vi émettre des sons inintelligibles.

gibberish |'dʒɪbərɪʃ| n charabia m.

gibe |dʒaɪb| n sarcasme m ♦ vi: to ~ at railler.

giblets |'dʒɪblɪts| npl abats mpl.

Gibraltar |dʒɪ'brɔːltə*| n Gibraltar m.

giddiness |'gɪdɪnɪs| n vertige m.

giddy |'gɪdɪ| adj (dizzy): to be (or feel) ~ avoir le vertige; (height) vertigineux(euse); (thoughtless) sot(te), étourdi(e).

gift |gɪft| n cadeau m, présent m; (donation) don m; (COMM: also: free ~) cadeau (-réclame) m; (talent): to have a ~ for sth avoir des dons pour or le don de qch.

gifted |'gɪftɪd| adj doué(e).

gift token, gift voucher n bon m d'achat.

gig |gɪg| n (col: of musician) gig f.

gigabyte |'dʒɪgəbaɪt| n gigaoctet m.

gigantic |dʒaɪ'gæntɪk| adj gigantesque.

giggle |'gɪgl| vi pouffer, ricaner sottement ♦ n petit rire sot, ricanement m.

GIGO |'gaɪgəʊ| abbr (COMPUT: col: = garbage in, garbage out) qualité d'entrée = qualité de sortie.

gild |gɪld| vt dorer.

gill |dʒɪl| n (measure) = 0.25 pints (BRIT = 0.148 l; US = 0.118 l).

gills |gɪlz| npl (of fish) ouïes fpl, branchies fpl.

gilt |gɪlt| n dorure f ♦ adj doré(e).

gilt-edged |'gɪltɛdʒd| adj (stocks, securities) de premier ordre.

gimlet |'gɪmlɪt| n vrille f.

gimmick |'gɪmɪk| n truc m; sales ~ offre promotionnelle.

gin |dʒɪn| n gin m.

ginger |'dʒɪndʒə*| n gingembre m.

▶**ginger up** vt secouer; animer.

ginger ale, ginger beer n boisson gazeuse au gingembre.

gingerbread |'dʒɪndʒəbrɛd| n pain m d'épices.

ginger group n (BRIT) groupe m de pression.

ginger-haired |'dʒɪndʒə'hɛəd| adj roux(rousse).

gingerly |'dʒɪndʒəlɪ| adv avec précaution.

gingham |'gɪŋəm| n vichy m.

ginseng |'dʒɪnsɛŋ| n ginseng m.

gipsy |'dʒɪpsɪ| n gitan/e, bohémien/ne ♦ cpd: ~ caravan n roulotte f.

giraffe |dʒɪ'rɑːf| n girafe f.

girder |'gɜːdə*| n poutrelle f.

girdle |'gɜːdl| n (corset) gaine f ♦ vt ceindre.

girl |gɜːl| n fille f, fillette f; (young unmarried woman) jeune fille; (daughter) fille; an English ~ une jeune Anglaise; a little English ~ une petite Anglaise.

girlfriend |'gɜːlfrɛnd| n (of girl) amie f; (of boy) petite amie.

girlish |'gɜːlɪʃ| adj de jeune fille.

Girl Scout n (US) guide f.

Giro |'dʒaɪrəʊ| n: the National ~ (BRIT) ≈ les comptes chèques postaux.

giro |'dʒaɪrəʊ| n (bank ~) virement m bancaire; (post office ~) mandat m.

girth |gɜːθ| n circonférence f; (of horse) sangle f.

gist |dʒɪst| n essentiel m.

give |gɪv| n (of fabric) élasticité f ♦ vb (pt gave, pp given |geɪv, 'gɪvn|) vt donner ♦ vi (break) céder; (stretch: fabric) se prêter; to ~ sb sth, ~ sth to sb donner qch à qn; to ~ a cry/sigh pousser un cri/un soupir; how much did you ~ for it? combien (l')avez-vous payé?; 12 o'clock, ~ or take a few minutes midi, à quelques minutes près; to ~ way vi céder; (BRIT AUT) donner la priorité.

▶**give away** vt donner; (give free) faire cadeau de; (betray) trahir; (disclose) révéler; (bride) conduire à l'autel.

▶**give back** vt rendre.

▶**give in** vi céder ♦ vt donner.

▶**give off** vt dégager.

▶**give out** vt (food etc) distribuer; (news) annoncer ♦ vi (be exhausted: supplies) s'épuiser; (fail) lâcher.

▶**give up** vi renoncer ♦ vt renoncer à; to ~ up smoking arrêter de fumer; to ~ o.s. up se rendre.

give-and-take |'gɪvənd'teɪk| n concessions mutuelles.

giveaway |'gɪvəweɪ| n (col): her expression was a ~ son expression la trahissait; the exam was a ~! cet examen, c'était du gâteau! ♦ cpd: ~ prices prix sacrifiés.

given ['gɪvn] pp of **give** ♦ adj (fixed: time, amount) donné(e), déterminé(e) ♦ conj: ~ **the circumstances ...** étant donné les circonstances ..., vu les circonstances ...; ~ **that ...** étant donné que ....

glacial ['gleɪsɪəl] adj (GEO) glaciaire; (wind, weather) glacial(e).

glacier ['glæsɪə*] n glacier m.

glad [glæd] adj content(e); **to be ~ about sth/ that** être heureux(euse) or bien content de qch/que; **I was ~ of his help** j'étais bien content de (pouvoir compter sur) son aide or qu'il m'aide.

gladden ['glædn] vt réjouir.

glade [gleɪd] n clairière f.

gladioli [glædɪ'əʊlaɪ] npl glaïeuls mpl.

gladly ['glædlɪ] adv volontiers.

glamorous ['glæmərəs] adj séduisant(e).

glamour ['glæmə*] n éclat m, prestige m.

glance [glɑːns] n coup m d'œil ♦ vi: **to ~ at** jeter un coup d'œil à.

▶**glance off** vt fus (bullet) ricocher sur.

glancing ['glɑːnsɪŋ] adj (blow) oblique.

gland [glænd] n glande f.

glandular ['glændjʊlə*] adj: ~ **fever** (BRIT) mononucléose infectieuse.

glare [glɛə*] n lumière éblouissante ♦ vi briller d'un éclat aveuglant; **to ~ at** lancer un or des regard(s) furieux à.

glaring ['glɛərɪŋ] adj (mistake) criant(e), qui saute aux yeux.

glasnost ['glæznɒst] n glasnost f.

glass [glɑːs] n verre m; (also: **looking ~**) miroir m.

glass-blowing ['glɑːsbləʊɪŋ] n soufflage m (du verre).

glass ceiling n (fig) plafond dans l'échelle hiérarchique au-dessus duquel les femmes ou les membres d'une minorité ethnique ne semblent pouvoir s'élever.

glasses ['glɑːsəz] npl lunettes fpl.

glass fibre n fibre f de verre.

glasshouse ['glɑːshaus] n serre f.

glassware ['glɑːswɛə*] n verrerie f.

glassy ['glɑːsɪ] adj (eyes) vitreux(euse).

Glaswegian [glæs'wiːdʒən] adj de Glasgow ♦ n habitant/e de Glasgow; natif/ive de Glasgow.

glaze [gleɪz] vt (door) vitrer; (pottery) vernir; (CULIN) glacer ♦ n vernis m; (CULIN) glaçage m.

glazed [gleɪzd] adj (eye) vitreux(euse); (pottery) verni(e); (tiles) vitrifié(e).

glazier ['gleɪzɪə*] n vitrier m.

gleam [gliːm] n lueur f ♦ vi luire, briller; **a ~ of hope** une lueur d'espoir.

gleaming ['gliːmɪŋ] adj luisant(e).

glean [gliːn] vt (information) recueillir.

glee [gliː] n joie f.

gleeful ['gliːful] adj joyeux(euse).

glen [glɛn] n vallée f.

glib [glɪb] adj qui a du bagou; facile.

glide [glaɪd] vi glisser; (AVIAT, bird) planer ♦ n glissement m; vol plané.

glider ['glaɪdə*] n (AVIAT) planeur m.

gliding ['glaɪdɪŋ] n (AVIAT) vol m à voile.

glimmer ['glɪmə*] vi briller ♦ n lueur f.

glimpse [glɪmps] n vision passagère, aperçu m ♦ vt entrevoir, apercevoir; **to catch a ~ of** entrevoir.

glint [glɪnt] n éclair m ♦ vi étinceler.

glisten ['glɪsn] vi briller, luire.

glitter ['glɪtə*] vi scintiller, briller ♦ n scintillement m.

glitz [glɪts] n (col) clinquant m.

gloat [gləʊt] vi: **to ~ (over)** jubiler (à propos de).

global ['gləʊbl] adj (world-wide) mondial(e); (overall) global(e).

global warming [-'wɔːmɪŋ] n réchauffement m de la planète.

globe [gləʊb] n globe m.

globe-trotter ['gləʊbtrɒtə*] n globe-trotter m.

globule ['glɒbjuːl] n (ANAT) globule m; (of water etc) gouttelette f.

gloom [gluːm] n obscurité f; (sadness) tristesse f, mélancolie f.

gloomy ['gluːmɪ] adj sombre, triste, mélancolique; **to feel ~** avoir or se faire des idées noires.

glorification [glɔːrɪfɪ'keɪʃən] n glorification f.

glorify ['glɔːrɪfaɪ] vt glorifier.

glorious ['glɔːrɪəs] adj glorieux(euse); (beautiful) splendide.

glory ['glɔːrɪ] n gloire f; splendeur f ♦ vi: **to ~ in** se glorifier de.

glory hole n (col) capharnaüm m.

Glos abbr (BRIT) = Gloucestershire.

gloss [glɒs] n (shine) brillant m, vernis m; (also: ~ **paint**) peinture brillante or laquée.

▶**gloss over** vt fus glisser sur.

glossary ['glɒsərɪ] n glossaire m, lexique m.

glossy ['glɒsɪ] adj brillant(e), luisant(e) ♦ n (also: ~ **magazine**) revue f de luxe.

glove [glʌv] n gant m.

glove compartment n (AUT) boîte f à gants, vide-poches m inv.

glow [gləʊ] vi rougeoyer; (face) rayonner ♦ n rougeoiement m.

glower ['glauə*] vi lancer des regards mauvais.

glowing ['gləʊɪŋ] adj (fire) rougeoyant(e); (complexion) éclatant(e); (report, description etc) dithyrambique.

glow-worm ['gləʊwəːm] n ver luisant.

glucose ['gluːkəʊs] n glucose m.

glue [gluː] n colle f ♦ vt coller.

glue-sniffing ['gluːsnɪfɪŋ] n inhalation f de colle.

glum [glʌm] adj maussade, morose.

glut [glʌt] n surabondance f ♦ vt rassasier; (market) encombrer.

glutinous ['gluːtɪnəs] adj visqueux(euse).

glutton ['glʌtn] n glouton/ne; **a ~ for work** un

bourreau de travail.

gluttonous [ˈglʌtənəs] *adj* glouton(ne).

gluttony [ˈglʌtənɪ] *n* gloutonnerie *f*; (*sin*) gourmandise *f*.

glycerin(e) [ˈglɪsəriːn] *n* glycérine *f*.

gm *abbr* (= *gram*) g.

GMAT *n abbr* (*US*: = *Graduate Management Admissions Test*) *examen d'admission dans le 2e cycle de l'enseignement supérieur.*

GMB *n abbr* (*BRIT*) = *General Municipal and Boilermakers (Union)*.

GMT *abbr* (= *Greenwich Mean Time*) GMT.

gnarled [nɑːld] *adj* noueux(euse).

gnash [næʃ] *vt*: **to ~ one's teeth** grincer des dents.

gnat [næt] *n* moucheron *m*.

gnaw [nɔː] *vt* ronger.

gnome [nəum] *n* gnome *m*, lutin *m*.

GNP *n abbr* = *gross national product*.

go [gəu] *vb* (*pt* **went**, *pp* **gone** [wɛnt, gɔn]) *vi* aller; (*depart*) partir, s'en aller; (*work*) marcher; (*be sold*): **to ~ for £10** se vendre 10 livres; (*fit, suit*): **to ~ with** aller avec; (*become*): **to ~ pale/mouldy** pâlir/moisir; (*break etc*) céder ♦ *n* (*pl*: ~**es**): **to have a ~ (at)** essayer (de faire); **to be on the ~** être en mouvement; **whose ~ is it?** à qui est-ce de jouer?; **to ~ by car/on foot** aller en voiture/à pied; **he's ~ing to do** il va faire, il est sur le point de faire; **to ~ for a walk** aller se promener; **to ~ dancing/shopping** aller danser/faire les courses; **to ~ looking for sb/sth** aller *or* partir à la recherche de qn/qch; **to ~ to sleep** s'endormir; **to ~ and see sb, to ~ to see sb** aller voir qn; **how is it ~ing?** comment ça marche?; **how did it ~?** comment est-ce que ça s'est passé?; **to ~ round the back/by the shop** passer par derrière/devant le magasin; **my voice has gone** j'ai une extinction de voix; **the cake is all gone** il n'y a plus de gâteau; **I'll take whatever is ~ing** (*BRIT*) je prendrai ce qu'il y a (*or* ce que vous avez); **... to ~** (*US*: *food*) ... à emporter.

▶**go about** *vi* (*also*: ~ **around**) aller çà et là; (: *rumour*) se répandre ♦ *vt fus*: **how do I ~ about this?** comment dois-je m'y prendre (pour faire ceci)?; **to ~ about one's business** s'occuper de ses affaires.

▶**go after** *vt fus* (*pursue*) poursuivre, courir après; (*job, record etc*) essayer d'obtenir.

▶**go against** *vt fus* (*be unfavourable to*) être défavorable à; (*be contrary to*) être contraire à.

▶**go ahead** *vi* (*make progress*) avancer; (*get going*) y aller.

▶**go along** *vi* aller, avancer ♦ *vt fus* longer, parcourir; **as you ~** (*with your work*) au fur et à mesure (de votre travail); **to ~ along with** (*accompany*) accompagner; (*agree with: idea*) être d'accord sur; (: *person*) suivre.

▶**go away** *vi* partir, s'en aller.

▶**go back** *vi* rentrer; revenir; (*go again*) retourner.

▶**go back on** *vt fus* (*promise*) revenir sur.

▶**go by** *vi* (*years, time*) passer, s'écouler ♦ *vt fus* s'en tenir à; (*believe*) en croire.

▶**go down** *vi* descendre; (*ship*) couler; (*sun*) se coucher ♦ *vt fus* descendre; **that should ~ down well with him** (*fig*) ça devrait lui plaire.

▶**go for** *vt fus* (*fetch*) aller chercher; (*like*) aimer; (*attack*) s'en prendre à; attaquer.

▶**go in** *vi* entrer.

▶**go in for** *vt fus* (*competition*) se présenter à; (*like*) aimer.

▶**go into** *vt fus* entrer dans; (*investigate*) étudier, examiner; (*embark on*) se lancer dans.

▶**go off** *vi* partir, s'en aller; (*food*) se gâter; (*bomb*) sauter; (*lights etc*) s'éteindre; (*event*) se dérouler ♦ *vt fus* ne plus aimer, ne plus avoir envie de; **the gun went off** le coup est parti; **to ~ off to sleep** s'endormir; **the party went off well** la fête s'est bien passée *or* était très réussie.

▶**go on** *vi* continuer; (*happen*) se passer; (*lights*) s'allumer ♦ *vt fus* (*be guided by: evidence etc*) se fonder sur; **to ~ on doing** continuer à faire; **what's ~ing on here?** qu'est-ce qui se passe ici?

▶**go on at** *vt fus* (*nag*) tomber sur le dos de qn.

▶**go on with** *vt fus* poursuivre, continuer.

▶**go out** *vi* sortir; (*fire, light*) s'éteindre; (*tide*) descendre; **to ~ out with sb** sortir avec qn.

▶**go over** *vi* (*ship*) chavirer ♦ *vt fus* (*check*) revoir, vérifier; **to ~ over sth in one's mind** repasser qch dans son esprit.

▶**go round** *vi* (*circulate: news, rumour*) circuler; (*revolve*) tourner; (*visit*): **to ~ round to sb's** passer chez qn; aller chez qn; (*make a detour*): **to ~ round (by)** faire un détour (par); (*suffice*) suffire (pour tout le monde).

▶**go through** *vt fus* (*town etc*) traverser; (*search through*) fouiller; (*examine: list, book*) lire *or* regarder en détail, éplucher; (*perform: lesson*) réciter; (: *formalities*) remplir; (: *programme*) exécuter.

▶**go through with** *vt fus* (*plan, crime*) aller jusqu'au bout de.

▶**go under** *vi* (*sink: also fig*) couler; (: *person*) succomber.

▶**go up** *vi* monter; (*price*) augmenter ♦ *vt fus* gravir; **to ~ up in flames** flamber, s'enflammer brusquement.

▶**go without** *vt fus* se passer de.

goad [gəud] *vt* aiguillonner.

go-ahead [ˈgəuəhɛd] *adj* dynamique, entreprenant(e) ♦ *n* feu vert.

goal [gəul] *n* but *m*.

goal difference *n* différence *f* de buts.

goalie [ˈgəulɪ] *n* (*col*) goal *m*.

goalkeeper ['gəʊkiːpə*] n gardien m de but.
goal post n poteau m de but.
goat [gəʊt] n chèvre f.
gobble ['gɔbl] vt (also: ~ **down**, ~ **up**)
engloutir.
go-between ['gəʊbɪtwiːn] n médiateur m.
Gobi Desert ['gəʊbɪ-] n désert m de Gobi.
goblet ['gɔblɪt] n goblet m.
goblin ['gɔblɪn] n lutin m.
go-cart ['gəʊkɑːt] n kart m ♦ cpd: ~ **racing** n
karting m.
god [gɔd] n dieu m; **G~** Dieu.
god-awful [gɔd'ɔːfəl] adj (col) franchement
atroce.
godchild ['gɔdtʃaɪld] n filleul/e.
goddamn(ed) ['gɔddæm(d)] excl (esp US col):
goddamn (it)! nom de Dieu! ♦ adj satané(e),
sacré(e) ♦ adv sacrément.
goddaughter ['gɔddɔːtə*] n filleule f.
goddess ['gɔdɪs] n déesse f.
godfather ['gɔdfɑːðə*] n parrain m.
god-fearing ['gɔdfɪərɪŋ] adj croyant(e).
god-forsaken ['gɔdfəseɪkən] adj maudit(e).
godmother ['gɔdmʌðə*] n marraine f.
godparents ['gɔdpɛərənts] npl: **the** ~ le
parrain et la marraine.
godsend ['gɔdsɛnd] n aubaine f.
godson ['gɔdsʌn] n filleul m.
goes [gəʊz] vb see **go**.
gofer ['gəʊfə*] n coursier/ière.
go-getter ['gəʊgɛtə*] n arriviste m/f.
goggle ['gɔgl] vi: **to** ~ **at** regarder avec des
yeux ronds.
goggles ['gɔglz] npl lunettes (protectrices)
(de motocycliste etc).
going ['gəʊɪŋ] n (conditions) état m du terrain
♦ adj: **the** ~ **rate** le tarif (en vigueur); **a** ~
concern une affaire prospère; **it was slow** ~
les progrès étaient lents, ça n'avançait pas
vite.
going-over [gəʊɪŋ'əʊvə*] n vérification f,
révision f; (col: beating) passage m à tabac.
goings-on ['gəʊɪŋz'ɔn] npl (col) manigances
fpl.
go-kart ['gəʊkɑːt] n = **go-cart**.
gold [gəʊld] n or m ♦ adj en or; (reserves) d'or.
golden ['gəʊldən] adj (made of gold) en or;
(gold in colour) doré(e).
golden age n âge m d'or.
golden handshake n (BRIT) prime f de
départ.
golden rule n règle f d'or.
goldfish ['gəʊldfɪʃ] n poisson m rouge.
gold leaf n or m en feuille.
gold medal n (SPORT) médaille f d'or.
goldmine ['gəʊldmaɪn] n mine f d'or.
gold-plated ['gəʊld'pleɪtɪd] adj plaqué(e) or
inv.
goldsmith ['gəʊldsmɪθ] n orfèvre m.
gold standard n étalon-or m.
golf [gɔlf] n golf m.
golf ball n balle f de golf; (on typewriter)

boule f.
golf club n club m de golf; (stick) club m,
crosse f de golf.
golf course n terrain m de golf.
golfer ['gɔlfə*] n joueur/euse de golf.
golfing ['gɔlfɪŋ] n golf m.
gondola ['gɔndələ] n gondole f.
gondolier [gɔndə'lɪə*] n gondolier m.
gone [gɔn] pp of **go** ♦ adj parti(e).
goner ['gɔnə*] n (col): **to be a** ~ être fichu(e)
or foutu(e).
gong [gɔŋ] n gong m.
good [gʊd] adj bon(ne); (kind) gentil(le);
(child) sage ♦ n bien m; ~! bon!, très bien!; **to
be** ~ **at** être bon en; **it's** ~ **for you** c'est bon
pour vous; **it's a** ~ **thing you were there**
heureusement que vous étiez là; **she is** ~
with children/her hands elle sait bien
s'occuper des enfants/sait se servir de ses
mains; **to feel** ~ se sentir bien; **it's** ~ **to see
you** ça me fait plaisir de vous voir, je suis
content de vous voir; **he's up to no** ~ il
prépare quelque mauvais coup; **it's no** ~
complaining cela ne sert à rien de se
plaindre; **for the common** ~ dans l'intérêt
commun; **for** ~ (for ever) pour de bon, une
fois pour toutes; **would you be** ~ **enough to
...?** auriez-vous la bonté or l'amabilité de
...?; **that's very** ~ **of you** c'est très gentil de
votre part; **is this any** ~? (will it do?) est-ce
que ceci fera l'affaire?; (what's it like?) qu'est-ce
que cela peut vous rendre service?; (what's it like?) qu'est-
ce que ça vaut?; **a** ~ **deal (of)** beaucoup (de);
a ~ **many** beaucoup (de); ~ **morning/
afternoon!** bonjour!; ~ **evening!** bonsoir!; ~
night! bonsoir!; (on going to bed) bonne nuit!
goodbye [gʊd'baɪ] excl au revoir!; **to say** ~ **to**
dire au revoir à.
good faith n bonne foi.
good-for-nothing ['gʊdfənʌθɪŋ] adj bon(ne)
or propre à rien.
Good Friday n Vendredi saint.
good-humoured ['gʊd'hjuːməd] adj (person)
jovial(e); (remark, joke) sans malice.
good-looking ['gʊd'lʊkɪŋ] adj bien inv.
good-natured ['gʊd'neɪtʃəd] adj (person) qui a
un bon naturel; (discussion) enjoué(e).
goodness ['gʊdnɪs] n (of person) bonté f; **for** ~
sake! je vous en prie!; ~ **gracious!** mon
Dieu!
goods [gʊdz] npl marchandise f, articles mpl;
(COMM etc) marchandises; ~ **and chattels**
biens mpl et effets mpl.
goods train n (BRIT) train m de
marchandises.
goodwill [gʊd'wɪl] n bonne volonté; (COMM)
réputation f (auprès de la clientèle).
goody-goody ['gʊdɪgʊdɪ] n (pej) petit saint,
sainte nitouche.
gooey ['guːɪ] adj (BRIT col) gluant(e).
goose, pl geese [guːs, giːs] n oie f.
gooseberry ['gʊzbərɪ] n groseille f à

maquereau; **to play** ~ (*BRIT*) tenir la chandelle.

gooseflesh ['guːsfleʃ] *n*, **goosepimples** ['guːspɪmplz] *npl* chair *f* de poule.

goose step *n* (*MIL*) pas *m* de l'oie.

GOP *n abbr* (*US POL*: *col*: = Grand Old Party) parti républicain.

gopher ['gəʊfə*] *n* = **gofer**.

gore [gɔː*] *vt* encorner ♦ *n* sang *m*.

gorge [gɔːdʒ] *n* gorge *f* ♦ *vt*: **to** ~ **o.s. (on)** se gorger (de).

gorgeous ['gɔːdʒəs] *adj* splendide, superbe.

gorilla [gə'rɪlə] *n* gorille *m*.

gormless ['gɔːmlɪs] *adj* (*BRIT col*) lourdaud(e).

gorse [gɔːs] *n* ajoncs *mpl*.

gory ['gɔːrɪ] *adj* sanglant(e).

go-slow ['gəʊ'sləʊ] *n* (*BRIT*) grève perlée.

gospel ['gɔspl] *n* évangile *m*.

gossamer ['gɔsəmə*] *n* (*cobweb*) fils *mpl* de la vierge; (*light fabric*) étoffe très légère.

gossip ['gɔsɪp] *n* bavardages *mpl*; (*malicious*) commérage *m*, cancans *mpl*; (*person*) commère *f* ♦ *vi* bavarder; cancaner, faire des commérages; **a piece of** ~ un ragot, un racontar.

gossip column *n* (*PRESS*) échos *mpl*.

got [gɔt] *pt, pp of* **get**.

Gothic ['gɔθɪk] *adj* gothique.

gotten ['gɔtn] (*US*) *pp of* **get**.

gouge [gaʊdʒ] *vt* (*also*: ~ **out**: *hole etc*) évider; (: *initials*) tailler; **to** ~ **sb's eyes out** crever les yeux à qn.

gourd [gʊəd] *n* calebasse *f*, gourde *f*.

gourmet ['gʊəmeɪ] *n* gourmet *m*, gastronome *m/f*.

gout [gaʊt] *n* goutte *f*.

govern ['gʌvən] *vt* (*gen, LING*) gouverner.

governess ['gʌvənɪs] *n* gouvernante *f*.

governing ['gʌvənɪŋ] *adj* (*POL*) au pouvoir, au gouvernement; ~ **body** conseil *m* d'administration.

government ['gʌvnmənt] *n* gouvernement *m*; (*BRIT*: *ministers*) ministère *m* ♦ *cpd* de l'État; **local** ~ administration locale.

governmental [gʌvn'mentl] *adj* gouvernemental(e).

government housing *n* (*US*) logements sociaux.

government stock *n* titres *mpl* d'État.

governor ['gʌvənə*] *n* (*of colony, state, bank*) gouverneur *m*; (*of school, hospital etc*) administrateur/trice; (*BRIT*: *of prison*) directeur/trice.

Govt *abbr* (= **government**) gvt.

gown [gaʊn] *n* robe *f*; (*of teacher; BRIT*: *of judge*) toge *f*.

GP *n abbr* (*MED*) = **general practitioner**.

GPMU *n abbr* (*BRIT*) = Graphical, Paper and Media Union.

GPO *n abbr* (*BRIT*: *old*) = General Post Office; (*US*) = Government Printing Office.

gr. *abbr* (*COMM*) = **gross**.

grab [græb] *vt* saisir, empoigner; (*property, power*) se saisir de ♦ *vi*: **to** ~ **at** essayer de saisir.

grace [greɪs] *n* grâce *f* ♦ *vt* honorer; **5 days'** ~ répit *m* de 5 jours; **to say** ~ dire le bénédicité; (*after meal*) dire les grâces; **with a good/bad** ~ de bonne/mauvaise grâce; **his sense of humour is his saving** ~ il se rachète par son sens de l'humour.

graceful ['greɪsful] *adj* gracieux(euse), élégant(e).

gracious ['greɪʃəs] *adj* (*kind*) charmant(e), bienveillant(e); (*elegant*) plein(e) d'élégance, d'une grande élégance; (*formal: pardon etc*) miséricordieux(euse) ♦ *excl*: **(good)** ~! mon Dieu!

gradation [grə'deɪʃən] *n* gradation *f*.

grade [greɪd] *n* (*COMM*) qualité *f*; calibre *m*; catégorie *f*; (*in hierarchy*) grade *m*, échelon *m*; (*US: SCOL*) note *f*, classe *f*; (: *gradient*) pente *f* ♦ *vt* classer; calibrer; graduer; **to make the** ~ (*fig*) réussir.

grade crossing *n* (*US*) passage *m* à niveau.

grade school *n* (*US*) école *f* primaire.

gradient ['greɪdɪənt] *n* inclinaison *f*, pente *f*; (*GEOM*) gradient *m*.

gradual ['grædjuəl] *adj* graduel(le), progressif(ive).

gradually ['grædjuəlɪ] *adv* peu à peu, graduellement.

graduate *n* ['grædjuɪt] diplômé/e d'université (*US*) diplômé/e de fin d'études ♦ *vi* ['grædjueɪt] obtenir un diplôme d'université (*or de fin d'études*).

graduated pension ['grædjueɪtɪd-] *n* retraite calculée en fonction des derniers salaires.

graduation [grædju'eɪʃən] *n* cérémonie *f* de remise des diplômes.

graffiti [grə'fiːtɪ] *npl* graffiti *mpl*.

graft [grɑːft] *n* (*AGR, MED*) greffe *f*; (*bribery*) corruption *f* ♦ *vt* greffer; **hard** ~ (*col*) boulot acharné.

grain [greɪn] *n* grain *m*; (*no pl: cereals*) céréale *fpl*; (*US: corn*) blé *m*; **it goes against the** ~ cela va à l'encontre de sa (*or ma etc*) nature.

gram [græm] *n* gramme *m*.

grammar ['græmə*] *n* grammaire *f*.

grammar school *n* (*BRIT*) ≈ lycée *m*.

grammatical [grə'mætɪkl] *adj* grammatical(e)

gramme [græm] *n* = **gram**.

gramophone ['græməfəʊn] *n* (*BRIT*) gramophone *m*.

granary ['grænərɪ] *n* grenier *m*.

grand [grænd] *adj* splendide, imposant(e); (*terrific*) magnifique, formidable; (*also humorous: gesture etc*) noble ♦ *n* (*col: thousand*) mille livres *fpl* (*or dollars mpl*).

grandchildren ['græntʃɪldrən] *npl* petits-enfants *mpl*.

granddad ['grændæd] *n* grand-papa *m*.

granddaughter ['grændɔːtə*] *n* petite-fille *f*.

grandeur ['grændjə*] n magnificence f, splendeur f; (of position etc) éminence f.
grandfather ['grændfɑːðə*] n grand-père m.
grandiose ['grændɪəus] adj grandiose; (pej) pompeux(euse).
grand jury n (US) jury m d'accusation (formé de 12 à 23 jurés).
grandma ['grænmɑː] n grand-maman f.
grandmother ['grænmʌðə*] n grand-mère f.
grandpa ['grænpɑː] n = granddad.
grandparent ['grændpɛərənt] n grand-père/grand-mère.
grand piano n piano m à queue.
Grand Prix ['grɑ̃ːˈpriː] n (AUT) grand prix automobile.
grandson ['grænsʌn] n petit-fils m.
grandstand ['grændstænd] n (SPORT) tribune f.
grand total n total général.
granite ['grænɪt] n granit m.
granny ['grænɪ] n grand-maman f.
grant [grɑːnt] vt accorder; (a request) accéder à; (admit) concéder ♦ n (SCOL) bourse f; (ADMIN) subside m, subvention f; **to take sth for ~ed** considérer qch comme acquis; **to ~ that** admettre que.
granulated ['grænjuleɪtɪd] adj: **~ sugar** sucre m en poudre.
granule ['grænjuːl] n granule m.
grape [greɪp] n raisin m; **a bunch of ~s** une grappe de raisin.
grapefruit ['greɪpfruːt] n pamplemousse m.
grapevine ['greɪpvaɪn] n vigne f; **I heard it on the ~** (fig) je l'ai appris par le téléphone arabe.
graph [grɑːf] n graphique m, courbe f.
graphic ['græfɪk] adj graphique; (vivid) vivant(e).
graphic designer n graphiste m/f.
graphic equalizer n égaliseur m graphique.
graphics ['græfɪks] n (art) arts mpl graphiques; (process) graphisme m; (pl: drawings) illustrations fpl.
graphite ['græfaɪt] n graphite m.
graph paper n papier millimétré.
grapple ['græpl] vi: **to ~ with** être aux prises avec.
grappling iron ['græplɪŋ-] n (NAUT) grappin m.
rasp [grɑːsp] vt saisir, empoigner; (understand) saisir, comprendre ♦ n (grip) prise f; (fig) compréhension f, connaissance f; **to have sth within one's ~** avoir qch à sa portée; **to have a good ~ of sth** (fig) bien comprendre qch.
grasp at vt fus (rope etc) essayer de saisir; (fig: opportunity) sauter sur.
rasping ['grɑːspɪŋ] adj avide.
rass [grɑːs] n herbe f; (BRIT col: informer) mouchard/e; (: ex-terrorist) balanceur/euse.
rasshopper ['grɑːshɔpə*] n sauterelle f.
rassland ['grɑːslænd] n prairie f.
rass roots npl (fig) base f.

grass snake n couleuvre f.
grassy ['grɑːsɪ] adj herbeux(euse).
grate [greɪt] n grille f de cheminée ♦ vi grincer ♦ vt (CULIN) râper.
grateful ['greɪtful] adj reconnaissant(e).
gratefully ['greɪtfəlɪ] adv avec reconnaissance.
grater ['greɪtə*] n râpe f.
gratification [grætɪfɪˈkeɪʃən] n satisfaction f.
gratify ['grætɪfaɪ] vt faire plaisir à; (whim) satisfaire.
gratifying ['grætɪfaɪɪŋ] adj agréable; satisfaisant(e).
grating ['greɪtɪŋ] n (iron bars) grille f ♦ adj (noise) grinçant(e).
gratitude ['grætɪtjuːd] n gratitude f.
gratuitous [grəˈtjuːɪtəs] adj gratuit(e).
gratuity [grəˈtjuːɪtɪ] n pourboire m.
grave [greɪv] n tombe f ♦ adj grave, sérieux(euse).
gravedigger ['greɪvdɪgə*] n fossoyeur m.
gravel ['grævl] n gravier m.
gravely ['greɪvlɪ] adv gravement, sérieusement; **~ ill** gravement malade.
gravestone ['greɪvstəun] n pierre tombale.
graveyard ['greɪvjɑːd] n cimetière m.
gravitate ['græviteɪt] vi graviter.
gravity ['grævɪtɪ] n (PHYSICS) gravité f; pesanteur f; (seriousness) gravité, sérieux m.
gravy ['greɪvɪ] n jus m (de viande); sauce f (au jus de viande).
gravy boat n saucière f.
gravy train n (col): **to ride the ~** avoir une bonne planque.
gray [greɪ] adj (US) = grey.
graze [greɪz] vi paître, brouter ♦ vt (touch lightly) frôler, effleurer; (scrape) écorcher ♦ n écorchure f.
grazing ['greɪzɪŋ] n (pasture) pâturage m.
grease [griːs] n (fat) graisse f; (lubricant) lubrifiant m ♦ vt graisser; lubrifier; **to ~ the skids** (US: fig) huiler les rouages.
grease gun n graisseur m.
greasepaint ['griːspeɪnt] n produits mpl de maquillage.
greaseproof paper ['griːspruːf-] n (BRIT) papier sulfurisé.
greasy ['griːsɪ] adj gras(se), graisseux(euse); (hands, clothes) graisseux; (BRIT: road, surface) glissant(e).
great [greɪt] adj grand(e); (heat, pain etc) très fort(e), intense; (col) formidable; **they're ~ friends** ils sont très amis, ce sont de grands amis; **we had a ~ time** nous nous sommes bien amusés; **it was ~!** c'était fantastique or super!; **the ~ thing is that ...** ce qu'il y a de vraiment bien c'est que ...
Great Barrier Reef n: **the ~** la Grande Barrière.
Great Britain n Grande-Bretagne f.
great-grandchild, pl **-children** [greɪtˈgræntʃaɪld, -tʃɪldrən] n arrière-petit(e)-

enfant.

great-grandfather [greɪt'grænfɑːðə*] *n* arrière-grand-père *m*.

great-grandmother [greɪt'grænmʌðə*] *n* arrière-grand-mère *f*.

Great Lakes *npl*: **the ~** les Grands Lacs.

greatly ['greɪtlɪ] *adv* très, grandement; (*with verbs*) beaucoup.

greatness ['greɪtnɪs] *n* grandeur *f*.

Grecian ['griːʃən] *adj* grec(grecque).

Greece [griːs] *n* Grèce *f*.

greed [griːd] *n* (*also*: **~iness**) avidité *f*; (*for food*) gourmandise *f*.

greedily ['griːdɪlɪ] *adv* avidement; avec gourmandise.

greedy ['griːdɪ] *adj* avide; gourmand(e).

Greek [griːk] *adj* grec(grecque) ♦ *n* Grec/ Grecque; (*LING*) grec *m*; **ancient/modern ~** grec classique/moderne.

green [griːn] *adj* vert(e); (*inexperienced*) (bien) jeune, naïf(ïve); (*ecological: product etc*) écologique ♦ *n* (*colour, of golf course*) vert *m*; (*stretch of grass*) pelouse *f*; (*also*: **village ~**) ≈ place *f* du village; **~s** *npl* légumes verts; **to have ~ fingers** *or* (*US*) **a ~ thumb** (*fig*) avoir le pouce vert; **G~** (*POL*) écologiste (*m/f*); **the G~ Party** le parti écologiste.

green belt *n* (*round town*) ceinture verte.

green card *n* (*AUT*) carte verte.

greenery ['griːnərɪ] *n* verdure *f*.

greenfly ['griːnflaɪ] *n* (*BRIT*) puceron *m*.

greengage ['griːngeɪdʒ] *n* reine-claude *f*.

greengrocer ['griːngrəusə*] *n* (*BRIT*) marchand *m* de fruits et légumes.

greenhouse ['griːnhaus] *n* serre *f*.

greenhouse effect *n*: **the ~** l'effet *m* de serre.

greenhouse gas *n* gaz *m* contribuant à l'effet de serre.

greenish ['griːnɪʃ] *adj* verdâtre.

Greenland ['griːnlənd] *n* Groenland *m*.

Greenlander ['griːnləndə*] *n* Groenlandais/e.

green light *n*: **to give sb/sth the ~** donner le feu vert à qn/qch.

green pepper *n* poivron (vert).

green pound *n* (*ECON*) livre verte.

greet [griːt] *vt* accueillir.

greeting ['griːtɪŋ] *n* salutation *f*; **Christmas/ birthday ~s** souhaits *mpl* de Noël/de bon anniversaire.

greeting(s) card *n* carte *f* de vœux.

gregarious [grə'gɛərɪəs] *adj* grégaire; sociable.

grenade [grə'neɪd] *n* (*also*: **hand ~**) grenade *f*.

grew [gruː] *pt of* **grow**.

grey [greɪ] *adj* gris(e); (*dismal*) sombre; **to go ~** (commencer à) grisonner.

grey-haired [greɪ'hɛəd] *adj* aux cheveux gris.

greyhound ['greɪhaund] *n* lévrier *m*.

grid [grɪd] *n* grille *f*; (*ELEC*) réseau *m*; (*US AUT*) intersection *f* (*matérialisée par des marques au sol*).

griddle [grɪdl] *n* (*on cooker*) plaque chauffante.

gridiron ['grɪdaɪən] *n* gril *m*.

gridlock ['grɪdlɔk] *n* (*traffic jam*) embouteillage *m*.

grief [griːf] *n* chagrin *m*, douleur *f*; **to come to ~** (*plan*) échouer; (*person*) avoir un malheur.

grievance ['griːvəns] *n* doléance *f*, grief *m*; (*cause for complaint*) grief.

grieve [griːv] *vi* avoir du chagrin; se désoler ♦ *vt* faire de la peine à, affliger; **to ~ at** se désoler de; pleurer.

grievous ['griːvəs] *adj* grave; cruel(le); **~ bodily harm** (*LAW*) coups *mpl* et blessures *fpl*.

grill [grɪl] *n* (*on cooker*) gril *m* ♦ *vt* (*BRIT*) griller; (*question*) interroger longuement, cuisiner.

grille [grɪl] *n* grillage *m*; (*AUT*) calandre *f*.

grill(room) ['grɪl(rum)] *n* rôtisserie *f*.

grim [grɪm] *adj* sinistre, lugubre.

grimace [grɪ'meɪs] *n* grimace *f* ♦ *vi* grimacer, faire une grimace.

grime [graɪm] *n* crasse *f*.

grimy ['graɪmɪ] *adj* crasseux(euse).

grin [grɪn] *n* large sourire *m* ♦ *vi* sourire; **to ~ (at)** faire un grand sourire (à).

grind [graɪnd] *vb* (*pt, pp* **ground** [graund]) *vt* écraser; (*coffee, pepper etc*) moudre; (*US: meat*) hacher; (*make sharp*) aiguiser; (*polish: gem, lens*) polir ♦ *vi* (*car gears*) grincer ♦ *n* (*work*) corvée *f*; **to ~ one's teeth** grincer des dents; **to ~ to a halt** (*vehicle*) s'arrêter dans un grincement de freins; (*fig*) s'arrêter, s'immobiliser; **the daily ~** (*col*) le train-train quotidien.

grinder ['graɪndə*] *n* (*machine: for coffee*) moulin *m* (à café); (: *for waste disposal etc*) broyeur *m*.

grindstone ['graɪndstəun] *n*: **to keep one's nose to the ~** travailler sans relâche.

grip [grɪp] *n* (*control, grasp*) étreinte *f*; (*hold*) prise *f*; (*handle*) poignée *f*; (*holdall*) sac *m* de voyage ♦ *vt* saisir, empoigner; étreindre; **to come to ~s with** se colleter avec, en venir aux prises avec; **to ~ the road** (*AUT*) adhérer à la route; **to lose one's ~** lâcher prise; (*fig*) perdre les pédales, être dépassé(e).

gripe [graɪp] *n* (*MED*) coliques *fpl*; (*col: complaint*) ronchonnement *m*, rouspétance *f* ♦ *vi* (*col*) râler.

gripping ['grɪpɪŋ] *adj* prenant(e), palpitant(e).

grisly ['grɪzlɪ] *adj* sinistre, macabre.

grist [grɪst] *n* (*fig*): **it's (all) ~ to his mill** ça l'arrange, ça apporte de l'eau à son moulin.

gristle ['grɪsl] *n* cartilage *m* (*de poulet etc*).

grit [grɪt] *n* gravillon *m*; (*courage*) cran *m* ♦ *vt* (*road*) sabler; **to ~ one's teeth** serrer les dents; **to have a piece of ~ in one's eye** avoir une poussière *or* saleté dans l'œil.

grits [grɪts] *npl* (*US*) gruau *m* de maïs.

grizzle ['grɪzl] *vi* (*BRIT*) pleurnicher.

grizzly ['grɪzlɪ] *n* (*also*: **~ bear**) grizzli *m*, ours gris.

roan [grəun] n gémissement m; grognement m ♦ vi gémir; grogner.

rocer ['grəusə*] n épicier m; **at the ~'s** à l'épicerie, chez l'épicier.

roceries ['grəusəriz] npl provisions fpl.

rocery ['grəusəri] n (shop) épicerie f.

rog [grɔg] n grog m.

roggy ['grɔgi] adj groggy inv.

roin [grɔin] n aine f.

room [gru:m] n palefrenier m; (also: **bride~**) marié m ♦ vt (horse) panser; (fig): **to ~ sb for** former qn pour.

roove [gru:v] n sillon m, rainure f.

rope [grəup] vi tâtonner; **to ~ for** vt fus chercher à tâtons.

ross [grəus] adj grossier(ière); (COMM) brut(e) ♦ n (pl inv) (twelve dozen) grosse f ♦ vt (COMM): **to ~ £500,000** gagner 500 000 livres avant impôt.

ross domestic product (GDP) n produit brut intérieur (PIB).

rossly ['grəusli] adv (greatly) très, grandement.

ross national product (GNP) n produit national brut (PNB).

rotesque [grə'tɛsk] adj grotesque.

rotto ['grɔtəu] n grotte f.

rotty ['grɔti] adj (BRIT col) minable.

rouch [grautʃ] (col) vi rouspéter ♦ n (person) rouspéteur/euse.

round [graund] pt, pp of grind ♦ n sol m, terre f; (land) terrain m, terres fpl; (SPORT) terrain; (reason: gen pl) raison f; (US: also: **~ wire**) terre f ♦ vt (plane) empêcher de décoller, retenir au sol; (US ELEC) équiper d'une prise de terre, mettre à la terre ♦ vi (ship) s'échouer ♦ adj (coffee etc) moulu(e); (US: meat) haché(e); **~s** npl (gardens etc) parc m, domaine m; (of coffee) marc m; **on the ~,** to the **~** par terre; **below ~** sous terre; **to gain/lose ~** gagner/perdre du terrain; **common ~** terrain d'entente; **he covered a lot of ~ in his lecture** sa conférence a traité un grand nombre de questions or la question en profondeur.

ound cloth n (US) = **groundsheet**.

ound control n (AVIAT, SPACE) centre m de contrôle (au sol).

ound floor n (BRIT) rez-de-chaussée m.

ounding ['graundiŋ] n (in education) connaissances fpl de base.

oundless ['graundlis] adj sans fondement.

oundnut ['graundnʌt] n arachide f.

ound rent n (BRIT) fermage m.

ound rules npl: **the ~** les principes mpl de base.

oundsheet ['graundʃi:t] n (BRIT) tapis m de sol.

oundsman ['graundzmən], (US)

groundskeeper ['graundzki:pə*] n (SPORT) gardien m de stade.

ground staff n équipage m au sol.

groundswell ['graundswɛl] n lame f or vague f de fond.

ground-to-air ['grauntu'ɛə*] adj (MIL) sol-air inv.

ground-to-ground ['grauntə'graund] adj (MIL) sol-sol inv.

groundwork ['graundwə:k] n préparation f.

group [gru:p] n groupe m ♦ vt (also: ~ **together**) grouper ♦ vi (also: ~ **together**) se grouper.

groupie ['gru:pi] n groupie f.

group therapy n thérapie f de groupe.

grouse [graus] n (pl inv) (bird) grouse f (sorte de coq de bruyère) ♦ vi (complain) rouspéter, râler.

grove [grəuv] n bosquet m.

grovel ['grɔvl] vi (fig): **to ~ (before)** ramper (devant).

grow, pt **grew,** pp **grown** [grəu, gru:, grəun] vi (plant) pousser, croître; (person) grandir; (increase) augmenter, se développer; (become): **to ~ rich/weak** s'enrichir/s'affaiblir ♦ vt cultiver, faire pousser.
▶**grow apart** vi (fig) se détacher (l'un de l'autre).
▶**grow away from** vt fus (fig) s'éloigner de.
▶**grow on** vt fus: **that painting is ~ing on me** je finirai par aimer ce tableau.
▶**grow out of** vt fus (clothes) devenir trop grand pour; (habit) perdre (avec le temps); **he'll ~ out of it** ça lui passera.
▶**grow up** vi grandir.

grower ['grəuə*] n producteur m; (AGR) cultivateur/trice.

growing ['grəuiŋ] adj (fear, amount) croissant(e), grandissant(e); **~ pains** (MED) fièvre f de croissance; (fig) difficultés fpl de croissance.

growing pains npl (fig) difficultés fpl de croissance.

growl [graul] vi grogner.

grown [grəun] pp of **grow** ♦ adj adulte.

grown-up [grəun'ʌp] n adulte m/f, grande personne.

growth [grəuθ] n croissance f, développement m; (what has grown) pousse f; poussée f; (MED) grosseur f, tumeur f.

growth rate n taux m de croissance.

GRSM n abbr (BRIT) = Graduate of the Royal Schools of Music.

grub [grʌb] n larve f; (col: food) bouffe f.

grubby ['grʌbi] adj crasseux(euse).

grudge [grʌdʒ] n rancune f ♦ vt: **to ~ sb sth** donner qch à qn à contre-cœur; reprocher qch à qn; **to bear sb a ~ (for)** garder rancune or en vouloir à qn (de); **he ~s spending** il rechigne à dépenser.

grudgingly ['grʌdʒiŋli] adv à contre-cœur, de mauvaise grâce.

gruelling ['gruəliŋ] adj exténuant(e).

gruesome ['gru:səm] adj horrible.

gruff [grʌf] *adj* bourru(e).

grumble ['grʌmbl] *vi* rouspéter, ronchonner.

grumpy ['grʌmpɪ] *adj* grincheux(euse).

grunge [grʌndʒ] *n* (*MUS, style*) grunge *m*.

grunt [grʌnt] *vi* grogner ♦ *n* grognement *m*.

G-string ['dʒiːstrɪŋ] *n* (*garment*) cache-sexe *m inv*.

GSUSA *n abbr* = *Girl Scouts of the United States of America.*

GU *abbr* (*US*) = *Guam.*

guarantee [gærən'tiː] *n* garantie *f* ♦ *vt* garantir; **he can't ~ (that) he'll come** il n'est pas absolument certain de pouvoir venir.

guarantor [gærən'tɔː*] *n* garant/e.

guard [gɑːd] *n* garde *f*, surveillance *f*; (*squad, BOXING, FENCING*) garde *f*; (*one man*) garde *m*; (*BRIT RAIL*) chef *m* de train; (*safety device: on machine*) dispositif *m* de sûreté; (*also:* **fire~**) garde-feu *m inv* ♦ *vt* garder, surveiller; (*protect*): **to ~ (against or from)** protéger (contre); **to be on one's ~** (*fig*) être sur ses gardes.

▶**guard against** *vi*: **to ~ against doing sth** se garder de faire qch.

guard dog *n* chien *m* de garde.

guarded ['gɑːdɪd] *adj* (*fig*) prudent(e).

guardian ['gɑːdɪən] *n* gardien/ne; (*of minor*) tuteur/trice.

guard's van ['gɑːdz-] *n* (*BRIT RAIL*) fourgon *m*.

Guatemala [gwɑːtɪ'mɑːlə] *n* Guatémala *m*.

Guernsey ['gɜːnzɪ] *n* Guernesey *m or f*.

guerrilla [gə'rɪlə] *n* guérillero *m*.

guerrilla warfare *n* guérilla *f*.

guess [gɛs] *vi* deviner ♦ *vt* deviner; (*US*) croire, penser ♦ *n* supposition *f*, hypothèse *f*; **to take or have a ~** essayer de deviner; **to keep sb ~ing** laisser qn dans le doute or l'incertitude, tenir qn en haleine.

guesstimate ['gɛstɪmɪt] *n* (*col*) estimation *f*.

guesswork ['gɛswɜːk] *n* hypothèse *f*, **I got the answer by ~** j'ai deviné la réponse.

guest [gɛst] *n* invité/e; (*in hotel*) client/e; **be my ~** faites comme chez vous.

guest-house ['gɛsthaus] *n* pension *f*.

guest room *n* chambre *f* d'amis.

guff [gʌf] *n* (*col*) bêtises *fpl*.

guffaw [gʌ'fɔː] *n* gros rire ♦ *vi* pouffer de rire.

guidance ['gaɪdəns] *n* conseils *mpl*; **under the ~ of** conseillé(e) or encadré(e) par, sous la conduite de; **vocational ~** orientation professionnelle; **marriage ~** conseils conjugaux.

guide [gaɪd] *n* (*person, book etc*) guide *m*; (*also:* **girl ~**) guide *f* ♦ *vt* guider; **to be ~d by sb/sth** se laisser guider par qn/qch.

guidebook ['gaɪdbuk] *n* guide *m*.

guided missile ['gaɪdɪd-] *n* missile téléguidé.

guide dog *n* chien *m* d'aveugle.

guide lines *npl* (*fig*) instructions générales, conseils *mpl*.

guild [gɪld] *n* corporation *f*; cercle *m*, association *f*.

guildhall ['gɪldhɔːl] *n* (*BRIT*) hôtel *m* de ville.

guile [gaɪl] *n* astuce *f*.

guileless ['gaɪllɪs] *adj* candide.

guillotine ['gɪlətiːn] *n* guillotine *f*; (*for paper*) massicot *m*.

guilt [gɪlt] *n* culpabilité *f*.

guilty ['gɪltɪ] *adj* coupable; **to plead ~/not ~** plaider coupable/non coupable; **to feel ~ about doing sth** avoir mauvaise conscience à faire qch.

Guinea ['gɪnɪ] *n*: **Republic of ~** (République *f* de) Guinée *f*.

guinea ['gɪnɪ] *n* (*BRIT*) guinée *f* (= 21 shillings: cette monnaie de compte ne s'emploie plus).

guinea pig *n* cobaye *m*.

guise [gaɪz] *n* aspect *m*, apparence *f*.

guitar [gɪ'tɑː*] *n* guitare *f*.

guitarist [gɪ'tɑːrɪst] *n* guitariste *m/f*.

gulch [gʌltʃ] *n* (*US*) ravin *m*.

gulf [gʌlf] *n* golfe *m*; (*abyss*) gouffre *m*; **the (Persian) G~** le golfe Persique.

Gulf States *npl*: **the ~** (*in Middle East*) les pays *mpl* du Golfe.

Gulf Stream *n*: **the ~** le Gulf Stream.

gull [gʌl] *n* mouette *f*.

gullet [gʌlɪt] *n* gosier *m*.

gullibility [gʌlɪ'bɪlɪtɪ] *n* crédulité *f*.

gullible ['gʌlɪbl] *adj* crédule.

gully ['gʌlɪ] *n* ravin *m*; ravine *f*; couloir *m*.

gulp [gʌlp] *vi* avaler sa salive; (*from emotion*) avoir la gorge serrée, s'étrangler ♦ *vt* (*also:* **~ down**) avaler ♦ *n* (*of drink*) gorgée *f*; **at one ~** d'un seul coup.

gum [gʌm] *n* (*ANAT*) gencive *f*; (*glue*) colle *f*; (*sweet*) boule *f* de gomme; (*also:* **chewing-~**) chewing-gum *m* ♦ *vt* coller.

▶**gum up** *vt*: **to ~ up the works** (*col*) bousiller tout.

gumboil ['gʌmbɔɪl] *n* abcès *m* dentaire.

gumboots ['gʌmbuːts] *npl* (*BRIT*) bottes *fpl* en caoutchouc.

gumption ['gʌmpʃən] *n* bon sens, jugeote *f*.

gun [gʌn] *n* (*small*) revolver *m*, pistolet *m*; (*rifle*) fusil *m*, carabine *f*; (*cannon*) canon *m* ♦ *vt* (*also:* **~ down**) abattre; **to stick to one's ~s** (*fig*) ne pas en démordre.

gunboat ['gʌnbəut] *n* canonnière *f*.

gun dog *n* chien *m* de chasse.

gunfire ['gʌnfaɪə*] *n* fusillade *f*.

gunk [gʌŋk] *n* (*col*) saleté *f*.

gunman ['gʌnmən] *n* bandit armé.

gunner ['gʌnə*] *n* artilleur *m*.

gunpoint ['gʌnpɔɪnt] *n*: **at ~** sous la menace du pistolet (*or* fusil).

gunpowder ['gʌnpaudə*] *n* poudre *f* à canon.

gunrunner ['gʌnrʌnə*] *n* trafiquant *m* d'armes.

gunrunning ['gʌnrʌnɪŋ] *n* trafic *m* d'armes.

gunshot ['gʌnʃɔt] *n* coup *m* de feu; **within ~** portée de fusil.

gunsmith ['gʌnsmɪθ] *n* armurier *m*.

gurgle ['gəːgl] *n* gargouillis *m* ♦ *vi* gargouiller.
guru ['guruː] *n* gourou *m*.
gush [gʌʃ] *n* jaillissement *m*, jet *m* ♦ *vi* jaillir; (*fig*) se répandre en effusions.
gushing ['gʌʃɪŋ] *adj* (*person*) trop exubérant(e) *or* expansif(ive); (*compliments*) exagéré(e).
gusset ['gʌsɪt] *n* gousset *m*, soufflet *m*; (*in tights, pants*) entre-jambes *m*.
gust [gʌst] *n* (*of wind*) rafale *f*; (*of smoke*) bouffée *f*.
gusto ['gʌstəu] *n* enthousiasme *m*.
gusty ['gʌstɪ] *adj* venteux(euse); ~ **winds** des rafales de vent.
gut [gʌt] *n* intestin *m*, boyau *m*; (*MUS etc*) boyau ♦ *vt* (*poultry, fish*) vider; (*building*) ne laisser que les murs de; ~**s** *npl* boyaux *mpl*; (*col: courage*) cran *m*; **to hate sb's** ~**s** ne pas pouvoir voir qn en peinture *or* sentir qn.
gut reaction *n* réaction instinctive.
gutsy ['gʌtsɪ] *adj* (*person*) qui a du cran; (*style*) qui a du punch.
gutted ['gʌtɪd] *adj*: **I was** ~ (*col: disappointed*) j'étais carrément dégoûté.
gutter ['gʌtə*] *n* (*of roof*) gouttière *f*; (*in street*) caniveau *m*; (*fig*) ruisseau *m*.
gutter press *n*: **the** ~ la presse de bas étage *or* à scandale.
guttural ['gʌtərl] *adj* guttural(e).
guy [gaɪ] *n* (*also*: ~**rope**) corde *f*; (*col: man*) type *m*; (*figure*) effigie de Guy Fawkes.
Guyana [gaɪˈænə] *n* Guyane *f*.

> **Guy Fawkes' Night**, que l'on appelle également "bonfire night", commémore l'échec du complot (le "Gunpowder Plot") contre James Ist et son parlement le 5 novembre 1605. L'un des conspirateurs, Guy Fawkes, avait été surpris dans les caves du parlement alors qu'il s'apprêtait à y mettre le feu. Chaque année pour le 5 novembre, les enfants préparent à l'avance une effigie de Guy Fawkes et ils demandent aux passants "un penny pour le guy" avec lequel ils pourront s'acheter des fusées de feu d'artifice. Beaucoup de gens font encore un feu dans leur jardin sur lequel ils brûlent le "guy".

guzzle ['gʌzl] *vi* s'empiffrer ♦ *vt* avaler gloutonnement.
gym [dʒɪm] *n* (*also*: **gymnasium**) gymnase *m*; (*also*: **gymnastics**) gym *f*.
gymkhana [dʒɪmˈkɑːnə] *n* gymkhana *m*.
gymnasium [dʒɪmˈneɪzɪəm] *n* gymnase *m*.
gymnast ['dʒɪmnæst] *n* gymnaste *m/f*.
gymnastics [dʒɪmˈnæstɪks] *n*, *npl* gymnastique *f*.
gym shoes *npl* chaussures *fpl* de gym(nastique).
gym slip *n* (*BRIT*) tunique *f* (d'écolière).
gynaecologist, (*US*) **gynecologist** [gaɪnɪˈkɔlədʒɪst] *n* gynécologue *m/f*.

gynaecology, (*US*) **gynecology** [gaɪnəˈkɔlədʒɪ] *n* gynécologie *f*.
gypsy ['dʒɪpsɪ] *n* = **gipsy**.
gyrate [dʒaɪˈreɪt] *vi* tournoyer.
gyroscope ['dʒaɪərəskəup] *n* gyroscope *m*.

H h

H, h [eɪtʃ] *n* (*letter*) H, h *m*; **H for Harry**, (*US*) **H for How** H comme Henri.
habeas corpus ['heɪbɪəsˈkɔːpəs] *n* (*LAW*) habeas corpus *m*.
haberdashery [hæbəˈdæʃərɪ] *n* (*BRIT*) mercerie *f*.
habit ['hæbɪt] *n* habitude *f*; (*costume*) habit *m*, tenue *f*; **to get out of/into the** ~ **of doing sth** perdre/prendre l'habitude de faire qch.
habitable ['hæbɪtəbl] *adj* habitable.
habitat ['hæbɪtæt] *n* habitat *m*.
habitation [hæbɪˈteɪʃən] *n* habitation *f*.
habitual [həˈbɪtjuəl] *adj* habituel(le); (*drinker, liar*) invétéré(e).
habitually [həˈbɪtjuəlɪ] *adv* habituellement, d'habitude.
hack [hæk] *vt* hacher, tailler ♦ *n* (*cut*) entaille *f*; (*blow*) coup *m*; (*pej: writer*) nègre *m*; (*old horse*) canasson *m*.
hackles ['hæklz] *npl*: **to make sb's** ~ **rise** (*fig*) mettre qn hors de soi.
hackney cab ['hæknɪ-] *n* fiacre *m*.
hackneyed ['hæknɪd] *adj* usé(e), rebattu(e).
hacksaw ['hæksɔː] *n* scie *f* à métaux.
had [hæd] *pt*, *pp of* **have**.
haddock, *pl* ~ *or* ~**s** ['hædək] *n* églefin *m*; **smoked** ~ haddock *m*.
hadn't ['hædnt] = **had not**.
haematology, (*US*) **hematology** ['hiːməˈtɔlədʒɪ] *n* hématologie *f*.
haemoglobin, (*US*) **hemoglobin** ['hiːməˈgləubɪn] *n* hémoglobine *f*.
haemophilia, (*US*) **hemophilia** ['hiːməˈfɪlɪə] *n* hémophilie *f*.
haemorrhage, (*US*) **hemorrhage** ['hɛmərɪdʒ] *n* hémorragie *f*.
haemorrhoids, (*US*) **hemorrhoids** ['hɛmərɔɪdz] *npl* hémorroïdes *fpl*.
hag [hæg] *n* (*ugly*) vieille sorcière; (*nasty*) chameau *m*, harpie *f*; (*witch*) sorcière.
haggard ['hægəd] *adj* hagard(e), égaré(e).
haggis ['hægɪs] *n* haggis *m*.
haggle ['hægl] *vi* marchander; **to** ~ **over** chicaner sur.
haggling ['hæglɪŋ] *n* marchandage *m*.
Hague [heɪg] *n*: **The** ~ La Haye.
hail [heɪl] *n* grêle *f* ♦ *vt* (*call*) héler; (*greet*)

acclamer ♦ _vi_ grêler; (_originate_): **he ~s from Scotland** il est originaire d'Écosse.

hailstone ['heɪlstəun] _n_ grêlon _m_.

hailstorm ['heɪlstɔːm] _n_ averse _f_ de grêle.

hair [hɛə*] _n_ cheveux _mpl_; (_on body_) poils _mpl_, pilosité _f_; (_single hair: on head_) cheveu _m_; (: _on body_) poil _m_; **to do one's ~** se coiffer.

hairbrush ['hɛəbrʌʃ] _n_ brosse _f_ à cheveux.

haircut ['hɛəkʌt] _n_ coupe _f_ (de cheveux).

hairdo ['hɛəduː] _n_ coiffure _f_.

hairdresser ['hɛədresə*] _n_ coiffeur/euse.

hair-dryer ['hɛədraɪə*] _n_ sèche-cheveux _m_.

-haired [hɛəd] _suffix_: **fair/long~** aux cheveux blonds/longs.

hair gel _n_ gel _m_ pour cheveux.

hairgrip ['hɛəgrɪp] _n_ pince _f_ à cheveux.

hairline ['hɛəlaɪn] _n_ naissance _f_ des cheveux.

hairline fracture _n_ fêlure _f_.

hairnet ['hɛənet] _n_ résille _f_.

hair oil _n_ huile _f_ capillaire.

hairpiece ['hɛəpiːs] _n_ postiche _m_.

hairpin ['hɛəpɪn] _n_ épingle _f_ à cheveux.

hairpin bend, (_US_) **hairpin curve** _n_ virage _m_ en épingle à cheveux.

hairraising ['hɛəreɪzɪŋ] _adj_ à (vous) faire dresser les cheveux sur la tête.

hair remover _n_ dépilateur _m_.

hair spray _n_ laque _f_ (pour les cheveux).

hairstyle ['hɛəstaɪl] _n_ coiffure _f_.

hairy ['hɛərɪ] _adj_ poilu(e); chevelu(e); (_fig_) effrayant(e).

Haiti ['heɪtɪ] _n_ Haïti _m_.

hake [heɪk] _n_ colin _m_, merlu _m_.

halcyon ['hælsɪən] _adj_ merveilleux(euse).

hale [heɪl] _adj_: **~ and hearty** robuste, en pleine santé.

half [hɑːf] _n_ (_pl_ **halves** [hɑːvz]) moitié _f_; (_SPORT: of match_) mi-temps _f_; (: _of ground_) moitié (du terrain) ♦ _adj_ demi(e) ♦ _adv_ (à) moitié, à demi; **~-an-hour** une demi-heure; **~ a dozen** une demi-douzaine; **~ a pound** une demi-livre, ≈ 250 g; **two and a ~** deux et demi; **a week and a ~** une semaine et demie; **~ (of it)** la moitié; **~ (of)** la moitié de; **~ the amount of** la moitié de; **to cut sth in ~** couper qch en deux; **~ past three** trois heures et demie; **~ empty/closed** à moitié vide/fermé; **to go halves (with sb)** se mettre de moitié avec qn.

half-back ['hɑːfbæk] _n_ (_SPORT_) demi _m_.

half-baked ['hɑːf'beɪkt] _adj_ (_col: idea, scheme_) qui ne tient pas debout.

half-breed ['hɑːfbriːd] _n_ = **halfcaste**.

half-brother ['hɑːfbrʌðə*] _n_ demi-frère _m_.

half-caste ['hɑːfkɑːst] _n_ métis/se.

half-hearted ['hɑːf'hɑːtɪd] _adj_ tiède, sans enthousiasme.

half-hour [hɑːf'auə*] _n_ demi-heure _f_.

half-mast ['hɑːf'mɑːst] _n_: **at ~** (_flag_) en berne, à mi-mât.

halfpenny ['heɪpnɪ] _n_ demi-penny _m_.

half-price ['hɑːf'praɪs] _adj_ à moitié prix ♦ _adv_

(_also_: **at ~**) à moitié prix.

half term _n_ (_BRIT SCOL_) congé _m_ de demi-trimestre.

half-time [hɑːf'taɪm] _n_ mi-temps _f_.

halfway ['hɑːf'weɪ] _adv_ à mi-chemin; **to meet sb ~** (_fig_) parvenir à un compromis avec qn.

halfway house _n_ (_hostel_) centre _m_ de réadaptation (_pour anciens prisonniers, malades mentaux etc_); (_fig_): **a ~ (between)** une étape intermédiaire (entre).

half-wit ['hɑːfwɪt] _n_ (_col_) idiot/e, imbécile _m/f_.

half-yearly [hɑːf'jɪəlɪ] _adv_ deux fois par an ♦ _adj_ semestriel(le).

halibut ['hælɪbət] _n_ (_pl inv_) flétan _m_.

halitosis [hælɪ'təusɪs] _n_ mauvaise haleine.

hall [hɔːl] _n_ salle _f_; (_entrance way_) hall _m_, entrée _f_; (_corridor_) couloir _m_; (_mansion_) château _m_, manoir _m_; **~ of residence** _n_ (_BRIT_) pavillon _m or_ résidence _f_ universitaire.

hallmark ['hɔːlmɑːk] _n_ poinçon _m_; (_fig_) marque _f_.

hallo [hə'ləu] _excl_ = **hello**.

Hallowe'en ['hæləu'iːn] _n_ veille _f_ de la Toussaint.

Selon la tradition, **Hallowe'en** _est la nuit des fantômes et des sorcières. En Écosse et aux États-Unis surtout (beaucoup moins en Angleterre) les enfants, pour fêter Hallowe'en, se déguisent ce soir-là et ils vont ainsi de porte en porte en demandant de petits cadeaux (du chocolat, une pomme etc)._

hallucination [həluːsɪ'neɪʃən] _n_ hallucination _f_.

hallucinogenic [həluːsɪnəu'dʒɛnɪk] _adj_ hallucinogène.

hallway ['hɔːlweɪ] _n_ vestibule _m_; couloir _m_.

halo ['heɪləu] _n_ (_of saint etc_) auréole _f_; (_of sun_) halo _m_.

halt [hɔːlt] _n_ halte _f_, arrêt _m_ ♦ _vt_ faire arrêter ♦ _vi_ faire halte, s'arrêter; **to call a ~ to sth** (_fig_) mettre fin à qch.

halter ['hɔːltə*] _n_ (_for horse_) licou _m_.

halterneck ['hɔːltənɛk] _adj_ (_dress_) (avec) dos nu _inv_.

halve [hɑːv] _vt_ (_apple etc_) partager _or_ diviser en deux; (_reduce by half_) réduire de moitié.

halves [hɑːvz] _npl of_ **half**.

ham [hæm] _n_ jambon _m_; (_col: also_: **radio ~**) radio-amateur _m_; (: _also_: **~ actor**) cabotin/e.

Hamburg ['hæmbəːg] _n_ Hambourg.

hamburger ['hæmbəːgə*] _n_ hamburger _m_.

ham-fisted ['hæm'fɪstɪd], (_US_) **ham-handed** ['hæm'hændɪd] _adj_ maladroit(e).

hamlet ['hæmlɪt] _n_ hameau _m_.

hammer ['hæmə*] _n_ marteau _m_ ♦ _vt_ (_fig_) éreinter, démolir ♦ _vi_ (_at door_) frapper à coups redoublés; **to ~ a point home to sb** faire rentrer qch dans la tête de qn.

▶**hammer out** _vt_ (_metal_) étendre au marteau; (_fig: solution_) élaborer.

hammock ['hæmək] n hamac m.
hamper ['hæmpə*] vt gêner ♦ n panier m (d'osier).
hamster ['hæmstə*] n hamster m.
hamstring ['hæmstrɪŋ] n (ANAT) tendon m du jarret.
hand [hænd] n main f; (of clock) aiguille f; (handwriting) écriture f; (at cards) jeu m; (measurement: of horse) paume f; (worker) ouvrier/ière ♦ vt passer, donner; **to give sb a ~** donner un coup de main à qn; **at ~** à portée de la main; **in ~** en main; (work) en cours; **we have the situation in ~** nous avons la situation bien en main; **to be on ~** (person) être disponible; (emergency services) se tenir prêt(e) (à intervenir); **to ~** (information etc) sous la main, à portée de la main; **to force sb's ~** forcer la main à qn; **to have a free ~** avoir carte blanche; **to have sth in one's ~** tenir qch à la main; **on the one ~ ..., on the other ~** d'une part ..., d'autre part.
►**hand down** vt passer; (tradition, heirloom) transmettre; (US: sentence, verdict) prononcer.
►**hand in** vt remettre.
►**hand out** vt distribuer.
►**hand over** vt remettre; (powers etc) transmettre.
►**hand round** vt (BRIT: information) faire circuler; (: chocolates etc) faire passer.
handbag ['hændbæg] n sac m à main.
hand baggage n bagages mpl à main; **one item of ~** un bagage à main.
handball ['hændbɔ:l] n handball m.
handbasin ['hændbeɪsn] n lavabo m.
handbook ['hændbuk] n manuel m.
handbrake ['hændbreɪk] n frein m à main.
h & c abbr (BRIT) = hot and cold (water).
hand cream n crème f pour les mains.
handcuffs ['hændkʌfs] npl menottes fpl.
handful ['hændful] n poignée f.
hand-held ['hænd'held] adj à main.
handicap ['hændɪkæp] n handicap m ♦ vt handicaper; **mentally/physically ~ped** handicapé(e) mentalement/physiquement.
handicraft ['hændɪkrɑːft] n travail m d'artisanat, technique artisanale.
handiwork ['hændɪwəːk] n ouvrage m; **this looks like his ~** (pej) ça a tout l'air d'être son œuvre.
handkerchief ['hæŋkətʃɪf] n mouchoir m.
handle ['hændl] n (of door etc) poignée f; (of cup etc) anse f; (of knife etc) manche m; (of saucepan etc) queue f; (for winding) manivelle f ♦ vt toucher, manier; (deal with) s'occuper de; (treat: people) prendre; "**~ with care**" "fragile".
handlebar(s) ['hændlbɑ:(z)] n(pl) guidon m.
handling ['hændlɪŋ] n (AUT) maniement m; (treatment): **his ~ of the matter** la façon dont il a traité l'affaire.

handling charges npl frais mpl de manutention; (BANKING) agios mpl.
hand-luggage ['hændlʌgɪdʒ] n bagages mpl à main.
handmade ['hænd'meɪd] adj fait(e) à la main.
handout ['hændaut] n documentation f, prospectus m; (press ~) communiqué m de presse.
hand-picked ['hænd'pɪkt] adj (produce) cueilli(e) à la main; (staff etc) trié(e) sur le volet.
handrail ['hændreɪl] n (on staircase etc) rampe f, main courante.
handset ['hændset] n (TEL) combiné m.
handshake ['hændʃeɪk] n poignée f de main; (COMPUT) établissement m de la liaison.
handsome ['hænsəm] adj beau(belle); (gift) généreux(euse); (profit) considérable.
hands-on [hændz'ɔn] adj (training, experience) sur le tas; **she has a very ~ approach** sa politique est de mettre la main à la pâte.
handstand ['hændstænd] n: **to do a ~** faire l'arbre droit.
hand-to-mouth ['hændtə'mauθ] adj (existence) au jour le jour.
handwriting ['hændraɪtɪŋ] n écriture f.
handwritten ['hændrɪtn] adj manuscrit(e), écrit(e) à la main.
handy ['hændɪ] adj (person) adroit(e); (close at hand) sous la main; (convenient) pratique; **to come in ~** être (or s'avérer) utile.
handyman ['hændɪmæn] n bricoleur m; (servant) homme m à tout faire.
hang, pt, pp hung [hæŋ, hʌŋ] vt accrocher; (criminal: pt, pp hanged) pendre ♦ vi pendre; (hair, drapery) tomber ♦ n: **to get the ~ of (doing) sth** (col) attraper le coup pour faire qch.
►**hang about** vi flâner, traîner.
►**hang back** vi (hesitate): **to ~ back (from doing)** être réticent(e) (pour faire).
►**hang on** vi (wait) attendre ♦ vt fus (depend on) dépendre de; **to ~ on to** (keep hold of) ne pas lâcher; (keep) garder.
►**hang out** vt (washing) étendre (dehors) ♦ vi pendre; (col: live) habiter, percher.
►**hang together** vi (argument etc) se tenir, être cohérent(e).
►**hang up** vi (TEL) raccrocher ♦ vt accrocher, suspendre; **to ~ up on sb** (TEL) raccrocher au nez de qn.
hangar ['hæŋə*] n hangar m.
hangdog ['hæŋdɔg] adj (look, expression) de chien battu.
hanger ['hæŋə*] n cintre m, portemanteau m.
hanger-on [hæŋər'ɔn] n parasite m.
hang-glider ['hæŋglaɪdə*] n deltaplane m.
hang-gliding ['hæŋglaɪdɪŋ] n vol m libre or sur aile delta.
hanging ['hæŋɪŋ] n (execution) pendaison f.
hangman ['hæŋmən] n bourreau m.
hangover ['hæŋəuvə*] n (after drinking) gueule

f de bois.

hang-up ['hæŋʌp] *n* complexe *m*.

hank [hæŋk] *n* écheveau *m*.

hanker ['hæŋkə*] *vi*: **to ~ after** avoir envie de.

hankering ['hæŋkərɪŋ] *n*: **to have a ~ for/to do sth** avoir une grande envie de/de faire qch.

hankie, hanky ['hæŋkɪ] *n abbr* = **handkerchief**.

Hants *abbr* (*BRIT*) = Hampshire.

haphazard [hæp'hæzəd] *adj* fait(e) au hasard, fait(e) au petit bonheur.

hapless ['hæplɪs] *adj* malheureux(euse).

happen ['hæpən] *vi* arriver, se passer, se produire; **what's ~ing?** que se passe-t-il?; **she ~ed to be free** il s'est trouvé (*or* se trouvait) qu'elle était libre; **if anything ~ed to him** s'il lui arrivait quoi que ce soit; **as it ~s** justement.

▶**happen (up)on** *vt fus* tomber sur.

happening ['hæpnɪŋ] *n* événement *m*.

happily ['hæpɪlɪ] *adv* heureusement.

happiness ['hæpɪnɪs] *n* bonheur *m*.

happy ['hæpɪ] *adj* heureux(euse); **~ with** (*arrangements etc*) satisfait(e) de; **yes, I'd be ~ to** oui, avec plaisir *or* (bien) volontiers; **~ birthday!** bon anniversaire!; **~ Christmas/ New Year!** joyeux Noël/bonne année!

happy-go-lucky ['hæpɪgəu'lʌkɪ] *adj* insouciant(e).

happy hour *n* l'heure *f* de l'apéritif, *heure pendant laquelle les consommations sont à prix réduit*.

harangue [hə'ræŋ] *vt* haranguer.

harass ['hærəs] *vt* accabler, tourmenter.

harassed ['hærəst] *adj* tracassé(e).

harassment ['hærəsmənt] *n* tracasseries *fpl*.

harbour, (*US*) **harbor** ['hɑːbə*] *n* port *m* ♦ *vt* héberger, abriter; (*hopes, suspicions*) entretenir; **to ~ a grudge against sb** en vouloir à qn.

harbo(u)r dues *npl* droits *mpl* de port.

harbo(u)r master *n* capitaine *m* du port.

hard [hɑːd] *adj* dur(e) ♦ *adv* (*work*) dur; (*think, try*) sérieusement; **to look ~ at** regarder fixement; regarder de près; **to drink ~** boire sec; **~ luck!** pas de veine!; **no ~ feelings!** sans rancune!; **to be ~ of hearing** être dur(e) d'oreille; **to be ~ done by** être traité(e) injustement; **to be ~ on sb** être dur(e) avec qn; **I find it ~ to believe that ...** je n'arrive pas à croire que ....

hard-and-fast ['hɑːdən'fɑːst] *adj* strict(e), absolu(e).

hardback ['hɑːdbæk] *n* livre relié.

hardboard ['hɑːdbɔːd] *n* Isorel *m* ®.

hard-boiled egg ['hɑːd'bɔɪld-] *n* œuf dur.

hard cash *n* espèces *fpl*.

hard copy *n* (*COMPUT*) sortie *f or* copie *f* papier.

hard-core ['hɑːd'kɔː*] *adj* (*pornography*) (dit(e)) dur(e); (*supporters*) inconditionnel(le).

hard court *n* (*TENNIS*) court *m* en dur.

hard disk *n* (*COMPUT*) disque dur.

harden ['hɑːdn] *vt* durcir; (*steel*) tremper; (*fig*) endurcir ♦ *vi* (*substance*) durcir.

hardened ['hɑːdnd] *adj* (*criminal*) endurci(e); **to be ~ to sth** être endurci(e) à qch, être (devenu(e)) insensible à qch.

hardening ['hɑːdnɪŋ] *n* durcissement *m*.

hard-headed ['hɑːd'hɛdɪd] *adj* réaliste; décidé(e).

hard-hearted ['hɑːd'hɑːtɪd] *adj* dur(e), impitoyable.

hard-hitting ['hɑːd'hɪtɪŋ] *adj* (*speech, article*) sans complaisances.

hard labour *n* travaux forcés.

hardliner [hɑːd'laɪnə*] *n* intransigeant/e, dur/e.

hard-luck story [hɑːd'lʌk-] *n* histoire larmoyante.

hardly ['hɑːdlɪ] *adv* (*scarcely*) à peine; (*harshly*) durement; **it's ~ the case** ce n'est guère le cas; **~ anywhere/ever** presque nulle part/ jamais; **I can ~ believe it** j'ai du mal à le croire.

hardness ['hɑːdnɪs] *n* dureté *f*.

hard-nosed ['hɑːd'nəuzd] *adj* impitoyable, dur(e).

hard-pressed ['hɑːd'prɛst] *adj* sous pression.

hard sell *n* vente agressive.

hardship ['hɑːdʃɪp] *n* épreuves *fpl*; privations *fpl*.

hard shoulder *n* (*BRIT AUT*) accotement stabilisé.

hard-up [hɑːd'ʌp] *adj* (*col*) fauché(e).

hardware ['hɑːdwɛə*] *n* quincaillerie *f*; (*COMPUT*) matériel *m*.

hardware shop *n* quincaillerie *f*.

hard-wearing [hɑːd'wɛərɪŋ] *adj* solide.

hard-won ['hɑːd'wʌn] *adj* (si) durement gagné(e).

hard-working [hɑːd'wəːkɪŋ] *adj* travailleur(euse), consciencieux(euse).

hardy ['hɑːdɪ] *adj* robuste; (*plant*) résistant(e) au gel.

hare [hɛə*] *n* lièvre *m*.

hare-brained ['hɛəbreɪnd] *adj* farfelu(e); écervelé(e).

harelip ['hɛəlɪp] *n* (*MED*) bec-de-lièvre *m*.

harem [hɑː'riːm] *n* harem *m*.

hark back [hɑːk-] *vi*: **to ~ to** (en) revenir toujours à.

harm [hɑːm] *n* mal *m*; (*wrong*) tort *m* ♦ *vt* (*person*) faire du mal *or* du tort à; (*thing*) endommager; **to mean no ~** ne pas avoir de mauvaises intentions; **there's no ~ in trying** on peut toujours essayer; **out of ~'s way** à l'abri du danger, en lieu sûr.

harmful ['hɑːmful] *adj* nuisible.

harmless ['hɑːmlɪs] *adj* inoffensif(ive); sans méchanceté.

harmonic [hɑː'mɒnɪk] *adj* harmonique.

harmonica [hɑː'mɒnɪkə] *n* harmonica *m*.

harmonics [hɑː'mɒnɪks] *npl* harmoniques *mpl*

or fpl.

harmonious [haː'məunɪəs] *adj* harmonieux(euse).

harmonium [haː'məunɪəm] *n* harmonium *m*.

harmonize ['haːmənaɪz] *vt* harmoniser ♦ *vi* s'harmoniser.

harmony ['haːmənɪ] *n* harmonie *f*.

harness ['haːnɪs] *n* harnais *m* ♦ *vt* (*horse*) harnacher; (*resources*) exploiter.

harp [haːp] *n* harpe *f* ♦ *vi:* **to ~ on about** parler tout le temps de.

harpist ['haːpɪst] *n* harpiste *m/f*.

harpoon [haː'puːn] *n* harpon *m*.

harpsichord ['haːpsɪkɔːd] *n* clavecin *m*.

harrow ['hærəu] *n* (*AGR*) herse *f*.

harrowing ['hærəuɪŋ] *adj* déchirant(e).

harry ['hærɪ] *vt* (*MIL, fig*) harceler.

harsh [haːʃ] *adj* (*hard*) dur(e), sévère; (*rough: surface*) rugueux(euse); (: *sound*) discordant(e); (: *taste*) âpre.

harshly ['haːʃlɪ] *adv* durement, sévèrement.

harshness ['haːʃnɪs] *n* dureté *f*, sévérité *f*.

harvest ['haːvɪst] *n* (*of corn*) moisson *f*; (*of fruit*) récolte *f*; (*of grapes*) vendange *f* ♦ *vi, vt* moissonner; récolter; vendanger.

harvester ['haːvɪstə*] *n* (*machine*) moissonneuse *f*; (*also:* **combine ~**) moissonneuse-batteuse(-lieuse *f*) *f*; (*person*) moissonneur/euse.

has [hæz] *vb see* **have**.

has-been ['hæzbiːn] *n* (*col: person*): **he/she's a ~** il/elle a fait son temps *or* est fini(e).

hash [hæʃ] *n* (*CULIN*) hachis *m*; (*fig: mess*) gâchis *m* ♦ *n abbr* (*col*) = **hashish**.

hashish ['hæʃɪʃ] *n* haschisch *m*.

hasn't ['hæznt] = **has not**.

hassle ['hæsl] *n* (*col: fuss*) histoire(s) *f(pl)*.

haste [heɪst] *n* hâte *f*, précipitation *f*; **in ~** à la hâte, précipitamment.

hasten ['heɪsn] *vt* hâter, accélérer ♦ *vi* se hâter, s'empresser; **I ~ to add that ...** je m'empresse d'ajouter que ....

hastily ['heɪstɪlɪ] *adv* à la hâte, précipitamment.

hasty ['heɪstɪ] *adj* hâtif(ive), précipité(e).

hat [hæt] *n* chapeau *m*.

hatbox ['hætbɔks] *n* carton *m* à chapeau.

hatch [hætʃ] *n* (*NAUT: also:* ~**way**) écoutille *f*; (*BRIT: also:* **service ~**) passe-plats *m inv* ♦ *vi* éclore ♦ *vt* faire éclore; (*fig: scheme*) tramer, ourdir.

hatchback ['hætʃbæk] *n* (*AUT*) modèle *m* avec hayon arrière.

hatchet ['hætʃɪt] *n* hachette *f*.

hatchet job *n* (*col*) démolissage *m*.

hatchet man *n* (*col*) homme *m* de main.

hate [heɪt] *vt* haïr, détester ♦ *n* haine *f*; **to ~ to do** *or* **doing** détester faire; **I ~ to trouble you, but ...** désolé de vous déranger, mais ....

hateful ['heɪtful] *adj* odieux(euse), détestable.

hatred ['heɪtrɪd] *n* haine *f*.

hat trick *n* (*BRIT SPORT, also fig*): **to get a ~** réussir trois coups (*or* gagner trois matchs *etc*) consécutifs.

haughty ['hɔːtɪ] *adj* hautain(e), arrogant(e).

haul [hɔːl] *vt* traîner, tirer; (*by lorry*) camionner; (*NAUT*) haler ♦ *n* (*of fish*) prise *f*; (*of stolen goods etc*) butin *m*.

haulage ['hɔːlɪdʒ] *n* transport routier.

haulage contractor *n* (*BRIT: firm*) entreprise *f* de transport (routier); (: *person*) transporteur routier.

haulier ['hɔːlɪə*], (*US*) **hauler** ['hɔːlə*] *n* transporteur (routier), camionneur *m*.

haunch [hɔːntʃ] *n* hanche *f*; ~ **of venison** cuissot *m* de chevreuil.

haunt [hɔːnt] *vt* (*subj: ghost, fear*) hanter; (: *person*) fréquenter ♦ *n* repaire *m*.

haunted ['hɔːntɪd] *adj* (*castle etc*) hanté(e); (*look*) égaré(e), hagard(e).

haunting ['hɔːntɪŋ] *adj* (*sight, music*) obsédant(e).

Havana [hə'vænə] *n* La Havane.

═══════════════════ *KEYWORD*

have [hæv] (*pt, pp* **had**) *aux vb* **1** (*gen*) avoir; être; **to ~ arrived/gone** être arrivé(e)/ allé(e); **to ~ eaten/slept** avoir mangé/dormi; **he has been promoted** il a été promu

2 (*in tag questions*): **you've done it, ~n't you?** vous l'avez fait, n'est-ce pas?

3 (*in short answers and questions*): **no I ~n't!/yes we ~!** mais non!/mais si!; **so I ~!** ah oui!, oui c'est vrai!; **I've been there before, ~ you?** j'y suis déjà allé, et vous?

♦ *modal aux vb* (*be obliged*): **to ~ (got) to do sth** devoir faire qch; être obligé(e) de faire qch; **she has (got) to do it** elle doit le faire, il faut qu'elle le fasse; **you ~n't to tell her** vous ne devez pas le lui dire

♦ *vt* **1** (*possess, obtain*) avoir; **he has (got) blue eyes/dark hair** il a les yeux bleus/les cheveux bruns; **may I ~ your address?** puis-je avoir votre adresse?

2 (*+noun: take, hold etc*): **to ~ breakfast/a bath/a shower** prendre le petit déjeuner/un bain/une douche; **to ~ dinner/lunch** dîner/ déjeuner; **to ~ a swim** nager; **to ~ a meeting** se réunir; **to ~ a party** organiser une fête; **let me ~ a try** laissez-moi essayer

3: **to ~ sth done** faire faire qch; **to ~ one's hair cut** se faire couper les cheveux; **to ~ sb do sth** faire faire qch à qn

4 (*experience, suffer*) avoir; **to ~ a cold/flu** avoir un rhume/la grippe; **to ~ an operation** se faire opérer; **I won't ~ it** cela ne se passera pas ainsi

5 (*inf: dupe*) avoir; **he's been had** il s'est fait avoir *or* rouler

▶**have out** *vt:* **to ~ it out with sb** (*settle a problem etc*) s'expliquer (franchement) avec qn.

haven ['heɪvn] *n* port *m*; (*fig*) havre *m*.
haversack ['hævəsæk] *n* sac *m* à dos.
haves [hævz] *npl* (*col*): **the ~ and have-nots** les riches et les pauvres.
havoc ['hævək] *n* ravages *mpl*, dégâts *mpl*; **to play ~ with** (*fig*) désorganiser complètement; détraquer.
Hawaii [hə'waɪiː] *n* (îles *fpl*) Hawaii *m*.
Hawaiian [hə'waɪjən] *adj* hawaïen(ne) ♦ *n* Hawaïen/ne; (*LING*) hawaïen *m*.
hawk [hɔːk] *n* faucon *m* ♦ *vt* (*goods for sale*) colporter.
hawker ['hɔːkə*] *n* colporteur *m*.
hawkish ['hɔːkɪʃ] *adj* belliciste.
hawthorn ['hɔːθɔːn] *n* aubépine *f*.
hay [heɪ] *n* foin *m*.
hay fever *n* rhume *m* des foins.
haystack ['heɪstæk] *n* meule *f* de foin.
haywire ['heɪwaɪə*] *adj* (*col*): **to go ~** perdre la tête; mal tourner.
hazard ['hæzəd] *n* (*chance*) hasard *m*, chance *f*; (*risk*) danger *m*, risque *m* ♦ *vt* risquer, hasarder; **to be a health/fire ~** présenter un risque d'incendie/pour la santé; **to ~ a guess** émettre *or* hasarder une hypothèse.
hazardous ['hæzədəs] *adj* hasardeux(euse), risqué(e).
hazard pay *n* (*US*) prime *f* de risque.
hazard warning lights *npl* (*AUT*) feux *mpl* de détresse.
haze [heɪz] *n* brume *f*.
hazel [heɪzl] *n* (*tree*) noisetier *m* ♦ *adj* (*eyes*) noisette *inv*.
hazelnut ['heɪzlnʌt] *n* noisette *f*.
hazy ['heɪzɪ] *adj* brumeux(euse); (*idea*) vague; (*photograph*) flou(e).
H-bomb ['eɪtʃbɔm] *n* bombe *f* H.
HE *abbr* = high explosive; (*REL, DIPLOMACY*) = His (or Her) Excellency.
he [hiː] *pron id*; **it is ~ who** ... c'est lui qui ...; **here ~ is** le voici; **~-bear** *etc* ours *etc* mâle.
head [hed] *n* tête *f*; (*leader*) chef *m* ♦ *vt* (*list*) être en tête de; (*group*) être à la tête de; **~s** (*on coin*) (le côté) face; **~s or tails** pile ou face; **~ over heels in love** follement *or* éperdument amoureux(euse); **to ~ the ball** faire une tête; **10 francs a ~ or per ~** 10 F par personne; **to sit at the ~ of the table** présider la tablée; **to have a ~ for business** avoir des dispositions pour les affaires; **to have no ~ for heights** être sujet(te) au vertige; **to come to a ~** (*fig: situation etc*) devenir critique.
▶**head for** *vt fus* se diriger vers.
▶**head off** *vt* (*threat, danger*) détourner.
headache ['hedeɪk] *n* mal *m* de tête; **to have a ~** avoir mal à la tête.
headband ['hedbænd] *n* bandeau *m*.
headboard ['hedbɔːd] *n* dosseret *m*.
head cold *n* rhume *m* de cerveau.
headdress ['heddres] *n* coiffure *f*.
headed notepaper ['hedɪd-] *n* papier *m* à lettres à en-tête.
header ['hedə*] *n* (*BRIT col*: *FOOTBALL*) (coup *m* de) tête *f*; (: *fall*) chute *f* (*or* plongeon *m*) la tête la première.
head-first ['hed'fəːst] *adv* (*lit*) la tête la première.
headhunt ['hedhʌnt] *vt*: **she was ~ed** elle a été recrutée par un chasseur de têtes.
headhunter ['hedhʌntə*] *n* chasseur *m* de têtes.
heading ['hedɪŋ] *n* titre *m*; (*subject title*) rubrique *f*.
headlamp ['hedlæmp] *n* (*BRIT*) = **headlight**.
headland ['hedlənd] *n* promontoire *m*, cap *m*.
headlight ['hedlaɪt] *n* phare *m*.
headline ['hedlaɪn] *n* titre *m*.
headlong ['hedlɔŋ] *adv* (*fall*) la tête la première; (*rush*) tête baissée.
headmaster [hed'mɑːstə*] *n* directeur *m*, proviseur *m*.
headmistress [hed'mɪstrɪs] *n* directrice *f*.
head office *n* siège *m*, direction *f* (générale).
head-on [hed'ɔn] *adj* (*collision*) de plein fouet.
headphones ['hedfəunz] *npl* casque *m* (à écouteurs).
headquarters (HQ) ['hedkwɔːtəz] *npl* (*of business*) siège *m*, direction *f* (générale); (*MIL*) quartier général.
head-rest ['hedrest] *n* appui-tête *m*.
headroom ['hedrum] *n* (*in car*) hauteur *f* de plafond; (*under bridge*) hauteur limite; dégagement *m*.
headscarf ['hedskɑːf] *n* foulard *m*.
headset ['hedset] *n* = **headphones**.
headstone ['hedstəun] *n* (*on grave*) pierre tombale.
headstrong ['hedstrɔŋ] *adj* têtu(e), entêté(e).
head waiter *n* maître *m* d'hôtel.
headway ['hedweɪ] *n*: **to make ~** avancer, faire des progrès.
headwind ['hedwɪnd] *n* vent *m* contraire.
heady ['hedɪ] *adj* capiteux(euse); enivrant(e).
heal [hiːl] *vt*, *vi* guérir.
health [helθ] *n* santé *f*; **Department of H~** (*US*) ≈ ministère *m* de la Santé; **Department of H~ (DH)** (*BRIT*) ≈ ministère *m* de la Santé.
health care *n* services médicaux.
health centre *n* (*BRIT*) centre *m* de santé.
health food(s) *n(pl)* aliment(s) naturel(s).
health food shop *n* magasin *m* diététique.
health hazard *n* risque *m* pour la santé.
Health Service *n*: **the ~** (*BRIT*) ≈ la Sécurité Sociale.
healthy ['helθɪ] *adj* (*person*) en bonne santé; (*climate, food, attitude etc*) sain(e).
heap [hiːp] *n* tas *m*, monceau *m* ♦ *vt* entasser, amonceler; **~s (of)** (*col*: *lots*) des tas (de); **to ~ favours/praise/gifts etc on sb** combler qn de faveurs/d'éloges/de cadeaux *etc*.
hear, *pt*, *pp* **heard** [hɪə*, həːd] *vt* entendre;

(*news*) apprendre; (*lecture*) assister à, écouter ♦ *vi* entendre; **to ~ about** entendre parler de; (*have news of*) avoir des nouvelles de; **did you ~ about the move?** tu es au courant du déménagement?; **to ~ from sb** recevoir des nouvelles de qn; **I've never heard of that book** je n'ai jamais entendu parler de ce livre.

►**hear out** *vt* écouter jusqu'au bout.

hearing ['hɪərɪŋ] *n* (*sense*) ouïe *f*; (*of witnesses*) audition *f*; (*of a case*) audience *f*; (*of committee*) séance *f*; **to give sb a ~** (*BRIT*) écouter ce que qn a à dire.

hearing aid *n* appareil *m* acoustique.

hearsay ['hɪəseɪ] *n* on-dit *mpl*, rumeurs *fpl*; **by ~** *adv* par ouï-dire.

hearse [hə:s] *n* corbillard *m*.

heart [hɑ:t] *n* cœur *m*; **~s** *npl* (*CARDS*) cœur *m*; **at ~** au fond; **by ~** (*learn, know*) par cœur; **to have a weak ~** avoir le cœur malade, avoir des problèmes de cœur; **to lose ~** perdre courage, se décourager; **to take ~** prendre courage; **to set one's ~ on sth/on doing sth** vouloir absolument qch/faire qch; **the ~ of the matter** le fond du problème.

heartache ['hɑ:teɪk] *n* chagrin *m*, douleur *f*.

heart attack *n* crise *f* cardiaque.

heartbeat ['hɑ:tbi:t] *n* battement *m* de cœur.

heartbreak ['hɑ:tbreɪk] *n* immense chagrin *m*.

heartbreaking ['hɑ:tbreɪkɪŋ] *adj* navrant(e), déchirant(e).

heartbroken ['hɑ:tbrəukən] *adj*: **to be ~** avoir beaucoup de chagrin.

heartburn ['hɑ:tbə:n] *n* brûlures *fpl* d'estomac.

-hearted ['hɑ:tɪd] *suffix*: **kind~** généreux(euse), qui a bon cœur.

heartening ['hɑ:tnɪŋ] *adj* encourageant(e), réconfortant(e).

heart failure *n* (*MED*) arrêt *m* du cœur.

heartfelt ['hɑ:tfɛlt] *adj* sincère.

hearth [hɑ:θ] *n* foyer *m*, cheminée *f*.

heartily ['hɑ:tɪlɪ] *adv* chaleureusement; (*laugh*) de bon cœur; (*eat*) de bon appétit; **to agree ~** être entièrement d'accord; **to be ~ sick of** (*BRIT*) en avoir ras le bol de.

heartland ['hɑ:tlænd] *n* centre *m*, cœur *m*; **France's ~s** la France profonde.

heartless ['hɑ:tlɪs] *adj* sans cœur, insensible; cruel(le).

heartstrings ['hɑ:tstrɪŋz] *npl*: **to tug (at) sb's ~** toucher *or* faire vibrer les cordes sensibles de qn.

heartthrob ['hɑ:tθrɔb] *n* idole *f*.

heart-to-heart ['hɑ:t'tə'hɑ:t] *adj, adv* à cœur ouvert.

heart transplant *n* greffe *f* du cœur.

heartwarming ['hɑ:twɔ:mɪŋ] *adj* réconfortant(e).

hearty ['hɑ:tɪ] *adj* chaleureux(euse); robuste; vigoureux(euse).

heat [hi:t] *n* chaleur *f*; (*fig*) ardeur *f*; feu *m*;

(*SPORT: also*: **qualifying ~**) éliminatoire *f*; (*ZOOL*): **in** *or* (*BRIT*) **on ~** en chaleur ♦ *vt* chauffer.

►**heat up** *vi* (*liquids*) chauffer; (*room*) se réchauffer ♦ *vt* réchauffer.

heated ['hi:tɪd] *adj* chauffé(e); (*fig*) passionné(e); échauffé(e), excité(e).

heater ['hi:tə*] *n* appareil *m* de chauffage; radiateur *m*.

heath [hi:θ] *n* (*BRIT*) lande *f*.

heathen ['hi:ðn] *adj, n* païen(ne).

heather ['hɛðə*] *n* bruyère *f*.

heating ['hi:tɪŋ] *n* chauffage *m*.

heat-resistant ['hi:trɪzɪstənt] *adj* résistant(e) à la chaleur.

heat-seeking ['hi:tsi:kɪŋ] *adj* guidé(e) par infrarouge.

heatstroke ['hi:tstrəuk] *n* coup *m* de chaleur.

heatwave ['hi:tweɪv] *n* vague *f* de chaleur.

heave [hi:v] *vt* soulever (avec effort) ♦ *vi* se soulever; (*retch*) avoir des haut-le-cœur ♦ *n* (*push*) poussée *f*; **to ~ a sigh** pousser un gros soupir.

heaven ['hɛvn] *n* ciel *m*, paradis *m*; **~ forbid!** surtout pas!; **thank ~!** Dieu merci!; **for ~'s sake!** (*pleading*) je vous en prie!; (*protesting*) mince alors!

heavenly ['hɛvnlɪ] *adj* céleste, divin(e).

heavily ['hɛvɪlɪ] *adv* lourdement; (*drink, smoke*) beaucoup; (*sleep, sigh*) profondément.

heavy ['hɛvɪ] *adj* lourd(e); (*work, rain, user, eater*) gros(se); (*drinker, smoker*) grand(e); **it's ~ going** ça ne va pas tout seul, c'est pénible.

heavy cream *n* (*US*) crème fraîche épaisse.

heavy-duty ['hɛvɪ'dju:tɪ] *adj* à usage intensif.

heavy goods vehicle (HGV) *n* (*BRIT*) poids lourd *m* (P.L.).

heavy-handed ['hɛvɪ'hændɪd] *adj* (*fig*) maladroit(e), qui manque de tact.

heavy metal *n* (*MUS*) heavy metal *m*.

heavy-set ['hɛvɪ'sɛt] *adj* (*esp US*) costaud(e).

heavyweight ['hɛvɪweɪt] *n* (*SPORT*) poids lourd.

Hebrew ['hi:bru:] *adj* hébraïque ♦ *n* (*LING*) hébreu *m*.

Hebrides ['hɛbrɪdɪːz] *n*: **the ~** les Hébrides *fpl*.

heck [hɛk] *n* (*col*): **why the ~ ...?** pourquoi diable ...?; **a ~ of a lot** une sacrée quantité; **he has done a ~ of a lot for us** il a vraiment beaucoup fait pour nous.

heckle ['hɛkl] *vt* interpeller (*un orateur*).

heckler ['hɛklə*] *n* interrupteur *m*; élément perturbateur.

hectare ['hɛktɑ:*] *n* (*BRIT*) hectare *m*.

hectic ['hɛktɪk] *adj* agité(e), trépidant(e); (*busy*) trépidant.

hector ['hɛktə*] *vt* rudoyer, houspiller.

he'd [hi:d] = **he would, he had**.

hedge [hɛdʒ] *n* haie *f* ♦ *vi* se défiler ♦ *vt*: **to ~ one's bets** (*fig*) se couvrir; **as a ~ against inflation** pour se prémunir contre l'inflation.

▶**hedge in** *vt* entourer d'une haie.
hedgehog ['hɛdʒhɔg] *n* hérisson *m*.
hedgerow ['hɛdʒrəu] *n* haie(s) *f(pl)*.
hedonism ['hiːdənɪzəm] *n* hédonisme *m*.
heed [hiːd] *vt* (*also*: **take ~ of**) tenir compte de, prendre garde à.
heedless ['hiːdlɪs] *adj* insouciant(e).
heel [hiːl] *n* talon *m* ♦ *vt* (*shoe*) retalonner; **to bring to ~** (*dog*) faire venir à ses pieds; (*fig: person*) rappeler à l'ordre; **to take to one's ~s** prendre ses jambes à son cou.
hefty ['hɛftɪ] *adj* (*person*) costaud(e); (*parcel*) lourd(e); (*piece, price*) gros(se).
heifer ['hɛfə*] *n* génisse *f*.
height [haɪt] *n* (*of person*) taille *f*, grandeur *f*; (*of object*) hauteur *f*; (*of plane, mountain*) altitude *f*; (*high ground*) hauteur, éminence *f*; (*fig: of glory*) sommet *m*; (: *of stupidity*) comble *m*; **what ~ are you?** combien mesurez-vous?, quelle est votre taille?; **of average ~** de taille moyenne; **to be afraid of ~s** être sujet(te) au vertige; **it's the ~ of fashion** c'est le dernier cri.
heighten ['haɪtn] *vt* hausser, surélever; (*fig*) augmenter.
heinous ['heɪnəs] *adj* odieux(euse), atroce.
heir [ɛə*] *n* héritier *m*.
heir apparent *n* héritier présomptif.
heiress ['ɛərɛs] *n* héritière *f*.
heirloom ['ɛəluːm] *n* meuble *m* (*or* bijou *m or* tableau *m*) de famille.
heist [haɪst] *n* (*US col: hold-up*) casse *m*.
held [hɛld] *pt, pp of* **hold**.
helicopter ['hɛlɪkɔptə*] *n* hélicoptère *m*.
heliport ['hɛlɪpɔːt] *n* (*AVIAT*) héliport *m*.
helium ['hiːlɪəm] *n* hélium *m*.
hell [hɛl] *n* enfer *m*; **a ~ of a** ... (*col*) un(e) sacré(e) ...; **oh ~!** (*col*) merde!
he'll [hiːl] = **he will, he shall**.
hell-bent [hɛl'bɛnt] *adj* (*col*): **to be ~ on doing sth** vouloir à tout prix faire qch.
hellish ['hɛlɪʃ] *adj* infernal(e).
hello [hə'ləu] *excl* bonjour!; salut! (*to sb one addresses as "tu"*); (*surprise*) tiens!
helm [hɛlm] *n* (*NAUT*) barre *f*.
helmet ['hɛlmɪt] *n* casque *m*.
helmsman ['hɛlmzmən] *n* timonier *m*.
help [hɛlp] *n* aide *f*; (*charwoman*) femme *f* de ménage; (*assistant etc*) employé/e ♦ *vt* aider; **~!** au secours!; **~ yourself** (**to bread**) servez-vous (de pain); **can I ~ you?** (*in shop*) vous désirez?; **with the ~ of** (*person*) avec l'aide de; (*tool etc*) à l'aide de; **to be of ~ to sb** être utile à qn; **to ~ sb (to) do sth** aider qn à faire qch; **I can't ~ saying** je ne peux pas m'empêcher de dire; **he can't ~ it** il n'y peut rien.
helper ['hɛlpə*] *n* aide *m/f*, assistant/e.
helpful ['hɛlpful] *adj* serviable, obligeant(e); (*useful*) utile.
helping ['hɛlpɪŋ] *n* portion *f*.
helping hand *n* coup *m* de main; **to give sb a**

~ prêter main-forte à qn.
helpless ['hɛlplɪs] *adj* impuissant(e); (*baby*) sans défense.
helplessly ['hɛlplɪslɪ] *adv* (*watch*) sans pouvoir rien faire.
helpline ['hɛlplaɪn] *n numéro téléphonique que l'on peut appeler pour obtenir une assistance sociale, médicale, judiciaire etc ou des renseignements sur un produit commercial.*
Helsinki ['hɛlsɪŋkɪ] *n* Helsinki.
helter-skelter ['hɛltə'skɛltə*] *n* (*BRIT: at amusement park*) toboggan *m*.
hem [hɛm] *n* ourlet *m* ♦ *vt* ourler.
▶**hem in** *vt* cerner; **to feel ~med in** (*fig*) avoir l'impression d'étouffer, se sentir oppressé(e) *or* écrasé(e).
he-man ['hiːmæn] *n* (*col*) macho *m*.
hematology ['hiːmə'tɔlədʒɪ] *n* (*US*) = **haematology**.
hemisphere ['hɛmɪsfɪə*] *n* hémisphère *m*.
hemlock ['hɛmlɔk] *n* cigüe *f*.
hemoglobin ['hiːmə'gləubɪn] *n* (*US*) = **haemoglobin**.
hemophilia ['hiːmə'fɪlɪə] *n* (*US*) = **haemophilia**.
hemorrhage ['hɛmərɪdʒ] *n* (*US*) = **haemorrhage**.
hemorrhoids ['hɛmərɔɪdz] *npl* (*US*) = **haemorrhoids**.
hemp [hɛmp] *n* chanvre *m*.
hen [hɛn] *n* poule *f*; (*female bird*) femelle *f*.
hence [hɛns] *adv* (*therefore*) d'où, de là; **2 years ~** d'ici 2 ans.
henceforth [hɛns'fɔːθ] *adv* dorénavant.
henchman ['hɛntʃmən] *n* (*pej*) acolyte *m*, séide *m*.
henna ['hɛnə] *n* henné *m*.
hen party *n* (*col*) réunion *f or* fête *f* entre femmes.
henpecked ['hɛnpɛkt] *adj* dominé par sa femme.
hepatitis [hɛpə'taɪtɪs] *n* hépatite *f*.
her [həː*] *pron* (*direct*) la, l' + *vowel or h mute*; (*indirect*) lui; (*stressed, after prep*) elle; *see note at* **she** ♦ *adj* son(sa), ses *pl*; **I see ~** je la vois; **give ~ a book** donne-lui un livre; **after ~** après elle.
herald ['hɛrəld] *n* héraut *m* ♦ *vt* annoncer.
heraldic [hɛ'rældɪk] *adj* héraldique.
heraldry ['hɛrəldrɪ] *n* héraldique *f*; (*coat of arms*) blason *m*.
herb [həːb] *n* herbe *f*; **~s** *npl* (*CULIN*) fines herbes.
herbaceous [həː'beɪʃəs] *adj* herbacé(e).
herbal ['həːbl] *adj* à base de plantes; **~ tea** tisane *f*.
herbicide ['həːbɪsaɪd] *n* herbicide *m*.
herd [həːd] *n* troupeau *m*; (*of wild animals, swine*) troupeau, troupe *f* ♦ *vt* (*drive: animals, people*) mener, conduire; (*gather*) rassembler; **~ed together** parqués (comme du bétail).

here [hɪə*] *adv* ici ♦ *excl* tiens!, tenez!; ~!
présent!; ~ **is**, ~ **are** voici; ~'**s my sister**
voici ma sœur; ~ **he/she is** le/la voici; ~ **she**
comes la voici qui vient; **come** ~! viens ici!;
~ **and there** ici et là.

hereabouts ['hɪərə'bauts] *adv* par ici, dans les
parages.

hereafter [hɪər'ɑ:ftə*] *adv* après, plus tard;
ci-après ♦ *n*: **the** ~ l'au-delà *m*.

hereby [hɪə'baɪ] *adv* (*in letter*) par la présente.

hereditary [hɪ'rɛdɪtrɪ] *adj* héréditaire.

heredity [hɪ'rɛdɪtɪ] *n* hérédité *f*.

heresy ['hɛrəsɪ] *n* hérésie *f*.

heretic ['hɛrətɪk] *n* hérétique *m/f*.

heretical [hɪ'rɛtɪkl] *adj* hérétique.

herewith [hɪə'wɪð] *adv* avec ceci, ci-joint.

heritage ['hɛrɪtɪdʒ] *n* héritage *m*, patrimoine
m; **our national** ~ notre patrimoine national.

hermetically [hə:'mɛtɪklɪ] *adv* hermétiquement; ~ **sealed** hermétiquement fermé *or*
clos.

hermit ['hə:mɪt] *n* ermite *m*.

hernia ['hə:nɪə] *n* hernie *f*.

hero, *pl* ~**es** ['hɪərəu] *n* héros *m*.

heroic [hɪ'rəuɪk] *adj* héroïque.

heroin ['hɛrəuɪn] *n* héroïne *f*.

heroin addict *n* héroïnomane *m/f*.

heroine ['hɛrəuɪn] *n* héroïne *f* (*femme*).

heroism ['hɛrəuɪzəm] *n* héroïsme *m*.

heron ['hɛrən] *n* héron *m*.

hero worship *n* culte *m* (du héros).

herring ['hɛrɪŋ] *n* hareng *m*.

hers [hə:z] *pron* le(la) sien(ne), les
siens(siennes); **a friend of** ~ un(e) ami(e) à
elle, un(e) de ses ami(e)s; **this is** ~ c'est à
elle, c'est le sien.

herself [hə:'sɛlf] *pron* (*reflexive*) se; (*emphatic*)
elle-même; (*after prep*) elle.

Herts [hɑ:ts] *abbr* (*BRIT*) = Hertfordshire.

he's [hi:z] = **he is**, **he has**.

hesitant ['hɛzɪtənt] *adj* hésitant(e), indécis(e);
to be ~ **about doing sth** hésiter à faire qch.

hesitate ['hɛzɪteɪt] *vi*: **to** ~ (**about/to do**)
hésiter (sur/à faire).

hesitation [hɛzɪ'teɪʃən] *n* hésitation *f*; **I have**
no ~ **in saying (that)** ... je n'hésiterai pas à
dire (que) ....

hessian ['hɛsɪən] *n* (*toile f de*) jute *m*.

heterogeneous ['hɛtərə'dʒi:nɪəs] *adj*
hétérogène.

heterosexual ['hɛtərəu'sɛksjuəl] *adj*, *n*
hétérosexuel(le).

het up [hɛt'ʌp] *adj* (*col*) agité(e), excité(e).

HEW *n abbr* (*US*: = *Department of Health,*
Education and Welfare) *ministère de la santé*
publique, de l'enseignement et du bien-être.

hew [hju:] *vt* tailler (*à la hache*).

hex [hɛks] (*US*) *n* sort *m* ♦ *vt* jeter un sort sur.

hexagon ['hɛksəgən] *n* hexagone *m*.

hexagonal [hɛk'sægənl] *adj* hexagonal(e).

hey [heɪ] *excl* hé!

heyday ['heɪdeɪ] *n*: **the** ~ **of** l'âge *m* d'or de,

les beaux jours de.

HF *n abbr* (= *high frequency*) HF *f*.

HGV *n abbr* = **heavy goods vehicle**.

HI *abbr* (*US*) = **Hawaii**.

hi [haɪ] *excl* salut!

hiatus [haɪ'eɪtəs] *n* trou *m*, lacune *f*; (*LING*)
hiatus *m*.

hibernate ['haɪbəneɪt] *vi* hiberner.

hibernation [haɪbə'neɪʃən] *n* hibernation *f*.

hiccough, hiccup ['hɪkʌp] *vi* hoqueter ♦ *n*
hoquet *m*; **to have (the)** ~**s** avoir le hoquet.

hick [hɪk] *n* (*US col*) plouc *m*, péquenaud/e.

hid [hɪd] *pt of* **hide**.

hidden ['hɪdn] *pp of* **hide** ♦ *adj*: **there are no** ~
extras absolument tout est compris dans le
prix; ~ **agenda** intentions non déclarées.

hide [haɪd] *n* (*skin*) peau *f* ♦ *vb* (*pt* **hid**, *pp* **hidden**
[hɪd, 'hɪdn]) *vt*: **to** ~ **sth (from sb)** cacher qch
(à qn); (*feelings, truth*) dissimuler qch (à qn)
♦ *vi*: **to** ~ (**from sb**) se cacher de qn.

hide-and-seek ['haɪdən'si:k] *n* cache-cache *m*.

hideaway ['haɪdəweɪ] *n* cachette *f*.

hideous ['hɪdɪəs] *adj* hideux(euse); atroce.

hide-out ['haɪdaut] *n* cachette *f*.

hiding ['haɪdɪŋ] *n* (*beating*) correction *f*, volée *f*
de coups; **to be in** ~ (*concealed*) se tenir
caché(e).

hiding place *n* cachette *f*.

hierarchy ['haɪərɑ:kɪ] *n* hiérarchie *f*.

hieroglyphic [haɪərə'glɪfɪk] *adj*
hiéroglyphique; ~**s** *npl* hiéroglyphes *mpl*.

hi-fi ['haɪfaɪ] *adj*, *n abbr* (= *high fidelity*) hi-fi (*f*)
inv.

higgledy-piggledy ['hɪgldɪ'pɪgldɪ] *adv* pêle-
mêle, dans le plus grand désordre.

high [haɪ] *adj* haut(e); (*speed, respect, number*)
grand(e); (*price*) élevé(e); (*wind*) fort(e),
violent(e); (*voice*) aigu(aiguë); (*col: person:*
on drugs) défoncé(e), fait(e); (*: on drink*)
soûl(e), bourré(e); (*BRIT CULIN: meat, game*)
faisandé(e); (*: spoilt*) avarié(e) ♦ *adv* haut, en
haut ♦ *n*: **exports have reached a new** ~ les
exportations ont atteint un nouveau record;
20 m ~ haut(e) de 20 m; **to pay a** ~ **price for**
sth payer cher pour qch.

highball ['haɪbɔ:l] *n* (*US*) whisky *m* à l'eau
avec des glaçons.

highboy ['haɪbɔɪ] *n* (*US*) grande commode.

highbrow ['haɪbrau] *adj*, *n* intellectuel(le).

highchair ['haɪtʃɛə*] *n* chaise haute (*pour*
enfant).

high-class ['haɪ'klɑ:s] *adj* (*neighbourhood,*
hotel) chic *inv*, de grand standing;
(*performance etc*) de haut niveau.

High Court *n* (*LAW*) cour *f* suprême.

> *La* **High Court** *en Grande-Bretagne est la plus*
> *haute cour de justice à laquelle les affaires les*
> *plus graves telles que le meurtre et le viol sont*
> *soumises et où elles sont jugées devant un*
> *jury.*

higher ['haɪə*] *adj* (*form of life, study etc*)
supérieur(e) ♦ *adv* plus haut.
higher education *n* études supérieures.
highfalutin [haɪfə'luːtɪn] *adj* (*col*) affecté(e).
high finance *n* la haute finance.
high-flier, high-flyer [haɪ'flaɪə*] *n* (*fig:
ambitious*) ambitieux/euse; (*: gifted*)
personne particulièrement douée et
promise à un avenir brillant.
high-flying [haɪ'flaɪɪŋ] *adj* (*fig*)
ambitieux(euse), de haut niveau.
high-handed [haɪ'hændɪd] *adj* très autoritaire;
très cavalier(ière).
high-heeled [haɪ'hiːld] *adj* à hauts talons.
highjack ['haɪdʒæk] *n, vt* = **hijack**.
high jump *n* (*SPORT*) saut *m* en hauteur.
highlands ['haɪləndz] *npl* région
montagneuse; **the H~** (*in Scotland*) les
Highlands *mpl*.
high-level ['haɪlɛvl] *adj* (*talks etc*) à un haut
niveau; ~ **language** (*COMPUT*) langage
évolué.
highlight ['haɪlaɪt] *n* (*fig: of event*) point
culminant ♦ *vt* faire ressortir, souligner; ~**s**
npl (*hairstyle*) reflets *mpl*.
highlighter ['haɪlaɪtə*] *n* (*pen*) surligneur
(lumineux).
highly ['haɪlɪ] *adv* très, fort, hautement; ~
paid très bien payé(e); **to speak ~ of** dire
beaucoup de bien de.
highly-strung ['haɪlɪ'strʌŋ] *adj* nerveux(euse),
toujours tendu(e).
High Mass *n* grand-messe *f*.
highness ['haɪnɪs] *n* hauteur *f*; **Her H~** son
Altesse *f*.
high-pitched [haɪ'pɪtʃt] *adj* aigu(ë).
high point *n*: **the ~ (of)** le clou (de), le point
culminant (de).
high-powered ['haɪ'pauəd] *adj* (*engine*)
performant(e); (*fig: person*) dynamique;
(*: job, businessman*) très important(e).
high-pressure ['haɪprɛʃə*] *adj* à haute
pression.
high-rise block ['haɪraɪz-] *n* tour *f*
(d'habitation).
high school *n* lycée *m*; (*US*) établissement *m*
d'enseignement supérieur.

Une **high school** *est un établissement
d'enseignement secondaire. Aux États-Unis, il
y a la Junior High School, qui correspond au
collège, et la Senior High School, qui
correspond au lycée. En Grande-Bretagne,
c'est un nom que l'on donne parfois aux écoles
secondaires; voir* **elementary school**

---

high season *n* (*BRIT*) haute saison.
high spirits *npl* pétulance *f*; **to be in ~** être
plein(e) d'entrain.
high street *n* (*BRIT*) grand-rue *f*.
highway ['haɪweɪ] *n* grand'route *f*, route
nationale; **the information ~** l'autoroute *f* de
l'information.
Highway Code *n* (*BRIT*) code *m* de la route.
highwayman ['haɪweɪmən] *n* voleur *m* de
grand chemin.
hijack ['haɪdʒæk] *vt* détourner (*par la force*) ♦ *n*
(*also: ~ing*) détournement *m* (d'avion).
hijacker ['haɪdʒækə*] *n* auteur *m* d'un
détournement d'avion, pirate *m* de l'air.
hike [haɪk] *vi* aller à pied ♦ *n* excursion *f* à
pied, randonnée *f*; (*col: in prices etc*)
augmentation *f* ♦ *vt* (*col*) augmenter.
hiker ['haɪkə*] *n* promeneur/euse,
excursionniste *m/f*.
hiking ['haɪkɪŋ] *n* excursions *fpl* à pied,
randonnée *f*.
hilarious [hɪ'lɛərɪəs] *adj* (*behaviour, event*)
désopilant(e).
hilarity [hɪ'lærɪtɪ] *n* hilarité *f*.
hill [hɪl] *n* colline *f*; (*fairly high*) montagne *f*; (*on
road*) côte *f*.
hillbilly ['hɪlbɪlɪ] *n* (*US*) montagnard/e du sud
des USA; (*pej*) péquenaud *m*.
hillock ['hɪlək] *n* petite colline, butte *f*.
hillside ['hɪlsaɪd] *n* (flanc *m* de) coteau *m*.
hill start *n* (*AUT*) démarrage *m* en côte.
hilly ['hɪlɪ] *adj* vallonné(e); montagneux(euse);
(*road*) à fortes côtes.
hilt [hɪlt] *n* (*of sword*) garde *f*; **to the ~** (*fig:
support*) à fond.
him [hɪm] *pron* (*direct*) le, l' + *vowel or h mute*;
(*stressed, indirect, after prep*) lui; **I see ~** je le
vois; **give ~ a book** donne-lui un livre; **after
~** après lui.
Himalayas [hɪmə'leɪəz] *npl*: **the ~** l'Himalaya
m.
himself [hɪm'sɛlf] *pron* (*reflexive*) se; (*emphatic*)
lui-même; (*after prep*) lui.
hind [haɪnd] *adj* de derrière ♦ *n* biche *f*.
hinder ['hɪndə*] *vt* gêner; (*delay*) retarder;
(*prevent*): **to ~ sb from doing** empêcher qn
de faire.
hindquarters ['haɪnd'kwɔːtəz] *npl* (*ZOOL*)
arrière-train *m*.
hindrance ['hɪndrəns] *n* gêne *f*, obstacle *m*.
hindsight ['haɪndsaɪt] *n* bon sens après coup;
with the benefit of ~ avec du recul,
rétrospectivement.
Hindu ['hɪnduː] *n* Hindou/e.
hinge [hɪndʒ] *n* charnière *f* ♦ *vi* (*fig*): **to ~ on**
dépendre de.
hint [hɪnt] *n* allusion *f*; (*advice*) conseil *m* ♦ *vt*:
to ~ that insinuer que ♦ *vi*: **to ~ at** faire une
allusion à; **to drop a ~** faire une allusion *or*
insinuation; **give me a ~** (*clue*) mettez-moi
sur la voie, donnez-moi une indication.
hip [hɪp] *n* hanche *f*; (*BOT*) fruit *m* de
l'églantier *or* du rosier.
hip flask *n* flacon *m* (pour la poche).
hip hop *n* hip hop *m*.
hippie, hippy ['hɪpɪ] *n* hippie *m/f*.
hip pocket *n* poche-revolver *f*.
hippopotamus, *pl* ~**es** *or* **hippopotami**

[hɪpə'pɒtəməs, -'pɒtəmaɪ] n hippopotame m.
hippy ['hɪpɪ] n = **hippie**.
hire ['haɪə*] vt (BRIT: car, equipment) louer;
(worker) embaucher, engager ♦ n location f;
for ~ à louer; (taxi) libre; **on** ~ en location.
▶**hire out** vt louer.
hire(d) car ['haɪə(d)-] n (BRIT) voiture louée.
hire purchase (H.P.) n (BRIT) achat m (or
vente f) à tempérament or crédit; **to buy sth
on** ~ acheter qch en location-vente.
his [hɪz] pron le(la) sien(ne), les siens(siennes)
♦ adj son(sa), ses pl; **this is** ~ c'est à lui,
c'est le sien.
hiss [hɪs] vi siffler ♦ n sifflement m.
histogram ['hɪstəgræm] n histogramme m.
historian [hɪ'stɔːrɪən] n historien/ne.
historic(al) [hɪ'stɔrɪk(l)] adj historique.
history ['hɪstərɪ] n histoire f; **medical** ~ (of
patient) passé médical.
histrionics [hɪstrɪ'ɒnɪks] n gestes mpl
dramatiques, cinéma m (fig).
hit [hɪt] vt (pt, pp hit) frapper; (knock against)
cogner; (reach: target) atteindre, toucher;
(collide with: car) entrer en collision avec,
heurter; (fig: affect) toucher; (find) tomber
sur ♦ n coup m; (success) coup réussi; succès
m; (song) chanson f à succès, tube m; **to** ~ **it
off with sb** bien s'entendre avec qn; **to** ~
the headlines être à la une des journaux; **to**
~ **the road** (col) se mettre en route.
▶**hit back** vi: **to** ~ **back at sb** prendre sa
revanche sur qn.
▶**hit out at** vt fus envoyer un coup à; (fig)
attaquer.
▶**hit (up)on** vt fus (answer) trouver (par
hasard); (solution) tomber sur (par hasard).
hit-and-miss ['hɪtænd'mɪs] adj au petit
bonheur (la chance).
hit-and-run driver ['hɪtænd'rʌn-] n chauffard
m.
hitch [hɪtʃ] vt (fasten) accrocher, attacher;
(also: ~ **up**) remonter d'une saccade ♦ n
(knot) nœud m; (difficulty) anicroche f,
contretemps m; **to** ~ **a lift** faire du stop;
technical ~ incident m technique.
▶**hitch up** vt (horse, cart) atteler; see also **hitch**.
hitch-hike ['hɪtʃhaɪk] vi faire de l'auto-stop.
hitch-hiker ['hɪtʃhaɪkə*] n auto-stoppeur/
euse.
hi-tech ['haɪ'tɛk] adj de pointe ♦ n high-tech m.
hitherto [hɪðə'tuː] adv jusqu'ici, jusqu'à
présent.
hit list n liste noire.
hitman ['hɪtmæn] n (col) tueur m à gages.
hit-or-miss ['hɪtə'mɪs] adj au petit bonheur (la
chance); **it's** ~ **whether** ... il est loin d'être
certain que ... + sub.
hit parade n hit parade m.
HIV n abbr (= human immunodeficiency virus)
HIV m, VIH m; ~-**negative/-positive**
séronégatif(ive)/séropositif(ive).
hive [haɪv] n ruche f; **the shop was a** ~ **of**
activity (fig) le magasin était une véritable
ruche.
▶**hive off** vt (col) mettre à part, séparer.
hl abbr (= hectolitre) hl.
HM abbr (= His (or Her) Majesty) SM.
HMG abbr (BRIT) = His (or Her) Majesty's
Government.
HMI n abbr (BRIT SCOL) = His (or Her) Majesty's
Inspector.
HMO n abbr (US: = health maintenance
organization) organisme médical assurant
un forfait entretien de santé.
HMS abbr (BRIT) = His (or Her) Majesty's Ship.
HMSO n abbr (BRIT: = His (or Her) Majesty's
Stationery Office) ≈ Imprimerie nationale.
HNC n abbr (BRIT: = Higher National Certificate)
≈ DUT m.
HND n abbr (BRIT: = Higher National Diploma)
≈ licence f de sciences et techniques.
hoard [hɔːd] n (of food) provisions fpl,
réserves fpl; (of money) trésor m ♦ vt
amasser.
hoarding ['hɔːdɪŋ] n (BRIT) panneau m
d'affichage or publicitaire.
hoarfrost ['hɔːfrɒst] n givre m.
hoarse [hɔːs] adj enroué(e).
hoax [həʊks] n canular m.
hob [hɒb] n plaque chauffante.
hobble ['hɒbl] vi boitiller.
hobby ['hɒbɪ] n passe-temps favori.
hobby-horse ['hɒbɪhɔːs] n cheval m à bascule;
(fig) dada m.
hobnail(ed) boot ['hɒbneɪl(d)-] n chaussure
(à semelle) cloutée.
hobnob ['hɒbnɒb] vi: **to** ~ **with** frayer avec,
fréquenter.
hobo ['həʊbəʊ] n (US) vagabond m.
hock [hɒk] n (BRIT: wine) vin m du Rhin; (of
animal, CULIN) jarret m; (col): **to be in** ~
(person) avoir des dettes; (object) être en
gage or au clou.
hockey ['hɒkɪ] n hockey m.
hocus-pocus ['həʊkəs'pəʊkəs] n (trickery)
supercherie f; (words: of magician) formules
fpl magiques; (: jargon) galimatias m.
hod [hɒd] n oiseau m, hotte f.
hodgepodge ['hɒdʒpɒdʒ] n = **hotchpotch**.
hoe [həʊ] n houe f, binette f ♦ vt (ground) biner;
(plants etc) sarcler.
hog [hɒg] n porc (châtré) m ♦ vt (fig) accaparer;
to go the whole ~ aller jusqu'au bout.
Hogmanay [hɒgmə'neɪ] n (Scottish) réveillon
m du jour de l'An, Saint-Sylvestre f.
hogwash ['hɒgwɒʃ] n (col) foutaises fpl.
hoist [hɔɪst] n palan m ♦ vt hisser.
hoity-toity [hɔɪtɪ'tɔɪtɪ] adj (col)
prétentieux(euse), qui se donne
de grands airs.
hold [həʊld] vb (pt, pp held [hɛld]) vt tenir;
(contain) contenir; (keep back) retenir;
(believe) maintenir; considérer; (possess)
avoir; détenir ♦ vi (withstand pressure) tenir

(bon); (*be valid*) valoir ♦ *n* prise *f*; (*fig*)
influence *f*; (*NAUT*) cale *f*; **to catch** *or* **get (a)**
~ of saisir; **to get ~ of** (*fig*) trouver; **to get**
~ of o.s. se contrôler; **~ the line!** (*TEL*) ne
quittez pas!; **to ~ one's own** (*fig*) (bien) se
défendre; **to ~ office** (*POL*) avoir un
portefeuille; **to ~ firm** *or* **fast** tenir bon; **he**
~s the view that ... il pense *or* estime que ...,
d'après lui ...; **to ~ sb responsible for sth**
tenir qn pour responsable de qch.
▶**hold back** *vt* retenir; (*secret*) cacher; **to ~**
sb back from doing sth empêcher qn de
faire qch.
▶**hold down** *vt* (*person*) maintenir à terre;
(*job*) occuper.
▶**hold forth** *vi* pérorer.
▶**hold off** *vt* tenir à distance ♦ *vi* (*rain*): **if the**
rain ~s off s'il ne pleut pas, s'il ne se met
pas à pleuvoir.
▶**hold on** *vi* tenir bon; (*wait*) attendre; **~ on!**
(*TEL*) ne quittez pas!
▶**hold on to** *vt fus* se cramponner à; (*keep*)
conserver, garder.
▶**hold out** *vt* offrir ♦ *vi* (*resist*): **to ~ out**
(against) résister (devant), tenir bon
(devant).
▶**hold over** *vt* (*meeting etc*) ajourner,
reporter.
▶**hold up** *vt* (*raise*) lever; (*support*) soutenir;
(*delay*) retarder; (: *traffic*) ralentir; (*rob*)
braquer.
holdall ['həʊldɔːl] *n* (*BRIT*) fourre-tout *m inv*.
holder ['həʊldə*] *n* (*of ticket, record*)
détenteur/trice; (*of office, title, passport etc*)
titulaire *m/f*.
holding ['həʊldɪŋ] *n* (*share*) intérêts *mpl*; (*farm*)
ferme *f*.
holding company *n* holding *m*.
holdup ['həʊldʌp] *n* (*robbery*) hold-up *m*;
(*delay*) retard *m*; (*BRIT*: *in traffic*)
embouteillage *m*.
hole [həʊl] *n* trou *m* ♦ *vt* trouer, faire un trou
dans; **~ in the heart** (*MED*) communication *f*
interventriculaire; **to pick ~s (in)** (*fig*)
chercher des poux (dans).
▶**hole up** *vi* se terrer.
holiday ['hɔlədɪ] *n* (*BRIT*: *vacation*) vacances *fpl*;
(*day off*) jour *m* de congé; (*public*) jour férié;
to be on ~ être en congé; **tomorrow is a ~**
demain c'est fête, on a congé demain.
holiday camp *n* (*BRIT*: *for children*) colonie *f* de
vacances; (: *also*: **holiday centre**) camp *m* de
vacances.
holidaymaker ['hɔlədɪmeɪkə*] *n* (*BRIT*)
vacancier/ière.
holiday pay *n* paie *f* des vacances.
holiday resort *n* centre *m* de villégiature *or*
de vacances.
holiday season *n* période *f* des vacances.
holiness ['həʊlɪnɪs] *n* sainteté *f*.
holistic [həʊ'lɪstɪk] *adj* holiste, holistique.
Holland ['hɔlənd] *n* Hollande *f*.

holler ['hɔlə*] *vi* (*col*) brailler.
hollow ['hɔləʊ] *adj* creux(euse); (*fig*)
faux(fausse) ♦ *n* creux *m*; (*in land*)
dépression *f* (de terrain), cuvette *f*
♦ *vt*: **to ~ out** creuser, évider.
holly ['hɔlɪ] *n* houx *m*.
hollyhock ['hɔlɪhɔk] *n* rose trémière.
holocaust ['hɔləkɔːst] *n* holocauste *m*.
hologram ['hɔləgræm] *n* hologramme *m*.
hols [hɔlz] *npl* (*col*) vacances *fpl*.
holster ['həʊlstə*] *n* étui *m* de revolver.
holy ['həʊlɪ] *adj* saint(e); (*bread, water*)
bénit(e); (*ground*) sacré(e).
Holy Communion *n* la (sainte) communion.
Holy Ghost, Holy Spirit *n* Saint-Esprit *m*.
Holy Land *n*: **the ~** la Terre Sainte.
holy orders *npl* ordres (majeurs).
homage ['hɔmɪdʒ] *n* hommage *m*; **to pay ~ to**
rendre hommage à.
home [həʊm] *n* foyer *m*, maison *f*; (*country*)
pays natal, patrie *f*; (*institution*) maison ♦ *adj*
de famille; (*ECON, POL*) national(e),
intérieur(e); (*SPORT*: *team*) qui reçoit;
(: *match, win*) sur leur (*or* notre) terrain
♦ *adv* chez soi, à la maison; au pays natal;
(*right in*: *nail etc*) à fond; **at ~** chez soi, à la
maison; **to go** (*or* **come**) **~** rentrer (chez
soi), rentrer à la maison (*or* au pays); **make**
yourself at ~ faites comme chez vous; **near**
my ~ près de chez moi.
▶**home in on** *vt fus* (*missiles*) se diriger
automatiquement vers *or* sur.
home address *n* domicile permanent.
home-brew [həʊm'bruː] *n* vin *m* (*or* bière *f*)
maison.
homecoming ['həʊmkʌmɪŋ] *n* retour *m* (au
bercail).
home computer *n* ordinateur *m* domestique.
Home Counties *npl* les comtés autour de
Londres.
home economics *n* économie *f* domestique.
home ground *n*: **to be on ~** être sur son
terrain.
home-grown ['həʊmgrəʊn] *adj* (*not foreign*) du
pays; (*from garden*) du jardin.
home help *n* (*BRIT*) aide-ménagère *f*.
homeland ['həʊmlænd] *n* patrie *f*.
homeless ['həʊmlɪs] *adj* sans foyer, sans abri;
the ~ *npl* les sans-abri *mpl*.
home loan *n* prêt *m* sur hypothèque.
homely ['həʊmlɪ] *adj* simple, sans prétention;
accueillant(e).
home-made [həʊm'meɪd] *adj* fait(e) à la
maison.
Home Office *n* (*BRIT*) ministère *m* de
l'Intérieur.
homeopathy *etc* [həʊmɪ'ɔpəθɪ] (*US*)
= **homoeopathy** *etc*.
homeowner ['həʊməʊnə*] *n* propriétaire
occupant.
home rule *n* autonomie *f*.
Home Secretary *n* (*BRIT*) ministre *m* de

l'Intérieur.

homesick ['həumsɪk] *adj*: **to be** ~ avoir le mal du pays; (*missing one's family*) s'ennuyer de sa famille.

homestead ['həumsted] *n* propriété *f*; (*farm*) ferme *f*.

home town *n* ville natale.

home truth *n*: **to tell sb a few** ~**s** dire ses quatre vérités à qn.

homeward ['həumwəd] *adj* (*journey*) du retour ♦ *adv* = **homewards**.

homewards ['həumwədz] *adv* vers la maison.

homework ['həumwəːk] *n* devoirs *mpl*.

homicidal [hɔmɪ'saɪdl] *adj* homicide.

homicide ['hɔmɪsaɪd] *n* (*US*) homicide *m*.

homily ['hɔmɪlɪ] *n* homélie *f*.

homing ['həumɪŋ] *adj* (*device, missile*) à tête chercheuse; ~ **pigeon** pigeon voyageur.

homoeopath, (*US*) **homeopath** ['həumɪəupæθ] *n* homéopathe *m/f*.

homoeopathy, (*US*) **homeopathy** [həumɪ'ɔpəθɪ] *n* homéopathie *f*.

homogeneous [hɔməu'dʒiːnɪəs] *adj* homogène.

homogenize [hə'mɔdʒənaɪz] *vt* homogénéiser.

homosexual [hɔməu'seksjuəl] *adj, n* homosexuel(le).

Hon. *abbr* (= honourable, honorary) dans un titre.

Honduras [hɔn'djuərəs] *n* Honduras *m*.

hone [həun] *n* pierre *f* à aiguiser ♦ *vt* affûter, aiguiser.

honest ['ɔnɪst] *adj* honnête; (*sincere*) franc(franche); **to be quite** ~ **with you** ... à dire vrai ....

honestly ['ɔnɪstlɪ] *adv* honnêtement; franchement.

honesty ['ɔnɪstɪ] *n* honnêteté *f*.

honey ['hʌnɪ] *n* miel *m*; (*US col: darling*) chéri/e.

honeycomb ['hʌnɪkəum] *n* rayon *m* de miel; (*pattern*) nid *m* d'abeilles, motif alvéolé ♦ *vt* (*fig*): **to** ~ **with** cribler de.

honeymoon ['hʌnɪmuːn] *n* lune *f* de miel, voyage *m* de noces.

honeysuckle ['hʌnɪsʌkl] *n* chèvrefeuille *m*.

Hong Kong ['hɔŋ'kɔŋ] *n* Hong Kong.

honk [hɔŋk] *n* (*AUT*) coup *m* de klaxon ♦ *vi* klaxonner.

Honolulu [hɔnə'luːluː] *n* Honolulu.

honorary ['ɔnərərɪ] *adj* honoraire; (*duty, title*) honorifique.

honour, (*US*) **honor** ['ɔnə*] *vt* honorer ♦ *n* honneur *m*; **in** ~ **of** en l'honneur de.

hono(u)rable ['ɔnərəbl] *adj* honorable.

hono(u)r-bound ['ɔnə'baund] *adj*: **to be** ~ **to do** se devoir de faire.

hono(u)rs degree ['ɔnəz-] *n* (*SCOL*) ≈ licence *f*.

Un **honours degree** *est un diplôme universitaire que l'on reçoit après trois années d'études en Angleterre et quatre années en Écosse. Les mentions qui l'accompagnent sont, par ordre décroissant: "first class" (très bien/ bien), "upper second class" (assez bien), "lower second class" (passable), et "third class" (diplôme sans mention). Le titulaire d'un honours degree a un titre qu'il peut mettre à la suite de son nom, par exemple: Peter Jones BA Hons; voir* **ordinary degree**

---

honours list *n* (*BRIT*): **the** ~ la liste de distinctions honorifiques conférées par le monarque.

---

*L'***honours list** *est la liste des titres et décorations que le souverain confère à certains citoyens du Royaume-Uni et du Commonwealth. Cette liste est préparée par le Premier ministre et paraît deux fois par an, au Nouvel An et lors de l'anniversaire officiel du règne du souverain. Des personnes qui se sont distinguées dans le monde des affaires, des sports et des médias, ainsi que dans les forces armées, mais également des citoyens "ordinaires" qui se consacrent à des œuvres de charité sont ainsi récompensées.*

Hons. *abbr* (*SCOL*) = hono(u)rs degree.

hood [hud] *n* capuchon *m*; (*BRIT AUT*) capote *f*; (*US AUT*) capot *m*; (*col*) truand *m*.

hoodlum ['huːdləm] *n* truand *m*.

hoodwink ['hudwɪŋk] *vt* tromper.

hoof, *pl* ~**s** *or* **hooves** [huːf, huːvz] *n* sabot *m*.

hook [huk] *n* crochet *m*; (*on dress*) agrafe *f*; (*for fishing*) hameçon *m* ♦ *vt* accrocher; (*dress*) agrafer; ~ **and eye** agrafe; **by** ~ **or by crook** de gré ou de force, coûte que coûte; **to be** ~**ed (on)** (*col*) être accroché(e) (par); (*person*) être dingue (de).

►**hook up** *vt* (*RADIO, TV etc*) faire un duplex entre.

hooligan ['huːlɪgən] *n* voyou *m*.

hoop [huːp] *n* cerceau *m*; (*of barrel*) cercle *m*.

hoot [huːt] *vi* (*AUT*) klaxonner; (*siren*) mugir; (*owl*) hululer ♦ *vt* (*jeer at*) huer ♦ *n* huée *f*; coup *m* de klaxon; mugissement *m*; hululement *m*; **to** ~ **with laughter** rire aux éclats.

hooter ['huːtə*] *n* (*BRIT AUT*) klaxon *m*; (*NAUT, factory*) sirène *f*.

hoover ['huːvə*] *n* ® (*BRIT*) aspirateur *m* ♦ *vt* (*room*) passer l'aspirateur dans; (*carpet*) passer l'aspirateur sur.

hooves [huːvz] *npl of* hoof.

hop [hɔp] *vi* sauter; (*on one foot*) sauter à cloche-pied ♦ *n* saut *m*.

hope [həup] *vt, vi* espérer ♦ *n* espoir *m*; **I** ~ **so** je l'espère; **I** ~ **not** j'espère que non.

hopeful ['həupful] *adj* (*person*) plein(e)

d'espoir; (*situation*) prometteur(euse), encourageant(e); **I'm ~ that she'll manage to come** j'ai bon espoir qu'elle pourra venir.

hopefully ['həupfulɪ] *adv* avec espoir, avec optimisme; **~, they'll come back** espérons bien qu'ils reviendront.

hopeless ['həuplɪs] *adj* désespéré(e), sans espoir; (*useless*) nul(le).

hopelessly ['həuplɪslɪ] *adv* (*live etc*) sans espoir; **~ confused** *etc* complètement désorienté *etc*.

hopper ['hɔpə*] *n* (*chute*) trémie *f*.

hops [hɔps] *npl* houblon *m*.

horde [hɔːd] *n* horde *f*.

horizon [hə'raɪzn] *n* horizon *m*.

horizontal [hɔrɪ'zɔntl] *adj* horizontal(e).

hormone ['hɔːməun] *n* hormone *f*.

hormone replacement therapy *n* hormonothérapie substitutive, traitement hormono-supplétif.

horn [hɔːn] *n* corne *f*; (*MUS*) cor *m*; (*AUT*) klaxon *m*.

horned [hɔːnd] *adj* (*animal*) à cornes.

hornet ['hɔːnɪt] *n* frelon *m*.

horny ['hɔːnɪ] *adj* corné(e); (*hands*) calleux(euse); (*col: aroused*) excité(e).

horoscope ['hɔrəskəup] *n* horoscope *m*.

horrendous [hə'rendəs] *adj* horrible, affreux(euse).

horrible ['hɔrɪbl] *adj* horrible, affreux(euse).

horrid ['hɔrɪd] *adj* méchant(e), désagréable.

horrific [hɔ'rɪfɪk] *adj* horrible.

horrify ['hɔrɪfaɪ] *vt* horrifier.

horrifying ['hɔrɪfaɪɪŋ] *adj* horrifiant(e).

horror ['hɔrə*] *n* horreur *f*.

horror film *n* film *m* d'épouvante.

horror-struck ['hɔrəstrʌk], **horror-stricken** ['hɔrəstrɪkn] *adj* horrifié(e).

hors d'œuvre [ɔː'dəːvrə] *n* hors d'œuvre *m*.

horse [hɔːs] *n* cheval *m*.

horseback ['hɔːsbæk]: **on ~** *adj, adv* à cheval.

horsebox ['hɔːsbɔks] *n* van *m*.

horse chestnut *n* marron *m* (d'Inde).

horse-drawn ['hɔːsdrɔːn] *adj* tiré(e) par des chevaux.

horsefly ['hɔːsflaɪ] *n* taon *m*.

horseman ['hɔːsmən] *n* cavalier *m*.

horsemanship ['hɔːsmənʃɪp] *n* talents *mpl* de cavalier.

horseplay ['hɔːspleɪ] *n* chahut *m* (*blagues etc*).

horsepower (hp) ['hɔːspauə*] *n* puissance *f* (en chevaux); cheval-vapeur *m* (CV).

horse-racing ['hɔːsreɪsɪŋ] *n* courses *fpl* de chevaux.

horseradish ['hɔːsrædɪʃ] *n* raifort *m*.

horseshoe ['hɔːsʃuː] *n* fer *m* à cheval.

horse show *n* concours *m* hippique.

horse-trading ['hɔːstreɪdɪŋ] *n* maquignonage *m*.

horse trials *npl* = **horse show**.

horsewhip ['hɔːswɪp] *vt* cravacher.

horsewoman ['hɔːswumən] *n* cavalière *f*.

horsey ['hɔːsɪ] *adj* féru(e) d'équitation *or* de cheval; (*appearance*) chevalin(e).

horticulture ['hɔːtɪkʌltʃə*] *n* horticulture *f*.

hose [həuz] *n* tuyau *m*; (*also*: **garden ~**) tuyau d'arrosage.

▶**hose down** *vt* laver au jet.

hosepipe ['həuzpaɪp] *n* tuyau *m*; (*in garden*) tuyau d'arrosage; (*for fire*) tuyau d'incendie.

hosiery ['həuzɪərɪ] *n* (*in shop*) (rayon *m* des) bas *mpl*.

hospice ['hɔspɪs] *n* hospice *m*.

hospitable ['hɔspɪtəbl] *adj* hospitalier(ière).

hospital ['hɔspɪtl] *n* hôpital *m*; **in ~**, (*US*) **in the ~** à l'hôpital.

hospitality [hɔspɪ'tælɪtɪ] *n* hospitalité *f*.

hospitalize ['hɔspɪtəlaɪz] *vt* hospitaliser.

host [həust] *n* hôte *m*; (*in hotel etc*) patron *m*; (*TV, RADIO*) présentateur/trice, animateur/trice; (*large number*): **a ~ of** une foule de; (*REL*) hostie *f* ♦ *vt* (*TV programme*) présenter, animer.

hostage ['hɔstɪdʒ] *n* otage *m*.

host country *n* pays *m* d'accueil, pays-hôte *m*.

hostel ['hɔstl] *n* foyer *m*; (*also*: **youth ~**) auberge *f* de jeunesse.

hostelling ['hɔstlɪŋ] *n*: **to go (youth) ~** faire une virée *or* randonnée en séjournant dans des auberges de jeunesse.

hostess ['həustɪs] *n* hôtesse *f*; (*AVIAT*) hôtesse de l'air; (*in nightclub*) entraîneuse *f*.

hostile ['hɔstaɪl] *adj* hostile.

hostility [hɔ'stɪlɪtɪ] *n* hostilité *f*.

hot [hɔt] *adj* chaud(e); (*as opposed to only warm*) très chaud; (*spicy*) fort(e); (*fig*) acharné(e); brûlant(e); violent(e), passionné(e); **to be ~** (*person*) avoir chaud; (*thing*) être (très) chaud; (*weather*) faire chaud.

▶**hot up** (*BRIT col*) *vi* (*situation*) devenir tendu(e); (*party*) s'animer ♦ *vt* (*pace*) accélérer, forcer; (*engine*) gonfler.

hot-air balloon [hɔt'ɛə-] *n* montgolfière *f*, ballon *m*.

hotbed ['hɔtbed] *n* (*fig*) foyer *m*, pépinière *f*.

hotchpotch ['hɔtʃpɔtʃ] *n* (*BRIT*) mélange *m* hétéroclite.

hot dog *n* hot-dog *m*.

hotel [həu'tel] *n* hôtel *m*.

hotelier [həu'telɪə*] *n* hôtelier/ière.

hotel industry *n* industrie hôtelière.

hotel room *n* chambre *f* d'hôtel.

hot flush *n* (*BRIT*) bouffée *f* de chaleur.

hotfoot ['hɔtfut] *adv* à toute vitesse.

hothead ['hɔthed] *n* (*fig*) tête brûlée.

hotheaded [hɔt'hedɪd] *adj* impétueux(euse).

hothouse ['hɔthaus] *n* serre chaude.

hot line *n* (*POL*) téléphone *m* rouge, ligne directe.

hotly ['hɔtlɪ] *adv* passionnément, violemment.

hotplate ['hɔtpleɪt] *n* (*on cooker*) plaque

chauffante.

hotpot ['hɔtpɔt] n (BRIT CULIN) ragoût m.

hot potato n (BRIT col) sujet brûlant; **to drop sb/sth like a ~** laisser tomber qn/qch brusquement.

hot seat n (fig) poste chaud.

hot spot n point chaud.

hot spring n source thermale.

hot-tempered ['hɔt'tɛmpəd] adj emporté(e).

hot-water bottle [hɔt'wɔːtə-] n bouillotte f.

hot-wire ['hɔtwaɪə*] vt (col: car) démarrer en faisant se toucher les fils de contact.

hound [haund] vt poursuivre avec acharnement ♦ n chien courant; **the ~s** la meute.

hour ['auə*] n heure f; **at 30 miles an ~** ≈ à 50 km à l'heure; **lunch ~** heure du déjeuner; **to pay sb by the ~** payer qn à l'heure.

hourly ['auəlɪ] adj toutes les heures; (rate) horaire; **~ paid** adj payé(e) à l'heure.

house n [haus] (pl: ~s ['hauzɪz]) maison f; (POL) chambre f; (THEAT) salle f; auditoire m ♦ vt [hauz] (person) loger, héberger; **at (or to) my ~** chez moi; **the H~ of Commons/of Lords** (BRIT) la Chambre des communes/des lords; **the H~ (of Representatives)** (US) la Chambre des représentants; **on the ~** (fig) aux frais de la maison.

Le parlement en Grande-Bretagne est constitué de deux assemblées:
  -La **House of Lords**, présidée par le Lord Chancellor et composée de membres du haut clergé et de lords séculiers dont le titre est, soit héréditaire, soit attribué par le souverain (dans ce dernier cas, il peut être héréditaire ou à vie); elle peut amender certains projets de loi votés par la Chambre des communes, mais elle n'est pas habilitée à débattre des projets de lois de finances. La Chambre des lords fait également office de la juridiction suprême en Angleterre et au Pays de Galles.
  -La **House of Commons**, présidée par le **Speaker** et composée de plus de 600 députés (les **MP**) élus au suffrage universel direct. Ceux-ci reçoivent tous un salaire. La Chambre des communes siège environ 175 jours par an.

Aux États-Unis, le parlement, appelé le **Congress**, est constitué du **Senate** et de la **House of Representatives**. Cette dernière comprend 435 membres, le nombre de ces représentants par Etat étant proportionnel à la densité de population de cet Etat. Ils sont élus pour deux ans au suffrage universel direct et siègent au **Capitol**, à Washington D.C.

house arrest n assignation f à domicile.

houseboat ['hausbəut] n bateau (aménagé en habitation).

housebound ['hausbaund] adj confiné(e) chez soi.

housebreaking ['hausbreɪkɪŋ] n cambriolage m (avec effraction).

house-broken ['hausbrəukn] adj (US) = **house-trained**.

housecoat ['hauskəut] n peignoir m.

household ['haushəuld] n ménage m; (people) famille f, maisonnée f; **~ name** nom connu de tout le monde.

householder ['haushəuldə*] n propriétaire m/f; (head of house) chef m de ménage or de famille.

househunting ['haushʌntɪŋ] n: **to go ~** se mettre en quête d'une maison (or d'un appartement).

housekeeper ['hauskiːpə*] n gouvernante f.

housekeeping ['hauskiːpɪŋ] n (work) ménage m; (also: ~ **money**) argent m du ménage; (COMPUT) gestion f (des disques).

houseman ['hausmən] n (BRIT MED) ≈ interne m.

house-owner ['hausəunə*] n propriétaire m/f (de maison ou d'appartement).

house-proud ['hauspraud] adj qui tient à avoir une maison impeccable.

house-to-house ['haustə'haus] adj (enquiries etc) chez tous les habitants (du quartier etc).

house-train ['haustreɪn] vt (pet) apprendre à être propre à.

house-trained ['haustreɪnd] adj (BRIT: animal) propre.

house-warming ['hauswɔːmɪŋ] n (also: ~ **party**) pendaison f de crémaillère.

housewife ['hauswaɪf] n ménagère f; femme f du foyer.

housework ['hauswəːk] n (travaux mpl du) ménage m.

housing ['hauzɪŋ] n logement m ♦ cpd (problem, shortage) de or du logement.

housing association n fondation f charitable fournissant des logements.

housing benefit n (BRIT) ≈ allocations fpl logement.

housing conditions npl conditions fpl de logement.

housing development, (BRIT) **housing estate** n cité f; lotissement m.

hovel ['hɔvl] n taudis m.

hover ['hɔvə*] vi planer; **to ~ round sb** rôder or tourner autour de qn.

hovercraft ['hɔvəkrɑːft] n aéroglisseur m.

hoverport ['hɔvəpɔːt] n hoverport m.

how [hau] adv comment; **~ are you?** comment allez-vous?; **~ do you do?** bonjour; (on being introduced) enchanté(e); **~ far is it to ...?** combien y a-t-il jusqu'à ...?; **~ long have you been here?** depuis combien de temps êtes-vous là?; **~ lovely!** que or comme c'est joli!; **~ many/much?** combien?; **~ many people/much milk** combien de gens/lait; **~ old are you?** quel âge avez-vous?; **~'s life?** (col) comment ça va?; **~ about a drink?** si on

buvait quelque chose?; ~ **is it that ...?**
comment se fait-il que ... + *sub*?
however [hau'evə*] *conj* pourtant, cependant
♦ *adv* de quelque façon *or* manière que
+ *sub*; (+ *adjective*) quelque *or* si ... que + *sub*;
(*in questions*) comment.
howitzer ['hauɪtsə*] *n* (*MIL*) obusier *m*.
howl [haul] *n* hurlement *m* ♦ *vi* hurler.
howler ['haulə*] *n* gaffe *f*, bourde *f*.
howling ['haulɪŋ] *adj*: **a ~ wind** *or* **gale** un
vent à décorner les bœufs.
HP *n abbr* (*BRIT*) = **hire purchase**.
hp *abbr* (*AUT*) = **horsepower**.
HQ *n abbr* (= *headquarters*) QG *m*.
HR *n abbr* (*US*) = **House of Representatives**.
HRH *abbr* (= *His (or Her) Royal Highness*) SAR.
hr(s) *abbr* = *hour(s)*) h.
HRT *n abbr* = **hormone replacement therapy**.
HS *abbr* (*US*) = **high school**.
HST *abbr* (*US*: = *Hawaiian Standard Time*) *heure*
de Hawaii.
hub [hʌb] *n* (*of wheel*) moyeu *m*; (*fig*) centre *m*,
foyer *m*.
hubbub ['hʌbʌb] *n* brouhaha *m*.
hub cap *n* (*AUT*) enjoliveur *m*.
HUD *n abbr* (*US*: = *Department of Housing and
Urban Development*) *ministère de
l'urbanisme et du logement*.
huddle ['hʌdl] *vi*: **to ~ together** se blottir les
uns contre les autres.
hue [hju:] *n* teinte *f*, nuance *f*; **~ and cry** *n* tollé
(général), clameur *f*.
huff [hʌf] *n*: **in a ~** fâché(e); **to take the ~**
prendre la mouche.
huffy ['hʌfɪ] *adj* (*col*) froissé(e).
hug [hʌg] *vt* serrer dans ses bras; (*shore, kerb*)
serrer ♦ *n* étreinte *f*; **to give sb a ~** serrer
qn dans ses bras.
huge [hju:dʒ] *adj* énorme, immense.
hulk [hʌlk] *n* (*ship*) vieux rafiot; (*car, building*)
carcasse *f*; (*person*) mastodonte *m*, malabar
m.
hulking ['hʌlkɪŋ] *adj* balourd(e).
hull [hʌl] *n* (*of ship, nuts*) coque *f*; (*of peas*)
cosse *f*.
hullabaloo ['hʌləbə'lu:] *n* (*col*: *noise*) tapage *m*,
raffut *m*.
hullo [hə'ləu] *excl* = **hello**.
hum [hʌm] *vt* (*tune*) fredonner ♦ *vi* fredonner;
(*insect*) bourdonner; (*plane, tool*) vrombir ♦ *n*
fredonnement *m*; bourdonnement *m*;
vrombissement *m*.
human ['hju:mən] *adj* humain(e) ♦ *n* (*also*: ~
being) être humain.
humane [hju:'meɪn] *adj* humain(e),
humanitaire.
humanism ['hju:mənɪzəm] *n* humanisme *m*.
humanitarian [hju:mænɪ'tɛərɪən] *adj*
humanitaire.
humanity [hju:'mænɪtɪ] *n* humanité *f*.
humanly ['hju:mənlɪ] *adv* humainement.
humanoid ['hju:mənɔɪd] *adj*, *n* humanoïde

(*m/f*).
human rights *npl* droits *mpl* de l'homme.
humble ['hʌmbl] *adj* humble, modeste ♦ *vt*
humilier.
humbly ['hʌmblɪ] *adv* humblement,
modestement.
humbug ['hʌmbʌg] *n* fumisterie *f*; (*BRIT*:
sweet) bonbon *m* à la menthe.
humdrum ['hʌmdrʌm] *adj* monotone,
routinier(ière).
humid ['hju:mɪd] *adj* humide.
humidifier [hju:'mɪdɪfaɪə*] *n* humidificateur
m.
humidity [hju:'mɪdɪtɪ] *n* humidité *f*.
humiliate [hju:'mɪlɪeɪt] *vt* humilier.
humiliation [hju:mɪlɪ'eɪʃən] *n* humiliation *f*.
humility [hju:'mɪlɪtɪ] *n* humilité *f*.
humorist ['hju:mərɪst] *n* humoriste *m/f*.
humorous ['hju:mərəs] *adj* humoristique;
(*person*) plein(e) d'humour.
humour, (*US*) **humor** ['hju:mə*] *n* humour *m*;
(*mood*) humeur *f* ♦ *vt* (*person*) faire plaisir à;
se prêter aux caprices de; **sense of ~** sens
m de l'humour; **to be in a good/bad ~** être
de bonne/mauvaise humeur.
humo(u)rless ['hu:məlɪs] *adj* dépourvu(e)
d'humour.
hump [hʌmp] *n* bosse *f*.
humpback ['hʌmpbæk] *n* bossu/e; (*BRIT*: *also*:
~ **bridge**) dos-d'âne *m*.
humus ['hju:məs] *n* humus *m*.
hunch [hʌntʃ] *n* bosse *f*; (*premonition*) intuition
f, **I have a ~ that** j'ai (comme une vague)
idée que.
hunchback ['hʌntʃbæk] *n* bossu/e.
hunched [hʌntʃt] *adj* arrondi(e), voûté(e).
hundred ['hʌndrəd] *num* cent; **about a ~
people** une centaine de personnes; **~s of
people** des centaines de gens; **I'm a ~ per
cent sure** j'en suis absolument certain.
hundredweight ['hʌndrɪdweɪt] *n* (*BRIT*) = 50.8
kg; 112 lb; (*US*) = 45.3 *kg; 100 lb*.
hung [hʌŋ] *pt, pp of* **hang**.
Hungarian [hʌŋ'gɛərɪən] *adj* hongrois(e) ♦ *n*
Hongrois/e; (*LING*) hongrois *m*.
Hungary ['hʌŋgərɪ] *n* Hongrie *f*.
hunger ['hʌŋgə*] *n* faim *f* ♦ *vi*: **to ~ for** avoir
faim de, désirer ardemment.
hunger strike *n* grève *f* de la faim.
hungover [hʌŋ'əuvə*] *adj* (*col*): **to be ~** avoir
la gueule de bois.
hungrily ['hʌŋgrəlɪ] *adv* voracement; (*fig*)
avidement.
hungry ['hʌŋgrɪ] *adj* affamé(e); **to be ~** avoir
faim; **~ for** (*fig*) avide de.
hung up *adj* (*col*) complexé(e), bourré(e) de
complexes.
hunk [hʌŋk] *n* gros morceau; (*col*: *man*) beau
mec.
hunt [hʌnt] *vt* (*seek*) chercher; (*SPORT*)
chasser ♦ *vi* chasser ♦ *n* chasse *f*.
►**hunt down** *vt* pourchasser.

hunter ['hʌntə*] n chasseur m; (BRIT: horse) cheval m de chasse.
hunting ['hʌntɪŋ] n chasse f.
hurdle ['hə:dl] n (for fences) claie f; (SPORT) haie f; (fig) obstacle m.
hurl [hə:l] vt lancer (avec violence).
hurling ['hə:lɪŋ] n (SPORT) genre de hockey joué en Irlande.
hurly-burly ['hə:lɪ'bə:lɪ] n tohu-bohu m inv; brouhaha m.
hurrah, hurray [hu'rɑ:, hu'reɪ] n hourra m.
hurricane ['hʌrɪkən] n ouragan m.
hurried ['hʌrɪd] adj pressé(e), précipité(e); (work) fait(e) à la hâte.
hurriedly ['hʌrɪdlɪ] adv précipitamment, à la hâte.
hurry ['hʌrɪ] n hâte f, précipitation f ♦ vi se presser, se dépêcher ♦ vt (person) faire presser, faire se dépêcher; (work) presser; **to be in a** ~ être pressé(e); **to do sth in a** ~ faire qch en vitesse; **to** ~ **in/out** entrer/ sortir précipitamment; **to** ~ **home** se dépêcher de rentrer.
►**hurry along** vi marcher d'un pas pressé.
►**hurry away, hurry off** vi partir précipitamment.
►**hurry up** vi se dépêcher.
hurt [hə:t] vb (pt, pp hurt) vt (cause pain to) faire mal à; (injure, fig) blesser; (damage: business, interests etc) nuire à, faire du tort à ♦ vi faire mal ♦ adj blessé(e); **I** ~ **my arm** je me suis fait mal au bras; **where does it** ~? où avez- vous mal?, où est-ce que ça vous fait mal?
hurtful ['hə:tful] adj (remark) blessant(e).
hurtle ['hə:tl] vt lancer (de toutes ses forces) ♦ vi: **to** ~ **past** passer en trombe; **to** ~ **down** dégringoler.
husband ['hʌzbənd] n mari m.
hush [hʌʃ] n calme m, silence m ♦ vt faire taire; ~! chut!
►**hush up** vt (fact) étouffer.
hush-hush [hʌʃ'hʌʃ] adj (col) ultra- secret(ète).
husk [hʌsk] n (of wheat) balle f; (of rice, maize) enveloppe f; (of peas) cosse f.
husky ['hʌskɪ] adj rauque; (burly) costaud(e) ♦ n chien m esquimau or de traîneau.
hustings ['hʌstɪŋz] npl (BRIT POL) plate-forme électorale.
hustle ['hʌsl] vt pousser, bousculer ♦ n bousculade f; ~ **and bustle** n tourbillon m (d'activité).
hut [hʌt] n hutte f; (shed) cabane f.
hutch [hʌtʃ] n clapier m.
hyacinth ['haɪəsɪnθ] n jacinthe f.
hybrid ['haɪbrɪd] adj, n hybride (m).
hydrant ['haɪdrənt] n prise f d'eau; (also: **fire** ~) bouche f d'incendie.
hydraulic [haɪ'drɔ:lɪk] adj hydraulique.
hydraulics [haɪ'drɔ:lɪks] n hydraulique f.
hydrochloric ['haɪdrəu'klɔrɪk] adj: ~ **acid** acide m chlorhydrique.

hydroelectric ['haɪdrəuɪ'lɛktrɪk] adj hydro- électrique.
hydrofoil ['haɪdrəfɔɪl] n hydrofoil m.
hydrogen ['haɪdrədʒən] n hydrogène m.
hydrogen bomb n bombe f à hydrogène.
hydrophobia ['haɪdrə'fəubɪə] n hydrophobie f.
hydroplane ['haɪdrəpleɪn] n (seaplane) hydravion m; (jetfoil) hydroglisseur m.
hyena [haɪ'i:nə] n hyène f.
hygiene ['haɪdʒi:n] n hygiène f.
hygienic [haɪ'dʒi:nɪk] adj hygiénique.
hymn [hɪm] n hymne m; cantique m.
hype [haɪp] n (col) matraquage m publicitaire or médiatique.
hyperactive ['haɪpər'æktɪv] adj hyperactif(ive).
hypermarket ['haɪpəmɑ:kɪt] n (BRIT) hypermarché m.
hypertension ['haɪpə'tɛnʃən] n (MED) hypertension f.
hyphen ['haɪfn] n trait m d'union.
hypnosis [hɪp'nəusɪs] n hypnose f.
hypnotic [hɪp'nɔtɪk] adj hypnotique.
hypnotism ['hɪpnətɪzəm] n hypnotisme m.
hypnotist ['hɪpnətɪst] n hypnotiseur/euse.
hypnotize ['hɪpnətaɪz] vt hypnotiser.
hypoallergenic ['haɪpəuæelə'dʒɛnɪk] adj hypoallergique.
hypochondriac [haɪpə'kɔndrɪæk] n hypocondriaque m/f.
hypocrisy [hɪ'pɔkrɪsɪ] n hypocrisie f.
hypocrite ['hɪpəkrɪt] n hypocrite m/f.
hypocritical [hɪpə'krɪtɪkl] adj hypocrite.
hypodermic [haɪpə'də:mɪk] adj hypodermique ♦ n (syringe) seringue f hypodermique.
hypotenuse [haɪ'pɔtɪnju:z] n hypoténuse f.
hypothermia [haɪpə'θə:mɪə] n hypothermie f.
hypothesis [haɪ'pɔθɪsɪs], pl **hypotheses** [haɪ'pɔθɪsi:z] n hypothèse f.
hypothetic(al) [haɪpəu'θɛtɪk(l)] adj hypothétique.
hysterectomy [hɪstə'rɛktəmɪ] n hystérectomie f.
hysteria [hɪ'stɪərɪə] n hystérie f.
hysterical [hɪ'stɛrɪkl] adj hystérique; **to become** ~ avoir une crise de nerfs.
hysterics [hɪ'stɛrɪks] npl (violente) crise de nerfs; (laughter) crise de rire; **to have** ~ avoir une crise de nerfs; attraper un fou rire.
Hz abbr (= hertz) Hz.

I i

I, i [aɪ] n (letter) I, i m; **I for Isaac**, (US) **I for Item** I comme Irma.

I [aɪ] pron je; (before vowel) j'; (stressed) moi ♦ abbr (= island, isle) I.

IA, Ia. abbr (US) = Iowa.

IAEA n abbr = International Atomic Energy Agency.

IBA n abbr (BRIT: = Independent Broadcasting Authority) ≈ CNCL f (= Commission nationale de la communication audio-visuelle).

Iberian [aɪˈbɪərɪən] adj ibérique, ibérien(ne).

Iberian Peninsula n: **the ~** la péninsule Ibérique.

IBEW n abbr (US: = International Brotherhood of Electrical Workers) syndicat international des électriciens.

i/c abbr (BRIT) = **in charge**.

ICBM n abbr (= intercontinental ballistic missile) ICBM m, engin m balistique à portée intercontinentale.

ICC n abbr (= International Chamber of Commerce) CCI f; (US = Interstate Commerce Commission.

ice [aɪs] n glace f; (on road) verglas m ♦ vt (cake) glacer; (drink) faire rafraîchir ♦ vi (also: ~ over) geler; (also: ~ up) se givrer; **to put sth on ~** (fig) mettre qch en attente.

Ice Age n ère f glaciaire.

ice axe n piolet m.

iceberg [ˈaɪsbəːg] n iceberg m; **the tip of the ~** (also fig) la partie émergée de l'iceberg.

icebox [ˈaɪsbɒks] n (US) réfrigérateur m; (BRIT) compartiment m à glace; (insulated box) glacière f.

icebreaker [ˈaɪsbreɪkə*] n brise-glace m.

ice bucket n seau m à glace.

ice-cap [ˈaɪskæp] n calotte f glaciaire.

ice-cold [aɪsˈkəʊld] adj glacé(e).

ice cream n glace f.

ice cube n glaçon m.

iced [aɪst] adj (drink) frappé(e); (coffee, tea, also cake) glacé(e).

ice hockey n hockey m sur glace.

Iceland [ˈaɪslənd] n Islande f.

Icelander [ˈaɪsləndə*] n Islandais/e.

Icelandic [aɪsˈlændɪk] adj islandais(e) ♦ n (LING) islandais m.

ice lolly [-ˈlɔlɪ] n (BRIT) esquimau m.

ice pick n pic m à glace.

ice rink n patinoire f.

ice-skate [ˈaɪsskeɪt] n patin m à glace ♦ vi faire du patin à glace.

ice-skating [ˈaɪsskeɪtɪŋ] n patinage m (sur glace).

icicle [ˈaɪsɪkl] n glaçon m (naturel).

icing [ˈaɪsɪŋ] n (AVIAT etc) givrage m; (CULIN) glaçage m.

icing sugar n (BRIT) sucre m glace.

ICJ n abbr = **International Court of Justice**.

icon [ˈaɪkɔn] n icône f.

ICR n abbr (US) = Institute for Cancer Research.

ICRC n abbr (= International Committee of the Red Cross) CICR m.

ICU n abbr = **intensive care unit**.

icy [ˈaɪsɪ] adj glacé(e); (road) verglacé(e); (weather, temperature) glacial(e).

ID abbr (US) = Idaho.

I'd [aɪd] = **I would**, **I had**.

Ida. abbr (US) = Idaho.

ID card n = **identity card**.

IDD n abbr (BRIT TEL: = international direct dialling) automatique international.

idea [aɪˈdɪə] n idée f; **good ~!** bonne idée!; **to have an ~ that ...** avoir idée que ...; **I haven't the least ~** je n'ai pas la moindre idée.

ideal [aɪˈdɪəl] n idéal m ♦ adj idéal(e).

idealist [aɪˈdɪəlɪst] n idéaliste m/f.

ideally [aɪˈdɪəlɪ] adv idéalement, dans l'idéal; **~ the book should have ...** l'idéal serait que le livre ait ....

identical [aɪˈdɛntɪkl] adj identique.

identification [aɪdɛntɪfɪˈkeɪʃən] n identification f; **means of ~** pièce f d'identité.

identify [aɪˈdɛntɪfaɪ] vt identifier ♦ vi: **to ~ with** s'identifier à.

Identikit [aɪˈdɛntɪkɪt] n ®: **~ (picture)** portrait-robot m.

identity [aɪˈdɛntɪtɪ] n identité f.

identity card n carte f d'identité.

identity parade n (BRIT) parade f d'identification.

ideological [aɪdɪəˈlɔdʒɪkl] adj idéologique.

ideology [aɪdɪˈɔlədʒɪ] n idéologie f.

idiocy [ˈɪdɪəsɪ] n idiotie f, stupidité f.

idiom [ˈɪdɪəm] n langue f, idiome m; (phrase) expression f idiomatique.

idiomatic [ɪdɪəˈmætɪk] adj idiomatique.

idiosyncrasy [ɪdɪəuˈsɪŋkrəsɪ] n particularité f, caractéristique f.

idiot [ˈɪdɪət] n idiot/e, imbécile m/f.

idiotic [ɪdɪˈɔtɪk] adj idiot(e), bête, stupide.

idle [ˈaɪdl] adj sans occupation, désœuvré(e); (lazy) oisif(ive), paresseux(euse); (unemployed) au chômage; (machinery) au repos; (question, pleasures) vain(e), futile ♦ vi (engine) tourner au ralenti; **to lie ~** être arrêté, ne pas fonctionner.

▶**idle away** vt: **to ~ away one's time** passer son temps à ne rien faire.

idleness [ˈaɪdlnɪs] n désœuvrement m; oisiveté f.

idler [ˈaɪdlə*] n désœuvré/e; oisif/ive.

idle time n (COMM) temps mort.

idol ['aɪdl] *n* idole *f.*

idolize ['aɪdəlaɪz] *vt* idolâtrer, adorer.

idyllic [ɪ'dɪlɪk] *adj* idyllique.

i.e. *abbr* (= *id est: that is*) c. à d., c'est-à-dire.

if [ɪf] *conj* si ♦ *n*: **there are a lot of ~s and buts** il y a beaucoup de si *mpl* et de mais *mpl*; **I'd be pleased ~ you could do it** je serais très heureux si vous pouviez le faire; **~ necessary** si nécessaire, le cas échéant; **~ only he were here** si seulement il était là; **~ only to show him my gratitude** ne serait-ce que pour lui témoigner ma gratitude.

iffy ['ɪfɪ] *adj* (*col*) douteux(euse).

igloo ['ɪgluː] *n* igloo *m.*

ignite [ɪg'naɪt] *vt* mettre le feu à, enflammer ♦ *vi* s'enflammer.

ignition [ɪg'nɪʃən] *n* (*AUT*) allumage *m*; **to switch on/off the ~** mettre/couper le contact.

ignition key *n* (*AUT*) clé *f* de contact.

ignoble [ɪg'nəubl] *adj* ignoble, indigne.

ignominious [ɪgnə'mɪnɪəs] *adj* honteux(euse), ignominieux(euse).

ignoramus [ɪgnə'reɪməs] *n* personne *f* ignare.

ignorance ['ɪgnərəns] *n* ignorance *f*; **to keep sb in ~ of sth** tenir qn dans l'ignorance de qch.

ignorant ['ɪgnərənt] *adj* ignorant(e); **to be ~ of** (*subject*) ne rien connaître en; (*events*) ne pas être au courant de.

ignore [ɪg'nɔː*] *vt* ne tenir aucun compte de, ne pas relever; (*person*) faire semblant de ne pas reconnaître, ignorer; (*fact*) méconnaître.

ikon ['aɪkɔn] *n* = **icon**.

IL *abbr* (*US*) = *Illinois*.

ILA *n abbr* (*US*: = *International Longshoremen's Association*) *syndicat international des dockers.*

ill [ɪl] *adj* (*sick*) malade; (*bad*) mauvais(e) ♦ *n* mal *m* ♦ *adv*: **to speak/think ~ of sb** dire/penser du mal de qn; **to take** *or* **be taken ~** tomber malade.

Ill. *abbr* (*US*) = *Illinois*.

I'll [aɪl] = **I will, I shall.**

ill-advised [ɪləd'vaɪzd] *adj* (*decision*) peu judicieux(euse); (*person*) malavisé(e).

ill-at-ease [ɪlət'iːz] *adj* mal à l'aise.

ill-considered [ɪlkən'sɪdəd] *adj* (*plan*) inconsidéré(e), irréfléchi(e).

ill-disposed [ɪldɪs'pəuzd] *adj*: **to be ~ towards sb/sth** être mal disposé(e) envers qn/qch.

illegal [ɪ'liːgl] *adj* illégal(e).

illegally [ɪ'liːgəlɪ] *adv* illégalement.

illegible [ɪ'lɛdʒɪbl] *adj* illisible.

illegitimate [ɪlɪ'dʒɪtɪmət] *adj* illégitime.

ill-fated [ɪl'feɪtɪd] *adj* malheureux(euse); (*day*) néfaste.

ill-favoured, (*US*) **ill-favored** [ɪl'feɪvəd] *adj* déplaisant(e).

ill feeling *n* ressentiment *m*, rancune *f.*

ill-gotten ['ɪlgɔtn] *adj* (*gains etc*) mal acquis(e).

ill health *n* mauvaise santé.

illicit [ɪ'lɪsɪt] *adj* illicite.

ill-informed [ɪlɪn'fɔːmd] *adj* (*judgment*) erroné(e); (*person*) mal renseigné(e).

illiterate [ɪ'lɪtərət] *adj* illettré(e); (*letter*) plein(e) de fautes.

ill-mannered [ɪl'mænəd] *adj* impoli(e), grossier(ière).

illness ['ɪlnɪs] *n* maladie *f.*

illogical [ɪ'lɔdʒɪkl] *adj* illogique.

ill-suited [ɪl'suːtɪd] *adj* (*couple*) mal assorti(e); **he is ~ to the job** il n'est pas vraiment fait pour ce travail.

ill-timed [ɪl'taɪmd] *adj* inopportun(e).

ill-treat [ɪl'triːt] *vt* maltraiter.

ill-treatment [ɪl'triːtmənt] *n* mauvais traitement.

illuminate [ɪ'luːmɪneɪt] *vt* (*room, street*) éclairer; (*building*) illuminer; **~d sign** enseigne lumineuse.

illuminating [ɪ'luːmɪneɪtɪŋ] *adj* éclairant(e).

illumination [ɪluːmɪ'neɪʃən] *n* éclairage *m*; illumination *f.*

illusion [ɪ'luːʒən] *n* illusion *f*; **to be under the ~ that** avoir l'illusion que.

illusive, illusory [ɪ'luːsɪv, ɪ'luːsərɪ] *adj* illusoire.

illustrate ['ɪləstreɪt] *vt* illustrer.

illustration [ɪlə'streɪʃən] *n* illustration *f.*

illustrator ['ɪləstreɪtə*] *n* illustrateur/trice.

illustrious [ɪ'lʌstrɪəs] *adj* illustre.

ill will *n* malveillance *f.*

ILO *n abbr* (= *International Labour Organization*) OIT *f.*

ILWU *n abbr* (*US*: = *International Longshoremen's and Warehousemen's Union*) *syndicat international des dockers et des magaziniers.*

I'm [aɪm] = **I am.**

image ['ɪmɪdʒ] *n* image *f*; (*public face*) image de marque.

imagery ['ɪmɪdʒərɪ] *n* images *fpl.*

imaginable [ɪ'mædʒɪnəbl] *adj* imaginable.

imaginary [ɪ'mædʒɪnərɪ] *adj* imaginaire.

imagination [ɪmædʒɪ'neɪʃən] *n* imagination *f.*

imaginative [ɪ'mædʒɪnətɪv] *adj* imaginatif(ive), plein(e) d'imagination.

imagine [ɪ'mædʒɪn] *vt* s'imaginer; (*suppose*) imaginer, supposer.

imbalance [ɪm'bæləns] *n* déséquilibre *m.*

imbecile ['ɪmbəsiːl] *n* imbécile *m/f.*

imbue [ɪm'bjuː] *vt*: **to ~ sth with** imprégner qch de.

IMF *n abbr* = **International Monetary Fund.**

imitate ['ɪmɪteɪt] *vt* imiter.

imitation [ɪmɪ'teɪʃən] *n* imitation *f.*

imitator ['ɪmɪteɪtə*] *n* imitateur/trice.

immaculate [ɪ'mækjulət] *adj* impeccable; (*REL*) immaculé(e).

immaterial [ɪmə'tɪərɪəl] *adj* sans importance, insignifiant(e).

immature [ɪməˈtjuə*] *adj* (*fruit*) qui n'est pas mûr(e); (*person*) qui manque de maturité.
immaturity [ɪməˈtjuərɪtɪ] *n* immaturité *f*.
immeasurable [ɪˈmɛʒrəbl] *adj* incommensurable.
immediacy [ɪˈmiːdɪəsɪ] *n* (*of events etc*) caractère *or* rapport immédiat; (*of needs*) urgence *f*.
immediate [ɪˈmiːdɪət] *adj* immédiat(e).
immediately [ɪˈmiːdɪətlɪ] *adv* (*at once*) immédiatement; ~ **next to** juste à côté de.
immense [ɪˈmɛns] *adj* immense; énorme.
immensity [ɪˈmɛnsɪtɪ] *n* immensité *f*.
immerse [ɪˈmɜːs] *vt* immerger, plonger; **to** ~ **sth in** plonger qch dans.
immersion heater [ɪˈmɜːʃən-] *n* (*BRIT*) chauffe-eau *m* électrique.
immigrant [ˈɪmɪɡrənt] *n* immigrant/e; (*already established*) immigré/e.
immigration [ɪmɪˈɡreɪʃən] *n* immigration *f*.
immigration authorities *npl* service *m* de l'immigration.
immigration laws *npl* lois *fpl* sur l'immigration.
imminent [ˈɪmɪnənt] *adj* imminent(e).
immobile [ɪˈməubaɪl] *adj* immobile.
immobilize [ɪˈməubɪlaɪz] *vt* immobiliser.
immoderate [ɪˈmɔdərət] *adj* immodéré(e), démesuré(e).
immodest [ɪˈmɔdɪst] *adj* (*indecent*) indécent(e); (*boasting*) pas modeste, présomptueux(euse).
immoral [ɪˈmɔrl] *adj* immoral(e).
immorality [ɪmɔˈrælɪtɪ] *n* immoralité *f*.
immortal [ɪˈmɔːtl] *adj*, *n* immortel(le).
immortalize [ɪˈmɔːtlaɪz] *vt* immortaliser.
immovable [ɪˈmuːvəbl] *adj* (*object*) fixe; immobilier(ière); (*person*) inflexible; (*opinion*) immuable.
immune [ɪˈmjuːn] *adj*: ~ (**to**) immunisé(e) (contre).
immune system *n* système *m* immunitaire.
immunity [ɪˈmjuːnɪtɪ] *n* immunité *f*; **diplomatic** ~ immunité diplomatique.
immunization [ɪmjunaɪˈzeɪʃən] *n* immunisation *f*.
immunize [ˈɪmjunaɪz] *vt* immuniser.
imp [ɪmp] *n* (*small devil*) lutin *m*; (*child*) petit diable.
impact [ˈɪmpækt] *n* choc *m*, impact *m*; (*fig*) impact.
impair [ɪmˈpɛə*] *vt* détériorer, diminuer.
impaired [ɪmˈpɛəd] *adj* (*organ, vision*) abimé(e), détérioré(e); **his memory/ circulation is** ~ il a des problèmes de mémoire/circulation; **visually** ~ malvoyant(e); **hearing** ~ malentendant(e); **mentally/physically** ~ intellectuellement/ physiquement diminué(e).
impale [ɪmˈpeɪl] *vt* empaler.
impart [ɪmˈpɑːt] *vt* (*make known*) communiquer, transmettre; (*bestow*)

confier, donner.
impartial [ɪmˈpɑːʃl] *adj* impartial(e).
impartiality [ɪmpɑːʃɪˈælɪtɪ] *n* impartialité *f*.
impassable [ɪmˈpɑːsəbl] *adj* infranchissable; (*road*) impraticable.
impasse [æmˈpɑːs] *n* (*fig*) impasse *f*.
impassioned [ɪmˈpæʃənd] *adj* passionné(e).
impassive [ɪmˈpæsɪv] *adj* impassible.
impatience [ɪmˈpeɪʃəns] *n* impatience *f*.
impatient [ɪmˈpeɪʃənt] *adj* impatient(e); **to get** *or* **grow** ~ s'impatienter.
impeach [ɪmˈpiːtʃ] *vt* accuser, attaquer; (*public official*) mettre en accusation.
impeachment [ɪmˈpiːtʃmənt] *n* (*LAW*) (mise *f* en) accusation *f*.
impeccable [ɪmˈpɛkəbl] *adj* impeccable, parfait(e).
impecunious [ɪmpɪˈkjuːnɪəs] *adj* sans ressources.
impede [ɪmˈpiːd] *vt* gêner.
impediment [ɪmˈpɛdɪmənt] *n* obstacle *m*; (*also:* **speech** ~) défaut *m* d'élocution.
impel [ɪmˈpɛl] *vt* (*force*): **to** ~ **sb** (**to do sth**) forcer qn (à faire qch).
impending [ɪmˈpɛndɪŋ] *adj* imminent(e).
impenetrable [ɪmˈpɛnɪtrəbl] *adj* impénétrable.
imperative [ɪmˈpɛrətɪv] *adj* nécessaire; urgent(e), pressant(e); (*tone*) impérieux(euse) ♦ *n* (*LING*) impératif *m*.
imperceptible [ɪmpəˈsɛptɪbl] *adj* imperceptible.
imperfect [ɪmˈpəːfɪkt] *adj* imparfait(e); (*goods etc*) défectueux(euse) ♦ *n* (*LING: also:* ~ **tense**) imparfait *m*.
imperfection [ɪmpəːˈfɛkʃən] *n* imperfection *f*; défectuosité *f*.
imperial [ɪmˈpɪərɪəl] *adj* impérial(e); (*BRIT: measure*) légal(e).
imperialism [ɪmˈpɪərɪəlɪzəm] *n* impérialisme *m*.
imperil [ɪmˈpɛrɪl] *vt* mettre en péril.
imperious [ɪmˈpɪərɪəs] *adj* impérieux(euse).
impersonal [ɪmˈpəːsənl] *adj* impersonnel(le).
impersonate [ɪmˈpəːsəneɪt] *vt* se faire passer pour; (*THEAT*) imiter.
impersonation [ɪmpəːsəˈneɪʃən] *n* (*LAW*) usurpation *f* d'identité; (*THEAT*) imitation *f*.
impersonator [ɪmˈpəːsəneɪtə*] *n* imposteur *m*; (*THEAT*) imitateur/trice.
impertinence [ɪmˈpəːtɪnəns] *n* impertinence *f*, insolence *f*.
impertinent [ɪmˈpəːtɪnənt] *adj* impertinent(e), insolent(e).
imperturbable [ɪmpəˈtəːbəbl] *adj* imperturbable.
impervious [ɪmˈpəːvɪəs] *adj* imperméable; (*fig*): ~ **to** insensible à; inaccessible à.
impetuous [ɪmˈpɛtjuəs] *adj* impétueux(euse), fougueux(euse).
impetus [ˈɪmpətəs] *n* impulsion *f*; (*of runner*) élan *m*.
impinge [ɪmˈpɪndʒ]: **to** ~ **on** *vt fus* (*person*)

affecter, toucher; (*rights*) empiéter sur.
impish ['ɪmpɪʃ] *adj* espiègle.
implacable [ɪm'plækəbl] *adj* implacable.
implant [ɪm'plɑ:nt] *vt* (*MED*) implanter; (*fig*) inculquer.
implausible [ɪm'plɔ:zɪbl] *adj* peu plausible.
implement *n* ['ɪmplɪmənt] outil *m*, instrument *m*; (*for cooking*) ustensile *m* ♦ *vt* ['ɪmplɪment] exécuter, mettre à effet.
implicate ['ɪmplɪkeɪt] *vt* impliquer, compromettre.
implication [ɪmplɪ'keɪʃən] *n* implication *f*; **by** ~ indirectement.
implicit [ɪm'plɪsɪt] *adj* implicite; (*complete*) absolu(e), sans réserve.
implicitly [ɪm'plɪsɪtlɪ] *adv* implicitement; absolument, sans réserve.
implore [ɪm'plɔ:*] *vt* implorer, supplier.
imply [ɪm'plaɪ] *vt* (*hint*) suggérer, laisser entendre; (*mean*) indiquer, supposer.
impolite [ɪmpə'laɪt] *adj* impoli(e).
imponderable [ɪm'pɒndərəbl] *adj* impondérable.
import *vt* [ɪm'pɔ:t] importer ♦ *n* ['ɪmpɔ:t] (*COMM*) importation *f*; (*meaning*) portée *f*, signification *f* ♦ *cpd* (*duty, licence etc*) d'importation.
importance [ɪm'pɔ:tns] *n* importance *f*; **to be of great/little** ~ avoir beaucoup/peu d'importance.
important [ɪm'pɔ:tnt] *adj* important(e); **it is** ~ **that** il importe que, il est important que; **it's not** ~ c'est sans importance, ce n'est pas important.
importantly [ɪm'pɔ:tntlɪ] *adv* (*with an air of importance*) d'un air important; (*essentially*): **but, more** ~ ... mais, (ce qui est) plus important encore ....
importation [ɪmpɔ:'teɪʃən] *n* importation *f*.
imported [ɪm'pɔ:tɪd] *adj* importé(e), d'importation.
importer [ɪm'pɔ:tə*] *n* importateur/trice.
impose [ɪm'pəuz] *vt* imposer ♦ *vi*: **to** ~ **on sb** abuser de la gentillesse de qn.
imposing [ɪm'pəuzɪŋ] *adj* imposant(e), impressionnant(e).
imposition [ɪmpə'zɪʃən] *n* (*of tax etc*) imposition *f*; **to be an** ~ **on** (*person*) abuser de la gentillesse *or* de la bonté de.
impossibility [ɪmpɒsə'bɪlɪtɪ] *n* impossibilité *f*.
impossible [ɪm'pɒsɪbl] *adj* impossible; **it is** ~ **for me to leave** il m'est impossible de partir.
impostor [ɪm'pɒstə*] *n* imposteur *m*.
impotence ['ɪmpətns] *n* impuissance *f*.
impotent ['ɪmpətnt] *adj* impuissant(e).
impound [ɪm'paund] *vt* confisquer, saisir.
impoverished [ɪm'pɒvərɪʃt] *adj* pauvre, appauvri(e).
impracticable [ɪm'præktɪkəbl] *adj* impraticable.
impractical [ɪm'præktɪkl] *adj* pas pratique;

(*person*) qui manque d'esprit pratique.
imprecise [ɪmprɪ'saɪs] *adj* imprécis(e).
impregnable [ɪm'prɛgnəbl] *adj* (*fortress*) imprenable; (*fig*) inattaquable; irréfutable.
impregnate ['ɪmprɛgneɪt] *vt* imprégner; (*fertilize*) féconder.
impresario [ɪmprɪ'sɑ:rɪəu] *n* impresario *m*.
impress [ɪm'prɛs] *vt* impressionner, faire impression sur; (*mark*) imprimer, marquer; **to** ~ **sth on sb** faire bien comprendre qch à qn.
impression [ɪm'prɛʃən] *n* impression *f*; (*of stamp, seal*) empreinte *f*; **to make a good/ bad** ~ **on sb** faire bonne/mauvaise impression sur qn; **to be under the** ~ **that** avoir l'impression que.
impressionable [ɪm'prɛʃnəbl] *adj* impressionnable, sensible.
impressionist [ɪm'prɛʃənɪst] *n* impressionniste *m/f*.
impressive [ɪm'prɛsɪv] *adj* impressionnant(e).
imprint ['ɪmprɪnt] *n* empreinte *f*; (*PUBLISHING*) notice *f*; (*: label*) nom *m* (de collection *or* d'éditeur).
imprinted [ɪm'prɪntɪd] *adj*: ~ **on** imprimé(e) sur; (*fig*) imprimé(e) *or* gravé(e) dans.
imprison [ɪm'prɪzn] *vt* emprisonner, mettre en prison.
imprisonment [ɪm'prɪznmənt] *n* emprisonnement *m*.
improbable [ɪm'prɒbəbl] *adj* improbable; (*excuse*) peu plausible.
impromptu [ɪm'prɒmptju:] *adj* impromptu(e) ♦ *adv* impromptu.
improper [ɪm'prɒpə*] *adj* (*wrong*) incorrect(e); (*unsuitable*) déplacé(e), de mauvais goût; indécent(e).
impropriety [ɪmprə'praɪətɪ] *n* inconvenance *f*; (*of expression*) impropriété *f*.
improve [ɪm'pru:v] *vt* améliorer ♦ *vi* s'améliorer; (*pupil etc*) faire des progrès.
▶**improve (up)on** *vt fus* (*offer*) enchérir sur.
improvement [ɪm'pru:vmənt] *n* amélioration *f*; (*of pupil etc*) progrès *m*; **to make** ~**s to** apporter des améliorations à.
improvisation [ɪmprəvaɪ'zeɪʃən] *n* improvisation *f*.
improvise ['ɪmprəvaɪz] *vt, vi* improviser.
imprudence [ɪm'pru:dns] *n* imprudence *f*.
imprudent [ɪm'pru:dnt] *adj* imprudent(e).
impudent ['ɪmpjudnt] *adj* impudent(e).
impugn [ɪm'pju:n] *vt* contester, attaquer.
impulse ['ɪmpʌls] *n* impulsion *f*; **on** ~ impulsivement, sur un coup de tête.
impulse buy *n* achat *m* d'impulsion.
impulsive [ɪm'pʌlsɪv] *adj* impulsif(ive).
impunity [ɪm'pju:nɪtɪ] *n*: **with** ~ impunément.
impure [ɪm'pjuə*] *adj* impur(e).
impurity [ɪm'pjuərɪtɪ] *n* impureté *f*.
IN *abbr* (*US*) = Indiana.

═══════════════════════ KEYWORD

in [ɪn] *prep* **1** (*indicating place, position*) dans; ~ **the house/the fridge** dans la maison/le frigo; ~ **the garden** dans le *or* au jardin; ~ **town** en ville; ~ **the country** à la campagne; ~ **school** à l'école; ~ **here/there** ici/là
2 (*with place names: of town, region, country*): ~ **London** à Londres; ~ **England** en Angleterre; ~ **Japan** au Japon; ~ **the United States** aux États-Unis
3 (*indicating time: during*): ~ **spring** au printemps; ~ **summer** en été; ~ **May/1992** en mai/1992; ~ **the afternoon** (dans) l'après-midi; **at 4 o'clock** ~ **the afternoon** à 4 heures de l'après-midi
4 (*indicating time: in the space of*) en; (: *future*) dans; **I did it** ~ **3 hours/days** je l'ai fait en 3 heures/jours; **I'll see you** ~ **2 weeks** *or* ~ **2 weeks' time** je te verrai dans 2 semaines; **once** ~ **a hundred years** une fois tous les cent ans
5 (*indicating manner etc*) à; ~ **a loud/soft voice** à voix haute/basse; ~ **pencil** au crayon; ~ **writing** par écrit; ~ **French** en français; **to pay** ~ **dollars** payer en dollars; **the boy** ~ **the blue shirt** le garçon à *or* avec la chemise bleue
6 (*indicating circumstances*): ~ **the sun** au soleil; ~ **the shade** à l'ombre; ~ **the rain** sous la pluie
7 (*indicating mood, state*): ~ **tears** en larmes; ~ **anger** sous le coup de la colère; ~ **despair** au désespoir; ~ **good condition** en bon état; **to live** ~ **luxury** vivre dans le luxe
8 (*with ratios, numbers*): **1** ~ **10 (households)**, **1 (household)** ~ **10** 1 (ménage) sur 10; **20 pence** ~ **the pound** 20 pence par livre sterling; **they lined up** ~ **twos** ils se mirent en rangs (deux) par deux; ~ **hundreds** par centaines
9 (*referring to people, works*) chez; **the disease is common** ~ **children** c'est une maladie courante chez les enfants; ~ **(the works of) Dickens** chez Dickens, dans (l'œuvre de) Dickens
10 (*indicating profession etc*) dans; **to be** ~ **teaching** être dans l'enseignement
11 (*after superlative*) de; **the best pupil** ~ **the class** le meilleur élève de la classe
12 (*with present participle*): ~ **saying this** en disant ceci
♦ *adv*: **to be** ~ (*person: at home, work*) être là; (*train, ship, plane*) être arrivé(e); (*in fashion*) être à la mode; **to ask sb** ~ inviter qn à entrer; **to run/limp** *etc* ~ entrer en courant/boitant *etc*; **their party is** ~ leur parti est au pouvoir
♦ *n*: **the** ~**s and outs (of)** (*of proposal, situation etc*) les tenants et aboutissants (de).

in. *abbr* = **inch(es)**.

inability [ɪnə'bɪlɪtɪ] *n* incapacité *f*; ~ **to pay** incapacité de payer.
inaccessible [ɪnək'sɛsɪbl] *adj* inaccessible.
inaccuracy [ɪn'ækjurəsɪ] *n* inexactitude *f*; manque *m* de précision.
inaccurate [ɪn'ækjurət] *adj* inexact(e); (*person*) qui manque de précision.
inaction [ɪn'ækʃən] *n* inaction *f*, inactivité *f*.
inactivity [ɪnæk'tɪvɪtɪ] *n* inactivité *f*.
inadequacy [ɪn'ædɪkwəsɪ] *n* insuffisance *f*.
inadequate [ɪn'ædɪkwət] *adj* insuffisant(e), inadéquat(e).
inadmissible [ɪnəd'mɪsəbl] *adj* (*behaviour*) inadmissible; (*LAW: evidence*) irrecevable.
inadvertent [ɪnəd'vɜːtnt] *adj* (*mistake*) commis(e) par inadvertance.
inadvertently [ɪnəd'vɜːtntlɪ] *adv* par mégarde.
inadvisable [ɪnəd'vaɪzəbl] *adj* à déconseiller; **it is** ~ **to** il est déconseillé de.
inane [ɪ'neɪn] *adj* inepte, stupide.
inanimate [ɪn'ænɪmət] *adj* inanimé(e).
inapplicable [ɪn'æplɪkəbl] *adj* inapplicable.
inappropriate [ɪnə'prəuprɪət] *adj* inopportun(e), mal à propos; (*word, expression*) impropre.
inapt [ɪn'æpt] *adj* inapte; peu approprié(e).
inaptitude [ɪn'æptɪtjuːd] *n* inaptitude *f*.
inarticulate [ɪnɑː'tɪkjulət] *adj* (*person*) qui s'exprime mal; (*speech*) indistinct(e).
inasmuch [ɪnəz'mʌtʃ] *adv*: ~ **as** vu que, en ce sens que.
inattention [ɪnə'tɛnʃən] *n* manque *m* d'attention.
inattentive [ɪnə'tɛntɪv] *adj* inattentif(ive), distrait(e); négligent(e).
inaudible [ɪn'ɔːdɪbl] *adj* inaudible.
inaugural [ɪ'nɔːgjurəl] *adj* inaugural(e).
inaugurate [ɪ'nɔːgjureɪt] *vt* inaugurer; (*president, official*) investir de ses fonctions.
inauguration [ɪnɔːgju'reɪʃən] *n* inauguration *f*; investiture *f*.
inauspicious [ɪnɔːs'pɪʃəs] *adj* peu propice.
in-between [ɪnbɪ'twiːn] *adj* entre les deux.
inborn [ɪn'bɔːn] *adj* (*feeling*) inné(e); (*defect*) congénital(e).
inbred [ɪn'brɛd] *adj* inné(e), naturel(le); (*family*) consanguin(e).
inbreeding [ɪn'briːdɪŋ] *n* croisement *m* d'animaux de même souche; unions consanguines.
Inc. *abbr* = **incorporated**.
Inca ['ɪŋkə] *adj* (*also*: ~**n**) inca *inv* ♦ *n* Inca *m/f*.
incalculable [ɪn'kælkjuləbl] *adj* incalculable.
incapability [ɪnkeɪpə'bɪlɪtɪ] *n* incapacité *f*.
incapable [ɪn'keɪpəbl] *adj*: ~ **(of)** incapable (de).
incapacitate [ɪnkə'pæsɪteɪt] *vt*: **to** ~ **sb from doing** rendre qn incapable de faire.
incapacitated [ɪnkə'pæsɪteɪtɪd] *adj* (*LAW*) frappé(e) d'incapacité.
incapacity [ɪnkə'pæsɪtɪ] *n* incapacité *f*.
incarcerate [ɪn'kɑːsəreɪt] *vt* incarcérer.

incarnate *adj* [ɪnˈkɑːnɪt] incarné(e) ♦ *vt* [ˈɪnkɑːneɪt] incarner.
incarnation [ɪnkɑːˈneɪʃən] *n* incarnation *f*.
incendiary [ɪnˈsɛndɪərɪ] *adj* incendiaire ♦ *n* (*bomb*) bombe *f* incendiaire.
incense *n* [ˈɪnsɛns] encens *m* ♦ *vt* [ɪnˈsɛns] (*anger*) mettre en colère.
incense burner *n* encensoir *m*.
incentive [ɪnˈsɛntɪv] *n* encouragement *m*, raison *f* de se donner de la peine.
incentive scheme *n* système *m* de primes d'encouragement.
inception [ɪnˈsɛpʃən] *n* commencement *m*, début *m*.
incessant [ɪnˈsɛsnt] *adj* incessant(e).
incessantly [ɪnˈsɛsntlɪ] *adv* sans cesse, constamment.
incest [ˈɪnsɛst] *n* inceste *m*.
inch [ɪntʃ] *n* pouce *m* (= 25 mm; 12 in a foot); **within an ~ of** à deux doigts de; **he wouldn't give an ~** (*fig*) il n'a pas voulu céder d'un pouce *or* faire la plus petite concession.
►**inch forward** *vi* avancer petit à petit.
inch tape *n* (*BRIT*) centimètre *m* (de couturière).
incidence [ˈɪnsɪdns] *n* (*of crime, disease*) fréquence *f*.
incident [ˈɪnsɪdnt] *n* incident *m*; (*in book*) péripétie *f*.
incidental [ɪnsɪˈdɛntl] *adj* accessoire; (*unplanned*) accidentel(le); **~ to** qui accompagne; **~ expenses** faux frais *mpl*.
incidentally [ɪnsɪˈdɛntəlɪ] *adv* (*by the way*) à propos.
incidental music *n* musique *f* de fond.
incident room *n* (*POLICE*) salle *f* d'opérations.
incinerate [ɪnˈsɪnəreɪt] *vt* incinérer.
incinerator [ɪnˈsɪnəreɪtə*] *n* incinérateur *m*.
incipient [ɪnˈsɪpɪənt] *adj* naissant(e).
incision [ɪnˈsɪʒən] *n* incision *f*.
incisive [ɪnˈsaɪsɪv] *adj* incisif(ive); mordant(e).
incisor [ɪnˈsaɪzə*] *n* incisive *f*.
incite [ɪnˈsaɪt] *vt* inciter, pousser.
incl. *abbr* = **including, inclusive (of)**.
inclement [ɪnˈklɛmənt] *adj* inclément(e), rigoureux(euse).
inclination [ɪnklɪˈneɪʃən] *n* inclination *f*.
incline *n* [ˈɪnklaɪn] pente *f*, plan incliné ♦ *vb* [ɪnˈklaɪn] *vt* incliner ♦ *vi*: **to ~ to** avoir tendance à; **to be ~d to** de do être enclin(e) à faire; (*have a tendency to do*) avoir tendance à faire; **to be well ~d towards sb** être bien disposé(e) à l'égard de qn.
include [ɪnˈkluːd] *vt* inclure, comprendre; **the tip is/is not ~d** le service est compris/n'est pas compris.
including [ɪnˈkluːdɪŋ] *prep* y compris; **~ tip** service compris.
inclusion [ɪnˈkluːʒən] *n* inclusion *f*.
inclusive [ɪnˈkluːsɪv] *adj* inclus(e), compris(e); **£50 ~ of all surcharges** 50 livres tous frais compris.

inclusive terms *npl* (*BRIT*) prix tout compris.
incognito [ɪnkɔgˈniːtəu] *adv* incognito.
incoherent [ɪnkəuˈhɪərənt] *adj* incohérent(e).
income [ˈɪnkʌm] *n* revenu *m*; **gross/net ~** revenu brut/net; **~ and expenditure account** compte *m* de recettes et de dépenses.
income support *n* (*BRIT*) ≈ revenu *m* minimum d'insertion, RMI *m*.
income tax *n* impôt *m* sur le revenu.
income tax inspector *n* inspecteur *m* des contributions directes.
income tax return *n* déclaration *f* des revenus.
incoming [ˈɪnkʌmɪŋ] *adj* (*passengers, mail*) à l'arrivée; (*government, tenant*) nouveau(nouvelle); **~ tide** marée montante.
incommunicado [ˈɪnkəmjunɪˈkɑːdəu] *adj*: **to hold sb ~** tenir qn au secret.
incomparable [ɪnˈkɔmpərəbl] *adj* incomparable.
incompatible [ɪnkəmˈpætɪbl] *adj* incompatible.
incompetence [ɪnˈkɔmpɪtns] *n* incompétence *f*, incapacité *f*.
incompetent [ɪnˈkɔmpɪtnt] *adj* incompétent(e), incapable.
incomplete [ɪnkəmˈpliːt] *adj* incomplet(ète).
incomprehensible [ɪnkɔmprɪˈhɛnsɪbl] *adj* incompréhensible.
inconceivable [ɪnkənˈsiːvəbl] *adj* inconcevable.
inconclusive [ɪnkənˈkluːsɪv] *adj* peu concluant(e); (*argument*) peu convaincant(e).
incongruous [ɪnˈkɔŋgruəs] *adj* peu approprié(e); (*remark, act*) incongru(e), déplacé(e).
inconsequential [ɪnkɔnsɪˈkwɛnʃl] *adj* sans importance.
inconsiderable [ɪnkənˈsɪdərəbl] *adj*: **not ~** non négligeable.
inconsiderate [ɪnkənˈsɪdərət] *adj* (*action*) inconsidéré(e); (*person*) qui manque d'égards.
inconsistency [ɪnkənˈsɪstənsɪ] *n* (*of actions etc*) inconséquence *f*; (*of work*) irrégularité *f*; (*of statement etc*) incohérence *f*.
inconsistent [ɪnkənˈsɪstnt] *adj* inconséquent(e); irregulier(ière); peu cohérent(e); **~ with** en contradiction avec.
inconsolable [ɪnkənˈsəuləbl] *adj* inconsolable.
inconspicuous [ɪnkənˈspɪkjuəs] *adj* qui passe inaperçu(e); (*colour, dress*) discret(ète); **to make o.s. ~** ne pas se faire remarquer.
inconstant [ɪnˈkɔnstnt] *adj* inconstant(e); variable.
incontinence [ɪnˈkɔntɪnəns] *n* incontinence *f*.
incontinent [ɪnˈkɔntɪnənt] *adj* incontinent(e).
incontrovertible [ɪnkɔntrəˈvəːtəbl] *adj* irréfutable.
inconvenience [ɪnkənˈviːnjəns] *n* inconvénient *m*; (*trouble*) dérangement *m*

♦ *vt* déranger; **don't ~ yourself** ne vous dérangez pas.

inconvenient [ɪnkən'viːnjənt] *adj* malcommode; (*time, place*) mal choisi(e), qui ne convient pas; **that time is very ~ for me** c'est un moment qui ne me convient pas du tout.

incorporate [ɪn'kɔːpəreɪt] *vt* incorporer; (*contain*) contenir ♦ *vi* fusionner; (*two firms*) se constituer en société.

incorporated [ɪn'kɔːpəreɪtɪd] *adj*: **~ company** (*US: abbr* **Inc.**) ≈ société *f* anonyme (S.A.).

incorrect [ɪnkə'rɛkt] *adj* incorrect(e); (*opinion, statement*) inexact(e).

incorrigible [ɪn'kɔrɪdʒɪbl] *adj* incorrigible.

incorruptible [ɪnkə'rʌptɪbl] *adj* incorruptible.

increase *n* ['ɪnkriːs] augmentation *f* ♦ *vi, vt* [ɪn'kriːs] augmenter; **an ~ of 5%** une augmentation de 5%; **to be on the ~** être en augmentation.

increasing [ɪn'kriːsɪŋ] *adj* croissant(e).

increasingly [ɪn'kriːsɪŋlɪ] *adv* de plus en plus.

incredible [ɪn'krɛdɪbl] *adj* incroyable.

incredulous [ɪn'krɛdjuləs] *adj* incrédule.

increment ['ɪnkrɪmənt] *n* augmentation *f*.

incriminate [ɪn'krɪmɪneɪt] *vt* incriminer, compromettre.

incriminating [ɪn'krɪmɪneɪtɪŋ] *adj* compromettant(e).

incrust [ɪn'krʌst] *vt* = **encrust**.

incubate ['ɪnkjubeɪt] *vt* (*egg*) couver, incuber ♦ *vi* (*eggs*) couver; (*disease*) couver.

incubation [ɪnkju'beɪʃən] *n* incubation *f*.

incubation period *n* période *f* d'incubation.

incubator ['ɪnkjubeɪtə*] *n* incubateur *m*; (*for babies*) couveuse *f*.

inculcate ['ɪnkʌlkeɪt] *vt*: **to ~ sth in sb** inculquer qch à qn.

incumbent [ɪn'kʌmbənt] *adj*: **it is ~ on him to ...** il lui incombe *or* appartient de ... ♦ *n* titulaire *m/f*.

incur [ɪn'kə:*] *vt* (*expenses*) encourir; (*anger, risk*) s'exposer à; (*debt*) contracter; (*loss*) subir.

incurable [ɪn'kjuərəbl] *adj* incurable.

incursion [ɪn'kəːʃən] *n* incursion *f*.

Ind. *abbr* (*US*) = **Indiana**.

indebted [ɪn'dɛtɪd] *adj*: **to be ~ to sb (for)** être redevable à qn (de).

indecency [ɪn'diːsnsɪ] *n* indécence *f*.

indecent [ɪn'diːsnt] *adj* indécent(e), inconvenant(e).

indecent assault *n* (*BRIT*) attentat *m* à la pudeur.

indecent exposure *n* outrage *m* public à la pudeur.

indecipherable [ɪndɪ'saɪfərəbl] *adj* indéchiffrable.

indecision [ɪndɪ'sɪʒən] *n* indécision *f*.

indecisive [ɪndɪ'saɪsɪv] *adj* indécis(e); (*discussion*) peu concluant(e).

indeed [ɪn'diːd] *adv* en effet, effectivement; (*furthermore*) d'ailleurs; **yes ~!** certainement!

indefatigable [ɪndɪ'fætɪgəbl] *adj* infatigable.

indefensible [ɪndɪ'fɛnsɪbl] *adj* (*conduct*) indéfendable.

indefinable [ɪndɪ'faɪnəbl] *adj* indéfinissable.

indefinite [ɪn'dɛfɪnɪt] *adj* indéfini(e); (*answer*) vague; (*period, number*) indéterminé(e).

indefinitely [ɪn'dɛfɪnɪtlɪ] *adv* (*wait*) indéfiniment; (*speak*) vaguement, avec imprécision.

indelible [ɪn'dɛlɪbl] *adj* indélébile.

indelicate [ɪn'dɛlɪkɪt] *adj* (*tactless*) indélicat(e), grossier(ière); (*not polite*) inconvenant(e), malséant(e).

indemnify [ɪn'dɛmnɪfaɪ] *vt* indemniser, dédommager.

indemnity [ɪn'dɛmnɪtɪ] *n* (*insurance*) assurance *f*, garantie *f*; (*compensation*) indemnité *f*.

indent [ɪn'dɛnt] *vt* (*text*) commencer en retrait.

indentation [ɪndɛn'teɪʃən] *n* découpure *f*; (*TYP*) alinéa *m*; (*on metal*) bosse *f*.

indenture [ɪn'dɛntʃə*] *n* contrat *m* d'emploi-formation.

independence [ɪndɪ'pɛndns] *n* indépendance *f*.

---

*L'**Independence Day** est la fête nationale aux États-Unis, le 4 juillet. Il commémore l'adoption de la déclaration d'Indépendance, en 1776, écrite par Thomas Jefferson et proclamant la séparation des 13 colonies américaines de la Grande-Bretagne.*

---

independent [ɪndɪ'pɛndnt] *adj* indépendant(e); **to become ~** s'affranchir.

independently [ɪndɪ'pɛndntlɪ] *adv* de façon indépendante; **~ of** indépendamment de.

in-depth ['ɪndɛpθ] *adj* approfondi(e).

indescribable [ɪndɪ'skraɪbəbl] *adj* indescriptible.

indeterminate [ɪndɪ'təːmɪnɪt] *adj* indéterminé(e).

index ['ɪndɛks] *n* (*pl*: **~es**: *in book*) index *m*; (: *in library etc*) catalogue *m*; (*pl*: **indices** ['ɪndɪsiːz]) (*ratio, sign*) indice *m*.

index card *n* fiche *f*.

index finger *n* index *m*.

index-linked ['ɪndɛks'lɪŋkt], (*US*) **indexed** ['ɪndɛkst] *adj* indexé(e) (sur le coût de la vie *etc*).

India ['ɪndɪə] *n* Inde *f*.

Indian ['ɪndɪən] *adj* indien(ne) ♦ *n* Indien/ne.

Indian ink *n* encre *f* de Chine.

Indian Ocean *n*: **the ~** l'océan Indien.

Indian summer *n* (*fig*) été indien, beaux jours en automne.

India paper *n* papier *m* bible.

India rubber *n* gomme *f*.

indicate ['ɪndɪkeɪt] *vt* indiquer ♦ *vi* (*BRIT AUT*):

to ~ **left/right** mettre son clignotant à gauche/à droite.

indication [ɪndɪ'keɪʃən] n indication f, signe m.

indicative [ɪn'dɪkətɪv] adj indicatif(ive) ♦ n (LING) indicatif m; **to be ~ of sth** être symptomatique de qch.

indicator ['ɪndɪkeɪtə*] n (sign) indicateur m; (AUT) clignotant m.

indices ['ɪndɪsiːz] npl of **index**.

indict [ɪn'daɪt] vt accuser.

indictable [ɪn'daɪtəbl] adj (person) passible de poursuites; ~ **offence** délit m tombant sous le coup de la loi.

indictment [ɪn'daɪtmənt] n accusation f.

indifference [ɪn'dɪfrəns] n indifférence f.

indifferent [ɪn'dɪfrənt] adj indifférent(e); (poor) médiocre, quelconque.

indigenous [ɪn'dɪdʒɪnəs] adj indigène.

indigestible [ɪndɪ'dʒɛstɪbl] adj indigeste.

indigestion [ɪndɪ'dʒɛstʃən] n indigestion f, mauvaise digestion.

indignant [ɪn'dɪgnənt] adj: ~ **(at sth/with sb)** indigné(e) (de qch/contre qn).

indignation [ɪndɪg'neɪʃən] n indignation f.

indignity [ɪn'dɪgnɪtɪ] n indignité f, affront m.

indigo ['ɪndɪgəu] adj indigo inv ♦ n indigo m.

indirect [ɪndɪ'rɛkt] adj indirect(e).

indirectly [ɪndɪ'rɛktlɪ] adv indirectement.

indiscreet [ɪndɪ'skriːt] adj indiscret(ète); (rash) imprudent(e).

indiscretion [ɪndɪ'skrɛʃən] n (see indiscreet) indiscrétion f; imprudence f.

indiscriminate [ɪndɪ'skrɪmɪnət] adj (person) qui manque de discernement; (admiration) aveugle; (killings) commis(e) au hasard.

indispensable [ɪndɪ'spɛnsəbl] adj indispensable.

indisposed [ɪndɪ'spəuzd] adj (unwell) indisposé(e), souffrant(e).

indisposition [ɪndɪspə'zɪʃən] n (illness) indisposition f, malaise m.

indisputable [ɪndɪ'spjuːtəbl] adj incontestable, indiscutable.

indistinct [ɪndɪ'stɪŋkt] adj indistinct(e); (memory, noise) vague.

indistinguishable [ɪndɪ'stɪŋgwɪʃəbl] adj impossible à distinguer.

individual [ɪndɪ'vɪdjuəl] n individu m ♦ adj individuel(le); (characteristic) particulier(ière), original(e).

individualist [ɪndɪ'vɪdjuəlɪst] n individualiste m/f.

individuality [ɪndɪvɪdju'ælɪtɪ] n individualité f.

individually [ɪndɪ'vɪdjuəlɪ] adv individuellement.

indivisible [ɪndɪ'vɪzɪbl] adj indivisible; (MATH) insécable.

Indo-China ['ɪndəu'tʃaɪnə] n Indochine f.

indoctrinate [ɪn'dɔktrɪneɪt] vt endoctriner.

indoctrination [ɪndɔktrɪ'neɪʃən] n endoctrinement m.

indolent ['ɪndələnt] adj indolent(e),

nonchalant(e).

Indonesia [ɪndə'niːzɪə] n Indonésie f.

Indonesian [ɪndə'niːzɪən] adj indonésien(ne) ♦ n Indonésien/ne; (LING) indonésien m.

indoor ['ɪndɔ:*] adj d'intérieur; (plant) d'appartement; (swimming pool) couvert(e); (sport, games) pratiqué(e) en salle.

indoors [ɪn'dɔ:z] adv à l'intérieur; (at home) à la maison.

indubitable [ɪn'djuːbɪtəbl] adj indubitable, incontestable.

induce [ɪn'djuːs] vt persuader; (bring about) provoquer; **to ~ sb to do sth** inciter or pousser qn à faire qch.

inducement [ɪn'djuːsmənt] n incitation f; (incentive) but m; (pej: bribe) pot-de-vin m.

induct [ɪn'dʌkt] vt établir dans ses fonctions; (fig) initier.

induction [ɪn'dʌkʃən] n (MED: of birth) accouchement provoqué.

induction course n (BRIT) stage m de mise au courant.

indulge [ɪn'dʌldʒ] vt (whim) céder à, satisfaire; (child) gâter ♦ vi: **to ~ in sth** s'offrir qch, se permettre qch; se livrer à qch.

indulgence [ɪn'dʌldʒəns] n fantaisie f (que l'on s'offre); (leniency) indulgence f.

indulgent [ɪn'dʌldʒənt] adj indulgent(e).

industrial [ɪn'dʌstrɪəl] adj industriel(le); (injury) du travail; (dispute) ouvrier(ière).

industrial action n action revendicative.

industrial estate n (BRIT) zone industrielle.

industrialist [ɪn'dʌstrɪəlɪst] n industriel m.

industrialize [ɪn'dʌstrɪəlaɪz] vt industrialiser.

industrial park n (US) zone industrielle.

industrial relations npl relations fpl dans l'entreprise.

industrial tribunal n (BRIT) ≈ conseil m de prud'hommes.

industrial unrest n (BRIT) agitation sociale, conflits sociaux.

industrious [ɪn'dʌstrɪəs] adj travailleur(euse).

industry ['ɪndəstrɪ] n industrie f; (diligence) zèle m, application f.

inebriated [ɪ'niːbrɪeɪtɪd] adj ivre.

inedible [ɪn'ɛdɪbl] adj immangeable; (plant etc) non comestible.

ineffective [ɪnɪ'fɛktɪv], **ineffectual** [ɪnɪ'fɛktʃuəl] adj inefficace; incompétent(e).

inefficiency [ɪnɪ'fɪʃənsɪ] n inefficacité f.

inefficient [ɪnɪ'fɪʃənt] adj inefficace.

inelegant [ɪn'ɛlɪgənt] adj peu élégant(e), inélégant(e).

ineligible [ɪn'ɛlɪdʒɪbl] adj (candidate) inéligible; **to be ~ for sth** ne pas avoir droit à qch.

inept [ɪ'nɛpt] adj inepte.

ineptitude [ɪ'nɛptɪtjuːd] n ineptie f.

inequality [ɪnɪ'kwɔlɪtɪ] n inégalité f.

inequitable [ɪn'ɛkwɪtəbl] adj inéquitable, inique.

ineradicable [ɪnɪ'rædɪkəbl] *adj* indéracinable, tenace.

inert [ɪ'nəːt] *adj* inerte.

inertia [ɪ'nəːʃə] *n* inertie *f*.

inertia-reel seat belt [ɪ'nəːʃə'riːl-] *n* ceinture *f* de sécurité à enrouleur.

inescapable [ɪnɪ'skeɪpəbl] *adj* inéluctable, inévitable.

inessential [ɪnɪ'sɛnʃl] *adj* superflu(e).

inestimable [ɪn'ɛstɪməbl] *adj* inestimable, incalculable.

inevitable [ɪn'ɛvɪtəbl] *adj* inévitable.

inevitably [ɪn'ɛvɪtəblɪ] *adv* inévitablement, fatalement.

inexact [ɪnɪg'zækt] *adj* inexact(e).

inexcusable [ɪnɪks'kjuːzəbl] *adj* inexcusable.

inexhaustible [ɪnɪg'zɔːstɪbl] *adj* inépuisable.

inexorable [ɪn'ɛksərəbl] *adj* inexorable.

inexpensive [ɪnɪk'spɛnsɪv] *adj* bon marché *inv*.

inexperience [ɪnɪk'spɪərɪəns] *n* inexpérience *f*, manque *m* d'expérience.

inexperienced [ɪnɪk'spɪərɪənst] *adj* inexpérimenté(e); **to be ~ in sth** manquer d'expérience dans qch.

inexplicable [ɪnɪk'splɪkəbl] *adj* inexplicable.

inexpressible [ɪnɪk'sprɛsɪbl] *adj* inexprimable; indicible.

inextricable [ɪnɪk'strɪkəbl] *adj* inextricable.

infallibility [ɪnfælə'bɪlɪtɪ] *n* infaillibilité *f*.

infallible [ɪn'fælɪbl] *adj* infaillible.

infamous ['ɪnfəməs] *adj* infâme, abominable.

infamy ['ɪnfəmɪ] *n* infamie *f*.

infancy ['ɪnfənsɪ] *n* petite enfance, bas âge; (*fig*) enfance, débuts *mpl*.

infant ['ɪnfənt] *n* (*baby*) nourrisson *m*; (*young child*) petit(e) enfant.

infantile ['ɪnfəntaɪl] *adj* infantile.

infant mortality *n* mortalité *f* infantile.

infantry ['ɪnfəntrɪ] *n* infanterie *f*.

infantryman ['ɪnfəntrɪmən] *n* fantassin *m*.

infant school *n* (*BRIT*) classes *fpl* préparatoires (*entre 5 et 7 ans*).

infatuated [ɪn'fætjueɪtɪd] *adj*: **~ with** entiché(e) de; **to become ~ (with sb)** s'enticher (de qn).

infatuation [ɪnfætju'eɪʃən] *n* toquade *f*; engouement *m*.

infect [ɪn'fɛkt] *vt* infecter, contaminer; (*fig: pej*) corrompre; **~ed with** (*illness*) atteint(e) de; **to become ~ed** (*wound*) s'infecter.

infection [ɪn'fɛkʃən] *n* infection *f*; contagion *f*.

infectious [ɪn'fɛkʃəs] *adj* infectieux(euse); (*also fig*) contagieux(euse).

infer [ɪn'fəː*] *vt*: **to ~ (from)** conclure (de), déduire (de).

inference ['ɪnfərəns] *n* conclusion *f*, déduction *f*.

inferior [ɪn'fɪərɪə*] *adj* inférieur(e); (*goods*) de qualité inférieure ♦ *n* inférieur/e; (*in rank*) subalterne *m/f*; **to feel ~** avoir un sentiment d'infériorité.

inferiority [ɪnfɪərɪ'ɔrətɪ] *n* infériorité *f*.

inferiority complex *n* complexe *m* d'infériorité.

infernal [ɪn'fəːnl] *adj* infernal(e).

infernally [ɪn'fəːnəlɪ] *adv* abominablement.

inferno [ɪn'fəːnəu] *n* enfer *m*; brasier *m*.

infertile [ɪn'fəːtaɪl] *adj* stérile.

infertility [ɪnfəː'tɪlɪtɪ] *n* infertilité *f*, stérilité *f*.

infested [ɪn'fɛstɪd] *adj*: **~ (with)** infesté(e) (de).

infidelity [ɪnfɪ'dɛlɪtɪ] *n* infidélité *f*.

in-fighting ['ɪnfaɪtɪŋ] *n* querelles *fpl* internes.

infiltrate ['ɪnfɪltreɪt] *vt* (*troops etc*) faire s'infiltrer; (*enemy line etc*) s'infiltrer dans ♦ *vi* s'infiltrer.

infinite ['ɪnfɪnɪt] *adj* infini(e); (*time, money*) illimité(e).

infinitely ['ɪnfɪnɪtlɪ] *adv* infiniment.

infinitesimal [ɪnfɪnɪ'tɛsɪməl] *adj* infinitésimal(e).

infinitive [ɪn'fɪnɪtɪv] *n* infinitif *m*.

infinity [ɪn'fɪnɪtɪ] *n* infinité *f*; (*also MATH*) infini *m*.

infirm [ɪn'fəːm] *adj* infirme.

infirmary [ɪn'fəːmərɪ] *n* hôpital *m*; (*in school, factory*) infirmerie *f*.

infirmity [ɪn'fəːmɪtɪ] *n* infirmité *f*.

inflamed [ɪn'fleɪmd] *adj* enflammé(e).

inflammable [ɪn'flæməbl] *adj* (*BRIT*) inflammable.

inflammation [ɪnflə'meɪʃən] *n* inflammation *f*.

inflammatory [ɪn'flæmətərɪ] *adj* (*speech*) incendiaire.

inflatable [ɪn'fleɪtəbl] *adj* gonflable.

inflate [ɪn'fleɪt] *vt* (*tyre, balloon*) gonfler; (*fig*) grossir; gonfler; faire monter.

inflated [ɪn'fleɪtɪd] *adj* (*style*) enflé(e); (*value*) exagéré(e).

inflation [ɪn'fleɪʃən] *n* (*ECON*) inflation *f*.

inflationary [ɪn'fleɪʃənərɪ] *adj* inflationniste.

inflection [ɪn'flɛkʃən] *n* inflexion *f*; (*ending*) désinence *f*.

inflexible [ɪn'flɛksɪbl] *adj* inflexible, rigide.

inflict [ɪn'flɪkt] *vt*: **to ~ on** infliger à.

infliction [ɪn'flɪkʃən] *n* infliction *f*; affliction *f*.

in-flight ['ɪnflaɪt] *adj* (*refuelling*) en vol; (*service etc*) à bord.

inflow ['ɪnfləu] *n* afflux *m*.

influence ['ɪnfluəns] *n* influence *f* ♦ *vt* influencer; **under the ~ of** sous l'effet de; **under the ~ of drink** en état d'ébriété.

influential [ɪnflu'ɛnʃl] *adj* influent(e).

influenza [ɪnflu'ɛnzə] *n* grippe *f*.

influx ['ɪnflʌks] *n* afflux *m*.

inform [ɪn'fɔːm] *vt*: **to ~ sb (of)** informer *or* avertir qn (de) ♦ *vi*: **to ~ on sb** dénoncer qn, informer contre qn; **to ~ sb about** renseigner qn sur, mettre qn au courant de.

informal [ɪn'fɔːml] *adj* (*person, manner*) simple, sans cérémonie; (*announcement, visit*) non officiel(le); **"dress ~"** "tenue de ville".

informality [ɪnfɔː'mælɪtɪ] *n* simplicité *f*,

absence f de cérémonie; caractère non officiel.

informal language n langage m de la conversation.

informally [ɪn'fɔːməlɪ] adv sans cérémonie, en toute simplicité; non officiellement.

informant [ɪn'fɔːmənt] n informateur/trice.

information [ɪnfə'meɪʃən] n information(s) f(pl); renseignements mpl; (knowledge) connaissances fpl; **to get ~ on** se renseigner sur; **a piece of ~** un renseignement; **for your ~** à titre d'information.

information bureau n bureau m de renseignements.

information processing n traitement m de l'information.

information retrieval n recherche f (informatique) de renseignements.

information technology (IT) n informatique f.

informative [ɪn'fɔːmətɪv] adj instructif(ive).

informed [ɪn'fɔːmd] adj (bien) informé(e); **an ~ guess** une hypothèse fondée sur la connaissance des faits.

informer [ɪn'fɔːmə*] n dénonciateur/trice; (also: **police ~**) indicateur/trice.

infra dig ['ɪnfrə'dɪg] adj abbr (col: = infra dignitatem) au-dessous de ma (or sa etc) dignité.

infra-red [ɪnfrə'red] adj infrarouge.

infrastructure ['ɪnfrəstrʌktʃə*] n infrastructure f.

infrequent [ɪn'friːkwənt] adj peu fréquent(e), rare.

infringe [ɪn'frɪndʒ] vt enfreindre ♦ vi: **to ~ on** empiéter sur.

infringement [ɪn'frɪndʒmənt] n: ~ **(of)** infraction f (à).

infuriate [ɪn'fjuərɪeɪt] vt mettre en fureur.

infuriating [ɪn'fjuərɪeɪtɪŋ] adj exaspérant(e).

infuse [ɪn'fjuːz] vt: **to ~ sb with sth** (fig) insuffler qch à qn.

infusion [ɪn'fjuːʒən] n (tea etc) infusion f.

ingenious [ɪn'dʒiːnjəs] adj ingénieux(euse).

ingenuity [ɪndʒɪ'njuːɪtɪ] n ingéniosité f.

ingenuous [ɪn'dʒɛnjuəs] adj franc(franche), ouvert(e).

ingot ['ɪŋgət] n lingot m.

ingrained [ɪn'greɪnd] adj enraciné(e).

ingratiate [ɪn'greɪʃɪeɪt] vt: **to ~ o.s. with** s'insinuer dans les bonnes grâces de, se faire bien voir de.

ingratiating [ɪn'greɪʃɪeɪtɪŋ] adj (smile, speech) insinuant(e); (person) patelin(e).

ingratitude [ɪn'grætɪtjuːd] n ingratitude f.

ingredient [ɪn'griːdɪənt] n ingrédient m; élément m.

ingrowing ['ɪngrəuɪŋ], **ingrown** ['ɪngrəun] adj: ~ **toenail** ongle incarné.

inhabit [ɪn'hæbɪt] vt habiter.

inhabitable [ɪn'hæbɪtəbl] adj habitable.

inhabitant [ɪn'hæbɪtnt] n habitant/e.

inhale [ɪn'heɪl] vt inhaler; (perfume) respirer ♦ vi (in smoking) avaler la fumée.

inhaler [ɪn'heɪlə*] n inhalateur m.

inherent [ɪn'hɪərənt] adj: ~ **(in or to)** inhérent(e) (à).

inherently [ɪn'hɪərəntlɪ] adv (easy, difficult) en soi; (lazy) fondamentalement.

inherit [ɪn'herɪt] vt hériter (de).

inheritance [ɪn'herɪtəns] n héritage m; **law of ~** droit m de la succession.

inhibit [ɪn'hɪbɪt] vt (PSYCH) inhiber; **to ~ sb from doing** empêcher or retenir qn de faire.

inhibited [ɪn'hɪbɪtɪd] adj (person) inhibé(e).

inhibiting [ɪn'hɪbɪtɪŋ] adj gênant(e).

inhibition [ɪnhɪ'bɪʃən] n inhibition f.

inhospitable [ɪnhɔs'pɪtəbl] adj inhospitalier(ière).

in-house ['ɪn'haus] adj (system) interne; (training) effectué(e) sur place or dans le cadre de la compagnie ♦ adv (train, produce) sur place.

inhuman [ɪn'hjuːmən] adj inhumain(e).

inhumane [ɪnhjuː'meɪn] adj inhumain(e).

inimitable [ɪ'nɪmɪtəbl] adj inimitable.

iniquity [ɪ'nɪkwɪtɪ] n iniquité f.

initial [ɪ'nɪʃl] adj initial(e) ♦ n initiale f ♦ vt parafer; ~**s** npl initiales fpl; (as signature) parafe m.

initialize [ɪ'nɪʃəlaɪz] vt (COMPUT) initialiser.

initially [ɪ'nɪʃəlɪ] adv initialement, au début.

initiate [ɪ'nɪʃɪeɪt] vt (start) entreprendre; amorcer; lancer; (person) initier; **to ~ sb into a secret** initier qn à un secret; **to ~ proceedings against sb** (LAW) intenter une action à qn, engager des poursuites contre qn.

initiation [ɪnɪʃɪ'eɪʃən] n (into secret etc) initiation f.

initiative [ɪ'nɪʃətɪv] n initiative f; **to take the ~** prendre l'initiative.

inject [ɪn'dʒɛkt] vt (liquid, fig: money) injecter; (person) faire une piqûre à.

injection [ɪn'dʒɛkʃən] n injection f, piqûre f; **to have an ~** se faire faire une piqûre.

injudicious [ɪndʒu'dɪʃəs] adj peu judicieux(euse).

injunction [ɪn'dʒʌŋkʃən] n (LAW) injonction f, ordre m.

injure ['ɪndʒə*] vt blesser; (wrong) faire du tort à; (damage: reputation etc) compromettre; (feelings) heurter; **to ~ o.s.** se blesser.

injured ['ɪndʒəd] adj (person, leg etc) blessé(e); (tone, feelings) offensé(e); ~ **party** (LAW) partie lésée.

injurious [ɪn'dʒuərɪəs] adj: ~ **(to)** préjudiciable (à).

injury ['ɪndʒərɪ] n blessure f; (wrong) tort m; **to escape without ~** s'en sortir sain et sauf.

injury time n (SPORT) arrêts mpl de jeu.

injustice [ɪn'dʒʌstɪs] n injustice f; **you do me an ~** vous êtes injuste envers moi.

ink [ɪŋk] n encre f.

ink-jet printer ['ɪŋkdʒɛt-] *n* imprimante *f* à jet d'encre.

inkling ['ɪŋklɪŋ] *n* soupçon *m*, vague idée *f*.

inkpad ['ɪŋkpæd] *n* tampon *m* encreur.

inky ['ɪŋkɪ] *adj* taché(e) d'encre.

inlaid ['ɪnleɪd] *adj* incrusté(e); (*table etc*) marqueté(e).

inland *adj* ['ɪnlənd] intérieur(e) ♦ *adv* [ɪn'lænd] à l'intérieur, dans les terres; ~ **waterways** canaux *mpl* et rivières *fpl*.

Inland Revenue *n* (*BRIT*) fisc *m*.

in-laws ['ɪnlɔːz] *npl* beaux-parents *mpl*; belle famille.

inlet ['ɪnlɛt] *n* (*GEO*) crique *f*.

inlet pipe *n* (*TECH*) tuyau *m* d'arrivée.

inmate ['ɪnmeɪt] *n* (*in prison*) détenu/e; (*in asylum*) interné/e.

inmost ['ɪnməʊst] *adj* le(la) plus profond(e).

inn [ɪn] *n* auberge *f*.

innards ['ɪnədz] *npl* (*col*) entrailles *fpl*.

innate [ɪ'neɪt] *adj* inné(e).

inner ['ɪnə*] *adj* intérieur(e).

inner city *n* (vieux quartiers du) centre urbain (*souffrant souvent de délabrement, d'embouteillages etc*).

innermost ['ɪnəməʊst] *adj* le(la) plus profond(e).

inner tube *n* (*of tyre*) chambre *f* à air.

innings ['ɪnɪŋz] *n* (*CRICKET*) tour *m* de batte; (*BRIT fig*): **he has had a good** ~ il (en) a bien profité.

innocence ['ɪnəsns] *n* innocence *f*.

innocent ['ɪnəsnt] *adj* innocent(e).

innocuous [ɪ'nɔkjuəs] *adj* inoffensif(ive).

innovation [ɪnəʊ'veɪʃən] *n* innovation *f*.

innuendo, ~**es** [ɪnju'ɛndəʊ] *n* insinuation *f*, allusion (malveillante).

innumerable [ɪ'njuːmrəbl] *adj* innombrable.

inoculate [ɪ'nɔkjuleɪt] *vt*: **to** ~ **sb with sth** inoculer qch à qn; **to** ~ **sb against sth** vacciner qn contre qch.

inoculation [ɪnɔkju'leɪʃən] *n* inoculation *f*.

inoffensive [ɪnə'fɛnsɪv] *adj* inoffensif(ive).

inopportune [ɪn'ɔpətjuːn] *adj* inopportun(e).

inordinate [ɪ'nɔːdɪnət] *adj* démesuré(e).

inordinately [ɪ'nɔːdɪnətlɪ] *adv* démesurément.

inorganic [ɪnɔː'gænɪk] *adj* inorganique.

in-patient ['ɪnpeɪʃənt] *n* malade hospitalisé(e).

input ['ɪnpʊt] *n* (*ELEC*) énergie *f*, puissance *f*; (*of machine*) consommation *f*; (*of computer*) information fournie ♦ *vt* (*COMPUT*) introduire, entrer.

inquest ['ɪnkwɛst] *n* enquête (criminelle).

inquire [ɪn'kwaɪə*] *vi* demander ♦ *vt* demander, s'informer de; **to** ~ **about** s'informer de, se renseigner sur; **to** ~ **when/where/whether** demander quand/où/si.

▶**inquire after** *vt fus* demander des nouvelles de.

▶**inquire into** *vt fus* faire une enquête sur.

inquiring [ɪn'kwaɪərɪŋ] *adj* (*mind*) curieux(euse), investigateur(trice).

inquiry [ɪn'kwaɪərɪ] *n* demande *f* de renseignements; (*LAW*) enquête *f*, investigation *f*; **to hold an** ~ **into sth** enquêter sur qch.

inquiry desk *n* (*BRIT*) guichet *m* de renseignements.

inquiry office *n* (*BRIT*) bureau *m* de renseignements.

inquisition [ɪnkwɪ'zɪʃən] *n* enquête *f*, investigation *f*; (*REL*): **the I**~ l'Inquisition *f*.

inquisitive [ɪn'kwɪzɪtɪv] *adj* curieux(euse).

inroads ['ɪnrəʊdz] *npl*: **to make** ~ **into** (*savings, supplies*) entamer.

ins *abbr* = **inches**.

insane [ɪn'seɪn] *adj* fou(folle); (*MED*) aliéné(e).

insanitary [ɪn'sænɪtərɪ] *adj* insalubre.

insanity [ɪn'sænɪtɪ] *n* folie *f*; (*MED*) aliénation (mentale).

insatiable [ɪn'seɪʃəbl] *adj* insatiable.

inscribe [ɪn'skraɪb] *vt* inscrire; (*book etc*): **to** ~ **(to sb)** dédicacer (à qn).

inscription [ɪn'skrɪpʃən] *n* inscription *f*; (*in book*) dédicace *f*.

inscrutable [ɪn'skruːtəbl] *adj* impénétrable.

inseam ['ɪnsiːm] *n* (*US*): ~ **measurement** hauteur *f* d'entre-jambe.

insect ['ɪnsɛkt] *n* insecte *m*.

insect bite *n* piqûre *f* d'insecte.

insecticide [ɪn'sɛktɪsaɪd] *n* insecticide *m*.

insect repellent *n* crème *f* anti-insectes.

insecure [ɪnsɪ'kjuə*] *adj* peu solide; peu sûr(e); (*person*) anxieux(euse).

insecurity [ɪnsɪ'kjuərɪtɪ] *n* insécurité *f*.

insensible [ɪn'sɛnsɪbl] *adj* insensible; (*unconscious*) sans connaissance.

insensitive [ɪn'sɛnsɪtɪv] *adj* insensible.

insensitivity [ɪnsɛnsɪ'tɪvɪtɪ] *n* insensibilité *f*.

inseparable [ɪn'sɛprəbl] *adj* inséparable.

insert *vt* [ɪn'səːt] insérer ♦ *n* ['ɪnsəːt] insertion *f*.

insertion [ɪn'səːʃən] *n* insertion *f*.

in-service ['ɪn'səːvɪs] *adj* (*training*) continu(e); (*course*) d'initiation; de perfectionnement; de recyclage.

inshore [ɪn'ʃɔː*] *adj* côtier(ière) ♦ *adv* près de la côte; vers la côte.

inside ['ɪnsaɪd] *n* intérieur *m*; (*of road: BRIT*) côté *m* gauche (*de la route*); (*: US, Europe etc*) côté droit (*de la route*) ♦ *adj* intérieur(e) ♦ *adv* à l'intérieur, dedans ♦ *prep* à l'intérieur de; (*of time*): ~ **10 minutes** en moins de 10 minutes; ~**s** *npl* (*col*) intestins *mpl*; ~ **out** *adv* à l'envers; **to turn sth** ~ **out** retourner qch; **to know sth** ~ **out** connaître qch à fond *or* comme sa poche; ~ **information** renseignements *mpl* à la source; ~ **story** histoire racontée par un témoin.

inside forward *n* (*SPORT*) intérieur *m*.

inside lane *n* (*AUT: in Britain*) voie *f* de gauche; (*: in US, Europe*) voie *f* de droite.

inside leg measurement n (BRIT) hauteur f d'entre-jambe.

insider [ɪn'saɪdə*] n initié/e.

insider dealing, insider trading n (STOCK EXCHANGE) délit m d'initiés.

insidious [ɪn'sɪdɪəs] adj insidieux(euse).

insight ['ɪnsaɪt] n perspicacité f; (glimpse, idea) aperçu m; **to gain (an) ~ into** parvenir à comprendre.

insignia [ɪn'sɪgnɪə] npl insignes mpl.

insignificant [ɪnsɪg'nɪfɪknt] adj insignifiant(e).

insincere [ɪnsɪn'sɪə*] adj hypocrite.

insincerity [ɪnsɪn'serɪtɪ] n manque m de sincérité, hypocrisie f.

insinuate [ɪn'sɪnjueɪt] vt insinuer.

insinuation [ɪnsɪnju'eɪʃən] n insinuation f.

insipid [ɪn'sɪpɪd] adj insipide, fade.

insist [ɪn'sɪst] vi insister; **to ~ on doing** insister pour faire; **to ~ that** insister pour que; (claim) maintenir or soutenir que.

insistence [ɪn'sɪstəns] n insistance f.

insistent [ɪn'sɪstənt] adj insistant(e), pressant(e).

insofar [ɪnsəu'fɑ:*]: **~ as** conj dans la mesure où.

insole ['ɪnsəul] n semelle intérieure; (fixed part of shoe) première f.

insolence ['ɪnsələns] n insolence f.

insolent ['ɪnsələnt] adj insolent(e).

insoluble [ɪn'sɔljubl] adj insoluble.

insolvency [ɪn'sɔlvənsɪ] n insolvabilité f; faillite f.

insolvent [ɪn'sɔlvənt] adj insolvable; (bankrupt) en faillite.

insomnia [ɪn'sɔmnɪə] n insomnie f.

insomniac [ɪn'sɔmnɪæk] n insomniaque m/f.

inspect [ɪn'spekt] vt inspecter; (BRIT: ticket) contrôler.

inspection [ɪn'spekʃən] n inspection f; contrôle m.

inspector [ɪn'spektə*] n inspecteur/trice; contrôleur/euse.

inspiration [ɪnspə'reɪʃən] n inspiration f.

inspire [ɪn'spaɪə*] vt inspirer.

inspired [ɪn'spaɪəd] adj (writer, book etc) inspiré(e); **in an ~ moment** dans un moment d'inspiration.

inspiring [ɪn'spaɪərɪŋ] adj inspirant(e).

inst. abbr (BRIT COMM: = instant): **of the 16th ~** du 16 courant.

instability [ɪnstə'bɪlɪtɪ] n instabilité f.

install [ɪn'stɔ:l] vt installer.

installation [ɪnstə'leɪʃən] n installation f.

installment plan n (US) achat m (or vente f) à tempérament or crédit.

instalment, (US) installment [ɪn'stɔ:lmənt] n acompte m, versement partiel; (of TV serial etc) épisode m; **in ~s** (pay) à tempérament; (receive) en plusieurs fois.

instance ['ɪnstəns] n exemple m; **for ~** par exemple; **in many ~s** dans bien des cas; **in that ~** dans ce cas; **in the first ~** tout d'abord, en premier lieu.

instant ['ɪnstənt] n instant m ♦ adj immédiat(e); urgent(e); (coffee, food) instantané(e), en poudre; **the 10th ~** le 10 courant.

instantaneous [ɪnstən'teɪnɪəs] adj instantané(e).

instantly ['ɪnstəntlɪ] adv immédiatement, tout de suite.

instant replay n (US TV) retour m sur une séquence.

instead [ɪn'sted] adv au lieu de cela; **~ of** au lieu de; **~ of sb** à la place de qn.

instep ['ɪnstep] n cou-de-pied m; (of shoe) cambrure f.

instigate ['ɪnstɪgeɪt] vt (rebellion, strike, crime) inciter à; (new ideas etc) susciter.

instigation [ɪnstɪ'geɪʃən] n instigation f; **at sb's ~** à l'instigation de qn.

instil [ɪn'stɪl] vt: **to ~ (into)** inculquer (à); (courage) insuffler (à).

instinct ['ɪnstɪŋkt] n instinct m.

instinctive [ɪn'stɪŋktɪv] adj instinctif(ive).

instinctively [ɪn'stɪŋktɪvlɪ] adv instinctivement.

institute ['ɪnstɪtju:t] n institut m ♦ vt instituer, établir; (inquiry) ouvrir; (proceedings) entamer.

institution [ɪnstɪ'tju:ʃən] n institution f; (school) établissement m (scolaire); (for care) établissement (psychiatrique etc).

institutional [ɪnstɪ'tju:ʃənl] adj institutionnel(le); **~ care** soins fournis par un établissement médico-social.

instruct [ɪn'strʌkt] vt instruire, former; **to ~ sb in sth** enseigner qch à qn; **to ~ sb to do** charger qn or ordonner à qn de faire.

instruction [ɪn'strʌkʃən] n instruction f; **~s** npl directives fpl; **~s for use** mode m d'emploi.

instruction book n manuel m d'instructions.

instructive [ɪn'strʌktɪv] adj instructif(ive).

instructor [ɪn'strʌktə*] n professeur m; (for skiing, driving) moniteur m.

instrument ['ɪnstrumənt] n instrument m.

instrumental [ɪnstru'mentl] adj (MUS) instrumental(e); **to be ~ in sth/in doing sth** contribuer à qch/à faire qch.

instrumentalist [ɪnstru'mentəlɪst] n instrumentiste m/f.

instrument panel n tableau m de bord.

insubordinate [ɪnsə'bɔ:dənɪt] adj insubordonné(e).

insubordination [ɪnsəbɔ:də'neɪʃən] n insubordination f.

insufferable [ɪn'sʌfrəbl] adj insupportable.

insufficient [ɪnsə'fɪʃənt] adj insuffisant(e).

insufficiently [ɪnsə'fɪʃəntlɪ] adv insuffisamment.

insular ['ɪnsjulə*] adj insulaire; (outlook) étroit(e); (person) aux vues étroites.

insulate ['ɪnsjuleɪt] vt isoler; (against sound) insonoriser.

insulating tape ['ɪnsjuleɪtɪŋ-] *n* ruban isolant.
insulation [ɪnsju'leɪʃən] *n* isolation *f*;
insonorisation *f*.
insulin ['ɪnsjulɪn] *n* insuline *f*.
insult *n* ['ɪnsʌlt] insulte *f*, affront *m* ♦ *vt*
[ɪn'sʌlt] insulter, faire un affront à.
insulting [ɪn'sʌltɪŋ] *adj* insultant(e),
injurieux(euse).
insuperable [ɪn'sju:prəbl] *adj* insurmontable.
insurance [ɪn'ʃuərəns] *n* assurance *f*; **fire/life**
~ assurance-incendie/-vie; **to take out** ~
(against) s'assurer (contre).
insurance agent *n* agent *m* d'assurances.
insurance broker *n* courtier *m* en
assurances.
insurance policy *n* police *f* d'assurance.
insurance premium *n* prime *f* d'assurance.
insure [ɪn'ʃuə*] *vt* assurer; **to** ~ **sb/sb's life**
assurer qn/la vie de qn; **to be** ~**d for £5000**
être assuré(e) pour 5 000 livres.
insured [ɪn'ʃuəd] *n*: **the** ~ l'assuré/e.
insurer [ɪn'ʃuərə*] *n* assureur *m*.
insurgent [ɪn'sə:dʒənt] *adj*, *n* insurgé(e).
insurmountable [ɪnsə'mauntəbl] *adj*
insurmontable.
insurrection [ɪnsə'rɛkʃən] *n* insurrection *f*.
intact [ɪn'tækt] *adj* intact(e).
intake ['ɪnteɪk] *n* (*TECH*) admission *f*;
adduction *f*; (*of food*) consommation *f*; (*BRIT*
SCOL): **an** ~ **of 200 a year** 200 admissions
par an.
intangible [ɪn'tændʒɪbl] *adj* intangible; (*assets*)
immatériel(le).
integral ['ɪntɪɡrəl] *adj* intégral(e); (*part*)
intégrant(e).
integrate ['ɪntɪɡreɪt] *vt* intégrer ♦ *vi*
s'intégrer.
integrated circuit ['ɪntɪɡreɪtɪd-] *n* (*COMPUT*)
circuit intégré.
integration [ɪntɪ'ɡreɪʃən] *n* intégration *f*; **racial**
~ intégration raciale.
integrity [ɪn'tɛɡrɪtɪ] *n* intégrité *f*.
intellect ['ɪntəlɛkt] *n* intelligence *f*.
intellectual [ɪntə'lɛktjuəl] *adj*, *n*
intellectuel(le).
intelligence [ɪn'tɛlɪdʒəns] *n* intelligence *f*; (*MIL*
etc) informations *fpl*, renseignements *mpl*.
intelligence quotient (IQ) *n* quotient
intellectuel (QI).
Intelligence Service *n* services *mpl* de
renseignements.
intelligence test *n* test *m* d'intelligence.
intelligent [ɪn'tɛlɪdʒənt] *adj* intelligent(e).
intelligently [ɪn'tɛlɪdʒəntlɪ] *adv*
intelligemment.
intelligible [ɪn'tɛlɪdʒɪbl] *adj* intelligible.
intemperate [ɪn'tɛmpərət] *adj* immodéré(e);
(*drinking too much*) adonné(e) à la boisson.
intend [ɪn'tɛnd] *vt* (*gift etc*): **to** ~ **sth for**
destiner qch à; **to** ~ **to do** avoir l'intention
de faire.
intended [ɪn'tɛndɪd] *adj* (*insult*) intention-

nel(le); (*journey*) projeté(e); (*effect*) voulu(e).
intense [ɪn'tɛns] *adj* intense; (*person*)
véhément(e).
intensely [ɪn'tɛnslɪ] *adv* intensément; (*moving*)
profondément.
intensify [ɪn'tɛnsɪfaɪ] *vt* intensifier.
intensity [ɪn'tɛnsɪtɪ] *n* intensité *f*.
intensive [ɪn'tɛnsɪv] *adj* intensif(ive).
intensive care *n*: **to be in** ~ être en
réanimation; ~ **unit** *n* service *m* de
réanimation.
intent [ɪn'tɛnt] *n* intention *f* ♦ *adj* attentif(ive),
absorbé(e); **to all** ~**s and purposes** en fait,
pratiquement; **to be** ~ **on doing sth** être
(bien) décidé à faire qch.
intention [ɪn'tɛnʃən] *n* intention *f*.
intentional [ɪn'tɛnʃənl] *adj* intentionnel(le),
délibéré(e).
intently [ɪn'tɛntlɪ] *adv* attentivement.
inter [ɪn'tə:*] *vt* enterrer.
interact [ɪntər'ækt] *vi* avoir une action
réciproque.
interaction [ɪntər'ækʃən] *n* interaction *f*.
interactive [ɪntər'æktɪv] *adj* (*group*)
interactif(ive); (*COMPUT*) interactif,
conversationnel(le).
intercede [ɪntə'si:d] *vi*: **to** ~ **with sb/on behalf**
of sb intercéder auprès de qn/en faveur de
qn.
intercept [ɪntə'sɛpt] *vt* intercepter; (*person*)
arrêter au passage.
interception [ɪntə'sɛpʃən] *n* interception *f*.
interchange *n* ['ɪntətʃeɪndʒ] (*exchange*)
échange *m*; (*on motorway*) échangeur *m* ♦ *vt*
[ɪntə'tʃeɪndʒ] échanger; mettre à la place
l'un(e) de l'autre.
interchangeable [ɪntə'tʃeɪndʒəbl] *adj*
interchangeable.
intercity [ɪntə'sɪtɪ] *adj*: ~ **(train)** train *m*
rapide.
intercom ['ɪntəkɔm] *n* interphone *m*.
interconnect [ɪntəkə'nɛkt] *vi* (*rooms*)
communiquer.
intercontinental ['ɪntəkɔntɪ'nɛntl] *adj*
intercontinental(e).
intercourse ['ɪntəkɔ:s] *n* rapports *mpl*; **sexual**
~ rapports sexuels.
interdependent [ɪntədɪ'pɛndənt] *adj*
interdépendant(e).
interest ['ɪntrɪst] *n* intérêt *m*; (*COMM: stake*,
share) participation *f*, intérêts *mpl* ♦ *vt*
intéresser; **compound/simple** ~ intérêt
composé/simple; **British** ~**s in the Middle**
East les intérêts britanniques au Moyen-
Orient; **his main** ~ **is** ... ce qui l'intéresse le
plus est ....
interested ['ɪntrɪstɪd] *adj* intéressé(e); **to be** ~
in s'intéresser à.
interest-free ['ɪntrɪst'fri:] *adj* sans intérêt.
interesting ['ɪntrɪstɪŋ] *adj* intéressant(e).
interest rate *n* taux *m* d'intérêt.
interface ['ɪntəfeɪs] *n* (*COMPUT*) interface *f*.

interfere [ɪntə'fɪə*] vi: **to ~ in** (quarrel, other people's business) se mêler à; **to ~ with** (object) tripoter, toucher à; (plans) contrecarrer; (duty) être en conflit avec; **don't ~** mêlez-vous de vos affaires.

interference [ɪntə'fɪərəns] n (gen) intrusion f; (PHYSICS) interférence f; (RADIO, TV) parasites mpl.

interfering [ɪntə'fɪərɪŋ] adj importun(e).

interim ['ɪntərɪm] adj provisoire; (post) intérimaire ♦ n: **in the ~** dans l'intérim.

interior [ɪn'tɪərɪə*] n intérieur m ♦ adj intérieur(e).

interior decorator, interior designer n décorateur/trice d'intérieur.

interjection [ɪntə'dʒɛkʃən] n interjection f.

interlock [ɪntə'lɔk] vi s'enclencher ♦ vt enclencher.

interloper ['ɪntələupə*] n intrus/e.

interlude ['ɪntəluːd] n intervalle m; (THEAT) intermède m.

intermarry [ɪntə'mærɪ] vi former des alliances entre familles (or tribus); former des unions consanguines.

intermediary [ɪntə'miːdɪərɪ] n intermédiaire m/f.

intermediate [ɪntə'miːdɪət] adj intermédiaire; (SCOL: course, level) moyen(ne).

interment [ɪn'tɜːmənt] n inhumation f, enterrement m.

interminable [ɪn'tɜːmɪnəbl] adj sans fin, interminable.

intermission [ɪntə'mɪʃən] n pause f; (THEAT, CINE) entracte m.

intermittent [ɪntə'mɪtnt] adj intermittent(e).

intermittently [ɪntə'mɪtntlɪ] adv par intermittence, par intervalles.

intern vt [ɪn'tɜːn] interner ♦ n ['ɪntɜːn] (US) interne m/f.

internal [ɪn'tɜːnl] adj interne; (dispute, reform etc) intérieur(e); **~ injuries** lésions fpl internes.

internally [ɪn'tɜːnəlɪ] adv intérieurement; "**not to be taken ~**" "pour usage externe".

Internal Revenue (Service) (IRS) n (US) fisc m.

international [ɪntə'næʃənl] adj international(e) ♦ n (BRIT SPORT) international m.

International Atomic Energy Agency (IAEA) n Agence Internationale de l'Énergie Atomique (AIEA).

International Court of Justice (ICJ) n Cour internationale de justice (CIJ).

international date line n ligne f de changement de date.

internationally [ɪntə'næʃnəlɪ] adv dans le monde entier.

International Monetary Fund (IMF) n Fonds monétaire international (FMI).

international relations npl relations internationales.

internecine [ɪntə'niːsaɪn] adj mutuellement

destructeur(trice).

internee [ɪntɜː'niː] n interné/e.

internment [ɪn'tɜːnmənt] n internement m.

interplay ['ɪntəpleɪ] n effet m réciproque, jeu m.

Interpol ['ɪntəpɔl] n Interpol m.

interpret [ɪn'tɜːprɪt] vt interpréter ♦ vi servir d'interprète.

interpretation [ɪntɜːprɪ'teɪʃən] n interprétation f.

interpreter [ɪn'tɜːprɪtə*] n interprète m/f.

interpreting [ɪn'tɜːprɪtɪŋ] n (profession) interprétariat m.

interrelated [ɪntərɪ'leɪtɪd] adj en corrélation, en rapport étroit.

interrogate [ɪn'tɛrəugeɪt] vt interroger; (suspect etc) soumettre à un interrogatoire.

interrogation [ɪntɛrəu'geɪʃən] n interrogation f; interrogatoire m.

interrogative [ɪntə'rɔgətɪv] adj interrogateur(trice) ♦ n (LING) interrogatif m.

interrogator [ɪn'tɛrəgeɪtə*] n interrogateur/trice.

interrupt [ɪntə'rʌpt] vt interrompre.

interruption [ɪntə'rʌpʃən] n interruption f.

intersect [ɪntə'sɛkt] vt couper, croiser; (MATH) intersecter ♦ vi se croiser, se couper; s'intersecter.

intersection [ɪntə'sɛkʃən] n intersection f; (of roads) croisement m.

intersperse [ɪntə'spəːs] vt: **to ~ with** parsemer de.

intertwine [ɪntə'twaɪn] vt entrelacer ♦ vi s'entrelacer.

interval ['ɪntəvl] n intervalle m; (BRIT: SCOL) récréation f; (: THEAT) entracte m; (: SPORT) mi-temps f; **bright ~s** (in weather) éclaircies fpl; **at ~s** par intervalles.

intervene [ɪntə'viːn] vi (time) s'écouler (entre-temps); (event) survenir; (person) intervenir.

intervention [ɪntə'vɛnʃən] n intervention f.

interview ['ɪntəvjuː] n (RADIO, TV etc) interview f; (for job) entrevue f ♦ vt interviewer; avoir une entrevue avec.

interviewee [ɪntəvjuː'iː] n (for job) candidat m (qui passe un entretien); (TV etc) invité/e, personne interviewée.

interviewer ['ɪntəvjuə*] n interviewer m.

intestate [ɪn'tɛsteɪt] adj intestat f inv.

intestinal [ɪn'tɛstɪnl] adj intestinal(e).

intestine [ɪn'tɛstɪn] n intestin m; **large ~** gros intestin; **small ~** intestin grêle.

intimacy ['ɪntɪməsɪ] n intimité f.

intimate adj ['ɪntɪmət] intime; (knowledge) approfondi(e) ♦ vt ['ɪntɪmeɪt] suggérer, laisser entendre; (announce) faire savoir.

intimately ['ɪntɪmətlɪ] adv intimement.

intimation [ɪntɪ'meɪʃən] n annonce f.

intimidate [ɪn'tɪmɪdeɪt] vt intimider.

intimidation [ɪntɪmɪ'deɪʃən] n intimidation f.

into ['ɪntu] *prep* dans; ~ **pieces/French** en morceaux/français; **to change pounds** ~ **dollars** changer des livres en dollars.
intolerable [ɪn'tɔlərəbl] *adj* intolérable.
intolerance [ɪn'tɔlərns] *n* intolérance *f*.
intolerant [ɪn'tɔlərnt] *adj*: ~ **(of)** intolérant(e) (de); (*MED*) intolérant (à).
intonation [ɪntəu'neɪʃən] *n* intonation *f*.
intoxicate [ɪn'tɔksɪkeɪt] *vt* enivrer.
intoxicated [ɪn'tɔksɪkeɪtɪd] *adj* ivre.
intoxication [ɪntɔksɪ'keɪʃən] *n* ivresse *f*.
intractable [ɪn'træktəbl] *adj* (*child, temper*) indocile, insoumis(e); (*problem*) insoluble; (*illness*) incurable.
intransigent [ɪn'trænsɪdʒənt] *adj* intransigeant(e).
intransitive [ɪn'trænsɪtɪv] *adj* intransitif(ive).
intra-uterine device (IUD) ['ɪntrə'juːtəraɪn-] *n* dispositif intra-utérin (DIU), stérilet *m*.
intravenous [ɪntrə'viːnəs] *adj* intraveineux(euse).
in-tray ['ɪntreɪ] *n* courrier *m* "arrivée".
intrepid [ɪn'trepɪd] *adj* intrépide.
intricacy ['ɪntrɪkəsɪ] *n* complexité *f*.
intricate ['ɪntrɪkət] *adj* complexe, compliqué(e).
intrigue [ɪn'triːg] *n* intrigue *f* ♦ *vt* intriguer ♦ *vi* intriguer, comploter.
intriguing [ɪn'triːgɪŋ] *adj* fascinant(e).
intrinsic [ɪn'trɪnsɪk] *adj* intrinsèque.
introduce [ɪntrə'djuːs] *vt* introduire; **to** ~ **sb (to sb)** présenter qn (à qn); **to** ~ **sb to** (*pastime, technique*) initier qn à; **may I** ~ ...? je vous présente ....
introduction [ɪntrə'dʌkʃən] *n* introduction *f*; (*of person*) présentation *f*; **a letter of** ~ une lettre de recommendation.
introductory [ɪntrə'dʌktərɪ] *adj* préliminaire, introductif(ive); ~ **remarks** remarques *fpl* liminaires; **an** ~ **offer** une offre de lancement.
introspection [ɪntrəu'spekʃən] *n* introspection *f*.
introspective [ɪntrəu'spektɪv] *adj* introspectif(ive).
introvert ['ɪntrəuvəːt] *adj, n* introverti(e).
intrude [ɪn'truːd] *vi* (*person*) être importun(e); **to** ~ **on** *or* **into** (*conversation etc*) s'immiscer dans; **am I intruding?** est-ce que je vous dérange?
intruder [ɪn'truːdə*] *n* intrus/e.
intrusion [ɪn'truːʒən] *n* intrusion *f*.
intrusive [ɪn'truːsɪv] *adj* importun(e), gênant(e).
intuition [ɪntjuː'ɪʃən] *n* intuition *f*.
intuitive [ɪn'tjuːɪtɪv] *adj* intuitif(ive).
inundate ['ɪnʌndeɪt] *vt*: **to** ~ **with** inonder de.
inure [ɪn'juə*] *vt*: **to** ~ **(to)** habituer (à).
invade [ɪn'veɪd] *vt* envahir.
invader [ɪn'veɪdə*] *n* envahisseur *m*.
invalid *n* ['ɪnvəlɪd] malade *m/f*; (*with disability*) invalide *m/f* ♦ *adj* [ɪn'vælɪd] (*not valid*) invalide, non valide.
invalidate [ɪn'vælɪdeɪt] *vt* invalider, annuler.
invalid chair ['ɪnvəlɪd-] *n* (*BRIT*) fauteuil *m* d'infirme.
invaluable [ɪn'væljuəbl] *adj* inestimable, inappréciable.
invariable [ɪn'vɛərɪəbl] *adj* invariable; (*fig*) immanquable.
invariably [ɪn'vɛərɪəblɪ] *adv* invariablement; **she is** ~ **late** elle est toujours en retard.
invasion [ɪn'veɪʒən] *n* invasion *f*.
invective [ɪn'vektɪv] *n* invective *f*.
inveigle [ɪn'viːgl] *vt*: **to** ~ **sb into (doing) sth** amener qn à (faire) qch (par la ruse *or* la flatterie).
invent [ɪn'vent] *vt* inventer.
invention [ɪn'venʃən] *n* invention *f*.
inventive [ɪn'ventɪv] *adj* inventif(ive).
inventiveness [ɪn'ventɪvnɪs] *n* esprit inventif *or* d'invention.
inventor [ɪn'ventə*] *n* inventeur/trice.
inventory ['ɪnvəntrɪ] *n* inventaire *m*.
inventory control *n* (*COMM*) contrôle *m* des stocks.
inverse [ɪn'vəːs] *adj* inverse ♦ *n* inverse *m*, contraire *m*; **in** ~ **proportion (to)** inversement proportionel(le) (à).
inversely [ɪn'vəːslɪ] *adv* inversement.
invert [ɪn'vəːt] *vt* intervertir; (*cup, object*) retourner.
invertebrate [ɪn'vəːtɪbrət] *n* invertébré *m*.
inverted commas [ɪn'vəːtɪd-] *npl* (*BRIT*) guillemets *mpl*.
invest [ɪn'vest] *vt* investir; (*endow*): **to** ~ **sb with sth** conférer qch à qn ♦ *vi* faire un investissement, investir; **to** ~ **in** placer de l'argent *or* investir dans; (*acquire*) s'offrir, faire l'acquisition de.
investigate [ɪn'vestɪgeɪt] *vt* étudier, examiner; (*crime*) faire une enquête sur.
investigation [ɪnvestɪ'geɪʃən] *n* examen *m*; (*of crime*) enquête *f*, investigation *f*.
investigative [ɪn'vestɪgeɪtɪv] *adj*: ~ **journalism** enquête-reportage *f*, journalisme *m* d'enquête.
investigator [ɪn'vestɪgeɪtə*] *n* investigateur/trice; **private** ~ détective privé.
investiture [ɪn'vestɪtʃə*] *n* investiture *f*.
investment [ɪn'vestmənt] *n* investissement *m*, placement *m*.
investment income *n* revenu *m* de placement.
investment trust *n* société *f* d'investissements.
investor [ɪn'vestə*] *n* épargnant/e; (*shareholder*) actionnaire *m/f*.
inveterate [ɪn'vetərət] *adj* invétéré(e).
invidious [ɪn'vɪdɪəs] *adj* injuste; (*task*) déplaisant(e).
invigilate [ɪn'vɪdʒɪleɪt] (*BRIT*) *vt* surveiller ♦ *vi* être de surveillance.
invigilator [ɪn'vɪdʒɪleɪtə*] *n* (*BRIT*) surveillant

m (d'examen).
invigorating [ɪn'vɪgəreɪtɪŋ] *adj* vivifiant(e);
  stimulant(e).
invincible [ɪn'vɪnsɪbl] *adj* invincible.
inviolate [ɪn'vaɪələt] *adj* inviolé(e).
invisible [ɪn'vɪzɪbl] *adj* invisible.
invisible assets *npl* (*BRIT*) actif incorporel.
invisible ink *n* encre *f* sympathique.
invisible mending *n* stoppage *m*.
invitation [ɪnvɪ'teɪʃən] *n* invitation *f*; **by ~
  only** sur invitation; **at sb's ~** à la demande
  de qn.
invite [ɪn'vaɪt] *vt* inviter; (*opinions etc*)
  demander; (*trouble*) chercher; **to ~ sb (to
  do)** inviter qn (à faire); **to ~ sb to dinner**
  inviter qn à dîner.
▶**invite out** *vt* inviter (à sortir).
▶**invite over** *vt* inviter (chez soi).
inviting [ɪn'vaɪtɪŋ] *adj* engageant(e),
  attrayant(e); (*gesture*) encourageant(e).
invoice ['ɪnvɔɪs] *n* facture *f* ♦ *vt* facturer; **to ~
  sb for goods** facturer des marchandises à
  qn.
invoke [ɪn'vəuk] *vt* invoquer.
involuntary [ɪn'vɔləntrɪ] *adj* involontaire.
involve [ɪn'vɔlv] *vt* (*entail*) impliquer;
  (*concern*) concerner; (*require*) nécessiter; **to
  ~ sb in** (*theft etc*) impliquer qn dans;
  (*activity, meeting*) faire participer qn à.
involved [ɪn'vɔlvd] *adj* complexe; **to feel ~** se
  sentir concerné(e); **to become ~** (*in love etc*)
  s'engager.
involvement [ɪn'vɔlvmənt] *n* (*personal role*)
  participation *f*; (*of resources, funds*) mise *f* en
  jeu.
invulnerable [ɪn'vʌlnərəbl] *adj* invulnérable.
inward ['ɪnwəd] *adj* (*movement*) vers
  l'intérieur; (*thought, feeling*) profond(e),
  intime ♦ *adv* = **inwards**.
inwardly ['ɪnwədlɪ] *adv* (*feel, think etc*)
  secrètement, en son for intérieur.
inwards ['ɪnwədz] *adv* vers l'intérieur.
I/O *abbr* (*COMPUT*: = *input/output*) E/S.
IOC *n abbr* (= *International Olympic Committee*)
  CIO *m* (= *Comité international olympique*).
iodine ['aɪəudiːn] *n* iode *m*.
ion ['aɪən] *n* ion *m*.
Ionian Sea [aɪ'əunɪən-] *n*: **the ~** la mer
  Ionienne.
ioniser ['aɪənaɪzə*] *n* ioniseur *m*.
iota [aɪ'əutə] *n* (*fig*) brin *m*, grain *m*.
IOU *n abbr* (= *I owe you*) reconnaissance *f* de
  dette.
IOW *abbr* (*BRIT*) = *Isle of Wight*.
IPA *n abbr* (= *International Phonetic Alphabet*)
  A.P.I. *m*.
IQ *n abbr* = **intelligence quotient**.
IRA *n abbr* (= *Irish Republican Army*) IRA *f*; (*US*)
  = *individual retirement account*.
Iran [ɪ'rɑːn] *n* Iran *m*.
Iranian [ɪ'reɪnɪən] *adj* iranien(ne) ♦ *n* Iranien/
  ne; (*LING*) iranien *m*.

Iraq [ɪ'rɑːk] *n* Irak *m*.
Iraqi [ɪ'rɑːkɪ] *adj* irakien(ne) ♦ *n* Irakien/ne.
irascible [ɪ'ræsɪbl] *adj* irascible.
irate [aɪ'reɪt] *adj* courroucé(e).
Ireland ['aɪələnd] *n* Irlande *f*; **Republic of ~**
  République *f* d'Irlande.
iris, ~es ['aɪrɪs, -ɪz] *n* iris *m*.
Irish ['aɪrɪʃ] *adj* irlandais(e) ♦ *n* (*LING*) irlandais
  m; **the ~** *npl* les Irlandais.
Irishman ['aɪrɪʃmən] *n* Irlandais *m*.
Irish Sea *n*: **the ~** la mer d'Irlande.
Irishwoman ['aɪrɪʃwumən] *n* Irlandaise *f*.
irk [əːk] *vt* ennuyer.
irksome ['əːksəm] *adj* ennuyeux(euse).
IRN *n abbr* (= *Independent Radio News*) agence
  de presse radiophonique.
IRO *n abbr* (*US*) = *International Refugee
  Organization*.
iron ['aɪən] *n* fer *m*; (*for clothes*) fer *m* à
  repasser ♦ *adj* de or en fer ♦ *vt* (*clothes*)
  repasser; **~s** *npl* (*chains*) fers *mpl*, chaînes *fpl*.
▶**iron out** *vt* (*crease*) faire disparaître au fer;
  (*fig*) aplanir; faire disparaître.
Iron Curtain *n*: **the ~** le rideau de fer.
iron foundry *n* fonderie *f* de fonte.
ironic(al) [aɪ'rɔnɪk(l)] *adj* ironique.
ironically [aɪ'rɔnɪklɪ] *adv* ironiquement.
ironing ['aɪənɪŋ] *n* repassage *m*.
ironing board *n* planche *f* à repasser.
ironmonger ['aɪənmʌŋgə*] *n* (*BRIT*)
  quincailler *m*; **~'s (shop)** quincaillerie *f*.
iron ore *n* minerai *m* de fer.
ironworks ['aɪənwəːks] *n* usine *f*
  sidérurgique.
irony ['aɪrənɪ] *n* ironie *f*.
irrational [ɪ'ræʃənl] *adj* irrationnel(le);
  déraisonnable; qui manque de logique.
irreconcilable [ɪrɛkən'saɪləbl] *adj*
  irréconciliable; (*opinion*): **~ with**
  inconciliable avec.
irredeemable [ɪrɪ'diːməbl] *adj* (*COMM*) non
  remboursable.
irrefutable [ɪrɪ'fjuːtəbl] *adj* irréfutable.
irregular [ɪ'rɛgjulə*] *adj* irrégulier(ière).
irregularity [ɪrɛgju'lærɪtɪ] *n* irrégularité *f*.
irrelevance [ɪ'rɛləvəns] *n* manque *m* de
  rapport or d'à-propos.
irrelevant [ɪ'rɛləvənt] *adj* sans rapport, hors
  de propos.
irreligious [ɪrɪ'lɪdʒəs] *adj* irréligieux(euse).
irreparable [ɪ'rɛprəbl] *adj* irréparable.
irreplaceable [ɪrɪ'pleɪsəbl] *adj* irremplaçable.
irrepressible [ɪrɪ'prɛsəbl] *adj* irrépressible.
irreproachable [ɪrɪ'prəutʃəbl] *adj*
  irréprochable.
irresistible [ɪrɪ'zɪstɪbl] *adj* irrésistible.
irresolute [ɪ'rɛzəluːt] *adj* irrésolu(e),
  indécis(e).
irrespective [ɪrɪ'spɛktɪv]: **~ of** *prep* sans tenir
  compte de.
irresponsible [ɪrɪ'spɔnsɪbl] *adj* (*act*)
  irréfléchi(e); (*person*) qui n'a pas le sens des

responsabilités.
irretrievable [ɪrɪ'triːvəbl] *adj* irréparable, irrémédiable; (*object*) introuvable.
irreverent [ɪ'rɛvərnt] *adj* irrévérencieux(euse).
irrevocable [ɪ'rɛvəkəbl] *adj* irrévocable.
irrigate ['ɪrɪgeɪt] *vt* irriguer.
irrigation [ɪrɪ'geɪʃən] *n* irrigation *f*.
irritable ['ɪrɪtəbl] *adj* irritable.
irritate ['ɪrɪteɪt] *vt* irriter.
irritation [ɪrɪ'teɪʃən] *n* irritation *f*.
IRS *n abbr* (*US*) = **Internal Revenue Service**.
is [ɪz] *vb see* **be**.
ISBN *n abbr* (= *International Standard Book Number*) ISBN *m*.
Islam ['ɪzlɑːm] *n* Islam *m*.
island ['aɪlənd] *n* île *f*; (*also*: **traffic ~**) refuge *m* (pour piétons).
islander ['aɪləndə*] *n* habitant/e d'une île, insulaire *m/f*.
isle [aɪl] *n* île *f*.
isn't ['ɪznt] = **is not**.
isolate ['aɪsəleɪt] *vt* isoler.
isolated ['aɪsəleɪtɪd] *adj* isolé(e).
isolation [aɪsə'leɪʃən] *n* isolement *m*.
isolationism [aɪsə'leɪʃənɪzəm] *n* isolationnisme *m*.
isotope ['aɪsəutəup] *n* isotope *m*.
Israel ['ɪzreɪl] *n* Israël *m*.
Israeli [ɪz'reɪlɪ] *adj* israélien(ne) ♦ *n* Israélien/ne.
issue ['ɪʃuː] *n* question *f*, problème *m*; (*outcome*) résultat *m*, issue *f*; (*of banknotes etc*) émission *f*; (*of newspaper etc*) numéro *m*; (*offspring*) descendance *f* ♦ *vt* (*rations, equipment*) distribuer; (*orders*) donner; (*book*) faire paraître, publier; (*banknotes, cheques, stamps*) émettre, mettre en circulation ♦ *vi*: **to ~ from** provenir de; **at ~** en jeu, en cause; **to avoid the ~** éluder le problème; **to take ~ with sb (over sth)** exprimer son désaccord avec qn (sur qch); **to make an ~ of sth** faire de qch un problème; **to confuse** *or* **obscure the ~** embrouiller la question.
Istanbul [ɪstæn'buːl] *n* Istamboul, Istanbul.
isthmus ['ɪsməs] *n* isthme *m*.
IT *n abbr* = **information technology**.

===================== *KEYWORD*

it [ɪt] *pron* **1** (*specific: subject*) il(elle); (: *direct object*) le(la, l'); (: *indirect object*) lui; **~'s on the table** c'est *or* il (*or* elle) est sur la table; **about/from/of ~** en; **I spoke to him about ~** je lui en ai parlé; **what did you learn from ~?** qu'est-ce que vous en avez retiré?; **I'm proud of ~** j'en suis fier; **I've come from ~** j'en viens; **in/to ~** y; **put the book in ~** mettez-y le livre; **it's on ~** c'est dessus; **he agreed to ~** il y a consenti; **did you go to ~?** (*party, concert etc*) est-ce que vous y êtes

allé(s)?; **above ~**, **over ~** (au-)dessus; **below ~**, **under ~** (en-)dessous; **in front of/behind ~** devant/derrière
2 (*impersonal*) il; ce, cela, ça; **~'s raining** il pleut; **~'s Friday tomorrow** demain c'est vendredi *or* nous sommes vendredi; **~'s 6 o'clock** il est 6 heures; **~'s 2 hours by train** c'est à 2 heures de train; **who is ~? — ~'s me** qui est-ce? — c'est moi.

ITA *n abbr* (*BRIT*: = *initial teaching alphabet*) alphabet en partie phonétique utilisé pour l'enseignement de la lecture.
Italian [ɪ'tæljən] *adj* italien(ne) ♦ *n* Italien/ne; (*LING*) italien *m*.
italic [ɪ'tælɪk] *adj* italique; **~s** *npl* italique *m*.
Italy ['ɪtəlɪ] *n* Italie *f*.
itch [ɪtʃ] *n* démangeaison *f* ♦ *vi* (*person*) éprouver des démangeaisons; (*part of body*) démanger; **I'm ~ing to do** l'envie me démange de faire.
itching ['ɪtʃɪŋ] *n* démangeaison *f*.
itchy ['ɪtʃɪ] *adj* qui démange; **my back is ~** j'ai le dos qui me démange.
it'd ['ɪtd] = **it would**; **it had**.
item ['aɪtəm] *n* (*gen*) article *m*; (*on agenda*) question *f*, point *m*; (*in programme*) numéro *m*; (*also*: **news ~**) nouvelle *f*; **~s of clothing** articles vestimentaires.
itemize ['aɪtəmaɪz] *vt* détailler, spécifier.
itemized bill ['aɪtəmaɪzd-] *n* facture détaillée.
itinerant [ɪ'tɪnərənt] *adj* itinérant(e); (*musician*) ambulant(e).
itinerary [aɪ'tɪnərərɪ] *n* itinéraire *m*.
it'll ['ɪtl] = **it will**, **it shall**.
ITN *n abbr* (*BRIT*: = *Independent Television News*) chaîne de télévision commerciale.
its [ɪts] *adj* son(sa), ses *pl* ♦ *pron* le(la) sien(ne), les siens(siennes).
it's [ɪts] = **it is**, **it has**.
itself [ɪt'sɛlf] *pron* (*emphatic*) lui-même(elle-même); (*reflexive*) se.
ITV *n abbr* (*BRIT*: = *Independent Television*) chaîne de télévision commerciale.

> **ITV** est une chaîne de télévision britannique financée par la publicité. Les actualités, documentaires, débats, etc, constituent environ un tiers des émissions de ITV, le reste étant partagé entre les sports, les films, les feuilletons, les jeux, les séries, etc. Des compagnies indépendantes fournissent des émissions au niveau régional.

IUD *n abbr* = **intra-uterine device**.
I've [aɪv] = **I have**.
ivory ['aɪvərɪ] *n* ivoire *m*.
Ivory Coast *n* Côte *f* d'Ivoire.
ivory tower *n* (*fig*) tour *f* d'ivoire.
ivy ['aɪvɪ] *n* lierre *m*.

L'**Ivy League** *regroupe les huit universités les plus prestigieuses du nord-est des États-Unis, ainsi surnommées à cause de leurs murs recouverts de lierre. Elles organisent des compétitions sportives entre elles. Ces universités sont: Brown, Columbia, Cornell, Dartmouth College, Harvard, Princeton, l'université de Pennsylvanie et Yale.*

J j

J, j [dʒeɪ] *n (letter)* J, j *m*; **J for Jack**, *(US)* **J for Jig** J comme Joseph.
JA *n abbr* = **judge advocate**.
J/A *abbr* = **joint account**.
jab [dʒæb] *vt*: **to ~ sth into** enfoncer *or* planter qch dans ♦ *n* coup *m*; *(MED: col)* piqûre *f*.
jabber ['dʒæbə*] *vt, vi* bredouiller, baragouiner.
jack [dʒæk] *n (AUT)* cric *m*; *(BOWLS)* cochonnet *m*; *(CARDS)* valet *m*.
►**jack in** *vt (col)* laisser tomber.
►**jack up** *vt* soulever (au cric).
jackal ['dʒækl] *n* chacal *m*.
jackass ['dʒækæs] *n (also fig)* âne *m*.
jackdaw ['dʒækdɔː] *n* choucas *m*.
jacket ['dʒækɪt] *n* veste *f*, veston *m*; *(of boiler etc)* enveloppe *f*; *(of book)* couverture *f*, jaquette *f*.
jacket potato *n* pomme *f* de terre en robe des champs.
jack-in-the-box ['dʒækɪnðəbɔks] *n* diable *m* à ressort.
jack-knife ['dʒæknaɪf] *n* couteau *m* de poche
♦ *vi*: **the lorry ~d** la remorque (du camion) s'est mise en travers.
jack-of-all-trades ['dʒækəv'ɔːltreɪdz] *n* bricoleur *m*.
jack plug *n (BRIT)* jack *m*.
jackpot ['dʒækpɔt] *n* gros lot.
Jacuzzi [dʒə'kuːzɪ] *n ®* jacuzzi *m ®*.
jade [dʒeɪd] *n (stone)* jade *m*.
jaded ['dʒeɪdɪd] *adj* éreinté(e), fatigué(e).
JAG *n abbr* = **Judge Advocate General**.
jagged ['dʒægɪd] *adj* dentelé(e).
jaguar ['dʒægjuə*] *n* jaguar *m*.
jail [dʒeɪl] *n* prison *f* ♦ *vt* emprisonner, mettre en prison.
jailbird ['dʒeɪlbəːd] *n* récidiviste *m/f*.
jailbreak ['dʒeɪlbreɪk] *n* évasion *f*.
jailer ['dʒeɪlə*] *n* geôlier/ière.
jalopy [dʒə'lɔpɪ] *n (col)* vieux clou.

jam [dʒæm] *n* confiture *f*; *(of shoppers etc)* cohue *f*; *(also: **traffic ~**)* embouteillage *m* ♦ *vt* *(passage etc)* encombrer, obstruer; *(mechanism, drawer etc)* bloquer, coincer; *(RADIO)* brouiller ♦ *vi (mechanism, sliding part)* se coincer, se bloquer; *(gun)* s'enrayer; **to get sb out of a ~** *(col)* sortir qn du pétrin; **to ~ sth into** entasser *or* comprimer qch dans; enfoncer qch dans; **the telephone lines are ~med** les lignes (téléphoniques) sont encombrées.
Jamaica [dʒə'meɪkə] *n* Jamaïque *f*.
Jamaican [dʒə'meɪkən] *adj* jamaïquain(e) ♦ *n* Jamaïquain/e.
jamb ['dʒæm] *n* jambage *m*.
jam-packed [dʒæm'pækt] *adj*: **~ (with)** bourré(e) (de).
jam session *n* jam session *f*.
Jan. *abbr (= January)* janv.
jangle ['dʒæŋgl] *vi* cliqueter.
janitor ['dʒænɪtə*] *n (caretaker)* huissier *m*; concierge *m*.
January ['dʒænjuərɪ] *n* janvier *m*; *for phrases see also* **July**.
Japan [dʒə'pæn] *n* Japon *m*.
Japanese [dʒæpə'niːz] *adj* japonais(e) ♦ *n (pl inv)* Japonais/e; *(LING)* japonais *m*.
jar [dʒɑː*] *n (container)* pot *m*, bocal *m* ♦ *vi (sound)* produire un son grinçant *or* discordant; *(colours etc)* détonner, jurer ♦ *vt (shake)* ébranler, secouer.
jargon ['dʒɑːgən] *n* jargon *m*.
jarring ['dʒɑːrɪŋ] *adj (sound, colour)* discordant(e).
Jas. *abbr* = **James**.
jasmin(e) ['dʒæzmɪn] *n* jasmin *m*.
jaundice ['dʒɔːndɪs] *n* jaunisse *f*.
jaundiced ['dʒɔːndɪst] *adj (fig)* envieux(euse), désapprobateur(trice).
jaunt [dʒɔːnt] *n* balade *f*.
jaunty ['dʒɔːntɪ] *adj* enjoué(e); désinvolte.
Java ['dʒɑːvə] *n* Java *f*.
javelin ['dʒævlɪn] *n* javelot *m*.
jaw [dʒɔː] *n* mâchoire *f*.
jawbone ['dʒɔːbəun] *n* maxillaire *m*.
jay [dʒeɪ] *n* geai *m*.
jaywalker ['dʒeɪwɔːkə*] *n* piéton indiscipliné.
jazz [dʒæz] *n* jazz *m*.
►**jazz up** *vt* animer, égayer.
jazz band *n* orchestre *or* groupe *m* de jazz.
jazzy ['dʒæzɪ] *adj* bariolé(e), tapageur(euse).
JCB *n ®* excavatrice *f*.
JCS *n abbr (US)* = **Joint Chiefs of Staff**.
JD *n abbr (US: = Doctor of Laws)* titre universitaire; *(: = Justice Department)* ministère de la Justice.
jealous ['dʒɛləs] *adj* jaloux(ouse).
jealously ['dʒɛləslɪ] *adv* jalousement.
jealousy ['dʒɛləsɪ] *n* jalousie *f*.
jeans [dʒiːnz] *npl* (blue-)jean *m*.
Jeep [dʒiːp] *n ®* jeep *f*.
jeer [dʒɪə*] *vi*: **to ~ (at)** huer; se moquer

cruellement (de), railler.

jeering ['dʒɪərɪŋ] _adj_ railleur(euse), moqueur(euse) ♦ _n_ huées _fpl_.

jeers ['dʒɪəz] _npl_ huées _fpl_; sarcasmes _mpl_.

jelly ['dʒɛlɪ] _n_ gelée _f_.

jellyfish ['dʒɛlɪfɪʃ] _n_ méduse _f_.

jeopardize ['dʒɛpədaɪz] _vt_ mettre en danger _or_ péril.

jeopardy ['dʒɛpədɪ] _n_: **in ~** en danger _or_ péril.

jerk [dʒə:k] _n_ secousse _f_; saccade _f_; sursaut _m_, spasme _m_; (_col_) pauvre type _m_ ♦ _vt_ donner une secousse à ♦ _vi_ (_vehicles_) cahoter.

jerkin ['dʒə:kɪn] _n_ blouson _m_.

jerky ['dʒə:kɪ] _adj_ saccadé(e); cahotant(e).

jerry-built ['dʒɛrɪbɪlt] _adj_ de mauvaise qualité.

jerry can ['dʒɛrɪ-] _n_ bidon _m_.

Jersey ['dʒə:zɪ] _n_ Jersey _f_.

jersey ['dʒə:zɪ] _n_ tricot _m_; (_fabric_) jersey _m_.

Jerusalem [dʒə'ru:sləm] _n_ Jérusalem.

jest [dʒɛst] _n_ plaisanterie _f_, **in ~** en plaisantant.

jester ['dʒɛstə*] _n_ (_HIST_) plaisantin _m_.

Jesus ['dʒi:zəs] _n_ Jésus; **~ Christ** Jésus-Christ.

jet [dʒɛt] _n_ (_of gas, liquid_) jet _m_; (_AUT_) gicleur _m_; (_AVIAT_) avion _m_ à réaction, jet _m_.

jet-black ['dʒɛt'blæk] _adj_ (d'un noir) de jais.

jet engine _n_ moteur _m_ à réaction.

jet lag _n_ décalage _m_ horaire.

jetsam ['dʒɛtsəm] _n_ objets jetés à la mer (et rejetés sur la côte).

jet-setter ['dʒɛtsɛtə*] _n_ membre _m_ du _or_ de la jet set.

jettison ['dʒɛtɪsn] _vt_ jeter par-dessus bord.

jetty ['dʒɛtɪ] _n_ jetée _f_, digue _f_.

Jew [dʒu:] _n_ Juif _m_.

jewel ['dʒu:əl] _n_ bijou _m_, joyau _m_.

jeweller ['dʒu:ələ*] _n_ bijoutier/ière, joaillier _m_; **~'s (shop)** _n_ bijouterie _f_, joaillerie _f_.

jewellery ['dʒu:əlrɪ] _n_ bijoux _mpl_.

Jewess ['dʒu:ɪs] _n_ Juive _f_.

Jewish ['dʒu:ɪʃ] _adj_ juif(juive).

JFK _n abbr_ (_US_) = _John Fitzgerald Kennedy International Airport._

jib [dʒɪb] _n_ (_NAUT_) foc _m_; (_of crane_) flèche _f_ ♦ _vi_ (_horse_) regimber; **to ~ at doing sth** rechigner à faire qch.

jibe [dʒaɪb] _n_ sarcasme _m_.

jiffy ['dʒɪfɪ] _n_ (_col_): **in a ~** en un clin d'œil.

jig [dʒɪg] _n_ (_dance, tune_) gigue _f_.

jigsaw ['dʒɪgsɔ:] _n_ (_also:_ **~ puzzle**) puzzle _m_; (_tool_) scie sauteuse.

jilt [dʒɪlt] _vt_ laisser tomber, plaquer.

jingle ['dʒɪŋgl] _n_ (_advertising ~_) couplet _m_ publicitaire ♦ _vi_ cliqueter, tinter.

jingoism ['dʒɪŋgəuɪzəm] _n_ chauvinisme _m_.

jinx [dʒɪŋks] _n_ (_col_) (mauvais) sort.

jitters ['dʒɪtəz] _npl_ (_col_): **to get the ~** avoir la trouille _or_ la frousse.

jittery ['dʒɪtərɪ] _adj_ (_col_) nerveux(euse); **to be ~** avoir les nerfs en pelote.

jiujitsu [dʒu:'dʒɪtsu:] _n_ jiu-jitsu _m_.

job [dʒɔb] _n_ travail _m_; (_employment_) emploi _m_, poste _m_, place _f_; **a part-time/full-time ~** un emploi à temps partiel/à plein temps; **he's only doing his ~** il fait son boulot; **it's a good ~ that ...** c'est heureux _or_ c'est une chance que ...; **just the ~!** (c'est) juste _or_ exactement ce qu'il faut!

jobber ['dʒɔbə*] _n_ (_BRIT STOCK EXCHANGE_) négociant _m_ en titres.

jobbing ['dʒɔbɪŋ] _adj_ (_BRIT: workman_) à la tâche, à la journée.

Jobcentre ['dʒɔbsɛntə*] _n_ agence _f_ pour l'emploi.

job creation scheme _n_ plan _m_ pour la création d'emplois.

job description _n_ description _f_ du poste.

jobless ['dʒɔblɪs] _adj_ sans travail, au chômage ♦ _npl_: **the ~** les sans-emploi _m inv_, les chômeurs _mpl_.

job lot _n_ lot _m_ (d'articles divers).

job satisfaction _n_ satisfaction professionnelle.

job security _n_ sécurité _f_ de l'emploi.

job specification _n_ caractéristiques _fpl_ du poste.

Jock [dʒɔk] _n_ (_col: Scotsman_) Écossais _m_.

jockey ['dʒɔkɪ] _n_ jockey _m_ ♦ _vi_: **to ~ for position** manœuvrer pour être bien placé.

jockey box _n_ (_US AUT_) boîte _f_ à gants, vide-poches _m inv_.

jockstrap ['dʒɔkstræp] _n_ slip _m_ de sport.

jocular ['dʒɔkjulə*] _adj_ jovial(e), enjoué(e); facétieux(euse).

jog [dʒɔg] _vt_ secouer ♦ _vi_ (_SPORT_) faire du jogging; **to ~ along** cahoter; trotter; **to ~ sb's memory** rafraîchir la mémoire de qn.

jogger ['dʒɔgə*] _n_ jogger _m/f_.

jogging ['dʒɔgɪŋ] _n_ jogging _m_.

john [dʒɔn] _n_ (_US col_): **the ~** (_toilet_) les cabinets _mpl_.

join [dʒɔɪn] _vt_ unir, assembler; (_become member of_) s'inscrire à; (_meet_) rejoindre, retrouver; se joindre à ♦ _vi_ (_roads, rivers_) se rejoindre, se rencontrer ♦ _n_ raccord _m_; **will you ~ us for dinner?** vous dînerez bien avec nous?; **I'll ~ you later** je vous rejoindrai plus tard; **to ~ forces (with)** s'associer (à).

▶**join in** _vi_ se mettre de la partie ♦ _vt_ se mêler à.

▶**join up** _vi_ s'engager.

joiner ['dʒɔɪnə*] _n_ menuisier _m_.

joinery ['dʒɔɪnərɪ] _n_ menuiserie _f_.

joint [dʒɔɪnt] _n_ (_TECH_) jointure _f_; joint _m_; (_ANAT_) articulation _f_, jointure; (_BRIT: CULIN_) rôti _m_; (_col: place_) boîte _f_ ♦ _adj_ commun(e); (_committee_) mixte, paritaire; **~ responsibility** coresponsabilité _f_.

joint account (J/A) _n_ compte joint.

jointly ['dʒɔɪntlɪ] _adv_ ensemble, en commun.

joint ownership _n_ copropriété _f_.

joint-stock company ['dʒɔɪntstɔk-] _n_ société _f_ par actions.

joint venture n entreprise commune.
joist [dʒɔɪst] n solive f.
joke [dʒəʊk] n plaisanterie f; (also: **practical ~**) farce f ♦ vi plaisanter; **to play a ~ on** jouer un tour à, faire une farce à.
joker ['dʒəʊkə*] n plaisantin m, blagueur/euse; (CARDS) joker m.
joking ['dʒəʊkɪŋ] n plaisanterie f.
jollity ['dʒɔlɪtɪ] n réjouissances fpl, gaieté f.
jolly ['dʒɔlɪ] adj gai(e), enjoué(e) ♦ adv (BRIT col) rudement, drôlement ♦ vt (BRIT): **to ~ sb along** amadouer qn, convaincre or entraîner qn à force d'encouragements; **~ good!** (BRIT) formidable!
jolt [dʒəʊlt] n cahot m, secousse f ♦ vt cahoter, secouer.
Jordan [dʒɔ:dən] n (country) Jordanie f; (river) Jourdain m.
Jordanian [dʒɔ:'deɪnɪən] adj jordanien(ne) ♦ n Jordanien/ne.
joss stick ['dʒɔsstɪk] n bâton m d'encens.
jostle ['dʒɔsl] vt bousculer, pousser ♦ vi jouer des coudes.
jot [dʒɔt] n: **not one ~** pas un brin.
▶**jot down** vt inscrire rapidement, noter.
jotter ['dʒɔtə*] n (BRIT) cahier m (de brouillon); bloc-notes m.
journal ['dʒə:nl] n journal m.
journalese [dʒə:nə'li:z] n (pej) style m journalistique.
journalism ['dʒə:nəlɪzəm] n journalisme m.
journalist ['dʒə:nəlɪst] n journaliste m/f.
journey ['dʒə:nɪ] n voyage m; (distance covered) trajet m; **a 5-hour ~** un voyage de 5 heures ♦ vi voyager.
jovial ['dʒəʊvɪəl] adj jovial(e).
jowl [dʒaʊl] n mâchoire f (inférieure); bajoue f.
joy [dʒɔɪ] n joie f.
joyful ['dʒɔɪful], **joyous** ['dʒɔɪəs] adj joyeux(euse).
joyride ['dʒɔɪraɪd] vi: **to go joyriding** faire une virée dans une voiture volée.
joyrider ['dʒɔɪraɪdə*] n voleur/euse de voiture (qui fait une virée dans le véhicule volé).
joystick ['dʒɔɪstɪk] n (AVIAT) manche m à balai; (COMPUT) manche à balai, manette f (de jeu).
JP n abbr = **Justice of the Peace**.
Jr. abbr = **junior**.
JTPA n abbr (US: = Job Training Partnership Act) programme gouvernemental de formation.
jubilant ['dʒu:bɪlnt] adj triomphant(e); réjoui(e).
jubilation [dʒu:bɪ'leɪʃən] n jubilation f.
jubilee ['dʒu:bɪli:] n jubilé m; **silver ~** (jubilé du) vingt-cinquième anniversaire.
judge [dʒʌdʒ] n juge m ♦ vt juger; (estimate: weight, size etc) apprécier; (consider) estimer ♦ vi: **judging** or **to ~ by his expression** d'après son expression; **as far as I can ~** autant que je puisse en juger; **I ~d it necessary to inform him** j'ai jugé nécessaire

de l'informer.
judge advocate (JA) n (MIL) magistrat m militaire.
judg(e)ment ['dʒʌdʒmənt] n jugement m; (punishment) châtiment m; **in my ~** à mon avis; **to pass ~ on** (LAW) prononcer un jugement (sur).
judicial [dʒu:'dɪʃl] adj judiciaire; (fair) impartial(e).
judiciary [dʒu:'dɪʃɪərɪ] n (pouvoir m) judiciaire m.
judicious [dʒu:'dɪʃəs] adj judicieux(euse).
judo ['dʒu:dəu] n judo m.
jug [dʒʌg] n pot m, cruche f.
jugged hare ['dʒʌgd-] n (BRIT) civet m de lièvre.
juggernaut ['dʒʌgənɔ:t] n (BRIT: huge truck) mastodonte m.
juggle ['dʒʌgl] vi jongler.
juggler ['dʒʌglə*] n jongleur m.
Jugoslav ['ju:gəu'sla:v] adj, n = **Yugoslav**.
jugular ['dʒʌgjulə*] adj: **~ (vein)** veine f jugulaire.
juice [dʒu:s] n jus m; (col: petrol): **we've run out of ~** c'est la panne sèche.
juicy ['dʒu:sɪ] adj juteux(euse).
jukebox ['dʒu:kbɔks] n juke-box m.
Jul. abbr (= July) juil.
July [dʒu:'laɪ] n juillet m; **the first of ~** le premier juillet; **(on) the eleventh of ~** le onze juillet; **in the month of ~** au mois de juillet; **at the beginning/end of ~** au début/à la fin (du mois) de juillet, début/fin juillet; **in the middle of ~** au milieu (du mois) de juillet, à la mi-juillet; **during ~** pendant le mois de juillet; **in ~ of next year** en juillet de l'année prochaine; **each** or **every ~** tous les ans or chaque année en juillet; **~ was wet this year** il a beaucoup plu cette année en juillet.
jumble ['dʒʌmbl] n fouillis m ♦ vt (also: **~ up**, **~ together**) mélanger, brouiller.
jumble sale n (BRIT) vente f de charité.

Les **jumble sales** ont lieu dans les églises, salles des fêtes ou halls d'écoles, et l'on y vend des articles de toutes sortes, en général bon marché et surtout d'occasion, pour collecter des fonds pour une œuvre de charité, une école (par exemple, pour acheter un ordinateur), ou encore une église (pour réparer un toit etc).

---

jumbo ['dʒʌmbəu] adj: **~ jet** (avion) gros porteur (à réaction); **~ size** format maxi or extra-grand.
jump [dʒʌmp] vi sauter, bondir; (start) sursauter; (increase) monter en flèche ♦ vt sauter, franchir ♦ n saut m, bond m; sursaut m; (fence) obstacle m; **to ~ the queue** (BRIT) passer avant son tour.
▶**jump about** vi sautiller.

▶**jump at** *vt fus* (*fig*) sauter sur; **he ~ed at the offer** il s'est empressé d'accepter la proposition.

▶**jump down** *vi* sauter (pour descendre).

▶**jump up** *vi* se lever (d'un bond).

jumped-up ['dʒʌmptʌp] *adj* (*BRIT pej*) parvenu(e).

jumper ['dʒʌmpə*] *n* (*BRIT: pullover*) pull-over *m*; (*US: pinafore dress*) robe-chasuble *f*; (*SPORT*) sauteur/euse.

jump leads, (*US*) **jumper cables** *npl* câbles *mpl* de démarrage.

jump-start ['dʒʌmpstɑːt] *vt* (*car: push*) démarrer en poussant; (*: with jump leads*) démarrer avec des câbles (de démarrage); (*fig: project, situation*) faire redémarrer promptement.

jumpy ['dʒʌmpɪ] *adj* nerveux(euse), agité(e).

Jun. *abbr* = **June; junior.**

Junr *abbr* = **junior.**

junction ['dʒʌŋkʃən] *n* (*BRIT: of roads*) carrefour *m*; (*of rails*) embranchement *m*.

juncture ['dʒʌŋktʃə*] *n*: **at this ~** à ce moment-là, sur ces entrefaites.

June [dʒuːn] *n* juin *m*; *for phrases see also* **July.**

jungle ['dʒʌŋgl] *n* jungle *f*.

junior ['dʒuːnɪə*] *adj, n*: **he's ~ to me (by 2 years), he's my ~ (by 2 years)** il est mon cadet (de 2 ans), il est plus jeune que moi (de 2 ans); **he's ~ to me** (*seniority*) il est en dessous de moi (dans la hiérarchie), j'ai plus d'ancienneté que lui.

junior executive *n* cadre moyen.

junior high school *n* (*US*) ≈ collège *m* d'enseignement secondaire.

junior minister *n* (*BRIT*) ministre *m* sous tutelle.

junior partner *n* associé(-adjoint) *m*.

junior school *n* (*BRIT*) école *f* primaire, cours moyen.

junior sizes *npl* (*COMM*) tailles *fpl* fillettes/ garçonnets.

juniper ['dʒuːnɪpə*] *n*: **~ berry** baie *f* de genièvre.

junk [dʒʌŋk] *n* (*rubbish*) bric-à-brac *m inv*; (*ship*) jonque *f* ♦ *vt* (*col*) abandonner, mettre au rancart.

junk bond *n* (*COMM*) obligation hautement spéculative utilisée dans les OPA agressives.

junk dealer *n* brocanteur/euse.

junket ['dʒʌŋkɪt] *n* (*CULIN*) lait caillé; (*BRIT col*): **to go on a ~**, **go ~ing** voyager aux frais de la princesse.

junk food *n* snacks vite prêts (*sans valeur nutritive*).

junkie ['dʒʌŋkɪ] *n* (*col*) junkie *m*, drogué/e.

junk mail *n* prospectus *mpl*.

junk room *n* (*US*) débarras *m*.

junk shop *n* (boutique *f* de) brocanteur *m*.

junta ['dʒʌntə] *n* junte *f*.

Jupiter ['dʒuːpɪtə*] *n* (*planet*) Jupiter *f*.

jurisdiction [dʒuərɪs'dɪkʃən] *n* juridiction *f*; **it falls** *or* **comes within/outside our ~** cela est/n'est pas de notre compétence *or* ressort.

jurisprudence [dʒuərɪs'pruːdəns] *n* jurisprudence *f*.

juror ['dʒuərə*] *n* juré *m*.

jury ['dʒuərɪ] *n* jury *m*.

jury box *n* banc *m* des jurés.

juryman ['dʒuərɪmən] *n* = **juror.**

just [dʒʌst] *adj* juste ♦ *adv*: **he's ~ done it/left** il vient de le faire/partir; **~ as I expected** exactement *or* précisément comme je m'y attendais; **~ right/two o'clock** exactement *or* juste ce qu'il faut/ deux heures; **we were ~ going** nous partions; **I was ~ about to phone** j'allais téléphoner; **~ as he was leaving** au moment *or* à l'instant précis où il partait; **~ before/ enough/here** juste avant/assez/là; **it's ~ me/a mistake** ce n'est que moi/(rien) qu'une erreur; **~ missed/caught** manqué/attrapé de justesse; **~ listen to this!** écoutez un peu ça!; **~ ask someone the way** vous n'avez qu'à demander votre chemin à quelqu'un; **it's ~ as good** c'est (vraiment) aussi bon; **it's ~ as well that you ...** heureusement que vous ...; **not ~ now** pas tout de suite; **~ a minute!**, **~ one moment!** un instant (s'il vous plaît)!

justice ['dʒʌstɪs] *n* justice *f*; **Lord Chief J~** (*BRIT*) premier président de la cour d'appel; **this photo doesn't do you ~** cette photo ne vous avantage pas.

Justice of the Peace (JP) *n* juge *m* de paix.

justifiable [dʒʌstɪ'faɪəbl] *adj* justifiable.

justifiably [dʒʌstɪ'faɪəblɪ] *adv* légitimement, à juste titre.

justification [dʒʌstɪfɪ'keɪʃən] *n* justification *f*.

justify ['dʒʌstɪfaɪ] *vt* justifier; **to be justified in doing sth** être en droit de faire qch.

justly ['dʒʌstlɪ] *adv* avec raison, justement.

justness ['dʒʌstnɪs] *n* justesse *f*.

jut [dʒʌt] *vi* (*also*: **~ out**) dépasser, faire saillie.

jute [dʒuːt] *n* jute *m*.

juvenile ['dʒuːvənaɪl] *adj* juvénile; (*court, books*) pour enfants ♦ *n* adolescent/e.

juvenile delinquency *n* délinquance *f* juvénile.

juxtapose ['dʒʌkstəpəuz] *vt* juxtaposer.

juxtaposition ['dʒʌkstəpə'zɪʃən] *n* juxtaposition *f*.

Kk

K, k [keɪ] *n* (*letter*) K, k *m*; **K for King** K comme Kléber.

K *abbr* (= *kilobyte*) Ko; (*BRIT*: = *Knight*) *titre honorifique* ♦ *n abbr* (= *one thousand*) K.

kaftan ['kæftæn] *n* cafetan *m*.

Kalahari Desert [kælə'hɑːrɪ-] *n* désert *m* de Kalahari.

kale [keɪl] *n* chou frisé.

kaleidoscope [kə'laɪdəskəup] *n* kaléidoscope *m*.

kamikaze [kæmɪ'kɑːzɪ] *adj* kamikaze.

Kampala [kæm'pɑːlə] *n* Kampala.

Kampuchea [kæmpu'tʃɪə] *n* Kampuchéa *m*.

kangaroo [kæŋgə'ruː] *n* kangourou *m*.

Kans. *abbr* (*US*) = *Kansas*.

kaput [kə'put] *adj* (*col*) kapout, capout.

karaoke [kɑːrə'əukɪ] *n* karaoke *m*.

karate [kə'rɑːtɪ] *n* karaté *m*.

Kashmir [kæʃ'mɪə*] *n* Cachemire *m*.

Kazakhstan [kɑːzɑːk'stæn] *n* Kazakhstan *m*.

KC *n abbr* (*BRIT LAW*: = *King's Counsel*) *titre donné à certains avocats*; *see also* **QC**.

kd *abbr* (*US*: = *knocked down*) en pièces détachées.

kebab [kə'bæb] *n* kébab *m*.

keel [kiːl] *n* quille *f*; **on an even ~** (*fig*) à flot.
▸**keel over** *vi* (*NAUT*) chavirer, dessaler; (*person*) tomber dans les pommes.

keen [kiːn] *adj* (*interest, desire, competition*) vif(vive); (*eye, intelligence*) pénétrant(e); (*edge*) effilé(e); (*eager*) plein(e) d'enthousiasme; **to be ~ to do** *or* **on doing sth** désirer vivement faire qch, tenir beaucoup à faire qch; **to be ~ on sth/sb** aimer beaucoup qch/qn; **I'm not ~ on going** je ne suis pas chaud pour aller, je n'ai pas très envie d'y aller.

keenly ['kiːnlɪ] *adv* (*enthusiastically*) avec enthousiasme; (*feel*) vivement, profondément; (*look*) intensément.

keenness ['kiːnnɪs] *n* (*eagerness*) enthousiasme *m*; **~ to do** vif désir de faire.

keep [kiːp] *vb* (*pt, pp* **kept** [kɛpt]) *vt* (*retain, preserve*) garder; (*hold back*) retenir; (*a shop, the books, a diary*) tenir; (*feed: one's family etc*) entretenir, assurer la subsistance de; (*a promise*) tenir; (*chickens, bees, pigs etc*) élever ♦ *vi* (*food*) se conserver; (*remain: in a certain state or place*) rester ♦ *n* (*of castle*) donjon *m*; (*food etc*): **enough for his ~** assez pour (assurer) sa subsistance; **to ~ doing sth** continuer à faire qch; faire qch

continuellement; **to ~ sb from doing/sth from happening** empêcher qn de faire *or* que qn (ne) fasse/que qch (n')arrive; **to ~ sb happy/a place tidy** faire que qn soit content/qu'un endroit reste propre; **to ~ sb waiting** faire attendre qn; **to ~ an appointment** ne pas manquer un rendez-vous; **to ~ a record of sth** prendre note de qch; **to ~ sth to o.s.** garder qch pour soi, tenir qch secret; **to ~ sth (back) from sb** cacher qch à qn; **to ~ time** (*clock*) être à l'heure, ne pas retarder.
▸**keep away** *vt*: **to ~ sth/sb away from sb** tenir qch/qn éloigné de qn ♦ *vi*: **to ~ away (from)** ne pas s'approcher (de).
▸**keep back** *vt* (*crowds, tears, money*) retenir ♦ *vi* rester en arrière.
▸**keep down** *vt* (*control: prices, spending*) empêcher d'augmenter, limiter; (*retain: food*) garder ♦ *vi* (*person*) rester assis(e); rester par terre.
▸**keep in** *vt* (*invalid, child*) garder à la maison; (*SCOL*) consigner ♦ *vi* (*col*): **to ~ in with sb** rester en bons termes avec qn.
▸**keep off** *vi* ne pas s'approcher; "**~ off the grass**" "pelouse interdite".
▸**keep on** *vi* continuer; **to ~ on doing** continuer à faire.
▸**keep out** *vt* empêcher d'entrer ♦ *vi* rester en dehors; "**~ out**" "défense d'entrer".
▸**keep up** *vi* se maintenir; (*fig: in comprehension*) suivre ♦ *vt* continuer, maintenir; **to ~ up with** se maintenir au niveau de; **to ~ up with sb** (*in race etc*) aller aussi vite que qn, être du même niveau que qn.

keeper ['kiːpə*] *n* gardien/ne.

keep-fit [kiːp'fɪt] *n* gymnastique *f* de maintien.

keeping ['kiːpɪŋ] *n* (*care*) garde *f*; **in ~ with** à l'avenant de; en accord avec.

keeps [kiːps] *n*: **for ~** (*col*) pour de bon, pour toujours.

keepsake ['kiːpseɪk] *n* souvenir *m*.

keg [kɛg] *n* barrique *f*, tonnelet *m*.

Ken. *abbr* (*US*) = *Kentucky*.

kennel ['kɛnl] *n* niche *f*; **~s** *npl* chenil *m*.

Kenya ['kɛnjə] *n* Kenya *m*.

Kenyan ['kɛnjən] *adj* kenyen(ne) ♦ *n* Kenyen/ne.

kept [kɛpt] *pt, pp* of **keep**.

kerb [kɑːb] *n* (*BRIT*) bordure *f* du trottoir.

kerb crawler [-krɔːlə*] *n personne qui accoste les prostitué(e)s en voiture*.

kernel ['kəːnl] *n* amande *f*; (*fig*) noyau *m*.

kerosene ['kɛrəsiːn] *n* kérosène *m*.

ketchup ['kɛtʃəp] *n* ketchup *m*.

kettle ['kɛtl] *n* bouilloire *f*.

kettle drums *npl* timbales *fpl*.

key [kiː] *n* (*gen, MUS*) clé *f*; (*of piano, typewriter*) touche *f*; (*on map*) légende *f* ♦ *cpd* (-)clé.
▸**key in** *vt* (*text*) introduire au clavier.

keyboard ['ki:bɔ:d] *n* clavier *m* ♦ *vt* (*text*) saisir.
keyboarder ['ki:bɔ:də*] *n* claviste *m/f*.
keyed up [ki:d'ʌp] *adj*: **to be (all)** ~ être surexcité(e).
keyhole ['ki:həul] *n* trou *m* de la serrure.
keyhole surgery *n* chirurgie très minutieuse où l'incision est minimale.
keynote ['ki:nəut] *n* (*MUS*) tonique *f*; (*fig*) note dominante.
keypad ['ki:pæd] *n* pavé *m* numérique.
key ring *n* porte-clés *m*.
keystroke ['ki:strəuk] *n* frappe *f*.
kg *abbr* (= *kilogram*) K.
KGB *n abbr* KGB *m*.
khaki ['kɑ:kɪ] *adj*, *n* kaki (*m*).
kibbutz [kɪ'buts] *n* kibboutz *m*.
kick [kɪk] *vt* donner un coup de pied à ♦ *vi* (*horse*) ruer ♦ *n* coup *m* de pied; (*of rifle*) recul *m*; (*col: thrill*): **he does it for** ~**s** il le fait parce que ça l'excite, il le fait pour le plaisir.
► **kick around** *vi* (*col*) traîner.
► **kick off** *vi* (*SPORT*) donner le coup d'envoi.
kick-off ['kɪkɔf] *n* (*SPORT*) coup *m* d'envoi.
kick-start ['kɪkstɑ:t] *n* (*also*: ~**er**) lanceur *m* au pied.
kid [kɪd] *n* (*col: child*) gamin/e, gosse *m/f*; (*animal, leather*) chevreau *m* ♦ *vi* (*col*) plaisanter, blaguer.
kid gloves *npl*: **to treat sb with** ~ traiter qn avec ménagement.
kidnap ['kɪdnæp] *vt* enlever, kidnapper.
kidnapper ['kɪdnæpə*] *n* ravisseur/euse.
kidnapping ['kɪdnæpɪŋ] *n* enlèvement *m*.
kidney ['kɪdnɪ] *n* (*ANAT*) rein *m*; (*CULIN*) rognon *m*.
kidney bean *n* haricot *m* rouge.
kidney machine *n* (*MED*) rein artificiel.
Kilimanjaro [kɪlɪmən'dʒɑ:rəu] *n*: **Mount** ~ Kilimandjaro *m*.
kill [kɪl] *vt* tuer; (*fig*) faire échouer; détruire; supprimer ♦ *n* mise *f* à mort; **to** ~ **time** tuer le temps.
► **kill off** *vt* exterminer; (*fig*) éliminer.
killer ['kɪlə*] *n* tueur/euse; meurtrier/ière.
killer instinct *n* combativité *f*; **to have the** ~ avoir un tempérament de battant.
killing ['kɪlɪŋ] *n* meurtre *m*; tuerie *f*, massacre *m*; (*col*): **to make a** ~ se remplir les poches, réussir un beau coup ♦ *adj* (*col*) tordant(e).
kill-joy ['kɪldʒɔɪ] *n* rabat-joie *m inv*.
kiln [kɪln] *n* four *m*.
kilo ['ki:ləu] *n abbr* (= *kilogram*) kilo *m*.
kilobyte ['kɪləubaɪt] *n* kilo-octet *m*.
kilogram(me) ['kɪləugræm] *n* kilogramme *m*.
kilometre, (*US*) **kilometer** ['kɪləmi:tə*] *n* kilomètre *m*.
kilowatt ['kɪləuwɔt] *n* kilowatt *m*.
kilt [kɪlt] *n* kilt *m*.
kilter ['kɪltə*] *n*: **out of** ~ déréglé(e), détraqué(e).

kimono [kɪ'məunəu] *n* kimono *m*.
kin [kɪn] *n see* **next-of-kin**, **kith**.
kind [kaɪnd] *adj* gentil(le), aimable ♦ *n* sorte *f*, espèce *f*; (*species*) genre *m*; **to be two of a** ~ se ressembler; **would you be** ~ **enough to ...?**, **would you be so** ~ **as to ...?** auriez-vous la gentillesse *or* l'obligeance de ...?; **it's very** ~ **of you (to do)** c'est très aimable à vous (de faire); **in** ~ (*COMM*) en nature; (*fig*): **to repay sb in** ~ rendre la pareille à qn.
kindergarten ['kɪndəgɑ:tn] *n* jardin *m* d'enfants.
kind-hearted [kaɪnd'hɑ:tɪd] *adj* bon(bonne).
kindle ['kɪndl] *vt* allumer, enflammer.
kindling ['kɪndlɪŋ] *n* petit bois.
kindly ['kaɪndlɪ] *adj* bienveillant(e), plein(e) de gentillesse ♦ *adv* avec bonté; **will you** ~ **...** auriez-vous la bonté *or* l'obligeance de ...; **he didn't take it** ~ il l'a mal pris.
kindness ['kaɪndnɪs] *n* bonté *f*, gentillesse *f*.
kindred ['kɪndrɪd] *adj* apparenté(e); ~ **spirit** âme *f* sœur.
kinetic [kɪ'nɛtɪk] *adj* cinétique.
king [kɪŋ] *n* roi *m*.
kingdom ['kɪŋdəm] *n* royaume *m*.
kingfisher ['kɪŋfɪʃə*] *n* martin-pêcheur *m*.
kingpin ['kɪŋpɪn] *n* (*TECH*) pivot *m*; (*fig*) cheville ouvrière.
king-size(d) ['kɪŋsaɪz(d)] *adj* (*cigarette*) (*format*) extra-long(longue).
kink [kɪŋk] *n* (*of rope*) entortillement *m*; (*in hair*) ondulation *f*; (*col: fig*) aberration *f*.
kinky ['kɪŋkɪ] *adj* (*fig*) excentrique; (*pej*) aux goûts spéciaux.
kinship ['kɪnʃɪp] *n* parenté *f*.
kinsman ['kɪnzmən] *n* parent *m*.
kinswoman ['kɪnzwumən] *n* parente *f*.
kiosk ['ki:ɔsk] *n* kiosque *m*; (*BRIT: also*: **telephone** ~) cabine *f* (téléphonique); (: *also*: **newspaper** ~) kiosque à journaux.
kipper ['kɪpə*] *n* hareng fumé et salé.
Kirghizia [kə:'gɪzɪə] *n* Kirghizistan *m*.
kiss [kɪs] *n* baiser *m* ♦ *vt* embrasser; **to** ~ (**each other**) s'embrasser; **to** ~ **sb goodbye** dire au revoir à qn en l'embrassant; ~ **of life** *n* (*BRIT*) bouche à bouche *m*.
kissagram ['kɪsəgræm] *n* baiser envoyé à l'occasion d'une célébration par l'intermédiaire d'une personne employée à cet effet.
kit [kɪt] *n* équipement *m*, matériel *m*; (*set of tools etc*) trousse *f*; (*for assembly*) kit *m*; **tool** ~ nécessaire *m* à outils.
► **kit out** *vt* (*BRIT*) équiper.
kitbag ['kɪtbæg] *n* sac *m* de voyage *or* de marin.
kitchen ['kɪtʃɪn] *n* cuisine *f*.
kitchen garden *n* jardin *m* potager.
kitchen sink *n* évier *m*.
kitchen unit *n* (*BRIT*) élément *m* de cuisine.
kitchenware ['kɪtʃɪnwɛə*] *n* vaisselle *f*; ustensiles *mpl* de cuisine.

kite [kaɪt] *n* (*toy*) cerf-volant *m*; (*ZOOL*) milan *m*.

kith [kɪθ] *n*: ~ **and kin** parents et amis *mpl*.

kitten ['kɪtn] *n* petit chat, chaton *m*.

kitty ['kɪtɪ] *n* (*money*) cagnotte *f*.

kiwi ['kiːwiː] *n*: ~ (**fruit**) kiwi *m*.

KKK *n abbr* (*US*) = Ku Klux Klan.

Kleenex ['kliːnɛks] *n* ® Kleenex *m* ®.

kleptomaniac [klɛptəʊ'meɪnɪæk] *n* kleptomane *m/f*.

km *abbr* (= *kilometre*) km.

km/h *abbr* (= *kilometres per hour*) km/h.

knack [næk] *n*: **to have the** ~ (**of doing**) avoir le coup (pour faire); **there's a** ~ il y a un coup à prendre *or* une combine.

knackered ['nækəd] *adj* (*col*) crevé(e), nase.

knapsack ['næpsæk] *n* musette *f*.

knave [neɪv] *n* (*CARDS*) valet *m*.

knead [niːd] *vt* pétrir.

knee [niː] *n* genou *m*.

kneecap ['niːkæp] *n* rotule *f* ♦ *vt* tirer un coup de feu dans la rotule de.

knee-deep ['niː'diːp] *adj*: **the water was** ~ l'eau arrivait aux genoux.

kneel, *pt*, *pp* **knelt** [niːl, nɛlt] *vi* (*also*: ~ **down**) s'agenouiller.

kneepad ['niːpæd] *n* genouillère *f*.

knell [nɛl] *n* glas *m*.

knelt [nɛlt] *pt*, *pp of* **kneel**.

knew [njuː] *pt of* **know**.

knickers ['nɪkəz] *npl* (*BRIT*) culotte *f* (de femme).

knick-knack ['nɪknæk] *n* colifichet *m*.

knife [naɪf] *n* (*pl* **knives**) couteau *m* ♦ *vt* poignarder, frapper d'un coup de couteau; ~, **fork and spoon** couvert *m*.

knife-edge ['naɪfɛdʒ] *n*: **to be on a** ~ être sur le fil du rasoir.

knight [naɪt] *n* chevalier *m*; (*CHESS*) cavalier *m*.

knighthood ['naɪthud] *n* chevalerie *f*; (*title*): **to get a** ~ être fait chevalier.

knit [nɪt] *vt* tricoter; (*fig*): **to** ~ **together** unir ♦ *vi* (*broken bones*) se ressouder.

knitted ['nɪtɪd] *adj* en tricot.

knitting ['nɪtɪŋ] *n* tricot *m*.

knitting machine *n* machine *f* à tricoter.

knitting needle *n* aiguille *f* à tricoter.

knitting pattern *n* modèle *m* (pour tricot).

knitwear ['nɪtwɛə*] *n* tricots *mpl*, lainages *mpl*.

knives [naɪvz] *npl of* **knife**.

knob [nɔb] *n* bouton *m*; (*BRIT*): **a** ~ **of butter** une noix de beurre.

knobbly ['nɔblɪ], (*US*) **knobby** ['nɔbɪ] *adj* (*wood, surface*) noueux(euse); (*knees*) noueux.

knock [nɔk] *vt* frapper; (*make: hole etc*): **to** ~ **a hole in** faire un trou dans, trouer; (*force: nail etc*): **to** ~ **a nail into** enfoncer un clou dans; (*fig: col*) dénigrer ♦ *vi* (*engine*) cogner; (*at door etc*): **to** ~ **at/on** frapper à/sur ♦ *n* coup *m*; **he** ~**ed at the door** il frappa à la porte.

►**knock down** *vt* renverser; (*price*) réduire.

►**knock off** *vi* (*col: finish*) s'arrêter (de travailler) ♦ *vt* (*vase, object*) faire tomber; (*col: steal*) piquer; (*fig: from price etc*): **to** ~ **off £10** faire une remise de 10 livres.

►**knock out** *vt* assommer; (*BOXING*) mettre k.-o.

►**knock over** *vt* (*object*) faire tomber; (*pedestrian*) renverser.

knockdown ['nɔkdaun] *adj* (*price*) sacrifié(e).

knocker ['nɔkə*] *n* (*on door*) heurtoir *m*.

knocking ['nɔkɪŋ] *n* coups *mpl*.

knock-kneed [nɔk'niːd] *adj* aux genoux cagneux.

knockout ['nɔkaut] *n* (*BOXING*) knock-out *m*, K.-O. *m*.

knockout competition *n* (*BRIT*) compétition *f* avec épreuves éliminatoires.

knock-up ['nɔkʌp] *n* (*TENNIS*): **to have a** ~ faire des balles.

knot [nɔt] *n* (*gen*) nœud *m* ♦ *vt* nouer; **to tie a** ~ faire un nœud.

knotty ['nɔtɪ] *adj* (*fig*) épineux(euse).

know [nəʊ] *vt* (*pt* **knew**, *pp* **known** [njuː, nəʊn]) savoir; (*person, place*) connaître; **to** ~ **that** savoir que; **to** ~ **how to do** savoir faire; **to** ~ **about/of sth** être au courant de/connaître qch; **to get to** ~ **sth** (*fact*) apprendre qch; (*place*) apprendre à connaître qch; **I don't** ~ **him** je ne le connais pas; **to** ~ **right from wrong** distinguer le bon du mauvais; **as far as I** ~ ... à ma connaissance ..., autant que je sache ....

know-all ['nəʊɔːl] *n* (*BRIT pej*) je-sais-tout *m/f*.

know-how ['nəʊhau] *n* savoir-faire *m*, technique *f*, compétence *f*.

knowing ['nəʊɪŋ] *adj* (*look etc*) entendu(e).

knowingly ['nəʊɪŋlɪ] *adv* sciemment; d'un air entendu.

know-it-all ['nəʊɪtɔːl] *n* (*US*) = **know-all**.

knowledge ['nɔlɪdʒ] *n* connaissance *f*; (*learning*) connaissances, savoir *m*; **to have no** ~ **of** ignorer; **not to my** ~ pas à ma connaissance; **without my** ~ à mon insu; **to have a working** ~ **of French** se débrouiller en français; **it is common** ~ **that** ... chacun sait que ...; **it has come to my** ~ **that** ... j'ai appris que ....

knowledgeable ['nɔlɪdʒəbl] *adj* bien informé(e).

known [nəʊn] *pp of* **know** ♦ *adj* (*thief, facts*) notoire; (*expert*) célèbre.

knuckle ['nʌkl] *n* articulation *f* (des phalanges), jointure *f*.

►**knuckle down** *vi* (*col*) s'y mettre.

►**knuckle under** *vi* (*col*) céder.

knuckleduster ['nʌkldʌstə*] *n* coup-de-poing américain.

KO *abbr* (= *knock out*) *n* K.-O. *m* ♦ *vt* mettre K.-O.

koala [kəʊ'ɑːlə] *n* (*also*: ~ **bear**) koala *m*.

kook [kuːk] *n* (*US col*) loufoque *m/f*.

Koran [kɔ'rɑːn] *n* Coran *m*.
Korea [kə'rɪə] *n* Corée *f*; **North/South** ~ Corée du Nord/Sud.
Korean [kə'rɪən] *adj* coréen(ne) ♦ *n* Coréen/ne.
kosher ['kəuʃə*] *adj* kascher *inv*.
kowtow ['kau'tau] *vi*: **to** ~ **to sb** s'aplatir devant qn.
Kremlin ['krɛmlɪn] *n*: **the** ~ le Kremlin.
KS *abbr* (*US*) = *Kansas*.
Kt *abbr* (*BRIT*: = *Knight*) titre honorifique.
Kuala Lumpur ['kwɑːlə'lumpuə*] *n* Kuala Lumpur.
kudos ['kjuːdɔs] *n* gloire *f*, lauriers *mpl*.
Kurd [kəːd] *n* Kurde *m/f*.
Kuwait [ku'weɪt] *n* Koweït *f*, Kuweit *f*.
Kuwaiti [ku'weɪtɪ] *adj* koweïtien(ne) ♦ *n* Koweïtien/ne.
kW *abbr* (= *kilowatt*) kW.
KY, Ky. *abbr* (*US*) = *Kentucky*.

L l

L, l [ɛl] *n* (*letter*) L, l *m*; **L for Lucy**, (*US*) **L for Love** L comme Louis.
L *abbr* (= *lake, large*); (= *left*) g; (*BRIT AUT*: = *learner*) signale un conducteur débutant.
l *abbr* (= *litre*) l.
LA *n abbr* (*US*) = *Los Angeles* ♦ *abbr* (*US*) = *Louisiana*.
La. *abbr* (*US*) = *Louisiana*.
lab [læb] *n abbr* (= *laboratory*) labo *m*.
Lab. *abbr* (*Canada*) = *Labrador*.
label ['leɪbl] *n* étiquette *f*; (*brand: of record*) marque *f* ♦ *vt* étiqueter; **to** ~ **sb a ...** qualifier qn de ....
labor *etc* ['leɪbə*] (*US*) = **labour** *etc*.
laboratory [lə'bɔrətərɪ] *n* laboratoire *m*.
Labor Day *n* (*US, Canada*) fête *f* du travail (*le premier lundi de septembre*).
laborious [lə'bɔːrɪəs] *adj* laborieux(euse).
labor union *n* (*US*) syndicat *m*.
Labour ['leɪbə*] *n* (*BRIT POL*: *also*: **the** ~ **Party**) le parti travailliste, les travaillistes *mpl*.
labour, (*US*) **labor** ['leɪbə*] *n* (*task*) travail *m*; (*workmen*) main-d'œuvre *f*; (*MED*) travail, accouchement *m* ♦ *vi*: **to** ~ **(at)** travailler dur (à), peiner (sur); **in** ~ (*MED*) en travail.
labo(u)r camp *n* camp *m* de travaux forcés.
labo(u)r cost *n* coût *m* de la main-d'œuvre; coût de la façon.
labo(u)red ['leɪbəd] *adj* lourd(e), laborieux(euse); (*breathing*) difficile, pénible; (*style*) lourd, embarrassé(e).
labo(u)rer ['leɪbərə*] *n* manœuvre *m*; (*on farm*) ouvrier *m* agricole.

labo(u)r force *n* main-d'œuvre *f*.
labo(u)r-intensive [leɪbərɪn'tɛnsɪv] *adj* intensif(ive) en main-d'œuvre.
labo(u)r market *n* marché *m* du travail.
labo(u)r pains *npl* douleurs *fpl* de l'accouchement.
labo(u)r relations *npl* relations *fpl* dans l'entreprise.
labo(u)r-saving ['leɪbəseɪvɪŋ] *adj* qui simplifie le travail.
labo(u)r unrest *n* agitation sociale.
labyrinth ['læbɪrɪnθ] *n* labyrinthe *m*, dédale *m*.
lace [leɪs] *n* dentelle *f*; (*of shoe etc*) lacet *m* ♦ *vt* (*shoe*) lacer; (*drink*) arroser, corser.
lacemaking ['leɪsmeɪkɪŋ] *n* fabrication *f* de dentelle.
laceration [læsə'reɪʃən] *n* lacération *f*.
lace-up ['leɪsʌp] *adj* (*shoes etc*) à lacets.
lack [læk] *n* manque *m* ♦ *vt* manquer de; **through** *or* **for** ~ **of** faute de, par manque de; **to be** ~**ing** manquer, faire défaut; **to be** ~**ing in** manquer de.
lackadaisical [lækə'deɪzɪkl] *adj* nonchalant(e), indolent(e).
lackey ['lækɪ] *n* (*also fig*) laquais *m*.
lacklustre ['læklʌstə*] *adj* terne.
laconic [lə'kɔnɪk] *adj* laconique.
lacquer ['lækə*] *n* laque *f*.
lacy ['leɪsɪ] *adj* comme de la dentelle, qui ressemble à de la dentelle.
lad [læd] *n* garçon *m*, gars *m*; (*BRIT*: *in stable etc*) lad *m*.
ladder ['lædə*] *n* échelle *f*; (*BRIT*: *in tights*) maille filée ♦ *vt, vi* (*BRIT*: *tights*) filer.
laden ['leɪdn] *adj*: ~ **(with)** chargé(e) (de); **fully** ~ (*truck, ship*) en pleine charge.
ladle ['leɪdl] *n* louche *f*.
lady ['leɪdɪ] *n* dame *f*; **L**~ **Smith** lady Smith; **the ladies' (room)** les toilettes *fpl* des dames; **a** ~ **doctor** une doctoresse, une femme médecin.
ladybird ['leɪdɪbəːd], (*US*) **ladybug** ['leɪdɪbʌg] *n* coccinelle *f*.
lady-in-waiting ['leɪdɪn'weɪtɪŋ] *n* dame *f* d'honneur.
ladykiller ['leɪdɪkɪlə*] *n* don Juan *m*.
ladylike ['leɪdɪlaɪk] *adj* distingué(e).
ladyship ['leɪdɪʃɪp] *n*: **your L**~ Madame la comtesse (*or* la baronne *etc*).
lag [læg] *n* = **time** ~ ♦ *vi* (*also*: ~ **behind**) rester en arrière, traîner ♦ *vt* (*pipes*) calorifuger.
lager ['lɑːgə*] *n* bière blonde.
lager lout *n* (*BRIT col*) jeune voyou *m* (*porté su la boisson*).
lagging ['lægɪŋ] *n* enveloppe isolante, calorifuge *m*.
lagoon [lə'guːn] *n* lagune *f*.
Lagos ['leɪgɔs] *n* Lagos.
laid [leɪd] *pt, pp of* **lay**.
laid-back [leɪd'bæk] *adj* (*col*) relaxe, décontracté(e).
lain [leɪn] *pp of* **lie**.

air [lɛə*] n tanière f, gîte m.
issez-faire [lɛseɪ'fɛə*] n libéralisme m.
ity ['leɪtɪ] n laïques mpl.
ake [leɪk] n lac m.
ake District n: the ~ (BRIT) la région des lacs.
amb [læm] n agneau m.
amb chop n côtelette f d'agneau.
ambskin ['læmskɪn] n (peau f d')agneau m.
ambswool ['læmzwul] n laine f d'agneau.
ame [leɪm] adj boiteux(euse); ~ **duck** (fig) canard boiteux.
amely ['leɪmlɪ] adv (fig) sans conviction.
ament [lə'mɛnt] n lamentation f ♦ vt pleurer, se lamenter sur.
amentable ['læməntəbl] adj déplorable, lamentable.
aminated ['læmɪneɪtɪd] adj laminé(e); (windscreen) (en verre) feuilleté.
amp [læmp] n lampe f.
amplight ['læmplaɪt] n: **by** ~ à la lumière de la (or d'une) lampe.
ampoon [læm'puːn] n pamphlet m.
amppost ['læmppəʊst] n (BRIT) réverbère m.
ampshade ['læmpʃeɪd] n abat-jour m inv.
ance [lɑːns] n lance f ♦ vt (MED) inciser.
ance corporal n (BRIT) (soldat m de) première classe m.
ancet ['lɑːnsɪt] n (MED) bistouri m.
ancs [læŋks] abbr (BRIT) = Lancashire.
and [lænd] n (as opposed to sea) terre f (ferme); (country) pays m; (soil) terre; terrain m; (estate) terre(s), domaine(s) m(pl) ♦ vi (from ship) débarquer; (AVIAT) atterrir; (fig: fall) (re)tomber ♦ vt (passengers, goods) débarquer; (obtain) décrocher; **to go/travel by** ~ se déplacer par voie de terre; **to own** ~ être propriétaire foncier; **to** ~ **on one's feet** (also fig) retomber sur ses pieds.
land up vi atterrir, (finir par) se retrouver.
nded gentry ['lændɪd-] n (BRIT) propriétaires terriens or fonciers.
ndfill site ['lændfɪl-] n centre m d'enfouissement des déchets.
nding ['lændɪŋ] n (from ship) débarquement m; (AVIAT) atterrissage m; (of staircase) palier m.
nding card n carte f de débarquement.
nding craft n péniche f de débarquement.
nding gear n train m d'atterrissage.
nding stage n (BRIT) débarcadère m, embarcadère m.
nding strip n piste f d'atterrissage.
ndlady ['lændleɪdɪ] n propriétaire f, logeuse f.
ndlocked ['lændlɒkt] adj entouré(e) de terre(s), sans accès à la mer.
ndlord ['lændlɔːd] n propriétaire m, logeur m; (of pub etc) patron m.
ndlubber ['lændlʌbə*] n terrien/ne.
ndmark ['lændmɑːk] n (point m de) repère m; **to be a** ~ (fig) faire date or époque.

landowner ['lændəʊnə*] n propriétaire foncier or terrien.
landscape ['lænskeɪp] n paysage m.
landscape architect, landscape gardener n paysagiste m/f.
landscape painting n (ART) paysage m.
landslide ['lændslaɪd] n (GEO) glissement m (de terrain); (fig: POL) raz-de-marée (électoral).
lane [leɪn] n (in country) chemin m; (in town) ruelle f; (AUT) voie f; file f; (in race) couloir m; **shipping** ~ route f maritime or de navigation.
language ['læŋgwɪdʒ] n langue f; (way one speaks) langage m; **bad** ~ grossièretés fpl, langage grossier.
language laboratory n laboratoire m de langues.
languid ['læŋgwɪd] adj languissant(e); langoureux(euse).
languish ['læŋgwɪʃ] vi languir.
lank [læŋk] adj (hair) raide et terne.
lanky ['læŋkɪ] adj grand(e) et maigre, efflanqué(e).
lanolin(e) ['lænəlɪn] n lanoline f.
lantern ['læntn] n lanterne f.
Laos [laʊs] n Laos m.
lap [læp] n (of track) tour m (de piste); (of body): **in** or **on one's** ~ sur les genoux ♦ vt (also: ~ **up**) laper ♦ vi (waves) clapoter.
▶**lap up** vt (fig) boire comme du petit-lait, se gargariser de; (: lies etc) gober.
La Paz [læ'pæz] n La Paz.
lapdog ['læpdɒg] n chien m d'appartement.
lapel [lə'pɛl] n revers m.
Lapland ['læplænd] n Laponie f.
lapse [læps] n défaillance f; (in behaviour) écart m (de conduite) ♦ vi (LAW) cesser d'être en vigueur; se périmer; **to** ~ **into bad habits** prendre de mauvaises habitudes; ~ **of time** laps m de temps, intervalle m; **a** ~ **of memory** un trou de mémoire.
laptop ['læptɒp] n (also: ~ **computer**) ordinateur portatif.
larceny ['lɑːsənɪ] n vol m.
lard [lɑːd] n saindoux m.
larder ['lɑːdə*] n garde-manger m inv.
large [lɑːdʒ] adj grand(e); (person, animal) gros(grosse); **to make** ~r agrandir; **a** ~ **number of people** beaucoup de gens; **by and** ~ en général; **on a** ~ **scale** sur une grande échelle; **at** ~ (free) en liberté; (generally) en général; pour la plupart.
largely ['lɑːdʒlɪ] adv en grande partie.
large-scale ['lɑːdʒ'skeɪl] adj (map, drawing etc) à grande échelle; (fig) important(e).
lark [lɑːk] n (bird) alouette f; (joke) blague f, farce f.
▶**lark about** vi faire l'idiot, rigoler.
larva, pl **larvae** ['lɑːvə, -iː] n larve f.
laryngitis [lærɪn'dʒaɪtɪs] n laryngite f.
larynx ['lærɪŋks] n larynx m.

lasagne [lə'zænjə] n lasagne f.
lascivious [lə'sıvıəs] adj lascif(ive).
laser ['leızə*] n laser m.
laser beam n rayon m laser.
laser printer n imprimante f laser.
lash [læʃ] n coup m de fouet; (also: **eye~**) cil m
  ♦ vt fouetter; (tie) attacher.
▶**lash down** vt attacher; amarrer; arrimer
  ♦ vi (rain) tomber avec violence.
▶**lash out** vi: **to ~ out (at** or **against sb/sth)**
  attaquer violemment (qn/qch); **to ~ out (on**
  sth) (col: spend) se fendre (de qch).
lashing ['læʃıŋ] n: **~s of** (BRIT col: cream etc)
  des masses de.
lass [læs] n (jeune) fille f.
lasso [læ'su:] n lasso m ♦ vt prendre au lasso.
last [lɑ:st] adj dernier(ière) ♦ adv en dernier
  ♦ vi durer; **~ week** la semaine dernière; **~**
  night hier soir; la nuit dernière; **at ~** enfin;
  ~ but one avant-dernier(ière); **the ~ time** la
  dernière fois; **it ~s (for) 2 hours** ça dure 2
  heures.
last-ditch ['lɑ:st'dıtʃ] adj ultime, désespéré(e).
lasting ['lɑ:stıŋ] adj durable.
lastly ['lɑ:stlı] adv en dernier lieu, pour finir.
last-minute ['lɑ:stmınıt] adj de dernière
  minute.
latch [lætʃ] n loquet m.
▶**latch on to** vt (cling to: person) s'accrocher
  à; (: idea) trouver bon(ne).
latchkey ['lætʃki:] n clé f (de la porte
  d'entrée).
late [leıt] adj (not on time) en retard; (far on in
  day etc) dernier(ière); tardif(ive); (recent)
  récent(e), dernier; (former) ancien(ne);
  (dead) défunt(e) ♦ adv tard; (behind time,
  schedule) en retard; **to be ~** avoir du retard;
  to be 10 minutes ~ avoir 10 minutes de
  retard; **to work ~** travailler tard; **~ in life**
  sur le tard, à un âge avancé; **of ~**
  dernièrement; **in ~ May** vers la fin (du
  mois) de mai, fin mai; **the ~ Mr X** feu M. X.
latecomer ['leıtkʌmə*] n retardataire m/f.
lately ['leıtlı] adv récemment.
lateness ['leıtnıs] n (of person) retard m; (of
  event) heure tardive.
latent ['leıtnt] adj latent(e); **~ defect** vice
  caché.
later ['leıtə*] adj (date etc) ultérieur(e);
  (version etc) plus récent(e) ♦ adv plus tard; **~**
  on today plus tard dans la journée.
lateral ['lætərl] adj latéral(e).
latest ['leıtıst] adj tout(e) dernier(ière); **the ~**
  news les dernières nouvelles; **at the ~** au
  plus tard.
latex ['leıtɛks] n latex m.
lath, ~s [læθ, læðz] n latte f.
lathe [leıð] n tour m.
lather ['lɑ:ðə*] n mousse f (de savon) ♦ vt
  savonner ♦ vi mousser.
Latin ['lætın] n latin m ♦ adj latin(e).
Latin America n Amérique latine.

Latin American adj latino-américain(e),
  d'Amérique latine ♦ n Latino-Américain/e.
latitude ['lætıtju:d] n (also fig) latitude f.
latrine [lə'tri:n] n latrines fpl.
latter ['lætə*] adj deuxième, dernier(ière) ♦ n:
  the ~ ce dernier, celui-ci.
latterly ['lætəlı] adv dernièrement,
  récemment.
lattice ['lætıs] n treillis m; treillage m.
lattice window n fenêtre treillissée, fenêtr
  à croisillons.
Latvia ['lætvıə] n Lettonie f.
Latvian ['lætvıən] adj letton(ne) ♦ n Letton/ne
  (LING) letton m.
laudable ['lɔ:dəbl] adj louable.
laudatory ['lɔ:dətrı] adj élogieux(euse).
laugh [lɑ:f] n rire m ♦ vi rire.
▶**laugh at** vt fus se moquer de; (joke) rire de.
▶**laugh off** vt écarter or rejeter par une
  plaisanterie or par une boutade.
laughable ['lɑ:fəbl] adj risible, ridicule.
laughing ['lɑ:fıŋ] adj rieur(euse); **this is no ~**
  matter il n'y a pas de quoi rire, ça n'a rien
  d'amusant.
laughing gas n gaz hilarant.
laughing stock n: **the ~ of** la risée de.
laughter ['lɑ:ftə*] n rire m; (people laughing)
  rires mpl.
launch [lɔ:ntʃ] n lancement m; (boat) chaloup
  f; (also: **motor ~**) vedette f ♦ vt (ship, rocket,
  plan) lancer.
▶**launch out** vi: **to ~ out (into)** se lancer
  (dans).
launching ['lɔ:ntʃıŋ] n lancement m.
launch(ing) pad n rampe f de lancement.
launder ['lɔ:ndə*] vt blanchir.
Launderette [lɔ:n'drɛt], (US) **Laundromat**
  ['lɔ:ndrəmæt] n ® laverie f (automatique).
laundry ['lɔ:ndrı] n blanchisserie f; (clothes)
  linge m; **to do the ~** faire la lessive.
laureate ['lɔ:rıət] adj see **poet laureate**.
laurel ['lɔrl] n laurier m; **to rest on one's ~s s**
  reposer sur ses lauriers.
lava ['lɑ:və] n lave f.
lavatory ['lævətərı] n toilettes fpl.
lavatory paper n (BRIT) papier m hygiénique
lavender ['lævəndə*] n lavande f.
lavish ['lævıʃ] adj copieux(euse);
  somptueux(euse); (giving freely): **~ with**
  prodigue de ♦ vt: **to ~ sth on sb** prodiguer
  qch à qn.
lavishly ['lævıʃlı] adv (give, spend) sans
  compter; (furnished) luxueusement.
law [lɔ:] n loi f; (science) droit m; **against the**
  contraire à la loi; **to study ~** faire du droit
  to go to ~ (BRIT) avoir recours à la justice,
  ~ and order n l'ordre public.
law-abiding ['lɔ:əbaıdıŋ] adj
  respectueux(euse) des lois.
lawbreaker ['lɔ:breıkə*] n personne f qui
  transgresse la loi.
law court n tribunal m, cour f de justice.

lawful ['lɔːful] adj légal(e); permis(e).
lawfully ['lɔːfəlɪ] adv légalement.
lawless ['lɔːlɪs] adj sans loi.
Law Lord n (BRIT) juge siégant à la Chambre des Lords.
lawmaker ['lɔːmeɪkə*] n législateur/trice.
lawn [lɔːn] n pelouse f.
lawnmower ['lɔːnməuə*] n tondeuse f à gazon.
lawn tennis n tennis m.
law school n faculté f de droit.
law student n étudiant/e en droit.
lawsuit ['lɔːsuːt] n procès m; **to bring a ~ against** engager des poursuites contre.
lawyer ['lɔːjə*] n (consultant, with company) juriste m; (for sales, wills etc) ≈ notaire m; (partner, in court) ≈ avocat m.
lax [læks] adj relâché(e).
laxative ['læksətɪv] n laxatif m.
laxity ['læksɪtɪ] n relâchement m.
lay [leɪ] pt of **lie** ♦ adj laïque; profane ♦ vt (pt, pp **laid** [leɪd]) poser, mettre; (eggs) pondre; (trap) tendre; (plans) élaborer; **to ~ the table** mettre la table; **to ~ the facts/one's proposals before sb** présenter les faits/ses propositions à qn; **to get laid** (col!) baiser (!); se faire baiser (!).
lay aside , lay by vt mettre de côté.
lay down vt poser; **to ~ down the law** (fig) faire la loi.
lay in vt accumuler, s'approvisionner en.
lay into vi (col: attack) tomber sur; (: scold) passer une engueulade à.
lay off vt (workers) licencier.
lay on vt (water, gas) mettre, installer; (provide: meal etc) fournir; (paint) étaler.
lay out vt (design) dessiner, concevoir; (display) disposer; (spend) dépenser.
lay up vt (to store) amasser; (car) remiser; (ship) désarmer; (subj: illness) forcer à s'aliter.
layabout ['leɪəbaut] n fainéant/e.
lay-by ['leɪbaɪ] n (BRIT) aire f de stationnement (sur le bas-côté).
lay days npl (NAUT) estarie f.
layer ['leɪə*] n couche f.
layette ['leɪɛt] n layette f.
layman ['leɪmən] n laïque m; profane m.
lay-off ['leɪɔf] n licenciement m.
layout ['leɪaut] n disposition f, plan m, agencement m; (PRESS) mise f en page.
laze [leɪz] vi paresser.
laziness ['leɪzɪnɪs] n paresse f.
lazy ['leɪzɪ] adj paresseux(euse).
LB abbr (Canada) = Labrador.
lb. abbr (= libra: pound) unité de poids.
lbw abbr (CRICKET: = leg before wicket) faute dans laquelle le joueur a la jambe devant le guichet.
LC n abbr (US) = Library of Congress.
lc abbr (TYP: = lower case) b.d.c.
L/C abbr = **letter of credit**.

LCD n abbr = **liquid crystal display**.
Ld abbr (BRIT: = lord) titre honorifique.
LDS n abbr (= Licentiate in Dental Surgery) diplôme universitaire; (= Latter-day Saints) Église de Jésus-Christ des Saints du dernier jour.
LEA n abbr (BRIT: = local education authority) services locaux de l'enseignement.
lead¹ [liːd] n (front position) tête f; (distance, time ahead) avance f; (clue) piste f; (to battery) raccord m; (ELEC) fil m; (for dog) laisse f; (THEAT) rôle principal ♦ vb (pt, pp **led** [lɛd]) vt mener, conduire; (induce) amener; (be leader of) être à la tête de; (SPORT) être en tête de; (orchestra: BRIT) être le premier violon de; (: US) diriger ♦ vi mener, être en tête; **to ~** to mener à; (result in) conduire à; aboutir à; **to ~ sb astray** détourner qn du droit chemin; **to be in the ~** (SPORT: in race) mener, être en tête; (: match) mener (à la marque); **to take the ~** (SPORT) passer en tête, prendre la tête; mener; (fig) prendre l'initiative; **to ~ sb to believe that ...** amener qn à croire que ...; **to ~ sb to do sth** amener qn à faire qch.
▶**lead away** vt emmener.
▶**lead back** vt ramener.
▶**lead off** vi (in game etc) commencer.
▶**lead on** vt (tease) faire marcher; **to ~ sb on to** (induce) amener qn à.
▶**lead up to** vt conduire à.
lead² [lɛd] n (chemical) plomb m; (in pencil) mine f.
leaded ['lɛdɪd] adj (windows) à petits carreaux.
leaden ['lɛdn] adj de or en plomb.
leader ['liːdə*] n (of team) chef m; (of party etc) dirigeant/e, leader m; (in newspaper) éditorial m; **they are ~s in their field** (fig) ils sont à la pointe du progrès dans leur domaine; **the L~ of the House** (BRIT) le chef de la majorité ministérielle.
leadership ['liːdəʃɪp] n direction f; **under the ~ of ...** sous la direction de ...; **qualities of ~** qualités fpl de chef or de meneur.
lead-free ['lɛdfriː] adj sans plomb.
leading ['liːdɪŋ] adj de premier plan; (main) principal(e); **a ~ question** une question tendancieuse; **~ role** rôle prépondérant or de premier plan.
leading lady n (THEAT) vedette (féminine).
leading light n (person) sommité f, personnalité f de premier plan.
leading man n (THEAT) vedette (masculine).
lead pencil [lɛd-] n crayon noir or à papier.
lead poisoning [lɛd-] n saturnisme m.
lead time [liːd-] n (COMM) délai m de livraison.
lead weight [lɛd-] n plomb m.
leaf, pl **leaves** [liːf, liːvz] n feuille f; (of table) rallonge f; **to turn over a new ~** (fig) changer de conduite or d'existence; **to take**

a ~ out of sb's book (*fig*) prendre exemple sur qn.
▶**leaf through** *vt* (*book*) feuilleter.
leaflet ['li:flɪt] *n* prospectus *m*, brochure *f*; (*POL, REL*) tract *m*.
leafy ['li:fɪ] *adj* feuillu(e).
league [li:g] *n* ligue *f*, (*FOOTBALL*) championnat *m*; (*measure*) lieue *f*; **to be in ~ with** avoir partie liée avec, être de mèche avec.
league table *n* classement *m*.
leak [li:k] *n* (*out, also fig*) fuite *f*; (*in*) infiltration *f* ♦ *vi* (*pipe, liquid etc*) fuir; (*shoes*) prendre l'eau ♦ *vt* (*liquid*) répandre; (*information*) divulguer.
▶**leak out** *vi* fuir; (*information*) être divulgué(e).
leakage ['li:kɪdʒ] *n* (*also fig*) fuite *f*.
leaky ['li:kɪ] *adj* (*pipe, bucket*) qui fuit, percé(e); (*roof*) qui coule; (*shoe*) qui prend l'eau; (*boat*) qui fait eau.
lean [li:n] *adj* maigre ♦ *n* (*of meat*) maigre *m* ♦ *vb* (*pt, pp* **leaned** *or* **leant** [lɛnt]) *vt*: **to ~ sth on** appuyer qch sur ♦ *vi* (*slope*) pencher; (*rest*): **to ~ against** s'appuyer contre; être appuyé(e) contre; **to ~ on** s'appuyer sur.
▶**lean back** *vi* se pencher en arrière.
▶**lean forward** *vi* se pencher en avant.
▶**lean out** *vi*: **to ~ out (of)** se pencher au dehors (de).
▶**lean over** *vi* se pencher.
leaning ['li:nɪŋ] *adj* penché(e) ♦ *n*: ~ **(towards)** penchant *m* (pour); **the L~ Tower of Pisa** la tour penchée de Pise.
leant [lɛnt] *pt, pp of* **lean**.
lean-to ['li:ntu:] *n* appentis *m*.
leap [li:p] *n* bond *m*, saut *m* ♦ *vi* (*pt, pp* **leaped** *or* **leapt** [lɛpt]) bondir, sauter; **to ~ at an offer** saisir une offre.
▶**leap up** *vi* (*person*) faire un bond; se lever d'un bond.
leapfrog ['li:pfrɒg] *n* jeu *m* de saute-mouton.
leapt [lɛpt] *pt, pp of* **leap**.
leap year *n* année *f* bissextile.
learn, *pt, pp* **learned** *or* **learnt** [lə:n, -t] *vt, vi* apprendre; **to ~ how to do sth** apprendre à faire qch; **we were sorry to ~ that ...** nous apprenons avec regret que ...; **to ~ about sth** (*SCOL*) étudier qch; (*hear*) apprendre qch.
learned ['lə:nɪd] *adj* érudit(e), savant(e).
learner ['lə:nə*] *n* débutant/e; (*BRIT: also:* ~ **driver**) (conducteur/trice) débutant(e).
learning ['lə:nɪŋ] *n* savoir *m*.
lease [li:s] *n* bail *m* ♦ *vt* louer à bail; **on ~** en location.
▶**lease back** *vt* vendre en cession-bail.
leaseback ['li:sbæk] *n* cession-bail *f*.
leasehold ['li:shəuld] *n* (*contract*) bail *m* ♦ *adj* loué(e) à bail.
leash [li:ʃ] *n* laisse *f*.
least [li:st] *adj*: **the ~** + *noun* le(la) plus petit(e),

le(la) moindre; (*smallest amount of*) le moins de; **the ~** + *adjective* le(la) moins; **the ~ money** le moins d'argent; **the ~ expensive** le moins cher; **at ~** au moins; **not in the ~** pas le moins du monde.
leather ['lɛðə*] *n* cuir *m* ♦ *cpd* en *or* de cuir; **~ goods** maroquinerie *f*.
leave [li:v] *vb* (*pt, pp* **left** [lɛft]) *vt* laisser; (*go away from*) quitter ♦ *vi* partir, s'en aller ♦ *n* (*time off*) congé *m*; (*MIL, also: consent*) permission *f*; **to be left** rester; **there's some milk left over** il reste du lait; **to ~ school** quitter l'école, terminer sa scolarité; ~ **it to me!** laissez-moi faire!, je m'en occupe!; **on ~** en permission; **to take one's ~ of** prendre congé de; ~ **of absence** *n* congé exceptionnel; (*MIL*) permission spéciale.
▶**leave behind** *vt* (*also fig*) laisser; (*opponent in race*) distancer; (*forget*) laisser, oublier.
▶**leave off** *vt* (*cover, lid, heating*) ne pas (re)mettre; (*light*) ne pas (r)allumer, laisser éteint(e); (*BRIT col: stop*): **to ~ off (doing sth)** s'arrêter (de faire qch).
▶**leave on** *vt* (*coat etc*) garder, ne pas enlever; (*lid*) laisser dessus; (*light, fire, cooker*) laisser allumé(e).
▶**leave out** *vt* oublier, omettre.
leaves [li:vz] *npl of* **leaf**.
leavetaking ['li:vteɪkɪŋ] *n* adieux *mpl*.
Lebanese [lɛbə'ni:z] *adj* libanais(e) ♦ *n* (*pl inv*) Libanais/e.
Lebanon ['lɛbənən] *n* Liban *m*.
lecherous ['lɛtʃərəs] *adj* lubrique.
lectern ['lɛktə:n] *n* lutrin *m*, pupitre *m*.
lecture ['lɛktʃə*] *n* conférence *f*; (*SCOL*) cours (magistral) ♦ *vi* donner des cours; enseigne ♦ *vt* (*reprove*) sermonner, réprimander; **to ~ on** faire un cours (*or* son cours) sur; **to give a ~ (on)** faire une conférence (sur); faire un cours (sur).
lecture hall *n* amphithéâtre *m*.
lecturer ['lɛktʃərə*] *n* (*speaker*) conférencier/ière *m*; (*BRIT: at university*) professeur *m* (d'université), ≈ maître assistant, maître de conférences; **assistant ~** (*BRIT*) ≈ assistant/e; **senior ~** (*BRIT*) ≈ chargé/e d'enseignement.
lecture theatre *n* = **lecture hall**.
LED *n abbr* (= *light-emitting diode*) LED *f*, diode électroluminescente.
led [lɛd] *pt, pp of* **lead**[1].
ledge [lɛdʒ] *n* (*of window, on wall*) rebord *m*; (*of mountain*) saillie *f*, corniche *f*.
ledger ['lɛdʒə*] *n* registre *m*, grand livre.
lee [li:] *n* côté *m* sous le vent; **in the ~ of** à l'abri de.
leech [li:tʃ] *n* sangsue *f*.
leek [li:k] *n* poireau *m*.
leer [lɪə*] *vi*: **to ~ at sb** regarder qn d'un air mauvais *or* concupiscent, lorgner qn.
leeward ['li:wəd] *adj, adv* sous le vent ♦ *n* côté *m* sous le vent; **to ~** sous le vent.

eeway ['liːweɪ] *n* (*fig*): **to make up ~** rattraper son retard; **to have some ~** avoir une certaine liberté d'action.

eft [lɛft] *pt, pp of* **leave ♦** *adj* gauche **♦** *adv* à gauche **♦** *n* gauche *f*; **on the ~, to the ~** à gauche; **the L~** (*POL*) la gauche.

eft-hand drive ['lɛfthænd-] *n* (*BRIT*) conduite *f* à gauche.

eft-handed [lɛft'hændɪd] *adj* gaucher(ère); (*scissors etc*) pour gauchers.

eft-hand side ['lɛfthænd-] *n* gauche *f*, côté *m* gauche.

eftie ['lɛftɪ] *n* (*col*) gaucho *m/f*, gauchiste *m/f*.

eftist ['lɛftɪst] *adj* (*POL*) gauchiste, de gauche.

eft-luggage (office) [lɛft'lʌgɪdʒ(-)] *n* (*BRIT*) consigne *f*.

eft-overs ['lɛftəuvəz] *npl* restes *mpl*.

eft wing *n* (*MIL, SPORT*) aile *f* gauche; (*POL*) gauche *f* **♦** *adj*: **left-wing** (*POL*) de gauche.

eft-winger ['lɛft'wɪŋgə*] *n* (*POL*) membre *m* de la gauche; (*SPORT*) ailier *m* gauche.

efty ['lɛftɪ] *n* (*col*) = **leftie**.

eg [lɛg] *n* jambe *f*; (*of animal*) patte *f*; (*of furniture*) pied *m*; (*CULIN: of chicken*) cuisse *f*; **lst/2nd ~** (*SPORT*) match *m* aller/retour; (*of journey*) 1ère/2ème étape; **~ of lamb** (*CULIN*) gigot *m* d'agneau; **to stretch one's ~s** se dégourdir les jambes.

egacy ['lɛgəsɪ] *n* (*also fig*) héritage *m*, legs *m*.

egal ['liːgl] *adj* légal(e); **to take ~ action** *or* **proceedings against sb** poursuivre qn en justice.

egal adviser *n* conseiller/ère juridique.

egality [lɪ'gælɪtɪ] *n* légalité *f*.

egalize ['liːgəlaɪz] *vt* légaliser.

egally ['liːgəlɪ] *adv* légalement; **~ binding** juridiquement contraignant(e).

egal tender *n* monnaie légale.

egation [lɪ'geɪʃən] *n* légation *f*.

egend ['lɛdʒənd] *n* légende *f*.

egendary ['lɛdʒəndərɪ] *adj* légendaire.

egged ['lɛgɪd] *suffix*: **two~** à deux pattes (*or* jambes *or* pieds).

eggings ['lɛgɪŋz] *npl* jambières *fpl*, guêtres *fpl*.

eggy ['lɛgɪ] *adj* aux longues jambes.

egibility [lɛdʒɪ'bɪlɪtɪ] *n* lisibilité *f*.

egible ['lɛdʒəbl] *adj* lisible.

egibly ['lɛdʒəblɪ] *adv* lisiblement.

egion ['liːdʒən] *n* légion *f*.

egionnaire [liːdʒə'nɛə*] *n* légionnaire *m*; **~'s disease** maladie *f* du légionnaire.

egislate ['lɛdʒɪsleɪt] *vi* légiférer.

egislation [lɛdʒɪs'leɪʃən] *n* législation *f*; **a piece of ~** un texte de loi.

egislative ['lɛdʒɪslətɪv] *adj* législatif(ive).

egislator ['lɛdʒɪsleɪtə*] *n* législateur/trice.

egislature ['lɛdʒɪslətʃə*] *n* corps législatif.

egitimacy [lɪ'dʒɪtɪməsɪ] *n* légitimité *f*.

egitimate [lɪ'dʒɪtɪmət] *adj* légitime.

egitimize [lɪ'dʒɪtɪmaɪz] *vt* légitimer.

egless ['lɛglɪs] *adj* (*BRIT col*) bourré(e).

leg-room ['lɛgruːm] *n* place *f* pour les jambes.

Leics *abbr* (*BRIT*) = *Leicestershire*.

leisure ['lɛʒə*] *n* (*time*) loisir *m*, temps *m*; (*free time*) temps libre, loisirs *mpl*; **at ~** (tout) à loisir; **à tête reposée**.

leisure centre *n* centre *m* de loisirs.

leisurely ['lɛʒəlɪ] *adj* tranquille; fait(e) sans se presser.

leisure suit *n* (*BRIT*) survêtement *m* (mode).

lemon ['lɛmən] *n* citron *m*.

lemonade [lɛmə'neɪd] *n* limonade *f*.

lemon cheese *n*, **lemon curd** *n* crème *f* de citron.

lemon juice *n* jus *m* de citron.

lemon squeezer [-skwiːzə*] *n* presse-citron *m inv*.

lemon tea *n* thé *m* au citron.

lend, *pt, pp* **lent** [lɛnd, lɛnt] *vt*: **to ~ sth (to sb)** prêter qch (à qn); **to ~ a hand** donner un coup de main.

lender ['lɛndə*] *n* prêteur/euse.

lending library ['lɛndɪŋ-] *n* bibliothèque *f* de prêt.

length [lɛŋθ] *n* longueur *f*; (*section: of road, pipe etc*) morceau *m*; (*of time*) durée *f*; **what ~ is it?** quelle longueur fait-il?; **it is 2 metres in ~** cela fait 2 mètres de long; **to fall full ~** tomber de tout son long; **at ~** (*at last*) enfin, à la fin; (*lengthily*) longuement; **to go to any ~(s) to do sth** faire n'importe quoi pour faire qch, ne reculer devant rien pour faire qch.

lengthen ['lɛŋθn] *vt* allonger, prolonger **♦** *vi* s'allonger.

lengthways ['lɛŋθweɪz] *adv* dans le sens de la longueur, en long.

lengthy ['lɛŋθɪ] *adj* (très) long(longue).

leniency ['liːnɪənsɪ] *n* indulgence *f*, clémence *f*.

lenient ['liːnɪənt] *adj* indulgent(e), clément(e).

leniently ['liːnɪəntlɪ] *adv* avec indulgence *or* clémence.

lens [lɛnz] *n* lentille *f*; (*of spectacles*) verre *m*; (*of camera*) objectif *m*.

Lent [lɛnt] *n* Carême *m*.

lent [lɛnt] *pt, pp of* **lend**.

lentil ['lɛntl] *n* lentille *f*.

Leo ['liːəu] *n* le Lion; **to be ~** être du Lion.

leopard ['lɛpəd] *n* léopard *m*.

leotard ['liːətɑːd] *n* maillot *m* (*de danseur etc*).

leper ['lɛpə*] *n* lépreux/euse.

leper colony *n* léproserie *f*.

leprosy ['lɛprəsɪ] *n* lèpre *f*.

lesbian ['lɛzbɪən] *n* lesbienne *f* **♦** *adj* lesbien(ne).

lesion ['liːʒən] *n* (*MED*) lésion *f*.

Lesotho [lɪ'suːtuː] *n* Lesotho *m*.

less [lɛs] *adj* moins de **♦** *pron, adv* moins; **~ than that/you** moins que cela/vous; **~ than half** moins de la moitié; **~ than one/a kilo/3 metres** moins de un/d'un kilo/de 3 mètres; **~ and ~** de moins en moins; **the ~ he works ...**

lessee [lɛˈsiː] *n* locataire *m/f* (à bail), preneur/euse du bail.

lessen [ˈlɛsn] *vi* diminuer, s'amoindrir, s'atténuer ♦ *vt* diminuer, réduire, atténuer.

lesser [ˈlɛsə*] *adj* moindre; **to a ~ extent** *or* **degree** à un degré moindre.

lesson [ˈlɛsn] *n* leçon *f*; **a maths ~** une leçon *or* un cours de maths; **to give ~s in** donner des cours de; **it taught him a ~** (*fig*) cela lui a servi de leçon.

lessor [ˈlɛsɔː*, lɛˈsɔː*] *n* bailleur/eresse.

lest [lɛst] *conj* de peur de + *infinitive*, de peur que + *sub*.

let, *pt, pp* **let** [lɛt] *vt* laisser; (*BRIT: lease*) louer; **to ~ sb do sth** laisser qn faire qch; **to ~ sb know sth** faire savoir qch à qn, prévenir qn de qch; **he ~ me go** il m'a laissé partir; **~ the water boil and ...** faites bouillir l'eau et ...; **~'s go** allons-y; **~ him come** qu'il vienne; **"to ~"** "à louer".

▶**let down** *vt* (*lower*) baisser; (*dress*) rallonger; (*hair*) défaire; (*BRIT: tyre*) dégonfler; (*disappoint*) décevoir.

▶**let go** *vi* lâcher prise ♦ *vt* lâcher.

▶**let in** *vt* laisser entrer; (*visitor etc*) faire entrer; **what have you ~ yourself in for?** à quoi t'es-tu engagé?

▶**let off** *vt* (*allow to leave*) laisser partir; (*not punish*) ne pas punir; (*subj: taxi driver, bus driver*) déposer; (*firework etc*) faire partir; (*smell etc*) dégager; **to ~ off steam** (*fig: col*) se défouler, décharger sa rate *or* bile.

▶**let on** *vi* (*col*): **to ~ on that ...** révéler que ..., dire que ....

▶**let out** *vt* laisser sortir; (*dress*) élargir; (*scream*) laisser échapper; (*rent out*) louer.

▶**let up** *vi* diminuer, s'arrêter.

let-down [ˈlɛtdaun] *n* (*disappointment*) déception *f*.

lethal [ˈliːθl] *adj* mortel(le), fatal(e).

lethargic [lɛˈθɑːdʒɪk] *adj* léthargique.

lethargy [ˈlɛθədʒɪ] *n* léthargie *f*.

letter [ˈlɛtə*] *n* lettre *f*; **~s** *npl* (*LITERATURE*) lettres; **small/capital ~** minuscule *f*/majuscule *f*; **~ of credit** lettre *f* de crédit.

letter bomb *n* lettre piégée.

letterbox [ˈlɛtəbɔks] *n* (*BRIT*) boîte *f* aux *or* à lettres.

letterhead [ˈlɛtəhɛd] *n* en-tête *m*.

lettering [ˈlɛtərɪŋ] *n* lettres *fpl*; caractères *mpl*.

letter opener *n* coupe-papier *m*.

letterpress [ˈlɛtəprɛs] *n* (*method*) typographie *f*.

letter quality *n* qualité *f* "courrier".

letters patent *npl* brevet *m* d'invention.

lettuce [ˈlɛtɪs] *n* laitue *f*, salade *f*.

let-up [ˈlɛtʌp] *n* répit *m*, détente *f*.

leukaemia, (*US*) **leukemia** [luːˈkiːmɪə] *n* leucémie *f*.

level [ˈlɛvl] *adj* plat(e), plan(e), uni(e); horizontal(e) ♦ *n* niveau *m*; (*flat place*) terrain plat; (*also*: **spirit ~**) niveau à bulle ♦ *vt* niveler, aplanir; (*gun*) pointer, braquer; (*accusation*): **to ~ (against)** lancer *or* porter (contre) ♦ *vi* (*col*): **to ~ with sb** être franc(franche) avec qn; **"A" ~s** *npl* (*BRIT: formerly*) ≈ baccalauréat *m*; **"O" ~s** *npl* (*BRIT: formerly*) *examens passés à l'âge de 16 ans sanctionnant les connaissances de l'élève*, ≈ brevet *m* des collèges; **a ~ spoonful** (*CULIN*) une cuillerée à raser; **to be ~ with** être au même niveau que; **to draw ~ with** (*team*) arriver à égalité de points avec, égaliser avec; arriver au même classement que; (*runner, car*) arriver à la hauteur de, rattraper; **on the ~** à l'horizontale; (*fig: honest*) régulier(ière).

▶**level off, level out** *vi* (*prices etc*) se stabiliser ♦ *vt* (*ground*) aplanir, niveler.

level crossing *n* (*BRIT*) passage *m* à niveau.

level-headed [lɛvlˈhɛdɪd] *adj* équilibré(e).

levelling, (*US*) **leveling** [ˈlɛvlɪŋ] *adj* (*process, effect*) de nivellement.

level playing field *n*: **to compete on a ~** jouer sur un terrain d'égalité.

lever [ˈliːvə*] *n* levier *m* ♦ *vt*: **to ~ up/out** soulever/extraire au moyen d'un levier.

leverage [ˈliːvərɪdʒ] *n*: **~ (on *or* with)** prise *f* (sur).

levity [ˈlɛvɪtɪ] *n* manque *m* de sérieux, légèreté *f*.

levy [ˈlɛvɪ] *n* taxe *f*, impôt *m* ♦ *vt* prélever, imposer; percevoir.

lewd [luːd] *adj* obscène, lubrique.

lexicographer [lɛksɪˈkɔgrəfə*] *n* lexicographe *m/f*.

lexicography [lɛksɪˈkɔgrəfɪ] *n* lexicographie *f*.

LGV *n abbr* (= *Large Goods Vehicle*) poids lourd.

LI *abbr* (*US*) = *Long Island*.

liabilities [laɪəˈbɪlətɪz] *npl* (*COMM*) obligations *fpl*, engagements *mpl*; (*on balance sheet*) passif *m*.

liability [laɪəˈbɪlətɪ] *n* responsabilité *f*; (*handicap*) handicap *m*.

liable [ˈlaɪəbl] *adj* (*subject*): **~ to** sujet(te) à; passible de; (*responsible*): **~ (for)** responsable (de); (*likely*): **~ to do** susceptible de faire; **to be ~ to a fine** être passible d'une amende.

liaise [liːˈeɪz] *vi*: **to ~ with** rester en liaison avec.

liaison [liːˈeɪzɔn] *n* liaison *f*.

liar [ˈlaɪə*] *n* menteur/euse.

libel [ˈlaɪbl] *n* écrit *m* diffamatoire; diffamation *f* ♦ *vt* diffamer.

libellous [ˈlaɪbləs] *adj* diffamatoire.

liberal [ˈlɪbərl] *adj* libéral(e); (*generous*): **~ with** prodigue de, généreux(euse) avec ♦ *n*: **L~** (*POL*) libéral/e.

Liberal Democrat *n* démocrate *m/f*.

liberality [lɪbəˈrælɪtɪ] *n* (*generosity*) générosité *f*, libéralité *f*.

liberalize [ˈlɪbərəlaɪz] *vt* libéraliser.

liberal-minded ['lɪbərl'maɪndɪd] *adj* libéral(e), tolérant(e).

liberate ['lɪbəreɪt] *vt* libérer.

liberation [lɪbə'reɪʃən] *n* libération *f*.

liberation theology *n* théologie *f* de libération.

Liberia [laɪ'bɪərɪə] *n* Libéria *m*, Liberia *m*.

Liberian [laɪ'bɪərɪən] *adj* libérien(ne) ♦ *n* Libérien/ne.

liberty ['lɪbətɪ] *n* liberté *f*; **at ~ to do** libre de faire; **to take the ~ of** prendre la liberté de, se permettre de.

libido [lɪ'biːdəʊ] *n* libido *f*.

Libra ['liːbrə] *n* la Balance; **to be ~** être de la Balance.

librarian [laɪ'brɛərɪən] *n* bibliothécaire *m/f*.

library ['laɪbrərɪ] *n* bibliothèque *f*.

library book *n* livre *m* de bibliothèque.

libretto [lɪ'brɛtəʊ] *n* livret *m*.

Libya ['lɪbɪə] *n* Libye *f*.

Libyan ['lɪbɪən] *adj* libyen(ne), de Libye ♦ *n* Libyen/ne.

ice [laɪs] *npl of* louse.

icence, (*US*) **license** ['laɪsns] *n* autorisation *f*, permis *m*; (*COMM*) licence *f*; (*RADIO, TV*) redevance *f*; (*also*: **driving ~**, (*US*) **driver's ~**) permis *m* (de conduire); (*excessive freedom*) licence; **import ~** licence d'importation; **produced under ~** fabriqué(e) sous licence.

icence number *n* (*BRIT AUT*) numéro *m* d'immatriculation.

icense ['laɪsns] *n* (*US*) = **licence** ♦ *vt* donner une licence à; (*car*) acheter la vignette de; délivrer la vignette de.

icensed ['laɪsnst] *adj* (*for alcohol*) patenté(e) pour la vente des spiritueux, qui a une patente de débit de boissons.

icensee [laɪsən'siː] *n* (*BRIT*: *of pub*) patron/ne, gérant/e.

icense plate *n* (*esp US AUT*) plaque *f* minéralogique.

icentious [laɪ'sɛnʃəs] *adj* licentieux(euse).

ichen ['laɪkən] *n* lichen *m*.

ick [lɪk] *vt* lécher; (*col: defeat*) écraser, flanquer une piquette *or* raclée a ♦ *n* coup *m* de langue; **a ~ of paint** un petit coup de peinture.

icorice ['lɪkərɪs] *n* = **liquorice**.

id [lɪd] *n* couvercle *m*; **to take the ~ off sth** (*fig*) exposer *or* étaler qch au grand jour.

ido ['laɪdəʊ] *n* piscine *f* en plein air; complexe *m* balnéaire.

ie [laɪ] *n* mensonge *m* ♦ *vi* mentir; (*pt* **lay**, *pp* **lain** [leɪ, leɪn]) (*rest*) être étendu(e) *or* allongé(e) *or* couché(e); (*in grave*) être enterré(e), reposer; (*of object: be situated*) se trouver, être; **to ~ low** (*fig*) se cacher, rester caché(e); **to tell ~s** mentir.

lie about, lie around *vi* (*things*) traîner; (*person*) traînasser, flemmarder.

lie back *vi* se renverser en arrière.

▶**lie down** *vi* se coucher, s'étendre.

▶**lie up** *vi* (*hide*) se cacher.

Liechtenstein ['lɪktənstaɪn] *n* Liechtenstein *m*.

lie detector *n* détecteur *m* de mensonges.

lie-down ['laɪdaʊn] *n* (*BRIT*): **to have a ~** s'allonger, se reposer.

lie-in ['laɪɪn] *n* (*BRIT*): **to have a ~** faire la grasse matinée.

lieu [luː]: **in ~ of** *prep* au lieu de, à la place de.

Lieut. *abbr* (= *lieutenant*) Lt.

lieutenant [lɛf'tɛnənt, (*US*) luː'tɛnənt] *n* lieutenant *m*.

lieutenant-colonel [lɛf'tɛnənt'kəːnl, (*US*) luː'tɛnənt'kəːnl] *n* lieutenant-colonel *m*.

life, *pl* **lives** [laɪf, laɪvz] *n* vie *f* ♦ *cpd* de vie; de la vie; à vie; **true to ~** réaliste, fidèle à la réalité; **to paint from ~** peindre d'après nature; **to be sent to prison for ~** être condamné(e) (à la réclusion criminelle) à perpétuité; **country/city ~** la vie à la campagne/à la ville.

life annuity *n* pension *f*, rente viagère.

life assurance *n* (*BRIT*) = **life insurance**.

lifebelt ['laɪfbɛlt] *n* (*BRIT*) bouée *f* de sauvetage.

lifeblood ['laɪfblʌd] *n* (*fig*) élément moteur.

lifeboat ['laɪfbəʊt] *n* canot *m* or chaloupe *f* de sauvetage.

lifebuoy ['laɪfbɔɪ] *n* bouée *f* de sauvetage.

life expectancy *n* espérance *f* de vie.

lifeguard ['laɪfɡɑːd] *n* surveillant *m* de baignade.

life imprisonment *n* prison *f* à vie; (*LAW*) réclusion *f* à perpétuité.

life insurance *n* assurance-vie *f*.

life jacket *n* gilet *m* or ceinture *f* de sauvetage.

lifeless ['laɪflɪs] *adj* sans vie, inanimé(e); (*dull*) qui manque de vie or de vigueur.

lifelike ['laɪflaɪk] *adj* qui semble vrai(e) or vivant(e); ressemblant(e).

lifeline ['laɪflaɪn] *n* corde *f* de sauvetage.

lifelong ['laɪflɒŋ] *adj* de toute une vie, de toujours.

life preserver [-prɪ'zɔːvə*] *n* (*US*) gilet *m* or ceinture *f* de sauvetage.

lifer ['laɪfə*] *n* (*col*) condamné/e à perpète.

life-raft ['laɪfrɑːft] *n* radeau *m* de sauvetage.

life-saver ['laɪfseɪvə*] *n* surveillant *m* de baignade.

life sentence *n* condamnation *f* à vie or à perpétuité.

life-sized ['laɪfsaɪzd] *adj* grandeur nature *inv*.

life span *n* (durée *f* de) vie *f*.

life style *n* style *m* de vie.

life support system *n* (*MED*) respirateur artificiel.

lifetime ['laɪftaɪm]: **in his ~** de son vivant; **the chance of a ~** la chance de ma (*or* sa *etc*) vie, une occasion unique.

lift [lɪft] *vt* soulever, lever; (*steal*) prendre, voler ♦ *vi* (*fog*) se lever ♦ *n* (*BRIT*: *elevator*)

ascenseur *m*; **to give sb a** ~ (*BRIT*) emmener *or* prendre qn en voiture.
▶**lift off** *vi* (*rocket, helicopter*) décoller.
▶**lift out** *vt* sortir; (*troops, evacuees etc*) évacuer par avion *or* hélicoptère.
▶**lift up** *vt* soulever.
lift-off ['lɪftɔf] *n* décollage *m*.
ligament ['lɪgəmənt] *n* ligament *m*.
light [laɪt] *n* lumière *f*, (*daylight*) lumière, jour *m*; (*lamp*) lampe *f*; (*AUT: traffic* ~, *rear* ~) feu *m*; (*: headlamp*) phare *m*; (*for cigarette etc*): **have you got a** ~? avez-vous du feu? ♦ *vt* (*pt, pp* **lighted** *or* **lit** [lɪt]) (*candle, cigarette, fire*) allumer; (*room*) éclairer ♦ *adj* (*room, colour*) clair(e); (*not heavy, also fig*) léger(ère) ♦ *adv* (*travel*) avec peu de bagages; **to turn the** ~ **on/off** allumer/éteindre; **to cast** *or* **shed** *or* **throw** ~ **on** éclaircir; **to come to** ~ être dévoilé(e) *or* découvert(e); **in the** ~ **of** à la lumière de; étant donné; **to make** ~ **of sth** (*fig*) prendre qch à la légère, faire peu de cas de qch.
▶**light up** *vi* s'allumer; (*face*) s'éclairer ♦ *vt* (*illuminate*) éclairer, illuminer.
light bulb *n* ampoule *f*.
lighten ['laɪtn] *vi* s'éclairer ♦ *vt* (*give light to*) éclairer; (*make lighter*) éclaircir; (*make less heavy*) alléger.
lighter ['laɪtə*] *n* (*also:* **cigarette** ~) briquet *m*; (*: in car*) allume-cigare *m inv*; (*boat*) péniche *f*.
light-fingered [laɪt'fɪŋgəd] *adj* chapardeur(euse).
light-headed [laɪt'hɛdɪd] *adj* étourdi(e), écervelé(e).
light-hearted [laɪt'hɑːtɪd] *adj* gai(e), joyeux(euse), enjoué(e).
lighthouse ['laɪthaus] *n* phare *m*.
lighting ['laɪtɪŋ] *n* (*on road*) éclairage *m*; (*in theatre*) éclairages.
lighting-up time [laɪtɪŋ'ʌp-] *n* (*BRIT*) *heure officielle de la tombée du jour.*
lightly ['laɪtlɪ] *adv* légèrement; **to get off** ~ s'en tirer à bon compte.
light meter *n* (*PHOT*) photomètre *m*, cellule *f*.
lightness ['laɪtnɪs] *n* clarté *f*; (*in weight*) légèreté *f*.
lightning ['laɪtnɪŋ] *n* éclair *m*, foudre *f*.
lightning conductor, (*US*) **lightning rod** *n* paratonnerre *m*.
lightning strike *n* (*BRIT*) grève *f* surprise.
light pen *n* crayon *m* optique.
lightship ['laɪtʃɪp] *n* bateau-phare *m*.
lightweight ['laɪtweɪt] *adj* (*suit*) léger(ère); (*boxer*) poids léger *inv*.
light year ['laɪtjɪə*] *n* année-lumière *f*.
like [laɪk] *vt* aimer (bien) ♦ *prep* comme ♦ *adj* semblable, pareil(le) ♦ *n*: **the** ~ un(e) pareil(le) *or* semblable; le(la) pareil(le); (*pej*) (d')autres du même genre *or* acabit; **his** ~s **and dislikes** ses goûts *mpl or* préférences *fpl*; **I would** ~, **I'd** ~ je voudrais, j'aimerais; **would you** ~ **a coffee?** voulez-

vous du café?; **to be/look** ~ **sb/sth** ressembler à qn/qch; **what's he** ~? comment est-il?; **what's the weather** ~? quel temps fait-il?; **that's just** ~ **him** c'est bien de lui, ça lui ressemble; **something** ~ **that** quelque chose comme ça; **I feel** ~ **a drink** je boirais bien quelque chose; **if you** ~ si vous voulez; **there's nothing** ~ ... il n'y a rien de tel que ....
likeable ['laɪkəbl] *adj* sympathique, agréable.
likelihood ['laɪklɪhud] *n* probabilité *f*; **in all** ~ selon toute vraisemblance.
likely ['laɪklɪ] *adj* (*result, outcome*) probable; (*excuse*) plausible; **he's** ~ **to leave** il va sûrement partir, il risque fort de partir; **not** ~! (*col*) pas de danger!
like-minded ['laɪk'maɪndɪd] *adj* de même opinion.
liken ['laɪkən] *vt*: **to** ~ **sth to** comparer qch à.
likeness ['laɪknɪs] *n* ressemblance *f*.
likewise ['laɪkwaɪz] *adv* de même, pareillement.
liking ['laɪkɪŋ] *n* affection *f*, penchant *m*; goût *m*; **to take a** ~ **to sb** se prendre d'amitié pour qn; **to be to sb's** ~ être au goût de qn, plaire à qn.
lilac ['laɪlək] *n* lilas *m* ♦ *adj* lilas *inv*.
Lilo ['laɪləu] *n* ® matelas *m* pneumatique.
lilt [lɪlt] *n* rythme *m*, cadence *f*.
lilting ['lɪltɪŋ] *adj* aux cadences mélodieuses; chantant(e).
lily ['lɪlɪ] *n* lis *m*; ~ **of the valley** muguet *m*.
Lima ['liːmə] *n* Lima.
limb [lɪm] *n* membre *m*; **to be out on a** ~ (*fig*) être isolé(e).
limber ['lɪmbə*]: **to** ~ **up** *vi* se dégourdir, se mettre en train.
limbo ['lɪmbəu] *n*: **to be in** ~ (*fig*) être tombé(e) dans l'oubli.
lime [laɪm] *n* (*tree*) tilleul *m*; (*fruit*) citron vert, lime *f*; (*GEO*) chaux *f*.
lime juice *n* jus *m* de citron vert.
limelight ['laɪmlaɪt] *n*: **in the** ~ (*fig*) en vedette, au premier plan.
limerick ['lɪmərɪk] *n* petit poème humoristique.
limestone ['laɪmstəun] *n* pierre *f* à chaux; (*GEO*) calcaire *m*.
limit ['lɪmɪt] *n* limite *f* ♦ *vt* limiter; **weight/ speed** ~ limite de poids/de vitesse.
limitation [lɪmɪ'teɪʃən] *n* limitation *f*, restriction *f*.
limited ['lɪmɪtɪd] *adj* limité(e), restreint(e); ~ **edition** édition *f* à tirage limité.
limited (liability) company (Ltd) *n* (*BRIT*) ≈ société *f* anonyme (SA).
limitless ['lɪmɪtlɪs] *adj* illimité(e).
limousine ['lɪməziːn] *n* limousine *f*.
limp [lɪmp] *n*: **to have a** ~ boiter ♦ *vi* boiter ♦ *adj* mou(molle).
limpet ['lɪmpɪt] *n* patelle *f*; **like a** ~ (*fig*) comme une ventouse.

limpid ['lɪmpɪd] *adj* limpide.
linchpin ['lɪntʃpɪn] *n* esse *f*; (*fig*) pivot *m*.
Lincs [lɪŋks] *abbr* (*BRIT*) = Lincolnshire.
line [laɪn] *n* (*gen*) ligne *f*; (*rope*) corde *f*; (*wire*) fil *m*; (*of poem*) vers *m*; (*row, series*) rangée *f*; file *f*, queue *f*; (*COMM: series of goods*) article(s) *m(pl)*, ligne de produits ♦ *vt* (*clothes*): **to ~ (with)** doubler (de); (*box*): **to ~ (with)** garnir *or* tapisser (de); (*subj: trees, crowd*) border; **to cut in ~** (*US*) passer avant son tour; **in his ~ of business** dans sa partie, dans son rayon; **on the right ~s** sur la bonne voie; **a new ~ in cosmetics** une nouvelle ligne de produits de beauté; **hold the ~ please** (*BRIT TEL*) ne quittez pas; **to be in ~ for sth** (*fig*) être en lice pour qch; **in ~ with** en accord avec, en conformité avec; **to bring sth into ~ with sth** aligner qch sur qch; **to draw the ~ at (doing) sth** (*fig*) se refuser à (faire) qch; ne pas tolérer *or* admettre (qu'on fasse) qch; **to take the ~ that ...** être d'avis *or* de l'opinion que ....
▶**line up** *vi* s'aligner, se mettre en rang(s) ♦ *vt* aligner; (*set up, have ready*) prévoir; trouver; **to have sb/sth ~d up** avoir qn/qch en vue *or* de prévu(e).
linear ['lɪnɪə*] *adj* linéaire.
lined [laɪnd] *adj* (*paper*) réglé(e); (*face*) marqué(e), ridé(e); (*clothes*) doublé(e).
line feed *n* (*COMPUT*) interligne *m*.
lineman ['laɪnmən] *n* (*US: RAIL*) poseur *m* de rails; (: *TEL*) ouvrier *m* de ligne; (: *FOOTBALL*) avant *m*.
linen ['lɪnɪn] *n* linge *m* (de corps *or* de maison); (*cloth*) lin *m*.
line printer *n* imprimante *f* (ligne par) ligne.
liner ['laɪnə*] *n* paquebot *m* de ligne.
linesman ['laɪnzmən] *n* (*TENNIS*) juge *m* de ligne; (*FOOTBALL*) juge de touche.
line-up ['laɪnʌp] *n* file *f*; (*also:* **police ~**) parade *f* d'identification; (*SPORT*) (composition *f* de l'équipe *f*.
linger ['lɪŋgə*] *vi* s'attarder; traîner; (*smell, tradition*) persister.
lingerie ['læ̃ʒəriː] *n* lingerie *f*.
lingering ['lɪŋgərɪŋ] *adj* persistant(e); qui subsiste; (*death*) lent(e).
lingo, ~es ['lɪŋgəu] *n* (*pej*) jargon *m*.
linguist ['lɪŋgwɪst] *n* linguiste *m/f*; personne douée pour les langues.
linguistic [lɪŋ'gwɪstɪk] *adj* linguistique.
linguistics [lɪŋ'gwɪstɪks] *n* linguistique *f*.
lining ['laɪnɪŋ] *n* doublure *f*; (*TECH*) revêtement *m*; (: *of brakes*) garniture *f*.
link [lɪŋk] *n* (*of a chain*) maillon *m*; (*connection*) lien *m*, rapport *m* ♦ *vt* relier, lier, unir; **rail ~** liaison *f* ferroviaire.
▶**link up** *vt* relier ♦ *vi* se rejoindre; s'associer.
links [lɪŋks] *npl* (terrain *m* de) golf *m*.
link-up ['lɪŋkʌp] *n* lien *m*, rapport *m*; (*of roads*) jonction *f*, raccordement *m*; (*of spaceships*) arrimage *m*; (*RADIO, TV*) liaison *f*;

(: *programme*) duplex *m*.
linoleum [lɪ'nəuliəm] *n* linoléum *m*.
linseed oil ['lɪnsiːd-] *n* huile *f* de lin.
lint [lɪnt] *n* tissu ouaté (*pour pansements*).
lintel ['lɪntl] *n* linteau *m*.
lion ['laɪən] *n* lion *m*.
lion cub *n* lionceau *m*.
lioness ['laɪənɪs] *n* lionne *f*.
lip [lɪp] *n* lèvre *f*; (*of cup etc*) rebord *m*; (*insolence*) insolences *fpl*.
liposuction ['lɪpəusʌkʃən] *n* liposuccion *f*.
lipread ['lɪpriːd] *vi* lire sur les lèvres.
lip salve [-sælv] *n* pommade *f* pour les lèvres, pommade rosat.
lip service *n*: **to pay ~ to sth** ne reconnaître le mérite de qch que pour la forme *or* qu'en paroles.
lipstick ['lɪpstɪk] *n* rouge *m* à lèvres.
liquefy ['lɪkwɪfaɪ] *vt* liquéfier ♦ *vi* se liquéfier.
liqueur [lɪ'kjuə*] *n* liqueur *f*.
liquid ['lɪkwɪd] *n* liquide *m* ♦ *adj* liquide.
liquid assets *npl* liquidités *fpl*, disponibilités *fpl*.
liquidate ['lɪkwɪdeɪt] *vt* liquider.
liquidation [lɪkwɪ'deɪʃən] *n* liquidation *f*; **to go into ~** déposer son bilan.
liquidator ['lɪkwɪdeɪtə*] *n* liquidateur *m*.
liquid crystal display (LCD) *n* affichage *m* à cristaux liquides.
liquidize ['lɪkwɪdaɪz] *vt* (*BRIT CULIN*) passer au mixer.
liquidizer ['lɪkwɪdaɪzə*] *n* (*BRIT CULIN*) mixer *m*.
liquor ['lɪkə*] *n* spiritueux *m*, alcool *m*.
liquorice ['lɪkərɪs] *n* (*BRIT*) réglisse *f*.
Lisbon ['lɪzbən] *n* Lisbonne.
lisp [lɪsp] *n* zézaiement *m*.
lissom ['lɪsəm] *adj* souple, agile.
list [lɪst] *n* liste *f*; (*of ship*) inclinaison *f* ♦ *vt* (*write down*) inscrire; faire la liste de; (*enumerate*) énumérer; (*COMPUT*) lister ♦ *vi* (*ship*) gîter, donner de la bande; **shopping ~** liste des courses.
listed building ['lɪstɪd-] *n* (*ARCHIT*) monument classé.
listed company ['lɪstɪd-] *n* société cotée en Bourse.
listen ['lɪsn] *vi* écouter; **to ~ to** écouter.
listener ['lɪsnə*] *n* auditeur/trice.
listeria [lɪs'tɪərɪə] *n* listéria *f*.
listing ['lɪstɪŋ] *n* (*COMPUT*) listage *m*; (: *hard copy*) liste *f*, listing *m*.
listless ['lɪstlɪs] *adj* indolent(e), apathique.
listlessly ['lɪstlɪslɪ] *adv* avec indolence *or* apathie.
list price *n* prix *m* de catalogue.
lit [lɪt] *pt, pp of* **light**.
litany ['lɪtənɪ] *n* litanie *f*.
liter ['liːtə*] *n* (*US*) = **litre**.
literacy ['lɪtərəsɪ] *n* degré *m* d'alphabétisation, fait *m* de savoir lire et écrire.
literal ['lɪtərl] *adj* littéral(e).

literally ['lɪtrəlɪ] *adv* littéralement.
literary ['lɪtərərɪ] *adj* littéraire.
literate ['lɪtərət] *adj* qui sait lire et écrire, instruit(e).
literature ['lɪtrɪtʃə*] *n* littérature *f*; (*brochures etc*) copie *f* publicitaire, prospectus *mpl*.
lithe [laɪð] *adj* agile, souple.
lithography [lɪ'θɒɡrəfɪ] *n* lithographie *f*.
Lithuania [lɪθju'eɪnɪə] *n* Lituanie *f*.
Lithuanian [lɪθju'eɪnɪən] *adj* lituanien(ne) ◆ *n* Lituanien/ne; (*LING*) lituanien *m*.
litigate ['lɪtɪɡeɪt] *vt* mettre en litige ◆ *vi* plaider.
litigation [lɪtɪ'ɡeɪʃən] *n* litige *m*; contentieux *m*.
litmus ['lɪtməs] *n*: ~ **paper** papier *m* de tournesol.
litre, (*US*) **liter** ['liːtə*] *n* litre *m*.
litter ['lɪtə*] *n* (*rubbish*) détritus *mpl*, ordures *fpl*; (*young animals*) portée *f* ◆ *vt* éparpiller; laisser des détritus dans; ~**ed with** jonché(e) de, couvert(e) de.
litter bin *n* (*BRIT*) boîte *f* à ordures, poubelle *f*.
litter lout, (*US*) **litterbug** ['lɪtəbʌɡ] *n* personne qui jette des détritus par terre.
little ['lɪtl] *adj* (*small*) petit(e); (*not much*): **it's ~** c'est peu ◆ *adv* peu; ~ **milk** peu de lait; **a ~** un peu (de); **a ~ milk** un peu de lait; **for a ~ while** pendant un petit moment; **with ~ difficulty** sans trop de difficulté; **as ~ as possible** le moins possible; ~ **by** ~ petit à petit, peu à peu; **to make** ~ **of** faire peu de cas de.
little-known ['lɪtl'nəun] *adj* peu connu(e).
liturgy ['lɪtədʒɪ] *n* liturgie *f*.
live *vi* [lɪv] vivre; (*reside*) vivre, habiter ◆ *adj* [laɪv] (*animal*) vivant(e), en vie; (*wire*) sous tension; (*broadcast*) (transmis(e)) en direct; (*issue*) d'actualité, brûlant(e); (*unexploded*) non explosé(e); **to ~ in London** habiter (à) Londres; **to ~ together** vivre ensemble, cohabiter; ~ **ammunition** munitions *fpl* de combat.
►**live down** *vt* faire oublier (avec le temps).
►**live in** *vi* être logé(e) et nourri(e); être interne.
►**live off** *vt* (*land, fish etc*) vivre de; (*pej*: *parents etc*) vivre aux crochets de.
►**live on** *vt fus* (*food*) vivre de ◆ *vi* survivre; **to ~ on £50 a week** vivre avec 50 livres par semaine.
►**live out** *vi* (*BRIT*: *students*) être externe ◆ *vt*: **to ~ out one's days** *or* **life** passer sa vie.
►**live up** *vt*: **to ~ it up** (*col*) faire la fête; mener la grande vie.
►**live up to** *vt fus* se montrer à la hauteur de.
live-in ['lɪvɪn] *adj* (*nanny*) à demeure; ~ **partner** concubin/e.
livelihood ['laɪvlɪhud] *n* moyens *mpl* d'existence.
liveliness ['laɪvlɪnəs] *n* vivacité *f*, entrain *m*.
lively ['laɪvlɪ] *adj* vif(vive), plein(e) d'entrain.

liven up ['laɪvn-] *vt* (*room etc*) égayer; (*discussion, evening*) animer.
liver ['lɪvə*] *n* foie *m*.
liverish ['lɪvərɪʃ] *adj* qui a mal au foie; (*fig*) grincheux(euse).
Liverpudlian [lɪvə'pʌdlɪən] *adj* de Liverpool ◆ *n* habitant/e de Liverpool; natif/ive de Liverpool.
livery ['lɪvərɪ] *n* livrée *f*.
lives [laɪvz] *npl of* **life**.
livestock ['laɪvstɒk] *n* cheptel *m*, bétail *m*.
live wire [laɪv-] *n* (*col, fig*): **to be a (real) ~** péter le feu.
livid ['lɪvɪd] *adj* livide, blafard(e); (*furious*) furieux(euse), furibond(e).
living ['lɪvɪŋ] *adj* vivant(e), en vie ◆ *n*: **to earn** *or* **make a ~** gagner sa vie; **cost of ~** coût *m* de la vie; **within ~ memory** de mémoire d'homme.
living conditions *npl* conditions *fpl* de vie.
living expenses *npl* dépenses courantes.
living room *n* salle *f* de séjour.
living wage *n* salaire *m* permettant de vivre (décemment).
lizard ['lɪzəd] *n* lézard *m*.
llama ['lɑːmə] *n* lama *m*.
LLB *n abbr* (= *Bachelor of Laws*) titre universitaire.
LLD *n abbr* (= *Doctor of Laws*) titre universitaire.
LMT *abbr* (*US*: = *Local Mean Time*) heure locale.
load [ləud] *n* (*weight*) poids *m*; (*thing carried*) chargement *m*, charge *f*; (*ELEC, TECH*) charge ◆ *vt* (*lorry, ship*): **to ~ (with)** charger (de); (*gun, camera*): **to ~ (with)** charger (avec); (*COMPUT*) charger; **a ~ of,** ~**s of** (*fig*) un *or* des tas de, des masses de.
loaded ['ləudɪd] *adj* (*dice*) pipé(e); (*question*) insidieux(euse); (*col: rich*) bourré(e) de fric; (*: drunk*) bourré(e).
loading bay ['ləudɪŋ-] *n* aire *f* de chargement.
loaf, loaves [ləuf, ləuvz] *n* pain *m*, miche *f* ◆ *vi* (*also:* ~ **about,** ~ **around**) fainéanter, traîner.
loam [ləum] *n* terreau *m*.
loan [ləun] *n* prêt *m* ◆ *vt* prêter; **on ~** prêté(e), en prêt; **public ~** emprunt public.
loan account *n* compte *m* de prêt.
loan capital *n* capital-obligations *m*.
loan shark *n* (*col, pej*) usurier *m*.
loath [ləuθ] *adj*: **to be ~ to do** répugner à faire.
loathe [ləuð] *vt* détester, avoir en horreur.
loathing ['ləuðɪŋ] *n* dégoût *m*, répugnance *f*.
loathsome ['ləuðsəm] *adj* répugnant(e), détestable.
loaves [ləuvz] *npl of* **loaf**.
lob [lɒb] *vt* (*ball*) lober.
lobby ['lɒbɪ] *n* hall *m*, entrée *f*; (*POL*) groupe *m* de pression, lobby *m* ◆ *vt* faire pression sur.
lobbyist ['lɒbɪɪst] *n* membre *m/f* d'un groupe de pression.

lobe [ləub] n lobe m.
lobster ['lɔbstə*] n homard m.
lobster pot n casier m à homards.
local ['ləukl] adj local(e) ♦ n (BRIT: pub) pub m or café m du coin; **the ~s** npl les gens mpl du pays or du coin.
local anaesthetic n anesthésie locale.
local authority n collectivité locale, municipalité f.
local call n (TEL) communication urbaine.
local government n administration locale or municipale.
locality [ləu'kælɪtɪ] n région f, environs mpl; (position) lieu m.
localize ['ləukəlaɪz] vt localiser.
locally ['ləukəlɪ] adv localement; dans les environs or la région.
locate [ləu'keɪt] vt (find) trouver, repérer; (situate) situer.
location [ləu'keɪʃən] n emplacement m; **on ~** (CINE) en extérieur.
loch [lɔx] n lac m, loch m.
lock [lɔk] n (of door, box) serrure f; (of canal) écluse f; (of hair) mèche f, boucle f ♦ vt (with key) fermer à clé; (immobilize) bloquer ♦ vi (door etc) fermer à clé; (wheels) se bloquer; **~ stock and barrel** (fig) en bloc; **on full ~** (BRIT AUT) le volant tourné à fond.
▶**lock away** vt (valuables) mettre sous clé; (criminal) mettre sous les verrous, enfermer.
▶**lock out** vt enfermer dehors; (on purpose) mettre à la porte; (: workers) lock-outer.
▶**lock up** vi tout fermer (à clé).
locker ['lɔkə*] n casier m.
locket ['lɔkɪt] n médaillon m.
lockjaw ['lɔkdʒɔ:] n tétanos m.
lockout ['lɔkaut] n (INDUSTRY) lock-out m, grève patronale.
locksmith ['lɔksmɪθ] n serrurier m.
lock-up ['lɔkʌp] n (prison) prison f; (cell) cellule f provisoire; (also: ~ **garage**) box m.
locomotive [ləukə'məutɪv] n locomotive f.
locum ['ləukəm] n (MED) suppléant/e (de médecin).
locust ['ləukəst] n locuste f, sauterelle f.
lodge [lɔdʒ] n pavillon m (de gardien); (FREEMASONRY) loge f ♦ vi (person): **to ~ with** être logé(e) chez, être en pension chez ♦ vt (appeal etc) présenter; déposer; **to ~ a complaint** porter plainte; **to ~ (itself) in/ between** se loger dans/entre.
lodger ['lɔdʒə*] n locataire m/f; (with room and meals) pensionnaire m/f.
lodging ['lɔdʒɪŋ] n logement m; see also **board**.
lodging house n (BRIT) pension f de famille.
lodgings ['lɔdʒɪŋz] npl chambre f, meublé m.
loft [lɔft] n grenier m; (US) grenier aménagé (en appartement) (gén dans ancien entrepôt ou fabrique).
lofty ['lɔftɪ] adj élevé(e); (haughty) hautain(e); (sentiments, aims) noble.

log [lɔg] n (of wood) bûche f; (book) = **logbook** ♦ n abbr (= logarithm) log m ♦ vt enregistrer.
▶**log in, log on** vi (COMPUT) ouvrir une session, entrer dans le système.
▶**log off, log out** vi (COMPUT) clore une session, sortir du système.
logarithm ['lɔgərɪðm] n logarithme m.
logbook ['lɔgbuk] n (NAUT) livre m or journal m de bord; (AVIAT) carnet m de vol; (of lorry driver) carnet de route; (of events, movement of goods etc) registre m; (of car) ≈ carte grise.
log cabin n cabane f en rondins.
log fire n feu m de bois.
logger ['lɔgə*] n bûcheron m.
loggerheads ['lɔgəhɛdz] npl: **at ~ (with)** à couteaux tirés (avec).
logic ['lɔdʒɪk] n logique f.
logical ['lɔdʒɪkl] adj logique.
logically ['lɔdʒɪkəlɪ] adv logiquement.
logistics [lɔ'dʒɪstɪks] n logistique f.
logjam ['lɔgdʒæm] n: **to break the ~** créer une ouverture dans l'impasse.
logo ['ləugəu] n logo m.
loin [lɔɪn] n (CULIN) filet m, longe f; **~s** npl reins mpl.
loin cloth n pagne m.
loiter ['lɔɪtə*] vi s'attarder; **to ~ (about)** traîner, musarder; (pej) rôder.
loll [lɔl] vi (also: ~ **about**) se prélasser, fainéanter.
lollipop ['lɔlɪpɔp] n sucette f.

Les **lollipop men/ladies** sont employés pour aider les enfants à traverser la rue à proximité des écoles à l'heure où ils entrent en classe et à la sortie. On les repère facilement à cause de leur long ciré blanc et ils portent une pancarte ronde pour faire signe aux automobilistes de s'arrêter. On les appelle ainsi car la forme circulaire de cette pancarte rappelle une sucette.

---

lollop ['lɔləp] vi (BRIT) avancer (or courir) maladroitement.
lolly ['lɔlɪ] n (col: ice) esquimau m; (: lollipop) sucette f; (: money) fric m.
Lombardy ['lɔmbədɪ] n Lombardie f.
London ['lʌndən] n Londres.
Londoner ['lʌndənə*] n Londonien/ne.
lone [ləun] adj solitaire.
loneliness ['ləunlɪnɪs] n solitude f, isolement m.
lonely ['ləunlɪ] adj seul(e); (childhood etc) solitaire; (place) solitaire, isolé(e); **to feel ~** se sentir seul.
lonely hearts adj: **~ ad** petite annonce (personnelle); **~ club** club m de rencontres (pour personnes seules).
lone parent n parent m unique.
loner ['ləunə*] n solitaire m/f.
lonesome ['ləunsəm] adj seul(e); solitaire.
long [lɔŋ] adj long(longue) ♦ adv longtemps

♦ n: the ~ and the short of it is that ... (fig) le fin mot de l'histoire c'est que ... ♦ vi: to ~ for sth/to do avoir très envie de qch/de faire; attendre qch avec impatience/impatience de faire; **he had ~ understood that ...** il avait compris depuis longtemps que ...; **how ~ is this river/course?** quelle est la longueur de ce fleuve/la durée de ce cours?; **6 metres ~** (long) de 6 mètres; **6 months ~** qui dure 6 mois, de 6 mois; **all night ~** toute la nuit; **he no ~er comes** il ne vient plus; **~ before** longtemps avant; **before ~** (+ future) avant peu, dans peu de temps; (+ past) peu de temps après; **~ ago** il y a longtemps; **don't be ~!** fais vite!, dépêche-toi!; **I shan't be ~** je n'en ai pas pour longtemps; **at ~ last** enfin; **in the ~ run** à la longue; finalement; **so** or **as ~ as** pourvu que.

long-distance [lɔŋ'dɪstəns] adj (race) de fond; (call) interurbain(e).

long-haired ['lɔŋ'hɛəd] adj (person) aux cheveux longs; (animal) aux longs poils.

longhand ['lɔŋhænd] n écriture normale or courante.

longing ['lɔŋɪŋ] n désir m, envie f, nostalgie f ♦ adj plein(e) d'envie or de nostalgie.

longingly ['lɔŋɪŋlɪ] adv avec désir or nostalgie.

longitude ['lɔŋgɪtjuːd] n longitude f.

long johns [-dʒɔnz] npl caleçons longs.

long jump n saut m en longueur.

long-lost ['lɔŋlɔst] adj perdu(e) depuis longtemps.

long-playing ['lɔŋpleɪɪŋ] adj: ~ **record (LP)** (disque m) 33 tours m inv.

long-range ['lɔŋ'reɪndʒ] adj à longue portée; (weather forecast) à long terme.

longshoreman ['lɔŋʃɔːmən] n (US) docker m, débardeur m.

long-sighted ['lɔŋ'saɪtɪd] adj (BRIT) presbyte; (fig) prévoyant(e).

long-standing ['lɔŋ'stændɪŋ] adj de longue date.

long-suffering [lɔŋ'sʌfərɪŋ] adj empreint(e) d'une patience résignée; extrêmement patient(e).

long-term ['lɔŋtəːm] adj à long terme.

long wave n (RADIO) grandes ondes, ondes longues.

long-winded [lɔŋ'wɪndɪd] adj intarissable, interminable.

loo [luː] n (BRIT col) w.-c. mpl, petit coin.

loofah ['luːfə] n sorte d'éponge végétale.

look [luk] vi regarder; (seem) sembler, paraître, avoir l'air; (building etc) to ~ **south/on to the sea** donner au sud/sur la mer ♦ n regard m; (appearance) air m, allure f, aspect m; ~**s** npl physique m, beauté f; **to ~ like** ressembler à; **it ~s like him** on dirait que c'est lui; **it ~s about 4 metres long** je dirais que ça fait 4 mètres de long, à vue de nez, ça fait 4 mètres de long; **it ~s all right**

to me ça me paraît bien; **to have a ~ at sth** jeter un coup d'œil à qch; **to have a ~ for sth** chercher qch; **to ~ ahead** regarder devant soi; (fig) envisager l'avenir.

►**look after** vt fus s'occuper de, prendre soin de; (luggage etc: watch over) garder, surveiller.

►**look around** vi regarder autour de soi.

►**look at** vt fus regarder.

►**look back** vi: to ~ **back at sth/sb** se retourner pour regarder qch/qn; **to look back on** (event, period) évoquer, repenser à.

►**look down on** vt fus (fig) regarder de haut, dédaigner.

►**look for** vt fus chercher.

►**look forward to** vt fus attendre avec impatience; **I'm not ~ing forward to it** cette perspective ne me réjouit guère; **~ing forward to hearing from you** (in letter) dans l'attente de vous lire.

►**look in** vi: to ~ **in on sb** passer voir qn.

►**look into** vt fus (matter, possibility) examiner, étudier.

►**look on** vi regarder (en spectateur).

►**look out** vi (beware): to ~ **out (for)** prendre garde (à), faire attention (à).

►**look out for** vt fus être à la recherche de; guetter.

►**look over** vt (essay) jeter un coup d'œil à; (town, building) visiter (rapidement); (person) jeter un coup d'œil à; examiner de la tête aux pieds.

►**look round** vi (turn) regarder derrière soi, se retourner; **to ~ round for sth** chercher qch.

►**look through** vt fus (papers, book) examiner; (: briefly) parcourir; (telescope) regarder à travers.

►**look to** vt fus veiller à; (rely on) compter sur.

►**look up** vi lever les yeux; (improve) s'améliorer ♦ vt (word) chercher; (friend) passer voir.

►**look up to** vt fus avoir du respect pour.

look-out ['lukaut] n poste m de guet; guetteur m; **to be on the ~ (for)** guetter.

look-up table ['lukʌp-] n (COMPUT) table f à consulter.

LOOM n abbr (US: = Loyal Order of Moose) association charitable.

loom [luːm] n métier m à tisser ♦ vi surgir; (fig) menacer, paraître imminent(e).

loony ['luːnɪ] adj, n (col) timbré(e), cinglé(e) (m/f).

loop [luːp] n boucle f; (contraceptive) stérilet m.

loophole ['luːphəul] n porte f de sortie (fig); échappatoire f.

loose [luːs] adj (knot, screw) desserré(e); (stone) branlant(e); (clothes) vague, ample, lâche; (animal) en liberté, échappé(e); (life) dissolu(e); (morals, discipline) relâché(e); (thinking) peu rigoureux(euse), vague; (translation) approximatif(ive) ♦ vt (free:

animal) lâcher; (: *prisoner*) relâcher, libérer; (*slacken*) détendre, relâcher; desserrer; défaire; donner du mou a; donner du ballant à; (*BRIT: arrow*) tirer; ~ **connection** (*ELEC*) mauvais contact; **to be at a ~ end** *or* (*US*) **at ~ ends** (*fig*) ne pas trop savoir quoi faire; **to tie up ~ ends** (*fig*) mettre au point *or* régler les derniers détails.

loose change *n* petite monnaie.

loose-fitting ['luːsfɪtɪŋ] *adj* (*clothes*) ample.

loose-leaf ['luːsliːf] *adj*: ~ **binder** *or* **folder** classeur *m* à feuilles *or* feuillets mobiles.

loose-limbed [luːs'lɪmd] *adj* agile, souple.

loosely ['luːslɪ] *adv* sans serrer; approximativement.

loosely-knit ['luːslɪ'nɪt] *adj* élastique.

loosen ['luːsn] *vt* desserrer, relâcher, défaire.

▶**loosen up** *vi* (*before game*) s'échauffer; (*col: relax*) se détendre, se laisser aller.

loot [luːt] *n* butin *m* ♦ *vt* piller.

looter ['luːtə*] *n* pillard *m*, casseur *m*.

looting ['luːtɪŋ] *n* pillage *m*.

lop [lɔp]: **to ~ off** *vt* couper, trancher.

lop-sided ['lɔp'saɪdɪd] *adj* de travers, asymétrique.

lord [lɔːd] *n* seigneur *m*; **L~ Smith** lord Smith; **the L~** (*REL*) le Seigneur; **the (House of) L~s** (*BRIT*) la Chambre des Lords.

lordly ['lɔːdlɪ] *adj* noble, majestueux(euse); (*arrogant*) hautain(e).

lordship ['lɔːdʃɪp] *n* (*BRIT*): **your L~** Monsieur le comte (*or* le baron *or* le Juge).

lore [lɔː*] *n* tradition(s) *f(pl)*.

lorry ['lɔrɪ] *n* (*BRIT*) camion *m*.

lorry driver *n* (*BRIT*) camionneur *m*, routier *m*.

lose, *pt, pp* **lost** [luːz, lɔst] *vt* perdre; (*opportunity*) manquer, perdre; (*pursuers*) distancer, semer ♦ *vi* perdre; **to ~** (*time*) (*clock*) retarder; **to ~ no time (in doing sth)** ne pas perdre de temps (à faire qch); **to get lost** *vi* (*person*) se perdre; **my watch has got lost** ma montre est perdue.

loser ['luːzə*] *n* perdant/e; **to be a good/bad ~** être beau/mauvais joueur.

loss [lɔs] *n* perte *f*; **to cut one's ~es** limiter les dégâts; **to make a ~** enregistrer une perte; **to sell sth at a ~** vendre qch à perte; **to be at a ~** être perplexe *or* embarrassé(e); **to be at a ~ to do** se trouver incapable de faire.

loss adjuster *n* (*INSURANCE*) responsable *m/f* de l'évaluation des dommages.

loss leader *n* (*COMM*) article sacrifié.

lost [lɔst] *pt, pp of* **lose** ♦ *adj* perdu(e); ~ **in thought** perdu dans ses pensées; ~ **and found property** *n* (*US*) objets trouvés; ~ **and found** *n* (*US*) (bureau *m* des) objets trouvés.

lost property *n* (*BRIT*) objets trouvés; ~ **office** *or* **department** (bureau *m* des) objets trouvés.

lot [lɔt] *n* (*at auctions*) lot *m*; (*destiny*) sort *m*, destinée *f*; **the ~** le tout; tous *mpl*, toutes *fpl*;

a ~ beaucoup; **a ~ of** beaucoup de; ~**s of** des tas de; **to draw ~s (for sth)** tirer (qch) au sort.

lotion ['ləʊʃən] *n* lotion *f*.

lottery ['lɔtərɪ] *n* loterie *f*.

loud [laʊd] *adj* bruyant(e), sonore, fort(e); (*gaudy*) voyant(e), tapageur(euse) ♦ *adv* (*speak etc*) fort; **out ~** tout haut.

loudhailer [laʊd'heɪlə*] *n* (*BRIT*) porte-voix *m inv*.

loudly ['laʊdlɪ] *adv* fort, bruyamment.

loudspeaker [laʊd'spiːkə*] *n* haut-parleur *m*.

lounge [laʊndʒ] *n* salon *m*; (*of airport*) salle *f* ♦ *vi* se prélasser, paresser.

lounge bar *n* (salle *f* de) bar *m*.

lounge suit *n* (*BRIT*) complet *m*; (: *on invitation*) "tenue de ville".

louse, *pl* **lice** [laʊs, laɪs] *n* pou *m*.

▶**louse up** *vt* (*col*) gâcher.

lousy ['laʊzɪ] *adj* (*fig*) infect(e), moche.

lout [laʊt] *n* rustre *m*, butor *m*.

louvre, (*US*) **louver** ['luːvə*] *adj* (*door, window*) à claire-voie.

lovable ['lʌvəbl] *adj* très sympathique; adorable.

love [lʌv] *n* amour *m* ♦ *vt* aimer; aimer beaucoup; **to ~ to do** aimer beaucoup *or* adorer faire; **I'd ~ to come** cela me ferait très plaisir (de venir); **"15 ~"** (*TENNIS*) "15 à rien *or* zéro"; **to be/fall in ~ with** être/tomber amoureux(euse) de; **to make ~** faire l'amour; ~ **at first sight** le coup de foudre; **to send one's ~ to sb** adresser ses amitiés à qn; ~ **from Anne, ~, Anne** affectueusement, Anne.

love affair *n* liaison (amoureuse).

love child *n* enfant *m/f* illégitime *or* naturel(le).

loved ones ['lʌvdwʌnz] *npl* proches *mpl* et amis chers.

love-hate relationship [lʌv'heɪt-] *n* rapport ambigu; **they have a ~** ils s'aiment et se détestent à la fois.

love letter *n* lettre *f* d'amour.

love life *n* vie sentimentale.

lovely ['lʌvlɪ] *adj* (*pretty: girl, house, garden*) ravissant(e); (*friend, wife*) charmant(e); (*holiday, surprise*) très agréable, merveilleux(euse); **we had a ~ time** c'était vraiment très bien, nous avons eu beaucoup de plaisir.

lover ['lʌvə*] *n* amant *m*; (*amateur*): **a ~ of** un(e) ami(e) de, un(e) amoureux(euse) de.

lovesick ['lʌvsɪk] *adj* qui se languit d'amour.

lovesong ['lʌvsɒŋ] *n* chanson *f* d'amour.

loving ['lʌvɪŋ] *adj* affectueux(euse), tendre, aimant(e).

low [ləʊ] *adj* bas(basse) ♦ *adv* bas ♦ *n* (*METEOROLOGY*) dépression *f* ♦ *vi* (*cow*) mugir; **to feel ~** se sentir déprimé(e); **he's very ~** (*ill*) il est bien bas *or* très affaibli; **to turn (down) ~** *vt* baisser; **to reach a new** *or*

an all-time ~ tomber au niveau le plus bas.
low-alcohol [ləʊˈælkəhɒl] *adj* à faible teneur en alcool, peu alcoolisé(e).
lowbrow [ˈləʊbraʊ] *adj* sans prétentions intellectuelles.
low-calorie [ˈləʊˈkælərɪ] *adj* hypocalorique.
low-cut [ˈləʊkʌt] *adj* (*dress*) décolleté(e).
low-down [ˈləʊdaʊn] *n* (*col*): **he gave me the ~ (on it)** il m'a mis au courant ♦ *adj* (*mean*) méprisable.
lower [ˈləʊə*] *adj, adv comparative of* **low** ♦ *vt* baisser; (*resistance*) diminuer ♦ *vi* [ˈlaʊə*] (*person*): **to ~ at sb** jeter un regard mauvais *or* noir à qn; (*sky, clouds*) être menaçant.
low-fat [ˈləʊˈfæt] *adj* maigre.
low-key [ˈləʊˈkiː] *adj* modéré(e); discret(ète).
lowland [ˈləʊlənd] *n* plaine *f*.
low-level [ˈləʊlɛvl] *adj* bas(basse); (*flying*) à basse altitude.
low-loader [ˈləʊləʊdə*] *n* semi-remorque *f* à plate-forme surbaissée.
lowly [ˈləʊlɪ] *adj* humble, modeste.
low-lying [ˈləʊˈlaɪɪŋ] *adj* à faible altitude.
low-paid [ˈləʊˈpeɪd] *adj* mal payé(e), aux salaires bas.
low-rise [ˈləʊraɪz] *adj* bas(se), de faible hauteur.
low-tech [ˈləʊtɛk] *adj* sommaire.
loyal [ˈlɔɪəl] *adj* loyal(e), fidèle.
loyalist [ˈlɔɪəlɪst] *n* loyaliste *m/f*.
loyalty [ˈlɔɪəltɪ] *n* loyauté *f*, fidélité *f*.
lozenge [ˈlɒzɪndʒ] *n* (*MED*) pastille *f*; (*GEOM*) losange *m*.
LP *n abbr* = **long-playing record**.
L-plates [ˈɛlpleɪts] *npl* (*BRIT*) plaques *fpl* (obligatoires) d'apprenti conducteur.

*Les **L-plates** sont des carrés blancs portant un "L" rouge que l'on met à l'avant et à l'arrière de sa voiture pour montrer qu'on n'a pas encore son permis de conduire. Jusqu'à l'obtention du permis, l'apprenti conducteur a un permis provisoire et n'a le droit de conduire que si un conducteur qualifié est assis à côté de lui. Il est interdit aux apprentis conducteurs de circuler sur les autoroutes, même s'ils sont accompagnés.*

lubricant [ˈluːbrɪkənt] *n* lubrifiant *m*.
lubricate [ˈluːbrɪkeɪt] *vt* lubrifier, graisser.

lucid [ˈluːsɪd] *adj* lucide.
lucidity [luːˈsɪdɪtɪ] *n* lucidité *f*.
luck [lʌk] *n* chance *f*; **bad ~** malchance *f*, malheur *m*; **to be in ~** avoir de la chance; t**c be out of ~** ne pas avoir de chance; **good ~** bonne chance!
luckily [ˈlʌkɪlɪ] *adv* heureusement, par bonheur.
luckless [ˈlʌklɪs] *adj* (*person*) malchanceux(euse); (*trip*) marqué(e) par la malchance.
lucky [ˈlʌkɪ] *adj* (*person*) qui a de la chance; (*coincidence*) heureux(euse); (*number etc*) qui porte bonheur.
lucrative [ˈluːkrətɪv] *adj* lucratif(ive), rentable, qui rapporte.
ludicrous [ˈluːdɪkrəs] *adj* ridicule, absurde.
ludo [ˈluːdəʊ] *n* jeu *m* des petits chevaux.
lug [lʌg] *vt* traîner, tirer.
luggage [ˈlʌgɪdʒ] *n* bagages *mpl*.
luggage lockers *npl* consigne *f* automatique.
luggage rack *n* (*in train*) porte-bagages *m inv*; (: *made of string*) filet *m* à bagages; (*on car*) galerie *f*.
luggage van, (*US*) **luggage car** *n* (*RAIL*) fourgon *m* (à bagages).
lugubrious [luˈguːbrɪəs] *adj* lugubre.
lukewarm [ˈluːkwɔːm] *adj* tiède.
lull [lʌl] *n* accalmie *f* ♦ *vt* (*child*) bercer; (*person, fear*) apaiser, calmer.
lullaby [ˈlʌləbaɪ] *n* berceuse *f*.
lumbago [lʌmˈbeɪgəʊ] *n* lumbago *m*.
lumber [ˈlʌmbə*] *n* bric-à-brac *m inv* ♦ *vt* (*BRIT col*): **to ~ sb with sth/sb** coller *or* refiler qch/qn à qn ♦ *vi* (*also:* ~ **about**, ~ **along**) marcher pesamment.
lumberjack [ˈlʌmbədʒæk] *n* bûcheron *m*.
lumber room *n* (*BRIT*) débarras *m*.
lumber yard *n* entrepôt *m* de bois.
luminous [ˈluːmɪnəs] *adj* lumineux(euse).
lump [lʌmp] *n* morceau *m*; (*in sauce*) grumeau *m*; (*swelling*) grosseur *f* ♦ *vt* (*also:* ~ **together**) réunir, mettre en tas.
lump sum *n* somme globale *or* forfaitaire.
lumpy [ˈlʌmpɪ] *adj* (*sauce*) qui a des grumeaux.
lunacy [ˈluːnəsɪ] *n* démence *f*, folie *f*.
lunar [ˈluːnə*] *adj* lunaire.
lunatic [ˈluːnətɪk] *n* fou/folle, dément/e ♦ *adj* fou(folle), dément(e).
lunatic asylum *n* asile *m* d'aliénés.
lunch [lʌntʃ] *n* déjeuner *m* ♦ *vi* déjeuner; **it is his ~ hour** c'est l'heure où il déjeune; **to invite sb to** *or* **for ~** inviter qn à déjeuner.
luncheon [ˈlʌntʃən] *n* déjeuner *m*.
luncheon meat *n* sorte de saucisson.
luncheon voucher *n* chèque-repas *m*, ticket-repas *m*.
lunchtime [ˈlʌntʃtaɪm] *n* l'heure *f* du déjeuner.
lung [lʌŋ] *n* poumon *m*.
lung cancer *n* cancer *m* du poumon.

lunge [lʌndʒ] *vi* (*also*: ~ **forward**) faire un mouvement brusque en avant; **to ~ at sb** envoyer *or* assener un coup à qn.

lupin ['luːpɪn] *n* lupin *m*.

lurch [ləːtʃ] *vi* vaciller, tituber ♦ *n* écart *m* brusque, embardée *f*; **to leave sb in the ~** laisser qn se débrouiller *or* se dépêtrer tout(e) seul(e).

lure [luə*] *n* appât *m*, leurre *m* ♦ *vt* attirer *or* persuader par la ruse.

lurid ['luərɪd] *adj* affreux(euse), atroce.

lurk [ləːk] *vi* se tapir, se cacher.

luscious ['lʌʃəs] *adj* succulent(e); appétissant(e).

lush [lʌʃ] *adj* luxuriant(e).

lust [lʌst] *n* luxure *f*; lubricité *f*; désir *m*; (*fig*): ~ **for** soif *f* de.

▶**lust after** *vt fus* convoiter, désirer.

luster ['lʌstə*] *n* (*US*) = **lustre**.

lustful ['lʌstful] *adj* lascif(ive).

lustre, (*US*) **luster** ['lʌstə*] *n* lustre *m*, brillant *m*.

lusty ['lʌstɪ] *adj* vigoureux(euse), robuste.

lute [luːt] *n* luth *m*.

Luxembourg ['lʌksəmbəːg] *n* Luxembourg *m*.

luxuriant [lʌgˈzjuərɪənt] *adj* luxuriant(e).

luxurious [lʌgˈzjuərɪəs] *adj* luxueux(euse).

luxury ['lʌkʃərɪ] *n* luxe *m* ♦ *cpd* de luxe.

LV *n abbr* (*BRIT*) = **luncheon voucher**.

LW *abbr* (*RADIO*: = *long wave*) GO.

Lycra ['laɪkrə] *n* ® Lycra *m* ®.

lying ['laɪɪŋ] *n* mensonge(s) *m(pl)* ♦ *adj* (*statement, story*) mensonger(ère), faux(fausse); (*person*) menteur(euse).

lynch [lɪntʃ] *vt* lyncher.

lynx [lɪŋks] *n* lynx *m inv*.

Lyons ['laɪənz] *n* Lyon *m*.

lyre ['laɪə*] *n* lyre *f*.

lyric ['lɪrɪk] *adj* lyrique; ~**s** *npl* (*of song*) paroles *fpl*.

lyrical ['lɪrɪkl] *adj* lyrique.

lyricism ['lɪrɪsɪzəm] *n* lyrisme *m*.

M m

M, m [ɛm] *n* (*letter*) M, m *m*; **M for Mary**, (*US*) **M for Mike** M comme Marcel.

M *n abbr* (*BRIT*: = *motorway*): **the M8** ≈ l'A8 ♦ *abbr* (= *medium*) M.

m *abbr* (= *metre*) m; (= *million*) M; (= *mile*) mi.

MA *n abbr* (*SCOL*) = **Master of Arts** ♦ *abbr* (*US*) = *military academy*; (*US*) = *Massachusetts*.

mac [mæk] *n* (*BRIT*) imper(méable *m*) *m*.

macabre [məˈkɑːbrə] *adj* macabre.

macaroni [mækəˈrəʊnɪ] *n* macaronis *mpl*.

macaroon [mækəˈruːn] *n* macaron *m*.

mace [meɪs] *n* masse *f*; (*spice*) macis *m*.

Macedonia [mæsɪˈdəʊnɪə] *n* Macédoine *f*.

Macedonian [mæsɪˈdəʊnɪən] *adj* macédonien(ne) ♦ *n* Macédonien/ne; (*LING*) macédonien *m*.

machinations [mækɪˈneɪʃənz] *npl* machinations *fpl*, intrigues *fpl*.

machine [məˈʃiːn] *n* machine *f* ♦ *vt* (*dress etc*) coudre à la machine; (*TECH*) usiner.

machine code *n* (*COMPUT*) code *m* machine.

machine gun *n* mitrailleuse *f*.

machine language *n* (*COMPUT*) langage *m* machine.

machine-readable [məˈʃiːnriːdəbl] *adj* (*COMPUT*) exploitable par une machine.

machinery [məˈʃiːnərɪ] *n* machinerie *f*, machines *fpl*; (*fig*) mécanisme(s) *m(pl)*.

machine shop *n* atelier *m* d'usinage.

machine tool *n* machine-outil *f*.

machine washable *adj* (*garment*) lavable en machine.

machinist [məˈʃiːnɪst] *n* machiniste *m/f*.

macho ['mætʃəʊ] *adj* macho *inv*.

mackerel ['mækrl] *n* (*pl inv*) maquereau *m*.

mackintosh ['mækɪntɒʃ] *n* (*BRIT*) imperméable *m*.

macro... ['mækrəʊ] *prefix* macro....

macro-economics ['mækrəʊiːkəˈnɒmɪks] *n* macro-économie *f*.

mad [mæd] *adj* fou(folle); (*foolish*) insensé(e); (*angry*) furieux(euse); **to go ~** devenir fou; **to be ~ (keen) about** *or* **on sth** (*col*) être follement passionné de qch, être fou de qch.

madam ['mædəm] *n* madame *f*; **yes ~** oui Madame; **M~ Chairman** Madame la Présidente.

madcap ['mædkæp] *adj* (*col*) écervelé(e).

mad cow disease *n* maladie *f* des vaches folles.

madden ['mædn] *vt* exaspérer.

maddening ['mædnɪŋ] *adj* exaspérant(e).

made [meɪd] *pt, pp of* **make**.

Madeira [məˈdɪərə] *n* (*GEO*) Madère *f*; (*wine*) madère *m*.

made-to-measure ['meɪdtəˈmɛʒə*] *adj* (*BRIT*) fait(e) sur mesure.

madhouse ['mædhaʊs] *n* (*also fig*) maison *f* de fous.

madly ['mædlɪ] *adv* follement.

madman ['mædmən] *n* fou *m*, aliéné *m*.

madness ['mædnɪs] *n* folie *f*.

Madrid [məˈdrɪd] *n* Madrid.

Mafia ['mæfɪə] *n* maf(f)ia *f*.

mag. [mæg] *n abbr* (*BRIT col*) = **magazine** (*PRESS*).

magazine [mægəˈziːn] *n* (*PRESS*) magazine *m*, revue *f*; (*MIL*: *store*) dépôt *m*, arsenal *m*; (*of firearm*) magasin *m*.

maggot ['mægət] *n* ver *m*, asticot *m*.

magic ['mædʒɪk] *n* magie *f* ♦ *adj* magique.

magical ['mædʒɪkl] *adj* magique.
magician [mə'dʒɪʃən] *n* magicien/ne.
magistrate ['mædʒɪstreɪt] *n* magistrat *m*; juge *m*; ~**s' court** (*BRIT*) ≈ tribunal *m* d'instance.
magnanimous [mæg'nænɪməs] *adj* magnanime.
magnate ['mægneɪt] *n* magnat *m*.
magnesium [mæg'ni:zɪəm] *n* magnésium *m*.
magnet ['mægnɪt] *n* aimant *m*.
magnetic [mæg'nɛtɪk] *adj* magnétique.
magnetic disk *n* (*COMPUT*) disque *m* magnétique.
magnetic tape *n* bande *f* magnétique.
magnetism ['mægnɪtɪzəm] *n* magnétisme *m*.
magnification [mægnɪfɪ'keɪʃən] *n* grossissement *m*.
magnificence [mæg'nɪfɪsns] *n* magnificence *f*.
magnificent [mæg'nɪfɪsnt] *adj* superbe, magnifique.
magnify ['mægnɪfaɪ] *vt* grossir; (*sound*) amplifier.
magnifying glass ['mægnɪfaɪɪŋ-] *n* loupe *f*.
magnitude ['mægnɪtjuːd] *n* ampleur *f*.
magnolia [mæg'nəʊlɪə] *n* magnolia *m*.
magpie ['mægpaɪ] *n* pie *f*.
mahogany [mə'hɔgənɪ] *n* acajou *m* ♦ *cpd* en (bois d')acajou.
maid [meɪd] *n* bonne *f*; **old** ~ (*pej*) vieille fille.
maiden ['meɪdn] *n* jeune fille *f* ♦ *adj* (*aunt etc*) non mariée; (*speech, voyage*) inaugural(e).
maiden name *n* nom *m* de jeune fille.
mail [meɪl] *n* poste *f*; (*letters*) courrier *m* ♦ *vt* envoyer (par la poste); **by** ~ par la poste.
mailbag ['meɪlbæg] *n* (*US*) sac postal; (*postman's*) sacoche *f*.
mailbox ['meɪlbɔks] *n* (*US: for letters etc*, *COMPUT*) boîte *f* aux lettres.
mailing list ['meɪlɪŋ-] *n* liste *f* d'adresses.
mailman ['meɪlmæn] *n* (*US*) facteur *m*.
mail-order ['meɪlɔːdə*] *n* vente *f* or achat *m* par correspondance ♦ *cpd*: ~ **firm** or **house** maison *f* de vente par correspondance.
mailshot ['meɪlʃɔt] *n* (*BRIT*) mailing *m*.
mail train *n* train postal.
mail truck *n* (*US AUT*) = **mail van**.
mail van *n* (*BRIT: AUT*) voiture *f* or fourgonnette *f* des postes; (*: RAIL*) wagon-poste *m*.
maim [meɪm] *vt* mutiler.
main [meɪn] *adj* principal(e) ♦ *n* (*pipe*) conduite principale, canalisation *f*; **the** ~**s** (*ELEC*) le secteur; **in the** ~ dans l'ensemble.
main course *n* (*CULIN*) plat *m* de résistance.
mainframe ['meɪnfreɪm] *n* (*also*: ~ **computer**) (gros) ordinateur, unité centrale.
mainland ['meɪnlənd] *n* continent *m*.
mainline ['meɪnlaɪn] *adj* (*RAIL*) de grande ligne ♦ *vb* (*drugs slang*) *vt* se shooter à ♦ *vi* se shooter.
main line *n* (*RAIL*) grande ligne.
mainly ['meɪnlɪ] *adv* principalement, surtout.
main road *n* grand axe, route nationale.

mainstay ['meɪnsteɪ] *n* (*fig*) pilier *m*.
mainstream ['meɪnstriːm] *n* (*fig*) courant principal.
maintain [meɪn'teɪn] *vt* entretenir; (*continue*) maintenir, préserver; (*affirm*) soutenir; **to** ~ **that ...** soutenir que ....
maintenance ['meɪntənəns] *n* entretien *m*; (*LAW: alimony*) pension *f* alimentaire.
maintenance contract *n* contrat *m* d'entretien.
maintenance order *n* (*LAW*) obligation *f* alimentaire.
maisonette [meɪzə'nɛt] *n* (*BRIT*) appartement *m* en duplex.
maize [meɪz] *n* maïs *m*.
Maj. *abbr* (*MIL*) = **major**.
majestic [mə'dʒɛstɪk] *adj* majestueux(euse).
majesty ['mædʒɪstɪ] *n* majesté *f*.
major ['meɪdʒə*] *n* (*MIL*) commandant *m* ♦ *adj* important(e), principal(e); (*MUS*) majeur(e) ♦ *vi* (*US SCOL*): **to** ~ **(in)** se spécialiser (en); **a** ~ **operation** (*MED*) une grosse opération.
Majorca [mə'jɔːkə] *n* Majorque *f*.
major general *n* (*MIL*) général *m* de division.
majority [mə'dʒɔrɪtɪ] *n* majorité *f* ♦ *cpd* (*verdict, holding*) majoritaire.
make [meɪk] *vt* (*pt, pp* **made** [meɪd]) faire; (*manufacture*) faire, fabriquer; (*cause to be*): **to** ~ **sb sad** *etc* rendre qn triste *etc*; (*force*): **to** ~ **sb do sth** obliger qn à faire qch, faire faire qch à qn; (*equal*): **2 and 2** ~ **4** 2 et 2 font 4 ♦ *n* fabrication *f*; (*brand*) marque *f*; **to** ~ **it** (*in time etc*) y arriver; (*succeed*) réussir; **what time do you** ~ **it?** quelle heure avez-vous?; **to** ~ **good** *vi* (*succeed*) faire son chemin, réussir ♦ *vt* (*deficit*) combler; (*losses*) compenser; **to** ~ **do with** se contenter de; se débrouiller avec.
▶**make for** *vt fus* (*place*) se diriger vers.
▶**make off** *vi* filer.
▶**make out** *vt* (*write out*) écrire; (*understand*) comprendre; (*see*) distinguer; (*claim, imply*) prétendre, vouloir faire croire; **to** ~ **out a case for sth** présenter des arguments solides en faveur de qch.
▶**make over** *vt* (*assign*): **to** ~ **over (to)** céder (à), transférer (au nom de).
▶**make up** *vt* (*invent*) inventer, imaginer; (*parcel*) faire ♦ *vi* se réconcilier; (*with cosmetics*) se maquiller, se farder; **to be made up of** se composer de.
▶**make up for** *vt fus* compenser; racheter.
make-believe ['meɪkbɪliːv] *n*: **a world of** ~ un monde de chimères *or* d'illusions; **it's just** ~ c'est de la fantaisie; c'est une illusion.
maker ['meɪkə*] *n* fabricant *m*.
makeshift ['meɪkʃɪft] *adj* provisoire, improvisé(e).
make-up ['meɪkʌp] *n* maquillage *m*.
make-up bag *n* trousse *f* de maquillage.
make-up remover *n* démaquillant *m*.
making ['meɪkɪŋ] *n* (*fig*): **in the** ~ en

formation *or* gestation; **he has the ~s of an actor** il a l'étoffe d'un acteur.

maladjusted [mælə'dʒʌstɪd] *adj* inadapté(e).

malaise [mæ'leɪz] *n* malaise *m*.

malaria [mə'lɛərɪə] *n* malaria *f*, paludisme *m*.

Malawi [mə'lɑːwɪ] *n* Malawi *m*.

Malay [mə'leɪ] *adj* malais(e) ♦ *n* (*person*) Malais/e; (*language*) malais *m*.

Malaya [mə'leɪə] *n* Malaisie *f*.

Malayan [mə'leɪən] *adj*, *n* = **Malay**.

Malaysia [mə'leɪzɪə] *n* Malaisie *f*.

Malaysian [mə'leɪzɪən] *adj* malaisien(ne) ♦ *n* Malaisien/ne.

Maldives ['mɔːldaɪvz] *npl*: **the ~** les Maldives *fpl*.

male [meɪl] *n* (*BIOL*, *ELEC*) mâle *m* ♦ *adj* (*sex*, *attitude*) masculin(e); mâle; (*child etc*) du sexe masculin; **~ and female students** étudiants et étudiantes.

male chauvinist *n* phallocrate *m*.

male nurse *n* infirmier *m*.

malevolence [mə'lɛvələns] *n* malveillance *f*.

malevolent [mə'lɛvələnt] *adj* malveillant(e).

malfunction [mæl'fʌŋkʃən] *n* fonctionnement défectueux.

malice ['mælɪs] *n* méchanceté *f*, malveillance *f*.

malicious [mə'lɪʃəs] *adj* méchant(e), malveillant(e); (*LAW*) avec intention criminelle.

malign [mə'laɪn] *vt* diffamer, calomnier.

malignant [mə'lɪɡnənt] *adj* (*MED*) malin(igne).

malingerer [mə'lɪŋɡərə*] *n* simulateur/trice.

mall [mɔːl] *n* (*also*: **shopping ~**) centre commercial.

malleable ['mælɪəbl] *adj* malléable.

mallet ['mælɪt] *n* maillet *m*.

malnutrition [mælnjuːˈtrɪʃən] *n* malnutrition *f*.

malpractice [mæl'præktɪs] *n* faute professionnelle; négligence *f*.

malt [mɔːlt] *n* malt *m* ♦ *cpd* (*whisky*) pur malt.

Malta ['mɔːltə] *n* Malte *f*.

Maltese [mɔːl'tiːz] *adj* maltais(e) ♦ *n* (*pl inv*) Maltais/e; (*LING*) maltais *m*.

maltreat [mæl'triːt] *vt* maltraiter.

mammal ['mæml] *n* mammifère *m*.

mammoth ['mæməθ] *n* mammouth *m* ♦ *adj* géant(e), monstre.

man, *pl* **men** [mæn, mɛn] *n* homme *m*; (*CHESS*) pièce *f*, (*DRAUGHTS*) pion *m* ♦ *vt* garnir d'hommes; servir, assurer le fonctionnement de; être de service à; **an old ~** un vieillard; **~ and wife** mari et femme.

Man. *abbr* (*Canada*) = **Manitoba**.

manacles ['mænəklz] *npl* menottes *fpl*.

manage ['mænɪdʒ] *vi* se débrouiller; y arriver, réussir ♦ *vt* (*business*) gérer; (*team*, *operation*) diriger; (*device, things to do, carry etc*) arriver à se débrouiller avec, s'en tirer avec; **to ~ to do** se débrouiller pour faire; (*succeed*) réussir à faire.

manageable ['mænɪdʒəbl] *adj* maniable; (*task*

etc) faisable.

management ['mænɪdʒmənt] *n* administration *f*, direction *f*; (*persons: of business, firm*) dirigeants *mpl*, cadres *mpl*; (*: of hotel, shop, theatre*) direction; **"under new ~"** "changement de gérant", "changement de propriétaire".

management accounting *n* comptabilité *f* de gestion.

management consultant *n* conseiller/ère de direction.

manager ['mænɪdʒə*] *n* (*of business*) directeur *m*; (*of institution etc*) administrateur *m*; (*of department, unit*) responsable *m/f*, chef *m*; (*of hotel etc*) gérant *m*; (*of artist*) impresario *m*; **sales ~** responsable *m* des ventes.

manageress [mænɪdʒə'rɛs] *n* directrice *f*; (*of hotel etc*) gérante *f*.

managerial [mænɪ'dʒɪərɪəl] *adj* directorial(e); **~ staff** cadres *mpl*.

managing director (MD) ['mænɪdʒɪŋ-] *n* directeur général.

Mancunian [mæŋ'kjuːnɪən] *adj* de Manchester ♦ *n* habitant/e de Manchester; natif/ive de Manchester.

mandarin ['mændərɪn] *n* (*also:* **~ orange**) mandarine *f*; (*person*) mandarin *m*.

mandate ['mændeɪt] *n* mandat *m*.

mandatory ['mændətərɪ] *adj* obligatoire; (*powers etc*) mandataire.

mandolin(e) ['mændəlɪn] *n* mandoline *f*.

mane [meɪn] *n* crinière *f*.

maneuver *etc* [mə'nuːvə*] (*US*) = **manoeuvre** *etc*.

manfully ['mænfəlɪ] *adv* vaillamment.

manganese [mæŋɡə'niːz] *n* manganèse *m*.

mangetout ['mɔnʒ'tuː] *n* mange-tout *m inv*.

mangle ['mæŋɡl] *vt* déchiqueter; mutiler ♦ *n* essoreuse *f*; calandre *f*.

mango, ~es ['mæŋɡəu] *n* mangue *f*.

mangrove ['mæŋɡrəuv] *n* palétuvier *m*.

mangy ['meɪndʒɪ] *adj* galeux(euse).

manhandle ['mænhændl] *vt* (*mistreat*) maltraiter, malmener; (*move by hand*) manutentionner.

manhole ['mænhəul] *n* trou *m* d'homme.

manhood ['mænhud] *n* âge *m* d'homme; virilité *f*.

man-hour ['mænauə*] *n* heure-homme *f*, heure *f* de main-d'œuvre.

manhunt ['mænhʌnt] *n* chasse *f* à l'homme.

mania ['meɪnɪə] *n* manie *f*.

maniac ['meɪnɪæk] *n* maniaque *m/f*.

manic ['mænɪk] *adj* maniaque.

manic-depressive ['mænɪkdɪ'prɛsɪv] *adj, n* (*PSYCH*) maniaco-dépressif(ive).

manicure ['mænɪkjuə*] *n* manucure *f* ♦ *vt* (*person*) faire les mains à.

manicure set *n* trousse *f* à ongles.

manifest ['mænɪfɛst] *vt* manifester ♦ *adj* manifeste, évident(e) ♦ *n* (*AVIAT, NAUT*) manifeste *m*.

manifestation [mænɪfɛsˈteɪʃən] *n* manifestation *f*.

manifesto [mænɪˈfɛstəu] *n* manifeste *m* (POL).

manifold [ˈmænɪfəuld] *adj* multiple, varié(e) ♦ *n* (AUT etc): **exhaust** ~ collecteur *m* d'échappement.

Manila [məˈnɪlə] *n* Manille, Manila.

manila [məˈnɪlə] *adj*: ~ **paper** papier *m* bulle.

manipulate [məˈnɪpjuleɪt] *vt* manipuler.

manipulation [mənɪpjuˈleɪʃən] *n* manipulation *f*.

mankind [mænˈkaɪnd] *n* humanité *f*, genre humain.

manliness [ˈmænlɪnɪs] *n* virilité *f*.

manly [ˈmænlɪ] *adj* viril(e); courageux(euse).

man-made [ˈmænˈmeɪd] *adj* artificiel(le).

manna [ˈmænə] *n* manne *f*.

mannequin [ˈmænɪkɪn] *n* mannequin *m*.

manner [ˈmænə*] *n* manière *f*, façon *f*; **(good)** ~**s** (bonnes) manières; **bad** ~**s** mauvaises manières; **all** ~ **of** toutes sortes de.

mannerism [ˈmænərɪzəm] *n* particularité *f* de langage (or de comportement), tic *m*.

mannerly [ˈmænəlɪ] *adj* poli(e), courtois(e).

manoeuvrable, (US) **maneuverable** [məˈnuːvrəbl] *adj* facile à manœuvrer.

manoeuvre, (US) **maneuver** [məˈnuːvə*] *vt, vi* manœuvrer ♦ *n* manœuvre *f*; **to** ~ **sb into doing sth** manipuler qn pour lui faire faire qch.

manor [ˈmænə*] *n* (also: ~ **house**) manoir *m*.

manpower [ˈmænpauə*] *n* main-d'œuvre *f*.

manservant, *pl* **menservants** [ˈmænsəːvənt, ˈmɛn-] *n* domestique *m*.

mansion [ˈmænʃən] *n* château *m*, manoir *m*.

manslaughter [ˈmænslɔːtə*] *n* homicide *m* involontaire.

mantelpiece [ˈmæntlpiːs] *n* cheminée *f*.

mantle [ˈmæntl] *n* cape *f*; (fig) manteau *m*.

man-to-man [ˈmæntəˈmæn] *adj, adv* d'homme à homme.

manual [ˈmænjuəl] *adj* manuel(le) ♦ *n* manuel *m*.

manual worker *n* travailleur manuel.

manufacture [mænjuˈfæktʃə*] *vt* fabriquer ♦ *n* fabrication *f*.

manufactured goods [mænjuˈfæktʃəd-] *npl* produits manufacturés.

manufacturer [mænjuˈfæktʃərə*] *n* fabricant *m*.

manufacturing industries [mænju ˈfæktʃərɪŋ-] *npl* industries *fpl* de transformation.

manure [məˈnjuə*] *n* fumier *m*; (artificial) engrais *m*.

manuscript [ˈmænjuskrɪpt] *n* manuscrit *m*.

many [ˈmɛnɪ] *adj* beaucoup de, de nombreux(euses) ♦ *pron* beaucoup, un grand nombre; **how** ~? combien?; **a great** ~ un grand nombre (de); **too** ~ **difficulties** trop de difficultés; **twice as** ~ deux fois plus; ~ **a** ... bien des ..., plus d'un(e) ....

Maori [ˈmaurɪ] *n* Maori/e ♦ *adj* maori(e).

map [mæp] *n* carte *f* ♦ *vt* dresser la carte de.

▶**map out** *vt* tracer; (fig: career, holiday) organiser, préparer (à l'avance); (: essay) faire le plan de.

maple [ˈmeɪpl] *n* érable *m*.

Mar. *abbr* = **March**.

mar [maː*] *vt* gâcher, gâter.

marathon [ˈmærəθən] *n* marathon *m* ♦ *adj*: **a** ~ **session** une séance-marathon.

marathon runner *n* coureur/euse de marathon, marathonien/ne.

marauder [məˈrɔːdə*] *n* maraudeur/euse.

marble [ˈmaːbl] *n* marbre *m*; (toy) bille *f*; ~**s** *n* (game) billes.

March [maːtʃ] *n* mars *m*; for phrases see also **July**.

march [maːtʃ] *vi* marcher au pas; (demonstrators) défiler ♦ *n* marche *f*; (demonstration) rallye *m*; **to** ~ **out of/into** etc sortir de/entrer dans etc (de manière décidée ou impulsive).

marcher [ˈmaːtʃə*] *n* (demonstrator) manifestant/e, marcheur/euse.

marching [ˈmaːtʃɪŋ] *n*: **to give sb his** ~ **orders** (fig) renvoyer qn; envoyer promener qn.

march-past [ˈmaːtʃpaːst] *n* défilé *m*.

mare [mɛə*] *n* jument *f*.

marg. [maːdʒ] *n abbr* (col) = **margarine**.

margarine [maːdʒəˈriːn] *n* margarine *f*.

margin [ˈmaːdʒɪn] *n* marge *f*.

marginal [ˈmaːdʒɪnl] *adj* marginal(e); ~ **seat** (POL) siège disputé.

marginally [ˈmaːdʒɪnəlɪ] *adv* très légèrement, sensiblement.

marigold [ˈmærɪɡəuld] *n* souci *m*.

marijuana [mærɪˈwaːnə] *n* marijuana *f*.

marina [məˈriːnə] *n* marina *f*.

marinade *n* [mærɪˈneɪd] marinade *f* ♦ *vt* [ˈmærɪneɪd] = **marinate**.

marinate [ˈmærɪneɪt] *vt* (faire) mariner.

marine [məˈriːn] *adj* marin(e) ♦ *n* fusilier marin; (US) marine *m*.

marine insurance *n* assurance *f* maritime.

marital [ˈmærɪtl] *adj* matrimonial(e); ~ **status** situation *f* de famille.

maritime [ˈmærɪtaɪm] *adj* maritime.

maritime law *n* droit *m* maritime.

marjoram [ˈmaːdʒərəm] *n* marjolaine *f*.

mark [maːk] *n* marque *f*; (of skid etc) trace *f*; (BRIT SCOL) note *f*; (SPORT) cible *f*; (currency) mark *m*; (BRIT TECH): **M**~ **2/3** 2ème/3ème série *f* or version *f* ♦ *vt* (also SPORT: player) marquer; (stain) tacher; (BRIT SCOL) noter; corriger; **punctuation** ~**s** signes *mpl* de ponctuation; **to** ~ **time** marquer le pas; **to be quick off the** ~ **(in doing)** (fig) ne pas perdre de temps (pour faire); **up to the** ~ (in efficiency) à la hauteur.

▶**mark down** *vt* (prices, goods) démarquer, réduire le prix de.

▶**mark off** *vt* (tick off) cocher, pointer.

▶**mark out** *vt* désigner.

mark up vt (price) majorer.
marked [mɑːkt] adj marqué(e), net(te).
markedly ['mɑːkɪdlɪ] adv visiblement, manifestement.
marker ['mɑːkə*] n (sign) jalon m; (bookmark) signet m.
market ['mɑːkɪt] n marché m ♦ vt (COMM) commercialiser; **to be on the** ~ être sur le marché; **on the open** ~ en vente libre; **to play the** ~ jouer à la or spéculer en Bourse.
marketable ['mɑːkɪtəbl] adj commercialisable.
market analysis n analyse f de marché.
market day n jour m de marché.
market demand n besoins mpl du marché.
market economy n économie f de marché.
market forces npl tendances fpl du marché.
market garden n (BRIT) jardin maraîcher.
marketing ['mɑːkɪtɪŋ] n marketing m.
marketplace ['mɑːkɪtpleɪs] n place f du marché; (COMM) marché m.
market price n prix marchand.
market research n étude f de marché.
market value n valeur marchande; valeur du marché.
marking ['mɑːkɪŋ] n (on animal) marque f, tache f; (on road) signalisation f.
marksman ['mɑːksmən] n tireur m d'élite.
marksmanship ['mɑːksmənʃɪp] n adresse f au tir.
mark-up ['mɑːkʌp] n (COMM: margin) marge f (bénéficiaire); (: increase) majoration f.
marmalade ['mɑːməleɪd] n confiture f d'oranges.
maroon [mə'ruːn] vt (fig): **to be** ~ed (in or at) être bloqué(e) (à) ♦ adj bordeaux inv.
marquee [mɑː'kiː] n chapiteau m.
marquess, marquis ['mɑːkwɪs] n marquis m.
Marrakech, Marrakesh [mærə'kɛʃ] n Marrakech.
marriage ['mærɪdʒ] n mariage m.
marriage bureau n agence matrimoniale.
marriage certificate n extrait m d'acte de mariage.
marriage guidance, (US) marriage counseling n conseils conjugaux.
marriage of convenience n mariage m de convenance.
married ['mærɪd] adj marié(e); (life, love) conjugal(e).
marrow ['mærəu] n moelle f; (vegetable) courge f.
marry ['mærɪ] vt épouser, se marier avec; (subj: father, priest etc) marier ♦ vi (also: **get married**) se marier.
Mars [mɑːz] n (planet) Mars f.
Marseilles [mɑː'seɪlz] n Marseille.
marsh [mɑːʃ] n marais m, marécage m.
marshal ['mɑːʃl] n maréchal m; (US: fire, police) ≈ capitaine m; (for demonstration, meeting) membre m du service d'ordre ♦ vt rassembler.

marshalling yard ['mɑːʃlɪŋ-] n (RAIL) gare f de triage.
marshmallow [mɑːʃ'mæləu] n (BOT) guimauve f; (sweet) (pâte f de) guimauve.
marshy ['mɑːʃɪ] adj marécageux(euse).
marsupial [mɑː'suːpɪəl] adj marsupial(e) ♦ n marsupial m.
martial ['mɑːʃl] adj martial(e).
martial arts npl arts martiaux.
martial law n loi martiale.
Martian ['mɑːʃən] n Martien/ne.
martin ['mɑːtɪn] n (also: **house** ~) martinet m.
martyr ['mɑːtə*] n martyr/e ♦ vt martyriser.
martyrdom ['mɑːtədəm] n martyre m.
marvel ['mɑːvl] n merveille f ♦ vi: **to** ~ (at) s'émerveiller (de).
marvellous, (US) marvelous ['mɑːvləs] adj merveilleux(euse).
Marxism ['mɑːksɪzəm] n marxisme m.
Marxist ['mɑːksɪst] adj, n marxiste (m/f).
marzipan ['mɑːzɪpæn] n pâte f d'amandes.
mascara [mæs'kɑːrə] n mascara m.
mascot ['mæskət] n mascotte f.
masculine ['mæskjulɪn] adj masculin(e) ♦ n masculin m.
masculinity [mæskju'lɪnɪtɪ] n masculinité f.
MASH [mæʃ] n abbr (US MIL) = mobile army surgical hospital.
mash [mæʃ] vt (CULIN) faire une purée de.
mashed [mæʃt] adj: ~ **potatoes** purée f de pommes de terre.
mask [mɑːsk] n masque m ♦ vt masquer.
masochism ['mæsəukɪzəm] n masochisme m.
masochist ['mæsəukɪst] n masochiste m/f.
mason ['meɪsn] n (also: **stone**~) maçon m; (also: **free**~) franc-maçon m.
masonic [mə'sɔnɪk] adj maçonnique.
masonry ['meɪsnrɪ] n maçonnerie f.
masquerade [mæskə'reɪd] n bal masqué; (fig) mascarade f ♦ vi: **to** ~ **as** se faire passer pour.
mass [mæs] n multitude f, masse f; (PHYSICS) masse; (REL) messe f ♦ vi se masser; **the** ~**es** les masses; **to go to** ~ aller à la messe.
Mass. abbr (US) = Massachusetts.
massacre ['mæsəkə*] n massacre m ♦ vt massacrer.
massage ['mæsɑːʒ] n massage m ♦ vt masser.
masseur [mæ'sə:*] n masseur m.
masseuse [mæ'sə:z] n masseuse f.
massive ['mæsɪv] adj énorme, massif(ive).
mass market n marché m grand public.
mass media npl mass-media mpl.
mass meeting n rassemblement m de masse.
mass-produce ['mæsprə'djuːs] vt fabriquer en série.
mass production n fabrication f en série.
mast [mɑːst] n mât m; (RADIO, TV) pylône m.
mastectomy [mæs'tɛktəmɪ] n mastectomie f.
master ['mɑːstə*] n maître m; (in secondary school) professeur m; (title for boys): **M~ X** Monsieur X ♦ vt maîtriser; (learn)

apprendre à fond; (*understand*) posséder parfaitement *or* à fond; ~ **of ceremonies (MC)** n maître des cérémonies; **M~ of Arts/ Science (MA/MSc)** n ≈ titulaire m/f d'une maîtrise (en lettres/science); **M~ of Arts/ Science degree (MA/MSc)** n ≈ maîtrise f; **M~'s degree** n ≈ maîtrise.

Le **Master's degree** est un diplôme que l'on prépare en général après le **Bachelor's degree**, bien que certaines universités décernent un *Master's* au lieu d'un *Bachelor's*. Il consiste soit à suivre des cours, soit à rédiger un mémoire à partir d'une recherche personnelle, soit encore les deux. Les principaux masters sont le MA (*Master of Arts*), et le MSc (*Master of Science*), qui comprennent cours et mémoire, et le MLitt (*Master of Letters*) et le MPhil (*Master of Philosophy*), qui reposent uniquement sur le mémoire; voir **doctorate**

master disk n (*COMPUT*) disque original.
masterful ['mɑːstəful] adj autoritaire, impérieux(euse).
master key n passe-partout m inv.
masterly ['mɑːstəlɪ] adj magistral(e).
mastermind ['mɑːstəmaɪnd] n esprit supérieur ♦ vt diriger, être le cerveau de.
masterpiece ['mɑːstəpiːs] n chef-d'œuvre m.
master plan n stratégie f d'ensemble.
master stroke n coup m de maître.
mastery ['mɑːstərɪ] n maîtrise f; connaissance parfaite.
mastiff ['mæstɪf] n mastiff m.
masturbate ['mæstəbeɪt] vi se masturber.
masturbation [mæstə'beɪʃən] n masturbation f.
mat [mæt] n petit tapis; (*also*: **door~**) paillasson m ♦ adj = **matt**.
match [mætʃ] n allumette f; (*game*) match m, partie f; (*fig*) égal/e; mariage m; parti m ♦ vt assortir; (*go well with*) aller bien avec, s'assortir à; (*equal*) égaler, valoir ♦ vi être assorti(e); **to be a good ~** être bien assorti(e).
▶**match up** vt assortir.
matchbox ['mætʃbɒks] n boîte f d'allumettes.
matching ['mætʃɪŋ] adj assorti(e).
matchless ['mætʃlɪs] adj sans égal.
mate [meɪt] n camarade m/f de travail; (*col*) copain/copine; (*animal*) partenaire m/f, mâle/femelle; (*in merchant navy*) second m ♦ vi s'accoupler ♦ vt accoupler.
material [mə'tɪərɪəl] n (*substance*) matière f, matériau m; (*cloth*) tissu m, étoffe f ♦ adj matériel(le); (*important*) essentiel(le); **~s** npl matériaux mpl; **reading ~** de quoi lire, de la lecture.
materialistic [mətɪərɪə'lɪstɪk] adj matérialiste.
materialize [mə'tɪərɪəlaɪz] vi se matérialiser, se réaliser.

materially [mə'tɪərɪəlɪ] adv matériellement; essentiellement.
maternal [mə'təːnl] adj maternel(le).
maternity [mə'təːnɪtɪ] n maternité f ♦ cpd de maternité, de grossesse.
maternity benefit n prestation f de maternité.
maternity hospital n maternité f.
matey ['meɪtɪ] adj (*BRIT col*) copain-copain inv.
math. [mæθ] n abbr (*US*: = mathematics) maths fpl.
mathematical [mæθə'mætɪkl] adj mathématique.
mathematician [mæθəmə'tɪʃən] n mathématicien/ne.
mathematics [mæθə'mætɪks] n mathématiques fpl.
maths [mæθs] n abbr (*BRIT*: = mathematics) maths fpl.
matinée ['mætɪneɪ] n matinée f.
mating ['meɪtɪŋ] n accouplement m.
mating call n appel m du mâle.
mating season n saison f des amours.
matriarchal [meɪtrɪ'ɑːkl] adj matriarcal(e).
matrices ['meɪtrɪsiːz] npl of **matrix**.
matriculation [mətrɪkju'leɪʃən] n inscription f
matrimonial [mætrɪ'məunɪəl] adj matrimonial(e), conjugal(e).
matrimony ['mætrɪmənɪ] n mariage m.
matrix, pl **matrices** ['meɪtrɪks, 'meɪtrɪsiːz] n matrice f.
matron ['meɪtrən] n (*in hospital*) infirmière-chef f; (*in school*) infirmière f.
matronly ['meɪtrənlɪ] adj de matrone; imposant(e).
matt [mæt] adj mat(e).
matted ['mætɪd] adj emmêlé(e).
matter ['mætə*] n question f; (*PHYSICS*) matière f, substance f; (*content*) contenu m, fond m; (*MED: pus*) pus m ♦ vi importer; **it doesn't ~** cela n'a pas d'importance; (*I don't mind*) cela ne fait rien; **what's the ~?** qu'est-ce qu'il y a?, qu'est-ce qui ne va pas?; **no ~ what** quoiqu'il arrive; **that's another ~** c'est une autre affaire; **as a ~ of course** tout naturellement; **as a ~ of fact** en fait; **it's a ~ of habit** c'est une question d'habitude; **printed ~** imprimés mpl; **reading ~** (*BRIT*) de quoi lire, de la lecture.
matter-of-fact ['mætərəv'fækt] adj terre à terre, neutre.
matting ['mætɪŋ] n natte f.
mattress ['mætrɪs] n matelas m.
mature [mə'tjuə*] adj mûr(e); (*cheese*) fait(e) ♦ vi mûrir; se faire.
mature student n étudiant/e plus âgé(e) que la moyenne.
maturity [mə'tjuərɪtɪ] n maturité f.
maudlin ['mɔːdlɪn] adj larmoyant(e).
maul [mɔːl] vt lacérer.
Mauritania [mɔːrɪ'teɪnɪə] n Mauritanie f.
Mauritius [mə'rɪʃəs] n l'île f Maurice.

mausoleum [mɔːsəˈlɪəm] *n* mausolée *m*.
mauve [məuv] *adj* mauve.
maverick [ˈmævrɪk] *n* (*fig*) franc-tireur *m*, non-conformiste *m/f*.
mawkish [ˈmɔːkɪʃ] *adj* mièvre; fade.
max. *abbr* = **maximum**.
maxim [ˈmæksɪm] *n* maxime *f*.
maxima [ˈmæksɪmə] *npl of* **maximum**.
maximize [ˈmæksɪmaɪz] *vt* (*profits etc, chances*) maximiser.
maximum [ˈmæksɪməm] *adj* maximum ♦ *n* (*pl* **maxima** [ˈmæksɪmə]) maximum *m*.
May [meɪ] *n* mai *m*; *for phrases see also* **July**.
may [meɪ] *vi* (*conditional*: **might**) (*indicating possibility*): **he ~ come** il se peut qu'il vienne; (*be allowed to*): **~ I smoke?** puis-je fumer?; (*wishes*): **~ God bless you!** (que) Dieu vous bénisse!; **~ I sit here?** vous permettez que je m'assoie ici?; **he might be there** il pourrait bien y être, il se pourrait qu'il y soit; **I might as well go** je ferais aussi bien d'y aller, autant y aller; **you might like to try** vous pourriez (peut-être) essayer.
maybe [ˈmeɪbiː] *adv* peut-être; **~ he'll** ... peut-être qu'il ...; **~ not** peut-être pas.
May Day *n* le Premier mai.
mayday [ˈmeɪdeɪ] *n* S.O.S. *m*.
mayhem [ˈmeɪhɛm] *n* grabuge *m*.
mayonnaise [meɪəˈneɪz] *n* mayonnaise *f*.
mayor [mɛə*] *n* maire *m*.
mayoress [ˈmɛərɛs] *n* maire *m*; épouse *f* du maire.
maypole [ˈmeɪpəul] *n* mât enrubanné (*autour duquel on danse*).
maze [meɪz] *n* labyrinthe *m*, dédale *m*.
MB *abbr* (*COMPUT*) = **megabyte**; (*Canada*) = Manitoba.
MBA *n abbr* (= *Master of Business Administration*) *titre universitaire*.
MBBS, MBChB *n abbr* (*BRIT*: = *Bachelor of Medicine and Surgery*) *titre universitaire*.
MBE *n abbr* (*BRIT*: = *Member of the Order of the British Empire*) *titre honorifique*.
MC *n abbr* = **master of ceremonies**.
MCAT *n abbr* (*US*) = *Medical College Admissions Test*.
MCP *n abbr* (*BRIT col*: = *male chauvinist pig*) phallocrate *m*.
MD *n abbr* (= *Doctor of Medicine*) *titre universitaire*; (*COMM*) = **managing director** ♦ *abbr* (*US*) = Maryland.
Md. *abbr* (*US*) = Maryland.
MDT *abbr* (*US*: = *Mountain Daylight Time*) *heure d'été des Montagnes Rocheuses*.
ME *n abbr* (*US*: = *medical examiner*) médecin légiste *m/f*; (*MED*: = *myalgic encephalomyelitis*) encéphalomyélite *f* myalgique ♦ *abbr* (*US*) = Maine.
me [miː] *pron* me, m' + *vowel*; (*stressed, after prep*) moi; **it's ~** c'est moi; **it's for ~** c'est pour moi.
meadow [ˈmɛdəu] *n* prairie *f*, pré *m*.

meagre, (*US*) **meager** [ˈmiːgə*] *adj* maigre.
meal [miːl] *n* repas *m*; (*flour*) farine *f*; **to go out for a ~** sortir manger.
meals on wheels *npl* (*BRIT*) *repas livrés à domicile aux personnes âgées ou handicapées*.
mealtime [ˈmiːltaɪm] *n* heure *f* du repas.
mealy-mouthed [ˈmiːlɪmauðd] *adj* mielleux(euse).
mean [miːn] *adj* (*with money*) avare, radin(e); (*unkind*) mesquin(e), méchant(e); (*US col*: *animal*) méchant, vicieux(euse); (: *person*) vache; (*average*) moyen(ne) ♦ *vt* (*pt, pp* **meant** [mɛnt]) (*signify*) signifier, vouloir dire; (*intend*): **to ~ to do** avoir l'intention de faire ♦ *n* moyenne *f*; **to be meant for** être destiné(e) à; **do you ~ it?** vous êtes sérieux?; **what do you ~?** que voulez-vous dire?
meander [mɪˈændə*] *vi* faire des méandres; (*fig*) flâner.
meaning [ˈmiːnɪŋ] *n* signification *f*, sens *m*.
meaningful [ˈmiːnɪŋful] *adj* significatif(ive); (*relationship*) valable.
meaningless [ˈmiːnɪŋlɪs] *adj* dénué(e) de sens.
meanness [ˈmiːnnɪs] *n* avarice *f*; mesquinerie *f*.
means [miːnz] *npl* moyens *mpl*; **by ~ of** par l'intermédiaire de; au moyen de; **by all ~** je vous en prie.
means test *n* (*ADMIN*) contrôle *m* des conditions de ressources.
meant [mɛnt] *pt, pp of* **mean**.
meantime [ˈmiːntaɪm] *adv*, **meanwhile** [ˈmiːnwaɪl] *adv* (*also*: **in the ~**) pendant ce temps.
measles [ˈmiːzlz] *n* rougeole *f*.
measly [ˈmiːzlɪ] *adj* (*col*) minable.
measurable [ˈmɛʒərəbl] *adj* mesurable.
measure [ˈmɛʒə*] *vt, vi* mesurer ♦ *n* mesure *f*; (*ruler*) règle (graduée); **a litre ~** un litre; **some ~ of success** un certain succès; **to take ~s to do sth** prendre des mesures pour faire qch.
▶**measure up** *vi*: **to ~ up (to)** être à la hauteur (de).
measured [ˈmɛʒəd] *adj* mesuré(e).
measurement [ˈmɛʒəmənt] *n*: **chest/hip ~** tour *m* de poitrine/hanches; **~s** *npl* mesures *fpl*; **to take sb's ~s** prendre les mesures de qn.
meat [miːt] *n* viande *f*; **cold ~s** (*BRIT*) viandes froides; **crab ~** crabe *f*.
meatball [ˈmiːtbɔːl] *n* boulette *f* de viande.
meat pie *n* pâté *m* en croûte.
meaty [ˈmiːtɪ] *adj* (*flavour*) de viande; (*fig: argument, book*) étoffé(e), substantiel(le).
Mecca [ˈmɛkə] *n* la Mecque; (*fig*): **a ~ (for)** la Mecque (de).
mechanic [mɪˈkænɪk] *n* mécanicien *m*.
mechanical [mɪˈkænɪkl] *adj* mécanique.
mechanical engineering *n* (*science*)

mécanique *f*; (*industry*) construction *f* mécanique.
mechanics [mə'kænɪks] *n* mécanique *f* ♦ *npl* mécanisme *m*.
mechanism ['mɛkənɪzəm] *n* mécanisme *m*.
mechanization [mɛkənaɪ'zeɪʃən] *n* mécanisation *f*.
MEd *n abbr* (= *Master of Education*) *titre universitaire*.
medal ['mɛdl] *n* médaille *f*.
medallion [mɪ'dælɪən] *n* médaillon *m*.
medallist, (*US*) **medalist** ['mɛdlɪst] *n* (*SPORT*) médaillé/e.
meddle ['mɛdl] *vi*: **to ~ in** se mêler de, s'occuper de; **to ~ with** toucher à.
meddlesome ['mɛdlsəm], **meddling** ['mɛdlɪŋ] *adj* indiscret(ète), qui se mêle de ce qui ne le (*or* la) regarde pas; touche-à-tout *inv*.
media ['miːdɪə] *npl* media *mpl*.
media circus *n* (*event*) battage *m* médiatique; (*group of journalists*) cortège *m* médiatique.
mediaeval [mɛdɪ'iːvl] *adj* = **medieval**.
median ['miːdɪən] *n* (*US: also:* ~ **strip**) bande médiane.
media research *n* étude *f* de l'audience.
mediate ['miːdɪeɪt] *vi* s'interposer; servir d'intermédiaire.
mediation [miːdɪ'eɪʃən] *n* médiation *f*.
mediator ['miːdɪeɪtə*] *n* médiateur/trice.
Medicaid ['mɛdɪkeɪd] *n* (*US*) *assistance médicale aux indigents.*
medical ['mɛdɪkl] *adj* médical(e) ♦ *n* (*also:* ~ **examination**) visite médicale; examen médical.
medical certificate *n* certificat médical.
medical student *n* étudiant/e en médecine.
Medicare ['mɛdɪkɛə*] *n* (*US*) *régime d'assurance maladie.*
medicated ['mɛdɪkeɪtɪd] *adj* traitant(e), médicamenteux(euse).
medication [mɛdɪ'keɪʃən] *n* (*drugs etc*) médication *f*.
medicinal [mɛ'dɪsɪnl] *adj* médicinal(e).
medicine ['mɛdsɪn] *n* médecine *f*; (*drug*) médicament *m*.
medicine chest *n* pharmacie *f* (*murale ou portative*).
medicine man *n* sorcier *m*.
medieval [mɛdɪ'iːvl] *adj* médiéval(e).
mediocre [miːdɪ'əukə*] *adj* médiocre.
mediocrity [miːdɪ'ɔkrɪtɪ] *n* médiocrité *f*.
meditate ['mɛdɪteɪt] *vi*: **to ~ (on)** méditer (sur).
meditation [mɛdɪ'teɪʃən] *n* méditation *f*.
Mediterranean [mɛdɪtə'reɪnɪən] *adj* méditerranéen(ne); **the ~ (Sea)** la (mer) Méditerranée.
medium ['miːdɪəm] *adj* moyen(ne) ♦ *n* (*pl* **media**) (*means*) moyen *m*; (*pl* **mediums**) (*person*) médium *m*; **the happy ~** le juste milieu.
medium-dry ['miːdɪəm'draɪ] *adj* demi-sec.

medium-sized ['miːdɪəm'saɪzd] *adj* de taille moyenne.
medium wave *n* (*RADIO*) ondes moyennes, petites ondes.
medley ['mɛdlɪ] *n* mélange *m*.
meek [miːk] *adj* doux(douce), humble.
meet, *pt, pp* **met** [miːt, mɛt] *vt* rencontrer; (*by arrangement*) retrouver, rejoindre; (*for the first time*) faire la connaissance de; (*go and fetch*): **I'll ~ you at the station** j'irai te chercher à la gare; (*problem*) faire face à; (*requirements*) satisfaire à, répondre à; (*bill, expenses*) régler, honorer ♦ *vi* se rencontrer; se retrouver; (*in session*) se réunir; (*join: objects*) se joindre ♦ *n* (*BRIT: HUNTING*) rendez-vous *m* de chasse; (*US SPORT*) rencontre *f*, meeting *m*; **pleased to ~ you!** enchanté!
▶**meet up** *vi*: **to ~ up with sb** rencontrer qn.
▶**meet with** *vt fus* rencontrer.
meeting ['miːtɪŋ] *n* rencontre *f*; (*session: of club etc*) réunion *f*; (*formal*) assemblée *f*; (*SPORT: rally*) rencontre, meeting *m*; (*interview*) entrevue *f*; **she's at a ~** (*COMM*) elle est en conférence; **to call a ~** convoquer une réunion.
meeting place *n* lieu *m* de (la) réunion; (*for appointment*) lieu de rendez-vous.
megabyte ['mɛgəbaɪt] *n* (*COMPUT*) méga-octet *m*.
megalomaniac [mɛgələ'meɪnɪæk] *n* mégalomane *m/f*.
megaphone ['mɛgəfəun] *n* porte-voix *m inv*.
megawatt ['mɛgəwɔt] *n* mégawatt *m*.
melancholy ['mɛlənkəlɪ] *n* mélancolie *f* ♦ *adj* mélancolique.
mellow ['mɛləu] *adj* velouté(e); doux(douce); (*colour*) riche et profond(e); (*fruit*) mûr(e) ♦ *vi* (*person*) s'adoucir.
melodious [mɪ'ləudɪəs] *adj* mélodieux(euse).
melodrama ['mɛləudrɑːmə] *n* mélodrame *m*.
melodramatic [mɛlədrə'mætɪk] *adj* mélodramatique.
melody ['mɛlədɪ] *n* mélodie *f*.
melon ['mɛlən] *n* melon *m*.
melt [mɛlt] *vi* fondre; (*become soft*) s'amollir; (*fig*) s'attendrir ♦ *vt* faire fondre.
▶**melt away** *vi* fondre complètement.
▶**melt down** *vt* fondre.
meltdown ['mɛltdaun] *n* fusion *f* (du cœur d'un réacteur nucléaire).
melting point ['mɛltɪŋ-] *n* point *m* de fusion.
melting pot ['mɛltɪŋ-] *n* (*fig*) creuset *m*; **to be in the ~** être encore en discussion.
member ['mɛmbə*] *n* membre *m*; (*of club, political party*) membre, adhérent/e ♦ *cpd*: **~ country/state** *n* pays *m*/état *m* membre; **M~ of Parliament (MP)** *n* (*BRIT*) député *m*; **M~ of the European Parliament (MEP)** *n* Eurodéputé *m*; **M~ of the House of Representatives (MHR)** *n* (*US*) membre de la Chambre des représentants.
membership ['mɛmbəʃɪp] *n* (*becoming a*

member) adhésion *f*; admission *f*; (*being a member*) qualité *f* de membre, fait *m* d'être membre; (*the members*) membres *mpl*, adhérents *mpl*; (*number of members*) nombre *m* des membres *or* adhérents.

membership card *n* carte *f* de membre.

membrane ['mɛmbreɪn] *n* membrane *f*.

memento [mə'mɛntəu] *n* souvenir *m*.

memo ['mɛməu] *n* note *f* (de service).

memoir ['mɛmwɑ:*] *n* mémoire *m*, étude *f*; ~s *npl* mémoires.

memo pad *n* bloc-notes *m*.

memorable ['mɛmərəbl] *adj* mémorable.

memorandum, *pl* **memoranda** [mɛmə'rændəm, -də] *n* note *f* (de service); (*DIPLOMACY*) mémorandum *m*.

memorial [mɪ'mɔ:rɪəl] *n* mémorial *m* ♦ *adj* commémoratif(ive).

Memorial Day *est un jour férié aux États-Unis, le dernier lundi de mai dans la plupart des États, à la mémoire des soldats américains morts au combat.*

---

memorize ['mɛməraɪz] *vt* apprendre *or* retenir par cœur.

memory ['mɛmərɪ] *n* mémoire *f*; (*recollection*) souvenir *m*; **to have a good/bad** ~ avoir une bonne/mauvaise mémoire; **loss of** ~ perte *f* de mémoire; **in** ~ **of** à la mémoire de.

men [mɛn] *npl of* **man**.

menace ['mɛnɪs] *n* menace *f*; (*col: nuisance*) peste *f*, plaie *f* ♦ *vt* menacer; **a public** ~ un danger public.

menacing ['mɛnɪsɪŋ] *adj* menaçant(e).

menagerie [mɪ'nædʒərɪ] *n* ménagerie *f*.

mend [mɛnd] *vt* réparer; (*darn*) raccommoder, repriser ♦ *n* reprise *f*; **on the** ~ en voie de guérison.

mending ['mɛndɪŋ] *n* raccommodages *mpl*.

menial ['mi:nɪəl] *adj* de domestique, inférieur(e); subalterne.

meningitis [mɛnɪn'dʒaɪtɪs] *n* méningite *f*.

menopause ['mɛnəupɔ:z] *n* ménopause *f*.

menservants ['mɛnsə:vənts] *npl of* **manservant**.

men's room *n*: **the** ~ (*esp US*) les toilettes *fpl* pour hommes.

menstruate ['mɛnstrueɪt] *vi* avoir ses règles.

menstruation [mɛnstru'eɪʃən] *n* menstruation *f*.

menswear ['mɛnzwɛə*] *n* vêtements *mpl* d'hommes.

mental ['mɛntl] *adj* mental(e); ~ **illness** maladie mentale.

mental hospital *n* hôpital *m* psychiatrique.

mentality [mɛn'tælɪtɪ] *n* mentalité *f*.

mentally ['mɛntlɪ] *adv*: **to be** ~ **handicapped** être handicapé/e mental(e).

menthol ['mɛnθɔl] *n* menthol *m*.

mention ['mɛnʃən] *n* mention *f* ♦ *vt* mentionner, faire mention de; **don't** ~ **it!** je

vous en prie, il n'y a pas de quoi!; **I need hardly** ~ **that** ... est-il besoin de rappeler que ...?; **not to** ~ ..., **without** ~**ing** ... sans parler de ..., sans compter ....

mentor ['mɛntɔ:*] *n* mentor *m*.

menu ['mɛnju:] *n* (*in restaurant, COMPUT*) menu *m*; (*printed*) carte *f*.

menu-driven ['mɛnju:drɪvn] *adj* (*COMPUT*) piloté(e) par menu.

MEP *n abbr* = **Member of the European Parliament.**

mercantile ['mə:kəntaɪl] *adj* marchand(e); (*law*) commercial(e).

mercenary ['mə:sɪnərɪ] *adj* mercantile ♦ *n* mercenaire *m*.

merchandise ['mə:tʃəndaɪz] *n* marchandises *fpl* ♦ *vt* commercialiser.

merchandiser ['mə:tʃəndaɪzə*] *n* marchandiseur *m*.

merchant ['mə:tʃənt] *n* négociant *m*, marchand *m*; **timber/wine** ~ négociant en bois/vins, marchand de bois/vins.

merchant bank *n* (*BRIT*) banque *f* d'affaires.

merchantman ['mə:tʃəntmən] *n* navire marchand.

merchant navy, (*US*) **merchant marine** *n* marine marchande.

merciful ['mə:sɪful] *adj* miséricordieux(euse), clément(e).

mercifully ['mə:sɪflɪ] *adv* avec clémence; (*fortunately*) par bonheur, Dieu merci.

merciless ['mə:sɪlɪs] *adj* impitoyable, sans pitié.

mercurial [mə:'kjuərɪəl] *adj* changeant(e); (*lively*) vif(vive).

mercury ['mə:kjurɪ] *n* mercure *m*.

mercy ['mə:sɪ] *n* pitié *f*, merci *f*; (*REL*) miséricorde *f*; **to have** ~ **on sb** avoir pitié de qn; **at the** ~ **of** à la merci de.

mercy killing *n* euthanasie *f*.

mere [mɪə*] *adj* simple.

merely ['mɪəlɪ] *adv* simplement, purement.

merge [mə:dʒ] *vt* unir; (*COMPUT*) fusionner, interclasser ♦ *vi* se fondre; (*COMM*) fusionner.

merger ['mə:dʒə*] *n* (*COMM*) fusion *f*.

meridian [mə'rɪdɪən] *n* méridien *m*.

meringue [mə'ræŋ] *n* meringue *f*.

merit ['mɛrɪt] *n* mérite *m*, valeur *f* ♦ *vt* mériter.

meritocracy [mɛrɪ'tɔkrəsɪ] *n* méritocratie *f*.

mermaid ['mə:meɪd] *n* sirène *f*.

merrily ['mɛrɪlɪ] *adv* joyeusement, gaiement.

merriment ['mɛrɪmənt] *n* gaieté *f*.

merry ['mɛrɪ] *adj* gai(e); **M**~ **Christmas!** joyeux Noël!

merry-go-round ['mɛrɪgəuraund] *n* manège *m*.

mesh [mɛʃ] *n* maille *f*; filet *m* ♦ *vi* (*gears*) s'engrener; **wire** ~ grillage *m* (métallique), treillis *m* (métallique).

mesmerize ['mɛzməraɪz] *vt* hypnotiser; fasciner.

mess [mɛs] *n* désordre *m*, fouillis *m*, pagaille *f*;

(*MIL*) mess *m*, cantine *f*; **to be (in) a** ~ être en désordre; **to be/get o.s. in a** ~ (*fig*) être/se mettre dans le pétrin.

▶**mess about, mess around** *vi* (*col*) perdre son temps.

▶**mess about** *or* **around with** *vt fus* (*col*) chambarder, tripoter.

▶**mess up** *vt* salir; chambarder; gâcher.

message ['mɛsɪdʒ] *n* message *m*; **to get the** ~ (*fig: col*) saisir, piger.

message switching [-swɪtʃɪŋ] *n* (*COMPUT*) commutation *f* de messages.

messenger ['mɛsɪndʒə*] *n* messager *m*.

Messiah [mɪ'saɪə] *n* Messie *m*.

Messrs, Messrs. ['mɛsəz] *abbr* (*on letters*: = *messieurs*) MM.

messy ['mɛsɪ] *adj* sale; en désordre.

Met [mɛt] *n abbr* (*US*) = *Metropolitan Opera*.

met [mɛt] *pt, pp of* **meet** ♦ *adj abbr* (= *meteorological*) météo *inv*.

metabolism [mɛ'tæbəlɪzəm] *n* métabolisme *m*.

metal ['mɛtl] *n* métal *m* ♦ *vt* empierrer.

metallic [mɛ'tælɪk] *adj* métallique.

metallurgy [mɛ'tælədʒɪ] *n* métallurgie *f*.

metalwork ['mɛtlwə:k] *n* (*craft*) ferronnerie *f*.

metamorphosis, pl -ses [mɛtə'mɔ:fəsɪs, -si:z] *n* métamorphose *f*.

metaphor ['mɛtəfə*] *n* métaphore *f*.

metaphysics [mɛtə'fɪzɪks] *n* métaphysique *f*.

mete [mi:t]: **to** ~ **out** *vt fus* infliger.

meteor ['mi:tɪə*] *n* météore *m*.

meteoric [mi:tɪ'ɔrɪk] *adj* (*fig*) fulgurant(e).

meteorite ['mi:tɪəraɪt] *n* météorite *m or f*.

meteorological [mi:tɪərə'lɔdʒɪkl] *adj* météorologique.

meteorology [mi:tɪə'rɔlədʒɪ] *n* météorologie *f*.

meter ['mi:tə*] *n* (*instrument*) compteur *m*; (*also*: **parking** ~) parc(o)mètre *m*; (*US*) = **metre**.

methane ['mi:θeɪn] *n* méthane *m*.

method ['mɛθəd] *n* méthode *f*; ~ **of payment** mode *m or* modalité *f* de paiement.

methodical [mɪ'θɔdɪkl] *adj* méthodique.

Methodist ['mɛθədɪst] *adj, n* méthodiste (*m/f*).

methylated spirit ['mɛθɪleɪtɪd-] *n* (*BRIT*: *also*: **meths**) alcool *m* à brûler.

meticulous [mɛ'tɪkjuləs] *adj* méticuleux(euse).

metre, (*US*) meter ['mi:tə*] *n* mètre *m*.

metric ['mɛtrɪk] *adj* métrique; **to go** ~ adopter le système métrique.

metrical ['mɛtrɪkl] *adj* métrique.

metrication [mɛtrɪ'keɪʃən] *n* conversion *f* au système métrique.

metric system *n* système *m* métrique.

metric ton *n* tonne *f*.

metronome ['mɛtrənəum] *n* métronome *m*.

metropolis [mɪ'trɔpəlɪs] *n* métropole *f*.

metropolitan [mɛtrə'pɔlɪtən] *adj* métropolitain(e).

Metropolitan Police *n* (*BRIT*): **the** ~ la police londonienne.

mettle ['mɛtl] *n* courage *m*.

mew [mju:] *vi* (*cat*) miauler.

mews [mju:z] *n* (*BRIT*): ~ **cottage** maisonnette aménagée dans une ancienne écurie ou remise.

Mexican ['mɛksɪkən] *adj* mexicain(e) ♦ *n* Mexicain/e.

Mexico ['mɛksɪkəu] *n* Mexique *m*.

Mexico City *n* Mexico.

mezzanine ['mɛtsəni:n] *n* mezzanine *f*; (*of shops, offices*) entresol *m*.

MFA *n abbr* (*US*: = *Master of Fine Arts*) titre universitaire.

mfr *abbr* = **manufacture, manufacturer**.

mg *abbr* (= *milligram*) mg.

Mgr *abbr* (= *Monseigneur, Monsignor*) Mgr; (= *manager*) dir.

MHR *n abbr* (*US*) = **Member of the House of Representatives.**

MHz *abbr* (= *megahertz*) MHz.

MI *abbr* (*US*) = *Michigan*.

MI5 *n abbr* (*BRIT*: = *Military Intelligence 5*) ≈ DST *f*.

MI6 *n abbr* (*BRIT*: = *Military Intelligence 6*) ≈ DGSE *f*.

MIA *abbr* (= *missing in action*) disparu au combat.

miaow [mi:'au] *vi* miauler.

mice [maɪs] *npl of* **mouse.**

Mich. *abbr* (*US*) = *Michigan*.

microbe ['maɪkrəub] *n* microbe *m*.

microbiology [maɪkrəbaɪ'ɔlədʒɪ] *n* microbiologie *f*.

microchip ['maɪkrəutʃɪp] *n* (*ELEC*) puce *f*.

micro(computer) ['maɪkrəu(kəm'pju:tə*)] *n* micro(-ordinateur *m*) *m*.

microcosm ['maɪkrəukɔzəm] *n* microcosme *m*.

microeconomics ['maɪkrəui:kə'nɔmɪks] *n* micro-économie *f*.

microfiche ['maɪkrəufi:ʃ] *n* microfiche *f*.

microfilm ['maɪkrəufɪlm] *n* microfilm *m* ♦ *vt* microfilmer.

microlight ['maɪkrəulaɪt] *n* ULM *m*.

micrometer [maɪ'krɔmɪtə*] *n* palmer *m*, micromètre *m*.

microphone ['maɪkrəfəun] *n* microphone *m*.

microprocessor ['maɪkrəu'prəusɛsə*] *n* microprocesseur *m*.

microscope ['maɪkrəskəup] *n* microscope *m*; **under the** ~ au microscope.

microscopic [maɪkrə'skɔpɪk] *adj* microscopique.

microwave ['maɪkrəuweɪv] *n* (*also*: ~ **oven**) four *m* à micro-ondes.

mid [mɪd] *adj*: ~ **May** la mi-mai; ~ **afternoon** le milieu de l'après-midi; **in** ~ **air** en plein ciel; **he's in his** ~ **thirties** il a dans les trente-cinq ans.

midday [mɪd'deɪ] *n* midi *m*:

middle ['mɪdl] *n* milieu *m*; (*waist*) ceinture *f*, taille *f* ♦ *adj* du milieu; **in the** ~ **of the night** au milieu de la nuit; **I'm in the** ~ **of reading**

it je suis (justement) en train de le lire.
middle age n tranche d'âge aux limites floues, entre la quarantaine et le début du troisième âge.
middle-aged ['mɪdl'eɪdʒd] adj (people: see middle age) d'un certain âge, ni vieux ni jeune; (pej: values, outlook) conventionnel(le), rassis(e).
Middle Ages npl: the ~ le moyen âge.
middle class n: the ~(es) ≈ les classes moyennes ♦ adj (also: middle-class) ≈ (petit(e)-)bourgeois(e).
Middle East n: the ~ le Proche-Orient, le Moyen-Orient.
middleman ['mɪdlmæn] n intermédiaire m.
middle management n cadres moyens.
middle name n second prénom.
middle-of-the-road ['mɪdləvðə'rəud] adj (policy) modéré(e), du juste milieu; (music etc) plutôt classique, assez traditionnel(le).
middleweight ['mɪdlweɪt] n (BOXING) poids moyen.
middling ['mɪdlɪŋ] adj moyen(ne).
Middx abbr (BRIT) = Middlesex.
midge [mɪdʒ] n moucheron m.
midget ['mɪdʒɪt] n nain/e ♦ adj minuscule.
midi system ['mɪdɪ-] n chaîne f midi.
Midlands ['mɪdləndz] npl comtés du centre de l'Angleterre.
midnight ['mɪdnaɪt] n minuit m; at ~ à minuit.
midriff ['mɪdrɪf] n estomac m, taille f.
midst [mɪdst] n: in the ~ of au milieu de.
midsummer [mɪd'sʌmə*] n milieu m de l'été.
midway [mɪd'weɪ] adj, adv: ~ (between) à mi-chemin (entre).
midweek [mɪd'wiːk] adj du milieu de la semaine ♦ adv au milieu de la semaine, en pleine semaine.
midwife, midwives ['mɪdwaɪf, -vz] n sage-femme f.
midwifery ['mɪdwɪfərɪ] n obstétrique f.
midwinter [mɪd'wɪntə*] n milieu m de l'hiver.
miffed [mɪft] adj (col) fâché(e), vexé(e).
might [maɪt] vb see **may** ♦ n puissance f, force f.
mighty ['maɪtɪ] adj puissant(e) ♦ adv (col) rudement.
migraine ['miːgreɪn] n migraine f.
migrant ['maɪgrənt] n (bird, animal) migrateur m; (person) migrant/e; nomade m/f ♦ adj migrateur(trice); migrant(e); nomade; (worker) saisonnier(ière).
migrate [maɪ'greɪt] vi émigrer.
migration [maɪ'greɪʃən] n migration f.
mike [maɪk] n abbr (= microphone) micro m.
Milan [mɪ'læn] n Milan.
mild [maɪld] adj doux(douce); (reproach) léger(ère); (illness) bénin(igne) ♦ n bière légère.
mildew ['mɪldjuː] n mildiou m.
mildly ['maɪldlɪ] adv doucement; légèrement;

to put it ~ (col) c'est le moins qu'on puisse dire.
mildness ['maɪldnɪs] n douceur f.
mile [maɪl] n mil(l)e m (= 1609 m); to do 30 ~s per gallon ≈ faire 9,4 litres aux cent.
mileage ['maɪlɪdʒ] n distance f en milles, ≈ kilométrage m.
mileage allowance n ≈ indemnité f kilométrique.
mileometer [maɪ'lɔmɪtə*] n (BRIT) = milometer.
milestone ['maɪlstəun] n borne f; (fig) jalon m.
milieu ['miːljəː] n milieu m.
militant ['mɪlɪtnt] adj, n militant(e).
militarism ['mɪlɪtərɪzəm] n militarisme m.
militaristic [mɪlɪtə'rɪstɪk] adj militariste.
military ['mɪlɪtərɪ] adj militaire ♦ n: the ~ l'armée f, les militaires mpl.
military service n service m (militaire ou national).
militate ['mɪlɪteɪt] vi: to ~ against militer contre.
militia [mɪ'lɪʃə] n milice f.
milk [mɪlk] n lait m ♦ vt (cow) traire; (fig) dépouiller, plumer.
milk chocolate n chocolat m au lait.
milk float n (BRIT) voiture f or camionnette f du or de laitier.
milking ['mɪlkɪŋ] n traite f.
milkman ['mɪlkmən] n laitier m.
milk shake n milk-shake m.
milk tooth n dent f de lait.
milk truck n (US) = milk float.
milky ['mɪlkɪ] adj lacté(e); (colour) laiteux(euse).
Milky Way n Voie lactée.
mill [mɪl] n moulin m; (factory) usine f, fabrique f; (spinning ~) filature f; (flour ~) minoterie f ♦ vt moudre, broyer ♦ vi (also: ~ about) grouiller.
millennium, pl ~s or **millennia** [mɪ'lɛnɪəm, -'lɛnɪə] n millénaire m.
miller ['mɪlə*] n meunier m.
millet ['mɪlɪt] n millet m.
milli... ['mɪlɪ] prefix milli....
milligram(me) ['mɪlɪgræm] n milligramme m.
millilitre, (US) **milliliter** ['mɪlɪliːtə*] n millilitre m.
millimetre, (US) **millimeter** ['mɪlɪmiːtə*] n millimètre m.
milliner ['mɪlɪnə*] n modiste f.
millinery ['mɪlɪnərɪ] n modes fpl.
million ['mɪljən] n million m.
millionaire [mɪljə'neə*] n millionnaire m.
millipede ['mɪlɪpiːd] n mille-pattes m inv.
millstone ['mɪlstəun] n meule f.
millwheel ['mɪlwiːl] n roue f de moulin.
milometer [maɪ'lɔmɪtə*] n (BRIT) ≈ compteur m kilométrique.
mime [maɪm] n mime m ♦ vt, vi mimer.
mimic ['mɪmɪk] n imitateur/trice ♦ vt, vi imiter, contrefaire.

mimicry ['mɪmɪkrɪ] *n* imitation *f*; (*ZOOL*) mimétisme *m*.

Min. *abbr* (*BRIT POL*) = **ministry**.

min. *abbr* (= *minute*) mn.; (= *minimum*) min.

minaret [mɪnə'rɛt] *n* minaret *m*.

mince [mɪns] *vt* hacher ♦ *vi* (*in walking*) marcher à petits pas maniérés ♦ *n* (*BRIT CULIN*) viande hachée, hachis *m*; **he does not ~ (his) words** il ne mâche pas ses mots.

mincemeat ['mɪnsmiːt] *n* hachis de fruits secs utilisés en pâtisserie.

mince pie *n* sorte de tarte aux fruits secs.

mincer ['mɪnsə*] *n* hachoir *m*.

mincing ['mɪnsɪŋ] *adj* affecté(e).

mind [maɪnd] *n* esprit *m* ♦ *vt* (*attend to, look after*) s'occuper de; (*be careful*) faire attention à; (*object to*): **I don't ~ the noise** je ne crains pas le bruit, le bruit ne me dérange pas; **do you ~ if ...?** est-ce que cela vous gêne si ...?; **I don't ~ cela ne me dérange pas; ~ you, ... remarquez, ...; never ~ peu importe, ça ne fait rien; it is on my ~** cela me préoccupe; **to change one's ~** changer d'avis; **to be in two ~s about sth** (*BRIT*) être indécis(e) *or* irrésolu(e) en ce qui concerne qch; **to my ~** à mon avis, selon moi; **to be out of one's ~** ne plus avoir toute sa raison; **to keep sth in ~** ne pas oublier qch; **to bear sth in ~** tenir compte de qch; **to have sb/sth in ~** avoir qn/qch en tête; **to have in ~ to do** avoir l'intention de faire; **it went right out of my ~** ça m'est complètement sorti de la tête; **to bring** *or* **call sth to ~** se rappeler qch; **to make up one's ~** se décider; **"~ the step"** "attention à la marche".

mind-boggling ['maɪndbɔglɪŋ] *adj* (*col*) époustouflant(e), ahurissant(e).

-minded ['maɪndɪd] *adj*: **fair~** impartial(e); **an industrially~ nation** une nation orientée vers l'industrie.

minder ['maɪndə*] *n* (*child ~*) gardienne *f*; (*bodyguard*) ange gardien (*fig*).

mindful ['maɪndful] *adj*: **~ of** attentif(ive) à, soucieux(euse) de.

mindless ['maɪndlɪs] *adj* irréfléchi(e); (*violence, crime*) insensé(e).

mine [maɪn] *pron* le(la) mien(ne), les miens(miennes); **this book is ~** ce livre est à moi ♦ *n* mine *f* ♦ *vt* (*coal*) extraire; (*ship, beach*) miner.

mine detector *n* détecteur *m* de mines.

minefield ['maɪnfiːld] *n* champ *m* de mines.

miner ['maɪnə*] *n* mineur *m*.

mineral ['mɪnərəl] *adj* minéral(e) ♦ *n* minéral *m*; **~s** *npl* (*BRIT*: *soft drinks*) boissons gazeuses (sucrées).

mineralogy [mɪnə'rælədʒɪ] *n* minéralogie *f*.

mineral water *n* eau minérale.

minesweeper ['maɪnswiːpə*] *n* dragueur *m* de mines.

mingle ['mɪŋgl] *vt* mêler, mélanger ♦ *vi*: **to ~ with** se mêler à.

mingy ['mɪndʒɪ] *adj* (*col*) radin(e).

miniature ['mɪnətʃə*] *adj* (en) miniature ♦ *n* miniature *f*.

minibus ['mɪnɪbʌs] *n* minibus *m*.

minicab ['mɪnɪkæb] *n* (*BRIT*) minitaxi *m*.

minicomputer ['mɪnɪkəm'pjuːtə*] *n* mini-ordinateur *m*.

minim ['mɪnɪm] *n* (*MUS*) blanche *f*.

minima ['mɪnɪmə] *npl of* **minimum**.

minimal ['mɪnɪml] *adj* minimal(e).

minimalist ['mɪnɪməlɪst] *adj*, *n* minimaliste (*m/f*).

minimize ['mɪnɪmaɪz] *vt* minimiser.

minimum ['mɪnɪməm] *n* (*pl*: **minima** ['mɪnɪmə]) minimum *m* ♦ *adj* minimum; **to reduce to a ~** réduire au minimum.

minimum lending rate (MLR) *n* (*ECON*) taux *m* de crédit minimum.

mining ['maɪnɪŋ] *n* exploitation minière ♦ *adj* minier(ière); de mineurs.

minion ['mɪnjən] *n* (*pej*) laquais *m*; favori/te.

mini-series ['mɪnɪsɪəriːz] *n* téléfilm *m* en plusieurs parties.

miniskirt ['mɪnɪskəːt] *n* mini-jupe *f*.

minister ['mɪnɪstə*] *n* (*BRIT POL*) ministre *m*; (*REL*) pasteur *m* ♦ *vi*: **to ~ to sb** donner ses soins à qn; **to ~ to sb's needs** pourvoir aux besoins de qn.

ministerial [mɪnɪs'tɪərɪəl] *adj* (*BRIT POL*) ministériel(le).

ministry ['mɪnɪstrɪ] *n* (*BRIT POL*) ministère *m*; (*REL*): **to go into the ~** devenir pasteur.

mink [mɪŋk] *n* vison *m*.

mink coat *n* manteau *m* de vison.

Minn. *abbr* (*US*) = **Minnesota**.

minnow ['mɪnəu] *n* vairon *m*.

minor ['maɪnə*] *adj* petit(e), de peu d'importance; (*MUS*) mineur(e) ♦ *n* (*LAW*) mineur/e.

Minorca [mɪ'nɔːkə] *n* Minorque *f*.

minority [maɪ'nɔrɪtɪ] *n* minorité *f*; **to be in a ~** être en minorité.

minster ['mɪnstə*] *n* église abbatiale.

minstrel ['mɪnstrəl] *n* trouvère *m*, ménestrel *m*.

mint [mɪnt] *n* (*plant*) menthe *f*; (*sweet*) bonbon *m* à la menthe ♦ *vt* (*coins*) battre; **the (Royal) M~**, (*US*) **the (US) M~** ≈ l'hôtel *m* de la Monnaie; **in ~ condition** à l'état de neuf.

mint sauce *n* sauce *f* à la menthe.

minuet [mɪnju'ɛt] *n* menuet *m*.

minus ['maɪnəs] *n* (*also*: **~ sign**) signe *m* moins ♦ *prep* moins.

minuscule ['mɪnəskjuːl] *adj* minuscule.

minute *adj* [maɪ'njuːt] minuscule; (*detailed*) minutieux(euse) ♦ *n* ['mɪnɪt] minute *f*; (*official record*) procès-verbal *m*, compte rendu; **~s** *npl* procès-verbal; **it is 5 ~s past 3** il est 3 heures 5; **wait a ~!** (attendez) un instant!; **at the last ~** à la dernière minute; **up to the ~** (*fashion*) dernier cri; (*news*) de dernière

minute; (*machine, technology*) de pointe; **in ~ detail** par le menu.
minute book *n* registre *m* des procès-verbaux.
minute hand *n* aiguille *f* des minutes.
minutely [maɪ'njuːtlɪ] *adv* (*by a small amount*) de peu, de manière infime; (*in detail*) minutieusement, dans les moindres détails.
minutiae [mɪ'njuːʃiiː] *npl* menus détails.
miracle ['mɪrəkl] *n* miracle *m*.
miraculous [mɪ'rækjuləs] *adj* miraculeux(euse).
mirage ['mɪrɑːʒ] *n* mirage *m*.
mire ['maɪə*] *n* bourbe *f*, boue *f*.
mirror ['mɪrə*] *n* miroir *m*, glace *f* ♦ *vt* refléter.
mirror image *n* image inversée.
mirth [mɜːθ] *n* gaieté *f*.
misadventure [mɪsəd'vɛntʃə*] *n* mésaventure *f*; **death by ~** (*BRIT*) décès accidentel.
misanthropist [mɪ'zænθrəpɪst] *n* misanthrope *m/f*.
misapply [mɪsə'plaɪ] *vt* mal employer.
misapprehension ['mɪsæprɪ'hɛnʃən] *n* malentendu *m*, méprise *f*.
misappropriate [mɪsə'prəuprɪeɪt] *vt* détourner.
misappropriation ['mɪsəprəuprɪ'eɪʃən] *n* escroquerie *f*, détournement *m*.
misbehave [mɪsbɪ'heɪv] *vi* se conduire mal.
misbehaviour, (*US*) **misbehavior** [mɪsbɪ'heɪvjə*] *n* mauvaise conduite.
misc. *abbr* = **miscellaneous**.
miscalculate [mɪs'kælkjuleɪt] *vt* mal calculer.
miscalculation ['mɪskælkju'leɪʃən] *n* erreur *f* de calcul.
miscarriage ['mɪskærɪdʒ] *n* (*MED*) fausse couche; **~ of justice** erreur *f* judiciaire.
miscarry [mɪs'kærɪ] *vi* (*MED*) faire une fausse couche; (*fail: plans*) échouer, mal tourner.
miscellaneous [mɪsɪ'leɪnɪəs] *adj* (*items, expenses*) divers(es); (*selection*) varié(e).
miscellany [mɪ'sɛlənɪ] *n* recueil *m*.
mischance [mɪs'tʃɑːns] *n* malchance *f*; **by (some) ~** par malheur.
mischief ['mɪstʃɪf] *n* (*naughtiness*) sottises *fpl*; (*harm*) mal *m*, dommage *m*; (*maliciousness*) méchanceté *f*.
mischievous ['mɪstʃɪvəs] *adj* (*naughty*) coquin(e), espiègle; (*harmful*) méchant(e).
misconception ['mɪskən'sɛpʃən] *n* idée fausse.
misconduct [mɪs'kɔndʌkt] *n* inconduite *f*; **professional ~** faute professionnelle.
misconstrue [mɪskən'struː] *vt* mal interpréter.
miscount [mɪs'kaunt] *vt*, *vi* mal compter.
misdeed ['mɪs'diːd] *n* méfait *m*.
misdemeanour, (*US*) **misdemeanor** [mɪsdɪ'miːnə*] *n* écart *m* de conduite; infraction *f*.
misdirect [mɪsdɪ'rɛkt] *vt* (*person*) mal renseigner; (*letter*) mal adresser.

miser ['maɪzə*] *n* avare *m/f*.
miserable ['mɪzərəbl] *adj* malheureux(euse); (*wretched*) misérable; **to feel ~** avoir le cafard.
miserably ['mɪzərəblɪ] *adv* (*smile, answer*) tristement; (*live, pay*) misérablement; (*fail*) lamentablement.
miserly ['maɪzəlɪ] *adj* avare.
misery ['mɪzərɪ] *n* (*unhappiness*) tristesse *f*; (*pain*) souffrances *fpl*; (*wretchedness*) misère *f*.
misfire [mɪs'faɪə*] *vi* rater; (*car engine*) avoir des ratés.
misfit ['mɪsfɪt] *n* (*person*) inadapté/e.
misfortune [mɪs'fɔːtʃən] *n* malchance *f*, malheur *m*.
misgiving(s) [mɪs'gɪvɪŋ(z)] *n(pl)* craintes *fpl*, soupçons *mpl*; **to have ~s about sth** avoir des doutes quant à qch.
misguided [mɪs'gaɪdɪd] *adj* malavisé(e).
mishandle [mɪs'hændl] *vt* (*treat roughly*) malmener; (*mismanage*) mal s'y prendre pour faire *or* résoudre *etc*.
mishap ['mɪshæp] *n* mésaventure *f*.
mishear [mɪs'hɪə*] *vt*, *vi irreg* mal entendre.
mishmash ['mɪʃmæʃ] *n* (*col*) fatras *m*, méli-mélo *m*.
misinform [mɪsɪn'fɔːm] *vt* mal renseigner.
misinterpret [mɪsɪn'təːprɪt] *vt* mal interpréter.
misinterpretation ['mɪsɪntəːprɪ'teɪʃən] *n* interprétation erronée, contresens *m*.
misjudge [mɪs'dʒʌdʒ] *vt* méjuger, se méprendre sur le compte de.
mislay [mɪs'leɪ] *vt irreg* égarer.
mislead [mɪs'liːd] *vt irreg* induire en erreur.
misleading [mɪs'liːdɪŋ] *adj* trompeur(euse).
misled [mɪs'lɛd] *pt*, *pp of* **mislead**.
mismanage [mɪs'mænɪdʒ] *vt* mal gérer; mal s'y prendre pour faire *or* résoudre *etc*.
mismanagement [mɪs'mænɪdʒmənt] *n* mauvaise gestion.
misnomer [mɪs'nəumə*] *n* terme *or* qualificatif trompeur *or* peu approprié.
misogynist [mɪ'sɔdʒɪnɪst] *n* misogyne *m/f*.
misplace [mɪs'pleɪs] *vt* égarer; **to be ~d** (*trust etc*) être mal placé(e).
misprint ['mɪsprɪnt] *n* faute *f* d'impression.
mispronounce [mɪsprə'nauns] *vt* mal prononcer.
misquote ['mɪs'kwəut] *vt* citer erronément *or* inexactement.
misread [mɪs'riːd] *vt irreg* mal lire.
misrepresent [mɪsrɛprɪ'zɛnt] *vt* présenter sous un faux jour.
Miss [mɪs] *n* Mademoiselle; **Dear ~ Smith** Chère Mademoiselle Smith.
miss [mɪs] *vt* (*fail to get*) manquer, rater; (*appointment, class*) manquer; (*escape, avoid*) échapper à, éviter; (*notice loss of: money etc*) s'apercevoir de l'absence de; (*regret the absence of*): **I ~ him/it** il/cela me manque

♦ *vi* manquer ♦ *n* (*shot*) coup manqué; **the bus just ~ed the wall** le bus a évité le mur de justesse; **you're ~ing the point** vous êtes à côté de la question.

►**miss out** *vt* (*BRIT*) oublier.

►**miss out on** *vt fus* (*fun, party*) rater, manquer; (*chance, bargain*) laisser passer.

Miss. *abbr* (*US*) = **Mississippi**.

missal ['mɪsl] *n* missel *m*.

misshapen [mɪs'ʃeɪpən] *adj* difforme.

missile ['mɪsaɪl] *n* (*AVIAT*) missile *m*; (*object thrown*) projectile *m*.

missile base *n* base *f* de missiles.

missile launcher [-lɔːntʃə*] *n* lance-missiles *m*.

missing ['mɪsɪŋ] *adj* manquant(e); (*after escape, disaster: person*) disparu(e); **to go ~** disparaître; **~ person** personne disparue, disparu/e.

mission ['mɪʃən] *n* mission *f*; **on a ~ to sb** en mission auprès de qn.

missionary ['mɪʃənrɪ] *n* missionnaire *m/f*.

missive ['mɪsɪv] *n* missive *f*.

misspell ['mɪs'spɛl] *vt* (*irreg: like* **spell**) mal orthographier.

misspent ['mɪs'spɛnt] *adj*: **his ~ youth** sa folle jeunesse.

mist [mɪst] *n* brume *f*, brouillard *m* ♦ *vi* (*also: ~ over, ~ up*) devenir brumeux(euse); (*BRIT: windows*) s'embuer.

mistake [mɪs'teɪk] *n* erreur *f*, faute *f* ♦ *vt* (*irreg: like* **take**) (*meaning*) mal comprendre; (*intentions*) se méprendre sur; **to ~ for** prendre pour; **by ~** par erreur, par inadvertance; **to make a ~** (*in writing*) faire une faute; (*in calculating etc*) faire une erreur; **to make a ~ about sb/sth** se tromper sur le compte de qn/sur qch.

mistaken [mɪs'teɪkən] *pp of* **mistake** ♦ *adj* (*idea etc*) erroné(e); **to be ~** faire erreur, se tromper.

mistaken identity *n* erreur *f* d'identité.

mistakenly [mɪs'teɪkənlɪ] *adv* par erreur, par mégarde.

mister ['mɪstə*] *n* (*col*) Monsieur *m*; *see* **Mr**.

mistletoe ['mɪsltəu] *n* gui *m*.

mistook [mɪs'tuk] *pt of* **mistake**.

mistranslation [mɪstræns'leɪʃən] *n* erreur *f* de traduction, contresens *m*.

mistreat [mɪs'triːt] *vt* maltraiter.

mistress ['mɪstrɪs] *n* maîtresse *f*; (*BRIT: in primary school*) institutrice *f*; *see* **Mrs**.

mistrust [mɪs'trʌst] *vt* se méfier de ♦ *n*: **~ (of)** méfiance *f* (à l'égard de).

mistrustful [mɪs'trʌstful] *adj*: **~ (of)** méfiant(e) (à l'égard de).

misty ['mɪstɪ] *adj* brumeux(euse).

misty-eyed ['mɪstɪ'aɪd] *adj* les yeux embués de larmes; (*fig*) sentimental(e).

misunderstand [mɪsʌndə'stænd] *vt, vi irreg* mal comprendre.

misunderstanding ['mɪsʌndə'stændɪŋ] *n*

méprise *f*, malentendu *m*.

misunderstood [mɪsʌndə'stud] *pt, pp of* **misunderstand**.

misuse *n* [mɪs'juːs] mauvais emploi; (*of power*) abus *m* ♦ *vt* [mɪs'juːz] mal employer; abuser de.

MIT *n abbr* (*US*) = **Massachusetts Institute of Technology**.

mite [maɪt] *n* (*small quantity*) grain *m*, miette *f*; (*BRIT: small child*) petit/e.

mitigate ['mɪtɪgeɪt] *vt* atténuer; **mitigating circumstances** circonstances atténuantes.

mitigation [mɪtɪ'geɪʃən] *n* atténuation *f*.

mitre, (*US*) miter ['maɪtə*] *n* mitre *f*; (*CARPENTRY*) onglet *m*.

mitt(en) ['mɪt(n)] *n* mitaine *f*; moufle *f*.

mix [mɪks] *vt* mélanger ♦ *vi* se mélanger ♦ *n* mélange *m*; dosage *m*; **to ~ sth with sth** mélanger qch à qch; **to ~ business with pleasure** unir l'utile à l'agréable; **cake ~** préparation *f* pour gâteau.

►**mix in** *vt* incorporer, mélanger.

►**mix up** *vt* mélanger; (*confuse*) confondre; **to be ~ed up in sth** être mêlé(e) à qch or impliqué(e) dans qch.

mixed [mɪkst] *adj* (*assorted*) assortis(ies); (*school etc*) mixte.

mixed-ability ['mɪkstə'bɪlɪtɪ] *adj* (*class etc*) sans groupes de niveaux.

mixed bag *n*: **it's a (bit of a) ~** il y a (un peu) de tout.

mixed blessing *n*: **it's a ~** cela a du bon et du mauvais.

mixed doubles *npl* (*SPORT*) double *m* mixte.

mixed economy *n* économie *f* mixte.

mixed grill *n* (*BRIT*) assortiment *m* de grillades.

mixed marriage *n* mariage *m* mixte.

mixed-up [mɪkst'ʌp] *adj* (*person*) désorienté(e) (*fig*).

mixer ['mɪksə*] *n* (*for food*) batteur *m*, mixeur *m*; (*person*): **he is a good ~** il est très sociable.

mixer tap *n* (robinet *m*) mélangeur *m*.

mixture ['mɪkstʃə*] *n* assortiment *m*, mélange *m*; (*MED*) préparation *f*.

mix-up ['mɪksʌp] *n* confusion *f*.

MK *abbr* (*BRIT TECH*) = **mark**.

mk *abbr* = **mark** (*currency*).

mkt *abbr* = **market**.

MLitt *n abbr* (= *Master of Literature, Master of Letters*) titre universitaire.

MLR *n abbr* (*BRIT*) = **minimum lending rate**.

mm *abbr* (= *millimetre*) mm.

MN *abbr* (*BRIT*) = **Merchant Navy**; (*US*) = **Minnesota**.

MO *n abbr* (*MED*) = **medical officer**; (*US col*: = *modus operandi*) méthode *f* ♦ *abbr* (*US*) = **Missouri**.

Mo. *abbr* (*US*) = **Missouri**.

m.o. *abbr* = **money order**.

moan [məun] *n* gémissement *m* ♦ *vi* gémir;

(col: complain): **to** ~ **(about)** se plaindre (de).

moaner ['məunə*] n (col) rouspéteur/euse, râleur/euse.

moaning ['məunɪŋ] n gémissements mpl.

moat [məut] n fossé m, douves fpl.

mob [mɔb] n foule f; (disorderly) cohue f; (pej): **the** ~ la populace ♦ vt assaillir.

mobile ['məubaɪl] adj mobile ♦ n (ART) mobile m; **applicants must be** ~ (BRIT) les candidats devront être prêts à accepter tout déplacement.

mobile home n caravane f.

mobile phone n téléphone portatif.

mobile shop n (BRIT) camion m magasin.

mobility [məu'bɪlɪtɪ] n mobilité f.

mobilize ['məubɪlaɪz] vt, vi mobiliser.

moccasin ['mɔkəsɪn] n mocassin m.

mock [mɔk] vt ridiculiser, se moquer de ♦ adj faux(fausse).

mockery ['mɔkərɪ] n moquerie f, raillerie f; **to make a** ~ **of** ridiculiser, tourner en dérision.

mocking ['mɔkɪŋ] adj moqueur(euse).

mockingbird ['mɔkɪŋbəːd] n moqueur m.

mock-up ['mɔkʌp] n maquette f.

MOD n abbr (BRIT) = **Ministry of Defence**; see **defence**.

mod cons ['mɔd'kɔnz] npl abbr (BRIT) = **modern conveniences**; see **convenience**.

mode [məud] n mode m; (of transport) moyen m.

model ['mɔdl] n modèle m; (person: for fashion) mannequin m; (: for artist) modèle ♦ vt modeler ♦ vi travailler comme mannequin ♦ adj (railway: toy) modèle réduit inv; (child, factory) modèle; **to** ~ **clothes** présenter des vêtements; **to** ~ **sb/sth on** modeler qn/qch sur.

modeller, (US) **modeler** ['mɔdlə*] n modeleur m; (model maker) maquettiste m/f; fabricant m de modèles réduits.

modem ['məudɛm] n modem m.

moderate adj, n ['mɔdərət] adj modéré(e) ♦ n (POL) modéré/e ♦ vb ['mɔdəreɪt] vi se modérer, se calmer ♦ vt modérer.

moderately ['mɔdərətlɪ] adv (act) avec modération or mesure; (expensive, difficult) moyennement; (pleased, happy) raisonnablement, assez; ~ **priced** à un prix raisonnable.

moderation [mɔdə'reɪʃən] n modération f, mesure f; **in** ~ à dose raisonnable, pris(e) or pratiqué(e) modérément.

moderator ['mɔdəreɪtə*] n (REL): **M**~ président m (de l'Assemblée générale de l'Église presbytérienne); (POL) modérateur m.

modern ['mɔdən] adj moderne; ~ **languages** langues vivantes.

modernization [mɔdənaɪ'zeɪʃən] n modernisation f.

modernize ['mɔdənaɪz] vt moderniser.

modest ['mɔdɪst] adj modeste.

modesty ['mɔdɪstɪ] n modestie f.

modicum ['mɔdɪkəm] n: **a** ~ **of** un minimum de.

modification [mɔdɪfɪ'keɪʃən] n modification f; **to make** ~**s** faire or apporter des modifications.

modify ['mɔdɪfaɪ] vt modifier.

modish ['məudɪʃ] adj à la mode.

Mods [mɔdz] n abbr (BRIT: = (Honour) Moderations) premier examen universitaire (à Oxford).

modular ['mɔdjulə*] adj (filing, unit) modulaire.

modulate ['mɔdjuleɪt] vt moduler.

modulation [mɔdju'leɪʃən] n modulation f.

module ['mɔdjuːl] n module m.

mogul ['məugl] n (fig) nabab m; (SKI) bosse f.

MOH n abbr (BRIT) = **Medical Officer of Health**.

mohair ['məuhɛə*] n mohair m.

Mohammed [mə'hæmɛd] n Mahomet m.

moist [mɔɪst] adj humide, moite.

moisten ['mɔɪsn] vt humecter, mouiller légèrement.

moisture ['mɔɪstʃə*] n humidité f; (on glass) buée f.

moisturize ['mɔɪstʃəraɪz] vt (skin) hydrater.

moisturizer ['mɔɪstʃəraɪzə*] n produit hydratant.

molar ['məulə*] n molaire f.

molasses [məu'læsɪz] n mélasse f.

mold [məuld] n, vt (US) = **mould**.

Moldavia [mɔl'deɪvɪə], **Moldova** [mɔl'dəuvə] n Moldavie f.

Moldavian [mɔl'deɪvɪən], **Moldovan** [mɔl'dəuvən] adj moldave.

mole [məul] n (animal) taupe f; (spot) grain m de beauté.

molecule ['mɔlɪkjuːl] n molécule f.

molehill ['məulhɪl] n taupinière f.

molest [məu'lɛst] vt tracasser; molester.

mollusc ['mɔləsk] n mollusque m.

mollycoddle ['mɔlɪkɔdl] vt chouchouter, couver.

Molotov cocktail ['mɔlətɔf-] n cocktail m Molotov.

molt [məult] vi (US) = **moult**.

molten ['məultən] adj fondu(e).

mom [mɔm] n (US) = **mum**.

moment ['məumənt] n moment m, instant m; (importance) importance f; **at the** ~ en ce moment; **for the** ~ pour l'instant; **in a** ~ dans un instant; "**one** ~ **please**" (TEL) "ne quittez pas".

momentarily ['məuməntrɪlɪ] adv momentanément; (US: soon) bientôt.

momentary ['məuməntərɪ] adj momentané(e), passager(ère).

momentous [məu'mɛntəs] adj important(e), capital(e).

momentum [məu'mɛntəm] n élan m, vitesse acquise; **to gather** ~ prendre de la vitesse.

mommy ['mɔmɪ] n (US: mother) maman f.

Mon. *abbr* (= *Monday*) l.
Monaco ['mɔnəkəʊ] *n* Monaco *f*.
monarch ['mɔnək] *n* monarque *m*.
monarchist ['mɔnəkɪst] *n* monarchiste *m/f*.
monarchy ['mɔnəkɪ] *n* monarchie *f*.
monastery ['mɔnəstərɪ] *n* monastère *m*.
monastic [mə'næstɪk] *adj* monastique.
Monday ['mʌndɪ] *n* lundi *m*; *for phrases see also* **Tuesday.**
monetarist ['mʌnɪtərɪst] *n* monétariste *m/f*.
monetary ['mʌnɪtərɪ] *adj* monétaire.
money ['mʌnɪ] *n* argent *m*; **to make** ~ (*person*) gagner de l'argent; (*business*) rapporter; **I've got no** ~ **left** je n'ai plus d'argent, je n'ai plus un sou.
moneyed ['mʌnɪd] *adj* riche.
moneylender ['mʌnɪlendə*] *n* prêteur/euse.
moneymaker ['mʌnɪmeɪkə*] *n* (*BRIT col: business*) affaire lucrative.
moneymaking ['mʌnɪmeɪkɪŋ] *adj* lucratif(ive), qui rapporte (de l'argent).
money market *n* marché financier.
money order *n* mandat *m*.
money-spinner ['mʌnɪspɪnə*] *n* (*col*) mine *f* d'or (*fig*).
money supply *n* masse *f* monétaire.
Mongol ['mɔŋgəl] *n* Mongol/e; (*LING*) mongol *m*.
mongol ['mɔŋgəl] *adj*, *n* (*MED*) mongolien(ne).
Mongolia [mɔŋ'gəʊlɪə] *n* Mongolie *f*.
Mongolian [mɔŋ'gəʊlɪən] *adj* mongol(e) ♦ *n* Mongol/e; (*LING*) mongol *m*.
mongoose ['mɔŋguːs] *n* mangouste *f*.
mongrel ['mʌŋgrəl] *n* (*dog*) bâtard *m*.
monitor ['mɔnɪtə*] *n* (*BRIT SCOL*) chef *m* de classe; (*US SCOL*) surveillant *m* (d'examen); (*TV, COMPUT*) écran *m*, moniteur *m* ♦ *vt* contrôler; (*foreign station*) être à l'écoute de.
monk [mʌŋk] *n* moine *m*.
monkey ['mʌŋkɪ] *n* singe *m*.
monkey nut *n* (*BRIT*) cacahuète *f*.
monkey wrench *n* clé *f* à molette.
mono ['mɔnəʊ] *adj* mono *inv*.
mono... ['mɔnəʊ] *prefix* mono....
monochrome ['mɔnəkrəʊm] *adj* monochrome.
monocle ['mɔnəkl] *n* monocle *m*.
monogamous [mɔ'nɔgəməs] *adj* monogame.
monogamy [mɔ'nɔgəmɪ] *n* monogamie *f*.
monogram ['mɔnəgræm] *n* monogramme *m*.
monolith ['mɔnəlɪθ] *n* monolithe *m*.
monologue ['mɔnəlɔg] *n* monologue *m*.
monoplane ['mɔnəpleɪn] *n* monoplan *m*.
monopolize [mə'nɔpəlaɪz] *vt* monopoliser.
monopoly [mə'nɔpəlɪ] *n* monopole *m*; **Monopolies and Mergers Commission** (*BRIT*) *commission britannique d'enquête sur les monopoles.*
monorail ['mɔnəʊreɪl] *n* monorail *m*.
monosodium glutamate [mɔnə'səʊdɪəm 'gluːtəmeɪt] *n* glutamate *m* de sodium.
monosyllabic [mɔnəsɪ'læbɪk] *adj* monosyllabique; (*person*) laconique.

monosyllable ['mɔnəsɪləbl] *n* monosyllabe *m*.
monotone ['mɔnətəʊn] *n* ton *m* (*or* voix *f*) monocorde; **to speak in a** ~ parler sur un ton monocorde.
monotonous [mə'nɔtənəs] *adj* monotone.
monotony [mə'nɔtənɪ] *n* monotonie *f*.
monoxide [mɔ'nɔksaɪd] *n*: **carbon** ~ oxyde *m* de carbone.
monsoon [mɔn'suːn] *n* mousson *f*.
monster ['mɔnstə*] *n* monstre *m*.
monstrosity [mɔns'trɔsɪtɪ] *n* monstruosité *f*, atrocité *f*.
monstrous ['mɔnstrəs] *adj* (*huge*) gigantesque; (*atrocious*) monstrueux(euse), atroce.
Mont. *abbr* (*US*) = *Montana.*
montage [mɔn'tɑːʒ] *n* montage *m*.
Mont Blanc [mɔ̃blɑ̃] *n* Mont Blanc *m*.
month [mʌnθ] *n* mois *m*; **every** ~ tous les mois; **300 dollars a** ~ 300 dollars par mois.
monthly ['mʌnθlɪ] *adj* mensuel(le) ♦ *adv* mensuellement ♦ *n* (*magazine*) mensuel *m*, publication mensuelle; **twice** ~ deux fois par mois.
Montreal [mɔntrɪ'ɔːl] *n* Montréal.
monument ['mɔnjumənt] *n* monument *m*.
monumental [mɔnju'mentl] *adj* monumental(e).
monumental mason *n* marbrier *m*.
moo [muː] *vi* meugler, beugler.
mood [muːd] *n* humeur *f*, disposition *f*; **to be in a good/bad** ~ être de bonne/mauvaise humeur; **to be in the** ~ **for** être d'humeur à, avoir envie de.
moody ['muːdɪ] *adj* (*variable*) d'humeur changeante, lunatique; (*sullen*) morose, maussade.
moon [muːn] *n* lune *f*.
moonbeam ['muːnbiːm] *n* rayon *m* de lune.
moon landing *n* alunissage *m*.
moonlight ['muːnlaɪt] *n* clair *m* de lune ♦ *vi* travailler au noir.
moonlighting ['muːnlaɪtɪŋ] *n* travail *m* au noir.
moonlit ['muːnlɪt] *adj* éclairé(e) par la lune; **a** ~ **night** une nuit de lune.
moonshot ['muːnʃɔt] *n* (*SPACE*) tir *m* lunaire.
moonstruck ['muːnstrʌk] *adj* fou(folle), dérangé(e).
moony ['muːnɪ] *adj*: **to have** ~ **eyes** avoir l'air dans la lune *or* rêveur.
Moor [mʊə*] *n* Maure/Mauresque.
moor [mʊə*] *n* lande *f* ♦ *vt* (*ship*) amarrer ♦ *vi* mouiller.
moorings ['mʊərɪŋz] *npl* (*chains*) amarres *fpl*; (*place*) mouillage *m*.
Moorish ['mʊərɪʃ] *adj* maure(mauresque).
moorland ['mʊələnd] *n* lande *f*.
moose [muːs] *n* (*pl inv*) élan *m*.
moot [muːt] *vt* soulever ♦ *adj*: ~ **point** point *m* discutable.
mop [mɔp] *n* balai *m* à laver ♦ *vt* éponger,

essuyer; ~ **of hair** tignasse f.
▸**mop up** vt éponger.
mope [məup] vi avoir le cafard, se
morfondre.
▸**mope about, mope around** vi broyer du
noir, se morfondre.
moped ['məuped] n cyclomoteur m.
moquette [mɔ'kɛt] n moquette f.
MOR adj abbr (MUS: = middle-of-the-road) tous
publics.
moral ['mɔrl] adj moral(e) ♦ n morale f; ~**s** npl
moralité f.
morale [mɔ'rɑːl] n moral m.
morality [mə'rælɪtɪ] n moralité f.
moralize ['mɔrəlaɪz] vi: **to** ~ **(about)** moraliser
(sur).
morally ['mɔrəlɪ] adv moralement.
moral victory n victoire morale.
morass [mə'ræs] n marais m, marécage m.
moratorium [mɔrə'tɔːrɪəm] n moratoire m.
morbid ['mɔːbɪd] adj morbide.

======= KEYWORD

more [mɔː*] adj 1 (greater in number etc) plus
(de), davantage; ~ **people/work (than)** plus
de gens/de travail (que)
2 (additional) encore (de); **do you want
(some)** ~ **tea?** voulez-vous encore du thé?; **I
have no** or **I don't have any** ~ **money** je n'ai
plus d'argent; **it'll take a few** ~ **weeks** ça
prendra encore quelques semaines
♦ pron plus, davantage; ~ **than 10** plus de 10;
it cost ~ **than we expected** cela a coûté plus
que prévu; **I want** ~ j'en veux plus or
davantage; **is there any** ~? est-ce qu'il en
reste?; **there's no** ~ il n'y en a plus; **a little**
~ un peu plus; **many/much** ~ beaucoup
plus, bien davantage
♦ adv: ~ **dangerous/easily (than)** plus
dangereux/facilement (que); ~ **and** ~
expensive de plus en plus cher; ~ **or less**
plus ou moins; ~ **than ever** plus que jamais;
once ~ encore une fois, une fois de plus;
and what's ~ ... et de plus ..., et qui plus
est ...

moreover [mɔː'rəuvə*] adv de plus.
morgue [mɔːg] n morgue f.
MORI ['mɔːrɪ] n abbr (BRIT: = Market & Opinion
Research Institute) institut de sondage.
moribund ['mɔrɪbʌnd] adj moribond(e).
morning ['mɔːnɪŋ] n matin m; (as duration)
matinée f; **in the** ~ le matin; **7 o'clock in the**
~ 7 heures du matin; **this** ~ ce matin.
morning-after pill ['mɔːnɪŋ'ɑːftə-] n pilule f
du lendemain.
morning sickness n nausées matinales.
Moroccan [mə'rɔkən] adj marocain(e) ♦ n
Marocain/e.
Morocco [mə'rɔkəu] n Maroc m.
moron ['mɔːrɔn] n idiot/e, minus m/f.
moronic [mə'rɔnɪk] adj idiot(e), imbécile.

morose [mə'rəus] adj morose, maussade.
morphine ['mɔːfiːn] n morphine f.
morris dancing ['mɔrɪs-] n (BRIT) danses
folkloriques anglaises.
Morse [mɔːs] n (also: ~ **code**) morse m.
morsel ['mɔːsl] n bouchée f.
mortal ['mɔːtl] adj, n mortel(le).
mortality [mɔː'tælɪtɪ] n mortalité f.
mortality rate n (taux m de) mortalité f.
mortar ['mɔːtə*] n mortier m.
mortgage ['mɔːgɪdʒ] n hypothèque f; (loan)
prêt m (or crédit m) hypothécaire ♦ vt
hypothéquer; **to take out a** ~ prendre une
hypothèque, faire un emprunt.
mortgage company n (US) société f de
crédit immobilier.
mortgagee [mɔːgə'dʒiː] n prêteur/euse (sur
hypothèque).
mortgagor ['mɔːgədʒə*] n emprunteur/euse
(sur hypothèque).
mortician [mɔː'tɪʃən] n (US) entrepreneur m
de pompes funèbres.
mortified ['mɔːtɪfaɪd] adj mortifié(e).
mortise lock ['mɔːtɪs-] n serrure encastrée.
mortuary ['mɔːtjuərɪ] n morgue f.
mosaic [məu'zeɪɪk] n mosaïque f.
Moscow ['mɔskəu] n Moscou.
Moslem ['mɔzləm] adj, n = **Muslim.**
mosque [mɔsk] n mosquée f.
mosquito, ~**es** [mɔs'kiːtəu] n moustique m.
mosquito net n moustiquaire f.
moss [mɔs] n mousse f.
mossy ['mɔsɪ] adj moussu(e).
most [məust] adj la plupart de; le plus de
♦ pron la plupart ♦ adv le plus; (very) très,
extrêmement; **the** ~ (also: + adjective) le
plus; ~ **fish** la plupart des poissons; ~ **of** la
plus grande partie de; ~ **of them** la plupart
d'entre eux; **I saw** ~ j'en ai vu la plupart;
c'est moi qui en ai vu le plus; **at the (very)** ~
au plus; **to make the** ~ **of** profiter au
maximum de.
mostly ['məustlɪ] adv surtout, principalement.
MOT n abbr (BRIT: = Ministry of Transport): **the** ~
(test) visite technique (annuelle) obligatoire
des véhicules à moteur.
motel [məu'tɛl] n motel m.
moth [mɔθ] n papillon m de nuit; mite f.
mothball ['mɔθbɔːl] n boule f de naphtaline.
moth-eaten ['mɔθiːtn] adj mité(e).
mother ['mʌðə*] n mère f ♦ vt (care for)
dorloter.
mother board n (COMPUT) carte-mère f.
motherhood ['mʌðəhud] n maternité f.
mother-in-law ['mʌðərɪnlɔː] n belle-mère f.
motherly ['mʌðəlɪ] adj maternel(le).
mother-of-pearl ['mʌðərəv'pəːl] n nacre f.
mother's help n aide f or auxiliaire f
familiale.
mother-to-be ['mʌðətə'biː] n future maman.
mother tongue n langue maternelle.
mothproof ['mɔθpruːf] adj traité(e) à

l'antimite.

motif [məʊ'tiːf] *n* motif *m*.

motion ['məʊʃən] *n* mouvement *m*; (*gesture*) geste *m*; (*at meeting*) motion *f*; (*BRIT: also*: **bowel** ~) selles *fpl* ♦ *vt, vi*: **to** ~ **(to) sb to do** faire signe à qn de faire; **to be in** ~ (*vehicle*) être en marche; **to set in** ~ mettre en marche; **to go through the** ~**s of doing sth** (*fig*) faire qch machinalement *or* sans conviction.

motionless ['məʊʃənlɪs] *adj* immobile, sans mouvement.

motion picture *n* film *m*.

motivate ['məʊtɪveɪt] *vt* motiver.

motivated ['məʊtɪveɪtɪd] *adj* motivé(e).

motivation [məʊtɪ'veɪʃən] *n* motivation *f*.

motive ['məʊtɪv] *n* motif *m*, mobile *m* ♦ *adj* moteur(trice); **from the best (of)** ~**s** avec les meilleures intentions (du monde).

motley ['mɒtlɪ] *adj* hétéroclite; bigarré(e), bariolé(e).

motor ['məʊtə*] *n* moteur *m*; (*BRIT col: vehicle*) auto *f* ♦ *adj* moteur(trice).

motorbike ['məʊtəbaɪk] *n* moto *f*.

motorboat ['məʊtəbəʊt] *n* bateau *m* à moteur.

motorcade ['məʊtəkeɪd] *n* cortège *m* d'automobiles *or* de voitures.

motorcar ['məʊtəkɑː] *n* (*BRIT*) automobile *f*.

motorcoach ['məʊtəkəʊtʃ] *n* (*BRIT*) car *m*.

motorcycle ['məʊtəsaɪkl] *n* vélomoteur *m*.

motorcyclist ['məʊtəsaɪklɪst] *n* motocycliste *m/f*.

motoring ['məʊtərɪŋ] (*BRIT*) *n* tourisme *m* automobile ♦ *adj* (*accident*) de voiture, de la route; ~ **holiday** vacances *fpl* en voiture; ~ **offence** infraction *f* au code de la route.

motorist ['məʊtərɪst] *n* automobiliste *m/f*.

motorize ['məʊtəraɪz] *vt* motoriser.

motor oil *n* huile *f* de graissage.

motor racing *n* (*BRIT*) course *f* automobile.

motor scooter *n* scooter *m*.

motor vehicle *n* véhicule *m* automobile.

motorway ['məʊtəweɪ] *n* (*BRIT*) autoroute *f*.

mottled ['mɒtld] *adj* tacheté(e), marbré(e).

motto, ~es ['mɒtəʊ] *n* devise *f*.

mould, (*US***) mold** [məʊld] *n* moule *m*; (*mildew*) moisissure *f* ♦ *vt* mouler, modeler; (*fig*) façonner.

mo(u)lder ['məʊldə*] *vi* (*decay*) moisir.

mo(u)lding ['məʊldɪŋ] *n* (*ARCHIT*) moulure *f*.

mo(u)ldy ['məʊldɪ] *adj* moisi(e).

moult, (*US***) molt** [məʊlt] *vi* muer.

mound [maʊnd] *n* monticule *m*, tertre *m*.

mount [maʊnt] *n* mont *m*, montagne *f*; (*horse*) monture *f*; (*for jewel etc*) monture ♦ *vt* monter; (*exhibition*) organiser, monter; (*picture*) monter sur carton; (*stamp*) coller dans un album ♦ *vi* (*also*: ~ **up**) s'élever, monter.

mountain ['maʊntɪn] *n* montagne *f* ♦ *cpd* de (la) montagne; **to make a** ~ **out of a molehill** (*fig*) se faire une montagne d'un rien.

mountain bike *n* VTT *m*, vélo *m* tout terrain.

mountaineer [maʊntɪ'nɪə*] *n* alpiniste *m/f*.

mountaineering [maʊntɪ'nɪərɪŋ] *n* alpinisme *m*; **to go** ~ faire de l'alpinisme.

mountainous ['maʊntɪnəs] *adj* montagneux(euse).

mountain range *n* chaîne *f* de montagnes.

mountain rescue team *n* colonne *f* de secours.

mountainside ['maʊntɪnsaɪd] *n* flanc *m or* versant *m* de la montagne.

mounted ['maʊntɪd] *adj* monté(e).

Mount Everest *n* le mont Everest.

mourn [mɔːn] *vt* pleurer ♦ *vi*: **to** ~ (**for**) se lamenter (sur).

mourner ['mɔːnə*] *n* parent/e *or* ami/e du défunt; personne *f* en deuil *or* venue rendre hommage au défunt.

mournful ['mɔːnful] *adj* triste, lugubre.

mourning ['mɔːnɪŋ] *n* deuil *m* ♦ *cpd* (*dress*) de deuil; **in** ~ en deuil.

mouse, *pl* mice [maʊs, maɪs] *n* (*also COMPUT*) souris *f*.

mousetrap ['maʊstræp] *n* souricière *f*.

moussaka [mu'sɑːkə] *n* moussaka *f*.

mousse [muːs] *n* mousse *f*.

moustache [məs'tɑːʃ] *n* moustache(s) *f(pl)*.

mousy ['maʊsɪ] *adj* (*person*) effacé(e); (*hair*) d'un châtain terne.

mouth, ~s [maʊθ, -ðz] *n* bouche *f*; (*of dog, cat*) gueule *f*; (*of river*) embouchure *f*; (*of bottle*) goulot *m*; (*opening*) orifice *m*.

mouthful ['maʊθful] *n* bouchée *f*.

mouth organ *n* harmonica *m*.

mouthpiece ['maʊθpiːs] *n* (*of musical instrument*) bec *m*, embouchure *f*; (*spokesman*) porte-parole *m inv*.

mouth-to-mouth ['maʊθtə'maʊθ] *adj*: ~ **resuscitation** bouche à bouche *m*.

mouthwash ['maʊθwɒʃ] *n* eau *f* dentifrice.

mouth-watering ['maʊθwɔːtərɪŋ] *adj* qui met l'eau à la bouche.

movable ['muːvəbl] *adj* mobile.

move [muːv] *n* (*movement*) mouvement *m*; (*in game*) coup *m*; (*: turn to play*) tour *m*; (*change of house*) déménagement *m* ♦ *vt* déplacer, bouger; (*emotionally*) émouvoir; (*POL: resolution etc*) proposer ♦ *vi* (*gen*) bouger, remuer; (*traffic*) circuler; (*also*: ~ **house**) déménager; **to** ~ **towards** se diriger vers; **to** ~ **sb to do sth** pousser *or* inciter qn à faire qch; **to get a** ~ **on** se dépêcher, se remuer.

▶**move about, move around** *vi* (*fidget*) remuer; (*travel*) voyager, se déplacer.

▶**move along** *vi* se pousser.

▶**move away** *vi* s'en aller, s'éloigner.

▶**move back** *vi* revenir, retourner.

▶**move forward** *vi* avancer ♦ *vt* avancer; (*people*) faire avancer.

▶**move in** *vi* (*to a house*) emménager.

▶**move off** *vi* s'éloigner, s'en aller.

▶**move on** *vi* se remettre en route ♦ *vt* (*onlookers*) faire circuler.

▶**move out** *vi* (*of house*) déménager.

▶**move over** *vi* se pousser, se déplacer.

▶**move up** *vi* avancer; (*employee*) avoir de l'avancement.

movement ['mu:vmənt] *n* mouvement *m*; ~ (**of the bowels**) (*MED*) selles *fpl*.

mover ['mu:və*] *n* auteur *m* d'une proposition.

movie ['mu:vɪ] *n* film *m*; **the ~s** le cinéma.

movie camera *n* caméra *f*.

moviegoer ['mu:vɪgəuə*] *n* (*US*) cinéphile *m/f*.

moving ['mu:vɪŋ] *adj* en mouvement; (*touching*) émouvant(e) ♦ *n* (*US*) déménagement *m*.

mow, *pt* **mowed**, *pp* **mowed** *or* **mown** [məu, -n] *vt* faucher; (*lawn*) tondre.

▶**mow down** *vt* faucher.

mower ['məuə*] *n* (*also:* **lawn~**) tondeuse *f* à gazon.

Mozambique [məuzəm'bi:k] *n* Mozambique *m*.

MP *n abbr* (= *Military Police*) PM; (*BRIT*) = **Member of Parliament**; (*Canada*) = Mounted Police.

mpg *n abbr* = *miles per gallon* (*30 mpg = 9,4 l. aux 100 km*).

mph *abbr* = *miles per hour* (*60 mph = 96 km/h*).

MPhil *n abbr* (*US*: = *Master of Philosophy*) *titre universitaire.*

MPS *n abbr* (*BRIT*) = *Member of the Pharmaceutical Society.*

Mr, Mr. ['mɪstə*] *n*: ~ **X** Monsieur X, M. X.

MRC *n abbr* (*BRIT*: = *Medical Research Council*) *conseil de la recherche médicale.*

MRCP *n abbr* (*BRIT*) = *Member of the Royal College of Physicians.*

MRCS *n abbr* (*BRIT*) = *Member of the Royal College of Surgeons.*

MRCVS *n abbr* (*BRIT*) = *Member of the Royal College of Veterinary Surgeons.*

Mrs, Mrs. ['mɪsɪz] *n*: ~ **X** Madame X, Mme X.

MS *n abbr* (= *manuscript*) ms; (= *multiple sclerosis*) SEP *f*; (*US*: = *Master of Science*) *titre universitaire* ♦ *abbr* (*US*) = Mississippi.

Ms, Ms. [mɪz] *n* (= *Miss or Mrs*): ~ **X** Madame X, Mme X.

MSA *n abbr* (*US*: = *Master of Science in Agriculture*) *titre universitaire.*

MSc *n abbr* = **Master of Science.**

MSG *n abbr* = **monosodium glutamate.**

MST *abbr* (*US*: = *Mountain Standard Time*) *heure d'hiver des Montagnes Rocheuses.*

MSW *n abbr* (*US*: = *Master of Social Work*) *titre universitaire.*

MT *n abbr* (= *machine translation*) TM ♦ *abbr* (*US*) = Montana.

Mt *abbr* (*GEO*: = *mount*) Mt.

MTV *n abbr* = *music television.*

much [mʌtʃ] *adj* beaucoup de ♦ *adv, n or pron* beaucoup; ~ **milk** beaucoup de lait; **how** ~

is it? combien est-ce que ça coûte?; **it's not** ~ ce n'est pas beaucoup; **too** ~ trop (de); **so** ~ tant (de); **I like it very/so** ~ j'aime beaucoup/tellement ça; **thank you very** ~ merci beaucoup; ~ **to my amazement** ... à mon grand étonnement ....

muck [mʌk] *n* (*mud*) boue *f*; (*dirt*) ordures *fpl*.

▶**muck about** *vi* (*col*) faire l'imbécile; (: *waste time*) traînasser; (: *tinker*) bricoler; tripoter.

▶**muck in** *vi* (*BRIT col*) donner un coup de main.

▶**muck out** *vt* (*stable*) nettoyer.

▶**muck up** *vt* (*col*: *ruin*) gâcher, esquinter; (: *dirty*) salir.

muckraking ['mʌkreɪkɪŋ] *n* (*fig*: *col*) déterrement *m* d'ordures.

mucky ['mʌkɪ] *adj* (*dirty*) boueux(euse), sale.

mucus ['mju:kəs] *n* mucus *m*.

mud [mʌd] *n* boue *f*.

muddle ['mʌdl] *n* pagaille *f*; désordre *m*, fouillis *m* ♦ *vt* (*also*: ~ **up**) brouiller, embrouiller; **to be in a** ~ (*person*) ne plus savoir ou l'on en est; **to get in a** ~ (*while explaining etc*) s'embrouiller.

▶**muddle along** *vi* aller son chemin tant bien que mal.

▶**muddle through** *vi* se débrouiller.

muddle-headed [mʌdl'hɛdɪd] *adj* (*person*) à l'esprit embrouillé *or* confus, dans le brouillard.

muddy ['mʌdɪ] *adj* boueux(euse).

mud flats *npl* plage *f* de vase.

mudguard ['mʌdgɑːd] *n* garde-boue *m inv*.

mudpack ['mʌdpæk] *n* masque *m* de beauté.

mud-slinging ['mʌdslɪŋɪŋ] *n* médisance *f*, dénigrement *m*.

muesli ['mju:zlɪ] *n* muesli *m*.

muff [mʌf] *n* manchon *m* ♦ *vt* (*col*: *shot, catch etc*) rater, louper; **to** ~ **it** rater *or* louper son coup.

muffin ['mʌfɪn] *n petit pain rond et plat.*

muffle ['mʌfl] *vt* (*sound*) assourdir, étouffer; (*against cold*) emmitoufler.

muffled ['mʌfld] *adj* étouffé(e), voilé(e).

muffler ['mʌflə*] *n* (*scarf*) cache-nez *m inv*; (*US AUT*) silencieux *m*.

mufti ['mʌftɪ] *n*: **in** ~ en civil.

mug [mʌg] *n* (*cup*) tasse *f* (*sans soucoupe*); (: *for beer*) chope *f*; (*col*: *face*) bouille *f*; (: *fool*) poire *f* ♦ *vt* (*assault*) agresser; **it's a** ~**'s game** (*BRIT*) c'est bon pour les imbéciles.

▶**mug up** *vt* (*BRIT col*: *also*: ~ **up on**) bosser, bûcher.

mugger ['mʌgə*] *n* agresseur *m*.

mugging ['mʌgɪŋ] *n* agression *f*.

muggins ['mʌgɪnz] *n* (*col*) ma pomme.

muggy ['mʌgɪ] *adj* lourd(e), moite.

mug shot *n* (*col*: *POLICE*) photo *f* de criminel; (: *gen*: *photo*) photo d'identité.

mulatto, ~**es** [mju:'lætəu] *n* mulâtre/esse.

mulberry ['mʌlbrɪ] *n* (*fruit*) mûre *f*; (*tree*)

mûrier *m*.
mule [mjuːl] *n* mule *f*.
mull [mʌl]: **to ~ over** *vt* réfléchir à, ruminer.
mulled [mʌld] *adj*: **~ wine** vin chaud.
multi... ['mʌltɪ] *prefix* multi....
multi-access ['mʌltɪ'æksɛs] *adj* (*COMPUT*) à accès multiple.
multicoloured, (*US*) **multicolored** ['mʌltɪkʌləd] *adj* multicolore.
multifarious [mʌltɪ'fɛərɪəs] *adj* divers(es); varié(e).
multilateral [mʌltɪ'lætərl] *adj* (*POL*) multilatéral(e).
multi-level ['mʌltɪlɛvl] *adj* (*US*) = **multistorey**.
multimillionaire [mʌltɪmɪljə'nɛə*] *n* milliardaire *m/f*.
multinational [mʌltɪ'næʃənl] *n* multinationale *f* ♦ *adj* multinational(e).
multiple ['mʌltɪpl] *adj* multiple ♦ *n* multiple *m*; (*BRIT: also*: **~ store**) magasin *m* à succursales (multiples).
multiple choice *adj* à choix multiple.
multiple crash *n* carambolage *m*.
multiple sclerosis *n* sclérose *f* en plaques.
multiplex ['mʌltɪplɛks] *n* (*also*: **~ cinema**) (cinéma *m*) multisalles *m*.
multiplication [mʌltɪplɪ'keɪʃən] *n* multiplication *f*.
multiplication table *n* table *f* de multiplication.
multiplicity [mʌltɪ'plɪsɪtɪ] *n* multiplicité *f*.
multiply ['mʌltɪplaɪ] *vt* multiplier ♦ *vi* se multiplier.
multiracial [mʌltɪ'reɪʃl] *adj* multiracial(e).
multistorey ['mʌltɪ'stɔːrɪ] *adj* (*BRIT: building*) à étages; (*: car park*) à étages *or* niveaux multiples.
multitude ['mʌltɪtjuːd] *n* multitude *f*.
mum [mʌm] *n* (*BRIT*) maman *f* ♦ *adj*: **to keep ~** ne pas souffler mot; **~'s the word!** motus et bouche cousue!
mumble ['mʌmbl] *vt, vi* marmotter, marmonner.
mumbo jumbo ['mʌmbəu-] *n* (*col*) baragouin *m*, charabia *m*.
mummify ['mʌmɪfaɪ] *vt* momifier.
mummy ['mʌmɪ] *n* (*BRIT: mother*) maman *f*; (*embalmed*) momie *f*.
mumps [mʌmps] *n* oreillons *mpl*.
munch [mʌntʃ] *vt, vi* mâcher.
mundane [mʌn'deɪn] *adj* banal(e), terre à terre *inv*.
municipal [mjuː'nɪsɪpl] *adj* municipal(e).
municipality [mjuːnɪsɪ'pælɪtɪ] *n* municipalité *f*.
munitions [mjuː'nɪʃənz] *npl* munitions *fpl*.
mural ['mjuərl] *n* peinture murale.
murder ['məːdə*] *n* meurtre *m*, assassinat *m* ♦ *vt* assassiner; **to commit ~** commettre un meurtre.
murderer ['məːdərə*] *n* meurtrier *m*, assassin *m*.

murderess ['məːdərɪs] *n* meurtrière *f*.
murderous ['məːdərəs] *adj* meurtrier(ière).
murk [məːk] *n* obscurité *f*.
murky ['məːkɪ] *adj* sombre, ténébreux(euse).
murmur ['məːmə*] *n* murmure *m* ♦ *vt, vi* murmurer; **heart ~** (*MED*) souffle *m* au cœur.
MusB(ac) *n abbr* (= *Bachelor of Music*) titre universitaire.
muscle ['mʌsl] *n* muscle *m*.
▶**muscle in** *vi* s'imposer, s'immiscer.
muscular ['mʌskjulə*] *adj* musculaire; (*person, arm*) musclé(e).
muscular dystrophy *n* dystrophie *f* musculaire.
MusD(oc) *n abbr* (= *Doctor of Music*) titre universitaire.
muse [mjuːz] *vi* méditer, songer ♦ *n* muse *f*.
museum [mjuː'zɪəm] *n* musée *m*.
mush [mʌʃ] *n* bouillie *f*; (*pej*) sentimentalité *f* à l'eau de rose.
mushroom ['mʌʃrum] *n* champignon *m* ♦ *vi* (*fig*) pousser comme un (*or* des) champignon(s).
mushy ['mʌʃɪ] *adj* (*vegetables, fruit*) en bouillie; (*movie etc*) à l'eau de rose.
music ['mjuːzɪk] *n* musique *f*.
musical ['mjuːzɪkl] *adj* musical(e); (*person*) musicien(ne) ♦ *n* (*show*) comédie musicale.
music(al) box *n* boîte *f* à musique.
musical chairs *npl* chaises musicales; (*fig*) **to play ~** faire des permutations.
musical instrument *n* instrument *m* de musique.
music centre *n* chaîne compacte.
music hall *n* music-hall *m*.
musician [mjuː'zɪʃən] *n* musicien/ne.
music stand *n* pupitre *m* à musique.
musk [mʌsk] *n* musc *m*.
musket ['mʌskɪt] *n* mousquet *m*.
muskrat ['mʌskræt] *n* rat musqué.
musk rose *n* (*BOT*) rose *f* muscade.
Muslim ['mʌzlɪm] *adj, n* musulman(e).
muslin ['mʌzlɪn] *n* mousseline *f*.
musquash ['mʌskwɔʃ] *n* loutre *f*; (*fur*) rat *m* d'Amérique, ondatra *m*.
mussel ['mʌsl] *n* moule *f*.
must [mʌst] *aux vb* (*obligation*): **I ~ do it** je dois le faire, il faut que je le fasse; (*probability*): **he ~ be there by now** il doit y être maintenant, il y est probablement maintenant; **I ~ have made a mistake** j'ai dû me tromper ♦ *n* nécessité *f*, impératif *m*; **it's a ~** c'est indispensable.
mustache ['mʌstæʃ] *n* (*US*) = **moustache**.
mustard ['mʌstəd] *n* moutarde *f*.
mustard gas *n* ypérite *f*, gaz *m* moutarde.
muster ['mʌstə*] *vt* rassembler; (*also*: **~ up**: *strength, courage*) rassembler.
mustiness ['mʌstɪnɪs] *n* goût *m* de moisi; odeur *f* de moisi *or* de renfermé.
mustn't ['mʌsnt] = **must not**.

musty ['mʌstɪ] adj qui sent le moisi or le
renfermé.
mutant ['mju:tənt] adj mutant(e) ♦ n mutant
m.
mutate [mju:'teɪt] vi subir une mutation.
mutation [mju:'teɪʃən] n mutation f.
mute [mju:t] adj, n muet(te).
muted ['mju:tɪd] adj (noise) sourd(e),
assourdi(e); (criticism) voilé(e); (MUS) en
sourdine; (: trumpet) bouché(e).
mutilate ['mju:tɪleɪt] vt mutiler.
mutilation [mju:tɪ'leɪʃən] n mutilation f.
mutinous ['mju:tɪnəs] adj (troops) mutiné(e);
(attitude) rebelle.
mutiny ['mju:tɪnɪ] n mutinerie f ♦ vi se
mutiner.
mutter ['mʌtə*] vt, vi marmonner, marmotter.
mutton ['mʌtn] n mouton m.
mutual ['mju:tʃuəl] adj mutuel(le),
réciproque.
mutually ['mju:tʃuəlɪ] adv mutuellement,
réciproquement.
Muzak ['mju:zæk] n ® (often pej) musique f
d'ambiance.
muzzle ['mʌzl] n museau m; (protective
device) muselière f; (of gun) gueule f ♦ vt
museler.
MVP n abbr (US SPORT) = most valuable player.
MW abbr (= medium wave) PO.
my [maɪ] adj mon(ma), mes pl.
Myanmar ['maɪænmɑ:*] n Myanmar m.
myopic [maɪ'ɔpɪk] adj myope.
myriad ['mɪrɪəd] n myriade f.
myself [maɪ'sɛlf] pron (reflexive) me; (emphatic)
moi-même; (after prep) moi.
mysterious [mɪs'tɪərɪəs] adj
mystérieux(euse).
mystery ['mɪstərɪ] n mystère m.
mystery story n roman m à suspense.
mystic ['mɪstɪk] n mystique m/f ♦ adj
(mysterious) ésotérique.
mystical ['mɪstɪkl] adj mystique.
mystify ['mɪstɪfaɪ] vt mystifier; (puzzle)
ébahir.
mystique [mɪs'ti:k] n mystique f.
myth [mɪθ] n mythe m.
mythical ['mɪθɪkl] adj mythique.
mythological [mɪθə'lɔdʒɪkl] adj
mythologique.
mythology [mɪ'θɔlədʒɪ] n mythologie f.

N n

N, n [ɛn] n (letter) N, n m; **N for Nellie,** (US) **N
for Nan** N comme Nicolas.
N abbr (= north) N.
NA n abbr (US: = Narcotics Anonymous)
association d'aide aux drogués; (US)
= National Academy.
n/a abbr (= not applicable) n.a.; (COMM etc) = no
account.
NAACP n abbr (US) = National Association for
the Advancement of Colored People.
NAAFI ['næfɪ] n abbr (BRIT: = Navy, Army & Air
Force Institute) organisme responsable des
magasins et cantines de l'armée.
nab [næb] vt (col) pincer, attraper.
NACU n abbr (US) = National Association of
Colleges and Universities.
nadir ['neɪdɪə*] n (ASTRONOMY) nadir m; (fig)
fond m, point m extrême.
nag [næg] vt (person) être toujours après,
reprendre sans arrêt ♦ n (pej: horse)
canasson m; (person): **she's an awful** ~ elle
est constamment après lui (or eux etc), elle
est terriblement casse-pieds.
nagging ['nægɪŋ] adj (doubt, pain)
persistant(e) ♦ n remarques continuelles.
nail [neɪl] n (human) ongle m; (metal) clou m
♦ vt clouer; **to** ~ **sb down to a date/price**
contraindre qn à accepter or donner une
date/un prix; **to pay cash on the** ~ (BRIT)
payer rubis sur l'ongle.
nailbrush ['neɪlbrʌʃ] n brosse f à ongles.
nailfile ['neɪlfaɪl] n lime f à ongles.
nail polish n vernis m à ongles.
nail polish remover n dissolvant m.
nail scissors npl ciseaux mpl à ongles.
nail varnish n (BRIT) = nail polish.
Nairobi [naɪ'rəubɪ] n Nairobi.
naïve [naɪ'i:v] adj naïf(ïve).
naïveté [naɪ'i:vteɪ], **naivety** [naɪ'i:vɪtɪ] n
naïveté f.
naked ['neɪkɪd] adj nu(e); **with the** ~ **eye** à
l'œil nu.
nakedness ['neɪkɪdnɪs] n nudité f.
NAM n abbr (US) = National Association of
Manufacturers.
name [neɪm] n nom m; (reputation) réputation f
♦ vt nommer; citer; (price, date) fixer,
donner; **by** ~ par son nom; de nom; **in the** ~
of au nom de; **what's your** ~? quel est votre
nom?; **my** ~ **is Peter** je m'appelle Peter; **to
take sb's** ~ **and address** relever l'identité de
qn or les nom et adresse de qn; **to make a** ~

for o.s. se faire un nom; **to get (o.s.) a bad** ~ se faire une mauvaise réputation; **to call sb** ~**s** traiter qn de tous les noms.

name dropping n mention (pour se faire valoir) du nom de personnalités qu'on connaît (ou prétend connaître).

nameless ['neɪmlɪs] adj sans nom; (witness, contributor) anonyme.

namely ['neɪmlɪ] adv à savoir.

nameplate ['neɪmpleɪt] n (on door etc) plaque f.

namesake ['neɪmseɪk] n homonyme m.

nan bread [nɑːn-] n nan m.

nanny ['nænɪ] n bonne f d'enfants.

nanny goat n chèvre f.

nap [næp] n (sleep) (petit) somme ♦ vi: **to be caught** ~**ping** être pris(e) à l'improviste or en défaut.

NAPA n abbr (US: = National Association of Performing Artists) syndicat des gens du spectacle.

napalm ['neɪpɑːm] n napalm m.

nape [neɪp] n: ~ **of the neck** nuque f.

napkin ['næpkɪn] n serviette f (de table).

Naples ['neɪplz] n Naples.

Napoleonic [nəpəulɪ'ɒnɪk] adj napoléonien(ne).

nappy ['næpɪ] n (BRIT) couche f (gen pl).

nappy liner n (BRIT) protège-couche m.

narcissistic [nɑːsɪ'sɪstɪk] adj narcissique.

narcissus, pl **narcissi** [nɑː'sɪsəs, -saɪ] n narcisse m.

narcotic [nɑː'kɒtɪk] n (MED) narcotique m; ~**s** npl (drugs) stupéfiants mpl.

nark [nɑːk] vt (BRIT col) mettre en rogne.

narrate [nə'reɪt] vt raconter, narrer.

narration [nə'reɪʃən] n narration f.

narrative ['nærətɪv] n récit m ♦ adj narratif(ive).

narrator [nə'reɪtə*] n narrateur/trice.

narrow ['nærəu] adj étroit(e); (fig) restreint(e), limité(e) ♦ vi devenir plus étroit, se rétrécir; **to have a** ~ **escape** l'échapper belle; **to** ~ **sth down to** réduire qch à.

narrow gauge adj (RAIL) à voie étroite.

narrowly ['nærəulɪ] adv: **he** ~ **missed injury/ the tree** il a failli se blesser/rentrer dans l'arbre; **he only** ~ **missed the target** il a manqué la cible de peu or de justesse.

narrow-minded [nærəu'maɪndɪd] adj à l'esprit étroit, borné(e).

NAS n abbr (US) = National Academy of Sciences.

NASA ['næsə] n abbr (US: = National Aeronautics and Space Administration) NASA f.

nasal ['neɪzl] adj nasal(e).

Nassau ['næsɔː] n (in Bahamas) Nassau.

nastily ['nɑːstɪlɪ] adv (say, act) méchamment.

nastiness ['nɑːstɪnɪs] n (of person, remark) méchanceté f.

nasturtium [nəs'təːʃəm] n capucine f.

nasty ['nɑːstɪ] adj (person) méchant(e); très désagréable; (smell) dégoûtant(e); (wound, situation) mauvais(e), vilain(e); (weather) affreux(euse); **to turn** ~ (situation) mal tourner; (weather) se gâter; (person) devenir méchant; **it's a** ~ **business** c'est une sale affaire.

NAS/UWT n abbr (BRIT: = National Association of Schoolmasters/Union of Women Teachers) syndicat enseignant.

nation ['neɪʃən] n nation f.

national ['næʃənl] adj national(e) ♦ n (abroad) ressortissant/e; (when home) national/e.

national anthem n hymne national.

National Curriculum n (BRIT) programme scolaire commun à toutes les écoles publiques en Angleterre et au Pays de Galles comprenant dix disciplines.

national debt n dette publique.

national dress n costume national.

National Guard n (US) milice f (de volontaires dans chaque État).

National Health Service (NHS) n (BRIT) service national de santé, ≈ Sécurité Sociale.

National Insurance n (BRIT) ≈ Sécurité Sociale.

nationalism ['næʃnəlɪzəm] n nationalisme m.

nationalist ['næʃnəlɪst] adj, n nationaliste (m/f).

nationality [næʃə'nælɪtɪ] n nationalité f.

nationalization [næʃnəlaɪ'zeɪʃən] n nationalisation f.

nationalize ['næʃnəlaɪz] vt nationaliser.

nationally ['næʃnəlɪ] adv du point de vue national; dans le pays entier.

national park n parc national.

national press n presse nationale.

National Security Council n (US) conseil national de sécurité.

national service n (MIL) service m militaire.

Le **National Trust** est un organisme indépendant, à but non lucratif, dont la mission est de protéger et de mettre en valeur les monuments et les sites britanniques en raison de leur intérêt historique ou de leur beauté naturelle.

nation-wide ['neɪʃənwaɪd] adj s'étendant à l'ensemble du pays; (problem) à l'échelle du pays entier ♦ adv à travers or dans tout le pays.

native ['neɪtɪv] n habitant/e du pays, autochtone m/f; (in colonies) indigène m/f ♦ adj du pays, indigène; (country) natal(e); (language) maternel(le); (ability) inné(e); **a** ~ **of Russia** une personne originaire de Russie; **a** ~ **speaker of French** une personne de langue maternelle française.

Native American n Indien/ne d'Amérique.

Nativity [nə'tɪvɪtɪ] n (REL): **the** ~ la Nativité.

nativity play n mystère m or miracle m de la

Nativité.

NATO ['neɪtəʊ] *n abbr* (= *North Atlantic Treaty Organization*) OTAN *f*.

natter ['nætə*] *vi* (*BRIT*) bavarder.

natural ['nætʃrəl] *adj* naturel(le); **to die of ~ causes** mourir d'une mort naturelle.

natural childbirth *n* accouchement *m* sans douleur.

natural gas *n* gaz naturel.

natural history *n* histoire naturelle.

naturalist ['nætʃrəlɪst] *n* naturaliste *m/f*.

naturalization ['nætʃrəlaɪ'zeɪʃən] *n* naturalisation *f*; acclimatation *f*.

naturalize ['nætʃrəlaɪz] *vt* naturaliser; (*plant*) acclimater; **to become ~d** (*person*) se faire naturaliser.

naturally ['nætʃrəlɪ] *adv* naturellement.

naturalness ['nætʃrəlnɪs] *n* naturel *m*.

natural resources *npl* ressources naturelles.

natural selection *n* sélection naturelle.

natural wastage *n* (*INDUSTRY*) départs naturels et volontaires.

nature ['neɪtʃə*] *n* nature *f*; **by ~** par tempérament, de nature; **documents of a confidential ~** documents à caractère confidentiel.

-natured ['neɪtʃəd] *suffix*: **ill~** qui a un mauvais caractère.

nature reserve *n* (*BRIT*) réserve naturelle.

nature trail *n* *sentier de découverte de la nature*.

naturist ['neɪtʃərɪst] *n* naturiste *m/f*.

naught [nɔːt] *n* = **nought**.

naughtiness ['nɔːtɪnɪs] *n* (*of child*) désobéissance *f*; (*of story etc*) grivoiserie *f*.

naughty ['nɔːtɪ] *adj* (*child*) vilain(e), pas sage; (*story, film*) grivois(e).

nausea ['nɔːsɪə] *n* nausée *f*.

nauseate ['nɔːsɪeɪt] *vt* écœurer, donner la nausée à.

nauseating ['nɔːsɪeɪtɪŋ] *adj* écœurant(e), dégoûtant(e).

nauseous ['nɔːsɪəs] *adj* nauséabond(e), écœurant(e); (*feeling sick*): **to be ~** avoir des nausées.

nautical ['nɔːtɪkl] *adj* nautique.

nautical mile *n* mille marin (= *1853 m*).

naval ['neɪvl] *adj* naval(e).

naval officer *n* officier *m* de marine.

nave [neɪv] *n* nef *f*.

navel ['neɪvl] *n* nombril *m*.

navigable ['nævɪgəbl] *adj* navigable.

navigate ['nævɪgeɪt] *vt* diriger, piloter ♦ *vi* naviguer; (*AUT*) indiquer la route à suivre.

navigation [nævɪ'geɪʃən] *n* navigation *f*.

navigator ['nævɪgeɪtə*] *n* navigateur *m*.

navvy ['nævɪ] *n* (*BRIT*) terrassier *m*.

navy ['neɪvɪ] *n* marine *f*; **Department of the N~** (*US*) ministère *m* de la Marine.

navy(-blue) ['neɪvɪ('bluː)] *adj* bleu marine *inv*.

Nazareth ['næzərɪθ] *n* Nazareth.

Nazi ['nɑːtsɪ] *adj* nazi(e) ♦ *n* Nazi/e.

NB *abbr* (= *nota bene*) NB; (*Canada*) = *New Brunswick*.

NBA *n abbr* (*US*) = *National Basketball Association, National Boxing Association*.

NBC *n abbr* (*US*: = *National Broadcasting Company*) chaîne de télévision.

NBS *n abbr* (*US*: = *National Bureau of Standards*) office de normalisation.

NC *abbr* (*COMM etc*) = *no charge*; (*US*) = *North Carolina*.

NCC *n abbr* (*BRIT*: = *Nature Conservancy Council*) organisme de protection de la nature; (*US*) = *National Council of Churches*.

NCCL *n abbr* (*BRIT*: = *National Council for Civil Liberties*) association de défense des libertés publiques.

NCO *n abbr* = **non-commissioned officer**.

ND, N. Dak. *abbr* (*US*) = *North Dakota*.

NE *abbr* (*US*) = *Nebraska, New England*.

NEA *n abbr* (*US*) = *National Education Association*.

neap [niːp] *n* (*also*: **~tide**) mortes-eaux *fpl*.

Neapolitan [nɪə'pɔlɪtən] *adj* napolitain(e) ♦ *n* Napolitain/e.

near [nɪə*] *adj* proche ♦ *adv* près ♦ *prep* (*also*: **~ to**) près de ♦ *vt* approcher de; **~ here/there** près d'ici/non loin de là; **£25,000 or ~est offer** (*BRIT*) 25 000 livres à débattre; **in the ~ future** dans un proche avenir; **the building is ~ing completion** le bâtiment est presque terminé; **to come ~** *vi* s'approcher.

nearby [nɪə'baɪ] *adj* proche ♦ *adv* tout près, à proximité.

Near East *n*: **the ~** le Proche-Orient.

nearer ['nɪərə*] *adj* plus proche ♦ *adv* plus près.

nearly ['nɪəlɪ] *adv* presque; **I ~ fell** j'ai failli tomber; **it's not ~ big enough** ce n'est vraiment pas assez grand, c'est loin d'être assez grand.

near miss *n* collision évitée de justesse; (*when aiming*) coup manqué de peu *or* de justesse.

nearness ['nɪənɪs] *n* proximité *f*.

nearside ['nɪəsaɪd] (*AUT*) *n* (*right-hand drive*) côté *m* gauche; (*left-hand drive*) côté droit ♦ *adj* de gauche; de droite.

near-sighted [nɪə'saɪtɪd] *adj* myope.

neat [niːt] *adj* (*person, work*) soigné(e); (*room etc*) bien tenu(e) *or* rangé(e); (*solution, plan*) habile; (*spirits*) pur(e); **I drink it ~** je le bois sec *or* sans eau.

neatly ['niːtlɪ] *adv* avec soin *or* ordre; habilement.

neatness ['niːtnɪs] *n* (*tidiness*) netteté *f*; (*skilfulness*) habileté *f*.

Nebr. *abbr* (*US*) = *Nebraska*.

nebulous ['nɛbjuləs] *adj* nébuleux(euse).

necessarily ['nɛsɪsrɪlɪ] *adv* nécessairement; **not ~** pas nécessairement *or* forcément.

necessary ['nɛsɪsrɪ] *adj* nécessaire; **if ~** si besoin est, le cas échéant.

necessitate [nɪ'sɛsɪteɪt] *vt* nécessiter.
necessity [nɪ'sɛsɪtɪ] *n* nécessité *f*; chose nécessaire *or* essentielle; **in case of** ~ en cas d'urgence.
neck [nɛk] *n* cou *m*; (*of horse, garment*) encolure *f*; (*of bottle*) goulot *m* ♦ *vi* (*col*) se peloter; ~ **and** ~ à égalité; **to stick one's** ~ **out** (*col*) se mouiller.
necklace ['nɛklɪs] *n* collier *m*.
neckline ['nɛklaɪn] *n* encolure *f*.
necktie ['nɛktaɪ] *n* (*esp US*) cravate *f*.
nectar ['nɛktə*] *n* nectar *m*.
nectarine ['nɛktərɪn] *n* brugnon *m*, nectarine *f*.
NEDC *n abbr* (*BRIT*: = *National Economic Development Council*) conseil national pour le développement économique.
Neddy ['nɛdɪ] *n abbr* (*BRIT col*) = **NEDC**.
née [neɪ] *adj*: ~ **Scott** née Scott.
need [niːd] *n* besoin *m* ♦ *vt* avoir besoin de; **to** ~ **to do** devoir faire; avoir besoin de faire; **you don't** ~ **to go** vous n'avez pas besoin *or* vous n'êtes pas obligé de partir; **a signature is** ~**ed** il faut une signature; **to be in** ~ **of** *or* **have** ~ **of** avoir besoin de; **£10 will meet my immediate** ~**s** 10 livres suffiront pour mes besoins immédiats; **in case of** ~ en cas de besoin, au besoin; **there's no** ~ **to do ...** il n'y a pas lieu de faire ..., il n'est pas nécessaire de faire ...; **there's no** ~ **for that** ce n'est pas la peine, cela n'est pas nécessaire.
needle ['niːdl] *n* aiguille *f*; (*on record player*) saphir *m* ♦ *vt* (*col*) asticoter, tourmenter.
needlecord ['niːdlkɔːd] *n* (*BRIT*) velours *m* milleraies.
needless ['niːdlɪs] *adj* inutile; ~ **to say**, ... inutile de dire que ....
needlessly ['niːdlɪslɪ] *adv* inutilement.
needlework ['niːdlwəːk] *n* (*activity*) travaux *mpl* d'aiguille; (*object*) ouvrage *m*.
needn't ['niːdnt] = **need not**.
needy ['niːdɪ] *adj* nécessiteux(euse).
negation [nɪ'geɪʃən] *n* négation *f*.
negative ['nɛgətɪv] *n* (*PHOT, ELEC*) négatif *m*; (*LING*) terme *m* de négation ♦ *adj* négatif(ive); **to answer in the** ~ répondre par la négative.
negative equity *n* situation dans laquelle la valeur d'une maison est inférieure à celle de l'emprunt-logement contracté pour la payer.
neglect [nɪ'glɛkt] *vt* négliger ♦ *n* (*of person, duty, garden*) le fait de négliger; (*state of*) ~ abandon *m*; **to** ~ **to do sth** négliger *or* omettre de faire qch.
neglected [nɪ'glɛktɪd] *adj* négligé(e), à l'abandon.
neglectful [nɪ'glɛktful] *adj* (*gen*) négligent(e); **to be** ~ **of sb/sth** négliger qn/qch.
negligee ['nɛglɪʒeɪ] *n* déshabillé *m*.
negligence ['nɛglɪdʒəns] *n* négligence *f*.
negligent ['nɛglɪdʒənt] *adj* négligent(e).

negligently ['nɛglɪdʒəntlɪ] *adv* par négligence; (*offhandedly*) négligemment.
negligible ['nɛglɪdʒɪbl] *adj* négligeable.
negotiable [nɪ'gəuʃɪəbl] *adj* négociable; **not** ~ (*cheque*) non négociable.
negotiate [nɪ'gəuʃɪeɪt] *vi* négocier ♦ *vt* (*COMM*) négocier; (*obstacle*) franchir, négocier; (*bend in road*) négocier; **to** ~ **with sb for sth** négocier avec qn en vue d'obtenir qch.
negotiating table [nɪ'gəuʃɪeɪtɪŋ-] *n* table *f* des négociations.
negotiation [nɪgəuʃɪ'eɪʃən] *n* négociation *f*, pourparlers *mpl*; **to enter into** ~**s with sb** engager des négociations avec qn.
negotiator [nɪ'gəuʃɪeɪtə*] *n* négociateur/trice.
Negress ['niːgrɪs] *n* négresse *f*.
Negro ['niːgrəu] *adj* (*gen*) noir(e); (*music, arts*) nègre, noir ♦ *n* (*pl*: ~**es**) Noir/e.
neigh [neɪ] *vi* hennir.
neighbour, (*US*) **neighbor** ['neɪbə*] *n* voisin/e.
neighbo(u)rhood ['neɪbəhud] *n* quartier *m*; voisinage *m*.
neighbourhood watch *n* (*BRIT*: *also*: ~ **scheme**) *système de surveillance, assuré par les habitants d'un même quartier*.
neighbo(u)ring ['neɪbərɪŋ] *adj* voisin(e), avoisinant(e).
neighbo(u)rly ['neɪbəlɪ] *adj* obligeant(e); (*relations*) de bon voisinage.
neither ['naɪðə*] *adj, pron* aucun(e) (des deux), ni l'un(e) ni l'autre ♦ *conj*: **I didn't move and** ~ **did Claude** je n'ai pas bougé, (et) Claude non plus ♦ *adv*: ~ **good nor bad** ni bon ni mauvais; ..., ~ **did I refuse** ..., (et *or* mais) je n'ai pas non plus refusé.
neo... ['niːəu] *prefix* néo-.
neolithic [niːəu'lɪθɪk] *adj* néolithique.
neologism [nɪ'ɔlədʒɪzəm] *n* néologisme *m*.
neon ['niːɔn] *n* néon *m*.
neon light *n* lampe *f* au néon.
neon sign *n* enseigne (lumineuse) au néon.
Nepal [nɪ'pɔːl] *n* Népal *m*.
nephew ['nɛvjuː] *n* neveu *m*.
nepotism ['nɛpətɪzəm] *n* népotisme *m*.
nerd [nəːd] *n* (*col*) pauvre mec *m*, ballot *m*.
nerve [nəːv] *n* nerf *m*; (*bravery*) sang-froid *m*, courage *m*; (*cheek*) aplomb *m*, toupet *m*; **he gets on my** ~**s** il m'énerve; **to have a fit of** ~**s** avoir le trac; **to lose one's** ~ (*self-confidence*) perdre son sang-froid.
nerve centre *n* (*ANAT*) centre nerveux; (*fig*) centre névralgique.
nerve gas *n* gaz *m* neuroplégique.
nerve-racking ['nəːvrækɪŋ] *adj* angoissant(e).
nervous ['nəːvəs] *adj* nerveux(euse); (*apprehensive*) inquiet(ète), plein(e) d'appréhension.
nervous breakdown *n* dépression nerveuse.
nervously ['nəːvəslɪ] *adv* nerveusement.
nervousness ['nəːvəsnɪs] *n* nervosité *f*, inquiétude *f*, appréhension *f*.

nervous wreck *n*: **to be a** ~ être une boule de nerfs.

nervy ['nɜːvɪ] *adj*: **he's very** ~ il a les nerfs à fleur de peau *or* à vif.

nest [nɛst] *n* nid *m* ♦ *vi* (se) nicher, faire son nid; ~ **of tables** table *f* gigogne.

nest egg *n* (*fig*) bas *m* de laine, magot *m*.

nestle ['nɛsl] *vi* se blottir.

nestling ['nɛstlɪŋ] *n* oisillon *m*.

net [nɛt] *n* (*also* fabric) filet *m* ♦ *adj* net(te) ♦ *vt* (*fish etc*) prendre au filet; (*money: subj: person*) toucher; (: *deal, sale*) rapporter; ~ **of tax** net d'impôt; **he earns £10,000** ~ **per year** il gagne 10 000 livres net par an.

netball ['nɛtbɔːl] *n* netball *m*.

net curtains *npl* voilages *mpl*.

Netherlands ['nɛðələndz] *npl*: **the** ~ les Pays-Bas *mpl*.

net profit *n* bénéfice net.

nett [nɛt] *adj* = **net**.

netting ['nɛtɪŋ] *n* (*for fence etc*) treillis *m*, grillage *m*; (*fabric*) voile *m*.

nettle ['nɛtl] *n* ortie *f*.

network ['nɛtwɜːk] *n* réseau *m* ♦ *vt* (*RADIO, TV*) diffuser sur l'ensemble du réseau; (*computers*) interconnecter.

neuralgia [njuəˈrældʒə] *n* névralgie *f*.

neurological [njuərəˈlɒdʒɪkl] *adj* neurologique.

neurosis, *pl* **neuroses** [njuəˈrəusɪs, -siːz] *n* névrose *f*.

neurotic [njuəˈrɒtɪk] *adj*, *n* névrosé(e).

neuter ['njuːtə*] *adj*, *n* neutre (*m*) ♦ *vt* (*cat etc*) châtrer, couper.

neutral ['njuːtrəl] *adj* neutre ♦ *n* (*AUT*) point mort.

neutrality [njuːˈtrælɪtɪ] *n* neutralité *f*.

neutralize ['njuːtrəlaɪz] *vt* neutraliser.

neutron bomb ['njuːtrɒn-] *n* bombe *f* à neutrons.

Nev. *abbr* (*US*) = *Nevada*.

never ['nɛvə*] *adv* (ne …) jamais; ~ **again** plus jamais; ~ **in my life** jamais de ma vie; *see also* **mind**.

never-ending [nɛvərˈɛndɪŋ] *adj* interminable.

nevertheless [nɛvəðəˈlɛs] *adv* néanmoins, malgré tout.

new [njuː] *adj* nouveau(nouvelle); (*brand new*) neuf(neuve); **as good as** ~ comme neuf.

New Age *n* New Age *m*.

newborn ['njuːbɔːn] *adj* nouveau-né(e).

newcomer ['njuːkʌmə*] *n* nouveau venu/nouvelle venue.

new-fangled ['njuːfæŋgld] *adj* (*pej*) ultramoderne (et farfelu(e)).

new-found ['njuːfaund] *adj* de fraîche date; (*friend*) nouveau/nouvelle.

Newfoundland ['njuːfənlənd] *n* Terre-Neuve *f*.

New Guinea *n* Nouvelle-Guinée *f*.

newly ['njuːlɪ] *adv* nouvellement, récemment.

newly-weds ['njuːlɪwɛdz] *npl* jeunes mariés *mpl*.

new moon *n* nouvelle lune.

newness ['njuːnɪs] *n* nouveauté *f*; (*of fabric, clothes etc*) état neuf.

New Orleans [-'ɔːliːənz] *n* la Nouvelle-Orléans.

news [njuːz] *n* nouvelle(s) *f(pl)*; (*RADIO, TV*) informations *fpl*; **a piece of** ~ une nouvelle; **good/bad** ~ bonne/mauvaise nouvelle; **financial** ~ (*PRESS, RADIO, TV*) page financière.

news agency *n* agence *f* de presse.

newsagent ['njuːzeɪdʒənt] *n* (*BRIT*) marchand *m* de journaux.

news bulletin *n* (*RADIO, TV*) bulletin *m* d'informations.

newscaster ['njuːzkɑːstə*] *n* (*RADIO, TV*) présentateur/trice.

newsdealer ['njuːzdiːlə*] *n* (*US*) = **newsagent**.

news flash *n* flash *m* d'information.

newsletter ['njuːzlɛtə*] *n* bulletin *m*.

newspaper ['njuːzpeɪpə*] *n* journal *m*; **daily** ~ quotidien *m*; **weekly** ~ hebdomadaire *m*.

newsprint ['njuːzprɪnt] *n* papier *m* (de) journal.

newsreader ['njuːzriːdə*] *n* = **newscaster**.

newsreel ['njuːzriːl] *n* actualités (filmées).

newsroom ['njuːzruːm] *n* (*PRESS*) salle *f* de rédaction; (*RADIO, TV*) studio *m*.

news stand *n* kiosque *m* à journaux.

newsworthy ['njuːzwɜːðɪ] *adj*: **to be** ~ valoir la peine d'être publié.

newt [njuːt] *n* triton *m*.

new town *n* (*BRIT*) ville nouvelle.

New Year *n* Nouvel An; **Happy** ~! Bonne Année!; **to wish sb a happy** ~ souhaiter la Bonne Année à qn.

New Year's Day *n* le jour de l'An.

New Year's Eve *n* la Saint-Sylvestre.

New York [-'jɔːk] *n* New York; (*also*: ~ **State**) New York *m*.

New Zealand [-'ziːlənd] *n* Nouvelle-Zélande *f* ♦ *adj* néo-zélandais(e).

New Zealander [-'ziːləndə*] *n* Néo-Zélandais/e.

next [nɛkst] *adj* (*seat, room*) voisin(e), d'à côté; (*meeting, bus stop*) suivant(e); prochain(e) ♦ *adv* la fois suivante; la prochaine fois; (*afterwards*) ensuite; ~ **to** *prep* à côté de; ~ **to nothing** presque rien; ~ **time** *adv* la prochaine fois; **the** ~ **day** le lendemain, le jour suivant *or* d'après; ~ **week** la semaine prochaine; **the** ~ **week** la semaine suivante; ~ **year** l'année prochaine; **"turn to the** ~ **page"** "voir page suivante"; **who's** ~? c'est à qui?; **the week after** ~ dans deux semaines; **when do we meet** ~? quand nous revoyons-nous?

next door *adv* à côté.

next-of-kin ['nɛkstəv'kɪn] *n* parent *m* le plus proche.

NF *n abbr* (*BRIT POL*: = *National Front*) ≈ FN

♦ *abbr* (*Canada*) = Newfoundland.
NFL *n abbr* (*US*) = National Football League.
Nfld. *abbr* (*Canada*) = Newfoundland.
NG *abbr* (*US*) = **National Guard.**
NGO *n abbr* (*US*: = *non-governmental organization*) ONG *f.*
NH *abbr* (*US*) = New Hampshire.
NHL *n abbr* (*US*) = National Hockey League.
NHS *n abbr* (*BRIT*) = **National Health Service.**
NI *abbr* = **Northern Ireland**; (*BRIT*) = **National Insurance.**
Niagara Falls [naɪˈægərə-] *npl*: **the** ~ les chutes *fpl* du Niagara.
nib [nɪb] *n* (*of pen*) (bec *m* de) plume *f.*
nibble [ˈnɪbl] *vt* grignoter.
Nicaragua [nɪkəˈrægjuə] *n* Nicaragua *m.*
Nicaraguan [nɪkəˈrægjuən] *adj* nicaraguayen(ne) ♦ *n* Nicaraguayen/ne.
nice [naɪs] *adj* (*holiday, trip, taste*) agréable; (*flat, picture*) joli(e); (*person*) gentil(le); (*distinction, point*) subtil(e).
nice-looking [ˈnaɪslukɪŋ] *adj* joli(e).
nicely [ˈnaɪslɪ] *adv* agréablement; joliment; gentiment; subtilement; **that will do** ~ ce sera parfait.
niceties [ˈnaɪsɪtɪz] *npl* subtilités *fpl.*
niche [niːʃ] *n* (*ARCHIT*) niche *f.*
nick [nɪk] *n* encoche *f*; (*BRIT col*): **in good** ~ en bon état ♦ *vt* (*cut*): **to** ~ **o.s.** se couper; (*col*: *steal*) faucher, piquer; (: *BRIT*: *arrest*) choper, pincer; **in the** ~ **of time** juste à temps.
nickel [ˈnɪkl] *n* nickel *m*; (*US*) pièce *f* de 5 cents.
nickname [ˈnɪkneɪm] *n* surnom *m* ♦ *vt* surnommer.
Nicosia [nɪkəˈsiːə] *n* Nicosie. *f.*
nicotine [ˈnɪkətiːn] *n* nicotine *f.*
nicotine patch *n* timbre *m* anti-tabac, patch *m.*
niece [niːs] *n* nièce *f.*
nifty [ˈnɪftɪ] *adj* (*col*: *car, jacket*) qui a du chic *or* de la classe; (: *gadget, tool*) astucieux(euse).
Niger [ˈnaɪdʒə*] *n* (*country, river*) Niger *m.*
Nigeria [naɪˈdʒɪərɪə] *n* Nigéria *m or f.*
Nigerian [naɪˈdʒɪərɪən] *adj* nigérien(ne) ♦ *n* Nigérien/ne.
niggardly [ˈnɪgədlɪ] *adj* (*person*) parcimonieux(euse), pingre; (*allowance, amount*) misérable.
nigger [ˈnɪgə*] *n* (*col!*: *highly offensive*) nègre/négresse.
niggle [ˈnɪgl] *vt* tracasser ♦ *vi* (*find fault*) trouver toujours à redire; (*fuss*) n'être jamais content(e).
niggling [ˈnɪglɪŋ] *adj* tatillon(ne); (*detail*) insignifiant(e); (*doubt, pain*) persistant(e).
night [naɪt] *n* nuit *f*; (*evening*) soir *m*; **at** ~ la nuit; **by** ~ de nuit; **in the** ~, **during the** ~ pendant la nuit; **the** ~ **before last** avant-hier soir.
night-bird [ˈnaɪtbəːd] *n* oiseau *m* nocturne; (*fig*) couche-tard *m inv*, noctambule *m/f.*

nightcap [ˈnaɪtkæp] *n* boisson prise avant le coucher.
night club *n* boîte *f* de nuit.
nightdress [ˈnaɪtdrɛs] *n* chemise *f* de nuit.
nightfall [ˈnaɪtfɔːl] *n* tombée *f* de la nuit.
nightie [ˈnaɪtɪ] *n* chemise *f* de nuit.
nightingale [ˈnaɪtɪŋgeɪl] *n* rossignol *m.*
night life *n* vie *f* nocturne.
nightly [ˈnaɪtlɪ] *adj* de chaque nuit *or* soir; (*by night*) nocturne ♦ *adv* chaque nuit *or* soir; nuitamment.
nightmare [ˈnaɪtmɛə*] *n* cauchemar *m.*
night porter *n* gardien *m* de nuit, concierge *m* de service la nuit.
night safe *n* coffre *m* de nuit.
night school *n* cours *mpl* du soir.
nightshade [ˈnaɪtʃeɪd] *n*: **deadly** ~ (*BOT*) belladone *f.*
nightshift [ˈnaɪtʃɪft] *n* équipe *f* de nuit.
night-time [ˈnaɪttaɪm] *n* nuit *f.*
night watchman *n* veilleur *m* de nuit; poste *m* de nuit.
nihilism [ˈnaɪɪlɪzəm] *n* nihilisme *m.*
nil [nɪl] *n* rien *m*; (*BRIT SPORT*) zéro *m.*
Nile [naɪl] *n*: **the** ~ le Nil.
nimble [ˈnɪmbl] *adj* agile.
nine [naɪn] *num* neuf.
nineteen [ˈnaɪnˈtiːn] *num* dix-neuf.
ninety [ˈnaɪntɪ] *num* quatre-vingt-dix.
ninth [naɪnθ] *num* neuvième.
nip [nɪp] *vt* pincer ♦ *vi* (*BRIT col*): **to** ~ **out/down/up** sortir/descendre/monter en vitesse ♦ *n* pincement *m*; (*drink*) petit verre; **to** ~ **into a shop** faire un saut dans un magasin.
nipple [ˈnɪpl] *n* (*ANAT*) mamelon *m*, bout *m* du sein.
nippy [ˈnɪpɪ] *adj* (*BRIT*: *person*) alerte, leste; (: *car*) nerveux(euse).
nit [nɪt] *n* (*in hair*) lente *f*; (*col*: *idiot*) imbécile *m/f*, crétin/e.
nit-pick [ˈnɪtpɪk] *vi* (*col*) être tatillon(ne).
nitrogen [ˈnaɪtrədʒən] *n* azote *m.*
nitroglycerin(e) [ˈnaɪtrəʊˈglɪsəriːn] *n* nitroglycérine *f.*
nitty-gritty [ˈnɪtɪˈgrɪtɪ] *n* (*fam*): **to get down to the** ~ en venir au fond du problème.
nitwit [ˈnɪtwɪt] *n* (*col*) nigaud/e.
NJ *abbr* (*US*) = New Jersey.
NLF *n abbr* (= *National Liberation Front*) FLN *m.*
NLQ *abbr* (= *near letter quality*) qualité *f* courrier.
NLRB *n abbr* (*US*: = *National Labor Relations Board*) *organisme de protection des travailleurs.*
NM, N. Mex. *abbr* (*US*) = New Mexico.

════════════════════════════ *KEYWORD*

no [nəʊ] (*pl* **-es**) *adv* (*opposite of "yes"*) non; **are you coming?** — ~ **(I'm not)** est-ce que vous venez? — non; **would you like some more?** — ~ **thank you** vous en voulez

encore? — non merci
♦ adj (not any) pas de, aucun(e) (used with "ne"); **I have ~ money/books** je n'ai pas d'argent/de livres; **~ student would have done it** aucun étudiant ne l'aurait fait; **"~ smoking"** "défense de fumer"; **"~ dogs"** "les chiens ne sont pas admis"
♦ n non m; **I won't take ~ for an answer** il n'est pas question de refuser.

no. abbr (= number) nº.

nobble ['nɔbl] vt (BRIT col: bribe: person) soudoyer, acheter; (: person: to speak to) mettre le grappin sur; (RACING: horse, dog) droguer (pour l'empêcher de gagner).

Nobel prize [nəu'bɛl-] n prix m Nobel.

nobility [nəu'bɪlɪtɪ] n noblesse f.

noble ['nəubl] adj noble.

nobleman ['nəublmən] n noble m.

nobly ['nəublɪ] adv noblement.

nobody ['nəubədɪ] pron personne (with negative).

no-claims bonus ['nəukleɪmz-] n bonus m.

nocturnal [nɔk'təːnl] adj nocturne.

nod [nɔd] vi faire un signe de (la) tête (affirmatif ou amical); (sleep) somnoler ♦ vt: **to ~ one's head** faire un signe de (la) tête; (in agreement) faire signe que oui ♦ n signe m de (la) tête; **they ~ded their agreement** ils ont acquiescé d'un signe de la tête.

nod off vi s'assoupir.

no-fly zone [nəu'flaɪ-] n zone interdite (aux avions et hélicoptères).

noise [nɔɪz] n bruit m.

noiseless ['nɔɪzlɪs] adj silencieux(euse).

noisily ['nɔɪzɪlɪ] adv bruyamment.

noisy ['nɔɪzɪ] adj bruyant(e).

nomad ['nəumæd] n nomade m/f.

nomadic [nəu'mædɪk] adj nomade.

no man's land n no man's land m.

nominal ['nɔmɪnl] adj (rent, fee) symbolique; (value) nominal(e).

nominate ['nɔmɪneɪt] vt (propose) proposer; (elect) nommer.

nomination [nɔmɪ'neɪʃən] n nomination f.

nominee [nɔmɪ'niː] n candidat agréé; personne nommée.

non- [nɔn] prefix non-.

nonalcoholic [nɔnælkə'hɔlɪk] adj non-alcoolisé(e).

nonbreakable [nɔn'breɪkəbl] adj incassable.

nonce word ['nɔns-] n mot créé pour l'occasion.

nonchalant ['nɔnʃələnt] adj nonchalant(e).

noncommissioned [nɔnkə'mɪʃənd] adj: **~ officer** sous-officier m.

noncommittal [nɔnkə'mɪtl] adj évasif(ive).

nonconformist [nɔnkən'fɔːmɪst] n non-conformiste m/f ♦ adj non-conformiste, dissident(e).

noncontributory [nɔnkən'trɪbjutərɪ] adj: **~ pension scheme** or (US) **plan** régime de retraite payée par l'employeur.

noncooperation ['nɔnkəuɔpə'reɪʃən] n refus m de coopérer, non-coopération f.

nondescript ['nɔndɪskrɪpt] adj quelconque, indéfinissable.

none [nʌn] pron aucun/e; **~ of you** aucun d'entre vous, personne parmi vous; **I have ~** je n'en ai pas; **I have ~ left** je n'en ai plus; **~ at all** (not one) aucun(e); **how much milk? — ~ at all** combien de lait? — pas du tout; **he's ~ the worse for it** il ne s'en porte pas plus mal.

nonentity [nɔ'nɛntɪtɪ] n personne insignifiante.

nonessential [nɔnɪ'sɛnʃl] adj accessoire, superflu(e) ♦ n: **~s** le superflu.

nonetheless ['nʌnðə'lɛs] adv néanmoins.

nonevent [nɔnɪ'vɛnt] n événement manqué.

nonexecutive [nɔnɪg'zɛkjutɪv] adj: **~ director** administrateur/trice, conseiller/ère de direction.

nonexistent [nɔnɪg'zɪstənt] adj inexistant(e).

nonfiction [nɔn'fɪkʃən] n littérature f non-romanesque.

nonflammable [nɔn'flæməbl] adj ininflammable.

nonintervention ['nɔnɪntə'vɛnʃən] n non-intervention f.

no-no ['nəunəu] n (col): **it's a ~** il n'en est pas question.

non obst. abbr (= non obstante: notwithstanding) nonobstant.

no-nonsense [nəu'nɔnsəns] adj (manner, person) plein(e) de bon sens.

nonpayment [nɔn'peɪmənt] n non-paiement m.

nonplussed [nɔn'plʌst] adj perplexe.

non-profit-making [nɔn'prɔfɪtmeɪkɪŋ] adj à but non lucratif.

nonsense ['nɔnsəns] n absurdités fpl, idioties fpl; **~!** ne dites pas d'idioties!; **it is ~ to say that ...** il est absurde de dire que ....

nonsensical [nɔn'sɛnsɪkl] adj absurde, qui n'a pas de sens.

nonshrink [nɔn'ʃrɪŋk] adj (BRIT) irrétrécissable.

nonskid [nɔn'skɪd] adj antidérapant(e).

nonsmoker ['nɔn'sməukə*] n non-fumeur m.

nonstarter [nɔn'stɑːtə*] n: **it's a ~** c'est voué à l'échec.

nonstick ['nɔn'stɪk] adj qui n'attache pas.

nonstop ['nɔn'stɔp] adj direct(e), sans arrêt (or escale) ♦ adv sans arrêt.

nontaxable [nɔn'tæksəbl] adj: **~ income** revenu m non imposable.

non-U ['nɔnjuː] adj abbr (BRIT col: = non-upper class) qui ne se dit (or se fait) pas.

nonvolatile [nɔn'vɔlətaɪl] adj: **~ memory** (COMPUT) mémoire rémanente or non volatile.

nonvoting [nɔn'vəutɪŋ] adj: **~ shares** actions fpl sans droit de vote.

non-white ['nɒn'waɪt] *adj* de couleur ♦ *n* personne *f* de couleur.

no-win situation [nəu'wɪn-] *n* impasse *f*; **we're in a** ~ nous sommes dans l'impasse.

noodles ['nuːdlz] *npl* nouilles *fpl*.

nook [nuk] *n*: ~**s and crannies** recoins *mpl*.

noon [nuːn] *n* midi *m*.

no one ['nəuwʌn] *pron* = **nobody**.

noose [nuːs] *n* nœud coulant; (*hangman's*) corde *f*.

nor [nɔː*] *conj* = **neither** ♦ *adv see* **neither**.

Norf *abbr* (*BRIT*) = *Norfolk*.

norm [nɔːm] *n* norme *f*.

normal ['nɔːml] *adj* normal(e) ♦ *n*: **to return to** ~ redevenir normal(e).

normality [nɔː'mælɪtɪ] *n* normalité *f*.

normally ['nɔːməlɪ] *adv* normalement.

Normandy ['nɔːməndɪ] *n* Normandie *f*.

north [nɔːθ] *n* nord *m* ♦ *adj* du nord, nord *inv* ♦ *adv* au *or* vers le nord.

North Africa *n* Afrique *f* du Nord.

North African *adj* nord-africain(e), d'Afrique du Nord ♦ *n* Nord-Africain/e.

North America *n* Amérique *f* du Nord.

North American *n* Nord-Américain/e ♦ *adj* nord-américain(e), d'Amérique du Nord.

Northants [nɔː'θænts] *abbr* (*BRIT*) = *Northamptonshire*.

northbound ['nɔːθbaund] *adj* (*traffic*) en direction du nord; (*carriageway*) nord *inv*.

Northd *abbr* (*BRIT*) = *Northumberland*.

north-east [nɔːθ'iːst] *n* nord-est *m*.

northerly ['nɔːðəlɪ] *adj* (*wind, direction*) du nord.

northern ['nɔːðən] *adj* du nord, septentrional(e).

Northern Ireland *n* Irlande *f* du Nord.

North Pole *n*: **the** ~ le pôle Nord.

North Sea *n*: **the** ~ la mer du Nord.

North Sea oil *n* pétrole *m* de la mer du Nord.

northward(s) ['nɔːθwəd(z)] *adv* vers le nord.

north-west [nɔːθ'wɛst] *n* nord-ouest *m*.

Norway ['nɔːweɪ] *n* Norvège *f*.

Norwegian [nɔː'wiːdʒən] *adj* norvégien(ne) ♦ *n* Norvégien/ne; (*LING*) norvégien *m*.

nos. *abbr* (= *numbers*) n°.

nose [nəuz] *n* nez *m*; (*fig*) flair *m* ♦ *vi* (*also*: ~ **one's way**) avancer précautionneusement; **to pay through the** ~ **(for sth)** (*col*) payer un prix excessif (pour qch).

▶**nose about, nose around** *vi* fouiner *or* fureter (partout).

nosebleed ['nəuzbliːd] *n* saignement *m* de nez.

nose-dive ['nəuzdaɪv] *n* (descente *f* en) piqué *m*.

nose drops *npl* gouttes *fpl* pour le nez.

nosey ['nəuzɪ] *adj* curieux(euse).

nostalgia [nɒs'tældʒɪə] *n* nostalgie *f*.

nostalgic [nɒs'tældʒɪk] *adj* nostalgique.

nostril ['nɒstrɪl] *n* narine *f*; (*of horse*) naseau *m*.

nosy ['nəuzɪ] *adj* = **nosey**.

not [nɒt] *adv* (ne ...) pas; **I hope** ~ j'espère que

non; ~ **at all** pas du tout; (*after thanks*) de rien; **you must** ~ *or* **mustn't do this** tu ne dois pas faire ça; **he isn't** ... il n'est pas ....

notable ['nəutəbl] *adj* notable.

notably ['nəutəblɪ] *adv* en particulier.

notary ['nəutərɪ] *n* (*also*: ~ **public**) notaire *m*.

notation [nəu'teɪʃən] *n* notation *f*.

notch [nɒtʃ] *n* encoche *f*.

▶**notch up** *vt* (*score*) marquer; (*victory*) remporter.

note [nəut] *n* note *f*; (*letter*) mot *m*; (*banknote*) billet *m* ♦ *vt* (*also*: ~ **down**) noter; (*notice*) constater; **just a quick** ~ **to let you know** ... juste un mot pour vous dire ...; **to take** ~**s** prendre des notes; **to compare** ~**s** (*fig*) échanger des (*or* leurs *etc*) impressions; **to take** ~ **of** prendre note de; **a person of** ~ une personne éminente.

notebook ['nəutbuk] *n* carnet *m*; (*for shorthand etc*) bloc-notes *m*.

note-case ['nəutkeɪs] *n* (*BRIT*) porte-feuille *m*.

noted ['nəutɪd] *adj* réputé(e).

notepad ['nəutpæd] *n* bloc-notes *m*.

notepaper ['nəutpeɪpə*] *n* papier *m* à lettres.

noteworthy ['nəutwɜːðɪ] *adj* remarquable.

nothing ['nʌθɪŋ] *n* rien *m*; **he does** ~ il ne fait rien; ~ **new** rien de nouveau; **for** ~ (*free*) pour rien, gratuitement; ~ **at all** rien du tout.

notice ['nəutɪs] *n* avis *m*; (*of leaving*) congé *m*; (*BRIT: review: of play etc*) critique *f*, compte rendu *m* ♦ *vt* remarquer, s'apercevoir de; **without** ~ sans préavis; **advance** ~ préavis *m*; **to give sb** ~ **of sth** notifier qn de qch; **at short** ~ dans un délai très court; **until further** ~ jusqu'à nouvel ordre; **to give** ~, **hand in one's** ~ (*subj: employee*) donner sa démission, démissionner; **to take** ~ **of** prêter attention à; **to bring sth to sb's** ~ porter qch à la connaissance de qn; **it has come to my** ~ **that** ... on m'a signalé que ...; **to escape** *or* **avoid** ~ (essayer de) passer inaperçu *or* ne pas se faire remarquer.

noticeable ['nəutɪsəbl] *adj* visible.

notice board *n* (*BRIT*) panneau *m* d'affichage.

notification [nəutɪfɪ'keɪʃən] *n* notification *f*.

notify ['nəutɪfaɪ] *vt*: **to** ~ **sth to sb** notifier qch à qn; **to** ~ **sb of sth** avertir qn de qch.

notion ['nəuʃən] *n* idée *f*; (*concept*) notion *f*.

notions ['nəuʃənz] *npl* (*US: haberdashery*) mercerie *f*.

notoriety [nəutə'raɪətɪ] *n* notoriété *f*.

notorious [nəu'tɔːrɪəs] *adj* notoire (*souvent en mal*).

notoriously [nəu'tɔːrɪəslɪ] *adj* notoirement.

Notts [nɒts] *abbr* (*BRIT*) = *Nottinghamshire*.

notwithstanding [nɒtwɪθ'stændɪŋ] *adv* néanmoins ♦ *prep* en dépit de.

nougat ['nuːgɑː] *n* nougat *m*.

nought [nɔːt] *n* zéro *m*.

noun [naun] *n* nom *m*.

nourish ['nʌrɪʃ] *vt* nourrir.

nourishing ['nʌrɪʃɪŋ] *adj* nourrissant(e).

nourishment ['nʌrɪʃmənt] *n* nourriture *f*.

Nov. *abbr* (= *November*) nov.

Nova Scotia ['nəuvə'skəuʃə] *n* Nouvelle-Écosse *f*.

novel ['nɔvl] *n* roman *m* ♦ *adj* nouveau(nouvelle), original(e).

novelist ['nɔvəlɪst] *n* romancier *m*.

novelty ['nɔvəltɪ] *n* nouveauté *f*.

November [nəu'vɛmbə*] *n* novembre *m*; *for phrases see also* **July**.

novice ['nɔvɪs] *n* novice *m/f*.

NOW [nau] *n abbr* (*US*) = National Organization for Women.

now [nau] *adv* maintenant ♦ *conj*: ~ **(that)** maintenant (que); **right** ~ tout de suite; **by** ~ à l'heure qu'il est; **just** ~: **that's the fashion just** ~ c'est la mode en ce moment *or* maintenant; **I saw her just** ~ je viens de la voir, je l'ai vue à l'instant; **I'll read it just** ~ je vais le lire à l'instant *or* dès maintenant; ~ **and then,** ~ **and again** de temps en temps; **from** ~ **on** dorénavant; **in 3 days from** ~ dans *or* d'ici trois jours; **between** ~ **and Monday** d'ici (à) lundi; **that's all for** ~ c'est tout pour l'instant.

nowadays ['nauədeɪz] *adv* de nos jours.

nowhere ['nəuwɛə*] *adv* nulle part; ~ **else** nulle part ailleurs.

noxious ['nɔkʃəs] *adj* toxique.

nozzle ['nɔzl] *n* (*of hose*) jet *m*, lance *f*.

NP *n abbr* = notary public.

NS *abbr* (*Canada*) = Nova Scotia.

NSC *n abbr* (*US*) = **National Security Council.**

NSF *n abbr* (*US*) = **National Science Foundation.**

NSPCC *n abbr* (*BRIT*) = National Society for the Prevention of Cruelty to Children.

NSW *abbr* (*Australia*) = New South Wales.

NT *n abbr* (= *New Testament*) NT *m* ♦ *abbr* (*Canada*) = Northwest Territories.

nth [ɛnθ] *adj*: **for the** ~ **time** (*col*) pour la énième fois.

nuance ['nju:ɑ̃ːns] *n* nuance *f*.

nubile ['nju:baɪl] *adj* nubile; (*attractive*) jeune et désirable.

nuclear ['nju:klɪə*] *adj* nucléaire.

nuclear disarmament *n* désarmement *m* nucléaire.

nuclear family *n* famille *f* nucléaire.

nuclear-free zone ['nju:klɪə'fri:-] *n* zone *f* où le nucléaire est interdit.

nucleus, *pl* **nuclei** ['nju:klɪəs, 'nju:klɪaɪ] *n* noyau *m*.

NUCPS *n abbr* (*BRIT*: = National Union of Civil and Public Servants) *syndicat des fonctionnaires.*

nude [nju:d] *adj* nu(e) ♦ *n* (*ART*) nu *m*; **in the** ~ (tout(e)) nu(e).

nudge [nʌdʒ] *vt* donner un (petit) coup de coude à.

nudist ['nju:dɪst] *n* nudiste *m/f*.

nudist colony *n* colonie *f* de nudistes.

nudity ['nju:dɪtɪ] *n* nudité *f*.

nugget ['nʌgɪt] *n* pépite *f*.

nuisance ['nju:sns] *n*: **it's a** ~ c'est (très) ennuyeux *or* gênant; **he's a** ~ il est assommant *or* casse-pieds; **what a** ~! quelle barbe!

NUJ *n abbr* (*BRIT*: = National Union of Journalists*) syndicat des journalistes.*

nuke [nju:k] *n* (*col*) bombe *f* atomique.

null [nʌl] *adj*: ~ **and void** nul(le) et non avenu(e).

nullify ['nʌlɪfaɪ] *vt* invalider.

NUM *n abbr* (*BRIT*: = National Union of Mineworkers*) syndicat des mineurs.*

numb [nʌm] *adj* engourdi(e) ♦ *vt* engourdir; ~ **with cold** engourdi(e) par le froid, transi(e) (de froid); ~ **with fear** transi de peur, paralysé(e) par la peur.

number ['nʌmbə*] *n* nombre *m*; (*numeral*) chiffre *m*; (*of house, car, telephone, newspaper*) numéro *m* ♦ *vt* numéroter; (*include*) compter; **a** ~ **of** un certain nombre de; **to be** ~**ed among** compter parmi; **the staff** ~**s 20** le nombre d'employés s'élève à *or* est de 20; **wrong** ~ (*TEL*) mauvais numéro.

numbered account ['nʌmbəd-] *n* (*in bank*) compte numéroté.

number plate *n* (*BRIT AUT*) plaque *f* minéralogique *or* d'immatriculation.

Number Ten *n* (*BRIT*: = 10 Downing Street) résidence du Premier ministre.

numbness ['nʌmnɪs] *n* torpeur *f*; (*due to cold*) engourdissement *m*.

numbskull ['nʌmskʌl] *n* (*col*) gourde *f*.

numeral ['nju:mərəl] *n* chiffre *m*.

numerate ['nju:mərɪt] *adj* (*BRIT*): **to be** ~ avoir des notions d'arithmétique.

numerical [nju:'mɛrɪkl] *adj* numérique.

numerous ['nju:mərəs] *adj* nombreux(euse).

nun [nʌn] *n* religieuse *f*, sœur *f*.

nunnery ['nʌnərɪ] *n* couvent *m*.

nuptial ['nʌpʃəl] *adj* nuptial(e).

nurse [nəːs] *n* infirmière *f*; (*also*: ~**maid**) bonne *f* d'enfants ♦ *vt* (*patient, cold*) soigner; (*baby*: *BRIT*) bercer (dans ses bras); (: *US*) allaiter, nourrir; (*hope*) nourrir *m*.

nursery ['nəːsərɪ] *n* (*room*) nursery *f*; (*institution*) pouponnière *f*; (*for plants*) pépinière *f*.

nursery rhyme *n* comptine *f*, chansonnette *f* pour enfants.

nursery school *n* école maternelle.

nursery slope *n* (*BRIT SKI*) piste *f* pour débutants.

nursing ['nəːsɪŋ] *n* (*profession*) profession *f* d'infirmière ♦ *adj* (*mother*) qui allaite.

nursing home *n* clinique *f*; maison *f* de convalescence.

nurture ['nəːtʃə*] *vt* élever.

NUS *n abbr* (*BRIT*: = National Union of Students) *syndicat des étudiants.*

NUT *n abbr* (*BRIT*: = *National Union of Teachers*) syndicat enseignant.

nut [nʌt] *n* (*of metal*) écrou *m*; (*fruit*) noix *f*, noisette *f*, cacahuète *f* (*terme générique en anglais*) ♦ *adj* (*chocolate etc*) aux noisettes; **he's ~s** (*col*) il est dingue.

nutcase ['nʌtkeɪs] *n* (*col*) dingue *m/f*.

nutcrackers ['nʌtkrækəz] *npl* casse-noix *m inv*, casse-noisette(s) *m*.

nutmeg ['nʌtmɛg] *n* (noix *f*) muscade *f*.

nutrient ['njuːtrɪənt] *adj* nutritif(ive) ♦ *n* substance nutritive.

nutrition [njuːˈtrɪʃən] *n* nutrition *f*, alimentation *f*.

nutritionist [njuːˈtrɪʃənɪst] *n* nutritionniste *m/f*.

nutritious [njuːˈtrɪʃəs] *adj* nutritif(ive), nourrissant(e).

nutshell ['nʌtʃɛl] *n* coquille *f* de noix; **in a ~** en un mot.

nutty ['nʌtɪ] *adj* (*flavour*) à la noisette; (*col: person*) cinglé(e), dingue.

nuzzle ['nʌzl] *vi*: **to ~ up to** fourrer son nez contre.

NV *abbr* (*US*) = *Nevada*.

NWT *abbr* (*Canada*) = *Northwest Territories*.

NY *abbr* (*US*) = *New York*.

NYC *abbr* (*US*) = *New York City*.

nylon ['naɪlɔn] *n* nylon *m* ♦ *adj* de *or* en nylon; **~s** *npl* bas *mpl* nylon.

nymph [nɪmf] *n* nymphe *f*.

nymphomaniac ['nɪmfəʊˈmeɪnɪæk] *adj, n* nymphomane (*f*).

NYSE *n abbr* (*US*) = *New York Stock Exchange*.

NZ *abbr* = **New Zealand**.

O o

O, o [əʊ] *n* (*letter*) O, o *m*; (*US SCOL*: = *outstanding*) tb (= *très bien*); **O for Oliver**, (*US*) **O for Oboe** O comme Oscar.

oaf [əʊf] *n* balourd *m*.

oak [əʊk] *n* chêne *m* ♦ *cpd* de *or* en (bois de) chêne.

O&M *n abbr* = *organization and method*.

OAP *n abbr* (*BRIT*) = **old age pensioner**.

oar [ɔː*] *n* aviron *m*, rame *f*; **to put** *or* **shove one's ~ in** (*fig: col*) mettre son grain de sel.

oarsman ['ɔːzmən], **oarswoman** ['ɔːzwʊmən] *n* rameur/euse; (*NAUT, SPORT*) nageur/euse.

OAS *n abbr* (= *Organization of American States*) OEA *f* (= *Organisation des États américains*).

oasis, *pl* oases [əʊˈeɪsɪs, əʊˈeɪsiːz] *n* oasis *f*.

oath [əʊθ] *n* serment *m*; (*swear word*) juron *m*;

to take the ~ prêter serment; **on** (*BRIT*) *or* **under ~** sous serment; assermenté(e).

oatmeal ['əʊtmiːl] *n* flocons *mpl* d'avoine.

oats [əʊts] *n* avoine *f*.

OAU *n abbr* (= *Organization of African Unity*) OUA *f* (= *Organisation de l'unité africaine*).

obdurate ['ɔbdjʊrɪt] *adj* obstiné(e); impénitent(e); intraitable.

OBE *n abbr* (*BRIT*: = *Order of the British Empire*) distinction honorifique.

obedience [əˈbiːdɪəns] *n* obéissance *f*; **in ~ to** conformément à.

obedient [əˈbiːdɪənt] *adj* obéissant(e); **to be ~ to sb/sth** obéir à qn/qch.

obelisk ['ɔbɪlɪsk] *n* obélisque *m*.

obese [əʊˈbiːs] *adj* obèse.

obesity [əʊˈbiːsɪtɪ] *n* obésité *f*.

obey [əˈbeɪ] *vt* obéir à; (*instructions, regulations*) se conformer à ♦ *vi* obéir.

obituary [əˈbɪtjuərɪ] *n* nécrologie *f*.

object *n* ['ɔbdʒɪkt] objet *m*; (*purpose*) but *m*, objet; (*LING*) complément *m* d'objet ♦ *vi* [əbˈdʒɛkt]: **to ~ to** (*attitude*) désapprouver; (*proposal*) protester contre, élever une objection contre; **I ~!** je proteste!; **he ~ed that ...** il a fait valoir *or* a objecté que ...; **do you ~ to my smoking?** est-ce que cela vous gêne si je fume?; **what's the ~ of doing that?** quel est l'intérêt de faire cela?; **money is no ~** l'argent n'est pas un problème.

objection [əbˈdʒɛkʃən] *n* objection *f*; (*drawback*) inconvénient *m*; **if you have no ~** si vous n'y voyez pas d'inconvénient; **to make** *or* **raise an ~** élever une objection.

objectionable [əbˈdʒɛkʃənəbl] *adj* très désagréable; choquant(e).

objective [əbˈdʒɛktɪv] *n* objectif *m* ♦ *adj* objectif(ive).

objectivity [ɔbdʒɪkˈtɪvɪtɪ] *n* objectivité *f*.

object lesson *n* (*fig*) (bonne) illustration.

objector [əbˈdʒɛktə*] *n* opposant/e.

obligation [ɔblɪˈgeɪʃən] *n* obligation *f*, devoir *m*; (*debt*) dette *f* (de reconnaissance); **"without ~"** "sans engagement".

obligatory [əˈblɪgətərɪ] *adj* obligatoire.

oblige [əˈblaɪdʒ] *vt* (*force*): **to ~ sb to do** obliger *or* forcer qn à faire; (*do a favour*) rendre service à, obliger; **to be ~d to sb for sth** être obligé(e) à qn de qch; **anything to ~!** (*col*) (toujours prêt à rendre) service!

obliging [əˈblaɪdʒɪŋ] *adj* obligeant(e), serviable.

oblique [əˈbliːk] *adj* oblique; (*allusion*) indirect(e) ♦ *n* (*BRIT TYP*): ~ **(stroke)** barre *f* oblique.

obliterate [əˈblɪtəreɪt] *vt* effacer.

oblivion [əˈblɪvɪən] *n* oubli *m*.

oblivious [əˈblɪvɪəs] *adj*: ~ **of** oublieux(euse) de.

oblong ['ɔblɔŋ] *adj* oblong(ue) ♦ *n* rectangle *m*

obnoxious [əbˈnɔkʃəs] *adj* odieux(euse);

(*smell*) nauséabond(e).

o.b.o. *abbr* (*US*: = *or best offer: in classified ads*) ≈ à débattre.

oboe ['əubəu] *n* hautbois *m*.

obscene [əb'siːn] *adj* obscène.

obscenity [əb'sɛnɪtɪ] *n* obscénité *f*.

obscure [əb'skjuə*] *adj* obscur(e) ♦ *vt* obscurcir; (*hide: sun*) cacher.

obscurity [əb'skjuərɪtɪ] *n* obscurité *f*.

obsequious [əb'siːkwɪəs] *adj* obséquieux(euse).

observable [əb'zəːvəbl] *adj* observable; (*appreciable*) notable.

observance [əb'zəːvns] *n* observance *f*, observation *f*; **religious ~s** observances religieuses.

observant [əb'zəːvnt] *adj* observateur(trice).

observation [ɔbzə'veɪʃən] *n* observation *f*; (*by police etc*) surveillance *f*.

observation post *n* (*MIL*) poste *m* d'observation.

observatory [əb'zəːvətrɪ] *n* observatoire *m*.

observe [əb'zəːv] *vt* observer; (*remark*) faire observer *or* remarquer.

observer [əb'zəːvə*] *n* observateur/trice.

obsess [əb'sɛs] *vt* obséder; **to be ~ed by** *or* **with sb/sth** être obsédé(e) par qn/qch.

obsession [əb'sɛʃən] *n* obsession *f*.

obsessive [əb'sɛsɪv] *adj* obsédant(e).

obsolescence [ɔbsə'lɛsns] *n* vieillissement *m*; obsolescence *f*; **built-in** *or* **planned ~** (*COMM*) désuétude calculée.

obsolescent [ɔbsə'lɛsnt] *adj* obsolescent(e), en voie d'être périmé(e).

obsolete ['ɔbsəliːt] *adj* dépassé(e), périmé(e).

obstacle ['ɔbstəkl] *n* obstacle *m*.

obstacle race *n* course *f* d'obstacles.

obstetrician [ɔbstə'trɪʃən] *n* obstétricien/ne.

obstetrics [ɔb'stɛtrɪks] *n* obstétrique *f*.

obstinacy ['ɔbstɪnəsɪ] *n* obstination *f*.

obstinate ['ɔbstɪnɪt] *adj* obstiné(e); (*pain, cold*) persistant(e).

obstreperous [əb'strɛpərəs] *adj* turbulent(e).

obstruct [əb'strʌkt] *vt* (*block*) boucher, obstruer; (*halt*) arrêter; (*hinder*) entraver.

obstruction [əb'strʌkʃən] *n* obstruction *f*; obstacle *m*.

obstructive [əb'strʌktɪv] *adj* obstructionniste.

obtain [əb'teɪn] *vt* obtenir ♦ *vi* avoir cours.

obtainable [əb'teɪnəbl] *adj* qu'on peut obtenir.

obtrusive [əb'truːsɪv] *adj* (*person*) importun(e); (*smell*) pénétrant(e); (*building etc*) trop en évidence.

obtuse [əb'tjuːs] *adj* obtus(e).

obverse ['ɔbvəːs] *n* (*of medal, coin*) côté *m* face; (*fig*) contrepartie *f*.

obviate ['ɔbvɪeɪt] *vt* parer à, obvier à.

obvious ['ɔbvɪəs] *adj* évident(e), manifeste.

obviously ['ɔbvɪəslɪ] *adv* manifestement; (*of course*): **~, he ... or he ~ ...** il est bien évident qu'il ...; **~!** bien sûr!; **~ not!** évidemment pas!, bien sûr que non!

OCAS *n abbr* (= *Organization of Central American States*) ODEAC *f* (= *Organisation des États d'Amérique centrale*).

occasion [ə'keɪʒən] *n* occasion *f*; (*event*) événement *m* ♦ *vt* occasionner, causer; **on that ~** à cette occasion; **to rise to the ~** se montrer à la hauteur de la situation.

occasional [ə'keɪʒənl] *adj* pris(e) (*or* fait(e) *etc*) de temps en temps; occasionnel(le).

occasionally [ə'keɪʒənəlɪ] *adv* de temps en temps; **very ~** (assez) rarement.

occasional table *n* table décorative.

occult [ɔ'kʌlt] *adj* occulte ♦ *n*: **the ~** le surnaturel.

occupancy ['ɔkjupənsɪ] *n* occupation *f*.

occupant ['ɔkjupənt] *n* occupant *m*.

occupation [ɔkju'peɪʃən] *n* occupation *f*; (*job*) métier *m*, profession *f*; **unfit for ~** (*house*) impropre à l'habitation.

occupational [ɔkju'peɪʃənl] *adj* (*accident, disease*) du travail; (*hazard*) du métier.

occupational guidance *n* (*BRIT*) orientation professionnelle.

occupational pension *n* retraite professionnelle.

occupational therapy *n* ergothérapie *f*.

occupier ['ɔkjupaɪə*] *n* occupant/e.

occupy ['ɔkjupaɪ] *vt* occuper; **to ~ o.s. with** *or* **by doing** s'occuper à faire; **to be occupied with sth** être occupé avec qch.

occur [ə'kəː*] *vi* se produire; (*difficulty, opportunity*) se présenter; (*phenomenon, error*) se rencontrer; **to ~ to sb** venir à l'esprit de qn.

occurrence [ə'kʌrəns] *n* présence *f*, existence *f*; cas *m*, fait *m*.

ocean ['əuʃən] *n* océan *m*; **~s of** (*col*) des masses de.

ocean bed *n* fond (sous-)marin.

ocean-going ['əuʃəngəuɪŋ] *adj* de haute mer.

Oceania [əuʃɪ'eɪnɪə] *n* Océanie *f*.

ocean liner *n* paquebot *m*.

ochre ['əukə*] *adj* ocre.

o'clock [ə'klɔk] *adv*: **it is 5 ~** il est 5 heures.

OCR *n abbr* = **optical character reader, optical character recognition**.

Oct. *abbr* (= *October*) oct.

octagonal [ɔk'tægənl] *adj* octogonal(e).

octane ['ɔkteɪn] *n* octane *m*; **high-~ petrol** *or* (*US*) **gas** essence *f* à indice d'octane élevé.

octave ['ɔktɪv] *n* octave *f*.

October [ɔk'təubə*] *n* octobre *m*; *for phrases see also* **July**.

octogenarian ['ɔktəudʒɪ'nɛərɪən] *n* octogénaire *m/f*.

octopus ['ɔktəpəs] *n* pieuvre *f*.

odd [ɔd] *adj* (*strange*) bizarre, curieux(euse); (*number*) impair(e); (*left over*) qui reste, en plus; (*not of a set*) dépareillé(e); **60-~** 60 et quelques; **at ~ times** de temps en temps; **the ~ one out** l'exception *f*.

oddball ['ɔdbɔːl] *n* (*col*) excentrique *m/f*.

oddity ['ɒdɪtɪ] n bizarrerie f; (person) excentrique m/f.

odd-job man [ɒd'dʒɔb-] n homme m à tout faire.

odd jobs npl petits travaux divers.

oddly ['ɒdlɪ] adv bizarrement, curieusement.

oddments ['ɒdmənts] npl (BRIT COMM) fins fpl de série.

odds [ɒdz] npl (in betting) cote f; **the ~ are against his coming** il y a peu de chances qu'il vienne; **it makes no ~** cela n'a pas d'importance; **to succeed against all the ~** réussir contre toute attente; **~ and ends** de petites choses; **at ~** en désaccord.

odds-on [ɒdz'ɔn] adj: **the ~ favourite** le grand favori; **it's ~ that he'll come** il y a toutes les chances or gros à parier qu'il vienne.

ode [əud] n ode f.

odious ['əudɪəs] adj odieux(euse), détestable.

odometer [ɔ'dɒmɪtə*] n odomètre m.

odour, (US) **odor** ['əudə*] n odeur f.

odo(u)rless ['əudəlɪs] adj inodore.

OECD n abbr (= Organization for Economic Cooperation and Development) OCDE f (= Organisation de coopération et de développement économique).

oesophagus, (US) **esophagus** [iː'sɒfəgəs] n œsophage m.

oestrogen, (US) **estrogen** ['iːstrəudʒən] n œstrogène m.

================================ KEYWORD

of [ɒv, əv] prep **1** (gen) de; **a friend ~ ours** un de nos amis; **a boy ~ 10** un garçon de 10 ans; **that was kind ~ you** c'était gentil de votre part

2 (expressing quantity, amount, dates etc) de; **a kilo ~ flour** un kilo de farine; **how much ~ this do you need?** combien vous en faut-il?; **there were 3 ~ them** (people) ils étaient 3; (objects) il y en avait 3; **3 ~ us went** 3 d'entre nous y sont allé(e)s; **the 5th ~ July** le 5 juillet; **a quarter ~ 4** (US) 4 heures moins le quart

3 (from, out of) en, de; **a statue ~ marble** une statue de or en marbre; **made ~ wood** (fait) en bois.

off [ɒf] adj, adv (engine) coupé(e); (tap) fermé(e); (BRIT: food) mauvais(e), avancé(e); (: milk) tourné(e); (absent) absent(e); (cancelled) annulé(e); (removed): **the lid was ~** le couvercle était retiré or n'était pas mis ♦ prep de; sur; **to be ~** (to leave) partir, s'en aller; **I must be ~** il faut que je file; **to be ~ sick** être absent pour cause de maladie; **a day ~** un jour de congé; **to have an ~ day** n'être pas en forme; **he had his coat ~** il avait enlevé son manteau; **the hook is ~** le crochet s'est détaché; le crochet n'est pas mis; **10% ~** (COMM) 10% de rabais; **5 km ~** (the road) à 5 km (de la route); **~ the coast** au large de la côte; **a house ~ the main road** une maison à l'écart de la grand-route; **it's a long way ~** c'est loin (d'ici); **I'm ~ meat** je ne mange plus de viande; je n'aime plus la viande; **on the ~ chance** à tout hasard; **to be well/badly ~** être bien/mal loti; (financially) être aisé/dans la gêne; **~ and on, on and ~** de temps à autre; **I'm afraid the chicken is ~** (BRIT: not available) je regrette, il n'y a plus de poulet; **that's a bit ~** (fig: col) c'est un peu fort.

offal ['ɒfl] n (CULIN) abats mpl.

offbeat ['ɒfbiːt] adj excentrique.

off-centre [ɒf'sɛntə*] adj décentré(e), excentré(e).

off-colour ['ɒf'kʌlə*] adj (BRIT: ill) malade, mal fichu(e); **to feel ~** être mal fichu.

offence, (US) **offense** [ə'fɛns] n (crime) délit m, infraction f; **to give ~ to** blesser, offenser; **to take ~ at** se vexer de, s'offenser de; **to commit an ~** commettre une infraction.

offend [ə'fɛnd] vt (person) offenser, blesser ♦ vi: **to ~ against** (law, rule) contrevenir à, enfreindre.

offender [ə'fɛndə*] n délinquant/e; (against regulations) contrevenant/e.

offending [ə'fɛndɪŋ] adj incriminé(e).

offense [ə'fɛns] n (US) = offence.

offensive [ə'fɛnsɪv] adj offensant(e), choquant(e); (smell etc) très déplaisant(e); (weapon) offensif(ive) ♦ n (MIL) offensive f.

offer ['ɒfə*] n offre f, proposition f ♦ vt offrir, proposer; **to make an ~ for sth** faire une offre pour qch; **to ~ sth to sb, ~ sb sth** offrir qch à qn; **to ~ to do sth** proposer de faire qch; **"on ~"** (COMM) "en promotion".

offering ['ɒfərɪŋ] n offrande f.

offhand [ɒf'hænd] adj désinvolte ♦ adv spontanément; **I can't tell you ~** je ne peux pas vous le dire comme ça.

office ['ɒfɪs] n (place) bureau m; (position) charge f, fonction f; **doctor's ~** (US) cabinet (médical); **to take ~** entrer en fonctions; **through his good ~s** (fig) grâce à ses bons offices; **O~ of Fair Trading** (BRIT) organisme de protection contre les pratiques commerciales abusives.

office automation n bureautique f.

office bearer n (of club etc) membre m du bureau.

office block, (US) **office building** n immeuble m de bureaux.

office boy n garçon m de bureau.

office hours npl heures fpl de bureau; (US MED) heures de consultation.

office manager n responsable administratif(ive).

officer ['ɒfɪsə*] n (MIL etc) officier m; (of organization) membre m du bureau directeur; (also: police ~) agent m (de police).

office work n travail m de bureau.
office worker n employé/e de bureau.
official [ə'fɪʃl] adj (authorized) officiel(le) ♦ n officiel m; (civil servant) fonctionnaire m/f; employé/e.
officialdom [ə'fɪʃldəm] n bureaucratie f.
officially [ə'fɪʃəlɪ] adv officiellement.
official receiver n administrateur m judiciaire, syndic m de faillite.
officiate [ə'fɪʃɪeɪt] vi (REL) officier; **to ~ as Mayor** exercer les fonctions de maire; **to ~ at a marriage** célébrer un mariage.
officious [ə'fɪʃəs] adj trop empressé(e).
offing ['ɔfɪŋ] n: **in the ~** (fig) en perspective.
off-key [ɔf'kiː] adj faux(fausse). ♦ adv faux.
off-licence ['ɔflaɪsns] n (BRIT: shop) débit m de vins et de spiritueux.

Un **off-licence** *est un magasin où l'on vend de l'alcool (à emporter) aux heures où les pubs sont fermés. On peut également y acheter des boissons non alcoolisées, des cigarettes, des chips, des bonbons, des chocolats etc.*

---

off-limits [ɔf'lɪmɪts] adj (esp US) dont l'accès est interdit.
off line adj (COMPUT) (en mode) autonome; (: switched off) non connecté(e).
off-load ['ɔfləud] vt: **to ~ sth (onto)** (goods) décharger qch (sur); (job) se décharger de qch (sur).
off-peak ['ɔf'piːk] adj aux heures creuses.
off-putting ['ɔfputɪŋ] adj (BRIT) rébarbatif(ive); rebutant(e), peu engageant(e).
off-season ['ɔf'siːzn] adj, adv hors-saison (inv).
offset ['ɔfsɛt] vt irreg (counteract) contrebalancer, compenser ♦ n (also: ~ printing) offset m.
offshoot ['ɔfʃuːt] n (fig) ramification f, antenne f; (: of discussion etc) conséquence f.
offshore [ɔf'ʃɔː*] adj (breeze) de terre; (island) proche du littoral; (fishing) côtier(ière); ~ **oilfield** gisement m pétrolifère en mer.
offside [ɔf'saɪd] n (AUT: with right-hand drive) côté droit; (: with left-hand drive) côté gauche ♦ adj (AUT) de droite; de gauche; (SPORT) hors jeu.
offspring ['ɔfsprɪŋ] n progéniture f.
offstage [ɔf'steɪdʒ] adv dans les coulisses.
off-the-cuff [ɔfðə'kʌf] adv au pied levé; de chic.
off-the-job ['ɔfðə'dʒɔb] adj: ~ **training** formation professionnelle extérieure.
off-the-peg ['ɔfðə'pɛg], (US) **off-the-rack** ['ɔfðə'ræk] adv en prêt-à-porter.
off-the-record ['ɔfðə'rɛkɔːd] adj (remark) confidentiel(le), sans caractère officiel ♦ adv officieusement.
off-white ['ɔfwaɪt] adj blanc cassé inv.
Ofgas ['ɔfgæs] n (BRIT: = Office of Gas Supply)

organisme qui surveille les activités des compagnies de gaz.
Oftel ['ɔftɛl] n (BRIT: = Office of Telecommunications) organisme qui supervise les télécommunications.
often ['ɔfn] adv souvent; **how ~ do you go?** vous y allez tous les combien?; **how ~ have you gone there?** vous y êtes allé combien de fois?; **as ~ as not** la plupart du temps.
Ofwat ['ɔfwɔt] n (BRIT: = Office of Water Services) organisme qui surveille les activités des compagnies des eaux.
ogle ['əugl] vt lorgner.
ogre ['əugə*] n ogre m.
OH abbr (US) = Ohio.
oh [əu] excl ô!, oh!, ah!
OHMS abbr (BRIT) = On His (or Her) Majesty's Service.
oil [ɔɪl] n huile f; (petroleum) pétrole m; (for central heating) mazout m ♦ vt (machine) graisser.
oilcan ['ɔɪlkæn] n burette f de graissage; (for storing) bidon m à huile.
oil change n vidange f.
oilfield ['ɔɪlfiːld] n gisement m de pétrole.
oil filter n (AUT) filtre m à huile.
oil-fired ['ɔɪlfaɪəd] adj au mazout.
oil gauge n jauge f de niveau d'huile.
oil industry n industrie pétrolière.
oil level n niveau m d'huile.
oil painting n peinture f à l'huile.
oil refinery n raffinerie f de pétrole.
oil rig n derrick m; (at sea) plate-forme f pétrolière.
oilskins ['ɔɪlskɪnz] npl ciré m.
oil slick n nappe f de mazout.
oil tanker n pétrolier m.
oil well n puits m de pétrole.
oily ['ɔɪlɪ] adj huileux(euse); (food) gras(se).
ointment ['ɔɪntmənt] n onguent m.
OK abbr (US) = Oklahoma.
O.K., okay ['əu'keɪ] (col) excl d'accord! ♦ vt approuver, donner son accord à ♦ n: **to give sth one's ~** donner son accord à qch ♦ adj en règle; en bon état; sain et sauf; acceptable; **is it ~?, are you ~?** ça va?; **are you ~ for money?** ça va or ira question argent?; **it's ~ with or by me** ça me va, c'est d'accord en ce qui me concerne.
Okla. abbr (US) = Oklahoma.
old [əuld] adj vieux(vieille); (person) vieux, âgé(e); (former) ancien(ne), vieux; **how ~ are you?** quel âge avez-vous?; **he's 10 years ~** il a 10 ans, il est âgé de 10 ans; **~er brother/sister** frère/sœur aîné(e); **any ~ thing will do** n'importe quoi fera l'affaire.
old age n vieillesse f.
old age pensioner (OAP) n (BRIT) retraité/e.
old-fashioned ['əuld'fæʃnd] adj démodé(e); (person) vieux jeu inv.
old maid n vieille fille.
old people's home n maison f de retraite.

old-style ['əuldstaɪl] *adj* à l'ancienne (mode).
old-time ['əuld'taɪm] *adj* du temps jadis, d'autrefois.
old-timer [əuld'taɪmə*] *n* ancien *m*.
old wives' tale *n* conte *m* de bonne femme.
O-level ['əulɛvl] *n* (*in England and Wales: formerly*) *examen passé à l'âge de 16 ans sanctionnant les connaissances de l'élève,* ≈ brevet *m* des collèges.
olive ['ɔlɪv] *n* (*fruit*) olive *f*; (*tree*) olivier *m* ♦ *adj* (*also:* ~-**green**) (vert) olive *inv*.
olive oil *n* huile *f* d'olive.
Olympic [əu'lɪmpɪk] *adj* olympique; **the ~ Games, the ~s** les Jeux *mpl* olympiques.
OM *n abbr* (*BRIT: = Order of Merit*) *titre honorifique.*
Oman [əu'mɑːn] *n* Oman *m*.
OMB *n abbr* (*US: = Office of Management and Budget*) *service conseillant le président en matière budgétaire.*
omelet(te) ['ɔmlɪt] *n* omelette *f*; **ham/cheese ~** omelette au jambon/fromage.
omen ['əumən] *n* présage *m*.
ominous ['ɔmɪnəs] *adj* menaçant(e), inquiétant(e); (*event*) de mauvais augure.
omission [əu'mɪʃən] *n* omission *f*.
omit [əu'mɪt] *vt* omettre; **to ~ to do sth** négliger de faire qch.
omnivorous [ɔm'nɪvrəs] *adj* omnivore.
ON *abbr* (*Canada*) = Ontario.

━━━━━━━━━━━━━━━━━ *KEYWORD*

on [ɔn] *prep* **1** (*indicating position*) sur; ~ **the table** sur la table; ~ **the wall** sur le *or* au mur; ~ **the left** à gauche; **I haven't any money** ~ **me** je n'ai pas d'argent sur moi
2 (*indicating means, method, condition etc*): ~ **foot** à pied; ~ **the train/plane** (*be*) dans le train/l'avion; (*go*) en train/avion; ~ **the telephone/radio/television** au téléphone/à la radio/à la télévision; **to be ~ drugs** se droguer; ~ **holiday,** (*US*) ~ **vacation** en vacances; ~ **the continent** sur le continent
3 (*referring to time*): ~ **Friday** vendredi; ~ **Fridays** le vendredi; ~ **June 20th** le 20 juin; **a week** ~ **Friday** vendredi en huit; ~ **arrival** à l'arrivée; ~ **seeing this** en voyant cela
4 (*about, concerning*) sur, de; **a book** ~ **Balzac/physics** un livre sur Balzac/de physique
5 (*at the expense of*): **this round is** ~ **me** c'est ma tournée
♦ *adv* **1** (*referring to dress, covering*): **to have one's coat** ~ avoir (mis) son manteau; **to put one's coat** ~ mettre son manteau; **what's she got** ~? qu'est-ce qu'elle porte?; **screw the lid** ~ **tightly** vissez bien le couvercle
2 (*further, continuously*): **to walk** *etc* ~ continuer à marcher *etc*; ~ **and off** de temps à autre; **from that day** ~ depuis ce jour

♦ *adj* **1** (*in operation: machine*) en marche; (: *radio, TV, light*) allumé(e); (: *tap, gas*) ouvert(e); (: *brakes*) mis(e); **is the meeting still ~?** (*not cancelled*) est-ce que la réunion a bien lieu?; (*in progress*) la réunion dure-t-elle encore?; **it was well ~ in the evening** c'était tard dans la soirée; **when is this film ~?** quand passe ce film?
2 (*col*): **that's not ~!** (*not acceptable*) cela ne se fait pas!; (*not possible*) pas question!

ONC *n abbr* (*BRIT: = Ordinary National Certificate*) ≈ BT *m*.
once [wʌns] *adv* une fois; (*formerly*) autrefois
♦ *conj* une fois que; ~ **he had left/it was done** une fois qu'il fut parti/que ce fut terminé; **at ~** tout de suite, immédiatement; (*simultaneously*) à la fois; **all at ~** *adv* tout d'un coup; ~ **a week** une fois par semaine; ~ **more** encore une fois; **I knew him** ~ je l'ai connu autrefois; ~ **and for all** une fois pour toutes; ~ **upon a time there was** ... il y avait une fois ..., il était une fois ....
oncoming ['ɔnkʌmɪŋ] *adj* (*traffic*) venant en sens inverse.
OND *n abbr* (*BRIT: = Ordinary National Diploma*) ≈ BTS *m*.

━━━━━━━━━━━━━━━━━ *KEYWORD*

one [wʌn] *num* un(e); ~ **hundred and fifty** cent cinquante; ~ **day** un jour
♦ *adj* **1** (*sole*) seul(e), unique; **the ~ book which** l'unique *or* le seul livre qui; **the ~ man who** le seul (homme) qui
2 (*same*) même; **they came in the ~ car** ils sont venus dans la même voiture
♦ *pron* **1**: **this** ~ celui-ci(celle-ci); **that** ~ celui-là(celle-là); **I've already got** ~/**a red** ~ j'en ai déjà un(e)/un(e) rouge; ~ **by** ~ un(e) à *or* par un(e); **which** ~ **do you want?** lequel voulez-vous?
2: ~ **another** l'un(e) l'autre; **to look at** ~ **another** se regarder
3 (*impersonal*) on; ~ **never knows** on ne sait jamais; **to cut** ~**'s finger** se couper le doigt
4 (*phrases*): **to be** ~ **up on sb** avoir l'avantage sur qn; **to be at** ~ **(with sb)** être d'accord (avec qn).

one-armed bandit ['wʌnɑːmd-] *n* machine *f* à sous.
one-day excursion ['wʌndeɪ-] *n* (*US*) billet *m* d'aller-retour (valable pour la journée).
One-hundred share index ['wʌnhʌndrəd-] *n* indice *m* Footsie des cent grandes valeurs.
one-man ['wʌn'mæn] *adj* (*business*) dirigé(e) *etc* par un seul homme.
one-man band *n* homme-orchestre *m*.
one-off [wʌn'ɔf] (*BRIT col*) *n* exemplaire *m* unique ♦ *adj* unique.
one-parent family ['wʌnpɛərənt-] *n* famille monoparentale.

one-piece ['wʌnpiːs] *adj:* ~ **bathing suit** maillot *m* une pièce.

onerous ['ɔnərəs] *adj* (*task, duty*) pénible; (*responsibility*) lourd(e).

oneself [wʌn'sɛlf] *pron* se; (*after prep, also emphatic*) soi-même; **by** ~ tout seul.

one-sided [wʌn'saɪdɪd] *adj* (*decision*) unilatéral(e); (*judgment, account*) partial(e); (*contest*) inégal(e).

one-time ['wʌntaɪm] *adj* d'autrefois.

one-to-one ['wʌntəwʌn] *adj* (*relationship*) univoque.

one-upmanship [wʌn'ʌpmənʃɪp] *n:* **the art of** ~ l'art de faire mieux que les autres.

one-way ['wʌnweɪ] *adj* (*street, traffic*) à sens unique.

ongoing ['ɔngəuɪŋ] *adj* en cours; suivi(e).

onion ['ʌnjən] *n* oignon *m*.

on line *adj* (*COMPUT*) en ligne; (*: switched on*) connecté(e).

onlooker ['ɔnlukə*] *n* spectateur/trice.

only ['əunlɪ] *adv* seulement ♦ *adj* seul(e), unique ♦ *conj* seulement, mais; **an** ~ **child** un enfant unique; **not** ~ non seulement; **I** ~ **took one** j'en ai seulement pris un, je n'en ai pris qu'un; **I saw her** ~ **yesterday** je l'ai vue hier encore; **I'd be** ~ **too pleased to help** je ne serais que trop content de vous aider; **I would come,** ~ **I'm very busy** je viendrais bien mais j'ai beaucoup à faire.

ono *abbr* (*BRIT*: = *or nearest offer: in classified ads*) ≈ à débattre.

onset ['ɔnsɛt] *n* début *m*; (*of winter, old age*) approche *f*.

onshore ['ɔnʃɔː*] *adj* (*wind*) du large.

onslaught ['ɔnslɔːt] *n* attaque *f*, assaut *m*.

Ont. *abbr* (*Canada*) = Ontario.

on-the-job ['ɔnðə'dʒɔb] *adj:* ~ **training** formation *f* sur place.

onto ['ɔntu] *prep* = on to.

onus ['əunəs] *n* responsabilité *f*; **the** ~ **is upon him to prove it** c'est à lui de le prouver.

onward(s) ['ɔnwəd(z)] *adv* (*move*) en avant.

onyx ['ɔnɪks] *n* onyx *m*.

oops [ups] *excl* houp!; ~**-a-daisy!** houp-là!

ooze [uːz] *vi* suinter.

opacity [əu'pæsɪtɪ] *n* opacité *f*.

opal ['əupl] *n* opale *f*.

opaque [əu'peɪk] *adj* opaque.

OPEC ['əupɛk] *n abbr* (= *Organization of Petroleum-Exporting Countries*) OPEP *f* (= *Organisation des pays exportateurs de pétrole*).

open ['əupn] *adj* ouvert(e); (*car*) découvert(e); (*road, view*) dégagé(e); (*meeting*) public(ique); (*admiration*) manifeste; (*question*) non résolu(e); (*enemy*) déclaré(e) ♦ *vt* ouvrir ♦ *vi* (*flower, eyes, door, debate*) s'ouvrir; (*shop, bank, museum*) ouvrir; (*book etc: commence*) commencer, débuter; **in the** ~ (*air*) en plein air; **the** ~ **sea** le large; ~ **ground** (*among trees*) clairière *f*; (*waste* *ground*) terrain *m* vague; **to have an** ~ **mind (on sth)** avoir l'esprit ouvert (sur qch).

▶**open on to** *vt fus* (*subj: room, door*) donner sur.

▶**open out** *vt* ouvrir ♦ *vi* s'ouvrir.

▶**open up** *vt* ouvrir; (*blocked road*) dégager ♦ *vi* s'ouvrir.

open-air [əupn'ɛə*] *adj* en plein air.

open-and-shut ['əupnən'ʃʌt] *adj:* ~ **case** cas *m* limpide.

open day *n* journée *f* portes ouvertes.

open-ended [əupn'ɛndɪd] *adj* (*fig*) non limité(e).

opener ['əupnə*] *n* (*also:* **can** ~, **tin** ~) ouvre-boîtes *m*.

open-heart surgery [əupn'hɑːt-] *n* chirurgie *f* à cœur ouvert.

opening ['əupnɪŋ] *n* ouverture *f*; (*opportunity*) occasion *f*; débouché *m*; (*job*) poste vacant.

opening night *n* (*THEAT*) première *f*.

open learning centre *n* centre ouvert à tous où l'on dispense un enseignement général à temps partiel.

openly ['əupnlɪ] *adv* ouvertement.

open-minded [əupn'maɪndɪd] *adj* à l'esprit ouvert.

open-necked ['əupnnɛkt] *adj* à col ouvert.

openness ['əupnnɪs] *n* (*frankness*) franchise *f*.

open-plan ['əupn'plæn] *adj* sans cloisons.

open prison *n* prison ouverte.

open sandwich *n* canapé *m*.

open shop *n* entreprise qui admet les travailleurs non syndiqués.

Open University *n* (*BRIT*) cours universitaires par correspondance.

L'**Open University** *a été fondée en 1969. Ce type d'enseignement comprend des cours (certaines plages horaires sont réservées à cet effet à la télévision et à la radio), des devoirs qui sont envoyés par l'étudiant à son directeur ou sa directrice d'études, et un séjour obligatoire en université d'été. Il faut couvrir un certain nombre d'unités de valeur pendant une période de temps déterminée et obtenir la moyenne à un certain nombre d'entre elles pour recevoir le diplôme visé.*

---

opera ['ɔpərə] *n* opéra *m*.

opera glasses *npl* jumelles *fpl* de théâtre.

opera house *n* opéra *m*.

opera singer *n* chanteur/euse d'opéra.

operate ['ɔpəreɪt] *vt* (*machine*) faire marcher, faire fonctionner; (*system*) pratiquer ♦ *vi* fonctionner; (*drug*) faire effet; **to** ~ **on sb (for)** (*MED*) opérer qn (de).

operatic [ɔpə'rætɪk] *adj* d'opéra.

operating ['ɔpəreɪtɪŋ] *adj* (*COMM: costs, profit*) d'exploitation; (*MED*): ~ **table/theatre** table *f*/salle *f* d'opération.

operating room *n* (*US*) salle *f* d'opération.

operating system *n* (*COMPUT*) système *m*

d'exploitation.
operation [ɔpə'reɪʃən] n opération f; (of machine) fonctionnement m; **to have an ~ (for)** se faire opérer (de); **to be in ~** (machine) être en service; (system) être en vigueur.
operational [ɔpə'reɪʃənl] adj opérationnel(le); (ready for use or action) en état de marche; **when the service is fully ~** lorsque le service fonctionnera pleinement.
operative ['ɔpərətɪv] adj (measure) en vigueur ♦ n (in factory) ouvrier/ière; **the ~ word** le mot clef.
operator ['ɔpəreɪtə*] n (of machine) opérateur/trice; (TEL) téléphoniste m/f.
operetta [ɔpə'rɛtə] n opérette f.
ophthalmologist [ɔfθæl'mɔlədʒɪst] n ophtalmologiste m/f, ophtalmologue m/f.
opinion [ə'pɪnjən] n opinion f, avis m; **in my ~** à mon avis; **to seek a second ~** demander un deuxième avis.
opinionated [ə'pɪnjəneɪtɪd] adj aux idées bien arrêtées.
opinion poll n sondage m d'opinion.
opium ['əupɪəm] n opium m.
opponent [ə'pəunənt] n adversaire m/f.
opportune ['ɔpətjuːn] adj opportun(e).
opportunist [ɔpə'tjuːnɪst] n opportuniste m/f.
opportunity [ɔpə'tjuːnɪtɪ] n occasion f; **to take the ~ to do** or **of doing** profiter de l'occasion pour faire.
oppose [ə'pəuz] vt s'opposer à; **~d to** adj opposé(e) à; **as ~d to** par opposition à.
opposing [ə'pəuzɪŋ] adj (side) opposé(e).
opposite ['ɔpəzɪt] adj opposé(e); (house etc) d'en face ♦ adv en face ♦ prep en face de ♦ n opposé m, contraire m; (of word) contraire m; **"see ~ page"** "voir ci-contre".
opposite number (BRIT) n homologue m/f.
opposite sex n: **the ~** l'autre sexe.
opposition [ɔpə'zɪʃən] n opposition f.
oppress [ə'prɛs] vt opprimer.
oppression [ə'prɛʃən] n oppression f.
oppressive [ə'prɛsɪv] adj oppressif(ive).
opprobrium [ə'prəubrɪəm] n (formal) opprobre m.
opt [ɔpt] vi: **to ~ for** opter pour; **to ~ to do** choisir de faire.
▶**opt out** vi (school, hospital) devenir autonome; (health service) devenir privé(e); **to ~ out of** choisir de quitter.
optical ['ɔptɪkl] adj optique; (instrument) d'optique.
optical character reader/recognition (OCR) n lecteur m/lecture f optique.
optical fibre n fibre f optique.
optician [ɔp'tɪʃən] n opticien/ne.
optics ['ɔptɪks] n optique f.
optimism ['ɔptɪmɪzəm] n optimisme m.
optimist ['ɔptɪmɪst] n optimiste m/f.
optimistic [ɔptɪ'mɪstɪk] adj optimiste.
optimum ['ɔptɪməm] adj optimum.

option ['ɔpʃən] n choix m, option f; (SCOL) matière f à option; (COMM) option; **to keep one's ~s open** (fig) ne pas s'engager; **I have no ~** je n'ai pas le choix.
optional ['ɔpʃənl] adj facultatif(ive); (COMM) en option; **~ extras** accessoires mpl en option, options fpl.
opulence ['ɔpjuləns] n opulence f; abondance f.
opulent ['ɔpjulənt] adj opulent(e); abondant(e).
OR abbr (US) = Oregon.
or [ɔː*] conj ou; (with negative): **he hasn't seen ~ heard anything** il n'a rien vu ni entendu; **~ else** sinon; ou bien, ou alors.
oracle ['ɔrəkl] n oracle m.
oral ['ɔːrəl] adj oral(e) ♦ n oral m.
orange ['ɔrɪndʒ] n (fruit) orange f ♦ adj orange inv.
orangeade [ɔrɪndʒ'eɪd] n orangeade f.
oration [ɔː'reɪʃən] n discours solennel.
orator ['ɔrətə*] n orateur/trice.
oratorio [ɔrə'tɔːrɪəu] n oratorio m.
orb [ɔːb] n orbe m.
orbit ['ɔːbɪt] n orbite f ♦ vt décrire une or des orbite(s) autour de; **to be in/go into ~ (round)** être/entrer en orbite (autour de).
orbital ['ɔːbɪtl] n (also: **~ motorway**) périphérique f.
orchard ['ɔːtʃəd] n verger m; **apple ~** verger de pommiers.
orchestra ['ɔːkɪstrə] n orchestre m; (US: seating) (fauteuils mpl d')orchestre.
orchestral [ɔː'kɛstrəl] adj orchestral(e); (concert) symphonique.
orchestrate ['ɔːkɪstreɪt] vt (MUS, fig) orchestrer.
orchid ['ɔːkɪd] n orchidée f.
ordain [ɔː'deɪn] vt (REL) ordonner; (decide) décréter.
ordeal [ɔː'diːl] n épreuve f.
order ['ɔːdə*] n ordre m; (COMM) commande f ♦ vt ordonner; (COMM) commander; **in ~** en ordre; (of document) en règle; **out of ~** hors service; (telephone) en dérangement; **a machine in working ~** une machine en état de marche; **in ~ of size** par ordre de grandeur; **in ~ to do/that** pour faire/que + sub; **to ~ sb to do** ordonner à qn de faire; **to place an ~ for sth with sb** commander qch auprès de qn, passer commande de qch à qn; **to be on ~** être en commande; **made to ~** fait sur commande; **to be under ~s to do sth** avoir ordre de faire qch; **a point of ~** un point de procédure; **to the ~ of** (BANKING) à l'ordre de.
order book n carnet m de commandes.
order form n bon m de commande.
orderly ['ɔːdəlɪ] n (MIL) ordonnance f ♦ adj (room) en ordre; (mind) méthodique; (person) qui a de l'ordre.
order number n numéro m de commande.

rdinal ['ɔːdɪnl] adj (number) ordinal(e).
rdinary ['ɔːdnrɪ] adj ordinaire, normal(e); (pej) ordinaire, quelconque; **out of the ~** exceptionnel(le).
rdinary degree n (SCOL) ≈ licence f libre.

> Un **ordinary degree** est un diplôme inférieur à l'**honours degree** que l'on obtient en général après trois années d'études universitaires. Il peut aussi être décerné en cas d'échec à l'**honours degree**.

rdinary seaman (OS) n (BRIT) matelot m.
rdinary shares npl actions fpl ordinaires.
rdination [ɔːdɪ'neɪʃən] n ordination f.
rdnance ['ɔːdnəns] n (MIL: unit) service m du matériel.
rdnance Survey map n (BRIT) ≈ carte f d'État-major.
re [ɔː*] n minerai m.
re(g). abbr (US) = Oregon.
rgan ['ɔːgən] n organe m; (MUS) orgue m, orgues fpl.
rganic [ɔː'gænɪk] adj organique; (crops etc) biologique, naturel(le).
rganism ['ɔːgənɪzəm] n organisme m.
rganist ['ɔːgənɪst] n organiste m/f.
rganization [ɔːgənaɪ'zeɪʃən] n organisation f.
rganization chart n organigramme m.
rganize ['ɔːgənaɪz] vt organiser; **to get ~d** s'organiser.
rganized crime ['ɔːgənaɪzd-] n crime organisé, grand banditisme.
rganized labour ['ɔːgənaɪzd-] n main-d'œuvre syndiquée.
rganizer ['ɔːgənaɪzə*] n organisateur/trice.
rgasm ['ɔːgæzəm] n orgasme m.
rgy ['ɔːdʒɪ] n orgie f.
rient ['ɔːrɪənt] n: **the ~** l'Orient m.
riental [ɔːrɪ'ɛntl] adj oriental(e) ♦ n Oriental/e.
rientate ['ɔːrɪənteɪt] vt orienter.
rifice ['ɔrɪfɪs] n orifice m.
rigin ['ɔrɪdʒɪn] n origine f; **country of ~** pays m d'origine.
riginal [ə'rɪdʒɪnl] adj original(e); (earliest) originel(le) ♦ n original m.
riginality [ərɪdʒɪ'nælɪtɪ] n originalité f.
riginally [ə'rɪdʒɪnəlɪ] adv (at first) à l'origine.
riginate [ə'rɪdʒɪneɪt] vi: **to ~ from** être originaire de; (suggestion) provenir de; **to ~ in** prendre naissance dans; avoir son origine dans.
riginator [ə'rɪdʒɪneɪtə*] n auteur m.
rkneys ['ɔːknɪz] npl: **the ~** (also: **the Orkney Islands**) les Orcades fpl.
rnament ['ɔːnəmənt] n ornement m; (trinket) bibelot m.
rnamental [ɔːnə'mɛntl] adj décoratif(ive); (garden) d'agrément.
rnamentation [ɔːnəmɛn'teɪʃən] n ornementation f.

ornate [ɔː'neɪt] adj très orné(e).
ornithologist [ɔːnɪ'θɒlədʒɪst] n ornithologue m/f.
ornithology [ɔːnɪ'θɒlədʒɪ] n ornithologie f.
orphan ['ɔːfn] n orphelin/e ♦ vt: **to be ~ed** devenir orphelin.
orphanage ['ɔːfənɪdʒ] n orphelinat m.
orthodox ['ɔːθədɒks] adj orthodoxe.
orthopaedic, (US) **orthopedic** [ɔːθə'piːdɪk] adj orthopédique.
OS abbr (BRIT: = Ordnance Survey) ≈ IGN m (= Institut géographique national); (: NAUT) = **ordinary seaman**; (: DRESS) = **outsize**.
O/S abbr = **out of stock**.
Oscar ['ɒskə*] n oscar m.
oscillate ['ɒsɪleɪt] vi osciller.
OSHA n abbr (US: = Occupational Safety and Health Administration) office de l'hygiène et de la sécurité au travail.
Oslo ['ɒzləu] n Oslo.
ostensible [ɒs'tɛnsɪbl] adj prétendu(e); apparent(e).
ostensibly [ɒs'tɛnsɪblɪ] adv en apparence.
ostentation [ɒstɛn'teɪʃən] n ostentation f.
ostentatious [ɒstɛn'teɪʃəs] adj prétentieux(euse); ostentatoire.
osteopath ['ɒstɪəpæθ] n ostéopathe m/f.
ostracize ['ɒstrəsaɪz] vt frapper d'ostracisme.
ostrich ['ɒstrɪtʃ] n autruche f.
OT n abbr (= Old Testament) AT m.
OTB n abbr (US: = off-track betting) paris pris en dehors du champ de course.
O.T.E. abbr (= on-target earnings) primes fpl sur objectifs inclus.
other ['ʌðə*] adj autre ♦ pron: **the ~ (one)** l'autre; **~s** (~ people) d'autres; **some ~ people have still to arrive** on attend encore quelques personnes; **the ~ day** l'autre jour; **~ than** autrement que; à part; **some actor or ~** un certain acteur, je ne sais quel acteur; **somebody or ~** quelqu'un; **the car was none ~ than John's** la voiture n'était autre que celle de John.
otherwise ['ʌðəwaɪz] adv, conj autrement; **an ~ good piece of work** par ailleurs, un beau travail.
OTT abbr (col) = **over the top**; see **top**.
otter ['ɒtə*] n loutre f.
OU n abbr (BRIT) = **Open University**.
ouch [autʃ] excl aïe!
ought, pt **ought** [ɔːt] aux vb: **I ~ to do it** je devrais le faire, il faudrait que je le fasse; **this ~ to have been corrected** cela aurait dû être corrigé; **he ~ to win** il devrait gagner; **you ~ to go and see it** vous devriez aller le voir.
ounce [auns] n once f (= 28.35g; 16 in a pound).
our ['auə*] adj notre, nos pl.
ours [auəz] pron le(la) nôtre, les nôtres.
ourselves [auə'sɛlvz] pron pl (reflexive, after preposition) nous; (emphatic) nous-mêmes; **we did it (all) by ~** nous avons fait ça tout

seuls.

oust [aust] *vt* évincer.

out [aut] *adv* dehors; (*published, not at home etc*) sorti(e); (*light, fire*) éteint(e); (*on strike*) en grève ♦ *vt*: **to ~ sb** révéler l'homosexualité de qn; **~ here** ici; **~ there** là-bas; **he's ~** (*absent*) il est sorti; (*unconscious*) il est sans connaissance; **to be ~ in one's calculations** s'être trompé dans ses calculs; **to run/back** *etc* **~** sortir en courant/en reculant *etc*; **to be ~ and about** *or* (*US*) **around again** être de nouveau sur pied; **before the week was ~** avant la fin de la semaine; **the journey ~** l'aller *m*; **the boat was 10 km ~** le bateau était à 10 km du rivage; **~ loud** *adv* à haute voix; **~ of** *prep* (*outside*) en dehors de; (*because of: anger etc*) par; (*from among*): **~ of 10** sur 10; (*without*): **~ of petrol** sans essence, à court d'essence; **made ~ of wood** en *or* de bois; **~ of order** (*machine*) en panne; (*TEL: line*) en dérangement; **~ of stock** (*COMM: article*) épuisé(e); (*: shop*) en rupture de stock.

outage ['autɪdʒ] *n* (*esp US: power failure*) panne *f or* coupure *f* de courant.

out-and-out ['autəndaut] *adj* véritable.

outback ['autbæk] *n* campagne isolée; (*in Australia*) intérieur *m*.

outbid [aut'bɪd] *irreg vt* surenchérir.

outboard ['autbɔːd] *n*: **~ (motor)** (moteur *m*) hors-bord *m*.

outbound ['autbaund] *adj*: **~ (from/for)** en partance (de/pour).

outbreak ['autbreɪk] *n* éruption *f*, explosion *f*; (*start*) déclenchement *m*.

outbuilding ['autbɪldɪŋ] *n* dépendance *f*.

outburst ['autbɜːst] *n* explosion *f*, accès *m*.

outcast ['autkɑːst] *n* exilé/e; (*socially*) paria *m*.

outclass [aut'klɑːs] *vt* surclasser.

outcome ['autkʌm] *n* issue *f*, résultat *m*.

outcrop ['autkrɔp] *n* affleurement *m*.

outcry ['autkraɪ] *n* tollé (général).

outdated [aut'deɪtɪd] *adj* démodé(e).

outdistance [aut'dɪstəns] *vt* distancer.

outdo [aut'duː] *vt irreg* surpasser.

outdoor [aut'dɔː] *adj* de *or* en plein air.

outdoors [aut'dɔːz] *adv* dehors; au grand air.

outer ['autə*] *adj* extérieur(e); **~ suburbs** grande banlieue.

outer space *n* espace *m* cosmique.

outfit ['autfɪt] *n* équipement *m*; (*clothes*) tenue *f*; (*col: COMM*) organisation *f*, boîte *f*.

outfitter ['autfɪtə*] *n* (*BRIT*): **"(gent's) ~'s"** "confection pour hommes".

outgoing ['autgəuɪŋ] *adj* (*president, tenant*) sortant(e); (*character*) ouvert(e), extraverti(e).

outgoings ['autgəuɪŋz] *npl* (*BRIT: expenses*) dépenses *fpl*.

outgrow [aut'grəu] *vt irreg* (*clothes*) devenir trop grand(e) pour.

outhouse ['authaus] *n* appentis *m*, remise *f*.

outing ['autɪŋ] *n* sortie *f*; excursion *f*.

outlandish [aut'lændɪʃ] *adj* étrange.

outlast [aut'lɑːst] *vt* survivre à.

outlaw ['autlɔː] *n* hors-la-loi *m inv* ♦ *vt* (*person*) mettre hors la loi; (*practice*) proscrire.

outlay ['autleɪ] *n* dépenses *fpl*; (*investment*) mise *f* de fonds.

outlet ['autlet] *n* (*for liquid etc*) issue *f*, sortie *f*; (*for emotion*) exutoire *m*; (*for goods*) débouché *m*; (*also: retail ~*) point *m* de vente; (*US: ELEC*) prise *f* de courant.

outline ['autlaɪn] *n* (*shape*) contour *m*; (*summary*) esquisse *f*, grandes lignes.

outlive [aut'lɪv] *vt* survivre à.

outlook ['autluk] *n* perspective *f*.

outlying ['autlaɪɪŋ] *adj* écarté(e).

outmanoeuvre [autmə'nuːvə*] *vt* (*rival etc*) avoir au tournant.

outmoded [aut'məudɪd] *adj* démodé(e); dépassé(e).

outnumber [aut'nʌmbə*] *vt* surpasser en nombre.

out-of-court [autəv'kɔːt] *adj, adv* à l'aimable.

out-of-date [autəv'deɪt] *adj* (*passport, ticket*) périmé(e); (*theory, idea*) dépassé(e); (*custom*) désuet(ète); (*clothes*) démodé(e).

out-of-the-way ['autəvðə'weɪ] *adj* loin de tout; (*fig*) insolite.

outpatient ['autpeɪʃənt] *n* malade *m/f* en consultation externe.

outpost ['autpəust] *n* avant-poste *m*.

outpouring ['autpɔːrɪŋ] *n* (*fig*) épanchement(s *m(pl)*.

output ['autput] *n* rendement *m*, production *f* ♦ *vt* (*COMPUT*) sortir.

outrage ['autreɪdʒ] *n* atrocité *f*, acte *m* de violence; scandale *m* ♦ *vt* outrager.

outrageous [aut'reɪdʒəs] *adj* atroce; scandaleux(euse).

outrider ['autraɪdə*] *n* (*on motorcycle*) motard *m*.

outright *adv* [aut'raɪt] complètement; catégoriquement; carrément; sur le coup ♦ *adj* ['autraɪt] complet(ète); catégorique.

outrun [aut'rʌn] *vt irreg* dépasser.

outset ['autset] *n* début *m*.

outshine [aut'ʃaɪn] *vt irreg* (*fig*) éclipser.

outside [aut'saɪd] *n* extérieur *m* ♦ *adj* extérieur(e); (*remote, unlikely*): **an ~ chance** une (très) faible chance ♦ *adv* (au) dehors, à l'extérieur ♦ *prep* hors de, à l'extérieur de; **at the ~** (*fig*) au plus *or* maximum; **~ left/right** *n* (*FOOTBALL*) ailier gauche/droit.

outside broadcast *n* (*RADIO, TV*) reportage *n*

outside lane *n* (*AUT: in Britain*) voie *f* de droite; (*: in US, Europe*) voie de gauche.

outside line *n* (*TEL*) ligne extérieure.

outsider [aut'saɪdə*] *n* (*in race etc*) outsider *m*; (*stranger*) étranger/ère.

outsize ['autsaɪz] *adj* énorme; (*clothes*) grand taille *inv*.

outskirts ['autskɜːts] *npl* faubourgs *mpl*.

outsmart [aut'smɑːt] *vt* se montrer plus malin(igne) *or* futé(e) que.

outspoken [aut'spəukən] *adj* très franc(franche).

outspread [aut'sprɛd] *adj* (*wings*) déployé(e).

outstanding [aut'stændɪŋ] *adj* remarquable, exceptionnel(le); (*unfinished*) en suspens; en souffrance; non réglé(e); **your account is still ~** vous n'avez pas encore tout remboursé.

outstay [aut'steɪ] *vt*: **to ~ one's welcome** abuser de l'hospitalité de son hôte.

outstretched [aut'strɛtʃt] *adj* (*hand*) tendu(e); (*body*) étendu(e).

outstrip [aut'strɪp] *vt* (*also fig*) dépasser.

out-tray ['auttreɪ] *n* courrier *m* "départ".

outvote [aut'vəut] *vt*: **to ~ sb (by)** mettre qn en minorité (par); **to ~ sth (by)** rejeter qch (par).

outward ['autwəd] *adj* (*sign, appearances*) extérieur(e); (*journey*) (d')aller.

outwardly ['autwədlɪ] *adv* extérieurement; en apparence.

outweigh [aut'weɪ] *vt* l'emporter sur.

outwit [aut'wɪt] *vt* se montrer plus malin que.

oval ['əuvl] *adj, n* ovale (*m*).

L'**Oval Office** est le bureau personnel du président des États-Unis à la Maison-Blanche, ainsi appelé du fait de sa forme ovale. Par extension, ce terme désigne la présidence elle-même.

ovarian [əu'vɛərɪən] *adj* ovarien(ne); (*cancer*) des ovaires.

ovary ['əuvərɪ] *n* ovaire *m*.

ovation [əu'veɪʃən] *n* ovation *f*.

oven ['ʌvn] *n* four *m*.

ovenproof ['ʌvnpruːf] *adj* allant au four.

oven-ready ['ʌvnrɛdɪ] *adj* prêt(e) à cuire.

ovenware ['ʌvnwɛə*] *n* plats *mpl* allant au four.

over ['əuvə*] *adv* (par-)dessus; (*excessively*) trop ♦ *adj* (*or adv*) (*finished*) fini(e), terminé(e); (*too much*) en plus ♦ *prep* sur; par-dessus; (*above*) au-dessus de; (*on the other side of*) de l'autre côté de; (*more than*) plus de; (*during*) pendant; (*about, concerning*): **they fell out ~ money/her** ils se sont brouillés pour des questions d'argent/à cause d'elle; **~ here** ici; **~ there** là-bas; **all ~** (*everywhere*) partout; (*finished*) fini(e); **~ and ~ (again)** à plusieurs reprises; **~ and above** en plus de; **to ask sb ~** inviter qn (à passer); **to go ~ to sb's** passer chez qn; **now ~ to our Paris correspondent** nous passons l'antenne à notre correspondant à Paris; **the world ~** dans le monde entier; **she's not ~ intelligent** (*BRIT*) elle n'est pas particulièrement intelligente.

over... ['əuvə*] *prefix*: **~abundant** surabondant(e).

overact [əuvər'ækt] *vi* (*THEAT*) outrer son rôle.

overall *adj, n* ['əuvərɔːl] *adj* (*length*) total(e); (*study*) d'ensemble ♦ *n* (*BRIT*) blouse *f* ♦ *adv* [əuvər'ɔːl] dans l'ensemble, en général; **~s** *npl* bleus *mpl* (de travail).

overall majority *n* majorité absolue.

overanxious [əuvər'æŋkʃəs] *adj* trop anxieux(euse).

overawe [əuvər'ɔː] *vt* impressionner.

overbalance [əuvə'bæləns] *vi* basculer.

overbearing [əuvə'bɛərɪŋ] *adj* impérieux(euse), autoritaire.

overboard ['əuvəbɔːd] *adv* (*NAUT*) par-dessus bord; **to go ~ for sth** (*fig*) s'emballer (pour qch).

overbook [əuvə'buk] *vi* faire du surbooking.

overcapitalize [əuvə'kæpɪtəlaɪz] *vt* surcapitaliser.

overcast ['əuvəkɑːst] *adj* couvert(e).

overcharge [əuvə'tʃɑːdʒ] *vt*: **to ~ sb for sth** faire payer qch trop cher à qn.

overcoat ['əuvəkəut] *n* pardessus *m*.

overcome [əuvə'kʌm] *vt irreg* triompher de; surmonter ♦ *adj* (*emotionally*) bouleversé(e); **~ with grief** accablé(e) de douleur.

overconfident [əuvə'kɔnfɪdənt] *adj* trop sûr(e) de soi.

overcrowded [əuvə'kraudɪd] *adj* bondé(e).

overcrowding [əuvə'kraudɪŋ] *n* surpeuplement *m*; (*in bus*) encombrement *m*.

overdo [əuvə'duː] *vt irreg* exagérer; (*overcook*) trop cuire; **to ~ it, to ~ things** (*work too hard*) en faire trop, se surmener.

overdose ['əuvədəus] *n* dose excessive.

overdraft ['əuvədrɑːft] *n* découvert *m*.

overdrawn [əuvə'drɔːn] *adj* (*account*) à découvert.

overdrive ['əuvədraɪv] *n* (*AUT*) (vitesse *f*) surmultipliée *f*.

overdue [əuvə'djuː] *adj* en retard; (*bill*) impayé(e); (*recognition*) tardif(ive); **that change was long ~** ce changement n'avait que trop tardé.

overemphasis [əuvər'ɛmfəsɪs] *n*: **to put an ~ on** accorder trop d'importance à.

overestimate [əuvər'ɛstɪmeɪt] *vt* surestimer.

overexcited [əuvərɪk'saɪtɪd] *adj* surexcité(e).

overexertion [əuvərɪg'zəːʃən] *n* surmenage *m* (physique).

overexpose [əuvərɪk'spəuz] *vt* (*PHOT*) surexposer.

overflow *vi* [əuvə'fləu] déborder ♦ *n* ['əuvəfləu] trop-plein *m*; (*also:* **~ pipe**) tuyau *m* d'écoulement, trop-plein *m*.

overfly [əuvə'flaɪ] *vt irreg* survoler.

overgenerous [əuvə'dʒɛnərəs] *adj* (*person*) prodigue; (*offer*) excessif(ive).

overgrown [əuvə'grəun] *adj* (*garden*) envahi(e) par la végétation; **he's just an ~ schoolboy** (*fig*) c'est un écolier attardé.

overhang ['əuvəhæŋ] *irreg vt* surplomber ♦ *vi* faire saillie.

overhaul *vt* [əuvə'hɔːl] réviser ♦ *n* ['əuvəhɔːl] révision *f*.

overhead *adv* [əuvə'hɛd] au-dessus ♦ *adj, n* ['əuvəhɛd] *adj* aérien(ne); (*lighting*) vertical(e) ♦ *n* (*US*) = **overheads**.

overheads ['əuvəhɛdz] *npl* (*BRIT*) frais généraux.

overhear [əuvə'hɪə*] *vt irreg* entendre (par hasard).

overheat [əuvə'hiːt] *vi* devenir surchauffé(e); (*engine*) chauffer.

overjoyed [əuvə'dʒɔɪd] *adj* ravi(e), enchanté(e).

overkill ['əuvəkɪl] *n* (*fig*): **it would be** ~ ce serait de trop.

overland ['əuvəlænd] *adj, adv* par voie de terre.

overlap *vi* [əuvə'læp] se chevaucher ♦ *n* ['əuvəlæp] chevauchement *m*.

overleaf [əuvə'liːf] *adv* au verso.

overload [əuvə'ləud] *vt* surcharger.

overlook [əuvə'luk] *vt* (*have view of*) donner sur; (*miss*) oublier, négliger; (*forgive*) fermer les yeux sur.

overlord ['əuvəlɔːd] *n* chef *m* suprême.

overmanning [əuvə'mænɪŋ] *n* sureffectif *m*, main-d'œuvre *f* pléthorique.

overnight *adv* [əuvə'naɪt] (*happen*) durant la nuit; (*fig*) soudain ♦ *adj* [əuvənaɪt] d'une (*or* de) nuit; soudain(e); **he stayed there** ~ il y a passé la nuit; **if you travel** ~ ... si tu fais le voyage de nuit ...; **he'll be away** ~ il ne rentrera pas ce soir.

overpass ['əuvəpɑːs] *n* pont autoroutier; (*US*) passerelle *f*, pont *m*.

overpay [əuvə'peɪ] *vt*: **to** ~ **sb by £50** donner à qn 50 livres de trop.

overplay [əuvə'pleɪ] *vt* exagérer; **to** ~ **one's hand** trop présumer de sa situation.

overpower [əuvə'pauə*] *vt* vaincre; (*fig*) accabler.

overpowering [əuvə'pauərɪŋ] *adj* irrésistible; (*heat, stench*) suffocant(e).

overproduction ['əuvəprə'dʌkʃən] *n* surproduction *f*.

overrate [əuvə'reɪt] *vt* surestimer.

overreact [əuvəriː'ækt] *vi* réagir de façon excessive.

override [əuvə'raɪd] *vt* (*irreg: like* **ride**) (*order, objection*) passer outre à; (*decision*) annuler.

overriding [əuvə'raɪdɪŋ] *adj* prépondérant(e).

overrule [əuvə'ruːl] *vt* (*decision*) annuler; (*claim*) rejeter.

overrun [əuvə'rʌn] *irreg vt* (*MIL: country etc*) occuper; (*time limit etc*) dépasser ♦ *vi* dépasser le temps imparti; **the town is** ~ **with tourists** la ville est envahie de touristes.

overseas [əuvə'siːz] *adv* outre-mer; (*abroad*) à l'étranger ♦ *adj* (*trade*) extérieur(e); (*visitor*) étranger(ère).

oversee [əuvə'siː] *vt irreg* surveiller.

overseer ['əuvəsɪə*] *n* (*in factory*) contremaître *m*.

overshadow [əuvə'ʃædəu] *vt* (*fig*) éclipser.

overshoot [əuvə'ʃuːt] *vt irreg* dépasser.

oversight ['əuvəsaɪt] *n* omission *f*, oubli *m*; **due to an** ~ par suite d'une inadvertance.

oversimplify [əuvə'sɪmplɪfaɪ] *vt* simplifier à l'excès.

oversleep [əuvə'sliːp] *vi irreg* se réveiller (trop) tard.

overspend [əuvə'spɛnd] *vi irreg* dépenser de trop; **we have overspent by 5,000 dollars** nous avons dépassé notre budget de 5 000 dollars, nous avons dépensé 5 000 dollars de trop.

overspill ['əuvəspɪl] *n* excédent *m* de population.

overstaffed [əuvə'stɑːft] *adj*: **to be** ~ avoir trop de personnel, être en surnombre.

overstate [əuvə'steɪt] *vt* exagérer.

overstatement [əuvə'steɪtmənt] *n* exagération *f*.

overstay [əuvə'steɪ] *vt*: **to** ~ **one's welcome (at sb's)** abuser de l'hospitalité de qn.

overstep [əuvə'stɛp] *vt*: **to** ~ **the mark** dépasser la mesure.

overstock [əuvə'stɔk] *vt* stocker en surabondance.

overstretched [əuvə'strɛtʃt] *adj* (*person*) débordé(e); **my budget is** ~ j'ai atteint les limites de mon budget.

overstrike *n* ['əuvəstraɪk] (*on printer*) superposition *f*, double frappe *f* ♦ *vt irreg* [əuvə'straɪk] surimprimer.

overt [əu'vəːt] *adj* non dissimulé(e).

overtake [əuvə'teɪk] *vt irreg* dépasser; (*AUT*) dépasser, doubler.

overtaking [əuvə'teɪkɪŋ] *n* (*AUT*) dépassement *m*.

overtax [əuvə'tæks] *vt* (*ECON*) surimposer; (*fig: strength, patience*) abuser de; **to** ~ **o.s.** se surmener.

overthrow [əuvə'θrəu] *vt irreg* (*government*) renverser.

overtime ['əuvətaɪm] *n* heures *fpl* supplémentaires; **to do** *or* **work** ~ faire des heures supplémentaires.

overtime ban *n* refus *m* de faire des heures supplémentaires.

overtone ['əuvətəun] *n* (*also*: ~**s**) note *f*, sous-entendus *mpl*.

overture ['əuvətʃuə*] *n* (*MUS, fig*) ouverture *f*.

overturn [əuvə'təːn] *vt* renverser ♦ *vi* se retourner.

overview ['əuvəvjuː] *n* vue *f* d'ensemble.

overweight [əuvə'weɪt] *adj* (*person*) trop gros(se); (*luggage*) trop lourd(e).

overwhelm [əuvə'wɛlm] *vt* accabler; submerger; écraser.

overwhelming [əuvə'wɛlmɪŋ] *adj* (*victory, defeat*) écrasant(e); (*desire*) irrésistible; **one's** ~ **impression is of heat** on a une impression dominante de chaleur.

overwhelmingly [əuvə'wɛlmɪŋlɪ] *adv* (*vote*) en masse; (*win*) d'une manière écrasante.

overwork [əuvə'wəːk] *n* surmenage *m* ♦ *vt* surmener ♦ *vi* se surmener.

overwrite [əuvə'raɪt] *vt irreg* (*COMPUT*) écraser.

overwrought [əuvə'rɔːt] *adj* excédé(e).

ovulation [ɔvju'leɪʃən] *n* ovulation *f*.

owe [əu] *vt* devoir; **to ~ sb sth, to ~ sth to sb** devoir qch à qn.

owing to ['əuɪŋtuː] *prep* à cause de, en raison de.

owl [aul] *n* hibou *m*.

own [əun] *vt* posséder ♦ *vi* (*BRIT*): **to ~ to sth** reconnaître *or* avouer qch; **to ~ to having done sth** avouer avoir fait qch ♦ *adj* propre; **a room of my ~** une chambre à moi, ma propre chambre; **can I have it for my (very) ~?** puis-je l'avoir pour moi (tout) seul?; **to get one's ~ back** prendre sa revanche; **on one's ~** tout(e) seul(e); **to come into one's ~** trouver sa voie; trouver sa justification.
▶**own up** *vi* avouer.

own brand *n* (*COMM*) marque *f* de distributeur.

owner ['əunə*] *n* propriétaire *m/f*.

owner-occupier ['əunər'ɔkjupaɪə*] *n* propriétaire occupant.

ownership ['əunəʃɪp] *n* possession *f*; **it's under new ~** (*shop etc*) il y a eu un changement de propriétaire.

own goal *n*: **he scored an ~** (*SPORT*) il a marqué un but contre son camp; (*fig*) cela s'est retourné contre lui.

ox, *pl* **oxen** [ɔks, 'ɔksn] *n* bœuf *m*.

> *Oxbridge*, *nom formé à partir des mots Ox(ford) et (Cam)bridge, s'utilise pour parler de ces deux universités comme formant un tout, dans la mesure où elles sont toutes deux les universités britanniques les plus prestigieuses et mondialement connues.*

Oxfam ['ɔksfæm] *n abbr* (*BRIT*: = *Oxford Committee for Famine Relief*) *association humanitaire*.

oxide ['ɔksaɪd] *n* oxyde *m*.

Oxon. ['ɔksn] *abbr* (*BRIT*: = *Oxoniensis*) = *of Oxford*.

oxtail ['ɔksteɪl] *n*: **~ soup** soupe *f* à la queue de bœuf.

oxyacetylene ['ɔksɪə'sɛtɪliːn] *adj* oxyacétylénique; **~ burner, ~ lamp** chalumeau *m* oxyacétylénique.

oxygen ['ɔksɪdʒən] *n* oxygène *m*.

oxygen mask *n* masque *m* à oxygène.

oxygen tent *n* tente *f* à oxygène.

oyster ['ɔɪstə*] *n* huître *f*.

oz. *abbr* = **ounce**.

ozone ['əuzəun] *n* ozone *m*.

P p

P, p [piː] *n* (*letter*) P, p *m*; **P for Peter** P comme Pierre.

P *abbr* = **president, prince**.

p *abbr* (= *page*) p; (*BRIT*) = **penny, pence**.

PA *n abbr* = **personal assistant, public address system** ♦ *abbr* (*US*) = **Pennsylvania**.

pa [paː] *n* (*col*) papa *m*.

Pa. *abbr* (*US*) = **Pennsylvania**.

p.a. *abbr* = **per annum**.

PAC *n abbr* (*US*) = *political action committee*.

pace [peɪs] *n* pas *m*; (*speed*) allure *f*; vitesse *f* ♦ *vi*: **to ~ up and down** faire les cent pas; **to keep ~ with** aller à la même vitesse que; (*events*) se tenir au courant de; **to set the ~** (*running*) donner l'allure; (*fig*) donner le ton; **to put sb through his ~s** (*fig*) mettre qn à l'épreuve.

pacemaker ['peɪsmeɪkə*] *n* (*MED*) stimulateur *m* cardiaque.

pacific [pə'sɪfɪk] *adj* pacifique ♦ *n*: **the P~ (Ocean)** le Pacifique, l'océan *m* Pacifique.

pacification [pæsɪfɪ'keɪʃən] *n* pacification *f*.

pacifier ['pæsɪfaɪə*] *n* (*US*: *dummy*) tétine *f*.

pacifist ['pæsɪfɪst] *n* pacifiste *m/f*.

pacify ['pæsɪfaɪ] *vt* pacifier; (*soothe*) calmer.

pack [pæk] *n* paquet *m*; ballot *m*; (*of hounds*) meute *f*; (*of thieves, wolves etc*) bande *f*; (*of cards*) jeu *m* ♦ *vt* (*goods*) empaqueter, emballer; (*in suitcase etc*) emballer; (*box*) remplir; (*cram*) entasser; (*press down*) tasser; damer; (*COMPUT*) grouper, tasser ♦ *vi*: **to ~ (one's bags)** faire ses bagages; **to ~ into** (*room, stadium*) s'entasser dans; **to send sb ~ing** (*col*) envoyer promener qn.
▶**pack in** (*BRIT col*) *vi* (*machine*) tomber en panne ♦ *vt* (*boyfriend*) plaquer; **~ it in!** laisse tomber!
▶**pack off** *vt* (*person*) envoyer (promener), expédier.
▶**pack up** *vi* (*BRIT col*: *machine*) tomber en panne; (*: person*) se tirer ♦ *vt* (*belongings*) ranger; (*goods, presents*) empaqueter, emballer.

package ['pækɪdʒ] *n* paquet *m*; (*of goods*) emballage *m*, conditionnement *m*; (*also*: **~ deal**) marché global; forfait *m*; (*COMPUT*) progiciel *m* ♦ *vt* (*goods*) conditionner.

package holiday *n* (*BRIT*) vacances organisées.

package tour *n* voyage organisé.

packaging ['pækɪdʒɪŋ] *n* conditionnement *m*.

packed [pækt] *adj* (*crowded*) bondé(e); **~ lunch**

(*BRIT*) repas froid.
packer ['pækə*] n (*person*) emballeur/euse;
conditionneur/euse.
packet ['pækɪt] n paquet m.
packet switching [-swɪtʃɪŋ] n (*COMPUT*)
commutation f de paquets.
pack ice ['pækaɪs] n banquise f.
packing ['pækɪŋ] n emballage m.
packing case n caisse f (d'emballage).
pact [pækt] n pacte m, traité m.
pad [pæd] n bloc(-notes m) m; (*for inking*)
tampon m encreur; (*col: flat*) piaule f ♦ vt
rembourrer ♦ vi: **to ~ in/about** *etc* entrer/
aller et venir *etc* à pas feutrés.
padded cell ['pædɪd-] n cellule capitonnée.
padding ['pædɪŋ] n rembourrage m; (*fig*)
délayage m.
paddle ['pædl] n (*oar*) pagaie f ♦ vi barboter,
faire trempette ♦ vt: **to ~ a canoe** *etc*
pagayer.
paddle steamer n bateau m à aubes.
paddling pool ['pædlɪŋ-] n petit bassin.
paddock ['pædək] n enclos m; paddock m.
paddy ['pædɪ] n (*also: ~ field*) rizière f.
padlock ['pædlɔk] n cadenas m ♦ vt
cadenasser.
padre ['pɑːdrɪ] n aumônier m.
paediatrician, (*US*) **pediatrician**
[piːdɪə'trɪʃən] n pédiatre m/f.
paediatrics, (*US*) **pediatrics** [piːdɪ'ætrɪks] n
pédiatrie f.
paedophile, (*US*) **pedophile** ['piːdəufaɪl] n
pédophile m.
pagan ['peɪgən] adj, n païen(ne).
page [peɪdʒ] n (*of book*) page f; (*also: ~ boy*)
groom m, chasseur m; (*at wedding*) garçon m
d'honneur ♦ vt (*in hotel etc*) (faire) appeler.
pageant ['pædʒənt] n spectacle m historique;
grande cérémonie.
pageantry ['pædʒəntrɪ] n apparat m, pompe f.
page break n fin f or saut m de page.
pager ['peɪdʒə*] n système m de téléappel, bip
m.
paginate ['pædʒɪneɪt] vt paginer.
pagination [pædʒɪ'neɪʃən] n pagination f.
pagoda [pə'gəudə] n pagode f.
paid [peɪd] pt, pp of **pay** ♦ adj (*work, official*)
rémunéré(e); **to put ~ to** (*BRIT*) mettre fin à,
mettre par terre.
paid-up ['peɪdʌp], (*US*) **paid-in** ['peɪdɪn] adj
(*member*) à jour de sa cotisation; (*shares*)
libéré(e); **~ capital** capital versé.
pail [peɪl] n seau m.
pain [peɪn] n douleur f; **to be in ~** souffrir,
avoir mal; **to have a ~ in** avoir mal à or une
douleur à or dans; **to take ~s to do** se
donner du mal pour faire; **on ~ of death**
sous peine de mort.
pained ['peɪnd] adj peiné(e), chagrin(e).
painful ['peɪnful] adj douloureux(euse);
(*difficult*) difficile, pénible.
painfully ['peɪnfəlɪ] adv (*fig: very*)

terriblement.
painkiller ['peɪnkɪlə*] n calmant m.
painless ['peɪnlɪs] adj indolore.
painstaking ['peɪnzteɪkɪŋ] adj (*person*)
soigneux(euse); (*work*) soigné(e).
paint [peɪnt] n peinture f ♦ vt peindre; (*fig*)
dépeindre; **to ~ the door blue** peindre la
porte en bleu; **to ~ in oils** faire de la
peinture à l'huile.
paintbox ['peɪntbɔks] n boîte f de couleurs.
paintbrush ['peɪntbrʌʃ] n pinceau m.
painter ['peɪntə*] n peintre m.
painting ['peɪntɪŋ] n peinture f; (*picture*)
tableau m.
paint-stripper ['peɪntstrɪpə*] n décapant m.
paintwork ['peɪntwɔːk] n (*BRIT*) peintures fpl;
(*: of car*) peinture f.
pair [peə*] n (*of shoes, gloves etc*) paire f;
(*couple*) couple m; (*twosome*) duo m; **~ of
scissors** (paire de) ciseaux mpl; **~ of trousers**
pantalon m.
▶**pair off** vi se mettre par deux.
pajamas [pə'dʒɑːməz] npl (*US*) pyjama(s) m(pl).
Pakistan [pɑːkɪ'stɑːn] n Pakistan m.
Pakistani [pɑːkɪ'stɑːnɪ] adj pakistanais(e) ♦ n
Pakistanais/e.
PAL [pæl] n abbr (*TV*: = *phase alternation line*)
PAL m.
pal [pæl] n (*col*) copain/copine.
palace ['pæləs] n palais m.
palatable ['pælɪtəbl] adj bon(bonne), agréable
au goût.
palate ['pælɪt] n palais m (*ANAT*).
palatial [pə'leɪʃəl] adj grandiose, magnifique.
palaver [pə'lɑːvə*] n palabres fpl or mpl;
histoire(s) f(pl).
pale [peɪl] adj pâle ♦ vi pâlir ♦ n: **to be beyond
the ~** être au ban de la société; **to grow** or
turn ~ (*person*) pâlir; **~ blue** adj bleu pâle
inv; **to ~ into insignificance (beside)** perdre
beaucoup d'importance (par rapport à).
paleness ['peɪlnɪs] n pâleur f.
Palestine ['pælɪstaɪn] n Palestine f.
Palestinian [pælɪs'tɪnɪən] adj palestinien(ne)
♦ n Palestinien/ne.
palette ['pælɪt] n palette f.
paling ['peɪlɪŋ] n (*stake*) palis m; (*fence*)
palissade f.
palisade [pælɪ'seɪd] n palissade f.
pall [pɔːl] n (*of smoke*) voile m ♦ vi: **to ~ (on)**
devenir lassant (pour).
pallet ['pælɪt] n (*for goods*) palette f.
pallid ['pælɪd] adj blême.
pallor ['pælə*] n pâleur f.
pally ['pælɪ] adj (*col*) copain(copine).
palm [pɑːm] n (*ANAT*) paume f; (*also: ~ tree*)
palmier m; (*leaf, symbol*) palme f ♦ vt: **to ~
sth off on sb** (*col*) refiler qch à qn.
palmist ['pɑːmɪst] n chiromancien/ne.
Palm Sunday n le dimanche des Rameaux.
palpable ['pælpəbl] adj évident(e), manifeste.
palpitation [pælpɪ'teɪʃən] n palpitation f.

paltry ['pɔ:ltrɪ] *adj* dérisoire; piètre.
pamper ['pæmpə*] *vt* gâter, dorloter.
pamphlet ['pæmflət] *n* brochure *f*; (*political etc*) tract *m*.
pan [pæn] *n* (*also:* **sauce~**) casserole *f*; (*also:* **frying ~**) poêle *f*; (*of lavatory*) cuvette *f* ♦ *vi* (*CINE*) faire un panoramique ♦ *vt* (*col: book, film*) éreinter; **to ~ for gold** laver du sable aurifère.
panacea [pænə'sɪə] *n* panacée *f*.
Panama ['pænəmɑ:] *n* Panama *m*.
Panama canal *n* canal *m* de Panama.
pancake ['pænkeɪk] *n* crêpe *f*.
Pancake Day *n* (*BRIT*) mardi gras.
pancake roll *n* rouleau *m* de printemps.
pancreas ['pæŋkrɪəs] *n* pancréas *m*.
panda ['pændə] *n* panda *m*.
panda car *n* (*BRIT*) ≈ voiture *f* pie *inv*.
pandemonium [pændɪ'məunɪəm] *n* tohu-bohu *m*.
pander ['pændə*] *vi:* **to ~ to** flatter bassement; obéir servilement à.
p&h *abbr* (*US:* = postage and handling) frais *mpl* de port.
P&L *abbr* = profit and loss.
p&p *abbr* (*BRIT:* = postage and packing) frais *mpl* de port.
pane [peɪn] *n* carreau *m* (de fenêtre).
panel ['pænl] *n* (*of wood, cloth etc*) panneau *m*; (*RADIO, TV*) panel *m*, invités *mpl*; (*of experts*) table ronde, comité *m*.
panel game *n* (*BRIT*) jeu *m* (radiophonique/ télévisé).
panelling, (*US*) **paneling** ['pænəlɪŋ] *n* boiseries *fpl*.
panellist, (*US*) **panelist** ['pænəlɪst] *n* invité/e (*d'un panel*), membre d'un panel.
pang [pæŋ] *n:* **~s of remorse** pincements *mpl* de remords; **~s of hunger/conscience** tiraillements *mpl* d'estomac/de la conscience.
panhandler ['pænhændlə*] *n* (*US col*) mendiant/e.
panic ['pænɪk] *n* panique *f*, affolement *m* ♦ *vi* s'affoler, paniquer.
panic buying [-baɪɪŋ] *n* achats *mpl* de précaution.
panicky ['pænɪkɪ] *adj* (*person*) qui panique *or* s'affole facilement.
panic-stricken ['pænɪkstrɪkən] *adj* affolé(e).
pannier ['pænɪə*] *n* (*on animal*) bât *m*; (*on bicycle*) sacoche *f*.
panorama [pænə'rɑ:mə] *n* panorama *m*.
panoramic [pænə'ræmɪk] *adj* panoramique.
pansy ['pænzɪ] *n* (*BOT*) pensée *f*; (*col*) tapette *f*, pédé *m*.
pant [pænt] *vi* haleter.
pantechnicon [pæn'tɛknɪkən] *n* (*BRIT*) (grand) camion de déménagement.
panther ['pænθə*] *n* panthère *f*.
panties ['pæntɪz] *npl* slip *m*, culotte *f*.
pantihose ['pæntɪhəuz] *n* (*US*) collant *m*.

panto ['pæntəu] *n* = **pantomime**.
pantomime ['pæntəmaɪm] *n* (*BRIT*) spectacle *m* de Noël.

Une **pantomime** (à ne pas confondre avec le mot tel qu'on l'utilise en français), que l'on appelle également de façon familière "panto", est un genre de farce où le personnage principal est souvent un jeune garçon et où il y a toujours une **dame**, c'est-à-dire une vieille femme jouée par un homme, et un méchant. La plupart du temps, l'histoire est basée sur un conte de fées comme Cendrillon ou Le Chat botté, et le public est encouragé à participer en prévenant le héros d'un danger imminent. Ce genre de spectacle, qui s'adresse surtout aux enfants, vise également un public d'adultes au travers des nombreuses plaisanteries faisant allusion à des faits d'actualité.

pantry ['pæntrɪ] *n* garde-manger *m inv*; (*room*) office *m*.
pants [pænts] *n* (*BRIT: woman's*) culotte *f*, slip *m*; (: *man's*) slip, caleçon *m*; (*US: trousers*) pantalon *m*.
pantsuit ['pæntsu:t] *n* (*US*) tailleur-pantalon *m*.
papacy ['peɪpəsɪ] *n* papauté *f*.
papal ['peɪpəl] *adj* papal(e), pontifical(e).
paparazzi [pæpə'rætsi:] *npl* paparazzi *mpl*.
paper ['peɪpə*] *n* papier *m*; (*also:* **wall~**) papier peint; (*also:* **news~**) journal *m*; (*study, article*) article *m*; (*exam*) épreuve écrite ♦ *adj* en *or* de papier ♦ *vt* tapisser (de papier peint); **a piece of ~** (*odd bit*) un bout de papier; (*sheet*) une feuille de papier; **to put sth down on ~** mettre qch par écrit.
paper advance *n* (*on printer*) avance *f* (du) papier.
paperback ['peɪpəbæk] *n* livre *m* de poche; livre broché *or* non relié ♦ *adj:* **~ edition** édition brochée.
paper bag *n* sac *m* en papier.
paperboy ['peɪpəbɔɪ] *n* (*selling*) vendeur *m* de journaux; (*delivering*) livreur *m* de journaux.
paper clip *n* trombone *m*.
paper handkerchief *n* mouchoir *m* en papier.
paper mill *n* papeterie *f*.
paper money *n* papier-monnaie *m*.
paper profit *n* profit *m* théorique.
papers ['peɪpəz] *npl* (*also:* **identity ~**) papiers *mpl* (d'identité).
paper shop *n* (*BRIT*) marchand *m* de journaux.
paperweight ['peɪpəweɪt] *n* presse-papiers *m inv*.
paperwork ['peɪpəwə:k] *n* paperasserie *f*.
papier-mâché ['pæpɪeɪ'mæʃeɪ] *n* papier mâché.
paprika ['pæprɪkə] *n* paprika *m*.
Pap test, Pap smear ['pæp-] *n* (*MED*)

frottis *m*.

par [pɑː*] *n* pair *m*; (*GOLF*) normale *f* du parcours; **on a ~ with** à égalité avec, au même niveau que; **at ~** au pair; **above/ below ~** au-dessus/au-dessous du pair; **to feel below** *or* **under** *or* **not up to ~** ne pas se sentir en forme.

parable ['pærəbl] *n* parabole *f* (*REL*).

parabola [pə'ræbələ] *n* parabole *f* (*MATH*).

parachute ['pærəʃuːt] *n* parachute *m* ♦ *vi* sauter en parachute.

parachute jump *n* saut *m* en parachute.

parachutist ['pærəʃuːtɪst] *n* parachutiste *m/f*.

parade [pə'reɪd] *n* défilé *m*; (*inspection*) revue *f*; (*street*) boulevard *m* ♦ *vt* (*fig*) faire étalage de ♦ *vi* défiler; **a fashion ~** (*BRIT*) un défilé de mode.

parade ground *n* terrain *m* de manœuvre.

paradise ['pærədaɪs] *n* paradis *m*.

paradox ['pærədɔks] *n* paradoxe *m*.

paradoxical [pærə'dɔksɪkl] *adj* paradoxal(e).

paradoxically [pærə'dɔksɪklɪ] *adv* paradoxalement.

paraffin ['pærəfɪn] *n* (*BRIT*): **~ (oil)** pétrole (lampant); **liquid ~** huile *f* de paraffine.

paraffin heater *n* (*BRIT*) poêle *m* à mazout.

paraffin lamp *n* (*BRIT*) lampe *f* à pétrole.

paragon ['pærəgən] *n* parangon *m*.

paragraph ['pærəgrɑːf] *n* paragraphe *m*; **to begin a new ~** aller à la ligne.

Paraguay ['pærəgwaɪ] *n* Paraguay *m*.

Paraguayan [pærə'gwaɪən] *adj* paraguayen(ne) ♦ *n* Paraguayen/ne.

parallel ['pærəlɛl] *adj*: **~ (with** *or* **to)** parallèle (à); (*fig*) analogue (à) ♦ *n* (*line*) parallèle *f*; (*fig*, *GEO*) parallèle *m*.

paralysis, *pl* **paralyses** [pə'rælɪsɪs, -siːz] *n* paralysie *f*.

paralytic [pærə'lɪtɪk] *adj* paralytique; (*BRIT col*: *drunk*) ivre mort(e).

paralyze ['pærəlaɪz] *vt* paralyser.

paramedic [pærə'mɛdɪk] *n* auxiliaire *m/f* médical(e).

parameter [pə'ræmɪtə*] *n* paramètre *m*.

paramilitary [pærə'mɪlɪtərɪ] *adj* paramilitaire.

paramount ['pærəmaunt] *adj*: **of ~ importance** de la plus haute *or* grande importance.

paranoia [pærə'nɔɪə] *n* paranoïa *f*.

paranoid ['pærənɔɪd] *adj* (*PSYCH*) paranoïaque; (*neurotic*) paranoïde.

paranormal [pærə'nɔːml] *adj* paranormal(e).

paraphernalia [pærəfə'neɪlɪə] *n* attirail *m*, affaires *fpl*.

paraphrase ['pærəfreɪz] *vt* paraphraser.

paraplegic [pærə'pliːdʒɪk] *n* paraplégique *m/f*.

parapsychology [pærəsaɪ'kɔlədʒɪ] *n* parapsychologie *f*.

parasite ['pærəsaɪt] *n* parasite *m*.

parasol ['pærəsɔl] *n* ombrelle *f*; (*at café etc*) parasol *m*.

paratrooper ['pærətruːpə*] *n* parachutiste *m* (*soldat*).

parcel ['pɑːsl] *n* paquet *m*, colis *m* ♦ *vt* (*also*: **~ up**) empaqueter.

▶**parcel out** *vt* répartir.

parcel bomb *n* (*BRIT*) colis piégé.

parcel post *n* service *m* de colis postaux.

parch [pɑːtʃ] *vt* dessécher.

parched [pɑːtʃt] *adj* (*person*) assoiffé(e).

parchment ['pɑːtʃmənt] *n* parchemin *m*.

pardon ['pɑːdn] *n* pardon *m*; grâce *f* ♦ *vt* pardonner à; (*LAW*) gracier; **~!** pardon!; **~ me!** excusez-moi!; **(I beg your) ~!** pardon!, je suis désolé!; **(I beg your) ~?**, (*US*) **~ me?** pardon?

pare [pɛə*] *vt* (*BRIT*: *nails*) couper; (*fruit etc*) peler; (*fig*: *costs etc*) réduire.

parent ['pɛərənt] *n* père *m* *or* mère *f*; **~s** *npl* parents *mpl*.

parentage ['pɛərəntɪdʒ] *n* naissance *f*; **of unknown ~** de parents inconnus.

parental [pə'rɛntl] *adj* parental(e), des parents.

parent company *n* société *f* mère.

parenthesis, *pl* **parentheses** [pə'rɛnθɪsɪs, -siːz] *n* parenthèse *f*; **in parentheses** entre parenthèses.

parenthood ['pɛərənthud] *n* paternité *f* *or* maternité *f*.

parenting ['pɛərəntɪŋ] *n* le métier de parent, le travail d'un parent.

Paris ['pærɪs] *n* Paris.

parish ['pærɪʃ] *n* paroisse *f*; (*civil*) ≈ commune *f* ♦ *adj* paroissial(e).

parish council *n* (*BRIT*) ≈ conseil municipal.

parishioner [pə'rɪʃənə*] *n* paroissien/ne.

Parisian [pə'rɪzɪən] *adj* parisien(ne) ♦ *n* Parisien/ne.

parity ['pærɪtɪ] *n* parité *f*.

park [pɑːk] *n* parc *m*, jardin public ♦ *vt* garer ♦ *vi* se garer.

parka ['pɑːkə] *n* parka *m*.

parking ['pɑːkɪŋ] *n* stationnement *m*; **"no ~"** "stationnement interdit".

parking lights *npl* feux *mpl* de stationnement.

parking lot *n* (*US*) parking *m*, parc *m* de stationnement.

parking meter *n* parc(o)mètre *m*.

parking offence, (*US*) **parking violation** *n* infraction *f* au stationnement.

parking place *n* place *f* de stationnement.

parking ticket *n* P.-V. *m*.

Parkinson's ['pɑːkɪnsənz] *n* (*also*: **~ disease**) maladie *f* de Parkinson, parkinson *m*.

parkway ['pɑːkweɪ] *n* (*US*) route *f* express (*en site vert ou aménagé*).

parlance ['pɑːləns] *n*: **in common/modern ~** dans le langage courant/actuel.

parliament ['pɑːləmənt] *n* parlement *m*.

Le **Parliament** *est l'assemblée législative britannique; elle est composée de deux chambres: la* **House of Commons** *et la* **House o Lords.** *Ses bureaux sont les "Houses of*

Parliament" au palais de Westminster à Londres. Chaque Parliament est en général élu pour cinq ans. Les débats du Parliament sont maintenant retransmis à la télévision.

parliamentary [pɑ:ləˈmɛntərɪ] *adj* parlementaire.

parlour, (US) **parlor** [ˈpɑ:lə*] *n* salon *m*.

parlous [ˈpɑ:ləs] *adj (formal)* précaire.

Parmesan [pɑ:mɪˈzæn] *n (also: ~ cheese)* Parmesan *m*.

parochial [pəˈrəukɪəl] *adj* paroissial(e); *(pej)* à l'esprit de clocher.

parody [ˈpærədɪ] *n* parodie *f*.

parole [pəˈrəul] *n*: **on ~** en liberté conditionnelle.

paroxysm [ˈpærəksɪzəm] *n (MED, of grief)* paroxysme *m*; *(of anger)* accès *m*.

parquet [ˈpɑ:keɪ] *n*: **~ floor(ing)** parquet *m*.

parrot [ˈpærət] *n* perroquet *m*.

parrot fashion *adv* comme un perroquet.

parry [ˈpærɪ] *vt* esquiver, parer à.

parsimonious [pɑ:sɪˈməunɪəs] *adj* parcimonieux(euse).

parsley [ˈpɑ:slɪ] *n* persil *m*.

parsnip [ˈpɑ:snɪp] *n* panais *m*.

parson [ˈpɑ:sn] *n* ecclésiastique *m*; *(Church of England)* pasteur *m*.

parsonage [ˈpɑ:snɪdʒ] *n* presbytère *m*.

part [pɑ:t] *n* partie *f*; *(of machine)* pièce *f*; *(THEAT etc)* rôle *m*; *(MUS)* voix *f*; partie ♦ *adj* partiel(le) ♦ *adv* = **partly** ♦ *vt* séparer ♦ *vi (people)* se séparer; *(roads)* se diviser; **to take ~ in** participer à, prendre part à; **to take sb's ~** prendre le parti de qn, prendre parti pour qn; **on his ~** de sa part; **for my ~** en ce qui me concerne; **for the most ~** en grande partie; dans la plupart des cas; **for the better ~ of the day** pendant la plus grande partie de la journée; **to be ~ and parcel of** faire partie de; **to take sth in good/bad ~** prendre qch du bon/mauvais côté; **~ of speech** *(LING)* partie *f* du discours.
▶**part with** *vt fus* se séparer de; se défaire de.

partake [pɑ:ˈteɪk] *vi irreg (formal)*: **to ~ of sth** prendre part à qch, partager qch.

part exchange *n (BRIT)*: **in ~** en reprise.

partial [ˈpɑ:ʃl] *adj* partiel(le); *(unjust)* partial(e); **to be ~ to** aimer, avoir un faible pour.

partially [ˈpɑ:ʃəlɪ] *adv* en partie, partiellement; partialement.

participant [pɑ:ˈtɪsɪpənt] *n*: **~ (in)** participant/e (à).

participate [pɑ:ˈtɪsɪpeɪt] *vi*: **to ~ (in)** participer (à), prendre part (à).

participation [pɑ:tɪsɪˈpeɪʃən] *n* participation *f*.

participle [ˈpɑ:tɪsɪpl] *n* participe *m*.

particle [ˈpɑ:tɪkl] *n* particule *f*.

particular [pəˈtɪkjulə*] *adj (specific)* particulier(ière); *(special)* particulier, spécial(e); *(fussy)* difficile, exigeant(e); méticuleux(euse); **~s** *npl* détails *mpl*; *(information)* renseignements *mpl*; **in ~** surtout, en particulier.

particularly [pəˈtɪkjuləlɪ] *adv* particulièrement; *(in particular)* en particulier.

parting [ˈpɑ:tɪŋ] *n* séparation *f*; *(BRIT: in hair)* raie *f* ♦ *adj* d'adieu; **his ~ shot was** ... il lança en partant ....

partisan [pɑ:tɪˈzæn] *n* partisan/e ♦ *adj* partisan(e); de parti.

partition [pɑ:ˈtɪʃən] *n (POL)* partition *f*, division *f*; *(wall)* cloison *f*.

partly [ˈpɑ:tlɪ] *adv* en partie, partiellement.

partner [ˈpɑ:tnə*] *n (COMM)* associé/e; *(SPORT)* partenaire *m/f*; *(at dance)* cavalier/ière ♦ *vt* être l'associé *or* le partenaire *or* le cavalier de.

partnership [ˈpɑ:tnəʃɪp] *n* association *f*; **to go into ~ (with), form a ~ (with)** s'associer (avec).

part payment *n* acompte *m*.

partridge [ˈpɑ:trɪdʒ] *n* perdrix *f*.

part-time [pɑ:tˈtaɪm] *adj, adv* à mi-temps, à temps partiel.

part-timer [pɑ:tˈtaɪmə*] *n (also: part-time worker)* travailleur/euse à temps partiel.

party [ˈpɑ:tɪ] *n (POL)* parti *m*; *(team)* équipe *f*; groupe *m*; *(LAW)* partie *f*; *(celebration)* réception *f*; soirée *f*; réunion *f*, fête *f*; **dinner ~** dîner *m*; **to give** *or* **throw a ~** donner une réception; **we're having a ~ next Saturday** nous organisons une soirée *or* réunion entre amis samedi prochain; **it's for our son's birthday ~** c'est pour la fête *(or le goûter)* d'anniversaire de notre garçon; **to be a ~ to a crime** être impliqué(e) dans un crime.

party line *n (POL)* ligne *f* politique; *(TEL)* ligne partagée.

party piece *n* numéro habituel.

party political broadcast *n émission réservée à un parti politique.*

pass [pɑ:s] *vt (time, object)* passer; *(place)* passer devant; *(car, friend)* croiser; *(exam)* être reçu(e) à, réussir; *(candidate)* admettre; *(overtake, surpass)* dépasser; *(approve)* approuver, accepter; *(law)* promulguer ♦ *vi* passer; *(SCOL)* être reçu(e) *or* admis(e), réussir ♦ *n (permit)* laissez-passer *m inv*; carte *f* d'accès *or* d'abonnement; *(in mountains)* col *m*; *(SPORT)* passe *f*; *(SCOL: also: ~ mark)*: **to get a ~** être reçu(e) (sans mention); **she could ~ for 25** on lui donnerait 25 ans; **to ~ sth through a ring** *etc* (faire) passer qch dans un anneau *etc*; **could you ~ the vegetables round?** pourriez-vous faire passer les légumes?; **things have come to a pretty ~** *(BRIT)* voilà où on en est!; **to make a ~ at sb** *(col)* faire des avances à qn.
▶**pass away** *vi* mourir.

►**pass by** vi passer ♦ vt négliger.
►**pass down** vt (customs, inheritance) transmettre.
►**pass on** vi (die) s'éteindre, décéder ♦ vt (hand on): **to ~ on (to)** transmettre (à); (: illness) passer (à); (: price rises) répercuter (sur).
►**pass out** vi s'évanouir; (BRIT MIL) sortir (d'une école militaire).
►**pass over** vt (ignore) passer sous silence.
►**pass up** vt (opportunity) laisser passer.
passable ['pɑːsəbl] adj (road) praticable; (work) acceptable.
passage ['pæsɪdʒ] n (also: ~**way**) couloir m; (gen, in book) passage m; (by boat) traversée f.
passenger ['pæsɪndʒə*] n passager/ère.
passer-by [pɑːsə'baɪ] n passant/e.
passing ['pɑːsɪŋ] adj (fig) passager(ère); **in ~** en passant.
passing place n (AUT) aire f de croisement.
passion ['pæʃən] n passion f; **to have a ~ for sth** avoir la passion de qch.
passionate ['pæʃənɪt] adj passionné(e).
passion fruit n fruit m de la passion.
passion play n mystère m de la Passion.
passive ['pæsɪv] adj (also LING) passif(ive).
passive smoking n tabagisme passif.
passkey ['pɑːskiː] n passe m.
Passover ['pɑːsəuvə*] n Pâque juive.
passport ['pɑːspɔːt] n passeport m.
passport control n contrôle m des passeports.
password ['pɑːswɔːd] n mot m de passe.
past [pɑːst] prep (further than) au delà de, plus loin que; après; (later than) après ♦ adj passé(e); (president etc) ancien(ne) ♦ n passé m; **quarter/half ~ four** quatre heures et quart/demie; **ten/twenty ~ four** quatre heures dix/vingt; **he's ~ forty** il a dépassé la quarantaine, il a plus de or passé quarante ans; **it's ~ midnight** il est plus de minuit, il est passé minuit; **for the ~ few/3 days** depuis quelques/3 jours; ces derniers/3 derniers jours; **to run ~** passer en courant; **he ran ~ me** il m'a dépassé en courant; il a passé devant moi en courant; **in the ~** (gen) dans le temps, autrefois; (LING) au passé; **I'm ~ caring** je ne m'en fais plus; **to be ~ it** (BRIT col: person) avoir passé l'âge.
pasta ['pæstə] n pâtes fpl.
paste [peɪst] n (glue) colle f (de pâte); (jewellery) strass m; (CULIN) pâté m (à tartiner); pâté f ♦ vt coller; **tomato ~** concentré m de tomate, purée f de tomate.
pastel ['pæstl] adj pastel inv.
pasteurized ['pæstəraɪzd] adj pasteurisé(e).
pastille ['pæstl] n pastille f.
pastime ['pɑːstaɪm] n passe-temps m inv, distraction f.
past master n (BRIT): **to be a ~ at** être expert en.

pastor ['pɑːstə*] n pasteur m.
pastoral ['pɑːstərl] adj pastoral(e).
pastry ['peɪstrɪ] n pâte f; (cake) pâtisserie f.
pasture ['pɑːstʃə*] n pâturage m.
pasty n ['pæstɪ] petit pâté (en croûte) ♦ adj ['peɪstɪ] pâteux(euse); (complexion) terreux(euse).
pat [pæt] vt donner une petite tape à ♦ n: **a ~ of butter** une noisette de beurre; **to give sb/o.s. a ~ on the back** (fig) congratuler qn/ se congratuler; **he knows it (off) ~**, (US) **he has it down ~** il sait cela sur le bout des doigts.
patch [pætʃ] n (of material) pièce f; (spot) tache f; (of land) parcelle f ♦ vt (clothes) rapiécer; **a bad ~** (BRIT) une période difficile.
►**patch up** vt réparer.
patchwork ['pætʃwɜːk] n patchwork m.
patchy ['pætʃɪ] adj inégal(e).
pate [peɪt] n: **a bald ~** un crâne chauve or dégarni.
pâté ['pæteɪ] n pâté m, terrine f.
patent ['peɪtnt] n brevet m (d'invention) ♦ vt faire breveter ♦ adj patent(e), manifeste.
patent leather n cuir verni.
patently ['peɪtntlɪ] adv manifestement.
patent medicine n spécialité f pharmaceutique.
patent office n bureau m des brevets.
paternal [pə'tɜːnl] adj paternel(le).
paternity [pə'tɜːnɪtɪ] n paternité f.
paternity suit n (LAW) action f en recherche de paternité.
path [pɑːθ] n chemin m, sentier m; allée f; (of planet) course f; (of missile) trajectoire f.
pathetic [pə'θetɪk] adj (pitiful) pitoyable; (very bad) lamentable, minable; (moving) pathétique.
pathological [pæθə'lɒdʒɪkl] adj pathologique.
pathologist [pə'θɒlədʒɪst] n pathologiste m/f.
pathology [pə'θɒlədʒɪ] n pathologie f.
pathos ['peɪθɒs] n pathétique m.
pathway ['pɑːθweɪ] n chemin m, sentier m.
patience ['peɪʃns] n patience f; (BRIT: CARDS) réussite f; **to lose (one's) ~** perdre patience.
patient ['peɪʃnt] n patient/e; (in hospital) malade m/f ♦ adj patient(e).
patiently ['peɪʃntlɪ] adv patiemment.
patio ['pætɪəu] n patio m.
patriot ['peɪtrɪət] n patriote m/f.
patriotic [pætrɪ'ɒtɪk] adj patriotique; (person) patriote.
patriotism ['pætrɪətɪzəm] n patriotisme m.
patrol [pə'trəul] n patrouille f ♦ vt patrouiller dans; **to be on ~** être de patrouille.
patrol boat n patrouilleur m.
patrol car n voiture f de police.
patrolman [pə'trəulmən] n (US) agent m de police.
patron ['peɪtrən] n (in shop) client/e; (of charity) patron/ne; **~ of the arts** mécène m.
patronage ['pætrənɪdʒ] n patronage m,

appui m.

patronize ['pætrənaɪz] vt être (un) client or un habitué de; (fig) traiter avec condescendance.

patronizing ['pætrənaɪzɪŋ] adj condescendant(e).

patron saint n saint(e) patron/ne.

patter ['pætə*] n crépitement m, tapotement m; (sales talk) boniment m ♦ vi crépiter, tapoter.

pattern ['pætən] n modèle m; (SEWING) patron m; (design) motif m; (sample) échantillon m; **behaviour** ~ mode m de comportement.

patterned ['pætənd] adj à motifs.

paucity ['pɔːsɪtɪ] n pénurie f, carence f.

paunch [pɔːntʃ] n gros ventre, bedaine f.

pauper ['pɔːpə*] n indigent/e; ~'s grave fosse commune.

pause [pɔːz] n pause f, arrêt m; (MUS) silence m ♦ vi faire une pause, s'arrêter; **to ~ for breath** reprendre son souffle; (fig) faire une pause.

pave [peɪv] vt paver, daller; **to ~ the way for** ouvrir la voie à.

pavement ['peɪvmənt] n (BRIT) trottoir m; (US) chaussée f.

pavilion [pə'vɪlɪən] n pavillon m; tente f; (SPORT) stand m.

paving ['peɪvɪŋ] n pavage m, dallage m.

paving stone n pavé m.

paw [pɔː] n patte f ♦ vt donner un coup de patte à; (subj: person: pej) tripoter.

pawn [pɔːn] n gage m; (CHESS, also fig) pion m ♦ vt mettre en gage.

pawnbroker ['pɔːnbrəukə*] n prêteur m sur gages.

pawnshop ['pɔːnʃɔp] n mont-de-piété m.

pay [peɪ] n salaire m; (of manual worker) paie f ♦ vb (pt, pp **paid** [peɪd]) vt payer; (be profitable to: also fig) rapporter à ♦ vi payer; (be profitable) être rentable; **how much did you ~ for it?** combien l'avez-vous payé?, vous l'avez payé combien?; **I paid £5 for that record** j'ai payé ce disque 5 livres; **to ~ one's way** payer sa part; (company) couvrir ses frais; **to ~ dividends** (fig) porter ses fruits, s'avérer rentable; **it won't ~ you to do that** vous ne gagnerez rien à faire cela; **to ~ attention (to)** prêter attention (à).

▶**pay back** vt rembourser.

▶**pay in** vt verser.

▶**pay off** vt (debts) régler, acquitter; (creditor, mortgage) rembourser; (workers) licencier ♦ vi (plan, patience) se révéler payant(e); **to ~ sth off in instalments** payer qch à tempérament.

▶**pay out** vt (money) payer, sortir de sa poche; (rope) laisser filer.

▶**pay up** vt (debts) régler; (amount) payer.

payable ['peɪəbl] adj payable; **to make a cheque ~ to sb** établir un chèque à l'ordre de qn.

pay award n augmentation f.

pay day n jour m de paie.

PAYE n abbr (BRIT: = pay as you earn) système de retenue des impôts à la source.

payee [peɪ'iː] n bénéficiaire m/f.

pay envelope n (US) (enveloppe f de) paie f.

paying ['peɪɪŋ] adj payant(e); ~ **guest** hôte payant.

payload ['peɪləud] n charge f utile.

payment ['peɪmənt] n paiement m; (of bill) règlement m; (of deposit, cheque) versement m; **advance** ~ (part sum) acompte m; (total sum) paiement anticipé; **deferred** ~, ~ **by instalments** paiement par versements échelonnés; **monthly** ~ mensualité f; **in** ~ **for, in** ~ **of** en règlement de; **on** ~ **of £5** pour 5 livres.

pay packet n (BRIT) paie f.

payphone ['peɪfəun] n cabine f téléphonique, téléphone public.

payroll ['peɪrəul] n registre m du personnel; **to be on a firm's** ~ être employé par une entreprise.

pay slip n (BRIT) bulletin m de paie, feuille f de paie.

pay station n (US) cabine f téléphonique.

PBS n abbr (US: = Public Broadcasting Service) groupement d'aide à la réalisation d'émissions pour la TV publique.

PC n abbr = **personal computer**; (BRIT) = **police constable** ♦ adj abbr = **politically correct** ♦ abbr (BRIT) = Privy Councillor.

pc abbr = **per cent, postcard**.

p/c abbr = **petty cash**.

PCB n abbr = **printed circuit board**.

PD n abbr (US) = **police department**.

pd abbr = **paid**.

PDSA n abbr (BRIT) = People's Dispensary for Sick Animals.

PDT abbr (US: = Pacific Daylight Time) heure d'été du Pacifique.

PE n abbr (= physical education) EPS f ♦ abbr (Canada) = Prince Edward Island.

pea [piː] n (petit) pois.

peace [piːs] n paix f; (calm) calme m, tranquillité f; **to be at** ~ **with sb/sth** être en paix avec qn/qch; **to keep the** ~ (subj: policeman) assurer le maintien de l'ordre; (: citizen) ne pas troubler l'ordre.

peaceable ['piːsəbl] adj paisible, pacifique.

peaceful ['piːsful] adj paisible, calme.

peacekeeper ['piːskiːpə*] n (force) force gardienne de la paix.

peacekeeping ['piːskiːpɪŋ] n maintien m de la paix.

peacekeeping force n forces fpl qui assurent le maintien de la paix.

peace offering n gage m de réconciliation; (humorous) gage de paix.

peach [piːtʃ] n pêche f.

peacock ['piːkɔk] n paon m.

peak [piːk] n (mountain) pic m, cime f; (fig:

highest level) maximum *m*; (: *of career, fame)* apogée *m*.

peak-hour ['piːkauə*] *adj (traffic etc)* de pointe.

peak hours *npl* heures *fpl* d'affluence.

peak period *n* période *f* de pointe.

peak rate *n* plein tarif.

peaky ['piːkɪ] *adj (BRIT col)* fatigué(e).

peal [piːl] *n (of bells)* carillon *m*; ~**s of laughter** éclats *mpl* de rire.

peanut ['piːnʌt] *n* arachide *f*, cacahuète *f*.

peanut butter *n* beurre *m* de cacahuète.

pear [pɛə*] *n* poire *f*.

pearl [pəːl] *n* perle *f*.

peasant ['pɛznt] *n* paysan/ne.

peat [piːt] *n* tourbe *f*.

pebble ['pɛbl] *n* galet *m*, caillou *m*.

peck [pɛk] *vt (also:* ~ **at)** donner un coup de bec à; *(food)* picorer ♦ *n* coup *m* de bec; *(kiss)* bécot *m*.

pecking order ['pɛkɪŋ-] *n* ordre *m* hiérarchique.

peckish ['pɛkɪʃ] *adj (BRIT col)*: **I feel** ~ je mangerais bien quelque chose, j'ai la dent.

peculiar [pɪ'kjuːlɪə*] *adj (odd)* étrange, bizarre, curieux(euse); *(particular)* particulier(ière); ~ **to** particulier à.

peculiarity [pɪkjuːlɪ'ærɪtɪ] *n* bizarrerie *f*, particularité *f*.

pecuniary [pɪ'kjuːnɪərɪ] *adj* pécuniaire.

pedal ['pɛdl] *n* pédale *f* ♦ *vi* pédaler.

pedal bin *n (BRIT)* poubelle *f* à pédale.

pedantic [pɪ'dæntɪk] *adj* pédant(e).

peddle ['pɛdl] *vt* colporter; *(drugs)* faire le trafic de.

peddler ['pɛdlə*] *n* colporteur *m*; camelot *m*.

pedestal ['pɛdəstl] *n* piédestal *m*.

pedestrian [pɪ'dɛstrɪən] *n* piéton *m* ♦ *adj* piétonnier(ière); *(fig)* prosaïque, terre à terre *inv*.

pedestrian crossing *n (BRIT)* passage clouté.

pedestrian precinct *n (BRIT)* zone piétonne.

pediatrics [piːdɪ'ætrɪks] *n (US)* = **paediatrics**.

pedigree ['pɛdɪgriː] *n* ascendance *f*; *(of animal)* pedigree *m* ♦ *cpd (animal)* de race.

pedlar ['pɛdlə*] *n* = **peddler**.

pee [piː] *vi (col)* faire pipi, pisser.

peek [piːk] *vi* jeter un coup d'œil (furtif).

peel [piːl] *n* pelure *f*, épluchure *f*; *(of orange, lemon)* écorce *f* ♦ *vt* peler, éplucher ♦ *vi (paint etc)* s'écailler; *(wallpaper)* se décoller.

▶**peel back** *vt* décoller.

peeler ['piːlə*] *n (potato etc* ~) éplucheur *m*.

peelings ['piːlɪŋz] *npl* pelures *fpl*, épluchures *fpl*.

peep [piːp] *n (BRIT: look)* coup d'œil furtif; *(sound)* pépiement *m* ♦ *vi (BRIT)* jeter un coup d'œil (furtif).

▶**peep out** *vi (BRIT)* se montrer (furtivement).

peephole ['piːphəul] *n* judas *m*.

peer [pɪə*] *vi*: **to** ~ **at** regarder attentivement, scruter ♦ *n (noble)* pair *m*; *(equal)* pair,

égal/e.

peerage ['pɪərɪdʒ] *n* pairie *f*.

peerless ['pɪəlɪs] *adj* incomparable, sans égal.

peeved [piːvd] *adj* irrité(e), ennuyé(e).

peevish ['piːvɪʃ] *adj* grincheux(euse), maussade.

peg [pɛg] *n* cheville *f*; *(for coat etc)* patère *f*; *(BRIT: also:* **clothes** ~) pince *f* à linge ♦ *vt (clothes)* accrocher; *(BRIT: groundsheet)* fixer (avec des piquets); *(fig: prices, wages)* contrôler, stabiliser.

pejorative [pɪ'dʒɔrətɪv] *adj* péjoratif(ive).

Pekin [piː'kɪn] *n*, **Peking** [piː'kɪŋ] *n* Pékin.

pekingese [piːkɪ'niːz] *n* pékinois *m*.

pelican ['pɛlɪkən] *n* pélican *m*.

pelican crossing *n (BRIT AUT)* feu *m* à commande manuelle.

pellet ['pɛlɪt] *n* boulette *f*; *(of lead)* plomb *m*.

pell-mell ['pɛl'mɛl] *adv* pêle-mêle.

pelmet ['pɛlmɪt] *n* cantonnière *f*; lambrequin *m*.

pelt [pɛlt] *vt*: **to** ~ **sb (with)** bombarder qn (de) ♦ *vi (rain)* tomber à seaux ♦ *n* peau *f*.

pelvis ['pɛlvɪs] *n* bassin *m*.

pen [pɛn] *n (for writing)* stylo *m*; *(for sheep)* parc *m*; *(US col: prison)* taule *f*; **to put** ~ **to paper** prendre la plume.

penal ['piːnl] *adj* pénal(e).

penalize ['piːnəlaɪz] *vt* pénaliser; *(fig)* désavantager.

penal servitude [-'səːvɪtjuːd] *n* travaux forcés.

penalty ['pɛnltɪ] *n* pénalité *f*; sanction *f*; *(fine)* amende *f*; *(SPORT)* pénalisation *f*; *(FOOTBALL: also:* ~ **kick)** penalty *m*.

penalty area *n (BRIT SPORT)* surface *f* de réparation.

penalty clause *n* clause pénale.

penalty kick *n (FOOTBALL)* penalty *m*.

penalty shoot-out [-'ʃuːtaut] *n (FOOTBALL)* épreuve *f* des penalties.

penance ['pɛnəns] *n* pénitence *f*.

pence [pɛns] *npl (BRIT) see* **penny**.

penchant ['pãːʃãːŋ] *n* penchant *m*.

pencil ['pɛnsl] *n* crayon *m* ♦ *vt*: **to** ~ **sth in** noter qch provisoirement.

pencil case *n* trousse *f* (d'écolier).

pencil sharpener *n* taille-crayon(s) *m inv*.

pendant ['pɛndnt] *n* pendentif *m*.

pending ['pɛndɪŋ] *prep* en attendant ♦ *adj* en suspens.

pendulum ['pɛndjuləm] *n* pendule *m*; *(of clock)* balancier *m*.

penetrate ['pɛnɪtreɪt] *vt* pénétrer dans; pénétrer.

penetrating ['pɛnɪtreɪtɪŋ] *adj* pénétrant(e).

penetration [pɛnɪ'treɪʃən] *n* pénétration *f*.

penfriend ['pɛnfrɛnd] *n (BRIT)* correspondant/e.

penguin ['pɛŋgwɪn] *n* pingouin *m*.

penicillin [pɛnɪ'sɪlɪn] *n* pénicilline *f*.

peninsula [pə'nɪnsjulə] *n* péninsule *f*.

enis ['pi:nɪs] n pénis m, verge f.

enitence ['penɪtns] n repentir m.

enitent ['penɪtnt] adj repentant(e).

enitentiary [penɪ'tenʃərɪ] n (US) prison f.

enknife ['pennaɪf] n canif m.

enn(a). abbr (US) = Pennsylvania.

en name n nom m de plume, pseudonyme m.

ennant ['penənt] n flamme f, banderole f.

enniless ['penɪlɪs] adj sans le sou.

ennines ['penaɪnz] npl: **the ~** les Pennines fpl.

enny, pl **pennies** or **pence** ['penɪ, 'penɪz, pens] n penny m (pl pennies) (new: 100 in a pound; old: 12 in a shilling; on tend à employer "pennies" ou "two-pence piece" etc pour les pièces, "pence" pour la valeur); (US) = **cent.**

enpal ['penpæl] n correspondant/e.

enpusher ['penpʊʃe*] n (pej) gratte-papier m inv.

ension ['penʃən] n retraite f; (MIL) pension f.

pension off vt mettre à la retraite.

ensionable ['penʃnəbl] adj qui a droit à une retraite.

ensioner ['penʃənə*] n (BRIT) retraité/e.

ension fund n caisse f de retraite.

ensive ['pensɪv] adj pensif(ive).

entagon ['pentəgən] n pentagone m; **the P~** (US POL) le Pentagone.

> Le **Pentagon** est le nom donné aux bureaux du ministère de la Défense américain, situés à Arlington en Virginie, à cause de la forme pentagonale du bâtiment dans lequel ils se trouvent. Par extension, ce terme est également utilisé en parlant du ministère lui-même.

entecost ['pentɪkɒst] n Pentecôte f.

enthouse ['penthaus] n appartement m (de luxe) en attique.

ent-up ['pentʌp] adj (feelings) refoulé(e).

enultimate [pɪ'nʌltɪmət] adj pénultième, avant-dernier(ière).

enury ['penjʊrɪ] n misère f.

eople ['pi:pl] npl gens mpl; personnes fpl; (citizens) peuple m ♦ n (nation, race) peuple m ♦ vt peupler; **several ~ came** plusieurs personnes sont venues; **I know ~ who** ... je connais des gens qui ...; **the room was full of ~** la salle était pleine de monde or de gens; **~ say that** ... on dit or les gens disent que ...; **old ~** les personnes âgées; **young ~** les jeunes; **a man of the ~** un homme du peuple.

EP [pep] n (= personal equity plan) ≈ CEA m (= compte d'épargne en actions)

ep [pep] n (col) entrain m, dynamisme m.

pep up vt (col) remonter.

epper ['pepə*] n poivre m; (vegetable) poivron m ♦ vt poivrer.

eppermint ['pepəmɪnt] n (plant) menthe poivrée; (sweet) pastille f de menthe.

pepperoni [pepə'rəʊnɪ] n saucisson sec de porc et de bœuf très poivré.

pepperpot ['pepəpɒt] n poivrière f.

peptalk ['peptɔːk] n (col) (petit) discours d'encouragement.

per [pə:*] prep par; **~ hour** (miles etc) à l'heure; (fee) (de) l'heure; **~ kilo** etc le kilo etc; **~ day/person** par jour/personne; **as ~ your instructions** conformément à vos instructions.

per annum adv par an.

per capita adj, adv par habitant, par personne.

perceive [pə'si:v] vt percevoir; (notice) remarquer, s'apercevoir de.

per cent adv pour cent; **a 20 ~ discount** une réduction de 20 pour cent.

percentage [pə'sentɪdʒ] n pourcentage m; **on a ~ basis** au pourcentage.

percentage point n: **ten ~s** dix pour cent.

perceptible [pə'septɪbl] adj perceptible.

perception [pə'sepʃən] n perception f; (insight) sensibilité f.

perceptive [pə'septɪv] adj (remark, person) perspicace.

perch [pə:tʃ] n (fish) perche f; (for bird) perchoir m ♦ vi (se) percher.

percolate ['pə:kəleɪt] vt, vi passer.

percolator ['pə:kəleɪtə*] n percolateur m; cafetière f électrique.

percussion [pə'kʌʃən] n percussion f.

peremptory [pə'remptərɪ] adj péremptoire.

perennial [pə'renɪəl] adj perpétuel(le); (BOT) vivace ♦ n plante f vivace.

perfect adj, n ['pə:fɪkt] adj parfait(e) ♦ n (also: **~ tense**) parfait m ♦ vt [pə'fekt] parfaire; mettre au point; **he's a ~ stranger to me** il m'est totalement inconnu.

perfection [pə'fekʃən] n perfection f.

perfectionist [pə'fekʃənɪst] n perfectionniste m/f.

perfectly ['pə:fɪktlɪ] adv parfaitement; **I'm ~ happy with the situation** cette situation me convient parfaitement; **you know ~ well** vous le savez très bien.

perforate ['pə:fəreɪt] vt perforer, percer.

perforated ulcer ['pə:fəreɪtɪd-] n (MED) ulcère perforé.

perforation [pə:fə'reɪʃən] n perforation f; (line of holes) pointillé m.

perform [pə'fɔːm] vt (carry out) exécuter, remplir; (concert etc) jouer, donner ♦ vi jouer.

performance [pə'fɔːməns] n représentation f, spectacle m; (of an artist) interprétation f; (of player etc) prestation f; (of car, engine) performance f; **the team put up a good ~** l'équipe a bien joué.

performer [pə'fɔːmə*] n artiste m/f.

performing [pə'fɔːmɪŋ] adj (animal) savant(e).

performing arts npl: **the ~** les arts mpl du spectacle.

perfume ['pə:fjuːm] n parfum m ♦ vt

parfumer.

perfunctory [pə'fʌŋktərı] adj négligent(e), pour la forme.

perhaps [pə'hæps] adv peut-être; ~ **he'll** ... peut-être qu'il ...; ~ **so/not** peut-être que oui/que non.

peril ['perıl] n péril m.

perilous ['perıləs] adj périlleux(euse).

perilously ['perıləslı] adv: **they came ~ close to being caught** ils ont été à deux doigts de se faire prendre.

perimeter [pə'rımıtə*] n périmètre m.

perimeter wall n mur m d'enceinte.

period ['pıərıəd] n période f; (HISTORY) époque f; (SCOL) cours m; (full stop) point m; (MED) règles fpl ♦ adj (costume, furniture) d'époque; **for a ~ of three weeks** pour (une période de) trois semaines; **the holiday ~** (BRIT) la période des vacances.

periodic [pıərı'ɔdık] adj périodique.

periodical [pıərı'ɔdıkl] adj périodique ♦ n périodique m.

periodically [pıərı'ɔdıklı] adv périodiquement.

period pains npl (BRIT) douleurs menstruelles.

peripatetic [perıpə'tetık] adj (salesman) ambulant; (BRIT: teacher) qui travaille dans plusieurs établissements.

peripheral [pə'rıfərəl] adj périphérique ♦ n (COMPUT) périphérique m.

periphery [pə'rıfərı] n périphérie f.

periscope ['perıskəup] n périscope m.

perish ['perıʃ] vi périr, mourir; (decay) se détériorer.

perishable ['perıʃəbl] adj périssable.

perishables ['perıʃəblz] npl denrées fpl périssables.

perishing ['perıʃıŋ] adj (BRIT col: cold) glacial(e).

peritonitis [perıtə'naıtıs] n péritonite f.

perjure ['pə:dʒə*] vt: **to ~ o.s.** se parjurer.

perjury ['pə:dʒərı] n (LAW: in court) faux témoignage; (breach of oath) parjure m.

perk [pə:k] n (col) avantage m, à-côté m.
▶**perk up** vi (col: cheer up) se ragaillardir.

perky ['pə:kı] adj (cheerful) guilleret(te), gai(e).

perm [pə:m] n (for hair) permanente f ♦ vt: **to have one's hair ~ed** se faire faire une permanente.

permanence ['pə:mənəns] n permanence f.

permanent ['pə:mənənt] adj permanent(e); (job, position) permanent, fixe; (dye, ink) indélébile; **I'm not ~ here** je ne suis pas ici à titre définitif; ~ **address** adresse habituelle.

permanently ['pə:mənəntlı] adv de façon permanente.

permeable ['pə:mıəbl] adj perméable.

permeate ['pə:mıeıt] vi s'infiltrer ♦ vt s'infiltrer dans; pénétrer.

permissible [pə'mısıbl] adj permis(e), acceptable.

permission [pə'mıʃən] n permission f, autorisation f; **to give sb ~ to do sth** donner à qn la permission de faire qch.

permissive [pə'mısıv] adj tolérant(e); **the ~ society** la société de tolérance.

permit n ['pə:mıt] permis m; (entrance pass) autorisation f, laisser-passer m; (for goods) licence f ♦ vt [pə'mıt] permettre; **to ~ sb to do** autoriser qn à faire, permettre à qn de faire; **weather ~ting** si le temps le permet.

permutation [pə:mju'teıʃən] n permutation f.

pernicious [pə:'nıʃəs] adj pernicieux(euse), nocif(ive).

pernickety [pə'nıkıtı] adj (col) pointilleux(euse), tatillon(ne); (task) minutieux(euse).

perpendicular [pə:pən'dıkjulə*] adj, n perpendiculaire (f).

perpetrate ['pə:pıtreıt] vt perpétrer, commettre.

perpetual [pə'petjuəl] adj perpétuel(le).

perpetuate [pə'petjueıt] vt perpétuer.

perpetuity [pə:pı'tju:ıtı] n: **in ~** à perpétuité.

perplex [pə'pleks] vt rendre perplexe; (complicate) embrouiller.

perplexing [pə:'pleksıŋ] adj embarrassant(e).

perquisites ['pə:kwızıts] npl (also: perks) avantages mpl annexes.

persecute ['pə:sıkju:t] vt persécuter.

persecution [pə:sı'kju:ʃən] n persécution f.

perseverance [pə:sı'vıərns] n persévérance f, ténacité f.

persevere [pə:sı'vıə*] vi persévérer.

Persia ['pə:ʃə] n Perse f.

Persian ['pə:ʃən] adj persan(e) ♦ n (LING) persan m; **the (~) Gulf** le golfe Persique.

Persian cat n chat persan.

persist [pə'sıst] vi: **to ~ (in doing)** persister (à faire), s'obstiner (à faire).

persistence [pə'sıstəns] n persistance f, obstination f; opiniâtreté f.

persistent [pə'sıstənt] adj persistant(e), tenace; (lateness, rain) persistant; ~ **offender** (LAW) multirécidiviste m/f.

persnickety [pə'snıkıtı] adj (US col) = **pernickety**.

person ['pə:sn] n personne f; **in ~** en personne; **on or about one's ~** sur soi; **to ~ call** (TEL) appel m avec préavis.

personable ['pə:snəbl] adj de belle prestance, au physique attrayant.

personal ['pə:snl] adj personnel(le); ~ **belongings**, ~ **effects** effets personnels; ~ **hygiene** hygiène f intime; **a ~ interview** un entretien.

personal allowance n (TAX) part f du revenu non imposable.

personal assistant (PA) n secrétaire personnel(le).

personal call n (TEL) communication f avec préavis.

personal column n annonces personnelles.

personal computer (PC) n ordinateur individuel, PC m.

personal details npl (on form etc) coordonnées fpl.

personal identification number (PIN) n (COMPUT, BANKING) numéro m d'identification personnel.

personality [pɜːsəˈnælɪtɪ] n personnalité f.

personally [ˈpɜːsnəlɪ] adv personnellement.

personal organizer n agenda (personnel) (style Filofax); (electronic) agenda électronique.

personal property n biens personnels.

personal stereo n walkman m ®, baladeur m.

personify [pɜːˈsɔnɪfaɪ] vt personnifier.

personnel [pɜːsəˈnɛl] n personnel m.

personnel department n service m du personnel.

personnel manager n chef m du personnel.

perspective [pəˈspɛktɪv] n perspective f; **to get sth into** ~ ramener qch à sa juste mesure.

perspex [ˈpɜːspɛks] n ® (BRIT) Plexiglas m ®.

perspicacity [pɜːspɪˈkæsɪtɪ] n perspicacité f.

perspiration [pɜːspɪˈreɪʃən] n transpiration f.

perspire [pəˈspaɪə*] vi transpirer.

persuade [pəˈsweɪd] vt: **to** ~ **sb to do sth** persuader qn de faire qch, amener or décider qn à faire qch; **to** ~ **sb of sth/that** persuader qn de qch/que.

persuasion [pəˈsweɪʒən] n persuasion f; (creed) conviction f.

persuasive [pəˈsweɪsɪv] adj persuasif(ive).

pert [pɜːt] adj coquin(e), mutin(e).

pertaining [pɜːˈteɪnɪŋ]: ~ **to** prep relatif(ive) à.

pertinent [ˈpɜːtɪnənt] adj pertinent(e).

perturb [pəˈtɜːb] vt troubler, inquiéter.

perturbing [pəˈtɜːbɪŋ] adj troublant(e).

Peru [pəˈruː] n Pérou m.

perusal [pəˈruːzl] n lecture (attentive).

Peruvian [pəˈruːvjən] adj péruvien(ne) ♦ n Péruvien/ne.

pervade [pəˈveɪd] vt se répandre dans, envahir.

pervasive [pəˈveɪsɪv] adj (smell) pénétrant(e); (influence) insidieux(euse); (gloom, ideas) diffus(e).

perverse [pəˈvɜːs] adj pervers(e); (stubborn) entêté(e), contrariant(e).

perversion [pəˈvɜːʃən] n perversion f.

perversity [pəˈvɜːsɪtɪ] n perversité f.

pervert n [ˈpɜːvɜːt] perverti/e ♦ vt [pəˈvɜːt] pervertir.

pessimism [ˈpɛsɪmɪzəm] n pessimisme m.

pessimist [ˈpɛsɪmɪst] n pessimiste m/f.

pessimistic [pɛsɪˈmɪstɪk] adj pessimiste.

pest [pɛst] n animal m (or insecte m) nuisible; (fig) fléau m.

pest control n lutte f contre les nuisibles.

pester [ˈpɛstə*] vt importuner, harceler.

pesticide [ˈpɛstɪsaɪd] n pesticide m.

pestilence [ˈpɛstɪləns] n peste f.

pestle [ˈpɛsl] n pilon m.

pet [pɛt] n animal familier; (favourite) chouchou m ♦ vt choyer ♦ vi (col) se peloter; ~ **lion** etc lion etc apprivoisé.

petal [ˈpɛtl] n pétale m.

peter [ˈpiːtə*]: **to** ~ **out** vi s'épuiser; s'affaiblir.

petite [pəˈtiːt] adj menu(e).

petition [pəˈtɪʃən] n pétition f ♦ vt adresser une pétition à ♦ vi: **to** ~ **for divorce** demander le divorce.

pet name n (BRIT) petit nom.

petrified [ˈpɛtrɪfaɪd] adj (fig) mort(e) de peur.

petrify [ˈpɛtrɪfaɪ] vt pétrifier.

petrochemical [pɛtrəˈkɛmɪkl] adj pétrochimique.

petrodollars [ˈpɛtrəʊdɔləz] npl pétrodollars mpl.

petrol [ˈpɛtrəl] n (BRIT) essence f.

petrol bomb n cocktail m Molotov.

petrol can n (BRIT) bidon m à essence.

petrol engine n (BRIT) moteur m à essence.

petroleum [pəˈtrəʊlɪəm] n pétrole m.

petroleum jelly n vaseline f.

petrol pump n (BRIT: in car, at garage) pompe f à essence.

petrol station n (BRIT) station-service f.

petrol tank n (BRIT) réservoir m d'essence.

petticoat [ˈpɛtɪkəʊt] n jupon m.

pettifogging [ˈpɛtɪfɔgɪŋ] adj chicanier(ière).

pettiness [ˈpɛtɪnɪs] n mesquinerie f.

petty [ˈpɛtɪ] adj (mean) mesquin(e); (unimportant) insignifiant(e), sans importance.

petty cash n caisse f des dépenses courantes, petite caisse.

petty officer n second-maître m.

petulant [ˈpɛtjʊlənt] adj irritable.

pew [pjuː] n banc m (d'église).

pewter [ˈpjuːtə*] n étain m.

Pfc abbr (US MIL) = private first class.

PG n abbr (CINE: = parental guidance) avis des parents recommandé.

PGA n abbr = Professional Golfers Association.

PH n abbr (US MIL: = Purple Heart) décoration accordée aux blessés de guerre.

PHA n abbr (US: = Public Housing Administration) organisme d'aide à la construction.

phallic [ˈfælɪk] adj phallique.

phantom [ˈfæntəm] n fantôme m; (vision) fantasme m.

Pharaoh [ˈfɛərəʊ] n pharaon m.

pharmaceutical [faːməˈsjuːtɪkl] adj pharmaceutique ♦ n: ~**s** produits mpl pharmaceutiques.

pharmacist [ˈfaːməsɪst] n pharmacien/ne.

pharmacy [ˈfaːməsɪ] n pharmacie f.

phase [feɪz] n phase f, période f ♦ vt: **to** ~ **sth in/out** introduire/supprimer qch progressivement.

PhD *abbr* (= *Doctor of Philosophy*) title
 ≈ Docteur *m* en Droit *or* Lettres *etc* ♦ *n*
 ≈ doctorat *m*; titulaire *m* d'un doctorat; *see
 also* **doctorate**.
pheasant ['fɛznt] *n* faisan *m*.
phenomenon, *pl* **phenomena** [fə'nɔmɪnən,
 -nə] *n* phénomène *m*.
phew [fjuː] *excl* ouf!
phial ['faɪəl] *n* fiole *f*.
philanderer [fɪ'lændərə*] *n* don Juan *m*.
philanthropic [fɪlən'θrɔpɪk] *adj*
 philanthropique.
philanthropist [fɪ'lænθrəpɪst] *n* philanthrope
 m/f.
philatelist [fɪ'lætəlɪst] *n* philatéliste *m/f*.
philately [fɪ'lætəlɪ] *n* philatélie *f*.
Philippines ['fɪlɪpiːnz] *npl* (*also*: **Philippine
 Islands**): **the** ~ les Philippines *fpl*.
philosopher [fɪ'lɔsəfə*] *n* philosophe *m*.
philosophical [fɪlə'sɔfɪkl] *adj* philosophique.
philosophy [fɪ'lɔsəfɪ] *n* philosophie *f*.
phlegm [flɛm] *n* flegme *m*.
phlegmatic [flɛg'mætɪk] *adj* flegmatique.
phobia ['fəubjə] *n* phobie *f*.
phone [fəun] *n* téléphone *m* ♦ *vt* téléphoner à
 ♦ *vi* téléphoner; **to be on the** ~ avoir le
 téléphone; (*be calling*) être au téléphone.
▶**phone back** *vt*, *vi* rappeler.
phone book *n* annuaire *m*.
phone box, **phone booth** *n* cabine *f*
 téléphonique.
phone call *n* coup *m* de fil *or* de téléphone.
phonecard ['fəunkɑːd] *n* télécarte *f*.
phone-in ['fəunɪn] *n* (*BRIT RADIO, TV*)
 programme *m* à ligne ouverte.
phone tapping [-tæpɪŋ] *n* mise *f* sur écoutes
 téléphoniques.
phonetics [fə'nɛtɪks] *n* phonétique *f*.
phoney ['fəunɪ] *adj* faux(fausse), factice ♦ *n*
 (*person*) charlatan *m*; fumiste *m/f*.
phonograph ['fəunəɡrɑːf] *n* (*US*)
 électrophone *m*.
phony ['fəunɪ] *adj*, *n* = **phoney**.
phosphate ['fɔsfeɪt] *n* phosphate *m*.
phosphorus ['fɔsfərəs] *n* phosphore *m*.
photo ['fəutəu] *n* photo *f*.
photo... ['fəutəu] *prefix* photo....
photocall ['fəutəukɔːl] *n* séance *f* de photos
 pour la presse.
photocopier ['fəutəukɔpɪə*] *n* copieur *m*.
photocopy ['fəutəukɔpɪ] *n* photocopie *f* ♦ *vt*
 photocopier.
photoelectric [fəutəui'lɛktrɪk] *adj*
 photoélectrique; ~ **cell** cellule *f*
 photoélectrique.
Photofit ['fəutəufɪt] *n* ® portrait-robot *m*.
photogenic [fəutəu'dʒɛnɪk] *adj* photogénique.
photograph ['fəutəɡræf] *n* photographie *f* ♦ *vt*
 photographier; **to take a** ~ **of sb** prendre qn
 en photo.
photographer [fə'tɔɡrəfə*] *n* photographe *m/f*.
photographic [fəutə'ɡræfɪk] *adj*

photographique.
photography [fə'tɔɡrəfɪ] *n* photographie *f*.
photo opportunity *n occasion, souvent
 arrangée, pour prendre des photos d'une
 personnalité.*
Photostat ['fəutəustæt] *n* ® photocopie *f*,
 photostat *m*.
photosynthesis [fəutəu'sɪnθəsɪs] *n*
 photosynthèse *f*.
phrase [freɪz] *n* expression *f*; (*LING*) locution *f*
 ♦ *vt* exprimer; (*letter*) rédiger.
phrasebook ['freɪzbuk] *n* recueil *m*
 d'expressions (pour touristes).
physical ['fɪzɪkl] *adj* physique; ~ **examination**
 examen médical; ~ **education** éducation
 physique; ~ **exercises** gymnastique *f*.
physically ['fɪzɪklɪ] *adv* physiquement.
physician [fɪ'zɪʃən] *n* médecin *m*.
physicist ['fɪzɪsɪst] *n* physicien/ne.
physics ['fɪzɪks] *n* physique *f*.
physiological [fɪzɪə'lɔdʒɪkl] *adj* physiologique.
physiology [fɪzɪ'ɔlədʒɪ] *n* physiologie *f*.
physiotherapist [fɪzɪəu'θɛrəpɪst] *n*
 kinésithérapeute *m/f*.
physiotherapy [fɪzɪəu'θɛrəpɪ] *n* kinésithérapie
physique [fɪ'ziːk] *n* (*appearance*) physique *m*;
 (*health etc*) constitution *f*.
pianist ['piːənɪst] *n* pianiste *m/f*.
piano [pɪ'ænəu] *n* piano *m*.
piano accordion *n* (*BRIT*) accordéon *m* à
 touches.
Picardy ['pɪkədɪ] *n* Picardie *f*.
piccolo ['pɪkələu] *n* piccolo *m*.
pick [pɪk] *n* (*tool: also*: ~**-axe**) pic *m*, pioche *f*
 ♦ *vt* choisir; (*gather*) cueillir; (*scab, spot*)
 gratter, écorcher; **take your** ~ faites votre
 choix; **the** ~ **of** le(la) meilleur(e) de; **to** ~ **a
 bone** ronger un os; **to** ~ **one's nose** se
 mettre le doigt dans le nez; **to** ~ **one's teeth**
 se curer les dents; **to** ~ **sb's brains** faire
 appel aux lumières de qn; **to** ~ **pockets**
 pratiquer le vol à la tire; **to** ~ **a quarrel/
 fight with sb** chercher querelle à/la bagarre
 avec qn.
▶**pick off** *vt* (*kill*) (viser soigneusement et)
 abattre.
▶**pick on** *vt fus* (*person*) harceler.
▶**pick out** *vt* choisir; (*distinguish*) distinguer.
▶**pick up** *vi* (*improve*) remonter, s'améliorer
 ♦ *vt* ramasser; (*telephone*) décrocher;
 (*collect*) passer prendre; (*AUT: give lift to*)
 prendre; (*learn*) apprendre; (*RADIO, TV, TEL*)
 capter; **to** ~ **up speed** prendre de la vitesse
 to ~ **o.s. up** se relever; **to** ~ **up where one
 left off** reprendre là où l'on s'est arrêté.
pickaxe, (*US*) **pickax** ['pɪkæks] *n* pioche *f*.
picket ['pɪkɪt] *n* (*in strike*) gréviste *m/f*
 participant à un piquet de grève; piquet *m*
 de grève ♦ *vt* mettre un piquet de grève
 devant.
picket line *n* piquet *m* de grève.
pickings ['pɪkɪŋz] *npl*: **there are rich** ~ **to be**

had in ... il y a gros à gagner dans ....

ickle ['pɪkl] n (also: ~s: as condiment) pickles mpl; (fig): **in a ~** dans le pétrin ♦ vt conserver dans du vinaigre or dans de la saumure.

ick-me-up ['pɪkmiːʌp] n remontant m.

ickpocket ['pɪkpɔkɪt] n pickpocket m.

ickup ['pɪkʌp] n (BRIT: on record player) bras m pick-up; (small truck: also: ~ truck, ~ van) camionnette f.

icnic ['pɪknɪk] n pique-nique m ♦ vi pique-niquer.

icnicker ['pɪknɪkə*] n pique-niqueur/euse.

ictorial [pɪk'tɔːrɪəl] adj illustré(e).

icture ['pɪktʃə*] n (also TV) image f; (painting) peinture f, tableau m; (photograph) photo(graphie) f; (drawing) dessin m; (film) film m ♦ vt se représenter; (describe) dépeindre, représenter; **the ~s** (BRIT) le cinéma; **to take a ~ of sb/sth** prendre qn/ qch en photo; **the overall ~** le tableau d'ensemble; **to put sb in the ~** mettre qn au courant.

icture book n livre m d'images.

icturesque [pɪktʃə'rɛsk] adj pittoresque.

icture window n baie vitrée, fenêtre f panoramique.

iddling ['pɪdlɪŋ] adj (col) insignifiant(e).

idgin ['pɪdʒɪn] adj: ~ **English** pidgin m.

ie [paɪ] n tourte f; (of meat) pâté m en croûte.

iebald ['paɪbɔːld] adj pie inv.

iece [piːs] n morceau m; (of land) parcelle f; (item): **a ~ of furniture/advice** un meuble/ conseil; (DRAUGHTS etc) pion m ♦ vt: **to ~ together** rassembler; **in ~s** (broken) en morceaux, en miettes; (not yet assembled) en pièces détachées; **to take to ~s** démonter; **in one ~** (object) intact(e); **to get back all in one ~** (person) rentrer sain et sauf; **a 10p ~** (BRIT) une pièce de 10p; **~ by ~** morceau par morceau; **a six-~ band** un orchestre de six musiciens; **to say one's ~** réciter son morceau.

iecemeal ['piːsmiːl] adv par bouts.

iece rate n taux m or tarif m à la pièce.

iecework ['piːswəːk] n travail m aux pièces or à la pièce.

ie chart n graphique m à secteurs, camembert m.

iedmont ['piːdmɔnt] n Piémont m.

ier [pɪə*] n jetée f; (of bridge etc) pile f.

ierce [pɪəs] vt percer, transpercer; **to have one's ears ~d** se faire percer les oreilles.

iercing ['pɪəsɪŋ] adj (cry) perçant(e).

iety ['paɪətɪ] n piété f.

iffling ['pɪflɪŋ] adj insignifiant(e).

ig [pɪg] n cochon m, porc m.

igeon ['pɪdʒən] n pigeon m.

igeonhole ['pɪdʒənhəul] n casier m.

igeon-toed ['pɪdʒəntəud] adj marchant les pieds en dedans.

iggy bank ['pɪgɪ-] n tirelire f.

igheaded ['pɪg'hɛdɪd] adj entêté(e), têtu(e).

piglet ['pɪglɪt] n petit cochon, porcelet m.

pigment ['pɪgmənt] n pigment m.

pigmentation [pɪgmən'teɪʃən] n pigmentation f.

pigmy ['pɪgmɪ] n = **pygmy**.

pigskin ['pɪgskɪn] n (peau f de) porc m.

pigsty ['pɪgstaɪ] n porcherie f.

pigtail ['pɪgteɪl] n natte f, tresse f.

pike [paɪk] n (spear) pique f; (fish) brochet m.

pilchard ['pɪltʃəd] n pilchard m (sorte de sardine).

pile [paɪl] n (pillar, of books) pile f; (heap) tas m; (of carpet) épaisseur f ♦ vb (also: ~ **up**) vt empiler, entasser ♦ vi s'entasser; **in a ~** en tas.

▶**pile on** vt: **to ~ it on** (col) exagérer.

piles [paɪlz] npl hémorroïdes fpl.

pileup ['paɪlʌp] n (AUT) télescopage m, collision f en série.

pilfer ['pɪlfə*] vt chaparder ♦ vi commettre des larcins.

pilfering ['pɪlfərɪŋ] n chapardage m.

pilgrim ['pɪlgrɪm] n pèlerin m.

pilgrimage ['pɪlgrɪmɪdʒ] n pèlerinage m.

pill [pɪl] n pilule f; **the ~** la pilule; **to be on the ~** prendre la pilule.

pillage ['pɪlɪdʒ] vt piller.

pillar ['pɪlə*] n pilier m.

pillar box n (BRIT) boîte f aux lettres (publique).

pillion ['pɪljən] n (of motor cycle) siège m arrière; **to ride ~** être derrière; (on horse) être en croupe.

pillory ['pɪlərɪ] n pilori m ♦ vt mettre au pilori.

pillow ['pɪləu] n oreiller m.

pillowcase ['pɪləukeɪs], **pillowslip** ['pɪləuslɪp] n taie f d'oreiller.

pilot ['paɪlət] n pilote m ♦ cpd (scheme etc) pilote, expérimental(e) ♦ vt piloter.

pilot boat n bateau-pilote m.

pilot light n veilleuse f.

pimento [pɪ'mɛntəu] n piment m.

pimp [pɪmp] n souteneur m, maquereau m.

pimple ['pɪmpl] n bouton m.

pimply ['pɪmplɪ] adj boutonneux(euse).

PIN n abbr = **personal identification number**.

pin [pɪn] n épingle f; (TECH) cheville f; (BRIT: drawing ~) punaise f; (in grenade) goupille f; (BRIT ELEC: of plug) broche f ♦ vt épingler; **~s and needles** fourmis fpl; **to ~ sb against/to** clouer qn contre/à; **to ~ sth on sb** (fig) mettre qch sur le dos de qn.

▶**pin down** vt (fig): **to ~ sb down** obliger qn à répondre; **there's something strange here but I can't quite ~ it down** il y a quelque chose d'étrange ici, mais je n'arrive pas exactement à savoir quoi.

pinafore ['pɪnəfɔː*] n tablier m.

pinafore dress n robe-chasuble f.

pinball ['pɪnbɔːl] n flipper m.

pincers ['pɪnsəz] npl tenailles fpl.

pinch [pɪntʃ] n pincement m; (of salt etc)

pincée *f* ♦ *vt* pincer; (*col: steal*) piquer,
chiper ♦ *vi* (*shoe*) serrer; **at a ~** à la rigueur;
to feel the ~ (*fig*) se ressentir des
restrictions (*or* de la récession *etc*).
pinched [pɪntʃt] *adj* (*drawn*) tiré(e); **~ with
cold** transi(e) de froid; **~ for** (*short of*): **~ for
money** à court d'argent; **~ for space** à
l'étroit.
pincushion ['pɪnkuʃən] *n* pelote *f* à épingles.
pine [paɪn] *n* (*also:* **~ tree**) pin *m* ♦ *vi*: **to ~ for**
aspirer à, désirer ardemment.
▶**pine away** *vi* dépérir.
pineapple ['paɪnæpl] *n* ananas *m*.
pine cone *n* pomme *f* de pin.
pine needle *n* aiguille *f* de pin.
ping [pɪŋ] *n* (*noise*) tintement *m*.
Ping-Pong ['pɪŋpɔŋ] *n* ® ping-pong *m* ®.
pink [pɪŋk] *adj* rose ♦ *n* (*colour*) rose *m*; (*BOT*)
œillet *m*, mignardise *f*.
pinking shears ['pɪŋkɪŋ-] *npl* ciseaux *mpl* à
denteler.
pin money *n* (*BRIT*) argent *m* de poche.
pinnacle ['pɪnəkl] *n* pinacle *m*.
pinpoint ['pɪnpɔɪnt] *vt* indiquer (avec
précision).
pinstripe ['pɪnstraɪp] *n* rayure très fine.
pint [paɪnt] *n* pinte *f* (*BRIT = 0.57 l; US* = 0.47 l);
(*BRIT col*) ≈ demi *m*, ≈ pot *m*.
pinup ['pɪnʌp] *n* pin-up *f inv*.
pioneer [paɪə'nɪə*] *n* explorateur/trice; (*early
settler*) pionnier *m*; (*fig*) pionnier,
précurseur *m* ♦ *vt* être un pionnier de.
pious ['paɪəs] *adj* pieux(euse).
pip [pɪp] *n* (*seed*) pépin *m*; (*BRIT: time signal on
radio*) top *m*.
pipe [paɪp] *n* tuyau *m*, conduite *f*; (*for smoking*)
pipe *f*; (*MUS*) pipeau *m* ♦ *vt* amener par
tuyau; **~s** *npl* (*also:* **bag~s**) cornemuse *f*.
▶**pipe down** *vi* (*col*) se taire.
pipe cleaner *n* cure-pipe *m*.
piped music [paɪpt-] *n* musique *f* de fond.
pipe dream *n* chimère *f*, utopie *f*.
pipeline ['paɪplaɪn] *n* (*for gas*) gazoduc *m*,
pipeline *m*; (*for oil*) oléoduc *m*, pipeline; **it is
in the ~** (*fig*) c'est en route, ça va se faire.
piper ['paɪpə*] *n* joueur/euse de pipeau (*or* de
cornemuse).
pipe tobacco *n* tabac *m* pour la pipe.
piping ['paɪpɪŋ] *adv*: **~ hot** très chaud(e).
piquant ['piːkənt] *adj* piquant(e).
pique [piːk] *n* pique *f*.
piracy ['paɪərəsɪ] *n* piraterie *f*.
pirate ['paɪərət] *n* pirate *m* ♦ *vt* (*record, video,
book*) pirater.
pirate radio *n* (*BRIT*) radio *f* pirate.
pirouette [pɪru'ɛt] *n* pirouette *f* ♦ *vi* faire une
or des pirouette(s).
Pisces ['paɪsiːz] *n* les Poissons *mpl*; **to be ~**
être des Poissons.
piss [pɪs] *vi* (*col!*) pisser (*!*); **~ off!** tire-toi! (*!*).
pissed [pɪst] *adj* (*BRIT col: drunk*) bourré(e).
pistol ['pɪstl] *n* pistolet *m*.

piston ['pɪstən] *n* piston *m*.
pit [pɪt] *n* trou *m*, fosse *f*; (*also:* **coal ~**)
puits *m* de mine; (*also:* **orchestra ~**) fosse
d'orchestre ♦ *vt*: **to ~ sb against sb** opposer
qn à qn; **to ~ o.s. against** se mesurer à; **~s**
npl (*in motor racing*) aire *f* de service.
pitapat ['pɪtə'pæt] *adv* (*BRIT*): **to go ~** (*heart*)
battre la chamade; (*rain*) tambouriner.
pitch [pɪtʃ] *n* (*throw*) lancement *m*; (*MUS*) ton
m; (*of voice*) hauteur *f*; (*fig: degree*) degré *m*;
(*also:* **sales ~**) baratin *m*, boniment *m*; (*BRIT
SPORT*) terrain *m*; (*NAUT*) tangage *m*; (*tar*)
poix *f* ♦ *vt* (*throw*) lancer; (*tent*) dresser; (*set
price, message*) adapter, positionner ♦ *vi*
(*NAUT*) tanguer; (*fall*): **to ~ into/off** tomber
dans/de; **to be ~ed forward** être projeté(e)
en avant; **at this ~** à ce rythme.
pitch-black ['pɪtʃ'blæk] *adj* noir(e) comme
poix.
pitched battle [pɪtʃt-] *n* bataille rangée.
pitcher ['pɪtʃə*] *n* cruche *f*.
pitchfork ['pɪtʃfɔːk] *n* fourche *f*.
piteous ['pɪtɪəs] *adj* pitoyable.
pitfall ['pɪtfɔːl] *n* trappe *f*, piège *m*.
pith [pɪθ] *n* (*of plant*) moelle *f*; (*of orange*)
intérieur *m* de l'écorce; (*fig*) essence *f*;
vigueur *f*.
pithead ['pɪthɛd] *n* (*BRIT*) bouche *f* de puits.
pithy ['pɪθɪ] *adj* piquant(e); vigoureux(euse).
pitiable ['pɪtɪəbl] *adj* pitoyable.
pitiful ['pɪtɪful] *adj* (*touching*) pitoyable;
(*contemptible*) lamentable.
pitifully ['pɪtɪfəlɪ] *adv* pitoyablement;
lamentablement.
pitiless ['pɪtɪlɪs] *adj* impitoyable.
pittance ['pɪtns] *n* salaire *m* de misère.
pitted ['pɪtɪd] *adj*: **~ with** (*chickenpox*) grêlé(e)
par; (*rust*) piqué(e) de.
pity ['pɪtɪ] *n* pitié *f* ♦ *vt* plaindre; **what a ~!**
quel dommage!; **it is a ~ that you can't
come** c'est dommage que vous ne puissiez
venir; **to have** *or* **take ~ on sb** avoir pitié de
qn.
pitying ['pɪtɪɪŋ] *adj* compatissant(e).
pivot ['pɪvət] *n* pivot *m* ♦ *vi* pivoter.
pixel ['pɪksl] *n* (*COMPUT*) pixel *m*.
pixie ['pɪksɪ] *n* lutin *m*.
pizza ['piːtsə] *n* pizza *f*.
placard ['plækɑːd] *n* affiche *f*.
placate [plə'keɪt] *vt* apaiser, calmer.
placatory [plə'keɪtərɪ] *adj* d'apaisement,
lénifiant(e).
place [pleɪs] *n* endroit *m*, lieu *m*; (*proper
position, rank, seat*) place *f*; (*house*) maison *f*,
logement *m*; (*in street names*): **Laurel ~** ≈ ru
des Lauriers; (*home*): **at/to his ~** chez lui
♦ *vt* (*position*) placer, mettre; (*identify*)
situer; reconnaître; **to take ~** avoir lieu;
(*occur*) se produire; **from ~ to ~** d'un
endroit à l'autre; **all over the ~** partout; **out
of ~** (*not suitable*) déplacé(e), inopportun(e)
I feel out of ~ here je ne me sens pas à ma

place ici; **in the first** ~ d'abord, en premier; **to put sb in his** ~ (*fig*) remettre qn à sa place; **he's going** ~**s** (*fig: col*) il fait son chemin; **it is not my** ~ **to do it** ce n'est pas à moi de le faire; **to** ~ **an order with sb (for)** (*COMM*) passer commande à qn (de); **to be** ~**d** (*in race, exam*) se placer; **how are you** ~**d next week?** comment ça se présente pour la semaine prochaine?

●**lacebo** [plə'siːbəu] *n* placebo *m*.

●**lace mat** *n* set *m* de table; (*in linen etc*) napperon *m*.

●**lacement** ['pleɪsmənt] *n* placement *m*; poste *m*.

●**lace name** *n* nom *m* de lieu.

●**lacenta** [plə'sɛntə] *n* placenta *m*.

●**lacid** ['plæsɪd] *adj* placide.

●**lacidity** [plə'sɪdɪtɪ] *n* placidité *f*.

●**lagiarism** ['pleɪdʒjərɪzəm] *n* plagiat *m*.

●**lagiarist** ['pleɪdʒjərɪst] *n* plagiaire *m/f*.

●**lagiarize** ['pleɪdʒjəraɪz] *vt* plagier.

●**lague** [pleɪg] *n* fléau *m*; (*MED*) peste *f* ♦ *vt* (*fig*) tourmenter; **to** ~ **sb with questions** harceler qn de questions.

●**laice** [pleɪs] *n* (*pl inv*) carrelet *m*.

●**laid** [plæd] *n* tissu écossais.

●**lain** [pleɪn] *adj* (*clear*) clair(e), évident(e); (*simple*) simple, ordinaire; (*frank*) franc(franche); (*not handsome*) quelconque, ordinaire; (*cigarette*) sans filtre; (*without seasoning etc*) nature *inv*; (*in one colour*) uni(e) ♦ *adv* franchement, carrément ♦ *n* plaine *f*; **in** ~ **clothes** (*police*) en civil; **to make sth** ~ **to sb** faire clairement comprendre qch à qn.

●**lain chocolate** *n* chocolat *m* à croquer.

●**lainly** ['pleɪnlɪ] *adv* clairement; (*frankly*) carrément, sans détours.

●**lainness** ['pleɪnnɪs] *n* simplicité *f*.

●**lain speaking** *n* propos *mpl* sans équivoque; **she has a reputation for** ~ elle est bien connue pour son franc parler *or* sa franchise.

●**laintiff** ['pleɪntɪf] *n* plaignant/e.

●**laintive** ['pleɪntɪv] *adj* plaintif(ive).

●**lait** [plæt] *n* tresse *f*, natte *f* ♦ *vt* tresser, natter.

●**lan** [plæn] *n* plan *m*; (*scheme*) projet *m* ♦ *vt* (*think in advance*) projeter; (*prepare*) organiser ♦ *vi* faire des projets; **to** ~ **to do** projeter de faire; **how long do you** ~ **to stay?** combien de temps comptez-vous rester?

●**lane** [pleɪn] *n* (*AVIAT*) avion *m*; (*tree*) platane *m*; (*tool*) rabot *m*; (*ART, MATH etc*) plan *m* ♦ *adj* plan(e), plat(e) ♦ *vt* (*with tool*) raboter.

●**lanet** ['plænɪt] *n* planète *f*.

●**lanetarium** [plænɪ'tɛərɪəm] *n* planétarium *m*.

●**lank** [plæŋk] *n* planche *f*; (*POL*) point *m* d'un programme.

●**lankton** ['plæŋktən] *n* plancton *m*.

●**lanned economy** [plænd-] *n* économie

planifiée.

planner ['plænə*] *n* planificateur/trice; (*chart*) planning *m*; **town** *or* (*US*) **city** ~ urbaniste *m/f*.

planning ['plænɪŋ] *n* planification *f*; **family** ~ planning familial.

planning permission *n* (*BRIT*) permis *m* de construire.

plant [plɑːnt] *n* plante *f*; (*machinery*) matériel *m*; (*factory*) usine *f* ♦ *vt* planter; (*bomb*) déposer, poser.

plantation [plæn'teɪʃən] *n* plantation *f*.

plant pot *n* (*BRIT*) pot *m* de fleurs.

plaque [plæk] *n* plaque *f*.

plasma ['plæzmə] *n* plasma *m*.

plaster ['plɑːstə*] *n* plâtre *m*; (*BRIT: also:* **sticking** ~) pansement adhésif ♦ *vt* plâtrer; (*cover*): **to** ~ **with** couvrir de; **in** ~ (*BRIT: leg etc*) dans le plâtre; ~ **of Paris** plâtre à mouler.

plasterboard ['plɑːstəbɔːd] *n* Placoplâtre *m* ®.

plaster cast *n* (*MED*) plâtre *m*; (*model, statue*) moule *m*.

plastered ['plɑːstəd] *adj* (*col*) soûl(e).

plasterer ['plɑːstərə*] *n* plâtrier *m*.

plastic ['plæstɪk] *n* plastique *m* ♦ *adj* (*made of plastic*) en plastique; (*flexible*) plastique, malléable; (*art*) plastique.

plastic bag *n* sac *m* en plastique.

plastic bullet *n* balle *f* de plastique.

plastic explosive *n* plastic *m*.

plasticine ['plæstɪsiːn] *n* ® pâte *f* à modeler.

plastic surgery *n* chirurgie *f* esthétique.

plate [pleɪt] *n* (*dish*) assiette *f*; (*sheet of metal, on door, PHOT*) plaque *f*; (*TYP*) cliché *m*; (*in book*) gravure *f*; (*AUT: number* ~) plaque minéralogique; **gold/silver** ~ (*dishes*) vaisselle *f* d'or/d'argent.

plateau, ~**s** *or* ~**x** ['plætəu, -z] *n* plateau *m*.

plateful ['pleɪtful] *n* assiette *f*, assiettée *f*.

plate glass *n* verre *m* à vitre, vitre *f*.

platen ['plætən] *n* (*on typewriter, printer*) rouleau *m*.

plate rack *n* égouttoir *m*.

platform ['plætfɔːm] *n* (*at meeting*) tribune *f*; (*BRIT: of bus*) plate-forme *f*; (*stage*) estrade *f*; (*RAIL*) quai *m*; **the train leaves from** ~ **7** le train part de la voie 7.

platform ticket *n* (*BRIT*) billet *m* de quai.

platinum ['plætɪnəm] *n* platine *m*.

platitude ['plætɪtjuːd] *n* platitude *f*, lieu commun.

platoon [plə'tuːn] *n* peloton *m*.

platter ['plætə*] *n* plat *m*.

plaudits ['plɔːdɪts] *npl* applaudissements *mpl*.

plausible ['plɔːzɪbl] *adj* plausible; (*person*) convaincant(e).

play [pleɪ] *n* jeu *m*; (*THEAT*) pièce *f* (de théâtre) ♦ *vt* (*game*) jouer à; (*team, opponent*) jouer contre; (*instrument*) jouer de; (*part, piece of music, note*) jouer ♦ *vi* jouer; **to bring** *or* **call into** ~ faire entrer en jeu; ~ **on words** jeu de mots; **to ~ a trick on sb** jouer un tour à qn; **they're ~ing at soldiers** ils jouent aux soldats; **to ~ for time** (*fig*) chercher à gagner du temps; **to ~ into sb's hands** (*fig*) faire le jeu de qn.

▶**play about, play around** *vi* (*person*) s'amuser.

▶**play along** *vi* (*fig*): **to ~ along with** (*person*) entrer dans le jeu de ♦ *vt* (*fig*): **to ~ sb along** faire marcher qn.

▶**play back** *vt* repasser, réécouter.

▶**play down** *vt* minimiser.

▶**play on** *vt fus* (*sb's feelings, credulity*) jouer sur; **to ~ on sb's nerves** porter sur les nerfs de qn.

▶**play up** *vi* (*cause trouble*) faire des siennes.

playact ['pleiækt] *vi* jouer la comédie.

playboy ['pleibɔi] *n* playboy *m*.

played-out ['pleid'aut] *adj* épuisé(e).

player ['pleiə*] *n* joueur/euse; (*THEAT*) acteur/trice; (*MUS*) musicien/ne.

playful ['pleiful] *adj* enjoué(e).

playgoer ['pleigəuə*] *n* amateur/trice de théâtre, habitué(e) des théâtres.

playground ['pleigraund] *n* cour *f* de récréation.

playgroup ['pleigru:p] *n* garderie *f*.

playing card ['pleiŋ-] *n* carte *f* à jouer.

playing field ['pleiŋ-] *n* terrain *m* de sport.

playmaker ['pleimeikə*] *n* (*SPORT*) *joueur qui crée des occasions de marquer des buts pour ses coéquipiers.*

playmate ['pleimeit] *n* camarade *m/f*, copain/copine.

play-off ['pleiɔf] *n* (*SPORT*) belle *f*.

playpen ['pleipen] *n* parc *m* (pour bébé).

playroom ['pleiru:m] *n* salle *f* de jeux.

plaything ['pleiθiŋ] *n* jouet *m*.

playtime ['pleitaim] *n* (*SCOL*) récréation *f*.

playwright ['pleirait] *n* dramaturge *m*.

plc *abbr* (*BRIT*) = **public limited company**.

plea [pli:] *n* (*request*) appel *m*; (*excuse*) excuse *f*; (*LAW*) défense *f*.

plea bargaining *n* (*LAW*) *négociations entre le procureur, l'avocat de la défense et parfois le juge, pour réduire la gravité des charges.*

plead [pli:d] *vt* plaider; (*give as excuse*) invoquer ♦ *vi* (*LAW*) plaider; (*beg*): **to ~ with sb (for sth)** implorer qn (d'accorder qch); **to ~ for sth** implorer qch; **to ~ guilty/not guilty** plaider coupable/non coupable.

pleasant ['pleznt] *adj* agréable.

pleasantly ['plezntli] *adv* agréablement.

pleasantry ['plezntri] *n* (*joke*) plaisanterie *f*; **pleasantries** *npl* (*polite remarks*) civilités *fpl*.

please [pli:z] *vt* plaire à ♦ *vi* (*think fit*): **do as you ~** faites comme il vous plaira; **~! s'il te** (*or vous*) **plaît; my bill, ~** l'addition, s'il vous plaît; **~ don't cry!** je t'en prie, ne pleure pas!; **~ yourself!** (faites) comme vous voulez!

pleased [pli:zd] *adj*: **~ (with)** content(e) (de); **~ to meet you** enchanté (de faire votre connaissance); **we are ~ to inform you that ...** nous sommes heureux de vous annoncer que ....

pleasing ['pli:ziŋ] *adj* plaisant(e), qui fait plaisir.

pleasurable ['pleʒərəbl] *adj* très agréable.

pleasure ['pleʒə*] *n* plaisir *m*; **"it's a ~"** "je vous en prie"; **with ~** avec plaisir; **is this trip for business or ~?** est-ce un voyage d'affaires ou d'agrément?

pleasure cruise *n* croisière *f*.

pleat [pli:t] *n* pli *m*.

plebiscite ['plebisit] *n* plébiscite *m*.

plebs [plebz] *npl* (*pej*) bas peuple.

plectrum ['plektrəm] *n* plectre *m*.

pledge [pledʒ] *n* gage *m*; (*promise*) promesse *f* ♦ *vt* engager; promettre; **to ~ support for sb** s'engager à soutenir qn; **to ~ sb to secrecy** faire promettre à qn de garder le secret.

plenary ['pli:nəri] *adj*: **in ~ session** en séance plénière.

plentiful ['plentiful] *adj* abondant(e), copieux(euse).

plenty ['plenti] *n* abondance *f*; **~ of** beaucoup de; (*sufficient*) (bien) assez de; **we've got ~ of time** nous avons largement le temps.

pleurisy ['pluərisi] *n* pleurésie *f*.

Plexiglas ['pleksiglɑ:s] *n* ® (*US*) Plexiglas *m* ®.

pliable ['plaiəbl] *adj* flexible; (*person*) malléable.

pliers ['plaiəz] *npl* pinces *fpl*.

plight [plait] *n* situation *f* critique.

plimsolls ['plimsəlz] *npl* (*BRIT*) (chaussures *fpl* tennis *fpl*.

plinth [plinθ] *n* socle *m*.

PLO *n abbr* (= *Palestine Liberation Organization*) OLP *f*.

plod [plɔd] *vi* avancer péniblement; (*fig*) peiner.

plodder ['plɔdə*] *n* bûcheur/euse.

plodding ['plɔdiŋ] *adj* pesant(e).

plonk [plɔŋk] (*col*) *n* (*BRIT: wine*) pinard *m*, piquette *f* ♦ *vt*: **to ~ sth down** poser brusquement qch.

plot [plɔt] *n* complot *m*, conspiration *f*; (*of story, play*) intrigue *f*; (*of land*) lot *m* de terrain, lopin *m* ♦ *vt* (*mark out*) pointer; relever; (*conspire*) comploter ♦ *vi* comploter; **a vegetable ~** (*BRIT*) un carré de légumes.

plotter ['plɔtə*] *n* conspirateur/trice; (*COMPUT*) traceur *m*.

plough, (*US*) **plow** [plau] *n* charrue *f* ♦ *vt* (*earth*) labourer.

▶**plough back** *vt* (*COMM*) réinvestir.

▶**plough through** *vt fus* (*snow etc*) avancer péniblement dans.

ploughing, (*US*) **plowing** ['plauiŋ] *n* labourage *m*.

ploughman, (*US*) **plowman** ['plaumən] *n*

laboureur m; ~'s lunch (BRIT) repas sommaire de pain et de fromage.

ploy [plɔɪ] n stratagème m.

pluck [plʌk] vt (fruit) cueillir; (musical instrument) pincer; (bird) plumer ♦ n courage m, cran m; **to ~ one's eyebrows** s'épiler les sourcils; **to ~ up courage** prendre son courage à deux mains.

plucky ['plʌkɪ] adj courageux(euse).

plug [plʌg] n bouchon m, bonde f; (ELEC) prise f de courant; (AUT: also: **spark(ing)** ~) bougie f ♦ vt (hole) boucher; (col: advertise) faire du battage pour, matraquer; **to give sb/sth a ~** (col) faire de la pub pour qn/qch.

▶**plug in** (ELEC) vt brancher ♦ vi se brancher.

plughole ['plʌghəʊl] n (BRIT) trou m (d'écoulement).

plum [plʌm] n (fruit) prune f ♦ adj: ~ **job** (col) travail m en or.

plumage ['pluːmɪdʒ] n plumage m.

plumb [plʌm] adj vertical(e) ♦ n plomb m ♦ adv (exactly) en plein ♦ vt sonder.

▶**plumb in** vt (washing machine) faire le raccordement de.

plumber ['plʌmə*] n plombier m.

plumbing ['plʌmɪŋ] n (trade) plomberie f; (piping) tuyauterie f.

plumbline ['plʌmlaɪn] n fil m à plomb.

plume [pluːm] n plume f, plumet m.

plummet ['plʌmɪt] vi plonger, dégringoler.

plump [plʌmp] adj rondelet(te), dodu(e), bien en chair ♦ vt: **to ~ sth (down) on** laisser tomber qch lourdement sur.

▶**plump for** vt fus (col: choose) se décider pour.

▶**plump up** vt (cushion) battre (pour lui redonner forme).

plunder ['plʌndə*] n pillage m ♦ vt piller.

plunge [plʌndʒ] n plongeon m ♦ vt plonger ♦ vi (fall) tomber, dégringoler; **to take the ~** se jeter à l'eau; **to ~ a room into darkness** plonger une pièce dans l'obscurité.

plunger ['plʌndʒə*] n piston m; (for blocked sink) (débouchoir m à) ventouse f.

plunging ['plʌndʒɪŋ] adj (neckline) plongeant(e).

pluperfect [pluː'pɜːfɪkt] n plus-que-parfait m.

plural ['plʊərl] adj pluriel(le) ♦ n pluriel m.

plus [plʌs] n (also: ~ **sign**) signe m plus ♦ prep plus; **ten/twenty ~** plus de dix/vingt; **it's a ~** c'est un atout.

plus fours npl pantalon m (de) golf.

plush [plʌʃ] adj somptueux(euse) ♦ n peluche f.

plutonium [pluː'təʊnɪəm] n plutonium m.

ply [plaɪ] n (of wool) fil m; (of wood) feuille f, épaisseur f ♦ vt (tool) manier; (a trade) exercer ♦ vi (ship) faire la navette; **three ~ (wool)** n laine f trois fils; **to ~ sb with drink** donner continuellement à boire à qn.

plywood ['plaɪwʊd] n contre-plaqué m.

PM n abbr (BRIT) = **prime minister**.

p.m. adv abbr (= post meridiem) de l'après-midi.

PMS n abbr (= premenstrual syndrome) syndrome prémenstruel.

PMT n abbr = **premenstrual tension.**

pneumatic [njuː'mætɪk] adj pneumatique; ~ **drill** marteau-piqueur m.

pneumonia [njuː'məʊnɪə] n pneumonie f.

PO n abbr (= Post Office) PTT fpl; (MIL) = **petty officer.**

po abbr = **postal order.**

POA n abbr (BRIT) = **Prison Officers' Association.**

poach [pəʊtʃ] vt (cook) pocher; (steal) pêcher (or chasser) sans permis ♦ vi braconner.

poached [pəʊtʃt] adj (egg) poché(e).

poacher ['pəʊtʃə*] n braconnier m.

poaching ['pəʊtʃɪŋ] n braconnage m.

PO box n abbr = **post office box.**

pocket ['pɒkɪt] n poche f ♦ vt empocher; **to be (£5) out of ~** (BRIT) en être de sa poche (pour 5 livres).

pocketbook ['pɒkɪtbʊk] n (wallet) portefeuille m; (notebook) carnet m; (US: handbag) sac m à main.

pocket knife n canif m.

pocket money n argent m de poche.

pockmarked ['pɒkmɑːkt] adj (face) grêlé(e).

pod [pɒd] n cosse f ♦ vt écosser.

podgy ['pɒdʒɪ] adj rondelet(te).

podiatrist [pɒ'diːətrɪst] n (US) pédicure m/f.

podiatry [pɒ'diːətrɪ] n (US) pédicurie f.

podium ['pəʊdɪəm] n podium m.

POE n abbr = **port of embarkation, port of entry.**

poem ['pəʊɪm] n poème m.

poet ['pəʊɪt] n poète m.

poetic [pəʊ'etɪk] adj poétique.

poet laureate n poète lauréat.

En Grande-Bretagne, le **poet laureate** est un poète qui reçoit un traitement en tant que poète de la cour et qui est officier de la maison royale à vie. Le premier d'entre eux fut Ben Jonson, en 1616. Jadis, le poète lauréat écrivait des poèmes lors des grandes occasions, mais cette tradition n'est plus guère observée.

poetry ['pəʊɪtrɪ] n poésie f.

poignant ['pɔɪnjənt] adj poignant(e); (sharp) vif(vive).

point [pɔɪnt] n (tip) pointe f; (in time) moment m; (in space) endroit m; (GEOM, SCOL, SPORT, on scale) point m; (subject, idea) point, sujet m; (also: **decimal** ~): **2 ~ 3 (2.3)** 2 virgule 3 (2,3); (BRIT ELEC: also: **power** ~) prise f (de courant) ♦ vt (show) indiquer; (wall, window) jointoyer; (gun etc): **to ~ sth at** braquer or diriger qch sur ♦ vi montrer du doigt; **to ~ to** montrer du doigt; (fig) signaler; ~**s** npl (AUT) vis platinées f; (RAIL) aiguillage m; **good** ~**s** qualités fpl; **the train stops at Carlisle and all** ~**s south** le train dessert Carlisle et toutes les gares vers le sud; **to make a ~** faire une remarque; **to make a ~ of doing**

sth ne pas manquer de faire qch; **to make one's** ~ se faire comprendre; **to get the** ~ comprendre, saisir; **to come to the** ~ en venir au fait; **when it comes to the** ~ le moment venu; **there's no** ~ **(in doing)** cela ne sert à rien (de faire); **to be on the** ~ **of doing sth** être sur le point de faire qch; **that's the whole** ~! précisément!; **to be beside the** ~ être à côté de la question; **you've got a** ~ **there!** (c'est) juste!; **in** ~ **of fact** en fait, en réalité; ~ **of departure** (*also fig*) point de départ; ~ **of order** point de procédure; ~ **of sale** (*COMM*) point de vente; ~ **of view** point de vue.
►**point out** *vt* faire remarquer, souligner.
point-blank ['pɔɪnt'blæŋk] *adv* (*also:* **at** ~ **range**) à bout portant ♦ *adj* (*fig*) catégorique.
point duty *n* (*BRIT*): **to be on** ~ diriger la circulation.
pointed ['pɔɪntɪd] *adj* (*shape*) pointu(e); (*remark*) plein(e) de sous-entendus.
pointedly ['pɔɪntɪdlɪ] *adv* d'une manière significative.
pointer ['pɔɪntə*] *n* (*stick*) baguette *f*; (*needle*) aiguille *f*; (*dog*) chien *m* d'arrêt; (*clue*) indication *f*; (*advice*) tuyau *m*.
pointless ['pɔɪntlɪs] *adj* inutile, vain(e).
poise [pɔɪz] *n* (*balance*) équilibre *m*; (*of head, body*) port *m*; (*calmness*) calme *m* ♦ *vt* placer en équilibre; **to be** ~**d for** (*fig*) être prêt à.
poison ['pɔɪzn] *n* poison *m* ♦ *vt* empoisonner.
poisoning ['pɔɪznɪŋ] *n* empoisonnement *m*.
poisonous ['pɔɪznəs] *adj* (*snake*) venimeux(euse); (*substance etc*) vénéneux(euse); (*fumes*) toxique; (*fig*) pernicieux(euse).
poke [pəʊk] *vt* (*fire*) tisonner; (*jab with finger, stick etc*) piquer; pousser du doigt; (*put*): **to** ~ **sth into** fourrer *or* enfoncer qch dans ♦ *n* (*jab*) (petit) coup; (*to fire*) coup *m* de tisonnier; **to** ~ **one's head out of the window** passer la tête par la fenêtre; **to** ~ **fun at sb** se moquer de qn.
►**poke about** *vi* fureter.
poker ['pəʊkə*] *n* tisonnier *m*; (*CARDS*) poker *m*.
poker-faced ['pəʊkə'feɪst] *adj* au visage impassible.
poky ['pəʊkɪ] *adj* exigu(ë).
Poland ['pəʊlənd] *n* Pologne *f*.
polar ['pəʊlə*] *adj* polaire.
polar bear *n* ours blanc.
polarize ['pəʊləraɪz] *vt* polariser.
Pole [pəʊl] *n* Polonais/e.
pole [pəʊl] *n* (*of wood*) mât *m*, perche *f*; (*ELEC*) poteau *m*; (*GEO*) pôle *m*.
poleaxe ['pəʊlæks] *vt* (*fig*) terrasser.
pole bean *n* (*US*) haricot *m* (à rames).
polecat ['pəʊlkæt] *n* putois *m*.
Pol. Econ. ['pɒlɪkɒn] *n abbr* = **political economy**.
polemic [pɒ'lemɪk] *n* polémique *f*.
pole star ['pəʊlstɑ:*] *n* étoile *f* polaire.

pole vault ['pəʊlvɔːlt] *n* saut *m* à la perche.
police [pə'liːs] *npl* police *f* ♦ *vt* maintenir l'ordre dans; **a large number of** ~ **were hurt** de nombreux policiers ont été blessés.
police car *n* voiture *f* de police.
police constable *n* (*BRIT*) agent *m* de police.
police department *n* (*US*) services *mpl* de police.
police force *n* police *f*, forces *fpl* de l'ordre.
policeman [pə'liːsmən] *n* agent *m* de police, policier *m*.
police officer *n* agent *m* de police.
police record *n* casier *m* judiciaire.
police state *n* état policier.
police station *n* commissariat *m* de police.
policewoman [pə'liːswʊmən] *n* femme-agent *f*.
policy ['pɒlɪsɪ] *n* politique *f*; (*also:* **insurance** ~) police *f* (d'assurance); (*of newspaper, company*) politique générale; **to take out a** ~ (*INSURANCE*) souscrire une police d'assurance.
policy holder *n* assuré/e.
policy-making ['pɒlɪsɪmeɪkɪŋ] *n* élaboration *f* de nouvelles lignes d'action.
polio ['pəʊlɪəʊ] *n* polio *f*.
Polish ['pəʊlɪʃ] *adj* polonais(e) ♦ *n* (*LING*) polonais *m*.
polish ['pɒlɪʃ] *n* (*for shoes*) cirage *m*; (*for floor*) cire *f*, encaustique *f*; (*for nails*) vernis *m*; (*shine*) éclat *m*, poli *m*; (*fig: refinement*) raffinement *m* ♦ *vt* (*put polish on: shoes, wood*) cirer; (*make shiny*) astiquer, faire briller; (*fig: improve*) perfectionner.
►**polish off** *vt* (*work*) expédier; (*food*) liquider.
polished ['pɒlɪʃt] *adj* (*fig*) raffiné(e).
polite [pə'laɪt] *adj* poli(e); **it's not** ~ **to do that** ça ne se fait pas.
politely [pə'laɪtlɪ] *adv* poliment.
politeness [pə'laɪtnɪs] *n* politesse *f*.
politic ['pɒlɪtɪk] *adj* diplomatique.
political [pə'lɪtɪkl] *adj* politique.
political asylum *n* asile *m* politique.
politically [pə'lɪtɪklɪ] *adv* politiquement.
politically correct *adj* politiquement correct(e).
politician [pɒlɪ'tɪʃən] *n* homme/femme politique, politicien/ne.
politics ['pɒlɪtɪks] *n* politique *f*.
polka ['pɒlkə] *n* polka *f*.
polka dot *n* pois *m*.
poll [pəʊl] *n* scrutin *m*, vote *m*; (*also:* **opinion** ~) sondage *m* (d'opinion) ♦ *vt* obtenir; **to go to the** ~**s** (*voters*) aller aux urnes; (*government*) tenir des élections.
pollen ['pɒlən] *n* pollen *m*.
pollen count *n* taux *m* de pollen.
pollination [pɒlɪ'neɪʃən] *n* pollinisation *f*.
polling ['pəʊlɪŋ] *n* (*BRIT POL*) élections *fpl*; (*TEL*) invitation *f* à émettre.
polling booth *n* (*BRIT*) isoloir *m*.

polling day n (BRIT) jour m des élections.
polling station n (BRIT) bureau m de vote.
pollster ['pəulstə*] n sondeur m, enquêteur/euse.
poll tax n (BRIT: formerly) ≈ impôts locaux.
pollutant [pə'lu:tənt] n polluant m.
pollute [pə'lu:t] vt polluer.
pollution [pə'lu:ʃən] n pollution f.
polo ['pəuləu] n polo m.
poloneck ['pəuləunɛk] n col roulé ♦ adj à col roulé.
poly ['pɔlɪ] n abbr (BRIT) = **polytechnic**.
poly bag n (BRIT col) sac m en plastique.
polyester [pɔlɪ'ɛstə*] n polyester m.
polygamy [pə'lɪgəmɪ] n polygamie f.
polygraph ['pɔlɪgrɑ:f] n détecteur m de mensonges.
Polynesia [pɔlɪ'ni:zɪə] n Polynésie f.
Polynesian [pɔlɪ'ni:zɪən] adj polynésien(ne) ♦ n Polynésien/ne.
polyp ['pɔlɪp] n (MED) polype m.
polystyrene [pɔlɪ'staɪri:n] n polystyrène m.
polytechnic [pɔlɪ'tɛknɪk] n (college) IUT m, Institut m universitaire de technologie.
polythene ['pɔlɪθi:n] n polyéthylène m.
polythene bag n sac m en plastique.
polyurethane [pɔlɪ'juərɪθeɪn] n polyuréthane m.
pomegranate ['pɔmɪgrænɪt] n grenade f.
pommel ['pɔml] n pommeau m ♦ vt = **pummel**.
pomp [pɔmp] n pompe f, faste f, apparat m.
pompom ['pɔmpɔm] n pompon m.
pompous ['pɔmpəs] adj pompeux(euse).
pond [pɔnd] n étang m; (stagnant) mare f.
ponder ['pɔndə*] vi réfléchir ♦ vt considérer, peser.
ponderous ['pɔndərəs] adj pesant(e), lourd(e).
pong [pɔŋ] (BRIT col) n puanteur f ♦ vi schlinguer.
pontiff ['pɔntɪf] n pontife m.
pontificate [pɔn'tɪfɪkeɪt] vi (fig): to ~ (about) pontifier (sur).
pontoon [pɔn'tu:n] n ponton m; (BRIT: CARDS) vingt-et-un m.
pony ['pəunɪ] n poney m.
ponytail ['pəunɪteɪl] n queue f de cheval.
pony trekking [-trɛkɪŋ] n (BRIT) randonnée f équestre or à cheval.
poodle ['pu:dl] n caniche m.
pooh-pooh ['pu:'pu:] vt dédaigner.
pool [pu:l] n (of rain) flaque f; (pond) mare f; (artificial) bassin m; (also: **swimming** ~) piscine f; (sth shared) fonds commun; (money at cards) cagnotte f; (billiards) poule f; (COMM: consortium) pool m; (US: monopoly trust) trust m ♦ vt mettre en commun; **typing** ~, (US) **secretary** ~ pool m dactylographique; **to do the (football)** ~s (BRIT) ≈ jouer au loto sportif; see also **football pools**.
poor [puə*] adj pauvre; (mediocre) médiocre, faible, mauvais(e) ♦ npl: **the** ~ les pauvres mpl.

poorly ['puəlɪ] adv pauvrement; médiocrement ♦ adj souffrant(e), malade.
pop [pɔp] n (noise) bruit sec; (MUS) musique f pop; (col: drink) soda m; (US col: father) papa m ♦ vt (put) fourrer, mettre (rapidement) ♦ vi éclater; (cork) sauter; **she ~ped her head out of the window** elle passa la tête par la fenêtre.
▶**pop in** vi entrer en passant.
▶**pop out** vi sortir.
▶**pop up** vi apparaître, surgir.
pop concert n concert m pop.
popcorn ['pɔpkɔ:n] n pop-corn m.
pope [pəup] n pape m.
poplar ['pɔplə*] n peuplier m.
poplin ['pɔplɪn] n popeline f.
popper ['pɔpə*] n (BRIT) bouton-pression m.
poppy ['pɔpɪ] n coquelicot m; pavot m.
poppycock ['pɔpɪkɔk] n (col) balivernes fpl.
Popsicle ['pɔpsɪkl] n ® (US) esquimau m (glace).
populace ['pɔpjuləs] n peuple m.
popular ['pɔpjulə*] adj populaire; (fashionable) à la mode; **to be** ~ **(with)** (person) avoir du succès (auprès de); (decision) être bien accueilli(e) (par).
popularity [pɔpju'lærɪtɪ] n popularité f.
popularize ['pɔpjuləraɪz] vt populariser; (science) vulgariser.
populate ['pɔpjuleɪt] vt peupler.
population [pɔpju'leɪʃən] n population f.
population explosion n explosion f démographique.
populous ['pɔpjuləs] adj populeux(euse).
porcelain ['pɔ:slɪn] n porcelaine f.
porch [pɔ:tʃ] n porche m.
porcupine ['pɔ:kjupaɪn] n porc-épic m.
pore [pɔ:*] n pore m ♦ vi: **to** ~ **over** s'absorber dans, être plongé(e) dans.
pork [pɔ:k] n porc m.
pork chop n côte f de porc.
porn [pɔ:n] adj, n (col) porno (m).
pornographic [pɔ:nə'græfɪk] adj pornographique.
pornography [pɔ:'nɔgrəfɪ] n pornographie f.
porous ['pɔ:rəs] adj poreux(euse).
porpoise ['pɔ:pəs] n marsouin m.
porridge ['pɔrɪdʒ] n porridge m.
port [pɔ:t] n (harbour) port m; (opening in ship) sabord m; (NAUT: left side) bâbord m; (wine) porto m; (COMPUT) port m, accès m ♦ cpd portuaire, du port; **to** ~ (NAUT) à bâbord; ~ **of call** (port d')escale f.
portable ['pɔ:təbl] adj portatif(ive).
portal ['pɔ:tl] n portail m.
portcullis [pɔ:t'kʌlɪs] n herse f.
portend [pɔ:'tɛnd] vt présager, annoncer.
portent ['pɔ:tɛnt] n présage m.
porter ['pɔ:tə*] n (for luggage) porteur m; (doorkeeper) gardien/ne; portier m.
portfolio [pɔ:t'fəuliəu] n portefeuille m; (of artist) portfolio m.

porthole ['pɔ:θəul] n hublot m.
portico ['pɔ:tɪkəu] n portique m.
portion ['pɔ:ʃən] n portion f, part f.
portly ['pɔ:tlɪ] adj corpulent(e).
portrait ['pɔ:treɪt] n portrait m.
portray [pɔ:'treɪ] vt faire le portrait de; (in writing) dépeindre, représenter.
portrayal [pɔ:'treɪəl] n portrait m, représentation f.
Portugal ['pɔ:tjugl] n Portugal m.
Portuguese [pɔ:tju'gi:z] adj portugais(e) ♦ n (pl inv) Portugais/e; (LING) portugais m.
Portuguese man-of-war [-mænəv'wɔ:*] n (jellyfish) galère f.
pose [pəuz] n pose f; (pej) affectation f ♦ vi poser; (pretend): **to ~ as** se poser en ♦ vt poser, créer; **to strike a ~** poser (pour la galerie).
poser ['pəuzə*] n question difficile or embarrassante; (person) = **poseur**.
poseur [pəu'zə:*] n (pej) poseur/euse.
posh [pɔʃ] adj (col) chic inv; **to talk ~** parler d'une manière affectée.
position [pə'zɪʃən] n position f; (job) situation f ♦ vt mettre en place or en position; **to be in a ~ to do sth** être en mesure de faire qch.
positive ['pɔzɪtɪv] adj positif(ive); (certain) sûr(e), certain(e); (definite) formel(le), catégorique; (clear) indéniable, réel(le).
posse ['pɔsɪ] n (US) détachement m.
possess [pə'zɛs] vt posséder; **like one ~ed** comme un fou; **whatever can have ~ed you?** qu'est-ce qui vous a pris?
possession [pə'zɛʃən] n possession f; **to take ~ of sth** prendre possession de qch.
possessive [pə'zɛsɪv] adj possessif(ive).
possessiveness [pə'zɛsɪvnɪs] n possessivité f.
possessor [pə'zɛsə*] n possesseur m.
possibility [pɔsɪ'bɪlɪtɪ] n possibilité f; **he's a ~ for the part** c'est un candidat possible pour le rôle.
possible ['pɔsɪbl] adj possible; (solution) envisageable, éventuel(le); **it is ~ to do it** il est possible de le faire; **as far as ~** dans la mesure du possible, autant que possible; **if ~** si possible; **as big as ~** aussi gros que possible.
possibly ['pɔsɪblɪ] adv (perhaps) peut-être; **if you ~ can** si cela vous est possible; **I cannot ~ come** il m'est impossible de venir.
post [pəust] n (BRIT: mail) poste f; (: collection) levée f; (: letters, delivery) courrier m; (job, situation) poste m; (pole) poteau m; (trading ~) comptoir (commercial) ♦ vt (BRIT: send by post, MIL) poster; (BRIT: appoint): **to ~ to** affecter à; (notice) afficher; **by ~** (BRIT) par la poste; **by return of ~** (BRIT) par retour du courrier; **to keep sb ~ed** tenir qn au courant.
post... [pəust] prefix post...; **~ 1990** adj d'après 1990 ♦ adv après 1990.
postage ['pəustɪdʒ] n affranchissement m; **~**

paid port payé; **~ prepaid** (US) franco (de port).
postage stamp n timbre-poste m.
postal ['pəustl] adj postal(e).
postal order n mandat(-poste m) m.
postbag ['pəustbæg] n (BRIT) sac postal; (postman's) sacoche f.
postbox ['pəustbɔks] n (BRIT) boîte f aux lettres (publique).
postcard ['pəustkɑ:d] n carte postale.
postcode ['pəustkəud] n (BRIT) code postal.
postdate ['pəust'deɪt] vt (cheque) postdater.
poster ['pəustə*] n affiche f.
poste restante [pəust'rɛstɑ̃:nt] n (BRIT) poste restante.
posterior [pɔs'tɪərɪə*] n (col) postérieur m, derrière m.
posterity [pɔs'tɛrɪtɪ] n postérité f.
poster paint n gouache f.
post exchange (PX) n (US MIL) magasin m de l'armée.
post-free [pəust'fri:] adj (BRIT) franco (de port).
postgraduate ['pəust'grædjuət] n ≈ étudiant/e de troisième cycle.
posthumous ['pɔstjuməs] adj posthume.
posthumously ['pɔstjuməslɪ] adv après la mort de l'auteur, à titre posthume.
posting ['pəustɪŋ] n (BRIT) affectation f.
postman ['pəustmən] n facteur m.
postmark ['pəustmɑ:k] n cachet m (de la poste).
postmaster ['pəustmɑ:stə*] n receveur m des postes.
Postmaster General n ≈ ministre m des Postes et Télécommunications.
postmistress ['pəustmɪstrɪs] n receveuse f des postes.
post-mortem [pəust'mɔ:təm] n autopsie f.
postnatal ['pəust'neɪtl] adj post-natal(e).
post office n (building) poste f; (organization) postes fpl.
post office box (PO box) n boîte postale (B.P.).
post-paid ['pəust'peɪd] adj (BRIT) port payé.
postpone [pəs'pəun] vt remettre (à plus tard), reculer.
postponement [pəs'pəunmənt] n ajournement m, renvoi m.
postscript ['pəustskrɪpt] n post-scriptum m.
postulate ['pɔstjuleɪt] vt postuler.
posture ['pɔstʃə*] n posture f, attitude f ♦ vi poser.
postwar ['pəust'wɔ:*] adj d'après-guerre.
posy ['pəuzɪ] n petit bouquet.
pot [pɔt] n (for cooking) marmite f; casserole f; (for plants, jam) pot m; (piece of pottery) poterie f; (col: marijuana) herbe f ♦ vt (plant) mettre en pot; **to go to ~** aller à vau-l'eau; **~s of** (BRIT col) beaucoup de, plein de.
potash ['pɔtæʃ] n potasse f.
potassium [pə'tæsɪəm] n potassium m.

potato, ~es [pə'teɪtəu] n pomme f de terre.
potato crisps, (US) potato chips npl chips mpl.
potato flour n fécule f.
potato peeler n épluche-légumes m.
potbellied ['pɒtbelɪd] adj (from overeating) bedonnant(e); (from malnutrition) au ventre ballonné.
potency ['pəutnsɪ] n puissance f, force f; (of drink) degré m d'alcool.
potent ['pəutnt] adj puissant(e); (drink) fort(e), très alcoolisé(e).
potentate ['pəutnteɪt] n potentat m.
potential [pə'tɛnʃl] adj potentiel(le) ♦ n potentiel m; **to have ~** être prometteur(euse); ouvrir des possibilités.
potentially [pə'tɛnʃəlɪ] adv potentiellement; **it's ~ dangerous** ça pourrait se révéler dangereux, il y a possibilité de danger.
pothole ['pɒthəul] n (in road) nid m de poule; (BRIT: underground) gouffre m, caverne f.
potholer ['pɒthəulə*] n (BRIT) spéléologue m/f.
potholing ['pɒthəulɪŋ] n (BRIT): **to go ~** faire de la spéléologie.
potion ['pəuʃən] n potion f.
potluck [pɒt'lʌk] n: **to take ~** tenter sa chance.
potpourri [pəu'puriː] n pot-pourri m.
pot roast n rôti m à la cocotte.
potshot ['pɒtʃɒt] n: **to take ~s at** canarder.
potted ['pɒtɪd] adj (food) en conserve; (plant) en pot; (fig: shortened) abrégé(e).
potter ['pɒtə*] n potier m ♦ vi (BRIT): **to ~ around, ~ about** bricoler; **~'s wheel** tour m de potier.
pottery ['pɒtərɪ] n poterie f; **a piece of ~** une poterie.
potty ['pɒtɪ] adj (BRIT col: mad) dingue ♦ n (child's) pot m.
potty-training ['pɒtɪtreɪnɪŋ] n apprentissage m de la propreté.
pouch [pautʃ] n (ZOOL) poche f; (for tobacco) blague f.
pouf(fe) [puːf] n (stool) pouf m.
poultice ['pəultɪs] n cataplasme m.
poultry ['pəultrɪ] n volaille f.
poultry farm n élevage m de volaille.
poultry farmer n aviculteur m.
pounce [pauns] vi: **to ~ (on)** bondir (sur), fondre (sur) ♦ n bond m, attaque f.
pound [paund] n livre f (weight = 453g, 16 ounces; money = 100 pence); (for dogs, cars) fourrière f ♦ vt (beat) bourrer de coups, marteler; (crush) piler, pulvériser; (with guns) pilonner ♦ vi (beat) battre violemment, taper; **half a ~ (of)** une demi-livre (de); **a five-~ note** un billet de cinq livres.
pounding ['paundɪŋ] n: **to take a ~** (fig) prendre une râclée.
pound sterling n livre f sterling.
pour [pɔː*] vt verser ♦ vi couler à flots; (rain) pleuvoir à verse; **to come ~ing in** (water) entrer à flots; (letters) arriver par milliers; (cars, people) affluer.
►**pour away, pour off** vt vider.
►**pour in** vi (people) affluer, se précipiter.
►**pour out** vi (people) sortir en masse ♦ vt vider; déverser; (serve: a drink) verser.
pouring ['pɔːrɪŋ] adj: **~ rain** pluie torrentielle.
pout [paut] n moue f ♦ vi faire la moue.
poverty ['pɒvətɪ] n pauvreté f, misère f.
poverty line n seuil m de pauvreté.
poverty-stricken ['pɒvətɪstrɪkn] adj pauvre, déshérité(e).
poverty trap n (BRIT) piège m de la pauvreté.
POW n abbr = **prisoner of war**.
powder ['paudə*] n poudre f ♦ vt poudrer; **~ one's nose** se poudrer; (euphemism) aller à la salle de bain; **~ed milk** lait m en poudre.
powder compact n poudrier m.
powder keg n (fig) poudrière f.
powder puff n houppette f.
powder room n toilettes fpl (pour dames).
powdery ['paudərɪ] adj poudreux(euse).
power ['pauə*] n (strength) puissance f, force f; (ability, POL: of party, leader) pouvoir m; (MATH) puissance; (of speech, thought) faculté f; (ELEC) courant m ♦ vt faire marcher, actionner; **to do all in one's ~ to help sb** faire tout ce qui est en son pouvoir pour aider qn; **the world ~s** les grandes puissances; **to be in ~** être au pouvoir.
powerboat ['pauəbəut] n (BRIT) hors-bord m.
power cut n (BRIT) coupure f de courant.
powered ['pauəd] adj: **~ by** actionné(e) par, fonctionnant à; **nuclear-~ submarine** sous-marin m (à propulsion) nucléaire.
power failure n panne f de courant.
powerful ['pauəful] adj puissant(e).
powerhouse ['pauəhaus] n (fig: person) fonceur m; **a ~ of ideas** une mine d'idées.
powerless ['pauəlɪs] adj impuissant(e).
power line n ligne f électrique.
power of attorney n procuration f.
power point n (BRIT) prise f de courant.
power station n centrale f électrique.
power steering n direction assistée.
powwow ['pauwau] n conciliabule m.
pox [pɒks] n see **chickenpox**.
pp abbr (= per procurationem: by proxy) p.p.
PPE n abbr (BRIT SCOL) = **philosophy, politics and economics**.
PPS n abbr (= post postscriptum) PPS; (BRIT: = parliamentary private secretary) parlementaire chargé de mission auprès d'un ministre.
PQ abbr (Canada: = Province of Quebec) PQ.
PR n abbr = **proportional representation, public relations** ♦ abbr (US) = **Puerto Rico**.
Pr. abbr (= prince) Pce.
practicability [præktɪkə'bɪlɪtɪ] n possibilité f de réalisation.
practicable ['præktɪkəbl] adj (scheme) réalisable.

practical ['præktɪkl] *adj* pratique.
practicality [præktɪ'kælɪtɪ] *n* (*of plan*) aspect *m* pratique; (*of person*) sens *m* pratique; **practicalities** *npl* détails *mpl* pratiques.
practical joke *n* farce *f*.
practically ['præktɪklɪ] *adv* (*almost*) pratiquement.
practice ['præktɪs] *n* pratique *f*; (*of profession*) exercice *m*; (*at football etc*) entraînement *m*; (*business*) cabinet *m*; clientèle *f* ♦ *vt, vi* (*US*) = **practise**; **in ~** (*in reality*) en pratique; **out of ~** rouillé(e); **2 hours' piano ~** 2 heures de travail *or* d'exercices au piano; **target ~** exercices de tir; **it's common ~** c'est courant, ça se fait couramment; **to put sth into ~** mettre qch en pratique.
practice match *n* match *m* d'entraînement.
practise, (*US*) **practice** ['præktɪs] *vt* (*work at: piano, one's backhand etc*) s'exercer à, travailler; (*train for: skiing, running etc*) s'entraîner à; (*a sport, religion, method*) pratiquer; (*profession*) exercer ♦ *vi* s'exercer, travailler; (*train*) s'entraîner; **to ~ for a match** s'entraîner pour un match.
practised, (*US*) **practiced** ['præktɪst] *adj* (*person*) expérimenté(e); (*performance*) impeccable; (*liar*) invétéré(e); **with a ~ eye** d'un œil exercé.
practising, (*US*) **practicing** ['præktɪsɪŋ] *adj* (*Christian etc*) pratiquant(e); (*lawyer*) en exercice; (*homosexual*) déclaré.
practitioner [præk'tɪʃənə*] *n* praticien/ne.
pragmatic [præg'mætɪk] *adj* pragmatique.
Prague [prɑːg] *n* Prague.
prairie ['preərɪ] *n* savane *f*; (*US*): **the ~s** la Prairie.
praise [preɪz] *n* éloge(s) *m(pl)*, louange(s) *f(pl)* ♦ *vt* louer, faire l'éloge de.
praiseworthy ['preɪzwɜːðɪ] *adj* digne de louanges.
pram [præm] *n* (*BRIT*) landau *m*, voiture *f* d'enfant.
prance [prɑːns] *vi* (*horse*) caracoler.
prank [præŋk] *n* farce *f*.
prat [præt] *n* (*BRIT col*) imbécile *m*, andouille *f*.
prattle ['prætl] *vi* jacasser.
prawn [prɔːn] *n* crevette *f* (rose).
pray [preɪ] *vi* prier.
prayer [preə*] *n* prière *f*.
prayer book *n* livre *m* de prières.
pre... ['priː] *prefix* pré...; **~-1970** *adj* d'avant 1970 ♦ *adv* avant 1970.
preach [priːtʃ] *vt, vi* prêcher; **to ~ at sb** faire la morale à qn.
preacher ['priːtʃə*] *n* prédicateur *m*; (*US: clergyman*) pasteur *m*.
preamble [prɪ'æmbl] *n* préambule *m*.
prearranged [priːə'reɪndʒd] *adj* organisé(e) *or* fixé(e) à l'avance.
precarious [prɪ'kɛərɪəs] *adj* précaire.
precaution [prɪ'kɔːʃən] *n* précaution *f*.
precautionary [prɪ'kɔːʃənrɪ] *adj* (*measure*) de

précaution.
precede [prɪ'siːd] *vt, vi* précéder.
precedence ['prɛsɪdəns] *n* préséance *f*.
precedent ['prɛsɪdənt] *n* précédent *m*; **to establish** *or* **set a ~** créer un précédent.
preceding [prɪ'siːdɪŋ] *adj* qui précède (*or* précédait).
precept ['priːsɛpt] *n* précepte *m*.
precinct ['priːsɪŋkt] *n* (*round cathedral*) pourtour *m*, enceinte *f*; (*US: district*) circonscription *f*, arrondissement *m*; **~s** *npl* (*neighbourhood*) alentours *mpl*, environs *mpl*; **pedestrian ~** zone piétonne; **shopping ~** (*BRIT*) centre commercial.
precious ['prɛʃəs] *adj* précieux(euse) ♦ *adv* (*col*): **~ little** *or* **few** fort peu; **your ~ dog** (*ironic*) ton chien chéri, ton chéri chien.
precipice ['prɛsɪpɪs] *n* précipice *m*.
precipitate *adj* [prɪ'sɪpɪtɪt] (*hasty*) précipité(e) ♦ *vt* [prɪ'sɪpɪteɪt] précipiter.
precipitation [prɪsɪpɪ'teɪʃən] *n* précipitation *f*.
precipitous [prɪ'sɪpɪtəs] *adj* (*steep*) abrupt(e), à pic.
précis, *pl* **précis** ['preɪsiː, -z] *n* résumé *m*.
precise [prɪ'saɪs] *adj* précis(e).
precisely [prɪ'saɪslɪ] *adv* précisément.
precision [prɪ'sɪʒən] *n* précision *f*.
preclude [prɪ'kluːd] *vt* exclure, empêcher; **to ~ sb from doing** empêcher qn de faire.
precocious [prɪ'kəʊʃəs] *adj* précoce.
preconceived [priːkən'siːvd] *adj* (*idea*) préconçu(e).
preconception [priːkən'sɛpʃən] *n* idée préconçue.
precondition ['priːkən'dɪʃən] *n* condition *f* nécessaire.
precursor [priː'kɜːsə*] *n* précurseur *m*.
predate ['priː'deɪt] *vt* (*precede*) antidater.
predator ['predətə*] *n* prédateur *m*, rapace *m*.
predatory ['predətərɪ] *adj* rapace.
predecessor ['priːdɪsɛsə*] *n* prédécesseur *m*.
predestination [priːdɛstɪ'neɪʃən] *n* prédestination *f*.
predetermine [priːdɪ'tɜːmɪn] *vt* déterminer à l'avance.
predicament [prɪ'dɪkəmənt] *n* situation *f* difficile.
predicate ['predɪkɪt] *n* (*LING*) prédicat *m*.
predict [prɪ'dɪkt] *vt* prédire.
predictable [prɪ'dɪktəbl] *adj* prévisible.
predictably [prɪ'dɪktəblɪ] *adv* (*behave, react*) de façon prévisible; **~ she didn't arrive** comme on pouvait s'y attendre, elle n'est pas venue.
prediction [prɪ'dɪkʃən] *n* prédiction *f*.
predispose [priːdɪs'pəʊz] *vt* prédisposer.
predominance [prɪ'dɒmɪnəns] *n* prédominance *f*.
predominant [prɪ'dɒmɪnənt] *adj* prédominant(e).
predominantly [prɪ'dɒmɪnəntlɪ] *adv* en majeure partie; surtout.

predominate [prɪ'dɔmɪneɪt] vi prédominer.
pre-eminent [pri:'ɛmɪnənt] adj prééminent(e).
pre-empt [pri:'ɛmt] vt (BRIT) acquérir par
droit de préemption; (fig) anticiper sur; **to
~ the issue** conclure avant même d'ouvrir
les débats.
pre-emptive [prɪ'ɛmtɪv] adj: **~ strike** attaque
(or action) préventive.
preen [pri:n] vt: **to ~ itself** (bird) se lisser les
plumes; **to ~ o.s.** s'admirer.
prefab ['pri:fæb] n bâtiment préfabriqué.
prefabricated [pri:'fæbrɪkeɪtɪd] adj
préfabriqué(e).
preface ['prɛfəs] n préface f.
prefect ['pri:fɛkt] n (BRIT: in school) élève
chargé de certaines fonctions de discipline;
(in France) préfet m.
prefer [prɪ'fə:*] vt préférer; (LAW): **to ~
charges** procéder à une inculpation; **to ~
coffee to tea** préférer le café au thé.
preferable ['prɛfrəbl] adj préférable.
preferably ['prɛfrəblɪ] adv de préférence.
preference ['prɛfrəns] n préférence f; **in ~ to
sth** plutôt que qch, de préférence à qch.
preference shares npl (BRIT) actions
privilégiées.
preferential [prɛfə'rɛnʃəl] adj préférentiel(le);
~ treatment traitement m de faveur.
preferred stock [prɪ'fə:d-] npl (US)
= preference shares.
prefix ['pri:fɪks] n préfixe m.
pregnancy ['prɛgnənsɪ] n grossesse f.
pregnancy test n test m de grossesse.
pregnant ['prɛgnənt] adj enceinte adj f; **3
months ~** enceinte de 3 mois.
prehistoric ['pri:hɪs'tɔrɪk] adj préhistorique.
prehistory ['pri:'hɪstərɪ] n préhistoire f.
prejudge [pri:'dʒʌdʒ] vt préjuger de.
prejudice ['prɛdʒudɪs] n préjugé m; (harm) tort
m, préjudice m ♦ vt porter préjudice à;
(bias): **to ~ sb in favour of/against** prévenir
qn en faveur de/contre.
prejudiced ['prɛdʒudɪst] adj (person) plein(e)
de préjugés; (view) préconçu(e), partial(e);
to be ~ against sb/sth avoir un parti-pris
contre qn/qch.
prelate ['prɛlət] n prélat m.
preliminaries [prɪ'lɪmɪnərɪz] npl préliminaires
mpl.
preliminary [prɪ'lɪmɪnərɪ] adj préliminaire.
prelude ['prɛljuːd] n prélude m.
premarital ['pri:'mærɪtl] adj avant le mariage.
premature ['prɛmətʃuə*] adj prématuré(e); **to
be ~ (in doing sth)** aller un peu (trop) vite
(en faisant qch).
premeditated [pri:'mɛdɪteɪtɪd] adj
prémédité(e).
premeditation [pri:mɛdɪ'teɪʃən] n
préméditation f.
premenstrual [pri:'mɛnstruəl] adj
prémenstruel(le).
premenstrual tension n irritabilité f avant

les règles.
premier ['prɛmɪə*] adj premier(ière),
principal(e) ♦ n (POL) premier ministre.
premiere ['prɛmɪɛə*] n première f.
premise ['prɛmɪs] n prémisse f.
premises ['prɛmɪsɪz] npl locaux mpl; **on the ~**
sur les lieux; sur place; **business ~** locaux
commerciaux.
premium ['pri:mɪəm] n prime f; **to be at a ~**
(fig: housing etc) être très demandé(e), être
rarissime; **to sell at a ~** (shares) vendre au-
dessus du pair.
premium bond n (BRIT) bon m à lots.

> Les **premium bonds** sont des bons du Trésor
> que le public peut acheter. Les intérêts ne sont
> pas versés, mais il y a chaque mois un tirage
> au sort par ordinateur. Les personnes dont le
> bon a été sélectionné gagnent une somme
> d'argent pouvant aller de quelques livres à
> plusieurs milliers de livres.

premium deal n (COMM) offre spéciale.
premium gasoline n (US) super m.
premonition [prɛmə'nɪʃən] n prémonition f.
preoccupation [pri:ɔkju'peɪʃən] n
préoccupation f.
preoccupied [pri:'ɔkjupaɪd] adj préoccupé(e).
prep [prɛp] adj abbr: **~ school** = **preparatory
school** ♦ n abbr (SCOL: = preparation) étude f.
prepackaged [pri:'pækɪdʒd] adj
préempaqueté(e).
prepaid [pri:'peɪd] adj payé(e) d'avance.
preparation [prɛpə'reɪʃən] n préparation f; **~s**
(for trip, war) préparatifs mpl; **in ~ for** en vue
de.
preparatory [prɪ'pærətərɪ] adj préparatoire; **~
to sth/to doing sth** en prévision de qch/
avant de faire qch.
preparatory school n école primaire privée;
(US) lycée privé.

> En Grande-Bretagne, une **preparatory school** -
> ou, plus familièrement, une **prep school** - est
> une école payante qui prépare les enfants de 7
> à 13 ans aux **public schools**.

prepare [prɪ'pɛə*] vt préparer ♦ vi: **to ~ for** se
préparer à.
prepared [prɪ'pɛəd] adj: **~ for** préparé(e) à; **~
to** prêt(e) à.
preponderance [prɪ'pɔndərns] n
prépondérance f.
preposition [prɛpə'zɪʃən] n préposition f.
prepossessing [pri:pə'zɛsɪŋ] adj avenant(e),
engageant(e).
preposterous [prɪ'pɔstərəs] adj absurde.
prep school n = **preparatory school**.
prerecord ['pri:rɪ'kɔːd] vt: **~ed broadcast**
émission f en différé; **~ed cassette** cassette
enregistrée.
prerequisite [pri:'rɛkwɪzɪt] n condition f

préalable.

prerogative [prɪˈrɔgətɪv] *n* prérogative *f*.

presbyterian [prezbɪˈtɪərɪən] *adj, n* presbytérien(ne).

presbytery [ˈprezbɪtərɪ] *n* presbytère *m*.

preschool [ˈpriːˈskuːl] *adj* préscolaire; (*child*) d'âge préscolaire.

prescribe [prɪˈskraɪb] *vt* prescrire; ~**d books** (*BRIT SCOL*) œuvres *fpl* au programme.

prescription [prɪˈskrɪpʃən] *n* prescription *f*; (*MED*) ordonnance *f*; **to make up** *or* (*US*) **fill a** ~ faire une ordonnance; **"only available on** ~" "uniquement sur ordonnance".

prescription charges *npl* (*BRIT*) participation *f* fixe au coût de l'ordonnance.

prescriptive [prɪˈskrɪptɪv] *adj* normatif(ive).

presence [ˈprezns] *n* présence *f*; ~ **of mind** présence d'esprit.

present [ˈpreznt] *adj* présent(e) ♦ *n* cadeau *m*; (*also:* ~ **tense**) présent *m* ♦ *vt* [prɪˈzent] présenter; (*give*): **to** ~ **sb with sth** offrir qch à qn; **to be** ~ **at** assister à; **those** ~ les présents; **at** ~ en ce moment; **to give sb a** ~ offrir un cadeau à qn; **to** ~ **sb (to sb)** présenter qn (à qn).

presentable [prɪˈzentəbl] *adj* présentable.

presentation [preznˈteɪʃən] *n* présentation *f*; (*gift*) cadeau *m*, présent *m*; (*ceremony*) remise *f* du cadeau; **on** ~ **of** (*voucher etc*) sur présentation de.

present-day [ˈprezntdeɪ] *adj* contemporain(e), actuel(le).

presenter [prɪˈzentə*] *n* (*BRIT RADIO, TV*) présentateur/trice.

presently [ˈprezntlɪ] *adv* (*soon*) tout à l'heure, bientôt; (*at present*) en ce moment; (*US: now*) maintenant.

preservation [prezəˈveɪʃən] *n* préservation *f*, conservation *f*.

preservative [prɪˈzɜːvətɪv] *n* agent *m* de conservation.

preserve [prɪˈzɜːv] *vt* (*keep safe*) préserver, protéger; (*maintain*) conserver, garder; (*food*) mettre en conserve ♦ *n* (*for game, fish*) réserve *f*; (*often pl: jam*) confiture *f*; (*: fruit*) fruits *mpl* en conserve.

preshrunk [priːˈʃrʌŋk] *adj* irrétrécissable.

preside [prɪˈzaɪd] *vi* présider.

presidency [ˈprezɪdənsɪ] *n* présidence *f*.

president [ˈprezɪdənt] *n* président/e; (*US: of company*) président-directeur général, PDG *m*.

presidential [prezɪˈdenʃl] *adj* présidentiel(le).

press [pres] *n* (*tool, machine, newspapers*) presse *f*; (*for wine*) pressoir *m*; (*crowd*) cohue *f*, foule *f* ♦ *vt* (*push*) appuyer sur; (*squeeze*) presser, serrer; (*clothes: iron*) repasser; (*pursue*) talonner; (*insist*): **to** ~ **sth on sb** presser qn d'accepter qch; (*urge, entreat*): **to** ~ **sb to do** *or* **into doing sth** pousser qn à faire qch ♦ *vi* appuyer, peser; se presser; **we are** ~**ed for time** le temps nous manque;

to ~ **for sth** faire pression pour obtenir q(
to ~ **sb for an answer** presser qn de répondre; **to** ~ **charges against sb** (*LAW*) engager des poursuites contre qn; **to go t** ~ (*newspaper*) aller à l'impression; **to be i** **the** ~ (*being printed*) être sous presse; (*in* newspapers) être dans le journal.
►**press ahead** *vi* = **press on**.
►**press on** *vi* continuer.

press agency *n* agence *f* de presse.

press clipping *n* coupure *f* de presse.

press conference *n* conférence *f* de press(

press cutting *n* = **press clipping**.

press-gang [ˈpresgæŋ] *vt* (*fig*): **to** ~ **sb into** **doing sth** faire pression sur qn pour qu'il fasse qch.

pressing [ˈpresɪŋ] *adj* urgent(e), pressant(e ♦ *n* repassage *m*.

press officer *n* attaché/e de presse.

press release *n* communiqué *m* de presse.

press stud *n* (*BRIT*) bouton-pression *m*.

press-up [ˈpresʌp] *n* (*BRIT*) traction *f*.

pressure [ˈpreʃə*] *n* pression *f*; (*stress*) tens *f* ♦ *vt* = **to put** ~ **on**; **to put** ~ **on sb (to do s** faire pression sur qn (pour qu'il fasse qc

pressure cooker *n* cocotte-minute *f*.

pressure gauge *n* manomètre *m*.

pressure group *n* groupe *m* de pression.

pressurize [ˈpreʃəraɪz] *vt* pressuriser; (*BRIT* *fig*): **to** ~ **sb (into doing sth)** faire pression sur qn (pour qu'il fasse qch).

pressurized [ˈpreʃəraɪzd] *adj* pressurisé(e).

Prestel [ˈprestel] *n* ® ≈ Minitel *m* ®.

prestige [presˈtiːʒ] *n* prestige *m*.

prestigious [presˈtɪdʒəs] *adj* prestigieux(eus

presumably [prɪˈzjuːməblɪ] *adv* vraisemblablement; ~ **he did it** c'est sans doute lui (qui a fait cela).

presume [prɪˈzjuːm] *vt* présumer, supposer **to** ~ **to do** (*dare*) se permettre de faire.

presumption [prɪˈzʌmpʃən] *n* supposition *f*, présomption *f*; (*boldness*) audace *f*.

presumptuous [prɪˈzʌmpʃəs] *adj* présomptueux(euse).

presuppose [priːsəˈpəʊz] *vt* présupposer.

pre-tax [priːˈtæks] *adj* avant impôt(s).

pretence, **(*US*) pretense** [prɪˈtens] *n* (*claim* prétention *f*; (*pretext*) prétexte *m*; **she is** **devoid of all** ~ elle n'est pas du tout prétentieuse; **to make a** ~ **of doing faire** semblant de faire; **on** *or* **under the** ~ **of** **doing sth** sous prétexte de faire qch.

pretend [prɪˈtend] *vt* (*feign*) feindre, simule ♦ *vi* (*feign*) faire semblant; (*claim*): **to** ~ **to** **sth** prétendre à qch; **to** ~ **to do** faire semblant de faire.

pretense [prɪˈtens] *n* (*US*) = **pretence**.

pretension [prɪˈtenʃən] *n* (*claim*) prétention **to have no** ~**s to sth/to being sth** n'avoir aucune prétention à qch/à être qch.

pretentious [prɪˈtenʃəs] *adj* prétentieux(eus

preterite [ˈpretərɪt] *n* prétérit *m*.

pretext ['priːtɛkst] n prétexte m; **on** or **under the ~ of doing sth** sous prétexte de faire qch.

pretty ['prɪtɪ] adj joli(e) ♦ adv assez.

prevail [prɪ'veɪl] vi (win) l'emporter, prévaloir; (be usual) avoir cours; (persuade): **to ~ (up)on sb to do** persuader qn de faire.

prevailing [prɪ'veɪlɪŋ] adj dominant(e).

prevalent ['prɛvələnt] adj répandu(e), courant(e); (fashion) en vogue.

prevarication [prɪværɪ'keɪʃən] n (usage m de) faux-fuyants mpl.

prevent [prɪ'vɛnt] vt: **to ~ (from doing)** empêcher (de faire).

preventable [prɪ'vɛntəbl] adj évitable.

preventative [prɪ'vɛntətɪv] adj préventif(ive).

prevention [prɪ'vɛnʃən] n prévention f.

preventive [prɪ'vɛntɪv] adj préventif(ive).

preview ['priːvjuː] n (of film) avant-première f; (fig) aperçu m.

previous ['priːvɪəs] adj (last) précédent(e); (earlier) antérieur(e); (question, experience) préalable; **I have a ~ engagement** je suis déjà pris(e); **~ to doing** avant de faire.

previously ['priːvɪəslɪ] adv précédemment, auparavant.

prewar [priː'wɔː*] adj d'avant-guerre.

prey [preɪ] n proie f ♦ vi: **to ~ on** s'attaquer à; **it was ~ing on his mind** ça le rongeait or minait.

price [praɪs] n prix m; (BETTING: odds) cote f ♦ vt (goods) fixer le prix de; tarifer; **what is the ~ of ...?** combien coûte ...?, quel est le prix de ...?; **to go up** or **rise in ~** augmenter; **to put a ~ on sth** chiffrer qch; **to be ~d out of the market** (article) être trop cher pour soutenir la concurrence; (producer, nation) ne pas pouvoir soutenir la concurrence; **what ~ his promises now?** (BRIT) que valent maintenant toutes ses promesses?; **he regained his freedom, but at a ~** il a retrouvé sa liberté, mais cela lui a coûté cher.

price control n contrôle m des prix.

price-cutting ['praɪskʌtɪŋ] n réductions fpl de prix.

priceless ['praɪslɪs] adj sans prix, inestimable; (col: amusing) impayable.

price list n tarif m.

price range n gamme f de prix; **it's within my ~** c'est dans mes prix.

price tag n étiquette f.

price war n guerre f des prix.

pricey ['praɪsɪ] adj (col) chérot inv.

prick [prɪk] n piqûre f; (col!) bitte f (!); connard m (!) ♦ vt piquer; **to ~ up one's ears** dresser or tendre l'oreille.

prickle ['prɪkl] n (of plant) épine f; (sensation) picotement m.

prickly ['prɪklɪ] adj piquant(e), épineux(euse); (fig: person) irritable.

prickly heat n fièvre f miliaire.

prickly pear n figue f de Barbarie.

pride [praɪd] n (feeling proud) fierté f; (: pej) orgueil m; (self-esteem) amour-propre m ♦ vt: **to ~ o.s. on** se flatter de; s'enorgueillir de; **to take (a) ~ in** être (très) fier(ère) de; **to take a ~ in doing** mettre sa fierté à faire; **to have ~ of place** (BRIT) avoir la place d'honneur.

priest [priːst] n prêtre m.

priestess ['priːstɪs] n prêtresse f.

priesthood ['priːsthud] n prêtrise f, sacerdoce m.

prig [prɪg] n poseur/euse, fat m.

prim [prɪm] adj collet monté inv, guindé(e).

primacy ['praɪməsɪ] n primauté f.

prima facie ['praɪmə'feɪʃɪ] adj: **to have a ~ case** (LAW) avoir une affaire qui paraît fondée.

primal ['praɪməl] adj (first in time) primitif(ive); (first in importance) primordial(e).

primarily ['praɪmərɪlɪ] adv principalement, essentiellement.

primary ['praɪmərɪ] adj primaire; (first in importance) premier(ière), primordial(e) ♦ n (US: election) (élection f) primaire f.

*Aux États-Unis, les **primaries** constituent un processus de sélection préliminaire des candidats qui seront choisis par les principaux partis lors de la campagne électorale pour les élections présidentielles. Elles ont lieu dans 35 États, de février à juin, l'année des élections. La plupart du temps, le nombre de **delegates** sera proportionnel au nombre de voix lors des conventions démocrate et républicaine en juillet-août, au cours desquelles on procède au choix final d'un candidat à la présidence.*

primary colour n couleur fondamentale.

primary school n (BRIT) école f primaire.

*Les **primary schools** en Grande-Bretagne accueillent les enfants de 5 à 11 ans. Elles marquent le début du cycle scolaire obligatoire et elles comprennent deux sections: la section des petits ("infant school") et la section des grands ("junior school"); voir **secondary school***

primate n (REL) ['praɪmɪt] primat m; (ZOOL) ['praɪmeɪt] primate m.

prime [praɪm] adj primordial(e), fondamental(e); (excellent) excellent(e) ♦ vt (gun, pump) amorcer; (fig) mettre au courant; **in the ~ of life** dans la fleur de l'âge.

prime minister n Premier ministre m.

primer ['praɪmə*] n (book) premier livre, manuel m élémentaire; (paint) apprêt m; (of gun) amorce f.

prime time n (RADIO, TV) heure(s) f(pl) de

grande écoute.
primeval [praɪˈmiːvl] *adj* primitif(ive).
primitive [ˈprɪmɪtɪv] *adj* primitif(ive).
primrose [ˈprɪmrəʊz] *n* primevère *f*.
primus (stove) [ˈpraɪməs-] *n* ® (*BRIT*) réchaud *m* de camping.
prince [prɪns] *n* prince *m*.
princess [prɪnˈsɛs] *n* princesse *f*.
principal [ˈprɪnsɪpl] *adj* principal(e) ♦ *n* (*headmaster*) directeur *m*, principal *m*; (*in play*) rôle principal; (*money*) principal *m*.
principality [prɪnsɪˈpælɪtɪ] *n* principauté *f*.
principally [ˈprɪnsɪplɪ] *adv* principalement.
principle [ˈprɪnsɪpl] *n* principe *m*; **in** ~ en principe; **on** ~ par principe.
print [prɪnt] *n* (*mark*) empreinte *f*; (*letters*) caractères *mpl*; (*fabric*) imprimé *m*; (*ART*) gravure *f*, estampe *f*; (*PHOT*) épreuve *f* ♦ *vt* imprimer; (*publish*) publier; (*write in capitals*) écrire en majuscules; **out of** ~ épuisé(e).
▶**print out** *vt* (*COMPUT*) imprimer.
printed circuit board (PCB) [ˈprɪntɪd-] *n* carte *f* à circuit imprimé.
printed matter [ˈprɪntɪd-] *n* imprimés *mpl*.
printer [ˈprɪntə*] *n* imprimeur *m*; (*machine*) imprimante *f*.
printhead [ˈprɪnthɛd] *n* tête *f* d'impression.
printing [ˈprɪntɪŋ] *n* impression *f*.
printing press *n* presse *f* typographique.
print-out [ˈprɪntaut] *n* listing *m*.
print wheel *n* marguerite *f*.
prior [ˈpraɪə*] *adj* antérieur(e), précédent(e) ♦ *n* (*REL*) prieur *m*; ~ **to doing** avant de faire; **without** ~ **notice** sans préavis; **to have a** ~ **claim to sth** avoir priorité pour qch.
priority [praɪˈɒrɪtɪ] *n* priorité *f*; **to have** or **take** ~ **over sth/sb** avoir la priorité sur qch/qn.
priory [ˈpraɪərɪ] *n* prieuré *m*.
prise [praɪz] *vt*: **to** ~ **open** forcer.
prism [ˈprɪzəm] *n* prisme *m*.
prison [ˈprɪzn] *n* prison *f*.
prison camp *n* camp *m* de prisonniers.
prisoner [ˈprɪznə*] *n* prisonnier/ière; **the** ~ **at the bar** l'accusé/e; **to take sb** ~ faire qn prisonnier; ~ **of war** prisonnier de guerre.
prissy [ˈprɪsɪ] *adj* bégueule.
pristine [ˈprɪstiːn] *adj* virginal(e).
privacy [ˈprɪvəsɪ] *n* intimité *f*, solitude *f*.
private [ˈpraɪvɪt] *adj* (*not public*) privé(e); (*personal*) personnel(le); (*house, car, lesson*) particulier(ière) ♦ *n* soldat *m* de deuxième classe; "~" (*on envelope*) "personnelle"; **in** ~ en privé; **in (his)** ~ **life** dans sa vie privée; **he is a very** ~ **person** il est très secret; **to be in** ~ **practice** être médecin (*or* dentiste *etc*) non conventionné; ~ **hearing** (*LAW*) audience *f* à huis-clos.
private enterprise *n* entreprise privée.
private eye *n* détective privé.
private limited company *n* (*BRIT*) société *f* à participation restreinte (*non cotée en Bourse*).

privately [ˈpraɪvɪtlɪ] *adv* en privé; (*within oneself*) intérieurement.
private parts *npl* parties (génitales).
private property *n* propriété privée.
private school *n* école privée.
privation [praɪˈveɪʃən] *n* privation *f*.
privatize [ˈpraɪvɪtaɪz] *vt* privatiser.
privet [ˈprɪvɪt] *n* troène *m*.
privilege [ˈprɪvɪlɪdʒ] *n* privilège *m*.
privileged [ˈprɪvɪlɪdʒd] *adj* privilégié(e); **to** ~ **to do sth** avoir le privilège de faire qch
privy [ˈprɪvɪ] *adj*: **to be** ~ **to** être au courant de.
privy council *n* conseil privé.

Le **privy council** *existe en Angleterre depuis l'avènement des Normands. À l'époque, ses membres étaient les conseillers privés du ro mais en 1688 le cabinet les a supplantés. Le ministres du cabinet sont aujourd'hui automatiquement conseillers du roi, et ce ti est également accordé aux personnes qui on occupé de hautes fonctions en politique, dan le clergé ou dans les milieux juridiques. Les pouvoirs de ces conseillers en tant que tels sont maintenant limités.*

prize [praɪz] *n* prix *m* ♦ *adj* (*example, idiot*) parfait(e); (*bull, novel*) primé(e) ♦ *vt* prise faire grand cas de.
prize-fighter [ˈpraɪzfaɪtə*] *n* boxeur professionnel.
prize giving *n* distribution *f* des prix.
prize money *n* argent *m* du prix.
prizewinner [ˈpraɪzwɪnə*] *n* gagnant/e.
prizewinning [ˈpraɪzwɪnɪŋ] *adj* gagnant(e); (*novel, essay etc*) primé(e).
PRO *n abbr* = **public relations officer**.
pro [prəʊ] *n* (*SPORT*) professionnel/le; **the** ~ **and cons** le pour et le contre.
pro- [prəʊ] *prefix* (*in favour of*) pro-.
pro-active [prəʊˈæktɪv] *adj* dynamique.
probability [prɒbəˈbɪlɪtɪ] *n* probabilité *f*; **in** ~ très probablement.
probable [ˈprɒbəbl] *adj* probable; **it is** ~/**hard** ~ **that ...** il est probable/peu probable que ....
probably [ˈprɒbəblɪ] *adv* probablement.
probate [ˈprəʊbɪt] *n* (*LAW*) validation *f*, homologation *f*.
probation [prəˈbeɪʃən] *n* (*in employment*) (période *f* d')essai *m*; (*LAW*) liberté surveillée; (*REL*) noviciat *m*, probation *f*; **o** ~ (*employee*) à l'essai; (*LAW*) en liberté surveillée.
probationary [prəˈbeɪʃənrɪ] *adj* (*period*) d'essai.
probe [prəʊb] *n* (*MED, SPACE*) sonde *f*; (*enqu* enquête *f*, investigation *f* ♦ *vt* sonder, explorer.
probity [ˈprəʊbɪtɪ] *n* probité *f*.
problem [ˈprɒbləm] *n* problème *m*; **to have**

with the car avoir des ennuis avec la voiture; **what's the ~?** qu'y a-t-il?, quel est le problème?; **I had no ~ in finding her** je n'ai pas eu de mal à la trouver; **no ~!** pas de problème!

problematic [prɔblə'mætɪk] *adj* problématique.

problem-solving ['prɔbləmsɔlvɪŋ] *n* résolution *f* de problèmes; **an approach to ~** une approche en matière de résolution de problèmes.

procedure [prə'siːdʒə*] *n* (*ADMIN, LAW*) procédure *f*; (*method*) marche *f* à suivre, façon *f* de procéder.

proceed [prə'siːd] *vi* (*go forward*) avancer; (*go about it*) procéder; (*continue*): **to ~ (with)** continuer, poursuivre; **to ~ to** aller à; passer à; **to ~ to do** se mettre à faire; **I am not sure how to ~** je ne sais pas exactement comment m'y prendre; **to ~ against sb** (*LAW*) intenter des poursuites contre qn.

proceedings [prə'siːdɪŋz] *npl* mesures *fpl*; (*LAW*) poursuites *fpl*; (*meeting*) réunion *f*, séance *f*; (*records*) compte rendu; actes *mpl*.

proceeds ['prəusiːdz] *npl* produit *m*, recette *f*.

process ['prəusɛs] *n* processus *m*; (*method*) procédé *m* ♦ *vt* traiter ♦ *vi* [prə'sɛs] (*BRIT formal: go in procession*) défiler; **in ~** en cours; **we are in the ~ of doing** nous sommes en train de faire.

processed cheese ['prəusɛst-] *n* ≈ fromage fondu.

processing ['prəusɛsɪŋ] *n* traitement *m*.

procession [prə'sɛʃən] *n* défilé *m*, cortège *m*; **funeral ~** cortège funèbre, convoi *m* mortuaire.

pro-choice [prəu'tʃɔɪs] *adj* en faveur de l'avortement.

proclaim [prə'kleɪm] *vt* déclarer, proclamer.

proclamation [prɔklə'meɪʃən] *n* proclamation *f*.

proclivity [prə'klɪvɪtɪ] *n* inclination *f*.

procrastination [prəukræstɪ'neɪʃən] *n* procrastination *f*.

procreation [prəukrɪ'eɪʃən] *n* procréation *f*.

Procurator Fiscal ['prɔkjureɪtə-] *n* (*Scottish*) ≈ procureur *m* (*de la République*).

procure [prə'kjuə*] *vt* (*for o.s.*) se procurer; (*for sb*) procurer.

procurement [prə'kjuəmənt] *n* achat *m*, approvisionnement *m*.

prod [prɔd] *vt* pousser ♦ *n* (*push, jab*) petit coup, poussée *f*.

prodigal ['prɔdɪgl] *adj* prodigue.

prodigious [prə'dɪdʒəs] *adj* prodigieux(euse).

prodigy ['prɔdɪdʒɪ] *n* prodige *m*.

produce *n* ['prɔdjuːs] (*AGR*) produits *mpl* ♦ *vt* [prə'djuːs] produire; (*to show*) présenter; (*cause*) provoquer, causer; (*THEAT*) monter, mettre en scène.

producer [prə'djuːsə*] *n* (*THEAT*) metteur *m* en scène; (*AGR, CINE*) producteur *m*.

product ['prɔdʌkt] *n* produit *m*.

production [prə'dʌkʃən] *n* production *f*; (*THEAT*) mise *f* en scène; **to put into ~** (*goods*) entreprendre la fabrication de.

production agreement *n* (*US*) accord *m* de productivité.

production line *n* chaîne *f* (de fabrication).

production manager *n* directeur/trice de la production.

productive [prə'dʌktɪv] *adj* productif(ive).

productivity [prɔdʌk'tɪvɪtɪ] *n* productivité *f*.

productivity agreement *n* (*BRIT*) accord *m* de productivité.

productivity bonus *n* prime *f* de rendement.

Prof. [prɔf] *abbr* (= *professor*) Prof.

profane [prə'feɪn] *adj* sacrilège; (*lay*) profane.

profess [prə'fɛs] *vt* professer; **I do not ~ to be an expert** je ne prétends pas être spécialiste.

professed [prə'fɛst] *adj* (*self-declared*) déclaré(e).

profession [prə'fɛʃən] *n* profession *f*; **the ~s** les professions libérales.

professional [prə'fɛʃənl] *n* (*SPORT*) professionnel/le ♦ *adj* professionnel(le); (*work*) de professionnel; **he's a ~ man** il exerce une profession libérale; **to take ~ advice** consulter un spécialiste.

professionalism [prə'fɛʃnəlɪzəm] *n* professionnalisme *m*.

professionally [prə'fɛʃnəlɪ] *adv* professionnellement; (*SPORT: play*) en professionnel; **I only know him ~** je n'ai avec lui que des relations de travail.

professor [prə'fɛsə*] *n* professeur *m* (*titulaire d'une chaire*); (*US: teacher*) professeur *m*.

professorship [prə'fɛsəʃɪp] *n* chaire *f*.

proffer ['prɔfə*] *vt* (*hand*) tendre; (*remark*) faire; (*apologies*) présenter.

proficiency [prə'fɪʃənsɪ] *n* compétence *f*, aptitude *f*.

proficient [prə'fɪʃənt] *adj* compétent(e), capable.

profile ['prəufaɪl] *n* profil *m*; **to keep a high/ low ~** (*fig*) rester *or* être très en évidence/ discret(ète).

profit ['prɔfɪt] *n* (*from trading*) bénéfice *m*; (*advantage*) profit *m* ♦ *vi*: **to ~ (by *or* from)** profiter (de); **~ and loss account** compte *m* de profits et pertes; **to make a ~** faire un *or* des bénéfice(s); **to sell sth at a ~** vendre qch à profit.

profitability [prɔfɪtə'bɪlɪtɪ] *n* rentabilité *f*.

profitable ['prɔfɪtəbl] *adj* lucratif(ive), rentable; (*fig: beneficial*) avantageux(euse); (*: meeting*) fructueux(euse).

profit centre *n* centre *m* de profit.

profiteering [prɔfɪ'tɪərɪŋ] *n* (*pej*) mercantilisme *m*.

profit-making ['prɔfɪtmeɪkɪŋ] *adj* à but lucratif.

profit margin *n* marge *f* bénéficiaire.

profit-sharing ['prɔfɪtʃɛərɪŋ] n intéressement m aux bénéfices.

profits tax n (BRIT) impôt m sur les bénéfices.

profligate ['prɔflɪgɪt] adj (behaviour, act) dissolu(e); (person) débauché(e); (extravagant): ~ **(with)** prodigue (de).

pro forma ['prəʊ'fɔːmə] adj: ~ **invoice** facture f pro-forma.

profound [prə'faund] adj profond(e).

profuse [prə'fjuːs] adj abondant(e).

profusely [prə'fjuːslɪ] adv abondamment; (thank etc) avec effusion.

profusion [prə'fjuːʒən] n profusion f, abondance f.

progeny ['prɔdʒɪnɪ] n progéniture f; descendants mpl.

programme, (US, also: BRIT COMPUT) **program** ['prəʊgræm] n programme m; (RADIO, TV) émission f ♦ vt programmer.

program(m)er ['prəʊgræmə*] n programmeur/euse.

program(m)ing ['prəʊgræmɪŋ] n programmation f.

program(m)ing language n langage m de programmation.

progress n ['prəʊgrɛs] progrès m ♦ vi [prə'grɛs] progresser, avancer; **in** ~ en cours; **to make** ~ progresser, faire des progrès, être en progrès; **as the match** ~ed au fur et à mesure que la partie avançait.

progression [prə'grɛʃən] n progression f.

progressive [prə'grɛsɪv] adj progressif(ive); (person) progressiste.

progressively [prə'grɛsɪvlɪ] adv progressivement.

progress report n (MED) bulletin m de santé; (ADMIN) rapport m d'activité; rapport sur l'état (d'avancement) des travaux.

prohibit [prə'hɪbɪt] vt interdire, défendre; **to** ~ **sb from doing sth** défendre or interdire à qn de faire qch; **"smoking** ~ed" "défense de fumer".

prohibition [prəʊɪ'bɪʃən] n prohibition f.

prohibitive [prə'hɪbɪtɪv] adj (price etc) prohibitif(ive).

project n ['prɔdʒɛkt] (plan) projet m, plan m; (venture) opération f, entreprise f; (gen SCOL: research) étude f, dossier m ♦ vb [prə'dʒɛkt] vt projeter ♦ vi (stick out) faire saillie, s'avancer.

projectile [prə'dʒɛktaɪl] n projectile m.

projection [prə'dʒɛkʃən] n projection f; (overhang) saillie f.

projectionist [prə'dʒɛkʃənɪst] n (CINE) projectionniste m/f.

projection room n (CINE) cabine f de projection.

projector [prə'dʒɛktə*] n (CINE etc) projecteur m.

proletarian [prəʊlɪ'tɛərɪən] adj prolétarien(ne) ♦ n prolétaire m/f.

proletariat [prəʊlɪ'tɛərɪət] n prolétariat m.

pro-life [prəʊ'laɪf] adj contre l'avortement.

proliferate [prə'lɪfəreɪt] vi proliférer.

proliferation [prəlɪfə'reɪʃən] n prolifération f.

prolific [prə'lɪfɪk] adj prolifique.

prologue ['prəʊlɔg] n prologue m.

prolong [prə'lɔŋ] vt prolonger.

prom [prɔm] n abbr = **promenade, promenade concert**; (US: ball) bal m d'étudiants.

promenade [prɔmə'nɑːd] n (by sea) esplanade f, promenade f.

promenade concert n concert m (de musique classique).

En Grande-Bretagne, un **promenade concert** (ou **prom**) est un concert de musique classique, ainsi appelé car, à l'origine, le public restait debout et se promenait au lieu de rester assis. De nos jours, une partie du public reste debout mais il y a également des places assises (plus chères). Les Proms les plus connus sont les Proms londoniens. La dernière séance (the Last Night of the Proms) est un grand événement médiatique où se jouent des airs traditionnels et patriotiques.
Aux États-Unis et au Canada, le **prom** ou **promenade** est un bal organisé par le lycée.

promenade deck n (NAUT) pont m promenade.

prominence ['prɔmɪnəns] n proéminence f; importance f.

prominent ['prɔmɪnənt] adj (standing out) proéminent(e); (important) important(e); **he is** ~ **in the field of** ... il est très connu dans le domaine de ....

prominently ['prɔmɪnəntlɪ] adv (display, set) bien en évidence; **he figured** ~ **in the case** il a joué un rôle important dans l'affaire.

promiscuity [prɔmɪs'kjuːɪtɪ] n (sexual) légèreté f de mœurs.

promiscuous [prə'mɪskjuəs] adj (sexually) de mœurs légères.

promise ['prɔmɪs] n promesse f ♦ vt, vi promettre; **to make sb a** ~ faire une promesse à qn; **to** ~ **(sb) to do sth** promettre (à qn) de faire qch; **a young man of** ~ un jeune homme plein d'avenir; **to** ~ **well** vi promettre.

promising ['prɔmɪsɪŋ] adj prometteur(euse).

promissory note ['prɔmɪsərɪ-] n billet m à ordre.

promontory ['prɔməntrɪ] n promontoire m.

promote [prə'məʊt] vt promouvoir; (venture, event) organiser, mettre sur pied; (new product) lancer; **the team was** ~d **to the second division** (BRIT FOOTBALL) l'équipe est montée en 2e division.

promoter [prə'məʊtə*] n (of event) organisateur/trice; (of cause etc) partisan/e, défenseur m.

promotion [prə'məʊʃən] n promotion f.

prompt [prɔmpt] adj rapide ♦ n (COMPUT)

message m (de guidage) ♦ vt inciter; (cause)
entraîner, provoquer; (THEAT) souffler (son
rôle or ses répliques) à; **they're very ~**
(punctual) ils sont ponctuels; **at 8 o'clock ~** à
8 heures précises; **he was ~ to accept** il a
tout de suite accepté; **to ~ sb to do** inciter
or pousser qn à faire.

prompter ['prɔmptə*] n (THEAT) souffleur m.

promptly ['prɔmptlɪ] adv rapidement, sans
délai; ponctuellement.

promptness ['prɔmptnɪs] n rapidité f;
promptitude f; ponctualité f.

promulgate ['prɔmǝlgeɪt] vt promulguer.

prone [prǝun] adj (lying) couché(e) (face
contre terre); (liable): **~ to** enclin(e) à; **to be
~ to illness** être facilement malade; **to be ~
to an illness** être sujet à une maladie; **she is
~ to burst into tears if** ... elle a tendance à
tomber en larmes si ....

prong [prɔŋ] n pointe f; (of fork) dent f.

pronoun ['prǝunaun] n pronom m.

pronounce [prǝ'nauns] vt prononcer ♦ vi: **to ~
(up)on** se prononcer sur; **they ~d him unfit
to drive** ils l'ont déclaré inapte à la
conduite.

pronounced [prǝ'naunst] adj (marked)
prononcé(e).

pronouncement [prǝ'naunsmǝnt] n
déclaration f.

pronunciation [prǝnʌnsɪ'eɪʃǝn] n
prononciation f.

proof [pru:f] n preuve f; (test, of book, PHOT)
épreuve f; (of alcohol) degré m ♦ adj: **~
against** à l'épreuve de ♦ vt (BRIT: tent, anorak)
imperméabiliser; **to be 70° ~** ≈ titrer 40
degrés.

proofreader ['pru:fri:də*] n correcteur/trice
(d'épreuves).

prop [prɔp] n support m, étai m ♦ vt (also: ~ **up**)
étayer, soutenir; (lean): **to ~ sth against**
appuyer qch contre or à.

Prop. abbr (COMM) = **proprietor**.

propaganda [prɔpǝ'gændǝ] n propagande f.

propagation [prɔpǝ'geɪʃǝn] n propagation f.

propel [prǝ'pel] vt propulser, faire avancer.

propeller [prǝ'pelǝ*] n hélice f.

propelling pencil [prǝ'pelɪŋ-] n (BRIT) porte-
mine m inv.

propensity [prǝ'pensɪtɪ] n propension f.

proper ['prɔpǝ*] adj (suited, right)
approprié(e), bon(bonne); (seemly)
correct(e), convenable; (authentic) vrai(e),
véritable; (col: real) fini(e), vrai(e); **to go
through the ~ channels** (ADMIN) passer par
la voie officielle.

properly ['prɔpǝlɪ] adv correctement,
convenablement; (really) bel et bien.

proper noun n nom m propre.

property ['prɔpǝtɪ] n (possessions) biens mpl;
(house etc) propriété f; (land) terres fpl,
domaine m; (CHEM etc: quality) propriété f;
it's their ~ cela leur appartient, c'est leur

propriété.

property developer n (BRIT) promoteur
immobilier.

property owner n propriétaire m.

property tax n impôt foncier.

prophecy ['prɔfɪsɪ] n prophétie f.

prophesy ['prɔfɪsaɪ] vt prédire ♦ vi
prophétiser.

prophet ['prɔfɪt] n prophète m.

prophetic [prǝ'fetɪk] adj prophétique.

proportion [prǝ'pɔ:ʃǝn] n proportion f; (share)
part f; partie f ♦ vt proportionner; **to be in/
out of ~ to** or **with sth** être à la mesure de/
hors de proportion avec qch; **to see sth in ~**
(fig) ramener qch à de justes proportions.

proportional [prǝ'pɔ:ʃǝnl], **proportionate**
[prǝ'pɔ:ʃǝnɪt] adj proportionnel(le).

proportional representation (PR) n (POL)
représentation proportionnelle.

proposal [prǝ'pǝuzl] n proposition f, offre f;
(plan) projet m; (of marriage) demande f en
mariage.

propose [prǝ'pǝuz] vt proposer, suggérer;
(have in mind): **to ~ sth/to do** or **doing sth**
envisager qch/de faire qch ♦ vi faire sa
demande en mariage; **to ~ to do** avoir
l'intention de faire.

proposer [prǝ'pǝuzǝ*] n (BRIT: of motion etc)
auteur m.

proposition [prɔpǝ'zɪʃǝn] n proposition f; **to
make sb a ~** faire une proposition à qn.

propound [prǝ'paund] vt proposer, soumettre.

proprietary [prǝ'praɪǝtǝrɪ] adj de marque
déposée; **~ article** article m or produit m de
marque; **~ brand** marque déposée.

proprietor [prǝ'praɪǝtǝ*] n propriétaire m/f.

propriety [prǝ'praɪǝtɪ] n (seemliness)
bienséance f, convenance f.

propulsion [prǝ'pʌlʃǝn] n propulsion f.

pro rata [prǝu'rɑ:tǝ] adv au prorata.

prosaic [prǝu'zeɪɪk] adj prosaïque.

Pros. Atty. abbr (US) = **prosecuting attorney**.

proscribe [prǝ'skraɪb] vt proscrire.

prose [prǝuz] n prose f; (SCOL: translation)
thème m.

prosecute ['prɔsɪkju:t] vt poursuivre.

prosecuting attorney (Pros. Atty.)
['prɔsɪkju:tɪŋ-] n (US) procureur m.

prosecution [prɔsɪ'kju:ʃǝn] n poursuites fpl
judiciaires; (accusing side) accusation f.

prosecutor ['prɔsɪkju:tǝ*] n procureur m;
(also: public ~) ministère public.

prospect n ['prɔspekt] perspective f; (hope)
espoir m, chances fpl ♦ vt, vi [prǝ'spekt]
prospecter; **we are faced with the ~ of
leaving** nous risquons de devoir partir;
there is every ~ of an early victory tout
laisse prévoir une victoire rapide.

prospecting [prǝ'spektɪŋ] n prospection f.

prospective [prǝ'spektɪv] adj (possible)
éventuel(le); (future) futur(e).

prospector [prǝ'spektǝ*] n prospecteur m;

gold ~ chercheur *m* d'or.
prospects ['prɔspɛkts] *npl* (*for work etc*)
possibilités *fpl* d'avenir, débouchés *mpl*.
prospectus [prə'spɛktəs] *n* prospectus *m*.
prosper ['prɔspə*] *vi* prospérer.
prosperity [prɔ'spɛrɪtɪ] *n* prospérité *f*.
prosperous ['prɔspərəs] *adj* prospère.
prostate ['prɔsteɪt] *n* (*also:* ~ **gland**) prostate
f.
prostitute ['prɔstɪtjuːt] *n* prostituée *f*; **male** ~
prostitué *m*.
prostitution [prɔstɪ'tjuːʃən] *n* prostitution *f*.
prostrate *adj* ['prɔstreɪt] prosterné(e); (*fig*)
prostré(e) ♦ *vt* [prɔ'streɪt]: **to** ~ **o.s. (before
sb)** se prosterner (devant qn).
protagonist [prə'tægənɪst] *n* protagoniste *m*.
protect [prə'tɛkt] *vt* protéger.
protection [prə'tɛkʃən] *n* protection *f*; **to be
under sb's** ~ être sous la protection de qn.
protectionism [prə'tɛkʃənɪzəm] *n*
protectionnisme *m*.
protection racket *n* racket *m*.
protective [prə'tɛktɪv] *adj* protecteur(trice);
~ **custody** (*LAW*) détention préventive.
protector [prə'tɛktə*] *n* protecteur/trice.
protégé ['prəuteʒeɪ] *n* protégé *m*.
protégée ['prəuteʒeɪ] *n* protégée *f*.
protein ['prəutiːn] *n* protéine *f*.
pro tem [prəu'tɛm] *adv abbr* (= *pro tempore: for
the time being*) provisoirement.
protest *n* ['prəutɛst] protestation *f* ♦ *vb*
[prə'tɛst] *vi*: **to** ~ **against/about** protester
contre/à propos de ♦ *vt* protester de.
Protestant ['prɔtɪstənt] *adj, n* protestant(e).
protester, protestor [prə'tɛstə*] *n* (*in
demonstration*) manifestant/e.
protest march *n* manifestation *f*.
protocol ['prəutəkɔl] *n* protocole *m*.
prototype ['prəutətaɪp] *n* prototype *m*.
protracted [prə'træktɪd] *adj* prolongé(e).
protractor [prə'træktə*] *n* (*GEOM*) rapporteur
m.
protrude [prə'truːd] *vi* avancer, dépasser.
protuberance [prə'tjuːbərəns] *n* protubérance
f.
proud [praud] *adj* fier(ère); (*pej*)
orgueilleux(euse); **to be** ~ **to do sth** être
fier de faire qch; **to do sb** ~ (*col*) faire
honneur à qn; **to do o.s.** ~ (*col*) ne se priver
de rien.
proudly ['praudlɪ] *adv* fièrement.
prove [pruːv] *vt* prouver, démontrer ♦ *vi*: **to** ~
correct *etc* s'avérer juste *etc*; **to** ~ **o.s.**
montrer ce dont on est capable; **to** ~ **o.s./
itself (to be) useful** *etc* se montrer *or* se
révéler utile *etc*; **he was** ~**d right in the end**
il s'est avéré qu'il avait raison.
proverb ['prɔvɔːb] *n* proverbe *m*.
proverbial [prə'vəːbɪəl] *adj* proverbial(e).
provide [prə'vaɪd] *vt* fournir; **to** ~ **sb with sth**
fournir qch à qn; **to be** ~**d with** (*person*)
disposer de; (*thing*) être équipé(e) *or*

muni(e) de.
►**provide for** *vt fus* (*person*) subvenir aux
besoins de; (*emergency*) prévoir.
provided [prə'vaɪdɪd] *conj*: ~ (**that**) à condition
que + *sub*.
Providence ['prɔvɪdəns] *n* la Providence.
providing [prə'vaɪdɪŋ] *conj* à condition que
+ *sub*.
province ['prɔvɪns] *n* province *f*.
provincial [prə'vɪnʃəl] *adj* provincial(e).
provision [prə'vɪʒən] *n* (*supply*) provision *f*;
(*supplying*) fourniture *f*; approvisionnement
m; (*stipulation*) disposition *f*; ~**s** *npl* (*food*)
provisions *fpl*; **to make** ~ **for** (*one's future*)
assurer; (*one's family*) assurer l'avenir de;
there's no ~ **for this in the contract** le
contrat ne prévoit pas cela.
provisional [prə'vɪʒənl] *adj* provisoire ♦ *n*: **P**~
(*Irish POL*) Provisional *m* (*membre de la
tendance activiste de l'IRA*).
provisional licence *n* (*BRIT AUT*) permis *m*
provisoire.
provisionally [prə'vɪʒnəlɪ] *adv*
provisoirement.
proviso [prə'vaɪzəu] *n* condition *f*; **with the** ~
that à la condition (expresse) que.
Provo ['prɔvəu] *n abbr* (*col*) = **Provisional**.
provocation [prɔvə'keɪʃən] *n* provocation *f*.
provocative [prə'vɔkətɪv] *adj*
provocateur(trice), provocant(e).
provoke [prə'vəuk] *vt* provoquer; **to** ~ **sb to
sth/to do** *or* **into doing sth** pousser qn à
qch/à faire qch.
provoking [prə'vəukɪŋ] *adj* énervant(e),
exaspérant(e).
provost ['prɔvəst] *n* (*BRIT: of university*)
principal *m*; (*Scottish*) maire *m*.
prow [prau] *n* proue *f*.
prowess ['prauɪs] *n* prouesse *f*.
prowl [praul] *vi* (*also:* ~ **about,** ~ **around**)
rôder ♦ *n*: **to be on the** ~ rôder.
prowler ['praulə*] *n* rôdeur/euse.
proximity [prɔk'sɪmɪtɪ] *n* proximité *f*.
proxy ['prɔksɪ] *n* procuration *f*; **by** ~ par
procuration.
PRP *n abbr* (= *performance related pay*) salaire *m*
au rendement.
prude [pruːd] *n* prude *f*.
prudence ['pruːdns] *n* prudence *f*.
prudent ['pruːdnt] *adj* prudent(e).
prudish ['pruːdɪʃ] *adj* prude, pudibond(e).
prune [pruːn] *n* pruneau *m* ♦ *vt* élaguer.
pry [praɪ] *vi*: **to** ~ **into** fourrer son nez dans.
PS *n abbr* (= *postscript*) PS *m*.
psalm [sɑːm] *n* psaume *m*.
PSAT *n abbr* (*US*) = *Preliminary Scholastic
Aptitude Test*.
PSBR *n abbr* (*BRIT*: = *public sector borrowing
requirement*) besoins *mpl* d'emprunts des
pouvoirs publics.
pseud [sjuːd] *n* (*BRIT col: intellectually*) pseudo-
intello *m*; (*: socially*) snob *m/f*.

pseudo- ['sju:dəu] *prefix* pseudo-.
pseudonym ['sju:dənɪm] *n* pseudonyme *m*.
PST *abbr* (*US*: = *Pacific Standard Time*) *heure d'hiver du Pacifique.*
PSV *n abbr* (*BRIT*) = **public service vehicle.**
psyche ['saɪkɪ] *n* psychisme *m*.
psychiatric [saɪkɪ'ætrɪk] *adj* psychiatrique.
psychiatrist [saɪ'kaɪətrɪst] *n* psychiatre *m/f*.
psychiatry [saɪ'kaɪətrɪ] *n* psychiatrie *f*.
psychic ['saɪkɪk] *adj* (*also*: ~**al**)
(méta)psychique; (*person*) doué(e) de télépathie *or* d'un sixième sens.
psycho ['saɪkəu] *n* (*col*) psychopathe *m/f*.
psychoanalyse [saɪkəu'ænəlaɪz] *vt* psychanalyser.
psychoanalysis, *pl* **-ses** [saɪkəuə'nælɪsɪs, -siːz] *n* psychanalyse *f*.
psychoanalyst [saɪkəu'ænəlɪst] *n* psychanalyste *m/f*.
psychological [saɪkə'lɔdʒɪkl] *adj* psychologique.
psychologist [saɪ'kɔlədʒɪst] *n* psychologue *m/f*.
psychology [saɪ'kɔlədʒɪ] *n* psychologie *f*.
psychopath ['saɪkəupæθ] *n* psychopathe *m/f*.
psychosis, *pl* **psychoses** [saɪ'kəusɪs, -siːz] *n* psychose *f*.
psychosomatic [saɪkəusə'mætɪk] *adj* psychosomatique.
psychotherapy [saɪkəu'θerəpɪ] *n* psychothérapie *f*.
psychotic [saɪ'kɔtɪk] *adj, n* psychotique (*m/f*).
PT *n abbr* (*BRIT*: = *physical training*) EPS *f*.
Pt. *abbr* (*in place names*: = *Point*) Pte.
pt *abbr* = **pint, point.**
PTA *n abbr* = *Parent-Teacher Association.*
Pte. *abbr* (*BRIT MIL*) = **private.**
PTO *abbr* (= *please turn over*) TSVP (= *tournez s'il vous plaît*).
PTV *n abbr* (*US*) = *pay television, public television.*
pub [pʌb] *n abbr* (= *public house*) pub *m*.

*Un **pub** comprend en général deux salles: l'une ("the lounge") est plutôt confortable, avec des fauteuils et des bancs capitonnés, tandis que l'autre ("the public bar") est simplement un bar où les consommations sont en général moins chères. Cette dernière est souvent aussi une salle de jeux, les jeux les plus courants étant les fléchettes, les dominos et le billard. Il y a parfois aussi une petite arrière-salle douillette appelée "the snug". Beaucoup de pubs servent maintenant des repas, surtout à l'heure du déjeuner, et c'est alors le seul moment où les enfants sont acceptés, à condition d'être accompagnés. Les pubs sont en général ouverts de 11 h à 23 h, mais cela peut varier selon leur licence; certains pubs ferment l'après-midi.*

pub crawl *n* (*BRIT col*): **to go on a** ~ faire la tournée des bars.
puberty ['pjuːbətɪ] *n* puberté *f*.
pubic ['pjuːbɪk] *adj* pubien(ne), du pubis.
public ['pʌblɪk] *adj* public(ique) ♦ *n* public *m*;
in ~ en public; **the general** ~ le grand public; **to be** ~ **knowledge** être de notoriété publique; **to go** ~ (*COMM*) être coté(e) en Bourse.
public address system (PA) *n* (système *m* de) sonorisation *f*, sono *f* (*col*).
publican ['pʌblɪkən] *n* patron *m or* gérant *m* de pub.
publication [pʌblɪ'keɪʃən] *n* publication *f*.
public company *n* société *f* anonyme (*cotée en Bourse*).
public convenience *n* (*BRIT*) toilettes *fpl*.
public holiday *n* (*BRIT*) jour férié.
public house *n* (*BRIT*) pub *m*.
publicity [pʌb'lɪsɪtɪ] *n* publicité *f*.
publicize ['pʌblɪsaɪz] *vt* faire connaître, rendre public.
public limited company (plc) *n* ≈ société *f* anonyme (SA) (*cotée en Bourse*).
publicly ['pʌblɪklɪ] *adv* publiquement, en public.
public opinion *n* opinion publique.
public ownership *n*: **to be taken into** ~ être nationalisé(e), devenir propriété de l'État.
public prosecutor *n* ≈ procureur *m* (*de la République*); ~**'s office** parquet *m*.
public relations (PR) *n or npl* relations publiques (RP).
public relations officer *n* responsable *m/f* des relations publiques.
public school *n* (*BRIT*) école privée; (*US*) école publique.

*Une **public school** est un établissement d'enseignement secondaire privé. Bon nombre d'entre elles sont des pensionnats. Beaucoup ont également une école primaire qui leur est rattachée (une **prep** ou **preparatory school**) pour préparer les élèves au cycle secondaire. Ces écoles sont en général prestigieuses, et les frais de scolarité sont très élevés dans les plus connues (Westminster, Eton, Harrow).
Beaucoup d'élèves vont ensuite à l'université, et un grand nombre entre à Oxford ou à Cambridge. Les grands industriels, les députés et les hauts fonctionnaires sortent souvent de ces écoles.
En Écosse et aux États-Unis, le terme "public school" désigne tout simplement une école publique gratuite.*

public sector *n* secteur public.
public service vehicle (PSV) *n* (*BRIT*) véhicule affecté au transport de personnes.
public-spirited [pʌblɪk'spɪrɪtɪd] *adj* qui fait preuve de civisme.
public transport, (*US*) **public transportation** *n* transports *mpl* en

commun.

public utility n service public.

public works npl travaux publics.

publish ['pʌblɪʃ] vt publier.

publisher ['pʌblɪʃə*] n éditeur m.

publishing ['pʌblɪʃɪŋ] n (industry) édition f; (of a book) publication f.

publishing company n maison f d'édition.

puce [pjuːs] adj puce.

puck [pʌk] n (elf) lutin m; (ICE HOCKEY) palet m.

pucker ['pʌkə*] vt plisser.

pudding ['pudɪŋ] n (BRIT: sweet) dessert m, entremets m; (sausage) boudin m; **rice** ~ ≈ riz m au lait; **black** ~, (US) **blood** ~ boudin (noir).

puddle ['pʌdl] n flaque f d'eau.

puerile ['pjuəraɪl] adj puéril(e).

Puerto Rico ['pwɜːtəuˈriːkəu] n Porto Rico f.

puff [pʌf] n bouffée f ◆ vt: **to** ~ **one's pipe** tirer sur sa pipe; (also: ~ **out:** sails, cheeks) gonfler ◆ vi sortir par bouffées; (pant) haleter; **to** ~ **out smoke** envoyer des bouffées de fumée.

puffed [pʌft] adj (col: out of breath) tout(e) essoufflé(e).

puffin ['pʌfɪn] n macareux m.

puff pastry, (US) **puff paste** n pâte feuilletée.

puffy ['pʌfɪ] adj bouffi(e), boursouflé(e).

pugnacious [pʌgˈneɪʃəs] adj pugnace, batailleur(euse).

pull [pul] n (of moon, magnet, the sea etc) attraction f; (fig) influence f ◆ vt tirer; (strain: muscle, tendon) se claquer ◆ vi tirer; **to give sth a** ~ (tug) tirer sur qch; **to** ~ **a face** faire une grimace; **to** ~ **to pieces** mettre en morceaux; **to** ~ **one's punches** (also fig) ménager son adversaire; **to** ~ **one's weight** y mettre du sien; **to** ~ **o.s. together** se ressaisir; **to** ~ **sb's leg** (fig) faire marcher qn; **to** ~ **strings (for sb)** intervenir (en faveur de qn).

▶**pull about** vt (BRIT: handle roughly: object) maltraiter; (: person) malmener.

▶**pull apart** vt séparer; (break) mettre en pièces, démantibuler.

▶**pull down** vt baisser, abaisser; (house) démolir; (tree) abattre.

▶**pull in** vi (AUT) se ranger; (RAIL) entrer en gare.

▶**pull off** vt enlever, ôter; (deal etc) conclure.

▶**pull out** vi démarrer, partir; (withdraw) se retirer; (AUT: come out of line) déboîter ◆ vt sortir; arracher; (withdraw) retirer.

▶**pull over** vi (AUT) se ranger.

▶**pull round** vi (unconscious person) revenir à soi; (sick person) se rétablir.

▶**pull through** vi s'en sortir.

▶**pull up** vi (stop) s'arrêter ◆ vt remonter; (uproot) déraciner, arracher; (stop) arrêter.

pulley ['pulɪ] n poulie f.

pull-out ['pulaut] n (of forces etc) retrait m

◆ cpd (magazine, pages) détachable.

pullover ['puləuvə*] n pull-over m, tricot m.

pulp [pʌlp] n (of fruit) pulpe f; (for paper) pâte à papier; (pej: also: ~ **magazines** etc) press f à sensation or de bas étage; **to reduce sth to (a)** ~ réduire qch en purée.

pulpit ['pulpɪt] n chaire f.

pulsate [pʌlˈseɪt] vi battre, palpiter; (music) vibrer.

pulse [pʌls] n (of blood) pouls m; (of heart) battement m; (of music, engine) vibrations fpl; **to feel** or **take sb's** ~ prendre le pouls à qn.

pulses ['pʌlsəz] npl (CULIN) légumineuses fpl

pulverize ['pʌlvəraɪz] vt pulvériser.

puma ['pjuːmə] n puma m.

pumice ['pʌmɪs] n (also: ~ **stone**) pierre f ponce.

pummel ['pʌml] vt rouer de coups.

pump [pʌmp] n pompe f; (shoe) escarpin m ◆ vt pomper; (fig: col) faire parler; **to** ~ **sb for information** essayer de soutirer des renseignements à qn.

▶**pump up** vt gonfler.

pumpkin ['pʌmpkɪn] n potiron m, citrouille f

pun [pʌn] n jeu m de mots, calembour m.

punch [pʌntʃ] n (blow) coup m de poing; (fig: force) vivacité f, mordant m; (tool) poinçon m; (drink) punch m ◆ vt (make a hole) poinçonner, perforer; (hit): **to** ~ **sb/sth** donner un coup de poing à qn/sur qch; **to** ~ **a hole (in)** faire un trou (dans).

▶**punch in** vi (US) pointer (en arrivant).

▶**punch out** vi (US) pointer (en partant).

punch-drunk ['pʌntʃdrʌŋk] adj (BRIT) sonné(e).

punch(ed) card [pʌntʃ(t)-] n carte perforée

punch line n (of joke) conclusion f.

punch-up ['pʌntʃʌp] n (BRIT col) bagarre f.

punctual ['pʌŋktjuəl] adj ponctuel(le).

punctuality [pʌŋktjuˈælɪtɪ] n ponctualité f.

punctually ['pʌŋktjuəlɪ] adv ponctuellement **it will start** ~ **at 6** cela commencera à 6 heures précises.

punctuate ['pʌŋktjueɪt] vt ponctuer.

punctuation [pʌŋktjuˈeɪʃən] n ponctuation f

punctuation mark n signe m de ponctuatic

puncture ['pʌŋktʃə*] n (BRIT) crevaison f ◆ v crever; **I have a** ~ (AUT) j'ai (un pneu) crevé.

pundit ['pʌndɪt] n individu m qui pontifie, pontife m.

pungent ['pʌndʒənt] adj piquant(e); (fig) mordant(e), caustique.

punish ['pʌnɪʃ] vt punir; **to** ~ **sb for sth/for doing sth** punir qn de qch/d'avoir fait qch

punishable ['pʌnɪʃəbl] adj punissable.

punishing ['pʌnɪʃɪŋ] adj (fig: exhausting) épuisant(e) ◆ n punition f.

punishment ['pʌnɪʃmənt] n punition f, châtiment m; (fig: col): **to take a lot of** ~ (boxer) encaisser; (car, person etc) être mis(e) à dure épreuve.

punk [pʌŋk] n (*person: also:* ~ **rocker**) punk *m/f*; (*music: also:* ~ **rock**) le punk; (*US col: hoodlum*) voyou *m*.

punt [pʌnt] n (*boat*) bachot *m*; (*IRELAND*) livre irlandaise ♦ vi (*BRIT: bet*) parier.

punter ['pʌntə*] n (*BRIT: gambler*) parieur/euse; (: *col*) Monsieur *m* tout le monde; type *m*.

puny ['pju:nɪ] adj chétif(ive).

pup [pʌp] n chiot *m*.

pupil ['pju:pl] n élève *m/f*; (*of eye*) pupille *f*.

puppet ['pʌpɪt] n marionnette *f*, pantin *m*.

puppet government n gouvernement *m* fantoche.

puppy ['pʌpɪ] n chiot *m*, petit chien.

purchase ['pəːtʃɪs] n achat *m*; (*grip*) prise *f* ♦ vt acheter; **to get a** ~ **on** trouver appui sur.

purchase order n ordre *m* d'achat.

purchase price n prix *m* d'achat.

purchaser ['pəːtʃɪsə*] n acheteur/euse.

purchase tax n (*BRIT*) taxe *f* à l'achat.

purchasing power ['pəːtʃɪsɪŋ-] n pouvoir *m* d'achat.

pure [pjuə*] adj pur(e); **a** ~ **wool jumper** un pull en pure laine; ~ **and simple** pur(e) et simple.

purebred ['pjuəbrɛd] adj de race.

purée ['pjuəreɪ] n purée *f*.

purely ['pjuəlɪ] adv purement.

purge [pəːdʒ] n (*MED*) purge *f*; (*POL*) épuration *f*, purge ♦ vt purger; (*fig*) épurer, purger.

purification [pjuərɪfɪ'keɪʃən] n purification *f*.

purify ['pjuərɪfaɪ] vt purifier, épurer.

purist ['pjuərɪst] n puriste *m/f*.

puritan ['pjuərɪtən] n puritain/e.

puritanical [pjuərɪ'tænɪkl] adj puritain(e).

purity ['pjuərɪtɪ] n pureté *f*.

purl [pəːl] n maille *f* à l'envers ♦ vt tricoter à l'envers.

purloin [pəː'lɔɪn] vt dérober.

purple ['pəːpl] adj violet(te); cramoisi(e).

purport [pəː'pɔːt] vi: **to** ~ **to be/do** prétendre être/faire.

purpose ['pəːpəs] n intention *f*, but *m*; **on** ~ exprès; **for illustrative** ~**s** à titre d'illustration; **for teaching** ~**s** dans un but pédagogique; **for the** ~**s of this meeting** pour cette réunion; **to no** ~ en pure perte.

purpose-built ['pəːpəs'bɪlt] adj (*BRIT*) fait(e) sur mesure.

purposeful ['pəːpəsful] adj déterminé(e), résolu(e).

purposely ['pəːpəslɪ] adv exprès.

purr [pəː*] n ronronnement *m* ♦ vi ronronner.

purse [pəːs] n porte-monnaie *m inv*, bourse *f*; (*US: handbag*) sac *m* (à main) ♦ vt serrer, pincer.

purser ['pəːsə*] n (*NAUT*) commissaire *m* du bord.

purse snatcher [-'snætʃə*] n (*US*) voleur *m* à l'arraché.

pursue [pə'sjuː] vt poursuivre; (*pleasures*) rechercher; (*inquiry, matter*) approfondir.

pursuer [pə'sjuːə*] n poursuivant/e.

pursuit [pə'sjuːt] n poursuite *f*; (*occupation*) occupation *f*, activité *f*; **scientific** ~**s** recherches *fpl* scientifiques; **in (the)** ~ **of sth** à la recherche de qch.

purveyor [pə'veɪə*] n fournisseur *m*.

pus [pʌs] n pus *m*.

push [puʃ] n poussée *f*; (*effort*) gros effort; (*drive*) énergie *f* ♦ vt pousser; (*button*) appuyer sur; (*thrust*): **to** ~ **sth (into)** enfoncer qch (dans); (*fig*) mettre en avant, faire de la publicité pour ♦ vi pousser; appuyer; **to** ~ **a door open/shut** pousser une porte (pour l'ouvrir/pour la fermer); **"**~**"** (*on door*) "pousser"; (*on bell*) "appuyer"; **to** ~ **for** (*better pay, conditions*) réclamer; **to be** ~**ed for time/money** être à court de temps/d'argent; **she is** ~**ing fifty** (*col*) elle frise la cinquantaine; **at a** ~ (*BRIT col*) à la limite, à la rigueur.

▶**push aside** vt écarter.

▶**push in** vi s'introduire de force.

▶**push off** vi (*col*) filer, ficher le camp.

▶**push on** vi (*continue*) continuer.

▶**push over** vt renverser.

▶**push through** vt (*measure*) faire voter.

▶**push up** vt (*total, prices*) faire monter.

push-bike ['puʃbaɪk] n (*BRIT*) vélo *m*.

push-button ['puʃbʌtn] n bouton(-poussoir *m*) *m*.

pushchair ['puʃtʃɛə*] n (*BRIT*) poussette *f*.

pusher ['puʃə*] n (*also: drug* ~) revendeur/euse (de drogue), ravitailleur/euse (en drogue).

pushover ['puʃəuvə*] n (*col*): **it's a** ~ c'est un jeu d'enfant.

push-up ['puʃʌp] n (*US*) traction *f*.

pushy ['puʃɪ] adj (*pej*) arriviste.

puss, pussy(-cat) [pus, 'pusɪ(kæt)] n minet *m*.

put [put], *pt, pp* **put** vt mettre; (*place*) poser, placer; (*say*) dire, exprimer; (*a question*) poser; (*estimate*) estimer; **to** ~ **sb in a good/bad mood** mettre qn de bonne/mauvaise humeur; **to** ~ **sb to bed** mettre qn au lit, coucher qn; **to** ~ **sb to a lot of trouble** déranger qn; **how shall I** ~ **it?** comment dirais-je?, comment dire?; **to** ~ **a lot of time into sth** passer beaucoup de temps à qch; **to** ~ **money on a horse** miser sur un cheval; **I** ~ **it to you that** ... (*BRIT*) je (vous) suggère que ..., je suis d'avis que ...; **to stay** ~ ne pas bouger.

▶**put about** vi (*NAUT*) virer de bord ♦ vt (*rumour*) faire courir.

▶**put across** vt (*ideas etc*) communiquer; faire comprendre.

▶**put aside** vt mettre de côté.

▶**put away** vt (*store*) ranger.

▶**put back** vt (*replace*) remettre, replacer; (*postpone*) remettre; (*delay, also: watch,* *clock*) retarder; **this will ~ us back ten years** cela nous ramènera dix ans en arrière.

►**put by** *vt* (*money*) mettre de côté, économiser.

►**put down** *vt* (*parcel etc*) poser, déposer; (*pay*) verser; (*in writing*) mettre par écrit, inscrire; (*suppress: revolt etc*) réprimer, écraser; (*attribute*) attribuer.

►**put forward** *vt* (*ideas*) avancer, proposer; (*date, watch, clock*) avancer.

►**put in** *vt* (*gas, electricity*) installer; (*application, complaint*) faire.

►**put in for** *vt fus* (*job*) poser sa candidature pour; (*promotion*) solliciter.

►**put off** *vt* (*light etc*) éteindre; (*postpone*) remettre à plus tard, ajourner; (*discourage*) dissuader.

►**put on** *vt* (*clothes, lipstick etc*) mettre; (*light etc*) allumer; (*play etc*) monter; (*extra bus, train etc*) mettre en service; (*food, meal*) servir; (*weight*) prendre; (*assume: accent, manner*) prendre; (*: airs*) se donner, prendre; (*brake*) mettre; (*col: tease*) faire marcher; (*inform, indicate*): **to ~ sb on to sb/sth** indiquer qn/qch à qn.

►**put out** *vt* mettre dehors; (*one's hand*) tendre; (*news, rumour*) faire courir, répandre; (*light etc*) éteindre; (*person: inconvenience*) déranger, gêner; (*BRIT: dislocate*) se démettre ♦ *vi* (*NAUT*): **to ~ out to sea** prendre le large; **to ~ out from Plymouth** quitter Plymouth.

►**put through** *vt* (*caller*) mettre en communication; (*call*) passer; **~ me through to Miss Blair** passez-moi Miss Blair.

►**put together** *vt* mettre ensemble; (*assemble: furniture, toy etc*) monter, assembler; (*meal*) préparer.

►**put up** *vt* (*raise*) lever, relever, remonter; (*pin up*) afficher; (*hang*) accrocher; (*build*) construire, ériger; (*a tent*) monter; (*increase*) augmenter; (*accommodate*) loger; (*incite*): **to ~ sb up to doing sth** pousser qn à faire qch; **to ~ sth up for sale** mettre qch en vente.

►**put upon** *vt fus*: **to be ~ upon** (*imposed on*) se laisser faire.

►**put up with** *vt fus* supporter.

putrid ['pju:trɪd] *adj* putride.

putt [pʌt] *vt, vi* putter ♦ *n* putt *m*.

putter ['pʌtə*] *n* (*GOLF*) putter *m*.

putting green ['pʌtɪŋ-] *n* green *m*.

putty ['pʌtɪ] *n* mastic *m*.

put-up ['pʊtʌp] *adj*: **~ job** coup monté.

puzzle ['pʌzl] *n* énigme *f*, mystère *m*; (*jigsaw*) puzzle *m*; (*also*: **crossword ~**) problème *m* de mots croisés ♦ *vt* intriguer, rendre perplexe ♦ *vi* se creuser la tête; **to ~ over** chercher à comprendre; **to be ~d about sth** être perplexe au sujet de qch.

puzzling ['pʌzlɪŋ] *adj* déconcertant(e), inexplicable.

PVC *n abbr* (= *polyvinyl chloride*) PVC *m*.

Pvt. *abbr* (*US MIL*) = **private**.

pw *abbr* (= *per week*) p.sem.

PX *n abbr* (*US MIL*) = **post exchange**.

pygmy ['pɪgmɪ] *n* pygmée *m/f*.

pyjamas [pɪ'dʒɑ:məz] *npl* (*BRIT*) pyjama *m*; **a pair of ~** un pyjama.

pylon ['paɪlən] *n* pylône *m*.

pyramid ['pɪrəmɪd] *n* pyramide *f*.

Pyrenean [pɪrə'ni:ən] *adj* pyrénéen(ne), des Pyrénées.

Pyrenees [pɪrə'ni:z] *npl*: **the ~** les Pyrénées *fpl*.

Pyrex ['paɪrɛks] *n* ® Pyrex *m* ® ♦ *cpd*: **~ dish** plat *m* en Pyrex.

python ['paɪθən] *n* python *m*.

Q q

Q, q [kju:] *n* (*letter*) Q, q *m*; **Q for Queen** Q comme Quintal.

Qatar [kæ'tɑ:*] *n* Qatar *m*, Katar *m*.

En Angleterre, un **QC** *ou* **Queen's Counsel** (*ou* **KC** *pour* **King's Counsel**, *sous le règne d'un roi*) *est un avocat qui reçoit un poste de haut fonctionnaire sur recommandation du Lord Chancellor. Il fait alors souvent suivre son nom des lettres QC, et lorsqu'il va au tribunal, il est toujours accompagné par un autre avocat (un "junior barrister").*

QED *abbr* (= *quod erat demonstrandum*) CQFD.

QM *n abbr* = **quartermaster**.

q.t. *n abbr* (*col*: = *quiet*): **on the ~** discrètement

qty *abbr* (= *quantity*) qté.

quack [kwæk] *n* (*of duck*) coin-coin *m inv*; (*pej: doctor*) charlatan *m* ♦ *vi* faire coin-coin.

quad [kwɔd] *n abbr* = **quadruple, quadruplet, quadrangle**.

quadrangle ['kwɔdræŋgl] *n* (*MATH*) quadrilatère *m*; (*courtyard: abbr*: **quad**) cour *f*.

quadruped ['kwɔdrupɛd] *n* quadrupède *m*.

quadruple [kwɔ'dru:pl] *adj, n* quadruple (*m*) ♦ *vt, vi* quadrupler.

quadruplet [kwɔ'dru:plɪt] *n* un/une des quadruplé(e)s.

quagmire ['kwæɡmaɪə*] *n* bourbier *m*.

quail [kweɪl] *n* (*ZOOL*) caille *f* ♦ *vi*: **to ~ at** *or* **before** se décourager devant.

quaint [kweɪnt] *adj* bizarre; (*old-fashioned*) désuet(ète); au charme vieillot, pittoresque

quake [kweɪk] *vi* trembler ♦ *n abbr* = **earthquake**.

Quaker ['kweɪkə*] n quaker/esse.

qualification [kwɔlɪfɪ'keɪʃən] n (degree etc) diplôme m; (ability) compétence f, qualification f; (limitation) réserve f, restriction f; **what are your ~s?** qu'avez-vous comme diplômes?; quelles sont vos qualifications?

qualified ['kwɔlɪfaɪd] adj diplômé(e); (able) compétent(e), qualifié(e); (limited) conditionnel(le); **it was a ~ success** ce fut un succès mitigé; **~ for/to do** qui a les diplômes requis pour/pour faire; qualifié pour/pour faire.

qualify ['kwɔlɪfaɪ] vt qualifier; (limit: statement) apporter des réserves à ♦ vi: **to ~ (as)** obtenir son diplôme (de); **to ~ (for)** remplir les conditions requises (pour); (SPORT) se qualifier (pour).

qualifying ['kwɔlɪfaɪɪŋ] adj: **~ exam** examen m d'entrée; **~ round** éliminatoires fpl.

qualitative ['kwɔlɪtətɪv] adj qualitatif(ive).

quality ['kwɔlɪtɪ] n qualité f ♦ cpd de qualité; **of good/poor ~** de bonne/mauvaise qualité.

quality control n contrôle m de qualité.

quality of life n qualité f de la vie.

quality papers npl (BRIT): **the ~** la presse d'information.

*Les **quality (news)papers** (ou la **quality press**) englobent les journaux sérieux, quotidiens ou hebdomadaires, par opposition aux journaux populaires (**tabloid press**). Ces journaux visent un public qui souhaite des informations détaillées sur un éventail très vaste de sujets et qui est prêt à consacrer beaucoup de temps à leur lecture. Les quality newspapers sont en général de grand format.*

qualm [kwɑːm] n doute m; scrupule m; **to have ~s about sth** avoir des doutes sur qch; éprouver des scrupules à propos de qch.

quandary ['kwɔndrɪ] n: **in a ~** devant un dilemme, dans l'embarras.

quango ['kwæŋgəu] n abbr (BRIT: = quasi-autonomous non-governmental organization) commission nommée par le gouvernement.

quantifiable [kwɔntɪ'faɪəbl] adj quantifiable.

quantitative ['kwɔntɪtətɪv] adj quantitatif(ive).

quantity ['kwɔntɪtɪ] n quantité f; **in ~** en grande quantité.

quantity surveyor n (BRIT) métreur vérificateur.

quantum leap ['kwɔntəm-] n (fig) bond m en avant.

quarantine ['kwɔrntiːn] n quarantaine f.

quark [kwɑːk] n quark m.

quarrel ['kwɔrl] n querelle f, dispute f ♦ vi se disputer, se quereller; **to have a ~ with sb** se quereller avec qn; **I've no ~ with him** je n'ai rien contre lui; **I can't ~ with that** je ne vois rien à y redire à cela.

quarrelsome ['kwɔrəlsəm] adj querelleur(euse).

quarry ['kwɔrɪ] n (for stone) carrière f; (animal) proie f, gibier m ♦ vt (marble etc) extraire.

quart [kwɔːt] n ≈ litre m.

quarter ['kwɔːtə*] n quart m; (of year) trimestre m; (district) quartier m; (US, Canada: 25 cents) (pièce f de) vingt-cinq cents m ♦ vt partager en quartiers or en quatre; (MIL) caserner, cantonner; **~s** npl logement m; (MIL) quartiers mpl, cantonnement m; **a ~ of an hour** un quart d'heure; **it's a ~ to 3,** (US) **it's a ~ of 3** il est 3 heures moins le quart; **it's a ~ past 3,** (US) **it's a ~ after 3** il est 3 heures et quart; **from all ~s** de tous côtés; **at close ~s** tout près.

quarterback ['kwɔːtəbæk] n (US FOOTBALL) quarterback m/f.

quarter-deck ['kwɔːtədɛk] n (NAUT) plage f arrière.

quarter final n quart m de finale.

quarterly ['kwɔːtəlɪ] adj trimestriel(le) ♦ adv tous les trois mois ♦ n (PRESS) revue trimestrielle.

quartermaster ['kwɔːtəmɑːstə*] n (MIL) intendant m militaire de troisième classe; (NAUT) maître m de manœuvre.

quartet(te) [kwɔː'tɛt] n quatuor m; (jazz players) quartette m.

quarto ['kwɔːtəu] adj, n in-quarto (m) inv.

quartz [kwɔːts] n quartz m ♦ cpd de or en quartz; (watch, clock) à quartz.

quash [kwɔʃ] vt (verdict) annuler, casser.

quasi- ['kweɪzaɪ] prefix quasi- + noun; quasi, presque + adjective.

quaver ['kweɪvə*] n (BRIT MUS) croche f ♦ vi trembler.

quay [kiː] n (also: ~side) quai m.

Que. abbr (Canada) = Quebec.

queasy ['kwiːzɪ] adj (stomach) délicat(e); **to feel ~** avoir mal au cœur.

Quebec [kwɪ'bɛk] n Québec m.

queen [kwiːn] n (gen) reine f; (CARDS etc) dame f.

queen mother n reine mère f.

*Le **Queen's speech** (ou **King's speech**) est le discours lu par le souverain à l'ouverture du **Parliament**, dans la **House of Lords**, en présence des lords et des députés. Il contient le programme de politique générale que propose le gouvernement pour la session, et il est préparé par le Premier ministre en consultation avec le cabinet.*

queer [kwɪə*] adj étrange, curieux(euse); (suspicious) louche; (BRIT: sick): **I feel ~** je me sens pas bien ♦ n (col) homosexuel m.

quell [kwɛl] vt réprimer, étouffer.

quench [kwɛntʃ] vt (flames) éteindre; **to ~ one's thirst** se désaltérer.

querulous ['kwɛruləs] adj (person)

récriminateur(trice); (_voice_) plaintif(ive).

query ['kwɪərɪ] _n_ question _f_; (_doubt_) doute _m_; (_question mark_) point _m_ d'interrogation ♦ _vt_ (_disagree with, dispute_) mettre en doute, questionner.

quest [kwɛst] _n_ recherche _f_, quête _f_.

question ['kwɛstʃən] _n_ question _f_ ♦ _vt_ (_person_) interroger; (_plan, idea_) mettre en question _or_ en doute; **to ask sb a ~, to put a ~ to sb** poser une question à qn; **to bring** _or_ **call sth into ~** remettre qch en question; **the ~ is ...** la question est de savoir ...; **it's a ~ of doing** il s'agit de faire; **there's some ~ of doing** il est question de faire; **beyond ~** sans aucun doute; **out of the ~** hors de question.

questionable ['kwɛstʃənəbl] _adj_ discutable.

questioner ['kwɛstʃənə*] _n_ personne _f_ qui pose une question (_or_ qui a posé la question _etc_).

questioning ['kwɛstʃənɪŋ] _adj_ interrogateur(trice) ♦ _n_ interrogatoire _m_.

question mark _n_ point _m_ d'interrogation.

questionnaire [kwɛstʃə'nɛə*] _n_ questionnaire _m_.

queue [kjuː] (_BRIT_) _n_ queue _f_, file _f_ ♦ _vi_ faire la queue; **to jump the ~** passer avant son tour.

quibble ['kwɪbl] _vi_ ergoter, chicaner.

quick [kwɪk] _adj_ rapide; (_reply_) prompt(e), rapide; (_mind_) vif(vive) ♦ _adv_ vite, rapidement ♦ _n_: **cut to the ~** (_fig_) touché(e) au vif; **be ~!** dépêche-toi!; **to be ~ to act** agir tout de suite.

quicken ['kwɪkən] _vt_ accélérer, presser; (_rouse_) stimuler ♦ _vi_ s'accélérer, devenir plus rapide.

quick fix _n_ solution _f_ de fortune.

quicklime ['kwɪklaɪm] _n_ chaux vive.

quickly ['kwɪklɪ] _adv_ (_fast_) vite, rapidement; (_immediately_) tout de suite.

quickness ['kwɪknɪs] _n_ rapidité _f_, promptitude _f_; (_of mind_) vivacité _f_.

quicksand ['kwɪksænd] _n_ sables mouvants.

quickstep ['kwɪkstɛp] _n_ fox-trot _m_.

quick-tempered [kwɪk'tɛmpəd] _adj_ emporté(e).

quick-witted [kwɪk'wɪtɪd] _adj_ à l'esprit vif.

quid [kwɪd] _n_ (_pl inv: BRIT col_) livre _f_.

quid pro quo ['kwɪdprəʊ'kwəʊ] _n_ contrepartie _f_.

quiet ['kwaɪət] _adj_ tranquille, calme; (_not noisy: engine_) silencieux(euse); (_reserved_) réservé(e); (_not busy: day, business_) calme; (_ceremony, colour_) discret(ète) ♦ _n_ tranquillité _f_, calme _m_ ♦ _vt, vi_ (_US_) **= quieten; keep ~!** tais-toi!; **on the ~** en secret, discrètement; **I'll have a ~ word with him** je lui en parlerai discrètement.

quieten ['kwaɪətn] (_also: ~ **down**_) _vi_ se calmer, s'apaiser ♦ _vt_ calmer, apaiser.

quietly ['kwaɪətlɪ] _adv_ tranquillement, calmement; discrètement.

quietness ['kwaɪətnɪs] _n_ tranquillité _f_, calme

_m_; silence _m_.

quill [kwɪl] _n_ plume _f_ (d'oie).

quilt [kwɪlt] _n_ édredon _m_; (_continental ~_) couette _f_.

quin [kwɪn] _n abbr_ **= quintuplet.**

quince [kwɪns] _n_ coing _m_; (_tree_) cognassier

quinine [kwɪ'niːn] _n_ quinine _f_.

quintet(te) [kwɪn'tɛt] _n_ quintette _m_.

quintuplet [kwɪn'tjuːplɪt] _n_ quintuplé/e.

quip [kwɪp] _n_ remarque piquante _or_ spirituelle, pointe _f_ ♦ _vt_: **... he ~ped** ... lança-t-il.

quire ['kwaɪə*] _n_ ≈ main _f_ (de papier).

quirk [kwəːk] _n_ bizarrerie _f_; **by some ~ of fa** par un caprice du hasard.

quit [kwɪt] _pt, pp_ **quit** _or_ **quitted** [kwɪt] _vt_ quitter ♦ _vi_ (_give up_) abandonner, renoncer; (_resig_ démissionner; **to ~ doing** arrêter de faire ~ **stalling!** (_US col_) arrête de te dérober!; **notice to ~** (_BRIT_) congé _m_ (signifié au locataire).

quite [kwaɪt] _adv_ (_rather_) assez, plutôt; (_entirely_) complètement, tout à fait; **~ nev** plutôt neuf; **tout à fait neuf; she's ~ prett** elle est plutôt jolie; **I ~ understand** je comprends très bien; **~ a few of them** un assez grand nombre d'entre eux; **that's ne** ~ **right** ce n'est pas tout à fait juste; **not ~ as many as last time** pas tout à fait autant que la dernière fois; **~ (so)!** exactement!

Quito ['kiːtəʊ] _n_ Quito.

quits [kwɪts] _adj_: ~ **(with)** quitte (envers); **le call it ~** restons-en là.

quiver ['kwɪvə*] _vi_ trembler, frémir ♦ _n_ (_for arrows_) carquois _m_.

quiz [kwɪz] _n_ (_on TV_) jeu-concours _m_ (télévisé); (_in magazine etc_) test _m_ de connaissances ♦ _vt_ interroger.

quizzical ['kwɪzɪkl] _adj_ narquois(e).

quoits [kwɔɪts] _npl_ jeu _m_ du palet.

quorum ['kwɔːrəm] _n_ quorum _m_.

quota ['kwəʊtə] _n_ quota _m_.

quotation [kwəʊ'teɪʃən] _n_ citation _f_; (_of sha_ etc) cote _f_, cours _m_; (_estimate_) devis _m_.

quotation marks _npl_ guillemets _mpl_.

quote [kwəʊt] _n_ citation _f_ ♦ _vt_ (_sentence, author_) citer; (_price_) donner, soumettre; (_shares_) coter ♦ _vi_: **to ~ from** citer; **to ~ fo** job établir un devis pour des travaux; ~**s** _npl_ (_col_) **= quotation marks; in ~s** entre guillemets; ~ **... unquote** (_in dictation_) ouvrez les guillemets ... fermez les guillemets.

quotient ['kwəʊʃənt] _n_ quotient _m_.

qv _abbr_ (= _quod vide: which see_) voir.

qwerty keyboard ['kwəːtɪ-] _n_ clavier _m_ QWERTY.

Rr

R, r [ɑː*] n (letter) R, r m; **R for Robert,** (US) **R for Roger** R comme Raoul.

R abbr (= right) dr; (= river) riv., fl.; (= Réaumur (scale)) R; (US CINE: = restricted) interdit aux moins de 17 ans; (US POL) = **republican**; (BRIT) = **Rex, Regina**.

RA abbr = **rear admiral** ♦ n abbr (BRIT) = **Royal Academy, Royal Academician**.

RAAF n abbr = Royal Australian Air Force.

Rabat [rə'bɑːt] n Rabat.

rabbi ['ræbaɪ] n rabbin m.

rabbit ['ræbɪt] n lapin m ♦ vi: **to ~ (on)** (BRIT) parler à n'en plus finir.

rabbit hole n terrier m (de lapin).

rabbit hutch n clapier m.

rabble ['ræbl] n (pej) populace f.

rabid ['ræbɪd] adj enragé(e).

rabies ['reɪbiːz] n rage f.

RAC n abbr (BRIT: = Royal Automobile Club) ≈ ACF m.

raccoon [rə'kuːn] n raton m laveur.

race [reɪs] n race f; (competition, rush) course f ♦ vt (person) faire la course avec; (horse) faire courir; (engine) emballer ♦ vi courir; (engine) s'emballer; **the human ~** la race humaine; **to ~ in/out** etc entrer/sortir etc à toute vitesse.

race car n (US) = **racing car**.

race car driver n (US) = **racing driver**.

racecourse ['reɪskɔːs] n champ m de courses.

racehorse ['reɪshɔːs] n cheval m de course.

race relations npl rapports mpl entre les races.

racetrack ['reɪstræk] n piste f.

racial ['reɪʃl] adj racial(e).

racialism ['reɪʃlɪzəm] n racisme m.

racialist ['reɪʃlɪst] adj, n raciste (m/f).

racing ['reɪsɪŋ] n courses fpl.

racing car n (BRIT) voiture f de course.

racing driver n (BRIT) pilote m de course.

racism ['reɪsɪzəm] n racisme m.

racist ['reɪsɪst] adj, n (pej) raciste (m/f).

rack [ræk] n (also: **luggage ~**) filet m à bagages; (also: **roof ~**) galerie f ♦ vt tourmenter; **magazine ~** porte-revues m inv; **shoe ~** étagère f à chaussures; **toast ~** porte-toast m; **to ~ one's brains** se creuser la cervelle; **to go to ~ and ruin** (building) tomber en ruine; (business) péricliter.

▶**rack up** vt accumuler.

racket ['rækɪt] n (for tennis) raquette f; (noise) tapage m, vacarme m; (swindle) escroquerie

f; (organized crime) racket m.

racketeer [rækɪ'tɪə*] n (esp US) racketteur m.

racoon [rə'kuːn] n = **raccoon**.

racquet ['rækɪt] n raquette f.

racy ['reɪsɪ] adj plein(e) de verve; osé(e).

RADA [rɑːdə] n abbr (BRIT) = Royal Academy of Dramatic Art.

radar ['reɪdɑː*] n radar m ♦ cpd radar inv.

radar trap n contrôle m radar.

radial ['reɪdɪəl] adj (also: **~-ply**) à carcasse radiale.

radiance ['reɪdɪəns] n éclat m, rayonnement m.

radiant ['reɪdɪənt] adj rayonnant(e); (PHYSICS) radiant(e).

radiate ['reɪdɪeɪt] vt (heat) émettre, dégager ♦ vi (lines) rayonner.

radiation [reɪdɪ'eɪʃən] n rayonnement m; (radioactive) radiation f.

radiation sickness n mal m des rayons.

radiator ['reɪdɪeɪtə*] n radiateur m.

radiator cap n bouchon m de radiateur.

radiator grill n (AUT) calandre f.

radical ['rædɪkl] adj radical(e).

radii ['reɪdɪaɪ] npl of **radius**.

radio ['reɪdɪəu] n radio f ♦ vi: **to ~ to sb** envoyer un message radio à qn ♦ vt (information) transmettre par radio; (one's position) signaler par radio; (person) appeler par radio; **on the ~** à la radio.

radioactive ['reɪdɪəu'æktɪv] adj radioactif(ive).

radioactivity ['reɪdɪəuæk'tɪvɪtɪ] n radioactivité f.

radio announcer n annonceur m.

radio-controlled ['reɪdɪəukən'trəuld] adj radioguidé(e).

radiographer [reɪdɪ'ɔgrəfə*] n radiologue m/f (technicien).

radiography [reɪdɪ'ɔgrəfɪ] n radiographie f.

radiologist [reɪdɪ'ɔlədʒɪst] n radiologue m/f (médecin).

radiology [reɪdɪ'ɔlədʒɪ] n radiologie f.

radio station n station f de radio.

radio taxi n radio-taxi m.

radiotelephone ['reɪdɪəu'tɛlɪfəun] n radiotéléphone m.

radiotherapist ['reɪdɪəu'θɛrəpɪst] n radiothérapeute m/f.

radiotherapy ['reɪdɪəu'θɛrəpɪ] n radiothérapie f.

radish ['rædɪʃ] n radis m.

radium ['reɪdɪəm] n radium m.

radius, pl **radii** ['reɪdɪəs, -ɪaɪ] n rayon m; (ANAT) radius m; **within a ~ of 50 miles** dans un rayon de 50 milles.

RAF n abbr (BRIT) = **Royal Air Force**.

raffia ['ræfɪə] n raphia m.

raffish ['ræfɪʃ] adj dissolu(e); canaille.

raffle ['ræfl] n tombola f ♦ vt mettre comme lot dans une tombola.

raft [rɑːft] n (craft; also: **life ~**) radeau m; (logs) train m de flottage.

rafter ['rɑːftə*] n chevron m.
rag [ræg] n chiffon m; (pej: newspaper) feuille f, torchon m; (for charity) attractions organisées par les étudiants au profit d'œuvres de charité ♦ vt (BRIT) chahuter, mettre en boîte; ~s npl haillons mpl; in ~s (person) en haillons; (clothes) en lambeaux.
rag-and-bone man [rægən'bəunmæn] n chiffonnier m.
ragbag ['rægbæg] n (fig) ramassis m.

Rag Day ou plus communément **Rag Week**, est un jour, une semaine, où les étudiants se déguisent et collectent de l'argent pour les œuvres de charité. Toutes sortes d'animations sont organisées à cette occasion (marches sponsorisées, spectacles de rue etc). Des magazines (les "rag mags") contenant des plaisanteries osées sont vendus dans les rues, également au profit des œuvres. Enfin, la plupart des universités organisent un bal (le "rag ball").

---

rag doll n poupée f de chiffon.
rage [reɪdʒ] n (fury) rage f, fureur f ♦ vi (person) être fou(folle) de rage; (storm) faire rage, être déchaîné(e); **to fly into a ~** se mettre en rage; **it's all the ~** cela fait fureur.
ragged ['rægɪd] adj (edge) inégal(e), qui accroche; (cuff) effiloché(e); (appearance) déguenillé(e).
raging ['reɪdʒɪŋ] adj (sea, storm) en furie; (fever, pain) violent(e); ~ **toothache** rage f de dents; **in a ~ temper** dans une rage folle.
rag trade n (col): **the ~** la confection.
raid [reɪd] n (MIL) raid m; (criminal) hold-up m inv; (by police) descente f, rafle f ♦ vt faire un raid sur or un hold-up dans or une descente dans.
raider ['reɪdə*] n malfaiteur m.
rail [reɪl] n (on stair) rampe f; (on bridge, balcony) balustrade f; (of ship) bastingage m; (for train) rail m; ~s npl rails mpl, voie ferrée; **by ~** par chemin de fer, par le train.
railcard ['reɪlkɑːd] n (BRIT) carte f de chemin de fer; **young person's ~** carte f jeune.
railing(s) ['reɪlɪŋ(z)] n(pl) grille f.
railway ['reɪlweɪ], (US) **railroad** ['reɪlrəud] n chemin m de fer.
railway engine n locomotive f.
railway line n ligne f de chemin de fer; (track) voie ferrée.
railwayman ['reɪlweɪmən] n cheminot m.
railway station n gare f.
rain [reɪn] n pluie f ♦ vi pleuvoir; **in the ~** sous la pluie; **it's ~ing** il pleut; **it's ~ing cats and dogs** il pleut à torrents.
rainbow ['reɪnbəu] n arc-en-ciel m.
raincoat ['reɪnkəut] n imperméable m.
raindrop ['reɪndrɔp] n goutte f de pluie.
rainfall ['reɪnfɔːl] n chute f de pluie;

(measurement) hauteur f des précipitations.
rainforest ['reɪnfɔrɪst] n forêt tropicale.
rainproof ['reɪnpruːf] adj imperméable.
rainstorm ['reɪnstɔːm] n pluie torrentielle.
rainwater ['reɪnwɔːtə*] n eau f de pluie.
rainy ['reɪnɪ] adj pluvieux(euse).
raise [reɪz] n augmentation f ♦ vt (lift) lever; hausser; (end: siege, embargo) lever; (build) ériger; (increase) augmenter; (a protest, doubt) provoquer, causer; (a question) soulever; (cattle, family) élever; (crop) faire pousser; (army, funds) rassembler; (loan) obtenir; **to ~ one's glass to sb/sth** porter un toast en l'honneur de qn/qch; **to ~ one's voice** élever la voix; **to ~ sb's hopes** donner de l'espoir à qn; **to ~ a laugh/a smile** faire rire/sourire.
raisin ['reɪzn] n raisin sec.
Raj [rɑːdʒ] n: **the ~** l'empire m (aux Indes).
rajah ['rɑːdʒə] n radja(h) m.
rake [reɪk] n (tool) râteau m; (person) débauché m ♦ vt (garden) ratisser; (fire) tisonner; (with machine gun) balayer ♦ vi: **to ~ through** (fig: search) fouiller (dans).
rake-off ['reɪkɔf] n (col) pourcentage m.
rakish ['reɪkɪʃ] adj dissolu(e); cavalier(ière).
rally ['rælɪ] n (POL etc) meeting m, rassemblement m; (AUT) rallye m; (TENNIS) échange m ♦ vt rassembler, rallier ♦ vi se rallier; (sick person) aller mieux; (Stock Exchange) reprendre.
►rally round vi venir en aide ♦ vt fus se rallier à; venir en aide à.
rallying point ['rælɪŋ-] n (MIL) point m de ralliement.
RAM [ræm] n abbr (COMPUT) = **random access memory**.
ram [ræm] n bélier m ♦ vt enfoncer; (soil) tasser; (crash into) emboutir; percuter; éperonner.
ramble ['ræmbl] n randonnée f ♦ vi (pej: also: ~ on) discourir, pérorer.
rambler ['ræmblə*] n promeneur/euse, randonneur/euse; (BOT) rosier grimpant.
rambling ['ræmblɪŋ] adj (speech) décousu(e); (house) plein(e) de coins et de recoins; (BOT) grimpant(e).
RAMC n abbr (BRIT) = **Royal Army Medical Corps**.
ramification [ræmɪfɪ'keɪʃən] n ramification f.
ramp [ræmp] n (incline) rampe f; dénivellation f; (in garage) pont m.
rampage [ræm'peɪdʒ] n: **to be on the ~** se déchaîner ♦ vi: **they went rampaging through the town** ils ont envahi les rues et ont tout saccagé sur leur passage.
rampant ['ræmpənt] adj (disease etc) qui sévit.
rampart ['ræmpɑːt] n rempart m.
ram raiding [-reɪdɪŋ] n pillage d'un magasin en enfonçant la vitrine avec une voiture volée.
ramshackle ['ræmʃækl] adj (house) délabré(e); (car etc) déglingué(e).

RAN n abbr = Royal Australian Navy.
ran [ræn] pt of **run**.
ranch [rɑːntʃ] n ranch m.
rancher ['rɑːntʃə*] n (owner) propriétaire m de ranch; (ranch hand) cowboy m.
rancid ['rænsɪd] adj rance.
rancour, (US) rancor ['ræŋkə*] n rancune f, rancœur f.
R&B n abbr = rhythm and blues.
R&D n abbr (= research and development) R-D f.
random ['rændəm] adj fait(e) or établi(e) au hasard; (COMPUT, MATH) aléatoire ♦ n: at ~ au hasard.
random access memory (RAM) n (COMPUT) mémoire vive, RAM f.
R&R n abbr (US MIL) = rest and recreation.
randy ['rændɪ] adj (BRIT col) excité(e); lubrique.
rang [ræŋ] pt of **ring**.
range [reɪndʒ] n (of mountains) chaîne f; (of missile, voice) portée f; (of products) choix m, gamme f; (also: **shooting** ~) champ m de tir; (: indoor) stand m de tir; (also: **kitchen** ~) fourneau m (de cuisine) ♦ vt (place) mettre en rang, placer; (roam) parcourir ♦ vi: to ~ over couvrir; to ~ from ... to aller de ... à; **price** ~ éventail m des prix; **do you have anything else in this price** ~? avez-vous autre chose dans ces prix?; **within (firing)** ~ à portée (de tir); ~**d left/right** (text) justifié à gauche/à droite.
ranger ['reɪndʒə*] n garde m forestier.
Rangoon [ræŋˈguːn] n Rangoon.
rank [ræŋk] n rang m; (MIL) grade m; (BRIT: also: **taxi** ~) station f de taxis ♦ vi: to ~ among compter or se classer parmi ♦ vt: I ~ him sixth je le place sixième ♦ adj (smell) nauséabond(e); (hypocrisy, injustice etc) flagrant(e); **he's a** ~ **outsider** il n'est vraiment pas dans la course; **the** ~**s** (MIL) la troupe; **the** ~ **and file** (fig) la masse, la base; **to close** ~**s** (MIL, fig) serrer les rangs.
rankle ['ræŋkl] vi (insult) rester sur le cœur.
ransack ['rænsæk] vt fouiller (à fond); (plunder) piller.
ransom ['rænsəm] n rançon f; **to hold sb to** ~ (fig) exercer un chantage sur qn.
rant [rænt] vi fulminer.
ranting ['ræntɪŋ] n invectives fpl.
rap [ræp] n petit coup sec; tape f ♦ vt frapper sur or à; taper sur.
rape [reɪp] n viol m; (BOT) colza m ♦ vt violer.
rape(seed) oil ['reɪp(siːd)-] n huile f de colza.
rapid ['ræpɪd] adj rapide.
rapidity [rəˈpɪdɪtɪ] n rapidité f.
rapidly ['ræpɪdlɪ] adv rapidement.
rapids ['ræpɪdz] npl (GEO) rapides mpl.
rapist ['reɪpɪst] n auteur m d'un viol.
rapport [ræˈpɔː*] n entente f.
rapt [ræpt] adj (attention) extrême; **to be** ~ **in contemplation** être perdu(e) dans la contemplation.

rapture ['ræptʃə*] n extase f, ravissement m; **to go into** ~**s over** s'extasier sur.
rapturous ['ræptʃərəs] adj extasié(e); frénétique.
rare [rɛə*] adj rare; (CULIN: steak) saignant(e).
rarebit ['rɛəbɪt] n see **Welsh rarebit**.
rarefied ['rɛərɪfaɪd] adj (air, atmosphere) raréfié(e).
rarely ['rɛəlɪ] adv rarement.
raring ['rɛərɪŋ] adj: **to be** ~ **to go** (col) être très impatient(e) de commencer.
rarity ['rɛərɪtɪ] n rareté f.
rascal ['rɑːskl] n vaurien m.
rash [ræʃ] adj imprudent(e), irréfléchi(e) ♦ n (MED) rougeur f, éruption f; **to come out in a** ~ avoir une éruption.
rasher ['ræʃə*] n fine tranche (de lard).
rasp [rɑːsp] n (tool) lime f ♦ vt (speak: also: ~ out) dire d'une voix grinçante.
raspberry ['rɑːzbərɪ] n framboise f.
raspberry bush n framboisier m.
rasping ['rɑːspɪŋ] adj: ~ **noise** grincement m.
Rastafarian [ræstəˈfɛərɪən] adj, n rastafari (m/f).
rat [ræt] n rat m.
ratable ['reɪtəbl] adj = **rateable**.
ratchet ['rætʃɪt] n: ~ **wheel** roue f à rochet.
rate [reɪt] n (ratio) taux m, pourcentage m; (speed) vitesse f, rythme m; (price) tarif m ♦ vt classer; évaluer; **to** ~ **sb/sth as** considérer qn/qch comme; **to** ~ **sb/sth among** classer qn/qch parmi; **to** ~ **sb/sth highly** avoir une haute opinion de qn/qch; **at a** ~ **of 60 kph** à une vitesse de 60 km/h; ~ **of exchange** taux or cours m du change; ~ **of flow** débit m; ~ **of return** (taux de) rendement m; **pulse** ~ fréquence f des pulsations.
rateable value ['reɪtəbl-] n (BRIT) valeur locative imposable.
ratepayer ['reɪtpeɪə*] n (BRIT) contribuable m/f (payant les impôts locaux).
rates ['reɪts] npl (BRIT) impôts locaux.
rather ['rɑːðə*] adv (somewhat) assez, plutôt; (to some extent) un peu; **it's** ~ **expensive** c'est assez cher; (too much) c'est un peu cher; **there's** ~ **a lot** il y en a beaucoup; **I would** or **I'd** ~ **go** j'aimerais mieux or je préférerais partir; **I had** ~ **go** il vaudrait mieux que je parte; **I'd** ~ **not leave** j'aimerais mieux ne pas partir; **or** ~ (more accurately) ou plutôt; **I** ~ **think he won't come** je crois bien qu'il ne viendra pas.
ratification [rætɪfɪˈkeɪʃən] n ratification f.
ratify ['rætɪfaɪ] vt ratifier.
rating ['reɪtɪŋ] n classement m; cote f; (NAUT: category) classe f; (: sailor: BRIT) matelot m; ~**s** npl (RADIO, TV) indice(s) m(pl) d'écoute.
ratio ['reɪʃɪəu] n proportion f; **in the** ~ **of 100 to 1** dans la proportion de 100 contre 1.
ration ['ræʃən] n (gen pl) ration(s) f(pl) ♦ vt rationner.
rational ['ræʃənl] adj raisonnable, sensé(e);

(*solution, reasoning*) logique; (*MED*) lucide.
rationale [ræʃəˈnɑːl] *n* raisonnement *m*;
justification *f*.
rationalization [ræʃnəlaɪˈzeɪʃən] *n*
rationalisation *f*.
rationalize [ˈræʃnəlaɪz] *vt* rationaliser;
(*conduct*) essayer d'expliquer *or* de motiver.
rationally [ˈræʃnəlɪ] *adv* raisonnablement;
logiquement.
rationing [ˈræʃnɪŋ] *n* rationnement *m*.
ratpack [ˈrætpæk] *n* (*BRIT col*) journalistes *mpl*
de la presse à sensation.
rat poison *n* mort-aux-rats *f inv*.
rat race *n* foire *f* d'empoigne.
rattan [ræˈtæn] *n* rotin *m*.
rattle [ˈrætl] *n* cliquetis *m*; (*louder*) bruit *m* de
ferraille; (*object: of baby*) hochet *m*; (: *of
sports fan*) crécelle *f* ♦ *vi* cliqueter; faire un
bruit de ferraille *or* du bruit ♦ *vt* agiter
(bruyamment); (*col: disconcert*)
décontenancer; (: *annoy*) embêter.
rattlesnake [ˈrætlsneɪk] *n* serpent *m* à
sonnettes.
ratty [ˈrætɪ] *adj* (*col*) en rogne.
raucous [ˈrɔːkəs] *adj* rauque.
raucously [ˈrɔːkəslɪ] *adv* d'une voix rauque.
raunchy [ˈrɔːntʃɪ] *adj* (*col: voice, image, act*)
sexy; (:*scenes, film*) lubrique.
ravage [ˈrævɪdʒ] *vt* ravager.
ravages [ˈrævɪdʒɪz] *npl* ravages *mpl*.
rave [reɪv] *vi* (*in anger*) s'emporter; (*with
enthusiasm*) s'extasier; (*MED*) délirer ♦ *n*: **a ~
(party)** une rave, une soirée techno ♦ *adj*
(*scene, culture, music*) rave, techno ♦ *cpd*: **~
review** (*col*) critique *f* dithyrambique.
raven [ˈreɪvən] *n* grand corbeau.
ravenous [ˈrævənəs] *adj* affamé(e).
ravine [rəˈviːn] *n* ravin *m*.
raving [ˈreɪvɪŋ] *adj*: **~ lunatic** *n* fou furieux/
folle furieuse.
ravings [ˈreɪvɪŋz] *npl* divagations *fpl*.
ravioli [rævɪˈəʊlɪ] *n* ravioli *mpl*.
ravish [ˈrævɪʃ] *vt* ravir.
ravishing [ˈrævɪʃɪŋ] *adj* enchanteur(eresse).
raw [rɔː] *adj* (*uncooked*) cru(e); (*not processed*)
brut(e); (*sore*) à vif, irrité(e); (*inexperienced*)
inexpérimenté(e); **~ deal** (*col: bad bargain*)
sale coup *m*; (: *unfair treatment*): **to get a ~
deal** être traité(e) injustement.
Rawalpindi [rɔːlˈpɪndɪ] *n* Rawalpindi.
raw material *n* matière première.
ray [reɪ] *n* rayon *m*; **~ of hope** lueur *f* d'espoir.
rayon [ˈreɪɔn] *n* rayonne *f*.
raze [reɪz] *vt* (*also*: **~ to the ground**) raser.
razor [ˈreɪzə*] *n* rasoir *m*.
razor blade *n* lame *f* de rasoir.
razzle(-dazzle) [ˈræzl(ˈdæzl)] *n* (*BRIT col*): **to
go on the ~** faire la bringue.
razzmatazz [ˈræzməˈtæz] *n* (*col*) tralala *m*,
tapage *m*.
RC *abbr* = **Roman Catholic**.
RCAF *n abbr* = **Royal Canadian Air Force**.

RCMP *n abbr* = **Royal Canadian Mounted Police**
RCN *n abbr* = **Royal Canadian Navy**.
RD *abbr* (*US*) = **rural delivery**.
Rd *abbr* = **road**.
RDC *n abbr* (*BRIT*) = **rural district council**.
RE *n abbr* (*BRIT*) = **religious education**; (*BRIT MI
= **Royal Engineers**.
re [riː] *prep* concernant.
reach [riːtʃ] *n* portée *f*, atteinte *f*; (*of river etc
étendue *f* ♦ *vt* atteindre, arriver à ♦ *vi*
s'étendre; (*stretch out hand*): **to ~ up/down
out** *etc* **(for sth)** lever/baisser/allonger *etc*
bras (pour prendre qch); **to ~ sb by phone**
joindre qn par téléphone; **out of/within ~**
(*object*) hors de/à portée; **within easy ~ (of
(*place*) à proximité (de), proche (de).
react [riːˈækt] *vi* réagir.
reaction [riːˈækʃən] *n* réaction *f*.
reactionary [riːˈækʃənrɪ] *adj, n* réactionnaire
(*m/f*).
reactor [riːˈæktə*] *n* réacteur *m*.
read, *pt, pp* **read** [riːd, rɛd] *vi* lire ♦ *vt* lire;
(*understand*) comprendre, interpréter;
(*study*) étudier; (*subj: instrument etc*)
indiquer, marquer; **to take sth as read** (*fig*
considérer qch comme accepté; **do you ~
me?** (*TEL*) est-ce que vous me recevez?
►**read out** *vt* lire à haute voix.
►**read over** *vt* relire.
►**read through** *vt* (*quickly*) parcourir;
(*thoroughly*) lire jusqu'au bout.
►**read up** *vt*, **read up on** *vt fus* étudier.
readable [ˈriːdəbl] *adj* facile *or* agréable à lir
reader [ˈriːdə*] *n* lecteur/trice; (*book*) livre *n
de lecture; (*BRIT: at university*) maître *m* de
conférences.
readership [ˈriːdəʃɪp] *n* (*of paper etc*) (*nombr
m de) lecteurs *mpl*.
readily [ˈrɛdɪlɪ] *adv* volontiers, avec
empressement; (*easily*) facilement.
readiness [ˈrɛdɪnɪs] *n* empressement *m*; **in ~**
(*prepared*) prêt(e).
reading [ˈriːdɪŋ] *n* lecture *f*; (*understanding*)
interprétation *f*; (*on instrument*) indication
fpl.
reading lamp *n* lampe *f* de bureau.
reading room *n* salle *f* de lecture.
readjust [riːəˈdʒʌst] *vt* rajuster; (*instrument*)
régler de nouveau ♦ *vi* (*person*): **to ~ (to)** s
réadapter (à).
ready [ˈrɛdɪ] *adj* prêt(e); (*willing*) prêt,
disposé(e); (*quick*) prompt(e); (*available*)
disponible ♦ *n*: **at the ~** (*MIL*) prêt à faire
feu; (*fig*) tout(e) prêt(e); **~ for use** prêt à
l'emploi; **to be ~ to do sth** être prêt à fair
qch; **to get ~** *vi* se préparer ♦ *vt* préparer.
ready cash *n* (argent *m*) liquide *m*.
ready-made [ˈrɛdɪˈmeɪd] *adj* tout(e) fait(e).
ready-mix [ˈrɛdɪmɪks] *n* (*for cakes etc*)
préparation *f* en sachet.
ready reckoner [-ˈrɛknə*] *n* (*BRIT*) barème *n*
ready-to-wear [ˈrɛdɪtəˈwɛə*] *adj* (en) prêt-à-

porter.

reagent [ri:'eɪdʒənt] n réactif m.

real [rɪəl] adj réel(le); (*genuine*) véritable; (*proper*) vrai(e) ♦ adv (*US col: very*) vraiment; **in ~ life** dans la réalité.

real ale n bière traditionnelle.

real estate n biens fonciers or immobiliers.

realism ['rɪəlɪzəm] n réalisme m.

realist ['rɪəlɪst] n réaliste m/f.

realistic [rɪə'lɪstɪk] adj réaliste.

reality [ri:'ælɪtɪ] n réalité f; **in ~** en réalité, en fait.

realization [rɪəlaɪ'zeɪʃən] n prise f de conscience; réalisation f.

realize ['rɪəlaɪz] vt (*understand*) se rendre compte de, prendre conscience de; (*a project, COMM: asset*) réaliser.

really ['rɪəlɪ] adv vraiment.

realm [rɛlm] n royaume m.

real-time ['ri:ltaɪm] adj (*COMPUT*) en temps réel.

Realtor ['rɪəltɔː*] n ® (*US*) agent immobilier.

ream [ri:m] n rame f (*de papier*); **~s** npl (*fig: col*) des pages et des pages.

reap [ri:p] vt moissonner; (*fig*) récolter.

reaper ['ri:pə*] n (*machine*) moissonneuse f.

reappear [ri:ə'pɪə*] vi réapparaître, reparaître.

reappearance [ri:ə'pɪərəns] n réapparition f.

reapply [ri:ə'plaɪ] vi: **to ~ for** (*job*) faire une nouvelle demande d'emploi concernant; reposer sa candidature à; (*loan, grant*) faire une nouvelle demande de.

reappraisal [ri:ə'preɪzl] n réévaluation f.

rear [rɪə*] adj de derrière, arrière inv; (*AUT: wheel etc*) arrière ♦ n arrière m, derrière m ♦ vt (*cattle, family*) élever ♦ vi (*also: ~ up: animal*) se cabrer.

rear admiral (RA) n vice-amiral m.

rear-engined ['rɪər'ɛndʒɪnd] adj (*AUT*) avec moteur à l'arrière.

rearguard ['rɪəgɑːd] n arrière-garde f.

rearm [ri:'ɑːm] vt, vi réarmer.

rearmament [ri:'ɑːməmənt] n réarmement m.

rearrange [ri:ə'reɪndʒ] vt réarranger.

rear-view ['rɪəvju:]: **~ mirror** n (*AUT*) rétroviseur m.

reason ['ri:zn] n raison f ♦ vi: **to ~ with sb** raisonner qn, faire entendre raison à qn; **the ~ for/why** la raison de/pour laquelle; **to have ~ to think** avoir lieu de penser; **it stands to ~ that** il va sans dire que; **she claims with good ~ that ...** elle affirme à juste titre que ...; **all the more ~ why** raison de plus pour + *infinitive* or pour que + *sub*.

reasonable ['ri:znəbl] adj raisonnable; (*not bad*) acceptable.

reasonably ['ri:znəblɪ] adv (*to behave*) raisonnablement; (*fairly*) assez; **one can ~ assume that ...** on est fondé à or il est permis de supposer que ....

reasoned ['ri:znd] adj (*argument*) raisonné(e).

reasoning ['ri:znɪŋ] n raisonnement m.

reassemble [ri:ə'sɛmbl] vt rassembler; (*machine*) remonter.

reassert [ri:ə'sə:t] vt réaffirmer.

reassurance [ri:ə'ʃuərəns] n assurance f, garantie f; (*comfort*) réconfort m.

reassure [ri:ə'ʃuə*] vt rassurer; **to ~ sb of** donner à qn l'assurance répétée de.

reassuring [ri:ə'ʃuərɪŋ] adj rassurant(e).

reawakening [ri:ə'weɪknɪŋ] n réveil m.

rebate ['ri:beɪt] n (*on product*) rabais m; (*on tax etc*) dégrèvement m; (*repayment*) remboursement m.

rebel n ['rɛbl] rebelle m/f ♦ vi [rɪ'bɛl] se rebeller, se révolter.

rebellion [rɪ'bɛljən] n rébellion f, révolte f.

rebellious [rɪ'bɛljəs] adj rebelle.

rebirth [ri:'bə:θ] n renaissance f.

rebound vi [rɪ'baund] (*ball*) rebondir ♦ n ['ri:baund] rebond m.

rebuff [rɪ'bʌf] n rebuffade f ♦ vt repousser.

rebuild [ri:'bɪld] vt irreg reconstruire.

rebuke [rɪ'bju:k] n réprimande f, reproche m ♦ vt réprimander.

rebut [rɪ'bʌt] vt réfuter.

rebuttal [rɪ'bʌtl] n réfutation f.

recalcitrant [rɪ'kælsɪtrənt] adj récalcitrant(e).

recall [rɪ'kɔːl] vt rappeler; (*remember*) se rappeler, se souvenir de ♦ n rappel m; **beyond ~** adj irrévocable.

recant [rɪ'kænt] vi se rétracter; (*REL*) abjurer.

recap [rɪ'kæp] n récapitulation f ♦ vt, vi récapituler.

recapture [ri:'kæptʃə*] vt reprendre; (*atmosphere*) recréer.

recd. abbr = received.

recede [rɪ'si:d] vi s'éloigner; reculer; redescendre.

receding [rɪ'si:dɪŋ] adj (*forehead, chin*) fuyant(e); **~ hairline** front dégarni.

receipt [rɪ'si:t] n (*document*) reçu m; (*for parcel etc*) accusé m de réception; (*act of receiving*) réception f; **~s** npl (*COMM*) recettes fpl; **to acknowledge ~ of** accuser réception de; **we are in ~ of ...** nous avons reçu ....

receivable [rɪ'si:vəbl] adj (*COMM*) recevable; (*: owing*) à recevoir.

receive [rɪ'si:v] vt recevoir; (*guest*) recevoir, accueillir; **"~d with thanks"** (*COMM*) "pour acquit".

*En Grande-Bretagne, la **received pronunciation** ou RP est une prononciation de la langue anglaise qui, récemment encore, était surtout associée à l'aristocratie et à la bourgeoisie, mais qui maintenant est en général considérée comme la prononciation correcte.*

receiver [rɪ'si:və*] n (*TEL*) récepteur m, combiné m; (*RADIO*) récepteur m; (*of stolen goods*) receleur m; (*COMM*) administrateur m judiciaire.

receivership [rɪ'siːvəʃɪp] n: **to go into** ~ être placé sous administration judiciaire.
recent ['riːsnt] adj récent(e); **in** ~ **years** au cours de ces dernières années.
recently ['riːsntlɪ] adv récemment; **as** ~ **as** pas plus tard que; **until** ~ jusqu'à il y a peu de temps encore.
receptacle [rɪ'septɪkl] n récipient m.
reception [rɪ'sepʃən] n réception f; (*welcome*) accueil m, réception.
reception centre n (*BRIT*) centre m d'accueil.
reception desk n réception f.
receptionist [rɪ'sepʃənɪst] n réceptionniste m/f.
receptive [rɪ'septɪv] adj réceptif(ive).
recess [rɪ'ses] n (*in room*) renfoncement m; (*for bed*) alcôve f; (*secret place*) recoin m; (*POL etc: holiday*) vacances fpl; (*US: LAW: short break*) suspension f d'audience; (*SCOL: esp US*) récréation f.
recession [rɪ'seʃən] n (*ECON*) récession f.
recharge [riː'tʃɑːdʒ] vt (*battery*) recharger.
rechargeable [riː'tʃɑːdʒəbl] adj rechargeable.
recipe ['resɪpɪ] n recette f.
recipient [rɪ'sɪpɪənt] n bénéficiaire m/f; (*of letter*) destinataire m/f.
reciprocal [rɪ'sɪprəkl] adj réciproque.
reciprocate [rɪ'sɪprəkeɪt] vt retourner, offrir en retour ♦ vi en faire autant.
recital [rɪ'saɪtl] n récital m.
recite [rɪ'saɪt] vt (*poem*) réciter; (*complaints etc*) énumérer.
reckless ['reklɪs] adj (*driver etc*) imprudent(e); (*spender etc*) insouciant(e).
recklessly ['reklɪslɪ] adv imprudemment; avec insouciance.
reckon ['rekən] vt (*count*) calculer, compter; (*consider*) considérer, estimer; (*think*): **I** ~ (**that**) ... je pense (que) ..., j'estime (que) ... ♦ vi: **he is somebody to be** ~**ed with** il ne faut pas le sous-estimer; **to** ~ **without sb/ sth** ne pas tenir compte de qn/qch.
▶**reckon on** vt fus compter sur, s'attendre à.
reckoning ['rekənɪŋ] n compte m, calcul m; estimation f; **the day of** ~ le jour du Jugement.
reclaim [rɪ'kleɪm] vt (*land*) amender; (*: from sea*) assécher; (*: from forest*) défricher; (*demand back*) réclamer (le remboursement or la restitution de).
reclamation [reklə'meɪʃən] n (*of land*) amendement m; assèchement m; défrichement m.
recline [rɪ'klaɪn] vi être allongé(e) or étendu(e).
reclining [rɪ'klaɪnɪŋ] adj (*seat*) à dossier réglable.
recluse [rɪ'kluːs] n reclus/e, ermite m.
recognition [rekəg'nɪʃən] n reconnaissance f; **in** ~ **of** en reconnaissance de; **to gain** ~ être reconnu(e); **transformed beyond** ~ méconnaissable.

recognizable ['rekəgnaɪzəbl] adj: ~ (**by**) reconnaissable (à).
recognize ['rekəgnaɪz] vt: **to** ~ (**by/as**) reconnaître (à/comme étant).
recoil [rɪ'kɔɪl] vi (*person*): **to** ~ (**from**) reculer (devant) ♦ n (*of gun*) recul m.
recollect [rekə'lekt] vt se rappeler, se souvenir de.
recollection [rekə'lekʃən] n souvenir m; **to th best of my** ~ autant que je m'en souvienne
recommend [rekə'mend] vt recommander; **she has a lot to** ~ **her** elle a beaucoup de choses en sa faveur.
recommendation [rekəmen'deɪʃən] n recommandation f.
recommended retail price (RRP) [rekə'mendɪd-] n (*BRIT*) prix conseillé.
recompense ['rekəmpens] vt récompenser; (*compensate*) dédommager ♦ n récompense f; dédommagement m.
reconcilable ['rekənsaɪləbl] adj (*ideas*) conciliable.
reconcile ['rekənsaɪl] vt (*two people*) réconcilier; (*two facts*) concilier, accorder; **to** ~ **o.s. to** se résigner à.
reconciliation [rekənsɪlɪ'eɪʃən] n réconciliation f; conciliation f.
recondite [rɪ'kɔndaɪt] adj abstrus(e), obscur(e).
recondition [riːkən'dɪʃən] vt remettre à neuf réviser entièrement.
reconnaissance [rɪ'kɔnɪsns] n (*MIL*) reconnaissance f.
reconnoitre, (*US*) reconnoiter [rekə'nɔɪtə*] (*MIL*) vt reconnaître ♦ vi faire une reconnaissance.
reconsider [riːkən'sɪdə*] vt reconsidérer.
reconstitute [riː'kɔnstɪtjuːt] vt reconstituer.
reconstruct [riːkən'strʌkt] vt (*building*) reconstruire; (*crime*) reconstituer.
reconstruction [riːkən'strʌkʃən] n reconstruction f; reconstitution f.
reconvene [riːkən'viːn] vt reconvoquer ♦ vi s réunir or s'assembler de nouveau.
record n ['rekɔːd] rapport m, récit m; (*of meeting etc*) procès-verbal m; (*register*) registre m; (*file*) dossier m; (*COMPUT*) articl m; (*also: police* ~) casier m judiciaire; (*MUS disc*) disque m; (*SPORT*) record m ♦ vt [rɪ'kɔːd (*set down*) noter; (*relate*) rapporter; (*MUS: song etc*) enregistrer; **in** ~ **time** dans un temps record *inv*; **public** ~**s** archives fpl; **to keep a** ~ **of** noter; **to keep the** ~ **straight** (*fig*) mettre les choses au point; **he is on** ~ **as saying that** ... il a déclaré en public que ...; **Italy's excellent** ~ les excellents résultats obtenus par l'Italie; **off the** ~ adj officieux(euse) ♦ adv officieusement.
record card n (*in file*) fiche f.
recorded delivery letter [rɪ'kɔːdɪd-] n (*BRIT POST*) ≈ lettre recommandée.
recorder [rɪ'kɔːdə*] n (*LAW*) avocat nommé à

la fonction de juge; (MUS) flûte f à bec.

•cord holder n (SPORT) détenteur/trice du record.

•cording [rɪ'kɔːdɪŋ] n (MUS) enregistrement m.

•cording studio n studio m d'enregistrement.

•cord library n discothèque f.

•cord player n électrophone m.

•count [rɪ'kaunt] vt raconter.

•-count n ['riːkaunt] (POL: of votes) nouveau décompte (des suffrages) ♦ vt [riː'kaunt] recompter.

•coup [rɪ'kuːp] vt: **to ~ one's losses** récupérer ce qu'on a perdu, se refaire.

•course [rɪ'kɔːs] n recours m; expédient m; **to have ~ to** recourir à, avoir recours à.

•cover [rɪ'kʌvə*] vt récupérer ♦ vi (from illness) se rétablir; (from shock) se remettre; (country) se redresser.

•-cover [riː'kʌvə*] vt (chair etc) recouvrir.

•covery [rɪ'kʌvərɪ] n récupération f; rétablissement m; redressement m.

•create [riːkrɪ'eɪt] vt recréer.

•creation [rɛkrɪ'eɪʃən] n récréation f, détente f.

•creational [rɛkrɪ'eɪʃnl] adj pour la détente, récréatif(ive).

creational drug n drogue que l'on prend pour le plaisir et non pour des raisons médicales ou par dépendance.

•creational vehicle (RV) n (US) camping-car m.

•crimination [rɪkrɪmɪ'neɪʃən] n récrimination f.

•cruit [rɪ'kruːt] n recrue f ♦ vt recruter.

•cruiting office [rɪ'kruːtɪŋ-] n bureau m de recrutement.

•cruitment [rɪ'kruːtmənt] n recrutement m.

•ctangle ['rɛktæŋgl] n rectangle m.

•ctangular [rɛk'tæŋgjulə*] adj rectangulaire.

•ctify ['rɛktɪfaɪ] vt (error) rectifier, corriger; (omission) réparer.

•ctor ['rɛktə*] n (REL) pasteur m; (in Scottish universities) personnalité élue par les étudiants pour les représenter.

•ctory ['rɛktərɪ] n presbytère m.

•ctum ['rɛktəm] n (ANAT) rectum m.

•cuperate [rɪ'kjuːpəreɪt] vi (from illness) se rétablir.

•cur [rɪ'kəː*] vi se reproduire; (idea, opportunity) se retrouver; (symptoms) réapparaître.

•currence [rɪ'kəːrns] n répétition f; réapparition f.

•current [rɪ'kəːrnt] adj périodique, fréquent(e).

•curring [rɪ'kəːrɪŋ] adj (MATH) périodique.

•cycle [riː'saɪkl] vt, vi recycler.

•d [rɛd] n rouge m; (POL: pej) rouge m/f ♦ adj rouge; **in the ~** (account) à découvert; (business) en déficit.

red alert n alerte f rouge.

red-blooded [rɛd'blʌdɪd] adj (col) viril, vigoureux(euse).

Une **redbrick university**, ainsi nommée à cause du matériau de construction répandu à l'époque (la brique), est une université britannique provinciale construite assez récemment, en particulier fin XIXe-début XXe siècle. Il y en a notamment une à Manchester, une à Liverpool et une à Bristol. Ce terme est utilisé pour établir une distinction avec les universités les plus anciennes et traditionnelles.

red carpet treatment n réception f en grande pompe.

Red Cross n Croix-Rouge f.

redcurrant ['rɛdkʌrənt] n groseille f (rouge).

redden ['rɛdn] vt, vi rougir.

reddish ['rɛdɪʃ] adj rougeâtre; (hair) plutôt roux(rousse).

redecorate [riː'dɛkəreɪt] vt refaire à neuf, repeindre et retapisser.

redecoration [riːdɛkə'reɪʃən] n remise f à neuf.

redeem [rɪ'diːm] vt (debt) rembourser; (sth in pawn) dégager; (fig, also REL) racheter.

redeemable [rɪ'diːməbl] adj rachetable; remboursable, amortissable.

redeeming [rɪ'diːmɪŋ] adj (feature) qui sauve, qui rachète (le reste).

redefine [riːdɪ'faɪn] vt redéfinir.

redemption [rɪ'dɛmʃən] n (REL) rédemption f; **past or beyond ~** (situation) irrémédiable; (place) qui ne peut plus être sauvé(e); (person) irrécupérable.

redeploy [riːdɪ'plɔɪ] vt (MIL) redéployer; (staff, resources) reconvertir.

redeployment [riːdɪ'plɔɪmənt] n redéploiement m; reconversion f.

redevelop [riːdɪ'vɛləp] vt rénover.

redevelopment [riːdɪ'vɛləpmənt] n rénovation f.

red-handed [rɛd'hændɪd] adj: **to be caught ~** être pris(e) en flagrant délit or la main dans le sac.

redhead ['rɛdhɛd] n roux/rousse.

red herring n (fig) diversion f, fausse piste.

red-hot [rɛd'hɔt] adj chauffé(e) au rouge, brûlant(e).

redirect [riːdaɪ'rɛkt] vt (mail) faire suivre.

redistribute [riːdɪ'strɪbjuːt] vt redistribuer.

red-letter day ['rɛdlɛtə-] n grand jour, jour mémorable.

red light n: **to go through a ~** (AUT) brûler un feu rouge.

red-light district ['rɛdlaɪt-] n quartier réservé.

red meat n viande f rouge.

redness ['rɛdnɪs] n rougeur f; (of hair) rousseur f.

redo [riːˈduː] *vt irreg* refaire.
redolent [ˈrɛdələnt] *adj*: ~ **of** qui sent; (*fig*) qui évoque.
redouble [riːˈdʌbl] *vt*: **to ~ one's efforts** redoubler d'efforts.
redraft [riːˈdrɑːft] *vt* remanier.
redress [rɪˈdrɛs] *n* réparation *f* ♦ *vt* redresser; **to ~ the balance** rétablir l'équilibre.
Red Sea *n*: **the ~** la mer Rouge.
redskin [ˈrɛdskɪn] *n* Peau-Rouge *m/f*.
red tape *n* (*fig*) paperasserie (administrative).
reduce [rɪˈdjuːs] *vt* réduire; (*lower*) abaisser; **"~ speed now"** (*AUT*) "ralentir"; **to ~ sth by/to** réduire qch de/à; **to ~ sb to tears** faire pleurer qn.
reduced [rɪˈdjuːst] *adj* réduit(e); **"greatly ~ prices"** "gros rabais"; **at a ~ price** (*goods*) au rabais; (*ticket etc*) à prix réduit.
reduction [rɪˈdʌkʃən] *n* réduction *f*; (*of price*) baisse *f*; (*discount*) rabais *m*; réduction.
redundancy [rɪˈdʌndənsɪ] *n* (*BRIT*) licenciement *m*, mise *f* au chômage; **compulsory ~** licenciement; **voluntary ~** départ *m* volontaire.
redundancy payment *n* (*BRIT*) indemnité *f* de licenciement.
redundant [rɪˈdʌndnt] *adj* (*BRIT: worker*) licencié(e), mis(e) au chômage; (*detail, object*) superflu(e); **to be made ~** (*worker*) être licencié, être mis au chômage.
reed [riːd] *n* (*BOT*) roseau *m*; (*MUS: of clarinet etc*) anche *f*.
re-educate [riːˈedjukeɪt] *vt* rééduquer.
reedy [ˈriːdɪ] *adj* (*voice, instrument*) ténu(e).
reef [riːf] *n* (*at sea*) récif *m*, écueil *m*.
reek [riːk] *vi*: **to ~ (of)** puer, empester.
reel [riːl] *n* bobine *f*; (*TECH*) dévidoir *m*; (*FISHING*) moulinet *m*; (*CINE*) bande *f* ♦ *vt* (*TECH*) bobiner; (*also*: **~ up**) enrouler ♦ *vi* (*sway*) chanceler; **my head is ~ing** j'ai la tête qui tourne.
▶**reel off** *vt* (*say*) énumérer, débiter.
re-election [riːɪˈlɛkʃən] *n* réélection *f*.
re-enter [riːˈentə*] *vt* (*also SPACE*) rentrer dans.
re-entry [riːˈentrɪ] *n* (*also SPACE*) rentrée *f*.
re-export *vt* [ˈriːɪksˈpɔːt] réexporter ♦ *n* [riːˈekspɔːt] marchandise réexportée; (*act*) réexportation *f*.
ref [rɛf] *n abbr* (*col*: = *referee*) arbitre *m*.
ref. *abbr* (*COMM*: = *with reference to*) réf.
refectory [rɪˈfɛktərɪ] *n* réfectoire *m*.
refer [rɪˈfəː*] *vt*: **to ~ sth to** (*dispute, decision*) soumettre qch à; **to ~ sb to** (*inquirer: for information*) adresser *or* envoyer qn à; (*reader: to text*) renvoyer qn à; **he ~red me to the manager** il m'a dit de m'adresser au directeur.
▶**refer to** *vt fus* (*allude to*) parler de, faire allusion à; (*apply to*) s'appliquer à; (*consult*) se reporter à; **~ring to your letter** (*COMM*)

en réponse à votre lettre.
referee [rɛfəˈriː] *n* arbitre *m*; (*TENNIS*) juge-arbitre *m*; (*BRIT: for job application*) répondant/e ♦ *vt* arbitrer.
reference [ˈrɛfrəns] *n* référence *f*, renvoi *m* (*mention*) allusion *f*, mention *f*; (*for job application: letter*) références; lettre *f* de recommandation; (*: person*) répondant/e; **with ~ to** en ce qui concerne; (*COMM: in letter*) me référant à; **"please quote this ~"** (*COMM*) "prière de rappeler cette référence".
reference book *n* ouvrage *m* de référence
reference library *n* bibliothèque *f* d'ouvra à consulter.
reference number *n* (*COMM*) numéro *m* d référence.
referendum, *pl* **referenda** [rɛfəˈrɛndəm, -ɑ référendum *m*.
referral [rɪˈfəːrəl] *n* soumission *f*; **she got a to a specialist** elle a été adressée à un spécialiste.
refill *vt* [riːˈfɪl] remplir à nouveau; (*pen, ligh etc*) recharger ♦ *n* [ˈriːfɪl] (*for pen etc*) recharge *f*.
refine [rɪˈfaɪn] *vt* (*sugar, oil*) raffiner; (*taste*) affiner.
refined [rɪˈfaɪnd] *adj* (*person, taste*) raffiné(e
refinement [rɪˈfaɪnmənt] *n* (*of person*) raffinement *m*.
refinery [rɪˈfaɪnərɪ] *n* raffinerie *f*.
refit (*NAUT*) *n* [ˈriːfɪt] remise *f* en état ♦ *vt* [riːˈfɪt] remettre en état.
reflate [riːˈfleɪt] *vt* (*economy*) relancer.
reflation [riːˈfleɪʃən] *n* relance *f*.
reflationary [riːˈfleɪʃənrɪ] *adj* de relance.
reflect [rɪˈflɛkt] *vt* (*light, image*) réfléchir, refléter; (*fig*) refléter ♦ *vi* (*think*) réfléchir méditer.
▶**reflect on** *vt fus* (*discredit*) porter atteinte faire tort à.
reflection [rɪˈflɛkʃən] *n* réflexion *f*; (*image*) reflet *m*; (*criticism*): ~ **on** critique *f* de; atteinte *f* à; **on ~** réflexion faite.
reflector [rɪˈflɛktə*] *n* (*also AUT*) réflecteur
reflex [ˈriːflɛks] *adj*, *n* réflexe (*m*).
reflexive [rɪˈflɛksɪv] *adj* (*LING*) réfléchi(e).
reform [rɪˈfɔːm] *n* réforme *f* ♦ *vt* réformer.
reformat [riːˈfɔːmæt] *vt* (*COMPUT*) reforma
Reformation [rɛfəˈmeɪʃən] *n*: **the ~** la Réforme.
reformatory [rɪˈfɔːmətərɪ] *n* (*US*) centre *m* d'éducation surveillée.
reformed [rɪˈfɔːmd] *adj* amendé(e), assagi(e
reformer [rɪˈfɔːmə*] *n* réformateur/trice.
refrain [rɪˈfreɪn] *vi*: **to ~ from doing** s'abste de faire ♦ *n* refrain *m*.
refresh [rɪˈfrɛʃ] *vt* rafraîchir; (*subj: food, sl etc*) redonner des forces à.
refresher course [rɪˈfrɛʃə-] *n* (*BRIT*) cours de recyclage.
refreshing [rɪˈfrɛʃɪŋ] *adj* rafraîchissant(e)

(*sleep*) réparateur(trice); (*fact,
idea etc*) qui réjouit par son originalité *or*
sa rareté.
efreshment [rɪ'frɛʃmənt] *n*: **for some ~**
(*eating*) pour se restaurer *or* sustenter; **in
need of ~** (*resting etc*) ayant besoin de
refaire ses forces; **~(s)** rafraîchissement(s)
m(pl).
efrigeration [rɪfrɪdʒə'reɪʃən] *n* réfrigération
f.
efrigerator [rɪ'frɪdʒəreɪtə*] *n* réfrigérateur
m, frigidaire *m*.
efuel [ri:'fjuəl] *vt* ravitailler en carburant ♦ *vi*
se ravitailler en carburant.
efuge ['rɛfju:dʒ] *n* refuge *m*; **to take ~ in** se
réfugier dans.
efugee [rɛfju'dʒi:] *n* réfugié/e.
efugee camp *n* camp *m* de réfugiés.
efund *n* ['ri:fʌnd] remboursement *m* ♦ *vt*
[rɪ'fʌnd] rembourser.
efurbish [ri:'fə:bɪʃ] *vt* remettre à neuf.
efurnish [ri:'fə:nɪʃ] *vt* remeubler.
efusal [rɪ'fju:zəl] *n* refus *m*; **to have first ~ on**
sth avoir droit de préemption sur qch.
efuse *n* ['rɛfju:s] ordures *fpl*, détritus *mpl* ♦ *vt,
vi* [rɪ'fju:z] refuser; **to ~ to do sth** refuser de
faire qch.
efuse collection *n* ramassage *m* d'ordures.
efuse disposal *n* élimination *f* des ordures.
efusenik [rɪ'fju:znɪk] *n* refuznik *m/f*.
efute [rɪ'fju:t] *vt* réfuter.
egain [rɪ'geɪn] *vt* regagner; retrouver.
egal ['ri:gl] *adj* royal(e).
egale [rɪ'geɪl] *vt*: **to ~ sb with sth** régaler qn
de qch.
egalia [rɪ'geɪlɪə] *n* insignes *mpl* de la royauté.
egard [rɪ'gɑ:d] *n* respect *m*, estime *f*,
considération *f* ♦ *vt* considérer; **to give one's
~s to** faire ses amitiés à; **"with kindest ~s"**
"bien amicalement"; **as ~s, with ~ to** en ce
qui concerne.
egarding [rɪ'gɑ:dɪŋ] *prep* en ce qui
concerne.
egardless [rɪ'gɑ:dlɪs] *adv* quand même; **~ of**
sans se soucier de.
egatta [rɪ'gætə] *n* régate *f*.
egency ['ri:dʒənsɪ] *n* régence *f*.
egenerate [rɪ'dʒɛnəreɪt] *vt* régénérer ♦ *vi* se
régénérer.
egent ['ri:dʒənt] *n* régent/e.
eggae ['rɛgeɪ] *n* reggae *m*.
égime [reɪ'ʒi:m] *n* régime *m*.
egiment *n* ['rɛdʒɪmənt] régiment *m* ♦ *vt*
['rɛdʒɪmɛnt] imposer une discipline trop
stricte à.
egimental [rɛdʒɪ'mɛntl] *adj* d'un *or* du
régiment.
egimentation [rɛdʒɪmɛn'teɪʃən] *n*
réglementation excessive.
egion ['ri:dʒən] *n* région *f*; **in the ~ of** (*fig*)
aux alentours de.
egional ['ri:dʒənl] *adj* régional(e).

En Écosse, le **regional council** *est une
assemblée délibérante régionale dont les
membres sont élus tous les quatre ans. Elle est
responsable, entre autres, de l'urbanisme, des
transports, de l'éducation, de la police et des
pompiers; voir* **district council**

regional development *n* aménagement *m*
du territoire.
register ['rɛdʒɪstə*] *n* registre *m*; (*also:
electoral ~) liste électorale ♦ *vt* enregistrer,
inscrire; (*birth*) déclarer; (*vehicle*)
immatriculer; (*luggage*) enregistrer; (*letter*)
envoyer en recommandé; (*subj: instrument*)
marquer ♦ *vi* se faire inscrire; (*at hotel*)
signer le registre; (*make impression*) être
(bien) compris(e); **to ~ for a course**
s'inscrire à un cours; **to ~ a protest**
protester.
registered ['rɛdʒɪstəd] *adj* (*design*) déposé(e);
(*BRIT: letter*) recommandé(e); (*student, voter*)
inscrit(e).
registered company *n* société
immatriculée.
registered nurse *n* (*US*) infirmier/ière
diplômé(e) d'État.
registered office *n* siège social.
registered trademark *n* marque déposée.
registrar ['rɛdʒɪstrɑ:*] *n* officier *m* de l'état
civil; secrétaire (général).
registration [rɛdʒɪs'treɪʃən] *n* (*act*)
enregistrement *m*; inscription *f*;
(*BRIT AUT: also: ~ **number**) numéro *m*
d'immatriculation.
registry ['rɛdʒɪstrɪ] *n* bureau *m* de
l'enregistrement.
registry office *n* (*BRIT*) bureau *m* de l'état
civil; **to get married in a ~** ≈ se marier à la
mairie.
regret [rɪ'grɛt] *n* regret *m* ♦ *vt* regretter; **to ~
that** regretter que + *sub*; **we ~ to inform you
that ...** nous sommes au regret de vous
informer que ....
regretfully [rɪ'grɛtfəlɪ] *adv* à *or* avec regret.
regrettable [rɪ'grɛtəbl] *adj* regrettable,
fâcheux(euse).
regrettably [rɪ'grɛtəblɪ] *adv* (*drunk, late*)
fâcheusement; **~, he ...** malheureusement,
il ....
regroup [ri:'gru:p] *vt* regrouper ♦ *vi* se
regrouper.
regt *abbr* = **regiment**.
regular ['rɛgjulə*] *adj* régulier(ière); (*usual*)
habituel(le), normal(e); (*listener, reader*)
fidèle; (*soldier*) de métier; (*COMM: size*)
ordinaire ♦ *n* (*client etc*) habitué/e.
regularity [rɛgju'lærɪtɪ] *n* régularité *f*.
regularly ['rɛgjuləlɪ] *adv* régulièrement.
regulate ['rɛgjuleɪt] *vt* régler.
regulation [rɛgju'leɪʃən] *n* (*rule*) règlement *m*;
(*adjustment*) réglage *m* ♦ *cpd* réglementaire.

rehabilitate [riːəˈbɪlɪteɪt] *vt* (*criminal*) réinsérer; (*drug addict*) désintoxiquer; (*invalid*) rééduquer.

rehabilitation [ˈriːəbɪlɪˈteɪʃən] *n* (*of offender*) réhabilitation *f*; (*of disabled*) rééducation *f*, réadaptation *f*.

rehash [riːˈhæʃ] *vt* (*col*) remanier.

rehearsal [rɪˈhəːsəl] *n* répétition *f*; **dress ~** (*répétition*) générale *f*.

rehearse [rɪˈhəːs] *vt* répéter.

rehouse [riːˈhauz] *vt* reloger.

reign [reɪn] *n* règne *m* ♦ *vi* régner.

reigning [ˈreɪnɪŋ] *adj* (*monarch*) régnant(e); (*champion*) actuel(le).

reimburse [riːɪmˈbəːs] *vt* rembourser.

rein [reɪn] *n* (*for horse*) rêne *f*; **to give sb free ~** (*fig*) donner carte blanche à qn.

reincarnation [riːɪnkɑːˈneɪʃən] *n* réincarnation *f*.

reindeer [ˈreɪndɪə*] *n* (*pl inv*) renne *m*.

reinforce [riːɪnˈfɔːs] *vt* renforcer.

reinforced concrete [riːɪnˈfɔst-] *n* béton armé.

reinforcement [riːɪnˈfɔːsmənt] *n* (*action*) renforcement *m*; **~s** *npl* (*MIL*) renfort(s) *m(pl)*.

reinstate [riːɪnˈsteɪt] *vt* rétablir, réintégrer.

reinstatement [riːɪnˈsteɪtmənt] *n* réintégration *f*.

reissue [riːˈɪʃjuː] *vt* (*book*) rééditer; (*film*) ressortir.

reiterate [riːˈɪtəreɪt] *vt* réitérer, répéter.

reject *n* [ˈriːdʒɛkt] (*COMM*) article *m* de rebut ♦ *vt* [rɪˈdʒɛkt] refuser; (*COMM: goods*) mettre au rebut; (*idea*) rejeter.

rejection [rɪˈdʒɛkʃən] *n* rejet *m*, refus *m*.

rejoice [rɪˈdʒɔɪs] *vi*: **to ~** (**at** *or* **over**) se réjouir (de).

rejoinder [rɪˈdʒɔɪndə*] *n* (*retort*) réplique *f*.

rejuvenate [rɪˈdʒuːvəneɪt] *vt* rajeunir.

rekindle [riːˈkɪndl] *vt* rallumer; (*fig*) raviver.

relapse [rɪˈlæps] *n* (*MED*) rechute *f*.

relate [rɪˈleɪt] *vt* (*tell*) raconter; (*connect*) établir un rapport entre ♦ *vi*: **to ~ to** (*connect*) se rapporter à; (*interact*) établir un rapport *or* une entente avec.

related [rɪˈleɪtɪd] *adj* apparenté(e).

relating [rɪˈleɪtɪŋ]: **~ to** *prep* concernant.

relation [rɪˈleɪʃən] *n* (*person*) parent/e; (*link*) rapport *m*, lien *m*; **diplomatic/international ~s** relations diplomatiques/internationales; **in ~ to** en ce qui concerne; par rapport à; **to bear no ~ to** être sans rapport avec.

relationship [rɪˈleɪʃənʃɪp] *n* rapport *m*, lien *m*; (*personal ties*) relations *fpl*, rapports *m*; (*also:* **family ~**) lien de parenté; (*affair*) liaison *f*; **they have a good ~** ils s'entendent bien.

relative [ˈrɛlətɪv] *n* parent/e ♦ *adj* relatif(ive); (*respective*) respectif(ive); **all her ~s** toute sa famille.

relatively [ˈrɛlətɪvlɪ] *adv* relativement.

relax [rɪˈlæks] *vi* se relâcher; (*person: unwind*) se détendre; (*calm down*) se calmer ♦ *vt* relâcher; (*mind, person*) détendre.

relaxation [riːlækˈseɪʃən] *n* relâchement *m*; détente *f*; (*entertainment*) distraction *f*.

relaxed [rɪˈlækst] *adj* relâché(e); détendu(e).

relaxing [rɪˈlæksɪŋ] *adj* délassant(e).

relay [ˈriːleɪ] *n* (*SPORT*) course *f* de relais ♦ *vt* (*message*) retransmettre, relayer.

release [rɪˈliːs] *n* (*from prison, obligation*) libération *f*; (*of gas etc*) émission *f*; (*of film etc*) sortie *f*; (*record*) disque *m*; (*device*) déclencheur *m* ♦ *vt* (*prisoner*) libérer; (*book, film*) sortir; (*report, news*) rendre public, publier; (*gas etc*) émettre, dégager; (*free: from wreckage etc*) dégager; (*TECH: catch, spring etc*) déclencher; (*let go*) relâcher; lâcher; desserrer; **to ~ one's grip** *or* **hold** lâcher prise; **to ~ the clutch** (*AUT*) débrayer.

relegate [ˈrɛləɡeɪt] *vt* reléguer; (*SPORT*): **to be ~d** descendre dans une division inférieure.

relent [rɪˈlɛnt] *vi* se laisser fléchir.

relentless [rɪˈlɛntlɪs] *adj* implacable.

relevance [ˈrɛləvəns] *n* pertinence *f*; **~ of sth to sth** rapport *m* entre qch et qch.

relevant [ˈrɛləvənt] *adj* approprié(e); (*fact*) significatif(ive); (*information*) utile, pertinent(e); **~ to** ayant rapport à, approprié à.

reliability [rɪlaɪəˈbɪlɪtɪ] *n* sérieux *m*; fiabilité

reliable [rɪˈlaɪəbl] *adj* (*person, firm*) sérieux(euse), fiable; (*method, machine*) fiable.

reliably [rɪˈlaɪəblɪ] *adv*: **to be ~ informed** savoir de source sûre.

reliance [rɪˈlaɪəns] *n*: **~ (on)** (*trust*) confiance (en); (*dependence*) besoin *m* (de), dépendance *f* (de).

reliant [rɪˈlaɪənt] *adj*: **to be ~ on sth/sb** dépendre de qch/qn.

relic [ˈrɛlɪk] *n* (*REL*) relique *f*; (*of the past*) vestige *m*.

relief [rɪˈliːf] *n* (*from pain, anxiety*) soulagement *m*; (*help, supplies*) secours *m(pl)*; (*of guard*) relève *f*; (*ART, GEO*) relief *m*; **by way of ligh ~** pour faire diversion.

relief map *n* carte *f* en relief.

relief road *n* (*BRIT*) route *f* de délestage.

relieve [rɪˈliːv] *vt* (*pain, patient*) soulager; (*bring help*) secourir; (*take over from: gen*) relayer; (*: guard*) relever; **to ~ sb of sth** débarrasser qn de qch; **to ~ sb of his command** (*MIL*) relever qn de ses fonctions; **to ~ o.s.** (*euphemism*) se soulager, faire ses besoins.

relieved [rɪˈliːvd] *adj* soulagé(e); **to be ~ that ...** être soulagé que ...; **I'm ~ to hear it** je suis soulagé de l'entendre.

religion [rɪˈlɪdʒən] *n* religion *f*.

religious [rɪˈlɪdʒəs] *adj* religieux(euse); (*book*) de piété.

eligious education n instruction religieuse.

elinquish [rɪ'lɪŋkwɪʃ] vt abandonner; (plan, habit) renoncer à.

elish ['rɛlɪʃ] n (CULIN) condiment m; (enjoyment) délectation f ♦ vt (food etc) savourer; **to ~ doing** se délecter à faire.

elive [ri:'lɪv] vt revivre.

eload [ri:'ləʊd] vt recharger.

elocate [ri:ləʊ'keɪt] vt (business) transférer ♦ vi se transférer, s'installer or s'établir ailleurs; **to ~ in** (déménager et) s'installer or s'établir à, se transférer à.

eluctance [rɪ'lʌktəns] n répugnance f.

eluctant [rɪ'lʌktənt] adj peu disposé(e), qui hésite; **to be ~ to do sth** hésiter à faire qch.

eluctantly [rɪ'lʌktəntlɪ] adv à contrecœur, sans enthousiasme.

ely [rɪ'laɪ]: **to ~ on** vt fus compter sur; (be dependent) dépendre de.

emain [rɪ'meɪn] vi rester; **to ~ silent** garder le silence; **I ~, yours faithfully** (BRIT: in letters) je vous prie d'agréer, Monsieur (etc), l'assurance de mes sentiments distingués.

emainder [rɪ'meɪndə*] n reste m; (COMM) fin f de série.

emaining [rɪ'meɪnɪŋ] adj qui reste.

emains [rɪ'meɪnz] npl restes mpl.

emand [rɪ'mɑ:nd] n: **on ~** en détention préventive ♦ vt: **to ~ in custody** écrouer; renvoyer en détention provisoire.

emand home n (BRIT) centre m d'éducation surveillée.

emark [rɪ'mɑ:k] n remarque f, observation f ♦ vt (faire) remarquer, dire; (notice) remarquer; **to ~ on sth** faire une or des remarque(s) sur qch.

emarkable [rɪ'mɑ:kəbl] adj remarquable.

emarry [ri:'mærɪ] vi se remarier.

emedial [rɪ'mi:dɪəl] adj (tuition, classes) de rattrapage.

emedy ['rɛmədɪ] n: **~ (for)** remède m (contre or à) ♦ vt remédier à.

emember [rɪ'mɛmbə*] vt se rappeler, se souvenir de; **I ~ seeing it, I ~ having seen it** je me rappelle l'avoir vu or que je l'ai vu; **she ~ed to do it** elle a pensé à le faire; **~ me to your wife** rappelez-moi au bon souvenir de votre femme.

emembrance [rɪ'mɛmbrəns] n souvenir m; mémoire f.

Remembrance Sunday ou **Remembrance Day** est le dimanche le plus proche du 11 novembre, jour où la Première Guerre mondiale a officiellement pris fin, et rend hommage aux victimes des deux guerres mondiales. À cette occasion, un silence de deux minutes est observé à 11 h, heure de la signature de l'armistice avec l'Allemagne en 1918; certains membres de la famille royale et du gouvernement déposent des gerbes de coquelicots au cénotaphe de Whitehall, et des couronnes sont placées sur les monuments aux morts dans toute la Grande-Bretagne; par ailleurs, les gens portent des coquelicots artificiels fabriqués et vendus par des membres de la légion britannique blessés au combat, au profit des blessés de guerre et de leur famille.

---

remind [rɪ'maɪnd] vt: **to ~ sb of sth** rappeler qch à qn; **to ~ sb to do** faire penser à qn à faire, rappeler à qn qu'il doit faire; **that ~s me!** j'y pense!

reminder [rɪ'maɪndə*] n rappel m; (note etc) pense-bête m.

reminisce [rɛmɪ'nɪs] vi: **to ~ (about)** évoquer ses souvenirs (de).

reminiscences [rɛmɪ'nɪsnsɪz] npl réminiscences fpl, souvenirs mpl.

reminiscent [rɛmɪ'nɪsnt] adj: **~ of** qui rappelle, qui fait penser à.

remiss [rɪ'mɪs] adj négligent(e); **it was ~ of me** c'était une négligence de ma part.

remission [rɪ'mɪʃən] n rémission f; (of debt, sentence) remise f; (of fee) exemption f.

remit [rɪ'mɪt] vt (send: money) envoyer.

remittance [rɪ'mɪtns] n envoi m, paiement m.

remnant ['rɛmnənt] n reste m, restant m; **~s** npl (COMM) coupons mpl; fins fpl de série.

remonstrate ['rɛmənstreɪt] vi: **to ~ (with sb about sth)** se plaindre (à qn de qch).

remorse [rɪ'mɔ:s] n remords m.

remorseful [rɪ'mɔ:sful] adj plein(e) de remords.

remorseless [rɪ'mɔ:slɪs] adj (fig) impitoyable.

remote [rɪ'məʊt] adj éloigné(e), lointain(e); (person) distant(e); **there is a ~ possibility that ...** il est tout juste possible que ....

remote control n télécommande f.

remote-controlled [rɪ'məʊtkən'trəʊld] adj téléguidé(e).

remotely [rɪ'məʊtlɪ] adv au loin; (slightly) très vaguement.

remoteness [rɪ'məʊtnɪs] n éloignement m.

remould ['ri:məʊld] n (BRIT: tyre) pneu rechapé.

removable [rɪ'mu:vəbl] adj (detachable) amovible.

removal [rɪ'mu:vəl] n (taking away) enlèvement m; suppression f; (BRIT: from house) déménagement m; (from office: dismissal) renvoi m; (MED) ablation f.

removal man n (BRIT) déménageur m.

removal van n (BRIT) camion m de déménagement.

remove [rɪ'mu:v] vt enlever, retirer; (employee) renvoyer; (stain) faire partir; (doubt, abuse) supprimer; **first cousin once ~d** cousin/e au deuxième degré.

remover [rɪ'mu:və*] n (for paint) décapant m; (for varnish) dissolvant m; **make-up ~** démaquillant m.

remunerate [rɪ'mju:nəreɪt] vt rémunérer.

remuneration [rɪmjuːnəˈreɪʃən] *n*
rémunération *f*.
rename [riːˈneɪm] *vt* rebaptiser.
rend, *pt, pp* **rent** [rɛnd, rɛnt] *vt* déchirer.
render [ˈrɛndə*] *vt* rendre; (*CULIN: fat*)
clarifier.
rendering [ˈrɛndərɪŋ] *n* (*MUS etc*)
interprétation *f*.
rendez-vous [ˈrɔndɪvuː] *n* rendez-vous *m inv*
♦ *vi* opérer une jonction, se rejoindre;
(*spaceship*) effectuer un rendez-vous (dans
l'espace); **to ~ with sb** rejoindre qn.
renegade [ˈrɛnɪgeɪd] *n* rénégat *m*.
renew [rɪˈnjuː] *vt* renouveler; (*negotiations*)
reprendre; (*acquaintance*) renouer.
renewable [rɪˈnjuːəbl] *adj* renouvelable; ~
energy, ~**s** énergies renouvelables.
renewal [rɪˈnjuːəl] *n* renouvellement *m*;
reprise *f*.
renounce [rɪˈnauns] *vt* renoncer à; (*disown*)
renier.
renovate [ˈrɛnəveɪt] *vt* rénover; (*work of art*)
restaurer.
renovation [rɛnəˈveɪʃən] *n* rénovation *f*;
restauration *f*.
renown [rɪˈnaun] *n* renommée *f*.
renowned [rɪˈnaund] *adj* renommé(e).
rent [rɛnt] *pt, pp of* **rend** ♦ *n* loyer *m* ♦ *vt* louer;
(*car, TV*) louer, prendre en location; (*also: ~
out: car, TV*) louer, donner en location.
rental [ˈrɛntl] *n* (*for television, car*) (prix *m* de)
location *f*.
rent boy *n* (*BRIT col*) jeune prostitué.
renunciation [rɪnʌnsɪˈeɪʃən] *n* renonciation *f*;
(*self-denial*) renoncement *m*.
reopen [riːˈəupən] *vt* rouvrir.
reopening [riːˈəupnɪŋ] *n* réouverture *f*.
reorder [riːˈɔːdə*] *vt* commander de nouveau;
(*rearrange*) réorganiser.
reorganize [riːˈɔːgənaɪz] *vt* réorganiser.
rep [rɛp] *n abbr* (*COMM*) = **representative**;
(*THEAT*) = **repertory**.
Rep. *abbr* (*US POL*) = **representative,**
republican.
repair [rɪˈpɛə*] *n* réparation *f* ♦ *vt* réparer; **in**
good/bad ~ en bon/mauvais état; **under ~**
en réparation.
repair kit *n* trousse *f* de réparations.
repair man *n* réparateur *m*.
repair shop *n* (*AUT etc*) atelier *m* de
réparations.
repartee [rɛpɑːˈtiː] *n* repartie *f*.
repast [rɪˈpɑːst] *n* (*formal*) repas *m*.
repatriate [riːˈpætrɪeɪt] *vt* rapatrier.
repay [riːˈpeɪ] *vt irreg* (*money, creditor*)
rembourser; (*sb's efforts*) récompenser.
repayment [riːˈpeɪmənt] *n* remboursement *m*;
récompense *f*.
repeal [rɪˈpiːl] *n* (*of law*) abrogation *f*; (*of
sentence*) annulation *f* ♦ *vt* abroger; annuler.
repeat [rɪˈpiːt] *n* (*RADIO, TV*) reprise *f* ♦ *vt*
répéter; (*pattern*) reproduire; (*promise,*

attack, also COMM: order) renouveler; (*SCO*
class) redoubler ♦ *vi* répéter.
repeatedly [rɪˈpiːtɪdlɪ] *adv* souvent, à
plusieurs reprises.
repel [rɪˈpɛl] *vt* repousser.
repellent [rɪˈpɛlənt] *adj* repoussant(e) ♦ *n*:
insect ~ insectifuge *m*; **moth ~** produit *m*
antimite(s).
repent [rɪˈpɛnt] *vi*: **to ~ (of)** se repentir (de)
repentance [rɪˈpɛntəns] *n* repentir *m*.
repercussion [riːpəˈkʌʃən] *n* (*consequence*)
répercussion *f*.
repertoire [ˈrɛpətwɑː*] *n* répertoire *m*.
repertory [ˈrɛpətərɪ] *n* (*also:* ~ **theatre**)
théâtre *m* de répertoire.
repertory company *n* troupe théâtrale
permanente.
repetition [rɛpɪˈtɪʃən] *n* répétition *f*.
repetitious [rɛpɪˈtɪʃəs] *adj* (*speech*) plein(e)
redites.
repetitive [rɪˈpɛtɪtɪv] *adj* (*movement, work*)
répétitif(ive); (*speech*) plein(e) de redites
replace [rɪˈpleɪs] *vt* (*put back*) remettre,
replacer; (*take the place of*) remplacer; (*TE*
"**~ the receiver**" "raccrochez".
replacement [rɪˈpleɪsmənt] *n* replacement *r*
remplacement *m*; (*person*) remplaçant/e.
replacement part *n* pièce *f* de rechange.
replay [ˈriːpleɪ] *n* (*of match*) match rejoué; (
tape, film*) répétition *f*.
replenish [rɪˈplɛnɪʃ] *vt* (*glass*) remplir (de
nouveau); (*stock etc*) réapprovisionner.
replete [rɪˈpliːt] *adj* rempli(e); (*well-fed*): ~
(**with**) rassasié(e) (de).
replica [ˈrɛplɪkə] *n* réplique *f*, copie exacte.
reply [rɪˈplaɪ] *n* réponse *f* ♦ *vi* répondre; **in ~**
(**to**) en réponse (à); **there's no ~** (*TEL*) ça r
répond pas.
reply coupon *n* coupon-réponse *m*.
report [rɪˈpɔːt] *n* rapport *m*; (*PRESS etc*)
reportage *m*; (*BRIT: also:* **school ~**) bulletin
(scolaire); (*of gun*) détonation *f* ♦ *vt*
rapporter, faire un compte rendu de; (*PR*
etc) faire un reportage sur; (*bring to notic*
occurrence) signaler; (*: person*) dénoncer ♦
(*make a report*): **to ~ (on)** faire un rapport
(sur); (*for newspaper*) faire un reportage
(sur); (*present o.s.*): **to ~ (to sb)** se présent
(chez qn); **it is ~ed that** on dit *or* annonce
que; **it is ~ed from Berlin that** on nous
apprend de Berlin que.
report card *n* (*US, Scottish*) bulletin *m*
(scolaire).
reportedly [rɪˈpɔːtɪdlɪ] *adv*: **she is ~ living ir**
Spain elle habiterait en Espagne; **he ~**
ordered them to ... il leur aurait ordonné
de ....
reported speech *n* (*LING*) discours indirec
reporter [rɪˈpɔːtə*] *n* reporter *m*.
repose [rɪˈpəuz] *n*: **in ~** en *or* au repos.
repossess [riːpəˈzɛs] *vt* saisir.
repossession order [riːpəˈzɛʃən-] *n* ordre *r*

de reprise de possession.

reprehensible [rɛprɪˈhɛnsɪbl] *adj* répréhensible.

represent [rɛprɪˈzɛnt] *vt* représenter; (*explain*): **to ~ to sb that** expliquer à qn que.

representation [rɛprɪzɛnˈteɪʃən] *n* représentation *f*; **~s** *npl* (*protest*) démarche *f*.

representative [rɛprɪˈzɛntətɪv] *n* représentant/e; (*COMM*) représentant/e (de commerce); (*US POL*) député *m* ♦ *adj*: **~ (of)** représentatif(ive) (de), caractéristique (de).

repress [rɪˈprɛs] *vt* réprimer.

repression [rɪˈprɛʃən] *n* répression *f*.

repressive [rɪˈprɛsɪv] *adj* répressif(ive).

reprieve [rɪˈpriːv] *n* (*LAW*) grâce *f*; (*fig*) sursis *m*, délai *m* ♦ *vt* gracier; accorder un sursis *or* un délai à.

reprimand [ˈrɛprɪmɑːnd] *n* réprimande *f* ♦ *vt* réprimander.

reprint *n* [ˈriːprɪnt] réimpression *f* ♦ *vt* [riːˈprɪnt] réimprimer.

reprisal [rɪˈpraɪzl] *n* représailles *fpl*; **to take ~s** user de représailles.

reproach [rɪˈprəʊtʃ] *n* reproche *m* ♦ *vt*: **to ~ sb with sth** reprocher qch à qn; **beyond ~** irréprochable.

reproachful [rɪˈprəʊtʃful] *adj* de reproche.

reproduce [riːprəˈdjuːs] *vt* reproduire ♦ *vi* se reproduire.

reproduction [riːprəˈdʌkʃən] *n* reproduction *f*.

reproductive [riːprəˈdʌktɪv] *adj* reproducteur(trice).

reproof [rɪˈpruːf] *n* reproche *m*.

reprove [rɪˈpruːv] *vt* (*action*) réprouver; (*person*): **to ~ (for)** blâmer (de).

reproving [rɪˈpruːvɪŋ] *adj* réprobateur(trice).

reptile [ˈrɛptaɪl] *n* reptile *m*.

Repub. *abbr* (*US POL*) = **republican**.

republic [rɪˈpʌblɪk] *n* république *f*.

republican [rɪˈpʌblɪkən] *adj, n* républicain(e).

repudiate [rɪˈpjuːdɪeɪt] *vt* (*ally, behaviour*) désavouer; (*accusation*) rejeter; (*wife*) répudier.

repugnant [rɪˈpʌgnənt] *adj* répugnant(e).

repulse [rɪˈpʌls] *vt* repousser.

repulsion [rɪˈpʌlʃən] *n* répulsion *f*.

repulsive [rɪˈpʌlsɪv] *adj* repoussant(e), répulsif(ive).

reputable [ˈrɛpjutəbl] *adj* de bonne réputation; (*occupation*) honorable.

reputation [rɛpjuˈteɪʃən] *n* réputation *f*; **to have a ~ for** être réputé(e) pour; **he has a ~ for being awkward** il a la réputation de ne pas être commode.

repute [rɪˈpjuːt] *n* (bonne) réputation.

reputed [rɪˈpjuːtɪd] *adj* réputé(e); **he is ~ to be rich/intelligent** *etc* on dit qu'il est riche/ intelligent *etc*.

reputedly [rɪˈpjuːtɪdlɪ] *adv* d'après ce qu'on dit.

request [rɪˈkwɛst] *n* demande *f*; (*formal*) requête *f* ♦ *vt*: **to ~ (of *or* from sb)** demander (à qn); **at the ~ of** à la demande de.

request stop *n* (*BRIT: for bus*) arrêt facultatif.

requiem [ˈrɛkwɪəm] *n* requiem *m*.

require [rɪˈkwaɪə*] *vt* (*need: subj: person*) avoir besoin de; (*: thing, situation*) nécessiter, demander; (*demand*) exiger, requérir; (*order*): **to ~ sb to do sth/sth of sb** exiger que qn fasse qch/qch de qn; **if ~d** s'il le faut; **what qualifications are ~d?** quelles sont les qualifications requises?; **~d by law** requis par la loi.

required [rɪˈkwaɪəd] *adj* requis(e), voulu(e).

requirement [rɪˈkwaɪəmənt] *n* exigence *f*; besoin *m*; condition *f* (requise).

requisite [ˈrɛkwɪzɪt] *n* chose *f* nécessaire ♦ *adj* requis(e), nécessaire; **toilet ~s** accessoires *mpl* de toilette.

requisition [rɛkwɪˈzɪʃən] *n*: **~ (for)** demande *f* (de) ♦ *vt* (*MIL*) réquisitionner.

reroute [riːˈruːt] *vt* (*train etc*) dérouter.

resale [ˈriːˈseɪl] *n* revente *f*.

resale price maintenance (RPM) *n* vente au détail à prix imposé.

rescind [rɪˈsɪnd] *vt* annuler; (*law*) abroger; (*judgment*) rescinder.

rescue [ˈrɛskjuː] *n* sauvetage *m*; (*help*) secours *mpl* ♦ *vt* sauver; **to come to sb's ~** venir au secours de qn.

rescue party *n* équipe *f* de sauvetage.

rescuer [ˈrɛskjuə*] *n* sauveteur *m*.

research [rɪˈsəːtʃ] *n* recherche(s) *f(pl)* ♦ *vt* faire des recherches sur ♦ *vi*: **to ~ (into sth)** faire des recherches (sur qch); **a piece of ~** un travail de recherche; **~ and development (R & D)** recherche-développement (R-D).

researcher [rɪˈsəːtʃə*] *n* chercheur/euse.

research work *n* recherches *fpl*.

resell [riːˈsɛl] *vt irreg* revendre.

resemblance [rɪˈzɛmbləns] *n* ressemblance *f*; **to bear a strong ~ to** ressembler beaucoup à.

resemble [rɪˈzɛmbl] *vt* ressembler à.

resent [rɪˈzɛnt] *vt* éprouver du ressentiment de, être contrarié(e) par.

resentful [rɪˈzɛntful] *adj* irrité(e), plein(e) de ressentiment.

resentment [rɪˈzɛntmənt] *n* ressentiment *m*.

reservation [rɛzəˈveɪʃən] *n* (*booking*) réservation *f*; (*doubt; protected area*) réserve *f*; (*BRIT AUT: also:* **central ~**) bande médiane; **to make a ~ (in an hotel/a restaurant/on a plane)** réserver *or* retenir une chambre/une table/une place; **with ~s** (*doubts*) avec certaines réserves.

reservation desk *n* (*US: in hotel*) réception *f*.

reserve [rɪˈzəːv] *n* réserve *f*; (*SPORT*) remplaçant/e ♦ *vt* (*seats etc*) réserver, retenir; **~s** *npl* (*MIL*) réservistes *mpl*; **in ~** en réserve.

reserve currency *n* monnaie *f* de réserve.

reserved [rɪ'zəːvd] *adj* réservé(e).
reserve price *n* (*BRIT*) mise *f* à prix, prix *m* de départ.
reserve team *n* (*BRIT SPORT*) deuxième équipe *f*.
reservist [rɪ'zəːvɪst] *n* (*MIL*) réserviste *m*.
reservoir ['rɛzəvwɑː*] *n* réservoir *m*.
reset [riː'sɛt] *vt irreg* remettre; (*clock, watch*) mettre à l'heure; (*COMPUT*) remettre à zéro.
reshape [riː'ʃeɪp] *vt* (*policy*) réorganiser.
reshuffle [riː'ʃʌfl] *n*: **Cabinet ~** (*POL*) remaniement ministériel.
reside [rɪ'zaɪd] *vi* résider.
residence ['rɛzɪdəns] *n* résidence *f*; **to take up ~** s'installer; **in ~** (*queen etc*) en résidence; (*doctor*) résidant(e).
residence permit *n* (*BRIT*) permis *m* de séjour.
resident ['rɛzɪdənt] *n* résident/e ♦ *adj* résidant(e).
residential [rɛzɪ'dɛnʃəl] *adj* de résidence; (*area*) résidentiel(le).
residue ['rɛzɪdjuː] *n* reste *m*; (*CHEM, PHYSICS*) résidu *m*.
resign [rɪ'zaɪn] *vt* (*one's post*) se démettre de ♦ *vi*: **to ~ (from)** démissionner (de); **to ~ o.s. to** (*endure*) se résigner à.
resignation [rɛzɪg'neɪʃən] *n* démission *f*; résignation *f*; **to tender one's ~** donner sa démission.
resigned [rɪ'zaɪnd] *adj* résigné(e).
resilience [rɪ'zɪlɪəns] *n* (*of material*) élasticité *f*; (*of person*) ressort *m*.
resilient [rɪ'zɪlɪənt] *adj* (*person*) qui réagit, qui a du ressort.
resin ['rɛzɪn] *n* résine *f*.
resist [rɪ'zɪst] *vt* résister à.
resistance [rɪ'zɪstəns] *n* résistance *f*.
resistant [rɪ'zɪstənt] *adj*: **~ (to)** résistant(e) (à).
resolute ['rɛzəluːt] *adj* résolu(e).
resolution [rɛzə'luːʃən] *n* résolution *f*; **to make a ~** prendre une résolution.
resolve [rɪ'zɔlv] *n* résolution *f* ♦ *vt* (*decide*): **to ~ to do** résoudre *or* décider de faire; (*problem*) résoudre.
resolved [rɪ'zɔlvd] *adj* résolu(e).
resonance ['rɛzənəns] *n* résonance *f*.
resonant ['rɛzənənt] *adj* résonnant(e).
resort [rɪ'zɔːt] *n* (*town*) station *f* (de vacances); (*recourse*) recours *m* ♦ *vi*: **to ~ to** avoir recours à; **seaside/winter sports ~** station balnéaire/de sports d'hiver; **in the last ~** en dernier ressort.
resound [rɪ'zaund] *vi*: **to ~ (with)** retentir (de).
resounding [rɪ'zaundɪŋ] *adj* retentissant(e).
resource [rɪ'sɔːs] *n* ressource *f*; **~s** *npl* ressources; **natural ~s** ressources naturelles; **to leave sb to his (or her) own ~s** (*fig*) livrer qn à lui-même (*or* elle-même).
resourceful [rɪ'sɔːsful] *adj* plein(e) de ressource, débrouillard(e).
resourcefulness [rɪ'sɔːsfəlnɪs] *n* ressource *f*.
respect [rɪs'pɛkt] *n* respect *m*; (*point, detail*): **in some ~s** à certains égards ♦ *vt* respecter; **~s** *npl* respects, hommages *mpl*; **to have** *or* **show ~ for sb/sth** respecter qn/qch; **out of ~ for** par respect pour; **with ~ to** en ce qui concerne; **in ~ of** sous le rapport de, quant à; **in this ~** sous ce rapport, à cet égard; **with due ~ I ... malgré le respect que je vous dois, je ....**
respectability [rɪspɛktə'bɪlɪtɪ] *n* respectabilité *f*.
respectable [rɪs'pɛktəbl] *adj* respectable; (*quite good: result etc*) honorable; (*player*) assez bon(bonne).
respectful [rɪs'pɛktful] *adj* respectueux(euse).
respective [rɪs'pɛktɪv] *adj* respectif(ive).
respectively [rɪs'pɛktɪvlɪ] *adv* respectivement.
respiration [rɛspɪ'reɪʃən] *n* respiration *f*.
respirator ['rɛspɪreɪtə*] *n* respirateur *m*.
respiratory ['rɛspərətərɪ] *adj* respiratoire.
respite ['rɛspaɪt] *n* répit *m*.
resplendent [rɪs'plɛndənt] *adj* resplendissant(e).
respond [rɪs'pɔnd] *vi* répondre; (*to treatment*) réagir.
respondent [rɪs'pɔndənt] *n* (*LAW*) défendeur/deresse.
response [rɪs'pɔns] *n* réponse *f*; (*to treatment*) réaction *f*; **in ~ to** en réponse à.
responsibility [rɪspɔnsɪ'bɪlɪtɪ] *n* responsabilité *f*; **to take ~ for sth/sb** accepter la responsabilité de qch/d'être responsable de qn.
responsible [rɪs'pɔnsɪbl] *adj* (*liable*): **~ (for)** responsable (de); (*person*) digne de confiance; (*job*) qui comporte des responsabilités; **to be ~ to sb (for sth)** être responsable devant qn (de qch).
responsibly [rɪs'pɔnsɪblɪ] *adv* avec sérieux.
responsive [rɪs'pɔnsɪv] *adj* qui n'est pas réservé(e) *or* indifférent(e).
rest [rɛst] *n* repos *m*; (*stop*) arrêt *m*, pause *f*; (*MUS*) silence *m*; (*support*) support *m*, appui *m*; (*remainder*) reste *m*, restant *m* ♦ *vi* se reposer; (*be supported*): **to ~ on** appuyer *or* reposer sur; (*remain*) rester ♦ *vt* (*lean*): **to ~ sth on/against** appuyer qch sur/contre; **the ~ of them** les autres; **to set sb's mind at ~** tranquilliser qn; **it ~s with him to** c'est à lui de; **~ assured that ...** soyez assuré que ....
restart [riː'stɑːt] *vt* (*engine*) remettre en marche; (*work*) reprendre.
restaurant ['rɛstərɔŋ] *n* restaurant *m*.
restaurant car *n* (*BRIT*) wagon-restaurant *m*.
rest cure *n* cure *f* de repos.
restful ['rɛstful] *adj* reposant(e).
rest home *n* maison *f* de repos.
restitution [rɛstɪ'tjuːʃən] *n* (*act*) restitution *f*; (*reparation*) réparation *f*.

estive ['rɛstɪv] adj agité(e), impatient(e); (horse) rétif(ive).

estless ['rɛstlɪs] adj agité(e); **to get ~** s'impatienter.

estlessly ['rɛstlɪslɪ] adv avec agitation.

estock [riː'stɔk] vt réapprovisionner.

estoration [rɛstə'reɪʃən] n restauration f; restitution f.

estorative [rɪ'stɔrətɪv] adj reconstituant(e) ♦ n reconstituant m.

estore [rɪ'stɔː*] vt (building) restaurer; (sth stolen) restituer; (peace, health) rétablir.

estorer [rɪ'stɔːrə*] n (ART etc) restaurateur/ trice (d'œuvres d'art).

estrain [rɪs'treɪn] vt (feeling) contenir; (person): **to ~ (from doing)** retenir (de faire).

estrained [rɪs'treɪnd] adj (style) sobre; (manner) mesuré(e).

estraint [rɪs'treɪnt] n (restriction) contrainte f; (moderation) retenue f; (of style) sobriété f; **wage ~** limitations salariales.

estrict [rɪs'trɪkt] vt restreindre, limiter.

estricted area [rɪs'trɪktɪd-] n (AUT) zone f à vitesse limitée.

estriction [rɪs'trɪkʃən] n restriction f, limitation f.

estrictive [rɪs'trɪktɪv] adj restrictif(ive).

estrictive practices npl (INDUSTRY) pratiques fpl entravant la libre concurrence.

est room n (US) toilettes fpl.

estructure [riː'strʌktʃə*] vt restructurer.

esult [rɪ'zʌlt] n résultat m ♦ vi: **to ~ (from)** résulter (de); **to ~ in** aboutir à, se terminer par; **as a ~ it is too expensive** il en résulte que c'est trop cher; **as a ~ of** à la suite de.

esultant [rɪ'zʌltənt] adj résultant(e).

esume [rɪ'zjuːm] vt (work, journey) reprendre; (sum up) résumer ♦ vi (work etc) reprendre.

esumé ['reɪzjuːmeɪ] n (summary) résumé m; (US: curriculum vitae) curriculum vitae m inv.

esumption [rɪ'zʌmpʃən] n reprise f.

esurgence [rɪ'səːdʒəns] n réapparition f.

esurrection [rɛzə'rɛkʃən] n résurrection f.

esuscitate [rɪ'sʌsɪteɪt] vt (MED) réanimer.

esuscitation [rɪsʌsɪ'teɪʃən] n réanimation f.

etail ['riːteɪl] n (vente f au) détail m ♦ cpd de or au détail ♦ vt vendre au détail ♦ vi: **to ~ at 10 francs** se vendre au détail à 10 francs.

etailer ['riːteɪlə*] n détaillant/e.

etail outlet n point m de vente.

etail price n prix m de détail.

etail price index n ≈ indice m des prix.

etain [rɪ'teɪn] vt (keep) garder, conserver; (employ) engager.

etainer [rɪ'teɪnə*] n (servant) serviteur m; (fee) acompte m, provision f.

etaliate [rɪ'tælɪeɪt] vi: **to ~ (against)** se venger (de); **to ~ (on sb)** rendre la pareille (à qn).

etaliation [rɪtælɪ'eɪʃən] n représailles fpl,

vengeance f; **in ~ for** par représailles pour.

retaliatory [rɪ'tælɪətərɪ] adj de représailles.

retarded [rɪ'tɑːdɪd] adj retardé(e).

retch [rɛtʃ] vi avoir des haut-le-cœur.

retentive [rɪ'tɛntɪv] adj: **~ memory** excellente mémoire.

rethink ['riː'θɪŋk] vt repenser.

reticence ['rɛtɪsns] n réticence f.

reticent ['rɛtɪsnt] adj réticent(e).

retina ['rɛtɪnə] n rétine f.

retinue ['rɛtɪnjuː] n suite f, cortège m.

retire [rɪ'taɪə*] vi (give up work) prendre sa retraite; (withdraw) se retirer, partir; (go to bed) (aller) se coucher.

retired [rɪ'taɪəd] adj (person) retraité(e).

retirement [rɪ'taɪəmənt] n retraite f.

retirement age n âge m de la retraite.

retiring [rɪ'taɪərɪŋ] adj (person) réservé(e); (chairman etc) sortant(e).

retort [rɪ'tɔːt] n (reply) riposte f; (container) cornue f ♦ vi riposter.

retrace [riː'treɪs] vt reconstituer; **to ~ one's steps** revenir sur ses pas.

retract [rɪ'trækt] vt (statement, claws) rétracter; (undercarriage, aerial) rentrer, escamoter ♦ vi se rétracter; rentrer.

retractable [rɪ'træktəbl] adj escamotable.

retrain [riː'treɪn] vt recycler ♦ vi se recycler.

retraining [riː'treɪnɪŋ] n recyclage m.

retread vt [riː'trɛd] (AUT: tyre) rechaper ♦ n ['riːtrɛd] pneu rechapé.

retreat [rɪ'triːt] n retraite f ♦ vi battre en retraite; (flood) reculer; **to beat a hasty ~** (fig) partir avec précipitation.

retrial [riː'traɪəl] n nouveau procès.

retribution [rɛtrɪ'bjuːʃən] n châtiment m.

retrieval [rɪ'triːvəl] n récupération f; réparation f; recherche f et extraction f.

retrieve [rɪ'triːv] vt (sth lost) récupérer; (situation, honour) sauver; (error, loss) réparer; (COMPUT) rechercher.

retriever [rɪ'triːvə*] n chien m d'arrêt.

retroactive [rɛtrəu'æktɪv] adj rétroactif(ive).

retrograde ['rɛtrəgreɪd] adj rétrograde.

retrospect ['rɛtrəspɛkt] n: **in ~** rétrospectivement, après coup.

retrospective [rɛtrə'spɛktɪv] adj (law) rétroactif(ive) ♦ n (ART) rétrospective f.

return [rɪ'təːn] n (going or coming back) retour m; (of sth stolen etc) restitution f; (recompense) récompense f; (FINANCE: from land, shares) rapport m; (report) relevé m, rapport ♦ cpd (journey) de retour; (BRIT: ticket) aller et retour; (match) retour ♦ vi (person etc: come back) revenir; (: go back) retourner ♦ vt rendre; (bring back) rapporter; (send back) renvoyer; (put back) remettre; (POL: candidate) élire; **~s** npl (COMM) recettes fpl; bénéfices mpl; (: ~ed goods) marchandises renvoyées; **many happy ~s (of the day)!** bon anniversaire!; **by ~ (of post)** par retour (du courrier); **in ~**

(for) en échange (de).
returnable [rɪ'tɜːnəbl] *adj* (*bottle etc*) consigné(e).
returner [rɪ'tɜːnə*] *n femme qui reprend un travail après avoir élevé ses enfants.*
returning officer [rɪ'tɜːnɪŋ-] *n* (*BRIT POL*) président *m* de bureau de vote.
return key *n* (*COMPUT*) touche *f* de retour.
reunion [riː'juːnɪən] *n* réunion *f.*
reunite [riːjuː'naɪt] *vt* réunir.
rev [rɛv] *n abbr* (= *revolution: AUT*) tour *m* ♦ *vb* (*also:* ~ **up**) *vt* emballer ♦ *vi* s'emballer.
Rev. *abbr* = **reverend**.
revaluation [riːvælju'eɪʃən] *n* réévaluation *f.*
revamp [riː'væmp] *vt* (*house*) retaper; (*firm*) réorganiser.
rev counter *n* (*BRIT*) compte-tours *m inv.*
Revd. *abbr* = **reverend**.
reveal [rɪ'viːl] *vt* (*make known*) révéler; (*display*) laisser voir.
revealing [rɪ'viːlɪŋ] *adj* révélateur(trice); (*dress*) au décolleté généreux *or* suggestif.
reveille [rɪ'vælɪ] *n* (*MIL*) réveil *m.*
revel ['rɛvl] *vi:* **to ~ in sth/in doing** se délecter de qch/à faire.
revelation [rɛvə'leɪʃən] *n* révélation *f.*
reveller ['rɛvlə*] *n* fêtard *m.*
revelry ['rɛvlrɪ] *n* festivités *fpl.*
revenge [rɪ'vɛndʒ] *n* vengeance *f*; (*in game etc*) revanche *f* ♦ *vt* venger; **to take ~** se venger.
revengeful [rɪ'vɛndʒful] *adj* vengeur(eresse); vindicatif(ive).
revenue ['rɛvənjuː] *n* revenu *m.*
reverberate [rɪ'vɜːbəreɪt] *vi* (*sound*) retentir, se répercuter; (*light*) se réverbérer.
reverberation [rɪvɜːbə'reɪʃən] *n* répercussion *f*; réverbération *f.*
revere [rɪ'vɪə*] *vt* vénérer, révérer.
reverence ['rɛvərəns] *n* vénération *f*, révérence *f.*
reverend ['rɛvərənd] *adj* vénérable; **the R~ John Smith** (*Anglican*) le révérend John Smith; (*Catholic*) l'abbé John Smith; (*Protestant*) le pasteur John Smith.
reverent ['rɛvərənt] *adj* respectueux(euse).
reverie ['rɛvərɪ] *n* rêverie *f.*
reversal [rɪ'vɜːsl] *n* (*of opinion*) revirement *m.*
reverse [rɪ'vɜːs] *n* contraire *m*, opposé *m*; (*back*) dos *m*, envers *m*; (*AUT: also:* ~ **gear**) marche *f* arrière ♦ *adj* (*order, direction*) opposé(e), inverse ♦ *vt* (*turn*) renverser, retourner; (*change*) renverser, changer complètement; (*LAW: judgment*) réformer ♦ *vi* (*BRIT AUT*) faire marche arrière; **to go into ~** faire marche arrière; **in ~ order** en ordre inverse.
reversed charge call [rɪ'vɜːst-] *n* (*BRIT TEL*) communication *f* en PCV.
reverse video *n* vidéo *m* inverse.
reversible [rɪ'vɜːsəbl] *adj* (*garment*) réversible; (*procedure*) révocable.
reversing lights [rɪ'vɜːsɪŋ-] *npl* (*BRIT AUT*)

feux *mpl* de marche arrière *or* de recul.
reversion [rɪ'vɜːʃən] *n* retour *m.*
revert [rɪ'vɜːt] *vi:* **to ~ to** revenir à, retourner à.
review [rɪ'vjuː] *n* revue *f*; (*of book, film*) critique *f* ♦ *vt* passer en revue; faire la critique de; **to come under ~** être révisé(e).
reviewer [rɪ'vjuːə*] *n* critique *m.*
revile [rɪ'vaɪl] *vt* injurier.
revise [rɪ'vaɪz] *vt* (*manuscript*) revoir, corriger; (*opinion*) réviser, modifier; (*study: subject, notes*) réviser; **~d edition** édition revue et corrigée.
revision [rɪ'vɪʒən] *n* révision *f*; (*revised version*) version corrigée.
revitalize [riː'vaɪtəlaɪz] *vt* revitaliser.
revival [rɪ'vaɪvəl] *n* reprise *f*; rétablissement *m*; (*of faith*) renouveau *m.*
revive [rɪ'vaɪv] *vt* (*person*) ranimer; (*custom*) rétablir; (*hope, courage*) redonner; (*play, fashion*) reprendre ♦ *vi* (*person*) reprendre connaissance; (*hope*) renaître; (*activity*) reprendre.
revoke [rɪ'vəuk] *vt* révoquer; (*promise, decision*) revenir sur.
revolt [rɪ'vəult] *n* révolte *f* ♦ *vi* se révolter, se rebeller.
revolting [rɪ'vəultɪŋ] *adj* dégoûtant(e).
revolution [rɛvə'luːʃən] *n* révolution *f*; (*of wheel etc*) tour *m*, révolution.
revolutionary [rɛvə'luːʃənrɪ] *adj*, *n* révolutionnaire (*m/f*).
revolutionize [rɛvə'luːʃənaɪz] *vt* révolutionner.
revolve [rɪ'vɔlv] *vi* tourner.
revolver [rɪ'vɔlvə*] *n* revolver *m.*
revolving [rɪ'vɔlvɪŋ] *adj* (*chair*) pivotant(e); (*light*) tournant(e).
revolving door *n* (porte *f* à) tambour *m.*
revue [rɪ'vjuː] *n* (*THEAT*) revue *f.*
revulsion [rɪ'vʌlʃən] *n* dégoût *m*, répugnance *f.*
reward [rɪ'wɔːd] *n* récompense *f* ♦ *vt:* **to ~ (for)** récompenser (de).
rewarding [rɪ'wɔːdɪŋ] *adj* (*fig*) qui (en) vaut la peine, gratifiant(e); **financially ~** financièrement intéressant(e).
rewind [riː'waɪnd] *vt irreg* (*watch*) remonter; (*ribbon etc*) réembobiner.
rewire [riː'waɪə*] *vt* (*house*) refaire l'installation électrique de.
reword [riː'wɜːd] *vt* formuler *or* exprimer différemment.
rewrite [riː'raɪt] *vt irreg* récrire.
Reykjavik ['reɪkjaviːk] *n* Reykjavik.
RFD *abbr* (*US POST*) = rural free delivery.
Rh *abbr* (= *rhesus*) Rh.
rhapsody ['ræpsədɪ] *n* (*MUS*) rhapsodie *f*; (*fig*) éloge délirant.
rhesus negative ['riːsəs-] *adj* (*MED*) de rhésus négatif.
rhesus positive ['riːsəs-] *adj* (*MED*) de rhésus

positif.

rhetoric ['rɛtərɪk] n rhétorique f.

rhetorical [rɪ'tɔrɪkl] adj rhétorique.

rheumatic [ru:'mætɪk] adj rhumatismal(e).

rheumatism ['ru:mətɪzəm] n rhumatisme m.

rheumatoid arthritis ['ru:mətɔɪd-] n polyarthrite f chronique.

Rhine [raɪn] n: **the ~** le Rhin.

rhinestone ['raɪnstəun] n faux diamant.

rhinoceros [raɪ'nɔsərəs] n rhinocéros m.

Rhodes [rəudz] n Rhodes f.

Rhodesia [rəu'di:ʒə] n Rhodésie f.

Rhodesian [rəu'di:ʒən] adj rhodésien(ne) ♦ n Rhodésien/ne.

rhododendron [rəudə'dɛndrn] n rhododendron m.

Rhône [rəun] n: **the ~** le Rhône.

rhubarb ['ru:bɑ:b] n rhubarbe f.

rhyme [raɪm] n rime f; (verse) vers mpl ♦ vi: to **~ (with)** rimer (avec); **without ~ or reason** sans rime ni raison.

rhythm ['rɪðm] n rythme m.

rhythmic(al) ['rɪðmɪk(l)] adj rythmique.

rhythmically ['rɪðmɪklɪ] adv avec rythme.

rhythm method n méthode f des températures.

RI n abbr (BRIT) = religious instruction ♦ abbr (US) = Rhode Island.

rib [rɪb] n (ANAT) côte f ♦ vt (mock) taquiner.

ribald ['rɪbəld] adj paillard(e).

ribbed [rɪbd] adj (knitting) à côtes; (shell) strié(e).

ribbon ['rɪbən] n ruban m; **in ~s** (torn) en lambeaux.

rice [raɪs] n riz m.

ricefield ['raɪsfi:ld] n rizière f.

rice pudding n riz m au lait.

rich [rɪtʃ] adj riche; (gift, clothes) somptueux(euse); **the ~** npl les riches mpl; **~es** npl richesses fpl; **to be ~ in sth** être riche en qch.

richly ['rɪtʃlɪ] adv richement; (deserved, earned) largement, grandement.

richness ['rɪtʃnɪs] n richesse f.

rickets ['rɪkɪts] n rachitisme m.

rickety ['rɪkɪtɪ] adj branlant(e).

rickshaw ['rɪkʃɔ:] n pousse(-pousse) m inv.

ricochet ['rɪkəʃeɪ] n ricochet m ♦ vi ricocher.

rid, pt, pp **rid** [rɪd] vt: **to ~ sb of** débarrasser qn de; **to get ~ of** se débarrasser de.

riddance ['rɪdns] n: **good ~!** bon débarras!

ridden ['rɪdn] pp of **ride**.

riddle ['rɪdl] n (puzzle) énigme f ♦ vt: **to be ~d with** être criblé(e) de.

ride [raɪd] n promenade f, tour m; (distance covered) trajet m ♦ vb (pt **rode**, pp **ridden** [rəud, 'rɪdn]) vi (as sport) monter (à cheval), faire du cheval; (go somewhere: on horse, bicycle) aller (à cheval or bicyclette etc); (journey: on bicycle, motor cycle, bus) rouler ♦ vt (a certain horse) monter; (distance) parcourir, faire; **we rode all day/all the way**

nous sommes restés toute la journée en selle/avons fait tout le chemin en selle or à cheval; **to ~ a horse/bicycle/camel** monter à cheval/à bicyclette/à dos de chameau; **can you ~ a bike?** est-ce que tu sais monter à bicyclette?; **to ~ at anchor** (NAUT) être à l'ancre; **horse/car ~** promenade or tour à cheval/en voiture; **to go for a ~** faire une promenade (en voiture or à bicyclette etc); **to take sb for a ~** (fig) faire marcher qn; rouler qn.

▶**ride out** vt: **to ~ out the storm** (fig) surmonter les difficultés.

rider ['raɪdə*] n cavalier/ière; (in race) jockey m; (on bicycle) cycliste m/f; (on motorcycle) motocycliste m/f; (in document) annexe f, clause additionnelle.

ridge [rɪdʒ] n (of hill) faîte m; (of roof, mountain) arête f; (on object) strie f.

ridicule ['rɪdɪkju:l] n ridicule m; dérision f ♦ vt ridiculiser, tourner en dérision; **to hold sb/ sth up to ~** tourner qn/qch en ridicule.

ridiculous [rɪ'dɪkjuləs] adj ridicule.

riding ['raɪdɪŋ] n équitation f.

riding school n manège m, école f d'équitation.

rife [raɪf] adj répandu(e); **~ with** abondant(e) en.

riffraff ['rɪfræf] n racaille f.

rifle ['raɪfl] n fusil m (à canon rayé) ♦ vt vider, dévaliser.

▶**rifle through** vt fus fouiller dans.

rifle range n champ m de tir; (indoor) stand m de tir.

rift [rɪft] n fente f, fissure f; (fig: disagreement) désaccord m.

rig [rɪg] n (also: oil ~: on land) derrick m; (: at sea) plate-forme pétrolière ♦ vt (election etc) truquer.

▶**rig out** vt (BRIT) habiller; (: pej) fringuer, attifer.

▶**rig up** vt arranger, faire avec des moyens de fortune.

rigging ['rɪgɪŋ] n (NAUT) gréement m.

right [raɪt] adj (true) juste, exact(e); (correctly chosen: answer, road etc) bon(bonne); (suitable) approprié(e), convenable; (just) juste, équitable; (morally good) bien inv; (not left) droit(e) ♦ n (title, claim) droit m; (not left) droite f ♦ adv (answer) correctement; (not on the left) à droite ♦ vt redresser ♦ excl bon!; **the ~ time** (precise) l'heure exacte; (not wrong) la bonne heure; **to be ~** (person) avoir raison; (answer) être juste or correct(e); **to get sth ~** ne pas se tromper sur qch; **let's get it ~ this time!** essayons de ne pas nous tromper cette fois-ci!; **you did the ~ thing** vous avez bien fait; **to put a mistake ~** (BRIT) rectifier une erreur; **~ now** en ce moment même; tout de suite; **~ before/after** juste avant/après; **~ against the wall** tout contre le mur; **~ ahead** tout droit; droit devant; ~ **in the middle** en plein milieu; ~ **away** immédiatement; **to go** ~ **to the end of sth** aller jusqu'au bout de qch; **by** ~**s** en toute justice; **on the** ~ à droite; ~ **and wrong** le bien et le mal; **to be in the** ~ avoir raison; **film** ~**s** droits d'adaptation cinématographique; ~ **of way** droit *m* de passage; (*AUT*) priorité *f*.

right angle *n* angle droit.

righteous ['raɪtʃəs] *adj* droit(e), vertueux(euse); (*anger*) justifié(e).

righteousness ['raɪtʃəsnɪs] *n* droiture *f*, vertu *f*.

rightful ['raɪtful] *adj* (*heir*) légitime.

rightfully ['raɪtfəlɪ] *adv* à juste titre, légitimement.

right-handed [raɪt'hændɪd] *adj* (*person*) droitier(ière).

right-hand man ['raɪthænd-] *n* bras droit (*fig*).

right-hand side ['raɪthænd-] *n* côté droit.

rightly ['raɪtlɪ] *adv* bien, correctement; (*with reason*) à juste titre; **if I remember** ~ (*BRIT*) si je me souviens bien.

right-minded ['raɪt'maɪndɪd] *adj* sensé(e), sain(e) d'esprit.

rights issue *n* (*STOCK EXCHANGE*) émission préférentielle *or* de droit de souscription.

right wing *n* (*MIL, SPORT*) aile droite; (*POL*) droite *f* ♦ *adj*: **right-wing** (*POL*) de droite.

right-winger [raɪt'wɪŋə*] *n* (*POL*) membre *m* de la droite; (*SPORT*) ailier droit.

rigid ['rɪdʒɪd] *adj* rigide; (*principle*) strict(e).

rigidity [rɪ'dʒɪdɪtɪ] *n* rigidité *f*.

rigidly ['rɪdʒɪdlɪ] *adv* rigidement; (*behave*) inflexiblement.

rigmarole ['rɪgmərəul] *n* galimatias *m*, comédie *f*.

rigor ['rɪgə*] *n* (*US*) = **rigour**.

rigor mortis ['rɪgə'mɔːtɪs] *n* rigidité *f* cadavérique.

rigorous ['rɪgərəs] *adj* rigoureux(euse).

rigorously ['rɪgərəslɪ] *adv* rigoureusement.

rigour, (*US*) **rigor** ['rɪgə*] *n* rigueur *f*.

rig-out ['rɪgaut] *n* (*BRIT col*) tenue *f*.

rile [raɪl] *vt* agacer.

rim [rɪm] *n* bord *m*; (*of spectacles*) monture *f*; (*of wheel*) jante *f*.

rimless ['rɪmlɪs] *adj* (*spectacles*) à monture invisible.

rind [raɪnd] *n* (*of bacon*) couenne *f*; (*of lemon etc*) écorce *f*.

ring [rɪŋ] *n* anneau *m*; (*on finger*) bague *f*; (*also*: **wedding** ~) alliance *f*; (*for napkin*) rond *m*; (*of people, objects*) cercle *m*; (*of spies*) réseau *m*; (*of smoke etc*) rond; (*arena*) piste *f*, arène *f*; (*for boxing*) ring *m*; (*sound of bell*) sonnerie *f*; (*telephone call*) coup *m* de téléphone ♦ *vb* (*pt* **rang**, *pp* **rung** [ræŋ, rʌŋ]) *vi* (*person, bell*) sonner; (*also*: ~ **out**: *voice, words*) retentir; (*TEL*) téléphoner ♦ *vt* (*BRIT TEL*: *also*: ~ **up**) téléphoner à; **to** ~ **the bell** sonner; **to give**

sb a ~ (*TEL*) passer un coup de téléphone *or* de fil à qn; **that has the** ~ **of truth about it** cela sonne vrai; **the name doesn't** ~ **a bell (with me)** ce nom ne me dit rien.

▶**ring back** *vt*, *vi* (*BRIT TEL*) rappeler.

▶**ring off** *vi* (*BRIT TEL*) raccrocher.

ring binder *n* classeur *m* à anneaux.

ring finger *n* annulaire *m*.

ringing ['rɪŋɪŋ] *n* (*of bell*) tintement *m*; (*louder, also of telephone*) sonnerie *f*; (*in ears*) bourdonnement *m*.

ringing tone *n* (*BRIT TEL*) sonnerie *f*.

ringleader ['rɪŋliːdə*] *n* (*of gang*) chef *m*, meneur *m*.

ringlets ['rɪŋlɪts] *npl* anglaises *fpl*.

ring road *n* (*BRIT*) route *f* de ceinture.

rink [rɪŋk] *n* (*also*: **ice** ~) patinoire *f*; (*for roller-skating*) skating *m*.

rinse [rɪns] *n* rinçage *m* ♦ *vt* rincer.

Rio (de Janeiro) ['riːəu(dədʒə'nɪərəu)] *n* Rio de Janeiro.

riot ['raɪət] *n* émeute *f*, bagarres *fpl* ♦ *vi* manifester avec violence; **a** ~ **of colours** une débauche *or* orgie de couleurs; **to run** ~ se déchaîner.

rioter ['raɪətə*] *n* émeutier/ière, manifestant/e.

riot gear *n*: **in** ~ casqué et portant un bouclier.

riotous ['raɪətəs] *adj* tapageur(euse); tordant(e).

riotously ['raɪətəslɪ] *adv*: ~ **funny** tordant(e).

riot police *n* forces *fpl* de police intervenant en cas d'émeute; **hundreds of** ~ des centaines de policiers casqués et armés.

RIP *abbr* (= *rest in peace*) RIP.

rip [rɪp] *n* déchirure *f* ♦ *vt* déchirer ♦ *vi* se déchirer.

▶**rip up** *vt* déchirer.

ripcord ['rɪpkɔːd] *n* poignée *f* d'ouverture.

ripe [raɪp] *adj* (*fruit*) mûr(e); (*cheese*) fait(e).

ripen ['raɪpn] *vt* mûrir ♦ *vi* mûrir; se faire.

ripeness ['raɪpnɪs] *n* maturité *f*.

rip-off ['rɪpɔf] *n* (*col*): **it's a** ~! c'est du vol manifeste!

riposte [rɪ'pɔst] *n* riposte *f*.

ripple ['rɪpl] *n* ride *f*, ondulation *f*; égrènement *m*, cascade *f* ♦ *vi* se rider, onduler ♦ *vt* rider, faire onduler.

rise [raɪz] *n* (*slope*) côte *f*, pente *f*; (*hill*) élévation *f*; (*increase: in wages*: *BRIT*) augmentation *f*; (: *in prices, temperature*) hausse *f*, augmentation; (*fig*) ascension *f* ♦ *vi* (*pt* **rose**, *pp* **risen** ['rəuz, rɪzn]) s'élever, monter; (*prices*) augmenter, monter; (*waters, river*) monter; (*sun, wind, person: from chair, bed*) se lever; (*also*: ~ **up**: *rebel*) se révolter; se rebeller; ~ **to power** montée *f* au pouvoir; **to give** ~ **to** donner lieu à; **to** ~ **to the occasion** se montrer à la hauteur.

rising ['raɪzɪŋ] *adj* (*increasing: number, prices*) en hausse; (*tide*) montant(e); (*sun, moon*) levant(e) ♦ n (*uprising*) soulèvement *m*, insurrection *f*.

rising damp n humidité *f* (montant des fondations).

rising star n (*also fig*) étoile montante.

risk [rɪsk] n risque *m*, danger *m*; (*deliberate*) risque ♦ vt risquer; **to take** *or* **run the ~ of doing** courir le risque de faire; **at ~** en danger; **at one's own ~** à ses risques et périls; **it's a fire/health ~** cela présente un risque d'incendie/pour la santé; **I'll ~ it** je vais risquer le coup.

risk capital n capital-risques *m*.

risky ['rɪskɪ] adj risqué(e).

risqué ['riːskeɪ] adj (*joke*) risqué(e).

rissole ['rɪsəul] n croquette *f*.

rite [raɪt] n rite *m*; **the last ~s** les derniers sacrements.

ritual ['rɪtjuəl] adj rituel(le) ♦ n rituel *m*.

rival ['raɪvl] n rival/e; (*in business*) concurrent/e ♦ adj rival(e); qui fait concurrence ♦ vt être en concurrence avec; **to ~ sb/sth in** rivaliser avec qn/qch de.

rivalry ['raɪvlrɪ] n rivalité *f*; concurrence *f*.

river ['rɪvə*] n rivière *f*; (*major, also fig*) fleuve *m* ♦ cpd (*port, traffic*) fluvial(e); **up/down ~** en amont/aval.

riverbank ['rɪvəbæŋk] n rive *f*, berge *f*.

riverbed ['rɪvəbed] n lit *m* (de rivière *or* de fleuve).

riverside ['rɪvəsaɪd] n bord *m* de la rivière *or* du fleuve.

rivet ['rɪvɪt] n rivet *m* ♦ vt riveter; (*fig*) river, fixer.

riveting ['rɪvɪtɪŋ] adj (*fig*) fascinant(e).

Riviera [rɪvɪ'ɛərə] n: **the (French) ~** la Côte d'Azur; **the Italian ~** la Riviera (italienne).

Riyadh [rɪ'jɑːd] n Riyad.

RMT n abbr (= Rail, Maritime and Transport) *syndicat des transports*.

RN n abbr (*BRIT*) = **Royal Navy**; (*US*) = **registered nurse**.

RNA n abbr (= ribonucleic acid) ARN *m*.

RNLI n abbr (*BRIT*: = Royal National Lifeboat Institution) ≈ SNSM *f*.

RNZAF n abbr = Royal New Zealand Air Force.

RNZN n abbr = Royal New Zealand Navy.

road [rəud] n route *f*; (*in town*) rue *f*; (*fig*) chemin, voie *f*; **main ~** grande route; **major ~** route principale *or* à priorité; **minor ~** voie secondaire; **it takes four hours by ~** il y a quatre heures de route; **"~ up"** (*BRIT*) "attention travaux".

roadblock ['rəudblɒk] n barrage routier.

road haulage n transports routiers.

roadhog ['rəudhɒg] n chauffard *m*.

road map n carte routière.

road safety n sécurité routière.

roadside ['rəudsaɪd] n bord *m* de la route, bas-côté *m* ♦ cpd (situé(e) etc) au bord de la route; **by the ~** au bord de la route.

roadsign ['rəudsaɪn] n panneau *m* de signalisation.

roadsweeper ['rəudswiːpə*] n (*BRIT*: person) balayeur/euse.

road user n usager *m* de la route.

roadway ['rəudweɪ] n chaussée *f*.

roadworks ['rəudwɜːks] npl travaux *mpl* (de réfection des routes).

roadworthy ['rəudwɜːðɪ] adj en bon état de marche.

roam [rəum] vi errer, vagabonder ♦ vt parcourir, errer par.

roar [rɔː*] n rugissement *m*; (*of crowd*) hurlements *mpl*; (*of vehicle, thunder, storm*) grondement *m* ♦ vi rugir; hurler; gronder; **to ~ with laughter** rire à gorge déployée.

roaring ['rɔːrɪŋ] adj: **a ~ fire** une belle flambée; **a ~ success** un succès fou; **to do a ~ trade** faire des affaires d'or.

roast [rəust] n rôti *m* ♦ vt (*meat*) (faire) rôtir.

roast beef n rôti *m* de bœuf, rosbif *m*.

roasting ['rəustɪŋ] n (*col*): **to give sb a ~** sonner les cloches à qn.

rob [rɒb] vt (*person*) voler; (*bank*) dévaliser; **to ~ sb of sth** voler *or* dérober qch à qn; (*fig: deprive*) priver qn de qch.

robber ['rɒbə*] n bandit *m*, voleur *m*.

robbery ['rɒbərɪ] n vol *m*.

robe [rəub] n (*for ceremony etc*) robe *f*; (*also: bath~*) peignoir *m* ♦ vt revêtir (d'une robe).

robin ['rɒbɪn] n rouge-gorge *m*.

robot ['rəubɒt] n robot *m*.

robotics [rə'bɒtɪks] n robotique *m*.

robust [rəu'bʌst] adj robuste; (*material, appetite*) solide.

rock [rɒk] n (*substance*) roche *f*, roc *m*; (*boulder*) rocher *m*; roche; (*BRIT*: sweet) ≈ sucre *m* d'orge ♦ vt (*swing gently: cradle*) balancer; (: *child*) bercer; (*shake*) ébranler, secouer ♦ vi (se) balancer; être ébranlé(e) *or* secoué(e); **on the ~s** (*drink*) avec des glaçons; (*ship*) sur les écueils; (*marriage etc*) en train de craquer; **to ~ the boat** (*fig*) jouer les trouble-fête.

rock and roll n rock (and roll) *m*, rock'n'roll *m*.

rock-bottom ['rɒk'bɒtəm] n (*fig*) niveau le plus bas ♦ adj (*fig: prices*) sacrifié(e); **to reach** *or* **touch ~** (*price, person*) tomber au plus bas.

rock climber n varappeur/euse.

rock climbing n varappe *f*.

rockery ['rɒkərɪ] n (jardin *m* de) rocaille *f*.

rocket ['rɒkɪt] n fusée *f*; (*MIL*) fusée, roquette *f* ♦ vi (*prices*) monter en flèche.

rocket launcher [-lɔːnʃə*] n lance-roquettes *m inv*.

rock face n paroi rocheuse.

rock fall n chute *f* de pierres.

rocking chair ['rɒkɪŋ-] n fauteuil *m* à bascule.

rocking horse ['rɒkɪŋ-] n cheval *m* à bascule.

rocky ['rɒkɪ] adj (*hill*) rocheux(euse); (*path*) rocailleux(euse); (*unsteady: table*) branlant(e).

Rocky Mountains *npl*: **the** ~ les (montagnes *fpl*) Rocheuses *fpl*.

rod [rɔd] *n* (*metallic*) tringle *f*; (*TECH*) tige *f*; (*wooden*) baguette *f*; (*also*: **fishing** ~) canne *f* à pêche.

rode [rəud] *pt of* **ride**.

rodent ['rəudnt] *n* rongeur *m*.

rodeo ['rəudɪəu] *n* rodéo *m*.

roe [rəu] *n* (*species: also*: ~ **deer**) chevreuil *m*; (*of fish: also*: **hard** ~) œufs *mpl* de poisson; **soft** ~ laitance *f*.

roe deer *n* chevreuil *m*; chevreuil femelle.

rogue [rəug] *n* coquin/e.

roguish ['rəugɪʃ] *adj* coquin(e).

role [rəul] *n* rôle *m*.

role model *n* modèle *m* à émuler.

role play, role playing *n* jeu *m* de rôle.

roll [rəul] *n* rouleau *m*; (*of banknotes*) liasse *f*; (*also*: **bread** ~) petit pain; (*register*) liste *f*; (*sound: of drums etc*) roulement *m*; (*movement: of ship*) roulis *m* ♦ *vt* rouler; (*also*: ~ **up**: *string*) enrouler; (*also*: ~ **out**: *pastry*) étendre au rouleau ♦ *vi* rouler; (*wheel*) tourner; **cheese** ~ ≈ sandwich *m* au fromage (*dans un petit pain*).

►**roll about** , **roll around** *vi* rouler çà et là; (*person*) se rouler par terre.

►**roll by** *vi* (*time*) s'écouler, passer.

►**roll in** *vi* (*mail, cash*) affluer.

►**roll over** *vi* se retourner.

►**roll up** *vi* (*col: arrive*) arriver, s'amener ♦ *vt* (*carpet, cloth, map*) rouler; (*sleeves*) retrousser; **to** ~ **o.s. up into a ball** se rouler en boule.

roll call *n* appel *m*.

rolled-gold ['rəuldgəuld] *adj* plaqué or *inv*.

roller ['rəulə*] *n* rouleau *m*; (*wheel*) roulette *f*.

roller blind *n* (*BRIT*) store *m*.

roller coaster *n* montagnes *fpl* russes.

roller skates *npl* patins *mpl* à roulettes.

rollicking ['rɔlɪkɪŋ] *adj* bruyant(e) et joyeux(euse); (*play*) bouffon(ne); **to have a** ~ **time** s'amuser follement.

rolling ['rəulɪŋ] *adj* (*landscape*) onduleux(euse).

rolling mill *n* laminoir *m*.

rolling pin *n* rouleau *m* à pâtisserie.

rolling stock *n* (*RAIL*) matériel roulant.

roll-on-roll-off ['rəulɔn'rəulɔf] *adj* (*BRIT: ferry*) transroulier(ière).

roly-poly ['rəulɪ'pəulɪ] *n* (*BRIT CULIN*) roulé *m* à la confiture.

ROM [rɔm] *n abbr* (*COMPUT*: = read-only memory*) mémoire morte, ROM *f*.

Roman ['rəumən] *adj* romain(e) ♦ *n* Romain/e.

Roman Catholic *adj*, *n* catholique (*m/f*).

romance [rə'mæns] *n* histoire *f* (*or* film *m or* aventure *f*) romanesque; (*charm*) poésie *f*; (*love affair*) idylle *f*.

Romanesque [rəumə'nɛsk] *adj* roman(e).

Romania [rəu'meɪnɪə] *n* Roumanie *f*.

Romanian [rəu'meɪnɪən] *adj* roumain(e) ♦ *n* Roumain/e; (*LING*) roumain *m*.

Roman numeral *n* chiffre romain.

romantic [rə'mæntɪk] *adj* romantique; (*play, attachment*) sentimental(e).

romanticism [rə'mæntɪsɪzəm] *n* romantisme *m*.

Romany ['rɔmənɪ] *adj* de bohémien ♦ *n* bohémien/ne; (*LING*) romani *m*.

Rome [rəum] *n* Rome.

romp [rɔmp] *n* jeux bruyants ♦ *vi* (*also*: ~ **about**) s'ébattre, jouer bruyamment; **to** ~ **home** (*horse*) arriver bon premier.

rompers ['rɔmpəz] *npl* barboteuse *f*.

rondo ['rɔndəu] *n* (*MUS*) rondeau *m*.

roof [ru:f] *n* toit *m*; (*of tunnel, cave*) plafond *m* ♦ *vt* couvrir (d'un toit); **the** ~ **of the mouth** la voûte du palais.

roof garden *n* toit-terrasse *m*.

roofing ['ru:fɪŋ] *n* toiture *f*.

roof rack *n* (*AUT*) galerie *f*.

rook [ruk] *n* (*bird*) freux *m*; (*CHESS*) tour *f* ♦ *vt* (*col: cheat*) rouler, escroquer.

rookie ['rukɪ] *n* (*col: esp MIL*) bleu *m*.

room [ru:m] *n* (*in house*) pièce *f*; (*also*: **bed**~) chambre *f* (à coucher); (*in school etc*) salle *f*; (*space*) place *f*; ~**s** *npl* (*lodging*) meublé *m*; **"~s to let"**, (*US*) **"~s for rent"** "chambres à louer"; **is there** ~ **for this?** est-ce qu'il y a de la place pour ceci?; **to make** ~ **for sb** faire de la place à qn; **there is** ~ **for improvement** on peut faire mieux.

rooming house ['ru:mɪŋ-] *n* (*US*) maison *f* de rapport.

roommate ['ru:mmeɪt] *n* camarade *m/f* de chambre.

room service *n* service *m* des chambres (*dans un hôtel*).

room temperature *n* température ambiante; **"serve at ~"** (*wine*) "servir chambré".

roomy ['ru:mɪ] *adj* spacieux(euse); (*garment*) ample.

roost [ru:st] *n* juchoir *m* ♦ *vi* se jucher.

rooster ['ru:stə*] *n* coq *m*.

root [ru:t] *n* (*BOT, MATH*) racine *f*; (*fig: of problem*) origine *f*, fond *m* ♦ *vi* (*plant*) s'enraciner; **to take** ~ (*plant, idea*) prendre racine.

►**root about** *vi* (*fig*) fouiller.

►**root for** *vt fus* (*col*) applaudir.

►**root out** *vt* extirper.

root beer *n* (*US*) sorte de limonade à base d'extraits végétaux.

rope [rəup] *n* corde *f*; (*NAUT*) cordage *m* ♦ *vt* (*box*) corder; (*climbers*) encorder; **to** ~ **sb in** (*fig*) embringuer qn; **to know the** ~**s** (*fig*) être au courant, connaître les ficelles.

rope ladder *n* échelle *f* de corde.

ropey ['rəupɪ] *adj* (*col*) pas fameux(euse) *or* brillant(e); **I feel a bit** ~ **today** c'est pas la forme aujourd'hui.

rosary ['rəuzərɪ] n chapelet m.

rose [rəuz] pt of **rise** ♦ n rose f; (also: ~**bush**) rosier m; (on watering can) pomme f ♦ adj rose.

rosé ['rəuzeɪ] n rosé m.

rosebed ['rəuzbed] n massif m de rosiers.

rosebud ['rəuzbʌd] n bouton m de rose.

rosebush ['rəuzbuʃ] n rosier m.

rosemary ['rəuzmərɪ] n romarin m.

rosette [rəu'zet] n rosette f; (larger) cocarde f.

ROSPA ['rɔspə] n abbr (BRIT) = Royal Society for the Prevention of Accidents.

roster ['rɔstə*] n: **duty** ~ tableau m de service.

rostrum ['rɔstrəm] n tribune f (pour un orateur etc).

rosy ['rəuzɪ] adj rose; **a** ~ **future** un bel avenir.

rot [rɔt] n (decay) pourriture f; (fig: pej) idioties fpl, balivernes fpl ♦ vt, vi pourrir; **to stop the** ~ (BRIT fig) rétablir la situation; **dry** ~ pourriture sèche (du bois); **wet** ~ pourriture (du bois).

rota ['rəutə] n liste f, tableau m de service; **on a** ~ **basis** par roulement.

rotary ['rəutərɪ] adj rotatif(ive).

rotate [rəu'teɪt] vt (revolve) faire tourner; (change round: crops) alterner; (: jobs) faire à tour de rôle ♦ vi (revolve) tourner.

rotating [rəu'teɪtɪŋ] adj (movement) tournant(e).

rotation [rəu'teɪʃən] n rotation f; **in** ~ à tour de rôle.

rote [rəut] n: **by** ~ machinalement, par cœur.

rotor ['rəutə*] n rotor m.

rotten ['rɔtn] adj (decayed) pourri(e); (dishonest) corrompu(e); (col: bad) mauvais(e), moche; **to feel** ~ (ill) être mal fichu(e).

rotting ['rɔtɪŋ] adj pourrissant(e).

rotund [rəu'tʌnd] adj rondelet(te); arrondi(e).

rouble, (US) **ruble** ['ru:bl] n rouble m.

rouge [ru:ʒ] n rouge m (à joues).

rough [rʌf] adj (cloth, skin) rêche, rugueux(euse); (terrain) accidenté(e); (path) rocailleux(euse); (voice) rauque, rude; (person, manner: coarse) rude, fruste; (: violent) brutal(e); (district, weather) mauvais(e); (plan) ébauché(e); (guess) approximatif(ive) ♦ n (GOLF) rough m ♦ vt: **to** ~ **it** vivre à la dure; **the sea is** ~ **today** la mer est agitée aujourd'hui; **to have a** ~ **time (of it)** en voir de dures; ~ **estimate** approximation f; **to play** ~ jouer avec brutalité; **to sleep** ~ (BRIT) coucher à la dure; **to feel** ~ (BRIT) être mal fichu(e).

▶**rough out** vt (draft) ébaucher.

roughage ['rʌfɪdʒ] n fibres fpl diététiques.

rough-and-ready ['rʌfən'redɪ] adj (accommodation, method) rudimentaire.

rough-and-tumble ['rʌfən'tʌmbl] n agitation f.

roughcast ['rʌfkɑːst] n crépi m.

rough copy, rough draft n brouillon m.

roughen ['rʌfn] vt (a surface) rendre rude or rugueux(euse).

rough justice n justice f sommaire.

roughly ['rʌflɪ] adv (handle) rudement, brutalement; (make) grossièrement; (approximately) à peu près, en gros; ~ **speaking** en gros.

roughness ['rʌfnɪs] n (of cloth, skin) rugosité f; (of person) rudesse f; brutalité f.

roughshod ['rʌfʃɔd] adv: **to ride** ~ **over** ne tenir aucun compte de.

rough work n (at school etc) brouillon m.

roulette [ru:'let] n roulette f.

Roumania etc [ru:'meɪnɪə] = **Romania** etc.

round [raund] adj rond(e) ♦ n rond m, cercle m; (BRIT: of toast) tranche f; (duty: of policeman, milkman etc) tournée f; (: of doctor) visites fpl; (game: of cards, in competition) partie f; (BOXING) round m; (of talks) série f ♦ vt (corner) tourner; (bend) prendre; (cape) doubler ♦ prep autour de ♦ adv: **right** ~, **all** ~ tout autour; **the long way** ~ (par) le chemin le plus long; **all the year** ~ toute l'année; **in** ~ **figures** en chiffres ronds; **it's just** ~ **the corner** c'est juste après le coin; (fig) c'est tout près; **to ask sb** ~ inviter qn (chez soi); **I'll be** ~ **at 6 o'clock** je serai là à 6 heures; **to go** ~ faire le tour or un détour; **to go** ~ **to sb's (house)** aller chez qn; **to go** ~ **an obstacle** contourner un obstacle; **go** ~ **the back** passez par derrière; **to go** ~ **a house** visiter une maison, faire le tour d'une maison; **enough to go** ~ assez pour tout le monde; **she arrived** ~ **(about) noon** (BRIT) elle est arrivée vers midi; **the clock 24 heures sur 24**; **to go the** ~**s** (disease, story) circuler; **the daily** ~ (fig) la routine quotidienne; ~ **of ammunition** cartouche f; ~ **of applause** ban m, applaudissements mpl; ~ **of drinks** tournée f; ~ **of sandwiches** (BRIT) sandwich m.

▶**round off** vt (speech etc) terminer.

▶**round up** vt rassembler; (criminals) effectuer une rafle de; (prices) arrondir (au chiffre supérieur).

roundabout ['raundəbaut] n (BRIT AUT) rond-point m (à sens giratoire); (at fair) manège m (de chevaux de bois) ♦ adj (route, means) détourné(e).

rounded ['raundɪd] adj arrondi(e); (style) harmonieux(euse).

rounders ['raundəz] npl (game) ≈ balle f au camp.

roundly ['raundlɪ] adv (fig) tout net, carrément.

round-robin ['raundrɔbɪn] n (SPORT: also: ~ **tournament**) tournoi où tous les joueurs se rencontrent.

round-shouldered ['raund'ʃəuldəd] adj au dos rond.

round trip n (voyage m) aller et retour m.

roundup ['raundʌp] n rassemblement m; (of

criminals) rafle *f*; **a ~ of the latest news** un rappel des derniers événements.

rouse [rauz] *vt* (*wake up*) réveiller; (*stir up*) susciter; provoquer; éveiller.

rousing ['rauzıŋ] *adj* (*welcome*) enthousiaste.

rout [raut] *n* (*MIL*) déroute *f* ♦ *vt* mettre en déroute.

route [ru:t] *n* itinéraire *m*; (*of bus*) parcours *m*; (*of trade, shipping*) route *f*; **"all ~s"** (*AUT*) "toutes directions"; **the best ~ to London** le meilleur itinéraire pour aller à Londres; **en ~ for** en route pour.

route map *n* (*BRIT: for journey*) croquis *m* d'itinéraire; (*for trains etc*) carte *f* du réseau.

routine [ru:'ti:n] *adj* (*work*) ordinaire, courant(e); (*procedure*) d'usage ♦ *n* routine *f*; (*THEAT*) numéro *m*; **daily ~** occupations journalières.

roving ['rəuvıŋ] *adj* (*life*) vagabond(e).

roving reporter *n* reporter volant.

row¹ [rəu] *n* (*line*) rangée *f*; (*of people, seats, KNITTING*) rang *m*; (*behind one another: of cars, people*) file *f* ♦ *vi* (*in boat*) ramer; (*as sport*) faire de l'aviron ♦ *vt* (*boat*) faire aller à la rame *or* à l'aviron; **in a ~** (*fig*) d'affilée.

row² [rau] *n* (*noise*) vacarme *m*; (*dispute*) dispute *f*, querelle *f*; (*scolding*) réprimande *f*, savon *m* ♦ *vi* (*also:* **to have a ~**) se disputer, se quereller.

rowboat ['rəubəut] *n* (*US*) canot *m* (à rames).

rowdiness ['raudınıs] *n* tapage *m*, chahut *m*; (*fighting*) bagarre *f*.

rowdy ['raudı] *adj* chahuteur(euse); bagarreur(euse) ♦ *n* voyou *m*.

rowdyism ['raudıızəm] *n* tendances *fpl* à la violence; actes *mpl* de violence.

rowing ['rəuıŋ] *n* canotage *m*; (*as sport*) aviron *m*.

rowing boat *n* (*BRIT*) canot *m* (à rames).

rowlock ['rɔlək] *n* (*BRIT*) dame *f* de nage, tolet *m*.

royal ['rɔıəl] *adj* royal(e).

La **Royal Academy** *ou* **Royal Academy of Arts**, *fondée en 1768 par George III pour encourager la peinture, la sculpture et l'architecture, est située à Burlington House, sur Piccadilly. Une exposition des œuvres d'artistes contemporains a lieu tous les étés. L'Académie dispense également des cours en peinture, sculpture et architecture.*

Royal Air Force (RAF) *n* (*BRIT*) *armée de l'air britannique.*

royal blue *adj* bleu roi *inv*.

royalist ['rɔıəlıst] *adj, n* royaliste (*m/f*).

Royal Navy (RN) *n* (*BRIT*) *marine de guerre britannique.*

royalty ['rɔıəltı] *n* (*royal persons*) (membres *mpl* de la) famille royale; (*payment: to author*) droits *mpl* d'auteur; (*: to inventor*) royalties *fpl*.

RP *n abbr* (*BRIT:* = *received pronunciation*) prononciation *f* standard.

rpm *abbr* (= *revolutions per minute*) t/mn (= *tours/minute*).

RR *abbr* (*US*) = **railroad**.

RSA *n abbr* (*BRIT:* = *Royal Society of Arts, Royal Scottish Academy*).

RSI *n abbr* (*MED:* = *repetitive strain injury*) microtraumatisme permanent.

RSPB *n abbr* (*BRIT:* = *Royal Society for the Protection of Birds*) ≈ LPO *f*.

RSPCA *n abbr* (*BRIT:* = *Royal Society for the Prevention of Cruelty to Animals*) ≈ SPA *f*.

RSVP *abbr* (= *répondez s'il vous plaît*) RSVP.

RTA *n abbr* (= *road traffic accident*) accident *m* de la route.

Rt Hon. *abbr* (*BRIT:* = *Right Honourable*) *titre donné aux députés de la Chambre des communes.*

Rt Rev. *abbr* (= *Right Reverend*) très révérend.

rub [rʌb] *n* (*with cloth*) coup *m* de chiffon *or* de torchon; (*on person*) friction *f* ♦ *vt* frotter; frictionner; **to ~ sb up** *or* (*US*) **~ sb the wrong way** prendre qn à rebrousse-poil.

▶**rub down** *vt* (*body*) frictionner; (*horse*) bouchonner.

▶**rub in** *vt* (*ointment*) faire pénétrer.

▶**rub off** *vi* partir; **to ~ off on** déteindre sur.

▶**rub out** *vt* effacer ♦ *vi* s'effacer.

rubber ['rʌbə*] *n* caoutchouc *m*; (*BRIT: eraser*) gomme *f* (à effacer).

rubber band *n* élastique *m*.

rubber bullet *n* balle *f* en caoutchouc.

rubber plant *n* caoutchouc *m* (*plante verte*).

rubber ring *n* (*for swimming*) bouée *f* (de natation).

rubber stamp *n* tampon *m*.

rubber-stamp [rʌbə'stæmp] *vt* (*fig*) approuver sans discussion.

rubbery ['rʌbərı] *adj* caoutchouteux(euse).

rubbish ['rʌbıʃ] *n* (*from household*) ordures *fpl*; (*fig: pej*) choses *fpl* sans valeur; camelote *f*; (*nonsense*) bêtises *fpl*, idioties *fpl* ♦ *vt* (*BRIT col*) dénigrer, rabaisser; **what you've just said is ~** tu viens de dire une bêtise.

rubbish bin *n* (*BRIT*) boîte *f* à ordures, poubelle *f*.

rubbish dump *n* (*in town*) décharge publique, dépotoir *m*.

rubbishy ['rʌbıʃı] *adj* (*BRIT col*) qui ne vaut rien, moche.

rubble ['rʌbl] *n* décombres *mpl*; (*smaller*) gravats *mpl*.

ruble ['ru:bl] *n* (*US*) = **rouble**.

ruby ['ru:bı] *n* rubis *m*.

RUC *n abbr* (*BRIT*) = *Royal Ulster Constabulary*.

rucksack ['rʌksæk] *n* sac *m* à dos.

ructions ['rʌkʃənz] *npl* grabuge *m*.

rudder ['rʌdə*] *n* gouvernail *m*.

ruddy ['rʌdı] *adj* (*face*) coloré(e); (*col: damned*)

sacré(e), fichu(e).

rude [ruːd] *adj* (*impolite: person*) impoli(e); (*: word, manners*) grossier(ière); (*shocking*) indécent(e), inconvenant(e); **to be ~ to sb** être grossier envers qn.

rudely ['ruːdlɪ] *adv* impoliment; grossièrement.

rudeness ['ruːdnɪs] *n* impolitesse *f*; grossièreté *f*.

rudiment ['ruːdɪmənt] *n* rudiment *m*.

rudimentary [ruːdɪ'mɛntərɪ] *adj* rudimentaire.

rue [ruː] *vt* se repentir de, regretter amèrement.

rueful ['ruːful] *adj* triste.

ruff [rʌf] *n* fraise *f*, collerette *f*.

ruffian ['rʌfɪən] *n* brute *f*, voyou *m*.

ruffle ['rʌfl] *vt* (*hair*) ébouriffer; (*clothes*) chiffonner; (*water*) agiter; (*fig: person*) émouvoir, faire perdre son flegme à.

rug [rʌg] *n* petit tapis; (*BRIT: for knees*) couverture *f*.

rugby ['rʌgbɪ] *n* (*also: ~ football*) rugby *m*.

rugged ['rʌgɪd] *adj* (*landscape*) accidenté(e); (*features, kindness, character*) rude; (*determination*) farouche.

rugger ['rʌgə*] *n* (*BRIT col*) rugby *m*.

ruin ['ruːɪn] *n* ruine *f* ♦ *vt* ruiner; (*spoil: clothes*) abîmer; **~s** *npl* ruine(s) *f*; **in ~s** en ruine.

ruination [ruːɪ'neɪʃən] *n* ruine *f*.

ruinous ['ruːɪnəs] *adj* ruineux(euse).

rule [ruːl] *n* règle *f*; (*regulation*) règlement *m*; (*government*) autorité *f*, gouvernement *m*; (*dominion etc*): **under British ~** sous l'autorité britannique ♦ *vt* (*country*) gouverner; (*person*) dominer; (*decide*) décider ♦ *vi* commander; décider; (*LAW*): **to ~ against/in favour of/on** statuer contre/en faveur de/sur; **to ~ that** (*umpire, judge etc*) décider que; **it's against the ~s** c'est contraire au règlement; **by ~ of thumb** à vue de nez; **as a ~** normalement, en règle générale.

▶**rule out** *vt* exclure; **murder cannot be ~d out** l'hypothèse d'un meurtre ne peut être exclue.

ruled [ruːld] *adj* (*paper*) réglé(e).

ruler ['ruːlə*] *n* (*sovereign*) souverain/e; (*leader*) chef *m* (d'État); (*for measuring*) règle *f*.

ruling ['ruːlɪŋ] *adj* (*party*) au pouvoir; (*class*) dirigeant(e) ♦ *n* (*LAW*) décision *f*.

rum [rʌm] *n* rhum *m* ♦ *adj* (*BRIT col*) bizarre.

Rumania *etc* [ruː'meɪnɪə] = **Romania** *etc*.

rumble ['rʌmbl] *n* grondement *m*; gargouillement *m* ♦ *vi* gronder; (*stomach, pipe*) gargouiller.

rumbustious [rʌm'bʌstʃəs], (*US*)
rumbunctious [rʌm'bʌŋkʃəs] *adj* (*person*) exubérant(e).

rummage ['rʌmɪdʒ] *vi* fouiller.

rumour, (*US*) **rumor** ['ruːmə*] *n* rumeur *f*, bruit *m* (qui court) ♦ *vt*: **it is ~ed that** le

bruit court que.

rump [rʌmp] *n* (*of animal*) croupe *f*; (*also: ~ steak*) romsteck *m*.

rumple ['rʌmpl] *vt* (*hair*) ébouriffer; (*clothes*) chiffonner, friper.

rumpus ['rʌmpəs] *n* (*col*) tapage *m*, chahut *m*; (*quarrel*) prise *f* de bec; **to kick up a ~** faire toute une histoire.

run [rʌn] *n* (*race etc*) course *f*; (*outing*) tour *m* or promenade *f* (en voiture); (*journey*) parcours *m*, trajet *m*; (*series*) suite *f*, série *f*; (*THEAT*) série de représentations; (*SKI*) piste *f*; (*in tights, stockings*) maille filée, échelle *f* ♦ *vb* (*pt* **ran**, *pp* **run** [ræn, rʌn]) *vt* (*business*) diriger; (*competition, course*) organiser; (*hotel, house*) tenir; (*COMPUT: program*) exécuter; (*force through: rope, pipe*): **to ~ sth through** faire passer qch à travers; (*to pass: hand, finger*): **to ~ sth over** promener or passer qch sur; (*water, bath*) faire couler ♦ *vi* courir; (*pass: road etc*) passer; (*work: machine, factory*) marcher; (*bus, train*) circuler; (*continue: play*) se jouer, être à l'affiche; (*: contract*) être valide or en vigueur; (*slide: drawer*) glisser; (*flow: river, bath*) couler; (*colours, washing*) déteindre; (*in election*) être candidat, se présenter; **to go for a ~** aller courir or faire un peu de course à pied; (*in car*) faire un tour or une promenade (en voiture); **to break into a ~** se mettre à courir; **a ~ of luck** une série de coups de chance; **to have the ~ of sb's house** avoir la maison de qn à sa disposition; **there was a ~ on** (*meat, tickets*) les gens se sont rués sur; **in the long ~** à longue échéance; à la longue; en fin de compte; **in the short ~** à brève échéance, à court terme; **on the ~** en fuite; **to make a ~ for it** s'enfuir; **I'll ~ you to the station** je vais vous emmener or conduire à la gare; **to ~ errands** faire des commissions; **the train ~s between Gatwick and Victoria** le train assure le service entre Gatwick et Victoria; **the bus ~s every 20 minutes** il y a un autobus toutes les 20 minutes; **it's very cheap to ~** (*car, machine*) c'est très économique; **to ~ on petrol** or (*US*) **gas/on diesel/off batteries** marcher à l'essence/au diesel/sur piles; **to ~ for president** être candidat à la présidence; **their losses ran into millions** leurs pertes se sont élevées à plusieurs millions; **to be ~ off one's feet** (*BRIT*) ne plus savoir où donner de la tête.

▶**run about** *vi* (*children*) courir çà et là.

▶**run across** *vt fus* (*find*) trouver par hasard.

▶**run away** *vi* s'enfuir.

▶**run down** *vi* (*clock*) s'arrêter (faute d'avoir été remonté) ♦ *vt* (*AUT*) renverser; (*BRIT: reduce: production*) réduire progressivement; (*: factory/shop*) réduire progressivement la production/l'activité de; (*criticize*) critiquer, dénigrer; **to be ~**

down être fatigué(e) *or* à plat.
▶**run in** *vt* (*BRIT: car*) roder.
▶**run into** *vt fus* (*meet: person*) rencontrer par hasard; (*: trouble*) se heurter à; (*collide with*) heurter; **to ~ into debt** contracter des dettes.
▶**run off** *vi* s'enfuir ♦ *vt* (*water*) laisser s'écouler.
▶**run out** *vi* (*person*) sortir en courant; (*liquid*) couler; (*lease*) expirer; (*money*) être épuisé(e).
▶**run out of** *vt fus* se trouver à court de; **I've ~ out of petrol** *or* (*US*) **gas** je suis en panne d'essence.
▶**run over** *vt* (*AUT*) écraser ♦ *vt fus* (*revise*) revoir, reprendre.
▶**run through** *vt fus* (*instructions*) reprendre, revoir.
▶**run up** *vt* (*debt*) laisser accumuler; **to ~ up against** (*difficulties*) se heurter à.
runaround ['rʌnəraund] *n* (*col*): **to give sb the ~** rester très évasif.
runaway ['rʌnəweɪ] *adj* (*horse*) emballé(e); (*truck*) fou(folle); (*inflation*) galopant(e).
rundown ['rʌndaun] *n* (*BRIT: of industry etc*) réduction progressive.
rung [rʌŋ] *pp of* **ring** ♦ *n* (*of ladder*) barreau *m*.
run-in ['rʌnɪn] *n* (*col*) accrochage *m*, prise *f* de bec.
runner ['rʌnə*] *n* (*in race: person*) coureur/euse; (*: horse*) partant *m*; (*on sledge*) patin *m*; (*for drawer etc*) coulisseau *m*; (*carpet: in hall etc*) chemin *m*.
runner bean *n* (*BRIT*) haricot *m* (à rames).
runner-up [rʌnər'ʌp] *n* second/e.
running ['rʌnɪŋ] *n* (*in race etc*) course *f*; (*of business*) direction *f*; (*of event*) organisation *f*; (*of machine etc*) marche *f*, fonctionnement *m* ♦ *adj* (*water*) courant(e); (*commentary*) suivi(e); **6 days ~ 6** jours de suite; **to be in/out of the ~ for sth** être/ne pas être sur les rangs pour qch.
running costs *npl* (*of business*) frais *mpl* de gestion; (*of car*): **the ~ are high** elle revient cher.
running head *n* (*TYP, WORD PROCESSING*) titre courant.
running mate *n* (*US POL*) *candidat à la vice-présidence*.
runny ['rʌnɪ] *adj* qui coule.
run-off ['rʌnɔf] *n* (*in contest, election*) deuxième tour *m*; (*extra race etc*) épreuve *f* supplémentaire.
run-of-the-mill ['rʌnəvðə'mɪl] *adj* ordinaire, banal(e).
runt [rʌnt] *n* (*also pej*) avorton *m*.
run-through ['rʌnθruː] *n* répétition *f*, essai *m*.
run-up ['rʌnʌp] *n* (*BRIT*): **~ to sth** période *f* précédant qch.
runway ['rʌnweɪ] *n* (*AVIAT*) piste *f* (d'envol *or* d'atterrissage).

rupee [ruː'piː] *n* roupie *f*.
rupture ['rʌptʃə*] *n* (*MED*) hernie *f* ♦ *vt*: **to ~ o.s.** se donner une hernie.
rural ['ruərl] *adj* rural(e).
ruse [ruːz] *n* ruse *f*.
rush [rʌʃ] *n* course précipitée; (*of crowd*) ruée *f*, bousculade *f*; (*hurry*) hâte *f*, bousculade; (*current*) flot *m*; (*BOT*) jonc *m*; (*for chair*) paille *f* ♦ *vt* transporter *or* envoyer d'urgence; (*attack: town etc*) prendre d'assaut; (*BRIT col: overcharge*) estamper; faire payer ♦ *vi* se précipiter; **don't ~ me!** laissez-moi le temps de souffler!; **to ~ sth off** (*do quickly*) faire qch à la hâte; (*send*) envoyer d'urgence; **is there any ~ for this?** est-ce urgent?; **we've had a ~ of orders** nous avons reçu une avalanche de commandes; **I'm in a ~ (to do)** je suis vraiment pressé (de faire); **gold ~** ruée vers l'or.
▶**rush through** *vt fus* (*work*) exécuter à la hâte ♦ *vt* (*COMM: order*) exécuter d'urgence.
rush hour *n* heures *fpl* de pointe *or* d'affluence.
rush job *n* travail urgent.
rush matting *n* natte *f* de paille.
rusk [rʌsk] *n* biscotte *f*.
Russia ['rʌʃə] *n* Russie *f*.
Russian ['rʌʃən] *adj* russe ♦ *n* Russe *m/f*; (*LING*) russe *m*.
rust [rʌst] *n* rouille *f* ♦ *vi* rouiller.
rustic ['rʌstɪk] *adj* rustique ♦ *n* (*pej*) rustaud/e.
rustle ['rʌsl] *vi* bruire, produire un bruissement ♦ *vt* (*paper*) froisser; (*US: cattle*) voler.
rustproof ['rʌstpruːf] *adj* inoxydable.
rustproofing ['rʌstpruːfɪŋ] *n* traitement *m* antirouille.
rusty ['rʌstɪ] *adj* rouillé(e).
rut [rʌt] *n* ornière *f*, (*ZOOL*) rut *m*; **to be in a ~** (*fig*) suivre l'ornière, s'encroûter.
rutabaga [ruːtə'beɪgə] *n* (*US*) rutabaga *m*.
ruthless ['ruːθlɪs] *adj* sans pitié, impitoyable.
ruthlessness ['ruːθlɪsnɪs] *n* dureté *f*, cruauté *f*.
RV *abbr* (= *revised version*) *traduction anglaise de la Bible de 1885* ♦ *n abbr* (*US*) = **recreational vehicle**.
rye [raɪ] *n* seigle *m*.
rye bread *n* pain *m* de seigle.

S s

S, s [ɛs] n (letter) S, s m; (US SCOL:
= satisfactory) ≈ assez bien; **S for Sugar** S
comme Suzanne.

S abbr (= south, small) S; (= saint) St.

SA n abbr = **South Africa, South America.**

Sabbath ['sæbəθ] n (Jewish) sabbat m;
(Christian) dimanche m.

sabbatical [sə'bætɪkl] adj: ~ **year** année f
sabbatique.

sabotage ['sæbətɑ:ʒ] n sabotage m ♦ vt
saboter.

saccharin(e) ['sækərɪn] n saccharine f.

sachet ['sæʃeɪ] n sachet m.

sack [sæk] n (bag) sac m ♦ vt (dismiss)
renvoyer, mettre à la porte; (plunder) piller,
mettre à sac; **to give sb the** ~ renvoyer qn,
mettre qn à la porte; **to get the** ~ être
renvoyé(e) or mis(e) à la porte.

sackful ['sækful] n: **a** ~ **of** un (plein) sac de.

sacking ['sækɪŋ] n toile f à sac; (dismissal)
renvoi m.

sacrament ['sækrəmənt] n sacrement m.

sacred ['seɪkrɪd] adj sacré(e).

sacred cow n (fig) chose sacro-sainte.

sacrifice ['sækrɪfaɪs] n sacrifice m ♦ vt
sacrifier; **to make ~s (for sb)** se sacrifier or
faire des sacrifices (pour qn).

sacrilege ['sækrɪlɪdʒ] n sacrilège m.

sacrosanct ['sækrəusæŋkt] adj sacro-saint(e).

sad [sæd] adj (unhappy) triste; (deplorable)
triste, fâcheux(euse).

sadden ['sædn] vt attrister, affliger.

saddle ['sædl] n selle f ♦ vt (horse) seller; **to be**
~d with sth (col) avoir qch sur les bras.

saddlebag ['sædlbæg] n sacoche f.

sadism ['seɪdɪzəm] n sadisme m.

sadist ['seɪdɪst] n sadique m/f.

sadistic [sə'dɪstɪk] adj sadique.

sadly ['sædlɪ] adv tristement; (regrettably)
malheureusement.

sadness ['sædnɪs] n tristesse f.

sado-masochism [seɪdəu'mæsəkɪzəm] n
sadomasochisme m.

sae abbr (BRIT: = stamped addressed envelope)
enveloppe affranchie pour la réponse.

safari [sə'fɑ:rɪ] n safari m.

safari park n réserve f.

safe [seɪf] adj (out of danger) hors de danger,
en sécurité; (not dangerous) sans danger;
(cautious) prudent(e); (sure: bet etc)
assuré(e) ♦ n coffre-fort m; ~ **from** à l'abri
de; ~ **and sound** sain(e) et sauf(sauve);

(just) **to be on the** ~ **side** pour plus de
sûreté, par précaution; **to play** ~ ne
prendre aucun risque; **it is** ~ **to say that** ...
on peut dire sans crainte que ...; ~ **journey!**
bon voyage!

safe bet n: **it was a** ~ ça ne comportait pas
trop de risques; **it's a** ~ **that he'll be late** il y
a toutes les chances pour qu'il soit en
retard.

safe-breaker ['seɪfbreɪkə*] n (BRIT) perceur m
de coffre-fort.

safe-conduct [seɪf'kɔndʌkt] n sauf-conduit m.

safe-cracker ['seɪfkrækə*] n = **safe-breaker.**

safe-deposit ['seɪfdɪpɔzɪt] n (vault) dépôt m de
coffres-forts; (box) coffre-fort m.

safeguard ['seɪfgɑ:d] n sauvegarde f,
protection f ♦ vt sauvegarder, protéger.

safe haven n zone f de sécurité.

safekeeping ['seɪf'ki:pɪŋ] n bonne garde.

safely ['seɪflɪ] adv sans danger, sans risque;
(without mishap) sans accident; **I can** ~ **say** ...
je peux dire à coup sûr ....

safe passage n: **to grant sb** ~ accorder un
laissez-passer à qn.

safe sex n rapports sexuels protégés.

safety ['seɪftɪ] n sécurité f; ~ **first!** la sécurité
d'abord!

safety belt n ceinture f de sécurité.

safety catch n cran m de sûreté or sécurité.

safety net n filet m de sécurité.

safety pin n épingle f de sûreté or de
nourrice.

safety valve n soupape f de sûreté.

saffron ['sæfrən] n safran m.

sag [sæg] vi s'affaisser, fléchir; pendre.

saga ['sɑ:gə] n saga f; (fig) épopée f.

sage [seɪdʒ] n (herb) sauge f, (man) sage m.

Sagittarius [sædʒɪ'tɛərɪəs] n le Sagittaire; **to**
be ~ être du Sagittaire.

sago ['seɪgəu] n sagou m.

Sahara [sə'hɑ:rə] n: **the** ~ **(Desert)** le (désert
du) Sahara m.

Sahel [sæ'hɛl] n Sahel m.

said [sɛd] pt, pp of **say.**

Saigon [saɪ'gɔn] n Saigon m.

sail [seɪl] n (on boat) voile f; (trip): **to go for a** ~
faire un tour en bateau ♦ vt (boat)
manœuvrer, piloter ♦ vi (travel: ship)
avancer, naviguer; (: passenger) aller or se
rendre (en bateau); (set off) partir, prendre
la mer; (SPORT) faire de la voile; **they ~ed**
into Le Havre ils sont entrés dans le port du
Havre.

▶**sail through** vi, vt fus (fig) réussir haut la
main.

sailboat ['seɪlbəut] n (US) bateau m à voiles,
voilier m.

sailing ['seɪlɪŋ] n (SPORT) voile f; **to go** ~ faire
de la voile.

sailing boat n bateau m à voiles, voilier m.

sailing ship n grand voilier.

sailor ['seɪlə*] n marin m, matelot m.

saint [seɪnt] *n* saint/e.

saintly ['seɪntlɪ] *adj* saint(e), plein(e) de bonté.

sake [seɪk] *n*: **for the ~ of** (*out of concern for*) pour, dans l'intérêt de; (*out of consideration for*) par égard pour; (*in order to achieve*) pour plus de, par souci de; **arguing for arguing's ~ discuter** pour (le plaisir de) discuter; **for the ~ of argument** à titre d'exemple; **for heaven's ~!** pour l'amour du ciel!

salad ['sæləd] *n* salade *f*; **tomato ~** salade de tomates.

salad bowl *n* saladier *m*.

salad cream *n* (*BRIT*) (sorte *f* de) mayonnaise *f*.

salad dressing *n* vinaigrette *f*.

salad oil *n* huile *f* de table.

salami [sə'lɑːmɪ] *n* salami *m*.

salaried ['sælərɪd] *adj* (*staff*) salarié(e), qui touche un traitement.

salary ['sælərɪ] *n* salaire *m*, traitement *m*.

salary scale *n* échelle *f* des traitements.

sale [seɪl] *n* vente *f*; (*at reduced prices*) soldes *mpl*; **"for ~"** "à vendre"; **on ~** en vente; **on ~ or return** vendu(e) avec faculté de retour; **closing-down** *or* (*US*) **liquidation ~** liquidation *f* (*avant fermeture*); **~ and lease back** *n* cession-bail *f*.

saleroom ['seɪlruːm] *n* salle *f* des ventes.

sales assistant *n* (*BRIT*) vendeur/euse.

sales clerk *n* (*US*) vendeur/euse.

sales conference *n* réunion *f* de vente.

sales drive *n* campagne commerciale, animation *f* des ventes.

sales force *n* (ensemble *m* du) service des ventes.

salesman ['seɪlzmən] *n* vendeur *m*; (*representative*) représentant *m* de commerce.

sales manager *n* directeur commercial.

salesmanship ['seɪlzmənʃɪp] *n* art *m* de la vente.

sales tax *n* (*US*) taxe *f* à l'achat.

saleswoman ['seɪlzwumən] *n* vendeuse *f*.

salient ['seɪlɪənt] *adj* saillant(e).

saline ['seɪlaɪn] *adj* salin(e).

saliva [sə'laɪvə] *n* salive *f*.

sallow ['sæləu] *adj* cireux(euse).

sally forth, sally out ['sælɪ-] *vi* partir plein(e) d'entrain.

salmon ['sæmən] *n* (*pl inv*) saumon *m*.

salmon trout *n* truite saumonée.

saloon [sə'luːn] *n* (*US*) bar *m*; (*BRIT AUT*) berline *f*; (*ship's lounge*) salon *m*.

SALT [sɔːlt] *n abbr* (= *Strategic Arms Limitation Talks/Treaty*) SALT *m*.

salt [sɔːlt] *n* sel *m* ♦ *vt* saler ♦ *cpd* de sel; (*CULIN*) salé(e); **an old ~** un vieux loup de mer.

▶**salt away** *vt* mettre de côté.

salt cellar *n* salière *f*.

salt-free ['sɔːlt'friː] *adj* sans sel.

saltwater ['sɔːlt'wɔːtə*] *adj* (*fish etc*) (d'eau) de mer.

salty ['sɔːltɪ] *adj* salé(e).

salubrious [sə'luːbrɪəs] *adj* salubre.

salutary ['sæljutərɪ] *adj* salutaire.

salute [sə'luːt] *n* salut *m* ♦ *vt* saluer.

salvage ['sælvɪdʒ] *n* (*saving*) sauvetage *m*; (*things saved*) biens sauvés *or* récupérés ♦ *vt* sauver, récupérer.

salvage vessel *n* bateau *m* de sauvetage.

salvation [sæl'veɪʃən] *n* salut *m*.

Salvation Army *n* Armée *f* du Salut.

salver ['sælvə*] *n* plateau *m* de métal.

salvo ['sælvəu] *n* salve *f*.

Samaritan [sə'mærɪtən] *n*: **the ~s** (*organization*) ≈ S.O.S. Amitié.

same [seɪm] *adj* même ♦ *pron*: **the ~** le(la) même, les mêmes; **the ~ book as** le même livre que; **on the ~ day** le même jour; **at the ~ time** en même temps; **all** *or* **just the ~** tout de même, quand même; **they're one and the ~** (*person/thing*) c'est une seule et même personne/chose; **to do the ~** faire de même, en faire autant; **to do the ~ as sb** faire comme qn; **and the ~ to you!** et à vous de même!; (*after insult*) toi-même!; **~ here!** moi aussi!; **the ~ again!** (*in bar etc*) la même chose!

sample ['sɑːmpl] *n* échantillon *m*; (*MED*) prélèvement *m* ♦ *vt* (*food, wine*) goûter; **to take a ~** prélever un échantillon; **free ~** échantillon gratuit.

sanatorium, *pl* **sanatoria** [sænə'tɔːrɪəm, -rɪə] *n* sanatorium *m*.

sanctify ['sæŋktɪfaɪ] *vt* sanctifier.

sanctimonious [sæŋktɪ'məunɪəs] *adj* moralisateur(trice).

sanction ['sæŋkʃən] *n* sanction *f* ♦ *vt* cautionner, sanctionner; **to impose economic ~s on** *or* **against** prendre des sanctions économiques contre.

sanctity ['sæŋktɪtɪ] *n* sainteté *f*, caractère sacré.

sanctuary ['sæŋktjuərɪ] *n* (*holy place*) sanctuaire *m*; (*refuge*) asile *m*; (*for wild life*) réserve *f*.

sand [sænd] *n* sable *m* ♦ *vt* sabler; (*also: ~ down: wood etc*) poncer.

sandal ['sændl] *n* sandale *f*.

sandbag ['sændbæg] *n* sac *m* de sable.

sandblast ['sændblɑːst] *vt* décaper à la sableuse.

sandbox ['sændbɒks] *n* (*US: for children*) tas *m* de sable.

sandcastle ['sændkɑːsl] *n* château *m* de sable.

sand dune *n* dune *f* de sable.

sander ['sændə*] *n* ponceuse *f*.

S&M *n abbr* (= *sadomasochism*) sadomasochisme *m*.

sandpaper ['sændpeɪpə*] *n* papier *m* de verre.

sandpit ['sændpɪt] *n* (*BRIT: for children*) tas *m* de sable.

sands [sændz] *npl* plage *f* (de sable).

sandstone ['sændstəun] *n* grès *m*.

andstorm ['sændstɔːm] n tempête f de sable.
andwich ['sændwɪtʃ] n sandwich m ♦ vt (also: ~ **in**) intercaler; ~**ed between** pris en sandwich entre; **cheese/ham** ~ sandwich au fromage/jambon.
andwich board n panneau m publicitaire (porté par un homme-sandwich).
andwich course n (BRIT) cours m de formation professionnelle.
andy ['sændɪ] adj sablonneux(euse); couvert(e) de sable; (colour) sable inv, blond roux inv.
ane [seɪn] adj (person) sain(e) d'esprit; (outlook) sensé(e), sain(e).
ang [sæŋ] pt of **sing**.
anguine ['sæŋgwɪn] adj optimiste.
anitarium, pl **sanitaria** [sænɪ'tɛərɪəm, -rɪə] n (US) = **sanatorium**.
anitary ['sænɪtərɪ] adj (system, arrangements) sanitaire; (clean) hygiénique.
anitary towel, (US) **sanitary napkin** n serviette f hygiénique.
anitation [sænɪ'teɪʃən] n (in house) installations fpl sanitaires; (in town) système m sanitaire.
anitation department n (US) service m de voirie.
anity ['sænɪtɪ] n santé mentale; (common sense) bon sens.
ank [sæŋk] pt of **sink**.
an Marino ['sænmə'riːnəu] n Saint-Marin m.
anta Claus [sæntə'klɔːz] n le Père Noël.
antiago [sæntɪ'ɑːgəu] n (also: ~ **de Chile**) Santiago (du Chili).
ap [sæp] n (of plants) sève f ♦ vt (strength) saper, miner.
apling ['sæplɪŋ] n jeune arbre m.
apphire ['sæfaɪə*] n saphir m.
arcasm ['sɑːkæzm] n sarcasme m, raillerie f.
arcastic [sɑː'kæstɪk] adj sarcastique.
arcophagus, pl **sarcophagi** [sɑː'kɔfəgəs, -gaɪ] n sarcophage m.
ardine [sɑː'diːn] n sardine f.
ardinia [sɑː'dɪnɪə] n Sardaigne f.
ardinian [sɑː'dɪnɪən] adj sarde ♦ n Sarde m/f; (LING) sarde m.
ardonic [sɑː'dɔnɪk] adj sardonique.
ari ['sɑːrɪ] n sari m.
artorial [sɑː'tɔːrɪəl] adj vestimentaire.
AS n abbr (BRIT MIL: = Special Air Service) ≈ GIGN m.
ASE n abbr (US: = self-addressed stamped envelope) enveloppe affranchie pour la réponse.
ash [sæʃ] n écharpe f.
ash window n fenêtre f à guillotine.
ask. abbr (Canada) = Saskatchewan.
AT n abbr (US) = Scholastic Aptitude Test.
at [sæt] pt, pp of **sit**.
at. abbr (= Saturday) sa.
atan ['seɪtn] n Satan m.
atanic [sə'tænɪk] adj satanique, démoniaque.

satchel ['sætʃl] n cartable m.
sated ['seɪtɪd] adj repu(e); blasé(e).
satellite ['sætəlaɪt] adj, n satellite (m).
satellite television n télévision f par satellite.
satiate ['seɪʃɪeɪt] vt rassasier.
satin ['sætɪn] n satin m ♦ adj en or de satin, satiné(e); **with a** ~ **finish** satiné(e).
satire ['sætaɪə*] n satire f.
satirical [sə'tɪrɪkl] adj satirique.
satirist ['sætɪrɪst] n (writer) auteur m satirique; (cartoonist) caricaturiste m/f.
satirize ['sætɪraɪz] vt faire la satire de, satiriser.
satisfaction [sætɪs'fækʃən] n satisfaction f.
satisfactory [sætɪs'fæktərɪ] adj satisfaisant(e).
satisfied ['sætɪsfaɪd] adj satisfait(e); **to be** ~ **with sth** être satisfait de qch.
satisfy ['sætɪsfaɪ] vt satisfaire, contenter; (convince) convaincre, persuader; **to** ~ **the requirements** remplir les conditions; **to** ~ **sb (that)** convaincre qn (que); **to** ~ **o.s. of sth** vérifier qch, s'assurer de qch.
satisfying ['sætɪsfaɪŋ] adj satisfaisant(e).
satsuma [sæt'suːmə] n satsuma f.
saturate ['sætʃəreɪt] vt: **to** ~ **(with)** saturer (de).
saturated fat ['sætʃəreɪtɪd-] n graisse saturée.
saturation [sætʃə'reɪʃən] n saturation f.
Saturday ['sætədɪ] n samedi m; for phrases see also **Tuesday**.
sauce [sɔːs] n sauce f.
saucepan ['sɔːspən] n casserole f.
saucer ['sɔːsə*] n soucoupe f.
saucy ['sɔːsɪ] adj impertinent(e).
Saudi Arabia ['saudɪ-] n Arabie f Saoudite or Séoudite.
Saudi (Arabian) ['saudɪ-] adj saoudien(ne) ♦ n Saoudien/ne.
sauna ['sɔːnə] n sauna m.
saunter ['sɔːntə*] vi: **to** ~ **to** aller en flânant or se balader jusqu'à.
sausage ['sɔsɪdʒ] n saucisse f; (salami etc) saucisson m.
sausage roll n friand m.
sauté ['səuteɪ] adj (CULIN: potatoes) sauté(e); (: onions) revenu(e) ♦ vt faire sauter; faire revenir.
savage ['sævɪdʒ] adj (cruel, fierce) brutal(e), féroce; (primitive) primitif(ive), sauvage ♦ n sauvage m/f ♦ vt attaquer férocement.
savagery ['sævɪdʒrɪ] n sauvagerie f, brutalité f, férocité f.
save [seɪv] vt (person, belongings) sauver; (money) mettre de côté, économiser; (time) (faire) gagner; (food) garder; (COMPUT) sauvegarder; (avoid: trouble) éviter ♦ vi (also: ~ **up**) mettre de l'argent de côté ♦ n (SPORT) arrêt m (du ballon) ♦ prep sauf, à l'exception de; **it will** ~ **me an hour** ça me fera gagner une heure; **to** ~ **face** sauver la face; **God** ~

the Queen! vive la Reine!

saving ['seɪvɪŋ] n économie f ♦ adj: **the ~ grace of** ce qui rachète; **~s** npl économies fpl; **to make ~s** faire des économies.

savings account n compte m d'épargne.

savings bank n caisse f d'épargne.

saviour, (US) **savior** ['seɪvjə*] n sauveur m.

savour, (US) **savor** ['seɪvə*] n saveur f, goût m ♦ vt savourer.

savo(u)ry ['seɪvərɪ] adj savoureux(euse); (dish: not sweet) salé(e).

savvy ['sævɪ] n (col) jugeote f.

saw [sɔ:] pt of **see** ♦ n (tool) scie f ♦ vt (pt **sawed**, pp **sawed** or **sawn** [sɔ:n]) scier; **to ~ sth up** débiter qch à la scie.

sawdust ['sɔ:dʌst] n sciure f.

sawmill ['sɔ:mɪl] n scierie f.

sawn-off ['sɔ:nɔf], (US) **sawed-off** ['sɔ:dɔf] adj: **~ shotgun** carabine f à canon scié.

saxophone ['sæksəfəun] n saxophone m.

say [seɪ] n: **to have one's ~** dire ce qu'on a à dire ♦ vt (pt, pp **said** [sed]) dire; **to have a ~** avoir voix au chapitre; **could you ~ that again?** pourriez-vous répéter ceci?; **to ~ yes/no** dire oui/non; **she said (that) I was to give you this** elle m'a chargé de vous remettre ceci; **my watch ~s 3 o'clock** ma montre indique 3 heures, il est 3 heures à ma montre; **shall we ~ Tuesday?** disons mardi?; **that doesn't ~ much for him** ce n'est pas vraiment à son honneur; **when all is said and done** en fin de compte, en définitive; **there is something** or **a lot to be said for it** cela a des avantages; **that is to ~** c'est-à-dire; **to ~ nothing of** sans compter; **~ that ...** mettons or disons que ...; **that goes without ~ing** cela va sans dire, cela va de soi.

saying ['seɪɪŋ] n dicton m, proverbe m.

SBA n abbr (US: = Small Business Administration) organisme d'aide aux PME.

SC n abbr (US) = **supreme court** ♦ abbr (US) = South Carolina.

s/c abbr = **self-contained**.

scab [skæb] n croûte f; (pej) jaune m.

scabby ['skæbɪ] adj croûteux(euse).

scaffold ['skæfəld] n échafaud m.

scaffolding ['skæfəldɪŋ] n échafaudage m.

scald [skɔ:ld] n brûlure f ♦ vt ébouillanter.

scalding ['skɔ:ldɪŋ] adj (also: ~ **hot**) brûlant(e), bouillant(e).

scale [skeɪl] n (of fish) écaille f; (MUS) gamme f; (of ruler, thermometer etc) graduation f, échelle (graduée); (of salaries, fees etc) barème m; (of map, also size, extent) échelle ♦ vt (mountain) escalader; (fish) écailler; **pay ~** échelle des salaires; **~ of charges** tarif m (des consultations or prestations etc); **on a large ~** sur une grande échelle, en grand; **to draw sth to ~** dessiner qch à l'échelle; **small-~ model** modèle réduit.

▶**scale down** vt réduire.

scaled-down [skeɪld'daun] adj à échelle réduite.

scale drawing n dessin m à l'échelle.

scale model n modèle m à l'échelle.

scales [skeɪlz] npl balance f; (larger) bascule f.

scallion ['skæljən] n oignon m; (US: shallot) échalote f; (: leek) poireau m.

scallop ['skɔləp] n coquille f Saint-Jacques.

scalp [skælp] n cuir chevelu ♦ vt scalper.

scalpel ['skælpl] n scalpel m.

scalper ['skælpə*] n (US col: of tickets) revendeur m de billets.

scam [skæm] n (col) arnaque f.

scamp [skæmp] vt bâcler.

scamper ['skæmpə*] vi: **to ~ away**, **~ off** détaler.

scampi ['skæmpɪ] npl langoustines (frites), scampi mpl.

scan [skæn] vt scruter, examiner; (glance at quickly) parcourir; (poetry) scander; (TV, RADAR) balayer ♦ n (MED) scanographie f.

scandal ['skændl] n scandale m; (gossip) ragots mpl.

scandalize ['skændəlaɪz] vt scandaliser, indigner.

scandalous ['skændələs] adj scandaleux(euse).

Scandinavia [skændɪ'neɪvɪə] n Scandinavie f.

Scandinavian [skændɪ'neɪvɪən] adj scandinave ♦ n Scandinave m/f.

scanner ['skænə*] n (RADAR, MED) scanner m, scanographe m.

scant [skænt] adj insuffisant(e).

scantily ['skæntɪlɪ] adv: **~ clad** or **dressed** vêtu(e) du strict minimum.

scanty ['skæntɪ] adj peu abondant(e), insuffisant(e), maigre.

scapegoat ['skeɪpgəut] n bouc m émissaire.

scar [skɑ:] n cicatrice f ♦ vt laisser une cicatrice or une marque à.

scarce [skɛəs] adj rare, peu abondant(e).

scarcely ['skɛəslɪ] adv à peine, presque pas; **~ anybody** pratiquement personne; **I can ~ believe it** j'ai du mal à le croire.

scarcity ['skɛəsɪtɪ] n rareté f, manque m, pénurie f.

scarcity value n valeur f de rareté.

scare [skɛə*] n peur f, panique f ♦ vt effrayer, faire peur à; **to ~ sb stiff** faire une peur bleue à qn; **bomb ~** alerte f à la bombe.

▶**scare away**, **scare off** vt faire fuir.

scarecrow ['skɛəkrəu] n épouvantail m.

scared ['skɛəd] adj: **to be ~** avoir peur.

scaremonger ['skɛəmʌŋgə*] n alarmiste m/f.

scarf, pl **scarves** [skɑ:f, skɑ:vz] n (long) écharpe f; (square) foulard m.

scarlet ['skɑ:lɪt] adj écarlate.

scarlet fever n scarlatine f.

scarper ['skɑ:pə*] vi (BRIT col) ficher le camp.

scarves [skɑ:vz] npl of **scarf**.

scary ['skɛərɪ] adj (col) qui fiche la frousse.

scathing ['skeɪðɪŋ] adj cinglant(e), acerbe; **to**

be ~ **about sth** être très critique vis-à-vis de qch.

scatter ['skætə*] vt éparpiller, répandre; (crowd) disperser ♦ vi se disperser.

scatterbrained ['skætəbreɪnd] adj écervelé(e), étourdi(e).

scattered ['skætəd] adj épars(e), dispersé(e).

scatty ['skætɪ] adj (BRIT col) loufoque.

scavenge ['skævəndʒ] vi (person): **to ~ (for)** faire les poubelles (pour trouver); **to ~ for food** (hyenas etc) se nourrir de charognes.

scavenger ['skævəndʒə*] n éboueur m.

SCE n abbr = Scottish Certificate of Education.

scenario [sɪ'nɑːrɪəu] n scénario m.

scene [siːn] n (THEAT, fig etc) scène f; (of crime, accident) lieu(x) m(pl), endroit m; (sight, view) spectacle m, vue f; **behind the ~s** (also fig) dans les coulisses; **to make a ~** (col: fuss) faire une scène or toute une histoire; **to appear on the ~** (also fig) faire son apparition, arriver; **the political ~** la situation politique.

scenery ['siːnərɪ] n (THEAT) décor(s) m(pl); (landscape) paysage m.

scenic ['siːnɪk] adj scénique; offrant de beaux paysages or panoramas.

scent [sɛnt] n parfum m, odeur f; (fig: track) piste f; (sense of smell) odorat m ♦ vt parfumer; (smell, also fig) flairer; **to put** or **throw sb off the ~** (fig) mettre or lancer qn sur une mauvaise piste.

sceptic, (US) **skeptic** ['skɛptɪk] n sceptique m/f.

sceptical, (US) **skeptical** ['skɛptɪkl] adj sceptique.

scepticism, (US) **skepticism** ['skɛptɪsɪzəm] n scepticisme m.

sceptre, (US) **scepter** ['sɛptə*] n sceptre m.

schedule ['ʃɛdjuːl, (US) 'skɛdjuːl] n programme m, plan m; (of trains) horaire m; (of prices etc) barème m, tarif m ♦ vt prévoir; **as ~d** comme prévu; **on ~** à l'heure (prévue); à la date prévue; **to be ahead of/behind ~** avoir de l'avance/du retard; **we are working to a very tight ~** notre programme de travail est très serré or intense; **everything went according to ~** tout s'est passé comme prévu.

scheduled ['ʃɛdjuːld, (US) 'skɛdjuːld] adj (date, time) prévu(e), indiqué(e); (visit, event) programmé(e), prévu; (train, bus, stop, flight) régulier(ière).

schematic [skɪ'mætɪk] adj schématique.

scheme [skiːm] n plan m, projet m; (method) procédé m; (dishonest plan, plot) complot m, combine f; (arrangement) arrangement m, classification f; (pension ~ etc) régime m ♦ vi comploter, manigancer; **colour ~** combinaison f de(s) couleurs.

scheming ['skiːmɪŋ] adj rusé(e), intrigant(e) ♦ n manigances fpl, intrigues fpl.

schism ['skɪzəm] n schisme m.

schizophrenia [skɪtsə'friːnɪə] n schizophrénie f.

schizophrenic [skɪtsə'frɛnɪk] adj schizophrène.

scholar ['skɒlə*] n érudit/e.

scholarly ['skɒləlɪ] adj érudit(e), savant(e).

scholarship ['skɒləʃɪp] n érudition f; (grant) bourse f (d'études).

school [skuːl] n (gen) école f; (in university) faculté f; (secondary school) collège m, lycée m; (of fish) banc m ♦ cpd scolaire ♦ vt (animal) dresser.

school age n âge m scolaire.

schoolbook ['skuːlbuk] n livre m scolaire or de classe.

schoolboy ['skuːlbɔɪ] n écolier m; collégien m, lycéen m.

schoolchild, pl **-children** ['skuːltʃaɪld, -'tʃɪldrən] n écolier/ière, collégien/ne, lycéen/ne.

schooldays ['skuːldeɪz] npl années fpl de scolarité.

schoolgirl ['skuːlgəːl] n écolière f; collégienne f, lycéenne f.

schooling ['skuːlɪŋ] n instruction f, études fpl.

school-leaver ['skuːlliːvə*] n (BRIT) jeune qui vient de terminer ses études secondaires.

schoolmaster ['skuːlmɑːstə*] n (primary) instituteur m; (secondary) professeur m.

schoolmistress ['skuːlmɪstrɪs] n (primary) institutrice f; (secondary) professeur m.

school report n (BRIT) bulletin m (scolaire).

schoolroom ['skuːlruːm] n (salle f de) classe f.

schoolteacher ['skuːltiːtʃə*] n (primary) instituteur/trice; (secondary) professeur m.

schoolyard ['skuːljɑːd] n (US) cour f de récréation.

schooner ['skuːnə*] n (ship) schooner m, goélette f; (glass) grand verre (à xérès).

sciatica [saɪ'ætɪkə] n sciatique f.

science ['saɪəns] n science f; **the ~s** les sciences; (SCOL) les matières fpl scientifiques.

science fiction n science-fiction f.

scientific [saɪən'tɪfɪk] adj scientifique.

scientist ['saɪəntɪst] n scientifique m/f; (eminent) savant m.

sci-fi ['saɪfaɪ] n abbr (col: = science fiction) SF f.

Scilly Isles ['sɪlɪ'aɪlz], **Scillies** ['sɪlɪz] npl: **the ~** les Sorlingues fpl, les îles fpl Scilly.

scintillating ['sɪntɪleɪtɪŋ] adj scintillant(e), étincelant(e); (wit etc) brillant(e).

scissors ['sɪzəz] npl ciseaux mpl; **a pair of ~** une paire de ciseaux.

sclerosis [sklɪ'rəusɪs] n sclérose f.

scoff [skɒf] vt (BRIT col: eat) avaler, bouffer ♦ vi: **to ~ (at)** (mock) se moquer (de).

scold [skəuld] vt gronder, attraper, réprimander.

scolding ['skəuldɪŋ] n réprimande f.

scone [skɒn] n sorte de petit pain rond au lait.

scoop [sku:p] *n* pelle *f* (à main); (*for ice cream*) boule *f* à glace; (*PRESS*) reportage exclusif *or* à sensation.
►**scoop out** *vt* évider, creuser.
►**scoop up** *vt* ramasser.
scooter ['sku:tə*] *n* (*motor cycle*) scooter *m*; (*toy*) trottinette *f*.
scope [skəup] *n* (*capacity: of plan, undertaking*) portée *f*, envergure *f*; (: *of person*) compétence *f*, capacités *fpl*; (*opportunity*) possibilités *fpl*; **within the ~ of** dans les limites de; **there is plenty of ~ for improvement** (*BRIT*) cela pourrait être beaucoup mieux.
scorch [skɔ:tʃ] *vt* (*clothes*) brûler (légèrement), roussir; (*earth, grass*) dessécher, brûler.
scorched earth policy ['skɔ:tʃt-] *n* politique *f* de la terre brûlée.
scorcher ['skɔ:tʃə*] *n* (*col: hot day*) journée *f* torride.
scorching ['skɔ:tʃɪŋ] *adj* torride, brûlant(e).
score [skɔ:*] *n* score *m*, décompte *m* des points; (*MUS*) partition *f*; (*twenty*) vingt ♦ *vt* (*goal, point*) marquer; (*success*) remporter; (*cut: leather, wood, card*) entailler, inciser ♦ *vi* marquer des points; (*FOOTBALL*) marquer un but; (*keep score*) compter les points; **on that ~** sur ce chapitre, à cet égard; **to have an old ~ to settle with sb** (*fig*) avoir un (vieux) compte à régler avec qn; **~s of** (*fig*) des tas de; **to ~ well/6 out of 10** obtenir un bon résultat/6 sur 10.
►**score out** *vt* rayer, barrer, biffer.
scoreboard ['skɔ:bɔ:d] *n* tableau *m*.
scorecard ['skɔ:kɑ:d] *n* (*SPORT*) carton *m*, feuille *f* de marque.
scoreline ['skɔ:laɪn] *n* (*SPORT*) score *m*.
scorer ['skɔ:rə*] *n* (*FOOTBALL*) auteur *m* du but; buteur *m*; (*keeping score*) marqueur *m*.
scorn [skɔ:n] *n* mépris *m*, dédain *m* ♦ *vt* mépriser, dédaigner.
scornful ['skɔ:nful] *adj* méprisant(e), dédaigneux(euse).
Scorpio ['skɔ:pɪəu] *n* le Scorpion; **to be ~** être du Scorpion.
scorpion ['skɔ:pɪən] *n* scorpion *m*.
Scot [skɔt] *n* Écossais/e.
Scotch [skɔtʃ] *n* whisky *m*, scotch *m*.
scotch [skɔtʃ] *vt* faire échouer; enrayer; étouffer.
Scotch tape *n* ® scotch *m* ®, ruban *m* adhésif.
scot-free ['skɔt'fri:] *adj*: **to get off ~** s'en tirer sans être puni(e) (*or* sans payer); s'en sortir indemne.
Scotland ['skɔtlənd] *n* Écosse *f*.
Scots [skɔts] *adj* écossais(e).
Scotsman ['skɔtsmən] *n* Écossais *m*.
Scotswoman ['skɔtswumən] *n* Écossaise *f*.
Scottish ['skɔtɪʃ] *adj* écossais(e); **the ~ National Party** le parti national écossais.
scoundrel ['skaundrl] *n* vaurien *m*.

scour ['skauə*] *vt* (*clean*) récurer; frotter; décaper; (*search*) battre, parcourir.
scourer ['skauərə*] *n* tampon abrasif *or* à récurer; (*powder*) poudre *f* à récurer.
scourge [skə:dʒ] *n* fléau *m*.
scout [skaut] *n* (*MIL*) éclaireur *m*; (*also*: **boy ~**) scout *m*.
►**scout around** *vi* chercher.
scowl [skaul] *vi* se renfrogner, avoir l'air maussade; **to ~ at** regarder de travers.
scrabble ['skræbl] *vi* (*claw*): **to ~ (at)** gratter; **to ~ about** *or* **around for sth** chercher qch à tâtons ♦ *n*: **S~** ® Scrabble *m* ®.
scraggy ['skrægɪ] *adj* décharné(e), efflanqué(e), famélique.
scram [skræm] *vi* (*col*) ficher le camp.
scramble ['skræmbl] *n* bousculade *f*, ruée *f* ♦ *vi* avancer tant bien que mal (à quatre pattes *or* en grimpant); **to ~ for** se bousculer *or* se disputer pour (avoir); **to go scrambling** (*SPORT*) faire du trial.
scrambled eggs ['skræmbld-] *npl* œufs brouillés.
scrap [skræp] *n* bout *m*, morceau *m*; (*fight*) bagarre *f*; (*also*: **~ iron**) ferraille *f* ♦ *vt* jeter, mettre au rebut; (*fig*) abandonner, laisser tomber; **~s** *npl* (*waste*) déchets *mpl*; **to sell sth for ~** vendre qch à la casse *or* à la ferraille.
scrapbook ['skræpbuk] *n* album *m*.
scrap dealer *n* marchand *m* de ferraille.
scrape [skreɪp] *vt, vi* gratter, racler ♦ *n*: **to get into a ~** s'attirer des ennuis.
►**scrape through** *vi* (*in exam etc*) réussir de justesse.
scraper ['skreɪpə*] *n* grattoir *m*, racloir *m*.
scrap heap *n* tas *m* de ferraille; (*fig*): **on the ~** au rancart *or* rebut.
scrap merchant *n* (*BRIT*) marchand *m* de ferraille.
scrap metal *n* ferraille *f*.
scrap paper *n* papier *m* brouillon.
scrappy ['skræpɪ] *adj* fragmentaire, décousu(e).
scrap yard *n* parc *m* à ferrailles; (*for cars*) cimetière *m* de voitures.
scratch [skrætʃ] *n* égratignure *f*, rayure *f*; éraflure *f*; (*from claw*) coup *m* de griffe ♦ *adj*: **~ team** équipe de fortune *or* improvisée ♦ *vt* (*record*) rayer; (*paint etc*) érafler; (*with claw, nail*) griffer; (*COMPUT*) effacer ♦ *vi* (se) gratter; **to start from ~** partir de zéro; **to be up to ~** être à la hauteur.
scrawl [skrɔ:l] *n* gribouillage *m* ♦ *vi* gribouiller.
scrawny ['skrɔ:nɪ] *adj* décharné(e).
scream [skri:m] *n* cri perçant, hurlement *m* ♦ *vi* crier, hurler; **to be a ~** (*col*) être impayable; **to ~ at sb to do sth** crier *or* hurler à qn de faire qch.
scree [skri:] *n* éboulis *m*.
screech [skri:tʃ] *n* cri strident, hurlement *m*;

(of tyres, brakes) crissement m, grincement m ♦ vi hurler; crisser, grincer.

screen [skriːn] n écran m, paravent m; (CINE, TV) écran; (fig) écran, rideau m ♦ vt masquer, cacher; (from the wind etc) abriter, protéger; (film) projeter; (candidates etc) filtrer; (for illness): **to ~ sb for sth** faire subir un test de dépistage de qch à qn.

screen editing [-'edɪtɪŋ] n (COMPUT) édition f or correction f sur écran.

screening ['skriːnɪŋ] n (of film) projection f; (MED) test m (or tests) de dépistage; (for security) filtrage m.

screen memory n (COMPUT) mémoire f écran.

screenplay ['skriːnpleɪ] n scénario m.

screen test n bout m d'essai.

screw [skruː] n vis f; (propeller) hélice f ♦ vt visser; (col!: woman) baiser (!); **to ~ sth to the wall** visser qch au mur; **to have one's head ~ed on** (fig) avoir la tête sur les épaules.

▶**screw up** vt (paper, material) froisser; (col: ruin) bousiller; **to ~ up one's face** faire la grimace.

screwdriver ['skruːdraɪvə*] n tournevis m.

screwed-up ['skruːd'ʌp] adj (col): **to be ~** être paumé(e).

screwy ['skruːɪ] adj (col) dingue, cinglé(e).

scribble ['skrɪbl] n gribouillage m ♦ vt gribouiller, griffonner; **to ~ sth down** griffonner qch.

scribe [skraɪb] n scribe m.

script [skrɪpt] n (CINE etc) scénario m, texte m; (in exam) copie f; (writing) (écriture f) script m.

scripted ['skrɪptɪd] adj (RADIO, TV) préparé(e) à l'avance.

Scripture ['skrɪptʃə*] n Écriture sainte.

scriptwriter ['skrɪptraɪtə*] n scénariste m/f, dialoguiste m/f.

scroll [skrəʊl] n rouleau m ♦ vt (COMPUT) faire défiler (sur l'écran).

scrotum ['skrəʊtəm] n scrotum m.

scrounge [skraʊndʒ] (col) vt: **to ~ sth (off or from sb)** se faire payer qch (par qn), emprunter qch (à qn) ♦ vi: **to ~ on sb** vivre aux crochets de qn.

scrounger ['skraʊndʒə*] n parasite m.

scrub [skrʌb] n (clean) nettoyage m (à la brosse); (land) broussailles fpl ♦ vt (floor) nettoyer à la brosse; (pan) récurer; (washing) frotter; (reject) annuler.

scrubbing brush ['skrʌbɪŋ-] n brosse dure.

scruff [skrʌf] n: **by the ~ of the neck** par la peau du cou.

scruffy ['skrʌfɪ] adj débraillé(e).

scrum(mage) ['skrʌm(ɪdʒ)] n mêlée f.

scruple ['skruːpl] n scrupule m; **to have no ~s about doing sth** n'avoir aucun scrupule à faire qch.

scrupulous ['skruːpjʊləs] adj

scrupuleux(euse).

scrupulously ['skruːpjʊləslɪ] adv scrupuleusement; **to be ~ honest** être d'une honnêteté scrupuleuse.

scrutinize ['skruːtɪnaɪz] vt scruter, examiner minutieusement.

scrutiny ['skruːtɪnɪ] n examen minutieux; **under the ~ of sb** sous la surveillance de qn.

scuba ['skuːbə] n scaphandre m (autonome).

scuba diving n plongée sous-marine (autonome).

scuff [skʌf] vt érafler.

scuffle ['skʌfl] n échauffourée f, rixe f.

scull [skʌl] n aviron m.

scullery ['skʌlərɪ] n arrière-cuisine f.

sculptor ['skʌlptə*] n sculpteur m.

sculpture ['skʌlptʃə*] n sculpture f.

scum [skʌm] n écume f, mousse f; (pej: people) rebut m, lie f.

scupper ['skʌpə*] vt (BRIT) saborder.

scurrilous ['skʌrɪləs] adj haineux(euse), virulent(e); calomnieux(euse).

scurry ['skʌrɪ] vi filer à toute allure; **to ~ off** détaler, se sauver.

scurvy ['skəːvɪ] n scorbut m.

scuttle ['skʌtl] n (NAUT) écoutille f; (also: **coal ~**) seau m (à charbon) ♦ vt (ship) saborder ♦ vi (scamper): **to ~ away, ~ off** détaler.

scythe [saɪð] n faux f.

SD, S. Dak. abbr (US) = South Dakota.

SDI n abbr (= Strategic Defense Initiative) IDS f.

SDLP n abbr (BRIT POL) = Social Democratic and Labour Party.

SDP n abbr (BRIT POL) = Social Democratic Party.

sea [siː] n mer f ♦ cpd marin(e), de (la) mer, maritime; **on the ~** (boat) en mer; (town) au bord de la mer; **by or beside the ~** (holiday) au bord de la mer; (village) près de la mer; **by ~** par mer, en bateau; **out to ~** au large; (**out) at ~** en mer; **heavy or rough ~(s)** grosse mer, mer agitée; **a ~ of faces** (fig) une multitude de visages; **to be all at ~** (fig) nager complètement.

sea bed n fond m de la mer.

sea bird n oiseau m de mer.

seaboard ['siːbɔːd] n côte f.

sea breeze n brise f de mer.

seafarer ['siːfeərə*] n marin m.

seafaring ['siːfeərɪŋ] adj (life) de marin; **~ people** les gens mpl de mer.

seafood ['siːfuːd] n fruits mpl de mer.

sea front n bord m de mer.

seagoing ['siːgəʊɪŋ] adj (ship) de haute mer.

seagull ['siːgʌl] n mouette f.

seal [siːl] n (animal) phoque m; (stamp) sceau m, cachet m; (impression) cachet, estampille f ♦ vt sceller; (envelope) coller; (: with seal) cacheter; (decide: sb's fate) décider (de); (: bargain) conclure; **~ of approval** approbation f.

▶**seal off** vt (close) condamner; (forbid entry

to) interdire l'accès de.
sea level *n* niveau *m* de la mer.
sealing wax ['si:lɪŋ-] *n* cire *f* à cacheter.
sea lion *n* lion *m* de mer.
sealskin ['si:lskɪn] *n* peau *f* de phoque.
seam [si:m] *n* couture *f*; (*of coal*) veine *f*, filon *m*; **the hall was bursting at the ~s** la salle était pleine à craquer.
seaman ['si:mən] *n* marin *m*.
seamanship ['si:mənʃɪp] *n* qualités *fpl* de marin.
seamless ['si:mlɪs] *adj* sans couture(s).
seamy ['si:mɪ] *adj* louche, mal famé(e).
seance ['seɪɔns] *n* séance *f* de spiritisme.
seaplane ['si:pleɪn] *n* hydravion *m*.
seaport ['si:pɔ:t] *n* port *m* de mer.
search [sə:tʃ] *n* (*for person, thing*) recherche(s) *f(pl)*; (*of drawer, pockets*) fouille *f*; (*LAW: at sb's home*) perquisition *f* ♦ *vt* fouiller; (*examine*) examiner minutieusement; scruter ♦ *vi*: **to ~ for** chercher; **in ~ of** à la recherche de; **"~ and replace"** (*COMPUT*) "rechercher et remplacer".
▶**search through** *vt fus* fouiller.
searcher ['sə:tʃə*] *n* chercheur/euse.
searching ['sə:tʃɪŋ] *adj* (*look, question*) pénétrant(e); (*examination*) minutieux(euse).
searchlight ['sə:tʃlaɪt] *n* projecteur *m*.
search party *n* expédition *f* de secours.
search warrant *n* mandat *m* de perquisition.
searing ['sɪərɪŋ] *adj* (*heat*) brûlant(e); (*pain*) aigu(ë).
seashore ['si:ʃɔ:*] *n* rivage *m*, plage *f*, bord *m* de (la) mer; **on the ~** sur le rivage.
seasick ['si:sɪk] *adj*: **to be ~** avoir le mal de mer.
seaside ['si:saɪd] *n* bord *m* de la mer.
seaside resort *n* station *f* balnéaire.
season ['si:zn] *n* saison *f* ♦ *vt* assaisonner, relever; **to be in/out of ~** être/ne pas être de saison; **the busy ~** (*for shops*) la période de pointe; (*for hotels etc*) la pleine saison; **the open ~** (*HUNTING*) la saison de la chasse.
seasonal ['si:znl] *adj* saisonnier(ière).
seasoned ['si:znd] *adj* (*wood*) séché(e); (*fig: worker, actor, troops*) expérimenté(e); **a ~ campaigner** un vieux militant, un vétéran.
seasoning ['si:znɪŋ] *n* assaisonnement *m*.
season ticket *n* carte *f* d'abonnement.
seat [si:t] *n* siège *m*; (*in bus, train: place*) place *f*; (*PARLIAMENT*) siège; (*buttocks*) postérieur *m*; (*of trousers*) fond *m* ♦ *vt* faire asseoir, placer; (*have room for*) avoir des places assises pour, pouvoir accueillir; **are there any ~s left?** est-ce qu'il reste des places?; **to take one's ~** prendre place; **to be ~ed** être assis; **please be ~ed** veuillez vous asseoir.
seat belt *n* ceinture *f* de sécurité.
seating capacity ['si:tɪŋ-] *n* nombre *m* de places assises.

SEATO ['si:təu] *n abbr* (= *Southeast Asia Treaty Organization*) OTASE *f* (= *Organisation du traité de l'Asie du Sud-Est*).
sea urchin *n* oursin *m*.
sea water *n* eau *f* de mer.
seaweed ['si:wi:d] *n* algues *fpl*.
seaworthy ['si:wə:ðɪ] *adj* en état de naviguer.
SEC *n abbr* (*US: = Securities and Exchange Commission*) ≈ COB *f* (= *Commission des opérations de Bourse*).
sec. *abbr* (= *second*) sec.
secateurs [sɛkə'tə:z] *npl* sécateur *m*.
secede [sɪ'si:d] *vi* faire sécession.
secluded [sɪ'klu:dɪd] *adj* retiré(e), à l'écart.
seclusion [sɪ'klu:ʒən] *n* solitude *f*.
second¹ ['sɛkənd] *num* deuxième, second(e) ♦ *adv* (*in race etc*) en seconde position ♦ *n* (*unit of time*) seconde *f*; (*in series, position*) deuxième *m/f*, second/e; (*BRIT SCOL*) ≈ licence *f* avec mention bien *or* assez bien; (*AUT: also:* **~ gear**) seconde *f*; (*COMM: imperfect*) article *m* de second choix ♦ *vt* (*motion*) appuyer; **Charles the S~** Charles II; **just a ~!** une seconde!, un instant!; (*stopping sb*) pas si vite!; **~ floor** (*BRIT*) deuxième (étage) *m*; (*US*) premier (étage) *m*; **to ask for a ~ opinion** (*MED*) demander l'avis d'un autre médecin; **to have ~ thoughts (about doing sth)** changer d'avis (à propos de faire qch); **on ~ thoughts** *or* (*US*) **thought** à la réflexion.
second² [sɪ'kɔnd] *vt* (*employee*) détacher, mettre en détachement.
secondary ['sɛkəndərɪ] *adj* secondaire.
secondary school *n* collège *m*, lycée *m*.

> Une **secondary school** est un établissement d'enseignement pour les élèves de 11 à 18 ans, certains d'entre eux arrêtant leurs études à 16 ans, âge de fin de scolarité. La plupart de ces écoles sont des **comprehensive schools**; mais certaines secondary schools sont encore à recrutement sélectif; voir **primary school**

second-best [sɛkənd'bɛst] *n* deuxième choix *m*; **as a ~** faute de mieux.
second-class ['sɛkənd'klɑ:s] *adj* de deuxième classe ♦ *adv*: **to send sth ~** envoyer qch à tarif réduit; **to travel ~** voyager en seconde; **~ citizen** citoyen/ne de deuxième classe.
second cousin *n* cousin/e issu(e) de germains.
seconder ['sɛkəndə*] *n* personne *f* qui appuie une motion.
second-guess ['sɛkənd'gɛs] *vt* (*predict*) (essayer d')anticiper; **they're still trying to ~ his motives** ils essaient toujours de comprendre ses raisons.
second hand *n* (*on clock*) trotteuse *f*.
secondhand ['sɛkənd'hænd] *adj* d'occasion ♦ *adv* (*buy*) d'occasion; **to hear sth ~** apprendre qch indirectement.

second-in-command ['sɛkəndɪnkə'mɑːnd] *n* (*MIL*) commandant *m* en second; (*ADMIN*) adjoint/e, sous-chef *m*.

secondly ['sɛkəndlɪ] *adv* deuxièmement.

secondment [sɪ'kɔndmənt] *n* (*BRIT*) détachement *m*.

second-rate ['sɛkənd'reɪt] *adj* de deuxième ordre, de qualité inférieure.

Second World War *n* Deuxième *or* Seconde Guerre mondiale.

secrecy ['siːkrəsɪ] *n* secret *m*; **in ~** en secret, dans le secret.

secret ['siːkrɪt] *adj* secret(ète) ♦ *n* secret *m*; **in ~** *adv* en secret, secrètement, en cachette; **to keep sth ~ from sb** cacher qch à qn, ne pas révéler qch à qn; **keep it ~** n'en parle à personne; **to make no ~ of sth** ne pas cacher qch.

secret agent *n* agent secret.

secretarial [sɛkrɪ'tɛərɪəl] *adj* de secrétaire, de secrétariat.

secretariat [sɛkrɪ'tɛərɪət] *n* secrétariat *m*.

secretary ['sɛkrətrɪ] *n* secrétaire *m/f*; (*COMM*) secrétaire général; **S~ of State** (*US POL*) ≈ ministre *m* des Affaires étrangères; **S~ of State (for)** (*BRIT POL*) ministre *m* (de).

secretary-general ['sɛkrətrɪ'dʒɛnərl] *n* secrétaire général.

secrete [sɪ'kriːt] *vt* (*ANAT, BIOL, MED*) sécréter; (*hide*) cacher.

secretion [sɪ'kriːʃən] *n* sécrétion *f*.

secretive ['siːkrətɪv] *adj* réservé(e); (*pej*) cachottier(ière), dissimulé(e).

secretly ['siːkrɪtlɪ] *adv* en secret, secrètement, en cachette.

secret police *n* police secrète.

secret service *n* services secrets.

sect [sɛkt] *n* secte *f*.

sectarian [sɛk'tɛərɪən] *adj* sectaire.

section ['sɛkʃən] *n* coupe *f*, section *f*; (*department*) section; (*COMM*) rayon *m*; (*of document*) section, article *m*, paragraphe *m* ♦ *vt* sectionner; **the business** *etc* ~ (*PRESS*) la page des affaires *etc*.

sectional ['sɛkʃənl] *adj* (*drawing*) en coupe.

sector ['sɛktə*] *n* secteur *m*.

secular ['sɛkjulə*] *adj* profane; laïque; séculier(ière).

secure [sɪ'kjuə*] *adj* (*free from anxiety*) sans inquiétude, sécurisé(e); (*firmly fixed*) solide, bien attaché(e) (*or* fermé(e) *etc*); (*in safe place*) en lieu sûr, en sûreté ♦ *vt* (*fix*) fixer, attacher; (*get*) obtenir, se procurer; (*COMM: loan*) garantir; **to make sth ~** bien fixer *or* attacher qch; **to ~ sth for sb** obtenir qch pour qn, procurer qch à qn.

secured creditor [sɪ'kjuəd-] *n* créancier/ière privilégié(e).

security [sɪ'kjuərɪtɪ] *n* sécurité *f*, mesures *fpl* de sécurité; (*for loan*) caution *f*, garantie *f*; **securities** *npl* (*STOCK EXCHANGE*) valeurs *fpl*, titres *mpl*; **to increase** *or* **tighten ~** renforcer les mesures de sécurité; ~ **of tenure** stabilité *f* d'un emploi, titularisation *f*.

Security Council *n*: **the ~** le Conseil de sécurité.

security forces *npl* forces *fpl* de sécurité.

security guard *n* garde chargé de la sécurité; (*transporting money*) convoyeur *m* de fonds.

security risk *n* menace *f* pour la sécurité de l'état (*or* d'une entreprise *etc*).

secy *abbr* (= *secretary*) secr.

sedan [sə'dæn] *n* (*US AUT*) berline *f*.

sedate [sɪ'deɪt] *adj* calme; posé(e) ♦ *vt* donner des sédatifs à.

sedation [sɪ'deɪʃən] *n* (*MED*) sédation *f*; **to be under ~** être sous calmants.

sedative ['sɛdɪtɪv] *n* calmant *m*, sédatif *m*.

sedentary ['sɛdntrɪ] *adj* sédentaire.

sediment ['sɛdɪmənt] *n* sédiment *m*, dépôt *m*.

sedition [sɪ'dɪʃən] *n* sédition *f*.

seduce [sɪ'djuːs] *vt* séduire.

seduction [sɪ'dʌkʃən] *n* séduction *f*.

seductive [sɪ'dʌktɪv] *adj* séduisant(e), séducteur(trice).

see [siː] *vb* (*pt* **saw**, *pp* **seen** [sɔː, siːn]) *vt* (*gen*) voir; (*accompany*): **to ~ sb to the door** reconduire *or* raccompagner qn jusqu'à la porte ♦ *vi* voir ♦ *n* évêché *m*; **to ~ that** (*ensure*) veiller à ce que + *sub*, faire en sorte que + *sub*, s'assurer que; **there was nobody to be ~n** il n'y avait pas un chat; **let me ~** (*show me*) fais(-moi) voir; (*let me think*) voyons (un peu); **to go and ~ sb** aller voir qn; ~ **for yourself** voyez vous-même; **I don't know what she ~s in him** je ne sais pas ce qu'elle lui trouve; **as far as I can ~** pour autant que je puisse en juger; ~ **you!** au revoir!, à bientôt!; ~ **you soon/later/ tomorrow!** à bientôt/plus tard/demain!

▶**see about** *vt fus* (*deal with*) s'occuper de.

▶**see off** *vt* accompagner (à la gare *or* à l'aéroport *etc*).

▶**see through** *vt* mener à bonne fin ♦ *vt fus* voir clair dans.

▶**see to** *vt fus* s'occuper de, se charger de.

seed [siːd] *n* graine *f*; (*fig*) germe *m*; (*TENNIS etc*) tête *f* de série; **to go to ~** monter en graine; (*fig*) se laisser aller.

seedless ['siːdlɪs] *adj* sans pépins.

seedling ['siːdlɪŋ] *n* jeune plant *m*, semis *m*.

seedy ['siːdɪ] *adj* (*shabby*) minable, miteux(euse).

seeing ['siːɪŋ] *conj*: ~ (**that**) vu que, étant donné que.

seek, *pt, pp* **sought** [siːk, sɔːt] *vt* chercher, rechercher; **to ~ advice/help from sb** demander conseil/de l'aide à qn.

▶**seek out** *vt* (*person*) chercher.

seem [siːm] *vi* sembler, paraître; **there ~s to be …** il semble qu'il y a …, on dirait qu'il y a …; **it ~s (that) …** il semble que …; **what ~s to be the trouble?** qu'est-ce qui ne va pas?

seemingly ['siːmɪŋlɪ] *adv* apparemment.
seen [siːn] *pp of* see.
seep [siːp] *vi* suinter, filtrer.
seer [sɪə*] *n* prophète/prophétesse, voyant/e.
seersucker ['sɪəsʌkə*] *n* cloqué *m*, étoffe cloquée.
seesaw ['siːsɔː] *n* (jeu *m* de) bascule *f*.
seethe [siːð] *vi* être en effervescence; **to ~ with anger** bouillir de colère.
see-through ['siːθruː] *adj* transparent(e).
segment ['sɛgmənt] *n* segment *m*.
segregate ['sɛgrɪgeɪt] *vt* séparer, isoler.
segregation [sɛgrɪ'geɪʃən] *n* ségrégation *f*.
Seine [seɪn] *n*: **the ~** la Seine.
seismic ['saɪzmɪk] *adj* sismique.
seize [siːz] *vt* (*grasp*) saisir, attraper; (*take possession of*) s'emparer de; (*LAW*) saisir.
▶**seize up** *vi* (*TECH*) se gripper.
▶**seize (up)on** *vt fus* saisir, sauter sur.
seizure ['siːʒə*] *n* (*MED*) crise *f*, attaque *f*; (*LAW*) saisie *f*.
seldom ['sɛldəm] *adv* rarement.
select [sɪ'lɛkt] *adj* choisi(e), d'élite; (*hotel, restaurant, club*) chic *inv*, sélect *inv* ♦ *vt* sélectionner, choisir; **a ~ few** quelques privilégiés.
selection [sɪ'lɛkʃən] *n* sélection *f*, choix *m*.
selection committee *n* comité *m* de sélection.
selective [sɪ'lɛktɪv] *adj* sélectif(ive); (*school*) à recrutement sélectif.
selector [sɪ'lɛktə*] *n* (*person*) sélectionneur/euse; (*TECH*) sélecteur *m*.
self [sɛlf] *n* (*pl* **selves** [sɛlvz]): **the ~** le moi *inv* ♦ *prefix* auto-.
self-addressed ['sɛlfə'drɛst] *adj*: **~ envelope** enveloppe *f* à mon (*or* votre *etc*) nom.
self-adhesive [sɛlfəd'hiːzɪv] *adj* autocollant(e).
self-assertive [sɛlfə'səːtɪv] *adj* autoritaire.
self-assurance [sɛlfə'ʃuərəns] *n* assurance *f*.
self-assured [sɛlfə'ʃuəd] *adj* sûr(e) de soi, plein(e) d'assurance.
self-catering [sɛlf'keɪtərɪŋ] *adj* (*BRIT: flat*) avec cuisine, où l'on peut faire sa cuisine; (: *holiday*) en appartement (*or* chalet *etc*) loué.
self-centred, (*US*) **self-centered** [sɛlf'sɛntəd] *adj* égocentrique.
self-cleaning [sɛlf'kliːnɪŋ] *adj* autonettoyant(e).
self-confessed [sɛlfkən'fɛst] *adj* (*alcoholic etc*) déclaré(e), qui ne s'en cache pas.
self-confidence [sɛlf'kɔnfɪdns] *n* confiance *f* en soi.
self-conscious [sɛlf'kɔnʃəs] *adj* timide, qui manque d'assurance.
self-contained [sɛlfkən'teɪnd] *adj* (*BRIT: flat*) avec entrée particulière, indépendant(e).
self-control [sɛlfkən'trəul] *n* maîtrise *f* de soi.
self-defeating [sɛlfdɪ'fiːtɪŋ] *adj* qui a un effet contraire à l'effet recherché.

self-defence, (*US*) **self-defense** [sɛlfdɪ'fɛns] *n* légitime défense *f*.
self-discipline [sɛlf'dɪsɪplɪn] *n* discipline personnelle.
self-employed [sɛlfɪm'plɔɪd] *adj* qui travaille à son compte.
self-esteem [sɛlfɪ'stiːm] *n* amour-propre *m*.
self-evident [sɛlf'ɛvɪdnt] *adj* évident(e), qui va de soi.
self-explanatory [sɛlfɪk'splænətrɪ] *adj* qui se passe d'explication.
self-governing [sɛlf'gʌvənɪŋ] *adj* autonome.
self-help ['sɛlf'hɛlp] *n* initiative personnelle, efforts personnels.
self-importance [sɛlfɪm'pɔːtns] *n* suffisance *f*.
self-indulgent [sɛlfɪn'dʌldʒənt] *adj* qui ne se refuse rien.
self-inflicted [sɛlfɪn'flɪktɪd] *adj* volontaire.
self-interest [sɛlf'ɪntrɪst] *n* intérêt personnel.
selfish ['sɛlfɪʃ] *adj* égoïste.
selfishness ['sɛlfɪʃnɪs] *n* égoïsme *m*.
selfless ['sɛlflɪs] *adj* désintéressé(e).
selflessly ['sɛlflɪslɪ] *adv* sans penser à soi.
self-made man ['sɛlfmeɪd-] *n* self-made man *m*.
self-pity [sɛlf'pɪtɪ] *n* apitoiement *m* sur soi-même.
self-portrait [sɛlf'pɔːtreɪt] *n* autoportrait *m*.
self-possessed [sɛlfpə'zɛst] *adj* assuré(e).
self-preservation ['sɛlfprɛzə'veɪʃən] *n* instinct *m* de conservation.
self-raising [sɛlf'reɪzɪŋ], (*US*) **self-rising** [sɛlf'raɪzɪŋ] *adj*: **~ flour** farine *f* pour gâteaux (*avec levure incorporée*).
self-reliant [sɛlfrɪ'laɪənt] *adj* indépendant(e).
self-respect [sɛlfrɪs'pɛkt] *n* respect *m* de soi, amour-propre *m*.
self-respecting [sɛlfrɪs'pɛktɪŋ] *adj* qui se respecte.
self-righteous [sɛlf'raɪtʃəs] *adj* satisfait(e) de soi, pharisaïque.
self-rising [sɛlf'raɪzɪŋ] *adj* (*US*) = **self-raising**.
self-sacrifice [sɛlf'sækrɪfaɪs] *n* abnégation *f*.
self-same ['sɛlfseɪm] *adj* même.
self-satisfied [sɛlf'sætɪsfaɪd] *adj* content(e) de soi, suffisant(e).
self-sealing [sɛlf'siːlɪŋ] *adj* (*envelope*) autocollant(e).
self-service [sɛlf'səːvɪs] *adj*, *n* libre-service (*m*), self-service (*m*).
self-styled ['sɛlfstaɪld] *adj* soi-disant *inv*.
self-sufficient [sɛlfsə'fɪʃənt] *adj* indépendant(e).
self-supporting [sɛlfsə'pɔːtɪŋ] *adj* financièrement indépendant(e).
self-taught [sɛlf'tɔːt] *adj* autodidacte.
self-test ['sɛlftɛst] *n* (*COMPUT*) test *m* automatique.
sell, *pt, pp* **sold** [sɛl, səuld] *vt* vendre ♦ *vi* se vendre; **to ~ at *or* for 10 F** se vendre 10 F; **to ~ sb an idea** (*fig*) faire accepter une idée à qn.

►**sell off** vt liquider.

►**sell out** vi: **to ~ out (to)** (COMM) vendre son fonds or son affaire (à) ♦ vt vendre tout son stock de; **the tickets are all sold out** il ne reste plus de billets.

►**sell up** vi vendre son fonds or son affaire.

sell-by date ['sɛlbaɪ-] n date f limite de vente.

seller ['sɛlə*] n vendeur/euse, marchand/e; **~'s market** marché m à la hausse.

selling price ['sɛlɪŋ-] n prix m de vente.

Sellotape ['sɛləuteɪp] n ® (BRIT) papier collant, scotch m ®.

sellout ['sɛlaut] n trahison f, capitulation f; (of tickets): **it was a ~** tous les billets ont été vendus.

selves [sɛlvz] npl of **self**.

semantic [sɪ'mæntɪk] adj sémantique.

semantics [sɪ'mæntɪks] n sémantique f.

semaphore ['sɛməfɔ:*] n signaux mpl à bras; (RAIL) sémaphore m.

semblance ['sɛmblns] n semblant m.

semen ['si:mən] n sperme m.

semester [sɪ'mɛstə*] n (esp US) semestre m.

semi... ['sɛmɪ] prefix semi-, demi-; à demi, à moitié ♦ n: **semi = semidetached (house)**.

semi-breve ['sɛmɪbri:v] n (BRIT) ronde f.

semicircle ['sɛmɪsə:kl] n demi-cercle m.

semicircular ['sɛmɪ'sə:kjulə*] adj en demi-cercle, semi-circulaire.

semicolon [sɛmɪ'kəulən] n point-virgule m.

semiconductor [sɛmɪkən'dʌktə*] n semiconducteur m.

semiconscious [sɛmɪ'kɔnʃəs] adj à demi conscient(e).

semidetached (house) [sɛmɪdɪ'tætʃt-] n (BRIT) maison jumelée or jumelle.

semifinal [sɛmɪ'faɪnl] n demi-finale f.

seminar ['sɛmɪnɑ:*] n séminaire m.

seminary ['sɛmɪnərɪ] n (REL: for priests) séminaire m.

semiprecious [sɛmɪ'prɛʃəs] adj semi-précieux(euse).

semiquaver ['sɛmɪkweɪvə*] n (BRIT) double croche f.

semiskilled [sɛmɪ'skɪld] adj: **~ worker** ouvrier/ière spécialisé(e).

semi-skimmed ['sɛmɪ'skɪmd] adj demi-écrémé(e).

semitone ['sɛmɪtəun] n (MUS) demi-ton m.

semolina [sɛmə'li:nə] n semoule f.

SEN n abbr (BRIT) = State Enrolled Nurse.

Sen., sen. abbr = senator, senior.

senate ['sɛnɪt] n sénat m.

Le **Senate** *est la chambre haute du* **Congress**, *le parlement des États-Unis. Il est composé de 100 sénateurs, 2 par État, élus au suffrage universel direct tous les 6 ans, un tiers d'entre eux étant renouvelé tous les 2 ans.*

---

senator ['sɛnɪtə*] n sénateur m.

send, pt, pp **sent** [sɛnd, sɛnt] vt envoyer; **to ~**

by post or (US) mail envoyer or expédier par la poste; **to ~ sb for sth** envoyer qn chercher qch; **to ~ word that ...** faire dire que ...; **she ~s (you) her love** elle vous adresse ses amitiés; **to ~ sb to Coventry** (BRIT) mettre qn en quarantaine; **to ~ sb to sleep** endormir qn; **to ~ sb into fits of laughter** faire rire qn aux éclats; **to ~ sth flying** envoyer valser qch.

►**send away** vt (letter, goods) envoyer, expédier.

►**send away for** vt fus commander par correspondance, se faire envoyer.

►**send back** vt renvoyer.

►**send for** vt fus envoyer chercher; faire venir; (by post) se faire envoyer, commander par correspondance.

►**send in** vt (report, application, resignation) remettre.

►**send off** vt (goods) envoyer, expédier; (BRIT SPORT: player) expulser or renvoyer du terrain.

►**send on** vt (BRIT: letter) faire suivre; (luggage etc: in advance) (faire) expédier à l'avance.

►**send out** vt (invitation) envoyer (par la poste); (emit: light, heat, signals) émettre.

►**send round** vt (letter, document etc) faire circuler.

►**send up** vt (person, price) faire monter; (BRIT: parody) mettre en boîte, parodier.

sender ['sɛndə*] n expéditeur/trice.

send-off ['sɛndɔf] n: **a good ~** des adieux chaleureux.

Senegal [sɛnɪ'gɔ:l] n Sénégal m.

Senegalese [sɛnɪgə'li:z] adj sénégalais(e) ♦ n (pl inv) Sénégalais/e.

senile ['si:naɪl] adj sénile.

senility [sɪ'nɪlɪtɪ] n sénilité f.

senior ['si:nɪə*] adj (older) aîné(e), plus âgé(e); (of higher rank) supérieur(e) ♦ n aîné/e; (in service) personne f qui a plus d'ancienneté; **P. Jones ~** P. Jones père.

senior citizen n personne âgée.

senior high school n (US) ≈ lycée m.

seniority [si:nɪ'ɔrɪtɪ] n priorité f d'âge, ancienneté f; (in rank) supériorité f (hiérarchique).

sensation [sɛn'seɪʃən] n sensation f; **to create a ~** faire sensation.

sensational [sɛn'seɪʃənl] adj qui fait sensation; (marvellous) sensationnel(le).

sense [sɛns] n sens m; (feeling) sentiment m; (meaning) signification f; (wisdom) bon sens ♦ vt sentir, pressentir; **~s** npl raison f; **it makes ~** c'est logique; **~ of humour** sens de l'humour; **there is no ~ in (doing)** that cela n'a pas de sens; **to come to one's ~s** (regain consciousness) reprendre conscience; (become reasonable) revenir à la raison; **to take leave of one's ~s** perdre la tête.

senseless ['sɛnslɪs] adj insensé(e), stupide;

(*unconscious*) sans connaissance.
sensibility [sɛnsɪ'bɪlɪtɪ] *n* sensibilité *f*;
sensibilities *npl* susceptibilité *f*.
sensible ['sɛnsɪbl] *adj* sensé(e), raisonnable;
(*shoes etc*) pratique.
sensitive ['sɛnsɪtɪv] *adj*: ~ **(to)** sensible (à); **he
is very ~ about it** c'est un point très
sensible (chez lui).
sensitivity [sɛnsɪ'tɪvɪtɪ] *n* sensibilité *f*.
sensual ['sɛnsjʊəl] *adj* sensuel(le).
sensuous ['sɛnsjʊəs] *adj* voluptueux(euse),
sensuel(le).
sent [sɛnt] *pt, pp of* **send**.
sentence ['sɛntns] *n* (*LING*) phrase *f*; (*LAW:
judgment*) condamnation *f*, sentence *f*;
(*: punishment*) peine *f* ♦ *vt*: **to ~ sb to death/
to 5 years** condamner qn à mort/à 5 ans; **to
pass ~ on sb** prononcer une peine contre
qn.
sentiment ['sɛntɪmənt] *n* sentiment *m*;
(*opinion*) opinion *f*, avis *m*.
sentimental [sɛntɪ'mɛntl] *adj* sentimental(e).
sentimentality [sɛntɪmɛn'tælɪtɪ] *n*
sentimentalité *f*, sensiblerie *f*.
sentry ['sɛntrɪ] *n* sentinelle *f*, factionnaire *m*.
sentry duty *n*: **to be on ~** être de faction.
Seoul [səʊl] *n* Séoul.
separable ['sɛprəbl] *adj* séparable.
separate *adj* ['sɛprɪt] séparé(e),
indépendant(e), différent(e) ♦ *vb* ['sɛpəreɪt]
vt séparer ♦ *vi* se séparer; ~ **from** distinct(e)
de; **under ~ cover** (*COMM*) sous pli séparé;
to ~ into diviser en.
separately ['sɛprɪtlɪ] *adv* séparément.
separates ['sɛprɪts] *npl* (*clothes*) coordonnés
mpl.
separation [sɛpə'reɪʃən] *n* séparation *f*.
Sept. *abbr* (= *September*) sept.
September [sɛp'tɛmbə*] *n* septembre *m*; *for
phrases see also* **July**.
septic ['sɛptɪk] *adj* septique; (*wound*)
infecté(e); **to go ~** s'infecter.
septicaemia [sɛptɪ'siːmɪə] *n* septicémie *f*.
septic tank *n* fosse *f* septique.
sequel ['siːkwl] *n* conséquence *f*, séquelles *fpl*;
(*of story*) suite *f*.
sequence ['siːkwəns] *n* ordre *m*, suite *f*; **in ~**
par ordre, dans l'ordre, les uns après les
autres; ~ **of tenses** concordance *f* des
temps.
sequential [sɪ'kwɛnʃəl] *adj*: ~ **access**
(*COMPUT*) accès séquentiel.
sequin ['siːkwɪn] *n* paillette *f*.
Serb [sɜːb] *adj, n* = **Serbian**.
Serbia ['sɜːbɪə] *n* Serbie *f*.
Serbian ['sɜːbɪən] *adj* serbe ♦ *n* Serbe *m/f*;
(*LING*) serbe *m*.
Serbo-Croat ['sɜːbəʊ'krəʊæt] *n* (*LING*) serbo-
croate *m*.
serenade [sɛrə'neɪd] *n* sérénade *f* ♦ *vt* donner
une sérénade à.
serene [sɪ'riːn] *adj* serein(e), calme, paisible.

serenity [sə'rɛnɪtɪ] *n* sérénité *f*, calme *m*.
sergeant ['sɑːdʒənt] *n* sergent *m*; (*POLICE*)
brigadier *m*.
sergeant major *n* sergent-major *m*.
serial ['sɪərɪəl] *n* feuilleton *m* ♦ *adj* (*COMPUT*:
interface, printer) série *inv*; (*: access*)
séquentiel(le).
serialize ['sɪərɪəlaɪz] *vt* publier (*or* adapter) en
feuilleton.
serial killer *n* meurtrier *m* tuant en série.
serial number *n* numéro *m* de série.
series ['sɪəriːz] *n* série *f*; (*PUBLISHING*)
collection *f*.
serious ['sɪərɪəs] *adj* sérieux(euse); (*accident
etc*) grave; **are you ~ (about it?)** parlez-vous
sérieusement?
seriously ['sɪərɪəslɪ] *adv* sérieusement,
gravement; ~ **rich/difficult** (*col: extremely*)
drôlement riche/difficile; **to take sth/sb ~**
prendre qch/qn au sérieux.
seriousness ['sɪərɪəsnɪs] *n* sérieux *m*, gravité
f.
sermon ['sɜːmən] *n* sermon *m*.
serrated [sɪ'reɪtɪd] *adj* en dents de scie.
serum ['sɪərəm] *n* sérum *m*.
servant ['sɜːvənt] *n* domestique *m/f*; (*fig*)
serviteur/servante.
serve [sɜːv] *vt* (*employer etc*) servir, être au
service de; (*purpose*) servir à; (*customer,
food, meal*) servir; (*apprenticeship*) faire,
accomplir; (*prison term*) faire; purger ♦ *vi*
(*also TENNIS*) servir; (*be useful*): **to ~ as/for/
to do** servir de/à/à faire ♦ *n* (*TENNIS*) service
m; **are you being ~d?** est-ce qu'on s'occupe
de vous?; **to ~ on a committee/jury** faire
partie d'un comité/jury; **it ~s him right** c'est
bien fait pour lui; **it ~s my purpose** cela fait
mon affaire.
▶**serve out, serve up** *vt* (*food*) servir.
service ['sɜːvɪs] *n* (*gen*) service *m*; (*AUT:
maintenance*) révision *f*; (*REL*) office *m* ♦ *vt*
(*car, washing machine*) réviser; **the S~s** *npl*
les forces armées; **to be of ~ to sb, to do sb
a ~** rendre service à qn; **to put one's car in
for ~** donner sa voiture à réviser; **dinner ~**
service de table.
serviceable ['sɜːvɪsəbl] *adj* pratique,
commode.
service area *n* (*on motorway*) aire *f* de
services.
service charge *n* (*BRIT*) service *m*.
service industries *npl* les industries *fpl* de
service, les services *mpl*.
serviceman ['sɜːvɪsmən] *n* militaire *m*.
service station *n* station-service *f*.
serviette [sɜːvɪ'ɛt] *n* (*BRIT*) serviette *f* (de
table).
servile ['sɜːvaɪl] *adj* servile.
session ['sɛʃən] *n* (*sitting*) séance *f*; (*SCOL*)
année *f* scolaire (*or* universitaire); **to be in
~** siéger, être en session *or* en séance.
session musician *n* musicien/ne de studio.

set [sɛt] n série f, assortiment m; (of tools etc)
jeu m; (RADIO, TV) poste m; (TENNIS) set m;
(group of people) cercle m, milieu m; (CINE)
plateau m; (THEAT: stage) scène f;
(: scenery) décor m; (MATH) ensemble m;
(HAIRDRESSING) mise f en plis ♦ adj (fixed)
fixe, déterminé(e); (ready) prêt(e) ♦ vb (pt, pp
set) vt (place) mettre, poser, placer; (fix,
establish) fixer; (: record) établir; (assign: task,
homework) donner; (adjust) régler; (decide:
rules etc) fixer, choisir; (TYP) composer ♦ vi
(sun) se coucher; (jam, jelly, concrete)
prendre; **to be ~ on doing** être résolu(e) à
faire; **to be all ~ to do** être (fin) prêt(e)
pour faire; **to be (dead) ~ against** être
(totalement) opposé à; **he's ~ in his ways** il
n'est pas très souple, il tient à ses
habitudes; **to ~ to music** mettre en
musique; **to ~ on fire** mettre le feu à; **to ~
free** libérer; **to ~ sth going** déclencher qch;
to ~ sail partir, prendre la mer; **a ~ phrase**
une expression toute faite, une locution; **a
~ of false teeth** un dentier; **a ~ of dining-
room furniture** une salle à manger.
►**set about** vt fus (task) entreprendre, se
mettre à; **to ~ about doing sth** se mettre à
faire qch.
►**set aside** vt mettre de côté.
►**set back** vt (in time): **to ~ back (by)** retarder
(de); (place): **a house ~ back from the road**
une maison située en retrait de la route.
►**set in** vi (infection, bad weather) s'installer;
(complications) survenir, surgir; **the rain has
~ in for the day** c'est parti pour qu'il pleuve
toute la journée.
►**set off** vi se mettre en route, partir ♦ vt
(bomb) faire exploser; (cause to start)
déclencher; (show up well) mettre en valeur,
faire valoir.
►**set out** vi: **to ~ out to do** entreprendre de
faire; avoir pour but or intention de faire
♦ vt (arrange) disposer; (state) présenter,
exposer; **to ~ out (from)** partir (de).
►**set up** vt (organization) fonder, constituer;
(monument) ériger; **to ~ up shop** (fig)
s'établir, s'installer.
setback ['sɛtbæk] n (hitch) revers m,
contretemps m; (in health) rechute f.
set menu n menu m.
set square n équerre f.
settee [sɛ'tiː] n canapé m.
setting ['sɛtɪŋ] n cadre m; (of jewel) monture f.
setting lotion n lotion f pour mise en plis.
settle ['sɛtl] vt (argument, matter, account)
régler; (problem) résoudre; (MED: calm)
calmer; (colonize: land) coloniser ♦ vi (bird,
dust etc) se poser; (sediment) se déposer;
(also: ~ **down**) s'installer, se fixer; (: become
calmer) se calmer; se ranger; **to ~ to sth** se
mettre sérieusement à qch; **to ~ for sth**
accepter qch, se contenter de qch; **to ~ on
sth** opter or se décider pour qch; **that's ~d**

then alors, c'est d'accord!; **to ~ one's
stomach** calmer des maux d'estomac.
►**settle in** vi s'installer.
►**settle up** vi: **to ~ up with sb** régler (ce que
l'on doit à) qn.
settlement ['sɛtlmənt] n (payment) règlement
m; (agreement) accord m; (colony) colonie f;
(village etc) établissement m; hameau m; **in ~
of our account** (COMM) en règlement de
notre compte.
settler ['sɛtlə*] n colon m.
setup ['sɛtʌp] n (arrangement) manière f dont
les choses sont organisées; (situation)
situation f, allure f des choses.
seven ['sɛvn] num sept.
seventeen [sɛvn'tiːn] num dix-sept.
seventh ['sɛvnθ] num septième.
seventy ['sɛvntɪ] num soixante-dix.
sever ['sɛvə*] vt couper, trancher; (relations)
rompre.
several ['sɛvərl] adj, pron plusieurs (m/fpl); **~ of
us** plusieurs d'entre nous; **~ times**
plusieurs fois.
severance ['sɛvərəns] n (of relations) rupture f.
severance pay n indemnité f de
licenciement.
severe [sɪ'vɪə*] adj sévère, strict(e); (serious)
grave, sérieux(euse); (hard)
rigoureux(euse), dur(e); (plain) sévère,
austère.
severely [sɪ'vɪəlɪ] adv sévèrement; (wounded,
ill) gravement.
severity [sɪ'vɛrɪtɪ] n sévérité f; gravité f;
rigueur f.
sew, pt **sewed**, pp **sewn** [səu, səud, səun] vt, vi
coudre.
►**sew up** vt (re)coudre; **it is all sewn up** (fig)
c'est dans le sac or dans la poche.
sewage ['suːɪdʒ] n vidange(s) f(pl).
sewage works n champ m d'épandage.
sewer ['suːə*] n égout m.
sewing ['səuɪŋ] n couture f.
sewing machine n machine f à coudre.
sewn [səun] pp of **sew**.
sex [sɛks] n sexe m; **to have ~ with** avoir des
rapports (sexuels) avec.
sex act n acte sexuel.
sex appeal n sex-appeal m.
sex education n éducation sexuelle.
sexism ['sɛksɪzəm] n sexisme m.
sexist ['sɛksɪst] adj sexiste.
sex life n vie sexuelle.
sex object n femme-objet f, objet sexuel.
sextet [sɛks'tɛt] n sextuor m.
sexual ['sɛksjuəl] adj sexuel(le); **~ assault**
attentat m à la pudeur; **~ harassment**
harcèlement sexuel; **~ intercourse** rapports
sexuels.
sexy ['sɛksɪ] adj sexy inv.
Seychelles [seɪ'ʃɛl(z)] npl: **the ~** les
Seychelles fpl.
SF n abbr (= science fiction) SF f.

SG *n abbr* (*US*) = **Surgeon General**.
Sgt *abbr* (= *sergeant*) Sgt.
shabbiness ['ʃæbɪnɪs] *n* aspect miteux; mesquinerie *f*.
shabby ['ʃæbɪ] *adj* miteux(euse); (*behaviour*) mesquin(e), méprisable.
shack [ʃæk] *n* cabane *f*, hutte *f*.
shackles ['ʃæklz] *npl* chaînes *fpl*, entraves *fpl*.
shade [ʃeɪd] *n* ombre *f*; (*for lamp*) abat-jour *m inv*; (*of colour*) nuance *f*, ton *m*; (*US: window* ~) store *m*; (*small quantity*): **a** ~ **of** un soupçon de ♦ *vt* abriter du soleil, ombrager; ~**s** *npl* (*US: sunglasses*) lunettes *fpl* de soleil; **in the** ~ à l'ombre; **a** ~ **smaller** un tout petit peu plus petit.
shadow ['ʃædəʊ] *n* ombre *f* ♦ *vt* (*follow*) filer; **without** *or* **beyond a** ~ **of doubt** sans l'ombre d'un doute.
shadow cabinet *n* (*BRIT POL*) cabinet parallèle formé par le parti qui n'est pas au pouvoir.
shadowy ['ʃædəʊɪ] *adj* ombragé(e); (*dim*) vague, indistinct(e).
shady ['ʃeɪdɪ] *adj* ombragé(e); (*fig: dishonest*) louche, véreux(euse).
shaft [ʃɑːft] *n* (*of arrow, spear*) hampe *f*; (*AUT, TECH*) arbre *m*; (*of mine*) puits *m*; (*of lift*) cage *f*; (*of light*) rayon *m*, trait *m*; **ventilator** ~ conduit *m* d'aération *or* de ventilation.
shaggy ['ʃægɪ] *adj* hirsute; en broussaille.
shake [ʃeɪk] *vb* (*pt* **shook**, *pp* **shaken** [ʃuk, 'ʃeɪkn]) *vt* secouer; (*bottle, cocktail*) agiter; (*house, confidence*) ébranler ♦ *vi* trembler ♦ *n* secousse *f*; **to** ~ **one's head** (*in refusal etc*) dire *or* faire non de la tête; (*in dismay*) secouer la tête; **to** ~ **hands with sb** serrer la main à qn.
▶**shake off** *vt* secouer; (*fig*) se débarrasser de.
▶**shake up** *vt* secouer.
shake-up ['ʃeɪkʌp] *n* grand remaniement.
shakily ['ʃeɪkɪlɪ] *adv* (*reply*) d'une voix tremblante; (*walk*) d'un pas mal assuré; (*write*) d'une main tremblante.
shaky ['ʃeɪkɪ] *adj* (*hand, voice*) tremblant(e); (*building*) branlant(e), peu solide; (*memory*) chancelant(e); (*knowledge*) incertain(e).
shale [ʃeɪl] *n* schiste argileux.
shall [ʃæl] *aux vb*: **I** ~ **go** j'irai.
shallot [ʃə'lɒt] *n* (*BRIT*) échalote *f*.
shallow ['ʃæləʊ] *adj* peu profond(e); (*fig*) superficiel(le), qui manque de profondeur.
sham [ʃæm] *n* frime *f*; (*jewellery, furniture*) imitation *f* ♦ *adj* feint(e), simulé(e) ♦ *vt* feindre, simuler.
shambles ['ʃæmblz] *n* confusion *f*, pagaïe *f*, fouillis *m*; **the economy is (in) a complete** ~ l'économie est dans la confusion la plus totale.
shambolic [ʃæm'bɒlɪk] *adj* (*col*) bordélique.
shame [ʃeɪm] *n* honte *f* ♦ *vt* faire honte à; **it is a** ~ **(that/to do)** c'est dommage (que + *sub*/de

faire); **what a** ~! quel dommage!; **to put sb/sth to** ~ (*fig*) faire honte à qn/qch.
shamefaced ['ʃeɪmfeɪst] *adj* honteux(euse), penaud(e).
shameful ['ʃeɪmful] *adj* honteux(euse), scandaleux(euse).
shameless ['ʃeɪmlɪs] *adj* éhonté(e), effronté(e); (*immodest*) impudique.
shampoo [ʃæm'puː] *n* shampooing *m* ♦ *vt* faire un shampooing à; ~ **and set** shampooing et mise *f* en plis.
shamrock ['ʃæmrɒk] *n* trèfle *m* (*emblème national de l'Irlande*).
shandy ['ʃændɪ] *n* bière panachée.
shan't [ʃɑːnt] = **shall not**.
shantytown ['ʃæntɪtaʊn] *n* bidonville *m*.
SHAPE [ʃeɪp] *n abbr* (= *Supreme Headquarters Allied Powers, Europe*) quartier général des forces alliées en Europe.
shape [ʃeɪp] *n* forme *f* ♦ *vt* façonner, modeler; (*clay, stone*) donner forme à; (*statement*) formuler; (*sb's ideas, character*) former; (*sb's life*) déterminer; (*course of events*) influer sur le cours de ♦ *vi* (*also*: ~ **up**: *events*) prendre tournure; (: *person*) faire des progrès, s'en sortir; **to take** ~ prendre forme *or* tournure; **in the** ~ **of a heart** en forme de cœur; **I can't bear gardening in any** ~ **or form** je déteste le jardinage sous quelque forme que ce soit; **to get o.s. into** ~ (re)trouver la forme.
-shaped [ʃeɪpt] *suffix*: **heart-**~ en forme de cœur.
shapeless ['ʃeɪplɪs] *adj* informe, sans forme.
shapely ['ʃeɪplɪ] *adj* bien proportionné(e), beau(belle).
share [ʃeə*] *n* (*thing received, contribution*) part *f*; (*COMM*) action *f* ♦ *vt* partager; (*have in common*) avoir en commun; **to** ~ **out** (**among** *or* **between**) partager (entre); **to** ~ **in** (*joy, sorrow*) prendre part à; (*profits*) participer à, avoir part à; (*work*) partager.
share capital *n* capital social.
share certificate *n* certificat *m* *or* titre *m* d'action.
shareholder ['ʃeəhəʊldə*] *n* actionnaire *m/f*.
share index *n* indice *m* de la Bourse.
shark [ʃɑːk] *n* requin *m*.
sharp [ʃɑːp] *adj* (*razor, knife*) tranchant(e), bien aiguisé(e); (*point*) aigu(ë); (*nose, chin*) pointu(e); (*outline*) net(te); (*curve, bend*) brusque; (*cold, pain*) vif(vive); (*MUS*) dièse; (*voice*) coupant(e); (*person: quick-witted*) vif(vive), éveillé(e); (: *unscrupulous*) malhonnête ♦ *n* (*MUS*) dièse *m* ♦ *adv*: **at 2 o'clock** ~ à 2 heures pile *or* tapantes; **turn** ~ **left** tournez immédiatement à gauche; **to be** ~ **with sb** être brusque avec qn; **look** ~! dépêche-toi!
sharpen ['ʃɑːpn] *vt* aiguiser; (*pencil*) tailler; (*fig*) aviver.
sharpener ['ʃɑːpnə*] *n* (*also*: **pencil** ~) taille-

crayon(s) *m inv*; (*also*: **knife** ~) aiguisoir *m*.

sharp-eyed [ʃɑːpˈaɪd] *adj* à qui rien n'échappe.

sharpish [ˈʃɑːpɪʃ] *adv* (*BRIT col: quickly*) en vitesse.

sharply [ˈʃɑːplɪ] *adv* (*abruptly*) brusquement; (*clearly*) nettement; (*harshly*) sèchement, vertement.

sharp-tempered [ʃɑːpˈtɛmpəd] *adj* prompt(e) à se mettre en colère.

sharp-witted [ʃɑːpˈwɪtɪd] *adj* à l'esprit vif, malin(igne).

shatter [ˈʃætə*] *vt* fracasser, briser, faire voler en éclats; (*fig: upset*) bouleverser; (*: ruin*) briser, ruiner ♦ *vi* voler en éclats, se briser, se fracasser.

shattered [ˈʃætəd] *adj* (*overwhelmed, grief-stricken*) bouleversé(e); (*col: exhausted*) éreinté(e).

shatterproof [ˈʃætəpruːf] *adj* incassable.

shave [ʃeɪv] *vt* raser ♦ *vi* se raser ♦ *n*: **to have a** ~ se raser.

shaven [ˈʃeɪvn] *adj* (*head*) rasé(e).

shaver [ˈʃeɪvə*] *n* (*also*: **electric** ~) rasoir *m* électrique.

shaving [ˈʃeɪvɪŋ] *n* (*action*) rasage *m*; ~s *npl* (*of wood etc*) copeaux *mpl*.

shaving brush *n* blaireau *m*.

shaving cream *n* crème *f* à raser.

shaving soap *n* savon *m* à barbe.

shawl [ʃɔːl] *n* châle *m*.

she [ʃiː] *pron* elle; **there** ~ **is** la voilà; ~-**elephant** *etc* éléphant *etc* femelle; *NB: for ships, countries follow the gender of your translation.*

sheaf, *pl* **sheaves** [ʃiːf, ʃiːvz] *n* gerbe *f*.

shear [ʃɪə*] *vt* (*pt* ~**ed**, *pp* ~**ed** *or* **shorn** [ʃɔːn]) (*sheep*) tondre.

▶**shear off** *vt* tondre; (*branch*) élaguer.

shears [ˈʃɪəz] *npl* (*for hedge*) cisaille(s) *f(pl)*.

sheath [ʃiːθ] *n* gaine *f*, fourreau *m*, étui *m*; (*contraceptive*) préservatif *m*.

sheathe [ʃiːð] *vt* gainer; (*sword*) rengainer.

sheath knife *n* couteau *m* à gaine.

sheaves [ʃiːvz] *npl of* **sheaf**.

shed [ʃɛd] *n* remise *f*, resserre *f*; (*INDUSTRY, RAIL*) hangar *m* ♦ *vt* (*pt, pp* **shed**) (*leaves, fur etc*) perdre; (*tears*) verser, répandre; **to** ~ **light on** (*problem, mystery*) faire la lumière sur.

she'd [ʃiːd] = **she had, she would**.

sheen [ʃiːn] *n* lustre *m*.

sheep [ʃiːp] *n* (*pl inv*) mouton *m*.

sheepdog [ˈʃiːpdɔg] *n* chien *m* de berger.

sheep farmer *n* éleveur *m* de moutons.

sheepish [ˈʃiːpɪʃ] *adj* penaud(e), timide.

sheepskin [ˈʃiːpskɪn] *n* peau *f* de mouton.

sheepskin jacket *n* canadienne *f*.

sheer [ʃɪə*] *adj* (*utter*) pur(e), pur et simple; (*steep*) à pic, abrupt(e); (*almost transparent*) extrêmement fin(e) ♦ *adv* à pic, abruptement; **by** ~ **chance** par pur hasard.

sheet [ʃiːt] *n* (*on bed*) drap *m*; (*of paper*) feuille *f*; (*of glass, metal*) feuille, plaque *f*.

sheet feed *n* (*on printer*) alimentation *f* en papier (feuille à feuille).

sheet lightning *n* éclair *m* en nappe(s).

sheet metal *n* tôle *f*.

sheet music *n* partition(s) *f(pl)*.

sheik(h) [ʃeɪk] *n* cheik *m*.

shelf, *pl* **shelves** [ʃɛlf, ʃɛlvz] *n* étagère *f*, rayon *m*; **set of shelves** rayonnage *m*.

shelf life *n* (*COMM*) durée *f* de conservation (avant la vente).

shell [ʃɛl] *n* (*on beach*) coquillage *m*; (*of egg, nut etc*) coquille *f*; (*explosive*) obus *m*; (*of building*) carcasse *f* ♦ *vt* (*crab, prawn etc*) décortiquer; (*peas*) écosser; (*MIL*) bombarder (d'obus).

▶**shell out** *vi* (*col*): **to** ~ **out** (**for**) casquer (pour).

she'll [ʃiːl] = **she will, she shall**.

shellfish [ˈʃɛlfɪʃ] *n* (*pl inv*) (*crab etc*) crustacé *m*; (*scallop etc*) coquillage *m*; (*pl: as food*) crustacés; coquillages.

shellsuit [ˈʃɛlsuːt] *n* survêtement *m*.

shelter [ˈʃɛltə*] *n* abri *m*, refuge *m* ♦ *vt* abriter, protéger; (*give lodging to*) donner asile à ♦ *vi* s'abriter, se mettre à l'abri; **to take** ~ (**from**) s'abriter (de).

sheltered [ˈʃɛltəd] *adj* (*life*) retiré(e), à l'abri des soucis; (*spot*) abrité(e).

shelve [ʃɛlv] *vt* (*fig*) mettre en suspens *or* en sommeil.

shelves [ˈʃɛlvz] *npl of* **shelf**.

shelving [ˈʃɛlvɪŋ] *n* (*shelves*) rayonnage(s) *m(pl)*.

shepherd [ˈʃɛpəd] *n* berger *m* ♦ *vt* (*guide*) guider, escorter.

shepherdess [ˈʃɛpədɪs] *n* bergère *f*.

shepherd's pie [ˈʃɛpədz-] *n* ≈ hachis *m* Parmentier.

sherbet [ˈʃəːbət] *n* (*BRIT: powder*) poudre acidulée; (*US: water ice*) sorbet *m*.

sheriff [ˈʃɛrɪf] *n* shérif *m*.

sherry [ˈʃɛrɪ] *n* xérès *m*, sherry *m*.

she's [ʃiːz] = **she is, she has**.

Shetland [ˈʃɛtlənd] *n* (*also*: **the** ~**s, the** ~ **Isles** *or* **Islands**) les îles *fpl* Shetland.

Shetland pony *n* poney *m* des îles Shetland.

shield [ʃiːld] *n* bouclier *m* ♦ *vt*: **to** ~ (**from**) protéger (de *or* contre).

shift [ʃɪft] *n* (*change*) changement *m*; (*of workers*) équipe *f*, poste *m* ♦ *vt* déplacer, changer de place; (*remove*) enlever ♦ *vi* changer de place, bouger; **the wind has** ~**ed to the south** le vent a tourné au sud; **a** ~ **in demand** (*COMM*) un déplacement de la demande.

shift key *n* (*on typewriter*) touche *f* de majuscule.

shiftless [ˈʃɪftlɪs] *adj* fainéant(e).

shift work *n* travail *m* par roulement; **to do** ~ travailler par roulement.

shifty [ˈʃɪftɪ] *adj* sournois(e); (*eyes*) fuyant(e).

Shiite ['ʃiːaɪt] n Chiite m/f ♦ adj chiite.
shilling ['ʃɪlɪŋ] n (BRIT) shilling m (= 12 old pence; 20 in a pound).
shilly-shally ['ʃɪlɪʃælɪ] vi tergiverser, atermoyer.
shimmer ['ʃɪmə*] n miroitement m, chatoiement m ♦ vi miroiter, chatoyer.
shin [ʃɪn] n tibia m ♦ vi: to ~ up/down a tree grimper dans un/descendre d'un arbre.
shindig ['ʃɪndɪg] n (col) bamboula f.
shine [ʃaɪn] n éclat m, brillant m ♦ vb (pt, pp **shone** [ʃɔn]) vi briller ♦ vt faire briller or reluire; (torch): to ~ on braquer sur.
shingle ['ʃɪŋgl] n (on beach) galets mpl; (on roof) bardeau m.
shingles ['ʃɪŋglz] n (MED) zona m.
shining ['ʃaɪnɪŋ] adj brillant(e).
shiny ['ʃaɪnɪ] adj brillant(e).
ship [ʃɪp] n bateau m; (large) navire m ♦ vt transporter (par mer); (send) expédier (par mer); (load) charger, embarquer; **on board** ~ à bord.
shipbuilder ['ʃɪpbɪldə*] n constructeur m de navires.
shipbuilding ['ʃɪpbɪldɪŋ] n construction navale.
ship canal n canal m maritime or de navigation.
ship chandler [-'tʃɑːndlə*] n fournisseur m maritime, shipchandler m.
shipment ['ʃɪpmənt] n cargaison f.
shipowner ['ʃɪpəunə*] n armateur m.
shipper ['ʃɪpə*] n affréteur m, expéditeur m.
shipping ['ʃɪpɪŋ] n (ships) navires mpl; (traffic) navigation f.
shipping agent n agent m maritime.
shipping company n compagnie f de navigation.
shipping lane n couloir m de navigation.
shipping line n = **shipping company**.
shipshape ['ʃɪpʃeɪp] adj en ordre impeccable.
shipwreck ['ʃɪprɛk] n épave f; (event) naufrage m ♦ vt: **to be ~ed** faire naufrage.
shipyard ['ʃɪpjɑːd] n chantier naval.
shire ['ʃaɪə*] n (BRIT) comté m.
shirk [ʃɜːk] vt esquiver, se dérober à.
shirt [ʃɜːt] n chemise f; **in ~ sleeves** en bras de chemise.
shirty ['ʃɜːtɪ] adj (BRIT col) de mauvais poil.
shit [ʃɪt] excl (col!) merde (!).
shiver ['ʃɪvə*] n frisson m ♦ vi frissonner.
shoal [ʃəul] n (of fish) banc m.
shock [ʃɔk] n (impact) choc m, heurt m; (ELEC) secousse f, décharge f; (emotional) choc; (MED) commotion f, choc ♦ vt (scandalize) choquer, scandaliser; (upset) bouleverser; **suffering from** ~ (MED) commotionné(e); **it gave us a** ~ ça nous a fait un choc; **it came as a** ~ **to hear that** ... nous avons appris avec stupeur que ....
shock absorber [-əbzɔːbə*] n amortisseur m.
shocker ['ʃɔkə*] n (col): **the news was a real** ~

to him il a vraiment été choqué par cette nouvelle.
shocking ['ʃɔkɪŋ] adj choquant(e), scandaleux(euse); (weather, handwriting) épouvantable.
shockproof ['ʃɔkpruːf] adj anti-choc inv.
shock therapy, shock treatment n (MED) (traitement m par) électrochoc(s) m(pl).
shock wave n (also fig) onde f de choc.
shod [ʃɔd] pt, pp of **shoe**; **well-**~ bien chaussé(e).
shoddy ['ʃɔdɪ] adj de mauvaise qualité, mal fait(e).
shoe [ʃuː] n chaussure f, soulier m; (also: **horse**~) fer m à cheval; (also: **brake** ~) mâchoire f de frein ♦ vt (pt, pp **shod** [ʃɔd]) (horse) ferrer.
shoebrush ['ʃuːbrʌʃ] n brosse f à chaussures.
shoehorn ['ʃuːhɔːn] n chausse-pied m.
shoelace ['ʃuːleɪs] n lacet m (de soulier).
shoemaker ['ʃuːmeɪkə*] n cordonnier m, fabricant m de chaussures.
shoe polish n cirage m.
shoeshop ['ʃuːʃɔp] n magasin m de chaussures.
shoestring ['ʃuːstrɪŋ] n: **on a** ~ (fig) avec un budget dérisoire; avec des moyens très restreints.
shoetree ['ʃuːtriː] n embauchoir m.
shone [ʃɔn] pt, pp of **shine**.
shoo [ʃuː] excl (allez,) ouste! ♦ vt (also: ~ **away**, ~ **off**) chasser.
shook [ʃuk] pt of **shake**.
shoot [ʃuːt] n (on branch, seedling) pousse f; (shooting party) partie f de chasse ♦ vb (pt, pp **shot** [ʃɔt]) vt (game: BRIT) chasser; tirer; abattre; (person) blesser (or tuer) d'un coup de fusil (or de revolver); (execute) fusiller; (CINE) tourner ♦ vi (with gun, bow): to ~ (at) tirer (sur); (FOOTBALL) shooter, tirer; **to** ~ **past sb** passer en flèche devant qn; **to** ~ **in/out** entrer/sortir comme une flèche.
▶**shoot down** vt (plane) abattre.
▶**shoot up** vi (fig) monter en flèche.
shooting ['ʃuːtɪŋ] n (shots) coups mpl de feu; (attack) fusillade f; (: murder) homicide m (à l'aide d'une arme à feu); (HUNTING) chasse f; (CINE) tournage m.
shooting range n stand m de tir.
shooting star n étoile filante.
shop [ʃɔp] n magasin m; (workshop) atelier m ♦ vi (also: **go** ~**ping**) faire ses courses or ses achats; **repair** ~ atelier de réparations; **to talk** ~ (fig) parler boutique.
▶**shop around** vi faire le tour des magasins (pour comparer les prix); (fig) se renseigner avant de choisir or décider.
shopaholic [ʃɔpə'hɔlɪk] n (col) personne qui achète sans pouvoir s'arrêter.
shop assistant n (BRIT) vendeur/euse.
shop floor n (BRIT: fig) ouvriers mpl.
shopkeeper ['ʃɔpkiːpə*] n marchand/e,

commerçant/e.
shoplift ['ʃɒplɪft] *vi* voler à l'étalage.
shoplifter ['ʃɒplɪftə*] *n* voleur/euse à l'étalage.
shoplifting ['ʃɒplɪftɪŋ] *n* vol *m* à l'étalage.
shopper ['ʃɒpə*] *n* personne *f* qui fait ses courses, acheteur/euse.
shopping ['ʃɒpɪŋ] *n* (*goods*) achats *mpl*, provisions *fpl*.
shopping bag *n* sac *m* (à provisions).
shopping centre *n* centre commercial.
shopping mall *n* centre commercial.
shop-soiled ['ʃɒpsɔɪld] *adj* défraîchi(e), qui a fait la vitrine.
shop steward *n* (*BRIT INDUSTRY*) délégué/e syndical(e).
shop window *n* vitrine *f*.
shore [ʃɔː*] *n* (*of sea, lake*) rivage *m*, rive *f* ♦ *vt*: **to ~ (up)** étayer; **on ~** à terre.
shore leave *n* (*NAUT*) permission *f* à terre.
shorn [ʃɔːn] *pp of* **shear** ♦ *adj*: **~ of** dépouillé(e) de.
short [ʃɔːt] *adj* (*not long*) court(e); (*soon finished*) court, bref(brève); (*person, step*) petit(e); (*curt*) brusque, sec(sèche); (*insufficient*) insuffisant(e) ♦ *n* (*also*: **~ film**) court métrage; **to be ~ of sth** être à court de *or* manquer de qch; **to be in ~ supply** manquer, être difficile à trouver; **I'm 3 ~** il m'en manque 3; **in ~** bref; en bref; **~ of doing** à moins de faire; **everything ~ of** tout sauf; **it is ~ for** c'est l'abréviation *or* le diminutif de; **a ~ time ago** il y a peu de temps; **in the ~ term** à court terme; **to cut ~** (*speech, visit*) abréger, écourter; (*person*) couper la parole à; **to fall ~ of** ne pas être à la hauteur de; **to stop ~** s'arrêter net; **to stop ~ of** ne pas aller jusqu'à.
shortage ['ʃɔːtɪdʒ] *n* manque *m*, pénurie *f*.
shortbread ['ʃɔːtbred] *n* ≈ sablé *m*.
short-change [ʃɔːt'tʃeɪndʒ] *vt*: **to ~ sb** ne pas rendre assez à qn.
short-circuit [ʃɔːt'sɜːkɪt] *n* court-circuit *m* ♦ *vt* court-circuiter ♦ *vi* se mettre en court-circuit.
shortcoming ['ʃɔːtkʌmɪŋ] *n* défaut *m*.
short(crust) pastry ['ʃɔːt(krʌst)-] *n* (*BRIT*) pâte brisée.
shortcut ['ʃɔːtkʌt] *n* raccourci *m*.
shorten ['ʃɔːtn] *vt* raccourcir; (*text, visit*) abréger.
shortening ['ʃɔːtnɪŋ] *n* (*CULIN*) matière grasse.
shortfall ['ʃɔːtfɔːl] *n* déficit *m*.
shorthand ['ʃɔːthænd] *n* (*BRIT*) sténo(graphie) *f*; **to take sth down in ~** prendre qch en sténo.
shorthand notebook *n* bloc *m* sténo.
shorthand typist *n* (*BRIT*) sténodactylo *m/f*.
short list *n* (*BRIT: for job*) liste *f* des candidats sélectionnés.
short-lived ['ʃɔːt'lɪvd] *adj* de courte durée.

shortly ['ʃɔːtlɪ] *adv* bientôt, sous peu.
shortness ['ʃɔːtnɪs] *n* brièveté *f*.
shorts [ʃɔːts] *npl* (*also*: **a pair of ~**) un short.
short-sighted [ʃɔːt'saɪtɪd] *adj* (*BRIT*) myope; (*fig*) qui manque de clairvoyance.
short-staffed [ʃɔːt'stɑːft] *adj* à court de personnel.
short story *n* nouvelle *f*.
short-tempered [ʃɔːt'tempəd] *adj* qui s'emporte facilement.
short-term ['ʃɔːttɜːm] *adj* (*effect*) à court terme.
short time *n*: **to work ~, to be on ~** (*INDUSTRY*) être en chômage partiel, travailler à horaire réduit.
short wave *n* (*RADIO*) ondes courtes.
shot [ʃɒt] *pt, pp of* **shoot** ♦ *n* coup *m* (de feu); (*shotgun pellets*) plombs *mpl*; (*person*) tireur *m*; (*try*) coup, essai *m*; (*injection*) piqûre *f*; (*PHOT*) photo *f*; **to fire a ~ at sb/sth** tirer sur qn/qch; **to have a ~ at (doing) sth** essayer de faire qch; **like a ~** comme une flèche; (*very readily*) sans hésiter; **to get ~ of sb/sth** (*col*) se débarrasser de qn/qch; **a big ~** (*col*) un gros bonnet.
shotgun ['ʃɒtgʌn] *n* fusil *m* de chasse.
should [ʃud] *aux vb*: **I ~ go now** je devrais partir maintenant; **he ~ be there now** il devrait être arrivé maintenant; **I ~ go if I were you** si j'étais vous j'irais; **I ~ like to** j'aimerais bien, volontiers; **~ he phone ...** si jamais il téléphone ....
shoulder ['ʃəʊldə*] *n* épaule *f*; (*BRIT: of road*): **hard ~** accotement *m* ♦ *vt* (*fig*) endosser, se charger de; **to look over one's ~** regarder derrière soi (en tournant la tête); **to rub ~s with sb** (*fig*) côtoyer qn; **to give sb the cold ~** (*fig*) battre froid à qn.
shoulder bag *n* sac *m* à bandoulière.
shoulder blade *n* omoplate *f*.
shoulder strap *n* bretelle *f*.
shouldn't ['ʃudnt] = **should not**.
shout [ʃaut] *n* cri *m* ♦ *vt* crier ♦ *vi* crier, pousser des cris; **to give sb a ~** appeler qn.
▶**shout down** *vt* huer.
shouting ['ʃautɪŋ] *n* cris *mpl*.
shouting match *n* (*col*) engueulade *f*, empoignade *f*.
shove [ʃʌv] *vt* pousser; (*col: put*): **to ~ sth in** fourrer *or* ficher qch dans ♦ *n* poussée *f*; **he ~d me out of the way** il m'a écarté en me poussant.
▶**shove off** *vi* (*NAUT*) pousser au large; (*fig: col*) ficher le camp.
shovel ['ʃʌvl] *n* pelle *f* ♦ *vt* pelleter, enlever (*or* enfourner) à la pelle.
show [ʃəʊ] *n* (*of emotion*) manifestation *f*, démonstration *f*; (*semblance*) semblant *m*, apparence *f*; (*exhibition*) exposition *f*, salon *m*; (*THEAT*) spectacle *m*, représentation *f*; (*CINE*) séance *f* ♦ *vb* (*pt* ~**ed**, *pp* **shown** [ʃəʊn]) *vt* montrer; (*courage etc*) faire preuve de,

manifester; (*exhibit*) exposer ♦ *vi* se voir,
être visible; **to ask for a ~ of hands**
demander que l'on vote à main levée; **to be
on ~** être exposé(e); **it's just for ~** c'est
juste pour l'effet; **who's running the ~
here?** (*col*) qui est-ce qui commande ici?; **to
~ sb to his seat/to the door** accompagner
qn jusqu'à sa place/la porte; **to ~ a profit/
loss** (*COMM*) indiquer un bénéfice/une perte;
it just goes to ~ that ... ça prouve bien
que ....
►**show in** *vt* faire entrer.
►**show off** *vi* (*pej*) crâner ♦ *vt* (*display*) faire
valoir; (*pej*) faire étalage de.
►**show out** *vt* reconduire à la porte.
►**show up** *vi* (*stand out*) ressortir; (*col: turn
up*) se montrer ♦ *vt* démontrer; (*unmask*)
démasquer, dénoncer.
showbiz ['ʃəubɪz] *n* (*col*) showbiz *m*.
show business *n* le monde du spectacle.
showcase ['ʃəukeɪs] *n* vitrine *f*.
showdown ['ʃəudaun] *n* épreuve *f* de force.
shower ['ʃauə*] *n* (*also:* ~ **bath**) douche *f*;
(*rain*) averse *f*; (*of stones etc*) pluie *f*, grêle *f*;
(*US: party*) réunion organisée pour la remise
de cadeaux ♦ *vi* prendre une douche, se
doucher ♦ *vt*: **to ~ sb with** (*gifts etc*) combler
qn de; (*abuse etc*) accabler qn de; (*missiles*)
bombarder qn de; **to have** *or* **take a ~**
prendre une douche, se doucher.
shower cap *n* bonnet *m* de douche.
showerproof ['ʃauəpruːf] *adj* imperméable.
showery ['ʃauərɪ] *adj* (*weather*)
pluvieux(euse).
showground ['ʃəugraund] *n* champ *m* de
foire.
showing ['ʃəuɪŋ] *n* (*of film*) projection *f*.
show jumping [-dʒʌmpɪŋ] *n* concours *m*
hippique.
showman ['ʃəumən] *n* (*at fair, circus*) forain *m*;
(*fig*) comédien *m*.
showmanship ['ʃəumənʃɪp] *n* art *m* de la
mise en scène.
shown ['ʃəun] *pp of* **show**.
show-off ['ʃəuɔf] *n* (*col: person*) crâneur/euse,
m'as-tu-vu/e.
showpiece ['ʃəupiːs] *n* (*of exhibition etc*) joyau
m, clou *m*; **that hospital is a ~** cet hôpital est
un modèle du genre.
showroom ['ʃəurum] *n* magasin *m or* salle *f*
d'exposition.
show trial *n* grand procès *m* médiatique (*qui
fait un exemple*).
showy ['ʃəuɪ] *adj* tapageur(euse).
shrank [ʃræŋk] *pt of* **shrink**.
shrapnel ['ʃræpnl] *n* éclats *mpl* d'obus.
shred [ʃrɛd] *n* (*gen pl*) lambeau *m*, petit
morceau; (*fig: of truth, evidence*) parcelle *f*
♦ *vt* mettre en lambeaux, déchirer;
(*documents*) détruire; (*CULIN*) râper; couper
en lanières.
shredder ['ʃrɛdə*] *n* (*for vegetables*) râpeur *m*;

(*for documents, papers*) déchiqueteuse *f*.
shrewd [ʃruːd] *adj* astucieux(euse),
perspicace.
shrewdness ['ʃruːdnɪs] *n* perspicacité *f*.
shriek [ʃriːk] *n* cri perçant *or* aigu, hurlement
m ♦ *vt, vi* hurler, crier.
shrift [ʃrɪft] *n*: **to give sb short ~** expédier qn
sans ménagements.
shrill [ʃrɪl] *adj* perçant(e), aigu(ë), strident(e).
shrimp [ʃrɪmp] *n* crevette grise.
shrine [ʃraɪn] *n* châsse *f*; (*place*) lieu *m* de
pèlerinage.
shrink [ʃrɪŋk], *pt* **shrank**, *pp* **shrunk** [ʃrɪŋk, ʃræŋk,
ʃrʌŋk] *vi* rétrécir; (*fig*) se réduire; se
contracter ♦ *vt* (*wool*) (faire) rétrécir ♦ *n*
(*col: pej*) psychanalyste *m/f*; **to ~ from
(doing) sth** reculer devant (la pensée de
faire) qch.
shrinkage ['ʃrɪŋkɪdʒ] *n* (*of clothes*)
rétrécissement *m*.
shrink-wrap ['ʃrɪŋkræp] *vt* emballer sous film
plastique.
shrivel ['ʃrɪvl] (*also:* ~ **up**) *vt* ratatiner, flétrir
♦ *vi* se ratatiner, se flétrir.
shroud [ʃraud] *n* linceul *m* ♦ *vt*: **~ed in mystery**
enveloppé(e) de mystère.
Shrove Tuesday ['ʃrəuv-] *n* (le) Mardi gras.
shrub [ʃrʌb] *n* arbuste *m*.
shrubbery ['ʃrʌbərɪ] *n* massif *m* d'arbustes.
shrug [ʃrʌg] *n* haussement *m* d'épaules ♦ *vt, vi*:
to ~ (one's shoulders) hausser les épaules.
►**shrug off** *vt* faire fi de; (*cold, illness*) se
débarrasser de.
shrunk [ʃrʌŋk] *pp of* **shrink**.
shrunken ['ʃrʌŋkn] *adj* ratatiné(e).
shudder ['ʃʌdə*] *n* frisson *m*, frémissement *m*
♦ *vi* frissonner, frémir.
shuffle ['ʃʌfl] *vt* (*cards*) battre; **to ~ (one's
feet)** traîner les pieds.
shun [ʃʌn] *vt* éviter, fuir.
shunt [ʃʌnt] *vt* (*RAIL: direct*) aiguiller; (*: divert*)
détourner ♦ *vi*: **to ~ (to and fro)** faire la
navette.
shunting yard ['ʃʌntɪŋ-] *n* voies *fpl* de garage
or de triage.
shush [ʃuʃ] *excl* chut!
shut [ʃʌt], *pt, pp* **shut** [ʃʌt] *vt* fermer ♦ *vi* (se)
fermer.
►**shut down** *vt* fermer définitivement;
(*machine*) arrêter ♦ *vi* fermer
définitivement.
►**shut off** *vt* couper, arrêter.
►**shut out** *vt* (*person, cold*) empêcher
d'entrer; (*noise*) éviter d'entendre; (*block:
view*) boucher; (*: memory of sth*) chasser de
son esprit.
►**shut up** *vi* (*col: keep quiet*) se taire ♦ *vt*
(*close*) fermer; (*silence*) faire taire.
shutdown ['ʃʌtdaun] *n* fermeture *f*.
shutter ['ʃʌtə*] *n* volet *m*; (*PHOT*) obturateur
m.
shuttle ['ʃʌtl] *n* navette *f*; (*also:* ~ **service**)

(service *m* de) navette *f* ♦ *vi* (*vehicle, person*) faire la navette ♦ *vt* (*passengers*) transporter par un système de navette.

shuttlecock ['ʃʌtlkɔk] *n* volant *m* (*de badminton*).

shuttle diplomacy *n* navettes *fpl* diplomatiques.

shy [ʃaɪ] *adj* timide; **to fight** ~ **of** se dérober devant; **to be** ~ **of doing sth** hésiter à faire qch, ne pas oser faire qch ♦ *vi*: **to** ~ **away from doing sth** (*fig*) craindre de faire qch.

shyness ['ʃaɪnɪs] *n* timidité *f*.

Siam [saɪ'æm] *n* Siam *m*.

Siamese [saɪə'miːz] *adj*: ~ **cat** chat siamois *mpl*; ~ **twins** (frères *mpl*) siamois *mpl*, (sœurs *fpl*) siamoises *fpl*.

Siberia [saɪ'bɪərɪə] *n* Sibérie *f*.

siblings ['sɪblɪŋz] *npl* (*formal*) enfants *mpl* d'un même couple.

Sicilian [sɪ'sɪlɪən] *adj* sicilien(ne) ♦ *n* Sicilien/ ne.

Sicily ['sɪsɪlɪ] *n* Sicile *f*.

sick [sɪk] *adj* (*ill*) malade; (*vomiting*): **to be** ~ vomir; (*humour*) noir(e), macabre; **to feel** ~ avoir envie de vomir, avoir mal au cœur; **to fall** ~ tomber malade; **to be (off)** ~ être absent(e) pour cause de maladie; **a** ~ **person** un(e) malade; **to be** ~ **of** (*fig*) en avoir assez de.

sickbag ['sɪkbæg] *n* sac *m* vomitoire.

sick bay *n* infirmerie *f*.

sick building syndrome *n* maladie dûe à la climatisation, l'éclairage artificiel etc des bureaux.

sicken ['sɪkn] *vt* écœurer ♦ *vi*: **to be** ~**ing for sth** (*cold, flu etc*) couver qch.

sickening ['sɪknɪŋ] *adj* (*fig*) écœurant(e), révoltant(e), répugnant(e).

sickle ['sɪkl] *n* faucille *f*.

sick leave *n* congé *m* de maladie.

sickle-cell anaemia ['sɪklsɛl-] *n* anémie *f* à hématies falciformes, drépanocytose *f*.

sickly ['sɪklɪ] *adj* maladif(ive), souffre-teux(euse); (*causing nausea*) écœurant(e).

sickness ['sɪknɪs] *n* maladie *f*; (*vomiting*) vomissement(s) *m(pl)*.

sickness benefit *n* (prestations *fpl* de l')assurance-maladie *f*.

sick pay *n* indemnité *f* de maladie (*versée par l'employeur*).

sickroom ['sɪkruːm] *n* infirmerie *f*.

side [saɪd] *n* côté *m*; (*of animal*) flanc *m*; (*of lake, road*) bord *m*; (*of mountain*) versant *m*; (*fig: aspect*) côté, aspect *m*; (*team: SPORT*) équipe *f* ♦ *cpd* (*door, entrance*) latéral(e) ♦ *vi*: **to** ~ **with sb** prendre le parti de qn, se ranger du côté de qn; **by the** ~ **of** au bord de; ~ **by** ~ côte à côte; **the right/wrong** ~ le bon/mauvais côté, l'endroit/l'envers *m*; **they are on our** ~ ils sont avec nous; **from all** ~**s** de tous côtés; **to take** ~**s (with)** prendre parti (pour); **a** ~ **of beef** ≈ un quartier de bœuf.

sideboard ['saɪdbɔːd] *n* buffet *m*.

sideboards ['saɪdbɔːdz] (*BRIT*), **sideburns** ['saɪdbɔːnz] *npl* (*whiskers*) pattes *fpl*.

sidecar ['saɪdkɑː*] *n* side-car *m*.

side dish *n* (plat *m* d')accompagnement *m*.

side drum *n* (*MUS*) tambour plat, caisse claire.

side effect *n* (*MED*) effet *m* secondaire.

sidekick ['saɪdkɪk] *n* (*col*) sous-fifre *m*.

sidelight ['saɪdlaɪt] *n* (*AUT*) veilleuse *f*.

sideline ['saɪdlaɪn] *n* (*SPORT*) (ligne *f* de) touche *f*; (*fig*) activité *f* secondaire.

sidelong ['saɪdlɔŋ] *adj*: **to give sb a** ~ **glance** regarder qn du coin de l'œil.

side plate *n* petite assiette.

side road *n* petite route, route transversale.

sidesaddle ['saɪdsædl] *adv* en amazone.

side show *n* attraction *f*.

sidestep ['saɪdstɛp] *vt* (*question*) éluder; (*problem*) éviter ♦ *vi* (*BOXING etc*) esquiver.

side street *n* rue transversale.

sidetrack ['saɪdtræk] *vt* (*fig*) faire dévier de son sujet.

sidewalk ['saɪdwɔːk] *n* (*US*) trottoir *m*.

sideways ['saɪdweɪz] *adv* de côté.

siding ['saɪdɪŋ] *n* (*RAIL*) voie *f* de garage.

sidle ['saɪdl] *vi*: **to** ~ **up (to)** s'approcher furtivement (de).

SIDS [sɪdz] *n abbr* (= *sudden infant death syndrome*) mort subite du nourrisson, mort *f* au berceau.

siege [siːdʒ] *n* siège *m*; **to lay** ~ **to** assiéger.

siege economy *n* économie *f* de (temps de) siège.

Sierra Leone [sɪ'ɛrəlɪ'əun] *n* Sierra Leone *f*.

sieve [sɪv] *n* tamis *m*, passoire *f* ♦ *vt* tamiser, passer (au tamis).

sift [sɪft] *vt* passer au tamis *or* au crible; (*fig*) passer au crible ♦ *vi* (*fig*): **to** ~ **through** passer en revue.

sigh [saɪ] *n* soupir *m* ♦ *vi* soupirer, pousser un soupir.

sight [saɪt] *n* (*faculty*) vue *f*; (*spectacle*) spectacle *m*; (*on gun*) mire *f* ♦ *vt* apercevoir; **in** ~ visible; (*fig*) en vue; **out of** ~ hors de vue; **at** ~ (*COMM*) à vue; **at first** ~ à première vue, au premier abord; **I know her by** ~ je la connais de vue; **to catch** ~ **of sb/ sth** apercevoir qn/qch; **to lose** ~ **of sb/sth** perdre qn/qch de vue; **to set one's** ~**s on sth** jeter son dévolu sur qch.

sighted ['saɪtɪd] *adj* qui voit; **partially** ~ qui a un certain degré de vision.

sightseeing ['saɪtsiːɪŋ] *n* tourisme *m*; **to go** ~ faire du tourisme.

sightseer ['saɪtsiːə*] *n* touriste *m/f*.

sign [saɪn] *n* (*gen*) signe *m*; (*with hand etc*) signe, geste *m*; (*notice*) panneau *m*, écriteau *m*; (*also: road* ~) panneau de signalisation ♦ *vt* signer; **as a** ~ **of** en signe de; **it's a good/bad** ~ c'est bon/mauvais signe; **plus/ minus** ~ signe plus/moins; **there's no** ~ **of a**

change of mind rien ne laisse présager un revirement; **he was showing ~s of improvement** il commençait visiblement à faire des progrès; **to ~ one's name** signer.
►**sign away** _vt_ (_rights etc_) renoncer officiellement à.
►**sign in** _vi_ signer le registre (en arrivant).
►**sign off** _vi_ (_RADIO, TV_) terminer l'émission.
►**sign on** _vi_ (_MIL_) s'engager; (_as unemployed_) s'inscrire au chômage; (_enrol_): **to ~ on for a course** s'inscrire pour un cours ♦ _vt_ (_MIL_) engager; (_employee_) embaucher.
►**sign out** _vi_ signer le registre (en partant).
►**sign over** _vt_: **to ~ sth over to sb** céder qch par écrit à qn.
►**sign up** (_MIL_) _vt_ engager ♦ _vi_ s'engager.
signal ['sɪgnl] _n_ signal _m_ ♦ _vi_ (_AUT_) mettre son clignotant ♦ _vt_ (_person_) faire signe à; (_message_) communiquer par signaux; **to ~ a left/right turn** (_AUT_) indiquer _or_ signaler que l'on tourne à gauche/droite; **to ~ to sb (to do sth)** faire signe à qn (de faire qch).
signal box _n_ (_RAIL_) poste _m_ d'aiguillage.
signalman ['sɪgnlmən] _n_ (_RAIL_) aiguilleur _m_.
signatory ['sɪgnətərɪ] _n_ signataire _m/f_.
signature ['sɪgnətʃə*] _n_ signature _f_.
signature tune _n_ indicatif musical.
signet ring ['sɪgnət-] _n_ chevalière _f_.
significance [sɪg'nɪfɪkəns] _n_ signification _f_; importance _f_; **that is of no ~** ceci n'a pas d'importance.
significant [sɪg'nɪfɪkənt] _adj_ significatif(ive); (_important_) important(e), considérable.
significantly [sɪg'nɪfɪkəntlɪ] _adv_ (_improve, increase_) sensiblement; (_smile_) d'un air entendu, éloquemment; **~, ...** fait significatif, ...
signify ['sɪgnɪfaɪ] _vt_ signifier.
sign language _n_ langage _m_ par signes.
signpost ['saɪnpəust] _n_ poteau indicateur.
silage ['saɪlɪdʒ] _n_ (_fodder_) fourrage vert; (_method_) ensilage _m_.
silence ['saɪlns] _n_ silence _m_ ♦ _vt_ faire taire, réduire au silence.
silencer ['saɪlənsə*] _n_ (_on gun, BRIT AUT_) silencieux _m_.
silent ['saɪlnt] _adj_ silencieux(euse); (_film_) muet(te); **to keep** _or_ **remain ~** garder le silence, ne rien dire.
silently ['saɪlntlɪ] _adv_ silencieusement.
silent partner _n_ (_COMM_) bailleur _m_ de fonds, commanditaire _m_.
silhouette [sɪlu:'ɛt] _n_ silhouette _f_ ♦ _vt_: **~d against** se profilant sur, se découpant contre.
silicon ['sɪlɪkən] _n_ silicium _m_.
silicon chip _n_ puce _f_ électronique.
silicone ['sɪlɪkəun] _n_ silicone _f_.
silk [sɪlk] _n_ soie _f_ ♦ _cpd_ de _or_ en soie.
silky ['sɪlkɪ] _adj_ soyeux(euse).
sill [sɪl] _n_ (_also:_ **window~**) rebord _m_ (de la fenêtre); (_of door_) seuil _m_; (_AUT_) bas _m_ de

marche.
silly ['sɪlɪ] _adj_ stupide, sot(te), bête; **to do something ~** faire une bêtise.
silo ['saɪləu] _n_ silo _m_.
silt [sɪlt] _n_ vase _f_; limon _m_.
silver ['sɪlvə*] _n_ argent _m_; (_money_) monnaie _f_ (en pièces d'argent); (_also:_ **~ware**) argenterie _f_ ♦ _cpd_ d'argent, en argent.
silver paper (_BRIT_), **silver foil** _n_ papier _m_ d'argent _or_ d'étain.
silver-plated [sɪlvə'pleɪtɪd] _adj_ plaqué(e) argent.
silversmith ['sɪlvəsmɪθ] _n_ orfèvre _m/f_.
silverware ['sɪlvəwɛə*] _n_ argenterie _f_.
silver wedding (anniversary) _n_ noces _fpl_ d'argent.
silvery ['sɪlvrɪ] _adj_ argenté(e).
similar ['sɪmɪlə*] _adj_: **~ (to)** semblable (à).
similarity [sɪmɪ'lærɪtɪ] _n_ ressemblance _f_, similarité _f_.
similarly ['sɪmɪləlɪ] _adv_ de la même façon, de même.
simile ['sɪmɪlɪ] _n_ comparaison _f_.
simmer ['sɪmə*] _vi_ cuire à feu doux, mijoter.
►**simmer down** _vi_ (_fig: col_) se calmer.
simper ['sɪmpə*] _vi_ minauder.
simpering ['sɪmpərɪŋ] _adj_ stupide.
simple ['sɪmpl] _adj_ simple; **the ~ truth** la vérité pure et simple.
simple interest _n_ (_MATH, COMM_) intérêts _mpl_ simples.
simple-minded [sɪmpl'maɪndɪd] _adj_ simplet(te), simple d'esprit.
simpleton ['sɪmpltən] _n_ nigaud/e, niais/e.
simplicity [sɪm'plɪsɪtɪ] _n_ simplicité _f_.
simplification [sɪmplɪfɪ'keɪʃən] _n_ simplification _f_.
simplify ['sɪmplɪfaɪ] _vt_ simplifier.
simply ['sɪmplɪ] _adv_ simplement; (_without fuss_) avec simplicité.
simulate ['sɪmjuleɪt] _vt_ simuler, feindre.
simulation [sɪmju'leɪʃən] _n_ simulation _f_.
simultaneous [sɪməl'teɪnɪəs] _adj_ simultané(e).
simultaneously [sɪməl'teɪnɪəslɪ] _adv_ simultanément.
sin [sɪn] _n_ péché _m_ ♦ _vi_ pécher.
Sinai ['saɪneɪaɪ] _n_ Sinaï _m_.
since [sɪns] _adv, prep_ depuis ♦ _conj_ (_time_) depuis que; (_because_) puisque, étant donné que, comme; **~ then** depuis ce moment-là; **~ Monday** depuis lundi; **(ever) ~ I arrived** depuis mon arrivée, depuis que je suis arrivé.
sincere [sɪn'sɪə*] _adj_ sincère.
sincerely [sɪn'sɪəlɪ] _adv_ sincèrement; **Yours ~** (_at end of letter_) veuillez agréer, Monsieur (_or_ Madame), l'expression de mes sentiments distingués _or_ les meilleurs.
sincerity [sɪn'sɛrɪtɪ] _n_ sincérité _f_.
sine [saɪn] _n_ (_MATH_) sinus _m_.
sinew ['sɪnju:] _n_ tendon _m_; **~s** _npl_ muscles _mpl_
sinful ['sɪnful] _adj_ coupable.

sing, *pt* **sang,** *pp* **sung** [sɪŋ, sæŋ, sʌŋ] *vt, vi* chanter.

Singapore [sɪŋgə'pɔː*] *n* Singapour *m*.

singe [sɪndʒ] *vt* brûler légèrement; (*clothes*) roussir.

singer ['sɪŋə*] *n* chanteur/euse.

Singhalese [sɪŋə'liːz] *adj* = Sinhalese.

singing ['sɪŋɪŋ] *n* (*of person, bird*) chant *m*; façon *f* de chanter; (*of kettle, bullet, in ears*) sifflement *m*.

single ['sɪŋgl] *adj* seul(e), unique; (*unmarried*) célibataire; (*not double*) simple ♦ *n* (*BRIT*: *also*: ~ **ticket**) aller *m* (simple); (*record*) 45 tours *m*; **not a** ~ **one was left** il n'en est pas resté un(e) seul(e); **every** ~ **day** chaque jour sans exception.
► **single out** *vt* choisir; distinguer.

single bed *n* lit *m* à une place.

single-breasted ['sɪŋglbrɛstɪd] *adj* droit(e).

Single European Market *n*: **the** ~ le marché unique européen.

single file *n*: **in** ~ en file indienne.

single-handed [sɪŋgl'hændɪd] *adv* tout(e) seul(e), sans (aucune) aide.

single-minded [sɪŋgl'maɪndɪd] *adj* résolu(e), tenace.

single parent *n* parent unique (*or* célibataire).

single room *n* chambre *f* à un lit *or* pour une personne.

singles ['sɪŋglz] *npl* (*TENNIS*) simple *m*; (*US*: *single people*) célibataires *m/fpl*.

singles bar *n* (*esp US*) bar *m* de rencontres pour célibataires.

single-sex school [sɪŋgl'sɛks-] *n* école *f* non mixte.

singlet ['sɪŋglɪt] *n* tricot *m* de corps.

singly ['sɪŋglɪ] *adv* séparément.

singsong ['sɪŋsɔŋ] *adj* (*tone*) chantant(e) ♦ *n* (*songs*): **to have a** ~ chanter quelque chose (ensemble).

singular ['sɪŋgjulə*] *adj* singulier(ière); (*odd*) singulier, étrange; (*LING*) (au) singulier, du singulier ♦ *n* (*LING*) singulier *m*; **in the feminine** ~ au féminin singulier.

singularly ['sɪŋgjuləlɪ] *adv* singulièrement; étrangement.

Sinhalese [sɪnhə'liːz] *adj* cingalais(e).

sinister ['sɪnɪstə*] *adj* sinistre.

sink [sɪŋk] *n* évier *m* ♦ *vb* (*pt* **sank,** *pp* **sunk** [sæŋk, sʌŋk]) *vt* (*ship*) (faire) couler, faire sombrer; (*foundations*) creuser; (*piles etc*): **to** ~ **sth into** enfoncer qch dans ♦ *vi* couler, sombrer; (*ground etc*) s'affaisser; **he sank into a chair/the mud** il s'est enfoncé dans un fauteuil/la boue; **a** ~**ing feeling** un serrement de cœur.
► **sink in** *vi* s'enfoncer, pénétrer; (*explanation*): **it took a long time to** ~ **in** il a fallu longtemps pour que ça rentre.

sinking ['sɪŋkɪŋ] *adj*: **that** ~ **feeling** un serrement de cœur.

sinking fund *n* fonds *mpl* d'amortissement.

sink unit *n* bloc-évier *m*.

sinner ['sɪnə*] *n* pécheur/eresse.

Sinn Féin [ʃɪn'feɪn] *n* Sinn Féin *m* (*parti politique irlandais qui soutient l'IRA*).

Sino- ['saɪnəu] *prefix* sino-.

sinuous ['sɪnjuəs] *adj* sinueux(euse).

sinus ['saɪnəs] *n* (*ANAT*) sinus *m inv*.

sip [sɪp] *n* petite gorgée ♦ *vt* boire à petites gorgées.

siphon ['saɪfən] *n* siphon *m* ♦ *vt* (*also*: ~ **off**) siphonner; (: *fig: funds*) transférer; (: *illegally*) détourner.

sir [sə*] *n* monsieur *m*; **S~ John Smith** sir John Smith; **yes** ~ oui Monsieur; **Dear S~** (*in letter*) Monsieur.

siren ['saɪərn] *n* sirène *f*.

sirloin ['səːlɔɪn] *n* aloyau *m*.

sirloin steak *n* bifteck *m* dans l'aloyau.

sirocco [sɪ'rɔkəu] *n* sirocco *m*.

sisal ['saɪsəl] *n* sisal *m*.

sissy ['sɪsɪ] *n* (*col: coward*) poule mouillée.

sister ['sɪstə*] *n* sœur *f*; (*nun*) religieuse *f*, (bonne) sœur; (*BRIT*: *nurse*) infirmière *f* en chef ♦ *cpd*: ~ **organization** organisation *f* sœur; ~ **ship** sister(-)ship *m*.

sister-in-law ['sɪstərɪnlɔː] *n* belle-sœur *f*.

sit, *pt, pp* **sat** [sɪt, sæt] *vi* s'asseoir; (*assembly*) être en séance, siéger; (*for painter*) poser; (*dress etc*) tomber ♦ *vt* (*exam*) passer, se présenter à; **to** ~ **on a committee** faire partie d'un comité; **to** ~ **tight** ne pas bouger.
► **sit about, sit around** *vi* être assis(e) *or* rester à ne rien faire.
► **sit back** *vi* (*in seat*) bien s'installer, se carrer.
► **sit down** *vi* s'asseoir; **to be** ~**ting down** être assis(e).
► **sit in** *vi*: **to** ~ **in on a discussion** assister à une discussion.
► **sit up** *vi* s'asseoir; (*not go to bed*) rester debout, ne pas se coucher.

sitcom ['sɪtkɔm] *n abbr* (*TV*: = *situation comedy*) série *f* comique.

sit-down ['sɪtdaun] *adj*: **a** ~ **strike** une grève sur le tas; **a** ~ **meal** un repas assis.

site [saɪt] *n* emplacement *m*, site *m*; (*also*: **building** ~) chantier *m* ♦ *vt* placer.

sit-in ['sɪtɪn] *n* (*demonstration*) sit-in *m inv*, occupation *f* de locaux.

siting ['saɪtɪŋ] *n* (*location*) emplacement *m*.

sitter ['sɪtə*] *n* (*for painter*) modèle *m*; (*also*: **baby**~) baby-sitter *m/f*.

sitting ['sɪtɪŋ] *n* (*of assembly etc*) séance *f*; (*in canteen*) service *m*.

sitting member *n* (*POL*) parlementaire *m/f* en exercice.

sitting room *n* salon *m*.

sitting tenant *n* (*BRIT*) locataire occupant(e).

situate ['sɪtjueɪt] *vt* situer.

situated ['sɪtjueɪtɪd] *adj* situé(e).
situation [sɪtju'eɪʃən] *n* situation *f*; *"~s*
vacant/wanted" (*BRIT*) "offres/demandes
d'emploi".
situation comedy *n* (*THEAT*) comédie *f* de
situation.
six [sɪks] *num* six.
six-pack ['sɪkspæk] *n* (*esp US*) pack *m* de six
canettes.
sixteen [sɪks'tiːn] *num* seize.
sixth ['sɪksθ] *adj* sixième; **the upper/lower** ~
(*BRIT SCOL*) la terminale/la première.
sixty ['sɪkstɪ] *num* soixante.
size [saɪz] *n* dimensions *fpl*; (*of person*) taille *f*;
(*of estate, area*) étendue *f*; (*of problem*)
ampleur *f*; (*of company*) importance *f*; (*of
clothing*) taille; (*of shoes*) pointure *f*; (*glue*)
colle *f*; **I take** ~ **14** (*of dress etc*) ≈ je prends
du 42 *or* la taille 42; **the small/large** ~ (*of
soap powder etc*) le petit/grand modèle; **it's
the** ~ **of** ... c'est de la taille (*or* grosseur) de
..., c'est grand (*or* gros) comme ...; **cut to** ~
découpé(e) aux dimensions voulues.
▶**size up** *vt* juger, jauger.
sizeable ['saɪzəbl] *adj* assez grand(e) *or*
gros(se); assez important(e).
sizzle ['sɪzl] *vi* grésiller.
SK *abbr* (*Canada*) = *Saskatchewan*.
skate [skeɪt] *n* patin *m*; (*fish: pl inv*) raie *f* ♦ *vi*
patiner.
▶**skate over, skate around** *vt* (*problem,
issue*) éluder.
skateboard ['skeɪtbɔːd] *n* skateboard *m*,
planche *f* à roulettes.
skater ['skeɪtə*] *n* patineur/euse.
skating ['skeɪtɪŋ] *n* patinage *m*.
skating rink *n* patinoire *f*.
skeleton ['skɛlɪtn] *n* squelette *m*; (*outline*)
schéma *m*.
skeleton key *n* passe-partout *m*.
skeleton staff *n* effectifs réduits.
skeptic *etc* ['skɛptɪk] (*US*) = **sceptic** *etc*.
sketch [skɛtʃ] *n* (*drawing*) croquis *m*, esquisse
f; (*THEAT*) sketch *m*, saynète *f* ♦ *vt* esquisser,
faire un croquis *or* une esquisse de.
sketch book *n* carnet *m* à dessin.
sketch pad *n* bloc *m* à dessin.
sketchy ['skɛtʃɪ] *adj* incomplet(ète),
fragmentaire.
skew [skjuː] *n* (*BRIT*): **on the** ~ de travers, en
biais.
skewer ['skjuːə*] *n* brochette *f*.
ski [skiː] *n* ski *m* ♦ *vi* skier, faire du ski.
ski boot *n* chaussure *f* de ski.
skid [skɪd] *n* dérapage *m* ♦ *vi* déraper; **to go
into a** ~ déraper.
skid mark *n* trace *f* de dérapage.
skier ['skiːə*] *n* skieur/euse.
skiing ['skiːɪŋ] *n* ski *m*; **to go** ~ (aller) faire du
ski.
ski instructor *n* moniteur/trice de ski.
ski jump *n* (*ramp*) tremplin *m*; (*event*) saut *m* à

skis.
skilful, (*US*) **skillful** ['skɪlful] *adj* habile,
adroit(e).
ski lift *n* remonte-pente *m inv*.
skill [skɪl] *n* (*ability*) habileté *f*, adresse *f*, talent
m; (*art, craft*) technique(s) *f(pl)*, compétences
fpl.
skilled [skɪld] *adj* habile, adroit(e); (*worker*)
qualifié(e).
skillet ['skɪlɪt] *n* poêlon *m*.
skillful *etc* ['skɪlful] (*US*) = **skilful** *etc*.
skil(l)fully ['skɪlfəlɪ] *adv* habilement,
adroitement.
skim [skɪm] *vt* (*milk*) écrémer; (*soup*) écumer;
(*glide over*) raser, effleurer ♦ *vi*: **to** ~
through (*fig*) parcourir.
skimmed milk [skɪmd-] *n* lait écrémé.
skimp [skɪmp] *vt* (*work*) bâcler, faire à la va-
vite; (*cloth etc*) lésiner sur.
skimpy ['skɪmpɪ] *adj* étriqué(e); maigre.
skin [skɪn] *n* peau *f* ♦ *vt* (*fruit etc*) éplucher;
(*animal*) écorcher; **wet** *or* **soaked to the** ~
trempé(e) jusqu'aux os.
skin cancer *n* cancer *m* de la peau.
skin-deep ['skɪn'diːp] *adj* superficiel(le).
skin diver *n* plongeur/euse sous-marin(e).
skin diving *n* plongée sous-marine.
skinflint ['skɪnflɪnt] *n* grippe-sou *m*.
skin graft *n* greffe *f* de peau.
skinhead ['skɪnhɛd] *n* skinhead *m*.
skinny ['skɪnɪ] *adj* maigre, maigrichon(ne).
skin test *n* cuti(-réaction *f*) *f*.
skintight ['skɪntaɪt] *adj* (*dress etc*) collant(e),
ajusté(e).
skip [skɪp] *n* petit bond *or* saut; (*container*)
benne *f* ♦ *vi* gambader, sautiller; (*with rope*)
sauter à la corde ♦ *vt* (*pass over*) sauter; **to** ~
school (*esp US*) faire l'école buissonnière.
ski pants *npl* pantalon *m* de ski.
ski pole *n* bâton *m* de ski.
skipper ['skɪpə*] *n* (*NAUT, SPORT*) capitaine *m*
♦ *vt* (*boat*) commander; (*team*) être le chef
de.
skipping rope ['skɪpɪŋ-] *n* (*BRIT*) corde *f* à
sauter.
ski resort *n* station *f* de sports d'hiver.
skirmish ['skəːmɪʃ] *n* escarmouche *f*,
accrochage *m*.
skirt [skəːt] *n* jupe *f* ♦ *vt* longer, contourner.
skirting board ['skəːtɪŋ-] *n* (*BRIT*) plinthe *f*.
ski run *n* piste *f* de ski.
ski suit *n* combinaison *f* de ski.
skit [skɪt] *n* sketch *m* satirique.
ski tow *n* = **ski lift**.
skittle ['skɪtl] *n* quille *f*; ~**s** (*game*) (jeu *m* de)
quilles *fpl*.
skive [skaɪv] *vi* (*BRIT col*) tirer au flanc.
skulk [skʌlk] *vi* rôder furtivement.
skull [skʌl] *n* crâne *m*.
skullcap ['skʌlkæp] *n* calotte *f*.
skunk [skʌŋk] *n* mouffette *f*; (*fur*) sconse *m*.
sky [skaɪ] *n* ciel *m*; **to praise sb to the skies**

porter qn aux nues.

sky-blue [skaɪ'bluː] *adj* bleu ciel *inv*.

skydiving ['skaɪdaɪvɪŋ] *n* parachutisme *m* (*en chute libre*).

sky-high ['skaɪ'haɪ] *adv* très haut ♦ *adj* exorbitant(e); **prices are** ~ les prix sont exorbitants.

skylark ['skaɪlɑːk] *n* (*bird*) alouette *f* (*des champs*).

skylight ['skaɪlaɪt] *n* lucarne *f*.

skyline ['skaɪlaɪn] *n* (*horizon*) (ligne *f* d')horizon *m*; (*of city*) ligne des toits.

skyscraper ['skaɪskreɪpə*] *n* gratte-ciel *m inv*.

slab [slæb] *n* plaque *f*; dalle *f*; (*of wood*) bloc *m*; (*of meat, cheese*) tranche épaisse.

slack [slæk] *adj* (*loose*) lâche, desserré(e); (*slow*) stagnant(e); (*careless*) négligent(e), peu sérieux(euse) *or* conscientieux(euse); (*COMM: market*) peu actif(ive); (*: demand*) faible; (*period*) creux(euse) ♦ *n* (*in rope etc*) mou *m*; **business is** ~ les affaires vont mal.

slacken ['slækn] (*also*: ~ **off**) *vi* ralentir, diminuer ♦ *vt* relâcher.

slacks [slæks] *npl* pantalon *m*.

slag [slæg] *n* scories *fpl*.

slag heap *n* crassier *m*.

slain [sleɪn] *pp of* **slay**.

slake [sleɪk] *vt* (*one's thirst*) étancher.

slalom ['slɑːləm] *n* slalom *m*.

slam [slæm] *vt* (*door*) (faire) claquer; (*throw*) jeter violemment, flanquer; (*criticize*) éreinter, démolir ♦ *vi* claquer.

slammer ['slæmə*] *n* (*col*): **the** ~ la taule.

slander ['slɑːndə*] *n* calomnie *f*; (*LAW*) diffamation *f* ♦ *vt* calomnier; diffamer.

slanderous ['slɑːndrəs] *adj* calomnieux(euse); diffamatoire.

slang [slæŋ] *n* argot *m*.

slanging match ['slæŋɪŋ-] *n* (*BRIT col*) engueulade *f*, empoignade *f*.

slant [slɑːnt] *n* inclinaison *f*; (*fig*) angle *m*, point *m* de vue.

slanted ['slɑːntɪd] *adj* tendancieux(euse).

slanting ['slɑːntɪŋ] *adj* en pente, incliné(e); couché(e).

slap [slæp] *n* claque *f*, gifle *f*; (*on the back*) tape *f* ♦ *vt* donner une claque *or* une gifle (*or* une tape) à ♦ *adv* (*directly*) tout droit, en plein.

slapdash ['slæpdæʃ] *adj* (*work*) fait(e) sans soin *or* à la va-vite; (*person*) insouciant(e), négligent(e).

slaphead ['slæphɛd] *n* (*BRIT col*) abruti/e, taré/e.

slapstick ['slæpstɪk] *n* (*comedy*) grosse farce (*style tarte à la crème*).

slap-up ['slæpʌp] *adj* (*BRIT*): **a** ~ **meal** un repas extra *or* fameux.

slash [slæʃ] *vt* entailler, taillader; (*fig: prices*) casser.

slat [slæt] *n* (*of wood*) latte *f*, lame *f*.

slate [sleɪt] *n* ardoise *f* ♦ *vt* (*fig: criticize*) éreinter, démolir.

slaughter ['slɔːtə*] *n* carnage *m*, massacre *m*; (*of animals*) abattage *m* ♦ *vt* (*animal*) abattre; (*people*) massacrer.

slaughterhouse ['slɔːtəhaus] *n* abattoir *m*.

Slav [slɑːv] *adj* slave.

slave [sleɪv] *n* esclave *m/f* ♦ *vi* (*also*: ~ **away**) trimer, travailler comme un forçat; **to** ~ **(away) at sth/at doing sth** se tuer à qch/à faire qch.

slave driver *n* (*col, pej*) négrier/ière.

slave labour *n* travail *m* d'esclave; **it's just** ~ (*fig*) c'est de l'esclavage.

slaver ['slævə*] *vi* (*dribble*) baver.

slavery ['sleɪvərɪ] *n* esclavage *m*.

Slavic ['slævɪk] *adj* slave.

slavish ['sleɪvɪʃ] *adj* servile.

slavishly ['sleɪvɪʃlɪ] *adv* (*copy*) servilement.

Slavonic [slə'vɔnɪk] *adj* slave.

slay, *pt* **slew**, *pp* **slain** [sleɪ, sluː, sleɪn] *vt* (*literary*) tuer.

sleazy ['sliːzɪ] *adj* miteux(euse), minable.

sledge [slɛdʒ] *n* luge *f*.

sledgehammer ['slɛdʒhæmə*] *n* marteau *m* de forgeron.

sleek [sliːk] *adj* (*hair, fur*) brillant(e), luisant(e); (*car, boat*) aux lignes pures *or* élégantes.

sleep [sliːp] *n* sommeil *m* ♦ *vi* (*pt, pp* **slept** [slɛpt]) dormir; (*spend night*) dormir, coucher ♦ *vt*: **we can** ~ **4** on peut coucher *or* loger 4 personnes; **to go to** ~ s'endormir; **to have a good night's** ~ passer une bonne nuit; **to put to** ~ (*patient*) endormir; (*animal: euphemism: kill*) piquer; **to** ~ **lightly** avoir le sommeil léger; **to** ~ **with sb** (*euphemism*) coucher avec qn.

▶**sleep in** *vi* (*lie late*) faire la grasse matinée; (*oversleep*) se réveiller trop tard.

sleeper ['sliːpə*] *n* (*person*) dormeur/euse; (*BRIT RAIL: on track*) traverse *f*; (*: train*) train *m* de voitures-lits; (*: carriage*) wagon-lits *m*, voiture-lits *f*; (*: berth*) couchette *f*.

sleepily ['sliːpɪlɪ] *adv* d'un air endormi.

sleeping ['sliːpɪŋ] *adj* qui dort, endormi(e).

sleeping bag *n* sac *m* de couchage.

sleeping car *n* wagon-lits *m*, voiture-lits *f*.

sleeping partner *n* (*BRIT COMM*) = **silent partner**.

sleeping pill *n* somnifère *m*.

sleeping sickness *n* maladie *f* du sommeil.

sleepless ['sliːplɪs] *adj*: **a** ~ **night** une nuit blanche.

sleeplessness ['sliːplɪsnɪs] *n* insomnie *f*.

sleepwalk ['sliːpwɔːk] *vi* marcher en dormant.

sleepwalker ['sliːpwɔːkə*] *n* somnambule *m/f*.

sleepy ['sliːpɪ] *adj* qui a envie de dormir; (*fig*) endormi(e); **to be** *or* **feel** ~ avoir sommeil, avoir envie de dormir.

sleet [sliːt] *n* neige fondue.

sleeve [sliːv] *n* manche *f*; (*of record*) pochette *f*.

sleeveless ['sliːvlɪs] *adj* (*garment*) sans

manches.

sleigh [sleɪ] *n* traîneau *m*.

sleight [slaɪt] *n*: ~ **of hand** tour *m* de passe-passe.

slender ['slɛndə*] *adj* svelte, mince; (*fig*) faible, ténu(e).

slept [slɛpt] *pt*, *pp of* **sleep**.

sleuth [slu:θ] *n* (*col*) détective (privé).

slew [slu:] *vi* (*also*: ~ **round**) virer, pivoter ♦ *pt of* **slay**.

slice [slaɪs] *n* tranche *f*; (*round*) rondelle *f* ♦ *vt* couper en tranches (*or* en rondelles); ~**d bread** pain *m* en tranches.

slick [slɪk] *adj* brillant(e) en apparence; mielleux(euse) ♦ *n* (*also*: **oil** ~) nappe *f* de pétrole, marée noire.

slid [slɪd] *pt*, *pp of* **slide**.

slide [slaɪd] *n* (*in playground*) toboggan *m*; (*PHOT*) diapositive *f*; (*BRIT*: *also*: **hair** ~) barrette *f*; (*microscope* ~) (lame *f*) porte-objet *m*; (*in prices*) chute *f*, baisse *f* ♦ *vb* (*pt*, *pp* **slid** [slɪd]) *vt* (faire) glisser ♦ *vi* glisser; **to let things** ~ (*fig*) laisser les choses aller à la dérive.

slide projector *n* (*PHOT*) projecteur *m* de diapositives.

slide rule *n* règle *f* à calcul.

sliding ['slaɪdɪŋ] *adj* (*door*) coulissant(e); ~ **roof** (*AUT*) toit ouvrant.

sliding scale *n* échelle *f* mobile.

slight [slaɪt] *adj* (*slim*) mince, menu(e); (*frail*) frêle; (*trivial*) faible, insignifiant(e); (*small*) petit(e), léger(ère) (*before n*) ♦ *n* offense *f*, affront *m* ♦ *vt* (*offend*) blesser, offenser; **the** ~**est** le (*or* la) moindre; **not in the** ~**est** pas le moins du monde, pas du tout.

slightly ['slaɪtlɪ] *adv* légèrement, un peu; ~ **built** fluet(te).

slim [slɪm] *adj* mince ♦ *vi* maigrir, suivre un régime amaigrissant.

slime [slaɪm] *n* vase *f*; substance visqueuse.

slimming [slɪmɪŋ] *n* amaigrissement *m* ♦ *adj* (*diet*, *pills*) amaigrissant(e), pour maigrir.

slimy ['slaɪmɪ] *adj* visqueux(euse), gluant(e); (*covered with mud*) vaseux(euse).

sling [slɪŋ] *n* (*MED*) écharpe *f* ♦ *vt* (*pt*, *pp* **slung** [slʌŋ]) lancer, jeter; **to have one's arm in a** ~ avoir le bras en écharpe.

slink, *pt*, *pp* **slunk** [slɪŋk, slʌŋk] *vi*: **to** ~ **away** *or* **off** s'en aller furtivement.

slinky ['slɪŋkɪ] *adj* (*clothes*) moulant(e).

slip [slɪp] *n* faux pas; (*mistake*) erreur *f*, bévue *f*; (*underskirt*) combinaison *f*; (*of paper*) petite feuille, fiche *f* ♦ *vt* (*slide*) glisser ♦ *vi* (*slide*) glisser; (*move smoothly*): **to** ~ **into/out of** se glisser *or* se faufiler dans/hors de; (*decline*) baisser; **to let a chance** ~ **by** laisser passer une occasion; **to** ~ **sth on/off** enfiler/enlever qch; **it** ~**ped from her hand** cela lui a glissé des mains; **to give sb the** ~ fausser compagnie à qn; **a** ~ **of the tongue** un lapsus.

►**slip away** *vi* s'esquiver.

►**slip in** *vt* glisser.

►**slip out** *vi* sortir.

slip-on ['slɪpɔn] *adj* facile à enfiler; ~ **shoes** mocassins *mpl*.

slipped disc [slɪpt-] *n* hernie discale.

slipper ['slɪpə*] *n* pantoufle *f*.

slippery ['slɪpərɪ] *adj* glissant(e); (*fig*: *person*) insaisissable.

slip road *n* (*BRIT*: *to motorway*) bretelle *f* d'accès.

slipshod ['slɪpʃɔd] *adj* négligé(e), peu soigné(e).

slip-up ['slɪpʌp] *n* bévue *f*.

slipway ['slɪpweɪ] *n* cale *f* (de construction *or* de lancement).

slit [slɪt] *n* fente *f*; (*cut*) incision *f*; (*tear*) déchirure *f* ♦ *vt* (*pt*, *pp* **slit**) fendre; couper; inciser; déchirer; **to** ~ **sb's throat** trancher la gorge à qn.

slither ['slɪðə*] *vi* glisser, déraper.

sliver ['slɪvə*] *n* (*of glass*, *wood*) éclat *m*; (*of cheese*, *sausage*) petit morceau.

slob [slɔb] *n* (*col*) rustaud/e.

slog [slɔg] *n* (*BRIT*) gros effort; tâche fastidieuse ♦ *vi* travailler très dur.

slogan ['sləugən] *n* slogan *m*.

slop [slɔp] *vi* (*also*: ~ **over**) se renverser; déborder ♦ *vt* répandre; renverser.

slope [sləup] *n* pente *f*; (*side of mountain*) versant *m*; (*slant*) inclinaison *f* ♦ *vi*: **to** ~ **down** être *or* descendre en pente; **to** ~ **up** monter.

sloping ['sləupɪŋ] *adj* en pente, incliné(e); (*handwriting*) penché(e).

sloppy ['slɔpɪ] *adj* (*work*) peu soigné(e), bâclé(e); (*appearance*) négligé(e), débraillé(e); (*film etc*) sentimental(e).

slosh [slɔʃ] *vi* (*col*): **to** ~ **about** *or* **around** (*children*) patauger; (*liquid*) clapoter.

sloshed [slɔʃt] *adj* (*col*: *drunk*) bourré(e).

slot [slɔt] *n* fente *f*; (*fig*: *in timetable*, *RADIO*, *TV*) créneau *m*, plage *f* ♦ *vt*: **to** ~ **into** encastrer *or* insérer dans ♦ *vi*: **to** ~ **into** s'encastrer *or* s'insérer dans.

sloth [sləuθ] *n* (*vice*) paresse *f*; (*ZOOL*) paresseux *m*.

slot machine *n* (*BRIT*: *vending machine*) distributeur *m* (automatique), machine *f* à sous; (*for gambling*) appareil *m* or machine à sous.

slot meter *n* (*BRIT*) compteur *m* à pièces.

slouch [slautʃ] *vi* avoir le dos rond, être voûté(e).

►**slouch about**, **slouch around** *vi* traîner à ne rien faire.

Slovak ['sləuvæk] *adj* slovaque ♦ *n* Slovaque *m/f*; (*LING*) slovaque *m*; **the** ~ **Republic** la République slovaque.

Slovakia [sləu'vækɪə] *n* Slovaquie *f*.

Slovakian [sləu'vækɪən] *adj*, *n* = **Slovak**.

Slovene [sləu'vi:n] *adj* slovène ♦ *n* Slovène *m/f*;

(*LING*) slovène *m*.

Slovenia [sləu'vi:nɪə] *n* Slovénie *f*.

Slovenian [sləu'vi:nɪən] *adj, n* = **Slovene**.

slovenly ['slʌvənlɪ] *adj* sale, débraillé(e), négligé(e).

slow [sləu] *adj* lent(e); (*watch*): **to be ~** retarder ♦ *adv* lentement ♦ *vt, vi* (*also*: **~ down, ~ up**) ralentir; " **~** " (*road sign*) "ralentir"; **at a ~ speed** à petite vitesse; **to be ~ to act/decide** être lent à agir/décider; **my watch is 20 minutes ~** ma montre retarde de 20 minutes; **business is ~** les affaires marchent au ralenti; **to go ~** (*driver*) rouler lentement; (*in industrial dispute*) faire la grève perlée.

slow-acting [sləu'æktɪŋ] *adj* qui agit lentement, à action lente.

slowcoach ['sləukəutʃ] *n* (*BRIT col*) lambin/e.

slowly ['sləulɪ] *adv* lentement.

slow motion *n*: **in ~** au ralenti.

slowness ['sləunɪs] *n* lenteur *f*.

slowpoke ['sləupəuk] *n* (*US col*) = **slowcoach**.

sludge [slʌdʒ] *n* boue *f*.

slug [slʌg] *n* limace *f*; (*bullet*) balle *f*.

sluggish ['slʌgɪʃ] *adj* mou(molle), lent(e); (*business, sales*) stagnant(e).

sluice [slu:s] *n* écluse *f*; (*also*: **~ gate**) vanne *f* ♦ *vt*: **to ~ down** *or* **out** laver à grande eau.

slum [slʌm] *n* taudis *m*.

slumber ['slʌmbə*] *n* sommeil *m*.

slump [slʌmp] *n* baisse soudaine, effondrement *m*; crise *f* ♦ *vi* s'effondrer, s'affaisser.

slung [slʌŋ] *pt, pp of* **sling**.

slunk [slʌŋk] *pt, pp of* **slink**.

slur [slə:*] *n* bredouillement *m*; (*smear*): **~ (on)** atteinte *f* (à); insinuation *f* (contre) ♦ *vt* mal articuler; **to be a ~ on** porter atteinte à.

slurp [slə:p] *vt, vi* boire à grand bruit.

slurred [slə:d] *adj* (*pronunciation*) inarticulé(e), indistinct(e).

slush [slʌʃ] *n* neige fondue.

slush fund *n* caisse noire, fonds secrets.

slushy ['slʌʃɪ] *adj* (*snow*) fondu(e); (*street*) couvert(e) de neige fondue; (*BRIT: fig*) à l'eau de rose.

slut [slʌt] *n* souillon *f*.

sly [slaɪ] *adj* rusé(e); sournois(e); **on the ~** en cachette.

smack [smæk] *n* (*slap*) tape *f*; (*on face*) gifle *f* ♦ *vt* donner une tape à; gifler; (*child*) donner la fessée à ♦ *vi*: **to ~ of** avoir des relents de, sentir ♦ *adv* (*col*): **it fell ~ in the middle** c'est tombé en plein milieu *or* en plein dedans; **to ~ one's lips** se lécher les babines.

smacker ['smækə*] *n* (*col: kiss*) bisou *m or* bise *f* sonore; (: *BRIT: pound note*) livre *f*; (: *US: dollar bill*) dollar *m*.

small [smɔ:l] *adj* petit(e); (*letter*) minuscule ♦ *n*: **the ~ of the back** le creux des reins; **to get** *or* **grow ~er** diminuer; **to make ~er** (*amount, income*) diminuer; (*object, garment*) rapetisser; **a ~ shopkeeper** un petit commerçant.

small ads *npl* (*BRIT*) petites annonces.

small arms *npl* armes individuelles.

small business *n* petit commerce, petite affaire.

small change *n* petite *or* menue monnaie.

smallholder ['smɔ:lhəuldə*] *n* (*BRIT*) petit cultivateur.

smallholding ['smɔ:lhəuldɪŋ] *n* (*BRIT*) petite ferme.

small hours *npl*: **in the ~** au petit matin.

smallish ['smɔ:lɪʃ] *adj* plutôt *or* assez petit(e).

small-minded [smɔ:l'maɪndɪd] *adj* mesquin(e).

smallpox ['smɔ:lpɔks] *n* variole *f*.

small print *n* (*in contract etc*) clause(s) imprimée(s) en petits caractères.

small-scale ['smɔ:lskeɪl] *adj* (*map, model*) à échelle réduite, à petite échelle; (*business, farming*) peu important(e), modeste.

small talk *n* menus propos.

small-time ['smɔ:ltaɪm] *adj* (*farmer etc*) petit(e); **a ~ thief** un voleur à la petite semaine.

small-town ['smɔ:ltaun] *adj* provincial(e).

smarmy ['smɑ:mɪ] *adj* (*BRIT pej*) flagorneur(euse), lécheur(euse).

smart [smɑ:t] *adj* élégant(e), chic *inv*; (*clever*) intelligent(e); (*pej*) futé(e); (*quick*) vif(vive), prompt(e) ♦ *vi* faire mal, brûler; **the ~ set** le beau monde; **to look ~** être élégant(e); **my eyes are ~ing** j'ai les yeux irrités *or* qui me piquent.

smartcard ['smɑ:tkɑ:d] *n* carte *f* à puce.

smarten up ['smɑ:tn–] *vi* devenir plus élégant(e), se faire beau(belle) ♦ *vt* rendre plus élégant(e).

smash [smæʃ] *n* (*also*: **~-up**) collision *f*, accident *m*; (*sound*) fracas *m* ♦ *vt* casser, briser, fracasser; (*opponent*) écraser; (*hopes*) ruiner, détruire; (*SPORT: record*) pulvériser ♦ *vi* se briser, se fracasser; s'écraser.

▶**smash up** *vt* (*car*) bousiller; (*room*) tout casser dans.

smash hit *n* (*grand*) succès.

smashing ['smæʃɪŋ] *adj* (*col*) formidable.

smattering ['smætərɪŋ] *n*: **a ~ of** quelques notions de.

smear [smɪə*] *n* tache *f*, salissure *f*; trace *f*; (*MED*) frottis *m*; (*insult*) calomnie *f* ♦ *vt* enduire; (*fig*) porter atteinte à; **his hands were ~ed with oil/ink** il avait les mains maculées de cambouis/d'encre.

smear campaign *n* campagne *f* de dénigrement.

smear test *n* (*BRIT MED*) frottis *m*.

smell [smɛl] *n* odeur *f*; (*sense*) odorat *m* ♦ *vb* (*pt, pp* **smelt** *or* **smelled** [smɛlt, smɛld]) *vt* sentir ♦ *vi* (*food etc*): **to ~ (of)** sentir; (*pej*) sentir mauvais; **it ~s good** ça sent bon.

smelly ['smɛlɪ] *adj* qui sent mauvais,

malodorant(e).
smelt [smɛlt] *pt, pp of* **smell** ♦ *vt* (*ore*) fondre.
smile [smaɪl] *n* sourire *m* ♦ *vi* sourire.
smiling ['smaɪlɪŋ] *adj* souriant(e).
smirk [smɜːk] *n* petit sourire suffisant *or* affecté.
smith [smɪθ] *n* maréchal-ferrant *m*; forgeron *m*.
smithy ['smɪðɪ] *n* forge *f*.
smitten ['smɪtn] *adj*: ~ **with** pris(e) de; frappé(e) de.
smock [smɒk] *n* blouse *f*, sarrau *m*.
smog [smɒg] *n* brouillard mêlé de fumée.
smoke [sməʊk] *n* fumée *f* ♦ *vt, vi* fumer; **to have a** ~ fumer une cigarette; **do you** ~? est-ce que vous fumez?; **to go up in** ~ (*house etc*) brûler; (*fig*) partir en fumée.
smoked ['sməʊkt] *adj* (*bacon, glass*) fumé(e).
smokeless fuel ['sməʊklɪs-] *n* combustible non polluant.
smokeless zone ['sməʊklɪs-] *n* (*BRIT*) zone *f* où l'usage du charbon est réglementé.
smoker ['sməʊkə*] *n* (*person*) fumeur/euse; (*RAIL*) wagon *m* fumeurs.
smoke screen *n* rideau *m or* écran *m* de fumée; (*fig*) paravent *m*.
smoke shop *n* (*US*) (bureau *m* de) tabac *m*.
smoking ['sməʊkɪŋ] *n*: "**no** ~" (*sign*) "défense de fumer"; **he's given up** ~ il a arrêté de fumer.
smoking compartment, (*US*) **smoking car** *n* wagon *m* fumeurs.
smoking room *n* fumoir *m*.
smoky ['sməʊkɪ] *adj* enfumé(e).
smolder ['sməʊldə*] *vi* (*US*) = **smoulder**.
smoochy ['smuːtʃɪ] *adj* (*col*) langoureux(euse).
smooth [smuːð] *adj* lisse, (*sauce*) onctueux(euse); (*flavour, whisky*) moelleux(euse); (*cigarette*) doux(douce); (*movement*) régulier(ière), sans à-coups *or* heurts; (*landing, takeoff*) en douceur; (*flight*) sans secousses; (*person*) doucereux(euse), mielleux(euse) ♦ *vt* lisser, défroisser; (*also*: ~ **out**: *creases, difficulties*) faire disparaître.
▶**smooth over** *vt*: **to** ~ **things over** (*fig*) arranger les choses.
smoothly ['smuːðlɪ] *adv* (*easily*) facilement, sans difficulté(s); **everything went** ~ tout s'est bien passé.
smother ['smʌðə*] *vt* étouffer.
smoulder, (*US*) **smolder** ['sməʊldə*] *vi* couver.
smudge [smʌdʒ] *n* tache *f*, bavure *f* ♦ *vt* salir, maculer.
smug [smʌg] *adj* suffisant(e), content(e) de soi.
smuggle ['smʌgl] *vt* passer en contrebande *or* en fraude; **to** ~ **in/out** (*goods etc*) faire entrer/sortir clandestinement *or* en fraude.
smuggler ['smʌglə*] *n* contrebandier/ière.
smuggling ['smʌglɪŋ] *n* contrebande *f*.

smut [smʌt] *n* (*grain of soot*) grain *m* de suie; (*mark*) tache *f* de suie; (*in conversation etc*) obscénités *fpl*.
smutty ['smʌtɪ] *adj* (*fig*) grossier(ière), obscène.
snack [snæk] *n* casse-croûte *m inv*; **to have a** ~ prendre un en-cas, manger quelque chose (de léger).
snack bar *n* snack(-bar) *m*.
snag [snæg] *n* inconvénient *m*, difficulté *f*.
snail [sneɪl] *n* escargot *m*.
snake [sneɪk] *n* serpent *m*.
snap [snæp] *n* (*sound*) claquement *m*, bruit sec; (*photograph*) photo *f*, instantané *m*; (*game*) sorte de jeu de bataille ♦ *adj* subit(e) fait(e) sans réfléchir ♦ *vt* faire claquer; (*break*) casser net; (*photograph*) prendre un instantané de ♦ *vi* se casser net *or* avec un bruit sec; (*fig: person*) craquer; **to** ~ **at sb** (*subj: person*) parler d'un ton brusque à qn; (: *dog*) essayer de mordre qn; **to** ~ **open/ shut** s'ouvrir/se refermer brusquement; **to** ~ **one's fingers at** (*fig*) se moquer de; **a cold** ~ (*of weather*) un refroidissement soudain de la température.
▶**snap off** *vt* (*break*) casser net.
▶**snap up** *vt* sauter sur, saisir.
snap fastener *n* bouton-pression *m*.
snappy ['snæpɪ] *adj* prompt(e); (*slogan*) qui a du punch; **make it** ~! (*col: hurry up*) grouille-toi!, magne-toi!
snapshot ['snæpʃɒt] *n* photo *f*, instantané *m*.
snare [snɛə*] *n* piège *m* ♦ *vt* attraper, prendre au piège.
snarl [snɑːl] *n* grondement *m or* grognement *m* féroce ♦ *vi* gronder ♦ *vt*: **to get** ~**ed up** (*wool, plans*) s'emmêler; (*traffic*) se bloquer.
snatch [snætʃ] *n* (*fig*) vol *m*; (*BRIT: small amount*): ~**es of** des fragments *mpl or* bribes *fpl* de ♦ *vt* saisir (*d'un geste vif*); (*steal*) voler ♦ *vi*: **don't** ~! doucement!; **to** ~ **a sandwich** manger *or* avaler un sandwich à la hâte; **to** ~ **some sleep** arriver à dormir un peu.
▶**snatch up** *vt* saisir, s'emparer de.
snazzy ['snæzɪ] *adj* (*col: clothes*) classe *inv*, chouette.
sneak [sniːk] *vi*: **to** ~ **in/out** entrer/sortir furtivement *or* à la dérobée ♦ *vt*: **to** ~ **a look at sth** regarder furtivement qch.
sneakers ['sniːkəz] *npl* chaussures *fpl* de tennis *or* basket.
sneaking ['sniːkɪŋ] *adj*: **to have a** ~ **feeling** *or* **suspicion that ...** avoir la vague impression que ....
sneaky ['sniːkɪ] *adj* sournois(e).
sneer [snɪə*] *n* ricanement *m* ♦ *vi* ricaner, sourire d'un air sarcastique; **to** ~ **at sb/sth** se moquer de qn/qch avec mépris.
sneeze [sniːz] *n* éternuement *m* ♦ *vi* éternuer.
snide [snaɪd] *adj* sarcastique, narquois(e).
sniff [snɪf] *n* reniflement *m* ♦ *vi* renifler ♦ *vt* renifler, flairer; (*glue, drug*) sniffer,

respirer.

▶**sniff at** vt fus: **it's not to be ~ed at** il ne faut pas cracher dessus, ce n'est pas à dédaigner.

sniffer dog ['snɪfə-] n (POLICE) chien dressé pour la recherche d'explosifs et de stupéfiants.

snigger ['snɪgə*] n ricanement m; rire moqueur ♦ vi ricaner; pouffer de rire.

snip [snɪp] n petit bout; (bargain) (bonne) occasion or affaire ♦ vt couper.

sniper ['snaɪpə*] n (marksman) tireur embusqué.

snippet ['snɪpɪt] n bribes fpl.

snivelling ['snɪvlɪŋ] adj larmoyant(e), pleurnicheur(euse).

snob [snɔb] n snob m/f.

snobbery ['snɔbərɪ] n snobisme m.

snobbish ['snɔbɪʃ] adj snob inv.

snog [snɔg] vi (col) se bécoter.

snooker ['snuːkə*] n sorte de jeu de billard.

snoop [snuːp] vi: **to ~ on sb** espionner qn; **to ~ about somewhere** fourrer son nez quelque part.

snooper ['snuːpə*] n fureteur/euse.

snooty ['snuːtɪ] adj snob inv, prétentieux(euse).

snooze [snuːz] n petit somme ♦ vi faire un petit somme.

snore [snɔː*] vi ronfler ♦ n ronflement m.

snoring ['snɔːrɪŋ] n ronflement(s) m(pl).

snorkel ['snɔːkl] n (of swimmer) tuba m.

snort [snɔːt] n grognement m ♦ vi grogner; (horse) renâcler ♦ vt (col: drugs) sniffer.

snotty ['snɔtɪ] adj morveux(euse).

snout [snaut] n museau m.

snow [snəu] n neige f ♦ vi neiger ♦ vt: **to be ~ed under with work** être débordé(e) de travail.

snowball ['snəubɔːl] n boule f de neige.

snowbound ['snəubaund] adj enneigé(e), bloqué(e) par la neige.

snow-capped ['snəukæpt] adj (peak, mountain) couvert(e) de neige.

snowdrift ['snəudrɪft] n congère f.

snowdrop ['snəudrɔp] n perce-neige m.

snowfall ['snəufɔːl] n chute f de neige.

snowflake ['snəufleɪk] n flocon m de neige.

snowman ['snəumæn] n bonhomme m de neige.

snowplough, (US) **snowplow** ['snəuplau] n chasse-neige m inv.

snowshoe ['snəuʃuː] n raquette f (pour la neige).

snowstorm ['snəustɔːm] n tempête f de neige.

snowy ['snəuɪ] adj neigeux(euse); (covered with snow) enneigé(e).

SNP n abbr (BRIT POL) = **Scottish National Party**.

snub [snʌb] vt repousser, snober ♦ n rebuffade f.

snub-nosed [snʌb'nəuzd] adj au nez

retroussé.

snuff [snʌf] n tabac m à priser ♦ vt (also: ~ **out**: candle) moucher.

snuff movie n (col) film pornographique qui se termine par le meurtre réel de l'un des acteurs.

snug [snʌg] adj douillet(te), confortable; **it's a ~ fit** c'est bien ajusté(e).

snuggle ['snʌgl] vi: **to ~ down in bed/up to sb** se pelotonner dans son lit/contre qn.

SO abbr (BANKING) = **standing order**.

═══════════════════════ KEYWORD

so [səu] adv 1 (thus, likewise) ainsi, de cette façon; **if ~** si oui; **~ do or have I** moi aussi; **it's 5 o'clock — ~ it is!** il est 5 heures — en effet! or c'est vrai!; **I hope/think ~** je l'espère/le crois; **~ far** jusqu'ici, jusqu'à maintenant; (in past) jusque-là; **quite ~!** exactement!, c'est bien ça!; **even ~** quand même, tout de même
2 (in comparisons etc: to such a degree) si, tellement; **~ big (that)** si or tellement grand (que); **she's not ~ clever as her brother** elle n'est pas aussi intelligente que son frère
3: **~ much** adj, adv tant (de); **I've got ~ much work** j'ai tant de travail; (in past) jusque-là; **I love you ~ much** je vous aime tant; **~ many** tant (de)
4 (phrases): **10 or ~** à peu près or environ 10; **~ long!** (inf: goodbye) au revoir!, à un de ces jours!; **~ (what)?** (col) (bon) et alors?, et après?

♦ conj 1 (expressing purpose): **~ as to do** pour or afin de faire; **~ (that)** pour que or afin que +sub
2 (expressing result) donc, par conséquent; **~ that** si bien que, de (telle) sorte que; **~ that's the reason!** c'est donc (pour) ça!

soak [səuk] vt faire or laisser tremper ♦ vi tremper; **to be ~ed through** être trempé(e) jusqu'aux os.

▶**soak in** vi pénétrer, être absorbé(e).

▶**soak up** vt absorber.

soaking ['səukɪŋ] adj (also: ~ **wet**) trempé(e).

so and so n un tel/une telle.

soap [səup] n savon m.

soapbox ['səupbɔks] n tribune improvisée (en plein air).

soapflakes ['səupfleɪks] npl paillettes fpl de savon.

soap opera n feuilleton télévisé (quotidienneté réaliste ou embellie).

soap powder n lessive f, détergent m.

soapsuds ['səupsʌdz] npl mousse f de savon.

soapy ['səupɪ] adj savonneux(euse).

soar [sɔː*] vi monter (en flèche), s'élancer; **~ing prices** prix qui grimpent.

sob [sɔb] n sanglot m ♦ vi sangloter.

s.o.b. n abbr (US col!: = son of a bitch) salaud m (!).

sober ['səubə*] adj qui n'est pas (or plus) ivre;

(*sedate*) sérieux(euse), sensé(e)); (*moderate*) mesuré(e); (*colour, style*) sobre, discret(ète).

▶**sober up** *vt* dégriser ♦ *vi* se dégriser.

sobriety [sə'braɪətɪ] *n* (*not being drunk*) sobriété *f*; (*seriousness, sedateness*) sérieux *m*.

sob story *n* (*col, pej*) histoire larmoyante.

Soc. *abbr* (= *society*) Soc.

so-called ['səu'kɔːld] *adj* soi-disant *inv*.

soccer ['sɔkə*] *n* football *m*.

soccer pitch *n* terrain *m* de football.

soccer player *n* footballeur *m*.

sociable ['səuʃəbl] *adj* sociable.

social ['səuʃl] *adj* social(e) ♦ *n* (petite) fête.

social climber *n* arriviste *m/f*.

social club *n* amicale *f*, foyer *m*.

Social Democrat *n* social-démocrate *m/f*.

social insurance *n* (*US*) sécurité sociale.

socialism ['səuʃəlɪzəm] *n* socialisme *m*.

socialist ['səuʃəlɪst] *adj, n* socialiste (*m/f*).

socialite ['səuʃəlaɪt] *n* personnalité mondaine.

socialize ['səuʃəlaɪz] *vi* voir *or* rencontrer des gens, se faire des amis; **to ~ with** fréquenter; lier connaissance *or* parler avec.

social life *n* vie sociale; **how's your ~?** est-ce que tu sors beaucoup?

socially ['səuʃəlɪ] *adv* socialement, en société.

social science *n* sciences humaines.

social security *n* aide sociale.

social services *npl* services sociaux.

social welfare *n* sécurité sociale.

social work *n* assistance sociale.

social worker *n* assistant/e social(e).

society [sə'saɪətɪ] *n* société *f*; (*club*) société, association *f*; (*also*: **high ~**) (haute) société, grand monde ♦ *cpd* (*party*) mondain(e).

socio-economic ['səusɪəuɪkə'nɔmɪk] *adj* socioéconomique.

sociological [səusɪə'lɔdʒɪkl] *adj* sociologique.

sociologist [səusɪ'ɔlədʒɪst] *n* sociologue *m/f*.

sociology [səusɪ'ɔlədʒɪ] *n* sociologie *f*.

sock [sɔk] *n* chaussette *f* ♦ *vt* (*col: hit*) flanquer un coup à; **to pull one's ~s up** (*fig*) se secouer (les puces).

socket ['sɔkɪt] *n* cavité *f*; (*ELEC: also*: **wall ~**) prise *f* de courant; (*: for light bulb*) douille *f*.

sod [sɔd] *n* (*of earth*) motte *f*; (*BRIT col!*) con *m* (*!*); salaud *m* (*!*).

▶**sod off** *vi*: **~ off!** (*BRIT col!*) fous le camp!, va te faire foutre! (*!*).

soda ['səudə] *n* (*CHEM*) soude *f*; (*also*: **~ water**) eau *f* de Seltz; (*US: also*: **~ pop**) soda *m*.

sodden ['sɔdn] *adj* trempé(e); détrempé(e).

sodium ['səudɪəm] *n* sodium *m*.

sodium chloride *n* chlorure *m* de sodium.

sofa ['səufə] *n* sofa *m*, canapé *m*.

Sofia ['səufɪə] *n* Sofia.

soft [sɔft] *adj* (*not rough*) doux(douce); (*not hard*) doux; mou(molle); (*not loud*) doux, léger(ère); (*kind*) doux, gentil(le); (*weak*) indulgent(e); (*stupid*) stupide, débile.

soft-boiled ['sɔftbɔɪld] *adj* (*egg*) à la coque.

soft drink *n* boisson non alcoolisée.

soft drugs *npl* drogues douces.

soften ['sɔfn] *vt* (r)amollir; adoucir; atténuer ♦ *vi* se ramollir; s'adoucir; s'atténuer.

softener ['sɔfnə*] *n* (*water ~*) adoucisseur *m*; (*fabric ~*) produit assouplissant.

soft fruit *n* (*BRIT*) baies *fpl*.

soft furnishings *npl* tissus *mpl* d'ameublement.

soft-hearted [sɔft'hɑːtɪd] *adj* au cœur tendre.

softly ['sɔftlɪ] *adv* doucement; légèrement; gentiment.

softness ['sɔftnɪs] *n* douceur *f*.

soft option *n* solution *f* de facilité.

soft sell *n* promotion *f* de vente discrète.

soft target *n* cible *f* facile.

soft toy *n* jouet *m* en peluche.

software ['sɔftwɛə*] *n* logiciel *m*, software *m*.

software package *n* progiciel *m*.

soggy ['sɔgɪ] *adj* trempé(e); détrempé(e).

soil [sɔɪl] *n* (*earth*) sol *m*, terre *f* ♦ *vt* salir; (*fig*) souiller.

soiled [sɔɪld] *adj* sale; (*COMM*) défraîchi(e).

sojourn ['sɔdʒəːn] *n* (*formal*) séjour *m*.

solace ['sɔlɪs] *n* consolation *f*, réconfort *m*.

solar ['səulə*] *adj* solaire.

solarium, *pl* **solaria** [sə'lɛərɪəm, -rɪə] *n* solarium *m*.

solar panel *n* panneau *m* solaire.

solar plexus [-'plɛksəs] *n* (*ANAT*) plexus *m* solaire.

solar power *n* énergie *f* solaire.

sold [səuld] *pt, pp of* **sell**.

solder ['səuldə*] *vt* souder (*au fil à souder*) ♦ *n* soudure *f*.

soldier ['səuldʒə*] *n* soldat *m*, militaire *m* ♦ *vi*: **to ~ on** persévérer, s'accrocher; **toy ~** petit soldat.

sold out *adj* (*COMM*) épuisé(e).

sole [səul] *n* (*of foot*) plante *f*; (*of shoe*) semelle *f*; (*fish: pl inv*) sole *f* ♦ *adj* seul(e), unique; **the ~ reason** la seule et unique raison.

solely ['səullɪ] *adv* seulement, uniquement; **I will hold you ~ responsible** je vous en tiendrai pour seul responsable.

solemn ['sɔləm] *adj* solennel(le); sérieux(euse), grave.

sole trader *n* (*COMM*) chef *m* d'entreprise individuelle.

solicit [sə'lɪsɪt] *vt* (*request*) solliciter ♦ *vi* (*prostitute*) racoler.

solicitor [sə'lɪsɪtə*] *n* (*BRIT: for wills etc*) ≈ notaire *m*; (*: in court*) ≈ avocat *m*.

solid ['sɔlɪd] *adj* (*not hollow*) plein(e), compact(e), massif(ive); (*strong, sound, reliable, not liquid*) solide; (*meal*) consistant(e), substantiel(le); (*vote*) unanime ♦ *n* solide *m*; **to be on ~ ground** être sur la terre ferme; (*fig*) être en terrain sûr; **we waited 2 ~ hours** nous avons attendu deux heures entières.

solidarity [sɔlɪ'dærɪtɪ] n solidarité f.
solid fuel n combustible m solide.
solidify [sə'lɪdɪfaɪ] vi se solidifier ♦ vt solidifier.
solidity [sə'lɪdɪtɪ] n solidité f.
solid-state ['sɔlɪdsteɪt] adj (ELEC) à circuits intégrés.
soliloquy [sə'lɪləkwɪ] n monologue m.
solitaire [sɔlɪ'tɛə*] n (gem, BRIT: game) solitaire m; (US: card game) réussite f.
solitary ['sɔlɪtərɪ] adj solitaire.
solitary confinement n (LAW) isolement m (cellulaire).
solitude ['sɔlɪtjuːd] n solitude f.
solo ['səuləu] n solo m.
soloist ['səuləuɪst] n soliste m/f.
Solomon Islands ['sɔləmən-] npl: **the ~** les (îles fpl) Salomon fpl.
solstice ['sɔlstɪs] n solstice m.
soluble ['sɔljubl] adj soluble.
solution [sə'luːʃən] n solution f.
solve [sɔlv] vt résoudre.
solvency ['sɔlvənsɪ] n (COMM) solvabilité f.
solvent ['sɔlvənt] adj (COMM) solvable ♦ n (CHEM) (dis)solvant m.
solvent abuse n usage m de solvants hallucinogènes.
Som. abbr (BRIT) = Somerset.
Somali [səu'maːlɪ] adj somali(e), somalien(ne) ♦ n Somali/e, Somalien/ne.
Somalia [səu'maːlɪə] n (République f de) Somalie f.
Somaliland [səu'maːlɪlænd] n Somaliland m.
sombre, (US) **somber** ['sɔmbə*] adj sombre, morne.

=========================== KEYWORD

some [sʌm] adj **1** (a certain amount or number of): **~ tea/water/ice cream** du thé/de l'eau/de la glace; **~ children/apples** des enfants/pommes
2 (certain: in contrasts): **~ people say that ...** il y a des gens qui disent que ...; **~ films were excellent, but most ...** certains films étaient excellents, mais la plupart ...
3 (unspecified): **~ woman was asking for you** il y avait une dame qui vous demandait; **he was asking for ~ book (or other)** il demandait un livre quelconque; **~ day** un de ces jours; **~ day next week** un jour la semaine prochaine; **after ~ time** après un certain temps; **at ~ length** assez longuement; **in ~ form or other** sous une forme ou une autre, sous une forme quelconque
♦ pron **1** (a certain number) quelques-un(e)s, certain(e)s; **I've got ~** (books etc) j'en ai (quelques-uns); **~ (of them) have been sold** certains ont été vendus
2 (a certain amount) un peu; **I've got ~** (money, milk) j'en ai un peu; **would you like ~?** est-ce que vous en voulez?, en voulez-

vous?
♦ adv: **~ 10 people** quelque 10 personnes, 10 personnes environ.

somebody ['sʌmbədɪ] pron quelqu'un; **~ or other** quelqu'un, je ne sais qui.
someday ['sʌmdeɪ] adv un de ces jours, un jour ou l'autre.
somehow ['sʌmhau] adv d'une façon ou d'une autre; (for some reason) pour une raison ou une autre.
someone ['sʌmwʌn] pron = **somebody**.
someplace ['sʌmpleɪs] adv (US) = **somewhere**.
somersault ['sʌməsɔːlt] n culbute f, saut périlleux ♦ vi faire la culbute or un saut périlleux; (car) faire un tonneau.
something ['sʌmθɪŋ] pron quelque chose m; **~ interesting** quelque chose d'intéressant; **~ to do** quelque chose à faire; **he's ~ like me** il est un peu comme moi; **it's ~ of a problem** il y a là un problème.
sometime ['sʌmtaɪm] adv (in future) un de ces jours, un jour ou l'autre; (in past): **~ last month** au cours du mois dernier.
sometimes ['sʌmtaɪmz] adv quelquefois, parfois.
somewhat ['sʌmwɔt] adv quelque peu, un peu.
somewhere ['sʌmwɛə*] adv quelque part; **~ else** ailleurs, autre part.
son [sʌn] n fils m.
sonar ['səunaː*] n sonar m.
sonata [sə'naːtə] n sonate f.
song [sɔŋ] n chanson f.
songbook ['sɔŋbuk] n chansonnier m.
songwriter ['sɔŋraɪtə*] n auteur-compositeur m.
sonic ['sɔnɪk] adj (boom) supersonique.
son-in-law ['sʌnɪnlɔ:] n gendre m, beau-fils m.
sonnet ['sɔnɪt] n sonnet m.
sonny ['sʌnɪ] n (col) fiston m.
soon [suːn] adv bientôt; (early) tôt; **~ afterwards** peu après; **quite ~** sous peu; **how ~ can you do it?** combien de temps vous faut-il pour le faire, au plus pressé?; **how ~ can you come back?** quand or dans combien de temps pouvez-vous revenir, au plus tôt; **see you ~!** à bientôt!; see also **as**.
sooner ['suːnə*] adv (time) plus tôt; (preference): **I would ~ do** j'aimerais autant or je préférerais faire; **~ or later** tôt ou tard; **no ~ said than done** sitôt dit, sitôt fait; **the ~ the better** le plus tôt sera le mieux; **no ~ had we left than ...** à peine étions-nous partis que ....
soot [sut] n suie f.
soothe [suːð] vt calmer, apaiser.
soothing ['suːðɪŋ] adj (ointment etc) lénitif(ive), lénifiant(e); (tone, words etc) apaisant(e); (drink, bath) relaxant(e).
SOP n abbr = standard operating procedure.
sop [sɔp] n: **that's only a ~** c'est pour nous (or

les *etc*) amadouer.

sophisticated [sə'fɪstɪkeɪtɪd] *adj* raffiné(e),
sophistiqué(e); (*system etc*) très
perfectionné(e), sophistiqué.

sophistication [səfɪstɪ'keɪʃən] *n* raffinement
m; (niveau *m* de) perfectionnement *m*.

sophomore ['sɔfəmɔ:*] *n* (*US*) étudiant/e de
seconde année.

soporific [sɔpə'rɪfɪk] *adj* soporifique ♦ *n*
somnifère *m*.

sopping ['sɔpɪŋ] *adj* (*also*: ~ **wet**) tout(e)
trempé(e).

soppy ['sɔpɪ] *adj* (*pej*) sentimental(e).

soprano [sə'prɑːnəu] *n* (*voice*) soprano *m*;
(*singer*) soprano *m/f*.

sorbet ['sɔ:beɪ] *n* sorbet *m*.

sorcerer ['sɔ:sərə*] *n* sorcier *m*.

sordid ['sɔ:dɪd] *adj* sordide.

sore [sɔ:*] *adj* (*painful*) douloureux(euse),
sensible; (*offended*) contrarié(e), vexé(e)
♦ *n* plaie *f*; **to have a ~ throat** avoir mal à la
gorge; **it's a ~ point** (*fig*) c'est un point
délicat.

sorely ['sɔ:lɪ] *adv* (*tempted*) fortement.

sorrel ['sɔrəl] *n* oseille *f*.

sorrow ['sɔrəu] *n* peine *f*, chagrin *m*.

sorrowful ['sɔrəuful] *adj* triste.

sorry ['sɔrɪ] *adj* désolé(e); (*condition, excuse,
tale*) triste, déplorable; (*sight*) désolant(e);
~**!** pardon!, excusez-moi!; **to feel ~ for sb**
plaindre qn; **I'm ~ to hear that** ... je suis
désolé(e) *or* navré(e) d'apprendre que ...; **to
be ~ about sth** regretter qch.

sort [sɔ:t] *n* genre *m*, espèce *f*, sorte *f*; (*make:
of coffee, car etc*) marque *f* ♦ *vt* (*also*: ~ **out**:
papers) trier; classer; ranger; (: *letters etc*)
trier; (: *problems*) résoudre, régler;
(*COMPUT*) trier; **what ~ do you want?** quelle
sorte *or* quel genre voulez-vous?; **what ~ of
car?** quelle marque de voiture?; **I'll do
nothing of the** ~**!** je ne ferai rien de tel!; **it's
~ of awkward** (*col*) c'est plutôt gênant.

sortie ['sɔ:tɪ] *n* sortie *f*.

sorting office ['sɔ:tɪŋ-] *n* (*POST*) bureau *m* de
tri.

SOS *n abbr* (= *save our souls*) SOS *m*.

so-so ['səusəu] *adv* comme ci comme ça.

soufflé ['su:fleɪ] *n* soufflé *m*.

sought [sɔ:t] *pt, pp* of **seek**.

sought-after ['sɔ:tɑ:ftə*] *adj* recherché(e).

soul [səul] *n* âme *f*; **the poor ~ had nowhere to
sleep** le pauvre n'avait nulle part où dormir;
I didn't see a ~ je n'ai vu (absolument)
personne.

soul-destroying ['səuldɪstrɔɪŋ] *adj*
démoralisant(e).

soulful ['səulful] *adj* plein(e) de sentiment.

soulless ['səullɪs] *adj* sans cœur, inhumain(e).

soul mate *n* âme *f* sœur.

soul-searching ['səulsə:tʃɪŋ] *n*: **after much ~,
I decided** ... j'ai longuement réfléchi avant
de décider ....

sound [saund] *adj* (*healthy*) en bonne santé,
sain(e); (*safe, not damaged*) solide, en bon
état; (*reliable, not superficial*) sérieux(euse),
solide; (*sensible*) sensé(e) ♦ *adv*: ~ **asleep**
dormant d'un profond sommeil ♦ *n* (*noise*)
son *m*; bruit *m*; (*GEO*) détroit *m*, bras *m* de
mer ♦ *vt* (*alarm*) sonner; (*also*: ~ **out**:
opinions) sonder ♦ *vi* sonner, retentir; (*fig:
seem*) sembler (être); **to be of ~ mind** être
sain(e) d'esprit; **I don't like the ~ of it** ça ne
me dit rien qui vaille; **to ~ one's horn** (*AUT*)
klaxonner, actionner son avertisseur; **to ~
like** ressembler à; **it ~s as if** ... il semblerait
que ..., j'ai l'impression que ....

▶**sound off** *vi* (*col*): **to ~ off (about)** la
ramener (sur).

sound barrier *n* mur *m* du son.

soundbite ['saundbaɪt] *n* phrase toute faite
(*pour être citée dans les médias*).

sound effects *npl* bruitage *m*.

sound engineer *n* ingénieur *m* du son.

sounding ['saundɪŋ] *n* (*NAUT etc*) sondage *m*.

sounding board *n* (*MUS*) table *f* d'harmonie;
(*fig*): **to use sb as a ~ for one's ideas** essayer
ses idées sur qn.

soundly ['saundlɪ] *adv* (*sleep*) profondément;
(*beat*) complètement, à plate couture.

soundproof ['saundpru:f] *vt* insonoriser ♦ *adj*
insonorisé(e).

sound system *n* sono(risation) *f*.

soundtrack ['saundtræk] *n* (*of film*) bande *f*
sonore.

sound wave *n* (*PHYSICS*) onde *f* sonore.

soup [su:p] *n* soupe *f*, potage *m*; **in the ~** (*fig*)
dans le pétrin.

soup course *n* potage *m*.

soup kitchen *n* soupe *f* populaire.

soup plate *n* assiette creuse *or* à soupe.

soupspoon ['su:pspu:n] *n* cuiller *f* à soupe.

sour ['sauə*] *adj* aigre, acide; (*milk*) tourné(e),
aigre; (*fig*) acerbe, aigre; revêche; **to go** *or*
turn ~ (*milk, wine*) tourner; (*fig: relationship,
plans*) mal tourner; **it's ~ grapes** c'est du
dépit.

source [sɔ:s] *n* source *f*; **I have it from a
reliable ~ that** je sais de source sûre que.

south [sauθ] *n* sud *m* ♦ *adj* sud *inv*, du sud ♦ *adv*
au sud, vers le sud; **(to the) ~ of** au sud de;
to travel ~ aller en direction du sud; **the S~
of France** le Sud de la France, le Midi.

South Africa *n* Afrique *f* du Sud.

South African *adj* sud-africain(e) ♦ *n* Sud-
Africain/e.

South America *n* Amérique *f* du Sud.

South American *adj* sud-américain(e) ♦ *n*
Sud-Américain/e.

southbound ['sauθbaund] *adj* en direction du
sud; (*carriageway*) sud *inv*.

south-east [sauθ'i:st] *n* sud-est *m*.

South-East Asia *n* le Sud-Est asiatique.

southerly ['sʌðəlɪ] *adj* du sud; au sud.

southern ['sʌðən] *adj* (du) sud; méridional(e);

with a ~ **aspect** orienté(e) or exposé(e) au
sud; **the** ~ **hemisphere** l'hémisphère sud or
austral.
South Pole n Pôle m Sud.
South Sea Islands npl: **the** ~ l'Océanie f.
South Seas npl: **the** ~ les mers fpl du Sud.
South Vietnam n Viêt-Nam m du Sud.
southward(s) ['sauθwəd(z)] adv vers le sud.
south-west [sauθ'wɛst] n sud-ouest m.
souvenir [su:və'nɪə*] n souvenir m (objet).
sovereign ['sɔvrɪn] adj, n souverain(e).
sovereignty ['sɔvrɪntɪ] n souveraineté f.
soviet ['səuvɪət] adj soviétique.
Soviet Union n: **the** ~ l'Union f soviétique.
sow n [sau] truie f ♦ vt [səu] (pt ~**ed**, pp **sown**
[səun]) semer.
soya ['sɔɪə], (US) **soy** [sɔɪ] n: ~ **bean** graine f
de soja; ~ **sauce** sauce f au soja.
sozzled ['sɔzld] adj (BRIT col) paf inv.
spa [spɑ:] n (town) station thermale; (US: also:
health ~) établissement m de cure de
rajeunissement.
space [speɪs] n (gen) espace m; (room) place f,
espace; (length of time) laps m de temps ♦ cpd
spatial(e) ♦ vt (also: ~ **out**) espacer; **to clear**
a ~ **for sth** faire de la place pour qch; **in a**
confined ~ dans un espace réduit or
restreint; **in a short** ~ **of time** dans peu de
temps; **(with)in the** ~ **of an hour** en l'espace
d'une heure.
space bar n (on typewriter) barre f
d'espacement.
spacecraft ['speɪskrɑ:ft] n engin spatial.
spaceman ['speɪsmæn] n astronaute m,
cosmonaute m.
spaceship ['speɪsʃɪp] n engin or vaisseau
spatial.
space shuttle n navette spatiale.
spacesuit ['speɪssu:t] n combinaison spatiale.
spacewoman ['speɪswumən] n astronaute f,
cosmonaute f.
spacing ['speɪsɪŋ] n espacement m; **single/**
double ~ (TYP etc) interligne m simple/
double.
spacious ['speɪʃəs] adj spacieux(euse),
grand(e).
spade [speɪd] n (tool) bêche f, pelle f; (child's)
pelle; ~**s** npl (CARDS) pique m.
spadework ['speɪdwə:k] n (fig) gros m du
travail.
spaghetti [spə'gɛtɪ] n spaghetti mpl.
Spain [speɪn] n Espagne f.
span [spæn] n (of bird, plane) envergure f; (of
arch) portée f; (in time) espace m de temps,
durée f ♦ vt enjamber, franchir; (fig)
couvrir, embrasser.
Spaniard ['spænjəd] n Espagnol/e.
spaniel ['spænjəl] n épagneul m.
Spanish ['spænɪʃ] adj espagnol(e), d'Espagne
♦ n (LING) espagnol m; **the** ~ npl les
Espagnols; ~ **omelette** omelette f à
l'espagnole.

spank [spæŋk] vt donner une fessée à.
spanner ['spænə*] n (BRIT) clé f (de
mécanicien).
spar [spɑ:*] n espar m ♦ vi (BOXING)
s'entraîner.
spare [spɛə*] adj de réserve, de rechange;
(surplus) de or en trop, de reste ♦ n (part)
pièce f de rechange, pièce détachée ♦ vt (do
without) se passer de; (afford to give) donner,
accorder, passer; (refrain from hurting)
épargner; (refrain from using) ménager; **to** ~
(surplus) en surplus, de trop; **there are 2**
going ~ (BRIT) il y en a 2 de disponible; **to** ~
no expense ne pas reculer devant la
dépense; **can you** ~ **the time?** est-ce que
vous avez le temps?; **there is no time to** ~ il
n'y a pas de temps à perdre; **I've a few**
minutes to ~ je dispose de quelques
minutes.
spare part n pièce f de rechange, pièce
détachée.
spare room n chambre f d'ami.
spare time n moments mpl de loisir.
spare tyre n (AUT) pneu m de rechange.
spare wheel n (AUT) roue f de secours.
sparing ['spɛərɪŋ] adj: **to be** ~ **with** ménager.
sparingly ['spɛərɪŋlɪ] adv avec modération.
spark [spɑ:k] n étincelle f; (fig) étincelle, lueur
f.
spark(ing) plug ['spɑ:k(ɪŋ)-] n bougie f.
sparkle ['spɑ:kl] n scintillement m,
étincellement m, éclat m ♦ vi étinceler,
scintiller; (bubble) pétiller.
sparkler ['spɑ:klə*] n cierge m magique.
sparkling ['spɑ:klɪŋ] adj étincelant(e),
scintillant(e); (wine) mousseux(euse),
pétillant(e).
sparring partner ['spɑ:rɪŋ-] n sparring-
partner m; (fig) vieil(le) ennemi/e.
sparrow ['spærəu] n moineau m.
sparse [spɑ:s] adj clairsemé(e).
spartan ['spɑ:tən] adj (fig) spartiate.
spasm ['spæzəm] n (MED) spasme m; (fig)
accès m.
spasmodic [spæz'mɔdɪk] adj (fig)
intermittent(e).
spastic ['spæstɪk] n handicapé/e moteur.
spat [spæt] pt, pp of **spit** ♦ n (US) prise f de bec.
spate [speɪt] n (fig): ~ **of** avalanche f or
torrent m de; **in** ~ (river) en crue.
spatial ['speɪʃl] adj spatial(e).
spatter ['spætə*] n éclaboussure(s) f(pl) ♦ vt
éclabousser ♦ vi gicler.
spatula ['spætjulə] n spatule f.
spawn [spɔ:n] vt pondre; (pej) engendrer ♦ vi
frayer ♦ n frai m.
SPCA n abbr (US: = Society for the Prevention of
Cruelty to Animals) ≈ SPA f.
SPCC n abbr (US) = Society for the Prevention of
Cruelty to Children.
speak, pt **spoke,** pp **spoken** [spi:k, spəuk,
'spəukn] vt (language) parler; (truth) dire ♦ vi

parler; (*make a speech*) prendre la parole; **to ~ to sb/of** *or* **about sth** parler à qn/de qch; **~ing!** (*on telephone*) c'est moi-même!; **to ~ one's mind** dire ce que l'on pense; **it ~s for itself** c'est évident; **~ up!** parle plus fort!; **he has no money to ~ of** il n'a pas d'argent.

▶**speak for** *vt fus*: **to ~ for sb** parler pour qn; **that picture is already spoken for** (*in shop*) ce tableau est déjà réservé.

speaker ['spiːkə*] *n* (*in public*) orateur *m*; (*also*: **loud~**) haut-parleur *m*; (*POL*): **the S~** le président de la Chambre des communes (*BRIT*) *or* des représentants (*US*); **are you a Welsh ~?** parlez-vous gallois?

speaking ['spiːkɪŋ] *adj* parlant(e); **French-~ people** les francophones; **to be on ~ terms** se parler.

spear [spɪə*] *n* lance *f* ♦ *vt* transpercer.

spearhead ['spɪəhɛd] *n* fer *m* de lance; (*MIL*) colonne *f* d'attaque ♦ *vt* (*attack etc*) mener.

spearmint ['spɪəmɪnt] *n* (*BOT etc*) menthe verte.

spec [spɛk] *n* (*BRIT col*): **on ~** à tout hasard; **to buy on ~** acheter avec l'espoir de faire une bonne affaire.

special ['spɛʃl] *adj* spécial(e) ♦ *n* (*train*) train spécial; **take ~ care** soyez particulièrement prudents; **nothing ~** rien de spécial; **today's ~** (*at restaurant*) le plat du jour.

special agent *n* agent secret.

special correspondent *n* envoyé spécial.

special delivery *n* (*POST*): **by ~** en exprès.

special effects *npl* (*CINE*) effets spéciaux.

specialist ['spɛʃəlɪst] *n* spécialiste *m/f*; **heart ~** cardiologue *m/f*.

speciality [spɛʃɪˈælɪtɪ] *n* spécialité *f*.

specialize ['spɛʃəlaɪz] *vi*: **to ~ (in)** se spécialiser (dans).

specially ['spɛʃlɪ] *adv* spécialement, particulièrement.

special offer *n* (*COMM*) réclame *f*.

specialty ['spɛʃəltɪ] *n* (*US*) = **speciality**.

species ['spiːʃiːz] *n* (*pl inv*) espèce *f*.

specific [spəˈsɪfɪk] *adj* (*not vague*) précis(e), explicite; (*particular*) particulier(ière); (*BOT, CHEM etc*) spécifique; **to be ~ to** être particulier à, être le *or* un caractère (*or* les caractères) spécifique(s) de.

specifically [spəˈsɪfɪklɪ] *adv* explicitement, précisément; (*intend, ask, design*) expressément, spécialement; (*exclusively*) exclusivement, spécifiquement.

specification [spɛsɪfɪˈkeɪʃən] *n* spécification *f*; stipulation *f*; **~s** *npl* (*of car, building etc*) spécification.

specify ['spɛsɪfaɪ] *vt* spécifier, préciser; **unless otherwise specified** sauf indication contraire.

specimen ['spɛsɪmən] *n* spécimen *m*, échantillon *m*; (*MED*) prélèvement *m*.

specimen copy *n* spécimen *m*.

specimen signature *n* spécimen *m* de signature.

speck [spɛk] *n* petite tache, petit point; (*particle*) grain *m*.

speckled ['spɛkld] *adj* tacheté(e), moucheté(e).

specs [spɛks] *npl* (*col*) lunettes *fpl*.

spectacle ['spɛktəkl] *n* spectacle *m*.

spectacle case *n* (*BRIT*) étui *m* à lunettes.

spectacles ['spɛktəklz] *npl* (*BRIT*) lunettes *fpl*.

spectacular [spɛkˈtækjulə*] *adj* spectaculair ♦ *n* (*CINE etc*) superproduction *f*.

spectator [spɛkˈteɪtə*] *n* spectateur/trice.

spectator sport *n*: **football is a great ~** le football est un sport qui passionne les foules.

spectra ['spɛktrə] *npl of* **spectrum**.

spectre, (*US*) **specter** ['spɛktə*] *n* spectre *m*, fantôme *m*.

spectrum, *pl* **spectra** ['spɛktrəm, -rə] *n* spectre *m*; (*fig*) gamme *f*.

speculate ['spɛkjuleɪt] *vi* spéculer; (*try to guess*): **to ~ about** s'interroger sur.

speculation [spɛkjuˈleɪʃən] *n* spéculation *f*; conjectures *fpl*.

speculative ['spɛkjulətɪv] *adj* spéculatif(ive)

speculator ['spɛkjuleɪtə*] *n* spéculateur/tric

speech [spiːtʃ] *n* (*faculty*) parole *f*; (*talk*) discours *m*, allocution *f*; (*manner of speaking*) façon *f* de parler, langage *m*; (*language*) langage *m*; (*enunciation*) élocution *f*.

speech day *n* (*BRIT SCOL*) distribution *f* des prix.

speech impediment *n* défaut *m* d'élocution

speechless ['spiːtʃlɪs] *adj* muet(te).

speech therapy *n* orthophonie *f*.

speed [spiːd] *n* vitesse *f*; (*promptness*) rapidit *f* ♦ *vi* (*pt, pp* **sped** [spɛd]): **to ~ along/by** *etc* aller/passer *etc* à toute vitesse; (*AUT: excee ~ limit*) faire un excès de vitesse; **at ~** (*BRI* rapidement; **at full** *or* **top ~** à toute vitesse *or* allure; **at a ~ of 70 km/h** à une vitesse d 70 km/h; **shorthand/typing ~s** nombre *m* de mots à la minute en sténographie/ dactylographie; **a five-~ gearbox** une boîte cinq vitesses.

▶**speed up**, *pt, pp* **~ed up** *vi* aller plus vite, accélérer ♦ *vt* accélérer.

speedboat ['spiːdbəut] *n* vedette *f*, hors-bor *m inv*.

speedily ['spiːdɪlɪ] *adv* rapidement, promptement.

speeding ['spiːdɪŋ] *n* (*AUT*) excès *m* de vitesse.

speed limit *n* limitation *f* de vitesse, vitesse maximale permise.

speedometer [spɪˈdɔmɪtə*] *n* compteur *m* (d vitesse).

speed trap *n* (*AUT*) piège *m* de police pour contrôle de vitesse.

speedway *n* (*SPORT*) piste *f* de vitesse pour motos; (*: also*: **~ racing**) épreuve(s) *f(pl)* de vitesse de motos.

speedy [spi:dɪ] *adj* rapide, prompt(e).
speleologist [spelɪˈɔlədʒɪst] *n* spéléologue *m/f*.
spell [spɛl] *n* (*also*: **magic ~**) sortilège *m*, charme *m*; (*period of time*) (courte) période ♦ *vt* (*pt*, *pp* **spelt** or **~ed** [spɛlt, spɛld]) (*in writing*) écrire, orthographier; (*aloud*) épeler; (*fig*) signifier; **to cast a ~ on sb** jeter un sort à qn; **he can't ~** il fait des fautes d'orthographe; **how do you ~ your name?** comment écrivez-vous votre nom?; **can you ~ it for me?** pouvez-vous me l'épeler?
spellbound [ˈspɛlbaund] *adj* envoûté(e), subjugué(e).
spelling [ˈspɛlɪŋ] *n* orthographe *f*.
spelt [spɛlt] *pt*, *pp of* **spell**.
spend, *pt*, *pp* **spent** [spend, spent] *vt* (*money*) dépenser; (*time*, *life*) passer; (*devote*): **to ~ time/money/effort on sth** consacrer du temps/de l'argent/de l'énergie à qch.
spending [ˈspendɪŋ] *n* dépenses *fpl*; **government ~** les dépenses publiques.
spending money *n* argent *m* de poche.
spending power *n* pouvoir *m* d'achat.
spendthrift [ˈspendθrɪft] *n* dépensier/ière.
spent [spent] *pt*, *pp of* **spend** ♦ *adj* (*patience*) épuisé(e), à bout; (*cartridge*, *bullets*) vide; **~ matches** vieilles allumettes.
sperm [spə:m] *n* spermatozoïde *m*; (*semen*) sperme *m*.
sperm bank *n* banque *f* du sperme.
sperm whale *n* cachalot *m*.
spew [spju:] *vt* vomir.
sphere [sfɪə*] *n* sphère *f*; (*fig*) sphère, domaine *m*.
spherical [ˈsfɛrɪkl] *adj* sphérique.
sphinx [sfɪŋks] *n* sphinx *m*.
spice [spaɪs] *n* épice *f* ♦ *vt* épicer.
spick-and-span [ˈspɪkənˈspæn] *adj* impeccable.
spicy [ˈspaɪsɪ] *adj* épicé(e), relevé(e); (*fig*) piquant(e).
spider [ˈspaɪdə*] *n* araignée *f*; **~'s web** toile *f* d'araignée.
spiel [spi:l] *n* laïus *m inv*.
spike [spaɪk] *n* pointe *f*; (*ELEC*) pointe de tension; **~s** *npl* (*SPORT*) chaussures *fpl* à pointes.
spike heel *n* (*US*) talon *m* aiguille.
spiky [ˈspaɪkɪ] *adj* (*bush*, *branch*) épineux(euse); (*animal*) plein(e) de piquants.
spill, *pt*, *pp* **spilt** or **~ed** [spɪl, -t, -d] *vt* renverser; répandre ♦ *vi* se répandre; **to ~ the beans** (*col*) vendre la mèche; (: *confess*) lâcher le morceau.
spill out *vi* sortir à flots, se répandre.
spill over *vi* déborder.
spillage [ˈspɪlɪdʒ] *n* (*of oil*) déversement *m* (accidentel).
spin [spɪn] *n* (*revolution of wheel*) tour *m*; (*AVIAT*) (*chute f en*) vrille *f*; (*trip in car*) petit tour, balade *f* ♦ *vb* (*pt*, *pp* **spun** [spʌn]) *vt* (*wool*

etc) filer; (*wheel*) faire tourner; (*BRIT: clothes*) essorer ♦ *vi* tourner, tournoyer; **to ~ a yarn** débiter une longue histoire; **to ~ a coin** (*BRIT*) jouer à pile ou face.
▶**spin out** *vt* faire durer.
spina bifida [ˈspaɪnəˈbɪfɪdə] *n* spina-bifida *m inv*.
spinach [ˈspɪnɪtʃ] *n* épinard *m*; (*as food*) épinards *mpl*.
spinal [ˈspaɪnl] *adj* vertébral(e), spinal(e).
spinal column *n* colonne vertébrale.
spinal cord *n* moelle épinière.
spindly [ˈspɪndlɪ] *adj* grêle, filiforme.
spin doctor *n* (*col*) personne employée pour présenter un parti politique sous un jour favorable.
spin-dry [ˈspɪnˈdraɪ] *vt* essorer.
spin-dryer [spɪnˈdraɪə*] *n* (*BRIT*) essoreuse *f*.
spine [spaɪn] *n* colonne vertébrale; (*thorn*) épine *f*, piquant *m*.
spine-chilling [ˈspaɪntʃɪlɪŋ] *adj* terrifiant(e).
spineless [ˈspaɪnlɪs] *adj* invertébré(e); (*fig*) mou(molle), sans caractère.
spinner [ˈspɪnə*] *n* (*of thread*) fileur/euse.
spinning [ˈspɪnɪŋ] *n* (*of thread*) filage *m*; (*by machine*) filature *f*.
spinning top *n* toupie *f*.
spinning wheel *n* rouet *m*.
spin-off [ˈspɪnɔf] *n* sous-produit *m*; avantage inattendu.
spinster [ˈspɪnstə*] *n* célibataire *f*; vieille fille.
spiral [ˈspaɪərl] *n* spirale *f* ♦ *adj* en spirale ♦ *vi* (*fig: prices etc*) monter en flèche; **the inflationary ~** la spirale inflationniste.
spiral staircase *n* escalier *m* en colimaçon.
spire [ˈspaɪə*] *n* flèche *f*, aiguille *f*.
spirit [ˈspɪrɪt] *n* (*soul*) esprit *m*, âme *f*; (*ghost*) esprit, revenant *m*; (*mood*) esprit, état *m* d'esprit; (*courage*) courage *m*, énergie *f*; **~s** *npl* (*drink*) spiritueux *mpl*, alcool *m*; **in good ~s** de bonne humeur; **in low ~s** démoralisé(e); **community ~** solidarité *f*; **public ~** civisme *m*.
spirit duplicator *n* duplicateur *m* à alcool.
spirited [ˈspɪrɪtɪd] *adj* vif(vive), fougueux(euse), plein(e) d'allant.
spirit level *n* niveau *m* à bulle.
spiritual [ˈspɪrɪtjuəl] *adj* spirituel(le); religieux(euse) ♦ *n* (*also*: **Negro ~**) spiritual *m*.
spiritualism [ˈspɪrɪtjuəlɪzəm] *n* spiritisme *m*.
spit [spɪt] *n* (*for roasting*) broche *f*; (*spittle*) crachat *m*; (*saliva*) salive *f* ♦ *vi* (*pt*, *pp* **spat** [spæt]) cracher; (*sound*) crépiter.
spite [spaɪt] *n* rancune *f*, dépit *m* ♦ *vt* contrarier, vexer; **in ~ of** en dépit de, malgré.
spiteful [ˈspaɪtful] *adj* malveillant(e), rancunier(ière).
spitroast [ˈspɪtˈrəust] *vt* faire rôtir à la broche.
spitting [ˈspɪtɪŋ] *n*: **"~ prohibited"** "défense

de cracher" ♦ _adj_: **to be the ~ image of sb** être le portrait tout craché de qn.

spittle ['spɪtl] _n_ salive _f_; bave _f_; crachat _m_.

spiv [spɪv] _n_ (_BRIT col_) chevalier _m_ d'industrie, aigrefin _m_.

splash [splæʃ] _n_ éclaboussement _m_; (_of colour_) tache _f_ ♦ _excl_ (_sound_) plouf! ♦ _vt_ éclabousser ♦ _vi_ (_also_: ~ **about**) barboter, patauger.

splashdown ['splæʃdaun] _n_ amerrissage _m_.

splay [spleɪ] _adj_: ~**footed** marchant les pieds en dehors.

spleen [spliːn] _n_ (_ANAT_) rate _f_.

splendid ['splendɪd] _adj_ splendide, superbe, magnifique.

splendour, (_US_) **splendor** ['splendə*] _n_ splendeur _f_, magnificence _f_.

splice [splaɪs] _vt_ épisser.

splint [splɪnt] _n_ attelle _f_, éclisse _f_.

splinter ['splɪntə*] _n_ (_wood_) écharde _f_; (_metal_) éclat _m_ ♦ _vi_ se fragmenter.

splinter group _n_ groupe dissident.

split [splɪt] _n_ fente _f_, déchirure _f_; (_fig: POL_) scission _f_ ♦ _vb_ (_pt, pp_ **split**) _vt_ fendre, déchirer; (_party_) diviser; (_work, profits_) partager, répartir ♦ _vi_ (_break_) se fendre, se briser; (_divide_) se diviser; **let's ~ the difference** coupons la poire en deux; **to do the ~s** faire le grand écart.

▶**split up** _vi_ (_couple_) se séparer, rompre; (_meeting_) se disperser.

split-level ['splɪtlevl] _adj_ (_house_) à deux or plusieurs niveaux.

split peas _npl_ pois cassés.

split personality _n_ double personnalité _f_.

split second _n_ fraction _f_ de seconde.

splitting ['splɪtɪŋ] _adj_: **a ~ headache** un mal de tête atroce.

splutter ['splʌtə*] _vi_ bafouiller; postillonner.

spoil, _pt, pp_ **spoilt** _or_ ~**ed** [spɔɪl, -t, -d] _vt_ (_damage_) abîmer; (_mar_) gâcher; (_child_) gâter; (_ballot paper_) rendre nul ♦ _vi_: **to be** ~**ing for a fight** chercher la bagarre.

spoils [spɔɪlz] _npl_ butin _m_.

spoilsport ['spɔɪlspɔːt] _n_ trouble-fête _m/f inv_, rabat-joie _m inv_.

spoilt [spɔɪlt] _pt, pp of_ **spoil** ♦ _adj_ (_child_) gâté(e); (_ballot paper_) nul(le).

spoke [spəuk] _pt of_ **speak** ♦ _n_ rayon _m_.

spoken ['spəukn] _pp of_ **speak**.

spokesman ['spəuksmən], **spokeswoman** [-wumən] _n_ porte-parole _m inv_.

spokesperson ['spəukspəːsn] _n_ porte-parole _m inv_.

sponge [spʌndʒ] _n_ éponge _f_; (_CULIN: also_: ~ **cake**) ≈ biscuit _m_ de Savoie ♦ _vt_ éponger ♦ _vi_: **to ~ on** _or_ (_US_) **off of** vivre aux crochets de.

sponge bag _n_ (_BRIT_) trousse _f_ de toilette.

sponge cake _n_ ≈ biscuit _m_ de Savoie.

sponger ['spʌndʒə*] _n_ (_pej_) parasite _m_.

spongy ['spʌndʒɪ] _adj_ spongieux(euse).

sponsor ['spɔnsə*] _n_ sponsor _m_, personne _f_ (or

organisme _m_) qui assure le parrainage; (_of new member_) parrain _m_/marraine _f_ ♦ _vt_ (_programme, competition etc_) parrainer, patronner, sponsoriser; (_POL: bill_) présenter (_new member_) parrainer; **I ~ed him at 3p a mile** (_in fund-raising race_) je me suis engagé à lui donner 3p par mile.

sponsorship ['spɔnsəʃɪp] _n_ patronage _m_, parrainage _m_.

spontaneity [spɔntə'neɪɪtɪ] _n_ spontanéité _f_.

spontaneous [spɔn'teɪnɪəs] _adj_ spontané(e).

spoof [spuːf] _n_ (_parody_) parodie _f_; (_trick_) canular _m_.

spooky ['spuːkɪ] _adj_ qui donne la chair de poule.

spool [spuːl] _n_ bobine _f_.

spoon [spuːn] _n_ cuiller _f_.

spoon-feed ['spuːnfiːd] _vt_ nourrir à la cuiller; (_fig_) mâcher le travail à.

spoonful ['spuːnful] _n_ cuillerée _f_.

sporadic [spə'rædɪk] _adj_ sporadique.

sport [spɔːt] _n_ sport _m_; (_amusement_) divertissement _m_; (_person_) chic type/chic fille ♦ _vt_ arborer; **indoor/outdoor ~s** sports en salle/de plein air; **to say sth in ~** dire qc pour rire.

sporting ['spɔːtɪŋ] _adj_ sportif(ive); **to give sb a ~ chance** donner sa chance à qn.

sport jacket _n_ (_US_) = **sports jacket**.

sports car _n_ voiture _f_ de sport.

sports ground _n_ terrain _m_ de sport.

sports jacket _n_ veste _f_ de sport.

sportsman ['spɔːtsmən] _n_ sportif _m_.

sportsmanship ['spɔːtsmənʃɪp] _n_ esprit sportif, sportivité _f_.

sports page _n_ page _f_ des sports.

sportswear ['spɔːtswɛə*] _n_ vêtements _mpl_ de sport.

sportswoman ['spɔːtswumən] _n_ sportive _f_.

sporty ['spɔːtɪ] _adj_ sportif(ive).

spot [spɔt] _n_ tache _f_; (_dot: on pattern_) pois _m_; (_pimple_) bouton _m_; (_place_) endroit _m_, coin _m_; (_also_: ~ **advertisement**) message _m_ publicitaire; (_small amount_): **a ~ of** un peu de ♦ _vt_ (_notice_) apercevoir, repérer; **on the ~** sur place, sur les lieux; (_immediately_) sur le champ; **to put sb on the ~** (_fig_) mettre qn dans l'embarras; **to come out in ~s** se couvrir de boutons, avoir une éruption de boutons.

spot check _n_ contrôle intermittent.

spotless ['spɔtlɪs] _adj_ immaculé(e).

spotlight ['spɔtlaɪt] _n_ projecteur _m_; (_AUT_) phare _m_ auxiliaire.

spot-on [spɔt'ɔn] _adj_ (_BRIT col_) en plein dans le mille.

spot price _n_ prix _m_ sur place.

spotted ['spɔtɪd] _adj_ tacheté(e), moucheté(e); à pois; ~ **with** tacheté(e) de.

spotty ['spɔtɪ] _adj_ (_face_) boutonneux(euse).

spouse [spauz] _n_ époux/épouse.

spout [spaut] _n_ (_of jug_) bec _m_; (_of liquid_) jet _m_

♦ *vi* jaillir.

sprain [spreɪn] *n* entorse *f*, foulure *f* ♦ *vt*: **to ~ one's ankle** se fouler *or* se tordre la cheville.

sprang [spræŋ] *pt of* **spring**.

sprawl [sprɔːl] *vi* s'étaler ♦ *n*: **urban ~** expansion urbaine; **to send sb ~ing** envoyer qn rouler par terre.

spray [spreɪ] *n* jet *m* (en fines gouttelettes); (*container*) vaporisateur *m*, bombe *f*; (*of flowers*) petit bouquet ♦ *vt* vaporiser, pulvériser; (*crops*) traiter ♦ *cpd* (*deodorant etc*) en bombe *or* atomiseur.

spread [spred] *n* (*distribution*) répartition *f*; (*CULIN*) pâte *f* à tartiner; (*PRESS, TYP: two pages*) double page *f* ♦ *vb* (*pt, pp* **spread**) *vt* (*paste, contents*) étendre, étaler; (*rumour, disease*) répandre, propager; (*repayments*) échelonner, étaler; (*wealth*) répartir ♦ *vi* s'étendre; se répandre; se propager; **middle-age ~** embonpoint *m* (pris avec l'âge).

spread-eagled ['spredi:gld] *adj*: **to be** *or* **lie ~** être étendu(e) bras et jambes écartés.

spreadsheet ['spredʃi:t] *n* (*COMPUT*) tableur *m*.

spree [spri:] *n*: **to go on a ~** faire la fête.

sprig [sprɪg] *n* rameau *m*.

sprightly ['spraɪtlɪ] *adj* alerte.

spring [sprɪŋ] *n* (*leap*) bond *m*, saut *m*; (*coiled metal*) ressort *m*; (*bounciness*) élasticité *f*; (*season*) printemps *m*; (*of water*) source *f* ♦ *vb* (*pt* **sprang**, *pp* **sprung** [spræŋ, sprʌŋ]) *vi* bondir, sauter ♦ *vt*: **to ~ a leak** (*pipe etc*) se mettre à fuir; **he sprang the news on me** il m'a annoncé la nouvelle de but en blanc; **in ~, in the ~** au printemps; **to ~ from** provenir de; **to ~ into action** passer à l'action; **to walk with a ~ in one's step** marcher d'un pas souple.

spring up *vi* (*problem*) se présenter, surgir.

springboard ['sprɪŋbɔːd] *n* tremplin *m*.

spring-clean [sprɪŋ'kliːn] *n* (*also*: ~**ing**) grand nettoyage de printemps.

spring onion *n* (*BRIT*) ciboule *f*, cive *f*.

spring roll *n* rouleau *m* de printemps.

springtime ['sprɪŋtaɪm] *n* printemps *m*.

springy ['sprɪŋɪ] *adj* élastique, souple.

sprinkle ['sprɪŋkl] *vt* (*pour*) répandre; verser; **to ~ water etc on, ~ with water etc** asperger d'eau *etc*; **to ~ sugar etc on, ~ with sugar etc** saupoudrer de sucre *etc*; **~d with** (*fig*) parsemé(e) de.

sprinkler ['sprɪŋklə*] *n* (*for lawn etc*) arroseur *m*; (*to put out fire*) diffuseur *m* d'extincteur automatique d'incendie.

sprinkling ['sprɪŋklɪŋ] *n* (*of water*) quelques gouttes *fpl*; (*of salt*) pincée *f*; (*of sugar*) légère couche.

sprint [sprɪnt] *n* sprint *m* ♦ *vi* sprinter.

sprinter ['sprɪntə*] *n* sprinteur/euse.

sprite [spraɪt] *n* lutin *m*.

spritzer ['sprɪtsə*] *n* boisson à base de vin blanc et d'eau de Seltz.

sprocket ['sprɔkɪt] *n* (*on printer etc*) picot *m*.

sprout [spraʊt] *vi* germer, pousser.

sprouts [spraʊts] *npl* (*also*: **Brussels ~**) choux *mpl* de Bruxelles.

spruce [spru:s] *n* épicéa *m* ♦ *adj* net(te), pimpant(e).

▶**spruce up** *vt* (*smarten up: room etc*) apprêter; **to ~ o.s. up** se faire beau(belle).

sprung [sprʌŋ] *pp of* **spring**.

spry [spraɪ] *adj* alerte, vif(vive).

SPUC *n abbr* = *Society for the Protection of Unborn Children*.

spud [spʌd] *n* (*col: potato*) patate *f*.

spun [spʌn] *pt, pp of* **spin**.

spur [spɔː*] *n* éperon *m*; (*fig*) aiguillon *m* ♦ *vt* (*also*: ~ **on**) éperonner; aiguillonner; **on the ~ of the moment** sous l'impulsion du moment.

spurious ['spjʊərɪəs] *adj* faux(fausse).

spurn [spɔːn] *vt* repousser avec mépris.

spurt [spɔːt] *n* jet *m*; (*of energy*) sursaut *m* ♦ *vi* jaillir, gicler; **to put in** *or* **on a ~** (*runner*) piquer un sprint; (*fig: in work etc*) donner un coup de collier.

sputter ['spʌtə*] *vi* = **splutter**.

spy [spaɪ] *n* espion/ne ♦ *vi*: **to ~ on** espionner, épier ♦ *vt* (*see*) apercevoir ♦ *cpd* (*film, story*) d'espionnage.

spying ['spaɪɪŋ] *n* espionnage *m*.

Sq. *abbr* (*in address*) = **square**.

sq. *abbr* (*MATH etc*) = **square**.

squabble ['skwɔbl] *n* querelle *f*, chamaillerie *f* ♦ *vi* se chamailler.

squad [skwɔd] *n* (*MIL, POLICE*) escouade *f*, groupe *m*; (*FOOTBALL*) contingent *m*; **flying ~** (*POLICE*) brigade volante.

squad car *n* (*BRIT POLICE*) voiture *f* de police.

squaddie ['skwɔdɪ] *n* (*MIL col*) troufion *m*, bidasse *m*.

squadron ['skwɔdrn] *n* (*MIL*) escadron *m*; (*AVIAT, NAUT*) escadrille *f*.

squalid ['skwɔlɪd] *adj* sordide, ignoble.

squall [skwɔːl] *n* rafale *f*, bourrasque *f*.

squalor ['skwɔlə*] *n* conditions *fpl* sordides.

squander ['skwɔndə*] *vt* gaspiller, dilapider.

square [skwɛə*] *n* carré *m*; (*in town*) place *f*; (*US: block of houses*) îlot *m*, pâté *m* de maisons; (*instrument*) équerre *f* ♦ *adj* carré(e); (*honest*) honnête, régulier(ière); (*col: ideas, tastes*) vieux jeu *inv*, qui retarde ♦ *vt* (*arrange*) régler; arranger; (*MATH*) élever au carré; (*reconcile*) concilier ♦ *vi* (*agree*) cadrer, s'accorder; **all ~** quitte; à égalité; **a ~ meal** un repas convenable; **2 metres ~** (de) 2 mètres sur 2; **1 ~ metre** 1 mètre carré; **we're back to ~ one** (*fig*) on se retrouve à la case départ.

▶**square up** *vi* (*BRIT: settle*) régler; **to ~ up with sb** régler ses comptes avec qn.

square bracket *n* (*TYP*) crochet *m*.

squarely ['skwɛəlɪ] adv carrément; (honestly, fairly) honnêtement, équitablement.

square root n racine carrée.

squash [skwɔʃ] n (BRIT: drink): **lemon/orange** ~ citronnade/orangeade f; (SPORT) squash m; (vegetable) courge f ♦ vt écraser.

squat [skwɔt] adj petit(e) et épais(se), ramassé(e) ♦ vi s'accroupir; (on property) squatter, squattériser.

squatter ['skwɔtə*] n squatter m.

squawk [skwɔ:k] vi pousser un or des gloussement(s).

squeak [skwi:k] n (of hinge, wheel etc) grincement m; (of shoes) craquement m; (of mouse etc) petit cri aigu ♦ vi grincer, crier.

squeaky ['skwi:kɪ] adj grinçant(e); **to be ~ clean** (fig) être au-dessus de tout soupçon.

squeal [skwi:l] vi pousser un or des cri(s) aigu(s) or perçant(s).

squeamish ['skwi:mɪʃ] adj facilement dégoûté(e); facilement scandalisé(e).

squeeze [skwi:z] n pression f; (also: **credit** ~) encadrement m du crédit, restrictions fpl de crédit ♦ vt presser; (hand, arm) serrer ♦ vi: **to ~ past/under sth** se glisser avec (beaucoup de) difficulté devant/sous qch; **a ~ of lemon** quelques gouttes de citron.

▶**squeeze out** vt exprimer; (fig) soutirer.

squelch [skwɛltʃ] vi faire un bruit de succion; patauger.

squib [skwɪb] n pétard m.

squid [skwɪd] n calmar m.

squiggle ['skwɪgl] n gribouillis m.

squint [skwɪnt] vi loucher ♦ n: **he has a ~** il louche, il souffre de strabisme; **to ~ at sth** regarder qch du coin de l'œil; (quickly) jeter un coup d'œil à qch.

squire ['skwaɪə*] n (BRIT) propriétaire terrien.

squirm [skwə:m] vi se tortiller.

squirrel ['skwɪrəl] n écureuil m.

squirt [skwə:t] n jet m ♦ vi jaillir, gicler.

Sr abbr = **senior, sister** (REL).

SRC n abbr (BRIT: = Students' Representative Council) ≈ CROUS m.

Sri Lanka [srɪ'læŋkə] n Sri Lanka m or f.

SRN n abbr (BRIT) = **State Registered Nurse.**

SRO abbr (US) = **standing room only.**

SS abbr (= steamship) S/S.

SSA n abbr (US: = Social Security Administration) organisme de sécurité sociale.

SST n abbr (US) = **supersonic transport.**

ST abbr (US: = Standard Time) heure officielle.

St abbr (= saint) St; (= street) R.

stab [stæb] n (with knife etc) coup m (de couteau etc); (col: try): **to have a ~ at (doing) sth** s'essayer à (faire) qch ♦ vt poignarder; **to ~ sb to death** tuer qn à coups de couteau.

stabbing ['stæbɪŋ] n: **there's been a ~** quelqu'un a été attaqué à coups de couteau ♦ adj (pain, ache) lancinant(e).

stability [stə'bɪlɪtɪ] n stabilité f.

stabilization [steɪbəlaɪ'zeɪʃən] n stabilisation f.

stabilize ['steɪbəlaɪz] vt stabiliser ♦ vi se stabiliser.

stabilizer ['steɪbəlaɪzə*] n stabilisateur m.

stable ['steɪbl] n écurie f ♦ adj stable; **riding ~** centre m d'équitation.

staccato [stə'kɑ:təu] adv staccato ♦ adj (MUS) piqué(e); (noise, voice) saccadé(e).

stack [stæk] n tas m, pile f ♦ vt empiler, entasser; **there's ~s of time** (BRIT col) on a tout le temps.

stadium ['steɪdɪəm] n stade m.

staff [stɑ:f] n (work force) personnel m; (BRIT SCOL: also: **teaching ~**) professeurs mpl, enseignants mpl, personnel enseignant; (servants) domestiques mpl; (MIL) état-major m; (stick) perche f, bâton m ♦ vt pourvoir en personnel.

staffroom ['stɑ:fru:m] n salle f des professeurs.

Staffs abbr (BRIT) = **Staffordshire.**

stag [stæg] n cerf m; (BRIT STOCK EXCHANGE) loup m.

stage [steɪdʒ] n scène f; (profession): **the ~** le théâtre; (point) étape f, stade m; (platform) estrade f ♦ vt (play) monter, mettre en scène; (demonstration) organiser; (fig: recovery etc) effectuer; **in ~s** par étapes, par degrés; **to go through a difficult ~** traverser une période difficile; **in the early ~s** au début; **in the final ~s** à la fin.

stagecoach ['steɪdʒkəutʃ] n diligence f.

stage door n entrée f des artistes.

stage fright n trac m.

stagehand ['steɪdʒhænd] n machiniste m.

stage-manage ['steɪdʒmænɪdʒ] vt (fig) orchestrer.

stage manager n régisseur m.

stagger ['stægə*] vi chanceler, tituber ♦ vt (person) stupéfier; bouleverser; (hours, holidays) étaler, échelonner.

staggering ['stægərɪŋ] adj (amazing) stupéfiant(e), renversant(e).

staging post ['steɪdʒɪŋ-] n relais m.

stagnant ['stægnənt] adj stagnant(e).

stagnate [stæg'neɪt] vi stagner, croupir.

stagnation [stæg'neɪʃən] n stagnation f.

stag night, stag party n enterrement m de vie de garçon.

staid [steɪd] adj posé(e), rassis(e).

stain [steɪn] n tache f; (colouring) colorant m ♦ vt tacher; (wood) teindre.

stained glass window [steɪnd-] n vitrail m.

stainless ['steɪnlɪs] adj (steel) inoxydable.

stain remover n détachant m.

stair [stɛə*] n (step) marche f; **~s** npl escalier m; **on the ~s** dans l'escalier.

staircase ['stɛəkeɪs], **stairway** ['stɛəweɪ] n escalier m.

stairwell ['stɛəwɛl] n cage f d'escalier.

stake [steɪk] n pieu m, poteau m; (BETTING) enjeu m ♦ vt risquer, jouer; (also: ~ **out:**

area) marquer, délimiter; **to be at** ~ être en jeu; **to have a** ~ **in sth** avoir des intérêts (en jeu) dans qch; **to** ~ **a claim (to sth)** revendiquer (qch).

stakeout ['steɪkaut] *n* surveillance *f*; **to be on a** ~ effectuer une surveillance.

stalactite ['stæləktaɪt] *n* stalactite *f*.

stalagmite ['stæləgmaɪt] *n* stalagmite *f*.

stale [steɪl] *adj* (*bread*) rassis(e); (*beer*) éventé(e); (*smell*) de renfermé.

stalemate ['steɪlmeɪt] *n* pat *m*; (*fig*) impasse *f*.

stalk [stɔːk] *n* tige *f* ♦ *vt* traquer ♦ *vi*: **to** ~ **in/ out** *etc* entrer/sortir *etc* avec raideur.

stall [stɔːl] *n* (*BRIT: in street, market etc*) éventaire *m*, étal *m*; (*in stable*) stalle *f* ♦ *vt* (*AUT*) caler ♦ *vi* (*AUT*) caler; (*fig*) essayer de gagner du temps; ~**s** *npl* (*BRIT: in cinema, theatre*) orchestre *m*; **a newspaper/flower** ~ un kiosque à journaux/de fleuriste.

stallholder ['stɔːlhəuldə*] *n* (*BRIT*) marchand/e en plein air.

stallion ['stæljən] *n* étalon *m* (*cheval*).

stalwart ['stɔːlwət] *n* partisan *m* fidèle.

stamen ['steɪmɛn] *n* étamine *f*.

stamina ['stæmɪnə] *n* vigueur *f*, endurance *f*.

stammer ['stæmə*] *n* bégaiement *m* ♦ *vi* bégayer.

stamp [stæmp] *n* timbre *m*; (*mark, also fig*) empreinte *f*; (*on document*) cachet *m* ♦ *vi* (*also:* ~ **one's foot**) taper du pied ♦ *vt* tamponner, estamper; (*letter*) timbrer; ~**ed addressed envelope (s.a.e.)** enveloppe affranchie pour la réponse.

stamp out *vt* (*fire*) piétiner; (*crime*) éradiquer; (*opposition*) éliminer.

stamp album *n* album *m* de timbres(-poste).

stamp collecting [-kələktɪŋ] *n* philatélie *f*.

stamp duty *n* (*BRIT*) droit *m* de timbre.

stampede [stæm'piːd] *n* ruée *f*; (*of cattle*) débandade *f*.

stamp machine *n* distributeur *m* de timbres-poste.

stance [stæns] *n* position *f*.

stand [stænd] *n* (*position*) position *f*; (*MIL*) résistance *f*; (*structure*) guéridon *m*; support *m*; (*COMM*) étalage *m*, stand *m*; (*SPORT*) tribune *f*; (*also:* **music** ~) pupitre *m* ♦ *vb* (*pt, pp* **stood** [stud]) *vi* être *or* se tenir (debout); (*rise*) se lever, se mettre debout; (*be placed*) se trouver ♦ *vt* (*place*) mettre, poser; (*tolerate, withstand*) supporter; **to make a** ~ prendre position; **to take a** ~ **on an issue** prendre position sur un problème; **to** ~ **for parliament** (*BRIT*) se présenter aux élections (*comme candidat à la députation*); **to** ~ **guard** *or* **watch** (*MIL*) monter la garde; **it** ~**s to reason** c'est logique; cela va de soi; **as things** ~ dans l'état actuel des choses; **to** ~ **sb a drink/meal** payer à boire/à manger à qn; **I can't** ~ **him** je ne peux pas le voir.

stand aside *vi* s'écarter.

stand by *vi* (*be ready*) se tenir prêt(e) ♦ *vt fus*

(*opinion*) s'en tenir à.

▶**stand down** *vi* (*withdraw*) se retirer; (*LAW*) renoncer à ses droits.

▶**stand for** *vt fus* (*signify*) représenter, signifier; (*tolerate*) supporter, tolérer.

▶**stand in for** *vt fus* remplacer.

▶**stand out** *vi* (*be prominent*) ressortir.

▶**stand up** *vi* (*rise*) se lever, se mettre debout.

▶**stand up for** *vt fus* défendre.

▶**stand up to** *vt fus* tenir tête à, résister à.

stand-alone ['stændələun] *adj* (*COMPUT*) autonome.

standard ['stændəd] *n* (*reference*) norme *f*; (*level*) niveau *m*; (*flag*) étendard *m* ♦ *adj* (*size etc*) ordinaire, normal(e); (*model, feature*) standard *inv*; (*practice*) courant(e); (*text*) de base; ~**s** *npl* (*morals*) morale *f*, principes *mpl*; **to be** *or* **come up to** ~ être du niveau voulu *or* à la hauteur; **to apply a double** ~ avoir *or* appliquer deux poids deux mesures; ~ **of living** niveau de vie.

standardization [stændədaɪ'zeɪʃən] *n* standardisation *f*.

standardize ['stændədaɪz] *vt* standardiser.

standard lamp *n* (*BRIT*) lampadaire *m*.

standard time *n* heure légale.

stand-by ['stændbaɪ] *n* remplaçant/e ♦ *adj* (*provisions*) de réserve; **to be on** ~ se tenir prêt(e) (à intervenir); (*doctor*) être de garde.

stand-by generator *n* générateur *m* de secours.

stand-by passenger *n* passager/ère en stand-by *or* en attente.

stand-by ticket *n* billet *m* stand-by.

stand-in ['stændɪn] *n* remplaçant/e; (*CINE*) doublure *f*.

standing ['stændɪŋ] *adj* debout *inv*; (*permanent: rule*) immuable; (*army*) de métier; (*grievance*) constant(e), de longue date ♦ *n* réputation *f*, rang *m*, standing *m*; (*duration*): **of 6 months'** ~ qui dure depuis 6 mois; **of many years'** ~ qui dure *or* existe depuis longtemps; **he was given a** ~ **ovation** on s'est levé pour l'acclamer; **it's a** ~ **joke** c'est un vieux sujet de plaisanterie; **a man of some** ~ un homme estimé.

standing committee *n* commission permanente.

standing order *n* (*BRIT: at bank*) virement permanent; ~**s** *npl* (*MIL*) règlement *m*.

standing room *n* places *fpl* debout.

stand-off ['stændɔf] *n* (*esp US: stalemate*) impasse *f*.

stand-offish [stænd'ɔfɪʃ] *adj* distant(e), froid(e).

standpat ['stændpæt] *adj* (*US*) inflexible, rigide.

standpipe ['stændpaɪp] *n* colonne *f* d'alimentation.

standpoint ['stændpɔɪnt] *n* point *m* de vue.

standstill ['stændstɪl] n: **at a ~** à l'arrêt; (fig) au point mort; **to come to a ~** s'immobiliser, s'arrêter.

stank [stæŋk] pt of **stink**.

stanza ['stænzə] n strophe f; couplet m.

staple ['steɪpl] n (for papers) agrafe f; (chief product) produit m de base ♦ adj (food, crop, industry etc) de base, principal(e) ♦ vt agrafer.

stapler ['steɪplə*] n agrafeuse f.

star [stɑ:*] n étoile f; (celebrity) vedette f ♦ vi: **to ~ (in)** être la vedette (de) ♦ vt (CINE) avoir pour vedette; **4-~ hotel** hôtel m 4 étoiles; **2-~ petrol** (BRIT) essence f ordinaire; **4-~ petrol** (BRIT) super m.

star attraction n grande attraction.

starboard ['stɑ:bəd] n tribord m; **to ~** à tribord.

starch [stɑ:tʃ] n amidon m.

starched ['stɑ:tʃt] adj (collar) amidonné(e), empesé(e).

starchy ['stɑ:tʃɪ] adj riche en féculents; (person) guindé(e).

stardom ['stɑ:dəm] n célébrité f.

stare [stɛə*] n regard m fixe ♦ vi: **to ~ at** regarder fixement.

starfish ['stɑ:fɪʃ] n étoile f de mer.

stark [stɑ:k] adj (bleak) désolé(e), morne; (simplicity, colour) austère; (reality, poverty) nu(e) ♦ adv: **~ naked** complètement nu(e).

starkers ['stɑ:kəz] adj: **to be ~** (BRIT col) être à poil.

starlet ['stɑ:lɪt] n (CINE) starlette f.

starlight ['stɑ:laɪt] n: **by ~** à la lumière des étoiles.

starling ['stɑ:lɪŋ] n étourneau m.

starlit ['stɑ:lɪt] adj étoilé(e); illuminé(e) par les étoiles.

starry ['stɑ:rɪ] adj étoilé(e).

starry-eyed [stɑ:rɪ'aɪd] adj (innocent) ingénu(e).

Stars and Stripes npl: **the ~** la bannière étoilée.

star sign n signe zodiacal or du zodiaque.

star-studded ['stɑ:stʌdɪd] adj: **a ~ cast** une distribution prestigieuse.

start [stɑ:t] n commencement m, début m; (of race) départ m; (sudden movement) sursaut m; (advantage) avance f ♦ vt commencer; (found: business, newspaper) lancer, créer ♦ vi partir, se mettre en route; (jump) sursauter; **at the ~** au début; **for a ~** d'abord, pour commencer; **to make an early ~** partir or commencer de bonne heure; **to ~ doing sth** se mettre à faire qch; **to ~ (off) with ...** (firstly) d'abord ...; (at the beginning) au commencement ....

▶**start off** vi commencer; (leave) partir.

▶**start over** vi (US) recommencer.

▶**start up** vi commencer; (car) démarrer ♦ vt déclencher; (car) mettre en marche.

starter ['stɑ:tə*] n (AUT) démarreur m; (SPORT:

official) starter m; (: runner, horse) partant m; (BRIT CULIN) entrée f.

starting handle ['stɑ:tɪŋ-] n (BRIT) manivelle f.

starting point ['stɑ:tɪŋ-] n point m de départ.

starting price ['stɑ:tɪŋ-] n prix initial.

startle ['stɑ:tl] vt faire sursauter; donner un choc à.

startling ['stɑ:tlɪŋ] adj surprenant(e), saisissant(e).

star turn n (BRIT) vedette f.

starvation [stɑ:'veɪʃən] n faim f, famine f; **to die of ~** mourir de faim or d'inanition.

starve [stɑ:v] vi mourir de faim; être affamé(e) ♦ vt affamer; **I'm starving** je meurs de faim.

stash [stæʃ] vt (col): **to ~ sth away** planquer qch.

state [steɪt] n état m; (pomp): **in ~** en grande pompe ♦ vt (declare) déclarer, affirmer; (specify) indiquer, spécifier; **to be in a ~** être dans tous ses états; **~ of emergency** état d'urgence; **~ of mind** état d'esprit; **the ~ of the art** l'état actuel de la technologie (or des connaissances).

state control n contrôle m de l'État.

stated ['steɪtɪd] adj fixé(e), prescrit(e).

State Department n (US) Département m d'État, ≈ ministère m des Affaires étrangères.

state education n (BRIT) enseignement public.

stateless ['steɪtlɪs] adj apatride.

stately ['steɪtlɪ] adj majestueux(euse), imposant(e).

statement ['steɪtmənt] n déclaration f; (LAW) déposition f; (ECON) relevé m; **official ~** communiqué officiel; **~ of account, bank ~** relevé de compte.

state-owned ['steɪtəund] adj étatisé(e).

States [steɪts] npl: **the ~** les États-Unis mpl.

state school n école publique.

state secret n secret m d'État.

statesman ['steɪtsmən] n homme m d'État.

statesmanship ['steɪtsmənʃɪp] n qualités fpl d'homme d'État.

static ['stætɪk] n (RADIO) parasites mpl; (also: ~ electricity) électricité f statique ♦ adj statique.

station ['steɪʃən] n gare f; (MIL, POLICE) poste m (militaire or de police etc); (rank) condition f, rang m ♦ vt placer, poster; **action ~s** postes de combat; **to be ~ed in** (MIL) être en garnison à.

stationary ['steɪʃnərɪ] adj à l'arrêt, immobile.

stationer ['steɪʃənə*] n papetier/ière; **~'s (shop)** papeterie f.

stationery ['steɪʃnərɪ] n papier m à lettres, petit matériel de bureau.

station master n (RAIL) chef m de gare.

station wagon n (US) break m.

statistic [stə'tɪstɪk] n statistique f.

statistical [stə'tɪstɪkl] adj statistique.

statistics [stə'tɪstɪks] n (science) statistique f.

statue ['stætjuː] n statue f.

statuesque [stætju'ɛsk] adj sculptural(e).

statuette [stætju'ɛt] n statuette f.

stature ['stætʃə*] n stature f; (fig) envergure f.

status ['steɪtəs] n position f, situation f; (prestige) prestige m; (ADMIN, official position) statut m.

status quo [-'kwəu] n: **the ~** le statu quo.

status symbol n marque f de standing, signe extérieur de richesse.

statute ['stætjuːt] n loi f; **~s** npl (of club etc) statuts mpl.

statute book n ≈ code m, textes mpl de loi.

statutory ['stætjutrɪ] adj statutaire, prévu(e) par un article de loi; **~ meeting** assemblée constitutive or statutaire.

staunch [stɔːntʃ] adj sûr(e), loyal(e) ♦ vt étancher.

stave [steɪv] n (MUS) portée f ♦ vt: **to ~ off** (attack) parer; (threat) conjurer.

stay [steɪ] n (period of time) séjour m; (LAW): **~ of execution** sursis m à statuer ♦ vi rester; (reside) loger; (spend some time) séjourner; **to ~ put** ne pas bouger; **to ~ with friends** loger chez des amis; **to ~ the night** passer la nuit.

▶**stay behind** vi rester en arrière.

▶**stay in** vi (at home) rester à la maison.

▶**stay on** vi rester.

▶**stay out** vi (of house) ne pas rentrer; (strikers) rester en grève.

▶**stay up** vi (at night) ne pas se coucher.

staying power ['steɪɪŋ-] n endurance f.

STD n abbr (BRIT: = subscriber trunk dialling) l'automatique m; (= sexually transmitted disease) MST f.

stead [stɛd] n (BRIT): **in sb's ~** à la place de qn; **to stand sb in good ~** être très utile or servir beaucoup à qn.

steadfast ['stɛdfɑːst] adj ferme, résolu(e).

steadily ['stɛdɪlɪ] adv régulièrement; fermement; d'une voix etc ferme.

steady ['stɛdɪ] adj stable, solide, ferme; (regular) constant(e), régulier(ière); (person) calme, pondéré(e) ♦ vt assurer, stabiliser; (voice) assurer; **to ~ oneself** reprendre son aplomb.

steak [steɪk] n (meat) bifteck m, steak m; (fish) tranche f.

steakhouse ['steɪkhaus] n ≈ grill-room m.

steal, pt **stole**, pp **stolen** [stiːl, stəul, 'stəuln] vt, vi voler.

▶**steal away, steal off** vi s'esquiver.

stealth [stɛlθ] n: **by ~** furtivement.

stealthy ['stɛlθɪ] adj furtif(ive).

steam [stiːm] n vapeur f ♦ vt passer à la vapeur; (CULIN) cuire à la vapeur ♦ vi fumer; (ship): **to ~ along** filer; **under one's own ~** (fig) par ses propres moyens; **to run out of ~** (fig: person) caler; être à bout; **to let off ~** (fig: col) se défouler.

▶**steam up** vi (window) se couvrir de buée; **to get ~ed up about sth** (fig: col) s'exciter à propos de qch.

steam engine n locomotive f à vapeur.

steamer ['stiːmə*] n (bateau m à) vapeur m; (CULIN) ≈ couscoussier m.

steam iron n fer m à repasser à vapeur.

steamroller ['stiːmrəulə*] n rouleau compresseur.

steamy ['stiːmɪ] adj embué(e), humide.

steed [stiːd] n (literary) coursier m.

steel [stiːl] n acier m ♦ cpd d'acier.

steel band n steel band m.

steel industry n sidérurgie f.

steel mill n aciérie f, usine f sidérurgique.

steelworks ['stiːlwəːks] n aciérie f.

steely ['stiːlɪ] adj (determination) inflexible; (eyes, gaze) d'acier.

steep [stiːp] adj raide, escarpé(e); (price) très élevé(e), excessif(ive) ♦ vt (faire) tremper.

steeple ['stiːpl] n clocher m.

steeplechase ['stiːpltʃeɪs] n steeple(-chase) m.

steeplejack ['stiːpldʒæk] n réparateur m de clochers et de hautes cheminées.

steeply ['stiːplɪ] adv en pente raide.

steer [stɪə*] n bœuf m ♦ vt diriger, gouverner; (lead) guider ♦ vi tenir le gouvernail; **to ~ clear of sb/sth** (fig) éviter qn/qch.

steering ['stɪərɪŋ] n (AUT) conduite f.

steering column n (AUT) colonne f de direction.

steering committee n comité m d'organisation.

steering wheel n volant m.

stellar ['stɛlə*] adj stellaire.

stem [stɛm] n (of plant) tige f; (of leaf, fruit) queue f; (of glass) pied m ♦ vt contenir, endiguer, juguler.

▶**stem from** vt fus provenir de, découler de.

stench [stɛntʃ] n puanteur f.

stencil ['stɛnsl] n stencil m; pochoir m ♦ vt polycopier.

stenographer [stɛ'nɔgrəfə*] n (US) sténographe m/f.

stenography [stɛ'nɔgrəfɪ] n (US) sténo(graphie) f.

step [stɛp] n pas m; (stair) marche f; (action) mesure f, disposition f ♦ vi: **to ~ forward** faire un pas en avant, avancer; **~s** npl (BRIT) = **stepladder**; **~ by ~** pas à pas; (fig) petit à petit; **to be in ~ (with)** (fig) aller dans le sens (de); **to be out of ~ (with)** (fig) être déphasé(e) (par rapport à).

▶**step down** vi (fig) se retirer, se désister.

▶**step in** vi (fig) intervenir.

▶**step off** vt fus descendre de.

▶**step over** vt fus enjamber.

▶**step up** vt augmenter; intensifier.

step aerobics npl ® step m ®.

stepbrother ['stɛpbrʌðə*] n demi-frère m.

stepchild ['stɛptʃaɪld] *n* beau-fils/belle-fille.

stepdaughter ['stɛpdɔːtə*] *n* belle-fille *f*.

stepfather ['stɛpfɑːðə*] *n* beau-père *m*.

stepladder ['stɛplædə*] *n* (*BRIT*) escabeau *m*.

stepmother ['stɛpmʌðə*] *n* belle-mère *f*.

stepping stone ['stɛpɪŋ-] *n* pierre *f* de gué; (*fig*) tremplin *m*.

step Reebok [-'riːbɔk] *n* ® step *m* ®.

stepsister ['stɛpsɪstə*] *n* demi-sœur *f*.

stepson ['stɛpsʌn] *n* beau-fils *m*.

stereo ['stɛrɪəu] *n* (*system*) stéréo *f*; (*record player*) chaîne *f* stéréo ♦ *adj* (*also*: ~**phonic**) stéréophonique; **in** ~ en stéréo.

stereotype ['stɪərɪətaɪp] *n* stéréotype *m* ♦ *vt* stéréotyper.

sterile ['stɛraɪl] *adj* stérile.

sterility [stɛ'rɪlɪtɪ] *n* stérilité *f*.

sterilization [stɛrɪlaɪ'zeɪʃən] *n* stérilisation *f*.

sterilize ['stɛrɪlaɪz] *vt* stériliser.

sterling ['stɜːlɪŋ] *adj* sterling *inv*; (*silver*) de bon aloi, fin(e); (*fig*) à toute épreuve, excellent(e) ♦ *n* (*currency*) livre *f* sterling *inv*; **a pound** ~ une livre sterling.

sterling area *n* zone *f* sterling *inv*.

stern [stɜːn] *adj* sévère ♦ *n* (*NAUT*) arrière *m*, poupe *f*.

sternum ['stɜːnəm] *n* sternum *m*.

steroid ['stɪərɔɪd] *n* stéroïde *m*.

stethoscope ['stɛθəskəup] *n* stéthoscope *m*.

stevedore ['stiːvədɔː*] *n* docker *m*, débardeur *m*.

stew [stjuː] *n* ragoût *m* ♦ *vt, vi* cuire à la casserole; ~**ed tea** thé trop infusé; ~**ed fruit** fruits cuits *or* en compote.

steward ['stjuːəd] *n* (*AVIAT, NAUT, RAIL*) steward *m*; (*in club etc*) intendant *m*; (*also*: **shop** ~) délégué syndical.

stewardess ['stjuːədɛs] *n* hôtesse *f*.

stewardship ['stjuːədʃɪp] *n* intendance *f*.

stewing steak ['stjuːɪŋ-], (*US*) **stew meat** *n* bœuf *m* à braiser.

St. Ex. *abbr* = **stock exchange**.

stg *abbr* = **sterling**.

stick [stɪk] *n* bâton *m*; (*of chalk etc*) morceau *m* ♦ *vb* (*pt, pp* **stuck** [stʌk]) *vt* (*glue*) coller; (*thrust*): **to** ~ **sth into** piquer *or* planter *or* enfoncer qch dans; (*col: put*) mettre, fourrer; (: *tolerate*) supporter ♦ *vi* (*adhere*) coller; (*remain*) rester; (*get jammed: door, lift*) se bloquer; **to get hold of the wrong end of the** ~ (*BRIT fig*) comprendre de travers; **to** ~ **to** (*one's word, promise*) s'en tenir à; (*principles*) rester fidèle à.

▶**stick around** *vi* (*col*) rester (dans les parages).

▶**stick out** *vi* dépasser, sortir ♦ *vt*: **to** ~ **it out** (*col*) tenir le coup.

▶**stick up** *vi* dépasser, sortir.

▶**stick up for** *vt fus* défendre.

sticker ['stɪkə*] *n* auto-collant *m*.

sticking plaster ['stɪkɪŋ-] *n* sparadrap *m*, pansement adhésif.

sticking point ['stɪkɪŋ-] *n* (*fig*) point *m* de friction.

stickleback ['stɪklbæk] *n* épinoche *f*.

stickler ['stɪklə*] *n*: **to be a** ~ **for** être pointilleux(euse) sur.

stick shift *n* (*US AUT*) levier *m* de vitesses.

stick-up ['stɪkʌp] *n* (*col*) braquage *m*, hold-up *m*.

sticky ['stɪkɪ] *adj* poisseux(euse); (*label*) adhésif(ive).

stiff [stɪf] *adj* (*gen*) raide, rigide; (*door, brush*) dur(e); (*difficult*) difficile, ardu(e); (*cold*) froid(e), distant(e); (*strong, high*) fort(e), élevé(e); **to be** *or* **feel** ~ (*person*) avoir des courbatures; **to have a** ~ **back** avoir mal au dos; ~ **upper lip** (*BRIT: fig*) flegme *m* (*typiquement britannique*).

stiffen ['stɪfn] *vt* raidir, renforcer ♦ *vi* se raidir; se durcir.

stiffness ['stɪfnɪs] *n* raideur *f*.

stifle ['staɪfl] *vt* étouffer, réprimer.

stifling ['staɪflɪŋ] *adj* (*heat*) suffocant(e).

stigma, *pl* (*BOT, MED, REL*) ~**ta**, (*fig*) ~**s** ['stɪgmə, stɪg'mɑːtə] *n* stigmate *m*.

stile [staɪl] *n* échalier *m*.

stiletto [stɪ'lɛtəu] *n* (*BRIT: also*: ~ **heel**) talon *m* aiguille.

still [stɪl] *adj* (*motionless*) immobile; (*calm*) calme, tranquille; (*BRIT: orange drink etc*) non gazeux(euse) ♦ *adv* (*up to this time*) encore, toujours; (*even*) encore; (*nonetheless*) quand même, tout de même ♦ *n* (*CINE*) photo *f*; **to stand** ~ rester immobile, ne pas bouger; **keep** ~! ne bouge pas!; **he** ~ **hasn't arrived** il n'est pas encore arrivé, il n'est toujours pas arrivé.

stillborn ['stɪlbɔːn] *adj* mort-né(e).

still life *n* nature morte.

stilt [stɪlt] *n* échasse *f*; (*pile*) pilotis *m*.

stilted ['stɪltɪd] *adj* guindé(e), emprunté(e).

stimulant ['stɪmjulənt] *n* stimulant *m*.

stimulate ['stɪmjuleɪt] *vt* stimuler.

stimulating ['stɪmjuleɪtɪŋ] *adj* stimulant(e).

stimulation [stɪmju'leɪʃən] *n* stimulation *f*.

stimulus, *pl* **stimuli** ['stɪmjuləs, 'stɪmjulaɪ] *n* stimulant *m*; (*BIOL, PSYCH*) stimulus *m*.

sting [stɪŋ] *n* piqûre *f*; (*organ*) dard *m*; (*col: confidence trick*) arnaque *m* ♦ *vt* (*pt, pp* **stung** [stʌŋ]) piquer ♦ *vi* piquer; **my eyes are** ~**ing** j'ai les yeux qui piquent.

stingy ['stɪndʒɪ] *adj* avare, pingre, chiche.

stink [stɪŋk] *n* puanteur *f* ♦ *vi* (*pt* **stank**, *pp* **stunk** [stæŋk, stʌŋk]) puer, empester.

stinker ['stɪŋkə*] *n* (*col: problem, exam*) vacherie *f*; (: *person*) dégueulasse *m/f*.

stinking ['stɪŋkɪŋ] *adj* (*fig: col*) infect(e); ~ **rich** bourré(e) de pognon.

stint [stɪnt] *n* part *f* de travail ♦ *vi*: **to** ~ **on** lésiner sur, être chiche de.

stipend ['staɪpɛnd] *n* (*of vicar etc*) traitement *m*.

stipendiary [staɪ'pɛndɪərɪ] *adj*: ~ **magistrate**

juge *m* de tribunal d'instance.

stipulate ['stɪpjuleɪt] *vt* stipuler.

stipulation [stɪpju'leɪʃən] *n* stipulation *f*, condition *f*.

stir [stə:*] *n* agitation *f*, sensation *f* ♦ *vt* remuer ♦ *vi* remuer, bouger; **to give sth a** ~ remuer qch; **to cause a** ~ faire sensation.

stir up *vt* exciter.

stir-fry ['stə:'fraɪ] *vt* faire sauter ♦ *n*: **vegetable** ~ légumes sautés à la poêle.

stirring ['stə:rɪŋ] *adj* excitant(e); émouvant(e).

tirrup ['stɪrəp] *n* étrier *m*.

titch [stɪtʃ] *n* (SEWING) point *m*; (KNITTING) maille *f*; (MED) point de suture; (pain) point de côté ♦ *vt* coudre, piquer; suturer.

toat [stəut] *n* hermine *f* (avec son pelage d'été).

tock [stɔk] *n* réserve *f*, provision *f*; (COMM) stock *m*; (AGR) cheptel *m*, bétail *m*; (CULIN) bouillon *m*; (FINANCE) valeurs *fpl*, titres *mpl*; (RAIL: also: **rolling** ~) matériel roulant; (descent, origin) souche *f* ♦ *adj* (fig: reply etc) courant(e); classique ♦ *vt* (have in stock) avoir, vendre; **well-~ed** bien approvisionné(e) or fourni(e); **in** ~ en stock, en magasin; **out of** ~ épuisé(e); **to take** ~ (fig) faire le point; ~**s and shares** valeurs (mobilières), titres; **government** ~ fonds publics.

stock up *vi*: **to** ~ **up (with)** s'approvisionner (en).

tockade [stɔ'keɪd] *n* palissade *f*.

tockbroker ['stɔkbrəukə*] *n* agent *m* de change.

tock control *n* (COMM) gestion *f* des stocks.

tock cube *n* (BRIT CULIN) bouillon-cube *m*.

tock exchange *n* Bourse *f* (des valeurs).

tockholder ['stɔkhəuldə*] *n* actionnaire *m/f*.

Stockholm ['stɔkhəum] *n* Stockholm.

tocking ['stɔkɪŋ] *n* bas *m*.

tock-in-trade ['stɔkɪn'treɪd] *n* (fig): **it's his** ~ c'est sa spécialité.

tockist ['stɔkɪst] *n* (BRIT) stockiste *m*.

tock market *n* (BRIT) Bourse *f*, marché financier.

tock phrase *n* cliché *m*.

tockpile ['stɔkpaɪl] *n* stock *m*, réserve *f* ♦ *vt* stocker, accumuler.

tockroom ['stɔkru:m] *n* réserve *f*, magasin *m*.

tocktaking ['stɔkteɪkɪŋ] *n* (BRIT COMM) inventaire *m*.

tocky ['stɔkɪ] *adj* trapu(e), râblé(e).

todgy ['stɔdʒɪ] *adj* bourratif(ive), lourd(e).

toic ['stəuɪk] *n* stoïque *m/f*.

toical ['stəuɪkl] *adj* stoïque.

toke [stəuk] *vt* garnir, entretenir; chauffer.

toker ['stəukə*] *n* (RAIL, NAUT etc) chauffeur *m*.

tole [stəul] *pt of* **steal** ♦ *n* étole *f*.

tolen ['stəuln] *pp of* **steal**.

tolid ['stɔlɪd] *adj* impassible, flegmatique.

stomach ['stʌmək] *n* estomac *m*; (abdomen) ventre *m* ♦ *vt* supporter, digérer.

stomach ache *n* mal *m* à l'estomac or au ventre.

stomach pump *n* pompe stomacale.

stomach ulcer *n* ulcère *m* à l'estomac.

stomp [stɔmp] *vi*: **to** ~ **in/out** entrer/sortir d'un pas bruyant.

stone [stəun] *n* pierre *f*; (pebble) caillou *m*, galet *m*; (in fruit) noyau *m*; (MED) calcul *m*; (BRIT: weight) = 6.348 kg; 14 pounds ♦ *cpd* de or en pierre ♦ *vt* dénoyauter; **within a** ~'s **throw of the station** à deux pas de la gare.

Stone Age *n*: **the** ~ l'âge *m* de pierre.

stone-cold ['stəun'kəuld] *adj* complètement froid(e).

stoned [stəund] *adj* (col: drunk) bourré(e); (: on drugs) défoncé(e).

stone-deaf ['stəun'dɛf] *adj* sourd(e) comme un pot.

stonemason ['stəunmeɪsn] *n* tailleur *m* de pierre(s).

stonewall [stəun'wɔ:l] *vi* faire de l'obstruction ♦ *vt* faire obstruction à.

stonework ['stəunwə:k] *n* maçonnerie *f*.

stony ['stəunɪ] *adj* pierreux(euse), rocailleux(euse).

stood [stud] *pt*, *pp of* **stand**.

stooge [stu:dʒ] *n* (col) larbin *m*.

stool [stu:l] *n* tabouret *m*.

stoop [stu:p] *vi* (also: **have a** ~) être voûté(e); (bend) se baisser, se courber; (fig): **to** ~ **to sth/doing sth** s'abaisser jusqu'à qch/ jusqu'à faire qch.

stop [stɔp] *n* arrêt *m*; (short stay) halte *f*; (in punctuation) point *m* ♦ *vt* arrêter; (break off) interrompre; (also: **put a** ~ **to**) mettre fin à; (prevent) empêcher ♦ *vi* s'arrêter; (rain, noise etc) cesser, s'arrêter; **to** ~ **doing sth** cesser or arrêter de faire qch; **to** ~ **sb (from) doing sth** empêcher qn de faire qch; **to** ~ **dead** *vi* s'arrêter net; ~ **it!** arrête!

▶**stop by** *vi* s'arrêter (au passage).

▶**stop off** *vi* faire une courte halte.

▶**stop up** *vt* (hole) boucher.

stopcock ['stɔpkɔk] *n* robinet *m* d'arrêt.

stopgap ['stɔpgæp] *n* (person) bouche-trou *m*; (also: ~ **measure**) mesure *f* intérimaire.

stoplights ['stɔplaɪts] *npl* (AUT) signaux *mpl* de stop, feux *mpl* arrière.

stopover ['stɔpəuvə*] *n* halte *f*; (AVIAT) escale *f*.

stoppage ['stɔpɪdʒ] *n* arrêt *m*; (of pay) retenue *f*; (strike) arrêt de travail.

stopper ['stɔpə*] *n* bouchon *m*.

stop press *n* nouvelles *fpl* de dernière heure.

stopwatch ['stɔpwɔtʃ] *n* chronomètre *m*.

storage ['stɔ:rɪdʒ] *n* emmagasinage *m*; (of nuclear waste etc) stockage *m*; (in house) rangement *m*; (COMPUT) mise *f* en mémoire or réserve.

storage heater *n* (BRIT) radiateur *m*

électrique par accumulation.

store [stɔ:*] *n* provision *f*, réserve *f*; (*depot*) entrepôt *m*; (*BRIT: large shop*) grand magasin *m*; (*US: shop*) magasin *m* ♦ *vt* emmagasiner; (*nuclear waste etc*) stocker; (*in filing system*) classer, ranger; (*COMPUT*) mettre en mémoire; **~s** *npl* provisions; **who knows what is in ~ for us?** qui sait ce que l'avenir nous réserve *or* ce qui nous attend?; **to set great/little ~ by sth** faire grand cas/peu de cas de qch.

▶**store up** *vt* mettre en réserve, emmagasiner.

storehouse ['stɔ:haus] *n* entrepôt *m*.

storekeeper ['stɔ:ki:pə*] *n* (*US*) commerçant/e.

storeroom ['stɔ:ru:m] *n* réserve *f*, magasin *m*.

storey, (*US*) **story** ['stɔ:rɪ] *n* étage *m*.

stork [stɔ:k] *n* cigogne *f*.

storm [stɔ:m] *n* tempête *f*; (*also*: **electric ~**) orage *m* ♦ *vi* (*fig*) fulminer ♦ *vt* prendre d'assaut.

storm cloud *n* nuage *m* d'orage.

storm door *n* double-porte (extérieure).

stormy ['stɔ:mɪ] *adj* orageux(euse).

story ['stɔ:rɪ] *n* histoire *f*; récit *m*; (*PRESS: article*) article *m*; (: *subject*) affaire *f*; (*US*) = **storey**.

storybook ['stɔ:rɪbuk] *n* livre *m* d'histoires *or* de contes.

storyteller ['stɔ:rɪtɛlə*] *n* conteur/euse.

stout [staut] *adj* solide; (*brave*) intrépide; (*fat*) gros(se), corpulent(e) ♦ *n* bière brune.

stove [stəuv] *n* (*for cooking*) fourneau *m*; (: *small*) réchaud *m*; (*for heating*) poêle *m*; **gas/electric ~** (*cooker*) cuisinière *f* à gaz/ électrique.

stow [stəu] *vt* ranger; cacher.

stowaway ['stəuəweɪ] *n* passager/ère clandestin(e).

straddle ['strædl] *vt* enjamber, être à cheval sur.

strafe [strɑ:f] *vt* mitrailler.

straggle ['strægl] *vi* être (*or* marcher) en dé- sordre; **~d along the coast** disséminé(e) tout au long de la côte.

straggler ['stræglə*] *n* traînard/e.

straggling ['stræglɪŋ], **straggly** ['stræglɪ] *adj* (*hair*) en désordre.

straight [streɪt] *adj* droit(e); (*frank*) honnête, franc(franche); (*plain, uncomplicated*) simple; (*THEAT: part, play*) sérieux(euse); (*col: not bent*) normal(e); réglo *inv* ♦ *adv* (tout) droit; (*drink*) sec, sans eau ♦ *n*: **the ~** (*SPORT*) la ligne droite; **to put** *or* **get ~** mettre en ordre, mettre de l'ordre dans; **let's get this ~** mettons les choses au point; **10 ~ wins** 10 victoires d'affilée; **to go ~ home** rentrer directement à la maison; **~ away, ~ off** (*at once*) tout de suite; **~ off, ~ out** sans hésiter.

straighten ['streɪtn] *vt* (*also*: **~ out**) redresser;

to ~ things out arranger les choses.

straight-faced [streɪt'feɪst] *adj* impassible ♦ *adv* en gardant son sérieux.

straightforward [streɪt'fɔ:wəd] *adj* simple; (*frank*) honnête, direct(e).

strain [streɪn] *n* (*TECH*) tension *f*; pression *f*; (*physical*) effort *m*; (*mental*) tension (nerveuse); (*MED*) entorse *f*; (*streak, trace*) tendance *f*; élément *m*; (*breed*) variété *f*; (*of virus*) souche *f*; **~s** *npl* (*of music*) accents *mpl*, accords *mpl* ♦ *vt* tendre fortement; mettre à l'épreuve; (*filter*) passer, filtrer ♦ *vi* peiner, fournir un gros effort; **he's been under a lot of ~** il a traversé des moments très difficiles, il est très éprouvé nerveusement.

strained [streɪnd] *adj* (*laugh etc*) forcé(e), contraint(e); (*relations*) tendu(e).

strainer ['streɪnə*] *n* passoire *f*.

strait [streɪt] *n* (*GEO*) détroit *m*; **to be in dire ~s** (*fig*) être dans une situation désespérée.

straitjacket ['streɪtdʒækɪt] *n* camisole *f* de force.

strait-laced [streɪt'leɪst] *adj* collet monté *inv*.

strand [strænd] *n* (*of thread*) fil *m*, brin *m* ♦ *vt* (*boat*) échouer.

stranded ['strændɪd] *adj* en rade, en plan.

strange [streɪndʒ] *adj* (*not known*) inconnu(e); (*odd*) étrange, bizarre.

strangely ['streɪndʒlɪ] *adv* étrangement, bizarrement.

stranger ['streɪndʒə*] *n* (*unknown*) inconnu/e; (*from somewhere else*) étranger/ère; **I'm a ~ here** je ne suis pas d'ici.

strangle ['stræŋgl] *vt* étrangler.

stranglehold ['stræŋglhəuld] *n* (*fig*) emprise totale, mainmise *f*.

strangulation [stræŋgju'leɪʃən] *n* strangulation *f*.

strap [stræp] *n* lanière *f*, courroie *f*, sangle *f*; (*of slip, dress*) bretelle *f* ♦ *vt* attacher (avec une courroie *etc*).

straphanging ['stræphæŋɪŋ] *n* (fait *m* de) voyager debout (dans le métro *etc*).

strapless ['stræplɪs] *adj* (*bra, dress*) sans bretelles.

strapped [stræpt] *adj*: **to be ~ for cash** (*col*) être à court d'argent.

strapping ['stræpɪŋ] *adj* bien découplé(e), costaud(e).

Strasbourg ['stræzbɔ:g] *n* Strasbourg.

strata ['strɑ:tə] *npl of* **stratum**.

stratagem ['strætɪdʒəm] *n* stratagème *m*.

strategic [strə'ti:dʒɪk] *adj* stratégique.

strategist ['strætɪdʒɪst] *n* stratège *m*.

strategy ['strætɪdʒɪ] *n* stratégie *f*.

stratosphere ['strætəsfɪə*] *n* stratosphère *f*.

stratum, *pl* **strata** ['strɑ:təm, 'strɑ:tə] *n* strate *f*, couche *f*.

straw [strɔ:] *n* paille *f*; **that's the last ~!** ça c'est le comble!

strawberry ['strɔ:bərɪ] *n* fraise *f*; (*plant*) fraisier *m*.

stray [streɪ] adj (animal) perdu(e), errant(e)
♦ vi s'égarer; ~ **bullet** balle perdue.

streak [striːk] n raie f, bande f, filet m; (fig: of
madness etc): **a** ~ **of** une or des tendance(s)
à ♦ vt zébrer, strier ♦ vi: **to** ~ **past** passer à
toute allure; **to have** ~**s in one's hair** s'être
fait faire des mèches; **a winning/losing** ~
une bonne/mauvaise série or période.

streaker ['striːkə*] n personne qui traverse
une foule en courant toute nue.

streaky ['striːkɪ] adj zébré(e), strié(e).

streaky bacon n (BRIT) ≈ lard m (maigre).

stream [striːm] n (brook) ruisseau m; (current)
courant m, flot m; (of people) défilé
ininterrompu, flot ♦ vt (SCOL) répartir par
niveau ♦ vi ruisseler; **to** ~ **in/out** entrer/
sortir à flots; **against the** ~ à contre
courant; **on** ~ (new power plant etc) en
service.

streamer ['striːmə*] n serpentin m, banderole
f.

stream feed n (on photocopier etc)
alimentation f en continu.

streamline ['striːmlaɪn] vt donner un profil
aérodynamique à; (fig) rationaliser.

streamlined ['striːmlaɪnd] adj (AVIAT)
fuselé(e), profilé(e); (AUT) aérodynamique;
(fig) rationalisé(e).

street [striːt] n rue f; **the back** ~**s** les quartiers
pauvres; **to be on the** ~**s** (homeless) être à
la rue or sans abri; (as prostitute) faire le
trottoir.

streetcar ['striːtkɑː*] n (US) tramway m.

street cred [-krɛd] n (col): **to have** ~ être
branché(e).

street lamp n réverbère m.

street lighting n éclairage public.

street map, street plan n plan m des rues.

street market n marché m à ciel ouvert.

streetwise ['striːtwaɪz] adj (col) futé(e),
réaliste.

strength [strɛŋθ] n force f; (of girder, knot etc)
solidité f; (of chemical solution) titre m; (of
wine) degré m d'alcool; **on the** ~ **of** en vertu
de; **at full** ~ au grand complet; **below** ~ à
effectifs réduits.

strengthen ['strɛŋθn] vt renforcer; (muscle)
fortifier.

strenuous ['strɛnjuəs] adj vigoureux(euse),
énergique; (tiring) ardu(e), fatigant(e).

stress [strɛs] n (force, pressure) pression f;
(mental strain) tension (nerveuse); (accent)
accent m; (emphasis) insistance f ♦ vt insister
sur, souligner; **to lay great** ~ **on sth** insister
beaucoup sur qch; **to be under** ~ être
stressé(e).

stressful ['strɛsful] adj (job) stressant(e).

stretch [strɛtʃ] n (of sand etc) étendue f; (of
time) période f ♦ vi s'étirer; (extend): **to** ~ **to**
or **as far as** s'étendre jusqu'à; (be enough:
money, food): **to** ~ **to** aller pour ♦ vt tendre,
étirer; (spread) étendre; (fig) pousser (au

maximum); **at a** ~ sans discontinuer, sans
interruption; **to** ~ **a muscle** se distendre un
muscle; **to** ~ **one's legs** se dégourdir les
jambes.

▶**stretch out** vi s'étendre ♦ vt (arm etc)
allonger, tendre; (to spread) étendre; **to** ~
out for sth allonger la main pour prendre
qch.

stretcher ['strɛtʃə*] n brancard m, civière f.

stretcher-bearer ['strɛtʃəbɛərə*] n
brancardier m.

stretch marks npl (on skin) vergetures fpl.

strewn [struːn] adj: ~ **with** jonché(e) de.

stricken ['strɪkən] adj très éprouvé(e);
dévasté(e); (ship) très endommagé(e); ~
with frappé(e) or atteint(e) de.

strict [strɪkt] adj strict(e); **in** ~ **confidence** tout
à fait confidentiellement.

strictly ['strɪktlɪ] adv strictement; ~
confidential strictement confidentiel(le); ~
speaking à strictement parler.

strictness ['strɪktnɪs] n sévérité f.

stride [straɪd] n grand pas, enjambée f ♦ vi (pt
strode, pp **stridden** [strəud, 'strɪdn]) marcher
à grands pas; **to take in one's** ~ (fig: changes
etc) accepter sans sourciller.

strident ['straɪdnt] adj strident(e).

strife [straɪf] n conflit m, dissensions fpl.

strike [straɪk] n grève f; (of oil etc) découverte
f; (attack) raid m ♦ vb (pt, pp **struck** [strʌk]) vt
frapper; (oil etc) trouver, découvrir; (make:
agreement, deal) conclure ♦ vi faire grève;
(attack) attaquer; (clock) sonner; **to go on** or
come out on ~ se mettre en grève, faire
grève; **to** ~ **a match** frotter une allumette;
to ~ **a balance** (fig) trouver un juste milieu.

▶**strike back** vi (MIL, fig) contre-attaquer.

▶**strike down** vt (fig) terrasser.

▶**strike off** vt (from list) rayer; (: doctor etc)
radier.

▶**strike out** vt rayer.

▶**strike up** vt (MUS) se mettre à jouer; **to** ~
up a friendship with se lier d'amitié avec.

strikebreaker ['straɪkbreɪkə*] n briseur m de
grève.

striker ['straɪkə*] n gréviste m/f; (SPORT)
buteur m.

striking ['straɪkɪŋ] adj frappant(e),
saisissant(e).

strimmer ['strɪmə*] n ® (BRIT) coupe-
bordures m.

string [strɪŋ] n ficelle f, fil m; (row: of beads)
rang m; (: of onions, excuses) chapelet m; (: of
people, cars) file f; (MUS) corde f; (COMPUT)
châine f ♦ vt (pt, pp **strung** [strʌŋ]): **to** ~ **out**
échelonner; **to** ~ **together** enchaîner; **the** ~**s**
(MUS) les instruments mpl à cordes; **to get a
job by pulling** ~**s** obtenir un emploi en
faisant jouer le piston; **with no** ~**s attached**
(fig) sans conditions.

string bean n haricot vert.

string(ed) instrument [strɪŋ(d)-] n (MUS)

instrument _m_ à cordes.
stringent ['strɪndʒənt] _adj_ rigoureux(euse);
(_need_) impérieux(euse).
string quartet _n_ quatuor _m_ à cordes.
strip [strɪp] _n_ bande _f_; (_SPORT_): **wearing the
Celtic** ~ en tenue du Celtic ♦ _vt_ déshabiller;
(_fig_) dégarnir, dépouiller; (_also_: ~ **down**:
machine) démonter ♦ _vi_ se déshabiller.
strip cartoon _n_ bande dessinée.
stripe [straɪp] _n_ raie _f_, rayure _f_.
striped ['straɪpt] _adj_ rayé(e), à rayures.
strip light _n_ (_BRIT_) (tube _m_ au) néon _m_.
stripper ['strɪpə*] _n_ strip-teaseuse _f_.
strip-search ['strɪpsəːtʃ] _n_ fouille corporelle
(_en faisant se déshabiller la personne_) ♦ _vt_: **to** ~
sb fouiller qn (_en le faisant se déshabiller_).
striptease ['strɪptiːz] _n_ strip-tease _m_.
strive, _pt_ **strove**, _pp_ **striven** [straɪv, strəuv,
'strɪvn] _vi_: **to** ~ **to do** s'efforcer de faire.
strobe [strəub] _n_ (_also_: ~ **light**) stroboscope _m_.
strode [strəud] _pt of_ **stride**.
stroke [strəuk] _n_ coup _m_; (_MED_) attaque _f_;
(_caress_) caresse _f_; (_SWIMMING: style_) (sorte _f_
de) nage _f_; (_of piston_) course _f_ ♦ _vt_ caresser;
at a ~ d'un (seul) coup; **on the** ~ **of 5** à 5
heures sonnantes; **a** ~ **of luck** un coup de
chance; **a 2-** ~ **engine** un moteur à 2 temps.
stroll [strəul] _n_ petite promenade ♦ _vi_ flâner,
se promener nonchalamment; **to go for a** ~
aller se promener _or_ faire un tour.
stroller ['strəulə*] _n_ (_US_) poussette _f_.
strong [strɔŋ] _adj_ (_gen_) fort(e); (_healthy_)
vigoureux(euse); (_object, material_) solide;
(_distaste, desire_) vif(vive); (_drugs, chemicals_)
puissant(e) ♦ _adv_: **to be going** ~ (_company_)
marcher bien; (_person_) être toujours solide;
they are 50 ~ ils sont au nombre de 50.
strong-arm ['strɔŋaːm] _adj_ (_tactics, methods_)
musclé(e).
strongbox ['strɔŋbɔks] _n_ coffre-fort _m_.
stronghold ['strɔŋhəuld] _n_ bastion _m_.
strongly ['strɔŋlɪ] _adv_ fortement, avec force;
vigoureusement; solidement; **I feel** ~ **about
it** c'est une question qui me tient
particulièrement à cœur; (_negatively_) j'y
suis profondément opposé(e).
strongman ['strɔŋmæn] _n_ hercule _m_, colosse
_m_; (_fig_) homme _m_ à poigne.
strongroom ['strɔŋruːm] _n_ chambre forte.
stroppy ['strɔpɪ] _adj_ (_BRIT col_) contrariant(e),
difficile.
strove [strəuv] _pt of_ **strive**.
struck [strʌk] _pt_, _pp of_ **strike**.
structural ['strʌktʃrəl] _adj_ structural(e);
(_CONSTR_) de construction; affectant les
parties portantes.
structurally ['strʌktʃrəlɪ] _adv_ du point de vue
de la construction.
structure ['strʌktʃə*] _n_ structure _f_; (_building_)
construction _f_.
struggle ['strʌgl] _n_ lutte _f_ ♦ _vi_ lutter, se battre;
to have a ~ **to do sth** avoir beaucoup de mal

à faire qch.
strum [strʌm] _vt_ (_guitar_) gratter de.
strung [strʌŋ] _pt_, _pp of_ **string**.
strut [strʌt] _n_ étai _m_, support _m_ ♦ _vi_ se
pavaner.
strychnine ['strɪkniːn] _n_ strychnine _f_.
stub [stʌb] _n_ bout _m_; (_of ticket etc_) talon _m_ ♦ _vt_:
to ~ **one's toe (on sth)** se heurter le doigt
de pied (contre qch).
▶**stub out** _vt_ écraser.
stubble ['stʌbl] _n_ chaume _m_; (_on chin_) barbe _f_
de plusieurs jours.
stubborn ['stʌbən] _adj_ têtu(e), obstiné(e),
opiniâtre.
stubby ['stʌbɪ] _adj_ trapu(e); gros(se) et
court(e).
stucco ['stʌkəu] _n_ stuc _m_.
stuck [stʌk] _pt_, _pp of_ **stick** ♦ _adj_ (_jammed_)
bloqué(e), coincé(e); **to get** ~ se bloquer _or_
coincer.
stuck-up [stʌk'ʌp] _adj_ prétentieux(euse).
stud [stʌd] _n_ clou _m_ (à grosse tête); (_collar_ ~)
bouton _m_ de col; (_of horses_) écurie _f_, haras _m_;
(_also_: ~ **horse**) étalon _m_ ♦ _vt_ (_fig_): ~**ded with**
parsemé(e) _or_ criblé(e) de.
student ['stjuːdənt] _n_ étudiant/e ♦ _cpd_
estudiantin(e); universitaire; d'étudiant;
law/medical ~ étudiant en droit/médecine.
student driver _n_ (_US_) (conducteur/trice)
débutant(e).
students' union _n_ (_BRIT: association_) ≈ union
_f_ des étudiants; (: _building_) ≈ foyer _m_ des
étudiants.
studied ['stʌdɪd] _adj_ étudié(e), calculé(e).
studio ['stjuːdɪəu] _n_ studio _m_, atelier _m_.
studio flat, (_US_) **studio apartment** _n_ studio
_m_.
studious ['stjuːdɪəs] _adj_ studieux(euse),
appliqué(e); (_deliberate_) étudié(e).
studiously ['stjuːdɪəslɪ] _adv_ (_carefully_)
soigneusement.
study ['stʌdɪ] _n_ étude _f_; (_room_) bureau _m_ ♦ _vt_
étudier ♦ _vi_ étudier, faire ses études; **to
make a** ~ **of sth** étudier qch, faire une
étude de qch; **to** ~ **for an exam** préparer un
examen.
stuff [stʌf] _n_ (_gen_) chose(s) _f(pl)_, truc _m_;
(_belongings_) affaires _fpl_, trucs; (_substance_)
substance _f_ ♦ _vt_ rembourrer; (_CULIN_) farcir;
(_animal: for exhibition_) empailler; **my nose is**
~**ed up** j'ai le nez bouché; **get** ~**ed!** (_col!_) va
te faire foutre! (_!_); ~**ed toy** jouet _m_ en
peluche.
stuffing ['stʌfɪŋ] _n_ bourre _f_, rembourrage _m_;
(_CULIN_) farce _f_.
stuffy ['stʌfɪ] _adj_ (_room_) mal ventilé(e) _or_
aéré(e); (_ideas_) vieux jeu _inv_.
stumble ['stʌmbl] _vi_ trébucher.
▶**stumble across** _vt fus_ (_fig_) tomber sur.
stumbling block ['stʌmblɪŋ-] _n_ pierre _f_
d'achoppement.
stump [stʌmp] _n_ souche _f_; (_of limb_) moignon _r_

♦ *vt*: **to be ~ed** sécher, ne pas savoir que répondre.

stun [stʌn] *vt* (*subj: blow*) étourdir; (: *news*) abasourdir, stupéfier.

stung [stʌŋ] *pt, pp of* **sting**.

stunk [stʌŋk] *pp of* **stink**.

stunning ['stʌnɪŋ] *adj* étourdissant(e); (*fabulous*) stupéfiant(e), sensationnel(le).

stunt [stʌnt] *n* tour *m* de force; truc *m* publicitaire; (*AVIAT*) acrobatie *f* ♦ *vt* retarder, arrêter.

stunted ['stʌntɪd] *adj* rabougri(e).

stuntman ['stʌntmæn] *n* cascadeur *m*.

stupefaction [stjuːpɪ'fækʃən] *n* stupéfaction *f*, stupeur *f*.

stupefy ['stjuːpɪfaɪ] *vt* étourdir; abrutir; (*fig*) stupéfier.

stupendous [stjuː'pɛndəs] *adj* prodigieux(euse), fantastique.

stupid ['stjuːpɪd] *adj* stupide, bête.

stupidity [stjuː'pɪdɪtɪ] *n* stupidité *f*, bêtise *f*.

stupidly ['stjuːpɪdlɪ] *adv* stupidement, bêtement.

stupor ['stjuːpə*] *n* stupeur *f*.

sturdy ['stəːdɪ] *adj* robuste, vigoureux(euse); solide.

sturgeon ['stəːdʒən] *n* esturgeon *m*.

stutter ['stʌtə*] *n* bégaiement *m* ♦ *vi* bégayer.

sty [staɪ] *n* (*of pigs*) porcherie *f*.

stye [staɪ] *n* (*MED*) orgelet *m*.

style [staɪl] *n* style *m*; (*of dress etc*) genre *m*; (*distinction*) allure *f*, cachet *m*, style; **in the latest ~** à la dernière mode; **hair ~** coiffure *f*.

stylish ['staɪlɪʃ] *adj* élégant(e), chic *inv*.

stylist ['staɪlɪst] *n* (*hair ~*) coiffeur/euse; (*literary ~*) styliste *m/f*.

stylized ['staɪlaɪzd] *adj* stylisé(e).

stylus, *pl* **styli** *or* **styluses** ['staɪləs, -laɪ] *n* (*of record player*) pointe *f* de lecture.

Styrofoam ['staɪrəfəum] *n* ® (*US*) polystyrène expansé ♦ *adj* en polystyrène.

suave [swɑːv] *adj* doucereux(euse), onctueux(euse).

sub [sʌb] *n abbr* = **submarine, subscription**.

sub... [sʌb] *prefix* sub..., sous-.

subcommittee ['sʌbkəmɪtɪ] *n* sous-comité *m*.

subconscious [sʌb'kɔnʃəs] *adj* subconscient(e) ♦ *n* subconscient *m*.

subcontinent [sʌb'kɔntɪnənt] *n*: **the (Indian) ~** le sous-continent indien.

subcontract *n* ['sʌb'kɔntrækt] contrat *m* de sous-traitance ♦ *vt* [sʌbkən'trækt] sous-traiter.

subcontractor ['sʌbkən'træktə*] *n* sous-traitant *m*.

subdivide [sʌbdɪ'vaɪd] *vt* subdiviser.

subdivision ['sʌbdɪvɪʒən] *n* subdivision *f*.

subdue [səb'djuː] *vt* subjuguer, soumettre.

subdued [səb'djuːd] *adj* contenu(e), atténué(e); (*light*) tamisé(e); (*person*) qui a perdu de son entrain.

sub-editor ['sʌb'ɛdɪtə*] *n* (*BRIT*) secrétaire *m/f* de (la) rédaction.

subject *n* ['sʌbdʒɪkt] sujet *m*; (*SCOL*) matière *f* ♦ *vt* [səb'dʒɛkt]: **to ~ to** soumettre à; exposer à; **to be ~ to** (*law*) être soumis(e) à; (*disease*) être sujet(te) à; **~ to confirmation in writing** sous réserve de confirmation écrite; **to change the ~** changer de conversation.

subjection [səb'dʒɛkʃən] *n* soumission *f*, sujétion *f*.

subjective [səb'dʒɛktɪv] *adj* subjectif(ive).

subject matter *n* sujet *m*; contenu *m*.

sub judice [sʌb'djuːdɪsɪ] *adj* (*LAW*) devant les tribunaux.

subjugate ['sʌbdʒugeɪt] *vt* subjuguer.

subjunctive [səb'dʒʌŋktɪv] *adj* subjonctif(ive) ♦ *n* subjonctif *m*.

sublet [sʌb'lɛt] *vt* sous-louer.

sublime [sə'blaɪm] *adj* sublime.

subliminal [sʌb'lɪmɪnl] *adj* subliminal(e).

submachine gun ['sʌbmə'ʃiːn-] *n* mitraillette *f*.

submarine [sʌbmə'riːn] *n* sous-marin *m*.

submerge [səb'məːdʒ] *vt* submerger; immerger ♦ *vi* plonger.

submersion [səb'məːʃən] *n* submersion *f*; immersion *f*.

submission [səb'mɪʃən] *n* soumission *f*; (*to committee etc*) présentation *f*.

submissive [səb'mɪsɪv] *adj* soumis(e).

submit [səb'mɪt] *vt* soumettre ♦ *vi* se soumettre.

subnormal [sʌb'nɔːml] *adj* au-dessous de la normale; (*person*) arriéré(e).

subordinate [sə'bɔːdɪnət] *adj, n* subordonné(e).

subpoena [səb'piːnə] (*LAW*) *n* citation *f*, assignation *f* ♦ *vt* citer *or* assigner (à comparaître).

subroutine [sʌbruː'tiːn] *n* (*COMPUT*) sousprogramme *m*.

subscribe [səb'skraɪb] *vi* cotiser; **to ~ to** (*opinion, fund*) souscrire à; (*newspaper*) s'abonner à; être abonné(e) à.

subscriber [səb'skraɪbə*] *n* (*to periodical, telephone*) abonné/e.

subscript ['sʌbskrɪpt] *n* (*TYP*) indice inférieur.

subscription [səb'skrɪpʃən] *n* (*to fund*) souscription *f*; (*to magazine etc*) abonnement *m*; (*membership dues*) cotisation *f*; **to take out a ~ to** s'abonner à.

subsequent ['sʌbsɪkwənt] *adj* ultérieur(e), suivant(e); **~ to** *prep* à la suite de.

subsequently ['sʌbsɪkwəntlɪ] *adv* par la suite.

subservient [səb'səːvɪənt] *adj* obséquieux(euse).

subside [səb'saɪd] *vi* s'affaisser; (*flood*) baisser; (*wind*) tomber.

subsidence [səb'saɪdns] *n* affaissement *m*.

subsidiarity [səbsɪdɪ'ærɪtɪ] *n* (*POL*) subsidiarité *f*.

subsidiary [səb'sɪdɪərɪ] *adj* subsidiaire;

accessoire; (*BRIT SCOL: subject*) complémentaire ♦ *n* filiale *f*.

subsidize ['sʌbsɪdaɪz] *vt* subventionner.

subsidy ['sʌbsɪdɪ] *n* subvention *f*.

subsist [səb'sɪst] *vi*: **to ~ on sth** (arriver à) vivre avec *or* subsister avec qch.

subsistence [səb'sɪstəns] *n* existence *f*, subsistance *f*.

subsistence allowance *n* indemnité *f* de séjour.

subsistence level *n* niveau *m* de vie minimum.

substance ['sʌbstəns] *n* substance *f*; (*fig*) essentiel *m*; **a man of ~** un homme jouissant d'une certaine fortune; **to lack ~** être plutôt mince (*fig*).

substance abuse *n* abus *m* de substances toxiques.

substandard [sʌb'stændəd] *adj* (*goods*) de qualité inférieure, qui laisse à désirer; (*housing*) inférieur(e) aux normes requises.

substantial [səb'stænʃl] *adj* substantiel(le); (*fig*) important(e).

substantially [səb'stænʃəlɪ] *adv* considérablement; en grande partie.

substantiate [səb'stænʃɪeɪt] *vt* étayer, fournir des preuves à l'appui de.

substitute ['sʌbstɪtjuːt] *n* (*person*) remplaçant/e; (*thing*) succédané *m* ♦ *vt*: **to ~ sth/sb for** substituer qch/qn à, remplacer par qch/qn.

substitute teacher *n* (*US*) suppléant/e.

substitution [sʌbstɪ'tjuːʃən] *n* substitution *f*.

subterfuge ['sʌbtəfjuːdʒ] *n* subterfuge *m*.

subterranean [sʌbtə'reɪnɪən] *adj* souterrain(e).

subtitle ['sʌbtaɪtl] *n* (*CINE*) sous-titre *m*.

subtle ['sʌtl] *adj* subtil(e).

subtlety ['sʌtltɪ] *n* subtilité *f*.

subtly ['sʌtlɪ] *adv* subtilement.

subtotal [sʌb'təutl] *n* total partiel.

subtract [səb'trækt] *vt* soustraire, retrancher.

subtraction [səb'trækʃən] *n* soustraction *f*.

subtropical [sʌb'trɔpɪkl] *adj* subtropical(e).

suburb ['sʌbəːb] *n* faubourg *m*; **the ~s** la banlieue.

suburban [sə'bəːbən] *adj* de banlieue, suburbain(e).

suburbia [sə'bəːbɪə] *n* la banlieue.

subvention [səb'vɛnʃən] *n* (*subsidy*) subvention *f*.

subversion [səb'vəːʃən] *n* subversion *f*.

subversive [səb'vəːsɪv] *adj* subversif(ive).

subway ['sʌbweɪ] *n* (*US*) métro *m*; (*BRIT*) passage souterrain.

sub-zero [sʌb'zɪərəu] *adj* au-dessous de zéro.

succeed [sək'siːd] *vi* réussir ♦ *vt* succéder à; **to ~ in doing** réussir à faire.

succeeding [sək'siːdɪŋ] *adj* suivant(e), qui suit (*or* suivent *or* suivront *etc*).

success [sək'sɛs] *n* succès *m*; réussite *f*.

successful [sək'sɛsful] *adj* qui a du succès;

(*candidate*) choisi(e), agréé(e); (*business*) prospère, qui réussit; (*attempt*) couronné(e) de succès; **to be ~ (in doing)** réussir (à faire).

successfully [sək'sɛsfəlɪ] *adv* avec succès.

succession [sək'sɛʃən] *n* succession *f*; **in ~** successivement; **3 years in ~** 3 ans de suite.

successive [sək'sɛsɪv] *adj* successif(ive); **on 3 ~ days** 3 jours de suite *or* consécutifs.

successor [sək'sɛsə*] *n* successeur *m*.

succinct [sək'sɪŋkt] *adj* succinct(e), bref(brève).

succulent ['sʌkjulənt] *adj* succulent(e) ♦ *n* (*BOT*): **~s** plantes grasses.

succumb [sə'kʌm] *vi* succomber.

such [sʌtʃ] *adj* tel(telle); (*of that kind*): **~ a book** un livre de ce genre *or* pareil, un tel livre ♦ *adv* si; **~ books** des livres de ce genre *or* pareils, de tels livres; (*so much*): **~ courage** un tel courage; **~ a long trip** un si long voyage; **~ good books** de si bons livres; **~ a long trip that** un voyage si *or* tellement long que; **~ a lot of** tellement *or* tant de; **making ~ a noise that** faisant un tel bruit que *or* tellement de bruit que; **~ a long time ago** il y a si *or* tellement longtemps; **~ as** (*like*) tel(telle) que, comme; **a noise ~ as** to un bruit de nature à; **~ books as I have** les quelques livres que j'ai; **as ~** *adv* en tant que tel(telle), à proprement parler.

such-and-such ['sʌtʃənsʌtʃ] *adj* tel(telle) ou tel(telle).

suchlike ['sʌtʃlaɪk] *pron* (*col*): **and ~** et le reste.

suck [sʌk] *vt* sucer; (*breast, bottle*) téter; (*subj: pump, machine*) aspirer.

sucker ['sʌkə*] *n* (*BOT, ZOOL, TECH*) ventouse *f*; (*col*) naïf/ïve, poire *f*.

suckle ['sʌkl] *vt* allaiter.

sucrose ['suːkrəuz] *n* saccharose *m*.

suction ['sʌkʃən] *n* succion *f*.

suction pump *n* pompe aspirante.

Sudan [su'dɑːn] *n* Soudan *m*.

Sudanese [suːdə'niːz] *adj* soudanais(e) ♦ *n* Soudanais/e.

sudden ['sʌdn] *adj* soudain(e), subit(e); **all of a ~** soudain, tout à coup.

sudden-death [sʌdn'dɛθ] *n*: **~ play-off** partie *supplémentaire pour départager les adversaires*.

suddenly ['sʌdnlɪ] *adv* brusquement, tout à coup, soudain.

suds [sʌdz] *npl* eau savonneuse.

sue [suː] *vt* poursuivre en justice, intenter un procès à ♦ *vi*: **to ~ (for)** intenter un procès (pour); **to ~ for divorce** engager une procédure de divorce; **to ~ sb for damages** poursuivre qn en dommages-intérêts.

suede [sweɪd] *n* daim *m*, cuir suédé ♦ *cpd* de daim.

suet ['suɪt] *n* graisse *f* de rognon *or* de bœuf.

Suez Canal ['suːɪz-] n canal m de Suez.
Suff. abbr (BRIT) = Suffolk.
suffer ['sʌfə*] vt souffrir, subir; (bear) tolérer, supporter, subir ♦ vi souffrir; **to ~ from** (illness) souffrir de, avoir; **to ~ from the effects of alcohol/a fall** se ressentir des effets de l'alcool/des conséquences d'une chute.
sufferance ['sʌfərns] n: **he was only there on ~** sa présence était seulement tolérée.
sufferer ['sʌfərə*] n malade m/f; victime m/f.
suffering ['sʌfərɪŋ] n souffrance(s) f(pl).
suffice [sə'faɪs] vi suffire.
sufficient [sə'fɪʃənt] adj suffisant(e); **~ money** suffisamment d'argent.
sufficiently [sə'fɪʃəntlɪ] adv suffisamment, assez.
suffix ['sʌfɪks] n suffixe m.
suffocate ['sʌfəkeɪt] vi suffoquer; étouffer.
suffocation [sʌfə'keɪʃən] n suffocation f; (MED) asphyxie f.
suffrage ['sʌfrɪdʒ] n suffrage m; droit m de suffrage or de vote.
suffuse [sə'fjuːz] vt baigner, imprégner; **the room was ~d with light** la pièce baignait dans la lumière or était imprégnée de lumière.
sugar ['ʃugə*] n sucre m ♦ vt sucrer.
sugar beet n betterave sucrière.
sugar bowl n sucrier m.
sugar cane n canne f à sucre.
sugar-coated ['ʃugə'kəutɪd] adj dragéifié(e).
sugar lump n morceau m de sucre.
sugar refinery n raffinerie f de sucre.
sugary ['ʃugərɪ] adj sucré(e).
suggest [sə'dʒɛst] vt suggérer, proposer; (indicate) laisser supposer, suggérer; **what do you ~ I do?** que vous me suggérez de faire?
suggestion [sə'dʒɛstʃən] n suggestion f.
suggestive [sə'dʒɛstɪv] adj suggestif(ive).
suicidal [suɪ'saɪdl] adj suicidaire.
suicide ['suɪsaɪd] n suicide m; **to commit ~** se suicider.
suicide attempt, suicide bid n tentative f de suicide.
suit [suːt] n (man's) costume m, complet m; (woman's) tailleur m, ensemble m; (CARDS) couleur f; (law~) procès m ♦ vt aller à; convenir à; (adapt): **to ~ sth to** adapter or approprier qch à; **to be ~ed to sth** (suitable for) être adapté(e) or approprié(e) à qch; **well ~ed** (couple) faits l'un pour l'autre, très bien assortis; **to bring a ~ against sb** intenter un procès contre qn; **to follow ~** (fig) faire de même.
suitable ['suːtəbl] adj qui convient; approprié(e), adéquat(e); **would tomorrow be ~?** est-ce que demain vous conviendrait?; **we found somebody ~** nous avons trouvé la personne qu'il nous faut.
suitably ['suːtəblɪ] adv comme il se doit (or se

devait etc), convenablement.
suitcase ['suːtkeɪs] n valise f.
suite [swiːt] n (of rooms, also MUS) suite f; (furniture): **bedroom/dining room ~** (ensemble m de) chambre f à coucher/salle f à manger; **a three-piece ~** un salon (canapé et deux fauteuils).
suitor ['suːtə*] n soupirant m, prétendant m.
sulfate ['sʌlfeɪt] n (US) = **sulphate**.
sulfur etc ['sʌlfə*] (US) = **sulphur** etc.
sulk [sʌlk] vi bouder.
sulky ['sʌlkɪ] adj boudeur(euse), maussade.
sullen ['sʌlən] adj renfrogné(e), maussade; morne.
sulphate, (US) sulfate ['sʌlfeɪt] n sulfate m; **copper ~** sulfate de cuivre.
sulphur, (US) sulfur ['sʌlfə*] n soufre m.
sulphur dioxide n anhydride sulfureux.
sulphuric, (US) sulfuric [sʌl'fjuərɪk] adj: **~ acid** acide m sulfurique.
sultan ['sʌltən] n sultan m.
sultana [sʌl'tɑːnə] n (fruit) raisin (sec) de Smyrne.
sultry ['sʌltrɪ] adj étouffant(e).
sum [sʌm] n somme f; (SCOL etc) calcul m.
►**sum up** vt résumer; (evaluate rapidly) récapituler ♦ vi résumer.
Sumatra [su'mɑːtrə] n Sumatra.
summarize ['sʌməraɪz] vt résumer.
summary ['sʌmərɪ] n résumé m ♦ adj (justice) sommaire.
summer ['sʌmə*] n été m ♦ cpd d'été, estival(e); **in (the) ~** en été, pendant l'été.
summer camp n (US) colonie f de vacances.
summerhouse ['sʌməhaus] n (in garden) pavillon m.
summertime ['sʌmətaɪm] n (season) été m.
summer time n (by clock) heure f d'été.
summery ['sʌmərɪ] adj estival(e); d'été.
summing-up [sʌmɪŋ'ʌp] n résumé m, récapitulation f.
summit ['sʌmɪt] n sommet m; (also: **~ conference**) (conférence f au) sommet m.
summon ['sʌmən] vt appeler, convoquer; **to ~ a witness** citer or assigner un témoin.
►**summon up** vt rassembler, faire appel à.
summons ['sʌmənz] n citation f, assignation f ♦ vt citer, assigner; **to serve a ~ on sb** remettre une assignation à qn.
sumo ['suːməu] n: **~ wrestling** sumo m.
sump [sʌmp] n (BRIT AUT) carter m.
sumptuous ['sʌmptjuəs] adj somptueux(euse).
sun [sʌn] n soleil m; **in the ~** au soleil; **to catch the ~** prendre le soleil; **everything under the ~** absolument tout.
Sun. abbr (= Sunday) dim.
sunbathe ['sʌnbeɪð] vi prendre un bain de soleil.
sunbeam ['sʌnbiːm] n rayon m de soleil.
sunbed ['sʌnbed] n lit pliant; (with sun lamp) lit à ultra-violets.

sunburn ['sʌnbəːn] *n* coup *m* de soleil.
sunburnt ['sʌnbəːnt], **sunburned** ['sʌnbəːnd] *adj* bronzé(e), hâlé(e); (*painfully*) brûlé(e) par le soleil.
sun cream *n* crème *f* (anti-)solaire.
sundae ['sʌndeɪ] *n* sundae *m*, coupe glacée.
Sunday ['sʌndɪ] *n* dimanche *m*; *for phrases see also* **Tuesday.**
Sunday paper *n* journal *m* du dimanche.

Les **Sunday papers** *sont une véritable institution en Grande-Bretagne. Il y a des "quality" Sunday papers des "popular" Sunday papers, et la plupart des quotidiens ont un journal du dimanche qui leur est associé, bien que leurs équipes de rédacteurs soient différentes. Les quality Sunday papers ont plusieurs suppléments et magazines; voir* **quality press** *et* **tabloid press**

Sunday school *n* ≈ catéchisme *m*.
sundial ['sʌndaɪəl] *n* cadran *m* solaire.
sundown ['sʌndaun] *n* coucher *m* du soleil.
sundries ['sʌndrɪz] *npl* articles divers.
sundry ['sʌndrɪ] *adj* divers(e), différent(e); **all and** ~ tout le monde, n'importe qui.
sunflower ['sʌnflauə*] *n* tournesol *m*.
sung [sʌŋ] *pp of* **sing.**
sunglasses ['sʌnglɑːsɪz] *npl* lunettes *fpl* de soleil.
sunk [sʌŋk] *pp of* **sink.**
sunken ['sʌŋkn] *adj* (*rock, ship*) submergé(e); (*eyes, cheeks*) creux(euse); (*bath*) encastré(e).
sunlamp ['sʌnlæmp] *n* lampe *f* à rayons ultra-violets.
sunlight ['sʌnlaɪt] *n* (lumière *f* du) soleil *m*.
sunlit ['sʌnlɪt] *adj* ensoleillé(e).
sunny ['sʌnɪ] *adj* ensoleillé(e); (*fig*) épanoui(e), radieux(euse); **it is** ~ il fait (du) soleil, il y a du soleil.
sunrise ['sʌnraɪz] *n* lever *m* du soleil.
sun roof *n* (*AUT*) toit ouvrant.
sunscreen ['sʌnskriːn] *n* crème *f* solaire.
sunset ['sʌnset] *n* coucher *m* du soleil.
sunshade ['sʌnʃeɪd] *n* (*lady's*) ombrelle *f*; (*over table*) parasol *m*.
sunshine ['sʌnʃaɪn] *n* (lumière *f* du) soleil *m*.
sunspot ['sʌnspɒt] *n* tache *f* solaire.
sunstroke ['sʌnstrəuk] *n* insolation *f*, coup *m* de soleil.
suntan ['sʌntæn] *n* bronzage *m*.
suntanned ['sʌntænd] *adj* bronzé(e).
suntan oil *n* huile *f* solaire.
suntrap ['sʌntræp] *n* coin très ensoleillé.
super ['suːpə*] *adj* (*col*) formidable.
superannuation [suːpərænjuˈeɪʃən] *n* cotisations *fpl* pour la pension.
superb [suːˈpəːb] *adj* superbe, magnifique.
Super Bowl *n* (*US SPORT*) Super Bowl *m*.
supercilious [suːpəˈsɪlɪəs] *adj* hautain(e), dédaigneux(euse).

superconductor [suːpəkənˈdʌktə*] *n* supraconducteur *m*.
superficial [suːpəˈfɪʃəl] *adj* superficiel(le).
superficially [suːpəˈfɪʃəlɪ] *adv* superficiellement.
superfluous [suˈpəːfluəs] *adj* superflu(e).
superglue ['suːpəgluː] *n* colle forte.
superhighway ['suːpəhaɪweɪ] *n* (*US*) voie *f* express (à plusieurs files); **the information** ~ la super-autoroute de l'information.
superhuman [suːpəˈhjuːmən] *adj* surhumain(e).
superimpose ['suːpərɪmˈpəuz] *vt* superposer.
superintend [suːpərɪnˈtend] *vt* surveiller.
superintendent [suːpərɪnˈtendənt] *n* directeur/trice; (*POLICE*) ≈ commissaire *m*.
superior [suˈpɪərɪə*] *adj* supérieur(e); (*COMM: goods, quality*) de qualité supérieure; (*smug*) condescendant(e), méprisant(e) ♦ *n* supérieur/e; **Mother S**~ (*REL*) Mère supérieure.
superiority [supɪərɪˈɒrɪtɪ] *n* supériorité *f*.
superlative [suˈpəːlətɪv] *adj* sans pareil(le), suprême ♦ *n* (*LING*) superlatif *m*.
superman ['suːpəmæn] *n* surhomme *m*.
supermarket ['suːpəmɑːkɪt] *n* supermarché *m*.
supermodel ['suːpəmɒdl] *n* top model *m*.
supernatural [suːpəˈnætʃərəl] *adj* surnaturel(le).
supernova [suːpəˈnəuvə] *n* supernova *f*.
superpower ['suːpəpauə*] *n* (*POL*) superpuissance *f*.
supersede [suːpəˈsiːd] *vt* remplacer, supplanter.
supersonic ['suːpəˈsɒnɪk] *adj* supersonique.
superstar ['suːpəstɑː*] *n* (*CINE etc*) superstar *f*; (*SPORT*) superchampion/ne ♦ *adj* (*status, lifestyle*) de superstar.
superstition [suːpəˈstɪʃən] *n* superstition *f*.
superstitious [suːpəˈstɪʃəs] *adj* superstitieux(euse).
superstore ['suːpəstɔː*] *n* (*BRIT*) hypermarché *m*, grand surface.
supertanker ['suːpətæŋkə*] *n* pétrolier géant, superpétrolier *m*.
supertax ['suːpətæks] *n* tranche supérieure de l'impôt.
supervise ['suːpəvaɪz] *vt* (*children etc*) surveiller; (*organization, work*) diriger.
supervision [suːpəˈvɪʒən] *n* surveillance *f*; direction *f*; **under medical** ~ sous contrôle du médecin.
supervisor ['suːpəvaɪzə*] *n* surveillant/e; (*in shop*) chef *m* de rayon; (*SCOL*) directeur/trice de thèse.
supervisory ['suːpəvaɪzərɪ] *adj* de surveillance.
supine ['suːpaɪn] *adj* couché(e) *or* étendu(e) sur le dos.
supper ['sʌpə*] *n* dîner *m*; (*late*) souper *m*; **to have** ~ dîner; souper.

supplant [sə'plɑːnt] *vt* supplanter.

supple ['sʌpl] *adj* souple.

supplement *n* ['sʌplɪmənt] supplément *m* ♦ *vt* [sʌplɪ'mɛnt] ajouter à, compléter.

supplementary [sʌplɪ'mɛntərɪ] *adj* supplémentaire.

supplementary benefit *n* (BRIT) allocation *f* supplémentaire d'aide sociale.

supplier [sə'plaɪə*] *n* fournisseur *m*.

supply [sə'plaɪ] *vt* (goods): **to ~ sth (to sb)** fournir qch (à qn); (people, organization): **to ~ sb (with sth)** approvisionner *or* ravitailler qn (en qch); fournir qn (en qch), fournir qch à qn; (system, machine): **to ~ sth (with sth)** alimenter qch (en qch); (a need) répondre à ♦ *n* provision *f*, réserve *f*; (supplying) approvisionnement *m*; (TECH) alimentation *f*; **supplies** *npl* (food) vivres *mpl*; (MIL) subsistances *fpl*; **office supplies** fournitures *fpl* de bureau; **the electricity/water/gas ~** l'alimentation en électricité/eau/gaz; **~ and demand** l'offre *f* et la demande; **it comes supplied with an adaptor** il (or elle) est pourvu(e) d'un adaptateur.

supply teacher *n* (BRIT) suppléant/e.

support [sə'pɔːt] *n* (moral, financial etc) soutien *m*, appui *m*; (TECH) support *m*, soutien ♦ *vt* soutenir, supporter; (financially) subvenir aux besoins de; (uphold) être pour, être partisan de, appuyer; (SPORT: team) être pour; **to ~ o.s.** (financially) gagner sa vie.

supporter [sə'pɔːtə*] *n* (POL etc) partisan/e; (SPORT) supporter *m*.

supporting [sə'pɔːtɪŋ] *adj* (wall) d'appui.

supporting actor/actress *n* second rôle *m/f*.

supporting role *n* second rôle *m*.

supportive [sə'pɔːtɪv] *adj*: **my family were very ~** ma famille m'a été d'un grand soutien.

suppose [sə'pəuz] *vt, vi* supposer; imaginer; **to be ~d to do/be** être censé(e) faire/être; **I don't ~ she'll come** je suppose qu'elle ne viendra pas, cela m'étonnerait qu'elle vienne.

supposedly [sə'pəuzɪdlɪ] *adv* soi-disant.

supposing [sə'pəuzɪŋ] *conj* si, à supposer que + *sub*.

supposition [sʌpə'zɪʃən] *n* supposition *f*, hypothèse *f*.

suppository [sə'pɔzɪtrɪ] *n* suppositoire *m*.

suppress [sə'prɛs] *vt* (revolt, feeling) réprimer; (publication) supprimer; (scandal) étouffer.

suppression [sə'prɛʃən] *n* suppression *f*, répression *f*.

suppressor [sə'prɛsə*] *n* (ELEC etc) dispositif *m* antiparasite.

supremacy [su'prɛməsɪ] *n* suprématie *f*.

supreme [su'priːm] *adj* suprême.

Supreme Court *n* (US) Cour *f* suprême.

supremo [su'priːməu] *n* grand chef.

supt. *abbr* (POLICE) = **superintendent**.

surcharge ['sɜːtʃɑːdʒ] *n* surcharge *f*; (extra tax) surtaxe *f*.

sure [ʃuə*] *adj* (gen) sûr(e); (definite, convinced) sûr, certain(e) ♦ *adv* (col: esp US): **that ~ is pretty, that's ~ pretty** c'est drôlement joli(e); **~!** (of course) bien sûr!; **~ enough** effectivement; **I'm not ~ how/why/when** je ne sais pas très bien comment/pourquoi/quand; **to be ~ of o.s.** être sûr de soi; **to make ~ of** s'assurer de; vérifier.

sure-fire ['ʃuəfaɪə*] *adj* (col) certain(e), infaillible.

sure-footed [ʃuə'futɪd] *adj* au pied sûr.

surely ['ʃuəlɪ] *adv* sûrement; certainement; **~ you don't mean that!** vous ne parlez pas sérieusement!

surety ['ʃuərətɪ] *n* caution *f*; **to go or stand ~ for sb** se porter caution pour qn.

surf [sɜːf] *n* ressac *m*.

surface ['sɜːfɪs] *n* surface *f* ♦ *vt* (road) poser le revêtement de ♦ *vi* remonter à la surface; faire surface; **on the ~** (fig) au premier abord.

surface area *n* superficie *f*, aire *f*.

surface mail *n* courrier *m* par voie de terre (or maritime).

surface-to-surface ['sɜːfɪstə'sɜːfɪs] *adj* (MIL) sol-sol *inv*.

surfboard ['sɜːfbɔːd] *n* planche *f* de surf.

surfeit ['sɜːfɪt] *n*: **a ~ of** un excès de; une indigestion de.

surfer ['sɜːfə*] *n* surfiste *m/f*.

surfing ['sɜːfɪŋ] *n* surf *m*.

surge [sɜːdʒ] *n* vague *f*, montée *f*; (ELEC) pointe *f* de courant ♦ *vi* déferler; **to ~ forward** se précipiter (en avant).

surgeon ['sɜːdʒən] *n* chirurgien *m*.

Surgeon General *n* (US) chef *m* du service fédéral de la santé publique.

surgery ['sɜːdʒərɪ] *n* chirurgie *f*; (BRIT: room) cabinet *m* (de consultation); (: session) consultation *f*; (: of MP etc) permanence *f* (où le député etc reçoit les électeurs etc); **to undergo ~** être opéré(e).

surgery hours *npl* (BRIT) heures *fpl* de consultation.

surgical ['sɜːdʒɪkl] *adj* chirurgical(e).

surgical spirit *n* (BRIT) alcool *m* à 90°.

surly ['sɜːlɪ] *adj* revêche, maussade.

surmise [sɜː'maɪz] *vt* présumer, conjecturer.

surmount [sɜː'maunt] *vt* surmonter.

surname ['sɜːneɪm] *n* nom *m* de famille.

surpass [sɜː'pɑːs] *vt* surpasser, dépasser.

surplus [sɜː'pləs] *n* surplus *m*, excédent *m* ♦ *adj* en surplus, de trop; **it is ~ to our requirements** cela dépasse nos besoins; **~ stock** surplus *m*.

surprise [sə'praɪz] *n* (gen) surprise *f*; (astonishment) étonnement *m* ♦ *vt* surprendre; étonner; **to take by ~** (person) prendre au dépourvu; (MIL: town, fort) prendre par surprise.

surprising [sə'praɪzɪŋ] *adj* surprenant(e), étonnant(e).

surprisingly [sə'praɪzɪŋlɪ] *adv* (*easy, helpful*) étonnamment, étrangement; (**somewhat**) ~, **he agreed** curieusement, il a accepté.

surrealism [sə'rɪəlɪzəm] *n* surréalisme *m*.

surrealist [sə'rɪəlɪst] *adj, n* surréaliste (*m/f*).

surrender [sə'rɛndə*] *n* reddition *f*, capitulation *f* ♦ *vi* se rendre, capituler ♦ *vt* (*claim, right*) renoncer à.

surrender value *n* valeur *f* de rachat.

surreptitious [sʌrəp'tɪʃəs] *adj* subreptice, furtif(ive).

surrogate ['sʌrəgɪt] *n* (*BRIT: substitute*) substitut *m* ♦ *adj* de substitution, de remplacement; **a food** ~ un succédané alimentaire; ~ **coffee** ersatz *m or* succédané *m* de café.

surrogate mother *n* mère porteuse *or* de substitution.

surround [sə'raund] *vt* entourer; (*MIL etc*) encercler.

surrounding [sə'raundɪŋ] *adj* environnant(e).

surroundings [sə'raundɪŋz] *npl* environs *mpl*, alentours *mpl*.

surtax ['sɔːtæks] *n* surtaxe *f*.

surveillance [sɔː'veɪləns] *n* surveillance *f*.

survey *n* ['sɔːveɪ] enquête *f*, étude *f*; (*in house buying etc*) inspection *f*, (rapport *m* d')expertise *f*; (*of land*) levé *m*; (*comprehensive view: of situation etc*) vue *f* d'ensemble ♦ *vt* [sɔː'veɪ] passer en revue; enquêter sur; inspecter; (*building*) expertiser; (*land*) faire le levé de.

surveying [sɔː'veɪɪŋ] *n* arpentage *m*.

surveyor [sɔː'veɪə*] *n* (*of building*) expert *m*; (*of land*) (arpenteur *m*) géomètre *m*.

survival [sə'vaɪvl] *n* survie *f*; (*relic*) vestige *m* ♦ *cpd* (*course, kit*) de survie.

survive [sə'vaɪv] *vi* survivre, (*custom etc*) subsister ♦ *vt* survivre à, réchapper de; (*person*) survivre à.

survivor [sə'vaɪvə*] *n* survivant/e.

susceptible [sə'sɛptəbl] *adj*: ~ **(to)** sensible (à); (*disease*) prédisposé(e) (à).

suspect *adj, n* ['sʌspɛkt] suspect(e) ♦ *vt* [sə'spɛkt] soupçonner, suspecter.

suspected [sə'spɛktɪd] *adj*: **a** ~ **terrorist** une personne soupçonnée de terrorisme; **he had a** ~ **broken arm** il avait une supposée fracture du bras.

suspend [sə'spɛnd] *vt* suspendre.

suspended animation [sə'spɛndɪd-] *n*: **in a state of** ~ en hibernation.

suspended sentence [sə'spɛndɪd-] *n* condamnation *f* avec sursis.

suspender belt [sə'spɛndə-] *n* (*BRIT*) porte-jarretelles *m inv*.

suspenders [sə'spɛndəz] *npl* (*BRIT*) jarretelles *fpl*; (*US*) bretelles *fpl*.

suspense [sə'spɛns] *n* attente *f*; (*in film etc*) suspense *m*.

suspension [səs'pɛnʃən] *n* (*gen, AUT*) suspension *f*; (*of driving licence*) retrait *m* provisoire.

suspension bridge *n* pont suspendu.

suspicion [səs'pɪʃən] *n* soupçon(s) *m(pl)*; **to be under** ~ être considéré(e) comme suspect(e), être suspecté(e); **arrested on** ~ **of murder** arrêté sur présomption de meurtre.

suspicious [səs'pɪʃəs] *adj* (*suspecting*) soupçonneux(euse), méfiant(e); (*causing suspicion*) suspect(e); **to be** ~ **of** *or* **about sb/sth** avoir des doutes à propos de qn/sur qch, trouver qn/qch suspect(e).

suss out ['sʌs'aut] *vt* (*BRIT col: discover*) supputer; (: *understand*) piger.

sustain [səs'teɪn] *vt* supporter; soutenir; corroborer; (*suffer*) subir; recevoir.

sustainable [səs'teɪnəbl] *adj* (*rate, growth*) qui peut être maintenu(e); (*agriculture, development*) durable.

sustained [səs'teɪnd] *adj* (*effort*) soutenu(e), prolongé(e).

sustenance ['sʌstɪnəns] *n* nourriture *f*; moyens *mpl* de subsistance.

suture ['suːtʃə*] *n* suture *f*.

SW *abbr* (= *short wave*) OC.

swab [swɔb] *n* (*MED*) tampon *m*; prélèvement *m* ♦ *vt* (*NAUT: also:* ~ **down**) nettoyer.

swagger ['swægə*] *vi* plastronner, parader.

swallow ['swɔləu] *n* (*bird*) hirondelle *f*; (*of food etc*) gorgée *f* ♦ *vt* avaler; (*fig*) gober.

swam [swæm] *pt of* **swim**.

swamp [swɔmp] *n* marais *m*, marécage *m* ♦ *vt* submerger.

swampy ['swɔmpɪ] *adj* marécageux(euse).

swan [swɔn] *n* cygne *m*.

swank [swæŋk] *vi* (*col*) faire de l'épate.

swan song *n* (*fig*) chant *m* du cygne.

swap [swɔp] *n* échange *m*, troc *m* ♦ *vt*: **to** ~ **(for)** échanger (contre), troquer (contre).

SWAPO ['swɑːpəu] *n abbr* (= *South-West Africa People's Organization*) SWAPO *f*.

swarm [swɔːm] *n* essaim *m* ♦ *vi* essaimer; fourmiller, grouiller.

swarthy ['swɔːðɪ] *adj* basané(e), bistré(e).

swashbuckling ['swɔʃbʌklɪŋ] *adj* (*film*) de cape et d'épée.

swastika ['swɔstɪkə] *n* croix gammée.

SWAT *n abbr* (*US:* = *Special Weapons and Tactics*) ≈ CRS *f*.

swat [swɔt] *vt* écraser ♦ *n* (*BRIT: also:* **fly** ~) tapette *f*.

swathe [sweɪð] *vt*: **to** ~ **in** (*bandages, blankets*) embobiner de.

swatter ['swɔtə*] *n* (*also:* **fly** ~) tapette *f*.

sway [sweɪ] *vi* se balancer, osciller; tanguer ♦ *vt* (*influence*) influencer ♦ *n* (*rule, power*): (**over**) emprise *f* (sur); **to hold** ~ **over sb** avoir de l'emprise sur qn.

Swaziland ['swɑːzɪlænd] *n* Swaziland *m*.

wear, *pt* **swore,** *pp* **sworn** [swɛə*, swɔ:*, swɔ:n] *vi* jurer; **to ~ to sth** jurer de qch; **to ~ an oath** prêter serment.

swear in *vt* assermenter.

wearword ['swɛəwə:d] *n* gros mot, juron *m*.

weat [swɛt] *n* sueur *f*, transpiration *f* ♦ *vi* suer; **in a ~** en sueur.

weatband ['swɛtbænd] *n* (SPORT) bandeau *m*.

weater ['swɛtə*] *n* tricot *m*, pull *m*.

weatshirt ['swɛtʃə:t] *n* sweat-shirt *m*.

weatshop ['swɛtʃɔp] *n* atelier *m* où les ouvriers sont exploités.

weaty ['swɛti] *adj* en sueur, moite *or* mouillé(e) de sueur.

wede [swi:d] *n* Suédois/e.

wede [swi:d] *n* (BRIT) rutabaga *m*.

weden ['swi:dn] *n* Suède *f*.

wedish ['swi:dɪʃ] *adj* suédois(e) ♦ *n* (LING) suédois *m*.

weep [swi:p] *n* coup *m* de balai; (curve) grande courbe; (range) champ *m*; (also: **chimney ~**) ramoneur *m* ♦ *vb* (pt, pp **swept** [swɛpt]) *vt* balayer; (fashion, craze) se répandre dans ♦ *vi* avancer majestueusement *or* rapidement; s'élancer; s'étendre.

sweep away *vt* balayer; entraîner; emporter.

sweep past *vi* passer majestueusement *or* rapidement.

sweep up *vt*, *vi* balayer.

weeper ['swi:pə*] *n* (person) balayeur *m*; (machine) balayeuse *f*; (FOOTBALL) libéro *m*.

weeping ['swi:pɪŋ] *adj* (gesture) large; circulaire; (changes, reforms) radical(e); **a ~ statement** une généralisation hâtive.

weepstake ['swi:psteɪk] *n* sweepstake *m*.

weet [swi:t] *n* (BRIT) dessert *m*; (candy) bonbon *m* ♦ *adj* doux(douce); (not savoury) sucré(e); (fresh) frais(fraîche), pur(e); (kind) gentil(le); (cute) mignon(ne) ♦ *adv*: **to smell ~** sentir bon; **to taste ~** avoir un goût sucré; **~ and sour** *adj* aigre-doux(douce).

weetbread ['swi:tbrɛd] *n* ris *m* de veau.

weetcorn ['swi:tkɔ:n] *n* maïs doux.

weeten ['swi:tn] *vt* sucrer; (fig) adoucir.

weetener ['swi:tnə*] *n* (CULIN) édulcorant *m*.

weetheart ['swi:thɑ:t] *n* amoureux/euse.

weetly ['swi:tli] *adv* (smile) gentiment; (sing, play) mélodieusement.

weetness ['swi:tnɪs] *n* douceur *f*; (of taste) goût sucré.

weet pea *n* pois *m* de senteur.

weet potato *n* patate douce.

weetshop ['swi:tʃɔp] *n* (BRIT) confiserie *f*.

weet tooth *n*: **to have a ~** aimer les sucreries.

well [swɛl] *n* (of sea) houle *f* ♦ *adj* (col: excellent) chouette ♦ *vb* (pt ~**ed**, pp **swollen** or ~**ed** ['swəulən]) *vt* augmenter; grossir ♦ *vi* grossir, augmenter; (sound) s'enfler; (MED) enfler.

welling ['swɛlɪŋ] *n* (MED) enflure *f*; grosseur *f*.

sweltering ['swɛltərɪŋ] *adj* étouffant(e), oppressant(e).

swept [swɛpt] *pt*, *pp of* **sweep**.

swerve [swə:v] *vi* faire une embardée *or* un écart; dévier.

swift [swɪft] *n* (bird) martinet *m* ♦ *adj* rapide, prompt(e).

swiftly ['swɪftlɪ] *adv* rapidement, vite.

swiftness ['swɪftnɪs] *n* rapidité *f*.

swig [swɪg] *n* (col: drink) lampée *f*.

swill [swɪl] *n* pâtée *f* ♦ *vt* (also: **~ out**, **~ down**) laver à grande eau.

swim [swɪm] *n*: **to go for a ~** aller nager *or* se baigner ♦ *vb* (pt **swam**, pp **swum** [swæm, swʌm]) *vi* nager; (SPORT) faire de la natation; (fig: head, room) tourner ♦ *vt* traverser (à la nage); (distance) faire (à la nage); **to ~ a length** nager une longueur; **to go ~ming** aller nager.

swimmer ['swɪmə*] *n* nageur/euse.

swimming ['swɪmɪŋ] *n* nage *f*, natation *f*.

swimming baths *npl* (BRIT) piscine *f*.

swimming cap *n* bonnet *m* de bain.

swimming costume *n* (BRIT) maillot *m* (de bain).

swimmingly ['swɪmɪŋlɪ] *adv*: **to go ~** (wonderfully) se dérouler à merveille.

swimming pool *n* piscine *f*.

swimming trunks *npl* maillot *m* de bain.

swimsuit ['swɪmsu:t] *n* maillot *m* (de bain).

swindle ['swɪndl] *n* escroquerie *f* ♦ *vt* escroquer.

swindler ['swɪndlə*] *n* escroc *m*.

swine [swaɪn] *n* (pl inv) pourceau *m*, porc *m*; (col!) salaud *m* (!).

swing [swɪŋ] *n* balançoire *f*; (movement) balancement *m*, oscillations *fpl*; (MUS) swing *m*; rythme *m* ♦ *vb* (pt, pp **swung** [swʌŋ]) *vt* balancer, faire osciller; (also: **~ round**) tourner, faire virer ♦ *vi* se balancer, osciller; (also: **~ round**) virer, tourner; **a ~ to the left** (POL) un revirement en faveur de la gauche; **to be in full ~** battre son plein; **to get into the ~ of things** se mettre dans le bain; **the road ~s south** la route prend la direction sud.

swing bridge *n* pont tournant.

swing door *n* (BRIT) porte battante.

swingeing ['swɪndʒɪŋ] *adj* (BRIT) écrasant(e); considérable.

swinging ['swɪŋɪŋ] *adj* rythmé(e); entraînant(e); (fig) dans le vent; **~ door** (US) porte battante.

swipe [swaɪp] *n* grand coup; gifle *f* ♦ *vt* (hit) frapper à toute volée; gifler; (col: steal) piquer; (credit card etc) faire passer (dans la machine).

swirl [swə:l] *n* tourbillon *m* ♦ *vi* tourbillonner, tournoyer.

swish [swɪʃ] *adj* (BRIT col: smart) rupin(e) ♦ *vi* (whip) siffler; (skirt, long grass) bruire.

Swiss [swɪs] *adj* suisse ♦ *n (pl inv)* Suisse/esse.
Swiss French *adj* suisse romand(e).
Swiss German *adj* suisse-allemand(e).
Swiss roll *n* gâteau roulé.
switch [swɪtʃ] *n (for light, radio etc)* bouton *m*; *(change)* changement *m*, revirement *m* ♦ *vt (change)* changer; *(exchange)* intervertir; *(invert)*: **to ~ (round** *or* **over)** changer de place.
▶**switch off** *vt* éteindre; *(engine)* arrêter.
▶**switch on** *vt* allumer; *(engine, machine)* mettre en marche; *(BRIT: water supply)* ouvrir.
switchback ['swɪtʃbæk] *n (BRIT)* montagnes *fpl* russes.
switchblade ['swɪtʃbleɪd] *n (also: ~ knife)* couteau *m* à cran d'arrêt.
switchboard ['swɪtʃbɔːd] *n (TEL)* standard *m*.
switchboard operator *n (TEL)* standardiste *m/f*.
Switzerland ['swɪtsələnd] *n* Suisse *f*.
swivel ['swɪvl] *vi (also: ~ round)* pivoter, tourner.
swollen ['swəulən] *pp of* **swell** ♦ *adj (ankle etc)* enflé(e).
swoon [swuːn] *vi* se pâmer.
swoop [swuːp] *n (by police etc)* rafle *f*, descente *f*; *(of bird etc)* descente *f* en piqué ♦ *vi (also: ~ down)* descendre en piqué, piquer.
swop [swɔp] *n, vt* = **swap**.
sword [sɔːd] *n* épée *f*.
swordfish ['sɔːdfɪʃ] *n* espadon *m*.
swore [swɔː*] *pt of* **swear**.
sworn [swɔːn] *pt of* **swear**.
swot [swɔt] *vt, vi* bûcher, potasser.
swum [swʌm] *pp of* **swim**.
swung [swʌŋ] *pt, pp of* **swing**.
sycamore ['sɪkəmɔː*] *n* sycomore *m*.
sycophant ['sɪkəfænt] *n* flagorneur/euse.
sycophantic [sɪkə'fæntɪk] *adj* flagorneur(euse).
Sydney ['sɪdnɪ] *n* Sydney.
syllable ['sɪləbl] *n* syllabe *f*.
syllabus ['sɪləbəs] *n* programme *m*; **on the ~** au programme.
symbol ['sɪmbl] *n* symbole *m*.
symbolic(al) [sɪm'bɔlɪk(l)] *adj* symbolique.
symbolism ['sɪmbəlɪzəm] *n* symbolisme *m*.
symbolize ['sɪmbəlaɪz] *vt* symboliser.
symmetrical [sɪ'mɛtrɪkl] *adj* symétrique.
symmetry ['sɪmɪtrɪ] *n* symétrie *f*.
sympathetic [sɪmpə'θɛtɪk] *adj (showing pity)* compatissant(e); *(understanding)* bienveillant(e), compréhensif(ive); **~ towards** bien disposé(e) envers.
sympathetically [sɪmpə'θɛtɪklɪ] *adv* avec compassion *or* bienveillance.
sympathize ['sɪmpəθaɪz] *vi*: **to ~ with sb** *(in grief)* être de tout cœur avec qn, compatir à la douleur de qn; *(in predicament)* partager les sentiments de qn; **to ~ with** *(sb's*

feelings) comprendre.
sympathizer ['sɪmpəθaɪzə*] *n (POL)* sympathisant/e.
sympathy ['sɪmpəθɪ] *n* compassion *f*; **in ~ with** en accord avec; *(strike)* en *or* par solidarité avec; **with our deepest ~** en vous priant d'accepter nos sincères condoléances.
symphonic [sɪm'fɔnɪk] *adj* symphonique.
symphony ['sɪmfənɪ] *n* symphonie *f*.
symphony orchestra *n* orchestre *m* symphonique.
symposium [sɪm'pəuzɪəm] *n* symposium *m*.
symptom ['sɪmptəm] *n* symptôme *m*; indice *m*.
symptomatic [sɪmptə'mætɪk] *adj* symptomatique.
synagogue ['sɪnəgɔg] *n* synagogue *f*.
sync [sɪŋk] *n (col)*: **in/out of ~** bien/mal synchronisé(e); **they're in ~ with each other** *(fig)* le courant passe bien entre eux.
synchromesh [sɪŋkrəu'mɛʃ] *n (AUT)* synchronisation *f*.
synchronize ['sɪŋkrənaɪz] *vt* synchroniser ♦ *vi* **to ~ with** se produire en même temps que.
synchronized swimming ['sɪŋkrənaɪzd-] *n* natation synchronisée.
syncopated ['sɪŋkəpeɪtɪd] *adj* syncopé(e).
syndicate ['sɪndɪkɪt] *n* syndicat *m*, coopérative *f*; *(PRESS)* agence *f* de presse.
syndrome ['sɪndrəum] *n* syndrome *m*.
synonym ['sɪnənɪm] *n* synonyme *m*.
synonymous [sɪ'nɔnɪməs] *adj*: **~ (with)** synonyme (de).
synopsis, *pl* **synopses** [sɪ'nɔpsɪs, -siːz] *n* résumé *m*, synopsis *m or f*.
syntax ['sɪntæks] *n* syntaxe *f*.
synthesis, *pl* **syntheses** ['sɪnθəsɪs, -siːz] *n* synthèse *f*.
synthesizer ['sɪnθəsaɪzə*] *n (MUS)* synthétiseur *m*.
synthetic [sɪn'θɛtɪk] *adj* synthétique ♦ *n* matière *f* synthétique; **~s** *npl* textiles artificiels.
syphilis ['sɪfɪlɪs] *n* syphilis *f*.
syphon ['saɪfən] *n, vb* = **siphon**.
Syria ['sɪrɪə] *n* Syrie *f*.
Syrian ['sɪrɪən] *adj* syrien(ne) ♦ *n* Syrien/ne.
syringe [sɪ'rɪndʒ] *n* seringue *f*.
syrup ['sɪrəp] *n* sirop *m*; *(BRIT: also:* **golden ~)** mélasse raffinée.
syrupy ['sɪrəpɪ] *adj* sirupeux(euse).
system ['sɪstəm] *n* système *m*; *(order)* méthode *f*; *(ANAT)* organisme *m*.
systematic [sɪstə'mætɪk] *adj* systématique; méthodique.
system disk *n (COMPUT)* disque *m* système.
systems analyst *n* analyste-programmeur *m/f*.

T t

T, t [tiː] n (*letter*) T, t m; **T for Tommy** T comme Thérèse.

TA n abbr (*BRIT*) = *Territorial Army.*

ta [tɑː] excl (*BRIT col*) merci!

tab [tæb] n abbr = **tabulator** ♦ n (*loop on coat etc*) attache f; (*label*) étiquette f; **to keep ~s on** (*fig*) surveiller.

tabby ['tæbɪ] n (*also: ~ cat*) chat/te tigré(e).

tabernacle ['tæbənækl] n tabernacle m.

table ['teɪbl] n table f ♦ vt (*BRIT: motion etc*) présenter; **to lay** or **set the ~** mettre le couvert or la table; **to clear the ~** débarrasser la table; **league ~** (*BRIT FOOTBALL, RUGBY*) classement m (du championnat); **~ of contents** table des matières.

tablecloth ['teɪblklɔθ] n nappe f.

table d'hôte [taːblˈdəut] adj (*meal*) à prix fixe.

table football n baby-foot m.

table lamp n lampe décorative.

tablemat ['teɪblmæt] n (*for plate*) napperon m, set m; (*for hot dish*) dessous-de-plat m inv.

table salt n sel fin or de table.

tablespoon ['teɪblspuːn] n cuiller f de service; (*also: ~ful: as measurement*) cuillerée f à soupe.

tablet ['tæblɪt] n (*MED*) comprimé m; (*: for sucking*) pastille f; (*for writing*) bloc m; (*of stone*) plaque f; **~ of soap** (*BRIT*) savonnette f.

table tennis n ping-pong m, tennis m de table.

table wine n vin m de table.

tabloid ['tæblɔɪd] n (*newspaper*) tabloïde m; **the ~s** les journaux mpl populaires.

Le terme **tabloid press** désigne les journaux populaires de demi-format où l'on trouve beaucoup de photos et qui adoptent un style très concis. Ce type de journaux vise des lecteurs s'intéressant aux faits divers ayant un parfum de scandale; voir **quality press**

taboo [təˈbuː] adj, n tabou (m).

tabulate ['tæbjuleɪt] vt (*data, figures*) mettre sous forme de table(s).

tabulator ['tæbjuleɪtə*] n tabulateur m.

tachograph ['tækəgrɑːf] n tachygraphe m.

tachometer [tæˈkɔmɪtə*] n tachymètre m.

tacit ['tæsɪt] adj tacite.

taciturn ['tæsɪtɜːn] adj taciturne.

tack [tæk] n (*nail*) petit clou; (*stitch*) point m de bâti; (*NAUT*) bord m, bordée f ♦ vt clouer; bâtir ♦ vi tirer un or des bord(s); **to change ~** virer de bord; **on the wrong ~** (*fig*) sur la mauvaise voie; **to ~ sth on to (the end of) sth** (*of letter, book*) rajouter qch à la fin de qch.

tackle ['tækl] n matériel m, équipement m; (*for lifting*) appareil m de levage; (*FOOTBALL, RUGBY*) plaquage m ♦ vt (*difficulty*) s'attaquer à; (*FOOTBALL, RUGBY*) plaquer.

tacky ['tækɪ] adj collant(e); pas sec(sèche); (*col: shabby*) moche.

tact [tækt] n tact m.

tactful ['tæktful] adj plein(e) de tact.

tactfully ['tæktfəlɪ] adv avec tact.

tactical ['tæktɪkl] adj tactique; **~ error** erreur f de tactique.

tactical voting n vote m tactique.

tactician [tækˈtɪʃən] n tacticien/ne.

tactics ['tæktɪks] n, npl tactique f.

tactless ['tæktlɪs] adj qui manque de tact.

tactlessly ['tæktlɪslɪ] adv sans tact.

tadpole ['tædpəul] n têtard m.

Tadzhikistan [tædʒɪkɪˈstɑːn] n = **Tajikistan.**

taffy ['tæfɪ] n (*US*) (bonbon m au) caramel m.

tag [tæg] n étiquette f; **price/name ~** étiquette (portant le prix/le nom).

▶**tag along** vi suivre.

Tahiti [tɑːˈhiːtɪ] n Tahiti m.

tail [teɪl] n queue f; (*of shirt*) pan m ♦ vt (*follow*) suivre, filer; **to turn ~** se sauver à toutes jambes; *see also* **head.**

▶**tail away, tail off** vi (*in size, quality etc*) baisser peu à peu.

tailback ['teɪlbæk] n (*BRIT*) bouchon m.

tail coat n habit m.

tail end n bout m, fin f.

tailgate ['teɪlgeɪt] n (*AUT*) hayon m arrière.

tail light n (*AUT*) feu m arrière.

tailor ['teɪlə*] n tailleur m (*artisan*) ♦ vt: **to ~ sth (to)** adapter qch exactement (à); **~'s (shop)** (boutique f de) tailleur m.

tailoring ['teɪlərɪŋ] n (*cut*) coupe f.

tailor-made ['teɪləˈmeɪd] adj fait(e) sur mesure; (*fig*) conçu(e) spécialement.

tailwind ['teɪlwɪnd] n vent m arrière inv.

taint [teɪnt] vt (*meat, food*) gâter; (*fig: reputation*) salir.

tainted ['teɪntɪd] adj (*food*) gâté(e); (*water, air*) infecté(e); (*fig*) souillé(e).

Taiwan ['taɪˈwɑːn] n Taiwan (*no article*).

Tajikistan [tædʒɪkɪˈstɑːn] n Tadjikistan m/f.

take [teɪk] vb (*pt* **took**, *pp* **taken** [tuk, 'teɪkn]) vt prendre; (*gain: prize*) remporter; (*require: effort, courage*) demander; (*tolerate*) accepter, supporter; (*hold: passengers etc*) contenir; (*accompany*) emmener, accompagner; (*bring, carry*) apporter, emporter; (*exam*) passer, se présenter à; (*conduct: meeting*) présider ♦ vi (*dye, fire etc*) prendre ♦ n (*CINE*) prise f de vues; **to ~ sth from** (*drawer etc*) prendre qch dans; (*person*) prendre qch à; **I ~ it that** je suppose que; **I took him for a doctor** je l'ai pris pour un docteur; **to ~ sb's hand** prendre qn par la main; **to ~ for a walk** (*child, dog*) emmener promener; **to be taken ill** tomber malade; **to ~ it upon o.s. to do sth** prendre sur soi de faire qch; **~ the first (street) on the left** prenez la première à gauche; **it won't ~ long** ça ne prendra pas longtemps; **I was quite taken with her/it** elle/cela m'a beaucoup plu.

▶**take after** *vt fus* ressembler à.

▶**take apart** *vt* démonter.

▶**take away** *vt* emporter; (*remove*) enlever; (*subtract*) soustraire ♦ *vi*: **to ~ away from** diminuer.

▶**take back** *vt* (*return*) rendre, rapporter; (*one's words*) retirer.

▶**take down** *vt* (*building*) démolir; (*dismantle: scaffolding*) démonter; (*letter etc*) prendre, écrire.

▶**take in** *vt* (*deceive*) tromper, rouler; (*understand*) comprendre, saisir; (*include*) couvrir, inclure; (*lodger*) prendre; (*orphan, stray dog*) recueillir; (*dress, waistband*) reprendre.

▶**take off** *vi* (AVIAT) décoller ♦ *vt* (*remove*) enlever; (*imitate*) imiter, pasticher.

▶**take on** *vt* (*work*) accepter, se charger de; (*employee*) prendre, embaucher; (*opponent*) accepter de se battre contre.

▶**take out** *vt* sortir; (*remove*) enlever; (*licence*) prendre, se procurer; **to ~ sth out of** enlever qch de; prendre qch dans; **don't ~ it out on me!** ne t'en prends pas à moi!

▶**take over** *vt* (*business*) reprendre ♦ *vi*: **to ~ over from sb** prendre la relève de qn.

▶**take to** *vt fus* (*person*) se prendre d'amitié pour; (*activity*) prendre goût à; **to ~ to doing sth** prendre l'habitude de faire qch.

▶**take up** *vt* (*one's story, a dress*) reprendre; (*occupy: time, space*) prendre, occuper; (*engage in: hobby etc*) se mettre à; (*accept: offer, challenge*) accepter; (*absorb: liquids*) absorber ♦ *vi*: **to ~ up with sb** se lier d'amitié avec qn.

takeaway ['teɪkəweɪ] *adj* (BRIT: *food*) à emporter.

take-home pay ['teɪkhəum-] *n* salaire net.

taken ['teɪkən] *pp of* **take**.

takeoff ['teɪkɔf] *n* (AVIAT) décollage *m*.

takeout ['teɪkaut] *adj* (US) = **takeaway**.

takeover ['teɪkəuvə*] *n* (COMM) rachat *m*.

takeover bid *n* offre publique d'achat, OPA *f*.

takings ['teɪkɪŋz] *npl* (COMM) recette *f*.

talc [tælk] *n* (*also:* ~**um powder**) talc *m*.

tale [teɪl] *n* (*story*) conte *m*, histoire *f*; (*account*) récit *m*; (*pej*) histoire; **to tell ~s** (*fig*) rapporter.

talent ['tælnt] *n* talent *m*, don *m*.

talented ['tæləntɪd] *adj* doué(e), plein(e) de talent.

talent scout *n* découvreur *m* de vedettes (*or* joueurs *etc*).

talisman ['tælɪzmən] *n* talisman *m*.

talk [tɔːk] *n* propos *mpl*; (*gossip*) racontars *mpl* (*pej*); (*conversation*) discussion *f*; (*interview*) entretien *m*; (*a speech*) causerie *f*, exposé *m* ♦ *vi* (*chatter*) bavarder; **~s** *npl* (POL *etc*) entretiens *mpl*; conférence *f*; **to give a ~** faire un exposé; **to ~ about** parler de; (*converse*) s'entretenir *or* parler de; **~ing of films, have you seen ...?** à propos de films, avez-vous vu ...?; **to ~ sb out of/into doing** persuader qn de ne pas faire/de faire; **to ~ shop** parler métier *or* affaires.

▶**talk over** *vt* discuter (de).

talkative ['tɔːkətɪv] *adj* bavard(e).

talker ['tɔːkə*] *n* causeur/euse; (*pej*) bavard/e.

talking point ['tɔːkɪŋ-] *n* sujet *m* de conversation.

talking-to ['tɔːkɪŋtu] *n*: **to give sb a good ~** passer un savon à qn.

talk show *n* (TV, RADIO) causerie (télévisée *or* radiodiffusée).

tall [tɔːl] *adj* (*person*) grand(e); (*building, tree*) haut(e); **to be 6 feet ~** ≈ mesurer 1 mètre 80; **how ~ are you?** combien mesurez-vous?

tallboy ['tɔːlbɔɪ] *n* (BRIT) grande commode.

tallness ['tɔːlnɪs] *n* grande taille; hauteur *f*.

tall story *n* histoire *f* invraisemblable.

tally ['tælɪ] *n* compte *m* ♦ *vi*: **to ~** (**with**) correspondre (à); **to keep a ~ of sth** tenir le compte de qch.

talon ['tælən] *n* griffe *f*; (*of eagle*) serre *f*.

tambourine [tæmbə'riːn] *n* tambourin *m*.

tame [teɪm] *adj* apprivoisé(e); (*fig: story, style*) insipide.

Tamil ['tæmɪl] *adj* tamoul(e) *or* tamil(e) ♦ *n* Tamoul/e *or* Tamil/e; (LING) tamoul *m* *or* tamil *m*.

tamper ['tæmpə*] *vi*: **to ~ with** toucher à (*en cachette ou sans permission*).

tampon ['tæmpɔn] *n* tampon *m* hygiénique *or* périodique.

tan [tæn] *n* (*also:* **sun~**) bronzage *m* ♦ *vt*, *vi* bronzer, brunir ♦ *adj* (*colour*) brun roux *inv*; **to get a ~** bronzer.

tandem ['tændəm] *n* tandem *m*.

tandoori [tæn'duərɪ] *adj* tandouri.

tang [tæŋ] *n* odeur (*or* saveur) piquante.

tangent ['tændʒənt] *n* (MATH) tangente *f*; **to go off at a ~** (*fig*) changer complètement de direction.

tangerine [tændʒə'riːn] *n* mandarine *f*.

tangible ['tændʒəbl] *adj* tangible; **~ assets** biens réels.

Tangier [tæn'dʒɪə*] *n* Tanger.

tangle ['tæŋgl] *n* enchevêtrement *m* ♦ *vt* enchevêtrer; **to get in(to) a ~** s'emmêler.

tango ['tæŋgəu] *n* tango *m*.

tank [tæŋk] *n* réservoir *m*; (*for processing*) cuve *f*; (*for fish*) aquarium *m*; (MIL) char *m* d'assaut, tank *m*.

tankard ['tæŋkəd] n chope f.

tanker ['tæŋkə*] n (ship) pétrolier m, tanker m; (truck) camion-citerne m; (RAIL) wagon-citerne m.

tanned [tænd] adj bronzé(e).

tannin ['tænɪn] n tanin m.

tanning ['tænɪŋ] n (of leather) tannage m.

tannoy ['tænɔɪ] n ® (BRIT) haut-parleur m; **over the** ~ par haut-parleur.

tantalizing ['tæntəlaɪzɪŋ] adj (smell) extrêmement appétissant(e); (offer) terriblement tentant(e).

tantamount ['tæntəmaunt] adj: ~ **to** qui équivaut à.

tantrum ['tæntrəm] n accès m de colère; **to throw a** ~ piquer une colère.

Tanzania [tænzə'nɪə] n Tanzanie f.

Tanzanian [tænzə'nɪən] adj tanzanien(ne) ♦ n Tanzanien/ne.

tap [tæp] n (on sink etc) robinet m; (gentle blow) petite tape ♦ vt frapper or taper légèrement; (resources) exploiter, utiliser; (telephone) mettre sur écoute; **on** ~ (beer) en tonneau; (fig: resources) disponible.

tap-dancing ['tæpdɑːnsɪŋ] n claquettes fpl.

tape [teɪp] n ruban m; (also: magnetic ~) bande f (magnétique) ♦ vt (record) enregistrer (au magnétophone or sur bande); **on** ~ (song etc) enregistré(e).

tape deck n platine f d'enregistrement.

tape measure n mètre m à ruban.

taper ['teɪpə*] n cierge m ♦ vi s'effiler.

tape-record ['teɪprɪkɔːd] vt enregistrer (au magnétophone or sur bande).

tape recorder n magnétophone m.

tape recording n enregistrement m (au magnétophone).

tapered ['teɪpəd], **tapering** ['teɪpərɪŋ] adj fuselé(e), effilé(e).

tapestry ['tæpɪstrɪ] n tapisserie f.

tape-worm ['teɪpwəːm] n ver m solitaire, ténia m.

tapioca [tæpɪ'əukə] n tapioca m.

tappet ['tæpɪt] n (AUT) poussoir m (de soupape).

tar [tɑː] n goudron m; **low-/middle-**~ **cigarettes** cigarettes fpl à faible/moyenne teneur en goudron.

tarantula [tə'ræntjulə] n tarentule f.

tardy ['tɑːdɪ] adj tardif(ive).

target ['tɑːgɪt] n cible f; (fig: objective) objectif m; **to be on** ~ (project) progresser comme prévu.

target practice n exercices mpl de tir (à la cible).

tariff ['tærɪf] n (COMM) tarif m; (taxes) tarif douanier.

tariff barrier n barrière douanière.

tarmac ['tɑːmæk] n (BRIT: on road) macadam m; (AVIAT) aire f d'envol ♦ vt (BRIT) goudronner.

tarnish ['tɑːnɪʃ] vt ternir.

tarot ['tærəu] n tarot m.

tarpaulin [tɑː'pɔːlɪn] n bâche goudronnée.

tarragon ['tærəgən] n estragon m.

tart [tɑːt] n (CULIN) tarte f; (BRIT col: pej: woman) poule f ♦ adj (flavour) âpre, aigrelet(te).

▶**tart up** vt (col): **to** ~ **o.s. up** se faire beau(belle); (: pej) s'attifer.

tartan ['tɑːtn] n tartan m ♦ adj écossais(e).

tartar ['tɑːtə*] n (on teeth) tartre m.

tartar sauce n sauce f tartare.

task [tɑːsk] n tâche f; **to take to** ~ prendre à partie.

task force n (MIL, POLICE) détachement spécial.

taskmaster ['tɑːskmɑːstə*] n: **he's a hard** ~ il est très exigeant dans le travail.

Tasmania [tæz'meɪnɪə] n Tasmanie f.

tassel ['tæsl] n gland m; pompon m.

taste [teɪst] n goût m; (fig: glimpse, idea) idée f, aperçu m ♦ vt goûter ♦ vi: **to** ~ **of** (fish etc) avoir le or un goût de; **it** ~s **like fish** ça a un or le goût de poisson, on dirait du poisson; **what does it** ~ **like?** quel goût ça a?; **you can** ~ **the garlic (in it)** on sent bien l'ail; **can I have a** ~ **of this wine?** puis-je goûter un peu de ce vin?; **to have a** ~ **of sth** goûter (à) qch; **to have a** ~ **for sth** aimer qch, avoir un penchant pour qch; **to be in good/bad** or **poor** ~ être de bon/mauvais goût.

taste bud n papille f.

tasteful ['teɪstful] adj de bon goût.

tastefully ['teɪstfəlɪ] adv avec goût.

tasteless ['teɪstlɪs] adj (food) qui n'a aucun goût; (remark) de mauvais goût.

tasty ['teɪstɪ] adj savoureux(euse), délicieux(euse).

tattered ['tætəd] adj see **tatters**.

tatters ['tætəz] npl: **in** ~ (also: **tattered**) en lambeaux.

tattoo [tə'tuː] n tatouage m; (spectacle) parade f militaire ♦ vt tatouer.

tatty ['tætɪ] adj (BRIT col) défraîchi(e), en piteux état.

taught [tɔːt] pt, pp of **teach**.

taunt [tɔːnt] n raillerie f ♦ vt railler.

Taurus ['tɔːrəs] n le Taureau; **to be** ~ être du Taureau.

taut [tɔːt] adj tendu(e).

tavern ['tævən] n taverne f.

tawdry ['tɔːdrɪ] adj (d'un mauvais goût) criard.

tawny ['tɔːnɪ] adj fauve (couleur).

tax [tæks] n (on goods etc) taxe f; (on income) impôts mpl, contributions fpl ♦ vt taxer; imposer; (fig: strain: patience etc) mettre à l'épreuve; **before/after** ~ avant/après l'impôt; **free of** ~ exonéré(e) d'impôt.

taxable ['tæksəbl] adj (income) imposable.

tax allowance n part f du revenu non imposable, abattement m à la base.

taxation [tæk'seɪʃən] n taxation f; impôts mpl,

contributions *fpl*; **system of** ~ système fiscal.

tax avoidance *n* évasion fiscale.

tax collector *n* percepteur *m*.

tax disc *n* (*BRIT AUT*) vignette *f* (automobile).

tax evasion *n* fraude fiscale.

tax exemption *n* exonération fiscale, exemption *f* d'impôts.

tax exile *n personne qui s'expatrie pour raisons fiscales.*

tax-free ['tæksfriː] *adj* exempt(e) d'impôts.

tax haven *n* paradis fiscal.

taxi ['tæksɪ] *n* taxi *m* ♦ *vi* (*AVIAT*) rouler (lentement) au sol.

taxidermist ['tæksɪdəːmɪst] *n* empailleur/euse (*d'animaux*).

taxi driver *n* chauffeur *m* de taxi.

tax inspector *n* (*BRIT*) percepteur *m*.

taxi rank (*BRIT*), **taxi stand** *n* station *f* de taxis.

tax payer [-peɪə*] *n* contribuable *m/f*.

tax rebate *n* ristourne *f* d'impôt.

tax relief *n* dégrèvement *or* allègement fiscal, réduction *f* d'impôt.

tax return *n* déclaration *f* d'impôts *or* de revenus.

tax year *n* année fiscale.

TB *n abbr* = **tuberculosis**.

TD *n abbr* (*US*) = **Treasury Department**; (: *FOOTBALL*) = **touchdown**.

tea [tiː] *n* thé *m*; (*BRIT*: *snack: for children*) goûter *m*; **high** ~ (*BRIT*) *collation combinant goûter et dîner.*

tea bag *n* sachet *m* de thé.

tea break *n* (*BRIT*) pause-thé *f*.

teacake ['tiːkeɪk] *n* (*BRIT*) ≈ petit pain aux raisins.

teach, *pt, pp* **taught** [tiːtʃ, tɔːt] *vt*: **to** ~ **sb sth**, ~ **sth to sb** apprendre qch à qn; (*in school etc*) enseigner qch à qn ♦ *vi* enseigner; **it taught him a lesson** (*fig*) ça lui a servi de leçon.

teacher ['tiːtʃə*] *n* (*in secondary school*) professeur *m*; (*in primary school*) instituteur/trice; **French** ~ professeur de français.

teacher training college *n* (*for primary schools*) ≈ école normale d'instituteurs; (*for secondary schools*) collège *m* de formation pédagogique (*pour l'enseignement secondaire*).

teaching ['tiːtʃɪŋ] *n* enseignement *m*.

teaching aids *npl* supports *mpl* pédagogiques.

teaching hospital *n* (*BRIT*) C.H.U. *m*, centre *m* hospitalo-universitaire.

teaching staff *n* (*BRIT*) enseignants *mpl*.

tea cosy *n* couvre-théière *m*.

teacup ['tiːkʌp] *n* tasse *f* à thé.

teak [tiːk] *n* teck *m* ♦ *adj* en *or* de teck.

tea leaves *npl* feuilles *fpl* de thé.

team [tiːm] *n* équipe *f*; (*of animals*) attelage *m*.

►**team up** *vi*: **to** ~ **up (with)** faire équipe (avec).

team games *npl* jeux *mpl* d'équipe.

teamwork ['tiːmwəːk] *n* travail *m* d'équipe.

tea party *n* thé *m* (*réception*).

teapot ['tiːpɔt] *n* théière *f*.

tear[1] *n* [tɛə*] déchirure *f* ♦ *vb* (*pt* **tore**, *pp* **torn** [tɔː*, tɔːn]) *vt* déchirer ♦ *vi* se déchirer; **to** ~ **to pieces** *or* **to bits** *or* **to shreds** mettre en pièces; (*fig*) démolir.

►**tear along** *vi* (*rush*) aller à toute vitesse.

►**tear apart** *vt* (*also fig*) déchirer.

►**tear away** *vt*: **to** ~ **o.s. away (from sth)** (*fig*) s'arracher (de qch).

►**tear out** *vt* (*sheet of paper, cheque*) arracher.

►**tear up** *vt* (*sheet of paper etc*) déchirer, mettre en morceaux *or* pièces.

tear[2] ['tɪə*] *n* larme *f*; **in** ~**s** en larmes; **to burst into** ~**s** fondre en larmes.

tearaway ['tɛərəweɪ] *n* (*col*) casse-cou *m inv*.

teardrop ['tɪədrɔp] *n* larme *f*.

tearful ['tɪəful] *adj* larmoyant(e).

tear gas ['tɪə-] *n* gaz *m* lacrymogène.

tearoom ['tiːruːm] *n* salon *m* de thé.

tease [tiːz] *n* taquin/e ♦ *vt* taquiner; (*unkindly*) tourmenter.

tea set *n* service *m* à thé.

teashop ['tiːʃɔp] *n* (*BRIT*) pâtisserie-salon de thé *f*.

Teasmade ['tiːzmeɪd] *n* ® machine *f* à faire le thé.

teaspoon ['tiːspuːn] *n* petite cuiller; (*also*: ~**ful**: *as measurement*) ≈ cuillerée *f* à café.

tea strainer *n* passoire *f* (à thé).

teat [tiːt] *n* tétine *f*.

teatime ['tiːtaɪm] *n* l'heure *f* du thé.

tea towel *n* (*BRIT*) torchon *m* (à vaisselle).

tea urn *n* fontaine *f* à thé.

tech [tɛk] *n abbr* (*col*) = **technology, technical college**.

technical ['tɛknɪkl] *adj* technique.

technical college *n* C.E.T. *m*, collège *m* d'enseignement technique.

technicality [tɛknɪˈkælɪtɪ] *n* technicité *f*; (*detail*) détail *m* technique; **on a legal** ~ à cause de (*or* grâce à) l'application à la lettre d'une subtilité juridique; pour vice de forme.

technically ['tɛknɪklɪ] *adv* techniquement; (*strictly speaking*) en théorie, en principe.

technician [tɛkˈnɪʃən] *n* technicien/ne.

technique [tɛkˈniːk] *n* technique *f*.

techno ['tɛknəu] *n* (*MUS*) techno *f*.

technocrat ['tɛknəkræt] *n* technocrate *m/f*.

technological [tɛknəˈlɔdʒɪkl] *adj* technologique.

technologist [tɛkˈnɔlədʒɪst] *n* technologue *m/f*.

technology [tɛkˈnɔlədʒɪ] *n* technologie *f*.

teddy (bear) ['tɛdɪ-] *n* ours *m* (en peluche).

tedious ['tiːdɪəs] *adj* fastidieux(euse).

tedium ['tiːdɪəm] *n* ennui *m*.

tee [tiː] *n* (*GOLF*) tee *m*.

teem [tiːm] *vi*: **to** ~ **(with)** grouiller (de); **it is**

~**ing (with rain)** il pleut à torrents.

teenage ['ti:neɪdʒ] *adj (fashions etc)* pour jeunes, pour adolescents.

teenager ['ti:neɪdʒə*] *n* jeune *m/f*, adolescent/e.

teens [ti:nz] *npl:* **to be in one's** ~ être adolescent(e).

tee-shirt ['ti:ʃə:t] *n* = **T-shirt**.

teeter ['ti:tə*] *vi* chanceler, vaciller.

teeth [ti:θ] *npl of* **tooth**.

teethe [ti:ð] *vi* percer ses dents.

teething ring ['ti:ðɪŋ-] *n* anneau *m (pour bébé qui perce ses dents).*

teething troubles ['ti:ðɪŋ-] *npl (fig)* difficultés initiales.

teetotal ['ti:'təutl] *adj (person)* qui ne boit jamais d'alcool.

teetotaller, *(US)* **teetotaler** ['ti:'təutlə*] *n* personne *f* qui ne boit jamais d'alcool.

TEFL ['tɛfl] *n abbr* = *Teaching of English as a Foreign Language.*

Teflon ['tɛflɔn] *n* ® Téflon *m* ®.

Teheran [tɛə'rɑ:n] *n* Téhéran.

tel. *abbr* (= *telephone*) tél.

Tel Aviv ['tɛlə'vi:v] *n* Tel Aviv.

telecast ['tɛlɪkɑ:st] *vt* télédiffuser, téléviser.

telecommunications ['tɛlɪkəmju:nɪ'keɪʃənz] *n* télécommunications *fpl.*

telegram ['tɛlɪgræm] *n* télégramme *m.*

telegraph ['tɛlɪgrɑ:f] *n* télégraphe *m.*

telegraphic [tɛlɪ'græfɪk] *adj* télégraphique.

telegraph pole *n* poteau *m* télégraphique.

telegraph wire *n* fil *m* télégraphique.

telepathic [tɛlɪ'pæθɪk] *adj* télépathique.

telepathy [tə'lɛpəθɪ] *n* télépathie *f.*

telephone ['tɛlɪfəun] *n* téléphone *m* ♦ *vt (person)* téléphoner à; *(message)* téléphoner; **to have a** ~, *(BRIT)* **to be on the** ~ *(subscriber)* être abonné(e) au téléphone; **to be on the** ~ *(be speaking)* être au téléphone.

telephone booth, *(BRIT)* **telephone box** *n* cabine *f* téléphonique.

telephone call *n* appel *m* téléphonique, communication *f* téléphonique.

telephone directory *n* annuaire *m* (du téléphone).

telephone exchange *n* central *m* (téléphonique).

telephone number *n* numéro *m* de téléphone.

telephone operator *n* téléphoniste *m/f*, standardiste *m/f.*

telephone tapping [-tæpɪŋ] *n* mise *f* sur écoute.

telephonist [tə'lɛfənɪst] *n (BRIT)* téléphoniste *m/f.*

telephoto ['tɛlɪfəutəu] *adj:* ~ **lens** téléobjectif *m.*

teleprinter ['tɛlɪprɪntə*] *n* téléscripteur *m.*

Teleprompter ['tɛlɪprɔmptə*] *n* ® *(US)* prompteur *m.*

telesales ['tɛlɪseɪlz] *npl* télévente *f.*

telescope ['tɛlɪskəup] *n* télescope *m* ♦ *vi* se télescoper ♦ *vt* télescoper.

telescopic [tɛlɪ'skɔpɪk] *adj* télescopique; *(umbrella)* à manche télescopique.

Teletext ['tɛlɪtɛkst] *n* ® télétexte *m.*

telethon ['tɛlɪθɔn] *n* téléthon *m.*

televise ['tɛlɪvaɪz] *vt* téléviser.

television ['tɛlɪvɪʒən] *n* télévision *f.*

television licence *n (BRIT)* redevance *f* (de l'audio-visuel).

television programme *n* émission *f* de télévision.

television set *n* poste *m* de télévision, téléviseur *m.*

telex ['tɛlɛks] *n* télex *m* ♦ *vt (message)* envoyer par télex; *(person)* envoyer un télex à ♦ *vi* envoyer un télex.

tell, *pt, pp* **told** [tɛl, təuld] *vt* dire; *(relate: story)* raconter; *(distinguish):* **to** ~ **sth from** distinguer qch de ♦ *vi (talk):* **to** ~ **(of)** parler (de); *(have effect)* se faire sentir, se voir; **to** ~ **sb to do** dire à qn de faire; **to** ~ **sb about sth** *(place, object etc)* parler de qch à qn; *(what happened etc)* raconter qch à qn; **to** ~ **the time** *(know how to)* savoir lire l'heure; **can you** ~ **me the time?** pourriez-vous me dire l'heure?; **(I)** ~ **you what ...** écoute, ...; **I can't** ~ **them apart** je n'arrive pas à les distinguer.

►**tell off** *vt* réprimander, gronder.

►**tell on** *vt fus (inform against)* dénoncer, rapporter contre.

teller ['tɛlə*] *n (in bank)* caissier/ière.

telling ['tɛlɪŋ] *adj (remark, detail)* révélateur(trice).

telltale ['tɛlteɪl] *n* rapporteur/euse ♦ *adj (sign)* éloquent(e), révélateur(trice).

telly ['tɛlɪ] *n abbr (BRIT col:* = *television)* télé *f.*

temerity [tə'mɛrɪtɪ] *n* témérité *f.*

temp [tɛmp] *abbr (BRIT col:* = *temporary) n* intérimaire *m/f* ♦ *vi* travailler comme intérimaire.

temper ['tɛmpə*] *n (nature)* caractère *m*; *(mood)* humeur *f*; *(fit of anger)* colère *f* ♦ *vt (moderate)* tempérer, adoucir; **to be in a** ~ être en colère; **to lose one's** ~ se mettre en colère; **to keep one's** ~ rester calme.

temperament ['tɛmprəmənt] *n (nature)* tempérament *m.*

temperamental [tɛmprə'mɛntl] *adj* capricieux(euse).

temperance ['tɛmpərns] *n* modération *f*; *(in drinking)* tempérance *f.*

temperate ['tɛmprət] *adj* modéré(e); *(climate)* tempéré(e).

temperature ['tɛmprətʃə*] *n* température *f*; **to have** *or* **run a** ~ avoir de la fièvre.

temperature chart *n (MED)* feuille *f* de température.

tempered ['tɛmpəd] *adj (steel)* trempé(e).

tempest ['tɛmpɪst] *n* tempête *f.*

tempestuous [tɛm'pɛstjuəs] *adj (fig)*

orageux(euse); (: *person*) passionné(e).

tempi ['tɛmpiː] *npl of* **tempo**.

template ['tɛmplɪt] *n* patron *m*.

temple ['tɛmpl] *n* (*building*) temple *m*; (ANAT) tempe *f*.

templet ['tɛmplɪt] *n* = **template**.

tempo, ~s *or* **tempi** ['tɛmpəu, 'tɛmpiː] *n* tempo *m*; (*fig: of life etc*) rythme *m*.

temporal ['tɛmpərl] *adj* temporel(le).

temporarily ['tɛmpərərɪlɪ] *adv* temporairement; provisoirement.

temporary ['tɛmpərərɪ] *adj* temporaire, provisoire; (*job, worker*) temporaire; ~ **secretary** (secrétaire *f*) intérimaire *f*; **a** ~ **teacher** un professeur remplaçant *or* suppléant.

temporize ['tɛmpəraɪz] *vi* atermoyer; transiger.

tempt [tɛmpt] *vt* tenter; **to ~ sb into doing** induire qn à faire; **to be ~ed to do sth** être tenté(e) de faire qch.

temptation [tɛmp'teɪʃən] *n* tentation *f*.

tempting ['tɛmptɪŋ] *adj* tentant(e).

ten [tɛn] *num* dix ♦ *n*: ~**s of thousands** des dizaines *fpl* de milliers.

tenable ['tɛnəbl] *adj* défendable.

tenacious [tə'neɪʃəs] *adj* tenace.

tenacity [tə'næsɪtɪ] *n* ténacité *f*.

tenancy ['tɛnənsɪ] *n* location *f*; état *m* de locataire.

tenant ['tɛnənt] *n* locataire *m/f*.

tend [tɛnd] *vt* s'occuper de; (*sick etc*) soigner ♦ *vi*: **to ~ to do** avoir tendance à faire; (*colour*): **to ~ to** tirer sur.

tendency ['tɛndənsɪ] *n* tendance *f*.

tender ['tɛndə*] *adj* tendre; (*delicate*) délicat(e); (*sore*) sensible; (*affectionate*) tendre, doux(douce) ♦ *n* (COMM: *offer*) soumission *f*; (*money*): **legal** ~ cours légal ♦ *vt* offrir; **to ~ one's resignation** donner *or* remettre sa démission; **to put in a** ~ **(for)** faire une soumission (pour); **to put work out to** ~ (BRIT) mettre un contrat en adjudication.

tenderize ['tɛndəraɪz] *vt* (CULIN) attendrir.

tenderly ['tɛndəlɪ] *adv* tendrement.

tenderness ['tɛndənɪs] *n* tendresse *f*; (*of meat*) tendreté *f*.

tendon ['tɛndən] *n* tendon *m*.

tenement ['tɛnəmənt] *n* immeuble *m* (de rapport).

Tenerife [tɛnə'riːf] *n* Ténérife *f*.

tenet ['tɛnət] *n* principe *m*.

Tenn. *abbr* (US) = *Tennessee*.

tenner ['tɛnə*] *n* (BRIT col) billet *m* de dix livres.

tennis ['tɛnɪs] *n* tennis *m* ♦ *cpd* (*club, match, racket, player*) de tennis.

tennis ball *n* balle *f* de tennis.

tennis court *n* (court *m* de) tennis *m*.

tennis elbow *n* (MED) synovite *f* du coude.

tennis shoes *npl* (chaussures *fpl* de)

tennis *mpl*.

tenor ['tɛnə*] *n* (MUS) ténor *m*; (*of speech etc*) sens général.

tenpin bowling ['tɛnpɪn-] *n* (BRIT) bowling *m* (à 10 quilles).

tense [tɛns] *adj* tendu(e); (*person*) tendu, crispé(e) ♦ *n* (LING) temps *m* ♦ *vt* (*tighten: muscles*) tendre.

tenseness ['tɛnsnɪs] *n* tension *f*.

tension ['tɛnʃən] *n* tension *f*.

tent [tɛnt] *n* tente *f*.

tentacle ['tɛntəkl] *n* tentacule *m*.

tentative ['tɛntətɪv] *adj* timide, hésitant(e); (*conclusion*) provisoire.

tenterhooks ['tɛntəhuks] *npl*: **on** ~ sur des charbons ardents.

tenth [tɛnθ] *num* dixième.

tent peg *n* piquet *m* de tente.

tent pole *n* montant *m* de tente.

tenuous ['tɛnjuəs] *adj* ténu(e).

tenure ['tɛnjuə*] *n* (*of property*) bail *m*; (*of job*) période *f* de jouissance; statut *m* de titulaire.

tepid ['tɛpɪd] *adj* tiède.

Ter. *abbr* = **terrace**.

term [təːm] *n* (*limit*) terme *m*; (*word*) terme, mot *m*; (SCOL) trimestre *m*; (LAW) session *f* ♦ *vt* appeler; ~**s** *npl* (*conditions*) conditions *fpl*; (COMM) tarif *m*; ~ **of imprisonment** peine *f* de prison; **his** ~ **of office** la période où il était en fonction; **in the short/long** ~ à court/long terme; **"easy ~s"** (COMM) "facilités de paiement"; **to come to** ~**s with** (*problem*) faire face à; **to be on good** ~**s with** bien s'entendre avec, être en bons termes avec.

terminal ['təːmɪnl] *adj* terminal(e); (*disease*) dans sa phase terminale ♦ *n* (ELEC) borne *f*; (*for oil, ore etc, also* COMPUT) terminal *m*; (*also*: **air** ~) aérogare *f*; (BRIT: *also*: **coach** ~) gare routière.

terminate ['təːmɪneɪt] *vt* mettre fin à ♦ *vi*: **to ~ in** finir en *or* par.

termination [təːmɪ'neɪʃən] *n* fin *f*; cessation *f*; (*of contract*) résiliation *f*; ~ **of pregnancy** (MED) interruption *f* de grossesse.

termini ['təːmɪnaɪ] *npl of* **terminus**.

terminology [təːmɪ'nɔlədʒɪ] *n* terminologie *f*.

terminus, *pl* **termini** ['təːmɪnəs, 'təːmɪnaɪ] *n* terminus *m inv*.

termite ['təːmaɪt] *n* termite *m*.

term paper *n* (US UNIVERSITY) dissertation trimestrielle.

Terr. *abbr* = **terrace**.

terrace ['tɛrəs] *n* terrasse *f*; (BRIT: *row of houses*) rangée *f* de maisons (*attenantes les unes aux autres*); **the ~s** (BRIT SPORT) les gradins *mpl*.

terraced ['tɛrəst] *adj* (*garden*) en terrasses; (*in a row: house, cottage etc*) attenant(e) aux maisons voisines.

terracotta ['tɛrə'kɔtə] *n* terre cuite.

terrain [tɛ'reɪn] n terrain m (sol).

terrible ['tɛrɪbl] adj terrible, atroce; (weather, work) affreux(euse), épouvantable.

terribly ['tɛrɪblɪ] adv terriblement; (very badly) affreusement mal.

terrier ['tɛrɪə*] n terrier m (chien).

terrific [tə'rɪfɪk] adj fantastique, incroyable, terrible; (wonderful) formidable, sensationnel(le).

terrify ['tɛrɪfaɪ] vt terrifier.

territorial [tɛrɪ'tɔːrɪəl] adj territorial(e).

territorial waters npl eaux territoriales.

territory ['tɛrɪtərɪ] n territoire m.

terror ['tɛrə*] n terreur f.

terrorism ['tɛrərɪzəm] n terrorisme m.

terrorist ['tɛrərɪst] n terroriste m/f.

terrorize ['tɛrəraɪz] vt terroriser.

terse [təːs] adj (style) concis(e); (reply) laconique.

tertiary ['təːʃərɪ] adj tertiaire; ~ **education** (BRIT) enseignement m postscolaire.

Terylene ['tɛrɪliːn] n ® (BRIT) tergal m ®.

TESL ['tɛsl] n abbr = Teaching of English as a Second Language.

TESSA ['tɛsə] n abbr (BRIT: = Tax Exempt Special Savings Account) compte de dépôt aux intérêts exempts d'impôts si le capital reste bloqué.

test [tɛst] n (trial, check) essai m; (: of goods in factory) contrôle m; (of courage etc) épreuve f; (MED) examens mpl; (CHEM) analyses fpl; (exam: of intelligence etc) test m (d'aptitude); (: in school) interrogation f de contrôle; (also: driving ~) (examen du) permis m de conduire ♦ vt essayer; contrôler; mettre à l'épreuve; examiner; analyser; tester; faire subir une interrogation (de contrôle) à; **to put sth to the** ~ mettre qch à l'épreuve.

testament ['tɛstəmənt] n testament m; **the Old/New T~** l'Ancien/le Nouveau Testament.

test ban n (also: nuclear ~) interdiction f des essais nucléaires.

test case n (LAW, fig) affaire-test f.

testes ['tɛstiːz] npl testicules mpl.

test flight n vol m d'essai.

testicle ['tɛstɪkl] n testicule m.

testify ['tɛstɪfaɪ] vi (LAW) témoigner, déposer; **to** ~ **to sth** (LAW) attester qch; (gen) témoigner de qch.

testimonial [tɛstɪ'məunɪəl] n (BRIT: reference) recommandation f; (gift) témoignage m d'estime.

testimony ['tɛstɪmənɪ] n (LAW) témoignage m, déposition f.

testing ['tɛstɪŋ] adj (situation, period) difficile.

test match n (CRICKET, RUGBY) match international.

testosterone [tɛs'tɔstərəun] n testostérone f.

test paper n (SCOL) interrogation écrite.

test pilot n pilote m d'essai.

test tube n éprouvette f.

test-tube baby ['tɛsttjuːb-] n bébé-éprouvette m.

testy ['tɛstɪ] adj irritable.

tetanus ['tɛtənəs] n tétanos m.

tetchy ['tɛtʃɪ] adj hargneux(euse).

tether ['tɛðə*] vt attacher ♦ n: **at the end of one's** ~ à bout (de patience).

Tex. abbr (US) = Texas.

text [tɛkst] n texte m.

textbook ['tɛkstbuk] n manuel m.

textile ['tɛkstaɪl] n textile m.

textual ['tɛkstjuəl] adj textuel(le).

texture ['tɛkstʃə*] n texture f; (of skin, paper etc) grain m.

TGIF abbr (col) = thank God it's Friday.

TGWU n abbr (BRIT: = Transport and General Workers' Union) syndicat de transporteurs.

Thai [taɪ] adj thaïlandais(e) ♦ n Thaïlandais/e; (LING) thaï m.

Thailand ['taɪlænd] n Thaïlande f.

thalidomide [θə'lɪdəmaɪd] n ® thalidomide f ®.

Thames [tɛmz] n: **the** ~ la Tamise.

than [ðæn, ðən] conj que; (with numerals): **more** ~ **10/once** plus de 10/d'une fois; **I have more/less** ~ **you** j'en ai plus/moins que toi; **she has more apples** ~ **pears** elle a plus de pommes que de poires; **it is better to phone** ~ **to write** il vaut mieux téléphoner (plutôt) qu'écrire; **no sooner did he leave** ~ **the phone rang** il venait de partir quand le téléphone a sonné.

thank [θæŋk] vt remercier, dire merci à; ~ **you (very much)** merci (beaucoup); ~ **heavens**, ~ **God** Dieu merci.

thankful ['θæŋkful] adj: ~ **(for)** reconnaissant(e) (de); ~ **for/that** (relieved) soulagé(e) de/que.

thankfully ['θæŋkfəlɪ] adv avec reconnaissance; avec soulagement; ~ **there were few victims** il y eut fort heureusement peu de victimes.

thankless ['θæŋklɪs] adj ingrat(e).

thanks [θæŋks] npl remerciements mpl ♦ excl merci!; ~ **to** prep grâce à.

Thanksgiving (Day) ['θæŋksgɪvɪŋ-] n jour m d'action de grâce.

Thanksgiving Day est un jour de congé aux États-Unis, le quatrième jeudi du mois de novembre, commémorant la bonne récolte que les Pèlerins venus de Grande-Bretagne ont eue en 1621; traditionnellement, c'était un jour où l'on remerciait Dieu et où l'on organisait un grand festin.
Une fête semblable, mais qui n'a aucun rapport avec les Pères Pèlerins, a lieu au Canada le deuxième lundi d'octobre.

================================ *KEYWORD*

that [ðæt] *adj* (*demonstrative*: *pl* **those**) ce, cet *+vowel or h mute*, *f* cette; ~ **man/woman/book** cet homme/cette femme/ce livre; (*not this*) cet homme-là/cette femme-là/ce livre-là; ~ **one** celui-là(celle-là)

♦ *pron* **1** (*demonstrative*: *pl* **those**) ce; (*not this one*) cela, ça; (*the one*) celui(celle); **who's ~?** qui est-ce?; **what's ~?** qu'est-ce que c'est?; **is ~ you?** c'est toi?; **I prefer this to ~** je préfère ceci à cela *or* ça; ~**'s what he said** c'est *or* voilà ce qu'il a dit; **all ~** tout cela, tout ça; ~ **is (to say)** c'est-à-dire, à savoir; **at** *or* **with ~, she ...** là-dessus, elle ...; **do it like ~** fais-le comme ça

2 (*relative*: *subject*) qui; (: *object*) que; (: *indirect*) lequel(laquelle), lesquels (lesquelles) *pl*; **the book ~ I read** le livre que j'ai lu; **the books ~ are in the library** les livres qui sont dans la bibliothèque; **all ~ I have** tout ce que j'ai; **the box ~ I put it in** la boîte dans laquelle je l'ai mis; **the people ~ I spoke to** les gens auxquels *or* à qui j'ai parlé; **not ~ I know of** pas à ma connaissance

3 (*relative*: *of time*) où; **the day ~ he came** le jour où il est venu

♦ *conj* que; **he thought ~ I was ill** il pensait que j'étais malade

♦ *adv* (*demonstrative*): **I can't work ~ much** je ne peux pas travailler autant que cela; **I didn't know it was ~ bad** je ne savais pas que c'était si *or* aussi mauvais; ~ **high** aussi haut; si haut; **it's about ~ high** c'est à peu près de cette hauteur.

thatched [θætʃt] *adj* (*roof*) de chaume; ~ **cottage** chaumière *f*.
Thatcherism ['θætʃərɪzəm] *n* thatchérisme *m*.
thaw [θɔː] *n* dégel *m* ♦ *vi* (*ice*) fondre; (*food*) dégeler ♦ *vt* (*food*) (faire) dégeler; **it's ~ing** (*weather*) il dégèle.

================================ *KEYWORD*

the [ðiː, ðə] *def art* **1** (*gen*) le, la *f*, l' *+vowel or h mute*, les *pl*; (NB: **à** *+le(s)* = au(x); **de** *+ le* = du; **de** *+les* = des); ~ **boy/girl/ink** le garçon/la fille/l'encre; ~ **children** les enfants; ~ **history of ~ world** l'histoire du monde; **give it to ~ postman** donne-le au facteur; **to play ~ piano/flute** jouer du piano/de la flûte; ~ **rich and ~ poor** les riches et les pauvres
2 (*in titles*): **Elizabeth ~ First** Elisabeth première; **Peter ~ Great** Pierre le Grand
3 (*in comparisons*): ~ **more he works,** ~ **more he earns** plus il travaille, plus il gagne de l'argent; ~ **sooner ~ better** le plus tôt sera le mieux.

theatre, (*US*) **theater** ['θɪətə*] *n* théâtre *m*.
theatre-goer ['θɪətəgəuə*] *n* habitué/e du théâtre.
theatrical [θɪ'ætrɪkl] *adj* théâtral(e); ~ **company** troupe *f* de théâtre.
theft [θɛft] *n* vol *m* (*larcin*).
their [ðɛə*] *adj* leur, leurs *pl*.
theirs [ðɛəz] *pron* le(la) leur, les leurs; **it is ~** c'est à eux; **a friend of ~** un de leurs amis.
them [ðɛm, ðəm] *pron* (*direct*) les; (*indirect*) leur; (*stressed, after prep*) eux(elles); **I see ~** je les vois; **give ~ the book** donne-leur le livre; **give me a few of ~** donnez m'en quelques unes (*or* quelques unes).
theme [θiːm] *n* thème *m*.
theme park *n* parc *m* à thème.
theme song *n* chanson principale.
themselves [ðəm'sɛlvz] *pl pron* (*reflexive*) se; (*emphatic*) eux-mêmes(elles-mêmes); **between ~** entre eux(elles).
then [ðɛn] *adv* (*at that time*) alors, à ce moment-là; (*next*) puis, ensuite; (*and also*) et puis ♦ *conj* (*therefore*) alors, dans ce cas
♦ *adj*: **the ~ president** le président d'alors *or* de l'époque; **by ~** (*past*) à ce moment-là; (*future*) d'ici là; **from ~ on** dès lors; **before ~** avant; **until ~** jusqu'à ce moment-là, jusque-là; **and ~ what?** et puis après?; **what do you want me to do ~?** (*afterwards*) que veux-tu que je fasse ensuite?; (*in that case*) bon alors, qu'est-ce que je fais?
theologian [θɪə'ləudʒən] *n* théologien/ne.
theological [θɪə'lɔdʒɪkl] *adj* théologique.
theology [θɪ'ɔlədʒɪ] *n* théologie *f*.
theorem ['θɪərəm] *n* théorème *m*.
theoretical [θɪə'rɛtɪkl] *adj* théorique.
theorize ['θɪəraɪz] *vi* élaborer une théorie; (*pej*) faire des théories.
theory ['θɪərɪ] *n* théorie *f*.
therapeutic(al) [θɛrə'pjuːtɪk(l)] *adj* thérapeutique.
therapist ['θɛrəpɪst] *n* thérapeute *m/f*.
therapy ['θɛrəpɪ] *n* thérapie *f*.

================================ *KEYWORD*

there [ðɛə*] *adv* **1**: ~ **is,** ~ **are** il y a; ~ **are 3 of them** (*people, things*) il y en a 3; ~ **has been an accident** il y a eu un accident
2 (*referring to place*) là, là-bas; **it's ~** c'est là(-bas); **in/on/up/down ~** là-dedans/là-dessus/là-haut/en bas; **he went ~ on Friday** il y est allé vendredi; **to go ~ and back** faire l'aller et retour; **I want that book ~** je veux ce livre-là; ~ **he is!** le voilà!
3: ~, ~ (*esp to child*) allons, allons!

thereabouts ['ðɛərə'bauts] *adv* (*place*) par là, près de là; (*amount*) environ, à peu près.
thereafter [ðɛər'ɑːftə*] *adv* par la suite.
thereby ['ðɛəbaɪ] *adv* ainsi.
therefore ['ðɛəfɔː*] *adv* donc, par conséquent.
there's ['ðɛəz] = **there is, there has**.
thereupon [ðɛərə'pɔn] *adv* (*at that point*) sur ce; (*formal: on that subject*) à ce sujet.

thermal ['θə:ml] *adj* thermique; ~ **paper/ printer** papier *m*/imprimante *f* thermique.

thermodynamics ['θə:məʊdaɪ'næmɪks] *n* thermodynamique *f*.

thermometer [θə'mɒmɪtə*] *n* thermomètre *m*.

thermonuclear ['θə:məʊ'nju:klɪə*] *adj* thermonucléaire.

thermos ['θə:məs] *n* ® (*also:* ~ **flask**) thermos *m or f inv* ®.

thermostat ['θə:məʊstæt] *n* thermostat *m*.

thesaurus [θɪ'sɔ:rəs] *n* dictionnaire *m* synonymique.

these [ði:z] *pl pron* ceux-ci(celles-ci) ♦ *pl adj* ces; (*not those*): ~ **books** ces livres-ci.

thesis, *pl* **theses** ['θi:sɪs, 'θi:si:z] *n* thèse *f*.

they [ðeɪ] *pl pron* ils(elles); (*stressed*) eux(elles); ~ **say that** ... (*it is said that*) on dit que ....

they'd [ðeɪd] = **they had, they would.**

they'll [ðeɪl] = **they shall, they will.**

they're [ðɛə*] = **they are.**

they've [ðeɪv] = **they have.**

thick [θɪk] *adj* épais(se); (*crowd*) dense; (*stupid*) bête, borné(e) ♦ *n*: **in the** ~ **of** au beau milieu de, en plein cœur de; **it's 20 cm** ~ ça a 20 cm d'épaisseur.

thicken ['θɪkn] *vi* s'épaissir ♦ *vt* (*sauce etc*) épaissir.

thicket ['θɪkɪt] *n* fourré *m*, hallier *m*.

thickly ['θɪklɪ] *adv* (*spread*) en couche épaisse; (*cut*) en tranches épaisses; ~ **populated** à forte densité de population.

thickness ['θɪknɪs] *n* épaisseur *f*.

thickset [θɪk'sɛt] *adj* trapu(e), costaud(e).

thickskinned [θɪk'skɪnd] *adj* (*fig*) peu sensible.

thief, *pl* **thieves** [θi:f, θi:vz] *n* voleur/euse.

thieving ['θi:vɪŋ] *n* vol *m* (*larcin*).

thigh [θaɪ] *n* cuisse *f*.

thighbone ['θaɪbəʊn] *n* fémur *m*.

thimble ['θɪmbl] *n* dé *m* (à coudre).

thin [θɪn] *adj* mince; (*person*) maigre; (*soup*) peu épais(se); (*hair, crowd*) clairsemé(e); (*fog*) léger(ère) ♦ *vt* (*hair*) éclaircir; (*also:* ~ **down**: *sauce, paint*) délayer ♦ *vi* (*fog*) s'éclaircir; (*also:* ~ **out**: *crowd*) se disperser; **his hair is** ~**ning** il se dégarnit.

thing [θɪŋ] *n* chose *f*; (*object*) objet *m*; (*contraption*) truc *m*; ~**s** *npl* (*belongings*) affaires *fpl*; **first** ~ (**in the morning**) à la première heure, tout de suite (le matin); **last** ~ (**at night**), **he** ... juste avant de se coucher, il ...; **the** ~ **is** ... c'est que ...; **for one** ~ d'abord; **the best** ~ **would be to** le mieux serait de; **how are** ~**s?** comment ça va?; **she's got a** ~ **about** ... elle déteste ...; **poor** ~! le (*or* la) pauvre!

think [θɪŋk], *pt, pp* **thought** [θɪŋk, θɔ:t] *vi* penser, réfléchir ♦ *vt* penser, croire; (*imagine*) s'imaginer; **to** ~ **of** penser à; **what do you** ~ **of it?** qu'en pensez-vous?; **what did you** ~ **of them?** qu'avez-vous pensé d'eux?; **to** ~ **about sth/sb** penser à qch/qn; **I'll** ~ **about it**

je vais y réfléchir; **to** ~ **of doing** avoir l'idée de faire; **I** ~ **so/not** je crois *or* pense que oui/non; **to** ~ **well of** avoir une haute opinion de; ~ **again!** attention, réfléchis bien!; **to** ~ **aloud** penser tout haut.

►**think out** *vt* (*plan*) bien réfléchir à; (*solution*) trouver.

►**think over** *vt* bien réfléchir à; **I'd like to** ~ **things over** (*offer, suggestion*) j'aimerais bien y réfléchir un peu.

►**think through** *vt* étudier dans tous les détails.

►**think up** *vt* inventer, trouver.

thinking ['θɪŋkɪŋ] *n*: **to my (way of)** ~ selon moi.

think tank *n* groupe *m* de réflexion.

thinly ['θɪnlɪ] *adv* (*cut*) en tranches fines; (*spread*) en couche mince.

thinness ['θɪnnɪs] *n* minceur *f*; maigreur *f*.

third [θə:d] *num* troisième *m/f*; (*fraction*) tiers *m*; (*BRIT SCOL: degree*) ≈ licence *f* avec mention passable; **a** ~ **of** le tiers de.

third-degree burns ['θə:ddɪgri:-] *npl* brûlures *fpl* au troisième degré.

thirdly ['θə:dlɪ] *adv* troisièmement.

third party insurance *n* (*BRIT*) assurance *f* au tiers.

third-rate ['θə:d'reɪt] *adj* de qualité médiocre.

Third World *n*: **the** ~ le Tiers-Monde.

thirst [θə:st] *n* soif *f*.

thirsty ['θə:stɪ] *adj* qui a soif, assoiffé(e); **to be** ~ avoir soif.

thirteen [θə:'ti:n] *num* treize.

thirtieth ['θə:tɪɪθ] *num* trentième.

thirty ['θə:tɪ] *num* trente.

===================================== *KEYWORD*

this [ðɪs] *adj* (*demonstrative*: *pl* **these**) ce, cet +*vowel or h mute*, cette *f*; ~ **man/woman/book** cet homme/cette femme/ce livre; (*not that*) cet homme-ci/cette femme-ci/ce livre-ci; ~ **one** celui-ci(celle-ci); ~ **time** cette fois-ci; ~ **time last year** l'année dernière à la même époque; ~ **way** (*in this direction*) par ici; (*in this fashion*) de cette façon, ainsi
♦ *pron* (*demonstrative*: *pl* **these**) ce; (*not that one*) celui-ci(celle-ci), ceci; **who's** ~? qui est-ce?; **what's** ~? qu'est-ce que c'est?; **I prefer** ~ **to that** je préfère ceci à cela; **they were talking of** ~ **and that** ils parlaient de choses et d'autres; ~ **is what he said** voici ce qu'il a dit; ~ **is Mr Brown** (*in introduction*) je vous présente Mr Brown; (*in photo*) c'est Mr Brown; (*on telephone*) ici Mr Brown
♦ *adv* (*demonstrative*): **it was about** ~ **big** c'était à peu près de cette grandeur *or* grand comme ça; **I didn't know it was** ~ **bad** je ne savais pas que c'était si *or* aussi mauvais.

thistle ['θɪsl] *n* chardon *m*.

thong [θɒŋ] *n* lanière *f*.

thorn [θɔːn] *n* épine *f*.

thorny ['θɔːnɪ] *adj* épineux(euse).

thorough ['θʌrə] *adj* (*search*) minutieux(euse); (*knowledge, research*) approfondi(e); (*work*) consciencieux(euse); (*cleaning*) à fond.

thoroughbred ['θʌrəbrɛd] *n* (*horse*) pur-sang *m inv*.

thoroughfare ['θʌrəfɛə*] *n* rue *f*; **"no ~"** (*BRIT*) "passage interdit".

thoroughgoing ['θʌrəgəuɪŋ] *adj* (*analysis*) approfondi(e); (*reform*) profond(e).

thoroughly ['θʌrəlɪ] *adv* minutieusement; en profondeur; à fond; **he ~ agreed** il était tout à fait d'accord.

thoroughness ['θʌrənɪs] *n* soin (méticuleux).

those [ðəuz] *pl pron* ceux-là(celles-là) ♦ *pl adj* ces; (*not these*): **~ books** ces livres-là.

though [ðəu] *conj* bien que + *sub*, quoique + *sub* ♦ *adv* pourtant; **even ~** quand bien même + *conditional*; **it's not easy, ~** pourtant, ce n'est pas facile.

thought [θɔːt] *pt, pp of* **think** ♦ *n* pensée *f*; (*opinion*) avis *m*; (*intention*) intention *f*; **after much ~** après mûre réflexion; **I've just had a ~** je viens de penser à quelque chose; **to give sth some ~** réfléchir à qch.

thoughtful ['θɔːtful] *adj* pensif(ive); (*considerate*) prévenant(e).

thoughtfully ['θɔːtfəlɪ] *adv* pensivement; avec prévenance.

thoughtless ['θɔːtlɪs] *adj* étourdi(e); qui manque de considération.

thoughtlessly ['θɔːtlɪslɪ] *adv* inconsidérément.

thought-provoking ['θɔːtprəvəukɪŋ] *adj* stimulant(e).

thousand ['θauzənd] *num* mille; **one ~** mille; **~s of** des milliers de.

thousandth ['θauzəntθ] *num* millième.

thrash [θræʃ] *vt* rouer de coups; donner une correction à; (*defeat*) battre à plate(s) couture(s).

▶**thrash about** *vi* se débattre.

▶**thrash out** *vt* débattre de.

thrashing ['θræʃɪŋ] *n*: **to give sb a ~ = to thrash sb**.

thread [θrɛd] *n* fil *m*; (*of screw*) pas *m*, filetage *m* ♦ *vt* (*needle*) enfiler; **to ~ one's way between** se faufiler entre.

threadbare ['θrɛdbɛə*] *adj* râpé(e), élimé(e).

threat [θrɛt] *n* menace *f*; **to be under ~ of** être menacé(e) de.

threaten ['θrɛtn] *vi* (*storm*) menacer ♦ *vt*: **to ~ sb with sth/to do** menacer qn de qch/de faire.

threatening ['θrɛtnɪŋ] *adj* menaçant(e).

three [θriː] *num* trois.

three-dimensional [θriːdɪ'mɛnʃənl] *adj* à trois dimensions; (*film*) en relief.

threefold ['θriːfəuld] *adv*: **to increase ~** tripler.

three-piece ['θriːpiːs]: **~ suit** *n* complet *m*

(avec gilet); **~ suite** *n* salon *m* comprenant un canapé et deux fauteuils assortis.

three-ply [θriː'plaɪ] *adj* (*wood*) à trois épaisseurs; (*wool*) trois fils *inv*.

three-quarters [θriː'kwɔːtəz] *npl* trois-quarts *mpl*; **~ full** aux trois-quarts plein.

three-wheeler [θriː'wiːlə*] *n* (*car*) voiture *f* à trois roues.

thresh [θrɛʃ] *vt* (*AGR*) battre.

threshing machine ['θrɛʃɪŋ-] *n* batteuse *f*.

threshold ['θrɛʃhəuld] *n* seuil *m*; **to be on the ~ of** (*fig*) être au seuil de.

threshold agreement *n* (*ECON*) accord *m* d'indexation des salaires.

threw [θruː] *pt of* **throw**.

thrift [θrɪft] *n* économie *f*.

thrifty ['θrɪftɪ] *adj* économe.

thrill [θrɪl] *n* frisson *m*, émotion *f* ♦ *vi* tressaillir, frissonner ♦ *vt* (*audience*) électriser; **to be ~ed** (*with gift etc*) être ravi(e).

thriller ['θrɪlə*] *n* film *m* (*or* roman *m or* pièce *f*) à suspense.

thrilling ['θrɪlɪŋ] *adj* (*book, play etc*) saisissant(e); (*news, discovery*) excitant(e).

thrive, *pt* **thrived, throve,** *pp* **thrived, thriven** [θraɪv, θrəuv, 'θrɪvn] *vi* pousser *or* se développer bien; (*business*) prospérer; **he ~s on it** cela lui réussit.

thriving ['θraɪvɪŋ] *adj* vigoureux(euse), (*industry etc*) prospère.

throat [θrəut] *n* gorge *f*; **to have a sore ~** avoir mal à la gorge.

throb [θrɒb] *n* (*of heart*) pulsation *f*; (*of engine*) vibration *f*; (*of pain*) élancement *m* ♦ *vi* (*heart*) palpiter; (*engine*) vibrer; (*pain*) lanciner; (*wound*) causer des élancements; **my head is ~bing** j'ai des élancements dans la tête.

throes [θrəuz] *npl*: **in the ~ of** au beau milieu de; en proie à; **in the ~ of death** à l'agonie.

thrombosis [θrɔm'bəusɪs] *n* thrombose *f*.

throne [θrəun] *n* trône *m*.

throng ['θrɔŋ] *n* foule *f* ♦ *vt* se presser dans.

throttle ['θrɒtl] *n* (*AUT*) accélérateur *m* ♦ *vt* étrangler.

through [θruː] *prep* à travers; (*time*) pendant, durant; (*by means of*) par, par l'intermédiaire de; (*owing to*) à cause de ♦ *adj* (*ticket, train, passage*) direct(e) ♦ *adv* à travers; **(from) Monday ~ Friday** (*US*) de lundi à vendredi; **to let sb ~** laisser passer qn; **to put sb ~ to sb** (*TEL*) passer qn à qn; **to be ~** (*TEL*) avoir la communication; (*have finished*) avoir fini; **"no ~ traffic"** (*US*) "passage interdit"; **"no ~ way"** (*BRIT*) "impasse".

throughout [θruː'aut] *prep* (*place*) partout dans; (*time*) durant tout(e) le(la) ♦ *adv* partout.

throughput ['θruːput] *n* (*of goods, materials*) quantité de matières premières utilisée;

(COMPUT) débit m.
throve [θrəʊv] pt of **thrive**.
throw [θrəʊ] n jet m; (SPORT) lancer m ♦ vt (pt
threw, pp thrown [θruː, θrəʊn]) lancer, jeter;
(SPORT) lancer; (rider) désarçonner; (fig)
décontenancer; (pottery) tourner; **to ~ a
party** donner une réception.
▶**throw about, throw around** vt (litter etc)
éparpiller.
▶**throw away** vt jeter.
▶**throw off** vt se débarrasser de.
▶**throw out** vt jeter dehors; (reject) rejeter.
▶**throw together** vt (clothes, meal etc)
assembler à la hâte; (essay) bâcler.
▶**throw up** vi vomir.
throwaway ['θrəʊəweɪ] adj à jeter.
throwback ['θrəʊbæk] n: **it's a ~ to** ça nous
etc ramène à.
throw-in ['θrəʊɪn] n (SPORT) remise f en jeu.
thru [θruː] prep, adj, adv (US) = **through**.
thrush [θrʌʃ] n (ZOOL) grive f; (MED: esp in
children) muguet m; (: BRIT: in women) muguet
vaginal.
thrust [θrʌst] n (TECH) poussée f ♦ vt (pt, pp
thrust) pousser brusquement; (push in)
enfoncer.
thrusting ['θrʌstɪŋ] adj dynamique; qui se met
trop en avant.
thud [θʌd] n bruit sourd.
thug [θʌg] n voyou m.
thumb [θʌm] n (ANAT) pouce m ♦ vt (book)
feuilleter; **to ~ a lift** faire de l'auto-stop,
arrêter une voiture; **to give sb/sth the ~s
up/~s down** donner/refuser de donner le
feu vert à qn/qch.
thumb index n répertoire m (à onglets).
thumbnail ['θʌmneɪl] n ongle m du pouce.
thumbnail sketch n croquis m.
thumbtack ['θʌmtæk] n (US) punaise f (clou).
thump [θʌmp] n grand coup; (sound) bruit
sourd ♦ vt cogner sur ♦ vi cogner, frapper.
thunder ['θʌndə*] n tonnerre m ♦ vi tonner;
(train etc): **to ~ past** passer dans un
grondement or un bruit de tonnerre.
thunderbolt ['θʌndəbəʊlt] n foudre f.
thunderclap ['θʌndəklæp] n coup m de
tonnerre.
thunderous ['θʌndrəs] adj étourdissant(e).
thunderstorm ['θʌndəstɔːm] n orage m.
thunderstruck ['θʌndəstrʌk] adj (fig)
abasourdi(e).
thundery ['θʌndərɪ] adj orageux(euse).
Thur(s). abbr (= Thursday) jeu.
Thursday ['θəːzdɪ] n jeudi m; for phrases see also
Tuesday.
thus [ðʌs] adv ainsi.
thwart [θwɔːt] vt contrecarrer.
thyme [taɪm] n thym m.
thyroid ['θaɪrɔɪd] n thyroïde f.
tiara [tɪˈɑːrə] n (woman's) diadème m.
Tibet [tɪˈbɛt] n Tibet m.
Tibetan [tɪˈbɛtən] adj tibétain(e) ♦ n

Tibétain/e; (LING) tibétain m.
tibia ['tɪbɪə] n tibia m.
tic [tɪk] n tic (nerveux).
tick [tɪk] n (sound: of clock) tic-tac m; (mark)
coche f; (ZOOL) tique f; (BRIT col): **in a ~** dans
un instant; (BRIT col: credit): **to buy sth on ~**
acheter qch à crédit ♦ vi faire tic-tac ♦ vt
cocher; **to put a ~ against sth** cocher qch.
▶**tick off** vt cocher; (person) réprimander,
attraper.
▶**tick over** vi (BRIT: engine) tourner au ralenti;
(: fig) aller or marcher doucettement.
ticker tape ['tɪkə-] n bande f de téléscripteur;
(US: in celebrations) ≈ serpentin m.
ticket ['tɪkɪt] n billet m; (for bus, tube) ticket m;
(in shop: on goods) étiquette f; (: from cash
register) reçu m, ticket; (for library) carte f;
(US POL) liste électorale (soutenue par un
parti); **to get a (parking) ~** (AUT) attraper
une contravention (pour stationnement
illégal).
ticket agency n (THEAT) agence f de
spectacles.
ticket collector n contrôleur/euse.
ticket holder n personne munie d'un billet.
ticket inspector n contrôleur/euse.
ticket office n guichet m, bureau m de vente
des billets.
tickle ['tɪkl] n chatouillement m ♦ vt
chatouiller; (fig) plaire à; faire rire.
ticklish ['tɪklɪʃ] adj (person)
chatouilleux(euse); (which tickles:
blanket) qui chatouille; (: cough)
qui irrite.
tidal ['taɪdl] adj à marée.
tidal wave n raz-de-marée m inv.
tidbit ['tɪdbɪt] n (esp US) = **titbit**.
tiddlywinks ['tɪdlɪwɪŋks] n jeu m de puce.
tide [taɪd] n marée f; (fig: of events) cours m
♦ vt: **to ~ sb over** dépanner qn; **high/low ~**
marée haute/basse.
tidily ['taɪdɪlɪ] adv avec soin, soigneusement.
tidiness ['taɪdɪnɪs] n bon ordre; goût m de
l'ordre.
tidy ['taɪdɪ] adj (room) bien rangé(e); (dress,
work) net(nette), soigné(e); (person)
ordonné(e), qui a de l'ordre; (: in character)
soigneux(euse); (mind) méthodique ♦ vt
(also: ~ up) ranger; **to o.s. up** s'arranger.
tie [taɪ] n (string etc) cordon m; (BRIT: also:
neck~) cravate f; (fig: link) lien m; (SPORT:
draw) égalité f de points; match nul;
(: match) rencontre f; (US RAIL) traverse f ♦ vt
(parcel) attacher; (ribbon) nouer ♦ vi (SPORT)
faire match nul; finir à égalité de points;
"black/white ~" "smoking/habit de
rigueur"; **family ~s** liens de famille; **to ~
sth in a bow** faire un nœud à or avec qch; **to
~ a knot in sth** faire un nœud à qch.
▶**tie down** vt attacher; (fig): **to ~ sb down to**
contraindre qn à accepter.
▶**tie in** vi: **to ~ in (with)** (correspond)

correspondre (à).

▶**tie on** *vt* (*BRIT: label etc*) attacher (avec une ficelle).

▶**tie up** *vt* (*parcel*) ficeler; (*dog, boat*) attacher; (*arrangements*) conclure; **to be ~d up** (*busy*) être pris *or* occupé.

tie-break(er) ['taɪbreɪk(ə*)] *n* (*TENNIS*) tie-break *m*; (*in quiz*) question *f* subsidiaire.

tie-on ['taɪɔn] *adj* (*BRIT: label*) qui s'attache.

tie-pin ['taɪpɪn] *n* (*BRIT*) épingle *f* de cravate.

tier [tɪə*] *n* gradin *m*; (*of cake*) étage *m*.

Tierra del Fuego [tɪˈerədɛlˈfweɪgəu] *n* Terre *f* de Feu.

tie tack *n* (*US*) épingle *f* de cravate.

tiff [tɪf] *n* petite querelle.

tiger ['taɪgə*] *n* tigre *m*.

tight [taɪt] *adj* (*rope*) tendu(e), raide; (*clothes*) étroit(e), très juste; (*budget, programme, bend*) serré(e); (*control*) strict(e), sévère; (*col: drunk*) ivre, rond(e) ♦ *adv* (*squeeze*) très fort; (*shut*) à bloc, hermétiquement; **to be packed ~** (*suitcase*) être bourré(e); (*people*) être serré(e); **everybody hold ~!** accrochez-vous bien!

tighten ['taɪtn] *vt* (*rope*) tendre; (*screw*) resserrer; (*control*) renforcer ♦ *vi* se tendre; se resserrer.

tight-fisted [taɪtˈfɪstɪd] *adj* avare.

tight-lipped ['taɪtˈlɪpt] *adj*: **to be ~ (about sth)** (*silent*) ne pas desserrer les lèvres *or* les dents (au sujet de qch); **she was ~ with anger** elle pinçait les lèvres de colère.

tightly ['taɪtlɪ] *adv* (*grasp*) bien, très fort.

tight-rope ['taɪtrəup] *n* corde *f* raide.

tight-rope walker *n* funambule *m/f*.

tights [taɪts] *npl* (*BRIT*) collant *m*.

tigress ['taɪgrɪs] *n* tigresse *f*.

tilde ['tɪldə] *n* tilde *m*.

tile [taɪl] *n* (*on roof*) tuile *f*; (*on wall or floor*) carreau *m* ♦ *vt* (*floor, bathroom etc*) carreler.

tiled [taɪld] *adj* en tuiles; carrelé(e).

till [tɪl] *n* caisse (enregistreuse) ♦ *vt* (*land*) cultiver ♦ *prep, conj* = **until**.

tiller ['tɪlə*] *n* (*NAUT*) barre *f* (du gouvernail).

tilt [tɪlt] *vt* pencher, incliner ♦ *vi* pencher, être incliné(e) ♦ *n* (*slope*) inclinaison *f*; **to wear one's hat at a ~** porter son chapeau incliné sur le côté; **(at) full ~** à toute vitesse.

timber ['tɪmbə*] *n* (*material*) bois *m* de construction; (*trees*) arbres *mpl*.

time [taɪm] *n* temps *m*; (*epoch: often pl*) époque *f*, temps; (*by clock*) heure *f*; (*moment*) moment *m*; (*occasion, also MATH*) fois *f*; (*MUS*) mesure *f* ♦ *vt* (*race*) chronométrer; (*programme*) minuter; (*remark etc*) choisir le moment de; **a long ~** un long moment, longtemps; **for the ~ being** pour le moment; **from ~ to ~** de temps en temps; **~ after ~,** **~ and again** bien des fois; **in ~** (*soon enough*) à temps; (*after some time*) avec le temps, à la longue; (*MUS*) en mesure; **in a week's ~** dans une semaine; **in no ~** en un

rien de temps; **on ~** à l'heure; **to be 30 minutes behind/ahead of ~** avoir 30 minutes de retard/d'avance; **by the ~ he arrived** quand il est arrivé, le temps qu'il arrive *sub*; **5 ~s 5** 5 fois 5; **what ~ is it?** quelle heure est-il?; **what ~ do you make it?** quelle heure avez-vous?; **to have a good ~** bien s'amuser; **we** (*or* **they** *etc*) **had a hard ~** ça a été difficile *or* pénible; **~'s up!** c'est l'heure!; **I've no ~ for it** (*fig*) cela m'agace; **he'll do it in his own (good) ~** (*without being hurried*) il le fera quand il en aura le temps; **he'll do it in** *or* **on his own ~** (*out of working hours*) il le fera à ses heures perdues; **to be behind the ~s** retarder (sur son temps).

time-and-motion study ['taɪmənd'məuʃən-] *n* étude *f* des cadences.

time bomb *n* bombe *f* à retardement.

time clock *n* horloge pointeuse.

time-consuming ['taɪmkənsju:mɪŋ] *adj* qui prend beaucoup de temps.

time difference *n* décalage *m* horaire.

time frame *n* délais *mpl*.

time-honoured, (*US*) **time-honored** ['taɪmɔnəd] *adj* consacré(e).

timekeeper ['taɪmki:pə*] *n* (*SPORT*) chronomètre *m*.

time lag *n* (*BRIT*) décalage *m*; (*: in travel*) décalage horaire.

timeless ['taɪmlɪs] *adj* éternel(le).

time limit *n* limite *f* de temps, délai *m*.

timely ['taɪmlɪ] *adj* opportun(e).

time off *n* temps *m* libre.

timer ['taɪmə*] *n* (*in kitchen*) compte-minutes *m inv*; (*TECH*) minuteur *m*.

time-saving ['taɪmseɪvɪŋ] *adj* qui fait gagner du temps.

time scale *n* délais *mpl*.

time-sharing ['taɪmʃɛərɪŋ] *n* (*COMPUT*) temps partagé.

time sheet *n* feuille *f* de présence.

time signal *n* signal *m* horaire.

time switch *n* (*BRIT*) minuteur *m*; (*: for lighting*) minuterie *f*.

timetable ['taɪmteɪbl] *n* (*RAIL*) (indicateur *m*) horaire *m*; (*SCOL*) emploi *m* du temps; (*programme of events etc*) programme *m*.

time zone *n* fuseau *m* horaire.

timid ['tɪmɪd] *adj* timide; (*easily scared*) peureux(euse).

timidity [tɪˈmɪdɪtɪ] *n* timidité *f*.

timing ['taɪmɪŋ] *n* minutage *m*; chrono-métrage *m*; **the ~ of his resignation** le moment choisi pour sa démission.

timing device *n* (*on bomb*) mécanisme *m* de retardement.

timpani ['tɪmpənɪ] *npl* timbales *fpl*.

tin [tɪn] *n* étain *m*; (*also:* **~ plate**) fer-blanc *m*; (*BRIT: can*) boîte *f* (de conserve); (*: for baking*) moule *m* (à gâteau); **a ~ of paint** un pot de peinture.

tin foil n papier m d'étain.
tinge [tɪndʒ] n nuance f ♦ vt: ~d with teinté(e) de.
tingle ['tɪŋgl] n picotement m; frisson m ♦ vi picoter.
tinker ['tɪŋkə*] n rétameur ambulant; (gipsy) romanichel m.
▶**tinker with** vt fus bricoler, rafistoler.
tinkle ['tɪŋkl] vi tinter ♦ n (col): **to give sb a ~** passer un coup de fil à qn.
tin mine n mine f d'étain.
tinned [tɪnd] adj (BRIT: food) en boîte, en conserve.
tinnitus ['tɪnɪtəs] n (MED) acouphène m.
tinny ['tɪnɪ] adj métallique.
tin opener [-'əupnə*] n (BRIT) ouvre-boîte(s) m.
tinsel ['tɪnsl] n guirlandes fpl de Noël (argentées).
tint [tɪnt] n teinte f; (for hair) shampooing colorant ♦ vt (hair) faire un shampooing colorant à.
tinted ['tɪntɪd] adj (hair) teint(e); (spectacles, glass) teinté(e).
tiny ['taɪnɪ] adj minuscule.
tip [tɪp] n (end) bout m; (protective: on umbrella etc) embout m; (gratuity) pourboire m; (BRIT: for coal) terril m; (: for rubbish) décharge f; (advice) tuyau m ♦ vt (waiter) donner un pourboire à; (tilt) incliner; (overturn: also: ~ over) renverser; (empty: also: ~ out) déverser; (predict: winner etc) pronostiquer; **he ~ped out the contents of the box** il a vidé le contenu de la boîte.
▶**tip off** vt prévenir, avertir.
tip-off ['tɪpɔf] n (hint) tuyau m.
tipped ['tɪpt] adj (BRIT: cigarette) (à bout) filtre inv; **steel-~** à bout métallique, à embout de métal.
Tipp-Ex ['tɪpɛks] n ® (BRIT) Tipp-Ex m ®.
tipple ['tɪpl] (BRIT) vi picoler ♦ n: **to have a ~** boire un petit coup.
tipster ['tɪpstə*] n (RACING) pronostiqueur m.
tipsy ['tɪpsɪ] adj un peu ivre, éméché(e).
tiptoe ['tɪptəu] n: **on ~** sur la pointe des pieds.
tiptop ['tɪptɔp] adj: **in ~ condition** en excellent état.
tirade [taɪ'reɪd] n diatribe f.
tire ['taɪə*] n (US) = **tyre** ♦ vt fatiguer ♦ vi se fatiguer.
▶**tire out** vt épuiser.
tired ['taɪəd] adj fatigué(e); **to be/feel/look ~** être/se sentir/avoir l'air fatigué; **to be ~ of** en avoir assez de, être las(lasse) de.
tiredness ['taɪədnɪs] n fatigue f.
tireless ['taɪəlɪs] adj infatigable, inlassable.
tiresome ['taɪəsəm] adj ennuyeux(euse).
tiring ['taɪərɪŋ] adj fatigant(e).
tissue ['tɪʃuː] n tissu m; (paper handkerchief) mouchoir m en papier, kleenex m ®.
tissue paper n papier m de soie.

tit [tɪt] n (bird) mésange f; (col: breast) nichon m; **to give ~ for tat** rendre coup pour coup.
titanium [tɪ'teɪnɪəm] n titane m.
titbit ['tɪtbɪt] n (food) friandise f; (before meal) amuse-gueule m inv; (news) potin m.
titillate ['tɪtɪleɪt] vt titiller, exciter.
titivate ['tɪtɪveɪt] vt pomponner.
title ['taɪtl] n titre m; (LAW: right): ~ **(to)** droit m (à).
title deed n (LAW) titre (constitutif) de propriété.
title page n page f de titre.
title role n rôle principal.
titter ['tɪtə*] vi rire (bêtement).
tittle-tattle ['tɪtltætl] n bavardages mpl.
titular ['tɪtjulə*] adj (in name only) nominal(e).
tizzy ['tɪzɪ] n: **to be in a ~** être dans tous ses états.
T-junction ['tiː'dʒʌŋkʃən] n croisement m en T.
TM n abbr = **trademark**, **transcendental meditation**.
TN abbr (US) = **Tennessee**.
TNT n abbr (= trinitrotoluene) TNT m.

———————————————— KEYWORD

to [tuː, tə] prep **1** (direction) à; (towards) vers; envers; **to go ~ France/Portugal/London/school** aller en France/au Portugal/à Londres/à l'école; **to go ~ Claude's/the doctor's** aller chez Claude/le docteur; **the road ~ Edinburgh** la route d'Édimbourg
2 (as far as) (jusqu')à); **to count ~ 10** compter jusqu'à 10; **from 40 ~ 50 people** de 40 à 50 personnes
3 (with expressions of time): **a quarter ~ 5** 5 heures moins le quart; **it's twenty ~ 3** il est 3 heures moins vingt
4 (for, of) de; **the key ~ the front door** la clé de la porte d'entrée; **a letter ~ his wife** une lettre (adressée) à sa femme
5 (expressing indirect object): **to give sth ~ sb** donner qch à qn; **to talk ~ sb** parler à qn; **it belongs ~ him** cela lui appartient, c'est à lui
6 (in relation to) à; **3 goals ~ 2** 3 (buts) à 2; **30 miles ~ the gallon** ≈ 9,4 litres aux cent (km)
7 (purpose, result): **to come ~ sb's aid** venir au secours de qn, porter secours à qn; **to sentence sb ~ death** condamner qn à mort; **~ my surprise** à ma grande surprise
♦ with vb **1** (simple infinitive): ~ **go/eat** aller/manger
2 (following another vb): **to want/try/start ~ do** vouloir/essayer de/commencer à faire
3 (with vb omitted): **I don't want ~** je ne veux pas
4 (purpose, result) pour; **I did it ~ help you** je l'ai fait pour vous aider
5 (equivalent to relative clause): **I have things ~ do** j'ai des choses à faire; **the main thing**

is ~ **try** l'important est d'essayer
6 (*after adjective etc*): **ready** ~ **go** prêt(e) à
partir; **too old/young** ~ ... trop vieux/jeune
pour ...
♦ *adv*: **push/pull the door** ~ tirez/poussez la
porte; **to go** ~ **and fro** aller et venir.

toad [təud] *n* crapaud *m*.
toadstool ['təudstuːl] *n* champignon
(vénéneux).
toady ['təudɪ] *vi* flatter bassement.
toast [təust] *n* (*CULIN*) pain grillé, toast *m*;
(*drink, speech*) toast ♦ *vt* (*CULIN*) faire griller;
(*drink to*) porter un toast à; **a piece** *or* **slice of**
~ un toast.
toaster ['təustə*] *n* grille-pain *m inv*.
toastmaster ['təustmɑːstə*] *n* animateur *m*
pour réceptions.
toast rack *n* porte-toast *m inv*.
tobacco [tə'bækəu] *n* tabac *m*; **pipe** ~ tabac à
pipe.
tobacconist [tə'bækənɪst] *n* marchand/e de
tabac; ~**'s (shop)** (bureau *m* de) tabac *m*.
Tobago [tə'beɪɡəu] *n see* **Trinidad and Tobago**.
toboggan [tə'bɒɡən] *n* toboggan *m*; (*child's*)
luge *f*.
today [tə'deɪ] *adv, n* (*also fig*) aujourd'hui (*m*);
what day is it ~? quel jour sommes-nous
aujourd'hui?; **what date is it** ~? quelle est la
date aujourd'hui?; ~ **is the 4th of March**
aujourd'hui nous sommes le 4 mars; **a week**
ago ~ il y a huit jours aujourd'hui.
toddler ['tɒdlə*] *n* enfant *m/f* qui commence à
marcher, bambin *m*.
toddy ['tɒdɪ] *n* grog *m*.
to-do [tə'duː] *n* (*fuss*) histoire *f*, affaire *f*.
toe [təu] *n* doigt *m* de pied, orteil *m*; (*of shoe*)
bout *m* ♦ *vt*: **to** ~ **the line** (*fig*) obéir, se
conformer; **big** ~ gros orteil; **little** ~ petit
orteil.
TOEFL *n abbr* = *Test(ing) of English as a Foreign*
Language.
toehold ['təuhəuld] *n* prise *f*.
toenail ['təuneɪl] *n* ongle *m* de l'orteil.
toffee ['tɒfɪ] *n* caramel *m*.
toffee apple *n* (*BRIT*) pomme caramélisée.
tofu ['təufuː] *n* fromage *m* de soja.
toga ['təuɡə] *n* toge *f*.
together [tə'ɡɛðə*] *adv* ensemble; (*at same*
time) en même temps; ~ **with** *prep* avec.
togetherness [tə'ɡɛðənɪs] *n* camaraderie *f*;
intimité *f*.
toggle switch ['tɒɡl-] *n* (*COMPUT*)
interrupteur *m* à bascule.
Togo ['təuɡəu] *n* Togo *m*.
togs [tɒɡz] *npl* (*col: clothes*) fringues *fpl*.
toil [tɔɪl] *n* dur travail, labeur *m* ♦ *vi* travailler
dur; peiner.
toilet ['tɔɪlət] *n* (*BRIT: lavatory*) toilettes *fpl*,
cabinets *mpl* ♦ *cpd* (*bag, soap etc*) de toilette;
to go to the ~ aller aux toilettes.
toilet bag *n* (*BRIT*) nécessaire *m* de toilette.

toilet bowl *n* cuvette *f* des W.-C.
toilet paper *n* papier *m* hygiénique.
toiletries ['tɔɪlətrɪz] *npl* articles *mpl* de
toilette.
toilet roll *n* rouleau *m* de papier hygiénique.
toilet water *n* eau *f* de toilette.
to-ing and fro-ing ['tuːɪŋən'frəuɪŋ] *n* (*BRIT*)
allées et venues *fpl*.
token ['təukən] *n* (*sign*) marque *f*, témoignage
m; (*voucher*) bon *m*, coupon *m* ♦ *cpd* (*fee,*
strike) symbolique; **by the same** ~ (*fig*) de
même; **book/record** ~ (*BRIT*) chèque-livre/
-disque *m*.
tokenism ['təukənɪzəm] *n* (*POL*): **it's just** ~
c'est une politique de pure forme.
Tokyo ['təukjəu] *n* Tokyo.
told [təuld] *pt, pp of* **tell**.
tolerable ['tɒlərəbl] *adj* (*bearable*) tolérable;
(*fairly good*) passable.
tolerably ['tɒlərəblɪ] *adv*: ~ **good** tolérable.
tolerance ['tɒlrns] *n* (*also TECH*) tolérance *f*.
tolerant ['tɒlrnt] *adj*: ~ (**of**) tolérant(e) (à
l'égard de).
tolerate ['tɒləreɪt] *vt* supporter; (*MED, TECH*)
tolérer.
toleration [tɒlə'reɪʃən] *n* tolérance *f*.
toll [təul] *n* (*tax, charge*) péage *m* ♦ *vi* (*bell*)
sonner; **the accident** ~ **on the roads** le
nombre des victimes de la route.
tollbridge ['təulbrɪdʒ] *n* pont *m* à péage.
toll call *n* (*US TEL*) appel *m* (à) longue
distance.
toll-free ['təul'friː] *adj* (*US*) gratuit(e) ♦ *adv*
gratuitement.
tomato, ~**es** [tə'mɑːtəu] *n* tomate *f*.
tomb [tuːm] *n* tombe *f*.
tombola [tɒm'bəulə] *n* tombola *f*.
tomboy ['tɒmbɔɪ] *n* garçon manqué.
tombstone ['tuːmstəun] *n* pierre tombale.
tomcat ['tɒmkæt] *n* matou *m*.
tomorrow [tə'mɒrəu] *adv, n* (*also fig*) demain
(*m*); **the day after** ~ après-demain; **a week** ~
demain en huit; ~ **morning** demain matin.
ton [tʌn] *n* tonne *f* (*Brit: = 1016 kg; US = 907 kg;*
metric = 1000 kg); (*NAUT: also:* **register** ~)
tonneau *m* (= *2.83 cu.m*); ~**s of** (*col*) des tas
de.
tonal ['təunl] *adj* tonal(e).
tone [təun] *n* ton *m*; (*of radio, BRIT TEL*) tonalité
f ♦ *vi* s'harmoniser.
▶**tone down** *vt* (*colour, criticism*) adoucir;
(*sound*) baisser.
▶**tone up** *vt* (*muscles*) tonifier.
tone-deaf [təun'dɛf] *adj* qui n'a pas d'oreille.
toner ['təunə*] *n* (*for photocopier*) encre *f*.
Tonga [tɒŋə] *n* îles *fpl* Tonga.
tongs [tɒŋz] *npl* pinces *fpl*; (*for coal*) pincettes
fpl; (*for hair*) fer *m* à friser.
tongue [tʌŋ] *n* langue *f*; ~ **in cheek** *adv*
ironiquement.
tongue-tied ['tʌŋtaɪd] *adj* (*fig*) muet(te).
tongue-twister ['tʌŋtwɪstə*] *n* phrase *f* très

difficile à prononcer.

tonic ['tɔnɪk] n (MED) tonique m; (MUS) tonique f; (also: ~ **water**) tonic m.

tonight [tə'naɪt] adv, n cette nuit; (this evening) ce soir; **(I'll) see you ~!** à ce soir!

tonnage ['tʌnɪdʒ] n (NAUT) tonnage m.

tonne [tʌn] n (BRIT: metric ton) tonne f.

tonsil ['tɔnsl] n amygdale f; **to have one's ~s out** se faire opérer des amygdales.

tonsillitis [tɔnsɪ'laɪtɪs] n amygdalite f; **to have ~** avoir une angine or une amygdalite.

too [tuː] adv (excessively) trop; (also) aussi; **it's ~ sweet** c'est trop sucré; **I went ~** moi aussi, j'y suis allé; **~ much** adv trop ♦ adj trop de; **~ many** adj trop de; **~ bad!** tant pis!

took [tuk] pt of **take**.

tool [tuːl] n outil m; (fig) instrument m ♦ vt travailler, ouvrager.

tool box n boîte f à outils.

tool kit n trousse f à outils.

toot [tuːt] n coup m de sifflet (or de klaxon) ♦ vi siffler; (with car-horn) klaxonner.

tooth, pl **teeth** [tuːθ, tiːθ] n (ANAT, TECH) dent f; **to have a ~ out** or (US) **pulled** se faire arracher une dent; **to brush one's teeth** se laver les dents; **by the skin of one's teeth** (fig) de justesse.

toothache ['tuːθeɪk] n mal m de dents; **to have ~** avoir mal aux dents.

toothbrush ['tuːθbrʌʃ] n brosse f à dents.

toothpaste ['tuːθpeɪst] n (pâte f) dentifrice m.

toothpick ['tuːθpɪk] n cure-dent m.

tooth powder n poudre f dentifrice.

top [tɔp] n (of mountain, head) sommet m; (of page, ladder) haut m; (of list, queue) commencement m; (of box, cupboard, table) dessus m; (lid: of box, jar) couvercle m; (: of bottle) bouchon m; (toy) toupie f; (DRESS: blouse etc) haut; (of pyjamas) veste f ♦ adj du haut; (in rank) premier(ière); (best) meilleur(e) ♦ vt (exceed) dépasser; (be first in) être en tête de; **the ~ of the milk** (BRIT) la crème du lait; **at the ~ of the stairs/ page/ street** en haut de l'escalier/de la page/de la rue; **on ~ of** sur; (in addition to) en plus de; **from ~ to toe** (BRIT) de la tête aux pieds; **at the ~ of the list** en tête de liste; **at the ~ of one's voice** à tue-tête; **at ~ speed** à toute vitesse; **over the ~** (col: behaviour etc) qui dépasse les limites.

▶**top up**, (US) **top off** vt remplir.

topaz ['təupæz] n topaze f.

top-class ['tɔp'klɑːs] adj (MED) de première classe; (SPORT) de haute compétition.

topcoat ['tɔpkəut] n pardessus m.

topflight ['tɔpflaɪt] adj excellent(e).

top floor n dernier étage.

top hat n haut-de-forme m.

top-heavy [tɔp'hevɪ] adj (object) trop lourd(e) du haut.

topic ['tɔpɪk] n sujet m, thème m.

topical ['tɔpɪkl] adj d'actualité.

topless ['tɔplɪs] adj (bather etc) aux seins nus; **~ swimsuit** monokini m.

top-level ['tɔplevl] adj (talks) à l'échelon le plus élevé.

topmost ['tɔpməust] adj le(la) plus haut(e).

top-notch ['tɔp'nɔtʃ] adj (col) de premier ordre.

topography [tə'pɔgrəfɪ] n topographie f.

topping ['tɔpɪŋ] n (CULIN) couche de crème, fromage etc qui recouvre un plat.

topple ['tɔpl] vt renverser, faire tomber ♦ vi basculer; tomber.

top-ranking ['tɔpræŋkɪŋ] adj très haut placé(e).

top-secret ['tɔp'siːkrɪt] adj ultra-secret(ète).

top-security ['tɔpsə'kjuərɪtɪ] adj (BRIT) de haute sécurité.

topsy-turvy ['tɔpsɪ'təːvɪ] adj, adv sens dessus-dessous.

top-up ['tɔpʌp] n: **would you like a ~?** je vous en remets or rajoute?

top-up loan n (BRIT) prêt m complémentaire.

torch [tɔːtʃ] n torche f; (BRIT: electric) lampe f de poche.

tore [tɔː*] pt of **tear**.

torment n ['tɔːment] tourment m ♦ vt [tɔː'ment] tourmenter; (fig: annoy) agacer.

torn [tɔːn] pp of **tear** ♦ adj: **~ between** (fig) tiraillé(e) entre.

tornado, **~es** [tɔː'neɪdəu] n tornade f.

torpedo, **~es** [tɔː'piːdəu] n torpille f.

torpedo boat n torpilleur m.

torpor ['tɔːpə*] n torpeur f.

torrent ['tɔrnt] n torrent m.

torrential [tɔ'renʃl] adj torrentiel(le).

torrid ['tɔrɪd] adj torride; (fig) ardent(e).

torso ['tɔːsəu] n torse m.

tortoise ['tɔːtəs] n tortue f.

tortoiseshell ['tɔːtəʃel] adj en écaille.

tortuous ['tɔːtjuəs] adj tortueux(euse).

torture ['tɔːtʃə*] n torture f ♦ vt torturer.

torturer ['tɔːtʃərə*] n tortionnaire m.

Tory ['tɔːrɪ] adj (BRIT POL) tory (pl tories), conservateur(trice) ♦ n tory m/f, conservateur/trice.

toss [tɔs] vt lancer, jeter; (BRIT: pancake) faire sauter; (head) rejeter en arrière ♦ vi: **to ~ up for sth** (BRIT) jouer qch à pile ou face ♦ n (movement: of head etc) mouvement soudain; (of coin) tirage m à pile ou face; **to ~ a coin** jouer à pile ou face; **to ~ and turn** (in bed) se tourner et se retourner; **to win/lose the ~** gagner/perdre à pile ou face; (SPORT) gagner/perdre le tirage au sort.

tot [tɔt] n (BRIT: drink) petit verre m; (child) bambin m.

▶**tot up** vt (BRIT: figures) additionner.

total ['təutl] adj total(e) ♦ n total m ♦ vt (add up) faire le total de, totaliser; (amount to) s'élever à; **in ~** au total.

totalitarian [təutælɪ'tɛərɪən] adj totalitaire.

totality [təu'tælɪtɪ] n totalité f.

totally ['təutəlɪ] *adv* totalement.
tote bag [təut-] *n* fourre-tout *m inv*.
totem pole ['təutəm-] *n* mât *m* totémique.
totter ['tɔtə*] *vi* chanceler; (*object, government*) être chancelant(e).
touch [tʌtʃ] *n* contact *m*, toucher *m*; (*sense, also skill: of pianist etc*) toucher; (*fig: note, also FOOTBALL*) touche *f* ♦ *vt* (*gen*) toucher; (*tamper with*) toucher à; **the personal** ~ la petite note personnelle; **to put the finishing ~es to sth** mettre la dernière main à qch; **a ~ of** (*fig*) un petit peu de; une touche de; **in ~ with** en contact *or* rapport avec; **to get in ~ with** prendre contact avec; **I'll be in ~** je resterai en contact; **to lose ~** (*friends*) se perdre de vue; **to be out of ~ with events** ne pas être au courant de ce qui se passe.
▶**touch on** *vt fus* (*topic*) effleurer, toucher.
▶**touch up** *vt* (*paint*) retoucher.
touch-and-go ['tʌtʃən'gəu] *adj* incertain(e); **it was ~ whether we did it** nous avons failli ne pas le faire.
touchdown ['tʌtʃdaun] *n* atterrissage *m*; (*on sea*) amerrissage *m*; (*US FOOTBALL*) essai *m*.
touched [tʌtʃt] *adj* touché(e); (*col*) cinglé(e).
touching ['tʌtʃɪŋ] *adj* touchant(e), attendrissant(e).
touchline ['tʌtʃlaɪn] *n* (*SPORT*) (ligne *f* de) touche *f*.
touch-sensitive ['tʌtʃsɛnsɪtɪv] *adj* (*keypad*) à effleurement; (*screen*) tactile.
touch-type ['tʌtʃtaɪp] *vi* taper au toucher.
touchy ['tʌtʃɪ] *adj* (*person*) susceptible.
tough [tʌf] *adj* dur(e); (*resistant*) résistant(e), solide; (*meat*) dur, coriace; (*journey*) pénible; (*task, problem, situation*) difficile; (*rough*) dur ♦ *n* (*gangster etc*) dur *m*; ~ **luck!** pas de chance!; tant pis!
toughen ['tʌfn] *vt* rendre plus dur(e) (*or* plus résistant(e) *or* plus solide).
toughness ['tʌfnɪs] *n* dureté *f*; résistance *f*; solidité *f*.
toupee ['tuːpeɪ] *n* postiche *m*.
tour ['tuə*] *n* voyage *m*; (*also:* **package ~**) voyage organisé; (*of town, museum*) tour *m*, visite *f*; (*by artist*) tournée *f* ♦ *vt* visiter; **to go on a ~ of** (*museum, region*) visiter; **to go in ~** partir en tournée.
touring ['tuərɪŋ] *n* voyages *mpl* touristiques, tourisme *m*.
tourism ['tuərɪzm] *n* tourisme *m*.
tourist ['tuərɪst] *n* touriste *m/f* ♦ *adv* (*travel*) en classe touriste ♦ *cpd* touristique; **the ~ trade** le tourisme.
tourist class *n* (*AVIAT*) classe *f* touriste.
tourist office *n* syndicat *m* d'initiative.
tournament ['tuənəmənt] *n* tournoi *m*.
tourniquet ['tuənɪkeɪ] *n* (*MED*) garrot *m*.
tour operator *n* (*BRIT*) organisateur *m* de voyages, tour-opérateur *m*.
tousled ['tauzld] *adj* (*hair*) ébouriffé(e).
tout [taut] *vi:* **to ~ for** essayer de raccrocher,

racoler; **to ~ sth (around)** (*BRIT*) essayer de placer *or* (re)vendre qch ♦ *n* (*BRIT: ticket ~*) revendeur *m* de billets.
tow [təu] *n:* **to give sb a ~** (*AUT*) remorquer qn ♦ *vt* remorquer; **"on ~"**, (*US*) **"in ~"** (*AUT*) "véhicule en remorque".
toward(s) [tə'wɔːd(z)] *prep* vers; (*of attitude*) envers, à l'égard de; (*of purpose*) pour; ~ **noon/the end of the year** vers midi/la fin de l'année; **to feel friendly ~ sb** être bien disposé envers qn.
towel ['tauəl] *n* serviette *f* (de toilette); (*also:* **tea ~**) torchon *m*; **to throw in the ~** (*fig*) jeter l'éponge.
towelling ['tauəlɪŋ] *n* (*fabric*) tissu-éponge *m*.
towel rail, (*US*) **towel rack** *n* porte-serviettes *m inv*.
tower ['tauə*] *n* tour *f* ♦ *vi* (*building, mountain*) se dresser (majestueusement); **to ~ above** *or* **over sb/sth** dominer qn/qch.
tower block *n* (*BRIT*) tour *f* (d'habitation).
towering ['tauərɪŋ] *adj* très haut(e), imposant(e).
towline ['təulaɪn] *n* (*câble m de*) remorque *f*.
town [taun] *n* ville *f*; **to go to ~** aller en ville; (*fig*) y mettre le paquet; **in the ~** dans la ville, en ville; **to be out of ~** (*person*) être en déplacement.
town centre *n* centre *m* de la ville, centre-ville *m*.
town clerk *n* ≈ secrétaire *m/f* de mairie.
town council *n* conseil municipal.
town crier [-'kraɪə*] *n* (*BRIT*) crieur public.
town hall *n* ≈ mairie *f*.
townie ['taunɪ] *n* (*BRIT col*) citadin/e.
town plan *n* plan *m* de ville.
town planner *n* urbaniste *m/f*.
town planning *n* urbanisme *m*.
township ['taunʃɪp] *n* banlieue noire (*établie sous le régime de l'apartheid*).
townspeople ['taunzpiːpl] *npl* citadins *mpl*.
towpath ['təupɑːθ] *n* (chemin *m* de) halage *m*.
towrope ['təurəup] *n* (*câble m de*) remorque *f*.
tow truck *n* (*US*) dépanneuse *f*.
toxic ['tɔksɪk] *adj* toxique.
toxin ['tɔksɪn] *n* toxine *f*.
toy [tɔɪ] *n* jouet *m*.
▶**toy with** *vt fus* jouer avec; (*idea*) caresser.
toyshop ['tɔɪʃɔp] *m* magasin *m* de jouets.
trace [treɪs] *n* trace *f* ♦ *vt* (*draw*) tracer, dessiner; (*follow*) suivre la trace de; (*locate*) retrouver; **without ~** (*disappear*) sans laisser de traces; **there was no ~ of it** il n'y en avait pas trace.
trace element *n* oligo-élément *m*.
trachea [trə'kɪə] *n* (*ANAT*) trachée *f*.
tracing paper ['treɪsɪŋ-] *n* papier-calque *m*.
track [træk] *n* (*mark*) trace *f*; (*path: gen*) chemin *m*, piste *f*; (: *of bullet etc*) trajectoire *f*; (: *of suspect, animal*) piste *f*; (*RAIL*) voie ferrée, rails *mpl*; (*on tape, COMPUT, SPORT*) piste *f*; (*on record*) plage *f* ♦ *vt* suivre la trace

or la piste de; **to keep ~ of** suivre; **to be on the right ~** (*fig*) être sur la bonne voie.

▶**track down** *vt* (*prey*) trouver et capturer; (*sth lost*) finir par retrouver.

tracked [trækt] *adj* (*AUT*) à chenille.

tracker dog ['trækə-] *n* (*BRIT*) *chien dressé pour suivre une piste.*

track events *npl* (*SPORT*) épreuves *fpl* sur piste.

tracking station ['trækɪŋ-] *n* (*SPACE*) centre *m* d'observation de satellites.

track meet *n* (*US*) réunion sportive sur piste.

track record *n*: **to have a good ~** (*fig*) avoir fait ses preuves.

track suit *n* survêtement *m*.

tract [trækt] *n* (*GEO*) étendue *f*, zone *f*; (*pamphlet*) tract *m*; **respiratory ~** (*ANAT*) système *m* respiratoire.

traction ['trækʃən] *n* traction *f*.

tractor ['træktə*] *n* tracteur *m*.

trade [treɪd] *n* commerce *m*; (*skill, job*) métier *m* ♦ *vi* faire du commerce; **to ~ with/in** faire du commerce avec/le commerce de; **foreign ~** commerce extérieur; **Department of T~ and Industry (DTI)** (*BRIT*) ministère *m* du Commerce et de l'Industrie.

▶**trade in** *vt* (*old car etc*) faire reprendre.

trade barrier *n* barrière commerciale.

trade deficit *n* déficit extérieur.

Trade Descriptions Act *n* (*BRIT*) *loi contre les appellations et la publicité mensongères.*

trade discount *n* remise *f* au détaillant.

trade fair *n* foire(-exposition) commerciale.

trade-in ['treɪdɪn] *n* reprise *f*.

trade-in price *n* prix *m* à la reprise.

trademark ['treɪdmɑːk] *n* marque *f* de fabrique.

trade mission *n* mission commerciale.

trade name *n* marque déposée.

trade-off ['treɪdɔf] *n* (*exchange*) échange *f*; (*balancing*) équilibre *m*.

trader ['treɪdə*] *n* commerçant/e, négociant/e.

trade secret *n* secret *m* de fabrication.

tradesman ['treɪdzmən] *n* (*shopkeeper*) commerçant *m*; (*skilled worker*) ouvrier qualifié.

trade union *n* syndicat *m*.

trade unionist [-'juːnjənɪst] *n* syndicaliste *m/f*.

trade wind *n* alizé *m*.

trading ['treɪdɪŋ] *n* affaires *fpl*, commerce *m*.

trading estate *n* (*BRIT*) zone industrielle.

trading stamp *n* timbre-prime *m*.

tradition [trə'dɪʃən] *n* tradition *f*; **~s** *npl* coutumes *fpl*, traditions.

traditional [trə'dɪʃənl] *adj* traditionnel(le).

traffic ['træfɪk] *n* trafic *m*; (*cars*) circulation *f* ♦ *vi*: **to ~ in** (*pej: liquor, drugs*) faire le trafic de.

traffic calming [-'kɑːmɪŋ] *n* ralentissement *m* de la circulation.

traffic circle *n* (*US*) rond-point *m*.

traffic island *n* refuge *m* (pour piétons).

traffic jam *n* embouteillage *m*.

trafficker ['træfɪkə*] *n* trafiquant/e.

traffic lights *npl* feux *mpl* (de signalisation).

traffic offence *n* (*BRIT*) infraction *f* au code de la route.

traffic sign *n* panneau *m* de signalisation.

traffic violation *n* (*US*) = **traffic offence**.

traffic warden *n* contractuel/le.

tragedy ['trædʒədɪ] *n* tragédie *f*.

tragic ['trædʒɪk] *adj* tragique.

trail [treɪl] *n* (*tracks*) trace *f*, piste *f*; (*path*) chemin *m*, piste; (*of smoke etc*) traînée *f* ♦ *vt* traîner, tirer; (*follow*) suivre ♦ *vi* traîner; **to be on sb's ~** être sur la piste de qn.

▶**trail away, trail off** *vi* (*sound, voice*) s'évanouir; (*interest*) disparaître.

▶**trail behind** *vi* traîner, être à la traîne.

trailer ['treɪlə*] *n* (*AUT*) remorque *f*; (*US*) caravane *f*; (*CINE*) bande-annonce *f*.

trailer truck *n* (*US*) (camion *m*) semi-remorque *m*.

train [treɪn] *n* train *m*; (*in underground*) rame *f*; (*of dress*) traîne *f*; (*BRIT: series*): **~ of events** série *f* d'événements ♦ *vt* (*apprentice, doctor etc*) former; (*sportsman*) entraîner; (*dog*) dresser; (*memory*) exercer; (*point: gun etc*): **to ~ sth on** braquer qch sur ♦ *vi* recevoir sa formation; s'entraîner; **one's ~ of thought** le fil de sa pensée; **to go by ~** voyager par le train *or* en train; **to ~ sb to do sth** apprendre à qn à faire qch; (*employee*) former qn à faire qch.

train attendant *n* (*US*) employé/e des wagons-lits.

trained [treɪnd] *adj* qualifié(e), qui a reçu une formation; dressé(e).

trainee [treɪˈniː] *n* stagiaire *m/f*; (*in trade*) apprenti/e.

trainer ['treɪnə*] *n* (*SPORT*) entraîneur/euse; (*of dogs etc*) dresseur/euse; **~s** *npl* (*shoes*) chaussures *fpl* de sport.

training ['treɪnɪŋ] *n* formation *f*; entraînement *m*; dressage *m*; **in ~** (*SPORT*) à l'entraîne-ment; (*fit*) en forme.

training college *n* école professionnelle; (*for teachers*) ≈ école normale.

training course *n* cours *m* de formation professionnelle.

traipse [treɪps] *vi* (se) traîner, déambuler.

trait [treɪt] *n* trait *m* (de caractère).

traitor ['treɪtə*] *n* traître *m*.

trajectory [trə'dʒɛktərɪ] *n* trajectoire *f*.

tram [træm] *n* (*BRIT: also*: **~car**) tram(way) *m*.

tramline ['træmlaɪn] *n* ligne *f* de tram(way).

tramp [træmp] *n* (*person*) vagabond/e, clochard/e; (*col: pej: woman*): **to be a ~** coureuse ♦ *vi* marcher d'un pas lourd ♦ *vt* (*walk through: town, streets*) parcourir à pied.

trample ['træmpl] *vt*: **to ~** (**underfoot**) piétiner; (*fig*) bafouer.

trampoline ['træmpəliːn] *n* trampolino *m*.

trance [trɑːns] *n* transe *f*; (*MED*) catalepsie *f*;
to go into a ~ entrer en transe.
tranquil ['træŋkwɪl] *adj* tranquille.
tranquillity [træŋ'kwɪlɪtɪ] *n* tranquillité *f*.
tranquillizer ['træŋkwɪlaɪzə*] *n* (*MED*)
tranquillisant *m*.
transact [træn'zækt] *vt* (*business*) traiter.
transaction [træn'zækʃən] *n* transaction *f*; **~s**
npl (*minutes*) actes *mpl*; **cash ~** transaction
au comptant.
transatlantic ['trænzət'læntɪk] *adj* transatlantique.
transcend [træn'sɛnd] *vt* transcender; (*excel
over*) surpasser.
transcendental [trænsɛn'dɛntl] *adj*: **~
meditation** méditation transcendantale.
transcribe [træn'skraɪb] *vt* transcrire.
transcript ['trænskrɪpt] *n* transcription *f*
(*texte*).
transcription [træn'skrɪpʃən] *n* transcription
f.
transept ['trænsɛpt] *n* transept *m*.
transfer *n* ['trænsfə*] (*gen, also SPORT*)
transfert *m*; (*POL: of power*) passation *f*; (*of
money*) virement *m*; (*picture, design*)
décalcomanie *f*; (*: stick-on*) autocollant *m* ♦ *vt*
[træns'fɔː*] transférer; passer; virer;
décalquer; **to ~ the charges** (*BRIT TEL*)
téléphoner en P.C.V.; **by bank ~** par
virement bancaire.
transferable [træns'fəːrəbl] *adj* transmissible,
transférable; **"not ~"** "personnel".
transfix [træns'fɪks] *vt* transpercer; (*fig*): **~ed
with fear** paralysé(e) par la peur.
transform [træns'fɔːm] *vt* transformer.
transformation [trænsfə'meɪʃən] *n*
transformation *f*.
transformer [træns'fɔːmə*] *n* (*ELEC*)
transformateur *m*.
transfusion [træns'fjuːʒən] *n* transfusion *f*.
transgress [træns'grɛs] *vt* transgresser.
transient ['trænzɪənt] *adj* transitoire,
éphémère.
transistor [træn'zɪstə*] *n* (*ELEC; also*: **~ radio**)
transistor *m*.
transit ['trænzɪt] *n*: **in ~** en transit.
transit camp *n* camp *m* de transit.
transition [træn'zɪʃən] *n* transition *f*.
transitional [træn'zɪʃənl] *adj* transitoire.
transitive ['trænzɪtɪv] *adj* (*LING*) transitif(ive).
transit lounge *n* (*AVIAT*) salle *f* de transit.
transitory ['trænzɪtərɪ] *adj* transitoire.
translate [trænz'leɪt] *vt*: **to ~ (from/into)**
traduire (du/en).
translation [trænz'leɪʃən] *n* traduction *f*;
(*SCOL: as opposed to prose*) version *f*.
translator [trænz'leɪtə*] *n* traducteur/trice.
translucent [trænz'luːsnt] *adj* translucide.
transmission [trænz'mɪʃən] *n* transmission *f*.
transmit [trænz'mɪt] *vt* transmettre; (*RADIO,
TV*) émettre.
transmitter [trænz'mɪtə*] *n* émetteur *m*.

transparency [træns'pɛərnsɪ] *n* (*BRIT PHOT*)
diapositive *f*.
transparent [træns'pærnt] *adj* transparent(e).
transpire [træns'paɪə*] *vi* (*become known*): **it
finally ~d that** ... on a finalement appris que
...; (*happen*) arriver.
transplant *vt* [træns'plɑːnt] transplanter;
(*seedlings*) repiquer ♦ *n* ['trænsplɑːnt] (*MED*)
transplantation *f*; **to have a heart ~** subir
une greffe du cœur.
transport *n* ['trænspɔːt] transport *m* ♦ *vt*
[træns'pɔːt] transporter; **public ~** transports
en commun; **Department of T~** (*BRIT*)
ministère *m* des Transports.
transportation [trænspɔː'teɪʃən] *n* (*moyen m
de*) transport *m*; (*of prisoners*) transportation
f; **Department of T~** (*US*) ministère *m* des
Transports.
transport café *n* (*BRIT*) ≈ restaurant *m* de
routiers.
transpose [træns'pəuz] *vt* transposer.
transsexual [trænz'sɛksjuəl] *adj, n*
transsexuel(le).
transverse ['trænzvəːs] *adj* transversal(e).
transvestite [trænz'vɛstaɪt] *n* travesti/e.
trap [træp] *n* (*snare, trick*) piège *m*; (*carriage*)
cabriolet *m* ♦ *vt* prendre au piège;
(*immobilize*) bloquer; (*jam*) coincer; **to set** *or*
lay a ~ (for sb) tendre un piège (à qn); **to
shut one's ~** (*col*) la fermer.
trap door *n* trappe *f*.
trapeze [trə'piːz] *n* trapèze *m*.
trapper ['træpə*] *n* trappeur *m*.
trappings ['træpɪŋz] *npl* ornements *mpl*;
attributs *mpl*.
trash [træʃ] *n* (*pej: goods*) camelote *f*;
(*: nonsense*) sottises *fpl*; (*US: rubbish*) ordures
fpl.
trash can *n* (*US*) boîte *f* à ordures.
trashy ['træʃɪ] *adj* (*col*) de camelote, qui ne
vaut rien.
trauma ['trɔːmə] *n* traumatisme *m*.
traumatic [trɔː'mætɪk] *adj* traumatisant(e).
travel ['trævl] *n* voyage(s) *m(pl)* ♦ *vi* voyager;
(*move*) aller, se déplacer ♦ *vt* (*distance*)
parcourir; **this wine doesn't ~ well** ce vin
voyage mal.
travel agency *n* agence *f* de voyages.
travel agent *n* agent *m* de voyages.
travel brochure *n* brochure *f* touristique.
traveller, (*US*) **traveler** ['trævlə*] *n*
voyageur/euse; (*COMM*) représentant *m* de
commerce.
traveller's cheque, (*US*) **traveler's check** *n*
chèque *m* de voyage.
travelling, (*US*) **traveling** ['trævlɪŋ] *n*
voyage(s) *m(pl)* ♦ *adj* (*circus, exhibition*)
ambulant(e) ♦ *cpd* (*bag, clock*) de voyage;
(*expenses*) de déplacement.
travel(l)ing salesman *n* voyageur *m* de
commerce.
travelogue ['trævəlɔg] *n* (*book, talk*) récit *m* de

voyage; (*film*) documentaire *m* de voyage.

travel sickness *n* mal *m* de la route (*or* de mer *or* de l'air).

traverse ['trævəs] *vt* traverser.

travesty ['trævəstı] *n* parodie *f*.

trawler ['trɔːlə*] *n* chalutier *m*.

tray [treı] *n* (*for carrying*) plateau *m*; (*on desk*) corbeille *f*.

treacherous ['tretʃərəs] *adj* traître(sse); **road conditions are** ~ l'état des routes est dangereux.

treachery ['tretʃərı] *n* traîtrise *f*.

treacle ['triːkl] *n* mélasse *f*.

tread [tred] *n* pas *m*; (*sound*) bruit *m* de pas; (*of tyre*) chape *f*, bande *f* de roulement ♦ *vi* (*pt* trod, *pp* trodden [trɔd, 'trɔdn]) marcher.
▶ **tread on** *vt fus* marcher sur.

treadle ['tredl] *n* pédale *f* (*de machine*).

treas. *abbr* = **treasurer**.

treason ['triːzn] *n* trahison *f*.

treasure ['treʒə*] *n* trésor *m* ♦ *vt* (*value*) tenir beaucoup à; (*store*) conserver précieusement.

treasure hunt *n* chasse *f* au trésor.

treasurer ['treʒərə*] *n* trésorier/ière.

treasury ['treʒərı] *n* trésorerie *f*; **the T**~, (*US*) **the T~ Department** ≈ le ministère des Finances.

treasury bill *n* bon *m* du Trésor.

treat [triːt] *n* petit cadeau, petite surprise ♦ *vt* traiter; **it was a** ~ ça m'a (*or* nous a *etc*) vraiment fait plaisir; **to** ~ **sb to sth** offrir qch à qn; **to** ~ **sth as a joke** prendre qch à la plaisanterie.

treatise ['triːtız] *n* traité *m* (*ouvrage*).

treatment ['triːtmənt] *n* traitement *m*; **to have** ~ **for sth** (*MED*) suivre un traitement pour qch.

treaty ['triːtı] *n* traité *m*.

treble ['trebl] *adj* triple ♦ *n* (*MUS*) soprano *m* ♦ *vt*, *vi* tripler.

treble clef *n* clé *f* de sol.

tree [triː] *n* arbre *m*.

tree-lined ['triːlaınd] *adj* bordé(e) d'arbres.

treetop ['triːtɔp] *n* cime *f* d'un arbre.

tree trunk *n* tronc *m* d'arbre.

trek [trek] *n* voyage *m*; randonnée *f*; (*tiring walk*) tirée *f* ♦ *vi* (*as holiday*) faire de la randonnée.

trellis ['trelıs] *n* treillis *m*, treillage *m*.

tremble ['trembl] *vi* trembler.

trembling ['tremblıŋ] *n* tremblement *m* ♦ *adj* tremblant(e).

tremendous [trı'mendəs] *adj* énorme, formidable; (*excellent*) fantastique, formidable.

tremendously [trı'mendəslı] *adv* énormément, extrêmement + *adjective*; formidablement.

tremor ['tremə*] *n* tremblement *m*; (*also:* **earth** ~) secousse *f* sismique.

trench [trentʃ] *n* tranchée *f*.

trench coat *n* trench-coat *m*.

trench warfare *n* guerre *f* de tranchées.

trend [trend] *n* (*tendency*) tendance *f*; (*of events*) cours *m*; (*fashion*) mode *f*; ~ **towards/away from doing** tendance à faire/ à ne pas faire; **to set the** ~ donner le ton; **to set a** ~ lancer une mode.

trendy ['trendı] *adj* (*idea*) dans le vent; (*clothes*) dernier cri *inv*.

trepidation [trepı'deıʃən] *n* vive agitation.

trespass ['trespəs] *vi*: **to** ~ **on** s'introduire sans permission dans; (*fig*) empiéter sur; "**no** ~**ing**" "propriété privée", "défense d'entrer".

trespasser ['trespəsə*] *n* intrus/e; "~**s will be prosecuted**" "interdiction d'entrer sous peine de poursuites".

tress [tres] *n* boucle *f* de cheveux.

trestle ['tresl] *n* tréteau *m*.

trestle table *n* table *f* à tréteaux.

trial ['traıəl] *n* (*LAW*) procès *m*, jugement *m*; (*test: of machine etc*) essai *m*; (*hardship*) épreuve *f*; (*worry*) souci *m*; ~**s** *npl* (*SPORT*) épreuves éliminatoires; **horse** ~**s** concours *m* hippique; ~ **by jury** jugement par jury; **to be sent for** ~ être traduit(e) en justice; **to be on** ~ passer en jugement; **by** ~ **and error** par tâtonnements.

trial balance *n* (*COMM*) balance *f* de vérification.

trial basis *n*: **on a** ~ pour une période d'essai.

trial run *n* essai *m*.

triangle ['traıæŋgl] *n* (*MATH, MUS*) triangle *m*.

triangular [traı'æŋgjulə*] *adj* triangulaire.

triathlon [traı'æθlən] *n* triathlon *m*.

tribal ['traıbl] *adj* tribal(e).

tribe [traıb] *n* tribu *f*.

tribesman ['traıbzmən] *n* membre *m* de la tribu.

tribulation [trıbju'leıʃən] *n* tribulation *f*, malheur *m*.

tribunal [traı'bjuːnl] *n* tribunal *m*.

tributary ['trıbjutərı] *n* (*river*) affluent *m*.

tribute ['trıbjuːt] *n* tribut *m*, hommage *m*; **to pay** ~ **to** rendre hommage à.

trice [traıs] *n*: **in a** ~ en un clin d'œil.

trick [trık] *n* ruse *f*; (*clever act*) astuce *f*; (*joke*) tour *m*; (*CARDS*) levée *f* ♦ *vt* attraper, rouler; **to play a** ~ **on sb** jouer un tour à qn; **to** ~ **sb into doing sth** persuader qn par la ruse de faire qch; **to** ~ **sb out of sth** obtenir qch de qn par la ruse; **it's a** ~ **of the light** c'est une illusion d'optique causée par la lumière; **that should do the** ~ (*col*) ça devrait faire l'affaire.

trickery ['trıkərı] *n* ruse *f*.

trickle ['trıkl] *n* (*of water etc*) filet *m* ♦ *vi* couler en un filet *or* goutte à goutte; **to** ~ **in/out** (*people*) entrer/sortir par petits groupes.

trick question *n* question-piège *f*.

trickster ['trıkstə*] *n* arnaqueur/euse, filou *m*.

tricky ['trıkı] *adj* difficile, délicat(e).

tricycle ['traisikl] n tricycle m.

trifle ['traifl] n bagatelle f; (CULIN)
≈ diplomate m ♦ adv: **a ~ long** un peu long
♦ vi: **to ~ with** traiter à la légère.

trifling ['traiflin] adj insignifiant(e).

trigger ['trigə*] n (of gun) gâchette f.
▶**trigger off** vt déclencher.

trigonometry [trigə'nɔmətri] n trigonométrie
f.

trilby ['trilbi] n (BRIT: also: ~ **hat**) chapeau
mou, feutre m.

trill [tril] n (of bird, MUS) trille m.

trilogy ['trilədʒi] n trilogie f.

trim [trim] adj net(te); (house, garden) bien
tenu(e); (figure) svelte ♦ n (haircut etc) légère
coupe; (embellishment) finitions fpl; (on car)
garnitures fpl ♦ vt couper légèrement;
(decorate): **to ~ (with)** décorer (de); (NAUT: a
sail) gréer; **to keep in (good) ~** maintenir en
(bon) état.

trimmings ['triminz] npl décorations fpl;
(extras: gen CULIN) garniture f.

Trinidad and Tobago ['trinidæd-] n Trinité
et Tobago f.

Trinity ['triniti] n: **the ~** la Trinité.

trinket ['triŋkit] n bibelot m; (piece of jewellery)
colifichet m.

trio ['triːəʊ] n trio m.

trip [trip] n voyage m; (excursion) excursion f;
(stumble) faux pas ♦ vi faire un faux pas,
trébucher; (go lightly) marcher d'un pas
léger; **on a ~** en voyage.
▶**trip up** vi trébucher ♦ vt faire un croc-en-
jambe à.

tripartite [trai'pɑːtait] adj triparti(e).

tripe [traip] n (CULIN) tripes fpl; (pej: rubbish)
idioties fpl.

triple ['tripl] adj triple ♦ adv: **~ the distance/
the speed** trois fois la distance/la vitesse.

triple jump n triple saut m.

triplets ['triplits] npl triplés/ées.

triplicate ['triplikət] n: **in ~** en trois
exemplaires.

tripod ['traipɔd] n trépied m.

Tripoli ['tripəli] n Tripoli.

tripper ['tripə*] n (BRIT) touriste m/f;
excursionniste m/f.

tripwire ['tripwaiə*] n fil m de déclenchement.

trite [trait] adj banal(e).

triumph ['traiʌmf] n triomphe m ♦ vi: **to ~
(over)** triompher (de).

triumphal [trai'ʌmfl] adj triomphal(e).

triumphant [trai'ʌmfənt] adj triomphant(e).

trivia ['triviə] npl futilités fpl.

trivial ['triviəl] adj insignifiant(e); (commonplace) banal(e).

triviality [trivi'æliti] n caractère insignifiant;
banalité f.

trivialize ['triviəlaiz] vt rendre banal(e).

trod [trɔd] pt of **tread**.

trodden ['trɔdn] pp of **tread**.

trolley ['trɔli] n chariot m.

trolley bus n trolleybus m.

trollop ['trɔləp] n prostituée f.

trombone [trɔm'bəʊn] n trombone m.

troop [truːp] n bande f, groupe m ♦ vi: **to ~ in/
out** entrer/sortir en groupe; **~ing the colour**
(BRIT: ceremony) le salut au drapeau.

troop carrier n (plane) avion m de transport
de troupes; (NAUT: also: **troopship**) transport
m (navire).

trooper ['truːpə*] n (MIL) soldat m de
cavalerie; (US: policeman) ≈ gendarme m.

troops [truːps] npl (MIL) troupes fpl; (: men)
hommes mpl, soldats mpl.

troopship ['truːpʃip] n transport m (navire).

trophy ['trəʊfi] n trophée m.

tropic ['trɔpik] n tropique m; **in the ~s** sous
les tropiques; **T~ of Cancer/Capricorn**
tropique du Cancer/Capricorne.

tropical ['trɔpikl] adj tropical(e).

trot [trɔt] n trot m ♦ vi trotter; **on the ~** (BRIT:
fig) d'affilée.
▶**trot out** vt (excuse, reason) débiter; (names,
facts) réciter les uns après les autres.

trouble ['trʌbl] n difficulté(s) f(pl),
problème(s) m(pl); (worry) ennuis mpl, soucis
mpl; (bother, effort) peine f; (POL) conflit(s)
m(pl), troubles mpl; (MED): **stomach etc ~**
troubles gastriques etc ♦ vt déranger,
gêner; (worry) inquiéter ♦ vi: **to ~ to do**
prendre la peine de faire; **~s** npl (POL etc)
troubles; **to be in ~** avoir des ennuis; (ship,
climber etc) être en difficulté; **to have ~
doing sth** avoir du mal à faire qch; **to go to
the ~ of doing** se donner le mal de faire; **it's
no ~!** je vous en prie!; **please don't ~
yourself** je vous en prie, ne vous dérangez
pas!; **the ~ is ...** le problème, c'est que ...;
what's the ~? qu'est-ce qui ne va pas?

troubled [trʌbld] adj (person) inquiet(ète);
(epoch, life) agité(e).

trouble-free ['trʌblfriː] adj sans problèmes or
ennuis.

troublemaker ['trʌblmeikə*] n élément
perturbateur, fauteur m de troubles.

troubleshooter ['trʌblʃuːtə*] n (in conflict)
conciliateur m.

troublesome ['trʌblsəm] adj ennuyeux(euse),
gênant(e).

trouble spot n point chaud (fig).

troubling ['trʌbliŋ] adj (times, thought)
inquiétant(e).

trough [trɔf] n (also: **drinking ~**) abreuvoir m;
(also: **feeding ~**) auge f; (channel) chenal m;
~ of low pressure (METEOROLOGY)
dépression f.

trounce [trauns] vt (defeat) battre à plates
coutures.

troupe [truːp] n troupe f.

trouser press n presse-pantalon m inv.

trousers ['trauzəz] npl pantalon m; **short ~**
(BRIT) culottes courtes.

trouser suit n (BRIT) tailleur-pantalon m.

trousseau, pl ~**x** or ~**s** ['tru:səu, -z] n
trousseau m.

trout [traut] n (pl inv) truite f.

trowel ['trauəl] n truelle f.

truant ['truənt] n: **to play** ~ (BRIT) faire l'école
buissonnière.

truce [tru:s] n trêve f.

truck [trʌk] n camion m; (RAIL) wagon m à
plate-forme; (for luggage) chariot m (à
bagages).

truck driver n camionneur m.

trucker ['trʌkə*] n (esp US) camionneur m.

truck farm n (US) jardin maraîcher.

trucking ['trʌkɪŋ] n (esp US) transport routier.

trucking company n (US) entreprise f de
transport (routier).

truck stop (US) routier m, restaurant m de
routiers.

truculent ['trʌkjulənt] adj agressif(ive).

trudge [trʌdʒ] vi marcher lourdement, se
traîner.

true [tru:] adj vrai(e); (accurate) exact(e);
(genuine) vrai, véritable; (faithful) fidèle;
(wall) d'aplomb; (beam) droit(e); (wheel)
dans l'axe; **to come** ~ se réaliser; ~ **to life**
réaliste.

truffle ['trʌfl] n truffe f.

truly ['tru:lɪ] adv vraiment, réellement;
(truthfully) sans mentir; (faithfully)
fidèlement; **yours** ~ (in letter) je vous prie
d'agréer, Monsieur (or Madame etc),
l'expression de mes sentiments
respectueux.

trump [trʌmp] n atout m; **to turn up** ~**s** (fig)
faire des miracles.

trump card n atout m; (fig) carte maîtresse f.

trumped-up [trʌmp't ʌp] adj inventé(e) (de
toutes pièces).

trumpet ['trʌmpɪt] n trompette f.

truncated [trʌŋ'keɪt ɪd] adj tronqué(e).

truncheon ['trʌntʃən] n bâton m (d'agent de
police); matraque f.

trundle ['trʌndl] vt, vi: **to** ~ **along** rouler
bruyamment.

trunk [trʌŋk] n (of tree, person) tronc m; (of
elephant) trompe f; (case) malle f; (US AUT)
coffre m.

trunk call n (BRIT TEL) communication
interurbaine.

trunk road n (BRIT) ≈ (route f) nationale f.

trunks [trʌŋks] npl (also: **swimming** ~) maillot
m or slip m de bain.

truss [trʌs] n (MED) bandage m herniaire ♦ vt:
to ~ (**up**) (CULIN) brider.

trust [trʌst] n confiance f; (LAW) fidéicommis
m; (COMM) trust m ♦ vt (rely on) avoir
confiance en; (entrust): **to** ~ **sth to sb** confier
qch à qn; (hope): **to** ~ (**that**) espérer (que);
to take sth on ~ accepter qch sans
garanties (or sans preuves); **in** ~ (LAW) par
fidéicommis.

trust company n société f fiduciaire.

trusted ['trʌstɪd] adj en qui l'on a confiance.

trustee [trʌs'ti:] n (LAW) fidéicommissaire m/f;
(of school etc) administrateur/trice.

trustful ['trʌstful] adj confiant(e).

trust fund n fonds m en fidéicommis.

trusting ['trʌstɪŋ] adj confiant(e).

trustworthy ['trʌstwə:ðɪ] adj digne de
confiance.

trusty ['trʌstɪ] adj fidèle.

truth, ~**s** [tru:θ, tru:ðz] n vérité f.

truthful ['tru:θful] adj (person) qui dit la
vérité; (description) exact(e), vrai(e).

truthfully ['tru:θfəlɪ] adv sincèrement, sans
mentir.

truthfulness ['tru:θfəlnɪs] n véracité f.

try [traɪ] n essai m, tentative f; (RUGBY) essai
♦ vt (LAW) juger; (test: sth new) essayer,
tester; (strain) éprouver ♦ vi essayer; **to** ~ **to
do** essayer de faire; (seek) chercher à faire;
to ~ **one's (very) best** or **one's (very) hardest**
faire de son mieux; **to give sth a** ~ essayer
qch.

▶**try on** vt (clothes) essayer; **to** ~ **it on** (fig)
tenter le coup, bluffer.

▶**try out** vt essayer, mettre à l'essai.

trying ['traɪɪŋ] adj pénible.

tsar [zɑ:*] n tsar m.

T-shirt ['ti:ʃə:t] n tee-shirt m.

T-square ['ti:skwɛə*] n équerre f en T.

TT adj abbr (BRIT col) = **teetotal** ♦ abbr (US) =
Trust Territory.

tub [tʌb] n cuve f; baquet m; (bath) baignoire f.

tuba ['tju:bə] n tuba m.

tubby ['tʌbɪ] adj rondelet(te).

tube [tju:b] n tube m; (BRIT: underground)
métro m; (for tyre) chambre f à air; (col:
television): **the** ~ la télé.

tubeless ['tju:blɪs] adj (tyre) sans chambre à
air.

tuber ['tju:bə*] n (BOT) tubercule m.

tuberculosis [tjubə:kju'ləusɪs] n tuberculose f.

tube station n (BRIT) station f de métro.

tubing ['tju:bɪŋ] n tubes mpl; **a piece of** ~ un
tube.

tubular ['tju:bjulə*] adj tubulaire.

TUC n abbr (BRIT: = Trades Union Congress)
confédération f des syndicats britanniques.

tuck [tʌk] n (SEWING) pli m, rempli m ♦ vt (put)
mettre.

▶**tuck away** vt cacher, ranger.

▶**tuck in** vt rentrer; (child) border ♦ vi (eat)
manger de bon appétit; attaquer le repas.

▶**tuck up** vt (child) border.

tuck shop n (BRIT SCOL) boutique f à
provisions.

Tue(s). abbr (= Tuesday) ma.

Tuesday ['tju:zdɪ] n mardi m; **(the date) today
is** ~ **23rd March** nous sommes aujourd'hui
le mardi 23 mars; **on** ~ mardi; **on** ~**s** le
mardi; **every** ~ tous les mardis, chaque
mardi; **every other** ~ un mardi sur deux;
last/next ~ mardi dernier/prochain; ~ **next**

mardi qui vient; **the following** ~ le mardi suivant; **a week/fortnight on** ~, ~ **week/fortnight** mardi en huit/quinze; **the** ~ **before last** l'autre mardi; **the** ~ **after next** mardi en huit; ~ **morning/lunchtime/afternoon/evening** mardi matin/midi/après-midi/soir; ~ **night** mardi soir; (*overnight*) la nuit de mardi (à mercredi); ~**'s newspaper** le journal de mardi.

tuft [tʌft] *n* touffe *f*.

tug [tʌg] *n* (*ship*) remorqueur *m* ♦ *vt* tirer (sur).

tug-of-love [tʌgəv'lʌv] *n* lutte acharnée entre parents divorcés pour avoir la garde d'un enfant.

tug-of-war [tʌgəv'wɔ:*] *n* lutte *f* à la corde.

tuition [tju:'ɪʃən] *n* (*BRIT: lessons*) leçons *fpl*; (*US: fees*) frais *mpl* de scolarité.

tulip ['tju:lɪp] *n* tulipe *f*.

tumble ['tʌmbl] *n* (*fall*) chute *f*, culbute *f* ♦ *vi* tomber, dégringoler; (*somersault*) faire une *or* des culbute(s) ♦ *vt* renverser, faire tomber; **to** ~ **to sth** (*col*) réaliser qch.

tumbledown ['tʌmbldaun] *adj* délabré(e).

tumble dryer *n* (*BRIT*) séchoir *m* (à linge) à air chaud.

tumbler ['tʌmblə*] *n* verre (droit), gobelet *m*.

tummy ['tʌmɪ] *n* (*col*) ventre *m*.

tumour, (*US*) **tumor** ['tju:mə*] *n* tumeur *f*.

tumult ['tju:mʌlt] *n* tumulte *m*.

tumultuous [tju:'mʌltjuəs] *adj* tumultueux(euse).

tuna ['tju:nə] *n* (*pl inv*) (*also:* ~ **fish**) thon *m*.

tune [tju:n] *n* (*melody*) air *m* ♦ *vt* (*MUS*) accorder; (*RADIO, TV, AUT*) régler, mettre au point; **to be in/out of** ~ (*instrument*) être accordé/désaccordé; (*singer*) chanter juste/faux; **to be in/out of** ~ **with** (*fig*) être en accord/désaccord avec; **she was robbed to the** ~ **of £10,000** (*fig*) on lui a volé la jolie somme de 10 000 livres.

▶**tune in** *vi* (*RADIO, TV*): **to** ~ **in (to)** se mettre à l'écoute (de).

▶**tune up** *vi* (*musician*) accorder son instrument.

tuneful ['tju:nful] *adj* mélodieux(euse).

tuner ['tju:nə*] *n* (*radio set*) radio-préamplificateur *m*; **piano** ~ accordeur *m* de pianos.

tuner amplifier *n* radio-ampli *m*.

tungsten ['tʌŋstn] *n* tungstène *m*.

tunic ['tju:nɪk] *n* tunique *f*.

tuning ['tju:nɪŋ] *n* réglage *m*.

tuning fork *n* diapason *m*.

Tunis ['tju:nɪs] *n* Tunis.

Tunisia [tju:'nɪzɪə] *n* Tunisie *f*.

Tunisian [tju:'nɪzɪən] *adj* tunisien(ne) ♦ *n* Tunisien/ne.

tunnel ['tʌnl] *n* tunnel *m*; (*in mine*) galerie *f* ♦ *vi* creuser un tunnel (*or* une galerie).

tunnel vision *n* (*MED*) rétrécissement *m* du champ visuel; (*fig*) vision étroite des choses.

tunny ['tʌnɪ] *n* thon *m*.

turban ['tɜ:bən] *n* turban *m*.

turbid ['tɜ:bɪd] *adj* boueux(euse).

turbine ['tɜ:baɪn] *n* turbine *f*.

turbo ['tɜ:bəu] *n* turbo *m*.

turbojet [tɜ:bəu'dʒɛt] *n* turboréacteur *m*.

turboprop [tɜ:bəu'prɔp] *n* (*engine*) turbopropulseur *m*.

turbot ['tɜ:bət] *n* (*pl inv*) turbot *m*.

turbulence ['tɜ:bjuləns] *n* (*AVIAT*) turbulence *f*.

turbulent ['tɜ:bjulənt] *adj* turbulent(e); (*sea*) agité(e).

tureen [tə'ri:n] *n* soupière *f*.

turf [tɜ:f] *n* gazon *m*; (*clod*) motte *f* (de gazon) ♦ *vt* gazonner; **the T**~ le turf, les courses *fpl*.

▶**turf out** *vt* (*col*) jeter; jeter dehors.

turf accountant *n* (*BRIT*) bookmaker *m*.

turgid ['tɜ:dʒɪd] *adj* (*speech*) pompeux(euse).

Turin [tjuə'rɪn] *n* Turin.

Turk [tɜ:k] *n* Turc/Turque.

Turkey ['tɜ:kɪ] *n* Turquie *f*.

turkey ['tɜ:kɪ] *n* dindon *m*, dinde *f*.

Turkish ['tɜ:kɪʃ] *adj* turc(turque) ♦ *n* (*LING*) turc *m*.

Turkish bath *n* bain turc.

Turkish delight *n* loukoum *m*.

turmeric ['tɜ:mərɪk] *n* curcuma *m*.

turmoil ['tɜ:mɔɪl] *n* trouble *m*, bouleversement *m*.

turn [tɜ:n] *n* tour *m*; (*in road*) tournant *m*; (*tendency: of mind, events*) tournure *f*; (*performance*) numéro *m*; (*MED*) crise *f*, attaque *f* ♦ *vt* tourner; (*collar, steak*) retourner; (*milk*) faire tourner; (*change*): **to** ~ **sth into** changer qch en; (*shape: wood, metal*) tourner ♦ *vi* tourner; (*person: look back*) se (re)tourner; (*reverse direction*) faire demi-tour; (*change*) changer; (*become*) devenir; **to** ~ **into** se changer en, se transformer en; **a good** ~ un service; **a bad** ~ un mauvais tour; **it gave me quite a** ~ ça m'a fait un coup; **"no left** ~**"** (*AUT*) "défense de tourner à gauche"; **it's your** ~ c'est (à) votre tour; **in** ~ à son tour; à tour de rôle; **to take** ~**s** se relayer; **to take** ~**s at** faire à tour de rôle; **at the** ~ **of the year/century** à la fin de l'année/du siècle; **to take a** ~ **for the worse** (*situation, events*) empirer; **his health** *or* **he has taken a** ~ **for the worse** son état s'est aggravé.

▶**turn about** *vi* faire demi-tour; faire un demi-tour.

▶**turn away** *vi* se détourner, tourner la tête ♦ *vt* (*reject: person*) renvoyer; (*: business*) refuser.

▶**turn back** *vi* revenir, faire demi-tour.

▶**turn down** *vt* (*refuse*) rejeter, refuser; (*reduce*) baisser; (*fold*) rabattre.

▶**turn in** *vi* (*col: go to bed*) aller se coucher ♦ *vt* (*fold*) rentrer.

►**turn off** *vi* (*from road*) tourner ♦ *vt* (*light, radio etc*) éteindre; (*engine*) arrêter.

►**turn on** *vt* (*light, radio etc*) allumer; (*engine*) mettre en marche.

►**turn out** *vt* (*light, gas*) éteindre; (*produce: goods, novel, good pupils*) produire ♦ *vi* (*appear, attend: troops, doctor etc*) être présent(e); **to ~ out to be ...** s'avérer ..., se révéler ....

►**turn over** *vi* (*person*) se retourner ♦ *vt* (*object*) retourner; (*page*) tourner.

►**turn round** *vi* faire demi-tour; (*rotate*) tourner.

►**turn up** *vi* (*person*) arriver, se pointer; (*lost object*) être retrouvé(e) ♦ *vt* (*collar*) remonter; (*increase: sound, volume etc*) mettre plus fort.

turnabout ['tɜːnəbaut], **turnaround** ['tɜːnəraund] *n* volte-face *f inv*.

turncoat ['tɜːnkəut] *n* renégat/e.

turned-up ['tɜːndʌp] *adj* (*nose*) retroussé(e).

turning ['tɜːnɪŋ] *n* (*in road*) tournant *m*; **the first ~ on the right** la première (rue *or* route) à droite.

turning circle *n* (*BRIT*) rayon *m* de braquage.

turning point *n* (*fig*) tournant *m*, moment décisif.

turning radius *n* (*US*) = **turning circle**.

turnip ['tɜːnɪp] *n* navet *m*.

turnout ['tɜːnaut] *n* (nombre *m* de personnes dans l')assistance *f*.

turnover ['tɜːnəuvə*] *n* (*COMM: amount of money*) chiffre *m* d'affaires; (*: of goods*) roulement *m*; (*CULIN*) sorte de chausson; **there is a rapid ~ in staff** le personnel change souvent.

turnpike ['tɜːnpaɪk] *n* (*US*) autoroute *f* à péage.

turnstile ['tɜːnstaɪl] *n* tourniquet *m* (*d'entrée*).

turntable ['tɜːnteɪbl] *n* (*on record player*) platine *f*.

turn-up ['tɜːnʌp] *n* (*BRIT: on trousers*) revers *m*.

turpentine ['tɜːpəntaɪn] *n* (*also:* **turps**) (essence *f* de) térébenthine *f*.

turquoise ['tɜːkwɔɪz] *n* (*stone*) turquoise *f* ♦ *adj* turquoise *inv*.

turret ['tʌrɪt] *n* tourelle *f*.

turtle ['tɜːtl] *n* tortue marine.

turtleneck (sweater) ['tɜːtlnɛk-] *n* pullover *m* à col montant.

Tuscany ['tʌskənɪ] *n* Toscane *f*.

tusk [tʌsk] *n* défense *f* (*d'éléphant*).

tussle ['tʌsl] *n* bagarre *f*, mêlée *f*.

tutor ['tjuːtə*] *n* (*BRIT SCOL*) directeur/trice d'études; (*private teacher*) précepteur/trice.

tutorial [tjuːˈtɔːrɪəl] *n* (*SCOL*) (séance *f* de) travaux *mpl* pratiques.

tuxedo [tʌkˈsiːdəu] *n* (*US*) smoking *m*.

TV [tiːˈviː] *n abbr* (= *television*) télé *f*, TV *f*.

TV dinner *n* plateau-repas surgelé.

twaddle ['twɔdl] *n* balivernes *fpl*.

twang [twæŋ] *n* (*of instrument*) son vibrant; (*of voice*) ton nasillard ♦ *vi* vibrer ♦ *vt* (*guitar*) pincer les cordes de.

tweak [twiːk] *vt* (*nose*) tordre; (*ear, hair*) tirer.

tweed [twiːd] *n* tweed *m*.

tweezers ['twiːzəz] *npl* pince *f* à épiler.

twelfth [twelfθ] *num* douzième.

Twelfth Night *n* la fête des Rois.

twelve [twelv] *num* douze; **at ~** (*o'clock*) à midi; (*midnight*) à minuit.

twentieth ['twentɪɪθ] *num* vingtième.

twenty ['twentɪ] *num* vingt.

twerp [twəːp] *n* (*col*) imbécile *m/f*.

twice [twaɪs] *adv* deux fois; **~ as much** deux fois plus; **~ a week** deux fois par semaine; **she is ~ your age** elle a deux fois ton âge.

twiddle ['twɪdl] *vt, vi*: **to ~ (with) sth** tripoter qch; **to ~ one's thumbs** (*fig*) se tourner les pouces.

twig [twɪg] *n* brindille *f* ♦ *vt, vi* (*col*) piger.

twilight ['twaɪlaɪt] *n* crépuscule *m*; (*morning*) aube *f*; **in the ~** dans la pénombre.

twill [twɪl] *n* sergé *m*.

twin [twɪn] *adj, n* jumeau(elle) ♦ *vt* jumeler.

twin(-bedded) room ['twɪn('bedɪd)-] *n* chambre *f* à deux lits.

twin beds *npl* lits *mpl* jumeaux.

twin-carburettor ['twɪŋkɑːbjuˈrɛtə*] *adj* à double carburateur.

twine [twaɪn] *n* ficelle *f* ♦ *vi* (*plant*) s'enrouler.

twin-engined [twɪnˈɛndʒɪnd] *adj* bimoteur; **~ aircraft** bimoteur *m*.

twinge [twɪndʒ] *n* (*of pain*) élancement *m*; (*of conscience*) remords *m*.

twinkle ['twɪŋkl] *n* scintillement *m*; pétillement *m* ♦ *vi* scintiller; (*eyes*) pétiller.

twin town *n* ville jumelée.

twirl [twəːl] *n* tournoiement *m* ♦ *vt* faire tournoyer ♦ *vi* tournoyer.

twist [twɪst] *n* torsion *f*, tour *m*; (*in wire, flex*) tortillon *m*; (*bend: in road*) tournant *m*; (*in story*) coup *m* de théâtre ♦ *vt* tordre; (*weave*) entortiller; (*roll around*) enrouler; (*fig*) déformer ♦ *vi* s'entortiller; s'enrouler; (*road*) serpenter; **to ~ one's ankle/wrist** (*MED*) se tordre la cheville/le poignet.

twisted ['twɪstɪd] *adj* (*wire, rope*) entortillé(e); (*ankle, wrist*) tordu(e), foulé(e); (*fig: logic, mind*) tordu.

twit [twɪt] *n* (*col*) crétin/e.

twitch [twɪtʃ] *n* saccade *f*; (*nervous*) tic *m* ♦ *vi* se convulser; avoir un tic.

two [tuː] *num* deux; **~ by ~, in ~s** par deux; **to put ~ and ~ together** (*fig*) faire le rapport.

two-bit [tuːˈbɪt] *adj* (*esp US col, pej*) de pacotille.

two-door [tuːˈdɔː*] *adj* (*AUT*) à deux portes.

two-faced [tuːˈfeɪst] *adj* (*pej: person*) faux(fausse).

twofold ['tuːfəuld] *adv*: **to increase ~** doubler ♦ *adj* (*increase*) de cent pour cent; (*reply*) en deux parties.

two-piece ['tuːˈpiːs] *n* (*also:* **~ suit**) (costume

m) deux-pièces *m inv*; (*also*: ~ **swimsuit**)
(maillot *m* de bain) deux-pièces.
two-seater [tuːˈsiːtə*] *n* (*plane*) (avion *m)*
biplace *m*; (*car*) voiture *f* à deux places.
twosome [ˈtuːsəm] *n* (*people*) couple *m*.
two-stroke [ˈtuːstrəuk] *n* (*also*: ~ **engine**)
moteur *m* à deux temps ♦ *adj* à deux
temps.
two-tone [ˈtuːˈtəun] *adj* (*in colour*) à deux
tons.
two-way [ˈtuːweɪ] *adj* (*traffic*) dans les deux
sens; ~ **radio** émetteur-récepteur *m*.
TX *abbr* (*US*) = *Texas.*
tycoon [taɪˈkuːn] *n*: (**business**) ~ gros homme
d'affaires.
type [taɪp] *n* (*category*) genre *m*, espèce *f*;
(*model*) modèle *m*; (*example*) type *m*; (*TYP*)
type, caractère *m* ♦ *vt* (*letter etc*) taper (à la
machine); **what** ~ **do you want?** quel genre
voulez-vous?; **in bold/italic** ~ en caractères
gras/en italiques.
typecast [ˈtaɪpkɑːst] *adj* condamné(e) à
toujours jouer le même rôle.
typeface [ˈtaɪpfeɪs] *n* police *f* (de caractères).
typescript [ˈtaɪpskrɪpt] *n* texte
dactylographié.
typeset [ˈtaɪpset] *vt* composer (*en imprimerie*).
typesetter [ˈtaɪpsetə*] *n* compositeur *m*.
typewriter [ˈtaɪpraɪtə*] *n* machine *f* à écrire.
typewritten [ˈtaɪprɪtn] *adj* dactylographié(e).
typhoid [ˈtaɪfɔɪd] *n* typhoïde *f*.
typhoon [taɪˈfuːn] *n* typhon *m*.
typhus [ˈtaɪfəs] *n* typhus *m*.
typical [ˈtɪpɪkl] *adj* typique, caractéristique.
typify [ˈtɪpɪfaɪ] *vt* être caractéristique de.
typing [ˈtaɪpɪŋ] *n* dactylo(graphie) *f*.
typing error *n* faute *f* de frappe.
typing pool *n* pool *m* de dactylos.
typist [ˈtaɪpɪst] *n* dactylo *m/f*.
typo [ˈtaɪpəu] *n abbr* (*col*: = *typographical error*)
coquille *f*.
typography [taɪˈpɔgrəfɪ] *n* typographie *f*.
tyranny [ˈtɪrənɪ] *n* tyrannie *f*.
tyrant [ˈtaɪərnt] *n* tyran *m*.
tyre, (*US*) **tire** [ˈtaɪə*] *n* pneu *m*.
tyre pressure *n* pression *f* (de gonflage).
Tyrol [tɪˈrəul] *n* Tyrol *m*.
Tyrolean [tɪrəˈliːən], **Tyrolese** [tɪrəˈliːz] *adj*
tyrolien(ne) ♦ *n* Tyrolien/ne.
Tyrrhenian Sea [tɪˈriːnɪən-] *n*: **the** ~ la mer
Tyrrhénienne.
tzar [zɑː*] *n* = **tsar**.

U u

U, u [juː] *n* (*letter*) U, u *m*; **U for Uncle** U
comme Ursule.
U *n abbr* (*BRIT CINE*: = *universal*) ≈ tous publics.
UAW *n abbr* (*US*: = *United Automobile Workers*)
syndicat des ouvriers de l'automobile.
UB40 *n abbr* (*BRIT*: = *unemployment benefit form
40*) numéro de référence d'un formulaire
d'inscription au chômage: par extension, le
bénéficiaire.
U-bend [ˈjuːbend] *n* (*BRIT AUT*) coude *m*,
virage *m* en épingle à cheveux; (*in pipe*)
coude.
ubiquitous [juːˈbɪkwɪtəs] *adj* doué(e)
d'ubiquité, omniprésent(e).
UCAS [ˈjuːkæs] *n abbr* (*BRIT*) = *Universities and
Colleges Admissions Service.*
UDA *n abbr* (*BRIT*) = *Ulster Defence Association.*
UDC *n abbr* (*BRIT*) = *Urban District Council.*
udder [ˈʌdə*] *n* pis *m*, mamelle *f*.
UDI *n abbr* (*BRIT POL*) = *unilateral declaration of
independence.*
UDR *n abbr* (*BRIT*) = *Ulster Defence Regiment.*
UEFA [juːˈeɪfə] *n abbr* (= *Union of European
Football Associations*) UEFA *f*.
UFO [ˈjuːfəu] *n abbr* (= *unidentified flying object*)
ovni *m* (= *objet volant non identifié*).
Uganda [juːˈgændə] *n* Ouganda *m*.
Ugandan [juːˈgændən] *adj* ougandais(e) ♦ *n*
Ougandais/e.
UGC *n abbr* (*BRIT*: = *University Grants
Committee*) commission d'attribution des
dotations aux universités.
ugh [əːh] *excl* pouah!
ugliness [ˈʌglɪnɪs] *n* laideur *f*.
ugly [ˈʌglɪ] *adj* laid(e), vilain(e); (*fig*)
répugnant(e).
UHF *abbr* (= *ultra-high frequency*) UHF.
UHT *adj abbr* (= *ultra-heat treated*): ~ **milk** lait *m*
UHT *or* longue conservation.
UK *n abbr* = **United Kingdom.**
Ukraine [juːˈkreɪn] *n* Ukraine *f*.
Ukrainian [juːˈkreɪnɪən] *adj* ukrainien(ne) ♦ *n*
Ukrainien/ne; (*LING*) ukrainien *m*.
ulcer [ˈʌlsə*] *n* ulcère *m*; **mouth** ~ aphte *f*.
Ulster [ˈʌlstə*] *n* Ulster *m*.
ulterior [ʌlˈtɪərɪə*] *adj* ultérieur(e); ~ **motive**
arrière-pensée *f*.
ultimate [ˈʌltɪmət] *adj* ultime, final(e);
(*authority*) suprême ♦ *n*: **the** ~ **in luxury** le
summum du luxe.
ultimately [ˈʌltɪmətlɪ] *adv* (*in the end*) en fin de
compte; (*at last*) finalement; (*eventually*) par

la suite.

ultimatum, pl ~**s** or **ultimata** [ʌltɪ'meɪtəm, -tə] n ultimatum m.

ultrasonic ['ʌltrə'sɔnɪk] adj ultrasonique.

ultrasound ['ʌltrəsaund] n (MED) ultrason m.

ultraviolet ['ʌltrə'vaɪəlɪt] adj ultraviolet(te).

umbilical [ʌmbɪ'laɪkl] adj: ~ **cord** cordon ombilical.

umbrage ['ʌmbrɪdʒ] n: **to take** ~ prendre ombrage, se froisser.

umbrella [ʌm'brɛlə] n parapluie m; (fig): **under the** ~ **of** sous les auspices de; chapeauté(e) par.

umlaut ['umlaut] n tréma m.

umpire ['ʌmpaɪə*] n arbitre m; (TENNIS) juge m de chaise ♦ vt arbitrer.

umpteen [ʌmp'tiːn] adj je ne sais combien de; **for the** ~**th time** pour la nième fois.

UMW n abbr (= United Mineworkers of America) syndicat des mineurs.

UN n abbr = **United Nations**.

unabashed [ʌnə'bæʃt] adj nullement intimidé(e).

unabated [ʌnə'beɪtɪd] adj non diminué(e).

unable [ʌn'eɪbl] adj: **to be** ~ **to** ne (pas) pouvoir, être dans l'impossibilité de; (not capable) être incapable de.

unabridged [ʌnə'brɪdʒd] adj complet(ète), intégral(e).

unacceptable [ʌnək'sɛptəbl] adj (behaviour) inadmissible; (price, proposal) inacceptable.

unaccompanied [ʌnə'kʌmpənɪd] adj (child, lady) non accompagné(e); (singing, song) sans accompagnement.

unaccountably [ʌnə'kauntəblɪ] adv inexplicablement.

unaccounted [ʌnə'kauntɪd] adj: **two passengers are** ~ **for** on est sans nouvelles de deux passagers.

unaccustomed [ʌnə'kʌstəmd] adj inaccoutumé(e), inhabituel(le); **to be** ~ **to sth** ne pas avoir l'habitude de qch.

unacquainted [ʌnə'kweɪntɪd] adj: **to be** ~ **with** ne pas connaître.

unadulterated [ʌnə'dʌltəreɪtɪd] adj pur(e), naturel(le).

unaffected [ʌnə'fɛktɪd] adj (person, behaviour) naturel(le); (emotionally): **to be** ~ **by** ne pas être touché(e) par.

unafraid [ʌnə'freɪd] adj: **to be** ~ ne pas avoir peur.

unaided [ʌn'eɪdɪd] adj sans aide, tout(e) seul(e).

unanimity [juːnə'nɪmɪtɪ] n unanimité f.

unanimous [juː'nænɪməs] adj unanime.

unanimously [juː'nænɪməslɪ] adv à l'unanimité.

unanswered [ʌn'ɑːnsəd] adj (question, letter) sans réponse.

unappetizing [ʌn'æpɪtaɪzɪŋ] adj peu appétissant(e).

unappreciative [ʌnə'priːʃɪətɪv] adj indif-

férent(e).

unarmed [ʌn'ɑːmd] adj (person) non armé(e); (combat) sans armes.

unashamed [ʌnə'ʃeɪmd] adj sans honte; impudent(e).

unassisted [ʌnə'sɪstɪd] adj non assisté(e) ♦ adv sans aide, tout(e) seul(e).

unassuming [ʌnə'sjuːmɪŋ] adj modeste, sans prétentions.

unattached [ʌnə'tætʃt] adj libre, sans attaches.

unattended [ʌnə'tɛndɪd] adj (car, child, luggage) sans surveillance.

unattractive [ʌnə'træktɪv] adj peu attrayant(e).

unauthorized [ʌn'ɔːθəraɪzd] adj non autorisé(e), sans autorisation.

unavailable [ʌnə'veɪləbl] adj (article, room, book) (qui n'est) pas disponible; (person) (qui n'est) pas libre.

unavoidable [ʌnə'vɔɪdəbl] adj inévitable.

unavoidably [ʌnə'vɔɪdəblɪ] adv inévitablement.

unaware [ʌnə'wɛə*] adj: **to be** ~ **of** ignorer, ne pas savoir, être inconscient(e) de.

unawares [ʌnə'wɛəz] adv à l'improviste, au dépourvu.

unbalanced [ʌn'bælənst] adj déséquilibré(e).

unbearable [ʌn'bɛərəbl] adj insupportable.

unbeatable [ʌn'biːtəbl] adj imbattable.

unbeaten [ʌn'biːtn] adj invaincu(e); (record) non battu(e).

unbecoming [ʌnbɪ'kʌmɪŋ] adj (unseemly: language, behaviour) malséant(e), inconvenant(e); (unflattering: garment) peu seyant(e).

unbeknown(st) [ʌnbɪ'nəun(st)] adv: ~ **to** à l'insu de.

unbelief [ʌnbɪ'liːf] n incrédulité f.

unbelievable [ʌnbɪ'liːvəbl] adj incroyable.

unbelievingly [ʌnbɪ'liːvɪŋlɪ] adv avec incrédulité.

unbend [ʌn'bend] vb (irreg) vi se détendre ♦ vt (wire) redresser, détordre.

unbending [ʌn'bendɪŋ] adj (fig) inflexible.

unbias(s)ed [ʌn'baɪəst] adj impartial(e).

unblemished [ʌn'blemɪʃt] adj impeccable.

unblock [ʌn'blɔk] vt (pipe) déboucher; (road) dégager.

unborn [ʌn'bɔːn] adj à naître.

unbounded [ʌn'baundɪd] adj sans bornes, illimité(e).

unbreakable [ʌn'breɪkəbl] adj incassable.

unbridled [ʌn'braɪdld] adj débridé(e), déchaîné(e).

unbroken [ʌn'brəukn] adj intact(e); (line) continu(e); (record) non battu(e).

unbuckle [ʌn'bʌkl] vt déboucler.

unburden [ʌn'bəːdn] vt: **to** ~ **o.s.** s'épancher, se livrer.

unbutton [ʌn'bʌtn] vt déboutonner.

uncalled-for [ʌn'kɔːldfɔː*] adj déplacé(e),

injustifié(e).

uncanny [ʌnˈkænɪ] *adj* étrange, troublant(e).

unceasing [ʌnˈsiːsɪŋ] *adj* incessant(e), continu(e).

unceremonious [ˌʌnserɪˈməʊnɪəs] *adj* (*abrupt, rude*) brusque.

uncertain [ʌnˈsəːtn] *adj* incertain(e); **we were ~ whether** ... nous ne savions pas vraiment si ...; **in no ~ terms** sans équivoque possible.

uncertainty [ʌnˈsəːtntɪ] *n* incertitude *f*, doutes *mpl*.

unchallenged [ʌnˈtʃælɪndʒd] *adj* (*gen*) incontesté(e); (*information*) non contesté(e); **to go ~** ne pas être contesté.

unchanged [ʌnˈtʃeɪndʒd] *adj* inchangé(e).

uncharitable [ʌnˈtʃærɪtəbl] *adj* peu charitable.

uncharted [ʌnˈtʃɑːtɪd] *adj* inexploré(e).

unchecked [ʌnˈtʃɛkt] *adj* non réprimé(e).

uncivilized [ʌnˈsɪvɪlaɪzd] *adj* non civilisé(e); (*fig*) barbare.

uncle [ˈʌŋkl] *n* oncle *m*.

unclear [ʌnˈklɪə*] *adj* (qui n'est) pas clair(e) *or* évident(e); **I'm still ~ about what I'm supposed to do** je ne sais pas encore exactement ce que je dois faire.

uncoil [ʌnˈkɔɪl] *vt* dérouler ♦ *vi* se dérouler.

uncomfortable [ʌnˈkʌmfətəbl] *adj* inconfortable; (*uneasy*) mal à l'aise, gêné(e); (*situation*) désagréable.

uncomfortably [ʌnˈkʌmfətəblɪ] *adv* inconfortablement; d'un ton *etc* gêné *or* embarrassé; désagréablement.

uncommitted [ˌʌnkəˈmɪtɪd] *adj* (*attitude, country*) non engagé(e).

uncommon [ʌnˈkɔmən] *adj* rare, singulier(ière), peu commun(e).

uncommunicative [ˌʌnkəˈmjuːnɪkətɪv] *adj* réservé(e).

uncomplicated [ʌnˈkɔmplɪkeɪtɪd] *adj* simple, peu compliqué(e).

uncompromising [ʌnˈkɔmprəmaɪzɪŋ] *adj* intransigeant(e), inflexible.

unconcerned [ˌʌnkənˈsəːnd] *adj* (*unworried*): **to be ~ (about)** ne pas s'inquiéter (de).

unconditional [ˌʌnkənˈdɪʃənl] *adj* sans conditions.

uncongenial [ˌʌnkənˈdʒiːnɪəl] *adj* peu agréable.

unconnected [ˌʌnkəˈnɛktɪd] *adj* (*unrelated*): **~ (with)** sans rapport (avec).

unconscious [ʌnˈkɔnʃəs] *adj* sans connaissance, évanoui(e); (*unaware*) inconscient(e) ♦ *n*: **the ~** l'inconscient *m*; **to knock sb ~** assommer qn.

unconsciously [ʌnˈkɔnʃəslɪ] *adv* inconsciemment.

unconstitutional [ˌʌnkɔnstɪˈtjuːʃənl] *adj* anticonstitutionnel(le).

uncontested [ˌʌnkənˈtɛstɪd] *adj* (*champion*) incontesté(e); (*POL: seat*) non disputé(e).

uncontrollable [ˌʌnkənˈtrəʊləbl] *adj* (*child, dog*) indiscipliné(e); (*emotion*) irrépressible.

uncontrolled [ˌʌnkənˈtrəʊld] *adj* (*laughter, price rises*) incontrôlé(e).

unconventional [ˌʌnkənˈvɛnʃənl] *adj* non conventionnel(le).

unconvinced [ˌʌnkənˈvɪnst] *adj*: **to be ~** ne pas être convaincu(e).

unconvincing [ˌʌnkənˈvɪnsɪŋ] *adj* peu convaincant(e).

uncork [ʌnˈkɔːk] *vt* déboucher.

uncorroborated [ˌʌnkəˈrɔbəreɪtɪd] *adj* non confirmé(e).

uncouth [ʌnˈkuːθ] *adj* grossier(ière), fruste.

uncover [ʌnˈkʌvə*] *vt* découvrir.

unctuous [ˈʌŋktjuəs] *adj* onctueux(euse), mielleux(euse).

undamaged [ʌnˈdæmɪdʒd] *adj* (*goods*) intact(e), en bon état; (*fig: reputation*) intact.

undaunted [ʌnˈdɔːntɪd] *adj* non intimidé(e), inébranlable.

undecided [ˌʌndɪˈsaɪdɪd] *adj* indécis(e), irrésolu(e).

undelivered [ˌʌndɪˈlɪvəd] *adj* non remis(e), non livré(e).

undeniable [ˌʌndɪˈnaɪəbl] *adj* indéniable, incontestable.

under [ˈʌndə*] *prep* sous; (*less than*) (de) moins de; au-dessous de; (*according to*) selon, en vertu de ♦ *adv* au-dessous; en dessous; **from ~ sth** de dessous *or* de sous qch; **~ there** là-dessous; **in ~ 2 hours** en moins de 2 heures; **~ anaesthetic** sous anesthésie; **~ discussion** en discussion; **~ the circumstances** étant donné les circonstances; **~ repair** en (cours de) réparation.

under... [ˈʌndə*] *prefix* sous-.

under-age [ˌʌndərˈeɪdʒ] *adj* qui n'a pas l'âge réglementaire.

underarm [ˈʌndərɑːm] *adv* par en-dessous ♦ *adj* (*throw*) par en-dessous; (*deodorant*) pour les aisselles.

undercapitalized [ˌʌndəˈkæpɪtəlaɪzd] *adj* sous-capitalisé(e).

undercarriage [ˈʌndəkærɪdʒ] *n* (*BRIT AVIAT*) train *m* d'atterrissage.

undercharge [ˌʌndəˈtʃɑːdʒ] *vt* ne pas faire payer assez à.

underclass [ˈʌndəklɑːs] *n* ≈ quart-monde *m*.

underclothes [ˈʌndəkləʊðz] *npl* sous-vêtements *mpl*; (*women's only*) dessous *mpl*.

undercoat [ˈʌndəkəʊt] *n* (*paint*) couche *f* de fond.

undercover [ˌʌndəˈkʌvə*] *adj* secret(ète), clandestin(e).

undercurrent [ˈʌndəkʌrnt] *n* courant sous-jacent.

undercut [ˌʌndəˈkʌt] *vt irreg* vendre moins cher que.

underdeveloped [ˈʌndədɪˈvɛləpt] *adj* sous-développé(e).

underdog [ˈʌndədɔg] *n* opprimé *m*.

underdone [ˌʌndəˈdʌn] *adj* (*food*) pas assez cuit(e).

underemployment [ˌʌndərɪm'plɔɪmənt] n sous-emploi m.

underestimate ['ʌndər'ɛstɪmeɪt] vt sous-estimer, mésestimer.

underexposed ['ʌndərɪks'pəuzd] adj (PHOT) sous-exposé(e).

underfed [ʌndə'fɛd] adj sous-alimenté(e).

underfoot [ʌndə'fut] adv sous les pieds.

under-funded ['ʌndə'fʌndɪd] adj: **to be ~** (organization) ne pas être doté(e) de fonds suffisants.

undergo [ʌndə'gəu] vt irreg subir; (treatment) suivre; **the car is ~ing repairs** la voiture est en réparation.

undergraduate [ʌndə'grædjuɪt] n étudiant/e (qui prépare la licence) ♦ cpd: **~ courses** cours mpl préparant à la licence.

underground ['ʌndəgraund] adj souterrain(e); (fig) clandestin(e) ♦ n (BRIT) métro m; (POL) clandestinité f.

undergrowth ['ʌndəgrəuθ] n broussailles fpl, sous-bois m.

underhand(ed) [ʌndə'hænd(ɪd)] adj (fig) sournois(e), en dessous.

underinsured [ʌndərɪn'ʃuəd] adj sous-assuré(e).

underlie [ʌndə'laɪ] vt irreg être à la base de; **the underlying cause** la cause sous-jacente.

underline [ʌndə'laɪn] vt souligner.

underling ['ʌndəlɪŋ] n (pej) sous-fifre m, subalterne m.

undermanning [ʌndə'mænɪŋ] n pénurie f de main-d'œuvre.

undermentioned [ʌndə'mɛnʃənd] adj mentionné(e) ci-dessous.

undermine [ʌndə'maɪn] vt saper, miner.

underneath [ʌndə'niːθ] adv (en) dessous ♦ prep sous, au-dessous de.

undernourished [ʌndə'nʌrɪʃt] adj sous-alimenté(e).

underpaid [ʌndə'peɪd] adj sous-payé(e).

underpants ['ʌndəpænts] npl caleçon m, slip m.

underpass ['ʌndəpaːs] n (BRIT) passage souterrain; (: on motorway) passage inférieur.

underpin [ʌndə'pɪn] vt (argument, case) étayer.

underplay [ʌndə'pleɪ] vt (BRIT) minimiser.

underpopulated [ʌndə'pɔpjuleɪtɪd] adj sous-peuplé(e).

underprice [ʌndə'praɪs] vt vendre à un prix trop bas.

underprivileged [ʌndə'prɪvɪlɪdʒd] adj défavorisé(e), déshérité(e).

underrate [ʌndə'reɪt] vt sous-estimer, mésestimer.

underscore [ʌndə'skɔː*] vt souligner.

underseal [ʌndə'siːl] vt (BRIT) traiter contre la rouille.

undersecretary ['ʌndə'sɛkrətrɪ] n sous-secrétaire m.

undersell [ʌndə'sɛl] vt (competitors) vendre

moins cher que.

undershirt ['ʌndəʃəːt] n (US) tricot m de corps.

undershorts ['ʌndəʃɔːts] npl (US) caleçon m, slip m.

underside ['ʌndəsaɪd] n dessous m.

undersigned ['ʌndə'saɪnd] adj, n soussigné(e) (m/f).

underskirt ['ʌndəskəːt] n (BRIT) jupon m.

understaffed [ʌndə'stɑːft] adj qui manque de personnel.

understand [ʌndə'stænd] vb (irreg: like **stand**) vt, vi comprendre; **I ~ that ...** je me suis laissé dire que ...; je crois comprendre que ...; **to make o.s. understood** se faire comprendre.

understandable [ʌndə'stændəbl] adj compréhensible.

understanding [ʌndə'stændɪŋ] adj compréhensif(ive) ♦ n compréhension f; (agreement) accord m; **to come to an ~ with sb** s'entendre avec qn; **on the ~ that ...** à condition que ....

understate [ʌndə'steɪt] vt minimiser.

understatement ['ʌndəsteɪtmənt] n: **that's an ~** c'est (bien) peu dire, le terme est faible.

understood [ʌndə'stud] pt, pp of **understand** ♦ adj entendu(e); (implied) sous-entendu(e).

understudy ['ʌndəstʌdɪ] n doublure f.

undertake [ʌndə'teɪk] vt irreg (job, task) entreprendre; (duty) se charger de; **to ~ to do sth** s'engager à faire qch.

undertaker ['ʌndəteɪkə*] n entrepreneur m des pompes funèbres, croque-mort m.

undertaking ['ʌndəteɪkɪŋ] n entreprise f; (promise) promesse f.

undertone ['ʌndətəun] n (low voice): **in an ~** à mi-voix; (of criticism etc) nuance cachée.

undervalue [ʌndə'væljuː] vt sous-estimer.

underwater [ʌndə'wɔːtə*] adv sous l'eau ♦ adj sous-marin(e).

underwear ['ʌndəwɛə*] n sous-vêtements mpl; (women's only) dessous mpl.

underweight [ʌndə'weɪt] adj d'un poids insuffisant; (person) (trop) maigre.

underworld ['ʌndəwəːld] n (of crime) milieu m, pègre f.

underwrite [ʌndə'raɪt] vt (FINANCE) garantir; (INSURANCE) souscrire.

underwriter ['ʌndəraɪtə*] n (INSURANCE) souscripteur m.

undeserving [ʌndɪ'zəːvɪŋ] adj: **to be ~ of** ne pas mériter.

undesirable [ʌndɪ'zaɪərəbl] adj peu souhaitable; indésirable.

undeveloped [ʌndɪ'vɛləpt] adj (land, resources) non exploité(e).

undies ['ʌndɪz] npl (col) dessous mpl, lingerie f.

undiluted ['ʌndaɪ'luːtɪd] adj pur(e), non dilué(e).

undiplomatic ['ʌndɪplə'mætɪk] adj peu diplomatique, maladroit(e).

undischarged ['ʌndɪs'tʃɑːdʒd] *adj*: ~ **bankrupt** failli/e non réhabilité(e).
undisciplined [ʌn'dɪsɪplɪnd] *adj* indiscipliné(e).
undisguised ['ʌndɪs'gaɪzd] *adj* (*dislike, amusement etc*) franc(franche).
undisputed ['ʌndɪs'pjuːtɪd] *adj* incontesté(e).
undistinguished ['ʌndɪs'tɪŋgwɪʃt] *adj* médiocre, quelconque.
undisturbed [ʌndɪs'tɜːbd] *adj* (*sleep*) tranquille, paisible; **to leave** ~ ne pas déranger.
undivided [ʌndɪ'vaɪdɪd] *adj*: **can I have your** ~ **attention?** puis-je avoir toute votre attention?
undo [ʌn'duː] *vt irreg* défaire.
undoing [ʌn'duːɪŋ] *n* ruine *f*, perte *f*.
undone [ʌn'dʌn] *pp of* **undo**; **to come** ~ se défaire.
undoubted [ʌn'daʊtɪd] *adj* indubitable, certain(e).
undoubtedly [ʌn'daʊtɪdlɪ] *adv* sans aucun doute.
undress [ʌn'drɛs] *vi* se déshabiller ♦ *vt* déshabiller.
undrinkable [ʌn'drɪŋkəbl] *adj* (*unpalatable*) imbuvable; (*poisonous*) non potable.
undue [ʌn'djuː] *adj* indu(e), excessif(ive).
undulating ['ʌndjuleɪtɪŋ] *adj* ondoyant(e), onduleux(euse).
unduly [ʌn'djuːlɪ] *adv* trop, excessivement.
undying [ʌn'daɪɪŋ] *adj* éternel(le).
unearned [ʌn'ɜːnd] *adj* (*praise, respect*) immérité(e); ~ **income** rentes *fpl*.
unearth [ʌn'ɜːθ] *vt* déterrer; (*fig*) dénicher.
unearthly [ʌn'ɜːθlɪ] *adj* surnaturel(le); (*hour*) indu(e), impossible.
uneasy [ʌn'iːzɪ] *adj* mal à l'aise, gêné(e); (*worried*) inquiet(ète); **to feel** ~ **about doing sth** se sentir mal à l'aise à l'idée de faire qch.
uneconomic(al) ['ʌniːkə'nɔmɪk(l)] *adj* peu économique; peu rentable.
uneducated [ʌn'ɛdjukeɪtɪd] *adj* sans éducation.
unemployed [ʌnɪm'plɔɪd] *adj* sans travail, au chômage ♦ *n*: **the** ~ les chômeurs *mpl*.
unemployment [ʌnɪm'plɔɪmənt] *n* chômage *m*.
unemployment benefit, (*US*) **unemployment compensation** *n* allocation *f* de chômage.
unending [ʌn'endɪŋ] *adj* interminable.
unenviable [ʌn'ɛnvɪəbl] *adj* peu enviable.
unequal [ʌn'iːkwəl] *adj* inégal(e).
unequalled, (*US*) **unequaled** [ʌn'iːkwəld] *adj* inégalé(e).
unequivocal [ʌnɪ'kwɪvəkl] *adj* (*answer*) sans équivoque; (*person*) catégorique.
unerring [ʌn'ɜːrɪŋ] *adj* infaillible, sûr(e).
UNESCO [juː'nɛskəʊ] *n abbr* (= *United Nations Educational, Scientific and Cultural*

Organization) UNESCO *f*.
unethical [ʌn'ɛθɪkl] *adj* (*methods*) immoral(e); (*doctor's behaviour*) qui ne respecte pas l'éthique.
uneven [ʌn'iːvn] *adj* inégal(e); irrégulier(ière).
uneventful [ʌnɪ'vɛntful] *adj* tranquille, sans histoires.
unexceptional [ʌnɪk'sɛpʃənl] *adj* banal(e), quelconque.
unexciting [ʌnɪk'saɪtɪŋ] *adj* pas passionnant(e).
unexpected [ʌnɪk'spɛktɪd] *adj* inattendu(e), imprévu(e).
unexpectedly [ʌnɪk'spɛktɪdlɪ] *adv* contre toute attente; (*arrive*) à l'improviste.
unexplained [ʌnɪk'spleɪnd] *adj* inexpliqué(e).
unexploded [ʌnɪk'spləʊdɪd] *adj* non explosé(e) *or* éclaté(e).
unfailing [ʌn'feɪlɪŋ] *adj* inépuisable; infaillible.
unfair [ʌn'fɛə*] *adj*: ~ **(to)** injuste (envers); **it'** ~ **that** ... il n'est pas juste que ....
unfair dismissal *n* licenciement abusif.
unfairly [ʌn'fɛəlɪ] *adv* injustement.
unfaithful [ʌn'feɪθful] *adj* infidèle.
unfamiliar [ʌnfə'mɪlɪə*] *adj* étrange, inconnu(e); **to be** ~ **with sth** mal connaître qch.
unfashionable [ʌn'fæʃnəbl] *adj* (*clothes*) démodé(e); (*district*) déshérité(e), pas à la mode.
unfasten [ʌn'fɑːsn] *vt* défaire; détacher.
unfathomable [ʌn'fæðəməbl] *adj* insondable.
unfavourable, (*US*) **unfavorable** [ʌn'feɪvrəbl] *adj* défavorable.
unfavo(u)rably [ʌn'feɪvrəblɪ] *adv*: **to look** ~ **upon** ne pas être favorable à.
unfeeling [ʌn'fiːlɪŋ] *adj* insensible, dur(e).
unfinished [ʌn'fɪnɪʃt] *adj* inachevé(e).
unfit [ʌn'fɪt] *adj* (*physically*) pas en forme; (*incompetent*): ~ **(for)** impropre (à); (*work, service*) inapte (à).
unflagging [ʌn'flægɪŋ] *adj* infatigable, inlassable.
unflappable [ʌn'flæpəbl] *adj* imperturbable.
unflattering [ʌn'flætərɪŋ] *adj* (*dress, hairstyle*) qui n'avantage pas; (*remark*) peu flatteur(euse).
unflinching [ʌn'flɪntʃɪŋ] *adj* stoïque.
unfold [ʌn'fəʊld] *vt* déplier; (*fig*) révéler, exposer ♦ *vi* se dérouler.
unforeseeable [ʌnfɔː'siːəbl] *adj* imprévisible
unforeseen ['ʌnfɔː'siːn] *adj* imprévu(e).
unforgettable [ʌnfə'gɛtəbl] *adj* inoubliable.
unforgivable [ʌnfə'gɪvəbl] *adj* impardonnable
unformatted [ʌn'fɔːmætɪd] *adj* (*disk, text*) non formaté(e).
unfortunate [ʌn'fɔːtʃnət] *adj* malheureux(euse); (*event, remark*) malencontreux(euse).
unfortunately [ʌn'fɔːtʃnətlɪ] *adv* malheureusement.

unfounded [ʌn'faundɪd] *adj* sans fondement.
unfriendly [ʌn'frɛndlɪ] *adj* froid(e), inamical(e).
unfulfilled [ʌnful'fɪld] *adj* (*ambition, prophecy*) non réalisé(e); (*desire*) insatisfait(e); (*promise*) non tenu(e); (*terms of contract*) non rempli(e); (*person*) qui n'a pas su se réaliser.
unfurl [ʌn'fəːl] *vt* déployer.
unfurnished [ʌn'fəːnɪʃt] *adj* non meublé(e).
ungainly [ʌn'geɪnlɪ] *adj* gauche, dégingandé(e).
ungodly [ʌn'gɔdlɪ] *adj* impie; **at an ~ hour** à une heure indue.
ungrateful [ʌn'greɪtful] *adj* qui manque de reconnaissance, ingrat(e).
unguarded [ʌn'gɑːdɪd] *adj*: ~ **moment** moment *m* d'inattention.
unhappily [ʌn'hæpɪlɪ] *adv* tristement; (*unfortunately*) malheureusement.
unhappiness [ʌn'hæpɪnɪs] *n* tristesse *f*, peine *f*.
unhappy [ʌn'hæpɪ] *adj* triste, malheureux(euse); (*unfortunate: remark etc*) malheureux(euse); (*not pleased*): ~ **with** mécontent(e) de, peu satisfait(e) de.
unharmed [ʌn'hɑːmd] *adj* indemne, sain(e) et sauf(sauve).
UNHCR *n abbr* (= *United Nations High Commission for Refugees*) HCR *m*.
unhealthy [ʌn'hɛlθɪ] *adj* (*gen*) malsain(e); (*person*) maladif(ive).
unheard-of [ʌn'həːdɔv] *adj* inouï(e), sans précédent.
unhelpful [ʌn'hɛlpful] *adj* (*person*) peu serviable; (*advice*) peu utile.
unhesitating [ʌn'hɛzɪteɪtɪŋ] *adj* (*loyalty*) spontané(e); (*reply, offer*) immédiat(e).
unholy [ʌn'həulɪ] *adj*: **an ~ alliance** une alliance contre nature; **he got home at an ~ hour** il est rentré à une heure impossible.
unhook [ʌn'huk] *vt* décrocher; dégrafer.
unhurt [ʌn'həːt] *adj* indemne, sain(e) et sauf(sauve).
unhygienic ['ʌnhaɪ'dʒiːnɪk] *adj* antihygiénique.
UNICEF ['juːnɪsɛf] *n abbr* (= *United Nations International Children's Emergency Fund*) UNICEF *m*, FISE *m*.
unicorn ['juːnɪkɔːn] *n* licorne *f*.
unidentified [ʌnaɪ'dɛntɪfaɪd] *adj* non identifié(e).
uniform ['juːnɪfɔːm] *n* uniforme *m* ♦ *adj* uniforme.
uniformity [juːnɪ'fɔːmɪtɪ] *n* uniformité *f*.
unify ['juːnɪfaɪ] *vt* unifier.
unilateral [juːnɪ'lætərəl] *adj* unilatéral(e).
unimaginable [ʌnɪ'mædʒɪnəbl] *adj* inimaginable, inconcevable.
unimaginative [ʌnɪ'mædʒɪnətɪv] *adj* sans imagination.
unimpaired [ʌnɪm'pɛəd] *adj* intact(e).

unimportant [ʌnɪm'pɔːtənt] *adj* sans importance.
unimpressed [ʌnɪm'prɛst] *adj* pas impressionné(e).
uninhabited [ʌnɪn'hæbɪtɪd] *adj* inhabité(e).
uninhibited [ʌnɪn'hɪbɪtɪd] *adj* sans inhibitions; sans retenue.
uninjured [ʌn'ɪndʒəd] *adj* indemne.
uninspiring [ʌnɪn'spaɪərɪŋ] *adj* peu inspirant(e).
unintelligent [ʌnɪn'tɛlɪdʒənt] *adj* inintelligent(e).
unintentional [ʌnɪn'tɛnʃənəl] *adj* involontaire.
unintentionally [ʌnɪn'tɛnʃnəlɪ] *adv* sans le vouloir.
uninvited [ʌnɪn'vaɪtɪd] *adj* (*guest*) qui n'a pas été invité(e).
uninviting [ʌnɪn'vaɪtɪŋ] *adj* (*place*) peu attirant(e); (*food*) peu appétissant(e).
union ['juːnjən] *n* union *f*; (*also: trade ~*) syndicat *m* ♦ *cpd* du syndicat, syndical(e).
unionize ['juːnjənaɪz] *vt* syndiquer.
Union Jack *n* drapeau du Royaume-Uni.
Union of Soviet Socialist Republics (USSR) *n* (*formerly*) Union *f* des républiques socialistes soviétiques (URSS).
union shop *n* entreprise où tous les travailleurs doivent être syndiqués.
unique [juː'niːk] *adj* unique.
unisex ['juːnɪsɛks] *adj* unisexe.
Unison ['juːnɪsn] *n* (*trade union*) grand syndicat des services publics en Grande-Bretagne.
unison ['juːnɪsn] *n*: **in ~** à l'unisson, en chœur.
unit ['juːnɪt] *n* unité *f*; (*section: of furniture etc*) élément *m*, bloc *m*; (*team, squad*) groupe *m*, service *m*; **production ~** atelier *m* de fabrication; **sink ~** bloc-évier *m*.
unit cost *n* coût *m* unitaire.
unite [juː'naɪt] *vt* unir ♦ *vi* s'unir.
united [juː'naɪtɪd] *adj* uni(e); unifié(e); (*efforts*) conjugué(e).
United Arab Emirates *npl* Émirats Arabes Unis.
United Kingdom (UK) *n* Royaume-Uni *m* (R.U.).
United Nations (Organization) (UN, UNO) *n* (Organisation *f* des) Nations unies (ONU).
United States (of America) (US, USA) *n* États-Unis *mpl*.
unit price *n* prix *m* unitaire.
unit trust *n* (*BRIT COMM*) fonds commun de placement, FCP *m*.
unity ['juːnɪtɪ] *n* unité *f*.
Univ. *abbr* = **university**.
universal [juːnɪ'vəːsl] *adj* universel(le).
universe ['juːnɪvəːs] *n* univers *m*.
university [juːnɪ'vəːsɪtɪ] *n* université *f* ♦ *cpd* (*student, professor*) d'université; (*education, year, degree*) universitaire.
unjust [ʌn'dʒʌst] *adj* injuste.

unjustifiable [ʌnˈdʒʌstɪˈfaɪəbl] *adj* injustifiable.

unjustified [ʌnˈdʒʌstɪfaɪd] *adj* injustifié(e); (*text*) non justifié(e).

unkempt [ʌnˈkɛmpt] *adj* mal tenu(e), débraillé(e); mal peigné(e).

unkind [ʌnˈkaɪnd] *adj* peu gentil(le), méchant(e).

unkindly [ʌnˈkaɪndlɪ] *adv* (*treat, speak*) avec méchanceté.

unknown [ʌnˈnəʊn] *adj* inconnu(e); ~ **to me** sans que je le sache; ~ **quantity** (*MATH, fig*) inconnue *f*.

unladen [ʌnˈleɪdn] *adj* (*ship, weight*) à vide.

unlawful [ʌnˈlɔːful] *adj* illégal(e).

unleaded [ʌnˈlɛdɪd] *n* (*also*: ~ **petrol**) essence *f* sans plomb.

unleash [ʌnˈliːʃ] *vt* détacher; (*fig*) déchaîner, déclencher.

unleavened [ʌnˈlɛvnd] *adj* sans levain.

unless [ʌnˈlɛs] *conj*: ~ **he leaves** à moins qu'il (ne) parte; ~ **we leave** à moins de partir, à moins que nous (ne) partions; ~ **otherwise stated** sauf indication contraire; ~ **I am mistaken** si je ne me trompe.

unlicensed [ʌnˈlaɪsnst] *adj* (*BRIT*) non patenté(e) pour la vente des spiritueux.

unlike [ʌnˈlaɪk] *adj* dissemblable, différent(e) ♦ *prep* à la différence de, contrairement à.

unlikelihood [ʌnˈlaɪklɪhud] *adj* improbabilité *f*.

unlikely [ʌnˈlaɪklɪ] *adj* (*result, event*) improbable; (*explanation*) invraisemblable.

unlimited [ʌnˈlɪmɪtɪd] *adj* illimité(e).

unlisted [ˈʌnˈlɪstɪd] *adj* (*US TEL*) sur la liste rouge; (*STOCK EXCHANGE*) non coté(e) en Bourse.

unlit [ʌnˈlɪt] *adj* (*room*) non éclairé(e).

unload [ʌnˈləʊd] *vt* décharger.

unlock [ʌnˈlɔk] *vt* ouvrir.

unlucky [ʌnˈlʌkɪ] *adj* malchanceux(euse); (*object, number*) qui porte malheur; **to be** ~ (*person*) ne pas avoir de chance.

unmanageable [ʌnˈmænɪdʒəbl] *adj* (*unwieldy: tool, vehicle*) peu maniable; (: *situation*) inextricable.

unmanned [ʌnˈmænd] *adj* sans équipage.

unmannerly [ʌnˈmænəlɪ] *adj* mal élevé(e), impoli(e).

unmarked [ʌnˈmɑːkt] *adj* (*unstained*) sans marque; ~ **police car** voiture de police banalisée.

unmarried [ʌnˈmærɪd] *adj* célibataire.

unmask [ʌnˈmɑːsk] *vt* démasquer.

unmatched [ʌnˈmætʃt] *adj* sans égal(e).

unmentionable [ʌnˈmɛnʃnəbl] *adj* (*topic*) dont on ne parle pas; (*word*) qui ne se dit pas.

unmerciful [ʌnˈmɜːsɪful] *adj* sans pitié.

unmistakable [ʌnmɪsˈteɪkəbl] *adj* indubitable; qu'on ne peut pas ne pas reconnaître.

unmitigated [ʌnˈmɪtɪgeɪtɪd] *adj* non mitigé(e), absolu(e), pur(e).

unnamed [ʌnˈneɪmd] *adj* (*nameless*) sans nom; (*anonymous*) anonyme.

unnatural [ʌnˈnætʃrəl] *adj* non naturel(le); contre nature.

unnecessary [ʌnˈnɛsəsərɪ] *adj* inutile, superflu(e).

unnerve [ʌnˈnəːv] *vt* faire perdre son sang-froid à.

unnoticed [ʌnˈnəʊtɪst] *adj* inaperçu(e); **to go** ~ passer inaperçu.

UNO [ˈjuːnəʊ] *n abbr* = **United Nations Organization**.

unobservant [ʌnəbˈzəːvnt] *adj* pas observateur(trice).

unobtainable [ʌnəbˈteɪnəbl] *adj* (*TEL*) impossible à obtenir.

unobtrusive [ʌnəbˈtruːsɪv] *adj* discret(ète).

unoccupied [ʌnˈɔkjupaɪd] *adj* (*seat, table, also MIL*) libre; (*house*) inoccupé(e).

unofficial [ʌnəˈfɪʃl] *adj* non officiel(le); (*strike*) ≈ non sanctionné(e) par la centrale.

unopposed [ʌnəˈpəʊzd] *adj* sans opposition.

unorthodox [ʌnˈɔːθədɔks] *adj* peu orthodoxe.

unpack [ʌnˈpæk] *vi* défaire sa valise, déballer ses affaires.

unpaid [ʌnˈpeɪd] *adj* (*bill*) impayé(e); (*holiday*) non-payé(e), sans salaire; (*work*) non rétribué(e); (*worker*) bénévole.

unpalatable [ʌnˈpælətəbl] *adj* (*truth*) désagréable (à entendre).

unparalleled [ʌnˈpærəlɛld] *adj* incomparable, sans égal.

unpatriotic [ˈʌnpætrɪˈɔtɪk] *adj* (*person*) manquant de patriotisme; (*speech, attitude*) antipatriotique.

unplanned [ʌnˈplænd] *adj* (*visit*) imprévu(e); (*baby*) non prévu(e).

unpleasant [ʌnˈplɛznt] *adj* déplaisant(e), désagréable.

unplug [ʌnˈplʌg] *vt* débrancher.

unpolluted [ʌnpəˈluːtɪd] *adj* non pollué(e).

unpopular [ʌnˈpɔpjulə*] *adj* impopulaire; **to make o.s.** ~ (**with**) se rendre impopulaire (auprès de).

unprecedented [ʌnˈprɛsɪdəntɪd] *adj* sans précédent.

unpredictable [ʌnprɪˈdɪktəbl] *adj* imprévisible.

unprejudiced [ʌnˈprɛdʒudɪst] *adj* (*not biased*) impartial(e); (*having no prejudices*) qui n'a pas de préjugés.

unprepared [ʌnprɪˈpɛəd] *adj* (*person*) qui n'est pas suffisamment préparé(e); (*speech*) improvisé(e).

unprepossessing [ˈʌnpriːpəˈzɛsɪŋ] *adj* peu avenant(e).

unpretentious [ʌnprɪˈtɛnʃəs] *adj* sans prétention(s).

unprincipled [ʌnˈprɪnsɪpld] *adj* sans principes.

unproductive [ʌnprəˈdʌktɪv] *adj* improductif(ive); (*discussion*) stérile.

unprofessional [ʌnprəˈfɛʃənl] *adj* (*conduct*) contraire à la déontologie.

unprofitable [ʌn'prɔfɪtəbl] *adj* non rentable.

UNPROFOR [ʌn'prəʊfɔː*] *n abbr* (= *United Nations Protection Force*) FORPRONU *f*.

unprotected ['ʌnprə'tɛktɪd] *adj* (*sex*) non protégé(e).

unprovoked [ʌnprə'vəʊkt] *adj* (*attack*) sans provocation.

unpunished [ʌn'pʌnɪʃt] *adj* impuni(e); **to go ~** rester impuni.

unqualified [ʌn'kwɔlɪfaɪd] *adj* (*teacher*) non diplômé(e), sans titres; (*success*) sans réserve, total(e).

unquestionably [ʌn'kwɛstʃənəblɪ] *adv* incontestablement.

unquestioning [ʌn'kwɛstʃənɪŋ] *adj* (*obedience, acceptance*) inconditionnel(le).

unravel [ʌn'rævl] *vt* démêler.

unreal [ʌn'rɪəl] *adj* irréel(le).

unrealistic ['ʌnrɪə'lɪstɪk] *adj* (*idea*) irréaliste; (*estimate*) peu réaliste.

unreasonable [ʌn'riːznəbl] *adj* qui n'est pas raisonnable; **to make ~ demands on sb** exiger trop de qn.

unrecognizable [ʌn'rɛkəgnaɪzəbl] *adj* pas reconnaissable.

unrecognized [ʌn'rɛkəgnaɪzd] *adj* (*talent, genius*) méconnu(e); (*POL: régime*) non reconnu(e).

unrecorded [ʌnrɪ'kɔːdɪd] *adj* non enregistré(e).

unrefined [ʌnrɪ'faɪnd] *adj* (*sugar, petroleum*) non raffiné(e).

unrehearsed [ʌnrɪ'həːst] *adj* (*THEAT etc*) qui n'a pas été répété(e); (*spontaneous*) spontané(e).

unrelated [ʌnrɪ'leɪtɪd] *adj* sans rapport; sans lien de parenté.

unrelenting [ʌnrɪ'lɛntɪŋ] *adj* implacable; acharné(e).

unreliable [ʌnrɪ'laɪəbl] *adj* sur qui (*or* quoi) on ne peut pas compter, peu fiable.

unrelieved [ʌnrɪ'liːvd] *adj* (*monotony*) constant(e), uniforme.

unremitting [ʌnrɪ'mɪtɪŋ] *adj* inlassable, infatigable, acharné(e).

unrepeatable [ʌnrɪ'piːtəbl] *adj* (*offer*) unique, exceptionnel(le).

unrepentant [ʌnrɪ'pɛntənt] *adj* impénitent(e).

unrepresentative ['ʌnrɛprɪ'zɛntətɪv] *adj*: **~ (of)** peu représentatif(ive) (de).

unreserved [ʌnrɪ'zəːvd] *adj* (*seat*) non réservé(e); (*approval, admiration*) sans réserve.

unresponsive [ʌnrɪs'pɔnsɪv] *adj* insensible.

unrest [ʌn'rɛst] *n* agitation *f*, troubles *mpl*.

unrestricted [ʌnrɪ'strɪktɪd] *adj* illimité(e); **to have ~ access to** avoir librement accès *or* accès en tout temps à.

unrewarded [ʌnrɪ'wɔːdɪd] *adj* pas récompensé(e).

unripe [ʌn'raɪp] *adj* pas mûr(e).

unrivalled, (*US*) **unrivaled** [ʌn'raɪvəld] *adj* sans égal, incomparable.

unroll [ʌn'rəʊl] *vt* dérouler.

unruffled [ʌn'rʌfld] *adj* (*person*) imperturbable; (*hair*) qui n'est pas ébouriffé(e).

unruly [ʌn'ruːlɪ] *adj* indiscipliné(e).

unsafe [ʌn'seɪf] *adj* (*machine, wiring*) dangereux(euse); (*method*) hasardeux(euse); **~ to drink/eat** non potable/comestible.

unsaid [ʌn'sɛd] *adj*: **to leave sth ~** passer qch sous silence.

unsaleable, (*US*) **unsalable** [ʌn'seɪləbl] *adj* invendable.

unsatisfactory ['ʌnsætɪs'fæktərɪ] *adj* qui laisse à désirer.

unsavoury, (*US*) **unsavory** [ʌn'seɪvərɪ] *adj* (*fig*) peu recommandable, répugnant(e).

unscathed [ʌn'skeɪðd] *adj* indemne.

unscientific ['ʌnsaɪən'tɪfɪk] *adj* non scientifique.

unscrew [ʌn'skruː] *vt* dévisser.

unscrupulous [ʌn'skruːpjuləs] *adj* sans scrupules.

unseat [ʌn'siːt] *vt* (*rider*) désarçonner; (*fig: official*) faire perdre son siège à.

unsecured ['ʌnsɪ'kjuəd] *adj*: **~ creditor** créancier/ière sans garantie.

unseeded [ʌn'siːdɪd] *adj* (*SPORT*) non classé(e).

unseemly [ʌn'siːmlɪ] *adj* inconvenant(e).

unseen [ʌn'siːn] *adj* (*person*) invisible; (*danger*) imprévu(e).

unselfish [ʌn'sɛlfɪʃ] *adj* désintéressé(e).

unsettled [ʌn'sɛtld] *adj* (*restless*) perturbé(e); (*unpredictable*) instable; incertain(e); (*not finalized*) non résolu(e).

unsettling [ʌn'sɛtlɪŋ] *adj* qui a un effet perturbateur.

unshak(e)able [ʌn'ʃeɪkəbl] *adj* inébranlable.

unshaven [ʌn'ʃeɪvn] *adj* non *or* mal rasé(e).

unsightly [ʌn'saɪtlɪ] *adj* disgracieux(euse), laid(e).

unskilled [ʌn'skɪld] *adj*: **~ worker** manœuvre *m*.

unsociable [ʌn'səʊʃəbl] *adj* (*person*) peu sociable; (*behaviour*) qui manque de sociabilité.

unsocial [ʌn'səʊʃl] *adj* (*hours*) en dehors de l'horaire normal.

unsold [ʌn'səʊld] *adj* invendu(e), non vendu(e).

unsolicited [ʌnsə'lɪsɪtɪd] *adj* non sollicité(e).

unsophisticated [ʌnsə'fɪstɪkeɪtɪd] *adj* simple, naturel(le).

unsound [ʌn'saʊnd] *adj* (*health*) chancelant(e); (*floor, foundations*) peu solide; (*policy, advice*) peu judicieux(euse).

unspeakable [ʌn'spiːkəbl] *adj* indicible; (*awful*) innommable.

unspoken [ʌn'spəʊkn] *adj* (*word*) qui n'est pas prononcé(e); (*agreement, approval*) tacite.

unsteady [ʌn'stɛdɪ] *adj* mal assuré(e), chancelant(e), instable.
unstinting [ʌn'stɪntɪŋ] *adj* (*support*) total(e), sans réserve; (*generosity*) sans limites.
unstuck [ʌn'stʌk] *adj*: **to come** ~ se décoller; (*fig*) faire fiasco.
unsubstantiated ['ʌnsəb'stænʃɪeɪtɪd] *adj* (*rumour*) qui n'est pas confirmé(e); (*accusation*) sans preuve.
unsuccessful [ʌnsək'sɛsful] *adj* (*attempt*) infructueux(euse); (*writer, proposal*) qui n'a pas de succès; (*marriage*) malheureux(euse), qui ne réussit pas; **to be** ~ (*in attempting sth*) ne pas réussir; ne pas avoir de succès; (*application*) ne pas être retenu(e).
unsuccessfully [ʌnsək'sɛsfəlɪ] *adv* en vain.
unsuitable [ʌn'su:təbl] *adj* qui ne convient pas, peu approprié(e); inopportun(e).
unsuited [ʌn'su:tɪd] *adj*: **to be** ~ **for** *or* **to** être inapte *or* impropre à.
unsung ['ʌnsʌŋ] *adj*: **an** ~ **hero** un héros méconnu.
unsupported [ʌnsə'pɔ:tɪd] *adj* (*claim*) non soutenu(e); (*theory*) qui n'est pas corroboré(e).
unsure [ʌn'ʃuə*] *adj* pas sûr(e); **to be** ~ **of o.s.** ne pas être sûr de soi, manquer de confiance en soi.
unsuspecting [ʌnsə'spɛktɪŋ] *adj* qui ne se méfie pas.
unsweetened [ʌn'swi:tnd] *adj* non sucré(e).
unswerving [ʌn'swə:vɪŋ] *adj* inébranlable.
unsympathetic ['ʌnsɪmpə'θɛtɪk] *adj* hostile; (*unpleasant*) antipathique; ~ **to** indifférent(e) à.
untangle [ʌn'tæŋgl] *vt* démêler, débrouiller.
untapped [ʌn'tæpt] *adj* (*resources*) inexploité(e).
untaxed [ʌn'tækst] *adj* (*goods*) non taxé(e); (*income*) non imposé(e).
unthinkable [ʌn'θɪŋkəbl] *adj* impensable, inconcevable.
unthinkingly [ʌn'θɪŋkɪŋlɪ] *adv* sans réfléchir.
untidy [ʌn'taɪdɪ] *adj* (*room*) en désordre; (*appearance*) désordonné(e), débraillé(e); (*person*) sans ordre, désordonné; débraillé; (*work*) peu soigné(e).
untie [ʌn'taɪ] *vt* (*knot, parcel*) défaire; (*prisoner, dog*) détacher.
until [ən'tɪl] *prep* jusqu'à; (*after negative*) avant ♦ *conj* jusqu'à ce que + *sub*, en attendant que + *sub*; (*in past, after negative*) avant que + *sub*; ~ **now** jusqu'à présent, jusqu'ici; ~ **then** jusque-là; **from morning** ~ **night** du matin au soir *or* jusqu'au soir.
untimely [ʌn'taɪmlɪ] *adj* inopportun(e); (*death*) prématuré(e).
untold [ʌn'təuld] *adj* incalculable; indescriptible.
untouched [ʌn'tʌtʃt] *adj* (*not used etc*) tel(le) quel(le), intact(e); (*safe: person*) indemne; (*unaffected*): ~ **by** indifférent(e) à.

untoward [ʌntə'wɔ:d] *adj* fâcheux(euse), malencontreux(euse).
untrained ['ʌn'treɪnd] *adj* (*worker*) sans formation; (*troops*) sans entraînement; **to the** ~ **eye** à l'œil non exercé.
untrammelled [ʌn'træmld] *adj* sans entraves.
untranslatable [ʌntrænz'leɪtəbl] *adj* intraduisible.
untrue [ʌn'tru:] *adj* (*statement*) faux(fausse).
untrustworthy [ʌn'trʌstwə:ðɪ] *adj* (*person*) pas digne de confiance, peu sûr(e).
unusable [ʌn'ju:zəbl] *adj* inutilisable.
unused *adj* [ʌn'ju:zd] (*new*) neuf(neuve); [ʌn'ju:st]: **to be** ~ **to sth/to doing sth** ne pas avoir l'habitude de qch/de faire qch.
unusual [ʌn'ju:ʒuəl] *adj* insolite, exceptionnel(le), rare.
unusually [ʌn'ju:ʒuəlɪ] *adv* exceptionnelle-ment, particulièrement.
unveil [ʌn'veɪl] *vt* dévoiler.
unwanted [ʌn'wɔntɪd] *adj* non désiré(e).
unwarranted [ʌn'wɔrəntɪd] *adj* injustifié(e).
unwary [ʌn'wɛərɪ] *adj* imprudent(e).
unwavering [ʌn'weɪvərɪŋ] *adj* inébranlable.
unwelcome [ʌn'wɛlkəm] *adj* importun(e); **to feel** ~ se sentir de trop.
unwell [ʌn'wɛl] *adj* indisposé(e), souffrant(e); **to feel** ~ ne pas se sentir bien.
unwieldy [ʌn'wi:ldɪ] *adj* difficile à manier.
unwilling [ʌn'wɪlɪŋ] *adj*: **to be** ~ **to do** ne pas vouloir faire.
unwillingly [ʌn'wɪlɪŋlɪ] *adv* à contrecœur, contre son gré.
unwind [ʌn'waɪnd] *vb* (*irreg*) *vt* dérouler ♦ *vi* (*relax*) se détendre.
unwise [ʌn'waɪz] *adj* imprudent(e), peu judicieux(euse).
unwitting [ʌn'wɪtɪŋ] *adj* involontaire.
unworkable [ʌn'wə:kəbl] *adj* (*plan etc*) inexploitable.
unworthy [ʌn'wə:ðɪ] *adj* indigne.
unwrap [ʌn'ræp] *vt* défaire; ouvrir.
unwritten [ʌn'rɪtn] *adj* (*agreement*) tacite.
unzip [ʌn'zɪp] *vt* ouvrir (la fermeture éclair de).

================================ *KEYWORD*

up [ʌp] *prep*: **he went** ~ **the stairs/the hill** il a monté l'escalier/la colline; **the cat was** ~ **a tree** le chat était dans un arbre; **they live further** ~ **the street** ils habitent plus haut dans la rue
♦ *vi* (*col*): **she** ~**ped and left** elle a fichu le camp sans plus attendre
♦ *adv* **1** en haut; en l'air; (*upwards, higher*): ~ **in the sky/the mountains** (là-haut) dans le ciel/les montagnes; **put it a bit higher** ~ mettez-le un peu plus haut; ~ **there** là-haut; ~ **above** au-dessus; **"this side** ~**"** "haut"
2: **to be** ~ (*out of bed*) être levé(e); (*prices*) avoir augmenté *or* monté; (*finished*): **when the year was** ~ à la fin de l'année; **time's** ~

c'est l'heure
3: ~ **to** (as far as) jusqu'à; ~ **to now** jusqu'à présent
4: **to be** ~ **to** (depending on): **it's** ~ **to you** c'est à vous de décider; (equal to): **he's not** ~ **to it** (job, task etc) il n'en est pas capable; (inf: be doing): **what is he** ~ **to?** qu'est-ce qu'il peut bien faire?
5 (phrases): **he's well** ~ **in** or **on** ... (BRIT: knowledgeable) il s'y connaît en ...; ~ **with Leeds United!** vive Leeds United!; **what's** ~**?** (col) qu'est-ce qui ne va pas?; **what's** ~ **with him?** (col) qu'est-ce qui lui arrive?
♦ n: ~**s and downs** hauts et bas mpl.

up-and-coming [ʌpənd'kʌmɪŋ] adj plein(e) d'avenir or de promesses.
upbeat ['ʌpbiːt] n (MUS) levé m; (in economy, prosperity) amélioration f ♦ adj (optimistic) optimiste.
upbraid [ʌp'breɪd] vt morigéner.
upbringing ['ʌpbrɪŋɪŋ] n éducation f.
upcoming ['ʌpkʌmɪŋ] adj tout(e) prochain(e).
update [ʌp'deɪt] vt mettre à jour.
upend [ʌp'ɛnd] vt mettre debout.
up-front [ʌp'frʌnt] adj franc(franche) ♦ adv (pay) d'avance.
upgrade [ʌp'greɪd] vt (person) promouvoir; (job) revaloriser; (property, equipment) moderniser.
upheaval [ʌp'hiːvl] n bouleversement m; branle-bas m; crise f.
uphill [ʌp'hɪl] adj qui monte; (fig: task) difficile, pénible ♦ adv (face, look) en amont, vers l'amont; (go, move) vers le haut, en haut; **to go** ~ monter.
uphold [ʌp'həuld] vt irreg maintenir; soutenir.
upholstery [ʌp'həulstərɪ] n rembourrage m; (of car) garniture f.
upkeep ['ʌpkiːp] n entretien m.
up-market [ʌp'mɑːkɪt] adj (product) haut de gamme inv.
upon [ə'pɔn] prep sur.
upper ['ʌpə*] adj supérieur(e); du dessus ♦ n (of shoe) empeigne f.
upper class n: **the** ~ ≈ la haute bourgeoisie ♦ adj: **upper-class** (district) élégant(e), huppé(e); (accent, attitude) caractéristique des classes supérieures.
uppercut ['ʌpəkʌt] n uppercut m.
upper hand n: **to have the** ~ avoir le dessus.
Upper House n: **the** ~ (in Britain) la Chambre des Lords, la Chambre haute; (in France, in the US etc) le Sénat.
uppermost ['ʌpəməust] adj le(la) plus haut(e); en dessus; **it was** ~ **in my mind** j'y pensais avant tout autre chose.
Upper Volta [-'vɔltə] n Haute Volta f.
upright ['ʌpraɪt] adj droit(e); vertical(e); (fig) droit, honnête ♦ n montant m.
uprising ['ʌpraɪzɪŋ] n soulèvement m, insurrection f.

uproar ['ʌprɔː*] n tumulte m, vacarme m.
uproarious [ʌp'rɔːrɪəs] adj (event etc) désopilant(e); ~ **laughter** un brouhaha de rires.
uproot [ʌp'ruːt] vt déraciner.
upset n ['ʌpsɛt] dérangement m ♦ vt [ʌp'sɛt] (irreg: like set) (glass etc) renverser; (plan) déranger; (person: offend) contrarier; (: grieve) faire de la peine à; bouleverser ♦ adj [ʌp'sɛt] contrarié(e); peiné(e); (stomach) détraqué(e), dérangé(e); **to get** ~ (sad) devenir triste; (offended) se vexer; **to have a stomach** ~ (BRIT) avoir une indigestion.
upset price n (US, Scottish) mise f à prix, prix m de départ.
upsetting [ʌp'sɛtɪŋ] adj (offending) vexant(e); (annoying) ennuyeux(euse).
upshot ['ʌpʃɔt] n résultat m; **the** ~ **of it all was that** ... il a résulté de tout cela que ....
upside down ['ʌpsaɪd-] adv à l'envers.
upstage ['ʌp'steɪdʒ] vt: **to** ~ **sb** souffler la vedette à qn.
upstairs [ʌp'stɛəz] adv en haut ♦ adj (room) du dessus, d'en haut ♦ n: **there's no** ~ il n'y a pas d'étage.
upstart ['ʌpstɑːt] n parvenu/e.
upstream [ʌp'striːm] adv en amont.
upsurge ['ʌpsəːdʒ] n (of enthusiasm etc) vague f.
uptake ['ʌpteɪk] n: **he is quick/slow on the** ~ il comprend vite/est lent à comprendre.
uptight [ʌp'taɪt] adj (col) très tendu(e), crispé(e).
up-to-date ['ʌptə'deɪt] adj moderne; très récent(e).
upturn ['ʌptəːn] n (in economy) reprise f.
upturned ['ʌptəːnd] adj (nose) retroussé(e).
upward ['ʌpwəd] adj ascendant(e); vers le haut ♦ adv see **upwards**.
upwardly-mobile ['ʌpwədlɪ'məubaɪl] adj à mobilité sociale ascendante.
upwards ['ʌpwədz] adv vers le haut; **and** ~ et plus, et au-dessus.
URA n abbr (US) = **Urban Renewal Administration**.
Ural Mountains ['juərəl-] npl: **the** ~ (also: **the Urals**) les monts mpl Oural, l'Oural m.
uranium [juə'reɪnɪəm] n uranium m.
Uranus [juə'reɪnəs] n Uranus f.
urban ['əːbən] adj urbain(e).
urbane [əː'beɪn] adj urbain(e), courtois(e).
urbanization [əːbənaɪ'zeɪʃən] n urbanisation f.
urchin ['əːtʃɪn] n gosse m, garnement m.
Urdu ['uəduː] n ourdou m.
urge [əːdʒ] n besoin (impératif), envie (pressante) ♦ vt (caution etc) recommander avec insistance; (person): **to** ~ **sb to do** presser qn de faire, recommander avec insistance à qn de faire.
▶**urge on** vt pousser, presser.
urgency ['əːdʒənsɪ] n urgence f; (of tone) insistance f.

urgent ['ə:dʒənt] *adj* urgent(e); (*plea, tone*) pressant(e).

urgently ['ə:dʒəntlɪ] *adv* d'urgence, de toute urgence; (*need*) sans délai.

urinal ['juərɪnl] *n* (*BRIT*) urinoir *m*.

urinate ['juərɪneɪt] *vi* uriner.

urine ['juərɪn] *n* urine *f*.

urn [ə:n] *n* urne *f*; (*also:* **tea ~**) fontaine *f* à thé.

Uruguay ['juərəgwaɪ] *n* Uruguay *m*.

Uruguayan [juərə'gwaɪən] *adj* uruguayen(ne) ♦ *n* Uruguayen/ne.

US *n abbr* = **United States**.

us [ʌs] *pron* nous.

USA *n abbr* = **United States of America**; (*MIL*) = United States Army.

usable ['ju:zəbl] *adj* utilisable.

USAF *n abbr* = United States Air Force.

usage ['ju:zɪdʒ] *n* usage *m*.

USCG *n abbr* = United States Coast Guard.

USDA *n abbr* = United States Department of Agriculture.

USDAW ['ʌzdɔ:] *n abbr* (*BRIT*: = Union of Shop, Distributive and Allied Workers*) syndicat du commerce de détail et de la distribution.

USDI *n abbr* = United States Department of the Interior.

use *n* [ju:s] emploi *m*, utilisation *f*; usage *m* ♦ *vt* [ju:z] se servir de, utiliser, employer; **in ~** en usage; **out of ~** hors d'usage; **to be of ~** servir, être utile; **to make ~ of sth** utiliser qch; **ready for ~** prêt à l'emploi; **it's no ~** ça ne sert à rien; **to have the ~ of** avoir l'usage de; **what's this ~d for?** à quoi est-ce que ça sert?; **she ~d to do it** elle le faisait (autrefois), elle avait coutume de le faire; **to be ~d to** avoir l'habitude de, être habitué(e) à; **to get ~d to** s'habituer à.

▶**use up** *vt* finir, épuiser; (*food*) consommer.

used [ju:zd] *adj* (*car*) d'occasion.

useful ['ju:sful] *adj* utile; **to come in ~** être utile.

usefulness ['ju:sfəlnɪs] *n* utilité *f*.

useless ['ju:slɪs] *adj* inutile.

user ['ju:zə*] *n* utilisateur/trice, usager *m*.

user-friendly ['ju:zə'frɛndlɪ] *adj* convivial(e), facile d'emploi.

USES *n abbr* = United States Employment Service.

usher ['ʌʃə*] *n* placeur *m* ♦ *vt:* **to ~ sb in** faire entrer qn.

usherette [ʌʃə'rɛt] *n* (*in cinema*) ouvreuse *f*.

USIA *n abbr* = United States Information Agency.

USM *n abbr* = United States Mail, United States Mint.

USN *n abbr* = United States Navy.

USPHS *n abbr* = United States Public Health Service.

USPO *n abbr* = United States Post Office.

USS *abbr* = United States Ship (*or* Steamer).

USSR *n abbr* = **Union of Soviet Socialist Republics**.

usu. *abbr* = **usually**.

usual ['ju:ʒuəl] *adj* habituel(le); **as ~** comme d'habitude.

usually ['ju:ʒuəlɪ] *adv* d'habitude, d'ordinaire.

usurer ['ju:ʒərə*] *n* usurier/ière.

usurp [ju:'zə:p] *vt* usurper.

UT *abbr* (*US*) = Utah.

utensil [ju:'tɛnsl] *n* ustensile *m*; **kitchen ~s** batterie *f* de cuisine.

uterus ['ju:tərəs] *n* utérus *m*.

utilitarian [ju:tɪlɪ'tɛərɪən] *adj* utilitaire.

utility [ju:'tɪlɪtɪ] *n* utilité *f*; (*also:* **public ~**) service public.

utility room *n* buanderie *f*.

utilization [ju:tɪlaɪ'zeɪʃən] *n* utilisation *f*.

utilize ['ju:tɪlaɪz] *vt* utiliser; exploiter.

utmost ['ʌtməust] *adj* extrême, le(la) plus grand(e) ♦ *n:* **to do one's ~** faire tout son possible; **of the ~ importance** d'une importance capitale, de la plus haute importance.

utter ['ʌtə*] *adj* total(e), complet(ète) ♦ *vt* prononcer, proférer; émettre.

utterance ['ʌtrns] *n* paroles *fpl*.

utterly ['ʌtəlɪ] *adv* complètement, totalement.

U-turn ['ju:'tə:n] *n* demi-tour *m*; (*fig*) volte-face *f inv*.

Uzbekistan [ʌzbɛkɪ'stɑ:n] *n* Ouzbékistan *m*.

V v

V, v [vi:] *n* (*letter*) V, v *m*; **V for Victor** V comme Victor.

v *abbr* (= *verse*, = *vide: see*) v.; (= *versus*) c.; (= *volt*) V.

VA, Va. *abbr* (*US*) = Virginia.

vac [væk] *n abbr* (*BRIT col*) = **vacation**.

vacancy ['veɪkənsɪ] *n* (*BRIT: job*) poste vacant; (*room*) chambre *f* disponible; **"no vacancies"** "complet".

vacant ['veɪkənt] *adj* (*post*) vacant(e); (*seat etc*) libre, disponible; (*expression*) distrait(e).

vacant lot *n* terrain inoccupé; (*for sale*) terrain à vendre.

vacate [və'keɪt] *vt* quitter.

vacation [və'keɪʃən] *n* (*esp US*) vacances *fpl*; **to take a ~** prendre des vacances; **on ~** en vacances.

vacation course *n* cours *mpl* de vacances.

vaccinate ['væksɪneɪt] *vt* vacciner.

vaccination [væksɪ'neɪʃən] *n* vaccination *f*.

vaccine ['væksi:n] *n* vaccin *m*.

vacuum ['vækjum] *n* vide *m*.

vacuum bottle *n* (*US*) = **vacuum flask**.

vacuum cleaner *n* aspirateur *m*.

vacuum flask *n* (*BRIT*) bouteille *f* thermos ®.

vacuum-packed ['vækjumpækt] *adj* emballé(e) sous vide.

vagabond ['vægəbɒnd] *n* vagabond/e; (*tramp*) chemineau *m*, clochard/e.

vagary ['veɪgərɪ] *n* caprice *m*.

vagina [və'dʒaɪnə] *n* vagin *m*.

vagrancy ['veɪgrənsɪ] *n* vagabondage *m*.

vagrant ['veɪgrənt] *n* vagabond/e, mendiant/e.

vague [veɪg] *adj* vague, imprécis(e); (*blurred: photo, memory*) flou(e); **I haven't the ~st idea** je n'en ai pas la moindre idée.

vaguely ['veɪglɪ] *adv* vaguement.

vain [veɪn] *adj* (*useless*) vain(e); (*conceited*) vaniteux(euse); **in ~** en vain.

valance ['væləns] *n* (*of bed*) tour *m* de lit.

valedictory [vælɪ'dɪktərɪ] *adj* d'adieu.

valentine ['væləntaɪn] *n* (*also: ~ card*) carte *f* de la Saint-Valentin.

valet ['vælɪt] *n* valet *m* de chambre.

valet parking *n* parcage *m* par les soins du personnel (de l'hôtel *etc*).

valet service *n* (*for clothes*) pressing *m*; (*for car*) nettoyage complet.

valiant ['vælɪənt] *adj* vaillant(e), courageux(euse).

valid ['vælɪd] *adj* valide, valable; (*excuse*) valable.

validate ['vælɪdeɪt] *vt* (*contract, document*) valider; (*argument, claim*) prouver la justesse de, confirmer.

validity [və'lɪdɪtɪ] *n* validité *f*.

valise [və'liːz] *n* sac *m* de voyage.

valley ['vælɪ] *n* vallée *f*.

valour, (US) valor ['vælə*] *n* courage *m*.

valuable ['væljuəbl] *adj* (*jewel*) de grande valeur; (*time*) précieux(euse); **~s** *npl* objets *mpl* de valeur.

valuation [vælju'eɪʃən] *n* évaluation *f*, expertise *f*.

value ['væljuː] *n* valeur *f* ♦ *vt* (*fix price*) évaluer, expertiser; (*cherish*) tenir à; **you get good ~ (for money) in that shop** vous en avez pour votre argent dans ce magasin; **to lose (in) ~** (*currency*) baisser; (*property*) se déprécier; **to gain (in) ~** (*currency*) monter; (*property*) prendre de la valeur; **to be of great ~ to sb** (*fig*) être très utile à qn.

value added tax (VAT) [-'ædɪd-] *n* (*BRIT*) taxe *f* à la valeur ajoutée (TVA).

valued ['væljuːd] *adj* (*appreciated*) estimé(e).

valuer ['væljuə*] *n* expert *m* (en estimations).

valve [vælv] *n* (*in machine*) soupape *f*; (*on tyre*) valve *f*; (*in radio*) lampe *f*.

vampire ['væmpaɪə*] *n* vampire *m*.

van [væn] *n* (*AUT*) camionnette *f*; (*BRIT RAIL*) fourgon *m*.

V and A *n abbr* (*BRIT*) = Victoria and Albert Museum.

vandal ['vændl] *n* vandale *m/f*.

vandalism ['vændəlɪzəm] *n* vandalisme *m*.

vandalize ['vændəlaɪz] *vt* saccager.

vanguard ['vængɑːd] *n* avant-garde *m*.

vanilla [və'nɪlə] *n* vanille *f* ♦ *cpd* (*ice cream*) à la vanille.

vanish ['vænɪʃ] *vi* disparaître.

vanity ['vænɪtɪ] *n* vanité *f*.

vanity case *n* sac *m* de toilette.

vantage ['vɑːntɪdʒ] *n*: **~ point** bonne position.

vaporize ['veɪpəraɪz] *vt* vaporiser ♦ *vi* se vaporiser.

vapour, (US) vapor ['veɪpə*] *n* vapeur *f*; (*on window*) buée *f*.

vapo(u)r trail *n* (*AVIAT*) traînée *f* de condensation.

variable ['vɛərɪəbl] *adj* variable; (*mood*) changeant(e) ♦ *n* variable *f*.

variance ['vɛərɪəns] *n*: **to be at ~ (with)** être en désaccord (avec); (*facts*) être en contradiction (avec).

variant ['vɛərɪənt] *n* variante *f*.

variation [vɛərɪ'eɪʃən] *n* variation *f*; (*in opinion*) changement *m*.

varicose ['værɪkəus] *adj*: **~ veins** varices *fpl*.

varied ['vɛərɪd] *adj* varié(e), divers(e).

variety [və'raɪətɪ] *n* variété *f*; (*quantity*): **a wide ~ of ...** une quantité *or* un grand nombre de ... (différent(e)s *or* divers(es)); **for a ~ of reasons** pour de diverses raisons.

variety show *n* (spectacle *m* de) variétés *fpl*.

various ['vɛərɪəs] *adj* divers(e), différent(e); (*several*) divers, plusieurs; **at ~ times** (*different*) en diverses occasions; (*several*) à plusieurs reprises.

varnish ['vɑːnɪʃ] *n* vernis *m*; (*for nails*) vernis (à ongles) ♦ *vt* vernir; **to ~ one's nails** se vernir les ongles.

vary ['vɛərɪ] *vt, vi* varier, changer; **to ~ with** *or* **according to** varier selon.

varying ['vɛərɪŋ] *adj* variable.

vase [vɑːz] *n* vase *m*.

vasectomy [væ'sɛktəmɪ] *n* vasectomie *f*.

Vaseline ['væsɪliːn] *n* ® vaseline *f*.

vast [vɑːst] *adj* vaste, immense; (*amount, success*) énorme.

vastly ['vɑːstlɪ] *adv* infiniment, extrêmement.

vastness ['vɑːstnɪs] *n* immensité *f*.

VAT [væt] *n abbr* (*BRIT*) = value added tax.

vat [væt] *n* cuve *f*.

Vatican ['vætɪkən] *n*: **the ~** le Vatican.

vatman ['vætmæn] *n* (*BRIT col*) contrôleur *m* de la T.V.A.

vault [vɔːlt] *n* (*of roof*) voûte *f*; (*tomb*) caveau *m*; (*in bank*) salle *f* des coffres; chambre forte; (*jump*) saut *m* ♦ *vt* (*also: ~ over*) sauter (d'un bond).

vaunted ['vɔːntɪd] *adj*: **much-~** tant célébré(e).

VC *n abbr* = vice-chairman; (*BRIT*: = Victoria Cross) distinction militaire.

VCR *n abbr* = video cassette recorder.

VD *n abbr* = venereal disease.

VDU *n abbr* = visual display unit.

veal [viːl] *n* veau *m*.

veer [vɪə*] *vi* tourner; virer.

veg. [vɛdʒ] *n abbr* (*BRIT col*) = **vegetable(s)**.
vegan ['viːgən] *n* végétalien/ne.
vegeburger ['vɛdʒɪbɔːgə*] *n* burger végétarien.
vegetable ['vɛdʒtəbl] *n* légume *m* ♦ *adj* végétal(e).
vegetable garden *n* (jardin *m*) potager *m*.
vegetarian [vɛdʒɪ'tɛərɪən] *adj, n* végétarien(ne).
vegetate ['vɛdʒɪteɪt] *vi* végéter.
vegetation [vɛdʒɪ'teɪʃən] *n* végétation *f*.
vegetative ['vɛdʒɪtətɪv] *adj* (*lit*) végétal(e); (*fig*) végétatif(ive).
veggieburger ['vɛdʒɪbɔːgə*] *n* = **vegeburger**.
vehemence ['viːɪməns] *n* véhémence *f*, violence *f*.
vehement ['viːɪmənt] *adj* violent(e), impétueux(euse); (*impassioned*) ardent(e).
vehicle ['viːɪkl] *n* véhicule *m*.
vehicular [vɪ'hɪkjulə*] *adj*: **"no ~ traffic"** "interdit à tout véhicule".
veil [veɪl] *n* voile *m* ♦ *vt* voiler; **under a ~ of secrecy** (*fig*) dans le plus grand secret.
veiled [veɪld] *adj* voilé(e).
vein [veɪn] *n* veine *f*; (*on leaf*) nervure *f*; (*fig: mood*) esprit *m*.
Velcro ['vɛlkrəu] ® *n* velcro *m* ®.
vellum ['vɛləm] *n* (*writing paper*) vélin *m*.
velocity [vɪ'lɔsɪtɪ] *n* vitesse *f*, vélocité *f*.
velour(s) [və'luə*] *n* velours *m*.
velvet ['vɛlvɪt] *n* velours *m*.
vending machine ['vɛndɪŋ-] *n* distributeur *m* automatique.
vendor ['vɛndə*] *n* vendeur/euse; **street ~** marchand ambulant.
veneer [və'nɪə*] *n* placage *m* de bois; (*fig*) vernis *m*.
venerable ['vɛnərəbl] *adj* vénérable.
venereal [vɪ'nɪərɪəl] *adj*: **~ disease (VD)** maladie vénérienne.
Venetian [vɪ'niːʃən] *adj*: **~ blind** store vénitien.
Venezuela [vɛnɛ'zweɪlə] *n* Venezuela *m*.
Venezuelan [vɛnɛ'zweɪlən] *adj* vénézuélien(ne) ♦ *n* Vénézuélien/ne.
vengeance ['vɛndʒəns] *n* vengeance *f*; **with a ~** (*fig*) vraiment, pour de bon.
vengeful ['vɛndʒful] *adj* vengeur(geresse).
Venice ['vɛnɪs] *n* Venise.
venison ['vɛnɪsn] *n* venaison *f*.
venom ['vɛnəm] *n* venin *m*.
venomous ['vɛnəməs] *adj* venimeux(euse).
vent [vɛnt] *n* conduit *m* d'aération; (*in dress, jacket*) fente *f* ♦ *vt* (*fig: one's feelings*) donner libre cours à.
ventilate ['vɛntɪleɪt] *vt* (*room*) ventiler, aérer.
ventilation [vɛntɪ'leɪʃən] *n* ventilation *f*, aération *f*.
ventilation shaft *n* conduit *m* de ventilation *or* d'aération.
ventilator ['vɛntɪleɪtə*] *n* ventilateur *m*.
ventriloquist [vɛn'trɪləkwɪst] *n* ventriloque

m/f.
venture ['vɛntʃə*] *n* entreprise *f* ♦ *vt* risquer, hasarder ♦ *vi* s'aventurer, se risquer; **a business ~** une entreprise commerciale; **to ~ to do sth** se risquer à faire qch.
venture capital *n* capital-risques *m*.
venue ['vɛnjuː] *n* (*of conference etc*) lieu *m* de la réunion (*or* manifestation *etc*); (*of match*) lieu de la rencontre.
Venus ['viːnəs] *n* (*planet*) Vénus *f*.
veracity [və'ræsɪtɪ] *n* véracité *f*.
veranda(h) [və'rændə] *n* véranda *f*.
verb [vəːb] *n* verbe *m*.
verbal ['vəːbl] *adj* verbal(e); (*translation*) littéral(e).
verbally ['vəːbəlɪ] *adv* verbalement.
verbatim [vəː'beɪtɪm] *adj, adv* mot pour mot.
verbose [vəː'bəus] *adj* verbeux(euse).
verdict ['vəːdɪkt] *n* verdict *m*; **~ of guilty/not guilty** verdict de culpabilité/de non-culpabilité.
verge [vəːdʒ] *n* bord *m*; **"soft ~s"** (*BRIT*) "accotements non stabilisés"; **on the ~ of doing** sur le point de faire.
▶**verge on** *vt fus* approcher de.
verger ['vəːdʒə*] *n* (*REL*) bedeau *m*.
verification [vɛrɪfɪ'keɪʃən] *n* vérification *f*.
verify ['vɛrɪfaɪ] *vt* vérifier.
veritable ['vɛrɪtəbl] *adj* véritable.
vermin ['vəːmɪn] *npl* animaux *mpl* nuisibles; (*insects*) vermine *f*.
vermouth ['vəːməθ] *n* vermouth *m*.
vernacular [və'nækjulə*] *n* langue *f* vernaculaire, dialecte *m*.
versatile ['vəːsətaɪl] *adj* polyvalent(e).
verse [vəːs] *n* vers *mpl*; (*stanza*) strophe *f*; (*in bible*) verset *m*; **in ~** en vers.
versed [vəːst] *adj*: **(well-)~ in** versé(e) dans.
version ['vəːʃən] *n* version *f*.
versus ['vəːsəs] *prep* contre.
vertebra, *pl* **~e** ['vəːtɪbrə, -briː] *n* vertèbre *f*.
vertebrate ['vəːtɪbrɪt] *n* vertébré *m*.
vertical ['vəːtɪkl] *adj* vertical(e) ♦ *n* verticale *f*.
vertically ['vəːtɪklɪ] *adv* verticalement.
vertigo ['vəːtɪgəu] *n* vertige *m*; **to suffer from ~** avoir des vertiges.
verve [vəːv] *n* brio *m*; enthousiasme *m*.
very ['vɛrɪ] *adv* très ♦ *adj*: **the ~ book which** le livre même que; **the ~ thought (of it) ...** rien que d'y penser ...; **at the ~ end** tout à la fin; **the ~ last** le tout dernier; **at the ~ least** au moins; **~ well** très bien; **~ little** très peu; **~ much** beaucoup.
vespers ['vɛspəz] *npl* vêpres *fpl*.
vessel ['vɛsl] *n* (*ANAT, NAUT*) vaisseau *m*; (*container*) récipient *m*.
vest [vɛst] *n* (*BRIT*) tricot *m* de corps; (*US*) gilet *m* ♦ *vt*: **to ~ sb with sth, to ~ sth in sb** investir qn de qch.
vested interest *n*: **to have a ~ in doing** avoir tout intérêt à faire; **~s** *npl* (*COMM*) droits acquis.

vestibule ['vɛstɪbjuːl] n vestibule m.
vestige ['vɛstɪdʒ] n vestige m.
vestry ['vɛstrɪ] n sacristie f.
Vesuvius [vɪ'suːvɪəs] n Vésuve m.
vet [vɛt] n abbr (= veterinary surgeon)
vétérinaire m/f ♦ vt examiner minutieusement; (text) revoir; (candidate) se
renseigner soigneusement sur, soumettre à
une enquête approfondie.
veteran ['vɛtərn] n vétéran m; (also: war ~)
ancien combattant ♦ adj: she's a ~
campaigner for ... cela fait très longtemps
qu'elle lutte pour ... .
veteran car n voiture f d'époque.
veterinarian [vɛtrɪ'nɛərɪən] n (US) = veterinary
surgeon.
veterinary ['vɛtrɪnərɪ] adj vétérinaire.
veterinary surgeon n (BRIT) vétérinaire m/f.
veto ['viːtəu] n (pl ~es) veto m ♦ vt opposer son
veto à; **to put a ~ on** mettre (or opposer)
son veto à.
vetting ['vɛtɪŋ] n: **positive ~** enquête f de
sécurité.
vex [vɛks] vt fâcher, contrarier.
vexed [vɛkst] adj (question) controversé(e).
VFD n abbr (US) = voluntary fire department.
VG n abbr (BRIT: SCOL etc: = very good) tb (= très
bien).
VHF abbr (= very high frequency) VHF.
VI abbr (US) = Virgin Islands.
via ['vaɪə] prep par, via.
viability [vaɪə'bɪlɪtɪ] n viabilité f.
viable ['vaɪəbl] adj viable.
viaduct ['vaɪədʌkt] n viaduc m.
vial ['vaɪəl] m fiole f.
vibes [vaɪbz] npl (col): **I get good/bad ~ about
it** je le sens bien/ne le sens pas; **there are
good/bad ~ between us** entre nous le
courant passe bien/ne passe pas.
vibrant ['vaɪbrnt] adj (sound, colour)
vibrant(e).
vibraphone ['vaɪbrəfəun] n vibraphone m.
vibrate [vaɪ'breɪt] vi: **to ~ (with)** vibrer (de);
(resound) retentir (de).
vibration [vaɪ'breɪʃən] n vibration f.
vibrator [vaɪ'breɪtə*] n vibromasseur m.
vicar ['vɪkə*] n pasteur m (de l'Église anglicane).
vicarage ['vɪkərɪdʒ] n presbytère m.
vicarious [vɪ'kɛərɪəs] adj (pleasure, experience)
indirect(e).
vice [vaɪs] n (evil) vice m; (TECH) étau m.
vice- [vaɪs] prefix vice-.
vice-chairman [vaɪs'tʃɛəmən] n vice-
président/e.
vice-chancellor [vaɪs'tʃɑːnsələ*] n (BRIT)
≈ président/e d'université.
vice-president [vaɪs'prɛzɪdənt] n vice-
président/e.
viceroy ['vaɪsrɔɪ] n vice-roi m.
vice squad n ≈ brigade mondaine.
vice versa ['vaɪsɪ'vəːsə] adv vice versa.
vicinity [vɪ'sɪnɪtɪ] n environs mpl, alentours

mpl.
vicious ['vɪʃəs] adj (remark) cruel(le),
méchant(e); (blow) brutal(e); **a ~ circle** un
cercle vicieux.
viciousness ['vɪʃəsnɪs] n méchanceté f,
cruauté f; brutalité f.
vicissitudes [vɪ'sɪsɪtjuːdz] npl vicissitudes fpl.
victim ['vɪktɪm] n victime f; **to be the ~ of**
être victime de.
victimization [vɪktɪmaɪ'zeɪʃən] n brimades fpl;
représailles fpl.
victimize ['vɪktɪmaɪz] vt brimer; exercer des
représailles sur.
victor ['vɪktə*] n vainqueur m.
Victorian [vɪk'tɔːrɪən] adj victorien(ne).
victorious [vɪk'tɔːrɪəs] adj victorieux(euse).
victory ['vɪktərɪ] n victoire f; **to win a ~ over
sb** remporter une victoire sur qn.
video ['vɪdɪəu] n (~ film) vidéo f; (also: ~
cassette) vidéocassette f; (also: ~ cassette
recorder) magnétoscope m ♦ cpd vidéo inv.
video camera n caméra f vidéo inv.
video cassette n vidéocassette f.
video (cassette) recorder n magnétoscope
m.
videodisc ['vɪdɪəudɪsk] n vidéodisque m.
video game n jeu m vidéo inv.
video nasty n vidéo à caractère violent ou
pornographique.
videophone ['vɪdɪəufəun] n visiophone m,
vidéophone m.
video recording n enregistrement m (en)
vidéo inv.
video tape n bande f vidéo inv; (cassette)
vidéocassette f.
vie [vaɪ] vi: **to ~ with** lutter avec, rivaliser
avec.
Vienna [vɪ'ɛnə] n Vienne.
Vietnam, Viet Nam ['vjɛt'næm] n Viet-Nam m
or Vietnam m.
Vietnamese [vjɛtnə'miːz] adj vietnamien(ne)
♦ n (pl inv) Vietnamien/ne; (LING) vietnamien
m.
view [vjuː] n vue f; (opinion) avis m, vue ♦ vt
(situation) considérer; (house) visiter; **on ~**
(in museum etc) exposé(e); **in full ~ of sb**
sous les yeux de qn; **to be within ~ (of sth)**
être à portée de vue (de qch); **an overall ~
of the situation** une vue d'ensemble de la
situation; **in my ~** à mon avis; **in ~ of the
fact that** étant donné que; **with a ~ to doing
sth** dans l'intention de faire qch.
viewdata ['vjuːdeɪtə] n (BRIT) télétexte m
(version téléphonique).
viewer ['vjuːə*] n (viewfinder) viseur m; (small
projector) visionneuse f; (TV) téléspectateur/
trice.
viewfinder ['vjuːfaɪndə*] n viseur m.
viewpoint ['vjuːpɔɪnt] n point m de vue.
vigil ['vɪdʒɪl] n veille f; **to keep ~** veiller.
vigilance ['vɪdʒɪləns] n vigilance f.
vigilance committee n comité m

d'autodéfense.

vigilant ['vɪdʒɪlənt] *adj* vigilant(e).

vigilante [vɪdʒɪ'læntɪ] *n justicier ou membre d'un groupe d'autodéfense.*

vigorous ['vɪgərəs] *adj* vigoureux(euse).

vigour, *(US)* **vigor** ['vɪgə*] *n* vigueur *f*.

vile [vaɪl] *adj* (*action*) vil(e); (*smell*) abominable; (*temper*) massacrant(e).

vilify ['vɪlɪfaɪ] *vt* calomnier, vilipender.

villa ['vɪlə] *n* villa *f*.

village ['vɪlɪdʒ] *n* village *m*.

villager ['vɪlɪdʒə*] *n* villageois/e.

villain ['vɪlən] *n* (*scoundrel*) scélérat *m*; (*criminal*) bandit *m*; (*in novel etc*) traître *m*.

VIN *n abbr* (*US*) = *vehicle identification number*.

vinaigrette [vɪneɪ'grɛt] *n* vinaigrette *f*.

vindicate ['vɪndɪkeɪt] *vt* défendre avec succès; justifier.

vindication [vɪndɪ'keɪʃən] *n*: **in ~ of** pour justifier.

vindictive [vɪn'dɪktɪv] *adj* vindicatif(ive), rancunier(ière).

vine [vaɪn] *n* vigne *f*; (*climbing plant*) plante grimpante.

vinegar ['vɪnɪgə*] *n* vinaigre *m*.

vine grower *n* viticulteur *m*.

vine-growing ['vaɪngrəʊɪŋ] *adj* viticole ♦ *n* viticulture *f*.

vineyard ['vɪnjɑːd] *n* vignoble *m*.

vintage ['vɪntɪdʒ] *n* (*year*) année *f*, millésime *m*; **the 1970 ~** le millésime 1970.

vintage car *n* voiture ancienne.

vintage wine *n* vin *m* de grand cru.

vinyl ['vaɪnl] *n* vinyle *m*.

viola [vɪ'əʊlə] *n* alto *m*.

violate ['vaɪəleɪt] *vt* violer.

violation [vaɪə'leɪʃən] *n* violation *f*; **in ~ of** (*rule, law*) en infraction à, en violation de.

violence ['vaɪələns] *n* violence *f*; (*POL etc*) incidents violents.

violent ['vaɪələnt] *adj* violent(e); **a ~ dislike of sb/sth** une aversion profonde pour qn/qch.

violently ['vaɪələntlɪ] *adv* violemment; (*ill, angry*) terriblement.

violet ['vaɪələt] *adj* (*colour*) violet(te) ♦ *n* (*plant*) violette *f*.

violin [vaɪə'lɪn] *n* violon *m*.

violinist [vaɪə'lɪnɪst] *n* violoniste *m/f*.

VIP *n abbr* (= *very important person*) VIP *m*.

viper ['vaɪpə*] *n* vipère *f*.

viral ['vaɪərəl] *adj* viral(e).

virgin ['vɜːdʒɪn] *n* vierge *f* ♦ *adj* vierge; **she is a ~** elle est vierge; **the Blessed V~** la Sainte Vierge.

virginity [vɜː'dʒɪnɪtɪ] *n* virginité *f*.

Virgo ['vɜːgəʊ] *n* la Vierge; **to be ~** être de la Vierge.

virile ['vɪraɪl] *adj* viril(e).

virility [vɪ'rɪlɪtɪ] *n* virilité *f*.

virtual ['vɜːtjuəl] *adj* (*COMPUT, PHYSICS*) virtuel(le); (*in effect*): **it's a ~ impossibility** c'est quasiment impossible; **the ~ leader** le

chef dans la pratique.

virtually ['vɜːtjuəlɪ] *adv* (*almost*) pratiquement; **it is ~ impossible** c'est quasiment impossible.

virtual reality *n* réalité virtuelle.

virtue ['vɜːtjuː] *n* vertu *f*; (*advantage*) mérite *m*, avantage *m*; **by ~ of** par le fait de.

virtuosity [vɜːtju'ɔsɪtɪ] *n* virtuosité *f*.

virtuoso [vɜːtju'əʊzəʊ] *n* virtuose *m/f*.

virtuous ['vɜːtjuəs] *adj* vertueux(euse).

virulent ['vɪrulənt] *adj* virulent(e).

virus ['vaɪərəs] *n* virus *m*.

visa ['viːzə] *n* visa *m*.

vis-à-vis [viːzə'viː] *prep* vis-à-vis de.

viscount ['vaɪkaunt] *n* vicomte *m*.

viscous ['vɪskəs] *adj* visqueux(euse), gluant(e).

vise [vaɪs] *n* (*US TECH*) = **vice**.

visibility [vɪzɪ'bɪlɪtɪ] *n* visibilité *f*.

visible ['vɪzəbl] *adj* visible; **~ exports/imports** exportations/importations *fpl* visibles.

visibly ['vɪzəblɪ] *adv* visiblement.

vision ['vɪʒən] *n* (*sight*) vue *f*, vision *f*; (*foresight, in dream*) vision *f*.

visionary ['vɪʒənrɪ] *n* visionnaire *m/f*.

visit ['vɪzɪt] *n* visite *f*; (*stay*) séjour *m* ♦ *vt* (*person*) rendre visite à; (*place*) visiter; **on a private/official ~** en visite privée/officielle.

visiting ['vɪzɪtɪŋ] *adj* (*speaker, team*) invité(e), de l'extérieur.

visiting card *n* carte *f* de visite.

visiting hours *npl* heures *fpl* de visite.

visiting professor *n* ≈ professeur associé.

visitor ['vɪzɪtə*] *n* visiteur/euse; (*in hotel*) client/e.

visitors' book *n* livre *m* d'or; (*in hotel*) registre *m*.

visor ['vaɪzə*] *n* visière *f*.

VISTA ['vɪstə] *n abbr* (= *Volunteers in Service to America*) programme d'assistance bénévole aux régions pauvres.

vista ['vɪstə] *n* vue *f*, perspective *f*.

visual ['vɪzjuəl] *adj* visuel(le).

visual aid *n* support visuel (pour l'enseignement).

visual arts *npl* arts *mpl* plastiques.

visual display unit (VDU) *n* console *f* de visualisation, visuel *m*.

visualize ['vɪzjuəlaɪz] *vt* se représenter; (*foresee*) prévoir.

visually ['vɪzjuəlɪ] *adv* visuellement; **~ handicapped** handicapé(e) visuel(le).

vital ['vaɪtl] *adj* vital(e); **of ~ importance (to sb/sth)** d'une importance capitale (pour qn/qch).

vitality [vaɪ'tælɪtɪ] *n* vitalité *f*.

vitally ['vaɪtəlɪ] *adv* extrêmement.

vital statistics *npl* (*of population*) statistiques *fpl* démographiques; (*col: woman's*) mensurations *fpl*.

vitamin ['vɪtəmɪn] *n* vitamine *f*.

vitiate ['vɪʃɪeɪt] *vt* vicier.

vitreous ['vɪtrɪəs] *adj* (*china*) vitreux(euse); (*enamel*) vitrifié(e).

vitriolic [vɪtrɪ'ɔlɪk] *adj* (*fig*) venimeux(euse).

viva ['vaɪvə] *n* (*also*: ~ **voce**) (examen) oral.

vivacious [vɪ'veɪʃəs] *adj* animé(e), qui a de la vivacité.

vivacity [vɪ'væsɪtɪ] *n* vivacité *f*.

vivid ['vɪvɪd] *adj* (*account*) frappant(e); (*light, imagination*) vif(vive).

vividly ['vɪvɪdlɪ] *adv* (*describe*) d'une manière vivante; (*remember*) de façon précise.

vivisection [vɪvɪ'sekʃən] *n* vivisection *f*.

vixen ['vɪksn] *n* renarde *f*; (*pej*: *woman*) mégère *f*.

viz [vɪz] *abbr* (= *vide licet*: namely) à savoir, c. à d.

VLF *abbr* = *very low frequency*.

V-neck ['viːnɛk] *n* décolleté *m* en V.

VOA *n abbr* (= *Voice of America*) voix *f* de l'Amérique (*émissions de radio à destination de l'étranger*).

vocabulary [vəu'kæbjulərɪ] *n* vocabulaire *m*.

vocal ['vəukl] *adj* vocal(e); (*articulate*) qui n'hésite pas à s'exprimer, qui sait faire entendre ses opinions; ~**s** *npl* voix *fpl*.

vocal cords *npl* cordes vocales.

vocalist ['vəukəlɪst] *n* chanteur/euse.

vocation [vəu'keɪʃən] *n* vocation *f*.

vocational [vəu'keɪʃənl] *adj* professionnel(le); ~ **guidance/training** orientation/formation professionnelle.

vociferous [və'sɪfərəs] *adj* bruyant(e).

vodka ['vɔdkə] *n* vodka *f*.

vogue [vəug] *n* mode *f*; (*popularity*) vogue *f*; **to be in** ~ être en vogue *or* à la mode.

voice [vɔɪs] *n* voix *f*; (*opinion*) avis *m* ♦ *vt* (*opinion*) exprimer, formuler; **in a loud/soft** ~ à voix haute/basse; **to give** ~ **to** exprimer.

voice-over ['vɔɪsəuvə*] *n* voix off *f*.

void [vɔɪd] *n* vide *m* ♦ *adj* (*invalid*) nul(le); (*empty*): ~ **of** vide de, dépourvu(e) de.

voile [vɔɪl] *n* voile *m* (*tissu*).

vol. *abbr* (= *volume*) vol.

volatile ['vɔlətaɪl] *adj* volatil(e); (*fig*) versatile.

volcanic [vɔl'kænɪk] *adj* volcanique.

volcano, ~**es** [vɔl'keɪnəu] *n* volcan *m*.

volition [və'lɪʃən] *n*: **of one's own** ~ de son propre gré.

volley ['vɔlɪ] *n* (*of gunfire*) salve *f*; (*of stones etc*) pluie *f*, volée *f*; (*TENNIS etc*) volée.

volleyball ['vɔlɪbɔːl] *n* volley(-ball) *m*.

volt [vəult] *n* volt *m*.

voltage ['vəultɪdʒ] *n* tension *f*, voltage *m*; **high/low** ~ haute/basse tension.

voluble ['vɔljubl] *adj* volubile.

volume ['vɔljuːm] *n* volume *m*; (*of tank*) capacité *f*; ~ **one/two** (*of book*) tome un/deux; **his expression spoke** ~**s** son expression en disait long.

volume control *n* (*RADIO, TV*) bouton *m* de réglage du volume.

volume discount *n* (*COMM*) remise *f* sur la quantité.

voluminous [və'luːmɪnəs] *adj* volumineux(euse).

voluntarily ['vɔləntrɪlɪ] *adv* volontairement; bénévolement.

voluntary ['vɔləntərɪ] *adj* volontaire; (*unpaid*) bénévole.

voluntary liquidation *n* (*COMM*) dépôt *m* de bilan.

voluntary redundancy *n* (*BRIT*) départ *m* volontaire (*en cas de licenciements*).

volunteer [vɔlən'tɪə*] *n* volontaire *m/f* ♦ *vi* (*MIL*) s'engager comme volontaire; **to** ~ **to do** se proposer pour faire.

voluptuous [və'lʌptjuəs] *adj* voluptueux(euse).

vomit ['vɔmɪt] *n* vomissure *f* ♦ *vt, vi* vomir.

voracious [və'reɪʃəs] *adj* vorace; (*reader*) avide.

vote [vəut] *n* vote *m*, suffrage *m*; (*cast*) voix *f*, vote; (*franchise*) droit *m* de vote ♦ *vt* (*bill*) voter; (*chairman*) élire ♦ *vi* voter; **to put sth to the** ~, **to take a** ~ **on sth** mettre qch aux voix, procéder à un vote sur qch; ~ **for** *or* **in favour of/against** vote pour/contre; **to** ~ **to do sth** voter en faveur de faire qch; ~ **of censure** motion *f* de censure; ~ **of thanks** discours *m* de remerciement.

voter ['vəutə*] *n* électeur/trice.

voting ['vəutɪŋ] *n* scrutin *m*.

voting paper *n* (*BRIT*) bulletin *m* de vote.

voting right *n* droit *m* de vote.

vouch [vautʃ]: **to** ~ **for** *vt fus* se porter garant de.

voucher ['vautʃə*] *n* (*for meal, petrol*) bon *m*; (*receipt*) reçu *m*; **travel** ~ bon *m* de transport.

vow [vau] *n* vœu *m*, serment *m* ♦ *vi* jurer; **to take** *or* **make a** ~ **to do sth** faire le vœu de faire qch.

vowel ['vauəl] *n* voyelle *f*.

voyage ['vɔɪɪdʒ] *n* voyage *m* par mer, traversée *f*.

voyeur [vwaː'jə:*] *n* voyeur *m*.

VP *n abbr* = *vice-president*.

vs *abbr* (= *versus*) c.

VSO *n abbr* (*BRIT*: = *Voluntary Service Overseas*) ≈ coopération civile.

VT, Vt. *abbr* (*US*) = *Vermont*.

vulgar ['vʌlgə*] *adj* vulgaire.

vulgarity [vʌl'gærɪtɪ] *n* vulgarité *f*.

vulnerability [vʌlnərə'bɪlɪtɪ] *n* vulnérabilité *f*.

vulnerable ['vʌlnərəbl] *adj* vulnérable.

vulture ['vʌltʃə*] *n* vautour *m*.

W w

W, w ['dʌblju:] *n* (*letter*) W, w *m*; **W for William** W comme William.

W *abbr* (= *west*) O; (*ELEC*: = *watt*) W.

WA *abbr* (*US*) = Washington.

wad [wɔd] *n* (*of cotton wool, paper*) tampon *m*; (*of banknotes etc*) liasse *f*.

wadding ['wɔdıŋ] *n* rembourrage *m*.

waddle ['wɔdl] *vi* se dandiner.

wade [weıd] *vi*: **to ~ through** marcher dans, patauger dans ♦ *vt* passer à gué.

wafer ['weıfə*] *n* (*CULIN*) gaufrette *f*; (*REL*) pain *m* d'hostie; (*COMPUT*) tranche *f* (de silicium).

wafer-thin ['weıfə'θın] *adj* ultra-mince, mince comme du papier à cigarette.

waffle ['wɔfl] *n* (*CULIN*) gaufre *f*; (*col*) rabâchage *m*; remplissage *m* ♦ *vi* parler pour ne rien dire; faire du remplissage.

waffle iron *n* gaufrier *m*.

waft [wɔft] *vt* porter ♦ *vi* flotter.

wag [wæg] *vt* agiter, remuer ♦ *vi* remuer; **the dog ~ged its tail** le chien a remué la queue.

wage [weıdʒ] *n* (*also*: ~**s**) salaire *m*, paye *f* ♦ *vt*: **to ~ war** faire la guerre; **a day's ~s** un jour de salaire.

wage claim *n* demande *f* d'augmentation de salaire.

wage differential *n* éventail *m* des salaires.

wage earner [-ə:nə*] *n* salarié/e; (*breadwinner*) soutien *m* de famille.

wage freeze *n* blocage *m* des salaires.

wage packet *n* (*BRIT*) (enveloppe *f* de) paye *f*.

wager ['weıdʒə*] *n* pari *m* ♦ *vt* parier.

waggle ['wægl] *vt, vi* remuer.

wag(g)on ['wægən] *n* (*horse-drawn*) chariot *m*; (*BRIT RAIL*) wagon *m* (de marchandises).

wail [weıl] *n* gémissement *m*; (*of siren*) hurlement *m* ♦ *vi* gémir; hurler.

waist [weıst] *n* taille *f*, ceinture *f*.

waistcoat ['weıskəut] *n* (*BRIT*) gilet *m*.

waistline ['weıstlaın] *n* (tour *m* de) taille *f*.

wait [weıt] *n* attente *f* ♦ *vi* attendre; **to ~ for sb/sth** attendre qn/qch; **to keep sb ~ing** faire attendre qn; **~ a minute!** un instant!; **"repairs while you ~"** "réparations minute"; **I can't ~ to ...** (*fig*) je meurs d'envie de ...; **to lie in ~ for** guetter.

▶**wait behind** *vi* rester (à attendre).

▶**wait on** *vt fus* servir.

▶**wait up** *vi* attendre, ne pas se coucher; **don't ~ up for me** ne m'attendez pas pour aller vous coucher.

waiter ['weıtə*] *n* garçon *m* (de café), serveur *m*.

waiting ['weıtıŋ] *n*: **"no ~"** (*BRIT AUT*) "stationnement interdit".

waiting list *n* liste *f* d'attente.

waiting room *n* salle *f* d'attente.

waitress ['weıtrıs] *n* serveuse *f*.

waive [weıv] *vt* renoncer à, abandonner.

waiver ['weıvə*] *n* dispense *f*.

wake [weık] *vb* (*pt* **woke**, ~**d**, *pp* **woken**, ~**d** [wəuk, 'wəukn]) *vt* (*also*: ~ **up**) réveiller ♦ *vi* (*also*: ~ **up**) se réveiller ♦ *n* (*for dead person*) veillée *f* mortuaire; (*NAUT*) sillage *m*; **to ~ up to sth** (*fig*) se rendre compte de qch; **in the ~ of** (*fig*) à la suite de; **to follow in sb's ~** (*fig*) marcher sur les traces de qn.

waken ['weıkn] *vt, vi* = **wake**.

Wales [weılz] *n* pays *m* de Galles.

walk [wɔ:k] *n* promenade *f*; (*short*) petit tour; (*gait*) démarche *f*; (*pace*): **at a quick ~** d'un pas rapide; (*path*) chemin *m*; (*in park etc*) allée *f* ♦ *vi* marcher; (*for pleasure, exercise*) se promener ♦ *vt* (*distance*) faire à pied; (*dog*) promener; **10 minutes' ~ from** à 10 minutes de marche de; **to go for a ~** se promener; faire un tour; **I'll ~ you home** je vais vous raccompagner chez vous; **from all ~s of life** de toutes conditions sociales.

▶**walk out** *vi* (*go out*) sortir; (*as protest*) partir (en signe de protestation); (*strike*) se mettre en grève; **to ~ out on sb** quitter qn.

walkabout ['wɔ:kəbaut] *n*: **to go (on a) ~** (*VIP*) prendre un bain de foule.

walker ['wɔ:kə*] *n* (*person*) marcheur/euse.

walkie-talkie ['wɔ:kı'tɔ:kı] *n* talkie-walkie *m*.

walking ['wɔ:kıŋ] *n* marche *f* à pied; **it's within ~ distance** on peut y aller à pied.

walking holiday *n* vacances passées à faire de la randonnée.

walking shoes *npl* chaussures *fpl* de marche.

walking stick *n* canne *f*.

Walkman ['wɔ:kmən] *n* ® Walkman *m* ®.

walk-on ['wɔ:kɔn] *adj* (*THEAT*: *part*) de figurant/e.

walkout ['wɔ:kaut] *n* (*of workers*) grève-surprise *f*.

walkover ['wɔ:kəuvə*] *n* (*col*) victoire *f* or examen *m etc* facile.

walkway ['wɔ:kweı] *n* promenade *f*, cheminement piéton.

wall [wɔ:l] *n* mur *m*; (*of tunnel, cave*) paroi *f*; **to go to the ~** (*fig*: *firm etc*) faire faillite.

▶**wall in** *vt* (*garden etc*) entourer d'un mur.

wall cupboard *n* placard mural.

walled [wɔ:ld] *adj* (*city*) fortifié(e).

wallet ['wɔlıt] *n* portefeuille *m*.

wallflower ['wɔ:lflauə*] *n* giroflée *f*; **to be a ~** (*fig*) faire tapisserie.

wall hanging *n* tenture (murale), tapisserie *f*.

wallop ['wɔləp] *vt* (*BRIT col*) taper sur, cogner.

wallow ['wɔləu] *vi* se vautrer; **to ~ in one's**

grief se complaire à sa douleur.

wallpaper ['wɔːlpeɪpə*] n papier peint.

wall-to-wall ['wɔːltə'wɔːl] adj: ~ **carpeting** moquette f.

wally [wɒlɪ] n (col) imbécile m/f.

walnut ['wɔːlnʌt] n noix f; (tree) noyer m.

walrus, pl ~ or ~**es** ['wɔːlrəs] n morse m.

waltz [wɔːlts] n valse f ♦ vi valser.

wan [wɒn] adj pâle; triste.

wand [wɒnd] n (also: **magic** ~) baguette f (magique).

wander ['wɒndə*] vi (person) errer, aller sans but; (thoughts) vagabonder; (river) serpenter ♦ vt errer dans.

wanderer ['wɒndərə*] n vagabond/e.

wandering ['wɒndrɪŋ] adj (tribe) nomade; (minstrel, actor) ambulant(e).

wane [weɪn] vi (moon) décroître; (reputation) décliner.

wangle ['wæŋgl] (BRIT col) vt se débrouiller pour avoir; carotter ♦ n combine f, magouille f.

wanker ['wæŋkə*] n (col!) branleur m (!).

want [wɒnt] vt vouloir; (need) avoir besoin de; (lack) manquer de ♦ n (poverty) pauvreté f, besoin m; ~**s** npl (needs) besoins mpl; **for** ~ **of** par manque de, faute de; **to** ~ **to do** vouloir faire; **to** ~ **sb to do** vouloir que qn fasse; **you're** ~**ed on the phone** on vous demande au téléphone; **"cook** ~**ed"** "on demande un cuisinier".

want ads npl (US) petites annonces.

wanting ['wɒntɪŋ] adj: **to be** ~ (**in**) manquer (de); **to be found** ~ ne pas être à la hauteur.

wanton ['wɒntn] adj capricieux(euse); dévergondé(e).

war [wɔː*] n guerre f; **to go to** ~ se mettre en guerre.

warble ['wɔːbl] n (of bird) gazouillis m ♦ vi gazouiller.

war cry n cri m de guerre.

ward [wɔːd] n (in hospital) salle f; (POL) section électorale; (LAW: child) pupille m/f.

►**ward off** vt parer, éviter.

warden ['wɔːdn] n (BRIT: of institution) directeur/trice; (of park, game reserve) gardien/ne; (BRIT: also: **traffic** ~) contractuel/le.

warder ['wɔːdə*] n (BRIT) gardien m de prison.

wardrobe ['wɔːdrəub] n (cupboard) armoire f; (clothes) garde-robe f; (THEAT) costumes mpl.

warehouse ['wɛəhaus] n entrepôt m.

wares [wɛəz] npl marchandises fpl.

warfare ['wɔːfɛə*] n guerre f.

war game n jeu m de stratégie militaire.

warhead ['wɔːhed] n (MIL) ogive f.

warily ['wɛərɪlɪ] adv avec prudence, avec précaution.

warlike ['wɔːlaɪk] adj guerrier(ière).

warm [wɔːm] adj chaud(e); (person, greeting, welcome, applause) chaleureux(euse);

(supporter) ardent(e), enthousiaste; **it's** ~ il fait chaud; **I'm** ~ j'ai chaud; **to keep sth** ~ tenir qch au chaud; **with my** ~**est thanks/ congratulations** avec mes remerciements/ mes félicitations les plus sincères.

►**warm up** vi (person, room) se réchauffer; (water) chauffer; (athlete, discussion) s'échauffer ♦ vt réchauffer; chauffer; (engine) faire chauffer.

warm-blooded ['wɔːm'blʌdɪd] adj (ZOOL) à sang chaud.

war memorial n monument m aux morts.

warm-hearted [wɔːm'hɑːtɪd] adj affectueux(euse).

warmly ['wɔːmlɪ] adv chaudement; chaleureusement.

warmonger ['wɔːmʌŋgə*] n belliciste m/f.

warmongering ['wɔːmʌŋgrɪŋ] n propagande f belliciste, bellicisme m.

warmth [wɔːmθ] n chaleur f.

warm-up ['wɔːmʌp] n (SPORT) période f d'échauffement.

warn [wɔːn] vt avertir, prévenir; **to** ~ **sb not to do sth** or **against doing sth** prévenir qn de ne pas faire qch.

warning ['wɔːnɪŋ] n avertissement m; (notice) avis m; **without (any)** ~ (suddenly) inopinément; (without notifying) sans prévenir; **gale** ~ (METEOROLOGY) avis de grand vent.

warning light n avertisseur lumineux.

warning triangle n (AUT) triangle m de présignalisation.

warp [wɔːp] n (TEXTILES) chaîne f ♦ vi (wood) travailler, se voiler or gauchir ♦ vt voiler; (fig) pervertir.

warpath ['wɔːpɑːθ] n: **to be on the** ~ (fig) être sur le sentier de la guerre.

warped [wɔːpt] adj (wood) gauchi(e); (fig) perverti(e).

warrant ['wɒrnt] n (guarantee) garantie f; (LAW: to arrest) mandat m d'arrêt; (: to search) mandat de perquisition ♦ vt (justify, merit) justifier.

warrant officer n (MIL) adjudant m; (NAUT) premier-maître m.

warranty ['wɒrəntɪ] n garantie f; **under** ~ (COMM) sous garantie.

warren ['wɒrən] n (of rabbits) terriers mpl, garenne f.

warring ['wɔːrɪŋ] adj (nations) en guerre; (interests etc) contradictoire, opposé(e).

warrior ['wɒrɪə*] n guerrier/ière.

Warsaw ['wɔːsɔː] n Varsovie f.

warship ['wɔːʃɪp] n navire m de guerre.

wart [wɔːt] n verrue f.

wartime ['wɔːtaɪm] n: **in** ~ en temps de guerre.

wary ['wɛərɪ] adj prudent(e); **to be** ~ **about** or **of doing sth** hésiter beaucoup à faire qch.

was [wɒz] pt of **be**.

wash [wɒʃ] vt laver; (sweep, carry: sea etc)

emporter, entraîner; (: *ashore*) rejeter ♦ *vi*
se laver ♦ *n* (*paint*) badigeon *m*; (*washing
programme*) lavage *m*; (*of ship*) sillage *m*; **to
give sth a** ~ laver qch; **to have a** ~ se laver,
faire sa toilette; **he was** ~**ed overboard** il a
été emporté par une vague.
▶**wash away** *vt* (*stain*) enlever au lavage;
(*subj: river etc*) emporter.
▶**wash down** *vt* laver; laver à grande eau.
▶**wash off** *vi* partir au lavage.
▶**wash up** *vi* faire la vaisselle; (*US: have a
wash*) se débarbouiller.
Wash. *abbr* (*US*) = *Washington*.
washable ['wɔʃəbl] *adj* lavable.
washbasin ['wɔʃbeɪsn] *n* lavabo *m*.
washcloth ['wɔʃklɔθ] *n* (*US*) gant *m* de
toilette.
washer ['wɔʃə*] *n* (*TECH*) rondelle *f*, joint *m*.
washing ['wɔʃɪŋ] *n* (*BRIT: linen etc*) lessive *f*.
washing line *n* (*BRIT*) corde *f* à linge.
washing machine *n* machine *f* à laver.
washing powder *n* (*BRIT*) lessive *f* (en
poudre).
Washington ['wɔʃɪŋtən] *n* (*city, state*)
Washington *m*.
washing-up [wɔʃɪŋˈʌp] *n* (*BRIT*) vaisselle *f*.
washing-up liquid *n* (*BRIT*) produit *m* pour la
vaisselle.
wash-out ['wɔʃaut] *n* (*col*) désastre *m*.
washroom ['wɔʃrum] *n* toilettes *fpl*.
wasn't ['wɔznt] = was not.
Wasp, WASP [wɔsp] *n abbr* (*US col*: = *White
Anglo-Saxon Protestant*) surnom, *souvent
péjoratif, donné à l'américain de souche
anglo-saxonne, aisé et de tendance
conservatrice*.
wasp [wɔsp] *n* guêpe *f*.
waspish ['wɔspɪʃ] *adj* irritable.
wastage ['weɪstɪdʒ] *n* gaspillage *m*; (*in
manufacturing, transport etc*) déchet *m*.
waste [weɪst] *n* gaspillage *m*; (*of time*) perte *f*;
(*rubbish*) déchets *mpl*; (*also:* **household** ~)
ordures *fpl* ♦ *adj* (*material*) de rebut; (*energy,
heat*) perdu(e); (*food*) inutilisé(e); (*land,
ground: in city*) à l'abandon; (: *in country*)
inculte, en friche ♦ *vt* gaspiller; (*time,
opportunity*) perdre; ~**s** *npl* étendue *f*
désertique; **it's a** ~ **of money** c'est de
l'argent jeté en l'air; **to go to** ~ être
gaspillé(e); **to lay** ~ (*destroy*) dévaster.
▶**waste away** *vi* dépérir.
wastebasket ['weɪstbɑːskɪt] *n* = **wastepaper
basket**.
waste disposal (unit) *n* (*BRIT*) broyeur *m*
d'ordures.
wasteful ['weɪstful] *adj* gaspilleur(euse);
(*process*) peu économique.
waste ground *n* (*BRIT*) terrain *m* vague.
wasteland ['weɪstlənd] *n* terres *fpl* à
l'abandon; (*in town*) terrain(s) *m(pl)*
vague(s).
wastepaper basket ['weɪstpeɪpə-] *n* corbeille

f à papier.
waste pipe *n* (tuyau *m* de) vidange *f*.
waste products *npl* (*INDUSTRY*) déchets *mpl*
(de fabrication).
waster ['weɪstə*] *n* (*col*) bon/ne à rien.
watch [wɔtʃ] *n* montre *f*; (*act of watching*)
surveillance *f*, guet *m*; (*guard: MIL*) sentinelle
f, (: *NAUT*) homme *m* de quart; (*NAUT: spell of
duty*) quart *m* ♦ *vt* (*look at*) observer;
(: *match, programme*) regarder; (*spy on,
guard*) surveiller; (*be careful of*) faire
attention à
♦ *vi* regarder; (*keep guard*) monter la garde;
to keep a close ~ **on sb/sth** surveiller qn/
qch de près; ~ **what you're doing** fais
attention à ce que tu fais.
▶**watch out** *vi* faire attention.
watchband ['wɔtʃbænd] *n* (*US*) bracelet *m* de
montre.
watchdog ['wɔtʃdɔg] *n* chien *m* de garde; (*fig*)
gardien/ne.
watchful ['wɔtʃful] *adj* attentif(ive),
vigilant(e).
watchmaker ['wɔtʃmeɪkə*] *n* horloger/ère.
watchman ['wɔtʃmən] *n* gardien *m*; (*also:*
night ~) veilleur *m* de nuit.
watch stem *n* (*US*) remontoir *m*.
watch strap *n* bracelet *m* de montre.
watchword ['wɔtʃwəːd] *n* mot *m* de passe.
water ['wɔːtə*] *n* eau *f* ♦ *vt* (*plant*) arroser ♦ *vi*
(*eyes*) larmoyer; **a drink of** ~ un verre d'eau;
in British ~**s** dans les eaux territoriales
Britanniques; **to pass** ~ uriner; **to make
sb's mouth** ~ mettre l'eau à la bouche de
qn.
▶**water down** *vt* (*milk*) couper d'eau; (*fig:
story*) édulcorer.
water closet *n* (*BRIT*) w.-c. *mpl*, waters *mpl*.
watercolour, (*US*) **watercolor** ['wɔːtəkʌlə*]
n aquarelle *f*; ~**s** *npl* couleurs *fpl* pour
aquarelle.
water-cooled ['wɔːtəkuːld] *adj* à
refroidissement par eau.
watercress ['wɔːtəkrɛs] *n* cresson *m* (de
fontaine).
waterfall ['wɔːtəfɔːl] *n* chute *f* d'eau.
waterfront ['wɔːtəfrʌnt] *n* (*seafront*) front *m*
de mer; (*at docks*) quais *mpl*.
water heater *n* chauffe-eau *m*.
water hole *n* mare *f*.
water ice *n* (*BRIT*) sorbet *m*.
watering can ['wɔːtərɪŋ-] *n* arrosoir *m*.
water level *n* niveau *m* de l'eau; (*of flood*)
niveau des eaux.
water lily *n* nénuphar *m*.
waterline ['wɔːtəlaɪn] *n* (*NAUT*) ligne *f* de
flottaison.
waterlogged ['wɔːtələgd] *adj* détrempé(e);
imbibé(e) d'eau.
water main *n* canalisation *f* d'eau.
watermark ['wɔːtəmɑːk] *n* (*on paper*) filigrane
m.

watermelon ['wɔːtəmɛlən] *n* pastèque *f*.
water polo *n* water-polo *m*.
waterproof ['wɔːtəpruːf] *adj* imperméable.
water-repellent ['wɔːtərɪ'pɛlnt] *adj*
  hydrofuge.
watershed ['wɔːtəʃɛd] *n* (GEO) ligne *f* de
  partage des eaux; (*fig*) moment *m* critique,
  point décisif.
water-skiing ['wɔːtəskiːɪŋ] *n* ski *m* nautique.
water softener *n* adoucisseur *m* d'eau.
water tank *n* réservoir *m* d'eau.
watertight ['wɔːtətaɪt] *adj* étanche.
water vapour *n* vapeur *f* d'eau.
waterway ['wɔːtəweɪ] *n* cours *m* d'eau
  navigable.
waterworks ['wɔːtəwɔːks] *npl* station *f*
  hydraulique.
watery ['wɔːtərɪ] *adj* (*colour*) délavé(e);
  (*coffee*) trop faible.
watt [wɔt] *n* watt *m*.
wattage ['wɔtɪdʒ] *n* puissance *f* or
  consommation *f* en watts.
wattle ['wɔtl] *n* clayonnage *m*.
wave [weɪv] *n* vague *f*; (*of hand*) geste *m*, signe
  m; (RADIO) onde *f*; (*in hair*) ondulation *f*; (*fig:
  of enthusiasm, strikes etc*) vague ♦ *vi* faire
  signe de la main; (*flag*) flotter au vent ♦ *vt*
  (*handkerchief*) agiter; (*stick*) brandir; (*hair*)
  onduler; **to ~ goodbye to sb** dire au revoir
  de la main à qn; **short/medium ~** (RADIO)
  ondes courtes/moyennes; **long ~** (RADIO)
  grandes ondes; **the new ~** (CINE, MUS) la
  nouvelle vague.
▶**wave aside, wave away** *vt* (*person*): **to ~
  sb aside** faire signe à qn de s'écarter; (*fig:
  suggestion, objection*) rejeter, repousser;
  (*: doubts*) chasser.
waveband ['weɪvbænd] *n* bande *f* de
  fréquences.
wavelength ['weɪvlɛŋθ] *n* longueur *f* d'ondes.
waver ['weɪvə*] *vi* vaciller; (*voice*) trembler;
  (*person*) hésiter.
wavy ['weɪvɪ] *adj* ondulé(e); onduleux(euse).
wax [wæks] *n* cire *f*; (*for skis*) fart *m* ♦ *vt* cirer;
  (*car*) lustrer ♦ *vi* (*moon*) croître.
waxen ['wæksn] *adj* cireux(euse).
waxworks ['wækswɔːks] *npl* personnages *mpl*
  de cire; musée *m* de cire.
way [weɪ] *n* chemin *m*, voie *f*; (*path, access*)
  passage *m*; (*distance*) distance *f*; (*direction*)
  chemin, direction *f*; (*manner*) façon *f*,
  manière *f*; (*habit*) habitude *f*, façon;
  (*condition*) état *m*; **which ~? — this ~** par où
  or de quel côté? — par ici; **to crawl one's ~
  to ...** ramper jusqu'à ...; **to lie one's ~ out of
  it** s'en sortir par un mensonge; **to lose one's
  ~** perdre son chemin; **on the ~** (**to**) en route
  (pour); **to be on one's ~** être en route; **to be
  in the ~** bloquer le passage; (*fig*) gêner; **to
  keep out of sb's ~** éviter qn; **it's a long ~
  away** c'est loin d'ici; **the village is rather out
  of the ~** le village est plutôt à l'écart *or*

isolé; **to go out of one's ~ to do** (*fig*) se
donner beaucoup de mal pour faire; **to be
under ~** (*work, project*) être en cours; **to
make ~ (for sb/sth)** faire place (à qn/qch),
s'écarter pour laisser passer (qn/qch); **to
get one's own ~** arriver à ses fins; **put it the
right ~ up** (BRIT) mettez-le dans le bon sens;
to be the wrong ~ round être à l'envers, ne
pas être dans le bon sens; **he's in a bad ~** il
va mal; **in a ~** d'un côté; **in some ~s** à
certains égards; d'un côté; **in the ~ of** en
fait de, comme; **by ~ of** (*through*) en passant
par, via; (*as a sort of*) en guise de; **"~ in"**
(BRIT) "entrée"; **"~ out"** (BRIT) "sortie"; **the
~ back** le chemin du retour; **this ~ and that**
par-ci par-là; **"give ~"** (BRIT AUT) "cédez la
priorité"; **no ~!** (*col*) pas question!
waybill ['weɪbɪl] *n* (COMM) récépissé *m*.
waylay [weɪ'leɪ] *vt irreg* attaquer; (*fig*): **I got
  waylaid** quelqu'un m'a accroché.
wayside ['weɪsaɪd] *n* bord *m* de la route; **to fall
  by the ~** (*fig*) abandonner; (*morally*) quitter
  le droit chemin.
way station *n* (US RAIL) petite gare; (*: fig*)
  étape *f*.
wayward ['weɪwəd] *adj* capricieux(euse),
  entêté(e).
WC *n abbr* (BRIT: = *water closet*) w.-c. *mpl*,
  waters *mpl*.
WCC *n abbr* (= *World Council of Churches*) COE
  m (= *Conseil œcuménique des Églises*).
we [wiː] *pl pron* nous.
weak [wiːk] *adj* faible; (*health*) fragile; (*beam
  etc*) peu solide; (*tea, coffee*) léger(ère); **to
  grow ~(er)** s'affaiblir, faiblir.
weaken ['wiːkn] *vi* faiblir ♦ *vt* affaiblir.
weak-kneed ['wiːk'niːd] *adj* (*fig*) lâche, faible.
weakling ['wiːklɪŋ] *n* gringalet *m*; faible *m/f*.
weakly ['wiːklɪ] *adj* chétif(ive) ♦ *adv*
  faiblement.
weakness ['wiːknɪs] *n* faiblesse *f*; (*fault*) point
  m faible.
wealth [wɛlθ] *n* (*money, resources*) richesse(s)
  f(pl); (*of details*) profusion *f*.
wealth tax *n* impôt *m* sur la fortune.
wealthy ['wɛlθɪ] *adj* riche.
wean [wiːn] *vt* sevrer.
weapon ['wɛpən] *n* arme *f*.
wear [wɛə*] *n* (*use*) usage *m*; (*deterioration
  through use*) usure *f*; (*clothing*): **sports/baby~**
  vêtements *mpl* de sport/pour bébés; **town/
  evening ~** tenue *f* de ville/de soirée ♦ *vb* (*pt
  wore, pp worn* [wɔː*, wɔːn]) *vt* (*clothes*)
  porter; (*beard etc*) avoir; (*damage: through
  use*) user ♦ *vi* (*last*) faire de l'usage; (*rub etc
  through*) s'user; **~ and tear** usure *f*; **to ~ a
  hole in sth** faire (à la longue) un trou dans
  qch.
▶**wear away** *vt* user, ronger ♦ *vi* s'user, être
  rongé(e).
▶**wear down** *vt* user; (*strength*) épuiser.
▶**wear off** *vi* disparaître.

▶**wear on** *vi* se poursuivre; passer.

▶**wear out** *vt* user; (*person, strength*) épuiser.

wearable ['wɛərəbl] *adj* mettable.

wearily ['wɪərɪlɪ] *adv* avec lassitude.

weariness ['wɪərɪnɪs] *n* épuisement *m*, lassitude *f*.

wearisome ['wɪərɪsəm] *adj* (*tiring*) fatigant(e); (*boring*) ennuyeux(euse).

weary ['wɪərɪ] *adj* (*tired*) épuisé(e); (*dispirited*) las(lasse); abattu(e) ♦ *vt* lasser ♦ *vi*: **to ~ of** se lasser de.

weasel ['wiːzl] *n* (*ZOOL*) belette *f*.

weather ['wɛðə*] *n* temps *m* ♦ *vt* (*wood*) faire mûrir; (*tempest, crisis*) essuyer, être pris(e) dans; survivre à, tenir le coup durant; **what's the ~ like?** quel temps fait-il?; **under the ~** (*fig: ill*) mal fichu(e).

weather-beaten ['wɛðəbiːtn] *adj* (*person*) hâlé(e); (*building*) dégradé(e) par les intempéries.

weather cock *n* girouette *f*.

weather forecast *n* prévisions *fpl* météorologiques, météo *f*.

weatherman ['wɛðəmæn] *n* météorologue *m*.

weatherproof ['wɛðəpruːf] *adj* (*garment*) imperméable; (*building*) étanche.

weather report *n* bulletin *m* météo, météo *f*.

weather vane [-veɪn] *n* = **weather cock.**

weave, *pt* **wove,** *pp* **woven** [wiːv, wəuv, 'wəuvn] *vt* (*cloth*) tisser; (*basket*) tresser ♦ *vi* (*fig: pt, pp* ~**d**: *move in and out*) se faufiler.

weaver ['wiːvə*] *n* tisserand/e.

weaving ['wiːvɪŋ] *n* tissage *m*.

web [wɛb] *n* (*of spider*) toile *f*; (*on foot*) palmure *f*; (*fabric, also fig*) tissu *m*.

webbed [wɛbd] *adj* (*foot*) palmé(e).

webbing ['wɛbɪŋ] *n* (*on chair*) sangles *fpl*.

wed [wɛd] *vt* (*pt, pp* **wedded**) épouser ♦ *n*: **the newly-~s** les jeunes mariés.

Wed. *abbr* (= *Wednesday*) me.

we'd [wiːd] = **we had, we would.**

wedded ['wɛdɪd] *pt, pp of* **wed.**

wedding ['wɛdɪŋ] *n* mariage *m*.

wedding anniversary *n* anniversaire *m* de mariage; **silver/golden ~** noces *fpl* d'argent/ d'or.

wedding day *n* jour *m* du mariage.

wedding dress *n* robe *f* de mariée.

wedding present *n* cadeau *m* de mariage.

wedding ring *n* alliance *f*.

wedge [wɛdʒ] *n* (*of wood etc*) coin *m*; (*under door etc*) cale *f*; (*of cake*) part *f* ♦ *vt* (*fix*) caler; (*push*) enfoncer, coincer.

wedge-heeled shoes ['wɛdʒhiːld-] *npl* chaussures *fpl* à semelles compensées.

wedlock ['wɛdlɔk] *n* (*union f du*) mariage *m*.

Wednesday ['wɛdnzdɪ] *n* mercredi *m*; *for phrases see also* **Tuesday.**

wee [wiː] *adj* (*Scottish*) petit(e); tout(e) petit(e).

weed [wiːd] *n* mauvaise herbe ♦ *vt* désherber.

▶**weed out** *vt* éliminer.

weed-killer ['wiːdkɪlə*] *n* désherbant *m*.

weedy ['wiːdɪ] *adj* (*man*) gringalet.

week [wiːk] *n* semaine *f*; **once/twice a ~** une fois/deux fois par semaine; **in two ~s' time** dans quinze jours; **Tuesday ~, a ~ on Tuesday** mardi en huit.

weekday ['wiːkdeɪ] *n* jour *m* de semaine; (*COMM*) jour ouvrable; **on ~s** en semaine.

weekend [wiːk'ɛnd] *n* week-end *m*.

weekend case *n* sac *m* de voyage.

weekly ['wiːklɪ] *adv* une fois par semaine, chaque semaine ♦ *adj*, *n* hebdomadaire (*m*).

weep, *pt, pp* **wept** [wiːp, wɛpt] *vi* (*person*) pleurer; (*MED: wound etc*) suinter.

weeping willow ['wiːpɪŋ-] *n* saule pleureur.

weepy ['wiːpɪ] *n* (*col: film*) mélo *m*.

weft [wɛft] *n* (*TEXTILES*) trame *f*.

weigh [weɪ] *vt, vi* peser; **to ~ anchor** lever l'ancre; **to ~ the pros and cons** peser le pour et le contre.

▶**weigh down** *vt* (*branch*) faire plier; (*fig: with worry*) accabler.

▶**weigh out** *vt* (*goods*) peser.

▶**weigh up** *vt* examiner.

weighbridge ['weɪbrɪdʒ] *n* pont-bascule *m*.

weighing machine ['weɪɪŋ-] *n* balance *f*, bascule *f*.

weight [weɪt] *n* poids *m* ♦ *vt* alourdir; (*fig: factor*) pondérer; **sold by ~** vendu au poids; **to put on/lose ~** grossir/maigrir; **~s and measures** poids et mesures.

weighting ['weɪtɪŋ] *n*: **~ allowance** indemnité *f* de résidence.

weightlessness ['weɪtlɪsnɪs] *n* apesanteur *f*.

weightlifter ['weɪtlɪftə*] *n* haltérophile *m*.

weight training *n* musculation *f*.

weighty ['weɪtɪ] *adj* lourd(e).

weir [wɪə*] *n* barrage *m*.

weird [wɪəd] *adj* bizarre; (*eerie*) surnaturel(le).

weirdo ['wɪədəu] *n* (*col*) type *m* bizarre.

welcome ['wɛlkəm] *adj* bienvenu(e) ♦ *n* accueil *m* ♦ *vt* accueillir; (*also: bid ~*) souhaiter la bienvenue à; (*be glad of*) se réjouir de; **to be ~** être le(la) bienvenu(e); **to make sb ~** faire bon accueil à qn; **you're ~ to try** vous pouvez essayer si vous voulez; **you're ~!** (*after thanks*) de rien, il n'y a pas de quoi.

welcoming ['wɛlkəmɪŋ] *adj* accueillant(e); (*speech*) d'accueil.

weld [wɛld] *n* soudure *f* ♦ *vt* souder.

welder ['wɛldə*] *n* (*person*) soudeur *m*.

welding ['wɛldɪŋ] *n* soudure *f* (autogène).

welfare ['wɛlfɛə*] *n* bien-être *m*.

welfare state *n* État-providence *m*.

welfare work *n* travail social.

well [wɛl] *n* puits *m* ♦ *adv* bien ♦ *adj*: **to be ~** aller bien ♦ *excl* eh bien!; bon!; enfin!; **~ done!** bravo!; **I don't feel ~** je ne me sens pas bien; **get ~ soon!** remets-toi vite!; **to do ~ in sth** bien réussir en or dans qch; **to**

think ~ **of sb** penser du bien de qn; **as ~** (in addition) aussi, également; **you might as ~ tell me** tu ferais aussi bien de me le dire; **as ~ as** aussi bien que or as; en plus de; **~, as I was saying ...** donc, comme je disais ....

▶**well up** vi (tears, emotions) monter.

we'll [wi:l] = **we will, we shall.**

well-behaved ['wɛlbɪ'heɪvd] adj sage, obéissant(e).

well-being ['wɛl'bi:ɪŋ] n bien-être m.

well-bred ['wɛl'brɛd] adj bien élevé(e).

well-built ['wɛl'bɪlt] adj (house) bien construit(e); (person) bien bâti(e).

well-chosen ['wɛl'tʃəuzn] adj (remarks, words) bien choisi(e), pertinent(e).

well-developed ['wɛldɪ'vɛləpt] adj (girl) bien fait(e).

well-disposed ['wɛldɪs'pəuzd] adj: **~ to(wards)** bien disposé(e) envers.

well-dressed ['wɛl'drɛst] adj bien habillé(e), bien vêtu(e).

well-earned ['wɛl'ə:nd] adj (rest) bien mérité(e).

well-groomed ['wɛl'gru:md] adj très soigné(e) de sa personne.

well-heeled ['wɛl'hi:ld] adj (col: wealthy) fortuné(e), riche.

well-informed ['wɛlɪn'fɔ:md] adj (having knowledge of sth) bien renseigné(e); (having general knowledge) cultivé(e).

Wellington ['wɛlɪŋtən] n Wellington.

wellingtons ['wɛlɪŋtənz] npl (also: **wellington boots**) bottes fpl de caoutchouc.

well-kept ['wɛl'kɛpt] adj (house, grounds) bien tenu(e), bien entretenu(e); (secret) bien gardé(e); (hair, hands) soigné(e).

well-known ['wɛl'nəun] adj (person) bien connu(e).

well-mannered ['wɛl'mænəd] adj bien élevé(e).

well-meaning ['wɛl'mi:nɪŋ] adj bien intentionné(e).

well-nigh ['wɛl'naɪ] adv: **~ impossible** pratiquement impossible.

well-off ['wɛl'ɔf] adj aisé(e), assez riche.

well-read ['wɛl'rɛd] adj cultivé(e).

well-spoken ['wɛl'spəukn] adj (person) qui parle bien; (words) bien choisi(e).

well-stocked ['wɛl'stɔkt] adj bien approvisionné(e).

well-timed ['wɛl'taɪmd] adj opportun(e).

well-to-do ['wɛltə'du:] adj aisé(e), assez riche.

well-wisher ['wɛlwɪʃə*] n ami/e, admirateur/trice; **scores of ~s had gathered** de nombreux amis et admirateurs s'étaient rassemblés; **letters from ~s** des lettres d'encouragement.

well-woman clinic ['wɛlwumən-] n service de check-up pour les femmes dans un cabinet médical.

Welsh [wɛlʃ] adj gallois(e) ♦ n (LING) gallois m; **the ~** npl les Gallois.

Welshman, Welshwoman ['wɛlʃmən, -wumən] n Gallois/e.

Welsh rarebit n croûte f au fromage.

welter ['wɛltə*] n fatras m.

went [wɛnt] pt of **go**.

wept [wɛpt] pt, pp of **weep**.

were [wə:*] pt of **be**.

we're [wɪə*] = **we are**.

weren't [wə:nt] = **were not**.

werewolf, pl **-wolves** ['wɪəwulf, -wulvz] n loup-garou m.

west [wɛst] n ouest m ♦ adj ouest inv, de or à l'ouest ♦ adv à or vers l'ouest; **the W~** l'Occident m, l'Ouest.

westbound ['wɛstbaund] adj (traffic) en direction de l'ouest; (carriageway) ouest inv.

West Country n: **the ~** le sud-ouest de l'Angleterre.

westerly ['wɛstəlɪ] adj (situation) à l'ouest; (wind) d'ouest.

western ['wɛstən] adj occidental(e), de or à l'ouest ♦ n (CINE) western m.

westerner ['wɛstənə*] n occidental/e.

westernized ['wɛstənaɪzd] adj occidentalisé(e).

West German (formerly) adj ouest-allemand(e) ♦ n Allemand/e de l'Ouest.

West Germany n (formerly) Allemagne f de l'Ouest.

West Indian adj antillais(e) ♦ n Antillais/e.

West Indies [-'ɪndɪz] npl: **the ~** les Antilles fpl.

Westminster ['wɛstmɪnstə*] n (BRIT PARLIAMENT) Westminster m.

westward(s) ['wɛstwəd(z)] adv vers l'ouest.

wet [wɛt] adj mouillé(e); (damp) humide; (soaked) trempé(e); (rainy) pluvieux(euse) ♦ vt: **to ~ one's pants** or **o.s.** mouiller sa culotte, faire pipi dans sa culotte; **to get ~** se mouiller; **"~ paint"** "attention peinture fraîche".

wet blanket n (fig) rabat-joie m inv.

wetness ['wɛtnɪs] n humidité f.

wet suit n combinaison f de plongée.

we've [wi:v] = **we have**.

whack [wæk] vt donner un grand coup à.

whacked [wækt] adj (BRIT col: tired) crevé(e).

whale [weɪl] n (ZOOL) baleine f.

whaler ['weɪlə*] n (ship) baleinier m.

whaling ['weɪlɪŋ] n pêche f à la baleine.

wharf, pl **wharves** [wɔ:f, wɔ:vz] n quai m.

═══════════════════════════ **KEYWORD**

what [wɔt] adj quel(le); **~ size is he?** quelle taille fait-il?; **~ colour is it?** de quelle couleur est-ce?; **~ books do you need?** quels livres vous faut-il?; **~ a mess!** quel désordre!

♦ pron 1 (interrogative) que, prep +quoi; **~ are you doing?** que faites-vous?, qu'est-ce que vous faites?; **~ is happening?** qu'est-ce qui se passe?, que se passe-t-il?; **~ are you talking about?** de quoi parlez-vous?; **~ is it**

called? comment est-ce que ça s'appelle?; ~
about me? et moi?; ~ **about doing ...?** et si
on faisait ...?
2 (relative: subject) ce qui; (: direct object) ce
que; (: indirect object) ce +prep +quoi, ce dont;
I saw ~ you did/was on the table j'ai vu ce
que vous avez fait/ce qui était sur la table;
tell me ~ you remember dites-moi ce dont
vous vous souvenez; ~ **I want is a cup of tea**
ce que je veux, c'est une tasse de thé
♦ excl (disbelieving) quoi!, comment!

whatever [wɔt'ɛvə*] adj: ~ **book** quel que soit
le livre que (or qui) + sub; n'importe quel
livre ♦ pron: **do ~ is necessary** faites (tout)
ce qui est nécessaire; ~ **happens** quoi qu'il
arrive; **no reason ~** or **whatsoever** pas la
moindre raison; **nothing ~** or **whatsoever**
rien du tout.
whatsoever [wɔtsəu'ɛvə*] adj see **whatever**.
wheat [wi:t] n blé m, froment m.
wheatgerm ['wi:tdʒə:m] n germe m de blé.
wheatmeal ['wi:tmi:l] n farine bise.
wheedle ['wi:dl] vt: **to ~ sb into doing sth**
cajoler or enjôler qn pour qu'il fasse qch;
to ~ sth out of sb obtenir qch de qn par des
cajoleries.
wheel [wi:l] n roue f; (AUT: also: **steering ~**)
volant m; (NAUT) gouvernail m ♦ vt pousser,
rouler ♦ vi (also: ~ **round**) tourner.
wheelbarrow ['wi:lbærəu] n brouette f.
wheelbase ['wi:lbeis] n empattement m.
wheelchair ['wi:ltʃɛə*] n fauteuil roulant.
wheel clamp n (AUT) sabot m (de Denver).
wheeler-dealer ['wi:lə'di:lə*] n (pej)
combinard/e, affairiste m/f.
wheelie-bin ['wi:lɪbɪn] n (BRIT) poubelle f à
roulettes.
wheeling ['wi:lɪŋ] n: ~ **and dealing** (pej)
manigances fpl, magouilles fpl.
wheeze [wi:z] n respiration bruyante
(d'asthmatique) ♦ vi respirer bruyamment.
wheezy ['wi:zɪ] adj sifflant(e).

=========================== KEYWORD

when [wen] adv quand; ~ **did he go?** quand
est-ce qu'il est parti?
♦ conj **1** (at, during, after the time that) quand,
lorsque; **she was reading ~ I came in** elle
lisait quand or lorsque je suis entré
2 (on, at which): **on the day ~ I met him** le
jour où je l'ai rencontré
3 (whereas) alors que; **I thought I was
wrong ~ in fact I was right** j'ai cru que
j'avais tort alors qu'en fait j'avais raison.

whenever [wɛn'ɛvə*] adv quand donc ♦ conj
quand; (every time that) chaque fois que; **I go
~ I can** j'y vais quand or chaque fois que je
le peux.
where [wɛə*] adv, conj où; **this is ~** c'est là
que; ~ **are you from?** d'où venez vous?

whereabouts ['wɛərəbauts] adv où donc ♦ n:
sb's ~ l'endroit où se trouve qn.
whereas [wɛər'æz] conj alors que.
whereby [wɛə'baɪ] adv (formal) par lequel (or
laquelle etc).
whereupon [wɛərə'pɔn] adv sur quoi, et sur
ce.
wherever [wɛər'ɛvə*] adv où donc ♦ conj où
que + sub; **sit ~ you like** asseyez-vous (là) où
vous voulez.
wherewithal ['wɛəwɪðɔ:l] n: **the ~ (to do sth)**
les moyens mpl (de faire qch).
whet [wɛt] vt aiguiser.
whether ['wɛðə*] conj si; **I don't know ~ to
accept or not** je ne sais pas si je dois
accepter ou non; **it's doubtful ~** il est peu
probable que; ~ **you go or not** que vous y
alliez ou non.
whey ['weɪ] n petit-lait m.

=========================== KEYWORD

which [wɪtʃ] adj **1** (interrogative: direct, indirect)
quel(le); ~ **picture do you want?** quel
tableau voulez-vous?; ~ **one?**
lequel(laquelle)?
2: **in ~ case** auquel cas
♦ pron **1** (interrogative) lequel(laquelle),
lesquels(lesquelles) pl; **I don't mind ~** peu
importe lequel; ~ **(of these) are yours?**
lesquels sont à vous?; **tell me ~ you want**
dites-moi lesquels or ceux que vous voulez
2 (relative: subject) qui; (: object) que, prep
+lequel(laquelle); (NB: à + lequel = auquel;
de + lequel = duquel); **the apple ~ you ate/~
is on the table** la pomme que vous avez
mangée/qui est sur la table; **the chair on ~
you are sitting** la chaise sur laquelle vous
êtes assis; **the book of ~ you spoke** le livre
dont vous avez parlé; **he knew, ~ is true/I
feared** il le savait, ce qui est vrai/ce que je
craignais; **after ~** après quoi.

whichever [wɪtʃ'ɛvə*] adj: **take ~ book you
prefer** prenez le livre que vous préférez,
peu importe lequel; ~ **book you take** quel
que soit le livre que vous preniez; ~ **way
you** de quelque façon que vous + sub.
whiff [wɪf] n bouffée f; **to catch a ~ of sth**
sentir l'odeur de qch.
while [waɪl] n moment m ♦ conj pendant que;
(as long as) tant que; (as, whereas) alors que;
(though) quoique + sub; **for a ~** pendant
quelque temps; **in a ~** dans un moment; **all
the ~** pendant tout ce temps-là; **we'll make
it worth your ~** nous vous récompenserons
de votre peine.
► **while away** vt (time) (faire) passer.
whilst [waɪlst] conj = **while**.
whim [wɪm] n caprice m.
whimper ['wɪmpə*] n geignement m ♦ vi
geindre.
whimsical ['wɪmzɪkl] adj (person)

capricieux(euse); (look) étrange.

whine [waɪn] n gémissement m ♦ vi gémir, geindre; pleurnicher.

whip [wɪp] n fouet m; (for riding) cravache f; (POL: person) chef m de file (assurant la discipline dans son groupe parlementaire) ♦ vt fouetter; (snatch) enlever (or sortir) brusquement.

▶ **whip up** vt (cream) fouetter; (col: meal) préparer en vitesse; (stir up: support) stimuler; (: feeling) attiser, aviver.

Un **whip** est un député dont le rôle est, entre autres, de s'assurer que les membres de son parti sont régulièrement présents à la **House of Commons**, surtout lorsque les votes ont lieu. Les convocations que les whips envoient se distinguent, selon leur degré d'importance, par le fait qu'elles sont soulignées 1, 2 ou 3 fois (les "1-, 2-, ou 3-line whips").

whiplash ['wɪplæʃ] n (MED: also: ~ injury) coup m du lapin.

whipped cream [wɪpt-] n crème fouettée.

whipping boy ['wɪpɪŋ-] n (fig) bouc m émissaire.

whip-round ['wɪpraʊnd] n (BRIT) collecte f.

whirl [wəːl] n tourbillon m ♦ vt faire tourbillonner; faire tournoyer ♦ vi tourbillonner.

whirlpool ['wəːlpuːl] n tourbillon m.

whirlwind ['wəːlwɪnd] n tornade f.

whirr [wəː*] vi bruire; ronronner; vrombir.

whisk [wɪsk] n (CULIN) fouet m ♦ vt fouetter, battre; **to ~ sb away** or **off** emmener qn rapidement.

whiskers ['wɪskəz] npl (of animal) moustaches fpl; (of man) favoris mpl.

whisky, (Irish, US) **whiskey** ['wɪskɪ] n whisky m.

whisper ['wɪspə*] n chuchotement m; (fig: of leaves) bruissement m; (rumour) rumeur f ♦ vt, vi chuchoter; **to ~ sth to sb** chuchoter qch à (l'oreille de) qn.

whispering ['wɪspərɪŋ] n chuchotement(s) m(pl).

whist [wɪst] n (BRIT) whist m.

whistle ['wɪsl] n (sound) sifflement m; (object) sifflet m ♦ vi siffler ♦ vt siffler, siffloter.

whistle-stop ['wɪslstɔp] adj: **to make a ~ tour of** (POL) faire la tournée électorale des petits patelins de.

Whit [wɪt] n la Pentecôte.

white [waɪt] adj blanc(blanche); (with fear) blême ♦ n blanc m; (person) blanc/blanche; **to turn** or **go ~** (person) pâlir, blêmir; (hair) blanchir; **the ~s** (washing) le linge blanc; **tennis ~s** tenue f de tennis.

whitebait ['waɪtbeɪt] n blanchaille f.

white coffee n (BRIT) café m au lait, (café) crème m.

white-collar worker ['waɪtkɔlə-] n employé/e de bureau.

white elephant n (fig) objet dispendieux et superflu.

white goods npl (appliances) (gros) électro-ménager m; (linen etc) linge m de maison.

white-hot [waɪt'hɔt] adj (metal) incandescent(e).

White House n (US): **the ~** la Maison-Blanche.

La **White House** est un grand bâtiment blanc situé à Washington D.C. où réside le Président des États-Unis. Par extension, ce terme désigne l'exécutif américain.

white lie n pieux mensonge.

whiteness ['waɪtnɪs] n blancheur f.

white noise n son m blanc.

whiteout ['waɪtaʊt] n jour blanc.

white paper n (POL) livre blanc.

whitewash ['waɪtwɔʃ] n (paint) lait m de chaux ♦ vt blanchir à la chaux; (fig) blanchir.

whiting ['waɪtɪŋ] n (pl inv) (fish) merlan m.

Whit Monday n le lundi de Pentecôte.

Whitsun ['wɪtsn] n la Pentecôte.

whittle ['wɪtl] vt: **to ~ away**, **~ down** (costs) réduire, rogner.

whizz [wɪz] vi aller (or passer) à toute vitesse.

whizz kid n (col) petit prodige.

WHO n abbr (= World Health Organization) OMS f (= Organisation mondiale de la Santé).

who [huː] pron qui.

whodunit [huː'dʌnɪt] n (col) roman policier.

whoever [huː'ɛvə*] pron: **~ finds it** celui(celle) qui le trouve (, qui que ce soit), quiconque le trouve; **ask ~ you like** demandez à qui vous voulez; **~ he marries** qui que ce soit or quelle que soit la personne qu'il épouse; **~ told you that?** qui a bien pu vous dire ça?, qui donc vous a dit ça?

whole [həʊl] adj (complete) entier(ère), tout(e); (not broken) intact(e), complet(ète) ♦ n (total) totalité f; (sth not broken) tout m; **the ~ lot (of it)** tout; **the ~ lot (of them)** tous (sans exception); **the ~ of the time** tout le temps; **the ~ of the town** la ville tout entière; **~ villages were destroyed** des villages entiers ont été détruits; **on the ~**, **as a ~** dans l'ensemble.

wholehearted [həʊl'hɑːtɪd] adj sans réserve(s), sincère.

wholemeal ['həʊlmiːl] adj (BRIT: flour, bread) complet(ète).

whole note n (US) ronde f.

wholesale ['həʊlseɪl] n (vente f en) gros m ♦ adj de gros; (destruction) systématique.

wholesaler ['həʊlseɪlə*] n grossiste m/f.

wholesome ['həʊlsəm] adj sain(e); (advice) salutaire.

wholewheat ['həʊlwiːt] adj = **wholemeal**.

wholly ['həulɪ] *adv* entièrement, tout à fait.

================== *KEYWORD*

whom [hu:m] *pron* **1** (*interrogative*) qui; ~ **did you see?** qui avez-vous vu?; **to ~ did you give it?** à qui l'avez-vous donné?
2 (*relative*) que, *prep* + qui; **the man ~ I saw/ to ~ I spoke** l'homme que j'ai vu/à qui j'ai parlé.

whooping cough ['hu:pɪŋ-] *n* coqueluche *f*.
whoops [wu:ps] *excl* (*also*: ~-**a-daisy**) oups!, houp-là!
whoosh [wuʃ] *n, vi*: **the skiers ~ed past, the skiers came by with a ~** les skieurs passèrent dans un glissement rapide.
whopper ['wɔpə*] *n* (*col: lie*) gros bobard; (*: large thing*) monstre *m*, phénomène *m*.
whopping ['wɔpɪŋ] *adj* (*col: big*) énorme.
whore [hɔ:*] *n* (*col: pej*) putain *f*.

================== *KEYWORD*

whose [hu:z] *adj* **1** (*possessive: interrogative*): ~ **book is this?** à qui est ce livre?; ~ **pencil have you taken?** à qui est le crayon que vous avez pris?, c'est le crayon de qui que vous avez pris?; ~ **daughter are you?** de qui êtes-vous la fille?
2 (*possessive: relative*): **the man ~ son you rescued** l'homme dont *or* de qui vous avez sauvé le fils; **the girl ~ sister you were speaking to** la fille à la sœur de qui *or* de laquelle vous parliez; **the woman ~ car was stolen** la femme dont la voiture a été volée
♦ *pron* à qui; ~ **is this?** à qui est ceci?; **I know ~ it is** je sais à qui c'est.

Who's Who ['hu:z'hu:] *n* ≈ Bottin Mondain.
why [waɪ] *adv* pourquoi ♦ *excl* eh bien!, tiens!; **the reason** ~ la raison pour laquelle; ~ **is he late?** pourquoi est-il en retard?
whyever [waɪ'ɛvə*] *adv* pourquoi donc, mais pourquoi.
WI *n abbr* (*BRIT*: = *Women's Institute*) amicale de femmes au foyer ♦ *abbr* (*GEO*) = **West Indies**; (*US*) = **Wisconsin**.
wick [wɪk] *n* mèche *f* (*de bougie*).
wicked ['wɪkɪd] *adj* foncièrement mauvais(e), inique; (*mischievous: grin, look*) espiègle, malicieux(euse); (*terrible: prices, weather*) épouvantable.
wicker ['wɪkə*] *n* osier *m*; (*also*: ~**work**) vannerie *f*.
wicket ['wɪkɪt] *n* (*CRICKET*) guichet *m*; espace compris entre les deux guichets.
wicket keeper *n* (*CRICKET*) gardien *m* de guichet.
wide [waɪd] *adj* large; (*region, knowledge*) vaste, très étendu(e); (*choice*) grand(e)
♦ *adv*: **to open** ~ ouvrir tout grand; **to shoot**

~ tirer à côté; **it is 3 metres** ~ cela fait 3 mètres de large.
wide-angle lens ['waɪdæŋgl-] *n* objectif *m* grand-angulaire.
wide-awake [waɪdə'weɪk] *adj* bien éveillé(e).
wide-eyed [waɪd'aɪd] *adj* aux yeux écarquillés; (*fig*) naïf(ïve), crédule.
widely ['waɪdlɪ] *adv* (*different*) radicalement; (*spaced*) sur une grande étendue; (*believed*) généralement; **to be** ~ **read** (*author*) être beaucoup lu(e); (*reader*) avoir beaucoup lu, être cultivé(e).
widen ['waɪdn] *vt* élargir.
wideness ['waɪdnɪs] *n* largeur *f*.
wide open *adj* grand(e) ouvert(e).
wide-ranging [waɪd'reɪndʒɪŋ] *adj* (*survey, report*) vaste; (*interests*) divers(e).
widespread ['waɪdsprɛd] *adj* (*belief etc*) très répandu(e).
widow ['wɪdəu] *n* veuve *f*.
widowed ['wɪdəud] *adj* (qui est devenu(e)) veuf(veuve).
widower ['wɪdəuə*] *n* veuf *m*.
width [wɪdθ] *n* largeur *f*; **it's 7 metres in** ~ cela fait 7 mètres de large.
widthways ['wɪdθweɪz] *adv* en largeur.
wield [wi:ld] *vt* (*sword*) manier; (*power*) exercer.
wife, *pl* **wives** [waɪf, waɪvz] *n* femme (mariée), épouse *f*.
wig [wɪg] *n* perruque *f*.
wigging ['wɪgɪŋ] *n* (*BRIT col*) savon *m*, engueulade *f*.
wiggle ['wɪgl] *vt* agiter, remuer ♦ *vi* (*loose screw etc*) branler; (*worm*) se tortiller.
wiggly ['wɪglɪ] *adj* (*line*) ondulé(e).
wild [waɪld] *adj* sauvage; (*sea*) déchaîné(e); (*idea, life*) fou(folle); extravagant(e); (*col: angry*) hors de soi, furieux(euse); (*: enthusiastic*): **to be** ~ **about** être fou(folle) *or* dingue de ♦ *n*: **the** ~ la nature; ~**s** *npl* régions *fpl* sauvages.
wild card *n* (*COMPUT*) caractère *m* de remplacement.
wildcat ['waɪldkæt] *n* chat *m* sauvage.
wildcat strike *n* grève *f* sauvage.
wilderness ['wɪldənɪs] *n* désert *m*, région *f* sauvage.
wildfire ['waɪldfaɪə*] *n*: **to spread like** ~ se répandre comme une traînée de poudre.
wild-goose chase [waɪld'gu:s-] *n* (*fig*) fausse piste.
wildlife ['waɪldlaɪf] *n* faune *f* (et flore *f*) sauvage(s).
wildly ['waɪldlɪ] *adv* (*applaud*) frénétiquement; (*hit, guess*) au hasard; (*happy*) follement.
wiles [waɪlz] *npl* ruses *fpl*, artifices *mpl*.
wilful, (*US*) **willful** ['wɪlful] *adj* (*person*) obstiné(e); (*action*) délibéré(e); (*crime*) prémédité(e).

will [wɪl] (vt: pt, pp **willed**) aux vb **1** (forming future tense): **I ~ finish it tomorrow** je le finirai demain; **I ~ have finished it by tomorrow** je l'aurai fini d'ici demain; **~ you do it? — yes I ~/no I won't** le ferez-vous? — oui/non; **you won't lose it, ~ you?** vous ne le perdrez pas, n'est-ce pas?
2 (in conjectures, predictions): **he ~ or he'll be there by now** il doit être arrivé à l'heure qu'il est; **that ~ be the postman** ça doit être le facteur
3 (in commands, requests, offers): **~ you be quiet!** voulez-vous bien vous taire!; **~ you help me?** est-ce que vous pouvez m'aider?; **~ you have a cup of tea?** voulez-vous une tasse de thé?; **I won't put up with it!** je ne le tolérerai pas!
♦ vt: **to ~ sb to do** souhaiter ardemment que qn fasse; **he ~ed himself to go on** par un suprême effort de volonté, il continua
♦ n volonté f; testament m; **to do sth of one's own free ~** faire qch de son propre gré; **against one's ~** à contre-cœur.

willful ['wɪlful] adj (US) = **wilful**.
willing ['wɪlɪŋ] adj de bonne volonté, serviable ♦ n: **to show ~** faire preuve de bonne volonté; **he's ~ to do it** il est disposé à le faire, il veut bien le faire.
willingly ['wɪlɪŋlɪ] adv volontiers.
willingness ['wɪlɪŋnɪs] n bonne volonté.
will-o'-the-wisp ['wɪlǝðǝ'wɪsp] n (also fig) feu follet m.
willow ['wɪlǝu] n saule m.
will power n volonté f.
willy-nilly ['wɪlɪ'nɪlɪ] adv bon gré mal gré.
wilt [wɪlt] vi dépérir.
Wilts [wɪlts] abbr (BRIT) = **Wiltshire**.
wily ['waɪlɪ] adj rusé(e).
wimp [wɪmp] n (col) mauviette f.
win [wɪn] n (in sports etc) victoire f ♦ vb (pt, pp **won** [wʌn]) vt (battle, money) gagner; (prize, contract) remporter; (popularity) acquérir ♦ vi gagner.
▶**win over**, (BRIT) **win round** vt gagner, se concilier.
wince [wɪns] n tressaillement m ♦ vi tressaillir.
winch [wɪntʃ] n treuil m.
Winchester disk ['wɪntʃɪstǝ-] n (COMPUT) disque m Winchester.
wind¹ [wɪnd] n (also MED) vent m ♦ vt (take breath away) couper le souffle à; **the ~(s)** (MUS) les instruments mpl à vent; **into or against the ~** contre le vent; **to get ~ of sth** (fig) avoir vent de qch; **to break ~** avoir des gaz.
wind², pt, pp **wound** [waɪnd, waund] vt enrouler; (wrap) envelopper; (clock, toy) remonter ♦ vi (road, river) serpenter

▶**wind down** vt (car window) baisser; (fig: production, business) réduire progressivement.
▶**wind up** vt (clock) remonter; (debate) terminer, clôturer.
windbreak ['wɪndbreɪk] n brise-vent m inv.
windcheater ['wɪndtʃiːtǝ*], (US) **windbreaker** ['wɪndbreɪkǝ*] n anorak m.
winder ['waɪndǝ*] n (BRIT: on watch) remontoir m.
windfall ['wɪndfɔːl] n coup m de chance.
winding ['waɪndɪŋ] adj (road) sinueux(euse); (staircase) tournant(e).
wind instrument n (MUS) instrument m à vent.
windmill ['wɪndmɪl] n moulin m à vent.
window ['wɪndǝu] n fenêtre f; (in car, train, also: ~pane) vitre f; (in shop etc) vitrine f.
window box n jardinière f.
window cleaner n (person) laveur/euse de vitres.
window dressing n arrangement m de la vitrine.
window envelope n enveloppe f à fenêtre.
window frame n châssis m de fenêtre.
window ledge n rebord m de la fenêtre.
window pane n vitre f, carreau m.
window-shopping ['wɪndǝuʃɔpɪŋ] n: **to go ~** faire du lèche-vitrines.
windowsill ['wɪndǝusɪl] n (inside) appui m de la fenêtre; (outside) rebord m de la fenêtre.
windpipe ['wɪndpaɪp] n gosier m.
wind power n énergie éolienne.
windscreen ['wɪndskriːn], (US) **windshield** ['wɪndʃiːld] n pare-brise m inv.
windscreen washer n lave-glace m inv.
windscreen wiper [-waɪpǝ*] n essuie-glace m inv.
windsurfing ['wɪndsǝːfɪŋ] n planche f à voile.
windswept ['wɪndswɛpt] adj balayé(e) par le vent.
wind tunnel n soufflerie f.
windy ['wɪndɪ] adj venté(e), venteux(euse); **it's ~** il y a du vent.
wine [waɪn] n vin m ♦ vt: **to ~ and dine sb** offrir un dîner bien arrosé à qn.
wine bar n bar m à vin.
wine cellar n cave f à vins.
wine glass n verre m à vin.
wine list n carte f des vins.
wine merchant n marchand/e de vins.
wine tasting [-teɪstɪŋ] n dégustation f (de vins).
wine waiter n sommelier m.
wing [wɪŋ] n aile f; (in air force) groupe m d'escadrilles; **~s** npl (THEAT) coulisses fpl.
winger ['wɪŋǝ*] n (SPORT) ailier m.
wing mirror n (BRIT) rétroviseur latéral.
wing nut n papillon m, écrou m à ailettes.
wingspan ['wɪŋspæn] n, **wingspread** ['wɪŋsprɛd] n envergure f.
wink [wɪŋk] n clin m d'œil ♦ vi faire un clin

d'œil; (*blink*) cligner des yeux.

winkle ['wɪŋkl] *n* bigorneau *m*.

winner ['wɪnə*] *n* gagnant/e.

winning ['wɪnɪŋ] *adj* (*team*) gagnant(e); (*goal*) décisif(ive); (*charming*) charmeur(euse).

winning post *n* poteau *m* d'arrivée.

winnings ['wɪnɪŋz] *npl* gains *mpl*.

winsome ['wɪnsəm] *adj* avenant(e), engageant(e).

winter ['wɪntə*] *n* hiver *m* ♦ *vi* hiverner.

winter sports *npl* sports *mpl* d'hiver.

wintry ['wɪntrɪ] *adj* hivernal(e).

wipe [waɪp] *n* coup *m* de torchon (*or* de chiffon *or* d'éponge) ♦ *vt* essuyer; **to give sth a ~** donner un coup de torchon à qch; **to ~ one's nose** se moucher.

▶**wipe off** *vt* essuyer.

▶**wipe out** *vt* (*debt*) régler; (*memory*) oublier; (*destroy*) anéantir.

▶**wipe up** *vt* essuyer.

wire ['waɪə*] *n* fil *m* (de fer); (*ELEC*) fil électrique; (*TEL*) télégramme *m* ♦ *vt* (*fence*) grillager; (*house*) faire l'installation électrique de; (*also:* **~ up**) brancher.

wire brush *n* brosse *f* métallique.

wire cutters [-kʌtəz] *npl* cisaille *f*.

wireless ['waɪəlɪs] *n* (*BRIT*) télégraphie *f* sans fil; (*set*) T.S.F. *f*.

wire netting *n* treillis *m* métallique, grillage *m*.

wire service *n* (*US*) revue *f* de presse (*par téléscripteur*).

wire-tapping ['waɪə'tæpɪŋ] *n* écoute *f* téléphonique.

wiring ['waɪərɪŋ] *n* (*ELEC*) installation *f* électrique.

wiry ['waɪərɪ] *adj* noueux(euse), nerveux(euse).

Wis. *abbr* (*US*) = Wisconsin.

wisdom ['wɪzdəm] *n* sagesse *f*; (*of action*) prudence *f*.

wisdom tooth *n* dent *f* de sagesse.

wise [waɪz] *adj* sage, prudent(e), judicieux(euse); **I'm none the ~r** je ne suis pas plus avancé(e) pour autant.

▶**wise up** *vi* (*col*): **to ~ up to** commencer à se rendre compte de.

...wise [waɪz] *suffix*: **time~** en ce qui concerne le temps, question temps.

wisecrack ['waɪzkræk] *n* sarcasme *m*.

wish [wɪʃ] *n* (*desire*) désir *m*; (*specific desire*) souhait *m*, vœu *m* ♦ *vt* souhaiter, désirer, vouloir; **best ~es** (*on birthday etc*) meilleurs vœux; **with best ~es** (*in letter*) bien amicalement; **give her my best ~es** faites-lui mes amitiés; **to ~ sb goodbye** dire au revoir à qn; **he ~ed me well** il me souhaitait de réussir; **to ~ to do/sb to do** désirer *or* vouloir faire/que qn fasse; **to ~ for** souhaiter; **to ~ sth on sb** souhaiter qch à qn.

wishbone ['wɪʃbəun] *n* fourchette *f*.

wishful ['wɪʃful] *adj*: **it's ~ thinking** c'est prendre ses désirs pour des réalités.

wishy-washy ['wɪʃɪ'wɔʃɪ] *adj* (*col: person*) qui manque de caractère, falot(e); (*: ideas, thinking*) faiblard(e).

wisp [wɪsp] *n* fine mèche (*de cheveux*); (*of smoke*) mince volute *f*; **a ~ of straw** un fétu de paille.

wistful ['wɪstful] *adj* mélancolique.

wit [wɪt] *n* (*gen pl: intelligence*) intelligence *f*, esprit *m*; (*presence of mind*) présence *f* d'esprit; (*wittiness*) esprit; (*person*) homme/femme d'esprit; **to be at one's ~s' end** (*fig*) ne plus savoir que faire; **to have one's ~s about one** avoir toute sa présence d'esprit, ne pas perdre la tête; **to ~** *adv* à savoir.

witch [wɪtʃ] *n* sorcière *f*.

witchcraft ['wɪtʃkrɑːft] *n* sorcellerie *f*.

witch doctor *n* sorcier *m*.

witch-hunt ['wɪtʃhʌnt] *n* chasse *f* aux sorcières.

========================= *KEYWORD*

with [wɪð, wɪθ] *prep* **1** (*in the company of*) avec; (*at the home of*) chez; **we stayed ~ friends** nous avons logé chez des amis; **I'll be ~ you in a minute** je suis à vous dans un instant

2 (*descriptive*): **a room ~ a view** une chambre avec vue; **the man ~ the grey hat/ blue eyes** l'homme au chapeau gris/aux yeux bleus

3 (*indicating manner, means, cause*): **~ tears in her eyes** les larmes aux yeux; **to walk ~ a stick** marcher avec une canne; **red ~ anger** rouge de colère; **to shake ~ fear** trembler de peur; **to fill sth ~ water** remplir qch d'eau

4: **I'm ~ you** (*I understand*) je vous suis; **to be ~ it** (*col: up-to-date*) être dans le vent.

withdraw [wɪθ'drɔː] *irreg vt* retirer ♦ *vi* se retirer; (*go back on promise*) se rétracter; **to ~ into o.s.** se replier sur soi-même.

withdrawal [wɪθ'drɔːəl] *n* retrait *m*; (*MED*) état *m* de manque.

withdrawal symptoms *npl*: **to have ~** être en état de manque, présenter les symptômes *mpl* de sevrage.

withdrawn [wɪθ'drɔːn] *pp of* withdraw ♦ *adj* (*person*) renfermé(e).

wither ['wɪðə*] *vi* se faner.

withered ['wɪðəd] *adj* fané(e), flétri(e); (*limb*) atrophié(e).

withhold [wɪθ'həuld] *vt irreg* (*money*) retenir; (*decision*) remettre; (*permission*): **to ~ (from)** refuser (à); (*information*): **to ~ (from)** cacher (à).

within [wɪð'ɪn] *prep* à l'intérieur de ♦ *adv* à l'intérieur; **~ sight of** en vue de; **~ a mile of** à moins d'un mille de; **~ the week** avant la fin de la semaine; **~ an hour from now** d'ici une heure; **to be ~ the law** être légal(e) *or* dans les limites de la légalité.

without [wɪð'aut] prep sans; ~ **anybody knowing** sans que personne le sache; **to go** or **do** ~ **sth** se passer de qch.

withstand [wɪθ'stænd] vt irreg résister à.

witness ['wɪtnɪs] n (person) témoin m; (evidence) témoignage m ♦ vt (event) être témoin de; (document) attester l'authenticité de; **to bear** ~ **to sth** témoigner de qch; ~ **for the prosecution/defence** témoin à charge/à décharge; **to** ~ **to sth/ having seen sth** témoigner de qch/d'avoir vu qch.

witness box, (US) **witness stand** n barre f des témoins.

witticism ['wɪtɪsɪzəm] n mot m d'esprit.

witty ['wɪtɪ] adj spirituel(le), plein(e) d'esprit.

wives [waɪvz] npl of **wife.**

wizard ['wɪzəd] n magicien m.

wizened ['wɪznd] adj ratatiné(e).

wk abbr = **week.**

Wm. abbr = **William.**

WO n abbr = **warrant officer.**

wobble ['wɔbl] vi trembler; (chair) branler.

wobbly ['wɔblɪ] adj tremblant(e); branlant(e).

woe [wəu] n malheur m.

woeful ['wəuful] adj (sad) malheureux(euse); (terrible) affligeant(e).

wok [wɔk] n wok m.

woke [wəuk] pt of **wake.**

woken ['wəukn] pp of **wake.**

wolf, pl **wolves** [wulf, wulvz] n loup m.

woman, pl **women** ['wumən, 'wɪmɪn] n femme f ♦ cpd: ~ **doctor** femme f médecin; ~ **friend** amie f; ~ **teacher** professeur m femme; **young** ~ jeune femme; **women's page** (PRESS) page f des lectrices.

womanize ['wumənaɪz] vi jouer les séducteurs.

womanly ['wumənlɪ] adj féminin(e).

womb [wu:m] n (ANAT) utérus m.

women ['wɪmɪn] npl of **woman.**

Women's (Liberation) Movement n (also: **women's lib**) mouvement m de libération de la femme, MLF m.

won [wʌn] pt, pp of **win.**

wonder ['wʌndə*] n merveille f, miracle m; (feeling) émerveillement m ♦ vi: **to** ~ **whether** se demander si; **to** ~ **at** s'étonner de; s'émerveiller de; **to** ~ **about** songer à; **it's no** ~ **that** il n'est pas étonnant que + sub.

wonderful ['wʌndəful] adj merveilleux(euse).

wonderfully ['wʌndəfəlɪ] adv (+ adj) merveilleusement; (+ vb) à merveille.

wonky ['wɔŋkɪ] adj (BRIT col) qui ne va or ne marche pas très bien.

wont [wəunt] n: **as is his/her** ~ comme de coutume.

won't [wəunt] = **will not.**

woo [wu:] vt (woman) faire la cour à.

wood [wud] n (timber, forest) bois m ♦ cpd de bois, en bois.

wood carving n sculpture f en or sur bois.

wooded ['wudɪd] adj boisé(e).

wooden ['wudn] adj en bois; (fig) raide; inexpressif(ive).

woodland ['wudlənd] n forêt f, région boisée.

woodpecker ['wudpɛkə*] n pic m (oiseau).

wood pigeon n ramier m.

woodwind ['wudwɪnd] n (MUS) bois m; **the** ~ (MUS) les bois.

woodwork ['wudwə:k] n menuiserie f.

woodworm ['wudwə:m] n ver m du bois; **the table has got** ~ la table est piquée des vers.

woof [wuf] n (of dog) aboiement m ♦ vi aboyer; ~, ~! oua, oua!

wool [wul] n laine f; **to pull the** ~ **over sb's eyes** (fig) en faire accroire à qn.

woollen, (US) **woolen** ['wulən] adj de laine; (industry) lainier(ière) ♦ n: ~**s** lainages mpl.

woolly, (US) **wooly** ['wulɪ] adj laineux(euse); (fig: ideas) confus(e).

woozy ['wu:zɪ] adj (col) dans les vapes.

word [wə:d] n mot m; (spoken) mot, parole f; (promise) parole; (news) nouvelles fpl ♦ vt rédiger, formuler; ~ **for** ~ (repeat) mot pour mot; (translate) mot à mot; **what's the** ~ **for "pen" in French?** comment dit-on "pen" en français?; **to put sth into** ~**s** exprimer qch; **in other** ~**s** en d'autres termes; **to have a** ~ **with sb** toucher un mot à qn; **to have** ~**s with sb** (quarrel etc) avoir des mots avec qn; **to break/keep one's** ~ manquer à/tenir sa parole; **I'll take your** ~ **for it** je vous crois sur parole; **to send** ~ **of** prévenir de; **to leave** ~ (with sb/for sb) that ... laisser un mot (à qn/pour qn) disant que ....

wording ['wə:dɪŋ] n termes mpl, langage m; libellé m.

word of mouth n: **by** or **through** ~ de bouche à oreille.

word-perfect ['wə:d'pə:fɪkt] adj: **he was** ~ (in his speech etc), **his speech etc was** ~ il savait son discours etc sur le bout du doigt.

word processing n traitement m de texte.

word processor [-prəusɛsə*] n machine f de traitement de texte.

wordwrap ['wə:dræp] n (COMPUT) retour m (automatique) à la ligne.

wordy ['wə:dɪ] adj verbeux(euse).

wore [wɔ:*] pt of **wear.**

work [wə:k] n travail m; (ART, LITERATURE) œuvre f ♦ vi travailler; (mechanism) marcher, fonctionner; (plan etc) marcher; (medicine) agir ♦ vt (clay, wood etc) travailler; (mine etc) exploiter; (machine) faire marcher or fonctionner; **to go to** ~ aller travailler; **to set to** ~, **to start** ~ se mettre à l'œuvre; **to be at** ~ (on sth) travailler (sur qch); **to be out of** ~ être au chômage; **to** ~ **hard** travailler dur; **to** ~ **loose** se défaire, se desserrer.

▶**work on** vt fus travailler à; (principle) se baser sur.

▶**work out** *vi* (*plans etc*) marcher; (*SPORT*) s'entraîner ♦ *vt* (*problem*) résoudre; (*plan*) élaborer; **it ~s out at £100** ça fait 100 livres.

workable ['wəːkəbl] *adj* (*solution*) réalisable.

workaholic [wəːkə'hɒlɪk] *n* bourreau *m* de travail.

workbench ['wəːkbɛntʃ] *n* établi *m*.

worked up [wəːkt-] *adj*: **to get ~** se mettre dans tous ses états.

worker ['wəːkə*] *n* travailleur/euse, ouvrier/ière; **office ~** employé/e de bureau.

work force *n* main-d'œuvre *f*.

work-in ['wəːkɪn] *n* (*BRIT*) occupation *f* d'usine *etc* (*sans arrêt de la production*).

working ['wəːkɪŋ] *adj* (*day, tools etc, conditions*) de travail; (*wife*) qui travaille; (*partner, population*) actif(ive); **in ~ order** en état de marche; **a ~ knowledge of English** une connaissance toute pratique de l'anglais.

working capital *n* (*COMM*) fonds *mpl* de roulement.

working class *n* classe ouvrière ♦ *adj*: **working-class** ouvrier(ière), de la classe ouvrière.

working man *n* travailleur *m*.

working party *n* (*BRIT*) groupe *m* de travail.

working week *n* semaine *f* de travail.

work-in-progress ['wəːkɪn'prəugrɛs] *n* (*COMM*) en-cours *m inv*; (: *value*) valeur *f* des en-cours.

workload ['wəːkləud] *n* charge *f* de travail.

workman ['wəːkmən] *n* ouvrier *m*.

workmanship ['wəːkmənʃɪp] *n* métier *m*, habileté *f*; facture *f*.

workmate ['wəːkmeɪt] *n* collègue *m/f*.

workout ['wəːkaut] *n* (*SPORT*) séance *f* d'entraînement.

work permit *n* permis *m* de travail.

works [wəːks] *n* (*BRIT*: *factory*) usine *f* ♦ *npl* (*of clock, machine*) mécanisme *m*; **road ~** travaux *mpl* (d'entretien des routes).

works council *n* comité *m* d'entreprise.

work sheet *n* (*COMPUT*) feuille *f* de programmation.

workshop ['wəːkʃɔp] *n* atelier *m*.

work station *n* poste *m* de travail.

work study *n* étude *f* du travail.

worktop ['wəːktɔp] *n* plan *m* de travail.

work-to-rule ['wəːktə'ruːl] *n* (*BRIT*) grève *f* du zèle.

world [wəːld] *n* monde *m* ♦ *cpd* (*champion*) du monde; (*power, war*) mondial(e); **all over the ~** dans le monde entier, partout dans le monde; **to think the ~ of sb** (*fig*) ne jurer que par qn; **what in the ~ is he doing?** qu'est-ce qu'il peut bien être en train de faire?; **to do sb a ~ of good** faire le plus grand bien à qn; **W~ War One/Two, the First/Second W~ War** la Première/Deuxième Guerre mondiale; **out of this ~** *adj* extraordinaire.

World Cup *n*: **the ~** (*FOOTBALL*) la Coupe du monde.

world-famous [wəːld'feɪməs] *adj* de renommée mondiale.

worldly ['wəːldlɪ] *adj* de ce monde.

world music *n* world music *f*.

World Series *n*: **the ~** (*US: BASEBALL*) le championnat national de baseball.

world-wide ['wəːld'waɪd] *adj* universel(le) ♦ *adv* dans le monde entier.

worm [wəːm] *n* ver *m*.

worn [wɔːn] *pp of* **wear** ♦ *adj* usé(e).

worn-out ['wɔːnaut] *adj* (*object*) complètement usé(e); (*person*) épuisé(e).

worried ['wʌrɪd] *adj* inquiet(ète); **to be ~ about sth** être inquiet au sujet de qch.

worrier ['wʌrɪə*] *n* inquiet/ète.

worrisome ['wʌrɪsəm] *adj* inquiétant(e).

worry ['wʌrɪ] *n* souci *m* ♦ *vt* inquiéter ♦ *vi* s'inquiéter, se faire du souci; **to ~ about** *or* **over sth/sb** se faire du souci pour *or* à propos de qch/qn.

worrying ['wʌrɪɪŋ] *adj* inquiétant(e).

worse [wəːs] *adj* pire, plus mauvais(e) ♦ *adv* plus mal ♦ *n* pire *m*; **to get ~** (*condition, situation*) empirer, se dégrader; **a change for the ~** une détérioration; **he is none the ~ for it** il ne s'en porte pas plus mal; **so much the ~ for you!** tant pis pour vous!

worsen ['wəːsn] *vt*, *vi* empirer.

worse off *adj* moins à l'aise financièrement; (*fig*): **you'll be ~ this way** ça ira moins bien de cette façon; **he is now ~ than before** il se retrouve dans une situation pire qu'auparavant.

worship ['wəːʃɪp] *n* culte *m* ♦ *vt* (*God*) rendre un culte à; (*person*) adorer; **Your W~** (*BRIT*: *to mayor*) Monsieur le Maire; (: *to judge*) Monsieur le Juge.

worshipper ['wəːʃɪpə*] *n* adorateur/trice; (*in church*) fidèle *m/f*.

worst [wəːst] *adj* le(la) pire, le(la) plus mauvais(e) ♦ *adv* le plus mal ♦ *n* pire *m*; **at ~** au pis aller; **if the ~ comes to the ~** si le pire doit arriver.

worst-case ['wəːstkeɪs] *adj*: **the ~ scenario** le pire scénario *or* cas de figure.

worsted ['wustɪd] *n*: **(wool) ~** laine peignée.

worth [wəːθ] *n* valeur *f* ♦ *adj*: **to be ~** valoir; **how much is it ~?** ça vaut combien?; **it's ~ it** cela en vaut la peine; **50 pence ~ of apples** (pour) 50 pence de pommes.

worthless ['wəːθlɪs] *adj* qui ne vaut rien.

worthwhile ['wəːθ'waɪl] *adj* (*activity*) qui en vaut la peine; (*cause*) louable; **a ~ book** un livre qui vaut la peine d'être lu.

worthy ['wəːðɪ] *adj* (*person*) digne; (*motive*) louable; **~ of** digne.

═══════════════════════ *KEYWORD*

would [wud] *aux vb* **1** (*conditional tense*): **if you asked him he ~ do it** si vous le lui demandiez, il le ferait; **if you had asked him**

he ~ **have done it** si vous le lui aviez demandé, il l'aurait fait

2 (*in offers, invitations, requests*): ~ **you like a biscuit?** voulez-vous *or* voudriez-vous un biscuit?; ~ **you close the door please?** voulez-vous fermer la porte, s'il vous plaît?

3 (*in indirect speech*): **I said I** ~ **do it** j'ai dit que je le ferais

4 (*emphatic*): **it WOULD have to snow today!** naturellement il neige aujourd'hui! *or* il fallait qu'il neige aujourd'hui!

5 (*insistence*): **she** ~**n't do it** elle n'a pas voulu *or* elle a refusé de le faire

6 (*conjecture*): **it** ~ **have been midnight** il devait être minuit

7 (*indicating habit*): **he** ~ **go there on Mondays** il y allait le lundi.

would-be ['wudbiː] *adj* (*pej*) soi-disant.

wound *vb* [waund] *pt, pp of* **wind** ♦ *n, vt* [wuːnd] *n* blessure *f* ♦ *vt* blesser; ~**ed in the leg** blessé à la jambe.

wove [wəuv] *pt of* **weave**.

woven ['wəuvn] *pp of* **weave**.

WP *n abbr* = **word processing, word processor** ♦ *abbr* (*BRIT col*) = **weather permitting**.

WPC *n abbr* (*BRIT*) = **woman police constable**.

wpm *abbr* (= *words per minute*) mots/minute.

WRAC *n abbr* (*BRIT*: = *Women's Royal Army Corps*) auxiliaires *féminines de l'armée de terre*.

WRAF *n abbr* (*BRIT*: = *Women's Royal Air Force*) auxiliaires féminines de l'armée de l'air.

wrangle ['ræŋgl] *n* dispute *f* ♦ *vi* se disputer.

wrap [ræp] *n* (*stole*) écharpe *f*; (*cape*) pèlerine *f* ♦ *vt* (*also:* ~ **up**) envelopper; **under** ~**s** (*fig: plan, scheme*) secret(ète).

wrapper ['ræpə*] *n* (*BRIT: of book*) couverture *f*; (*on chocolate etc*) papier *m*.

wrapping paper ['ræpɪŋ-] *n* papier *m* d'emballage; (*for gift*) papier cadeau.

wrath [rɔθ] *n* courroux *m*.

wreak [riːk] *vt* (*destruction*) entraîner; **to** ~ **havoc** faire des ravages; **to** ~ **vengeance on** se venger de, exercer sa vengeance sur.

wreath, ~**s** [riːθ, riːðz] *n* couronne *f*.

wreck [rɛk] *n* (*sea disaster*) naufrage *m*; (*ship*) épave *f*; (*pej: person*) loque (humaine) ♦ *vt* démolir; (*ship*) provoquer le naufrage de; (*fig*) briser, ruiner.

wreckage ['rɛkɪdʒ] *n* débris *mpl*; (*of building*) décombres *mpl*; (*of ship*) naufrage *m*.

wrecker ['rɛkə*] *n* (*US: breakdown van*) dépanneuse *f*.

WREN [rɛn] *n abbr* (*BRIT*) membre du WRNS.

wren [rɛn] *n* (*ZOOL*) troglodyte *m*.

wrench [rɛntʃ] *n* (*TECH*) clé *f* (à écrous); (*tug*) violent mouvement de torsion; (*fig*) arrachement *m* ♦ *vt* tirer violemment sur, tordre; **to** ~ **sth from** arracher qch (violemment) à *or* de.

wrest [rɛst] *vt*: **to** ~ **sth from sb** arracher *or* ravir qch à qn.

wrestle ['rɛsl] *vi*: **to** ~ **(with sb)** lutter (avec qn); **to** ~ **with** (*fig*) se débattre avec, lutter contre.

wrestler ['rɛslə*] *n* lutteur/euse.

wrestling ['rɛslɪŋ] *n* lutte *f*; (*also:* **all-in** ~: *BRIT*) catch *m*.

wrestling match *n* rencontre *f* de lutte (*or* de catch).

wretch [rɛtʃ] *n* pauvre malheureux/euse; **little** ~! (*often humorous*) petit(e) misérable!

wretched ['rɛtʃɪd] *adj* misérable; (*col*) maudit(e).

wriggle ['rɪgl] *n* tortillement *m* ♦ *vi* se tortiller.

wring, *pt, pp* **wrung** [rɪŋ, rʌŋ] *vt* tordre; (*wet clothes*) essorer; (*fig*): **to** ~ **sth out of** arracher qch à.

wringer ['rɪŋə*] *n* essoreuse *f*.

wringing ['rɪŋɪŋ] *adj* (*also:* ~ **wet**) tout mouillé(e), trempé(e).

wrinkle ['rɪŋkl] *n* (*on skin*) ride *f*; (*on paper etc*) pli *m* ♦ *vt* rider, plisser ♦ *vi* se plisser.

wrinkled ['rɪŋkld] *adj*, **wrinkly** ['rɪŋklɪ] *adj* (*fabric, paper*) froissé(e), plissé(e); (*surface*) plissé; (*skin*) ridé(e), plissé.

wrist [rɪst] *n* poignet *m*.

wristband ['rɪstbænd] *n* (*BRIT: of shirt*) poignet *m*; (*: of watch*) bracelet *m*.

wrist watch *n* montre-bracelet *f*.

writ [rɪt] *n* acte *m* judiciaire; **to issue a** ~ **against sb, serve a** ~ **on sb** assigner qn en justice.

write, *pt* **wrote,** *pp* **written** [raɪt, rəut, 'rɪtn] *vt, vi* écrire; **to** ~ **sb a letter** écrire une lettre à qn.

▶**write away** *vi*: **to** ~ **away for** (*information*) (écrire pour) demander; (*goods*) (écrire pour) commander.

▶**write down** *vt* noter; (*put in writing*) mettre par écrit.

▶**write off** *vt* (*debt*) passer aux profits et pertes; (*depreciate*) amortir; (*smash up: car etc*) démolir complètement.

▶**write out** *vt* écrire; (*copy*) recopier.

▶**write up** *vt* rédiger.

write-off ['raɪtɔf] *n* perte totale; **the car is a** ~ la voiture est bonne pour la casse.

write-protect ['raɪtprə'tɛkt] *vt* (*COMPUT*) protéger contre l'écriture.

writer ['raɪtə*] *n* auteur *m*, écrivain *m*.

write-up ['raɪtʌp] *n* (*review*) critique *f*.

writhe [raɪð] *vi* se tordre.

writing ['raɪtɪŋ] *n* écriture *f*; (*of author*) œuvres *fpl*; **in** ~ par écrit; **in my own** ~ écrit(e) de ma main.

writing case *n* nécessaire *m* de correspondance.

writing desk *n* secrétaire *m*.

writing paper *n* papier *m* à lettres.

written ['rɪtn] *pp of* **write**.

WRNS *n abbr* (*BRIT*: = *Women's Royal Naval*

Service) auxiliaires féminines de la marine.
wrong [rɔŋ] *adj* faux(fausse); (*incorrectly chosen: number, road etc*) mauvais(e); (*not suitable*) qui ne convient pas; (*wicked*) mal; (*unfair*) injuste ♦ *adv* faux ♦ *n* tort *m* ♦ *vt* faire du tort à, léser; **to be ~** (*answer*) être faux(fausse); (*in doing/saying*) avoir tort (de dire/faire); **you are ~ to do it** tu as tort de le faire; **it's ~ to steal, stealing is ~** c'est mal de voler; **you are ~ about that, you've got it ~** tu te trompes; **to be in the ~** avoir tort; **what's ~?** qu'est-ce qui ne va pas?; **there's nothing ~** tout va bien; **what's ~ with the car?** qu'est-ce qu'elle a, la voiture?; **to go ~** (*person*) se tromper; (*plan*) mal tourner; (*machine*) se détraquer.
wrongdoer ['rɔŋduːə*] *n* malfaiteur *m*.
wrong-foot [rɔŋ'fut] *vt* (*SPORT*) prendre à contre-pied; (*fig*) prendre au dépourvu.
wrongful ['rɔŋful] *adj* injustifié(e); **~ dismissal** (*INDUSTRY*) licenciement abusif.
wrongly ['rɔŋlɪ] *adv* à tort; (*answer, do, count*) mal, incorrectement; (*treat*) injustement.
wrong number *n* (*TEL*): **you have the ~** vous vous êtes trompé de numéro.
wrong side *n* (*of cloth*) envers *m*.
wrote [rəut] *pt of* **write**.
wrought [rɔːt] *adj*: **~ iron** fer forgé.
wrung [rʌŋ] *pt, pp of* **wring**.
WRVS *n abbr* (*BRIT*: = Women's Royal Voluntary Service*) auxiliaires féminines bénévoles au service de la collectivité.
wry [raɪ] *adj* désabusé(e).
wt. *abbr* (= *weight*) pds.
WV, W. Va. *abbr* (*US*) = West Virginia.
WY, Wyo. *abbr* (*US*) = Wyoming.
WYSIWYG ['wɪzɪwɪg] *abbr* (*COMPUT*: = *what you see is what you get*) ce que vous voyez est ce que vous aurez.

X x

X, x [ɛks] *n* (*letter*) X, x *m*; (*BRIT CINE: formerly*) film interdit aux moins de 18 ans; **X for Xmas** X comme Xavier.
Xerox ['zɪərɔks] *n* ® (*also*: **~ machine**) photocopieuse *f*; (*photocopy*) photocopie *f* ♦ *vt* photocopier.
XL *abbr* (= *extra large*) XL.
Xmas ['ɛksməs] *n abbr* = **Christmas**.
X-rated ['ɛks'reɪtɪd] *adj* (*US: film*) interdit(e) aux moins de 18 ans.
X-ray [ɛks'reɪ] *n* rayon *m* X; (*photograph*) radio(graphie) *f* ♦ *vt* radiographier.
xylophone ['zaɪləfəun] *n* xylophone *m*.

Y y

Y, y [waɪ] *n* (*letter*) Y, y *m*; **Y for Yellow**, (*US*) **Y for Yoke** Y comme Yvonne.
yacht [jɔt] *n* voilier *m*; (*motor, luxury ~*) yacht *m*.
yachting ['jɔtɪŋ] *n* yachting *m*, navigation *f* de plaisance.
yachtsman ['jɔtsmən] *n* yacht(s)man *m*.
yam [jæm] *n* igname *f*.
Yank [jæŋk], **Yankee** ['jæŋkɪ] *n* (*pej*) Amerloque *m/f*, Ricain/e.
yank [jæŋk] *vt* tirer d'un coup sec.
yap [jæp] *vi* (*dog*) japper.
yard [jɑːd] *n* (*of house etc*) cour *f*; (*US: garden*) jardin *m*; (*measure*) yard *m* (= *914 mm; 3 feet*); **builder's ~** chantier *m*.
yardstick ['jɑːdstɪk] *n* (*fig*) mesure *f*, critère *m*.
yarn [jɑːn] *n* fil *m*; (*tale*) longue histoire.
yawn [jɔːn] *n* bâillement *m* ♦ *vi* bâiller.
yawning ['jɔːnɪŋ] *adj* (*gap*) béant(e).
yd *abbr* = **yard**.
yeah [jɛə] *adv* (*col*) ouais.
year [jɪə*] *n* an *m*, année *f*; (*SCOL etc*) année; **every ~** tous les ans, chaque année; **this ~** cette année; **a** *or* **per ~** par an; **~ in, ~ out** année après année; **to be 8 ~s old** avoir 8 ans; **an eight-~-old child** un enfant de huit ans.
yearbook ['jɪəbuk] *n* annuaire *m*.
yearly ['jɪəlɪ] *adj* annuel(le) ♦ *adv* annuellement; **twice ~** deux fois par an.
yearn [jəːn] *vi*: **to ~ for sth/to do** aspirer à qch/à faire, languir après qch.
yearning ['jəːnɪŋ] *n* désir ardent, envie *f*.
yeast [jiːst] *n* levure *f*.
yell [jɛl] *n* hurlement *m*, cri *m* ♦ *vi* hurler.
yellow ['jɛləu] *adj, n* jaune (*m*).
yellow fever *n* fièvre *f* jaune.
yellowish ['jɛləuɪʃ] *adj* qui tire sur le jaune, jaunâtre (*pej*).
Yellow Pages *npl* ® pages *fpl* jaunes.
Yellow Sea *n*: **the ~** la mer Jaune.
yelp [jɛlp] *n* jappement *m*; glapissement *m* ♦ *vi* japper; glapir.
Yemen ['jɛmən] *n* Yémen *m*.
yen [jɛn] *n* (*currency*) yen *m*; (*craving*): **~ for/to do** grand(e) envie *f* or désir *m* de/de faire.
yeoman ['jəumən] *n*: **Y~ of the Guard** hallebardier *m* de la garde royale.
yes [jɛs] *adv* oui; (*answering negative question*) si ♦ *n* oui *m*; **to say ~ (to)** dire oui (à).
yesterday ['jɛstədɪ] *adv, n* hier (*m*); **~**

morning/evening hier matin/soir; **the day before** ~ avant-hier; **all day** ~ toute la journée d'hier.

yet [jɛt] adv encore; déjà ♦ conj pourtant, néanmoins; **it is not finished** ~ ce n'est pas encore fini or toujours pas fini; **must you go just** ~? dois-tu déjà partir?; **the best** ~ le meilleur jusqu'ici or jusque-là; **as** ~ jusqu'ici, encore; **a few days** ~ encore quelques jours; ~ **again** une fois de plus.

yew [ju:] n if m.

Y-fronts ['waɪfrʌnts] npl ® (BRIT) slip m kangourou.

YHA n abbr (BRIT) = Youth Hostels Association.

Yiddish ['jɪdɪʃ] n yiddish m.

yield [ji:ld] n production f, rendement m; (FINANCE) rapport m ♦ vt produire, rendre, rapporter; (surrender) céder ♦ vi céder; (US AUT) céder la priorité; **a** ~ **of 5%** un rendement de 5%.

YMCA n abbr (= Young Men's Christian Association) ≈ union chrétienne de jeunes gens (UCJG).

yob(bo) ['jɔb(əʊ)] n (BRIT col) loubar(d) m.

yodel ['jəʊdl] vi faire des tyroliennes, jodler.

yoga ['jəʊgə] n yoga m.

yog(h)ourt, yog(h)urt ['jəʊgət] n yaourt m.

yoke [jəʊk] n joug m ♦ vt (also: ~ **together**: oxen) accoupler.

yolk [jəʊk] n jaune m (d'œuf).

yonder ['jɔndə*] adv là(-bas).

yonks [jɔŋks] npl (col): **for** ~ très longtemps; **we've been here for** ~ ça fait une éternité qu'on est ici; **we were there for** ~ on est resté là pendant des lustres.

Yorks [jɔ:ks] abbr (BRIT) = Yorkshire.

========================= KEYWORD

you [ju:] pron **1** (subject) tu; (polite form) vous; (plural) vous; ~ **French enjoy your food** vous autres Français, vous aimez bien manger; ~ **and I will go** toi et moi or vous et moi, nous irons

2 (object: direct, indirect) te, t' +vowel; vous; **I know** ~ je te or vous connais; **I gave it to** ~, je vous l'ai donné, je te l'ai donné

3 (stressed) toi; vous; **I told YOU to do it** c'est à toi or vous que j'ai dit de le faire

4 (after prep, in comparisons) toi; vous; **it's for** ~ c'est pour toi or vous; **she's younger than** ~ elle est plus jeune que toi or vous

5 (impersonal: one) on; **fresh air does** ~ **good** l'air frais fait du bien; ~ **never know** on ne sait jamais.

you'd [ju:d] = you had, you would.

you'll [ju:l] = you will, you shall.

young [jʌŋ] adj jeune ♦ npl (of animal) petits mpl; (people): **the** ~ les jeunes, la jeunesse; **a** ~ **man** un jeune homme; **a** ~ **lady** (unmarried) une jeune fille, une demoiselle; (married) une jeune femme or dame; **my** ~**er**

brother mon frère cadet; **the** ~**er generation** la jeune génération.

youngish ['jʌŋɪʃ] adj assez jeune.

youngster ['jʌŋstə*] n jeune m/f, (child) enfant m/f.

your [jɔ:*] adj ton(ta), tes pl; (polite form, pl) votre, vos pl.

you're [juə*] = you are.

yours [jɔ:z] pron le(la) tien(ne), les tiens(tiennes); (polite form, pl) le(la) vôtre, les vôtres; **is it** ~? c'est à toi (or à vous)?; **a friend of** ~ un(e) de tes (or de vos) amis.

yourself [jɔ:'sɛlf] pron (reflexive) te; (: polite form) vous; (after prep) toi; vous; (emphatic) toi-même; vous-même; **you** ~ **told me** c'est vous qui me l'avez dit, vous me l'avez dit vous-même.

yourselves [jɔ:'sɛlvz] pl pron vous; (emphatic) vous-mêmes.

youth [ju:θ] n jeunesse f; (young man: pl ~**s** [ju:ðz]) jeune homme m; **in my** ~ dans ma jeunesse, quand j'étais jeune.

youth club n centre m de jeunes.

youthful ['ju:θful] adj jeune; (enthusiasm etc) juvénile; (misdemeanour) de jeunesse.

youthfulness ['ju:θəlnɪs] n jeunesse f.

youth hostel n auberge f de jeunesse.

youth movement n mouvement m de jeunes.

you've [ju:v] = you have.

yowl [jaul] n hurlement m; miaulement m ♦ vi hurler; miauler.

YT abbr (Canada) = Yukon Territory.

Yugoslav ['ju:gəʊslɑ:v] adj yougoslave ♦ n Yougoslave m/f.

Yugoslavia [ju:gəʊ'slɑ:vɪə] n Yougoslavie f.

Yugoslavian [ju:gəʊ'slɑ:vɪən] adj yougoslave.

Yule [ju:l]: ~ **log** n bûche f de Noël.

yuppie ['jʌpɪ] n yuppie m/f.

YWCA n abbr (= Young Women's Christian Association) union chrétienne féminine.

Z z

Z, z [zɛd, (US) zi:] n (letter) Z, z m; **Z for Zebra** Z comme Zoé.

Zaïre [zɑ:'i:ə*] n Zaïre m.

Zambia ['zæmbɪə] n Zambie f.

Zambian ['zæmbɪən] adj zambien(ne) ♦ n Zambien/ne.

zany ['zeɪnɪ] adj farfelu(e), loufoque.

zap [zæp] vt (COMPUT) effacer.

zeal [zi:l] n (revolutionary etc) ferveur f; (keenness) ardeur f, zèle m.

zealot ['zɛlət] n fanatique m/f.

zealous ['zɛləs] *adj* fervent(e); ardent(e), zélé(e).

zebra ['zi:brə] *n* zèbre *m*.

zebra crossing *n* (*BRIT*) passage *m* pour piétons.

zenith ['zɛnɪθ] *n* (*ASTRONOMY*) zénith *m*; (*fig*) zénith, apogée *m*.

zero ['zɪərəu] *n* zéro *m* ♦ *vi*: **to ~ in on** (*target*) se diriger droit sur; **5° below ~** 5 degrés au-dessous de zéro.

zero hour *n* l'heure *f* H.

zero option *n* (*POL*): **the ~** l'option *f* zéro.

zero-rated ['zi:rəureɪtɪd] *adj* (*BRIT*) exonéré(e) de TVA.

zest [zɛst] *n* entrain *m*, élan *m*; (*of lemon etc*) zeste *m*.

zigzag ['zɪgzæg] *n* zigzag *m* ♦ *vi* zigzaguer, faire des zigzags.

Zimbabwe [zɪm'bɑ:bwɪ] *n* Zimbabwe *m*.

Zimbabwean [zɪm'bɑ:bwɪən] *adj* zimbabwéen(ne) ♦ *n* Zimbabwéen/ne.

Zimmer ['zɪmə*] *n* ® (*also*: **~ frame**) déambulateur *m*.

zinc [zɪŋk] *n* zinc *m*.

Zionism ['zaɪənɪzəm] *n* sionisme *m*.

Zionist ['zaɪənɪst] *adj* sioniste ♦ *n* Sioniste *m/f*.

zip [zɪp] *n* (*also*: **~ fastener,** (*US*) **~per**) fermeture *f* éclair ® *or* à glissière; (*energy*) entrain *m* ♦ *vt* (*also*: **~ up**) fermer (avec une fermeture éclair ®).

zip code *n* (*US*) code postal.

zither ['zɪðə*] *n* cithare *f*.

zodiac ['zəudɪæk] *n* zodiaque *m*.

zombie ['zɔmbɪ] *n* (*fig*): **like a ~** avec l'air d'un zombie, comme un automate.

zone [zəun] *n* zone *f*.

zonked [zɔŋkt] *adj* (*col*) crevé(e), claqué(e).

zoo [zu:] *n* zoo *m*.

zoological [zuə'lɔdʒɪkl] *adj* zoologique.

zoologist [zu'ɔlədʒɪst] *n* zoologiste *m/f*.

zoology [zu:'ɔlədʒɪ] *n* zoologie *f*.

zoom [zu:m] *vi*: **to ~ past** passer en trombe; **to ~ in (on sb/sth)** (*PHOT, CINE*) zoomer (sur qn/qch).

zoom lens *n* zoom *m*, objectif *m* à focale variable.

zucchini [zu:'ki:nɪ] *n(pl)* (*US*) courgette(s) *f(pl)*.

Zulu ['zu:lu:] *adj* zoulou ♦ *n* Zoulou *m/f*.

Zürich ['zjuərɪk] *n* Zurich.

TABLE DES MATIÈRES   CONTENTS